Pocket Oxford Russian Dictionary

Using this dictionary

Russian–English section

Stress

In Russian there are some classes of words—prepositions, conjunctions, particles—which are normally unstressed. Stress is indicated for all other words, except monosyllables, by the placing of a stress mark (´) over the vowel of the stressed syllable. Except in a few compound words, the vowel ё is always stressed and so has no stress mark. When two stress marks are found in the same word or form (as in о́бли́тый) either of the two syllables may be stressed.

Treatment of entries

Articles consist of a word, prefix or other lexical element, or occasionally of two or more synonymous words or forms, or corresponding masculine and feminine forms, with basic grammatical information, translation(s), and sometimes usage examples. To save space related and alphabetically consecutive words may be grouped in paragraphs, as may consecutive but unrelated entries each consisting only of a cross-reference, and compound words of which the first element is a prefix or other combining form. All headwords, including those together in paragraphs, are printed in enlarged bold type. Conjugational and declensional information, as well as all usage examples, are printed in smaller bold type.

The swung dash (∼) may be substituted in the body of an article for the whole of the headword or, in a list of compound words, for the prefix or other combining form which is common to all of them. In some headwords the ending may be separated from the stem by a thin vertical stroke; the swung dash will then represent the stem only, and the appropriate form of the ending will be appended to it, as in са́харн|ый sugar; sugary; ∼ая голова́ sugar loaf; ∼ый заво́д sugar refinery.

The headword of an article is usually the nominative case of nouns or pronouns, the nominative singular masculine of adjectives, or the infinitive of verbs. The genitive ending of every noun is given and is followed by that of any case showing an irregularity of ending or a change of stress. In the singular any case is named, but in the plural the cases can be identified by their endings. The alternative genitive ending in -y is given in parentheses immediately after the genitive (see examples below); the term locative (abbreviated to *loc.*) is used for the prepositional form ending in -у́ after в or на. In the case of those pronouns for which a list of case endings is given, the accusative is never included and the cases are shown in the order: genitive, dative, instrumental, and prepositional. Since the gender of Russian nouns can usually be deduced from the endings of the nominative and genitive it is indicated here only in exceptional instances, as in the case of masculine nouns ending in -a or -я and neuter nouns ending in -мя. Nouns ending in a soft sign (-ь) should be assumed to be feminine unless labelled *m*. All verbs are labelled *impf.* or *pf.* or, when bi-aspectual, *impf. & pf.* The form and stress of the first person singular of the present or future tense are indicated immediately after the infinitive and other forms of the present (or future) and past tenses are given if they show a change of stress or an irregularity of ending or contain the vowel **ё**. When a perfective verb is formed by the addition of a prefix to a simple imperfective, the prefix is divided from the rest of the infinitive by a thin vertical stroke. A single parenthesis, (, before the reflexive ending of an infinitive indicates, especially in cross-references, that the cross-reference etc. applies to both the active and the reflexive infinitive. When the construction of a verb demands the use of a case other than the accusative or genitive the case required is indicated, as in **маха́ть**... *impf.*, **махну́ть**... *pf.+i.* wave; brandish.

Some adjectives have mobile stress in the short forms; in these the full nominative singular masculine form of the headword is followed immediately by a semicolon and then by the short forms.

The following examples illustrate many of the points made above:

адресова́ть, -су́ю *impf. & pf.* address, send; **~ся** address o.s.

нали́ть, -лью́, -льёшь; на́ли́л, -а́, -о *pf.* (*impf.* **налива́ть**) pour (out).

пла́мя, -мени *nt.* flame; fire, blaze.

· **по́вод**[2], -а (-у), *loc.* -у́; *pl.* -о́дья, -ьев rein.

по|проси́ть(ся, -ошу́(сь, -о́сишь(ся *pf.*

прозва́ть, -зову́, -зовёшь; -а́л, -а́, -о *pf.* (*impf.* **прозыва́ть**) nickname, name.

проси́ть, -ошу́, -о́сишь *impf.* (*pf.* **по~**) ask; beg; invite; **~ся** ask; apply.

про|слу́шать, -аю *pf.*, **прослу́шивать**, -аю *impf.* hear; listen to.

сестра́, -ы́; *pl.* сёстры, сестёр, сёстрам sister.

сок, -а (-у), *loc.* -у́ juice; sap; **в (по́лном) ~у́** in the prime of life.

худо́й; худ, -а́, -о thin, lean.

English–Russian section

General

To save space several headwords are sometimes included in the same paragraph. They are printed in enlarged bold type and separated by full stops. Phrases and usage examples are printed in smaller bold type and separated by semicolons.

When a headword is used in a phrase or usage example it is replaced by a swung dash (~), e.g. **crash** ... **~ landing**. The swung dash is also used as a space-saving device in the Russian text, where it stands for the preceding Russian word, e.g. **Georgian** ... грузи́н, **~ка** (where **~ка** indicates грузи́нка) and **sing** ... петь *impf.*, про**~**, с**~** *pf.* (where про**~**, с**~** indicates пропе́ть, спеть).

In giving grammatical forms a hyphen is often used to stand for the whole or a part of the preceding or following Russian word, e.g. **grey** ... седо́й (сед, -а́, -о) = седо́й (сед, седа́, седо); **come** ... приходи́ть (-ожу́, -о́дишь) = приходи́ть (прихожу́, прихо́дишь); **prepare** ... при-, под-, гото́вливаться = пригото́вливаться, подгото́вливаться. Superscript numerals are used to distinguish unrelated headwords spelt alike, and glosses may follow in parentheses, e.g. **bank**[1] *n.* (*of river*), **bank**[2] *n.* (*econ.*).

Stress

For guidance on the use of the stress indicator (') in the English text see *Pronunciation* below.

The stress of each Russian word is indicated above the vowel of the stressed syllable. It is not given for monosyllables, except those which bear the main stress in a phrase, e.g. **be** ... нé бы́ло; **year** ... год óт году; here, the stressed monosyllable and the next word are pronounced as one.

The vowel ё has no stress mark since it is almost always stressed; when the stress falls elsewhere this is shown, e.g. **quarterly** ... трёхмéсячный.

The presence of two stress marks indicates that either of the marked syllables may be stressed.

Changes of stress which take place in conjugation, or declension, or in the short forms of adjectives, are shown as follows:

(i) **suggest** ... предложи́ть (-жу́, -жишь). Here, the absence of a stress mark on the second person singular indicates that the stress is on the preceding syllable: предло́жишь.

(ii) **begin** ... нача́ть (-чну́, -чнёшь; нáчал, -á, -о). When the stress of the two preceding forms is not identical as it is in (i) above, the final form takes the stress of the first of these: нáчало. Forms not shown at all, e.g. the rest of the conjugation of предложи́ть, and the rest of the future and the past plural of нача́ть, are stressed like the last form given: предло́жит etc., начнёт etc., нáчали.

(iii) **boring²** ... ску́чный (-чен, -чнá, -чно) = (ску́чен, скучнá, ску́чно, ску́чны); where the ending (e.g. -чны here) is not given, the stress is the same as for the previous form.

(iv) **rain** ... дождь (-дя́). The single form in parentheses is the genitive (see *Declension* below) and all other forms have the same stressed syllable. If only one case-labelled form is given in the singular it is an exception to the regular paradigm. For example, **leg** ... ногá (*a.* -гу; *pl.* -ги, -г, -гáм); the other singular forms have end-stress, while the unmentioned plural forms follow the stress of the last form given: ногáми, ногáх.

Pronunciation

For the convenience of users whose native language is not English all main headwords, i.e. those starting a paragraph, are transcribed into the International Phonetic Alphabet, a key to which is supplied below. To save space within the paragraph the transcription of a word is not given where its pronunciation can be deduced from that of a preceding word. It is also omitted in the case of compound words whose second element is listed elsewhere in the dictionary. Where the stress of an untranscribed word changes this is indicated by means of a stress indicator (') immediately before the stressed syllable.

In the case of abbreviations transcriptions are not supplied where the component letters are pronounced individually, e.g. **BBC**, or where the expanded form or key word therein is treated elsewhere as a separate entry.

Where the pronunciation of a word varies according to its part of speech both transcriptions are supplied, separated by a semicolon. The order of the transcriptions is the same as the order in which the parts of speech are treated (see **conduct**).

Nouns

Gender This can usually be deduced from the ending of the nominative singular: a final consonant or -й indicates a masculine noun, -a or -я or -ь feminine, -e or -o neuter. Gender is shown explicitly for masculine nouns ending in -a, -я or -ь, neuter nouns in -мя, and indeclinable nouns. If a noun is given only as a plural form either the gender or the genitive plural is indicated.

Declension When a single inflected form is added in parentheses with no indication of case or number it is the genitive singular, e.g. **Indian** ... индеец (-ейца), and all other inflected cases have the genitive stem. Apart from changes in stress (see *Stress* above), the following irregularities are among those indicated:

(i) The mobile vowel in masculine nouns, e.g. **stub** ... окурок (-рка).

(ii) The alternative genitive singular in -y or -ю of masculine nouns, e.g. **cheese** ... сыр (-a(y)), i.e. сыра or сыру. For nouns denoting a substance, a number of objects, or a collective unit, the -y/-ю form has partitive value; with other nouns it is used only in certain set phrases.

(iii) The prepositional singular of masculine nouns, when ending in -ý (or -ю) after в or на. Here the term *locative* is used, e.g. **shore** ... берег (*loc.* -ý).

(iv) Substantivized adjectives are followed by *sb.* to show that they retain the adjectival declension.

Adjectives

The short forms of adjectives are shown when they are irregular, when the stress moves (see *Stress* above), and for all adjectives ending in -нный or -нний, e.g. **sickly** ... болезненный (-ен, -енна); **sincere** ... искренний (-нен, -нна, -нно & -нне).

Verbs

Persons and tenses treated as irregular, and changes of stress in conjugation, are shown in parentheses, e.g. **come** ... приходить (-ожу, -одишь) *impf.*, прийти (приду, -дёшь; пришёл, -шла) *pf.* The first two forms in parentheses are the first and second persons singular of the present or future tense; other persons and the past tense follow where necessary. Each verb is labelled with its aspect. The case construction is indicated for transitive verbs *not* followed by the accusative.

The conjugation of быть is given only under **be**. Irregularities of imperative, participial and gerundial forms are not usually shown.

The following changes in the first person singular of the present or future tense of verbs in -ить are treated as regular (and therefore not provided):

(i) Insertion of л after a stem in -б, -в, -м, -п, or -ф, e.g. **add** ... добавить: добавлю, добавишь.

(ii) Change of д or з to ж, к or т to ч, с or х to ш, ск or ст to щ, e.g. **annoy** ... досадить: досажу, досадишь; **answer** ... ответить: отвечу, ответишь; **paint** ... красить: крашу, красишь; **clean** ... чистить: чищу, чистишь.

The reflexive suffix -ся or -сь is placed in parentheses when the verb may be used with or without it, usually as an intransitive or a transitive verb respectively, e.g. **open** *v.t.* & *i.* открывать(ся) *impf.*, открыть(ся) (-рою(сь), -роешь(ся)) *pf.*

Phonetic symbols

Consonants

b	*b*ut	j	*y*es	p	*p*en	w	*w*e	ð	*th*is
d	*d*og	k	*c*at	r	*r*ed	z	*z*oo	ŋ	ri*ng*
f	*f*ew	l	*l*eg	s	*s*it	ʃ	*sh*e	x	lo*ch*
g	*g*et	m	*m*an	t	*t*op	ʒ	deci*s*ion	tʃ	*ch*ip
h	*h*e	n	*n*o	v	*v*oice	θ	*th*in	dʒ	*j*ar

Vowels

æ	c*a*t	iː	s*ee*	uː	t*oo*	əʊ	n*o*	aɪə	f*ire*
ɑː	*ar*m	ɒ	h*o*t	ə	*ago*	eə	h*air*	aʊə	s*our*
e	b*e*d	ɔː	s*aw*	aɪ	m*y*	ɪə	n*ear*		
ɜː	h*er*	ʌ	r*u*n	aʊ	h*ow*	ɔɪ	b*oy*		
ɪ	s*i*t	ʊ	p*u*t	eɪ	d*ay*	ʊə	p*oor*		

(ə) signifies the indeterminate sound as in gard*e*n, carn*a*l, and rhyth*m*.

(r) at the end of a word indicates an r that is sounded when a word beginning with a vowel follows, as in *clutter up* and *an acre of land*.

The mark ˜ indicates a nasalized sound, as in the following sounds that are not natural in English: æ̃ (*timbre*) ɑ̃ (*élan*) ɔ̃ (*garçon*)

The main or primary stress of a word is shown by ' preceding the relevant syllable; any secondary stress in words of three or more syllables is shown by , preceding the relevant syllable.

The Russian alphabet

Capital letters	Lower-case letters	Letter names	Capital letters	Lower-case letters	Letter names	Capital letters	Lower-case letters	Letter names
А	а	а	Л	л	эль	Ч	ч	че
Б	б	бэ	М	м	эм	Ш	ш	ша
В	в	вэ	Н	н	эн	Щ	щ	ща
Г	г	гэ	О	о	о	Ъ	ъ	твёрдый знак
Д	д	дэ	П	п	пэ			
Е	е	е	Р	р	эр	Ы	ы	ы
Ё	ё	ё	С	с	эс	Ь	ь	мягкий знак
Ж	ж	жэ	Т	т	тэ			
З	з	зэ	У	у	у	Э	э	э
И	и	и	Ф	ф	эф	Ю	ю	ю
Й	й	и кра́ткое	Х	х	ха	Я	я	я
К	к	ка	Ц	ц	цэ			

Abbreviations

a.	accusative	geom.	geometry	phot.	photography
abbr.	abbreviation (of)	gram.	grammar	phys.	physics
abs.	absolute			pl.	plural
adj., adjs.	adjective(s)	hist.	historical	poet.	poetical
adv., advs.	adverb(s)	hort.	horticulture	pol.	political
aeron.	aeronautics			poss.	possessive
agric.	agricultural	i.	instrumental;	pred.	predicate;
anat.	anatomy		intransitive		predicative
approx.	approximate(ly)	imper.	imperative	pref.	prefix
archaeol.	archaeology	impers.	impersonal	prep.	preposition
astron.	astronomy	impf.	imperfective	pres.	present (tense)
attr.	attributive	indecl.	indeclinable	print.	printing
aux.	auxiliary	indef.	indefinite	pron., prons.	pronoun(s)
		indet.	indeterminate	propr.	proprietary term
bibl.	biblical	inf.	infinitive	psych.	psychology
biol.	biology	int.	interjection		
bot.	botany	interrog.	interrogative	rail.	railway
				refl.	reflexive
c.g.	common gender	journ.	journalism	rel.	relative
chem.	chemistry			relig.	religion;
cin.	cinema(tography)	leg.	legal		religious
coll.	colloquial	ling.	linguistics	Russ.	Russian
collect.	collective(ly)	liter.	literary		
comb.	combination	loc.	locative	sb.	substantive
comm.	commerce			sg.	singular
comp.	comparative	m.	masculine	sl.	slang
comput.	computing	math.	mathematics	s.o.	someone
conj., conjs.	conjunction(s)	med.	medicine	sth.	something
cul.	culinary	meteor.	meteorology	superl.	superlative
		mil.	military		
d.	dative	min.	mineralogy	t.	transitive
def.	definite	mus.	music	tech.	technical
det.	determinate	myth.	mythology	theatr.	theatre
dim.	diminutive			theol.	theology
dipl.	diplomacy	n.	noun	trig.	trigonometry
		naut.	nautical		
eccl.	ecclesiastical	neg.	negative	univ.	university
econ.	economics	nn.	nouns	usu.	usually
elec.	electrical	nom.	nominative		
emph.	emphatic	nt.	neuter	v.	verb
esp.	especially			var.	various
etc.	etcetera	o.s.	oneself	v.aux	auxiliary verb
				vbl.	verbal
f.	feminine	p.	prepositional	vet.	veterinary
fig.	figurative	parl.	parliamentary	v.i.	intransitive verb
fut.	future (tense)	part.	particle	voc.	vocative
		pej.	pejorative	v.t.	transitive verb
g.	genitive	pers.	person	vv.	verbs
geog.	geography	pf.	perfective		
geol.	geology	phon.	phonetics	zool.	zoology

Russian–English dictionary

A

A *abbr.* (*of* **ампе́р**) amp, ampere.
a *nt.indecl.* the letter **a**.
a *conj.* and, but; **a (не) то́** or else, otherwise.
a *part.* eh?
a *int.* oh, ah.
абажу́р, -а lampshade.
абба́т, -a abbot; abbé. **аббати́са, -ы** abbess. **абба́тство, -a** abbey.
аббревиату́ра, -ы abbreviation; acronym.
абза́ц, -a indention; paragraph; **сде́лать ~** indent.
абонеме́нт, -a subscription, season ticket; **сверх ~a** extra. **абоне́нт, -a** subscriber; (*library*) borrower, reader; (*theatre etc.*) season-ticket holder. **абони́ровать, -рую** *impf. & pf.* subscribe for, subscribe to, take a (season-)ticket for; **~ся** subscribe, take out a subscription, be a subscriber.
абориге́н, -a aboriginal, native. **абориге́нный** aboriginal, native.
або́рт, -a abortion; abort, failure, cancellation; **подпо́льный ~** backstreet abortion; **сде́лать ~** have an abortion. **аборти́вный** abortive; causing abortion.
абрико́с, -a apricot.
а́брис, -a outline, contour.
абсолю́т, -a absolute. **абсолю́тно** *adv.* absolutely, utterly. **абсолю́тный** absolute; utter; **~ слух** perfect pitch.
абсу́рд, -a absurdity; the absurd. **абсу́рдный** absurd.
аванга́рд, -a advanced guard, van; vanguard; avant-garde. **авангарди́зм, -a** avant-gardism. **авангарди́ст, -a** avant-gardist. **авангарди́стский** avant-garde. **аванза́л, -a** anteroom. **аванпо́ст, -a** outpost; forward position.
ава́нс, -a advance, advance payment; *pl.* advances, overtures. **аванси́ровать, -рую** *impf. & pf.* advance. **ава́нсом** *adv.* in advance, on account.
авансце́на, -ы proscenium.
авантю́ра, -ы adventure; venture; escapade; shady, risky, or speculative enterprise. **авантюри́зм, -a** adventurism. **авантюри́ст, -a** adventurer. **авантюри́стка, -и** adventuress; (*sl.*) gold-digger. **авантю́рный** adventurous; adventure, of adventure.
авари́йно-спаса́тельный (emergency-)rescue, life-saving. **авари́йный** accident, breakdown, crash; emergency; spare; **~ сигна́л** distress signal. **ава́рия, -и** accident, crash, wreck; breakdown; damage; loss; **потерпе́ть ава́рию** have an accident.
а́вгуст, -a August.
а́виа *abbr.* (*of* **авиапо́чтой**) '(by) airmail'.
авиа... *abbr.* (*of* **авиацио́нный**) *in comb.* air-, aero-; aircraft; aviation. **авиабиле́т, -a** air-ticket. **~деса́нт, -a** airborne assault landing; airborne assault force. **~деса́нтник, -a** paratrooper. **~диспе́тчер, -a** air-traffic controller. **~каскадёр, -a** stunt flyer. **~катастро́фа, -ы** air crash. **~компа́ния, -и** airline. **~ли́ния, -и** air-route, airway. **~но́сец, -сца** aircraft carrier. **~пассажи́р, -a** airline passenger. **~письмо́, -а́;** *pl.* **-а, -сем** airmail letter; aerogram(me). **~по́чта, -ы** airmail. **~разве́дка, -и** air reconnaissance. **~спо́рт, -a** aerial sports. **~съёмка, -и** aerial survey.
авиацио́нно-косми́ческий aerospace. **авиацио́нный** aviation; flying; aircraft. **авиа́ция, -и** aviation; flying; aircraft; air-force.
авока́до *nt.indecl.* avocado (*tree*).
аво́сь *adv.* perhaps, maybe; **на ~** at random, on the off-chance. **аво́ська, -и** (*string*) shopping-bag.
авра́л, -a a work involving all hands; emergency; rush job; *int.* all hands on deck! all hands to the pump! **авра́льный** rush, emergency.
австрали́ец, -и́йца, австрали́йка, -и Australian. **австрали́йский** Australian. **Австра́лия, -и** Australia.
австри́ец, -и́йца, австри́йка, -и Austrian. **австри́йский** Austrian. **А́встрия, -и** Austria.
авто... *in comb.* self-; auto-; automatic; motor-; bus. **автоава́рия, -и** road, traffic accident. **~а́тлас, -a** road atlas. **~ба́за, -ы** motor-transport depot. **~биогра́фия, -и** autobiography. **автобус, -a** bus; coach. **~вокза́л, -a** bus, coach station. **~во́р, -a** car thief. **~го́нщик, -a** racing-driver. **~гра́ф, -a** autograph. **~да́ча, -и** mobile home, caravan, trailer. **~доро́га, -и** road; highway. **~запра́вочн|ый; ~ая ста́нция** petrol station. **~запра́вщик, -a** petrol tanker. **~ка́р, -a** motor trolley. **~каскадёр, -a** stunt driver. **~катастро́фа, -ы** road, traffic accident. **~кла́в, -a** autoclave. **~коло́нка, -и** petrol pump. **~коло́нна, -ы** motorcade; convoy. **~корри́дда, -ы** stock-car race; stock-car racing. **~кра́т, -a** autocrat. **~крати́ческий**

autocratic. ~лиха́ч, -а́ reckless driver, road-hog. ~магази́н, -а car dealer's, motorcar showroom. ~магистра́ль, -и (motor) high-way; скоростна́я ~ expressway. ~маши́на, -ы motor vehicle. ~мотодро́м, -а race-track. ~но́мия, -и autonomy. ~но́мный autonomous; self-contained. ~отве́тчик, -а answerphone. ~павильо́н, -а bus shelter. ~пило́т, -а automatic pilot. ~портре́т, -а self-portrait. ~прице́п, -а trailer, caravan; жило́й ~ camper, mobile home. ~ра́лли nt.indecl. (car) rally. ~ралли́ст, -а rallyist, rally driver. ~ру́чка, -и fountain-pen. ~спо́рт, -а motor sports. ~ста́нция, -и bus, coach station. ~сто́п, -а automatic brakes; hitch-hiking; hitch-hiking permit. ~стоя́нка, -и car park. ~стра́да, -ы motorway. ~суф-лёр, -а Autocue (propr.), teleprompter. ~трюка́ч, -а́ stunt driver. ~шко́ла, -ы driv-ing school.

автома́т, -а slot-machine; automatic device, weapon, etc.; sub-machine gun; robot; au-tomaton; де́нежный ~ cash dispenser; игро-во́й ~ slot machine; парко́вочный ~ park-ing meter; стира́льный ~ washing machine; суши́льный ~ dryer; (телефо́н-)~ dial tel-ephone, automatic telephone; public call-box. автоматиза́ция, -и automation. автоматизи́ровать, -рую impf. & pf. automate; make automatic; ~ся become automatic. автома-ти́ческий, автомати́чный, автома́тный automatic.

а́втор, -а author; composer, producer, inven-tor; (fig.) architect; ~ го́ла scorer; ~ предло-же́ния, ~ резолю́ции mover of a resolution. авториза́ция, -и authorization. авторизо́-ванный authorized. авторизова́ть, -зу́ю pf. & impf. authorize.

авторитари́зм, -а authoritarianism. автори-те́т, -а authority; prestige. авторите́тный authoritative.

а́вторск|ий author's; ~ий гонора́р royalty; ~ое пра́во copyright; «~ие права́ заяв-лены» 'all rights reserved'; ~ие sb., pl. roy-alties. а́вторско-правово́й copyright. а́в-торство, -а authorship.

ага́ int. ah; aha.

аге́нт, -а agent; attaché. аге́нтство, -а agency; ~ печа́ти news agency; бракопо-сре́дническое ~ marriage bureau. аген-ту́ра, -ы secret service; (network of) agents.

агит... abbr. (of агитацио́нный) in comb. agitation, campaign. агитпро́п, -а agitation and propaganda section. ~пункт, -а abbr. agitation centre; committee-rooms.

агита́тор, -а agitator, propagandist; canvasser, electioneer. агитацио́нный propaganda; campaign. агита́ция, -и propaganda, agita-tion; campaign; предвы́борная ~ election-eering. агити́ровать, -рую impf. (pf. с~) agitate, campaign; electioneer; (try to) per-suade, win over. аги́тка, -и piece of propa-ganda.

агонизи́ровать, -рую impf. & pf. be in the throes of death. аго́ния, -и agony of death, death-pangs.

агрега́т, -а aggregate; assembly, unit, outfit, set.

агресси́вность, -и aggression, aggressive-ness. агресси́вный aggressive. агре́ссия, -и (pol.) aggression. агре́ссор, -а aggressor.

агроло́гия, -и agrology, soil science.

агроно́м, -а, -но́мша, -и agronomist. агро-но́мия, -и agriculture. агроте́хник, -а agri-cultural technician. агроте́хника, -и agri-cultural technology.

ад, -а, loc. -у́ hell.

адвока́т, -а lawyer, advocate. адвокату́ра, -ы legal profession; lawyers.

аде́пт, -а adherent, follower, disciple.

адида́ски, -сок pl. (coll.) trainers.

администрати́вный administrative. адми-нистра́тор, -а administrator, manager. ад-министра́торская sb. (hotel) reception. ад-министра́ция, -и administration; manage-ment. администри́рование, -я bureauc-racy, red tape. администри́ровать, -рую impf. act as administrator or manager (of); send into exile.

адмира́л, -а admiral; (zool.) Red Admiral. адмиралте́йский Admiralty. адмирал-те́йство, -а Admiralty; naval dockyard. ад-мира́льский admiral's; flag. адмира́льша, -и admiral's wife.

а́дов adj. infernal, diabolical.

а́дрес, -а; pl. -а́, -о́в address; не по ~у to the wrong address. адреса́нт, -а sender. адре-са́т, -а addressee. а́дресн|ый address; ~ая кни́га directory; ~ый стол address bureau. адресова́ть, -су́ю impf. & pf. address, send; ~ся address o.s.

а́дский infernal, hellish, fiendish, devilish.

адъю́нкт, -а service student.

адъюта́нт, -а aide-de-camp; ста́рший ~ ad-jutant.

ажу́р, -а openwork; up-to-date; в ~е in or-der, (all) correct. ажу́рн|ый openwork; deli-cate, lacy; ~ая рабо́та openwork; tracery.

аза́рт, -а heat; excitement; fervour, ardour, passion. аза́ртн|ый reckless, venture-some; heated; excitable; ~ая игра́ game of chance.

а́збука, -и alphabet; ABC; дакти́льная ~ sign language; ~ Мо́рзе Morse code. а́збуч-ный alphabetical; elementary.

Азербайджа́н, -а Azerbaijan.

азиа́т, -а, азиа́тка, -и Asian. азиа́тский Asian. А́зия, -и Asia.

азо́т, -а nitrogen; за́кись ~а nitrous oxide.

а́ист, -а stork.

ай int. oh; oo; ай да молоде́ц! well done! good lad!

айва́, -ы quince, quinces.

айда́ int. come on! let's go!

акаде́мик, -а Academician; member or student of an academy. академи́ческий,

академи́чный academic. **акаде́мия, -и** academy.

аквала́нг, -а aqualung. **аквалангист, -а** skin-diver. **акварелист, -а** water-colour painter. **акваре́ль, -и** water-colour, water-colours. **аква́риум, -а** aquarium. **аквариумист, -а** aquarist. **акведу́к, -а** aqueduct.

аккомпанеме́нт, -а accompaniment; **под ~+g.** to the accompaniment of. **аккомпаниа́тор, -а, -а́торша, -и** accompanist. **аккомпани́ровать, -рую** *impf.+d.* accompany.

акко́рд, -а a chord; **взять ~** strike a chord.

акко́рдн|ый agreed, by agreement; **~ая рабо́та** piece-work.

аккредитив, -а a letter of credit; credentials. **аккредитова́ть, -тую** *impf. & pf.* accredit.

аккумуля́ция, -и accumulation.

аккура́тный accurate, neat, careful; punctual; exact, thorough.

акри́л, -а acrylic. **акри́ловый** acrylic.

аксельба́нт, -а aiguillette.

аксессуа́р, -а accessory; (stage) property.

аксио́ма, -ы axiom; truism.

акт, -а act; deed, document; **обвини́тельный ~** indictment.

актёр, -а actor. **актёрский** actor's. **актёрство, -а** acting; posing.

актив, -а activists; assets; advantages. **активиза́ция, -и** stirring up, making (more) active. **активизи́ровать, -рую** *impf. & pf.* make (more) active, stir up, arouse. **активный** active; **~ бала́нс** favourable balance.

акти́ровать, -рую *impf. & pf.* (*pf. also* **с~**) register, record, presence or absence of; (*sl.*) write off. **актиро́вка, -и** (*sl.*) writing off, write-off; cancellation.

а́ктов|ый; **~ая бума́га** official document, stamped paper; **~ый зал** assembly hall.

актри́са, -ы actress.

актуа́льный actual; up-to-date, topical, urgent.

аку́ла, -ы shark.

акупункту́ра, -ы acupuncture.

аку́стика, -и acoustics. **акусти́ческий** acoustic.

акуше́р, -а obstetrician. **акуше́рка, -и** midwife. **акуше́рский** obstetric, obstetrical. **акуше́рство, -а** obstetrics; midwifery.

акце́нт, -а accent, stress. **акценти́ровать, -рую** *impf. & pf.* accent; accentuate.

акци́з, -а duty; Excise. **акци́зный** excise.

акционе́р, -а shareholder; stockholder. **акционе́рн|ый** joint-stock; **~ое о́бщество** joint-stock company. **а́кция[1], -и** share; *pl.* stock. **а́кция[2], -и** action.

але́ть, -е́ет *impf.* (*pf.* **за~**) redden, flush; blush; show red.

алка́ш, -а́ (*sl.*) boozer.

алкоголи́зм, -а alcoholism. **алкого́лик, -а** alcoholic; drunkard. **алкоголи́ческий** alcoholic. **алкого́ль, -я** *m.* alcohol. **алкого́льный** alcoholic.

аллерге́н, -а allergen. **алле́ргик, -а** allergy sufferer. **аллерги́я, -и** allergy.

алле́я, -и avenue; path, walk.

алло́ *int.* hello!

аллю́р, -а pace, gait.

алма́з, -а diamond. **алма́зный** diamond; of diamonds.

алта́рь, -я́ *m.* altar; chancel, sanctuary.

алфави́т, -а alphabet. **алфави́тный** alphabetical; **~ указа́тель** index.

а́лчный greedy, grasping.

а́лый scarlet.

альбино́с, -а, альбино́ска, -и albino.

альбо́м, -а album; sketch-book.

альмана́х, -а literary miscellany; almanac.

альпи́йск|ий Alpine; **~ие луга́** alps, mountain meadows. **альпина́рий, -я** rock garden. **альпини́зм, -а** mountaineering. **альпини́ст, -а, альпини́стка, -и** (mountain) climber.

А́льпы, Альп *pl.* the Alps.

альт, -а́; *pl.* **-ы́** alto, contralto; viola. **альтера́ция, -и** change in pitch; **зна́ки альтера́ции** accidentals. **альти́ст, -а, -и́стка, -и** viola-player. **альто́вый** alto, contralto; viola.

альтруи́зм, -а altruism. **альтруи́ст, -а** altruist. **альтруисти́ческий** altruistic.

алья́нс, -а alliance.

алюми́ниевый aluminium. **алюми́ний, -я** aluminium.

Аля́ска, -и Alaska.

аляфурше́т, -а buffet.

Амазо́нка, -и the Amazon (*river*); **а~, -и** Amazon; horsewoman; riding-habit.

а́мба *f.indecl.* (*sl.*) finish, curtains, kibosh.

амба́р, -а barn; storehouse, warehouse. **амба́рный** barn.

амби́ция, -и pride; arrogance. **амбицио́зный** vainglorious, conceited; self-loving, egoistic.

а́мбра, -ы ambergris; scent, perfume, fragrance. **амбре́** *nt.indecl.* scent, perfume.

амбулато́рия, -и out-patients' department; surgery. **амбулато́рный**; **~ больно́й** out-patient.

Аме́рика, -и America. **америка́нец, -нца, америка́нка, -и** American. **америка́нск|ий** American; US; **~ие го́ры** Big Dipper, switchback; **~ий замо́к** Yale (*propr.*) lock; **~ий оре́х** Brazil nut.

амети́ст, -а amethyst.

ами́нь, -я *m.* amen; finis, finish, kibosh.

аммиа́к, -а ammonia. **аммиа́чный** ammonia, ammoniac, ammoniacal. **аммо́ний, -я** ammonium.

амнисти́ровать, -рую *impf. & pf.* amnesty. **амни́стия, -и** amnesty.

амора́льный amoral; immoral.

амортиза́тор, -а shock-absorber. **амортиза́ция, -и** depreciation, wear and tear; shock-absorption. **амортизи́ровать, -рую** *impf. & pf.* amortize; damp, make shock-proof.

ампе́р, -а; *g.pl.* **ампе́р** ampere.

ампи́р, -а Empire style. **ампи́рный** Empire.

амплуа *nt.indecl.* type; role; occupation, job.

ампутация, -и amputation. **ампутировать, -ую** *impf. & pf.* amputate.

амур, -а cupid; *pl.* amours, love-affairs. **амурный** love.

амфетамин, -а amphetamine.

амфитеатр, -а amphitheatre; circle.

АН *abbr.* (*of* **Академия Наук**) Academy of Sciences.

анализ, -а analysis; ~ **крови** blood test. **анализировать, -рую** *impf. & pf.* analyse. **аналитик, -а** analyst. **аналитический** analytical.

аналогичный analogous. **аналоги|я, -и** analogy; **по ~и** (с+*i.*) by analogy (with).

аналой, -я lectern.

ананас, -а pineapple. **ананасный, ананасовый** pineapple.

анархист, -а, -истка, -и anarchist. **анархический** anarchic, anarchical. **анархия, -и** anarchy.

анатомический anatomic(al). **анатомия, -и** anatomy.

анаша, -и (*sl.*) pot, hash. **анашист, -а** (*sl.*) pot smoker; hash-head.

ангар, -а hangar.

ангел, -а angel; **день ~а** name day. **ангельский** angels'; angelic.

ангина, -ы quinsy, tonsillitis, ulcerated sore throat.

англизировать, -рую *impf. & pf.* anglicize. **английск|ий** English; ~**ая булавка** safety-pin; ~**ая соль** Epsom salts; ~**ий рожок** cor anglais. **англикан|ец, -нца, англиканка, -нки** Anglican. **англицизм, -а** Anglicism, English loan-word. **англичанин, -а;** *pl.* **-чане, -чан** Englishman. **англичанка, -и** Englishwoman. **Англия, -и** England, Britain. **англоязычный** English-speaking, anglophone.

андреевский St. Andrew's.

Анды, Анд *pl.* the Andes.

анекдот, -а anecdote, story; funny thing. **анекдотический** anecdotal; unlikely; funny, comical. **анекдотичный** improbable; odd; amusing, funny.

анемический, анемичный anaemic. **анеми|я, -и** anaemia.

анестезиолог, -а anaesthetist. **анестезировать, -рую** *impf. & pf.* anaesthetize. **анестезирующ|ий** anaesthetizing, anaesthetic; ~**ее средство** anaesthetic. **анестезия, -и** anaesthesia.

анис, -а anise; variety of apple. **анисов|ый; ~ое семя** aniseed.

анкета, -ы questionnaire, (application-)form; (opinion) poll, inquiry, survey.

аннотация, -и annotation; blurb.

аннулировать, -рую *impf. & pf.* annul, nullify; cancel, repeal, revoke, abolish. **аннуляция, -и** annulment, nullification; cancellation, revocation, repeal.

аноним, -а anonymous author, work, letter. **анонимка, -и** poison-pen letter. **анонимный** anonymous. **анонимщик, -а** poison-pen writer.

анонс, -а announcement, notice; advertisement. **анонсировать, -рую** *impf. & pf.* announce, make an announcement.

анорекси|я, -и anorexia.

ансамбль, -я *m.* ensemble; company, troupe.

Антарктида, -ы Antarctica.

Антарктика, -и the Antarctic.

антенна, -ы antenna; aerial.

анти... *in comb.* anti-. **антиалкогольный** temperance. ~**вещество, -а** anti-matter. ~**детонатор, -а** anti-knock (compound). ~**детонационный** anti-knock. ~**патия, -и** antipathy. ~**пригарный** non-stick. ~**ракета, -ы** anti-missile missile. ~**ракетчик, -а** a ban-the-bomb campaigner. ~**санитарный** insanitary. ~**септик, -а** antiseptic; preservative. ~**септический** antiseptic. ~**тело, -а;** *pl.* **-а** antibody. ~**фриз, -а** antifreeze. ~**человеческий** inhuman.

антологи|я, -и anthology.

антракт, -а interval; entr'acte.

антрекот, -а entrecôte, steak.

антрепренёр, -а impresario.

антресол|и, -ей *pl.* mezzanine; attic floor; attics; gallery.

антрополог, -а anthropologist. **антропологический** anthropological. **антропология, -и** anthropology.

антропофаг, -а cannibal. **антропофагия, -и** cannibalism.

антураж, -а surroundings, environment; entourage, associates.

анфас *adv.* full face.

анфилада, -ы suite.

анчоус, -а anchovy.

аншлаг, -а 'house full' notice; **пройти с ~ом** play to full houses.

апартеид, -а apartheid.

апатичный apathetic. **апатия, -и** apathy.

апеллировать, -рую *impf. & pf.* appeal. **апелляционный;** ~ **суд** Court of Appeal. **апелляция, -и** appeal.

апельсин, -а orange; orange-tree. **апельсинный, апельсиновый** orange; **апельсинное варенье** (orange) marmalade.

аперитив, -а apéritif.

аппликé *indecl. adj.* plated; appliqué.

аплодировать, -рую *impf.+d.* **аплодисмент, -а** clap; *pl.* applause; **под ~ы** to applause.

АПН *abbr.* (*of* **Агентство печати «Новости»**) APN, Novosti Press Agency.

аполитизм, -а political apathy. **аполитичный** politically apathetic.

апостол, -а apostle; Acts and Epistles. **апостольский** apostolic.

аппара́т, -a apparatus, apparat; machinery, organs; staff, establishment; camera; ка́ссовый ~ cash register; копирова́льный ~ photocopier; ку́хонный ~ food processor; слухово́й ~ hearing aid; факси́ми́льный a. fax (machine). аппарату́ра, -ы apparatus, gear; (*comput.*) hardware. аппара́тчик, -a operator; apparatchnik, functionary.

аппе́ндикс, -a appendix. аппендици́т, -a appendicitis.

аппликату́ра, -ы fingering. апплика́ция, -и appliqué, appliqué-work. аппликацио́нный appliqué.

апре́ль, -я *m.* April; пе́рвое ~я April Fool's Day; c пе́рвым ~я! April Fool! апре́льский April.

апроба́ция, -и approval. апроби́ровать, -рую *impf. & pf.* approve.

апси́да, -ы apse.

апте́ка, -и (dispensing) chemist's; medicine chest; first-aid kit. апте́карский chemist's; pharmaceutical. апте́карь, -я *m.* chemist, pharmacist. апте́карша, -и pharmacist; chemist's wife. апте́чка, -и medicine chest; first-aid kit. апте́чный medicine, drug.

апчхи́ *int.* atishoo!

ара́б, -a, ара́бка, -и Arab. ара́бский Arab, Arabian, Arabic; arabic. арави́йский Arabian.

Ара́вия, -и Arabia.

ара́п, -a Negro; trickster, swindler.

ара́пник, -a (*huntsman's*) whip.

ара́хис, -a peanut, groundnut. ара́хисов|ый peanut, groundnut; ~ая па́ста peanut butter.

арба́, -ы́; *pl.* -ы (bullock-)cart.

арби́тр, -a arbitrator. арбитра́ж, -a arbitration.

арбу́з, -a water-melon.

арго́ *nt.indecl.* argot, slang. арготи́зм, -a slang expression. аргот и́ческий slang.

аргуме́нт, -a argument. аргумента́ция, -и reasoning; arguments. аргументи́ровать, -рую *impf. & pf.* argue, (try to) prove.

аре́на, -ы arena, ring.

аре́нда, -ы lease; rent; в аре́нду on lease. аренда́тор, -a leaseholder, tenant. арендова́ть, -ду́ю *impf. & pf.* lease, take or hold on lease.

аре́ст, -a arrest; seizure; sequestration. аресто́ант, -a, -а́нтка, -и prisoner. аресто́антская *sb.* lock-up, cells. арестова́ть, -ту́ю *pf.*, аресто́вывать, -аю *impf.* arrest; seize, sequestrate.

арифме́тика, -и arithmetic. арифмети́ческий arithmetical. арифмо́граф, -a, арифмо́метр, -a calculating machine.

а́рка, -и arch. арка́да, -ы arcade.

арка́н, -a lasso. арка́нить, -ню *impf.* (*pf.* за~) lasso.

А́рктика, -и the Arctic.

армади́л, -a armadillo.

армату́ра, -ы fittings, accessories; equipment;

reinforcement; armature; trophy (of arms). армату́рщик, -a fitter.

арме́ец, -е́йца soldier; *pl.* Soviet Army Sports-Club team. арме́йский army.

Арме́ния, -и Armenia.

а́рмия, -и army.

армя́к, -а́ peasant's heavy overcoat.

армяни́н, -a; *pl.* -я́не, -я́н, армя́нка, -и Armenian. армя́нский Armenian.

арома́т, -a scent, odour, aroma; fragrance; bouquet. ароматиза́тор, -a flavouring. аромати́ческий, аромати́чный, арома́тный aromatic, fragrant.

а́рочный arched, vaulted.

арсена́л, -a arsenal.

арта́читься, -чусь *impf.* jib, be restive; dig one's heels in; be pigheaded, be obstinate.

арте́ль, -и artel. арте́льный of an artel; common, collective. арте́льщик, -a, арте́льщица, -ы member, leader, of an artel.

артериа́льный arterial. арте́рия, -и artery.

артиллери́йский artillery, ordnance. артилле́рия, -и artillery.

арти́ст, -a, -и́стка, -и artiste, artist, performer; expert. артисти́зм, -a artistry. артисти́ческая *sb.* dressing-room, greenroom, artists' room. артисти́ческий artistic.

а́рфа, -ы harp. арфи́ст, -a, -и́стка, -и harpist.

археоло́г, -a archaeologist. археологи́ческий archaeological. археоло́гия, -и archaeology.

архи́в, -a archives. архива́риус, -a, архиви́ст, -a archivist. архи́вный archive, archival.

архидья́кон, -a archdeacon. архиепи́скоп, -a archbishop. архиере́й, -я bishop.

архите́ктор, -a architect. архитекту́ра, -ы architecture. архитекту́рный architectural.

арши́н, -a; *g.pl.* -ши́н(ов) arshin (*old Russ. measurement, equivalent to approx. 71 cm.*); arshin-rule; как бу́дто ~ проглоти́л bolt upright, as stiff as a poker.

асе́ссор, -a; колле́жский ~ Collegiate Assessor (*8th grade: see* чин).

аске́т, -a ascetic. аскети́зм, -a asceticism. аскети́ческий ascetic.

а́спид[1], -a an asp; viper.

а́спид[2], -a slate. а́спидн|ый; ~ая доска́ slate.

аспира́нт, -a, -а́нтка, -и post-graduate student. аспиранту́ра, -ы post-graduate course; post-graduate students.

ассигна́ция, -и banknote.

ассамбле́я, -и assembly; ball.

ассисте́нт, -a assistant; junior lecturer, research assistant. ассисти́ровать, -рую *impf.+d.* assist.

ассоциа́ция, -и association. ассоции́ровать, -рую *impf. & pf.* associate.

АССР *abbr.* (*of* автоно́мная сове́тская социалисти́ческая республика) ASSR, Autonomous Soviet Socialist Republic.

астро... *in comb.* astro-. **астрона́вт**, -a astronaut. **~на́втика**, -и space-travel. **~но́м**, -a astronomer. **~номи́ческий** astronomical. **~но́мия**, -и astronomy.

ась *int.* eh?

атама́н, -a ataman; Cossack chieftain, commander; (gang-)leader, robber chieftain.

ателье́ *nt.indecl.* studio; atelier; **портно́вское ~** tailor's shop; **телевизио́нное ~** TV repair workshop.

Атланти́ческий; ~ океа́н the Atlantic (Ocean).

а́тлас¹, -a atlas.

атла́с², -a satin. **атла́систый, атла́сный** satin; like satin, satiny.

атле́т, -a athlete; acrobat; (*circus*) strongman. **атлети́зм**, -a athleticism; body-building. **атле́тика**, -и athletics; **лёгкая ~** track and field sports; **тяжёлая ~** weight-lifting, boxing, wrestling. **атлети́ческий** athletic.

атмосфе́ра, -ы atmosphere. **атмосфери́ческий, атмосфе́рный** atmospheric; **атмосфе́рные оса́дки** rainfall.

а́том, -a atom. **атоми́стика**, -и atomics; atomic theory. **атомисти́ческий** atomistic. **а́томник**, -a atomic scientist. **а́томный** atomic.

аттеста́т, -a testimonial, recommendation, reference; certificate; pedigree. **аттеста́ция**, -и attestation; testimonial; confidential report. **аттестова́ть**, -ту́ю *impf. & pf.* attest; recommend.

аттракцио́н, -a sideshow; **парк ~ов** amusement park.

ау́ *int.* halloo, cooee.

аудито́рия, -и auditorium, lecture-room; audience.

ау́кать(ся, -аю(сь *impf.* **ау́кнуть(ся**, -ну(сь *pf.* halloo, cooee.

аукцио́н, -a auction. **аукционе́р**, -a bidder (*at auction*). **аукциони́ст**, -a auctioneer. **аукцио́нный** auction; **~ зал** auction room.

аул, -a aul, Caucasian or Central Asian village.

аутбо́рт, -a outboard motor.

ауто́псия, -и autopsy, post-mortem.

афга́нец, -нца Afghan, Afghani; «**~**» (*Soviet*) Afghan war vet(eran).

афи́нский Athenian.

Афи́ны, Афи́н *pl.* Athens. **афи́нянин**, -a; *pl.* -яне, **афи́нянка**, -и Athenian.

афи́ша, -и placard, poster. **афиши́ровать**, -рую *impf. & pf.* parade, advertise; **~ся** be exhibitionist, seek the limelight.

афори́зм, -a aphorism. **афористи́ческий, афористи́чный** aphoristic.

А́фрика, -и Africa. **африка́анс**, -a Afrikaans. **африка́нер**, -a Afrikaner. **африка́нец**, -нца, **африка́нка**, -и African. **африка́нский** African.

аффе́кт, -a fit of passion, rage, nervous excitement; temporary insanity.

ах *int.* ah, oh. **а́хи**, -ов; *pl.* ahs, ohs. **а́ханье**, -я sighing; exclamations. **а́хать**, -аю *impf.* (*pf.* **а́хнуть**) sigh; exclaim; gasp.

ахине́я, -и nonsense, rubbish; **нести́ ахине́ю** talk nonsense.

а́хнуть, -ну *pf.* (*impf.* **а́хать**) gasp, exclaim; bang; strike.

аэро... *in comb.* aero-, air-, aerial. **аэро́бика**, -и aerobics. **~би́ст**, -a, **~би́стка**, -и aerobicist. **аэро́б|ый** aerobic; **~ая гимна́стика** aerobics, aerobic exercises. **аэровокза́л**, -a air terminal, airport building. **~дро́м**, -a aerodrome, air-field. **~зо́ль**, -я *m.* aerosol, spray. **~на́вт**, -a aeronaut; balloonist. **~по́рт**, -a airport. **~по́чта**, -и air-mail. **~сни́мок**, -мка aerial photograph. **~ста́т**, -a balloon. **~съёмка**, -и aerial photography.

аэрокосми́ческий aerospace.

АЭС *abbr.* (*of* **а́томная электроста́нция**) atomic power station.

аятолла́, -ы́ ayatollah.

а/я *abbr.* (*of* **абонеме́нтный я́щик**) PO, Post Office box.

Б

б *letter*: *see* бэ

б *part.*: *see* бы

б. *abbr.* (*of* **бы́вший**) former, ex-, one-time.

ба *int.* expressing surprise.

ба́ба, -ы (*married*) peasant woman; woman; **ка́менная ~** ancient stone image; **снежная ~** snowman. **баб|ий**; **~ье ле́то** Indian summer; **~ьи ска́зки** old wives' tales. **ба́бка¹**, -и grandmother; (**повива́льная**) **~** midwife.

ба́бка², -и knucklebone; pastern; **игра́ть в ба́бки** play at knucklebones.

ба́бочка, -и butterfly; **ночна́я ~** moth.

ба́бушка, -и grandmother; granny.

бага́ж, -á luggage. **бага́жник**, -a carrier; luggage-rack, compartment; boot. **бага́жничек**, -чка glove compartment. **бага́жный** luggage; **~ ваго́н** luggage-van.

багрове́ть, -ею *impf.* (*pf.* **по~**) crimson, flush, go red. **багро́вый, багря́ный** crimson, purple.

бадминто́н, -a badminton. **бадминтони́ст**, -a badminton-player.

бадья́, -и́; *g.pl.* -де́й tub, bucket, pail.

ба́за, -ы base; centre; stock, stores; basis; **~ да́нных** database; **плаву́чая ~** factory ship.

база́р, -a market; fair; bazaar; row, din. **база́рный** market.

базировать, -рую *impf.* base; ~**ся** be based, rest (on).

байдарка, -и canoe; kayak. **байдарочник**, -а canoeist. **байдарочный** canoe.

байка[1], -и flannelette, flannel. **байковый** flannelette, flannel; ~ **платок** woollen shawl.

байка[2], -и fairy story, cock-and-bull story.

байт, -а (*comput.*) byte.

бак[1], -а tank, cistern; can, billy.

бак[2], -а forecastle, fo'c's'le.

бакалейный grocer's, grocery. **бакалейщик**, -а grocer. **бакалея**, -и groceries.

бакан, -а, **бакен**, -а buoy.

бакенбарды, -бард *pl.*, **бакены**, -ов *pl.* whiskers; side-whiskers. **баки**, бак *pl.* sideburns, (*short*) side-whiskers.

баклажан, -а; *g.pl.* -ов *or* -жан aubergine.

бактериальный, **бактерийный** bacterial. **бактериолог**, -а bacteriologist. **бактерия**, -и bacterium.

бал, -а, *loc.* -у́; *pl.* -ы́ dance, ball.

балаган, -а booth; side-show; popular show; farce, buffoonery. **балаганить**, -ню *impf.* play the fool. **балаганщик**, -а showman; clown, buffoon.

балалаечник, -а balalaika player. **балалайка**, -и balalaika.

баламут, -а trouble-maker. **баламутить**, -у́чу *impf.* (*pf.* вз~) stir up, trouble; disturb; upset.

баланда, -ы (*sl.*) watery soup, skilly, swill.

балансёр, -а rope-walker.

балансир, -а balance, balance-wheel. **балансировать**, -рую *impf.* (*pf.* с~) balance; keep one's balance.

балахон, -а loose overall; shapeless garment.

балбес, -а booby.

балдахин, -а canopy.

балерина, -ы ballerina. **балет**, -а ballet.

балка[1], -и beam, girder.

балка[2], -и ravine, gully.

балл, -а mark, number, point, degree; force; **высший** ~ top marks, an 'A'; **ветер в пять** ~**ов** wind force 5.

баллада, -ы ballad.

балласт, -а ballast; lumber.

баллон, -а container, carboy, cylinder; balloon tyre.

баллотировать, -рую *impf.* ballot, vote; put to the vote; ~**ся** stand, be a candidate (**в** *or* **на**+*a.* for). **баллотировка**, -и vote, ballot, poll; polling, voting.

балованный spoilt. **баловать**, -лую *impf.* (*pf.* из~) spoil; indulge, pamper; play about, play up; +*i.* play with, play at, amuse o.s. with; ~**ся** play about, get up to tricks; amuse o.s., play; +*i.* indulge in. **баловень**, -вня *m.* spoilt child; pet, favourite. **баловство**, -а́ spoiling, over-indulgence; pampering; monkey tricks, mischief.

балтийск|ий Б~**ое море** the Baltic (Sea).

бальза, -ы balsa(wood).

бальзам, -а balsam; balm; ~ **для волос** hair

conditioner. **бальзамировать**, -рую *impf.* (*pf.* на~) embalm.

бальный ball, dance.

балюстрада, -ы balustrade; banister. **балясина**, -ы baluster, banister. **балясы**; ~ **точить** jest, joke.

БАМ *abbr.* (*of* Байкало-Амурская (железнодорожная) магистраль) Baykal-Amur railway.

бамбук, -а bamboo. **бамбуков|ый** bamboo; ~**ое положение** awkward situation.

бан, -а, *loc.* -у́ (*sl.*) railway station.

банда, -ы band, gang.

бандаж, -а́ truss; belt, bandage; tyre.

бандероль, -и wrapper; printed matter, book-post.

бандит, -а bandit, brigand; gangster; **вооружённый** ~ armed robber. **бандитизм**, -а banditry, robbery; **воздушный** ~ air piracy.

банк, -а bank; **Всемирный** ~ World Bank.

банка[1], -и jar; tin.

банка[2], -и (sand-)bank, shoal.

банкет, -а banquet.

банкир, -а banker. **банкрот**, -а bankrupt.

бант, -а bow. **бантик**, -а bow; **губки** ~**ом** Cupid's bow. **бантов|ой**; ~**ая складка** box-pleat.

баня, -и bath, bath-house; **финская** ~ sauna.

бар, -а bar; snack-bar; **пивной** ~ pub.

барабан, -а drum. **барабанить**, -ню *impf.* drum, thump. **барабанн|ый** drum; ~**ая дробь** drum-roll; ~**ая перепонка** ear-drum. **барабанщик**, -а drummer.

барак, -а barrack; *pl.* hutments.

баран, -а ram; sheep. **бараний** sheep's; sheepskin; mutton. **баранина**, -ы mutton. **баранка**, -и baranka, ring-shaped roll; (steering-)wheel.

барахлить, -лю *impf.* pink, knock; talk rubbish.

барахло, -а́ old clothes, jumble; odds and ends; trash, junk; rubbish. **барахолка**, -и second-hand market, junk-stall.

барахтаться, -аюсь *impf.* flounder, wallow, thrash about.

барашек, -шка young ram; lamb; lambskin; wing nut; catkin; *pl.* white horses; fleecy clouds. **барашковый** lambskin.

баржа, -и *or* -и́; *g.pl.* барж(е́й) barge.

барин, -а; *pl.* -ре *or* -ры, бар barin; landowner; gentleman; master; sir.

барка, -и barge.

барочный baroque.

барс, -а ounce, snow-leopard.

барский gentleman's; lordly; grand. **барственный** lordly, grand, arrogant.

барсук, -а́ badger. **барсучий** badger; badger-skin.

бархан, -а sand-hill, dune.

бархат, -а (-у) velvet. **бархатистый** velvety. **бархатка**, -и velvet ribbon **бархатный** velvet; velvety.

барчо́нок, -нка; *pl.* -ча́та, -ча́т, барчу́к, -а́ barin's son; young master, young gentleman.

ба́рыня, -и barin's wife; lady; mistress; madam.

бары́ш, -а́ profit. бары́шник, -а dealer; buyer for re-sale; jobber; (ticket) speculator. бары́шничать, -аю *impf.* deal, speculate, job (+*i.* in).

ба́рышня, -и; *g.pl.* -шень barin's daughter; young lady, young mistress; miss.

барье́р, -а barrier; obstacle; bar; fence, jump, hurdle. барьери́ст, -а, -и́стка, -и hurdler. барье́рный hurdle; ∼ бег hurdle-race.

бас, -а; *pl.* -ы́ bass. баси́стый bass.

баскетбо́л, -а basket-ball. баскетболи́ст, -а, -и́стка, -и basket-ball player баскетбо́льный basket-ball. баске́тки, -ток *pl.* basketball boots.

баснопи́сец, -сца fabulist, writer of fables. басносло́вный mythical, legendary; fabulous. ба́сня, -и; *g.pl.* -сен fable; legend; fabrication.

басо́вый bass.

бассе́йн, -а basin; pool, pond; reservoir; swimming-pool; плеска́тельный ∼ paddling pool; каменноуго́льный ∼, у́гольный ∼ coal-field.

бастова́ть, -тую *impf.* be on strike.

батаре́ец, -е́йца gunner. батаре́йка, -и, батаре́я, -и battery; radiator.

бати́ст, -а (-у) batiste, cambric, lawn.

бато́н, -а long loaf; stick, bar. бато́нчик, -а stick, bar; шокола́дный ∼ bar of chocolate.

батра́к, -а́, батра́чка, -и farm-hand, farm-worker, farm labourer. батра́цкий farm, farm labourer's.

бату́т, -а trampoline. батути́ст, -а, бату́ти́стка, -и trampolinist.

ба́тька, -и *m.*, ба́тюшка, -и *m.*, ба́тя, -и *m.* father; my dear chap. ба́тюшки *int.* good gracious!

бах *int.* bang! ба́хать(ся, -аю(сь *impf. of* ба́хнуть(ся

бахва́л, -а boaster, braggart. бахва́льство, -а bragging, boasting.

ба́хнуть, -ну *pf.* (*impf.* ба́хать) bang; thump; ∼ся fall or bump heavily and noisily; let o.s. fall, plump down; ∼ся голово́й bang one's head.

бахрома́, -ы́ fringe. бахро́мчатый fringed.

бац *int.* bang! crack! ба́цать, -аю *impf.*, ба́цнуть, -ну *pf.* crack, bang, bash.

баци́лла, -ы bacillus. бациллоноси́тель, -я *m.* carrier.

ба́шенка, -и turret. ба́шенный tower, turret.

башка́, -и́ head. башкови́тый brainy.

ба́шли, -ей dosh, lolly.

башлы́к, -а́ hood.

башма́к, -а́ shoe; chock; под ∼ о́м у+*g.* under the thumb of.

ба́шня, -и; *g.pl.* -шен tower, turret.

баю́-ба́й, ба́юшки-баю́ *int.* hushabye, lullaby. баю́кать, -аю *impf.* (*pf.* у∼) lull, rock, sing to sleep.

бде́ние, -я vigil, wakefulness. бди́тельность, -и vigilance, watchfulness. бди́тельный vigilant, watchful.

бег, -а, *loc.* -у́; *pl.* -а́ run, running; double; race; оздорови́тельный ∼ jogging; *pl.* trotting-races. бе́гать, -аю *indet.* (*det.* бежа́ть) *impf.* run; move quickly.

бегемо́т, -а hippopotamus.

бегле́ц, -а́, бегля́нка, -и fugitive. бе́глость, -и speed, fluency, dexterity. бе́глый fugitive; quick, rapid, fluent; fleeting, cursory, passing; ∼ гла́сный fugitive vowel, fillvowel; *sb.* fugitive, runaway. бегови́к, -о́в *pl.* running shoes. бегово́й running; race; ∼ круг race-course, ring. бего́м *adv.* running, at a run, at the double. беготня́, -и́ running about; bustle. бе́гство, -а flight, hasty retreat; escape. бегу́н, -а́, бегу́нья, -и; *g.pl.* -ний runner.

беда́, -ы́; *pl.* -ы misfortune; calamity, disaster; trouble; ∼ в том, что the trouble is (that); ∼ как terribly, awfully; на беду́ unfortunately; не ∼ it doesn't matter; что за ∼! what does it matter? so what? бедне́ть, -е́ю *impf.* (*pf.* о∼) grow poor. бе́дность, -и poverty, the poor; у́ровень/поро́г бе́дности poverty line. бе́дный; -ден, -дна́, -дно poor; poverty-stricken. бедня́га, -и *m.*, бедня́жка, -и *c.g.* poor thing, poor creature. бедня́к, -а́, бедня́чка, -и poor peasant; poor man, poor woman. бедня́чество, -а poor peasants.

бе́дренный femoral, thigh-. бедро́, -а́; *pl.* бёдра, -дер thigh; hip; leg.

бе́дственный disastrous, calamitous. бе́дствие, -я disaster, calamity; райо́н бе́дствия disaster area. сигна́л бе́дствия distress signal. бе́дствовать, -твую *impf.* be in want, live in poverty.

бежа́ть, бегу́ *det.* (*indet.* бе́гать) *impf.* (*pf.* по∼) run; flow; fly; boil over; *impf. & pf.* escape. бе́женец, -нца, бе́женка, -и refugee.

без, безо *prep.*+*g.* without; in the absence of; minus, less, short of; ∼ вас in your absence; ∼ ма́лого almost, all but; ∼ пяти́ (мину́т) five (minutes) to; ∼ ума́ (от+*g.*) mad, crazy (about); ∼ че́тверти a quarter to.

без..., безъ..., бес... *in comb.* in-, un-; non-; -less. безава́рийный accident-free; without breakdowns. ∼алабе́рный disorderly, unsystematic; slovenly, careless. ∼алкого́льный non-alcoholic, soft. ∼апелляцио́нный without appeal; peremptory, categorical. ∼биле́тник, -а, -ница, -ы fare dodger; stowaway. ∼бо́жие, -я atheism, ∼бо́жный atheistic; irreligious, anti-religious; godless; shameless, scandalous, outrageous. ∼боле́зненный painless. ∼бра́чность, -и unmarried state, living in sin. ∼бра́чный celibate.

~бре́жный boundless. ~ве́рие, -я unbelief. ~ве́стный unknown; obscure. ~ве́тренный calm, windless. ~ви́нный guiltless, innocent. ~вку́сие, -я, ~вку́сица, -ы lack of taste; bad taste. ~вку́сный tasteless. ~вла́стие, -я anarchy. ~во́дный arid, waterless; anhydrous. ~возвра́тный irrevocable; irretrievable; irrecoverable. ~возме́здный free, gratis; unpaid. ~во́лие, -я weakness of will, lack of will-power. ~во́льный weak-willed, spineless. ~вре́дный harmless, innocuous; экологи́чески ~ eco-friendly. ~вре́менный untimely, premature. ~вы́ходный hopeless, desperate; without going out; uninterrupted. ~гла́зый one-eyed, eyeless. ~гла́сный silent, dumb; powerless to protest. ~голо́сный voiceless, unvoiced. ~гра́мотный illiterate; ignorant. ~грани́чный boundless, limitless, infinite. ~гре́шный innocent, sinless, without sin. ~да́рник, -a mediocrity, third-rater. ~да́рный ungifted, untalented; third-rate; ~ актёр ham; ~ певе́ц third-rate singer. ~де́йственный inactive; idle, passive. ~де́йствие, -я inaction, inactivity, inertia, idleness; negligence. ~де́йствовать, -твую impf. be idle, be inactive; stand idle, not work.

безде́лица, -ы, безде́лка, -и trifle, bagatelle. безделу́шка, -и trinket, knick-knack, toy. безде́льник, -a idler, loafer; ne'er-do-well. безде́льничать, -аю impf. idle, loaf. безде́льный idle; trifling.

бе́здна, -ы abyss, chasm; enormous numbers, a multitude, masses.

без... бездо́ждье, -я dry weather, drought. ~доказа́тельный unsupported, unsubstantiated, unproved. ~до́мный homeless; ~ая ко́шка stray cat. ~до́нный bottomless, fathomless. ~доро́жный without roads. ~доро́жье, -я lack of (good) roads; season when roads are impassable. ~ду́шный heartless, callous; soulless, lifeless. ~жа́лостный pitiless, ruthless. ~жи́зненный lifeless. ~забо́тный carefree, untroubled, careless. ~заве́тный selfless, wholehearted. ~зако́ние, -я lawlessness; unlawful act. ~зако́нный illegal, unlawful; lawless. ~засте́нчивый shameless, unblushing, barefaced. ~защи́тный defenceless, unprotected. ~земе́льный landless. ~зло́бный good-natured, kindly. ~ли́кий featureless, faceless, impersonal. ~ли́чный characterless, without personality, without individuality; impersonal. ~лу́нный moonless. ~лю́дный uninhabited; sparsely populated; lonely, solitary; empty, unfrequented.

безме́н, -a steelyard; spring balance.

без... безме́рный boundless, limitless. ~мо́зглый brainless. ~мо́лвие, -я silence. ~мо́лвный silent, mute. ~мото́рный engineless; ~мото́рный самолёт glider. ~мяте́жный serene, placid. ~надёжный hopeless. ~надзо́рный neglected. ~нака́-

занно adv. with impunity, unpunished. ~нака́занный unpunished. ~но́гий legless; one-legged. ~нра́вственный immoral.

безо prep.: see без

безобра́зие, -я ugliness; outrage; disgrace, scandal. безобра́зить, -а́жу impf. (pf. о~) disfigure, mutilate; create a disturbance, make a nuisance of o.s. безобра́зничать, -аю impf. behave outrageously; make a nuisance of o.s.

без... безоговоро́чный unconditional. ~опа́сность, -и safety, security; по́яс/реме́нь безопа́сности seat belt. ~опа́сный safe; secure; ~опа́сная бри́тва safety razor. ~ору́жный unarmed. ~оско́лочный unsplinterable; splinter-proof, shatter-proof. ~основа́тельный groundless. ~остано́вочный unceasing, continuous; without a break; sustained; non-stop. ~отве́тный meek, unanswering; unanswered; dumb. ~отве́тственный irresponsible. ~отка́зно adv. without a hitch. ~отка́зный trouble-free, smooth-(running). ~отлага́тельный, ~отло́жный urgent. ~отлу́чный uninterrupted; continual, continuous; ever-present. ~относи́тельно adv.+к+d. irrespective of. ~относи́тельный absolute, unconditional. ~отра́дный cheerless, dreary. ~отчётный uncontrolled; unaccountable; instinctive. ~оши́бочный unerring; faultless; correct. ~рабо́тица, -ы unemployment. ~рабо́тн|ый unemployed; постоя́нно ~ые the long-term unemployed. ~разде́льный undivided; whole-hearted; complete. ~разли́чие, -я indifference. ~разли́чно adv. indifferently; it is all the same. ~разли́чный indifferent; neutral. ~разме́рный one-size, stretch. ~рассу́дный reckless, foolhardy, imprudent. ~ро́дный alone in the world; without relatives; of unknown antecedents. ~ро́потный uncomplaining, unmurmuring; meek, resigned. ~рука́вка, -и sleeveless jacket, jerkin. ~ру́кий armless; one-armed; awkward. ~уда́рный unstressed, unaccented. ~у́держный unrestrained, uncontrolled; uncontrollable. ~укори́зненный irreproachable, impeccable.

безу́мец, -мца madman. безу́мие, -я madness, insanity; distraction. безу́мный mad, inane; crazy, senseless; terrible. ~у́мство, -a madness.

без... безупре́чный irreproachable, faultless. ~уря́дица, -ы disorder, confusion. ~уса́дочный pre-shrunk, shrinkproof. ~усло́вно adv. unconditionally, absolutely; of course, undoubtedly, certainly. ~усло́вный unconditional, absolute; undoubted, indisputable. ~успе́шный unsuccessful. ~уста́нный tireless; ceaseless, unremitting. ~уте́шный inconsolable. ~уча́стие, -я, ~уча́стность, -и indifference, apathy. ~уча́стный indifferent, apathetic, unconcerned. ~ъя́дерный nuclear-free, non-nuclear. ~ыде́йный without ideas or ideals; unideological; unprincipled. **~ызвестный** unknown, obscure. **~ымённый**, **~ымянный** nameless, anonymous; **~ымянный палец** third finger, ringfinger. **~ынтересный** uninteresting. **~ыскуственный**, **~ыскусный** artless, ingenuous, unsophisticated. **~ысходный** hopeless, inconsolable; irreparable; interminable.

бейсбол, -а baseball. **бейсболист**, -а baseball player.

Бейсик (*comput.*) Basic.

бекар, -а, **бекар** *indecl. adj.* natural.

бекас, -а snipe. **бекасинник**, -а small shot.

бекон, -а bacon.

Беларусь, -и Belarus.

белеть, **-ею** *impf.* (*pf.* **по~**) grow white, turn white; show white; **~ся** show white.

белизна, **-ы** whiteness. **белила**, **-ил** *pl.* whitewash, whiting; correction fluid, Tippex (*propr.*); ceruse. **белильный** bleaching.

белить, **-лю**, **белишь** *impf.* (*pf.* **вы~**, **на~**, **по~**) whitewash; whiten; bleach; **~ся** put ceruse on.

беличий squirrel, squirrel's. **белка**, **-и** squirrel.

белковый albuminous.

беллетрист, -а writer of fiction. **беллетристика**, -и fiction.

бело... *in comb.* white-, leuco-. **белогвардеец**, **-ейца** White Guard. **~деревец**, **-вца** joiner. **~кровие**, **-я** leukaemia. **~курый** fair, blonde. **~рус**, -а, **~руска**, **-и**, **~русский** Belorussian. **~рыбица** white salmon. **~снежный** snow-white.

беловик, **-а** fair copy. **беловой** clean, fair.

белок, **-лка** white; albumen, protein.

белошвейка, **-и** seamstress. **белошвейн|ый** linen; **~ая работа** plain sewing.

белуга, **-и** beluga, white sturgeon.

белуха, **-и** white whale.

бел|ый; **бел**, **-а**, **бело** white; clean, blank; **~ая берёза** silver birch; **~ый день** broad daylight; **~ое каление** white heat; **~ый медведь** polar bear; **~ые ночи** white nights, midnight sun; **~ые стихи** blank verse.

Бельгия, **-и** Belgium.

бельё, **-я** linen; bedclothes, underclothes, underclothing; washing; **дамское ~** lingerie.

бельмо, **-а**; *pl.* -а cataract; wall-eye.

бельэтаж, -а first floor; dress circle.

бемоль, **-я** *m.*, **бемоль** *indecl. adj.* flat.

бенефис, -а benefit (performance).

бензин, -а petrol; benzine; **неэтилированный ~** unleaded. **бензинов|ый** petrol; **~ая колонка** petrol pump. **бензиномер**, -а petrol-gauge **бензинопровод**, -а petrol pipe.

бензо... *in comb.* petrol. **бензобак**, -а petrol-tank. **~воз**, -а petrol tanker. **~заправка**, -и, **~заправочная** sb. filling-station, petrol-station. **~заправщик**, -а petrol bowser, **~колонка**, -и petrol pump. **~мер**, -а fuel gauge. **~очиститель**, -я *m.* petrol filter. **~провод**, -а petrol pipe, fuel line.

~хранилище, -а petrol (storage) tank. **~цистерна**, -ы petrol tanker.

бензол, -а benzene; benzol.

берёг *etc.: see* **беречь**

берег, -а, *loc.* -у; *pl.* -а bank, shore; coast; **на ~у моря** at the seaside. **берегов|ой** coast; coastal; **~ое судоходство** coastal shipping.

бережёшь *etc.: see* **беречь**. **бережливый** thrifty, economical; careful. **бережный** careful; cautious; solicitous.

берёза, -ы birch. **березник**, -а, **березняк**, -а birch grove, birch wood. **берёзовый** birch.

берейтор, -а horse-breaker; riding-master.

беременеть, -ею *impf.* (*pf.* **за~**) become pregnant; be pregnant. **беременный** pregnant (+*i.* with). **беременность**, -и pregnancy; gestation.

берет, -а a beret.

беречь, **-регу**, **-режёшь**; **-рёг**, **-ла** *impf.* take care of, look after; keep; cherish; husband; be sparing of; **~ся** be careful, take care; beware; **береги(те)сь!** look out.

Берлин, -а Berlin. **берлинск|ий** Berlin; **~ая лазурь** Prussian blue.

берлога, -и den, lair.

бермуды, **-ов** *pl.* Bermuda shorts.

беру *etc.: see* **брать**

бес, -а a devil; the devil.

бес... *see* **без...**

беседа, -ы talk, conversation; discussion; **~ по душам** heart-to-heart (talk). **беседка**, -и summer-house. **беседовать**, **-дую** *impf.* talk, converse.

бесить, **бешу**, **бесишь** *impf.* (*pf.* **вз~**) enrage, madden, infuriate; **~ся** go mad; rage, be furious.

бес... бесклассовый classless. **~конечный** endless; infinite; interminable; **~конечная дробь** recurring decimal. **~корыстие**, -я disinterestedness. **~корыстный** disinterested. **~кофейновый** decaffeinated. **~крайний** boundless. **~кровный** bloodless.

бесноватый like one possessed; raving, frenzied. **бесноваться**, **нуюсь** *impf.* rage, storm, rave; be possessed. **бесовский** devilish, devil's.

бес... беспамятный forgetful. **~память-ство**, -а unconsciousness; forgetfulness; delirium **~пардонный** shameless, brazen. **~партийный** non-party. **~перспективный** without prospects; hopeless. **~печность**, -и carelessness, unconcern. **~печный** carefree; careless, unconcerned. **~пилотный** unmanned. **~платно** *adv.* free. **~платный** free; rent-free; complimentary. **~плодие**, -я sterility, barrenness. **~плодность**, -и fruitlessness, futility. **~плодный** sterile, barren; fruitless, futile. **~поворотный** irrevocable, final. **~подобный** incomparable, superb, magnificent. **~позвоночный** invertebrate.

беспокóить, -óю *impf.* (*pf.* **о~, по~**) disturb, make anxious, make uneasy; trouble; **~ся** worry, be anxious; trouble, put o.s. out. **беспокóйный** restless; anxious; uneasy; troubled; disturbing; fidgety.

бес... бесполéзный useless. **~пóлый** sexless, asexual. **~помóщный** helpless, powerless; feeble. **~порóдный** mongrel, not thoroughbred. **~порóчный** blameless, irreproachable; immaculate. **~порядок, -дка** disorder; untidy state; *pl.* disorders, disturbances, rioting. **~порядочный** disorderly; untidy. **~посáдочный** non-stop. **~почвéнный** groundless; unsound. **~пóшлинный** duty-free; **~пóшлинная торгóвля** free trade. **~пощáдный** merciless, relentless. **~прáвный** wihout rights, deprived of civil rights. **~предéл, -а** chaos, mayhem. **~предéльный** boundless, infinite. **~предмéтный** aimless, purposeless; abstract. **~прекослóвный** unquestioning, absolute. **~препя́тственный** unhindered; free, clear, unimpeded. **~прерывный** continuous, uninterrupted. **~престáнный** continual, incessant. **~прибыльный** non-profit-making. **беспризóрник, -а, -ница, -ы** waif, homeless child. **беспризóрный** neglected, stray; homeless; *sb.* waif, homeless child or young person.

бес... беспримéрный unexampled, unparalleled **~пристрáстие -я, ~пристрáстность, -и** impartiality. **~пристрáстный** impartial, unbiased. **~приютный** homeless; not affording shelter. **~прóволочный** wireless. **~просвéтный** pitch-dark, pitch-black; hopeless, gloomy; unrelieved. **~путный** debauched, dissipated, dissolute. **~свя́зный** incoherent. **~семя́нный** seedless. **~сердéчие, -я, ~сердéчность, -и** heartlessness, callousness. **~сердéчный** heartless; callous, unfeeling, hard-hearted. **~си́лие, -я** impotence; debility, feebleness. **~си́льный** weak, feeble; impotent, powerless. **~слáвие, -я** infamy. **~слáвный** ignominious; infamous; inglorious. **~слéдно** *adv.* without trace; utterly, completely. **~слéдный** without leaving a trace, complete. **~словéсный** dumb, speechless; silent, unmurmuring, meek, humble; walking-on. **~смéнный** permanent, continuous. **~смéртие, -я** immortality. **~смéртный** immortal, undying. **~смы́сленный** senseless; foolish; meaningless, nonsensical. **~смы́слица, -ы** nonsense. **~сóвестный** unscrupulous; shameless. **~сознáтельный** unconscious; involuntary. **~сóнница, -ы** insomnia, sleeplessness. **~сóнный** sleepless. **~спóрный** indisputable, undeniable, unquestionable; incontrovertible. **~срóчный** indefinite; indeterminate; unlimited. **~стрáстный** impassive. **~стрáшный** intrepid, fearless. **~талáнный** untalented, without talent. **бестолкóвщина, -ы** muddle, confusion, disorder. **бестолкóвый** muddleheaded, slow,

stupid; confused, incoherent. **бестолóчь, -и** confusion, muddle; stupid creature; blockheads.

бес... бестрéпетный dauntless, undaunted, intrepid. **~фóрменный** shapeless, formless. **~харáктерный** weak, spineless. **~хи́тростный** artless; ingenuous; unsophisticated. **~цвéтный** colourless. **~цéльный** aimless; pointless. **~цéнный** priceless. **~цéнок; за ~цéнок** very cheap, for a song. **~церемóнный** unceremonious; cavalier; free and easy, familiar, off-hand. **~человéчный** inhuman. **~чéстить, -éщу** *impf.* (*pf.* **о~чéстить**) dishonour, disgrace. **~чéстный** dishonourable, disgraceful. **~чи́сленный** innumerable, countless.

бесчу́вственный insensible, unconscious; insensitive, unfeeling. **бесчу́вствие, -я** unconsciousness, insensibility; callousness, heartlessness; **пьян до бесчу́вствия** dead drunk.

бес... бесшóвный seamless. **~шу́мный** noiseless.

бетóн, -а concrete. **бетони́ровать, -рую** *impf.* (*pf.* **за~**) concrete. **бетóнный** concrete. **бетономешáлка, -и** concrete-mixer. **бетóнщик, -а** concrete-worker, concreter.

бечевá, -ы́ tow-rope; rope, cord, twine. **бечёвка, -и** twine, cord, string. **бечевни́к, -á** tow-path, towing-path. **бечев|óй** tow, towing; **~áя** *sb.* tow-path, towing-path.

бéшенство, -а hydrophobia, rabies; fury, rage. **бéшеный** rabid, mad; furious, violent.

бешу́ *etc.*: *see* **беси́ть**

биатлóн, -а biathlon. **биатлони́ст, -а** biathlete, biathlon competitor.

бибабó *nt.indecl.* glove puppet.

библéйский biblical. **библиóграф, -а** bibliographer. **библиографи́ческий** bibliographical. **библиотéка, -и** library; **~чи́тáльня** reading-room. **библиотéкарь, -я** *m.*, **-тéкарша, -и** librarian. **библиотéчный** library. **би́блия, -и** bible.

бивáк, -а bivouac, camp.

би́вень, -вня *m.* tusk.

бигль, -я beagle (*dog*).

бигуди́ *indecl. pl.* curlers.

бидé *nt.indecl.* bidet.

бидóн, -а can; milk-churn.

биéние, -я beating; beat.

бижутéрия, -и costume jewellery.

би́знес, -а business. **бизнесмéн, -а** businessman.

билéт, -а ticket; card; pass, permit; **креди́тный ~** bank-note. **билетёр, -а, -тёрша, -и** ticket-collector; usherette. **билéтный** ticket.

билья́рд, -а billiards. **билья́рди́ст, -а** *m.* billiards-player. **билья́рдная** *sb.* billiard-hall.

бинóкль, -я *m.* binoculars; **полевóй ~** field-glasses; **театрáльный ~** opera-glasses. **бинокуля́рный** binocular.

бинт, -á bandage. **бинтовáть, -ту́ю** *impf.* (*pf.* **за~**) bandage. **бинтóвка, -и** bandaging.

биóграф, -а biographer. **биографи́ческий**

biographical. **биогра́фия, -и** biography; curriculum vitae, CV.

био́лог, -а a biologist. **биологи́ческий** biological. **биоло́гия, -и** biology. **биоресу́рсы, -ов** *pl.* bioresources. **биори́тмы, -ов** *pl.* biorhythms. **биохими́ческий** biochemical. **биохи́мия, -и** biochemistry.

би́ржа, -и exchange.

би́рка, -и tally; name-plate; label.

бирюза́, -ы́ turquoise

бис *int.* encore; **спеть на ~** repeat as encore. **биси́ровать, -рую** *impf. & pf.* repeat; give an encore.

би́сер, -а glass beads, bugles. **би́серина, -ы, би́серинка, -и** (*small*) glass bead.

бискви́т, -а sponge cake; biscuit. **бискви́тный** sponge; biscuit.

бит, -а (*comput.*) bit.

би́тва, -ы battle.

битко́м *adv.*; **~ наби́т** crowded, packed.

битло́вка, -и polo-neck (sweater).

бито́к, -тка́ rissole, hamburger.

би́т|ый beaten; broken, cracked; **~ые сли́вки** whipped cream; **~ый час** a full hour; hours, ages. **бить, бью, бьёшь** *impf.* (*pf.* **за~, по~, про~, уда́рить**) beat; hit; defeat; strike; whip; sound; thump, bang; kill, slaughter; smash, shatter; fight, struggle, wage war (**по**+*d.* on, against); spurt, gush; shoot, fire; **~ в бараба́н** beat a drum; **~ в ладо́ши** clap one's hands; **~ (в) наба́т** sound, raise the alarm; **~ в цель** hit the target; **~ ключо́м** gush out, well up; be in full swing; **~ на**+*a.* strive for, after; have a range of; **~ отбо́й** beat a retreat; **~ по**+*d.* damage, injure, wound; **~ трево́гу** sound, raise, the alarm; **~ хвосто́м** lash its tail; **~ся** fight; beat; writhe, struggle; break; +*i.* knock, hit, strike; +**над**+*i.* struggle with, rack one's brains over; **~ голово́й об сте́ну** be up against a blank wall; **~ об закла́д** bet, wager. **битьё, -я́** beating, thrashing, thumping, banging; smashing.

бифште́кс, -а (beef)steak. **бифште́ксная** *sb.* steakhouse.

бич, -а́ whip, lash; scourge. **бичева́ть, -чую** *impf.* flog; lash, castigate.

бишь *part.* expressing effort to remember name, etc.: **как ~ его́?** what was the name again?; what's-his-name, thingamy; **то ~** that is to say.

бла́го, -а good; blessing; **всех благ!** all the best! **бла́го** *conj.* since.

бла́го... *in comb.* well-, good-. **Благове́щение, -я** Annunciation. **~ве́щенский** of the Annunciation. **~ви́дный** comely; plausible, specious. **~воле́ние, -я** goodwill; favour. **~воспи́танный** well-bred.

благодаре́ние, -я gratitude, thanks. **благодари́ть, -рю́** *impf.* (*pf.* **по~**) thank; **благодарю́ вас** thank you. **благода́рность, -и** gratitude; thanks; bribe; **не сто́ит благода́рности** don't mention it, not at all.

благода́рный grateful; rewarding, promising. **благода́рственный** of gratitude, of thanks; thanksgiving. **благодаря́** *prep.*+*d.* thanks to, owing to; because of.

благо... благоде́тель, -я *m.*, **-ница, -ы** benefactor. **~де́тельный** beneficial; beneficent. **~ду́шный** placid, equable; good-humoured. **~жела́тель, -я** *m.* well-wisher. **~жела́тельный** well-disposed; benevolent. **~зву́чный** melodious, harmonious. **~мы́слящий** right-thinking, right-minded. **~надёжный** reliable, trustworthy, sure; loyal. **~наме́ренный** well-intentioned. **~нра́вие, -я** good behaviour. **~нра́вный** well-behaved; high-principled. **~получие, -я** well-being; happiness. **~полу́чно** *adv.* all right, well; happily; safely. **~полу́чный** happy, successful; safe. **~присто́йный** decent, seemly, decorous. **~прия́тный** favourable. **~прия́тствовать** *impf.*+*d.* favour; **наибо́лее ~прия́тствуемая держа́ва** most-favoured nation. **~разу́мие, -я** sense; prudence. **~разу́мный** judicious; sensible, prudent. **~ро́дие, -я**; **ва́ше ~ро́дие** Your Honour. **~ро́дный** noble. **~ро́дство, -а** nobility. **~скло́нность, -и** favour, good graces. **~скло́нный** favourable; gracious. **~слови́ть, -влю́** *pf.*, **благослови́ть, -я́ю** *impf.* bless. **~состоя́ние, -я** prosperity. **~твори́тель, -я** *m.*, **-ница, -ы** philanthropist. **~твори́тельный** charitable, charity. **~тво́рный** salutary; beneficial; wholesome. **~устро́енный** well-equipped, well-arranged, well-planned; with all amenities.

блаже́нный blessed; blissful; simple-minded. **блаже́нство, -а** bliss, blessedness.

бланк, -а form; **анке́тный ~** questionnaire. **бла́нков|ый** form; **~ая на́дпись** endorsement.

блат, -а (*sl.*) thieves' cant, criminals' slang; pull, protection racket, fiddle; string-pulling, wangling. **блатн|о́й** criminal; soft, cushy; **~а́я му́зыка** thieves' cant; *sb.* criminal, thief.

бледне́ть, -е́ю *impf.* (*pf.* **по~**) grow pale; pale. **бледноли́цый** pale; *sb.* paleface. **бле́дность, -и** paleness, pallor. **бле́дный; -ден, -дна́, -о** pale; colourless; **~ как полотно́** as white as a sheet.

бле́йзер, -а blazer.

блёклый faded. **блёкнуть, -ну; блёк(нул)** *impf.* (*pf.* **по~**) fade, wither.

блеск, -а (-у) brightness, brilliance, lustre, shine; splendour, magnificence.

блесну́ть, -ну́, -нёшь *pf.* flash, gleam; shine. **блесте́ть, -ещу́, -сти́шь** *or* **бле́щешь** *impf.* shine; glitter, sparkle. **блёстка, -и** sparkle, flash; spangle, sequin. **блестя́щий** shining, bright; brilliant.

бле́яние, -я bleat, bleating. **бле́ять, -е́ет** *impf.* bleat.

ближа́йший nearest, closest; next; immediate; **~ ро́дственник** next of kin. **бли́же** *comp. of* **бли́зкий, бли́зко. ближневосто́чный**

Middle East; Middle Eastern. **ближний** near, close; neighbouring; *sb.* neighbour. **близ** *prep.+g.* near, close to, by. **близиться,** -зится *impf.* approach, draw near. **близкий;** -зок, -зка, -о near, close; imminent; intimate; ~кие *sb.*, *pl.* one's nearest and dearest, near relatives. **близко** *adv.* near, close (от+*g.* to); nearly, closely. **близнец,** -а twin; *pl.* Gemini. **близорукий** short-sighted. **близость,** -и nearness, closeness, proximity; intimacy.

блик, -a spot or patch of light; light, highlight.

блин, -а pancake. **блинная** *sb.* pancake parlour.

блиндаж, -а dug-out.

блистательный brilliant, splendid. **блистать,** -аю shine; glitter; sparkle.

блиц, -a flash (attachment).

блиц(-)... *in comb.* lightning ...; whirlwind ... **блицвизит** flying visit. **блицкриг,** -a blitzkrieg.

блок[1], -a block, pulley, sheave.

блок[2], -a bloc; block; section, unit; slab; module; carton. **блокадник,** -a victim of siege of Leningrad (1941–44). **блокировать,** -рую *impf. & pf.* blockade; block; ~ся form a bloc. **блокировка,** -и block system.

блокнот, -a writing-pad, note-pad, note-book. **блондин,** -a, **блондинка,** -и blond(e).

блоха, -й; *pl.* -и, -ам flea.

блочный modular.

блошиный flea. **блошки,** -шек *pl.* tiddlywinks.

блудница, -ы whore.

блуждать, -аю *impf.* roam, wander, rove. **блуждающ|ий** wandering; ~ий огонёк will-o'-the-wisp; ~ почка floating kidney.

блуза, -ы, **блузка,** -и blouse.

блюдечко, -a saucer; small dish; **на блюдечке** on a plate. **блюдо,** -a dish; course. **блюдолиз,** -a lickspittle. **блюдце,** -a saucer.

блюсти, -юду, -дёшь; блюл, -а *impf.* (*pf.* со~) guard, keep; watch over; observe. **блюститель,** -я *m.* keeper, guardian.

боб, -а bean. **бобов|ый** bean; ~ые *sb.*, *pl.* **бобок,** -бка leguminous plants.

бобр, -а beaver. **бобрик,** -a beaver-cloth; волосы ~ом crew cut. **бобровый** beaver.

бобслей, -я bobsleigh; bobsleighing. **бобслейст,** -a bobsleigher.

бобыль, -я *m.* poor landless peasant; solitary person.

Бог, бог, -а, *voc.* **Боже** God; god; **дай** ~ God grant; ~ **его знает** who knows? **не дай** ~ God forbid; **Боже (мой)!** my God! good God!; **ради** ~а for God's sake; **с** ~**ом!** good luck!; **слава** ~у thank God. **богадельня,** -и almshouse, workhouse.

богатей, -я rich man. **богатеть,** -ею *impf.* (*pf.* раз~) grow rich. **богатство,** -a riches, wealth; richness. **богатый** rich, wealthy; *sb.*

rich man. **богач,** -а rich man.

богиня, -и goddess. **Богоматерь,** -и Mother of God. **богомолец,** -льца, **богомолка,** -и devout person; pilgrim. **богомолье,** -я pilgrimage. **богомольный** religious, devout. **Богородица,** -ы the Virgin Mary. **богослов,** -a theologian. **богословие,** -я theology. **боготворить,** -рю *impf.* worship, idolize; deify. **Богоявление,** -я Epiphany.

бодать(ся, -аю(сь *impf.*, **боднуть,** -ну, -нёшь *pf.* (*pf. also* **забодать**) butt. **бодливый** inclined to butt.

бодрить, -рю *impf.* stimulate, invigorate, brace up; ~ся try to keep up one's spirits. **бодрость,** -и cheerfulness, good spirits, courage. **бодрствовать,** -твую be awake; stay awake, keep awake; sit up. **бодрый;** бодр, -а, -о cheerful, brisk, bright; hale and hearty. **бодрящий** invigorating, bracing.

боевик, -а active revolutionary, militant; smash hit. **боевитость,** -и fighting spirit. **боев|ой** fighting, battle, war; urgent; militant, determined, unyielding; ~ **ой клич** war-cry; ~**ое крещение** baptism of fire; ~**ой механизм** striking mechanism. **боеголовка,** -и warhead. **боеготовность,** -и combat readiness. **боеприпасы,** -ов *pl.* ammunition. **боец,** бойца soldier; fighter; warrior; butcher, slaughterer; *pl.* men.

Боже *see* **Бог. божеский** divine; fair, just. **божество,** -а deity; divinity. **бож|ий** God's; ~**ья коровка** ladybird; **каждый** ~**ий день** every blessed day. **божиться,** -жусь *impf.* (*pf.* по~) swear. **божок,** -жка idol.

бой, -я (-ю), *loc.* -ю; *pl.* -и, -ёв battle, action, fight; bout; fighting; killing, slaughtering; striking; breakage(s), broken glass, crockery, etc.; **барабанный** ~ drumbeat; ~ **быков** bullfight; ~ **китов** whaling; ~ **тюленей** sealing; **с бою** by force; **часы с боем** striking clock.

бой|кий; боек, бойка, -о bold, spry, smart, sharp; glib; lively, animated; busy.

бойница, -ы loophole, embrasure.

бойня, -и; *g.pl.* **боен** slaughter-house, abattoir, shambles; massacre, slaughter, butchery.

бойче *comp. of* **бойкий**

бок, -a (-у), *loc.* -ý; *pl.* -á side; flank; ~ **ó** ~ side by side; **в** ~ sideways; **на** ~ sideways, to the side; **на** ~**ý** on one side; **под** ~**ом** near by, close by; **с** ~**у** from the side, from the flank; **с** ~**у на бок** from side to side.

бокал, -a glass; goblet.

боковой side, flank; lateral; sidelong. **боком** *adv.* sideways.

бокс, -a boxing. **боксёр,** -a boxer. **боксёрский** boxing. **боксировать,** -рую *impf.* box.

болван, -a block; blockhead; twit; dummy; idol. **болванка,** -и block; pig; **железо в** ~**х** pig-iron.

Болгария, -и Bulgaria.

болевой of pain, painful.

более *adv.* more; ~ **всего** most of all; **тем** ~

especially as.

болéзнен|ный sickly; unhealthy; abnormal; morbid; painful. **болéзнь, -и** illness, disease, ailment; abnormality; ~ **рóста** growing pains.

болéльщик, -а, -щица, -ы fan, supporter. **болéть¹, -éю** *impf.* be ill, suffer; be worried; +**за**+*a.* support, be a fan of. **болéть², -лúт** *impf.* ache, hurt.

болóнья, -и (cape of) waterproof nylon.

болóтистый marshy, boggy, swampy. **болóто, -а** marsh, bog, swamp. **болóтный** marsh, bog.

болтáнка, -и air-pocket. **болтáть¹, -áю** *impf.* stir; shake; dangle; ~**ся** dangle, swing; hang loosely; hang about; fly bumpily, bump.

болтáть², -áю *impf.* chatter, jabber, natter. **болтлúвый** garrulous, talkative; indiscreet. **болтнýть, -нý, -нёшь** *pf.* blurt out. **болтовня, -й** talk chatter; gossip. **болтýн¹, -á, болтýнья, -и** talker, chatterer; chatterbox; gossip.

болтýн², -á addled egg.

болтýшка, -и scrambled eggs; mixture; swill, mash; whisk.

боль, -и pain; ache; ~ **в бокý** stitch. **больнúца, -ы** hospital. **больнúчный** hospital; ~ **листóк** medical certificate. **бóльно¹** *adv.* painfully, badly; *pred.*+*d.* it hurts. **бóльно²** *adv.* very, extremely, terribly. **больнóй; -лен, -льнá** ill, sick; diseased; sore; *sb.* patient, invalid.

большáк, -á high road. **бóльше** *comp. of* **большóй, велúкий, мнóго**; bigger, larger; greater; more; ~ **не** not any more, no more, no longer; ~ **тогó** and what is more; *adv.* for the most part. **бóльш|ий** greater, larger; ~**ей чáстью** for the most part; **сáмое** ~**ее** at most, at the utmost, at the outside. **большинствó, -á** majority; most people. **больш|óй** big, large; great; grown-up; ~**áя бýква** capital letter; ~**áя дорóга** high road; ~**óй пáлец** thumb; big toe; ~**óй свет** high society, the world; ~**úе** *sb.*, *pl.* grown-ups. **большýщий** huge, enormous.

болячка, -и sore, scab; defect, weakness.

бóмба, -ы bomb; **зажигáтельная** ~ petrol bomb, Molotov cocktail. **бомбардировáть, -рýю** *impf.* bombard; bomb. **бомбардирóвка, -и** bombardment, bombing. **бомбардирóвщик, -а** bomber; bomber pilot. **бомбёжка, -и** bombing. **бомбúть, -блю** bomb. **бомбовóз, -а** bomber. **бóмбовый** bomb. **бомбоубéжище, -а** bomb shelter.

бомж, -а *abbr.* (*of* **без определённого мéста жúтельства**) homeless person, vagrant.

бóна, -ы bond, bill; money order; *pl.* paper money.

бор, -а, *loc.* -ý; *pl.* -ы́ pine-wood, coniferous forest.

бордó *nt.indecl.* claret; red Bordeaux. **бордó** *indecl. adj.*, **бордóвый** wine-red, claret-coloured.

бордюр, -а border.

борéц, -рцá fighter; wrestler; campaigner; activist; ~ **за мир** peace campaigner.

борзáя *sb.* borzoi; **англúйская** ~ greyhound. **бóрзый** swift.

бормотáние, -я muttering, mumbling; mutter, mumble. **бормотáть, -очý, -óчешь** *impf.* (*pf.* **про**~) mutter, mumble.

бóрный boric, boracic.

бóров, -а hog.

боровúк, -á (edible) boletus.

бородá, -ы́, *a.* **бóроду**; *pl.* **бóроды, -рóд, -áм** beard; wattles. **бородáвка, -и** wart. **бородáтый** bearded. **бородáч, -á** bearded man. **борóдка, -и** small beard, tuft; key-bit; barb.

бороздá, -ы́; *pl.* **бóрозды, -óзд, -áм** furrow; fissure. **бороздúть, -зжý** *impf.* (*pf.* **вз**~) furrow; plough; leave wake or track on; score. **борóздка, -и** furrow, groove. **борóздчатый** furrowed; grooved, scored.

боронá, -ы́, *a.* **бóрону**; *pl.* **бóроны, -рóн, -áм** harrow. **боронúть, -ню** *impf.* (*pf.* **вз**~) harrow.

борóться, -рюсь, бóрешься *impf.* wrestle, grapple; struggle, fight.

борт, -а, *loc.* -ý; *pl.* -á, -óв side, ship's side; front; cushion; за ~, за ~ом overboard; на ~, на ~ý on board. **борт...** *in comb.* ship's; air, flight, flying.

бортов|óй ship's; side; onboard; flight, flying; ~**áя кáчка** rolling. **бортпроводнúк, -á** air steward. **бортпроводнúца, -ы** air hostess.

борщ, -á bor(t)sch.

борьбá, -ы́ wrestling; struggle, fight; conflict; **америкáнская** ~ all-in wrestling.

босикóм *adv.* barefoot. **босóй; бос, -á, -о, босонóгий** barefooted; **на бóсу нóгу** on one's bare feet; barefoot dancer; *pl.* sandals, mules. **босяк, -á, босячка, -и** tramp; down-and-out.

бот, -а, бóтик¹, -а small boat.

ботáник, -а botanist. **ботáника, -и** botany. **ботанический** botanical; ~ **сад** botanical gardens.

бóтик², -а high overshoe. **ботúнок, -нка** boot.

бóцман, -а boatswain, boatswain's mate.

бочáг, -á pool; deep puddle.

бочкóм *adv.* sideways.

бóчка, -и barrel, cask. **бочóнок, -нка** keg, small barrel.

боязлúвый timid, timorous. **боязнь, -и** fear, dread.

боя́рин, -а; *pl.* **-я́ре, -я́р** boyar. **боя́рск|ий** boyar's, boyars'; ~**ие дéти** small landowners.

боя́рышник, -а hawthorn.

боя́ться, боюсь *impf.*+*g.* be afraid of, fear; dislike, be intolerant of.

бр. *abbr.* (*of* **брáтья**) bros., brothers.

бра *nt. indecl.* sconce, bracket.

бра́га, **-и** home-brewed beer.

бра́к[1], **-а** marriage.

бра́к[2], **-а** defective goods, defect, defective part; reject, waste. **бракёр**, **-а** inspector. **бракова́ть**, **-ку́ю** *impf.* (*pf.* **за~**) reject. **бракоде́л**, **-а** bad workman.

бракоразво́дный divorce.

брандахлы́ст, **-а** slops, swill.

брани́ть, **-ню́** *impf.* (*pf.* **вы́~**) scold; abuse, curse; **~ся** (*pf.* **по~ся**) swear, curse; quarrel. **бра́нн|ый**[1] abusive, profane; **~ое сло́во** swear-word.

бра́нн|ый[2] martial, battle. **брань**[1], **-и** war; battle.

брань[2], **-и** swearing, bad language; abuse.

брасле́т, **-а** bracelet.

брасс, **-а** breast stroke. **брасси́ст**, **-а**, **-и́стка**, **-и** breast-stroke swimmer.

брат, **-а**; *pl.* **-тья**, **-тьев** brother; comrade; old man, my lad, mate; lay brother, monk, friar; *pl.* friends, boys; **на ~а** per head; **наш ~** we, the likes of us, our sort. **брата́ние**, **-я** fraternization. **брата́ться**, **-а́юсь** *impf.* (*pf.* **по~**) fraternize. **братва́**, **-ы́** comrades, friends. **бра́тия**, **-и**; *g.pl.* **-тий**, **бра́тья**, **-и** brotherhood, fraternity. **братоуби́йство**, **-а**, **братоуби́йца**, **-ы** *c.g.* fratricide. **бра́тский** brotherly, fraternal. **бра́тство**, **-а** brotherhood, fraternity.

брать, **беру́**, **-рёшь**; **брал**, **-а́**, **-о** *impf.* (*pf.* **взять**) take; get, obtain, book; hire; seize, grip; exact, demand, require; surmount, clear; work; be effective; take bribes; **+adv.** bear; **~ верх** get the upper hand; **~ в ско́бки** put in brackets; **~ на+a.** have a range of; **~ на букси́р** take in tow; **~ на пору́ки** go bail for; **~ но́ту** sing (play) a note; **~ под аре́ст** put under arrest; **~ своё** get one's (own) way; take its toll, tell; **~ сло́во** take the floor; **~ся+за+а.** touch; take hold of, seize; take up; get down to; **+за+а.** *or inf.* undertake, take on o.s.; appear, come; **~ся за ум** come to one's senses; **~ся нарасхва́т** go (sell) like hot cakes.

бра́чный marriage; mating.

бреве́нчатый log. **бревно́**, **-а́**; *pl.* **-ёвна**, **-вен** log, beam.

бред, **-а**, *loc.* **-у́** delirium; raving(s); gibberish; **соба́чий ~** twaddle, poppycock. **бре́дить**, **-е́жу** *impf.* be delirious, rave; **+i.** rave about, be infatuated with. **бре́дни**, **-ей** *pl.* ravings; fantasies. **бредово́й**, **бредо́вый** delirious; fantastic, nonsensical.

бреду́ *etc.: see* **брести́**. **бре́жу** *etc.: see* **бре́дить**

бре́згать, **-аю** *impf.* (*pf.* **по~**) **+inf. or i.** be squeamish about, be fastidious about; be nauseated by, be sickened by; shrink from, scruple or hesitate to. **брезгли́вый** squeamish, fastidious.

брезе́нт, **-а** tarpaulin.

бре́зжить(ся, **-ит(ся** *impf.* dawn; gleam faintly, glimmer.

брейк, **-а** break dancing. **бре́йкер**, **-а** break dancer.

брёл *etc.: see* **брести́**

брело́к, **-а** charm, trinket; **~ для ключе́й** key ring, fob.

бремени́ть, **-ню́** *impf.* (*pf.* **о~**) burden. **бре́мя**, **-мени** *nt.* burden; load.

бренча́ть, **-чу́** *impf.* strum; jingle.

брести́, **-еду́**, **-едёшь**; **брёл**, **-а́** *impf.* stroll, amble; struggle along, drag o.s. along.

брете́ль, **-и**, **брете́лька**, **-и** shoulder strap.

бре́ю *etc.: see* **брить**

брига́да, **-ы** brigade; squadron; crew, team, gang, squad. **бригади́р**, **-а** brigadier; brigade-leader; team-leader; foreman. **брига́дник**, **-а**, **-ница**, **-ы** member of brigade, crew, team.

бри́дер, **-а** breeder reactor.

бри́джи, **-ей** *pl.* breeches.

бриза́нтный high-explosive.

бриллиа́нт, **-а**, **брилья́нт**, **-а** brilliant, diamond.

брита́нец, **-нца**, **брита́нка**, **-и** Briton, British subject; Englishman, Englishwoman. **брита́нск|ий** British; **Б~ие острова́** *pl.* the British Isles.

бри́тва, **-ы** razor. **бри́твенный** shaving. **бри́тый** shaved; clean-shaven. **брить**, **бре́ю** *impf.* (*pf.* **по~**) shave; **~ся** shave (o.s.). **бритьё**, **-я́** shave; shaving.

бри́чка, **-и** britzka, trap.

бро́вка, **-и** brow; edge. **бровь**, **-и**; *pl.* **-и**, **-е́й** eyebrow; brow.

брод, **-а** ford.

броди́ть, **-ожу́**, **-о́дишь** *impf.* wander, roam, stray; amble, stroll; ferment. **бродя́га**, **-и** *c.g.* **бродя́жка**, **-и** *c.g.* tramp, vagrant, down-and-out; wanderer. **бродя́жничать**, **-аю** *impf.* be on the road, be a tramp. **бродя́жничество**, **-а** vagrancy. **бродя́чий** vagrant; wandering, roving, strolling; stray; restless.

броже́ние, **-я** ferment, fermentation.

бром, **-а** bromine; bromide. **броми́стый** bromic, bromidic; **~ ка́лий** potassium bromide. **бро́мный**, **бро́мовый** bromine.

броне... *in comb.* armoured, armour. **бронеба́йный** armour-piercing. **~ви́к**, **-а́** armoured car. **~во́й** armoured, armour. **~жиле́т**, **-а** bulletproof vest. **~но́сец**, **-сца** battleship, ironclad; armadillo. **~но́сный**, **~та́нковый** armoured.

бро́нза, **-ы** bronze; (collection of) bronzes. **бронзирова́ть**, **-ру́ю** *impf. & pf.* bronze. **бронзиро́вка**, **-и** bronzing. **бро́нзовый** bronze; bronzed.

брони́рованный armoured. **брони́ровать**[1], **-ру́ю** *impf. & pf.* (*pf. also* **за~**) armour.

брони́ровать[2], **-ру́ю** *impf. & pf.* (*pf. also* **за~**) reserve, book.

бронхи́т, **-а** bronchitis.

броня́[1], **-и́** armour.

бро́ня², **-и** reservation; commandeering; warrant, permit; exemption.

броса́ть, **-а́ю** *impf.*, **бро́сить**, **-о́шу** *pf.* throw, cast, fling; drop, throw down; leave, abandon, desert; give up, leave off; **бро́сь(те)!** stop it! drop it!; **~ся** throw o.s., fling o.s., rush; +*inf.* begin, start; +*i.* throw away, squander; throw at one another, pelt one another with; **~ся в глаза́** be striking, arrest the attention; **~ся на коле́ни** fall on one's knees; **~ся на по́мощь**+*d.* rush to the assistance of. **бро́ский** arresting, striking; loud, garish, glaring. **бро́сов|ый** worthless, rubbishy; **~ая цена́** giveaway price; **~ый э́кспорт** dumping. **бросо́к**, **-ска́** throw; burst; bound, spurt; thrust.

бро́шка, **-и**, **брошь**, **-и** brooch.

брошю́ра, **-ы** pamphlet, booklet, brochure. **брошюрова́ть**, **-рую** *impf.* (*pf.* **с~**) stitch. **брошюро́вка**, **-и** stitching. **брошюро́вщик**, **-а** stitcher.

брус, **-а**; *pl.* **-сья**, **-сьев** squared timber; beam, joist; bar; (**паралле́льные**) **~ья** parallel bars. **бруско́вый** bar.

брусни́ка, **-и** cowberry, red whortleberry; cowberries, red whortleberries.

брусо́к, **-ска́** bar; ingot; slug.

бру́ствер, **-а** breastwork, parapet.

бру́тто *indecl. adj.* gross.

бры́згалка, **-и** sprinkler; water-pistol.

бры́згать, **-зжу** *or* **-гаю** *impf.*, **бры́знуть**, **-ну** *pf.* splash, spatter; sprinkle; spurt, gush; **~ слюно́й** sputter, splutter; **~ся** splash o.s., splash one another; spray o.s. **бры́зги**, **брызг** *pl.* spray, splashes; fragments; sparks.

брыка́ть, **-а́ю** *impf.*, **брыкну́ть**, **-ну́**, **-нёшь** *pf.* kick; **~ся** kick, rebel.

брысь *int.* shoo!

брюзга́, **-и́** *c.g.* grumbler. **брюзгли́вый** grumbling, peevish. **брюзжа́ть**, **-жу́** *impf.* grumble.

брю́ква, **-ы** swede.

брю́ки, **брюк** *pl.* trousers; **~-ю́бка** culottes.

брюне́т, **-а** dark man, dark-haired man. **брюне́тка**, **-и** brunette.

Брюссе́ль, **-и** Brussels.

брюха́стый, **брюха́тый** big-bellied. **брю́хо**, **-а**; *pl.* **-и** belly; paunch, corporation; stomach.

брю́чный trouser; **~ костю́м** trouser suit. **брюшко́**, **-а́**; *pl.* **-и**, **-о́в** abdomen; paunch. **брюшно́й** abdominal; **~ тиф** typhoid.

бря́канье, **-я** clatter. **бря́кать**, **-аю** *impf.*, **бря́кнуть**, **-ну** *pf.* crash down, drop with a crash; blurt out; (+*i.*) clatter, make a clatter; **~ся** crash, fall heavily. **бряца́ние**, **-я** rattling, rattle; clanking, clank; clang. **бряца́ть**, **-а́ю** *impf.* rattle; clank, clang.

бу́бен, **-бна** tambourine. **бубене́ц**, **-нца́**, **бубе́нчик**, **-а** small bell.

бу́бны, **-бён**, **-бна́м** *pl.* diamonds. **бубно́вый** diamond; **~ вале́т** knave of diamonds.

буго́р, **-гра́** mound, hillock, knoll; bump,

lump. **бугоро́к**, **-рка́** small mound or lump; protuberance; tubercle. **бугорча́тка**, **-и** tuberculosis, consumption. **бугри́стый** hilly, bumpy.

бу́дет that's enough, that will do; +*inf.* it's time to stop; **~ вам писа́ть** don't do any more writing.

буди́льник, **-а** alarm-clock. **буди́ть**, **бужу́**, **бу́дишь** *impf.* (*pf.* **про~**, **раз~**) wake, awaken; rouse, arouse.

бу́дка, **-и** box, booth; hut; stall; **соба́чья ~** dog-kennel.

бу́дни, **-ней** *pl.* weekdays; workdays, working days; humdrum existence. **бу́дний**, **бу́дничный** weekday; everyday; dull, humdrum.

бу́дто *conj.* as if, as though; **~ (бы)**, **(как) ~** apparently, allegedly, ostensibly; *part.* really?

бу́ду *etc.*: see **быть**. **бу́дучи** being. **бу́дущ|ий** future; next, coming; to be, to come; **~ая мать** mother-to-be, expectant mother; **~ее** *sb.* future. **бу́дущность**, **-и** future.

будь(те) see **быть**

бу́ер, **-а**; *pl.* **-а́**, **-о́в** ice-boat, ice-yacht.

бужу́ see **буди́ть**

буза́, **-ы́** home brew; (*sl.*) row, shindy; rubbish.

бузина́, **-ы́** elder. **бузи́нник**, **-а** thicket of elders. **бузи́нный**, **бузи́новый** elder.

бузи́ть, **-и́шь** *impf.* (*sl.*) kick up a row.

бузотёр, **-а** (*sl.*) rowdy; trouble-maker.

буй, **-я**; *pl.* **-и́**, **-ёв** buoy.

бу́йвол, **-а** buffalo.

бу́йный; **бу́ен**, **буйна́**, **-о** violent, turbulent; tempestuous; ungovernable; wild; luxuriant, lush. **бу́йство**, **-а** tumult, uproar; unruly conduct, riotous behaviour. **бу́йствовать**, **-твую** *impf.* create uproar, behave violently.

бук, **-а** beech.

бука́шка, **-и** small insect.

бу́ква, **-ы**; *g.pl.* **букв** letter; **~ в бу́кву** literally, word for word. **буква́льно** *adv.* literally. **буква́льный** literal. **буква́рь**, **-я́** ABC. **бу́квенно-цифрово́й** alphanumeric. **буквое́д**, **-а** pedant. **буквое́дство**, **-а** pedantry.

букети́ровать, **-рую** *impf.* thin out.

букини́ст, **-а** second-hand bookseller.

букле́т, **-а** (fold-out) leaflet.

буклиро́ванн|ый bouclé; **~ая ткань** bouclé fabric. **бу́кля**, **-и** curl, ringlet.

бу́ковый beech, beech-wood.

букс, **-а** box(-tree).

букси́р, **-а** tug, tug-boat; tow-rope, hawser. **букси́ровать**, **-рую** *impf.* tow, be towing; have in tow.

буксова́ние, **-я** wheel-spin. **буксова́ть**, **-су́ет** *impf.* spin, slip.

булава́, **-ы́** mace. **була́вка**, **-и** pin; **англи́йская ~** safety-pin. **була́вочный** pin.

булими́я, **-и** bulimia.

бу́лка, **-и** roll; **сдо́бная ~** bun. **бу́лочная** *sb.* bakery; baker's shop. **бу́лочник**, **-а** baker.

булты́х *int.* splash, plump. **булты́ха́ться, -а́юсь** *impf.*, **булты́хну́ться, -ну́сь, -нёшься** *pf.* fall with heavy splash, plunge, plump.

булы́жник, -а cobble-stone, cobbles. **булы́жный** cobbled.

бульва́р, -а avenue; boulevard. **бульва́рный** boulevard, avenue; trashy, rubbishy; vulgar.

бу́льканье, -я gurgling, gurgle. **бу́лькать, -аю** *impf.* gurgle.

бульо́н, -а broth, stock.

бум, -а beam.

бума́га, -и cotton; paper; document; **почто́вая ~** notepaper; *pl.* securities. **бумагодержа́тель, -я** *m.* security-holder, bond-holder; paper-clip. **бума́жка, -и** piece of paper; paper; note. **бума́жник, -а** wallet; paper-maker. **бума́жн|ый** cotton; paper; **~ая волоки́та** red tape; **~ змей** kite; **~ая фа́брика** paper-mill. **бумажо́нка, -и** scrap of paper.

бунт¹, -а bale; package; bundle.

бунт², -а; *pl.* **-ы́** rebellion, revolt, rising; riot; mutiny. **бунта́рский** seditious, mutinous; rebellious; turbulent. **бунта́рь, -я́** *m.* rebel; insurgent; mutineer; rioter; inciter to rebellion or mutiny. **бунтова́ть(ся, -ту́ю(сь** *impf.* (*pf.* **вз~**) revolt, rebel; mutiny, riot; incite to rebellion or mutiny. **бунтовско́й** rebellious, mutinous. **бунтовщи́к, -а́, -щи́ца, -ы** rebel, insurgent; mutineer; rioter.

бур, -а auger; bore; drill.

бура́, -ы́ borax.

бура́в, -а́; *pl.* **-а́** auger; gimlet. **бура́вить, -влю** *impf.* (*pf.* **про~**) bore, drill. **бура́вчик, -а** gimlet.

бура́н, -а snowstorm.

бурда́, -ы́ (*sl.*) slops, swill, hog-wash.

буреве́стник, -а stormy petrel. **буревой** storm; stormy. **бурело́м, -а** wind-fallen trees.

буре́ние, -я boring, drilling.

буржуа́ *m.indecl.* bourgeois. **буржуази́я, -и** bourgeoisie. **буржуа́зный** bourgeois. **буржу́й, -я** bourgeois. **буржу́йка, -и** bourgeois; small stove. **буржу́йский** bourgeois.

бури́льный boring, drilling. **бури́льщик, -а** borer, driller, drill-operator. **бури́ть, -рю́** *impf.* bore, drill.

бу́ркать, -аю *impf.*, **бу́ркнуть, -ну** *pf.* growl, grumble, mutter.

бурли́вый stormy; seething, turbulent. **бурли́ть, -лю́** *impf.* boil, seethe.

бу́рный; -рен, -рна́, -о stormy, rough; impetuous; rapid; energetic.

буров|о́й boring, bore, drilling; **~ая вы́шка** derrick; **~ая (сква́жина)** borehole; **~о́й стано́к, ~ая устано́вка** drilling rig.

бурча́ть, -чу́ *impf.* (*pf.* **про~**) grumble; mumble, mutter; rumble; bubble.

бу́р|ый; бур, -а́, -о brown; (dark) chestnut; **~ая лиси́ца** red fox.

бурья́н, -а tall weeds.

бу́ря, -и storm; tempest; gale.

бу́сать, -аю *impf.* (*sl.*) drink, swallow.

бу́сина, -ы, бу́синка, -и bead. **бу́сы, бус** *pl.* beads.

бутафо́р, -а property-man, props. **бутафо́рия, -и** properties, props; window-dressing. **бутафо́рский** property.

бутербро́д, -а (open) sandwich; **зако́н ~а** Sod's Law, Murphy's Law. **бутербро́дная** *sb.* sandwich bar.

буто́н, -а bud. **бутонье́рка, -и** button-hole, spray of flowers.

бу́тсы, -ов *pl.* football boots.

буты́лка, -и bottle. **буты́лочный** bottle; **~ цвет** bottle green. **буты́ль, -и** large bottle; demijohn; carboy.

буфе́т, -а sideboard; buffet, refreshment room; bar, counter. **буфе́тная** *sb.* pantry. **буфе́тчик, -а** barman; steward. **буфе́тчица, -ы** barmaid; counter assistant.

бу́фы, буф *pl.* gathered fullness, close gathering, puffs.

бух *int.* thump, thud. **бу́хать, -аю** *impf.* (*pf.* **бу́хнуть**) thump, bang; drop noisily, bang down; thunder, thud; blurt out; **~ся** fall heavily; plump o.s. down.

бухга́лтер, -а book-keeper, accountant. **бухгалте́рия, -и** book-keeping, accountancy; counting-house; accounts office, department. **бухга́лтерский** book-keeping, account.

бу́хнуть¹, -ну; *fut.* swell.

бу́хнуть²(ся, -ну(сь *pf. of* **бу́хать(ся**

бу́хта, -ы bay, bight. **бу́хточка, -и** cove, creek, inlet.

бушева́ть, -шу́ю *impf.* rage, storm.

бушла́т, -а pea-jacket; wadded jacket; (*sl.*) **деревя́нный ~** coffin.

буя́н, -а rowdy, brawler. **буя́нить, -ню** *impf.* make row, create uproar, brawl. **буя́нство, -а** rowdyism, brawling.

бы, б *part.* **I.** +*past tense or inf.* indicates the conditional or subjunctive, expresses possibility, a wish, a polite suggestion or exhortation. **II.** (+**ни**) forms indef. prons. and conjs. see **е́сли, как, когда́, кто,** *etc.*

быва́ло *part.* used to, would; **мать быва́ло ча́сто пе́ла э́ту пе́сню** my mother would often sing this song. **быва́лый** experienced; worldly-wise; past, former; not new; habitual, familiar. **быва́ть, -а́ю** *impf.* be, be present; happen; take place; be inclined to be, tend to be; **как не быва́ло**+*g.* have completely disappeared; **как ни в чём не быва́ло** as if nothing had happened, as though everything was all right. **бы́вший** former, formerly, ex-.

бык, -а́ bull, ox; stag; pier.

были́на, -ы bylina. **были́нный** of byliny; epic, heroic.

бы́ло *part.* nearly, on the point of; (only) just; **чуть ~ не** very nearly, all but. **был|о́й** former, past, bygone; **~о́е** *sb.* the past. **быль, -и** the past, what really happened; true story, true happening.

быстрина́, **-ы́**; *pl.* **-ы** rapids. **быстроно́гий** swift-footed, fleet-footed; fast. **быстрота́**, **-ы́** quickness, swiftness, rapidity; speed. **быстроте́чный** fleeting, transient. **быстрохо́дный** fast, high-speed. **бы́стрый**; **быстр**, **-а́**, **-о** rapid, fast, quick; prompt.

быт, **-а**, *loc.* **-у́** way of life, life; everyday life; **слу́жба ~а** consumer services. **бытие́**, **-я́** being, existence; objective reality; **кни́га Бытия́** Genesis. **бытова́ть**, **-ту́ет** *impf.* exist; occur; be current. **бытово́|й** of everyday life; everyday; domestic; social; **~а́я жи́вопись** genre painting; **~о́е обслу́живание** consumer services; **~а́я ЭВМ** home computer; **~ы́е прибо́ры** domestic appliances.

бытописа́ние, **-я** annals, chronicles. **бытописа́тель**, **-я** *m.* annalist, chronicler; writer on social themes.

быть *pres.* 3rd sg. **есть**, *pl.* **суть**; *fut.* **бу́ду**; *past* **был**, **-а́**, **-о**; *imper.* **будь(те)** *impf.* be; exist; be situated; happen, take place; *impers.+d.* be sure to happen, be inevitable; **будь, что бу́дет** come what may; **~ беде́** there's sure to be trouble; **должно́ ~** probably, very likely; **как ~?** what is to be done?; **не будь его́** but for him, if it weren't for him; **так и ~** so be it; all right, very well, have it your own way.

быча́чий, **бы́чий** bull, ox. **бычо́к**[1], **-чка́** young ox, steer.

бычо́к[2], **-чка́** (*sl.*) cigarette end, fag-end.

бью *etc.*: *see* **бить**

бэ *nt.indecl.* the letter б.

бюллете́нь, **-я** *m.* bulletin; voting-paper, ballot-paper; medical certificate; **информаци́онный ~** newsletter; **быть на бюллете́не** be on the sick-list, be on sick-leave.

бюро́ *nt.indecl.* bureau; office; writing-desk; **тури́сти́ческое ~** travel agency. **бюрокра́т**, **-а** bureaucrat. **бюрократи́зм**, **-а** bureaucracy. **бюрократи́ческий** bureaucratic. **бюрокра́тия**, **-и** bureaucracy; bureaucrats. **бюст**, **-а** bust; bosom. **бюстга́льтер**, **-а** brassière, bra.

В

В *abbr.* (*of* **вольт**) volt; (*of* **восто́к**) E, East. **в** *letter*: *see* **вэ**

в, **во** *prep.* **I.** +*a.* into, to; on; at; within; for; as; through; **быть в** take after, be like; **в два ра́за бо́льше** twice as big, twice the size; **в на́ши дни** in our day; **войти́ в дом** go into the house; **в понеде́льник** on Monday; **в тече́ние**+*g.* during, in the course of; **в четы́ре** часа́ at four o'clock **высото́й в три ме́тра** three metres high; **игра́ть в ша́хматы** play chess; **моро́з в де́сять гра́дусов** ten degrees of frost; **пое́хать в Москву́** go to Moscow; **положи́ть в я́щик стола́** put in(to) a drawer; **преврати́ть во́ду в лёд** turn water into ice; **разби́ть в куски́** smash to pieces; **руба́шка в кле́тку** check(ed) shirt; **сесть в ваго́н** get into the carriage; **сказа́ть в шу́тку** say as a joke; **смотре́ть в окно́** look out of the window; **э́то мо́жно сде́лать в неде́лю** it can be done in a week. **II.** +*p.* in; on; at; of; at a distance of; **в двадца́том ве́ке** in the twentieth century; **в теа́тре** at the theatre; **в трёх киломе́трах от го́рода** three kilometres from the town; **в четвёртом часу́** between three (o'clock) and four; **в э́том году́** this year; **в январе́** in January; **лицо́ в весну́шках** freckled face; **пье́са в пяти́ а́ктах** a play in five acts, a five-act play; **роди́ться в Москве́** be born in Moscow; **са́хар в куска́х** lump sugar; **служи́ть в куха́рках** be a cook.

в. *abbr.* (*of* **век**) C, century.

в..., **во...**, **въ...** *vbl. pref. expressing direction of action or motion inwards or upwards*; *occurrence wholly within the agent.*

ваго́н, **-а** (railway-)carriage, coach; van; car; wagon-load; loads, stacks; **~-рестора́н** restaurant car, dining-car. **вагоне́тка**, **-и** truck, trolley. **вагоновожа́тый** *sb.* tram-driver.

ва́жничанье, **-я** airs. **ва́жничать**, **-аю** *impf.* give o.s. airs; +*i.* plume o.s., pride o.s., on. **ва́жность**, **-и** importance, consequence; significance; pomposity, pretentiousness. **ва́жный**; **-жен**, **-жна́**, **-о** important; weighty, consequential; pompous, pretentious.

ва́за, **-ы** vase, bowl.

ва́кса, **-ы** (shoe-)polish, blacking; **чи́стить ва́ксой** polish. **ва́ксить**, **-кшу** *impf.* (*pf.* **на~**) black, polish.

вал[1], **-а**, *loc.* **-у́**; *pl.* **-ы́** bank, earthen wall; rampart; billow, roller, wave; barrage.

вал[2], **-а**, *loc.* **-у́**; *pl.* **-ы́** shaft, spindle.

вал[3], **-а** gross output.

валанда́ться, **-аюсь** *impf.* loiter, hang about; mess about.

валёк, **-лька́** battledore; swingle-tree; roll; roller; flail; loom.

ва́ленок, **-нка**; *g.pl.* **-нок** felt boot. **ва́леный** felt.

вале́т, **-а** knave, Jack.

ва́лик, **-а** bolster; roller; cylinder; spindle, shaft; platen.

вали́ть[1], **-лю́т** *impf.* flock, throng; pour; **ва́лом ~** throng, flock; **вали́(те)!** go on! have a go!

вали́ть[2], **-лю́**, **-лишь** *impf.* (*pf.* **по~**, **с~**) throw down, bring down, knock down; overthrow; fell; lay low; heap, pile up; **~ся** fall, collapse; drop; topple; **у него́ всё из рук ва́лится** his fingers are all thumbs; he can't give his mind to anything.

ва́лка, -и felling. ва́лкий; -лок, -лка́, -о unsteady, shaky.

валово́й gross; wholesale.

валто́рна, -ы French-horn. валторни́ст, -a French-horn (player).

валу́н, -а́ boulder.

вальс, -a waltz. вальси́ровать, -и́рую *impf.* waltz.

вальцева́ть, -цу́ю *impf.* roll. вальцо́вка, -и rolling; rolling press. вальцо́вый rolling. вальцы́, *pl.* -о́в rolling press. вальцо́вщик, -a roller.

валю́та, -ы currency; foreign currency. валю́тчик, -a, -чица, -ы (foreign) currency speculator.

ва́ляный felt. валя́ть, -я́ю *impf.* (*pf.* на~, с~) drag; roll; shape; full; felt; botch, bungle; make a mess (of), mess about; ~ дурака́ play the fool; валя́й(те)! go ahead! carry on!; ~ся lie, lie about, loll; roll, wallow; ~ся в нога́х y+g. fall at the feet of.

вам, ва́ми *see* вы

вани́ль, -и vanilla, vanilla-pod.

ва́нна, -ы, ва́нночка, -и bath. ва́нный bath; ~ая *sb.* bathroom.

ва́нька, -и *m.* cabby.

ва́рвар, -a barbarian. варвари́зм, -a loanword; barbarism. ва́рварский barbarian; barbarous; barbaric. ва́рварство, -a barbarity; vandalism.

ва́режка, -и mitten.

варёный boiled; limp. варе́нье, -я jam, marmalade.

вариа́нт, -a reading, variant; version; option; scenario; model.

вари́ть, -рю́, -ришь *impf.* (*pf.* с~) boil; cook; brew; make; digest; ~ся boil; cook. ва́рка, -и boiling; cooking; making; brewing.

Варша́ва, -ы Warsaw.

вас *see* вы

василёк, -лька́ cornflower. василько́вый cornflower; cornflower blue.

ва́та, -ы cotton wool; wadding; са́харная ~ candyfloss.

вата́га, -и band, gang.

ватерли́ния, -и water-line. ватерпа́с, -a spirit-level.

Ватика́н, -a the Vatican.

вати́н, -a (sheet) wadding, quilting. ва́тник, -a quilted jacket. ва́тный quilted, wadded.

ватру́шка, -и open tart; curd tart, cheesecake.

ватт, -a; *g.pl.* ватт watt.

ва́учер, -a (privatization) voucher.

ва́фельный waffle. ва́фля, -и; *g.pl.* -фель waffle.

вахла́к, -а́ lout; sloven.

ва́хта, -ы watch. ва́хтенный watch; ~ журна́л log, log-book; ~ команди́р officer of the watch, duty officer.

ваш, -его *m.*, ва́ша, -ей *f.*, ва́ше, -его *nt.*, ва́ши, -их *pl.*, *pron.* your, yours.

Вашингто́н, -a Washington.

вая́ние, -я sculpture. вая́тель, -я *m.* sculptor. вая́ть, -я́ю *impf.* (*pf.* из~) sculpture; carve, model.

вбега́ть, -а́ю *impf.*, вбежа́ть, вбегу́ *pf.* run in, rush in.

вберу́ *etc.*: *see* вобра́ть

вбива́ть, -а́ю *impf.* of вбить. вби́вка, -и knocking in, driving in, hammering.

вбира́ть, -а́ю *impf.* of вобра́ть

вбить, вобью́, -бьёшь *pf.* (*impf.* вбива́ть) drive in, hammer in, knock in.

вблизи́ *adv.* (+от+g.) close (to), near (to), not far (from); closely.

вбок *adv.* sideways, to one side.

вбра́сывание, -я throw-in. вбра́сывать, -аю *impf.* of вбро́сить

вброд *adv.* by fording or wading; переходи́ть ~ ford, wade.

вбро́сить, -о́шу *pf.* (*impf.*, вбра́сывать) throw in.

вв. *abbr.* (*of* века́) centuries.

вва́ливать, -аю *impf.*, ввали́ть, -лю́, -лишь *pf.* throw heavily, heave, fling, bundle, tumble; ~ся fall heavily; sink, become hollow or sunken; burst in. ввали́вшийся sunken, hollow.

введе́ние, -я leading in; introduction. введу́ *etc.*: *see* ввести́

ввезти́, -зу́, -зёшь; ввёз, -ла́ *pf.* (*impf.* ввози́ть) import; bring in, take in, carry in.

ввек *adv.* ever; for ever.

вве́рить, -рю *pf.* (*impf.* вверя́ть) entrust, confide; ~ся+d. trust in, put one's faith in; put o.s. in the hands of.

ввернуть, -ну́, -нёшь *pf.*, ввёртывать, -аю *impf.* screw in; insert; put in.

вверх *adv.* up, upward(s); ~дном, ~ нога́ми, ~ тормашками upside down, topsy-turvy; ~ (по ле́стнице) upstairs; ~ (по тече́нию) upstream. вверху́ *adv.* above, overhead; upstairs; upstream; at the top.

вве́рять(ся, -я́ю(сь *impf. of* вве́рить(ся

ввести́, -еду́, -едёшь; ввёл, -а́ *pf.* (*impf.* вводи́ть) bring in, lead in; introduce; insert, interpolate, incorporate; administer.

ввиду́ *prep.*+g. in view of.

ввинти́ть, -нчу́ *pf.*, вви́нчивать, -аю *impf.* screw in.

ввод, -a bringing in, leading in; lead-in, lead; input, intake. вводи́ть, -ожу́, -о́дишь *impf.* of ввести́. вво́дн|ый introductory; parenthetic; ~ое предложе́ние, ~ое сло́во parenthesis; ~ый тон leading note.

ввожу́ *see* вводи́ть, ввози́ть

ввоз, -a importation, importing; import, imports. ввози́ть, -ожу́, -о́зишь *impf.* of ввезти́. вво́зный imported; import.

вво́лю *adv.* to one's heart's content; enough and to spare; ad lib.

ввосьмеро *adv.* eight times. ввосьмеро́м *adv.* eight together; мы ~ eight of us.

ВВС *abbr.* (*of* вое́нно-возду́шные си́лы) air force.

ввысь *adv.* up, upward(s).

ввяза́ть, **-яжу́**, **-я́жешь** *pf.*, **ввя́зывать**, **-аю** *impf.* knit in; involve; **~ся** meddle, get involved, get or be mixed up (in).

вгиб, **-а** inward bend; concavity, dent, sag. **вгиба́ть(ся**, **-а́ю(сь** *impf. of* **вогну́ть(ся**

вглубь *adv.* deep, deep into, into the depths.

вгляде́ться, **-яжу́сь** *pf.*, **вгля́дываться**, **-аюсь** *impf.* peer, look closely or intently (**в**+*a.* at).

вгоня́ть, **-я́ю** *impf. of* **вогна́ть**. **вдава́ться**, **вдаю́сь**, **-ёшься** *impf. of* **вда́ться**

вдави́ть, **-авлю́**, **-а́вишь** *pf.*, **вда́вливать**, **-аю** *impf.* press in, crush in; **~ся** give, give way; be crushed or pressed in; press in.

вдалеке́, **вдали́** *adv.* in the distance, far away; **~ от** a long way from. **вдаль** *adv.* into the distance.

вда́ться, **-а́мся**, **-а́шься**, **-а́стся**, **-ади́мся**; **-а́лся**, **-ла́сь** *pf.* (*impf.* **вдава́ться**) jut out; penetrate, go in; **~ в то́нкости** split hairs.

вдвига́ть(ся, **-а́ю(сь** *impf.*, **вдви́нуть(ся**, **-ну(сь** *pf.* push in, move in, thrust in.

вдво́е *adv.* twice; double; **~ бо́льше** twice as big, as much, as many. **вдвоём** *adv.* (the) two together, both. **вдвойне́** *adv.* twice as much, double; doubly.

вдева́ть, **-а́ю** *impf. of* **вдеть**

вдёжка, **-и** threading; thread, tape, cord, lace. **вде́лать**, **-аю** *pf.*, **вде́лывать**, **-аю** *impf.* set in, fit in.

вде́ржка, **-и** bodkin; threading. **вдёргивать**, **-аю** *impf.*, **вдёрнуть**, **-ну** *pf.* **в**+*a.* thread through, pull through.

вде́сятеро *adv.* ten times; **~ бо́льше** ten times as much, as many. **вдесятеро́м** *adv.* ten together; **мы ~** ten of us.

вдеть, **-е́ну** *pf.* (*impf.* **вдева́ть**) put in, thread.

ВДНХ *abbr.* (*of* **Вы́ставка достиже́ний наро́дного хозя́йства**) Exhibition of National Economic Achievements.

вдоба́вок *adv.* in addition; besides, as well, into the bargain.

вдова́, **-ы́**; *pl.* **-ы** widow. **вдове́ц**, **-вца́** widower. **вдо́вий** widow's, widows'. **вдови́ца**, **-ы** widow.

вдо́воль *adv.* enough; in abundance; plenty (of).

вдо́вствующая *sb.* dowager. **вдо́вый** widowed.

вдого́нку *adv.* (**за**+*i.*) after, in pursuit (of).

вдоль *adv.* lengthways, lengthwise; **~ и попере́к** in all directions, far and wide; minutely, in detail; *prep.*+*g. or* **по**+*d.* along.

вдох, **-а** breath. **вдохнове́ние**, **-я** inspiration, **вдохнове́нный** inspired. **вдохнови́тель**, **-я** *m.*, **-тельница**, **-ы** inspirer, inspiration. **вдохнови́ть**, **-влю́** *pf.*, **вдохновля́ть**, **-я́ю** *impf.* inspire. **вдохну́ть**, **-ну́**, **-нёшь** *pf.* (*impf.* **вдыха́ть**) breathe in, inhale; **+в**+*a.* inspire with, breathe into.

вдре́безги *adv.* to pieces, to smithereens; **~**

пьян blotto, plastered.

вдруг *adv.* suddenly; all at once; what if? suppose; **все ~** all together.

вдува́ть, **-а́ю** *impf. of* **вду́нуть**, **вдуть**

вду́маться, **-аюсь** *pf.*, **вду́мываться**, **-аюсь** *impf.* ponder, meditate; **+в**+*a.* think over. **вду́мчивый** thoughtful.

вду́нуть, **-ну** *pf.*, **вдуть**, **-у́ю** *pf.* (*impf.* **вдува́ть**) blow in, pump in.

вдыха́ние, **-я** inhalation, inspiration. **вдыха́тельный** respiratory. **вдыха́ть**, **-а́ю** *impf. of* **вдохну́ть**

веда́ть, **-аю** *impf.* know; **+i.** manage, handle; be in charge of. **ве́дение¹**, **-я** authority, jurisdiction; **в ве́дении**+*g.* under the jurisdiction of; **вне моего́ ве́дения** outside my province.

веде́ние², **-я** conducting, conduct, management; **~ книг** book-keeping.

ве́домость, **-и**; *g.pl.* **-е́й** list, register; *pl.* gazette. **ве́домственный** departmental. **ве́домство**, **-а** department.

ведро́, **-а́**; *pl.* **вёдра**, **-дер** bucket, pail; vedro (*old Russ. liquid measure, equivalent to approx. 12 litres*).

веду́ *etc.: see* **вести́**. **веду́щ|ий** leading; **~ее колесо́** driving-wheel.

ведь *part. and conj.* you see, you know; but; why; isn't it? is it?

ве́дьма, **-ы** witch; old bag, hag.

ве́ер, **-а**; *pl.* **-а́** fan. **веерообра́зный** fan-shaped; **~ свод** fan vault(ing).

ве́жливость, **-и** politeness, courtesy, civility. **ве́жливый** polite, courteous, civil.

везде́ *adv.* everywhere. **вездехо́д**, **-а** cross-country vehicle. **вездехо́дный** cross-country.

везе́ние, **-я** luck. **везу́чий** fortunate, lucky. **везти́**, **-зу́**, **-зёшь**; **вёз**, **-ла́** *impf.* (*pf.* **по~**) cart, convey, carry; bring, take; *impers.*+*d.* be lucky, be in luck, have luck; **ему́ не везло́** he was unlucky.

Везу́вий, **-я** (Mt.) Vesuvius.

век, **-а (-у)**, *loc.* **-у́**; *pl.* **-а́** century; age; life, lifetime; **испоко́н ~о́в** from time immemorial. **век** *adv.* for ages, for ever; always, constantly.

ве́ко, **-а**; *pl.* **-и**, **век** eyelid.

веко́вечный eternal, everlasting. **веково́й** ancient, age-old, secular.

ве́ксель, **-я**; *pl.* **-я́**, **-е́й** *m.* promissory note, bill (of exchange). **ве́ксельный**; **~ курс** rate of exchange.

вёл *etc.: see* **вести́**

веле́ть, **-лю́** *impf. & pf.* order, tell; **не ~** forbid, not allow.

велика́н, **-а** giant. **велика́нша**, **-и** giantess. **велика́нский** gigantic. **вели́к|ий**; **вели́к**, **-а** *or* **-а́** great; big, large; too big; **~ие держа́вы** Great Powers; **~ий князь** grand prince, grand duke; **~ий пост** Lent.

велико... *in comb.* great. **Великобрита́ния**, **-и** Great Britain. **~держа́вный** great-power.

~**ду́шие**, -я magnanimity, generosity. ~**ду́шный** magnanimous; generous. ~**ле́пие**, -я splendour, magnificence. ~**ле́пный** splendid, magnificent; excellent. ~**по́стный** Lenten. ~**ру́с**, -а, -**ру́ска**, -и Great Russian. ~**ру́сский** Great Russian.

велича́вый stately, majestic. **велича́йший** greatest, extreme, supreme. **вели́чественный** majestic, grand. **вели́чество**, -а Majesty. **вели́чие**, -я greatness, grandeur, sublimity. **величина́**, -ы́; pl. -ы size; quantity, magnitude; value; great figure.

велосипе́д, -а bicycle, bike; **трёхколёсный** ~ tricycle. **велосипеди́ст**, -а cyclist. **велотренажёр**, -а exercise bicycle.

вельве́т, -а velveteen, cotton velvet; ~ в ру́бчик corduroy. **вельве́товый** velveteen; corduroy.

вельмо́жа, -и m. grandee, dignitary, magnate.

Ве́на, -ы Vienna.

ве́на, -ы vein.

венге́рка, -и Hungarian; dolman; Hungarian ballroom dance. **венге́рский** Hungarian. **венгр**, -а Hungarian. **Ве́нгрия**, -и Hungary.

Вене́ра, -ы Venus. **вене́рин** adj. Venusian, of Venus; ~ **волосо́к** maidenhair fern. **венери́ческий** venereal.

вене́ц[1], -нца Viennese.

вене́ц[2], -нца́ crown; wreath, garland; corona; halo.

Вене́ция, -и Venice.

вене́чный coronal; coronary.

ве́нзель, -я; pl. -я, -ей m. monogram.

ве́ник, -а besom, (birch-)broom.

ве́нка, -и Viennese.

вено́зный venous.

вено́к, -нка́ wreath, garland.

ве́нский Viennese; ~ **стул** ballroom chair.

ве́нтиль, -я m. valve.

вентиля́тор, -а ventilator; extractor (fan).

венча́льный wedding. **венча́ние**, -я wedding; coronation. **венча́ть**, -а́ю impf. (pf. об~, по~, у~) crown; marry; ~**ся** be married, marry. **ве́нчик**, -а halo, nimbus; corolla; edge, rim; crown; ring, bolt.

ве́ра, -ы faith, belief; trust, confidence; **на** ~**у** on trust.

ве́рба, -ы willow, osier, pussy-willow; willow branch. **ве́рбн|ый**; ~**ое воскресе́нье** Palm Sunday.

верблю́д, -а, -**ю́дица**, -ы camel. **верблю́ж|ий** camel's; camelhair; ~**ья шерсть** camel's hair.

ве́рбный see **ве́рба**

вербова́ть, -бу́ю impf. (pf. за~) recruit, enlist. **вербо́вка**, -и recruitment.

ве́рбовый willow; osier; wicker.

верёвка, -и rope; string; cord. **верёвочный** rope.

верени́ца, -ы row, file, line, string.

ве́реск, -а heather.

веретено́, -а́; pl. -тёна spindle, shank, axle.

вереща́ть, -щу́ impf. squeal; chirp.

ве́рить, -рю impf. believe, have faith; +d. or в+a. trust (in), believe in; ~ **на́ сло́во** take on trust.

вермише́ль, -и vermicelli.

верне́е adv. rather. **вернопо́дданный** loyal, faithful. **ве́рно** part. probably, I suppose; that's right! **ве́рность**, -и faithfulness, loyalty; truth, correctness.

верну́ть, -ну́, -нёшь pf. (impf. возвраща́ть) give back, return; get back, recover, retrieve; ~**ся** return, revert. **ве́рный**, -рен, -рна́, -о faithful, loyal; true; correct; sure; reliable; certain.

ве́рование, -я belief; creed. **ве́ровать**, -рую impf. believe. **вероисповеда́ние**, -я religion; denomination. **вероло́мный** treacherous, perfidious. **вероотсту́пник**, -а apostate. **веротерпи́мость**, -и (religious) toleration. **вероя́тно** adv. probably. **вероя́тность**, -и probability. **вероя́тный** probable, likely.

Верса́ль, -и Versailles.

ве́рсия, -и version.

верста́, -ы́, а. -у́ or вёрсту; pl. вёрсты verst (old Russ. measurement, equivalent to approx. 1.06 km.); verst-post: **за́** ~у miles away.

верста́к, -а́ bench.

верстово́й verst (see **верста́**); ~ **столб** milestone.

ве́ртел, -а; pl. -а́ spit, skewer. **верте́ть**, -чу́, -тишь impf. turn (round); twirl; spin; ~**ся** rotate, turn (round), revolve, spin; move about, hang about, go round; fidget; turn and twist, dodge. **вёрткий** -ток, -тка nimble, agile. **вертлю́г**, -а́ swivel. **вертля́вый** restless, fidgety; flighty, frivolous.

вертодро́м, -а heliport. **вертолёт**, -а helicopter.

верту́н, -а́ fidget; tumbler-pigeon. **верту́шка**, -и revolving door, revolving stand; turntable; flibbertigibbet; coquette.

ве́рующий sb. believer.

верфь, -и dockyard, shipyard.

верх, -а (-у), loc. -у́; pl. -и́ or -а́ top; summit; height; upper part, upper side; upper reaches; bonnet, hood; upper hand; outside; right side; pl. upper ten, bosses, leadership, management, top brass; high notes. **ве́рхний** upper; outer; top. **верхо́вный** supreme. **верхово́й**[1] riding; sb. rider. **верхово́й**[2] upstream, up-river; upper. **верхо́вье**, -я; g.pl. -вьев upper reaches, head. **верхола́з**, -а steeple-jack. **верхо́м**[1] adv. on high ground; quite full, brim-full. **верхо́м**[2] adv. on horseback; astride; **е́здить** ~ ride. **верху́шка**, -и top, summit; apex; bosses, top brass, management.

верчу́ etc.: see **верте́ть**

вершина, -ы top, summit; peak; height; apex, vertex. **верши́ть**, -шу́ impf. top, top out; decide, settle; +i. manage, control, direct; control, sway.

вершо́к, -шка́ vershok (*old Russ. measurement, equivalent to approx. 4.4 cm.*); inch; smattering.

вес, -а (-у), *loc.* -ý; *pl.* -á weight; authority, influence; **на ~** by weight; **на ~ý** suspended, balanced.

весеље́ть, -е́ю *impf.* (*pf.* **по~**) cheer up, be cheerful. **весели́ть**, -лю́ *impf.* (*pf.* **раз~**) cheer up, gladden; amuse; **~ся** enjoy o.s.; amuse o.s. **ве́село** *adv.* gaily, merrily. **весёлость**, -и gaiety; cheerfulness. **весё́лый; ве́сел**, -á, -о gay, merry; cheerful, lively. **весе́лье**, -я gaiety, merriment.

весе́нн|ий spring; vernal; **~ее равноде́нствие** vernal equinox.

ве́сить, ве́шу *impf.* weigh. **ве́ский** weighty, solid.

весло́, -á; *pl.* вёсла, -сел oar; scull; paddle.

весна́, -ы́; *pl.* вёсны, -сен spring; spring-time. **весно́й, -о́ю** *adv.* in (the) spring. **весну́шка**, -и freckle. **весну́шчатый** freckled. **весня́нка**, -и mayfly.

весово́й weight, of weight; sold by weight. **весо́мый** heavy, weighty; ponderable.

вест, -а west; west wind.

ве́стерн, a western.

вести́, веду́, -дёшь; вёл, -á *impf.* (*pf.* **по~**) lead, take; conduct, carry on; be engaged in, drive; conduct; direct, run; keep; +*i.* pass, run (**по**+*d.* over, across); **~ кора́бль** navigate a ship; **~ (своё) нача́ло** originate; **~ ого́нь** fire; **~ самолёт** pilot an aircraft; **~ свой род от** be descended from; **~ себя́** behave, conduct o.s.; **~сь** be observed, be the the custom.

ве́стник, -a messenger, herald; bulletin. **вестово́й** signal; *sb.* orderly. **весть, и;** *g.pl.* -е́й news; *pl.* tales, talk, gossip; **без вести** without trace. **весть; Бог ~** God knows; **не ~** goodness knows, there's no knowing.

весы́, -о́в *pl.* scales, balance; Libra.

весь, всего́ *m.*, **вся, всей** *f.*, **всё, всего́** *nt.*, **все, всех** *pl.*, *pron.* all, the whole of; all gone; **бума́га вся** the paper has all gone, there's no paper left; **во ~ го́лос** at the top of one's voice; **во-всю** like anything; **вот и всё** that's all; **при всём том** for all that; moreover; **всего́ хоро́шего!** goodbye; all the best!; **всё** everything; **без всего́** without anything, with nothing; **все** everybody.

весьма́ *adv.* very, highly; very much.

ветви́стый spreading, (many-) branched, branching. **ветви́ться, -влю́сь** *impf.* branch. **ветвра́ч**, -á vet.

ветвь, -и; *g.pl.* -е́й branch; bough.

ве́тер, -тра (-у), *loc.* -ý; *g.pl.* ветро́в wind; *pl.* wind; **по ве́тру** before the wind; down wind; **подби́тый ве́тром** empty-headed; light, flimsy; **под ве́тром** (to) leeward; **про́тив ве́тра** close to the wind, against the wind. **ветеро́к, -рка́** breeze.

ве́тка, -и branch; twig.

ветла́, -ы́; *pl.* ветлы (white) willow.

ве́то *nt.indecl.* veto.

ве́точка, -и twig, sprig, shoot.

вето́шка, -и *rag.* **вето́шник**, -a old clothes dealer, rag-dealer. **ве́тошь, -и** old clothes, rags.

ветрене́ть, -е́ет *impf.* become windy, get windy. **ве́треный** windy; frivolous, inconstant, unstable. **ветров|о́й** wind, of wind; **~о́е окно́, ~о́е стекло́** windscreen. **ветроме́р**, -a anemometer. **ветроуказа́тель**, -я *m.* drogue, wind cone, wind sock. **ветра́к, -á** wind motor; windmill. **ветряно́й, ве́тряный** wind; **ве́тряная о́спа** chicken-pox.

ве́тхий; ветх, -á, -о old, ancient; dilapidated, ramshackle, tumbledown; decrepit; **В~ заве́т** Old Testament. **ветхозаве́тный** Old-Testament; antiquated, out-of-date. **ве́тхость**, -и decrepitude, dilapidation, decay.

ветчина́, -ы́ ham.

ветша́ть, -áю *impf.* (*pf.* **об~**) decay; become dilapidated.

ве́ха, -и landmark; marker post, stake.

ве́чер, -а; *pl.* -á evening; party; soirée. **вечерн|ий** evening; **~яя заря́** sunset; dusk. **вече́рник**, -a evening student, evening worker. **вече́рня, -и;** *g.pl.* -рен vespers. **ве́чером** *adv.* in the evening.

ве́чно *adv.* for ever, eternally; everlastingly. **вечнозелёный** evergreen. **ве́чность, -и** eternity; an age, ages. **ве́чн|ый** eternal, everlasting; endless; perpetual; **~ая мерзлота́** permafrost; **~ое перо́** fountain-pen.

ве́шалка, -и peg, rack, stand; hanger; cloakroom. **ве́шать, -аю** *impf.* (*pf.* **взве́сить, пове́сить, све́шать**) hang; weigh, weigh out; **~ся** be hung, be hanged; hang o.s.; weigh o.s.

ве́шний spring, vernal.

ве́шу *etc.*: *see* **ве́сить**

веща́ние, -я radio; prophecy. **веща́ть, -áю** *impf.* broadcast; prophesy; pontificate.

вещево́й clothing, kit; in kind; **~ мешо́к** knapsack; pack, hold-all, kit-bag; **~ склад** clothing store, stores. **веще́ственный** substantial, material, real. **вещество́, -á** substance; matter. **вещмешо́к, -шка́** rucksack. **вещь, -и;** *g.pl.* -е́й thing.

ве́ялка, -и winnowing-fan; winnowing-machine. **ве́яние, -я** winnowing; breathing, blowing; current, tendency, trend. **ве́ять, ве́ю** *impf.* (*pf.* **про~**) winnow, fan; blow, breathe; wave, flutter.

вз..., взо..., взъ..., вс... *vbl. pref. expressing direction of motion or action upwards or on to; rapidity or suddenness of occurrence; completion or finality of action.*

взад *adv.* backwards; **~ и вперёд** backwards and forwards, to and fro.

взаи́мность, -и reciprocity; requital, return. **взаи́мный** mutual, reciprocal.

взаи́мо... *in comb.* inter-. **взаимоде́йствие, -я** interaction; co-operation, coordination **~де́йствовать, -твую** *impf.* interact; cooperate. ~отношéние, -я interrelation; *pl.* relations. ~пóмощь, -и mutual aid. ~свя́зь, -и intercommunication; interdependence, correlation.

взаймы́ *adv.* as a loan; **взять ~** borrow; **дать ~** lend.

взамéн *prep.*+g. instead of; in return for, in exchange for.

взаперти́ *adv.* under lock and key; in seclusion, in isolation.

взапрáвду *adv.* in truth, really and truly.

вз|баламýтить, -ýчу *pf.*

взбáлмошный unbalanced, eccentric.

взбáлтывание, -я shaking (up). **взбáлтывать, -аю** *impf. of* **взболтáть**

взбегáть, -áю *impf.*, **взбежáть, -егý** *pf.* run up.

взберýсь *etc.*: see **взобрáться. вз|беси́ть(ся, -ешý(сь, -éсишь(ся** *pf.* **взбивáть, -áю** *impf. of* **взбить. взбирáться, -áюсь** *impf. of* **взобрáться**

взби́тый whipped, beaten. **взбить, взобью́, -бьёшь** *pf.* (*impf.* **взбивáть**) beat (up), whip; shake up, fluff up.

взболтáть, -áю *pf.* (*impf.* **взбáлтывать**) shake (up).

вз|бороздить, -зжý *pf.* **вз|борони́ть, -ню́** *pf.* **взбрáсывать, -аю** *impf. of* **взбро́сить**

взбредáть, -áю *impf.*, **взбрести́, -едý, -едёшь; -ёл, -елá** *pf.* +на+a. climb (up), mount, with difficulty; struggle up; **~ в гóлову, на ум** come into one's head.

взбро́сить, -óшу *pf.* (*impf.* **взбрáсывать**) throw up, toss up.

вз|будорáжить, -жу *pf.* **вз|бунтовáться, -тýюсь** *pf.*

взбухáть, -áет *impf.*, **взбýхнуть, -нет; -ух** *pf.* swell (out).

взвáливать, -аю *impf.*, **взвали́ть, -лю́, -лишь** *pf.* hoist, heave (up); load; +на+a. saddle with.

взвéсить, -éшу *pf.* (*impf.* **вéшать, взвéшивать**) weigh.

взвéсти, -едý, -едёшь; -ёл, -á *pf.* (*impf.* **взводи́ть**) lead up, take up; lift up, raise; cock, arm; +на+a. impute to, bring against.

взвесь, -и suspension. **взвéшенный** weighed; suspended, of suspension. **взвéшивать, -аю** *impf. of* **взвéсить**

взвивáть(ся, -áю(сь *impf. of* **взвить(ся**

взвизг, -а a scream, squeal, screech; yelp. **взви́згивать, -аю** *impf.*, **взви́згнуть, -ну** *pf.* let out screams, a scream; scream, screech; yelp.

взвинти́ть, -нчý *pf.*, **взви́нчивать, -аю** *impf.* excite, work up; inflate; **~ся** work o.s. up; spiral up. **взви́нченный** excited, worked up; nervy, on edge; highly strung; inflated.

взвить, взовью́, -ёшь; -ил, -á, -о *pf.* (*impf.* **взвивáть**) raise; **~ся** rise, be hoisted; fly up, soar.

взвод[1], -а platoon, troop.

взвод[2], -а cocking; notch; **на боевóм ~е** at half cock. **взводи́ть, -ожý, -óдишь** *impf. of* **взвéсти. взводнóй** cocking.

взвóдный platoon; *sb.* platoon commander.

вз|двóить, -ою́ *pf.*

взволнóванный agitated, disturbed; ruffled; anxious, troubled, worried. **вз|волновáть(ся, -нýю(сь** *pf.*

взвыть, взвóю *pf.* howl, set up a howl.

взгляд, -а look; glance; gaze, stare; view; opinion; **на ~** to judge from appearances; **на пéрвый ~, с пéрвого ~** at first sight. **взгля́дывать, -аю** *impf.*, **взгляну́ть, -яну́, -я́нешь** *pf.* look, glance.

взгóрок, -рка, взгóрье, -я hill, hillock.

взгромождáть, -áю *impf.*, **взгромозди́ть, -зжý** *pf.* pile up; **~ся** clamber up.

вздёргивать, -аю *impf.*, **вздёрнуть, -ну** *pf.* hitch up; jerk up; turn up; hang.

вздор, -а nonsense. **вздóрный** cantankerous, quarrelsome; foolish, stupid.

вздорожáние, -я rise in price. **вз|дорожáть, -áет** *pf.*

вздох, -а a sigh; deep breath. **вздохну́ть, -нý, -нёшь** *pf.* (*impf.* **вздыхáть**) sigh; heave a sigh; take a deep breath; take a breather, pause for breath.

вздрáгивать, -аю *impf.* (*pf.* **вздрóгнуть**) shudder, quiver.

вздремну́ть, -нý, -нёшь *pf.* have a nap, doze.

вздрóгнуть, -ну *pf.* (*impf.* **вздрáгивать**) start, jump; wince, flinch.

вздувáть(ся, -áю(сь *impf. of* **вздýть[1](ся**

вздýмать, -аю *pf.* take it into one's head; **не вздýмай(те)!** mind you don't, don't you dare! **вздýматься, -ается** *pf.*, *impers.* (+d.) come into one's head; **как вздýмается** as the fancy takes one, as one likes.

вздýтие, -я swelling; inflation. **вздýтый** swollen. **вздуть[1], -ýю** *pf.* (*impf.* **вздувáть**) blow up, swell, inflate; **~ся** swell.

вздуть[2], -ýю *pf.* thrash, lick, give a hiding.

вздыхáние, -я sighing; sigh. **вздыхáтель, -я** *m.* admirer, suitor. **вздыхáть, -áю** *impf.* (*pf.* **вздохну́ть**) breathe; sigh.

взимáть, -áю *impf.* levy, collect.

взлáмывать, -аю *impf. of* **взломáть**

вз|лелéять, -éю *pf.*

взлёт, -а flight; taking wing; take-off. **взлетáть, -áю** *impf.*, **взлетéть, -лечý** *pf.* fly (up); take off. **взлётный** flying; take-off; **взлётно-посáдочная полосá** runway, landing strip.

взлом, -а a breaking open, breaking in; break-in. **взломáть, -áю** *pf.* (*impf.* **взлáмывать**) break open, force; smash; break up, break through. **взлóмщик, -а** burglar, house-breaker.

взлохмáченный dishevelled, tousled.

взмах, -а stroke, sweep, wave, flap. **взмáхивать, -аю** *impf.*, **взмахну́ть, -нý, -нёшь** *pf.*+i. wave, flap.

взмóрье, -я (sea-)shore, coast; seaside, beach;

coastal waters.

вз|мути́ть, -учу́, -у́тишь *pf.*

взнос, -а payment; fee, dues; subscription; instalment.

взнузда́ть, -а́ю *pf.*, взну́здывать, -аю *impf.* bridle.

взо... *see* вз...

взобра́ться, взберу́сь, -ёшься; -а́лся, -ла́сь, -а́ло́сь *pf.* (*impf.* взбира́ться) на+*a.* climb (up), clamber up.

взобью́ *etc.*: *see* взбить. взовью́ *etc.*: *see* взвить

взойти́, -йду́, -йдёшь; -ошёл, -шла́ *pf.* (*impf.* вос-, всходи́ть) rise, go up, come up; на+*a.* mount, ascend; enter.

взор, -а look, glance.

взорва́ть, -ву́, -вёшь; -а́л, -а́, -о *pf.* (*impf.* взрыва́ть) blow up; blast; fire, explode, detonate; exasperate, madden; ~ся blow up, burst, explode.

взро́слый grown-up, adult.

взрыв, -а explosion; burst, outburst; plosion. взрыва́тель, -я *m.* fuse. взрыва́ть, -а́ю *impf.*, взрыть, -ро́ю *pf.* (*pf. also* взорва́ть) blow up; ~ся blow up, explode. взрывн|о́й explosive; explosion, blasting; plosive; ~а́я волна́ shock wave, blast. взрывча́тка, -и explosive. взры́вчатый explosive.

взъ... *see* вз...

взъеро́шенный tousled, dishevelled; ruffled. взъеро́шивать, -аю *impf.*, взъ|еро́шить, -шу *pf.* tousle, ruffle, rumple; ~ся become dishevelled, bristle up, stand on end.

взыва́ть, -а́ю *impf. of* воззва́ть

взыска́ние, -я penalty, punishment; recovery, exaction; prosecution. взыска́тельный exacting; demanding. взыска́ть, -ыщу́, -ы́щешь *pf.*, взы́скивать, -аю *impf.* exact, recover; call to account, make answer.

взя́тие, -я taking, capture, seizure. взя́тка, -и bribe; trick. взя́точничество, -а bribery, corruption. взять(ся), возьму́(сь), -мёшь(ся); -я́л(ся, -а́(сь, -о(сь *pf. of* брать(ся); ни дать ни ~ exactly, neither more nor less than; отку́да ни возьми́сь out of the blue, from nowhere.

вибра́ция, -и vibration. вибри́ровать, -рует *impf.* vibrate, oscillate.

вид[1], -а (-у), *loc.* -у́ look; appearance; air; shape, form; condition; view; prospect; sight; де́лать вид pretend; име́ть в ~у́ plan, intend; mean; bear in mind, not forget; из ~у out of sight; на ~у́ in the public eye; потеря́ть из ~у lose sight of; под ~ом under the pretext; при ~е at the sight.

вид[2], -а kind, sort; species.

ви́данный seen; heard of. вида́ть, -а́ю *impf.* (*pf.* по~, у~) see; ~ся meet; see one another. ви́дение[1], -я sight, vision. виде́ние[2], -я vision, apparition.

ви́део *in comb.* video. видеоза́пись, -и video recording. ~ка́мера, -ы video camera. ~кассе́та, -ы video cassette. ~ле́нта,

-ы videotape. ~магнитофо́н, -а video recorder. ~те́ка, -и video rental club. ~телефо́н, -а videophone.

ви́деть, ви́жу *impf.* (*pf.* у~) see; ~ во сне dream (of); ~ся see one another, meet; appear. ви́димо *adv.* visibly; evidently; seemingly. ви́димо-неви́димо *adv.* immense numbers of. ви́димость, -и visibility, vision; appearance, semblance, show; appearances. ви́димый visible, in sight; apparent, evident, seeming. видне́ться, -е́ется be visible. ви́дный; -ден, -дна́, -о, -ы *or* -ы́ visible; conspicuous; distinguished, prominent; stately, portly, dignified. видово́й[1] landscape; ~ фильм travelogue, travel-film.

видово́й[2] specific; aspectual.

видоизмене́ние, -я modification; alteration; variety. видоизмени́ть, -ню́ *pf.*, видоизменя́ть, -я́ю *impf.* modify, alter; ~ся alter; be modified, be altered.

видоиска́тель, -я *m.* view-finder.

ви́жу *see* ви́деть

ви́за, -ы visa; official stamp.

визг, -а squeal; scream; yelp. визгли́вый shrill; screaming, squealing, squalling. визжа́ть, -жу́ *impf.* squeal, scream, yelp, squeak.

визи́ровать, -рую *impf. & pf.* (*pf. also* за~) visa, visé.

визи́т, -а visit; call. визита́ция, -и call; round; search. визи́тка, -и morning coat.

викторина, -ы quiz.

ви́лка, -и fork; plug; bracket. вилообра́зный forked. ви́лочный fork-lift. ви́лы, вил *pl.* pitchfork.

вильну́ть, -ну́, -нёшь *pf.*, виля́ть, -я́ю *impf.* twist and turn; turn sharply; prevaricate, be evasive; +*i.* wag.

Ви́льнюс, -а Vilnius.

вина́, -ы́; *pl.* ви́ны fault, guilt; blame.

виндсёрфинг, -а windsurfing, sailboarding.

винегре́т, -а Russian salad; medley, farrago.

вини́тельный accusative. вини́ть, -ню́ *impf.* accuse, blame; reproach; ~ся (*pf.* по~) confess.

ви́нкель, -я; *pl.* -я́ *m.* set-square.

виннока́менный tartaric. ви́нн|ый wine; winy; vinous; ~ый ка́мень tartar; ~ая я́года fig. вино́, -а́; *pl.* -а wine; vodka.

винова́тый guilty; to blame; винова́т(а)! (I'm) sorry. вино́вник, -а author, initiator; culprit; ~ торжества́ founder of the feast. вино́вный guilty.

виногра́д, -а (-у) vine; grapes. виногра́дарь, -я *m.* wine-grower. виногра́дина, -ы grape. виногра́дник, -а vineyard. виногра́дный vine; grape; wine, vintage. виноку́р, -а distiller. винокуре́ние, -я distillation. виноку́ренный distilling; ~ заво́д distillery.

винт, -а́ screw; propeller; rotor; spiral; vint. винти́ть, -нчу́ *impf.* screw in; unscrew; turn. винто́вка, -и rifle. винтово́й screw; spiral; helical. винто́вочный rifle-. винто́м *adv.* spirally.

вира́ж, -а́ turn; bend, curve.

вис, -а hang, hanging. ви́селица, -ы gallows. висе́ть, вишу́ *impf.* hang; hover.

ви́ски *nt.indecl.* whisky; шотла́ндское ~ Scotch (whisky).

вислоу́хий lop-eared. ви́снуть, -ну; вис(нул) *impf.* hang; droop.

висо́к, -ска́ temple.

високо́сный; ~ год leap-year.

висо́чный temporal.

висю́лька, -и pendant. вися́чий hanging; ~ замо́к padlock; ~ мост suspension bridge.

витами́н, -а vitamin. витаминизи́ровать, -рую *impf. & pf.* fortify, enrich with vitamins. витами́нный vitamin; vitamin-rich.

витой twisted, spiral. вито́к, -тка́ turn, coil, loop; orbit.

витра́ж, -а́ stained-glass window, panel, etc. витри́на, -ы shop-window; showcase.

вить, вью, вьёшь; вил, -а́, -о *impf. (pf.* с~) twist, wind, weave; ~ гнездо́ build a nest; ~ верёвки из+*g.* twist round one's little finger; ~ся wind, twine; curl, wave; hover, circle; twist, turn; whirl, eddy; writhe.

вихо́р, -хра́ tuft. вихра́стый shaggy, wiry; shock-headed.

вихрево́й vortical. вихрь, -я *m.* whirlwind; whirl, eddy, vortex; сне́жный ~ blizzard.

ви́це- *pref.* vice-. ви́це-коро́ль, -я́ viceroy. ~президе́нт, -а vice-president.

вицмунди́р, -а *(dress)* uniform.

ВИЧ *abbr. (of* ви́рус иммунодефици́та челове́ка) HIV *(human immunodeficiency virus);* инфици́рованный ~ HIV-positive.

ви́шенник, -а, вишня́к, -а́ cherry-orchard; cherry-grove; wild cherry. вишнёвый cherry; cherry-coloured. ви́шня, -и; *g.pl.* -шен cherry, cherries; cherry-tree.

вишу́ *see* висе́ть

вишь *part.* look, just look; well!

вка́лывать, -аю *impf. (pf.* вколо́ть) *(sl.)* work hard, slave; get stuck in.

вка́пывать, -аю *impf. of* вкопа́ть

вкати́ть, -ачу́, -а́тишь *pf.,* вка́тывать, -аю *impf.* roll in, wheel in; roll up; put in, put on; administer; ~ся roll in; run in.

вкл. *(abbr. of* включи́тельно) incl., including.

вклад, -а deposit; investment; endowment; contribution. вкла́дка, -и, вкла́дыш, -а supplementary sheet, inset. вкладно́й deposit; supplementary, inserted; ~ лист loose leaf, insert. вкла́дчик, -а depositor; investor.

вкла́дывать, -аю *impf. of* вложи́ть. вкла́дыш *see* вкла́дка

вкле́ивать, -аю *impf.,* вкле́ить, -ею *pf.* stick in, glue in, paste in; put in. вкле́йка, -и sticking in; inset.

вкли́нивать, -аю *impf.,* вкли́нить, -ню *pf.* wedge in; put in; ~ся edge one's way in; drive a wedge (into).

включа́тель, -я *m.* switch. включа́ть, -а́ю *impf.,* включи́ть, -чу́ *pf.* include; insert; switch on, turn on, start; plug in, connect; engage, let in; ~ся join in, enter into. включа́я including. включе́ние, -я inclusion, insertion; switching on, turning on. включи́тельно *adv.* inclusive.

вкола́чивать, -аю *impf.,* вколоти́ть, -очу́, -о́тишь *pf.* hammer in, knock in.

вколо́ть, -олю́, -о́лешь *pf. (impf.* вка́лывать) stick (in), pin (in).

вконе́ц *adv.* completely, absolutely.

вко́панный dug in; rooted to the ground. вкопа́ть, -а́ю *pf. (impf.* вка́пывать) dig in.

вкорени́ть, -ню́ *pf.,* вкореня́ть, -я́ю *impf.* inculcate; ~ся take root.

вкось *adv.* obliquely, slantwise; ~ и вкривь, вкривь и ~ at random, all over the place; indiscriminately.

вкра́дчивый insinuating, ingratiating. вкра́дываться, -аюсь *impf.,* вкра́сться, -аду́сь, -адёшься *pf.* steal in, creep in; worm o.s., insinuate o.s., (into).

вкра́тце *adv.* briefly, succinctly.

вкривь *adv.* aslant; wrongly, perversely; ~ и вкось *see* вкось

вкруг *see* вокру́г

вкруту́ю *adv.* hard(-boiled).

вку́пе *adv.* together.

вкус, -а taste; manner, style; де́ло ~а a matter of taste. вкуси́ть, -ушу́, -у́сишь *pf.,* вкуша́ть, -а́ю *impf.* taste; partake of; savour, experience. вку́сный; -сен, -сна́, -о tasty, nice, good; appetizing.

вла́га, -и moisture, damp, liquid.

влага́лище, -а vagina; sheath.

влага́ть, -а́ю *impf. of* вложи́ть

владе́лец, -льца, -лица, -ы owner; proprietor. владе́ние, -я ownership; possession; property; domain, estate. владе́тель, -я *m.,* -ница, -ы possessor; sovereign. владе́тельный sovereign. владе́ть, -е́ю *impf.*+*i.* own, possess; control; be in possession of; have (a) command of; have the use of.

влады́ка, -и *m.* master, sovereign; Orthodox prelate; my Lord. влады́чество, -а dominion, rule, sway.

влажне́ть, -е́ет *impf. (pf.* по~) become humid, grow damp. вла́жный; -жен, -жна́, -о damp, moist, humid.

вла́мываться, -аюсь *impf. of* вломи́ться

вла́ствовать, -твую *impf.*+(над+) *i.* rule, hold sway over. власти́тель, -я *m.* sovereign, ruler. вла́стный imperious, commanding; masterful; empowered; competent. власть, -и; *g.pl.* -е́й power; authority; control; *pl.* authorities; ва́ша ~ as you like, please yourself, it's up to you.

вле́во *adv.* to the left.

влеза́ть, -а́ю *impf.,* влезть, -зу; влез *pf.* climb in, climb up; get in; fit in, go in, go on; ско́лько вле́зет as much as will go in, any amount.

влёк *etc.: see* влечь

влепи́ть, -плю́, -пишь *pf.*, влепля́ть, -я́ю *impf.* stick in, fasten in; ~ пощёчину+*d.* give a slap in the face.

влета́ть, -а́ю *impf.*, влете́ть, -ечу́ *pf.* fly in; rush in.

влече́ние, -я attraction; bent, inclination. влечь, -еку́, -ечёшь; влёк, -ла́ *impf.* draw, drag; attract; ~ за собо́й involve, entail; ~ся к+*d.* be drawn to, be attracted by.

влива́ть, -а́ю *impf.*, влить, волью́, -ёшь; влил, -а́, -о *pf.* pour in; infuse; instil; bring in; ~ся flow in.

влия́ние, -я influence. влия́тельный influential. влия́ть, -я́ю *impf.* (*pf.* по~) на+*a.* influence, have an influence on, affect.

вложе́ние, -я enclosure; investment. вложи́ть, -ожу́, -о́жишь *pf.* (*impf.* вкла́дывать, влага́ть) put in, insert; enclose; invest.

вломи́ться, -млю́сь, -мишься *pf.* (*impf.* вла́мываться) break in.

влюби́ть, -блю́, -бишь *pf.*, влюбля́ть, -я́ю *impf.* capture the heart of, make fall in love (в+*a.* with); ~ся fall in love, влюблённый; -лён, -а́ in love; loving, tender; *sb.* lover. влюбчивый amorous, susceptible.

вма́зать, -а́жу *pf.*, вма́зывать, -аю *impf.* cement in, putty in, mortar in.

вм. *abbr.* (*of* вме́сто) instead of, in place of.

вмени́ть, -ню́ *pf.*, вменя́ть, -я́ю *impf.* impute; ~ в вину́ lay to the charge of; ~ в обя́занность impose as a duty. вменя́емый responsible, liable; of sound-mind.

вме́сте *adv.* together; at the same time; ~ с тем at the same time, also.

вмести́лище, -а receptacle. вмести́мость, -и capacity; tonnage. вмести́тельный capacious; spacious, roomy. вмести́ть, -ещу́ *pf.* (*impf.* вмеща́ть) contain, hold, accommodate; find room for; put, place; ~ся go in.

вме́сто *prep.*+*g.* instead of, in place of.

вмеша́тельство, -а interference; intervention. вмеша́ть, -а́ю *pf.*, вме́шивать, -аю *impf.* mix in; mix up, implicate; ~ся interfere, meddle.

вмеща́ть(ся, -а́ю(сь *impf. of* вмести́ться

вмиг *adv.* in an instant, in a flash.

вмина́ть, -а́ю *impf.*, вмять, вомну́, -нёшь *pf.* crush in, press in, dent.

ВМФ *abbr.* (*of* вое́нно-морско́й флот) navy.

вмя́тина, -ы dent.

внаём, внаймы́ *adv.* to let; for hire; брать ~ hire, rent; отдава́ться ~ let, hire out, rent; сдава́ться ~ be to let.

внаки́дку *adv.* thrown over the shoulders.

внача́ле *adv.* at first, in the beginning.

вне *prep.*+*g.* outside; out of; without; ~ себя́ beside o.s.; ~ сомне́ния without doubt, undoubtedly.

вне... *pref.* extra-; situated outside, lying outside the province or scope of; -less. внебра́чный extra-marital; illegitimate,

born outside wedlock. ~вре́менный timeless. ~кла́ссный out-of-school, extracurricular. ~ма́точный extra-uterine. ~очередно́й out of turn, out of order; extraordinary; extra. ~парти́йный non-party. ~пи́ковый off-peak. ~служе́бный leisure-time, leisure. ~студи́йный outside. ~шко́льный adult; extra-scholastic; out-of-school. ~шта́тник, а freelancer; casual. ~шта́тный casual, part-time; untenured.

внедре́ние, -я introduction; inculcation, indoctrination; intrusion. внедри́ть, -рю́ *pf.*, внедря́ть, -я́ю *impf.* inculcate, instil; introduce; ~ся take root.

внеза́пно *adv.* suddenly, all of a sudden, all at once. внеза́пный sudden, unexpected; surprise.

вне́млю *etc.: see* внима́ть

внесе́ние, -я bringing in, carrying in; paying in, deposit; entry, insertion; moving, submission. внести́, -су́, -сёшь; внёс, -ла́ *pf.* (*impf.* вноси́ть) bring in, carry in; introduce, put in; pay in, deposit; move, table; insert, enter; bring about, cause.

вне́шне *adv.* outwardly. вне́шний outer, exterior; outward, external; outside; surface, superficial; foreign. вне́шность, -и exterior; surface; appearance.

вниз *adv.* down, downwards; downstream; ~ по+*d.* down; ~ по тече́нию downstream. внизу́ *adv.* below; downstairs; *prep.*+*g.* at the foot of, in the lower part of.

вника́ть, -а́ю *impf.*, вни́кнуть, -ну; вник *pf.*+в+*a.* go carefully into, investigate thoroughly, get to the heart or root of.

внима́ние, -я attention; notice, note; heed; consideration; attentions, kindness; ~! look out!; ~ на старт! get set! внима́тельный attentive; thoughtful, considerate, kind. внима́ть, -а́ю *or* вне́млю *impf.* (*pf.* внять) listen to, hear; heed.

вничью́ *adv.*; око́нчиться ~ end in a draw, be drawn; сыгра́ть ~ draw.

вноси́ть, -ошу́, -о́сишь *impf. of* внести́

внук, -а grandson; *pl.* grandchildren, descendants.

вну́тренн|ий inner, interior; internal; intrinsic; home, inland; ~ие дохо́ды inland revenue. вну́тренность, -и interior; *pl.* entrails, intestines; internal organs; viscera. внутри́ *adv.* & *prep.*+*g.* inside, within. внутрь *adv.* & *prep.*+*g.* inside, in; inwards.

внуча́та, -ча́т *pl.* grandchildren. внуча́тный, внуча́тый second, great-; ~ брат second cousin; ~ племя́нник great-nephew. вну́чка, -и grand-daughter; grandchild.

внуша́емость, -и suggestibility. внуша́ть, -а́ю *impf.*, внуши́ть, -шу́ *pf.* instil; suggest; +*d.* inspire with, fill with. внуше́ние, -я suggestion; reproof, reprimand. внуши́тельный inspiring, impressive; imposing, striking.

вня́тный distinct; intelligible. внять *no fut.*; -ял, -а́, -о *pf. of* внима́ть во *see* в[2]

во... *see* в...

вобра́ть, вберу́, -рёшь; -а́л, -а́, -о *pf.* (*impf.* вбира́ть) absorb, draw in, soak up, inhale.

вобью́ *etc.*: *see* вбить

вове́к, вовеки́ *adv.* for ever; ~ не never.

во́время *adv.* in time; on time; не ~ at the wrong time.

во́все *adv.* quite; ~ не not at all.

во-вторы́х *adv.* secondly, in the second place.

вогна́ть, вгоню́, -о́нишь; -гна́л, -а́, -о *pf.* (*impf.* вгоня́ть) drive in. во́гнутый concave; dented. вогну́ть, -ну́, -нёшь *pf.* (*impf.* вгиба́ть) bend or curve inwards; ~ся bend inwards, curve inwards.

...вод *in comb.* -breeder, -grower, -raiser.

вода́, -ы́, *a.* во́ду; *pl.* -ы water; *pl.* the waters; watering-place, spa.

водворе́ние, -я settlement; establishment. водвори́ть, -рю́ *pf.*, водворя́ть, -я́ю *impf.* settle, install, house; establish.

води́тель, -я *m.* driver; leader. води́тельница, -ы (*woman*) driver. води́тельство, -a leadership. води́ть, вожу́, во́дишь *impf.* lead; conduct; take; drive; +*i.* (по+*d.*) pass (over, across); ~ автомоби́ль, маши́ну drive a car; ~ глаза́ми по+*d.* cast one's eyes over; ~ся be, be found; associate, play (with); be the custom, happen.

во́дка, -и *a.* vodka. воднолы́жник, -a, -ница, -ы water-skier. во́дн|ый water; watery; aquatic; aqueous; ~ые лы́жи water-skiing; water-skis.

водо... *in comb.* water, water-; hydraulic; hydro-. водобоя́знь, -и hydrophobia. ~вмести́лище, -a reservoir. ~во́з, -a a water-carrier. ~воро́т, -a whirlpool, eddy; vortex, maelstrom, whirl. ~ём, -a reservoir. ~измеще́ние, -я displacement. ~ка́чка, -и water-tower, pump-house, pumping station. ~ла́з, -a diver; Newfoundland (*dog*). ~ла́зный diving. ~лей, -я Aquarius. ~непроница́емый watertight; waterproof. ~но́сный water-bearing. ~отво́д, -a drain, overflow. ~отво́дный drainage, overflow. ~отта́лкивающий water-repellent. ~па́д, -a a waterfall; falls, cataract. ~по́й, -я watering-place; water-supply; watering. ~прово́д, -a water-pipe, water-main; water supply. ~прово́дный water-main, mains; tap-. ~прово́дчик, -a plumber. ~разде́л, -a watershed. ~распыли́тель, -я *m.* sprinkler. ~ро́д, -a hydrogen. во́доросль, -и water-plant, water-weed; seaweed; alga. ~снабже́ние, -я water supply ~сто́к, -a a drain, gutter. ~усто́йчивый water-repellant.

во́дочный vodka.

водружа́ть, -а́ю *impf.*, водрузи́ть, -ужу́ *pf.* hoist; set up, fix up.

водяни́стый watery. водя́нка, -и dropsy. водяно́й water; aquatic; ~ знак watermark; *sb.* water-sprite. водя́ночный dropsical.

воева́ть, вою́ю *impf.* wage war, make war,

be at war; quarrel. воево́да, -ы *m.* voivode (*in ancient Russia, commander of army or governor of province*). воево́дство, -a office of voivode; voivode's province.

воедино́ *adv.* together, into one.

воен... *abbr.* (*of* вое́нный) *in comb.* military, war-. военко́м, -a military commissar. ~ко́р, -a war correspondent.

воениза́ция, -и militarization. военизи́рованный militarized, armed; paramilitary.

военно... *in comb.* military; war-. вое́нно-возду́шный air-, air-force; ~-возду́шные си́лы air force. вое́нно-морско́й naval; ~морско́й флот navy. ~пле́нный *sb.* prisoner of war. вое́нно-полево́й; ~-полево́й суд (drumhead) court-martial. ~слу́жащий *sb.* serviceman.

вое́нн|ый military; war; army; ~ое положе́ние martial law; ~ый суд court-martial; *sb.* soldier, serviceman; *pl.* the military.

вожа́к, -а́ guide; leader. вожа́тый *sb.* guide; leader; tram-driver. вожде́ние, -я leading; driving, steering, piloting. вождь, -я́ *m.* leader, chief.

вожжа́, -й; *pl.* -и, -éй reins.

вожу́ *etc.*: *see* води́ть, вози́ть

воз, -a (-y), *loc.* -ý; *pl.* -ы *or* -á cart, wagon; cart-load; loads, heaps.

воз..., возо..., вос... *vbl. pref. expressing direction or movement upwards*; *renewed action*; *action in response*; *beginning of action*; *intensity, excitement, solemnity.*

возбуди́мый excitable, irritable. возбуди́тель, -я *m.* agent; stimulus; stimulant; exciter; instigator. возбуди́ть, -ужу́ *pf.*, возбужда́ть, -а́ю *impf.* excite, rouse, arouse; stimulate, whet; stir up, incite; provoke; institute, bring, raise. возбужда́ющ|ий; ~ее сре́дство stimulant. возбужде́ние, -я excitement, agitation. возбуждённый excited, agitated.

возвести́, -еду́, -дёшь; -вёл, -ла́ *pf.* (*impf.* возводи́ть) elevate; raise; erect, put up; bring, advance, level; +к+*d.* trace to, derive from.

возвести́ть, -ещу́ *pf.*, возвеща́ть, -а́ю *impf.* proclaim, announce.

возводи́ть, -ожу́, -о́дишь *impf. of* возвести́

возвра́т, -a return; repayment; reimbursement; restitution; ~ боле́зни relapse; ~ со́лнца solstice. возврати́ть, -ащу́ *pf.*, возвраща́ть, -а́ю *impf.* (*pf. also* верну́ть) return, give back, restore; pay back; recover; retrieve; send back, bring back; ~ся return; go back, come back; revert. возвра́тный back, return; relapsing; recurrent; reflexive. возвраще́ние, -я return; recurrence; restoration, restitution.

возвы́сить, -ы́шу *pf.*, возвыша́ть, -а́ю *impf.* raise; ennoble; ~ся rise, go up; tower. возвыше́ние, -я rise; raising; eminence; raised place. возвы́шенность, -и height; eminence; loftiness, sublimity. возвы́шенный high, elevated; lofty, sublime.

возгла́вить, -влю *pf.*, **возглавля́ть**, -я́ю *impf.* head, be at the head of.

во́зглас, -а cry, exclamation. **возгласи́ть**, -ашу́ *pf.*, **возглаша́ть**, -а́ю *impf.* proclaim. **возглаше́ние**, -я proclamation; exclamation.

возгора́емость, -и inflammability. **возгора́емый** inflammable. **возгора́ние**, -я ignition; то́чка возгора́ния flash-point. **возгора́ться**, -а́юсь *impf.*, **возгоре́ться**, -рю́сь *pf.* flare up; be seized (with); be smitten.

воздава́ть, -даю́, -даёшь *impf.*, **возда́ть**, -а́м, -а́шь, -а́ст, -ади́м; -а́л, -а́, -о *pf.* render; ~ до́лжное+*d.* do justice to.

воздвига́ть, -а́ю *impf.*, **воздви́гнуть**, -ну; -дви́г *pf.* raise, erect; ~ся rise, arise.

возде́йствие, -я influence; физи́ческое ~ coercion. **возде́йствовать**, -твую *impf.* & *pf.* influence, affect; act on, work on.

возде́лать, -аю *pf.*, **возде́лывать**, -аю *impf.* cultivate, till.

воздержа́вшийся *sb.* abstainer; abstention. **воздержа́ние**, -я abstinence; abstention. **возде́ржанный**, **возде́ржный** abstemious; temperate; abstinent. **воздержа́ться**, -жу́сь, -жишься *pf.*, **возде́рживаться**, -аюсь *impf.* refrain; abstain; withhold acceptance, decline.

во́здух, -а air; в ~е in the air; на ~, на ~е out of doors. **воздуходу́вка**, -и blower. **воздухонепроница́емый** air-tight. **воздухоохлажда́емый** air-cooled. **возду́ш|ный** air, aerial; overhead; air-raid; airy, light; flimsy; ~ые за́мки castles in the air; ~ый змей kite; ~ая пе́тля chain (stitch); ~ый пиро́г soufflé; ~ый флот air force; ~ый шар balloon.

воззва́ние, -я appeal. **воззва́ть**, -зову́, -вёшь *pf.* (*impf.* **взыва́ть**) appeal, call (о+*p.* for).

воззре́ние, -я view, opinion, outlook.

вози́ть, вожу́, во́зишь *impf.* cart, convey; carry; bring, take; drive; draw; beat, flog; ~ся romp, run about, play noisily; take trouble, spend time, busy o.s.; potter about; tinker, fiddle about, mess about. **во́зка**, -и carting, carriage.

возлага́ть, -а́ю *impf. of* **возложи́ть**

во́зле *adv.* & *prep.*+*g.* by, near; near by; past.

возложи́ть, -жу́, -жишь *pf.* (*impf.* **возлага́ть**) lay; place.

возлю́бленный beloved; *sb.* boy-friend, girl-friend; lover, mistress.

возме́здие, -я retribution; requital; punishment.

возмести́ть, -ещу́ *pf.*, **возмеща́ть**, -а́ю *impf.* compensate for, make up for; refund, reimburse. **возмеще́ние**, -я compensation, indemnity; damages; replacement; refund, reimbursement.

возмо́жно *adv.* possibly; +*comp.* as ... as possible. **возмо́жность**, -и possibility; opportunity; *pl.* means, resources; potentialities; по (ме́ре) возмо́жности as far as possible; при

пе́рвой возмо́жности as soon as possible, at the first opportunity. **возмо́жный** possible; greatest possible.

возмужа́лость, -и maturity; manhood, womanhood. **возмужа́лый** mature; grown up. **возмужа́ть**, -а́ю *pf.* grow up, reach maturity; gain strength, become strong.

возмути́тельный disgraceful, scandalous; seditious, subversive. **возмути́ть**, -ущу́ *pf.*, **возмуща́ть**, -а́ю *impf.* disturb, trouble; stir up, incite; anger, rouse to indignation; ~ся be indignant, be roused to indignation; be exasperated; rebel, rise in revolt. **возмуще́ние**, -я indignation; revolt, rebellion; perturbation; disturbance. **возмущённый**; -щён, -щена́ indignant, troubled, disturbed.

вознагради́ть, -ажу́ *pf.*, **вознагражда́ть**, -а́ю *impf.* reward; recompense; make up to (за+*a.* for). **вознагражде́ние**, -я reward, recompense; compensation; fee, remuneration.

возненави́деть, -и́жу *pf.* conceive a hatred for, come to hate.

вознесе́ние, -я ascent; Ascension. **вознести́**, -несу́, -несёшь; -нёс, -ла́ *pf.* (*impf.* **возноси́ть**) raise, lift up; ~сь rise; ascend.

возника́ть, -а́ет *impf.*, **возни́кнуть**, -нет; -ни́к *pf.* arise, spring up. **возникнове́ние**, -я rise, beginning, origin.

возни́ца, -ы *m.* coachman, driver. **возни́чий** *sb.* coachman, driver.

возноси́ть(ся, -ошу́(сь, -о́сишь(ся *impf. of* **вознести́(сь. возноше́ние**, -я raising, elevation.

возня́, -и́ row, noise; horse-play; bother, trouble.

возобнови́ть, -влю́ *pf.*, **возобновля́ть**, -я́ю *impf.* renew, resume; restore; ~ся begin again. **возобновле́ние**, -я renewal, resumption; revival.

возража́ть, -а́ю *impf.*, **возрази́ть**, -ажу́ *pf.* object, have or raise an objection; take exception; retort; say. **возраже́ние**, -я objection; retort; answer.

во́зраст, -а age; на ~е grown up. **возраста́ние**, -я growth, increase; increment. **возраста́ть**, -а́ет *impf.*, **возрасти́**, -тёт; -ро́с, -ла́ *pf.* grow, increase.

возроди́ть, -ожу́ *pf.*, **возрожда́ть**, -а́ю *impf.* regenerate; revive; ~ся revive. **возрожде́ние**, -я rebirth; revival; Renaissance.

возро́с *etc.: see* **возрасти́. возро́сший** increased.

во́зчик, -а carter, carrier; drayman.

возьму́ *etc.: see* **взять**

во́ин, -а warrior; soldier; serviceman. **во́ин-ск|ий** military; soldierly; army, troop; ~ая пови́нность conscription. **во́инственный** warlike; bellicose. **вои́нствующий** militant.

вои́стину *adv.* indeed; verily.

вой, -я howl, howling; wail, wailing.

войду́ *etc.: see* **войти́**

во́йлок, -а felt; strip of felt. **во́йлочный** felt.

война́, -ы́; *pl.* -ы war.
во́йско, -а; *pl.* -а́ army; host; multitude; *pl.* troops, forces. войсково́й military; of the (Cossack) host.
войти́, -йду́, -йдёшь; вошёл, -шла́ *pf.* (*impf.* входи́ть) go in, come in, enter; get in(to); ~ в аза́рт grow heated; ~ в лета́ get on (in years); ~ в мо́ду become fashionable; ~ во вкус acquire a taste; ~ в си́лу come into force.
вокза́л, -а (railway-)station.
вокру́г *adv.* & *prep.*+*g.* round, around.
вол, -а́ ox, bullock.
вола́н, -а flounce; shuttlecock.
Во́лга, -и the Volga.
волды́рь, -я́ *m.* blister; lump, bump.
волево́й volitional; strong-willed. во́лей-нево́лей *adv.* willy-nilly.
во́лжский Volga, of the Volga.
волк, -а; *pl.* -и, -о́в wolf. волкода́в, -а wolfhound.
волна́, -ы́; *pl.* -ы, во́лнам wave. волне́ние, -я roughness, choppiness; agitation, disturbance; emotion, excitement; (*usu. pl.*) unrest. волни́стый wavy; undulating; corrugated; watered. волнова́ть, -ну́ю *impf.* (*pf.* вз~) disturb, agitate; excite; worry; ~ся be disturbed or agitated; fret, worry, be nervous, be excited; be in a state of ferment or unrest; be rough or choppy; ripple, wave. волноло́м, -а breakwater. волнообра́зный wavelike; undulatory; wavy, undulating. волноре́з, -а breakwater. волну́ющий disturbing, worrying; exciting, thrilling, stirring.
во́лок, -а; *pl.* -и or -а́ portage.
волоки́та, -ы red tape.
волокни́стый fibrous, stringy. волокно́, -а́; *pl.* -а fibre, filament.
волоку́ *etc.: see* воло́чь
во́лос, -а; *pl.* -ы or -а́, -о́с hair; *pl.* hair. волоса́тый hairy; hirsute; pilose. волоси́стый fibrous. волосно́й capillary. волосо́к, -ска́ hair, fine hair; hair-spring; filament.
волостно́й of a volost (*see* во́лость). во́лость, -и; *pl.* -и, -е́й volost (*smallest administrative division of tsarist Russia*).
волосяно́й hair.
волочи́ть, -очу́, -о́чишь *impf.* drag; draw; ~ся drag, trail; +за+*i.* run after. воло́чь, -оку́, -очёшь; -о́к, -ла́ *impf.* drag; ~ся drag, trail; drag o.s. along; shuffle.
волча́та *etc.: see* волчо́нок. во́лчий wolf, wolf's; wolfish. волчи́ха, -и, волчи́ца, -ы she-wolf.
волчо́к, -чка́ top; gyroscope.
волчо́нок, -нка; *pl.* -ча́та, -ча́т wolf cub.
волше́бник, -а magician; wizard. волше́бница, -ы enchantress. волше́бн|ый magic, magical; enchanted; bewitching, enchanting; ~ая па́лочка magic wand; ~ое ца́рство fairyland, enchanted kingdom. волшебство́, -а́ magic, enchantment.
во́льно *adv.* freely; ~! stand at ease!

вольнонаёмный civilian. во́льность, -и freedom, liberty; license; familiarity во́льный; -лен, -льна́, -о, -ы or -ы́ free; unrestricted; loose; free-style; familiar; private; at liberty; ~ ка́менщик Freemason.
вольт[1], -а volt.
вольт[2], -а, *loc.* -у́ vault; volte. вольтижёр, -а trick-rider. вольтижи́ровать, -рую *impf.* vault.
во́льтов *adj.* voltaic.
вольфра́м, -а tungsten; wolfram.
волью́ *etc.: see* влить
во́ля, -и will; volition; wish(es); freedom, liberty; ~ ва́ша as you please, as you like; дать во́лю+*d.* give rein, vent to; дать себе́ во́лю let o.s. go; на во́ле at liberty; не по свое́й во́ле against one's will; по до́брой во́ле freely, of one's own free will.
вомну́ *etc.: see* вмять
вон *adv.* out; off, away.
вон *part.* there, over there.
вонза́ть, -а́ю *impf.*, вонзи́ть, -нжу́ *pf.* plunge, thrust; ~ся в+*a.* pierce, penetrate.
вонь, -и stink, stench. воню́чий stinking, fetid. воню́чка, -и stinker; skunk. воня́ть, -я́ю stink, reek.
вообража́емый imaginary; fictitious. вообража́ть, -а́ю *impf.*, вообрази́ть, -ажу́ *pf.* imagine; fancy; ~ся imagine o.s. воображе́ние, -я imagination; fancy. вообрази́мый imaginable.
вообще́ *adv.* in general; generally (speaking); on the whole; always; altogether; at all; ~ говоря́ generally speaking; as a matter of fact.
воодушеви́ть, -влю́ *pf.*, воодушевля́ть, -я́ю *impf.* inspire, rouse; in spirit, hearten. воодушевле́ние, -я rousing; inspiration; inspiriting; animation; enthusiasm, fervour. воодушевлённый animated; enthusiastic, fervent.
вооружа́ть, -а́ю *impf.*, вооружи́ть, -жу́ *pf.* arm, equip; fit out; set turn; ~ про́тив себя́ antagonize; ~ся arm o.s., provide o.s. вооруже́ние, -я arming; arms, armament; equipment. вооружённый; -жён, -а́ armed; equipped.
воо́чию *adv.* with one's own eyes, for o.s.; clearly, plainly.
во-пе́рвых *adv.* first, first of all, in the first place.
вопи́ть, -плю́ *impf.* yell, howl, wail. вопию́щий crying, glaring; flagrant, scandalous. вопия́ть, -ию́, -ие́шь *impf.* cry out, clamour.
воплоти́ть, -ощу́ *pf.*, воплоща́ть, -а́ю *impf.* embody, incarnate; ~ в себе́ be the embodiment of. воплоще́ние, -я embodiment; incarnation. воплощённый; -щён, -щена́ incarnate; personified.
вопль, -я *m.* cry, wail; wailing, howling.
вопреки́ *prep.*+*d.* despite, in spite of; against, contrary to.
вопро́с, -а question; problem; matter; ~ по

существу́ substance of the matter; под ~ом in question, undecided; что за ~! of course! **вопроси́тельный** interrogative; questioning; ~ знак question-mark. **вопроша́ющий** questioning, inquiring.

вопью́ *etc.: see* впить

вор, -а; *pl.* -ы, -о́в thief; criminal.

ворва́ться, -ву́сь, -вёшься; -а́лся, -ла́сь, -а́лось *pf.* (*impf.* **врыва́ться**) burst in.

воркова́ть, -ку́ю *impf.* coo; bill and coo.

воркотня́, -й grumbling.

воробе́й, -ья́ sparrow. **воробьи́ный** sparrow's; sparrow; passerine.

воро́ванный stolen. **орова́тый** thievish; furtive. **ворова́ть**, -ру́ю *impf.* (*pf.* c~) steal; be a thief. **воро́вка**, -и (*woman*) thief. **воро́вский** *adv.* furtively. **воровско́й** thieves'; illegal. **воровство́**, -а́ stealing; theft.

во́рон, -а raven. **воро́на**, -ы crow. **вороне́ный** blued. **воро́ний** crow's; corvine. **ворони́ть**, -ню́ *impf.* blue.

воро́нка, -и funnel; crater.

вороно́й black; *sb.* black horse.

воро́нье, -я carrion crows.

во́рот[1], -а neckline; collar; neckband.

во́рот[2], -а winch; windlass.

воро́та, -ро́т *pl.* gate, gates; gateway; goal.

вороти́ть[1], -очу́, -о́тишь *impf.+i.* be in charge of; ~ нос turn up one's nose; меня́ воро́тит от э́того де́ла this business makes me sick.

вороти́ть[2], -очу́, -о́тишь *pf.* bring back, get back; turn back, send back; ~ся return, come back, go back.

воротни́к, -а́, **воротничо́к**, -чка́ collar. **воро́тн|ый** gate; ~ая ве́на portal vein.

во́рох, -а; *pl.* -а heap, pile; masses, lots, heaps.

воро́чать, -аю *impf.* turn (over); move, shift; +i. control, have control of; boss; ~ глаза́ми roll one's eyes; ~ миллио́нами deal in millions; ~ся move, turn; toss and turn.

ворочу́(сь *etc.: see* вороти́ть(ся

вороши́ть, -шу́ *impf.* stir up; turn (over); ~ся move about, stir.

ворс, -а nap, pile. **ворси́нка**, -и hair, nap, lint; fibre. **ворси́стый** fleecy.

ворча́ть, -чу́ *impf.* grumble, growl. **ворчли́вый** querulous, peevish; grumpy.

вос... *see* воз...

восвоя́си *adv.* home; отпра́виться ~ go back home.

восемна́дцатый eighteenth. **восемна́дцать**, -и eighteen. **во́семь**, -сьми́, *i.* -сьмью́ *or* -семью́ eight. **во́семьдесят**, -сьми́десяти eighty. **восемьсо́т**, -сьмисо́т, -ста́ми eight hundred. **во́семью** *adv.* eight times.

воск, -а (-у) wax, beeswax.

воскли́кнуть, -ну *pf.*, **восклица́ть**, -а́ю *impf.* exclaim. **восклица́ние**, -я exclamation. **восклица́тельный** exclamatory; ~ знак exclamation mark.

воско́вка, -и waxed paper; stencil. **воско́в|ой** wax, waxen; waxy; waxed; ~а́я бума́га greaseproof paper.

воскреса́ть, -а́ю *impf.*, **воскре́снуть**, -ну; -е́с *pf.* rise again, rise from the dead; revive. **воскресе́ние**, -я resurrection. **воскресе́нье**, -я Sunday. **воскреси́ть**, -ешу́ *pf.*, **воскреша́ть**, -а́ю *impf.* raise from the dead, resurrect; revive. **воскре́сник**, -а voluntary Sunday work. **воскре́сный** Sunday. **воскреше́ние**, -я raising from the dead, resurrection; revival.

воспале́ние, -я inflammation. **воспалённый**; -лён, -а́ inflamed; sore. **воспали́ть**, -лю́ *pf.* **воспаля́ть**, -я́ю *impf.* inflame; ~ся become inflamed.

воспита́ние, -я upbringing, education; training; (good) breeding. **воспита́нник**, -а, -ница, -ы pupil, schoolboy, schoolgirl; ward. **воспи́танность**, -и (good) breeding. **воспи́танный** well-brought-up. **воспита́тельный** educational; ~ дом foundling hospital. **воспита́ть**, -а́ю *pf.*, **воспи́тывать**, -аю *impf.* bring up, rear; cultivate, foster; inculcate; educate; train.

воспламени́ть, -ню́ *pf.*, **воспламеня́ть**, -я́ю *impf.* kindle, set on fire, ignite; fire, inflame; ~ся ignite, catch fire; blaze up; take fire, flare up. **воспламеня́емый** inflammable.

вос|по́льзоваться, -зуюсь *pf.*

воспомина́ние, -я recollection, memory; *pl.* memoirs; reminiscences.

вос|препя́тствовать, -твую *pf.*

воспрети́ть, -ещу́ *pf.*, **воспреща́ть**, -а́ю *impf.* forbid, prohibit. **воспреще́ние**, -я prohibition. **воспрещённый**; -щён, -а́ forbidden, prohibited.

восприе́мник, -а godfather. **восприе́мница**, -ы godmother. **восприи́мчивый** receptive, impressionable; susceptible. **воспринима́емый** perceptible, apprehensible. **воспринима́ть**, -а́ю *impf.*, **восприня́ть**, -иму́, -и́мешь; -и́нял, -а́, -о *pf.* perceive, apprehend; grasp, take in; interpret, take (как for). **восприя́тие**, -я perception.

воспроизведе́ние, -я reproduction. **воспроизвести́**, -еду́, -едёшь; -вёл, -а́ *pf.*, **воспроизводи́ть**, -ожу́, -о́дишь *impf.* reproduce; renew; recall. **воспроизводи́тельный** reproductive. **воспроизво́дство**, -а reproduction.

вос|проти́виться, -влюсь *pf.*

воссоедине́ние, -я reunion, reunification. **воссоедини́ть**, -ню́ *pf.*, **воссоединя́ть**, -я́ю *impf.* reunite.

восстава́ть, -таю́, -таёшь *impf. of* восста́ть. **восстана́вливать**, -аю *impf. of* восстанови́ть

восста́ние, -я rising, insurrection.

восстанови́тельный of restoration of, reconstruction. **восстанови́ть**, -влю́, -вишь *pf.* (*impf.* **восстана́вливать**) restore, renew, re-establish, reinstate; recall, recollect; reduce; ~ про́тив+g. set against; ~ про́тив себя́ antagonize. **восстановле́ние**, -я restoration, renewal, reinstatement; rehabilitation; reconstruction; reduction.

восста́ть, -а́ну *pf.* (*impf.* **восстава́ть**) rise (up), arise.

восто́к, -а east. **востокове́дение, -я** oriental studies.

восто́рг, -а delight, rapture; **в ~е от**+*g.* delighted with. **восторга́ть, -а́ю** *impf.* delight, enrapture; **~ся**+*i.* be delighted with, go into raptures over. **восто́рженный** enthusiastic. **восторжествова́ть, -тву́ю** *pf.* triumph.

восто́чник, -а orientalist. **восто́чный** east, eastern; oriental.

востре́бование, -я claiming, demand; **до востре́бования** to be called for, poste restante. **востре́бовать, -бую** *pf.* claim, call for.

восхвали́ть, -лю́, -лишь *pf.*, **восхваля́ть, -я́ю** *impf.* praise, extol.

восхити́тельный entrancing, ravishing; delightful; delicious. **восхити́ть, -хищу́** *pf.*, **восхища́ть, -а́ю** *impf.* carry away, delight, enrapture. **восхище́ние, -я** delight, rapture; admiration. **восхищённый; -щён, -а́** rapt, admiring.

восхо́д, -а rising; east. **восходи́ть, -ожу́, -о́дишь** *impf. of* **взойти́**; **~ к**+*d.* go back to, date from. **восходи́тель, -я** mountaineer, climber. **восхожде́ние, -я** ascent. **восходя́щий** rising.

восше́ствие, -я accession.

восьма́я *sb.* eighth; octave. **восьмёрка, -и** eight; No.8; figure of eight. **во́сьмеро, -ры́х** eight; eight pairs.

восьми... *in comb.* eight-; octo-. **восьмигра́нник, -а** octahedron. **~деся́тый** eightieth. **~кла́ссник, -а, -ница, -ы** eighth-year pupil. **~кра́тный** eightfold, octuple. **~ле́тний** eight-year; eight-year-old. **~со́тый** eight-hundredth. **~уго́льник, -а** octagon. **~уго́льный** octagonal. **~часово́й** eighthour.

восьмо́й eighth.

вот *part.* here (is), there (is); this (is); here's a ..! there's a ..!; well!; **~ ещё!** well, what next?; **~ и всё** and that's all; **~ как!** no! really! **~ та́к!** that's it! that's right! **~ тебе́!** take that!; **~ тебе́ и...** so much for ...; **~ что!** no! not really? **вот-во́т** *adv.* a moment more, and ...; this moment, just; *part.* that's it, that's right!

воткну́ть, -ну́, -нёшь *pf.* (*impf.* **втыка́ть**) stick in, drive in, thrust in.

вотру́ *etc.: see* **втере́ть**

воцаре́ние, -я accession. **воцари́ться, -и́тся** *pf.*, **воцаря́ться, -я́ется** *impf.* come to the throne; fall, set in, reign; establish o.s.

вошёл *etc.: see* **войти́**

вошь, вши; *g.pl.* **вшей** louse.

вошью́ *etc.: see* **вшить**

воща́нка, -и wax paper, wax(ed) cloth; cobbler's wax. **вощано́й** wax. **вощи́ть, -щу́** *impf.* (*pf.* **на~**) wax, wax-polish.

во́ю *etc.: see* **выть**

вою́ю *etc.: see* **воева́ть. вою́ющий** warring; belligerent.

впада́ть, -а́ю *impf.*, **впасть, -аду́** *pf.* fall, flow; lapse, sink; fall in; **+в**+*a.* verge on, approximate to. **впаде́ние, -я** confluence, (river-)mouth. **впа́дина, -ы** cavity, hollow; socket. **впа́лый** hollow, sunken.

впервой, впервы́е *adv.* for the first time, first.

вперёд *adv.* forward(s), ahead; in future; in advance; **идти́ ~** be fast. **впереди́** *adv.* in front, ahead; in (the) future; *prep.*+*g.* in front of, ahead of, before.

вперемешку *adv.* pell-mell, higgledy-piggledy.

впери́ть, -рю́ *pf.*, **впери́ть, -я́ю** *impf.* fix, fasten; direct; **~ся** be fixed; gaze fixedly, stare.

впечатле́ние, -я impression; effect. **впечатли́тельный** impressionable, sensitive.

впива́ть(ся, -а́ю(сь *impf. of* **впи́ть(ся**

вписа́ть, -ишу́, -и́шешь *pf.*, **впи́сывать, -аю** *impf.* enter, insert; inscribe; **~ся** be enrolled, join. **впи́ска, -и** entry; insertion.

впита́ть, -а́ю *pf.*, **впи́тывать, -аю** *impf.* absorb, take in; **~ся** soak.

впить, вопью́, -ьёшь; -и́л, -а́, -о *pf.* (*impf.* **впива́ть**) imbibe, absorb; **~ся** dig in, stick in; cling to; **~ся взо́ром, глаза́ми** fix one's gaze, one's eyes (on).

впи́хивать, -аю *impf.*, **впихну́ть, -ну́, -нёшь** *pf.* stuff in, cram in; shove in.

вплавь *adv.* (by) swimming; **перепра́виться ~** swim across.

вплести́, -ету́, -етёшь; -ёл, -а́ *pf.*, **вплета́ть, -а́ю** *impf.* plait in, intertwine; involve.

вплотну́ю *adv.* close; closely; in earnest. **вплоть** *adv.*; **~ до**+*g.* (right) up to; **~ к**+*d.* right against, close to, right up to.

вполго́лоса *adv.* under one's breath, in an undertone.

вполза́ть, -а́ю *impf.*, **вползти́, -зу́, -зёшь; -з, -ла́** *pf.* creep in, creep up, crawl in.

вполне́ *adv.* fully, entirely; quite.

вполови́ну *adv.* (by) half.

впопа́д *adv.* to the point; opportunely.

впопыха́х *adv.* in a hurry, hastily; in one's haste.

впо́ру *adv.* at the right time, opportune(ly); just right, exactly; **быть ~** (+*d.*) fit.

впосле́дствии *adv.* subsequently, afterwards.

впотьма́х *adv.* in the dark.

впра́вду *adv.* really.

впра́ве *adv.*; **быть ~** have a right.

впра́вить, -влю *pf.*, **вправля́ть, -я́ю** *impf.* set, reduce; tuck in. **впра́вка, -и** setting, reduction.

впра́во *adv.* to the right (**от**+*g.* of).

впредь *adv.* in (the) future; **~ до**+*g.* until.

впро́чем *conj.* however, but; though; or rather.

впры́гивать, -аю *impf.*, **впры́гнуть, -ну** *pf.* jump in, jump up (on).

впры́скивание, -я injection. **впры́скивать,**

-аю *impf.*, **впры́снуть, -ну** *pf.* inject.

впряга́ть, -а́ю *impf.* **впрячь, -ягу́, -я́жешь; -яг, -ла́** *pf.* harness.

впуск, -а admission, admittance. **впуска́ть, -а́ю** *impf.*, **впусти́ть, -ущу́, -у́стишь** *pf.* admit, let in. **впускно́й** admittance; inlet.

впусту́ю *adv.* for nothing, to no purpose, in vain.

впу́тать, -аю *perf,.* **впу́тывать, -аю** *impf.* entangle, involve, implicate; **~ся** get mixed up in.

впущу́ *etc.: see* **впусти́ть**

впя́теро *adv.* five times. **впятеро́м** *adv.* five (together).

враг, -а́ enemy; the Devil. **вражда́, -ы́** enmity, hostility. **вражде́бный** hostile; enemy. **враждова́ть, -ду́ю** be at war, be at enmity, be hostile, quarrel. **вра́жеский** enemy. **вра́жий** enemy, hostile.

вразби́вку *adv.* at random.

вразбро́д *adv.* separately, not in concert, disunitedly.

вразре́з *adv.* contrary; **идти́ ~ с+***i.* go against.

вразуми́тельный intelligible, clear; instructive; persuasive. **вразуми́ть, -млю́** *pf.*, **вразумля́ть, -я́ю** *impf.* make understand, make listen to reason, make see sense.

врасплóх *adv.* unexpectedly, unawares, by surprise.

враста́ть, -а́ет *impf.*, **врасти́, -тёт; врос, -ла́** *pf.* grow in; take root. **враста́ющий** ingrowing.

врата́рь, -я́ *m.* gate-keeper; goalkeeper.

врать, вру, врёшь; -ал, -а́, -о *impf.* (*pf.* **на~, со~**) lie, tell lies; talk nonsense.

врач, -а́ doctor; medical officer; **де́тский ~** paediatrician; **зубно́й ~** dentist. **враче́бный** medical.

враща́тельный rotary. **враща́ть, -а́ю** *impf.* turn, rotate, revolve; **~ глаза́ми** roll one's eyes; **~ся** turn, revolve, rotate; **~ся в худо́жественных круга́х** move in artistic circles. **враще́ние, -я** rotation, revolution, gyration.

вред, -а́ harm, hurt, injury; damage. **вреди́тель, -я** *m.* pest; wrecker, saboteur; *pl.* vermin. **вреди́тельство, -а** wrecking, (act of) sabotage. **вреди́ть, -ежу́** *impf.* (*pf.* **по~**) +*d.* injure, harm, hurt; damage. **вре́дный; -ден, -дна́, -о** harmful, injurious; unhealthy.

врежу́ *see* **вреди́ть. вре́жу(сь** *etc.: see* **вреза́ть(ся**

вре́зать, -е́жу *pf.*, **вреза́ть, -а́ю** *impf.* cut in, engrave; set in, fit in, insert; (*sl.*) +*d.* hit, smash; slang, curse; **~ся** cut, force one's way, run (into); be engraved; fall in love; **~ся в зе́млю** plunge to the ground. **вре́зной** inset; mortise; notch.

времена́ми *adv.* at times, now and then, from time to time.

временни́к, -а́ chronicle, annals. **вре́менно** *adv.* temporarily; **~ исполня́ющий обя́занности** acting; **~ пове́ренный в дела́х** acting chargé d'affaires. **временно́й** temporal;

time; of tense(s). **вре́менный** temporary; provisional; acting. **временщи́к, -а́** favourite. **вре́мя, -мени;** *pl.* **-мена́, -мён, -а́м** *nt.* time, times; tense; **~ го́да** season; **~ от вре́мени** at times, from time to time, now and then; **в своё ~** in one's time; once, at one time; in due course, in one's own time; **до того́ вре́мени** till then, till that time; **на ~** for a time; **са́мое ~** just the time, the (right) time; **ско́лько вре́мени?** what is the time? **тем вре́менем** meanwhile. **времянка, -и** portable or makeshift stove; temporary structure.

врид, -а *abbr.* (*of* **вре́менно исполня́ющий до́лжность**) temporary, acting (as).

вро́вень *adv.* level, on a level.

вро́де *prep.*+*g.* like; **не́что ~ а** sort of, a kind of; *part.* such as, like; apparently, seemingly.

врождённый; -дён, -а́ innate; congenital; inherent.

врознь, врозь *adv.* separately, apart.

врос *etc.: see* **врасти́. вро́ю(сь,** *etc.: see* **вры́ть(ся. вру,** *etc.: see* **врать**

врун, -а́, вру́нья, -и liar.

вруча́ть, -а́ю *impf.*, **вручи́ть, -чу́** *pf.* hand, deliver; entrust; serve. **вручи́тель, -я** *m.* bearer.

вручну́ю *adv.* by hand.

врыва́ть(ся, -а́ю(сь *impf. of* **ворва́ться, вры́ть(ся**

врыть, вро́ю *pf.* (*impf.* **врыва́ть**) dig in, bury; **~ся** dig in.

вряд (ли) *adv.* it's not likely; hardly, scarcely; **~ ли сто́ит** it's hardly worth while.

вс... see вз...

всади́ть, -ажу́, -а́дишь *pf.*, **вса́живать, -аю** *impf.* thrust in, plunge in; set in; put in, sink in. **вса́дник, -а** rider, horseman; knight. **вса́дница, -ы** rider, horsewoman.

вса́сывание, -я suction; absorption. **вса́сывать(ся, -аю(сь** *impf. of* **всоса́ть(ся**

всё, все *pron.: see* **весь. всё** *adv.* always, all the time; only, all; **~ (ещё)** still; **~ из-за тебя́** all because of you; **~ лу́чше и лу́чше** better and better; *conj.* however, nevertheless; **~ же** all the same.

все... *in comb.* all-, omni-. **всевозмо́жный** of every kind; all possible. **~во́лновый** all-wave. **~ме́рно** *adv.* in every way, to the utmost. **~ме́рный** of every kind, every possible kind of. **~ми́рный** world, world-wide, universal. **~могу́щий** omnipotent, all-powerful. **~наро́дно** *adv.* publicly. **~наро́дный** national; nation-wide, **~ору́жие; во всеору́жии** completely ready; fully armed, equipped. **~плане́тный** global, worldwide. **~побежда́ющий** all-conquering. **~пого́дный** all-weather. **~росси́йский** All-Russian. **~сезо́нный** year-round. **~си́льный** omnipotent, all-powerful. **~славя́нский** pan-Slav. **~сою́зный** All-Union. **~сторо́нний** all-round; thorough, detailed; comprehensive.

всегда́ always, ever. **всегда́шний** usual, habitual, customary.

всего́ *adv.* in all, all told; only.

вселе́ние, -я installation, moving in.

вселе́нная *sb.* universe. **вселе́нский** universal; ecumenical.

всели́ть, -лю́ *pf.*, **вселя́ть, -я́ю** *impf.* install, settle, lodge; move; inspire, instill; ~ся move in, install o.s., settle in; be implanted.

все́меро *adv.* seven times, **всемеро́м** *adv.* seven (together).

всеобу́ч, -а *abbr.* (*of* всео́бщее обуче́ние) compulsory education. **всео́бщий** general, universal.

всерьёз *adv.* seriously, in earnest.

всё-таки *conj. and part.* all the same, for all that, still. **всеце́ло** *adv.* completely; exclusively.

вска́кивать, -аю *impf. of* вскочи́ть

вс|кара́бкаться, -аюсь *pf.*, **вскара́бкиваться, -аюсь** *impf.* scramble up, clamber up.

вска́чь *adv.* at a gallop.

вски́дывать, -аю *impf.*, **вски́нуть, -ну** *pf.* throw up, toss; ~ся leap up; +на+*a.* turn on, go for.

вскипа́ть, -а́ю *impf.*, **вс|кипе́ть, -плю́** *pf.* boil up; flare up.

вс|кипяти́ть(ся, -ячу́(сь *pf.*

всклоко́чивать, -аю *impf.*, **всклоко́чить, -чу** *pf.* dishevel, tousle.

всколыхну́ть, -ну́, -нёшь *pf.* stir; stir up, rouse.

вско́льзь *adv.* slightly; in passing.

вско́ре *adv.* soon, shortly after.

вскочи́ть, -очу́, -о́чишь *pf.* (*impf.* вска́кивать) jump up, spring up, leap up; come up.

вскри́кивать, -аю *impf.*, **вскри́кнуть, -ну** *pf.* cry out, shriek, scream. **вскрича́ть, -чу́** *pf.* exclaim.

вскрыва́ть, -а́ю *impf.*, **вскрыть, -ро́ю** *pf.* open; reveal, disclose; turn up; lance; cut open, dissect; ~ся come to light, be revealed; become clear of ice, become open; burst. **вскры́тие, -я** opening; revelation, disclosure; lancing; dissection, post-mortem.

вслед *adv. & prep.+d.* after; ~ за+*i.* after, following. **всле́дствие** *prep.+g.* in consequence of, because of, on account of.

вслепу́ю *adv.* blindly; blindfold; печа́тать ~ to touch-type.

вслух *adv.* aloud.

вслу́шаться, -аюсь *pf.* **вслу́шиваться, -аюсь** *impf.* listen attentively, listen hard.

всма́триваться, -аюсь *impf.*, **всмотре́ться, -рю́сь, -ришься** *pf.* look closely, peer, look hard.

всмя́тку *adv.* soft(-boiled), lightly (boiled).

всо́вывать, -аю *impf. of* всу́нуть

всоса́ть, -су́, -сёшь *pf.* (*impf.* вса́сывать) suck in; absorb; imbibe; ~ся be absorbed, soak in; sink in.

вспа́рхивать, -аю *impf. of* вспорхну́ть

вспа́рывать, -аю *impf. of* вспоро́ть

вс|паха́ть, -ашу́, -а́шешь *pf.*, **вспа́хивать, -аю** *impf.* plough up. **вспа́шка, -и** ploughing.

вс|пе́нить, -ню *pf.*

всплеск, -а splash; blip. **вспле́скивать, -аю** *impf.*, **всплесну́ть, -ну́, -нёшь** *pf.* splash; ~ рука́ми fling up, throw up, one's hands.

всплыва́ть, -а́ю *impf.*, **всплыть, -ыву́, -ывёшь; -ыл, -а́, -о** *pf.* rise to the surface, surface; arise, come up; come to light, be revealed.

вс|полоши́ть(ся, -шу́(сь *pf.*

вспомна́ть, -а́ю *impf.*, **вспо́мнить, -ню** *pf.* remember, recall, recollect; ~ся *impers.*+*d.*: мне вспо́мнилось I remembered.

вспомога́тельный auxiliary; subsidiary, branch.

вспоро́ть, -орю́, -о́решь *pf.* (*impf.* вспа́рывать) rip open.

вспорхну́ть, -ну́, -нёшь *pf.* (*impf.* вспа́рхивать) take wing, start up, fly up.

вс|поте́ть, -е́ю *pf.*

вспры́гивать, -аю *impf.*, **вспры́гнуть, -ну** *pf.* jump up, spring up.

вспры́скивать, -аю *impf.*, **вспры́снуть, -ну** *pf.* sprinkle.

вспуха́ть, -а́ет *impf.*, **вс|пу́хнуть, -нет; -ух** *pf.* swell up.

вспыли́ть, -лю́ *pf.* flare up; fly into a rage (на+*a.* with) **вспы́льчивый** hot-tempered, irritable.

вспы́хивать, -аю *impf.*, **вспы́хнуть, -ну** *pf.* burst into flame, blaze up; flare up; break out; blush. **вспы́шка, -и** flash; flare, spurt; outburst, burst; outbreak.

встава́ние, -я rising, standing. **встава́ть, -таю́, -таёшь** *impf. of* встать

вста́вить, -влю *pf.*, **вставля́ть, -я́ю** *impf.* put in, set in, insert. **вста́вка, -и** fixing, insertion; framing, mounting; inset; front; interpolation. **вставн|о́й** inserted; set in; ~ые зу́бы false teeth; ~ые ра́мы double window-frames.

встать, -а́ну *pf.* (*impf.* встава́ть) get up, rise; stand up; stand; arise, come up; stop; go, fit (в+*a.* into); ~ на коле́ни kneel down; ~ с ле́вой ноги́ get out of bed on the wrong side.

встрево́женный *adj.* anxious, worried, alarmed. **вс|трево́жить, -жу** *pf.*

встрёпанный dishevelled.

встрепену́ться, -ну́сь, -нёшься *pf.* rouse o.s.; shake its wings; start, start up; beat faster, begin to thump.

встре́тить, -е́чу *pf.*, **встреча́ть, -а́ю** *impf.* meet, meet with, encounter; greet, welcome; receive; ~ся meet; be found, be met with. **встре́ча, -и** meeting; reception; encounter; match. **встре́чный** coming to meet; contrary, head; counter; ~ ве́тер head wind; ~ иск counter-claim; *sb.* person met with; ка́ждый ~ и попере́чный anybody and everybody, every Tom, Dick and Harry; пе́рвый

~ the first person you meet, anybody.
встря́ска, -и shaking; shock. **встря́хивать, -аю** *impf.*, **встряхну́ть, -ну́, -нёшь** *pf.* shake; shake up, rouse; ~**ся** shake o.s.; rouse o.s., pull o.s. together; have a good time.

вступа́ть, -а́ю *impf.*, **вступи́ть, -плю́, -пишь** *pf.*+**в**+*a.* enter, enter into, join, join in; come into; +**на**+*a.* go up, mount; ~ **в брак** marry; ~ **на престо́л** ascend the throne; ~**ся** intervene; +**за**+*a.* stand up for. **вступи́тельный** introductory; inaugural, opening; entrance. **вступле́ние, -я** entry, joining; accession; prelude, opening, introduction, preamble.

всу́нуть, -ну *pf.* (*impf.* **всо́вывать**) put in, stick in, push in, slip in.

всхли́пнуть, -ну *pf.*, **всхли́пывать, -аю** *impf.* sob. **всхли́пывание, -я** sobbing; sobs.

всходи́ть, -ожу́, -о́дишь *impf. of* **взойти́. всхо́ды, -ов** *pl.* new growth, shoots.

всхрапну́ть, -ну́, -нёшь *pf.*, **всхра́пывать, -аю** *impf.* snore; snort; have a nap.

всю *see* **весь**

всю́ду *adv.* everywhere.

вся *see* **весь**

вся́к|ий any; every, all kinds of; ~**ом слу́чае** in any case, anyhow, at any rate; **на** ~**ий слу́чай** just in case, to be on the safe side; *pron.* anyone, everyone; anything. **вся́чески** *adv.* in every possible way, in all ways. **вся́ческий** all kinds of.

Вт *abbr.* (*of* **ватт**) W, watt.

вта́йне *adv.* secretly, in secret.

вта́лкивать, -аю *impf. of* **втолкну́ть**

вта́птывать, -аю *impf. of* **втопта́ть**

вта́скивать, -аю *impf. of* **втащи́ть**

втача́ть, -а́ю *pf.*, **вта́чивать, -аю** *impf.* sew in, sew on; set in. **вта́чка, -и** sewing in, sewing on; patch. **вта́чанный, втачно́й** sewn in, sewn on; set in.

втащи́ть, -щу́, -щишь *pf.* (*impf.* **вта́скивать**) drag in, drag on, drag up; ~**ся** drag o.s.

втека́ть, -а́ет *impf. of* **втечь**

втере́ть, вотру́, вотрёшь; втёр *pf.* (*impf.* **втира́ть**) rub in; ~**ся** insinuate o.s., worm o.s.

втечь, -чёт; втёк, -ла́ *pf.* (*impf.* **втека́ть**) flow in.

втира́ние, -я rubbing in; embrocation, liniment. **втира́ть(ся, -а́ю(сь** *impf. of* **втере́ть(ся**

вти́скивать, -аю *impf.*, **вти́снуть, -ну** *pf.* squeeze in; ~**ся** squeeze (o.s.) in.

втихомо́лку, втиху́ю *advs.* surreptitiously; on the quiet.

втолкну́ть, -ну́, -нёшь *pf.* (*impf.* **вта́лкивать**) push in, shove in.

втопта́ть, -пчу́, -пчешь *pf.* (*impf.* **вта́птывать**) trample (in).

вто́ра, -ы second voice, violin, etc. **вто́рить, -рю** *impf.* play or sing second; +*d.* repeat, echo. **втори́чный** second, secondary. **вто́рник, -а** Tuesday. **втор|о́й** second; ~**о́е** *sb.* second course. **второочередно́й** secondary.

второстепе́нный secondary, minor.

в-тре́тьих *adv.* thirdly, in the third place. **втро́е** *adv.* three times, treble. **втро́ём** *adv.* three (together). **втройне́** *adv.* three times as much, treble.

втуз, -а *abbr.* (*of* **вы́сшее техни́ческое уче́бное заведе́ние**) technical college.

вту́лка, -и bush; plug; bung; liner, sleeve.

втыка́ть, -а́ю *impf. of* **воткну́ть. вты́чка, -и** thrusting in, driving in, driving in; plug, bung.

втя́гивать, -аю *impf.*, **втяну́ть, -ну́, -нешь** *pf.* draw in, up; pull in, up; absorb; take in; involve; ~**ся** sink, fall in; +**в**+*a.* draw into enter; get used to; get keen on.

вуале́тка, -и veil. **вуали́ровать, -рую** *impf.* (*pf.* **за~**) veil, draw a veil over; fog. **вуа́ль, -и** veil; fog.

вуз, -а *abbr.* (*of* **вы́сшее уче́бное заведе́ние**) higher educational establishment; university, college, institute. **ву́зовец, -вца, -овка, -и** student.

вулка́н, -а volcano. **вулкани́ческий** volcanic.

вульга́рность, -и vulgarity. **вульга́рный** vulgar.

вундерки́нд, -а infant prodigy.

вход, -а entrance; entry. **входи́ть, -ожу́, -о́дишь** *impf. of* **войти́. входн|о́й** entrance, input; ~**о́е отве́рстие** inlet, inlet port. **входя́щий** incoming, entering; reentrant; male.

вхолосту́ю *adv.* idle, free; **рабо́тать** ~ idle.

вцепи́ться, -плю́сь, -пишься *pf.*, **вцепля́ться, -я́юсь** *impf.* clutch, cling to; seize, catch hold of.

вчера́ *adv.* yesterday. **вчера́шний** yesterday's.

вчерне́ in rough, roughly.

вче́тверо *adv.* four times, by four, in four. **вчетверо́м** *adv.* four (together). **в-четвёртых** *adv.* fourthly, in the fourth place.

вши *etc.*: *see* **вошь**

вше́стеро *adv.* six times, by six. **вшестеро́м** *adv.* six (together).

вшива́ть, -а́ю *impf. of* **вшить. вши́вка, -и** sewing in; patch. **вшивно́й** sewn in, set in.

вши́вый lousy.

вширь *adv.* in breadth; widely.

вшить, вошью́, -ьёшь *pf.* (*impf.* **вшива́ть**) sew in, set in.

въ... *see* **в...**

въеда́ться, -а́ется *impf. of* **въе́сться. въе́дливый, въе́дчивый** *adjs.* corrosive; caustic; acid.

въезд, -а entry; entrance. **въезжа́ть, -а́ю** *impf. of* **въе́хать**

въе́сться, -е́стся, -едя́тся *pf.* (*impf.* **въеда́ться**) в+*a.* eat into, corrode.

въе́хать, -е́ду *pf.* (*impf.* **въезжа́ть**) ride in, up; drive in, up; +**в**+*a.* move into; run into.

въявь *adv.* in reality; before one's eyes, with one's own eyes.

вы, вас, вам, ва́ми, вас *pron.* you.

вы... *vbl. pref. expressing direction of mo-*

tion or action outwards; achievement or attainment by means of action; completion of action or process.

выбега́ть, -а́ю *impf.*, **вы́бежать**, -егу *pf.* run out.

вы́|белить, -лю *pf.* **вы́белка**, -и bleaching; whitening.

вы́беру *etc.*: see **вы́брать**. **выбива́ть(ся**, -а́ю(сь *impf. of* **вы́бить(ся**. **выбира́ть(ся**, -а́ю(сь *impf. of* **вы́брать(ся**

вы́бить, -бью *pf.* (*impf.* **выбива́ть**) knock out, kick out; dislodge; beat; beat down; beat out; stamp, strike; hammer out; ~**ся** get out; break loose; come out, show; ~**ся из сил** exhaust o.s., be exhausted.

вы́боина, -ы rut; pot-hole; dent; groove.

вы́бор, -а choice, option; selection, assortment; *pl.* election, elections, **вы́борка**, -и selection; excerpt. **вы́борн|ый** elective; electoral; elected; ~ бюллете́нь ballot-paper; ~ый, ~ая *sb.* delegate. **вы́борочный** selective.

вы́|бранить(ся, -ню(сь *pf.* **выбра́сывать(ся**, -аю(сь *impf. of* **вы́бросить(ся**

вы́брать, -беру *pf.* (*impf.* **выбира́ть**) choose, select, pick out; elect; take out; haul in; ~**ся** get out; move, remove; manage to go out.

выбрива́ть, -а́ю *impf.*, **вы́брить**, -рею *pf.* shave; ~**ся** shave (o.s.).

вы́брос, -а blip, pip. **вы́бросить**, -ошу *pf.* (*impf.* **выбра́сывать**) throw out; reject, discard, throw away; put out; ~**ся** throw o.s. out, leap out; ~**ся с парашю́том** bale out.

выбыва́ть, -а́ю *impf.*, **вы́быть**, -буду *pf.* из+g. leave, quit; be out of. **вы́бытие**, -я departure, removal, absence.

выва́ливать, -аю *impf.*, **вы́валить**, -лю *pf.* throw out; pour out; ~**ся** fall out; pour out.

выва́ривать, -аю *impf.*, **вы́варить**, -рю *pf.* boil out; extract by boiling; boil thoroughly. **вы́варка**, -и decoction, extraction; residue, concentrate.

вы́везти, -зу; -ез *pf.* (*impf.* **вывози́ть**) take out, remove; bring out; export; save, rescue.

вы́верить, -рю *pf.* (*impf.* **выверя́ть**) verify; regulate.

вы́вернуть, -ну *pf.*, **вывёртывать**, -аю *impf.* turn inside out; unscrew; pull out; twist, wrench; dislocate; ~**ся** come unscrewed; slip out; get out, extricate o.s., wriggle out; be dislocated; emerge. **вы́верт**, -а caper; mannerism; affectation.

выверя́ть, -я́ю *impf. of* **вы́верить**

вы́весить, -ешу *pf.* (*impf.* **выве́шивать**) weigh; hang out; put up, post up. **вы́веска**, -и sign, signboard; screen, pretext; mug.

вы́вести, -еду; -ел *pf.* (*impf.* **выводи́ть**) lead out, bring out; drive out; turn out, force out; remove; exterminate; deduce, conclude; hatch; grow, breed, raise; put up, erect; depict, portray; write, draw, trace out; ~**сь** go out of use; lapse; disappear; become extinct; come out; hatch out.

вlevel second column

выве́тривание, -я airing; weathering. **выве́тривать**, -аю *impf.*, **вы́ветрить**, -рю *pf.* air; drive out, remove, efface; weather, erode; ~**ся** weather; disappear, be driven out, be effaced.

выве́шивать, -аю *impf. of* **вы́весить**

вы́вих, -а dislocation; sprain; kink; oddity, quirk. **вы́вихнуть**, -ну *pf.* dislocate, put out; sprain.

вы́вод, -а deduction, conclusion; withdrawal, removal. **выводи́ть(ся**, -ожу́(сь, -о́дишь(ся *impf. of* **вы́вести(сь**. **вы́водка**, -и removal; exercising. **вы́водок**, -дка brood; hatch litter.

вывожу́ *see* **выводи́ть**, **вывози́ть**

вы́воз, -а export; removal. **вывози́ть**, -ожу́, -о́зишь *impf. of* **вы́везти**. **вы́возка**, -и carting out. **вывозно́й** export.

вы́гарки, -ов *pl.* slag, dross.

вы́гиб, -а a curve, curvature. **выгиба́ть(ся**, -а́ю(сь *impf. of* **вы́гнуть(ся**

вы́|гладить, -ажу *pf.*

вы́глядеть, -яжу *impf.* look, look like. **выгля́дывать**, -аю *impf.*, **вы́глянуть**, -ну *pf.* look out; peep out, emerge, become visible.

вы́гнать, -гоню *pf.* (*impf.* **выгоня́ть**) drive out; expel; distil; force.

вы́гнутый curved, convex. **вы́гнуть**, -ну *pf.* (*impf.* **выгиба́ть**) bend, arch; ~**ся** arch up.

выгова́ривать, -аю *impf.* **вы́говорить**, -рю *pf.* pronounce, utter, speak; reserve; stipulate for; +d. reprimand; ~**ся** speak out, have one's say out. **вы́говор**, -а accent, pronunciation; reprimand, rebuke.

вы́года, -ы advantage, benefit; profit, gain; interest. **вы́годн|ый** advantageous, beneficial; profitable; ~о it pays.

вы́гон, -а pasture, common. **вы́гонка**, -и distillation. **выгоня́ть**, -я́ю *impf. of* **вы́гнать**

выгора́живать, -аю *impf. of* **вы́городить**

выгора́ть, -а́ет *impf.*, **вы́гореть**, -рит *pf.* burn down; burn out; fade, bleach; turn out well, come off.

вы́городить, -ожу *pf.* (*impf.* **выгора́живать**) fence off; shield, screen.

вы́|гравировать, -рую *pf.*

выгружа́ть, -а́ю *impf.*, **вы́грузить**, -ужу *pf.* unload; discharge; disembark; ~**ся** unload; disembark; detrain, debus. **вы́грузка**, -и unloading; disembarkation.

выдава́ть, -даю́, -даёшь *impf.*, **вы́дать**, -ам, -ашь, -аст, -адим *pf.* give out, issue, produce; give away, betray; deliver up, extradite; +за+a. pass off as, give out to be; ~ за́муж give in marriage; ~**ся** protrude, project, jut out; stand out; present itself, happen to be. **вы́дача**, -и issuing; issue; payment; extradition. **выдаю́щийся** prominent; salient; eminent, outstanding.

выдвига́ть, -а́ю *impf.*, **вы́двинуть**, -ну *pf.* move out; pull out, open; put forward, advance; promote; nominate, propose; ~**ся** move forward, move out, come out; rise, get on. **выдвиже́нец, -нца, -же́нка, -и** worker promoted from rank and file. **выдвиже́ние, -я** nomination; promotion, advancement.

выделе́ние, -я secretion; excretion; isolation; apportionment. **вы́делить, -лю** *pf.*, **выде-ля́ть, -я́ю** *impf.* pick out, single out; detach; detail; assign, earmark; allot; secrete; excrete; isolate; ~ **курси́вом** italicize; ~**ся** take one's share; ooze out, exude; stand out, be noted (+*i.* for).

вы́держанный consistent; self-possessed; firm; matured, seasoned. **вы́держать, -жу** *pf.* **выде́рживать, -аю** *impf.* bear, hold; stand, stand up to, endure; contain o.s.; pass; keep; lay up; mature; season; maintain, sustain. **вы́держка¹, -и** endurance; self-possession; exposure.

вы́держка², -и extract, excerpt, quotation.

вы́дох, -а expiration. **вы́дохнуть, -ну** *pf.* (*impf.* **выдыха́ть**) breathe out; ~**ся** have lost fragrance or smell; be played out; be flat; be past one's best.

вы́дра, -ы otter.

вы́|драть, -деру *pf.* **вы́|дрессирова́ть, -рую** *pf.* **вы́|дубить, -блю** *pf.*

выдува́льщик, -а glass-blower. **выдува́ть, -а́ю** *impf. of* **вы́дуть. вы́дувка, -и** glass-blowing. **вы́дувной** blown.

вы́думанный made-up, invented, fabricated. **вы́думать, -аю** *pf.*, **выду́мывать, -аю** *impf.* invent; make up, fabricate. **вы́думка, -и** invention; idea, gadget, device; inventiveness; fabrication, fiction.

вы́|дуть, -ую *pf.* (*impf. also* **выдува́ть**) blow; blow out; blow up.

выдыха́ние, -я expiration. **выдыха́ть(ся, -а́ю(сь** *impf. of* **вы́дохнуть(ся**

вы́езд, -а departure; exit; turn-out, equipage; going out.

выездн|о́й going-out; travelling, visiting; exit; away; ~**о́й матч** away match; ~**а́я се́ссия суда́** assizes. **выезжа́ть, -а́ю** *impf. of* **вы́ехать**

вы́емка, -и taking out; seizure; collection; excavation; hollow, groove; fluting, flute; cutting, cut.

вы́ехать, -еду *pf.* (*impf.* **выезжа́ть**) go out, depart; drive out, ride out; move, remove, leave; +**на**+*p.* make use of, exploit, take advantage of.

вы́жать, -жму *pf.* (*impf.* **выжима́ть**) squeeze out; wring out, press out; lift, press-lift.

вы́ждать, -ду *pf.* (*impf.* **выжида́ть**) wait for, wait out.

вы́жечь, -жгу *pf.* (*impf.* **выжига́ть**) burn low, burn out; burn, scorch; cauterize. **вы́жженн|ый, ~ая земля́** scorched earth.

выжива́ние, -я survival. **выжива́ть, -а́ю** *impf. of* **вы́жить**

выжига́ние, -я burning out, scorching; cauterization; ~ **по де́реву** poker-work. **выжига́ть, -а́ю** *impf. of* **вы́жечь**

выжида́ние, -я waiting, temporizing. **вы-жида́тельный** waiting; expectant; temporizing. **выжида́ть, -а́ю** *impf. of* **вы́ждать**

вы́жим, -а press-up. **выжима́ние, -я** squeezing; wringing (out); (weight-)lifting. **выжима́ть, -а́ю** *impf. of* **вы́жать. вы́жимка, -и** squeezing, pressing, wringing; abstract, brief summary.

вы́жить, -иву *pf.* (*impf.* **выжива́ть**) survive; live through; stay alive, hold out, stick it out; drive out, hound out; get rid of; ~ **из ума́** become senile.

вы́звать, -зову *pf.* (*impf.* **вызыва́ть**) call, call out; send for; challenge; call forth, provoke; cause; stimulate, rouse; ~ **по телефо́ну** ring up; ~**ся** volunteer, offer.

выздора́вливать, -аю *impf.*, **вы́здороветь, -ею** *pf.* recover, get better. **выздоровле́ние, -я** recovery; convalescence.

вы́зов, -а call; summons; challenge.

вы́|золотить, -лочу *pf.* **вы́золоченный** gilt.

вызу́бривать, -аю *impf.*, **вы́|зубрить, -рю** *pf.* learn by heart, cram.

вызыва́ть(ся, -а́ю(сь *impf. of* **вы́звать(ся. вызыва́ющий** defiant; challenging, provocative.

вы́играть, -аю *pf.*, **выи́грывать, -аю** *impf.* win; gain. **вы́игрыш, -а** win; winning; winnings; gain; prize. **вы́игрышный** winning; premium; lottery; advantageous; effective.

вы́йти, -йду; -шел, -шла *pf.* (*impf.* **выходи́ть**) go out; come out; get out; appear; turn out; come to be used up; have expired; ~ **в свет** appear; ~ **в фина́л** reach the final; ~ **за́муж (за**+*a.*) marry; ~ **из грани́ц, ~ из преде́лов** exceed the bounds; ~ **из себя́** lose one's temper, be beside o.s.; ~ **на вы́зовы** take a call; ~ **на сце́ну** come onto the stage.

вы́казать, -ажу *pf.*, **выка́зывать, -аю** *impf.* show; display.

выка́лывать, -аю *impf. of* **вы́колоть**

выка́пчивать, -аю *impf. of* **вы́коптить**

выка́пывать, -аю *impf. of* **вы́копать**

вы́карабкаться, -аюсь *pf.*, **выкара́бки-ваться, -аюсь** *impf.* scramble out; get out.

вы́|катать, -аю *pf.*

вы́|качать, -аю *pf.*, **выка́чивать, -аю** *impf.* pump out.

выки́дывать, -аю *impf.*, **вы́кинуть, -ну** *pf.* throw out, reject; put out; miscarry, abort; ~ **флаг** hoist a flag. **вы́кидыш, -а** miscarriage, abortion.

вы́кладка, -и laying out; lay-out; facing; kit; computation, calculation. **выкла́дывать, -аю** *impf. of* **вы́ложить**

выклика́ть, -аю *impf.*, **вы́кликнуть, -ну** *pf.* call out.

выключа́тель, -я *m.* switch. **выключа́ть, -а́ю** *impf.*, **вы́ключить, -чу** *pf.* turn off, switch off; remove, exclude; justify.

вы́|клянчить, -чу *pf.*

выкола́чивать, -аю *impf.*, **вы́колотить, -лочу** *pf.* knock out, beat out; beat; extort; wring out.

вы́колоть, -лю *pf.* (*impf.* **выка́лывать**) put out; gouge out; tattoo.

вы́|копать, -аю *pf.* (*impf. also* **выка́пывать**) dig; dig up, dig out; exhume; unearth; ~ся dig o.s. out.

вы́коптить, -пчу *pf.* (*impf.* **выка́пчивать**) smoke.

вы́корчевать, -чую *pf.*, **выкорчёвывать**, -аю *impf.* uproot, root out; extirpate, eradicate.

выкра́ивать, -аю *impf. of* **вы́кроить**

вы́|красить, -ашу *pf.*, **выкра́шивать**, -аю *impf.* paint; dye.

вы́крик, -а cry, shout; yell. **выкри́кивать**, -аю *impf.*, **вы́крикнуть**, -ну *pf.* cry out; yell.

вы́кроить, -ою *pf.* (*impf.* **выкра́ивать**) cut out; (manage to) find. **вы́кройка**, -и pattern.

вы́крутить, -учу *pf.*, **выкру́чивать**, -аю *impf.* unscrew; twist; ~ся extricate o.s., get o.s. out.

вы́куп, -а ransom; redemption.

вы́|купать¹(ся, -аю(сь *pf.*

выкупа́ть², -а́ю *impf.*, **вы́купить**, -плю *pf.* ransom, redeem. **выкупно́й** ransom; redemption.

выку́ривать, -аю *impf.*, **вы́курить**, -рю *pf.* smoke; smoke out; distil.

выла́вливать, -аю *impf. of* **вы́ловить**

вы́лазка, -и sally, sortie; raid; ramble, excursion, outing.

вы́|лакать, -аю *pf.* **выла́мывать**, -аю *impf. of* **вы́ломать выла́щивать**, -аю *impf. of* **вы́лощить**

вылеза́ть, -а́ю *impf.*, **вы́лезти**, **вы́лезть**, -зу; -лез *pf.* crawl out; climb out; fall out; come out.

вы́|лепить, -плю *pf.*

вы́лет, -а flight; take-off, departure; emission; escape; overhang. **вылета́ть**, -а́ю *impf.*, **вы́лететь**, -ечу *pf.* fly out, off, away; take off; rush out, dash out; escape.

вылéчивать, -аю *impf.*, **вы́лечить**, -чу *pf.* cure, heal; ~ся recover, be cured; ~ся от+g. get over.

вылива́ть(ся, -а́ю(сь *pf. of* **вы́лить(ся**

вы́|линять, -яет *pf.*

вы́лить, -лью *pf.* (*impf.* **вылива́ть**) pour out; empty (out); cast, found; mould; ~ся run out, flow (out); be expressed, express itself.

вы́ловить, -влю *pf.* (*impf.* **выла́вливать**) fish out, catch.

вы́ложить, -жу *pf.* (*impf.* **выкла́дывать**) lay out, spread out; cover, lay, face; tell, reveal.

вы́лом, -а breaking down, in, out, open; breach, break, gap. **вы́ломать**, -аю *pf.*, **вы́ломить**, -млю *pf.* (*impf.* **выла́мывать**) break down, break out, break open. **вы́ломка**, -и breaking off.

вы́лощенный glossy; polished, smooth. **вы́лощить**, -щу *pf.* (*impf.* **выла́щивать**) polish.

вы́|лудить, -ужу *pf.* **вы́лью** *etc.*: *see* **вы́лить**

вы́|мазать, -мажу *pf.*, **выма́зывать**, -аю *impf.* smear, daub, dirty; ~ся get dirty, make o.s. dirty.

выма́ливать, -аю *impf. of* **вы́молить**

выма́нивать, -аю *impf.*, **вы́манить**, -ню *pf.* entice, lure; +y+g. swindle, cheat, out of; wheedle, coax out of.

вы́|марать, -аю *pf.* **вы́мени** *etc.*: *see* **вы́мя**

вы́мереть, -мрет; -мер *pf.* (*impf.* **вымира́ть**) die out; become extinct; be, become, deserted. **вы́мерший** extinct.

вымина́ть, -а́ю *impf. of* **вы́мять**. **вымира́ть**, -а́ю *impf. of* **вы́мереть**. **вы́мну** *etc.*: *see* **вы́мять**

вымога́тель, -я *m.*, **-ница**, -ы blackmailer, extortioner. **вымога́тельство**, -а blackmail, extortion. **вымога́ть**, -а́ю *impf.* extort, wring (out).

вымока́ть, -а́ю *impf.*, **вы́мокнуть**, -ну; -ок *pf.* be soaked, drenched, wet through; soak, steep; rot.

вымола́чивать, -аю *impf. of* **вы́молотить**

вы́молвить, -влю *pf.* say, utter.

вы́молить, -лю *pf.* (*impf.* **выма́ливать**) beg; obtain by prayer(s).

вы́молот, -а threshing; grain. **вы́молотить**, -очу *pf.* (*impf.* **вымола́чивать**) thresh. **вы́молотки**, -ток *or* -тков *pl.* chaff.

вы́|мостить, -ощу *pf.* **вы́мою** *etc.*: *see* **вы́мыть**

вы́мпел, -а pennant.

вы́мрет *see* **вы́мереть**. **вымыва́ть(ся** *impf. of* **вы́мыть(ся**

вы́мысел, -сла invention, fabrication; fantasy, flight of fancy. **вы́мыслить**, -лю *pf.* (*impf.* **вымышля́ть**) think up, make up, invent; imagine.

вы́|мыть, -мою *pf.* (*impf.* **вымыва́ть**) wash; wash out, off; wash away; ~ся wash, wash o.s.

вы́мышленный fictitious, imaginary. **вымышля́ть**, -я́ю *impf. of* **вы́мыслить**

вы́мя, -мени *nt.* udder.

вы́мять, -мну *pf.* (*impf.* **вымина́ть**) knead, work; trample down.

вы́нести, -су; -нес *pf.* (*impf.* **выноси́ть**) carry out, take out; take away; carry away; bear, stand, endure; pass; ~ **вопро́с** submit a question; ~ **на бе́рег** wash up; ~сь fly out, rush out.

вынима́ть(ся, -а́ю(сь *impf. of* **вы́нуть(ся**

вы́нос, -а carrying out; removal; drift; trace. **выноси́ть**, -ошу́, -о́сишь *impf. of* **вы́нести**; не ~ be unable to bear, to stand; ~ся *impf. of* **вы́нестись**. **вы́носка**, -и taking out, carrying out; removal; marginal note, footnote. **выно́сливость**, -и endurance, staying-power; hardiness.

вы́нудить, -ужу *pf.*, **вынужда́ть**, -а́ю *impf.* force, compel, oblige; extort. **вы́нужденный** forced, compulsory.

вы́нуть, -ну *pf.* (*impf.* **вынима́ть**) take out;

pull out; extract; draw out; ~**ся** come out, pull out.

вы́пад, -а attack; lunge, thrust. **выпада́ть, -а́ю** *impf. of* **вы́пасть. выпаде́ние, -я** falling out; fall-out; precipitation; prolapsus.

вы́па́лывать, -аю *impf. of* **вы́полоть**

выпа́ривать, -аю *impf.*, **вы́парить, -рю** evaporate.

выпа́рывать, -аю *impf. of* **вы́пороть²**

вы́пасть, -аду; -ал *pf.* (*impf.* **выпада́ть**) fall out; fall; occur, turn out; lunge, thrust.

выпека́ть, -а́ю *impf.*, **вы́печь, -еку; -ек** *pf.* bake. **вы́печка, -и** baking, batch.

выпива́ть, -а́ю *impf. of* **вы́пить**; enjoy a drink. **вы́пивка, -и** drinking; drinks.

выпи́ливать, -аю *impf.*, **вы́пилить, -лю** *pf.* saw, cut out, make with fretsaw.

вы́писать, -ишу *pf.*, **выпи́сывать, -аю** *impf.* copy out, excerpt; trace out; write out; order; subscribe to; send for, write for; strike off the list; ~ **из больни́цы** discharge from hospital; ~**ся** leave, be discharged. **вы́писка, -и** copying out, making extracts; writing out; extract, excerpt, cutting; ordering, subscription; discharge.

вы́|пить, -пью *pf.* (*impf. also* **выпива́ть**) drink; drink up, drink off.

вы́плавить, -влю *pf.*, **выплавля́ть, -я́ю** *impf.* smelt. **вы́плавка, -и** smelting; smelted metal.

вы́плата, -ы payment. **вы́платить, -ачу** *pf.*, **выпла́чивать, -аю** *impf.* pay out; pay off.

выплёвывать, -аю *impf. of* **вы́плюнуть**

вы́плести, -ету *pf.*, **выплета́ть, -а́ю** *impf.* undo, untie; unplait; weave.

выплыва́ть, -а́ю *impf.*, **вы́плыть, -ву** *pf.* swim out, sail out, come to surface, come up; emerge; appear, crop up.

вы́плюнуть, -ну *pf.* (*impf.* **выплёвывать**) spit out.

выполза́ть, -а́ю *impf.*, **вы́ползти, -зу; -олз** *pf.* crawl out, creep out.

выполне́ние, -я execution, carrying out; fulfilment. **выполни́мый** practical, feasible. **вы́полнить, -ню** *pf.*, **выполня́ть, -я́ю** *impf.* execute, carry out; fulfil; discharge.

вы́|полоскать, -ощу *pf.*

вы́|полоть, -лю *pf.* (*impf. also* **выпа́лывать**) weed out; weed.

вы́|пороть¹, -рю *pf.*

вы́пороть², -рю *pf.* (*impf.* **выпа́рывать**) rip out, rip up.

вы́|потрошить, -шу *pf.*

вы́править, -влю *pf.*, **выправля́ть, -я́ю** *impf.* straighten (out); correct; prove; get, obtain; ~**ся** become straight; improve. **вы́правка, -и** bearing; correction.

выпра́шивать, -аю *impf. of* **вы́просить, -шу** solicit.

выпрова́живать, -аю *impf.*, **вы́проводить, -ожу** *pf.* send packing; show the door.

вы́просить, -ошу *pf.* (*impf.* **выпра́шивать**) (*ask for and*) obtain, get.

выпряга́ть, -а́ю *impf. of* **вы́прячь**

выпрями́тель, -я *m.* rectifier. **вы́прямить, -млю** *pf.*, **выпрямля́ть, -я́ю** *impf.* straighten (out); rectify; ~**ся** come straight; straighten up, pull o.s. up.

вы́прячь, -ягу; -яг *pf.* (*impf.* **выпряга́ть**) unharness.

выпу́гивать, -аю *impf.*, **вы́пугнуть, -ну** *pf.* scare off; start.

вы́пукло *adv.* in relief. **вы́пукло-** convex-. **вы́пуклость, -и** protuberance; prominence; bulge; convexity; relief; clarity, distinctness. **вы́пуклый** protuberant; prominent, bulging; convex; in relief; clear, distinct.

вы́пуск, -а output; issue; discharge; part, number, instalment; final-year students, pupils; cut, omission; edging, piping. **выпуска́ть, -а́ю** *impf.*, **вы́пустить, -ущу** *pf.* let out, release; put out, issue; turn out, produce; cut, cut out, omit; let out, let down; show; see through the press. **выпускни́к, -а́** final-year student, pupil. **выпускн|о́й** output; discharge; exhaust; ~**о́й экза́мен** finals, final examination; ~**а́я цена́** market-price; ~**о́й** *sb.* final-year student.

вы́путать, -аю *pf.*, **выпу́тывать, -аю** *impf.* disentangle; ~**ся** disentangle o.s., extricate o.s.; ~**ся из беды́** get out of a scrape.

вы́пушка, -и edging, braid, piping.

вы́пытать, -аю *pf.*, **выпы́тывать, -аю** *impf.* elicit, worm out.

выпь, -и bittern.

вы́пью *etc.: see* **вы́пить**

вы́пятить(ся, -ячу(сь *pf.*, **выпя́чивать(ся, -аю(сь** *impf.* stick out, protrude.

выраба́тывать, -аю *impf.*, **вы́работать, -аю** *pf.* work out; work up; draw up; elaborate; manufacture; produce, make; earn. **вы́работка, -и** manufacture; production, making; working; working out, drawing up; output, yield; make.

выра́внивать(ся, -аю(сь *impf. of* **вы́ровнять(ся**

выража́ть, -а́ю *impf.*, **вы́разить, -ажу** *pf.* express; convey; voice; ~**ся** express o.s.; manifest itself; amount, come (**в**+*p.* to). **выраже́ние, -я** expression. **вы́раженный** pronounced, marked. **вырази́тель, -я** *m.* spokesman, exponent; voice. **вырази́тельный** expressive; significant.

выраста́ть, -а́ю *impf.*, **вы́расти, -ту; -рос** *pf.* grow, grow up; develop; increase; appear, rise up; ~ **из**+*g.* grow out of. **вы́растить, -ащу** *pf.*, **выра́щивать, -аю** *impf.* bring up; rear, breed; grow, cultivate.

вы́рвать¹, -ву *pf.* (*impf.* **вырыва́ть**) pull out, tear out; extort, wring out; ~**ся** tear o.s. away; break out, break loose, break free; get away; come loose, come out; break, burst, escape; shoot up, shoot (out).

вы́|рвать², -ву *pf.*

вы́рез, -а cut; notch; décolletage. **вы́резать, -ежу** *pf.*, **выреза́ть, -а́ю** *impf.*, **вырезы́-**

вать, -аю *impf.* cut out; excise; cut, carve; engrave; slaughter, butcher. **вы́резка**, -и cutting out, excision; carving; engraving; cutting; fillet. **вырезно́й** cut; carved; low-necked, décolleté. **вырéзывание**, -я cutting out; excision; carving; engraving.

вы́рисовать, -сую *pf.*, **вырисо́вывать**, -аю *impf.* draw carefully, draw in detail; ~ся appear; stand out.

выровня́ть, -яю *pf.* (*impf.* **выра́внивать**) smooth, level; straighten (out); draw up; ~ся become level, become even; form up; equalize; catch up, draw level; improve.

вы́родиться, -ится *pf.*, **вырожда́ться**, -áется *impf.* degenerate. **вы́родок**, -дка degenerate; black sheep. **вырождéнец**, -нца degenerate. **вырождéние**, -я degeneration. **вы́ронить**, -ню *pf.* drop.

вы́рос *etc.*: see **вы́расти. вы́рост**, -а growth, excrescence; offshoot. **вы́ростковый** calf.

вы́росток, -тка yearling; calf.

вы́рою *etc.*: see **вы́рыть**

выруба́ть, -áю *impf.*, **вы́рубить**, -блю *pf.* cut down, fell; hew out; cut (out); carve (out); ~ся cut one's way out. **вы́рубка**, -и cutting down, felling; hewing out; clearing.

вы́|ругать(ся, -аю(сь *pf.*

выру́ливать, -аю *impf.*, **вы́|рулить**, -лю *pf.* taxi.

выруча́ть, -áю *impf.*, **вы́ручить**, -чу *pf.* recue; help out; gain; make. **вы́ручка**, -и rescue, assistance; gain; proceeds; receipts; earnings.

вырыва́ние[1], -я pulling out, extraction; uprooting.

вырыва́ние[2], -я digging (up). **вырыва́ть**[2], -áю *impf.*, **вы́рыть**, -рою *pf.* dig up, dig out, unearth.

вырыва́ть[1](ся *impf. of* **вы́рвать(ся**

вы́садить, -ажу *pf.*, **выса́живать**, -аю *impf.* set down; help down; put off; detrain, debus; put ashore, land; plant out, transplant; smash; break in; ~ся alight, get off; land; disembark; detrain, debus. **вы́садка**, -и disembarkation; landing; transplanting, planting out.

выса́сывать, -аю *impf. of* **вы́сосать**

высвéрливать, -аю *impf.*, **вы́сверлить**, -лю *pf.* drill, bore.

вы́свободить, -божу *pf.*, **высвобожда́ть**, -áю *impf.* free; disengage, disentangle; release; help to escape.

высека́ть, -áю *impf. of* **вы́сечь**[2]. **вы́секу** *etc.*: see **вы́сечь**

выселéнец, -нца evacuee. **выселéние**, -я eviction. **вы́селить**, -лю *pf.*, **выселя́ть**, -я́ю *impf.* evict; evacuate, move; ~ся move, remove. **вы́селок**, -лка settlement.

вы́сечка, -и carving; hewing. **вы́|сечь**[1], -еку -сек *pf.* **вы́сечь**[2], -еку -сек (*impf.* **высека́ть**) cut, cut out; carve; hew.

вы́сидеть, -ижу *pf.*, **выси́живать**, -аю *impf.* sit out; stay; hatch, hand out.

вы́ситься, -сится *impf.* rise, tower.

вы́сказать, -кажу *pf.*, **выска́зывать**, -аю *impf.* express; state; ~ся speak out; speak one's mind, have one's say; speak. **выска́зывание**, -я utterance; pronouncement, opinion.

выска́кивать, -аю *impf. of* **вы́скочить**

выска́льзывать, -аю *impf. of* **вы́скользнуть**

вы́скоблить, -лю *pf.* scrape out; erase; remove.

вы́скользнуть, -ну *pf.* (*impf.* **выска́льзывать**) slip out.

вы́скочить, -чу *pf.* (*impf.* **выска́кивать**) jump out; leap out, spring out, rush out; come up; drop out, fall out; ~ c+*i.* come out with. **вы́скочка**, -и upstart, parvenu.

вы́сланный *sb.* exile, deportee. **вы́слать**, **вы́шлю** *pf.* (*impf.* **высыла́ть**) send, send out, dispatch; exile; deport.

вы́следить, -ежу *pf.*, **высле́живать**, -аю *impf.* trace, track; stalk; shadow.

вы́слуга, -и; ~ лет long service. **выслу́живать**, -аю *impf.*, **вы́служить**, -жу *pf.* qualify for, earn; serve (out); ~ся gain promotion, be promoted; curry favour, get in (with).

вы́слушать, -аю *pf.*, **выслу́шивать**, -аю *impf.* hear out; sound; listen to. **выслу́шивание**, -я auscultation.

вы́|смолить, -лю *pf.* **вы́|сморкать(ся**, -аю(сь *pf.* **высо́вывать(ся**, -аю(сь *impf. of* **вы́сунуть(ся**

высо́кий, -о́к, -á, -о́ко́ high; tall; lofty; elevated, sublime.

высоко... *in comb.* high-, highly. **высокоблагоро́дие**, -я (your) Honour, Worship. ~**во́льтный** high-tension. ~**го́рный** Alpine, mountain. ~**ка́чественный** high-quality. ~**ме́рие**, -я haughtiness, arrogance. ~**ме́рный** haughty, arrogant. ~**па́рный** high-flown, stilted; bombastic, turgid. ~**про́бный** sterling; standard; of high quality. ~**со́ртный** high-grade. ~**часто́тный** high-frequency.

вы́сосать, -осу *pf.* (*impf.* **выса́сывать**) suck out.

высота́, -ы́; *pl.* -ы height, altitude; pitch; eminence; high level; high quality. **высо́тник**, -а high-building worker; high-altitude flier. **высо́тный** high; high-altitude; tall, multistorey, high-rise; ~ое зда́ние tower block. **высотоме́р**, -а altimeter, height-finder.

вы́|сохнуть, -ну; -ох *pf.* (*impf. also* **высыха́ть**) dry, dry out; dry up; wither, fade; waste away, fade away. **вы́сохший** dried up; shrivelled; wizened.

вы́ставить, -влю *pf.*, **выставля́ть**, -я́ю *impf.* bring out, bring forward; display, exhibit; post; put forward; adduce; put down, set down; take out, remove; send out, turn out, throw out; +*i.* represent as, make out to be; ~ свою́ кандидату́ру stand for election; ~ся lean out, thrust o.s. forward; show off. **вы́ставка**, -и exhibition; show; display;

showcase, (shop-)window. **выставно́й** removable.

вы́|**стега́ть, -а́ю** pf. **вы́стелю** etc.: see **вы́стлать. выстила́ть, -а́ю** impf. of **вы́стлать. вы́**|**стира́ть, -а́ю** pf.

вы́стлать, -телю pf. (impf. **выстила́ть**) cover; line; pave.

вы́страдать, -аю pf. suffer, go through; gain through suffering.

выстра́ивать(ся, -аю(сь impf. of **вы́строиться. выстра́чивать, -аю** impf. of **вы́строчить**

вы́стрел, -а shot; report. **вы́стрелить, -лю** pf. shoot, fire.

вы́|**строгать, -аю** pf.

вы́строить, -ою pf. (impf. **выстра́ивать**) build; draw up, order, arrange; form up. **~ся** form up.

вы́строчить, -чу pf. (impf. **выстра́чивать**) hemstitch; stitch.

вы́стукать, -аю pf. **высту́кивать, -аю** impf. tap, percuss; tap out. **высту́кивание, -я** percuss'on; tapping.

вы́ступ, -а protuberance, projection, ledge; bulge, salient; lug. **выступа́ть, -а́ю** impf.

вы́ступить, -плю pf. come forward, go forward; come out; appear; perform; speak; +**из**+g. go beyond, exceed; ~ **из берего́в** overflow its banks; ~ **с докла́дом** give a talk; ~ **с ре́чью** make a speech. **выступле́ние, -я** appearance, performance; speech; setting out.

вы́сунуть, -ну pf. (impf. **высо́вывать**) put out, thrust out; **~ся** show o.s., thrust o.s. forward; ~ **ся в окно́** lean out of the window.

вы́|**сушить(ся, -шу(сь** pf.

вы́сш|**ий** highest; supreme; high; higher; **~ая то́чка** climax.

высыла́ть, -а́ю impf. of **вы́слать. вы́сылка, -и** sending, dispatching; expulsion, exile.

вы́сыпать, -плю pf, **высыпа́ть, -а́ю** impf. pour out; empty (out); spill; **~ся** pour out, spill.

высыха́ть, -а́ю impf. of **вы́сохнуть**

высь, -и height; summit.

выта́лкивать, -аю impf. of **вы́толкать, вы́толкнуть. вы́**|**таращить, -щу** pf. **выта́скивать, -аю** impf. of **вы́тащить. вы́**|**тачать, -аю** pf. **выта́чивать, -аю** impf. of **вы́точить**

вы́тачка, -и tuck; dart.

вы́|**тащить, -щу** pf. (impf. also **выта́скивать**) drag out; pull out, extract; steal, pinch.

вы́|**твердить, -ржу** pf.

вытека́ть, -а́ю impf. (pf. **вы́течь**); ~ **из**+g. flow from, out of; result from, follow from.

вы́|**теребить, -блю** pf.

вы́тереть, -тру; -тер pf. (impf. **вытира́ть**) wipe, wipe up; dry, rub dry; wear out.

вы́терпеть, -плю pf. bear, endure.

вы́тертый threadbare.

вытесне́ние, -я ousting; supplanting; dis-

placement. **вы́теснить, -ню** pf., **вытесня́ть, -я́ю** impf. crowd out; force out; oust; supplant; displace.

вы́течь, -чет; -ек pf. (impf. **вытека́ть**) flow out, run out.

вытира́ть, -а́ю impf. of **вы́тереть**

вы́тиснить, -ню pf., **вытисня́ть, -я́ю** impf. stamp, imprint, impress.

вы́толкать, -аю pf., **вы́толкнуть, -ну** pf. (impf. **выта́лкивать**) throw out, sling out; push down, force out.

вы́точенный turned; **сло́вно ~** chiselled; perfectly formed. **вы́**|**точить, -чу** pf. (impf., also **выта́чивать**) turn; sharpen; gnaw through.

вы́|**травить, -влю** pf., **вытра́вливать, -аю** impf., **вытравля́ть, -я́ю** impf. exterminate, destroy, poison; remove, get out; etch; trample down, damage.

вы́требовать, -бую pf. summon, send for; get on demand.

вытрезви́тель, -я m. detoxification centre. **вы́трезвить(ся, -влю(сь** pf., **вытрезвля́ть(ся, -я́ю(сь** impf. sober up.

вы́тру etc.: see **вы́тереть**

вытряса́ть, -а́ю impf., **вы́**|**трясти, -су; -яс** pf. shake out.

вытря́хивать, -аю impf., **вы́тряхнуть, -ну** pf. shake out.

выть, во́ю impf. howl; wail. **вытьё, -я́** howling; wailing.

вытя́гивать, -аю impf., **вы́тянуть, -ну** pf. stretch, stretch out; extend; draw out, extract; endure, stand, stick; weigh; **~ся** stretch, stretch out, stretch o.s.; grow, shoot up; draw o.s. up. **вы́тяжка, -и** drawing out, extraction; extract; stretching extension. **вытяжно́й** drawing; exhaust; ventilating; ~ **шкаф** fume chamber.

вы́|**утюжить, -жу** pf.

выу́чивать, -аю impf., **вы́**|**учить, -чу** pf. learn; teach; **~ся**+d. or inf. learn. **вы́учка, -и** teaching, training.

выха́живать, -аю impf. of **вы́ходить**

вы́хватить, -ачу pf., **выхва́тывать, -аю** impf. snatch out, up; snatch away; pull out, draw; tear out; take up.

вы́хлоп, -а exhaust.

выхлопа́тывать, -аю impf. of **вы́хлопота́ть**

выхлопно́й exhaust, discharge.

вы́хлопота́ть, -очу pf. (impf. **выхлопа́тывать**) obtain with much trouble.

вы́ход, -а going out; leaving, departure; way out, exit; outlet, vent; appearance; entrance; output, yield; outcrop; **все хо́ды и ~ы** all the ins and outs; ~ **в отста́вку** retirement; ~ **за́муж** marriage. **вы́ходец, -дца** emigrant; immigrant. **выходи́ть¹, -ожу́, -о́дишь** impf. of **вы́йти**; +**на**+a. look out on, give on, face.

вы́ходить², -ожу pf. (impf. **выха́живать**) tend, nurse; rear, bring up; grow.

вы́ходить³, -ожу *pf.* (*impf.* **выха́живать**) pass through; go all over.

вы́ходка, -и trick; escapade, prank.

выходн|о́й exit, outlet; going-out, outgoing; leaving, departure, discharge; publication. issue; output; ~**а́я дверь** street door; ~**о́й день** day off, free day, rest-day; ~**о́й лист** title-page; ~**а́я роль** walking-on part; ~**ые све́дения** imprint; ~**о́й** *sb.* person off duty; day off; ~**а́я** *sb.* person off duty. **вы́хожу** *etc.: see* **вы́ходить. выхожу́** *etc.: see* **выходи́ть**¹

выхола́щивать, -аю *impf.*, **вы́холостить**, -ощу *pf.* castrate, geld; emasculate.

вы́хухоль, -я *m.* musk-rat; musquash. **вы́хухолевый** musquash.

вы́царапать, -аю *pf.*, **выцара́пывать**, -аю *impf.* scratch; scratch out; extract, get out.

вы́цвести, -ветет *pf.*, **выцвета́ть**, -а́ет *impf.* fade. **вы́цветший** faded.

вы́цедить, -ежу *pf.*, **выце́живать**, -аю *impf.* filter, rack off; strain; decant; drink off, drain.

вычека́нивать, -аю *impf.*, **вы́|чеканить**, -ню *pf.* mint; strike.

вычёркивать, -аю *impf.*, **вы́черкнуть**, -ну *pf.* cross out, strike out; expunge, erase.

вы́черпать, -аю *pf.*, **выче́рпывать**, -аю *impf.* bale out.

вы́честь, -чту; -чел, -чла *pf.* (*impf.* **вычита́ть**) subtract; deduct, keep back. **вы́чет**, -а deduction; **за** ~**ом** except; less, minus, allowing for.

вычисле́ние, -я calculation. **вычисли́тель**, -я *m.* calculator; plotter; computer **вычисли́тельн|ый** calculating, computing; ~**ая маши́на** computer. **вы́числить**, -лю *pf.*, **вычисля́ть**, -яю *impf.* calculate, compute.

вы́|чистить, -ищу *pf.* (*impf. also* **вычища́ть**) clean, clean out; purge.

вычита́емое *sb.* subtrahend. **вычита́ние**, -я subtraction. **вычита́ть**, -а́ю *impf. of* **вы́честь**

вычища́ть, -а́ю *impf. of* **вы́чистить**

вы́чту *etc.: see* **вы́честь**

вы́швырнуть, -ну *pf.* **вышвы́ривать**, -аю *impf.* throw out, hurl out; chuck out.

вы́ше higher, taller; *prep.*+*g.* above, beyond; over; *adv.* above.

вы́ше... *in comb.* above-, afore-. **вышеизло́женный** foregoing. ~**на́званный** aforenamed. ~**означенный** aforesaid, above-mentioned. ~**ска́занный**, ~**ука́занный** aforesaid. ~**упомя́нутый** aforementioned.

вы́шел *etc.: see* **вы́йти**

вышиба́ла, -ы *m.* chucker-out, bouncer. **вышиба́ть**, -а́ю *impf.*, **вы́шибить**, -бу; -иб *pf.* knock out; chuck out.

вышива́льный embroidery. **вышива́льщица**, -ы embroideress, needlewoman. **вышива́ние**, -я embroidery, needlework. **вышива́ть**, -а́ю *impf. of* **вы́шить. вы́шивка**, -и embroidery.

вышина́, -ы́ height.

вы́шить, -шью *pf.* (*impf.* **вышива́ть**) embroider. **вы́шитый** embroidered.

вы́шка, -и turret; tower; (**бурова́я**) ~ derrick.

вы́|школить, -лю *pf.* **вы́шлю** *etc.: see* **вы́слать. вы́шью** *etc.: see* **вы́шить**

выщипа́ть, -плю *pf.* **вы́щипнуть**, -ну *pf.*, **выщи́пывать**, -аю *impf.* pluck out, pull out.

вы́явить, -влю *pf.*, **выявля́ть**, -я́ю *impf.* reveal; bring out; make known; display; show up, expose; ~**ся** appear, come to light, be revealed. **выявле́ние**, -я revelation; showing up, exposure.

выясне́ние, -я elucidation; explanation. **вы́яснить**, -ню *pf.* **выясня́ть**, -я́ю *impf.* elucidate; clear up, explain; ~**ся** become clear; turn out, prove.

Вьетна́м, -а Vietnam.

вью *etc.: see* **вить**

вью́га, -и snow-storm, blizzard.

вьюк, -а pack; load.

вьюно́к, -нка́ bindweed, convolvulus.

вью́чн|ый pack; ~**ое живо́тное** pack animal, beast of burden; ~**ая ло́шадь** pack-horse; ~**ое седло́** pack-saddle.

вью́шка, -и damper.

вью́щийся creeping, climbing; curly, frizzy.

вэ *nt.indecl.* the letter в.

вяжу́ *etc.: see* **вяза́ть. вя́жущий** binding, cementing; astringent.

вяз, -а elm.

вяза́льный knitting, crochet. **вяза́ние**, -я knitting, crocheting; binding, tying. **вя́занка**¹, -и knitted garment. **вяза́нка**², -и bundle, truss. **вя́заный** knitted, crocheted. **вяза́нье**, -я knitting; crochet(-work). **вяза́ть**, **вяжу́**, **вя́жешь** (*impf. pf.* **с~**) tie, bind; clamp; knit, crochet; be astringent; ~**ся** accord, agree; fit in, be in keeping, tally. **вя́зка**, -и tying, binding; knitting, crocheting; bunch, string.

вя́зкий; -зок, -зка́, -о viscous, glutinous, sticky; boggy; ductile, malleable; tough; astringent. **вя́знуть**, -ну; **вяз**(**нул**), -зла *impf.* (*pf.* **за~**, **у~**) stick, get stuck; sink.

вя́зовый elm.

вя́зчик, -а binder. **вязь**, -и ligature; arabesque.

вял *etc.: see* **вя́нуть**

вя́ление, -я dry-curing; drying. **вя́леный** dried; sun-cured. **вя́лить**, -лю *impf.* (*pf.* **про~**) dry, dry-cure. **вя́лый** flabby, flaccid; limp; sluggish; inert; slack. **вя́нуть**, -ну; **вял** *impf.* (*pf.* **за~**, **у~**) fade, wither; droop, flag.

Г

г *letter: see* **гэ**

г *abbr.* (*of* **грамм**) g, gr, gram(me)(s).

г. *abbr.* (*of* **год**) year; (*of* **гора́**) Mt., mountain; (*of* **го́род**) city, town; (*of* **господи́н**) Mr.

га *abbr.* (*of* **гекта́р**) ha., hectare.

габари́т, -а clearance; clearance diagram; size, dimension. **габари́тн|ый** clearance; overall; **~ые воро́та** loading gauge; **~ая высота́** headroom.

га́вань, -и harbour.

га́врик, -а (*sl.*) petty crook; man, fellow, mate.

га́га, -и eider(-duck).

гага́ра, -ы loon, diver. **гага́рка, -и** razorbill.

гага́т, -а jet.

гага́чий eider-; **~ пух** eiderdown.

гад, -а reptile, amphibian; vile creature; *pl.* vermin.

гада́лка, -и fortune-teller. **гада́ние, -я** fortune-telling, divination; guess-work. **гада́тельный** fortune-telling; problematical, conjectural, hypothetical. **гада́ть, -а́ю** *impf.* (*pf.* **по~**) tell fortunes; guess, conjecture, surmise.

га́дина, -ы reptile; vile creature; *pl.* vermin.

га́дить, га́жу *impf.* (*pf.* **на~**) **+в+***p.*, **на+***a.* foul, dirty, defile. **га́дкий; -док, -дка́, -о** nasty, vile, foul, loathsome; **~ утёнок** ugly duckling. **гадли́вость, -и** aversion, disgust. **гадли́вый** of disgust, disgusted. **га́дость, -и** filth, muck; dirty trick; *pl.* filthy expressions. **гадю́ка, -и** adder, viper; repulsive person.

га́ер, -а buffoon, clown. **га́ерничать, -аю** *impf.*, **га́ерствовать, -твую** *impf.* clown, play the fool.

га́ечный nut; **~ ключ** spanner, wrench.

га́же *comp. of* **га́дкий**

газ[1], -а gauze.

газ[2], -а (-у) gas; wind; **дать ~** step on the gas; **сба́вить ~** reduce speed; **на по́лном га́зе** at top speed. **газану́ть, -ну́, -нёшь** *pf.* (*impf.* **газова́ть**) accelerate; scram. **газа́ция, -и** aeration. **газго́льдер, -а** gasholder.

газе́ль, -и gazelle.

газе́та, -ы newspaper, paper. **газе́тный** newspaper, news. **газе́тчик, -а, -чица, -ы** journalist; newspaper-seller.

газиро́ванный aerated. **гази́ровать, -рую**

impf. aerate. **газиро́вка, -и** aeration; aerated water. **газова́ть, -зу́ю** *impf.* (*pf.* **газану́ть**) accelerate, step on it; scram. **га́зовый[1]** gas; **~ счётчик** gas-meter.

га́зовый[2] gauze.

газокали́льный incandescent. **газоли́н, -а** gasolene. **газоме́р, -а** gas-meter.

газо́н, -а lawn, turf, grass. **газонокоси́лка, -и** lawn-mower.

газообра́зный gaseous. **газопрово́д, -а** gas pipeline; gas-main. **газопрово́дный** gas.

ГАИ *abbr.* (*of* **Госуда́рственная автомоби́льная инспе́кция**) State Motor-vehicle Inspectorate.

га́йка, -и nut; female screw.

гала́ктика, -и galaxy.

галантере́йный haberdasher's, haberdashery. **галантере́я, -и** haberdashery, fancy goods.

галанти́р, -а galantine.

галдёж, -а́ din, racket, row. **галде́ть, -ди́шь** *impf.* make a din, make a row.

гале́ра, -ы galley.

галере́я, -и gallery. **галёрка, -и** gallery, gods.

галифе́ *indecl. pl.* riding-breeches; jodhpurs.

га́лка, -и jackdaw, daw.

галл, -а Gaul. **га́лльский** Gaulish; Gallic.

гало́п, -а gallop; galop. **галопи́ровать, -рую** *impf.* gallop.

га́лочий jackdaw's, daw's. **га́лочка, -и** tick.

гало́ша, -и galosh.

галс, -а tack.

га́лстук, -а tie; neckerchief.

галу́шка, -и dumpling.

га́лька, -и pebble; pebbles, shingle.

гам, -а (-у) din, uproar.

гама́к, -а́ hammock.

га́мбургер, -а (ham)burger. **га́мбургерная** *sb.* burger bar.

га́мма, -ы scale; gamut; range.

гангре́н, -а gangrene. **гангрено́зный** gangrenous.

гандбо́л, -а handball. **гандболи́ст, -а** handball-player.

ганте́ль, -и dumb-bell.

гара́ж, -а garage.

гаранти́ровать, -рую *impf. & pf.* guarantee, vouch for. **гара́нтия, -и** guarantee; safeguard.

гардеро́б, -а wardrobe; cloakroom. **гардеро́бная** *sb.* cloakroom. **гардеро́бщик, -а, -щица, -ы** cloakroom attendant.

гарди́на, -ы curtain.

гаре́в|ой, га́рев|ый cinder; **~ая доро́жка** cinder track, cinder-path.

га́ркать, -аю *impf.*, **га́ркнуть, -ну** *pf.* shout, bark.

гармо́ника, -и accordion, concertina; pleats; **гармо́никой** (accordion-)pleated, in pleats. **гармони́ческий** harmonic; harmonious; rhythmic. **гармони́чный** harmonious. **гармо́ния, -и** harmony; concord; accordion, concertina. **гармо́нь**, -и, **гармо́шка**, -и accordion, concertina.

гарнизо́н, -а garrison.

гарни́р, -а garnish; trimmings; vegetables.

гарниту́р, -а set; suite.

гарпу́н, -а́ harpoon.

гарт, -а type-metal.

гарь, -и burning; cinders, ashes.

гаси́льник, -а extinguisher, **гаси́тель**, -я m. extinguisher; damper; suppressor. **гаси́ть**, **гашу́**, **га́сишь** impf. (pf. **за∼**, **по∼**) put out, extinguish; slake; suppress, stifle; cancel; liquidate. **га́снуть**, -ну; гас impf. (pf. **за∼**, **по∼**, **у∼**) be extinguished, go out; grow dim; sink.

гастролёр, -а, **ёрша**, -и guest-artist; touring actor, actress; casual worker. **гастроли́ровать**, -рую impf. tour, be on tour. **гастро́ль**, -и tour; guest-appearance, performance; temporary engagement.

гастроно́м, -а gourmet; grocery, grocer's (shop). **гастрономи́ческий** gastronomic; provision. **гастроно́мия**, -и gastronomy; provisions; delicatessen.

га́убица, -ы howitzer.

гауптва́хта, -ы guardhouse, guardroom.

гаше́ние, -я extinguishing; slaking; cancellation, suppression. **гашёный** slaked.

гашётка, -и trigger; button.

гварде́ец, -е́йца guardsman. **гварде́йский** guards. **гва́рдия**, -и Guards.

гво́здик, -а tack; stiletto heel. **гвозди́ка**, -и pink(s), carnation(s); cloves. **гвоздь**, -я; pl. -и, -е́й m. nail; tack; peg; crux; highlight, hit.

гг. abbr. (of **го́ды**) years.

где adv. where; somewhere; anywhere; how; ∼ бы ни wherever; ∼ мне зна́ть? how should I know? **где́-либо** adv. anywhere. **где́-нибудь** adv. somewhere; anywhere. **где́-то** adv. somewhere.

ГДР abbr. **Герма́нская Демократи́ческая Респу́блика** German Democratic Republic.

некта́р, -а hectare. **гекто́...** in comb. hecto-.

ге́лий, -я helium.

геморро́й, -я haemorrhoids, piles.

гемофили́я, -и haemophilia.

ген, -а gene.

ген... abbr. (of **генера́льный**) in comb. general.

генеалоги́ческий genealogical. **генеало́гия**, -и genealogy.

генера́л, -а general; ∼-губерна́тор governor-general. **генералите́т**, -а generals; high command. **генера́льн|ый** general; radical, basic; ∼ая репети́ция dress rehearsal. **генера́льский** general's. **генера́льша**, -и general's wife.

генера́тор, -а generator. **генера́ция**, -и generation; oscillation.

гениа́льный of genius, great; brilliant. **ге́ний**, -я genius.

гео... in comb. geo-. **гео́граф**, -а geographer. ∼**графи́ческий** geographical. ∼**гра́фия**, -и

geography. **гео́лог**, -а geologist. ∼**логи́ческий** geological. ∼**ло́гия**, -и geology. **гео́метр**, -а geometrician. ∼**метри́ческий** geometric, geometrical. ∼**ме́трия**, -и geometry.

георги́н, -а, **георги́на**, -ы dahlia.

гепа́рд, -а cheetah.

гера́нь, -и geranium.

герб, -а́ arms, coat of arms. **ге́рбов|ый** heraldic; bearing coat of arms; stamped; ∼ая печа́ть official stamp; ∼ый сбо́р stamp-duty.

геркуле́с, -а Hercules; rolled oats. **геркуле́совский** Herculean.

герма́нец, -нца Teuton, German. **Герма́ния**, -и Germany. **герма́нский** Germanic, Teutonic; German.

герметм́ческий, **герметм́чный** hermetic, secret; hermetically sealed, air-tight, watertight, pressurized.

геро́изм, -а heroism. **геро́ика**, -и heroics; heroic spirit; heroic style. **герои́ня**, -и heroine. **герои́ческий** heroic. **геро́й**, -я hero. **геро́йский** heroic. **геро́йство**, -а heroism.

герц, -а; g.pl. герц hertz.

гетеросексуа́льный heterosexual.

ге́тман, -а hetman.

г-жа abbr. (of **госпожа́**) Mrs.; Miss; Ms.

гиаци́нт, -а hyacinth; jacinth.

ги́бель, -и death; destruction, ruin; loss; wreck; downfall. **ги́бельный** disastrous, fatal.

ги́бк|ий, -бок, -бка́, -бко flexible, pliant; floppy; lithe; adaptable, versatile, resourceful; tractable; ∼ий диск (comput.) floppy (disk). **ги́бкость**, -и flexibility, pliancy; suppleness.

ги́бнуть, -ну; ги́б(нул) impf. (pf. **по∼**) perish.

Гибралта́р, -а Gibraltar.

гига́нт, -а giant. **гига́нтский** gigantic.

гигие́на, -ы hygiene. **гигиени́ческ|ий** hygienic, sanitary; ∼ая повя́зка sanitary towel; ∼ая бума́га toilet paper.

гид, -а guide.

гидро... pf. hydro-. **гидро́лиз**, -а hydrolysis. ∼**о́кись**, -и hydroxide. ∼**ста́нция**, -и hydro-electric power-station. ∼**те́хник**, -а hydraulic engineer. ∼**те́хника**, -и hydraulic engineering. ∼**фо́н**, -а hydrophone.

гие́на, -ы hyena.

гик, -а whoop, whooping. **ги́кать**, -аю impf., **ги́кнуть**, -ну pf. whoop.

ги́льдия, -и guild.

ги́льза, -ы case; cartridge-case; sleeve; liner; (cigarette-)wrapper.

Гимала́и, -ев pl. the Himalayas.

гимн, -а hymn.

гимнази́ст, -а, **-и́стка**, -и grammar-school or high-school pupil. **гимна́зия**, -и grammar school, high school.

гимна́стика, -и gymnastics.

гипно́з, -а hypnosis. **гипнотизёр**, -а hypnotist. **гипнотизи́ровать**, -рую impf. (pf. **за∼**) hypnotize. **гипноти́зм**, -а hypnotism.

гипноти́ческий hypnotic.

гипо́теза, -ы hypothesis. **гипотети́ческий, гипотети́чный** hypothetical.

гиппопота́м, -а hippopotamus.

гипс, -а gypsum, plaster of Paris; plaster; plaster cast. **ги́псовый** plaster.

гиреви́к, -а́ weight-lifter.

гирля́нда, -ы garland.

ги́ря, -и weight.

гита́ра, -ы guitar.

гл. abbr. (of **глава́**) chapter.

глав... (abbr. of **гла́вный**) in comb. head, chief, main; **гла́вное управле́ние** central administration, central board. **главбу́х, -а** chief accountant. **главк, -а** chief directorate; central committee, central administration. **~ре́ж, -а** head producer, chief director.

глава́, -ы́; pl. **-ы** head; chief; chapter; cupola. **глава́рь, -я́** m. leader, ring-leader. **главе́нство, -а** supremacy. **главе́нствовать, -твую** impf. be in command, lead, dominate. **главнокома́ндующий** sb. commander-in-chief. **гла́вн|ый** chief, main, principal; head, senior; **~ая кни́га** ledger; **~ый нерв** nerve-centre; **~ым о́бразом** chiefly, mainly, for the most part; **~ое** sb. the chief thing, the main thing; the essentials; **и са́мое ~ое** and above all.

глаго́л, -а verb; word. **глаго́льный** verbal.

глади́льный ironing. **гла́дить, -а́жу** impf. (pf. **вы́~, по~**) stroke; iron, press. **гла́дкий** smooth; sleek; plain; fluent, facile. **гла́дко** adv. smoothly; swimmingly; **~ вы́бритый** clean-shaven. **гладь, -и** smooth surface; satin-stitch. **гла́же** comp. of **гла́дкий**, **гла́дко**. **гла́женье, -я** ironing.

глаз, -а (-у), loc. **-у́;** pl. **-а́, глаз** eye; eyesight; **в ~а́** to one's face; **за ~а́**+g. in the absence of, behind the back of; **на ~а́, на ~а́х** before one's eyes; **с ~у на ~** without witnesses; **смотре́ть во все ~а́** be all eyes. **глаза́стый** big-eyed; quick-sighted.

глазиро́ванный glazed; glossy; iced, glacé. **глазирова́ть, -рую** impf. & pf. glaze; candy; ice. **глазиро́вка, -и** glazing; icing.

глазни́к, -а́ oculist. **глазни́ца, -ы** eye-socket. **глазно́й** eye; optic; **~ врач** oculist, eye-specialist.

глазу́нья, -и fried eggs.

глазу́рь, -и glaze; syrup; icing.

гла́нда, -ы gland; tonsil.

глас, -а voice. **гласи́ть, -си́т** impf. announce; say, run. **гла́сность, -и** publicity; glasnost, openness. **гла́сный** open, public; vowel, vocalic; sb. vowel. **глаша́тай, -я** crier; herald.

гле́тчер, -а glacier.

гли́на, -ы clay. **гли́нистый** clay; clayey, argillaceous. **глинозём, -а** alumina. **гли́няный** clay; earthenware, pottery; clayey; **~ая посу́да** earthenware.

гли́ссер, -а speed-boat; hydroplane.

глоба́льный global; (fig.) extensive.

гл. обр. abbr. (of **гла́вным о́бразом**) chiefly, mainly.

гло́бус, -а globe.

глода́ть, -ожу́, -о́жешь impf. gnaw.

глота́ть, -а́ю impf. swallow. **гло́тка, -и** gullet; throat. **глото́к, -тка́** gulp; mouthful.

гло́хнуть, -ну; глох impf. (pf. **за~, о~**) become deaf; die away, subside; decay; die; grow wild, become a wilderness, run to seed.

глу́бже comp. of **глубо́кий, глубоко́. глубина́, -ы́;** pl. **-ы** depth; depths, deep places; heart, interior; recesses; profundity; intensity. **глуби́нный** deep; deep-laid; deep-sea; depth; remote, out-of-the-way. **глубо́к|ий; -о́к, -а́, -о́ко́** deep; profound; intense; thorough, thorough-going; considerable, serious; late, advanced, extreme; **~ий вира́ж** steep turn; **~ой о́сенью** in the late autumn; **~ая ста́рость** extreme old age; **~ая таре́лка** soup-plate. **глубоко́** adv. deep; deeply, profoundly. **глубоково́дный** deep-water, deep-sea. **глубокомы́слие, -я** profundity; perspicacity. **глубоме́р, -а** depth gauge. **глубоча́йший** superl. of **глубо́кий. глубь, -и** depth; (the) depths.

глуми́ться, -млю́сь impf. mock, jeer (**над**+i. at). **глумле́ние, -я** mockery; gibe, jeer. **глумли́вый** mocking; gibing, jeering.

глупе́ть, -е́ю impf. (pf. **по~**) grow stupid. **глупе́ц, -пца́** fool, blockhead. **глупи́ть, -плю́** impf. (pf. **с~**) make a fool of o.s.; do something foolish. **глупова́тый** silly; rather stupid. **глу́пость, -и** foolishness, stupidity; nonsense; **глу́пости!** (stuff and) nonsense! **глу́пый; глуп, -а́, -о** foolish, stupid, silly.

глуха́рь, -я́ m. capercailzie; deaf person; coach screw. **глухова́тый** somewhat deaf, hard of hearing. **глухо́й; глух, -а́, -о** muffled, confused, indistinct; obscure, vague; voiceless; thick, dense; wild; remote, lonely, deserted; god-forsaken; sealed; blank, blind; buttoned up, done up; not open; late; **~а́я крапи́ва** dead-nettle; **~о́й, ~а́я** sb. deaf man, deaf woman. **глухонемо́й** deaf and dumb; sb. deaf mute. **глухота́, -ы́** deafness.

глу́ше comp. of **глухо́й. глуши́лка, -и** jamming, jammer. **глуши́тель, -я** m. silencer, damper; suppressor; jammer. **глуши́ть, -шу́** impf. (pf. **за~, о~**) stun, stupefy; muffle; dull, deaden, damp; drown, jam; switch off; put out, extinguish; choke, stifle; suppress; soak up, swill. **глушь, -и** backwoods; solitary place.

глы́ба, -ы clod; lump, block.

гляде́ть, -яжу́ impf. (pf. **по~, гля́нуть**) look, gaze; heed, take notice; look for, seek; show, appear; **+за**+i. look after, see to; **+на**+a. look on (to), give on (to), face; take example from, imitate; **+i. or adv.** look, look like; **~ в о́ба** be on one's guard; **~ ко́со на** take a poor view of; **гляди́(те)** mind (out); **(того́ и) гляди́** it looks as if; I'm afraid; at any moment; **гля́дя по**+d. depending on; **не**

гля́дя на+*a.* unmindful of, heedless of; ~**ся** look at o.s.

гля́нец, -нца gloss, lustre; polish.

гля́нуть, -ну *pf.* (*impf.* **гляде́ть**) glance.

глянцеви́тый glossy, lustrous.

гм *int.* hm!

г-н *abbr.* (*of* **господи́н**) Mr.

гнать, гоню́, го́нишь; гнал, -а́, -о *impf.* drive; urge (on); whip up; drive hard; dash, tear; hunt, chase; persecute; turn out; distil; ~**ся** за+*i.* pursue; strive for, strive after; keep up with.

гнев, -а anger, rage; wrath. **гне́ваться**, -аюсь *impf.* (*pf.* **раз**~) be angry. **гневи́ть**, -влю́ *impf.* (*pf.* **про**~) anger, enrage. **гневли́вый** irascible. **гне́вный** angry, irate.

гнедо́й bay.

гнезди́ться, -зжу́сь *impf.* nest, build a nest; roost; have its seat; be lodged. **гнездо́**, -а́; *pl.* гнёзда nest; eyrie; den, lair; brood; cluster; socket; seat; housing. **гнездова́ние**, -я nesting.

гнести́, -ету́, -етёшь *impf.* oppress, weigh down; press. **гнёт**, -а press; weight; oppression. **гнету́щий** oppressive.

гни́да, -ы nit.

гние́ние, -я decay, putrefaction, rot. **гнило́й**; -ил, -а́, -о rotten; decayed; putrid; corrupt; damp, muggy. **гнить**, -ию́, -иёшь; -ил, -а́, -о *impf.* (*pf.* **с**~) rot, decay; decompose. **гное́ние**, -я suppuration. **гнои́ть**, -ою́ *impf.* (*pf.* **с**~) let rot, leave to rot; allow to decay; ~**ся** suppurate, discharge matter. **гной**, -я (-ю), *loc.* -ю́ pus, matter. **гнойни́к**, -а́ abscess; ulcer. **гно́йный** purulent.

гнуса́вить, -влю *impf.* talk, speak, through one's nose. **гнуса́вость**, -и nasal twang. **гнуса́вый**, **гнусли́вый** nasal.

гну́сный; -сен, -сна́, -о vile, foul.

гну́т|**ый** bent; ~**ая ме́бель** bentwood furniture. **гнуть**, гну, гнёшь *impf.* (*pf.* **со**~) bend, bow; drive at, aim at; ~**ся** bend; be bowed; stoop; be flexible. **гнутьё**, -я́ bending.

гнуша́ться, -а́юсь *impf.* (*pf.* **по**~) disdain; +*g. or i.* shun; abhor, have an aversion to.

гобеле́н, -а tapestry.

гобои́ст, -а oboist. **гобо́й**, -я oboe.

гове́нье, -я fasting. **гове́ть**, -е́ю *impf.* fast.

говно́, -а́ shit.

го́вор, -а sound of voices; murmur, babble; talk, rumour; pronunciation, accent; dialect. **говори́льня**, -и talking-shop. **говори́ть**, -рю́ *impf.* (*pf.* **сказа́ть**) speak, talk; say; tell; mean, convey, signify; point, testify; **говори́т Москва́** this is Moscow; ~ **в по́льзу**+*g.* tell in favour of; support, back; **не говоря́ уже́** о+*p.* not to mention; **не́чего (и)** ~ it goes without saying, needless to say; **что и** ~ it can't be denied; ~**ся; как говори́тся** as they say, as the saying goes. **говорли́вый** garrulous, talkative. **говору́н**, -а́, -ру́нья, -и talker, chatterer, chatterbox.

говя́дина, -ы beef. **говя́жий** beef.

го́гот, -а cackle; shouts of laughter. **гогота́нье**, -я cackling. **гогота́ть**, -очу́, -о́чешь *impf.* cackle; laugh aloud, shout with laughter.

год, -а (-у), *loc.* -ý; *pl.* -ы or -а́, *g.* -ов or лет year; *pl.* years, age, time; **без** ~**у неде́ля** only a few days; **в** ~**ы** in the days (of), during; **в** ~**а́х** advanced in years, getting on; ~ **от** ~**у** every year; **из** ~**а в** ~ year in, year out; **не по** ~**а́м** beyond one's years, precocious(ly). **года́ми** *adv.* for years (on end). **годи́на**, -ы time; period; year.

годи́ться, -жу́сь *impf.* be fit, suitable, suited; do, serve; +**в**+*nom. or a.* be cut out for, be old enough to be; **не годи́тся** it's no good, it won't do; +*inf.* it does not do to, one should not.

годи́чный lasting a year, a year's; annual, yearly.

го́дный; -ден, -дна́, -о, -ы or -ы́ fit, suitable, valid.

годова́лый a year-old; yearling. **годови́к**, -а́ yearling. **годово́й** annual, yearly. **годовщи́на**, -ы anniversary.

гожу́сь *etc.: see* **годи́ться**

гол, -а goal.

гола́вль, -я́ *m.* chub.

голена́ст|**ый** long-legged; ~**ые** *sb.*, *pl.* wading birds. **голени́ще**, -а (boot-)top. **го́лень**, -и shin.

голла́ндец, -дца Dutchman. **Голла́ндия**, -и Holland. **голла́ндка**, -и Dutchwoman; tiled stove; jumper. **голла́ндск**|**ий** Dutch; ~**ая печь** tiled stove; ~**ое полотно́** Holland.

голова́, -ы́, *a.* го́лову; *pl.* го́ловы, -о́в, -а́м head; brain, mind; wits; life; van; *c.g.* person in charge, head; **в пе́рвую го́лову** first of all; **городско́й** ~ mayor; ~ **сы́ру** a cheese; **на свою́ го́лову** to one's cost; **с головы́** per head. **голова́стик**, -а tadpole. **голо́вка**, -и head; cap, nose, tip; head-scarf; *pl.* vamp. **головн**|**о́й** head; brain, cerebral; leading, advance; ~**ая боль** headache; ~**о́й го́лос** head-voice, falsetto; ~**о́й мозг** brain, cerebrum; ~**о́й убо́р** headgear, headdress. **головокруже́ние**, -я giddiness, dizziness; vertigo. **головокружи́тельный** dizzy, giddy. **головоло́мка**, -и puzzle, riddle, conundrum. **головоло́мный** puzzling. **головомо́йка**, -и reprimand, dressing-down, telling-off. **головоре́з**, -а cut-throat; bandit; blackguard, ruffian, rascal. **головотя́п**, -а bungler, muddler.

го́лод, -а (-у) hunger; starvation; famine; dearth, acute shortage. **голода́ние**, -я starvation; fasting. **голода́ть**, -а́ю *impf.* go hungry, hunger, starve; fast, go without food. **голо́дный**; го́лоден, -дна́, -о, -ы or -ы́ hungry; hunger, starvation; meagre, scanty, poor. **голодо́вка**, -и starvation; hunger-strike.

голоно́гий bare-legged; bare-foot.

го́лос, -а (-у); *pl.* -а́, -о́в voice; part; word,

opinion; say; vote; **во весь** ~ at the top of one's voice; **подать** ~ **за**+*a*. vote for; **право** ~**a** vote, suffrage, franchise; **с** ~**a** by ear. **голосистый** loud-voiced; vociferous; loud. **голосить, -ошу** *impf.* sing loudly; cry; wail, keen.

голословный unsubstantiated, unfounded; unsupported by evidence.

голосование, -я voting; poll; hitching lifts, hitch-hiking; **всеобщее** ~ universal suffrage. **голосовать, -сую** *impf.* (*pf.* **про**~) vote; put to the vote, vote on; hitch lifts, hitch-hike. **голосовой** vocal.

голоштанник, -a ragamuffin.

голубеть, -еет *impf.* (*pf.* **по**~) turn blue, show blue. **голубизна, -ы** blueness. **голубка, -и** pigeon; (my) dear, darling. **голуб|ой** blue; light blue, pale blue; gay, homosexual; ~**ое топливо** natural gas; ~**ой экран** television screen. **голубчик, -a** my dear, my dear fellow; darling. **голубь, -я**; *pl.* **-и, -ей** *m.* pigeon, dove. **голубятник, -a** pigeon-fancier; dovecot. **голубятня, -и**; *g.pl.* **-тен** dovecot, pigeon-loft.

голый; гол, -ла, -ло naked, bare; poor; unmixed, unadorned; pure, neat. **голытьба, -ы** the poor. **голыш, -a** naked child, naked person; pauper; pebble, smooth round stone. **голышом** *adv.* stark naked. **голяк, -a** beggar, tramp.

гомеопат, -a homoeopath. **гомеопатический** homoeopathic. **гомеопатия, -и** homoeopathy.

гомогенный homogeneous.

гомон, -a (-y) hubbub. **гомонить, -ню** *impf.* shout, talk noisily.

гомосексуалист, -a homosexual, gay. **гомосексуальный** homosexual, gay.

гондола, -ы gondola; car; nacelle.

гонение, -я persecution. **гонитель, -я** *m.*, ~**ница, -ы** persecutor. **гонка, -и** race; dashing, rushing; haste, hurry. **гонкий; -нок, -нка, -нко** fast, swift; fast-growing.

Гонконг, -a Hong Kong.

гонорар, -a fee.

гоночный racing.

гончар, -a potter.

гонщик, -a racer; drover. **гоню** *etc.: see* **гнать**. **гонять, -яю** *impf.* drive; send on errands; ~**ся** race; +**за**+*i.* chase, pursue, hunt.

гор... *abbr.* (*of* **городской**) *in comb.* city, town. **горсовет, -a** city soviet, town soviet.

гора, -ы, *a.* **гору**; *pl.* **горы, -ам** mountain; hill; heap, pile, mass; **в гору** uphill; **под гору** downhill.

гораздо *adv.* much, far, by far.

горб, -a, *loc.* **-у** hump; protuberance, bulge. **горбатый** humpbacked, hunchbacked; ~ **нос** hooked nose. **горбить, -блю** *impf.* (*pf.* **с**~) arch, hunch; ~**ся** stoop, become bent. **горбоносый** hook-nosed. **горбун, -a** *m.*, **горбунья, -и**; *g.pl.* **-ний** humpback, hunch-

back. **горбушка, -и**; *g.pl.* **-шек** crust, heel of loaf.

горделивый haughty, proud. **гордиться, -ржусь** *impf.* put on airs, be haughty; +*i.* be proud of, pride o.s. on. **гордость, -и** pride. **гордый; горд, -а, -о, горды** proud. **гордыня, -и** pride, arrogance.

горе, -я grief, sorrow; distress; woe; misfortune, trouble. **горевать, -рюю** *impf.* grieve, mourn.

горелка, -и burner. **горелый** burnt. **горение, -я** burning, combustion; enthusiasm.

горестный sad, sorrowful; pitiful, mournful. **горесть, -и** sorrow, grief; *pl.* afflictions, misfortunes, troubles.

гореть, -рю *impf.* (*pf.* **с**~) burn; be on fire, be alight; glitter, shine.

горец, -рца mountain-dweller, highlander.

горечь, -и bitterness; bitter taste; bitter stuff.

горизонт, -a horizon; skyline. **горизонталь, -и** horizontal; contour line.

гористый mountainous, hilly. **горка, -и** hill; hillock; steep climb.

горлан, -a bawler. **горланить, -ню** *impf.* bawl, yell. **горластый** noisy, loud-mouthed. **горло, -a** throat; neck. **горловой** throat; of the throat; guttural; raucous. **горлышко, -a** neck.

горн¹, -a furnace, forge.

горн², -a bugle. **горнист, -a** bugler.

горничная *sb.* maid, chambermaid; stewardess.

горновой furnace, forge; *sb.* furnaceman. **горнозаводский** mining and metallurgical. **горнопромышленность, -и** mining industry. **горнопромышленный** mining. **горнорабочий** *sb.* miner.

горностаевый ermine. **горностай, -я** ermine.

горный mountain; mountainous; mineral; mining; ~ **лён** asbestos; ~ **хрусталь** rock crystal.

город, -a; *pl.* **-а** town; city; base, home. **городить, -ожу, -одишь** *impf.* fence, enclose; ~ **глупости** talk nonsense; **огород** ~ make a fuss. **городовой** *sb.* policeman. **городск|ой** urban; city; municipal; ~**ая ласточка** (house-)martin. **город-спутник, -a** satellite town. **горожанин, -a**; *pl.* **-ане, -ан** *m.*, **-жанка, -и** town-dweller; townsman, townswoman.

горох, -a (-y) pea, peas. **гороховый** pea. **горошек, -шка** spotted design (*on material*), polka dots; **душистый** ~ sweet peas; **зелёный** ~ green peas. **горошина, -ы** pea.

горсточка, -и, горсть, -и; *g.pl.* **-ей** handful.

гортанный guttural; laryngeal. **гортань, -и** larynx.

горче *comp. of* **горький**. **горчить, -чит** *impf.* taste bitter. **горчица, -ы** mustard. **горчичник, -a** mustard plaster. **горчичница, -ы** mustard-pot.

горшок, -шка pot; chamber-pot.

го́рький; -рек, -рька́, -о bitter; rancid; hapless, wretched.

горю́ч|ий combustible, inflammable; ~**ее** sb. fuel. **горю́чка**, -и motor fuel.

горячело́мкий hot-short. **горя́чий**; -ря́ч, -а́ hot; passionate; ardent, fervent; hot-tempered; mettlesome; heated; impassioned; busy; high-temperature.

горячи́ть, -чу́ impf. (pf. **раз~**) excite, irritate; ~**ся** get excited, become impassioned. **горя́чка**, -и fever; feverish activity; feverish haste; c.g. hothead; firebrand; **поро́ть горя́чку** hurry, bustle; rush headlong. **горя́чность**, -и zeal, fervour, enthusiasm.

гос... abbr. (of **госуда́рственный**) in comb. state. **Госдепарта́мент**, -а State Department. ~**пла́н**, -а State Planning Commission (in former USSR). ~**стра́х** State Insurance.

го́спиталь, -я m. (military) hospital.

го́споди int. good Lord! good gracious! **господи́н**, -а; pl. -ода́, -о́д, -а́м master; gentleman; Mr.; Messrs. **госпо́дский** seigniorial, manorial; ~ **дом** manor-house; the big house.

госпо́дство, -а supremacy, dominion, mastery; predominance. **госпо́дствовать**, -твую impf. hold sway, exercise dominion; predominate, prevail; ~ **над**+i. command, dominate; tower above. **госпо́дствующий** ruling; predominant, prevailing; commanding. **Госпо́дь**, **Го́спода**, voc. **Го́споди** m. God, the Lord. **госпожа́**, -й mistress; lady; Mrs., Miss, Ms.

гостево́й guest, guests'. **гостеприи́мный** hospitable. **гостеприи́мство**, -а hospitality. **гости́ная** sb. drawing-room, sitting-room; drawing-room suite. **гости́ница**, -ы hotel; inn. **гости́ный**; ~ **двор** arcade, bazaar. **гости́ть**, гощу́ impf. stay, be on a visit. **гость**, -я; g.pl. -е́й m., **го́стья**, -и; g.pl. -ий guest, visitor.

госуда́рственный State, public. **госуда́рство**, -а State. **госуда́рыня**, -и, **госуда́рь**, -я m. sovereign; Your Majesty.

гот, -а Goth. **готи́ческий** Gothic; ~ **шрифт** Gothic (type), black letter.

гото́вить, -влю impf. (pf. **с~**) prepare, get ready; train; cook; lay in, store; have in store; ~**ся** get ready; prepare o.s., make preparations; be at hand, brewing, impending, imminent; loom ahead. **гото́вность**, -и readiness, preparedness, willingness. **гото́в|ый** ready, prepared; willing; on the point, on the verge; ready-made, finished; tight, plastered; **на всём ~ом** and all found.

гофриро́ванный corrugated; crimped, waved; pleated; goffered. **гофрирова́ть**, -ру́ю impf. & pf. corrugate; wave, crimp; goffer. **гофриро́вка**, -и corrugation; goffering; waving; waves.

гр. abbr. (of **граждани́н**, **гражда́нка**) citizen.

граб, -а hornbeam.

грабёж, -а́ robbery; pillage, plunder. **граби́тель**, -я m. robber. **граби́тельский** extor-

tionate, exorbitant. **граби́тельство**, -а robbery. **гра́бить**, -блю impf. (pf. **о~**) rob, pillage. **гра́бленый** stolen.

гра́бли, -бель or -блей pl. rake.

гра́бовый hornbeam.

гравёр, -а, **гравиро́вщик**, -а engraver, etcher. **гравёрный** engraver's, etcher's; engraving, etching.

гра́вий, -я gravel. **грави́йный** gravel.

гравирова́льный engraving, etching. **гравирова́ть**, -ру́ю impf. (pf. **вы́~**) engrave; etch. **грави́ровка**, -и engraving, print; etching.

гравю́ра, -ы engraving, print; etching; ~ **на де́реве** woodcut; ~ **на лино́лиуме** linocut.

град[1] a city, town.

град[2], -а hail; shower, torrent; volley; ~**ом** thick and fast. **гра́дина**, -ы hailstone.

гра́дирня, -и salt-pan; cooling-tower. **гради́ровать**, -рую impf. & pf. evaporate.

градово́й hail. **гра́дом** see **град**

градострои́тель, -я m. town-planner. **градострои́тельный**, **градострои́тельство**, -а town planning.

гра́дус, -а degree; pitch; stage. **гра́дусник**, -а thermometer. **гра́дусн|ый** degree; grade; ~**ая се́тка** grid.

граждани́н, -а; pl. **гра́ждане**, -дан, **гражда́нка**, -и citizen. **гражда́нский** civil; citizens'; civic; secular; civilian. **гражда́нство**, -а citizenship, nationality.

грамза́пись, -и gramophone recording.

грамм, -а gram(me).

грамма́тик, -а grammarian. **грамма́тика**, -и grammar; grammar-book. **граммати́ческий** grammatical.

гра́мота, -ы ability to read and write, reading and writing; official document; deed. **гра́мотность**, -и literacy. **гра́мотный** literate; grammatically correct; competent.

грампласти́нка, -и disc, gramophone record.

гран, -а; g.pl. **гран** grain.

грана́т, -а pomegranate; garnet. **грана́та**, -ы shell, grenade. **грана́тник**, -а pomegranate. **грана́товый** pomegranate; garnet; rich red.

гране́ние, -я cutting. **гранёный** cut, faceted; cut-glass. **грани́льный** lapidary; diamond-cutting. **грани́льня**, -и; g.pl. -лен diamond-cutter's workshop. **грани́льщик**, -а lapidary, diamond-cutter.

грани́т, -а granite.

грани́ть, -ню́ impf. cut, facet.

грани́ца, -ы frontier, border; boundary, limit, bound; **за грани́цей**, **за грани́цу** abroad. **грани́чить**, -чит impf. border; verge.

гра́нка, -и galley proof, galley, slip (proof).

грань, -и border, verge; brink; side, facet; edge; period.

граф, -а count; earl.

графа́, -ы́ column. **гра́фик**, -а graph; chart; schedule; draughtsman, graphic artist. **гра́фика**, -и drawing, graphic art; script.

графи́н, -а carafe; decanter.

графи́ня, -и countess.

графи́т, -а graphite, black-lead; (pencil-)lead.
графи́ть, -флю́ *impf.* (*pf.* **раз~**) rule.
графи́ческий graphic.
графлёный ruled.
гра́фство, -а title of earl or count; county.
грацио́зный graceful. **гра́ция**, -и grace.
грач, -а́ rook.
гребёнка, -и comb; rack; hackle. **гре́бень**, -бня *m.* comb; hackle; crest; ridge. **гребе́ц**, -бца́ rower, oarsman. **гребно́й** rowing. **гребо́к**, -бка́ stroke; blade. **гребу́** *etc.*: see **грести́**
грёза, -ы day-dream, dream. **грёзить**, -ёжу *impf.* dream.
гре́йдер, -а grader; unmetalled road.
грек, -а Greek.
гре́лка, -и heater; hot-water bottle, foot-warmer.
греме́ть, -млю́ *impf.* (*pf.* **про~**) thunder, roar; rumble; peal; rattle; resound, ring out. **грему́ч|ий** roaring, rattling; fulminating; ~**ий газ** fire-damp; ~**ая змея́** rattlesnake; ~**ая ртуть** fulminate of mercury; ~**ий сту́день** nitro-gelatine. **грему́шка**, -и rattle; sleigh-bell.
грести́, -ебу́, -ебёшь; грёб, -бла́ *impf.* row; scull, paddle; rake.
греть, -е́ю *impf.* warm, heat; give out heat; ~**ся** warm o.s., bask.
грех, -а́ sin. **грехопа́вный** sinful. **грехопаде́ние**, -я the Fall; fall.
Гре́ция, -и Greece. **гре́цкий** Greek, Grecian; ~ **оре́х** walnut. **греча́нка**, -и Greek. **гре́ческий** Greek, Grecian.
гречи́ха, -и buckwheat. **гре́чневый** buckwheat.
греши́ть, -шу́ *impf.* (*pf.* **по~**, **со~**) sin. **гре́шник**, -а, -**ница**, -ы sinner. **гре́шный**; -шен, -шна́, -о sinful; culpable.
гриб, -а́ mushroom, toadstool, fungus. **грибно́й** mushroom.
гри́ва, -ы mane; wooded ridge; spit, shelf, sandbank.
гри́венник, -а ten-copeck piece.
грим, -а make-up; grease-paint.
грима́с|а, -ы grimace; **де́лать** ~**ы** make, pull faces.
гримёр, -а, -**ёрша**, -и make-up artist. **гримирова́ть**, -рую *impf.* (*pf.* **за~**, **на~**) make up; +*i.* make up as; ~**ся** make up. **гримиро́вка**, -и making up, make-up.
грипп, -а influenza.
гриф[1], -а gryphon; vulture.
гриф[2], -а finger-board.
гриф[3], -а seal, stamp.
гри́фель, -я *m.* slate-pencil. **гри́фельн|ый** slate; ~**ая доска́** slate.
гроб, -а, *loc.* -у́; *pl.* -ы́ *or* -а́ coffin; grave. **гробану́ть**, -ну́, -нёшь *pf.* damage, break; ~**ся** have an accident, be killed in an accident. **гробово́й** coffin; deathly, sepulchral. **гробовщи́к**, -а́ coffin-maker; undertaker.
гроза́, -ы́; *pl.* -ы (thunder-)storm; calamity,

disaster; terror; threats.
гроздь, -и; *pl.* -ди *or* -дья , -де́й *or* -дьев cluster, bunch.
грози́ть(ся, -ожу́(сь *impf.* (*pf.* **по~**, **при~**) threaten; make a threatening gesture; ~ **кулако́м** +*d.* shake one's fist at. **гро́зный**; -зен, -зна́, -о menacing, threatening; dread, terrible; formidable; stern, severe. **грозово́й** storm, thunder.
гром, -а; *pl.* -ы, -о́в thunder.
грома́да, -ы mass; bulk, pile; heaps, **грома́дина**, -ы vast object. **грома́дный** huge, vast, enormous, colossal.
громи́ть, -млю́ *impf.* destroy; smash, rout; thunder, fulminate, against.
гро́мкий; -мок, -мка́, -о loud; famous; notorious; fine-sounding, specious. **гро́мко** *adv.* loud(ly); aloud. **громкоговори́тель**, -я *m.* loud-speaker. **громово́й** thunder, of thunder; thunderous, deafening; crushing, smashing. **громогла́сный** loud; loud-voiced; public, open.
громозди́ть, -зжу́ *impf.* (*pf.* **на~**) pile up, heap up; ~**ся** tower; clamber up. **громо́здкий** cumbersome, unwieldy.
гро́мче *comp. of* **гро́мкий**, **гро́мко**
громыха́ть, -а́ю *impf.* rumble, clatter.
гроссме́йстер, -а grand master.
грот, -а grotto.
гро́хать, -аю *impf.*, **гро́хнуть**, -ну *pf.* crash, bang; drop with a crash, bang down; ~**ся** fall with a crash. **гро́хот**[1], -а crash, din.
гро́хот[2], -а screen, sieve, riddle.
грохота́ть, -очу́, -о́чешь *impf.* (*pf.* **про~**) crash; roll, rumble; thunder, roar; roar (with laughter).
грош, -а́ half-copeck piece; farthing, brass farthing, penny. **грошо́вый** dirt-cheap, shoddy; insignificant, trifling.
грубе́ть, -е́ю *impf.* (*pf.* **за~**, **о~**, **по~**) grow coarse, coarsen; become rough. **груби́ть**, -блю́ *impf.* (*pf.* **на~**) be rude. **грубия́н**, -а boor. **грубия́нить**, -ню *impf.* (*pf.* **на~**) be rude; behave boorishly. **гру́бо** *adv.* coarsely, roughly; crudely; rudely. **гру́бость**, -и rudeness; coarseness; grossness; rude remark. **гру́бый**; груб, -а́, -о coarse; rough; crude, rude; gross, flagrant.
гру́да, -ы heap, pile.
груди́на, -ы breastbone. **груди́нка**, -и brisket; breast. **грудн|о́й** breast, chest; pectoral; ~**а́я жа́ба** angina pectoris; ~**о́й ребёнок** infant in arms. **грудобрю́шн|ый**; ~**ая прегра́да** diaphragm. **грудь**, -й *or* -и, *i.* -ю, *loc.* -й; *pl.* -и, -е́й breast; bosom, bust; chest; (shirt-)front.
груз, -а weight; load, cargo; freight; burden; bob. **грузи́ло**, -а sinker.
грузи́н, -а; *g.pl.* -и́н, **грузи́нка**, -и Georgian. **грузи́нский** Georgian.
грузи́ть, -ужу́, -у́зишь *impf.* (*pf.* **за~**, **на~**, **по~**) load, lade, freight; ~**ся** load, take on cargo.

Грузия, -и Georgia.

грузка, -и lading. **грузный; -зен, -зна, -о** weighty, bulky; unwieldy; corpulent. **грузовик, -а** lorry, truck. **грузовой** goods, cargo, freight, load. **грузопоток, -а** freight traffic, goods traffic. **грузотакси** *nt.indecl.* taxilorry. **грузчик, -а** stevedore, docker; loader.

грунт, -а ground, soil, earth; subsoil; bottom; priming, primer. **грунтовать, -тую** *impf.* (*pf.* **за~**) prime. **грунтовка, -и** priming, ground coat, ground. **грунтовой** soil, earth, ground; subsoil; bottom; priming; unpaved, unmetalled.

группа, -ы group. **группировать, -рую** *impf.* (*pf.* **с~**) group, classify; **~ся** group, form groups. **группировка, -и** grouping; classification; group. **групповой** group; team.

грустить, -ущу *impf.* grieve, mourn; +**по**+*d.* pine for. **грустный; -тен, -тна, -о** sad; melancholy; grievous, distressing. **грусть, -и** sadness, melancholy.

груша, -и pear; pear-shaped thing. **грушевый** pear; ~ **компот** stewed pears.

грыжа, -и hernia, rupture. **грыжевый** hernial; ~ **бандаж** truss.

грызня, -и dog-fight, fight; squabble. **грызть, -зу, -зёшь; грыз** *impf.* (*pf.* **раз~**) gnaw; nibble; nag; devour, consume; **~ся** fight; squabble, bicker. **грызун, -а** rodent.

гряда, -ы; *pl.* **-ы, -ам** ridge; bed; row, series; bank. **грядка, -и** (flower-)bed.

грядущий approaching; coming, future; to come; **на сон ~** at bedtime; last thing at night.

грязевой mud. **грязнить, -ню** *impf.* (*pf.* **за~, на~**) dirty, soil; sully, besmirch; make a mess, be untidy; **~ся** become dirty. **грязный; -зен, -зна, -о** muddy, mud-stained; dirty; untidy, slovenly; filthy; refuse, garbage, slop. **грязь, -и,** *loc.* **-и** mud; dirt, filth; *pl.* mud; mud-baths, mud-cure.

грянуть, -ну *pf.* burst out, crash out, ring out; strike up. **~ся** crash (down).

грясти, -яду, -ядёшь *impf.* approach.

губа, -ы; *pl.* **-ы, -ам** lip; *pl.* pincers. **губастый** thick-lipped.

губернатор, -а governor. **губерния, -и** (*hist.*) gubernia, province. **губернский** provincial; ~ **секретарь** Provincial Secretary (*12th grade: see* **чин**).

губительный destructive, ruinous; baneful, pernicious. **губить, -блю, -бишь** *impf.* (*pf.* **по~**) destroy; be the undoing of; ruin, spoil; **~ся** be destroyed; be wasted.

губка, -и sponge.

губн|ой lip; labial; **~ая гармоника** harmonica, mouth organ.

губчатый porous, spongy; ~ **каучук** foam rubber.

гувернантка, -и governess. **гувернёр, -а** tutor.

гугу; ни ~! not a sound!; mum's the word!

гудение, -я hum; drone; buzzing; hooting, hoot. **гудеть, гужу** *impf.* (*pf.* **про~**) hum;

drone; buzz; hoot. **гудок, -дка** hooter, siren, horn, whistle; hoot, hooting.

гудрон, -а tar. **гудронировать, -рую** *impf.* & *pf.* (*pf. also* **за~**) tar. **гудронный** tar, tarred.

гул, -а rumble; hum; boom. **гулкий; -лок, -лка, -о** resonant; booming, rumbling.

ГУЛАГ *abbr.* (*of Главное управление исправительно-трудовых лагерей*) GULAG, Main Administration for Corrective Labour Camps.

гулянье, -я; *g.pl.* **-ний** walking, going for a walk; walk; fête; outdoor party. **гулять, -яю** *impf.* (*pf.* **по~**) walk, stroll; go for a walk, take a walk; have time off, not be working; make merry, carouse, have a good time; +**с**+*i.* go with.

ГУМ, -а *abbr.* (*of Государственный универсальный магазин*) GUM, State Department Store.

гуманизм, -а humanism. **гуманист, -а** humanist. **гуманитарный** of the humanities; humane. **гуманный** humane.

гумно, -а; *pl.* **-а, -мен** *or* **-мён, -ам** threshing-floor; barn.

гурт, -а herd, drove; flock. **гуртовщик, -а** herdsman; drover. **гуртом** *adv.* wholesale; in bulk; together; in a body, en masse.

гусак, -а gander.

гусеница, -ы caterpillar; (caterpillar) track. **гусеничный** track, tracked.

гусёнок, -нка; *pl.* **-сята, -сят** gosling. **гусин|ый** goose; **~ая кожа** goose-flesh; **~ые лапки** crow's-feet.

густеть, -еет *impf.* (*pf.* **за~, по~**) thicken, get thicker. **густой; густ, -а, -о** thick, dense; deep, rich. **густота, -ы** thickness, density; deepness, richness.

гусыня, -и goose. **гусь, -я;** *pl.* **-и, -ей** *m.* goose. **гуськом** *adv.* in single file. **гусятина, -ы** goose.

гуталин, -а shoe-polish, boot-polish.

гуща, -и dregs, lees, grounds, sediment; thicket; thick, centre, heart. **гуще** *comp. of* **густой. гущина, -ы** thickness; thicket.

гэ *nt.indecl.* the letter **г**.

ГЭС *abbr.* (*of гидроэлектростанция*) hydroelectric power station.

Д

д *letter: see* **дэ**

д. *abbr.* (*of* **деревня**) village; (*of* **дом**) house.

да *conj.* and; but; **да (ещё)** and what is more;

да (и) and besides; **да и то́лько** and that's all.

да *part.* yes; yes? really? indeed; well; *+3rd pers. of v.*, may, let; **да здра́вствует...!** long live ..!

дава́ть, даю́, -ёшь *impf. of* **дать; дава́й(те)** let us, let's; come on; **~ся** yield; let o.s. be caught; come easy; **не ~ся+d.** dodge, evade; **ру́сский язы́к ему́ даётся легко́** Russian comes easy to him.

да́веча *adv.* lately, recently.

дави́ло, -а press. **дави́ть, -влю́, -вишь** *impf.* (*pf.* **за~, по~, раз~, у~**) press; squeeze; weigh, lie heavy; crush; oppress; trample; strangle; **~ся** choke; hang o.s. **да́вка, -и** crushing, squeezing; throng, crush. **давле́ние, -я** pressure.

да́вний ancient; of long standing. **давно́** *adv.* long ago; for a long time; long since. **давнопроше́дший** remote; long past; pluperfect. **да́вность, -и** antiquity; remoteness; long standing; prescription. **давны́м-давно́** *adv.* long long ago, ages ago.

дади́м *etc.*: *see* **дать. даю́** *etc.*: *see* **дава́ть**

да́же *adv.* even.

дакти́льн|ый; ~ая а́збука sign language.

да́лее *adv.* further; **и так ~** and so on, etc. **далёкий; -ёк, -а́, -ёко́** distant, remote; far (away). **далеко́, далёко** *adv.* far; far off; by a long way; **~ за** long after; **~ не** far from. **даль, -и**, *loc.* **-и́** distance. **да́льн|ий** distant, remote; long; **без ~их слов** without more ado; **~ Восто́к** the Far East. **дально-зо́ркий** long-sighted. **да́льность, -и** distance; range. **да́льше** *adv.* farther; further; then, next; longer.

дам *etc.*: *see* **дать**

да́ма, -ы lady; partner; queen.

да́мба, -ы dike, embankment; dam.

да́мка, -и king. **да́мский** ladies'.

Да́ния, -и Denmark.

да́нные *sb.*, *pl.* data; facts, information; qualities, gifts; grounds; **необрабо́танные ~** raw data. **да́нный** given, present; in question, this. **дань, -и** tribute; debt.

дар, -а; *pl.* **-ы́** gift; donation; grant. **даре́ние, -я** donation. **дари́тель, -я** *m.* donor. **дари́ть, -рю́, -ришь** *impf.* (*pf.* **по~**) *+d.* give, make a present.

дармое́д, -а, -е́дка, -и parasite, sponger, scrounger. **дармое́дничать, -аю** *impf.* sponge, scrounge.

дарова́ние, -я gift, talent. **дарова́ть, -ру́ю** *impf. & pf.* grant, confer. **дарови́тый** gifted, talented. **даровой** free, gratuitous. **да́ром** *adv.* free, gratis; in vain, to no purpose.

да́та, -ы date.

да́тельный dative.

дати́ровать, -рую *impf. & pf.* date.

да́тский Danish. **датча́нин, -а;** *pl.* **-а́не, -а́н, датча́нка, -и** Dane.

дать, дам, дашь, даст, дади́м; дал, -а́, да́ло *pf.* (*impf.* **дава́ть**) give; administer; grant;

let; **~ взаймы́** lend; **~ газ** step on the gas; **~ доро́гу** make way; **~ кля́тву** take an oath; **~ нача́ло+d.** give rise to; **~ сло́во** give one's word; *+d.* give the floor; **~ ход+d.** set in motion, get going; **~ся** *pf. of* **дава́ться**

да́ча, -и dacha; **на да́че** in the country; **на да́чу** (in)to the country. **да́чник, -а** (holiday) visitor.

два *m. & nt.*, **две** *f.*, **двух, -ум, -умя́, -ух** two; **~-три** two or three, a couple; **ка́ждые ~ дня** every other day. **двадцатиле́тний** twenty-year; twenty-year-old. **двадца́т|ый** twentieth; **~ые го́ды** the twenties. **два́дцать, -и,** *i.* **-ью** twenty. **два́дцатью** *adv.* twenty times. **два́жды** *adv.* twice; double. **двена́дцатый** twelfth. **двена́дцать, -и** twelve.

дверн|о́й door; **~а́я коро́бка** door-frame. **две́рца, -ы;** *g.pl.* **-рец** door, hatch. **дверь, -и,** *loc.* **-и́;** *pl.* **-и, -е́й,** *i.* **-я́ми** *or* **-ьми́** door; *pl.* doors, door.

две́сти, двухсо́т, -умста́м, -умяста́ми, -ухста́х two hundred.

дви́гатель, -я *m.* engine, motor; (prime) mover, motive force. **дви́гательный** motive; motor. **дви́гать, -аю** *or* **-ижу** *impf.*, **дви́нуть, -ну** *pf.* move; set in motion, get going; advance, further; **~ся** move; advance; start, get started. **движе́ние, -я** movement; motion; exercise; flow; traffic; promotion; advancement; impulse; **железнодоро́жное ~** train service. **дви́жимость, -и** movables, chattels; personal property. **дви́жимый** movable; moved, prompted, activated. **движко́в|ый** slide; **~ые регуля́торы** slide controls. **дви́жущий** motive; moving; driving.

дво́е, -и́х two; two pairs.

двое... *in comb.* two-; double(-). **двоебо́рец, -рца** competitor in double event. **~бо́рье, -я** double event. **~ду́шие, -я** duplicity, double-dealing. **~ду́шный** two-faced. **~же́нец, -нца** bigamist. **~му́жница, -ы** bigamist. **~же́нство, -а, ~му́жие, -я** bigamy. **~то́чие, -я** colon.

двои́ть, -ою́ *impf.* (*pf.* **вз~**) double; divide into two; **~ся** divide in two; appear double. **двои́чный** binary. **дво́йка, -и** two; figure 2; No. 2; pair-oar. **двойни́к, -а́** double; twin. **двойно́й** double, twofold; binary. **дво́йня, -и;** *g.pl.* **-ен** twins. **дво́йственный** double-dealing, two-faced; dual; bipartite.

двор, -а́ yard; courtyard; homestead; court; **на ~е́** out of doors, outside; **при ~е́** at court. **дворе́ц, -рца́** palace. **дворе́цкий** *sb.* butler; majordomo. **дво́рник, -а** yardman; windscreen-wiper. **дво́рницк|ий** dvornik's. **~ая** *sb.* dvornik's lodge. **дво́рня, -и** servants, menials. **дворо́вый** yard, courtyard; *sb.* house-serf. **дворо́вый** palace. **дворяни́н, -а;** *pl.* **-я́не, -я́н, дворя́нка, -и** member of the nobility or gentry. **дворя́нство, -а** nobility, gentry.

двою́родн|ый; ~ый брат, ~ая сестра́ (first)

cousin; **~ый дя́дя, ~ая тётка** first cousin once removed. **двоя́кий** double; ambiguous; in two ways, of two kinds. **двоя́ко...** double-, bi-, di-.

дву..., двух... *in comb.* two-; bi-, di-; double(-); diplo-. **двубо́ртный** double-breasted. **~гла́вый** two-headed. **~гла́сный** *sb.* diphthong. **~гри́венный** *sb.* twenty-copeck piece. **~жи́льный** strong; hardy; tough. **~зна́чный** two-digit. **~ли́кий** two-faced. **~ли́чие, -я** double-dealing, duplicity. **~ли́чный** two-faced; hypocritical. **~пла́нный** two-dimensional. **~по́лый** bisexual. **~ру́чный** two-handed; two-handled. **~ру́шник, -а** double-dealer. **~сло́жный** disyllabic. **~сме́нный** in two shifts, two-shift. **~смы́сленный** ambiguous, equivocal. **~(х)спа́льный** double. **~сторо́нний** double-sided; two-way; bilateral. **~хата́мный** diatomic. **~хгоди́чный** two-year. **~хкра́сочный** two-colour; two-tone. **~хле́тний** two-year; two-year-old; biennial. **~хме́стный** two-seater; two-berth. **~хмеся́чник, -а** bimonthly. **~хмото́рный** twin-engined, two-engined. **~хпала́тный** bicameral. **~хпарти́йный** bipartisan. **~хсотле́тие, -я** bicentenary. **~хсо́тый** two-hundredth. **~хта́ктный** two-beat; two-stroke. **~хъя́русный** two-layer, two-storey, two-tier, double-deck; two-lever. **~хэта́жный** two-storey, double-deck; **~член, -а** binomial. **~язы́чный** bilingual.

деба́ты, -ов *pl.* debate.
де́бет, -а debit. **дебетова́ть, -ту́ю** *impf. & pf.* debit.
де́бит, -а discharge, flow, yield, output.
де́бри, -ей *pl.* jungle; thickets; the wilds; maze, labyrinth.
дебю́т, -а a début; opening.
де́ва, -ы maid, maiden; girl; spinster; Virgo. **ста́рая ~** old maid.
девальва́ция, -и devaluation.
дева́ть(ся, -а́ю(сь *impf. of* **де́ть(ся**
деви́з, -а motto; device.
деви́ца, -ы spinster; girl. **деви́ческий, де́вич|ий** girlish, maidenly; **~ья фами́лия** maiden name. **де́вка, -и** girl, wench, lass; tart, whore. **де́вочка, -и** (little) girl. **де́вственник, -а, -ица, -ы** virgin. **де́вственный** virgin; virginal, innocent. **де́вушка, -и** girl; maid.
девяно́сто, -а ninety. **девяно́стый** ninetieth. **де́вятеро, -ых** nine; nine pairs. **девятисо́тый** nine-hundredth. **девя́тка, -и** nine; figure 9; No. 9; group of nine. **девятна́дцать, -и** nineteen. **девя́тый** ninth. **де́вять, -й, i. -ью** nine. **девятьсо́т, -тисо́т, -тиста́м, -тьюста́ми, -тиста́х** nine hundred. **де́вятью** *adv.* nine times.
дегенера́т, -а degenerate. **дегенерати́вный** degenerate. **дегенера́ция, -и** degeneration. **дегенери́ровать, -рую** *impf. & pf.* degenerate.

дёготь, -гтя tar, coal-tar, pitch. **дёгтебето́н, -а** tarmac, tar concrete. **дегтя́рный** tar, coal-tar, pich; tarry.
дед, -а grandfather; grandad, grandpa. **де́довский** grandfather's; old-world; old-fashioned. **де́душка, -и** grandfather; grandad.
дееприча́стие, -я gerund, adverbial participle.
дежу́рить, -рю *impf.* be on duty, be in (constant) attendance. **дежу́рный** duty; on duty. **дежу́рство, -а** (being on) duty.
дезинфе́кция, -и disinfection. **дезинфици́ровать, -рую** *impf. & pf.* disinfect.
дезерти́р, -а deserter. **дезерти́ровать, -рую** *impf. & pf.* desert. **дезерти́рство, -а** desertion.
дезодора́нт, -а deodorant; air freshener.
де́йственный efficacious; effective. **де́йствие, -я** action; operation; activity; functioning; effect; act; **под ~м** under the influence. **действи́тельно** *adv.* really; indeed. **действи́тельность, -и** reality; realities; conditions; validity; efficacy; **в действи́тельности** in reality, in fact. **действи́тельный** real, actual; true, authentic; valid, efficacious; effective; active. **де́йствовать, -твую** *impf.* (*pf.* **по~**) affect, have an effect; act; work, function; operate; +*i.* use; **не ~** be out of order, not be working. **де́йствующ|ий** active; in force; working; **~ее лицо́** character; active participant; **~ие ли́ца** dramatis personae, cast.
де́ка, -и sounding-board.
декабри́ст, -а Decembrist. **дека́брь, -я́** *m.* December. **дека́брьский** December.
дека́да, -ы ten days; (ten-day) festival.
дека́н, -а dean. **декана́т, -а** office of dean.
деклама́тор, -а reciter, declaimer. **деклама́ция, -и** recitation, declamation. **деклами́ровать, -рую** *impf.* (*pf.* **про~**) recite, declaim. **деклара́ция, -и** declaration; **нало́говая ~** tax return.
декорати́вный decorative, ornamental. **декора́тор, -а** decorator; scene-painter. **декора́ция, -и** scenery, décor; window-dressing.
декре́т, -а a decree; maternity leave; **уйти́ в ~** take maternity leave. **декрети́ровать, -ую** *impf. & pf.* decree. **декре́тный; ~ о́тпуск** maternity leave.
де́ланный artificial, forced, affected. **де́лать, -аю** *impf.* (*pf.* **с~**) make; do; give, produce; **~ вид** pretend, feign; **~ предложе́ние** propose; **~ честь**+*d.* honour; do credit to; **~ся** become, get, grow; happen; be going on; break out, appear.
делега́т, -а delegate. **делега́ция, -и** delegation; group. **делеги́ровать, -ую** *impf. & pf.* delegate.
делёж, -á, делёжка, -и sharing, division; partition. **деле́ние, -я** division; point, degree, unit.
деле́ц, -льца́ business man, dealer; smart operator.

деликатность, -и delicacy. **деликатный** delicate.

делимое sb. dividend. **делимость**, -и divisibility. **делитель**, -я m. divisor. **делить**, -лю, -лишь impf. (pf. **по~**, **раз~**) divide; share; ~ **шесть на три** divide six by three; ~**ся** divide; be divisible; +i. share; communicate, impart.

дело, -а; pl. -á business; affair, affairs; cause; occupation; matter; point; fact; deed; thing; case, action; file, dossier; battle, fighting; **в самом деле** really, indeed; ~ **в том** the point is; **в том то и** ~ that's just the point; ~ **за вами** it's up to you; **как (ваши) дела?** how are things going? how are you getting on? **на самом деле** in actual fact, as a matter of fact; **по делу, по делам** on business; **то и** ~ continually, time and again. **деловитый** business-like, efficient. **деловой** business, work; business-like. **дельный** efficient, business-like; sensible, practical.

дельтаплан, -а hang-glider (craft). **дельта-планерист**, -а hang-glider (pers.).

дельфин, -а dolphin.

демагог, -а demagogue. **демагогический** demagogic. **демагогия**, -и demagogy.

демократ, -а democrat; plebeian. **демократизировать**, -рую impf. & pf. democratize. **демократический** democratic; plebeian. **демократия**, -и democracy; common people, lower classes.

демонстрация, -и demonstration; (public) showing; display, show.

дендрарий, -я arboretum.

денежн|ый monetary; money; moneyed; ~**ый перевод** money order, postal order; ~**ая реформа** currency reform; ~**ый штраф** fine.

дену etc.: see **деть**

день, **дня** m. day; afternoon; **днём** in the afternoon; **на днях** the other day; one of these days; **через** ~ every other day.

деньги, -нег, -ьгам pl. money.

департамент, -а department.

депо nt. indecl. depot.

депозитарий, -я m. depository.

депортант, -а deportee. **депортация**, -и deportation. **депортировать**, -ую impf. & pf. deport.

депутат, -а deputy; delegate. **депутация**, -и deputation.

дёргать, -аю impf. (pf. **дёрнуть**) pull, tug; pull out; harass, pester; +i. move sharply, jerk, shrug; ~**ся** twitch; jerk; move sharply.

дергач, -á corncrake, landrail.

деревенеть, -ею impf. (pf. **за~**, **о~**) grow stiff, grow numb. **деревенский** village; rural, country. **деревня**, -и; pl. -и, -вень, -вням village; the country. **дерево**, -а; pl. -евья, -ьев tree; wood. **деревушка**, -и hamlet. **деревянный** wood; wooden; expressionless, dead; dull.

держава, -ы power; orb. **державный** hold-

ing supreme power, sovereign; powerful.

держать, -жу, -жишь impf. hold; hold up, support; keep; ~ **корректуру** read proofs; ~ **пари** bet; ~ **себя** behave; ~ **экзамен** take an examination; ~**ся** hold; be held up, be supported; keep, stay, be; hold o.s.; behave; last; hold together; hold out, stand firm, hold one's ground; +g. keep to; adhere to, stick to; ~ **ся на ниточке** hang by a thread.

дерзание, -я daring. **дерзать**, -аю impf., **дерзнуть**, -ну, -нёшь pf. dare. **дерзкий** impertinent, impudent, cheeky; insolent; daring, audacious. **дерзновенный** audacious, daring. **дерзость**, -и impertinence; cheek; rudeness; insolence; daring, audacity.

дёрн, -а (-у) turf. **дерновый** turf. **дерновать**, -ную impf. turf, edge with turf.

дёрнуть(ся, -ну(сь pf. of **дёргать(ся**

деру etc.: see **драть**

десант, -а landing; landing force. **десантник**, -а paratrooper. **десантный** landing.

десна, -ы; pl. дёсны, -сен gum.

деспот, -а despot.

десятерой tenfold. **десятеро**, -ых ten. **десятилетие**, -я decade; tenth anniversary. **десятилетка**, -и ten-year (secondary) school. **десятилетний** ten-year, decennial; ten-year-old. **десятичный** decimal. **десятка**, -и ten; No. 10; group of ten; tenner (10-rouble note). **десяток**, -тка ten; ten years, decade. **десятник**, -а foreman. **десятский** sb. peasant policeman. **десятый** tenth. **десять**, -й, i. -ью ten. **десятью** adv. ten times.

дет... abbr. (of **детский**) in comb. children's. **детдом**, -а children's home. ~**площадка**, -и playground. ~**сад**, -а kindergarten, nursery school.

деталь, -и detail; part, component. **детальный** detailed; minute.

детвора, -ы children.

детектив, -а whodunit; detective story.

детёныш, -а young animal; cub, whelp, etc.; pl. young.

детергент, -а detergent.

дети, -тей, -тям, -тьми, -тях pl. children. **детская** sb. nursery. **детский** child's, children's; childish. **детство**, -а childhood.

деть, **дену** pf. (impf. **девать**) put; **куда ты дел моё перо?** what have you done with my pen?; ~**ся** get to, disappear to; **куда она делась?** what has become of her?

дефект, -а defect. **дефективный** defective; handicapped; ~ **ребёнок** (mentally or physically) handicapped child. **дефектный** imperfect, faulty.

дефис, -а hyphen; **писать через** ~ hyphenate.

дефицит, -а deficit; shortage, deficiency. **дефицитный** showing a loss; in short supply; scarce.

децимальный decimal.

дешеветь, -еет impf. (pf. **по~**) fall in price, get cheaper. **дешевизна**, -ы cheapness; low

price. **деше́вле** *comp. of* **дёшево, дешёвый. дёшево** *adv.* cheap, cheaply; lightly.
деше́вый; дёшев, -á, -о cheap; empty,
worthless.
дешифри́ровать, -рую *impf. & pf.* decipher,
decode. **дешифро́вка, -и** decipherment,
decifering, decoding.
дея́ние, -я act, deed. **де́ятель, -я** *m.*; **госуда́-
рственный ~** statesman; **~ нау́ки** scientific
worker, scientist; **обще́ственный ~** public
figure. **де́ятельность, -и** activity; activities;
work; operation. **де́ятельный** active, energetic.
джаз, -а jazz. **джаз-анса́мбль, -я** jazz-
combo. **джази́ст, -а** jazz musician.
джéмпер, -а jumper, pullover, jersey.
джинсо́вый denim. **джи́нсы, -ов** *pl.* jeans.
джип, -а jeep.
джо́ггинг, -а jogging, fun-running.
джо́йстик, -а (*comput.*) joystick.
джу́нгли, -ей *pl.* jungle.
ДЗУ *abbr.* (*of* **долговре́менное запомина́ю-
щее устро́йство**) (*comput.*) ROM (*read-only
memory*).
дзю(-)до́ *nt. indecl.* judo. **дзюдо́ист, -а**
judoist, judoka.
диа́гноз, -а diagnosis. **диагности́ровать,
-рую** *impf. & pf.* diagnose.
диагона́ль, -и diagonal; **по ~и** diagonally.
диагона́льный diagonal.
диагра́мма, -ы diagram; **кругова́я ~** pie
chart.
диале́кт, -а dialect. **диалекти́ческий, диа-
ле́ктный** dialectal.
диало́г, -а dialogue. **диало́говый** interactive.
диа́метр, -а diameter.
диапазо́н, -а diapason; range; compass; band.
диапозити́в, -а a slide, transparency.
диафра́гма, -ы diaphragm; (*phot.*) aperture.
дива́н, -а sofa; divan.
диверса́нт, -а saboteur. **диверсио́нный** di-
versionary; saboteur, wrecking. **диве́рсия,
-и** diversion; sabotage.
диви́зия, -и (*mil.*) division.
ди́вный amazing; marvellous, wonderful.
ди́во, -а a wonder, marvel.
дие́з, -а sharp.
дие́та, -ы diet. **диете́тика, -и** dietetics. **дие-
тети́ческий** dietetic; **~ магази́н** health food
shop. **дието́лог, -а** nutritionist.
ди́зель, -я *m.* diesel; diesel engine. **ди́зель-
ный** diesel.
дизентери́я, -и dysentery.
дика́рь, -я *m.*, **дика́рка, -и** savage; barbarian; shy person. **ди́кий** wild; savage; shy,
unsociable; queer, absurd; fantastic, preposterous, ridiculous. **дикобра́з, -а** porcupine.
дико́вина, -ы marvel, wonder. **дикорасту́-
щий** wild. **ди́кость, -и** wildness, savagery;
shyness, unsociableness; absurdity, queer-
ness.
дикта́нт, -а dictation.

дикта́тор, -а dictator. **дикта́торский** dictatorial. **диктату́ра, -ы** dictatorship.
диктова́ть, -ту́ю *impf.* (*pf.* **про~**) dictate.
дикто́вка, -и dictation. **ди́ктор, -а** announcer.
дилета́нт, -а dilettante, dabbler. **дилета́нт-
ство, -а** dilettantism.
дилижа́нс, -а stage-coach.
ди́на, -ы dyne.
дина́мик, -а loudspeaker. **дина́мика, -и** dynamics; action, movement.
диноза́вр, -а dinosaur.
дипло́м, -а diploma; degree; degree work, research; pedigree.
диплома́т, -а diplomat; attaché case. **дипло-
мати́ческий, дипломати́чный** diplomatic.
диплома́тия, -и diplomacy; **~ канонéрок**
gunboat diplomacy.
диплома́рованный graduate; professionally
qualified, certificated, diplomaed. **дипло́м-
ный** diploma, degree.
директи́ва, -ы instructions; directions, direc-
tives.
дире́ктор, -а; *pl.* **-á** director, manager; **~
шко́лы** head (master, mistress); principal.
дире́кция, -и management; board (of directors).
дирижа́бль, -я *m.* airship.
дирижёр, -а conductor. **дирижи́ровать,
-рую** *impf.+i.* conduct.
диск, -а disk, disk; discus; plate; dial; **ком-
па́ктный ~** compact disk.
ди́скант, -а treble.
диске́т, -а (*comput.*) diskette; **пусто́й ~**
blank diskette. **диск-жоке́й, -я** disc-jockey.
дисково́д, -а (*comput.*) disk drive.
дискре́тность, -и discreteness, discontinuity.
дискре́тн|ый discrete; digital; **~ая маши́на**
digital computer.
дискриминацио́нный discriminatory.
дискримина́ция, -и discrimination; **~ жéн-
щин** sexism.
дискуссио́нный discussion, debating; debatable, open to question. **диску́ссия, -и** discussion, debate. **дискути́ровать, -рую** *impf.
& pf.* discuss, debate.
диспансéр, -а clinic, (health) centre.
диспéтчер, -а controller, dispatcher. **диспéт-
черская** *sb.* controller's office; control
tower.
диссерта́ция, -и dissertation, thesis.
дистанцио́нн|ый distance, distant, remote;
remote-control; **~ый взрыва́тель** time fuse;
~ое управлéние remote control. **диста́н-
ция, -и** distance; range; division, region, sector.
дисципли́на, -ы discipline. **дисциплина́р-
ный** disciplinary. **дисциплини́ровать, -рую**
impf. & pf. discipline.
дитя́, -я́ти; *pl.* **дéти, -éй** *nt.* child; baby.
дифтери́т, -а, дифтери́я, -и diptheria.
дича́ть, -а́ю *impf.* (*pf.* **о~**) grow wild; become unsociable; run wild. **дичи́на, -ы** game.

дичи́ться, -чу́сь *impf.* be shy; +g. shun, fight shy of. **дичь**, -и, *loc.* -и́ game; wildfowl; wilderness, wilds.

длина́, -ы́ length; **длино́й** in length, long. **длинново́лновый** long-wave. **дли́нный**; -нен, -нна́, -о long; lengthy. **дли́тельность**, -и duration. **дли́тельный** long, protracted, long-drawn-out. **дли́ться**, -и́тся *impf.* (*pf.* про~) last, be protracted.

для *prep.*+g. for; for the sake of; to; of; ~ ви́ду for the sake of appearances; вре́дно ~ дете́й bad for children; высо́к ~ свои́х лет tall for his age; непроница́емый ~ воды́ waterproof, impervious to water; ~ того́, чтобы... in order to ...; э́то ~ вас this is for you; э́то типи́чно ~ них it is typical of them.

дневальный *sb.* orderly, man on duty. **дневни́к**, -а́ diary, journal. **дневн|о́й** day; daylight; day's, daily; ~áя сме́на day shift; ~о́й спекта́кль matinée. **днём** *adv.* in the daytime, by day; in the afternoon. **дни** *etc.*: *see* день

ДНК *abbr.* (*of* дезоксирибонуклеи́новая кислота́) DNA (*deoxyribonucleic acid*).

дно, дна; *pl.* до́нья, -ьев bottom.

до *nt.indecl.* C; doh.

до *prep.*+g. to, up to; as far as; until, till; before; to the point of; under; about, approximately; with regard to, concerning; дети до пяти́ лет children under five; до бо́ли until it hurt(s); до войны́ before the war; до на́шей э́ры B.C. до сих пор up to now, till now, hitherto; до тех пор till then, before; до того́, как before; до того́, что to such an extent that, to the point where; мне не до I don't feel like, I'm not in the mood for; от Санкт-Петербу́рга до Москвы́ from St. Petersburg to Moscow; что до меня́ as far as I am concerned; ю́бка до коле́н knee-length skirt.

до... *pref.* up (to); pre-; sub- *in comb.* **I.** *with vv., etc. expresses completion of action, indicates that action is carried to a certain point, expresses supplementary action; with refl. vv. expresses eventual attainment of object, or continuation of action with injurious consequences.* **II.** *with adjs. indicates priority in time sequence.*

доба́вить, -влю *pf.*, **добавля́ть**, -я́ю *impf.* (+a. or g.) add. **доба́вка**, -и addition; second-helping. **добавле́ние**, -я addition; appendix, addendum, supplement; extra. **доба́вочный** additional, supplementary; extra; extension, booster.

добега́ть, -а́ю *impf.*, **добежа́ть**, -егу́ *pf.*+до+g. run to, run as far as; reach.

добела́ *adv.* to white heat, white-hot; clean, white.

добива́ть, -а́ю *impf.*, **доби́ть**, -бью́, -бьёшь *pf.* finish (off), kill off, deal the final blow to; ~ся+g. get, obtain, secure; achieve; ~ся своего́ get one's way, gain one's end.

добира́ться, -а́юсь *impf. of* **добра́ться**

до́блестный valiant, valorous, brave. **до́блесть**, -и valour, prowess.

добра́ться, -беру́сь, -ёшься; -а́лся, -ла́сь, -а́ло́сь *pf.* (*impf.* **добира́ться**) +до+g. get to, reach.

добро́, -а́ good; good deed; goods, property; э́то не к добру́ it is a bad sign, it augurs ill.

добро́... *in comb.* good-, well-. **доброво́лец**, -льца volunteer. ~во́льно *adv.* voluntarily, of one's own free will. ~во́льный voluntary. ~де́тель, -и virtue. ~де́тельный virtuous. ~ду́шие, -я good nature. ~ду́шный good-natured; genial. ~жела́тельный benevolent. ~ка́чественный of good quality; benign. ~со́вестный conscientious.

доброта́, -ы́ goodness, kindness. **до́бр|ый**; добр, -а́, -о, до́бры good; kind; бу́дьте добры́+*imper.* please; would you be kind enough to; в ~ый час! good luck! по ~ой во́ле of one's own accord, of one's own free will.

добыва́ть, -а́ю *impf.*, **добы́ть**, -бу́ду; до́был, -а , -о *pf.* get, obtain, procure; extract, mine, quarry. **добы́ча**, -и output; extraction; mining, quarrying; booty, spoils, loot; bag, catch; mineral products.

добью *etc.*: *see* **доби́ть**. **доведу́** *etc.*: *see* **довести́**

довезти́, -зу́, -зёшь; -вёз, -ла́ *pf.* (*impf.* **довози́ть**) take (to), carry (to), drive (to).

дове́ренность, -и warrant; power of attorney; trust. **дове́ренн|ый** trusted; confidential; ~ое лицо́ confidential agent; ~ый *sb.* agent, proxy. **дове́рие**, -я trust, confidence. **дове́рить**, -рю *pf.* (*impf.* **доверя́ть**) entrust; trust, confide; ~ся+d. trust in; confide in. **дове́рчивый** trustful, credulous.

доверша́ть, -а́ю *impf.*, **доверши́ть**, -шу́ *pf.* complete. **доверше́ние**, -я completion, accomplishment; в ~ всего́ to crown all.

доверя́ть(ся, -я́ю(сь *impf. of* **дове́рить(ся**

дове́сок, -ска makeweight.

довести́, -еду́, -едёшь; -вёл, -а́ *pf.*, **доводи́ть**, -ожу́, -о́дишь *impf.* lead, take, accompany (to); bring, drive, reduce (to). **до́вод**, -а argument, reason.

довое́нный pre-war.

довози́ть, -ожу́, -о́зишь *impf. of* **довезти́**

дово́льно *adv.* enough; quite, fairly; rather; pretty. **дово́льный** contented, satisfied; content; pleased; considerable. **дово́льство**, -а content, contentment; ease, prosperity. **дово́льствоваться**, -ствуюсь *impf.* (*pf.* у~) be content, be satisfied.

дог, -а Great Dane; **далма́тский** ~ Dalmation.

догада́ться, -а́юсь *pf.*, **дога́дываться**, -аюсь *impf.* guess; suspect. **дога́дка**, -и surmise, conjecture; shrewdness; imagination. **дога́дливый** quick witted, shrewd.

до́гма, -ы dogma, dogmatic assertion. **догма́тизм**, -а dogmatism. **догмати́ческий** dogmatic.

догна́ть, -гоню́, -го́нишь; -гна́л, -а́, -о *pf.* (*impf.* догоня́ть) catch up (with); drive; push up.

догова́риваться, -аюсь *impf.*, договори́ться, -рю́сь *pf.* come to an agreement or understanding; arrange; negotiate, treat; догова́ривающиеся сто́роны contracting parties. догово́р, -а; *pl.* -ы *or* -а́, -о́в agreement; contract; treaty, pact. догово́рный contractual; agreed; fixed by treaty.

догоня́ть, -я́ю *impf. of* догна́ть

догора́ть, -а́ет *impf.*, догоре́ть, -ри́т *pf.* burn out, burn down.

дое́ду *etc.: see* дое́хать. доезжа́ть, -а́ю *impf. of* дое́хать

дое́ние, -я milking.

дое́хать, -е́ду *pf.* (*impf.* доезжа́ть) +до+*g.* reach, arrive at.

дожда́ться, -ду́сь, -дёшься; -а́лся, -ла́сь, -а́лось *pf.*+*g.* wait for, wait until.

дождеви́к, -а́ raincoat; puff-ball. дождево́й rain; rainy; ~ червь earthworm. до́ждик, -а shower. дождли́вый rainy. дождь, -я́ *m.* rain; shower, hail; ~ идёт it is raining.

дожива́ть, -а́ю *impf.*, дожи́ть, -иву́, -ивёшь; до́жил, -а́, -о *pf.* live out; spend; +до+*g.* live until; reach; come to, be reduced to.

до́за, -ы dose.

доза́тор, -а metering device; hopper, feeder, dispenser.

дозволе́ние, -я permission. дозво́ленный permitted; legal. дозво́лить, -лю *pf.*, дозволя́ть, -я́ю *impf.* permit, allow.

дозвони́ться, -ню́сь *pf.* get through, reach by telephone; ring (*doorbell etc.*) until one gets an answer.

дозо́р, -а patrol; ночно́й ~ night watch. дозо́рный patrol, scout.

дозрева́ть, -а́ет *impf.*, дозре́ть, -е́ет *pf.* ripen. дозре́лый fully ripe.

доистори́ческий prehistoric. доисто́рия, -и prehistory.

дои́ть, дою́, до́ишь *impf.* (*pf.* по~) milk; ~ся give milk. до́йка, -и milking. до́йный milch.

дойму́ *etc.: see* доня́ть

дойти́, дойду́, -дёшь; дошёл, -шла́ *pf.* (*impf.* доходи́ть) +до+*g.* reach; make an impression on, get through to, penetrate to, touch; come to, be a matter of.

док, -а dock.

доказа́тельный demonstrative, conclusive. доказа́тельство, -а proof, evidence; demonstration. доказа́ть, -ажу́ *pf.*, дока́зывать, -аю *impf.* demonstrate, prove; argue, try to show. доказу́емый demonstrable.

докати́ться, -ачу́сь, -а́тишься *pf.*, дока́тываться, -аюсь *impf.* roll; thunder, boom; +до+*g.* sink into, come to.

докла́д, -а report; lecture; paper; talk, address; announcement. докла́дчик, -а speaker, lecturer; rapporteur. докла́дывать(ся, -аю(сь *impf. of* доложи́ть(ся

до́красна́ *adv.* to red heat, to redness; red-hot, red.

до́ктор, -а; *pl.* -а́ doctor. доктора́льный didactic. доктора́нт, -а person working for doctorate. до́кторский doctor's; doctoral. до́кторша, -и woman doctor; doctor's wife.

доктри́на, -ы doctrine. доктринёр, -а doctrinaire. доктринёрский doctrinaire.

докуме́нт, -а document, paper; deed, instrument. документа́льный documentary. документа́ция, -и documentation; documents, papers.

долби́ть, -блю́ *impf.* hollow; chisel, gouge; repeat, say over and over again; swot up; learn by rote.

долг, -а (-у), *loc.* -у́; *pl.* -и́ duty; debt; в ~ on credit; в ~у́ indebted; взять в ~ borrow; дать в ~ lend.

до́лгий; до́лог, -лга́, -о long. до́лго *adv.* long, (for) a long time. долгове́чный lasting; durable.

долголе́тие, -я longevity. долголе́тний of many years; long-standing.

долгота́, -ы́; *pl.* -ы length; longitude.

долево́й lengthwise. до́лее *adv.* longer.

должа́ть, -а́ю *impf.* (*pf.* за~) borrow.

до́лжен, -жна́ *pred.*+*d.* in debt to; +*inf.* obliged, bound; likely; must, have to, ought to; он ~ мне три рубля́ he owes me three roubles; он ~ идти́ he must go; он ~ был отказа́ться he had to refuse; он ~ ско́ро прийти́ he should be here soon; должно́ быть probably. должни́к, -а́, -ница, -ы debtor. должностн|о́й official; ~о́е лицо́ official, functionary, public servant. до́лжность, -и; *g.pl.* -е́й post, appointment, office; duties. до́лжный due, fitting, proper.

доли́на, -ы valley.

до́ллар, -а dollar.

доложи́ть[1], -ожу́, -о́жишь *pf.* (*impf.* докла́дывать) add.

доложи́ть[2], -ожу́, -о́жишь *pf.* (*impf.* докла́дывать) +*a. or* о+*p.* report; give a report on; announce; ~ся announce one's arrival.

доло́й *adv.* away, off; +*a.* down with!; с глаз ~, из се́рдца вон out of sight, out of mind; с глаз мои́х ~! get out of my sight!

долото́, -а́; *pl.* -а chisel.

до́лька, -и segment, section; clove.

до́льше *adv.* longer.

до́ля, -и; *g.pl.* -е́й part, portion; share; quota, allotment; lobe; lot, fate.

дом, -а (-у), *loc.* -у́; *pl.* -а́ building, house; home; household; lineage; family; на ~у́ at home. до́ма *adv.* at home; in(doors). дома́шн|ий house; home; domestic; home-made, homespun, home-brewed; tame; ~яя рабо́та homework; housework; ~яя хозя́йка housewife; ~ие *sb., pl.* family, people.

до́менн|ый blast-furnace, ironmaking; ~ая печь blast-furnace.

домини́ровать, -рует *impf.* dominate, predominate; +над+*i.* dominate, command.

домкра́т, -а jack.

до́мна, -ы blast-furnace.

домовладе́лец, -льца, -лица, -ы house-owner; landlord. **домово́дство, -а** household management; domestic science. **домо́в|ый** house; household; housing; ~**ая кни́га** house-register, register of tenants; ~**ая конто́ра** house-manager's office; ~**ый трест** housing trust.

домога́тельство, -а solicitation, importunity; demand, bid. **домога́ться, -а́юсь** *impf.*+*g.* seek, solicit, covet, bid for.

домо́й *adv.* home, homewards. **домострое́ние, -я** housebuilding. **домострои́тельный** housebuilding. **домоуправле́ние, -я** house management (committee). **домохозя́йка, -и** housewife. **домрабо́тница, -ы** domestic servant, daily (maid).

дона́шиваться, -вается *impf. of* **доноси́ться²**

доне́льзя *adv.* in the extreme; to the utmost degree; **он ~ упря́м** he's as stubborn as a mule, he couldn't be more pigheaded.

донесе́ние, -я dispatch, report, message. **донести́, -су́, -сёшь; -нёс, -сла́** *pf.* (*impf.* **доноси́ть**) report, announce; +*d.* inform; +**на**+*a.* inform against, denounce; ~**сь** be heard; +**до**+*g.* reach, reach the ears of; carry as far as.

до́низу *adv.* to the bottom; **све́рху ~** from top to bottom.

донима́ть, -а́ю *impf. of* **доня́ть**

до́нный bottom, base; **~ лёд** ground ice.

до́нор, -а blood-donor.

доно́с, -а a denunciation, information. **доноси́ть(ся¹, -ношу́(сь, -но́сишь(ся** *impf. of* **донести́(сь**

доноси́ться², -но́сится *pf.* (*impf.* **дона́шиваться**) wear out, be worn out.

доно́счик, -а informer.

донско́й Don; **~ каза́к** Don Cossack.

до́нья *etc.: see* **дно**

до н.э. *abbr.* **до на́шей э́ры** B.C.

доня́ть, дойму́, -мёшь; до́нял, -а́, -о *pf.* (*impf.* **донима́ть**) weary to death, pester.

допла́та, -ы additional payment, extra charge, excess. **доплати́ть, -ачу́, -а́тишь** *pf.*, **допла́чивать, -аю** *impf.* pay in addition; pay the rest.

доплыва́ть, -а́ю *impf.*, **доплы́ть, -ыву́, -ывёшь; -ы́л, -а́, -о** *pf.* **до**+*g.* swim to, sail to; reach.

допо́длинно *adv.* for certain. **допо́длинный** authentic, genuine.

дополне́ние, -я supplement, addition; appendix; addendum; object. **дополни́тельно** *adv.* in addition. **дополни́тельн|ый** supplementary, additional, extra; complementary; ~**ые вы́боры** by-election. **допо́лнить, -ню** *pf.*, **дополня́ть, -я́ю** *impf.* supplement, add to, amplify; complete; complement.

допото́пный antediluvian.

допра́шивать, -аю *impf.*, **допроси́ть, -ошу́,** **-о́сишь** *pf.* interrogate, question, examine.

допро́с, -а interrogation, examination.

до́пуск, -а right of entry, admittance; tolerance. **допуска́ть, -а́ю** *impf.*, **допусти́ть,** **-ущу́, -у́стишь** *pf.* admit; allow, permit; tolerate; grant, assume, suppose. **допусти́мый** permissable, admissible, allowable, acceptable. **допуще́ние, -я** assumption.

доро́га, -и road; highway; way; journey; route; **в доро́ге** on the journey, on the way, en route; **по доро́ге** on the way; the same way; **туда́ ему́ и ~!** serves him right!

до́рого *adv.* dear, dearly. **дорогови́зна, -ы** expensiveness; high cost, high prices. **дорого́й; до́рог, -а́, -о** dear; expensive; costly.

доро́дный portly, corpulent, stout; healthy, strong.

дородово́й antenatal.

дорожа́ть, -а́ет *impf.* (*pf.* **вз~, по~**) rise in price, go up. **доро́же** *comp. of* **до́рого, дорого́й. дорожи́ть, -жу́** *impf.*+*i.* value; prize; care about.

доро́жка, -и path, walk; track; lane; runway; strip, runner, stair-carpet. **доро́жный** road; highway; travelling.

доса́да, -ы annoyance; disappointment; nuisance, pity. **досади́ть, -ажу́** *pf.*, **досажда́ть, -а́ю** *impf.*+*d.* annoy. **доса́дливый** annoyed, irritated, disappointed; of annoyance. **доса́дный** annoying; disappointing. **доса́довать, -дую** be annoyed (**на**+*a.* with).

досе́ле *adv.* up to now.

доска́, -и́, *a.* до́ску; *pl.* -и, -со́к, -ска́м board; plank; slab; plaque, plate.

досло́вный literal, verbatim; word-for-word.

досмо́тр, -а inspection, examination. **досмо́трщик, -а** inspector, examiner.

доспе́хи, -ов *pl.* armour.

досро́чный ahead of time, ahead of schedule, early.

достава́ть(ся, -таю́(сь, -ёшь(ся *impf. of* **доста́ть(ся**

доста́вить, -влю *pf.*, **доставля́ть, -я́ю** *impf.* deliver, convey; supply, furnish; cause, give. **доста́вка, -и** delivery; conveyance. **доста́вщик, -а** roundsman, delivery man.

доста́ну *etc.: see* **доста́ть**

доста́ток, -тка sufficiency; prosperity; *pl.* income. **доста́точно** *adv.* enough, sufficiently. **доста́точный** sufficient; adequate; prosperous, well-off.

доста́ть, -а́ну *pf.* (*impf.* **достава́ть**) fetch; get (out), take (out); obtain; +*g. or* **до**+*g.* touch; reach; *impers.* suffice, be sufficient; ~**ся**+*d.* pass to, be inherited by; fall to the lot of; **ему́ доста́нется** he'll catch it.

достига́ть, -а́ю *impf.*, **дости́гнуть, дости́чь, -и́гну; -сти́г** *pf.*+*g.* attain, achieve; +*g. or* **до**+*g.* reach. **достиже́ние, -я** achievement, attainment. **достижи́мый** accessible; attainable.

досто́... *in comb.* worthy (of). **достове́рный** reliable, trustworthy; authentic. **~па́мятный**

memorable. ~примеча́тельность, -и notable place or object; *pl.* sights; осма́тривать ~примеча́тельности go sightseeing. ~примеча́тельный noteworthy, remarkable, notable.

досто́инство, -а dignity; merit, virtue; value; rank, title. досто́йно *adv.* suitably, fittingly, adequately, properly; with dignity. досто́йный deserved; fitting, adequate; suitable, fit; worthy; +*g.* worthy of, deserving.

достоя́ние, -я property.

до́ступ, -а access; entrance; admission, admittance. досту́пный accessible; simple; easily understood; intelligible; approachable; moderate, reasonable; ~ для open to; available to.

досу́г, -а leisure, (spare) time. досу́жий leisure, spare; idle.

до́суха *adv.* dry.

досяга́емый attainable, accessible.

дота́ция, -и grant, subsidy.

дотла́ utterly, completely, out; to the ground.

дото́шный meticulous.

дотра́гиваться, -аюсь *impf.*, дотро́нуться, -нусь *pf.* +до+*g.* touch.

дотя́гивать, -аю *impf.*, дотяну́ть, -яну́, -я́нешь *pf.* draw out; stretch out; hold out; live, last; put off; +до+*g.* draw, drag, haul as far as; reach, make; ~ся stretch, reach; drag on; +до+*g.* reach, touch.

до́хлый dead; sickly, puny. до́хнуть, -нет; дох (*pf.* из~, по~, с~) die; croak, kick the bucket.

дохну́ть, -ну́, -нёшь *pf.* draw a breath.

дохо́д, -а income; receipts; revenue. доходи́ть, -ожу́, -о́дишь *impf. of* дойти. дохо́дность, -и profitability; income. дохо́дный profitable, lucrative, paying; income-producing, revenue-producing. дохо́дчивый intelligible, easy to understand.

до́чери *etc.: see* дочь

до́чиста *adv.* clean; completely.

до́чка, -и *pl.* daughter. дочь, -чери, *i.* -черью; *pl.* -чери, -чере́й, *i.* -черьми́ daughter.

дошёл *etc.: see* дойти

дошко́льник, -а, -ница, -ы preschooler. дошко́льный pre-school; nusery.

доща́тый plank, board, wooden. доще́чка, -и small plank, small board; door-plate, name-plate.

доя́рка, -и milkmaid.

др.: и ~ *abbr.* (*of* други́е) & co.; *et al.*

д-р *abbr.* (*of* до́ктор) Dr, Doctor; (*of* дире́ктор) Director.

драгоце́нность, -и jewel; gem; precious stone; treasure; *pl.* jewellery; valuables. драгоце́нный precious.

дразни́ть, -ню́, -нишь *impf.* tease.

дра́ка, -и fight; доходи́ть до дра́ки come to blows.

драко́н, -а dragon; wyvern.

дра́ма, -ы drama; tragedy, calamity. драмати́зм, -а dramatic effect; dramatic charac-

ter, dramatic quality; tension. драмати́ческий dramatic; drama, theatre, of the theatre; theatrical; tense. драмату́рг, -а playwright, dramatist. драматурги́я, -и dramatic art; dramatic composition, play-writing; drama, plays.

драп, -а heavy woollen cloth.

драпиро́вка, -и draping; curtain; hangings. драпиро́вщик, -а upholsterer. драпри́ *indecl. pl.* curtain(s), hangings.

дра́повый cloth.

драть, деру́, -рёшь; драл, -á, -о *impf.* (*pf.* вы́~, за~, со~) tear, tear up; sting, irritate; run away, make off; tear off; kill; beat, flog, thrash; tear out; +с+*g.* fleece; sting; ~ го́рло bawl; ~ у́ши +*d.* jar on; чёрт его́ (по)дери́! damn him! ~ся fight; use one's fists; struggle.

дре́безги *pl.*; в ~ to smithereens. дребезжа́ние, -я rattle, clink, jingle, tinkle. дребезжа́ть, -жи́т *impf.* rattle, jingle, tinkle, clink.

древеси́на, -ы wood; wood-pulp; timber. древе́сн|ый wood; ~ая ма́сса wood-pulp; ~ый пито́мник arboretum; ~ый у́голь charcoal.

дре́вко, -а; *pl.* -и, -ов pole, (flag-)staff; shaft.

древнееврейский Hebrew. древнеру́сский Old Russian. дре́вний ancient; very old, aged. дре́вность, -и antiquity.

дрезина, -ы trolley.

дрейф, -а drift; leeway. дрейфова́ть, -фу́ет *impf.* drift. дрейфу́ющий drifting; ~ лёд drift-ice.

дрема́, -ы, дрёма, -ы drowsiness, sleepiness. дрема́ть, -млю́, -млешь *impf.* doze; slumber; drowse; не ~ be wakeful; be wide awake, on the alert. дремо́та, -ы drowsiness, somnolence.

дрему́чий thick, dense.

дрессиро́ванный trained; performing. дрессирова́ть, -ру́ю *impf.* (*pf.* вы́~) train, school. дрессиро́вка, -и training. дрессиро́вщик, -а trainer.

дроби́льный crushing, grinding. дроби́на, -ы pellet. дроби́ть, -блю́ *impf.* (*pf.* раз~) break up, smash; crush, grind; divide, split up; ~ся break to pieces, smash; crumble; divide, split up. дроблёный splintered, crushed, ground, fragmented. дро́бный separate; subdivided, split up; minute; staccato, abrupt; fractional; ~ дождь fine rain. дробови́к, -á shot-gun. дробь, -и (small) shot, pellets; drumming; tapping; trilling; fraction.

дрова́, дров *pl.* firewood. дро́вни, дро́вней *pl.* wood-sledge.

дро́ги, дрог *pl.* dray; hearse.

дро́гнуть, -ну *pf.*, дрожа́ть, -жу́ *impf.* shake, move; tremble; shiver; quiver, quaver; flicker; waver, falter; +над+*i.* be concerned over, worry about; grudge.

дрожжево́й yeast. дро́жжи, -е́й *pl.* yeast.

дро́жки, -жек *pl.* droshky.

дрожь, -и shivering, trembling; tremor, quaver.

дрозд, -а́ thrush.

дро́ссель, -я *m.* throttle, choke.

дро́тик, -а javelin, dart.

друг[1], -а; *pl.* -узья́, -зе́й friend. **друг**[2]; ~ дру́га (дру́гу) each other, one another; ~ за ~ом one after another; in single file. **друго́й** other, another; different; second; **на** ~ **день** (the) next day. **дру́жба**, -ы friendship. **дружелю́бный, дру́жеский, дру́жественный** friendly. **дружи́ть**, -жу́, -у́жишь *impf.* be friends, be on friendly terms; ~ся (*pf.* по~ся) make friends. **дру́жно** *adv.* harmoniously, in concord; simultaneously, in concert; rapidly, smoothly. **дру́жный**; -жен, -жна́, -о amicable; harmonious; simultaneous, concerted.

друммо́ндов свет limelight.

дря́блый; дрябл, -а́, -о flabby; flaccid; sluggish.

дря́зги, -зг *pl.* squabbles; petty annoyances.

дрянно́й worthless, rotten; good-for-nothing. **дрянь**, -и trash, rubbish.

дряхле́ть, -е́ю *impf.* (*pf.* о~) become decrepit. **дря́хлый**; -хл, -ла́, -о decrepit, senile.

дуб, -а; *pl.* -ы́ oak; blockhead. **дуби́льный** tanning, tannic. **дуби́льня**, -и; *g.pl.* -лен tannery. **дуби́на**, -ы club, cudgel; blockhead. **дуби́нка**, -и truncheon, baton. **дуби́ть**, -блю́ *impf.* (*pf.* вы́~) tan.

дублёр, -а understudy; actor dubbing a part. **дубле́т**, -а, **дублика́т**, -а duplicate. **дубли́ровать**, -рую duplicate; understudy; dub. **дубова́тый** coarse; stupid; thick. **дубо́вый** oak; coarse; clumsy; thick.

Дувр, -а Dover.

дуга́, -и́; *pl.* -и shaft-bow; arc; arch.

ду́дка, -и pipe, fife. **ду́жка**, -и small arch or bow; handle; (croquet-)hoop; wishbone.

ду́ло, -а muzzle; barrel. **ду́льце**, -а; *g.pl.* -лец mouthpiece.

ду́ма, -ы thought; Duma; council. **ду́мать**, -аю *impf.* (*pf.* по~) think; +*inf.* think of, intend.

Дуна́й, -я the Danube.

дунове́ние, -я puff, breath. **ду́нуть**, -ну *pf.* *of* дуть

дупли́стый hollow. **дупло́**, -а́; *pl.* -а, -пел hollow; hole; cavity.

ду́ра, -ы, **дура́к**, -а́ fool. **дура́чить**, -чу *impf.* (*pf.* о~) fool, dupe; ~ся play the fool. **дуре́ть**, -е́ю *impf.* (*pf.* о~) grow stupid. **дурма́н**, -а datura; drug, narcotic; intoxicant. **дурма́нить**, -ню *impf.* (*pf.* о~) stupefy. **дурно́й**; -рен, -рна́, -о bad; evil; nasty; ill, faint; ugly; **мне ду́рно** I'm going to faint. **дурнота́**, -ы́ faintness; nausea.

ду́тый blown, blown up, hollow; inflated; pneumatic; exaggerated. **дуть**, ду́ю *impf.* (*pf.* вы́~, по~, ду́нуть) blow; **ду́ет** there is a draught. **дутьё**, -я́ blowing; draught; blast; glass-blowing. **ду́ться, ду́юсь** *impf.* pout; sulk, be sulky.

дух, -а (-у) spirit; spirits; heart; mind; breath; air; ghost; smell; **в** ~е in high spirits, in a good mood; **во весь** ~ at full speed, flat out; **не в моём** ~е not to my taste; **ни слу́ху ни** ~у no news, not a word, not a whisper; **одни́м** ~**ом** in one breath; at one go, at a stretch; **па́дать** ~**ом** lose heart, grow despondent. **духи́**, -о́в *pl.* scent, perfume. **Ду́хов день** Whit Monday. **духове́нство**, -а clergy, priesthood. **духови́дец**, -дца clairvoyant; medium. **духо́вка**, -и oven. **духо́вный** spiritual; inner, inward; ecclesiastical, church, religious. **духово́й** wind; air; steam; steamed. **духота́**, -ы́ stuffiness, closeness; stuffy heat.

душ, -а shower.

душа́, -и́, *a.* -у; *pl.* -и soul; heart; feeling; spirit; moving spirit; inspiration; **в глубине́ души́** in one's heart of hearts; **в душе́** inwardly, secretly; at heart; **за душо́й** to one's name; **на ду́шу** per head; **от всей души́** with all one's heart.

душева́я *sb.* shower-room.

душевнобольно́й mentally ill, insane; *sb.* mental patient; lunatic. **душе́вный** mental; of the mind; sincere, cordial, heartfelt.

души́стый fragrant; sweet-scented; ~ **горо́шек** sweet pea(s). **души́ть**[1], -шу́, -шишь *impf.* (*pf.* на~) scent, perfume; ~ся use scent, put on scent.

души́ть[2], -шу́, -шишь *impf.* (*pf.* за~) strangle; stifle, smother, suffocate; suppress; choke.

ду́шный; -шен, -шна́, -о stuffy, close; sultry; stifling, suffocating.

дуэли́ст, -а duellist. **дуэ́ль**, -и duel.

ды́бом *adv.* on end; **у меня́ во́лосы вста́ли** ~ my hair stood on end. **дыбы́: станови́ться на** ~ rear; resist, jib, dig one's heels in.

дым, -а (-у), *loc.* -у́; *pl.* -ы́ smoke. **дыми́ть**, -млю́ *impf.* (*pf.* на~) smoke; ~ся smoke, steam; billow. **ды́мка**, -и haze, mist. **ды́мный** smoky. **дымово́й** smoke; ~я **труба́** flue, chimney; smoke-stack, funnel. **дымо́к**, -мка́ puff of smoke. **дымохо́д**, -а flue. **ды́мчатый** smoky; smoked; smoke-coloured.

ды́ня, -и melon.

дыра́, -ы́; *pl.* -ы, **ды́рка**, -и; *g.pl.* -рок hole; gap. **дыря́вый** full of holes; holed, perforated.

дыха́ние, -я breathing, respiration; breath. **дыха́тельн|ый** respiratory; breathing, breather; ~ое **го́рло** windpipe. **дыша́ть**, -шу́, -шишь *impf.* breathe.

дья́вол, -а devil. **дья́вольский** devilish, diabolical; damnable.

дья́кон, -а; *pl.* -а́ deacon. **дьячо́к**, -чка́ sacristan, sexton; reader.

дю́жина, -ы dozen. **дю́жинный** ordinary, commonplace.

дэ *nt.indecl.* the letter **д.**

дюйм, -а inch.

дя́денька, -и *m.*, **дя́дюшка, -и** *m.* uncle. **дя́дя, -и**; *g.pl.* **-ей** uncle.

дя́тел, -тла woodpecker.

е *nt.indecl.* the letter **е.**

ев... *pref.* eu-. **евге́ника, -и** eugenics. **éвнух, -а** eunuch. **евразийский** Eurasian. **евста́хиев** Eustachian.

ева́нгелие, -я gospel; the Gospels. **евангели́ческий** evangelical. **ева́нгельский** gospel.

евре́й, -я Jew; Hebrew; **ве́рующий ~** Orthodox Jew. **евре́йка, -и** Jewess. **евре́йский** Jewish.

Евро́па, -ы Europe. **Европарла́мент, -а** Europarliament. **европе́ец, -е́йца, европе́йка, -е́йки** European. **европе́йский** European; Western.

ЕВС *abbr.* (*of* **Европе́йская валю́тная систе́ма**) EMS, European Monetary System. **Еги́пет, -а** Egypt. **еги́петский** Egyptian. **египтя́нин, -а**; *pl.* **-я́не, -я́н, египтя́нка, -и** Egyptian.

его́ *see* **он, оно́**; *pron.* his; its, of it.

еда́, -ы́ food; meal; eating.

едва́ *adv.* & *conj.* hardly, barely; only just; scarcely; **~...**, **как** no sooner ... than; **~ ли** hardly, scarcely; **~ (ли) не** nearly, almost, all but.

еди́м *etc.: see* **есть**[1]

едине́ние, -я unity. **едини́ца, -ы** one; figure one; unity; unit; individual. **едини́чность, -и** singleness; single occurrence. **едини́чный** single, unitary; solitary; isolated; individual.

едино... *in comb.* mono-, uni-; one; co-. **единобо́жие, -я** monotheism. **~бо́рство, -а** single combat. **~бра́чие, -я** monogamy. **~бра́чный** monogamous. **~вла́стие, -я** autocracy, absolute rule. **~вла́стный** autocratic; dictatorial; absolute. **~вре́менно** *adv.* only once; simultaneously. **~вре́менный** extraordinary; unique; +*d. or* c+*i.* simultaneous with. **~гла́сие, -я, ~ду́шие, -я** unanimity. **~гла́сный, ~ду́шный** unanimous. **~кро́вный** consanguineous; **~кровный брат** half-brother. **~мы́слие, -я** like-mindedness; agreement in opinion. **~мы́шленник, -а** like-minded person; accomplice; **мы с ним ~мы́шленники** we are in agreement, we think the same way. **~нача́лие, -я** unified management command. **~обра́зие, -я** uni-

formity. **~обра́зный** uniform. **~ро́г, -а** unicorn; narwhal. **~утро́бный** uterine; **~утро́бный брат** half-brother.

еди́нственно *adv.* only, solely. **еди́нственный** only, sole; singular; unique, unequalled. **еди́нство, -а** unity. **еди́ный** one; single, sole; united, unified; common.

éдкий; éдок, едка́, -о caustic, corrosive; acrid, pungent; sarcastic; **~ натр** caustic soda.

едо́к, -а́ mouth, head; eater.

éду *etc.: see* **éхать. éдче** *comp. of* **éдкий**

её *see* **она́**; *pron.* her, hers; its.

ёж, ежа́ hedgehog.

еже... *in comb.* every; -ly. **ежего́дник, -а** annual, year-book. **~го́дный** annual, yearly. **~дне́вный** daily; everyday; quotidian. **~кварта́льный** quarterly. **~ме́сячник, -а, ~ме́сячный** monthly. **~неде́льник, -а, ~неде́льный** weekly. **~но́щный** nightly.

ежеви́ка, -и blackberries; blackberry bush, bramble. **ежеви́чный** blackberry.

ёжиться, ёжусь *impf.* (*pf.* **съ~**) huddle up; shrivel; shrink away; hesitate.

езда́, -ы́ ride, riding; drive, driving; going; journey; traffic. **éздить, éзжу** *impf.* go; ride, drive; slip; **~ верхо́м** ride. **ездо́к, -а́** rider; horseman. ·

ей *see* **она́**

ей-бо́гу *int.* really! I swear (to God).

ел *etc.: see* **есть**[1]

éле *adv.* hardly, barely, scarcely; only just.

ёлка, -и fir, fir-tree, spruce; Christmas tree; Christmas party; herring-bone pattern. **ело́вый** fir, spruce; deal, white-wood. **ёлочка, -и** herring-bone pattern, herring-boning. **ёлочный** Christmas-tree; herring-bone; dendritic. **ель, -и** fir, fir-tree; spruce; deal, white wood. **éльник, -а** fir (spruce) plantation; fir-wood, fir-twigs.

ем *etc.: see* **есть**[1]

ёмкий capacious. **ёмкость, -и** capacity, cubic content; capacitance.

ему́ *see* **он, оно́**

ено́т, -а, ено́товый raccoon.

епи́скоп, -а bishop. **епи́скопский** episcopal.

éресь, -и heresy. **ерети́к, -а́** heretic. **ерети́ческий** heretical.

ёрзать, -аю *impf.* fidget.

еро́шить, -шу *impf.* (*pf.* **взъ~**) ruffle, rumple, tousle; dishevel; **~ся** bristle, stand on end, stick up.

ерунда́, -ы́ nonsense, rubbish; trifle, trifling matter.

éсли if; **~ бы** if only; **~ бы не** but for, if it were not for; **~ не** unless; **~ то́лько** provided; if only; **что, ~ бы** what about, how about.

ест *see* **есть**[1]

есте́ственно *adv.* naturally. **есте́ственный** natural. **естество́, -а́** nature; essence. **естествове́дение, -я, естествозна́ние, -я** (natural) science; natural history; nature study.

есть[1], **ем, ешь, ест, еди́м; ел** *impf.* (*pf.* **съ~**) eat; corrode, eat away; sting, make smart; torment, nag (at).

есть[2] *see* **быть**; is, are; there is, there are; **и ~** yes, indeed; **как ~** entirely, completely; *int.* yes, sir; very good, sir; aye, aye sir.

ефре́йтор, -а lance-corporal.

е́хать, е́ду *impf.* (*pf.* **по~**) go; ride, drive; travel, journey, voyage; **~ верхо́м** ride.

ехи́дный malicious, spiteful; venomous.

ешь *see* **есть**[1]

ещё *adv.* still; yet; (some) more; any more; yet, further; again; +*comp.* still, yet even; **всё ~** still; **~ бы!** of course! oh yes! can you ask?; **~ не, нет ~** not yet; **~ раз** once more, again; encore!; **пока́ ~** for the present, for the time being.

ЕЭС *abbr.* (*of* **Европе́йское экономи́ческое соо́бщество**) EEC, European Economic Community.

е́ю *see* **она́**

Ж

ж *letter*: *see* **жэ**

ж *conj.*: *see* **же**

жа́ба, -ы toad; quinsy.

жа́бра, -ы; *g.pl.* **-бр** gill, branchia.

жа́воронок, -нка lark.

жа́дничать, -аю *impf.* be greedy; be mean. **жа́дность, -и** greed; greediness; avidity; avarice, meanness. **жа́дный; -ден, -дна́, -о** greedy; avid; avaricious, mean.

жа́жда, -ы thirst; +*g.* thirst for, craving for. **жа́ждать, -ду** *impf.* thirst, long, yearn.

жаке́т, -а, жаке́тка, -и jacket.

жале́ть, -е́ю *impf.* (*pf.* **по~**) pity, feel sorry for; regret, be sorry; +*a. or g.* spare; grudge.

жа́лить, -лю *impf.* (*pf.* **у~**) sting, bite.

жа́лкий; -лок, -лка́, -о pitiful, pitiable, pathetic, wretched. **жа́лко** *pred.*: *see* **жаль**

жа́ло, -а a sting.

жа́лоба, -ы complaint. **жа́лобный** plaintive; doleful; mournful.

жа́лованн|ый granted, conferred; **~ая гра́мота** charter, letters patent. **жа́лованье, -я** salary, pay, wage(s); reward; donation. **жа́ловать, -лую** *impf.* (*pf.* **по~**) +*a. or d.* of person, *i. or a.* of thing, grant, bestow on, confer on; +**к**+*d.* come to see, visit; **~ся** complain (**на**+*a.* of, about).

жа́лостливый compassionate; sympathetic; pitiful. **жа́лостный** piteous; compassionate, sympathetic. **жа́лость, -и** pity, compassion. **жаль, жа́лко** *pred., impers.* (it is) a pity, a shame; +*d.* it grieves; +*d. & g.* regret; feel sorry for; +*g.* grudge; **ей ~ бы́ло себя́** she felt sorry for herself; **~, что вас там не́ было** it is a pity you were not there; **как ~ what** a pity; **мне ~ его́** I'm sorry for him.

жанр, -а genre; genre-painting. **жанри́ст, -а** genre-painter.

жар, -а (-у), *loc.* **-у́** heat; heat of the day; hot place; embers; fever; (high) temperature; ardour. **жара́, -ы́** heat; hot weather.

жарго́н, -а jargon; slang, cant.

жа́рен|ый roast grilled; fried; **~ый карто́фель** chips; **~ое** *sb.* roast (meat). **жа́рить, -рю** *impf.* (*pf.* **за~, из~**) roast; grill; fry; scorch, burn; **~ся** roast, fry; **~ся на со́лнце** sunbathe. **жа́рк|ий; -рок, -рка́, -о** hot; torrid; tropical; heated; ardent; passionate; **-о́е** *sb.* roast (meat). **жаро́вня, -и**; *g.pl.* **-вен** brazier. **жаропро́чный** ovenproof. **жар-пти́ца, -ы.** Firebird. **жа́рче** *comp. of* **жа́ркий**

жа́тва, -ы harvest. **жа́твенн|ый** harvest; reaping; **~ая маши́на** harvester, reaper. **жа́тка, -и** harvester, reaper. **жать**[1], **жну, жнёшь** *impf.* (*pf.* **с~**) reap, cut.

жать[2], **жму, жмёшь** *impf.* press, squeeze; pinch, be tight; oppress.

жва́чка, -и chewing, rumination; cud; chewing-gum. **жва́чн|ый** ruminant; **~ое** *sb.* ruminant.

жгу *etc.*: *see* **жечь**

жгут, -а́ plait; braid; tourniquet.

жгу́чий burning, smarting; scalding, baking; hot; caustic, corrosive. **жёг** *etc.*: *see* **жечь**

ж.д. *abbr.* (*of* **желе́зная доро́га**) railway.

ждать, жду, ждёшь; -ал, -а́, -о *impf.*+*g.* wait for, await; expect.

же, ж *conj.* but; and; however; also; *part.* giving emphasis or expressing identity; **мне же ка́жется** it seems to me, however; **на пе́рвом же шагу́** at the very first step; **оди́н и тот же** one and the same; **он же ваш брат** he's your brother, after all; **сего́дня же** this very day; **так же** in the same way; **тако́й же, тот же** the same, idem; **там же** in the same place, ibid.; **что же ты де́лаешь?** what on earth are you doing?

жева́тельн|ый chewing; **~ая рези́нка** chewing-gum. **жева́ть, жую́, жуёшь** *impf.* chew; masticate; ruminate.

жезл, -а́ rod; staff; baton; crozier.

жела́ние, -я wish, desire. **жела́нный** wished-for, longed-for; desired; beloved. **жела́тельный** desirable; advisable, preferable; optative. **жела́ть, -а́ю** *impf.* (*pf.* **по~**) +*g.* wish for, desire; want; +**что́бы** *or inf.* wish, want. **жела́ющие** *sb.*, *pl.* those who wish.

желе́ *nt.indecl.* jelly.

железа́, -ы́; *pl.* **же́лезы, -лёз, -за́м** gland; *pl.* tonsils. **желе́зистый**[1] glandular.

желе́зистый[2] iron; ferrous; ferriferous; chalybeate. **железнодоро́жник, -а** railwayman. **железнодоро́жн|ый** railway; **~ая ве́тка** branch line; **~ое полотно́** permanent way; ~ый у́зел junction. **желе́зн|ый** iron; ferric; reliable, dependable; ~ая доро́га railway; ~ый лом scrap iron. **желе́зо, -а** iron.

железо... in comb. iron, ferro-, ferri-, ferric. **железобето́н, -а** reinforced concrete, ferro-concrete. ~бето́нный reinforced-concrete. ~пла́вильный iron foundry. ~прока́тный steel-rolling; ~прока́тный заво́д rolling mill. ~ру́дный iron-ore.

же́лоб, -а; pl. **-а́** gutter; trough; chute; channel; groove. **желобо́к, -бка́** groove, channel, flute; slot; furrow.

желте́ть, -е́ю impf. (pf. **по~**) turn yellow; show yellow. **желтова́тый** yellowish; sallow. **желто́к, -тка́** yolk. **желту́ха, -и** jaundice. **желту́шный** jaundiced. **жёлт|ый;** жёлт, -а́, жёлто́ yellow; ~ая медь brass.

желу́док, -дка stomach. **желу́дочный** stomach; gastric.

жёлудь, -я; g.pl. **-е́й** m. acorn.

жёлчный bilious; bile, gall; peevish, irritable. **жёлчь, -и** bile, gall.

жема́ниться, -нюсь impf. mince, be affected, put on airs. **жема́нный** mincing, affected.

же́мчуг, -а; pl. **-а́** pearl, pearls. **жемчу́жина, -ы** pearl. **жемчу́жный** pearl; pearly.

жена́, -ы́; pl. **жёны** wife. **жена́тик, -а** married man; pl. married couple. **жена́тый** married.

Жене́ва, -ы Geneva.

жени́ть, -ню́, -нишь impf. & pf. (pf. also **по~**) marry. **жени́тьба, -ы** marriage, wedding. **жени́ться, -ню́сь, -нишься** impf. & pf. (+на+p.) marry, get married (to). **жени́х, -а́** fiancé; bridegroom. **же́нский** woman's; feminine; female. **же́нственный** womanly, feminine. **же́нщина, -ы** woman.

жердь, -и; g.pl. **-е́й** pole; stake.

жеребёнок, -нка; pl. **-бя́та, -бя́т** foal. **жеребе́ц, -бца́** stallion.

жеребьёвка, -и casting of lots.

жерло́, -а́; pl. **-а** a muzzle; vent, pipe, crater. **жёрнов, -а;** pl. **-а, -о́в** millstone.

же́ртва, -ы sacrifice; victim; пасть же́ртвой+g. fall victim to; принести́ в же́ртву sacrifice. **же́ртвенный** sacrificial. **же́ртвовать, -твую** impf. (pf. **по~**) present, donate, make a donation (of); +i. sacrifice, give up.

жест, -а gesture.

жёсткий; -ток, -тка́, -о hard, tough; rigid, strict.

жесто́кий; -то́к, -а́, -о cruel; brutal; severe, sharp. **жестокосе́рдный, -се́рдый** hard-hearted. **жесто́кость, -и** crulty, brutality.

жёстче comp. of **жёсткий**

жесть, -и tin(-plate). **жестя́нка, -и** tin, can; piece of tin. **жестя́н|ой** tin; ~ая посу́да tinware.

жето́н, -а medal; counter; token; проездно́й ~ travel token.

жечь, жгу, жжёшь; жёг, жгла impf. (pf. **с~**) burn; ~ся burn, sting; burn o.s. **жжёный**

burnt; scorched; ~ ко́фе roasted coffee.

живи́тельный invigorating, revivifying; bracing. **жи́во** adv. vividly; with animation; keenly; strikingly; quickly; promptly. **жив|о́й;** жив, -а́, -о living, live, alive; lively; keen; brisk; animated; vivacious; poignant; bright, sparkling; ~а́я и́згородь (quickset) hedge; ~о́й инвента́рь livestock; на ~ую ни́тку hastily, anyhow; шить на ~ую ни́тку tack; оста́ться в ~ых survive, escape with one's life. **живопи́сец, -сца** painter. **живопи́сн|ый** pictorial; picturesque; ~ое ме́сто beauty spot. **жи́вопись, -и** painting; paintings, art. **жи́вость, -и** liveliness, vivacity, animation.

живо́т, -а abdomen, belly; stomach. **живо́тик, -а** tummy. **животново́дство, -а** stock-breeding, animal husbandry. **живо́тное** sb. animal; beast; brute; ко́мнатное ~ pet. **живо́тный** animal.

живу́ etc.: see **жить. живу́чий** tenacious of life; hardy; firm, stable. **живьём** adv. alive.

жи́дк|ий; -док, -дка́, -о liquid; fluid; watery; weak, thin; sparse, scanty; feeble; ~ий криста́лл liquid crystal; ~ое те́ло liquid. **жи́дкостный** liquid, fluid; liquid-fuel. **жи́дкость, -и** liquid, fluid; liquor; wateriness, weakness, thinness. **жи́жа, -и, жи́жица, -ы** sludge, slurry; slush; wash, swill; liquid, liquor. **жи́же** comp. of **жи́дкий**

жи́зненный life, of life; vital; living; close to life; lifelike; vitally important; ~ые си́лы vitality, sap; ~ый у́ровень standard of living. **жизнеописа́ние, -я** biography. **жизнера́достный** full of the joy of living; cheerful, buoyant. **жизнеспосо́бный** capable of living; viable; vigorous, flourishing. **жизнь, -и** life; existence.

жил... abbr. (of **жили́щный, жило́й**) in comb. living; housing. **жилмасси́в, -а** housing estate. ~отде́л, -а housing department. ~пло́щадь, -и floor-space; housing, accommodation. ~строи́тельство, -а house building. ~фонд, -а housing, accommodation.

жи́ла, -ы vein; tendon, sinew; lode, seam; core, strand; catgut.

жиле́т, -а, жиле́тка, -и waistcoat.

жиле́ц, -льца́, жили́ца, -ы lodger; tenant; inhabitant; он не ~ (на бе́лом све́те) he is not long for this world.

жи́листый sinewy; stringy; wiry.

жили́ца see **жиле́ц. жили́ще, -а** dwelling, abode; lodging; (living) quarters. **жили́щн|ый** housing; living; ~ые усло́вия living conditions.

жи́лка, -и vein; fibre, rib; streak; bent.

жил|о́й dwelling; residential; inhabited; habitable, fit to live in; ~о́й дом dwelling house; block of flats; ~а́я пло́щадь floor-space; housing, accommodation. **жильё, -я́** habitation; dwelling; lodging; (living) accommodation.

жим, -а press.

жир, -а (-у), *loc.* -ý; *pl.* -ы́ fat; grease. **жире́ть**, -ре́ю *impf.* (*pf.* о~, раз~) grow fat, stout, plump. **жи́рный**; -рен, -рна́, -о fatty; greasy; rich; plump; lush; bold, heavy. **жирова́ть**, -ру́ю *impf.* lubricate, oil, grease; fatten, grow fat. **жирово́й** fatty; adipose; fat.

жите́йский worldly; of life, of the world; everyday. **жи́тель**, -я *m.* inhabitant; dweller. **жи́тельство**, -а residence; ме́сто жи́тельства residence, domicile; ме́сто постоя́нного жи́тельства permanent address. **жи́тница**, -ы granary. **жи́тный** cereal. **жи́то**, -а corn, cereal. **жить**, живу́, -вёшь; жил, -á, -о *impf.* live; +i. live for, live on, live in. **житьё**, -я́ life; existence; habitation, residence.

жму *etc.: see* **жать²**

жму́риться, -рюсь *impf.* (*pf.* за~) screw up one's eyes, frown. **жму́рки**, -рок *pl.* blindman's buff.

жмых, -á, жмыхи́, -óв *pl.* oil-cake.

жне́йка, -и reaper. **жнец**, -á, жни́ца, -ы reaper. **жну** *etc.: see* **жать¹**

жоке́й, -я jockey. **жоке́йка**, -и jockey cap.

жре́бий, -я lot; fate; destiny; ~ бро́шен the die is cast.

жрец, -á priest. **жре́ческий** priestly. **жри́ца**, -ы priestess.

жужжа́ние, -я humming, buzzing; hum, buzz, drone. **жужжа́ть**, -жжу́ hum, buzz, drone; whiz(z).

жук, -á beetle.

жу́лик, -а petty thief; cheat, swindler; cardsharper. **жу́льничать**, -аю *impf.* (*pf.* с~) cheat, swindle, defraud.

жура́вль, -я́ *m.* crane.

жури́ть, -рю *impf.* reprove, take to task.

журна́л, -а magazine, periodical; journal; diary; register; log; ~ заседа́ний minute-book. **журнали́ст**, -а journalist. **журнали́стика**, -и journalism. **журнали́стский** journalistic.

журча́ние, -я ripple, babble; murmur. **журча́ть**, -чи́т *impf.* babble, ripple, murmur.

жу́ткий; -ток, -тка́, -о awe-inspiring; uncanny; terrible, terrifying. **жу́тко** *adv.* terrifyingly; terribly, awfully.

жую́ *etc.: see* **жева́ть**

жэ *nt.indecl.* the letter ж.

жюри́ *nt.indecl.* jury, judges; umpire, referee; член ~ judge.

З

з *letter: see* **зэ**

з. *abbr.* (*of* за́пад) W, West.

за *prep.* **I.** +*a.* (*indicating motion or action*) or *i.* (*indicating rest or state*) behind; beyond; across, the other side of; at; to; вы́йти за́муж за+a. marry, get married to; за́мужем за+i. married to; за́ борт, за бо́ртом overboard; за́ городом out of town; за рубежо́м abroad; сесть за роя́ль sit down at the piano; сиде́ть за роя́лем be at the piano; за́ угол, за угло́м round the corner. **II.** +*a.* after; over; during, in the space of; by; for; to; боя́ться за fear for; за ва́ше здоро́вье! your health!; вести́ за́ руку lead by the hand; далеко́ за по́лночь long after midnight; за два дня до+g. two days before; ему́ уже́ за́ сорок he is over forty already; есть за трои́х eat enough for three; за́ три киломе́тра от дере́вни three kilometres from the village; за́ ночь during the night, overnight; плати́ть за биле́т pay for a ticket; за после́днее вре́мя recently, lately, of late. **III.** +*i.* after; for; on account of, because of; at; during; год за го́дом year after year; идти́ за молоко́м go for milk; за неиме́нием+g. for want of; за обе́дом at dinner; о́чередь за ва́ми it is your turn; посла́ть за до́ктором send for a doctor; следи́ть за look after; сле́довать за follow.

за... *pref. in comb.* **I.** *with vv. forms the perfective aspect; indicates beginning of action, direction of action beyond a given point, continuation of action to excess.* **II.** *with nn. and adjs.: trans-, beyond, on the far side.*

за|але́ть, -е́ет *pf.* **за|арка́нить**, -ню *pf.*

заба́ва, -ы amusement; game; pastime; fun. **забавля́ть**, -я́ю *impf.* amuse, entertain, divert; ~ся amuse o.s. **заба́вный** amusing, funny.

забаллоти́ровать, -рую *pf.* blackball, reject, fail to elect.

забастова́ть, -ту́ю *pf.* strike; go on strike, come out on strike. **забасто́вка**, -и strike; stoppage. **забасто́вщик**, -а, -щица, -ы striker.

забве́ние, -я oblivion; unconsciousness; drowsiness. **забве́нный** forgotten.

забе́г, -а heat, race; trial **забега́ть**, -а́ю *impf.* **забежа́ть**, -егу́ *pf.* run up; run off; stray; +к+d. drop in on, look in to see; ~ вперёд run ahead; anticipate.

забеле́ть(ся, -е́ет(ся *pf.* (begin to) turn white.

за|бере́менеть, -ею *pf.* become pregnant.

заберу́ *etc.: see* **забра́ть**. **за|бетони́ровать**, -рую *pf.*

забива́ние, -я jamming. **забива́ть(ся**, -а́ю(сь *impf. of* **заби́ть(ся¹**. **заби́вка**, -и driving in; blocking up, stopping up.

за|бинтова́ть, -ту́ю *pf.*, **забинто́вывать** *impf.* bandage; ~ся bandage o.s.

забира́ть(ся, -а́ю(сь *impf. of* **забра́ть(ся**

заби́тый cowed, downtrodden. **заби́ть¹**, -бью, -бьёшь *pf.* (*impf.* **забива́ть**) drive in, hammer in, ram in; score; seal, stop up, block up; obstruct; choke; jam; cram, stuff; beat up, knock senseless; render defenceless;

beat; outdo, surpass; slaughter; ~ себе́ в го́лову get it firmly fixed in one's head; ~ся hide, take refuge; become cluttered, become clogged; +в+a. get into, penetrate. за|би́ть(ся² *pf.* begin to beat. забия́ка, -и *c.g.* quarrelsome person; squabbler; troublemaker; bully.

заблаговре́менно *adv.* in good time; well in advance. заблаговре́менный timely, done in good time.

заблагорассу́диться, -ится *pf.*, *impers.* (+d.) come into one's head; seem good (to); он придёт, когда́ ему́ заблагорассу́дится he will come when he thinks fit, feels so disposed.

заблесте́ть, -ещу́, -ести́шь *or* -е́щешь *pf.* begin to shine, glitter, glow.

заблуди́ться, -ужу́сь, -у́дишься *pf.* lose one's way, get lost. заблу́дший lost, stray. заблужда́ться, -а́юсь *impf.* be mistaken. заблужде́ние, -я error; delusion.

за|бода́ть, -а́ю *pf.*

забо́й, -я (pit-)face. забо́йщик, -а faceworker, cutter.

заболева́емость, -и sickness rate; number of cases. заболева́ние, -я sickness, illness, disease; falling ill. заболева́ть¹, -а́ю *impf.*, заболе́ть¹, -е́ю *pf.* fall ill, fall sick; be taken ill; +i. go down with. заболева́ть², -а́ет *impf.*, заболе́ть², -ли́т *pf.* (begin to) ache, (begin to) hurt; у меня́ заболе́л зуб I have tooth-ache.

забо́р¹, -а fence. забо́ристый strong; pungent; risqué, racy. забо́рный fence; coarse, indecent; risqué.

забо́р², -а taking away; obtaining on credit.

забо́ртный outboard.

забо́та, -ы concern; care, attention(s); cares, trouble(s). забо́тить, -о́чу *impf.* (*pf.* o~) trouble, worry, cause anxiety to; ~ся *impf.* (*pf.* по~) worry, be troubled; take care (o+p. of); take trouble; care. забо́тливый solicitous, thoughtful, caring.

забрако́ванный rejected; ~ това́р rejects. за|бракова́ть, -ку́ю *pf.*

забра́сывать, -аю *impf. of* заброса́ть, забро́сить

забра́ть, -беру́, -берёшь; -а́л, -а́, -о *pf.* (*impf.* забира́ть) take; take away; seize; appropriate; take in, turn off, turn aside; come over; catch; stop up, block up; ~ся climb; get to, get into; hide, go into hiding.

забреда́ть, -а́ю *impf.*, забрести́, -еду́, -едёшь; -ёл, -а́ *pf.* stray, wander; drop in.

за|брони́ровать¹, -рую *pf.* за|брони́ровать², -рую *pf.*

заброса́ть, -а́ю *pf.* (*impf.* забра́сывать) fill up; shower, bespatter, deluge. забро́сить, -о́шу *pf.* (*impf.* забра́сывать) throw; fling; cast; throw up, give up, abandon; neglect, let go; take, bring; leave behind; mislay. забро́шенный neglected; deserted, desolate.

забры́згать, -аю *pf.*, забры́згивать, -аю *impf.* splash, spatter, bespatter.

забыва́ть, -а́ю *impf.*, забы́ть, -бу́ду *pf.* forget; ~ся doze off, drop off; lose consciousness; sink into a reverie; forget o.s. забы́вчивый forgetful; absent-minded. забытьё, -я́ unconsciousness; drowsiness.

забы́о *etc.*: *see* забы́ть

зав, -а *abbr.* (*of* заве́дующий) manager; chief, head.

зав... *abbr.* (*of* заве́дующий) *in comb.* manager, director, superintendent; заводско́й factory, works. завга́р, -а garage manager. ~ко́м, -а factory committee. за́вуч, -а director of studies.

зава́ливать, -аю *impf.*, завали́ть, -лю́, -лишь *pf.* block up, obstruct; fill; pile; cram; overload; knock down, demolish; make a mess of; ~ся fall, tumble; collapse; overturn, tip up; come to grief.

зава́ривать, -аю *impf.*, завари́ть, -арю́, -а́ришь *pf.* make; brew; scald; weld. зава́рка, -и brewing; scalding; welding.

заведе́ние, -я establishment, institution; custom, habit. заве́довать, -дую *impf.*+i. manage, superintend; be in charge of.

заве́домо *adv.* wittingly. заве́домый notorious, undoubted; well-known.

заведу́ *etc.*: *see* завести́

заве́дующий *sb.* (+i.) manager; head; director, superintendent; person in charge.

завезти́, -зу́, -зёшь; -ёз, -ла́ *pf.* (*impf.* завози́ть) convey, deliver; supply; leave.

за|вербова́ть, -бу́ю *pf.*

заве́ренный witnessed; certified; ~ая ко́пия certified true copy. заве́ритель, -я *m.* witness. заве́рить, -рю *pf.* (*impf.* заверя́ть) assure; certify; witness.

заверну́ть, -ну́, -нёшь *pf.* (*impf.* завёртывать, завора́чивать) wrap, wrap up; tuck up, roll up; screw tight, screw up; turn off; drop in, call in; turn; come on, come down; ~ся wrap o.s. up, wrap up, muffle o.s.

заверте́ться, -рчу́сь, -ртишься *pf.* begin to turn, begin to spin; become flustered, lose one's head.

завёртка, -и wrapping up; package. завёртывать(ся, -аю(сь *impf. of* заверну́ть(ся

заверша́ть, -а́ю *impf.*, заверши́ть, -шу́ *pf.* complete, conclude, crown. заверше́ние, -я completion; end, conclusion.

заверя́ть, -я́ю *impf. of* заве́рить

заве́са, -ы curtain; veil, screen. заве́сить, -е́шу *pf.* (*impf.* заве́шивать) cover; curtain, curtain off.

завести́, -еду́, -ёшь; -вёл, -а́ *pf.* (*impf.* заводи́ть) take, bring; leave, drop off; set up, start; acquire; institute, introduce; wind (up), crank; ~сь be; appear; be established, be set up; start.

заве́т, -а behest, bidding, ordinance; Testament. заве́тный cherished; intimate; secret.

заве́шивать, -аю *impf. of* заве́сить

завеща́ние, -я will, testament. завеща́ть,

-а́ю leave, bequeath; devise.

завзя́тый inveterate, out-and-out, downright; incorrigible.

завива́ть(ся, -а́ю(сь *impf. of* **зави́ть(ся. зави́вка**, -и waving; curling; wave.

зави́дно *impers.*+*d.*: **мне ~** I feel envious. **зави́дный** enviable. **зави́довать**, -дую *impf.* (*pf.* **по~**) +*d.* envy.

за|визи́ровать, -рую *pf.*

завинти́ть, -нчу́ *pf.*, **зави́нчивать**, -аю *impf.* screw up; **~ся** screw up.

зави́сеть, -и́шу *impf.* +**от**+*g.* depend on; lie in the power of. **зави́симость**, -и dependence; **в зави́симости от** depending on, subject to. **зави́симый** dependent.

зави́стливый envious. **за́висть**, -и envy.

завито́й; за́вит, -а́, -о curled, waved. **завито́к**, -тка́ curl, lock; flourish; volute, scroll; tendril; helix. **зави́ть**, -вью́, -вьёшь; -и́л, -а́, -о *pf.* (*impf.* **завива́ть**) curl, wave; twist, wind; **~ся** curl, wave, twine; curl, wave, one's hair; have one's hair waved.

завладева́ть, -а́ю *impf.*, **завладе́ть**, -е́ю *pf.*+*i.* take possession of; seize, capture.

завлека́тельный alluring; fascinating; captivating; attractive. **завлека́ть**, -а́ю *impf.*, **завле́чь**, -еку́, -ечёшь; -лёк, -ла́ *pf.* lure, entice; fascinate; captivate.

заво́д[1], -а factory; mill; works; plant; stud(farm). **заво́д**[2], -а winding up; winding mechanism. **заводи́ть(ся**, -ожу́(сь, -о́дишь(ся *impf. of* **завести́(сь. заво́дка**, -и winding up; starting, cranking. **заводно́й** clockwork, mechanical; winding, cranking, starting. **заво́дский, заводско́й** factory, works, mill; prefabricated; stud; *sb.* factory worker. **заводча́не**, -а́н *pl.* factory workers. **заво́дчик**, -а manufacturer, mill-owner, factory owner.

за́водь, -и backwater.

завоева́ние, -я winning; conquest; achievement, gain. **завоева́тель**, -я *m.* conqueror. **завоева́тельный** aggressive; of aggression. **завоева́ть**, -оюю́ *pf.*, **завоёвывать**, -аю *impf.* conquer; win, gain; try to get.

завожу́ *etc.: see* **заводи́ть, завози́ть**

заво́з, -а delivery; carriage. **завози́ть**, -ожу́, -о́зишь *impf. of* **завезти́**

завора́чивать(ся, -аю(сь *impf. of* **заверну́ть(ся. заворо́т**[1], -а a turn, turning; sharp bend. **за́ворот**[2], -а; **~ кишо́к** twisted intestines, volvulus.

заво́ю *etc.: see* **завы́ть**

завсегда́ *adv.* always. **завсегда́тай**, -я habitué, frequenter.

за́втра tomorrow. **за́втрак**, -а breakfast; lunch; **второ́й ~** elevenses, mid-morning snack. **за́втракать**, -аю *impf.* (*pf.* **по~**) have breakfast; have lunch. **за́втрашний** tomorrow's; **~ день** tomorrow, the morrow; **the (near) future.**

за|вуали́ровать, -рую *pf.*

завыва́ть, -а́ю *impf.*, **завы́ть**, -во́ю *pf.* (be-

gin to) howl.

завяза́ть, -яжу́, -я́жешь *pf.* (*impf.* **завя́зывать**) tie, tie up; knot; bind, bind up; start; **~ся** start; arise; (of fruit) set. **завя́зка**, -и string, lace, band; beginning, start; opening; plot.

за|вя́знуть, -ну; -я́з *pf.* **завя́зывать(ся**, -аю(сь *impf. of* **завяза́ть(ся**

завя́лый withered, faded; dead. **за|вя́нуть**, -ну; -я́л *pf.*

загада́ть, -а́ю *pf.*, **зага́дывать**, -аю *impf.* think of; plan ahead, look ahead; guess at the future; **~ зага́дку** ask a riddle. **зага́дка**, -и riddle; enigma, mystery. **зага́дочный** enigmatic, mysterious.

зага́р, -а sunburn, tan.

за|гаси́ть, -ашу́, -а́сишь *pf.* **за|га́снуть**, -ну *pf.*

загво́здка, -и snag, obstacle; difficulty.

заги́б, -а fold; bend; exaggeration; deviation. **загиба́ть(ся**, -а́ю(сь *impf. of* **загну́ть(ся. заги́бщик**, -а deviationist.

за|гипнотизи́ровать, -рую *pf.*

загла́вие, -я title; heading. **загла́вн|ый** title; **~ая бу́ква** capital letter; **~ая роль** title-role, name-part.

загла́дить, -а́жу *pf.*, **загла́живать**, -аю *impf.* iron, iron out, press; make up for; expiate; **~ся** iron out, become smooth; fade.

за|гло́хнуть, -ну; -гло́х *pf.*

заглуша́ть, -а́ю *impf.*, **за|глуши́ть**, -шу́ *pf.* drown, deaden, muffle; jam; choke; suppress, stifle; alleviate, soothe. **заглу́шка**, -и choke, plug, stopper.

загляде́нье, -я lovely sight. **загляде́ться**, -я́жусь *pf.*, **загля́дываться**, -аюсь *impf.* **на**+*a.* stare at; be lost in admiration of. **загля́дывать**, -аю *impf.*, **загляну́ть**, -ну́, -нешь *pf.* peep; glance; look in, drop in.

за́гнанный driven, at the end of one's tether; tired out, exhausted; downtrodden, cowed. **загна́ть**, -гоню́, -го́нишь; -а́л, -а́, -о *pf.* (*impf.* **загоня́ть**) drive in, drive home; drive; exhaust; sell, flog.

загнива́ние, -я rotting, putrescence; decay; suppuration. **загнива́ть**, -а́ю *impf.*, **загни́ть**, -ию́, -иёшь; -и́л, -а́, -о *pf.* rot; decay; fester.

загну́ть, -ну́, -нёшь *pf.* (*impf.* **загиба́ть**) turn up, turn down; bend, fold; crease; utter; **~ся** turn up, stick up; turn down; turn up one's toes.

загова́ривать, -аю *impf.*, **заговори́ть**, -рю́ *pf.* begin to talk; begin to speak; talk to death, tire out with talk; cast a spell over; protect with a charm (**от**+*g.* against); **~ с**+*i.* speak to. **за́говор**, -а a plot, conspiracy; charm, spell. **загово́рщик**, -а conspirator.

заголо́вок, -вка title; heading; headline.

заго́н, -а enclosure, pen; driving in; rounding up. **заго́нщик**, -а beater. **загоня́ть**[1], -я́ю *impf. of* **загна́ть. загоня́ть**[2], -я́ю *pf.* tire out; work to death; grill.

загора́живать(ся, -аю(сь *impf. of* **загороди́ть**

загора́ть, -а́ю *impf.*, **загоре́ть, -рю́** *pf.* become sunburnt, brown, tan; **~ся** catch fire; blaze, break out, start; *impers.+d.* become eager, want very much.

за́город, -а suburbs; **~ом** in the suburbs.

загороди́ть, -рожу́, -ро́ди́шь *pf.* (*impf.* **загора́живать**) enclose, fence in; barricade; bar; obstruct, block. **загоро́дка, -и** fence, enclosure.

за́городный out-of-town; country; suburban.

загота́вливать, -аю *impf.*, **заготовля́ть, -я́ю** *impf.*, **загото́вить, -влю** *pf.* lay in; lay in a stock of, stockpile, store; prepare. **загото́вка, -и** (State) procurement, purchase; laying in; stocking up, stockpiling; semi-finished product.

загради́тельный defensive; barrage; mine-laying. **загради́ть, -ажу́** *pf.*, **загражда́ть, -а́ю** *impf.* block, obstruct; bar. **загражде́ние, -я** blocking; obstruction; obstacle, barrier.

загра́ни́ца, -ы abroad, foreign parts. **заграни́чный** foreign.

загреба́ть, -а́ю *impf.*, **загрести́, -ебу́, -ебёшь; -ёб, -ла́** *pf.* rake up, gather; rake in.

загри́вок, -вка withers; nape (of the neck).

за|гримирова́ть(ся, -ру́ю(сь *pf.*

загроможда́ть, -а́ю *impf.*, **загромозди́ть, -зжу́** *pf.* block up, encumber; pack, cram; overload.

загрубе́лый coarsened, callous. **за|грубе́ть, -е́ю** *pf.*

загружа́ть, -а́ю *impf.*, **за|грузи́ть, -ужу́, -у́зи́шь** *pf.* load; overload; feed; keep fully occupied; **~ся+i.** load up with, take on. **загру́зка, -и** loading, feeding; charge, load, capacity.

за|грунтова́ть, -ту́ю *pf.*

загрусти́ть, -ущу́ *pf.* grow sad.

загрязне́ние, -я soiling; pollution; contamination. **за|грязни́ть, -ню́** *pf.*, **загрязня́ть, -я́ю** *impf.* soil, make dirty; contaminate, pollute; **~ся** make o.s. dirty, become dirty; be polluted.

загс, -а *abbr.* (*of* **отде́л за́писи а́ктов гражда́нского состоя́ния**) registry office.

загуби́ть, -блю́, -бишь *pf.* ruin; squander, waste.

за|гудрони́ровать, -рую *pf.*

загуля́ть, -я́ю *pf.*, **загу́ливать, -аю** *impf.* take to drink.

за|густе́ть, -е́ет *pf.* thicken, grow thick.

зад, -а (-у), *loc.* **-у́;** *pl.* **-ы́** back; hindquarters; buttocks, seat; croup, rump; *pl.* back-yard(s); **~ом наперёд** back to front; **е́хать ~ом** to reverse, back up.

зада́бривать, -аю *impf. of* **задо́брить**

задава́ть(ся, -даю́(сь *impf. of* **зада́ть(ся**

задави́ть, -влю́, -вишь *pf.* crush; run over; knock down.

задади́м *etc.*, **за́дал** *etc.*, **зада́м** *etc.: see* **зада́ть**

зада́ние, -я task, job; commission, assignment.

зада́ривать, -аю *impf.*, **задари́ть, -рю́, -ришь** *pf.* load with presents; bribe.

зада́тки, -тков *pl.* instincts, inclinations.

зада́ток, -тка deposit, advance.

зада́ть, -а́м, -а́шь, -а́ст, -ади́м; за́дал, -а́, -о *pf.* (*impf.* **задава́ть**) set; give; put; **~ вопро́с** ask a question; **~ тя́гу** take to one's heels; **я ему́ зада́м!** I'll give him what-for!; **~ся** turn out well; work out, succeed; **~ся мы́слью, це́лью** set o.s., make up one's mind. **зада́ча, -и** problem, sum; task; mission.

задвига́ть, -а́ю *impf.*, **задви́нуть, -ну** *pf.* bolt; bar; close; push, slide; **~ задви́жку** shoot a bolt; **~ за́навес** draw a curtain; **~ся** shut; slide. **задви́жка, -и** bolt; catch, fastening; slide-valve. **задвижно́й** sliding.

задво́рки, -рок *pl.* back-yard; back parts; out-of-the-way place, backwoods.

задева́ть, -а́ю *impf. of* **заде́ть**

заде́лать, -аю *pf.*, **заде́лывать, -аю** *impf.* do up; block up, close up; wall up; stop (up). **заде́лка, -и** doing up; blocking up, stopping up.

заде́ну *etc.: see* **заде́ть. задёргивать, -аю** *impf. of* **задёрнуть. за|деревене́ть, -е́ю** *pf.*

задержа́ние, -я detention, arrest; retention; suspension. **задержа́ть, -жу́, -жишь** *pf.*, **заде́рживать, -аю** *impf.* detain; delay; withhold, keep back; retard; arrest; **~ дыха́ние** hold one's breath; **~ся** stay too long; linger.

задёрнуть, -ну *pf.* (*impf.* **задёргивать**) pull; draw; cover; curtain off.

задеру́ *etc.: see* **задра́ть**

заде́ть, -е́ну *pf.* (*impf.* **задева́ть**) touch, brush (against), graze; offend, wound; catch (against), catch on; **~ за живо́е** touch on the raw.

задира, -ы *c.g.* bully; trouble-maker. **задира́ть(ся, -а́ю(сь** *impf. of* **задра́ть(ся. задири́стый** provocative, pugnacious; cocky, pert.

за́дн|ий back, rear; hind; **дать ~ий ход** back, reverse; **~яя мысль** ulterior motive; **~ий план** background; **~ий прохо́д** anus, back passage; **~ий фона́рь** tail-light. **за́дник, -а** back; back drop.

задо́брить, -рю *pf.* (*impf.* **задо́бривать**) cajole; coax; win over.

задо́к, -дка́ back.

задо́лго *adv.* long before.

за|должа́ть, -а́ю *pf.*; **~ся** run into debt. **задо́лженность, -и** debts; liabilities.

задо́р, -а fervour, ardour; enthusiasm; passion; temper. **задо́рный** provocative; fervent, ardent; impassioned; quick-tempered.

задохну́ться, -ну́сь, -нёшься; -о́хся *or* **-у́лся** *pf.* (*impf.* **задыха́ться**) suffocate; choke; pant; gasp for breath.

за|дра́ть, -деру́, -дерёшь; -а́л, -а́, -о *pf.* (*impf. also* **задира́ть**) tear to pieces, kill; lift up, stretch up; break, split; provoke, insult; **~ нос** put on airs; **~ся** break; split; ride up.

задрема́ть, -млю́, -млешь *pf.* doze off, begin to nod.

задува́ть, -а́ю *impf. of* заду́ть

заду́мать, -аю *pf.*, заду́мывать, -аю *impf.* plan; intend; think of; conceive the idea (of); ~ся become thoughtful, pensive; meditate; ponder. заду́мчивость, -и thoughtfulness; reverie. заду́мчивый thoughtful, pensive.

заду́ть, -у́ю *pf.* (*impf.* задува́ть) blow out; blow in; begin to blow.

задуше́вный sincere; cordial; intimate; ~ разгово́р heart-to-heart (talk).

за|души́ть, -ушу́, -у́шишь *pf.* зады́ *etc.: see* зад

задыха́ться, -а́юсь *impf. of* задохну́ться

заеда́ние, -я jamming. заеда́ть, -а́ю *impf. of* зае́сть. заеди́м *etc.: see* зае́сть

зае́зд, -а calling in; lap, round, heat. зае́здить, -зжу *pf.* override; wear out; work too hard. заезжа́ть, -а́ю *impf. of* зае́хать. зае́зженный hackneyed, trite; worn out. зае́зж|ий visiting; ~ий двор wayside inn; ~ая тру́ппа touring company.

заём, за́йма loan. заёмный loan. заёмщик, -а, -щица, -ы borrower, debtor.

зае́сть, -е́м, -е́шь, -е́ст, -еди́м *pf.* (*impf.* заеда́ть) torment, oppress; jam; foul; +*i.* take with.

зае́хать, -е́ду *pf.* (*impf.* заезжа́ть) call in; enter, ride in, drive in; land o.s.; reach; +за+*a.* go beyond, go past; +за+*i.* call for, fetch.

за|жа́рить(ся, -рю(сь *pf.*

зажа́ть, -жму́, -жмёшь *pf.* (*impf.* зажима́ть) squeeze; press; clutch; grip; suppress.

заже́чь, -жгу́, -жжёшь; -жёг, -жгла́ *pf.* (*impf.* зажига́ть) set fire to; kindle; light; strike; inflame; ~ся catch fire; light up; flame up.

зажива́ть(ся, -а́ю(сь *impf. of* зажи́ть(ся. заживи́ть, -влю́ *pf.*, заживля́ть, -я́ю *impf.* heal. за́живо *adv.* alive. заживу́ *etc.: see* зажи́ть

зажига́лка, -и lighter; incendiary. зажига́ние, -я ignition. зажига́тельн|ый inflammatory; incendiary; ~ая свеча́ sparking-plug. зажига́ть(ся, -а́ю(сь *impf. of* заже́чь(ся

зажи́м, -а clamp; clutch; clip; (screw) terminal; suppression, clamping down. зажима́ть, -а́ю *impf. of* зажа́ть. зажи́мистый strong, powerful; tight-fisted; stingy. зажимно́й tight-fisted. зажи́мщик, -а suppressor.

зажи́точность, -и prosperity. зажи́точный well-to-do; prosperous. зажи́ть, -иву́, -ивёшь; -ил, -а́, -о *pf.* (*impf.* зажива́ть) heal; close up; begin to live; ~ся live to a great age; live too long.

зажму́ *etc.: see* зажа́ть. за|жму́риться, -рюсь *pf.*

зазелене́ть, -е́ет *pf.* turn green.

заземле́ние, -я earthing; earth. заземли́ть, -лю́ *pf.*, заземля́ть, -я́ю *impf.* earth.

зазнава́ться, -наю́сь, -наёшься *impf.*, зазна́ться, -а́юсь *pf.* give o.s. airs, become conceited.

зазу́бренный notched, jagged, serrated. за-

зу́брина, -ы notch, jag. за|зубри́ть[1], -рю́ *pf.* за|зубри́ть[2], -рю́, -у́бришь *pf.*

заи́грывать, -аю *impf.* make advances; flirt.

заи́ка, -и *c.g.* stammerer, stutterer. заика́ние, -я stammer, stutter; stammering, stuttering. заика́ться, -а́юсь *impf.*, заикну́ться, -ну́сь, -нёшься *pf.* stammer, stutter; +o+*p.* hint at, mention, touch on.

заимообра́зно *adv.* on credit, on loan. заи́мствование, -я borrowing, adoption. заи́мствованн|ый borrowed, taken over; ~ое сло́во loan-word. заи́мствовать, -твую *impf. & pf.* (*pf. also* по~) borrow, take over, adopt.

заинтересо́ванный interested, concerned. заинтересова́ть, -су́ю *pf.*, заинтересо́вывать, -аю *impf.* interest; excite the curiosity of; ~ся+*i.* become interested in, take an interest in.

заи́скивать, -аю *impf.* make up (to), ingratiate o.s.

зайду́ *etc.: see* зайти́. займу́ *etc.: see* заня́ть

зайти́, -йду́, -йдёшь; зашёл, -шла́ *pf.* (*impf.* заходи́ть) call; look in, drop in; go, go on; set; wane; +в+*a.* get to, reach; +за+*a.* go behind, turn; +за+*i.* call for, go for, fetch.

за́яц *etc.: see* за́яц. за́йчик, -а (dear) little hare; reflection of sunlight. за́йчиха, -и doe (*of hare*). зайчо́нок, -нка; *pl.* -ча́та, -ча́т leveret.

закабали́ть, -лю́ *pf.*, закабаля́ть, -я́ю *impf.* enslave.

закавка́зский Transcaucasian. Закавка́зье, -я Transcaucasia.

закады́чный intimate, bosom.

зака́з, -а order; prohibition; на ~ to order. заказа́ть, -ажу́, -а́жешь *pf.*, зака́зывать, -аю *impf.* order; reserve, book. зака́зник, -а reserve; preserve. заказн|о́й made to order, made to measure; bespoke; registered; ~о́е (письмо́) registered letter. зака́зчик, -а customer, client.

зака́л, -а temper, tempering; stamp, cast; strength of character, backbone. закалённый tempered, hardened, hard; seasoned; tough; fully trained. зака́ливать, -аю *impf.*, закали́ть, -лю́ *pf.* (*impf. also* закаля́ть) temper; harden, case-harden; harden off. зака́лка, -и tempering, hardening; temper, calibre.

зака́лывать, -аю *impf. of* заколо́ть

закаля́ть, -я́ю *impf. of* закали́ть. зака́нчивать(ся, -аю(сь *impf. of* зако́нчить(ся

зака́пать, -аю *pf.*, зака́пывать[1], -аю *impf.* begin to drip; rain, fall in drops; pour in drops; spot, spatter.

зака́пывать[2](ся, -аю(сь *impf. of* закопа́ть(ся

зака́т, -а setting; sunset; decline; на ~е at sunset; на ~е дней in one's declining years. заката́ть, -а́ю *pf.*, зака́тывать[1], -аю *impf.* begin to roll; roll up; roll out; ~ в тюрьму́ throw into prison. закати́ть, -ачу́, -а́тишь *pf.*, **закáтывать²**, **-аю** *impf.* roll; **~ся** roll; set; wane; vanish, disappear; go off; **~ся смéхом** burst out laughing.

закáтный sunset.

заквáсить, **-áшу** *pf.*, **заквáшивать**, **-аю** *impf.* ferment; leaven. **заквáска**, **-и** ferment; leaven.

закидáть, **-áю** *pf.*, **закúдывать¹**, **-аю** *impf.* shower; cover up; fill up; spatter, bespatter; **~ вопрóсами** ply with questions; **~ грязью** fling mud at.

закúдывать², **-аю** *impf.*, **закúнуть**, **-ну** *pf.* throw; throw out, away; fling, cast, toss.

закипáть, **-áет** *impf.*, **закипéть**, **-пúт** *pf.* begin to boil, simmer; be in full swing.

закисáть, **-áю** *impf.*, **закúснуть**, **-ну; -úс**, **-ла** *pf.* turn sour; become apathetic. **зáкись**, **-и** oxide, protoxide; **~ азóта** nitrous oxide.

заклáд, **-а** pawn; pledge; mortgage; bet, wager; **бúться об ~** bet, wager; **в ~е** in pawn. **заклáдка**, **-и** laying, laying down; batch, charge; bookmark. **закладнáя** *sb.* mortgage. **закладнóй** mortgage; pawn. **заклáдывать**, **-аю** *impf. of* **заложúть**

заклéивать, **-аю** *impf.*, **заклéить**, **-éю** *pf.* glue up; stick up; seal; **~ся** stick.

заклеймúть, **-млю** *pf.*

заклепáть, **-áю** *pf.*, **заклёпывать**, **-аю** *impf.* rivet. **заклёпка**, **-и** rivet; riveting.

заклинáние, **-я** incantation; spell, charm; exorcism. **заклинáтель**, **-я** *m.* exorcist; **~ змей** snake-charmer. **заклинáть**, **-áю** *impf.* conjure; invoke; exorcize; adjure, entreat.

заключáть, **-áю** *impf.*, **заключúть**, **-чý** *pf.* conclude; end; infer; enter into; contain; enclose; comprise; confine. **заключáться**, **-áется** consist; lie, be; be contained. **заключéние**, **-я** conclusion; end; inference; resolution, decision; confinement, detention. **заключённый** *sb.* prisoner, convict. **заключúтельный** final, concluding.

заклятие, **-я** oath, pledge. **заклятый** sworn, inveterate; enchanted; bewitched.

заковáть, **-кую**, **-куёшь** *pf.*, **закóвывать**, **-аю** *impf.* chain; shackle, put in irons.

заколáчивать, **-аю** *impf. of* **заколотúть**

заколдóванный bewitched, enchanted; spellbound; **~ круг** vicious circle. **заколдовáть**, **-дую** *pf.* bewitch, enchant; lay a spell on.

закóлка, **-и** hairpin; hair-grip; hair-slide.

заколотúть, **-лочý**, **-лóтишь** *pf.* (*impf.* **заколáчивать**) board up; nail up; knock in, drive in; beat the life out of, knock insensible.

заколóть, **-олю**, **-óлешь** *pf.* (*impf. also* **закáлывать**) stab, spear, stick; kill; pin, pin up; fasten; (*impers.*) **у меня заколóло в бокý** I have a stitch in my side; **~ся** stab o.s.

закóн, **-а** law; **~ бóжий** scripture, divinity. **законнорождённый** legitimate. **закóнный** lawful, legal; legitimate, rightful.

законо... *in comb.* law, legal. **законоведéние**, **-я** law, jurisprudence. **~дáтельный** legislative. **~мéрность**, **-и** regularity, normality. **~мéрный** regular, natural. **~положéние**, **-я** statute. **~проéкт**, **-а** bill.

за|конопáтить, **-áчу** *pf.* **за|консервúровать**, **-рую** *pf.* **за|конспектúровать**, **-рую** *pf.* **за|контрактовáть(ся**, **-тýю(сь** *pf.*

закóнченность, **-и** finish; completeness. **закóнченный** finished; complete; consummate. **закóнчить**, **-чу** *pf.* (*impf.* **закáнчивать**) end, finish; **~ся** end, finish; come to an end.

закопáть, **-áю** *pf.* (*impf.* **закáпывать**) begin to dig; bury; **~ся** begin to rummage; bury o.s.; dig (o.s.) in.

закоптéлый sooty, grimy. **за|коптéть**, **-тúт** *pf.* **за|коптúть**, **-пчý** *pf.*

закоренéлый deep-rooted; ingrained; inveterate.

закóрки, **-рок** *pl.* back, shoulders.

закоснéлый deep-rooted; incorrigible, inveterate. **за|коснéть**, **-éю** *pf.*

закостенéлый ossified; stiff.

закоýлок, **-лка** back street, alley, passage; secluded corner, nook; **знать все закоýлки** know all the ins and outs.

закоченéлый numb with cold. **за|коченéть**, **-éю** *pf.*

закрáдываться, **-аюсь** *impf. of* **закрáсться**. **закрáивать**, **-аю** *impf. of* **закрóйть**

закрáсить, **-áшу** *pf.* (*impf.* **закрáшивать**) paint over, paint out.

закрáсться, **-адýсь**, **-адёшься** *pf.* (*impf.* **закрáдываться**) steal in, creep in.

закрáшивать, **-аю** *impf. of* **закрáсить**

закрéпа, **-ы** catch; fastener. **закрепúтель**, **-я** *m.* fastener; fixative, fixing agent, fixer. **закрепúть**, **-плю** *pf.*, **закреплять**, **-яю** *impf.* fasten, secure; make fast; fix; consolidate; **+за+i.** allot to, assign to; appoint to, attach to; **~ за собóй** secure; **~ ся**, **на+а.** consolidate one's hold on.

закрепостúть, **-ощý** *pf.* **закрепощáть**, **-áю** *impf.* enslave; make a serf of. **закрепощéние**, **-я** enslavement; slavery, serfdom.

закричáть, **-чý** *pf.* cry out; begin to shout; give a shout.

закрóйть, **-ою** *pf.* (*impf.* **закрáивать**) cut out, groove. **закрóй**, **-я** cutting out; cut, style; groove. **закрóйный** cutting, cutting out. **закрóйщик**, **-а** cutter.

закрóм, **-а**; *pl.* **-á** corn-bin.

закрóю *etc.: see* **закрыть**. **закрою** *etc.: see* **закрóйть**

закруглéние, **-я** rounding, curving; curve; curvature; well-rounded period. **закруглённый**, **-ён**, **-á** rounded; well-rounded. **закруглúть**, **-лю** *pf.*, **закруглять**, **-яю** *impf.* make round; round off; **~ся** become round.

закружúться, **-ужýсь**, **-ýжишься** *pf.* begin to whirl, begin to go round; be in a whirl.

за|крутúть, **-учý**, **-ýтишь** *pf.*, **закрýчивать**, **-аю** *impf.* twist, twirl, whirl round; wind round; roll; turn; screw in; turn the head of;

~ся twist, twirl, whirl; wind round; begin to whirl.

закрыва́ть, -а́ю *impf.* **закры́ть**, -ро́ю *pf.* close, shut; shut off, turn off; close down, shut down; cover; ~ся close, shut; end; close down; cover o.s., take cover; find shelter, shelter. **закры́тие**, -я closing; shutting; closing down; shelter, cover. **закры́т|ый** closed, shut; private; ~ое голосова́ние secret ballot; ~ое заседа́ние private meeting; closed session; ~ое мо́ре inland sea; ~ое пла́тье high-necked dress; ~ый просмо́тр private view.

закули́сный behind the scenes; secret; underhand, under-cover.

закупа́ть, -а́ю *impf.*, **закупи́ть**, -плю́, -пишь *pf.* buy up; lay in; stock up with; bribe. **заку́пка**, -и purchase. **закупно́й** bought, purchased.

заку́поривать, -аю *impf.*, **заку́порить**, -рю *pf.* cork; stop up; plug, clog; shut up; coop up. **заку́порка**, -и corking; embolism, thrombosis.

заку́почный purchase. **заку́пщик**, -а, -щица, -ы purchaser; buyer.

заку́ривать, -аю *impf.*, **закури́ть**, -рю́, -ришь *pf.* light; light up; begin to smoke.

закуси́ть, -ушу́, -у́сишь *pf.*, **заку́сывать**, -аю *impf.* have a snack; have a bite; +*i.* have a bit of; ~ удила́ take the bit between one's teeth. **заку́ска**, -и hors-d'oeuvre; appetizer, snack, titbit. **заку́сочная** *sb.* snack-bar.

за|ку́тать, -аю *pf.*, **заку́тывать**, -аю *impf.* wrap up; muffle; tuck up; ~ся wrap o.s. up.

зал, -а a hall, room; ~ ожида́ния waiting-room.

залёг *etc.: see* **зале́чь. залега́ние**, -я bedding; bed, seam. **залега́ть**, -а́ю *impf. of* **зале́чь**

за|ледене́ть, -е́ю *pf.*

залежа́лый stale, long unused. **залежа́ться**, -жу́сь *pf.*, **залёживаться**, -аюсь *impf.* lie too long; lie idle a long time; find no market; become stale. **за́лежь**, -и deposit, bed, seam; stale goods.

залеза́ть, -а́ю *impf.*, **зале́зть**, -зу; -е́з *pf.* climb, climb up; get in; creep in; ~ в долги́ run into debt.

за|лепи́ть, -плю́, -пишь *pf.*, **залепля́ть**, -я́ю *impf.* paste up, paste over; glue up, stick up.

залета́ть, -а́ю *impf.*, **залете́ть**, -ечу́ *pf.* fly; +в+*a.* fly into; land at; +за+*a.* fly over, fly beyond. **залётн|ый** flown in; ~ая пти́ца bird of passage.

зале́чивать, -аю *impf.*, **залечи́ть**, -чу́, -чишь *pf.* heal, cure; ~ся heal, heal up.

зале́чь, -ля́гу, -ля́жешь; -залёг, -ла́ *pf.* (*impf.* **залега́ть**) lie down; lie low; lie in wait; lie, be deposited; take root, become ingrained; become blocked.

зали́в, -а bay; gulf; creek, cove. **залива́ть**, -а́ю *impf.*, **зали́ть**, -лью́, -льёшь; за́лил, -а́, -о *pf.* flood, inundate; quench, extinguish, put out; lay, spread; stop holes in; +*i.* pour over,

spill on; ~ ска́терть черни́лами spill ink on the tablecloth; ~ ту́шью ink in; ~ся be flooded; pour, spill; +*i.* break into, burst into; ~ ся слеза́ми burst into tears, dissolve in tears.

зало́г, -а deposit; pledge; security, mortgage; token; voice. **заложи́ть**, -жу́, -жишь *pf.* (*impf.* **закла́дывать**) lay; put; mislay; pile up, heap up; block up; pawn, mortgage; harness; lay in, store, put by. **зало́жник**, -а hostage.

залп, -а volley, salvo; ~ом without pausing for breath, at one gulp.

залью́ *etc.: see* **зали́ть. заля́гу** *etc.: see* **зале́чь**

зам, -а *abbr.* (*of* **замести́тель**) assistant, deputy.

зам... *abbr.* (*of* **замести́тель**) *in comb.* assistant, deputy; vice-. **замдире́ктора** deputy director; vice-principal, assistant head. ~мини́стра deputy minister. ~председа́теля vice-chairman.

за|ма́зать, -а́жу *pf.*, **зама́зывать**, -аю *impf.* paint over; efface; slur over; putty; daub, smear; soil; ~ся smear o.s.; get dirty. **зама́зка**, -и putty, paste, cement; puttying.

зама́лчивать, -аю *impf. of* **замолча́ть**

зама́нивать, -аю *impf.*, **замани́ть**, -ню́, -нишь *pf.* entice, lure; attract; decoy. **зама́нчивость**, -и allurements. **зама́нчивый** tempting, alluring.

за|мара́ть(ся, -а́ю(сь *pf.* **за|маринова́ть**, -ну́ю *pf.*

замаскиро́ванный masked; disguised; concealed. **за|маскирова́ть**, -ру́ю *pf.*, **замаски́ровывать**, -аю *impf.* mask; disguise; camouflage; conceal; ~ся disguise o.s.

зама́х, -а threatening gesture. **зама́хиваться**, -аюсь *impf.*, **замахну́ться**, -ну́сь, -нёшься *pf.* threaten; +*i.* raise threateningly; ~ руко́й на+*a.* lift one's hand against.

зама́чивать, -аю *impf. of* **замочи́ть**

зама́щивать, -аю *impf. of* **замости́ть**

замедле́ние, -я slowing down, deceleration; delay. **заме́дленный** retarded, delayed. **заме́длить**, -лю *pf.*, **замедля́ть**, -я́ю *impf.* slow down, retard; reduce, slacken; delay; hold back; be slow (to), be long (in); ~ся slow down; slacken, grow slower.

замёл *etc.: see* **замести́**

заме́на, -ы substitution; replacement; commutation; substitute. **замени́мый** replaceable. **замени́тель**, -я *m.* (+*g.*) substitute (for). **замени́ть**, -ню́, -нишь *pf.*, **заменя́ть**, -я́ю *impf.* replace; take the place of; be a substitute for.

замере́ть, -мру́, -мрёшь; за́мер, -ла́, -о *pf.* (*impf.* **замира́ть**) stand still; freeze, be rooted to the spot; die down, die away; die.

замерза́ние, -я freezing. **замерза́ть**, -а́ю *impf.*, **за|мёрзнуть**, -ну *pf.* freeze, freeze up; freeze to death.

заме́рить, -рю *pf.* (*impf.* **замеря́ть**) measure, gauge. **заме́рн|ый** gauge, measuring;

~ая ре́йка dip-stick, gauge rod.
за́мертво *adv.* like one dead, in a dead faint.
замеря́ть, -я́ю *impf. of* заме́рить
замеси́ть, -ешу́, -е́сишь *pf.* (*impf.* заме́шивать) knead.

замести́, -ету́, -ете́шь; -мёл, -а́ *pf.* (*impf.* замета́ть) sweep up; cover; ~ следы́ cover one's traces.
замести́тель, -я *m.*, ~ница, -ы substitute; assistant, deputy, vice-. замести́ть, -ещу́ *pf.* (*impf.* замеща́ть) replace, be substitute for; deputize for, act for; serve in place of.
замета́ть[1], -а́ю *impf. of* замести́
замета́ть[2], -а́ю *pf.* (*impf.* замётывать) tack, baste.
заме́тить, -е́чу *pf.* (*impf.* замеча́ть) notice; take notice of, make a note of; remark, observe. заме́тка, -и paragraph; mark; note. заме́тный noticeable; appreciable; outstanding.
замётывать, -аю *impf. of* замета́ть[2]
замеча́ние, -я remark, observation; reprimand, reproof. замеча́тельный remarkable; splendid, wonderful. замеча́ть, -а́ю *impf. of* заме́тить. заме́ченный discovered; noticed; detected.
замеша́тельство, -а confusion; embarrassment. замеша́ть, -а́ю *pf.*, заме́шивать, -аю *impf.* mix up, entangle; ~ся become mixed up, become entangled; mix, mingle. заме́шивать, -аю *impf. of* замеси́ть, замеша́ть
заме́шка, -и delay. заме́шкаться, -аюсь *pf.* linger, loiter.
замеща́ть, -а́ю *impf. of* замести́ть. замеще́ние, -я substitution; filling.
замина́ть, -а́ю *impf. of* замя́ть. зами́нка, -и hitch; hesitation.
замира́ние, -я dying out, dying down; sinking. замира́ть, -а́ю *impf. of* замере́ть
за́мкнутость, -и reserve, reticence. за́мкнутый reserved; closed, exclusive. замкну́ть, -ну́, -нёшь *pf.* (*impf.* замыка́ть) lock; close; ~ся close; shut o.s. up; become reserved; ~ся в себя́ shrink into o.s.
замну́ *etc.: see* замя́ть
за́мок[1], -мка castle.
замо́к[2], -мка́ lock; padlock; keystone; bolt; clasp, clip; запере́ть на ~ lock; под замко́м under lock and key.
замо́лвить, -влю *pf.*; ~ слове́чко put in a word.
замолка́ть, -а́ю *impf.*, замо́лкнуть, -ну; -мо́лк *pf.* fall silent; stop, cease. замолча́ть, -чу́ *pf.* (*impf.* зама́лчивать) fall silent; cease corresponding; keep silent about, hush up.
замора́живание, -я freezing; chilling, refrigeration; congealing; quenching. замора́живать, -аю *impf.*, заморо́зить, -ро́жу *pf.* freeze; refrigerate; ice, chill. заморо́женный frozen; iced. за́морозки, -ов *pl.* (slight) frosts.
замо́рский overseas.
замо́рыш, -а weakling, puny creature; runt.

за|мости́ть, -ощу́ *pf.* (*impf. also* зама́щивать) pave.
за|мочи́ть, -чу́, -чишь *pf.* (*impf. also* зама́чивать) wet; soak; ret.
замо́чн|ый lock; ~ая сква́жина keyhole.
замру́ *etc.: see* замере́ть
за́муж *adv.*; вы́йти ~ (за+*a.*) marry; вы́дать ~ за+*a.* marry (off) to. за́мужем *adv.* married (за+*i.* to). заму́жество, -а marriage.
замурова́ть, -ру́ю *pf.*, замуро́вывать, -аю *impf.* brick up; wall up; immure.
за|мути́ть(ся, -учу́(сь, -у́ти́шь(ся *pf.*
заму́чивать, -аю *impf.*, за|му́чить, -чу *pf.* torment; wear out; plague the life out of, bore to tears. за|му́читься, -чусь *pf.*
за́мша, -и suede; chamois leather, shammy. замшеви́дный suedette, suede-cloth.
замыка́ние, -я locking, closing; closure; short circuit, shorting. замыка́ть(ся, -а́ю(сь *impf. of* замкну́ть(ся замыка́ющ|ий; идти́ ~им bring up the rear.
за́мысел, -сла project, plan; design; scheme; idea. замы́слить, -лю *pf.*, замышля́ть, -я́ю *impf.* plan; contemplate, intend, think of. замыслова́тый intricate, complicated.
замя́ть, -мну́, -мнёшь *pf.* (*impf.* замина́ть) hush up, stifle, smother; suppress; put a stop to; distract attention from; ~ся falter; stumble; stop short.
за́навес, -а, занаве́ска, -и curtain. занаве́сить, -е́шу *pf.*, занаве́шивать, -аю *impf.* curtain; hang; cover.
за|неме́ть, -е́ю *pf.*
занесённый сне́гом snowbound. занести́, -су́, -сёшь; -ёс, -ла́ *pf.* (*impf.* заноси́ть) bring; leave, drop; raise, lift; note down, put down, enter; cover with snow, sand, etc.; ~ в протоко́л place on record, record in the minutes; ~сь be carried away.
занима́тельный entertaining, diverting; absorbing. занима́ть, -а́ю *impf.* (*pf.* заня́ть) occupy; interest; engage, secure; take, take up; borrow; ~ся+*i.* be occupied with, be engaged in; work at, work on; study; busy o.s. with; devote o.s. to.
зано́за, -ы splinter. занози́ть, -ожу́ *pf.* get a splinter in.
зано́с, -а drift, accumulation; raising; lifting; skid, skidding. заноси́ть(ся, -ошу́(сь, -о́сишь(ся *impf. of* занести́(сь зано́сный alien, foreign, imported. зано́счивый arrogant, haughty.
за|нумерова́ть, -ру́ю *pf.*
заня́тие, -я occupation; pursuit; *pl.* studies, work. за́нятный entertaining, amusing; interesting. за́нято *adv.* engaged, number engaged. занято́й busy. за́нятый; -нят, -а́, -о occupied; taken; engaged; employed; busy. заня́ть(ся, займу́(сь, -мёшь(ся; за́нял(ся, -а́(сь, -о(сь *pf. of* занима́ть(ся
заодно́ *adv.* in concert; at one; at the same time.
заострённый pointed, sharp. заостри́ть, -рю́

pf., **заостря́ть**, **-я́ю** *impf.* sharpen; stress, emphasize; **~ся** grow sharp; become pointed.

забо́чник, **-а**, **-ница**, **-ы** student taking correspondence course; external student. **забо́чно** *adv.* in one's absence; by correspondence course. **забо́чн|ый**; **~ый курс** correspondence course. **~ое обуче́ние** postal tuition; **~ый пригово́р** judgement by default.

за́пад, **-а** west; the West, the Occident. **за́падный** west, western; westerly.

западня́, **-й́**; *g.pl.* **-не́й** trap; pitfall, snare.

запа́здывать, **-аю** *impf. of* **запозда́ть**

запа́ивать, **-аю** *impf. of* **запая́ть**. **запа́йка**, **-и** soldering; sealing (off), seal.

за|пакова́ть, **-ку́ю** *pf.*, **запако́вывать**, **-аю** *impf.* pack; wrap up, do up.

за|па́костить, **-ощу** *pf.*

запа́л, **-а** ignition; fuse; detonator. **запа́ливать**, **-аю** *impf.*, **запали́ть**, **-лю́** light, ignite, kindle; set fire to. **запа́льн|ый** ignition; detonating; **~ая свеча́** (sparking-)plug. **запа́льчивый** quick-tempered.

за|паркова́ть(ся, **-ку́ю(сь** *pf.*

запа́с, **-а** reserve; stock, supply; hem; *pl.* turnings; **вы́пустить ~** let out; **отложи́ть про ~** put by; **про ~** for an emergency; **прове́рить ~** take stock; **~ слов** vocabulary. **запаса́ть**, **-а́ю** *impf.*, **запасти́**, **-су́**, **-сёшь**; **-а́с**, **-ла́** *pf.* stock, store; lay in stock of; **~ся+*i.* provide o.s. with; stock up with; arm o.s. with. **запа́сливый** thrifty; provident. **запа́сник**, **-а**, **запасно́й** *sb.* reservist. **запасно́й**, **запа́сный** spare; reserve; **~ вы́ход** emergency exit; **~ путь** siding.

за́пах[1], **-а** smell.

запа́х[2], **-а** wrapover. **запа́хивать**, **-аю** *impf.*, **запахну́ть**[2], **-ну́**, **-нёшь** *pf.* wrap up; **~ся** wrap (o.s.) up.

запа́хнуть[1], **-ну**; **-а́х** *pf.* begin to smell.

за|па́чкать, **-аю** *pf.*

запа́шка, **-и** ploughing in, ploughing up; plough-land, arable land.

запая́ть, **-я́ю** *pf.* (*impf.* **запа́ивать**) solder; seal, seal off.

запе́в, **-а** a solo part. **запева́ла**, **-ы** *c.g.* singer of solo part; leader of chorus; leader, instigator. **запева́ть**, **-а́ю** *impf.* (*pf.* **запе́ть**) lead the singing, set the tune.

запека́нка, **-и** baked pudding, baked dish; spiced brandy. **запека́ть(ся**, **-а́ю** *impf. of* **запе́чь(ся**. **запеку́** *etc.: see* **запе́чь**

за|пелена́ть, **-а́ю** *pf.*

запере́ть, **-пру́**, **-прёшь**; **за́пер**, **-ла́**, **-ло** *pf.* (*impf.* **запира́ть**) lock; lock in; shut up; bar; block up; **~ на засо́в** bolt; **~ся** lock o.s. in; shut (o.s.) up; **+в+*p.* refuse to admit, refuse to speak about.

запе́ть, **-пою́**, **-поёшь** *pf.* (*impf.* **запева́ть**) begin to sing; **~ друго́е** change one's tune; **~ пе́сню** strike up a song; plug a song.

запеча́тать, **-аю** *pf.*, **запеча́тывать**, **-аю** *impf.* seal. **запечатлева́ть**, **-а́ю** *impf.* **запечат-**

-ле́ть, **-е́ю** *pf.* imprint, impress, engrave; **~ся** imprint, stamp, impress, itself.

запе́чь, **-еку́**, **-ечёшь**; **-пёк**, **-ла́** *pf.* (*impf.* **запека́ть**) bake; **~ся** bake; become parched; clot, coagulate.

запива́ть, **-а́ю** *impf. of* **запи́ть**

запина́ться, **-а́юсь** *impf. of* **запну́ться**. **запи́нка**, **-и** hesitation; **без запи́нки** smoothly.

запира́тельство, **-а** denial, disavowal. **запира́ть(ся**, **-а́ю(сь** *impf. of* **запере́ть(ся**

записа́ть, **-ишу́**, **-и́шешь** *pf.* **запи́сывать**, **-аю** *impf.* note, make a note of, take notes; take down; record; enter, register, enrol; make over (to); begin to write, begin to correspond; **~ся** register, enter one's name, enrol; **~ся в клуб** join a club; **~ся к врачу́** make an appointment with the doctor. **запи́ска**, **-и** note; minute, memorandum; *pl.* notes; memoirs; transactions. **записн|о́й** note, writing; regular; inveterate; **~а́я кни́жка** notebook. **за́пись**, **-и** writing down; recording; registration; entry, record; deed.

запи́ть, **-пью**, **-пьёшь**; **за́пил**, **-а́**, **-о** *pf.* (*impf.* **запива́ть**) begin drinking, take to drink; wash down (with), take (with).

запиха́ть, **-а́ю** *pf.*, **запи́хивать**, **-аю** *impf.*, **запихну́ть**, **-ну́**, **-нёшь** *pf.* push in, cram in.

запишу́ *etc.: see* **записа́ть**

запла́канный tear-stained; in tears. **запла́кать**, **-а́чу** *pf.* begin to cry.

за|плани́ровать, **-рую** *pf.*

запла́та, **-ы** patch. **запла́танный** patched, mended.

за|плати́ть, **-ачу́**, **-а́тишь** *pf.* pay; **+за+*а.* pay for; **~ по счёту** settle an account.

запла́чу *etc.: see* **запла́кать**. **заплачу́** *see* **заплати́ть**

заплесневе́лый mouldy, mildewed. **за|плесневе́ть**, **-веет** *pf.*

заплести́, **-ету́**, **-етёшь**; **-ёл**, **-а́** *pf.*, **заплета́ть**, **-а́ю** *impf.* plait, braid; **~сь** stumble; be unsteady in one's gait; falter.

за|пломбирова́ть, **-рую** *pf.*

заплы́в, **-а** heat, round. **заплыва́ть**, **-а́ю** *impf.*, **заплы́ть**, **-ыву́**, **-ывёшь**; **-ы́л**, **-а́**, **-о** *pf.* swim in, sail in; swim out, sail out; be swollen, be bloated.

запну́ться, **-ну́сь**, **-нёшься** *pf.* (*impf.* **запина́ться**) hesitate; stumble, halt; stammer; **~ ного́й** trip (up).

запове́дник, **-а** reserve; preserve; **госуда́рственный ~** national park. **запове́дный** prohibited; **~ лес** forest reserve. **за́поведь**, **-и** precept; commandment.

заподо́зривать, **-аю** *impf.*, **заподо́зрить**, **-рю** *pf.* suspect (**в+*p.* of); be suspicious of.

запое́м *see* **запо́й**

запозда́лый belated; late; delayed. **запозда́ть**, **-а́ю** *pf.* (*impf.* **запа́здывать**) be late.

запо́й, **-я** hard drinking; alcoholism; **кури́ть запое́м** smoke like a chimney; **пить запое́м** have bouts of heavy drinking. **запо́йный** *adj.*; **~ пья́ница** chronic drunk; old soak.

заползать, -аю, заползти, -зу, -зёшь; -олз, -зла creep in, creep under; crawl in, crawl under.

заполнить, -ню *pf.*, заполнять, -яю *impf.* fill (in, up).

заполярный polar; trans-polar. заполярье, -я polar regions.

запоминать, -аю *impf.*, запомнить, -ню *pf.* remember, keep in mind; memorize; ~ся be retained in memory, stay in one's mind. запоминающ|ий; ~ее устройство (*comput.*) storage device.

запонка, -и cuff-link; (collar-)stud.

запор, -а bolt; lock; closing, locking, bolting; constipation; на ~е be locked, bolted.

запорошить, -шит *pf.* powder, dust, scatter.

запотелый misted, dim. за|потеть, -еет *pf.* mist over.

запою *etc.*: *see* запеть

заправила, -ы boss. заправить, -влю *pf.*, заправлять, -яю *impf.* insert, tuck in; prepare, set up; fuel, refuel, fill up; season, dress, flavour; ins ~ лампу trim a lamp; за-правлять делами boss the show; ~ся refuel. заправка, -и refuelling, filling; servicing, setting up; seasoning, dressing, flavouring.

запрашивать, -аю *impf. of* запросить

запрет, -а prohibition, ban; под ~ом banned, prohibited. запретительный prohibitive. запретить, -ещу *pf.*, запрещать, -аю *impf.* prohibit, forbid, ban. запретный forbidden, prohibited. запрещение, -я prohibition; distraint. запрещённый forbidden, illicit.

за|приходовать, -ую *pf.* за|программировать, -ую *pf.*

запрокидывать, -аю *impf.*, запрокинуть, -ну *pf.* throw back; ~ся throw o.s. back; fall back, sink back.

запрос, -а inquiry; overcharging; *pl.* requirements, needs. запросить, -ошу, -осишь *pf.* (*impf.* запрашивать) inquire; inquire of, question; ask (*a high price*).

запросто *adv.* without ceremony, without formality.

за|протоколировать, -рую *pf.* запрошу *etc.*: *see* запросить. запру *etc.*: *see* запереть

запруда, -ы dam, weir; mill-pond. за|прудить, -ужу, -удишь *pf.*, запруживать, -аю *impf.* block; dam; fill to overflowing, cram, jam.

запрягать, -аю *impf. of* запрячь. запрягу *etc.*: *see* запрячь. запряжка, -и harnessing; harness, team.

запрятать(ся, -ячу(сь *pf.*, запрятывать(ся, -аю(сь *impf.* hide.

запрячь, -ягу, -яжёшь; -яг, -яла *pf.* (*impf.* запрягать) harness; yoke.

запуганный cowed, intimidated, broken-spirited. запугать, -аю *pf.*, запугивать, -аю *impf.* cow, intimidate.

запускать, -аю *impf.*, запустить, -ущу,

-устишь *pf.* thrust (in), push (in), dig (in); start, start up; launch; (+*a. or i.*) throw, fling; neglect, let go. запустелый neglected; desolate. запустение, -я neglect; desolation.

запутанный tangled; intricate, involved, knotty. за|путать, -аю *pf.*, запутывать, -аю *impf.* tangle; confuse; complicate; muddle; involve; ~ся get tangled, get entangled; be involved, get involved; become complicated.

запущенный neglected. запущу *etc.*: *see* запустить

запчасть, -и; *g.pl.* -ей *abbr.* (*of* запасная часть) spare part, spare.

за|пылить(ся, -лю(сь *pf.*

запыхаться, -аюсь *pf.* be out of breath.

запью *etc.*: *see* запить

запястье, -я wrist; bracelet.

запятая *sb.* comma; difficulty, snag.

за|пятнать, -аю *pf.*

зарабатывать, -аю *impf.*, заработать, -аю *pf.* earn; start (up), begin to work; ~ся overwork. заработн|ый; ~ая плата wages; pay, salary. заработок, -тка earnings.

заражать, -аю *impf.*, заразить, -ажу *pf.* infect; ~ся+*i.* be infected with, catch. зараза, -ы infection, contagion; pest, plague. заразительный infectious; catching. заразный infectious, contagious; *sb.* infectious case.

заранее *adv.* beforehand; in good time; in advance.

зарастать, -аю *impf.*, зарасти, -ту, -тёшь; -рос, -ла *pf.* be overgrown; heal, skin over.

зарево, -а glow.

за|регистрировать(ся, -рую(сь *pf.*

за|регулировать, -рую *pf.*

зарез, -а (-у) disaster; до ~у desperately, badly, urgently. за|резать, -ежу *pf.* kill, knife; slaughter; ~ся cut one's throat.

зарекаться, -аюсь *impf. of* заречься

зарекомендовать, -дую *pf.*; ~ себя show o.s., present o.s.; +*i.* prove o.s., show o.s., to be.

заречься, -екусь, -ечёшься; -ёкся, -еклась *pf.* (*impf.* зарекаться) +*inf.* renounce; swear off, promise to give up.

за|ржаветь, -еет *pf.* заржавленный rusty.

зарисовать, -сую *pf.*, зарисовывать, -аю *impf.* sketch. зарисовка, -и sketching; sketch.

зарница, -ы summer lightning.

зародить, -ожу *pf.*, зарождать, -аю *impf.* generate, engender; ~ся be born; arise. зародыш, -а foetus; bud; embryo, germ. зародышевый embryonic. зарождение, -я conception; origin.

зарок, -а (solemn) promise, vow, pledge, undertaking.

зарос *etc.*: *see* зарасти. заросль, -и thicket; brushwood.

зарою *etc.*: *see* зарыть

зарплата, -ы *abbr.* (*of* заработная плата) wages; pay; salary.

зарубать, -аю *impf. of* зарубить

зарубе́жный foreign.

заруби́ть, -блю́, -бишь *pf.* (*impf.* **заруба́ть, -а́ю**) kill, cut down; notch, cut in. **зару́бка, -и** notch, incision.

за|румя́нить(ся, -ню(сь *pf.*

заруча́ться, -а́юсь *impf.*, **заручи́ться, -учу́сь** *pf.+i.* secure. **зару́чка, -и** pull, protection.

зарыва́ть, -а́ю *impf.*, **зары́ть, -ро́ю** *pf.* bury; ∼**ся** bury o.s.; dig in.

заря́, -и́; *pl.* **зо́ри, зорь** dawn, daybreak; sunset, nightfall; reveille, retreat.

заря́д, -а charge; cartridge; fund, supply. **заряди́ть, -яжу́, -я́ди́шь** *pf.*, **заряжа́ть, -а́ю** *impf.* load; charge; stoke; ∼**ся** be loaded; be charged. **заря́дка, -и** loading; charging; exercises, drill. **заряжа́ющий** *sb.* loader.

заса́да, -ы ambush. **засади́ть, -ажу́, -а́дишь** *pf.*, **заса́живать, -аю** *impf.* plant; plunge, drive; shut in, confine; keep in; set (**за**+*a.* to); ∼ (**в тюрьму́**) put in prison, lock up. **заса́дка, -и** planting. **заса́живаться, -аюсь** *impf. of* **засе́сть**

заса́ливать[1], -аю *impf. of* **засоли́ть**

заса́ливать[2], -аю *impf.*, **заса́лить, -лю** *pf.* soil, make greasy.

заса́сывать, -аю *impf. of* **засоса́ть**

заса́харенный candied, crystallized.

засвети́ть, -ечу́, -е́тишь *pf.* light; ∼**ся** light up. **за́светло** *adv.* before nightfall, before dark.

за|свиде́тельствовать, -твую *pf.*

засе́в, -а sowing; seed, seed-corn; sown area. **засева́ть, -а́ю** *impf. of* **засе́ять**

заседа́ние, -я meeting; session, sitting; conference. **заседа́тель, -я** *m.* assessor. **заседа́ть, -а́ю** *impf.* sit, meet, be in session.

засе́ивать, -аю *impf. of* **засе́ять. засёк** *etc.: see* **засе́чь засека́ть, -а́ю** *impf. of* **засе́чь**

засекре́тить, -е́чу *pf.*, **засекре́чивать, -аю** *impf.* classify; restrict; make secret; clear, give access to secret material. **засекре́ченный** classified; cleared; hush-hush, secret.

засеку́ *etc.: see* **засе́чь. засёл** *etc.: see* **засе́сть заселе́ние, -я** settlement; colonization. **заселённый; -ён, -ена́** populated, inhabited. **засели́ть, -лю́** *pf.*, **заселя́ть, -я́ю** *impf.* settle; colonize; populate; occupy.

засе́сть, -ся́ду; -сёл *pf.* (*impf.* **заса́живаться**) sit down (**за**+*a.* to); sit firm, sit tight; ensconce o.s.; lodge in, stick in.

засе́чка, -и notch, indentation, mark; intersection; fix; serif. **засе́чь, -еку́, -ечёшь; -ёк, -ла́** *pf.* (*impf.* **засека́ть**) flog to death; notch; intersect; locate; fix.

засе́ять, -ею *pf.* **засева́ть, засе́ивать**) sow.

засиде́ться, -ижу́сь *pf.*, **заси́живаться, -аюсь** *impf.* sit too long, stay too long; sit up late; stay late. **заси́женный** fly-specked, fly-blown.

за|силосова́ть, -су́ю *pf.*

заси́лье, -я dominance, sway.

засла́ть, зашлю́, -шлёшь *pf.* (*impf.* **засыла́ть**) send.

засло́н, -а screen; barrier, road-block; (*furnace, oven*) door. **заслони́ть, -оню́** *pf.*, **заслоня́ть, -я́ю** *impf.* cover; shield, screen; hide, push into the background. **засло́нка, -и** (stove-)lid; damper; slide; baffle-plate; (*furnace, oven*) door.

заслу́га, -и merit, desert; service. **заслу́женный, заслужённый** deserved, merited; meritorious, of merit, distinguished; Honoured; time-honoured, good old. **заслу́живать, -аю** *impf.*, **заслужи́ть, -ужу́, -у́жишь** *pf.* deserve, merit; win, earn; +*g.* be worthy or deserving of.

заслу́шать, -аю *pf.*, **заслу́шивать, -аю** *impf.* listen to, hear; ∼**ся** (+*g.*) listen spellbound (to).

засме́ивать, -аю *impf.*, **засмея́ть, -ею́, -еёшь** *pf.* ridicule; ∼**ся** begin to laugh; burst out laughing.

засмоли́ть, -лю́ *pf.* tar, pitch.

засну́ть, -ну́, -нёшь *pf.* (*impf.* **засыпа́ть**) go to sleep, fall asleep; die down.

засо́в, -а bolt, bar.

засо́вывать, -аю *impf. of* **засу́нуть**

засо́л, -а salting, pickling. **засоли́ть, -олю́, -о́ли́шь** *pf.* (*impf.* **заса́ливать**) salt, corn, pickle. **засо́лка, -и** salting, pickling; brine, pickle.

засоре́ние, -я littering; pollution, contamination; obstruction, clogging up. **засори́ть, -рю́** *pf.*, **засоря́ть, -я́ю** *impf.* litter; get dirt into; clog, block up, stop.

засоса́ть, -осу́, -осёшь *pf.* (*impf.* **заса́сывать**) suck in; engulf, swallow up.

за|со́хнуть, -ну; -со́х *pf.* (*impf. also* **засыха́ть**) dry, dry up; wither.

за́спанный sleepy.

заста́ва, -ы gate, gates; barrier; picket, picquet; outpost; **пограни́чная** ∼ frontier post.

застава́ть, -таю́, -таёшь *impf. of* **заста́ть**

заста́вить[1], -влю *pf.*, **заставля́ть, -я́ю** *impf.* cram; fill; block up, obstruct.

заста́вить[2], -влю *pf.*, **заставля́ть, -я́ю** *impf.* make; compel, force.

заста́иваться, -ается *impf. of* **застоя́ться.**

заста́ну *etc.: see* **заста́ть**

застаре́лый chronic; rooted.

заста́ть, -а́ну *pf.* (*impf.* **застава́ть**) find; catch.

застёгивать, -аю *impf.*, **застегну́ть, -ну́, -нёшь** *pf.* fasten, do up; button up, hook up. **застёжка, -и** fastening; clasp, buckle; hasp; ∼**-мо́лния** zip fastener, zip.

застекли́ть, -лю́ *pf.*, **застекля́ть, -я́ю** *impf.* glaze, fit with glass.

застелю́ *etc.: see* **застла́ть засте́нчивый** shy.

застига́ть, -а́ю *impf.*, **засти́гнуть, засти́чь, -и́гну; -сти́г** *pf.* catch; take unawares.

застила́ть, -а́ю *impf. of* **застла́ть. засти́лка, -и** covering; floor-covering.

засти́чь *see* **засти́гнуть**

застла́ть, -телю́, -те́лешь *pf.* (*impf.* застила́ть) cover; spread over; cloud; ~ ковро́м carpet.

засто́й, -я stagnation; standstill; depression. засто́йный stagnant; sluggish, immobile.

засто́льн|ый table-; ~ая речь after-dinner speech.

за|сто́порить, -рю *pf.*

застоя́ться, -и́тся *pf.* (*impf.* заста́иваться) stagnate, stand too long, get stale.

застра́ивать, -аю *impf. of* застро́ить

застрахо́ванный insured. за|страхова́ть, -ху́ю *pf.*, застрахо́вывать, -аю *impf.* insure (от+*g.* against).

застрева́ть, -а́ю *impf. of* застря́ть

застрели́ть, -елю́, -е́лишь *pf.* shoot (dead); ~ся shoot o.s.; blow one's brains out.

застре́льщик, -а pioneer, leader.

застро́ить, -о́ю *pf.* (*impf.* застра́ивать) build over, build on, build up. застро́йка, -и building.

застря́ть, -я́ну *pf.* (*impf.* застрева́ть) stick; get stuck; be held up; be bogged down.

за|студене́ть, -е́ет *pf.*

застуди́ть, -ужу́, -у́дишь *pf.*, засту́живать, -аю *impf.* expose to cold, chill; ~ся catch cold.

за́ступ, -а spade.

заступа́ться, -а́юсь *impf.*, заступи́ться, -плю́сь, -пишься *pf.* +за+*a.* stand up for, take the part of; plead for. засту́пник, -а defender; protector. засту́пничество, -а protection; intercession, defence.

застыва́ть, -а́ю *impf.*, засты́ть, -ы́ну *pf.* congeal; thicken, harden, set; become stiff; freeze; be petrified, be paralysed. засты́лый congealed; stiff.

засу́нуть, -ну *pf.* (*impf.* засо́вывать) thrust in, push in, shove in; stuff in; tuck in.

за́суха, -и drought.

засу́чивать, -аю *impf.*, засучи́ть, -чу́, -чишь *pf.* roll up.

засу́шивать, -аю *impf.*, засуши́ть, -шу́, -шишь *pf.* dry up, shrivel. засу́шливый arid, dry, drought.

засыла́ть, -а́ю *impf. of* засла́ть

засыпа́ть[1], -плю *pf.*, засыпа́ть, -а́ю *impf.* fill up, fill in; cover, strew; put in, add; ~ вопро́сами bombard with questions.

засыпа́ть[2](ся, -а́ю(сь *impf. of* засну́ть, засы́пать(ся

засы́паться, -плюсь *pf.* (*impf.* засыпа́ться) be caught; come to grief; slip up; fail an examination.

засы́пка, -и filling; backfilling; filling up, charging; covering, strewing; putting in.

засыха́ть, -а́ю *impf. of* засо́хнуть

зася́ду *etc.: see* засе́сть

затаённый; -ён, -ена́ secret; repressed, suppressed. зата́ивать, -аю *impf.*, затаи́ть, -аю́ *pf.* suppress, repress; conceal; harbour, cherish; ~ дыха́ние hold one's breath; ~ оби́ду nurse a grievance, bear a grudge.

зата́лкивать, -аю *impf. of* затолка́ть. зата́пливать, -аю *impf. of* затопи́ть. зата́птывать, -аю *impf. of* затопта́ть

зата́сканный worn; threadbare; hackneyed, trite. затаска́ть, -а́ю *pf.*, зата́скивать[1], -аю *impf.* wear out; make hackneyed, make trite; drag about; ~ по суда́м drag through the courts; ~ся wear (out), get dirty or threadbare with use.

зата́скивать[2], -аю *impf.*, затащи́ть, -щу́, -щишь *pf.* drag in; drag off, drag away.

затвердева́ть, -а́ет *impf.*, за|тверде́ть, -е́ет *pf.* harden, become hard; set; solidify; freeze. затверде́вший, затверде́лый hardened; solidified, set, congealed. затверде́ние, -я hardening; induration, callosity; callus. за|тверди́ть, -ржу́ *pf.*

затво́р, -а bolt, bar; lock; breech-block; shutter; water-gate, flood-gate. затвори́ть, -рю́, -ришь *pf.*, затворя́ть, -я́ю *impf.* shut, close; ~ся shut o.s. up, lock o.s. in. затво́рник, -а hermit, anchorite, recluse.

затева́ть, -а́ю *impf. of* зате́ять. зате́йливый ingenious; intricate, involved; original.

затёк *etc.: see* зате́чь. затека́ть, -а́ет *impf. of* зате́чь

зате́м *adv.* then, after that, next; for that reason; ~ что because, since, as.

затемне́ние, -я darkening, obscuring; blacking out; black-out; fade-out. затемни́ть, -ню́ *pf.*, затемня́ть, -я́ю *impf.* darken, obscure; black out. за́темно *adv.* before dawn.

затере́ть, -тру́, -трёшь; -тёр *pf.* (*impf.* затира́ть) rub out; block, jam; су́дно затёрло льда́ми the ship was ice bound.

зате́рянный lost; forgotten, forsaken. затеря́ть, -я́ю *pf.* lose, mislay; ~ся be lost; be mislaid; be forgotten.

зате́чь, -ечёт, -еку́т; -тёк, -кла́ *pf.* (*impf.* затека́ть) pour, flow; leak; swell up; become numb.

зате́я, -и undertaking, enterprise, venture; escapade; joke. зате́ять, -е́ю *pf.* (*impf.* затева́ть) undertake, venture; organize; ~ дра́ку start a fight.

затира́ть, -а́ю *impf. of* затере́ть

затиха́ть, -а́ю *impf.*, зати́хнуть, -ну; -ти́х *pf.* die down, abate; die away, fade; become quiet. зати́шье, -я calm; lull; sheltered corner; backwater.

заткну́ть, -ну́, -нёшь *pf.* (*impf.* затыка́ть) stop up; plug; stick, thrust; ~ про́бкой cork.

затмева́ть, -а́ю *impf.*, затми́ть, -ми́шь *pf.* darken, obscure; eclipse; overshadow. затме́ние, -я eclipse; darkening; black-out.

зато́ *conj.* but then, but on the other hand.

затова́ренность, -и, затова́ривание, -я overstocking; glut.

затолка́ть, -а́ю *pf.* (*impf.* зата́лкивать) jostle.

зато́н, -а backwater; boat-yard. затону́ть, -о́нет *pf.* sink, be submerged.

затопи́ть[1], -плю́, -пишь *pf.* (*impf.* затап-

ли́вать) light; turn on the heating.

затопи́ть², **-плю́**, **-пишь** *pf.*, **затопля́ть**, **-я́ю** *impf.* flood, submerge; sink, scuttle.

затопта́ть, **-пчу́**, **-пчешь** *pf.* (*impf.* **зата́птывать**) trample, trample down; trample underfoot.

зато́р, **-а** obstruction, block, jam; congestion.

за|тормози́ть, **-ожу́** *pf.*

заточа́ть, **-а́ю** *impf.*, **заточи́ть**, **-чу́** *pf.* confine, shut up; incarcerate, imprison. **заточе́ние**, **-я** confinement; incarceration, captivity.

за|трави́ть, **-влю́**, **-вишь** *pf.*, **затра́вливать**, **-аю** *impf.* hunt down, bring to bay; persecute, harass, harry; badger.

затра́гивать, **-аю** *impf. of* **затро́нуть**

затра́та, **-ы** expense; outlay. **затра́тить**, **-а́чу** *pf.*, **затра́чивать**, **-аю** *impf.* expend, spend.

затре́бовать, **-бую** *pf.* request, require; ask for.

затро́нуть, **-ну** *pf.* (*impf.* **затра́гивать**) affect; touch, graze; touch on.

затрудне́ние, **-я** difficulty. **затрудни́тельный** difficult; embarrassing. **затрудни́ть**, **-ню́** *pf.*, **затрудня́ть**, **-я́ю** *impf.* trouble; cause trouble to; embarrass; make difficult; hamper; **~ся** be in difficulties; +*inf. or i.* find difficulty in.

затума́нивать, **-аю** *impf.*, **за|тума́нить**, **-ит** *pf.* befog; cloud, dim, obscure.

за|тупи́ть, **-плю́**, **-пишь** *pf.*

за|тушева́ть, **-шу́ю** *pf.*, **затушёвывать**, **-аю** *impf.* shade; conceal; draw a veil over.

за|туши́ть, **-шу́**, **-шишь** *pf.* put out, extinguish; suppress.

за́тхлый musty, mouldy; stuffy, close; stagnant.

затыка́ть, **-а́ю** *impf. of* **заткну́ть**

заты́лок, **-лка** back of the head; occiput; scrag, scrag-end. **заты́лочный** occipital.

затя́гивать, **-аю** *impf.*, **затяну́ть**, **-ну́**, **-нешь** *pf.* tighten; lace up; cover; close, heal; drag out, draw out, spin out; **~ся** be covered; close, skin over; be delayed; linger; be drawn out, drag on; inhale. **затя́жка**, **-и** inhaling; prolongation; dragging on; drawing out; delaying, putting off; lagging. **затяжно́й** long-drawn-out; lingering.

зауны́вный mournful, doleful.

заура́дный ordinary, commonplace; mediocre.

заусе́нец, **-нца**, **заусе́ница**, **-ы** agnail, hangnail, wire-edge, burr.

за|фарширова́ть, **-ру́ю** *pf.* **за|фикси́ровать**, **-рую** *pf.* **за|фрахтова́ть**, **-ту́ю** *pf.*

захва́т, **-а** seizure, capture; usurpation; clamp, claw. **захвати́ть**, **-ачу́**, **-а́тишь** *pf.* **захва́тывать**, **-аю** *impf.* take; seize, capture; carry away; thrill, excite; catch; **у меня́ захвати́ло дух** it took my breath away. **захва́тнический** predatory; aggressive. **захва́тчик**, **-а** invader; aggressor. **захва́тывающий** gripping; **~ дух** breath-taking.

захвора́ть, **-а́ю** *pf.* fall ill, be taken ill.

за|хире́ть, **-е́ю** *pf.*

захлебну́ться, **-ну́сь**, **-нёшься** *pf.*, **захлёбываться**, **-аюсь** *impf.* choke (**от**+*g.* with).

захлестну́ть, **-ну́**, **-нёшь** *pf.* **захлёстывать**, **-аю** *impf.* flow over, swamp, overwhelm; overflow.

захло́пнуть, **-ну** *pf.*, **захло́пывать**, **-аю** *impf.* slam, bang; **~ся** slam (to), bang (to), shut with a bang.

захо́д, **-а** setting, sunset; stopping, calling, putting in. **заходи́ть**, **-ожу́**, **-о́дишь** *impf. of* **зайти́**. **захо́жий** newly-arrived.

захолу́стный remote, out-of-the-way, provincial. **захолу́стье**, **-я** backwoods; godforsaken hole.

за|хорони́ть, **-ню́**, **-нишь** *pf.* **за|хоте́ть(ся**, **-очу́(сь**, **-о́чешь(ся**, **-оти́м(ся** *pf.*

захуда́лый impoverished, poor, shabby; emaciated.

зацвести́, **-ете́т**, **-вёл**, **-а́** *pf.*, **зацвета́ть**, **-а́ет** *impf.* burst into flower, come into bloom.

зацепи́ть, **-плю́**, **-пишь** *pf.*, **зацепля́ть**, **-я́ю** *impf.* hook; engage; sting; catch (**за**+*a.* on); **~ся за**+*a.* catch on; catch hold of. **заце́пка**, **-и** catch, hook, peg; hooking; hitch, catch; pull, protection.

зачасту́ю *adv.* often, frequently.

зача́тие, **-я** conception. **зача́ток**, **-тка** embryo; rudiment; beginning, germ. **зача́точный** rudimentary. **зача́ть**, **-чну́**, **-чнёшь**; **-ча́л**, **-а́**, **-о** *pf.* (*impf.* **зачина́ть**) conceive; begin.

за|ча́хнуть, **-ну**; **-ча́х** *pf.* **зачёл** *etc.*: *see* **заче́сть**

зачем *adv.* why; what for. **заче́м-то** *adv.* for some reason.

зачёркивать, **-аю** *impf.*, **зачеркну́ть**, **-ну́**, **-нёшь** *pf.* cross out, strike out; delete.

за|черни́ть, **-ню́** *pf.*

зачерпну́ть, **-ну́**, **-нёшь** *pf.*, **заче́рпывать**, **-аю** *impf.* scoop up; ladle; draw up.

зачерстве́лый stale; hard-hearted. **за|черстве́ть**, **-е́ет** *pf.*

заче́сть, **-чту́**, **-чтёшь**; **-чёл**, **-чла́** *pf.* (*impf.* **зачи́тывать**) take into account, reckon as credit. **зачёт**, **-а** reckoning; instalment; test; **в ~ пла́ты** in payment, on account; **получи́ть**, **сдать ~ по**+*d.* pass a test in; **поста́вить ~ по**+*d.* pass in. **зачётн**|**ый**; **~ая квита́нция** receipt; **~ая кни́жка** (student's) record book.

за|чехли́ть, **-лю́** *pf.*

зачина́тель, **-я** founder, author. **зачина́ть**, **-а́ю** *impf. of* **зача́ть**. **зачи́нщик**, **-а** instigator, ringleader.

зачи́слить, **-лю** *pf.*, **зачисля́ть**, **-я́ю** *impf.* include; enter; enrol, enlist; **~ся** join, enter.

зачи́тывать, **-аю** *impf. of* **заче́сть**

зачну́ *etc.*: *see* **зача́ть**. **зачту́** *etc.*: *see* **заче́сть**. **зашёл** *etc.*: *see* **зайти́**

зашива́ть, **-а́ю** *impf.*·**заши́ть**, **-шью́**, **-шьёшь** *pf.* sew up; suture; put stitches in.

зашифро́ванный encoded, in cipher **за|шифрова́ть**, **-ру́ю** *pf.* **зашифро́вывать**, **-аю**

impf. encipher, encode.

зашлю́ *etc.*: *see* **засла́ть**

за|шнурова́ть, -ру́ю *pf.*, **зашнуро́вывать, -аю** *impf.* lace up.

за|шпаклева́ть, -лю́ю *pf.* **за|штемпелева́ть, -лю́ю** *pf.* **за|што́пать, -аю** *pf.* **за|штрихова́ть, -ху́ю** *pf.*

зашью́ *etc.*: *see* **заши́ть**

защипну́ть, -ну́, -нёшь *pf.*, **защи́пывать, -аю** *impf.* pinch, nip, tweak; take; curl; punch.

защи́та, -ы defence; protection; the defence. **защити́ть, -ищу́** *pf.*, **защища́ть, -а́ю** *impf.* defend, protect; stand up for.

заяви́ть, -влю́, -вишь *pf.*, **завля́ть, -я́ю** *impf.* announce, declare; claim; show, attest; **~ся** appear, turn up. **зая́вка, -и** claim; demand, request. **заявле́ние, -я** statement, declaration; application.

зая́длый inveterate, confirmed.

за́яц, за́йца hare; stowaway; gate-crasher; **е́хать за́йцем** travel without a ticket. **за́ячий** hare, hare's; **~ щаве́ль** wood sorrel.

зва́ние, -я calling, profession; rank; title. **зва́ный** invited; **~ ве́чер** guest-night; **~ гость** guest; **~ обе́д** banquet, dinner, dinner-party. **зва́тельный** vocative. **звать, зову́, -вёшь; звал, -á, -о** *impf.* (*pf.* по**~**) call; ask, invite; **как вас зову́т?** what is your name?; **~ся** be called.

звезда́, -ы́; *pl.* **звёзды** star. **звёздный** star; starry; starlit; stellar. **звездообра́зный** star-shaped; radial; stellate. **звездочёт, -á** astrologer. **звёздочка, -и** little star; asterisk.

звене́ть, -ню́ *impf.* ring; +*i.* jingle, clink.

звено́, -á; *pl.* **зве́нья, -ьев** link; bond; team, group, section, flight; unit; component, element; network. **звеньево́й** *sb.* team leader; section leader.

звери́нец, -нца menagerie. **звери́ный** wild-animal, wild-beast. **зверобо́й** hunter, sealer. **зверово́дство, -а** fur farming. **звероло́в, -а** trapper. **зве́рски** *adv.* brutally, bestially; terribly, awfully. **зве́рский** brutal, bestial; terrific, tremendous. **зве́рство, -а** brutality; atrocity. **зве́рствовать, -твую** *impf.* commit atrocities. **зверь, -я;** *pl.* **-и, -éй** *m.* wild animal, wild beast; brute. **зверьё, -я́** wild animals; wild beasts.

звон, -а ringing; ringing sound, chime, peal, chink, clink. **звони́ть, -ню́** *impf.* (*pf.* по**~**) ring; ring up; **~ в колокола́** ring the bells; **~ кому́-нибудь (по телефо́ну)** ring s.o. up, telephone s.o.; **вы не туда́ звони́те** you've got the wrong number; **звоня́т** the telephone's ringing; there's s.o. at the door; **~ся** ring the (door-)bell, ring. **зво́нк|ий; -нок, -нка́, -о** ringing, clear; voiced; **~ая моне́та** hard cash, coin. **звоно́к, -нка́** bell; **~ по телефо́ну** (telephone) call. **зво́нче, звонче́е** *comp. of* **зво́нкий, зво́нко**

звук, -а sound; **ни ~а** not a sound.

звуко... *in comb.* sound. **звукоза́пись, -и** sound recording. **~изоля́ция, -и** sound-

proofing. **~непроница́емый** sound-proof. **~подража́тельный** onomatopoeic. **~прово́дный** sound conducting. **~снима́тель, -я** *m.* pick-up. **~ула́вливатель, -я** *m.* sound locator. **~часто́тный** audio, audio-frequency.

звуково́й sound; audio; acoustical, acoustic. **звуча́ние, -я** sound vibration; phonation. **звуча́ть, -чи́т** *impf.* be heard; sound; +*i.* express, convey; **~ и́скренно** ring true. **зву́чный; -чен, -чна́, -о** sonorous.

звя́канье, -я jingling; tinkling. **звя́кать, -аю** *impf.*, **звя́кнуть, -ну** *pf.* (+*i.*) jingle; tinkle.

зда́ние, -я building.

здесь *adv.* here; at this point; in this. **зде́шний** local; **не ~** a stranger here.

здоро́ваться, -аюсь *impf.* (*pf.* по**~**) exchange greetings; **~ за́ руку** shake hands. **здо́рово** *adv.* splendidly, magnificently; well done! fine! **здоро́вый** healthy, strong; well; health-giving, wholesome, sound. **здоро́вье, -я** health; **за ва́ше ~!** your health! **как ва́ше ~?** how are you? **здра́вица, -ы** toast. **здра́вница, -ы** sanatorium. **здра́во** *adv.* soundly; sensibly.

здра́во... *in comb.* health; sound, sensible. **здравомы́слящий** sensible, judicious. **~охране́ние, -я** public health; health service. **~охрани́тельный** public-health.

здравпу́нкт, -а medical post, medical centre. **здра́вствовать, -твую** *impf.* be healthy; thrive, prosper; **здра́вствуй(те)!** how do you do?; good morning, afternoon, evening; **да здра́вствует!** long live! **здра́в|ый** sensible; healthy; **в ~ом уме́** in one's right mind; **~ый смысл** common sense.

зе́бра, -ы zebra; zebra crossing.

зев, -а pharynx; jaws. **зева́ка, -и** *c.g.* idler, gaper. **зева́ть, -а́ю** *impf.*, **зевну́ть, -нёшь** *pf.* (*pf. also* про**~**) yawn; gape; miss, let slip; lose. **зево́к, -вка́** **зево́та, -ы** yawn.

зелене́ть, -éет *impf.* (*pf.* по**~**) turn green, go green; show green. **зеленн|о́й** **~ая ла́вка** greengrocer's. **зеленова́тый** greenish. **зелён|ый; зе́лен, -á, -о** green; **~ый лук** spring onions; **~ая у́лица** go, green light. **зе́лень, -и** green; greenery, vegetation; greens; vegetables.

земле... *in comb.* land; earth. **землеве́дение, -я** physical geography. **~владе́лец, -льца** landowner. **~де́лец, -льца** farmer. **~де́лие, -я** farming, agriculture. **~де́льческий** agricultural. **~ко́п, -а** navvy. **~ме́р, -а** land-surveyor. **~ме́рный** surveying, surveyor's. **~ро́йный** earth-moving, excavating. **~трясе́ние, -я** earthquake. **~черпа́лка, -и** mechanical dredger, bucket dredger. **~черпа́ние, -я** dredging.

земли́стый earthy; sallow. **земля́, -и́, *a.* -ю;** *pl.* **-и, земе́ль, -ям** earth; land; soil. **земля́к, -á** fellow-countryman. **земляни́ка, -и** strawberries; wild strawberries. **земля́нка, -и** dug-out; mud hut. **землян|о́й** earthen; earth;

earthy; ~ая груша Jerusalem artichoke.
землячка, -и country-woman. **земной**
earthly; terrestrial; ground; mundane; ~ шар
the globe.

зенит, -а zenith. **зенитный** zenith; anti-aircraft.

зеркало, -а; *pl.* -á looking-glass; mirror; re-
flector. **зеркальн|ый** mirror; looking-glass;
reflecting; smooth; plate, plate-glass; ~ое
изображение mirror image.

зернист|ый granular, granulated; grainy; ~ая
икра unpressed caviare. **зерно**, -á; *pl.* **зёрна**,
зёрен grain; seed; kernel, core; corn; **кофе**
в зёрнах coffee beans. **зерновидный** granular. **зерновой** grain, corn, seed. **зерно-
вые** *sb.*, *pl.* cereals; grain crop. **зернохра-
нилище**, -а granary.

зерцало, -а looking-glass; *pl.* breast-plate.

зигзаг, -а zigzag.

зима, -ы, *a.* -у; *pl.* -ы winter. **зимний** winter,
wintry. **зимовать**, -мую *impf.* (*pf.* пере~,
про~) winter, spend the winter; hibernate.
зимовка, -и wintering, winter stay; hibernation; polar station. **зимовщик**, -а win-
terer. **зимовье**, -я winter quarters. **зимой**
adv. in winter. **зимостойкий** hardy.

зияние, -я gaping, yawning; gap; hiatus.
зиять, -яет *impf.* gape, yawn.

злак, -а grass; cereal. **злаковый** grassy, herbaceous; cereal, grain.

злейший *superl.* of **злой**; ~враг worst enemy. **злить**, злю *impf.* (*pf.* обо~, о~,
разо~) anger; irritate; ~ся be angry, be in
a bad temper; rage. **зло**, -а; *g.pl.* зол evil;
harm; misfortune, disaster; malice, spite;
vexation. **зло** *adv.* maliciously, spitefully.

зло... *in comb.* evil, harm, malice; wicked,
malicious; bad-tempered. **зловещий** ominous, ill-omened. ~воние, -я stink, stench.
~вонный fetid, stinking. ~вредный pernicious; noxious. ~качественный malignant; pernicious. ~намеренный ill-inten-
tioned. ~памятный rancorous, unforgiving.
~получный unlucky, ill-starred. ~радный
malevolent, gloating. ~словие, -я malicious
gossip; backbiting. ~умышленник, -а mal-
efactor, criminal; plotter. ~умышленный
with criminal intent. ~язычие, -я slander,
backbiting. ~язычный slanderous.

злоба, -ы malice; spite; anger; ~ дня topic
of the day, latest news. **злобный** malicious,
spiteful; bad-tempered. **злободневн|ый**
topical; ~ые вопросы burning issues, top-
ics of the day. **злодей**, -я villain; scoundrel.
злодейский villainous. **злодейство**, -а villainy; crime, evil deed. **злодеяние**, -я crime,
evil deed. **злой**; зол, зла evil; bad; wicked;
malicious; malevolent; vicious; bad-tempered;
savage; dangerous; severe, cruel; bad, nasty;
«злая собака» 'beware of the dog'. **злост-
н|ый** malicious; conscious, intentional; per-
sistent, hardened; ~ное банкротство
fraudulent bankruptcy. **злость**, -и malice,

spite; fury. **злоупотребить**, -блю *pf.*, **зло-
употреблять**, -яю *impf.*+i. abuse. **злоупот-
ребление**, -я+i. abuse of; ~ доверием
breach of confidence.

змейный snake; snake's; cunning, crafty;
wicked. **змейстый** serpentine; sinuous.
змей, -я snake; dragon; kite. **змея**, -й; *pl.* -и
snake. **змий**, -я serpent, dragon.

знак, -а sign; mark; token, symbol; omen; signal; ~и препинания punctuation marks; ~и
различия insignia, badges of rank.
знакомить, -млю *impf.* (*pf.* о~, по~) acquaint; introduce; ~ся become acquainted,
acquaint o.s.; get to know; introduce o.s.;
study, investigate; +c+i. meet, make the acquaintance of. **знакомство**, -а acquaintance;
(circle of) acquaintances; knowledge (c+i.
of). **знаком|ый** familiar; **быть** ~ым c+i. be
acquainted with, know; ~ый, ~ая *sb.* acquaintance, friend.

знаменатель, -я *m.* denominator; **привести**
к одному знаменателю reduce to a common denominator. **знаменательный** significant, important; principal. **знамение**, -я
sign. **знаменитость**, -и celebrity. **знаменитый** celebrated, famous, renowned; outstanding, superlative. **знаменовать**, -ную
impf. signify, mark. **знаменосец**, -сца standard-bearer. **знамя**, -мени; *pl.* -мёна *nt.* banner; flag; standard.

знание, -я knowledge; *pl.* learning; accom-
plishments; **со знанием дела** capably, com-
petently.

знатный; -тен, -тна, -о distinguished; outstanding, notable; noble, aristocratic; splendid.

знаток, -á expert; connoisseur. **знать**, -аю
impf. know; **дать** ~ inform, let know; **дайте**
мне ~ **о вас** let me hear from you; **дать**
себе ~ make itself felt; ~ **в лицо** know by
sight; ~ **меру** know where to stop; ~ **себе**
цену know one's own value; ~ **толк в**+*p.* be
knowledgeable about; ~ся associate.

значение, -я meaning; significance; importance; value. **значит** so then; that means.
значительный considerable, sizeable; important; significant; meaningful. **значить**,
-чу *impf.* mean; signify; have significance, be
of importance; ~ся be; be mentioned, appear. **значок**, -чка badge; mark.

знающий expert; learned, erudite; knowledgeable; well-informed.

знобить, -ит *impf.*, *impers.*+a.; **меня**, *etc.*,
знобит I feel shivery, feverish.

зной, -я intense heat. **знойный** hot, sultry;
burning.

зов, -а (-у) call, summons; invitation. **зову**
etc.: *see* **звать**

зодческий architecture, architectural. **зод-
чество**, -а architecture. **зодчий** *sb.* architect.

зол *see* **зло**, **злой**

зола, -ы ashes, cinders.

золо́вка, -и sister-in-law, husband's sister.
золоти́стый golden. **золоти́ть, -очу́** *impf.* (*pf.* **вы~, по~**) gild. **зо́лото, -а** gold. **золот|о́й** gold; golden; **~бе дно** gold-mine; **~о́й запа́с** gold reserves; **~о́й песо́к** gold-dust; **~ы́е про́мыслы** gold-fields. **золото-но́сный** auriferous; gold-bearing.
золоту́ха, -и scrofula. **золоту́шный** scrofulous.
золоче́ние, -я gilding. **золочёный** gilt, gilded.
зо́на, -ы zone; region; band, belt. **зона́льный** zonal, zone; regional.
зонд, -а probe; bore; sonde. **зонди́ровать, -рую** *impf.* sound, probe.
зонт, -а́ umbrella; awning. **зо́нтик, -а** umbrella; sunshade; umbrel. **зо́нтичный** umbellate, umbelliferous.
зоо́лог, -а zoologist. **зоологи́ческий** zoological. **зооло́гия, -и** zoology. **зоомагази́н, -а** pet-shop. **зоопа́рк, -а** zoo, zoological gardens. **зоофе́рма, -ы** fur farm.
зо́ри *etc.*: *see* **заря́**
зо́ркий; -рок, -рка́, -о sharp-sighted; perspicacious, penetrating; vigilant.
зрачо́к, -чка́ pupil.
зре́лище, -а sight; spectacle; show; pageant.
зре́лость, -и ripeness; maturity; **аттеста́т зре́лости** school-leaving certificate. **зре́лый; зрел, -а́, -о** ripe, mature.
зре́ние, -я sight, eyesight, vision; **обма́н зре́ния** optical illusion; **по́ле зре́ния** field of vision, field of view; **то́чка зре́ния** point of view; **у́гол зре́ния** viewing angle, camera angle.
зреть, -е́ю *impf.* (*pf.* **со~**) ripen; mature.
зри́мый visible. **зри́тель, -я** *m.* spectator, observer; onlooker; *pl.* audience. **зри́тельный** visual; optic; **~ зал** hall, auditorium.
зря *adv.* to no purpose, for nothing, in vain.
зря́чий sighted, seeing.
зуб, -а; *pl.* **-ы** *or* **-бья, -бв** *or* **-бьев** tooth; cog. **зуба́стый** large-toothed; sharp-tongued. **зубе́ц, -бца́** tooth, cog, tine; blip. **зуби́ло, -а** chisel. **зубно́й** dental; tooth; **~ врач** dentist. **зубоврачо́бный** dentists', dental; **~ кабине́т** dental surgery. **зубоврача́вание, -я** dentistry. **зубо́к, -бка́;** *pl.* **-бки́** tooth; cog; clove. **зубоска́л, -а** scoffer. **зубочи́стка, -и** toothpick.
зубр, -а (European) bison, aurochs; die-hard. **зубри́ть¹, -рю** *impf.* (*pf.* **за~**) notch, serrate. **зубри́ть², -рю, зу́бришь** *impf.* (*pf.* **вы~, за~**) cram, learn by rote.
зубча́тка, -и sprocket; gear-wheel; gear; rack-wheel. **зубча́тый** toothed, cogged; gear, gear-wheel; serrate, serrated; jagged, indented.
зуд, -а itch. **зуда́, -ы́** *c.g.* bore. **зуде́ть, -и́т** itch.
ЗУПВ *abbr.* (*of* **запомина́ющее устро́йство с произво́льной вы́боркой**) (*comput.*) RAM, (*random-access memory*).
зы́бкий; -бок, -бка́, -о unsteady, shaky; un-

stable, shifting; vacillating. **зыбу́ч|ий** unsteady, shifting, shifting; **~ие пески́** quick-sands. **зыбь, -и;** *g.pl.* **-е́й** ripple, rippling.
зы́чный loud, stentorian.
зэ *nt.indecl.* the letter **з**.
зюйд, -а south; south wind.
зя́бкий chilly, sensitive to cold.
зя́блик, -а chaffinch.
зя́блый frozen; damaged by frost.
зя́бнуть, -ну; зяб *impf.* suffer from cold, feel the cold.
зять, -я; *pl.* **-тья, -тьёв** son-in-law; brother-in-law, sister's husband.

И

и *nt.indecl.* the letter **и**; **и с кра́ткой, и кра́ткое** the letter **й**.
и *conj.* and; and so; even; just; too; as well; (*with neg.*) either; **в то́м-то и де́ло** that's just it, that's the whole point; **и... и** both ... and; **и он не знал** he didn't know either; **и про́чее, и так да́лее** etc., etcetera, and so on and so forth; **и тому́ подо́бное** and the like; **и тот и друго́й** both.
и́бо *conj.* for; because, since.
и́ва, -ы willow. **ивня́к, -а́** osier-bed; osiers, osier. **и́вовый** willow.
и́волга, -и oriole.
игла́, -ы́; *pl.* **-ы** needle; thorn; spine; quill.
иглотерапе́вт, -а acupuncturist. **иглотера-пи́я, -и** acupuncture.
и́го, -а yoke.
иго́лка, -и needle. **иго́лочка, -и** *dim.*: **с иго́-лочки** brand-new, spick and span. **иго́ль-ник, -а** needle-case. **иго́льный** needle, needle's. **иго́льчатый** needle-shaped; acicular; needle; **~ при́нтер** dot-matrix printer.
иго́рный gaming, gambling. **игра́, -ы́;** *pl.* **-ы** play, playing; game; hand; turn, lead; **~ приро́ды** sport, freak (of nature); **~ слов** *pun.* **игра́льный** playing; **~ ко́сти** dice. **игра́ть, -а́ю** *impf.* (*pf.* **сыгра́ть**) play; act; **~ в+a.** play (*game*); **~ на+p.** play (*an instrument*), play on; **+i. or c+i.** play with, toy with, trifle with; **~ в билья́рд, на билья́рде** play billiards; **э́то не игра́ет ро́ли** it is of no importance, of no significance. **игри́вый** playful. **игри́стый** sparkling. **игро́к, -а́** player; gambler. **игру́шечный** toy. **игру́ш-ка, -и** toy; plaything.
идеа́л, -а ideal. **идеализи́ровать, -рую** *impf. & pf.* idealize. **идеали́зм, -а** idealism. **идеали́ст, -а** idealist. **идеалисти́ческий, идеалисти́чный** idealistic.

идеа́льн|ый ideal, perfect; **~ое состоя́ние** mint condition.

иде́йность, -и principle, integrity; ideological content. **иде́йный** high-principled; acting on principle; ideological.

идео́лог, -а ideologist. **идеологи́ческий** ideological. **идеоло́гия, -и** ideology.

идёт *etc.: see* **идти́**

иде́|я, -и idea; notion, concept; **счастли́вая ~** happy thought.

идилли́ческий idyllic. **иди́ллия, -и** idyll.

идио́ма, -ы idiom. **идиомати́ческий** idiomatic.

идио́т, -а idiot, imbecile. **идиоти́зм, -а** idiocy, imbecility. **идиоти́ческий, идио́тский** idiotic, imbecile.

йдол, -а idol. **идолопокло́нник, -а** idolater. **идолопокло́ннический** idolatrous.

идти́, иду́, идёшь; шёл, шла *impf. (pf.* **пойти́)** go; come; go round; run, work; pass; go on, be in progress; be on, be showing; fall; **+в+**nom.-a. become; **+в+**a. be used for, go for; **+(к+)**d. suit, become; **+на+**a. enter; go to make, go on; **+о+**p. be about; **+**i. or **с+**g. play, lead, move; **ей идёт тридца́тый год** she is in her thirtieth year; **~ в лётчики** become a flyer; **~ в лом** go for scrap; **~ на сме́ну+**d. take the place of, succeed; **~ ферзём** move the queen; **~ с черве́й** lead a heart; **хорошо́ ~** be selling well, be going well; **шли го́ды** years passed; **э́та шля́па ей не идёт** that hat doesn't suit her.

иезуи́т, -а Jesuit. **иезуи́тский** Jesuit.

иере́й, -я priest. **иере́йство, -а** priesthood.

иеро́глиф, -а hieroglyph; ideogram, ideograph. **иероглифи́ческий** hieroglyphic.

иждиве́нец, -нца, -ве́нка, -и dependant. **иждиве́ние, -я** maintenance; means, funds; **на иждиве́нии** at the expense of; **жить на своём иждиве́нии** keep o.s.; **жить на иждиве́нии роди́телей** live on one's parents. **иждиве́нчество, -а** dependence.

из, изо *prep.+*g. from, out of, of; **вы́йти из до́ма** go out, leave the house; **изо всех сил** with all one's might; **из достове́рных исто́чников** from reliable sources, on good authority; **ло́жки из серебра́** silver spoons; **обе́д из трёх блюд** a three-course dinner; **оди́н из ста** one in a hundred.

из..., изо..., изъ..., ис... *vbl. pref. expressing motion outwards; action over entire surface of object, in all directions; expenditure of instrument or object in course of action; continuation or repetition of action to extreme point; exhaustiveness of action.*

изба́, -ы́; *pl.* **-ы** izba; **~-чита́льня** village reading-room.

изба́витель, -я *m.* deliverer. **изба́вить, -влю** *pf.,* **избавля́ть, -я́ю** *impf.* save, deliver; **изба́ви Бог!** God forbid! **~ся** be saved, escape; **~ся от** get rid of; get out of. **избавле́ние, -я** deliverance.

избало́ванный spoilt. **из|балова́ть, -лу́ю**

pf., **избало́вывать, -аю** *impf.* spoil.

изба́ч, -а́ village librarian.

избега́ть, -а́ю *impf.,* **избе́гнуть, -ну; -бе́г(нул)** *pf.,* **избежа́ть, -егу́** *pf.+*g. *or inf.* avoid; shun, escape, evade. **избежа́ние, -я; во ~+**g. (in order) to avoid.

изберу́ *etc.: see* **избра́ть**

избива́ть, -а́ю *impf. of* **изби́ть. избие́ние, -я** slaughter, massacre; beating, beating-up.

избира́тель, -я *m.,* **~ница, -ы** elector, voter. **избира́тельн|ый** electoral; election; selective; **~ый бюллете́нь** voting-paper; **~ая у́рна** ballot-box; **~ый уча́сток** polling station. **избира́ть, -а́ю** *impf. of* **избра́ть**

изби́тый beaten, beaten up; hackneyed, trite. **изби́ть, изобью́, -бьёшь** *pf. (impf.* **избива́ть)** beat unmercifully, beat up; slaughter, massacre; wear down, ruin.

избра́ние, -я election. **и́збранн|ый** selected; select; **~ые** *sb., pl.* the elite. **избра́ть, -беру́, -берёшь; -а́л, -а́, -о** *pf. (impf.* **избира́ть)** elect; choose.

избу́шка, -и small hut.

избы́ток, -тка surplus, excess; abundance, plenty. **избы́точный** surplus; abundant, plentiful.

изва́яние, -я statue, sculpture. **изва́ять, -я́ю** *pf.*

изве́дать, -аю *pf.,* **изве́дывать, -аю** *impf.* come to know, learn the meaning of.

изведу́ *etc.,* **изве́л** *etc.: see* **извести́**

и́зверг, -а monster. **изверга́ть, -а́ю** *impf.,* **изве́ргнуть, -ну; -е́рг** *pf.* disgorge; eject; throw out; excrete; expel; **~ся** erupt. **изверже́ние, -я** eruption; ejection, expulsion; excretion.

извернуться, -ну́сь, -нёшься *pf.,* **изверты́ваться, -аюсь** *impf. (impf. also* **изворачиваться)** dodge, take evasive action; be evasive.

извести́, -еду́, -едёшь; -ёл, -ела́ *pf. (impf.* **изводи́ть)** use (up); waste; destroy, exterminate; exhaust; torment.

изве́стие, -я news; information; intelligence; *pl.* proceedings, transactions. **извести́ть, -ещу́** *pf. (impf.* **извеща́ть)** inform, notify.

изве́стка, -и lime. **известкова́ть, -ку́ю** *impf. & pf.* lime. **известко́вый** lime; limestone; calcareous.

изве́стно it is (well) known; of course, certainly; **как ~** as everybody knows; **наско́лько мне ~** as far as I know. **изве́стность, -и** fame, reputation; repute; notoriety. **изве́стн|ый** known; well-known, famous; notorious; certain; **в ~ых слу́чаях** in certain cases.

известня́к, -а́ limestone. **и́звесть, -и** lime.

извеща́ть, -а́ю *impf. of* **извести́ть. извеще́ние, -я** notification, notice; advice.

изги́в, -а winding, bend. **извива́ть, -а́ю** *impf. of* **изви́ть; ~ся** coil; wriggle, writhe; twist, wind; meander. **изви́лина, -ы** bend, twist, winding; convolution. **изви́листый** winding;

tortuous; sinuous; meandering.

извинéние, -я excuse; apology, pardon.
извинительный excusable, pardonable; apologetic. **извинить,** -ню *pf.*, **извинять,** -яю *impf.* excuse; **извините (меня)** I beg your pardon, excuse me, (I'm) sorry; **извините, что я опоздáл** sorry I'm late; ~**ся** apologize; make excuses, excuse o.s.; **извиняюсь** I apologize, (I'm) sorry; **извинитесь за меня** present my apologies, make my excuses.

извить, изовью, -вьёшь; -ил, -á, -о *pf.* (*impf.* **извивáть**) coil; twist; wind; ~**ся** coil; writhe, twist.

извлекáть, -áю *impf.*, **извлéчь,** -еку, -ечёшь; -ёк, -лá *pf.* extract; derive, elicit; extricate; ~ **урóк из** learn a lesson from. **извлечéние,** -я extraction; extract, excerpt.

извне *adv.* from outside.

изводить, -ожу, -óдишь *impf. of* **известй**

извóзчик, -а cabman, cabby; carrier, carter, drayman; cab.

изволить, -лю *impf.*+*inf. or g.* wish, desire; +*inf.* deign, be pleased; **извóльте** if you wish; all right; with pleasure.

изворáчиваться, -аюсь *impf. of* **извернуться. изворóт,** -а bend, twist; *pl.* tricks, wiles. **изворóтливый** resourceful, artful; wily, shrewd.

извратить, -ащу *pf.*, **извращáть,** -áю *impf.* distort; pervert; misinterpret, misconstrue. **извращéние,** -я perversion; misinterpretation, distortion. **извращённый** perverted, unnatural.

изгáдить, -áжу *pf.* befoul, soil; spoil, make a mess of.

изгиб, -а bend, twist; winding; inflexion, nuance. **изгибáть(ся,** -áю(сь *impf. of* **изогнуть(ся**

изглáдить, -áжу *pf.*, **изглáживать,** -аю *impf.* efface, wipe out, blot out.

изгнáние, -я banishment; expulsion; exile. **изгнáнник,** -а exile. **изгнáть,** -гоню, -гóнишь; -áл, -á, -о *pf.* (*impf.* **изгонять**) banish, expel, exile; oust, do away with.

изголóвье, -я bed-head; bedside; **служить изголóвьем** serve as a pillow.

изголодáться, -áюсь be famished, starve; +**по**+*d.* thirst for, yearn for.

изгоню *etc.: see* **изгнáть. изгонять,** -яю *impf. of* **изгнáть**

изгорóдь, -и fence, hedge.

изготáвливать, -аю *impf.*, **изготóвить,** -влю *pf.*, **изготовлять,** -яю *impf.* make, manufacture, produce; prepare; cook; ~**ся** get ready, make ready. **изготовитель,** -я manufacturer, producer. **изготóвка,** -и, **изготовлéние,** -я making, manufacture, production; preparation.

издавáть, -даю, -даёшь *impf. of* **издáть**

издавна *adv.* from time immemorial; for a very long time.

издадим *etc.: see* **издáть**

издалекá, издалёка, издали *advs.* from afar, from far away, from a distance.

издáние, -я publication; edition; promulgation. **издáтель,** -я *m.*, ~**ница,** -ы publisher. **издáтельство,** -а publishing house, press, publisher's. **издáть,** -áм, -áшь, -áст, -адим; -áл, -á, -о *pf.* (*impf.* **издавáть**) publish; promulgate; issue; produce; emit; let out, utter; ~**ся** be published.

издевáтельский mocking. **издевáтельство,** -а mocking, scoffing; mockery; taunt, insult. **издевáться,** -áюсь *impf.* (+**над**+*i.*) mock, scoff (at). **издёвка,** -и taunt, insult.

издéлие, -я make, work; article; *pl.* wares.

издержáть, -жу, -жишь *pf.* spend; ~**ся** spend all one's money; be spent up. **издéржки,** -жек *pl.* expenses; costs; cost.

издеру *etc.: see* **изодрáть. издирáть,** -áю *impf. of* **изодрáть**

из|дóхнуть, -ну; -дóх *pf.*, **издыхáть,** -áю *impf.* die; peg out, kick the bucket. **издыхáние,** -я; **послéднее** ~ last breath, last gasp.

из|жáрить(ся, -рю(сь *pf.*

изживáть, -áю *impf.*, **изжить,** -иву, -вёшь; -ил, -á, -о *pf.* overcome, get over; eliminate, get rid of.

изжóга, -и heartburn.

из-за *prep.*+*g.* from behind, from beyond; because of, through; **жениться** ~ **дéнег** marry for money.

излагáть, -áю *impf. of* **изложить**

излáмывать, -аю *impf. of* **изломáть**

излечéние, -я treatment; recovery; cure. **излéчивать,** -аю *impf.*, **излечить,** -чу, -чишь cure; ~**ся** be cured, make a complete recovery; +**от**+*g.* rid o.s. of, shake off.

изливáть, -áю *impf.*, **излить,** изолью, -льёшь; -ил, -á, -о *pf.* pour out, give vent to; ~ **душу** unbosom o.s.; unburden one's heart.

излишек, -шка surplus; remainder; excess; **с излишком** enough and to spare. **излишество,** -а excess; over-indulgence. **излишний,** -шен, -шня superfluous; excessive; unnecessary.

излияние, -я outpouring, outflow, effusion; discharge.

изловчиться, -чусь *pf.* contrive, manage.

изложéние, -я exposition; account. **изложить,** -жу, -жишь *pf.* (*impf.* **излагáть**) expound, state; set forth; word, draft; ~ **на бумáге** commit to paper.

излóм, -а break, fracture; sharp bend; salient point. **излóманный** broken, fractured; winding, tortuous; worn out. **изломáть,** -áю *pf.* (*impf.* **излáмывать**) break; smash; wear out; warp, corrupt.

излучáть, -áю *impf.* radiate, emit; ~**ся** be emitted, be radiated; emanate. **излучéние,** -я radiation; emanation.

излучина, -ы bend, curve, meander. **излучистый** winding, meandering.

излюбленный favourite.

из|мáзать, -áжу *pf.*, dirty, smear all over; use up; ~ся get dirty, smear o.s. all over.

из|марáть, -áю *pf.* из|мельчáть, -áю *pf.* из|мельчи́ть, -чý *pf.*

измéна, -ы betrayal; treachery, treason; infidelity.

изменéние, -я change, alteration; inflexion.

измени́ть[1], -ню́, -нишь *pf.* (*impf.* изменя́ть) change, alter; ~ся change, alter; vary; ~ся в лицé change countenance.

измени́ть[2], -ню́, -нишь *pf.* (*impf.* изменя́ть) +*d.* betray; be unfaithful to; fail. измéнник, -a traitor измéннический treacherous, traitorous.

измéнчивый changeable; inconstant, fickle. изменя́емый variable. изменя́ть(ся, -я́ю(сь *impf. of* измени́ть(ся

измерéние, -я measurement, measuring; mensuration; sounding, fathoming; metering; gauging; taking; dimension. измери́мый measurable. измери́тель, -я *m.* gauge, meter; index. измери́тельный measuring; standard. измéрить, -рю *pf.*, измеря́ть, -я́ю *impf.* measure, gauge; sound; survey.

измождённый; -ён, -енá emaciated; worn out.

й́зморозь, -и hoar-frost; rime.

измучáть, -áю *pf.*, измýчивать, -аю *impf.*, из|мýчить, -чу *pf.* torment; tire out, exhaust; ~ся be tired out, be exhausted. измýченный worn out, tired out.

измы́слить, -лю *pf.*, измышля́ть, -я́ю *impf.* fabricate, invent; contrive. измышлéние, -я fabrication, invention.

измя́тый crumpled, creased; haggard, jaded. из|мя́ть(ся, изомнý(сь, -нёшь(ся *pf.*

изнáнка, -и wrong side; under side; reverse; seamy side. изнáночн|ый; ~ая петля́ purl (stitch).

из|наси́ловать, -лую *pf.* rape, assault, violate.

изнáшивание, -я wear (and tear). изнáшивать(ся, -аю(сь *impf. of* износи́ть(ся

изнéженный pampered; delicate; soft, effete; effeminate. изнéживать, -аю *impf.*, изнéжить, -жу *pf.* pamper, coddle; make effeminate; ~ся go soft, grow effete; become effeminate.

изнемогáть, -áю *impf.*, изнемóчь, -огý, -óжешь; -óг, -лá *pf.* be exhausted, be dead tired. изнеможéние, -я exhaustion. изнеможённый; -ён, -á exhausted.

изнóс, -a (-у) wear; wear and tear; deterioration; не знать ~у wear well, stand hard wear. износи́ть, -ошý, -óсишь *pf.* (*impf.* изнáшивать) wear out; ~ся wear out; be used up, be played out; age (*prematurely*). износостóйкий hard-wearing. изнóшенный worn out; threadbare; worn; aged.

изнóю *etc.: see* изны́ть

изнурéние, -я exhaustion; emaciation. изнурённый; -ён, -енá exhausted, worn out; jaded; ~ гóлодом faint with hunger. изну-

ри́тельный exhausting. изнури́ть, -рю́ *pf.*, изнуря́ть, -я́ю *impf.* exhaust, wear out.

изнутри́ *adv.* from inside, from within.

изнывáть, -áю *impf.*, изны́ть, -нóю *pf.* languish, be exhausted; ~ от жáжды be tormented by thirst; ~ по+*d.* pine for.

изо *see* из изо...[1] *see* из... . изо...[2] iso-.

изоби́лие, -я abundance, plenty, profusion. изоби́ловать, -лует *impf.*+*i.* abound in, be rich in. изоби́льный abundant; +*i.* abounding in.

изобличáть, -áю *impf.*, изобличи́ть, -чý *pf.* expose; unmask; reveal, show. изобличéние, -я exposure; conviction. изобличи́тельн|ый damning; ~ые докумéнты documentary evidence.

изобрести́, -етý, -етёшь; -ёл, -á *pf.*, изобретáть, -áю *impf.* invent; devise, contrive. изобретáтель, -я *m.* inventor. изобретáтельный inventive; resourceful. изобретéние, -я invention.

изображáть, -áю *impf.*, изобрази́ть, -ажý *pf.* represent, depict, portray (+*i.* as); imitate, take off; ~ из себя́+*a.* make o.s. out to be, represent o.s. as; ~ся appear, show itself. изображéние, -я image; representation; portrayal; imprint. изобрази́тельн|ый graphic; decorative; ~ые искýсства fine arts.

изобью́ *etc.: see* изби́ть. изовью́ *etc.: see* изви́ть

изóгнутый bent, curved; winding. изогнýть(ся, -нý(сь, -нёшь(ся *pf.* (*impf.* изгибáть(ся) bend, curve.

изóдранный tattered. изодрáть, издерý, -дерёшь; -áл, -á, -о *pf.* (*impf.* издирáть) tear to pieces; scratch all over.

изолгáться, -лгýсь, -лжёшься; -áлся, -áсь, -ось *pf.* become a hardened liar.

изоли́рованный isolated; separate; insulated. изоли́ровать, -рую *impf. & pf.* isolate; quarantine; insulate. изолирóвка, -и insulation; insulating tape.

изолью́ *etc.: see* излить

изоля́тор, -a insulator; isolation ward; solitary confinement cell. изоля́ция, -и isolation; quarantine; insulation.

изомнý(сь *etc.: see* измя́ть

изóрванный tattered, torn. изорвáть, -вý, -вёшь; -áл, -á, -о *pf.* tear, tear to pieces; ~ся be in tatters.

изотрý *etc.: see* истерéть

изощрённый; -рён, -á refined; keen. изощри́ть, -рю́ *pf.*, изощря́ть, -я́ю *impf.* sharpen; cultivate, refine, develop; ~ся acquire refinement; excel.

из-под *prep.*+*g.* from under; from near; from; буты́лка ~ молокá milk-bottle.

изразéц, -зцá tile. изразцóвый tile; tiled.

Изрáиль, -я *m.* Israel.

из|расхóдовать(ся, -дую(сь *pf.*

и́зредка *adv.* now and then; occasionally; from time to time.

изрéзанный cut up; indented, rugged.

изре́зать, -е́жу *pf.*, **изре́зывать**, -аю *impf.* cut up; cut to pieces; indent.

изрека́ть, -а́ю *impf.*, **изре́чь**, -еку́, -ече́шь; -е́к, -ла́ *pf.* speak solemnly; utter. **изрече́ние**, -я dictum, saying.

изро́ю *etc.*: *see* **изры́ть**

изруба́ть, -а́ю *impf.*, **изруби́ть**, -блю́, -бишь *pf.* cut (up); chop, chop up; mince; cut down, cut to pieces.

изруга́ть, -а́ю *pf.* abuse, swear at, curse.

изрыва́ть, -а́ю *impf.*, **изры́ть**, -ро́ю *pf.* dig up, tear up, plough up. **изры́тый** pitted; cratered; torn up.

изря́дно *adv.* fairly, pretty; tolerably. **изря́дный** fair, handsome; fairly large.

изуве́чивать, -аю *impf.*, **изуве́чить**, -чу *pf.* maim, mutilate.

изуми́тельный amazing, astounding. **изуми́ть**, -млю́ *pf.* **изумля́ть**, -я́ю *impf.* amaze, astonish; **~ся** be amazed. **изумле́ние**, -я amazement. **изумлённый**; -лён, -а́ amazed, astonished; dumbfounded.

изумру́д, -а emerald.

изуро́дованный maimed, mutilated; disfigured. **из|уро́довать**, -дую *pf.*

изуча́ть, -а́ю *impf.*, **изучи́ть**, -чу́, -чишь *pf.* learn, study; master; come to know (very well). **изуче́ние**, -я study.

изъ... *see* **из...**

изъе́здить, -зжу *pf.* travel all over; wear out. **изъе́зженный** much-travelled, well-worn; rutted.

изъяви́тельн|ый; **~ое наклоне́ние** indicative (mood). **изъяви́ть**, -влю, -вишь *pf.*, **изъявля́ть**, -я́ю *impf.* express; **~ согла́сие** give consent. **изъявле́ние**, -я expression.

изъя́н, -а (-у) defect, flaw.

изъя́тие, -я withdrawal; removal; exception. **изъя́ть**, изыму́, -мешь *pf.* **изыма́ть**, -а́ю *impf.* withdraw; remove; confiscate.

изыска́ние, -я investigation, research; prospecting; survey. **изы́сканный** refined; recherché. **изыска́тель**, -я *m.* project surveyor; prospector. **изыска́ть**, -ыщу́, -ы́щешь *pf.*, **изы́скивать**, -аю *impf.* search (successfully) for, search out; (try to) find; prospect for.

изю́м, -а (-у) raisins; sultanas. **изю́мина**, -ы raisin. **изю́минка**, -и zest, go, spirit; sparkle; **с изю́минкой** spirited, piquant.

изя́щество, -а elegance, grace. **изя́щный** elegant, graceful.

ика́ние, -я hiccupping. **ика́ть**, -а́ю *impf.*, **икну́ть**, -ну́, -нёшь *pf.* hiccup.

ико́на, -ы icon. **иконогра́фия**, -и iconography; portraiture, portraits. **иконопи́сец**, -сца icon-painter. **и́конопись**, -и icon-painting.

ико́та, -ы hiccup, hiccups.

икра́[1], -ы́ (hard) roe; spawn; caviare; pâté, paste.

икра́[2], -ы́; *pl.* -ы calf.

икс, -а (letter) x.

ил, -а silt, mud, ooze; sludge.

и́ли, **иль** *conj.* or; **~...~** either ... or.

и́листый muddy, silty, oozy.

иллюзиони́ст, -а illusionist; conjurer, magician. **иллю́зия**, -и illusion. **иллюзо́рный** illusory.

иллюмина́тор, -а porthole.

иллюстри́рованный illustrated. **иллюстри́ровать**, -рую *impf.* & *pf.* illustrate.

иль *see* **и́ли**. **им** *see* **он**, **они́**, **оно́**

им. *abbr.* (*of* **и́мени**) named after.

и́мени *etc.*: *see* **и́мя**

име́ние, -я estate; property, possessions.

имени́ны, -и́н *pl.* name-day (party). **имени́тельный** nominative. **и́менно** *adv.* namely; to wit, viz.; just, exactly, precisely; to be exact; **вот ~!** exactly! precisely! **именно́й** named, nominal; bearing the owner's name; inscribed, autographed; name. **именова́ть**, -ну́ю *impf.* (*pf.* **на~**) name; **~ся**+*i.* be called; be termed. **имену́емый** called.

име́ть, -е́ю *impf.* have; **~ в виду́** bear in mind, think of, mean; **~ де́ло** с+*i.* have dealings with, have to do with; **~ значе́ние** be of importance, matter; **~ ме́сто** take place; **~ся** be; be present, be available.

и́ми *see* **они́**

иммигра́нт, -а immigrant. **иммиграцио́нный** immigration. **иммигра́ция**, -и immigration. **иммигри́ровать**, -рую *impf.* & *pf.* immigrate.

иммуниза́ция, -и immunization. **иммунизи́ровать**, -рую *impf.* & *pf.* immunize. **иммуните́т**, -а immunity. **иммунный** (к+*d.*) immune (to).

импера́тор, -а emperor. **импера́торский** imperial. **императри́ца**, -ы empress. **империали́зм**, -а imperialism. **импе́рия**, -и empire.

импони́ровать, -рую *impf.*+*d.* impress.

и́мпорт, -а import; foreign goods. **импортёр**, -а importer. **импорти́ровать**, -ую *impf.* & *pf.* import. **и́мпортный** imported, foreign.

импровиза́ция, -и improvisation. **импровизи́ровать**, -рую *impf.* (*pf.* **сымпровизи́ровать**) improvise; extemporize.

и́мпульс, -а impulse, impetus. **импульси́вный** impulsive.

иму́щественный property. **иму́щество**, -а property, belongings; stock; stores, equipment. **иму́щий** propertied; well off, wealthy.

и́мя, **и́мени**; *pl.* **имена́**, -ён *nt.* name; first name, christian name; reputation; noun; **во ~**+*g.* in the name of; **~ прилага́тельное** adjective; **~ существи́тельное** noun, substantive; **~ числи́тельное** numeral; **от и́мени**+*g.* on behalf of; **по и́мени** by name; in name, nominally; **Теа́тр и́мени Го́рького** the Gorky Theatre.

ин... *abbr.* (*of* **иностра́нный**) *in comb.* foreign. **инвалю́та**, -ы foreign currency. **инотде́л**, -а foreign department.

инакомы́слие, -я nonconformism, heterodoxy. **инакомы́слящий** nonconformist.

йна́че *adv.* differently, otherwise; **так йли** ~ in either case, in any event, at all events; *conj.* otherwise, or, or else.

инвали́д, -а disabled person; invalid. **инвали́дность, -и** disablement, disability.

инвента́рн|ый inventory, stock; ~**ая о́пись** inventory. **инвента́рь, -я** *m.* stock; equipment, appliances; inventory.

инве́стор, -а investor.

инде́ец, -е́йца (*American*) Indian. **инде́йка, -и**; *g.pl.* **-е́ек** turkey(-hen). **инде́йский** (*American*) Indian; ~ **пету́х** turkey-cock. **индиа́нка, -и** (*American*) Indian.

индивидуа́льность, -и individuality. **индивидуа́льный** individual. **индиви́дуум, -а** individual.

инди́ец, -и́йца Indian. **инди́йский** Indian. **Йндия, -и** India.

Индоне́зия, -и Indonesia.

инду́с, -а, инду́ска, -и Hindu. **инду́сский** Hindu.

индустриализа́ция, -и industrialization. **индустриализи́ровать, -рую** *impf. & pf.* industrialize. **индустриа́льный** industrial. **инду́стрия, -и** industry.

индю́к, -а́, индю́шка, -и turkey.

и́ней, -я hoar-frost, rime.

ине́ртность, -и inertness, inertia; sluggishness, inaction, passivity. **ине́ртный** inert; passive; sluggish, inactive. **ине́рция, -и** inertia.

инжене́р, -а engineer; ~**-меха́ник** mechanical engineer; ~**-строи́тель** civil engineer. **инжене́рн|ый** engineering; ~**ые войска́** Engineers; ~**ое де́ло** engineering.

инициа́лы, -ов *pl.* initials.

инициати́в|а, -ы initiative; **по со́бственной** ~**е** on one's own initiative. **инициати́вный** enterprising, go-getting.

ин-ква́рто *nt.indecl.* quarto.

инкруста́ция, -и inlaid work, inlay. **инкрусти́ровать, -рую** *impf. & pf.* inlay.

ино́... *in comb.* other, different; hetero-. **иногоро́дн|ый** of, from, for, another town. ~**зе́мец, -мца** foreigner. ~**зе́мный** foreign. ~**плане́та́рный** alien, extraterrestrial. ~**планетя́нин, -а,** *pl.* **-я́не, -я́н** alien, extraterrestrial. ~**ро́дец, -дца** non-Russian. ~**ро́дный** foreign. ~**сказа́ние, -я** allegory. ~**сказа́тельный** allegorical. ~**стра́нец, -нца,** ~**стра́нка, -и;** *g.pl.* **-нок** foreigner. ~**стра́нный** foreign. ~**язы́чный** speaking, belonging to, another language; non-native, foreign.

иногда́ *adv.* sometimes.

ино́й different; other; some; ~ **раз** sometimes; **ины́ми слова́ми** in other words.

и́нок, -а monk. **и́нокиня, -и** nun.

ин-окта́во *nt.indecl.* octavo.

инотде́л *see* **ин...**

йноходь, -и amble.

инспе́ктор, -а inspector; ~ **мане́жа** ringmaster; **порто́вый** ~ harbourmaster.

инспе́кция, -и inspection; inspectorate.

инсти́нкт, -а instinct. **инстинкти́вный** instinctive.

институ́т, -а institution; institute; young ladies' boarding school. **институ́тка, -и** boarding-school miss; innocent, unsophisticated girl.

инструкти́ровать, -рую *impf. & pf.* (*pf. also* **про~**) instruct, give instructions to; brief. **инстру́кция, -и** instructions; directions.

инструме́нт, -а instrument; tool, implement; tools, implements.

инсцени́ровать, -рую *impf. & pf.* dramatize, adapt; stage. **инсцениро́вка, -и** dramatization, adaptation; pretence, act.

интелле́кт, -а intellect; **иску́сственный** ~ (*comput.*) artificial intelligence. **интеллектуа́льный** intellectual.

интеллиге́нт, -а intellectual, member of intelligentsia. **интеллиге́нтный** cultured, educated. **интеллиге́нтский** dilettante. **интеллиге́нция, -и** intelligentsia.

интенда́нт, -а commissary, quartermaster.

интенси́вный intensive. **интенсифици́ровать, -рую** *impf. & pf.* intensify.

интерва́л, -а interval.

интерве́нция, -и (*pol.*) intervention.

интервью́ *nt.indecl.* interview; ~ **в прямо́м эфи́ре** live (*TV or radio*) interview. **интервью́е́р, -а** interviewer. **интервью́и́ровать, -рую** *impf. & pf.* interview.

интере́с, -а interest. **интере́сный** interesting; striking, attractive. **интересова́ть, -су́ю** *impf.* interest; ~**ся** be interested (+*i.* in).

интерна́т, -а boarding-school.

интернационализа́ция, -и internationalization. **интернационализи́ровать, -рую** *impf. & pf.* internationalize. **интернационали́зм, -а** internationalism. **итнернационали́ст, -а** internationalist. **интернациона́льный** international.

интерни́ровать, -ую *impf. & pf.* intern.

интерфе́йс, -а (*comput.*) interface.

инти́мность, -и intimacy. **инти́мный** intimate.

интри́га, -и intrigue; plot.

интуити́вный intuitive. **интуи́ция, -и** intuition.

инфа́ркт, -а infarct; coronary (thrombosis), heart attack.

инфля́ция, -и inflation.

инфекцио́нн|ый infectious; ~**ая больни́ца** isolation hospital. **инфе́кция, -и** infection.

инфля́ция, -и inflation.

ин-фо́лио *nt.indecl.* folio.

информа́тик, -а information scientist. **информа́тика, -и** information science. **информацио́нный** news. **информа́ция, -и** information; news item.

и.о. *abbr.* (*of* **исполня́ющий обя́занности**) acting.

иод *etc.: see* **йод**

ипподро́м, -а hippodrome; racecourse.

Ира́к, -а Iraq.

Ира́н, -а Iran.

и́рис¹, -а (*bot.*) iris.

ири́с², -а toffee. **ири́ска, -и** (a) toffee.

ирла́ндец, -дца Irishman. **Ирла́ндия, -и** Ireland. **ирла́ндка, -и** Irishwoman. **ирла́ндский** Irish.

ирони́ческий, ирони́чный ironic(al). **иро́ния, -и** irony.

ис... *see* **из...**

иск, -а suit, action.

искажа́ть, -а́ю *impf.*, **исказ́ить, -ажу́** *pf.* distort, pervert, twist; misrepresent. **искаже́ние, -я** distortion, perversion. **искажённый; -ён, -ена́** distorted, perverted.

искале́ченный crippled, maimed. **искале́чивать, -аю** *impf.*, **ис|кале́чить, -чу** *pf.* cripple, maim; break, damage; **~ся** become a cripple; be crippled.

иска́ние, -я search, quest; *pl.* strivings. **иска́тель, -я** seeker; searcher; view-finder; selector; scanner. **иска́ть, ищу́, и́щешь** *impf.* (+*a.* or *g.*) seek, look for, search for.

исключа́ть, -а́ю *impf.*, **исключи́ть, -чу́** *pf.* exclude; eliminate; expel; dismiss; rule out. **исключа́я** *prep.*+*g.* except, excepting, with the exception of; **~ прису́тствующих** present company excepted. **исключе́ние, -я** exception; exclusion; expulsion; elimination; **за исключе́нием**+*g.* with the exception of. **исключи́тельно** *adv.* exceptionally; exclusively, solely; exclusive. **исключи́тельный** exceptional; exclusive, sole; excellent.

искове́рканный corrupt, corrupted; broken; spoilt. **ис|кове́ркать, -аю** *pf.*

исколеси́ть, -ешу́ *pf.* travel all over.

ис|ко́мкать, -аю *pf.*

ископа́емое mineral; fossil. **ископа́емый** fossilized, fossil.

искорене́ние, -я eradication. **искорени́ть, -ню́** *pf.*, **искореня́ть, -я́ю** *impf.* eradicate.

и́скоса *adv.* sideways; sidelong; askance.

и́скра, -ы spark; flash; glimmer.

и́скренний sincere, candid. **и́скренно** *adv.* sincerely; candidly. **и́скренность, -и** sincerity; candour.

искриви́ть, -влю́ *pf.*, **искривля́ть, -я́ю** *impf.* bend; curve; distort, twist, warp. **искривле́ние, -я** bend; distortion, warping.

искри́стый sparkling. **искри́ть, -и́т** *impf.* spark; **~ся** sparkle; scintillate. **искрово́й** spark.

ис|кромса́ть, -а́ю *pf.* **ис|кроши́ть(ся, -шу́(сь, -ши́шь(ся** *pf.*

ис|купа́ть¹(ся, -а́ю(сь *pf.*

искупа́ть², -а́ю *impf.*, **искупи́ть, -плю́, -пишь** *pf.* expiate, atone for; make up for, compensate for. **искупи́тель, -я** *m.* redeemer. **искупле́ние, -я** redemption, expiation, atonement.

искуси́ть, -ушу́ *pf. of* **искуша́ть**

иску́сный skilful; expert. **иску́сственный** artificial; synthetic; feigned, pretended. **иску́сство, -а** art; craftsmanship, skill.

искуша́ть, -а́ю *impf.* (*pf.* **искуси́ть**) tempt; seduce. **искуше́ние, -я** temptation, seduction. **искушённый; -ён, -ена́** experienced; tested.

исла́м, -а Islam.

ис|па́костить, -ощу *pf.*

испа́нец, -нца, испа́нка, -и Spaniard. **Испа́ния, -и** Spain. **испа́нский** Spanish.

испаре́ние, -я evaporation; *pl.* fumes. **испа́рина, -ы** perspiration. **испари́тель, -я** *m.* evaporator; vaporizer. **испари́ть, -рю́** *pf.*, **испаря́ть, -я́ю** *impf.* evaporate, volatilize; exhale; **~ся** evaporate, vaporize; be evaporated.

ис|па́чкать, -аю *pf.* **ис|пе́чь, -еку́, -ечёшь** *pf.*

испещрённый; -рён, -рена́ speckled. **испещри́ть, -рю́** *pf.*, **испещря́ть, -я́ю** *impf.* speckle, spot; mark all over, cover.

исписа́ть, -ишу́, -и́шешь *pf.*, **испи́сывать, -аю** *impf.* cover, fill with writing; use up.

испито́й haggard, gaunt; hollow-cheeked.

испове́довать, -дую *impf.* & *pf.* confess; profess; **~ся** confess; make one's confession; +*в*+*p.* unburden o.s. of, acknowledge. **и́споведь, -и** confession.

исподло́бья *adv.* sullenly, distrustfully.

исподтишка́ *adv.* in an underhand way; on the quiet, on the sly; **смея́ться ~** laugh in one's sleeve.

испоко́н веко́в, ве́ку *see* **век**

исполи́н, -а giant. **исполи́нский** gigantic.

исполко́м, -а *abbr.* (*of* **исполни́тельный комите́т**) executive committee.

исполне́ние, -я fulfilment, execution, discharge; performance; **привести́ в ~** carry out, execute. **исполни́мый** feasible, practicable. **исполни́тель, -я** *m.*, **-тельница, -ы** executor; performer. **исполни́тельный** executive; assiduous, careful, attentive; **~ лист** writ, court order. **испо́лнить, -ню** *pf.*, **исполня́ть, -я́ю** *impf.* carry out, execute; fulfil; perform; **~ обеща́ние** keep a promise; **~ про́сьбу** grant a request; **~ся** be fulfilled; *impers.* (+*d.*); **исполнилось пять лет с тех пор, как** it is five years since; **ему́ исполнилось семь лет** he is seven years old. **исполня́ющий; ~ обя́занности**+*g.* acting.

испо́льзование, -я utilization; **повто́рное ~** recycling. **испо́льзовать, -зую** *impf.* & *pf.* make (good) use of, utilize; turn to account.

ис|по́ртить(ся, -рчу(сь *pf.* **испо́рченность, -и** depravity. **испо́рченный** depraved; corrupted; spoiled; bad, rotten.

исправи́тельный correctional; corrective; **~ дом** reformatory. **испра́вить, -влю** *pf.*, **исправля́ть, -я́ю** *impf.* rectify, correct; emendate; repair, mend; reform, improve, amend; **~ся** improve, reform. **исправле́ние, -я** correcting; repairing; improvement; correction; emendation. **испра́вленный** improved, corrected; revised; reformed.

испра́вник, -а district police superintendent. **испра́вность, -и** good repair, good condition; punctuality; preciseness; meticulousness. **испра́вный** in good order; punctual; precise; meticulous.

ис|про́бовать, -бую *pf.*

испу́г, -а (-у) fright; alarm. **испу́ганный** frightened, scared, startled. **ис|пуга́ть(ся, -а́ю(сь** *pf.*

испуска́ть, -а́ю *impf.*, **испусти́ть, -ущу́, -у́стишь** *pf.* emit, let out; utter; ~ **вздох** heave a sigh; ~ **дух** breathe one's last.

испыта́ние, -я test; trial; ordeal; examination. **испы́танный** tried, well-tried; tested. **испыта́тельный** test, trial; examining; experimental; probationary. **испыта́ть, -а́ю** *pf.*, **испы́тывать, -аю** *impf.* test; try; feel, experience.

йссера- in comb. grey-, greyish; ~**голубо́й** grey-blue.

йссиня- in comb. blue-, bluish.

иссле́дование, -я investigation; research; analysis; exploration; paper; study. **иссле́дователь, -я** *m.* researcher; investigator; explorer. **иссле́довательский** research. **иссле́довать, -дую** *impf.* & *pf.* investigate, examine; research into; explore, analyse.

йсстари *adv.* from of old; **так** ~ **ведётся** it is an old custom.

исступле́ние, -я frenzy, transport. **исступлённый** frenzied; ecstatic.

иссуша́ть, -а́ю *impf.*, **иссуши́ть, -шу́, -шишь** *pf.* dry up; consume, waste.

иссяка́ть, -а́ет *impf.*, **исся́кнуть, -нет; -я́к** *pf.* run dry, dry up; run low, fail.

иста́сканный worn out; threadbare; worn; haggard. **истаска́ть, -а́ю** *pf.*, **иста́скивать, -аю** *impf.* wear out; ~**ся** wear out; be worn out.

истека́ть, -а́ет *impf. of* **исте́чь. исте́кший** past, last; preceding, previous.

истере́ть, изотру́, -трёшь; истёр *pf.* (*impf.* **истира́ть**) grate; wear away, wear down; ~**ся** wear out; wear away, be worn away.

истёрзанный tattered, lacerated; tormented.

исте́рик, -а, истери́чка, -и hysterical subject. **исте́рика, -и** hysterics. **истери́чный** hysterical. **истери́я, -и** hysteria.

исте́ц, -тца́, истица, -ы plaintiff; petitioner.

истече́ние, -я outflow; expiry, expiration; ~ **кро́ви** haemorrhage. **исте́чь, -ечёт; -тёк, -ла́** *pf.* (*impf.* **истека́ть**) flow out; elapse; expire.

истина, -ы truth. **истинный** true.

истира́ние, -я abrasion. **истира́ть(ся, -а́ю(сь** *impf. of* **истере́ть(ся**

истица *see* **исте́ц**

истлева́ть, -а́ю *impf.*, **истле́ть, -е́ю** *pf.* rot, decay; be reduced to ashes, smoulder away.

исто́к, -а source.

истолкова́ть, -ку́ю *pf.*, **истолко́вывать, -аю** *impf.* interpret, expound; comment on.

ис|толо́чь, -лку́ -лчёшь; -ло́к, -лкла́ *pf.*

исто́ма, -ы lassitude; languor. **ис|томи́ть, -млю́** *pf.*, **истомля́ть, -я́ю** *impf.* exhaust, weary; ~**ся** be exhausted, be worn out; be weary. **истомлённый; -ён, -ена́** exhausted,

tired out, worn out.

истопни́к, -а́ stoker, boilerman.

исторга́ть, -а́ю *impf.*, **исто́ргнуть, -ну; -орг** *pf.* throw out, expel; wrest, wrench; force, extort.

исто́рик, -а historian. **истори́ческий** historical; historic. **исто́ричный** historical. **исто́рия, -и** history; story; incident, event; **заба́вная** ~ a funny thing.

исто́чник, -а spring; source.

истоща́ть, -а́ю *impf.*, **истощи́ть, -щу́** *pf.* exhaust; drain, sap; deplete; emaciate. **истоще́ние, -я** emaciation; exhaustion; depletion. **истощённый; -ён, -ена́** emaciated; exhausted.

ис|тра́тить, -а́чу *pf.*

истреби́тель, -я *m.* destroyer; fighter. **истреби́тельный** destructive; fighter. **истреби́ть, -блю́** *pf.*, **истребля́ть, -я́ю** *impf.* destroy; exterminate, extirpate.

истрёпанный torn, frayed; worn. **ис|трепа́ть, -плю́, -плешь** *pf.*

истука́н, -а idol, image.

ис|тупи́ть, -плю, -пишь *pf.*

йстый true, genuine.

истяза́ние, -я torture. **истяза́ть, -а́ю** *impf.* torture.

исхо́д, -а outcome, issue; end; Exodus; **на** ~**е** nearing the end, coming to an end; **на** ~**е дня** towards evening. **исходи́ть, -ожу́, -о́дишь** *impf.* (+**из** *or* **от**+*g.*) issue (from), come (from); emanate (from); proceed (from), base o.s. (on). **исхо́дный** initial, original, starting; departure, of departure.

исхуда́лый emaciated, wasted. **исхуда́ть, -а́ю** *pf.* grow thin, become wasted.

исцеле́ние, -я healing, cure; recovery. **исцели́мый** curable. **исцели́ть, -лю́** *pf.*, **исцеля́ть, -я́ю** *impf.* heal, cure.

исчеза́ть, -а́ю *impf.*, **исче́знуть, -ну; -е́з** *pf.* disappear, vanish. **исчезнове́ние, -я** disappearance.

йсчерна- in comb. blackish-.

исче́рпать, -аю *pf.*, **исче́рпывать, -аю** *impf.* exhaust, drain; settle, conclude. **исче́рпывающий** exhaustive.

исчисле́ние, -я calculation; calculus. **исчи́слить, -лю** *pf.*, **исчисля́ть, -я́ю** *impf.* calculate, compute; estimate. **исчисля́ться, -яется** *impf.+i. or* **в**+*a.* amount to, come to; be calculated at.

ита́к *conj.* thus; so then; and so.

Ита́лия, -и Italy. **италья́нец, -нца, италья́нка, -и** Italian. **италья́нск|ий** Italian; ~**ая забасто́вка** sit-down strike, work-to-rule, go-slow.

ито́г, -а sum; total; result, upshot. **итого́** *adv.* in all, altogether. **ито́говый** total, final.

иуде́й, -я, иуде́йка, -и Jew. **иуде́йский** Judaic.

их *see* **они́. их, йхний** their, theirs.

ихтиоза́вр, -а ichthyosaurus. **ихтиоло́гия, -и** ichthyology.

ишáк, -á donkey, ass; hinny.
ищéйка, -и bloodhound; police dog; sleuth.
ищý *etc.*: *see* **искáть**
июль, -я *m.* July. **июльский** July.
июнь, -я *m.* June. **июньский** June.

Й

й *letter: see* **и**
йéти *m. indecl.* yeti, abominable snowman.
йог, -а Yogi.
йóга, -и yoga.
йогýрт, -а yog(h)urt.
йод, -а iodine.
йóта, -ы iota.

К

к *letter: see* **ка**
к, **ко** *prep.+d.* to, towards; by; for; on; on the occasion of; **к лýчшему** for the better; **к (не)счáстью** (un)fortunately, (un)luckily; **к пéрвому января** by the first of January; **к срóку** on time; **к томý врéмени** by then, by that time; **к томý же** besides, moreover; **к чемý?** what for?; **лицóм к лицý** face to face; **ни к чемý** no good, no use.
к. *abbr.* (*of* **кóмната**) room; (*of* **копéйка**) copeck.
ка *nt.indecl.* the letter **к**.
-ка *part. modifying force of imper. or expressing decision or intention*; **дáйте-ка пройти** let me pass, please; **скажи-ка мне** do tell me.
кабáк, -а a tavern, drinking-shop; pub.
кабалá, -ы servitude, bondage. **кабалить**, -лю *impf.* enslave.
кабáн, -á wild boar.
кабарé *nt.indecl.* cabaret.
кабачóк[1], -чкá *dim. of* **кабáк**
кабачóк[2], -чкá vegetable marrow.
кáбель, -я *m.* cable. **кáбельный** *adj.* **кáбельтов**, -а cable, hawser; cable's length.
кабина, -ы cabin; booth; cockpit; cab. **кабинéт**, -а study; consulting-room, surgery; room, classroom, laboratory, office; cabinet. **кабинéтский** cabinet.

каблýк, -а heel. **каблучóк**, -чкá heel; ogee; ~-шпилька stiletto heel.
каботáж, -а cabotage; coastal shipping. **каботáжник**, -а a coaster. **каботáжный** cabotage; coastal, coasting, coastwise. **кавалéр**, -а knight; partner, gentleman. **кавалергáрд**, -а horse-guardsman. **кавалерийский** cavalry. **кавалерист**, -а cavalryman. **кавалéрия**, -и cavalry.
кáверза, -ы chicanery; mean trick, dirty trick. **кáверзный** tricky, ticklish.
Кавкáз, -а Caucasus. **кавкáзец**, -зцá, **кавкáзка**, -и Caucasian. **кавкáзский** Caucasian.
кавычки, -чек *pl.* inverted commas, quotation marks; **открыть** ~ quote; **закрыть** ~ unquote.
кадéт, -а cadet. **кадéтский** cadet; ~ **кóрпус** military school.
кáдка, -и tub, vat.
кадр, -а a frame, still; close-up; cadre; *pl.* establishment; staff; personnel; specialists, skilled workers. **кадровик**, -á member of permanent establishment, professional body, etc. **кáдровый** regular; experienced, skilled; trained.
кадык, -á Adam's apple.
каёмка, -и (narrow) border, (narrow) edging. **каёмчатый** with a border.
каждодневный daily, everyday. **кáждый** each, every; *sb.* everybody, everyone.
кáжется *etc.*: *see* **казáться**
казáк, -á; *pl.* -áки, -áкóв, **казáчка**, -и Cossack. **Казахстáн**, -а Kazakhstan.
казáрма, -ы barracks; barrack.
казáться, **кажýсь**, **кáжешься** *impf.* (*pf.* **по~**) seem, appear; *impers.* (+*d.*) **кáжется**, **казáлось** apparently; **казáлось бы** it would seem, one would think; **мне кáжется** it seems to me; I think.
казáцкий, **казáчий** Cossack. **казáчка** *see* **казáк**. **казачóк**, -чкá page-boy.
казённый State; government; fiscal; public; bureaucratic, formal; banal, undistinguished, conventional; ~ **язык** official jargon; **на** ~ **счёт** at the public expense. **казнá**, -ы Exchequer, Treasury; public purse; the State; money, property. **казначéй**, -я treasurer, bursar; paymaster; purser.
казнить, -ню *impf. & pf.* execute, put to death; punish, chastise; castigate. **казнь**, -и execution.
каймá, -ы; *g.pl.* **каём** border, edging; hem; selvage.
как *adv.* how; what; all of a sudden, all at once; **вот** ~! not really! you don't say!; ~ **вы дýмаете?** what do you think?; ~ **вы поживáете?** how are you? ~ **делá?** how are you getting on? ~ **егó зовýт?** what is his name? what is he called?; ~ **есть** complete(ly), utter(ly); ~ **же** naturally, of course; ~ **же так?** how is that?; ~ **ни** however; ~-**никáк** nevertheless, for all that; ~ **есть**

дура́к he's a complete fool. **как** *conj.* as; like; when; since; +*neg.* but, except, than; **бу́дьте ~ до́ма** make yourself at home; **в то вре́мя ~** while, whereas; **~ вдруг** when suddenly; **~ мо́жно, ~ нельзя́**+*comp.* as ... as possible; **~ мо́жно скоре́е** as soon as possible; **~ нельзя́ лу́чше** as well as possible; **~ наро́чно** as luck would have it; **~..., так и** both ... and; **~ то́лько** as soon as, when; **ме́жду тем, ~** while, whereas; **я ви́дел, ~ она́ ушла́** I saw her go. **как бу́дто** *conj.* as if, as though; *part.* apparently, it would seem. **как бы** how; as if, as though; **как бы... не** what if, supposing; **бою́сь, как бы он не́ был в дурно́м настрое́нии** I am afraid he may be in a bad temper; **как бы не так!** not likely, certainly not; **как бы... ни** however. **ка́к-либо** *adv.* somehow. **ка́к-нибудь** *adv.* somehow; in some way or other; anyhow; some time. **как раз** *adv.* just, exactly. **ка́к-то** *adv.* somehow; once, one day.

кака́о *nt.indecl.* cocoa. **кака́ов|ый; ~ые бобы́** cocoa-beans.

како́в *m.*, **какова́** *f.*, **каково́** *nt.*, **каковы́** *pl. pron.* what, what sort (of); **~ он?** what is he like?; **~ он собо́й?** what does he look like?; **пого́да-то какова́!** what weather! **каково́** *adv.* how. **како́й** *pron.* what; (such) as; which; **~... ни** whatever, whichever; **каки́м о́бразом?** how?; **~ тако́й?** which (exactly)?; **како́е тако́й?** nothing of the kind, quite the contrary. **како́й-либо, како́й-нибудь** *prons.* some; any; only. **како́й-то** *pron.* some; a; a kind of; something like.

как раз, ка́к-то *see* как

каламбу́р, -а pun. **каламбури́ст, -а** punster. **каламбу́рить, -ю** *impf.* (*pf.* с~) pun. **каланча́, -й** watch-tower. **кале́ка, -и** *c.g.* cripple. **календа́рь, -я́** *m.* calendar. **кале́ние, -я** incandescence. **кале́чить, -чу** *impf.* (*pf.* ис~, по~) cripple, maim, mutilate; twist, pervert; **~ся** become a cripple, be crippled. **кали́бр, -а** calibre; bore; gauge. **ка́лий, -я** potassium. **кали́тка, -и** wicket, (wicket-)gate. **калори́йность, -и** calorie content. **калори́йный** high-calorie; fattening. **кало́рия, -и** calorie. **кало́ша, -и** galosh. **ка́лька, -и** tracing-paper; tracing; calque. **калькуля́тор, -а** calculator. **калькуля́ция, -и** calculation. **кальсо́ны, кальсо́н** *pl.* (under)pants, drawers. **ка́льций, -я** calcium. **ка́мбала, -ы** flat-fish; plaice; flounder. **камени́стый** stony, rocky. **каменноуго́льный** coal; **~ бассе́йн** coal-field. **ка́менн|ый** stone; rock; stony; hard, immovable; **~ый век** Stone Age; **~ая соль** rock-salt; **~ у́голь** coal. **каменоло́мня, -и;** *g.pl.* quarry. **ка-**

ме́нщик, -а (stone)mason; bricklayer. **ка́мень, -мня;** *pl.* **-мни, -мне́й** *m.* stone.
ка́мера, -ы chamber; compartment; cell, ward; camera; inner tube, (foot-ball) bladder; **~ хране́ния (багажа́)** cloak-room, left-luggage office. **ка́мерный** chamber. **камерто́н, -а** tuning-fork.
ками́н, -а fireplace; fire.
камко́рдер, -а camcorder.
камо́рка, -и closet, very small room.
кампа́ния, -и campaign; cruise.
камфара́, -ы́ camphor.
камы́ш, -а́ reed, rush; cane.
кана́ва, -ы ditch; gutter; drain; trench; inspection pit.
Кана́да, -ы Canada. **кана́дец, -дца, кана́дка, -и** Canadian. **кана́дский** Canadian.
кана́л, -а canal; channel; duct; bore. **канализа́ция, -и** sewerage, sewerage system; drainage; underground cable system.
канаре́ечный canary; canary-coloured.
канаре́йка, -и canary.
кана́т, -а rope; cable, hawser. **канатохо́дец, -дца** rope-walker.
канва́, -ы́ canvas; groundwork; outline, design. **канво́вый** canvas.
кандалы́, -о́в *pl.* shackles, fetters, irons.
кандида́т, -а candidate; kandidat (*in former USSR, holder of first higher degree, awarded on dissertation*). **кандида́тская** *sb.* doctoral thesis. **кандидату́ра, -ы** candidature.
кани́кулы, -ул *pl.* vacation; holidays. **каникуля́рный** holiday.
кани́стра, -ы can, canister.
канифо́ль, -и rosin.
канниба́л, -а cannibal. **каннибали́зм, -а** cannibalism.
кано́ист, -а canoeist.
канона́да, -ы cannonade.
каноне́рка, -и gunboat. **каноне́рск|ий; ~ая ло́дка** gunboat. **кано́нир, -а** gunner.
кано́э *nt.indecl.* canoe.
кант, -а edging, piping; welt; mount. **канто-ва́ть, -ту́ю** *impf.* (*pf.* о~) border, pipe; mount.
кану́н, -а eve; vigil, watch-night.
ка́нуть, -ну *pf.* drop, sink; **~ в ве́чность** sink into oblivion; **как в во́ду ~** vanish into thin air, disappear without trace.
канцеля́рия, -и office. **канцеля́рск|ий** office; clerical; **~ие принадле́жности** stationery. **канцеля́рщина, -ы** office-work; red-tape.
канцероге́н, -а carcinogen. **канцероге́н-н|ый** carcinogenic; **~ое вещество́** carcinogen.
ка́нцлер, -а chancellor.
канцтова́р|ы, -ов *pl. abbr.* (*of* **канцеля́рские това́ры**) office supplies.
ка́пать, -аю *or* **-плю** *impf.* (*pf.* **ка́пнуть, на~**) drip, drop; trickle, dribble; fall in drops; pour out in drops; +*i.* spill. **ка́пелька, -и** small drop, droplet; a little; a bit, a grain,

a whit; ~ росы́ dew-drop.

капельме́йстер, -а conductor; bandmaster.

ка́пельный drip, drop, drip-feed, trickle; tiny.

капита́л, -а capital. **капиталисти́ческий** capitalist, capitalistic. **капита́льный** capital; main, fundamental; most important; ~ ремо́нт capital repairs, major overhaul.

капита́н, -а captain; master, skipper.

капите́ль, -и capital; small caps.

капитуля́ция, -и capitulation.

капка́н, -а trap. **капка́нный** trap; trapping.

ка́пля, -и; *g.pl.* -пель drop; bit, scrap; ни ка́пли not a bit, not a scrap, not a whit; по ка́пле drop by drop. **ка́пнуть, -ну** *pf. of* ка́пать

ка́пор, -а hood, bonnet.

капо́т, -а hood, cowl, cowling; bonnet; (*loose*) dressing-gown, house-coat.

капри́з, -а caprice, whim; vagary; ~ судьбы́ twist of fate. **капри́зник, -а** capricious person, child. **капри́зничать, -аю** *impf.* behave capriciously; (*of a child*) play up, be naughty. **капри́зный** capricious; naughty; wilful.

капу́ста, -ы cabbage; кормова́я ~ kale; спа́ржевая ~ broccoli.

капюшо́н, -а hood.

ка́ра, -ы punishment, retribution.

караби́н, -а carbine. **карабине́р, -а** car(a)bineer.

кара́бкаться, -аюсь *impf.* (*pf.* вс~) clamber, scramble up.

карава́й, -я round loaf, cob; pudding.

карава́н, -а caravan; convoy.

кара́куль, -я *m.* Persian lamb.

кара́куля, -и scrawl, scribble.

карамбо́ль, -я *m.* cannon.

караме́ль, -и caramel; caramels. **караме́лька, -и** caramel.

каранда́ш, -а́ pencil.

карапу́з, -а chubby little fellow.

кара́сь, -я́ *m.* crucian carp.

кара́тельный punitive. **кара́ть, -аю** *impf.* (*pf.* по~) punish, chastise.

карау́л, -а guard; watch; ~! help!; нести́ ~ be on guard. **карау́лить, -лю** *impf.* guard; watch for, lie in wait for. **карау́льный** guard; *sb.* sentry, sentinel, guard.

карбо́ловый carbolic.

карбу́нкул, -а carbuncle.

карбюра́тор, -а carburettor.

кардио́лог, -а cardiologist. **кардиостимуля́тор, -а** pacemaker.

каре́та, -ы carriage, coach; ~ ско́рой по́мощи ambulance.

ка́рий brown; hazel.

карикату́ра, -ы caricature; cartoon.

карка́с, -а frame; framework.

ка́ркать, -аю *impf.*, **ка́ркнуть, -ну** *pf.* (*pf. also* на~) caw, croak.

ка́рлик, -а, ка́рлица, -ы dwarf; pygmy. **ка́рликовый** dwarf, dwarfish; pygmy.

карма́н, -а pocket. **карма́нный** *adj.* pocket; ~ вор pickpocket.

карнава́л, -а carnival.

карни́з, -а cornice; ledge.

ка́рта, -ы map; chart; (playing-)card.

карта́вить, -влю *impf.* burr. **карта́вость, -и** burr. **карта́вый** burring.

ка́ртер, -а gear casing, crank-case.

карте́чь, -и case-shot, grape-shot; buckshot.

карти́на, -ы picture; scene. **карти́нка, -и** picture; illustration; ~-зага́дка jig-saw puzzle. **карти́нный** picturesque; picture.

карто́н, -а cardboard, pasteboard; cartoon. **карто́нка, -и** cardboard box; hat-box, bandbox.

картоте́ка, -и card-index.

картофелечи́стка, -и potato peeler. **карто́фелина, -ы** potato. **карто́фель, -я (-ю)** *m.* potatoes; potato(-plant). **карто́фельн|ый** potato; ~ая запека́нка shepherd's pie; ~ый крахма́л potato flour; ~ое пюре́ mashed potatoes.

ка́рточка, -и card; season ticket; photograph; ~ вин wine-list; ~ ку́шаний menu, bill of fare. **ка́рточный** card; ~ до́мик house of cards.

карто́шка, -и potatoes; potato.

карту́з, -а́ (peaked) cap.

карусе́ль, -и roundabout, merry-go-round.

ка́рцер, -а cell, lock-up.

карье́р[1], -а full gallop.

карье́р[2], -а quarry; sand-pit.

карье́ра, -ы career. **карьери́зм, -а** careerism. **карьери́ст, -а** careerist.

каса́ние, -я contact. **каса́тельная** *sb.* tangent. **каса́ться, -а́юсь** *impf.* (*pf.* косну́ться) +*g. or* до+*g.* touch; touch on; concern, relate to; что каса́ется as to, as regards, with regard to.

ка́ска, -и helmet.

Каспи́йск|ий: ~ое мо́ре the Caspian (Sea).

ка́сса, -ы till; cash-box; booking-office; box-office; cash-desk; cash; case; ~-автома́т slot-machine, ticket-machine; ~ взаимопо́мощи benefit fund, mutual aid fund, friendly society.

кассе́та, -ы cassette; plate-holder.

касси́р, -а, касси́рша, -и cashier. **ка́ссовый** cash; box-office; ~ аппара́т cash rgister. ~ счёт cash-account; ~ успе́х box-office success.

кастра́т, -а eunuch. **кастра́ция, -и** castration. **кастри́ровать, -рую** *impf. & pf.* castrate, geld.

кастрю́ля, -и saucepan.

ката́лка, -и; де́тская ~ baby buggy, push-chair.

катало́г, -а catalogue. **каталогизи́ровать, -рую** *impf. & pf.* catalogue.

ката́ние, -я rolling; driving; ~ верхо́м riding; ~ на конька́х skating; ~ на ро́ликах roller skating; ~ с гор tobogganing.

ката́ть, -а́ю *impf.* (*pf.* вы́~, с~) roll; wheel; trundle; drive, take for a drive, take out; roll out; mangle; ~ся roll, roll about; go for a drive; ~ся верхо́м ride, go riding; ~ся на конька́х skate, go skating; ~ся со́ смеху split one's sides.

катастро́фа, -ы catastrophe, disaster; accident, crash.

катафа́лк, -а catafalque; hearse.

категори́ческий categorical.

ка́тер, -а; pl. -а́ cutter; boat, motorboat, launch.

кати́ть, -ачу́, -а́тишь impf. bowl along, rip, tear; ~ся rush, tear; flow, stream, roll; ~ся по́д гору go downhill; ~ся с горы́ slide downhill; кати́сь, кати́тесь get out! clear off!

като́д, -а cathode. като́дн|ый; ~ые лучи́ cathode rays; ~ая тру́бка cathode-ray tube.

като́к, -тка́ skating-rink; roller; mangle.

като́лик, -а (Roman) Catholic. католи́чка, -и (Roman) Catholic. католици́зм, -а (Roman) Catholicism. католи́ческий (Roman) Catholic.

ка́торга, -и penal servitude, hard labour.

каторжа́нин, -а convict, ex-convict. ка́торжник, -а convict. ка́торжн|ый penal, convict; ~ые рабо́ты hard labour; drudgery.

кату́шка, -и reel, bobbin; spool; coil.

каучу́к, -а rubber.

кафе́ nt.indecl. café; ~-моро́женое ice-cream parlour.

ка́федра, -ы pulpit; rostrum, platform; chair; department.

кача́лка, -и rocking-chair; конь-~ rocking-horse. кача́ние, -я rocking, swinging, swing; pumping. кача́ть, -а́ю impf. (pf. качну́ть) +a. or i. rock, swing; shake; lift up, chair; pump; ~ся rock, swing; roll, pitch; reel, stagger. каче́ли, -ей pl. swing; see-saw.

ка́чественный qualitative; high-quality. ка́чество, -а quality; в ка́честве+g. as, in the capacity or character of; вы́играть ~, потеря́ть ~ gain, lose, by an exchange.

ка́чка, -и rocking; tossing.

качну́ть(ся, -ну́(сь, -нёшь(ся pf. of кача́ть(ся. качу́ etc.: see кати́ть

ка́ша, -и kasha; gruel, porridge; завари́ть ка́шу stir up trouble. кашева́р, -а cook.

ка́шель, -шля cough. ка́шлянуть, -ну pf., ка́шлять, -яю impf. cough; have a cough.

кашне́ nt.indecl. scarf, muffler.

кашта́н, -а chestnut. кашта́новый chestnut.

каю́та, -ы cabin, stateroom. каю́т-компа́ния, -и wardroom; passengers' lounge.

ка́ющийся repentant, contrite, penitent. ка́яться, ка́юсь impf. (pf. по~, рас~) repent; confess; ка́юсь I am sorry to say, I (must) confess.

кв. abbr. (of квадра́тный) square; (of кварти́ра) flat, apartment.

квадра́т, -а square; quad; в квадра́те squared; возвести́ в ~ square. квадра́тный square; quadratic. квадрату́ра, -ы squaring; quadrature.

ква́канье, -я croaking. ква́кать, -аю impf., ква́кнуть, -ну pf. croak.

квалифика́ция, -и qualification. квалифици́рованный qualified, skilled, trained, spe-

cialized. квалифици́ровать, -рую impf. & pf. check, test; qualify (as).

квант, -а, ква́нта, -ы quantum.

кварта́л, -а block; quarter. кварта́льный quarterly; sb. police officer.

кварти́ра, -ы flat; lodging(s); apartment(s); quarters, billets. квартира́нт, -а, -ра́нтка, -и lodger; tenant. кварти́рн|ый; ~ая пла́та, квартпла́та, -ы rent.

кварц, -а quartz.

квас, -а (-у); pl. ~ы́ kvass (sour Russ. beer). ква́сить, -а́шу impf. sour; ferment; pickle; leaven. квасцо́вый alum. квасцы́, -о́в pl. alum. ква́шен|ый sour, fermented; ~ая капу́ста sauerkraut.

вве́рху adv. up, upwards.

квит, кви́ты quits.

квита́нция, -и receipt. квито́к, -тка́ ticket, check.

кВт abbr. (of килова́тт) kW, kilowatt.

кг abbr. (of кило́, килогра́мм) k, kg, kilo(s), kilogram(s).

КГБ abbr. (of Комите́т госуда́рственной безопа́сности) KGB, State Security Committee.

кеба́б, -а kebab. кеба́бная sb. kebab house.

кегельба́н, -а bowling alley; skittle alley.

кегль, -я m. point size, body size.

ке́гля, -и skittle.

кедр, -а cedar. кедро́вый cedar.

ке́ды, -ов or кед pl. sports shoes, plimsolls.

кекс, -а cake; fruit-cake.

Кёльн, -а Cologne.

ке́лья, -и; g.pl. -лий cell.

кем see кто

ке́мпинг, -а a camp-site.

кенгуру́ m.indecl. kangaroo.

кенота́ф, -а cenotaph.

ке́пка, -и cap, cloth cap.

кера́мика, -и ceramics. керами́ческий ceramic.

керога́з, -а oil pressure stove. кероси́н, -а paraffin, kerosene. кероси́нка, -и oil-stove.

ке́та, -ы Siberian salmon. ке́тов|ый; ~ая икра́ red caviare.

кефи́р, -а kefir.

киберне́тика, -и cybernetics. кибернети́ческий cybernetic.

киби́тка, -и covered wagon; nomad tent.

кива́ть, -а́ю impf., кивну́ть, -ну́, -нёшь pf. (голово́й) nod, nod one's head; (+на+a.) motion (to). киво́к, -вка́ nod.

кида́ть, -а́ю impf. (pf. ки́нуть) throw, fling, cast; ~ся throw o.s., fling o.s.; rush; +i. throw, fling, shy.

Ки́ев, -а Kiev. ки́евский Kiev; Kievan.

кий, -я́; pl. -и́, -ёв (billiard) cue.

киле́в|о́й keel; ~áя ка́чка pitching.

кило́ nt.indecl. kilogram(me).

кило... in comb. kilo-. килоба́йт, -а kilobyte. ~ва́тт, -а kilowatt. ~гра́мм, -а kilogram(me). ~ме́тр, -а kilometre.

киль, -я m. keel; fin. кильва́тер, -а wake.

ки́лька, -и sprat.

кинжа́л, -а dagger.

кино́ *nt.indecl.* cinema.

кино́... *in comb.* film-, cine-. **киноаппара́т,** -а cinecamera. ~арти́ст, -а, ~арти́стка, -и film actor, actress. ~ателье́ *nt.indecl.* film studio. ~ве́дение, -я film studies. ~журна́л, -а news-reel. ~звезда́, -ы́ film-star. ~зри́тель, -я *m.* film-goer. ~карти́на, -ы film, picture. ~меха́ник, -а projectionist. ~опера́тор, -а cameraman. ~плёнка, -и film. ~прока́тчик, -а film distributor. ~режиссёр, -а film director. ~съёмка, -и filming, shooting. ~теа́тр, -а cinema. ~хро́ника, -и news-reel.

ки́нуть(ся, -ну(сь *pf. of* кида́ть(ся

кио́ск, -а kiosk, stall, stand.

ки́па, -ы pile, stack; pack, bale.

кипари́с, -а cypress.

кипе́ние, -я boiling. кипе́ть, -плю́ *impf.* (*pf.* вс~) boil, seethe; **рабо́та кипе́ла** work was in full swing.

Кипр, -а Cyprus.

кипу́чий boiling, seething; ebullient, turbulent. кипяти́льник, -а kettle, boiler. кипяти́льный boiling, boiler. кипяти́ть, -ячу́ *impf.* (*pf.* вс~) boil; ~ся boil; get excited, be enraged, be in a rage. кипято́к, -тка́ boiling water. кипячёный boiled.

Кирги́зия, -и Kirghizia.

кири́ллица, -ы Cyrillic alphabet.

кирка́, -й pickaxe, pick.

кирпи́ч, -а́ brick; bricks; 'no-entry' sign. кирпи́чный brick; brick-red; ~ заво́д brickworks, brick-field, brick-yard.

кисе́йный muslin.

кисе́ль, -я́ *m.* kissel (*kind of blancmange*).

кисе́т, -а tobacco-pouch.

кисея́, -й muslin.

ки́ска, -и pussy.

кислоро́д, -а oxygen. кислота́, -ы́; *pl.* -ы acid; sourness, acidity. кисло́тный acid. ки́слый sour; acid; ~ая капу́ста sauerkraut. ки́снуть, -ну; кис *impf.* (*pf.* про~) turn sour, go sour; mope.

ки́сточка, -и brush; tassel. кисть, -и; *g.pl.* -е́й cluster, bunch; brush; tassel; hand.

кит, -а́ whale.

кита́ец, -а́йца; *pl.* -цы, -цев, кита́янка, -и Chinese. Кита́й, -я China. кита́йка, -и nankeen. кита́йск|ий Chinese; ~ая тушь Indian ink.

китобо́й, -я whaler, whaling ship. кито́вый whale; ~ ус whalebone. китобо́йный whaling. китообра́зный cetacean.

кичи́ться, -чу́сь *impf.* plume o.s.; strut. кичли́вость, -и conceit; arrogance. кичли́вый conceited, arrogant, haughty, strutting.

кише́ть, -ши́т *impf.* swarm, teem.

кише́чник, -а bowels, intestines. кише́чный intestinal. кишка́, -и́ gut, intestine; hose.

кишмя́ *adv.*; ~ кише́ть swarm.

к.-л. *abbr.* (*of* како́й-либо) some.

клавеси́н, -а harpsichord. клавиату́ра, -ы keyboard. кла́виш, -а, кла́виша, -ы key. кла́вишн|ый; ~ые инструме́нты keyboard instruments.

клад, -а treasure.

кла́дбище, -а cemetery, graveyard, churchyard.

кла́дка, -и laying; masonry, walling. кладова́я *sb.* pantry, larder; store-room. кладовщи́к, -а́ storeman; shopman. кладу́ *etc.*: *see* клас́ть. кла́дчик, -а bricklayer.

кла́няться, -яюсь *impf.* (*pf.* поклони́ться) +d. bow to; greet; send, convey greetings; humble o.s.; go cap in hand to.

кла́пан, -а valve; vent; flap.

кларне́т, -а clarinet.

класс, -а class; form; class-room; *pl.* hopscotch. кла́ссн|ый class; classroom; high-class; first-class; ~ый ваго́н passenger coach; ~ая доска́ blackboard; ~ая каю́та private cabin. кла́ссовый class.

класть, -аду́, -адёшь; -ал *impf.* (*pf.* положи́ть, сложи́ть) lay; put; place; construct, build.

клаустрофо́бия, -и claustrophobia.

клева́ть, клюю́, клюёшь *impf.* (*pf.* клюну́ть) peck; bite; ~ но́сом nod.

кле́вер, -а; *pl.* -а́ clover.

клевета́, -ы́ slander; calumny, aspersion; libel. клевета́ть, -ещу́, -е́щешь *impf.* (*pf.* на~) +на+a. slander, calumniate; libel. клеветни́к, -а́, -ни́ца, -ы slanderer. клеветни́ческий slanderous; libellous, defamatory.

клеево́й glue; adhesive; size. клеёнка, -и oilcloth; oilskin. кле́ить, -е́ю *impf.* (*pf.* с~) glue; gum; paste; stick; ~ся stick; become sticky; get on, go well. клей, -я (-ю), *loc.* -ю́; *pl.* -й glue, adhesive, gum; size. кле́йк|ий sticky; ~ая ле́нта adhesive tape.

клеймёный branded. клейми́ть, -млю́ *impf.* (*pf.* за~) brand; stamp; stigmatize. клеймо́, -а́; *pl.* -а brand; stamp; mark.

клемма, -ы clamp, clip; terminal.

клён, -а maple.

клёпаный riveted. клепа́ть, -а́ю *impf.* rivet.

кле́тка, -и cage; coop; hutch; square; check; cell. кле́точка, -и cell; cellule. кле́точный cell; cell, cellular. клетча́тка, -и cellulose. кле́тчатый checked; squared; cellular.

клёш, -а flare; брю́ки ~ flares, bell-bottoms; ю́бка ~ flared skirt.

клешня́, -й; *g.pl.* -е́й claw.

клещ, -а́, -е́й *pl.* pincers, tongs; pincer-movement.

клие́нт, -а client; customer. клиенту́ра, -ы clientèle.

кли́зма, -ы enema.

клик, -а cry, call. кли́кать, -и́чу *impf.*, кли́кнуть, -ну *pf.* call, hail; honk.

кли́макс, -а, климакте́рий, -я menopause.

клин, -а; *pl.* -нья, -ньев wedge; quoin; gore; gusset; field.

кли́ника, -и clinic. клиници́ст, -а clinician. клини́ческий clinical.

клинóк, -нкá blade. клѝнопись, -и cuneiform.

клѝрос, -a choir.

клич, -a call. клѝчка, -и name; alias; nickname. клѝчу *etc.*: *see* клѝкать

клишé *nt.indecl.* cliché.

клок, -á; *pl.* -óчья, -ьев *or* -ѝ, -óв rag, shred;
tuft; ~ сéна wisp of hay.

клóкот, -a bubbling; gurgling. клокотáть,
-óчет *impf.* bubble; gurgle; boil up.

клонѝровать, -рую *impf. & pf.* clone.

клонѝть, -ню́, -нишь *impf.* bend; incline;
+к+*d.* lead; drive at; ~ся bow, bend; +к+*d.*
near, approach, lead up to, head for; день
клонѝлся к вéчеру the day was declining.

клоп, -á bug.

клóун, -a clown.

клочóк, -чкá scrap, shred, wisp; plot. клóчья
etc.: *see* клок

клуб¹, -a club; ~ здорóвья keep-fit club;
офицéрский ~ officers' mess.

клуб², -a; *pl.* -ы́ puff; ~ы́ пы́ли clouds of
dust.

клýбень, -бня *m.* tuber.

клубѝться, -ѝтся *impf.* swirl; wreathe, curl.
клубнѝка, -и strawberry; strawberries. клуб-
нѝчный strawberry.

клубóк, -бкá ball; tangle, mass; ~ в гóрле
lump in the throat.

клýмба, -ы (flower-)bed.

клык, -á fang; tusk; canine (*tooth*).

клюв, -a beak.

клю́ква, -ы cranberry; cranberries; развé-
систая ~ traveller's tale, tall story.

клю́нуть, -ну *pf. of* клевáть

ключ¹, -á key; clue; keystone; clef; wrench,
spanner; заперéть на ~ lock.

ключ², -á spring; source; бить ~óм spout,
jet; be in full swing.

ключевóй key; ~ знак clef; ~ кáмень keystone. ключѝца, -ы collarbone, clavicle.

клю́шка, -и (hockey) stick; (golf-)club.

клюю́ *etc.*: *see* клевáть

кля́кса, -ы blot, smudge.

кляну́ *etc.*: *see* кля́сть

кляня́ть, -чу́ *impf.* (*pf.* вы́~) beg.

кля́сть, -яну́, -янёшь; -ял, -á, -о *impf.* curse;
~ся (*pf.* по~ся) swear, vow. кля́тва, -ы
oath, vow; дать кля́тву take an oath. кля́т-
венный sworn, on oath.

км *abbr.* (*of* километр) km, kilometre.

к.-н. *abbr.* (*of* какóй-нибудь) some, any.

кнѝга, -и book.

кнѝго... *in comb.* book, biblio-. кнѝговéде-
ние¹, -я bibliography. ~вéдение², -я book-
keeping. ~держáтель, -я *m.* book-end.
~éд, -a bookworm. ~издáтель, -я *m.* publisher. ~лю́б, -a bibliophile, book-lover.
~хранѝлище, -a library; book-stack; book-
storage, shelving.

кнѝжечка, -и booklet. кнѝжка, -и book;
note-book; bank-book. кнѝжн|ый book;
~ая пóлка bookshelf; ~ый червь book-

worm; ~ый шкаф bookcase.

книзу *adv.* downwards.

кнóпка, -и drawing-pin; press-stud; knob,
(push-)button. кнóпочный; ~ телефóн
push-button telephone.

кнут, -á whip; knout.

княгѝня, -и princess. кня́жество, -a princi-
pality. княжня́, -ы́; *g.pl.* -жóн princess.
князь, -я; *pl.* -зья́, -зéй *m.* prince.

К° *abbr.* (*of* компáния) Co., Company.

ко *see* к *prep.*

коалѝция, -и coalition.

кобурá, -ы́ holster.

кобы́ла, -ы mare; (vaulting-)horse. кобы́л-
ка, -и filly; bridge.

кóваный forged; hammered; wrought; iron-
bound, iron-tipped; terse.

ковáрный insidious, crafty; perfidious,
treacherous. ковáрство, -a insidiousness,
craftiness; perfidy, treachery.

ковáть, кую́, -ёшь *impf.* (*pf.* под~) forge;
hammer; shoe.

ковёр, -врá carpet; rug; ~-самолёт magic
carpet.

ковéркать, -аю *impf.* (*pf.* ис~) distort, mangle, mispronounce; spoil, ruin.

кóвка, -и forging; shoeing. кóвкий; -вок, -вкá
-вко malleable, ductile.

коврѝга, -и loaf. коврѝжка, -и honeycake,
gingerbread.

кóврик, -a rug, mat. ковроочистѝтель, -я
carpet cleaner. коврочѝстка, -и carpet
sweeper.

ковш, -á scoop, ladle, dipper; bucket.

ковы́ль, -я *m.* feather-grass.

ковыля́ть, -я́ю *impf.* hobble; stump; toddle.

ковырну́ть, -ну́, -нёшь *pf.*, ковыря́ть, -я́ю
impf. dig into; tinker, potter; +в+*p.* pick; pick
at; ~ в зубáх pick one's teeth; ~ся rummage; tinker, potter.

когдá *adv.* when; ~..., ~ sometimes ...., sometimes; ~ (бы) ни whenever; ~ как it depends; *conj.* when; while, as; if; ~ так if so,
if that is the case. когдá-либо, когдá-
нибудь *advs.* some time, some day; ever.
когдá-то *adv.* once, at one time; at some
time; formerly; some day, some time.

когó *see* кто

кóготь, -гтя; *pl.* -гти, -гтéй *m.* claw; talon;
показáть свой кóгти show one's teeth.

код, -a code; персонáльный ~ personal identification number; PIN.

кóдекс, -a code; codex.

кодоскóп, -a an overhead projector.

кóе-гдé *adv.* here and there, in places. кóе-
кáк *adv.* anyhow; somehow (or other), just.
кóе-какóй *pron.* some. кóе-ктó, -когó
pron. somebody; some people. кóе-чтó, -чегó
pron. something; a little.

кóжа, -и skin, hide; leather; peel, rind; epi-
dermis. кожáн, -á leather coat. кóжанка, -и
leather jacket, leather coat. кóжаный leather.
кожéвенный leather; tanning, leather-dress-

ing; ~ заво́д tannery. **коже́вник, -а** tanner, leather-dresser, currier. **ко́жица, -ы** thin skin; film, pellicle; peel, skin. **ко́жный** skin; cutaneous. **кожура́, -ы́** rind, peel, skin.

коза́, -ы́; *pl.* **-ы** she-goat, nanny-goat, **козёл, -зла́** goat; he-goat, billy-goat. **козеро́г, -а** ibex; Capricorn. **ко́зий** goat; ~ пух angora. **козлёнок, -нка;** *pl.* **-ля́та, -ля́т** kid. **ко́зловый** goatskin.

ко́злы, -зел *pl.* (coach-)box; trestle(s); sawhorse.

ко́зни, -ей *pl.* machinations, intrigues.

козырёк, -рька́ peak; eye-shade; **взять под** ~+*d.* salute.

козырно́й trump, of trumps. **козырну́ть, -ну́, -нёшь** *pf.,* **козыря́ть, -я́ю** *impf.* lead trumps; trump; play one's trump card; salute. **ко́зырь, -я;** *pl.* **-и, -е́й** *m.* trump; **откры́ть свои́ ко́зыри** put one's cards on the table.

ко́йка, -и; *g.pl.* **ко́ек** berth, bunk; hammock; bed.

коке́тка, -и coquette. **коке́тливый** coquettish. **коке́тничать, -ю** *impf.* (с+*i.*) flirt (with); (+*i.*) show off, flaunt. **коке́тство, -а** coquetry.

коклю́ш, -а whooping-cough.

ко́кон, -а cocoon.

коко́с, -а coco(-tree); coconut. **коко́сов|ый** coconut; ~ый оре́х coconut; ~ая па́льма coconut tree.

кокс, -а coke.

кокте́йль, -я *m.* cocktail; моло́чный ~ milk shake.

кол, -а́; *pl.* **-лья, -ьев** stake, picket; ни ~а́ ни двора́ neither house nor home.

ко́лба, -ы retort.

колбаса́, -ы́; *pl.* **-ы** sausage; кровяна́я ~ black pudding.

колго́тки, -ток *pl.* tights.

колдовство́, -а́ witchcraft, sorcery, magic. **колду́н, -а́** sorcerer, magician, wizard. **колду́нья, -и;** *g.pl.* **-ний** witch, sorceress.

колеба́ние, -я oscillation, vibration; fluctuation, variation; hesitation; wavering, vacillation. **колеба́тельный** oscillatory, vibratory. **колеба́ть, -е́блю** *impf.* (*pf.* по~) shake; ~ся oscillate, vibrate, swing; shake; fluctuate, vary; hesitate; waver.

коленко́р, -а calico. **коленко́ровый** calico.

коле́но, -а; *pl.* **-и** *or* **-а** *or* **-нья, -ей** *or* **-лен** *or* **-ньев** knee, joint, node; bend, elbow, crank; по ~, по коле́ни knee deep, up to one's knees; стать на коле́ни kneel (down); стоя́ть на коле́нях be kneeling, be on one's knees. **коле́нчатый** crank, cranked; bent, elbow; ~ вал crankshaft.

коле́сник, -а wheelwright. **колесни́ца, -ы** chariot. **колёсный** wheel; wheeled. **колесо́, -а́;** *pl.* **-ёса** wheel.

коле́чко, -а ringlet.

коле́я, -и́ rut; track, gauge.

коли́бри *c.g. indecl.* humming-bird.

коли́чественн|ый quantitative; ~ое числи-

тельное cardinal number. **коли́чество, -а** quantity, amount; number.

ко́лкий; -лок, -лка́, -о prickly; sharp, biting, caustic.

колла́ж, -а collage.

колле́га, -и colleague. **коллегиа́льный** joint, collective; corporate. **колле́гия, -и** board; college. **колле́жский** collegiate; ~ асе́ссор, регистра́тор, секрета́рь, сове́тник (*8th, 14th, 10th, 6th grade: see* чин).

коллекти́в, -а group, body, team. **коллективиза́ция, -и** collectivization. **коллективизи́ровать, -рую** *impf. & pf.* collectivize. **коллективи́зм, -а** collectivism; team spirit. **коллекти́вн|ый** collective; joint; ~ое владе́ние joint ownership; ~ое хозя́йство collective farm; ~ое руково́дство collective leadership.

колле́ктор, -а commutator; manifold.

коллекционе́р, -а collector. **коллекциони́ровать, -рую** *impf.* collect. **колле́кция, -и** collection.

колли́зия, -и clash, conflict, collision.

коло́да, -ы block; log; pack (*of cards*).

коло́дезный well; well-deck. **коло́дец, -дца** well; shaft.

коло́дка, -и last; block, chock.

ко́локол, -а; *pl.* **-а́, -о́в** bell. **колоко́льный** bell; ~ звон peal, chime. **колоко́льня, -и** bell-tower. **колоко́льчик, -а** small bell; handbell; campanula, harebell.

колониа́льный colonial. **колониза́ция, -и** colonization. **колонизова́ть, -у́ю** *impf. & pf.* colonize. **колони́ст, -а** colonist. **коло́ния, -и** colony; settlement.

коло́нка, -и geyser; (street) fountain; standpipe; column; бензи́новая ~ petrol pump. **коло́нна, -ы** column. **коло́нный** columned. **колонти́тул, -а** a running title, catchword. **колонци́фра, -ы** page number, folio.

колори́т, -а colouring, colour. **колори́тный** colourful, picturesque, graphic.

ко́лос, -а; -о́сья, -ьев ear, spike. **колоси́ться, -и́тся** *impf.* form ears.

колосники́, -о́в *pl.* fire-bars; grate; flies.

колоти́ть, -очу́, -о́тишь *impf.* (*pf.* по~) beat; batter, pound; thrash, drub; break, smash; shake; ~ся pound, thump; shake; +о+*a.* beat; strike, against.

коло́ть[1], -лю́, -лешь *impf.* (*pf.* рас~) break, chop, split; ~ оре́хи crack nuts.

коло́ть[2], -лю́, -лешь *impf.* (*pf.* за~, кольну́ть) prick; stab; sting; taunt; slaughter; ~ся prick.

колпа́к, -а cap; lamp-shade; hood, cover, cowl.

колу́н, -а́ axe, chopper.

колхо́з, -а *abbr.* (*of* коллекти́вное хозя́йство) collective farm.

колыбе́ль, -и cradle.

колыха́ть, -ы́шу *impf.,* **колыхну́ть, -ну́, -нёшь** *pf.* sway, rock; ~ся sway, heave; flutter, flicker.

ко́лышек, -шка peg.

кольну́ть, -ну́, -нёшь *pf. of* коло́ть

кольцева́ть, -цу́ю *impf.* (*pf.* о~) ring. кольцево́й annular; circular. кольцо́, -á; *pl.* -а, -ле́ц, -льцам ring; hoop.

колю́ч|ий prickly; thorny; sharp, biting; ~ая про́волока barbed wire. колю́чка, -и prickle; thorn; quill; burr.

коля́ска, -и carriage; side-car; де́тская ~ pram; pushchair; инвали́дная ~ wheelchair; ~-су́мка shopping trolley, shopper.

ком, -а; *pl.* -мья, -мьев lump; ball; clod.

ком *see* кто

ком... *abbr.* (*of* коммунисти́ческий, кома́ндир, кома́ндный) *in comb.* Communist; commander; command. комба́т, -а battalion commander. ~ди́в, -а divisional commander. ~инте́рн, -а Comintern. ~па́ртия, -и Communist Party. ~сомо́л, -а Komsomol, Young Communist League. ~сомо́лец, -льца, -о́лка, -и member of Komsomol.

кома́нда, -ы command; order; party, detachment; crew; ship's company, team. команди́р, -а commander, commanding officer; captain. командирова́ть, -рую *impf. & pf.* post, send, dispatch on mission, on official business. командиро́вка, -и posting, dispatching; mission, commission, business trip; warrant; authority. командиро́вочн|ый *adj.*; ~ые де́ньги travelling allowance; ~ые *sb.*, *pl.* travelling allowance, expenses. кома́ндн|ый command; commanding; control; ~ая вы́шка control tower; ~ый пункт command post; ~ый соста́в officers; executive (*body*). кома́ндование, -я commanding; command; headquarters. кома́ндовать, -дую *impf.* (*pf.* с~) give orders; be in command; +*i.* command; +*i. or* над+*i.* order about; +над+*i.* command. кома́ндующий *sb.* commander.

кома́р, -á mosquito.

комба́йн, -а combine, multi-purpose machine; зерново́й ~ combine harvester; ку́хонный ~ food processor.

комбина́т, -а industrial complex; combine; training centre. комбина́ция, -и combination; merger; scheme, system; manoeuvre; combinations, slip. комбинезо́н, -а overalls, boiler suit; dungarees. комбини́ровать, -рую *impf.* (*pf.* с~) combine.

коме́дия, -и comedy; play-acting; farce.

комеда́нт, -а commandant; manager; warden; superintendent. комендату́ра, -ы commandant's office.

коме́та, -ы comet.

коми́зм, -а humour; the funny side, the comic element; the comic. ко́мик, -а comic actor; comedian. ко́микс, -а comic, comic strip, comic book; *pl.* the funnies.

комисса́р, -а commissar. комиссариа́т, -а ministry department.

комиссионе́р, -а (commission-)agent, factor,

broker. комиссио́нн|ый commission; committee, board; ~ый магази́н second-hand shop; ~ые *sb.*, *pl.* commission. коми́ссия, -и commission; committee, board.

комите́т, -а committee.

коми́ческий comic; comical, funny. коми́чный comical, funny.

ко́мкать, -аю *impf.* (*pf.* ис~, с~) crumple; make a hash of, muff.

коммента́рий, -я commentary; *pl.* comment. коммента́тор, -а commentator. комменти́ровать, -рую *impf. & pf.* comment (upon).

коммерса́нт, -а merchant; businessman комме́рция, -и commerce, trade. комме́рческий commercial, mercantile.

комму́на, -ы commune. коммуна́льн|ый communal; municipal; ~ые услу́ги public utilities. коммуна́р, -а Communard. коммуни́зм, -а communism.

коммуникацио́нн|ый; ~ая ли́ния line of communication. коммуника́ция, -и communication.

коммуни́ст, -а communist. коммунисти́ческий communist.

коммута́тор, -а commutator; switchboard.

ко́мната, -ы room. ко́мнатный room; indoor.

комо́д, -а chest of drawers.

комо́к, -мка́ lump; ~ не́рвов bundle of nerves.

компа́кт-ди́ск, -а compact disk, CD; про́игрыватель *m.* ~ов compact disk, CD player.

компа́ния, -и company. компаньо́н, -а, -о́нка, -и companion; partner.

ко́мпас, -а compass.

компенса́ция, -и compensation. компенси́ровать, -рую *impf. & pf.* compensate; indemnify; equilibrate.

компете́нтный competent. компете́нция, -и competence.

ко́мплексный complex, compound, composite; combined; over-all, all-in; ~ обе́д table d'hote dinner. компле́кт, -а complete set; complement; specified number; ~ белья́ bedclothes. компле́ктный complete, комплектова́ть, -ту́ю *impf.* (*pf.* с~, у~) complete; replenish; bring up to strength, (re)man. компле́кция, -и build; constitution.

комплиме́нт, а compliment.

компози́тор, -а composer. компози́ция, -и composition.

компо́стер, -а punch. компости́ровать, -рую *impf.* (*pf.* про~) punch.

компре́сс, -а compress.

компромети́ровать, -рую *impf.* (*pf.* с~) compromise. компроми́сс, -а compromise.

компью́тер, -а computer; ИБМ-совмести́мый ~ IBM(*propr.*)-compatible computer; ~-калькуля́тор scientific calculator; наколе́нный ~ laptop (computer). компью́терный computer; computerized.

кому́ *see* кто

комфо́рт, -а comfort. комфорта́бельный comfortable.

конве́йер, -а conveyor.

конвенциона́льный conventional. конве́нция, -и convention, agreement.

конве́рт, -а envelope; sleeve.

конво́йр, -а escort. конво́йровать, -рую *impf.* escort, convoy. конво́й, -я escort, convoy.

конгре́сс, -а congress.

конденса́тор, -а a capacitor; condenser.

конди́терская *sb.* confectioner's, sweetshop, cake shop.

кондиционе́р, -а air-conditioner. кондиционный air-conditioning.

конду́ктор, -а; *pl.* -а́, -торша, -и conductor; guard.

конево́дство, -а horse-breeding. конево́дческий horse-breeding. конёк, -нька́ *dim. of* конь; hobby-horse, hobby.

коне́ц, -нца́ end; distance, way; в конце́ концо́в in the end, after all; в о́ба конца́ there and back; в оди́н ~ one way; и концы́ в во́ду and nobody any the wiser оди́н ~ it comes to the same thing in the end; своди́ть концы́ с конца́ми make (both) ends meet; со всех концо́в from all quarters. коне́чно *adv.* of course, certainly; no doubt. коне́чность, -и extremity. коне́чн|ый final, last; ultimate; terminal; finite; ~ая остано́вка, ~ая ста́нция terminus.

кони́на, -ы horse-meat.

кони́ческий conic, conical.

конкре́тный concrete; specific.

конку́р, -а showjumping.

конкуре́нт, -а competitor. конкуре́нция, -и competition; вне конкуре́нции *hors concours*. конкури́ровать, -рую *impf.* compete. ко́нкурс, -а competition; вне ~а *hors concours*. конкурса́нт, -а competitor; contestant. ко́нкурсный competitive.

ко́нник, -а cavalryman; rider, equestrian. ко́нница, -ы cavalry; horse. конногварде́ец, -е́йца horse-guardsman; life-guard. коннозаво́дство, -а horse-breeding; stud, stud-farm. ко́нный horse; mounted; equestrian; ~ заво́д stud.

конопа́тить, -а́чу *impf.* (*pf.* за~) caulk.

конопля́, -й hemp.

консе́нсус, -а consensus.

консерва́нт, -а a preservative.

консервати́вный conservative. консервати́зм, -а conservatism. консерва́тор, -а conservative.

консервато́рия, -и conservatoire, academy of music.

консерва́ция, -и conservation; temporary closing down. консерви́ровать, -рую *impf.* & *pf.* (*pf. also* за~) preserve; can, bottle, pot; close down temporarily. консе́рвн|ый preserving; ~ая ба́нка tin; can. консервоткрыва́тель, -я *m.* tin, can opener. кон-

се́рвы, -ов *pl.* tinned goods; goggles.

конси́лиум, -а consultation.

консо́ль, -и console; cantilever; pedestal.

конспе́кт, -а synopsis, summary, abstract, précis. конспекти́вный concise, summary. конспекти́ровать, -рую *impf.* (*pf.* за~, про~) make an abstract of.

конспирати́вный secret, clandestine. конспира́тор, -а conspirator.

конста́ция, -и ascertaining; verification, establishment. констати́ровать, -рую *impf.* & *pf.* ascertain; verify, establish; certify.

конструи́ровать, -рую *impf.* & *pf.* (*pf. also* с~) construct; design; form (*government, etc.*). конструкти́вный structural; constructional; constructive. констру́ктор, -а a designer, constructor. констру́кция, -и construction; structure; design.

ко́нсул, -а consul. ко́нсульский consular. ко́нсульство, -а consulate.

консульта́ция, -и consultation; advice; advice bureau; clinic, surgery; tutorial; supervision. консульти́ровать, -рую *impf.* (*pf.* про~) advise; act as tutor (to); +c+i. consult; ~ся have a consultation; obtain advice; +c+i. be a pupil of; consult.

конта́кт, -а contact; touch. конта́ктный contact; ~ рельс live rail.

конте́йнер, -а a container. контейнерово́з, -а container ship, carrier.

континге́нт, -а quota; contingent; batch; ~ во́йск a military force.

контине́нт, -а continent. континента́льный continental.

конто́ра, -ы office. конто́рск|ий office; ~ая кни́га account-book, ledger. конто́рщик, -а clerk.

контр... *in comb.* counter-.

контраба́нда, -ы contraband, smuggling. контраба́ндист, -а a smuggler. контраба́ндный contraband; bootleg.

контраба́с, -а double-bass.

контраге́нт, -а a contracting party; subcontractor. контра́кт, -а a contract. контрактова́ть, -ту́ю *impf.* (*pf.* за~) contract for; engage; ~ся contract, undertake.

контрама́рка, -и complimentary ticket.

контрапу́нкт, -а a counterpoint. контрапункти́ческий, контрапу́нктный contrapuntal.

контра́ст, -а, контра́стность, -и contrast.

контрата́ка, -и counter-attack. контратакова́ть, -ву́ю *impf.* & *pf.* counter-attack.

контрибу́ция, -и indemnity; contribution.

контрнаступле́ние, -я counter-offensive.

контролёр, -а a inspector; ticket-collector. контроли́ровать, -рую *impf.* (*pf.* про~) check; inspect. контро́ль, -я *m.* control; check, checking; inspection; inspectors. контро́льн|ый control; check; monitoring; reference; ~ая вы́шка conning-tower; ~ая рабо́та test.

контрразве́дка, -и counter-intelligence; security service, secret service. контрразве́дчик,

-a counter-intelligence agent.

контршпиона́ж, -a counterespionage.

конту́женный contused, bruised; shell-shocked, **конту́зить, -у́жу** *pf.* contuse, bruise; shell-shock. **конту́зия, -и** contusion; shell-shock.

ко́нтур, -a contour, outline; circuit.

конура́, -ы́ kennel.

ко́нус, -a cone. **конусообра́зный** conical.

конферансье́ *m.indecl.* compère, master of ceremonies, MC.

конфере́нц-за́л, -a conference room. **конфере́нция, -и** conference.

конфе́т|а, -ы sweet, chocolate; ~**ы-соса́лки** fruit drops. **конфе́тница, -ы** sweet bowl, dish.

конфиденциа́льный confidential.

конфли́кт, -a clash, conflict; dispute.

конфронта́ция, -и confrontation, showdown.

конфу́з, -a discomfiture, embarrassment. **конфу́зить, -у́жу** *impf.* (*pf.* с~) confuse, embarrass; place in an awkward or embarrassing position; ~**ся** feel awkward or embarrassed; be shy. **конфу́зливый** bashful; shy. **конфу́зный** awkward, embarrassing.

концентра́т, -a concentrate. **концентрацио́нный** concentration. **концентра́ция, -и** concentration. **концентри́ровать, -рую** *impf.* (*pf.* с~) concentrate; mass.

конце́рт, -a concert; recital; concerto. **концерта́нт, -a, -а́нтка, -и** performer. **концерти́на, -ы** concertina. **концертме́йстер, -a** first violin; leader; soloist; accompanist. **конце́ртный** concert.

концла́герь, -я *abbr.* (*of* **концентрацио́нный ла́герь**) concentration camp.

концо́вка, -и tail-piece; colophon; ending.

конча́ть, -а́ю *impf.*, **ко́нчить, -чу** *pf.* finish; end; +*inf.* stop; ~**ся** end, finish; come to an end; be over; expire. **ко́нчен|ый** finished; decided, settled; **всё** ~**о** it's all over; it's all up. **ко́нчик, -a** tip; point. **кончи́на, -ы** decease, demise; end.

конь, -я́; *pl.* **-и, -е́й** horse; vaulting-horse; knight; ~**-кача́лка** rocking-horse. **конь́ки, -о́в** *pl.* skates; ~ **на ро́ликах** roller skates. **конькобе́жец, -жца** skater. **конькобе́жный** skating. **ко́нюх, -a** groom, stable-boy. **коню́шня, -и**; *g.pl.* **-шен** stable.

кооперати́в, -a cooperative society. **кооперати́вный** cooperative. **коопера́тор, -a** co-operator, member of the co-operative society. **коопера́ция, -и** cooperation. **коопери́ровать, -рую** *impf. & pf.* organize on co-operative lines. **коопери́роваться, -руюсь** *impf. & pf.* cooperate.

координа́ция, -и co-ordination. **координи́ровать, -рую** *impf. & pf.* co-ordinate.

копа́ть, -а́ю *impf.* (*pf.* **копну́ть, вы́~**) dig; dig up; dig out; root; dawdle.

копе́ечный worth, costing, a copeck; cheap;

petty, trifling. **копе́йка, -и** copeck.

Копенга́ген, -a Copenhagen.

ко́пи, -ей *pl.* mines.

копи́лка, -и money-box.

копи́рка, -и carbon paper; copying paper. **копирова́льный** copying. **копи́ровать, -рую** *impf.* (*pf.* с~) copy; imitate, mimic. **копиро́вка, -и** copying. **копиро́вщик, -a, -щица, -ы** copyist.

копи́ть, -плю́, -пишь *impf.* (*pf.* **на~**) save (up); accumulate, amass; store up; ~**ся** accumulate.

ко́пия, -и copy; duplicate; replica; **печа́тная** ~ (*comput.*) hard copy; **резе́рвная** ~ (*comput.*) backup.

копна́, -ы́; *pl.* **-ы, -пён** shock, stook; heap, pile; ~ **се́на** hay-cock. **копни́ть, -ню́** *impf.* (*pf.* с~) shock, stook; cock.

копну́ть, -ну́, -нёшь *pf. of* **копа́ть**

ко́поть, -и soot; lamp-black.

копоши́ться, -шу́сь *impf.* swarm; potter (about).

копте́ть, -и́т *impf.* (*pf.* **за~**) be covered with soot; smoke. **копти́лка, -и** oil-lamp. **копти́ть, -пчу́** *impf.* (*pf.* **за~, на~**) smoke, (smoke-)cure; blacken with smoke; cover with soot. **копче́ние, -я** smoking, curing; smoked foods. **копчёный** smoked, cured.

копы́тный hoof; hoofed, ungulate. **копы́то, -a** hoof.

копьё, -я́; *pl.* **-я, -пий** spear, lance.

кора́, -ы́ bark, rind; cortex; crust.

кора́бельный ship's, ship; marine, naval. **корабе́льщик, -a** shipwright. **кораблевожде́ние, -я** navigation. **кораблекруше́ние, -я** shipwreck. **кораблестрое́ние, -я** shipbuilding. **кораблестрои́тель, -я** *m.* shipbuilder, naval architect. **кора́бль, -я́** *m.* ship, vessel; nave.

кора́лл, -a coral.

коревой measles.

коре́ец, -е́йца, корея́нка, -и Korean. **коре́йский** Korean.

корена́стый thickset, stocky. **корени́ться, -и́тся** *impf.* be rooted. **коренн|о́й** radical, fundamental; ~**о́й жи́тель** native; ~**о́й зуб** molar; ~**а́я ло́шадь** shaft-horse; ~**о́е населе́ние** indigenous population. **ко́рень, -рня**; *pl.* **-и, -е́й** *m.* root; radical. **коре́нья, -ьев** *pl.* root vegetables. **корешо́к, -шка́** rootlet; root; back, spine; counterfoil; pal, mate.

Коре́я, -и Korea. **корея́нка** *see* **коре́ец**

корзи́на, -ы, корзи́нка, -и basket. **корзи́нный** basket.

коридо́р, -a corridor, passage.

кори́нка, -и currants.

кори́ца, -ы cinnamon.

кори́чневый brown.

ко́рка, -и crust; rind, peel; scab.

корм, -a (-у), *loc.* **-у́;** *pl.* **-á** fodder, food, feed; forage.

корма́, -ы́ stern, poop.

корми́лец, -льца bread-winner; benefactor.

кормилица, -ы wet-nurse; benefactress.

кормить, -млю, -мишь *impf.* (*pf.* на~, по~, про~) feed; keep, maintain; ~ся eat, feed; +*i.* live on, make a living by. **кормление**, -я feeding. **кормов|ой**[1] fodder, forage; ~ая свёкла mangel-wurzel.

кормовой[2] stern, poop; after.

корневище, -а rhizome. **корневой** root; radical. **корнеплоды**, -ов root-crops.

корнишон, -а gherkin.

коробить, -блю *impf.* (*pf.* по~) warp; jar upon, grate upon; ~ся (*pf. also* с~ся) warp, buckle.

коробка, -и box, case; ~ скоростей gear-box.

корова, -ы cow. **коров|ий** cow, cow's; ~ье масло butter. **коровник**, -а cow-shed.

королева, -ы queen. **королевич**, -а king's son. **королевна**, -ы king's daughter. **королевский** royal; king's; regal, kingly. **королевство**, -а kingdom. **королёк**, -лька петти king, kinglet; gold-crest; blood-orange. **король**, -я *m.* king.

коромысло, -а a yoke; beam; rocking shaft, rocker (arm); balance arm.

корона, -ы crown; coronet; corona.

коронаротромбоз, -а coronary thrombosis; coronary. **коронарный** coronary.

коронка, -и crown. **коронный** crown, of state. **короновать**, -ную *impf. & pf.* crown.

коростель, -я corncrake.

коротать, -аю *impf.* (*pf.* с~) while away, pass. **коротк|ий**; короток, -тка, коротко, коротки short; brief; close, intimate; ~ая расправа short shrift; на ~ой ноге on intimate terms. **коротко** *adv.* briefly; intimately; ~ говоря in short. **коротковолновый** short-wave. **короче** *comp. of* корот* кий*, коротко

корпеть, -плю *impf.* sweat, pore (над+*i.* over).

корпус, -а; *pl.* -ы, -ов *or* -а, -ов corps; services high school; building; hull; housing, frame, case; long primer; body; trunk, torso; length.

корректив, -а amendment, correction. **корректировать**, -рую *impf.* (*pf.* про~, с~) correct, read, edit. **корректный** correct, proper. **корректор**, -а; *pl.* -а proof-reader, corrector. **корректура**, -ы proof-reading; proof.

корреспондент, -а correspondent. **корреспонденция**, -и correspondence; заказная, простая ~ registered, non-registered mail. **корреспондировать**, -рую *impf.* correspond.

корсет, -а corset.

корт, -а (tennis-)court.

кортик, -а dirk.

корточки, -чек *pl.*; сесть на ~, сидеть на корточках squat.

корчевать, -чую *impf.* grub up, root out. **корчёвка**, -и grubbing up, rooting out.

корчить, -чу *impf.* (*pf.* с~) contort; ~ гримасы, рожи make faces, pull faces; ~ дурака play the fool; ~ из себя pose as; *impers.*+*a.* convulse; make writhe; его корчит от боли he is writhing in pain; ~ся writhe.

коршун, -а kite.

корыстный mercenary. **корыстолюбивый** self-interested, mercenary. **корыстолюбие**, -я self-interest, cupidity. **корысть**, -и cupidity, avarice; profit, gain.

корыто, -а trough; wash-tub.

корь, -и measles.

корявый rough, uneven; gnarled; clumsy, uncouth; pock-marked.

коса[1], -ы, *a.* -у; *pl.* -ы plait, tress, braid.

коса[2], -ы, *a.* косу; *pl.* -ы spit.

коса[3], -ы, *a.* косу; *pl.* -ы scythe. **косарь**, -я *m.* mower, hay-maker.

косвенн|ый indirect; oblique; ~ые улики circumstantial evidence.

косилка, -и mower, mowing-machine. **косить**[1], кошу, косишь *impf.* (*pf.* с~) mow; cut; mow down.

косить[2], кошу *impf.* (*pf.* по~, с~) squint; be crooked; ~ся slant; look sideways; look askance.

косица, -ы lock; pigtail.

косматый shaggy.

косметика, -и cosmetics, make-up. **космети́ческ|ий** cosmetic; ~ий кабинет beauty parlour; ~ая маска face-pack; ~ая сумочка vanity bag, case; ~ий ремонт redecoration; refurbishment.

косми́ческ|ий cosmic; space; ~ий корабль spaceship, spacecraft; ~ое пространство (outer) space; ~ое телевидение satellite television broadcasting. **космодром**, -а cosmodrome, launching-site (*for spacecraft*). **космолёт**, -а (space) shuttle. **космонавтика**, -и astronautics, space exploration. **космотехника**, -и space technology. **космонавт**, -а, -навтка, -и spaceman, cosmonaut, astronaut. **космос**, -а cosmos; (outer) space. **космотехника**, -и space technology.

коснеть, -ею *impf.* (*pf.* за~) stagnate; stick. **косноязычный** tongue-tied.

коснуться, -нусь, -нёшься *pf. of* касаться

косный inert, sluggish; stagnant.

косо *adv.* slantwise, aslant, askew; sidelong, obliquely. **косоглазие**, -я squint, cast. **косоглазый** cross-eyed, squint-eyed. **косогор**, -а slope, hillside. **косой** кос, -а, -о slanting; oblique; sloping; sidelong; squinting, cross-eyed; скроенный по ~ cut on the cross. **косолапый** pigeon-toed; clumsy, awkward.

костёр, -тра bonfire; camp-fire.

костистый, **костлявый** bony; костный bone, bony, osseous. **косточка**, -и *dim. of* кость bone; kernel, stone, pip.

костыль, -я *m.* crutch; tail-skid.

кость, -и, *loc.* й; *pl.* -и, -ей bone; die; играть в кости dice.

костюм, -а dress, clothes; suit; costume;

англи́йский ~ tailor-made (coat and skirt); **вече́рний** ~ dress suit; **купа́льный** ~ swim-suit; **маскара́дный** ~ fancy-dress. **костюмёр**, -a wardrobe master. **костюми́рованный** in costume; fancy-dress; ~ **бал**, **вёчер** fancy-dress ball. **костю́мн|ый** adj.; ~**ая пье́са** period play, costume play.

костя́к, -á skeleton; backbone. **костяно́й** bone; ivory.

косы́нк|а, -и (three-cornered) head-scarf, shawl.

кот, -á tom-cat.

котёл, -тла́ boiler; copper, cauldron. **котело́к**, -лка́ pot; mess-tin; bowler (hat); noddle, head. **коте́льная** sb. boiler-room, boiler-house.

котёнок, -нка; pl. -тя́та, -тя́т kitten. **ко́тик**, -a fur-seal; sealskin. **ко́тиковый** sealskin.

котле́та, -ы rissole, croquette; **отбивна́я** ~ cutlet, chop.

котлова́н, -a foundation pit, excavation. **котлови́на**, -ы basin, hollow; trough.

кото́мка, -и knapsack.

кото́рый pron. which, what; who; that; **в кото́ром часу́** (at) what time; **кото́рые...**, **кото́рые** some ..., some; ~ **раз** how many times; ~ **час?** what time is it? **кото́рый-либо**, **кото́рый-нибудь** prons. some; one or other.

котя́та etc.: see **котёнок**

ко́фе m.indecl. coffee; **раствори́мый** ~ instant coffee. **кофева́рка**, -и coffee-maker. **кофеи́н**, -a caffeine. **кофе́йник**, -a coffee-pot. **кофе́йный** coffee. **кофемо́лка**, -и coffee-mill, coffee-grinder.

ко́фта, -ы, **ко́фточка**, -и blouse.

коча́н, -á or -чна́ (cabbage-)head.

кочева́ть, -чу́ю impf. lead a nomadic life; rove, wander; migrate. **кочёвка**, -и nomad camp; wandering, migration; nomadic existence. **коче́вник**, -a nomad. **кочево́й** nomadic; migratory. **коче́вье**, -я; g.pl. -вий nomad encampment; nomad territory.

кочега́р, -a stoker, fireman. **кочега́рка**, -и stokehold, stokehole.

кочене́ть, -е́ю impf. (pf. за~, о~) grow numb; stiffen.

кочерга́, -й; g.pl. -рёг poker.

кочеры́жка, -и cabbage-stalk.

ко́чка, -и hummock; tussock. **кочкова́тый** hummocky, tussocky.

коша́чий cat, cat's; catlike; feline; ~ **конце́рт** caterwauling; hooting, barracking.

кошелёк, -лька́ purse.

коше́рный kosher.

ко́шка, -и cat; grapnel, drag; pl. climbing-irons; cat(-o'-nine-tails).

кошма́р, -a nightmare. **кошма́рный** nightmarish; horrible, awful.

кошу́ etc.: see **коси́ть**

кощу́нственный blasphemous. **кощу́нство**, -a blasphemy.

коэффицие́нт, -a coefficient, factor; ~

у́мственных спосо́бностей intelligence quotient, IQ.

КП abbr. (of **Коммунисти́ческая па́ртия**) Communist Party. **КПСС** abbr. (of **Коммунисти́ческая па́ртия Сове́тского Сою́за**) CPSU, Communist Party of the Soviet Union.

кра́деный stolen. **краду́** etc.: see **красть**. **кра́дучись** adv. stealthily, furtively.

краеве́дение, -я regional studies.

краеуго́льный; ~ **ка́мень** corner-stone.

кра́жа, -и theft; **магази́нная** ~ shoplifting; ~ **со взло́мом** burglary.

край, -я (-ю), loc. -ю́; pl. -я́, -ёв edge; brim; brink; land, country; territory, region; side (of meat); **в чужи́х края́х** in foreign parts; **на краю́ све́та** at the world's end; **че́рез** ~ overmuch, beyond measure. **кра́йне** adv. extremely. **кра́йний** extreme; last; uttermost; outside, wing. **кра́йность**, -и extreme; extremity.

крал etc.: see **кра́сть**

кран, -a tap, cock, faucet; crane.

крапи́ва, -ы nettle. **крапи́вница**, -ы nettle-rash. **крапи́вный** nettle.

кра́пина, -ы, **кра́пинка**, -и speck, spot. **краплёный** marked.

краса́вец, -вца handsome man; Adonis. **краса́вица**, -ы beauty. **краси́вость**, -и (mere) prettiness. **краси́вый** beautiful; handsome; fine.

краси́льн|ый dye; dyeing. **краси́льня**, -и; g.pl. -лен dye-house, dye-works. **краси́льщик**, -a dyer. **краси́тель**, -я m. dye, dye-stuff. **кра́сить**, -а́шу impf. (pf. вы́~, о~, по~) paint; colour; dye; stain; ~**ся** (pf. на~) make-up. **кра́ска**, -и paint, dye; colour; painting, colouring, dyeing; (printer's) ink; ~ **для ресни́ц** mascara; **(водо-)эму́льсио́нная** ~ emulsion (paint). **краскораспыли́тель**, -я m. paint sprayer, spray-gun.

красне́ть, -е́ю impf. (pf. по~) blush; redden, grow red; show red; colour; ~**ся** show red.

красно... in comb. red; beautiful. **красноарме́ец**, -е́йца Red Army man. ~**арме́йский** Red Army. ~**ва́тый** reddish. ~**гварде́ец**, -е́йца Red Guard. ~**дере́вец**, -вца, ~**дере́вщик**, -a a cabinet-maker. ~**знамённый** Red-Banner. ~**ко́жий** red-skinned; sb. redskin. ~**речи́вый** eloquent; expressive. ~**ре́чие**, -я eloquence; oratory.

краснота́, -ы́ redness; red spot. **кра́сн|ый**; -сен, -сна́, -о red; beautiful; fine; of high quality or value; ~**ое де́рево** mahogany; ~**ый лес** coniferous forest; ~**ая строка́** (first line of) new paragraph; ~**ый у́гол** place of honour; ~**ый уголо́к** Red Corner.

красова́ться, -су́юсь impf. (pf. по~) stand in beauty; show off; +i. flaunt. **красота́**, -ы́; pl. -ы beauty. **кра́сочный** paint; ink; colourful, (highly) coloured.

красть, -аду́, -адёшь; крал impf. (pf. у~) steal; ~**ся** steal, creep, sneak.

кра́тк|ий; -ток, -тка́, -о short; brief; concise;

~ое содержа́ние summary. **кра́тко** *adv.* briefly. **кратковре́менный** short, brief; short-lived; transitory. **краткосро́чный** short-term.

кра́тное *sb.* multiple.

кратча́йший *superl. of* **кра́ткий. кра́тче** *comp. of* **кра́ткий, кра́тко**

крах, -а crash; failure.

крахма́л, -а starch. **крахма́лить, -лю** *impf.* (*pf.* на~) starch. **крахма́льный** starched.

кра́ше *comp. of* **краси́вый, краси́во**

кра́шеный painted; coloured; dyed; made up, wearing make-up. **кра́шу** *etc.: see* **кра́сить**

краю́ха, -и hunk, thick slice.

креве́тка, -и shrimp; prawn. **креветколо́в|ный; ~ое су́дно** shrimper, shrimp boat.

креди́т, -а credit. **креди́тка, -и** credit card. **креди́тный** credit, on credit. **кредитова́ть, -ту́ю** *impf. & pf.* credit, give credit (to). **креди́тор, -а** creditor; ~ по закладно́й mortgagee. **кредитоспосо́бность, -и** credit-worthiness, credit rating.

кре́йсер, -а; pl. -а́, -о́в cruiser. **кре́йсерский** cruiser, cruising. **крейси́ровать, -рую** *impf.* cruise.

крем, -а cream.

креме́нь, -мня́ *m.*, **кремешо́к, -шка́** flint.

кремлеве́д, -а Kremlinologist. **кремлеве́дение, -я** Kremlinology. **кремлёвский** Kremlin. **кремль, -я́** *m.* citadel; Kremlin.

кремнёв|ый flint; silicon; siliceous; ~ое ружьё flint-lock. **кремнезём, -а** silica. **кре́мний, -я** silicon. **кремни́стый** siliceous; stony.

кре́мовый cream; cream-coloured.

крен, -а list, heel; bank. **крени́ть, -ню** *impf.* (*pf.* на~) heel; bank; ~ся heel over, list; bank.

креп, -а crêpe; crape.

крепи́ть, -плю́ *impf.* strengthen; support, shore up timber; make fast, hitch, lash; furl; constipate, make costive; ~ся hold out. **кре́пк|ий; -пок, -пка́, -о** strong; sound; sturdy, robust; firm; ~ий моро́з hard frost; ~ие напи́тки spirits; ~ое сло́во, словцо́ swear-word, curse. **кре́пко** *adv.* strongly; firmly; soundly. **крепле́ние, -я** strengthening; fastening; binding; timbering, shoring up; lashing, furling.

кре́пнуть, -ну; -еп *impf.* (*pf.* о~) get stronger.

крепостни́чество, -а serfdom. **крепостн|о́й** serf; ~о́е пра́во serfdom; ~о́й *sb.* serf.

кре́пость, -и fortress; strength. **крепча́ть, -а́ет** *impf.* (*pf.* по~) strengthen; get stronger, get harder, get up. **кре́пче** *comp. of* **кре́пкий, кре́пко**

кре́сло, -а; g.pl. -сел arm-chair, easy-chair; stall; высо́кое ~ (*child's*) high chair; инвали́дное ~ wheelchair; ~-кача́лка rocking chair.

крест, -а́ cross; поста́вить ~ на+*p.* give up for lost. **крести́ны, -и́н** *pl.* christening.

крести́ть, крещу́, -е́стишь *impf. & pf.* (*pf. also* о~, пере~) baptize, christen; nickname; make sign of the cross over; ~ся cross o.s.; be baptized, be christened. **кре́стна́крест** *adv.* crosswise. **кре́стник, -а, кре́стница, -ы** god-child. **крёстн|ый; ~ая (мать)** godmother; ~ый оте́ц godfather. **кресто́вый** of the cross; ~ похо́д crusade. **крестоно́сец, -сца** crusader. **крестообра́зный** cruciform.

крестья́нин, -а; pl. -я́не, -я́н, крестья́нка, -и peasant. **крестья́нский** peasant. **крестья́нство, -а** peasants, peasantry.

креще́ние, -я baptism, christening; K~ Epiphany. **крещён|ый; -ён, -ена́** baptized; *sb.* Christian. **крещу́** *etc.: see* **крести́ть**

крива́я *sb.* curve. **кривизна́, -ы́** crookedness; curvature. **криви́ть, -влю́** *impf.* (*pf.* по~, с~) bend, distort; ~ душо́й go against one's conscience; ~ся become crooked or bent; make a wry face. **кривля́ка, -и** *c.g.* poseur; affected person. **кривля́нье, -я** affectation. **кривля́ться, -я́юсь** *impf.* be affected, give o.s. airs.

криво... *in comb.* curved, crooked; one-sided. **кривобо́кий** lopsided. **~гла́зый** blind in one eye; one-eyed. **~лине́йный** curvilinear. **~но́гий** bandy-legged. **~то́лки, -ов** *pl.* false rumours. **~ши́п, -а** crank; crankshaft.

криво́й; крив, -а́, -о crooked; curved; one-eyed.

крик, -а cry, shout; *pl.* clamour, outcry. **крикли́вый** clamorous, shouting; bawling; loud; penetrating; blatant. **кри́кнуть, -ну** *pf. of* **крича́ть. крику́н, -а́** shouter, bawler; babbler.

криста́лл, -а crystal; маги́ческий ~ crystal ball; (*comput.*) (silicon) chip.

кри́тик, -а critic. **кри́тика, -и** criticism; critique. **критикова́ть, -ку́ю** *impf.* criticize. **крити́ческий** critical.

крича́ть, -чу́ *impf.* (*pf.* кри́кнуть) cry, shout; yell, scream. **крича́щий** loud; blatant.

кров, -а roof; shelter; лишённый ~а homeless.

крова́вый bloody.

крова́ть, -и bed; bedstead.

кро́вельный roof, roofing.

кровено́сный blood-; circulatory. **крови́нка, -и** drop of blood.

кро́вля, -и; g.pl. -вель roof.

кро́вн|ый blood; thoroughbred; vital, deep, intimate; deadly; ~ая месть blood-feud.

крово... *in comb.* blood, sangui-, haemo-. **кровожа́дный** bloodthirsty. **~излия́ние, -я** haemorrhage. **~обраще́ние, -я** circulation. **~подтёк, -а** bruise. **~проли́тие, -я** bloodshed. **~проли́тный** bloody; sanguinary. **~со́с, -а** a vampire-bat; bloodsucker. **~тече́ние, -я** bleeding; haemorrhage. **~точи́вость, -и** haemophilia. **~точи́ть, -чи́т** *impf.* bleed. **~ха́ркание, -я** spitting of blood; haemoptysis.

кровь, -и, *loc.* -и́ blood. **кровяно́й** blood.

кро́йть, крою́ *impf.* (*pf.* с~) cut, cut out.

кро́йка, -и cutting out.

крокоди́л, -а crocodile.

кро́кус, -а crocus.

кро́лик, -а rabbit. **кроликово́дство, -а** rabbit-breeding. **кро́ликовый, кро́личий** rabbit.

кроль, -я *m.* crawl(-stroke).

крольча́тник, -а rabbit-hutch; rabbit farm. **крольчи́ха, -и** doe, she-rabbit.

кро́ме *prep.*+g. except; besides, in addition to; ~ того́ besides, moreover, furthermore; ~ шу́ток joking apart.

кро́мка, -и edge; selvage; rim; brim.

кромса́ть, -а́ю *impf.* (*pf.* ис~) cut up carelessly, hack to pieces; shred.

кро́на¹, -ы crown, top.

кро́на², -ы (*coin*) crown.

кроншты́йн, -а bracket; corbel.

кропотли́вый painstaking; minute; laborious; precise.

кросс, -а cross-country race.

кроссво́рд, -а crossword.

кроссме́н, -а cross-country runner.

крот, -а́ mole, moleskin.

кро́ткий, -ток, -тка́, -тко meek, gentle; mild. **кро́тость, -и** gentleness; mildness, meekness.

кроха́, -и́, а. -у; *pl.* -и, -ох, -а́м crumb. **кро́хотный, кро́шечный** tiny, minute. **кро́шево, -а** hash; medley. **кроши́ть, -шу́, -шишь** *impf.* (*pf.* ис~, на~, рас~) crumble; chop, hack; hack to pieces; +i. drop crumbs of; ~ся crumble; break up small. **кро́шка, -и** crumb; a bit.

круасса́н, -а croissant.

круг, -а (-у), *loc.* -у́; *pl.* -и́ circle; ring; circuit, lap; sphere; range; compass; на ~ on average, taking it all round. **круглогоди́чный** year-round. **круглосу́точный** round-the-clock, 24-hour. **кру́гл|ый; кругл, -а́, -о** round; complete, utter, perfect; ~ый год all the year round; ~ый, ~ая сирота́ (complete) orphan; ~ые су́тки day and night. **кругов|о́й** circular; all-round; cyclic; ~а́я пору́ка mutual responsibility guarantee; ~а́я ча́ша loving-cup. **кругозо́р, -а** prospect; outlook, horizon, range of interests. **круго́м** *adv.* round, around; round about; completely; entirely; *prep.*+g. round, around. **кругооборо́т, -а** circulation. **кругосве́тный** round-the-world.

кружевно́й lace; lacy. **кру́жево, -а;** *pl.* -а́, -ев, -а́м lace.

кружи́ть, -ужу́, -у́жишь *impf.* whirl, spin round; circle; wander; ~ся whirl, spin round, go round.

кру́жка, -и mug; tankard; collecting-box.

кружно́й roundabout, circuitous. **кружо́к, -жка́** circle, society, group; disc; washer.

круи́з, -а cruise.

крупа́, -ы́; *pl.* -ы groats; sleet. **крупи́нка, -и** grain. **крупи́ца, -ы** grain, fragment, atom.

крупно... *in comb.* large, coarse, macro-, megalo-; **крупномасшта́бный** large-scale; ambitious; **кру́пн|ый** large, big; large-scale; coarse; important; serious; prominent, outstanding; ~ый план close-up; ~ый разгово́р high words; ~ый шаг coarse pitch; ~ым ша́гом at a round pace.

крупча́тка, -и finest (white) flour. **крупча́тый** granular.

крутизна́, -ы́ steepness; steep slope.

крути́льный torsion, torsional; doubling. **крути́ть, -учу́, -у́тишь** *impf.* (*pf.* за~, с~) twist, twirl; roll; turn, wind; whirl; ~ся turn, spin, revolve; whirl; be in a whirl.

кру́то *adv.* steeply; suddenly; abruptly; sharply; sternly, severely; drastically; thoroughly. **крут|о́й; крут, -а́, -о** steep; sudden; abrupt, sharp; stern, severe; drastic; thick; well-done; ~о́е яйцо́ hard-boiled egg. **кру́ча, -и** steep slope, cliff. **кру́че** *comp. of* круто́й, кру́то

кручу́ *etc.: see* крути́ть

круше́ние, -я wreck; crash; ruin; collapse.

крыжо́венный gooseberry. **крыжо́вник, -а** gooseberries; gooseberry bush.

крыла́тый winged. **крыло́, -а́;** *pl.* -лья, -льев wing; sail, vane; splashboard, mudguard.

крыльцо́, -а́; *pl.* -а, -ле́ц, -ца́м porch; (front, back) steps.

Крым, -а the Crimea. **кры́мский** Crimean.

кры́са, -ы rat. **крысоло́в, -а** rat-catcher. **крысоло́вка, -и** rat-trap.

кры́тый covered. **крыть, кро́ю** *impf.* cover; roof; coat; trump; ~ся be, lie; be concealed. **кры́ша, -и** roof. **кры́шка, -и** lid; cover.

крюк, -а́ (-у); *pl.* -ки́, -ко́в *or* -ю́чья, -чьев hook; detour. **крючкова́тый** hooked. **крючо́к, -чка́** hook; hitch, catch.

кря́ду *adv.* in succession, running.

кряж, -а a ridge.

кря́кать, -аю *impf.* **кря́кнуть, -ну** *pf.* quack; grunt.

кряхте́ть, -хчу́ *impf.* groan.

ксероко́пия, -и xerox (copy). **ксе́рокс, -а** Xerox(*propr.*)(-machine); xerox.

кста́ти *adv.* to the point, to the purpose; opportunely; at the same time, incidentally; by the way.

кто, кого́, кому́, кем, ком *pron.* who; anyone, anybody; кому́ как tastes differ; ~ (бы) ни whoever; whosoever; ~ идёт? who goes there?; ~ кого́? who will win, who will come out on top?; ~... ~ some ..., others; ~ куда́ in all directions; ~ что лю́бит tastes differ. **кто́-либо, кто́-нибудь** *prons.* anyone, anybody; someone, somebody. **кто́-то** *pron.* someone, somebody.

куб, -а; *pl.* -ы́ cube; cubic metre; boiler, water-heater, urn; still; vat; в ~е cubed.

куб. *abbr.* (*of* куби́ческий) cubic.

ку́барем *adv.* head over heels; headlong.

кубату́ра, -ы cubic content. **ку́бик, -а** brick, block; cubic centimetre.

куби́нец, -нца, **куби́нка**, -и Cuban. **куби́нский** Cuban.

куби́ческий cubic, cubical; cube.

ку́бовый indigo.

ку́бок, -бка goblet, bowl, beaker; cup; **встре́ча на ~** cup-tie.

кубоме́тр, -a cubic metre.

кувши́н, -a jug; pitcher. **кувши́нка**, -и water-lily.

кувырка́ться, -а́юсь *impf.*, **кувыркну́ться**, -ну́сь *pf.* turn somersaults, go head over heels; **кувырко́м** *adv.* head over heels; topsy-turvy.

куда́ *adv.* where, where to; what for; +*comp.* much, far; **~ (бы) ни** wherever; **~ бы то ни́ было** anywhere; **~ лу́чше** much better; **хоть ~** fine, excellent. **куда́-либо**, **куда́-нибудь** *adv.* anywhere, somewhere. **куда́-то** *adv.* somewhere.

куда́хтанье, -я cackling, clucking. **куда́хтать**, -хчу *impf.* cackle, cluck.

ку́дри, -е́й *pl.* curls. **кудря́в|ый** curly; curly-headed; leafy, bushy; flowery, florid, ornate; **~ая капу́ста** curly kale. **кудря́шки**, -шек *pl.* ringlets.

кузне́ц, -а́ smith, blacksmith. **кузне́чик**, -a grasshopper. **кузне́чный** blacksmith's; **~ мех** bellows; **~ мо́лот** sledge-hammer. **ку́зница**, -ы forge, smithy.

ку́зов, -a; *pl.* -а́ basket; body.

кукаре́кать, -ает *impf.*, **кукаре́кнуть**, -нет *pf.* (*pf. also* **про~**) crow. **кукареку́** cock-a-doodle-doo.

ку́киш, -a fico, fig.

ку́кла, -ы doll; puppet; **теа́тр ку́кол** puppet theatre.

кукова́ть, -ку́ю *impf.* (*pf.* **про~**) cuckoo.

ку́колка, -и dolly; chrysalis, pupa. **ку́кольник**, -a puppeteer. **ку́кольный** doll's; doll-like; puppet.

кукуру́за, -ы (Indian) corn, maize; **возду́шная ~** popcorn.

куку́шка, -и cuckoo.

кула́к, -а́ fist; striking force; kulak. **кула́цкий** kulak, kulak's. **кула́чный** fist.

кулёк, -лька́ bag.

кули́к, -а́ sandpiper.

кули́сы, -и́с wings; **за кули́сами** behind the scenes.

кули́ч, -а́ Easter cake.

кулуа́ры, -ов *pl.* lobby.

ку́льман, -a drawing-board.

культ... *abbr.* (*of* **культу́рно-**, **культу́рный**) *in comb.* cultural, educational, recreational. **культба́за**, -ы recreation centre. **~отде́л**, -a Cultural Section. **~похо́д**, -a cultural crusade; cultural outing. **~рабо́та**, -ы cultural and educational work.

культу́ра, -ы culture; standard, level; cultivation, growing.

культури́зм, -a body-building. **культури́ст**, -a body-builder.

культу́рно *adv.* in a civilized manner. **культурность**, -и (level of) culture. **культу́рный** cultured; cultivated; cultural.

культя́, -й, **культя́пка**, -и stump.

кум, -а; *pl.* **-мовья́**, **-ьёв**, **кума́**, **-ы́** god-parent of one's child.

кума́ч, -а́ red calico.

куми́р, -a idol.

кумы́с, -a koumiss (*fermented mare's milk*).

ку́ний marten(-fur). **куни́ца**, -ы marten.

кун-фу́ *nt. indecl.* kung-fu.

купа́льный bathing, swimming. **купа́льня**, -и bathing-place. **купа́льщик**, -a, **-щица**, -ы bather. **купа́ть**, -а́ю *impf.* (*pf.* **вы́**, **ис~**) bathe; bath; **~ся** bathe; take a bath.

купе́ *nt.indecl.* compartment.

купе́ц, -пца́ merchant. **купе́ческий** merchant, mercantile. **купе́чество**, -a merchant class. **купи́ть**, -плю́, **-пишь** *pf.* (*impf.* **покупа́ть**) buy.

купле́т, -a stanza, strophe.

ку́пля, -и buying, purchase.

ку́пол, -a; *pl.* -а́ cupola, dome.

купо́н, -a a coupon.

купоро́с, -a vitriol.

купчи́ха, -и merchant's wife; woman of merchant class.

кура́нты, -ов *pl.* chiming clock; chimes.

курга́н, -a barrow; tumulus.

куре́ние, -я smoking; incense. **кури́льница**, -ы censer; incense-burner. **кури́льщик**, -a, **-щица**, -ы smoker.

кури́н|ый hen's; chicken's.

кури́тельн|ый smoking; **~ая бума́га** cigarette paper. **кури́ть**, -рю́, **-ришь** *impf.* (*pf.* **по~**) smoke; distil; +*a. or i.* burn; **~ся** burn; smoke; +*i.* produce, emit.

ку́рица, -ы; *pl.* **ку́ры**, **кур** hen, chicken.

курно́сый snub; snub-nosed.

куро́к, -рка́ cock, cocking-piece; **взвести́ ~** cock a gun; **спусти́ть ~** pull the trigger.

куропа́тка, -и partridge; ptarmigan.

куро́рт, -a health-resort; spa.

курс, -a course; policy; year; rate (of exchange). **курса́нт**, -a student.

курси́в, -a italics; **~ом** in italics. **курси́вный** italic.

курси́ровать, -рую *impf.* ply.

курси́стка, -и woman student.

ку́ртка, -и jacket.

курча́виться, -ится *impf.* curl. **курча́вый** curly; curly-headed.

ку́ры *etc.*: *see* **ку́рица**

курьёз, -a a funny thing; **для ~а**, **ра́ди ~а** for a joke, for amusement. **курьёзный** curious; funny.

курье́р, -a messenger; courier. **курье́рский** fast, express.

куря́тина, -ы chicken. **куря́тник**, -a hen-house, hen-coop.

куря́щий *sb.* smoker; **ваго́н для куря́щих** smoking-carriage, smoker.

куса́ть, -а́ю *impf.* bite; sting; **~ся** bite; bite one another.

кусково́й in lumps; lump. кусо́к, -ска́ piece, bit; slice; lump; cake.

куст, -а́ bush, shrub. куста́рник, -а shrubbery; bush, shrub; bushes, shrubs.

куста́рн|ый hand-made, home-made; handicrafts; amateurish, primitive; ~ая промы́шленность cottage industry. куста́рь, -я́ m. handicraftsman.

ку́тать, -аю impf. (pf. за~) wrap up, muffle up; ~ся muffle o.s. up.

кутёж, -а́ drinking-bout; drunken revel, binge.

кутерьма́, -ы́ commotion, stir, bustle. кути́ть, кучу́, ку́тишь impf., кутну́ть, -ну́, -нёшь pf. drink, carouse; go on a binge, the spree.

куха́рка, -и cook. ку́хня, -и; g.pl. -хонь kitchen; cook-house; cooking, cuisine. ку́хон|ый kitchen; ~ая посу́да kitchen utensils.

ку́цый tailless; bob-tailed; short; limited, abbreviated.

ку́ча, -и heap, pile; heaps, piles, lots. кучево́й cumulus.

ку́чер, -а; pl. -а́ coachman, driver. кучерско́й coachman's.

ку́чка, -и small heap; small group. ку́чный closely-grouped.

кучу́ see кути́ть

куша́к, -а́ sash; (plaited) girdle; belt.

ку́шанье, -я food; dish. ку́шать, -аю impf. (pf. по~, с~) eat, take, have.

кушётка, -и couch, chaise-longue.

кую́ etc.: see кова́ть

кюве́т, -а ditch, drain; tray, dish, bath.

Л

л letter: see эль

л abbr. (of литр) l., litre(s).

лабири́нт, -а labyrinth, maze.

лабора́нт, -а, -а́нтка, -и laboratory assistant. лаборато́рия, -и laboratory. лаборато́рный laboratory.

ла́ва, -ы lava.

лави́на, -ы avalanche.

ла́вка, -и bench; shop. ла́вочка, -и small shop. ла́вочник, -а, -ница, -ы shopkeeper, retailer.

лавр, -а bay-tree, laurel; pl. laurels.

ла́вра, -ы monastery.

ла́вро́вый laurel, bay; ~ вено́к laurel wreath, laurels.

ла́герник, -а camp inmate. ла́герн|ый camp; ~ая жизнь nomad existence; ~ый сбор annual camp. ла́герь, -я; pl. -я́ or -и, -е́й or -ей m. camp.

лад, -а (-у), loc. -у́; pl. -ы́, -о́в harmony, con-

cord; manner, way; stop, fret key, stud; в ~, не в ~ in, out of, tune; идти́ на ~ go well, be successful; на свой ~ in one's own way, after one's own fashion; не в ~а́х at odds, at variance; они́ не в ~а́х they don't get on.

ла́дан, -а incense; дыша́ть на ~ have one foot in the grave.

ла́дить, ла́жу impf. get on, be on good terms; ~ся go well, succeed. ла́дно adv. harmoniously; well; all right; very well! ла́дный fine, excellent; harmonious.

ладо́нный palmar. ладо́нь, -и palm.

ладья́[1], -ьи́ rook, castle.

ладья́[2], -ьи́ boat, barge.

ла́жу etc.: see ла́дить, ла́зить

лазаре́т, -а (mil.) field hospital; sick quarters; sick-bay; infirmary.

ла́зать see ла́зить. лазе́йка, -и hole, gap; loop-hole.

ла́зер, -а laser. ла́зерный laser; ~ при́нтер laser printer.

ла́зить, ла́жу, ла́зать, -аю impf. climb, clamber; ~в+a. climb into, get into.

лазу́рный sky-blue, azure. лазу́рь, -и azure.

лазу́тчик, -а scout; spy.

лай, -а bark, barking. ла́йка[1], -и husky.

ла́йка[2], -и kid. ла́йковый kid; kidskin.

ла́йнер, -а liner, airliner.

лак, -а (-у) varnish, lacquer; ~ для воло́с hair spray.

лака́ть, -а́ю impf. (pf. вы́~) lap.

лаке́й, -я footman, man-servant; lackey, flunkey. лаке́йский man-servant's; servile.

лакиро́ванн|ый varnished, lacquered; ~ая ко́жа patent leather. лакирова́ть, -ру́ю impf. (pf. от~) varnish; lacquer. лакиро́вка, -и varnishing, lacquering; varnish; gloss, polish.

ла́кмус, -а litmus. ла́кмусов|ый litmus; ~ая бума́га litmus paper.

ла́ков|ый varnished, lacquered; ~ая ко́жа patent leather.

ла́комить, -млю impf. (pf. по~) regale, treat; ~ся+i. treat o.s. to. ла́комка, -и c.g. gourmand; lover of sweet things. ла́комство, -а delicacy; pl. dainties, sweet things. ла́комый dainty, tasty; +до fond of, partial to.

лакони́ческий laconic.

Ла-Ма́нш, -а the (English) Channel.

ла́мпа, -ы lamp; valve, tube. ла́мпочка, -и lamp; bulb; light.

ландша́фт, -а landscape.

ла́ндыш, -а lily of the valley.

лань, -и fallow deer; doe.

ла́па, -ы paw; tenon, dovetail; fluke; (sl.) bribe; попа́сть в ла́пы к+d. fall into the clutches of.

ла́поть, -птя; pl. -и, -е́й m. bast shoe, bast sandal.

ла́почка, -и (my) darling, sweetheart (form of direct address).

ла́пчатый palmate; web-footed.

лапша́, -и́ noodles; noodle soup.

ларёк, -рька́ stall. **ларёчник, -а** stall-keeper. **ларь, -я́** *m.* chest, coffer; bin; stall.

ла́ска, -и caress, endearment; kindness. **ласка́тельн|ый** caressing; affectionate; ~**ое и́мя** pet name. **ласка́ть, -а́ю** *impf.* caress, fondle, pet; comfort, console; ~**ся+к+***d.* make up to; snuggle up to; coax; fawn upon. **ла́сковый** affectionate, tender.

ла́стик, -а (india-)rubber, eraser.

ла́сточка, -и swallow.

Ла́твия, -и Latvia.

ла́текс, -а latex.

лати́нский Latin.

лату́нный brass. **лату́нь, -и** brass.

ла́ты, лат *pl.* armour.

латы́нь, -и Latin.

латы́ш, -а́, латы́шка, -и Latvian, Lett. **латы́шский** Latvian, Lettish.

лауреа́т, -а prize-winner.

лафе́т, -а a gun-carriage.

ла́цкан, -а lapel.

лачу́га, -и hovel, shack.

ла́ять, ла́ю *impf.* bark; bay.

лба *etc.: see* **лоб**

лгать, лгу, лжёшь; лгал, -а́, -о *impf.* (*pf.* **на~, со~**) lie; tell lies; +**на**+*a.* slander. **лгун, -а́, лгу́нья, -и** liar.

лебедёнок, -нка; *pl.* **-дя́та, -дя́т** cygnet. **лебеди́ный** swan, swan's. **лебёдка, -и** swan, pen; winch, windlass. **ле́бедь, -я;** *pl.* **-и, -е́й** *m.* swan, cob.

лебези́ть, -ежу́ *impf.* fawn, cringe.

лев, льва lion.

левко́й, -я stock.

ле́во... *in comb.* left, left-hand. **левобере́жный** left-bank. **левша́, -и́;** *g.pl.* **-е́й** *c.g.* left-handed person, left-hander, southpaw. **ле́в|ый** *adj.* left; left-hand; port; left-wing; unofficial, illegal; ~**ая сторона́** left-hand side, near side, wrong side.

лёг *etc.: see* **лечь**

легализа́ция, -и legalization.

легализова́ть, -у́ю *impf. & pf.* legalize. **легализова́ться, -зу́юсь** *impf. & pf.* become legalized. **лега́льный** legal.

леге́нда, -ы legend. **легенда́рный** legendary.

легио́н, -а legion; **иностра́нный** ~ the Foreign Legion; **о́рден почётного** ~**а** Legion of Honour. **легионе́р, -а** legionary, legionnaire.

лёгк|ий; -гок, -гка́, лёгки́ light; easy; slight, mild; ~**ая атле́тика** field and track events; **лёгок на поми́не** talk of the devil! **у него́** ~**ая рука́** he brings luck. **легко́** *adv.* easily, lightly, slightly.

легко́... *in comb.* light, light-weight; easy, easily, readily. **легкове́рие, -я** credulity, gullibility. ~**ве́рный** credulous, gullible. ~**ве́с, -а, ~ве́сный** light-weight. ~**ву́шка, -и** (private) car. ~**мы́сленный** light-minded; thoughtless, careless, irresponsible; flippant, frivolous, superficial. ~**мы́слие, -я** flippancy,

frivolity, levity.

легков|о́й; ~о́й автомоби́ль, ~а́я маши́на (private) car. **лёгкое** *sb.* lung; lights. **лёгкость, -и** lightness; easiness. **лего́нько** *adv.* slightly; gently. **лёгочный** lung, pulmonary. **ле́гче** *comp. of* **лёгкий, легко́**

лёд, льда (-у), *loc.* **-у** ice. **леденёть, -е́ю** *impf.* (*pf.* **за~, о~**) freeze; grow numb with cold. **ледене́ц, -нца́** fruit-drop. **ледени́стый** frozen; icy. **ледени́ть, -и́т** *impf.* (*pf.* **о~**) freeze; chill. **леденя́щий** chilling, icy.

ле́дник[1], -а ice-house; ice-box; **ваго́н-~** refrigerator van. **ледни́к[2], -а́** glacier. **ледняко́вый** glacial; glacier; ice; refrigerator; ~ **пери́од** Ice Age. **ледоко́л, -а** ice-breaker. **ледору́б, -а** ice-axe. **ледян|о́й** ice; icy; ice-cold; ~**а́я гора́** tobogganing run, ice slope; iceberg.

лежа́ть, -жу́ *impf.* lie; be, be situated. **лежа́чий** lying (down); ~ **больно́й** bed-patient.

ле́звие, -я (cutting) edge; blade.

лезть, -зу; лез *impf.* (*pf.* **по~**) climb; clamber, crawl; make one's way; come on, keep on; creep, get, go; fall out; come to pieces; ~ **в пе́тлю** stick one's neck out; ~ **на́ стену** climb up the wall; **не** ~ **за сло́вом в карма́н** not be at a loss for words.

лейбори́ст, -а Labourite. **лейбори́стский** Labour.

ле́йка, -и watering-can; pourer; funnel.

лейтена́нт, -а a lieutenant.

лека́рственный medicinal. **лека́рство, -а** medicine, drug.

ле́ксика, -и vocabulary. **лексико́н, -а** lexicon; vocabulary. **лекси́ческий** lexical.

ле́ктор, -а lecturer. **лекцио́нный** lecture. **ле́кция, -и** lecture; **чита́ть ле́кцию** lecture, deliver a lecture.

леле́ять, -е́ю *impf.* (*pf.* **вз~**) cherish, foster; coddle, pamper.

лён, льна flax.

лени́вый lazy, idle; sluggish.

Ленингра́д, -а Leningrad.

лени́ться, -ню́сь, -нишься *impf.* (*pf.* **по~**) be lazy, be idle; +*inf.* be too lazy to.

ле́нта, -ы ribbon; band; tape; film; belt; track.

лентя́й, -я, -я́йка, -и lazy-bones; sluggard. **лентя́йничать, -аю** *impf.* be lazy, be idle, loaf, be idle; **лень, -и** laziness, idleness; indolence; **ей** ~ **встать** she is too lazy to get up.

леопа́рд, -а a leopard.

леота́рд, -а leotard.

лепесто́к, -тка́ petal.

ле́пет, -а babble; prattle. **лепета́ть, -ечу́, -е́чешь** *impf.* (*pf.* **про~**) babble, prattle.

лепёшка, -и scone; tablet, lozenge, pastille.

лепи́ть, -плю́, -пишь *impf.* (*pf.* **вы~, за~, на~, с~**) model, fashion; mould; stick; ~**ся** cling; crawl. **ле́пка, -и** modelling. **лепн|о́й** modelled, moulded; ~**о́е украше́ние** stucco moulding.

лес, -а (-у), *loc.* **-у́;** *pl.* **-а́** forest, wood, woods;

timber; **тропи́ческий** ~ rainforest; *pl.* scaffold, scaffolding.

ле́са́, -ы *or* -ы́; *pl.* **ле́сы** fishing-line.

лесби́йский lesbian. **лесбия́нка**, -и lesbian.

леси́стый wooded, forest, woodland. **лесни́к**, -а́ forester; gamekeeper. **лесни́чество**, -а forestry area. **лесни́чий** *sb.* forestry officer; forest warden; gamekeeper. **лесно́й** forest, forestry; timber.

лесо... *in comb.* forest, forestry; timber wood. **лесово́дство**, -а forestry. ~**загото́вка**, -и logging, lumbering. ~**защи́тный** forest-protection. ~**насажде́ние**, -я afforestation; (forest) plantation. ~**пи́лка**, -и, ~**пи́льня**, -и; *g.pl.* -**лен** sawmill. ~**руб**, -а woodcutter, logger. ~**спла́в**, -а (timber) rafting. ~**степь**, -и partially wooded steppe. ~**ту́ндра**, -ы forest-tundra.

ле́стница, -ы stairs, staircase; ladder; steps. **ле́стничн|ый**; ~**ая кле́тка** (stair-)well.

ле́стный flattering; complimentary. **лесть**, -и flattery; adulation.

лёт, -а, *loc.* -у́ flight, flying; **на** ~**у́** in the air, on the wing; hurriedly, in passing.

лета́, **лет** *pl.* years; age; **в** ~**х** elderly, getting on (in years); **на ста́рости лет** in one's old age; **прошло́ мно́го лет** many years passed; **ско́лько вам лет?** how old are you? **сре́дних лет** middle-aged.

лета́тельный flying. **лета́ть**, -а́ю *impf.*, **лете́ть**, **лечу́** *impf.* (*pf.* **полете́ть**) fly; rush, tear; fall, drop.

ле́тний summer. **ле́тник**, -а annual.

лётный flying, flight; ~ **соста́в** air-crew.

ле́то, -а; *pl.* -а́ summer; *pl.* years. **ле́том** *adv.* in summer.

летопи́сец, -сца chronicler, annalist. **ле́топись**, -и chronicle, annals.

летосчисле́ние, -я (system of) chronology; era.

лету́н, -а́, **лету́нья**, -и flyer; rolling stone, drifter. **лету́ч|ий** flying; passing, ephemeral; brief; volatile; ~**ий листо́к** leaflet; ~**ий ми́тинг** emergency meeting, extraordinary meeting, impromptu meeting; ~**ая мышь** bat; hurricane lamp. **лету́чка**, -и leaflet; emergency meeting; mobile detachment, road patrol; mobile dressing station. **лётчик**, -а, -**чица**, -ы pilot; aviator, flyer; ~-**испыта́тель** test pilot.

лече́бница, -ы clinic, hospital. **лече́бный** medical; medicinal. **лече́ние**, -я (medical) treatment; cure. **лечи́ть**, -чу́, -чишь *impf.* treat (**от** for); ~**ся** be given, have treatment (**от** for); +*i.* take a course of.

лечу́ *etc.*: see **лете́ть**, **лечи́ть**

лечь, **ля́гу**, **ля́жешь**; **лёг**, -ла́ *pf.* (*impf.* **ложи́ться**) lie, lie down; go to bed, turn in; +**на**+*a.* fall on, rest on, lie on.

лещ, -а́ bream.

лже... *in comb.* false, pseudo-, mock-. **лженау́ка**, -и pseudo-science. ~**свиде́тель**, -я *m.*, ~**ница**, -ы perjuror, perjured witness.

~**свиде́тельство**, -а false witness. ~**уче́ние**, -я false doctrine.

лжец, -а́ liar. **лжи́вый** lying; mendacious; false, deceitful.

ли, **ль** *interrog. part.* & *conj.* whether, if; **ли**,... **ли** whether ... or; **ра́но ли**, **по́здно ли** sooner or later.

либера́л, -а liberal. **либерали́зм**, -а liberalism; tolerance. **либера́льный** liberal; tolerant.

ли́бо *conj.* or; ~... ~ either ... or.

ли́вень, -вня *m.* heavy shower, downpour, rainstorm; cloud-burst; hail.

ливре́йный livery, liveried. **ливре́я**, -и livery.

ли́га, -и league.

ли́дер, -а leader; flotilla leader. **ли́дерство**, -а leadership; first place, lead. **лиди́ровать**, -рую *impf.* & *pf.* be in the lead.

лиза́ть, **лижу́**, -ешь *impf.*, **лизну́ть**, -ну́, -нёшь *pf.* lick.

лик, -а face.

ликвида́тор, -а liquidator. **ликвида́ция**, -и liquidation; elimination, abolition; ~ **долго́в** settlement of debts. **ликвиди́ровать**, -рую *impf.* & *pf.* liquidate, wind up; eliminate, abolish.

ликёр, -а liqueur.

ликова́ние, -я rejoicing, exultation, triumph. **ликова́ть**, -ку́ю *impf.* rejoice, exult, triumph.

лиле́йный lily-white; liliaceous. **ли́лия**, -и lily.

лило́вый mauve, violet.

лима́н, -а estuary.

лими́т, -а quota; limit. **лимити́ровать**, -рую *impf.* & *pf.* establish a quota, maximum in respect of.

лимо́н, -а lemon. **лимона́д**, -а lemonade; fruit squash. **лимо́нн|ый** lemon; ~**ая кислота́** citric acid.

ли́мфа, -ы lymph.

лингви́ст, -а linguist. **лингви́стика**, -и linguistics. **лингвисти́ческий** linguistic.

лине́йка, -и ruler; rule; line. **лине́йный** linear, line; of the line; ~ **кора́бль** battleship.

ли́нза, -ы lens.

ли́ния, -и line. **лино́ваный** lined, ruled. **линова́ть**, -ну́ю *impf.* (*pf.* **на**~) rule.

линогравю́ра, -ы linocut.

лино́леум, -а lino(leum).

Линч, -а; **зако́н** ~**а**, **суд** ~**а** lynch law.

линю́чий liable to fade, not fast. **линя́лый** faded, discoloured; moulted.

линя́ть, -я́ет *impf.* (*pf.* **вы́**~, **по**~, **с**~) fade, lose colour; run; cast the coat, skin; shed hair; moult; slough.

ли́па, -ы lime(-tree).

ли́пкий; -пок, -пка́, -о sticky, adhesive. **ли́пнуть**, -ну; **лип** *impf.* stick, adhere.

липня́к, -а́ lime-grove. **ли́повый** lime, linden.

ли́ра, -ы lyre. **ли́рик**, -а lyric poet. **ли́рика**, -и lyric poetry. **лири́ческий** lyric; lyrical.

лири́чный lyrical.

лиса́, **-ы́**; *pl.* **-ы** fox. **лисёнок**, **-нка**; *pl.* **-ся́та**, **-ся́т** fox-cub. **ли́сий** fox, fox's. **лиси́ца**, **-ы** fox.

лист, **-а́**; *pl.* **-ы́** *or* **-ья́**, **-о́в** *or* **-ев** leaf; sheet; quire; page; form; certificate; **в ~** in folio; **игра́ть с ~а́** play at sight; **корректу́ра в ~а́х** page proofs. **листа́ть**, **-а́ю** *impf.* leaf through, turn over the pages of. **листва́**, **-ы́** leaves, foliage. **ли́ственный** deciduous. **листо́вка**, **-и** leaflet. **листово́й** sheet, plate; leaf. **листо́к**, **-тка́** *dim.* of **лист**; leaflet; form, pro-forma. **листопа́д**, **-а** fall of the leaves.

лит... *abbr.* (*of* **литерату́ра**, **-ту́рный**) *in comb.* literature, literary.

Литва́, **-ы́** Lithuania.

лите́йная *sb.* foundry, smelting house. **лите́йный** founding, casting. **лите́йщик**, **-а** founder. **ли́тера**, **-ы** type, letter. **литера́тор**, **-а** literary man, man of letters. **литерату́ра**, **-ы** literature. **литерату́рн|ый** literary; **~ое воро́вство** plagiarism.

ли́тий, **-я** lithium.

лито́вец, **-вца**, **лито́вка**, **-и** Lithuanian. **лито́вский** Lithuanian.

литой cast.

литр, **-а** litre. **литро́вый** litre.

лить, **лью**, **льёшь**; **лил**, **-а́**, **-о** *impf.* (*pf.* **с~**) pour; shed, spill; found, cast, mould. **литьё**, **-я́** founding, casting; moulding; castings, mouldings. **ли́ться**, **льётся**; **ли́лся**, **-ась**, **ли́ло́сь** *impf.* flow; stream, pour.

лиф, **-а** bodice.

лифт, **-а** lift, elevator. **лифтёр**, **-а** lift operator.

ли́фчик, **-а** bodice; bra.

лиха́ч, **-а́** (driver of) smart cab; reckless driver, road-hog. **лихо́й**[1]; **лих**, **-а́**, **-о** dashing, spirited.

лихо́й[2]; **лих**, **-а́**, **-о**, **ли́хи** evil.

лихора́дка, **-и** fever. **лихора́дочный** feverish.

лицева́ть, **-цу́ю** *impf.* (*pf.* **пере~**) turn. **лицев|о́й** facial; exterior; **~ая ру́копись** illuminated manuscript; **~ая пе́тля** plain (stitch); **~ая сторона́** facade, front; right side; obverse.

лицеме́р, **-а** hypocrite, dissembler. **лицеме́рие**, **-я** hypocrisy, dissimulation. **лицеме́рный** hypocritical.

лице́нзия, **-и** licence.

лицо́, **-а́**; *pl.* **-а** face; exterior; right side; person; **быть к лицу́**+*d.* suit, become; befit; **в лице́**+*g.* in the person of; **знать в ~** know by sight; **~м к лицу́** face to face; **на нём лица́ нет** he looks awful; **невзира́я на ли́ца** without respect of persons; **от лица́**+*g.* in the name of, on behalf of; **сказа́ть в ~**+*d.* say to his, *etc.*, face; **черты́ лица́** features. **личи́на**, **-ы** mask; guise; escutcheon, key-plate. **личи́нка**, **-и** larva, grub; maggot. **ли́чно** *adv.* personally, in person. **ли́чно́й**

face; facial. **ли́чность**, **-и** personality; person, individual; *pl.* personalities, personal remarks. **ли́чный** personal; individual; private; **~ секрета́рь** private secretary; **~ соста́в** staff, personnel.

лиша́й, **-я** lichen; herpes; **опоя́сывающий ~** shingles. **лиша́йник**, **-а** lichen.

лиша́ть(ся, **-а́ю(сь** *impf. of* **лиши́ть(ся**

ли́шек, **-шка** (**-у**) surplus; **с ли́шком** odd, and more, just over.

лише́нец, **-нца** disfranchised person. **лише́ние**, **-я** deprivation; privation, hardship; **гражда́нских прав** disfranchisement. **лишённый**; **-ён**, **-ена́**+*g.* lacking in, devoid of.

лиши́ть, **-шу́** *pf.* (*impf.* **лиша́ть**) +*g.* deprive of; **~ себя́ жи́зни** take one's own life; **~ся**+*g.* lose, be deprived of. **ли́шн|ий** superfluous; unnecessary; left over; spare, odd; **~ раз** once more; **с ~им** odd, and more.

лишь *adv.* only; *conj.* as soon as; **~ бы** if only, provided that; **~ (то́лько)** as soon as.

лоб, **лба**, *loc.* **лбу** forehead; brow.

ло́бби *nt. indecl.* lobby. **лобби́ст**, **-а** lobbyist.

ло́бзик, **-а** fret-saw.

ло́бн|ый frontal; front; **~ое ме́сто** place of execution. **лобово́й** frontal, front.

ловец, **-ца́** fisherman; hunter. **лови́ть**, **-влю́**, **-вишь** *impf.* (*pf.* **пойма́ть**) catch, try to catch; **~ на сло́ве** take at his, *etc.*, word; **~ ста́нцию** try to pick up a (radio-)station.

ло́вкий; **-вок**, **-вка́**, **-о** adroit, dexterous, deft; cunning, smart; comfortable. **ло́вкость**, **-и** adroitness, dexterity, deftness; cunning, smartness.

ло́вля, **-и**; *g.pl.* **-вель** catching, hunting; fishing-ground. **лову́шка**, **-и** snare, trap.

ло́вче *comp.* of **ло́вкий**

логари́фм, **-а** logarithm. **логарифми́ческ|ий**; **~ая лине́йка** slide-rule.

ло́гика, **-и** logic. **логи́ческий** logical. **логи́чность**, **-и** logicality.

ло́говище, **-а**, **ло́гово**, **-а** den, lair.

логопе́д, **-а** speech therapist. **логопе́дия**, **-и** speech therapy.

ло́дка, **-и**, **ло́дочка**, **-и** boat. **ло́дочник**, **-а** boatman. **ло́дочный** boat-.

ло́дырничать, **-аю** *impf.* loaf, idle about. **ло́дырь**, **-я** *m.* loafer, idler.

ло́жа, **-и** box; (masonic) lodge.

ложби́на, **-ы** hollow.

ло́же, **-а** couch; bed; channel; gun-stock.

ложи́ться, **-жу́сь** *impf. of* **лечь**

ло́жка, **-и** spoon; spoonful.

ло́жн|ый false, erroneous; sham, dummy. **ложь**, **лжи** lie, falsehood.

лоза́, **-ы́**; *pl.* **-ы** vine. **лозня́к**, **-а́** willow-bush. **ло́зунг**, **-а** slogan, catchword; watchword; pass-word.

локомоти́в, **-а** locomotive.

ло́кон, **-а** lock, curl, ringlet.

локотни́к, **-а́** (chair-, sofa-)arm. **ло́коть**, **-ктя**; *pl.* **-и**, **-е́й** *m.* elbow.

лом, -а; *pl.* -ы, - óв crowbar; scrap, waste.
лóманый broken. **ломáть,** -áю *impf.* (*pf.* **по~, с~**) break; fracture; rack, cause to ache; ~ **кáмень** quarry stone; ~ **рýки** wring one's hands; ~ **себé гóлову** rack one's brains; **меня всегó ломáло** I was aching all over; **~ся** break; crack; pose, put on airs; make difficulties, be obstinate.
ломбáрд, -а pawnshop. **ломбáрдн|ый; ~ая квитáнция** pawn-ticket.
лóмберный; ~ **стол** card-table.
ломúть, лóмит *impf.* break; break through, rush; *impers.* cause to ache; **у меня лóмит спúну** my back aches; **~ся** be (near to) breaking; +**в**+*a.* force; +**от**+*g.* be bursting, crammed, loaded, with. **лóмка,** -и breaking; *pl.* quarry. **лóмкий;** -мок, -мкá, -о fragile, brittle.
ломов|óй dray, draught; **~óй извóзчик** drayman, carter; **~áя лóшадь** cart-horse, dray-horse, draught-horse.
ломóта, -ы ache (in one's bones).
ломóть, -мтя; *pl.* -мтú *m.* large slice, round; hunk; chunk. **лóмтик,** -а slice.
Лóндон, -а London. **лóндонец,** -ца, **лóндонка,** -ки Londoner. **лóндонский** London.
лóно, -а bosom, lap.
лопáрь, -я *m.*, **лопáрка,** -и Lapp, Lapplander. **лопáрский** Lapp, Lappish.
лóпасть, -и; *pl.* -и, -éй blade; fan, vane; paddle; lamina; ~ **осú** axle-tree.
лопáта, -ы spade; shovel. **лопáтка,** -и shoulder-blade; shovel; trowel; blade.
лóпаться, -аюсь *impf.*, **лóпнуть,** -ну *pf.* burst; split, crack; break; fail, be a failure; go bankrupt, crash.
лопоýхий lop-eared.
лопýх, -á burdock.
лосúна, -ы elk-skin, chamois leather; elk-meat; *pl.* buckskins. **лосúный** elk, elk-.
лоск, -а (-у) lustre, gloss, shine.
лоскýт, -á; *pl.* -ы *or* -ья, -óв *or* -ьев rag, shred, scrap. **лоскýтн|ый** scrappy; made of scraps, patchwork; **~ое одеяло** patchwork quilt.
лоснúться, -нюсь *impf.* be glossy, shine.
лососúна, -ы salmon. **лосóсь,** -я *m.* salmon.
лось, -я; *pl.* -и, -éй *m.* elk.
лосьóн, -а lotion; aftershave; make-up remover.
лот, -а lead, plummet.
лотерéйный lottery, raffle. **лотерéя,** -и lottery, raffle.
лотó *nt. indecl.* lotto, bingo.
лотóк, -ткá hawker's stand; hawker's tray; chute; gutter; trough. **лотóчник,** -а, **-ница,** -ы hawker.
лохáнка, -и, **лохáнь,** -и (wash-)tub.
лохмáтить, -áчу *impf.* (*pf.* **раз~**) tousle, ruffle; **~ся** become tousled, be dishevelled.
лохмáтый shaggy(-haired); dishevelled, tousled.
лохмóтья, -ьев *pl.* rags.

лóцман, -а pilot; pilot-fish.
лошадúн|ый horse; equine; **~ая сúла** horse-power. **лошáдка,** -и (small) horse; hobby-horse; rocking-horse; **лóшадь,** -и; *pl.* -и, -éй, *i.* -дьмú *or* -дями horse.
лощёный glossy, polished.
лощúна, -ы hollow, depression.
лощúть, -щý *impf.* (*pf.* **на~**) polish; gloss, glaze.
лоя́льность, -и fairness; honesty; loyalty. **лоя́льный** fair; honest; loyal.
л.с. *abbr.* (*of* **лошадúная сúла**) horsepower.
луб, -а bast. **лубóк,** -бкá splint; wood-block; popular print. **лубóчн|ый; ~ая картúнка** popular print.
луг, -а, *loc.* -ý; *pl.* -á meadow.
лудúть, лужý, лýдишь *impf.* (*pf.* **вы́~, по~**) tin.
лýжа, -и puddle, pool.
лужáйка, -и grass-plot, lawn, (forest-)glade.
лужéние, -я tinning. **лужёный** tinned, tin-plate. **лужý** *etc.*: *see* **лудúть**
лýза, -ы pocket.
лук[1], -а (-у) onions; **зелёный лук** spring onions; **~-шнитт** chives.
лук[2], -а bow.
лукáвить, -влю *impf.* (*pf.* **с~**) be cunning. **лукáвство,** -а craftiness; slyness. **лукáвый** crafty, sly, cunning; arch.
лукóвица, -ы onion; bulb; onion dome. **лýковичный** onion-shaped; bulbous.
лукомóрье, -я cove, bay.
лунá, -ы́; *pl.* -ы moon. **лунáтик,** -а sleepwalker, somnambulist.
лукóшко, -а; *pl.* -и punnet, bast basket.
лýнка, -и hole; socket, alveolus.
лýнник, -а lunar probe. **лýнн|ый** moon; lunar; **~ый кáмень** moonstone; **~ая ночь** moonlit night; **~ый свет** moonlight. **лунохóд,** -а lunar rover, Moon buggy.
лýпа, -ы magnifying-glass.
лупúть, -плю, -пишь *impf.* (*pf.* **об~, с~**) peel (off); bark; fleece; **~ся** peel (off); scale; come off, chip.
луч, -á ray; beam. **лучевóй** ray, beam; radial, radiating; radiation. **лучезáрный** radiant, resplendent. **лучеиспускáние,** -я radiation. **лучепреломлéние,** -я refraction.
лучúна, -ы spill; chip; splinter.
лучúстый radiant; radial.
лýчше better; ~ **всегó,** ~ **всех** best of all; **нам** ~ **вернýться** we had better go back; **тем** ~ so much the better. **лýчш|ий** better; best; **в** ~**ем слýчае** at best; **всегó** ~**его!** all the (very) best! **к** ~**ему** for the better.
лущёный; -ён, -енá hulled, shelled, husked. **лущúть,** -щý *impf.* (*pf.* **об~**) shell, husk, hull, pod.
лы́жа, -и ski; snow-shoe. **лы́жник,** -а skier. **лы́жный** ski, skiing; ~ **спорт** skiing. **лы́жня, -и** ski-track.
лы́ко, -а bast.
лысéть, -éю *impf.* (*pf.* **об~, по~**) grow bald.

лы́сина, -ы bald spot, bald patch; blaze, star, patch. **лы́сый**; лыс, -á, -о bald.

ль *see* **ли**

льва *etc.: see* **лев. львёнок**, -нка; *pl.* **львя́та**, -я́т lion-cub. **льви́ный** lion, lion's; ~ зев snapdragon. **льви́ца**, -ы lioness.

льгóта, -ы privilege; advantage. **льгóтн|ый** privileged; favourable; ~ый биле́т complimentary ticket, free ticket; на ~ых усло́виях on easy terms.

льда *etc.: see* **лёд. льди́на**, -ы block of ice; ice-floe. **льди́нка**, -и piece of ice. **льди́стый** icy; ice-covered.

льна *etc.: see* **лён. льновóдство**, -a flax-growing. **льнопряде́ние**, -я flax-spinning. **льнопряди́льный** flax-spinning. **льнопряди́льня**, -и; *g.pl.* -лен flax-mill.

льнуть, -ну, -нёшь *impf.* (*pf.* при~) +к+*d.* cling to, stick to; have a weakness for; make up to, try to get in with.

льнянóй flax, flaxen; linen; linseed.

льстéц, -á flatterer. **льсти́вый** flattering; smooth-tongued. **льсти́ть**, льщу *impf.* (*pf.* по~) +*d.* flatter; gratify; +*a.* delude; ~ся+на+*a.* be tempted by.

лью *etc.: see* **лить**

любéзность, -и courtesy; politeness, civility; kindness; compliment. **любéзн|ый** courteous; polite; obliging; kind, amiable; бу́дьте ~ы be so kind (as to).

люби́мец, -мца, **-мица**, -ы pet, favourite. **люби́мый** beloved, loved; favourite. **люби́тель**, -я *m.*, **-ница**, -ы lover; amateur. **люби́тельский** amateurish; choice. **люби́ть**, -блю́, -бишь *impf.* love; like, fond of; need, require.

любовáться, -бу́юсь *impf.* (*pf.* по~) admire; feast one's eyes (на+*a.* on).

любóвник, -а lover. **любóвница**, -ы mistress. **любóвный** love-; loving. **любóвь**, -бви́, *i.* -бóвью love.

любознáтельный inquisitive.

любóй any; either; *sb.* anyone, anybody.

любопы́тн|ый curious; inquisitive; prying; interesting; ~о знать it would be interesting to know. **любопы́тство**, -a curiosity. **любопы́тствовать**, -твую *impf.* (*pf.* по~) be curious.

любя́щий loving, affectionate; ~ вас yours affectionately.

лю́ди, -éй, -ям, -дьми́, -ях *pl.* people; men; servants; в ~ away from home; на лю́дях in the presence of others, in company. **лю́дный** populous; crowded. **людоéд**, -a cannibal; ogre. **людскóй** human; servants'.

люк, -a hatch, hatchway; trap; manhole.

люкс, -a luxury (class).

Люксембу́рг, -a Luxemburg.

лю́ксовый luxury(-class).

лю́лька, -и cradle.

лю́стра, -ы chandelier.

лю́тик, -a buttercup.

лю́тый; лют, -á, -о ferocious, fierce, cruel.

люцéрна, -ы lucerne.

ля *nt.indecl.* A; lah.

лягáть, -áю *impf.*, **лягну́ть**, -ну́, -нёшь *pf.* kick; ~ся kick.

ля́гу *etc.: see* **лечь**

лягушáтник, -a paddling-pool. **лягу́шка**, -и frog.

ля́жка, -и thigh, haunch.

ля́згать, -аю *impf.* clank, clang; +*i.* rattle, clatter; он ля́згал зуба́ми his teeth were chattering.

ля́мка, -и strap; тяну́ть ля́мку toil, sweat, drudge.

ля́пис, -a silver nitrate, lunar caustic.

ля́псус, -a blunder; slip (*of the tongue, of the pen*).

M

м *letter: see* **эм**

м *abbr.* (*of* **метр**) m, metre(s).

м. *abbr.* (*of* **мину́та**) min., minute(s).

мавзолéй, -я mausoleum.

мавр, -а, **маврита́нка**, -и Moor. **маврита́нский** Moorish; Moresque; Mauretanian.

магази́н, -a shop; store; depot; magazine. **магази́нный** *adj.*; ~ вор shoplifter.

маги́стерский master's. **маги́стр**, -а (holder of) master's degree; head of knightly or monastic order.

магистрáль, -и main; main line, main road.

маги́ческий magic, magical. **ма́гия**, -и magic.

ма́гний, -я magnesium.

магни́т, -a magnet. **магни́тный** magnetic. **магнитóла**, -ы radio cassette (recorder). **магнитолéнта**, -ы magnetic tape. **магнитотéка**, -и tape library. **магнитофóн**, -a tape-recorder; видеокассéтный ~ video recorder. **магнитофóнн|ый**; ~ая за́пись tape-recording.

мадáм *f.indecl.* madam, madame; governess; dressmaker.

мадемуазéль, -и mademoiselle; governess.

Мадри́д, -a Madrid.

мадья́р, -a; *pl.* -ы, -я́р, **мадья́рка**, -и Magyar, Hungarian. **мадья́рский** Magyar.

мажóр, -a major (key); cheerful mood, good spirits. **мажóрный** major; cheerful.

ма́заный dirty, soiled; cob, daub, clay. **ма́зать**, ма́жу *impf.* (*pf.* вы́~, за~, из~, на~, по~, про~) oil, grease, lubricate; smear; spread; soil, dirty; daub; miss; ~ся get dirty; soil; make up. **мазóк**, -зкá touch, dab; smear; miss. **мазу́т**, -a fuel oil. **мазь**, -и ointment; grease.

майс, -а maize. **майсов|ый**; ~ая ка́ша polenta.

май, -я May.

ма́йка, -и singlet, vest, T-shirt; **се́тчатая** ~ string vest.

майоне́з, -а mayonnaise.

майо́р, -а major.

майора́н, -а marjoram.

ма́йский May; May-day; ~ жук cockchafer.

мак, -а (-у) poppy; poppy-seeds.

мака́ть, -а́ю *impf.* (*pf.* **макну́ть**) dip.

маке́т, -а model; dummy.

макну́ть, -ну́, -нёшь *pf. of* **мака́ть**

ма́ковка, -и poppy-head; crown; cupola. **ма́ковый** poppy; poppy-seed.

макре́ль, -и mackerel.

максима́льный maximum. **ма́ксимум**, -а maximum; at most.

макулату́ра, -ы paper for recycling.

маку́шка, -и top, summit; crown.

мал *etc.: see* **ма́лый**

малева́ть, -лю́ю *impf.* (*pf.* **на**~). paint.

мале́йший least, slightest. **ма́ленький** little; small; slight; young.

мали́на, -ы raspberries; raspberry-bush, raspberry-cane; raspberry tea. **мали́нник**, -а raspberry-bushes. **мали́новый** raspberry; crimson.

ма́ло *adv.* little, few; not enough; ~ кто few (people); ~ ли что! what does it matter? ~ ли что мо́жет случи́ться who knows what may happen; ~ того́ moreover; ~ того́ что... not only ..., it is not enough that ...; э́того ма́ло this is not enough.

мало... *in comb.* (too) little, small-, low-, under-. **малова́жный** of little importance, insignificant. ~**вероя́тный** unlikely, improbable. ~**ве́сный** light, light-weight. ~**во́дье**, -я shortage of water. ~**во́льтный** low-voltage. ~**гра́мотный** semi-literate; crude, ignorant. ~**достове́рный** improbable; not well-founded. ~**ду́шие**, -я faint-heartedness, cowardice. ~**ду́шный** faint-hearted, cowardly. ~**жи́рный** low-fat. ~**заме́тный** barely visible, hardly noticeable; ordinary, undistinguished. ~**земе́лье**, -я shortage of (arable) land. ~**земе́льный** without enough (arable) land; land-hungry. ~**изве́данный** little-known. ~**иму́щий** needy, indigent, poor. ~**калори́йный** low-calorie. ~**кро́вие**, -я anaemia. ~**кро́вный** anaemic. ~**ле́тний** young; juvenile; minor, under-age. ~**ле́тство**, -а infancy; nonage, minority. ~**лю́дный** not crowded, unfrequented; poorly attended; thinly populated. ~**обеспе́ченный** needy, poverty-stricken. ~**опла́чиваемый** low-paid, badly-paid. ~**ро́слый** undersized, stunted. ~**содержа́тельный** empty, shallow. ~**употреби́тельный** infrequent, rarely used. ~**форма́тный** miniature. ~**це́нный** of little value. ~**чи́сленный** small (in number), few.

мало-ма́льски *adv.* in the slightest degree; at all. **маломальский** slightest, most insignificant. **мало-пома́лу** *adv.* little by little, bit by bit.

мал|ый; **мал**, -а́ little, (too) small; без ~ого almost, all but; са́мое ~ое at the least; с ~ых лет from childhood; *sb.* fellow, chap; lad, boy. **малы́ш**, -а́ child, kiddy; little boy.

ма́льчик, -а boy, lad; child; apprentice. **мальчико́вый** boy's, boys'. **мальчи́шеский** boyish; childish, puerile. **мальчи́шка**, -и *m.* urchin, boy. **мальчуга́н**, -а little boy.

малю́тка, -и *c.g.* baby, little one.

маля́р, -а́ (house-)painter, decorator.

маляри́я, -и malaria.

ма́ма, -ы mother, mummy, mamma. **мама́ша**, -и, **ма́менька**, -и mummy, mamma. **ма́менькин**, **ма́мин** mother's.

ма́монт, -а mammoth.

мандари́н, -а mandarin, tangerine.

манда́т, -а warrant; mandate, credentials. **манда́тн|ый** mandate, mandated; ~ая систе́ма голосова́ния card-vote system.

мане́вр, -а manoeuvre; shunting. **манёвренный** manoeuvre, manoeuvring, manoeuvrable; shunting, switching. **маневри́ровать**, -рую *impf.* (*pf.* **с**~) manoeuvre; shunt; +*i.* make good use of, use to advantage. **маневро́вый** shunting.

мане́ж, -а a riding-school, manège; (*circus*) ring; инспе́ктор ~а ringmaster; спорти́вный ~ sports hall; (де́тский) ~ play-pen. **мане́жик**, -а play-pen.

манеке́н, -а a lay figure; dummy; mannequin. **манеке́нщик**, -а, **-щица**, -ы model, mannequin.

мане́р, -а, **мане́ра**, -ы manner, way; style. **мане́рный** affected; precious.

манже́та, -ы cuff.

маникю́рша, -ы manicurist.

манипули́ровать, -рую *impf.* manipulate. **манипуля́ция**, -и manipulation; machination, intrigue.

мани́ть, -ню́, -нишь *impf.* (*pf.* **по**~) beckon; attract; lure, allure.

манифе́ст, -а manifesto. **манифеста́нт**, -а demonstrator. **манифеста́ция**, -и demonstration. **манифести́ровать**, -рую *impf.* demonstrate.

мани́шка, -и false shirt-front, dickey.

ма́ния, -и mania; passion, craze; ~ величия megalomania.

манки́ровать, -рую *impf. & pf.* be absent; +*i.* neglect; +*d.* be impolite to.

ма́нн|ый; ~ая ка́ша, ~ая крупа́ semolina.

мано́метр, -а pressure-gauge, manometer.

ма́нтия, -и cloak; mantle; robe, gown.

мануфакту́ра, -ы manufacture; textiles; workshop; (textile) mill.

мара́тель, -я *m.* dauber; scribbler. **мара́ть**, -а́ю *impf.* (*pf.* **вы**~, **за**~, **из**~, **на**~) soil, stain; daub; scribble; cross out, strike out; ~**ся** get dirty; soil one's hands.

марафо́нец, -ца marathon runner. марафо́н-
ский; ~ бег marathon.

ма́рганец, -нца manganese.

маргари́тка, -и daisy.

марино́ванный pickled. маринова́ть, -ную
impf. (*pf.* за~) pickle, marinate; delay, hold
up, shelve.

марионе́тка, -и puppet, marionette. марио-
не́точный puppet, marionette.

ма́рка, -и stamp; mark; counter; brand, make;
trade-mark; grade, sort; name, reputation.

ма́ркетинг, -а marketing.

ма́ркий easily soiled. маркирова́ть, -ру́ю
impf. & pf. mark; brand.

ма́рлевый gauze. ма́рля, -и gauze; butter
muslin, cheesecloth.

мармела́д, -а fruit jellies. мармела́дка, -и
fruit jelly.

мармори́ровать, -рую *impf. & pf.* marble.

Марс, -а Mars.

Марсе́ль, -я Marseilles.

марсиа́нин, -а; *pl.* -а́не, -а́н, марсиа́нка, -и
Martian. марсиа́нский Martian.

март, -а March. ма́ртовский March.

марты́шка, -и marmoset; monkey.

марш, -а march; ~ проте́ста protest march.

маршрова́ть, -ру́ю *impf.* march; ~ на ме́сте
mark time. марширо́вка, -и marching.

маршру́т, -а route, itinerary. маршру́тка, -и,
маршру́тное та́кси fixed-route taxi.

ма́ска, -и mask. маскара́д, -а masked ball;
masquerade. маскирова́ть, -ру́ю *impf.* (*pf.*
за~) mask, disguise; camouflage. маски-
ро́вка, -и masking, disguise; camouflage.
маскиро́вщик, -а camouflage expert.

Ма́сленица, -ы Shrovetide; (Mardi Gras) carnival. маслёнка, -и butter-dish; oil-can.
ма́слен|ый buttered; oiled; oily; unctuous;
~ая неде́ля Shrovetide. масли́на, -ы olive. ма́слить, -лю *impf.* (*pf.* на~, по~) butter; oil, grease. ма́сло, -а; *pl.* -а́, ма́сел, -
сла́м butter; oil; oil paints, oils; как по
ма́слу swimmingly. маслобо́йка, -и churn;
oil press. маслобо́йный заво́д, масло-
бо́йня, -и; *g.pl.* -о́ен, маслозаво́д, -а
creamery; dairy; oil-mill. масломе́р, -а oil
gauge; dipstick. масляни́стый oily. ма́сля-
ный oil; butter.

ма́сса, -ы mass; paste, pulp; a lot, lots.

масса́ж, -а massage; то́чечный ~ shiatsu,
acupressure.

масси́в, -а massif; expanse, tract. масси́в-
ный massive.

массо́вка, -и mass-meeting; outing; crowd
scene. ма́ссов|ый mass; popular; bulk; ~ая
поста́вка bulk delivery; ~ые сце́ны crowd
scenes.

мастаќ, -а́ expert, past master. ма́стер, -а;
pl. -а́, масте́р|ица, -ы foreman, forewoman;
master craftsman, skilled worker; expert,
master; (*sport*) vet(eran); ~ по ремо́нту ре-
пайрман; телевизио́нный ~ TV repairman;
~ на все ру́ки jack of all trades. мастери́ть,

-рю́ *impf.* (*pf.* с~) make, build, construct.

мастерска́я *sb.* workshop; shop; studio.

мастерско́й masterly. мастерство́, -а́
trade, craft; skill, craftsmanship.

масти́ка, -и mastic; putty; floor-polish.

масти́тый venerable.

масть, -и; *pl.* -и, -е́й colour; suit; ходи́ть в ~
follow suit.

масшта́б, -а scale. масшта́бность, -и (large)
scale, range, dimensions. масшта́бный
scale; large-scale.

мат, -а checkmate, mate; объяви́ть ~ mate,
checkmate.

матема́тик, -а mathematician. матема́тика,
-и mathematics. математи́ческ|ий mathe-
matical; ~ое обеспе́чение (computer) software.

материа́л, -а material; stuff. материа́льный
material; physical; financial, pecuniary, economic.

матери́к, -а́ continent; mainland; subsoil.
материко́вый continental.

матери́нский maternal, motherly. матери́н-
ство, -а maternity, motherhood.

мате́рия, -и material, cloth, stuff; matter; pus;
subject, topic.

ма́тка, -и uterus, womb; female, queen; (submarine) tender, depot ship.

ма́тов|ый matt; dull; suffused; ~ое стекло́
frosted glass.

матра́с, -а, матра́ц, -а mattress; надувно́й
~ air bed, inflatable mattress.

ма́трица, -ы matrix; die, mould.

матро́с, -а sailor, seaman. матро́ска, -и sail-
or's wife; sailor's blouse, sailor blouse.
матро́сский sailor's, sailors', seaman's,
seamens'; ~ воротни́к sailor collar.

ма́тушка, -и mother; priest's wife.

матч, -а match; междунаро́дный ~ test
(match); повто́рный ~ return match.

мать, ма́тери, *i.* -рью; *pl.* -те́ри, -ре́й mother;
бу́дущая ~ expectant mother; ~-одино́чка
single mother.

ма́фия, -и Mafia.

мах, -а (-у) swing, stroke; дать ~у let a chance
slip, make a blunder; одни́м ~ом at one
stroke, in a trice; с ~у rashly, without thinking. маха́ть, машу́, ма́шешь *impf.*, махну́ть,
-ну́, -нёшь *pf.+i.* wave; brandish; wag; flap;
go, travel; rush, leap; jump. маховиќ, -а́ fly-
wheel. махово́|й; ~о́е колесо́ fly-wheel;
~ые пе́рья wing-feathers.

ма́хонький very little, small, tiny.

махро́в|ый double-dyed, dyed-in-the-
wool; terry; ~ая ткань terry-towelling.

ма́чеха, -и stepmother.

ма́чта, -ы mast.

маши́на, -ы machine; mechanism; engine;
(motor) vehicle; car; bicycle; train; (посу́до)-
мо́ечная ~ dishwasher; ~ «ско́рой по́мощи»
ambulance. машина́льный mechanical; automatic, absent-minded; machine-like. маши-
низи́ровать, -рую *impf. & pf.* mechanize.

машинист, -а operator, engineer; engine-driver; scene-shifter. **машинистка**, -и typist; **~стенографистка** shorthand-typist. **машинка**, -и machine; typewriter; sewing-machine; clippers. **машинно-тракторн|ый**; **~ая станция** machine and tractor station. **машинн|ый** machine, engine; mechanical, mechanized; power-driven; **~ое бюро** typing bureau; **~ая графика** computer graphics; **~ый зал** engine-room; machine-room; **~ое обучение** computer-aided learning. **машинописный** typewritten; **~ текст** typescript. **машинопись**, -и typewriting; typescript. **машиностроение**, -я mechanical engineering, machine-building.

маяк, -а lighthouse; beacon.

маятник, -а pendulum. **маять**, **маю** impf. wear out, exhaust, weary; **~ся** suffer, languish; loaf, loiter about.

маячить, **-чу** impf. loom, loom up; appear indistinctly.

мг abbr. (of **миллиграмм**) mg, milligram(s).

мгла, -ы haze; mist; gloom, darkness. **мглистый** hazy.

мгновение, -я instant, moment. **мгновенный** instantaneous, momentary.

МГУ abbr. (of **Московский государственный университет**) Moscow State University.

мебель, -и furniture. **мебельщик**, -а upholsterer; furniture-dealer. **меблированный** furnished. **меблировать**, **-рую** impf. & pf. furnish. **меблировка**, -и furnishing; furniture.

мег..., **мега...** in comb. meg-, mega-. **мегаватт**, -а; g.pl. **-атт** megawatt. **~герц**, -а megacycle. **мегом**, -а megohm. **~тонна**, -ы megaton.

мёд, -а (-у), loc. **-у**; pl. **-ы** honey; mead.

мед... abbr. (of **медицинский**) in comb. of medicine, medical. **медбрат**, -а a male nurse. **~вуз**, -а medical school, school of medicine. **~институт**, -а medical school. **~осмотр**, -а medical (examination), check-up; **пройти ~** to have a checkup. **~пункт**, -а a first aid post, medical station; surgery. **~сестра**, -ы (hospital) nurse.

медалист, -а a medallist; medal winner. **медаль**, -и medal. **медальон**, -а medallion, locket.

медведица, -ы she-bear; Bear, Ursa. **медведь**, -я m. bear; **бамбуковый ~** giant panda. **медвежий** bear; bear's; bearskin; bear-like. **медвежонок**, -нка; pl. **-жата**, **-жат** bear cub; **плюшевый ~** teddy bear.

медеплавильный copper-smelting.

медик, -а medical student; doctor. **медикамент**, -а medicine; pl. medical supplies.

медитация, -и meditation. **медитировать**, **-рую** impf. to meditate.

медицина, -ы medicine. **медицинск|ий** medical; **~ое обслуживание** medical attendance, medical care; **~ий пункт** dressing-station, first-aid post. **медичка**, -и medical student.

медленно adv. slowly. **медленный** slow. **медлительный** sluggish; slow, tardy. **медлить**, **-лю** impf. linger; tarry; be slow.

медник, -а coppersmith; tinker. **медный** copper; brass, brazen; cupric, cuprous.

медовый honey; honeyed; **~ месяц** honeymoon.

медуза, -ы jellyfish, medusa.

медь, -и copper.

меж prep.+i. between.

меж... in comb. inter-; between. **межгородской** intercity. **~континентальный** intercontinental. **~личностный** interpersonal. **~национальный** interethnic. **~планетный** interplanetary. **~расовый** interracial. **~сезонье**, -я off season.

межа, -й; pl. **-и**, **меж**, **-ам** boundary; boundary-strip.

междометие, -я interjection.

между prep.+i. between; among, amongst; **~ нами (говоря)** between ourselves, between you and me; **~ прочим** incidentally, by the way; **~ тем** meanwhile; all the same; **~ тем как** while, whereas.

между... in comb. inter-, between. **междугородный** inter-urban, inter-city; **~городный телефон** trunk-line. **~народный** international.

мезонин, -а attic (storey); mezzanine (floor).

Мексика, -и Mexico.

мел, -а, loc. **-у** chalk; whiting; whitewash.

мёл etc.: see **мести**

меланхолик, -а melancholic person. **меланхолический** melancholy. **меланхолия**, -и melancholy.

мелеть, **-еет** impf. (pf. **об~**) grow shallow.

мелить, **-лю** impf. (pf. **на~**) chalk.

мелк|ий; **-лок**, **-лка**, **-о** small; shallow; shallow-draught; fine; petty, small-minded; **~ая тарелка** flat plate. **мелко** adv. fine, small.

мелко... in comb. small; fine, finely; petty; shallow. **мелкобуржуазный** petty-bourgeois. **~водный** shallow. **~водье**, -я shallow water; shallow. **~зернистый** fine-grained, small-grained **~собственнический** relating to small property holders.

мелок, **-лка** chalk.

мелочность, -и pettiness, small-mindedness, meanness. **мелочный** petty, trifling; paltry; small-minded. **мелочь**, -и; pl. **-ей** small items; small fry; small coin; (small) change; pl. minutiae; trifles, trivialities.

мель, -и, loc. **-й** shoal; bank; **на мели** aground; on the rocks in low water; **сесть на ~** run aground.

мелькать, **-аю** impf., **мелькнуть**, **-ну**, **-нёшь** pf. be glimpsed fleetingly; flash, gleam (for a moment). **мельком** adv. in passing; for a moment.

мельник, -а miller. **мельница**, -ы mill. **мельничный** mill; **~ лоток** mill-race.

мельчайший superl. of **мелкий**. **мельчать**, **-аю** impf. (pf. **из~**) grow shallow; become

small(er); become petty. **ме́льче** *comp. of*
ме́лкий, ме́лко. мельчи́ть, -чу́ *impf. (pf.*
из~, раз~) crush, crumble; pulverize; grind;
mill; reduce size or significance of. **мелюзга́,
-й** small fry.

мелю́ *etc.: see* **моло́ть**

мембра́на, -ы membrane; diaphragm.

мемуа́ры, -ов *pl.* memoirs.

ме́на, -ы exchange, barter.

ме́неджер, -а manager; **~ по сбы́ту** sales
manager.

ме́нее *adv.* less; **~ всего́** least of all; **тем не
~** none the less, all the same.

мензу́рка, -и measuring-glass; graduated
measure.

меново́й exchange; barter.

ме́ньше smaller; less. **ме́ньш|ий** lesser, small-
er; younger; **по ~ей ме́ре** at least; **са́мое
~ее** at the least. **меньшинство́, -а́** minority.

меню́ *nt.indecl.* menu, bill of fare.

меня́ *see* **я** *pron.*

меня́ть, -я́ю *impf. (pf.* **об~, по~)** change;
exchange; **~ся** change; +*i.* exchange.

ме́ра, -ы measure; **в ме́ру** fairly, moderately;
в ме́ру+*g.* to the extent of; **по ме́ре воз-
мо́жности** as far as possible; **по ме́ре того́,
как** (in proportion) as; **не в ме́ру, сверх
ме́ры, чрез ме́ру** excessively, immoderately.

мере́жка, -и hem-stitching, open-work.

мере́щиться, -щусь *impf. (pf.* **по~)** seem,
appear; appear dimly, glimmer.

мерза́вец, -вца blackguard, scoundrel. **мерз-
кий; -зок, -зка́, -о** disgusting, loathsome;
abominable, foul.

мерзлота́, -ы́; ве́чная ~ permafrost. **мёрз-
лый** frozen, congealed. **мёрзнуть, -ну** *мёрз*
impf. (pf. **за~)** freeze.

ме́рзость, -и vileness, loathsomeness; loathsome thing, nasty thing; abomination.

мери́ло, -а standard, criterion. **мери́льный**
measuring.

ме́рить, -рю *impf. (pf.* **по~, с~)** measure;
try on; **~ся**+*i.* measure. **ме́рка, -и** measure.

ме́ркнуть, -нет; мерк(нул) *impf. (pf.* **по~)**
grow dark, grow dim; fade.

ме́рный measured; rhythmical; measuring.

мероприя́тие, -я measure.

ме́ртвенный deathly, ghastly. **мертве́ть, -е́ю**
impf. (pf. **о~, по~)** grow numb; mortify; be
benumbed. **мертве́ц, -а́** corpse, dead man.
мертве́цкая *sb.* mortuary, morgue. **мёрт-
в|ый; мёртв, -а́, мёртво́** dead; **~ая зыбь**
swell; **~ая петля́** loop; noose; **спать ~ым
сном** sleep like the dead.

мерца́ть, -а́ет *impf.* twinkle; shimmer, glimmer; flicker.

ме́сиво, -а mash; medley; jumble. **меси́ть,
мешу́, ме́сишь** *impf. (pf.* **с~)** knead.

места́ми *adv.* here and there, in places.
месте́чко, -а; *pl.* -и, -чек small town.

мести́, мету́, -тёшь; мёл, -а́ *impf.* sweep;
whirl; **метёт** there is a snow-storm.

местко́м, -а *abbr. (of* **ме́стный комите́т)** local (trade-union) committee. **ме́стность, -и**
locality, district; area; ground, country, terrain. **ме́стный** local; localized; locative.
...ме́стный *in comb.* -berth, -seater, -place.
ме́сто, -а; *pl.* -а́ place; site; seat; berth; space,
room; post, situation, job; passage; piece of
luggage; *pl.* the provinces; the country; **без
ме́ста** out of work; **име́ть ~** take place; **~
де́йствия** scene (of action); **на ме́сте
преступле́ния** in the act, red-handed; **не к
ме́сту** out of place; **ни с ме́ста!** don't move!
stay where you are! **местожи́тельство, -а**
(place of) residence; **без определённого
местожи́тельства** of no fixed abode. **место-
име́ние, -я** pronoun. **местоиме́нный** pronominal. **местонахожде́ние, -я** location,
whereabouts. **местопребыва́ние, -я** abode,
residence. **месторожде́ние, -я** birthplace;
deposit; bed; layer; **~ угля́** coal-field.

месть, -и vengeance, revenge.

ме́сяц, -а month; moon. **ме́сячный** monthly.

метаболи́зм, -а metabolism.

мета́лл, -а metal. **металли́ст, -а** metal-
worker. **металли́ческий** metal, metallic.
металлоиска́тель, -я *m.* metal-detector.
металлоло́м, -а scrap(-metal).

мета́ние, -я throwing, casting, flinging; **~
копья́** throwing the javelin. **мета́тель, -я**
m. thrower. **мета́ть[1], мечу́, ме́чешь** *impf.*
(pf. **метну́ть)** throw, cast, fling; **~ банк** keep
the bank; **~ икру́** spawn; **~ся** rush about;
toss (and turn).

мета́ть[2], -а́ю *impf. (pf.* **на~, с~)** tack, baste.

метёлка, -и whisk; panicle.

мете́ль, -и snow-storm; blizzard.

метео... *abbr. (of* **метеорологи́ческий)** *in
comb.* meteorological; weather-. **метео-
сво́дка, -и** weather report. **~слу́жба, -ы**
weather service. **~ста́нция** weather-station.
~усло́вия weather conditions.

метео́р, -а meteor; hydrofoil.

метеоро́лог, -а a meteorologist; weatherman.
метеорологи́ческ|ий meteorological; **~ая
сво́дка** weather report **метеороло́гия, -и**
meteorology.

ме́тить[1], -чу *impf. (pf.* **на~, по~)** mark.

ме́тить[2], ме́чу *impf. (pf.* **на~)** aim; +*в*+*a. pl.*
aim at, aspire to; +*в or* **на**+*a.* drive at, mean.

ме́тка, -и marking, mark.

ме́ткий; -ток, -тка́, -о well-aimed, accurate.
ме́ткость, -и marksmanship; accuracy; neat-
ness, pointedness.

метла́, -ы́; *pl.* мётлы, -тел broom.

метну́ть, -ну́, -нёшь *pf. of* **мета́ть[1]**

ме́тод, -а method. **мето́дика, -и** method(s);
system; principles; methodology. **методи́-
ческий** methodical, systematic. **методи́ч-
ный** methodical, orderly.

метр, -а metre. **метра́ж, -а́** metric area;
length in metres.

ме́трика, -и birth-certificate. **метри́ческ|ий[1];
~ая кни́га** register of births deaths and

marriages; ~**ое свиде́тельство** birth-certificate.

метри́ческий[2] metric; metrical.

метро́ *nt.indecl.* metro; underground; **на** ~ by metro, by underground.

мету́ *etc.: see* **мести́**

ме́тче *comp. of* **ме́ткий**

мех[1], **-а**, *loc.* **-у́**; *pl.* **-а́** fur; **на** ~**у́** fur lined.

мех[2], **-а**; *pl.* **-и́** wine-skin, water-skin; *pl.* bellows.

механиза́ция, -и mechanization. **механизи́рованный** mechanized. **механизи́ровать, -рую** *impf. & pf.* mechanize. **механи́зм, -а** mechanism; gear, gearing; *pl.* machinery. **меха́ник, -а** mechanic. **меха́ника, -и** mechanics; trick; knack. **механи́ческий** mechanical; power-driven; of mechanics; mechanistic; ~ **моме́нт** momentum; ~ **цех** machine shop. **механи́чный** mechanical, automatic.

мехово́й fur. **меховщи́к, -а́** furrier.

меч, -а́ sword.

ме́ченый marked; labelled, tagged; ~ **а́том** tracer, tracer element.

мече́ть, -и mosque.

мечта́, -ы́ dream, day-dream. **мечта́тельный** dreamy. **мечта́ть, -а́ю** *impf.* dream.

ме́чу *etc.: see* **ме́тить**. **мечу́** *etc.: see* **мета́ть**

меша́лка, -и mixer, stirrer.

меша́ть[1], **-а́ю** *impf.* (*pf.* **по**~) +*d.* hinder, impede, hamper; prevent; disturb; **не меша́ло бы**+*inf.* it would do no harm to, it would not be a bad thing to.

меша́ть[2], **-а́ю** *impf.* (*pf.* **по**~, **с**~) stir; agitate; mix, blend, confuse, mix up; ~**ся** (**в**+*a.*) interfere (in), meddle (with).

ме́шкать, -аю *impf.* linger, delay; loiter.

мешкова́тый baggy; awkward, clumsy. **мешкови́на, -ы** sacking, hessian. **мешо́к, -шка́** bag; sack; clumsy fellow.

меща́нин, -а; *pl.* **-а́не, -а́н** petty bourgeois; Philistine. **меща́нский** lower middle-class; bourgeois, vulgar, narrow-minded; Philistine. **меща́нство, -а** petty bourgeoisie, lower middle-class; philistinism, vulgarity, narrow-mindedness.

ми *nt.indecl.* E; me.

миг, -а moment, instant.

мига́ть, -а́ю *impf.*, **мигну́ть, -ну́, -нёшь** *pf.* blink; wink, twinkle; +*d.* wink at.

ми́гом *adv.* in a flash; in a jiffy.

мигре́нь, -и migraine.

ми́дия, -и mussel.

мизе́рный scanty, wretched.

мизи́нец, -нца little finger; little toe.

микро... *in comb.* micro-; small. **микроавто́бус, -а** minibus. ~**ампе́р, -а** microampere. ~**во́лнов|ый**; ~**ая пе́чка** microwave (oven). ~**ди́ск, -а** (*comput.*) floppy (disk), diskette. ~**компью́тер, -а** microcomputer. ~**органи́зм, -а** micro-organism. ~**ско́п, -а** microscope. ~**скопи́ческий**, ~**скопи́чный** microscopic. ~**фо́н, -а** microphone.

микро́н, -а micron.

ми́ксер, -а (*cul.*) blender, liquidizer.

миксту́ра, -ы medicine, mixture.

ми́ленький pretty; nice; sweet; dear, darling.

милитари́зм, -а militarism. **милитари́ст, -а** militarist. **милитаристи́ческий** militaristic.

милиционе́р, -а militiaman, policeman. **мили́ция, -и** militia, police force.

милли... *in comb.* milli-. **миллигра́мм, -а** milligram(me). ~**ли́тр, -а** millilitre. ~**ме́тр, -а** millimetre.

миллиа́рд, -а billion, a thousand millions. **миллиарде́р, -а** multi-millionaire. **миллио́н, -а** million. **миллионе́р, -а** millionaire. **миллио́нный** millionth; worth, numbered in, millions.

милосе́рдие, -я mercy, charity; **сестра́ милосе́рдия** (*hospital*) nurse. **милосе́рдный** merciful, charitable.

ми́лостив|ый gracious, kind; ~**ый госуда́рь** sir; (Dear) Sir; ~**ая госуда́рыня** madam; (Dear) Madam. **ми́лостыня, -и** alms. **ми́лость, -и** favour, grace; mercy; charity; **ва́ша** ~ your worship; **ми́лости про́сим!** welcome!; you are always welcome; come and see us.

ми́лочка, -и dear, darling. **ми́лый; мил, -а́, -о** nice; kind; sweet, lovable; dear, darling.

ми́ля, -и mile.

ми́мика, -и (facial) expression; miming.

ми́мо *adv. & prep.*+*g.* by, past. **мимое́здом** *adv.* in passing. **мимолётный** fleeting, transient. **мимохо́дом** *adv.* in passing.

мин. *abbr.* (*of* **мину́та**) min., minute(s).

ми́на[1], **-ы** mine; bomb; rocket.

ми́на[2], **-ы** expression; face, countenance.

миндалеви́дн|ый almond-shaped. **минда́лина, -ы** almond; tonsil. **минда́ль, -я́** *m.* almond(-tree); almonds. **минда́льн|ый** almond; ~**ое пече́нье** macaroon.

минера́л, -а mineral. **минерало́гия, -и** mineralogy. **минера́льный** mineral.

мини- *in comb.* mini-. **мини-трусы́, -о́в** *pl.* briefs, panties. ~**футбо́л, -а** five-a-side (football). ~**ю́бка, -и** miniskirt.

миниатю́рный diminutive, tiny, dainty.

минима́льный minimum. **ми́нимум, -а** minimum; at the least.

министе́рский ministerial. **министе́рство, -а** ministry. **мини́стр, -а** minister.

минова́ть, -ну́ю *impf. & pf.* pass, pass by, pass over; be over, be past; *impers.*+*d.* escape, avoid; **тебе́ э́того не** ~ you can't escape it.

миномёт, -а mortar. **мино́носец, -сца** torpedo-boat.

мино́р, -а minor (key); blues.

мину́вш|ий past; ~**ее** *sb.* the past.

ми́нус, -а minus; defect, shortcoming. **ми́нусовый** negative.

мину́та minute. **мину́тный** minute; momentary; transient, ephemeral, brief.

мину́ть, -нешь; ми́нул *pf.* pass; pass by; be over, be past; **ему́ ми́нуло два́дцать лет** he is turned twenty.

мир[1], -а; *pl.* -ы́ world; universe; mir (*Russ. village community*); живо́тный ~ fauna; расти́тельный ~ flora; престу́пный ~ the underworld.

мир[2], -а peace. **мири́ть, -рю́** *impf.* (*pf.* по~, при~) reconcile; ~ся be reconciled, make it up; reconcile o.s. (с+*i.* to). **ми́рный** peace; peaceful; peaceable.

мировоззре́ние, -я (world-)outlook; philosophy. **миров|о́й** world; ~а́я держа́ва world power.

миролюби́вость, -и peaceable disposition. **миролюби́вый** peace-loving, peaceful.

ми́ска, -и basin, bowl, tureen.

миссионе́р, -а missionary.

ми́ссия, -и mission; legation.

мисте́рия, -и mystery(-play).

ми́стика, -и mysticism.

мистифика́тор, -а hoaxer. **мистифика́ция, -и** hoax, leg-pull.

мисти́ческий mystic, mystical.

ми́тинг, -а mass meeting. **митингова́ть, -гу́ю** *impf.* hold a mass meeting; discuss endlessly.

миф, -а myth. **мифи́ческий** mythical. **мифологи́ческий** mythological. **мифоло́гия, -и** mythology.

мише́нь, -и target.

ми́шка, -и bear; Teddy bear.

мишура́, -ы́ tinsel; tawdriness, show. **мишу́рный** tinsel; trumpery, tawdry.

мл *abbr.* (*of* **миллили́тр**) ml, millilitre(s).

младе́нец, -нца baby; infant. **младе́нческий** infantile. **младе́нчество, -а** infancy, babyhood. **мла́дший** younger; youngest; junior; ~ кома́ндный соста́в non-commissioned officers; ~ офице́рский соста́в junior officers.

млекопита́ющие *sb.*, *pl.* mammals. **мле́чный** milk; lactic; ~ Путь Milky Way, Galaxy.

млн. *abbr.* (*of* **миллио́н**) m, million(s).

млрд. *abbr.* (*of* **миллиа́рд**) b., billion(s) (= thousand million).

мм *abbr.* (*of* **миллиме́тр**) mm., millimetre(s).

мне *see* **я** *pron.*

мне́ние, -я opinion; по моему́ мне́нию in my opinion.

мни́мый imaginary; sham, pretended. **мни́тельный** hypochondriac; mistrustful, suspicious. **мнить, мню** *impf.* think, imagine; мно́го мнить о себе́ think a lot of o.s.

мно́г|ий much; many; ~ие *sb.*, *pl.* many (people); ~ое *sb.* much, a great deal, many things; во мно́гом in many respects. **мно́го** *adv.*+*g.* much; many; a great deal; a lot of; ~ лу́чше much better; на ~ by far; ни ~ ни ма́ло neither more nor less (than), no less (than).

мно́го... *in comb.* many-, poly-, multi-, multiple-. **многобо́жие, -я** polytheism. ~бо́рец, -рца multi-eventer; all-rounder. ~бо́рье, -я multi-discipline event. ~бра́чие, -я polygamy. ~веково́й centuries-old.

~во́дный full, in spate; well-watered, abounding in water. ~гра́нник, -а polyhedron. ~гра́нный polyhedral; many-sided. ~де́тный having many children. ~же́нец, -нца polygamist. ~же́нство, -а polygamy. ~значи́тельный significant. ~зна́чный multi-digit; polysemantic. ~каска́дный multi-stage. ~кра́тный repeated, re-iterated; multiple; frequentative, iterative. ~ле́тний lasting, living, many years; of many years' standing; perennial. ~ле́тник, -а perennial. ~лю́дный populous; crowded. ~му́жие, -я polyandry. ~национа́льный multinational. ~обеща́ющий promising, hopeful; significant. ~обра́зие, -я variety, diversity. ~обра́зный varied, diverse. ~ра́совый multiracial. ~семе́йный having a large family. ~сло́вный verbose, prolix. ~сло́жный complex, complicated; polysyllabic. ~сло́йный multi-layer; multi-ply; ~сло́йная фане́ра plywood. ~сторо́нний polygonal; multi-lateral; many-sided; versatile. ~ступе́нчатый multistage. ~тира́жка, -и factory newspaper; house organ. ~то́мный multi-volume. ~то́чие, -я ellipsis, suspension points. ~уважа́емый respected; Dear. ~уго́льник, -а polygon. ~уго́льный polygonal. ~цве́тный many-coloured, multi-coloured; polychromatic; multiflorous, floribunda. ~целево́й multipurpose. ~чи́сленный numerous. ~член, -а polynomial. ~эта́жный multi-storey. ~язы́чный polyglot; multilingual.

мно́жественный plural. **мно́жество, -а** great number; value; set; aggregate; great quantities; multitude. **мно́жимое** *sb.* multiplicand. **мно́житель, -я** *m.* multiplier; factor. **мно́жить, -жу** *impf.* (*pf.* по~, у~) multiply; increase, augment; ~ся multiply, increase.

мной *etc.*: *see* **я** *pron.* **мог** *etc.*: *see* **мочь.** **мну** *etc.*: *see* **мять**

мобилиза́ция, -и mobilization. **мобилизова́ть, -зу́ю** *impf.* & *pf.* (на+*a.*) mobilize (for).

моби́льный mobile.

моги́ла, -ы grave. **моги́льник, -а** burial ground, cemetery. **моги́льн|ый** grave; of the grave; sepulchral; ~ая плита́ tombstone, gravestone, headstone. **моги́льщик, -а** grave-digger.

могу́ *etc.*: *see* **мочь. могу́чий** mighty, powerful. **могу́щественный** powerful. **могу́щество, -а** power, might.

мо́да, -ы fashion, vogue.

модели́ровать, -рую *impf.* & *pf.* design. **моде́ль, -и** model; pattern. **модельё́р, -а** dress-designer. **моде́льный** model; fashionable.

мо́дем, -а modem.

модерниза́ция, -и modernization; updating. **модернизи́ровать, -рую** *impf.* & *pf.* modernize; update.

моди́стка, -и milliner; modiste.

модификáция, **-и** modification. **модифицировать**, **-рую** *impf.* & *pf.* modify.

мóдный; **-ден**, **-днá**, **-о** fashionable, stylish; fashion.

мóжет *see* **мочь**

можжевéльник, **-а** juniper.

мóжно one may, one can; it is permissible; it is possible; **как** **~**+*comp.* as ... as possible; **как ~ лýчше** as well as possible, to the best of one's abilities; **как ~ скорéе** as soon as possible.

мозáика, **-и** mosaic; inlay. **мозаи́чный** in-laid, mosaic.

мозг, **-а (-у)**, *loc.* **-ý**; *pl.* **-и́** brain; marrow; **шевели́ть ~áми** use one's head. **мозгови́тый** brainy. **мозгово́й** cerebral; brain.

мозо́листый calloused; horny. **мозо́ль**, **-и** corn; callus, callosity.

мой, **моего́** *m.*, **моя́**, **мое́й** *f.*, **моё**, **моего́** *nt.*, **мой**, **-и́х** *pl. pron.* my; mine; **по-мо́ему** in my opinion, I think; in my way; as I wish, as I think right.

мо́йщик, **-а** washer; cleaner; **~ о́кон** window-cleaner.

мо́кнуть, **-ну; мок** *impf.* get wet, get soaked; soak. **мокрова́тый** moist, damp. **мокро́та**[1], **-ы** phlegm. **мокрота́**[2], **-ы́** humidity, damp. **мо́крый** wet, damp; soggy.

мол, **-а**, *loc.* **-ý** mole, pier.

молва́, **-ы́** rumour, talk. **мо́лвить**, **-влю** *impf.* & *pf.* utter; say.

Молда́вия, **-и** Moldavia.

моле́кула, **-ы** molecule. **молекуля́рный** molecular.

моле́ние, **-я** prayer; entreaty, supplication. **моли́тва**, **-ы** prayer. **моли́ть**, **-лю́**, **-лишь** *impf.* pray; entreat, supplicate, beg (**о**+*p.* for); **~ся** (*pf.* **по~ся**) pray, offer prayers; say one's prayers; **+на**+*a.* idolize.

мо́лкнуть, **-ну; молк** *impf.* fall silent.

молниено́сн|ый lightning; **~ая война́** blitzkrieg. **молниеотво́д**, **-а** lighning-conductor. **мо́лния**, **-и** lightning; zip(-fastener); **(телегра́мма-)~** express telegram.

молодёжь, **-и** youth, young people; the younger generation. **молоде́ть**, **-е́ю** *impf.* (*pf.* **по~**) get younger, look younger. **молоде́ц**, **-дца́** fine fellow; brick; **~! well** done! good man!; **вести́ себя́ молодцо́м** put up a good show. **молоде́цкий** dashing, spirited. **молодня́к**, **-а́** saplings; young animals; youth, young people. **молод|о́й; мо́лод**, **-а́**, **-о** young, youthful; **~о́й карто́фель** new potatoes; **~о́й ме́сяц** new moon; **~о́й** *sb.* bridegroom; **~а́я** *sb.* bride; **~ы́е** *sb.*, *pl.* young couple, newly-weds. **мо́лодость**, **-и** youth; youthfulness. **моложа́вый** young-looking; **име́ть ~ вид** look young for one's age. **моло́же** *comp. of* **молодо́й**

молоко́, **-а́** milk. **молокосо́с**, **-а** greenhorn; raw youth.

мо́лот, **-а** hammer. **молоти́лка**, **-и** threshing-machine. **молоти́ть**, **-очу́**, **-о́тишь** *impf.*

(*pf.* **с~**) thresh; hammer. **молото́к**, **-тка́** hammer; **отбо́йный ~** pneumatic drill.

мо́лотый ground. **моло́ть**, **мелю́**, **ме́лешь** *impf.* (*pf.* **с~**) grind, mill; **~ вздор** talk nonsense, talk rot.

молотьба́, **-ы́** threshing.

моло́чник, **-а** milk-jug, milk-can; milkman. **моло́чница**, **-ы** milkwoman, milk-seller. **моло́чн|ый** milk; dairy; milky; lactic; **~ый брат** foster-brother; **~ое стекло́** frosted-glass, opal glass; **~ое хозя́йство** dairy farm(ing); **~я** *sb.* dairy; creamery.

мо́лча *adv.* silently, in silence. **молчали́вый** silent, taciturn; tacit; unspoken. **молча́ние**, **-я** silence. **молча́ть**, **-чу́** *impf.* be silent, keep silence.

моль, **-и** (clothes-)moth.

мольба́, **-ы́** entreaty, supplication.

мольбе́рт, **-а** easel.

моме́нт, **-а** moment; instant; feature, element, factor. **момента́льно** *adv.* in a moment, instantly. **момента́льный** instantaneous; **~ сни́мок** snap(shot). **моме́нтами** *adv.* now and then.

мона́рх, **-а** monarch. **монархи́зм**, **-а** monarchism. **монархи́ст**, **-а** monarchist. **монархи́ческий** monarchic(al). **мона́рхия**, **-и** monarchy.

монасты́рь, **-я́** *m.* monastery; convent. **мона́х**, **-а** monk; friar. **мона́хиня**, **-и** nun. **мона́шеский** monastic; monkish.

Монбла́н, **-а** Mont Blanc.

Монго́лия, **-и** Mongolia.

моне́та, **-ы** coin; **приня́ть за чи́стую моне́ту** take at face value, take in good faith. **монетари́ст**, **-а** (*econ.*) monetarist. **монетари́стский** monetarist. **моне́тный** monetary; **~ двор** mint.

монито́ринг, **-а** monitoring.

монога́мия, **-и** monogamy. **монога́мный** monogamous.

моноли́т, **-а** monilith. **моноли́тность**, **-и** monolithic character; solidity. **моноли́тный** monolithic; massive, united.

моноло́г, **-а** monologue, soliloquy.

монополиза́ция, **-и** monopolization. **монополизи́ровать**, **-рую** *impf.* & *pf.* monopolize. **монополи́ст**, **-а** monopolist. **монополисти́ческий** monopolistic. **монопо́лия**, **-и** monopoly.

моното́нный monotonous. **монохро́мный** monochrome. **моноци́кл**, **-а** unicycle.

монта́ж, **-а́** assembling, mounting, installation; montage; editing, cutting; arrangement. **монта́жник**, **-а** rigger, erector, fitter. **монтёр**, **-а** fitter, maintenance man, mechanic. **монти́ровать**, **-рую** *impf.* (*pf.* **с~**) mount; install, fit; erect; edit, cut.

мор, **-а** pestilence, plague.

мора́ль, **-и** moral; morals, ethics. **мора́льн|ый** moral; ethical; **~ое состоя́ние** morale.

морга́ть, **-а́ю** *impf.*, **моргну́ть**, **-ну́**, **-нёшь** *pf.* blink; wink.

мо́рда, -ы snout, muzzle; face, (ugly) mug.

мо́ре, -я; *pl.* -я́, -е́й sea; в откры́том мо́ре on the open sea; за́ мо́рем oversea(s).

море́на, -ы moraine.

морепла́вание, -я navigation; voyaging.

морепла́ватель, -я *m.* navigator, seafarer.

морепла́вательный nautical, navigational.

морехо́д, -а seafarer.

морж, -а́, моржи́ха, -и walrus; (*open-air*) winter bather. моржо́вый walrus, walrus-hide.

Мо́рзе Morse; а́збука ~ Morse code. морзя́нка, -и Morse code.

мори́ть, -рю́ *impf.* (*pf.* по~, у~) exterminate; exhaust; wear out; ~ го́лодом starve.

морко́вка, -и carrot. морко́вный carrot; carroty. морко́вь, -и carrots.

моро́женое *sb.* ice-cream, ice. моро́женый frozen, chilled. моро́з, -а frost; *pl.* intensely cold weather. морози́лка, -и freezer compartment; freezer. моро́зить, -о́жу freeze. моро́зный cold, frosty. морозоусто́йчивый frost-resistant, hardy.

мороси́ть, -и́т *impf.* drizzle.

морс, -а fruit-juice, fruit syrup; fruit drink.

морск|о́й sea; maritime; marine, nautical; shipping; naval; ~о́й волк old salt; ~а́я звезда́ starfish; ~о́й конёк sea-horse; ~а́я пе́нка meerschaum; ~а́я пехо́та marines; ~о́й разбо́йник pirate; ~а́я свинья́ porpoise; ~о́й флот navy, fleet.

мо́рфий, -я morphia, morphine.

морфоло́гия, -и morphology; accidence.

морщи́на, -ы wrinkle; crease. морщи́нистый wrinkled, lined; creased. мо́рщить[1], -щу *impf.* (*pf.* на~, по~, с~) wrinkle; pucker; ~ лоб knit one's brow; ~ся make a wry face; knit one's brow; wince; crease, wrinkle. морщи́ть[2], -и́т *impf.* crease; ruck up.

моря́к, -а́ sailor, seaman.

Москва́, -ы́ Moscow; the Moskva (*river*). москви́ч, -а́, москви́чка, -и Muscovite.

моски́т, -а mosquito.

моско́вский Moscow, of Moscow.

мост, мо́ста (-у), *loc.* -у́; *pl.* -ы́ bridge. мо́стик, -а bridge. мости́ть, -ощу́ *impf.* (*pf.* вы́~, за~, на~) pave; lay. мостки́, -о́в *pl.* planked footway, board-walk; wooden platform. мостова́я *sb.* roadway; pavement. мостово́й bridge.

мота́льный winding. мота́ть[1], -а́ю *impf.* (*pf.* мотну́ть, на~) wind, reel; shake.

мота́ть[2], -а́ю *impf.* (*pf.* про~) squander.

мота́ться, -а́юсь *impf.* dangle; wander; rush about; ~ по́ свету knock about the world.

моти́в, -а motive; reason; tune; motif. мотиви́ровать, -рую *impf.* & *pf.* give reasons for, justify. мотивиро́вка, -и reason(s); motivation; justification.

мотну́ть, -ну́, -нёшь *pf. of* мота́ть

мото... in *comb.* motor-, engine-; motor cycle; motorized; power. мотого́нки, -нок *pl.* motor-cycle races. ~дро́м, -а motor cycle race-track. ~кро́сс, -а motocross. ~пе́д, -а moped. ~пехо́та, -ы motorized infantry. ~пила́, -ы́ power saw. ~планёр, -а powered glider. ~ро́ллер, -а (motor-)scooter. ~спо́рт, -а motorcycle racing. ~ци́кл, -а, ~цикле́т, -а motor cycle. ~цикли́ст, -а motorcyclist, biker; ~ свя́зи despatch-rider.

мотовско́й wasteful, extravagant. мотовство́, -а́ wastefulness, extravagance, prodigality.

мото́к, -тка́ skein, hank.

мото́р, -а motor, engine. мотори́ст, -а motor-mechanic. мото́рка, -и motorboat. мото́рный motor; engine.

моты́га, -и hoe, mattock. моты́жить, -жу *impf.* hoe.

мотылёк, -лька́ butterfly, moth.

мох, мха *or* мо́ха, *loc.* мху; *pl.* мхи, мхов moss. мохна́т|ый hairy, shaggy; ~ое полоте́нце Turkish towel.

моцио́н, -а exercise.

моча́, -и́ urine; water.

моча́лка, -и loofah. моча́ло, -а bast.

мочеви́на, -ы urea. мочево́й urinary; uric; ~ пузы́рь bladder. мо́ченный wetted; steeped; soused. мочёный soaked, steeped. мочи́ть, -чу́, -чишь *impf.* (*pf.* за~, на~) wet, moisten; soak; steep, macerate; ~ся (*pf.* по~ся) urinate, make water.

мочь, могу́, мо́жешь; мог, -ла́ *impf.* (*pf.* с~) be able; мо́жет (быть) perhaps, maybe; не могу́ знать I don't know. мочь, -и power, might; во всю ~, изо всей мо́чи, что есть мо́чи with all one's might and main.

моше́нник, -а rogue, scoundrel; swindler. моше́нничать, -аю *impf.* (*pf.* с~) play the rogue, cheat, swindle. моше́ннический rascally, swindling.

мо́шка, -и midge. мошкара́, -ы́ (swarm of) midges.

мощёный paved.

мо́щность, -и power; capacity; rating; output. мо́щный, -щен, -щна́, -о powerful; vigorous.

мощу́ *etc.: see* мости́ть

мощь, -и power, might.

мо́ю *etc.: see* мыть. мо́ющий washing; detergent.

мрак, -а darkness, gloom. мракобе́с, -а obscurantist. мракобе́сие, -я obscurantism.

мра́мор, -а marble. мра́морный marble; marbled; marmoreal.

мрачне́ть, -е́ю *impf.* (*pf.* по~) grow dark; grow gloomy. мра́чный dark, sombre; gloomy, dismal.

мсти́тель, -я *m.* avenger. мсти́тельный vindictive. мстить, мщу *impf.* (*pf.* ото~) take vengeance on, revenge o.s.; +за+*a.* avenge.

мудрёный; -рён, -а́ strange, queer, odd; difficult, abstruse, complicated; не мудрено́, что no wonder (that). мудре́ц, -а́ sage, wise man. мудри́ть, -рю́ *impf.* (*pf.* на~, с~) subtilize, complicate matters unnecessarily.

мудрость, -и wisdom. **мудрый; -др, -а, -о** wise, sage.

муж, -а; *pl.* **-жья** or **-и** husband; man. **мужать, -аю** *impf.* grow up; mature, ripen; grow strong; **~ся** take heart, take courage. **мужеподобный** mannish; masculine. **мужеский** male; masculine. **мужественный** manly, steadfast. **мужество, -а** courage, fortitude.

мужик, -а muzhik, moujik (*Russ. peasant*); peasant; man, fellow.

мужск|ой masculine; male; **~ой род** masculine gender; **~ая школа** boys' school. **мужчина, -ы** *m.* man.

музей, -я museum.

музыка, -и music; instrumental music; band; business, affair. **музыкальность, -и** melodiousness; musical talent. **музыкальный** musical. **музыкант, -а** musician; **уличный ~** busker.

мука¹, -и torment; torture; suffering; pangs, throes.

мука², -й meal; flour. **мукомол, -а** miller.

мул, -а mule.

мультипликатор, -а multiplier; multiplying camera; animator, animated-cartoon artist. **мультипликационный** cartoon, animated-cartoon **мультипликация, -и, мультфильм, -а** cartoon (*film*).

мумия, -и mummy (*embalmed corpse*).

мундир, -а (full-dress) uniform; **картофель в ~е** baked potatoes, jacket-potatoes.

мундштук, -а mouthpiece; cigarette-holder, cigar-holder; curb.

муравей, -вья ant. **муравейник, -а** ant-hill; ant-bear. **мурашка, -и** small ant; **мурашки по спине бегают** it sends a shiver down one's spine.

мурлыкать, -ычу or **-каю** *impf.* purr; hum.

мускат, -а nutmeg; muscat, muscatel. **мускатный; ~ орех** nutmeg; **~ цвет** mace.

мускул, -а a muscle. **мускулистый** muscular, sinewy, brawny. **мускульный** muscular.

мусор, -а refuse; sweepings; dust; rubbish; garbage; debris. **мусорн|ый; ~ая повозка** dust-cart; **~ая свалка** rubbish heap; **~ый ящик** dustbin. **мусородробилка, -и** waste-disposal unit. **мусоропровод, -а** refuse chute. **мусоросжигатель, -я** incinerator.

муссон, -а monsoon.

мусульманин, -ина; *pl.* **-ане, -ан** Muslim, Moslem. **мусульманский** Muslim, Moslem. **мусульманство, -а** Islam, Mohammedanism.

мутант, -а mutant.

мутить, мучу, мутишь *impf.* (*pf.* **вз~, за~, по~**) trouble, make muddy; stir up, upset; dull, make dull; **~ся** grow turbid, muddy, dull; dim. **мутнеть, -еет** *impf.* (*pf.* **по~**) grow or become turbid, muddy, dull. **мутность, -и** turbidity; dullness. **мутный; -тен, -тна, -о** turbid, troubled; dull, dulled, lacklustre; confused.

муфта, -ы muff; sleeve, coupling, clutch; **~ сцепления** clutch.

муха, -и fly. **мухомор, -а** fly-agaric, toadstool.

мучение, -я torment, torture. **мученик, -а, мученица, -ы** martyr. **мучитель, -я** *m.* torturer; tormentor. **мучить, -чу** *impf.* (*pf.* **за~, из~**) torment; worry, harass; **~ся** torment o.s.; worry, feel unhappy; suffer agonies; **~ся от боли** be racked with pain.

мучнистый farinaceous, starchy; mealy, floury. **мучной** flour, meal; farinaceous, starchy; **~ое** *sb.* starchy foods.

мха *etc.: see* **мох**

МХАТ, -а, *abbr.* (*of* **Московский художественный (академический) театр**) Moscow Arts Theatre.

мчать, мчу *impf.* rush along, whirl along; **~ся** rush, race, tear along.

мшистый mossy.

мщение, -я vengeance.

мщу *etc.: see* **мстить**

мы, нас, нам, нами, нас *pron.* we; **мы с вами, мы с тобой** you and I.

мылить, -лю *impf.* (*pf.* **на~**) soap, lather; **~ся** soap o.s.; lather, make a lather. **мылкий** lathering easily; soapy. **мыло, -а;** *pl.* **-а** soap; foam, lather. **мыловарение, -я** soap-boiling, soap-making. **мыловаренный** soap-making; **~ завод** soap works. **мыльница, -ы** soap-dish; soap-box. **мыльн|ый** soap, soapy; **~ый камень** soapstone; **~ые хлопья** soap-flakes.

мыс, -а cape, promontory.

мысленный mental. **мыслимый** conceivable, thinkable. **мыслитель, -я** *m.* thinker. **мыслительный** intellectual; thought, of thought. **мыслить, -лю** *impf.* think; reason; conceive, think up. **мысль, -и** thought; idea. **мыслящий** thinking.

мыть, мою *impf.* (*pf.* **вы~, по~**) wash; **~ся** wash (o.s.); **~ся в ванне** have a bath; **~ся под душем** take a shower.

мычать, -чу *impf.* (*pf.* **про~**) low, moo; bellow; mumble.

мышеловка, -и mousetrap.

мышечный muscular.

мышление, -я thinking, thought.

мышца, -ы muscle.

мышь, -и; *g.pl.* **-ей** mouse. **мышьяк, -а (-у)** arsenic.

мэр, -а mayor. **мэрия, -и** town council; town hall.

Мюнхен, -а Munich.

мягк|ий; -гок, -гка, -о soft; mild; gentle; **~ий вагон** 'soft-class' carriage, sleeping-car, sleeper; **~ий знак** soft sign, the letter ь; **~ое кресло** easy-chair; **~ий хлеб** new bread. **мягко** *adv.* softly; mildly; gently. **мягче** *comp. of* **мягкий, мягко. мякиш, -а** soft part (of loaf), crumb. **мякнуть, -нет;** мяк *impf.* (*pf.* **раз~**) soften, become soft. **мякоть, -и** fleshy part, flesh; pulp.

мямлить, -лю *impf.* (*pf.* **про~**) mumble; vacillate; procrastinate.

мясистый fleshy; meaty; pulpy. **мясник**, -á butcher. **мясн|ой** meat; **~ые консервы** tinned meat; **~áя** *sb.* butcher's (shop). **мясо**, -а flesh; meat; beef. **мясорубка**, -и mincer.

мята, -ы mint; peppermint.

мятеж, -á mutiny, revolt. **мятежник**, -а mutineer, rebel. **мятежный** rebellious, mutinous; restless; stormy.

мятный mint, peppermint.

мятый crushed; rumpled, crumpled; **~ пар** exhaust steam. **мять, мну, мнёшь** *impf.* (*pf.* **из~, раз~, с~**) work up; knead; crumple, rumple; **~ся** become crumpled; get creased, get crushed; crush (easily); hesitate, vacillate; hum and haw.

мяукать, -аю *impf.* mew, miaow.

мяч, -á, **мячик**, -a ball.

Н

н *letter*: *see* **эн**

на *prep.* **I.** +*a.* on; on to, to, into; at; till, until; for; by; **комната на двоих** a room for two; **короче на дюйм** shorter by an inch, an inch shorter; **на беду** unfortunately; **на вес** by weight; **на другой день** (the) next day; **на зиму** for the winter; **на Новый год** on New Year's Day; **на рубль марок** a rouble's worth of stamps; **на север от** to (the) north of; **на солнце** in the sun; **на чёрный день** for a rainy day; **на что это вам нужно?** what do you want it for? **на этот раз** this time, for this once; **отложить на завтра** put off till tomorrow; **перевести на** translate into; **сесть на** get on, get in, go on board. **II.** +*p.* on, upon; in; at; **жарить на масле** fry (in butter); **играть на рояле** play the piano; **на вате** padded; **на дворе**, **на улице** out of doors; **на его памяти** within his recollection; **на каникулах** during the holidays, in the holidays; **на концерте** at a concert; **на лету** in flight; **на людях** in public; **на моих глазах** in my presence; **на море** at sea; **на работе** at work; **на этих днях** one of these days; **на этой неделе** this week; **работать на нефти** run on oil.

на *part.* here; here you are; here, take it.

на... *pref.* **I.** of *vv.*, *forms the perfective aspect*; *indicates direction on to, action applied to a surface, or to a certain quantity or number, or continued to sufficiency, excess, or the point of satisfaction or exhaustion.* **II.** *of nn. and adjs.*: on. **III.** *of advs.*: extremely, very.

наб. *abbr.* (*of* **набережная**) embankment, quay.

набавить, -влю *pf.*, **набавлять**, -яю *impf.* add; add to, increase, raise. **набавка**, -и adding, addition, increase, rise. **набавочный** extra, additional.

набалдашник, -а knob.

на|бальзамировать, -рую *pf.*

набат, -а alarm, alarm-bell; **бить в ~** sound the alarm, raise an alarm.

набег, -а a raid, foray. **набегать**, -аю *impf.*, **набежать**, -егу *pf.* run against, run into; come running, pour in; spring up; *impers.* pucker, wrinkle.

набекрень *adv.* on one side, over one ear.

на|белить(ся, -елю(сь, -елишь(ся *pf.* **набело** *adv.*; **переписать ~** make a fair copy of.

набережная *sb.* embankment, quay.

наберу *etc.*: *see* **набрать**

набивать(ся, -аю(сь *impf. of* **набить(ся**. **набивка**, -и stuffing, padding, packing; (textile) printing. **набивной** printed.

набирать(ся, -аю(сь *impf. of* **набрать(ся**

набит|ый packed, stuffed, filled; crowded; **битком ~** crammed, packed out; **~ый дурак** utter fool. **набить, -бью, -бьёшь** *pf.* (*impf.* **набивать**) stuff, pack in, fill; break to pieces, smash; kill, bag; print; beat, hammer, drive, knock; **~ оскомину** set the teeth on edge; **~ руку** get one's hand in, become skilled; **~ цену** put up the price; bid up; **~ся** crowd in; be crowded; +*d.* impose or force o.s. on.

наблюдатель, -я *m.* observer; spectator. **наблюдательность**, -и (power of) observation. **наблюдательный** observant; observation. **наблюдать**, -аю *impf.* observe, watch; +**за**+*i.* take care of, look after; supervise, superintend, control. **наблюдение**, -я observation; supervision, superintendence, control.

набожный devout, pious.

набойка, -и print; printed fabric; printed pattern; (*rubber etc.*) heel.

набок *adv.* on one side, crooked.

наболевший sore, painful; **~ вопрос** burning question, pressing problem. **наболеть, -еет** *pf.* ache, be painful.

набор, -а recruiting, enlisting, engaging; collection, set; setting up, composing; matter set up; metal plaques, (horse-)brasses; **~ слов** mere verbiage. **наборная** *sb.* composing room. **наборщик**, -а compositor.

набрасывать(ся, -аю(сь *impf. of* **набросать, набросить(ся**

набрать, -беру, -берёшь; -áл, -á, -о *pf.* (*impf.* **набирать**) gather, collect, assemble; enlist, engage; compose, set up; **~ высоту** gain height; **~ номер** dial a number; **~ скорость** pick up speed, gather speed; **~ся** assemble, collect; +*g.* find, acquire, pick up; **~ся смелости** pluck up courage.

набрести, -еду, -дёшь; -ёл, -елá *pf.* +**на**+*a.* come across, hit upon.

наброса́ть, -а́ю *pf.* (*impf.* набра́сывать) throw, throw down; sketch, outline; jot down. набро́сить, -о́шу *pf.* (*impf.* набра́сывать) throw; ~ся throw o.s., fling o.s.; ~ся на attack, assail. набро́сок, -ска sketch, outline, (rough) draft.

набуха́ть, -а́ет *impf.*, набу́хнуть, -нет; -у́х *pf.* swell.

набью́ *etc.*: *see* наби́ть

наважде́ние, -я delusion, hallucination.

на|ва́ксить, -кшу *pf.*

нава́ливать, -аю *impf.*, навали́ть, -лю́, -лишь *pf.* heap, pile up; put on top; load, overload; ~ся lean, bring one's weight to bear; +на+*a.* fall (up)on. нава́лка, -и loading; list, listing; в нава́лку in bulk, loose. нава́лом *adv.* in bulk, loose.

на|валя́ть, -я́ю *pf.*

нава́р, -а fat; goodness. нава́ристый, нава́рный rich and nourishing. нава́ривать, -аю *impf.*, навари́ть, -рю́, -ришь *pf.* weld (on); boil, cook. наварно́й welded.

навева́ть, -а́ю *impf.* of наве́ять

наве́даться, -аюсь *pf.*, наве́дываться, -аюсь *impf.* call, look in.

наведе́ние, -я laying, laying on; placing; induction; ~ спра́вок making inquiries; ~ поря́дка putting in order.

наведу́ *etc.*: *see* навести́

навезти́, -зу́, -зёшь; -вёз, -ла́ *pf.* (*impf.* навози́ть) cart, bring in; +на+*a.* drive against, drive into.

наве́ивать, -аю *impf.* of наве́ять

наве́к, наве́ки *adv.* for ever, for good.

навёл *etc.*: *see* навести́

наве́рно, наве́рное *adv.* probably, most likely; certainly, for sure. наверняка́ *adv.* certainly, for sure; safely; держа́ть пари́ ~ bet on a certainty.

наверста́ть, -а́ю *pf.*, навёрстывать, -аю *impf.* make up for, compensate for.

наве́рх *adv.* up, upwards; upstairs; to the top. наверху́ *adv.* above; upstairs.

наве́с, -а awning, roof, canopy; penthouse; (*open*) shed; car-port.

навеселе́ *adv.* merry, a bit tight.

наве́систый overhanging, jutting. наве́сить, -е́шу *pf.* (*impf.* наве́шивать) hang, hang up. наве́ска, -и hanging; hinge. навесн|о́й hanging; ~а́я дверь hinged door.

навести́, -еду́, -едёшь; -вёл, -а́ *pf.* (*impf.* наводи́ть) direct, lead; aim; cover, coat; cover with, spread; introduce, bring, produce; make; cause; ~ красоту́ make up; ~ спра́вку make inquiries.

навести́ть, -ещу́ *pf.* (*impf.* навеща́ть) visit, call on.

наве́тренный windward, exposed to the wind.

наве́чно *adv.* for ever; in perpetuity.

наве́шать, -аю *pf.* наве́шивать[1], -аю *impf.* hang, hang out; weigh out.

наве́шивать[2], -аю *impf.* of наве́сить

навеща́ть, -а́ю *impf.* of навести́ть

наве́ять, -е́ю *pf.* (*impf.* навева́ть, наве́ивать) blow; cast, bring, bring about; winnow.

навзничь *adv.* backwards, on one's back.

навзры́д *adv.*; пла́кать ~ sob.

нависа́ть, -а́ет *impf.*, нави́снуть, -нет; -ви́с *pf.* hang, overhang, hang over; threaten, impend. нави́слый, нави́сший beetling, overhanging.

навлека́ть, -а́ю *impf.*, навле́чь, -еку́, -ечёшь; -ёк, -ла́ *pf.* bring, draw, call down; incur.

наводи́ть, -ожу́, -о́дишь *impf.* of навести́; наводя́щий вопро́с leading question. наво́дка, -и aiming, directing; applying.

наводне́ние, -я flood. наводни́ть, -ню́ *pf.*, наводня́ть, -я́ю *impf.* flood; inundate.

наво́жу *see* навози́ть. навожу́ *see* навози́ть

наво́з, -а (-у) dung, manure, muck. наво́зить[1], -о́жу *impf.* (*pf.* у~) manure. наво́зн|ый dung-, muck-; ~ая ку́ча dunghill.

навози́ть[2], -ожу́, -о́зишь *impf.* of навезти́

на́волока, -и, на́волочка, -и pillowcase.

навостри́ть, -рю́ *pf.* sharpen; prick up; ~ лы́жи clear off, clear out; ~ся train o.s., grow skilful, become good.

на|вощи́ть, -щу́ *pf.*

на|вра́ть, -ру́, -рёшь; -а́л, -а́, -о *pf.* tell lies, romance; talk nonsense; +в+*p.* make a mistake (mistakes) in; get wrong.

навреди́ть, -ежу́ *pf.*+*d.* harm.

навсегда́ *adv.* for ever, for good; раз ~ once and for all.

навстре́чу *adv.* to meet; идти́ ~ go to meet; meet halfway; compromise with; consider sympathetically.

навы́ворот *adv.* inside out; back to front.

на́вык, -а habit; knack; experience, skill.

навы́кат(е) *adv.* protuberant, bulging.

навы́лет *adv.* right through.

навы́нос *adv.* to take away; for consumption off the premises, off-licence.

навы́пуск *adv.* worn outside.

навы́тяжку *adv.*; стоя́ть ~ stand at attention.

навью́чивать, -аю *impf.*, на|вью́чить, -чу *pf.* load.

навяза́ть[1], -а́ет *impf.*, навя́знуть, -нет; -я́з *pf.* stick; э́то навя́зло у меня́ в зуба́х I'm sick and tired of it.

навяза́ть[2], -яжу́, -я́жешь *pf.*, навя́зывать, -аю *impf.* tie, fasten; knit; thrust, force, foist, press; ~ся thrust o.s., intrude; be importunate. навя́зчив|ый importunate, intrusive; persistent; ~ая иде́я fixed idea, obsession.

нагада́ть, -а́ю *pf.* predict, foretell.

на|га́дить, -а́жу *pf.*

нага́йка, -и whip; riding-crop.

нага́н, -а revolver.

нага́р, -а snuff, scale.

нагиба́ть(ся, -а́ю(сь *impf.* of нагну́ть(ся

нагишо́м *adv.* stark naked.

нагла́зник, -а blinker; eye-shade, patch.

нагле́ц, -а́ impudent fellow. на́глость, -и

impudence, insolence, effrontery.

на́глухо *adv.* tightly, hermetically.

нагля́дн|ый clear, graphic; visual; **~ые посо́бия** visual aids; **~ый уро́к** object-lesson.

нагна́ть, -гоню́, -го́нишь; -а́л, -а́, -о *pf.* (*impf.* **нагоня́ть**) overtake, catch up (with); drive; inspire, arouse, cause.

нагнести́, -ету́, -етёшь *pf.*, **нагнета́ть, -а́ю** *impf.* compress; supercharge. **нагнета́тель, -я** *m.* supercharger.

на́глый; -гл, -а́, -о impudent, insolent, impertinent; bold-faced, brazen.

нагное́ние, -я suppuration. **нагнои́ться, -и́тся** *pf.* fester, suppurate.

нагну́ть, -ну́, -нёшь *pf.* (*impf.* **нагиба́ть**) bend; **~ся** bend, stoop.

нагова́ривать, -аю *impf.*, **наговори́ть, -рю́** *pf.* slander, calumniate; talk a lot (of); record; **~ пласти́нку** make a record; **~ся** talk o.s. out.

наго́й; наг, -а́, -о naked, bare.

на́голо́ *adv.* naked, bare; **остри́женный на́голо** close-cropped; **с ша́шками наголо́** with drawn swords.

нагоня́й, -я scolding, telling-off. **нагоня́ть, -я́ю** *impf. of* **нагна́ть**

нагора́живать, -аю *impf. of* **нагороди́ть**

нагора́ть, -а́ет *impf.*, **нагоре́ть, -ри́т** *pf.* gutter; be consumed; *impers.+d.* catch it, be told off; **ему́ за э́то нагоре́ло** he was told off for it.

наго́рн|ый upland, mountain; mountainous; **~ая про́поведь** Sermon on the Mount.

нагороди́ть, -ожу́, -о́ди́шь *pf.* (*impf.* **нагора́живать**) pile up; erect; build; **~ вздо́р(а)** talk a lot of nonsense.

нагота́, -ы́ nakedness, nudity, bareness.

нагота́вливать, -аю *impf.*, **нагото́вить, -влю** *pf.* get in, lay in; prepare. **нагото́ве** *adv.* in readiness, ready.

награ́бить, -блю *pf.* amass by dishonest means; acquire as loot.

награ́да, -ы reward; award; decoration; prize. **награди́ть, -ажу́** *pf.*, **награжда́ть, -а́ю** *impf.* reward; decorate; award prize to. **наградны́е** *sb.*, *pl.* bonus. **награжде́ние, -я** rewarding; award, decoration.

нагрева́тельный heating. **нагрева́ть, -а́ю** *impf.*, **нагре́ть, -е́ю** *pf.* warm, heat; **~ся** get hot, warm up.

на|гримирова́ть, -ру́ю *pf.*

нагроможда́ть, -а́ю *impf.*, **на|громозди́ть, -зжу́** *pf.* heap up, pile up.

на|груби́ть, -блю́ *pf.* **на|грубия́нить, -ню** *pf.*

нагру́дник, -а bib; breastplate. **нагру́дный** breast; pectoral; **~ крест** pectoral cross.

нагружа́ть, -а́ю *impf.*, **на|грузи́ть, -ужу́, -у́зишь** *pf.* load, burden; **~ся** load o.s., burden; o.s. **нагру́зка, -и** loading; load; work; commitments, obligation(s).

на|грязни́ть, -ню́ *pf.*

нагря́нуть, -ну *pf.* appear unexpectedly; +**на**+*a.* descend on, take unawares.

над, надо *prep.+i.* over, above; on, at; **~**

голово́й overhead; **рабо́тать ~ диссерта́цией** be working on a dissertation; **смея́ться над** laugh at.

над..., надо... *pref. in comb.* I. *with vv.* indicates increase, addition; incomplete or partial action, superficiality, slightness. II. *with nn. and adjs.*: over-, super-, above-. **надво́дный** above-water, surface-. **~гро́бие** a epitaph. **~гро́бный** on or over a grave. **~ду́в, -а** supercharge, boost; pressurization. **~зе́мный** overground; surface-. **~по́чечник, -а** adrenal (gland). **~по́чечный** adrenal.

надави́ть, -влю́, -вишь *pf.*, **нада́вливать, -аю** *impf.* press; squeeze out; crush.

надба́вить, -влю *pf.*, **надбавля́ть, -я́ю** *impf.* add; add to, increase, raise. **надба́вка, -и** addition, increase; rise.

надвига́ть, -а́ю *impf.*, **надви́нуть, -ну** *pf.* move, pull, push; **~ся** approach, advance, draw near.

на́двое *adv.* in two; ambiguously.

надво́рный; ~ сове́тник Court Councillor (*7th grade: see* **чин**).

наде́ванный worn, used. **надева́ть, -а́ю** *impf. of* **наде́ть**

наде́жда, -ы hope; **в наде́жде**+*inf. or* **на**+*a.* in the hope of. **надёжный** reliable, trustworthy, safe.

наде́л, -а allotment.

наде́лать, -аю *pf.* make; cause; do.

надели́ть, -лю́, -лишь *pf.*, **наделя́ть, -я́ю** *impf.* endow, provide; allot to, give to.

наде́ть, -е́ну *pf.* (*impf.* **надева́ть**) put on.

наде́яться, -е́юсь *impf.* (*pf.* **по~**) hope, expect; rely.

надзира́тель, -я *m.* overseer, supervisor, superintendent; (police) inspector. **надзира́ть, -а́ю** *impf.*+**за**+*i.* supervise, superintend, oversee.

надзо́р, -а supervision; surveillance; inspectorate.

надла́мывать(ся, -аю(сь *impf. of* **надломи́ть(ся**

надлежа́щ|ий fitting, proper, appropriate; **~им о́бразом** properly. **надлежи́т; -жа́ло** *impers.* (+*d.*) it is necessary, required; **вам ~ яви́ться в де́сять часо́в** you are (required) to present yourself at ten o'clock; **~ э́то сде́лать** it must be done.

надло́м, -а break; fracture; crack; breakdown, crack-up. **надломи́ть, -млю́, -мишь** *pf.* (*impf.* **надла́мывать**) break; fracture; crack; breakdown; **~ся** break, crack, breakdown. **надло́мленный** broken, cracked.

надме́нный haughty, arrogant, supercilious.

на дня́х *adv.* one of these days; the other day, recently, lately.

на́до[1], на́добно (+*d.*) it is necessary; I, *etc.*, must, ought to; I, *etc.*, need; **так ему́ и ~** serve him right!; **~ быть** probably. **на́добность, -и** necessity, need; **в слу́чае на́добности** in case of need.

надо[2] *see* **над. надо...** *see* **над...**

надоеда́ть, -а́ю *impf.*, **надое́сть, -е́м, -е́шь,**

-е́ст, -еди́м *pf.*+*d.* bore, bother, pester, plague; annoy. **надое́дливый** boring, tiresome.

надо́лго *adv.* for a long time, for long.

надорва́ть, -ву́, -вёшь; -а́л, -а́, -о *pf.* (*impf.* **надрыва́ть**) tear; strain, overtax; ~ся tear; overstrain o.s., rupture o.s.

надоу́мить, -млю *pf.*, **надоу́мливать**, -аю *impf.* advise, suggest an idea to.

надошью́ *etc.*: *see* **надши́ть**

надписа́ть, -ишу́, -и́шешь *pf.*, **надпи́сывать**, -аю *impf.* inscribe, write. **на́дпись**, -и inscription; notice; writing, legend; superscription, address.

надре́з, -а cut, incision; notch. **надре́зать**, -е́жу *pf.*, **надреза́ть**, -а́ю *impf.*, **надре́зывать**, -аю *impf.* make an incision in.

надруга́тельство, -а outrage. **надруга́ться**, -а́юсь *pf.*+**над**+*i.* outrage, insult, abuse.

надры́в, -а tear; strain; breakdown; outburst. **надрыва́ть(ся**, -а́ю(сь *impf. of* **надорва́ть(ся**. **надры́вный** violent, hysterical; heartrending.

надсмо́тр, -а supervision; surveillance. **надсмо́трщик**, -а, -щица, -ы overseer; supervisor.

надста́вить, -влю *pf.*, **надставля́ть**, -я́ю *impf.* lengthen. **надста́вка**, -и lengthening; piece put on.

надстра́ивать, -аю *impf.*, **надстро́ить**, -о́ю *pf.* build on top; extend upwards. **надстро́йка**, -и building upwards; superstructure.

надува́ла, -ы *c.g.* swindler, cheat. **надува́тельство**, -а swindle, cheating, trickery. **надува́ть(ся**, -а́ю(сь *impf. of* **наду́ть(ся**. **надувно́й** pneumatic, inflatable.

наду́манный far-fetched, artificial, invented. **наду́мать**, -аю *pf.*, **наду́мывать**, -аю *impf.* make up one's mind; think up, make up.

наду́тый swollen, inflated; haughty; sulky. **наду́ть**, -у́ю *pf.* (*impf.* **надува́ть**) inflate, blow up; puff out; dupe, swindle; ~ гу́бы pout; ~ся fill out, swell out; be puffed up; pout, sulk.

надуше́нный scented, perfumed. **наду|ши́ть(ся**, -ушу́(сь, -у́шишь(ся *pf.*

надшива́ть, -а́ю *impf.*, **надши́ть**, -дошью́, -дошьёшь *pf.* lengthen; sew on.

на|дыми́ть, -млю *pf.* **наеда́ться**, -а́юсь *impf. of* **нае́сться**

наедине́ *adv.* privately, alone.

нае́зд, -а flying visit; raid. **нае́здить**, -зжу *pf.*, **нае́зживать**, -аю *impf.* travel; cover; travel over; make by driving; break in. **нае́здник**, -а a horseman, rider; jockey. **нае́здница**, -ы horsewoman, rider. **наез|жа́ть**, -а́ю *impf. of* **нае́здить**, **нае́хать** pay occasional visits. **нае́зженный** well-travelled. **нае́зжий** newly-arrived.

наём, на́йма hire, hiring; renting; **взять в** ~ rent; **сдать в** ~ let. **наёмник**, -а hireling; mercenary. **наёмный** hired, rented. **наёмщик**, -а tenant, lessee.

нае́сться, -е́мся, -е́шься, -е́стся, -еди́мся *pf.* (*impf.* **наеда́ться**) eat one's fill; stuff o.s.

нае́хать, -е́ду *pf.* (*impf.* **наезжа́ть**) come down, arrive unexpectedly; +**на**+*a.* run into, collide with.

нажа́ть[1], -жму́, -жмёшь *pf.* (*impf.* **нажима́ть**) press; squeeze; press on; put pressure (on).

нажа́ть[2], -жну́, -жнёшь *pf.* (*impf.* **нажина́ть**) reap harvest.

наждаќ, -а́ emery. **наждачн|ый**, ~ая бума́га emery paper.

нажи́ва, -ы profit, gain.

нажива́ть(ся, -а́ю(сь *impf. of* **нажи́ть(ся**

нажи́м, -а pressure; clamp. **нажима́ть**, -а́ю *impf. of* **нажа́ть**[1] **нажи́мистый** exacting. **нажимно́й**, **нажи́мный** pressure.

нажина́ть, -а́ю *impf. of* **нажа́ть**[2]

нажи́ть, -иву́, -ивёшь; на́жил, -а́, -о *pf.* (*impf.* **нажива́ть**) acquire, gain; contract, incur; ~ враго́в make enemies; ~ся; -жи́лся, -а́сь get rich, make a fortune.

нажму́ *etc.*: *see* **нажа́ть**[1]. **нажну́** *etc.*: *see* **нажа́ть**[2]

наза́втра *adv.* (the) next day.

наза́д *adv.* back, backwards; **(тому́)** ~ ago. **назади́** *adv.* behind.

назва́ние, -я name; title. **на́званый** adopted; sworn. **назва́ть**, -зову́, -зовёшь; -а́л, -а́, -о *pf.* (*impf.* **называ́ть**) call, name; invite; ~ся be called; call o.s.; give one's name.

назе́мный ground, surface. **на́земь** *adv.* to the ground.

назида́ние, -я edification. **назида́тельный** edifying.

на́зло́ *adv.* out of spite; to spite.

назнача́ть, -а́ю *impf.*, **назна́чить**, -чу *pf.* appoint; nominate; fix, set; prescribe.

назову́ *etc.*: *see* **назва́ть**

назо́йливый importunate, persistent; tiresome.

назрева́ть, -а́ет *impf.*, **назре́ть**, -е́ет *pf.* ripen, mature; become urgent, imminent, inevitable.

назубо́к *adv.*; **знать** ~ know by heart.

называ́емый; **так** ~ so-called. **называ́ть(ся**, -а́ю(сь *impf. of* **назва́ть(ся**; **что называ́ется** as they say.

наи... *pref. used with comparatives and superlatives to signify the very highest degree.*

наибо́лее *adv.* (the) most. **~бо́льший** greatest, biggest; **~бо́льший о́бщий дели́тель** highest common factor. **~вы́сший** highest. **~лу́чший** best. **~ме́нее** *adv.* (the) least. **~ме́ньший** least, smallest; **~ме́ньшее о́бщее кра́тное** lowest common multiple. **~ху́дший** worst.

наи́гранный put on, assumed; forced. **наи|гра́ть**, -а́ю *pf.*, **наи́грывать**, -аю *impf.* win; play, strum, pick out; ~ **пласти́нку** make a recording. **наи́грыш**, -а folk-tune; artificiality, staginess.

наизна́нку *adv.* inside out.

наизу́сть *adv.* by heart.

наименова́ние, -я name; title. **на|имено-ва́ть, -ную** *pf.*

наискосо́к, на́искось *adv.* obliquely, diagonally, aslant.

найтие, -я inspiration; influence; **по найтию** instinctively, by intuition.

найдёныш, -а foundling.

наймит, -а hireling.

найму́ *etc.: see* **наня́ть**

найти́, -йду́, -йдёшь; нашёл, -шла́, -шло́ *pf.* (*impf.* **находи́ть**) find; find out, discover; gather, collect; **+на**+*a.* come across, come over, come upon; **~сь** be found; be, be situated; turn up; rise to the occasion, find the right thing (*to do, say, etc.*); **не ~сь** be at a loss.

нака́з, -а order, instructions; mandate. **наказа́ние, -я** punishment. **наказа́ть, -ажу́, -а́жешь** *pf.*, **нака́зывать, -аю** *impf.* punish; order, tell. **наказу́емый** punishable.

нака́л, -а heating; incandescence, (white-)heat. **накалённый** heated; red-hot, white-hot; incandescent; strained, tense. **накали́ваться, -аю** *impf.*, **накали́ть, -лю́** *pf.*, **накаля́ть, -я́ю** *impf.* heat; make red-hot, white-hot; strain, make tense; **~ся** glow, become incandescent; heat up; become strained, become tense.

нака́лывать(ся, -аю(сь *impf. of* **наколо́ть(ся**

накану́не *adv.* the day before; *prep.*+*g.* on the eve of the day before.

на|ка́пать, -аю *pf.* (*impf.* **нака́пывать**) pour out (*drop by drop*), measure out; +*i.* spill.

нака́пливать(ся, -аю(сь *impf. of* **накопи́ть(ся нака́пывать, -аю** *impf. of* **нака́пать. на|ка́ркать, -аю** *pf.*

накача́ть, -а́ю *pf.*, **нака́чивать, -аю** *impf.* pump; pump up; **~ся** get tight.

наки́д, -а loop; made stitch. **накида́ть, -а́ю** *pf.*, **наки́дывать, -аю** *impf.* throw, throw down. **наки́дка, -и** cloak, cape; wrap; pillow-cover; increase, extra charge. **наки́нуть, -ну** *pf.*, **наки́дывать, -аю** *impf.* throw; throw on, slip on; **~ся** throw o.s., fling o.s.; **~ся на** attack, assail.

накипа́ть, -а́ет *impf.*, **накипе́ть, -пи́т** *pf.* form a scum, form a scale; boil up. **на́кипь, -и** scum; scale, fur, deposit.

накла́дка, -и bracket; hair piece, wig; appliqué. **накладна́я** *sb.* invoice, way-bill. **накладн|о́й** laid on; false; **~о́е зо́лото** rolled gold; **~о́й карма́н** patch pocket; **~о́е серебро́** plated silver, (silver) plate; **~ые расхо́ды** overheads. **накла́дывать, -аю** *impf. of* **наложи́ть**

на|клевета́ть, -ещу́, -е́щешь *pf.* **наклёвываться, -а́ется** *impf. of* **наклюну́ться наклеи́вать, -аю** *impf.*, **накле́ить, -е́ю** *pf.* stick on, paste on. **накле́йка, -и** sticking (on, up); sticker; label; patch.

наклепа́ть, -а́ю *pf.*, **наклёпывать, -аю** *impf.*

rivet; make roughly, knock together.

накло́н, -а slope, inclination, incline; bend. **наклоне́ние, -я** inclination; mood. **накло-ни́ть, -ню́, -нишь** *pf.* **наклоня́ть, -я́ю** *impf.* incline, bend; **~ся** stoop, bend; bow. **на-кло́нность, -и** learning, inclination, propensity. **накло́нный** inclined, sloping.

наклю́нуться, -нется *pf.* (*impf.* **наклёвываться**) peck its way out of the shell; turn up.

накова́льня, -и anvil.

нако́жный cutaneous, skin.

нако́лка, -и pinning, sticking; head-dress; tattooing, tattoo. **наколо́ть¹, -лю́, -лешь** *pf.* (*impf.* **нака́лывать**) prick; pin; stick; **~ся** prick o.s.

наколо́ть², -лю́, -лешь *pf.* (*impf.* **нака́лывать**) chop, split.

наконе́ц *adv.* at last; in the end; finally. **нако-не́чник, -а** tip, point. **наконе́чный** final; on the end.

на|копи́ть, -плю́, -пишь *pf.*, **накопля́ть, -я́ю** *impf.* (*impf. also* **нака́пливать**) accumulate, amass, pile up, store; **~ся** accumulate. **на-копле́ние, -я** accumulation; storage; build-up; **~ да́нных** data storage.

на|копти́ть, -пчу́ *pf.* **на|корми́ть, -млю́, -мишь** *pf.*

накра́пывать, -ает *impf.* spit, drizzle.

на|кра́сить, -а́шу *pf.* (*impf.* **накра́шивать**) paint; make up. **на|кра́ситься, -а́шусь** *pf.*

на|крахма́лить, -лю *pf.* **накра́шивать, -аю** *impf. of* **накра́сить**

на|крени́ть, -ню́ *pf.* **накрени́ться, -ни́тся** *pf.*, **накреня́ться, -я́ется** *impf.* tilt; list, take a list, heel.

на́крепко *adv.* fast, tight; strictly.

на́крест *adv.* crosswise.

накрича́ть, -чу́ *pf.* (+на+*a.*) shout (at). **на|кроши́ть, -шу́, -шишь** *pf.* **накро́ю** *etc.: see* **накры́ть**

накрути́ть, -учу́, -у́тишь *pf.*, **накру́чивать, -аю** *impf.* wind, twist.

накрыва́ть, -а́ю *impf.*, **накры́ть, -ро́ю** *pf.* cover; catch; **~ (на) стол** lay the table; **~ на ме́сте** catch red-handed; **~ся** cover o.s.

накупа́ть, -а́ю *impf.*, **накупи́ть, -плю́, -пишь** *pf.* buy up.

наку́ренный smoky, smoke-filled. **накури́ть, -рю́, -ришь** *pf.* fill with smoke; distil.

налага́ть, -а́ю *impf. of* **наложи́ть**

нала́дить, -а́жу *pf.* **нала́живать, -аю** *impf.* regulate, adjust; tune; repair; organize; **~ся** come right; get going.

на|лга́ть, -лгу́, -лжёшь; -а́л, -а́, -о *pf.*

нале́во *adv.* to the left; on the side.

налёт *etc.: see* **нале́чь**. **налега́ть, -а́ю** *impf. of* **нале́чь**

налегке́ *adv.* lightly dressed; without luggage.

на|лепи́ть, -плю́, -пишь *pf.*

налёт, -а raid, swoop; flight; thin coating, bloom, patina; touch, shade; **с ~а** suddenly, without warning or preparation, just like that.

налета́ть[1], **-а́ю** *pf.* have flown. **налета́ть**[2], **-а́ю** *impf.*, **налете́ть, -лечу́** *pf.* swoop down; come flying; spring up; +**на**+*a.* fly or drive into, run into. **налётчик, -а** raider, robber.

нале́чь, -ля́гу, -ля́жешь; -лёг, -ла́ *pf.* (*impf.* **налега́ть**) lean, apply one's weight, lie; apply o.s.; +**на**+*a.* put one's weight behind.

налжёшь *etc.: see* **налга́ть**

нали́в, -а pouring in; ripening, swelling. **налива́ть(ся, -а́ю(сь** *impf. of* **нали́ть(ся. нали́вка, -и** (*fruit-flavoured*) liqueur. **нали́вн|о́й** ripe, juicy; for carriage of liquids; overshot; ~**о́й док** wet dock; ~**о́е су́дно** tanker.

налинова́ть, -ну́ю *pf.*

налипа́ть, -а́ет *impf.*, **нали́пнуть, -нет; -и́п** *pf.* stick.

налито́й plump, juicy; ~ **кро́вью** bloodshot. **нали́ть, -лью, -льёшь; на́лил, -а́, -о** *pf.* (*impf.* **налива́ть**) pour (out), fill; pour on; ~**ся; -и́лся, -а́сь, -и́ло́сь** pour in, run in; ripen, swell.

налицо́ *adv.* present, manifest; available, on hand.

нали́чие, -я presence. **нали́чность, -и** presence; amount on hand; cash, ready money. **нали́чн|ый** on hand, in hand, available; cash; ~**ые (де́ньги)** cash, ready money.

наловчи́ться, -чу́сь *pf.* become skilful.

нало́г, -а tax. **нало́говый** tax. **налогоплате́льщик, -а** taxpayer. **нало́женн|ый**; ~**ым платежо́м** C.O.D. **наложи́ть, -жу́, -жишь** *pf.* (*impf.* **накла́дывать, налага́ть**) lay (in, on), put (in, on); apply; impose; ~ **отпеча́ток** leave traces; ~ **штраф** impose a fine; ~ **на себя́ ру́ки** lay hands on o.s., commit suicide.

на|лощи́ть, -щу́ *pf.* **налью́** *etc.: see* **нали́ть**

налюбова́ться, -бу́юсь *pf.*+*i. or* **на**+*a.* gaze one's fill at, admire (sufficiently).

наля́гу *etc.: see* **нале́чь**

нам *etc.: see* **мы**

на|ма́зать, -а́жу *pf.*, **нама́зывать, -аю** *impf.* oil, grease; smear, spread; daub; ~**ся** make up.

на|малева́ть, -лю́ю *pf.* **на|мара́ть, -а́ю** *pf.* **на|ма́слить, -лю** *pf.* **нама́тывать, -аю** *impf. of* **намота́ть. нама́чивать, -аю** *impf. of* **намочи́ть**

наме́дни *adv.* the other day, recently.

намёк, -а a hint. **намека́ть, -а́ю** *impf.*, **намекну́ть, -ну́, -нёшь** *pf.* hint, allude.

на|мели́ть, -лю́ *pf.*

намерева́ться, -а́юсь *impf.*+*inf.* intend to, mean to, be about to. **наме́рен** *pred.*; **я** ~+*inf.* I intend to, I mean to; **что она́** ~**а сде́лать?** what is she going to do? **наме́рение, -я** intention, purpose. **наме́ренный** intentional, deliberate.

на|мета́ть, -а́ю *pf.* **на|ме́тить**[1], **-е́чу** *pf.* **наме́тить**[2], **-е́чу** *pf.* (*impf.* **намеча́ть**) plan, project; outline; nominate, select; ~**ся** be outlined, take shape. **наме́тка**[1], **-и** draft,

preliminary outline.

наме́тка[2], **-и** tacking, basting; tacking thread. **намеча́ть(ся, -а́ю(сь** *impf. of* **наме́тить(ся**

намно́го *adv.* much, far.

намока́ть, -а́ю *impf.*, **намо́кнуть, -ну** *pf.* get wet.

намо́рдник, -а a muzzle.

на|мо́рщить(ся, -щу(сь *pf.* **на|мости́ть, -ощу́** *pf.*

на|мота́ть, -а́ю *pf.* (*impf. also* **нама́тывать**) wind, reel.

на|мочи́ть, -очу́, -о́чишь *pf.* (*impf. also* **нама́чивать**) wet; soak, steep; splash, spill.

намы́в, -а alluvium. **намывно́й** alluvial. **намы́ливать, -аю** *impf.*, **на|мы́лить, -лю** *pf.* soap. **намы́ть, -мо́ю** *pf.* wash; wash down, wash up.

нанести́, -су́, -сёшь; -ёс, -ла́ *pf.* (*impf.* **наноси́ть**) carry, bring; draw, plot; cause, inflict; ~ **оскорбле́ние** insult; ~ **уда́р**+*d.* deal a blow; hit, punch, strike; ~ **уще́рб** damage.

на|низа́ть, -ижу́, -и́жешь *pf.*, **нани́зывать, -аю** *impf.* string, thread.

нанима́тель, -я *m.* tenant; employer. **нанима́ть(ся, -а́ю(сь** *impf. of* **наня́ть(ся**

нано́с, -а alluvial deposit; drift. **наноси́ть, -ошу́, -о́сишь** *impf. of* **нанести́. нано́сный** alluvial; alien, borrowed.

наня́ть, найму́, -мёшь; на́нял, -а́, -о *pf.* (*impf.* **нанима́ть**) hire, engage; rent; ~**ся** get a job, get work.

наоборо́т *adv.* on the contrary; back to front; the other, the wrong, way (round); **и** ~ and vice versa.

наобу́м *adv.* without thinking, at random.

на́отмашь *adv.* with a wild swing (of the hand), violently, full.

наотре́з *adv.* flatly, point-blank.

напада́ть, -а́ю *impf. of* **напа́сть. напада́ющий** *sb.* forward. **нападе́ние, -я** attack; forwards. **напа́дки, -док** *pl.* attacks, accusations.

на|па́костить, -ощу *pf.*

напа́рник, -а co-driver, fellow-worker; team-mate; mate.

напа́сть, -аду́, -адёшь; -а́л *pf.* (*impf.* **напада́ть**) **на**+*a.* attack; descend on; grip, seize, come over; come upon, come across. **напа́сть, -и** misfortune, disaster.

на|па́чкать, -аю *pf.*

напе́в, -а melody, tune. **напева́ть, -а́ю** *impf. of* **напе́ть. напе́вный** melodious.

наперебо́й, наперерыв *adv.* interrupting, vying with, one another.

наперёд *adv.* in advance, beforehand.

напереко́р *adv.*+*d.* in defiance of, counter to.

наперерыв *see* **наперебо́й**

напёрсток, -тка thimble.

на|перчи́ть, -чу *pf.*

напе́ть, -пою́, -поёшь *pf.* (*impf.* **напева́ть**) sing; hum, croon; ~ **пласти́нку** make a record.

на|печа́тать(ся, -аю(сь *pf.* **напива́ться, -а́юсь** *impf. of* **напи́ться**

напи́лок, -лка, напи́льник, -а file.

на|писа́ть, -ишу́, -и́шешь *pf.*

напи́ток, -тка drink, bevarage. напи́ться, -пью́сь, -пьёшься; -и́лся, -а́сь, -и́ло́сь *pf.* (*impf.* напива́ться) quench one's thirst, drink; get drunk.

напиха́ть, -а́ю *pf.*, напи́хивать, -аю *impf.* cram, stuff.

на|плева́ть, -люю́, -люёшь *pf.*; ~! to hell with it! who cares?

напле́чник, -а shoulder strap. напле́чный shoulder-.

наплы́в, -а flow, influx; accumulation; dissolve; canker.

наплюю́ *etc.: see* наплева́ть

напова́л outright, on the spot.

наподо́бие *prep.*+*g.* like, not unlike.

на|пои́ть, -ою́, -о́ишь *pf.*

напока́з *adv.* for show; выставля́ть ~ display; show off.

наполне́ние, -я filling; inflation. наполни́тель, -я *m.* filler. напо́лнить(ся, -ню(сь *pf.*, наполня́ть(ся, -я́ю(сь *impf.* fill.

наполови́ну *adv.* half.

напомина́ние, -я reminder. напомина́ть, -а́ю *impf.*, напо́мнить, -мню *pf.* remind.

напо́р, -а pressure. напо́ристость, -и energy; push, go. напо́ристый energetic, pushing. напо́рный pressure.

напо́ртить, -рчу *pf.* spoil; damage; +*d.* injure, harm.

напосле́док *adv.* in the end; after all.

напою́ *etc.: see* напе́ть, напои́ть

напр. *abbr.* (*of* наприме́р) e.g., for example.

напра́вить, -влю *pf.*, направля́ть, -я́ю *impf.* direct; aim; send; refer; sharpen, whet; organize; ~ся make (for), go (towards); get going, get underway. напра́вка, -и setting, whetting. направле́ние, -я direction; trend, tendency, turn; order, warrant, directive; action, effect; sector. напра́вленный purposeful, unswerving; directional. направля́ющая *sb.* guide. направля́ющий guiding, guide; leading.

напра́во *adv.* to the right, on the right.

напра́сно *adv.* vainly, in vain, to no purpose, for nothing; wrong, unjustly, mistakenly. напра́сный vain, idle; unfounded, unjust.

напра́шиваться, -аюсь *impf. of* напроси́ться

наприме́р for example, for instance.

на|прока́зить, -а́жу *pf.* на|прока́зничать, -аю *pf.*

напрока́т *adv.* for hire, on hire; взять ~ hire.

напролёт *adv.* through, without a break; всю ночь ~ all night long.

напроло́м *adv.* straight, regardless of obstacles; идти́ ~ push one's way through.

на|проро́чить, -очу *pf.*

напроси́ться, -ошу́сь, -о́сишься *pf.* (*impf.* напра́шиваться) thrust o.s., force o.s.; suggest itself; ~ на ask for, invite; ~ на комплиме́нты fish for compliments.

напро́тив *adv.* opposite; on the contrary; +*d.* against, to spite. напро́тив *prep.*+*g.* opposite.

напру́живать, -аю *impf.*, напру́жить, -жу *pf.* strain; tense; ~ся become tense, become taut.

напряга́ть(ся, -а́ю(сь *impf. of* напря́чь(ся.

напряже́ние, -я tension; effort, exertion, strain; stress; voltage; ~ смеще́ния grid bias. напряжённый tense, strained; intense; intensive.

напрями́к *adv.* straight, straight out.

напря́чь, -ягу́, -яжёшь; -яг, -ла́ *pf.* (*impf.* напряга́ть) tense, strain; ~ся exert o.s., strain o.s.; become tense.

на|пуга́ть(ся, -а́ю(сь *pf.* на|пу́дрить(ся, -рю(сь *pf.*

на́пуск, -а letting in; slipping, letting loose; bloused or loosely hanging part. напуска́ть, -а́ю *impf.*, напусти́ть, -ущу́, -у́стишь *pf.* let in, admit; let loose, slip; ~ на себя́ affect, put on, assume; ~ся+на+*a.* fly at, go for. напускно́й assumed, put on, artificial.

напу́тать, -аю *pf.* +в+*p.* make a mess of, make a hash of; confuse; get wrong.

напу́тственный parting, farewell. напу́тствие, -я parting words, farewell speech.

напуха́ть, -а́ет *impf.*, напу́хнуть, -нет *pf.* swell (up).

на|пыли́ть, -лю́ *pf.*

напы́щенный pompous, bombastic, highflown.

напью́сь *etc.: see* напи́ться

наравне́ *adv.* level, keeping pace; equally; on an equal footing.

нараспа́шку *adv.* unbuttoned; у него́ душа́ ~ he wears his heart on his sleeve.

нараспе́в *adv.* in a sing-song (way).

нараста́ние, -я growth, accumulation; build-up. нараста́ть, -а́ет *impf.*, нарасти́, -тёт; -ро́с, -ла́ *pf.* grow, form; increase, swell; accumulate.

нарасхва́т *adv.* very quickly, like hot cakes; раскупа́ться ~ be in great demand.

нарва́ть[1], -рву́, -рвёшь; -а́л, -а́, -о *pf.* (*impf.* нарыва́ть) pick; tear up.

нарва́ть[2], -вёт; -а́л, -а́, -о *pf.* (*impf.* нарыва́ть) gather, come to a head.

нарва́ться, -ву́сь, -вёшься; -а́лся, -ала́сь, -а́ло́сь *pf.* (*impf.* нарыва́ться) +на+*a.* run into, run up against.

наре́з, -а thread, groove; rifling; plot. наре́зать, -е́жу *pf.*, нареза́ть, -а́ю *impf.* cut, cut up, slice, carve; thread, rifle; allot, parcel out. наре́зка, -и cutting, slicing; thread, rifling. нарезно́й rifled.

нарека́ние, -я censure.

наре́чие[1], -я dialect.

наре́чие[2], -я adverb. наре́чный adverbial.

на|рисова́ть, -су́ю *pf.*

нарица́тельн|ый nominal; и́мя ~ое common noun; ~ая сто́имость face value, nominal value.

наркоделе́ц, -ьца́ drug trafficker, pusher.
нарко́з, -a anaesthesia; narcosis; anaesthetic.
наркома́н, -a, -ма́нка, -и drug addict. нар-
кома́ния, -и drug addiction. наркосиндик-
а́т, -a drug ring. нарко́тик, -a narcotic,
drug.
наро́д, -a (-y) people.
народи́ться, -ожу́сь pf. (impf. нарож-
да́ться) be born; come into being, arise.
наро́дник, -a narodnik, populist. наро́дни-
ческий populist. наро́дность, -и nationality; people; national character. наро́дный
national; folk; popular; people's. народо-
населе́ние, -я population.
нарожда́ться, -а́юсь impf. of народи́ться.
нарожде́ние, -я birth, springing up.
наро́с etc.: see нарасти́. наро́ст, -a out-
growth, excrescence; burr, tumour; incrusta-
tion, scale.
нарочи́тый deliberate, intentional. наро́чно
adv. on purpose, purposely, deliberately; for
fun, jokingly. на́рочный sb. courier; express
messenger; special messenger; с ~м express
delivery.
на́рты, нарт pl., на́рта, -ы sledge.
нару́жно adv. outwardly, on the surface. на-
ру́жность, -и exterior, (outward) appearance. нару́жный external, exterior, outward; for external use only, not to be taken.
нару́жу adv. outside, out.
на|румя́нить(ся, -ню(сь pf.
нару́чник, -a handcuff, manacle. нару́чн|ый;
~ые часы́ wrist-watch.
наруше́ние, -я breach; infringement, violation; offence. наруши́тель, -я m. transgressor, infringer, violator; ~ грани́цы illegal entrant. нару́шить, -шу pf., наруша́ть,
-а́ю impf. break; disturb, infringe, violate,
transgress.
на́ры, нар pl. plank-bed.
нары́в, -a abscess, boil. нарыва́ть(ся, -а́ю(сь
impf. of нарва́ть(ся
наря́д¹, -a order, warrant; duty; detail.
наря́д², -a attire; apparel; dress. наряди́ть,
-яжу́ pf. (impf. наряжа́ть) dress array; dress
up; ~ся dress up, array o.s. наря́дный well-
dressed, elegant, smart.
наряду́ adv. alike, equally; side by side; ~ с
э́тим at the same time.
наряжа́ть(ся, -а́ю(сь impf. of наряди́ть(ся
нас see мы
НАСА NASA abbr. (of National Aeronautics
and Space Administration).
насади́ть, -ажу́, -а́дишь pf., насажда́ть,
-а́ю impf. (impf. also наса́живать) plant;
seat; propagate; implant, inculcate; set; fix,
stick, pin. наса́дка, -и setting, fixing, putting
on; hafting; bait; nozzle, mouthpiece. наса-
жа́ть, -а́ю pf. (impf. наса́живать) plant,
seat. насажде́ние, -я planting; plantation
stand, wood; spreading, dissemination, pro-
pagation. наса́живать, -аю impf. of наса-
ди́ть, насажа́ть

наса́ливать, -аю impf. of насоли́ть
наса́сывать, -аю impf. of насоса́ть
насви́стывать, -аю impf. whistle.
наседа́ть, -а́ю impf. (pf. насе́сть) press; settle, collect. насе́дка, -и sitting hen.
насека́ть, -а́ю impf. of насе́чь. насеко́мое
sb. insect. насеку́ etc.: see насе́чь
населе́ние, -я population, inhabitants; settling, peopling. населённость, -и density
of population. населённый populated, settled, inhabited; thickly populated, populous;
~ пункт settlement; inhabited place; built-
up area. насели́ть, -лю́ pf., населя́ть, -я́ю
impf. settle, people, inhabit. насе́льник, -a
inhabitant.
насе́ст, -a roost, perch. насе́сть, -ся́ду, -се́л
pf. of наседа́ть
насе́чка, -и incision, cut; notch; inlay. на-
се́чь, -еку́, -ечёшь; -ёк, -ла́ pf. (impf.
насека́ть) cut; cut up; incise; damascene.
насиде́ть, -ижу́ pf., наси́живать, -аю impf.
hatch; warm. наси́женн|ый long occupied;
~ое ме́сто old haunt, old home.
наси́лие, -я violence, force, aggression. наси́-
ловать, -лую impf. (pf. из~) coerce, constrain; rape. наси́лу adv. with difficulty,
hardly. наси́льник, -a aggressor, user of violence, violator. наси́льно adv. by force, forcibly. наси́льственный violent, forcible.
наска́кивать, -аю impf. of наскочи́ть
на|сканда́лить, -лю pf.
насквозь adv. through, throughout.
наско́лько adv. how much? how far?; as far
as, so far as.
на́скоро adv. hastily, hurriedly.
наскочи́ть, -очу́, -о́чишь pf. (impf. наска́-
кивать) +на+a. run into, collide with; fly
at.
наскреба́ть, -а́ю impf., наскрести́, -ебу́,
-ебёшь; -ёб, -ла́ pf. scrape up, scrape together.
наскучи́ть, -чу pf. bore.
наслади́ть, -ажу́ pf., наслажда́ть, -а́ю impf.
delight, please; ~ся enjoy, take pleasure,
delight. наслажде́ние, -я delight, pleasure,
enjoyment.
насла́иваться, -ается impf. of наслои́ться
насле́дие, -я legacy; heritage. на|следи́ть,
-ежу́ pf. насле́дник, -a heir, legatee; successor. насле́дница, -ы heiress. насле́д-
ный next in succession; ~ принц crown
prince. насле́дование, -я inheritance, succession. насле́довать, -дую impf. & pf. (pf.
also y~) inherit, succeed to. насле́дст-
венный hereditary, inherited. насле́дство,
-a inheritance, legacy; heritage.
наслое́ние, -я stratification; stratum, layer,
deposit. наслои́ться, наслои́тся pf. (impf.
насла́иваться) form a layer or stratum, be
deposited.
наслы́шаться, -шусь pf. have heard a lot.
наслы́шка, -и; по наслы́шке by hearsay.
на́смерть adv. to death; to the death.

насмеха́ться, -а́юсь *impf.* jeer, gibe; +над+*i.* ridicule. на|смеши́ть, -шу́ *pf.* насме́шка, -и mockery, ridicule; gibe. насме́шливый mocking, derisive; sarcastic.

на́сморк, -а a cold in the head.

насмотре́ться, -рю́сь, -ришься *pf.* see a lot; ~ на see enough of, have looked enough at.

насоли́ть, -олю́, -о́лишь *pf.* (*impf.* наса́ливать) salt, pickle; oversalt; annoy, spite, injure.

на|сори́ть, -рю́ *pf.*

насо́с, -а pump. насоса́ть, -осу́, -осёшь *pf.* (*impf.* наса́сывать) pump; suck; ~ся suck one's fill; drink o.s. drunk. насо́сный pumping.

на́спех *adv.* hastily.

на|спле́тничать, -аю *pf.* настава́ть, -таёт *impf. of* наста́ть

настави́тельный edifying, instructive. наста́вить[1], -влю *pf.* (*impf.* наставля́ть) edify; exhort, admonish.

наста́вить[2], -влю *pf.* (*impf.* наставля́ть) lengthen; add, add on; aim, point; set up, place. наста́вка, -и addition. наставле́ние, -я exhortation, admonition; directions, instructions, manual.

наставля́ть, -я́ю *impf. of* наста́вить

наста́вник, -а tutor, teacher, mentor; кла́ссный ~ form-master. наста́вничество, -а tutorship, tutelage.

наставно́й lengthened; added.

наста́ивать(ся, -аю(сь *impf. of* настоя́ть(ся

наста́ть, -а́нет *pf.* (*impf.* настава́ть) come, begin, set in.

на́стежь *adv.* wide, wide open.

настелю́ *etc.: see* настла́ть

насте́нн|ый hanging; ~ые часы́ wall-clock.

настига́ть, -а́ю *impf.,* настигну́ть, настичь, -и́гну; -и́г *pf.* catch up with, overtake.

насти́л, -а flooring, planking. настила́ть, -а́ю *impf. of* настла́ть

насти́чь *see* настига́ть

настла́ть, -телю́, -те́лешь *pf.* (*impf.* настила́ть) lay, spread.

насто́й, -я infusion; (*fruit-flavoured*) liqueur, cordial. насто́йка, -и (*fruit-flavoured*) liqueur, cordial.

насто́йчивый persistent; urgent, insistent.

насто́лько *adv.* so, so much; ~, наско́лько as much as.

насто́льник, -а table-lamp, desk-lamp. насто́льный table, desk; for constant reference, in constant use.

настора́живать, -аю *impf.,* насторожи́ть, -жу́ *pf.* set; prick up, strain; ~ся prick up one's ears. насторожé *adv.* on the alert, on one's guard. насторо́женный; -ен, -енна, насторожённый; -ён, -ена́ *or* -ённа guarded; alert.

настоя́ние, -я insistence. настоя́тельный persistent, insistent; urgent, pressing. настоя́ть[1], -ою́ *pf.* (*impf.* наста́ивать) insist.

настоя́ть[2], -ою́ *pf.* (*impf.* наста́ивать) brew,

draw, infuse; ~ся draw, stand; stand a long time.

настоя́щее *sb.* the present. настоя́щий (the) present, this; real, genuine.

настра́ивать(ся, -аю(сь *impf. of* настро́ить(ся

настри́г, -а shearing, clipping; clip. настри́чь, -игу́, -ижёшь; -и́г *pf.* shear, clip.

на́строго *adv.* strictly.

настрое́ние, -я mood, temper, humour; ~ умо́в public feeling, general mood.

настро́ить, -о́ю *pf.* (*impf.* настра́ивать) tune, tune in; dispose, incline; incite; ~ся dispose o.s., incline, settle; make up one's mind. настро́йка, -и tuning; tuning in; tuning signal. настро́йщик, -а tuner.

на|строчи́ть, -чу́ *pf.*

настря́пать, -аю *pf.* cook; cook up.

наступа́тельный offensive; aggressive. наступа́ть[1], -а́ю *impf. of* наступи́ть[1]

наступа́ть[2], -а́ет *impf. of* наступи́ть[2]. наступа́ющий coming, beginning.

наступа́ющий *sb.* attacker.

наступи́ть[1], -плю́, -пишь *pf.* (*impf.* наступа́ть) tread, step; attack; advance.

наступи́ть[2], -у́пит *pf.* (*impf.* наступа́ть) come, set in; fall; наступи́ла ночь night had fallen; наступи́ла тишина́ silence fell. наступле́ние[1], -я coming, approach; с ~м но́чи at nightfall.

наступле́ние[2], -я offensive, attack.

насу́питься, -плюсь *pf.,* насу́пливаться, -аюсь *impf.* frown, knit one's brows.

насу́хо *adv.* dry. насуши́ть, -шу́, -шишь *pf.* dry.

насу́щность, -и urgency. насу́щный urgent, vital, essential; хлеб ~ daily bread.

насчёт *prep.*+*g.* about, concerning; as regards.

насчита́ть, -а́ю *pf.,* насчи́тывать, -аю *impf.* count; hold, contain; ~ся+*g.* number.

насы́пать, -плю *pf.,* насыпа́ть, -а́ю *impf.* pour in, pour on; fill; spread, scatter; raise, heap up. насы́пка, -и pouring; filling. насыпно́й bulk; piled up; ~ холм artificial mound. на́сыпь, -и embankment.

насы́тить, -ы́щу *pf.,* насыща́ть, -а́ю *impf.* sate, satiate; saturate, impregnate; ~ся be full, be sated; be saturated. насы́щенный saturated; rich, concentrated.

насяду *etc.: see* насе́сть

ната́лкивать(ся, -аю(сь *impf. of* натолкну́ть(ся ната́пливать, -аю *impf. of* натопи́ть

натаска́ть, -а́ю *pf.,* ната́скивать, -аю *impf.* train; coach, cram; bring in, lay in; fish out, drag out, fetch out.

натвори́ть, -рю́ *pf.* do, get up to.

натере́ть, -тру́, -трёшь; -тёр *pf.* (*impf.* натира́ть) rub on, rub in; polish; chafe, rub; grate; ~ся rub o.s.

натерпе́ться, -плю́сь, -пишься *pf.* have suffered much, have gone through a great deal.

натира́ть(ся, -а́ю(сь *impf. of* натере́ть(ся

на́тиск, -а onslaught, charge, onset; pressure; impress, impression. **нати́скать, -аю** *pf.* impress; cram in; shove, push about.

наткну́ться, -ну́сь, -нёшься *pf.* (*impf.* **натыка́ться**) +**на**+*a.* run against, run into; strike, stumble on, come across.

HATO NATO *abbr.* (*of* North Atlantic Treaty Organization).

натолкну́ть, -ну́, -нёшь *pf.* (*impf.* **ната́лкивать**) push, lead; ~ **на** suggest; ~**ся** run against, run across.

натопи́ть, -плю́, -пишь *pf.* (*impf.* **ната́пливать**) heat, heat up; stoke up; melt.

на|точи́ть, -чу́, -чишь *pf.*

натоща́к *adv.* on an empty stomach.

натр, -а natron, soda; **е́дкий** ~ caustic soda.

натрави́ть, -влю́, -вишь *pf.*, **натра́вливать, -аю** *impf.*, **натравля́ть, -яю** *impf.* set (on); stir up; etch; exterminate (*by poison*).

натрениро́ванный trained. **на|трениро-ва́ть(ся, -ру́ю(сь** *pf.*

на́трий, -я sodium.

нату́га, -и effort, strain. **на́туго** *adv.* tight, tightly. **нату́жный** strained, forced.

нату́ра, -ы nature; kind; model; **на нату́ре** on location; **плати́ть нату́рой** pay in kind; **с нату́ры** from life. **натура́льно** *adv.* naturally, of course. **натура́льный** natural; real; genuine; in kind; ~ **обме́н** barter. **нату́рный** life, from life; on location.

натуропа́т, -а naturopath. **натуропа́тия, -и** naturopathy.

нату́рщик, -а, -щица, -ы artist's model.

натыка́ть(ся, -а́ю(сь *impf. of* **наткну́ть(ся**

натюрмо́рт, -а still life.

натя́гивать, -аю *impf.*, **натяну́ть, -ну́, -нешь** *pf.* stretch; draw; pull tight, tauten; pull on; ~**ся** stretch. **натя́жка, -и** stretching, straining; tension; stretch; **допусти́ть натя́жку** stretch a point; **с натя́жкой** be stretching a point, at a pinch. **натяжно́й** tension. **натя́нутость, -и** tension. **натя́нутый** tight; strained, forced.

науга́д *adv.* at random; by guesswork.

нау́ка, -и science; learning, scholarship; study; lesson. **наукообра́зный** scientific; pseudo-scientific.

наутёк *adv.*: **пусти́ться** ~ take to one's heels, take to flight.

нау́тро *adv.* (the) next morning.

на|учи́ть, -чу́, -чишь *pf.*

нау́чн|ый scientific; ~**ая фанта́стика** science fiction.

нау́шник, -а ear-flap, ear-muff; ear-phone; head-phone; informer, tale-bearer. **нау́шничать, -аю** *impf.* tell tales, inform.

нафтали́н, -а (-у) naphthalene. **нафтали́новый** ~ **ша́рик** moth-ball.

наха́л, -а, -ха́лка, -и impudent creature, brazen creature; lout, hussy. **наха́льный** impudent, impertinent, cheeky; brazen, bold-faced. **наха́льство, -а** impudence, effrontery.

нахвата́ть, -а́ю *pf.*, **нахва́тывать, -аю** *impf.* pick up, get hold of, come by; ~**ся**+*g.* pick up, get a smattering of.

нахле́бник, -а parasite, hanger-on; boarder, paying guest.

нахлобу́чивать, -аю *impf.*, **нахлобу́чить, -чу** *pf.* pull down; +*d.* tell off, dress down. **нахлобу́чка, -и** telling-off, dressing-down.

нахлы́нуть, -нет *pf.* well up; surge; flow, gush; crowd.

нахму́ренный frowning, scowling. **на|хму́-рить(ся, -рю(сь** *pf.*

находи́ть(ся, -ожу́(сь, -о́дишь(ся *impf. of* **найти́(сь. нахо́дка, -и** find; godsend. **нахо́дчивый** resourceful, ready, quick-witted.

на|холоди́ть, -ожу́ *pf.*

нацеди́ть, -ежу́, -е́дишь *pf.*, **наце́живать, -аю** *impf.* strain.

наце́ливать, -аю *impf.*, **на|це́лить, -лю** *pf.* aim, level, direct; ~**ся** aim, take aim.

наце́нка, -и extra, addition; additional charge.

национализи́ровать, -рую *impf. & pf.* nationalize. **националисти́ческий** nationalist, nationalistic. **национа́льность, -и** nationality; ethnic group; national character. **национа́льный** national. **на́ция, -и** nation. **нацме́н, -а, -ме́нка, -и** member of national minority. **нацменьши́нство, -а** *abbr.* national minority.

на|чади́ть, -ажу́ *pf.*

нача́ло, -а beginning, start; origin, source; principle, basis; command, authority; **для нача́ла** to start with; **с нача́ла** at, from, the beginning. **нача́льник, -а** head, chief; superior, boss. **нача́льный** initial, first; primary. **нача́льственный** overbearing, domineering. **нача́льство, -а** the authorities; command, direction; head, boss. **нача́льство-вание, -я** command. **нача́льствовать, -твую** *impf.* be in command; +**над**+*i.* command. **на-ча́тки, -ков** *pl.* rudiments, elements. **нача́ть, -чну́, -чнёшь; на́чал, -а́, -о** *pf.* (*impf.* **начи-на́ть**) begin, start; ~**ся** begin, start.

начеку́ *adv.* on the alert, ready.

на|черни́ть, -ню́ *pf.* **на́черно** *adv.* roughly, in rough.

начерта́ние, -я tracing; outline. **начерта́-тельн|ый**; ~**ая геоме́трия** descriptive geometry. **начерта́ть, -а́ю** *pf.* trace, inscribe. **на|черти́ть, -рчу́, -ртишь** *pf.*

начина́ние, -я undertaking; project; initiative. **начина́тель, -я** *m.*, **-тельница, -ы** originator, initiator. **начина́тельный** inchoative, inceptive. **начина́ть(ся, -а́ю(сь** *impf. of* **нача́ть(ся. начина́ющий** *sb.* beginner. **на-чина́я с** *prep.*+*g.* as from, starting with.

начи́нивать, -аю *impf.*, **начини́ть[1], -ню́, -нишь** *pf.* mend; sharpen.

начиня́ть[2], -ню́ *pf.*, **начиня́ть, -я́ю** *impf.* stuff, fill. **начи́нка, -и** stuffing, filling.

начисле́ние, -я extra charge, supplement, addition. **начи́слить, -лю** *pf.*, **начисля́ть, -я́ю** *impf.* add.

начи́стить, -и́щу *pf.* (*impf.* **начища́ть**) clean;

polish, shine; peel. **нáчисто** adv. flatly, decidedly; openly, frankly; **переписáть** ~ make a clean copy (of). **начистотý, начистýю** adv. openly, frankly.

начи́танность, -и learning, erudition; wide reading. **начи́танный** well-read; **начитáть, -áю** pf. have read; ~**ся** have read (too) much, have read enough.

начищáть, -áю impf. of **начи́стить**

наш, -его m., **нáша, -ей** f., **нáше, -его** nt., **нáши, -их** pl., pron. our, ours; ~**а взялá** we've won; ~**его** (after comp.) than we (have etc.); ~**и** our (own) people; **оди́н из** ~**их** one of us; **служи́ть, угождáть, и** ~**им и вáшим** run with the hare and hunt with the hounds.

нашаты́рный; ~ **спирт** ammonia. **нашаты́рь, -я́** m. sal-ammoniac; ammonia.

нашёл etc.: see **найти́**

нашептáть, -пчý, -пчешь pf., **нашёптывать, -аю** impf. whisper; cast a spell.

нашéствие, -я invasion.

нашивáть, -áю impf., **наши́ть, -шью, -шьёшь** pf. sew on. **наши́вка, -и** stripe, chevron; tab. **нашивнóй** sewn on; ~ **кармáн** patch pocket.

нашинковáть, -кýю pf., **нашинкóвывать, -аю** impf. shred, chop.

нашпи́ливать, -аю impf., **нашпи́лить, -лю** pf. pin on.

нашлёпать, -аю impf. slap.

нашумéть, -млю pf. make a din; cause a sensation.

нашью́ etc.: see **наши́ть**

нащýпать, -аю pf., **нащýпывать, -аю** impf. grope for, fumble for, feel (about) for; grope one's way to, find by groping.

на|электризовáть, -зýю pf.

на|я́бедничать, -аю pf.

наявý adv. awake; in reality; **сон** ~ waking dream.

не part. not; **не раз** more than once.

не... pref. un-, in-, non-, mis-, dis-; -less; not. **неаккурáтный** careless, inaccurate; unpunctual; untidy.

Неáполь, -я Naples.

небезопáсный unsafe. **небезразли́чный** not indifferent. **небезызвéстн|ый** not unknown; notorious; well-known; ~**о, что** it is no secret that; **нам** ~**о** we are not unaware. **небезынтерéсный** not without interest.

небесá etc.: see **нéбо²**. **небéсный** heavenly, of heaven; celestial.

не... **небесполéзный** of some use, useful. **неблагодáрный** ungrateful, thankless. **неблагожелáтельный** malevolent, ill-disposed. **неблагозвýчие, -я** disharmony, dissonance. **неблагозвýчный** inharmonious, discordant. **неблагонадёжный** unreliable. **неблагополýчие, -я** trouble. **неблагополýчный** unsuccessful, bad, unfavourable. **неблагопристóйный** obscene, indecent, improper. **неблагоразýмный** imprudent,

ill-advised, unwise. **неблагорóдный** ignoble, base.

нёбный palatal, palatine. **нёбо¹, -а** palate. **нéбо², -а;** pl. **-бесá, -бéс** sky; heaven.

не... небогáтый of modest means, modest. **небольшóй** small, not great; **с небольши́м** a little over.

небосвóд, -а firmament, vault of heaven. **небосклóн, -а** horizon. **небоскрёб, -а** skyscraper.

небóсь adv. I dare say; probably, very likely; I suppose.

не... небрéжничать, -аю impf. be careless. **небрéжный** careless, negligent; slipshod; offhand. **небывáлый** unprecedented; fantastic, imaginary; inexperienced. **небыли́ца, -ы** fable, cock-and-bull story. **небытиé, -я́** non-existence. **небью́щийся** unbreakable.

Невá, -ы́ the Neva.

невáжно adv. not too well, indifferently. **невáжный** unimportant, insignificant; poor, indifferent. **невдалекé** adv. not far away. **невéдение, -я** ignorance. **невéдомо** adv. God (only) knows. **невéдомый** unknown; mysterious. **невéжа, -и** c.g. boor, lout. **невéжда, -ы** c.g. ignoramus. **невéжественный** ignorant. **невéжество, -а** ignorance; rudeness, bad manners, discourtesy. **невéжливый** rude, impolite, ill-mannered. **невели́кий, -и́к, -á, -и́кó** small, short; slight, insignificant. **невéрие, -я** unbelief, atheism; lack of faith, scepticism. **невéрный; -рен, -рнá, -о** incorrect, wrong; inaccurate, uncertain, unsteady; false; faithless, disloyal; unfaithful; **Фомá** ~ doubting Thomas. **невероя́тный** improbable, unlikely; incredible, unbelievable. **невéрующий** unbelieving; sb. unbeliever, atheist. **невесёлый** joyless, sad. **невесóмость, -и** weightlessness. **невесóмый** weightless; imponderable, insignificant. **невéста, -ы** fiancée; bride. **невéстка, -и** daughter-in-law; brother's wife, sister-in-law.

не... невзгóда, -ы adversity, misfortune. **невзирáя на** prep.+a. in spite of; regardless of. **невзначáй** adv. by chance, unexpectedly. **невзрáчный** unattractive, plain. **невзыскáтельный** unexacting, undemanding. **невидаль, -и** wonder, prodigy. **невиданный** unprecedented, unheard-of; mysterious. **невиди́мый** invisible. **невидя́щий** unseeing. **неви́нность, -и** innocence. **неви́нный** innocent. **невинóвный** innocent, not guilty. **невкýсный** tasteless, unappetizing, not nice. **невменя́емый** irresponsible, not responsible; beside o.s. **невмешáтельство, -а** non-intervention; non-interference. **невмоготý, невмóчь** advs. unbearable, unendurable, too much (for). **невнимáние, -я** inattention; carelessness; lack of consideration. **невнимáтельный** inattentive, thoughtless. **невня́тный** indistinct, incomprehensible.

нéвод, -а seine, seine-net.

не... **невозврати́мый, невозвра́тный** irrevocable, irrecoverable. **невозвраще́нец, -нца** defector. **невозде́ланный** untilled, waste. **невозде́ржанный, невозде́ржный** intemperate; incontinent; uncontrolled, unrestrained. **невозмо́жный** impossible; insufferable. **невозмути́мый** imperturbable; calm, unruffled. **невозобновля́емый** nonrenewable.

нево́лить, -лю impf. (pf. **при~**) force, compel. **нево́льник, -а, -ница, -ы** slave. **нево́льно** adv. involuntarily; unintentionally. **нево́льный** involuntary; unintentional; forced; **~ная поса́дка** forced landing. **нево́ля, -и** bondage, captivity; necessity.

не... **невообрази́мый** unimaginable, inconceivable. **невооружённ|ый** unarmed; **~ным гла́зом** with the naked eye. **невоспи́танность, -и** ill breeding, bad manners. **невоспи́танный** ill-bred. **невоспламеня́емый** non-inflammable. **невоспри́мчивый** unreceptive; immune. **невпопа́д** adv. out of place; irrelevant, inopportune.

невралги́ческий neuralgic. **невралги́|я, -и** neuralgia.

невреди́мый safe, unharmed, uninjured.

неври́т, -а neuritis. **невро́з, -а** neurosis. **неврологи́ческий** neurological. **невроло́гия, -и** neurology. **невро́тик, -а** neurotic. **невроти́ческий** neurotic.

не... **невруче́ние, -я** non-delivery. **невы́года, -ы** disadvantage, loss. **невы́годный** disadvantageous, unfavourable; unprofitable, unremunerative. **невы́держанный** lacking self-control; unmatured. **невыноси́мый** unbearable, insufferable, intolerable. **невыполне́ние, -я** non-fulfilment, non-compliance. **невыполни́мый** impracticable. **невырази́мый** inexpressible, unmentionable. **невысо́кий; -со́к, -а́, -око́** not high, low; not tall, short. **невы́ясненный** obscure, uncertain. **неувя́зка, -и** discrepancy.

не́га, -и luxury; bliss, delight; voluptuousness.

негашён|ый unslaked; **~ая и́звесть** quicklime.

не́где adv. there is nowhere.

не... **неги́бкий; -бок, -бка́, -о** inflexible, stiff. **негла́сный** secret. **неглубо́кий; -о́к, -а́, -о** rather shallow; superficial. **неглу́п|ый; -у́п, -а́, -о** sensible, quite intelligent; **он ~** he is no fool. **него́дник, -а** a reprobate, scoundrel, good-for-nothing. **него́дный; -ден, -дна́, -о** unfit, unsuitable; worthless. **негодова́ние, -я** indignation. **негодова́ть, -ду́ю** impf. be indignant. **негоду́ющий** indignant. **негодя́й, -я** scoundrel, rascal. **негостеприи́мный** inhospitable.

негр, -а Negro.

негра́мотность, -и illiteracy. **негра́мотный** illiterate.

негритёнок, -нка; pl. **-тя́та, -тя́т** Negro child. **негритя́нка, -и** Negress. **негритя́нский, не́грский** Negro.

не... **неда́вний** recent. **неда́вно** adv. recently. **недалёкий; -ёк, -а́, -ёко́** not far away, near; short; not bright, dull-witted. **недалёко** adv. not far, near. **неда́ром** adv. not for nothing, not without reason, not without purpose. **недви́жимость, -и** real property, real estate. **недви́жимый** immovable; motionless. **недвусмы́сленный** unequivocal. **недействи́тельный** ineffective, ineffectual; invalid, null and void. **недели́мый** indivisible.

неде́льный of a week, week's. **неде́ля, -и** week.

не... **недёшево** adv. not cheap(ly), dear(ly). **недоброжела́тель, -я** m. ill-wisher **недоброжела́тельность, -и, недоброжела́тельство, -а** hostility, ill-will, malevolence. **недоброжела́тельный** ill-disposed, hostile, malevolent. **недоброка́чественный** of poor quality, low-grade; bad. **недобросо́вестный** unscrupulous; not conscientious, careless. **недо́брый; -о́бр, -бра́, -о** unkind, unfriendly; bad; evil, wicked. **недове́рие, -я** distrust; mistrust; lack of confidence. **недове́рчивый** distrustful, not confident, mistrustful. **недове́с, -а** short weight. **недово́льный** dissatisfied, discontented, displeased; sb. malcontent. **недово́льство, -а** dissatisfaction, discontent, displeasure. **недога́дливый** slow-witted. **недогляде́ть, -яжу́** pf. overlook; take insufficient care of. **недоеда́ние, -я** malnutrition. **недоеда́ть, -а́ю** impf. be undernourished, be underfed, not eat enough. **недозво́ленный** unlawful; illicit.

недои́мка, -и arrears. **недои́мочность, -и** non-payment. **недои́мщик, -а** defaulter, person in arrears.

не... **недо́лг|ий; -лог, -лга́, -о** short, brief; **вот и вся ~а** that's all there is to it. **недо́лго** adv. not long. **недолгове́чный** short-lived, ephemeral. **недоме́р, -а** short measure. **недоме́рок, -рка** undersized object; small size. **недомога́ние, -я** indisposition. **недомога́ть, -а́ю** impf. be unwell, be indisposed. **недомо́лвка, -и** reservation, omission. **недомы́слие, -я** thoughtlessness. **недоно́сок, -ска** premature child. **недоно́шенный** premature. **недооце́нивать, -аю** impf., **недооцени́ть, -ню́, -нишь** pf. underestimate, underrate. **недооце́нка, -и** underestimation. **недопроизво́дство, -а** underproduction. **недопусти́мый** inadmissible, intolerable. **недоразуме́ние, -я** misunderstanding. **недорого́й, -до́рог, -а́, -о** not dear, inexpensive; reasonable, modest. **недоро́д, -а** crop failure, bad harvest. **недосмо́тр, -а** oversight. **недосмотре́ть, -рю́, -ришь** pf. overlook, miss; take insufficient care. **недоспа́ть, -плю́; -а́л, -а́, -о** pf. (impf. **недосыпа́ть**) not have enough sleep.

недостава́ть, -таёт impf., **недоста́ть, -а́нет** pf. impers. be missing, be lacking, be want ing. **недоста́ток**, **-тка** shortage, lack, deficiency, want; shortcoming, defect. **недоста́точно** *adv.* insufficiently, not enough. **недоста́точный** insufficient, inadequate; ~ **глаго́л** defective verb. **недоста́ча**, **-и** lack, shortage, deficit.

не... недостижи́мый unattainable. **недостове́рный** not authentic, doubtful, apocryphal. **недосто́йный** unworthy, **недосту́пный** inaccessible. **недосу́г**, **-а** lack of time, being too busy; **за** ~**ом** for lack of time. **недосчита́ться**, **-а́юсь** *pf.* **недосчи́тываться**, **-аюсь** *impf.* miss, find missing, be short (of). **недосыпа́ть**, **-а́ю** *impf. of* **недоспа́ть**. **недосяга́емый** unattainable. **недотро́га**, **-и** *c.g.* touchy person; *f.* mimosa.

недоумева́ть, **-а́ю** *impf.* be puzzled, be at a loss, be bewildered. **недоуме́ние**, **-я** perplexity, bewilderment. **недоуме́нный** puzzled, perplexed.

не... недоу́чка, **-и** *c.g.* half-educated person. **недохва́тка**, **-и** shortage, lack. **недочёт**, **-а** deficit, shortage; shortcoming, defect.

не́дра, **недр** *pl.* depths, heart, bowels; **бога́тство недр** mineral wealth.

не... недре́млющий unsleeping, watchful, vigilant. **не́друг**, **-а** enemy. **недружелю́бный** unfriendly.

неду́г, **-а** illness, disease.

недурно́й not bad; not bad looking.

недю́жинный out of the ordinary, outstanding, exceptional.

не... неесте́ственный unnatural. **нежда́нно** *adv.* unexpectedly; ~**-нега́данно** quite unexpectedly. **нежда́нный** unexpected, unlooked-for. **нежела́ние**, **-я** unwillingness, disinclination. **нежела́тельный** undesirable, unwanted. **нежена́тый** unmarried. **не́женка**, **-и** *c.g.* mollycoddle.

нежило́й uninhabited; not habitable.

не́жить, **-жу** *impf.* pamper; indulge; caress; ~**ся** luxuriate, bask. **не́жничать**, **-аю** *impf.* bill and coo; be soft, be over-indulgent. **не́жность**, **-и** tenderness; delicacy; *pl.* endearments, display of affection, compliments, flattery. **не́жный** tender; delicate; affectionate.

не... незабве́нный unforgettable. **незабу́дка**, **-и** forget-me-not. **незабыва́емый** unforgettable. **незаве́ренный** uncertified. **незави́симо** *adv.* independently; ~ **от** irrespective of. **незави́симый** independent; sovereign. **незави́сящ|ий**; **по** ~**им от нас обстоя́тельствам** owing to circumstances beyond our control. **незада́ча**, **-и** ill luck, bad luck. **незада́чливый** unlucky; luckless. **незадо́лго** *adv.* not long. **незако́нн|ый** illegal, illicit, unlawful; illegitimate; ~**ая жена́** common-law wife. **незако́нченный** unfinished, incomplete. **незамени́мый** irreplaceable, indispensable. **незамерза́ю|щий** ice-free; anti-freeze; ~**ая смесь** anti-freeze. **незаме́тно** *adv.* imperceptibly, insensibly. **незаме́тный** imperceptible; incon-

spicuous, insignificant. **незаму́жняя** unmarried, single. **незамыслова́тый** simple, uncomplicated. **незапа́мятный** immemorial. **незапя́тнанный** unstained, unsullied. **незара́зный** non-contagious. **незаслу́женный** unmerited, undeserved. **незастро́енный** not built on, undeveloped; vacant. **незате́йливый** simple, plain; modest. **незауря́дный** uncommon, outstanding, out of the ordinary.

не́зачем *adv.* there is no need; it is useless, pointless, no use.

не... незащищённый unprotected. **незва́ный** uninvited. **нездоро́виться**, **-ится** *impf.*, *impers.*+*d.*; **мне нездоро́вится** I don't feel well, I am not well. **нездоро́вый** unhealthy, sickly; morbid; unwholesome; unwell. **нездоро́вье**, **-я** indisposition; ill health. **неземно́й** not of the earth; unearthly. **незло́бивый** gentle, mild, forgiving. **незнако́мец**, **-мца**, **незнако́мка**, **-и** stranger. **незнако́мый** unknown, unfamiliar; unacquainted. **незна́ние**, **-я** ignorance. **незна́чащий**, **незначи́тельный** insignificant, unimportant, of no consequence. **незре́лый** unripe, immature. **незри́мый** invisible. **незы́блемый** unshakable, stable, firm. **неизбе́жный** inevitable, unavoidable, inescapable. **неизве́данный** unknown, unexplored; not experienced before.

неизве́стное *sb.* unknown quantity. **неизве́стность**, **-и** uncertainty; ignorance; obscurity. **неизве́стный** unknown; *sb.* stranger, unknown.

не... неизглади́мый indelible, uneffaceable. **неи́зданный** unpublished. **неизлечи́мый** incurable. **неизме́нный** unchanged, unchanging; devoted, true. **неизменя́емый** invariable, unalterable. **неизмери́мый** immeasurable, immense. **неизу́ченный** unstudied; obscure, unknown; unexplored. **неиме́ние**, **-я** lack, want; absence; **за** ~**м**+*g.* for want of. **неимове́рный** incredible, unbelievable. **неиму́щий** indigent, needy, poor. **нейскренний** insincere; false. **неиску́сный** unskilful, inexpert. **неискушённый** inexperienced, innocent, unsophisticated. **неисполне́ние**, **-я** non-performance, non-observance, non-execution. **неисполни́мый** impracticable, unrealizable. **неисправи́мый** incorrigible; irremediable, irreparable. **неиспра́вность**, **-и** disrepair, fault, defect; carelessness. **неиспра́вный** out of order, faulty, defective; careless. **неиссле́дованный** unexplored, uninvestigated. **неиссяка́емый** inexhaustible. **неи́стовство**, **-а** fury, frenzy; violence; savagery, atrocity. **неи́стовый** furious, frenzied, uncontrolled. **неистощи́мый**, **неисчерпа́емый** inexhaustible. **неисчисли́мый** innumerable, incalculable.

нейло́н, **-а**, **нейло́новый** nylon.

нейро́н, **-а** neuron.

нейтрализа́ция, -и neutralization. **нейтра-лизова́ть**, -зу́ю *impf. & pf.* neutralize.
нейтралите́т, -а, **нейтра́льность**, -и neutrality. **нейтра́льный** neutral. **нейтри́но**, -а neutrino. **нейтро́н**, -а neutron.

неквалифици́рованный unskilled; unqualified.

не́кий *pron.* a certain, some.

не́когда[1] *adv.* once, long ago, in the old days.

не́когда[2] *adv.* there is no time; мне ~ I have no time.

не́кого, не́кому, не́кем, не́ о ком *pron.* (*with separable pref.*) there is nobody.

неколеби́мый unshakeable.

некомпете́нтный not competent, unqualified.

не́котор|ый *pron.* some; ~ым о́бразом somehow, in a way; ~ые *sb.*, *pl.* some, some people.

некраси́вый plain, ugly, unsightly, unpleasant.

некро́з, -а necrosis. **некроло́г**, -а obituary (notice). **некрома́нтия**, -и necromancy; telling fortunes.

некры́тый roofless.

некста́ти *adv.* malapropos, unseasonably, at the wrong time, out of place.

не́кто *pron.* somebody; one, a certain.

не́куда *adv.* there is nowhere.

не... **некульту́рный** uncivilized, uncultured; uncultivated; barbarous, ill-mannered, uncouth, boorish. **некуря́щий** *sb.* non-smoker. **нела́дн|ый** wrong; здесь что́-то ~о something is wrong here; будь он ~ен! blast him! **нела́ды**, -о́в *pl.* discord, disagreement; trouble, something wrong. **нелега́льный** illegal. **нелега́льщина**, -ы illegal literature, illegal activity. **нелёгкая** *sb.* the devil, the deuce. **нелёгкий** difficult, not easy; heavy, not light. **неле́пость**, -и absurdity, nonsense. **неле́пый** absurd, ridiculous. **нело́вк|ий** awkward, clumsy, gauche; uncomfortable, embarrassing; мне ~о I'm uncomfortable. **нело́вко** *adv.* awkwardly, uncomfortably. **нело́вкость**, -и awkwardness, gaucherie, clumsiness; blunder. **нельзя́** *adv.* it is impossible, it is not allowed; one ought not, one should not, one can't; здесь кури́ть ~ smoking is not allowed here; как ~ лу́чше in the best possible way.

не... **нелюбе́зный** ungracious; discourteous. **нелюби́мый** unloved. **нелюди́м**, -а, **нелюди́мка**, -и unsociable person. **нелюди́мый** unsociable; unpeopled, lonely. **нема́ло** *adv.* not a little, not a few; a considerable amount or number. **немалова́жный** of no small importance. **нема́лый** no small, considerable. **неме́дленно** *adv.* immediately, at once, without delay. **неме́дленный** immediate.

неме́ть, -е́ю *impf.* (*pf.* за~, о~) become dumb; grow numb. **не́мец**, -мца German. **неме́цк|ий** German; ~ая овча́рка Alsation (*dog*).

неми́лость, -и disgrace, disfavour.

немину́емый inevitable, unavoidable.

не́мка, -и German.

немно́г|ий a little; not much; (a) few; ~ие *sb.*, *pl.* few, a few. **немно́го** *adv.* a little; some, not much; a few; somewhat, slightly. **немногосло́вный** laconic, brief, terse. **немно́жко** *adv.* a little, a bit, a trifle.

немну́щийся uncrushable, crease-resistant.

нем|о́й; нем, -а́, -о dumb, mute, (utterly) silent; ~о́й а́збука deaf-and-dumb alphabet; ~о́й согла́сный voiceless consonant; ~о́й фильм silent film. **немота́**, -ы́ dumbness. **не́мощный** feeble, ill, sick. **не́мощь**, -и sickness; feebleness, infirmity.

ненави́деть, -и́жу *impf.* hate, detest, loathe. **ненави́стник**, -а a hater. **ненави́стный** hated, hateful. **не́нависть**, -и hatred.

не... **ненагля́дный** dear, beloved. **ненадёжный** insecure; unreliable, untrustworthy. **нена́добность**, -и uselessness. **ненадо́лго** *adv.* for a short time, not for long. **ненападе́ние**, -я non-aggression. **ненаруши́мый** inviolable. **ненаси́лие**, -я non-violence. **ненаси́льственный** non-violent. **нена́стный** bad, foul, rainy. **нена́стье**, -я bad weather, wet weather. **ненастоя́щий** artificial, imitation, counterfeit. **ненасы́тный** insatiable. **ненорма́льность**, -и abnormality. **ненорма́льный** abnormal; deranged. **нену́жный** unnecessary, superfluous.

нео... *pref.* neo-. **неозо́йский** neozoic. ~**класси́цизм**, -а neo-classicism. ~**колониали́зм**, -а neo-colonialism. ~**фаши́стский** neo-fascist. ~**фи́т**, -а neophyte.

не... **необду́манный** thoughtless, hasty, precipitate. **необеспе́ченный** without means, unprovided for, not provided (with). **необита́емый** uninhabited; ~ о́стров desert island. **необозна́ченный** not indicated, not marked. **необозри́мый** boundless, immense. **необосно́ванный** unfounded, groundless. **необрабо́танный** uncultivated, untilled; raw, crude; unpolished, untrained. **необразо́ванный** uneducated. **необу́зданный** unbridled, ungovernable. **необу́ченный** untrained.

необходи́мость, -и necessity; по необходи́мости of necessity, perforce. **необходи́мый** necessary, essential.

не... **необъясни́мый** inexplicable, unaccountable. **необъя́тный** immense, unbounded. **необыкнове́нный** unusual, uncommon. **необыча́йный** extraordinary, exceptional, unaccustomed. **необы́чный** unusual, singular. **необяза́тельный** optional. **неограни́ченный** unlimited, absolute. **неодно-кра́тно** *adv.* repeatedly, more than once. **неоднокра́тный** repeated. **неодобре́ние**, -я disapproval. **неодобри́тельный** disapproving. **неодушевлённый** inanimate.

неожи́данность, -и unexpectedness, suddenness; surprise. **неожи́данный** unexpected, sudden.

не... неоконча́тельный inconclusive. **неоко́нченный** unfinished. **неопису́емый** indescribable. **неопла́тный** that cannot be repaid; insolvent. **неопла́ченный** unpaid. **неопра́вданный** unjustified, unwarranted. **неопределённый** indefinite, indeterminate; infinitive; vague, uncertain. **неопредели́мый** indefinable. **неопроверж́имый** irrefutable; incontestable. **неопря́тный** slovenly, untidy, sloppy. **неопублико́ванный** unpublished. **нео́пытность, -и** inexperience. **нео́пытный** inexperienced. **неосведомлённый** ill-informed. **неосе́длый** nomadic. **неосла́бный** unremitting, unabated, untiring. **неосмотри́тельный** imprudent, incautious; indiscreet. **неоснова́тельный** unfounded, unwarranted; frivolous. **неоспори́мый** unquestionable, incontestable, indisputable. **неосторо́жный** careless, imprudent, indiscreet, incautious. **неосуществи́мый** impracticable, unrealizable. **неося́заемый** intangible. **неотврати́мый** inevitable. **неотвя́зный, неотвя́зчивый** importunate; obsessive. **неотёсанный** rough, undressed; unpolished, uncouth. **не́откуда** adv. there is nowhere; there is no reason; мне ~ э́то получи́ть there is nowhere I can get it from.

не... неотло́жн|ый urgent, pressing; ~ая по́мощь first aid. **неотлу́чно** adv. constantly, continually, unremittingly; permanent. **неотлу́чный** continual, constant, permanent. **неотрази́мый** irresistible; incontrovertible, irrefutable. **неотсту́пный** persistent, importunate. **неотъе́млемый** inalienable; inseparable, integral. **неохо́та, -ы** reluctance. **неохо́тно** adv. reluctantly; unwillingly. **неоцени́мый** inestimable, invaluable. **неощути́мый** imperceptible. **непа́рный** odd. **непарти́йный** non-party; unbefitting a member of the (Communist) Party. **непереводи́мый** untranslatable. **непередава́емый** incommunicable, inexpressible. **непереходно́й** intransitive. **непеча́тный** unprintable.

неплатёж, -ежа́ non-payment. **неплатёжеспосо́бный** insolvent. **неплате́льщик, -а** defaulter; person in arrears.

не... неплодоро́дный infertile. **непло́хо** adv. not badly, quite well. **неплохо́й** not bad, quite good. **непобеди́мый** invincible. **неповинове́ние, -я** insubordination, disobedience. **неповоро́тливый** clumsy, awkward; sluggish, slow. **неповтори́мый** inimitable, unique. **непого́да, -ы** bad weather. **непогреши́мый** infallible. **неподалёку** adv. not far(away). **неподат́ливый** stubborn, intractable, unyielding. **неподви́жный** motionless, immobile, immovable; fixed, stationary. **неподде́льный**

genuine; sincere, unfeigned. **неподку́пный** incorruptible, unbribable. **неподража́емый** inimitable. **неподходя́щий** unsuitable, inappropriate. **непоко́йный** troubled, disturbed, restless. **непоколеби́мый** unshakable, steadfast. **непоко́рный** recalcitrant, unruly, insubordinate. **непокры́тый** uncovered, bare.

не... непола́дки, -док pl. defects. **неполноце́нность, -и; ко́мплекс неполноце́нности** inferiority complex. **неполноце́нный** defective, imperfect; inadequate. **непо́лный** incomplete; defective; not quite, not (a) full. **непоме́рный** excessive, inordinate. **непонима́ние, -я** incomprehension, lack of understanding. **непоня́тливый** slow-witted, stupid, dull. **непоня́тный** unintelligible, incomprehensible. **непоправи́мый** irreparable, irremediable. **непоря́док, -дка** disorder. **непоря́дочный** dishonourable. **непосвящённый** uninitiated. **непосе́да, -ы** c.g. fidget, restless person. **непоси́льный** beyond one's strength, excessive. **непосле́довательный** inconsistent; inconsequent. **непослуша́ние, -я** disobedience. **непослу́шный** disobedient, naughty. **непосре́дственный** immediate, direct; spontaneous; ingenuous. **непостижи́мый** incomprehensible. **непостоя́нный** inconstant, changeable. **непостоя́нство, -а** inconstancy. **непотопля́емый** unsinkable. **непотре́бный** obscene, indecent; useless; bad. **непоча́тый** untouched, not begun; ~ край, у́гол a lot, a wealth, no end. **непочте́ние, -я** disrespect. **непочти́тельный** disrespectful.

не... непра́вда, -ы untruth, falsehood, lie. **неправдоподо́бие, -я** improbability, unlikelihood. **неправдоподо́бный** improbable, unlikely, implausible. **непра́вильно** adv. wrong; irregularly; incorrectly; erroneously. **непра́вильность, -и** irregularity; anomaly; incorrectness. **непра́вильн|ый** irregular; anomalous; incorrect, erroneous, wrong, mistaken; ~ая дробь improper fraction. **неправомо́чный** incompetent; not entitled. **неправоспосо́бный** disqualified. **неправота́, -ы́** error; injustice. **непра́вый** wrong, mistaken; unjust. **непракти́чный** unpractical. **непревзойдённый** unsurpassed, matchless. **непредви́денный** unforeseen. **непредубеждённый** unprejudiced. **непредусмо́тренный** unforeseen; unprovided for. **непредусмотри́тельный** improvident, short-sighted. **непрекло́нный** inflexible, unbending; inexorable, adamant. **непрело́жный** immutable, unalterable; indisputable.

не... непреме́нно adv. without fail; certainly; absolutely. **непреме́нный** indispensable, necessary; ~ секрета́рь permanent secretary. **непреодоли́мый** insuperable, insurmountable; irresistible. **непреры́вно** adv. uninterruptedly, continuously. **непреры́вный** uninterrupted, unbroken; continuous. **непрестанный** incessant, continual. **неприветливый** unfriendly, ungracious; bleak. **непривлекательный** unattractive. **непривычный** unaccustomed, unwonted, unusual. **неприглядный** unattractive, unsightly. **непригодный** unfit, unserviceable, useless; ineligible. **неприемлемый** unacceptable. **неприкосновенность, -и** inviolability, immunity. **неприкосновенный** inviolable; to be kept intact; reserve, emergency. **неприкрашенный** plain, unadorned, unvarnished. **неприличный** indecent, improper; unseemly, unbecoming. **неприменимый** inapplicable. **непримиримый** irreconcilable. **непринуждённый** unconstrained; natural, relaxed, easy; spontaneous. **неприспособленный** unadapted; maladjusted. **непристойный** obscene, indecent. **неприступный** inaccessible, impregnable; unapproachable, haughty. **непритворный** unfeigned. **непритязательный, неприхотливый** modest, unpretentious, simple, plain. **неприязненный** hostile, inimical. **неприязнь, -и** hostility, enmity. **неприятель, -я** *m.* enemy. **неприятельский** hostile, enemy. **неприятный** unpleasant, disagreeable; annoying, troublesome; obnoxious.

не... **непроверенный** unverified, unchecked. **непроводник, -а** non-conductor. **непроводящий** non-conducting. **непроглядный** impenetrable; pitch-dark. **непродолжительный** short, short-lived. **непродуманный** rash, unconsidered. **непроезжий** impassable. **непрозрачный** opaque. **непроизводительный** unproductive; wasteful. **непроизвольный** involuntary. **непролазный** impassable, impenetrable. **непромокаемый** waterproof. **непроницаемый** impenetrable, impervious; inscrutable; +для+g. proof against. **непростительный** unforgivable, unpardonable, inexcusable. **непроходимый** impassable; complete, utter, hopeless. **непрочный; -чен, -чна, -о** fragile, flimsy; precarious, unstable; not durable. **не прочь** *pred.* not averse; я ∼ пойти туда I wouldn't mind going there.

не... **непрошеный** uninvited, unasked(-for). **неработоспособный** incapacitated, disabled. **нерабочий** ∼ день day of rest, free day. **неравенство, -а** inequality, disparity. **неравномерный** uneven, irregular. **неравный** unequal. **нерадивый** negligent, indolent, careless, remiss. **неразбериха, -и** muddle, confusion. **неразборчивый** not fastidious; unscrupulous; illegible. **неразвитой; -развит, -а, -о** undeveloped; backward. **неразговорчивый** taciturn, not talkative. **неразделимый, нераздельный** indivisible, inseparable. **неразличимый** indistinguishable. **неразлучный** inseparable. **неразрешённый** unsolved; forbidden, prohibited. **неразрешимый** insoluble. **нераз-**

рывный indissoluble, inseparable. **неразумный** unwise, unreasonable. **нерасположение, -я** dislike; disinclination. **нерасположенный** ill-disposed; unwilling, disinclined. **нерастворимый** insoluble. **нерасчётливый** extravagant, wasteful; improvident.

нерв, -а nerve; **главный** ∼ nerve-centre. **нервировать, -рую** *impf.* get on s.o.'s nerves, irritate. **нервничать, -аю** *impf.* be fidgety, fret; be irritable. **нервический** nervous. **нервнобольной** *sb.* neurotic, nervous case. **нервный; -вен, -вна, -о** nervous; neural; irritable, highly strung; ∼ **узел** ganglion. **нервозный** nervy, irritable, excitable. **нервюра, -ы** rib.

не... **нереальный** unreal; unrealistic. **нередкий; -док, -дка, -о** not infrequent, not uncommon. **нередко** not infrequently. **нерешимость, -и, нерешительность, -и** indecision; irresolution. **нерешительный** indecisive, irresolute, undecided. **нержавеющий** rustless; ∼**ая сталь** stainless steel. **неровный; -вен, -вна, -о** uneven, rough; unequal, irregular. **нерукотворный** not made with hands. **нерушимый** inviolable, indestructible, indissoluble.

неряха, -и *c.g.* sloven; slattern, slut. **неряшливый** slovenly, untidy, slatternly; careless, slipshod.

не... **несбыточн|ый** unrealizable; ∼**ые мечты** castles in the air; ∼**ые надежды** vain hopes. **несварение, -я;** ∼ **желудка** indigestion. **несвежий; -еж, -а** not fresh; stale; tainted; weary, washed-out. **несвоевременный** ill-timed, inopportune; overdue, not at the right time. **несвойственный** not characteristic, unusual, unlike. **несвязный** disconnected, incoherent. **несгибаемый** unbending, inflexible. **несговорчивый** intractable. **несгораемый** fireproof; ∼ **шкаф** safe.

несессер, -а dressing-case.

нескладный incoherent; ungainly, awkward; absurd.

несклоняемый indeclinable.

несколько, -их *pron.* some, several; a number, a few; *adv.* somewhat, a little, rather.

не... **нескончаемый** interminable, never-ending. **нескромный; -мен, -мна, -о** immodest; vain; indelicate, tactless, indiscreet. **несложный** simple. **неслыханный** unheard-of, unprecedented. **неслышный** inaudible; noiseless. **несметный** countless, incalculable, innumerable. **несминаемый** uncrushable, crease-resistant. **несмолкаемый** ceaseless, unremitting.

несмотря на *prep.+a.* in spite of, despite, notwithstanding.

не... **несносный** intolerable, insupportable, unbearable. **несоблюдение, -я** non-observance. **несовершеннолетие, -я** minority.

несовершеннолéтний under-age; *sb.* minor. несовершéнный imperfect, incomplete; imperfective. несовмести́мость, -и incompatibility. несовмести́мый incompatible. несоглáсие, -я disagreement, difference; discord, variance; refusal. несоглáсный not agreeing; inconsistent, incompatible; discordant; not consenting. несогласовáние, -я non-agreement. несоглáсо́ванный uncoordinated. несознáтельный irresponsible. несоизмери́мый incommensurable. несокруши́мый indestructible; unconquerable. несóлоно; уйти́ ~ хлебáвши get nothing for one's pains, go away empty-handed. несомнéнно *adv.* undoubtedly, doubtless, beyond question. несомнéнный undoubted, indubitable, unquestionable. несообрáзный incongruous, incompatible; absurd. несоотвéтствие, -я disparity, incongruity. несоразмéрный disproportionate. несостоя́тельный insolvent, bankrupt; not wealthy, of modest means; groundless, unsupported. неспéлый unripe. неспокóйный restless; uneasy. неспосóбный dull, not able; incapable, not competent. несправедли́вый unjust, unfair; incorrect, unfounded. неспростá *adv.* not without purpose; with an ulterior motive. несравнéнно *adv.* incomparably, matchlessly; far, by far. несравнéнный; -éнен, -éнна incomparable, matchless. несравни́мый not comparable; incomparable, unmatched. нестерпи́мый unbearable, unendurable.

нести́, -сý, -сёшь; нёс, -лá *impf.* (*pf.* по~, с~) carry; bear; bring, take; support; suffer; incur; perform; talk; lay; *impers.+i.* stink of, reek of; ~сь rush, tear, fly; float, drift, be carried; skim; spread, be diffused; lay, lay eggs.

не... нестóйкий unstable. нестроеви́к, -á non-combatant. нестроевóй non-combatant. нестрóйный; -óен, -óйнá, -о discordant, dissonant; disorderly; clumsily built. несудохóдный unnavigable. несущéственный immaterial, inessential.

несý *etc.*: *see* нести́. несýщий supporting, carrying, bearing, lifting.

несхóдный unlike, dissimilar; unreasonable.

несчастли́вец, -вца, -вица, -ы unlucky person; unfortunate. несчастли́вый unfortunate, unlucky; unhappy. несчáстный unhappy, unfortunate, unlucky; *sb.* wretch, unfortunate; к несчáстью unfortunately.

несчётный innumerable, countless.

нет *part.* no, not; nothing; ~ да ~, ~ как ~ absolutely not; свести́ на ~ bring to naught; ~~~ да и from time to time, every now and then. нет, нéту there is not, there are not.

не... нетакти́чный tactless. нетвёрдый; -ёрд, -á, -о unsteady, shaky; not firm. нетерпели́вый impatient. нетерпéние, -я impa-

tience. нетерпи́мый intolerable, intolerant. нетóчный; -чен, -чнá, -о inaccurate, inexact. нетрадициóнный unconventional. нетрéбовательный not exacting, undemanding; unpretentious. нетрéзвый drunk, intoxicated. нетрóнутый untouched; chaste, virginal. нетрудовóй; ~ дохóд unearned income. нетрудоспосóбность, -и disablement, disability.

нéтто *indecl. adj. & adv.* net, nett.

нéту *see* нет

не... неубеди́тельный unconvincing. неуважéние, -я disrespect. неуважи́тельный inadequate; disrespectful. неувéренный uncertain; hesitant; ~ в себé diffident. неувядáемый, неувядáющий unfading, eternal, immortal. неувя́зка, -и lack of coordination; misunderstanding. неугаси́мый inextinguishable, unquenchable; never extinguished. неугомóнный restless; unsleeping, indefatigable. неудáча, -и failure. неудáчливый unlucky. неудáчник, -а, -ница, -ы unlucky person, failure. неудáчный unsuccessful, unfortunate. неудержи́мый irrepressible. неудóбный uncomfortable; inconvenient, awkward, embarrassing. неудóбство, -а discomfort, inconvenience, embarrassment. неудовлетворéние, -я dissatisfaction. неудовлетворённый dissatisfied, discontented. неудовлетвори́тельный unsatisfactory. неудовóльствие, -я displeasure.

неужéли? *part.* indeed? really? surely not? ~ он так дýмает? does he really think that? не... неузнавáемый unrecognizable. неуклóнный steady, steadfast; undeviating, unswerving, strict. неуклю́жий clumsy, awkward. неукроти́мый ungovernable, untameable. неукрощённый; -ён, -á untamed. неулови́мый elusive, difficult to catch; imperceptible, subtle. неумéлый unskilful; clumsy. неумéренный immoderate; excessive. неумéстный inappropriate; out of place, misplaced; irrelevant. неумоли́мый implacable, inexorable. неумы́шленный unintentional.

не... неуплáта, -ы non-payment. неупотреби́тельный not in use, not current. неуравновéшенный unbalanced. неурожáй, -я bad harvest, crop failure. неурóчный untimely, unseasonable, inopportune. неуряди́ца, -ы disorder, mess; squabbling, squabble. неуспевáемость, -и poor progress; underachievement. неуспевáющий backward; underachieving. неуспéх, -а failure. неустóйка, -и forfeit, penalty; failure. неустóйчивый unstable; unsteady. неустраши́мый fearless, intrepid. неуступчи́вый unyielding, uncompromising. неусы́пный vigilant, unremitting. неутéшный inconsolable, disconsolate. неутоли́мый unquenchable; unappeasable; insatiable. неутоми́мый tireless, indefatigable. нéуч, -а ignoramus.

неучти́вый discourteous, impolite. **неуязви́мый** invulnerable; unassailable.

неф, -а nave.

нефри́т, -а jade.

нефте... in comb. oil, petroleum. **нефтево́з, -а** tanker. **~но́сный** oil-bearing. **~перего́нный заво́д** oil refinery. **~прово́д, -а** (oil) pipeline. **~проду́кты, -ов** pl. petroleum products. **~та́нкер, -а** oil-tanker (ship). **~хими́ческий** petrochemical.

нефть, -и oil, petroleum; **~сыре́ц** crude oil. **нефтян|о́й** oil, petroleum; oil-fired; **~о́е покрыва́ло, -а́я плёнка** oil-slick.

не... **нехва́тка, -и** shortage, deficiency. **нехорошо́** adv. badly. **нехоро́ш|ий; -о́ш, -а́** bad; **~о́** it is bad, it is wrong; **как ~о́!** what a shame!; **чу́вствовать себя́ ~о́** feel unwell. **не́хотя** adv. reluctantly, unwillingly; unintentionally. **нецелесообра́зн|ый** inexpedient; purposeless, pointless; **~ая тра́та** waste. **нецензу́рный** unprintable. **неча́янный** unexpected; accidental; unintentional.

не́чего, не́чему, ~чем, не́ о чем pron. (with separate pref.) (there is) nothing; it's no good, it's no use; there is no need; **~ де́лать** there is nothing to be done; it can't be helped; **~ сказа́ть!** well, really! well, I must say!; **от ~ де́лать** for want of something better to do, idly.

нечелове́ческий inhuman, superhuman.

нече́стивый impious, profane. **нече́стно** adv. dishonestly, unfairly. **нече́стный** dishonest, unfair.

не́чет, -а odd number. **нечётный** odd.

нечистопло́тный dirty; slovenly; unscrupulous. **нечистота́, -ы́;** pl. **-о́ты, -о́т** dirtiness, dirt, filth; pl. sewage. **нечи́стый; -и́ст, -а́, -о** dirty, unclean; impure; adulterated; careless, inaccurate; dishonourable, dishonest; sb. the evil one, the devil. **не́чисть, -и** evil spirits; scum, vermin.

нечленоразде́льный inarticulate.

не́что pron. something.

не... pref. **нешу́точн|ый** grave, serious; **~ое де́ло** no joke, no laughing matter. **неща́дный** merciless, pitiless. **ненвка, -и** non-appearance, absence. **неядови́тый** non-poisonous, non-toxic. **ненсный; -сен, -сна́, -о** unclear; vague, obscure.

ни part. not a; **ни оди́н (одна́, одно́)** not one, not a single; (with prons. and pronominal advs.) -ever; **как... ни** however; **кто... ни** whoever; **что... ни** whatever; **како́й ни на есть** any whatsoever. **ни** conj.; **ни... ни** neither ... nor; **ни за что ни про что** for no reason, without rhyme or reason; **ни ры́ба ни мя́со** neither fish, flesh, nor good red herring; **ни с того́, ни с сего́** all of a sudden, for no apparent reason; **ни то ни сё** neither one thing nor the other.

ни́ва, -ы cornfield, field.

нивели́р, -а level. **нивели́ровать, -рую** impf. & pf. level; survey, contour. **ниве-**

лиро́вщик, -а surveyor.

нигде́ adv. nowhere.

нидерла́ндец, -дца; g.pl. **-дцев** Dutchman. **нидерла́ндка, -и** Dutchwoman. **нидерла́ндский** Dutch.

Нидерла́нды, -ов pl. the Netherlands.

нижа́йший lowest, humblest; very low, very humble. **ни́же** adj. lower, humbler; adv. below; prep.+g. below, beneath. **нижеподписа́вшийся** (the) undersigned. **нижеследу́ющий** following. **нижестоя́щий** subordinate. **нижеупомя́нутый** (the) undermentioned. **ни́жн|ий** lower, under-; **~ее бельё** underclothes; **~ий эта́ж** ground floor. **низ, -а (-у),** loc. **-у́;** pl. **-ы́** bottom; ground floor; pl. lower classes; low notes.

низ..., нис... vbl. pref. down, downward(s).

низа́ть, нижу́, ни́жешь impf. (pf. **на~**) string, thread.

низверга́ть, -а́ю impf., **низве́ргнуть, -ну; -е́рг** pf. precipitate; throw down, overthrow; **~ся** crash down; be overthrown. **низверже́ние, -я** overthrow.

низи́на, -ы depression, hollow. **ни́зкий; -зок, -зка́, -о** low; humble; base, mean. **ни́зко** adv. low; basely, meanly, despicably. **низкопокло́нник, -а** a toady, crawler. **низкопокло́нничать, -аю** impf. crawl, cringe, grovel. **низкопокло́нство, -а** obsequiousness, cringing, servility. **низкопро́бный** base; low-grade; inferior. **низкоро́слый** undersized, stunted, dwarfish. **низкосо́ртный** low-grade, of inferior quality.

ни́зменность, -и lowland; baseness. **ни́зменный** low-lying; low, base, vile.

низово́й lower; down-stream; from lower down the Volga; local. **низо́вье, -я;** g.pl. **-ьев** the lower reaches; **низо́вья Во́лги** the lower Volga. **ни́зость, -и** lowness; baseness, meanness. **ни́зш|ий** lower, lowest; **~ее образова́ние** primary education; **~ий сорт** inferior quality.

никако́й pron. no; no ... whatever

ни́кель, -я m. nickel.

нике́м see **никто́. никогда́** adv. never. **ник|о́й** no; **~о́им о́бразом** by no means, in no way. **никто́, -кого́, -кому́, -ке́м, ни о ко́м** pron. (with separable pref.) nobody, no one. **никуда́** nowhere; **~ не годи́тся** (it) is worthless, (it) is no good at all, (it) won't do. **никуды́шный** useless, worthless, good-for-nothing. **никчёмный** pointless, useless; no good. **нима́ло** adv. not at all, not in the least.

нимб, -а halo, nimbus.

ни́мфа, -ы nymph; pupa. **нимфома́нка, -и** nymphomaniac.

ниотку́да adv. from nowhere; not from anywhere.

нипочём adv. it is nothing; for nothing, dirt cheap; never, in no circumstances.

ни́ппель, -я; pl. **-я** nipple.

нис... *see* низ...

ниско́лько *adv.* not at all, not in the least.

ниспроверга́ть, -а́ю *impf.*, ниспрове́ргнуть, -ну; -е́рг *pf.* overthrow, overturn. ниспроверже́ние, -я overthrow.

нисходя́щий descending, of descent; falling.

ни́тка, -и thread; string; до ни́тки to the skin; на живу́ю ни́тку hastily, carelessly, anyhow. ни́точка, -и thread. ни́точный thread; spinning.

нитро... *in comb.* nitro-. нитробензо́л, -а nitrobenzene. ~глицери́н, -а nitroglycerine. ~клетча́тка, -и nitrocellulose.

ни́тчатый filiform. нить, -и thread; filament; suture; (путево́дная) ~ clue. нитяно́й, ни́тяный cotton, thread.

Ни́цца, -ы Nice.

ничего́ *etc.: see* ничто́. ничего́ *adv.* all right; so-so, passably, not too badly; *as indecl. adj.* not bad, passable. ниче́й, -чья́, -чьё *pron.* nobody's, no-one's; ничья́ земля́ no man's land. ничья́ *sb.* draw, drawn game; tie; dead heat.

ничко́м *adv.* face downwards, prone.

ничто́, -чего́, -чему́, -чём, ни о чём *pron.* (*with separable pref.*) nothing; naught; nil; ничего́! that's all right! it doesn't matter! never mind! ничто́жество, -а a nonentity, nobody; nothingness. ничто́жный insignificant; paltry, worthless.

ничу́ть *adv.* not at all, not in the least, not a bit.

ничьё *etc.: see* ниче́й

ни́ша, -и niche, recess; bay.

ни́щенка, -и beggar-woman. ни́щенский beggarly. ни́щенствовать, -твую *impf.* beg, be a beggar; be destitute. нищета́, -ы́ destitution, indigence, poverty; beggars, the poor. ни́щий; нищ, -а́, -е destitute, indigent, poverty-stricken, poor; *sb.* beggar, mendicant, pauper.

НЛО *abbr.* (*of* неопо́знанный лета́ющий объе́кт) UFO, unidentified flying object.

но *conj.* but; still, nevertheless; *sb.* snag, difficulty.

но *int.* gee up!

нова́тор, -а innovator. нова́торство, -а innovation.

Но́вая Зела́ндия, -ой -и New Zealand.

нове́йший newest, latest.

нове́лла, -ы short story. новелли́ст, -а short-story writer.

но́веньк|ий brand-new; ~ий, ~ая *sb.* new boy, new girl.

новизна́, -ы́ novelty; newness. нови́нка, -и novelty. новичо́к, -чка́ novice, beginner, tyro; new recruit, new boy, new girl.

но́во... *in comb.* new, newly; recent, recently; modern. новобра́нец, -нца new recruit. ~бра́чный bridegroom; ~бра́чная bride; ~бра́чные *sb., pl.* newly-weds. ~введе́ние, -я innovation. ~го́дний new year's, new-year. ~зела́ндец, -дца; *g.pl.* -дцев,

~зела́ндка, -и New-Zealander. ~зела́ндский New Zealand. ~лу́ние, -я new moon. ~мо́дный up-to-date, fashionable; new-fangled. ~прибы́вший newly-arrived; *sb.* newcomer. ~рождённый newborn; *sb.* neonate. ~сёл, -а, ~сёлка, -и new settler. ~се́лье, -я new home; house-warming.

но́вость, -и news; novelty. но́вшество, -а innovation, novelty. но́вый; нов, -а́, -о new, novel, fresh; modern, recent; ~ год New Year's Day. новь, -и virgin soil.

нога́, -и́, *a.* но́гу; *pl.* но́ги, нога́м foot, leg; без (за́дних) ног dead beat; встать с ле́вой ноги́ get out of bed on the wrong side; дать но́гу get in step; идти́ в но́гу c+*i.* keep in step with; на коро́ткой ноге́ c+*i.* intimate with, on good terms with; на широ́кую (большу́ю, ба́рскую) но́гу in style, like a lord; протяну́ть но́ги turn up one's toes; сбить с ног knock down; сби́ться с ноги́ get out of step; со всех ног as fast as one's legs will carry one; стать на́ ноги, стоя́ть на нога́х stand on one's own feet.

ного́ть, -гтя́ nail; marigold. но́готь, -гтя *pl.* -и *m.* finger-nail, toe-nail.

нож, -а́ knife; на ~а́х at daggers drawn. ножев|о́й knife; ~ы́е изде́лия, ~о́й това́р cutlery; ~о́й ма́стер cutler.

но́жка, -и small foot or leg; leg; stem, stalk.

но́жницы, -иц *pl.* scissors, shears.

ножно́й foot, pedal, treadle.

но́жны, -жен *pl.* sheath, scabbard.

ножо́вка, -и saw, hacksaw.

ножо́вщик, -а cutler.

ноздрева́тый porous, spongy. ноздря́, -и́; *pl.* -и, -е́й nostril.

нока́ут, -а knock-out. нокаути́ровать, -рую *impf. & pf.* knock out.

нолево́й, нулево́й zero. ноль, -я́, нуль, -я́ *m.* nought, zero, nil, love; cipher; абсолю́тный ~ absolute zero; в семна́дцать ~~ at seventeen hundred hours, at five p.m.

но́мер, -а; *pl.* -а́ number; size; (hotel-)room; item, turn; trick. номера́тор *etc.: see* нуме́ра́тор *etc.* номерно́й *sb.* floor waiter, hotel servant. номеро́к, -рка́ tag; label, ticket; small room.

номина́л, -а face value. номина́льный nominal; rated, indicated.

нора́, -ы́; *pl.* -ы burrow, hole; lair, form.

Норве́гия, -и Norway. норве́жец, -жца, норве́жка, -и Norwegian. норве́жский Norwegian.

норд, -а north; north wind. норд-ве́ст, -а north-west, north-wester. норд-о́ст, -а north-east, north-easter.

но́рка, -и mink.

но́рма, -ы standard, norm; rate; ~ вре́мени time limit. нормализа́ция, -и standardization. нормализова́ть, -зу́ю *impf. & pf.* standardize. норма́льный normal; standard.

Норма́ндск|ий; ~ие острова́ *pl.* the Channel Islands.

норматив, -а norm, standard **нормирова́ние**, -я, **нормиро́вка**, -и regulation, normalization; rate-fixing. **нормирова́ть**, -ру́ю *impf. & pf.* regulate, standardize, normalize. **нормиро́вщик**, -а, -щица, -ы rate-fixer, rate-setter.

нос, -а (-у), *loc.* -у́; *pl.* -ы́ nose; beak; bow, prow; **на** ~у́ near (at hand), imminent; **оста́вить с** ~ом dupe, make a fool of; **пове́сить** ~ be crestfallen, be discouraged. **но́сик**, -а (small) nose; toe; spout.

носи́лки, -лок *pl.* stretcher; litter; hand-barrow. **носи́льщик**, -а porter. **носи́тель**, -я *m.*, **-тельница**, -ы bearer; carrier; vehicle. **носи́ть**, -ошу́, -о́сишь *impf.* carry, bear; wear; ~ **на рука́х** make much of, make a fuss of, spoil; ~ся rush, tear along, fly; float, drift, be carried; wear; +c+*i.* make much of, make a fuss of. **но́ска**, -и carrying, bearing, wearing; laying. **но́ский** hard-wearing, durable; laying, that lays well.

носово́й of or for the nose; nasal; bow, fore; ~ **плато́к** (pocket) handkerchief. **носо́к**, -ска́ little nose; toe; sock. **носоро́г**, -а rhinoceros.

но́та, -ы note; *pl.* music.

нота́риус, -а notary.

нота́ция, -и notation; lecture, reprimand.

ночева́ть, -чу́ю *impf.* (*pf.* **пере**~) spend the night. **ночёвка**, -и spending the night. **ночле́г**, -а shelter for the night, a night's lodging; passing the night. **ночле́жка**, -и, **ночле́жный дом** doss-house, common lodging-house. **ночни́к**, -а́ night-light. **ночн|о́й** night, nocturnal; ~**а́я ба́бочка** moth; ~**а́я руба́шка** nightdress, nightgown, nightshirt; ~**о́й сто́лик** bedside table; ~**ые ту́фли** bedroom slippers. **ночь**, -и, *loc.* -и́; *g.pl.* -е́й night; **глуха́я** ~ dead of night. **но́чью** *adv.* at night, by night.

но́ша, -и burden. **но́шеный** in use, worn; part-worn, second-hand.

но́ю *etc.: see* **ныть**

ноя́брь, -я́ *m.* November. **ноя́брьский** November.

нрав, -а disposition, temper; *pl.* manners, customs, ways; **по** ~у to one's taste, pleasing. **нра́виться**, -влюсь *impf.* (*pf.* **по**~) +*d.* please; **мне нра́вится** I like. **нравоуче́ние**, -я moralizing, moral lecture; moral. **нравоучи́тельный** edifying. **нра́вственность**, -и morality, morals. **нра́вственный** moral.

н. ст. *abbr.* (*of* **но́вый стиль**) NS, New Style (*of calendar*).

ну *int. & part.* well, well then; what?; really; what a ..!; there's a ..!; **а ну́**+*g.* to hell with; **(да) ну́?** not really?; **ну́ как**+*fut.* suppose, what if?

ну́дный tedious, boring.

нужда́, -ы́; *pl.* -ы want, straits; need; indigence; necessity; call of nature; **нужды́ нет** never mind, it doesn't matter. **нужда́ться**, -а́юсь *impf.* be in want, be poor, be hard up;

+в+*p.* need, require, want. **ну́жник**, -а lavatory, public convenience, latrine. **ну́жн|ый**; -жен, -жна́, -о, **ну́жны́** necessary, requisite; ~**о** it is necessary; +*d.* I, *etc.*, must, ought to, should, need.

нуклеи́новый nucleic.

нулево́й, нуль *see* **нолево́й, ноль**

нумера́тор, ном-, -а numberer, numbering machine; annunciation. **нумера́ция, ном-**, -и numeration; numbering. **нумерова́ть, ном-**, -ру́ю *impf.* (*pf.* **за**~, **про**~) number.

нутро́, -а́ inside, interior; core, kernel; instinct(s), intuition; **всем** ~**м** with one's whole being, completely; **по нутру́**+*d.* to the liking of. **нутряно́й** internal.

ны́не *adv.* now; today. **ны́нешний** the present, this; today's. **ны́нче** *adv.* today; now.

нырну́ть, -ну́, -нёшь *pf.*, **ныря́ть**, -я́ю *impf.* dive, plunge; duck. **ныро́к**, -рка́ dive, plunge; duck, ducking; diver. **ныря́ло**, -а plunger.

ны́тик, -а whiner, moaner. **ныть**, **но́ю** *impf.* ache; whine, moan. **нытьё**, -я́ whining, moaning.

Нью-Йо́рк, -а New York.

н.э. *abbr.* (*of* **на́шей э́ры**) AD; **до н. э.** BC.

нюх, -а scent; nose, flair. **ню́хательный таба́к** snuff. **ню́хать**, -аю *impf.* (*pf.* **по**~) smell, sniff; ~ **таба́к** take snuff.

ня́нчить, -чу *impf.* nurse, look after; dandle; ~ся c+*i.* be nurse to, act as nurse to; fuss over, make a fuss of. **ня́нька**, -и nanny. **ня́ня**, -и (*children's*) nurse, nanny; hospital nurse; **приходя́щая** ~ babysitter; childminder.

О

о *nt.indecl.* the letter o.

о, об, обо *prep.* **I.** +*p.* of, about, concerning; on; with, having; **стол о трёх но́жках** a three-legged table. **II.** +*a.* against; on, upon; **бок о бок** side by side; **опере́ться о сте́ну** lean against the wall; **рука́ о́б руку** hand in hand; **споткну́ться о ка́мень** stumble against a stone. **III.** +*a. or p.* on, at, about; **об э́ту по́ру** about this time; **о заре́** about dawn.

о *int.* oh!

о. *abbr.* (*of* **о́стров**) Is., Island, Isle.

о..., об..., обо..., объ... *vbl. pref. indicates transformation, process of becoming, action applied to entire surface of object or to series of objects.*

об *see* **о** *prep.*

об..., обо..., объ... *vbl. pref.* = **о...** *or indicates action or motion about an object.*

óба, обо́их *m.* & *nt.*, о́бе, обе́их *f.* both; обе́ими рука́ми with both hands; very willingly, readily; смотре́ть в óба keep one's eyes open, be on one's guard.

обагри́ть, -рю́ *pf.*, обагря́ть, -я́ю *impf.* crimson, incarnadine; ~ кро́вью stain with blood; ~ ру́ки в крови́ steep one's hands in blood; ~ся be crimsoned; ~ся (кро́вью) be stained with blood.

обалдева́ть, -а́ю *impf.*, обалде́ть, -е́ю *pf.* go crazy; become dulled; be stunned.

обанкро́титься, -о́чусь *pf.* go bankrupt.

обая́ние, -я fascination, charm. обая́тельный fascinating, charming.

обва́л, -a fall, falling, crumbling; collapse; caving-in; landslide; (сне́жный) ~ avalanche. обва́ливать(ся, -аю(сь *impf.* of обвали́ть(ся, обваля́ть. обва́листый liable to fall, liable to cave in. обвали́ть, -лю́, -лишь *pf.* (*impf.* обва́ливать) cause to fall, cause to collapse; crumble; heap round; ~ся fall, collapse, cave in; crumble.

обваля́ть, -я́ю *pf.* (*impf.* обва́ливать) roll; ~ в сухаря́х roll in bread-crumbs.

обва́ривать, -аю *impf.*, обвари́ть, -рю́, -ришь *pf.* pour boiling water over; scald; ~ся scald o.s.

обведу́ *etc.*: see обвести́. обвёл *etc.*: see обвести́ об|венча́ть(ся, -а́ю(сь *pf.*

обверну́ть, -ну́, -нёшь *pf.*, обвёртывать, -аю *impf.* wrap, wrap up.

обве́с, -a short weight. обве́сить, -е́шу *pf.* (*impf.* обве́шивать) give short weight (to); cheat in weighing.

обвести́, -еду́, -едёшь; -ёл, -ела́ *pf.* (*impf.* обводи́ть) lead round, take round; encircle; surround; outline; dodge, get past; deceive, fool, cheat; ~ взо́ром, глаза́ми look round (at), take in; ~ вокру́г па́льца twist round one's little finger.

обве́тренный weather-beaten; chapped. обветша́лый decrepit, decayed; dilapidated. об|ветша́ть, -а́ю *pf.*

обве́шивать, -аю *impf.* of обве́сить

обвива́ть(ся, -а́ю(сь *impf.* of обви́ть(ся

обвине́ние, -я charge, accusation; prosecution; вы́нести ~ в+*p.* find guilty of. обвини́тель, -я *m.* accuser; prosecutor. обвини́тельн|ый accusatory; ~ый акт indictment; ~ый пригово́р verdict of guilty; ~ая речь speech for the prosecution. обвини́ть, -ню́ *pf.*, обвиня́ть, -я́ю *impf.* prosecute, indict; +в+*p.* accuse of, charge with. обвиня́емый *sb.* the accused; defendant.

обвиса́ть, -а́ет *impf.*, обви́снуть, -нет; -ви́с *pf.* sag; droop; grow flabby. обви́слый flabby; hanging, drooping.

обви́ть, обовью́, обовьёшь; обви́л, -а́, -о *pf.* (*impf.* обвива́ть) wind round, entwine; ~ся wind round, twine o.s. round.

обво́д, -a enclosing, surrounding; outlining. обводи́ть, -ожу́, -о́дишь *impf. of* обвести́ обводне́ние, -я irrigation; filling up. обвод-

ни́тельный irrigation. обводни́ть, -ню́ *pf.*, обводня́ть, -ня́ю *impf.* irrigate; fill with water.

обво́дный bypass, leading round.

обвора́живать, -аю *impf.*, обворожи́ть, -жу́ *pf.* charm, fascinate, enchant. обворожи́тельный charming, fascinating, enchanting.

обвяза́ть, -яжу́, -я́жешь *pf.*, обвя́зывать, -аю *impf.* tie round; edge; ~ся+*i.* tie round o.s.

обгла́дывать, -аю *impf.*, обглода́ть, -ожу́, -о́жешь *pf.* pick, gnaw (round). обгло́док, -дка bare bone.

обго́н, -a passing. обгоня́ть, -я́ю *impf. of* обогна́ть

обгора́ть, -а́ю *impf.*, обгоре́ть, -рю́ *pf.* be burnt, be scorched. обгоре́лый burnt, charred, scorched.

обдава́ть, -даю́, -даёшь *impf.*, обда́ть, -а́м, -а́шь, -а́ст, -ади́м; о́бдал, -а́, -о *pf.*+*i.* pour over, cover with; overcome, overwhelm with; ~ся+*i.* pour over o.s.

обде́лать, -аю *pf.* (*impf.* обде́лывать) finish; cut, polish, set; manage, arrange; cheat. обдели́ть, -лю́, -лишь *pf.* (*impf.* обделя́ть) +*i.* do out of one's (fair) share of. обде́лывать, -аю *impf. of* обде́лать обделя́ть, -я́ю *impf. of* обдели́ть

обдеру́ *etc.*: see ободра́ть. обдира́ть, -а́ю *impf. of* ободра́ть. обди́рка, -и peeling; hulling, shelling; skinning, flaying; groats. обди́рный peeled, hulled.

обдува́ла, -ы *c.g.* cheat, trickster. обдува́ть, -а́ю *impf. of* обду́ть

обду́манно *adv.* after careful consideration, deliberately. обду́манный deliberate, well-considered, well-weighed, carefully-thought-out. обду́мать, -аю *pf.*, обду́мывать, -аю *impf.* consider, think over, weigh.

обду́ть, -у́ю *pf.* (*impf.* обдува́ть) blow on, blow round; cheat, fool, dupe.

о́бе see óба. обега́ть, -а́ю *impf. of* обежа́ть. обегу́ *etc.*: see обежа́ть

обе́д, -a dinner; пе́ред ~ом in the morning; по́сле ~a in the afternoon. обе́дать, -аю *impf.* (*pf.* по~) have dinner, dine. обе́денный dinner; перерыв dinner hour.

обедне́вший, обедне́лый impoverished. обедне́ние, -я impoverishment. о|бедне́ть, -е́ю *pf.*, обедни́ть, -ню́ *pf.*, обедня́ть, -я́ю *impf.* impoverish.

обе́дня, -и; *g.pl.* -ден mass.

обежа́ть, -егу́ *pf.* (*impf.* обега́ть) run round; run past; outrun, pass.

обезбо́ливание, -я anaesthetization. обезбо́ливать, -аю *impf.*, обезбо́лить, -лю *pf.* anaesthetize.

обезвре́дить, -е́жу *pf.*, обезвре́живать, -аю *impf.* render harmless; neutralize.

обездо́ленный deprived; unfortunate, hapless. обездо́ливать, -аю *impf.*, обездо́лить, -лю *pf.* deprive of one's share.

обеззара́живать, -аю *impf.*, обеззара́зить,

-а́жу *pf.* disinfect. **обеззара́живающий** disinfectant.

обезле́сение, -я deforestation.

обезли́ченный depersonalized; generalized, reduced to a standard; mechanical. **обезли́чивать, -аю** *impf.*, **обезли́чить, -чу** *pf.* deprive of individuality, depersonalize; do away with personal responsibility for. **обезли́чка, -и** lack of personal responsibility.

обезобра́живать, -аю *impf.*, **о|безобра́зить, -а́жу** *pf.* disfigure, mutilate.

обезопа́сить, -а́шу *pf.* secure, make safe; **~ся** secure o.s.

обезору́живание, -я disarmament. **обезору́живать, -аю** *impf.*, **обезору́жить, -жу** *pf.* disarm.

обезу́меть, -ею *pf.* lose one's senses, lose one's head; **~ от испу́га** become panic-stricken.

обезья́на, -ы monkey; ape. **обезья́ний** monkey; simian; ape-like. **обезья́нник, -а** monkey-house. **обезья́нничать, -аю** *impf.* (*pf.* **с~**) ape.

обели́ть, -лю *pf.*, **обеля́ть, -я́ю** *impf.* vindicate, prove the innocence of; clear of blame; whitewash; **~ся** vindicate o.s., prove one's innocence.

оберега́ть, -а́ю *impf.*, **обере́чь, -егу́, -ежёшь; -рёг, -ла́** *pf.* guard; protect; **~ся** guard o.s., protect o.s.

обернуть, -ну́, -нёшь *pf.*, **обёртывать, -аю** *impf.* (*impf. also* **обора́чивать**) wind, twist; wrap up; turn; turn over; **~ кни́гу** jacket a book; cover a book; **~ся** turn, turn around; turn out; come back; manage, get by; +*i. or* в+*a.* turn into; **~ся лицо́м к** turn towards. **обёртка, -и** wrapper; envelope; (dust-)jacket, cover. **обёрточн|ый** wrapping; **~ая бума́га** brown paper, wrapping paper.

оберу́ *etc.: see* **обобра́ть**

обескура́живать, -аю *impf.*, **обескура́жить, -жу** *pf.* discourage; dismay.

обескро́вить, -влю *pf.*, **обескро́вливать, -аю** *impf.* drain of blood, bleed white; render lifeless. **обескро́вленный** bloodless; pallid, anaemic, lifeless.

обеспе́чение, -я securing, guaranteeing; ensuring; providing, provision; guarantee; security; safeguard(s); protection. **обеспе́ченность, -и** security; +*i.* being provided with, provision of. **обеспе́ченный** well-to-do; well provided for. **обеспе́чивать, -аю** *impf.*, **обеспе́чить, -чу** *pf.* provide for; secure, guarantee; ensure, assure; safeguard, protect; +*i.* provide with, guarantee supply of.

о|беспоко́ить(ся, -о́ю(сь *pf.*

обесси́леть, -ею *pf.* grow weak, lose one's strength; collapse, break down. **обесси́ливать, -аю** *impf.*, **обесси́лить, -лю** *pf.* weaken.

о|бессла́вить, -влю *pf.*

обессме́ртить, -рчу *pf.* immortalize.

обесцве́тить, -е́чу *pf.*, **обесцве́чивать, -аю** *impf.* fade, deprive of colour; make colourless, tone down; **~ся** fade; become colourless.

обесцене́ние, -я depreciation; loss of value. **обесце́нивать, -аю** *impf.*, **обесце́нить, -ню** *pf.* depreciate; cheapen; **~ся** depreciate, lose value.

о|бесче́стить, -е́щу *pf.*

обе́т, -а vow, promise. **обетова́нный** promised. **обеща́ние, -я** promise; **дать ~** give a promise, give one's word; **сдержа́ть ~** keep a promise, keep one's word. **обеща́ть, -а́ю** *impf. & pf.* (*pf. also* **по~**) promise.

обжа́лование, -я appeal. **обжа́ловать, -лую** *pf.* appeal against, lodge a complaint against.

обже́чь, обожгу́, обожжёшь; обжёг, обожгла́ *pf.*, **обжига́ть, -а́ю** *impf.* burn; scorch; bake; fire, calcine; sting; **~ся** burn o.s.; scald o.s.; burn one's fingers; **~ся крапи́вой** be stung by a nettle. **обжига́тельн|ый** glazing; baking; roasting; **~ая печь** kiln.

обжо́ра, -ы *c.g.* glutton, gormandizer. **обжо́рливый** gluttonous. **обжо́рство, -а** gluttony.

обзаведе́ние, -я providing, fitting out; establishment; fittings, appointments; bits and pieces. **обзавести́сь, -еду́сь, -едёшься; -вёлся, -ла́сь** *pf.*, **обзаводи́ться, -ожу́сь, -о́дишься** *impf.* +*i.* provide o.s. with; set up.

обзову́ *etc.: see* **обозва́ть**

обзо́р, -а survey, review.

обзыва́ть, -а́ю *impf. of* **обозва́ть**

обива́ть, -а́ю *impf. of* **оби́ть. оби́вка, -и** upholstering; upholstery.

оби́да, -ы offence, injury, insult; annoying thing, nuisance; **не в оби́ду будь ска́зано** no offence meant; **не дать себя́ в оби́ду** stand up for o.s. **оби́деть, -и́жу** *pf.*, **обижа́ть, -а́ю** *impf.* offend; hurt, wound; **му́хи не оби́дит** he would not harm a fly; **~ся** take offence, take umbrage; feel hurt; **~ся на+**а. resent; **не обижа́йтесь** don't be offended. **оби́дный** offensive; annoying, tiresome; **мне оби́дно** I feel hurt, it pains me; **оби́дно** it is a pity, it is a nuisance. **оби́дчивый** touchy, sensitive. **оби́женный** offended, hurt, aggrieved.

оби́лие, -я abundance, plenty. **оби́льный** abundant, plentiful; +*i.* rich in.

обиня́к, -а́ circumlocution; hint, evasion; **без ~о́в** plainly, in plain terms; **говори́ть ~а́ми** beat about the bush.

обира́ть, -а́ю *impf. of* **обобра́ть**

обита́емый inhabited. **обита́тель, -я** *m.* inhabitant; resident; inmate. **обита́ть, -а́ю** *impf.* live, dwell, reside.

оби́ть, обобью́, -ьёшь *pf.* (*impf.* **обива́ть**) upholster, cover; knock off, knock down; **~ гвоздя́ми** stud; **~ желе́зом** bind with iron.

обихо́д, -а custom, (general) use, practice; **в дома́шнем ~е** in domestic use, in the household. **обихо́дный** everyday.

обката́ть, -а́ю *pf.*, **обка́тывать, -аю** *impf.*

roll; roll smooth; run in. **обка́тка, -и** running in.

обкла́дка, -и facing; ~ **дёрном** turfing. **обкла́дывать(ся, -аю(сь** *impf. of* **обло-жи́ть(ся**

обко́м, -а *abbr.* (*of* **областно́й комите́т**) regional committee.

обкра́дывать, -аю *impf. of* **обокра́сть**

обл. *abbr.* (*of* **о́бласть**) oblast, region.

обла́ва, -ы raid, swoop; round-up; cordon, cordoning off; battue.

облага́емый taxable. **облага́ть(ся, -а́ю(сь** *impf. of* **обложи́ть(ся;** ~**ся нало́гом** be liable to tax, be taxable.

облагора́живать, -аю *impf.*, **облагоро́-дить, -о́жу** *pf.* ennoble.

облада́ние, -я possession. **облада́тель, -я** *m.* possessor. **облада́ть, -а́ю** *impf.+i.* possess, be possessed of; ~ **пра́вом** have the right; ~ **хоро́шим здоро́вьем** enjoy good health.

о́блако, -а; *pl.* **-а́, -о́в** cloud.

обла́мывать(ся, -аю(сь *impf. of* **обло-ма́ть(ся, обломи́ться**

обласка́ть, -а́ю *pf.* treat with affection, show much kindness or consideration to.

областно́й oblast; provincial; regional; dialectal. **о́бласть, -и;** *g.pl.* **-е́й** oblast, province; region; district; belt; tract; field, sphere, realm, domain.

обла́тка, -и wafer; capsule; paper seal.

о́блачко, -а; *pl.* **-а́, -о́в** *dim. of* **о́блако. о́блачность, -и** cloudiness; cloud. **о́блач-ный** cloudy.

облёг *etc.: see* **обле́чь. облега́ть, -а́ет** *impf. of* **обле́чь облега́ющий** tight-fitting.

облегча́ть, -а́ю *impf.*, **облегчи́ть, -чу́** *pf.* lighten; relieve; alleviate, mitigate; commute; facilitate. **облегче́ние, -я** relief.

обледене́лый ice-covered. **обледене́ние, -я** icing over; **пери́од обледене́ния** Ice Age. **обледене́ть, -ее́т** *pf.* ice over, become covered with ice.

облеза́ть, -а́ет *impf.*, **обле́зть, -зет; -ле́з** *pf.* come out, fall out, come off; grow bare, grow mangy; peel off. **обле́злый** shabby, bare; mangy.

облека́ть(ся, -а́ю(сь *impf. of* **обле́чь²(ся. облеку́** *etc.: see* **обле́чь²**

облени́ваться, -аюсь *impf.*, **облени́ться, -ню́сь, -нишься** *pf.* grow lazy, get lazy.

облепи́ть, -плю́, -пишь *pf.*, **облепля́ть, -я́ю** *impf.* stick to, cling to; surround, throng round; paste all over, plaster.

облета́ть, -а́ю *impf.*, **облете́ть, -лечу́** fly (round); spread (round, all over); fall.

обле́чь¹, -ля́жет; -лёг, -ла́ *pf.* (*impf.* **облега́ть**) cover, surround, envelop; fit tightly.

обле́чь², -еку́, -ечёшь; -ёк, -кла́ *pf.* (*impf.* **облека́ть**) clothe, invest; wrap, shroud; ~**ся** clothe o.s., dress o.s.; +*g.* take the form of, assume the shape of.

облива́ние, -я spilling over, pouring over; shower-bath; sponge down. **облива́ть(ся,**

-а́ю(сь *impf. of* **обли́ть(ся; се́рдце у меня́ кро́вью облива́ется** my heart bleeds. **обли́вка, -и** glazing; glaze. **обливно́й** glazed.

облига́ция, -и bond, debenture.

обли́занный smooth. **облиза́ть, -ижу́, -и́жешь** *pf.*, **обли́зывать, -аю** *impf.* lick (all over); lick clean; ~**ся** smack one's lips; lick itself.

о́блик, -а look, aspect, appearance; cast of mind, temper.

облисполко́м, -а *abbr.* (*of* **областно́й испол-ни́тельный комите́т**) regional executive committee.

о́блитый; о́блит, -а́, -о covered, enveloped; ~ **све́том луны́** bathed in moonlight. **обли́ть, оболью́, -льёшь; о́блил, -ила́, -о** *pf.* (*impf.* **облива́ть**) pour, sluice, spill; glaze; ~**ся** sponge down, take a shower; pour over o.s., spill over o.s.; ~**ся по́том** be bathed in sweat; ~**ся слеза́ми** melt into tears.

облицева́ть, -цу́ю *pf.*, **облицо́вывать, -аю** *impf.* face, revet. **облицо́вка, -и** facing, revetment; lining, coating.

облича́ть, -а́ю *impf.*, **обличи́ть, -чу́** *pf.* expose, unmask, denounce; reveal, display, manifest; point to. **обличе́ние, -я** exposure, unmasking, denunciation. **обличи́тельн|ый** denunciatory; ~**ая речь**, ~**ая статья́** diatribe, tirade.

обложе́ние, -я taxation; assessment, rating. **обложи́ть, -жу́, -жишь** *pf.* (*impf.* **обкла́-дывать, облага́ть**) put round; edge; surface; face; cover; surround; close round, corner; assess; **круго́м обложи́ло (не́бо)** the sky is completely overcast; ~ **ме́стным нало́гом** rate; ~ **нало́гом** tax; **обложи́ло язы́к** the tongue is furred; ~**ся**+*i.* put round o.s., surround o.s. with. **обло́жка, -и** (dust-)cover; folder.

облока́чиваться, -аюсь *impf.*, **облокоти́ться, -очу́сь, -о́тишься** *pf.* **на**+*a.* lean one's elbows on.

обло́м, -а breaking off; break; profile. **облома́ть, -а́ю** *pf.* (*impf.* **обла́мывать**) break off; make yield; ~**ся** break off, snap. **обломи́ться, -ло́мится** *pf.* (*impf.* **обла́мы-ваться**) break off. **обло́мок, -мка** fragment; debris, wreckage.

об|лупи́ть, -плю, -пишь *pf.*, **облу́пливать, -аю** *impf.* peel; shell; fleece; ~**ся** peel, peel off, scale; come off, chip. **облу́пленный** chipped.

облучи́ть, -чу́ *pf.*, **облуча́ть, -а́ю** *impf.* irradiate. **облуче́ние, -я** irradiation.

об|лущи́ть, -щу́ *pf.* **об|лысе́ть, -е́ю** *pf.*

облюбова́ть, -бу́ю *pf.*, **облюбо́вывать, -аю** *impf.* pick, choose, select.

обля́жет *etc.: see* **обле́чь¹**

обма́зать, -а́жу *pf.*, **обма́зывать, -аю** *impf.* coat; putty; soil, besmear. ~**ся**+*i.* besmear o.s. with, get covered with. **обма́зка, -и** coating, puttying.

обма́кивать, -аю *impf.*, **обмакну́ть, -ну́, -нёшь** *pf.* dip.

обма́н, -а fraud, deception; illusion; ~ зре́ния optical illusion. обма́нный fraudulent, deceitful. обману́ть, -ну́, -нешь pf., обма́нывать, -аю impf. deceive; cheat, swindle; betray, disappoint; ~ся be deceived, be disappointed. обма́нчивый deceptive, delusive. обма́нщик, -а deceiver; cheat, fraud.

обма́тывать(ся, -аю(сь impf. of обмота́ть(ся

обма́хивать, -аю impf., обмахну́ть, -ну́, -нёшь pf. brush off, dust (off); fan; ~ся fan o.s.

обмёл etc.: see обмести́

обмеле́ние, -я shallowing, shoaling. об|меле́ть, -е́ет pf. become shallow, shoal; run aground.

обме́н, -а exchange, interchange; barter; в ~ за+a. in exchange for; ~ веще́ств metabolism; ~ мне́ниями exchange of opinions. обме́нивать, -аю impf., обмени́ть, -ню́, -нишь pf., об|меня́ть, -я́ю pf. exchange; barter; swap; ~ся+i. exchange; обменя́ться впечатле́ниями compare notes. обме́нный exchange; metabolic.

обме́р, -а measurement; false measure. обмере́ть, обомру́, -рёшь; о́бмер, -ла́, -ло pf. (impf. обмира́ть) faint; ~ от у́жаса be horror-struck; я о́бмер my heart stood still.

обме́ривать, -аю impf., обме́рить, -рю pf. measure; cheat in measuring, give short measure (to); ~ся make a mistake in measuring.

обмести́, -ету́, -ете́шь; -мёл, -а́ pf., обмета́ть[1], -а́ю impf. sweep off, dust.

обмета́ть[2], -ечу́ or -а́ю, -е́чешь or -а́ешь pf. (impf. обмётывать) oversew, overcast, whip; blanket-stitch.

обмету́ etc.: see обмести́. обмётывать, -аю impf. of обмета́ть. обмира́ть, -а́ю impf. of обмере́ть

обмозгова́ть, -гу́ю pf., обмозго́вывать, -аю impf. think over, turn over (in one's mind).

обмола́чивать, -аю impf. of обмолоти́ть

обмо́лвиться, -влюсь pf. make a slip of the tongue; +i. say, utter. обмо́лвка, -и slip of the tongue.

обмоло́т, -а threshing. обмолоти́ть, -лочу́, -ло́тишь pf. (impf. обмола́чивать) thresh.

обмора́живать, -аю impf., обморо́зить, -ро́жу pf. expose to frost, subject to frostbite, get frost-bite; я обморо́зил себе́ ру́ки I have got my hands frost-bitten; ~ся suffer frost-bite, be frost-bitten. обморо́женный frost-bitten.

о́бморок, -а fainting-fit, swoon; syncope.

обмота́ть, -а́ю pf. (impf. обма́тывать) wind round; ~ся+i. wrap o.s. in. обмо́тка, -и winding; lagging; taping; pl. puttees, leg-wrappings.

обмо́ю etc.: see обмы́ть

обмундирова́ние, -я, обмундиро́вка, -и fitting out (with uniform), issuing of uniform; uniform. обмундирова́ть, -ру́ю pf., обмун-

диро́вывать, -аю impf. fit out (with uniform), issue with clothing; ~ся fit o.s. out; draw uniform. обмундиро́вочный; ~ые де́ньги uniform allowance.

обмыва́ние, -я bathing, washing. обмыва́ть, -а́ю impf., обмы́ть, -мо́ю pf. bathe, wash; sponge down. ~ся wash, bathe; sponge down.

обмяка́ть, -а́ю impf., обмя́кнуть, -ну; -мя́к pf. become soft; go limp, become flabby.

обнадёживать, -аю impf., обнадёжить, -жу pf. give hope to, reassure.

обнажа́ть, -а́ю impf., обнажи́ть, -жу́ pf. bare, uncover; unsheathe; lay bare, reveal. обнажённый; -ён, -ена́ naked, bare; nude.

обнаро́дование, -я publication, promulgation. обнаро́довать, -дую impf. & pf. publish, promulgate.

обнаруже́ние, -я disclosure; displaying, revealing; discovery; detection. обнару́живать, -аю impf., обнару́жить, -жу pf. disclose; display; reveal, betray; discover, bring to light; detect; ~ся be revealed, come to light.

обнести́, -су́, -сёшь; -нёс, -ла́ pf. (impf. обноси́ть) enclose; +i. serve round, pass round; pass over, leave out; меня́ обнесли́ вино́м I have not been offered wine; ~ и́згородью fence (in); ~ пери́лами rail in, rail off.

обнима́ть(ся, -а́ю(сь impf. of обня́ть(ся. обниму́ etc.: see обня́ть

обнища́лый impoverished; beggarly. обнища́ние, -я impoverishment.

обнови́ть, -влю́ pf., обновля́ть, -я́ю impf. renovate; renew; re-form; repair, restore; use or wear for the first time; ~ся revive, be restored. обно́вка, -и new acquisition, new toy; new dress. обновле́ние, -я renovation, renewal; вне́шнее ~ face-lift.

обноси́ть, -ошу́, -о́сишь impf. of обнести́; ~ся have worn out one's clothes; be out at the elbow. обно́ски, -ов pl. old clothes, cast-offs.

обнюхать, -аю pf., обню́хивать, -аю impf. smell, sniff at.

обня́ть, -ниму́, -ни́мешь; о́бнял, -á, -о pf. (impf. обнима́ть) embrace; clasp in one's arms; take in; ~ взгля́дом survey; ~ умо́м comprehend, take in; ~ся embrace; hug one another.

обо see o prep. обо... see o...

обобра́ть, оберу́, -рёшь; обобра́л, -á, -о pf. (impf. обира́ть) rob; clean out; pick; gather all of.

обобща́ть, -а́ю impf., обобщи́ть, -щу́ pf. generalize. обобще́ние, -я generalization. обобществи́ть, -влю́ pf., обобществля́ть, -я́ю impf. socialize; collectivize. обобществле́ние, -я socialization; collectivization.

обобью́ etc.: see оби́ть. обовью́ etc.: see обви́ть

обогати́ть, -ащу́ pf., обогаща́ть, -а́ю impf.

enrich; concentrate; ~ся become rich; enrich o.s. **обогаще́ние, -я** enrichment; concentration.

обогна́ть, обгоню́, -о́нишь; обогна́л, -á, -o *pf.* (*impf.* **обгоня́ть**) pass, leave behind; outstrip, outdistance. **обогну́ть, -ну́, -нёшь** *pf.* (*impf.* **огиба́ть**) round, skirt; double; bend round.

обогре́в, -a heating. **обогрева́ние, -я** heating, warming. **обогрева́тель, -я** *m.* heater. **обогрева́ть, -а́ю** *impf.,* **обогре́ть, -е́ю** *pf.* heat, warm; ~ся warm o.s.; warm up.

о́бод, -a; *pl.* -о́дья, -ьев rim; felloe. **ободо́к, -дка́** thin rim, narrow border; fillet.

ободра́нец, -нца ragamuffin, ragged fellow. **обо́дранный** ragged. **ободра́ть, обдеру́, -рёшь; -а́л, -á, -o** *pf.* (*impf.* **обдира́ть**) strip; skin, flay; peel; fleece.

ободре́ние, -я encouragement, reassurance. **ободри́тельный** encouraging, reassuring. **ободри́ть, -рю́** *pf.,* **ободря́ть, -я́ю** *impf.* cheer up; encourage, reassure; ~ся cheer up, take heart.

обожа́ние, -я adoration. **обожа́тель, -я** *m.* adorer; admirer. **обожа́ть, -а́ю** *impf.* adore, worship.

обожгу́ *etc.: see* **обже́чь**

обожестви́ть, -влю́ *pf.,* **обожествля́ть, -я́ю** *impf.* deify; worship, idolize. **обожествле́ние, -я** deification, worship.

обожжённый; -ён, -ена́ burnt, scorched; scalded; stung.

обо́з, -a string of carts, string of sledges; transport; collection of vehicles.

обозва́ть, обзову́, -вёшь; -а́л, -á, -o *pf.* (*impf.* **обзыва́ть**) call; call names; ~ дурако́м call a fool.

обозлённый; -ён, -á angered; embittered. **обо|зли́ть, -лю́** *pf.,* **о|зли́ть, -лю́** *pf.* enrage, anger; embitter; ~ся get angry, grow angry.

обознача́ть, -а́ю *impf.,* **обозна́чить, -чу** *pf.* mean; mark; reveal; emphasize; ~ся appear, reveal o.s. **обозначе́ние, -я** marking; sign, symbol.

обо́зник, -a driver.

обозрева́тель, -я *m.* reviewer, observer; columnist; **полити́ческий ~** political correspondent. **обозрева́ть, -а́ю** *impf.,* **обозре́ть, -рю́** *pf.* survey; view; look round; (pass in) review. **обозре́ние, -я** surveying; viewing; looking round; survey; review; revue. **обозри́мый** visible.

обо́и, -ев *pl.* wallpaper.

обо́йма, -ы; *g.pl.* **-о́йм** cartridge clip.

обойти́, -йду́, -йдёшь; -ошёл, -ошла́ *pf.* (*impf.* **обходи́ть**) go round, pass; make the round of, go (all) round; avoid; leave out; pass over; ~ молча́нием pass over in silence; ~сь соме to; manage, make do; turn out, end; +c+i. treat.

обо́йщик, -a upholsterer.

обокра́сть, обкраду́, -дёшь *pf.* (*impf.* **об-кра́дывать**) rob.

оболо́чка, -и casing; membrane; cover, envelope, jacket; shell; coat.

обо́лтус, -a blockhead, booby.

обольсти́тель, -я *m.* seducer. **обольсти́тельный** seductive, captivating. **обольсти́ть, -льщу́** *pf.,* **обольща́ть, -а́ю** *impf.* captivate; seduce. **обольще́ние, -я** seduction; delusion.

оболью́ *etc.: see* **обли́ть**

обомле́ть, -е́ю *pf.* be stupefied, be stunned.

обомру́ *etc.: see* **обмере́ть**

обомше́лый moss-grown.

обоня́ние, -я (sense of) smell. **обоня́тельный** olfactory. **обоня́ть, -я́ю** *impf.* smell.

обопру́ *etc.: see* **опере́ть**

обора́чиваемость, -и turnover. **обора́чивать(ся, -аю(сь** *impf. of* **оберну́ть(ся, оборо́тить(ся**

оборва́нец, -нца ragamuffin, ragged fellow. **обо́рванный** torn, ragged. **оборва́ть, -ву́, -вёшь; -а́л, -á, -o** *pf.* (*impf.* **обрыва́ть**) tear off, pluck; strip; break; snap; cut short, interrupt; ~ся break; snap; fall; come away; stop suddenly, stop short.

обо́рка, -и frill, flounce.

оборо́на, -ы defence; defences. **оборони́тельный** defensive. **оборони́ть, -ню́** *pf.,* **обороня́ть, -я́ю** *impf.* defend; ~ся defend o.s. **оборо́нный** defence, defensive. **обороноспосо́бность, -и** defensive capability.

оборо́т, -a a turn; revolution, rotation; circulation; turnover; back; ~ ре́чи (turn of) phrase; locution; **смотри́ на ~e** P.T.O., please turn over; see other side. **оборо́тистый** resourceful. **оборо́тить, -рочу́, -ро́тишь** *pf.* (*impf.* **обора́чивать**) turn; ~ся turn (round); +i. or в+a. turn into. **оборо́тливый** resourceful. **оборо́тн|ый** circulating, working; turn-round; reverse; ~ый капита́л working capital; ~ая сторона́ reverse side; verso; з ~oe the letter э.

обору́дование, -я equipping; equipment; **вспомога́тельное ~** (*comput.*) peripherals. **обору́довать, -дую** *impf. & pf.* equip, fit out; manage, arrange.

обоснова́ние, -я basing; basis, ground. **обосно́ванный** well-founded, well-grounded. **обоснова́ть, -ну́ю, -нуёшь** *or* **-ну́ю, -ну́ешь** *pf.,* **обосно́вывать, -аю** *impf.* ground, base; substantiate; ~ся settle down.

обосо́бить, -блю *pf.,* **обособля́ть, -я́ю** *impf.* isolate; ~ся stand apart; keep aloof. **обособле́ние, -я** isolation. **обосо́бленный** isolated, solitary.

обостре́ние, -я aggravation, exacerbation. **обострённый** keen; strained, tense; sharp, pointed. **обостри́ть, -рю́** *pf.,* **обостря́ть, -я́ю** *impf.* sharpen, intensify; strain; aggravate, exacerbate; ~ся become sharp, become pointed; become keener, become more sensitive; become strained; be aggravated; become acute.

оботру́ *etc.*: *see* **обтере́ть**

обо́чина, -ы verge; shoulder, edge, side.

обошёл *etc.*: *see* **обойти́. обошью́** *etc.*: *see* **обши́ть**

обою́дность, -и mutuality, reciprocity. **обою́дный** mutual, reciprocal. **обоюдоо́стрый** double-edged, two-edged.

обраба́тывать, -аю *impf.*, **обрабо́тать, -аю** *pf.* till, cultivate; work, work up; treat, process; machine; polish, perfect; work upon, win round. **обраба́тывающ|ий; ~ая промы́шленность** manufacturing industry. **обрабо́тка, -и** working (up); treatment, processing; cultivation.

обра́довать(ся, -дую(сь *pf.*

о́браз, -а shape, form; appearance; image; type; figure; mode, manner; way; icon; **гла́вным ~ом** mainly, chiefly, largely; **каки́м ~ом?** how?; **~ де́йствий** line of action, policy; **~ жи́зни** way of life; **~ мы́слей** way of thinking; **~ правле́ния** form of government; **таки́м ~ом** thus. **образе́ц, -зца́** model; pattern; example; specimen, sample. **о́бразный** picturesque, graphic; figurative; employing images. **образова́ние, -я** formation; education. **образо́ванный** educated. **образова́тельный** educational. **образова́ть, -зу́ю** *impf. & pf.*, **образо́вывать, -аю** *impf.* form; make (up); organize; educate; **~ся** form; arise; turn out well.

образу́мить, -млю *pf.* bring to reason; make listen to reason; **~ся** come to one's senses, see reason.

образцо́вый model; exemplary. **обра́зчик, -а** specimen, sample; pattern.

обра́мить, -млю *pf.*, **обрамля́ть, -я́ю** *impf.* frame. **обрамле́ние, -я** framing; frame; setting.

обраста́ть, -а́ю *impf.*, **обрасти́, -ту́, -тёшь; -ро́с, -ла́** *pf.* be overgrown; be covered, surrounded, cluttered; +*i.* acquire, accumulate.

обрати́м|ый reversible, convertible; **~ая валю́та** convertible currency. **обрати́ть, -ащу́** *pf.*, **обраща́ть, -а́ю** *impf.* turn; convert; **~ в бе́гство** put to flight; **~ внима́ние на**+*a.* pay attention to, take notice of, notice; call, draw, attention to; **~ на себя́ внима́ние** attract attention (to o.s.); **~ в шу́тку** turn into a joke; **~ся** turn; revert; appeal; apply; accost, address; circulate; +*в*+*a.* turn into, become; +*с*+*i.* treat; handle, manage; **~ся в бе́гство** take to flight; **~ся в слух** be all ears; **~ся** prick up one's ears. **обра́тно** *adv.* back; backwards; conversely; inversely; **~ пропорциона́льный** inversely proportional; **туда́ и ~** there and back. **обра́тн|ый** reverse; return; opposite; inverse; **в ~ую сто́рону** in the opposite direction; **~ый а́дрес** sender's address, return address; **~ая вспы́шка** backfiring; **~ой по́чтой** by return (of post); **~ый уда́р** backfire; **~ый ход** reverse motion, back stroke. **обраще́ние, -я** appeal, address; conversion; circulation; manner; (+*с*+*i.*)

treatment (of); handling (of); use (of).

об|ревизова́ть, -зу́ю *pf.*

обре́з, -а edge, side; sawn-off gun; **в ~**+*g.* only just enough; **де́нег у меня́ в ~** I haven't a penny to spare. **обре́зать, -е́жу** *pf.*, **обреза́ть, -а́ю** *impf.* cut; cut off; clip, trim; pare; prune; bevel; circumcise; cut short, snub; **~ся** cut o.s. **обре́зок, -зка** scrap; remnant; *pl.* ends; clippings.

обрека́ть, -а́ю *impf. of* **обре́чь. обреку́** *etc.*: *see* **обре́чь обрёл** *etc.*: *see* **обрести́**

обремени́тельный burdensome, onerous. **о|бремени́ть, -ню́** *pf.*, **обременя́ть, -я́ю** *impf.* burden.

обрести́, -ету́, -етёшь; -рёл, -а́ *pf.*, **обрета́ть, -а́ю** *impf.* find. **обрета́ться, -а́юсь** *impf.* be; live.

обрече́ние, -я doom. **обречённый** doomed. **обре́чь, -еку́, -ечёшь; -ёк, -ла́** *pf.* (*impf.* **обрека́ть**) condemn, doom.

обрисова́ть, -су́ю *pf.*, **обрисо́вывать, -аю** *impf.* outline, delineate, depict; **~ся** appear (in outline), take shape.

оброќ, -а quit-rent.

оброни́ть, -ню́, -нишь *pf.* drop; let drop, let fall.

обро́с *etc.*: *see* **обрасти́. обро́сший** overgrown.

обруба́ть, -а́ю *impf.*, **обруби́ть, -блю́, -бишь** *pf.* chop off; lop off, cut off; dock; hem seam. **обру́бок, -бка** stump.

об|руга́ть, -а́ю *pf.*

о́бруч, -а; *pl.* **-и, -е́й** hoop. **обруча́льн|ый** engagement, betrothal; **~ое кольцо́** betrothal ring, wedding ring. **обруча́ть, -а́ю** *impf.*, **обручи́ть, -чу́** betroth; **~ся**+*с*+*i.* become engaged to. **обруче́ние, -я** betrothal.

обру́шивать, -аю *impf.*, **об|ру́шить, -шу** *pf.* bring down, rain down; **~ся** come down, collapse, cave in; +**на**+*a.* beat down on; come down on, fall on, pounce on.

обры́в, -а precipice; break, rupture. **обрыва́ть(ся, -а́ю(сь** *impf. of* **оборва́ть(ся. обры́вистый** steep, precipitous; abrupt. **обры́вок, -вка** scrap; snatch.

обры́згать, -аю *pf.*, **обры́згивать, -аю** *impf.*, **обры́знуть, -ну** *pf.* splash, spatter; sprinkle.

обрю́зглый, обрю́згший flabby.

обря́д, -а rite, ceremony. **обря́дный, обря́довый** ritual, ceremonial.

обслу́живание, -я service; servicing, maintenance; **бытово́е ~** consumer service(s); **медици́нское ~** medical attendance, medical care. **обслу́живать, -аю** *impf.*, **обслужи́ть, -жу́, -жишь** *pf.* serve, attend to; service; mind, operate; **обслу́живающий персона́л** staff; assistants, attendants.

обсле́дование, -я inspection; inquiry; investigation. **обсле́дователь, -я** *m.* inspector, investigator. **обсле́довать, -дую** *impf. & pf.* inspect; investigate; examine.

обсо́хнуть, -ну; -ох *pf.* (*impf.* **обсыха́ть**) dry, dry up.

обста́вить, -влю *pf.*, обставля́ть, -я́ю *impf.* surround, encircle; furnish; arrange; organize; ~ся establish o.s., furnish one's home. обстано́вка, -и furniture; décor; situation, conditions; environment; set-up.

обстоя́тельный thorough, reliable; detailed, circumstantial. обстоя́тельственный adverbial. обстоя́тельство, -a circumstance; adverbial modifier, adverb, adverbial phrase. обстоя́ть, -ои́т *impf.* be; get on go; как обстои́т де́ло? how is it going? how are things going?

обстра́гивать, -аю *impf. of* обстрога́ть

обстра́ивать(ся, -аю(сь *impf. of* обстро́ить(ся

обстре́л, -a firing, fire; под ~ом under fire. обстре́ливать, -аю *impf.*, обстреля́ть, -я́ю *pf.* fire at, fire on; bombard; ~ся become seasoned (in battle); receive one's baptism of fire. обстре́лянный seasoned, experienced.

обстрога́ть, -а́ю, обструга́ть, -а́ю *pf.* (*impf.* обстра́гивать) plane; whittle.

обстро́ить, -о́ю *pf.* (*impf.* обстра́ивать) build up, build round; ~ся be built; spring up; build for o.s.

обструга́ть *see* обстрога́ть

обступа́ть, -а́ет *impf.*, обступи́ть, -у́пит *pf.* surround; cluster round.

обсуди́ть, -ужу́, -у́дишь *pf.*, обсужда́ть, -а́ю *impf.* discuss; consider. обсужде́ние, -я discussion.

обсчита́ть, -а́ю *pf.*, обсчи́тывать, -аю *impf.* cheat (*in reckoning*); ~ся make a mistake (*in counting*), miscalculate; вы обсчита́лись на шесть копе́ек you were six copecks out.

обсы́пать, -плю *pf.* обсыпа́ть, -а́ю *impf.* strew; sprinkle.

обсыха́ть, -а́ю *impf. of* обсо́хнуть. обта́чивать, -аю *impf. of* обточи́ть

обтека́емый streamlined, streamline. обтека́тель, -я *m.* fairing, cowling.

обтере́ть, оботру́, -трёшь; обтёр *pf.* (*impf.* обтира́ть) wipe; wipe dry; rub; ~ся wipe o.s. dry, dry o.s.; sponge down.

обтерпе́ться, -плю́сь, -пишься *pf.* become acclimatized, get used.

о(б)теса́ть, -ешу́, -е́шешь *pf.*, о(б)тёсывать, -аю *impf.* square; rough-hew; dress, trim; lick into shape.

обтира́ние, -я sponge-down; lotion. обтира́ть(ся, -а́ю(сь *pf. of* обтере́ть(ся

обточи́ть, -чу́, -чишь *pf.* (*impf.* обта́чивать) grind; turn, machine, round off. обто́чка, -и turning, machining, rounding off.

обтрёпанный frayed; shabby. обтрепа́ть, -плю́, -плешь *pf.* fray; ~ся fray; become frayed; get shabby.

обтя́гивать, -аю *impf.*, обтяну́ть, -ну́, -нешь *pf.* cover; fit close, fit tight. обтя́жка, -и cover; skin; в обтя́жку close-fitting.

обува́ть(ся, -а́ю(сь *impf. of* обу́ть(ся. обу́вка, -и boots, shoes. обувно́й shoe. о́бувь, -и footwear; boots, shoes.

обу́гливание, -я carbonization. обу́гливать, -аю *impf.*, обу́глить, -лю *pf.* char; carbonize; ~ся char, become charred.

обу́живать, -аю *impf. of* обу́зить

обу́за, -ы burden, encumbrance.

обузда́ть, -а́ю *pf.*, обу́здывать, -аю *impf.* bridle, curb; restrain, control.

обу́зить, -у́жу *pf.* (*impf.* обу́живать) make too tight, too narrow.

обурева́емый possessed; +*i.* a prey to. обурева́ть, -а́ет *impf.* shake; grip; possess.

обусло́вить, -влю *pf.*, обусло́вливать, -аю *impf.* cause, bring about; +*i.* make conditional on, limit by; ~ся+*i.* be conditioned by, be conditional on; depend on.

обу́тый shod. обу́ть, -у́ю *pf.* (*impf.* обува́ть) put boots, shoes on; provide with boots, shoes; ~ся put on one's boots, shoes.

о́бух, -a *or* -а́ butt, back.

обуча́ть, -а́ю *impf.*, обу́|чи́ть, -чу́, -чишь *pf.* teach; train, instruct; ~ся+*d. or inf.* learn. обуче́ние, -я teaching; instruction, training.

обхва́т, -a girth; в ~е in circumference. обхвати́ть, -ачу́, -а́тишь *pf.*, обхва́тывать, -аю *impf.* embrace; clasp.

обхо́д, -a round; beat; roundabout way; by-pass; evasion, circumvention. обходи́тельный amiable; courteous; pleasant. обходи́ть(ся, -ожу́(сь, -о́дишь(ся *impf. of* обойти́(сь. обхо́дный roundabout, circuitous; ~ путь detour. обхожде́ние, -я manners; treatment; behaviour.

обша́ривать, -аю *impf.*, обша́рить, -рю *pf.* rummage through, ransack.

обшива́ть, -а́ю *impf. of* обши́ть. обши́вка, -и edging, bordering; trimming, facing; boarding, panelling; sheathing; plating; ~ фане́рой veneering.

обши́рный extensive; spacious; vast.

обши́ть, обошью́, -шьёшь *pf.* (*impf.* обшива́ть) edge, border; sew round; trim, face; fit out, make outfit(s) for; plank; panel; sheathe, plate.

обшла́г, -а́; *pl.* -а́, -о́в cuff.

обща́ться, -а́юсь *impf.* associate, mix.

обще... *in comb.* common(ly), general(ly). общедосту́пный moderate in price; popular. ~жи́тие, -я hostel; community; communal life. ~изве́стный well-known, generally known; notorious. ~наро́дный general, national, public; ~наро́дный пра́здник public holiday. ~образова́тельный general, of general education. ~при́нятый generally accepted. ~сою́зный All-Union. ~употреби́тельный in general use. ~челове́ческий common to all mankind; human; universal, general, ordinary.

обще́ние, -я intercourse; relations, links; ли́чное ~ personal contact.

обще́ственник, -a, -ица, -ы social activist, public-spirited person. обще́ственность, -и (the) public; public opinion; community;

communal organizations; **дух общественности** public spirit. **общественн|ый** social, public; voluntary, unpaid, amateur; **на ~ых началах** voluntary, unpaid; **~ые науки** social sciences; **~ое питание** public catering. **общество, -а** society; association; company; **научное ~** learned body.

общ|ий general; common; **в ~ем** on the whole, in general, in sum; **~ий итог, ~ая сумма** sum total. **община, -ы** community; commune. **общинный** communal; common.

об|щипать, -плю, -плешь pf.

общительный sociable. **общность, -и** community.

объ... see **о..., об...**

объедать(ся, -аю(сь impf. of **объесть(ся**

объединение, -я unification; merger; union, association. **объединённый; -ён, -а** united. **объединительный** unifying, uniting. **объединить, -ню** pf., **объединять, -яю** impf. unite; join; pool, combine; **~ся** unite.

объедки, -ов pl. leavings, leftovers, scraps.

объездить, -зжу, -здишь pf. (impf. **объезжать**) travel over; break in.

объезжать, -аю impf. of **объездить, объехать. объезжий** roundabout, circuitous.

объект, -а object; objective; establishment, works. **объектив, -а** objective, lens. **объективный** objective; unbiased.

объём, -а volume; bulk, size, capacity. **объёмистый** voluminous, bulky. **объёмный** by volume, volumetric.

объесть, -ем, -ешь, -ест, -едим pf. (impf. **объедать**) gnaw (round), nibble; **~ся** overeat.

объехать, -еду pf. (impf. **объезжать**) drive round; go round; go past, skirt; visit, make the round of; travel over.

объявить, -влю, -вишь pf., **объявлять, -яю** impf. declare, announce; publish, proclaim; advertise; **~ся** turn up, appear; +i. announce o.s., declare o.s. **объявление, -я** declaration, announcement; notice; avertisement.

объяснение, -я explanation; **~ в любви** declaration of love. **объяснимый** explicable, explainable. **объяснительный** explanatory. **объяснить, -ню** pf., **объяснять, -яю** impf. explain; **~ся** explain o.s.; become clear, be explained; speak, make o.s. understood; +c+i. have a talk with; have it out with; +i. be explained, accounted for, by.

объятие, -я embrace.

обыватель, -я m. man in the street; inhabitant, resident. **обывательский** commonplace; of the local inhabitants; narrowminded.

обыграть, -аю pf., **обыгрывать, -аю** impf. beat; win; use with effect, play up; turn to advantage, turn to account.

обыденный ordinary, usual; commonplace; everyday.

обыкновение, -я habit, wont; **иметь ~+inf.** be in the habit of; **по обыкновению** as usual.

обыкновенно adv. usually; as a rule. **обыкновенный** usual; ordinary; commonplace; everyday.

обыск, -а search. **обыскать, -ыщу, -ыщешь** pf. **обыскивать, -аю** impf. search.

обычай, -я custom; usage. **обычно** adv. usually, as a rule. **обычный** usual, ordinary.

обязанность, -и duty; responsibility; **исполняющий обязанности** acting. **обязанный** (+inf.) obliged, bound; +d. obliged to, indebted to (+i. for). **обязательно** adv. without fail; **он ~ там будет** he is sure to be there, he is bound to be there. **обязательный** obligatory; compulsory; binding; obliging, kind. **обязательство, -а** obligation; engagement; pl. liabilities; **взять на себя ~** pledge o.s., undertake. **обязать, -яжу, -яжешь** pf., **обязывать, -аю** impf. bind; commit; oblige; **~ся** bind o.s., pledge o.s., undertake; **не хочу ни перед кем обязываться** I do not want to be beholden to anybody.

овдовевший widowed. **овдоветь, -ею** pf. become a widow, widower.

овен, овна Aries, the Ram.

овёс, овса oats.

овечий sheep, sheep's. **овечка, -и** dim. of **овца**; lamb, harmless person, gentle creature.

овин, -а barn.

овладевать, -аю impf., **овладеть, -ею** pf.+i. take possession of; master; seize; **~ собой** get control of o.s., regain self-control. **овладение, -я** mastery; mastering.

о-во abbr. (of **общество**) Soc., Society.

овод, -а; pl. **-ы** or **-а, оводов** gadfly.

овощ, -а; pl. **-и, -ей** vegetable, vegetables. **овощной** vegetable; **~ магазин** greengrocer's, greengrocery.

овраг, -а ravine, gully.

овсянка, -и oatmeal; porridge. **овсяной** oat, of oats. **овсян|ый** oat, oatmeal; **~ая крупа** (coarse) oatmeal.

овца, -ы; pl. **-ы, овец, овцам** sheep; ewe. **овцеводство, -а** sheep-breeding. **овчар, -а** shepherd. **овчарка, -и** sheep-dog. **овчина, -ы** sheepskin. **овчинный** sheepskin.

огарок, -рка candle-end.

огибать, -аю impf. of **обогнуть**

оглавление, -я table of contents.

огласить, -ашу pf., **оглашать, -аю** impf. proclaim; announce; divulge; make public; fill (with sound); **~ся** resound, ring. **огласка, -и** publicity; **получить огласку** be given publicity. **оглашение, -я** proclaiming, publication; **не подлежит оглашению** confidential, not for publication.

оглобля, -и; g.pl. **-бель** shaft.

о|глохнуть, -ну; -ох pf.

оглушать, -аю impf., **о|глушить, -шу** pf. deafen; stun. **оглушительный** deafening.

оглядеть, -яжу pf., **оглядывать, -аю** impf., **оглянуть, -ну, -нешь** pf. look round; look over, examine, inspect; **~ся** look round, look about; look back; turn to look; adapt o.s., become acclimatized. **огля́дка, -и** looking round, looking back; care, caution; **бежа́ть без огля́дки** run for one's life.

огнево́й fire; fiery; igneous. **огнебезопа́сный** non-inflammable. **огнемёт, -а** flame-thrower. **о́гненный** fiery. **огнеопа́сный** inflammable. **огнеприпа́сы, -ов** *pl.* ammunition. **огнесто́йкий** fire-proof, fire-resistant. **огнестре́льн|ый; ~ое ору́жие** fire-arm(s). **огнетуши́тель, -я** fire-extinguisher. **огнеупо́рн|ый** fire-resistant, fire-proof; refractory; **~ая гли́на** fire-clay; **~ый кирпи́ч** fire brick.

ого́ *int.* oho!

огова́ривать, -аю *impf.*, **оговори́ть, -рю** *pf.* slander; stipulate (for); fix, agree on; **~ся** make a reservation, make a proviso; make a slip (of the tongue); **я оговори́лся** it was a slip of the tongue. **огово́р, -а** slander. **огово́рка, -и** reservation, proviso; slip of the tongue; **без огово́рок** without reserve.

оголённый bare, nude; uncovered, exposed. **оголи́ть, -лю** *pf.* (*impf.* **оголя́ть**) bare; strip, uncover; **~ся** strip, strip o.s.; become exposed.

оголте́лый wild, frantic; frenzied; unbridled.

оголя́ть(ся, -я́ю(сь *impf. of* **оголи́ть(ся**

огонёк, -нька́ (*small*) light; zest, spirit. **ого́нь, огня́** *m.* fire; firing; light.

огора́живать, -аю *impf.*, **огороди́ть, -рожу́, -ро́ди́шь** *pf.* fence in, enclose; **~ся** fence o.s. in. **огоро́д, -а** kitchen-garden; market-garden. **огоро́дник, -а** market-gardener. **огоро́дничество, -а** market-gardening. **огоро́дный** kitchen-garden, market-garden.

огоро́шить, -шу *pf.* take aback, dumbfound; startle.

огорча́ть, -а́ю *impf.*, **огорчи́ть, -чу́** *pf.* grieve, distress, pain; **~ся** grieve, distress o.s., be distressed, be pained. **огорче́ние, -я** grief, affliction; chagrin. **огорчи́тельный** distressing.

о|гра́бить, -блю *pf.* **ограбле́ние, -я** robbery; burglary; **у́личное ~** mugging.

огра́да, -ы fence. **огради́ть, -ажу́** *pf.*, **огражда́ть, -а́ю** *impf.* guard, protect; enclose, fence in; **~ся** defend o.s., protect o.s., guard o.s.

ограниче́ние, -я limitation, restriction. **ограни́ченный** limited, narrow. **ограни́чивать, -аю** *impf.*, **ограни́чить, -чу** *pf.* limit, restrict, cut down; **~ся+i.** limit o.s. to, confine o.s. to; be limited, be confined to.

огро́мный huge; vast; enormous.

огрубе́лый coarse, hardened, rough. **о|грубе́ть, -е́ю** *pf.*

огрыза́ться, -а́юсь *impf.*, **огрызну́ться, -ну́сь, -нёшься** *pf.* snap (**на+a.** at).

огры́зок, -зка bit, end; stub, stump.

огу́зок, -зка rump.

огу́лом *adv.* all together; wholesale, indiscriminately. **огу́льно** *adv.* without grounds.

огу́льный wholesale, indiscriminate; unfounded, groundless.

огуре́ц, -рца́ cucumber.

одарённый gifted, talented. **ода́ривать, -аю** *impf.*, **одари́ть, -рю́** *pf.*, **одаря́ть, -я́ю** *impf.* give presents (to); **+i.** endow with.

одева́ть(ся, -а́ю(сь *impf. of* **оде́ть(ся**

оде́жда, -ы clothes; garments; clothing; revetment; surfacing.

одеколо́н, -а eau-de-Cologne.

одели́ть, -лю́ *pf.*, **оделя́ть, -я́ю** *impf.* (**+i.**) present (with); endow (with).

оде́ну *etc.: see* **оде́ть. одёргивать, -аю** *impf. of* **одёрнуть**

одеревене́лый numb; lifeless. **о|деревене́ть, -е́ю** *pf.*

одержа́ть, -жу́, -жишь *pf.*, **оде́рживать, -аю** *impf.* gain, win; **~ верх** gain the upper hand, prevail. **одержи́мый** possessed.

одёрнуть, -ну *pf.* (*impf.* **одёргивать**) pull down, straighten; call to order; silence.

оде́тый dressed; clothed. **оде́ть, -е́ну** *pf.* (*impf.* **одева́ть**) dress; clothe; **~ся** dress (o.s.); **+в+a.** put on. **одея́ло, -а** blanket; coverlet; **~-гре́лка** electric blanket. **одея́ние, -я** garb, attire.

оди́н, одного́, одна́, одно́й, одно́, одного́; *pl.* **одни́, одни́х** *num.* one; a, an; a certain; alone; only; by o.s.; nothing but; same; **в оди́н го́лос** with one voice, with one accord; **все до одного́** (all) to a man; **мне э́то всё одно́** it is all one to me; **одни́..., други́е** some ..., others; **оди́н за други́м** one after the other; **оди́н и тот же** one and the same; **одно́ и то же** the same thing; **оди́н на оди́н** in private, tête-à-tête; face to face; **одни́ но́жницы** one pair of scissors; **оди́н раз** once; **одни́м сло́вом** in a word, in short; **по одному́** one by one, one at a time; in single file.

одина́ково *adv.* equally. **одина́ковый** identical, the same, equal. **одина́рный** single.

оди́ннадцатый eleventh. **оди́ннадцать, -и** eleven.

одино́кий solitary; lonely; single. **одино́чество, -а** solitude; loneliness, **одино́чка, -и** *c.g.* (one) person alone; **в одино́чку** alone, on one's own; **мать-~** unmarried mother; **по одино́чке** one by one. **одино́чкой** *adv.* alone, by o.s., by itself. **одино́чн|ый** individual; one-man; single; **~ое заключе́ние** solitary confinement. **одино́чник, -а** individual competitor; skiff.

одио́зный odious.

одича́лый wild, gone wild. **одича́ние, -я** running wild. **о|дича́ть, -а́ю** *pf.*

одна́жды *adv.* once; one day; once upon a time; **~ у́тром, ~ ве́чером, ~ но́чью** one morning, evening, night.

одна́ко *conj.* however; but; though; *int.* you don't say so! not really!

одно́... *in comb.* single, one; uni-, mono-, homo-. **однобо́кий** one-sided. **~бо́ртный**

single-breasted. **~вре́менно** *adv.* simultaneously, at the same time. **~го́док, -дка,** **~го́дка, -и** person of the same age (c+i. as). **~дне́вный** one-day. **~звꙋ́чный** monotonous. **~зна́чащий** synonymous; monosemantic. **~зна́чный** synonymous; monosemantic; simple; one-digit. **~име́нный** of the same name; eponymous. **~кла́ссник** classmate. **~кле́точный** unicellular. **~коле́йный** single-track. **~кра́тный** single; **~кра́тный вид** momentary aspect. **~ле́тний** oneyear; annual. **~ле́тник, -а** annual. **~ле́ток, -тка, ~ле́тка, -и** (person) of the same age (c+i. as). **~ме́стный** for one (person); single-seater. **~мото́рный** single-engined. **~обра́зие, -я, ~обра́зность, -и** monotony. **~обра́зный** monotonous. **~по́люсный** unipolar. **~пу́тка, -и** single-track railway. **~пу́тный** one-way. **~ро́дность, -и** homogeneity, uniformity; similar. **~ро́дный** homogeneous, uniform; similar. **~сло́жный** monosyllabic; terse, abrupt. **~сло́йный** single-layer; one-ply, single-ply. **~сторо́нний** one-sided; unilateral; one-way; one-track. **~та́ктный** one-stroke; single-cycle. **~ти́пный** of the same type; of the same kind. **~то́мник, -а** one-volume edition. **~то́мный** one-volume. **~фами́лец, -льца** person bearing the same surname; namesake. **~цве́тный** one-colour; monochrome. **~эта́жный** single-stage; one-storeyed. **~язы́чный** monolingual. **~я́русный** single-tier, single-deck; single-layer.

одобре́ние, -я approval. **одобри́тельный** approving. **одо́брить, -рю** *pf.,* **одобря́ть, -я́ю** *impf.* approve of, approve.

одолева́ть, -а́ю *impf.,* **одоле́ть, -е́ю** *pf.* overcome, conquer; master, cope with.

одолжа́ть, -а́ю *impf.,* **одолжи́ть, -жꙋ́** *pf.* lend; +y+g. borrow from; **~ся** be obliged, be beholden; borrow, get into debt. **одолже́ние, -я** favour, service.

одома́шненный domesticated. **одома́шнивать, -аю** *impf.,* **одома́шнить, -ню** *pf.* domesticate, tame.

о|дряхле́ть, -е́ю *pf.*

одува́нчик, -а dandelion.

оду́маться, -аюсь *pf.,* **оду́мываться, -аюсь** *impf.* change one's mind; think better of it; have time to think. **одꙋ́рачивать, -аю** *impf.,* **о|дꙋра́чить, -чу** *pf.* fool, make a fool of.

одꙋре́лый stupid. **одꙋре́ние, -я** stupefaction, torpor. **о|дꙋре́ть, -е́ю** *pf.*

одꙋрма́нивать, -аю *impf.,* **о|дꙋрма́нить, -ню** *pf.* stupefy. **о́дꙋрь, -и** stupefaction, torpor. **одꙋря́ть, -я́ю** *impf.* stupefy; **одꙋря́ющий за́пах** overpowering scent.

одꙋхотворённый inspired; spiritual. **одꙋхотвори́ть, -рю** *pf.,* **одꙋхотворя́ть, -я́ю** *impf.* inspire.

одꙋшеви́ть, -влю *pf.,* **одꙋшевля́ть, -я́ю** *impf.* animate; **~ся** be animated. **одꙋшевле́ние, -я** animation. **одꙋшевлённый** animated; animate.

оды́шка, -и shortness of breath; **страда́ть оды́шкой** be short-winded.

ожере́лье, -я necklace.

ожесточа́ть, -а́ю *impf.,* **ожесточи́ть, -чꙋ́** *pf.* embitter, harden; **~ся** become embittered, become hard. **ожесточе́ние, -я, ожесточённость, -и** bitterness; hardness. **ожесточённый** bitter, embittered; hard.

ожива́ть, -а́ю *impf. of* **ожи́ть**

оживи́ть, -влю *pf.,* **оживля́ть, -я́ю** *impf.* revive; enliven, vivify, animate; **~ся** become animated, liven up. **оживле́ние, -я** animation, gusto; reviving; enlivening. **оживлённый** animated, lively.

ожида́ние, -я expectation; waiting; **в ожида́нии** expecting; +g. pending; **про́тив ожида́ния** unexpectedly; **сверх ожида́ния** beyond expectation. **ожида́ть, -а́ю** *impf.+g.* wait for; expect, anticipate.

ожире́ние, -я obesity. **о|жире́ть, -е́ю** *pf.*

ожи́ть, -ивꙋ́, -ивёшь; о́жил, -а́, -о *pf.* (*impf.* **ожива́ть**) come to life, revive.

ожо́г, -а burn, scald.

оз. *abbr.* (*of* **о́зеро**) L., Lake.

о|забо́тить, -о́чу *pf.,* **озабо́чивать, -аю** *impf.* trouble, worry; cause anxiety to; **~ся** attend to, see to. **озабо́ченность, -и** preoccupation; anxiety. **озабо́ченный** preoccupied; anxious, worried.

озагла́вить, -лю *pf.,* **озагла́вливать, -аю** *impf.* entitle, call; head. **озада́ченный** perplexed, puzzled. **озада́чивать, -аю** *impf.,* **озада́чить, -чу** *pf.* perplex, puzzle; take aback.

озари́ть, -рю *pf.,* **озаря́ть, -я́ю** *impf.* light up, illuminate; **их озари́ло** it dawned on them; **~ся** light up. **озвере́лый** brutal; brutalized. **о|звере́ть, -е́ю** *pf.*

озвꙋ́ченный фильм sound film.

оздорови́тельный sanitary; fitness, keep-fit; **~ бег** jogging; **~ ла́герь** health camp. **оздорови́ть, -влю** *pf.,* **оздоровля́ть, -я́ю** *impf.* render (more) healthy; improve sanitary conditions of.

озелени́ть, -ню *pf.,* **озеленя́ть, -я́ю** *impf.* plant (*with trees, grass, etc.*).

озёрный lake; **~ райо́н** lake district. **о́зеро, -а; pl. озёра** lake.

ози́мые *sb., pl.* winter crops. **ози́мый** winter. **о́зимь, -и** winter crop.

озира́ться, -а́юсь *impf.* look round; look back.

о|зли́ть(ся *see* **обозли́ть(ся**

озло́бить, -блю *pf.,* **озлобля́ть, -я́ю** *impf.* embitter; **~ся** grow bitter, be embittered. **озлобле́ние, -я** bitterness, animosity. **озло́бленный** embittered, bitter; angry.

о|знако́мить, -млю *pf.,* **ознакомля́ть, -я́ю** *impf.* c+i. acquaint with; **~ся** c+i. familiarize o.s. with.

ознаменова́ние, -я marking, commemoration; **в ~+g.** to mark, to commemorate, in commemoration of. **ознаменова́ть, -нꙋ́ю**

pf., **ознамено́вывать**, **-аю** *impf.* mark, commemorate; celebrate.

означа́ть, **-а́ет** *impf.* mean, signify, stand for. **озна́ченный** aforesaid.

озно́б, **-а** shivering, chill.

озо́н, **-а** ozone. **озо́нный**; ~ **слой** ozone layer. **озонобезвре́дный** ozone-friendly.

озо́рник, **-а́** naughty child, mischievous child; rowdy. **озорнича́ть**, **-а́ю** *impf.* (*pf.* **с~**) be naughty, get up to mischief. **озорно́й** naughty, mischievous; rowdy. **озорство́**, **-а́** naughtiness, mischief.

озя́бнуть, **-ну**; **озя́б** *pf.* be cold, be freezing. **ой** *int.* oh; ow!; ouch!; oops!

ок. *abbr.* (*of* **о́коло**) approx., c., circa.

оказа́ть, **-ажу́**, **-а́жешь** *pf.* (*impf.* **ока́зывать**) render, show; ~ **влия́ние на**+*a.* influence, exert influence on; ~ **де́йствие** have an effect, take effect; ~ **предпочте́ние** show preference; ~ **услу́гу** do a service, do a good turn; ~ **честь** do honour; ~**ся** turn out, prove; find o.s., be found.

ока́зия, **-и** opportunity; unexpected happening, funny thing.

ока́зывать(ся, **-аю(сь** *impf. of* **оказа́ть(ся**

окайми́ть, **-млю́** *pf.*, **окаймля́ть**, **-я́ю** *impf.* border, edge.

окамене́лость, **-и** fossil. **окамене́лый** fossil; fossilized; petrified. **о**|**камене́ть**, **-е́ю** *pf.*

о|**кантова́ть**, **-ту́ю** *pf.* **оканто́вка**, **-и** mount; edge.

ока́нчивать(ся, **-аю(сь** *impf. of* **око́нчить(ся ока́пывать(ся**, **-аю(сь** *impf. of* **окопа́ть(ся**

ока́янный damned, cursed.

океа́н, **-а** ocean. **океа́нский** ocean; oceanic; ocean-going; ~ **парохо́д** ocean liner.

оки́дывать, **-аю** *impf.*, **оки́нуть**, **-ну** *pf.* cast round; ~ **взгля́дом** take in at a glance, glance over.

о́кисел, **-сла** oxide. **окисле́ние**, **-я** oxidation. **окисли́ть**, **-лю́** *pf.* **окисля́ть**, **-я́ю** *impf.* oxidize; ~**ся** oxidize. **о́кись**, **-и** oxide.

оккупа́нт, **-а** invader; *pl.* occupying forces, occupiers. **оккупа́ция**, **-и** occupation. **окку-пи́ровать**, **-рую** *impf. & pf.* occupy.

окла́д, **-а** salary scale; (basic) pay; tax(-rate); metal overlay, setting.

оклевета́ть, **-ещу́**, **-е́щешь** *pf.* slander, calumniate, defame.

окле́ивать, **-аю** *impf.*, **окле́ить**, **-е́ю** *pf.* cover; glue over, paste over; ~ **обо́ями** paper.

окно́, **-а́**; *pl.* **о́кна** window; port; gap; aperture; interval, free period.

о́ко, **-а**; *pl.* **о́чи**, **оче́й** eye; **в мгнове́ние о́ка** in the twinkling of an eye.

окова́ть, **окую́**, **-ёшь** *pf.*, **око́вывать**, **-аю** *impf.* bind; fetter, shackle. **око́вы**, **око́в** *pl.* fetters.

окола́чиваться, **-аюсь** *impf.* lounge about, kick one's heels.

околдова́ть, **-ду́ю** *pf.*, **околдо́вывать**, **-аю** *impf.* bewitch, entrance, enchant.

околева́ть, **-а́ю** *impf.*, **околе́ть**, **-е́ю** *pf.* die. **околе́лый** dead.

о́коло *adv. & prep.*+*g.* by; close (to); near; around; about; **где́-нибудь** ~ hereabouts, somewhere here; ~ **э́того**, ~ **того́** thereabouts.

око́лыш, **-а** cap-band.

око́льн|**ый** roundabout; ~**ым путём** in a roundabout way.

о|**кольцева́ть**, **-цу́ю** *pf.*

око́нный window; ~ **переплёт** sash.

оконча́ние, **-я** end; conclusion, termination; ending; ~ **сле́дует** to be concluded. **оконча́тельно** *adv.* finally, definitively; completely. **оконча́тельный** final; definitive, decisive. **око́нчить**, **-чу** *pf.* (*impf.* **ока́нчивать**) finish, end; ~**ся** finish, end, terminate; be over.

око́п, **-а** trench; entrenchment. **окопа́ть**, **-а́ю** *pf.* (*impf.* **ока́пывать**) dig up, dig round; ~**ся** entrench o.s., dig in. **око́пн**|**ый** trench; ~**ая война́** trench warfare.

о́корок, **-а**; *pl.* **-а́**, **-о́в** ham, gammon; leg.

окостенева́ть, **-а́ю** *impf.*, **окостене́ть**, **-е́ю** *pf.* ossify; stiffen. **окостене́лый** ossified; stiff.

окочене́лый stiff with cold. **о**|**кочене́ть**, **-е́ю** *pf.*

око́шечко, **-а**, **око́шко**, **-а** (small) window; opening.

окра́ина, **-ы** outskirts, outlying districts; borders, marches.

о|**кра́сить**, **-а́шу** *pf.*, **окра́шивать**, **-аю** *impf.* paint, colour; dye; stain. **окра́ска**, **-и** painting; colouring; dyeing, staining; colouration; tinge, tint, touch, slant.

о|**кре́пнуть**, **-ну** *pf.* **о**|**крести́ть(ся**, **-ещу́(сь**, **-е́стишь(ся** *pf.*

окре́стность, **-и** environs; neighbourhood, vicinity. **окре́стный** neighbouring, surrounding.

о́крик, **-а** hail, call; cry, shout. **окри́кивать**, **-аю** *impf.*, **окри́кнуть**, **-ну** *pf.* hail, call, shout to.

окрова́вленный blood-stained, bloody.

окро́шка, **-и** okroshka (*a cold soup*); hotchpotch, jumble.

о́круг, **-а** okrug; region; district; circuit. **окру́га**, **-и** neighbourhood. **округлённый**; **-лён**, **-а́** rounded. **округли́ть**, **-лю́** *pf.*, **округля́ть**, **-я́ю** *impf.* round; round off; express in round numbers; ~**ся** become rounded; be expressed in round numbers. **окру́глый** rounded, roundish. **окружа́ть**, **-а́ю** *impf.*, **окружи́ть**, **-жу́** *pf.* surround; encircle. **окружа́ющ**|**ий** surrounding; ~**ая среда́** environment; ~**ее** *sb.* environment; ~**ие** *sb., pl.* associates; entourage. **окруже́ние**, **-я** encirclement; surroundings; environment; milieu; **в окруже́нии**+*g.* accompanied by; surrounded by, in the midst of. **окружн**|**о́й** okrug, district, circuit; circle;

~а́я желе́зная доро́га circle line. **окру́жность**, **-и** circumference; circle; neighbourhood; **на три ми́ли в окру́жности** within a radius of three miles, for three miles round. **окру́жный** neighbouring.

окрыли́ть, **-лю́** *pf.*, **окрыля́ть**, **-я́ю** *impf.* inspire, encourage.

окта́н, **-а** octane. **окта́нов|ый** octane; ~ое **число́** octane rating.

октя́брь, **-я́** *m.* October. **октя́брьский** October.

окуна́ть, **-а́ю** *impf.*, **окуну́ть**, **-ну́**, **-нёшь** *pf.* dip; ~**ся** dip; plunge; become absorbed, become engrossed.

о́кунь, **-я**; *pl.* **-и**, **-е́й** *m.* perch.

окупа́ть, **-а́ю** *impf.*, **окупи́ть**, **-плю́**, **-пишь** *pf.* compensate, repay, make up for; ~**ся** be compensated, be repaid, pay for itself; pay; be justified, be requited, be rewarded.

оку́ривание, **-я** fumigation. **оку́ривать**, **-аю** *impf.*, **окури́ть**, **-рю́**, **-ришь** *pf.* fumigate. **оку́рок**, **-рка** cigarette-end; (cigar-)stub.

оку́тать, **-аю** *pf.*, **оку́тывать**, **-аю** *impf.* wrap up; shroud, cloak; ~**ся** wrap up; be shrouded, be cloaked.

оку́чивать, **-аю** *impf.*, **оку́чить**, **-чу** earth up. **ола́дья**, **-и**; *g.pl.* **-ий** fritter; girdle scone, drop-scone.

оледене́лый frozen. **о|ледене́ть**, **-е́ю** *pf.* **о|ледени́ть**, **-и́т** *pf.*

оле́н|ий deer, deer's; reindeer; hart, hart's; ~**ий мох** reindeer moss; ~**ьи рога́** antlers. **оле́нина**, **-ы** venison. **оле́нь**, **-я** *m.* deer; reindeer.

оли́ва, **-ы** olive. **оли́вковый** olive; olive(-coloured).

олимпиа́да, **-ы** olympiad; competition. **олимпи́йск|ий** Olympic; Olympian; ~**ие и́гры** Olympic games, Olympics. **олимпи́ец**, **-и́йца**, **олимпи́йка**, **-и** Olympian, Olympic contender.

оли́фа, **-ы** drying oil.

олицетворе́ние, **-я** personification; embodiment. **олицетворённый**; **-рён**, **-а́** personified. **олицетвори́ть**, **-рю́** *pf.*, **олицетворя́ть**, **-я́ю** *impf.* personify, embody.

о́лово, **-а** tin; stannic; ~**ая посу́да** tinware; pewter; ~**ая фольга́** tinfoil.

ом, **-а** ohm.

омерзе́ние, **-я** loathing. **омерзе́ть**, **-е́ю** *pf.* become loathsome. **омерзи́тельн|ый** loathsome, sickening; ~**ое настрое́ние** foul mood.

омертве́лость, **-и** stiffness, numbness; necrosis, mortification. **омертве́л|ый** stiff, numb; necrotic; ~**ая ткань** dead tissue. **омертве́ние**, **-я** necrosis. **о|мертве́ть**, **-е́ю** *pf.*

омле́т, **-а** omelette.

омоложе́ние, **-я** rejuvenation.

омо́ним, **-а** homonym.

омо́ю *etc.*: *see* **омы́ть**

омрача́ть, **-а́ю** *impf.*, **омрачи́ть**, **-чу́** *pf.* darken, cloud, overcloud; ~**ся** become darkened, become clouded.

о́мут, **-а** pool; whirlpool; whirl, maelstrom.

омыва́ть, **-а́ю** *impf.*, **омы́ть**, **омо́ю** *pf.* wash; wash away, wash out; wash down; ~**ся** be washed.

он, **его́**, **ему́**, **им**, **о нём** *pron.* he. **она́**, **её**, **ей**, **ей** (**е́ю**), **о ней** *pron.* she.

онда́тра, **-ы** musk-rat, musquash. **онда́тровый** musquash.

онеме́лый dumb; numb. **о|неме́ть**, **-е́ю** *pf.*

они́, **их**, **им**, **и́ми**, **о них** *pron.* they. **оно́**, **его́**, **ему́**, **им**, **о нём** *pron.* it; this, that.

ООН *abbr.* (*of* **Организа́ция объединённых на́ций**) UN(O), United Nations (Organization). **оо́новский** United Nations.

опада́ть, **-а́ет** *impf.* of **опа́сть**. **опада́ющий** deciduous.

опа́здывать, **-аю** *impf.* of **опозда́ть**

опа́ла, **-ы** disgrace, disfavour.

о|пали́ть, **-лю́** *pf.*

опа́ловый opal; opaline.

опа́лубка, **-и** shuttering, casing.

опаса́ться, **-а́юсь** *impf.* +*g.* fear, be afraid of; +*g. or inf.* beware (of); avoid, keep off. **опасе́ние**, **-я** fear; apprehension; misgiving(s). **опа́сливый** cautious; wary.

опа́сность, **-и** danger; peril. **опа́сный** dangerous, perilous.

опа́сть, **-адёт** *pf.* (*impf.* **опада́ть**) fall, fall off; subside, go down.

опе́ка, **-и** guardianship, tutelage; trusteeship; guardians, trustees; care; surveillance. **опека́емый** *sb.* ward. **опека́ть**, **-а́ю** *impf.* be guardian of; take care of, watch over. **опеку́н**, **-а́**, **-у́нша**, **-и** guardian; tutor; trustee.

операти́вность, **-и** drive, energy. **операти́вный** energetic; efficient; executive; operative, surgical; operation(s); operational; strategical. **опера́тор**, **-а** operator; cameraman. **опера́торная** *sb.* management and control centre. **операцио́нн|ый** operating; surgical; ~**ая** *sb.* operating theatre. **опера́ция**, **-и** operation.

опереди́ть, **-режу́** *pf.*, **опережа́ть**, **-а́ю** *impf.* outstrip, leave behind; forestall.

опере́ние, **-я** plumage. **оперённый**; **-ён**, **-а́** feathered.

опере́тта, **-ы**, **-е́тка**, **-и** musical comedy, operetta.

опере́ть, **обопру́**, **-прёшь**; **опёр**, **-ла́** *pf.* (*impf.* **опира́ть**) +**о**+*a.* lean against; ~**ся**, **на** *or* **о**+*a.* lean on, lean against.

опери́ровать, **-рую** *impf.* & *pf.* operate on; operate, act; +*i.* operate with; use, handle.

опери́ть, **-рю́** *pf.* (*impf.* **оперя́ть**) feather; adorn with feathers; ~**ся** be fledged; stand on one's own feet.

о́перный opera; operatic; ~ **теа́тр** opera-house.

оперуполномо́ченный *sb.* C.I.D. officer; security officer.

опершись на+*a.* leaning on.

оперя́ть(ся, **-я́ю(сь** *impf.* of **опери́ть(ся**

опеча́лить(ся, **-лю(сь** *pf.*

опеча́тать, -аю *pf.* (*impf.* опеча́тывать) seal up.

опеча́тка, -и misprint; спи́сок опеча́ток errata.

опеча́тывать, -аю *impf. of* опеча́тать

опе́шить, -шу *pf.* be taken aback.

опи́вки, -вок *pl.* dregs.

опи́лки, -лок *pl.* sawdust; (metal) filings.

опира́ть(ся, -а́ю(сь *impf. of* опере́ть(ся

описа́ние, -я description; account. опи́санный circumscribed. описа́тельный descriptive. описа́ть, -ишу́, -и́шешь *pf.*, описы́вать, -аю *impf.* describe; list, inventory; circumscribe; distrain; ~ся make a slip of the pen. о́пись, -и list, schedule; inventory.

опла́кать, -а́чу *pf.*, опла́кивать, -аю *impf.* mourn for; bewail, deplore.

опла́та, -ы pay, payment; remuneration. оплати́ть, -ачу́, -а́тишь *pf.*, опла́чивать, -аю *impf.* pay for, pay; ~ расхо́ды meet the expenses, foot the bill; ~ счёт settle the account, pay the bill. опла́ченн|ый paid; с ~ым отве́том reply-paid.

оплачу́ *etc.: see* опла́кать. оплачу́ *etc.: see* оплати́ть

оплева́ть, -люю, -люёшь *pf.*, оплёвывать, -аю *impf.* spit on; humiliate.

оплеу́ха, -и slap in the face.

о|плеши́веть, -ею *pf.*

оплодотворе́ние, -я impregnation, fecundation; fertilization. оплодотвори́тель, -я *m.* fertilizer. оплодотвори́ть, -рю́ *pf.*, оплодотворя́ть, -яю *impf.* impregnate, fecundate; fertilize.

о|пломбирова́ть, -ру́ю *pf.*

опло́т, -а stronghold, bulwark.

опло́шность, -и blunder, oversight. опло́шный mistaken, blundering.

оплюю́ *etc.: see* оплева́ть

оповести́ть, -ещу́ *pf.*, оповеща́ть, -а́ю *impf.* notify, inform. оповеще́ние, -я notification; warning.

о|пога́нить, -ню *pf.*

опозда́вший *sb.* late-comer. опозда́ние, -я being late, lateness; delay; без опозда́ния on time; с ~м на де́сять мину́т ten minutes late. опозда́ть, -а́ю *pf.* (*impf.* опа́здывать) be late; be overdue; be slow.

опознава́тельный distinguishing; ~ знак landmark, beacon; marking. опознава́ть, -наю́, -наёшь *impf.*, опозна́ть, -а́ю *pf.* identify. опозна́ние, -я identification.

опозо́рение, -я defamation. о|позо́рить(ся, -рю(сь *pf.*

ополоскиватель, -я *m.*: ~ (для воло́с) hair conditioner.

ополза́ть, -а́ет *impf.*, оползти́, -зёт; -о́лз, -ла́ *pf.* slip, slide. о́ползень, -зня *m.* landslide, landslip.

ополча́ться, -а́юсь *impf.*, ополчи́ться, -чу́сь *pf.* take up arms; be up in arms; +на+a. fall on, attack. ополче́нец, -нца militiaman. ополче́ние, -я militia; irregulars; levies.

опо́мниться, -нюсь *pf.* come to one's senses, collect o.s.

опо́р, -а; во весь ~ at full speed, at top speed, full tilt.

опо́ра, -ы support; bearing; pier; buttress; то́чка опо́ры fulcrum, bearing.

опора́жнивать, -аю *impf. of* опорожни́ть

опо́рн|ый support, supporting, supported; bearing; ~ый прыжо́к vault; ~ый пункт strong point; ~ая то́чка fulcrum.

опоро́жни́ть, -ню *or* -ню́ *pf.*, опорожня́ть, -яю *impf.* (*impf. also* опора́жнивать) empty; drain.

о|пороси́ться, -и́тся *pf.* о|поро́чить, -чу *pf.*

опохмели́ться, -лю́сь *pf.*, опохмеля́ться, -я́юсь *impf.* take a hair of the dog that bit you.

опо́шлить, -лю *pf.*, опошля́ть, -я́ю *impf.* vulgarize, debase.

опоя́сать, -я́шу *pf.*, опоя́сывать, -аю *impf.* gird on; girdle.

оппозицио́нный opposition, in opposition; antagonistic, of opposition. оппози́ция, -и opposition.

оппони́ровать, -рую *impf.* (+*d.*) oppose.

опра́ва, -ы setting, mounting; case; rim.

оправда́ние, -я justification; excuse; acquittal, discharge. оправда́тельный пригово́р verdict of not guilty. оправда́ть, -а́ю *pf.*, опра́вдывать, -аю *impf.* justify, warrant; vindicate; authorize; excuse; acquit, discharge; ~ся justify o.s.; vindicate o.s.; be justified.

опра́вить, -влю *pf.*, оправля́ть, -я́ю *impf.* put in order, set right; adjust; set, mount; ~ся put one's dress in order; recover; +от+g. get over.

опра́шивать, -аю *impf. of* опроси́ть

определе́ние, -я definition; determination; decision; attribute. определённый definite; determinate; fixed; certain. определи́мый definable. определи́ть, -лю́ *pf.*, определя́ть, -я́ю *impf.* define; determine; fix, appoint; allot, assign; ~ на слу́жбу appoint; ~ся be formed; take shape; be determined; obtain a fix, find one's position.

опроверга́ть, -а́ю *impf.*, опрове́ргнуть, -ну; -ве́рг *pf.* refute, disprove. опроверже́ние, -я refutation; disproof; denial.

опрокидн|о́й tipping, tip-up. опроки́дывать, -аю *impf.*, опроки́нуть, -ну *pf.* overturn; upset; topple; overthrow; overrun; refute; knock back; ~ся overturn; topple over, tip over, tip up; capsize.

опроме́тчивый precipitate, rash, hasty, unconsidered. о́прометью *adv.* headlong.

опро́с, -а interrogation; (cross-)examination; referendum; (opinion) poll. опроси́ть, -ошу́, -о́сишь *pf.* (*impf.* опра́шивать) interrogate, question; (cross-)examine. опро́сный interrogatory; ~ лист questionnaire.

опроти́веть, -ею *pf.* become loathsome, become repulsive.

опры́скать, -аю *pf.*, опры́скивать, -аю *impf.* sprinkle; spray. опры́скиватель, -я *m.* sprinkler, spray(er).

опря́тный neat, tidy.

о́птик, -а optician. о́птика, -и optics; optical instruments. опти́ческий optic, optical; ~ обма́н optical illusion.

опто́вый wholesale. о́птом *adv.* wholesale; ~ и в ро́зницу wholesale and retail.

опубликова́ние, -я publication; promulgation. о|публикова́ть, -ку́ю *pf.*, опублико́вывать, -аю *impf.* publish; promulgate.

опуска́ть(ся, -а́ю(сь *impf. of* опусти́ть(ся опускн|о́й movable; ~а́я дверь trap-door.

опусте́лый deserted. о|пусте́ть, -е́ет *pf.*

опусти́ть, -ущу́, -у́стишь *pf.* (*impf.* опуска́ть) lower; let down; turn down; omit; ~ глаза́ look down; ~ го́лову hang one's head; ~ ру́ки lose heart; ~ што́ры draw the blinds; ~ся lower o.s.; sink; fall; go down; let o.s. go, go to pieces.

опустоша́ть, -а́ю *impf.*, опустоши́ть, -шу́ *pf.* devastate, lay waste, ravage. опусто- ше́ние, -я devastation, ruin. опустоши́- тельный devastating.

опу́тать, -аю *pf.*, опу́тывать, -аю *impf.* enmesh, entangle; ensnare.

опуха́ть, -а́ю *impf.*, о|пу́хнуть, -ну; опу́х *pf.* swell, swell up. опу́хлый swollen. о́пухоль, -и swelling; tumour.

опущу́ *etc.: see* опусти́ть

опыле́ние, -я pollination. опыли́ть, -лю́ *pf.*, опыля́ть, -я́ю *impf.* pollinate.

о́пыт, -а experience; experiment; test, trial; attempt. о́пытный experienced; experimental.

опьяне́лый intoxicated. опьяне́ние, -я intoxication. о|пьяне́ть, -е́ю *pf.*, о|пьяни́ть, -и́т *pf.*, опьяня́ть, -я́ет *impf.* intoxicate, make drunk. опьяня́ющий intoxicating.

опя́ть *adv.* again.

ора́ва, -ы crowd, horde.

ора́кул, -а oracle.

ора́нжевый orange. оранжере́йный hothouse, greenhouse. оранжере́я, -и hothouse, greenhouse, conservatory.

ора́тор, -а orator, (public) speaker. ора́тор- ский orator's, speaker's; oratorical. ора́тор- ствовать, -твую *impf.* orate, harangue; speechify.

ора́ть, ору́, орёшь *impf.* bawl, yell.

орби́та, -ы orbit; (eye-)socket; вы́вести на орби́ту put into orbit; ~ влия́ния sphere of influence.

орг... *abbr. in comb.* organization, organizational.

о́рган[1], -а organ; organization; unit, element; department, body; исполни́тельный о́рган executive; agency. орга́н[2], -а (*mus.*) organ. организа́тор, -а organizer. организацио́н- ный organization, organizational. организа́- ция, -и organization; ~ Объединённых на́ций United Nations Organization.

органи́зм, -а organism.

организо́ванный organized; orderly, disciplined. организова́ть, -зу́ю *impf. & pf.* (*pf. also* с~) organize; ~ся be organized; organize. органи́ческий, органи́чный organic.

о́ргия, -и orgy.

оргте́хника, -и office equipment.

орда́, -ы́; *pl.* -ы horde.

о́рден, -а; *pl.* -а́ order. орденоно́сец, -сца holder of an order or decoration. ордено- но́сный decorated with an order.

о́рдер, -а; *pl.* -а́ order; warrant; writ.

ордина́рец, -рца orderly; batman.

ордина́тор, -а house-surgeon. ординату́ра, -ы house-surgeon's appointment; clinical studies.

орды́нский of the (Tartar) horde(s).

орёл, орла́ eagle; ~ и́ли ре́шка? heads or tails?

орео́л, -а halo, aureole.

оре́х, -а nut, nuts; nut-tree; walnut. оре́хо- вый nut; walnut. орехоко́лка, -и nut- crackers. оре́шник, -а hazel; hazel-thicket.

оригина́л, -а original; eccentric, oddity. ори- гина́льный original.

ориента́ция, -и orientation (на+*a.* towards); understanding, grasp (в+*p.* of). ориенти́р, -а landmark; reference point, guiding line. ориенти́рование, -я orienteering. ориен- ти́роваться, -руюсь *impf. & pf.* orient o.s.; find, get, one's bearings; +на+*a.* head for, make for; aim at. ориентиро́вка, -и orien- tation. ориентиро́вочный serving for ori- entation, position-finding; tentative; provi- sional; rough; approximate.

орке́стр, -а orchestra; band.

орли́ный eagle's, eagle; aquiline. орли́ца, -ы female eagle.

орна́мент, -а ornament; ornamental design; plaster cast.

орнито́лог, -а ornithologist; ~-люби́тель bird- watcher. орнитоло́гия, -и ornithology.

оробе́лый timid; frightened. о|робе́ть, -е́ю *pf.*

ороси́тельный irrigation. ороси́ть, -ошу́ *pf.*, ороша́ть, -а́ю *impf.* irrigate. ороше́ние, -я irrigation; поля́ ороше́ния sewage farm.

ору́ *etc.: see* ора́ть

ору́дие, -я instrument; implement; tool; gun. ору́дийный gun. ору́довать, -дую *impf.+i.* handle; be active in; run; он там всем ору́- дует he runs the whole show there. ору- же́йн|ый arms; gun; ~ый заво́д arms fac- tory; ~ая пала́та armoury. ору́жие, -я arm, arms; weapons.

орфографи́ческ|ий orthographic, ortho- graphical; ~ая оши́бка spelling mistake. орфогра́фия, -и orthography, spelling.

орхиде́я, -и orchid.

оса́, -ы́; *pl.* -ы wasp.

оса́да, -ы siege. осади́ть[1], -ажу́ *pf.* (*impf.* осажда́ть) besiege, lay siege to; beleaguer; ~ вопро́сами ply with questions; ~ про́сь- бами bombard with requests.

осади́ть[2], **-ажу́**, **-а́дишь** *pf.* (*impf.* **осажда́ть**) precipitate.

осади́ть[3], **-ажу́**, **-а́дишь** *pf.* (*impf.* **оса́живать**) check, halt; force back; rein in; put in his (her) place; take down a peg.

оса́дн|ый siege; ~ое положе́ние state of siege.

оса́док, **-дка** sediment; precipitate; fall-out; after-taste; *pl.* precipitation, fall-out. **оса́дочный** precipitation; sedimentary.

осажда́ть, **-а́ю** *impf. of* **осади́ть**. **осажда́ться**, **-а́ется** *impf.* fall; be precipitated, fall out.

оса́живать, **-аю** *impf. of* **осади́ть**. **осажу́** *see* **осади́ть**

оса́нистый portly. **оса́нка**, **-и** carriage, bearing.

осва́ивать(ся, **-аю(сь** *impf. of* **осво́ить(ся**

осведоми́тель, **-я** *m.* informer. **осведоми́тельный** informative; information. **осве́домить**, **-млю** *pf.*, **осведомля́ть**, **-я́ю** *impf.* inform; ~ся о+*p.* inquire about, ask after. **осведомле́ние**, **-я** informing, notification. **осведомлённость**, **-и** knowledge, information. **осведомлённый** well-informed, knowledgeable; conversant, versed.

освежа́ть, **-а́ю** *impf.*, **освежи́ть**, **-жу́** *pf.* refresh; freshen; air; revive. **освежи́тельный** refreshing.

освети́тельный lighting, illuminating. **освети́ть**, **-ещу́** *pf.*, **освеща́ть**, **-а́ю** *pf.* light; light up; illuminate, illumine; throw light on; ~ся light up, brighten; be lighted. **освеще́ние**, **-я** light, lighting, illumination. **освещённый**; **-ён**, **-а́** lit; ~ луно́й moonlit.

о|свиде́тельствовать, **-твую** *pf.*

освиста́ть, **-ищу́**, **-и́щешь** *pf.*, **осви́стывать**, **-аю** *impf.* hiss (off); boo, hoot; greet with catcalls.

освободи́тель, **-я** *m.* liberator. **освободи́тельный** liberation, emancipation. **освободи́ть**, **-ожу́** *pf.*, **освобожда́ть**, **-а́ю** *impf.* free, liberate; release, set free; emancipate; dismiss; vacate; clear, empty; ~ся free o.s.; become free. **освобожде́ние**, **-я** liberation; release; emancipation; discharge; dismissal; vacation. **освобождённый**; **-ён**, **-а́** freed, free; exempt; ~ от нало́га tax-free.

освое́ние, **-я** assimilation, mastery, familiarization; reclamation, opening up. **осво́ить**, **-о́ю** *pf.* (*impf.* **осва́ивать**) assimilate, master; cope with; become familiar with; acclimatize; ~ся familiarize o.s.; feel at home.

о|святи́ть, **-ящу́** *pf.* **освящённый**; **-ён**, **-ена́** consecrated; sanctified, hallowed; обы́чай, ~ века́ми time-honoured custom.

осево́й axle; axis; axial.

оседа́ние, **-я** settling, subsidence; settlement. **оседа́ть**, **-а́ю** *impf. of* **осе́сть**

осёдланный saddled. **о|седла́ть**, **-а́ю** *pf.*, **осёдлывать**, **-аю** *impf.* saddle.

осе́длый settled.

осека́ться, **-а́юсь** *impf. of* **осе́чься**

осёл, **-сла́** donkey; ass.

осело́к, **-лка́** touchstone; hone, whetstone, oil-stone.

осени́ть, **-ню́** *pf.* (*impf.* **осеня́ть**) cover; overshadow; shield; dawn upon, strike; ~ся кресто́м cross o.s.

осе́нний autumn, autumnal. **о́сень**, **-и** autumn. **о́сенью** *adv.* in autumn.

осеня́ть(ся, **-я́ю(сь** *impf. of* **осени́ть(ся**

осерди́ться, **-ржу́сь**, **-рди́шься** *pf.* (+на+*a.*) become angry (with).

осеребри́ть, **-рю́** *pf.* silver (over).

осе́сть, **ося́ду**; **осе́л** *pf.* (*impf.* **оседа́ть**) settle; subside; sink; form a sediment.

осётр, **-а́** sturgeon. **осетри́на**, **-ы** sturgeon. **осетро́вый** sturgeon, sturgeon's.

осе́чка, **-и** misfire. **осе́чься**, **-еку́сь**, **-ечёшься** *pf.* (*impf.* **осека́ться**) misfire; stop short, break (off).

оси́ливать, **-аю** *impf.*, **оси́лить**, **-лю** *pf.* overpower; master; manage.

оси́на, **-ы** aspen. **оси́новый** aspen.

оси́ный wasp, wasp's; hornets'.

оси́плый hoarse, husky. **о|си́пнуть**, **-ну**; **оси́п** get hoarse, grow hoarse.

осироте́лый orphaned. **осироте́ть**, **-е́ю** *pf.* be orphaned.

оска́ливать, **-аю** *impf.*, **о|ска́лить**, **-лю** *pf.*; ~ зу́бы, ~ся show one's teeth, bare one's teeth.

о|сканда́лить(ся, **-лю(сь** *pf.*

оскверне́ние, **-я** defilement; profanation. **оскверни́ть**, **-ню́** *pf.*, **оскверня́ть**, **-я́ю** *impf.* profane; defile.

оскла́биться, **-блюсь** *pf.* grin.

оско́лок, **-лка** splinter; fragment. **оско́лочный** *adj.* splinter; fragmentation.

оско́мина, **-ы** bitter taste (in the mouth); наби́ть оско́мину set the teeth on edge. **оско́мистый** sour, bitter.

оскорби́тельный insulting, abusive. **оскорби́ть**, **-блю́** *pf.*, **оскорбля́ть**, **-я́ю** *impf.* insult; offend; ~ся take offence; be offended, be hurt. **оскорбле́ние**, **-я** insult; ~ де́йствием assault and battery. **оскорблённ|ый**; **-ён**, **-а́** offended, insulted; ~ая неви́нность outraged innocence.

ослабева́ть, **-а́ю** *impf.*, **о|слабе́ть**, **-е́ю** *pf.* weaken, become weak; slacken; abate. **осла-бе́лый** weakened, enfeebled. **ослаби́ть**, **-блю** *pf.*, **ослабля́ть**, **-я́ю** *impf.* weaken; slacken, relax; loosen. **ослабле́ние**, **-я** weakening, slackening, relaxation.

ослепи́тельный blinding, dazzling. **ослепи́ть**, **-плю́** *pf.*, **ослепля́ть**, **-я́ю** *impf.* blind, dazzle. **ослепле́ние**, **-я** blinding, dazzling; blindness. **о|сле́пнуть**, **-ну**; **-е́п** *pf.*

осли́ный donkey; ass's, asses'; asinine. **осли́ца**, **-ы** she-ass.

осложне́ние, **-я** complication. **осложни́ть**, **-ню́** *pf.*, **осложня́ть**, **-я́ю** *impf.* complicate; ~ся become complicated.

ослуша́ние, **-я** disobedience. **ослу́шаться**,

-аюсь *pf.*, ослу́шиваться, -аюсь *impf.* disobey.

ослы́шаться, -шусь *pf.* mishear. ослы́шка, -и mishearing, mistake of hearing.

осма́тривать(ся, -аю(сь *impf. of* осмотре́ть(ся. осме́ивать, -аю *impf. of* осмея́ть

о|смеле́ть, -е́ю *pf.* осме́ливаться, -аюсь *impf.*, осме́литься, -люсь *pf.* dare; beg to, take the liberty of.

осмея́ть, -ею́, -еёшь *pf.* (*impf.* осме́ивать) mock, ridicule.

о|смоли́ть, -лю́ *pf.*

осмо́тр, -а examination, inspection. осмотре́ть, -рю́, -ришь *pf.* (*impf.* осма́тривать) examine, inspect; look round, look over; ~ся look round; take one's bearings, see how the land lies. осмотри́тельный circumspect. осмо́трщик, -а inspector.

осмы́сленный sensible, intelligent. осмы́сливать, -аю *impf.*, осмы́слить, -лю *pf.*, осмысля́ть, -я́ю *impf.* interpret, give a meaning to; comprehend.

оснасти́ть, -ащу́ *pf.*, оснаща́ть, -а́ю *impf.* rig; fit out, equip. осна́стка, -и rigging. оснаще́ние, -я rigging; fitting out; equipment.

осно́ва, -ы base, basis, foundation; *pl.* principles, fundamentals; stem (*of a word*); warp (*of cloth*); на осно́ве+g. on the basis of; положи́ть в осно́ву take as a principle. основа́ние, -я founding, foundation; base; basis; ground, reason; на како́м основа́нии? on what grounds?; разру́шить до основа́ния raze to the ground. основа́тель, -я *m.* founder. основа́тельный well-founded; just; solid, sound; thorough; bulky. основа́ть, -ную́, -нуёшь *pf.*, осно́вывать, -аю *impf.* found; base; ~ся settle; base o.s.; founded, be based. основно́й fundamental, basic; principal, main; primary; в основно́м in the main, on the whole. основополо́жник, -а founder, initiator.

осо́ба, -ы person, individual, personage. осо́бенно *adv.* especially; particularly; unusually; не ~ not very, not particularly; not very much. осо́бенность, -и peculiarity; в осо́бенности especially, in particular; (more) particularly. осо́бенный special, particular, peculiar; ничего́ осо́бенного nothing in particular; nothing (very) much. особня́к, -а́ private residence; detached house. особняко́м *adv.* by o.s. осо́бо *adv.* apart, separately; particularly, especially. осо́бый special; particular; peculiar.

осовреме́нивать, -аю *impf.*, осовреме́нить, -ню, -нишь *pf.* modernize.

осознава́ть, -наю́, -наёшь *impf.*, осозна́ть, -а́ю *pf.* realize.

осо́ка, -и sedge.

о́спа, -ы smallpox; pock-marks; vaccination marks.

оспа́ривать, -аю *impf.*, оспо́рить, -рю *pf.* dispute, question; challenge, contest; contend for.

о|срами́ть(ся, -млю́(сь *pf.*

ост, -а east; east wind.

оставаться, -таю́сь, -таёшься *impf. of* остаться

оста́вить, -влю *pf.*, оставля́ть, -я́ю *impf.* leave; abandon, give up; reserve, keep; ~ в поко́е leave alone, let alone; ~ за собо́й пра́во reserve the right; ~ь(те)! stop it! stop that! lay off!

остальн|о́й the rest of; в ~о́м in other respects; ~о́е *sb.* the rest; ~ы́е *sb.*, *pl.* the others.

остана́вливать(ся, -аю(сь *impf. of* остановить(ся

оста́нки, -ов *pl.* remains.

остано́в, -а stop, stopper, ratchet-gear. останови́ть, -влю́, -вишь *pf.* (*impf.* остана́вливать) stop; interrupt; pull up, restrain; check; direct, concentrate; ~ся stop, come to a stop, come to a halt; stay, put up; +на+p. dwell on; settle on, rest on. остано́вка, -и stop; stoppage; hold-up; ~ за ва́ми you are holding us up.

оста́ток, -тка remainder; rest; residue; remnant; residuum; balance; *pl.* remains; leavings; leftovers. оста́точный residual. remaining. оста́ться, -а́нусь *pf.* (*impf.* оставаться) remain; stay; be left, be left over; за ним оста́лось пять рубле́й he owes five roubles; ~ в живы́х survive, come through; ~ на́ ночь stay the night; *impers.* (+d.) it is necessary; нам не остаётся ничего́ друго́го, как согласи́ться we have no choice but to agree.

о|стеклене́ть, -е́ет *pf.* остекли́ть, -лю́ *pf.*, остекля́ть, -я́ю *impf.* glaze.

остепени́ться, -ню́сь *pf.*, остепеня́ться, -я́юсь *impf.* settle down; become staid, become respectable; mellow.

остерега́ть, -а́ю *impf.*, остере́чь, -регу́, -режёшь; -рёг, -ла́ *pf.* warn, caution; ~ся (+g.) beware (of); be careful (of), be on one's guard (against).

о́стов, -а frame, framework; shell; hull; skeleton.

остолбене́лый dumbfounded. о|столбене́ть, -е́ю *pf.*

осторо́жно *adv.* carefully; cautiously; guardedly; ~! look out! 'with care'. осторо́жность, -и care, caution; prudence. осторо́жный careful, cautious; prudent.

острига́ть(ся, -а́ю(сь *impf. of* остри́чь(ся

острие́, -я́ point; spike; (cutting) edge. остри́ть[1], -рю́ *impf.* sharpen, whet. остри́ть[2], -рю́ *impf.* (*pf.* с~) be witty.

о|стри́чь, -игу́, -ижёшь; -иг *pf.* (*impf. also* острига́ть) cut, clip; ~ся cut one's hair; have one's hair cut.

остро... *in comb.* sharp, pointed. острогла́зый sharp-sighted, keen-eyed. ~коне́чный pointed. ~ли́ст, -а holly. ~но́сый sharp-nosed; pointed, tapered. ~сло́в, -а wit. ~уго́льный acute-angled. ~у́мие, -я wit. ~у́мный witty.

óстров, -а; *pl.* -á island; isle. **островнóй** island; insular. **островóк**, -вкá islet; ~ **безопáсности** (traffic) island.

острóта[1], -ы witticism, joke. **острота́**[2], -ы́ sharpness; keenness; acuteness; pungency; poignancy.

óстр|ый; остр, -á, -о sharp; pointed; acute; keen; ~ое положéние critical situation; ~ый сыр strong cheese; ~ый у́гол acute angle. **остря́к**, -á wit.

о|студи́ть, -ужу́, -у́дишь *pf.*, **остужа́ть**, -áю *impf.* cool.

оступáться, -áюсь *impf.*, **оступи́ться**, -плю́сь, -пишься *pf.* stumble.

остывáть, -áю *impf.*, **осты́ть**, -ы́ну *pf.* get cold; cool, cool down.

осуди́ть, -ужу́, -у́дишь *pf.*, **осужда́ть**, -áю *impf.* condemn, sentence; convict; censure, blame. **осужде́ние**, -я censure, condemnation; conviction. **осуждённый**; -ён, -á condemned, convicted; *sb.* convict, convicted person.

осу́нуться, -нусь *pf.* grow thin, get pinched-looking.

осуша́ть, -áю *impf.*, **осуши́ть**, -шу́, -шишь *pf.* drain; dry. **осуше́ние**, -я drainage. **осуши́тельный** drainage.

осуществи́мый practicable, realizable, feasible. **осуществи́ть**, -влю́ *pf.*, **осуществля́ть**, -я́ю *impf.* realize, bring about; accomplish, carry out; implement; ~ся be fulfilled, come true. **осуществле́ние**, -я realization; accomplishment; implementation.

осчастли́вить, -влю *pf.*, **осчастли́вливать**, -аю *impf.* make happy.

осыпать, -плю *pf.*, **осыпа́ть**, -áю *impf.* strew; shower; heap; pull down, knock down; ~ уда́рами rain blows on; ~ся crumble; fall. **óсыпь**, -и scree.

ось, -и; *g.pl.* -éй axis; axle; spindle; pin.

ося́ду *etc.: see* **осéсть**

осяза́емый tangible; palpable. **осяза́ние**, -я touch. **осяза́тельный** tactile, tactual; tangible, palpable, sensible. **осяза́ть**, -áю *impf.* feel.

от, ото *prep.*+*g.* from; of; for; against; **бли́зко от гóрода** near the town; **врéмя от врéмени** from time to time; **день ото дня** from day to day; **дрожа́ть от стра́ха** tremble with fear; **застрахова́ть от огня́** insure against fire; **ключ от две́ри** door-key; **на се́вер от Москвы́** north of Moscow; **от всей души́** with all one's heart; **от и́мени**+*g.* on behalf of; **от нача́ла до конца́** from beginning to end; **от ра́дости** for joy; **письмо́ от пе́рвого а́вгуста** letter of the first of August; **рабо́чий от станка́** machine operative; **сре́дство от** a remedy for; **сын от пре́жнего бра́ка** a son by a previous marriage; **умере́ть от го́лода** die of hunger; **це́ны от рубля́ и вы́ше** prices from a rouble upwards.

от..., **ото...**, **отъ...** *vbl. pref. indicating com-*

pletion of action or task, fulfilment of duty or obligation; action or motion away from a point; action continued through a certain time; (with vv. reflexive in form) action of negative character, cancelling or undoing of a state, omission, etc.

ота́пливать, -аю *impf. of* **отопи́ть**

отба́вить, -влю *pf.*, **отбавля́ть**, -я́ю *impf.* take away; pour off; **хоть отбавля́й** more than enough.

отберу́ *etc.: see* **отобра́ть**

отбива́ть(ся, -а́ю(сь *impf. of* **отби́ть(ся**. **отби́вка**, -и marking out, delineation; whetting, sharpening.

отбивн|óй; ~áя котле́та cutlet, chop.

отбира́ть, -а́ю *impf. of* **отобра́ть**

отби́тие, -я repulse; repelling. **отби́ть**, отобью́, -ёшь *pf.* (*impf.* **отбива́ть**) beat off, repulse, repel; parry; take; win over; break off, knock off; knock up; damage by knocks or blows; whet, sharpen; ~ся break off; drop behind, straggle; +от+*g.* defend o.s. against; repulse, beat off; ~ся от рук get out of hand.

от|бла́говестить, -ещу *pf.*

óтблеск, -а reflection.

отбóй, -я (-ю) repulse, repelling; retreat; ringing off; **бить** ~ beat a retreat; **дать** ~ ring off; ~ **возду́шной трево́ги** the all-clear; ~ **мяча́** return; **отбóю нет от** there is no getting rid of.

отбóр, -а selection. **отбóрный** choice, select(ed); picked. **отбóрочн|ый** selection; ~ая коми́ссия selection board; ~ое соревнова́ние knock-out competition.

отбра́сывать, -аю *impf.*, **отбрóсить**, -óшу *pf.* throw off; cast away; throw back, thrust back, hurl back, hurl back; give up, reject, discard; ~ **тень** cast a shadow. **отбрóс**, -а garbage, refuse; offal.

отбыва́ть, -áю *impf.*, **отбы́ть**, -бу́ду; óтбыл, -á, -о *pf.* depart, leave; serve, do; ~ **наказа́ние** serve one's sentence, do time.

отва́га, -и courage, bravery.

отва́дить, -а́жу *pf.*, **отва́живать**, -аю *impf.* scare away; +от+*g.* break of, cure of.

отва́живаться, -аюсь *impf.*, **отва́житься**, -жусь *pf.* dare, venture; have the courage. **отва́жный** courageous, brave.

отва́л, -а mould-board; dump, slag-heap; putting off, pushing off, casting off; **до** ~а to satiety; **нае́сться до** ~а eat one's fill, stuff o.s. **отва́ливать**, -аю *impf.*, **отвали́ть**, -лю́, -лишь *pf.* heave off; push aside; put off, push off, cast off; fork out, stump up.

отва́р, -а broth; decoction. **отва́ривать**, -аю *impf.*, **отвари́ть**, -рю́, -ришь *pf.* boil. **отварнóй** boiled.

отве́дать, -аю *pf.* (*impf.* **отве́дывать**) taste, try.

отведённый allotted. **отведу́** *etc.: see* **отвести́**

отве́дывать, -аю *impf. of* **отве́дать**

отвезти́, -зу́, -зёшь; -вёз, -ла́ *pf.* (*impf.* **отвози́ть**) take, take away; cart away.

отвёл *etc.*: *see* **отвести́**

отверга́ть, -а́ю *impf.*, **отве́ргнуть, -ну;** **-ве́рг** *pf.* reject, turn down; repudiate; spurn.

отвердева́ть, -а́ет *impf.*, **отверде́ть, -е́ет** *pf.* harden. **отверде́лость, -и** hardening; callus. **отверде́лый** hardened.

отве́рженец, -нца outcast. **отве́рженный** outcast.

отверну́ть, -ну́, -нёшь *pf.* (*impf.* **отвёрты-** **вать, отвора́чивать**) turn away, turn aside; turn down; turn on; unscrew; screw off, twist off; **~ся** turn away, turn aside; come on; come unscrewed.

отве́рстие, -я opening, aperture, orifice; hole; slot.

отверте́ть, -рчу́, -ртишь *pf.* (*impf.* **отвёрты-** **вать**) unscrew; screw off, twist off; **~ся** come unscrewed; get off; get out, wriggle out. **отвёртка, -и** screwdriver.

отвёртывать(ся, -аю(сь *impf. of* **отвер-** **ну́ть(ся, отверте́ть(ся**

отве́с, -а plumb, plummet; slope. **отве́сить,** **-е́шу** *pf.* (*impf.* **отве́шивать**) weigh out. **отве́сно** *adv.* plumb; sheer. **отве́сный** perpendicular, sheer.

отвести́, -еду́, -едёшь; -вёл, -а́ *pf.* (*impf.* **отводи́ть**) lead, take, conduct; draw aside; take aside; deflect; draw off; reject; challenge; allot, assign; **~ глаза́** look aside, look away; **~ глаза́ от** take one's eyes off; **~ ду́шу** unburden one's heart; **~ обвине́ние** justify o.s.

отве́т, -а answer, reply, response; responsibility; **быть в отве́те (за)** be answerable (for).

ответви́ться, -ится *pf.*, **ответвля́ться,** **-я́ется** *impf.* branch off. **ответвле́ние, -я** branch, offshoot; branch pipe; tap, shunt.

отве́тить, -е́чу *pf.*, **отвеча́ть, -а́ю** *impf.* answer, reply; **+на+**a. return; **+за+**a. answer for, pay for. **отве́тный** given in answer, answering. **отве́тственность, -и** responsibility; **привле́чь к отве́тственности** call to account, bring to book. **отве́тственный** responsible; crucial; **~ реда́ктор** editor-in-chief. **отве́тчик, -а** defendant, respondent; bearer of responsibility; **телефо́нный ~** answerphone, telephone answering machine.

отве́шивать, -аю *impf. of* **отве́сить. от-** **ве́шу** *etc.*: *see* **отве́сить**

отви́ливать, -аю *impf.*, **отвильну́ть, -ну́,** **-нёшь** *pf.* dodge.

отвинти́ть, -нчу́ *pf.*, **отви́нчивать, -аю** *impf.* unscrew; **~ся** unscrew, come unscrewed.

отвиса́ть, -а́ет *impf.*, **отви́снуть, -нет; -ис** *pf.* hang down, sag. **отви́сл|ый** hanging, baggy; **с ~ыми уша́ми** lop-eared.

отвлека́ть, -а́ю *impf.*, **отвле́чь, -еку́, -ечёшь;** **-влёк, -ла́** *pf.* distract, divert; draw away attention of; **~ся** be distracted; become abstracted. **отвлече́ние, -я** abstraction; dis-

traction. **отвлечённый** abstract.

отво́д, -а taking aside; deflection; diversion; leading, taking, conducting; withdrawal; rejection; challenge; allotment, allocation; tap, tapping. **отводи́ть, -ожу́, -о́дишь** *impf. of* **отвести́. отво́дка, -и** branch; diversion; shifting device, shifter. **отво́док, -дка** cutting, layer.

отвоева́ть, -ою́ю *pf.*, **отвоёвывать, -аю** *impf.* win back, reconquer; fight, spend in fighting; finish fighting, finish the war.

отвози́ть, -ожу́, -о́зишь *impf. of* **отвезти́. отвора́чивать(ся, -аю(сь** *impf. of* **отвер-** **ну́ть(ся**

отвори́ть, -рю́, -ришь *pf.* (*impf.* **отворя́ть**) open; **~ся** open.

отворо́т, -а lapel flap; top.

отворя́ть(ся, -я́ю(сь *impf. of* **отвори́ть(ся.** **отвою́ю** *etc.*: *see* **отвоева́ть**

отврати́тельный, отвра́тный repulsive, disgusting, loathsome; abominable. **отвра-** **ти́ть, -ащу́** *pf.*, **отвраща́ть, -а́ю** *impf.* avert, stave off; deter, stay the hand of. **отвра-** **ще́ние, -я** aversion, disgust, repugnance; loathing.

отвяза́ть, -яжу́, -я́жешь *pf.*, **отвя́зывать,** **-аю** *impf.* untie, unfasten; untether; **~ся** come untied, come loose; **+от+**g. get rid of, shake off, get shut of; leave alone, leave in peace; stop nagging at; **отвяжи́сь от меня́!** leave me alone!

отвыка́ть, -а́ю *impf.*, **отвы́кнуть, -ну; -вы́к** *pf.* **+от** *or inf.* break o.s. of, give up; lose the habit of; grow out of.

отгада́ть, -а́ю *pf.*, **отга́дывать, -аю** *impf.* guess. **отга́дка, -и** answer. **отга́дчик, -а** guesser, solver, diviner.

отгиба́ть(ся, -а́ю(сь *impf. of* **отогну́ть(ся** **отглаго́льный** verbal.

отгла́дить, -а́жу *pf.*, **отгла́живать, -аю** *impf.* iron (out).

отгова́ривать, -аю *impf.*, **отговори́ть, -рю́** *pf.* dissuade; talk out of; **~ся+**i. plead, excuse o.s. on the ground of. **отгово́рка, -и** excuse, pretext.

отголо́сок, -ска echo.

отго́н, -а driving off; distillation; distillate. **отго́нка, -и** driving off; distillation. **от-** **го́нн|ый; ~ые па́стбища** distant pastures. **отгоня́ть, -я́ю** *impf. of* **отогна́ть**

отгора́живать, -аю *impf.*, **отгороди́ть, -ожу́,** **-о́дишь** *pf.* fence off; partition off, screen off; **~ся** fence o.s. off; shut o.s. off, cut o.s. off.

отгрыза́ть, -а́ю *impf.*, **отгры́зть, -зу́, -зёшь** *pf.* gnaw off, bite off.

отдава́ть[1]**(ся, -даю́(сь** *impf. of* **отда́ть(ся.** **отдава́ть**[2]**, -аёт** *impf.*, *impers.+*i. taste of; smell of; smack of; **от него́ отдаёт во́дкой** he reeks of vodka.

отдави́ть, -влю́, -вишь *pf.* crush; **~ но́гу+**d. tread on the foot of.

отдале́ние, -я removal; estrangement; distance; **держа́ть в отдале́нии** keep at a distance. **отдалённость, -и** remoteness. **отдалённый** distant, remote. **отдали́ть, -лю́** *pf.*, **отдаля́ть, -я́ю** *impf.* remove; estrange, alienate; postpone, put off; **~ся** move away; digress.

отда́ние, -я giving back, returning. **отда́ть, -а́м, -а́шь, -а́ст, -ади́м; о́тдал, -а́, -о** *pf.* (*impf.* **отдава́ть**) give back, return; give; give up; devote; give in marriage; give away; put, place; make; sell, let have; recoil, kick; let go; cast off; **~ в шко́лу** send to school; **~ до́лжное**+*d.* render his due to; **~ под суд** prosecute; **~ прика́з** issue an order, give orders; **~ честь**+*d.* salute; **~ся** give o.s. (up); devote o.s.; resound; reverberate; ring. **отда́ча, -и** return; payment, reimbursement; letting go, casting off; efficiency, performance; output; recoil, kick.

отде́л, -а department; section, part.

отде́лать, -аю *pf.* (*impf.* **отде́лывать**) finish, put the finishing touches to; trim; decorate. **~ся**+*от*+*g.* get rid of, finish with; +*i.* escape with, get off with.

отделе́ние, -я separation; department, branch; compartment; section; part; **~ шка́фа** pigeon-hole. **отделённый** section; *sb.* section commander. **отделе́нский, отделе́нческий** department(al), branch. **отдели́мый** separable. **отдели́ть, -елю́, -е́лишь** *pf.* (*impf.* **отделя́ть**) separate, part; detach; separate off; cut off; **~ся** separate, part; detach o.s., itself; get detached; come apart; come off.

отде́лка, -и finishing; trimming; finish, decoration; décor. **отде́лочник, -а** (interior) decorator. **отде́лывать(ся, -аю(сь** *impf.* of **отде́лать(ся**

отде́льно separately; apart. **отде́льность, -и; в отде́льности** taken separately, individually. **отде́льный** separate, individual; independent. **отделя́ть(ся, -я́ю(сь** *impf.* of **отдели́ть(ся**

отдёргивать, -аю *impf.*, **отдёрнуть, -ну** *pf.* draw aside, pull aside; draw back, pull back; jerk back.

отдеру́ *etc.*: *see* **отодра́ть. отдира́ть, -а́ю** *impf. of* **отодра́ть**

отдохну́ть, -ну́, -нёшь *pf.* (*impf.* **отдыха́ть**) rest; have a rest, take a rest.

отду́шина, -ы air-hole, vent; safety-valve. **отду́шник, -а** air-hole, vent.

о́тдых, -а rest; relaxation; holiday. **отдыха́ть, -а́ю** *impf.* (*pf.* **отдохну́ть**) be resting; be on holiday. **отдыха́ющий** *sb.* holiday-maker.

отдыша́ться, -шу́сь, -шишься *pf.* recover one's breath.

отека́ть, -а́ю *impf. of* **оте́чь. о|тели́ться, -е́лится** *pf.* **оте́сать** *etc.*: *see* **обтеса́ть**

оте́ц, отца́ father; **~-одино́чка** single father. **оте́ческий** fatherly, paternal. **оте́чествен|ный** home, native; **~ая промы́шленность** home industry; **Вели́кая О~ая война́** Great

Patriotic War. **оте́чество, -а** native land, fatherland, home country.

оте́чь, -еку́, -ечёшь; отёк, -ла́ *pf.* (*impf.* **отека́ть**) swell, become swollen; gutter.

отжива́ть, -а́ю *impf.* **отжи́ть, -иву́, -ивёшь; о́тжил, -а́, -о** *pf.* become obsolete; become outmoded; **~ свой век** have had one's day; go out of fashion. **отжи́вший** obsolete; outmoded.

о́тзвук, -а echo.

о́тзыв[1], -а opinion, judgement; reference; testimonial; review; reply, response; **похва́льный ~** honourable mention. **отзы́в[2], -а** recall. **отзыва́ть(ся, -а́ю(сь** *impf. of* **отозва́ть(ся. отзывн|о́й; ~ые гра́моты** letters of recall. **отзы́вчивый** responsive.

отка́з, -а refusal; denial; repudiation; rejection; renunciation; giving up; failure; natural; **де́йствовать без ~а** run smoothly; **получи́ть ~** be refused, be turned down; **по́лный до ~а** full to capacity, cram-full. **отказа́ть, -ажу́, -а́жешь** *pf.*, **отка́зывать, -аю** *impf.* fail, break down; (+*d.* в+*p.*) refuse, deny; *от*+*g.* dismiss, discharge; **~ от до́ма** forbid the house; **~ся** (+*от*+*g.* *or* +*inf.*) refuse, decline; turn down; retract; renounce; give up; relinquish, abdicate; **~ся от свое́й по́дписи** repudiate one's signature; **~ся служи́ть** be out of order. **отка́зник, -а, отка́зница, -цы** refusenik.

отка́лывать(ся, -аю(сь *impf. of* **отколо́ть(ся. отка́пывать, -аю** *impf. of* **откопа́ть. отка́рмливать, -аю** *impf. of* **откорми́ть**

откати́ть, -ачу́, -а́тишь *pf.*, **отка́тывать, -аю** *impf.* roll away; **~ся** roll away; roll back, be forced back.

откача́ть, -а́ю *pf.*, **отка́чивать, -аю** *impf.* pump out; resuscitate, give artificial respiration to.

отка́шливаться, -аюсь *impf.*, **отка́шляться, -яюсь** *pf.* clear one's throat.

откидно́й folding, collapsible. **отки́дывать, -аю** *impf.*, **отки́нуть, -ну** *pf.* turn back, fold back; throw aside, cast away.

откла́дывать, -аю *impf. of* **отложи́ть**

откла́няться, -яюсь *pf.* take one's leave.

откле́ивать, -аю *impf.*, **откле́ить, -е́ю** *pf.* unstick; **~ся** come unstuck.

о́тклик, -а response; comment; echo; repercussion. **откликать́ся, -аюсь** *impf.*, **откли́кнуться, -нусь** *pf.* answer, respond.

отклоне́ние, -я deviation; divergence; declining, refusal; deflection, declination; error; diffraction; **~ в сто́рону** deviation; **~ от те́мы** digression. **отклони́ть, -ню́, -нишь** *pf.*, **отклоня́ть, -я́ю** *impf.* deflect; decline; **~ся** deviate; diverge; swerve.

отключа́ть, -а́ю *impf.*, **отключи́ть, -чу́** *pf.* cut off, disconnect.

отколоти́ть, -очу́, -о́тишь *pf.* knock off; beat up, thrash, give a good hiding.

отколо́ть, -лю́, -лешь *pf.* (*impf.* **отка́лы-**

вать) break off; chop off; unpin; ~ся break off; come unpinned; come undone; break away, cut o.s. off.

откопа́ть, -а́ю *pf.* (*impf.* **отка́пывать**) dig out; exhume, disinter; dig up, unearth.

откорми́ть, -млю́, -мишь *pf.* (*impf.* **отка́рмливать**) fatten, fatten up. **отко́рмленный** fat, fatted, fattened.

отко́с, -а slope; **пусти́ть под ~** derail.

открепи́ть, -плю́ *pf.*, **открепля́ть, -я́ю** *impf.* unfasten, untie; ~ся become unfastened.

открове́ние, -я revelation. **открове́нничать, -аю** *impf.* be candid, be frank; open one's heart. **открове́нный** candid, frank; blunt, outspoken; open, unconcealed; revealing. **откро́ю** *etc.*: *see* **откры́ть**

открути́ть, -учу́, -у́тишь *pf.*, **откру́чивать, -аю** *impf.* untwist, unscrew; ~ся come untwisted; +от+g. get out of.

открыва́лка, -и tin-, can-opener; corkscrew. **открыва́ть, -а́ю** *impf.*, **откры́ть, -ро́ю** *pf.* open; uncover, reveal, bare; discover; turn on; ~ **па́мятник** unveil a monument; ~ся open; come to light, be revealed; confide. **откры́тие, -я** discovery; revelation; opening; inauguration; unveiling. **откры́тка, -и** postcard. **откры́то** openly. **откры́тый** open; **на ~ом во́здухе, под ~ым не́бом** out of doors, in the open air; ~ое заседа́ние public sitting; ~ое письмо́ postcard; open letter.

отку́да *adv.* whence; where from; from which; ~ **вы об э́том зна́ете?** how do you come to know about that?; ~ **ни возьми́сь** quite unexpectedly, suddenly. **отку́да-либо, -нибу́дь** from somewhere or other. **отку́да-то** from somewhere.

отку́поривать, -аю *impf.*, **отку́порить, -рю** *pf.* uncork; open. **отку́порка, -и** opening, uncorking.

откуси́ть, -ушу́, -у́сишь *pf.*, **отку́сывать, -аю** *impf.* bite off; snap off, nip off.

отлага́тельство, -а delay; procrastination; **де́ло не те́рпит отлага́тельства** the matter is urgent. **отлага́ть(ся, -а́ю(сь** *impf. of* **отложи́ть(ся**

от|лакирова́ть, -ру́ю *pf.* **отла́мывать, -аю** *impf. of* **отлома́ть, отломи́ть**

отлежа́ть, -жу́ *pf.*, **отлёживать, -аю** *impf.*; **я отлежа́л но́гу** my foot has gone to sleep.

отлепи́ть, -плю́, -пишь *pf.*, **отлепля́ть, -я́ю** *impf.* unstick, take off; ~ся come unstuck, come off.

отлёт, -а flying away; departure; **на ~е** on the point of departure, about to leave; in one's outstretched hand; (standing) by itself. **отлета́ть, -а́ю** *impf.*, **отлете́ть, -лечу́** *pf.* fly, fly away, fly off; vanish; rebound, bounce back; come off, burst off.

отли́в, -а ebb, ebb-tide; tint; play of colours; **с золоты́м ~ом** shot with gold. **отлива́ть, -а́ю** *impf.*, **отли́ть, отолью́; о́тлил, -а́, -о** *pf.* pour off; pump out; cast, found; (*no pf.*)

+*i.* to be shot with. **отли́вка, -и** casting, founding; cast, ingot, moulding. **отливно́й** cast, casting; founded, moulded.

отлича́ть, -а́ю *impf.*, **отличи́ть, -чу́** *pf.* distinguish; single out; ~ **одно́ от друго́го** tell one (thing) from another; ~ся distinguish o.s., excel; differ; +*i.* be notable for. **отли́чие, -я** difference; distinction; **в ~ от** unlike, as distinguished from, in contradistinction to; **знак отли́чия** order, decoration; **с отли́чием** with honours. **отли́чник, -а** outstanding student, worker, etc. **отличи́тельный** distinctive; distinguishing. **отли́чно** *adv.* excellently; perfectly; extremely well. **отли́чный** different; excellent; perfect; extremely good.

отло́гий sloping. **отло́гость, -и** slope. **отло́же** *comp. of* **отло́гий**

отложе́ние, -я sediment, precipitation; deposit. **отложи́ть, -ожу́, -о́жишь** *pf.* (*impf.* **откла́дывать, отлага́ть**) put aside; put away, put by; put off, postpone; adjourn; turn back, turn down; unharness; deposit; ~ся detach o.s., separate; deposit, be deposited. **отложно́й воротни́к** turn-down collar.

отлома́ть, -а́ю, отломи́ть, -млю́, -мишь *pf.* (*impf.* **отла́мывать**) break off.

отлуча́ть, -а́ю *impf.*, **отлучи́ть, -чу́** *pf.* separate, remove; ~ **(от це́ркви)** excommunicate; ~ся absent o.s. **отлу́чка, -и** absence; **быть в отлу́чке** be absent, be away.

отлы́нивать, -аю *impf.*+от+g. shirk.

отма́лчиваться, -аюсь *impf. of* **отмолча́ться**

отма́хивать, -аю *impf.*, **отмахну́ть, -ну́, -нёшь** *pf.* brush off; wave away; ~ся от+g. brush off; brush aside.

отмежева́ться, -жу́юсь *pf.*, **отмежёвываться, -аюсь** *impf.* от+g. dissociate o.s. from; refuse to acknowledge.

о́тмель, -и bar, (sand-)bank; shallow.

отме́на, -ы abolition; abrogation, repeal, revocation; cancellation; countermand. **отмени́ть, -ню́, -нишь** *pf.*, **отменя́ть, -я́ю** *impf.* abrogate, repeal, revoke, rescind; abolish; cancel, countermand; disaffirm.

отмере́ть, отомрёт; о́тмер, -ла́, -ло *pf.* (*impf.* **отмира́ть**) die off; die out, die away.

отме́ривать, -аю *impf.*, **отме́рить, -рю** *pf.*, **отмеря́ть, -я́ю** *impf.* measure off.

отмести́, -ету́, -етёшь; -ёл, -а́ *pf.* (*impf.* **отмета́ть**) sweep aside.

отме́стка, -и revenge.

отмета́ть, -а́ю *impf. of* **отмести́**

отме́тина, -ы mark, notch; star, blaze. **отме́тить, -е́чу** *pf.*, **отмеча́ть, -а́ю** *impf.* mark, note; make a note of; point to, mention, record; celebrate, mark by celebration; ~ся sign one's name; sign out. **отме́тка, -и** note; mark; blip. **отме́тчик, -а** marker.

отмира́ние, -я dying off; dying away, fading away, withering away. **отмира́ть, -а́ет** *impf. of* **отмере́ть**

отмолча́ться, -чу́сь *pf.* (*impf.* **отма́лчиваться**) keep silent, say nothing.

отмора́живать, -аю *impf.*, **отморо́зить, -о́жу** *pf.* injure by frost-bite. **отморо́жение, -я** frost-bite. **отморо́женный** frost-bitten.

отмо́ю *etc.*: see **отмы́ть**

отмыва́ть, -а́ю *impf.*, **отмы́ть, -мо́ю** *pf.* wash clean; wash off, wash away; ~**ся** wash o.s. clean; come out, come off.

отмы́чка, -и picklock; master key.

отнёкиваться, -аюсь *impf.* refuse.

отнести́, -су́, -сёшь; -нёс, -ла́ *pf.* (*impf.* **относи́ть**) take; carry away, carry off; ascribe, attribute, refer; ~**сь к**+*d.* treat; regard; apply to; concern, have to do with; date from; **э́то к де́лу не отно́сится** that's beside the point, that is not relevant.

отнима́ть(ся, -а́ю(сь *impf. of* **отня́ть(ся**

относи́тельно *adv.* relatively; *prep.*+*g.* concerning, about, with regard to. **относи́тельность, -и** relativity. **относи́тельный** relative; ~**ое местоиме́ние** relative pronoun. **относи́ть¹(ся, -ошу́(сь, -о́сишь(ся** *impf. of* **отнести́(сь. относи́ть², -ошу́, -о́сишь** *pf.* stop wearing. **отноше́ние, -я** attitude; treatment; relation; respect; ratio; letter, memorandum; *pl.* relations; terms; **в не́которых отноше́ниях** in some respects; **в отноше́нии**+*g.*, **по отноше́нию к**+*d.* with respect to, with regard to; **в прямо́м (обра́тном) отноше́нии** in direct (inverse) ratio; **не име́ть отноше́ния к**+*d.* bear no relation to, have nothing to do with.

отны́не *adv.* henceforth, henceforward.

отня́тие, -я taking away; amputation. **отня́ть, -ниму́, -ни́мешь; о́тнял, -а́, -о** *pf.* (*impf.* **отнима́ть**) take (away); amputate; ~ **от груди́** wean; ~ **три от шести́** take three away from six; **э́то отня́ло у меня́ три часа́** it took me three hours; ~**ся** be paralysed; **у него́ отняла́сь пра́вая рука́** he has lost the use of his right arm.

ото *see* **от. ото... see от...**

отобража́ть, -а́ю *impf.*, **отобрази́ть, -ажу́** *pf.* reflect; represent. **отображе́ние, -я** reflection; representation.

отобра́ть, отберу́, -рёшь; отобра́л, -а́, -о *pf.* (*impf.* **отбира́ть**) take (away); seize; select, pick out.

отобью́ *etc.*: see **отби́ть**

отовсю́ду *adv.* from everywhere.

отогна́ть, отгоню́, -о́нишь; отогна́л, -а́, -о *pf.* (*impf.* **отгоня́ть**) drive away, off; keep off; distil (off).

отогну́ть, -ну́, -нёшь *pf.* (*impf.* **отгиба́ть**) bend back; flange; ~**ся** bend back.

отогрева́ть, -а́ю *impf.*, **отогре́ть, -е́ю** *pf.* warm; ~**ся** warm o.s.

отодвига́ть, -а́ю *impf.*, **отодви́нуть, -ну** *pf.* move aside; put off, put back; ~**ся** move aside.

отодра́ть, отдеру́, -рёшь; отодра́л, -а́, -о *pf.* (*impf.* **отдира́ть**) tear off, rip off; flog.

отож(д)естви́ть, -влю́ *pf.*, **отож(д)ествля́ть, -я́ю** *impf.* identify.

отожжённый, -ён, -а́ annealed.

отозва́ть, отзову́, -вёшь; отозва́л, -а́, -о *pf.* (*impf.* **отзыва́ть**) take aside; recall; ~**ся на**+*a.* answer; respond to; **о**+*a.* speak of; **на**+*a. or p.* tell on; have an affect on.

отойти́, -йду́, -йдёшь; отошёл, -шла́ *pf.* (*impf.* **отходи́ть**) move away; move off; leave, depart; withdraw; recede; fall back; digress, diverge; come out, come away, come off; recover; come to o.s., come round; pass, go; be lost.

отолью́ *etc.*: see **отли́ть. отомрёт** *etc.*: see **отмере́ть**

ото|мсти́ть, -мщу́ *pf.*

отопи́тельный heating. **отопи́ть, -плю́, -пишь** *pf.* (*impf.* **ота́пливать**) heat. **отопле́ние, -я** heating.

отопру́ *etc.*: see **отпере́ть. отопью́** *etc.*: see **отпи́ть**

ото́рванность, -и detachment, isolation; loneliness. **ото́рванный** cut off, isolated, out of touch. **оторва́ть, -ву́, -вёшь** *pf.* (*impf.* **отрыва́ть**) tear off; tear away; ~**ся** come off, be torn off; be cut off, lose touch, lose contact; break away; tear o.s. away; ~**ся от земли́** take off.

оторопе́лый dumbfounded. **оторопе́ть, -е́ю** *pf.* be struck dumb.

отосла́ть, -ошлю́, -ошлёшь *pf.* (*impf.* **отсыла́ть**) send (off), dispatch; send back; +**к**+*d.* refer to.

отошёл *etc.*: see **отойти́. отошлю́** *etc.*: see **отосла́ть**

отоща́лый emaciated. **о|тоща́ть, -а́ю** *pf.*

отпада́ть, -а́ет *impf. of* **отпа́сть. отпаде́ние, -я** falling away; defection.

от|пари́ровать, -рую *pf.* **отпа́рывать, -аю** *impf. of* **отпоро́ть**

отпа́сть, -адёт *pf.* (*impf.* **отпада́ть**) fall off, drop off; fall away; defect, drop away; pass, fade.

отпере́ть, отопру́, -прёшь; о́тпер, -ла́, -ло *pf.* (*impf.* **отпира́ть**) unlock; open; ~**ся** open; +**от**+*g.* deny; disown.

отпе́тый arrant, inveterate.

от|печа́тать, -аю *pf.*, **отпеча́тывать, -аю** *impf.* print (off); type (out); imprint; unseal, open (up); ~**ся** leave an imprint; be printed. **отпеча́ток, -тка** imprint, print; impress.

отпива́ть, -а́ю *impf. of* **отпи́ть**

отпи́ливать, -аю *impf.*, **отпили́ть, -лю́, -лишь** *pf.* saw off.

отпира́тельство, -а denial, disavowal. **отпира́ть(ся, -а́ю(сь** *impf. of* **отпере́ть(ся**

отпи́ть, отопью́, -пьёшь; о́тпил, -а́, -о *pf.* (*impf.* **отпива́ть**) sip, take a sip of.

отпи́хивать, -аю *impf.*, **отпихну́ть, -ну́, -нёшь** *pf.* push off; shove aside.

отпла́та, -ы repayment. **отплати́ть, -ачу́, -а́тишь** *pf.*, **отпла́чивать, -аю** *impf.*+*d.* pay back, repay, requite; ~ **той же моне́той** pay back in his own coin.

отплыва́ть, -а́ю *impf.*, **отплы́ть**, -ыву́, -ывёшь; -ы́л, -а́, -о *pf.* sail, set sail; swim off.

отплы́тие, -я sailing, departure.

о́тповедь, -и reproof, rebuke.

отполза́ть, -а́ю *impf.* **отползти́**, -зу́, -зёшь; -о́лз, -ла́ *pf.* crawl away.

от|полирова́ть, -ру́ю *pf.* **от|полоска́ть**, -ощу́ *pf.*

отпо́р, -а repulse; rebuff; **встре́тить** ~ meet with a rebuff; **дать** ~ repulse.

отпоро́ть[1], -рю́, -решь *pf.* (*impf.* **отпа́рывать**) rip off, rip out.

отпоро́ть[2], -рю́, -решь *pf.* flog, thrash, give a thrashing.

отправи́тель, -я *m.* sender. **отпра́вить**, -влю *pf.*, **отправля́ть**, -я́ю *impf.* send, forward, dispatch; ~**ся** set out, set off, start; leave, depart. **отпра́вка**, -и sending off, forwarding, dispatch. **отправле́ние**, -я sending; departure; exercise, performance; ~ **обя́занностей** performance of one's duties. **отправн|о́й**; ~**о́й пункт**, ~**а́я то́чка** starting-point.

от|пра́здновать, -ную *pf.*

отпра́шиваться, -аюсь *impf.*, **отпроси́ться**, -ошу́сь, -о́сишься *pf.* ask for leave, get leave.

отпры́гивать, -аю *impf.*, **отпры́гнуть**, -ну *pf.* jump back, spring back; jump aside, spring aside; bounce back.

о́тпрыск, -а offshoot, scion.

отпряга́ть, -а́ю *impf. of* **отпря́чь**

отпря́дывать, -аю *impf.*, **отпря́нуть**, -ну *pf.* recoil, start back.

отпря́чь, -ягу́, -яжёшь; -я́г, -ла́ *pf.* (*impf.* **отпряга́ть**) unharness.

отпу́гивать, -аю *impf.*, **отпугну́ть**, -ну́, -нёшь *pf.* frighten off, scare away.

о́тпуск, -а, *loc.* -у́; *pl.* -а́ leave, holiday(s); furlough; issue, delivery, distribution; tempering, drawing; **в** ~**е**, **в** ~**у́** on leave; ~ **по боле́зни** sick-leave. **отпуска́ть**, -а́ю *impf.*, **отпусти́ть**, -ущу́, -у́стишь *pf.* let go, let off; let out; set free; release; give leave (of absence); relax, slacken; (let) grow; issue, give out; serve; assign, allot; remit; forgive; temper, draw; ~ **шу́тку** crack a joke. **отпускни́к**, -а́ person on leave, holiday-maker; soldier on leave. **отпускн|о́й** holiday; leave; on leave; ~**ы́е де́ньги** holiday pay; ~**а́я цена́** (wholesale) selling price. **отпуще́ние**, -я remission; **козёл отпуще́ния** scapegoat. **отпу́щенник**, -а freedman.

отраба́тывать, -аю *impf.*, **отрабо́тать**, -аю *pf.* work off; work (for); finish work; finish working on; master. **отрабо́танный** worked out; waste, spent, exhaust.

отра́ва, -ы poison; bane. **отрави́тель**, -я *m.* poisoner. **отрави́ть**, -влю́, -вишь *pf.*, **отравля́ть**, -я́ю *impf.* poison; ~**ся** poison o.s.

отра́да, -ы joy, delight; comfort. **отра́дный** gratifying, pleasing; comforting.

отража́тель, -я *m.* reflector; scanner; ejec-

tor. **отража́тельный** reflecting, deflecting; reverberatory. **отража́ть**, -а́ю *impf.*, **отрази́ть**, -ажу́ *pf.* reflect; repulse, repel, parry; ward off; ~**ся** be reflected; reverberate; +**на**+*p.* affect, tell on.

отраслево́й branch. **о́трасль**, -и branch.

отраста́ть, -а́ет *impf.*, **отрасти́**, -тёт; отро́с, -ла́ *pf.* grow. **отрасти́ть**, -ащу́ *pf.*, **отра́щивать**, -аю *impf.* (let) grow.

от|реаги́ровать, -рую *pf.* **от|регули́ровать**, -рую *pf.* **от|редакти́ровать**, -рую *pf.*

отре́з, -а cut; length; ~ **на пла́тье** dress-length. **отреза́ть**, -е́жу *pf.*, **отреза́ть**, -а́ю *impf.* cut off; divide, apportion; snap.

о|трезве́ть, -ею *pf.* **отрезви́тельный** sobering. **отрезви́ть**, -влю́, -ви́шь *pf.*, **отрезвля́ть**, -я́ю *impf.* sober; ~**ся** become sober, sober up. **отрезвле́ние**, -я sobering (up).

отрезно́й cutting; tear-off, cut-off. **отре́зок**, -зка piece, cut; section; portion; segment; ~ **вре́мени** period, space of time.

отрека́ться, -а́юсь *impf. of* **отре́чься**

от|рекомендова́ть(ся, -ду́ю(сь *pf.* **отрёкся** *etc.: see* **отре́чься**. **от|ремонти́ровать**, -рую *pf.* **от|репети́ровать**, -рую *pf.*

отре́пье, -я, **отре́пья**, -ьев *pl.* rags.

от|реставри́ровать, -йрую *pf.*

отрече́ние, -я renunciation; ~ **от престо́ла** abdication. **отре́чься**, -еку́сь, -ечёшься *pf.* (*impf.* **отрека́ться**) renounce, disavow, give up.

отреша́ть, -а́ю *impf.*, **отреши́ть**, -шу́ *pf.* release; dismiss, suspend; ~**ся** renounce, give up; get rid of. **отрешённость**, -и estrangement, aloofness.

отрица́ние, -я denial; negation. **отрица́тельный** negative; bad, unfavourable. **отрица́ть**, -а́ю *impf.* deny; disclaim.

отро́г, -а spur.

отро́дье, -я race, breed, spawn.

отро́с *etc.: see* **отрасти́**. **отро́сток**, -тка shoot, sprout; branch, extension; appendix.

о́трочески adolescent. **о́трочество**, -а adolescence.

отруба́ть, -а́ю *impf. of* **отруби́ть**

о́труби, -ей *pl.* bran.

отруби́ть, -блю́, -бишь *pf.* (*impf.* **отруба́ть**) chop off; snap back.

от|руга́ть, -а́ю *pf.*

отры́в, -а tearing off; alienation, isolation; loss of contract, estrangement; **без** ~**а от произво́дства** while remaining at work; **в** ~**е от**+*g.* out of touch with; ~ **(от земли́)** take-off. **отрыва́ть(ся**, -а́ю(сь *impf. of* **оторва́ть(ся. отры́вистый** jerky, abrupt; curt. **отрывно́й** detachable, tear-off. **отры́вок**, -вка fragment, except; passage. **отры́вочный** fragmentary, scrappy.

отры́жка, -и belch; belching, eructation; survival, throw-back.

от|ры́ть, -ро́ю *pf.*

отря́д, -а detachment; order. **отряди́ть**, -яжу́ *pf.*, **отряжа́ть**, -а́ю *impf.* detach, detail, tell off.

отря́хивать, -аю *impf.*, отряхну́ть, -ну́, -нёшь *pf.* shake down, shake off; ~ся shake o.s. down.

от|салютова́ть, -ту́ю *pf.*

отса́сывание, -я suction. отса́сыватель, -я *m.* suction pump. отса́сывать, -аю *impf. of* отсоса́ть

о́тсвет, -a reflection; reflected light. отсве́чивать, -аю *impf.* be reflected; +*i.* shine with, reflect.

отсебя́тина, -ы words of one's own; ad-libbing.

отсе́в, -a sifting, selection; siftings, residue. отсева́ть(ся, -а́ю(сь, отсе́ивать(ся, -аю(сь *impf. of* отсе́ять(ся. отсе́вки, -ов *pl.* siftings, residue.

отсе́к, -a compartment. отсека́ть, -аю *impf.*, отсе́чь, -еку́, -ечёшь; -сёк, -ла́ *pf.* sever, chop off, cut off. отсече́ние, -я cutting off, severance; дать го́лову на ~ stake one's life. отсе́чка, -и cut-off.

отсе́ять, -е́ю *pf.* (*impf.* отсева́ть, отсе́ивать) sift, screen; eliminate; ~ся fall out, fall off; fall away, drop out.

отска́кивать, -аю *impf.*, отскочи́ть, -чу́, -чишь *pf.* jump aside, jump away; rebound, bounce back; come off, break off.

отслу́живать, -аю *impf.*, отслужи́ть, -жу́, -жишь *pf.* serve; serve one's time; have served its turn, be worn out.

отсове́товать, -тую *pf.*+*d.* dissuade.

отсоса́ть, -осу́, -осёшь *pf.* (*impf.* отса́сывать) suck off, draw off; filter by suction.

отсро́чивать, -аю *impf.*, отсро́чить, -чу *pf.* postpone, delay, defer; adjourn; extend (date of). отсро́чка, -и postponement, delay, deferment; adjournment; respite; extension.

отстава́ние, -я lag; lagging behind. отстава́ть, -таю́, -аёшь *impf. of* отста́ть

отста́вить, -влю *pf.*, отставля́ть, -я́ю *impf.* set aside, put aside; dismiss, discharge; rescind; ~! as you were! отста́вка, -и dismissal, discharge; resignation; retirement; в отста́вке retired, in retirement; вы́йти в отста́вку resign, retire. отставно́й retired.

отста́ивать(ся, -аю(сь *impf. of* отстоя́ть(ся

отста́лость, -и backwardness. отста́лый backward; у́мственно ~ mentally retarded; физи́чески ~ physically handicapped. отста́ть, -а́ну *pf.* (*impf.* отстава́ть) fall behind, drop behind; lag behind; be backward, be retarded; be behind(hand); be left behind, become detached; lose touch; break (off); break o.s.; be slow; come off; ~ на полчаса́ be half an hour late; ~ от break o.s. of, give up; leave alone.

от|стега́ть, -а́ю *pf.*

отстёгивать, -аю *impf.*, отстегну́ть, -ну́, -нёшь *pf.* unfasten, undo; unbutton; ~ся come unfastened, come undone.

отсто́й, -я sediment, deposit. отсто́йник, -a settling tank; sedimentation tank; cesspool.

отстоя́ть[1], -ою́ *pf.* (*impf.* отста́ивать) defend, save; stand up for; ~ свои́ права́ assert one's rights. отстоя́ть[2], -ои́т *impf.* be ... away; ста́нция отстои́т от це́нтра го́рода на два киломе́тра the station is two kilometres from the town centre. отстоя́ться, -ои́тся *pf.* (*impf.* отста́иваться) settle; precipitate; become stabilized, become fixed.

отстра́ивать(ся, -аю(сь *impf. of* отстро́ить(ся

отстране́ние, -я pushing aside; dismissal, discharge. отстрани́ть, -ню́ *pf.*, отстраня́ть, -я́ю *impf.* push aside, lay aside; dismiss, discharge, remove; suspend; ~ся move away; keep out of the way, keep aloof; ~ся от dodge; relinquish.

отстре́ливаться, -аюсь *impf.*, отстреля́ться, -я́юсь *pf.* fire back.

отстрига́ть, -а́ю *impf.*, отстри́чь, -игу́, -ижёшь; -и́г *pf.* cut off, clip.

отстро́ить, -о́ю *pf.* (*impf.* отстра́ивать) complete the construction of, finish building; build up; ~ся finish building; be built up.

отступа́ть, -а́ю *impf.*, отступи́ть, -плю́, -пишь *pf.* step back; recede; retreat, fall back; back down; ~ от+*g.* go back on; give up; swerve from, deviate from; ~ся от+*g.* give up, renounce; go back on. отступле́ние, -я retreat; deviation; digression. отсту́пник, -a apostate; recreant. отступн|о́й; ~ые де́ньги, -о́е *sb.* indemnity, compensation. отступя́ *adv.* (farther) off, away (от+*g.* from).

отсу́тствие, -я absence; lack, want; за ~м+*g.* in the absence of; for lack of, for want of; находи́ться в отсу́тствии be absent. отсу́тствовать, -твую *impf.* be absent; default. отсу́тствующий absent; *sb.* absentee.

отсчита́ть, -а́ю *pf.*, отсчи́тывать, -аю *impf.* count off, count out; read off.

отсыла́ть, -а́ю *impf. of* отосла́ть. отсы́лка, -и dispatch; reference; ~ де́нег remittance.

отсы́пать, -плю *pf.*, отсыпа́ть, -а́ю *impf.* pour off; measure off; ~ся pour out.

отсыре́лый damp. от|сыре́ть, -е́ет *pf.*

отсю́да *adv.* from here; hence; from this.

отта́ивать, -аю *impf. of* отта́ять

отта́лкивание, -я repulsion. отта́лкивать, -аю *impf. of* оттолкну́ть. отта́лкивающий repulsive, repellent.

отта́чивать, -аю *impf. of* отточи́ть

отта́ять, -а́ю *pf.* (*impf.* отта́ивать) thaw out.

оттени́ть, -ню́ *pf.*, оттеня́ть, -я́ю *impf.* shade, shade in; set off, make more prominent. отте́нок, -нка shade, nuance; tint, hue.

о́ттепель, -и thaw.

оттесни́ть, -ню́ *pf.*, оттесня́ть, -я́ю *impf.* drive back, press back; push aside, shove aside.

оттого́ *adv.* that is why; ~, что because.

о́ттиск, -a impression; off-print, reprint.

оттолкну́ть, -ну́, -нёшь *pf.* (*impf.* отта́лкивать) push away, push aside; antagonize, alienate; ~ся push off.

оттопы́ренный protruding, sticking out. **оттопы́ривать**, -аю *impf.*, **оттопы́рить**, -рю *pf.* stick out; ~ гу́бы pout; ~ся protrude, stick out; bulge.

отточи́ть, -чу́, -чишь *pf.* (*impf.* **отта́чивать**) sharpen, whet.

отту́да *adv.* from there.

оття́гивать, -аю *impf.*, **оттяну́ть**, -ну́, -нешь *pf.* draw out, pull away; draw off; delay. **оття́жка**, -и delay, procrastination; guyrope; strut, brace, stay.

отупе́лый stupefied, dulled. **отупе́ние**, -я stupefaction, dullness, torpor. **о|тупе́ть**, -е́ю *pf.* grow dull, sink into torpor.

от|утю́жить, -жу *pf.*

отуча́ть, -а́ю *impf.*, **отучи́ть**, -чу́, -чишь *pf.* break (of); ~ся break o.s. (of).

от|футбо́лить, -лю *pf.*, **отфутбо́ливать**, -аю *impf.* pass on; send on; send from pillar to post.

отха́ркать, -аю *pf.*, **отха́ркивать**, -аю expectorate. **отха́ркивающ|ий** *adv.*; ~ее (сре́дство) expectorant.

отхлебну́ть, -ну́, -нешь *pf.*, **отхлёбывать**, -аю *impf.* sip, take a sip of; take a mouthful of.

отхлы́нуть, -нет *pf.* flood back, rush back, rush away.

отхо́д, -а departure, sailing; withdrawal, retirement, falling back; ~ от deviation from; break with. **отходи́ть**, -ожу́, -о́дишь *impf. of* **отойти́**. **отхо́дчивый** not bearing grudges. **отхо́ды**, -ов *pl.* waste; siftings; screenings; tailings.

отцвести́, -ету́, -етёшь; -ёл, -а́ *pf.*, **отцвета́ть**, -а́ю *impf.* finish blossoming, fade.

отцепи́ть, -плю́, -пишь *pf.*, **отцепля́ть**, -я́ю *impf.* unhook; uncouple; ~ся come unhooked, come uncoupled; +от+g. leave alone. **отце́пка**, -и uncoupling.

отцо́вский father's; paternal. **отцо́вство**, -а paternity.

отча́иваться, -аюсь *impf. of* **отча́яться**

отча́ливать, -аю *impf.*, **отча́лить**, -лю *pf.* cast off; push off.

отча́сти *adv.* partly.

отча́яние, -я despair. **отча́янный** despairing; desperate; daredevil. **отча́яться**, -а́юсь *pf.* (*impf.* **отча́иваться**) despair.

отчего́ *adv.* why. **отчего́-либо**, **-нибу́дь** *adv.* for some reason or other. **отчего́-то** *adv.* for some reason.

от|чека́нить, -ню *pf.*

о́тчество, -а patronymic; как его́ по о́тчеству? what is his patronymic?

отчёт, -а account; дать ~ в+p. give an account of; report on; отда́ть себе́ ~ в+p. be aware of, realize. **отчётливый** distinct; precise; intelligible, clear. **отчётность**, -и bookkeeping; accounts. **отчётный** *adj.*; ~ год financial year, current year; ~ докла́д report.

отчи́зна, -ы country, native land; fatherland. **о́тчий** paternal. **о́тчим**, -а step-father.

отчисле́ние, -я deduction; assignment; dismissal. **отчи́слить**, -лю *pf.*, **отчисля́ть**, -я́ю *impf.* deduct; assign; dismiss.

отчита́ть, -а́ю *pf.*, **отчи́тывать**, -аю *impf.* scold, read a lecture, tell off; ~ся report back; +в+p. give an account of, report on.

отчужда́ть, -у́ж *pf.*, **отчужда́ть**, -а́ю *impf.* alienate; estrange. **отчужде́ние**, -я alienation; estrangement.

отшатну́ться, -ну́сь, -нёшься *pf.*, **отша́тываться**, -аюсь *impf.* start back, recoil; +от+g. give up, forsake, break with.

отшвы́ривать, -аю *impf.*, **отшвырну́ть**, -ну́, -нёшь *pf.* fling away; throw off.

отше́льник, -а hermit, anchorite; recluse.

от|шлифова́ть, -фу́ю *pf.* **от|штукату́рить**, -рю *pf.*

отшути́ться, -учу́сь, -у́тишься *pf.*, **отшу́чиваться**, -аюсь *impf.* reply with a joke; laugh it off.

отщепе́нец, -нца renegade.

отъ... *see* **от...**

отъе́зд, -а departure. **отъезжа́ть**, -а́ю *impf.*, **отъе́хать**, -е́ду *pf.* drive off, go off. **отъе́зжий** distant.

отъя́вленный thorough; inveterate.

отыгра́ть, -а́ю *pf.*, **оты́грывать**, -аю *impf.* win back; ~ся win, get, back what one has lost; get one's own back, get one's revenge.

отыска́ть, -ыщу́, -ы́щешь *pf.*, **оты́скивать**, -аю *impf.* find; track down, run to earth; look for, try to find; ~ся turn up, appear.

офице́р, -а officer. **офице́рский** officer's, officers'. **офице́рство**, -а officers; commissioned rank.

официа́льный official.

официа́нт, -а waiter. **официа́нтка**, -и waitress.

официо́з, -а semi-official organ (*of the press*). **официо́зный** semi-official.

офо́рмитель, -я *m.* decorator, stage-painter. **офо́рмить**, -млю *pf.*, **оформля́ть**, -я́ю *impf.* get up, mount, put into shape; register officially, legalize; ~ пье́су stage a play; ~ся take shape; be registered; legalize one's position; be taken on the staff, join the staff. **оформле́ние**, -я get-up; mounting, staging; registration, legalization.

офса́йд, -а (*sport*) offside.

ох *int.* oh! ah!

оха́пка, -и armful; взять в оха́пку take in one's arms.

о|характеризова́ть, -зу́ю *pf.*

о́хать, -аю *impf.* (*pf.* **о́хнуть**) moan, groan; sigh.

охва́т, -а scope, range; inclusion; outflanking, envelopment. **охвати́ть**, -ачу́, -а́тишь *pf.*, **охва́тывать**, -аю *impf.* envelop; enclose; grip, seize; comprehend, take in; outflank; +i. draw into, involve in. **охва́ченный** seized, gripped; ~ у́жасом terror-stricken.

охладева́ть, -а́ю *impf.*, **охладе́ть**, -е́ю *pf.* grow cold. **охладе́лый** cold; grown cold.

охлади́тельный cooling, cool. охлади́ть, -ажу́ *pf.*, охлажда́ть, -а́ю *impf.* cool, chill; refrigerate, freeze; ~ся become cool, cool down. охлажда́ющ|ий cooling, refrigerating; ~ая жи́дкость coolant. охлажде́ние, -я cooling, chilling; refrigerating; freezing; coolness; с возду́шным ~м air-cooled.

о|хмеле́ть, -е́ю *pf.* о́хнуть, -ну *pf.* of о́хать

охо́та[1], -ы hunt, hunting; chase.

охо́та[2], -ы desire, wish; inclination.

охо́титься, -о́чусь *impf.* hunt. охо́тник[1], -а hunter; sportsman.

охо́тник[2], -а volunteer; +до+*g. or inf.* lover of, enthusiast for.

охо́тничий hunting; sporting, shooting.

охо́тно *adv.* willingly, gladly, readily.

о́хра, -ы ochre.

охра́на, -ы guarding; protection; conservation, preservation; guard. охрани́ть, -ню́ *pf.*, охраня́ть, -я́ю *impf.* guard, protect; preserve. охра́нка, -и secret police. охра́нн|ый guard, protection; ~ая гра́мота, ~ый лист safe-conduct, pass.

охри́плый, охри́пший hoarse, husky. о|хри́пнуть, -ну; охри́п *pf.* become hoarse.

о|хроме́ть, -е́ю *pf.*

о|цара́пать(ся, -аю(сь *pf.*

оце́нивать, -аю *impf.*, оцени́ть, -ню́, -нишь *pf.* estimate, evaluate; appraise; appreciate. оце́нка, -и estimation, evaluation; appraisal; estimate; appreciation. оце́нщик, -а valuer.

оцепене́лый torpid, benumbed. о|цепене́ть, -е́ю *pf.*

оцепи́ть, -плю, -пишь *pf.*, оцепля́ть, -я́ю *impf.* surround; cordon off. оцепле́ние, -я surrounding; cordoning off; cordon.

оцинко́ванный galvanized.

оча́г, -а́ hearth; centre, seat; focus; nidus; дома́шний ~ hearth, home; ~ зара́зы nidus of affection; ~ землетрясе́ния focus of earthquake; ~ сопротивле́ния pocket of resistance.

очарова́ние, -я charm, fascination. очарова́тельный charming, fascinating. очарова́ть, -ру́ю *pf.*, очаро́вывать, -аю charm, fascinate.

очеви́дец, -дца eye-witness. очеви́дно *adv.* obviously, evidently. очеви́дный obvious, evident, manifest, patent.

о́чень *adv.* very; very much.

очередн|о́й next; next in turn; periodic, periodical; recurrent; usual, regular; routine; ~а́я зада́ча immediate task; ~о́й о́тпуск usual holiday. о́чередь, -и; *g.pl.* -е́й turn; queue, line; burst, salvo; на о́череди next (in turn); по о́череди in turn, in order, in rotation; в пе́рвую ~ in the first place, in the first instance; ~ за ва́ми it is your turn; стоя́ть в о́череди (за+*i*) queue (for), stand in line (for).

о́черк, -а essay, sketch, study; outline.

о|черни́ть, -ню́ *pf.*

очерстве́лый hardened, callous. о|черстве́ть, -е́ю *pf.*

очерта́ние, -я outline(s), contour(s). очерти́ть, -рчу́, -ртишь *pf.*, оче́рчивать, -аю *impf.* outline, trace.

очёски, -ов *pl.* combings; flocks.

оче́чник, -а spectacle case.

о́чи *etc.: see* о́ко

очи́нивать, -аю *impf.* о|чини́ть, -ню́, -нишь *pf.* sharpen, point.

очисти́тельный purifying, cleansing. о|чи́стить, -и́щу *pf.*, очища́ть, -а́ю *impf.* clean; cleanse, purify; refine; rectify; clear; free; peel; ~ся clear o.s.; become clear (от+*g.* of). очи́стка, -и cleaning; cleansing, purification; refinement, rectification; clearance; freeing; mopping up; для очи́стки со́вести for conscience sake. очи́стки, -ов *pl.* peelings. очище́ние, -я cleansing; purification.

очки́, -о́в *pl.* glasses, spectacles; goggles; защи́тные ~ protective goggles. очко́, -а́; *g.pl.* -о́в pip; point; hole. очко́в|ый[1]; ~ая систе́ма points system. очко́в|ый[2]; ~ая змея́ cobra.

очну́ться, -ну́сь, -нёшься *pf.* wake, wake up; come to (o.s.), regain consciousness.

о́чн|ый; ~ое обуче́ние internal courses; ~ая ста́вка confrontation.

очути́ться, -у́тишься *pf.* find o.s.; come to be.

о|швартова́ть, -ту́ю *pf.*

оше́йник, -а collar.

ошеломи́тельный stunning. ошеломи́ть, -млю́ *pf.*, ошеломля́ть, -я́ю *impf.* stun. ошеломле́ние, -я stupefaction.

ошиба́ться, -а́юсь *impf.*, ошиби́ться, -бу́сь, -бёшься; -и́бся *pf.* be mistaken, make a mistake, make mistakes; be wrong; err, be at fault. оши́бка, -и mistake; error; blunder; по оши́бке by mistake. оши́бочный erroneous, mistaken.

ошпа́ривать, -аю *impf.*, о|шпа́рить, -рю *pf.* scald.

о|штрафова́ть, -фу́ю *pf.* о|штукату́рить, -рю *pf.* о|щени́ться, -и́тся *pf.*

ощети́ниваться, -ается *impf.*, о|щети́ниться, -нится *pf.* bristle (up).

о|щипа́ть, -плю́, -плешь *pf.*, ощи́пывать, -аю *impf.* pluck.

ощу́пать, -аю *pf.*, ощу́пывать, -аю *impf.* feel, touch; grope about. о́щупь, -и; на ~ to the touch; by touch; идти́ на ~ grope one's way; feel one's way. о́щупью *adv.* gropingly, fumblingly; by touch; blindly; идти́ ~ grope one's way, feel one's way; иска́ть ~ grope for.

ощути́|мый, ощути́тельный perceptible, tangible, palpable; appreciable. ощути́ть, -ущу́ *pf.*, ощуща́ть, -а́ю *impf.* feel, sense, experience. ощуще́ние, -я sensation; feeling, sense.

П

п *letter: see* пэ

па *nt.indecl.* step, *pas.*

па́ва, -ы peahen.

павиа́н, -а baboon.

павильо́н, -а pavilion; film studio.

павли́н, -а peacock.

па́водок, -дка (sudden) flood, freshet.

па́вш|ий fallen; **~ие в бою́** (those) who fell in action.

па́губа, -ы ruin, destruction; bane. **па́губный** pernicious, ruinous; baneful; fatal.

па́даль, -и carrion.

па́дать, -аю *impf.* (*pf.* **пасть, упа́сть**) fall; sink; drop; decline; fall out, drop out; die; **~ ду́хом** lose heart, lose courage; **~ от уста́лости** be ready to drop. **па́дающ|ий** falling; incident; incoming; **~ие звёзды** shooting stars. **паде́ж, -á** case. **паде́ние, -я** fall; drop, sinking; degradation; slump; incidence; dip. **па́дкий на**+*a. or* **до**+*g.* having a weakness for; susceptible to; greedy for. **паду́ч|ий** falling; **~ая (боле́знь)** falling sickness, epilepsy.

па́дчерица, -ы step-daughter.

па́дш|ий fallen; **~ие** *sb., pl.* the fallen.

паёк, пайка́ ration.

па́зуха, -и bosom; sinus; axil; **за па́зухой** in one's bosom.

пай, -я; *pl.* **-и́, -ёв** share. **па́йщик, -а** shareholder.

пак, -а pack-ice.

Пакиста́н, -а Pakistan.

паке́т, -а parcel, package; packet; (*official*) letter; paper bag.

па́кля, -и tow; oakum.

накова́ть, -ку́ю *impf.* (*pf.* **за~, у~**) pack.

па́костить, -ощу *impf.* (*pf.* **за~, ис~, на~**) soil, dirty; spoil, mess up; +*d.* play dirty tricks on. **па́костный** dirty, mean, foul; nasty. **па́кость, -и** filth; dirty trick; obscenity, dirty word.

пакт, -а pact; **~ догово́ра** covenant; **~ о ненападе́нии** non-agression pact.

паланти́н, -а (fur) stole, cape.

пала́та, -ы ward; chamber, house; hall; *pl.* palace; **Оруже́йная ~** Armoury; **~ мер и весо́в** Board of Weights and Measures; **~ о́бщин** House of Commons; **торго́вая ~** Chamber of Commerce. **пала́тка, -и** tent; marquee; stall, booth; **в ~x** under canvas. **пала́тн|ый** ward; **~ая сестра́** (ward) sister.

пала́точный tent; tented, of tents.

пала́ч, -á hangman; executioner; butcher.

па́лец, -льца finger; toe; pin, peg; cam, cog, tooth; **знать как свои́ пять па́льцев** have at one's finger-tips; **он па́льцем никого́ не тро́нет** he wouldn't harm a fly; **~ о ~ не уда́рить** not lift a finger; **смотре́ть сквозь па́льцы на**+*a.* close one's eyes to.

палиса́д, -а paling; palisade, stockade. **палиса́дник, -а** (*small*) front garden.

палиса́ндр, -а rosewood.

пали́тра, -ы palette.

пали́ть[1], -лю́ *impf.* (*pf.* **о~, с~**) burn; scorch.

пали́ть[2], -лю́ *impf.* (*pf.* **вы́~, пальну́ть**) fire, shoot.

па́лка, -и stick; walking-stick, cane; staff; **из-под па́лки** under the lash, under duress; **~ о двух конца́х** double-edged weapon.

пало́мник, -а pilgrim. **пало́мничество, -а** pilgrimage.

па́лочка, -и stick; bacillus; **дирижёрская ~** (conductor's) baton. **па́лочковый** bacillary. **па́лочный** stick, cane.

па́луба, -ы deck. **па́лубный; ~ груз** deck cargo.

пальба́, -ы́ fire, cannonade.

па́льма, -ы palm(-tree). **па́льмов|ый** palm; **~ая ветвь** olive-branch; **~ое де́рево** boxwood.

пальну́ть, -ну́, -нёшь *pf. of* **пали́ть**

пальто́ *nt.indecl.* (over)coat; topcoat.

паля́щий burning, scorching.

па́мятник, -а monument; memorial; tombstone. **па́мятн|ый** memorable; memorial; **~ая кни́жка** notebook, memorandum book. **па́мять, -и** memory; recollection; remembrance; mind, consciousness; **без па́мяти** unconscious; **на ~** by heart; **по па́мяти** from memory; **подари́ть на ~** give as a keepsake.

пана́ма, -ы, пана́мка, -и panama (hat).

пане́ль, -и pavement, footpath; panel(ling); wainscot(ing). **пане́льн|ый** panelling; **~ая обши́вка** panelling, wainscot.

па́ника, -и panic. **паникёр, -а** panicmonger, scaremonger, alarmist.

панихи́да, -ы office for the dead; requiem; **гражда́нская ~** (civil) funeral. **панихи́дный** requiem; funereal.

пани́ческий panic; panicky.

панк, -а punk. **па́нковый** punk.

панно́ *nt.indecl.* panel.

пансио́н, -а boarding-school; boarding-house; board and lodging; **ко́мната с ~ом** room and board. **пансиона́т, -а** living in; holiday hotel. **пансионе́р, -а** boarder; guest.

пантало́ны, -о́н *pl.* trousers; knickers, panties.

панте́ра, -ы panther.

па́па[1], -ы *m.* (the) Pope.

па́па[2], -ы *m.,* **папа́ша, -и** *m.* daddy; papa.

папиро́са, -ы (*Russian*) cigarette. **папиро́сн|ый** *adj.;* **~ая бума́га** rice-paper.

па́пка, -и file; document case, folder; cardboard, pasteboard.

па́поротник, -а fern.

па́пский papal. па́пство, -а papacy.

пар¹, -а (-у), *loc.* -у́; *pl.* -ы́ steam; exhalation; на всех пара́х full steam ahead, at full speed.

пар², -а, *loc.* -у́; *pl.* -ы́ fallow.

па́ра, -ы pair, couple; (two-piece) suit.

пара́граф, -а paragraph.

пара́д, -а parade; review; возду́шный ~ air-display, fly-past. па́радность, -и magnificence; ostentation. пара́дн|ый parade; gala; main, front; ~ая дверь front door; ~ые ко́мнаты state rooms, (suite of) reception rooms; ~ый подъе́зд main entrance; ~ая фо́рма full dress (uniform).

парализо́ванный paralysed. парализова́ть, -зу́ю *impf. & pf.* paralyse. парали́ч, -а́ paralysis, palsy. парали́чный paralytic.

паралле́ль, -и parallel. паралле́льн|ый parallel; ~ые бру́сья parallel bars; ~ая медици́на alternative, complementary medicine.

пара́ф, -а flourish; initials. парафи́ровать, -рую *impf. & pf.* initial.

парашю́т, -а parachute; на ~е by parachute; прыжо́к с ~ом parachute jump. парашюти́ст, -а parachute jumper; paratrooper.

паре́ние, -я soaring.

па́рень, -рня; *g.pl.* -рне́й *m.* boy, lad; chap, fellow.

пари́ *nt.indecl.* bet; держа́ть ~ bet, lay a bet.

Пари́ж, -а Paris. парижа́нин, -а; *pl.* -а́не, -а́н, парижа́нка, -и Parisian. пари́жский Parisian.

пари́к, -а́ wig. парикма́хер, -а barber; hairdresser. парикма́херская *sb.* barber's, hairdresser's.

пари́ровать, -рую *impf. & pf.* (*pf. also* от~) parry, counter.

парите́т, -а parity. парите́тн|ый; на ~ых нача́лах on a par, on an equal footing.

пари́ть¹, -рю́ *impf.* soar, swoop, hover.

па́рить², -рю *impf.* steam, induce sweating in; stew; *impers.* па́рит it is sultry; ~ся (*pf.* по~ся) steam, sweat; stew.

парк, -а park; yard, depot; fleet; stock; pool; ваго́нный ~ rolling-stock.

па́рка, -и steaming; stewing.

парке́т, -а parquet.

па́ркий steamy.

па́ркинг, -а car park. паркова́ть, -ку́ю *impf.* (*pf.* за~) park. парко́вочный; ~ автома́т, ~ счётчик parking meter.

парла́мент, -а parliament. парламента́рный parliamentarian. парламенте́р, -а envoy; bearer of flag of truce. парламенте́рский; ~ флаг flag of truce. парла́ментский parliamentary; ~ зако́н Act of Parliament.

парни́к, -а́ hot bed, seed-bed; frame. парнико́в|ый *adj.*; ~ые расте́ния hothouse plants.

парни́шка, -и boy, lad.

парн|о́й fresh; steamy; ~о́е молоко́ milk fresh from the cow. па́рный¹ steamy.

па́рный² pair; forming a pair; twin; pair-horse.

паро... *in comb.* steam-. парово́з, -а locomotive, (steam-)engine. ~во́зник, -а engine-driver, engineer. ~во́зный engine. ~выпускно́й exhaust. ~непроница́емый steam-tight, steam-proof. ~обра́зный vaporous. ~прово́д, -а steam-pipe. ~силово́й steam-power. ~хо́д, -а steamer; steamship; колёсный ~ paddle-boat. ~хо́дный steam; steamship; ~хо́дное о́бщество steamship company. ~хо́дство, -а steam-navigation; steamship-line.

паров|о́й steam; steamed; ~а́я маши́на steam-engine; ~о́е отопле́ние steam heating; central heating.

пароди́ст, -а mimic, impressionist.

паро́ль, -я *m.* password, countersign.

паро́м, -а ferry(-boat). паро́мщик, -а ferryman.

паро́сский Parian.

парт... *abbr. in comb.* Party. партакти́в, -а Party activists. ~биле́т, -а Party (membership) card. ~кабине́т, -а Party educational centre. ~ко́м, -а Party committee. ~о́рг, -а Party organizer. ~организа́ция, -и Party organization. ~съезд, -а Party congress.

па́рта, -ы (*school*) desk.

парте́р, -а stalls; pit.

парти́ец, -и́йца Party member.

партиза́н, -а; *g.pl.* -а́н partisan; guerilla. партиза́нск|ий partisan, guerilla; unplanned, haphazard; ~ая война́ guerilla warfare; ~ое движе́ние Resistance (movement).

парти́йка, -и Party member. парти́йность, -и Party membership; Party spirit, Party principles. парти́йный party; Party; *sb.* Party member.

партиту́ра, -ы score.

па́ртия, -и party; group; batch; lot; consignment; game, set; part.

партнёр, -а partner. партнёрство, -а partnership.

па́рус, -а; *pl.* -а́, -о́в sail; идти́ под ~а́ми sail, be under sail; на всех ~а́х in full sail; подня́ть ~а́ set sail. паруси́на, -ы canvas, sail-cloth; duck. па́русник, -а sailing vessel. па́русный sail; ~ спорт sailing.

парфюме́рия, -и perfumery.

парча́, -и́; *g.pl.* -е́й brocade. парчо́вый brocade.

паря́щ|ий soaring, hovering; ~ая маши́на hovercraft.

пас¹, -а (*cards*) pass; в э́том де́ле я ~ (*coll.*) I'm no good at this.

пас², -а (*sport*) pass; ~ сюда́! pass!

па́сека, -и apiary, beehive. па́сечный *adj.* beekeeper's, beekeeping.

пасётся *see* пасти́сь

па́сквиль, -я *m.* libel, lampoon. па́сквильный libellous.

па́смурный dull, cloudy; overcast; gloomy, sullen. пасова́ть, -су́ю *impf.* (*pf.* с~) pass;

be unable to cope (with), give up, give in.

паспорт, -a; *pl.* -á passport; registration certificate.

пассáж, -a passage; arcade.

пассажúр, -a passenger. **пассажúрск|ий** passenger; ~ое движéние passenger services.

пассúв, -a (*gram.*) passive voice. **пассúвность**, -и passiveness, passivity. **пассúвный** passive.

пáста, -ы paste; purée.

пáстбище, -a pasture.

пастернáк, -a parsnip.

пастú, -сý, -сёшь; пас, -лá *impf.* graze, pasture; shepherd, tend.

пастúсь, -сётся; пáсся, -лáсь *impf.* graze; browse. **пастýх**, -á shepherd; herdsman. **пастýшеский** shepherd's, herdsman's; pastoral. **пастушóк**, -шкá shepherd. **пастýшка**, -и shepherdess.

пасть, -и mouth; jaws.

пасть, падý, -дёшь; пал *pf. of* пáдать

Пáсха, -и Easter; Passover. **пасхáльный** Easter, paschal.

пáсынок, -нка stepson, stepchild; outcast.

пат, -a stalemate.

патéнт, -a (на+a.) patent (for); licence (for); владéлец ~a patentee. **патентовáть**, -тýю *impf.* patent, take out a patent (for).

патетúческий, патетúчный pathetic.

патефóн, -a (*portable*) gramophone.

пáтока, -и treacle; syrup. **пáточный** treacle; treacly.

патриóт, -a patriot. **патриотúзм**, -a patriotism. **патриотúческий** patriotic.

патрóн, -a cartridge; chuck, holder; lamp-socket; lamp-holder; pattern.

патронáж, -a patronage; home health service. **патронáжн|ый**; ~ая сестрá health visitor, district nurse.

патрóнка, -и pattern.

патрóнный cartridge.

патрулúровать, -рую *impf.* patrol. **патрýль**, -я *m.* patrol.

пáуза, -ы pause; interval; rest.

паýк, -á spider. **паутúна**, -ы cobweb, spider's web; gossamer; web. **паýчий** spider, spider's.

пáфос, -a (excessive) feeling; zeal, enthusiasm; spirit.

пах, -a, *loc.* -ý groin.

пáханый ploughed. **пáхарь**, -я *m.* ploughman. **пахáть**, пашý, пáшешь *impf.* (*pf.* вс~) plough, till.

пáхнуть[1], -ну; пах *impf.*+*i.* smell of; reek of; savour of, smack of.

пахнýть[2], -нёт *pf.* puff, blow.

пáхота, -ы ploughing, tillage. **пáхотный** arable.

пахýчий odorous, strong-smelling.

пациéнт, -a patient.

пáчка, -и bundle; batch; packet, pack; tutu.

пáчкать, -аю *impf.* (*pf.* за~, ис~, на~) dirty, soil, stain, sully; daub. **пачкотня**, -й

daub. **пачкýн**, -á sloven; dauber.

пашý *etc.*: *see* пахáть. **пáшня**, -и; *g.pl.* -шен ploughed field.

пашóт, -a; яйцó-~ poached egg.

паштéт, -a pie; pâté.

паэ́лья, -и paella.

пáюсн|ый; ~ая икрá pressed caviare.

паяльник, -a soldering iron. **пая́льн|ый** soldering; ~ая лáмпа blow-lamp. **пая́льщик**, -a tinman, tinsmith. **пáяный** soldered. **пая́ть**, -я́ю *impf.* solder.

пая́ц, -a clown.

певéц, -вцá, **певúца**, -ы singer. **певýчий** melodious. **пéвч|ий** singing; ~ая птúца song-bird; *sb.* chorister.

пéгий skewbald, piebald.

пед... *abbr.* (*of* педагогúческий) *in comb.* pedagogic(al); teachers'; education, educational. **педвýз**, -a, ~инститýт, -a (teachers') training college. ~кýрсы, -ов *pl.* teachers' training courses. ~совéт, -a staff-meeting. ~фáк, -a education department.

педагóг, -a teacher; pedagogue, educationist. **педагóгика**, -и pedagogy, pedagogics. **педагогúческий** pedagogical; educational; ~ инститýт (teachers') training college; ~ факультéт education department.

педáль, -и pedal; treadle. **педáльный** pedal.

педáнт, -a pedant. **педантúческий** pedantic. **педантúчность**, -и pedantry.

пединститýт, -a teacher training college.

педофúл, -a paedophile.

пейзáж, -a landscape; scenery. **пейзажúст**, -a landscape painting.

пёк *see* печь. **пекáрный** baking, bakery. **пекáрня**, -и; *g.pl.* -рен bakery, bakehouse. **пéкарь**, -я; *pl.* -я, -éй *m.* baker.

Пекúн, -a Peking; Beijing.

пéкло, -a scorching heat; hell-fire. **пекý** *etc.*: *see* печь

пеленá, -ы́; *g.pl.* -лён shroud. **пеленáть**, -áю *impf.* (*pf.* за~, с~) swaddle; put nappy on, change.

пéленг, -a bearing. **пеленгáтор**, -a direction finder. **пеленговáть**, -гýю *impf. & pf.* take the bearings of.

пелёнка, -и napkin, nappy; *pl.* swaddling-clothes; с пелёнок from the cradle.

пельмéни, -ей *pl.* pelmeni (*kind of ravioli*).

пéмза, -ы pumice(-stone). **пéмзовый** pumice.

пéна, -ы foam, spume; scum; froth, head; lather; (мыльная) ~ soapsuds.

пенáл, -a pencil-box, pencil-case.

пéние, -я singing; ~ петухá crowing.

пéнист|ый foamy; frothy; ~ое винó sparkling wine. **пéнить**, -ню *impf.* (*pf.* вс~) froth; ~ся foam, froth.

пеницúллин, -a penicillin.

пéнка, -и skin; (морскáя) ~ meerschaum. **пéнковый** meerschaum. **пеноплáст**, -a foam plastic.

пенсионéр, -a pensioner. **пенсиóнный** pension; ~ вóзраст retirement age. пéнсия, -и pension; ~ по инвали́дности disability pension; ~ по стáрости old-age pension.

пенснé nt.indecl. pince-nez.

пень, пня m. stump, stub.

пенькá, -й hemp. пенькóвый hempen.

пéня, -и fine. пеня́ть, -я́ю impf. (pf. по~) +d. reproach; +на+a. blame.

пéпел, -пла ash, ashes. пепели́ще, -а site of fire; (hearth and) home; роднóе ~ old home. пéпельница, -ы ashtray. пéпельный ashy.

пер. abbr. (of переýлок) Street, Lane.

пéрвейший the first, the most important; first-class. пéрвенец, -нца first-born; first of its kind. пéрвенство, -а first place; championship; ~ по футбóлу football championship. пéрвенствовáть, -твую or -твýю impf. take first place; take precedence, take priority. перви́чный primary; initial.

перво... in comb. first, primary; prime, top; newly, just; arch-, archaeo-, proto-; prim(o)-. первобы́тный primitive; primordial; primeval; pristine. ~здáнный primordial; primitive, primary. ~истóчник, -а primary source; origin. ~категóрник, -а first-ranker. ~клáссный first-class, first-rate. ~кýрсник, -а first-year student, freshman. ~мáйский Mayday. ~начáло adv. originally. ~начáльный original; primary; initial; prime; elementary. ~обрáз, -а a prototype, original; protoplast. ~очереднóй, -очерёдный first and foremost, immediate. ~печáтный early printed, incunabular; first printed, first edition; ~печáтные кни́ги incunabula. ~причи́на, -ы first cause. ~разря́дный first-class, first-rank. ~рóдный first-born; primal original. ~рождённый first-born. ~сóртный best-quality; first-class, first-rate. ~степéнный paramount, of the first order.

пéрвое sb. first course. пéрво-нáперво adv. first of all. пéрв|ый first; former; earliest; быть ~ым, идти́ ~ым come first; lead; ~ое дéло, ~ым дéлом first of all, first thing; с ~ого рáза from the first.

пергáмент, -а parchment; greaseproof paper. пергáментный parchment; parchment-like; greaseproof.

пере... vbl. pref. indicating action across or through something; repetition of action; superiority, excess, etc.; extension of action to encompass many or all objects or cases of a given kind; division into two or more parts; reciprocity of action: trans-, re-, over-, out-.

переадресовáть, -сýю pf., переадресóвывать, -аю impf. re-address.

перебегáть, -áю impf., перебежáть, -бегý pf. run across; desert, go over. перебéжка, -и bound, rush; re-run. перебéжчик, -а deserter; turncoat.

перебéливать, -аю impf., перебели́ть, -елю́,

-éли́шь pf. re-whitewash; make a fair copy of.

переберý etc.: see перебрáть

перебивáть(ся, -áю(сь impf. of переби́ть-(ся. переби́вка, -и re-upholstering.

перебирáть(ся, -áю(сь impf. of перебрáть-(ся

переби́ть, -бью́, -бьёшь pf. (impf. перебивáть) interrupt; intercept; kill, slay, slaughter; beat; beat up again; break; re-upholster; ~ся break; make ends meet; get by. перебóй interruption, intermission; stoppage; hold-up; irregularity; misfire. перебóйный interrupted, intermittent.

перебóрка, -и sorting out; re-assembly; partition; bulkhead.

переборóть, -рю́, -решь pf. overcome; master.

переборщи́ть, -щý pf. go too far; overdo it.

перебрáнка, -и wrangle, squabble.

перебрáсывать(ся, -аю(сь impf. of перебрóсить(ся

перебрáть, -берý, -берёшь; -áл, -á, -о pf. (impf. перебирáть) sort out, pick over; look through, look over; turn over; turn over in one's mind; finger; dismantle and re-assemble; reset; take in excess; score more than enough; ~ся get over, cross; move.

перебрóсить, -óшу pf. (impf. перебрáсывать) throw over; transfer; ~ся fling o.s.; spread; +i. throw to one another; ~ся нéсколькими словáми exchange a few words. перебрóска, -и transfer.

перебью́ etc.: see переби́ть

перевáл, -а a passing, crossing; pass. перевáливать, -аю impf., перевали́ть, -лю́, -лишь pf. transfer, shift; cross, pass; impers. (+d.) перевали́ло зá полночь it is past midnight; ей перевали́ло зá сорок she's turned forty; ~ся waddle.

перевáривать, -аю impf., перевари́ть, -рю́, -ришь pf. boil again; reheat; overdo, overcook; digest; swallow, bear, stand.

переведý etc.: see перевести́

перевезти́, -зý, -зёшь; -вёз, -лá pf. (impf. перевози́ть) take across, put across; transport, convey; (re)move.

перевернýть, -нý, -нёшь pf., перевёртывать, -аю impf. (impf. also переворáчивать) turn (over); overturn, upset; turn inside out; ~ вверх дном turn upside-down; ~ся turn (over).

перевéс, -а preponderance; predominance; advantage, superiority; с ~ом в пять голосóв with a majority of five votes. перевéсить, -éшу pf. (impf. перевéшивать) re-weigh, weigh again; outweigh, outbalance; tip the scales; hang somewhere else.

перевести́, -ведý, -ведёшь; -вёл, -á pf. (impf. переводи́ть) take across; transfer, move, switch, shift; translate; convert, express; copy; ~ дух take breath; ~ часы́ вперёд (назáд) put a clock forward (back); ~сь be transferred; come to an end, run out; become extinct; **у меня́ перевели́сь де́ньги** my money ran out.

перевё́шивать, -аю *impf. of* **переве́сить**

перевира́ть, -а́ю *impf. of* **переврать**

перево́д, -а (-у) transfer, move, switch, shift; translation; version; conversion; spending, using up, waste; **нет ~у+***d.* there is no shortage of, there is an inexhaustible supply of. **переводи́ть(ся, -ожу́(сь, -о́дишь(ся** *impf. of* **перевести́(сь. переводн|о́й** transfer; ~**а́я бума́га** carbon paper, transfer paper; ~**а́я карти́нка** transfer. **перево́дный** transfer; translated. **перево́дчик, -а** translator; interpreter.

перево́з, -а transporting, conveyance; crossing; ferry. **перевози́ть, -ожу́, -о́зишь** *impf. of* **перевезти́. перево́зка, -и** conveyance, carriage. **перево́зчик, -а** ferryman; boatman; carrier, carter, removal man.

перевооружа́ть, -а́ю *impf.*, **перевооружи́ть, -жу́** *pf.* rearm; ~**ся** rearm. **перевооруже́ние, -я** rearmament.

перевоплоти́ть, -лощу́ *pf.*, **перевоплоща́ть, -а́ю** *impf.* reincarnate; transform; ~**ся** be reincarnated; transform o.s., be transformed. **перевоплоще́ние, -я** reincarnation; transformation.

перевора́чивать(ся, -аю(сь *impf. of* **переверну́ть(ся. переворо́т, -а** revolution; overturn; cataclysm; **госуда́рственный ~** coup d'état.

перевоспита́ние, -я re-education; rehabilitation. **перевоспита́ть, -а́ю** *pf.*, **перевоспи́тывать, -аю** *impf.* re-educate; rehabilitate.

переврать, -ру́, -рёшь; -а́л, -а́, -о *pf.* (*impf.* **перевира́ть**) garble, confuse; misinterpret; misquote.

перевыполне́ние, -я over-fulfilment. **перевы́полнить, -ню** *pf.*, **перевыполня́ть, -я́ю** *impf.* over-fulfil.

перевяза́ть, -яжу́, -я́жешь *pf.*, **перевя́зывать, -аю** *impf.* dress, bandage; tie up, cord; tie again, re-tie; knit again. **перевя́зка, -и** dressing, bandage. **перевя́зочный; ~ материа́л** dressing; **~ пункт** dressing station. **пе́ревязь, -и** cross-belt, shoulder-belt; sling.

переги́б, -а bend, twist; fold; exaggeration; **допусти́ть ~ в+***p.* carry too far. **перегиба́ть(ся, -а́ю(сь** *impf. of* **перегну́ть(ся**

перегля́дываться, -аюсь *impf.*, **перегляну́ться, -ну́сь, -нешься** *pf.* exchange glances.

перегна́ть, -гоню́, -го́нишь; -а́л, -а́, -о *pf.* (*impf.* **перегоня́ть**) outdistance, leave behind; overtake, surpass; drive; ferry; distil; sublimate.

перегно́й, -я humus.

перегну́ть, -ну́, -нёшь *pf.* (*impf.* **перегиба́ть**) bend; ~ **па́лку** go too far; ~**ся** bend; lean over.

переговаривать, -аю *impf.* **переговори́ть, -рю́** *pf.* talk, speak; silence, out-talk; +*о*+*p.*

talk over, discuss; ~**ся (с+***i.***)** exchange remarks (with). **перегово́р, -а** (telephone) call, conversation; *pl.* negotiations, parley; **вести́ ~ы** negotiate, conduct negotiations, parley. **переговорн|ый** *adj.*; ~**ая бу́дка** call-box, telephone booth; ~**ый пункт** public call-boxes; trunk-call office.

перего́н, -а driving; stage. **перего́нка, -и** distillation. **перего́нный** distilling, distillation; **~ заво́д** distillery; **~ куб** still. **перегоню́** *etc.: see* **перегна́ть. перегоня́ть, -я́ю** *impf. of* **перегна́ть**

перегора́живать, -аю *impf. of* **перегороди́ть**

перегора́ть, -а́ет *impf.*, **перегоре́ть, -ри́т** *pf.* burn out, fuse; burn through; rot through.

перегороди́ть, -рожу́, -ро́ди́шь *pf.* (*impf.* **перегора́живать**) partition off; block. **перегоро́дка, -и** partition; baffle (plate). **перегоро́женный** partitioned off; blocked.

перегре́в, -а overheating; superheating. **перегрева́ть, -а́ю** *impf.*, **перегре́ть, -е́ю** *pf.* overheat; ~**ся** overheat; burn, burn out, get burned.

перегружа́ть, -а́ю *impf.*, **перегрузи́ть, -ужу́, -у́зишь** *pf.* overload; transfer, trans-ship; overwork. **перегру́зка, -и** overload; overwork; transfer; reloading.

перегрыза́ть, -а́ю *impf.*, **перегры́зть, -зу́, -зёшь; -гры́з** *pf.* gnaw through, bite through; ~**ся** fight; quarrel, wrangle.

пе́ред, пе́редо, пред, пре́до *prep.*+*i.* before; in front of; in the face of; to; compared to, in comparison with; **извини́ться ~** apologize to. **пе́рёд, пе́реда,** *pl.* **-а́** front, forepart.

передава́ть, -даю́, -даёшь *impf.*, **переда́ть, -а́м, -а́шь, -а́ст, -ади́м; пе́редал, -а́, -о** *pf.* pass, hand, hand over; hand down; make over; tell; communicate; transmit, convey; pay too much, give too much; **вы пе́редали три рубля́** you have paid three roubles too much; ~ **де́ло в суд** take a matter to court, sue; ~ **приве́т** convey one's greetings, send one's regards; **переда́й(те) им приве́т** remember me to them; ~**ся** pass; be transmitted; be communicated; be inherited; +*d.* go over to. **переда́точн|ый; ~ый механи́зм** drive, driving mechanism, transmission; ~**ое число́** gear ratio. **переда́тчик, -а** transmitter, sender; conductor. **переда́ча, -и** passing; transmission; communication; broadcast; drive; gear, gearing; transfer; **пряма́я ~** live broadcast; **рекла́мная ~** commercial, advert.

передвига́ть, -а́ю *impf.*, **передви́нуть, -ну** *pf.* move, shift; ~ **часы́ вперёд (наза́д)** put the clock forward (back); ~ **сро́ки экза́менов** change the date of examinations; ~**ся** move, shift; travel. **передвиже́ние, -я** movement, moving; conveyance; travel; **сре́дства передвиже́ния** means of transport. **передви́жка, -и** movement; moving;

travel; *in comb.* travelling; itinerant; **библио-те́ка-~** travelling library, mobile library; **теа́тр-~** strolling players. **передвижно́й** movable, mobile; travelling, itinerant.

переде́л, -а re-partition; re-division, redistri-bution; re-allotment.

переде́лать, -аю *pf.*, **переде́лывать, -аю** *impf.* alter; change; refashion, recast; do. **переде́лка, -и** alteration; adaptation; **отда́ть в переде́лку** have altered; **попа́сть в переде́лку** get into a pretty mess.

передёргивать(ся, -аю(сь *impf. of* **передёрнуть(ся**

передержа́ть, -жу́, -жишь *pf.*, **переде́ржи-вать, -аю** *impf.* keep too long; overdo; over-cook; overexpose. **переде́ржка, -и** over-exposure.

передёрнуть, -ну *pf.* (*impf.* **передёрги-вать**) pull aside, pull across; cheat; distort, misrepresent; **~ фа́кты** juggle with facts; **~ся** flinch, wince.

пере́дний front, fore; anterior; first; leading; **~ план** foreground. **пере́дник, -а** apron; pinafore. **пере́дняя** *sb.* ante-room; (en-trance) hall, lobby. **пе́редо** *see* **пе́ред**. **передови́к, -а́** outstanding worker. **передови́ца, -ы** leading article, leader; editorial. **передово́|й** forward; advanced; foremost; **~ые взгля́ды** advanced views; **~о́й отря́д** advanced detachment; vanguard; **~а́я (статья́)** leading article, leader; editorial.

передозиро́вка, -и overdose.

передохну́ть, -ну́, -нёшь *pf.* pause for breath, take a breather.

передра́знивать, -аю *impf.*, **передразни́ть, -ню́, -нишь** *pf.* take off, mimic.

передря́га, -и scrape, tight corner; unpleas-antness.

переду́мать, -аю *pf.*, **переду́мывать, -аю** *impf.* change one's mind, think better of it; do a lot of thinking.

переды́шка, -и respite, breathing-space.

перее́зд, -а crossing; removal. **переезжа́ть, -аю** *impf.*, **перее́хать, -е́ду** *pf.* cross; run over, knock down; move, remove.

пережа́ренный overdone; burnt. **пережа́ри-вать, -аю** *impf.*, **пережа́рить, -рю** *pf.* overdo, overcook.

пережда́ть, -жду́, -ждёшь; -а́л, -а́, -о *pf.* (*impf.* **пережида́ть**) wait; wait through, wait for the end of.

пережёвывать, -аю *impf.* masticate, chew; repeat over and over again.

пережива́ние, -я experience. **пережива́ть, -аю** *impf. of* **пережи́ть**

пережида́ть, -аю *impf. of* **пережда́ть**

пережито́е *sb.* the past. **пережи́ток, -тка** survival; vestige. **пережи́ть, -иву́, -ивёшь; пе́режил, -а́, -о** *pf.* (*impf.* **пережива́ть**) live through; experience; go through; endure; suf-fer; outlive, outlast, survive.

перезаряди́ть, -яжу́, -я́дишь *pf.*, **перезаря-жа́ть, -а́ю** *impf.* recharge, reload. **пере-**

заря́дка, -и recharging, reloading.

перезво́н, -а ringing, chime.

пере|зимова́ть, -му́ю *pf.*

перезрева́ть, -а́ю *impf.*, **перезре́ть, -е́ю** *pf.* become overripe; be past one's prime. **пере-зре́лый** overripe; past one's first youth, past one's prime.

переизбира́ть, -а́ю *impf.*, **переизбра́ть, -беру́, -берёшь; -бра́л, -а́, -о** *pf.* re-elect. **переизбра́ние, -я** re-election.

переиздава́ть, -даю́, -даёшь *impf.*, **переиз-да́ть, -а́м, -а́шь, -а́ст, -ади́м; -а́л, -а́, -о** *pf.* republish, reprint. **переизда́ние, -я** re-publication; new edition, reprint.

переименова́ть, -ну́ю *pf.*, **переимено́вы-вать, -аю** *impf.* rename.

перейму́ *etc.: see* **переня́ть**

перейти́, -йду́, -йдёшь; перешёл, -шла́ *pf.* (*impf.* **переходи́ть**) cross; get across, get over, go over; pass; turn (**в**+*a.* to, into); **~ в наступле́ние** go over to the offensive; **~ грани́цу** cross the frontier; **~ из рук в ру́ки** change hands; **~ на другу́ю рабо́ту** change one's job; **~ че́рез мост** cross a bridge.

перека́рмливать, -аю *impf. of* **перекор-ми́ть**

переквалифика́ция, -и training for a new profession; retraining. **переквалифици́ро-ваться, -руюсь** *impf. & pf.* change one's profession; retrain.

перекидно́й, -я́ **мо́стик** footbridge, gangway; **~ календа́рь** loose-leaf calendar. **переки́-дывать, -аю** *impf.*, **переки́нуть, -ну** *pf.* throw over; **~ся** leap; spread; go over, de-fect; **~ся слова́ми** exchange a few remarks.

перекиса́ть, -а́ет *impf.*, **переки́снуть, -нет** *pf.* turn sour, go sour. **пе́рекись, -и** pero-xide.

перекла́дина, -ы cross-beam, cross-piece, transom; joist; horizontal bar.

перекла́дывать, -аю *impf. of* **переложи́ть**

переклика́ться, -а́юсь *impf.*, **перекли́к-нуться, -нусь** *pf.* call to one another. **перекли́чка, -и** roll-call, call-over; hook-up.

переключа́тель, -я *m.* switch. **переключа́ть, -а́ю** *impf.*, **переключи́ть, -чу́** *pf.* switch, switch over; **~ся** switch (over).

перекова́ть, -кую́, -куёшь *pf.*, **переко́вы-вать, -аю** *impf.* re-shoe; re-forge; hammer out, beat out.

переколоти́ть, -лочу́, -ло́тишь *pf.* break, smash.

перекорми́ть, -млю́, -мишь *pf.* (*impf.* **перека́рмливать**) overfeed, surfeit; feed.

перекоси́ть, -ошу́, -о́сишь *pf.* warp; distort; **~ся** warp, be warped; become distorted.

перекочева́ть, -чу́ю *pf.*, **перекочёвывать, -аю** *impf.* migrate, move on.

переко́шенный distorted, twisted.

перекра́ивать, -аю *impf. of* **перекро́йть**

перекра́сить, -а́шу *pf.*, **перекра́шивать, -аю** *impf.* (re-)colour, (re-)paint; (re-)dye; **~ся** change colour; turn one's coat.

пере|крести́ть, -ещу́, -е́стишь pf., перекре́-
щивать, -аю impf. cross; ~ся cross, inter-
sect; cross o.s. перекрёстн|ый cross; ~ый
допро́с cross-examination; ~ый ого́нь cross-
fire; ~ая ссы́лка cross-reference. перекрёсток, -тка cross-roads, crossing.
перекри́кивать, -аю impf., перекрича́ть,
-чу́ pf. out-shout, outroar; shout down.
перекро́ить, -ою́ pf. (impf. перекра́ивать)
cut out again; rehash; reshape.
перекрыва́ть, -а́ю impf., перекры́ть, -ро́ю
pf. re-cover; exceed; ~ реко́рд break a
record.
перекую́ etc.: see перекова́ть
перекупа́ть, -а́ю impf., перекупи́ть, -плю́,
-пишь pf. buy; buy up; buy secondhand.
переку́пщик, -а second-hand dealer.
перекуси́ть, -ушу́, -у́сишь pf., перекусы́-
вать, -аю impf. bite through; have a bite,
have a snack.
перелага́ть, -а́ю impf. of переложи́ть
перела́мывать, -аю impf. of переломи́ть
перелеза́ть, -а́ю impf., переле́зть, -зу; -е́з
pf. climb over, get over.
перелёт, -а migration; flight. перелета́ть,
-а́ю impf., перелете́ть, -лечу́ pf. fly over,
fly across; overshoot the mark. перелёт-
н|ый migratory; ~ая пти́ца bird of passage.
перелива́ние, -я decanting; transfusion; ~
кро́ви blood transfusion. перелива́ть, -а́ю
impf. of перели́ть. перелива́ться, -а́ется
impf. of перели́ться play; modulate. пере-
ли́вчатый iridescent; shot; modulating.
перелиста́ть, -а́ю pf., перели́стывать, -аю
impf. turn over, leaf through; look through,
glance at.
перели́ть, -лью́, -льёшь; -и́л, -а́, -о pf. (impf.
перелива́ть) pour; decant; let overflow;
transfuse. перели́ться, -льётся; -ли́лся,
-лила́сь, -ли́ло́сь pf. (impf. перелива́ться)
flow; overflow, run over.
пере|лицева́ть, -цу́ю pf., перелицо́вы-
вать, -аю impf. turn; have turned.
переложе́ние, -я arrangement. перело-
жи́ть, -жу́, -жишь pf. (impf. перекла́ды-
вать, перелага́ть) put somewhere else;
shift, move; transfer; interlay; re-set, re-lay;
put in too much; put, set, arrange; transpose;
~ в стихи́ put into verse; ~ на му́зыку set
to music.
перело́м, -а break, breaking; fracture; turning-point, crisis; sudden change; на ~е+g. on
the eve of. переломи́ть, -а́ю pf. break; ~ся
break, be broken. переломи́ть, -млю́, -мишь
pf. (impf. перела́мывать) break in two;
break; fracture; master; ~ себя́ master o.s.,
restrain one's feelings. перело́мный; ~
моме́нт critical moment, crucial moment.
перелью́ etc.: see перели́ть. перема́лы-
вать, -аю impf. of перемоло́ть
перема́нивать, -аю impf., перемани́ть, -ню́,
-нишь pf. win over; entice.
перемежа́ться, -а́ется impf. alternate; пере-

межа́ющаяся лихора́дка intermittent fever.
перемелю́ etc.: see перемоло́ть
переме́на, -ы change, alteration; change (of
clothes); interval, break. перемени́ть, -ню́,
-нишь pf., переменя́ть, -я́ю impf. change;
~ся change. переме́нный variable, changeable; ~ ток alternating current. переме́н-
чивый changeable.
перемести́ть, -мещу́ pf. (impf. переме-
ща́ть) move; transfer; ~ся move.
переме́шивать, -аю impf., перемеша́ть, -аю
impf. mix, intermingle; mix up; confuse; ~ся
get mixed; get mixed up.
перемеща́ть(ся, -а́ю(сь impf. of переме-
сти́ть(ся. перемеще́ние, -я movement,
shift; displacement; dislocation; travel. пере-
мещён|ый displaced; ~ые ли́ца displaced
persons.
перемиги́ваться, -аюсь impf., перемиг-
ну́ться, -ну́сь, -нёшься pf. wink at each
other; +с+i. wink at.
переми́рие, -я armistice, truce.
перемога́ть, -а́ю impf. (try to) overcome;
~ся struggle (against illness, tears, etc.).
перемоло́ть, -мелю́, -ме́лешь pf. (impf.
перема́лывать) grind, mill; pulverize.
перемыва́ть, -а́ю impf., перемы́ть, -мо́ю pf.
wash (up) again.
перенапряга́ть, -а́ю impf., перенапря́чь,
-ягу́, -яжёшь; -я́г, -ла́ pf. overstrain; ~ся
overstrain o.s.
перенаселе́ние, -я overpopulation. перенаселённый; -лён, -а́ overpopulated; overcrowded. перенасели́ть, -лю́ pf., перена-
селя́ть, -я́ю impf. overpopulate; overcrowd.
перенести́, -су́, -сёшь; -нёс, -ла́ pf. (impf.
переноси́ть) carry, move, take; transport;
transfer; carry over; take over; put off, postpone; endure, bear, stand; ~сь be carried;
be borne; be carried away.
перено́с, -а transfer; transportation; division
of words; знак ~а hyphen. переноси́мый
bearable, endurable. переноси́ть(ся, -ошу́(сь,
-о́сишь(ся impf. of перенести́(сь
перено́сица, -ы bridge (of the nose).
перено́ска, -и carrying over; transporting;
carriage. перено́сный portable; figurative,
metaphorical.
пере|ночева́ть, -чу́ю pf. переношу́ etc.: see
переноси́ть
переня́ть, -ейму́, -еймёшь; пе́реня́л, -а́, -о
pf. (impf. перенима́ть) imitate, copy; adopt.
переобору́довать, -дую impf. & pf. re-equip.
переоде́валка, -и changing-room.
переосвиде́тельствовать, -твую impf. &
pf. re-examine.
переоце́нивать, -аю impf., переоцени́ть,
-ню́, -нишь pf. overestimate; overrate; revalue;
reappraise. переоце́нка, -и overestimation;
revaluation, reappraisal.
перепа́чкать, -аю pf. dirty, make dirty; ~ся
get dirty.

пе́репел, -а; *pl.* -а́, **перепёлка**, -и quail.

перепеча́тать, -аю *pf.*, **перепеча́тывать**, -аю *impf.* reprint; type (out). **перепеча́тка**, -и reprinting; reprint.

перепи́ливать, -аю *impf.*, **перепили́ть**, -лю́, -лишь *pf.* saw in two.

переписа́ть, -ишу́, -и́шешь *pf.*, **перепи́сывать**, -аю *impf.* copy; type; re-write; list, make a list of. **перепи́ска**, -и copying; typing; correspondence; letters; **быть в перепи́ске** с+*i.* be in correspondence with. **перепи́счик**, -а, **-чица**, -ы copyist; typist. **перепи́сываться**, -аюсь *impf.* correspond. **пе́репись**, -и census; inventory.

перепла́вить, -влю *pf.*, **переплавля́ть**, -я́ю *impf.* smelt.

перепла́та, -ы overpayment; surplus. **переплати́ть**, -ачу́, -а́тишь *pf.*, **перепла́чивать**, -аю *impf.* overpay, pay too much.

переплести́, -лету́, -летёшь; -лёл, -а́ *pf.*, **переплета́ть**, -а́ю *impf.* bind; interlace, interknit; re-plait; **~ся** interlace, interweave; get mixed up. **переплёт**, -а binding; cover; transom; caning; mess, scrape. **переплётная** *sb.* bindery; bookbinder's. **переплётчик**, -а bookbinder.

переплыва́ть, -а́ю *impf.*, **переплы́ть**, -ыву́, -ывёшь; -ы́л, -а́, -о *pf.* swim (across); sail across, row across, cross.

переподгота́вливать, -аю *impf.*, **переподгото́вить**, -влю *pf.* retrain; give further training. **переподгото́вка**, -и further training; retraining; **ку́рсы по переподгото́вке** refresher courses.

переполза́ть, -а́ю *impf.*, **переползти́**, -зу́, -зёшь; -о́лз, -ла́ *pf.* crawl across; creep across.

переполне́ние, -я overfilling; overcrowding. **перепо́лненный** overcrowded; overfull. **переполнить**, -ню *pf.*, **переполня́ть**, -я́ю *impf.* overfill; overcrowd; **~ся** be overflowing; be overcrowded.

переполо́х, -а alarm; commotion, rumpus. **переполоши́ть**, -шу́ *pf.* alarm; arouse, alert; **~ся** take alarm, become alarmed.

перепо́нка, -и membrane; web. **перепо́нчатый** membranous; webbed; web-footed.

переправить, -влю *pf.*, **переправля́ть**, -я́ю *impf.* convey, transport; take across; forward; correct; **~ся** cross, get across.

перепродава́ть, -даю́, -даёшь *impf.*, **перепрода́ть**, -а́м, -а́шь, -а́ст, -адим; -про́дал, -а́, -о *pf.* re-sell. **перепрода́жа**, -и re-sale.

перепроизво́дство, -а overproduction.

перепры́гивать, -аю *impf.*, **перепры́гнуть**, -ну *pf.* jump, jump over.

перепу́г, -а (-у) fright. **перепуга́ть**, -а́ю *pf.* frighten, give a fright, give a turn; **~ся** get a fright.

пере|пу́тать, -аю *pf.*, **перепу́тывать**, -аю *impf.* entangle; confuse, mix up, muddle up.

перепу́тье, -я cross-roads.

перераба́тывать, -аю *impf.*, **перерабо́тать**, -аю *pf.* work up, make; convert; treat; remake; recast, re-shape; process; work overtime; overwork; **~ся** overwork.

перераспределе́ние, -я redistribution. **перераспредели́ть**, -лю́ *pf.*, **перераспределя́ть**, -я́ю *impf.* redistribute.

перераста́ние, -я outgrowing; escalation; growing (into); development (into). **перераста́ть**, -а́ю *impf.*, **перерасти́**, -ту́, -тёшь; -ро́с, -ла́ *pf.* outgrow, overtop; outstrip; be too old (for); +в+*a.* grow into, develop into, turn into.

перерасхо́д, -а over-expenditure; overdraft. **перерасхо́довать**, -дую *impf.* & *pf.* overspend, expend too much of; overdraw.

перерасчёт, -а recalculation, recomputation.

перерва́ть, -ву́, -вёшь; -а́л, -а́, -о *pf.* (*impf.* **перерыва́ть**) break, tear asunder; **~ся** break, come apart.

перерегистра́ция, -и re-registration. **перерегистри́ровать**, -рую *impf.* & *pf.* re-register.

перере́зать, -е́жу *pf.*, **перере́зать**, -а́ю *impf.*, **перере́зывать**, -аю *impf.* cut; cut off; cut across; break; kill, slaughter.

перереша́ть, -а́ю *impf.*, **перереши́ть**, -шу́ *pf.* re-solve; decide differently; change one's mind, reconsider one's decision.

перероди́ть, -ожу́ *pf.*, **перерожда́ть**, -а́ю *impf.* regenerate; **~ся** be reborn; be regenerated; degenerate. **перерожде́ние**, -я regeneration; degeneration.

перерос *etc.*: *see* **перерасти́**. **перерою** *etc.*: *see* **перерыть**

переруба́ть, -а́ю *impf.*, **переруби́ть**, -блю́, -бишь *pf.* chop in two; cut up, chop up.

переры́в, -а interruption; interval, break, intermission; **с ~ами** off and on.

перерыва́ть¹(ся, -а́ю(сь *impf. of* **перерва́ть(ся**

перерыва́ть², -а́ю *impf.*, **переры́ть**, -ро́ю *pf.* dig up; rummage through, search thoroughly.

пересади́ть, -ажу́, -а́дишь *pf.*, **переса́живать**, -аю *impf.* transplant; graft; seat somewhere else; make change, help change; **~ че́рез**+*a.* help across. **переса́дка**, -и transplantation; grafting; change, changing.

переса́живаться, -аюсь *impf. of* **пересе́сть**. **переса́ливать**, -аю *impf. of* **пересоли́ть**. **пересека́ть(ся**, -а́ю(сь *impf. of* **пересе́чь(ся**

переселе́нец, -нца settler; migrant, emigrant; immigrant. **переселе́ние**, -я migration, emigration; immigration, resettlement; move, removal. **пересели́ть**, -лю́ *pf.*, **переселя́ть**, -я́ю *impf.* move; transplant; resettle; **~ся** move; migrate.

пересе́сть, -ся́ду *pf.* (*impf.* **переса́живаться**) change one's seat; change (*trains etc.*).

пересече́ние, -я crossing, intersection. **пересе́чь**, -секу́, -сечёшь; -сёк, -ла́ *pf.* (*impf.*

пересека́ть) cross; traverse; intersect; cut, cut up; ~ся cross, intersect.

переси́ливать, -аю *impf.*, переси́лить, -лю *pf.* overpower; overcome, master.

переска́з, -а (re)telling; exposition. пересказа́ть, -ажу́, -а́жешь *pf.*, переска́зывать, -аю *impf.* tell, retell; expound; retail; relate.

переска́кивать, -аю *impf.*, перескочи́ть, -чу́, -чишь *pf.* jump (over), vault (over); skip (over).

пересла́ть, -ешлю́, -шлёшь *pf.* (*impf.* пересыла́ть) send; remit; send on, forward.

пересма́тривать, -аю *impf.*, пересмотре́ть, -трю́, -тришь *pf.* revise; reconsider; review. пересмо́тр, -а revision; reconsideration; review; re-trial.

пересоли́ть, -олю́, -о́ли́шь *pf.* (*impf.* переса́ливать) put too much salt in, over-salt; exaggerate, overdo it.

пересо́хнуть, -нет; -о́х *pf.* (*impf.* пересыха́ть) dry up, become parched; dry out.

переспа́ть, -плю́; -а́л, -а́, -о *pf.* oversleep; spend the night; ~ c+*i.* sleep with.

переспе́лый overripe.

переспо́рить, -рю *pf.* out-argue, defeat in argument.

переспра́шивать, -аю *impf.*, переспроси́ть, -ошу́, -о́сишь *pf.* ask again; ask to repeat.

пересо́риться, -рюсь *pf.* quarrel, fall out.

переставать, -таю́, -таёшь *impf. of* переста́ть

переста́вить, -влю *pf.*, переставля́ть, -я́ю *impf.* move, shift; re-arrange; transpose; ~ часы́ вперёд (наза́д) put the clock forward (back).

перестара́ться, -а́юсь *pf.* overdo it, try too hard.

переста́ть, -а́ну *pf.* (*impf.* переставать) stop, cease.

пострада́ть, -а́ю *pf.* have suffered, have gone through.

перестра́ивать(ся, -аю(сь *impf. of* перестро́ить(ся

перестре́лка, -и exchange of fire; firing; skirmish. перестреля́ть, -я́ю *pf.* shoot (down).

перестро́ить, -о́ю *pf.* (*impf.* перестра́ивать) rebuild, reconstruct; re-design, re-fashion, reshape; reorganize; retune; ~ся reform; reorganize o.s.; switch over, retune (на+*a.* to). перестро́йка, -и rebuilding, reconstruction; reorganization; retuning; (*pol.*) perestroika.

переступа́ть, -а́ю *impf.*, переступи́ть, -плю́, -пишь *pf.* step over; cross; overstep; ~ с ноги́ на́ ногу shuffle one's feet.

пересу́ды, -ов *pl.* gossip.

пересчита́ть, -а́ю *pf.*, пересчи́тывать, -аю *impf.* (*pf.* перече́сть) re-count; count; +на+*a.* convert to, express in terms of.

пересыла́ть, -а́ю *impf. of* пересла́ть. пересы́лка, -и sending, forwarding; ~ беспла́тно

post free; carriage paid; сто́имость пересы́лки postage. пересы́льный transit.

пересыха́ть, -а́ет *impf. of* пересо́хнуть

переся́ду *etc.*: *see* пересе́сть. перета́пливать, -аю *impf. of* перетопи́ть

перета́скивать, -аю *impf.*, перетащи́ть, -щу́, -щишь *pf.* drag (over, through); move, remove.

перетере́ть, -тру́, -трёшь; -тёр *pf.*, перетира́ть, -а́ю *impf.* wear out, wear down; grind; wipe, dry; ~ся wear out, wear through.

перетопи́ть, -плю́, -пишь *pf.* (*impf.* перета́пливать) melt.

перетру́ *etc.*: *see* перетере́ть

перетя́гивание, -я; ~ кана́та tug-of-war. перетя́гивать, -аю *impf.*, перетяну́ть, -ну́, -нешь *pf.* pull, draw; attract, win over; outbalance, outweigh; ~ на свою́ сто́рону win over.

переу́лок, -лка narrow street; cross-street; lane, passage.

переустро́йство, -а reconstruction, reorganization.

переутоми́ть, -млю́ *pf.*, переутомля́ть, -я́ю *impf.* overtire, overstrain; overwork; ~ся overtire o.s., overstrain o.s.; overwork; be run down. переутомле́ние, -я overstrain; overwork.

переформирова́ть, -ру́ю *pf.*, переформиро́вывать, -аю *impf.* re-form.

перехвати́ть, -ачу́, -а́тишь *pf.*, перехва́тывать, -аю *impf.* intercept, catch; snatch a bite (of); borrow; go too far, overdo it. перехва́тчик, -а interceptor.

перехитри́ть, -рю́ *pf.* outwit.

перехо́д, -а passage, transition; crossing; day's march; going over, conversion; подзе́мный ~ underpass, subway. переходи́ть, -ожу́, -о́дишь *impf. of* перейти́. перехо́дный transitional; transitive; transient. переходя́щий transient, transitory; intermittent; brought forward, carried over; ~ ку́бок challenge cup.

пе́рец, -рца pepper.

перечёл *etc.*: *see* перече́сть

пе́речень, -чня *m.* list, enumeration.

перечёркивать, -аю *impf.*, перечеркну́ть, -ну́, -нёшь *pf.* cross out, cancel.

перече́сть, -чту́, -чтёшь; -чёл, -чла́ *pf.*: *see* пересчита́ть, перечита́ть

перечисле́ние, -я enumeration; list; transfer, transferring. перечи́слить, -лю *pf.*, перечисля́ть, -я́ю *impf.* enumerate, list; transfer.

перечита́ть, -а́ю *pf.*, перечи́тывать, -аю *impf.* (*pf.* перече́сть) re-read.

пере́чить, -чу *impf.* contradict; cross, go against.

пе́речница, -ы pepper-pot. пе́речн|ый pepper; ~ая мя́та peppermint.

перечту́ *etc.*: *see* перече́сть. пере́чу *etc.*: *see* пере́чить

перешаги́вать, -аю *impf.*, перешагну́ть, -ну́,

-нёшь *pf.* step over; ~ порóг cross the threshold.

перешéек, -éйка isthmus, neck.

перешёл *etc.: see* перейти

перешёптываться, -аюсь *impf.* whisper (together), exchange whispers.

перешивáть, -áю *impf.*, перешить, -шью, -шьёшь *pf.* alter; have altered. перешивка, -и altering, alteration.

перешлю *etc.: see* пересла́ть

перещеголя́ть, -я́ю *pf.* outdo, surpass.

переэкзаменовáть, -ну́ю *pf.*, переэкзаменóвывать, -аю re-examine; ~ся take an examination again.

пери́ла, -и́л *pl.* rail, railing(s); handrail; banisters.

пери́на, -ы feather-bed.

пери́од, -а period. периóдика, -и periodicals, journals. периоди́ческ|ий periodic; periodical; recurring, recurrent; ~ая дробь recurring decimal.

пе́ристо-кучевóй cirro-cumulus. пе́рист|ый feathery; plumose; pinnate; ~ые облакá fleecy clouds; cirrus.

перифери́я, -и periphery; the provinces; outlying districts.

перл, -а pearl. перламу́тр, -а mother-of-pearl, nacre. перламу́тров|ый; ~ая пу́говица pearl button. перлóв|ый; ~ая крупá pearl barley.

перманéнт, -а permanent wave, perm. перманéнтный permanent.

пернáтый feathered. пернáтые *sb., pl.* birds. перó, -á; *pl.* пéрья, -ьев feather; pen; fin; blade, paddle. перочи́нный нож, нóжик penknife.

перрóн, -а platform.

перс, -а Persian. перси́дский Persian.

пéрсик, -а peach.

персия́нин, -а; *pl.* -я́не, -я́н, персия́нка, -и Persian.

персóна, -ы person; сóбственной персóной in person. персонáж, -а a character; personage. персонáл, -а personnel, staff. персонáльный personal; individual; ~ состáв staff, personnel.

перспекти́ва, -ы perspective; vista; prospect; outlook. перспекти́вный perspective; prospective, forward-looking; long-term; promising.

перст, -á finger. пéрстень, -тня *m.* ring; signet-ring.

перфокáрта, -ы punched card.

пéрхоть, -и dandruff, scurf.

перцóвый pepper.

перчáтка, -и glove; gauntlet.

перчи́нка, -и peppercorn. пéрчить, -чу *impf.* (*pf.* на~, по~) pepper.

перши́ть, -и́т *impf., impers.*; у меня́ перши́т в гóрле I have a tickle in my throat.

пёс, пса dog.

пéсенник, -а song-book; (choral) singer; song-writer. пéсенный song; of songs.

песéц, -сцá (polar) fox.

пéсий dog; dog's, dogs'; пéсья звездá dog-star, Sirius.

песнь, -и; *g.pl.* -ей song; canto, book; П~ Пéсней Song of Songs. пéсня, -и; *g.pl.* -сен song; air.

песóк, -скá (-у́) sand; *pl.* sands, stretches of sand. песóчница, -ы sand-box; sand-pit. песóчн|ый sand; sandy; short; ~ое печéнье, ~ое тéсто shortbread; ~ые часы́ sand-glass, hourglass.

пест, -á pestle. пéстик, -а pistil; pestle.

пестротá, -ы́ variegation, diversity of colours; mixed character. пёстрый motley, variegated, many-coloured, particoloured; colourful.

песчáник, -а sandstone. песчáный sand, sandy. песчи́нка, -и grain of sand.

петáрда, -ы petard; squib, cracker.

петли́ца, -ы buttonhole; tab. петля́, -и; *g.pl.* -тель loop; noose; button-hole; stitch; hinge.

петру́шка[1], -и parsley.

петру́шка[2], -и *m.* Punch; *f.* Punch-and-Judy show; foolishness, absurdity.

пету́х, -á cock; встать с ~áми be up with the lark; ~боéц fighting-cock. пету́ший, петуши́ный cock, cock's. петушóк, -шкá cockerel.

петь, пою́, поёшь *impf.* (*pf.* про~, с~) sing; chant, intone; crow; ~ вполгóлоса hum.

пехóта, -ы infantry, foot. пехоти́нец, -нца infantryman. пехóтный infantry.

печáлить, -лю *impf.* (*pf.* о~) grieve, sadden; ~ся grieve, be sad. печáль, -и grief, sorrow. печáльный sad, mournful, sorrowful; sorry, bad.

печáтание, -я printing. печáтать, -аю *impf.* (*pf.* на~, от~) print; type; ~ся write, be published; be at the printer's. печáтка, -и signet, seal, stamp. печáтн|ый printing; printer's; printed; ~ые бу́квы block letters, block capitals; ~ая крáска printer's ink; ~ый лист quire, sheet; ~ый станóк printing-press. печáть, -и seal, stamp; print; printing; type; press.

печéние, -я baking.

печёнка, -и liver.

печёный baked.

пéчень, -и liver.

печéнье, -я pastry; biscuit; cake. пéчка, -и stove. печнóй stove; oven; furnace; kiln. печь, -и, *loc.* -и́; *g.pl.* -éй stove; oven; furnace, kiln; ~ сверхвысóкой частоты́ microwave oven. печь, пеку́, -чёшь; пёк, -лá *impf.* (*pf.* ис~) bake; scorch, parch; ~ся bake; broil.

пешехóд, -а pedestrian. пешехóдн|ый pedestrian; foot; ~ая дорóжка, ~ая тропá foot-path; ~ый мост foot-bridge. пéшечный pawn, pawn's. пéший pedestrian; unmounted, foot. пéшка, -и pawn. пешкóм *adv.* on foot.

пеще́ра, -ы cave, cavern; grotto. **пеще́-ристый** cavernous. **пеще́рник**, -а caver, pot-holer. **пеще́рный** cave; ~ челове́к cave-man, cave-dweller.

ПЗУ *abbr.* (*of* постоя́нное запомина́ющее устро́йство) (*comput.*) ROM, (*read-only memory*).

пиани́но *nt.indecl.* (*upright*) piano.

пивна́я *sb.* pub; alehouse. **пивн|о́й** beer; ~ы́е дро́жжи brewer's yeast. **пи́во**, -а beer, ale. **пивова́р**, -а brewer.

пиджа́к, -а́ jacket, coat. **пиджа́чн|ый**; ~ый костю́м, ~ая па́ра (lounge-)suit.

пижа́ма, -ы pyjamas.

пик, -а peak; часы́ пик rush-hour.

пи́ка, -и pike, lance.

пика́нтный piquant; spicy; savoury.

пика́п, -а pick-up (*van*).

пике́ *nt.indecl.* dive.

пике́т, -а picket; piquet. **пике́тчик**, -а picket.

пи́ки, пик *pl.* spades.

пики́рование, -я dive, diving. **пики́ровать**, -рую *impf. & pf.* (*pf. also* с~) dive.

пики́роваться, -руюсь *impf.* exchange caustic remarks, cross swords. **пикиро́вка**, -и altercation, slanging match.

пикиро́вщик, -а dive-bomber. **пики́рующий** diving; ~ бомбардиро́вщик dive-bomber.

пи́кнуть, -ну *pf.* squeak, let out a squeak; make a sound.

пи́ковый of spades; awkward, unfavourable.

пила́, -ы́; *pl.* -ы saw; nagger. **пилёный** sawed, sawn; ~ са́хар lump sugar. **пили́ть**, -лю́, -лишь *impf.* saw; nag (at). **пи́лка**, -и sawing; fret-saw; nail-file. **пилообра́зный** serrated, notched.

пило́тка, -и forage-cap.

пилоти́ровать, -рую *impf.* pilot. **пилоти́руемый** manned.

пилю́ля, -и pill.

пина́ть, -а́ю *impf.* (*pf.* пнуть) kick.

пингви́н, -а penguin.

пино́к, -нка́ kick.

пинце́т, -а pincers, tweezers.

пио́н, -а peony.

пионе́р, -а pioneer. **пионе́рский** pioneer.

пир, -а, *loc.* -у́; *pl.* -ы́ feast, banquet.

пирами́да, -ы pyramid.

пира́т, -а pirate; возду́шный ~ air pirate, sky-jacker.

Пирене́и, -ев *pl.* the Pyrenees.

пирова́ть, -ру́ю *impf.* feast; celebrate.

пиро́г, -а́ pie; tart. **пиро́жное** *sb.* pastries; cake, pastry. **пирожо́к**, -жка́ patty, pastry, pie.

пиру́шка, -и party, celebration. **пи́ршество**, -а feast, banquet; celebration.

писа́ка, -и *c.g.* scribbler, quill-driver, pen-pusher. **пи́сан|ый** written, manuscript; ~ая краса́вица as pretty as a picture. **писа́рь**, -я; *pl.* -я́ *m.* clerk. **писа́тель**, -я *m.*, **писа́тельница**, -ы writer, author. **писа́ть**, пишу́, пи́шешь *impf.* (*pf.* на~) write; paint; ~

ма́слом paint in oils; ~ся be written, be spelt. **писе́ц**, -сца́ clerk; scribe.

писк, -а squeak, cheep, chirp, peep. **пискли́вый**, **пискля́вый** squeaky. **пи́скнуть**, -ну *pf. of* пища́ть

пистоле́т, -а pistol; gun; ~-пулемёт sub-machine gun.

писто́н, -а (percussion-)cap; piston; hollow rivet.

писчебума́жный writing-paper; stationery; ~ магази́н stationer's (shop). **пи́сч|ий** writing; ~ая бума́га writing paper. **пи́сьменно** *adv.* in writing. **пи́сьменн|ый** writing, written; в ~ом ви́де, в ~ой фо́рме in writing; ~ый знак letter; ~ый стол writing-table, desk. **письмо́**, -а́; *pl.* -а, -сем letter; writing; script; hand(-writing). **письмоно́сец**, -сца postman.

пита́ние, -я nourishment, nutrition; feeding; feed. **пита́тельн|ый** nourishing, nutritious; alimentary; feed, feeding; ~ая среда́ culture medium; breeding-ground. **пита́ть**, -а́ю *impf.* (*pf.* на~) feed; nourish; sustain; supply; ~ся be fed, eat; +*i.* feed on, live on.

пи́терский of St. Petersburg.

пито́мец, -мца foster-child, nursling; charge; pupil; alumnus. **пито́мник**, -а nursery.

пить, пью, пьёшь; пил, -а́, -о *impf.* (*pf.* вы́~) drink; have, take; мне хо́чется ~, я хочу́ ~ I am thirsty. **питьё**, -я́ drinking; drink, beverage. **питьев|о́й** drinkable; ~а́я вода́ drinking-water.

пи́хта, -ы (silver) fir.

пи́цца, -ы pizza. **пицце́ри|я**, -и pizza parlour, pizzeria.

пи́чкать, -аю *impf.* (*pf.* на~) stuff, cram.

пи́шущ|ий writing; ~ая маши́нка typewriter.

пи́ща, -и food.

пища́ть, -щу́ *impf.* (*pf.* пи́скнуть) squeak; cheep, peep; whine; sing.

пищеваре́ние, -я digestion; расстро́йство пищеваре́ния indigestion. **пищево́д**, -а oesophagus, gullet. **пищев|о́й** food; ~ые проду́кты foodstuffs; foods; eatables. **пище-комбина́т**, -а catering combine.

пия́вка, -и leech.

пл. *abbr.* (*of* пло́щадь) Sq., Square.

пла́вание, -я swimming; sailing; navigation; voyage; су́дно да́льнего пла́вания ocean-going ship. **пла́вательный** swimming, bathing; ~ бассе́йн swimming-bath, pool. **пла́вать**, -аю *impf.* swim; float; sail. **плавба́за**, -ы factory ship.

плави́льник, -а crucible. **плави́льный** melting, smelting; fusion. **плави́льня**, -и foundry. **плави́льщик**, -а founder, smelter. **пла́вить**, -влю *impf.* (*pf.* рас~) melt, smelt; fuse; ~ся melt; fuse. **пла́вка**, -и fusing; fusion.

пла́вки, -вок *pl.* bathing trunks.

пла́вк|ий fusible; fuse; ~ая вста́вка, ~ий предохрани́тель, ~ая про́бка fuse. **плавле́ние**, -я melting, fusion. **пла́вленый**; ~

сыр processed cheese.

плавни́к, -á fin; flipper. **пла́вный** smooth, flowing; liquid. **плаву́ч|ий** floating; buoyant; **~ая льди́на** ice-floe; **~ий мая́к** lightship, floating light; **~ий рыбозаво́д** factory ship.

плагиа́т, -а plagiarism. **плагиа́тор, -а** plagiarist.

плака́т, -а poster, bill; placard. **плакати́ст, -а** poster artist.

пла́кать, -áчу impf. cry, weep; cry for, weep for; mourn; **~ навзры́д** sob; **~ся** complain, lament; +**на**+a. complain of; lament, bewail, bemoan.

плакирова́ть, -ру́ю impf. & pf. plate. **плакиро́вка, -и** plating.

пла́кса, -ы cry-baby. **плакси́вый** whining; piteous, pathetic. **плаку́чий** weeping.

пла́менность, -и ardour. **пла́менный** flaming, fiery; ardent, burning. **пла́мя, -мени** nt. flame; fire, blaze.

план, -а plan; scheme; plane.

планёр, -а glider. **планери́зм, -а** gliding. **планери́ст, -а** glider-pilot. **планёрный** gliding; **~ спорт** gliding.

плане́та, -ы planet. **плане́тный** planetary.

плани́рование¹, -я planning.

плани́рование², -я gliding; glide.

плани́ровать¹, -рую impf. (pf. **за~**) plan.

плани́ровать², -рую impf. (pf. **с~**) glide, glide down.

пла́нка, -и lath, slat.

пла́новый planned, systematic; planning. **планоме́рный** systematic, planned, balanced, regular.

планта́тор, -а planter. **планта́ция, -и** plantation.

планше́т, -а plane-table; map-case.

пласт, -á layer; sheet; course; stratum, bed. **пласти́на, -ы** plate. **пласти́нка, -и** plate; (gramophone) record, disc.

пласти́ческий plastic. **пласти́чность, -и** plasticity. **пласти́чный** plastic; supple, pliant; rhythmical; fluent, flowing. **пластма́сса, -ы** plastic. **пластма́ссовый** plastic.

пла́та, -ы pay; salary; payment, charge; fee; fare. **платёж, -á** payment. **платёжеспосо́бный** solvent. **платёжный** payment; pay. **плате́льщик, -а** payer.

пла́тина, -ы platinum. **пла́тиновый** platinum.

плати́ть, -ачу́, -а́тишь impf. (pf. **за~, у~**) pay; +i. pay back, return; **~ся** (pf. **по~ся**) за+a. pay for. **пла́тн|ый** paid; requiring payment, chargeable; paying; **~ая доро́га** toll road.

плато́к, -тка́ shawl; head-scarf; handkerchief.

платфо́рма, -ы platform; truck.

пла́тье, -я g.pl. **-ьев** clothes, clothing; dress; gown, frock. **платяно́й** clothes; **~ шкаф** wardrobe.

плафо́н, -а ceiling; lamp shade, ceiling light; bowl.

плац, -а, loc. **-ý** parade-ground. **плацда́рм,** -а bridgehead, beach-head; base; springboard.

плацка́рта, -ы reserved-seat ticket.

плач, -а weeping, crying; wailing; keening; lament. **плаче́вный** mournful, sad; sorry; lamentable, deplorable. **пла́чу** etc.: see **пла́кать**

плачу́ etc.: see **плати́ть**

плашмя́ adv. flat, prone.

плащ, -á cloak; raincoat; waterproof cape.

плебисци́т, -а plebiscite.

плева́тельница, -ы spittoon. **плева́ть, плюю́, плюёшь** impf. (pf. **на~, плю́нуть**) spit; **~ в потоло́к** idle, fritter away the time; impers.+d.: **мне ~** I don't give a damn, a toss (**на**+a. about); **~ся** spit. **плево́к, -вка́** spit, spittle.

плеври́т, -а pleurisy.

плед, -а rug; plaid.

плее́р, -а personal stereo, Walkman (propr.).

плёл etc.: see **плести́**

племенно́й tribal; pedigree. **пле́мя, -мени;** pl. **-мена́, -мён** nt., tribe; breed; stock. **племя́нник, -а** nephew. **племя́нница, -ы** niece.

плен, -а, loc. **-ý** captivity.

плена́рный plenary.

плени́тельный captivating, fascinating, charming. **плени́ть, -ню́** pf. (impf. **пленя́ть**) take prisoner, take captive; captivate, fascinate, charm; **~ся** be captivated, be fascinated.

плёнка, -и film; pellicle.

пле́нник, -а prisoner, captive. **пле́нный** captive.

плёночный film; filmy.

пле́нум, -а plenum, plenary session.

пленя́ть(ся, -я́ю(сь impf. of **плени́ть(ся**

пле́сенный mouldy, musty. **пле́сень, -и** mould.

плеск, -а splash, plash. lapping. **плеска́тельный бассе́йн** paddling pool. **плеска́ть, -ещу́, -е́щешь** impf. (pf. **плесну́ть**) splash, plash; lap; **~ся** splash; lap.

пле́сневеть, -еет impf. (pf. **за~**) go mouldy, grow musty.

плесну́ть, -ну́, -нёшь pf. of **плеска́ть**

плести́, -ету́, -етёшь; плёл, -á impf. (pf. **с~**) plait, braid; weave; tat; spin; net; **~ вздор, ~ чепуху́** talk rubbish; **~сь** drag o.s. along; trudge; **~сь в хвосте́** lag behind. **плете́ние, -я** plaiting, braiding; wickerwork. **плетёнка, -и** (wicker) mat, basket; hurdle. **плетён|ый** woven; wattled; wicker. **плете́нь, -тня́** m. hurdle; wattle fencing. **плётка, -и, плеть, -и;** g.pl. **-ей** lash.

пле́чико, -а; pl. **-и, -ов** shoulder-strap; pl. coat-hanger; padded shoulders. **плечи́стый** broad-shouldered. **плечо́, -á;** pl. **-и, -а́м** shoulder; arm.

плеши́веть, -ею impf. (pf. **о~**) grow bald. **плеши́вый** bald. **плешина́, -ы, плешь, -и** bald patch; bare patch.

плещу́ etc.: see **плеска́ть**

пли́нтус, -а plinth; skirting-board.

плис, -а velveteen. **плисовый** velveteen.

плиссированный pleated. **плиссировать, -рую** *impf.* pleat.

плита́, -ы́; *pl.* **-ы** plate, slab; flag-(stone); stove, cooker; **моги́льная ~** gravestone, tombstone. **пли́тка, -и** tile; (thin) slab; stove, cooker; **~ шокола́да** bar, block, of chocolate. **пли́точный** tile, of tiles; **~ пол** tiled floor.

пловец́, -вца́, пловчи́ха, -и swimmer; **~ на доске́** surfer. **пловучий** floating; buoyant.

плод, -а́ fruit; **приноси́ть ~ы́** bear fruit. **плоди́ть, -ожу́** *impf.* (*pf.* **рас~**) produce, procreate; engender; **~ся** multiply; propagate. **пло́дный** fertile; fertilized.

плодо... *in comb.* fruit-. **плодови́тый** fruitful, prolific; fertile. **~во́дство, -а** fruit-growing. **~но́сный** fruit-bearing, fruitful. **~овощно́й** fruit and vegetable. **~ро́дный** fertile. **~сме́нн|ый; ~сме́нная систе́ма** rotation of crops. **~тво́рный** fruitful. **~я́дный** frugivorous.

пло́мба, -ы stamp, seal; stopping; filling. **пломбирова́ть, -рую** *impf.* (*pf.* **за~, о~**) seal; stop, fill.

пло́ский; -сок, -ска́, -о flat; plane; trivial, tame.

плоско... *in comb.* flat. **плоского́рье, -я** plateau; tableland. **~гру́дый** flat-chested. **~гу́бцы, -ев** *pl.* pliers. **~до́нный** flat-bottomed. **~сто́пие, -я** flat feet.

пло́скость, -и; *g.pl.* **-е́й** flatness; plane; platitude, triviality.

плот, -а́ raft.

плоти́на, -ы dam; weir; dike, dyke.

пло́тник, -а carpenter, joiner.

пло́тно *adv.* close(ly), tight(ly). **пло́тность, -и** thickness; compactness; solidity, strength; density. **пло́тный; -тен, -тна́, -о** thick; compact; dense; solid, strong; thickset, solidly built; tightly-filled; square, hearty.

плотоя́дный carnivorous; lustful. **плоть, -и** flesh.

пло́хо *adv.* badly; ill; bad; **~ ко́нчить** come to a bad end; **чу́вствовать себя́ ~** feel unwell, feel bad; *sb.* bad mark. **плохова́тый** rather bad, not too good. **плохо́й** bad; poor.

площа́дка, -и area, (sports) ground, playground; site; landing; platform; **киносъёмочная ~** (*film*) set. **пло́щадь, -и;** *g.pl.* **-е́й** area; space; square.

пло́ще *comp. of* **пло́ский**

плуг, -а; *pl.* **-и́** plough.

плут, -а́ cheat, swindler, knave; rogue. **плутова́тый** cunning. **плутова́ть, -ту́ю** *impf.* (*pf.* **с~**) cheat, swindle. **плутовско́й** knavish; roguish, mischievous; picaresque.

плыть, -ыву́, -ывёшь; плыл, -а́, -о *impf.* swim; float; drift; sail; **~ стоя́** tread water.

плю́нуть, -ну *pf. of* **плева́ть**

плюс, -а plus; advantage.

плюш, -а plush. **плю́шевый** plush; plush-covered.

плющ, -а́ ivy.

плюю *etc.: see* **плева́ть**

пляж, -а beach.

пляса́ть, -яшу́, -я́шешь *impf.* (*pf.* **с~**) dance. **пля́ска, -и** dance; dancing. **плясов|о́й** dancing; **~а́я** *sb.* dance tune, dancing song. **плясу́н, -а́, плясу́нья, -и;** *g.pl.* **-ий** dancer.

пневма́тик, -а pneumatic tyre. **пневмати́ческий** pneumatic.

пнуть, пну, пнёшь *pf. of* **пина́ть**

пня *etc.: see* **пень**

по *prep.* **I.** +*d.* on; along; round, about; by; over; according to; in accordance with; for; in; at; by (reason of); on account of; from; **жить по сре́дствам** live within one's means; **идти́ по следа́м**+*g.* follow in the track(s) of; **идти́ по траве́** walk on the grass; **лу́чший по ка́честву** better in quality; **переда́ть по ра́дио** broadcast; **по а́дресу**+*g.* to the address of; **по во́здуху** by air; **по де́лу** on business; **по и́мени** by name; **по любви́** for love; **по ма́тери** on the mother's side; **по оши́бке** by mistake; **по положе́нию** by one's position; ex officio; **по понеде́льникам** on Mondays; **по по́чте** by post; **по пра́ву** by right, by rights; **по происхожде́нию** by descent, by origin; **по профе́ссии** by profession; **по ра́дио** over the radio; **по рассе́янности** from absent mindedness; **по утра́м** in the mornings; **това́рищ по шко́ле** school fellow; **тоска́ по до́му, по ро́дине** homesickness; **чемпио́н по ша́хматам** chess champion. **II.** +*d. or a. of cardinal number, forms distributive number;* **по́ два, по́ двое** in twos, two by two; **по пять рубле́й шту́ка** at five roubles each; **по рублю́ шту́ка** one rouble each; **по ча́су в день** an hour a day. **III.** +*a.* to, up to; for, to get; **идти́ по грибы́** go to get mushrooms; **по пе́рвое сентября́** up to (and including) the first of September; **по по́яс** up to the waist; **по ту сто́рону** on that side. **IV.** +*p.* on, (immediately) after; for; **носи́ть тра́ур** be in mourning for; **по нём** to his liking; **по прибы́тии** on arrival.

по- *pref. in comb. with d. case of adjs., or with advs. ending in* **-и**, *indicates manner of action, conduct, etc., use of a named language, or accordance with the opinion or wish of;* **говори́ть по-ру́сски** speak Russian; **жить по-ста́рому** live in the old style; **по-мо́ему** in my opinion.

по...[1] *vbl. pref. forms the perfective aspect; indicates action of short duration or incomplete or indefinite character, and action repeated at intervals or of indeterminate duration.*

по...[2] *pref.* **I.** *in comb. with adjs. and nn., indicates situation along or near something.* **пово́лжский** situated on the Volga. **пово́лжье, -я** the Volga region. **помо́ры, -ов** *pl.* native Russian inhabitants of White-sea coasts. **помо́рье, -я** seaboard, coastal region. **II.** *in comb. with comp. of adjs., indicates a* smaller degree of comparison, *slightly more* (*or less*) ...; **поме́ньше** a little less; **помоло́же** rather younger.

по|багрове́ть, -е́ю *pf.*

поба́иваться, -аюсь *impf.* be rather afraid.

побе́г[1]**, -а** flight; escape.

побе́г[2]**, -а** sprout, shoot; sucker; set; graft.

побегу́шки; быть на побегу́шках у+g. run errands for; be at the beck and call of.

побе́да, -ы victory. **победи́тель, -я** *m.* victor, conqueror; winner. **победи́ть, -и́шь** *pf.* (*impf.* **побежда́ть**) conquer, vanquish; defeat; master, overcome. **побе́дный, побе-до-но́сный** victorious, triumphant.

побежда́ть, -а́ю *impf. of* **победи́ть**

по|беле́ть, -е́ю *pf.* **по|бели́ть, -лю́, -е́ли́шь** *pf.*

побере́жный coastal. **побере́жье, -я** seaboard, (sea-)coast, littoral.

по|беспоко́ить(ся), -о́ю(сь *pf.*

побира́ться, -а́юсь *impf.* beg; live by begging.

по|би́ть(ся), -бью́(сь, -бьёшь(ся *pf.*

по|благодари́ть, -рю́ *pf.*

побла́жка, -и indulgence.

по|бледне́ть, -е́ю *pf.* **по|блёкнуть, -ну; -блёк** *pf.*

поблизости *adv.* near at hand, hereabouts.

по|божи́ться, -жу́сь, -жи́шься *pf.*

побо́и, -ев *pl.* beating, blows. **побо́ище, -а** slaughter, carnage; bloody battle.

побо́рник, -а champion, upholder, advocate. **поборо́ть, -рю́, -решь** *pf.* overcome; fight down; beat.

побо́чн|ый secondary, accessory; collateral; ~**ый проду́кт** by-product; ~**ая рабо́та** sideline; ~**ый сын** natural son.

по|брани́ться, -ню́сь *pf.*

по|брата́ться, -а́юсь *pf.* **по-бра́тски** *adv.* like a brother; fraternally. **побрати́мы, -ов** *pl.* twin cities.

по|брезгать, -аю *pf.* **по|бри́ть(ся, -бре́ю(сь** *pf.*

побуди́тельный stimulating. **побуди́ть, -ужу́** *pf.*, **побужда́ть, -а́ю** *impf.* induce, impel, prompt, spur. **побужде́ние, -я** motive; inducement; incentive.

побыва́ть, -а́ю *pf.* have been, have visited; look in, visit. **побы́вка, -и** leave, furlough; **прие́хать на побы́вку** come on leave. **побы́ть, -бу́ду, -дешь; побыл, -а́, -о** *pf.* stay (for a short time).

побью́(сь *etc.: see* **поби́ть(ся**

пова́дить, -а́жу *pf.*, **пова́живать, -аю** *impf.* accustom; train; ~**ся** get into the habit (of). **пова́дка, -и** habit.

по|вали́ть(ся, -лю́(сь, -лишь(ся *pf.*

пова́льно *adv.* without exception. **пова́льный** general, mass; epidemic.

по́вар, -а; *pl.* -á cook, chef. **пова́ренный** culinary; cookery, cooking.

по-ва́шему *adv.* in your opinion; as you wish.

поведе́ние, -я conduct, behaviour.

поведу́ *etc.: see* **повести́. по|везти́, -зу́, -зёшь; -вёз, -ла́** *pf.* **повёл** *etc.: see* **повести́**

повелева́ть, -а́ю *impf.*+i. command, rule; +d. enjoin. **повеле́ние, -я** command, injunction. **повели́тельный** imperious, peremptory; authoritative; imperative.

по|венча́ть(ся, -а́ю(сь *pf.*

пове́ренная *sb.* confidante. **пове́ренный** *sb.* attorney; confidant; ~ **в дела́х** chargé d'affaires. **пове́рить, -рю** *pf.* (*impf.* **поверя́ть**) believe; check, verify; confide, entrust. **пове́рка, -и** check-up, check; verification; proof; roll-call; ~ **вре́мени** time-signal.

поверну́ть, -ну́, -нёшь *pf.*, **повёртывать, -аю** *impf.* (*impf. also* **повора́чивать**) turn; change; ~**ся** turn; ~**ся спино́й** к+d. turn one's back on.

пове́рх *prep.*+g. over, above. **пове́рхностн|ый** surface, superficial; shallow; perfunctory; ~**ое унаво́живание** top dressing. **пове́рхность, -и** surface.

пове́рье, -я; *g.pl.* **-ий** popular belief, superstition. **поверя́ть, -я́ю** *impf. of* **пове́рить**

по|веселе́ть, -е́ю *pf.* **повесить(ся, -вешу(сь** *pf. of* **ве́шать(ся**

повествова́ние, -я narrative, narration. **повествова́тельный** narrative. **повествова́ть, -тву́ю** *impf.* +o+p. narrate, recount, relate, tell about.

по|вести́, -еду́, -еде́шь; -вёл, -á *pf.* (*impf.* **поводи́ть**) +i. move; ~ **бровя́ми** raise one's eyebrows.

пове́стка, -и notice, notification; summons; writ; signal; last post; ~ **(дня)** agenda.

по́весть, -и; *g.pl.* **-е́й** story, tale.

пове́трие, -я epidemic; infection.

пове́шу *etc.: see* **пове́сить. по|вздо́рить, -рю** *pf.*

повива́льн|ый obstetric; ~**ая ба́бка** midwife.

по|вида́ть(ся, -а́ю(сь *pf.* **по|вини́ться, -ню́сь** *pf.*

пови́нность, -и duty, obligation; **во́инская** ~ conscription. **пови́нный** guilty; obliged, bound.

повинова́ться, -ну́юсь *impf. & pf.* obey. **повинове́ние, -я** obedience.

повиса́ть, -а́ю *impf.*, **по|ви́снуть, -ну; -вис** *pf.* hang on; hang down, droop; hang; ~ **в во́здухе** hang in mid-air.

по|влажне́ть, -е́ет *pf.*

повле́чь, -еку́, -ече́шь; -ёк, -ла́ *pf.* drag; pull behind one; ~ **(за собо́й)** entail, bring in its train.

по|влия́ть, -я́ю *pf.*

по́вод[1]**, -а** occasion, cause, ground; **по** ~**у**+g. apropos of, as regards, concerning.

по́вод[2]**, -а,** *loc.* **-у́;** *pl.* **-о́дья, -ьев** rein; **быть на** ~**у́** у+g. be under the thumb of. **поводи́ть, -ожу́, -о́дишь** *impf. of* **повести́. поводо́к, -дка́** rein; lead.

повозка, -и cart; vehicle, conveyance; (*unsprung*) carriage.

поволжский, поволжье *see* по...² I.

повора́чивать(ся, -аю(сь *impf. of* поверну́ть(ся, повороти́ть(ся; повора́чивайся, -айтесь! get a move on! look sharp! look lively!

по|ворожи́ть, -жу́ *pf.*

поворо́т, -а turn, turning; bend; turning-point. повороти́ть(ся, -рочу́(сь, -ро́тишь(ся *pf.* (*impf.* повора́чивать(ся) turn. поворо́тливый nimble, agile, quick; manoeuvrable. поворо́тный turning; rotary, rotating; revolving; ~ круг turntable; ~ мост swing bridge; ~ пункт turning point.

по|вреди́ть, -ежу́ *pf.*, поврежда́ть, -аю *impf.* damage; injure, hurt; ~ся be damaged; be injured, be hurt. поврежде́ние, -я damage, injury.

повремени́ть, -ню́ *pf.* wait a little; +c+*i.* linger over, delay. повреме́нный periodic, periodical; by time.

повседне́вно *adv.* daily, every day. повседне́вный everyday.

повсеме́стно *adv.* everywhere, in all parts. повсеме́стный universal, general.

повста́нец, -нца rebel, insurgent, insurrectionist. повста́нческий rebel; insurgent.

повсю́ду *adv.* everywhere.

повто́р, -а replay. повторе́ние, -я repetition; reiteration. повтори́тельный repeated; revision. повтори́ть, -рю́ *pf.*, повторя́ть, -я́ю *impf.* repeat; ~ся repeat o.s.; be repeated; recur. повто́рный repeated; recurring.

повы́сить, -ы́шу *pf.*, повыша́ть, -а́ю *impf.* raise, heighten; promote, prefer, advance; ~ вдво́е, втро́е double, treble; ~ го́лос, ~ тон raise one's voice; ~ся rise; improve; be promoted, receive advancement. повыше́ние, -я rise, increase; advancement. повы́шенн|ый heightened, increased; ~ое настрое́ние state of excitement; ~ая температу́ра high temperature.

повяза́ть, -яжу́, -я́жешь *pf.*, повя́зывать, -аю *impf.* tie. повя́зка, -и bandeau, fillet; bandage.

по|гада́ть, -а́ю *pf.*

пога́нец, -нца swine; scoundrel. пога́нить, -ню *impf.* (*pf.* о~) pollute, defile. пога́нка, -и toadstool. пога́ный foul; unclean; filthy, vile; ~ гриб toadstool, poisonous mushroom.

погаса́ть, -а́ю *impf.*, по|га́снуть, -ну *pf.* go out, be extinguished. по|гаси́ть, -ашу́, -а́сишь *pf.* погаша́ть, -а́ю *impf.* liquidate, cancel. пога́шенный used, cancelled, cashed.

погиба́ть, -а́ю *impf.*, по|ги́бнуть, -ну; -ги́б *pf.* perish; be lost. поги́бель, -и ruin, perdition. поги́бельный ruinous, fatal. поги́бший lost; ruined; killed; число́ поги́бших death-roll.

по|гла́дить, -а́жу *pf.*

поглоти́ть, -ощу́, -о́тишь *pf.*, поглоща́ть, -а́ю *impf.* swallow up; take up; absorb.

по|глупе́ть, -е́ю *pf.*

по|гляде́ть(ся, -яжу́(сь *pf.* погля́дывать, -аю *impf.* glance; look from time to time; +за+*i.* keep an eye on.

погна́ть, -гоню́, -го́нишь; -гна́л, -а́, -о *pf.* drive; begin to drive; ~ся за+*i.* run after; start in pursuit of, give chase to; strive for, strive after.

по|гну́ть(ся, -ну́(сь, -нёшь(ся *pf.* по|гнуша́ться, -а́юсь *pf.*

погово́рка, -и saying, proverb; byword.

пого́да, -ы weather.

погоди́ть, -ожу́ *pf.* wait a little, wait a bit; немно́го погодя́ a little later.

поголо́вно *adv.* one and all; to a man. поголо́вный general, universal, across-the-board; capitation, poll. поголо́вье, -я head, number.

по|голубе́ть, -е́ет *pf.*

пого́н, -а; *g.pl.* -о́н shoulder-strap; (rifle-)sling. пого́нщик, -а driver. погоню́ *etc.*: *see* погна́ть. пого́ня, -и pursuit, chase. погоня́ть, -я́ю *impf.* urge on, drive.

погоре́ть, -рю́ *pf.* burn down; be burnt out; lose everything in a fire. погоре́лец, -льца one who has lost all his possessions in a fire.

пограни́чник, -а frontier guard. пограни́чн|ый frontier; boundary; ~ая полоса́ border; ~ая стра́жа frontier guards.

по́греб, -а; *pl.* -а́ cellar. погреба́льн|ый funeral; ~ая колесни́ца hearse. погреба́ть, -а́ю *impf. of* погрести́. погребе́ние, -я burial.

погрему́шка, -и rattle.

погрести́¹, -ебу́, -ебёшь; -рёб, -ла́ *pf.* (*impf.* погреба́ть) bury.

погрести́², -ебу́, -ебёшь; -рёб, -ла́ *pf.* row for a while.

погре́ть, -е́ю *pf.* warm; ~ся warm o.s.

по|греши́ть, -шу́ *pf.* sin; err. погре́шность, -и error, mistake, inaccuracy.

по|грози́ть(ся, -ожу́(сь *pf.* по|грубе́ть, -е́ю *pf.*

погружа́ть, -а́ю *impf.*, по|грузи́ть, -ужу́, -у́зишь *pf.* load; ship; dip, plunge, immerse; submerge; duck; ~ся sink, plunge; submerge, dive; be plunged, absorbed, buried, lost. погруже́ние, -я sinking, submergence; immersion; dive, diving. погру́зка, -и loading, shipment.

погряза́ть, -а́ю *impf.*, по|гря́знуть, -ну; -я́з *pf.* be bogged down, be stuck.

по|губи́ть, -блю́, -бишь *pf.* по|гуля́ть, -я́ю *pf.* по|густе́ть, -е́ет *pf.*

под, подо *prep.* I. +*a. or i.* under; near, close to; быть ~ ружьём be under arms; взять под руку+*a.* take the arm of; ~ ви́дом+*g.* under the guise of; под го́ру downhill; ~ замко́м under lock and key; ~ землёй underground; ~ Москво́й in the neighbourhood of Moscow; ~ руко́й (close) at hand, to hand. II. +*i.* occupied by, used as; (meant, implied) by; in, with; говя́дина ~ хре́ном beef with horse-radish; **по́ле ~ карто́фелем** potato-field. **III.** +*a.* towards; on the eve of; to (the accompaniment of); in imitation of; on; for, to serve as; **ему́ ~ пятьдеся́т (лет)** he is getting on for fifty; **~ аплодисме́нты** to applause; **~ ве́чер** towards evening; **подде́лка ~ же́мчуг** fake pearls; **~ дикто́вку** from dictation; **~ зву́ки му́зыки** to the sound of music; **~ коне́ц** towards the end; **Но́вый год** on New Year's Eve; **шу́ба ~ ко́тик** imitation sealskin coat.

под..., подо..., подъ... *pref. in comb.* **I.** with *vv.* indicates action from beneath or affecting lower part of something, motion upwards or towards a point, slight or insufficient action or effect, supplementary action, underhand action. **II.** with *nn.* and *adjs.*: under-, sub-.

подава́льщик, -а waiter; supplier. **подава́льщица, -ы** waitress. **подава́ть(ся, -даю́(сь, -даёшь(ся** *impf. of* **пода́ть(ся**

подави́ть, -влю́, -вишь *pf.,* **подавля́ть, -я́ю** *impf.* suppress, put down; repress; depress; crush, overwhelm. **по|дави́ться, -влю́сь, -вишься** *pf.* **подавле́ние, -я** suppression; repression. **пода́вленность, -и** depression; blues. **пода́вленный** suppressed; depressed, dispirited. **подавля́ющ|ий** overwhelming; overpowering; **~ее большинство́** overwhelming majority.

пода́вно *adv.* much less, all the more.

пода́гра, -ы gout. **подагри́ческий** gouty.

пода́льше *adv.* a little further.

по|дари́ть, -рю́, -ришь *pf.* **пода́рок, -рка** present; gift.

пода́тель, -я *m.* bearer; **~ проше́ния** petitioner. **пода́тливый** pliant, pliable; complaisant. **по́дать, -и;** *g.pl.* **-ей** tax, duty, assessment. **пода́ть, -а́м, -а́шь, -а́ст, -ади́м; по́дал, -а́, -о** *pf.* (*impf.* **подава́ть**) serve; give; put, move, turn; put forward, present, hand in; display; **обе́д по́дан** dinner is served; **~ в отста́вку** send in one's resignation; **~ в суд на**+*a.* bring an action against; **~ го́лос** vote; **~ жа́лобу** lodge a complaint; **~ заявле́ние** hand in an application; **~ мяч** serve; **~ ру́ку** hold out one's hand; **~ телегра́мму** send a telegram; **~ся** move; give way; yield; cave in, collapse; +**на**+*a.* make for, set out for; **~ся в сто́рону** move aside; **~ся наза́д** draw back. **пода́ча, -и** giving, presenting; service, serve; feed, supply; introduction; **~ голосо́в** voting. **пода́чка, -и** (charitable) gift; pittance. **подаю́** *etc.: see* **подава́ть. подая́ние, -я** charity, alms; dole.

подбега́ть, -а́ю *impf.,* **подбежа́ть, -егу́** *pf.* run up, come running up.

подбива́ть, -а́ю *impf. of* **подби́ть. подби́вка, -и** lining; re-soling.

подберу́ *etc.: see* **подобра́ться. подбира́ть(ся, -а́ю(сь** *impf. of* **подобра́ть(ся**

подби́тый bruised; lined; padded; **~ глаз** black eye. **подби́ть, -добью́, -добьёшь** *pf.*

(*impf.* **подбива́ть**) line; pad, wad; re-sole; injure, bruise; put out of action, knock out, shoot down; incite, instigate.

подбодри́ть, -рю́ *pf.,* **подбодря́ть, -я́ю** *impf.,* cheer up, encourage; **~ся** cheer up, take heart.

подбо́йка, -и lining; re-soling.

подбо́р, -а a selection, assortment; **в ~** run on; **(как) на ~** choice, well-matched.

подборо́док, -дка chin.

подбоче́ниваться, -аюсь *impf.,* **подбоче́ниться, -нюсь** *pf.* place one's arms akimbo. **подбоче́нившись** *adv.* with arms akimbo, with hands on hips.

подбра́сывать, -аю *impf.,* **подбро́сить, -ро́шу** *pf.* throw up, toss up; throw in, throw on; abandon, leave surreptitiously.

подва́л, -а cellar; basement; (article appearing at) foot of page. **подва́льный** basement, cellar.

подведу́ *etc.: see* **подвести́**

подвезти́, -зу́, -зёшь; -вёз, -ла́ *pf.* (*impf.* **подвози́ть**) bring, take; give a lift.

подвене́чн|ый wedding; **~ое пла́тье** wedding-dress.

подверга́ть, -а́ю *impf.,* **подве́ргнуть, -ну; -ве́рг** *pf.* subject; expose; **~ опа́сности** expose to danger; **~ сомне́нию** call in question. **подве́рженный** subject, liable; susceptible.

подве́сить, -е́шу *pf.* (*impf.* **подве́шивать**) hang up, suspend; **~ся** hang, be suspended. **подвесно́й** hanging, suspended, pendant; overhead; suspension; **~ дви́гатель, мото́р** outboard motor, engine.

подвести́, -еду́, -едёшь; -вёл, -а́ *pf.* (*impf.* **подводи́ть**) lead up, bring up; place (under); bring under, subsume; put together; let down; **~ ито́ги** reckon up; sum up; **~ фунда́мент** underpin.

подве́шивать(ся, -аю(сь *impf. of* **подве́сить(ся**

по́двиг, -а exploit, feat; heroic deed.

подвига́ть(ся, -а́ю(сь *impf. of* **подви́нуть(ся**

подвижно́й mobile; movable; travelling; lively; agile; **~ соста́в** rolling-stock. **подви́жный** mobile; lively; agile.

подвиза́ться, -а́юсь *impf.* (**в** *or* **на**+*p.*) work (in), make a career (in).

подви́нуть, -ну *pf.* (*impf.* **подвига́ть**) move; push; advance, push forward; **~ся** move; advance, progress.

подвла́стный+*d.* subject to; under the jurisdiction of.

подво́да, -ы cart. **подводи́ть, -ожу́, -о́дишь** *impf. of* **подвести́**

подво́дник, -а a submariner. **подво́дн|ый** submarine; underwater; **~ая скала́** reef.

подво́з, -а transport; supply. **подвози́ть, -ожу́, -о́зишь** *impf. of* **подвезти́**

подворо́тня, -и; *g.pl.* **-тен** gateway.

подво́х, -а trick.

подвы́пивший tipsy, tiddly.

подвяза́ть, -яжу́, -я́жешь *pf.*, подвя́зывать, -аю *impf.* tie up; keep up. подвя́зка, -и garter; suspender.

подгиба́ть(ся, -а́ю(сь *impf. of* подогну́ть(ся

подгляде́ть, -яжу́ *pf.*, подгля́дывать, -аю *impf.* peep; spy, watch furtively.

подгова́ривать, -аю *impf.*, подговори́ть, -рю́ *pf.* put up, incite, instigate.

подголо́сок, -ска second part, supporting voice; yes-man.

подгоню́ *etc.: see* подогна́ть. подгоня́ть, -я́ю *impf. of* подогна́ть

подгора́ть, -а́ет *impf.*, подгоре́ть, -ри́т *pf.* get a bit burnt. подгоре́лый slightly burnt.

подготови́тельный preparatory. подгото́вить, -влю *pf.*, подготовля́ть, -я́ю *impf.* prepare; ~ по́чву pave the way; ~ся prepare, get ready. подгото́вка, -и preparation, training; grounding; schooling. подгото́вленность, -и preparedness.

поддава́ться, -даю́сь, -даёшься *impf. of* подда́ться

подда́кивать, -аю *impf.* agree, assent.

по́дданный *sb.* subject; national. по́дданство, -а citizenship, nationality. подда́ться, -а́мся, -а́шься, -а́стся, -ади́мся; -а́лся, -ла́сь *pf.* (*impf.* поддава́ться) yield, give way, give in; не ~ описа́нию beggar description.

подде́лать, -аю *pf.*, подде́лывать, -аю *impf.* counterfeit, falsify; fake; forge; fabricate. подде́лка, -и falsification; forgery; counterfeit; imitation, fake; ~ под же́мчуг artificial pearls. подде́льный false, counterfeit; forged; sham, spurious.

поддержа́ние, -я maintenance, support. поддержа́ть, -жу́, -жишь *pf.* подде́рживать, -аю *impf.* support; back up, second; keep up, maintain; bear; ~ поря́док maintain order. подде́ржка, -и support; encouragement; backing; seconding; prop, stay; при подде́ржке+g. with the support of.

поддра́знивать, -аю *impf.*, поддразни́ть, -ню́, -нишь *pf.* tease (slightly).

поддува́ло, -а ash-pit.

по|де́йствовать, -твую *pf.*

поде́лать, -аю *pf.* do; ничего́ не поде́лаешь it can't be helped, there's nothing to be done about it.

по|дели́ть(ся, -лю́(сь, -лишь(ся *pf.*

поде́лка, -и *pl.* small (hand-made) articles.

поде́лом *adv.*; ~ ему́, *etc.* it serves him, *etc.*, right.

подённо *adv.*, подённый by the day; подённая опла́та payment for the day. подёнщик, -а day-labourer, workman hired by the day. подёнщица, -ы daily, char.

подёргивание, -я twitch, twitching; jerk. подёргиваться, -аюсь *impf.* twitch.

подёржанный second-hand.

подёрнуть, -нет *pf.* cover, coat; ~ся be covered.

подеру́ *etc.: see* подра́ть. по|дешеве́ть, -е́ет *pf.*

поджа́ривать(ся, -аю(сь *impf.*, поджа́рить(ся, -рю(сь *pf.* fry, roast, grill; brown, toast. поджа́ристый brown, browned; crisp.

поджа́рый lean, wiry, sinewy.

поджа́ть, -дожму́, -дожмёшь *pf.* (*impf.* поджима́ть) draw in, draw under; ~ гу́бы purse one's lips; ~ хвост have one's tail between one's legs.

подже́чь, -дожгу́, -ожжёшь; -жёг, -дожгла́ *pf.*, поджига́ть, -а́ю *impf.* set fire to, set on fire; burn. поджига́тель, -я *m.* incendiary; instigator; ~ войны́ warmonger. поджига́тельский inflammatory.

поджида́ть, -а́ю *impf.* (+g.) wait (for); lie in wait (for).

поджима́ть, -а́ю *impf. of* поджа́ть

поджо́г, -а arson.

подзаголо́вок, -вка subtitle, sub-heading.

подзадо́ривать, -аю *impf.*, подзадо́рить, -рю *pf.* egg on, set on.

подзащи́тный *sb.* client.

подземе́лье, -я; *g.pl.* -лий cave; dungeon. подзе́мка, -и underground, tube. подзе́мный underground, subterranean.

подзо́рн|ый; ~ая труба́ telescope.

подзову́ *etc.: see* подозва́ть. подзыва́ть, -а́ю *impf. of* подозва́ть

подиви́ть, -влю́ *pf.* astonish, amaze. по|диви́ться, -влю́сь *pf.*

подка́пывать(ся, -аю(сь *impf. of* подкопа́ть(ся

подкара́уливать, -аю *impf.*, подкара́улить, -лю *pf.* be on the watch (for), lie in wait (for); catch.

подка́рмливать, -аю *impf. of* подкорми́ть

подкати́ть, -ачу́, -а́тишь *pf.*, подка́тывать, -аю *impf.* roll up, drive up; roll.

подка́шивать(ся, -аю(сь *impf. of* подкоси́ть(ся

подки́дывать, -аю *impf.*, подки́нуть, -ну *pf.* throw up, toss up; throw in, throw on; abandon. подки́дыш, -а foundling.

подкла́дка, -и lining; на шёлковой подкла́дке silk-lined. подкла́дочный lining.

подкла́дывать, -аю *impf. of* подложи́ть

подкле́ивать, -аю *impf.*, подкле́ить, -е́ю *pf.* glue, paste; glue up, paste up; stick together, mend. подкле́йка, -и glueing, pasting; sticking.

подко́ва, -ы (horse-)shoe. под|кова́ть, -кую́, -ёшь *pf.*, подко́вывать, -аю *impf.* shoe.

подко́жный subcutaneous, hypodermic.

подкоми́ссия, -и, подкомите́т, -а subcommittee.

подко́п, -а undermining; underground passage; intrigue, underhand plotting. подкопа́ть, -а́ю *pf.* (*impf.* подка́пывать) undermine, sap; ~ся под+a. undermine, sap; burrow under; intrigue against.

подкорми́ть, -млю́, -мишь *pf.* (*impf.* подка́рмливать) top-dress, give a top-dressing;

feed up. **подкóрмка, -и** top-dressing.

подкосúть, -ошý, -óсишь *pf.* (*impf.* **подкáшивать**) cut down; fell, lay low; **~ся** give way, fail one.

подкрáдываться, -аюсь *impf. of* **подкрáсться**

подкрáсить, -áшу *pf.* (*impf.* **подкрáшивать**) touch up; tint; colour; **~ся** make up lightly.

подкрáсться, -адýсь, -адёшься *pf.* (*imp* **подкрáдываться**) steal up, sneak up.

подкрáшивать(ся, -аю(сь *impf. of* **подкрáсить(ся. подкрáшу** *etc.: see* **подкрáсить**

подкрепúть, -плю *pf.*,**подкреплять, -яю** *impf.* reinforce; support; back; confirm, corroborate; fortify, recruit the strength of; **~ся** fortify o.s. **подкреплéние, -я** confirmation, corroboration; sustenance; reinforcement.

пóдкуп, -а bribery. **подкупáть, -áю** *impf.,* **подкупúть, -плю, -пишь** *pf.* bribe; suborn; win over.

подлáдиться, -áжусь *pf.,* **подлáживаться, -аюсь** *impf.* +к+d. adapt o.s. to, fit in with; humour; make up to.

подлáмываться, -ается *impf. of* **подломúться**

пóдле *prep.*+g. by the side of, beside.

подлежáть, -жý *impf.*+d. be liable to, be subject to; **не подлежúт сомнéнию** it is beyond doubt; unquestionably. **подлежáщее** *sb.* subject. **подлежáщий**+d. liable to, subject to; **не ~ оглашéнию** confidential, private; off the record.

подлезáть, -áю *impf.,* **подлéзть, -зу; -éз** *pf.* crawl (under), creep (under).

подлéц, -á scoundrel, villain.

подливáть, -áю *impf. of* **подлúть. подлúвка, -и** sauce, dressing; gravy. **подливн|óй; ~óе колесó** undershot wheel.

подлúза, -ы *c.g.* lickspittle, toady. **подлизáться, -ижýсь, -ижешься** *pf.,* **подлúзываться, -аюсь** *impf.* +к+d. make up to, suck up to; wheedle.

пóдлинник, -а original. **пóдлинно** *adv.* really; genuinely. **пóдлинн|ый** genuine; authentic; original; true; real; **с ~ым вéрно** certified true copy.

подлúть, -долью, -дольёшь; пóдлúл, -á, -о *pf.* (*impf.* **подливáть**) pour; add; **~ мáсла в огóнь** add fuel to the flames.

подлóг, -а forgery.

подлóдка, -и submarine; sub.

подложúть, -жý, -жишь *pf.* (*impf.* **подклáдывать**) add; +под+a. lay under; line.

подлóжный false, spurious; counterfeit, forged.

подломúться, -óмится *pf.* (*impf.* **подлáмываться**) break; give way under one.

пóдлость, -и meanness, baseness; mean trick, low trick.

пóдлый; подл, -á, -о mean, base, ignoble.

подмáзать, -áжу *pf.,* **подмáзывать, -аю**

impf. grease, oil; paint; give bribes, grease palms.

подмандáтный mandated.

подмастéрье, -я; *g.pl.* **-ьев** *m.* apprentice.

подмéн, -а, подмéна, -ы replacement. **подмéнивать, -аю** *impf.,* **подменúть, -ню, -нишь** *pf.,* **подменять, -яю** *impf.* replace.

подместú, -етý, -етёшь; -мёл, -á *pf.,* **подметáть[1], -áю** *impf.* sweep.

подметáть[2], -áю *pf.* (*impf.* **подмётывать**) baste, tack.

подмéтить, -éчу *pf.* (*impf.* **подмечáть**) notice.

подмётка, -и sole.

подмётывать, -аю *impf. of* **подметáть[2]**

подмечáть, -áю *impf. of* **подмéтить**

подмешáть, -áю *pf.,* **подмéшивать, -аю** *impf.* mix in, stir in.

подмúгивать, -аю *impf.,* **подмигнýть, -нý, -нёшь** *pf.*+d. wink at.

подмóга, -и help, assistance; **идтú на подмóгу** lend a hand.

подмокáть, -áет *impf.,* **подмóкнуть, -нет; -мóк** *pf.* get damp, get wet.

подморáживать, -ает *impf.,* **подморóзить, -зит** *pf.* freeze. **подморóженный** frost-bitten, frozen.

подмóстки, -ов *pl.* scaffolding, staging; stage.

подмóченный damp; tarnished, tainted; blemished.

подмыв, -а washing away, undermining. **подмывáть, -áю** *impf.,* **подмыть, -óю** *pf.* wash; wash away, undermine; **егó так и подмывáет** he feels an urge (to), he can hardly help (doing).

подмышка, -и armpit. **подмышник, -а** dress-preserver.

подневóльный dependent; subordinate; forced.

поднестú, -сý, -сёшь; -ёс, -лá *pf.* (*impf.* **подносúть**) present; take, bring.

поднимáть(ся, -áю(сь *impf. of* **подня́ть(ся**

подновúть, -влю *pf.,* **подновлять, -яю** *impf.* renew, renovate.

поднóжие, -я foot; pedestal. **поднóжка, -и** step; running-board. **поднóжный; ~ корм** pasture.

поднóс, -а tray; salver. **подносúть, -ошý, -óсишь** *impf. of* **поднестú. подношéние, -я** giving; present, gift.

подня́тие, -я raising; rise; rising. **подня́ть, -нимý, -нúмешь; пóднял, -á, -о** *pf.* (*impf.* **поднимáть, подымáть**) raise; lift (up); hoist; pick up; rouse, stir up; open up; improve, enhance; **~ на смех** hold up to ridicule; **~ пéтли** pick up stitches; **~ орýжие** take up arms; **~ целинý** break fresh ground; open up virgin lands; **~ся** rise; go up; get up; climb, ascend; arise; break out, develop; improve; recover.

подо *see* **под. подо...** *see* **под...**

подобáть, -áет *impf.* be becoming, be fitting. **подобáющий** proper, fitting.

подобие, -я likeness; similarity. **подобн|ый** like, similar; **и тому ~ое** and the like, and so on, and such like; **ничего ~ого!** nothing of the sort!

подобострастие, -я servility. **подобострастный** servile.

подобрать, -дберу, -дберёшь; -брал, -á, -о pf. (impf. **подбирать**) pick up; tuck up, put up; select, pick; **~ся** steal up, approach stealthily; make o.s. tidy.

подобью etc.: see **подбить**

подогнать, -дгоню, -дгонишь; -áл, -á, -о pf. (impf. **подгонять**) drive; drive on, urge on, hurry; adjust, fit.

подогнуть, -ну, -нёшь pf. (impf. **подгибáть**) tuck in; bend under; **~ся** bend.

подогревáть, -áю impf., **подогрéть, -éю** pf. warm up, heat up; arouse.

пододвигáть, -áю impf., **пододвúнуть, -ну** pf. move up, push up.

пододеяльник, -a quilt cover, blanket cover; top sheet.

подожгу etc.: see **поджéчь**

подождáть, -ду, -дёшь; -áл, -á, -о pf. wait (+g. or a. for).

подожму etc.: see **поджáть**

подозвáть, -дзову, -дзовёшь; -áл, -á, -о pf. (impf. **подзывáть**) call up; beckon.

подозревáемый suspected; suspect. **подозревáть, -áю** impf. suspect. **подозрéние, -я** suspicion. **подозрúтельный** suspicious; suspect; shady, fishy.

по|дойть, -ою, -óйшь pf. **подóйник, -a** milk-pail.

подойти, -йду, -йдёшь; -ошёл, -шлá pf. (impf. **подходúть**) approach; come up, go up; +d. do for; suit, fit.

подокóнник, -a window-sill.

подóл, -a hem; lower part, lower slopes, foot.

подóлгу adv. for a long time; for ages; for hours, etc., together.

подолью etc.: see **подлúть**

подóнки, -ов pl. dregs; scum.

подоплёка, -и underlying cause, hidden motive.

подопру etc.: see **подперéть**

подóпытный experimental; **~ крóлик** guinea-pig.

подорвáть, -рву, -рвёшь; -áл, -á, -о pf. (impf. **подрывáть**) undermine, sap; damage severely; blow up; blast.

по|дорожáть, -áет pf.

подорóжник, -a plantain; provisions for a journey. **подорóжный** on the road; along the road; **~ столб** milestone.

подослáть, -ошлю -ошлёшь pf. (impf. **подсылáть**) send (secretly).

подоспевáть, -áю impf. **подоспéть, -éю** pf. arrive, appear (at the right moment).

подостлáть, -дстелю -дстéлешь pf. (impf. **подстилáть**) lay underneath.

подотдéл, -a section, subdivision.

подотру etc.: see **подтерéть**

подотчётный accountable; on account.

по|дóхнуть, -ну pf. (impf. also **подыхáть**) die; peg out, kick the bucket.

подоходный; ~ налóг income-tax.

подóшва, -ы sole; foot; base.

подошёл etc.: see **подойти. подошлю** etc.: see **подослáть. подошью** etc.: see **подшúть. подпадáть, -áю** impf. of **подпáсть. подпáивать, -аю** impf. of **подпóить.**

подпáсть, -аду, -адёшь; -áл pf. (impf. **подпадáть**) **под**+a. fall under; **~ под влияние**+g. fall under the influence of.

подпевáла, -ы c.g. yes-man.

подперéть, -допру; -пёр pf. (impf. **подпирáть**) prop up.

подпúливать, -аю impf., **подпилúть, -лю, -лишь** pf. saw a little off; file, file down. **подпúлок, -лка** file.

подпирáть, -áю impf. of **подперéть**

подписáвший sb. signatory. **подписáние, -я** signing, signature. **подписáть, -ишу, -úшешь** pf., **подпúсывать, -аю** impf. sign; write underneath, add; **~ся** sign; subscribe. **подпúска, -и** subscription; engagement, written undertaking; signed statement. **подписнóй** subscription; **~ лист** subscription list. **подпúсчик, -a** a subscriber. **пóдпись, -и** signature; caption; inscription; **за ~ю**+g. signed by; **за ~ю и печáтью** signed and sealed.

подпóить, -ою, -óйшь pf. (impf. **подпáивать**) make tipsy.

подполкóвник, -a lieutenant-colonel.

подпóлье, -я cellar; underground. **подпóльный** under-floor; underground.

подпóра, -ы, подпóрка, -и prop, support; brace, strut.

подпрыгивать, -аю impf., **подпрыгнуть, -ну** pf. leap up, jump up.

подпускáть, -áю impf., **подпустúть, -ущу, -устишь** pf. allow to approach; add in; get in, put in; **~ шпúльку** sting.

подражáние, -я imitation. **подражáть, -áю** impf. imitate.

подраздéл, -a subsection. **подразделéние, -я** subdivision; sub-unit. **подразделúть, -лю** pf., **подразделять, -яю** subdivide.

подразумевáть, -áю impf. imply, mean; **~ся** be implied, be meant, be understood.

подрастáть, -áю impf. **подрастú, -ту, -тёшь; -рóс, -лá** pf. grow.

по|дрáть(ся, -деру(сь, -дерёшь(ся, -áл(ся, -лá(сь, -ó(сь or **-о(сь** pf.

подрезáть, -éжу pf., **подрезáть, -áю** impf. cut; clip, trim; prune, lop; +g. cut (off) more of.

подрóбно adv. minutely, in detail; at (great) length. **подрóбность, -и** detail; minuteness. **подрóбный** detailed, minute.

подрóвнять, -яю pf. level, even; trim.

подрóс etc.: see **подрастú. подрóсток, -тка** adolescent; teenager; youth, young girl.

подрóю etc.: see **подрыть**

подрубáть[1], -áю impf., **подрубúть, -блю,**

-бишь *pf.* chop down; cut short(er); hew.

подруба́ть², **-а́ю** *impf.*, **подруби́ть**, **-блю́, -бишь** *pf.* hem.

подру́га, **-и** friend. **по-дру́жески** *adv.* in a friendly way; as a friend. **по|дружи́ться, -жу́сь** *pf.*

подру́ливать, **-аю** *impf.*, **подрули́ть**, **-лю́** *pf.* taxi up.

подру́чный at hand, to hand; improvised, makeshift; *sb.* assistant, mate.

подры́в, **-а** undermining; injury, blow, detriment.

подрыва́ть¹, **-а́ю** *impf. of* **подорва́ть**

подрыва́ть², **-а́ю** *impf.*, **подры́ть**, **-ро́ю** undermine, sap. **подрывно́й** blasting, demolition; undermining, subversive.

подря́д *adv.* in succession; running; on end.

подря́д, **-а** contract. **подря́дный** (done by) contract. **подря́дчик**, **-а** contractor.

подса́живаться, **-аюсь** *impf. of* **подсе́сть**

подсве́чник, **-а** candlestick.

подсе́сть, **-ся́ду; -се́л** *pf.* (*impf.* **подса́живаться**) sit down, take a seat (к+*d.* by, near, next to).

под|сини́ть, **-ню́** *pf.*

подсказа́ть, **-ажу́, -а́жешь** *pf.*, **подска́зывать**, **-аю** *impf.* prompt; suggest. **подска́зка**, **-и** prompting.

подска́кивать, **-аю** *impf.*, **подскочи́ть**, **-чу́, -чишь** *pf.* jump (up), leap up, soar; run up, come running.

подслепова́тый weak-sighted.

подслу́шать, **-аю** *pf.*, **подслу́шивать**, **-аю** *impf.* overhear; eavesdrop, listen.

подсма́тривать, **-аю** *impf. of* **подсмотре́ть**

подсме́иваться, **-аюсь** *impf.* **над**+*i.* laugh at, make fun of.

подсмотре́ть, **-рю́, -ришь** *pf.* (*impf.* **подсма́тривать**) spy (on).

подсне́жник, **-а** snowdrop.

подсо́бный subsidiary, supplementary; secondary; auxiliary; accessory.

подсо́вывать, **-аю** *impf. of* **подсу́нуть**

подсозна́ние, **-я** subconscious (mind). **подсозна́тельный** subconscious.

подсо́лнечник, **-а** sunflower. **подсо́лнечн|ый** sunflower; **~ое ма́сло** sunflower(-seed) oil. **подсо́лнух**, **-а** sunflower; sunflower seed.

подсо́хнуть, **-ну** *pf.* (*impf.* **подсыха́ть**) get dry, dry out a little.

подспо́рье, **-я** help, support.

подста́вить, **-влю** *pf.*, **подставля́ть**, **-я́ю** *impf.* put (under); bring up, put up; hold up; expose, lay bare; substitute; **~ но́жку**+*d.* trip up. **подста́вка**, **-и** stand; support, rest, prop. **подставн|о́й** false; substitute; **~о́е лицо́** dummy, figure-head.

подстака́нник, **-а** a glass-holder.

подстелю́ *etc.: see* **подостла́ть**

подстерега́ть, **-а́ю** *impf.*, **подстере́чь**, **-егу́, -ежёшь; -рёг, -ла́** *pf.* be on the watch for, lie in wait for.

подстила́ть, **-а́ю** *impf. of* **подостла́ть. подсти́лка**, **-и** bedding; litter.

подстра́ивать, **-аю** *impf. of* **подстро́ить**

подстрека́тель, **-я** *m.* instigator. **подстрека́тельский** inflammatory. **подстрека́тельство**, **-а** instigation, incitement, setting-on. **подстрека́ть**, **-а́ю** *impf.*, **подстрекну́ть**, **-ну́, -нёшь** *pf.* instigate, incite, set on; excite.

подстре́ливать, **-аю** *impf.*, **подстрели́ть**, **-лю́, -лишь** *pf.* wound; wing.

подстрига́ть, **-а́ю** *impf.*, **подстри́чь**, **-игу́, -ижёшь; -иг** *pf.* cut; clip, trim; prune; **~ся** trim one's hair; have a hair-cut, a trim.

подстро́ить, **-о́ю** *pf.* (*impf.* **подстра́ивать**) build on; tune (up); arrange, contrive.

подстро́чн|ый interlinear; literal, word-for-word; **~ое примеча́ние** footnote.

по́дступ, **-а** approach. **подступа́ть**, **-а́ю** *impf.* **подступи́ть**, **-плю́, -пишь** *pf.* approach, come up, come near; **~ся** к+*d.* approach.

подсуди́мый *sb.* defendant; the accused. **подсу́дн|ый**+*d.* under the jurisdiction of, within the competence of; **~ое де́ло** punishable offence.

подсу́нуть, **-ну** *pf.* (*impf.* **подсо́вывать**) put, thrust, shove; slip, palm off.

подсчёт, **-а** calculation; count. **подсчита́ть**, **-а́ю** *pf.*, **подсчи́тывать**, **-аю** count (up); calculate.

подсыла́ть, **-а́ю** *impf. of* **подосла́ть**

подсыха́ть, **-а́ю** *impf. of* **подсо́хнуть**

подся́ду *etc.: see* **подсе́сть. подта́лкивать**, **-аю** *impf. of* **подтолкну́ть**

подтасова́ть, **-су́ю** *pf.*, **подтасо́вывать**, **-аю** *impf.* shuffle unfairly; garble, juggle with.

подта́чивать, **-аю** *impf. of* **подточи́ть**

подтверди́тельный confirmatory; of acknowledgement. **подтверди́ть**, **-ржу́** *pf.*, **подтвержда́ть**, **-а́ю** *impf.* confirm; corroborate, bear out; **~ получе́ние**+*g.* acknowledge receipt of. **подтвержде́ние**, **-я** confirmation, corroboration; acknowledgement.

подтёк, **-а** bruise. **подтека́ть**, **-а́ет** *impf. of* **подте́чь** leak, be leaking.

подтере́ть, **-дотру́, -дотрёшь; подтёр** *pf.* (*impf.* **подтира́ть**) wipe, wipe up.

подте́чь, **-ечёт; -тёк, -ла́** *pf.* (*impf.* **подтека́ть**) под+*a.* flow under, run under.

подтира́ть, **-а́ю** *impf. of* **подтере́ть**

подтолкну́ть, **-ну́, -нёшь** *pf.* (*impf.* **подта́лкивать**) push, nudge; urge on.

подточи́ть, **-чу́, -чишь** *pf.* (*impf.* **подта́чивать**) sharpen slightly, give an edge (to); eat away, gnaw; undermine.

подтру́нивать, **-аю** *impf.*, **подтруни́ть**, **-ню́** *pf.* над+*i.* chaff, tease.

подтя́гивать, **-аю** *impf.*, **подтяну́ть**, **-ну́, -нешь** *pf.* tighten; pull up, haul up; bring up; move up; take in hand, chase up; **~ся** tighten one's belt, etc.; pull o.s. up; move up, move in; pull o.s. together, take o.s. in hand.

подтя́жки, -жек *pl.* braces, suspenders. **подтя́нутый** smart.

по|ду́мать, -аю *pf.* think; think a little, think for a while. **поду́мывать**, -аю+*inf.* or о+*p.* think of, think about.

по|ду́ть, -у́ю *pf.*

поду́чивать, -аю *impf.*, **подучи́ть**, -чу́, -чишь *pf.*+*a.* study, learn; +*a.* and *d.* instruct in; ~ся (+*d.*) learn.

поду́шка, -и pillow; cushion.

подхали́м, -а *m.* toady, lickspittle. **подхали́мничать**, -аю *impf.* toady. **подхали́мство**, -а toadying, grovelling.

подхвати́ть, -ачу́, -а́тишь *pf.*, **подхва́тывать**, -аю *impf.* catch (up), pick up, take up; ~ пе́сню take up, join in a song.

подхо́д, -а approach. **подходи́ть**, -ожу́, -о́дишь *impf. of* **подойти́**. **подходя́щий** suitable, proper, appropriate.

подцепи́ть, -плю́, -пишь *pf.*, **подцепля́ть**, -я́ю *impf.* hook on, couple on; pick up.

подча́с *adv.* sometimes, at times.

подчёркивать, -аю *impf.*, **подчеркну́ть**, -ну́, -нёшь *pf.* underline; emphasize.

подчине́ние, -я subordination; submission, subjection. **подчинённый** subordinate; tributary; *sb.* subordinate. **подчини́ть**, -ню́ *pf.*, **подчиня́ть**, -я́ю subordinate, subject; place (under); ~ся+*d.* submit to, obey.

подше́фный aided, assisted; +*d.* under the patronage of, sponsored by.

подшива́ть, -а́ю *impf. of* **подши́ть**. **подши́вка**, -и hemming; lining; soling; hem, facing; filing, file.

подши́пник, -а bearing.

подши́ть, -дошью́, -дошьёшь *pf.* (*impf.* **подшива́ть**) hem, line, face; sole; sew underneath; file.

подшути́ть, -учу́, -у́тишь *pf.*, **подшу́чивать**, -аю *impf.* над+*i.* chaff, mock; play a trick on.

подъ... *see* **под...** . **подъе́ду** *etc.*: *see* **подъе́хать**

подъе́зд, -а porch, entrance, doorway; approach, approaches. **подъездно́й** approach; ~а́я алле́я drive; ~а́я доро́га access road; ~о́й путь spur (track). **подъе́здный** entrance. **подъезжа́ть**, -а́ю *impf. of* **подъе́хать**

подъём, -а lifting; raising; hoisting; ascent; climb; rise; upward slope; development; élan; enthusiasm, animation; instep; reveille; тяжёл (лёгок) на ~ slow (quick) off the mark, (not) easily persuaded to go somewhere. **подъёмник**, -а lift, elevator, hoist; jack. **подъёмн|ый** lifting; ~ые де́ньги removal allowance; travelling expenses; ~ кран crane, jenny, derrick; ~ маши́на lift; ~ мост drawbridge; ~ые *sb.*, *pl.* removal allowance, travelling expenses.

подъе́хать, -е́ду *pf.* (*impf.* **подъезжа́ть**) drive up, draw up; call; get round.

подыма́ть(ся, -а́ю(сь *impf. of* **подня́ть(ся**

подыска́ть, -ыщу́, -ы́щешь *pf.*, **подыски́вать**, -аю *impf.* seek (out), (try to) find.

подыто́живать, -аю *impf.*, **подыто́жить**, -жу *pf.* sum up.

подыха́ть, -а́ю *impf. of* **подо́хнуть**

подыша́ть, -шу́, -шишь *pf.* breathe; ~ све́жим во́здухом have, get, a breath of fresh air.

поеда́ть, -а́ю *impf. of* **пое́сть**

поеди́нок, -нка duel; single combat.

по́езд, -а; *pl.* -а́ train; convoy, procession; ~ом by train. **пое́здка**, -и journey; trip, excursion, outing, tour. **поездн|о́й** train; ~а́я брига́да train crew.

пое́сть, -е́м, -е́шь, -е́ст, -еди́м; -е́л *pf.* (*impf.* **поеда́ть**) eat, eat up; have a bite to eat.

по|е́хать, -е́ду *pf.* go; set off, depart.

по|жале́ть, -е́ю *pf.*

по|жа́ловать(ся, -лую(сь *pf.* **пожа́луй** *adv.* perhaps; very likely; it may be. **пожа́луйста** *part.* please; certainly! by all means! with pleasure!; not at all, don't mention it.

пожа́р, -а fire; conflagration. **пожа́рник**, -а, **пожа́рный** *sb.* fireman. **пожа́рн|ый** fire; ~ая кома́нда fire-brigade; ~ая ле́стница fire-escape; ~ая маши́на fire-engine.

пожа́тие, -я ~ руки́ handshake. **пожа́ть[1]**, -жму́, -жмёшь *pf.* (*impf.* **пожима́ть**) press, squeeze; ~ ру́ку+*d.* shake hands with; ~ плеча́ми shrug one's shoulders; ~ся shrink; huddle up, hug o.s.

пожа́ть[2], -жну́, -жнёшь *pf.* (*impf.* **пожина́ть**) reap.

пожела́ние, -я wish, desire. **по|жела́ть**, -а́ю *pf.*

пожелте́лый yellowed; gone yellow. **по|желте́ть**, -е́ю *pf.*

по|жени́ть, -ню́, -нишь *pf.* **пожени́ться**, -же́нимся *pf.* get married.

поже́ртвование, -я donation; sacrifice. **по|же́ртвовать**, -твую *pf.*

пожива́ть, -а́ю *impf.* live; как (вы) пожива́ете? how are you (getting on)?; ста́ли они́ жить-~ да добра́ нажива́ть they lived happily ever after. **пожи́ться**, -влю́сь *pf.* (+*i.*) profit (by), live (off). **пожи́вший** experienced. **пожило́й** middle-aged; elderly.

пожима́ть(ся, -а́ю(сь *impf. of* **пожа́ть[1](ся**. **пожина́ть**, -а́ю *impf. of* **пожа́ть[2]**

пожира́ть, -а́ю *impf. of* **пожра́ть**

пожи́тки, -ов *pl.* belongings, things; goods and chattels; со все́ми пожи́тками bag and baggage.

пожму́ *etc.*: *see* **пожа́ть[1]**. **пожну́** *etc.*: **пожа́ть[2]**

пожра́ть, -ру́, -рёшь; -а́л, -а́, -о *pf.* (*impf.* **пожира́ть**) devour.

по́за, -ы pose; attitude, posture.

по|забо́титься, -о́чусь *pf.* **по|зави́довать**, -дую *pf.* **по|за́втракать**, -аю *pf.*

позавчера́ *adv.* the day before yesterday.

позади́ *adv.* & *prep.*+*g.* behind.

по|заи́мствовать, -твую *pf.* **по|зва́ть**, -зову́,

-зовёшь; -а́л, -а́, -о *pf.*

позволе́ние, -я permission, leave; **с ва́шего позволе́ния** with your permission, by your leave; **с позволе́ния сказа́ть** if one may say so. **позволи́тельный** permissible. **позво́лить, -лю** *pf.*, **позволя́ть, -я́ю** *impf.+d. or a.* allow, permit; ∼ **себе́ пое́здку в Пари́ж** be able to afford a trip to Paris; **позво́ль(те)** allow me; excuse me.

по|звони́ться, -ню́(сь) *pf.*

позвоно́к, -нка́ vertebra. **позвоно́чник, -а** spine, backbone; spinal column. **позвоно́чн|ый** spinal, vertebral; vertebrate; ∼ые *sb., pl.* vertebrates.

поздне́е *adv.* later. **поздне́йший** latest. **по́здний** late; **по́здно** it is late. **по́здно** *adv.* late.

по|здоро́ваться, -аюсь *pf.* **поздра́вить, -влю** *pf.*, **поздравля́ть, -я́ю** *impf.* **с**+*i.* congratulate on; ∼ **с днём рожде́ния** wish many happy returns. **поздрави́тельн|ый** congratulatory; ∼ая ка́рточка greetings card. **позравле́ние, -я** congratulation.

по|зелене́ть, -е́ет *pf.*

поземе́льный land; ∼ **нало́г** land-tax.

по́зже *adv.* later (on.).

позицио́нн|ый positional, position; static; ∼ая война́ trench warfare. **пози́ция, -и** position; stand; **заня́ть пози́цию** take one's stand.

познава́емый cognizable, knowable. **познава́тельный** cognitive. **познава́ть, -наю́, -наёшь** *impf. of* **позна́ть**. **познава́ться, -наю́сь, -наёшься** *impf.* become known, be recognized.

по|знако́мить(ся, -млю(сь *pf.*

позна́ние, -я cognition; *pl.* knowledge. **позна́ть, -а́ю** *pf.* (*impf.* **познава́ть**) get to know, become acquainted with.

позоло́та, -ы gilding, gilt. **по|золоти́ть, -лочу́** *pf.*

позо́р, -а shame, disgrace; infamy, ignominy. **позо́рить, -рю** *pf.* (*pf.* **o**∼) disgrace; ∼ся disgrace o.s. **позо́рный** shameful, disgraceful; infamous, ignominious.

позы́в, -а urge, call; inclination. **позывн|о́й** call; ∼о́й сигна́л, ∼ые *sb., pl.* call sign.

поимённо *adv.* by name; **вызыва́ть** ∼ call over, call the roll of. **поимённый** nominal; ∼ **спи́сок** list of names.

по́иски, -ов *pl.* search; **в по́исках**+*g.* in search of, in quest of.

пои́стине *adv.* indeed, in truth.

пои́ть, пою́, по́ишь *impf.* (*pf.* **на**∼) give something to drink; water.

пойду́ *etc.*: *see* **пойти́**

по́йло, -а a swill, mash.

пойма́ть, -а́ю *pf. of* **лови́ть. пойму́** *etc.*: *see* **поня́ть**

пойти́, -йду́, -йдёшь; пошёл, -шла́ *pf. of* **идти́, ходи́ть;** go, walk; begin to walk; +*inf.* begin; +**в**+*a.* take after; **пошёл!** off you go! I'm off; **пошёл вон!** be off! get out!; **(так) не пойдёт** that won't work, that won't wash,

э́то ей не пойдёт it won't suit her.

пока́ *adv.* for the present, for the time being; ∼ **что** in the meanwhile. **пока́** *conj.* while; ∼ **не** until, till.

пока́з, -а showing, demonstration. **показа́ние, -я** testimony, evidence; deposition; affidavit; reading. **показа́тель, -я** *m.* index, exponent; showing. **показа́тельный** significant; instructive, revealing; model; demonstration; exponential; ∼ **суд** show-trial. **показа́ть, -ажу́, -а́жешь** *pf.*, **пока́зывать, -аю** *impf.* show; display, reveal; register, read; testify, give evidence; +**на**+*a.* point at, point to; ∼ **вид** pretend; ∼ **лу́чшее вре́мя** clock (make) the best time; ∼ **на дверь**+*d.* show the door (to). **по|каза́ться, -ажу́сь, -а́жешься** *pf.*, **пока́зываться, -аюсь** *impf.* show o.s. (itself); come in sight; appear; seem. **показно́й** for show; ostentatious.

по-како́вски *adv.* in what language?

по|кале́чить(ся, -чу(сь *pf.*

пока́мест *adv. & conj.* for the present; while; meanwhile.

по|кара́ть, -а́ю *pf.*

пока́тость, -и slope, incline. **пока́тый** sloping; slanting.

покача́ть, -а́ю *pf.* rock, swing; ∼ **голово́й** shake one's head. **пока́чивать, -аю** rock slightly; ∼ся rock; swing; stagger, totter. **покачну́ть, -ну́, -нёшь** shake; rock; ∼ся sway, totter, lurch.

покая́ние, -я confession; penitence, repentance. **покая́нный** penitential. **по|ка́яться, -а́юсь** *pf.*

поквита́ться, -а́юсь *pf.* be quits; get even.

покида́ть, -а́ю *impf.*, **поки́нуть, -ну** *pf.* leave; desert, abandon, forsake. **поки́нутый** deserted; abandoned.

покла́дистый complaisant, obliging; easy to get on with.

покла́жа, -и load; baggage; luggage.

поклёп, -а slander, calumny.

покло́н, -а bow; greeting; **переда́ть мой** ∼+*d.* remember me to, give my regards to; **посла́ть** ∼ send one's compliments, one's kind regards. **поклоне́ние, -я** worship. **поклони́ться, -ню́сь, -нишься** *pf. of* **кла́няться. покло́нник, -а** admirer; worshipper. **поклоня́ться, -я́юсь** *impf.+d.* worship.

по|кля́сться, -яну́сь, -нёшься; -я́лся, -ла́сь *pf.*

поко́иться, -о́юсь *impf.* rest, repose, be based; lie. **поко́й, -я** rest, peace; room, chamber. **поко́йник, -а** the deceased. **поко́йн|ый** calm, quiet; comfortable; restful; ∼ой но́чи! good night!

по|колеба́ть(ся, -е́блю(сь *pf.*

поколе́ние, -я generation.

по|колоти́ть(ся, -очу́(сь, -о́тишь(ся *pf.*

поко́нчить, -чу *pf.* **с**+*i.* finish; finish with, have done with; put an end to, do away with; ∼ **с собо́й** commit suicide; **с э́тим поко́нчено** that's done with.

покоре́ние, -я subjugation, subdual; conquest. покори́ть, -рю́ pf. (impf. покоря́ть) subjugate, subdue; conquer; ~ся submit, resign o.s.

по|корми́ть(ся, -млю́(сь, -мишь(ся pf.

поко́рно adv. humbly; submissively, obediently.

по|коро́бить(ся, -блю(сь pf. покоро́бленный warped.

покоря́ть(ся, -яю(сь impf. of покори́ть(ся

поко́с, -а mowing, haymaking; meadow(-land); второ́й ~ aftermath.

покоси́вшийся rickety, crazy, ramshackle; leaning. по|коси́ть(ся, -ошу́(сь pf.

покра́жа, -и theft; stolen goods.

по|кра́сить, -а́шу pf. покра́ска, -и painting, colouring.

по|красне́ть, -е́ю pf. по|красова́ться, -су́юсь pf. по|крепча́ть, -а́ет pf. по|криви́ть(ся, -влю́(сь pf.

покри́кивать, -аю impf. shout (на+a. at).

покро́в, -а cover; covering; pall; cloak, shroud; protection. покрови́тель, -я m., покрови́тельница, -ы patron; sponsor. покрови́тельственный protective; condescending, patronizing. покрови́тельство, -а protection, patronage. покрови́тельствовать, -твую impf.+d. protect, patronize.

покро́й, -я cut.

покроши́ть, -шу́, -шишь pf. crumble; mince, chop.

покрыва́ло, -а cover; bedspread, counterpane; shawl; veil. покрыва́ть, -а́ю impf., по|кры́ть, -ро́ю pf. cover; coat; roof; drown; shield, cover up for; hush up; discharge, pay off; ~ся cover o.s.; get covered. покры́тие, -я covering; surfacing; discharge, payment. покры́шка, -и cover, covering; outer cover.

покупа́тель, -я m. buyer, purchaser; customer, client. покупа́тельный purchasing. покупа́ть, -а́ю impf. of купи́ть. поку́пка, -и buying; purchasing; purchase. покупн|о́й bought, purchased; purchase, purchasing; ~а́я цена́ purchase price.

по|кури́ть, -рю́, -ришь pf., поку́ривать, -аю impf. smoke a little; have a smoke.

по|ку́шать, -аю pf.

пол¹, -а (-у), loc. -у́; pl. -ы́ floor

пол², -а sex.

пол... in comb. with n. in g., in oblique cases usu. полу... half. полвека half a century. ~го́да half a year, six months. ~доро́ги half-way. ~дю́жины half a dozen. ~миллио́на half a million. ~мину́ты half a minute. ~цены́ half price. ~часа́ half an hour.

пола́, -ы́; pl. -ы skirt, flap; из-под полы́ on the sly, under cover.

полага́ть, -а́ю impf. suppose, think, believe; lay, place. полага́ться, -а́юсь impf. of положи́ться; impers. полага́ется one is supposed to; не полага́ется it is not done; так полага́ется it is the custom, done thing; +d.

it is due to; нам э́то полага́ется it is our due; we have a right to it.

пола́дить, -а́жу pf. come to an understanding; get on good terms.

по|ла́комить(ся, -млю(сь pf.

по́лдень, -дня or -лу́дня m. noon, midday; south. полдне́вный adj.

по́ле, -я; pl. -я́ field; ground; margin; brim; ~ де́ятельности sphere of action. полев|о́й field; ~ы́е цветы́ wild flowers; ~о́й шпат feldspar.

поле́зн|ый useful; helpful; good, wholesome; effective; ~ая нагру́зка payload.

по|ле́зть, -зу; -ле́з pf.

поле́мика, -и controversy, dispute; polemics. полемизи́ровать, -рую impf. argue, debate, engage in controversy. полеми́ческий controversial; polemical.

по|лени́ться, -ню́сь, -нишься pf.

поле́но, -а; pl. -е́нья, -ьев log.

поле́сье, -я woodlands, wooded region.

полёт, -а flight; flying; вид с пти́чьего ~а bird's eye view. по|лете́ть, -лечу́ pf.

по́лзать, -аю indet. impf., ползти́, -зу́, -зёшь; полз, -ла́ det. impf. crawl, creep; ooze; spread; fray, ravel; slip, slide, collapse. ползу́ч|ий creeping; ~ие расте́ния creepers.

поли... in comb. poly-.

поли́ва, -ы glaze. полива́ть(ся, -а́ю(сь impf. of поли́ть(ся

поливитами́ны, -ов pl. multivitamins.

поли́вка, -и watering.

полиграфи́ст, -а printing trades worker. полиграфи́ческ|ий printing-trades; ~ая промы́шленность printing industry. полигра́фия, -и printing.

полиго́н, -а range; уче́бный ~ training ground.

поликли́ника, -и polyclinic; outpatients' (department).

полиненасы́щенный; ~ые жиры́ polyunsaturated fats.

полиня́лый faded, discoloured. по|линя́ть, -я́ет pf.

полирова́льн|ый polishing; ~ая бума́га sandpaper. полирова́ть, -ру́ю impf. (pf. от~) polish. полиро́вка, -и polishing; polish. полиро́вочный polishing; buffing. полиро́вщик, -а polisher.

по́лис, -а policy; страхово́й ~ insurance policy.

полит... abbr. (of полити́ческий) in comb. political. политбюро́ nt.indecl. Politburo (executive organ of Central Committee of CPSU). ~гра́мота, -ы elementary political education. ~заключённый sb. political prisoner. ~кружо́к, -жка́ political study circle. ~просве́т, а political education. ~рабо́тник, -а political worker.

полите́хник, -а polytechnic student. полите́хникум, -а polytechnic. политехни́ческий polytechnic, polytechnical.

поли́тика, -и policy; politics. **полити́ческий** political.

поли́ть, -лью́, -льёшь; по́лил, -á, -о *pf.* (*impf.* **полива́ть**) pour on, pour over; ~ **(водо́й)** water; ~**ся**+*i.* pour over o.s.

полихлорвини́л, -а PVC (*polyvinyl chloride*).

полице́йский police; *sb.* policeman. **поли́ция, -и** police.

поли́чн|ое *sb.*: с ~ым red-handed.

полк, -á, *loc.* **-ý** regiment.

по́лка[1], -и shelf; berth.

по́лка[2], -и weeding.

полко́вник, -а colonel. **полково́дец, -дца** commander; general. **полково́й** regimental.

поллюта́нт, -а pollutant.

полне́ть, -е́ю *impf.* (*pf.* **по~**) put on weight, fill out.

по́лно *adv.* that's enough! that will do! stop it! ~ **ворча́ть!** stop grumbling.

полно... *in comb.* full; completely. **полновла́стный** sovereign. ~**кро́вный** full-blooded. ~**лу́ние, -я** full moon. ~**метра́жный** full-length. ~**пра́вный** enjoying full rights; competent; ~**пра́вный член** full member. ~**сбо́рный** prefabricated. ~**це́нный** of full value.

полномо́чие, -я authority, power; plenary powers; commission; proxy; *pl.* terms of reference; credentials; **дать полномо́чия**+*d.* empower, commission; **превы́сить полномо́чия** exceed one's commission. **полномо́чный** plenipotentiary.

по́лностью *adv.* fully, in full; completely, utterly. **полнота́, -ы́** fullness, completeness; plenitude; stoutness, corpulence, plumpness.

по́лночь, -л(ý)ночи midnight; north; **за ~** after midnight.

по́лн|ый; -лон, -лна́, по́лно́ full; complete; entire, total; absolute; stout, portly; plump; **в ~ом соста́ве** in full force; in a body; ~ым **го́лосом** at the top of one's voice; ~ым-**полно́** chock-full, cram-full; ~ый **сбор** full house; ~ое **собра́ние сочине́ний** complete works; ~ый **стенографи́ческий отчёт** verbatim record.

полови́к, -á mat, matting; door-mat.

полови́на, -ы half; middle; **два с полови́ной** two and a half; ~ **(две́ри)** leaf; ~ **шесто́го** half past five. **полови́нка, -и** half; leaf. **полови́нчатый** halved; half-and-half; half-hearted; undecided; indeterminate.

полово́й[1] floor.

полово́й[2] sexual.

по́лог, -а curtains; cover, blanket.

поло́гий gently sloping.

положе́ние, -я position; whereabouts; posture; attitude; condition, state; situation; status, standing; circumstances; regulations, statute; thesis; tenet; clause, provisions; **быть на высоте́ положе́ния** rise to the situation; **по положе́нию** according to the regulations.

поло́женный agreed; determined. **поло́жим** let us assume; suppose; though, even if. **положи́тельный** positive; affirmative; favourable; complete, absolute; practical. **положи́ть, -жу́, -жишь** *pf.* (*impf.* **класть**) put, place; lay (down); decide; agree; propose, offer; fix; ~**ся** (*impf.* **полага́ться**) rely, count; pin one's hopes.

по́лоз, -а; *pl.* **-о́зья, -ьев** runner.

по|лома́ть(ся, -а́ю(сь *pf.* **поло́мка, -и** breakage.

полоса́, -ы́, *a.* **по́лосу;** *pl.* **по́лосы, -ло́с, -áм** stripe, streak; strip; band; region; zone, belt; period; phase; spell, run. **полоса́тый** striped, stripy.

полоска́ние, -я rinse, rinsing; gargle, gargling. **полоска́тельница, -ы** slop-basin. **полоска́ть, -ощу́, -о́щешь** *impf.* (*pf.* **вы́~, от~, про~**) rinse; ~ **го́рло** gargle; ~**ся** paddle; flap.

по́лость[1], -и; *g.pl.* **-е́й** cavity.

по́лость[2], -и; *g.pl.* **-е́й** carriage-rug.

полоте́нце, -а; *g.pl.* **-нец** towel.

полотёр, -а floor-polisher.

поло́тнище, -а width; panel. **полотно́, -á;** *pl.* **-а, -тен** linen; canvas. **полотня́ный** linen.

поло́ть, -лю́, -лешь *impf.* (*pf.* **вы́~**) weed.

полоши́ть, -шу́ *impf.* (*pf.* **вс~**) agitate, alarm; ~**ся** take alarm, take fright.

полощу́ *etc.*: *see* **полоска́ть**

полтерге́йст, -а poltergeist.

полти́на, -ы, полти́нник, -а fifty copecks; fifty-copeck piece.

полтора́, -лу́тора *m. & nt.*, **полторы́, -лу́тора** *f.* one and a half. **полтора́ста, полу́т-** a hundred and fifty.

полу...[1] *see* **пол...[1]**

полу...[2] *in comb.* half-, semi-, demi-. **полуботи́нок, -нка;** *g.pl.* **-нок** shoe. ~**вое́нный** paramilitary. ~**го́дие, -я** six months, half a year. ~**годи́чный** six months', lasting six months. ~**годова́лый** six-month-old. ~**годово́й** half-yearly, six-monthly. ~**гра́мотный** semi-literate. ~**гра́ция, -и** pantie-girdle. ~**гу́сеничный** half-track. ~**защи́та, -ы** half backs; **центр ~защи́ты** centre half. ~**защи́тник, -а** half-back. ~**комбина́ция, -и** half-slip, waist petticoat. ~**круг, -а** semicircle. ~**кру́глый** semicircular. ~**ме́ра, -ы** half-measure. ~**ме́сяц, -а** crescent (moon). ~**но́ски, -óв** *pl.* ankle socks. ~**оборо́т, -а** half-turn. ~**о́стров, -а** peninsula. ~**откры́тый** half-open; ajar. ~**официа́льный** semi-official. ~**подва́льный** semi-basement. ~**проводни́к, -á** semi-conductor, transistor. ~**проводнико́вый** transistor, transistorized. ~**со́нный** half-asleep; dozing. ~**ста́нок, -нка** halt. ~**то́нка, -и** half-ton lorry. ~**тьма́, -ы́** semi-darkness; twilight, dusk. ~**фабрика́т, -а** semi-finished product, convenience food. ~**фина́л, -а** semi-final. ~**ша́рие, -я** hemisphere. ~**шу́бок, -бка** sheepskin coat.

полу́да, -ы tinning. по|луди́ть, -ужу́, -у́дишь *pf.*

полу́денный midday.

полу́торка, -и thirty-hundredweight lorry.

получа́тель, -я *m.* recipient. получа́ть, -а́ю *impf.*, получи́ть, -чу́, -чишь *pf.* get, receive, obtain; ~ся come, arrive, turn up; turn out, prove, be; из э́того ничего́ не получи́лось nothing came of it; результа́ты получи́лись нева́жные the results are poor. получе́ние, -я receipt. полу́чка, -и receipt; pay(-packet).

полу́чше *adv.* rather better, a little better.

по́лчище, -a horde; mass, flock.

полы́нн|ый wormwood; ~ая во́дка absinthe. полы́нь, -и wormwood.

по|лысе́ть, -е́ю *pf.*

по́льза, -ы use; advantage, benefit, profit; в по́льзу+*g.* in favour of, on behalf of. по́льзовани|е, -я use; многокра́тного ~я re-usable. по́льзователь, -я *m.* user. по́льзоваться, -зуюсь *impf.* (*pf.* вос~) +*i.* make use of, utilize; profit by; enjoy; take advantage of; ~ дове́рием+*g.* enjoy the confidence of; ~ креди́том be credit-worthy; ~ слу́чаем take the opportunity; ~ уваже́нием be held in respect.

по́лька, -и Pole; polka. по́льский Polish; *sb.* polonaise.

по|льсти́ть(ся, -льщу́(сь *pf.*

По́льша, -и Poland.

полы́о *etc.*: *see* поли́ть

полюби́ть, -блю́, -бишь *pf.* come to like, take to; fall in love with.

по|любова́ться, -буюсь *pf.*

полюбо́вный amicable.

по|любопы́тствовать, -твую *pf.*

по́люс, -a pole.

поля́к, -a Pole.

поля́на, -ы glade, clearing.

поля́рник, -a polar explorer, member of polar expedition. поля́рн|ый polar, arctic; diametrically opposed; ~ая звезда́ pole-star; (се́верное) ~ое сия́ние aurora borealis, Northern Lights.

пом... *abbr.* (*of* помо́щник) *in comb.* assistant. помбу́х, -a assistant accountant. ~дире́ктор, -a assistant manager. ~нач, -a assistant chief, assistant head.

пома́да, -ы pomade; lipstick.

по|ма́зать(ся, -а́жу(сь *pf.* помазо́к, -зка́ small brush.

пома́леньку *adv.* gradually, little by little; gently; in a small way, modestly; tolerably, so-so.

пома́лкивать, -аю *impf.* hold one's tongue, keep mum.

по|мани́ть, -ню́, -нишь *pf.*

пома́рка, -и blot; pencil mark; correction.

по|ма́слить, -лю *pf.*

помаха́ть, -машу́, -ма́шешь *pf.*, пома́хивать, -аю *impf.*+*i.* wave; brandish, swing, wag.

поме́ньше somewhat smaller, rather smaller,

a little smaller; somewhat less, a little less, rather less.

по|меня́ть(ся, -я́ю(сь *pf.* по|мере́щиться, -щусь *pf.* по|ме́рить(ся, -рю(сь *pf.* по|ме́ркнуть, -нет; -ме́рк(нул) *pf.*

помертве́лый deathly pale. по|мертве́ть, -е́ю *pf.*

помести́тельный roomy; capacious; spacious. помести́ть, -ещу́ *pf.* (*impf.* помеща́ть) lodge, accommodate; put up; place, locate; invest; ~ статьёй publish an article; ~ся lodge; find room; put up; go in. поме́стье, -я; *g.pl.* -тий, -тьям estate.

по́месь, -и cross-breed, hybrid; cross; mongrel; mixture, hotch-potch.

поме́сячный monthly.

помёт, -a dung, excrement; droppings; litter, brood, farrow.

поме́та, -ы mark, note. по|ме́тить, -е́чу *pf.* (*impf. also* помеча́ть) mark; date; ~ га́лочкой tick.

помеха, -и hindrance; obstacle; encumbrance; *pl.* interference; быть (служи́ть) поме́хой+*d.* hinder, impede, stand in the way of. помехоусто́йчивый anti-static, anti-interference.

помеча́ть, -а́ю *impf. of* поме́тить

поме́шанный mad, crazy; insane; *sb.* madman, madwoman. помеша́тельство, -a madness, craziness; lunacy, insanity; craze. по|меша́ть, -а́ю *pf.* помеша́ться, -а́юсь *pf.* go made, go crazy.

поме́шивать, -аю *impf.* stir slowly.

помеща́ть, -а́ю *impf. of* помести́ть. помеща́ться, -а́юсь *impf. of* помести́ться be; be located, be situated; be housed; be accommodated, find room; в э́тот стадио́н помеща́ются се́мьдесят ты́сяч челове́к this stadium holds seventy thousand people. помеще́ние, -я premises; apartment, room, lodging; placing, location; investment; жило́е ~ housing, living accommodation. поме́щик, -a landowner, landlord. поме́щичий landowner's; ~ дом manor-house, gentleman's residence.

помидо́р, -a tomato.

поми́лование, -я forgiveness, pardon. поми́ловать, -лую *pf.* forgive, pardon.

поми́мо *prep.*+*g.* apart from; besides; without the knowledge of, unbeknown to.

поми́н, -a (-у) mention; лёгок на ~е talk of the devil. помина́ть, -а́ю *impf. of* помяну́ть; не ~ ли́хом remember kindly; not bear a grudge against; помина́й как зва́ли he, *etc.*, has vanished into thin air; ~ добро́м speak well of. поми́нки, -нок *pl.* funeral repast.

по|мири́ть(ся, -рю́(сь *pf.*

по́мнить, -ню *impf.* remember.

помножа́ть, -а́ю *impf.*, по|мно́жить, -жу *pf.* multiply; ~ два на́ три multiply two by three.

помога́ть, -а́ю *impf. of* помо́чь

по-мо́ему *adv.* I think; in my opinion; to my

mind, to my way of thinking; as I (would) wish, as I would have it.

помо́и, -ев *pl.* slops. помо́йка, -и; *g.pl.* -о́ек dustbin; rubbish heap, rubbish dump; cesspit. помо́йн|ый slop; ~ое ведро́ slop-pail.

помо́л, -а grinding, milling; grist.

помо́лвка, -и betrothal, engagement.

по|моли́ться, -лю́сь, -лишься *pf.*

по|молоде́ть, -е́ю *pf.*

помолча́ть, -чу́ *pf.* be silent for a time. pause.

помо́р, помо́рский *etc.: see* по...² I.

по|мори́ть, -рю́ *pf.* по|мо́рщиться, -щусь *pf.*

помо́ст, -а dais; platform, stage, rostrum; scaffold.

по|мочи́ться, -чу́сь, -чишься *pf.*

помо́чь, -огу́, -о́жешь; -о́г, -ла́ *pf.* (*impf.* помога́ть) help, aid, assist; relieve, bring relief. помо́щник, -а, помо́щница, -ы assistant, mate; help, helper, helpmeet. по́мощь, -и help, aid, assistance; relief; без посторо́нней по́мощи unaided, single-handed; на ~! help!; пода́ть ру́ку по́мощи lend a hand, give a helping hand; при по́мощи, с по́мощью+*g.* with the help of, by means of.

помо́ю *etc.: see* помы́ть

по́мпа, -ы pump.

по|мрачне́ть, -е́ю *pf.*

по|мути́ть(ся, -учу́(сь, -у́ти́шь(ся *pf.* помутне́ние, -я dimness, dullness, clouding. по|мутне́ть, -е́ет *pf.*

помча́ться, -чу́сь *pf.* dash, rush, tear; dart off.

помыка́ть, -а́ю *impf.*+*i.* order about.

по́мысел, -сла intention, design; thought.

по|мы́ть(ся, -мо́ю(сь *pf.*

помяну́ть, -ну́, -нешь *pf.* (*impf.* помина́ть) mention; remember in one's prayers; помяни́ мое́ сло́во mark my words.

помя́тый crushed; flabby, baggy. по|мя́ться, -мнётся *pf.*

по|наде́яться, -е́юсь *pf.* count, rely.

пона́добиться, -блюсь *pf.* become necessary, be needed; е́сли пона́добится if necessary.

понапра́сну *adv.* in vain.

понаслы́шке *adv.* by hearsay.

по-настоя́щему *adv.* in the right way, properly, truly.

понево́ле *adv.* willynilly; against one's will.

понеде́льник, -а Monday. понеде́льный weekly.

понемно́гу, понемно́жку *adv.* little by little; a little.

по|нести́(сь, -су́(сь, -сёшь(ся; -нёс(ся, -ла́(сь *pf.*

понижа́ть, -а́ю *impf.*, пони́зить, -ни́жу *pf.* lower; reduce; ~ся fall, drop, go down, fall off. пониже́ние, -я fall, drop; lowering; reduction.

поника́ть, -а́ю *impf.*, по|ни́кнуть, -ну; -ник *pf.* droop, flag, wilt; ~ голово́й hang one's head.

понима́ние, -я understanding; comprehen-

sion; interpretation, conception. понима́ть, -а́ю *impf. of* поня́ть

по-но́вому *adv.* in a new fashion; нача́ть жить ~ begin a new life, turn over a new leaf.

поно́с, -а diarrhoea.

поноси́ть¹, -ошу́, -о́сишь *pf.* carry; wear. поноси́ть², -ошу́, -о́сишь *impf.* abuse, revile. поно́сный abusive, defamatory.

поно́шенный worn; shabby, threadbare.

по|нра́виться, -влюсь *pf.*

понто́н, -а pontoon; pontoon bridge. понто́нный pontoon.

понуди́тельный compelling, pressing; coercive. пону́дить, -у́жу *pf.* понужда́ть, -а́ю *impf.* force, compel, coerce; impel.

понука́ть, -а́ю *impf.* urge on.

пону́рить, -рю *pf.*; ~ го́лову hang one's head. пону́рый downcast, depressed.

по|ню́хать, -аю *pf.* поню́шка, -и; ~ табаку́ pinch of snuff.

поня́тие, -я concept, conception; notion, idea. поня́тливость, -и comprehension, understanding. поня́тливый bright, quick. поня́тн|ый understandable; clear, intelligible; perspicuous; ~о of course, naturally; ~о? (do you) see? is that clear?; ~о! I see; I understand; quite! поня́ть, пойму́, -мёшь; по́нял, -á, -о *pf.* (*impf.* понима́ть) understand, comprehend; realize.

по|обе́дать, -аю *pf.* по|обеща́ть, -а́ю *pf.*

поо́даль *adv.* at some distance, a little way away.

поодино́чке *adv.* one by one, one at a time.

поочерёдно *adv.* in turn, by turns.

поощре́ние, -я encouragement; incentive; spur. поощри́ть, -рю́ *pf.*, поощря́ть, -я́ю *impf.* encourage.

поп, -á priest.

поп- *in comb.* pop-. поп-анса́мбль, -я *m.* pop group. ~-му́зыка, -и pop (music). ~-певе́ц, -ца́, ~-певи́ца, -ы pop singer.

попада́ние, -я hit. попада́ть(ся, -а́ю(ся *impf. of* попа́сть(ся

попадья́, -й priest's wife.

попа́ло *see* попа́сть. по|па́риться, -рюсь *pf.*

попа́рно *adv.* in pairs, two by two.

попа́сть, -аду́, -адёшь; -а́л *pf.* (*impf.* попада́ть) +в+*a.* hit; get to, get into, find o.s. in; +на+*a.* hit upon, come on; не туда́ ~ get the wrong number; ~ в плен be taken prisoner; ~ в цель hit the target; ~ на по́езд catch a train; ~ на рабо́ту land a job; ~ся be caught; find o.s.; turn up; пе́рвый попа́вшийся the first person one happens to meet; ~ся на у́дочку swallow the bait; что попадётся anything. попа́ло *with prons. and advs.*; где ~ anywhere; как ~ anyhow; helter-skelter; что ~ the first thing to hand.

по|пеня́ть, -я́ю *pf.*

попере́к *adv. & prep.*+*g.* across; вдоль и ~ far and wide; знать вдоль и ~ know inside out, know the ins and outs of; стать ~

го́рла+*d.* stick in the throat of; **стоя́ть ~ доро́ги**+*d.* be in the way of.

попереме́нно *adv.* in turns, by turn.

попере́чник, -а diameter. **попере́чн|ый** transverse, diametrical, cross; dihedral; **~ый разре́з, ~ое сече́ние** cross-section.

по|перчи́ть, -чу́ *pf.*

попече́ние, -я care; charge; **быть на попече́нии**+*g.* be under the charge of, be left to the care of. **попечи́тель, -я** *m.* guardian, trustee.

попира́ть, -а́ю *impf.* (*pf.* **попра́ть**) trample on; flout.

поплавко́в|ый float; **~ая ка́мера** float chamber. **поплаво́к, -вка́** float; floating restaurant.

попла́кать, -а́чу *pf.* cry a little; shed a few tears.

по|плати́ться, -чу́сь, -ти́шься *pf.*

попо́йка, -и drinking-bout.

попола́м *adv.* in two, in half; half-and-half; fifty-fifty.

поползнове́ние, -я feeble impulse; half-formed intention, half a mind; pretension(s).

пополне́ние, -я replenishment; re-stocking; re-fuelling; reinforcement. **по|полне́ть, -е́ю** *pf.* **попо́лнить, -ню** *pf.*, **пополня́ть, -я́ю** *impf.* replenish, supplement, fill up; re-stock; re-fuel; reinforce.

пополу́дни *adv.* in the afternoon, p.m.

пополу́ночи *adv.* after midnight, a.m.

попо́на, -ы horse-cloth.

поправи́мый reparable, remediable. **попра́вить, -влю** *pf.*, **поправля́ть, -я́ю** *impf.* mend, repair; correct, set right, put right; adjust, set straight, tidy; improve, better; **~ причёску** tidy one's hair; **~ся** correct o.s.; get better, recover; put on weight; look better; improve. **попра́вка, -и** correction, amendment; mending, repairing; adjustment; recovery.

попра́ть; -а́л *pf. of* **попира́ть**

по-пре́жнему *adv.* as before; as usual.

попрёк, -а reproach. **попрека́ть, -а́ю** *impf.*, **попрекну́ть, -ну́, -нёшь** *pf.* reproach.

по́прище, -а field; walk of life, profession, career.

по|про́бовать, -бую *pf.* **по|проси́ть(ся, -ошу́(сь, -о́сишь(ся** *pf.*

по́просту *adv.* simply; without ceremony.

попроша́йка, -и *c.g.* cadger; beggar. **попроша́йничать, -аю** *impf.* beg; cadge.

попуга́й, -я parrot.

популя́рность, -и popularity. **популя́рный** popular.

попусти́тельство, -а connivance; toleration; tolerance.

по-пусто́му, по́пусту *adv.* in vain, to no purpose.

попу́тно *adv.* at the same time; in passing; incidentally. **попу́тный** accompanying; following; passing; incidental; **~ ве́тер** fair wind. **попу́тчик, -а** fellow-traveller.

попыта́ть, -а́ю *pf.* try; **~ сча́стья** try one's luck. **по|пыта́ться, -а́юсь** *pf.* **попы́тка, -и** attempt, endeavour.

по|пяти́ться, -я́чусь *pf.* **попя́тный** backward; **идти́ на ~** go back on one's word.

пора́, -ы́, *a.* -у; *pl.* -ы, пор, -а́м time, season; it is time; **в (са́мую) по́ру** opportunely, at the right time; **давно́ ~** it is high time; **до поры́ до вре́мени** for the time being; **до каки́х пор?** till when? till what time? how long? **до сих пор** till now, up to now, so far; hitherto; **на пе́рвых ~х** at first; **с каки́х пор? с кото́рых пор?** since when?

порабо́тить, -ощу́ *pf.*, **порабоща́ть, -а́ю** *impf.* enslave. **порабоще́ние, -я** enslavement.

по|ра́довать(ся, -дую(сь *pf.*

поража́ть, -а́ю *impf.*, **по|рази́ть, -ажу́** *pf.* rout; hit; strike; defeat; affect; stagger, startle; **~ся** be astounded, be startled; be staggered. **пораже́нец, -нца** defeatist. **пораже́ние, -я** defeat; hitting; striking; affection; lesion; **~ в права́х** disfranchisement. **пораже́нчество, -а** defeatism. **порази́тельный** striking; staggering, startling.

пора́нить, -ню *pf.* wound; injure; hurt.

порва́ть, -ву́, -вёшь; -ва́л, -а́, -о *pf.* (*impf.* **порыва́ть**) tear (up); break, break off; **~ся** tear; break (off); snap; be broken off.

по|реде́ть, -е́ет *pf.*

поре́з, -а cut. **поре́зать, -е́жу** *pf.* cut; kill, slaughter; **~ся** cut o.s.

поре́й, -я leek.

по|рекомендова́ть, -ду́ю *pf.* **по|ржа́веть, -еет** *pf.*

по́ристый porous.

порица́ние, -я censure; reproof, reprimand; blame; **обще́ственное ~** public censure. **порица́тельный** disapproving; reproving. **порица́ть, -а́ю** *impf.* blame; censure.

по́ровну *adv.* equally, in equal parts.

поро́г, -а threshold; rapids.

поро́да, -ы breed, race, strain, species, stock; kind, sort, type; breeding; rock; layer, bed, stratum; matrix. **поро́дистый** thoroughbred, pedigree. **породи́ть, -ожу́** *pf.* (*impf.* **порожда́ть**) give birth to, beget; raise, generate, engender, give rise to.

породнённ|ый; ~ые города́ twin cities, **по|родни́ть(ся, -ню(сь** *pf.* **поро́дность, -и** race, breed; stock, strain, **поро́дный** pedigree.

порожда́ть, -а́ю *impf. of* **породи́ть**

поро́жний empty.

по́рознь *adv.* separately, apart.

поро́й, поро́ю *adv.* at times, now and then.

поро́к, -а vice; defect; flaw, blemish; **~ се́рдца** heart-disease.

пороло́н, -а foam rubber. **поропла́ст, -а** foam plastic.

порося́нок, -нка; *pl.* -ся́та, -ся́т piglet; sucking-pig. **пороси́ться, -и́тся** *impf.* (*pf.* о~) farrow.

по́росль, -и suckers, shoots; young wood.

пороть¹, -рю, -решь *impf.* (*pf.* вы́~) flog, thrash; whip, lash.

пороть², -рю, -решь *impf.* (*pf.* рас~) undo, unpick; rip (out); ~ вздор, ерунду́, чушь talk rot, talk nonsense; ~ горя́чку be in a frantic hurry; ~ся come unstitched, come undone.

по́рох, -а (-у); *pl.* ~á gunpowder, powder; он ~а не вы́думает he'll never set the Thames on fire. **пороховóй** powder; ~ погреб, ~ склад powder-magazine.

поро́чить, -чу *impf.* (*pf.* о~) discredit; bring into disrepute; defame, denigrate, blacken, smear. **поро́чный** vicious, depraved; wanton; faulty, defective, fallacious.

порошóк, -шкá powder.

порт, -а, *loc.* -ý; *pl.* -ы, -óв port; harbour; dockyard.

по́ртить, -рчу *impf.* (*pf.* ис~) spoil, mar; damage; corrupt; ~ся deteriorate; go bad, decay, rot; get out of order; be corrupted, become corrupt.

портни́ха, -и dressmaker, tailor. **портнóвский** tailor's, tailoring. **портнóй** *sb.* tailor.

портови́к, -á docker. **портóвый** port, harbour; ~ рабóчий docker.

портрéт, -а portrait; likeness.

портсигáр, -а cigarette-case; cigar-case.

Португáлия, -и Portugal.

портфéль, -я *m.* brief-case; portfolio.

портьéра, -ы curtain(s), portière.

портя́нка, -и foot-binding, puttee.

порýганный profaned, desecrated; outraged. **поругáть**, -áю *pf.* scold, swear at; ~ся curse, swear; fall out, quarrel.

порýка, -и bail; guarantee; surety; на порýки on bail.

по-рýсски *adv.* (in) Russian; говори́ть ~ speak Russian.

поручáть, -áю *impf. of* поручи́ть. **поручéнец**, -нца special messenger. **поручéние**, -я commission, errand; message; mission.

пóручень, -чня *m.* handrail.

поручи́к, -а lieutenant.

поручи́ть, -чý, -чишь *pf.* (*impf.* поручáть) charge, commission; entrust; instruct.

поручи́ться, -чýсь, -чишься *pf. of* ручáться

порхáть, -áю *impf.*, **порхнýть**, -нý, -нёшь *pf.* flutter, flit; fly about.

порциóн, -а ration. **порциóнный** à la carte.

пóрция, -и portion; helping.

пóрча, -и spoiling; damage; wear and tear.

пóршень, -шня *m.* piston; plunger. **поршневóй** piston, plunger; reciprocating; ~óе кольцó piston ring.

порыв¹, -а gust; rush; fit; uprush, upsurge; impulse.

порыв², -а breaking, snapping. **порывáть¹**, -áю(сь) *impf. of* порвáть(ся

порывáться², -áюсь *impf.* make jerky movements; try, endeavour, strive. **порывисто** *adv.* fitfully, by fits and starts. **порывистый** gusty; jerky; impetuous, violent; fitful.

порядкóвый ordinal. **поря́дком** *adv.* pretty, rather; properly, thoroughly. **поря́док**, -дка (-у) order; sequence; manner, way; procedure; *pl.* customs, usages, observances; в обязáтельном поря́дке without fail; всё в поря́дке everything is alright, it's all in order; в спéшном поря́дке quickly, in haste; не в поря́дке out of order; по поря́дку in order, in succession; ~ дня agenda, order of business, order of the day. **поря́дочно** *adv.* decently; honestly; respectably; fairly, pretty; a fair amount; fairly well, quite decently. **поря́дочный** decent; honest; respectable; fair, considerable.

пос. *abbr.* (*of* посёлок) settlement, housing estate.

посади́ть, -ажý, -áдишь *pf. of* сади́ть, сажáть. **посáдка**, -и planting; embarkation; boarding; landing; seat. **посáдочн|ый** planting; landing; ~ые огни́ flare-path; ~ фáры landing lights.

посажý *etc.*: *see* посади́ть. **по|сáхарить**, -рю *pf.* **по|сватáть(ся**, -аю(сь *pf.* **по|светжéть**, -éет *pf.* **по|свети́ть**, -ечý, -éтишь *pf.* **по|светлéть**, -éет *pf.*

пóсвист, -а whistle; whistling. **посви́стывать**, -аю *impf.* whistle.

по-свóему *adv.* (in) one's own way.

посвяти́ть, -ящý *pf.*, **посвящáть**, -áю *impf.* devote, give up; dedicate; initiate, let in; ordain, consecrate. **посвящéние**, -я dedication; initiation; consecration, ordination.

посéв, -а sowing; crops. **посевн|óй** sowing; ~áя плóщадь sown area, area under crops.

по|седéть, -éю *pf.* **посéкся** *etc.*: *see* посéчься

поселéнец, -нца settler; deportee, exile. **поселéние**, -я settling, settlement; deportation, exile. **по|сели́ть**, -лю́ *pf.*, **поселя́ть**, -я́ю *impf.* settle; lodge; inspire, arouse, engender; ~ся settle, take up residence, make one's home. **посёлок**, -лка settlement; housing estate.

посеребрённый; -рён, -á silver-plated; silvered. **по|серебри́ть**, -рю́ *pf.*

по|серéть, -éю *pf.*

посети́тель, -я *m.* visitor; caller; guest. **посети́ть**, -ещý *pf.* (*impf.* посещáть) visit; call on; attend.

по|сéтовать, -тую *pf.* **по|сéчься**, -ечётся, -екýтся; -сéкся, -лáсь *pf.*

посещáемость, -и attendance, (number of) visitors. **посещáть**, -áю *impf. of* посети́ть. **посещéние**, -я visiting; visit.

по|сéять, -éю *pf.*

поси́льн|ый within one's powers.

посинéлый gone blue. **по|сине́ть**, -éю *pf.*

по|скакáть, -ачý, -áчешь *pf.*

поскользнýться, -нýсь, -нёшься *pf.* slip.

поско́льку *conj.* as far as, as much as, (in) so far as; since.

по|скрóмничать, -аю *pf.* **по|скупи́ться**, -плю́сь *pf.*

послáнец, -нца messenger, envoy. послáние, -я message; epistle. послáнник, -а envoy, minister. послáть, -шлю́, -шлёшь *pf.* (*impf.* посылáть) send, dispatch; move, thrust; ~ за дóктором send for the doctor; ~ по пóчте post.

пóсле *adv. & prep.+g.* after; afterwards, later (on); since; ~ всегó after all, when all is said and done; ~ всех last (of all).

пóсле... *in comb.* post-; after-. послевоéнный post-war. ~зáвтра *adv.* the day after tomorrow. ~обéденный after-dinner. ~родовóй post-natal. ~слóвие, -я epilogue; concluding remarks. ~удáрный post-tonic.

послéдн|ий last; final; recent; latest; latter; (в) ~ее врéмя, за ~ее врéмя lately, recently; (в) ~ий раз for the last time; до ~его врéмени until very recently; ~яя кáпля the last straw; ~яя мóда the latest fashion. послéдователь, -я *m.* follower. послéдовательный successive, consecutive; consistent, logical. по|слéдовать, -дую *pf.* послéдствие, -я consequence, sequel; after-effect. послéдующий subsequent, succeeding, following, ensuing; consequent.

послóвица, -ы proverb, saying. послóвичный proverbial.

по|служи́ть, -жу́, -жишь *pf.* послужнóй service; ~ спи́сок service record.

послушáние, -я obedience. по|слýшать(ся, -аю(сь *pf.* послýшный obedient, dutiful.

по|слы́шаться, -шится *pf.*

посмáтривать, -аю *impf.* look from time to time (at), glance occasionally.

посмéиваться, -аюсь *impf.* chuckle, laugh softly.

посмéртный posthumous.

по|смéть, -éю *pf.*

посмéшище, -а a laughing-stock, butt. посмея́ние, -я mockery, ridicule. посмея́ться, -éюсь, -éёшься *pf.* laugh; +над+*i.* laugh at, ridicule, make fun of.

по|смотрéть(ся, -рю́(сь, -ришь(ся *pf.*

посóбие, -я aid, help, relief, assistance; allowance, benefit; textbook; (*educational*) aid; *pl.* teaching equipment; учéбные посóбия educational supplies. посóбник, -а accomplice; abettor.

по|совéтовать(ся, -тую(сь *pf.* по|содéйствовать, -твую *pf.*

посóл, -слá ambassador.

по|соли́ть, -олю́, -óли́шь *pf.*

посóльский ambassadorial, ambassador's; embassy. посóльство, -а embassy.

поспáть, -сплю́; -áл, -á, -о *pf.* sleep; have a nap.

поспевáть[1], -áет *impf.*, по|спéть[1], -éет *pf.* ripen; be done, be ready.

поспевáть[2], -áю *impf.*, по|спéть[2], -éю *pf.* have time; be in time; (к+*d.*, на+*a.* for); +за+*i.* keep up with, keep pace with; не ~ к пóезду miss the train; ~ на пóезд catch the train.

по|спеши́ть, -шý *pf.* поспéшно *adv.* in a hurry, hurriedly, hastily. поспéшный hasty, hurried.

по|спóрить, -рю *pf.* по|спосóбствовать, -твую *pf.*

посреди́ *adv. & prep.+g.* in the middle (of), in the midst (of). посреди́не *adv.* in the middle. посрéдник, -а mediator, intermediary; go-between; middleman; umpire. посрéдничество, -а mediation. посрéдственно *adv.* so-so, (only) fairly well; satisfactory. посрéдственность, -и mediocrity. посрéдственный mediocre, middling; fair, satisfactory. посрéдством *prep.+g.* by means of; by dint of; with the aid of.

по|ссóрить(ся, -рю(сь *pf.*

пост[1], -á, *loc.* -ý post; занимáть ~ occupy a post; на ~ý at one's post; on one's beat; on point duty.

пост[2], -á, *loc.* -ý fasting; abstinence; fast.

по|стáвить[1], -влю *pf.*

постáвить[2], -влю *pf.*, поставля́ть, -я́ю *impf.* supply, purvey. постáвка, -и supply; delivery. поставщи́к, -á supplier, purveyor, provider; caterer; outfitter.

постанови́ть, -влю́, -вишь *pf.* (*impf.* постановля́ть) decree, enact, ordain; decide, resolve.

постанóвка, -и staging; production; arrangement, organization; putting, placing, setting; erection, raising; ~ гóлоса voice training; ~ пáльцев fingering.

постановлéние, -я decree, enactment; decision, resolution. постановля́ть, -я́ю *impf. of* постанови́ть

постанóвочный stage, staging, production. постанóвщик, -а producer, stage-manager; (film) director.

по|старáться, -áюсь *pf.*

по|старéть, -éю *pf.* по-стáрому *adv.* as before; as of old.

постéль, -и bed; bottom. постéльн|ый bed; ~ое бельё bed-clothes; ~ режи́м confinement to bed. постéлю *etc.: see* постлáть

постепéнно *adv.* gradually, little by little. постепéнный gradual.

по|стесня́ться, -я́юсь *pf.*

постигáть, -áю *impf. of* пости́чь. пости́гнуть *see* пости́чь постижéние, -я comprehension, grasp. постижи́мый comprehensible.

постилáть, -áю *impf. of* постлáть. пости́лка, -и spreading, laying; bedding; litter.

пости́чь, пости́гнуть, -и́гну; -и́г(нул) *pf.* (*impf.* постигáть) comprehend, grasp; befall.

по|стлáть, -стелю́, -стéлешь *pf.* (*impf. also* постилáть) spread, lay; ~ постéль make a bed.

пóстн|ый lenten; lean; glum; ~ое мáсло vegetable oil.

постóй, -я billeting, quartering.

постóльку *conj.* to the same extent, to the same degree; (so).

по|сторонúться, -нюсь, -нишься *pf.* **посторóнн|ий** strange; foreign; extraneous, outside; *sb.* stranger, outsider; **~им вход запрещён** no admission; private.

постоя́нно *adv.* constantly, continually, perpetually, always. **постоя́нн|ый** permanent; constant; continual; invariable; steadfast, unchanging; **~ый áдрес** permanent address; **~ая (величина́)** constant; **~ый ток** direct current. **постоя́нство, -а** constancy; permanency.

по|стоя́ть, -ою́ *pf.* stand, stop; **+за+a.** stand up for.

пострада́вший *sb.* victim. **по|страда́ть, -а́ю** *pf.*

построéние, -я construction; building; formation. **по|стрóить(ся, -рóю(сь** *pf.* **постро́йка, -и** building; erection, construction; building-site.

пострóмка, -и trace; strap.

поступа́тельный progressive, forward, advancing. **поступа́ть, -а́ю** *impf.*, **поступи́ть, -плю́, -пишь** *pf.* act; do; come through, come in, be received; **+в** *or* **на+a.** enter, join, go to, go into; **+c+i.** treat, deal with; **~ в прода́жу** be on sale, come on the market; **~ в шкóлу** go to school, start school; **поступи́ла жа́лоба** a complaint has been received; **~ся+i.** waive, forgo; give up. **поступлéние, -я** entering, joining; receipt; entry. **постýпок, -пка** action; act, deed; *pl.* conduct, behaviour. **пóступь, -и** gait; step, tread.

по|стуча́ть(ся, -чу́(сь *pf.*

по|стыди́ться, -ыжу́сь *pf.* **посты́дный** shameful.

посýда, -ы crockery; plates and dishes; service; ware; utensils; vessel, crock. **посýдн|ый** china; dish; **~ое полотéнце** tea-towel; **~ый шкаф** dresser, china-cupboard.

по|сули́ть, -лю́ *pf.*

посýточный 24-hour, round-the-clock; by the day.

посчастли́виться, -ится *pf. impers.* (**+d.**) turn out well, go well (for); **ей посчастли́вилось+inf.** she had the luck to, she was lucky enough to.

посчита́ть, -а́ю *pf.* count (up). **по|счита́ться, -а́юсь** *pf.*

посыла́ть, -а́ю *impf. of* **посла́ть. посы́лка, -и** sending; parcel, package; errand; premise. **посы́лочн|ый** parcel; **~ая фи́рма** mail-order firm. **посы́льный** *sb.* messenger.

посыпа́ть, -плю, -плешь *pf.*, **посыпа́ть, -а́ю** *impf.* strew; sprinkle; powder.

посяга́тельство, -а encroachment; infringement. **посяга́ть, -а́ю** *impf.*, **посягну́ть, -ну́, -нёшь** *pf.* encroach, infringe; make an attempt (**на+a.** on).

пот, -а (-у), *loc.* **-ý;** *pl.* **-ы́** sweat, perspiration.
потаённый, потайнóй secret.
по-твóему *adv.* in your opinion; as you wish;

as you advise; **пусть бýдет ~** have it your own way; just as you think.

потака́ть, -а́ю *impf.+d.* indulge, pander to.
потасóвка, -и brawl, fight; hiding, beating.
потвóрствовать, -твую *impf.* (**+d.**) be indulgent (towards), connive (at), pander (to).

потёмки, -мок *pl.* darkness. **по|темнéть, -éет** *pf.*

по|теплéть, -éет *pf.*
потерпéвший *sb.* victim; survivor. **по|терпéть, -плю́, -пишь** *pf.*

потéря, -и loss; waste; *pl.* losses, casualties. **по|теря́ть(ся, -я́ю(сь** *pf.*

по|тесни́ться, -ню́ *pf.* **по|тесни́ться, -ню́сь** *pf.*; make room; sit closer, stand closer, squeeze up, move up.

потéть, -éю *impf.* (*pf.* **вс~, за~**) sweat, perspire; mist over, steam up; (**+над+i.**) sweat, toil (over).

потéха, -и fun, amusement. **по|тéшить(ся, -шу́(сь** *pf.* **потéшный** funny, amusing.

потира́ть, -а́ю *impf.* rub.

потихóньку *adv.* noiselessly, softly; secretly; by stealth, on the sly; slowly.

пóтн|ый, -тен, -тна́, -тно sweaty, damp with perspiration; misty, steamed up; **~ые рýки** clammy hands.

потóк, -а stream; flow; torrent; flood; production line; group; **потóк маши́н** traffic flow.

потолóк, -лка́ ceiling.
по|толстéть, -éю *pf.*

потóм *adv.* afterwards; later (on); then, after that. **потóмок, -мка** descendant; scion; offspring, progeny. **потóмство, -а** posterity, descendants.

потомý *adv.* that is why; **~ что** *conj.* because, as.

по|тонýть, -нý, -нешь *pf.* **потóп, -а** flood, deluge. **по|топи́ть, -плю́, -пишь** *pf.*, **потопля́ть, -я́ю** *impf.* sink. **потоплéние, -я** sinking.

по|топта́ть, -пчу́, -пчешь *pf.* **по|торопи́ть(ся, -плю́(сь, -пишь(ся** *pf.*

потóчн|ый continuous; production-line; **~ая ли́ния** production line; **~ое произвóдство** mass production.

по|тра́тить, -а́чу *pf.*

потреби́тель, -я *m.* consumer, user. **потреби́тельск|ий** consumer; consumer's, consumers'; **~ие това́ры** consumer goods. **потреби́ть, -блю́** *pf.*, **потребля́ть, -я́ю** *impf.* consume, use. **потреблéние, -я** consumption, use. **потрéбность, -и** need, want, necessity, requirement. **потрéбный** necessary, required, requisite. **по|трéбовать(ся, -бую(сь** *pf.*

по|тревóжить(ся, -жу(сь *pf.*
потрёпанный shabby; ragged, tattered; battered; worn, seedy. **по|трепа́ть(ся, -плю́(сь, -плешь(ся** *pf.*

по|трéскаться, -ается *pf.* **потрéскивать, -ает** *impf.* crackle.

потроха́, -о́в pl. giblets; pluck. потроши́ть, -шу́ impf. (pf. вы́~) disembowel, clean; draw.

потруди́ться, -ужу́сь, -у́дишься pf. take some pains, do some work; take the trouble.

потряса́ть, -а́ю impf., потрясти́, -су́, -сёшь; -я́с, -ла́ pf. shake; rock; stagger, stun; +a. or i. brandish; shake; ~ кулако́м shake one's fist. потряса́ющий staggering, stupendous, tremendous.

поту́га, -и muscular contraction; pl. labours, vain attempts; родовы́е поту́ги labour.

поту́пить, -плю pf., потупля́ть, -я́ю impf. lower, cast down; ~ся look down, cast down one's eyes.

потускне́лый tarnished; lack-lustre. по|туск-не́ть, -е́ет pf.

потуха́ть, -а́ет impf., по|ту́хнуть, -нет, -у́х pf. go out; die out. поту́хший extinct; lifeless, lack-lustre.

по|туши́ть, -шу́, -шишь pf. по|тяга́ться, -а́юсь pf.

потя́гиваться, -аюсь impf., по|тяну́ться, -ну́сь, -нешься pf. stretch o.s. по|тяну́ть, -ну́, -нешь pf.

по|у́жинать, -аю pf. по|умне́ть, -е́ю pf.

поучи́тельный instructive.

похвала́, -ы́ praise. по|хвали́ть(ся, -лю́(сь, -лишь(ся pf. похвальба́, -ы́ bragging, boasting. похва́льный praiseworthy, laudable, commendable; laudatory.

по|хва́стать(ся, -аю(сь pf.

похити́тель, -я m. kidnapper; abductor; thief. похи́тить, -хи́щу pf., похища́ть, -а́ю impf. kidnap; abduct, carry off; steal. похище́ние, -я theft; kidnapping; abduction.

похлёбка, -и broth, soup.

по|хлопота́ть, -очу́, -о́чешь pf.

похме́лье, -я hangover.

похо́д, -а campaign; march; cruise; (long) walk, hike; outing, excursion; вы́ступить в ~ take the field; set out; на ~е on the march.

по|хода́тайствовать, -твую pf.

походи́ть, -ожу́, -о́дишь impf. на+a. be like, look like, resemble.

похо́дка, -и gait, walk, step. похо́дн|ый mobile, field; marching, cruising; ~ая крова́ть camp-bed; ~ая ку́хня mobile kitchen, field kitchen; ~ый мешо́к kit-bag; ~ый поря́док marching order; ~ая ра́ция walkie-talkie. похожде́ние, -я adventure, escapade.

похо́жий similar, alike; ~ на like.

по|хорони́ть, -ню́, -нишь pf. похоро́нный funeral. по́хороны, -ро́н pl. funeral; burial.

по|хороше́ть, -е́ю pf.

по́хоть, -и lust.

по|худе́ть, -е́ю pf.

по|целова́ть(ся, -лу́ю(сь pf. поцелу́й, -я kiss.

по|церемо́ниться, -нюсь pf.

по́чва, -ы soil, earth; ground; basis, footing. по́чвенный soil, ground; ~ покро́в top-soil.

почём adv. how much; how; ~ знать? who

can tell? how is one to know?; ~ сего́дня я́блоки how much are apples today?; ~ я зна́ю? how should I know?

почему́ adv. why; (and) so, that's why. почему́-либо, -нибу́дь advs. for some reason or other. почему́-то adv. for some reason.

по́черк, -а hand(writing).

почерне́лый blackened, darkened. по|черне́ть, -е́ю pf.

почерпа́ть, -а́ю impf., почерпну́ть, -ну́, -нёшь pf. get, draw, scoop up; pick up.

по|черстве́ть, -е́ю pf. по|чеса́ть(ся, -ешу́(сь, -е́шешь(ся pf.

по́честь, -и honour. почёт, -а honour; respect, esteem. почётный honoured, respected, esteemed; of honour; honourable; honorary; ~ карау́л guard of honour.

по́чечный renal; kidney.

почива́ть, -а́ю impf. of почи́ть

почи́н, -а initiative; beginning, start.

по|чини́ть, -ню́, -нишь pf., починя́ть, -я́ю impf. repair, mend. почи́нка, -и repairing, mending.

по|чи́стить(ся, -и́щу(сь pf.

почита́ние, -я honouring; respect, esteem. почита́ть[1], -а́ю impf. honour, respect, esteem; revere; worship.

почита́ть[2], -а́ю pf. read for a while, look at.

почи́ть, -и́ю pf. (impf. почива́ть) rest, take one's rest; pass away; ~ на ла́врах rest on one's laurels.

по́чка[1], -и bud.

по́чка[2], -и kidney; иску́сственная ~ kidney machine.

по́чта, -ы post, mail; post-office; электро́нная ~ e-mail. почтальо́н, -а postman. почтальо́нша, -и postwoman. почта́мт, -а (head) post-office.

почте́ние, -я respect; esteem; deference. почтённый honourable; respectable, estimable; venerable; considerable.

почти́ adv. almost, nearly.

почти́тельный respectful, deferential; considerable. почти́ть, -чту́ pf. honour.

почто́в|ый post, mail; postal; ~ая каре́та stage coach, mail; ~ая ка́рточка postcard; ~ый перево́д postal order; ~ый по́езд mail (train); ~ый я́щик letter-box.

по|чу́диться, -ишься pf. по|шаба́шить, -шу pf.

пошатну́ть, -ну́, -нёшь pf. shake; ~ся shake; totter, reel, stagger; be shaken.

по|шевели́ть(ся, -елю́(сь, -ели́шь(ся pf. пошёл etc.: see пойти́

поши́вка, -и sewing. поши́вочный sewing.

по́шлина, -ы duty; customs.

по́шлость, -и vulgarity, commonness; triviality; triteness, banality. по́шлый vulgar, common; commonplace, trivial; trite, banal. пошля́к, -а́ vulgarian, Philistine.

пошту́чно adv. by the piece. пошту́чный by the piece; piece-work.

по|шути́ть, -учу́, -у́тишь pf.

пощáда, -ы mercy. **по|щадúть**, -ажý *pf.*
по|щекотáть, -очý, -óчешь *pf.*
пощёчина, -ы box on the ear; slap in the face.
по|щýпать, -аю *pf.*
поэ́зия, -и poetry. **поэ́ма**, -ы poem. **поэ́т**, -а poet.
поэ́тапный phased.
поэти́ческий poetic, poetical.
поэ́тому *adv.* therefore, and so.
пою́ *etc.*: see **петь, пойть**
появи́ться, -влю́сь, -вишься *pf.*, **появля́ться**, -я́юсь *impf.* appear; show up; emerge. **появле́ние**, -я appearance.
пóяс, -а; *pl.* -á belt; girdle; waist-band; waist; zone; **по ~** up to the waist, waist-deep, waist-high.
поясне́ние, -я explanation, elucidation. **поясни́тельный** explanatory. **поясни́ть**, -ню́ *pf.* (*impf.* **поясня́ть**) explain, elucidate.
поясни́ца, -ы small of the back. **поясн|óй** waist; to the waist, waist-high; zone, zonal; **~áя вáнна** hip-bath.
поясня́ть, -я́ю *impf. of* **поясни́ть**
пр. *abbr.* (*of* **проéзд**) passage, thoroughfare; (*of* **проспéкт**) Prospect, Avenue; **и ~** (*of* **и прóчее**) etc. etcetera; and so on; (*of* **и прóчие**) *et al.*, and Co.
пра... *pref.* original, first, oldest; great-. **прабáбушка**, -и great-grandmother. **прáвнук**, -а great-grandson. **прáвнучка**, -и great-granddaughter. **прáдед**, -а great-grandfather; *pl.* ancestors, forefathers. **~дéдовский** great-grandfather's; ancestral; ancient. **~дéдушка**, -и *m.* great-grandfather. **прáотец**, -тца forefather. **~прáдед**, -а great-great-grandfather. **~родúтель**, -я *m.* primogenitor; forefather.
прáвда, -ы (the) truth; true; justice; **всéми ~ми и непрáвдами** by fair means or foul, by hook or by crook; **э́то ~** that's true. **правди́вый** true; truthful; honest, upright. **правдоподóбный** probable, likely; plausible.
прáвило, -а rule; regulation; principle; **взять за ~, положúть за ~** make it a rule; **взять себé за ~** make a point of; **как ~** as a rule; **прáвила ýличного движе́ния** traffic regulations.
прáвильно *adv.* rightly; correctly; regularly. **прáвильн|ый** right, correct; regular; rectilinear, rectilineal; **~о!** that's right! exactly!
правúтельственный government, governmental. **правúтельство**, -а government. **прáвить**[1], -влю+*i.* rule, govern; drive.
прáвить[2], -влю *impf.* correct; **~ корректýру** read proofs, correct proofs. **прáвка**, -и correcting; (proof-)reading.
правле́ние, -я board, governing body; administration, management; governing, government.
прáвленый corrected.
прá|внук, **~внучка** see **пра...**
прáво, -а; *pl.* -á law; right; (**водúтельские**) **правá** driving licence; **на правáх**+*g.* in the capacity, character, or position of; **на правáх рýкописи** all rights reserved; **~ гóлоса** the vote, suffrage.
прáво *adv.* really, truly, indeed.
прáво...[1] *in comb.* law; right. **правовéд**, -а jurist; law-student. **~вéдение**, -я jurisprudence. **~вéрный** orthodox; *sb.* true believer (*esp. of Moslems*). **~мéрный** lawful, rightful. **~мóчие**, -я competence. **~мóчный** competent, authorized. **~наруше́ние**, -я infringement of the law, offence. **~нарушúтель**, -я *m.* offender, delinquent. **~писáние**, -я spelling, orthography. **~слáвный** orthodox; *sb.* member of Orthodox Church. **~сýдие**, -я justice.
прáво...[2] *in comb.* right, right-hand. **правобере́жный** on the right bank, right-bank. **~охранúтельн|ый** law-enforcement; **~ые óрганы** law-enforcement agencies. **~сторóнний** right; right-hand. **~флангóвый** right-flank, right-wing.
правовóй legal, of the law; lawful, rightful.
правотá, -ы́ rightness; innocence.
прáвый[1] right; right-hand; right-wing.
прáв|ый[2]; прав, -á, -о right, correct; righteous, just; innocent, not guilty; **~ое де́ло** a just cause.
прáвящий ruling.
Прáга, -и Prague.
прáдед *etc.*: see **пра...**
прáздник, -а (public) holiday; feast; festival; festive occasion. **празднова́ние**, -я celebration. **прáздновать**, -ную *impf.* (*pf.* **от~**) celebrate. **прáздность**, -и idleness, inactivity; emptiness. **прáздный** idle; inactive; empty; vain, useless.
прáктика, -и practice; practical work; **на прáктике** in practice. **практикова́ть**, -кýю *impf.* practise; apply in practice; **~ся** (*pf.* **на~ся**) practice; be used, be practised; +**в**+*p.* have practice in. **прáктикум**, -а practical work. **практúческий, практúчный** practical.
прáотец see **пра...**
прáпорщик, -а ensign.
прапрáдед *etc.*: see **пра...**
прах, -а dust; ashes, remains; **пойтú ~ом** go to rack and ruin.
прáчечная *sb.* laundry; wash-house; **~-автомáт** launderette. **прáчка**, -и laundress.
пре... *pref. in comb.* **I.** *with vv. indicates action in extreme degree or superior measure:* sur-, over-, out-. **II.** *with adjs. and advs. indicates superlative degree:* very, most, exceedingly.
пребыва́ние, -я stay; residence; tenure, period; **~ в дóлжности, ~ на постý** tenure of office, period in office. **пребыва́ть**, -áю *impf.* be; reside; **~ в неве́дении** be in the dark; **~ у влáсти** be in power.
превзойтú, -йдý, -йдёшь; -ошёл, -шлá *pf.* (*impf.* **превосходúть**) surpass; excel; **~**

самого́ себя́ surpass o.s.; ~ чи́сленностью outnumber.

превозмога́ть, -а́ю *impf.*, превозмо́чь, -огу́, -о́жешь; -о́г, -ла́ *pf.* overcome, surmount.

превознести́, -су́, -сёшь; -ёс, -ла́ *pf.*, превозноси́ть, -ошу́, -о́сишь *impf.* extol, praise.

превосходи́тельство, -а Excellency. превосходи́ть, -ожу́, -о́дишь *impf. of* превзойти́. превосхо́дн|ый superlative; superb, outstanding, excellent; superior; ~ая сте́пень superlative (degree). превосходя́щий superior.

преврати́ть, -ащу́ *pf.*, превраща́ть, -а́ю *impf.* convert, turn, reduce; transmute; ~ся turn, change. превра́тно *adv.* wrongly; ~ истолкова́ть misinterpret; ~ поня́ть misunderstand. превра́тный wrong, false; changeful, inconstant, perverse. превраще́ние, -я transformation, conversion; transmutation; metamorphosis.

превы́сить, -ышу *pf.*, превыша́ть, -а́ю *impf.* exceed. превыше́ние, -я exceeding, excess.

прегра́да, -ы obstacle; bar, barrier. прегради́ть, -ажу́ *pf.*, прегражда́ть, -а́ю *impf.* bar, obstruct, block.

пред *see* пе́ред

пред...[1], предъ... *pref.* pre-, fore-, ante-.

пред...[2] *abbr.* (*of* председа́тель) *in comb.* chairman.

...пре́д, -а *abbr.* (*of* председа́тель) *in comb.* representative, spokesman.

предава́ть(ся, -даю́(сь, -даёшь(ся *impf. of* преда́ть(ся

преда́ние, -я legend; tradition; handing over, committal. пре́данность, -и devotion; faithfulness; loyalty. пре́данный devoted, faithful. преда́тель, -я *m.* traitor; betrayer. преда́тельский traitorous; perfidious; treacherous. преда́тельство, -а treachery, betrayal, perfidy. преда́ть, -а́м, -а́шь, -а́ст, -ади́м; пре́дал, -а́, -о *pf.* (*impf.* предава́ть) hand over, commit; betray; ~ забве́нию bury in oblivion; ~ земле́ commit to the earth; ~ суду́ bring to trial; ~ся give o.s. up, abandon o.s.; give way, indulge; +*d.* go over to, put o.s. in the hands of.

предаю́ *etc.: see* предава́ть

предвари́тельн|ый preliminary; prior; по ~ому соглаше́нию by prior arrangement; ~ое заключе́ние detention before trial; ~ая прода́жа биле́тов advance sale of tickets, advance booking. предвари́ть, -рю́ *pf.*, предваря́ть, -я́ю *impf.* forestall, anticipate; forewarn, inform beforehand.

предве́стник, -а forerunner, precursor; herald, harbinger; presage, portent. предвеща́ть, -а́ю *impf.* foretell; herald, presage, portend; э́то предвеща́ет хоро́шее this augurs well.

предвзя́тый preconceived; prejudiced, biased.

предви́деть, -и́жу *impf.* foresee; ~ся be foreseen; be expected.

предвкуси́ть, -ушу́, -у́сишь *pf.*, предвку-

ша́ть, -а́ю *impf.* look forward to, anticipate (with pleasure).

предводи́тель, -я *m.* leader. предводи́тельствовать, -твую *impf.*+*i.* lead.

предвое́нный pre-war.

предвосхи́тить, -и́щу *pf.*, предвосхища́ть, -а́ю *impf.* anticipate.

предвы́борный (pre-)election.

предго́рье, -я foothills.

преде́л, -а limit; bound, boundary; end; *pl.* range; положи́ть ~+*d.* put an end to, terminate. преде́льн|ый boundary; limiting; maximum; utmost; critical; saturated; ~ый во́зраст age-limit; ~ое напряже́ние breaking load, maximum stress; ~ая ско́рость maximum speed; ~ый срок time-limit, deadline.

предзнаменова́ние, -я omen, augury. предзнаменова́ть, -ну́ю *impf.* bode, augur, portend.

предисло́вие, -я preface, foreword.

предлага́ть, -а́ю *impf. of* предложи́ть. предло́г[1], -а pretext; под ~ом+*g.* on the pretext of.

предло́г[2], -а preposition.

предложе́ние[1], -я sentence; clause; proposition.

предложе́ние[2], -я offer; proposition; proposal; motion; suggestion; supply; внести́ ~ move, introduce, put down, a motion; сде́лать ~+*d.* make an offer to; propose to; спрос и ~ supply and demand. предложи́ть, -жу́, -жишь *pf.* (*impf.* предлага́ть) offer; propose; suggest; put, set, propound; order, require; ~ резолю́цию move a resolution.

предло́жный prepositional.

предме́т, -а object; article, item; subject; topic, theme; *pl.* goods; на сей ~ to this end, with this object; ~ спо́ра point at issue; ~ы пе́рвой необходи́мости necessities. предме́тный object; ~ катало́г subject catalogue; ~ сто́лик stage; ~ уро́к object-lesson.

предназнача́ть, -а́ю *impf.*, предназна́чить, -чу destine, intend, mean; earmark, set aside. предназначе́ние, -я earmarking; destiny.

преднаме́ренный premeditated; aforethought; deliberate.

предо *see* пе́ред

предо́к, -дка forefather, ancestor; *pl.* forebears.

предоста́вить, -влю *pf.*, предоставля́ть, -я́ю *impf.* grant; leave; give; ~ в его́ распоряже́ние put at his disposal; ~ пра́во concede a right; ~ сло́во+*d.* give the floor to, call on to speak.

предостерега́ть, -а́ю *impf.*, предостере́чь, -егу́, -ежёшь; -ёг, -ла́ *pf.* warn, caution. предостереже́ние, -я warning, caution. предосторо́жность, -и caution; precaution; ме́ры предосторо́жности precautionary measures.

предосудительный wrong, reprehensible, blameworthy.

предотвратить, -щу *pf.*, **предотвращать, -аю** *impf.* avert, prevent; ward off, stave off.

предохранение, -я protection; preservation. **предохранитель, -я** *m.* guard; safety device, safety-catch; fuse. **предохранительный** preservative; preventive; safety; protective; ~**ый клапан** safety-valve; ~**ая коробка** fuse-box. **предохранить, -ню** *pf.*, **предохранять, -яю** *impf.* preserve, protect.

предписание, -я order, injunction; *pl.* directions, instructions; prescription; **согласно предписанию** by order. **предписать, -ишу, -ишешь** *pf.*, **предписывать, -аю** *impf.* order, direct, instruct; prescribe.

предполагаемый supposed, conjectural. **предполагать, -аю** *impf.*, **предположить, -жу, -ожишь** *pf.* suppose, assume; conjecture, surmise; intend, propose; contemplate; presuppose; **предполагается** *impers.* it is proposed, it is intended. **предположение, -я** supposition, assumption; intention. **предположительно** *adv.* supposedly, presumably; probably. **предположительный** conjectural; hypothetical.

предпоследний penultimate, last-but-one, next-to-last.

предпосылка, -и prerequisite, precondition; premise.

предпочесть, -чту, -чтёшь; -чёл, -чла *pf.*, **предпочитать, -аю** *impf.* prefer; **я предпочёл бы** I would rather. **предпочтение, -я** preference. **предпочтительный** preferable.

предприимчивость, -и enterprise. **предприимчивый** enterprising.

предприниматель, -я *m.* owner; employer; entrepreneur; contractor. **предпринимательство, -а** a business undertakings; **свободное** ~ free enterprise. **предпринимать, -аю** *impf.*, **предпринять, -иму, -имешь; -инял, -а, -о** *pf.* undertake; ~ **атаку** launch an attack; ~ **шаги** take steps. **предприятие, -я** undertaking, enterprise; business; concern; works; **рискованное** ~ venture, risky undertaking.

предрасположение, -я predisposition. **предрасположенный** predisposed.

предрассудок, -дка prejudice.

предрешать, -аю *impf.* **предрешить, -шу** *pf.* decide beforehand; predetermine.

предреш... see **пред...**[1]

председатель, -я *m.*, **председательница, -ы** chairman. **председательский** chairman's; ~**ое кресло** the chair. **председательствовать, -твую** *impf.* preside, be in the chair.

предсказание, -я prediction, forecast, prophecy; prognostication. **предсказатель, -я** *m.* foreteller, forecaster; soothsayer. **предсказать, -ажу, -ажешь** *pf.*, **предсказывать, -аю** *impf.* foretell, predict; forecast, prophesy.

предсмертный dying; ~ **час** one's last hour.

представать, -таю, -таёшь *impf. of* **предстать**

представитель, -я *m.* representative; spokesman; specimen. **представительный** representative; imposing. **представительство, -а** representation; representatives; delegation.

представить, -влю *pf.*, **представлять, -яю** *impf.* present; produce, submit; introduce; recommend, put forward; display; perform; play; represent; ~ **себе** imagine, fancy, picture, conceive; **представлять собой** represent, be; constitute; ~**ся** present itself, occur, arise; seem; introduce o.s.; +*i.* pretend to be, pass o.s. off as. **представление, -я** presentation, introduction; declaration; statement; representation; performance; idea, notion, conception.

предстать, -ану *pf.* (*impf.* **представать**) appear; ~ **перед судом** appear in court.

предстоять, -оит *impf.* be in prospect, lie ahead, be at hand; **мне предстоит пойти туда** I shall have to go there. **предстоящий** coming, forthcoming; impending, imminent.

предтеча, -и *c.g.* forerunner, precursor; **Иоанн** ~ John the Baptist.

предубеждение, -я prejudice, bias.

предугадать, -аю *pf.*, **предугадывать, -аю** *impf.* guess; foresee.

предупредительность, -и courtesy; attentiveness. **предупредительный** preventive; precautionary; courteous, attentive; obliging. **предупредить, -ежу** *pf.*, **предупреждать, -аю** *impf.* notify in advance, let know beforehand; warn; give notice; prevent, avert; anticipate, forestall. **предупреждение, -я** notice; notification; warning, caution; prevention; anticipation; forestalling.

предусматривать, -аю *impf.*, **предусмотреть, -рю, -ришь** *pf.* envisage, foresee; provide for, make provision for. **предусмотрительный** prudent; provident; far-sighted.

предчувствие, -я presentiment; foreboding, misgiving, premonition. **предчувствовать, -твую** *impf.* have a presentiment (about), have a premonition of.

предшественник, -а predecessor; forerunner, precursor. **предшествовать, -твую** *impf.*+*d.* go in front of; precede.

предъ... see **пред...**[1]

предъявитель, -я *m.* bearer; **акция на предъявителя** ordinary share. **предъявить, -влю, -вишь** *pf.*, **предъявлять, -яю** *impf.* show, produce, present; bring, bring forward; ~ **иск к**+*d.* bring suit against; ~ **обвинение**+*d.* charge; ~ **право на**+*a.* lay claim to.

предыдущий previous, preceding; ~**ее** *sb.* the foregoing.

преемник, -а successor. **преемственность, -и** succession; continuity.

прежде *adv.* before; first; formerly, in former times; ~ **чем** before; *prep.*+*g.* before; ~

всего́ first of all, to begin with; first and foremost. **преждевре́менный** premature, untimely. **пре́жний** previous, former.

презента́ция, -и presentation; launch.

презервати́в, -а condom.

президе́нт, -а president, **президе́нтский** presidential. **прези́диум, -а** presidium.

презира́ть, -а́ю *impf.* despise; hold in contempt; disdain; scorn. **презре́ние, -я** contempt; scorn. **презре́нный** contemptible, despicable. **прези́тельный** contemptuous, scornful.

преиму́щественно *adv.* mainly, chiefly, principally. **преиму́щественный** main, principal, primary; prime; preferential; priority. **преиму́щество, -а** advantage; preference; **по преиму́ществу** for the most part, chiefly.

прейскура́нт, -а price-list.

преклоне́ние, -я admiration, worship. **преклони́ть, -ню́** *pf.*, **преклоня́ть, -я́ю** *impf.* bow, bend; ~ го́лову bow; ~ коле́на genuflect, kneel; ~ся bow down; +*d.* or перед+*i.* admire, worship. **прекло́нный;** ~ во́зраст old age; declining years.

прекра́сно *adv.* excellently; perfectly well. **прекра́сный** beautiful; fine; excellent, capital, first-rate; **в оди́н** ~ **день** one fine day; ~ **пол** the fair sex.

прекрати́ть, -ащу́ *pf.*, **прекраща́ть, -а́ю** *impf.* stop, cease, discontinue; put a stop to, end; break off, sever, cut off; ~ войну́ end the war; ~ подпи́ску discontinue a subscription, stop subscribing; ~ся cease, end.

преле́стный charming, delightful, lovely. **пре́лесть, -и** charm; fascination.

преломи́ть, -млю́, -мишь *pf.*, **преломля́ть, -я́ю** *impf.* refract; ~ся be refracted. **преломле́ние, -я** refraction.

пре́лый fusty, musty; rotten. **прель, -и** mouldiness, mould, rot.

прельсти́ть, -льщу́ *pf.*, **прельща́ть, -а́ю** *impf.* attract; lure, entice; ~ся be attracted; be tempted; fall (+*i.* for).

прелю́дия, -и prelude.

премиа́льн|ый bonus; prize; ~ые *sb.*, *pl.* bonus.

премину́ть, -ну *pf. with neg.* (not) fail.

премирова́ть, -ру́ю *impf. & pf.* award a prize to; give a bonus. **пре́мия, -и** prize; bonus; bounty, gratuity; premium.

премье́р, -а prime minister; leading actor, lead. **премье́ра, -ы** première, first performance. **премье́рша, -и** leading lady, lead.

пренебрега́ть, -а́ю *impf.*, **пренебре́чь, -егу́, -ежёшь; -ёг, -ла́** *pf.*+*i.* scorn, despise; neglect, disregard. **пренебреже́ние, -я** scorn, contempt, disdain; neglect, disregard. **пренебрежи́тельный** scornful; slighting; disdainful.

пре́ния, -ий *pl.* debate; discussion; pleadings; **вы́ступить в** ~**х** take part in a discussion.

преоблада́ние, -я predominance. **преоблада́ть, -а́ет** *impf.* predominate; prevail.

преобража́ть, -а́ю *impf.*, **преобрази́ть, -ажу́** *pf.* transform. **преображе́ние, -я** transformation; Transfiguration. **преобразова́ние, -я** transformation; reform; reorganization. **преобразова́ть, -зу́ю** *pf.*, **преобразо́вывать, -аю** *impf.* transform; reform, reorganize.

преодолева́ть, -а́ю *impf.*, **преодоле́ть, -е́ю** *pf.* overcome, get over, surmount.

препара́т, -а preparation.

препина́ние, -я; зна́ки препина́ния punctuation marks.

препира́тельство, -а altercation, wrangling, squabbling. **препира́ться, -а́юсь** *impf.* wrangle, squabble.

преподава́ние, -я teaching, tuition, instruction. **преподава́тель, -я** *m.*, **-ница, -ы** teacher; lecturer, instructor. **преподава́тельский** teaching; teacher's, teachers'; ~ соста́в (teaching) staff. **преподава́ть, -даю́, -даёшь** *impf.* teach.

преподнести́, -су́, -сёшь; -ёс, -ла́ *pf.*, **преподноси́ть, -ошу́, -о́сишь** present with, make a present of.

препроводи́тельный accompanying. **препроводи́ть, -вожу́, -во́дишь** *pf.*, **препровожда́ть, -а́ю** *impf.* send, forward, dispatch.

препя́тствие, -я obstacle, impediment, hindrance; hurdle; **ска́чки (бег) с препя́тствиями** steeplechase; hurdle-race, obstacle-race. **препя́тствовать, -твую** *impf.* (*pf.* вос~) +*d.* hinder, impede, hamper; stand in the way of.

прерва́ть, -ву́, -вёшь; -а́л, -а́, -о *pf.* (*impf.* прерыва́ть) interrupt; break off; cut off, sever; cut short; **нас прерва́ли** we've been cut off; ~ся be interrupted; be broken off; break down; break.

пререка́ние, -я altercation, argument, wrangle. **пререка́ться, -а́юсь** *impf.* argue, wrangle, dispute.

прерыва́ть(ся, -а́ю(сь *impf. of* прерва́ть(ся

пресека́ть, -а́ю *impf.*, **пресе́чь, -еку́, -ечёшь; -ёк, -екла́** *pf.* stop, cut short; put an end to; ~ **в ко́рне** nip in the bud; ~ся stop; break.

пресле́дование, -я pursuit, chase; persecution, victimization; prosecution. **пресле́довать, -дую** *impf.* pursue, chase, be after; haunt; persecute, torment; victimize; prosecute.

пресловутый notorious.

пресмыка́ться, -а́юсь *impf.* grovel, cringe; creep, crawl. **пресмыка́ющееся** *sb.* reptile.

пре́сный fresh; unsalted; unleavened; flavourless, tasteless; insipid, vapid, flat.

пре́сса, -ы the press. **пресс-атташе́** *m.indecl.* press attaché. **пресс-бюро́** *nt.indecl.* press department. **пресс-конфере́нция, -и** press conference.

престаре́лый aged; advanced in years.

престо́л, -а throne; altar.

преступле́ние, -я crime, offence; felony; transgression. **престу́пник, -а** criminal, offender, delinquent; felon; **вое́нный** ~ war criminal. **престу́пность, -и** criminality; crime, delinquency. **престу́пный** criminal; felonious.

пресы́титься, -ы́щусь *pf.*, **пресыща́ться, -а́юсь** *impf.* be satiated, be surfeited. **пресыще́ние, -я** surfeit, satiety.

претвори́ть, -рю́ *pf.*, **претворя́ть, -я́ю** *impf.* (**в**+*a.*) turn, change, convert; ~ **в жизнь** put into practice, realize, carry out; ~**ся в**+*a.* turn into, become; ~ **в жизнь** be realized, come true.

претенде́нт, -а claimant; aspirant; candidate; contestant; pretender. **претендова́ть, -ду́ю** *impf.* **на**+*a.* claim, lay claim to; have pretensions to; aspire to. **прете́нзия, -и** claim; pretension; **быть в прете́нзии на**+*a.* have a grudge, a grievance against; bear a grudge.

претерпева́ть, -а́ю *impf.*, **претерпе́ть, -плю́, -пишь** *pf.* undergo; suffer, endure.

преувеличе́ние, -я exaggeration; overstatement. **преувели́чивать, -аю** *impf.*, **преувели́чить, -чу** *pf.* exaggerate; overstate.

преуменьша́ть, -а́ю *impf.*, **преуме́ньшить, -е́ньшу** *pf.* underestimate; minimize; belittle; understate.

преуспева́ть, -а́ю *impf.*, **преуспе́ть, -е́ю** *pf.* succeed, be successful; thrive, prosper, flourish.

преходя́щий transient.

при *prep.* +*p.* by, at; in the presence of; attached to, affiliated to, under the auspices of; with; about; on; for, notwithstanding; in the time of, in the days of; under; during; when, in case of; **би́тва** ~ **Бородине́** the battle of Borodino; ~ **всём том** with it all, moreover; for all that; ~ **де́тях** in front of the children; ~ **дневно́м све́те** by daylight; ~ **доро́ге** by the road(-side); ~ **Ива́не Гро́зном** in the reign of Ivan the Terrible; under Ivan the Terrible; **при мне** in my presence; ~ **перехо́де че́рез у́лицу** when crossing the street; ~ **Пу́шкине** in Pushkin's day; ~ **слу́чае** when the occasion arises; ~ **све́те ла́мпы** by lamplight; **у него́ не́ было** ~ **себе́ де́нег** he had no money on him.

при... *pref.* I. *with vv. indicates action or motion continued to a given terminal point; action of attaching or adding; direction of action towards speaker or from above downward; incomplete or tentative action; exhaustive action; action to an accompaniment.* II. *with nn. and adjs. indicates juxtaposition or proximity.*

приба́вить, -влю *pf.*, **прибавля́ть, -я́ю** add, put on; increase, augment; exaggerate, lay it on (thick); ~ (**в ве́се**) put on weight; ~ **хо́ду** put on speed; ~ **ша́гу** mend one's pace; ~**ся** increase; rise; wax; **день приба́вился** the days are getting longer, are drawing out. **приба́вка, -и** addition, augmentation; increase, supplement, rise. **прибавле́ние, -я** addition, augmentation; supplement, appendix. **приба́вочный** additional; surplus.

прибалти́йский Baltic. **Приба́лтика, -и** the Baltic States.

прибега́ть[1]**, -а́ю** *impf. of* **прибежа́ть**

прибега́ть[2]**, -а́ю** *impf.*, **прибе́гнуть, -ну; -бе́г** *pf.* +*k*+*d.* resort to, fall back on.

прибежа́ть, -егу́ *pf.* (*impf.* **прибега́ть**) come running, run up.

прибе́жище, -а refuge; **после́днее** ~ last resort.

прибере́га́ть, -а́ю *impf.*, **прибере́чь, -егу́, -ежёшь; -ёг, -ла́** *pf.* save (up), reserve.

приберу́ *etc.: see* **прибра́ть. прибива́ть, -а́ю** *impf. of* **приби́ть прибира́ть, -а́ю** *impf. of* **прибра́ть**

приби́ть, -бью́, -бьёшь *pf.* (*impf.* **прибива́ть**) nail, fix with nails; lay, flatten; drive, carry; beat up.

прибл. *abbr.* (*of* **приблизи́тельно**) approx., approximately.

приближа́ть, -а́ю *impf.*, **прибли́зить, -и́жу** *pf.* bring nearer, move nearer; hasten, advance; ~**ся** approach, draw near; draw (come) nearer. **приблизи́тельно** *adv.* approximately, roughly. **приблизи́тельный** approximate, rough.

прибо́й, -я surf, breakers.

прибо́р, -а instrument, device, apparatus, appliance, gadget; set, service, things; fittings; **бри́твенный** ~ shaving things; **ча́йный** ~ tea service, tea things. **прибо́рн|ый** instrument; ~**ая доска́** dash-board, instrument panel.

прибра́ть, -беру́, -берёшь; -а́л, -а́, -о *pf.* (*impf.* **прибира́ть**) tidy (up), clear up, clean up; put away; ~ **ко́мнату** do (out) a room; ~ **посте́ль** make a bed.

прибре́жн|ый coastal; littoral, riverside; riparian; ~**ые острова́** off-shore islands.

прибыва́ть, -а́ю *impf.*, **прибы́ть, -бу́ду; при́был, -а́, -о** *pf.* arrive; get in; increase, grow; rise, swell; wax. **при́быль, -и** profit, gain; return; increase, rise. **при́быльный** profitable, lucrative. **прибы́тие, -я** arrival.

прибью́ *etc.: see* **приби́ть**

прива́л, -а halt, stop; stopping-place.

приватиза́ция, -и privatization. **приватизи́ровать, -ую** *impf. & pf.* privatize.

приведу́ *etc.: see* **привести́**

привезти́, -зу́, -зёшь; -ёз, -ла́ (*impf.* **привози́ть**) bring.

привере́дливый fastidious, squeamish, hard to please. **привере́дничать, -аю** *impf.* be hard to please, be fastidious, be squeamish.

приве́рженец, -нца adherent; follower. **приве́рженный** attached, devoted.

приве́сить, -е́шу *pf.* (*impf.* **приве́шивать**) hang up, suspend.

привести́, -еду́, -едёшь; -ёл, -а́ *pf.* (*impf.* **приводи́ть**) bring; lead; take; reduce; adduce, cite; +*к*+*d.* lead to, bring to, conduce to, result in; +*в*+*a.* put in(to), set; ~ **в движе́ние, в де́йствие** set in motion, set going; ~ в изумле́ние astonish, astound; ~ в исполне́ние execute, carry out; ~ в отча́яние drive to despair; ~ в поря́док put in order, tidy (up); arrange, fix; ~ в у́жас horrify.

приве́т, -a greeting(s); regards; переда́йте ~+d. remember me to, my regards to; с серде́чным ~ом yours sincerely. приве́тливость, -и affability; cordiality. приве́тливый cordial, friendly; affable. приве́тствие, -я greeting, salutation; speech of welcome. приве́тствовать, -твую impf. & pf. greet, salute, hail; welcome; ~ сто́я give a standing ovation to).

приве́шивать, -аю impf. of приве́сить

привива́ть(ся, -а́ю(сь, -а́ешь(ся impf. of приви́ть(ся. приви́вка, -и inoculation; vaccination; grafting, graft.

привиде́ние, -я ghost, spectre; apparition. при|ви́деться, -дится pf.

привилегиро́ванн|ый privileged; ~ая а́кция preference share. привиле́гия, -и privilege.

привинти́ть, -нчу́ pf., приви́нчивать, -аю impf. screw on.

приви́ть, -вью́, -вьёшь; -и́л, -а́, -о pf. (impf. привива́ть) inoculate, vaccinate; graft; implant; inculcate; cultivate, foster; ~ о́спу+d. vaccinate; ~ся take; become established, find acceptance, catch on.

при́вкус, -a after-taste; smack.

привлека́тельный attractive. привлека́ть, -а́ю impf., привле́чь, -еку́, -ечёшь; -ёк, -ла́ pf. attract; draw; draw in, win over; have up; ~ внима́ние attract attention; ~ к суду́ sue, take to court; prosecute; put on trial.

при́вод, -a drive, driving-gear. приводи́ть, -ожу́, -о́дишь impf. of привести́. приводно́й driving.

привожу́ etc.: see приводи́ть, привози́ть

приво́з, -a bringing, supply; importation; import. привози́ть, -ожу́, -о́зишь impf. of привезти́. привозно́й, приво́зный imported.

приво́льный free.

привстава́ть, -таю́, -таёшь impf., привста́ть, -а́ну pf. half-rise; rise, stand up.

привыка́ть, -а́ю impf., привы́кнуть, -ну; -ы́к pf. get used, get accustomed; get into the habit, get into the way. привы́чка, -и habit. привы́чный habitual, usual, customary; accustomed, used; of habit.

привью́ etc.: see приви́ть

привя́занность, -и attachment; affection. привя́занный attached. привяза́ть, -яжу́, -я́жешь pf., привя́зывать, -аю impf. attach; tie, bind, fasten, secure, tether; ~ся become attached; attach o.s.; +к+d. pester, bother. привязно́й fastened, secured, tethered. привя́зчивый importunate, insistent, annoying; affectionate; susceptible. при́вязь, -и tie; lead, leash; tether.

пригласи́ть, -ашу́ pf., приглаша́ть, -а́ю impf. invite, ask; call (in); ~ на обе́д ask to dinner. приглаше́ние, -я invitation; offer.

пригляде́ться, -яжу́сь pf., пригля́дываться, -аюсь impf. look closely; +к+d. scutinize, examine; get used to, get accustomed to.

пригна́ть, -гоню́, -го́нишь; -а́л, -а́, -о pf. (impf. пригоня́ть) drive in, bring in; fit, adjust.

пригова́ривать[1], -аю impf. keep saying, keep (on) repeating.

пригова́ривать[2], -аю impf., приговори́ть, -рю́ pf. sentence, condemn.

пригоди́ться, -ожу́сь pf. prove useful; be of use; come in useful, come in handy. приго́дный fit, suitable, good; useful. приго́жий fine.

пригоня́ть, -я́ю impf. of пригна́ть

пригора́ть, -а́ет impf., пригоре́ть, -ри́т pf. be burnt. пригоре́лый burnt.

при́город, -a suburb. при́городный suburban.

приго́рок, -рка hillock, knoll.

при́го́ршня, -и; g.pl. -ей handful.

приготови́тельный preparatory. пригото́вить, -влю pf., приготовля́ть, -я́ю impf. prepare, cook, ~ роль learn a part; ~ся prepare; prepare o.s. приготовле́ние, -я preparation.

пригрева́ть, -а́ю impf. of пригре́ть

при|гре́зиться, -е́жусь pf.

пригре́ть, -е́ю pf. (impf. пригрева́ть) warm; cherish.

при|грози́ть, -ожу́ pf.

придава́ть, -даю́, -даёшь impf., прида́ть, -а́м, -а́шь, -а́ст, -ади́м; при́дал, -а́, -о pf. add; increase, strengthen; give, impart; attach; ~ значе́ние+d. attach importance to. прида́ча, -и adding; addition, supplement; в прида́чу into the bargain, in addition.

придвига́ть, -а́ю impf. придви́нуть, -ну pf. move up, draw up; ~ся move up, draw near. придво́рный court; sb. courtier.

приде́лать, -аю pf., приде́лывать, -аю impf. fix, attach.

приде́рживаться, -аюсь impf. hold on, hold; +g. hold to, keep to; stick to, adhere to; ~ пра́вой стороны́ keep to the right; ~ мне́ния be of the opinion.

придеру́сь etc.: see придра́ться. придира́ться, -а́юсь impf. of придра́ться. приди́рка, -и cavil, captious objection; fault-finding; carping. приди́рчивый niggling; captious.

придоро́жный roadside, wayside.

придра́ться, -деру́сь, -дерёшься; -а́лся, -а́сь, -а́лось pf. (impf. придира́ться) find fault, cavil, carp; seize; ~ к слу́чаю seize an opportunity.

приду́ etc.: see прийти́

приду́мать, -аю pf., приду́мывать, -аю impf. think up, devise, invent; think of.

придыха́тельное sb. aspirate.

приéду *etc.*: *see* **приéхать. приéзд,** -а arrival, coming. **приезжáть,** -áю *impf. of* **приéхать. приéзжий** newly arrived; *sb.* newcomer; visitor.

приём, -а receiving; reception; surgery; welcome; admittance; dose; go; motion, movement; method, way, mode; device, trick; hold, grip; **в одúн ~** at one go. **приéмлемый** acceptable; admissible. **приéмная** *sb.* waiting-room; reception room. **приéмник,** -а radio, wireless, receiver. **приёмн|ый** receiving; reception; entrance; foster, adoptive, adopted; **~ый день** visiting day; **~ая комúссия** selection board; **~ая мать** foster-mother; **~ые часы́** (business) hours; surgery (hours); **~ый экзáмен** entrance examination. **приёмо-передаю́щий** two-way. **приём-щик,** -а inspector, examiner. **приёмочный** inspection, examining.

приéхать, -éду *pf.* (*impf.* **приезжáть**) arrive, come.

прижáть, -жму́, -жмёшь *pf.* (*impf.* **прижимáть**) press; clasp; **~ся** press o.s.; cuddle up, snuggle up, nestle up.

прижéчь, -жгу́, -жжёшь; -жёг, -жгла́ *pf.* (*impf.* **прижигáть**) cauterize, sear.

приживáлка, -и, **приживáльщик,** -а dependant; hanger-on, sponger, parasite.

прижигáние, -я cauterization. **прижигáть,** -áю *impf. of* **прижéчь**

прижимáть(ся, -áю(сь *impf. of* **прижáть(ся. прижúмистый** tight-fisted, stingy. **прижму́** *etc.*: *see* **прижáть**

приз, -а; *pl.* -ы́ prize.

призадýматься, -аюсь *pf.*, **призадýмываться,** -аюсь *impf.* become thoughtful, become pensive.

призвáние, -я vocation, calling; **по призвáнию** by vocation. **призвáть,** -зову́, -зовёшь; -áл, -á, -о *pf.* (*impf.* **призывáть**) call, summon; call upon, appeal to; call up; **~ся** be called up.

призéмистый stocky, squat; thickset.

приземлéние, -я landing, touchdown. **приземлúться,** -лю́сь *pf.*, **приземля́ться,** -я́юсь *impf.* land, touch down.

призёр, -а, **призёрша,** -и prizewinner.

прúзма, -ы prism. **призматúческий** prismatic.

признавáть, -наю́, -наёшь *impf.*, **признáть,** -áю *pf.* recognize; spot, identify; admit, own, acknowledge; deem, vote; (**не**) **~ себя́ винóвным** plead (not) guilty; **~ся** confess, own; **~ся (сказáть)** to tell the truth. **прúзнак,** -а sign, symptom; indication. **признáние,** -я confession, declaration; admission; acknowledgement; recognition. **прúзнанный** acknowledged, recognized. **признáтельный** grateful.

призовý *etc.*: *see* **призвáть**

прúзрак, -а spectre, ghost, phantom, apparition. **прúзрачный** spectral, ghostly, phantasmal; illusory, imagined.

призы́в, -а call, appeal; slogan; call-up, conscription. **призывáть(ся,** -áю(сь *impf. of* **призвáть(ся. призывнóй** conscription; **~ вóзраст** military age; *sb.* conscript.

прúиск, -а mine; **золоты́е ~и** gold-field(s).

прийтú, придý, -дёшь; **пришёл,** -шлá *pf.* (*impf.* **приходúть**) come; arrive; **~ в себя́** come round, regain consciousness; **~ в ýжас** be horrified; **~ к концý** come to an end; **к заключéнию** come to the conclusion, arrive at a conclusion; **~сь+по**+*d.* fit; suit; **+на**+*a.* fall on; *impers.* (+*d.*) have to; happen (to), fall to the lot (of); **+на**+*a.* or **с**+*g.* be owing to, from; **нам пришлóсь верну́ться в Москвý** we had to return to Moscow; **как придётся** anyhow, at haphazard.

прикáз, -а order, command; order of the day; office, department. **приказáние,** -я order, command, injunction. **приказáть,** -ажу́, -áжешь *pf.*, **прикáзывать,** -аю *impf.* order, command; give orders, direct.

прикáлывать, -аю *impf. of* **приколóть**

прикасáться, -áюсь *impf. of* **прикосну́ться**

прикúдывать, -аю *impf.*, **прикúнуть,** -ну *pf.* throw in, add; weigh; estimate; calculate, reckon; **~ся**+*i.* pretend (to be), feign; **~ся больны́м** pretend to be ill, feign illness.

приклáд¹, -а butt.

приклáд², -а trimmings, findings. **прикладнóй** applied. **прикла́дывать(ся,** -аю(сь *impf. of* **приложúть(ся**

приклéивать, -аю *impf.*, **приклéить,** -éю *pf.* stick; glue; paste; affix; **~ся** stick, adhere.

приключáться, -áется *impf.*, **приключúться,** -úтся *pf.* happen, occur. **приключéние,** -я adventure. **приключéнческий** adventure.

прикóвать, -кую́, -куёшь *pf.*, **прикóвывать,** -аю *impf.* chain; rivet.

прикóл, -а stake; **на ~е** laid up, idle.

прикола́чивать, -аю *impf.*, **приколотúть,** -очу́, -óтишь *pf.* nail, fasten with nails; beat up.

приколóть, -лю́, -лешь *pf.* (*impf.* **прикáлывать**) pin, fasten with a pin; stab, transfix.

прикомандировáть, -ру́ю *pf.*, **прикомандирóвывать,** -аю *impf.* attach, second.

прикосновéние, -я touch, contact; concern. **прикосновéнный** concerned, involved, implicated (**к**+*d.* in). **прикосну́ться,** -ну́сь, -нёшься *pf.* (*impf.* **прикасáться**) **к**+*d.* touch.

прикрáсить, -áшу *pf.*, **прикрáшивать,** -аю *impf.* embellish, embroider.

прикрепúть, -плю́ *pf.*, **прикрепля́ть,** -я́ю *impf.* fasten, attach. **прикреплéние,** -я fastening; attachment; registration.

прикрывáть, -áю *impf.*, **прикры́ть,** -рóю *pf.* cover; screen; protect, shelter, shield; cover up, conceal; close down, wind up; **~ся** cover o.s.; close down, go out of business; +*i.* use as cover, take refuge in, shelter behind.

прику́ривать, -аю *impf.*, **прикури́ть**, -рю́, -ришь *pf.* get a light; light a cigarette from another.

прику́с, -а bite. **прикуси́ть**, -ушу́, -у́сишь *pf.*, **прику́сывать**, -аю *impf.* bite; ~ язы́к hold one's tongue, keep one's mouth shut.

прила́вок, -вка counter; **рабо́тник прила́вка** counter-hand; (shop) assistant.

прилага́тельн|ый adjective; ~ое *sb.* adjective. **прилага́ть**, -а́ю *impf. of* **приложи́ть**

прила́дить, -а́жу *pf.*, **прила́живать**, -аю *impf.* fit, adjust.

приласка́ть, -а́ю *pf.* caress, fondle, pet; ~ся snuggle up, nestle up.

прилега́ть, -а́ет *impf.* (*pf.* **приле́чь**) к+d. fit; adjoin, be adjacent to, border (on). **прилега́ющий** close-fitting, tight-fitting; adjoining, adjacent, contiguous.

прилежа́ние, -я diligence, industry; application. **приле́жный** diligent, industrious, assiduous.

прилепи́ть(ся, -плю́(сь, -пишь(ся *pf.*, **прилепля́ть(ся**, -я́ю(сь *impf.* stick.

прилёт, -а arrival. **прилета́ть**, -а́ю *impf.*, **прилете́ть**, -ечу́ *pf.* arrive, fly in; fly, come flying.

приле́чь, -ля́гу, -ля́жешь; -ёг, -гла́ *pf.* (*impf.* **прилега́ть**) lie down; be laid flat; +к+d. fit.

прили́в, -а flow, flood; rising tide; surge, influx; congestion; ~ кро́ви rush of blood; ~ эне́ргии burst of energy. **прилива́ть**, -а́ет *impf. of* **прили́ть**. **прили́вный** tidal.

прилипа́ть, -а́ет *impf.*, **прили́пнуть**, -нет; -ли́п *pf.* stick, adhere. **прили́пчивый** sticking, adhesive; clinging; not to be shaken off; tiresome; catching.

прили́ть, -лье́т; -и́л, -á, -о *pf.* (*impf.* **прилива́ть**) flow; rush.

прили́чие, -я decency, propriety; decorum. **прили́чный** decent; proper, decorous, seemly; tolerable, fair.

приложе́ние, -я application; affixing; enclosure; supplement; appendix; schedule, exhibit; apposition. **приложи́ть**, -жу́, -жишь *pf.* (*impf.* **прикла́дывать**, **прилага́ть**) put; apply; affix; add, join; enclose; ~ все стара́ния do one's best, try one's hardest; ~ся take aim; +i. put, apply; +к+d. kiss.

прилуни́ться, -ню́сь *pf.* land on the Moon.

прильё́т *etc.: see* **прили́ть**. **при|льну́ть**, -ну́, -нёшь *pf.* **приля́гу** *etc.: see* **приле́чь**

прима́нивать, -аю *impf.*, **примани́ть**, -ню́, -нишь *pf.* lure; entice, allure. **прима́нка**, -и bait, lure; enticement, allurement.

примене́ние, -я application; employment, use. **примени́ть**, -ню́, -нишь *pf.*, **применя́ть**, -я́ю *impf.* apply; employ, use; ~ на пра́ктике put into practice; ~ся adapt o.s., conform.

приме́р, -а example; instance; model; не в ~+d. unlike; +comp. far more, by far; **подава́ть** ~ set an example; **привести́ в** ~ cite as an example.

при|ме́рить, -рю *pf.* (*impf. also* **примеря́ть**) try on; fit. **приме́рка**, -и trying on; fitting.

приме́рно *adv.* in exemplary fashion; approximately, roughly. **приме́рный** exemplary, model; approximate, rough.

приме́рочная *sb.* fitting-room.

примеря́ть, -я́ю *impf. of* **приме́рить**

при́месь, -и admixture; dash; **без при́меси** unadulterated.

приме́та, -ы sign, token; mark. **приме́тный** perceptible, visible, noticeable; conspicuous, prominent.

примеча́ние, -я note, footnote; *pl.* comments.

примеша́ть, -а́ю *pf.*, **приме́шивать**, -аю *impf.* add, mix in.

примина́ть, -а́ю *impf. of* **примя́ть**

примире́ние, -я reconciliation. **примире́нчество**, -а appeasement, compromise. **примири́мый** reconcilable. **примири́тель**, -я *m.* reconciler, conciliator, peace-maker. **примири́тельный** conciliatory. **при|мири́ть**, -рю́ *pf.*, **примиря́ть**, -я́ю *impf.* reconcile; conciliate; ~ся be reconciled, make it up; +с+i. reconcile o.s. to, put up with.

примити́вный primitive; crude.

примкну́ть, -ну́, -нёшь *pf.* (*impf.* **примыка́ть**) join; fix, attach.

примну́ *etc.: see* **примя́ть**

примо́рский seaside; maritime. **примо́рье**, -я seaside; littoral.

примо́чка, -и wash, lotion.

приму́ *etc.: see* **приня́ть**

примча́ться, -чу́сь *pf.* come tearing along.

примыка́ние, -я contiguity; agglutination. **примыка́ть**, -а́ю *impf. of* **примкну́ть**; +к+d. adjoin, abut on, border on. **примыка́ющий** affiliated.

примя́ть, -мну́, -мнёшь *pf.* (*impf.* **примина́ть**) crush, flatten; trample down.

принадлежа́ть, -жу́ *impf.* belong. **принадле́жност|ь**, -и belonging; membership; *pl.* accessories, appurtenances; equipment; outfit, tackle; **туале́тные** ~и toiletries.

при|неволи́ть, -лю *pf.*

принести́, -су́, -сёшь *pf.* (*impf.* **приноси́ть**) bring; fetch; bear, yield; bring in; ~ в же́ртву sacrifice; ~ по́льзу be of use, be of benefit.

принима́ть(ся, -а́ю(сь *impf. of* **приня́ть(ся**; **принима́ющая сторона́** host country.

принора́вливать, -аю *impf.*, **приноро́вить**, -влю́ *pf.* fit, adapt, adjust; ~ся adapt o.s., accommodate o.s.

приноси́ть, -ошу́, -о́сишь *impf. of* **принести́**. **приноше́ние**, -я gift, offering.

при́нтер, -а a printer; **ла́зерный** ~ laser printer.

принуди́тельн|ый compulsory; forced, coercive; ~ые рабо́ты forced labour, hard labour. **прину́дить**, -у́жу *pf.*, **принужда́ть**, -а́ю *impf.* force, compel, coerce, constrain. **принужде́ние**, -я compulsion, constraint; duress. **принуждённый** constrained, forced.

при́нцип, -а principle. **принципиа́льно** *adv.* on principle; in principle. **принципиа́льный**

of principle; in principle; general.

принятие, -я taking; taking up; assumption; acceptance, adoption; admission, admittance. **принято** it is accepted, it is usual; **не** ~ it is not done. **принять**, -иму, -имешь; принял, -á, -о *pf.* (*impf.* **принимáть**) take; accept; take up; take over; pass, approve; admit; receive; +за+*a.* take for; ~ вáнну take (have) a bath; ~ в шкóлу admit to, accept for, a school; ~ закóн pass a law; ~ лекáрство take medicine; ~ мéры take measures; ~ резолюцию pass, adopt, carry a resolution; ~ учáстье take part; ~ся begin; start; take; take root, strike root; +за+*a.* take in hand; set to, get down to; ~ за рабóту set to work.

приободрить, -рю *pf.*, **приободрять**, -яю *impf.* cheer up, encourage, hearten; ~ся cheer up.

приобрести, -ету, -етёшь; -рёл, -á *pf.*, **приобретáть**, -áю *impf.* acquire, gain. **приобретéние**, -я acquisition; gain; bargain, find.

приобщáть, -áю *impf.*, **приобщить**, -щу *pf.* join, attach, unite; ~ к дéлу file; ~ся к+*d.* join in.

приозёрный lakeside, lakeland.

приостанáвливать, -аю *impf.* **приостановить**, -влю, -вишь *pf.* stop, suspend, check; ~ся halt, stop, pause. **приостанóвка**, -и halt, check, stoppage, suspension.

приотворить, -рю, -ришь *pf.*, **приотворять**, -яю *impf.* open slightly, half-open, set ajar.

припáдок, -дка fit; attack; paroxysm.

припасáть, -áю *impf.*, **припасти**, -су, -сёшь; -áс, -лá *pf.* store, lay in, lay up. **припáсы**, -ов *pl.* stores, supplies; provisions; munitions.

припéв, -а refrain, burden.

приписáть, -ишу, -ишешь *pf.*, **приписывать**, -аю *impf.* add; attribute, ascribe; put down, impute. **припúска**, -и addition; postscript; codicil.

приплáта, -ы extra pay; additional payment. **приплатить**, -ачу, -áтишь *pf.* **приплáчивать**, -аю *impf.* pay in addition.

приплóд, -а issue, increase.

приплывáть, -áю *impf.*, **приплыть**, -ыву, -ывёшь; -ыл, -á, -о *pf.* swim up, sail up.

приплюснуть, -ну *pf.*, **приплющивать**, -аю *impf.* flatten.

приподнимáть, -áю *impf.*, **приподнять**, -ниму, -нимешь; -однял, -á, -о *pf.* raise (a little); ~ся raise o.s. (a little), rise.

припóй, -я solder.

припоминáть, -áю *impf.*, **припóмнить**, -ню *pf.* remember, recollect, recall; +*d.* remind.

приправа, -ы seasoning, flavouring; relish, condiment, dressing. **приправить**, -влю *pf.*, **приправлять**, -яю *impf.* season, flavour, dress.

припрятать, -ячу *pf.*, **припрятывать**, -аю *impf.* secrete, put by.

припугивать, -аю *impf.*, **припугнуть**, -ну, -нёшь *pf.* intimidate, scare.

припуск, -а allowance, margin.

прирабáтывать, -аю *impf.*, **прирабóтать**, -аю *pf.* earn ... extra, earn in addition. **прирабóток**, -тка supplementary earnings, additional earnings.

прирáвнивать, -аю *impf.*, **приравнять**, -яю *pf.* equate, place on the same footing; compare (к+*d.* to).

прирастáть, -áю *impf.*, **прирасти**, -тёт; -рóс, -лá *pf.* adhere; take; increase; accrue; ~ к мéсту be rooted to the spot.

прирéчный riverside.

прирóда, -ы nature; character. **прирóдный** natural; native; born, by birth; inborn, innate. **природосберегáющий** environment-friendly. **прирождённый** inborn, innate; born.

прирóс etc.: see **прирасти**. **прирóст**, -а increase, growth.

приручáть, -áю *impf.*, **приручить**, -чу *pf.* tame; domesticate. **приручéние**, -я taming, domestication.

присáживаться, -аюсь *impf. of* **присéсть**

присвáивать, -аю *impf.*, **присвóить**, -ою *pf.* appropriate; give, award, confer; ~ имя+*d.* & g. name after.

приседáть, -áю *impf.*, **присéсть**, -сяду *pf.* (*impf. also* **присáживаться**) sit down, take a seat; squat; cower.

прискакáть, -ачу, -áчешь *pf.* come galloping, arrive at a gallop; rush, tear.

прискóрбный sorrowful, regrettable, lamentable.

прислáть, -ишлю, -ишлёшь *pf.* (*impf.* **присылáть**) send, dispatch.

прислонить(ся, -оню(сь, -óнишь(ся *pf.*, **прислонять(ся**, -яю(сь *impf.* lean, rest (к+*d.* against).

прислуга, -и maid, servant; servants, domestics; crew. **прислуживать**, -аю *impf.* (к+*d.*) wait (upon); ~ся к+*d.* fawn upon, cringe to.

прислушаться, -аюсь *pf.*, **прислушиваться**, -аюсь *impf.* listen; +к+*d.* listen to; heed, pay attention to; get used to (the sound of), cease to notice.

присмáтривать, -аю *impf.*, **присмотрéть**, -рю, -ришь *pf.* look for, find; +за+*i.* look after, keep an eye on; supervise, superintend; ~ за ребёнком mind the baby; ~ся (к+*d.*) look closely (at); get accustomed, get used (to).

присниться, -нюсь *pf.*

присовокупить, -плю *pf.*, **присовокуплять**, -яю *impf.* add; attach.

присоединéние, -я joining; addition; annexation; connection. **присоединить**, -ню *pf.* **присоединять**, -яю *impf.* join; add; annex; connect; ~ся к+*d.* join; associate o.s. with; ~ к мнéнию subscribe to an opinion.

приспосóбить, -блю *pf.*, **приспособлять**, -яю *impf.* fit, adjust, adapt, accommodate; ~ся adapt o.s., accommodate o.s. **приспособлéние**, -я adaptation, accommodation; device, contrivance; appliance, gadget. **приспосóбленность**, -и fitness, suitability. **приспособля́емость**, -и adaptability.

пристав, -а; *pl.* -á *or* -ы police officer, police sergeant.

пристава́ть, -таю, -таёшь *impf. of* **приста́ть**

приста́вить, -влю *pf.* (*impf.* **приставля́ть**) к+d. put, place, set to, against; lean against; add to; appoint to look after.

приста́вка, -и prefix.

приставля́ть, -я́ю *impf. of* **приста́вить**. **приставн|óй** added, attached; ~а́я ле́стница step-ladder.

приста́льный fixed, intent.

при́стань, -и; *g.pl.* -éй landing-stage, jetty; pier; wharf; refuge; haven.

приста́ть, -а́ну *pf.* (*impf.* **пристава́ть**) stick, adhere; attach o.s.; pester, bother, badger; put in, come alongside.

пристёгивать, -аю *impf.*, **пристегну́ть**, -ну́, -нёшь *pf.* fasten. **пристежнóй**; ~ воротничóк separate collar.

пристра́ивать(ся, -аю(сь *impf. of* **пристрóить(ся**

пристра́стие, -я weakness, predilection, passion; partiality, bias. **пристра́стный** partial, biased.

пристрóить, -óю *pf.* (*impf.* **пристра́ивать**) add, build on; place, settle, fix up; ~ся be placed, be settled, be fixed up, get a place; join up, form up. **пристрóйка**, -и annexe, extension; outhouse; lean-to.

при́ступ, -а assault, storm; fit, attack; bout, touch; access, approach. **приступи́ть**, -плю́, -пишь *pf.* к+d. set about, start; get down to; approach; importune, pester. **пристýпок**, -пка step.

при|стыди́ть, -ыжý *pf.* **пристыжённый**; -жён, -á ashamed.

при|стыкова́ться, -кýется *pf.*

пристя́жка, -и, **пристяжна́я** *sb.* trace-horse, outrunner.

присуди́ть, -ужý, -ýдишь *pf.*, **присужда́ть**, -áю *impf.* sentence, condemn; award; confer; ~ к штра́фу fine, impose a fine on. **присужде́ние**, -я awarding, adjudication; conferment.

присýтственн|ый; ~ое мéсто government office. **присýтствие**, -я presence; attendance; government office; ~ дýха presence of mind. **присýтствовать**, -твую be present, attend. **присýтствующ|ий** present; ~ие *sb.*, *pl.* those present, present company.

присýщий inherent; characteristic; distinctive.

присыла́ть, -áю *impf. of* **присла́ть**

прися́га, -и oath; привести́ к прися́ге swear in, administer the oath to. **присяга́ть**, -áю *impf.*, **присягну́ть**, -ну́, -нёшь *pf.* take one's oath, swear; ~ в вéрности swear allegiance.

прися́ду etc.: see **присе́сть**

прися́жный sworn; born, inveterate; ~ засе-

да́тель juror, juryman; ~ повéренный barrister.

притаи́ться, -аю́сь *pf.* hide, conceal o.s.

прита́скивать, -аю *impf.*, **притащи́ть**, -ащу́, -а́щишь *pf.* bring, drag, haul; ~ся drag o.s.

притвори́ться, -рю́сь *pf.*, **притворя́ться**, -я́юсь *impf.*+i. pretend to be; feign; sham; ~ больны́м pretend to be ill, feign illness. **притвóрный** pretended, feigned, sham. **притвóрство**, -а pretence, sham. **притвóрщик**, -а sham; dissembler, hypocrite.

притека́ть, -а́ю *impf. of* **прите́чь**

притесне́ние, -я oppression. **притесни́ть**, -ню́ *pf.*, **притесня́ть**, -я́ю *impf.* oppress.

прите́чь, -ечёт, -екýт; -ёк, -ла́ *pf.* (*impf.* **притека́ть**) flow in, pour in.

притиха́ть, -а́ю *impf.*, **прити́хнуть**, -ну; -их *pf.* quiet down, grow quiet, hush.

притóк, -а tributary; flow, influx; intake.

притóм *conj.* (and) besides.

притóн, -а den, haunt.

при́торный sickly-sweet, luscious, cloying.

притра́гиваться, -аюсь *impf.*, **притрóнуться**, -нусь *pf.* touch.

притупи́ть, -плю́, -пишь *pf.*, **притупля́ть**, -я́ю *impf.* blunt, dull; deaden; ~ся become blunt, lose its edge; become dull.

при́тча, -и parable.

притяга́тельный attractive, magnetic. **притя́гивать**, -аю *impf. of* **притяну́ть**

притяжа́тельный possessive.

притяже́ние, -я attraction; земнóе ~ gravity.

притяза́ние, -я claim, pretension. **притяза́ть**, -а́ю *impf.* на+a. lay claim to, have pretensions to.

притя́нутый; ~ за́ уши, за́ волосы far-fetched. **притяну́ть**, -ну́, -нешь *pf.* (*impf.* **притя́гивать**) draw, attract; drag (up) pull (up).

приуро́чивать, -аю *impf.*, **приуро́чить**, -чу *pf.* к+d. time for, time to coincide with.

приуса́дебный; ~ уча́сток personal plot, individual holding.

приуча́ть, -а́ю *impf.*, **приучи́ть**, -чу́, -чишь *pf.* accustom; train, school.

прихва́рывать, -аю *impf.*, **прихворну́ть**, -ну́, -нёшь *pf.* be unwell, be indisposed.

при́хвостень, -тня *m.* hanger-on.

прихлеба́тель, -я *m.* sponger, parasite.

прихóд, -а coming, arrival; advent; receipts; parish; ~ и расхóд credit and debit. **приходи́ть(ся**, -ожý(сь, -óдишь(ся *impf. of* **прийти́(сь. прихóдный** receipt. **прихóдовать**, -дую (*pf.* за~) credit. **прихóдящ|ий** non-resident; ~ий больнóй outpatient; ~ая домрабóтница daily (maid), char(woman).

прихотли́вый capricious, whimsical; fanciful; intricate. **при́хоть**, -и whim, caprice, fancy.

прихра́мывать, -аю limp (slightly).

прицéл, -а sight; aiming. **прицéливаться**, -аюсь *impf.*, **прицéлиться**, -люсь *pf.* aim, take aim.

прице́ниваться, -аюсь *impf.*, **прицени́ться, -ню́сь, -нишься (к+***d.***)** ask the price (of).

прице́п, -а a trailer. **прицепи́ть, -плю́, -пишь** *pf.*, **прицепля́ть, -я́ю** *impf.* hitch, hook on; couple; **~ся к+***d.* stick to, cling to; pester; nag at. **прице́пка, -и** hitching, hooking on; coupling; trailer; pestering; nagging. **прицепно́й**; **~ ваго́н** trailer.

прича́л, -а mooring, making fast; mooring line; berth, moorings. **прича́ливать, -аю** *impf.*, **прича́лить, -лю** *pf.* moor.

прича́стие¹, -я participle. **прича́стие², -я** communion.

прича́стный¹ participial. **прича́стный²** participating, concerned; involved; accessary, privy.

причём *conj.* moreover, and; while. **причём** *adv.* why? what for? **а ~ же я тут?** what has it to do with me?

причеса́ть, -ешу́, -е́шешь *pf.*, **причёсывать, -аю** *impf.* brush, comb; do the hair (of); **~ся** do one's hair, have one's hair done. **причёска, -и** hair-do, hair-style; haircut.

причи́на, -ы cause; reason. **причини́ть, -ню́** *pf.*, **причиня́ть, -я́ю** *impf.* cause; occasion.

причи́слить, -лю *pf.*, **причисля́ть, -я́ю** *impf.* reckon, number, rank (**к+***d.* among); add on; attach.

причита́ние, -я lamentation.

причита́ться, -а́ется *impf.* be due; **вам причита́ется два рубля́** you have two roubles to come; **с вас причита́ется два рубля́** you have two roubles to pay.

причу́да, -ы caprice, whim, fancy; oddity, vagary.

причу́|диться, -ится *pf.*

причу́дливый odd, queer; fantastic; capricious, whimsical.

при|швартова́ть, -ту́ю *pf.* **пришёл** *etc.*: *see* **прийти́**

пришиблённый crest-fallen, dejected.

пришива́ть, -а́ю *impf.*, **приши́ть, -шью́, -шьёшь** *pf.* sew on, attach; nail (on).

пришлю́ *etc.*: *see* **присла́ть**

пришпо́ривать, -аю *impf.*, **пришпо́рить, -рю** *pf.* spur (on).

прищеми́ть, -млю́ *pf.* **прищемля́ть, -я́ю** *impf.* pinch, squeeze.

прище́пка, -и, прище́пок, -пка clothes-peg.

прищу́риваться, -аюсь *impf.*, **прищу́риться, -рюсь** *pf.* screw up one's eyes.

прию́т, -а asylum, orphanage; shelter, refuge. **приюти́ть, -ючу́** *pf.* shelter, give refuge; **~ся** take shelter.

прия́тель, -я *m.*, **прия́тельница, -ы** friend. **прия́тельский** friendly, amicable. **прия́тный** nice, pleasant, agreeable, pleasing; **~ на вкус** nice, palatable, tasty.

про *prep.*+*a.* about; for; **~ себя́** to o.s.

про... *pref. in comb.* **I.** *with vv. indicates action through, across,* or *past object; action continued throughout given period of time; overall* or *exhaustive action* or *effect; loss or*

failure. **II.** *with nn. and adjs.*: pro-.

про́ба, -ы trial, test; try-out; assay; hallmark; sample; standard, measure of fineness of gold; **зо́лото 96-о́й про́бы** 24-carat gold, pure gold.

пробе́г, -а run; race; mileage, distance. **пробега́ть, -а́ю** *impf.*, **пробежа́ть, -егу́** *pf.* run; cover; pass, run past, run by; run through; run along, run over.

пробе́л, -а blank, gap; hiatus; lacuna; deficiency, flaw.

проберу́ *etc.*: *see* **пробра́ть**. **пробива́ть(ся, -а́ю(сь** *impf. of* **проби́ть(ся. пробира́ть(ся, -а́ю(сь** *impf. of* **пробра́ть(ся**

проби́рка, -и test-tube. **проби́рный** test, assay; **~ое клеймо́** hallmark. **проби́ровать, -рую** *impf.* test, assay.

про|би́ть, -бью́, -бьёшь *pf.* (*impf. also* **пробива́ть**) make a hole in; hole, pierce; punch; strike; **~ся** fight, force, make, one's way through; break through, strike through.

про́бка, -и cork; stopper; plug; fuse; (traffic) jam, blockage, congestion. **про́бковый** cork; **~ по́яс** life-belt, life-jacket.

пробле́ма, -ы problem. **проблемати́ческий** problematic(al).

про́блеск, -а flash; gleam, ray.

про́бный trial, test, experimental; hallmarked; **~ ка́мень** touchstone. **про́бовать, -бую** *impf.* (*pf.* **ис~, по~**) try; attempt, endeavour; test; taste, feel.

пробо́ина, -ы hole.

проболта́ться, -а́юсь *pf.* blab, let out a secret; hang about.

пробо́р, -а parting; **де́лать (себе́) ~** part one's hair.

про|бормота́ть, -очу́, -о́чешь *pf.*

пробра́ть, -беру́, -берёшь; -а́л, -а́, -о *pf.* (*impf.* **пробира́ть**) go through; scold, rate; clear, weed; **~ся** make one's way; force one's way; steal (through); **~ о́щупью** feel one's way.

пробу́ду *etc.*: *see* **пробы́ть**

про|буди́ть, -ужу́, -у́дишь *pf.*, **пробужда́ть, -а́ю** *impf.* wake (up); awaken, rouse, arouse; **~ся** wake, wake up. **пробужде́ние, -я** waking (up), awakening.

про|бура́вить, -влю *pf.*, **пробура́вливать, -аю** *impf.* bore (through), drill.

про|бурча́ть, -чу́ *pf.*

пробы́ть, -бу́ду; про́бы́л, -а́, -о *pf.* remain, stay; be.

пробью́ *etc.*: *see* **проби́ть**

прова́л, -а failure; flop; downfall; gap; funnel. **прова́ливать, -аю** *impf.*, **провали́ть, -лю́, -лишь** *pf.* cause to fall in, bring down; ruin, make a mess of; reject, fail; **~ся** collapse; fall in, come down; fall through; fail; disappear, vanish.

прова́нск|ий Provençal; **~ое ма́сло** olive oil.

прове́дать, -аю *pf.*, **прове́дывать, -аю** *impf.* come to see, call on; find out, learn.

провезти́, -зу́, -зёшь; -ёз, -ла́ *pf.* (*impf.*

провози́ть) convey, transport; smuggle (through, in, out); bring.

прове́рить, -рю *pf.* **проверя́ть, -я́ю** *impf.* check, check up on; verify; audit; control; test; ~ биле́ты examine tickets; ~ тетра́ди correct exercise-books; ~ на алкого́ль breathalyse. **прове́рка, -и** checking, check; examination; verification; control; testing.

про|вести́, -еду́, -еде́шь; -ёл, -а́ *pf.* (*impf. also* **проводи́ть**) lead, take; pilot; build; install; carry out, carry on; conduct, hold; carry through; carry; pass; advance, put forward; draw; spend; +*i.* pass over, run over; ~ в жизнь put into effect, put into practice; ~ водопрово́д lay on water; ~ вре́мя pass the time; ~ черту́ draw a line; хорошо́ ~ вре́мя have a good time.

прове́тривать, -аю *impf.* **прове́трить, -рю** *pf.* air; ventilate.

про|ве́ять, -е́ю *pf.*

провиде́ние, -я Providence. **прови́деть, -и́жу** *impf.* foresee.

прови́зия, -и provisions.

провизо́рный preliminary, provisional; temporary.

провини́ться, -ню́сь *pf.* be guilty; do wrong; ~ пе́ред+*i.* wrong.

провинциа́льный provincial. **прови́нция, -и** province; the provinces.

про́|вод, -а; *pl.* **-а́** wire, lead, conductor. **проводи́мость, -и** conductivity; conductance. **проводи́ть[1], -ожу́, -о́дишь** *impf. of* **провести́** conduct, be a conductor.

проводи́ть[2], -ожу́, -о́дишь *pf.* (*impf.* **провожа́ть**) accompany; see off; ~ глаза́ми follow with one's eyes; ~ домо́й see home.

прово́дка, -и leading, taking; building; installation; wiring, wires.

проводни́к[1], -а́ guide; conductor, guard.

проводни́к[2], -а́ conductor; bearer; transmitter. **проводно́й** wire, line.

про́воды, -ов *pl.* seeing off, send-off. **провожа́тый** *sb.* guide, escort. **провожа́ть, -а́ю** *impf. of* **проводи́ть**

прово́з, -а carriage, conveyance, transport.

провозгласи́ть, -ашу́ *pf.*, **провозглаша́ть, -а́ю** *impf.* proclaim, declare; announce; +*i.* proclaim, hail as; ~ тост propose a toast. **провозглаше́ние, -я** proclamation; declaration.

провози́ть, -ожу́, -о́зишь *impf. of* **провезти́**

провока́тор, -а agent provocateur; instigator, provoker. **провокацио́нный** provocative. **провока́ция, -и** provocation. **про́волока, -и** wire. **про́волочн|ый** wire; ~ая сеть wire netting.

прово́рный quick, swift, prompt; agile, nimble, adroit, dexterous. **прово́рство, -а** quickness, swiftness; agility, nimbleness, adroitness, dexterity.

провоци́ровать, -рую *impf. & pf.* (*pf.* с~) provoke.

про|вя́лить, -лю *pf.*

прогада́ть, -а́ю *pf.*, **прога́дывать, -аю** *impf.* miscalculate.

прога́лина, -ы glade; (clear) space.

прогла́тывать, -аю *impf.*, **проглоти́ть, -очу́, -о́тишь** *pf.* swallow.

прогляде́ть, -яжу́ *pf.*, **прогля́дывать[1], -аю** *impf.* overlook, miss; look through, glance through. **проглянуть, -я́нет** *pf.*, **прогля́дывать[2], -ает** *impf.* show, show through, peep out, peep through, appear.

прогна́ть, -гоню́, -го́нишь; -а́л, -а́, -о *pf.* (*impf.* **прогоня́ть**) drive away; banish; drive; sack, fire.

про|гневи́ть, -влю́ *pf.*

прогнива́ть, -а́ет *impf.*, **прогни́ть, -ниёт; -и́л, -а́, -о** *pf.* rot through, be rotten.

прогно́з, -а prognosis; (weather) forecast. **прогнози́рование, -я** forecasting. **прогнози́ст, -а** forecaster.

проголода́ться, -а́юсь *pf.* get hungry, grow hungry.

про|голосова́ть, -су́ю *pf.* **прогоня́ть, -я́ю** *impf. of* **прогна́ть**

прогора́ть, -а́ю *impf.*, **прогоре́ть, -рю́** *pf.* burn; burn out; get burnt; go bankrupt, go bust.

прого́рклый rancid, rank.

програ́мма, -ы programme; schedule; syllabus, curriculum. **программи́ровать, -рую** *impf.* (*pf.* за~) programme.

прогре́в, -а warming up. **прогрева́ть, -а́ю** *impf.*, **прогре́ть, -е́ю** *pf.* heat, warm thoroughly; warm up; ~ся get warmed through, get thoroughly warmed; warm up.

про|греме́ть, -млю́ *pf.*

прогре́сс, -а progress. **прогресси́вный** progressive. **прогресси́ровать, -рую** *impf.* progress, make progress.

про|грохота́ть, -очу́, -о́чешь *pf.*

прогрыза́ть, -а́ю *impf.*, **прогры́зть, -зу́, -зёшь; -ы́з** *pf.* gnaw through.

про|гуде́ть, -гужу́ *pf.*

прогу́л, -а absence (from work); absenteeism. **прогу́ливать, -аю** *impf.*, **прогуля́ть, -я́ю** *pf.* be absent from work; miss; take for a walk, walk; ~ уро́ки (play) truant; ~ся stroll, saunter; take a walk. **прогу́лка, -и** walk, stroll; ramble; outing. **прогу́льщик, -а** absentee, truant.

прод... *abbr.* (*of* **продово́льственный**) *in comb.* food-, provision-. **продма́г, -а** grocery; provision-shop. **~пу́нкт, -а** food centre. **~това́ры, -ов** *pl.* food products.

продава́ть, -даю́, -даёшь *impf.*, **прода́ть, -а́м, -а́шь, -а́ст, -ади́м; про́дал, -а́, -о** *pf.* sell. **продава́ться, -даётся** *impf.* be for sale; sell. **продаве́ц, -вца́** seller, vender; salesman; shop-assistant. **продавщи́ца, -ы** seller, vendor; saleswoman; shop-assistant, shop-girl. **прода́жа, -и** sale, selling. **прода́жный** for sale, to be sold; mercenary, venal.

продвига́ть, -а́ю *impf.*, **продви́нуть, -ну** *pf.* move forward, push forward; promote, further, advance; ~**ся** advance; move on, move forward; push on, push forward, forge ahead; be promoted.

про|декламировать, -рую *pf.*

проделать, -аю *pf.,* **проделывать, -аю** *impf.* do, perform, accomplish. **проделка, -и** trick; prank, escapade.

продёргивать, -аю *impf. of* **продёрнуть**

продержать, -жу, -жишь *pf.* hold; keep; ~**ся** hold out.

продёрнуть, -ну, -нешь *pf. (impf.* **продёргивать)** pass, run; put through; criticize, pull to pieces; ~ **нитку в иголку** thread a needle.

продешевить, -влю *pf.* sell too cheap.

про|диктовать, -тую *pf.*

продлевать, -аю *impf.,* **продлить, -лю** *pf.* extend, prolong. **продление, -я** extension, prolongation. **про|длиться, -ится** *pf.*

продмаг, -а grocer's (shop).

продовольственн|ый food, provision; ~**ая карточка** ration book, ration card; ~**ый магазин** grocery, provision shop. **продовольствие, -я** food, food-stuffs; provisions.

продолговатый oblong.

продолжатель, -я *m.* continuer, successor. **продолжать, -аю** *impf.,* **продолжить, -жу** *pf.* continue, go on (with), proceed (with); extend, prolong; ~**ся** continue, last, go on, be in progress. **продолжение, -я** continuation; sequel; extension, prolongation; **в** ~+*g.* in the course of, during, for, throughout; ~ **следует** to be continued. **продолжительность, -и** duration, length. **продолжительный** long; prolonged, protracted.

продольный longitudinal, lengthwise, linear.

продрогнуть, -ну; -óг *pf.* be chilled to the marrow, be half-frozen.

продукт, -а product; produce; provisions, food-stuffs; **натуральные** ~**ы** wholefoods. **продуктивно** *adv.* productively; to good effect, with a good result. **продуктивность, -и** productivity. **продуктивный** productive; fruitful. **продуктовый** food, provision; ~ **магазин** grocery, food-shop.

продукция, -и production, output.

продумать, -аю *pf.,* **продумывать, -аю** *impf.* think over; think out.

продырявить, -влю *pf.* make a hole in, pierce.

продюсер, -а (film-)producer.

проедать, -аю *impf. of* **проесть. проеду** *etc.: see* **проехать**

проезд, -а passage, thoroughfare; journey; «~**а нет»** 'no thoroughfare'. **проездить, -зжу** *pf. (impf.* **проезжать)** spend on a journey, spend in travelling; spend travelling (driving, riding). **проездн|ой** travelling; ~**ой билет** ticket; ~**ая плата** fare; ~**ые** *sb.,* *pl.* travelling expenses. **проездом** *adv.* en route, in transit, while passing through. **проезжать, -аю** *impf. of* **проездить, проехать. проезж|ий** passing (by); ~**ая дорога** highway, thoroughfare; ~**ий** *sb.* passer-by.

проект, -а project, scheme, design; draft; ~ **договора** draft treaty; ~ **резолюции** draft resolution. **проектировать, -рую** *impf. (pf.* **с~)** project; plan, design. **проектный** planning, designing; planned. **проектор, -а** projector.

проекционный; ~ **фонарь** projector. **проекция, -и** projection.

проесть, -ем, -ешь, -ест, -едим; -ел *pf. (impf.* **проедать)** eat through, corrode; spend on food.

проехать, -еду *pf. (impf.* **проезжать)** pass by, through; drive by, through; ride by, through; go past, pass; go, do, make, cover.

прожаренный well-done.

прожектор, -а; *pl.* **-ы** *or* **-á** searchlight; floodlight.

прожечь, -жгу, -жжёшь; -жёг, -жгла *pf. (impf.* **прожигать)** burn; burn through.

проживать, -аю *impf. of* **прожить**

прожигать, -аю *impf. of* **прожечь**

прожиточный enough to live on; ~ **минимум** living wage. **прожить, -иву, -ивёшь; -óжил, -á, -о** *pf. (impf.* **проживать)** live; spend; run through.

прожорливый voracious, gluttonous.

проза, -ы prose. **прозаический** prose; prosaic; prosy.

прозвание, -я, прозвище, -а nickname. **прозвать, -зову; -зовёшь; -ал, -á, -о** *pf. (impf.* **прозывать)** nickname, name.

про|зевать, -аю *pf.* **про|зимовать, -мую** *pf.* **прозову** *etc.: see* **прозвать**

прозодежда, -ы *abr.* working clothes; overalls.

прозорливый sagacious; perspicacious.

прозрачный transparent; limpid, pellucid.

прозывать, -аю *impf. of* **прозвать**

прозябание, -я vegetation. **прозябать, -аю** *impf.* vegetate.

проиграть, -аю *pf.,* **проигрывать, -аю** *impf.* lose; play; ~**ся** lose everything, gamble away all one's money. **проигрыватель, -я** *m.* record-player; ~ **компакт-дисков** CD player. **проигрыш, -а** loss.

произведение, -я work; production; product. **произвести, -еду, -едёшь; -ёл, -á** *pf.,* **производить, -ожу, -одишь** *impf.* make; carry out; execute; produce; cause; effect; give birth to; +**в**+*a./nom. pl.* promote to (the rank of); ~ **впечатление** make an impression, create an impression; ~ **на свет** bring into the world. **производительность, -и** productivity, output; productiveness. **производительный** productive; efficient. **производн|ый** derivative, derived; ~**ое слово** derivative. **производственный** industrial; production; commercial; ~ **стаж** industrial experience, industrial work record. **производство, -а** production, manufacture; factory, works; carrying out, execution.

произвол, -а arbitrariness; arbitrary rule; **оставить на** ~ **судьбы** leave to the mercy

of fate; **чини́ть** ~ impose arbitrary rule.
произво́льный arbitrary.
произнести́, -су́, -сёшь; -ёс, -ла́ *pf.*, **произно-
си́ть**, -ошу́, -о́сишь *impf.* pronounce; articulate; say, utter; ~ **речь** deliver a speech.
произношéние, -я pronunciation; articulation.
произойти́, -ойдёт; -ошёл, -шла́ *pf.* (*impf.*
происходи́ть) happen, occur, take place;
spring, arise, result; come, descend, be descended.
про|инструкти́ровать, -рую *pf.*
про́иски, -ов *pl.* intrigues; machinations,
schemes, underhand plotting.
проистека́ть, -а́ет *impf.*, **проистéчь**, -ечёт;
-ёк, -ла́ *pf.* spring, result; stem.
происходи́ть, -ожу́, -о́дишь *impf. of* **произо-
йти́**; go on, be going on. **происхождéние**, -я origin; provenance; parentage, descent, extraction, birth; **по происхождéнию**
by birth.
происшéствие, -я event, incident, happening, occurrence; accident.
пройти́, -йду́, -йдёшь; -ошёл, -шла́ *pf.* (*impf.*
проходи́ть) pass; go; go past, go by, elapse;
do, cover; be over; pass off, abate, let up; go
off; take, study, learn; go through, get
through; fall; ~ **в**+*a./nom. pl.*, become, be
made; be taken on; **емý э́то да́ром не
пройдёт** he will have to pay for it; ~ **ми́мо**
pass by, go by, go past; overlook, disregard;
~ **чéрез** pass, get through; э́то не пройдёт
it won't work; ~**сь** walk up and down; take
a stroll, a walk; pace.
прок, -а (-у) use benefit.
прокажённый *sb.* leper. **прока́за**[1], -ы leprosy.
прока́за[2], -ы mischief, prank, trick. **прока́-
зить**, -а́жу *impf.*, **прока́зничать**, -аю *impf.*
(*pf.* **на**~) be up to mischief, play pranks.
прока́зник, -а mischievous child.
прока́лывать, -аю *impf. of* **проколо́ть**
прока́т, -а hire.
прокати́ться, -ачу́сь, -а́тишься *pf.* roll; go
for a drive, go for a run.
прока́тный rolling; rolled; ~ **стан** rolling-mill.
прокипяти́ть, -ячу́ *pf.* boil; boil thoroughly.
прокиса́ть, -а́ет *impf.*, **про|ки́снуть**, -нет
pf. turn (sour).
прокла́дка, -и laying; building, construction;
washer, gasket; packing. **прокла́дывать**,
-аю *impf. of* **проложи́ть**
проклама́ция, -и proclamation, leaflet.
проклина́ть, -а́ю *impf.*, **прокля́сть**, -яну́,
-янёшь; -о́клял, -а́, -о *pf.* curse, damn; swear
at. **прокля́тие**, -я curse; damnation, perdition; imprecation. **прокля́тый**; -я́т, -а́, -о
accursed, damned; damnable, confounded.
проколо́ть, -лю́, -лешь *pf.* (*impf.* **про-
ка́лывать**) prick, pierce; perforate; run
through.
про|компости́ровать, -рую *pf.* **про|кон-
спекти́ровать**, -рую *pf.* **про|консульти́-**

ровать(ся, -рую(сь *pf.* **про|контроли́-
ровать**, -рую *pf.*
прокóрм, -а nourishment, sustenance.
про|корми́ть(ся, -млю́(сь, -мишь(ся *pf.*
про|корректи́ровать, -рую *pf.*
прокра́дываться, -аюсь *impf.*, **прокра́сть-
ся**, -аду́сь, -адёшься *pf.* steal in.
прокуро́р, -а public prosecutor; procurator;
investigating magistrate.
прокути́ть, -учу́, -у́тишь *pf.*, **проку́чивать**,
-аю *impf.* squander, dissipate; go on the
spree, go on the binge.
пролага́ть, -а́ю *impf. of* **проложи́ть**
пролега́ть, -а́ет *impf.* lie, run.
про́лежень, -жня *m.* bedsore.
пролеза́ть, -а́ю *impf.*, **проле́зть**, -зу; -лéз
pf. get through, climb through; get in, worm
o.s. in.
про|лепета́ть, -ечу́, -éчешь *pf.*
пролёт, -а span; stair-well; bay.
пролетариáт, -а a proletariat. **пролета́рий**, -я
proletarian; **пролета́рии всех стран, соеди-
ня́йтесь!** workers of the world, unite! **про-
лета́рский** proletarian.
пролета́ть, -а́ю *impf.*, **пролетéть**, -ечу́ *pf.*
fly; cover; fly by, fly past, fly through; flash,
flit.
проли́в, -а strait, sound. **пролива́ть**, -а́ю
impf., **проли́ть**, -лью, -льёшь; -о́лил, -а́, -о
pf. spill, shed; ~ **свет на**+*a.* throw light on;
shed light on.
проложи́ть, -жу́, -жишь *pf.* (*impf.* **прокла́-
дывать**, **пролага́ть**) lay; build, construct;
interlay; insert; interleave; ~ **доро́гу** build a
road; pave the way, blaze a trail; ~ **себé
доро́гу** carve one's way.
проло́м, -а breach, break; gap; fracture. **про-
лома́ть**, -а́ю *pf.* break, break through.
пролью *etc.*: *see* **проли́ть**
пром... *abbr.* (*of* **промы́шленный**) *in comb.*
industrial. **промтова́ры**, -ов *pl.* manufactured goods. ~**финпла́н**, -а industrial and
financial plan.
про|ма́зать, -а́жу *pf.* **прома́тывать(ся**,
-аю(сь *impf. of* **промота́ть(ся**
про́мах, -а miss; slip, blunder. **прома́хи-
ваться**, -аюсь *impf.*, **промахну́ться**, -ну́сь,
-нёшься *pf.* miss; miss the mark; miscue; be
wide of the mark, make a mistake, miss an
opportunity.
прома́чивать, -аю *impf. of* **промочи́ть**
промедлéние, -я delay; procrastination.
промéдлить, -лю *pf.* delay, dally; procrastinate.
промежу́ток, -тка interval; space. **проме-
жу́точный** intermediate; intervening; interval.
промелькну́ть, -ну́, -нёшь *pf.* flash; flash
past, fly by; be perceptible, be discernible.
промéнивать, -аю *impf.*, **променя́ть**, -я́ю
pf. exchange, trade, barter; change.

промерзáть, -áю *impf.*, промёрзнуть, -ну; -ёрз *pf.* freeze through. промёрзлый frozen.

промокáтельн|ый; ~ая бумáга blotting-paper. промокáть, -áю *impf.*, промóкнуть, -ну; -мóк *pf.* get soaked, get drenched.

промóлвить, -влю *pf.* say, utter.

про|мотáть, -áю *pf.* (*impf. also* промáтывать) squander; ~ся run through one's money.

промочить, -чý, -чишь *pf.* (*impf.* промáчивать) get wet (through); soak, drench; ~ нóги get one's feet wet.

промóю *etc.: see* промы́ть

промчáться, -чýсь *pf.* tear, dart, rush (by, past, through); fly.

промывáние, -я washing (out, down); bathing; irrigation. промывáть, -áю *impf. of* промы́ть

прóмысел, -сла trade, business; *pl.* works; гóрный ~ mining; охóтничий ~ hunting, trapping; ры́бный ~ fishing, fishery. промыслóв|ый producers'; business; hunters', trappers'; game; ~ая коoperáция producers' cooperative.

промы́ть, -мóю *pf.* (*impf.* промывáть) wash well, wash thoroughly; bathe, irrigate; wash; scrub; ~ мозги+*d.* brain-wash.

про|мычáть, -чý *pf.*

промы́шленник, -а manufacturer, industrialist. промы́шленность, -и industry. промы́шленный industrial.

про|мя́млить, -лю *pf.*

пронести́, -сý, -сёшь; -ёс, -лá *pf.* (*impf.* проноси́ть) carry; carry by, past, through; pass (over), be over, be past; ~сь rush by, past, through; scud (past); fly; be carried, spread; пронёсся слух there was a rumour.

пронзáть, -áю *impf.*, пронзи́ть, -нжý *pf.* pierce, run through, transfix. пронзи́тельный penetrating; piercing; shrill, strident.

пронизáть, -ижý, -и́жешь *pf.*, прони́зывать, -аю *impf.* pierce; permeate, penetrate; run through. прони́зывающий piercing, penetrating.

проникáть, -áю *impf.*, прони́кнуть, -ну; -и́к *pf.* penetrate; percolate; run through; ~ся be imbued, be filled. проникновéние, -я penetration; feeling; heartfelt conviction. проникновéнный full of feeling; heartfelt. прони́кнутый+*i.* imbued with, full of.

проница́емый permeable, pervious. проница́тельный penetrating; perspicacious; acute, shrewd.

проноси́ть(ся, -ошý(сь, -óсишь(ся *impf. of* пронести́(сь про|нумеровáть, -рýю *pf.*

проны́рливый pushful, pushing.

проню́хать, -аю *pf.*, проню́хивать, -аю *impf.* smell out, nose out, get wind of.

прообраз, -а a prototype.

пропагáнда, -ы propaganda. пропаганди́ровать, -рую *impf.* engage in propaganda (for); propagandize. пропаганди́ст, -а propagandist.

пропадáть, -áю *impf. of* пропáсть. пропáжа, -и loss; lost object, missing thing.

пропáлывать, -аю *impf. of* прополóть

пропáн, -а propane.

прóпасть, -и precipice; abyss; a mass, masses.

пропáсть, -адý, -адёшь *pf.* (*impf.* пропадáть) be missing; be lost; disappear, vanish; be done for, die; be wasted; мы пропáли we're lost, we're done for; ~ бéз вести be missing.

пропекáть(ся, -áю(сь *impf. of* пропéчь(ся. про|пéть, -пою́, -поёшь *pf.*

пропéчь, -екý, -ечёшь; -ёк, -лá *pf.* (*impf.* пропекáть) bake well, bake thoroughly; ~ся bake well; get baked through.

пропивáть, -áю *impf. of* пропи́ть

прописáть, -ишý, -и́шешь *pf.*, пропи́сывать, -аю *impf.* prescribe; register; ~ся register. пропи́ска, -и registration; residence permit. прописн|óй capital; commonplace, trivial; ~áя бýква capital letter; ~áя и́стина truism. прóпись, -и copy; copy-book maxim. прóписью *adv.* in words, in full; писáть цифры ~ write out figures in words.

пропитáние, -я subsistence, sustenance, food; зарабóтать себé на ~ earn one's living. пропитáть, -áю *pf.*, пропи́тывать, -аю *impf.* impregnate, saturate; soak, steep; keep, provide for; ~ся be saturated, be steeped; keep o.s.

пропи́ть, -пью, -пьёшь; -óпил, -á, -о *pf.* (*impf.* пропивáть) spend on drink, squander on drink.

проплы́в, -а (swimming) race, heat. проплывáть, -áю *impf.*, проплы́ть, -ывý, -ывёшь; -ы́л, -á, -о *pf.* swim, swim by, past, through; sail by, past, through; float; drift by, past, through; ~ стометрóвку swim the hundred metres.

проповéдовать, -дую *impf.* preach; advocate. прóповедь, -и sermon; homily; preaching, advocacy; нагóрная ~ Sermon on the Mount.

прополка, -и weeding. прополóть, -лю, -лешь *pf.* (*impf.* пропáлывать) weed.

про|полоскáть, -ощý, -óщешь *pf.*

пропорциональный proportional, proportionate. пропóрция, -и proportion; ratio.

прóпуск, -а; *pl.* -á *or* -и, -óв *or* -ов pass, permit; password; admission; omission, lapse; absence, non-attendance; blank, gap. пропускáть, -áю *impf.*, пропусти́ть, -ущý, -ýстишь *pf.* let pass, let through; let in, admit; absorb; pass; omit, leave out; skip; miss; let slip; ~ ми́мо ушéй pay no heed to, turn a deaf ear to; не пропускáть воды́ be waterproof; пропускáть вóду leak. пропускн|óй; ~áя бумáга blotting-paper; ~óй свет transmitted light; ~áя спосóбность capacity.

пропью́ *etc.: see* пропи́ть

прорабáтывать, -аю *impf.*, прорабóтать, -аю *pf.* work, work through; work at, study; get up; slate, pick holes in. проработка, -и study, studying, getting up; slating.

прораста́ть, -ает *impf.*, **прорасти́**, -тёт; -рóс, -лá *pf.* germinate, sprout, shoot.

прорва́ть, -ву́, -вёшь; -а́л, -á, -о *pf.* (*impf.* **прорыва́ть**) break through; tear, make a hole in; burst; ~ **блокáду** run the blockade; ~**ся** burst open, break; tear; break out, break through.

про|реаги́ровать, -рую *pf.*

прорéз, -a cut; slit, notch, nick. **про|рéзать**, -éжу *pf.*, **прореза́ть**, -áю *impf.* (*impf. also* **прорéзывать**) cut through; ~**ся** be cut, come through.

прорéзинивать, -аю *impf.*, **прорéзинить**, -ню *pf.* rubberize. **прорéзывать(ся**, -аю(сь *impf. of* **прорéзать(ся.** **про|репети́ровать**, -рую *pf.*

прорéха, -и rent, tear, slit; fly, flies; gap, deficiency.

про|рецензи́ровать, -рую *pf.*

проро́к, -a prophet.

проро́с *etc.: see* **прорасти́**

пророни́ть, -ню́, -нишь *pf.* utter, breathe, drop.

проро́ческий prophetic, oracular. **проро́чество**, -a prophecy **проро́чить**, -чу *impf.* (*pf.* **на~**) prophesy; predict.

проро́ю *etc.: see* **проры́ть**

проруба́ть, -áю *impf.*, **проруби́ть**, -блю́, -бишь *pf.* cut through, hack through; break. **прóрубь**, -и ice-hole.

проры́в, -a break; break-through, breach; hitch, hold-up. **ликвиди́ровать** ~ put things right; **пóлный** ~ breakdown. **прорыва́ть**[1](ся, -áю(сь *impf. of* **прорва́ть(ся**

прорыва́ть[2], -áю *impf.*, **проры́ть**, -рóю *pf.* dig through; ~**ся** dig one's way through, tunnel through.

проса́чиваться, -ается *impf. of* **просочи́ться**

просвéрливать, -аю *impf.*, **про|сверли́ть**, -лю́ *pf.* drill, bore; perforate, pierce.

просвéт, -a (clear) space; shaft of light; ray of hope; aperture, opening. **просвети́тельный** educational; cultural. **просвети́тельство**, -a educational activities, cultural activities. **просвети́ть**[1], -ещу́ *pf.* (*impf.* **просвеща́ть**) educate; enlighten.

просвети́ть[2], -ечу́, -éтишь *pf.* (*impf.* **просвéчивать**) X-ray.

просветлéние, -я clearing-up; brightening (up); clarity, lucidity. **просветлённый** clear, lucid. **про|светлéть**, -éет *pf.*

просвéчивание, -я fluoroscopy; radioscopy. **просвéчивать**, -аю *impf. of* **просвети́ть**; be translucent; be visible; show, appear, shine.

просвеща́ть, -áю *impf. of* **просвети́ть. просвещéние**, -я enlightenment; education, instruction; **наро́дное** ~ public education. **просвещённый** enlightened; educated, cultured.

про́седь, -и streak(s) of grey; **вóлосы с** ~**ю**

greying hair.

просéивать, -аю *impf. of* **просéять**

про́сека, -и cutting, ride.

просёлок, -лка country road, cart-track.

просéять, -éю *pf.* (*impf.* **просéивать**) sift, riddle, screen.

про|сигнализи́ровать, -рую *pf.*

просидéть, -ижу́ *pf.*, **проси́живать**, -аю *impf.* sit; ~ **всю ночь** sit up all night.

проси́тель, -я *m.* applicant; supplicant; petitioner. **проси́тельный** pleading. **проси́ть**, -ошу́, -óсишь *impf.* (*pf.* **по~**) ask; beg; plead, intercede; invite; «**прóсят не кури́ть**» 'No smoking, please'; ~**ся** ask; apply.

просия́ть, -я́ю *pf.* brighten; begin to shine; beam, light up.

проска́кивать, -аю *impf. of* **проскочи́ть**

проска́льзывать, -аю *impf.*, **проскользну́ть**, -ну́, -нёшь *pf.* slip in, creep in; ~ **ми́мо** slip past.

проскочи́ть, -чу́, -óчишь *pf.* (*impf.* **проска́кивать**) rush, tear; slip through; slip in, creep in.

про|сла́бить, -бит *pf.*

просла́вить, -влю *pf.*, **прославля́ть**, -я́ю *impf.* glorify; bring fame to; make famous; ~**ся** become famous, be renowned. **просла́вленный** famous, renowned, celebrated, illustrious.

проследи́ть, -ежу́ *pf.* track (down); trace.

прослези́ться, -ежу́сь *pf.* shed a tear, a few tears.

прослои́ть, -ою́ *pf.* layer; sandwich. **просло́йка**, -и layer, stratum; seam, streak.

про|слу́шать, -аю *pf.*, **прослу́шивать**, -аю *impf.* hear; listen to; miss, not catch.

про|слы́ть, -ыву́, -ывёшь; -ы́л, -á, -о *pf.*

просма́тривать, -аю *impf.*, **просмотрéть**, -рю́, -ришь *pf.* look over, look through; glance over, glance through; survey; view; run over; overlook, miss. **просмо́тр**, -a survey; view, viewing; examination; **закры́тый** ~ private view; **предвари́тельный** ~ preview.

просну́ться, -ну́сь, -нёшься *pf.* (*impf.* **просыпа́ться**) wake up, awake.

про́со, -a millet.

просо́вывать(ся, -аю(сь *impf. of* **просу́нуть(ся**

про|со́хнуть, -ну; -óх *pf.* (*impf. also* **просыха́ть**) get dry, dry out. **просо́хший** dried.

просочи́ться, -и́тся *pf.* (*impf.* **проса́чиваться**) percolate; filter; leak, ooze; seep out; filter through, leak out.

проспа́ть, -плю́; -а́л, -á, -о *pf.* (*impf.* **просыпа́ть**) sleep (for, through); oversleep; miss.

проспéкт, -a avenue; prospectus; summary.

проспо́рить, -рю *pf.* lose, lose a bet; argue.

про|спряга́ть, -áю *pf.*

просро́ченный overdue; out-of-date, expired; **па́спорт** ~ the passport is out of date. **просро́чивать**, -аю *impf.*, **просро́чить**, -чу *pf.* allow to run out; be behind with; overstay; ~ **óтпуск** overstay one's leave. **просро́чка, -и** delay; expiration of time limit.

проста́к, -а́ simpleton. **просте́йший** *superl. of* **просто́й**

просте́нок, -нка pier; partition.

простере́ться, -трётся; -тёрся *pf.,* **простира́ться, -а́ется** *impf.* stretch, extend.

прости́тельный pardonable, excusable, justifiable.

проститу́тка, -и prostitute. **проститу́ция, -и** prostitution.

прости́ть, -ощу́ *pf.* (*impf.* **проща́ть**) forgive, pardon; excuse; **~ся (с+*i*.)** say goodbye (to), take (one's) leave (of), bid farewell.

про́сто *adv.* simply; **~ так** for no particular reason.

просто... *in comb.* simple; open; mere. **простоволо́сый** bare-headed, with head uncovered. **~ду́шный** open-hearted; simple-hearted, simple-minded; ingenuous, artless. **~ква́ша, -и** (thick) sour milk, yoghurt. **~люди́н, -а** a man of the common people. **~наро́дный** of the common people. **~ре́чие, -я** popular speech; **в ~ре́чии** colloquially. **~ре́чный** popular, of popular speech. **~серде́чный** simple-hearted; frank; open.

просто́й, -я standing idle, enforced idleness; stoppage.

прост|о́й simple; easy; ordinary; plain; unaffected, unpretentious; mere; **~ым гла́зом** with the naked eye; **~ые лю́ди** ordinary people; **~о́й наро́д** the common people; **~о́е предложе́ние** simple sentence; **~о́е число́** prime number. **про́сто-на́просто** *adv.* simply.

просто́р, -а spaciousness; space, expanse; freedom, scope; elbow-room; **дать ~** give scope, free range, full play. **просто́рн|ый** spacious, roomy; ample; **здесь ~о** there is plenty of room here.

простота́, -ы́ simplicity.

простра́нный extensive, vast; diffuse; verbose. **простра́нственный** spatial. **простра́нство, -а** space; expanse; area.

простре́л, -а lumbago. **простре́ливать, -аю** *impf.,* **прострели́ть, -лю́, -лишь** *pf.* shoot through.

прострётся *etc.: see* **простере́ться**

про|строчи́ть, -очу́, -о́чишь *pf.*

просту́да, -ы cold; chill. **простуди́ть, -ужу́, -у́дишь** *pf.,* **простужа́ть, -а́ю** *impf.* let catch cold; **~ся** catch (a) cold, a chill.

просту́пок, -пка fault; misdemeanour.

простынн|ый sheet; **~ое полотно́** sheeting. **простыня́, -й;** *pl.* **про́стыни, -ы́нь, -ня́м** sheet.

просты́ть, -ы́ну *pf.* get cold; cool; catch cold.

просу́нуть, -ну *pf.* (*impf.* **просо́вывать**) push, shove, thrust; **~ся** push through, force one's way through.

просу́шивать, -аю *impf.,* **просуши́ть, -шу́, -шишь** *pf.* dry (*thoroughly, properly*); **~ся**

dry, get dry. **просу́шка, -и** drying.

просуществова́ть, -тву́ю *pf.* exist; last, endure.

просчита́ться, -а́юсь *pf.,* **просчи́тываться, -аюсь** *impf.* miscalculate.

про́сып, -а (-у); без ~у without waking, without stirring.

просыпа́ть, -плю *pf.,* **просыпа́ть[1], -а́ю** *impf.* spill; **~ся** spill, get spilt.

просыпа́ть[2], -а́ю *impf. of* **проспа́ть. просыпа́ться, -а́юсь** *impf. of* **просну́ться.**

просыха́ть, -а́ю *impf. of* **просо́хнуть**

про́сьба, -ы request; application, petition; **«~ не кури́ть»** 'No smoking, please'; **у меня́ к вам ~** I have a favour to ask you.

прота́лкивать, -аю *impf. of* **протолкну́ть.**

прота́пливать, -аю *impf. of* **протопи́ть**

прота́скивать, -аю *impf.,* **протащи́ть, -щу́, -щишь** *pf.* pull, drag, trail.

проте́з, -а artificial limb; (*artificial*) aid; prosthesis, prosthetic appliance; **зубно́й ~** false teeth, denture; **слухово́й ~** hearing aid. **проте́зный** prosthetic.

протека́ть, -а́ет *impf. of* **проте́чь. протёкший** past, last.

проте́кция, -и patronage, influence.

протере́ть, -тру́, -трёшь; -тёр *pf.* (*impf.* **протира́ть**) wipe (over); wipe dry; rub (through).

проте́ст, -а protest; objection.

протеста́нт, -а Protestant. **протеста́нтский** Protestant. **протеста́нтство, -а** Protestantism.

протестова́ть, -ту́ю *impf. & pf.* (**про́тив**+*g.*) protest (against), object (to).

проте́чь, -ечёт; -тёк, -ла́ *pf.* (*impf.* **протека́ть**) flow, run; leak; ooze, seep; elapse, pass; take its course.

про́тив *prep.*+*g.* against; opposite; facing; contrary to, as against; in proportion to, according to; **име́ть что́-нибудь ~** have something against, mind, object; **ничего́ не име́ть ~** not mind, not object.

про́тивень, -вня *m.* dripping-pan; meat-tin; girdle, griddle.

проти́виться, -влюсь *impf.* (*pf.* **вос~**) +*d.* oppose; resist, stand up against. **проти́вник, -а** opponent, adversary, antagonist; the enemy. **проти́вно** *prep.*+*d.* against; contrary to. **проти́вн|ый[1]** opposite; contrary; opposing, opposed; **в ~ом слу́чае** otherwise; **~ый ве́тер** contrary wind, head wind. **проти́вный[2]** nasty, offensive, disgusting; unpleasant, disagreeable; **мне проти́вно** I am disgusted.

противо... *in comb.* anti-, contra-, counter-. **противове́с, -а** counterbalance, counterpoise. **~возду́шный** anti-aircraft. **~га́з, -а** gas-mask, respirator. **~га́зовый** anti-gas. **~де́йствие, -я** opposition, counteraction. **~де́йствовать, -тву́ю** *impf.*+*d.* oppose, counteract. **~есте́ственный** unnatural. **~зако́нный** unlawful; illegal. **~зача́точ-**

ный contraceptive. **~лежа́щий** opposite. **~обще́ственный** anti-social. **~пожа́рный** fire-fighting, fire-prevention. **~поло́жность, -и** opposition; contrast; opposite, antithesis; **пряма́я ~поло́жность** exact opposite. **~поло́жный** opposite; opposed, contrary. **~поста́вить, -влю** *pf.*, **~поставля́ть, -я́ю** *impf.* oppose; contrast, set off. **~прига́рный** non-stick. **~раке́та, -ы** antimissile. **~раке́тный** anti-missile. **~речи́вый** contradictory; discrepant, conflicting. **~ре́чие, -я** contradiction; inconsistency; conflict, clash. **~ре́чить, -чу** *impf.+d.* contradict; be at variance with, conflict with, be contrary to, run counter to. **~стоя́ть, -ою** *impf.+d.* resist, withstand. **~та́нковый** anti-tank. **~уго́нный** anti-theft. **~хими́ческий** anti-gas. **~шу́мы, -ов** *pl.* earplugs. **~я́дие, -я** antidote.

протира́ть, -а́ю *impf. of* **протере́ть. проти́рка, -и** cleaning rag.

проткну́ть, -ну́, -нёшь *pf.* (*impf.* **протыка́ть**) pierce; transfix; spit, skewer.

протоко́л, -а minutes, record of proceedings; report; statement; charge-sheet; protocol; **вести́ ~** take, record, the minutes; **занести́ в ~** enter in the minutes. **протоколи́ровать, -рую** *impf. & pf.* (*pf. also* **за~**) minute, record. **протоко́льный** of protocol; exact, factual.

протолкну́ть, -ну́, -нёшь *pf.* (*impf.* **прота́лкивать**) push through.

протопи́ть, -плю́, -пишь *pf.* (*impf.* **прота́пливать**) heat (*thoroughly*).

проторённ|ый beaten, well-trodden; **~ая доро́жка** beaten track.

прото́чный flowing, running.

про|тра́лить, -лю *pf.* протру́ *etc.: see* **протере́ть. про|тру́бить, -блю** *pf.*

протуха́ть, -а́ет *impf.*, **проту́хнуть, -нет; -ух** *pf.* become foul, become rotten; go bad. **проту́хший** foul, rotten; bad, tainted.

протыка́ть, -а́ю *impf. of* **проткну́ть**

протя́гивать, -аю *impf.*, **протяну́ть, -ну́, -нешь** *pf.* stretch; extend; stretch out, hold out; reach out; protract; drawl out; last; **~ся** stretch out; reach out; extend, stretch, reach; last, go on. **протяже́ние, -я** extent; stretch; distance, expanse, area; space; **на всём протяже́нии+g.** along the whole length of, all along; **на протяже́нии** during, for the space of. **протяжённость, -и** extent, length. **протя́жность, -и** slowness; **~ ре́чи** drawl. **протя́жный** long-drawn-out; drawling.

проу́чивать, -аю *impf.*, **проучи́ть, -чу́, -чишь** *pf.* study, learn (up); teach a lesson, punish. **проф.** *abbr.* (*of* **профе́ссор**) professor. **проф...** *abbr.* (*of* **профессиона́льный, профсою́зный**) *in comb.* professional, occupational; trade-union. **профбиле́т, -а** trade-union card. **~боле́знь, -и** occupational disease. **~ко́м, -а** trade-union committee. **~о́рг, -а** trade-union organizer.

~ориента́ция, -и vocational guidance. **~рабо́тник, -а** trade-union official. **~сою́з, -а** trade-union. **~сою́зный** trade-union. **~техучи́лище, -а** a technical college. **~техшко́ла, -ы** trade school. **~шко́ла, -ы** trade-union school.

профа́н, -а layman; ignoramus. **профессиона́льн|ый** professional; occupational; **~ая ориента́ция** career guidance; **~ый риск** occupational hazard; **~ый сою́з** trade-union. **профе́ссия, -и** profession, occupation, trade.

профе́ссор, -а; *pl.* **~а́** professor. **профе́ссорский** professorial.

профила́ктика, -и prophylaxis; preventive measures, precautions. **профилакти́ческий** prophylactic; preventive, precautionary. **про́филь, -я** *m.* profile; side-view; outline; section; type.

профо́рма, -ы form, formality.

прохла́да, -ы coolness, cool. **прохлади́тельный** refreshing, cooling. **прохла́дный** cool, fresh.

прохо́д, -а (-у) passage; passageway; gangway; aisle; duct; **пра́во ~а** right of way; **«~а нет»** 'no thoroughfare'. **проходи́мец, -мца** rogue, rascal. **проходи́мый** passable. **проходи́ть, -ожу́, -о́дишь** *impf. of* **пройти́. прохо́дка, -и** going through, getting through; tunnelling, driving. **проходно́й** of passage; through; communciating. **прохо́жий** passing, in transit; *sb.* passer-by.

процвета́ние, -я prosperity, well-being; flourishing, thriving. **процвета́ть, -а́ю** *impf.* prosper, flourish, thrive.

процеди́ть, -ежу́, -е́дишь *pf.* (*impf.* **проце́живать**) filter, strain; **~ сквозь зу́бы** mutter, mumble.

процеду́ра, -ы procedure; treatment; **лече́бные процеду́ры** medical treatment.

проце́живать, -аю *impf. of* **процеди́ть**

проце́нт, -а percentage; per cent; interest; **сто ~ов** a hundred per cent.

проце́сс, -а process; trial; legal action, legal proceedings; lawsuit; cause, case. **проце́ссия, -и** procession.

проце́ссор, -а (*comput.*) processor.

процессуа́льный trial; legal.

про|цити́ровать, -рую *pf.*

прочёска, -и screening; combing.

проче́сть, -чту́, -чтёшь; -чёл, -чла́ *pf. of* **чита́ть**

про́ч|ий other; **и ~ее** etc., etcetera, and so on; **ме́жду ~им** incidentally, by the way; **~ие** *sb., pl.* (the) others.

прочи́стить, -и́щу *pf.* (*impf.* **прочища́ть**) clean; cleanse thoroughly.

про|чита́ть, -а́ю *pf.*, **прочи́тывать, -аю** *impf.* read (through).

прочища́ть, -а́ю *impf. of* **прочи́стить**

про́чно *adv.* firmly, soundly, solidly, well. **про́чн|ый; -чен, -чна́, -о** firm, sound, stable, solid; durable, lasting; enduring. **~ая**

кра́ска fast colour.

прочте́ние, -я reading; reciting; giving, delivering. прочту́ etc.: see проче́сть

прочу́вствовать, -твую pf. feel; feel deeply, acutely, keenly; experience, go through; get the feel of.

прочь adv. away, off; averse to; (поди́) ~! go away! be off!; (пошёл) ~ отсю́да! get out of here!; ~ с доро́ги! get out of the way!; ру́ки ~! hands off!; я не прочь I have no objection, I am not averse to, I am quite willing.

проше́дш|ий past; last; ~ее sb. the past.

прошёл etc.: see пройти́

проше́ние, -я application, petition.

прошепта́ть, -пчу́, -пчешь pf. whisper.

проше́ствие, -я; по проше́ствии+g. after the lapse of, after the expiration of.

прошива́ть, -а́ю impf., проши́ть, -шью, -шьёшь pf. sew, stitch. проши́вка, -и insertion.

прошлого́дний last year's. про́шл|ый past; of the past; bygone, former; last; в ~ом году́ last year; ~ое sb. the past.

про|шнурова́ть, -ру́ю pf. про|штуди́ровать, -рую pf. прошью́ etc.: see проши́ть

проща́й(те) goodbye; farewell. проща́льный parting, farewell. проща́ние, -я farewell; parting, leave-taking. проща́ть(ся, -а́ю(сь impf. of прости́ть(ся

про́ще simpler, plainer, easier.

проще́ние, -я forgiveness, pardon; прошу́ проще́ния I beg your pardon; (I'm) sorry.

прощу́пать, -аю pf., прощу́пывать, -аю impf. feel; detect; sound (out).

про|экзаменова́ть, -ную pf.

проявитель, -я m. developer. прояви́ть, -влю́, -вишь pf., проявля́ть, -я́ю impf. show, display, manifest, reveal; develop.

проя́снеть[1], -еет pf. clear; проясне́ло it cleared up. проясне́ть[2], -е́ет pf. brighten (up). проясни́ться, -и́тся pf., проясня́ться, -я́ется impf. clear, clear up.

пруд, -а́, loc. -у́ pond. пруди́ть, -ужу́, -у́дишь impf. (pf. за~) dam. прудово́й pond.

пружи́на, -ы spring. пружи́нистый springy, elastic. пружи́нка, -и mainspring; hairspring. пружи́нный spring.

пруса́к, -а́ cockroach.

прусса́к, -а́, прусса́чка, -и Prussian. пру́сский Prussian.

прут, -а or -а́; pl. -тья twig; switch; rod.

пры́галка, -и skipping-rope. пры́гать, -аю impf., пры́гнуть, -ну pf. jump, leap, spring; bound; hop; bounce; ~ со скака́лкой skip; ~ с упо́ром vault; ~ с шесто́м pole-vault. прыгу́н, -а́, прыгу́нья, -и; g.pl. -ний jumper. прыжко́в|ый; ~ая вы́шка diving board. прыжо́к, -жка́ jump; leap, spring, caper; прыжки́ jumping; прыжки́ на бату́те trampolining; прыжки́ в во́ду diving; ~ в высоту́ high jump; прыжки́ с пара-шю́том parachute-jumping, sky-diving; ~ с

разбе́га running jump; ~ с упо́ром vault, vaulting; ~ с шесто́м pole-vault.

пры́скать, -аю impf., пры́снуть, -ну pf. spurt, gush; ~ на or в+a. spray, sprinkle; ~ (со́ смеху) burst out laughing.

пры́ткий quick, lively, sharp. прыть, -и speed; quickness, liveliness, go.

прыщ, -а́, пры́щик, -а pimple; postule. прыща́вый pimply, pimpled.

пряде́ние, -я spinning. пря́деный spun. пряди́льный spinning. пряди́льня, -и; g.pl. -лен (spinning-)mill. пряди́льщик, -а spinner. пряду́ etc.: see прясть. прядь, -и lock; strand. пря́жа, -и yarn, thread.

пря́жка, -и buckle, clasp.

пря́лка, -и distaff; spinning-wheel.

пряма́я sb. straight line; по прямо́й on the straight. пря́мо adv. straight; straight on; directly; frankly, openly, bluntly; really.

прямо... in comb. straight-; direct; ortho-, rect(i)-, right. прямоду́шие, -я directness, frankness, straightforwardness. ~ду́шный direct, frank, straightforward. ~кры́лый orthopterous. ~лине́йный rectilinear; straightforward, forthright. ~сло́йный straight-grained. ~уго́льник, -а rectangle. ~уго́льный right-angled, rectangular.

прямо́й; -ям, -а́, -о straight; upright, erect; through; direct; straightforward; real.

пря́ник, -а spice cake; gingerbread; honey-cake. пря́ничный gingerbread. пря́ность, -и spice; spiciness. пря́ный spicy; heady.

прясть, -яду́, -ядёшь; -ял, -я́ла, -о impf. (pf. с~) spin.

пря́тать, -я́чу impf. (pf. с~) hide, conceal; ~ся hide, conceal o.s. пря́тки, -ток pl. hide-and-seek.

пря́ха, -и spinner.

пса etc.: see пёс

псало́м, -лма́ psalm. псало́мщик, -а (psalm-)reader; sexton.

псевдони́м, -а pseudonym; pen-name.

псих, -а madman, lunatic, crank. психбольни́ца, -ы mental hospital. психиа́тр, -а psychiatrist. психиатри́ческ|ий psychiatric(al); ~ая лече́бница mental hospital. психиатри́я, -и psychiatry. пси́хика, -и state of mind; psyche; psychology. психи́ческий mental, psychical.

психоана́лиз, -а psychoanalysis. психоанали́тик, -а psychoanalyst. психоаналити́ческий psychoanalytic(al). психо́з, -а psychosis. психо́лог, -а psychologist. психологи́ческий psychological. психоло́гия, -и psychology. психопа́т, -а psychopath; lunatic. психотерапе́вт, -а psychotherapist. психотерапи́я, -и psychotherapy.

псориа́з, -а psoriasis.

птене́ц, -нца́ nestling; fledgeling. пти́ца, -ы bird; ва́жная ~ big noise; дома́шняя ~ poultry. птицево́д, -а poultry-farmer, poultry-breeder. пти́ч|ий bird, bird's; poultry; вид с ~ьего полёта bird's-eye view; ~ий

двор poultry-yard. **птичка, -и** bird.

публика, -и public; audience. **публикация, -и** publication; notice, advertisement. **публиковать, -кую** impf. (pf. **о~**) publish. **публицист, -а** publicist; commentator on current affairs. **публицистика, -и** social and political journalism; writing on current affairs. **публицистический** publicistic. **публично** adv. publicly; in public; openly. **публичность, -и** publicity. **публичн|ый** public; ~**ый дом** brothel; ~**ая женщина** prostitute.

пугало, -а scarecrow. **пуганый** scared, frightened. **пугать, -аю** impf. (pf. **ис~, на~**) frighten, scare; intimidate; +i. threaten with; ~**ся** (+g.) be frightened (of), be scared (of); take fright (at); shy (at). **пугач, -а** toy pistol; screech owl. **пугливый** fearful, timorous; timid. **пугнуть, -ну, -нёшь** pf. scare, frighten; give a fright.

пуговица, -ы, пуговка, -и button.

пуд, -а; pl. **-ы** pood (old Russ. measurement, equivalent to approx. 16.38 kg). **пудовой, пудовый** one pood in weight.

пудра, -ы powder. **пудреный** powdered. **пудрить, -рю** impf. (pf. **на~**) powder; ~**ся** powder one's face, use powder.

пузатый big-bellied, pot-bellied.

пузырёк, -рька phial, vial; bubble; bleb. **пузырь, -я** m. bubble; blister; bladder.

пук, -а; pl. **-й** bunch, bundle; tuft; wisp.

пулевой bullet. **пулемёт, -а** machine-gun. **пулемётный** machine-gun. **пулемётчик, -а** machine-gunner. **пулестойкий** bullet-proof.

пульс, -а pulse. **пульсар, -а** pulsar. **пульсировать, -рует** impf. pulse; pulsate; beat, throb.

пульт, -а desk, stand; control panel.

пуля, -и bullet.

пункт, -а point; spot; post; centre; item; plank; **по всем** ~**ам** at all points. **пунктир, -а** dotted line. **пунктирный** dotted, broken.

пунктуальность, -и punctuality. **пунктуальный** punctual.

пунктуация, -и punctuation.

пунцовый crimson.

пунш, -а punch (drink).

пуп, -а navel; umbilicus; ~ **земли** hub of the universe. **пуповина, -ы** umbilical cord. **пупок, -пка** navel; gizzard. **пупочный** umbilical.

пурга, -и snow-storm, blizzard.

пурпур, -а purple, crimson. **пурпурный, пурпуровый** purple, crimson.

пуск, -а starting (up); setting in motion. **пускай** see **пусть. пускать(ся, -аю(сь** impf. of **пустить(ся. пусков|ой** starting; initial; ~**ая площадка** (rocket-)launching platform.

пустеть, -еет impf. (pf. **о~**) empty; become deserted.

пустить, пущу, пустишь pf. (impf. **пускать**) let go; set free; let in, allow to enter; let, allow, permit; start; set, put; send; set in mo-

tion, set going, set working; throw, shy; put forth, put out; **не** ~ keep out; ~ **воду** turn on the water; ~ **в ход** start, launch, set going, set in train; ~ **корни** take root; ~ **ростки** shoot, sprout; ~ **слух** start, spread, a rumour; ~ **фейерверк** let off fireworks; ~**ся** set out; start; begin; ~**ся в путь** set out, get on one's way.

пустобрёх, -а chatterbox, windbag.

пустовать, -тует impf. be empty, stand empty; lie fallow. **пуст|ой; -ст, -а, -о** empty; void; tenantless, vacant, uninhabited; deserted; idle; shallow; futile, frivolous; vain, ungrounded; ~**ое место** blank space; ~**ая отговорка** lame excuse, hollow pretence; ~**ые слова** mere words; ~**ой чай** just tea.

пустота, -ы; pl. **-ы** emptiness; void; vacuum; shallowness; futility, frivolousness. **пустотелый** hollow.

пустынник, -а hermit, anchorite. **пустынный** uninhabited; deserted; ~ **остров** desert island. **пустынь, -и** hermitage, monastery. **пустыня, -и** desert, wilderness. **пустырь, -я** m. waste land; vacant plot; desolate area.

пустышка, -и blank; hollow object; (baby's) dummy; empty-headed person.

пусть, пускай part. let; all right, very well; though, even if; ~ **будет так** so be it; ~ **х равен 3** let x = 3.

пустяк, -а trifle; bagatelle. **пустяковый** trifling, trivial.

путаница, -ы muddle, confusion; mess, tangle. **путаный** muddled, confused; tangled; confusing; muddle-headed. **путать, -аю** impf. (pf. **за~, пере~, с~**) tangle; confuse; muddle; mix up; ~**ся** get tangled; get confused; get muddled; get mixed up.

путёвка, -и pass, authorization; permit; **просить путёвку в санаторий** apply for a place in a sanatorium. **путеводитель, -я** m. guide, guide-book. **путеводн|ый** guiding; ~**ая звезда** guiding star; lodestar. **путев|ой** travelling, itinerary; ~**ая карта** road-map; ~**ая скорость** ground-speed. **путём** prep.+g. by means of, by dint of. **путепровод, -а** overpass; underpass; bridge. **путешественник, -а** traveller. **путешествие, -я** journey; trip; voyage; cruise; pl. travels. **путешествовать, -твую** impf. travel; voyage. **путь, -й,** i. **-ём,** p. **-й** way; track; path; road; course; journey; voyage; passage, duct; means; use, benefit; **водный** ~ water-way; **в пути** en route, on one's way; **в четырёх днях пути от** four day's journey from; **мирным путём** amicably, peaceably; **морские пути** shipping-routes, sea-lanes; **нам с вами по пути** we are going the same way; **на обратном пути** on the way back; **пойти по пути**+g. take, follow, the path of; **по пути** on the way; **пути сообщения** communications; **стоять на пути** be in the way.

путч, -а coup, putsch. **путчист, -а** coup-leader, putschist.

пух, -а (-у), *loc.* -у́ down; fluff; **разби́ть в ~ и прах** put to complete rout.

пу́хл|ый; -хл, -а́, -о chubby, plump. **пу́хнуть**, -ну; пух *impf.* (*pf.* вс~, о~) swell.

пухови́к, -а́ feather-bed; down quilt; eider-down. **пухо́вка**, -и powder-puff. **пухо́вый** downy.

пучегла́зый goggle-eyed.

пучи́на, -ы gulf, abyss; the deep.

пучо́к, -чка́ bunch, bundle; tuft, fascicle; wisp.

пу́шечн|ый gun, cannon; ~ое мя́со cannon-fodder.

пуши́нка, -и bit of fluff; ~ сне́га snowflake. **пуши́стый** fluffy, downy.

пу́шка, -и gun, cannon.

пушни́на, -ы furs, fur-skins, pelts. **пушно́й** fur; fur-bearing; ~ зверь fur-bearing animals.

пу́ще *adv.* more; ~ всего́ most of all.

пущу́ *etc.: see* **пусти́ть**

пчела́, -ы́; *pl.* -ёлы bee. **пчели́ный** bee, bee's, of bees; ~ воск beeswax. **пчелово́д**, -а bee-keeper, apiarist. **пче́льник**, -а apiary.

пшени́ца, -ы wheat. **пшени́чный** wheat, wheaten.

пшённый millet. **пшено́**, -а́ millet.

пыл, -а (-у), *loc.* -у́ heat, ardour, passion. **пыла́ть**, -а́ю *impf.* blaze, flame; burn; glow.

пылеви́дный powdered, pulverized. **пылесо́с**, -а vacuum cleaner. **пылесо́сить**, -сю *impf.* vacuum(-clean), hoover. **пыли́нка**, -и speck of dust. **пыли́ть**, -лю́ *impf.* (*pf.* за~, на~) raise a dust, raise the dust; cover with dust, make dusty; ~ся get dusty, get covered with dust.

пы́лкий ardent, passionate; fervent; fervid. **пы́лкость**, -и ardour, passion; fervency.

пыль, -и, *loc.* -и́ dust. **пы́льн|ый**; -лен, -льна́, -о dusty; ~ый котёл dust-bowl; ~ая тря́пка duster. **пыльца́**, -ы́ pollen.

пыта́ть, -а́ю *impf.* torture, torment. **пыта́ться**, -та́юсь *impf.* (*pf.* по~) try. **пы́тка**, -и torture, torment. **пытли́вый** inquisitive, searching.

пы́хать, **пы́шет** *impf.* blaze.

пыхте́ть, -хчу́ *impf.* puff, pant.

пы́шет *see* **пы́хать**

пы́шка, -и bun; doughnut; chubby child; plump woman.

пы́шность, -и splendour, magnificence. **пы́шн|ый**; -шен, -шна́, -шно splendid, magnificent; fluffy, light; luxuriant.

пьедеста́л, -а pedestal.

пье́ксы, -с *pl.* ski-boots.

пье́са, -ы play; piece.

пью *etc.: see* **пить**

пьяне́ть, -е́ю *impf.* (*pf.* о~) get drunk. **пьяни́ть**, -ни́т *impf.* (*pf.* о~) intoxicate, make drunk; go to one's head. **пья́ница**, -ы *c.g.* drunkard; tippler; toper. **пья́нство**, -а drunkenness; hard drinking. **пья́нствовать**, -твую *impf.* drink hard, drink heavily. **пья́ный**

drunk; drunken; tipsy, tight; intoxicated; heady, intoxicating.

пэ *nt.indecl.* the letter **п**.

пюпи́тр, -а desk; reading-desk; music-stand.

пюре́ *nt.indecl.* purée.

пядь, -и; *g.pl.* -е́й span; **ни пя́ди** not an inch.

пя́льцы, -лец *pl.* tambour; embroidery frame.

пята́, -ы́; *pl.* -ы, -а́м heel.

пята́к, -а́, **пятачо́к**, -чка́ five-copeck piece.

пятёрка, -и five; figure 5; No.5; group of five; fiver, five-rouble note. **пя́теро**, -ы́х five.

пяти... *in comb.* five; penta-. **пятибо́рье**, -я pentathlon. ~гла́вый five-headed; five-domed. ~две́рн|ый; ~ая маши́на hatch-back. ~десятиле́тие, -я fifty years; fiftieth anniversary; fiftieth birthday. П~деся́тница, -ы Pentecost. ~деся́тый fiftieth; ~деся́тые го́ды the fifties. ~кла́ссник, -а, ~ница, -ы, ~кла́шка, -и *c.g.* class-five pupil. ~кни́жие, -я Pentateuch. ~коне́чный five-pointed. ~кра́тный fivefold, quintuple. ~ле́тие, -я five years; fifth anniversary. ~ле́тка, -и five years; five-year plan; five-year-old. ~со́тенный five-hundred-rouble. ~сотле́тие, -я five centuries; quincentenary. ~со́тый five-hundredth. ~сто́пный penta-meter. ~то́нка, -и five-ton lorry. ~ты́сячный five-thousandth. ~уго́льник, -а penta-gon. ~уго́льный pentagonal.

пя́тка, -и heel.

пятна́дцатый fifteenth. **пятна́дцать**, -и fifteen.

пятна́ть, -а́ю *impf.* (*pf.* за~) spot, stain, smirch; tig, catch. **пятна́шки**, -шек *pl.* tag, tig. **пятни́стый** spotted, dappled.

пя́тница, -ы Friday.

пятно́, -а́; *pl.* -а, -тен stain; spot; patch; blot; stigma, blemish; **роди́мое ~** birth-mark.

пято́к, -тка́ five. **пя́тый** fifth. **пять**, -и́, *i.* -ью́ five. **пятьдеся́т**, -и́десяти, *i.* -ью́десятью fifty. **пятьсо́т**, -тисо́т, -тиста́м five hundred. **пя́тью** *adv.* five times.

Р

р *letter: see* **эр**

р. *abbr.* (*of* река́) R., River.; (*of* рубль) r., rouble(s).

раб, -а́ slave, bondsman.

раб... *abbr.* (*of* рабо́чий) *in comb.* worker. **рабко́р**, -а worker correspondent. ~селько́р, -а worker-peasant correspondent. ~си́ла, -ы manpower, labour force.

раба́, -ы́ slave; bondswoman. **рабовладе́лец**, -льца slave-owner. **рабовладе́ль-**

ческий slave-owning. **раболе́пие, -я** servility. **раболе́пный** servile. **раболе́пствовать, -твую** cringe, fawn.

рабо́та, -ы work; labour; job, employment; working; functioning; running; workmanship. **рабо́тать, -аю** *impf.* work; run, function; be open; +*i.* work, operate; **не ~** not work, be out of order; **~ над**+*i.* work at, work on. **рабо́тник, -а, рабо́тница, -ы** worker; workman; hand, labourer. **рабо́тный** working; **~ дом** workhouse. **работома́н, -а, работома́нка, -ки** workaholic. **работоспосо́бность, -и** capacity for work, efficiency. **работоспосо́бный** able-bodied, efficient. **работя́щий** hardworking, industrious. **рабо́чий** *sb.* worker; working man; workman; hand, labourer. **рабо́ч|ий** worker's; work; working; working-class; driving; **~ее движе́ние** working-class movement, labour movement; **~ий день** working day; **~ее колесо́** driving wheel; **~ая ло́шадь** draughthorse; **~ие ру́ки** hands; **~ая си́ла** manpower, labour force; labour.

ра́бский slave; servile. **ра́бство, -а** slavery, servitude.

равви́н, -а rabbi.

ра́венство, -а equality; **знак ра́венства** equals sign.

равио́ли *nt. & pl. indecl.* ravioli.

равне́ние, -я dressing, alignment; **~ напра́во!** eyes right! **равни́на, -ы** plain. **равни́нный** plain; level, flat.

равно́ *adv.* alike; equally; **~ как** as well as; and also, as also. **равно́** *pred.: see* **ра́вный**

равно... *in comb.* equi-, iso-. **равнобе́дренный** isosceles. **~ве́сие, -я** equilibrium; balance, equipoise; **привести́ в ~ве́сие** balance. **~де́йствующая** *sb.* resultant force. **~де́йствие, -я** equinox. **~ду́шие, -я** indifference. **~ду́шный** indifferent. **~зна́чащий, ~зна́чный** equivalent, equipollent. **~ме́рный** even; uniform. **~отстоя́щий** equidistant. **~пра́вие, -я** equality of rights. **~пра́вный** equal in rights, having equal rights. **~си́льный** of equal strength; equal, equivalent, tantamount. **~сторо́нний** equilateral. **~уго́льный** equiangular. **~це́нный** of equal value, of equal worth; equivalent.

ра́вн|ый; -вен, -вна́ equal; **на ~ых** as equals, on an equal footing; **при про́чих ~ых усло́виях** other things being equal; **~ым о́бразом** equally, likewise; **равно́** *pred.* make(s), equals; **всё ~о́** it is all the same, it makes no difference; all the same; **мне всё ~о́** I don't mind, it's all the same to me; **не всё́ ли ~о́?** what difference does it make? what does it matter? **равня́ть, -я́ю** *impf.* (*pf.* **с~**) make even; treat equally; +*c*+*i.* compare with, treat as equal to; **~ счёт** equalize; **~ся** compete, compare; be equal; be equivalent, be tantamount; dress; +*d.* equal, amount to; +*c*+*i.* compete with, match.

рагу́ *nt. indecl.* ragout; **кита́йское ~** chop suey.

рад, -а, -о *pred.* glad.

ра́ди *prep.* +*g.* for the sake of; **чего́ ~?** what for?

радиа́тор, -а radiator.

радиацио́нный radiation. **радиа́ция, -и** radiation.

ра́диевый radium. **ра́дий, -я** radium.

радика́л, -а radical. **радикали́зм, -а** radicalism. **радика́льность, -и** radicalism. **радика́льн|ый** radical, drastic; **~ые измене́ния** sweeping changes.

ра́дио *nt.indecl.* radio, wireless; radio set; **переда́ть по ~** broadcast; **слу́шать ~** listen in.

радио... *in comb.* radio-; radioactive. **радиоакти́вность, -и** radioactivity. **~акти́вный** radioactive. **~аппара́т, -а** radio set. **~бесе́да, -ы** phone-in. **~веща́ние, -я** broadcasting. **~веща́тельный** broadcasting. **~гра́мма, -ы** radiogram; wireless message. **~журнали́ст, -а** broadcaster. **~зо́нд, -а** radiosonde. **радио́лог, -а** radiologist. **~логи́ческий** radiological. **~ло́гия, -и** radiology. **~лока́тор, -а** a radar (set). **~люби́тель, -я** *m.* radio amateur, ham. **~мая́к, -á** radio beacon. **~мо́ст, -а** satellite (radio) link-up. **~переда́тчик, -а** transmitter. **~переда́ча, -и** transmission, broadcast. **~перекли́чка, -и** radio link-up. **~приёмник, -а** receiver radio (set). **~связь, -и** radio communication, radio link. **~слу́шатель, -я** *m.* listener. **~ста́нция, -и** radio station, set. **~те́хника, -и** radio-engineering. **~управля́емый** remote-controlled. **~фици́ровать, -рую** *impf. & pf.* instal radio in, equip with radio. **~хими́ческий** radiochemical. **~хи́мия, -и** radiochemistry. **~электро́ника, -и** radioelectronics.

радио́ла, -ы radiogram.

ради́ровать, -рую *impf. & pf.* radio. **ради́ст, -а** radio operator; telegraphist.

ра́диус, -а radius.

ра́довать, -дую *impf.* (*pf.* **об~, по~**) gladden, make glad, make happy; **~ся** be glad, be happy, rejoice. **ра́достный** glad, joyous, joyful. **ра́дость, -и** gladness, joy; **от ра́дости** for joy, with joy; **с ~ю** with pleasure, gladly.

ра́дуга, -и rainbow. **ра́дужн|ый** iridescent, opalescent, rainbow-coloured; cheerful; optimistic; **~ая оболо́чка** iris.

раду́шие, -я cordiality. **раду́шный** cordial; **~ приём** hearty welcome.

раёк, райка́ gallery; gods.

ражу́ *etc.: see* **рази́ть**

раз, -а; *pl.* **-ы́, раз** time, occasion; one; **в друго́й ~** another time, some other time; **в са́мый ~** at the right moment, just right; **ещё ~** (once) again, once more; **как ~** just, exactly; **как ~ то** the very thing; **в э́тот ~** this time, on this occasion, (for) this once; **не ~** more than once; time and again; **ни ~у** not once, never; **оди́н ~** once; **~ (и) навсегда́** once (and) for all. **раз** *adv.* once, one day. **раз** *conj.* if, since; ~ **так** in that case.

раз..., **разо...**, **разъ...**, **рас...** *vbl. pref.* indicating division into parts; distribution; action in different directions; action in reverse; termination of action or state; intensification of action: dis-, un-.

разба́вить, **-влю** *pf.*, **разбавля́ть**, **-я́ю** *impf.* dilute.

разбаза́ривание, **-я** squandering; sell-out. **разбаза́ривать**, **-аю** *impf.*, **разбаза́рить**, **-рю** *pf.* squander, waste.

разба́лтывать(ся, -аю(сь *impf. of* **разболта́ть(ся**

разбе́г, **-а (-у)** run, running start; **прыжо́к с разбе́га (-éгу)** running jump. **разбега́ться**, **-а́юсь** *impf.*, **разбежа́ться**, **-егу́сь** *pf.* take a run, run up; scatter, disperse; be scattered; **у меня́ разбежа́лись глаза́** I was dazzled.

разберу́ *etc.: see* **разобра́ть**

разбива́ть(ся, -а́ю(сь *impf. of* **разби́ть(ся. разби́вка**, **-и** laying out; spacing (out).

разбинтова́ть, **-ту́ю** *pf.*, **разбинто́вывать**, **-аю** *impf.* unbandage, remove a bandage from; ~**ся** remove one's bandage(s); come off, come undone; come unbandaged, lose its bandage.

разбира́тельство, **-а** examination, investigation. **разбира́ть**, **-а́ю** *impf. of* **разобра́ть**; be particular; **не разбира́я** indiscriminately; ~**ся** *impf. of* **разобра́ться**

разби́ть, **-зобью́, -зобьёшь** *pf.* (*impf.* **разбива́ть**) break; smash; break up, break down; divide (up), split; damage; fracture; beat, defeat; lay out, mark out; space (out); ~**ся** break, get broken, get smashed; hurt o.s. badly; smash o.s. up. **разби́тый** broken; jaded.

раз|благовести́ть, **-ещу́** *pf.* **раз|богате́ть**, **-éю** *pf.*

разбо́й, **-я** robbery, brigandage. **разбо́йник**, **-а** robber, brigand, bandit. **разбо́йнич|ий** robber; thieves'; ~**ья ша́йка** gang of robbers.

разболе́ться[1], **-ли́тся** *pf.* ache; **у меня́ разболе́лась голова́** I've got a (bad) headache. **разболе́ться**[2], **-éюсь** *pf.* become ill, lose one's health.

разболта́ть[1], **-а́ю** *pf.* (*impf.* **разба́лтывать**) divulge, let out, give away.

разболта́ть[2], **-а́ю** *pf.* (*impf.* **разба́лтывать**) shake up, stir up; loosen; ~**ся** mix; come loose, work loose; get slack, get out of hand.

разбомби́ть, **-блю́** *pf.* bomb, destroy by bombing.

разбо́р, **-а (-у)** analysis; parsing; criticism, critique; selectiveness, discrimination; investigation; stripping, dismantling; buying up; sorting out; sort, quality; **без ~у (-а)** indiscriminately. **разбо́рный** collapsible. **разбо́рчивость**, **-и** legibility; scrupulousness; fastidiousness. **разбо́рчивый** legible; scrupulous; fastidious, exacting; discriminating.

разбра́сывать, **-аю** *impf. of* **разброса́ть**

разбреда́ться, **-а́ется** *impf.*, **разбрести́сь**, **-едётся; -ёлся, -ла́сь** *pf.* disperse; straggle. **разбро́д**, **-а** disorder.

разбро́санный sparse, scattered; straggling; disconnected, incoherent. **разброса́ть**, **-а́ю** *pf.* (*impf.* **разбра́сывать**) throw about; scatter, spread, strew.

раз|буди́ть, **-ужу́, -у́дишь** *pf.*

разбуха́ние, **-я** swelling; ~ **шта́та** over-staffing. **разбуха́ть**, **-а́ет** *impf.*, **разбу́хнуть**, **-нет; -бу́х** *pf.* swell.

разбушева́ться, **-шу́юсь** *pf.* fly into a rage; blow up; run high.

разва́л, **-а** breakdown, disintegration, disruption; disorganization. **разва́ливать**, **-аю** *impf.*, **развали́ть**, **-лю́, -лишь** *pf.* pull down; break up; mess up; ~**ся** collapse; go to pieces, fall to pieces; fall down, tumble down; break down; sprawl, lounge. **разва́лина**, **-ы** ruin; wreck; **гру́да разва́лин** a heap of ruins.

разварно́й boiled soft.

ра́зве *part.* really?; ~ **вы не зна́ете?** don't you know?; ~ **(то́лько)**, ~ **(что)** only; perhaps; except that, only. **ра́зве** *conj.* unless.

развева́ться, **-а́ется** *impf.* fly, flutter.

развед... *abbr.* (*of* **разве́дывательный**) *in comb.* reconnaissance; intelligence. **разве́дгруппа**, **-ы** reconnaissance party. ~**о́рган**, **-а** intelligence agency; reconnaissance unit. ~**сво́дка**, **-и** intelligence summary. ~**слу́жба**, **-ы** intelligence service.

разве́дать, **-аю** *pf.* (*impf.* **разве́дывать**) find out; investigate; reconnoitre; prospect.

разведе́ние, **-я** breeding, rearing; cultivation. **разведённ|ый** divorced; ~**ый**, ~**ая** *sb.* divorcee.

разве́дка, **-и** intelligence; secret service, intelligence service; reconnaissance; prospecting; **идти́ в разве́дку** reconnoitre. **разве́дочный** prospecting, exploratory.

разведу́ *etc.: see* **развести́**

разве́дчик, **-а** intelligence officer; scout; prospector. **разве́дывать**, **-аю** *impf. of* **разве́дать**

развезти́, **-зу́, -зёшь; -ёз, -ла́** *pf.* (*impf.* **развози́ть**) convey, transport; deliver; exhaust, wear out; make impassable, make unfit for traffic.

разве́ивать(ся, -аю(сь *impf. of* **разве́ять(ся. развёл** *etc.: see* **развести́**

развенча́ть, **-а́ю** *pf.*, **разве́нчивать**, **-аю** *impf.* dethrone; debunk.

развёрнутый extensive, large-scale, all-out; detailed; deployed, extended. **разверну́ть**, **-ну́, -нёшь** *pf.* (*impf.* **развёртывать**, **развора́чивать**) unfold, unwrap, open; unroll; unfurl; deploy; expand; develop; turn, swing; scan; show, display; ~**ся** unfold, unroll, come unwrapped; deploy; develop; spread; expand; turn, swing.

разверста́ть, **-а́ю** *pf.*, **развёрстывать**, **-аю** *impf.* distribute, allot, apportion. **развёрстка**, **-и** allotment, apportionment; distribution.

развёртывать(ся, -аю(сь *impf. of* **развер-нуть(ся**

развес, -a weighing out.

раз|весели́ть, -лю *pf.* cheer up, amuse; **~ся** cheer up.

разве́систый branchy, spreading. **разве́-сить¹, -ешу** *pf.* (*impf.* **разве́шивать**) spread; hang (out).

разве́сить², -ешу *pf.* (*impf.* **разве́шивать**) weigh out. **развесно́й** sold by weight.

развести́, -еду́, -едёшь; -ёл, -а́ *pf.* (*impf.* **разводи́ть**) take, conduct; part, separate; divorce; dilute; dissolve; start; breed, rear; cultivate; **~ мост** raise a bridge, swing a bridge open; **~ ого́нь** light a fire; **~сь** be divorced; breed, multiply.

разветви́ться, -вится *pf.* **разветвля́ться, -йется** *impf.* branch; fork; ramify. **разветв-ле́ние, -я** branching, ramification, forking; branch; fork.

разве́шать, -аю *pf.*, **разве́шивать, -аю** *impf.* hang.

разве́шивать, -аю *impf. of* **разве́сить, разве́шать. разве́шу** *etc.: see* **разве́сить**

разве́ять, -ею *pf.* (*impf.* **разве́вать**) scatter, disperse; dispel; destroy; **~ся** disperse; be dispelled.

развива́ть(ся, -а́ю(сь *impf. of* **разви́ть(ся**

развинти́ть, -нчу́ *pf.*, **разви́нчивать, -аю** *impf.* unscrew. **разви́нченный** unstrung; unsteady; lurching.

разви́тие, -я development; evolution; progress; maturity. **развито́й; ра́звит, -а́, -о** developed; mature, adult. **разви́ть, -зовью́; -зовьёшь; -и́л, -а́, -о** *pf.* (*impf.* **развива́ть**) develop; unwind, untwist; **~ся** develop.

развлека́ть, -а́ю *impf.*, **развле́чь, -еку́, -ечёшь; -ёк, -ла́** *pf.* entertain, amuse; divert; **~ся** have a good time; amuse o.s.; be diverted, be distracted.

разво́д, -a divorce. **разводи́ть(ся, -ожу́(сь, -о́дишь(ся** *impf. of* **развести́(сь. разво́д-ка, -и** separation. **разводно́й; ~ ключ** adjustable spanner, monkey-wrench; **~ мост** drawbridge, swing bridge.

развози́ть, -ожу́, -о́зишь *impf. of* **развезти́**

разволнова́ть(ся, -ну́ю(сь *pf.* get excited, be agitated.

развора́чивать(ся, -аю(сь *impf. of* **развер-нуть(ся**

раз|вороши́ть, -шу́ *pf.*

развра́т, -a debauchery, depravity, dissipation. **разврати́ть, -ащу́** *pf.* **развраща́ть, -а́ю** *impf.* debauch, corrupt; deprave. **развра́т-ничать, -аю** *impf.* indulge in debauchery, lead a depraved life. **развра́тный** debauched, depraved, profligate; corrupt. **раз-вращённый; -ён, -а́** corrupt.

развяза́ть, -яжу́, -я́жешь *pf.*, **развя́зывать, -аю** *impf.* untie, unbind, undo; unleash; **~ся** come untied, come undone; **~ся с+i.** rid o.s. of, have done with. **развя́зка, -и** dénoue-ment; outcome, issue, upshot; (*motorway*)

junction; **де́ло идёт к развя́зке** things are coming to a head. **развя́зный** familiar; free-and-easy.

разгада́ть, -а́ю *pf.*, **разга́дывать, -аю** *impf.* solve, guess, puzzle out, make out; **~ сны** interpret dreams; **~ шифр** break a cipher. **разга́дка, -и** solution.

разга́р, -a height, peak, climax; **в по́лном ~е** in full swing; **в ~е ле́та** in the height of summer.

разгиба́ть(ся, -а́ю(сь *impf. of* **разогну́ть(ся**

разглаго́льствовать, -твую *impf.* hold forth, expatiate.

разгла́дить, -а́жу *pf.*, **разгла́живать, -аю** *impf.* smooth out; iron out, press.

разгласи́ть, -ашу́ *pf.*, **разглаша́ть, -а́ю** *impf.* divulge, give away, let out; +о+*p.* spread, broadcast; herald, trumpet. **разглаше́ние, -я** divulging, disclosure.

разгляде́ть, -яжу́ *pf.*, **разгля́дывать, -аю** *impf.* make out, discern, descry; examine closely, scrutinize.

разгне́ванный angry. **разгне́вать, -аю** *pf.* anger, incense. **раз|гне́ваться, -аюсь** *pf.*

разгова́ривать, -аю *impf.* talk, speak, converse. **разгово́р, -a (-у)** talk, conversation. **разгово́рник, -a** a phrase-book. **разгово́р-ный** colloquial; conversational. **разгово́р-чивый** talkative, loquacious.

разго́н, -a dispersal; breaking up; run, running start; distance; space. **разго́нистый** widely-spaced. **разгоня́ть(ся, -я́ю(сь** *impf. of* **разогна́ть(ся**

разгора́живать, -аю *impf. of* **разгороди́ть**

разгора́ться, -а́юсь *impf.*, **разгоре́ться, -рю́сь** *pf.* flame up, flare up; flush; **стра́сти разгоре́лись** feelings ran high, passions rose.

разгороди́ть, -ожу́, -о́дишь *pf.* (*impf.* **раз-гора́живать**) partition off.

раз|горячи́ть(ся, -чу́(сь *pf.*; **~ся от вина́** be flushed with wine.

разгра́бить, -блю *pf.* plunder, pillage, loot. **разграбле́ние, -я** plunder, pillage; looting.

разграниче́ние, -я demarcation, delimitation; differentiation. **разграни́чивать, -аю** *impf.*, **разграни́чить, -чу** *pf.* delimit, demarcate; differentiate, distinguish.

раз|графи́ть, -флю́ *pf.*, **разграфля́ть, -я́ю** *impf.* rule, square. **разграфле́ние, -я** ruling.

разгреба́ть, -а́ю *impf.*, **разгрести́, -ебу́, -ебёшь; -ёб, -ла́** *pf.* rake (away), shovel (away).

разгро́м, -a rout, crushing defeat; knock-out blow; havoc, devastation. **разгроми́ть, -млю́** *pf.* rout, defeat.

разгружа́ть, -а́ю *impf.*, **разгрузи́ть, -ужу́, -у́зишь** *pf.* unload; relieve; **~ся** unload; be relieved. **разгру́зка, -и** unloading; relief, relieving.

разгрыза́ть, -а́ю *impf.*, **раз|грызть, -зу́, -зёшь; -ы́з** *pf.* crack; bite through.

разгу́л, -a revelry, debauch; raging; (wild)

outburst. **разгу́ливать, -аю** *impf.* stroll about, walk about. **разгу́ливаться, -аюсь** *impf.*, **разгуля́ться, -я́юсь** *pf.* spread o.s.; have free scope; wake up, be wide awake; clear up; improve. **разгу́льный** loose, wild, rakish.

раздава́ть(ся, -даю́(сь, -даёшь(ся *impf. of* **разда́ть(ся**

раз|дави́ть, -влю́, -вишь *pf.* **разда́вливать, -аю** *impf.* crush; squash; run down, run over; overwhelm.

разда́ть, -а́м, -а́шь, -а́ст, -ади́м; ро́з- *or* **разда́л, -а́, -о** *pf.* (*impf.* **раздава́ть**) distribute, give out, serve out, dispense; **~ся** be heard; resound; ring out; make way; stretch, expand; put on weight. **разда́ча, -и** distribution. **раздаю́** *etc.: see* **раздава́ть**

раздва́ивать(ся, -аю(сь *impf. of* **раздво́ить(ся**

раздвига́ть, -аю *impf.*, **раздви́нуть, -ну** *pf.* move apart, slide apart; draw back; **~ стол** extend a table; **~ся** move apart, slide apart; be drawn back; **за́навес раздви́нулся** the curtain rose. **раздвижно́й** expanding; sliding; extensible.

раздвое́ние, -я division into two; bifurcation; **~ ли́чности** split personality. **раздво́енный, раздвоённый** forked; bifurcated; cloven; split. **раздво́ить, -ою́** *pf.* (*impf.* **раздва́ивать**) divide into two; bisect; **~ся** bifurcate, fork; split, become double.

раздева́лка, -и, раздева́льня, -и; *g.pl.* **-лен** cloakroom. **раздева́ть(ся, -а́ю(сь** *impf. of* **разде́ть(ся**

разде́л, -а division; partition; allotment; section, part.

разде́латься, -аюсь *pf.* +*c*+*i.* finish with, be through with; settle accounts with; pay off; get even with.

разделе́ние, -я division; **~ труда́** division of labour. **раздели́мый** divisible. **раз|дели́ть, -лю́, -лишь** *pf.*, **разделя́ть, -я́ю** *impf.* divide; separate; share; **~ся** divide; be divided; be divisible; separate, part. **разде́льный** separate; clear, distinct.

разде́ну *etc.: see* **разде́ть. раздеру́** *etc.: see* **раздира́ть**

разде́ть, -де́ну *pf.* (*impf.* **раздева́ть**) undress; **~ся** undress (o.s.), strip; take off one's coat, one's things.

раздира́ть, -а́ю *impf. of* **разодра́ть. раздира́ющий (ду́шу)** heart-rending, harrowing.

раздобыва́ть, -а́ю *impf.*, **раздобы́ть, -бу́ду** *pf.* get, procure, come by, get hold of.

раздо́лье, -я expanse; freedom, liberty. **раздо́льный** free.

раздо́р, -а discord, dissension; **се́ять ~** breed strife, sow discord.

раздоса́довать, -дую *pf.* vex.

раздража́ть, -а́ю *impf.*, **раздражи́ть, -жу́** *pf.* irritate; annoy, exasperate, put out; **~ся** lose one's temper, get annoyed; get irritated;

become inflamed. **раздраже́ние, -я** irritation; **в раздраже́нии** in a temper. **раздражи́тельный** irritable; short-tempered.

раздразни́ть, -ню́, -нишь *pf.* tease; arouse, stimulate.

раз|дроби́ть, -блю́ *pf.*, **раздробля́ть, -я́ю** *impf.* break; smash to pieces, splinter; turn, convert, reduce. **раздро́бленный, раздроблённый** shattered; small-scale; fragmented.

раздува́ть(ся, -а́ю(сь *impf. of* **разду́ть(ся**

разду́мать, -аю *pf.*, **разду́мывать, -аю** *impf.* change one's mind; +*inf.* decide not to; ponder, consider; hesitate; **не разду́мывая** without a moment's thought. **разду́мье, -я** meditation; thought, thoughtful mood; hesitation; **в глубо́ком ~** deep in thought.

разду́ть, -у́ю *pf.* (*impf.* **раздува́ть**) blow; fan; blow out; exaggerate; whip up; inflate, swell; blow about; **~ся** swell.

разева́ть, -а́ю *impf. of* **рази́нуть**

разжа́лобить, -блю *pf.* move (to pity).

разжа́ловать, -лую *pf.* degrade, demote.

разжа́ть, -зожму́, -мёшь *pf.* (*impf.* **разжима́ть**) unclasp, open; release, unfasten, undo.

разжева́ть, -жую́, -жуёшь *pf.*, **разжёвывать, -аю** *impf.* chew, masticate; chew over.

разже́чь, -зожгу́, -зожжёшь; -жёг, -зожгла́ *pf.*, **разжига́ть, -а́ю** *impf.* kindle; rouse, stir up.

разжима́ть, -а́ю *impf. of* **разжа́ть. раз|жире́ть, -е́ю** *pf.*

рази́нуть, -ну *pf.* (*impf.* **разева́ть**) open; **~ рот** gape; **рази́нув рот** open-mouthed. **рази́ня, -и** *c.g.* scatter-brain.

рази́тельный striking. **рази́ть, ражу́** *impf.* (*pf.* **по~**) strike.

разлага́ть(ся, -а́ю(сь *impf. of* **разложи́ть(ся**

разла́д, -а discord, dissension; disorder.

разла́мывать(ся, -аю(сь *impf. of* **разлома́ть(ся, разломи́ть(ся. разлёгся** *etc.: see* **разле́чься**

разлеза́ться, -а́ется *impf.*, **разле́зться, -зется; -ле́зся** *pf.* come to pieces; come apart, fall apart.

разлени́ться, -ню́сь, -нишься *pf.* get very lazy, sink into sloth.

разлета́ться, -а́юсь *impf.*, **разлете́ться, -лечу́сь** *pf.* fly away; fly about, scatter; shatter; vanish, be shattered; fly, rush; rush up.

разле́чься, -ля́гусь; -лёгся, -гла́сь *pf.* stretch out; sprawl.

разли́в, -а bottling; flood; overflow. **разлива́ть, -а́ю** *impf.*, **разли́ть, -золью́, -зольёшь; -и́л, -а́, -о** *pf.* pour out; spill; flood (with), drench (with); **~ся** spill; overflow, flood; spread. **разли́вка, -и** bottling. **разливн|о́й** on tap, on draught; **~о́е вино́** wine from the wood. **разли́тие, -я** flooding.

различа́ть, -а́ю *impf.*, **различи́ть, -чу́** *pf.* distinguish; tell the difference; discern, make out; **~ся** differ. **разли́чие, -я** distinction; difference; **зна́ки разли́чия** badges of rank.

различи́тельный distinctive, distinguishing. **разли́чный** different; various, diverse.

разложе́ние, -я breaking down; decomposition; decay; putrefaction; demoralization; corruption; disintegration; expansion; resolution. **разложи́ть, -жу́, -жишь** pf. (impf. **разлага́ть, раскла́дывать**) put away; lay out; spread (out); distribute, apportion; break down; decompose; expand; resolve; demoralize, corrupt; ~ **костёр** make a fire; ~**ся** decompose; rot, decay; become demoralized; be corrupted; disintegrate, crack up, go to pieces.

разло́м, -а breaking; break. **разлома́ть, -а́ю, разломи́ть, -млю́, -мишь** pf. (impf. **разла́мывать**) break, break to pieces; pull down; ~**ся** break to pieces.

раз|лохма́тить, -а́чу pf.

разлу́ка, -и separation; parting. **разлуча́ть, -а́ю** impf., **разлучи́ть, -чу́** pf. separate, part, sever; ~**ся** separate, part.

разлюби́ть, -блю́, -бишь pf. cease to love, stop loving; stop liking, no longer like.

разля́гусь etc.: see **разле́чься**

разма́зать, -а́жу pf., **разма́зывать, -аю** impf. spread, smear.

разма́лывать, -аю impf. of **размоло́ть**

разма́тывать, -аю impf. of **размота́ть**

разма́х, -а (-у) sweep; swing; span; amplitude; scope, range, scale. **разма́хивать, -аю** impf.+i. swing; brandish; ~ **рука́ми** gesticulate. **разма́хиваться, -аюсь** impf., **размахну́ться, -ну́сь, -нёшься** pf. swing one's arm. **разма́шистый** sweeping.

размежева́ние, -я demarcation, delimitation. **размежева́ть, -жу́ю** pf., **размежёвывать, -аю** impf. divide out, delimit; ~**ся** fix one's boundaries; delimit functions or spheres of action.

размёл etc.: see **размести́**

размельча́ть, -а́ю impf., **раз|мельчи́ть, -чу́** pf. crumble, crush, pulverize.

размелю́ etc.: see **размоло́ть**

размéн, -а exchange; changing. **разме́нивать, -аю** impf., **разменя́ть, -я́ю** pf. change; ~**ся**+i. exchange; dissipate. **разме́нн|ый** exchange; ~**ая моне́та** (small) change.

разме́р, -а dimension(s); size; measurement; rate, amount; scale, extent; metre; measure; pl. proportions. **разме́ренный** measured. **разме́рить, -рю** pf., **размеря́ть, -я́ю** impf. measure off; measure.

размести́, -ету́, -етёшь; -мёл, -а́ pf. (impf. **размета́ть**) sweep clear; clear; sweep away.

размести́ть, -ещу́ pf. (impf. **размеща́ть**) place, accommodate; quarter; stow; distribute; ~**ся** take one's seat.

размета́ть, -а́ю impf. of **размести́**

разме́тить, -е́чу pf., **размеча́ть, -а́ю** impf. mark.

размеша́ть, -а́ю pf., **разме́шивать, -аю** impf. stir (in).

размеща́ть(ся, -а́ю(сь impf. of **размес-**

ти́ть(ся. размеще́ние, -я placing; accommodation; distribution, disposal, allocation; investment. **размещу́** etc.: see **размести́ть**

размина́ть(ся, -а́ю(сь impf. of **размя́ть(ся**

размину́ться, -ну́сь, -нёшься pf. pass (one another); cross; +c+i. pass; miss.

размножа́ть, -а́ю impf., **размно́жить, -жу** pf. multiply, manifold, duplicate; breed, rear; ~**ся** propagate itself; breed; spawn.

размозжи́ть, -жу́ pf. smash.

размо́лвка, -и tiff, disagreement.

размоло́ть, -мелю́, -ме́лешь pf. (impf. **разма́лывать**) grind.

размора́живать, -аю impf., **разморо́зить, -о́жу** pf. unfreeze, defreeze, defrost; ~**ся** unfreeze; become defrozen, defrosted.

размота́ть, -а́ю pf. (impf. **разма́тывать**) unwind, unreel; squander.

размыва́ть, -а́ет impf., **размы́ть, -о́ет** pf. wash away; erode.

размышле́ние, -я reflection; meditation, thought. **размышля́ть, -я́ю** impf. reflect, ponder; think (things) over.

размягча́ть, -а́ю impf., **размягчи́ть, -чу́** pf. soften; ~**ся** soften, grow soft. **размягче́ние, -я** softening.

размяка́ть, -а́ю impf., **раз|мя́кнуть, -ну; -мя́к** pf. soften, become soft.

раз|мя́ть, -зомну́, -зомнёшь pf. (impf. also **размина́ть**) knead; mash; ~**ся** soften, grow soft; stretch one's legs; limber up, loosen up.

разна́шивать, -аю impf. of **разноси́ть**

разнести́, -су́, -сёшь; -ёс, -ла́ pf. (impf. **разноси́ть**) carry, convey; take round, deliver; spread; enter, note down; smash, break up, destroy; blow up; scatter, disperse; impers.+a. swell (up); **у меня́ щёку разнесло́** my cheek is swollen.

разнима́ть, -а́ю impf. of **разня́ть**

ра́зниться, -нюсь impf. differ. **ра́зница, -ы** difference; disparity; **кака́я ~?** what difference does it make?

разно... in comb. different, vari-, hetero-. **разнобо́й, -я** lack of co-ordination; difference, disagreement. **~вéс, -а** (set of) weights. **~ви́дность, -и** variety. **~гла́сие, -я** difference, disagreement; discrepancy. **~голо́сый** discordant. **~кали́берный** of different calibres; mixed, heterogeneous. **~мы́слие, -я** difference of opinions. **~обра́зие, -я** variety, diversity; **для ~обра́зия** for a change. **~обра́зить, -а́жу** impf. vary, diversify. **~обра́зный** various, varied, diverse. **~рабо́чий** sb. unskilled labourer. **~речи́вый** contradictory, conflicting. **~ро́дный** heterogeneous. **~склоня́емый** irregularly declined. **~сторо́нний** many-sided; versatile; all-round; scalene. **~хара́ктерный** diverse, varied. **~цве́тный** of different colours; many-coloured, variegated, motley. **~чте́ние, -я** variant reading. **~шёрстный, ~шёрстый** with coats of different colours; mixed, ill-assorted. **~язы́чный** polyglot.

разноси́ть[1], **-ошу́**, **-о́сишь** *pf.* (*impf.* **разна́шивать**) break in, wear in; **~ся** become comfortable with wear.

разноси́ть[2], **-ошу́**, **-о́сишь** *impf. of* **разнести́**. **разно́ска**, **-и** delivery. **разно́сный** delivery; abusive; **~ые слова́** swear-words. **ра́зность**, **-и** difference; diversity. **разно́счик**, **-а** pedlar, hawker.

разношу́ *etc.: see* **разноси́ть**

разну́зданный unbridled, unruly.

ра́зн|ый different, differing; various, diverse; **~ое** *sb.* different things; various matters, any other business.

разня́ть, **-ниму́**, **-ни́мешь**; **ро́з-** *or* **разня́л**, **-а́**, **-о** *pf.* (*impf.* **разнима́ть**) take to pieces, dismantle, disjoint; part, separate.

разо... *see* **раз...**

разоблача́ть, **-а́ю** *impf.*, **разоблачи́ть**, **-чу́** *pf.* expose, unmask. **разоблаче́ние**, **-я** exposure, unmasking.

разобра́ть, **-зберу́**, **-рёшь**; **-а́л**, **-а́**, **-о** *pf.* (*impf.* **разбира́ть**) take; take to pieces, strip, dismantle; buy up; sort out; investigate, look into; analyse, parse; make out, understand; **ничего́ нельзя́ ~** one can't make head or tail of it; **~ся** sort things out; **+в+***p.* investigate, look into; understand.

разобща́ть, **-а́ю** *impf.*, **разобщи́ть**, **-щу́** *pf.* separate; estrange, alienate; disconnect, uncouple, disengage. **разобще́ние**, **-я** disconnection, uncoupling. **разобще́нно** *adv.* apart, separately.

разобью́ *etc.: see* **разби́ть**. **разовью́** *etc.: see* **разви́ть**

разогна́ть, **-згоню́**, **-о́нишь**; **-гна́л**, **-а́**, **-о** *pf.* (*impf.* **разгоня́ть**) scatter, drive away; disperse; dispel; drive fast, race; space. **~ся** gather speed, gather momentum.

разогну́ть, **-ну́**, **-нёшь** *pf.* (*impf.* **разгиба́ть**) unbend, straighten; **~ся** straighten (o.s.) up.

разогрева́ть, **-а́ю** *impf.*, **разогре́ть**, **-е́ю** *pf.* warm up; **~ся** warm up, grow warm.

разоде́ть(ся, **-е́ну(сь** *pf.* dress up.

разодра́ть, **-здеру́**, **-рёшь**; **-а́л**, **-а́**, **-о** *pf.* (*impf.* **раздира́ть**) tear (up); lacerate, harrow.

разожгу́ *etc.: see* **разже́чь**. **разожму́** *etc.: see* **разжа́ть**

разо|зли́ть, **-лю́** *pf.* anger, enrage; **~ся** get angry, fly into a rage.

разойти́сь, **-йду́сь**, **-йдёшься**; **-оше́лся**, **-оша́сь** *pf.* (*impf.* **расходи́ться**) go away; break up, disperse; branch off, diverge; radiate; differ, be at variance, conflict; part, separate, be divorced; dissolve, melt; be spent; be sold out; be out of print; gather speed; be carried away.

разолью́ *etc.: see* **разли́ть**

ра́зом *adv.* all at once, all at one go.

разомну́ *etc.: see* **размя́ть**

разорва́ть, **-ву́**, **-вёшь**; **-а́л**, **-а́**, **-о** *pf.* (*impf.* **разрыва́ть**) tear; break (off); sever; blow up, burst; **~ся** tear, become torn; break, snap; blow up, burst; explode, go off.

разоре́ние, **-я** ruin; destruction, havoc. **разори́тельный** ruinous; wasteful. **разори́ть**, **-рю́** *pf.* (*impf.* **разоря́ть**) ruin, bring to ruin; destroy, ravage; **~ся** ruin o.s., be ruined.

разоружа́ть, **-а́ю** *impf.*, **разоружи́ть**, **-жу́** *pf.* disarm; **~ся** disarm. **разоруже́ние**, **-я** disarmament.

разоря́ть(ся, **-я́ю(сь** *impf. of* **разори́ть(ся**

разосла́ть, **-ошлю́**, **-ошлёшь** *pf.* (*impf.* **рассыла́ть**) send round, distribute, circulate; send out, dispatch.

разостла́ть, **расстели́ть**, **-сстелю́**, **-те́лешь** *pf.* (*impf.* **расстила́ть**) spread (out); lay; **~ся** spread.

разотру́ *etc.: see* **растере́ть**

разочарова́ние, **-я** disappointment. **разочаро́ванный** disappointed, disillusioned.

разочарова́ть, **-ру́ю** *pf.*, **разочаро́вывать**, **-аю** *impf.* disappoint, disillusion, disenchant; **~ся** be disappointed, be disillusioned.

разочту́ *etc.: see* **расче́сть**. **разошёлся** *etc.: see* **разойти́сь**. **разошлю́** *etc.: see* **разосла́ть**. **разошью́** *etc.: see* **расши́ть**

разраба́тывать, **-аю** *impf.*, **разрабо́тать**, **-аю** *pf.* cultivate; work, exploit; work out, work up; develop, elaborate. **разрабо́тка**, **-и** cultivation; working, exploitation; working out, working up; elaboration; field; pit, working, quarry.

разража́ться, **-а́юсь** *impf.*, **разрази́ться**, **-ажу́сь** *pf.* break out; burst out; **~ сме́хом** burst out laughing.

разраста́ться, **-а́ется** *impf.*, **разрасти́сь**, **-тётся**; **-ро́сся**, **-ла́сь** *pf.* grow, grow up; grow thickly; spread.

разрежённ|ый; **-ён**, **-а́** rarefied, rare; **~ое простра́нство** vacuum.

разре́з, **-а** cut; slit, slash; section; point of view; **в ~е+***g.* from the point of view of, in the context of; **в э́том ~е** in this connection. **разреза́ть**, **-е́жу** *pf.*, **разреза́ть**, **-а́ю** *impf.* cut; slit. **разрезно́й** cutting; slit, with slits; **~ нож** paper-knife.

разреша́ть, **-а́ю** *impf.*, **разреши́ть**, **-шу́** *pf.* (+*d.*) allow, permit; authorize; (+*a.*) release, absolve; solve; settle; **разреши́те пройти́** let me pass; do you mind letting me pass?; **~ся** be allowed; be solved; be settled; **~ся от бре́мени** be delivered of; **«кури́ть не разреша́ется»** 'No smoking'. **разреше́ние**, **-я** permission; authorization; permit; solution; settlement. **разреши́мый** solvable.

разро́зненный uncoordinated; odd; incomplete, broken.

разро́сся *etc.: see* **разрасти́сь**. **разро́ю** *etc.: see* **разры́ть**

разруба́ть, **-а́ю** *impf.*, **разруби́ть**, **-блю́**, **-бишь** *pf.* cut, cleave; hack; chop.

разру́ха, **-и** ruin, collapse. **разруша́ть**, **-а́ю** *impf.*, **разру́шить**, **-шу** *pf.* destroy; demolish, wreck; ruin; frustrate, blast, blight; **~ся**

go to ruin, collapse. **разрушение**, -я destruction. **разрушительный** destructive.

разрыв, -а breach; break; gap; rupture, severance; burst, explosion. **разрывать¹(ся**, -аю(сь *impf. of* **разорвать(ся**

разрывать², -аю *impf. of* **разрыть**

разрывной explosive, bursting.

разрыть, -рою *pf.* (*impf.* **разрывать**) dig (up); turn upside down, rummage through.

раз|рыхлить, -лю *pf.*, **разрыхлять**, -яю *impf.* loosen; hoe.

разряд¹, -а category, rank; sort; class, rating.

разряд², -а discharge. **разрядить**, -яжу, -ядишь *pf.* (*impf.* **разряжать**) unload; discharge; space out; **~ся** run down; clear, ease.

разрядка, -и spacing (out); discharging; unloading; **~** напряжённости lessening of tension, détente.

разрядник, -а, -ница, -ы ranking player or competitor.

разряжать(ся, -аю(сь *impf. of* **разрядить(ся**

разубедить, -ежу *pf.*, **разубеждать**, -аю *impf.* dissuade; **~ся** change one's mind, change one's opinion.

разуверить, -рю *pf.*, **разуверять**, -яю *impf.* dissuade, undeceive; +в+*p.* argue out of; **~ся** (в+*p.*) lose faith (in), cease to believe.

разузнавать, -наю, -наёшь *impf.*, **разузнать**, -аю *pf.* (try to) find out; make inquiries.

разукрасить, -ашу *pf.*, **разукрашивать**, -аю *impf.* adorn, decorate, embellish.

разукрупнить(ся, -ню(сь *pf.*, **разукрупнять(ся**, -яю(сь *impf.* break up into smaller units.

разум, -а reason; mind, intellect; у него ум за **~** зашёл he is (was) at his wit's end.

разуметься, -еется *impf.* be understood, be meant; (само собой) разумеется of course; it stands to reason, it goes without saying.

разумный possessing reason; judicious, intelligent; sensible; reasonable; wise.

разуться, -уюсь *pf.* (*impf.* **разуваться**) take off one's shoes.

разучивать, -аю *impf.*, **разучить**, -чу, -чишь *pf.* study; learn (up). **разучиваться**, -аюсь *impf.*, **разучиться**, -чусь, -чишься *pf.* forget (how to).

разъ... *see* **раз...**

разъедать, -ает *impf. of* **разъесть**

разъединить, -ню *pf.*, **разъединять**, -яю *impf.* separate, disunite; disconnect; нас разъединили we were cut off.

разъедусь *etc.: see* **разъехаться**

разъезд, -а departure; dispersal; passing loop, siding (track); mounted patrol; travelling (about), journeys. **разъездной** travelling.

разъезжать, -аю *impf.* drive about, ride about; travel, wander; **~ся** *impf. of* **разъехаться**

разъесть, -ест, -едят; -ел *pf.* (*impf.* **разъ-**

едать) eat away; corrode.

разъехаться, -едусь *pf.* (*impf.* **разъезжаться**) depart; disperse; separate; (be able to) pass; pass one another, miss one another; slide apart.

разъярённый; -ён, -а furious, in a furious temper, frantic with rage. **разъярить**, -рю *pf.*, **разъярять**, -яю *impf.* infuriate, rouse to fury; **~ся** get furious, become frantic with rage.

разъяснение, -я explanation, elucidation; interpretation. **разъяснительный** explanatory, elucidatory. **разъясниваться**, -ается *impf.*, **разъясниться**, -ится *pf.* clear (up).

разъяснить, -ню *pf.*, **разъяснять**, -яю *impf.* explain, elucidate; interpret; **~ся** become clear, be cleared up.

разыграть, -аю *pf.*, **разыгрывать**, -аю *impf.* play (through); perform; draw; raffle; play a trick on; **~ся** rise, get up; run high.

разыскать, -ыщу, -ыщешь *pf.* find. **разыскивать**, -аю *impf.* look for, search for; **~ся** be wanted.

рай, -я, *loc.* -ю paradise; garden of Eden.

рай... *abbr.* (*of* **районный**) *in comb.* district. **райком**, -а district committee. **~совет**, -а district soviet.

район, -а a region; area; zone; (*administrative*) district. **районный** district.

райский heavenly.

рак, -а crawfish, crayfish; cancer, canker; Crab; Cancer.

ракета¹, -ы, **ракетка**, -и racket.

ракета², -ы rocket; (*ballistic*) missile; flare; **~носитель**, -я carrier rocket, launch vehicle. **ракетный** rocket; jet.

раковина, -ы shell; sink.

раковый cancer; cancerous.

ралли *nt. indecl.* rally. **раллист**, -а rallier.

рама, -ы frame; chassis, carriage; вставить в раму frame.

рамазан, -а (*relig.*) Ramadan.

рамка, -и frame; *pl.* framework, limits; в рамке framed.

рампа, -ы footlights.

рана, -ы wound. **ранение**, -я wounding; wound, injury. **раненый** wounded; injured.

ранец, -нца knapsack, haversack; satchel.

ранить, -ню *impf. & pf.* wound; injure.

ранний early. **рано** *pred.* it is (too) early. **рано** *adv.* early; **~** или поздно sooner or later. **раньше** *adv.* earlier; before; formerly; first (of all).

рапира, -ы foil. **рапирист**, -а, **рапиристка**, -и fencer.

рапорт, -а report. **рапортовать**, -тую *impf. & pf.* report.

рапсодия, -и rhapsody.

рас... *see* **раз...** .

раса, -ы race. **расизм**, -а rac(ial)ism. **расист**, -а rac(ial)ist.

раскаиваться, -аюсь *impf. of* **раскаяться**

раскалённый; -ён, -а scorching, burning hot;

incandescent. **раскали́ть**, -лю́ *pf.* (*impf.* **раскаля́ть**) make very hot, make red-hot, white-hot; ∼**ся** heat up, glow, become red-hot, white-hot. **раска́лывать(ся**, -аю(сь *impf.* of **расколо́ть(ся раскаля́ть(ся**, -я́ю(сь *impf.* of **раскали́ть(ся**. **раска́пывать**, -аю *impf.* of **раскопа́ть**

раска́т, -а roll, peal. **раската́ть**, -а́ю *pf.*, **раска́тывать**, -аю *impf.* roll, roll out, smooth out, level; drive, ride, (about). **раска́тистый** rolling, booming. **раската́ться**, -ачу́сь, -а́тишься *pf.*, **раска́тываться**, -аюсь *impf.* gather speed; roll away; peal, boom.

раскача́ть, -а́ю *pf.*, **раска́чивать**, -аю *impf.* swing; rock; loosen, shake loose; shake up, stir up; ∼**ся** swing, rock; shake loose; bestir o.s.

раска́яние, -я repentance, remorse. **рас|ка́яться**, -а́юсь *pf.* (*impf. also* **раска́иваться**) repent.

раски́дывать, -аю *impf.*, **раски́нуть**, -ну *pf.* stretch (out); spread; scatter; set up, pitch; ∼ **умо́м** ponder, think things over, consider; ∼**ся** spread out, lie, sprawl.

раскла́дка, -и laying; putting up; allotment. **раскладн|о́й** folding; ∼**а́я крова́ть** camp-bed. **раскладу́шка**, -и camp-bed. **раскла́дывать**, -аю *impf.* of **разложи́ть**

раскла́няться, -яюсь *pf.* bow; exchange bows; take leave.

раскле́ивать, -аю *impf.*, **раскле́ить**, -е́ю *pf.* unstick; stick (up), paste (up); ∼**ся** come unstuck; fall through, fail to come off; feel seedy, be off colour.

раскле́шенный flared.

раско́л, -а a split, division; schism; dissent. **рас|коло́ть**, -лю́, -лешь *pf.* (*impf. also* **раска́лывать**) split; chop; break; disrupt, break up; ∼**ся** split; crack, break. **раско́льник**, -а dissenter, schismatic. **раско́льнический** dissenting, schismatic.

раскопа́ть, -а́ю *pf.* (*impf.* **раска́пывать**) dig up, unearth, excavate. **раско́пка**, -и digging up; *pl.* excavation, excavations.

раско́сый slanting, slant.

раскраду́ *etc.*: *see* **раскра́сть**. **раскра́дывать**, -аю *impf.* of **раскра́сть**. **раскра́ивать**, -аю *impf.* of **раскрои́ть**

раскра́сить, -а́шу *pf.* (*impf.* **раскра́шивать**) paint, colour. **раскра́ска**, -и painting, colouring; colours, colour scheme.

раскрасне́ться, -е́юсь *pf.* flush, go red.

раскра́сть, -аду́, -адёшь *pf.* (*impf.* **раскра́дывать**) loot, clean out.

раскра́шивать, -аю *impf.* of **раскра́сить**

раскрепости́ть, -ощу́ *pf.*, **раскрепоща́ть**, -а́ю *impf.* set free, liberate, emancipate. **раскрепоще́ние**, -я liberation, emancipation.

раскритикова́ть, -кую *pf.* criticize harshly, slate.

раскрои́ть, -ою́ *pf.* (*impf.* **раскра́ивать**) cut out; cut open.

рас|кроши́ть(ся, -шу́(сь, -шишь(ся *pf.* **раскрою́** *etc.*: *see* **раскры́ть**

раскрути́ть, -учу́, -у́тишь *pf.*, **раскру́чивать**, -аю *impf.* untwist, undo; ∼**ся** come untwisted, come undone.

раскрыва́ть, -а́ю *impf.*, **раскры́ть**, -о́ю *pf.* open; expose, bare; reveal, disclose, lay bare; discover; ∼**ся** open; uncover o.s.; come out, come to light, be discovered.

раскупа́ть, -а́ет *impf.*, **раскупи́ть**, -у́пит *pf.* buy up.

раску́поривать, -аю *impf.*, **раску́порить**, -рю *pf.* uncork, open.

раскуси́ть, -ушу́, -у́сишь *pf.*, **раску́сывать**, -аю *impf.* bite through; get to the core of; see through.

раску́тать, -аю *pf.* unwrap.

ра́совый racial.

распа́д, -а disintegration, break-up; collapse; decomposition. **распада́ться**, -а́ется *impf.* of **распа́сться**

распа́ивать, -аю *impf.* of **распая́ть**

распакова́ть, -ку́ю *pf.*, **распако́вывать**, -аю *impf.* unpack; ∼**ся** unpack; come undone.

распа́рывать(ся, -аю(сь *impf.* of **распоро́ть(ся**

распа́сться, -адётся *pf.* (*impf.* **распада́ться**) disintegrate, fall to pieces; break up; collapse; decompose, dissociate.

распаха́ть, -ашу́, -а́шешь *pf.*, **распа́хивать**[1], -аю *impf.* plough up.

распа́хивать[2], -аю *impf.*, **распахну́ть**, -ну́, -нёшь *pf.* open (wide); fling open, throw open; ∼**ся** open; fly open, swing open; throw open one's coat.

распая́ть, -я́ю *pf.* (*impf.* **распа́ивать**) unsolder; ∼**ся** come unsoldered.

распева́ть, -а́ю *impf.* sing.

распеча́тать, -аю *pf.*, **распеча́тывать**, -аю *impf.* open; unseal; print out. **распеча́тка**, -и printout.

распи́вочн|ый for consumption on the premises; ∼**ая** *sb.* tavern, bar.

распи́ливать, -аю *impf.*, **распили́ть**, -лю́, -лишь *pf.* saw up.

распина́ть, -а́ю *impf.* of **распя́ть**

расписа́ние, -я time-time, schedule. **расписа́ть**, -ишу́, -и́шешь *pf.*, **распи́сывать**, -аю *impf.* enter; assign, allot; paint; decorate; ∼**ся** sign; register one's marriage; +**в**+*p.* sign for; acknowledge; testify to. **распи́ска**, -и receipt. **расписно́й** painted, decorated.

рас|пла́вить, -влю *pf.*, **расплавля́ть**, -я́ю *impf.* melt, fuse. **расплавле́ние**, -я melting, fusion.

распла́каться, -а́чусь *pf.* burst into tears.

распласта́ть, -а́ю *pf.* spread; flatten; split; divide into layers; ∼**ся** sprawl.

распла́та, -ы payment; retribution; **час распла́ты** day of reckoning. **расплати́ться**, -ачу́сь, -а́тишься *pf.*, **распла́чиваться**,

-аюсь *impf.* (+**с**+*i.*) pay off; settle accounts, get even; +**за**+*a.* pay for.

расплеска́ть(ся, **-ещу́(сь**, **-е́щешь(ся** *pf.*, **расплёскивать(ся**, **-аю(сь** *impf.* spill.

расплести́, **-ету́**, **-етёшь**; **-ёл**, **-а́** *pf.*, **расплета́ть**, **-а́ю** *impf.* unplait; untwine, untwist, undo; **~сь** come unplaited, come undone; untwine, untwist.

рас|плоди́ть(ся, **-ожу́(сь** *pf.*

расплыва́ться, **-а́ется** *impf.*, **расплы́ться**, **-ывётся**; **-ы́лся**, **-а́сь** *pf.* run; spread. **расплы́вчатый** dim, indistinct; diffuse, vague.

расплю́щивать, **-аю** *impf.*, **расплю́щить**, **-щу** *pf.* flatten out, hammer out.

распну́ *etc.*: *see* **распя́ть**

распознава́емый recognizable, identifiable. **распознава́ть**, **-наю́**, **-наёшь** *impf.*, **распозна́ть**, **-а́ю** *pf.* recognize, identify; distinguish; diagnose.

располага́ть, **-а́ю** *impf.* (*pf.* **расположи́ть**) +*i.* dispose of, have at one's disposal, have available; **я не о́чень** ~ **вре́менем** I have no time to spare. **располага́ться**, **-а́юсь** *impf. of* **расположи́ться располага́ющий** prepossessing.

располза́ться, **-а́ется** *impf.*, **расползти́сь**, **-зётся**; **-о́лзся**, **-зла́сь** *pf.* crawl, crawl away; ravel out; give (at the seams).

расположе́ние, **-я** disposition; arrangement; situation, location; inclination; tendency, propensity; bias, penchant; favour, liking; sympathies; mood, humour. **располо́женный** well-disposed; disposed, inclined, in the mood; **я не о́чень располо́жен сего́дня рабо́тать** I don't feel much like working today. **расположи́ть**, **-жу́**, **-жишь** *pf.* (*impf.* **располага́ть**) dispose; arrange, set out; win over, gain; **~ся** settle down; compose o.s., make o.s. comfortable.

рас|поро́ть, **-рю́**, **-решь** *pf.* (*impf. also* **распа́рывать**) unpick, undo, rip; **~ся** rip, come undone.

распоряди́тель, **-я** *m.* manager. **распоряди́тельность**, **-и** good management; efficiency; **отсу́тствие распоряди́тельности** mismanagement. **распоряди́тельный** capable; efficient; active. **распоряди́ться**, **-яжу́сь** *pf.*, **распоряжа́ться**, **-а́юсь** *impf.* order, give orders; see; +*i.* manage, deal with, dispose of. **распоря́док**, **-дка** order; routine; **пра́вила вну́треннего распоря́дка на фа́брике** factory regulations. **распоряже́ние**, **-я** order; instruction, direction; disposal, command; **быть в распоряже́нии**+*g.* be at the disposal of; **до осо́бого распоряже́ния** until further notice.

распра́ва, **-ы** punishment, execution; violence; reprisal; **крова́вая** ~ massacre, butchery.

распра́вить, **-влю** *pf.*, **расправля́ть**, **-я́ю** *impf.* straighten; smooth out; spread, stretch; ~ **кры́лья** spread one's wings.

распра́виться, **-влюсь** *pf.*, **расправля́ться**,

-я́юсь *impf.* **с**+*i.* deal with, make short work of; give short shrift to.

распределе́ние, **-я** distribution; allocation, assignment. **распредели́тель**, **-я** *m.* distributor; retailer. **распредели́тельный** distributive, distributing; ~ **щит** switchboard. **распредели́ть**, **-лю́** *pf.*, **распределя́ть**, **-я́ю** *impf.* distribute; allocate, allot, assign; ~ **своё вре́мя** allocate one's time.

распродава́ть, **-даю́**, **-даёшь** *impf.*, **распрода́ть**, **-а́м**, **-а́шь**, **-а́ст**, **-ади́м**, **-о́дал**, **-а́**, **-о** *pf.* sell off; sell out. **распрода́жа**, **-и** sale; clearance sale.

распростёрт|**ый** outstretched; prostrate, prone; **с** ~**ыми объя́тиями** with open arms.

распрости́ться, **-ощу́сь** *pf.*, **распроща́ться**, **-а́юсь** *pf.* take leave, bid farewell.

распростране́ние, **-я** spreading, diffusion; dissemination; circulation. **распространённый**; **-ён**, **-а́** widespread, prevalent. **распространи́ть**, **-ню́** *pf.*, **распространя́ть**, **-я́ю** *impf.* spread; give currency to; diffuse; disseminate, propagate; popularize; extend; give off, give out; **~ся** spread; extend; apply; enlarge, expatiate, dilate (**о**+*p.* on).

распроща́ться *etc.*: *see* **распрости́ться**

ра́спря, **-и**; *g.pl.* **-ей** quarrel, feud.

распряга́ть, **-а́ю** *impf.*, **распря́чь**, **-ягу́**, **-яжёшь**; **-я́г**, **-ла́** *pf.* unharness.

распуска́ть, **-а́ю** *impf.*, **распусти́ть**, **-ущу́**, **-у́стишь** *pf.* dismiss; dissolve; disband; let out; relax; let get out of hand; spoil; dissolve; melt; spread; ~ **во́лосы** loosen one's hair; ~ **на кани́кулы** dismiss for the holidays; **~ся** open, come out; come loose; dissolve; melt; get out of hand; let o.s. go.

распу́тать, **-аю** *pf.* (*impf.* **распу́тывать**) disentangle, untangle; unravel; untie, loose; puzzle out.

распу́тица, **-ы** season of bad roads; slush.

распу́тный dissolute, dissipated, debauched.

распу́тывать, **-аю** *impf. of* **распу́тать**

распу́тье, **-я** crossroads; parting of the ways.

распуха́ть, **-а́ю** *impf.*, **распу́хнуть**, **-ну**; **-у́х** *pf.* swell (up).

распу́щенный undisciplined; spoilt; dissolute, dissipated.

распыле́ние, **-я** dispersion, scattering; spraying; atomization. **распыли́тель**, **-я** *m.* spray, atomizer. **распыли́ть**, **-лю́** *pf.*, **распыля́ть**, **-я́ю** *impf.* spray; atomize; pulverize; disperse; scatter; **~ся** disperse, get scattered.

распя́тие, **-я** crucifixion; crucifix, cross. **распя́ть**, **-пну́**, **-пнёшь** *pf.* (*impf.* **распина́ть**) crucify.

расса́да, **-ы** seedlings. **рассади́ть**, **-ажу́**, **-а́дишь** *pf.*, **расса́живать**, **-аю** *impf.* plant out, transplant; seat, offer seats; separate, seat separately.

расса́живаться, **-ается** *impf. of* **рассе́сться. расса́сываться**, **-ается** *impf. of* **рассоса́ться**

рассвести́, **-етёт**; **-ело́** *pf.*, **рассвета́ть**, **-а́ет**

impf. dawn; **рассветáет** day is breaking; **совершéнно рассвелó** it is (was) broad daylight. **рассвéт, -а** dawn, daybreak.

рас|свирипéть, -éю *pf.*

расседлáть, -áю *pf.* unsaddle.

рассéивание, -я dispersion; dispersal, scattering, dissipation. **рассéивать(ся, -аю(сь** *impf. of* **рассéять(ся**

рассекáть, -áю *impf. of* **рассéчь**

расселéние, -я settling, resettlement; separation.

рассéлина, -ы cleft, fissure; crevasse.

расселúть, -лю *pf.*, **расселя́ть, -я́ю** *impf.* settle, resettle; separate, settle apart.

рас|сердúть(ся, -жý(сь, -рдишь(ся *pf.* **рассéрженный** angry.

рассéсться, -ся́дусь *pf.* (*impf.* **рассáживаться**) take seats; sprawl.

рассéчь, -екý, -ечёшь; -ёк, -лá *pf.* (*impf.* **рассекáть**) cut, cut through; cleave.

рассéянность, -и absent-mindedness, distraction; diffusion; dispersion; dissipation. **рассéянный** absent-minded; diffused; scattered, dispersed; dissipated; ~ **свет** diffused light. **рассéять, -éю** *pf.* (*impf.* **рассéивать**) sow, broadcast; place at intervals, dot about; disperse, scatter; dispel; ~**ся** disperse, scatter; clear, lift; divert o.s., have some distraction.

расскáз, -а story, tale; account, narrative. **рассказáть, -ажý, -áжешь** *pf.*, **расскáзывать, -аю** *impf.* tell, narrate, recount. **рассскáзчик, -а** story-teller, narrator.

расслáбить, -блю *pf.*, **расслабля́ть, -я́ю** *impf.* weaken, enfeeble; enervate. **расслаблéние, -я** weakening, enfeeblement; relaxation.

расслáивать(ся, -аю(сь *impf. of* **расслоúть(ся**

расслéдование, -я investigation, examination; inquiry; **произвестú** ~+*g.* hold an inquiry into. **расслéдовать, -дую** *impf. & pf.* investigate, look into, hold an inquiry into.

расслоéние, -я stratification; exfoliation. **расслоúть, -ою** *pf.* (*impf.* **расслáивать**) divide into layers, stratify; ~**ся** become stratified; exfoliate, flake off.

расслы́шать, -шу *pf.* catch.

рассмáтривать, -аю *impf. of* **рассмотрéть**; examine, scrutinize; regard as, consider.

рас|смея́ться, -ею́сь, -еёшься *pf.* burst out laughing.

рассмотрéние, -я examination, scrutiny; consideration; **предстáвить на** ~ submit for consideration. **рассмотрéть, -рю́, -ришь** *pf.* (*impf.* **рассмáтривать**) examine, consider; descry, discern, make out.

рассовáть, -сую́, -суёшь *pf.*, **рассóвывать, -аю** *impf.* по+*d.* shove in, stuff into.

рассóл, -а (-у) brine; pickle.

рассóриться, -рюсь *pf.* с+*i.* fall out with, quarrel with.

рас|сортировáть, -рую́ *pf.*, **рассортирóвывать, -аю** *impf.* sort out.

рассосáться, -сётся *pf.* (*impf.* **рассáсываться**) resolve.

рассóхнуться, -нется; -óхся *pf.* (*impf.* **рассыхáться**) warp, crack, shrink.

расспрáшивать, -аю *impf.*, **расспросúть, -ошý, -óсишь** *pf.* question, make inquiries of.

рассрóчить, -чу *pf.* spread (over), divide into instalments. **рассрóчка, -и** instalment; **в рассрóчку** in instalments, by instalments.

расставáние, -я parting. **расставáться, -таю́сь, -таёшься** *impf. of* **расстáться**

расстáвить, -влю *pf.*, **расставля́ть, -я́ю** *impf.*, **расстанáвливать, -аю** *impf.* place, arrange, post; move apart, set apart; let out; ~ **часовы́х** post sentries. **расстанóвка, -и** placing; arrangement; pause; spacing; **говорúть с расстанóвкой** speak slowly and deliberately.

расстáться, -áнусь *pf.* (*impf.* **расставáться**) part, separate; +**с**+*i.* leave; give up.

расстёгивать, -аю *impf.*, **расстегнýть, -нý, -нёшь** *pf.* undo, unfasten; unbutton; unhook, unclasp, unbuckle; ~**ся** come undone; undo one's coat.

расстелúть(ся, *etc.: see* **разостлáть(ся. расстилáть(ся, -áю(сь** *impf. of* **разостлáть(ся**

расстоя́ние, -я distance, space, interval; **на далёком расстоя́нии** a long way off, in the far distance.

расстрáивать(ся, -аю(сь *impf. of* **расстрóить(ся**

расстрéл, -а execution, shooting. **расстрéливать, -аю** *impf.*, **расстреля́ть, -я́ю** *pf.* shoot.

расстрóенный disordered, deranged; upset; out of tune. **расстрóить, -ою** *pf.* (*impf.* **расстрáивать**) upset; thwart; frustrate; put out; disorder, derange; disturb; throw into confusion; unsettle; put out of tune; ~ **ряды́ протúвника** break the enemy's ranks; ~**ся** be frustrated; be shattered; be upset, be put out; get out of tune; fall into confusion, fall apart; fall through. **расстрóйство, -а** disorder, disarray; derangement; confusion; frustration; discomposure; ~ **желýдка** indigestion; diarrhoea.

расступáться, -áется *impf.*, **расступúться, -ýпится** *pf.* part, make way.

расстыковáться, -кýется *pf.* disengage, cast off. **расстыкóвка, -и** disengagement, casting off.

рассудúтельность, -и reasonableness; good sense. **рассудúтельный** reasonable; soberminded; sensible. **рассудúть, -ужý, -ýдишь** *pf.* judge, arbitrate; think, consider; decide. **рассýдок, -дка** reason; intellect, mind; good sense. **рассуждáть, -áю** *impf.* reason; deliberate; debate; argue; +**о**+*p.* discuss. **рассуждéние, -я** reasoning; discussion; debate; argument; **без рассуждéний** without arguing.

рассую́ *etc.*: *see* **рассова́ть**

рассчи́танный calculated, deliberate; meant, intended, designed. **рассчита́ть, -а́ю** *pf.*, **рассчи́тывать, -аю** *impf.*, **расче́сть, разочту́, -тёшь; расчёл, разочла́** *pf.* calculate; compute; rate; count, reckon; expect, hope; rely, depend; ~**ся** settle accounts, reckon.

рассыла́ть, -а́ю *impf. of* **разосла́ть. рассы́лка, -и** delivery, distribution. **рассы́льный** *sb.* messenger; delivery man.

рассыпа́ть, -плю *pf.*, **рассыпа́ть, -а́ю** *impf.* spill; strew, scatter; ~**ся** spill, scatter; spread out, deploy; crumble; go to pieces, disintegrate; be profuse; ~**ся в похвала́х**+*d.* shower praises on. **рассыпно́й** (sold) loose. **рассы́пчатый** friable; short, crumbly; floury.

рассыха́ться, -а́ется *impf. of* **рассо́хнуться. рассяду́сь** *etc.*: *see* **рассе́сться.**

раста́лкивать, -аю *impf. of* **растолка́ть растапливать(ся, -аю(сь** *impf. of* **растопи́ть(ся раста́птывать, -аю** *impf. of* **растопта́ть**

растаска́ть, -а́ю *pf.*, **раста́скивать, -аю** *impf.*, **растащи́ть, -щу́, -щишь** *pf.* pilfer, filch.

раста́чивать, -аю *impf. of* **расточи́ть. растащи́ть** *see* **растаска́ть. рас|та́ять, -а́ю** *pf.*

раство́р², -а (extent of) opening, span. **раство́р¹, -а** solution; mortar. **раствори́мый** soluble; ~ **ко́фе** instant coffee. **раствори́тель, -я** *m.* solvent. **раствори́ть¹, -рю́** *pf.* (*impf.* **растворя́ть**) dissolve; mix; ~**ся** dissolve.

раствори́ть², -рю́, -ришь *pf.* (*impf.* **растворя́ть**) open; ~**ся** open.

растворя́ть(ся, -я́ю(сь *impf. of* **раствори́ть(ся. растека́ться, -а́ется** *impf. of* **расте́чься**

расте́ние, -я plant.

растере́ть, разотру́, -трёшь; растёр *pf.* (*impf.* **растира́ть**) grind; pound; triturate; spread; rub; massage; ~**ся** rub o.s. briskly.

растерза́ть, -а́ю *pf.*, **расте́рзывать, -аю** *impf.* tear to pieces; lacerate, harrow.

расте́рянность, -и confusion, perplexity, dismay. **расте́рянный** confused, perplexed, dismayed. **растеря́ть, -я́ю** *pf.* lose; ~**ся** get lost; lose one's head, get confused.

расте́чься, -ечётся, -еку́тся; -тёкся, -ла́сь *pf.* (*impf.* **растека́ться**) spill; run; spread.

расти́, -ту́, -тёшь; рос, -ла́ *impf.* grow; increase; grow up; advance, develop.

растира́ние, -я grinding; rubbing, massage. **растира́ть(ся, -а́ю(сь** *impf. of* **растере́ть(ся**

расти́тельность, -и vegetation; hair. **расти́тельный** vegetable. **расти́ть, ращу́** *impf.* raise, bring up; train; grow, cultivate.

растолка́ть, -а́ю *pf.* (*impf.* **раста́лкивать**) push apart; shake. **растолкну́ть, -ну́, -нёшь** *pf.* part forcibly, push apart.

растолкова́ть, -ку́ю *pf.*, **растолко́вывать, -аю** *impf.* explain, make clear.

рас|толо́чь, -лку́, -лчёшь; -ло́к, -лкла́ *pf.*

растолсте́ть, -е́ю *pf.* put on weight, grow stout.

растопи́ть¹, -плю́, -пишь *pf.* (*impf.* **раста́пливать**) melt; thaw; ~**ся** melt.

растопи́ть², -плю́, -пишь *pf.* (*impf.* **раста́пливать**) light, kindle; ~**ся** begin to burn. **расто́пка, -и** lighting; kindling, firewood.

растопта́ть, -пчу́, -пчешь *pf.* (*impf.* **раста́птывать**) trample, stamp on, crush.

расторга́ть, -а́ю *impf.*, **расто́ргнуть, -ну; -о́рг** *pf.* cancel, dissolve, annul, abrogate. **расторже́ние, -я** cancellation, dissolution, annulment, abrogation.

растороп́ный quick, prompt, smart; efficient.

расточа́ть, -а́ю *impf.*, **расточи́ть¹, -чу́** *pf.* waste, squander, dissipate; lavish, shower. **расточи́тельный** extravagant, wasteful.

расточи́ть², -чу́, -чишь *pf.* (*impf.* **раста́чивать**) bore, bore out.

растрави́ть, -влю́, -вишь *pf.*, **растравля́ть, -я́ю** *impf.* irritate.

растра́та, -ы spending; waste; squandering; embezzlement. **растра́тить, -а́чу** *pf.*, **растра́чивать, -аю** *impf.* spend; waste, squander, dissipate; fritter away; embezzle. **растра́тчик, -а** embezzler.

растрёпанный tousled, dishevelled; tattered. **рас|трепа́ть, -плю́, -плешь** *pf.* disarrange; tousle, dishevel; tatter, tear; ~**ся** get tousled; be dishevelled; get tattered.

растре́скаться, -ается *pf.*, **растре́скиваться, -ается** *impf.* crack, chap.

растро́гать, -аю *pf.* move, touch; ~**ся** be moved.

растя́гивать, -аю *impf.*, **растяну́ть, -ну́, -нешь** *pf.* stretch (out); strain, sprain; prolong, drag out; ~ **себе́ мы́шцу** pull a muscle; ~**ся** stretch; lengthen; be prolonged, drag out; stretch o.s. out, sprawl; measure one's length, fall flat. **растяже́ние, -я** tension; stretch, stretching; strain, sprain. **растяжи́мость, -и** stretchability; tensility; extensibility. **растяжи́мый** tensile; extensible; stretchable. **растя́нутый** stretched; long-winded, prolix.

рас|фасова́ть, -су́ю *pf.*

расформирова́ние, -я breaking up; disbandment. **расформирова́ть, -ру́ю** *pf.*, **расформиро́вывать, -аю** *impf.* break up; disband.

расха́живать, -аю *impf.* walk about; pace up and down; ~ **по ко́мнате** pace the floor.

расхва́ливать, -аю *impf.*, **расхвали́ть, -лю́, -лишь** *pf.* lavish, shower, praises on.

расхва́рываться, -аюсь *impf. of* **расхвора́ться**

расхвата́ть, -а́ю *pf.*, **расхва́тывать, -аю** *impf.* seize on, buy up.

расхвора́ться, -а́юсь *pf.* (*impf.* **расхва́рываться**) fall (seriously) ill.

расхити́тель, -я *m.* plunderer. **расхи́тить, -и́щу** *pf.*, **расхища́ть, -а́ю** *impf.* plunder, misappropriate. **расхище́ние, -я** plundering, misappropriation.

расхляба́нный loose; unstable; lax, undisciplined.

расхо́д, -а expenditure; consumption; outlay; expenses; *pl.* expenses, outlay, cost; **списа́ть в ~** write off. **расходи́ться, -ожу́сь, -о́дишься** *impf. of* **разойти́сь. расхо́дование, -я** expense, expenditure. **расхо́довать, -дую** *impf.* (*pf.* **из~**) spend, expend; use up, consume; **~ся** spend money; be spent, be consumed. **расхожде́ние, -я** divergence; **~ во мне́ниях** difference of opinion.

расхола́живать, -аю *impf.*, **расхолоди́ть, -ожу́** *pf.* damp the ardour of.

расхоте́ть, -очу́, -о́чешь, -оти́м *pf.* cease to want, no longer want.

расхохота́ться, -очу́сь, -о́чешься *pf.* burst out laughing.

расцара́пать, -аю *pf.* scratch (all over).

расцвести́, -ету́, -ете́шь; -ёл, -а́ *pf.*, **расцвета́ть, -а́ю** *impf.* blossom, come into bloom; flourish. **расцве́т, -а** bloom, blossoming (out); flourishing; flowering, heyday; **в ~е сил** in the prime of life, in one's prime. **расцве́тка, -и** colours; colouring.

расце́нивать, -аю *impf.*, **расцени́ть, -ню́, -нишь** *pf.* estimate, assess, value; rate; consider, think. **расце́нка, -и** valuation; price; (wage-)rate.

расцепи́ть, -плю́, -пишь *pf.*, **расцепля́ть, -я́ю** *impf.* uncouple, unhook; disengage, release. **расцепле́ние, -я** uncoupling, unhooking; disengaging, release.

расчеса́ть, -ешу́, -е́шешь *pf.* (*impf.* **расчёсывать**) comb; scratch. **расчёска, -и** comb.

расче́сть *etc.: see* **рассчита́ть. расчёсывать, -аю** *impf. of* **расчеса́ть**

расчёт[1], -а calculation; computation; estimate, reckoning; gain, advantage; settling, settlement; dismissal, discharge; **быть в ~** be quits, be even; **дать ~**+*d.* dismiss, sack; **не принима́ть в ~** leave out of account; **приня́ть в ~** take into consideration. **расчётливый** economical, thrifty; careful. **расчётный** calculation, computation, reckoning; pay; accounts; rated, calculated, designed; **~ день** pay-day; **~ отде́л** accounts department.

расчи́стить, -и́щу *pf.*, **расчища́ть, -а́ю** *impf.* clear; **~ся** clear. **расчи́стка, -и** clearing.

расчлене́ние, -я dismemberment; partition. **расч|лени́ть, -ню́** *pf.*, **расчленя́ть, -я́ю** *impf.* dismember; partition; break up, divide.

расшата́ть, -а́ю *pf.*, **расша́тывать, -аю** *impf.* shake loose, make rickety; shatter, impair; **~ся** get loose, get rickety; go to pieces, crack up.

расшеве́ливать, -аю *impf.*, **расшевели́ть, -лю́, -е́лишь** *pf.* stir, shake; rouse.

расшиба́ть, -а́ю *impf.*, **расшиби́ть, -бу́,**

-бёшь; -и́б *pf.* break up, smash to pieces; hurt; knock, stub; **~ся** hurt o.s., knock o.s.; **~ся в лепёшку** go flat out.

расшива́ть, -а́ю *impf. of* **расши́ть. расшивно́й** embroidered.

расшире́ние, -я broadening, widening; expansion; extension; dilation, dilatation; distension. **расши́рить, -рю** *pf.*, **расширя́ть, -я́ю** *impf.* broaden, widen; enlarge; expand; extend; **~ся** broaden, widen, gain in breadth; extend; expand, dilate.

расши́ть, разошью́, -шьёшь *pf.* (*impf.* **расшива́ть**) embroider; undo, unpick.

расшифрова́ть, -ру́ю *pf.*, **расшифро́вывать, -аю** *impf.* decipher, decode; interpret.

расшнурова́ть, -ру́ю *pf.*, **расшнуро́вывать, -аю** *impf.* unlace, undo.

расще́дриться, -рюсь be generous, turn generous.

расще́лина, -ы cleft, crevice, crack.

расще́п, -а split. **расщепи́ть, -плю́** *pf.*, **расщепля́ть, -я́ю** *impf.* split; splinter; break up; **~ся** split, splinter. **расщепле́ние, -я** splitting; splintering; fission; break-up, disintegration; **~ ядра́** nuclear fission. **расщепля́емый, расщепля́ющийся** fissile, fissionable.

ратифика́ция, -и ratification. **ратифици́ровать, -рую** *impf. & pf.* ratify.

рафина́д, -а lump sugar.

рахи́т, -а rickets.

рационализа́тор, -а efficiency expert. **рационализа́торский** rationalization. **рационализа́ция, -и** rationalization, improvement. **рационализи́ровать, -рую** *impf. & pf.* rationalize, improve. **рациона́льный** rational; efficient.

ра́ция, -и portable radio transmitter; walkie-talkie.

рвану́ться, -ну́сь, -нёшься *pf.* dart, rush, dash.

рва́ный torn; lacerated. **рвать[1], рву, рвёшь; рвал, -а́, -о** *impf.* tear; rend; rip; pull out, tear out; pick, pluck; blow up; break off, sever; **~ и мета́ть** rant and rave; **~ся** break; tear, burst, explode; strive, be eager, be bursting; **~ с привязи** strain at the leash.

рвать[2], рвёт; рва́ло *impf.* (*pf.* **вы́~**), *impers.*+*a.* vomit, be sick, throw up; **его́ рвёт** he's vomiting.

рве́ние, -я zeal, fervour, ardour.

рво́та, -ы vomiting; retching; vomit. **рво́т|ный** emetic; **~ое** *sb.* emetic.

ре *nt. indecl.* (*mus.*) D; ray.

реабилита́ция, -и rehabilitation. **реабилити́ровать, -рую** *impf. & pf.* rehabilitate.

реаги́ровать, -рую *impf.* (*pf.* **от~, про~**) react; respond.

реакти́вный reactive; jet, jet-propelled; rocket; **~ самолёт** jet (plane). **реа́ктор, -а** reactor, pile.

реакционе́р, -а reactionary. **реакцио́нный** reactionary. **реа́кция, -и** reaction.

реали́зм, -а realism. реализова́ть, -зу́ю *impf. & pf.* realize (*assets*). реали́ст, -а realist. реалисти́ческий realistic. реа́льность, -и reality; practicability. реа́льный real; realizable, practicable, workable; realistic; practical.

ребёнок, -нка; *pl.* ребя́та, -я́т *and* де́ти, -е́й child; infant.

ребро́, -а́; *pl.* рёбра, -бер rib; fin; edge, verge; поста́вить вопро́с ∼м put a question point-blank.

ребя́та, -я́т *pl.* children; boys, lads. ребя́ческий child's; childish; infantile, puerile. ребя́чество, -а childishness, puerility. ребя́чий childish. ребя́читься, -чусь *impf.* behave like a child.

рёв, -а roar; bellow, howl.

рев... *abbr.* (*of* революцио́нный, ревизио́нный) *in comb.* revolutionary; inspection. ревко́м, -а revolutionary committee. ∼коми́ссия, -и Inspection Board.

рева́нш, -а revenge; return match.

реве́ть, -ву́, -вёшь *impf.* roar; bellow; howl.

ревизио́нный inspection; auditing. реви́зия, -и inspection; audit; revision. ревизова́ть, -зу́ю *impf. & pf.* (*pf. also* об∼) inspect; revise. ревизо́р, -а inspector.

ревмати́зм, -а rheumatism; rheumatics; суставно́й ∼ rheumatic fever. ревмати́ческий rheumatic; ∼ артри́т rheumatoid arthritis.

ревни́вый jealous. ревнова́ть, -ну́ю *impf.* (*pf.* при∼) be jealous. ре́вностный zealous, earnest, fervent. ре́вность, -и jealousy; zeal, earnestness, fervour.

револьве́р, -а revolver, pistol.

революционе́р, -а revolutionary. революцио́нный revolutionary. револю́ция, -и revolution.

ре́гби *nt. indecl.* rugby (football); люби́тельское ∼ rugby union; профессиона́льное ∼ rugby league.

реги́стр, -а register. регистра́тор, -а registrar. регистрату́ра, -ы registry. регистра́ция, -и registration. регистри́ровать, -рую *impf. & pf.* (*pf. also* за∼) register, record; ∼ся register; register one's marriage.

регла́мент, -а regulations; standing orders; time-limit; установи́ть ∼ agree on procedure. регламента́ция, -и regulation. регламенти́ровать, -рую *impf. & pf.* regulate.

регресси́вный regressive. регресси́ровать, -рую *impf.* regress.

регули́рование, -я regulation, control; adjustment. регули́ровать, -рую *impf.* (*pf.* за∼, от∼, у∼) regulate; control; adjust, tune. регулиро́вщик, -а traffic controller; man on point duty.

регуля́рность, -и regularity. регуля́рный regular. регуля́тор, -а regulator; control.

ред... *abbr.* (*of* редакцио́нный) *in comb.* editorial. редколле́гия, -и editorial board. ∼отде́л, -а editorial department. ∼сове́т,

-а editorial committee.

...ред *abbr.* (*of* реда́ктор) *in comb.* editor.

редакти́рование, -я editing. редакти́ровать, -рую *impf.* (*pf.* от∼) edit, be editor of; word. реда́ктор, -а editor; гла́вный ∼ editor-in-chief; ∼ отде́ла sub-editor. реда́кторский editorial. редакцио́нн|ый editorial, editing; ∼ая коми́ссия drafting committee. реда́кция, -и editorial staff; editorial office; editing; wording; под реда́кцией+g. edited by.

реде́ть, -е́ет *impf.* (*pf.* по∼) thin, thin out.

ре́дис, -а radishes. реди́ска, -и radish.

ре́дк|ий; -док, -дка́, -о thin; sparse; rare; uncommon. ре́дко *adv.* sparsely; far apart; rarely, seldom. ре́дкость, -и rarity; curiosity, curio.

ре́дька, -и black radish.

рее́стр, -а list, roll, register.

режи́м, -а régime; routine; procedure; regimen; mode of operation; conditions; rate; ∼ пита́ния diet.

режиссёр, -а producer; director. режисси́ровать, -рую *impf.* produce; direct.

ре́жущий cutting, sharp. ре́зать, -е́жу *impf.* (*pf.* за∼, про∼, с∼) cut; slice; carve; engrave; pass close to, shave; cut into; kill, slaughter, knife; speak bluntly; ∼ся be cut, come through; gamble.

резви́ться, -влю́сь *impf.* sport, gambol, play. ре́звый frisky, playful, sportive.

резе́рв, -а reserve(s); име́ть в ∼е have in reserve. резерва́ция, -и reservation. резерви́ровать, -рую *impf. & pf.* reserve. резерви́ст, -а reservist. резе́рвн|ый reserve; back-up; ∼ая ко́пия back-up copy. резервуа́р, -а reservoir, vessel, tank.

резе́ц, -зца́ cutter; cutting tool; chisel; incisor.

рези́на, -ы rubber. рези́нка, -и rubber; (piece of) elastic. рези́нов|ый rubber; elastic; ∼ые сапоги́ wellingtons, gum-boots.

ре́зкий sharp; harsh; abrupt; shrill. резно́й carved, fretted. резня́, -и́ slaughter, butchery, carnage.

резолю́ция, -и resolution.

резо́н, -а reason, basis; в э́том есть свой ∼ there is a reason for this. резона́нс, -а resonance; echo, response; име́ть ∼ have repercussions. резо́нный reasonable.

результа́т, -а result, outcome. результати́вный successful.

резьба́, -ы́ carving, fretwork.

резюме́ *nt. indecl.* summary, résumé. резюми́ровать, -рую *impf. & pf.* sum up, summarize.

рейд[1], -а roads, roadstead.

рейд[2], -а raid.

Рейн, -а the Rhine. рейнве́йн, -а (-у) hock. ре́йнский Rhine.

рейс, -а trip, run; voyage, passage; flight.

река́, -и́, *a.* ре́ку; *pl.* -и, ре́кам river.

реквизи́т, -а properties, props.

рекла́ма, -ы advertising, advertisement; publicity. **рекламировать**, **-рую** *impf. & pf.* advertise, publicize, push. **рекламный** publicity.

рекомендательн|ый of recommendation; ~**ое письмо** letter of introduction. **рекомендация**, **-и** recommendation; reference. **рекомендовать**, **-дую** *impf. & pf.* (*pf. also* **от~**, **по~**) recommend; speak well for; advise; ~**ся** introduce o.s.; be advisable.

реконструировать, **-рую** *impf. & pf.* reconstruct.

рекорд, **-а** record; **побить** ~ break, beat, a record. **рекордный** record, record-breaking. **рекордсмен**, **-а**, **-енка**, **-и** record-holder.

ректор, **-а** rector, vice-chancellor, principal (*head of a university*).

религиоведение, **-я** religious studies. **религиозный** religious; of religion; pious. **религия**, **-и** religion.

реликвия, **-и** relic.

рельеф, **-а** relief. **рельефно** *adv.* boldly. **рельефный** relief; raised, embossed, bold.

рельс, **-а** rail; **сойти с** ~**ов** be derailed, go off the rails. **рельсовый** rail, railway.

ремарка, **-и** stage direction.

ремень, **-мня** *m.* strap; belt; thong; ~ **безопасности** seat belt.

ремесленник, **-а** artisan, craftsman; hack. **ремесленничество**, **-а** workmanship, craftsmanship; hack-work. **ремесленн|ый** handicraft; trade; mechanical; stereotyped; ~**ое училище** trade school. **ремесло**, **-á**; *pl.* **-ёсла**, **-ёсел** handicraft; trade; profession.

ремонт, **-а** repair, repairs; maintenance; **косметический** ~ face-lift. **ремонтировать**, **-рую** *impf. & pf.* (*pf. also* **от~**) repair; refit; recondition, overhaul. **ремонтный** repair, repairing.

рента, **-ы** rent; income. **рентабельный** paying, profitable.

рентген, **-а** X-rays; roentgen. **рентгенизировать**, **-рую** *impf. & pf.* X-ray. **рентгеновский** X-ray. **рентгенолог**, **-а** radiologist. **рентгенология**, **-и** radiology.

реорганизация, **-и** reorganization. **реорганизовать**, **-зую** *impf. & pf.* reorganize.

репа, **-ы** turnip.

репарация, **-и** reparation.

репатриант, **-а** repatriate. **репатриация**, **-и** repatriation. **репатриировать**, **-рую** *impf.· & pf.* repatriate.

репеллент, **-а** insect repellant.

репертуар, **-а** repertoire.

репетировать, **-рую** *impf.* (*pf.* **от~**, **про~**, **с~**) rehearse; coach. **репетитор**, **-а** coach. **репетиция**, **-и** rehearsal; repeater mechanism; **часы с репетицией** repeater.

реплика, **-и** rejoinder, retort; cue.

репортаж, **-а** reporting; account. **репортёр**, **-а** reporter.

репрессалии, **-ий** *pl.* reprisals.

репрессивный repressive. **репрессировать**, **-рую** *impf. & pf.* subject to repression. **репрессия**, **-и** punitive measure.

репродуктор, **-а** loud-speaker.

республика, **-и** republic. **республиканец**, **-нца** republican. **республиканский** republican.

рессора, **-ы** spring. **рессорный** spring; sprung.

реставрация, **-и** restoration. **реставрировать**, **-рую** *impf. & pf.* (*pf. also* **от~**) restore.

ресторан, **-а** restaurant.

ресурс, **-а** resource; **последний** ~ the last resort.

ретивый zealous, ardent.

ретироваться, **-руюсь** *impf. & pf.* retire, withdraw; make off.

ретранслятор, **-а** (radio-)relay. **ретрансляция**, **-и** relaying, retransmission.

ретроракета, **-ы** retro-rocket.

ретушировать, **-рую** *impf. & pf.* (*pf. also* **от~**) retouch. **ретушь**, **-и** retouching.

реферат, **-а** synopsis, abstract; paper, essay.

реформа, **-ы** reform. **реформатор**, **-а** reformer. **Реформация**, **-и** (*hist.*) Reformation. **реформизм**, **-а** reformism. **реформировать**, **-рую** *impf. & pf.* reform. **реформист**, **-а** reformist.

рецензент, **-а** reviewer. **рецензировать**, **-рую** *impf.* (*pf.* **про~**) review, criticize. **рецензия**, **-и** review; notice.

рецепт, **-а** prescription; recipe; method, way, practice.

рецидив, **-а** recurrence; relapse; repetition. **рецидивист**, **-а** recidivist.

рециркуляция, **-и** recycling.

речевой speech; vocal.

речка, **-и** river. **речной** river; riverine; fluvial; ~ **вокзал** river-steamer and water-bus station; ~ **трамвай** water-bus.

речь, **-и**; *g.pl.* **-ей** speech; enunciation, way of speaking; language; discourse; oration; address; **выступить с** ~**ю** make a speech; **не об этом** ~ that's not the point; **об этом не может быть и речи** it is (quite) out of the question; **о чём** ~? what are you talking about? what is it all about?; ~ **идёт о том...** the question is ... .

решать(ся, **-аю(сь** *impf. of* **решить(ся**. **решающий** decisive, deciding; key; conclusive. **решение**, **-я** decision; decree; judgement; verdict; solution, answer; **вынести** ~ pass a resolution.

решётка, **-и** grating; grille; railing; lattice; trellis; fender, (fire)guard; (fire)-grate; tail. **решето**, **-á**; *pl.* **-ёта** sieve. **решётчатый** lattice, latticed; trellised.

решимость, **-и** resolution, resoluteness; resolve. **решительно** *adv.* resolutely; decidedly, definitely; absolutely; ~ **всё равно** it makes no difference whatever. **решительность**, **-и** resolution, determination, firmness. **решительный** resolute, determined; decided; firm; definite; decisive; crucial; absolute. **решить**, **-шу** *pf.* (*impf.* **решать**) decide, determine; make up one's mind; solve, settle; ~ся make up one's mind, resolve; bring o.s.; +g. lose, be deprived of.

решка; орёл или ~? heads or tails?

ржаветь, -еет impf. (pf. **за~, по~**) rust. **ржавчина, -ы** rust; mildew. **ржавый** rusty.

ржаной rye.

ржать, ржу, ржёшь impf. neigh.

Рига, -и Riga.

рига, -и (threshing-)barn.

Рим, -а Rome. **римлянин, -а;** pl. **-яне, -ян, римлянка, -и** Roman. **римск|ий** Roman; **папа ~ий** the Pope; **~ие цифры** Roman numerals.

ринуться, -нусь pf. rush, dash, dart.

рис, -а (-у) rice.

рис. abbr. (of **рисунок**) fig., figure.

риск, -а risk; hazard; **пойти на ~** run risks, take chances. **рискованный** risky; risqué. **рисковать, -кую** impf. run risks, take chances; +i. or inf. risk, take the risk of.

рисование, -я drawing. **рисовать, -сую** impf. (pf. **на~**) draw; paint, depict, portray; **~ся** be silhouetted; appear, present o.s.; pose, act.

рисов|ый rice; **~ая каша** rice pudding; boiled rice.

рисунок, -нка drawing; illustration; figure; pattern, design; outline; draughtsmanship.

ритм, -а rhythm. **ритмический, ритмичный** rhythmic(al).

риф, -а reef.

рифма, -ы rhyme. **рифмовать, -мую** impf. (pf. **с~**) rhyme; **~ся** rhyme. **рифмовка, -и** rhyming (system).

р-н abbr. (of **район**) district.

робеть, -ею impf. (pf. **о~**) be timid; be afraid, quail. **робкий; -бок, -бка, -о** timid, shy. **робость, -и** timidity, shyness.

роботехника, -и robotics.

робче comp. of **робкий**

ров, рва, loc. **-у** ditch.

ровесник, -а a person of the same age, coeval.

ровно adv. regularly, evenly; exactly; sharp; absolutely; just as, exactly like; **~ в час** at one sharp, on the stroke of one; **~ ничего** absolutely nothing, nothing at all. **ровный** flat; even; level; regular; equable; exact; equal. **ровня, ровній** c.g. equal; match. **ровнять, -яю** impf. (pf. **с~**) even, level; **~ с землёй** raze to the ground.

рог, -а; pl. **-а, -ов** horn; antler; bugle. **рогатый** horned. **роговица, -ы** cornea. **роговой** horn; horny; horn-rimmed.

рогожа, -ы bast mat(ting).

род, -а (-у), loc. **-у;** pl. **-ы** family, kin, clan; birth, origin, stock; generation; genus; sort, kind; **без ~у, без племени** without kith or kin; **в этом ~е** of this sort, of the kind; **ей десять лет от ~у** she is ten years old; **он своего ~а гений** he is a genius in his (own) way; **~ом** by birth; **своего ~а** a kind of, a sort of; **человеческий ~** mankind, the hu-

man race. **родильный** maternity; puerperal.

родина, -ы native land, mother country; home, homeland. **родинка, -и** birth-mark.

родитель, -я m. father; **~ница, -ы** mother; **родители, -ей** pl. parents. **родительный** genitive. **родительский** parental, parents'; paternal. **родить, -ию, -ил, -ила, -о** impf. & pf. (impf. also **рожать, рождать**) bear; give birth to; give rise to; **~ся** be born; arise, come into being; spring up, thrive.

родник, -а spring. **родниковый** spring.

роднить, -нит (pf. **по~**) make related, link; make similar, make alike; **~ся** become related, be linked. **родн|ой** own; native; home; **~ой брат** brother; **~ой язык** mother tongue; **~ые** sb., pl. relations, relatives, family.

родня, -й relation(s), relative(s); kinsfolk.

родовой clan, tribal; ancestral; generic; gender. **родоначальник, -а** ancestor, forefather; father. **родословн|ый** genealogical; **~ая** sb. genealogy, pedigree. **родственник, -а** relation, relative. **родственный** kindred, related; allied; cognate; familiar, intimate. **родство, -а** relationship, kinship; relations, relatives. **роды, -ов** pl. birth; childbirth, delivery; labour.

рожа, -и (ugly) mug; **строить рожи** pull faces.

рожать, -аю, рождать(ся, -аю(сь impf. of **родить(ся. рождаемость, -и** birth-rate. **рождение, -я** birth; birthday. **рождённый; -ён, -а** born. **Рождество, -а** Christmas.

рожь, ржи rye.

роза, -ы rose; rose-bush, rose-tree; rose window.

розга, -и; g.pl. **-зог** birch.

роздал etc.: see **раздать**

розетка, -и rosette; socket; wall-plug.

розмарин, -а rosemary.

розница, -ы retail; **в ~у** retail. **розничный** retail. **розно** adv. apart, separately. **рознь, -и** difference; dissension.

рознял etc.: see **разнять**

розовый pink; rose-coloured; rosy; rose.

розыгрыш, -а draw; drawing; drawn game; playing off; tournament, competition, championship.

розыск, -а search; inquiry; investigation.

ройться, -йтся swarm. **рой, -я,** loc. **-ю;** pl. **-й, -ёв** swarm.

рок, -а fate.

рокировать(ся, -рую(сь impf. & pf. castle. **рокировка, -и** castling.

рок-музыка, -и rock music. **рок-н-ролл, -а** rock 'n' roll.

роковой fateful; fated; fatal.

рокот, -а roar, rumble. **рокотать, -очет** impf. roar, rumble.

ролик, -а a roller; castor; pl. roller skates. **роликов|ый; ~ая доска** skateboard. **роликодром, -а** roller-skating rink. **роллер, -а** scooter. **роллинг, -а** skateboard; skateboarding.

роль, -и; *g.pl.* -**ей** role, part.

ром, -а (-у) rum.

рома́н, -а novel; romance; love affair. **рома-
ни́ст**, -а novelist.

рома́нс, -а song; romance.

рома́шка, -и, **рома́шковый** camomile.

роня́ть, -я́ю *impf.* (*pf.* **урони́ть**) drop, let
fall; shed; lower, injure, discredit.

ро́пот, -а murmur, grumble. **ропта́ть**, -пщу́,
-пщешь *impf.* murmur, grumble.

рос *etc.: see* **расти́**

роса́, -ы́; *pl.* -ы dew. **роси́стый** dewy.

роско́шный luxurious; sumptuous; luxuriant;
splendid. **ро́скошь**, -и luxury; luxuriance;
splendour.

ро́слый tall, strapping.

ро́спись, -и list, inventory; painting(s),
mural(s).

ро́спуск, -а dismissal; disbandment; breaking up.

росси́йский Russian. **Росси́я**, -и Russia.

россия́нин, -а; *pl.* -я́не, -я́н, **россия́нка**, -и
Russian.

ро́ссказни, -ей *pl.* old wives' tales, cock-and-
bull stories.

ро́ссыпь, -и scattering; *pl.* deposit; ~ю in
bulk, loose.

рост, -а (-у) growth; increase, rise; height, stature; **во весь** ~ upright, straight; ~ом in
height.

ростовщи́к, -а́ usurer, money-lender.

росто́к, -тка́ sprout, shoot; **пусти́ть ростки́**
put out shoots.

ро́счерк, -а flourish, **одни́м** ~**ом пера́** with
a stroke of the pen.

рот, рта (рту), *loc.* рту mouth.

ро́та, -ы company.

рота́тор, -а duplicator. **ротацио́нн|ый** ro-
tary; ~**ая маши́на** rotary press. **рота́ция**, -и
rotary press.

ро́тный company; *sb.* company commander.

ротозе́й, -я, -зе́йка, -и gaper, rubberneck;
scatter-brain. **ротозе́йство**, -а carelessness,
absent-mindedness.

ро́ща, -и, **ро́щица**, -ы grove.

ро́ю *etc.: see* **рыть**

роя́ль, -я *m.* (grand) piano; **игра́ть на роя́ле**
play the piano.

РСФСР *abbr.* (*of* **Росси́йская Сове́тская Феде-
рати́вная Социалисти́ческая Респу́блика**)
Russian Soviet Federal Socialist Republic.

рту́тный mercury, mercurial. **ртуть**, -и mercury; quicksilver.

руба́нок, -нка plane.

руба́шка, -и shirt; **ночна́я** ~ night-shirt,
nightgown, nightdress.

рубе́ж, -а́ boundary, border(line), frontier;
line; **за** ~**о́м** abroad.

рубе́ц, -бца́ scar, cicatrice; weal; hem; seam;
tripe.

руби́н, -а ruby. **руби́новый** ruby; ruby-col-
oured.

руби́ть, -блю́, -бишь *impf.* (*pf.* **с**~) fell; hew,
chop, hack; mince, chop up; build (of logs),
put up, erect.

ру́бище, -а rags, tatters.

ру́бка[1], -и felling; hewing, hacking; chopping;
mincing.

ру́бка[2], -и deck house, deck cabin; **боева́я** ~
conning-tower; **рулева́я** ~ wheelhouse.

рублёвка, -и one-rouble note. **рублёвый**
(one-)rouble.

ру́блен|ый minced, chopped; log, of logs;
~**ые котле́ты** rissoles; ~**ое мя́со** mince,
minced meat, hash.

рубль, -я́ *m.* rouble.

ру́брика, -и rubric, heading; column.

ру́бчатый ribbed. **ру́бчик**, -а scar, seam, rib.

ру́гань, -и abuse, bad language, swearing.
руга́тельн|ый abusive; ~**ые слова́** bad lan-
guage, swear-words. **руга́тельство**, -а oath,
swear-word. **руга́ть**, -а́ю *impf.* (*pf.* **вы́**~,
об~, **от**~) curse, swear at; abuse; tear to
pieces; criticize severely; ~**ся** curse, swear,
use bad language; swear at, abuse, one another.

руда́, -ы́; *pl.* -ы ore. **рудни́к**, -а́ mine, pit.
рудни́чный mine, pit; mining; ~ **газ** fire-
damp. **рудоко́п**, -а miner.

руже́йный rifle, gun; ~ **вы́стрел** rifle-shot.
ружьё, -ья́; *pl.* -ья, -жей, -ьям gun, rifle.

рука́, -и́, *a.* -у; *pl.* -и, рук, -а́м hand; arm; **в
со́бственные ру́ки** personal; **игра́ть в четы́-
ре руки́** play duets; **идти́ под руку с**+*i.*, walk
arm in arm with; **маха́ть руко́й** wave one's
hand; **махну́ть руко́й на**+*a.* give up as lost;
на ско́рую ру́ку hastily; extempore; **не
поднима́ется** ~+*inf.* one cannot bring o.s.
to; **под руко́й** at hand; **по рука́м!** done! it's
a bargain!; **приложи́ть ру́ку** append one's
signature; **рука́ми не тро́гать!** (please) don't
touch!; **ру́ки вверх!** hands up; **ру́ки прочь!**
hands off!; **руко́й пода́ть** a stone's throw
away; **у вас на** ~**х** on you; **чёткая** ~ a clear
hand; **э́то мне на́ руку** that suits me.

рука́в, -а́; *pl.* -а́, -о́в sleeve; branch, arm; hose;
пожа́рный ~ fire-hose. **рукави́ца**, -ы mitten; gauntlet.

руководи́тель, -я *m.* leader; manager; instructor; guide. **руководи́ть**, -ожу́ *impf.*+*i.*
lead; guide; direct, manage. **руково́дство**, -а
leadership; guidance; direction; guide; handbook, manual; instructions; leaders; governing body. **руково́дствоваться**, -твуюсь+*i.*
follow; be guided by, be influenced by. **руко-
водя́щ|ий** leading; guiding; ~**ая статья́**
leader; ~**ий комите́т** steering committee.

рукоде́лие, -я needlework; *pl.* hand-made
goods.

рукомо́йник, -а wash-stand.

рукопа́шн|ый hand-to-hand; ~**ая** *sb.* hand-
to-hand fighting.

рукопи́сный manuscript. **ру́копись**, -и manuscript.

рукоплеска́ние, -я applause. **рукопле-
ска́ть**, -ещу́, -е́щешь *impf.*+*d.* applaud, clap.

рукопожа́тие, **-я** handshake; **обменя́ться рукопожа́тиями** shake hands.

руко́ятка, **-и** handle; hilt; haft, helve; shaft; grip.

рулев|о́й steering; **~о́е колесо́** steering wheel; *sb*. helmsman, man at the wheel.

руле́тка, **-и** tape-measure; roulette.

рули́ть, **-лю́** *impf*. (*pf*. **вы́~**) taxi.

руль, **-я́** *m*. rudder; helm; (steering-)wheel; handlebar.

румы́н, **-а**; *g.pl*. **-ы́н**, **румы́нка**, **-и** Romanian, Rumanian. **Румы́ния**, **-и** Romania, Rumania. **румы́нский** Romanian, Rumanian.

румя́на, **-я́н** *pl*. rouge. **румя́нец**, **-нца** (high) colour; flush; blush. **румя́нить**, **-ню** *impf*. (*pf*. **за~**, **на~**) redden, bring colour to; rouge; **~ся** redden; glow; flush; use rouge, put on rouge. **румя́ный** rosy, ruddy; brown.

ру́пор, **-а** megaphone, speaking-trumpet; loud-hailer; mouthpiece.

руса́лка, **-и** mermaid. **руса́лочий** mermaid, mermaid's.

ру́сский Russian; *sb*. Russian.

ру́сый light brown.

рути́на, **-ы** routine; rut, groove. **рути́нный** routine.

ру́хлядь, **-и** junk, lumber.

ру́хнуть, **-ну** *pf*. crash down; fall heavily; crash (*to the ground*).

руча́тельство, **-а** guarantee; **с ~м** warranted, guaranteed. **руча́ться**, **-а́юсь** *impf*. (*pf*. **поручи́ться**) answer, vouch; **+за**+*a*. warrant, guarantee, certify.

руче́й, **-чья́** stream, brook.

ру́чка, **-и** handle; (door-)knob; (chair-)arm; pen; penholder. **ручн|о́й** hand; arm; manual; hand-made; tame; **~ы́е часы́** wrist-watch.

ру́шить, **-у** *impf*. (*pf*. **об~**) pull down; **~ся** fall, fall in; collapse.

ры́ба, **-ы** fish; *pl*. Pisces. **рыба́к**, **-а́** fisherman. **рыба́лка**, **-и** fishing. **рыба́цкий**, **рыба́чий** fishing. **ры́бий** fish; fishlike, fishy; **~ жир** cod-liver oil. **ры́бн|ый** fish; **~ые консе́рвы** tinned fish. **рыбово́дческ|ий**; **~ая фе́рма** fish farm. **рыболо́в**, **-а** fisherman; angler. **рыболо́вный** fishing. **рыбопито́мник**, **-а** fish hatchery.

рыво́к, **-вка́** jerk; dash, burst, spurt.

рыда́ние, **-я** sobbing, sobs. **рыда́ть**, **-а́ю** *impf*. sob.

ры́жий; **рыж**, **-а́**, **-е** red, red-haired; ginger; chestnut; reddish-brown, brown with age; gold.

ры́ло, **-а** snout; (ugly) mug.

ры́нок, **-нка** market; market-place. **ры́ночный** market.

рыса́к, **-а́** trotter.

ры́сий lynx.

рыси́стый trotting. **рыси́ть**, **-и́шь** *impf*. trot. **рысь**[1], **-и**, *loc*. **-и́** trot; **~ю**, **на рыся́х** at a trot. **рысь**[2], **-и** lynx.

ры́твина, **-ы** rut, groove. **рыть**, **ро́ю** *impf*. (*pf*. **вы́~**, **от~**) dig; rummage about (in),

ransack, burrow in; **~ся** dig; rummage.

рыхли́ть, **-лю́** *impf*. (*pf*. **вз~**, **раз~**) loosen, make friable. **ры́хлый**: **-л**, **-а́**, **-о** friable; loose; porous; pudgy, podgy.

ры́царский knightly; chivalrous. **ры́царь**, **-я** *m*. knight.

рыча́г, **-а́** lever.

рыча́ть, **-чу́** *impf*. growl, snarl.

рья́ный zealous, ardent.

ре́ггей *m*. *indecl*. reggae.

рюкза́к, **-а** rucksack, backpack. **рюкза́чник**, **-а** backpacker.

рю́мка, **-и** wineglass.

ряби́на[1], **-ы** rowan (tree), mountain ash; rowan-berry.

ряби́на[2], **-ы** pit, pock. **ряби́ть**, **-и́т** *impf*. ripple; *impers*. **у меня́ ряби́т в глаза́х** I am dazzled. **рябо́й** pitted, pock-marked; speckled. **ря́бчик**, **-а** hazel-hen, hazel grouse. **рябь**, **-и** ripple, ripples; dazzle.

ря́вкать, **-аю** *impf*., **ря́вкнуть**, **-ну** *pf*. bellow, roar.

ряд, **-а** (**-у**), *loc*. **-у́**; *pl*. **-ы́** row; line; file, rank; series; numbers; **из ~а вон выходя́щий** outstanding, exceptional, out of the common run; **пе́рвый ~** front row; **после́дний ~** back row; **стоя́ть в одно́м ~у́ с**+*i*. rank with. **рядово́й** ordinary; common; **~ соста́в** rank and file; men, other ranks; *sb*. private. **ря́дом** *adv*. alongside; near, close by, next door; **+с**+*i*. next to.

ря́са, **-ы** cassock.

С

С *abbr*. (*of* **се́вер**) N, North.

с *letter*: *see* **эс**

с, **со** *prep*. **I.** **+**g. from; since; off; for, with; on; by; **дово́льно с тебя́!** that's enough from you!; **перево́д с ру́сского** translation from Russian; **с большо́й бу́квы** with a capital letter; **сда́ча с рубля́** change for a rouble; **с ле́вой стороны́** on the left-hand side; **с одно́й стороны́, с друго́й стороны́** on the one hand, on the other hand; **со сна** just up, half awake; **со стыда́** for shame, with shame; **с пе́рвого взгля́да** at first sight; **с ра́дости** for joy; **с утра́** since morning. **II.** **+**a. about; the size of; **ма́льчик с па́льчик** Tom Thumb; **на́ша до́чка ро́стом с ва́шу** our daughter is about the same height as yours; **с неде́лю** for about a week. **III.** **+**i. with; and; **мы с ва́ми** you and I; **получи́ть с пе́рвой по́чтой** receive by the first post; **что с ва́ми?** what is the matter with you? what's up?

с. abbr. (of **село́**) village; (of **страни́ца**) p., page.

с..., со..., съ... vbl. pref. indicating perfective aspect; unification, joining, fastening; accompaniment, participation; comparison; copying; removal; movement away (from), to one side, downwards, down (from), off, there and back, directed to a point or centre; action in concert.

СА abbr. (of **Сове́тская А́рмия**) Soviet Army.

са́бельный sabre.

сабза́, -ы́ sultanas.

са́бля, -и; g.pl. **-бель** sabre; (cavalry) sword.

сабота́ж, -а sabotage. **сабота́жник, -а** saboteur. **саботи́ровать, -рую** impf. & pf. sabotage.

са́ван, -а shroud; blanket.

с|агити́ровать, -рую pf.

сад, -а, loc. **-у́;** pl. **-ы́** garden, gardens. **сади́ть, сажу́, са́дишь** impf. (pf. **по~**) plant; **~ на дие́ту** put on a diet. **сади́ться, сажу́сь** impf. of **сесть. садо́вник, -а, -ница, -ы** gardener. **садово́дство, -а** gardening; horticulture; nursery; garden(s). **садо́вый** garden; cultivated.

садо-мазохи́зм, -а sado-masochism.

са́жа, -и soot.

сажа́ть, -а́ю impf. (pf. **посади́ть**) plant; seat; set put; **~ в тюрьму́** put in prison, imprison, jail; **~ под аре́ст** put under arrest. **са́женец, -нца** seedling; sapling.

са́жень, -и; pl. **-и, -жен** or **-же́ней** sazhen (old Russ. measure of length, equivalent to 2.13 metres).

сажу́ etc.: see **сади́ть**

са́йка, -и roll.

саквоя́ж, -а travelling-bag, grip.

с|акти́ровать, -рую pf.

сала́зки, -зок pl. sled, toboggan.

сала́т, -а (-у) salad; **~-лату́к** lettuce. **сала́тник, -а, сала́тница, -ы** salad-dish, salad-bowl.

са́ло, -а fat, lard; suet; tallow.

сало́н, -а salon; saloon; **да́мский ~** beauty parlour.

салфе́тка, -и napkin, serviette.

са́льный greasy; fat; tallow; obscene, bawdy.

салю́т, -а salute. **салютова́ть, -ту́ю** impf. & pf. (pf. **от~**) +d. salute.

сам, -ого́ m., **сама́, -о́й,** a. **-оё** f., **само́, -ого́** nt., **са́ми, -их** pl., pron. -self, -selves; myself, etc., ourselves, etc.; **она́ — -á доброта́** she is kindness itself; **~ по себе́** in itself; by o.s., unassisted; **~ собо́й** of itself, of its own accord; **~ó собо́й (разуме́ется)** of course; it goes without saying.

са́мбо nt.indecl. abbr. (of **самозащи́та без ору́жия**) unarmed combat.

саме́ц, -мца́ male. **са́мка, -и** female.

само... in comb. self-, auto-. **самобы́тный** original, distinctive. **~внуше́ние, -я** auto-suggestion. **~возгора́ние, -я** spontaneous combustion. **~во́льный** wilful, self-willed; unauthorized; unwarranted. **~дви́жущийся** self-propelled. **~де́лка, -и** home-made product. **~де́льный** home-made; self-made. **~держа́вие, -я** autocracy. **~держа́вный** autocratic. **~де́ятельность, -и** amateur work, amateur performance; initiative. **~дово́льный** self-satisfied, smug, complacent. **~ду́р, -а** petty tyrant; wilful person. **~ду́рство, -а** petty tyranny, obstinate wilfulness. **~забве́ние, -я** selflessness. **~забве́нный** selfless. **~защи́та, -ы** self-defence. **~зва́нец, -нца** imposter, pretender. **~зва́нство, -а** imposture. **~ка́т, -а** scooter; bicycle. **~кри́тика, -и** self-criticism. **~люби́вый** proud; touchy. **~лю́бие, -я** pride, self-esteem. **~мне́ние, -я** conceit, self-importance. **~наде́янный** presumptuous. **~облада́ние, -я** self-control, self-possession; composure. **~обма́н, -а** self-deception. **~оборо́на, -ы** self-defence. **~образова́ние, -я** self-education. **~обслу́живание, -я** self-service. **~определе́ние, -я** self-determination. **~опроки́дывающийся** self-tipping; **~опроки́дывающийся грузови́к** tip-up lorry. **~отверже́ние, -я, ~отве́рженность, -и** selflessness. **~отве́рженный** selfless, self-sacrificing. **~пи́шущий** recording, registering; **~пи́шущее перо́** fountain-pen. **~поже́ртвование, -я** self-sacrifice. **~пу́ск, -а** self-starter. **~рекла́ма, -ы** self-advertisement. **~ро́дный** native. **~ро́док, -дка** nugget; rough diamond. **~сва́л, -а** tip-up lorry. **~созна́ние, -я** self-consciousness. **~сохране́ние, -я** self-preservation. **~стоя́тельно** adv. independently; on one's own. **~стоя́тельность, -и** independence. **~стоя́тельный** independent. **~су́д, -а** lynch law, mob law. **~тёк, -а** drift. **~тёком** adv. by gravity; haphazard of its own accord; **идти́ ~тёком** drift. **~уби́йственный** suicidal. **~уби́йство, -а** suicide (act). **~уби́йца, -ы** c.g. suicide (person). **~уве́ренность, -и** self-confidence, self-assurance. **~уве́ренный** self-confident, self-assured; cocksure. **~униже́ние, -я** self-abasement, self-disparagement. **~управле́ние, -я** self-government; local authority. **~управля́ющийся** self-governing. **~упра́вный** arbitrary. **~упра́вство, -а** arbitrariness. **~учи́тель, -я** m. (self-tuition) manual, self-instructor. **~учка, -и** c.g. self-taught person. **~хо́дный** self-propelled. **~чу́вствие, -я** general state; **как ва́ше ~чу́вствие?** how do you feel?

самова́р, -а samovar.

самолёт, -а aeroplane, aircraft, plane.

самоцве́т, -а semi-precious stone.

са́м|ый pron. (the) very (the) right; (the) same; (the) most; **в ~ое вре́мя** at the right time; **в ~ом де́ле** indeed; **в ~ом де́ле?** indeed? really? **в ~ый раз** just right; **на ~ом де́ле** actually, in fact; **~ый глу́пый** the stupidest, the most stupid; **~ые пустяки́** the merest trifles; **с ~ого нача́ла** from the very beginning, right from the start; **с ~ого утра́** since first thing.

сан, -а dignity, office.

сан... *abbr.* (*of* **санита́рный**) *in comb.* medical, hospital; sanitary. **санвра́ч, -а́** medical officer of health; sanitary inspector. **~по́езд, -а** a hospital train, ambulance train. **~пу́нкт, -а** medical centre; dressing-station, aid-post. **~у́зел, -зла́** sanitary unit; lavatory. **~ча́сть, -и** medical unit.

са́ни, -е́й *pl.* sledge, sleigh.

санита́р, -а medical orderly, hospital orderly, male nurse; stretcher-bearer. **санита́рия, -и** hygiene, public health. **санита́рка, -и** nurse. **санита́рн|ый** medical; hospital; (public) health; sanitary; **~ый автомоби́ль, ~ая каре́та, ~ая маши́на** ambulance; **~ый у́зел** sanitary unit; lavatory.

са́нки, -нок *pl.* sledge; toboggan.

Санкт-Петербу́рг, -а St. Petersburg. **санкт-петербу́ргский** St. Petersburg. **санкт-петербуржа́нка, -и, санкт-петербу́ржец, -ца** St. Petersburger.

санкциони́ровать, -рую *impf. & pf.* sanction. **са́нкция, -и** sanction, approval.

са́нный sledge, sleigh; **~ путь** sleigh-road.

сано́вник, -а dignitary, high official. **сано́вный** of exalted rank.

са́ночник, -а tobogganist.

сантиме́тр, -а centimetre; tape-measure; ruler.

сапёр, -а sapper; pioneer. **сапёрный** sapper, pioneer; engineer.

сапо́г, -а́; *g.pl.* **-о́г** boot; top-boot, jackboot. **сапо́жник, -а** shoemaker, bootmaker; cobbler. **сапо́жный** boot, shoe.

сапфи́р, -а sapphire.

сара́й, -я shed; barn, barrack.

саранча́, -й locust; locusts.

сарафа́н, -а sarafan (*Russ. peasant womens' dress, without sleeves and buttoning in front*); pinafore (dress).

сарде́лька, -и (*small, fat*) sausage.

сарди́н|а, -ы sardine, pilchard; **~ы в ма́сле** (tinned) sardines.

сатана́, -ы́ *m.* Satan. **сатани́нский** satanic.

сати́н, -а sateen. **сати́новый** sateen.

сати́ра, -ы satire. **сати́рик, -а** satirist. **сатири́ческий** satirical.

Сау́довская Ара́вия, -ой -и Saudi Arabia.

са́уна, -ы sauna.

сафа́ри *nt. indecl.* safari; **«~» зоопа́рк** safari park.

сафья́н, -а morocco. **сафья́новый** morocco.

са́хар, -а (-у) sugar.

Саха́ра, -ы the Sahara.

сахари́н, -а saccharine. **са́харистый** sugary; saccharine. **са́харить, -рю** *impf.* (*pf.* **по~**) sugar, sweeten. **са́харница, -ы** sugar-basin. **са́харн|ый** sugar; sugary; **~ая голова́** sugar-loaf; **~ый заво́д** sugar-refinery; **~ый песо́к** granulated sugar; **~ая пу́дра** castor sugar; **~ая свёкла** sugar-beet.

сачо́к, -чка́ net; landing net; butterfly-net.

сб. *abbr.* (*of* **сбо́рник**) collection.

сба́вить, -влю *pf.* **сбавля́ть, -я́ю** *impf.* take off, deduct; reduce; **~ в ве́се** lose weight; **~ газ** throttle down; **~ с цены́** reduce the price

с|баланси́ровать, -рую *pf.*

сбе́гать[1], -аю *pf.* run; **+за+i.** run for. **сбега́ть[2], -а́ю** *impf.*, **сбежа́ть, -егу́** *pf.* run down (from); run away; disappear, vanish; **~ся** come running; gather, collect.

сберега́тельн|ый; ~ая ка́сса savings bank. **сберега́ть, -а́ю** *impf.*, **сбере́чь, -егу́, -ежёшь; -ёг, -ла́** *pf.* save; save up, put aside; preserve, protect. **сбереже́ние, -я** economy; saving, preservation; savings. **сберка́сса, -ы** *abbr.* savings bank. **сберкни́жка, -и** savings book.

сбива́ть, -а́ю *impf.*, **с|бить, собью́, -бьёшь** *pf.* bring down, knock down, throw down; knock off, dislodge; put out; distract; deflect; wear down, tread down; knock together; churn; beat up, whip, whisk; **~ с доро́ги** misdirect; **~ с ног** knock down; **~ с то́лку** muddle, confuse; **~ це́ну** beat down the price; **~ся** be dislodged; slip; be deflected; go wrong; be confused; be inconsistent; **~ся в ку́чу, ~ся толпо́й** bunch, huddle; **~ся с доро́ги, ~ся с пути́** lose one's way, go astray; **~ся с ног** be run off one's feet; **~ся со счёта** lose count. **сби́вчивый** confused, indistinct; inconsistent, contradictory. **сби́т|ый; ~ые сли́вки** whipped cream.

сближа́ть, -а́ю *impf.*, **сбли́зить, -и́жу** *pf.* bring (closer) together, draw together; **~ся** draw together, converge; become good friends. **сближе́ние, -я** rapprochement; intimacy; approach, closing in.

сбо́ку *adv.* from one side; on one side; at the side.

сбор, -а collection; dues; duty; charge(s), fee, toll; takings, returns; salvage; assemblage, gathering; course of instruction; **быть в ~е** be assembled, be in session; **~ урожа́я** harvest. **сбо́рище, -а** crowd, mob. **сбо́рка, -и** assembling, assembly, erection; gather. **сбо́рник, -а** collection; **~ пра́вил** code of rules. **сбо́рн|ый** assembly; mixed, combined; that can be taken to pieces; prefabricated, sectional; detachable; **~ая кома́нда** combined team, representative team; picked team; scratch team; **~ый пункт** assembly point, rallying point. **сбо́рочный** assembly; **~ цех** assembly shop. **сбо́рчатый** gathered. **сбо́рщик, -а** collector; assembler, fitter, mounter.

сбра́сывать(ся, -аю(сь *impf. of* **сбро́сить(ся**

сбрива́ть, -а́ю *impf.*, **сбрить, сбре́ю** *pf.* shave off.

сброд, -а riff-raff, rabble.

сброс, -а fault, break. **сбро́сить, -о́шу** *pf.* (*impf.* **сбра́сывать**) throw down, drop; throw off; cast off; shed; throw away, discard; **~ся** throw o.s. down, leap (+g. off, from).

с|брошюрова́ть, -рую *pf.*

сбру́я, -и harness.

сбыва́ть, -а́ю *impf.*, **сбыть, сбу́ду; сбыл, -а́, -о** *pf.* sell, market; get rid of; dump; **~ с рук** get off one's hands; **~ся** come true, be realized; happen; **что сбу́дется с ней?** what will become of her? **сбыт, -а** sale; market. **сбытово́й** selling, marketing.

св. *abbr.* (*of* **свято́й**) St., Saint.

сва́дебный wedding; nuptial. **сва́дьба, -ы;** *g.pl.* **-деб** wedding.

сва́ливать, -аю *impf.*, **с|вали́ть, -лю́, -лишь** *pf.* throw down, bring down; overthrow; lay low; heap up, pile up; abate; **~ся** fall, fall down, collapse. **сва́лка, -и** dump; scrapheap, rubbish-heap; scuffle; **вы́бросить на сва́лку** dump.

с|валя́ть, -я́ю *pf.* **сваля́ться, -я́ется** *pf.* get tangled, get matted.

сва́ривать, -аю *impf.*, **с|вари́ть, -рю́, -ришь** *pf.* boil; cook; weld; **~ся** boil, cook; weld (together), unite. **сва́рка, -и** welding.

сварли́вый peevish; shrewish.

сварно́й welded. **сва́рочный** welding. **сва́рщик, -а** welder.

сва́тать, -аю *impf.* (*pf.* **по~, со~**) propose as a husband or wife; ask in marriage; **~ся к**+*d. or* **за**+*a.* ask, seek in marriage.

сва́я, -и pile.

све́дение, -я piece of information; knowledge; attention, notice; report, minute; *pl.* information, intelligence; knowledge. **све́дущий** knowledgeable; versed, experienced; **~ие ли́ца** experts, informed persons.

сведу́ *etc.: see* **свести́**

свежезаморо́женный fresh-frozen; chilled. **све́жесть, -и** freshness; coolness. **свеже́ть, -е́ет** *impf.* (*pf.* **по~**) become cooler; freshen. **све́ж|ий; -еж, -а́** fresh; **~ее бельё** clean underclothes; **~ие проду́кты** fresh food; **~ий хлеб** new bread.

свезти́, -зу́, -зёшь; свёз, -ла́ *pf.* (*impf.* **свози́ть**) take, convey; bring down, take down; take away, clear away.

свёкла, -ы beet, beetroot.

свёкор, -кра father-in-law. **свекро́вь, -и** mother-in-law.

свёл *etc.: see* **свести́**

сверга́ть, -а́ю *impf.*, **све́ргнуть, -ну; сверг** *pf.* throw down, overthrow. **сверже́ние, -я** overthrow; **~ с престо́ла** dethronement.

све́рить, -рю *pf.* (*impf.* **сверя́ть**) collate; check.

сверка́ние, -я sparkling, sparkle; twinkling, twinkle; glitter; glare. **сверка́ть, -а́ю** *impf.* sparkle, twinkle; glitter; gleam. **сверкну́ть, -ну́, -нёшь** *pf.* flash.

сверли́льный drill, drilling; boring. **сверли́ть, -лю́** *impf.* (*pf.* **про~**) drill; bore through; nag, gnaw. **сверло́, -а́** drill. **сверля́щий** nagging, gnawing, piercing.

сверну́ть, -ну́, -нёшь *pf.* (*impf.* **свёртывать, свора́чивать**) roll, roll up; turn; reduce, contract, curtail, cut down; wind up; **~ ла́герь** break camp; **~ ше́ю**+*d.* wring the neck of; **~ся** roll up, curl up; coil up; fold; curdle, coagulate, turn; contract.

све́рстник, -а person of the same age, coeval; **мы с ним ~и** he and I are the same age

свёрток, -тка package, parcel, bundle. **свёртывание, -я** rolling, rolling up; curdling, turning; coagulation; reduction; curtailment, cutting down, cuts. **свёртывать(ся, -аю(сь** *impf. of* **сверну́ть(ся**

сверх *prep.*+*g.* over, above, on top of; beyond; over and above; in addition to; in excess of; **~ того́** moreover, besides.

сверх... *in comb.* super-, supra-, extra-, over-, preter-, hyper-. **сверхзвезда́, -ы́** quasar. **~звуково́й** supersonic. **~пла́новый** over and above the plan. **~при́быль, -и** excess profit. **~проводни́к, -а́** superconductor. **~секре́тный** top-secret. **~совреме́нный** ultra-modern. **~уро́чный** overtime. **~уро́чные** *sb., pl.* overtime. **~челове́к, -а** superman. **~челове́ческий** superhuman. **~шпио́н, -а** super-spy. **~шта́тный** supernumerary. **~ъесте́ственный** supernatural, preternatural.

све́рху *adv.* from above; from the top; on the surface; **~ до́низу** from top to bottom.

сверчо́к, -чка́ cricket.

сверя́ть, -я́ю *impf. of* **све́рить**

свес, -а overhang. **све́сить, -е́шу** *pf.* (*impf.* **све́шивать**) let down, lower; dangle; weigh; **~ся** hang over, overhang; lean over.

свести́, -еду́, -едёшь; -ёл, -а́ *pf.* (*impf.* **своди́ть**) take; take down; take away, lead off; remove, take out; bring together, put together; unite; reduce, bring; cramp, convulse; **~ дру́жбу, ~ знако́мство** make friends; **~ концы́ с конца́ми** make (both) ends meet; **~ на нет** bring to naught; **~ с ума́** drive mad; **~ счёты** settle accounts, get even; **у меня́ свело́ но́гу** I've got cramp in the leg.

свет¹, -а (-у) light; daybreak; **при ~е**+*g.* by the light of.

свет², -а (-у) world; society, beau monde.

света́ть, -а́ет *impf., impers.* dawn; **~а́ет** day is breaking, it is getting light. **свете́лка, -и** attic. **свети́ло, -а** luminary. **свети́льный** illuminating; **~ газ** coal-gas. **свети́ть, -ечу́, -е́тишь** *impf.* (*pf.* **по~**) shine; +*d.* light; hold a light for, light the way for; **~ся** shine, gleam. **светле́ть, -е́ет** *impf.* (*pf.* **по~, про~**) brighten; grow lighter; clear up, brighten up. **све́тлый** light, light-coloured; radiant; joyous; pure, unclouded; lucid, clear. **светля́к, -а́, светлячо́к, -чка́** glow-worm; fire-fly.

свето... *in comb.* light, photo-. **светобоя́знь, -и** photophobia. **~ко́пия, -и** photocopy, Photostat (*propr.*); blueprint. **~маскиро́вка, -и** black-out. **~непроница́емый** light-proof, light-tight, opaque. **~си́ла, -ы** candlepower; rapidity, speed, focal ratio.

~фильтр, -а light filter; (colour) filter.
~фо́р, -а traffic light(s). ~чувстви́тельный photosensitive, light-sensitive, photographic, sensitized.

свето́в|о́й light, lighting; luminous; ~о́й год light-year; ~ая рекла́ма illuminated sign(s).

све́тский society, fashionable; genteel, refined; temporal, lay, secular; ~ челове́к man of the world, man of fashion.

светя́щийся luminous, luminescent, fluorescent, phosphorescent. свеча́, -й; pl. -и, -е́й candle; taper; (sparking-)plug. свече́ние, -я luminescence, fluorescence; phosphorescence. све́чка, -и candle. свечно́й candle; ~ ога́рок candle-end. свечу́ etc.: see свети́ть

с|ве́шать, -аю pf. све́шивать(ся, -аю(сь impf. of све́сить(ся. свива́ть, -а́ю impf. of свить

свида́ние, -я meeting; appointment; rendez-vous; date; до свида́ния! goodbye!; назна́чить ~ make an appointment; make a date.

свиде́тель, -я m., -ница, -ы witness. свиде́тельство, -а evidence; testimony; certificate; ~ о бра́ке marriage certificate; ~ о прода́же bill of sale. свиде́тельствовать, -твую impf. (pf. за~, о~) give evidence, testify; be evidence (of), show; witness; attest, certify; examine, inspect.

свина́рник, -а, свина́рня, -и pigsty.

свине́ц, -нца́ lead.

свини́на, -ы pork. свин|о́й pig; pork; ~ая ко́жа pigskin; ~ое са́ло lard.

свинцо́в|ый lead; leaden; lead-coloured; ~ые бели́ла white lead.

свинья́, -й; pl. -и, -е́й, -я́м pig, swine; hog; sow.

свире́ль, -и (reed-)pipe.

свирепе́ть, -е́ю impf. (pf. рас~) grow fierce, grow savage. свире́пствовать, -твую impf. rage; be rife. свире́пый fierce, ferocious, savage; violent.

свиса́ть, -а́ю impf., сви́снуть, -ну; -ис pf. hang down, droop, dangle; trail.

свист, -а whistle; whistling; singing, piping, warbling. свиста́ть, -ищу́, -и́щешь impf. whistle; sing, pipe, warble. свисте́ть, -ищу́ impf., сви́стнуть, -ну pf. whistle; hiss. свисто́к, -тка́ whistle.

сви́та, -ы suite; retinue; series, formation.

сви́тер, -а sweater; спорти́вный ~ sweatshirt.

сви́ток, -тка roll, scroll. с|вить, совью́, совьёшь; -ил, -а́, -о pf. (impf. also свива́ть) twist, wind; ~ся roll up, curl up, coil.

свищ, -а́ flaw; (knot-)hole; fistula.

свищу́ etc.: see свиста́ть, свисте́ть

свобо́да, -ы freedom, liberty; на свобо́де at leisure; at large, at liberty; ~ рук a free hand; ~ сло́ва freedom of speech. свобо́дно adv. freely; easily, with ease; fluently; loose, loosely. свобо́дн|ый free; easy; vacant; spare; free-and-easy; loose, loose-fitting;

flowing. ~ое вре́мя free time, time off; spare time; ~ый до́ступ easy access; ~ый уда́р free kick. свободолюби́вый freedom-loving. свободомы́слие, -я free-thinking. свободомы́слящий free-thinking; sb. free-thinker.

свод, -а code; collection; arch, vault; ~ зако́нов code of laws.

своди́ть, -ожу́, -о́дишь impf. of свести́

сво́дка, -и summary, résumé; report; communiqué; revise. сво́дный composite, combined; collated; step-; ~ брат step-brother.

сво́дчатый arched, vaulted.

своево́лие, -я self-will, wilfulness. своево́льный self-willed, wilful.

своевре́менно adv. in good time; opportunely. своевре́менный timely, opportune; well-timed.

своенра́вие, -я wilfulness, waywardness, capriciousness. своенра́вный wilful, wayward, capricious.

своеобра́зие, -я originality; peculiarity. своеобра́зный original; peculiar, distinctive.

свожу́ etc.: see своди́ть, свози́ть. свози́ть, -ожу́, -о́зишь impf. of свезти́

свой, своего́ m., своя́, свое́й f., своё, своего́ nt., свои́, свои́х pl., pron. one's (own); my, his, her, its; our, your, their; доби́ться своего́ get one's own way; она́ сама́ не своя́ she is not herself; он не в своём уме́ he is not in his right mind. сво́йственный peculiar, characteristic. сво́йство, -а property, quality, attribute, characteristic.

сво́ра, -ы leash, pair; pack; gang.

свора́чивать, -аю impf. of сверну́ть, свороти́ть. с|ворова́ть, -ру́ю pf.

свороти́ть, -очу́, -о́тишь pf. (impf. свора́чивать) dislodge, displace, shift; turn, swing; twist, dislocate.

свыка́ться, -а́юсь impf., свы́кнуться, -нусь; -ы́кся pf. get used, accustom o.s.

высока́ adv. haughtily; condescendingly. свы́ше adv. from above; from on high. свы́ше prep.+g. over, more than; beyond.

свя́занный constrained; combined, fixed; bound; coupled. с|вяза́ть, -яжу́, -я́жешь pf., свя́зывать, -аю impf. tie together; tie, bind; connect, link; associate; ~ся get in touch, communicate; get involved; get mixed up. связи́ст, -а, -и́стка, -и signaller; worker in communication services. свя́зка, -и sheaf, bunch, bundle; chord; ligament; copula. связно́й liaison, communication. свя́зный connected, coherent. свя́зующий connecting, linking; liaison. связь, -и, loc. -и́ connection; causation; link, tie, bond; liaison, association; communication(s); signals; tie, stay, brace, strut; coupling; pl. connections, contacts.

святи́лище, -а sanctuary. святи́тель, -я m. prelate. святи́ть, -ячу́ impf. (pf. о~) consecrate; bless, sanctify. **свя́тки**, -ток *pl.* Christmas-tide. **свя́то** *adv.* piously; religiously; ~ бере́чь treasure; ~ чти́ть hold sacred. **свят|о́й**, -я́т, -а́, -о holy; sacred; saintly; pious; ~о́й, ~а́я *sb.* saint. **свяще́нник**, -а priest. **свяще́нный** holy; sacred. **свяще́нство**, -а priesthood; priests.

сгиб, -а bend. **сгиба́емый** flexible, pliable. **сгиба́ть**, -а́ю *impf. of* **согну́ть**

сгла́дить, -а́жу *pf.*, **сгла́живать**, -аю *impf.* smooth out; smooth over, soften; ~ся smooth out, become smooth; be smoothed over, be softened; diminish, abate.

с|глупи́ть, -плю́ *pf.*

сгнива́ть, -а́ю *impf.*, **с|гни́ть**, -ию́, -иёшь; -и́л, -а́, -о *pf.* rot, decay.

с|гнои́ть, -ою́ *pf.*

сгова́риваться, -аюсь *impf.*, **сговори́ться**, -рю́сь *pf.* come to an arrangement, reach an understanding; arrange; make an appointment. **сго́вор**, -а agreement, compact, deal; betrothal. **сгово́рчивый** compliant, complaisant, tractable.

сгон, -а driving; herding, rounding-up. **сго́нка**, -и rafting, floating. **сго́нщик**, -а herdsman, drover; rafter. **сгоня́ть**, -я́ю *impf. of* **согна́ть**

сгора́ние, -я combustion; **дви́гатель вну́треннего сгора́ния** internal-combustion engine. **сгора́ть**, -а́ю *impf. of* **сгоре́ть**

с|го́рбить(ся, -блю(сь *pf.* **сго́рбленный** crooked, bent; hunchbacked.

с|горе́ть, -рю́ *pf.* (*impf. also* **сгора́ть**) burn down; be burnt out, be burnt down; be burned; be used up; burn; burn o.s. out; ~ **от стыда́** burn with shame. **сгоряча́** *adv.* in the heat of the moment; in a fit of temper.

с|гото́вить, -влю *pf.*

сгреба́ть, -а́ю *impf.*, **сгрести́**, -ебу́, -ебёшь; -ёб, -ла́ *pf.* rake up, rake together; shovel away, off.

сгружа́ть, -а́ю *impf.*, **сгрузи́ть**, -ужу́, -у́зишь *pf.* unload.

с|группирова́ть(ся, -ру́ю(сь *pf.*

сгусти́ть, -ущу́ *pf.*, **сгуща́ть**, -а́ю *impf.* thicken; condense; ~ся thicken; condense; clot. **сгу́сток**, -тка clot. **сгуще́ние**, -я thickening, condensation; clotting. **сгущённ|ый**, -ён, -а́ condensed; ~ое молоко́ condensed milk; evaporated milk.

сда́бривать, -аю *impf. of* **сдо́брить**

сдава́ть, сдаю́, сдаёшь *impf. of* **сдать**; ~ **экза́мен** take, sit for, an examination; ~ся *impf. of* **сда́ться**

сда́вить, -влю́, -вишь *pf.*, **сда́вливать**, -аю *impf.* squeeze. **сда́вленный** squeezed; constrained.

сда́точн|ый delivery; ~ая квита́нция receipt. **сдать**, -ам, -ашь, -аст, -ади́м; -ал, -а́, -о *pf.* (*impf.* **сдава́ть**) hand over; pass; let, let out, hire out; give in change; surrender; yield, give up; deal; ~ бага́ж на хране́ние deposit, leave, one's luggage; ~ экза́мен pass

an examination; ~ся surrender, yield. **сда́ча**, -и handing over; letting out, hiring out; surrender; change; deal; **дать сда́чи** give change; give as good as one gets.

сдвиг, -а displacement; fault, dislocation; change, improvement. **сдвига́ть**, -а́ю *impf.*, **сдви́нуть**, -ну *pf.* shift, move, displace; move together, bring together; ~ся move, budge; come together. **сдвижно́й** movable.

с|де́лать(ся, -аю(сь *pf.* **сде́лка**, -и transaction; deal, bargain; agreement. **сде́льн|ый** piece-work; ~ая рабо́та piece-work. **сде́льщик**, -а piece-worker. **сде́льщина**, -ы piece-work.

сдёргивать, -аю *impf. of* **сдёрнуть**

сде́ржанно *adv.* with restraint, with reserve. **сде́ржанный** restrained, reserved. **сдержа́ть**, -жу́, -жишь *pf.*, **сде́рживать**, -аю *impf.* hold, hold back; hold in check, contain; keep back, restrain; keep; ~ сло́во keep one's word.

сдёрнуть, -ну *pf.* (*impf.* **сдёргивать**) pull off.

сдеру́ *etc.: see* **содра́ть**. **сдира́ть**, -а́ю *impf. of* **содра́ть**

сдо́ба, -ы shortening; fancy bread, bun(s). **сдо́бн|ый**; -бен, -бна́, -о rich, short; ~ая бу́лка bun. **сдо́брить**, -рю *pf.* (*impf.* **сда́бривать**) flavour; spice; enrich.

с|до́хнуть, -нет; сдох *pf.* (*impf. also* **сдыха́ть**) die, croak, kick the bucket.

сдружи́ться, -жу́сь *pf.* become friends.

сдубли́рованный bonded.

сдува́ть, -а́ю *impf.*, **сду́нуть**, -ну *pf.*, **сдуть**, -у́ю *pf.* blow away, blow off; crib.

сдыха́ть, -а́ет *impf. of* **сдо́хнуть**

сеа́нс, -а performance; showing, house; sitting.

себесто́имость, -и prime cost; cost (price).

себя́, *d. & p.* себе́, *i.* собо́й *or* собо́ю *refl. pron.* oneself; myself, yourself, himself, *etc.*; собо́й -looking, in appearance; хоро́ш собо́й good-looking, nice-looking; ничего́ себе́ not bad; так себе́ so-so.

сев, -а sowing.

се́вер, -а north. **се́вернее** *adv.*+*g.* northwards of, to the north of. **се́верн|ый** north, northern; northerly; С~ый Ледови́тый океа́н the Arctic Ocean; ~ый оле́нь reindeer; ~ое сия́ние northern lights, aurora borealis. **се́веро-восто́к**, -а north-east **се́веро-восто́чный** north-east, north-eastern. **се́веро-за́пад**, -а north-west. **се́веро-за́падный** north-west, north-western. **северя́нин**, -а; *pl.* -я́не, -я́н northerner.

севооборо́т, -а rotation of crops.

сего́ *see* **сей. сего́дня** *adv.* today; ~ ве́чером this evening, tonight. **сего́дняшний** of today, today's.

седе́льник, -а saddler. **седе́льный** saddle.

седе́ть, -е́ю *impf.* (*pf.* по~) go grey, turn grey. **седе́ющий** grizzled, greying. **седина́**, -ы́; *pl.* -ы grey hairs; grey streak.

седла́ть, -а́ю *impf.* (*pf.* **о~**) saddle. **седло́, -а́**; *pl.* **сёдла, -дел** saddle. **седлови́на, -ы** arch; saddle; col.

седоборо́дый grey-bearded. **седовла́сый, седоволо́сый** grey-haired. **седо́й; сед, -а́, -о** grey; hoary; grey-haired; flecked with white.

седо́к, -а́ fare, passenger; rider, horseman.

седьмо́й seventh.

сезо́н, -а season. **сезо́нник, -а** seasonal worker. **сезо́нный** seasonal.

сей, сего́ *m.*, **сия́, сей** *f.*, **сие́, сего́** *nt.*, **сий, сих** *pl.*, *pron.* this; these; **на сей раз** this time, for this once; **сего́ ме́сяца** this month's; **сию́ мину́ту** this (very) minute; at once, instantly.

сейча́с *adv.* now, at present, at the (present) moment; just, just now; presently, soon; straight away, immediately.

сёк *etc.*: *see* **сечь**

сек. *abbr.* (*of* **секу́нда**) sec., second(s).

секре́т, -а secret; hidden mechanism; listening post; **по ~у** secretly; confidentially, in confidence.

секретариа́т, -а secretariat. **секрета́рский** secretarial; secretary's. **секрета́рша, -и, секрета́рь, -я́** *m.* secretary.

секре́тно *adv.* secretly, in secret; secret, confidential; **соверше́нно ~** top secret. **секре́тный** secret; confidential; **~ сотру́дник** secret agent, under-cover agent.

секс, -а sex; **~ вне бра́ка** extramarital sex. **сексапи́льность, -и** sex appeal. **сексапи́льный** sexy. **сексуа́льность, -и** sexuality. **сексуа́льный** sexual.

се́кта, -ы sect. **секта́нт, -а** sectarian, sectary. **секта́нтство, -а** sectarianism.

се́ктор, -а sector, section, part, sphere.

секу́ *etc.*: *see* **сечь**

секу́нда, -ы second; **сию́ секу́нду!** (in) just a moment! **секунда́нт, -а** second; second string. **секу́ндн|ый** second; **~ая стре́лка** second hand. **секундоме́р, -а** a stop-watch.

секцио́нный sectional. **се́кция, -и** section.

селёдка, -и herring. **селёдочный** herring, of herring(s).

се́лезень, -зня *m.* drake.

селе́ктор, -а intercom.

селе́ние, -я settlement, village.

сели́тра, -ы saltpetre, nitre. **сели́трян|ый** saltpetre; **~ая кислота́** nitric acid.

сели́ть, -лю́ *impf.* (*pf.* **по~**) settle; **~ся** settle. **сели́тебный** built-up; building, development. **сели́тьба, -ы**; *g.pl.* **-итьб** developed land; built-up area; settlement. **село́, -а́**; *pl.* **сёла** village.

сель... *abbr.* (*of* **се́льский**) *in comb.* village; country, rural. **селько́р, -а** rural correspondent. **~ма́г, -а, ~по́** *nt.indecl.* village shop. **~сове́т, -а** village soviet.

сельдере́й, -я celery.

сельдь, -и; *pl.* **-и, -е́й** herring. **сельдяно́й** herring.

се́льск|ий country, rural; village; **~ое хозя́йство** agriculture, farming. **сельскохозя́йственный** agricultural, farming.

семафо́р, -а semaphore; signal.

сёмга, -и salmon; smoked salmon.

семе́йный family; domestic; **~ челове́к** married man, family man. **семе́йство, -а** family.

се́мени *etc.*: *see* **се́мя**

семени́ть, -ню́ *impf.* mince.

семени́ться, -и́тся *impf.* seed. **семенни́к, -а́** testicle; pericarp, seed-vessel; seed-plant. **семенно́й** seed; seminal, spermatic.

семери́чный septenary. **семёрка, -и** seven; figure 7; No. 7; group of seven. **семерно́й** sevenfold, septuple. **се́меро, -ы́х** seven.

семе́стр, -а term, semester. **семестро́вый** terminal.

се́мечко, -а; *pl.* **-и** seed; *pl.* sunflower seeds.

семидесятиле́тие, -я seventy years; seventieth anniversary, birthday. **семидесяти-ле́тний** seventy-year, seventy years'; seventy-year-old. **семидеся́т|ый** seventieth; **~ые го́ды** the seventies. **семикра́тный** sevenfold, septuple. **семиле́тка, -и** seven-year school; seven-year plan; seven-year-old. **семиле́тний** seven-year; septennial; seven-year-old; **~ ребёнок** child of seven, seven-year-old.

семина́р, -а seminar.

семинари́ст, -а seminarist. **семина́рия, -и** seminary; training college.

семисо́тый seven-hundredth. **семиты́сяч-ный** seven-thousandth. **семиуго́льник, -а** heptagon. **семиуго́льный** heptagonal. **семна́дцатый** seventeenth. **семна́дцать, -и** seventeen. **семь, -ми́, -мью** seven. **се́мьдесят, -ми́десяти, -мьюдесятью** seventy. **семьсо́т, -мисо́т, i. -мьюста́ми** seven hundred. **се́мью** *adv.* seven times.

семья́, -и́; *pl.* **-и, -е́й, -ям** family. **семьяни́н, -а** family man.

се́мя, -мени; *pl.* **-мена́, -мя́н, -мена́м** seed; semen, sperm.

Се́на, -ы the Seine.

сена́т, -а senate. **сена́тор, -а** senator. **сена́-торский** senatorial.

се́ни, -е́й *pl.* (entrance-)hall; (*enclosed*) porch.

сенно́й hay. **се́но, -а** hay. **сенова́л, -а** hayloft, hay-mow. **сеноко́с, -а** mowing, haymaking; hayfield. **сенокоси́лка, -и** mowing-machine. **сеноко́сный** haymaking.

сенсацио́нный sensational. **сенса́ция, -и** sensation.

сентимента́льность, -и sentimentality. **сен-тимента́льный** sentimental.

сентя́брь, -я́ *m.*, **сентя́брьский** September.

сепарати́вный separatist. **сепарати́зм, -а** separatism. **сепарати́ст, -а** separatist. **сепара́тный** separate.

се́псис, -а sepsis, septicaemia. **септи́ческий** septic.

се́ра, -ы sulphur; brimstone; ear-wax.

серва́нт, -а sideboard.
серви́з, -а service, set. сервирова́ть, -ру́ю *impf. & pf.* serve; ~ стол lay a table. сервиро́вка, -и laying; serving, service.
серде́чник, -а core. серде́чность, -и cordiality; warmth. серде́чный heart; of the heart; cardiac; cordial, hearty; heartfelt, sincere; warm, warm-hearted. серди́тый angry, cross; irate; strong. серди́ть, -ржу́, -рдишь *impf. (pf.* рас~) anger, make angry; ~ся be angry, be cross. се́рдце, -а; *pl.* -á, -де́ц heart; в сердца́х in anger, in a fit of temper; от всего́ се́рдца from the bottom of one's heart, wholeheartedly. сердцебие́ние, -я palpitation. сердцеви́дный heart-shaped; cordate. сердцеви́на, -ы core, pith, heart.
серебрёный silver-plated. серебри́стый silvery. серебри́ть, -рю́ *impf. (pf.* по~) silver, silver-plate; ~ся silver, become silvery. серебро́, -á silver. сере́бряник, -а a silversmith. сере́бряный silver; ~ая сва́дьба silver wedding.
середи́на, -ы middle, midst; золота́я ~ golden mean. середи́нный middle, mean, intermediate. серёдка, -и middle, centre.
серёжка, -и earring; catkin.
сере́нький grey; dull, drab. сере́ть, -е́ю *impf. (pf.* по~) turn grey, go grey; show grey.
сержа́нт, -а sergeant.
сери́йный serial; ~ое произво́дство mass production. се́рия, -и series; range; part.
се́рный sulphur; sulphuric; ~ая кислота́ sulphuric acid.
серова́тый greyish. серогла́зый grey-eyed.
серп, -á sickle, reaping-hook; ~ луны́ crescent moon.
серпанти́н, -а paper streamer; serpentine road.
серпови́дный crescent(-shaped).
серсо́ *nt.indecl.* hoop.
се́рфинг, -а surfing. серфинги́ст, -а surfer.
се́рый; сер, -á, -о grey; dull; drab; dim; ignorant, uncouth, uneducated.
серьга́, -и́; *pl.* -и, -рёг earring.
серьёзно *adv.* seriously; earnestly; in earnest. серьёзный serious; earnest; grave.
се́ссия, -и session, sitting; conference, congress; term.
сестра́, -ы́; *pl.* сёстры, сестёр, сёстрам sister.
сесть, ся́ду *pf. (impf.* сади́ться) sit down; alight; settle; perch; land; set; shrink; +на+*a.* board, take, get on; ~ за рабо́ту set to work; ~ на кора́бль go on board, go aboard; ~ на ло́шадь mount a horse; ~ на по́езд board a train.
сетево́й net, netting, mesh. се́тка, -и net, netting; (luggage-)rack; string bag; grid; co-ordinates; scale.
се́товать, -тую *impf. (pf.* по~) complain; lament, mourn.
се́точный net; grid. сетча́тка, -и retina. се́тчатый netted, network; reticular. сеть,

-и, *loc.* -и́; *pl.* -и, -е́й net; network; circuit; system.
сече́ние, -я cutting; section. сечь, секу́, сечёшь; сек *impf. (pf.* вы́~) cut to pieces; beat, flog; ~ся *(pf.* по~ся) split; cut.
се́ялка, -и sowing-machine, seed drill. се́яльщик, -а, се́ятель, -я *m.* sower. се́ять, се́ю *impf. (pf.* по~) sow; throw about.
сжа́литься, -люсь *pf.* take pity (над+*i.*) on.
сжа́тие, -я pressing, pressure; grasp, grip; compression; condensation. сжа́тость, -и compression; conciseness, concision. сжа́тый compressed; condensed, compact; concise, brief.
с|жать[1], сожму́, -нёшь *pf.*
сжать[2], сожму́, -мёшь *pf. (impf.* сжима́ть) squeeze; compress; grip; clench; ~ зу́бы grit one's teeth; ~ся tighten, clench; shrink, contract.
с|жечь, сожгу́, сожжёшь; сжёг, сожгла́ *pf. (impf.* сжига́ть) burn; burn up, burn down; cremate.
сжива́ться, -а́юсь *impf. of* сжи́ться
сжига́ть, -а́ю *impf. of* сжечь
сжим, -а clip, grip, clamp. сжима́емость, -и compressibility, condensability. сжима́ть(ся *impf. of* сжа́ть[2](ся
сжи́ться, -иву́сь, -ивёшься; -и́лся, -а́сь *pf. (impf.* сжива́ться) с+*i.* get used to, get accustomed to.
с|жу́льничать, -аю *pf.*
сза́ди *adv.* from behind; behind; from the end; from the rear. сза́ди *prep.*+*g.* behind.
сзыва́ть, -а́ю *impf. of* созва́ть
си *nt.indecl.* B; te.
сиби́рский Siberian; ~ кедр Siberian pine. Сиби́рь, -и Siberia. сибиря́к, -á, сибиря́чка, -и Siberian.
сига́ра, -ы cigar. сигаре́та, -ы cigarette; small cigar. сига́рка, -и *(home-made)* cigarette. сига́рный cigar.
сигна́л, -а signal. сигнализа́ция, -и signalling. сигнализи́ровать, -рую *impf. & pf. (pf. also* про~) signal; give warning. сигна́льный signal. сигна́льщик, -а signaller, signal-man.
сиде́лка, -и *(untrained)* nurse, sick-nurse. сиде́ние, -я sitting. сиде́нье, -я seat. сиде́ть, -ижу́ *impf.* sit; be; fit; пла́тье хорошо́ сиди́т на ней the dress fits her; ~ без де́ла have nothing to do; ~ верхо́м be on horseback; ~ (в тюрьме́) be in prison; ~ на насе́сте roost, perch.
Си́дней, -я Sydney.
сидр, -а cider.
сидя́чий sitting; sedentary; sessile.
сие́ *etc.: see* сей
си́зый; сиз, -á, -о dove-coloured, (blue-)grey; bluish, blue.
сий *see* сей
сикх, -а Sikh. си́кхский Sikh.
си́ла, -ы strength; force; power; energy; quantity, multitude; point, essence; *pl.* force(s); в

силе in force, valid; **в силу**+g. on the strength of, by virtue of, because of; **имеющий силу** valid; **не по ~ам** beyond one's powers, beyond one's strength; **своими ~ами** unaided; **силой** by force. **силач, -а** strong man. **силиться, -люсь** impf. try, make efforts. **силов|ой** power; of force; **~ое поле** field of force; **~ая станция** power-station, power-house; **~ая установка** power-plant.

силок, -лка noose, snare.

силос, -а silo, silage. **силосовать, -сую** impf. & pf. (pf. also **за~**) silo, ensile.

сильно adv. strongly, violently; very much, greatly; badly. **сильный; -лен** or **-лён, -льна, -о** strong; powerful; intense, keen, hard; **он не силён в языках** he is not good at languages; **~ мороз** hard frost.

символ, -а symbol; emblem; **~ веры** creed. **символизировать, -рую** impf. symbolize. **символизм, -а** symbolism. **символический** symbolic.

симметрический symmetrical. **симметрия, -и** symmetry.

симпатизировать, -рую impf.+d. be in sympathy with, sympathize with. **симпатический** sympathetic. **симпатичный** likeable, attractive, nice. **симпатия, -и** liking; sympathy.

симулировать, -рую impf. & pf. simulate, feign, sham. **симулянт, -а** malingerer, sham. **симуляция, -и** simulation, pretence.

симфонический symphonic. **симфония, -и** symphony; concordance.

синагога, -и synagogue.

синдикат, -а syndicate. **синдицировать, -рую** impf. & pf. syndicate.

синева, -ы blue; **~ под глазами** dark rings under the eyes. **синеватый** bluish. **синеглазый** blue-eyed. **синеть, -ею** impf. (pf. **по~**) turn blue, become blue; show blue. **синий; синь, -ня, -не** (dark) blue. **синильная кислота** prussic acid. **синить, -ню** impf. (pf. **под~**) paint blue; blue.

синод, -а synod. **синодальный** synodal.

синоним, -а synonym. **синонимика, -и** synonymy; synonyms.

синоптик, -а weather-forecaster. **синоптика, -и** weather-forecasting.

синтаксис, -а syntax. **синтаксический** syntactical.

синтез, -а synthesis. **синтезатор, -а** synthesizer. **синтезировать, -рую** impf. & pf. synthesize. **синтетический** synthetic.

синус, -а a sine; sinus.

синхронизм, -а synchronism. **синхронизация, -и** synchronization. **синхронизировать, -рую** impf. & pf. synchronize. **синхронист, -а** simultaneous interpreter.

синь¹, -и blue. **синь²** see **синий**. **синька, -и** blue, blueing; blue-print. **синяк, -а** bruise; **~ (под глазом)** black eye.

сиплый hoarse, husky. **сипнуть, -ну;** сип impf. (pf. **о~**) become hoarse, become husky.

сирена, -ы siren; hooter.

сиреневый lilac(-coloured). **сирень, -и** lilac.

Сирия, -и Syria.

сироп, -а syrup.

сирота, -ы pl. **-ы** c.g. orphan. **сиротливый** lonely. **сиротский** orphan's, orphans'; **~ дом** orphanage.

система, -ы system; type. **систематизировать, -рую** impf. & pf. systematize. **систематика, -и** systematics; classification; taxonomy. **систематический, систематичный** systematic; methodical.

ситец, -тца (-тцу) (cotton) print, (printed) cotton; chintz.

сито, -а sieve; screen; riddle.

ситцевый print, chintz; chintz-covered.

сия see **сей**

сияние, -я radiance; halo. **сиять, -яю** impf. shine, beam; be radiant.

сказ, -а a tale, lay; skaz. **сказание, -я** story, tale, legend, lay. **сказать, -ажу, -ажешь** pf. (impf. **говорить**) say; speak; tell; **как ~** how shall I put it?; **сказано — сделано** no sooner said than done; **так сказать** so to say. **сказаться, -ажусь, -ажешься** pf., **сказываться, -аюсь** impf. give notice, give warning; tell (on); declare o.s.; **~ больным** report sick. **сказитель, -я** m. narrator, storyteller. **сказка, -и** tale; story; fairy-tale; fib. **сказочник, -а** story-teller. **сказочный** fairy-tale; fabulous, fantastic; **~ ая страна** fairyland. **сказуемое** sb. predicate.

скакалка, -и skipping-rope. **скакать, -ачу, -ачешь** impf. (pf. **по~**) skip; jump; hop; gallop. **скаковой** race, racing. **скакун, -а** fast horse, race-horse.

скала, -ы; pl. **-ы** rock face, crag; cliff; **подводная ~** reef. **скалистый** rocky; precipitous.

скалить, -лю impf. (pf. **о~**); **~ зубы** bare one's teeth; grin.

скалка, -и rolling-pin.

скалолаз, -а rock-climber. **скалолазание, -я** rock-climbing.

скалывать, -аю impf. of **сколоть**

скамеечка, -и footstool; small bench. **скамейка, -и** bench. **скамья, й;** pl. **скамьи, -ей** bench; **~ подсудимых** dock; **со школьной скамьи** straight from school.

скандал, -а scandal; disgrace; brawl, rowdy scene. **скандалист, -а** brawler; troublemaker; rowdy. **скандалить, -лю** impf. (pf. **на~, о~**) brawl; kick up a row; shame; **~ся** disgrace o.s.; cut a poor figure **скандальный** scandalous; rowdy; scandal.

Скандинавия, -и Scandinavia.

скандирование, -я scansion.

сканер, -а scanner.

скапливать(ся, -аю(сь impf. of **скопить(ся**

скарб, -а goods and chattels, bits and pieces.

ска́ред, -а, **ска́реда**, -ы *c.g.* miser. **ска́редничать**, -аю *impf.* be stingy. **ска́редный** stingy, miserly, niggardly.

скарлати́на, -ы scarlet fever, scarlatina.

скат, -а slope, incline; pitch.

с|ката́ть, -а́ю *pf.* (*impf.* **ска́тывать**) roll (up); furl.

ска́терть, -и; *pl.* -и, -ей table-cloth; ~ью доро́га! good riddance!

скати́ть, -ачу́, -а́тишь *pf.*, **ска́тывать**[1], -аю *impf.* roll down; ~ся roll down; slip, slide. **ска́тывать**[2], -аю *impf. of* **ската́ть**

скафа́ндр, -а a diving-suit; space-suit.

ска́чка, -и gallop, galloping. **ска́чки**, -чек *pl.* horse-race; races, race-meeting; ~ с препя́тствиями steeple-chase, obstacle-race. **скачкообра́зный** spasmodic; uneven. **скачо́к**, -чка́ jump, leap, bound.

ска́шивать, -аю *impf. of* **скоси́ть**

СКВ *abbr.* (*of* **свобо́дно конверти́руемая валю́та**) freely convertible currency, hard currency.

сква́жина, -ы slit, chink; bore-hole; well **сква́жистый**, **сква́жный** porous.

сквер, -а public garden; square.

скве́рно badly; bad, poorly. **скверносло́вить**, -влю *impf.* use foul language. **скве́рный** nasty, foul; bad.

сквози́ть, -и́т *impf.* be transparent, show light through; show through; **сквози́т** *impers.* there is a draught. **сквозно́й** through; all-round; transparent; ~ ве́тер draught. **сквозня́к**, -а́ draught. **сквозь** *prep.*+*g.* through.

скворе́ц, -рца́ starling.

скеле́т, -а skeleton.

ске́птик, -а sceptic. **скептици́зм**, -а scepticism. **скепти́ческий** sceptical.

скетч, -а (*theatr.*) sketch.

ски́дка, -и rebate, reduction, discount; allowance(s); **со ски́дкой в**+*a.* with a reduction of, at a discount of. **ски́дывать**, -аю *impf.*, **ски́нуть**, -ну *pf.* throw off, throw down; knock off.

ски́петр, -а sceptre.

скипида́р, -а (-у) turpentine.

скирд, -а́; *pl.* -ы́, **скирда́**, -ы́; *pl.* -ы, -а́м stack, rick.

скиса́ть, -а́ю *impf.*, **ски́снуть**, -ну; скис *pf.* go sour, turn (sour).

скита́лец, -льца wanderer. **скита́льческий** wandering. **скита́ться**, -а́юсь *impf.* wander.

скиф, -а Scythian. **ски́фский** Scythian.

склад[1], -а storehouse; depot; store.

склад[2], -а (-у) stamp, mould; turn; logical connection; ~ ума́ turn of mind, mentality.

скла́дка, -и fold; pleat, tuck; crease; wrinkle.

скла́дно *adv.* smoothly, coherently.

складн|о́й folding, collapsible; ~а́я крова́ть camp-bed; ~а́я ле́стница steps, step-ladder.

скла́дный; -ден, -дна, -о well-knit, well-built; well-made; rounded, smooth, coherent.

скла́дочный, **складско́й** storage, warehousing; **скла́дочное ме́сто** store-room, lumber-room, box-room.

скла́дчатый plicated, folded.

скла́дчина, -ы clubbing; pooling; **в скла́дчину** by clubbing together. **скла́дывать(ся**, -аю(сь *impf. of* **сложи́ть(ся**

скле́ивать, -аю *impf.*, **с|кле́ить**, -е́ю *pf.* stick together; glue together, paste together; ~ся stick together. **скле́йка**, -и glueing, pasting, together.

склеп, -а (burial) vault, crypt.

склепа́ть, -а́ю *pf.* **склёпывать**, -аю *impf.* rivet. **склёпка**, -и riveting.

склеро́з, -а sclerosis; **рассе́янный**, **мно́жественный** ~ multiple sclerosis.

скло́ка, -и squabble; row.

склон, -а slope; **на** ~**е лет** in one's declining years. **склоне́ние**, -я inclination; declination; declension. **склони́ть**, -ню́, -нишь *pf.*, **склоня́ть**, -я́ю *impf.* incline; bend, bow; win over, gain over; decline; ~ся bend, bow; give in, yield; decline, be declined. **скло́нность**, -и inclination; disposition; susceptibility; bent, penchant. **скло́нный**; -нен, -нна́, -нно inclined, disposed, susceptible, given, prone. **склоня́емый** declinable.

скло́чник, -а squabbler, trouble-maker. **скло́чный** troublesome, trouble-making.

скля́нка, -и phial; bottle; hour-glass; bell; **шесть скля́нок** six bells.

скоба́, -ы́; *pl.* -ы, -а́м cramp, clamp; staple; catch, fastening; shackle.

ско́бель, -я *m.* spoke-shave, draw(ing)-knife.

ско́бка, -и *dim. of* **скоба́**; bracket; *pl.* parenthesis, parentheses; **в** ~**х** in brackets; in parenthesis, by the way, incidentally.

скобли́ть, -облю́, -о́блишь *impf.* scrape, plane.

ско́бочн|ый cramp, clamp, staple, shackle; bracket; ~**ая маши́на** stapler, stapling machine.

ско́ванность, -и constraint. **ско́ванный** constrained; locked, bound; ~ **льда́ми** ice-bound. **скова́ть**, скую́, скуёшь *pf.* (*impf.* **ско́вывать**) forge; hammer out; chain; fetter, bind; pin down, hold, contain; lock; **лёд скова́л ре́ку** the river is ice-bound.

сковорода́, -ы́; *pl.* **ско́вороды**, -ро́д, -а́м, **сковоро́дка**, -и frying-pan.

ско́вывать, -аю *impf. of* **скова́ть**

скола́чивать, -аю *impf.*, **сколоти́ть**, -очу́, -о́тишь *pf.* knock together; knock up; put together.

сколо́ть, -лю́, -лешь *pf.* (*impf.* **ска́лывать**) split off, chop off; pin together.

скольже́ние, -я sliding, slipping; glide; ~ **на крыло́** side-slip. **скользи́ть**, -льжу́ *impf.*, **скользну́ть**, -ну́, -нёшь *pf.* slide; slip; glide. **скóльзкий**; -зок, -зка́, -о slippery. **скользя́щий** sliding; ~ **у́зел** slip-knot.

ско́лько *adv.* how much; how many; as far as, so far as; ~ **вам лет?** how old are you?; ~ **вре́мени?** what time is it? how long?; ~

раз? how many times? **ско́лько-нибудь**
adv. any.

с|кома́ндовать, -дую *pf.* с|комбини́ровать,
-рую *pf.* с|ко́мкать, -аю *pf.* с|комплекто-
ва́ть, -тую *pf.* с|компромети́ровать, -рую
pf.

сконфу́женный embarrassed, confused,
abashed, disconcerted. с|конфу́зить(ся,
-у́жу(сь *pf.*

с|концентри́ровать, -рую *pf.*

сконча́ние, -я end; passing, death. **скон-
ча́ться**, -а́юсь *pf.* pass away, die.

с|копи́ровать, -рую *pf.*

скопи́ть, -плю́, -пишь *pf.* (*impf.* **ска́пли-
вать**) save, save up; amass, pile up; ~ся
accumulate, pile up; gather, collect. **скоп-
ле́ние**, -я accumulation; crowd; concentration, conglomeration.

с|копни́ть, -ню́ *pf.* **ско́пом** *adv.* in a crowd,
in a bunch, en masse.

скорбе́ть, -блю́ *impf.* grieve, mourn, lament.
ско́рбный sorrowful, mournful, doleful.
скорбь, -и; *pl.* -и, -е́й sorrow, grief.

скоре́е, скоре́й *comp. of* **ско́ро, ско́рый**;
adv. rather, sooner; **как мо́жно ~** as soon
as possible; ~ **всего́** most likely, most probably.

скорлупа́, -ы́; *pl.* -ы shell.

скорня́жн|ый fur, fur-dressing; ~ое де́ло
furriery; ~ый това́р furs. **скорня́к**, -а́ furrier, fur-dresser.

ско́ро *adv.* quickly, fast; soon.

ско́ро... *in comb.* quick-, fast-. **скорова́рка**,
-и pressure-cooker. ~**гово́рка**, -и patter;
tongue-twister. ~**ду́м**, -а quick-witted person. ~**пи́сный** cursive. **ско́ропись**, -и cursive; shorthand. ~**подъёмность**, -и rate of
climb. ~**по́ртящийся** perishable. ~**по-
сти́жный** sudden. ~**спе́лый** early; fast-rip-
ening; premature; hasty. ~**стре́льный**
rapid-firing, quick-firing. ~**сшива́тель**, -я
m. loose-leaf binder; folder, file. ~**те́чный**
transient, short-lived; ~**те́чная чахо́тка** galloping consumption. ~**хо́д**, -а runner, messenger; fast runner; high-speed skater.

с|коро́биться, -ится *pf.*

скоростни́к, -а́ high-speed worker, performer. **скоростно́й** high-speed; ~ **авто́бус** express bus. **ско́рость**, -и; *g.pl.* -е́й speed; velocity; rate; **в ско́рости** soon, in the near
future; **коро́бка скоросте́й** gear-box.

с|корота́ть, -а́ю *pf.*

скорпио́н, -а scorpion; Scorpio.

с|корректи́ровать, -рую *pf.* с|ко́рчить(ся,
-чу(сь *pf.*

ско́р|ый; скор, -а́, -о quick, fast; rapid; near;
short; forthcoming; **в ~ом бу́дущем** in the
near future; **в ~ом вре́мени** shortly, before
long; **на ~ую ру́ку** off-hand, in a rough-and-
ready way; ~ый по́езд fast train, express;
~ая по́мощь first-aid; ambulance service.

скос, -а mowing. с|коси́ть[1], -ошу́, -о́сишь
pf. (*impf. also* **ска́шивать**) mow.

с|коси́ть[2], -ошу́ *pf.* (*impf. also* **ска́шивать**)
squint; be drawn to one side; cut on the cross.

скот, -а́, **скоти́на**, -ы cattle; livestock; beast,
swine. **ско́тник**, -а herdsman; cowman.
ско́тный cattle, livestock; ~ **двор** cattle-
yard, farmyard.

ско́то... *in comb.* cattle. **скотобо́йня**, -и;
g.pl. -о́ен slaughter-house. ~**во́д**, -а cattle-
breeder, stock-breeder. ~**во́дство**, -а cat-
tle-raising, stock-breeding. ~**кра́дство**, -а
cattle-stealing. ~**приго́нный двор** stockyard. ~**промы́шленник**, -а cattle-dealer.
~**сбра́сыватель**, -я *m.* cow-catcher.

ско́тский cattle; brutal, brutish, bestial.
ско́тство, -а brutish condition; brutality,
bestiality.

скра́сить, -а́шу *pf.*, **скра́шивать**, -аю *impf.*
smooth over; relieve, take the edge off; improve.

скребо́к, -бка́ scraper. **скребу́** *etc.: see*
скрести́

скре́жет, -а grating; gnashing, grinding. **скре-
жета́ть**, -ещу́, -е́щешь *impf.* grate, grit; +*i.*
scrape, grind, gnash.

скре́па, -ы tie, clamp, brace; counter-signa-
ture, authentication.

скре́пер, -а scraper.

скрепи́ть, -плю́ *pf.*, **скрепля́ть**, -я́ю *impf.*
fasten (together), make fast; pin (together);
clamp, brace; countersign, authenticate,
ratify; **скрепя́ се́рдце** reluctantly, grudgingly. **скре́пка**, -и paper-clip. **скрепле́-
ние**, -я fastening; clamping; tie, clamp.

скрести́, -ебу́, -ебёшь; -ёб, -ла́ *impf.* scrape;
scratch, claw; ~ся scratch.

скрести́сь, -ещу́ *pf.*, **скре́щивать**, -аю *impf.*
cross; interbreed; ~ся cross; clash; interbreed. **скреще́ние**, -я crossing; intersection.
скре́щивание, -я crossing; interbreeding.

с|криви́ть(ся, -влю́(сь *pf.*

скрип, -а squeak, creak. **скрипа́ч**, -а́ violinist; fiddler. **скрипе́ть**, -плю́ *impf.*, **скри́п-
нуть**, -ну *pf.* squeak, creak; scratch. **скрипи́-
чный** violin; ~ **ключ** treble clef. **скри́пка**,
-и violin, fiddle. **скрипу́чий** squeaking,
creaking; rasping, scratching.

с|крои́ть, -ою́ *pf.*

скро́мник, -а modest man. **скро́мничать**,
-аю *impf.* (*pf.* **по~**) be (too) modest. **скро́м-
ность**, -и modesty. **скро́мный**; -мен, -мна́,
-о modest.

скро́ю *etc.: see* **скрыть. скрою́** *etc.: see*
скрои́ть

скру́пул, -а scruple. **скрупулёзный** scrupulous.

с|крути́ть, -учу́, -у́тишь *pf.*, **скру́чивать**, -аю
impf. twist; roll; bind, tie up.

скрыва́ть, -а́ю *impf.*, **скрыть**, -о́ю *pf.* hide,
conceal; ~ся hide, go into hiding, be hid-
den; steal away, escape; disappear, vanish.
скры́тничать, -аю *impf.* be secretive, be
reticent. **скры́тный** reticent, secretive.
скры́тый secret, concealed, hidden; latent.

скря́га, -и *c.g.* miser. **скря́жничать, -аю** *impf.* pinch, scrape; be miserly.

ску́дный; -ден, -дна́, -о scanty, poor; slender, meagre; scant; +*i.* poor in, short of. **ску́дость, -и** scarcity, poverty.

ску́ка, -и boredom, tedium.

скула́, -ы́; *pl.* **-ы** cheek-bone. **скула́стый** with high cheek-bones.

скули́ть, -лю́ *impf.* whine, whimper.

ску́льптор, -а sculptor. **скульпту́ра, -ы** sculpture. **скульпту́рный** sculptural; statuesque.

ску́мбрия, -и mackerel.

скунс, -а skunk.

скупа́ть, -а́ю *impf. of* **скупи́ть**

скупе́ц, -пца́ miser.

скупи́ть, -плю́, -пишь *pf.* (*impf.* **скупа́ть**) buy (up); corner.

скупи́ться, -плю́сь *impf.* (*pf.* **по~**) pinch, scrape, be stingy, be miserly; be sparing; +**на**+*a.* stint, grudge; ~ **на де́ньги** be close-fisted.

ску́пка, -и buying (up); cornering.

ску́по *adv.* sparingly. **скупо́й; -п, -а́, -о** stingy, miserly, niggardly; inadequate. **ску́пость, -и** stinginess, miserliness, niggardliness.

ску́пщик, -а buyer (up); ~ **кра́деного** fence.

ску́тер, -а; *pl.* **-а́** outboard speed-boat.

скуча́ть, -а́ю *impf.* be bored; +**по**+*d.* or *p.* miss, yearn for.

ску́ченность, -и density, congestion; ~ **населе́ния** overcrowding. **ску́ченный** dense, congested. **ску́чивать, -аю** *impf.*, **ску́чить, -чу** *pf.* crowd (together); ~**ся** flock, cluster; crowd together, huddle together.

ску́чный; -чен, -чна́, -о boring, tedious, dull; bored; **мне ску́чно** I'm bored.

с|ку́шать, -аю *pf.* **скую́** *etc.: see* **скова́ть**

слабе́ть, -е́ю *impf.* (*pf.* **о~**) weaken, grow weak; slacken, droop. **слабина́, -ы́** slack; weak spot, weak point. **слаби́тельн|ый** laxative, purgative; ~**ое** *sb.* purge. **слаби́ть, -ит** *impf.* (*pf.* **про~**) purge, act as a laxative; *impers.*+*a.* **его́ сла́бит** he has diarrhoea.

слабо... *in comb.* weak, feeble, slight. **слабоалкого́льный** low-alcohol. **~во́лие, -я** weakness of will. **~во́льный** weak-willed. **~ду́шный** faint-hearted. **~не́рвный** nervy, nervous; neurasthenic. **~ра́звитый** underdeveloped. **~си́льный** weak, feeble; low-powered. **~то́чный** low-current, weak-current, low-power. **~у́мие, -я** feeble-mindedness, imbecility; dementia. **~у́мный** feeble-minded, imbecile. **~хара́ктерный** characterless, of weak character.

сла́бый; -б, -а́, -о weak; feeble; slack, loose; poor.

сла́ва, -ы glory; fame; name, repute, reputation; rumour; **на сла́ву** wonderfully well, excellently, famously. **сла́вить, -влю** *impf.* celebrate, hymn, sing the praises of; ~**ся** (+*i.*) be famous, famed, renowned, (for); have a reputation (for). **сла́вный** glorious, famous, renowned; nice, splendid.

славяни́н, -а; *pl.* **-я́не, -я́н, славя́нка, -и** Slav. **славянофи́л, -а** Slavophil(e). **славя́нский** Slav, Slavonic.

слага́емое *sb.* component, term, member. **слага́ть, -а́ю** *impf. of* **сложи́ть**

сла́дить, -а́жу *pf.* **с**+*i.* cope with, manage, handle; make, construct.

сла́дк|ий; -док, -дка́, -о sweet; sugary, sugared, honeyed; ~**кое мя́со** sweetbread; ~**ое** *sb.* sweet course. **сладостра́стник, -а** voluptuary. **сладостра́стный** voluptuous. **сла́дость, -и** joy; sweetness; sweetening; *pl.* sweets.

сла́женность, -и co-ordination, harmony, order. **сла́женный** co-ordinated, harmonious, orderly.

сла́нец, -нца shale, slate; schist. **сланцева́тый, сла́нцевый** shale; shaly, slaty, schistose.

сластёна *c.g.* person with a sweet tooth. **сласть, -и;** *pl.* **-и, -е́й** delight, pleasure; *pl.* sweets, sweet things.

слать, шлю, шлёшь *impf.* send.

слаща́вый sugary, sickly-sweet. **сла́ще** *comp. of* **сла́дкий**

сле́ва *adv.* from (the) left; on, to, the left; ~ **напра́во** from left to right.

слёг *etc.: see* **слечь**

слегка́ *adv.* slightly; lightly, gently; somewhat.

след, следа́ (-у), *d.* **-у,** *loc.* **-у́;** *pl.* **-ы́** track, trail, footprint, footstep; trace, sign, vestige. **следи́ть[1], -ежу́** *impf.* +**за**+*i.* watch; track; shadow; follow; keep up with; look after; keep an eye on. **следи́ть[2], -ежу́** *impf.* (*pf.* **на~**) leave traces, marks, footmarks, footprints. **сле́дование, -я** movement, proceeding. **сле́дователь, -я** *m.* investigator. **сле́довательно** *adv.* consequently, therefore, hence. **сле́довать, -дую** *impf.* (*pf.* **по~**) I. +*d.* or **за**+*i.* follow; go after; comply with; result; go, be bound; **по́езд сле́дует до Москвы́** the train goes to Moscow; II. *impers.* (+*d.*) ought, should; be owing, be owed; **вам сле́дует**+*inf.* you should, you ought to; **как и сле́довало ожида́ть** as was to be expected; **как сле́дует** properly, well; as it should be; **куда́ сле́дует** to the proper quarter; **ско́лько с меня́ сле́дует?** how much do I owe (you)? **сле́дом** *adv.* (**за**+*i.*) immediately after, behind, close behind. **следопы́т, -а** pathfinder, tracker. **сле́дственн|ый** investigation, inquiry; ~**ая коми́ссия** commission (committee) of inquiry. **сле́дствие[1], -я** consequence, result. **сле́дствие[2], -я** investigation. **сле́дующ|ий** following, next; **в ~ий раз** next time; **на ~ей неде́ле** next week; **~им о́бразом** in the following way. **слёжка, -и** *n* shadowing.

слеза́, -ы́; *pl.* **-ёзы, -а́м** tear.

слеза́ть, -а́ю *impf. of* **слезть**

слези́ться, -и́тся *impf.* water. **слезли́вый** tearful, lachrymose. **слёзный** tear; lachrymal; tearful, plaintive. **слезоточи́вый** watering, running; lachrymatory; ~ **газ** tear-gas.

слезть, -зу; слез *pf.* (*impf.* **слеза́ть**) climb down, get down; dismount, alight, get off; come off, peel.

сленг, -а slang. **сле́нговый** slang.

слепе́нь, -пня́ *m.* gadfly, horse-fly.

слепе́ц, -пца́ blind man. **слепи́ть**[1], -пи́т *impf.* blind; dazzle.

с|лепи́ть[2], -плю́, -пишь *pf.*, **слепля́ть**, -я́ю *impf.* stick together; mould, model.

слепну́ть, -ну; слеп *impf.* (*pf.* о~) go blind, become blind. **сле́по** *adv.* blindly; indistinctly. **слеп|о́й**; -п, -а́, -о blind; indistinct; ~**ы́е** *sb.*, *pl.* the blind.

слепо́к, -пка cast.

слепота́, -ы́ blindness.

сле́сарь, -я; *pl.* -я́ *or* -и *m.* metal worker; locksmith.

слёт, -а gathering, meeting; rally. **слета́ть**, -а́ю *impf.*, **слете́ть**, -ечу́ *pf.* fly down; fall down, fall off; fly away; ~**ся** fly together; congregate.

слечь, сля́гу, -я́жешь; слёг, -ла́ *pf.* take to one's bed.

сли́ва, -ы plum; plum-tree.

слива́ть(ся, -а́ю(сь *impf.* *of* **слить(ся**. **сли́вки**, -вок *pl.* cream. **сли́вочник**, -а cream-jug. **сли́вочн|ый** cream; creamy; ~**ое ма́сло** butter; ~**ое моро́женое** ice-cream.

сли́зистый mucous; slimy. **слизня́к**, -а́ slug. **слизь**, -и mucus; slime.

с|линя́ть, -я́ет *pf.*

слипа́ться, -а́ется *impf.*, **сли́пнуться**, -нется; -и́пся *pf.* stick together.

сли́тно together, as one word. **сли́ток**, -тка ingot, bar. **с|лить**, солью́, -ьёшь; -ил, -а́, -о *pf.* (*impf. also* **слива́ть**) pour, pour out, pour off; fuse, merge, amalgamate; ~**ся** flow together; blend, mingle; merge, amalgamate.

слича́ть, -а́ю *impf.*, **сличи́ть**, -чу́ *pf.* collate; check. **сличе́ние**, -я collation, checking. **сличи́тельный** checking, check.

сли́шком *adv.* too; too much.

слия́ние, -я confluence; blending, merging, amalgamation; merger.

слова́рный lexical; lexicographic(al), dictionary. **слова́рь**, -я́ *m.* dictionary; glossary; vocabulary. **слове́сник**, -а, -**ница**, -ы philologist; student of philology; (*Russian*) language and literature teacher. **слове́сность**, -и literature; philology. **слове́сный** verbal, oral; literary; philological. **сло́вник**, -а glossary; word-list, vocabulary. **сло́вно** *conj.* as if; like, as. **сло́во**, -а; *pl.* -а́ word; speech; speaking; address; lay, tale; **к сло́ву** by the way, by the by; **одни́м** ~**м** in a word. **сло́вом** *adv.* in a word, in short. **словообразова́ние**, -я word-formation. **словоохо́тливый** talkative, loquacious. **словосочета́ние**, -я word combination, word-group, phrase. **словоупотребле́ние**, -я use of words, usage. **словцо́**, -а́ word; apt word,

the right word; **для кра́сного словца́** for effect, to display one's wit.

слог[1], -а style.

слог[2], -а; *pl.* -и, -о́в syllable. **слогово́й** syllabic.

слое́ние, -я stratification. **слоён|ый** flaky; ~**ое те́сто** puff pastry, flaky pastry.

сложе́ние, -я adding; composition; addition; build, constitution. **сложи́ть**, -жу́, -жишь *pf.* (*impf.* **класть**, **скла́дывать**, **слага́ть**) (together), lay (together); pile, heap, stack; add, add up; fold (up); make up, compose; take off, put down, set down; lay down; **сложа́ ру́ки** with arms folded; idle; ~ **ве́щи** pack, pack up; ~ **наказа́ние** remit a punishment; ~**ся** form, turn out; take shape; arise; club together, pool one's resources. **сложно-сокращённ|ый**: ~**ое сло́во** acronym. **сло́жность**, -и complication; complexity; **в о́бщей сло́жности** all in all, in sum. **сло́жн|ый**; -жен, -жна́, -о compound; complex; multiple; complicated, intricate; ~**ое сло́во** compound (word).

сло́йстый stratified; lamellar; flaky, foliated; schistose. **слои́ть**, -ою́ *impf.* stratify; layer; make flaky. **слой**, -я; *pl.* -и́, -ёв layer; stratum; coat, coating, film.

слом, -а demolition, pulling down, breaking up; **пойти́ на** ~ be scrapped. **с|лома́ть(ся**, -а́ю(сь *pf.* **сломи́ть**, -млю́, -мишь *pf.* break, smash; overcome; **сломя́ го́лову** like mad, at breakneck speed; ~**ся** break.

слон, -а́ elephant; bishop. **слони́ха**, -и she-elephant. **слоно́в|ый** elephant; elephantine; ~**ая кость** ivory.

слою́ *etc.*: *see* **слои́ть**

слоня́ться, -я́юсь *impf.* loiter (about), mooch about.

слуга́, -и́; *pl.* -и *m.* man, (man)servant. **служа́нка**, -и servant, maid. **слу́жащий** *sb.* employee; *pl.* staff. **слу́жба**, -ы service; work; employment. **служе́бн|ый** service; office; official; work; auxiliary; secondary; ~**ый вход** staff entrance; ~**ое вре́мя** office hours; ~**ое де́ло** official business. **служе́ние**, -я service, serving. **служи́ть**, -жу́, -жишь *impf.* (*pf.* по~) serve; work, be employed; be; be used, do; be in use, do duty; +*d.* devote o.s. to; ~ **доказа́тельством**+*g.* serve as evidence of; ~ **при́знаком** indicate, be a sign of.

с|лука́вить, -влю *pf.* **с|лупи́ть**, -плю́, -пишь *pf.*

слух, -а hearing; ear; rumour, hearsay; **по** ~**у** be ear. **слуха́ч**, -а́ monitor. **слухов|о́й** acoustic, auditory, aural; ~**о́й аппара́т** hearing aid; ~**о́е окно́** dormer (window).

слу́чай, -я incident, occurrence, event; case; accident; opportunity, occasion; chance; **ни в ко́ем слу́чае** in no circumstances; **по слу́чаю** secondhand; +*g.* by reason of, on account of; on the occasion of. **случа́йно** *adv.* by chance, by accident, accidentally; by any

chance. **случайность**, -и chance; **по счаст-
ливой случайности** by a lucky chance, by
sheer luck. **случайн|ый** accidental, fortui-
tous; chance; casual, incidental; **~ая встреча**
chance meeting. **случаться**, -ается *impf.*,
случиться, -ится *pf.* happen; come about,
come to pass, befall; turn up show up; **что
случилось?** what has happened? what's up?
слушатель, -я *m.* hearer, listener; student;
pl. audience. **слушать**, -аю *impf. (pf.* **по~,
про~)** listen to; hear; attend lectures on; **(я)
слушаю!** hello!; very well, very good; yes,
sir; **~ся**+*g.* obey, listen to.
слыть, -ыву́ -ывёшь; -ыл, -á, -о *impf. (pf.*
про~) have the reputation, be known, be
said; pass (+*i. or* **за**+*a.* for).
слыхáть *impf.*, **слышать**, -шу *impf. (pf.* у~)
hear; notice; feel, sense. **слышаться**, -шится
impf. (pf. **по~)** be heard, be audible. **слы-
шимость**, -и audibility. **слышимый** aud-
ible. **слышно** *adv.* audibly. **слышн|ый** au-
dible; **~о** *pred.* *impers.* (+*d.*) one can hear;
it is said, they say; **нам никого не было ~о**
we could not hear anyone; **что ~о?** what's
new?
слюдá, -ы́ mica. **слюдяной** mica.
слюнá, -ы́; *pl.* -и, -ей saliva; spit; *pl.* slobber,
spittle. **слюнявый** dribbling, drivelling,
slavering.
сля́гу *etc.: see* **слечь**
сля́котный slushy. **слякоть**, -и slush.
см *abbr. (of* **сантиметр)** cm, centimetre(s).
см. *abbr. (of* **смотри)** see, *vide.*
смáзать, -áжу *pf.*, **смáзывать**, -аю *impf.* oil,
lubricate; grease; smudge; rub over; slur over.
смáзка, -и oiling, lubrication; oil, lubricant;
greasing; grease. **смáзочн|ый** oil; lubri-
cating; **~ое мáсло** lubricating oil. **смáзчик**,
-а greaser. **смáзывание**, -я oiling, lubrication; greasing; slurring over.
смак, -а (-у) relish, savour. **смаковáть**, -кую
impf. relish, enjoy; savour.
с|маневри́ровать, -рую *pf.*
смáнивать, -аю *impf.*, **сманить**, -ню́, -нишь
pf. entice, lure.
с|мастери́ть, -рю́ *pf.* **смáтывать**, -аю *impf.*
of **смотáть**
смáхивать, -аю *impf.*, **смахнýть**, -нý, -нёшь
pf. brush away, off; flick away, off.
смáчивать, -аю *impf. of* **смочить**
смéжный adjacent, contiguous, adjoining,
neighbouring.
смекáлка, -и native wit, mother wit; sharpness.
смёл *etc.: see* **смести**
смелéть, -éю *impf. (pf.* о~) grow bold, grow
bolder. **смéло** *adv.* boldly; easily, with ease.
смéлость, -и boldness, audacity, courage.
смéлый bold, audacious, courageous, daring. **смельчáк**, -á bold spirit; daredevil.
смелю́ *etc.: see* **смолóть**
смéна, -ы changing, change; replacement(s);
relief; shift; change; **идти на смéну**+*d.* take

the place of, relieve; **~ карáула** changing of
the guard. **сменить**, -ню́, -нишь *pf.*, **сме-
нять¹**, -яю *impf.* change; replace; relieve;
succeed; **~ся** hand over; be relieved; take
turns; +*i.* give place to. **смéнность**, -и shift
system; shiftwork. **смéнн|ый** shift; change-
able; **~ое колесó** spare wheel. **смéнщик**, -а
relief; *pl.* new shift. **сменяемый** removable,
interchangeable. **сменять²**, -яю *pf.* exchange.
с|мéрить, -рю *pf.*
смеркáться, -ается *impf.*, **смéркнуться**,
-нется *pf.* get dark.
смертéльно *adv.* mortally; extremely, terribly; **~ устáть** be dead tired. **смертéльный**
mortal, fatal, death; extreme, terrible. **смéрт-
ность**, -и mortality, death-rate. **смéртн|ый**
mortal; death; deadly; extreme; **~ая казнь**
death penalty; capital punishment; **~ый
приговóр** death sentence. **смерть**, -и; *g.pl.*
-éй death; decease; **дó смерти** to death;
умерéть своéй смéртью die a natural death;
~ как *adv.* awfully, terribly.
смерч, -а whirlwind, tornado; waterspout;
sandstorm.
смеси́тельный mixing. **с|меси́ть**, -ешу́,
-éсишь *pf.*
смести́, -ету́, -етёшь; -ёл, -á *per. (impf.* **сметáть)** sweep off, sweep (away).
смести́ть, -ещу́ *pf. (impf.* **смещáть)** displace;
remove; move; dismiss; **~ся** change position,
become displaced.
смесь, -и mixture; blend, miscellany, medley.
смéта, -ы estimate.
сметáна, -ы smetana, sour cream.
с|метáть¹, -áю *pf. (impf. also* **смётывать)**
tack (together).
сметáть², -áю *impf. of* **смести**
смётливый quick, sharp; resourceful.
смéтный estimated, budget, planned.
сметý *etc.: see* **смести**. **смётывать**, -аю
impf. of **сметáть**
сметь, -éю *impf. (pf.* **по~)** dare; have the
right.
смех, -а (-у) laughter; laugh; **~а рáди** for a
joke, for fun. **смехотвóрный** laughable, ludicrous, ridiculous.
смéшанн|ый mixed; combined; **~ое акцио-
нéрное óбщество** joint-stock company.
с|мешáть, -áю *pf.*, **смéшивать**, -аю *impf.*
mix, blend; lump together; confuse, mix up;
~ся mix, (inter)blend, blend in; mingle; become confused, get mixed up. **смешéние**,
-я mixture, blending, merging; confusion,
mixing up.
смеши́ть, -шý *impf. (pf.* **на~, рас~)** amuse,
make laugh. **смеши́вость**, -и risibility.
смешли́вый inclined to laugh, easily amu-
sed, given to laughing. **смешн|ой** funny;
amusing; absurd, ridiculous, ludicrous; **здесь
нет ничегó ~óго** there's nothing to laugh
at, it is no laughing matter; **~ó** *pred.* it is

funny; it makes one laugh.

смешу́ *etc.*: *see* **смеси́ть, смеши́ть**

смеща́ть(ся, -а́ю(сь *impf. of* **смести́ть(ся. смеще́ние, -я** displacement, removal; shifting, shift; drift; bias. **смещу́** *etc.*: *see* **смести́ть**

смея́ться, -ею́сь, -еёшься *impf.* laugh; +**над**+*i.* laugh at, make fun of.

смире́ние, -я humility, meekness. **смире́нный** humble, meek. **смири́тельн|ый; ~ая руба́шка** straitjacket. **смири́ть, -рю́** *pf.*, **смиря́ть, -я́ю** *impf.* restrain, subdue; humble; **~ся** submit; resign o.s. **сми́рно** *adv.* quietly; **~!** attention! **сми́рный** quiet; submissive.

см. на об. *abbr.* (*of* **смотри́ на оборо́те**) PTO (= *please turn over*), see over.

смогу́ *etc.*: *see* **смочь**

смо́кинг, -а dinner-jacket.

смола́, -ы́; *pl.* **-ы** resin; pitch, tar; rosin. **смолёный** resined; tarred, pitched. **смоли́стый** resinous. **смоли́ть, -лю́** *impf.* (*pf.* **вы́~, о~**) resin; tar, pitch.

смолка́ть, -а́ю *impf.*, **смо́лкнуть, -ну -олк** *pf.* fall silent, be silent; cease.

смо́лоду *adv.* from one's youth.

с|молоти́ть, -очу́ -о́тишь *pf.* **с|моло́ть, смелю́, сме́лешь** *pf.*

смоляно́й pitch, tar, resin.

с|монти́ровать, -рую *pf.*

сморка́ть, -а́ю *impf.* (*pf.* **вы́~**) blow; **~ся** blow one's nose.

сморо́дина, -ы currants; currant(-bush). **сморо́динный** currant.

смо́рщенный wrinkled. **с|мо́рщить(ся, -щу(сь** *pf.*

смота́ть, -а́ю *pf.* (*impf.* **сма́тывать**) wind, reel; **~ся** hurry (away); go, drop in.

смотр, -а, *loc.* **-у́**; *pl.* **-о́тры** review, inspection; public showing; **произвести́ ~**+*d.* inspect, review; **~ худо́жественной самоде́ятельности** amateur arts festival. **смотре́ть, -рю́, -ришь** *impf.* (*pf.* **по~**) look; see; watch; look through; examine; review, inspect; +**за**+*i.* look after; be in charge of, supervise; +**в**+*a.*, **на**+*a.* look on to, look over; +*i.* look (like); **смотри́(те)!** mind! take care!; **~ за поря́дком** keep order; **смотря́** it depends; **смотря́ по** depending on, in accordance with; **~ся** look at o.s. **смотри́тель, -я** *m.* supervisor; custodian keeper. **смотрово́й** review; observation, inspection, sight.

смочи́ть, -чу́, -чишь *pf.* (*impf.* **сма́чивать**) damp, wet, moisten.

с|мочь, -огу́, -о́жешь; смог, -ла́ *pf.* **с|моше́нничать, -аю** *pf.* **смо́ю** *etc.*: *see* **смы́ть**

смрад, -а stink stench. **смра́дный** stinking.

смуглоли́цый, сму́глый; -гл, -а́, -о dark-complexioned; swarthy.

с|мудри́ть, -рю́ *pf.*

сму́та, -ы disturbance, sedition. **смути́ть, -ущу́** *pf.*, **смуща́ть, -а́ю** *impf.* embarrass,

confuse; disturb, trouble; **~ся** be embarrassed, be confused. **сму́тн|ый** vague; confused; dim; disturbed, troubled; **~ое вре́мя** Time of Troubles. **смутья́н, -а** troublemaker. **смуще́ние, -я** embarrassment, confusion. **смущённый; -ён, -а́** embarrassed, confused.

смыва́ть(ся, -а́ю(сь *impf. of* **смыть(ся**

смыка́ть(ся, -а́ю(сь *impf. of* **сомкну́ть(ся**

смысл, -а sense; meaning; purport; point; **в по́лном ~е сло́ва** in the full sense of the word; **нет ~а** there is no sense, there is no point. **смы́слить, -лю** *impf.* understand. **смыслово́й** sense, semantic; of meaning.

смыть, смо́ю *pf.* (*impf.* **смыва́ть**) wash off; wash away; **~ся** wash off, come off; slip away, run away, disappear.

смы́чка, -и union; linking. **смычо́к, -чка́** bow.

смышлёный clever, bright.

смягча́ть, -а́ю *impf.*, **смягчи́ть, -чу́** *pf.* soften; mollify; ease, alleviate; assuage; palatalize; **~ся** soften, become soft, grow softer; be mollified; relent, relax; grow mild; ease (off).

смяте́ние, -я confusion, disarray; commotion; **приводи́ть в ~** confuse, perturb. **с|мять(ся, сомну́(сь, -нёшь(ся** *pf.*

снабди́ть, -бжу́ *pf.*, **снабжа́ть, -а́ю** *impf.*+*i.* supply with, furnish with, provide with. **снабже́ние, -я** supply, supplying, provision.

сна́добье, -я; *g.pl.* **-ий** drug; concoction.

сна́йпер, -а sniper; sharp-shooter.

снару́жи *adv.* on the outside; from (the) outside. **снаря́д, -а** projectile, missile; shell; contrivance, machine, gadget; tackle, gear. **снаряди́ть, -яжу́** *pf.*, **снаряжа́ть, -а́ю** *impf.* equip, fit out; **~ся** equip o.s., get ready. **снаря́дн|ый** shell, projectile; ammunition; apparatus. **снаряже́ние, -я** equipment, outfit.

снасть, -и; *g.pl.* **-е́й** tackle, gear; *pl.* rigging.

снача́ла *adv.* at first, at the beginning; all over again.

сна́шивать, -аю *impf. of* **сноси́ть**

СНГ *abbr.* (*of* **Сообщество незави́симых госуда́рств**) CIS, Commonwealth of Independent States.

снег, -а (-у); *pl.* **-а́** snow; **мо́крый ~** sleet.

снеги́рь, -я́ bullfinch.

снегово́й snow. **снегоочисти́тель, -я** *m.* snow-plough. **снегопа́д, -а** snowfall, fall of snow. **снегосту́пы, -ов** *pl.* snow-shoes. **снегохо́д, -а** a snow-tractor. **Снегу́рочка, -и** Snow Maiden. **снежи́нка, -и** snow-flake. **сне́жн|ый** snow; snowy; **~ая ба́ба** snowman. **снежо́к, -жка́** light snow; snowball.

снести́[1], -су́, -сёшь; -ёс, -ла́ *pf.* (*impf.* **сноси́ть**) take; bring together, pile up; bring down, fetch down; carry away; blow off; take off; demolish, take down, pull down; bear, endure, stand, put up with; **~сь** communicate (**с**+*i.* with).

с|нести²(сь, -су(сь, -сёшь(ся; снёс(ся, -сла(сь *pf.*

снижа́ть, -а́ю *impf.*, сни́зить, -и́жу *pf.* lower; bring down; reduce; ~ся descend; come down; lose height; fall, sink. сниже́ние, -я lowering; reduction; loss of height.

снизойти́, -йду́, -йдёшь, -ошёл, -шла́ *pf.* (*impf.* снисходи́ть) condescend, deign.

сни́зу *adv.* from below; from the bottom; ~ до́верху from top to bottom.

снима́ть(ся, -а́ю(сь *impf. of* снять(ся. сни́мок, -мка photograph; print. сниму́ *etc.: see* снять

сниска́ть, -ищу́, -и́щешь *pf.*, сни́скивать, -аю *impf.* gain, get, win.

снисходи́тельность, -и condescension; indulgence, tolerance, leniency. снисходи́тельный condescending; indulgent, tolerant, lenient. снисходи́ть, -ожу́, -о́дишь *impf. of* снизойти́. снисхожде́ние, -я indulgence, leniency.

сни́ться, снюсь *impf.* (*pf.* при~), *impers.+d.* dream; ей сни́лось she dreamed; мне сни́лся сон I had a dream.

сно́ва *adv.* again, anew, afresh.

сновиде́ние, -я dream.

сноп, -а́; ~ луче́й sheaf of light. сноповяза́лка, -и binder.

снорови́стый quick, smart, nimble, clever. сноро́вка, -и knack, skill.

снос, -а demolition, pulling down; drift; wear. сноси́ть¹, -ошу́, -о́сишь *pf.* (*impf.* сна́шивать) wear out. сноси́ть²(ся, -ошу́(сь, -о́сишь(ся *impf. of* снести́(сь. сно́ска, -и footnote. сно́сный *adv.* tolerably, so-so. сно́сный tolerable; fair, reasonable.

снотво́рн|ый soporific; ~ые *sb.*, *pl.* sleeping-pills.

сноха́, -и́; *pl.* -и daughter-in-law.

сноше́ние, -я intercourse; relations, dealings. сношу́ *etc.: see* сноси́ть

сня́тие, -я taking down; removal, lifting; raising; taking, making; ~ ко́пии copying. сня́т|о́й; ~о́е молоко́ skim milk. снять, сниму́, -и́мешь; -ял, -а́, -о *pf.* (*impf.* снима́ть) take off; take down; gather in; remove; withdraw, cancel; take; make; photograph; ~ запре́т lift a ban; ~ с рабо́ты discharge; sack; ~ с учёта strike off the register; ~ фильм shoot, make, a film; ~ся come off; move off; have one's photograph taken; ~ с я́коря weigh anchor; get under way.

со *see* с *prep.*

со...¹ *vbl.pref.* used instead of с... before и, й, о, *before two or more consonants, and before single consonants followed by* ь.

со...² *pref. in comb. with nn. and adjs.:* co-, joint. соа́втор, -а co-author, joint author. ~а́вторство, -а co-authorship, joint authorship. ~бра́т, -а; *pl.* -ья, -ьев colleague. ~владе́лец, -льца joint owner, joint proprietor. ~владе́ние, -я joint ownership. ~вме́стно *adv.* in common, jointly.

~вме́стный joint, combined; ~вме́стное обуче́ние co-education; ~вме́стная рабо́та team-work. ~вою́ющий co-belligerent. ~граждани́н, -а; *pl.* -а́ждане, -ан fellow-citizen. ~докла́д, -а supplementary report, paper. ~жи́тель, -я *m.* room-mate, flat-mate; cohabitee, lover. ~жи́тельница, -ы room-mate, flat-mate; cohabitee, mistress. ~жи́тельство, -а living together, lodging together; cohabitation. ~квартира́нт, -а co-tenant, sharer of flat or lodgings. ~насле́дник, -а co-heir. ~о́бщник, -а accomplice, confederate. ~оте́чественник, -а compatriot, fellow-countryman. ~племе́нник, -а fellow-tribesman. ~подчине́ние, -я co-ordination. ~преде́льный contiguous. ~прича́стность, -и complicity, participation. ~ра́тник, -а comrade-in-arms. ~служи́вец, -вца colleague, fellow-employee. ~существова́ние, -я co-existence. ~умы́шленник, -а accomplice. ~учени́к, -а́ schoolfellow. ~чле́н, -а fellow-member.

соба́ка, -и dog; hound; ~поводы́рь guide-dog. соба́чий dog, dog's; canine. соба́чка, -и little dog, doggie; trigger. соба́чник, -а dog-lover.

с|обезья́нничать, -аю *pf.*

соберу́ *etc.: see* собра́ть

СОБЕС, а *or* собе́с, а *abbr.* (*of* (отде́л) социа́льного обеспе́чения) social security department (*of local authority*).

собесе́дник, -а interlocutor, party to conversation, companion; он — заба́вный ~ he is amusing to talk to, amusing company.

собира́ние, -я collecting, collection. собира́тель, -я *m.* collector. собира́тельный collective. собира́ть(ся, -а́ю(сь *impf. of* собра́ть(ся

собла́зн, -а temptation. соблазни́тель, -я *m.* tempter; seducer. соблазни́тельница, -ы temptress. соблазни́тельный tempting; alluring; seductive; suggestive, corrupting. соблазни́ть, -ню́ *pf.*, соблазня́ть, -я́ю *impf.* tempt; seduce, entice.

соблюда́ть, -а́ю *impf.*, со|блюсти́, -юду́, -дёшь; -юл, -а́ *pf.* observe; keep (to), stick to. соблюде́ние, -я observance; maintenance.

собо́й, собо́ю *see* себя́

соболе́знование, -я sympathy, condolence(s). соболе́зновать, -ную *impf.+d.* sympathize with, condole with.

собо́лий, соболи́ный sable. со́боль, -я; *pl.* -и *or* -я́ *m.* sable.

собо́р, -а cathedral; council, synod, assembly. собо́рный cathedral; synod, council.

собра́ние, -я meeting; gathering; assembly; collection; ~ сочине́ний collected works. со́бранный collected; concentrated. собра́ть, -беру́, -берёшь; -ал, -а́, -о *pf.* (*impf.* собира́ть) gather; collect; pick; assemble, muster; convoke, convene; mount; obtain; poll; prepare, make ready, equip; make gath-

собственник, -a owner, proprietor. **собст-
веннический** proprietary; proprietorial,
possessive. **собственно** *adv.* strictly; ~
(**говоря**) strictly speaking, properly speaking, as a matter of fact. **собственноручно**
adv. personally, with one's own hand. **соб-
ственноручн|ый** done, made, written, with
one's own hand(s); ~**ая подпись** autograph.
собственность, -и property; possession,
ownership. **собственн|ый** (one's) own;
proper; true; natural; internal; **в** ~**ые руки**
personal; **имя** ~**ое** proper name; ~**ой
персоной** in person.

событие, -я event; **текущие события** current affairs.

собью *etc.*: *see* **сбить**

сов... *abbr.* (*of* **совет**) *in comb.* soviet, Soviet, council; **советский** Soviet. **совмин**, -a
Council of Ministers. ~**нарком**, -a Council
of People's Commissars. ~**нархоз**, -a (Regional) Economic Council. ~**хоз**, -a sovkhoz,
State farm.

сова, -ы; *pl.* -ы owl.

совать, **сую**, -**ёшь** *impf.* (*pf.* **сунуть**) thrust,
shove, poke; ~**ся** push, push in; poke one's
nose in, butt in.

совершать, -**аю** *impf.* **совершить**, -**шу** *pf.*
accomplish; carry out; perform; commit, perpetuate; complete, conclude; ~**ся** happen;
be accomplished; be completed. **совер-
шение**, -я accomplishment, fulfilment; per-
petration, commission. **совершенно** *adv.*
perfectly; absolutely, utterly, completely, totally. **совершеннолетие**, -я majority.
совершеннолетний of age. **совершён-
ный**[1] perfect; absolute, utter, complete, total. **совершенный**[2] perfective. **совершён-
ство**, -a perfection. **совершенствовать**,
-**твую** *impf.* (*pf.* **у**~) perfect; improve; ~**ся**
в+*i.* perfect o.s. in; pursue advanced studies
in.

совестливый conscientious. **совестно**
impers.+*d.* be ashamed; **ему было** ~ he was
ashamed. **совесть**, -и conscience; **по со-
вести** (**говоря**) to be honest.

совет, -a advice, counsel; opinion; council;
conference; soviet, Soviet; ~ **Безопасности**
Security Council. **советник**, -a adviser;
counsellor. **советовать**, -**тую** *impf.* (*pf.*
по~) advise; ~**ся** **с**+*i.* consult, ask advice
of, seek advice from. **советовед**, -a
Sovietologist. **советолог**, -a Kremlinologist,
Kremlin-watcher. **советск|ий** Soviet; of
soviets; of the Soviet Union; ~**ая власть** the
Soviet regime; ~**ий Союз** the Soviet Union.
советчик, -a adviser, counsellor.

совещание, -я conference, meeting. **совеща-
тельный** consultative, deliberative. **совещаться**, -**аюсь** *impf.* deliberate; consult;
confer.

совладать, -**аю** *pf.* **с**+*i.* control, cope with.

совместимый compatible. **совместитель**,
-я *m.* person holding more than one office,
combining jobs; pluralist. **совместить**, -**ещу**
pf., **совмещать**, -**аю** *impf.* combine; ~**ся**
coincide; be combined, combine. **совмест-
н|ый** joint, combined; ~**ое обучение** co-edu-
cation; ~**ое предприятие** joint venture.

совок, -**вка** shovel; scoop; dust-pan; **садовый**
~ trowel.

совокупить, -**плю** *pf.*, **совокуплять**, -**яю**
impf. combine, unite; ~**ся** copulate. **совоку-
пление**, -я copulation. **совокупно** *adv.*
in common, jointly. **совокупность**, -и aggregate, sum total; totality. **совокупный**
joint, combined, aggregate.

совпадать, -**ает** *impf.*, **совпасть**, -**адёт** *pf.*
coincide; agree, concur, tally.

совратить, -**ащу** *pf.* (*impf.* **совращать**) pervert, seduce; ~**ся** go astray.

со|врать, -**вру**, -**врёшь**; -**ал**, -**а**, -**о** *pf.*

совращать(ся, -**аю(сь** *impf.* *of* **совратить-
(ся**. **совращение**, -я perverting, seducing,
seduction.

современник, -a contemporary. **современ-
ность**, -и the present (time); contempo-
raneity. **современный** contemporary, present-day; modern; up-to-date; +*d.* con-
temporaneous with, of the time of.

совру *etc.*: *see* **соврать**

совсем *adv.* quite; entirely, completely, altogether; ~ **не** not at all, not in the least.

совью *etc.*: *see* **свить**

согласие, -я consent; assent; agreement; accordance; accord; concord, harmony. **согла-
сить**, -**ашу** *pf.* (*impf.* **соглашать**) reconcile; ~**ся** consent; agree; concur. **согласно**
adv. in accord, in harmony, in concord;
prep.+*d.* in accordance with; according to.
согласность, -и harmony, harmoniousness.
согласн|ый[1] agreeable (to); in agreement;
concordant; harmonious; **быть** ~**ым** agree
(with). **согласный**[2] consonant, consonan-
tal; *sb.* consonant.

согласование, -я co-ordination; concordance; agreement; concord. **согласован-
ность**, -и co-ordination; ~ **во времени** synchronization. **согласовать**, -**сую** *pf.*, **согла-
совывать**, -**аю** *impf.* co-ordinate; agree;
make agree; ~**ся** accord; conform; agree.

соглашатель, -я *m.* appeaser; compromiser.
соглашательский conciliatory. **соглаша-
тельство**, -a appeasement; compromise.
соглашать(ся, -**аю(сь** *impf.* *of* **согла-
сить(ся**. **соглашение**, -я agreement; understanding; covenant. **соглашу** *etc.*: *see* **со-
гласить**

согнать, **сгоню**, **сгонишь**; -**ал**, -**а**, -**о** *pf.* (*impf.*
сгонять) drive away; drive together; round
up.

со|гну́ть, -ну́, -нёшь *pf.* (*impf. also* **сгиба́ть**) bend, curve, crook; **~ся** bend (down), bow (down); stoop.

согрева́ть, -а́ю *impf.*, **согре́ть, -е́ю** *pf.* warm, heat; **~ся** get warm; warm o.s.

согреше́ние, -я sin, trespass. **со|греши́ть, -шу́** *pf.*

соде́йствие, -я assistance, help; good offices. **соде́йствовать, -твую** *impf. & pf.* (*pf. also* **по~**) +*d.* assist, help; further, promote; make for, contribute to.

содержа́ние, -я maintenance, upkeep; keeping; allowance; pay; content; matter, substance; contents; plot; table of contents; **быть на содержа́нии у**+*g.* be kept, supported, by. **содержа́нка, -и** kept woman. **содержа́тельный** rich in content; pithy. **содержа́ть, -жу́, -жишь** *impf.* keep; maintain; support; have, contain; **~ся** be kept; be maintained; be contained. **содержи́мое** *sb.* contents.

со|дра́ть, сдеру́, -рёшь; -а́л, -а́, -о *pf.* (*impf. also* **сдира́ть**) tear off, strip off; fleece.

содрога́ние, -я shudder. **содрога́ться, -а́юсь** *impf.*, **содрогну́ться, -ну́сь, -нёшься** *pf.* shudder, shake, quake.

содру́жество, -а concord; community, commonwealth.

со́евый soya.

соедине́ние, -я joining, conjunction, combination; joint, join, junction; compound; formation. **соединённ|ый; -ён, -á** united, joint. **С~ое Короле́вство** United Kingdom. **С~ые Шта́ты (Аме́рики)** United States (of America). **соедини́тельный** connective, connecting; copulative. **соедини́ть, -ню́** *pf.*, **соединя́ть, -я́ю** *impf.* join, unite; connect, link; combine; **~ (по телефо́ну)** put through; **~ся** join, unite; combine.

сожале́ние, -я regret; pity; **к сожале́нию** unfortunately. **сожале́ть, -е́ю** *impf.* regret, deplore.

сожгу́ *etc.: see* **сжечь. сожже́ние, -я** burning; cremation.

сожму́ *etc.: see* **сжать². сожну́** *etc.: see* **сжать¹ созва́ниваться, -аюсь** *impf. of* **созвони́ться**

созва́ть, -зову́, -зовёшь; -а́л, -á, -о *pf.* (*impf.* **сзыва́ть, созыва́ть**) call together; call; invite; summon; convoke, convene.

созве́здие, -я constellation.

созвони́ться, -ню́сь *pf.* (*impf.* **созва́ниваться**) ring up; speak on the telephone.

созву́чие, -я accord, consonance; assonance. **созву́чный** harmonious; +*d.* consonant with, in keeping with.

создава́ть, -даю́, -даёшь *impf.*, **созда́ть, -а́м, -а́шь, -а́ст, -ади́м; со́здал, -á, -о** *pf.* create; found, originate; set up, establish; **~ся** be created; arise, spring up. **созда́ние, -я** creation; making; work; creature. **созда́тель, -я** *m.* creator; founder, originator.

созерца́ние, -я contemplation. **созерца́-тельный** contemplative, meditative. **созер-**

-ца́ть, -а́ю *impf.* contemplate.

сознава́ть, -наю́, -наёшь *impf.*, **созна́ть, -а́ю** *pf.* be conscious of, realize; recognize, acknowledge; **~ся** confess; plead guilty. **созна́ние, -я** consciousness; recognition, acknowledgement; admission, confession; **прийти́ в ~** recover consciousness; **~ до́лга** sense of duty. **созна́тельность, -и** awareness, consciousness; intelligence, acumen; deliberation, deliberateness. **созна́тельный** conscious; politically conscious; intelligent; deliberate.

созову́ *etc.: see* **созва́ть. с|озорнича́ть, -а́ю** *pf.*

созрева́ть, -а́ю *impf.*, **со|зре́ть, -е́ю** *pf.* ripen, mature; come to a head.

созы́в, -а convocation; summoning, calling. **созыва́ть, -а́ю** *impf. of* **созва́ть**

соизво́лить, -лю *pf.*, **соизволя́ть, -я́ю** *impf.* deign, condescend, be pleased.

соизмери́мый commensurable.

соиска́ние, -я competition, candidacy. **со-иска́тель, -я** *m.*, **-ница, -ы** competitor, candidate.

сойти́, -йду́, -йдёшь; сошёл, -шла́ *pf.* (*impf.* **сходи́ть**) go down, come down; descend, get off, alight; leave; come off; pass, go off; +*за*+*a.* pass for, be taken for; **снег сошёл** the snow has melted; **сойдёт и так** it will do (as it is); **~ с доро́ги** get out of the way, step aside; **~ с ума́** go mad, go out of one's mind; **сошло́ благополу́чно** it went off all right; **~сь** meet; come together; gather; become friends; become intimate; agree; tally; **~сь хара́ктером** get on, hit it off.

сок, -а (-у), *loc.* -ý juice; sap; **в (по́лном) ~ý** in the prime of life. **соковыжима́лка, -и** juicer, juice-extractor.

со́кол, -а a falcon.

сократи́ть, -ащу́ *pf.*, **сокраща́ть, -а́ю** *impf.* shorten; curtail; abbreviate; abridge; reduce, cut down; dismiss, discharge, lay off; cancel; **~ся** grow shorter, get shorter; decrease, decline; cut down; be cancelled; contract. **сокраще́ние, -я** shortening; abridgement; abbreviation; reduction, cutting down; curtailment; cancellation; contraction; **~ шта́тов** staff reduction; **уво́лить по сокраще́нию шта́тов** dismiss as redundant. **сокращён-н|ый** brief; abbreviated; **~ое сло́во** abbreviation.

сокрове́нный secret, concealed; innermost. **сокро́вище, -а** treasure. **сокро́вищница, -ы** treasure-house, treasury.

сокруша́ть, -а́ю *impf.*, **сокруши́ть, -шу́** *pf.* shatter; smash; crush; distress, grieve; **~ся** grieve, be distressed. **сокруше́ние, -я** smashing, shattering; grief, distress. **сокру-шённый; -ён, -á** grief-stricken. **сокруши́-тельный** shattering; crippling, withering, destructive.

сокры́тие, -я concealment. **сокры́ть, -ро́ю** *pf.* conceal, hide, cover up; **~ся** hide, conceal o.s.

со|лга́ть, -лгу́, -лжёшь; -а́л, -а́, -о *pf.*

солда́т, -a; *g.pl.* -а́т soldier. **солда́тский** soldier's; army.

соле́ние, -я salting; pickling. **солёный; со́лон,** -а́, -o salty; salted; pickled; corned; spicy; hot. **соле́нье,** -я salted food(s); pickles.

солида́рность, -и solidarity; collective (joint) responsibility. **солида́рный** at one, in sympathy; collective, joint, solidary. **соли́дность,** -и solidity; reliability. **соли́дн|ый** solid; strong, sound; reliable; respectable; sizeable; ~ый во́зраст middle age; челове́к ~ых лет a middle-aged man.

соли́ст, -a, **соли́стка,** -и soloist.

солите́р, -a solitaire (diamond).

соли́ть, -лю́, со́лишь *impf.* (*pf.* по~) salt; pickle, corn.

со́лнечн|ый sun; solar; sunny; ~ый свет sunlight; sunshine; ~ый уда́р sunstroke; ~ые часы́ sundial. **со́лнце,** -a sun. **солнцепёк,** -a; на ~e right in the sun, in the full blaze of the sun. **солнцестоя́ние,** -я solstice.

солове́й, -вья́ nightingale. **соловьи́ный** nightingale's.

со́лод, -a (-y) malt.

соло́дка, -и liquorice. **солодко́вый** liquorice.

соло́ма, -ы straw; thatch. **соло́менн|ый** straw; straw-coloured; ~ая вдова́ grass widow; ~ая кры́ша thatch, thatched roof. **соло́минка,** -и straw.

со́лон *etc.*: see **солёный. солони́на,** -ы salted beef, corned beef. **соло́нка,** -и saltcellar. **солонча́к,** -а́ saline soil; *pl.* salt marshes. **соль¹,** -и; *pl.* -и, -е́й salt.

соль² *nt.indecl.* G; sol. soh.

со́льный solo.

со́лью *etc.*: see **слить**

соляно́й, соля́ный salt, saline; **соля́ная кислота́** hydrochloric acid.

со́мкнутый close; ~ строй close order. **сомкну́ть,** -ну́, -нёшь *pf.* (*impf.* **смыка́ть**) close; ~ся close, close up.

сомнева́ться, -а́юсь *impf.* doubt, have doubts; question; worry; не ~ в+*p.* have no doubts of. **сомне́ние,** -я doubt; uncertainty; без сомне́ния without doubt, undoubtedly. **сомни́тельн|ый** doubtful, questionable; dubious; equivocal; ~o it is doubtful, it is open to question.

сомну́ *etc.*: see **смять**

сон, сна sleep; dream; ви́деть во сне dream, dream about. **сонли́вость,** -и sleepiness, drowsiness; somnolence. **сонли́вый** sleepy, drowsy; somnolent. **со́нный** sleepy, drowsy; somnolent; slumberous; sleeping, soporific.

соображ́ать, -а́ю *impf.*, **сообрази́ть,** -ажу́ *pf.* consider, ponder, think out; weigh; understand, grasp; think up, arrange; have a quick one, have a round of drinks. **соображ́ительный** quick-witted, quick, sharp, bright. **сообра́зный** с+*i.* conformable to, in conformity with, consistent with. **сообразо-**

ва́ть, -зу́ю *impf.* & *pf.* conform, make conformable; adapt; ~ся conform, adapt o.s.

сообща́ *adv.* together, jointly. **сообща́ть,** -а́ю *impf.*, **сообщи́ть,** -щу́ *pf.* communicate, report, announce; impart; +*d.* inform of, tell that. **сообще́ние,** -я communication, report; information; announcement; connection.

сооруди́ть, -ужу́ *pf.*, **сооружа́ть,** -а́ю *impf.* build, erect. **сооруже́ние,** -я building; erection; construction; structure.

соотве́тственно *adv.* accordingly, correspondingly; *prep.*+*d.* according to, in accordance with, in conformity with, in compliance with. **соотве́тственный** corresponding. **соотве́тствие,** -я accordance, conformity, correspondence. **соотве́тствовать,** -твую *impf.* correspond, conform, be in keeping. **соотве́тствующий** corresponding; proper, appropriate, suitable.

сопе́рник, -a rival. **сопе́рничать,** -аю *impf.* be rivals; compete, vie. **сопе́рничество,** -a rivalry.

сопе́ть, -плю́ *impf.* breathe heavily; sniff; snuffle; huff and puff.

со́пка, -и knoll, hill, mound.

сопли́вый snotty.

сопоста́вимый comparable. **сопоста́вить,** -влю *pf.*, **сопоставля́ть,** -я́ю *impf.* compare. **сопоставле́ние,** -я comparison.

соприкаса́ться, -а́юсь *impf.*, **соприкосну́ться,** -ну́сь, -нёшься *pf.* adjoin, be contiguous (to); come into contact. **соприкоснове́ние,** -я contiguity; contact.

сопроводи́тель, -я *m.* escort. **сопроводи́тельный** accompanying. **сопроводи́ть,** -ожу́ *pf.*, **сопровожда́ть,** -а́ю *impf.* accompanying; escort. **сопровожде́ние,** -я accompaniment; escort; звуково́е ~ soundtrack.

сопротивле́ние, -я resistance; opposition. **сопротивля́ться,** -я́юсь *impf.*+*d.* resist, oppose.

сопу́тствовать, -твую *impf.*+*d.* accompany.

сопыюсь *etc.*: see **спи́ться**

сор, -a (-y) litter, dust, rubbish.

соразме́рить, -рю *pf.*, **соразмеря́ть,** -я́ю *impf.* proportion, balance, match. **соразме́рный** proportionate, commensurate.

сорва́ть, -ву́, -вёшь; -а́л, -а́, -o *pf.* (*impf.* **срыва́ть**) tear off, away, down; break off; pick, pluck; get, extract; break; smash, wreck, ruin, spoil; vent; ~ся break away, break loose; fall; fall, come down; fall through, fall to the ground, miscarry; ~ с ме́ста dart off; ~ с пете́ль come off its hinges.

с|организова́ть, -зу́ю *pf.*

соревнова́ние, -я competition; contest; tournament; event; emulation. **соревнова́ться,** -ну́юсь *impf.* compete, contend. **соревну́ющийся** *sb.* competitor, contestant, contender. **сори́ть,** -рю́ *impf.* (*pf.* на~) +*a.* or *i.* litter; throw about. **со́рн|ый** dust, rubbish, refuse; ~ая трава́ weed, weeds. **сорня́к,** -а́ weed.

cópoк, -á forty.

copóка, -и magpie.

coрокóв|о́й fortieth; **~ые го́ды** the forties.

coрóчка, -и shirt; blouse; shift.

copт, -a; *pl.* **-á** grade, quality; brand; sort, kind, variety. **сортирова́ть, -ру́ю** *impf.* (*pf.* **рас~**) sort, assort, grade, size. **сортиро́вка, -и** sorting, grading, sizing. **сортиро́вочный** sorting; **~ая** *sb.* marshalling-yard. **сорти-ро́вщик, -a** sorter. **со́ртность, -и** grade, quality. **со́ртный** of high quality. **сортово́й** high-grade, of high quality.

соса́ть, -су́, -сёшь *impf.* suck.

со|сва́тать, -аю *pf.*

сосе́д, -a; *pl.* **-и, сосе́дка, -и** neighbour; **~ по кварти́ре** flatmate. **сосе́дний** neighbouring; adjacent, next; **~ дом** the house next door. **сосе́дский** neighbours', neighbouring, next-door. **сосе́дство, -a** a neighbourhood, vicinity. **сосиска, -и** sausage; frankfurter.

со́ска, -и (*baby's*) dummy.

соска́кивать, -аю *impf. of* **соскочи́ть**

соска́льзывать, -аю *impf.*, **соскользну́ть, -ну́, -нёшь** *pf.* slide down, glide down; slip off, slide off.

соскочи́ть, -чу́, -чишь *pf.* (*impf.* **соска́ки-вать**) jump off, leap off; jump down, leap down; come off; vanish suddenly.

соску́читься, -чусь *pf.* get bored, be bored; **~ по** miss.

сослага́тельный subjunctive.

сосла́ть, сошлю́, -лёшь *pf.* (*impf.* **ссыла́ть**) exile, banish, deport; **~ся на**+*a.* refer to, allude to; cite, quote, plead, allege.

сосло́вие, -я estate; corporation, professional association.

сосна́, -ы́; *pl.* **-ы, -сен** pine(-tree). **сосно́вый** pine; deal.

соснýть, -нý, -нёшь *pf.* have a nap.

сосóк, -ска́ nipple, teat.

сосредото́ченность, -и concentration. **со-средото́ченный** concentrated. **сосредото́-чивать, -аю** *impf.*, **сосредото́чить, -чу** *pf.* concentrate; focus; **~ся** concentrate.

соста́в, -a composition, make-up; structure; compound; staff; personnel; membership; strength; train; **в ~e**+*g.* numbering, consisting of, amounting to; **в по́лном ~e** with its full complement; in, at, full strength; in a body. **соста́витель, -я** *m.* compiler, author. **соста́вить, -влю** *pf.*, **составля́ть, -я́ю** *impf.* put together; make (up); compose; draw up; compile; work out; construct; be, constitute; amount to, total; **~ в сре́днем** average; **~ся** form, be formed; come into being. **составно́й** compound, composite; sectional; component, constituent.

со|ста́рить(ся, -рю(сь *pf.*

состоя́ние, -я state, condition; position; status; fortune; **в состоя́нии**+*inf.* able to, in a position to. **состоя́тельный** solvent; well-off, well-to-do; well-grounded. **состоя́ть, -ою́** *impf.* be; +*из*+*g.* consist of, comprise,

be made up of; +*в*+*p.* consist in, lie in, be; **~ в до́лжности**+*g.* occupy the post of. **со-стоя́ться, -ойтся** *pf.* take place.

сострада́ние, -я compassion, sympathy. **со-страда́тельный** compassionate, sympathetic.

с|остри́ть, -рю́ *pf.* **со|стря́пать, -аю** *pf.*

со|стыкова́ть, -у́ю *pf.*, **состыко́вывать, -аю** *impf.* dock; **~ся** dock.

состяза́ние, -я competition, contest; match; уча́стник состяза́ния competitor. **состя-за́ться, -а́юсь** *impf.* compete, contend.

сосу́д, -a vessel.

сосу́лька, -и icicle.

со|счита́ть, -а́ю *pf.* **cот** *see* **сто. со|твори́ть, -рю́** *pf.*

со́тенная *sb.* hundred-rouble note.

со|тка́ть, -ку́, -кёшь; -áл, -áлá, -o *pf.*

со́тня, -и; *g.pl.* **-тен** a hundred.

сотови́дный honeycomb. **со́товый** honey-comb; **~ мёд** honey in the comb.

сотру́ *etc.: see* **стере́ть**

сотру́дник, -a collaborator; employee, assistant, official; contributor. **сотру́дничать, -аю** *impf.* collaborate; +*в*+*p.* contribute to. **со-тру́дничество, -a** collaboration; cooperation.

сотряса́ть, -а́ю *impf.*, **сотрясти́, -су́, -сёшь; -я́с, -ла́** *pf.* shake; **~ся** shake, tremble. **сотрясе́ние, -я** shaking; concussion.

со́ты, -ов *pl.* honeycomb; **мёд в со́тах** honey in the comb.

со́тый hundredth.

со́ул, -a; (му́зыка) ~ soul music.

со́ус, -a (-у) sauce; gravy; dressing.

соуча́стие, -я participation; taking part; complicity. **соуча́стник, -a** partner; participant; accessory, accomplice.

соха́, -и́; *pl.* **-и** (*wooden*) plough.

со́хнуть, -ну; сох *impf.* (*pf.* **вы́~, за~, про~**) dry, get dry; become parched; wither.

сохране́ние, -я preservation; conservation; care, custody, charge, keeping; retention. **сохрани́ть, -ню́** *pf.*, **сохраня́ть, -я́ю** *impf.* preserve, keep; keep safe; retain, reserve; **~ся** remain (intact); last out, hold out; be well preserved. **сохра́нность, -и** safety, undamaged state; safe-keeping. **сохра́нный** safe.

соц... *abbr.* (*of* **социа́льный, социали-сти́ческий**) *in comb.* social; socialist. **соц-реали́зм, -a** socialist realism. **~соревно-ва́ние, -я** socialist emulation. **~стра́х, -a** social insurance.

социа́л-демокра́т, -a Social Democrat. **социа́л-демократи́ческий** Social Democratic. **социализа́ция, -и** socialization. **социализи́ровать, -рую** *impf. & pf.* socialize. **социали́зм, -a** socialism. **социали́ст, -a** socialist. **социалисти́ческий** socialist. **социа́л|ьный** social; **~ое обеспе́чение** social security; **~ое положе́ние** social status; **~ое страхова́ние** social insurance.

социо́лог, -a sociologist. **социологи́ческий** sociological. **социоло́гия, -и** sociology.

соч. *abbr.* (*of* **сочинéния**) works.

сочетáние, -я combination. **сочетáть, -áю** *impf. & pf.* combine; +c+*i.* go with, harmonize with; match; ~ **брáком** marry; ~**ся** combine; harmonize; match; ~**ся брáком** be married.

сочинéние, -я composition; work; essay; coordination. **сочинúть, -ню** *pf.*, **сочинять, -яю** *impf.* compose; write; make up, fabricate.

сочúться, -úтся *impf.* ooze (out), trickle; ~ **крóвью** bleed.

сочленúть, -ню *pf.*, **сочленять, -яю** *impf.* join, couple.

сóчный; -чен, -чнá, -о juicy; succulent; rich; lush.

сочтý *etc.: see* **счесть**

сочýвственный sympathetic. **сочýвствие, -я** sympathy. **сочýвствовать, -твую** *impf.*+*d.* sympathize with, feel for.

сошёл *etc.: see* **сойтú. сошлю** *etc.: see* **сослáть. сошью** *etc.: see* **сшить**

сощýривать, -аю *impf.*, **со|щýрить, -рю** *pf.* screw up, narrow; ~**ся** screw up one's eyes; narrow.

союз[1], -а union; alliance; agreement; league. **союз[2], -а** conjunction. **союзник, -а** ally. **союзный** allied; of the (Soviet) Union.

сóя, -и soya bean.

спагéтти *nt. & pl. indecl.* spaghetti.

спад, -а slump, recession; abatement. **спадáть, -áет** *impf. of* **спасть**

спáивать, -аю *impf. of* **спаять, спойть**

спáйка, -и soldered joint; solidarity, unity.

с|палúть, -лю *pf.*

спáльник, -а sleeping-bag. **спáльн|ый** sleeping; ~**ый вагóн** sleeper, sleeping car; ~**ое мéсто** berth, bunk. **спáльня, -и;** *g.pl.* **-лен** bedroom; bedroom suite; ~**-гостúная** bedsitting room.

спáржа, -и asparagus.

спартакиáда, -ы sports meeting.

спáрывать, -аю *impf. of* **спорóть**

спасáние, -я rescuing, life-saving. **спасáтель, -я** *m.* (*at sea*) lifeguard; rescuer; (*pl.*) rescue party; lifeboat. **спасáтельн|ый** rescue, life-saving; ~**ый круг** lifebuoy; ~**ый пояс** lifebelt; ~**ая экспедúция** rescue party. **спасáть(ся, -áю(сь** *impf. of* **спастú(сь. спасéние, -я** rescuing, saving; rescue, escape; salvation.

спасúбо thanks; thank you.

спасúтель, -я *m.* rescuer, saver; saviour. **спасúтельный** saving; of rescue, of escape; salutary.

с|пасовáть, -сýю *pf.*

спастú, -сý, -сёшь; спас, -лá *pf.* (*impf.* **спасáть**) save; rescue; ~**сь** save o.s., escape; be saved.

спасть, -адёт *pf.* (*impf.* **спадáть**) fall (down); abate.

спать, сплю; -ал, -á, -о *impf.* sleep, be asleep; **лечь** ~ go to bed; **порá** ~ it is bedtime.

спáянность, -и cohesion, unity; solidarity. **спáянный** united. **спаять, -яю** *pf.* (*impf.* **спáивать**) solder together, weld; unite, knit together.

спектáкль, -я *m.* performance.

спектр, -а spectrum.

спекулúровать, -рую *impf.* speculate; profiteer; gamble; +на+*p.* gamble on, reckon on; profit by. **спекулянт, -а** speculator, profiteer. **спекуляция, -и** speculation; profiteering; gamble.

с|пеленáть, -áю *pf.*

спелеóлог, -а caver, pot-holer.

спéлый ripe.

спервá *adv.* at first; first.

спéреди *adv.* in front, at the front, from the front; *prep.*+*g.* (from) in front of.

спёртый close, stuffy.

спесúвый arrogant, haughty, lofty. **спесь, -и** arrogance, haughtiness, loftiness.

спеть[1], -éет *impf.* (*pf.* **по**~) ripen.

с|петь[2], спою, споёшь *pf.*

спец, -á; *pl.* **-ецы, -ев** *or* **-óв** *abbr.* (*of* **специалúст**) specialist, expert, authority.

спец... *abbr.* (*of* **специáльный**) *in comb.* special. **спецкóр, -а** special correspondent. ~**кýрс, -а** special course (of lectures). ~**одéжда, -ы** working clothes, protective clothing; overalls.

специализúроваться, -руюсь *impf. & pf.* specialize. **специалúст, -а** specialist, expert, authority. **специáльность, -и** speciality, special interest; profession; trade. **специáльный** special; specialist; ~ **тéрмин** technical term.

спецúфика, -и specific character. **специфúческий** specific.

спецóвка, -и protective clothing, working clothes; overall(s).

спешúть, -шý *impf.* (*pf.* **по**~) hurry, be in a hurry; make haste, hasten; hurry up; be fast. **спéшка, -и** hurry, haste, rush. **спéшн|ый** urgent, pressing; ~**ый закáз** rush order; ~**ая пóчта** express delivery.

спивáться, -áюсь *impf. of* **спúться**

СПИД, а *abbr.* (*of* **синдрóм приобретённого иммýнного дефицúта**) AIDS (*acquired immune deficiency syndrome*).

с|пикúровать, -рую *pf.*

спúливать, -аю *impf.*, **спилúть, -лю, -лишь** *pf.* saw down; saw off.

спинá, -ы́, *a.* **-у;** *pl.* **-ы** back. **спúнка, -и** back. **спиннóй** spinal; ~ **мозг** spinal cord; ~ **хребéт** spinal column.

спирт, -а (**-у**) alcohol, spirit(s). **спиртн|óй** spirituous; ~**ые напúтки** spirits; ~**óе** *sb.* spirits. **спиртóвка, -и** spirit-stove. **спиртовóй** spirit, spirituous.

спúсывать, -ишý, -úшешь *pf.*, **спúсывать, -аю** *impf.* copy; crib; write off; ~**ся** exchange letters. **спúсок, -ска** list; roll; record; manuscript copy; ~ **избирáтелей** voters' list, electoral roll; ~ **убúтых и рáненых** casualty list.

спи́ться, сопью́сь, -ьёшься; -и́лся, -ась *pf.* (*impf.* **спива́ться**) take to drink, become a drunkard.

спи́хивать, -аю *impf.*, **спихну́ть, -ну́, -нёшь** *pf.* push aside; push down.

спи́ца, -ы knitting-needle; spoke.

спи́чечн|ый match; **~ая коро́бка** match-box. **спи́чка, -и** match.

спишу́ *etc.: see* **списа́ть**

сплав[1], -а floating, rafting. **сплав[2], -а** alloy. **спла́вить[1], -влю** *pf.*, **сплавля́ть[1], -я́ю** *impf.* float; raft; get rid of. **спла́вить[2], -влю** *pf.*, **сплавля́ть[2], -я́ю** *impf.* alloy; **~ся** fuse, coalesce.

с|пла́нировать, -рую *pf.* **спла́чивать(ся, -аю(сь** *impf. of* **сплоти́ть(ся**

сплёвывать, -аю *impf. of* **сплю́нуть**

с|плести́, -ету́, -етёшь; -ёл, -а́ *pf.*, **сплета́ть, -а́ю** *impf.* weave; plait; interlace. **сплете́ние, -я** interlacing; plexus.

спле́тник, -а, -ница, -ы gossip, scandalmonger. **спле́тничать, -аю** *impf.* (*pf.* **на~**) gossip, tittle-tattle; talk scandal. **спле́тня, -и;** *gen pl.* **-тен** gossip, scandal.

сплоти́ть, -очу́ *pf.* (*impf.* **спла́чивать**) join; unite, rally; **~ ряды́** close the ranks; **~ся** unite, rally; close the ranks. **сплочённость, -и** cohesion, unity. **сплочённый; -ён, -а́** united, firm; unbroken.

сплошно́й solid; all-round, complete; unbroken, continuous; sheer, utter, unreserved. **сплошь** *adv.* all over; throughout; without a break; completely, utterly; without exception; **~ да ря́дом** nearly always; pretty often.

с|плутова́ть, -ту́ю *pf.*

сплыва́ть, -а́ет *impf.*, **сплыть, -ывёт; -ыл, -а́, -о** *pf.* sail down, float down; be carried away; overflow, run over; **бы́ло да сплы́ло** those were the days; it's all over. **~ся** run (together), merge, blend.

сплю *see* **спать**

сплю́нуть, -ну *pf.* (*impf.* **сплёвывать**) spit; spit out.

сплю́щенный flattened out. **сплю́щивать, -аю** *impf.*, **сплю́щить, -щу** *pf.* flatten; **~ся** become flat.

с|пляса́ть, -яшу́, -я́шешь *pf.*

сподви́жник, -а comrade-in-arms.

спои́ть, -ою́, -о́ишь *pf.* (*impf.* **спа́ивать**) accustom to drinking, make a drunkard of.

споко́йн|ый quiet; calm, tranquil; placid, serene; composed; comfortable; **~ой но́чи** good night! **споко́йствие, -я** quiet; tranquility; calm, calmness; order; composure, serenity.

спола́скивать, -аю *impf. of* **сполосну́ть**

сполза́ть, -а́ю *impf.*, **сползти́, -зу́, -зёшь; -олз, -ла́** *pf.* climb down; slip (down); fall away.

сполна́ *adv.* completely, in full.

сполосну́ть, -ну́, -нёшь *pf.* (*impf.* **спола́скивать**) rinse.

спо́нсор, -а sponsor, backer.

спор, -а (-у) argument; controversy; debate; dispute. **спо́рить, -рю** *impf.* (*pf.* **по~**) argue; dispute; debate; bet, have a bet. **спо́рный** disputable, debatable, questionable; disputed, at issue; **~ вопро́с** moot point, vexed question; **~ мяч** jump ball; held ball.

споро́ть, -рю́, -решь *pf.* (*impf.* **спа́рывать**) rip off.

спорт, -а sport, sports; **бату́тный ~** trampolining; **ко́нный ~** equestrianism; **лы́жный ~** skiing; **парашю́тный ~** parachute-jumping. **спорти́вн|ый** sports; **~ый зал** gymnasium; **~ая площа́дка** sports-ground, playing-field; **~ые состяза́ния** sports. **спортсме́н, -а, спортсме́нка, -и** athlete, player.

спо́рый; -ор, -а́, -о successful, profitable; skilful, efficient.

спо́соб, -а a way, manner, method; mode; means; **~ употребле́ния** directions for use; **таки́м ~ом** in this way. **спосо́бность, -и** ability, talent, aptitude, flair; capacity. **спосо́бный** able; talented, gifted, clever; capable. **спосо́бствовать, -твую** *impf.* (*pf.* **по~**) *+d.* assist; be conducive to, further, promote, make for.

споткну́ться, -ну́сь, -нёшься *pf.*, **спотыка́ться, -а́юсь** *impf.* stumble; get stuck, come to a stop.

спохвати́ться, -ачу́сь, -а́тишься *pf.*, **спохва́тываться, -аюсь** *impf.* remember suddenly.

спою́ *etc.: see* **спеть, спои́ть**

спра́ва *adv.* to the right.

справедли́вость, -и justice; equity; fairness; truth, correctness. **справедли́вый** just; equitable, fair; justified.

спра́вить, -влю *pf.*, **справля́ть, -я́ю** *impf.* celebrate. **спра́виться[1], -влюсь** *pf.* **справля́ться, -я́юсь** *impf.* *c+i.* cope with, manage; deal with. **спра́виться[2], -влюсь** *pf.*, **справля́ться, -я́юсь** *impf.* ask, inquire; inform o.s.; **~ в словаре́** consult a dictionary. **спра́вка, -и** information; reference; certificate; **навести́ спра́вку** inquire; **наводи́ть спра́вку** make inquiries. **спра́вочник, -а** reference-book, handbook, guide, directory. **спра́вочн|ый** inquiry, information; **~ая кни́га** reference-book, handbook.

спра́шивать(ся, -аю(сь *impf. of* **спроси́ть(ся. с|провоци́ровать, -рую** *pf.*

с|проекти́ровать, -рую *pf.*

спрос, -а (-у) demand; asking; **без ~у** without asking leave, without permission; **по́льзоваться (бо́льшим) ~ом** be in (great) demand; **~ на+a.** demand for, run on. **спроси́ть, -ошу́, -о́сишь** *pf.* (*impf.* **спра́шивать**) ask (for); inquire; ask to see; *+c+g.* make answer for, make responsible for; **~ся** ask permission.

спросо́нок *adv.* (being) only half-awake.

спры́гивать, -аю *impf.*, **спры́гнуть, -ну** *pf.*

jump off, jump down.

спры́скивать, -аю *impf.*, **спры́снуть, -ну** *pf.* sprinkle.

спряга́ть, -а́ю *impf.* (*pf.* **про~**) conjugate; **~ся** be conjugated. **спряже́ние, -я** conjugation.

с|прясть, -яду́, -ядёшь; -ял, -яла́, -о *pf.* **с|пря́тать(ся, -аю(сь** *pf.*

спу́гивать, -аю *impf.*, **спугну́ть, -ну́, -нёшь** *pf.* frighten off, scare off.

спуск, -а lowering, hauling down; descent; descending; landing; release; draining; slope. **спуска́ть, -а́ю** *impf.*, **спусти́ть, -ущу́, -у́стишь** *pf.* let down, lower; haul down; let go, let loose, release; let out, drain; send out; go down; forgive, let off, let go, let pass; lose; throw away, squander; **~ кора́бль** launch a ship; **~ куро́к** pull the trigger; **~ пе́тлю** drop a stitch; **~ с це́пи** unchain; **спустя́ рукава́** carelessly. **спускн|о́й** drain; **~а́я труба́** drain-pipe. **спусково́й** trigger. **спустя́** *prep.+a.* after; later; **немно́го ~** not long after.

с|пу́тать(ся, -аю(сь *pf.*

спу́тник, -а satellite, sputnik; (travelling) companion; fellow-traveller; concomitant.

спущу́ *etc.: see* **спусти́ть**

спя́чка, -и hibernation; sleepiness, lethargy.

ср. *abbr.* (*of* **сравни́**) cf., compare; (*of* **сре́дний**) mean.

сравне́ние, -я comparison; simile; **по сравне́нию** c+*i.* as compared with, as against.

сра́внивать, -аю *impf. of* **сравни́ть, сравня́ть**

сравни́тельно *adv.* comparatively; **~** c+*i.* compared with. **сравни́тельный** comparative. **сравни́ть, -ню́** *pf.* (*impf.* **сра́внивать**) compare; **~ся** c+*i.* compare with, come up to, touch.

с|равня́ть, -я́ю *pf.* (*impf. also* **сра́внивать**) make even, make equal; level.

сража́ть, -а́ю *impf.*, **срази́ть, -ажу́** *pf.* slay, strike down, fell; overwhelm, crush; **~ся** fight, join battle. **сраже́ние, -я** battle, engagement.

сра́зу *adv.* at once; straight away, right away.

срам, -а (-у) shame. **срами́ть, -млю** *impf.* (*pf.* **о~**) shame, put to shame; **~ся** cover o.s. with shame. **срамни́к, -а́** shameless person. **срамно́й** shameless. **срамота́, -ы́** shame.

сраста́ние, -я growing together; knitting. **сраста́ться, -а́ется** *impf.*, **срасти́сь, -тётся; сро́сся, -ла́сь** *pf.* grow together; knit.

сребролюби́вый money-grubbing. **среброно́сный** argentiferous.

среда́[1], -ы́; *pl.* **-ы** environment, surroundings; milieu; habitat; medium; **в на́шей среде́** in our midst, among us. **среда́[2], -ы́,** *a.* **-у;** *pl.* **-ы, -ам** *or* **-ам** Wednesday. **среди́** *prep.+g.* among, amongst; amidst; in the middle of; **~ бе́ла дня** in broad daylight.

Средизе́мное мо́ре, -ого -я the Medi-

terranean (Sea). **средиземномо́рский** Mediterranean.

среди́на, -ы middle. **сре́дне** *adv.* middling, so-so. **средневеко́вый** medieval. **средневеко́вье, -я** the Middle Ages. **средневи́к, -а́** middle-distance runner. **сре́дн|ий** middle; medium; mean; average; middling; secondary; neuter; **~ие века́** the Middle Ages; **~яя величина́** mean value; **~ий па́лец** middle finger, second finger; **~ее** *sb.* mean, average; **вы́ше ~его** above (the) average. **сре́дство, -а** means; remedy; *pl.* means; resources; credits; **жить не по сре́дствам** live beyond one's means.

срез, -а cut; section; shear, shearing; slice, slicing. **с|ре́зать, -е́жу** *pf.* **среза́ть, -а́ю** *impf.* cut off; slice, cut, chop, fail, plough; **~ся** fail, be ploughed.

с|репети́ровать, -рую *pf.*

срисова́ть, -су́ю *pf.*, **срисо́вывать, -аю** *impf.* copy.

с|рифмова́ть(ся, -му́ю(сь *pf.* **с|ровня́ть, -я́ю** *pf.*

сродство́, -а́ affinity.

срок, -а (-у) date; term; time, period; **в ~, к ~у** in time, to time; **~ хране́ния** shelf life.

сро́сся *etc.: see* **срасти́сь**

сро́чно *adv.* urgently; quickly. **сро́чность, -и** urgency; hurry; **что за ~?** what's the hurry? **сро́чный** urgent, pressing; at a fixed date; for a fixed period; periodic, routine; **~ зака́з** rush order.

сро́ю *etc.: see* **срыть**

сруб, -а felling; framework. **сруба́ть, -а́ю** *impf.*, **с|руби́ть, -блю́, -бишь** *pf.* fell, cut down; build (*of logs*).

срыв, -а disruption; derangement, frustration; foiling, spoiling, ruining, wrecking; **~ перегово́ров** breaking-off of talks, breakdown in negotiations. **срыва́ть[1](ся, -а́ю(сь** *impf. of* **сорва́ть(ся**

срыва́ть[2], -а́ю *impf.*, **срыть, сро́ю** *pf.* raze, level to the ground.

сря́ду *adv.* running.

сса́дина, -ы scratch, abrasion. **ссади́ть, -ажу́, -а́дишь** *pf.*, **сса́живать, -аю** *impf.* set down; help down, help to alight; put off, turn off.

ссо́ра, -ы quarrel; falling-out; slanging-match; **быть в ссо́ре** be on bad terms, have fallen out. **ссо́рить, -рю** *impf.* (*pf.* **по~**) cause to quarrel, embroil; **~ся** quarrel, fall out.

СССР *abbr.* (*of* **Сою́з Сове́тских Социалисти́ческих Респу́блик**) USSR, Union of Soviet Socialist Republics.

ссу́да, -ы loan. **ссуди́ть, -ужу́, -у́дишь** *pf.*, **ссужа́ть, -а́ю** *impf.* lend, loan.

с|сучи́ть, -чу́, -у́чишь *pf.*

ссыла́ть(ся, -а́ю(сь *impf. of* **сосла́ть(ся. ссы́лка[1], -и** exile, banishment; deportation. **ссы́лка[2], -и** reference. **ссы́льный, ссы́льная** *sb.* exile.

ссыпа́ть, -плю *pf.*, **ссыпа́ть, -а́ю** *impf.* pour. **ссыпно́й; ~ пункт** grain-collecting station.

ст. *abbr.* (*of* **статья́**) Art., Article (*of law, etc.*); (*of* **столе́тие**) c., century.

стабилиза́тор, -а stabilizer; tail-plane. **стабилизи́ровать, -рую** *impf. & pf.*, **стабилизова́ть, -зу́ю** *impf. & pf.* stabilize; **~ся** become stable. **стаби́льный** stable, firm; **~** уче́бник standard textbook.

ста́вень, -вня; *g.pl.* -вней *m.*, **ста́вня, -и;** *g.pl.* -вен shutter.

ста́вить, -влю *impf.* (*pf.* **по~**) put, place, set; stand; station; put up, erect; install; put in; put on; apply; present, stage, stake. **ста́вка¹, -и** rate; stake; **~** зарпла́ты rate of pay. **ста́вка², -и** headquarters.

ста́вня *see* **ста́вень**

стадио́н, -а stadium.

ста́дия, -и stage.

ста́дность, -и herd instinct. **ста́дный** gregarious. **ста́до, -а;** *pl.* -á herd, flock.

стаж, -а length of service; record; probation. **стажёр,** -а probationer, houseman; trainee. **стажирова́ть(ся, -ру́ю(сь** *impf.* go through period of training.

ста́ивать, -ает *impf. of* **ста́ять**

ста́йер, -а long-distance runner.

стака́н, -а glass, tumbler, beaker.

сталелите́йный steel-founding, steel-casting; **~** заво́д steel foundry. **сталеплави́льный** steel-making; **~** заво́д steel works. **сталепрока́тный** (steel-)rolling; **~** стан rolling-mill.

ста́лкивать(ся, -аю(сь *impf. of* **столкну́ть(ся**

ста́ло быть *conj.* consequently, therefore, so. **сталь, -и** steel. **стально́й** steel.

стаме́ска, -и chisel.

стан¹, -а figure, torso.

стан², -а camp.

стан³, -а mill.

станда́рт, -а standard. **стандартиза́ция, -и** standardization. **станда́ртный** standard.

станко́вый machine; mounted; (free-)standing. **станкострое́ние, -я** machine-tool engineering.

станови́ться, -влю́сь, -вишься *impf. of* **стать**

стано́к, -нка́ machine tool, machine; bench; mount, mounting.

ста́ну *etc.: see* **стать**

станцио́нный station. **ста́нция, -и** station.

ста́пель, -я; *pl.* -я́ *m.* stocks.

ста́птывать(ся, -аю(сь *impf. of* **стопта́ть(ся**

стара́ние, -я effort, endeavour, pains, diligence. **стара́тель, -я** *m.* prospector (*for gold*), (gold-)digger. **стара́тельность, -и** application, diligence. **стара́тельный** diligent, painstaking, assiduous. **стара́ться, -а́юсь** *impf.* (*pf.* **по~**) try, endeavour; take pains; make an effort.

старе́ть, -е́ю *impf.* (*pf.* **по~, у~**) grow old, age. **ста́рец, -рца** elder, (*venerable*) old man; hermit. **стари́к, -а́** old man. **старина́, -ы́**

antiquity, olden times; antique(s); old man, old fellow. **стари́нный** ancient; old; antique.

ста́рить, -рю *impf.* (*pf.* **со~**) age, make old; **~ся** age, grow old.

старо... *in comb.* old. **старове́р, -а** Old Believer. **~да́вний** ancient. **~жи́л, -а** old inhabitant; old resident. **~заве́тный** old-fashioned, conservative; antiquated. **~мо́дный** old-fashioned, out-moded; out-of-date. **~печа́тный; ~печа́тные кни́ги** early printed books. **~све́тский** old-world; old-fashioned. **~славя́нский** Old Slavonic.

ста́роста, -ы head; senior; monitor; churchwarden. **ста́рость, -и** old age.

старт, -а start; на **~!** on your marks! **ста́ртёр, -а** starter. **стартова́ть, -ту́ю** *impf. & pf.* start. **ста́ртовый** starting.

стару́ха, -и old woman. **ста́рческий** old man's; senile; **~ое слабоу́мие** senility, senile decay. **ста́рше** *comp. of* **ста́рый.** **ста́рш|ий** oldest, eldest; senior; superior; chief, head; upper, higher; **~ий адъюта́нт** adjutant; **~ие** *sb.*; *pl.* (one's) elders; **~ий** *sb.* chief; man in charge; кто здесь **~ий?** who is in charge here? **старшина́, -ы́** *m.* sergeant-major; petty officer; leader, senior representative, doyen, foreman. **старшинство́, -а́** seniority; по старшинству́ by right of, in order of, seniority. **ста́рый; -ар, -а́, -о** old. **старьё, -я́** old things, old clothes, old junk.

ста́скивать, -аю *impf. of* **стащи́ть**

с|тасова́ть, -су́ю *pf.*

стати́ст, -а super, extra.

стати́стика, -и statistics. **статисти́ческий** statistical.

ста́тный stately.

ста́тский civil, civilian; State; **~** сове́тник State Councillor (*5th grade: see* **чин**).

ста́туя, -и statue.

стать, -а́ну *pf.* (*impf.* **станови́ться**) stand; take up position; stop, come to a halt; cost; suffice, do; begin, start; *+i.* become, get, grow; *+c+i.* become of, happen to; **не ~** *impers.+g.* cease to be; disappear, be gone; его́ не ста́ло he is no more; её отца́ давно́ не ста́ло her father has been dead a long time; **~ в о́чередь** queue up; **~ в по́зу** strike an attitude; **~ на коле́ни** kneel; **~ на рабо́ту** begin work; часы́ ста́ли the clock (has) stopped.

стать, -и; *g.pl.* -е́й need, necessity; physique, build; points; быть под **~** be well-matched; *+d.* be like; с како́й ста́ти? why? what for?

ста́ться, -а́нется *pf.* happen; become; вполне́ мо́жет **~** it is quite possible.

статья́, -и; *g.pl.* -е́й article; clause; item; matter, job; class, rating; э́то осо́бая **~** that is another matter.

стациона́р, -а permanent establishment; hospital. **стациона́рный** stationary; permanent, fixed; **~** больно́й in-patient.

с|тача́ть, -а́ю *pf.*

ста́чечник, -а striker. **ста́чка**, -и strike.

с|тащи́ть, -щу́, -щишь *pf.* (*impf. also* **ста́скивать**) drag off, pull off; drag down; pinch, swipe, whip.

ста́я, -и flock, flight; school, shoal; pack.

ста́ять, -ает *pf.* (*impf.* **ста́ивать**) melt.

ствол, -а́ trunk; stem; bole, barrel; tube, pipe; shaft.

ство́рка, -и leaf, fold; door, gate, shutter. **ство́рчатый** folding; valved.

сте́бель, -бля; *g.pl.* -бле́й *m.* stem, stalk. **стебе́льчатый** stalky, stalk-like; ~ шов feather-stitch.

стёганка, -и quilted jacket. **стёган|ый** quilted; ~ое одея́ло quilt. **стега́ть**[1], -а́ю *impf.* (*pf.* вы́~) quilt.

стега́ть[2], -а́ю *impf.*, **стегну́ть**, -ну́ *pf.* (*pf. also* от~) whip, lash.

стежо́к, -жка́ stitch.

стёк *etc.*: *see* **стечь**. **стека́ть(ся**, -а́ет(ся *impf. of* **сте́чь(ся**

стекле́неть, -ест *impf.* (*pf.* о~) become glassy. **стекло́**, -а́; *pl.* -ёкла, -кол glass; lens; (window-)pane.

стекло́... *in comb.* glass. **стекловолокно́**, -а́ glass fibre. **~ду́в**, -а a glass-blower. **~ма́сса**, -ы molten glass. **~очисти́тель**, -я *m.* windscreen-wiper.

стекля́нн|ый glass; glassy; ~ый колпа́к bell-glass, glass case; ~ая посу́да glassware. **стеко́льный** glass; vitreous. **стеко́льщик**, -а glazier.

стели́ть *see* **стлать**

стелла́ж, -а́ shelves, shelving; rack, stand.

сте́лька, -и insole, sock.

сте́льная коро́ва cow in calf.

стелю́ *etc.*: *see* **стлать**

с|темне́ть, -еет *pf.*

стена́, *a.* -у; *pl.* -ы, -а́м wall. **стенгазе́та**, -ы wall newspaper. **стенно́й** wall; mural.

стеногра́мма, -ы shorthand record. **стено́граф**, -а, **стенографи́ст**, -а, **стенографи́стка**, -и stenographer, shorthand-writer. **стенографи́ровать**, -рую *impf. & pf.* take down in shorthand. **стенографи́ческий** shorthand. **стеногра́фия**, -и shorthand, stenography.

сте́нопись, -и mural.

степе́нный staid, steady; middle-aged.

сте́пень, -и; *g.pl.* -е́й degree; extent; power.

степно́й steppe. **степня́к**, -а́ steppe-dweller; steppe horse. **степь**, -и, *loc.* -и́; *g.pl.* -е́й steppe.

стерегу́ *etc.*: *see* **стере́чь**

стереоти́п, -а stereotype. **стереоти́пн|ый** stereotype; ~ая фра́за stock phrase.

стереофони́ческий stereophonic.

стере́ть, сотру́, сотрёшь; стёр *pf.* (*impf.* **стира́ть**) wipe off; rub out, erase; rub sore; grind down; ~ся rub off; fade; wear down; be effaced, be obliterated.

стере́чь, -регу́, -режёшь; -ёг, -ла́ *impf.* guard; watch (over); watch for.

сте́ржень, -жня *m.* pivot; shank, rod; core. **стержнево́й** pivoted; ~ вопро́с key question.

стерилиза́тор, -а sterilizer. **стерилиза́ция**, -и sterilization. **стерилизова́ть**, -зу́ю *impf. & pf.* sterilize. **стери́льность**, -и sterility. **стери́льный** sterile; germ-free.

сте́рлинг, -а sterling; фунт ~ов pound sterling.

сте́рлядь, -и; *g.pl.* -ей sterlet.

стеро́ид, -а steroid.

стерпе́ть, -плю́, -пишь *pf.* bear, suffer, endure.

стёртый worn, effaced.

стесне́ние, -я constraint. **стесни́тельный** shy; inhibited; difficult, inconvenient. **с|тесни́ть**, -ню́ *pf.*, **стесня́ть**, -я́ю *impf.* constrain; hamper; inhibit. **с|тесни́ться**, -ню́сь *pf.*, **стесня́ться**, -я́юсь *impf.* (*pf. also* по~) +*inf.* feel too shy to, be ashamed to; (+*g.*) feel shy (of).

стече́ние, -я confluence; ~ наро́да concourse; ~ обстоя́тельств coincidence. **стечь**, -чёт; -ёк, -ла́ *pf.* (*impf.* **стека́ть**) flow down; ~ся flow together; gather, throng.

стиль, -я *m.* style. **сти́льный** stylish; period.

сти́мул, -а stimulus, incentive. **стимули́ровать**, -рую *impf. & pf.* stimulate.

стипендиа́т, -а grant-aided student. **стипе́ндия**, -и grant.

стира́льный washing.

стира́ть[1](ся, -а́ю(сь *impf. of* **стере́ть(ся**

стира́ть[2], -а́ю *impf.* (*pf.* вы́~) wash, launder; ~ся wash. **сти́рка**, -и washing, wash, laundering, laundry.

сти́скивать, -аю *impf.*, **сти́снуть**, -ну *pf.* squeeze; clench; hug.

стих, -а́ verse; line; *pl.* verses, poetry.

стиха́ть, -а́ю *impf. of* **сти́хнуть**

стихи́йн|ый elemental; spontaneous, uncontrolled; ~ое бе́дствие disaster. **стихи́я**, -и element.

сти́хнуть, -ну; стих *pf.* (*impf.* **стиха́ть**) abate, subside; die down; calm down.

стихове́дение, -я prosody. **стихосложе́ние**, -я versification; prosody. **стихотворе́ние**, -я poem. **стихотво́рный** in verse form; of verse; poetic; ~ разме́р metre.

стлать, стели́ть, стелю́, сте́лешь *impf.* (*pf.* по~) spread; ~ посте́ль make a bed; ~ ска́терть lay the cloth; ~ся spread; drift, creep.

сто, ста; *g.pl.* сот a hundred.

стог, -а (*loc.* -е & -у́; *pl.* -а́ stack, rick.

стогра́дусный centigrade.

сто́имость, -и cost; value. **сто́ить**, -о́ю *impf.* cost; be worth; be worthy of, deserve; не сто́ит don't mention it; сто́ит it is worth while; ~ то́лько+*inf.* one has only to.

стой *see* **стоя́ть**

сто́йка, -и counter, bar; support, prop; stanchion, upright; strut; set; stand, stance.

стойкий firm; stable; persistent; steadfast, staunch, steady. **стойкость, -и** firmness, stability; steadfastness, staunchness; determination. **стойло, -a** stall. **стоймя** *adv.* upright.

сток, -a flow; drainage, outflow; drain, gutter; sewer.

Стокгольм, -a Stockholm.

стол, -á table; desk; board; cooking, cuisine; department, section; office, bureau.

столб, -á post, pole, pillar, column. **столбенеть, -ею** *impf.* (*pf.* **o~**) be rooted to the ground, be transfixed. **столбец, -бца** column. **столбик, -a** column; style; double crochet, treble. **столбняк, -á** stupor; tetanus. **столбовой** main, chief.

столетие, -я century; centenary. **столетний** of a hundred years; a hundred years old; ~ **старик** centenarian.

столица, -ы capital; metropolis. **столичный** capital; of the capital.

столкновение, -я collision; clash. **столкнуть, -ну, -нёшь** *pf.* (*impf.* **сталкивать**) push off, push away; cause to collide, bring into collision; bring together; ~**ся** collide, come into collision; clash, conflict; +**c**+*i.* run into, bump into.

столоваться, -луюсь *impf.* have meals, board, mess. **столовая** *sb.* dining-room; mess; canteen; dining-room suite. **столовый** table; dinner; feeding, catering, messing.

столп, -á pillar, column.

столпиться, -ится *pf.* crowd.

столь *adv.* so. **столько** *adv.* so much, so many.

столяр, -á joiner, carpenter. **столярный** joiner's, carpenter's.

стометровка, -и (the) hundred metres; hundred-metre event.

стон, -a groan, moan. **стонать, -ну, -нешь** *impf.* groan, moan.

стоп! *int.* stop!; *indecl. adj.* stop.

стопа¹, -ы; *pl.* **-ы** foot.

стопа², -ы; *pl.* **-ы** goblet.

стопа³, -ы; *pl.* **-ы** ream; pile, heap.

стопка¹, -и pile, heap.

стопка², -и small glass.

стопор, -a stop, catch, pawl. **стопорить, -рю** *impf.* (*pf.* **за~**) stop, lock; slow down, bring to a stop; ~**ся** slow down, come to a stop.

стопроцентный hundred-per-cent.

стоп-сигнал, -a brake-light.

стоптать, -пчу, -пчешь *pf.* (*impf.* **стаптывать**) wear down; trample; ~**ся** wear down, be worn down.

с|торговать(ся, -гую(сь *pf.*

сторож, -a; *pl.* **-á** watchman, guard. **сторожевой** watch; ~**ая будка** sentry-box; ~**ой корабль** escort vessel; ~**ое судно** patrol-boat. **сторожить, -жу** *impf.* guard, watch, keep watch over.

сторона, -ы, *a.* **сторону**; *pl.* **стороны, -рон, -ам** side; quarter; hand; feature, aspect; part;

party; land, place; parts; **в стороне** aside, aloof; **в сторону** aside; **на чужой стороне** in foreign parts; **по ту сторону**+*g.* across; on the other, the far, side of; **с моей стороны** for my part; **с одной стороны** on the one hand; **шутки в сторону** joking apart. **сторониться, -нюсь, -нишься** *impf.* (*pf.* **по~**) stand aside, make way; +*g.* shun, avoid. **сторонний** strange, foreign; detached; indirect. **сторонник, -a** supporter, adherent, advocate; ~ **мира** peace campaigner.

сточн|ый sewage, drainage; ~**ые воды** sewage; ~**ая труба** drainpipe, sewer.

стояк, -á post, stanchion, upright; stand-pipe; chimney. **стоянка, -и** stop; parking; stopping place, parking space; stand; rank; moorage; site; «~ **запрещена!**» 'No parking'; ~ **такси** taxi-rank. **стоять, -ою** *impf.* (*pf.* **по~**) stand; be; be situated, lie; continue; stay; be stationed; stop; have stopped, have come to a stop; +**за**+*a.* stand up for; **мой часы стоят** my watch has stopped; **работа стоит** work has come to a standstill; **стой(те)!** stop! halt!; ~ **во главе**+*g.* head, be at the head of; ~ **лагерем** be encamped, be under canvas; ~ **на коленях** kneel, be kneeling; ~ **у власти** be in power, be in office; **стояла хорошая погода** the weather kept fine. **стоячий** standing; upright, vertical; stagnant. **стоящий** deserving; worthwhile.

стр. *abbr.* (*of* **страница**) p., page.

страдалец, -льца sufferer. **страдание, -я** suffering. **страдательный** passive. **страдать, -аю** *or* **-ражду** *impf.* (*pf.* **по~**) suffer; be subject; be in pain; be weak, be poor; ~ **за**+*g.* feel for; ~ **по**+*d. or p.* miss, long for, pine for; ~ **от зубной боли** have toothache.

стража, -и guard, watch; **взять под стражу** take into custody; **под стражей** under arrest, in custody; **стоять на страже**+*g.* guard.

страна, -ы; *pl.* **-ы** country; land; ~ **света** cardinal point.

страница, -ы page.

странник, -a, странница, -ы wanderer; pilgrim.

странно *adv.* strangely, oddly. **странность, -и** strangeness; oddity, eccentricity, singularity. **странн|ый; -анен, -анна, -о** strange; funny, odd, queer.

странствие, -я wandering, journeying, travelling. **странствовать, -твую** *impf.* wander, journey, travel.

Страсбург, -a Strasbourg.

Страстн|ой of Holy Week; ~**ая пятница** Good Friday.

страстный; -тен, -тна, -о passionate; impassioned; ardent. **страсть, -и**; *g.pl.* **-ей** passion; +**к**+*d.* passion for; **до страсти** passionately. **страсть** *adv.* awfully, frightfully; an awful lot, a terrific number.

стратег, -a strategist. **стратегический** strategic. **стратегия, -и** strategy.

стратостат, -a stratosphere balloon. **страто-**

сфе́ра, -ы stratosphere. **стратосфе́рный** stratospheric.

стра́ус, -а ostrich. **стра́усовый** ostrich.

страх, -а (-у) fear; terror; risk, responsibility; **на свой ~** at one's own risk; **под ~ом сме́рти** on pain of death. **страх** *adv.* terribly.

страхка́сса, -ы insurance office. **страхова́-ние**, -я insurance; **~ жи́зни** life insurance; **~ от огня́** fire insurance. **страхова́ть**, -ху́ю *impf.* (*pf.* за**~**) insure (от+g. against); **~ся** insure o.s. **страхо́вка**, -и insurance; guarantee.

стра́шно *adv.* terribly, awfully. **стра́шн|ый;** -шен, -шна́, -о terrible, awful, dreadful, frightful, fearful; terrifying, frightening; **~ый сон** bad dream.

стрекоза́, -ы́; *pl.* -ы dragonfly.

стре́кот, -а, **стрекотня́**, -й chirr; rattle, chatter, clatter. **стрекота́ть**, -очу́, -о́чешь *impf.* chirr; rattle, chatter, clatter.

стрела́, -ы́; *pl.* -ы arrow; shaft; dart; arm, boom, jib; derrick. **стреле́ц**, -льца́ Sagittarius. **стре́лка**, -и pointer, indicator; needle; arrow; spit; points. **стрелко́вый** rifle; shooting, fire; small-arms; infantry. **стрело-ви́дность**, -и angle, sweep. **стреloви́д-н|ый** arrow-shaped; **~ое крыло́** swept-back wing. **стрело́к**, -лка́ shot; rifleman, gunner. **стре́лочник**, -а pointsman. **стрельба́**, -ы́; *pl.* -ы shooting, firing; shoot, fire. **стрель-ну́ть**, -ну́, -нёшь *pf.* fire, fire a shot; rush away. **стре́льчатый** lancet; arched, pointed. **стре́ляный** shot; used, fired, spent; that has been under fire. **стреля́ть**, -яю *impf.* shoot; fire; **~ глаза́ми** dart glances; make eyes; **~ кнуто́м** crack a whip.

стремгла́в *adv.* headlong.

стремено́й stirrup.

стреми́тельный swift, headlong; impetuous. **стреми́ться**, -млю́сь *impf.* strive; seek, aspire; try; rush, speed, charge. **стремле́ние**, -я striving, aspiration. **стремни́на**, -ы rapid, rapids; precipice.

стре́мя, -мени; *pl.* -мена́, -мя́н, -а́м *nt.* stirrup. **стремя́нка**, -и step-ladder, steps. **стре-мя́нный** stirrup.

стреха́, -й; *pl.* -и eaves.

стрига́льщик, -а shearer. **стри́женый** short; short-haired, cropped; shorn, sheared; clipped. **стри́жка**, -и hair-cut; cut; shearing; clipping. **стричь**, -игу́, -ижёшь; -иг *impf.* (*pf.* о**~**) cut, clip; cut the hair of; shear; cut into pieces; **~ся** cut one's hair, have one's hair cut; wear one's hair short.

строга́ль, -я́ *m.*, **строга́льщик**, -а plane operator, planer. **строга́льный** planing; **~ резе́ц** planer, cutter. **строга́ть**, -а́ю *impf.* (*pf.* вы**~**) plane, shave.

стро́гий strict; severe; stern. **стро́гость**, -и strictness; severity; *pl.* strong measures.

строев|о́й combatant; line; drill; **~а́я слу́жба** combatant service. **строе́ние**, -я building; structure; composition; texture.

строжа́йший, **стро́же** *superl.* & *comp.* of **стро́гий**

строи́тель, -я *m.* builder. **строи́тельн|ый** building, construction; **~ое иску́сство** civil engineering; **~ая площа́дка** building site. **строи́тельство**, -а building, construction; building site, construction site. **стро́ить**, -о́ю *impf.* (*pf.* по**~**) build; construct; make; formulate, express; base; draw up, form up; **~ся** be built, be under construction; draw up, form up; **стро́йся!** fall in! **строй**, -я, *loc.* -ю́; *pl.* -и *or* -й, -ев *or* -ёв system; order; régime; structure; pitch; formation; service, commission. **стро́йка**, -и building, construction; building-site. **стро́йность**, -и proportion; harmony; balance, order. **стро́йн|ый;** -о́ен, -ойна́, -о harmonious, well-balanced, orderly, well put together, well-proportioned, shapely.

строка́, -й, *a.* -о́ку́; *pl.* -и, -а́м line; **кра́сная ~** break-line, new paragraph.

строп, -а, **стро́па**, -ы sling; shroud line.

стропи́ло, -а rafter, truss, beam.

стропти́в|ый obstinate, refractory; **~ая** *sb.* shrew.

строфа́, -ы́; *pl.* -ы, -а́м stanza, strophe.

стро́чёный stitched; hem-stitched. **строчи́ть**, -чу́, -о́чишь *impf.* (*pf.* на**~**, про**~**) sew, stitch; back-stitch; scribble, dash off. **стро́ч-ка**, -и stitch; back-stitching; hem-stitching; line.

строчно́й lower-case, small.

стро́ю *etc.: see* **стро́ить**

струг, -а plane. **струга́ть**, -а́ю *impf.* (*pf.* вы**~**) plane, shave. **стру́жка**, -и shaving, filing.

струи́ться, -и́тся *impf.* stream, flow.

структу́ра, -ы structure. **структу́рный** structural; structured.

струна́, -ы́; *pl.* -ы string. **стру́нный** stringed.

с|тру́сить, -у́шу *pf.*

стручко́вый leguminous, podded; **~ пе́рец** capsicum; **~ горо́шек** peas in the pod. **стручо́к**, -чка́ pod.

струя́, -й; *pl.* -и, -уй jet, spurt, stream; current; spirit; impetus.

стря́пать, -аю *impf.* (*pf.* со**~**) cook; cook up; concoct. **стряпня́**, -й cooking. **стря-пу́ха**, -и cook.

стря́хивать, -аю *impf.*, **стряхну́ть**, -ну́, -нёшь *pf.* shake off.

ст. ст. *abbr.* (*of* ста́рый стиль) OS, Old Style (*of calendar*).

студене́ть, -е́ет *impf.* (*pf.* за**~**) thicken, set. **студени́стый** jelly-like.

студе́нт, -а, **студе́нтка**, -и student. **студе́н-ческий** student.

сту́день, -дня *m.* jelly; galantine; aspic.

студи́ец, -и́йца, **студи́йка**, -и student. **сту-ди́йный** studio.

студи́ть, -ужу́, -у́дишь *impf.* (*pf.* о**~**) cool.

сту́дия, -и studio, workshop; school.

стук, -а knock; tap; thump; rumble; clatter.

стУ́кать, -аю *impf.*, стУ́кнуть, -ну *pf.* knock; bang; tap; rap; hit, strike; ~ся knock (o.s.), bang, bump.

стул, -а; *pl.* -лья, -льев chair. стульчáк, -á (*lavatory*) seat. стУ́льчик, -а stool.

стУ́па, -ы mortar.

ступáть, -áю *impf.*, ступи́ть, -плю́, -пишь *pf.* step; tread; ступáй(те)! be off! clear out! ступéнчатый stepped, graduated, graded; multi-stage. ступéнь, -и; *g.pl.* -éнéй step, rung; stage, grade, level, phase. ступня́, -й foot; sole.

стучáть, -чý *impf.* (*pf.* по~) knock; bang; tap; rap; chatter; hammer, pulse, thump, pound; ~ся knock at.

стушевáться, -шýюсь *pf.* стушёвываться, -аюсь *impf.* efface o.s., retire to the background; be covered with confusion; shade off, fade out.

с|тушИ́ть, -шý, -шишь *pf.*

стыд, -á shame. стыди́ть, -ыжý *impf.* (*pf.* при~) shame, put to shame; ~ся (*pf.* по~ся) be ashamed. стыдли́вый bashful. стЫ́дн|ый shameful; ~о! (for) shame! ~о *impers.*+*d.* емý ~о he is ashamed; как тебé не ~о! you ought to be ashamed of yourself!

стык, -а joint; junction; meeting-point. стыковáть, -кУ́ю *impf.* (*pf.* со~) join end to end; dock; ~ся (*pf.* при~ся) dock. стыкóвка, -и docking. стыкóвочный docking.

стЫ́нуть, стыть, -Ы́ну; стыл *impf.* cool; get cold; run cold; freeze.

стЫ́чка, -и skirmish, clash; squabble.

стюардéсса, -ы stewardess; air hostess.

стя́гивать, -аю *impf.*, стяну́ть, -нý, -нешь *pf.* tighten; pull together; gather, assemble; pull off; pinch, steal; ~ся tighten; gird o.s. tightly; gather, assemble.

суббóта, -ы Saturday.

субсиди́ровать, -рую *impf.* & *pf.* subsidize. субси́дия, -и subsidy, grant.

субти́тр, -а subtitle.

субтропи́ческий subtropical.

субъéкт, -а subject; self, ego; person, individual; character, type. субъекти́вный subjective.

суверéн, -а sovereign. суверенитéт, -а sovereignty. суверéнный sovereign.

сугли́нок, -нка loam.

сугрóб, -а snowdrift.

сугУ́бо *adv.* especially, particularly; exclusively.

суд, -á court; law-court; legal proceedings; the judges; the bench; judgement, verdict; подáть в ~ на+*a.* bring an action against; ~ чéсти court of honour.

судá *etc.*: *see* суд, сУ́дно[1]

судáк, -á pike-perch.

судéбный judicial; legal; forensic. судéйский judge's; referee's, umpire's. судéйство, -а refereeing, umpiring; judging. суди́мость, -и previous convictions, record.

суди́ть, сужý, сУ́дишь *impf.* judge; form an opinion; try; pass judgement; referee, umpire; foreordain; ~ся go to law.

сУ́дно[1], -а; *pl.* -дá, -óв vessel, craft.

сУ́дно[2], -а; *g.pl.* -ден bed-pan.

судоводи́тель, -я *m.* navigator. судовождéние, -я navigation. судовóй ship's; marine.

судомóйка, -и kitchen-maid, scullery maid, washer-up; scullery.

судопроизвóдство, -а legal proceedings.

сУ́дорога, -и cramp, convulsion, spasm. сУ́дорожный convulsive, spasmodic.

судострóение, -я shipbuilding. судострóительный shipbuilding. судохóдный navigable; shipping; ~ канáл ship canal.

судьбá, -Ы́; *pl.* -ы, -дéб fate, fortune, destiny, lot; каки́ми судьбáми? how do you come to be here?

судья́, -й; *pl.* -и, -éй, -ям *m.* judge; referee; umpire.

суевéр, -а superstitious person. суевéрие, -я superstition. суевéрный superstitious.

суетá, -Ы́ bustle, fuss. суети́ться, -ечýсь *impf.* bustle, fuss. суетли́вый fussy, bustling.

суждéние, -я opinion; judgement.

сУ́женая *sb.* fiancée; intended (*wife*). сУ́женый *sb.* fiancé; intended (*husband*).

сужéние, -я narrowing; constriction. сУ́живать, -аю *impf.*, сУ́зить, -у́жу *pf.* narrow, contract; make too narrow; ~ся narrow; taper.

сук, -á, *loc.* -ý; *pl.* сУ́чья, -ьев *or* -й, -óв bough; knot.

сУ́ка, -и bitch. сУ́кин *adj.*; ~ сын son of a bitch.

сукнó, -á; *pl.* -а, -кон cloth; положи́ть под ~ shelve. сукóнный cloth; rough, clumsy, crude.

сули́ть, -лю́ *impf.* (*pf.* по~) promise.

султáн[1], -а sultan.

султáн[2], -а plume.

сумá, -Ы́ bag; pouch.

сумасбрóд, -а, сумасбрóдка, -и madcap. сумасбрóдный wild, extravagant. сумасбрóдство, -а extravagance, wild behaviour. сумасшéдш|ий mad; lunatic; ~ий *sb.* madman, lunatic; ~ая *sb.* madwoman, lunatic. сумасшéствие, -я madness, lunacy.

суматóха, -и hurly-burly, turmoil; bustle; confusion, chaos.

сумбУ́р, -а confusion, chaos. сумбУ́рный confused, chaotic.

сУ́меречный twilight; crepuscular. сУ́мерки, -рек *pl.* twilight, dusk; half-light.

сумéть, -éю *pf.*+*inf.* be able to, manage to.

сУ́мка, -и bag; handbag; shopping-bag; case; satchel; pouch.

сУ́мма, -ы sum. суммáрный summary; total. сумми́ровать, -рую *impf.* & *pf.* sum up, total up; summarize.

сУ́мрак, -а dusk, twilight; murk. сУ́мрачный gloomy; murky; dusky.

сумчатый marsupial.

сундук, -а trunk, box, chest.

сунуть(ся, -ну(сь pf. of **совать(ся**

суп, -а (-у); pl. **-ы** soup.

суперобложка, -и dust-jacket.

супов|ой soup; ~**ая ложка** soup-spoon; ~**ая миска** soup-tureen.

супруг, -а husband, spouse; pl. husband and wife, (married) couple. **супруга, -и** wife, spouse. **супружеск|ий** conjugal, matrimonial; ~**ая измена** infidelity. **супружество, -а** matrimony, wedlock.

сургуч, -а sealing-wax.

сурдинка, -и mute; **под сурдинку** on the quiet, on the sly. **сурдокамера, -ы** sound-proof room.

суровость, -и severity, sterness. **суров|ый** severe, stern; rigorous; bleak; unbleached, brown; ~**ое полотно** crash; brown holland.

сурок, -рка marmot.

суррогат, -а substitute.

суслик, -а ground-squirrel.

сусло, -а must; wort; grape-juice.

сустав, -а joint, articulation.

сутки, -ток pl. twenty-four hours; a day (and a night); **двое с половиной суток** sixty hours.

сутолока, -и commotion, hubbub, hurly-burly.

суточн|ый twenty-four hour; daily; per diem; round-the-clock; ~**ые деньги,** ~**ые** sb., pl. per diem allowance.

сутулиться, -люсь impf. stoop. **сутулый** round-shouldered, stooping.

суть, -и essence, main point; **по сути дела** as a matter of fact, in point of fact; ~ **дела** the heart of the matter.

суфлёр, -а prompter. **суфлёрск|ий** prompt; ~**ая будка** prompt-box. **суфлировать, -рую** impf.+d. prompt.

сухарь, -я m. rusk; pl. bread-crumbs. **сухо** adv. drily; coldly.

сухожилие, -я tendon, sinew.

сухой; сух, -а, -о dry; dried-up; arid; dried; withered; chilly, cold. **сухопутный** land. **сухость, -и** dryness, aridity; chilliness, coldness. **сухощавый** lean, skinny.

сучить, -чу, сучишь impf. (pf. **с~**) twist, spin; throw; roll out.

сучковатый knotty; gnarled. **сучок, -чка** twig; knot.

суша, -и (dry) land. **суше** comp. of **сухой.** **сушёный** dried. **сушилка, -и** dryer; drying-room. **сушильня, -и;** g.pl. **-лен** drying-room. **сушить, -шу, -шишь** impf. (pf. **вы~**) dry, dry out, dry up; ~**ся** dry, get dry.

существенный essential, vital; material; important. **существительное** sb. noun, substantive. **существо, -а** being, creature; essence. **существование, -я** existence. **существовать, -твую** impf. exist. **сущий** existing; real; absolute, utter, downright. **сущность, -и** essence; ~ **дела** the point; в

сущности in essence, at bottom; as a matter of fact.

сую etc.: see **совать.** **с|фабриковать, -кую** pf. **с|фальшивить, -влю** pf. **с|фантазировать, -рую** pf.

сфера, -ы sphere; realm; zone, area; ~ **влияния** sphere of influence. **сферический** spherical

с|формировать(ся, -рую(сь pf. **с|формовать, -мую** pf. **с|формулировать, -рую** pf. **с|фотографировать(ся, -рую(сь** pf.

с.-х. abbr. (of **сельское хозяйство**) agri-culture.

схватить, -ачу, -атишь pf. **схватывать, -аю** impf. (impf. also **хватать**) seize; catch; grasp, comprehend; clamp together; ~**ся** snatch, catch; grapple, come to grips. **схватка, -и** skirmish, fight, encounter; squabble; pl. contractions; fit, spasm; **родовые схватки** labour.

схема, -ы diagram, chart; sketch; outline, plan; circuit. **схематический** diagrammatic, schematic; sketchy, over-simplified. **схематичный** sketchy, over-simplified.

с|хитрить, -рю pf.

схлынуть, -нет pf. (break and) flow back; break up, rush away; subside, vanish.

сход, -а coming off, alighting; descent; gathering, assembly. **сходить¹(ся, -ожу(сь, -одишь(ся** impf. of **сойти(сь. с|ходить², -ожу, -одишь** pf. go; +за+i. go for, go to fetch. **сходка, -и** gathering, assembly, meeting. **сходный; -ден, -дна, -о** similar; reasonable, fair. **сходня, -и;** g.pl. **-ей** (usu. pl.) gangway, gang-plank. **сходство, -а** likeness, similarity, resemblance.

схоластика, -и scholasticism. **схоластический** scholastic.

с|хоронить(ся, -ню(сь, -нишь(ся pf.

сцедить, -ежу, -едишь pf., **сцеживать, -аю** impf. strain off, pour off, decant.

сцена, -ы stage; scene. **сценарий, -я** scenario; script; stage directions. **сценарист, -а** script-writer. **сценическ|ий** stage; ~**ая ремарка** stage direction. **сценичный** good theatre.

сцеп, -а coupling; drawbar. **сцепить, -плю, -пишь** pf., **сцеплять, -яю** impf. couple; ~**ся** be coupled; grapple, come to grips. **сцепка, -и** coupling. **сцепление, -я** coupling; adhesion; cohesion; accumulation, chain; clutch.

счастливец, -вца, счастливчик, -а lucky man. **счастливица, -ы** lucky woman. **счастлив|ый; счастлив** happy; lucky, fortunate; successful; ~**ая идея** happy thought; ~**ого пути,** ~**ого плавания** bon voyage, pleasant journey. **счастье, -я** happiness; luck, good fortune.

счесть(ся, сочту(сь, -тёшь(ся; счёл(ся, сочла(сь pf. of **считать(ся. счёт, -а (-у),** loc. **-у;** pl. **-а** bill; account; counting, calculation, reckoning; score; expense; **быть на хорошем** ~**у** be in good repute, stand well; **в два** ~**а**

in two ticks, in two shakes; **за** ~+g. at the expense of; **на** ~ on account; +g. on the account, to the account; **потеря́ть** ~+d. lose count of. **счётн|ый** counting, calculating, computing; accounts, accounting; ~**ая ли-не́йка** slide-rule; ~**ая маши́на** calculating machine. **счетово́д, -a** accountant, book-keeper. **счетово́дство, -a** accounting, book-keeping. **счётчик, -a, счётчица, -ы** teller; counter; meter. **счёты, -ов** pl. abacus.

счи́стить, -и́щу pf. (impf. **счища́ть**) clean off; clear away; ~**ся** come off, clean off.

счита́ть, -а́ю impf. (pf. **со**~, **счесть**) count; compute, reckon; consider, think; regard (as); ~**ся** (pf. also **по**~**ся**) settle accounts; be considered, be thought, be reputed; be regarded (as); +c+i. take into consideration; take into account, reckon with.

счища́ть(ся, -а́ю(сь impf. of **счи́стить(ся**

США abbr. (of **Соединённые Шта́ты Аме́рики**) USA, United States of America.

сшиба́ть, -а́ю impf., **сшиби́ть, -бу́, -бёшь; сшиб** pf. strike, hit, knock (off); ~ **с ног** knock down; ~**ся** collide; come to blows.

сшива́ть, -а́ю impf., **с|шить, сошью́, -ьёшь** pf. sew; sew together, sew up. **сши́вка, -и** sewing together.

съ... vbl. pref.: see с...

съеда́ть, -а́ю impf. of **съесть. съедо́бный** edible; eatable, nice.

съе́ду etc.: see **съе́хать**

съёживаться, -аюсь impf., **съ|ёжиться, -жусь** pf. huddle up; shrivel, shrink.

съезд, -a congress; conference, convention; arrival, gathering. **съе́здить, -зжу** pf. go, drive, travel.

съезжа́ть(ся, -а́ю(сь impf. of **съе́хать(ся**

съел etc.: see **съесть**

съём, -a removal. **съёмка, -и** removal; survey, surveying; plotting; exposure; shooting. **съёмный** detachable, removable. **съём-щик, -a, съёмщица, -ы** tenant, lessee; surveyor.

съестн|о́й food; ~**ы́е припа́сы**, ~**о́е** sb. food supplies, provisions, eatables, food-stuffs. **съ|есть, -ем, -ешь, -ест, -еди́м; съел** pf. (impf. also **съеда́ть**)

съе́хать, -е́ду pf. (impf. **съезжа́ть**) go down; come down; move, remove; slip; ~**ся** meet, arrive, gather, assemble.

съязви́ть, -влю pf.

сы́воротка, -и whey; serum. **сы́вороточ-ный** serum; serous.

сы́гранность, -и team-work. **сыгра́ть, -а́ю** pf. of **игра́ть**; ~**ся** play (well) together, play as a team.

сымпровизи́ровать, -рую pf. of **импрови-зи́ровать**

сын, -a; pl. **сыновья́, -е́й** or **-ы́, -о́в** son. **сыно́вий, сыно́вний** filial. **сыно́к, -нка́** little son, little boy; sonny.

сы́пать, -плю impf. pour; strew; pour forth; ~**ся** fall; pour out, run out; scatter; fly; rain

down; fray. **сыпно́й тиф** typhus. **сыпу́ч|ий** friable; free-flowing; shifting; **ме́ры** ~**их тел** dry measures; ~**ий песо́к** quicksand; shifting sand. **сыпь, -и** rash, eruption.

сыр, -a (-у), loc. **-ý;** pl. **-ы́** cheese.

сыре́ть, -е́ю impf. (pf. **от**~) become damp.

сыре́ц, -рца́ unfinished product, raw product; **шёлк-**~ raw silk.

сы́рник, -a curd fritter. **сы́рный** cheese; cheesy. **сырова́р, -a** cheese-maker. **сыро-варе́ние, -я, сыроде́лие, -я** cheese-making.

сыр|о́й; сыр, -á, -о damp; raw; uncooked; unfinished; green, unripe; ~**áя вода́** unboiled water; ~**ы́е материа́лы** raw materials. **сы́-рость, -и** dampness, humidity. **сырьё, -я́** raw material(s).

сыск, -a investigation, detection. **сыска́ть, сыщу́, сы́щешь** pf. find; ~**ся** be found, come to light. **сыскно́й** investigation.

сы́тный; -тен, -тна́, -о satisfying, substantial, copious. **сы́тость, -и** satiety, repletion. **сы́-тый; сыт, -á, -о** satisfied, replete, full; fat; ~ **по го́рло** full up; ~ **скот** fat stock.

сыч, -á little owl.

сы́щик, -a, сы́щица, -ы detective.

с|эконо́мить, -млю pf.

сюда́ adv. here, hither.

сюже́т, -a subject; plot; topic. **сюже́тный** subject; based on, having, a theme.

сюи́та, -ы (mus.) suite.

сюрпри́з, -a surprise.

сюрреали́зм, -a surrealism. **сюрреали́ст, -a** surrealist.

сюрту́к, -á frock-coat.

сюсю́кать, -аю impf. lisp.

сяк adv.: see **так сям** adv.: see **там**

Т

т letter: see **тэ**

т abbr. (of **то́нна**) t., ton(s), tonne(s).

т. abbr. (of **това́рищ**) Comrade; (of **том**) vol., volume.

та see **тот**

таба́к, -á (-ý) tobacco; snuff. **табаке́рка, -и** snuff-box. **таба́чн|ый** tobacco; ~**ого цве́та** snuff-coloured.

та́бель, -я; pl. **-и, -ей** or **-я́, -е́й** m. table, list, scale. **та́бельн|ый** table; time; ~**ые часы́** time-clock. **та́бельщик, -a, -щица, -ы** time-keeper.

табле́тка, -и tablet.

табли́ца, -ы table; list; plate; ~ **вы́игрышей** prize-list; **табли́цы логари́фмов** logarithm tables; ~ **Менделе́ева** periodic table; ~ **умноже́ния** multiplication table. **табли́чный** tabular; standard.

та́бор, -a camp; gipsy encampment. **та́борный** camp; gypsy.

табуля́тор, -a tabulator.

табу́н, -á herd.

табуре́т, -a, табуре́тка, -и stool.

таврёный branded. **тавро́, -á;** *pl.* **-a, -áм** brand.

Таджикиста́н, -a Tadzhikistan.

таёжник, -a, -ница, -ы taiga dweller. **таёжный** taiga.

таз, -a, *loc.* **-ý;** *pl.* **-ы́** basin; wash-basin; pelvis. **тазобе́дренный** hip; ~ **суста́в** hip-joint. **та́зовый** pelvic.

таи́нственный mysterious; enigmatic; secret; secretive. **таи́ть, таю́** *impf.* hide, conceal; harbour; **~ся** hide, be in hiding; lurk.

Тайва́нь, -я Taiwan.

тайга́, -й taiga.

тайко́м *adv.* in secret, surreptitiously, by stealth; ~ **от+g.** behind the back of.

тайм, -a half; period of play.

та́йна, -ы mystery; secret. **тайни́к, -á** hiding-place; *pl.* secret places, recesses. **тайно́пись, -и** cryptography. **та́йнопись, -и** cryptography, cryptogram. **та́йный** secret; clandestine; privy; ~ **сове́тник** Privy Councillor (*3rd grade: see* **чин**).

так *adv.* so; thus, in this way, like this; in such a way; as it should be; just like that; **и** ~ even so; as it is, as it stands; **и** ~ **да́лее** and so on, and so forth; **и** ~ **и сяк** this way and that; **мы сде́лали** ~ this is what we did, we did it this way; **не** ~ amiss, wrong; **про́сто** ~, ~ (**то́лько**) for no special reason, just for fun; ~ **же** in the same way; ~ **же... как** as ... as; ~ **и** simply, just; ~ **и быть** all right, right you are; ~ **и есть** I thought so!; ~ **ему́ и на́до** serves him right; ~ **и́ли ина́че** in any event, whatever happens; one way or another; ~ **себе́** so-so, middling, not too good; **что́-то бы́ло не совсе́м** ~ something was amiss, something was not quite right; **я** ~ **и забы́л** I clean forgot. **так** *conj.* then; so; **не сего́дня,** ~ **за́втра** if not today, then tomorrow; ~ **как** as, since. **так** *part.* yes.

такела́ж, -a rigging; tackle, gear. **такела́жник, -a** rigger, scaffolder. **такела́жный** rigging; scaffolding.

та́кже *adv.* also, too, as well.

-таки *part.* after all; **всё~** nevertheless; **опя́ть~** again; **та́к~** after all, really.

тако́в *m.,* **-á** *f.,* **-ó** *nt.,* **-ы́** *pl.,* *pron.* such; **все они́ ~ы́** they are all the same.

тако́|й *pron.* such; so; a kind of; **в ~о́м слу́чае** in that case; **кто он ~о́й?** who is he?; **~о́й же** the same; **~и́м о́бразом** thus, in this way; **что ~о́е?** what's that? what did you say?; **что э́то ~о́е?** what is this? **тако́й-то** *pron.* so-and-so; such-and-such.

та́кса, -ы fixed price, statutory price; tariff.

такса́тор, -a price-fixer; valuer. **такса́ция, -и** price-fixing; valuation.

такси́ *nt.indecl.* taxi.

такси́ровать, -рую *impf. & pf.* fix the price of, value.

такси́ст, -a taxi-driver. **таксомото́рный** taxi. **таксомото́рщик, -a** taxi-driver. **таксопа́рк, -a** taxi-depot, fleet of taxis.

такт, -a time; measure; bar; stroke; tact.

та́к-таки *see* **-таки**

та́ктик, -a a tactician. **та́ктика, -и** tactics. **такти́ческий** tactical. **такти́чность, -и** tact. **такти́чный** tactful.

та́ктов|ый time, timing; ~**ая черта́** bar-line.

тала́нт, -a a talent, gift; talented man. **тала́нтливый** talented, gifted.

та́лия, -и waist.

Та́ллин, -a Tallin(n).

тало́н, -a, тало́нчик, -a coupon; stub; ~ **на обе́д** luncheon voucher; **поса́дочный** ~ boarding pass; landing card.

та́л|ый thawed, melted; ~**ая вода́** melted snow; ~**ый снег** slush.

там *adv.* there; **и** ~ **и сям** here, there, and everywhere; ~ **же** in the same place; ibid, *ibidem.*

тамада́, -ы́ *m.* master of ceremonies; toast-master.

та́мбур[1], -a tambour; lobby; platform. **та́мбур[2], -a** tambour-stitch, chain-stitch. **та́мбурный** tambour; ~ **шов** tambour-stitch; chain-stitch.

тамо́женный customs. **тамо́жня, -и** custom-house.

тампо́н, -a (*med.*) tampon, plug; **гигиени́ческий** ~ sanitary towel, pad.

та́нгенс, -a tangent. **тангенциа́льный** tangential.

та́нец, -нца dance; dancing.

та́нковый tank, armoured.

танцева́льный dancing; ~ **ве́чер** dance. **танцева́ть, -цу́ю** *impf.* dance. **танцо́вщик, -a, танцо́вщица, -ы** (ballet) dancer. **танцо́р, -a, танцо́рка, -и** dancer.

та́пка, -и, та́почка, -и (*heelless*) slipper; sports shoe, gym shoe.

та́ра, -ы packing, packaging; tare.

тарака́н, -a cockroach; black-beetle.

тара́щить, -щу *impf.* (*pf.* **вы́~**); ~ **глаза́** goggle.

таре́лка, -и plate; disc; **быть не в свое́й таре́лке** feel uneasy, feel unsettled, be not quite o.s. **таре́льчатый** plate; disc.

тари́ф, -a tariff, rate. **тарифици́ровать, -рую** *impf. & pf.* tariff.

таска́ть, -áю *impf.* drag, lug; carry; pull; take; drag off; pull out; pinch, swipe; wear; ~**ся** drag, trail; roam about, hang about.

тасова́ть, -су́ю *impf.* (*pf.* **с~**) shuffle. **тасо́вка, -и** shuffle, shuffling.

ТАСС *abbr.* (*of* **Телегра́фное аге́нство Сове́тского Сою́за**) TASS, Telegraph Agency of the Soviet Union.

тафта́, -ы́ taffeta.

тахта́, -ы́ divan, ottoman.

тача́ть, -а́ю *impf. (pf.* вы́~, с~) stitch.

та́чка, -и wheelbarrow.

тащи́ть, -щу́, -щишь *impf. (pf.* вы́~, с~) pull; drag, lug; carry; take; drag off; pull out; pinch, swipe; ~ся drag o.s. along; drag, trail.

та́яние, -я thaw, thawing. та́ять, та́ю *impf. (pf.* рас~) melt; thaw; melt away, dwindle, wane; waste away.

Тбили́си *m.indecl.* Tbilisi.

тварь, -и creature; creatures; wretch.

твердѐть, -ѐет *impf. (pf.* за~) harden, become hard. тверди́ть, -ржу́ *impf. (pf.* вы́~, за~) repeat, say again and again; memorize, learn by heart. твѐрдо *adv.* hard; firmly, firm. твердоло́бый thick-skulled; diehard. твѐрд|ый hard; firm; solid; stable; steadfast; ~ый знак hard sign, ъ; ~ые це́ны fixed prices. тверды́ня, -и stronghold.

твой, -его́ *m.,* твоя́, -ѐй *f.,* твоё, -его́ *nt.,* твой, -и́х *pl.* your, yours; твой *sb., pl.* your people.

творе́ние, -я creation, work; creature; being. творе́ц, -рца́ creator. твори́тельный instrumental. твори́ть, -рю́ *impf. (pf.* со~) create; do; make; ~ чудеса́ work wonders; ~ся happen, go on; что тут твори́тся? what is going on here?

творо́г, -а́ (-у́) *or* -а (-у) curds; cottage cheese. творо́жный curd.

тво́рческий creative. тво́рчество, -а creation; creative work; works.

т.д.: и ~ *(of* так да́лее) etc., and so on.

те *see* тот

т.е. *abbr. (of* то есть) that is, i.e.

теа́тр, -а theatre; stage; plays, dramatic works. театра́л, -а theatre-goer, playgoer. театра́льн|ый theatre; theatrical; stagy; ~ая ка́сса box-office. театрове́дение, -я drama studies.

тебя́ *etc.: see* ты

те́зис, -а thesis; proposition, point.

тёзка, -и namesake.

тёк *see* течь

текст, -а a text; words, libretto, lyrics.

тексти́ль, -я *m.* textiles. тексти́льный textile. тексти́льщик, -а, -щица, -ы textile worker.

текстуа́льный verbatim, word-for-word; textual.

теку́честь, -и fluidity; fluctuation; instability. теку́чий fluid; fluctuating, unstable. теку́щ|ий current, of the present moment; instant; routine, ordinary; ~ий ремо́нт running repair(s), routine maintenance; ~ие собы́тия current affairs; ~ий счёт current account; 6-го числа́ ~его ме́сяца the 6th inst.

тел. *abbr. (of* телефо́н) tel., telephone.

теле... *in comb.* tele-; television. телеателье́ *nt.indecl.* TV repair workshop. ~ви́дение, -я television. ~визио́нный television, T.V.

~ви́зор, -а television (set). ~гра́мма, -ы telegram, wire. ~гра́ф, -а telegraph (office). ~графи́ровать, -рую *impf. & pf.* telegraph, wire. ~гра́фный telegraph; telegraphic; ~гра́фный столб telegraph-pole. ~журна́л, -а current affairs programme *(on TV).* ~зри́тель, -я *m.* (television) viewer. ~ма́н, -а TV addict. ~мо́ст, -а satellite (TV) link-up. ~объекти́в, -а telephoto lens. ~патичеческий telepathic. ~па́тия, -и telepathy. ~ско́п, -а telescope. ~скопи́ческий telescopic. ~ста́нция, -и television station. ~сту́дия, -и television studio. ~суфлёр, -а teleprompter, Autocue *(propr.).* ~управле́ние, -я remote control. ~фа́кс, -а fax (machine). ~фо́н, -а telephone; (telephone) number; (по)звони́ть по ~фо́ну+*d.* telephone, ring up; ~фо́н-автома́т, -а public telephone, call-box. ~фони́ровать, -рую *impf. & pf.* telephone. ~фони́ст, -а, -и́стка, -и telephonist, (switchboard) operator. ~фони́я, -и telephony. ~фо́нный telephone; ~фо́нная кни́га telephone directory; ~фо́нная ста́нция telephone exchange; ~фо́нная тру́бка handset, receiver. ~фотогра́фия, -и telephotography. ~це́нтр, -а television centre.

теле́га, -и cart, waggon. теле́жка, -и small cart; handcart; bogie, trolley. теле́жный cart.

телёнок, -нка; *pl.* -я́та, -я́т calf.

телѐсн|ый bodily; corporal; somatic; physical; corporeal; ~ое наказа́ние corporal punishment; ~ого цве́та flesh-coloured.

тели́ться, -ится *impf. (pf.* о~) calve. тёлка, -и heifer.

те́ло, -а; *pl.* -а́ body; держа́ть в чёрном те́ле ill-treat, maltreat. телогре́йка, -и quilted jacket, padded jacket. телодвиже́ние, -я movement, motion; gesture. телосложе́ние, -я build, frame. телохрани́тель, -я *m.* bodyguard. тельня́шка, -и vest.

теля́та *etc.: see* телёнок. теля́тина, -ы veal. теля́чий calf; veal.

тем *conj.* (so much) the; ~ лу́чше so much the better; ~ не ме́нее none the less, nevertheless.

тем *see* тот, тьма[2]

те́ма, -ы subject; topic; theme. тема́тика, -и subject-matter; themes, subjects. темати́ческий subject; thematic.

тембр, -а timbre.

Те́мза, -ы the Thames.

темнѐть, -ѐет *impf. (pf.* по~, с~) grow dark, become dark; darken; show dark; темне́ет it gets dark, it is getting dark. темни́ца, -ы dungeon. темно́ *pred.* it is dark. темноко́жий dark-skinned, dusky, swarthy. тёмно-си́ний dark blue. темнота́, -ы́ dark, darkness; ignorance; backwardness. тёмный dark; obscure; vague; sombre; shady, fishy, suspicious; ignorant, benighted.

темп, -а tempo; rate, speed, pace.

те́мпера, -ы distemper; tempera.

темпера́мент, -а temperament. **темпера́ментный** temperamental; spirited.

температу́ра, -ы temperature; ~ **кипе́ния** boiling-point; ~ **замерза́ния** freezing-point.

те́мя, -мени *nt.* crown, top of the head.

тенденцио́зный tendentious, biased. **тенде́нция, -и** tendency; bias.

те́ндер, -а tender.

тенево́й, тени́стый shady.

те́ннис, -а tennis. **тенниси́ст, -а, -и́стка, -и** tennis-player. **те́ннисн|ый** tennis; ~**ая площа́дка** tennis-court.

те́нор, -а; *pl.* **-á, -óв** (*mus.*) tenor.

тент, -а awning, canopy.

тень, -и, *loc.* **-и́;** *pl.* **-и, -éй** shade; shadow; phantom; ghost; particle, vestige, atom; suspicion.

теологи́ческий theological. **теоло́гия, -и** theology.

теоре́ма, -ы theorem. **теоретизи́ровать, -рую** *impf.* theorize. **теоре́тик, -а** theorist. **теорети́ческий** theoretical. **тео́рия, -и** theory.

теософи́ческий theosophical. **теосо́фия, -и** theosophy.

тепе́решн|ий present; **в** ~**ее вре́мя** at the present time, nowadays. **тепе́рь** *adv.* now; nowadays, today.

тепле́ть, -éет *impf.* (*pf.* **по**~) get warm. **те́плиться, -ится** *impf.* flicker; glimmer. **тепли́ца, -ы** greenhouse, hothouse, conservatory. **тепли́чный** hothouse. **тепло́, -á** heat; warmth. **тепло́** *adv.* warmly; *pred.* it is warm.

тепло... *in comb.* heat; thermal; thermo-. **теплово́з, -а** diesel locomotive. ~**во́зный** diesel. ~**ёмкость, -и** heat capacity, thermal capacity; heat. ~**кро́вный** warm-blooded. ~**обме́н, -а** heat exchange. ~**прово́д, -а** hot-water system. ~**прово́дный** heat-conducting. ~**сто́йкий** heat-proof, heat-resistant. ~**те́хник, -а** heating engineer. ~**те́хника, -и** heat engineering. ~**хо́д, -а** motor ship. ~**центра́ль, -и** (district) heating plant.

теплово́й heat; thermal; ~ **дви́гатель** heat-engine; ~ **уда́р** heat-stroke; thermal shock. **теплота́, -ы́** heat; warmth. **теплу́шка, -и** heated railway van. **тёплый; -пел, -пла́, тёпло́** warm; warmed, heated; cordial; kindly; affectionate; heartfelt.

терапе́вт, -а therapeutist. **терапи́я, -и** therapy; **интенси́вная** ~ intensive care.

тереби́ть, -блю́ *impf.* (*pf.* **вы́**~) pull, pick; pull at, pull about; pester, bother.

тере́ть, тру, трёшь; тёр *impf.* rub; grate, grind; chafe; ~**ся** rub o.s.; ~**ся о**+*a.* rub against; ~**ся о́коло**+*g.* hang about, hang around; ~**ся среди́**+*g.* mix with, hobnob with.

терза́ть, -а́ю *impf.* tear to pieces; pull about; torment, torture; ~**ся**+*i.* suffer; be a prey to.

тёрка, -и grater.

те́рмин, -а term. **терминоло́гия, -и** terminology.

терми́ческий thermic, thermal. **термодина́мика, -и** thermodynamics. **термодинами́ческий** thermodynamic. **термо́метр, -а** thermometer. **термоста́т, -а** thermostat. **те́рмос, -а** thermos (flask). **термоя́дерный** thermonuclear.

тёрн, -а, терно́вник, -а sloe, blackthorn. **терни́стый, терно́вый** thorny, prickly.

терпели́вый patient. **терпе́ние, -я** patience; endurance, perseverance; **запасти́сь** ~**м** be patient. **терпе́ть, -плю́, -пишь** *impf.* (*pf.* **по**~) suffer; undergo; bear, endure, stand; have patience; tolerate, put up with; **вре́мя не те́рпит** there is no time to be lost, time is getting short; **вре́мя те́рпит** there is plenty of time; ~ **не могу́** I can't stand, I hate. **терпе́ться, -пится** *impf., impers.*+*d.* **ему́ не те́рпится**+*inf.* he is impatient to. **терпи́мость, -и** tolerance; indulgence. **терпи́мый** tolerant; indulgent, forbearing; tolerable, bearable, supportable.

те́рпкий; -пок, -пка́, -о astringent; tart, sharp. **те́рпкость, -и** astringency; tartness, sharpness, acerbity.

терра́са, -ы terrace.

территориа́льный territorial. **террито́рия, -и** territory, confines, grounds; area.

терро́р, -а terror. **терроризи́ровать, -рую** *impf. & pf.* terrorize. **террори́зм, -а** terrorism; **возду́шный** ~ air piracy. **террори́ст, -а** terrorist; **возду́шный** ~ air pirate. **террористи́ческий** terrorist.

тёртый ground; grated; hardened, experienced.

теря́ть, -я́ю *impf.* (*pf.* **по**~, **у**~) lose; shred; ~ **в ве́се** lose weight; ~ **из ви́ду** lose sight of; ~ **си́лу** become invalid; ~**ся** get lost; disappear, vanish; fail, decline, decrease, weaken; become flustered; be at a loss; ~**ся в дога́дках** be at a loss.

тёс, -а (-у) boards, planks. **теса́ть, тешу́, те́шешь** *impf.* cut, hew; trim, square.

тесёмка, -и tape, ribbon, lace, braid. **тесёмчатый** ribbon, braid; ~ **глист** tapeworm.

тесни́ть, -ню́ *impf.* (*pf.* **по**~, **с**~) press; crowd; squeeze, constrict; be too tight; ~**ся** press through, push a way through; move up, make room; crowd, cluster, jostle. **те́сно** *adv.* closely; tightly; narrowly. **теснота́, -ы́** crowded state; narrowness; crush, squash. **те́сн|ый** crowded, cramped; narrow; (too) tight; close; compact; hard, difficult; ~**о** it is crowded, there is not enough room.

тесо́вый board, plank.

те́сто, -а dough; pastry; paste.

тесть, -я *m.* father-in-law.

тесьма́, -ы́ tape, ribbon, lace, braid.

те́терев, -а; *pl.* **-á** black grouse, blackcock. **тетёрка, -и** grey hen.

тётка, -и aunt.

тетра́дка, -и, тетра́дь, -и exercise book; copy-book; part, fascicule.

тётя, -и; *g.pl.* **-ей** aunt.

тех... *abbr.* (*of* **техни́ческий**) *in comb.* technical. **техми́нимум, -a** minimum (technical) qualifications. **~персона́л, -a** technical personnel. **~ре́д, -a** technical editor.

те́хник, -a technician. **те́хника, -и** machinery, technical equipment; technical devices; engineering; technology; technique, art. **те́хникум, -a** technical college, technical school. **техни́ческий** technical; engineering; maintenance; industrial; commercial(-grade); assistant, subordinate; **~ие усло́вия** specifications.

техно́лог, -a technologist. **технологи́ческий** technological. **техноло́гия, -и** technology; **высокосло́жная ~** high technology.

тече́ние, -я flow; course; current, stream; trend, tendency; **вверх по тече́нию** upstream.

течь, -чёт; тёк, -ла́ *impf.* flow; stream; pass; leak, be leaky.

те́шить, -шу *impf.* (*pf.* **по~**) amuse, entertain; gratify, please; **~ся** (+*i.*) amuse o.s. (with), play (with).

тешу́ *etc.: see* **теса́ть**

тёща, -и mother-in-law.

тигр, -a tiger. **тигри́ца, -ы** tigress. **тигро́вый** tiger.

ти́на, -ы slime, mud; mire. **ти́нистый** slimy, muddy.

тип, -a type. **типи́чный** typical. **типово́й** standard; model; type. **типогра́фия, -и** printing-house, press. **типогра́фск|ий** typographical; printing, printer's; **~ая кра́ска** printer's ink.

тир, -a shooting-range; shooting-gallery. **тира́да, -ы** tirade; sally.

тира́ж, -а́ draw; circulation; edition; **вы́йти в тира́ж** be drawn; have served one's turn, become redundant; be superannuated.

тира́н, -a tyrant **тирани́ческий** tyrannical. **тирани́я, -и** tyranny. **тира́нствовать, -вую** *impf.* (над+*i.*) tyrannize (over).

тире́ *nt.indecl.* dash.

ти́скать, -aю *impf.*, **ти́снуть, -ну** *pf.* press, squeeze; pull. **тиски́, -о́в** *pl.* vice; **в тиска́х**+*g.* in the grip of, in the clutches of. **тисне́ние, -я** stamping, printing; imprint; design. **тиснёный** stamped, printed.

ти́тул, -a title; title-page. **ти́тульный** title; **~ лист** title-page; **~ спи́сок** itemized list. **титуля́рный** titular; **~ сове́тник** Titular Councillor (*9th grade: see* **чин**).

тиф, -a, *loc.* **-у́** typhus; typhoid.

ти́хий; тих, -а́, -о quiet; low, soft, faint; silent, noiseless; still; calm; gentle; slow, slow-moving; **Т~ океа́н** the Pacific (Ocean); **~ ход** slow-speed, slow pace. **ти́хо** *adv.* quietly; softly; gently; silently; noiselessly; calmly; still; slowly. **тихоокеа́нский** Pacific. **ти́ше** *comp. of* **ти́хий, ти́хо;** ти́ше! quiet!

silence! hush! gently! careful! **тишина́, -ы́** quiet, silence; stillness; **нару́шить тишину́** break the silence; **соблюда́ть тишину́** keep quiet.

т. к. *abbr.* (*of* **так как**) as, since.

тка́невый tissue. **тка́ный** woven. **ткань, -и** fabric, cloth; tissue; substance, essence. **ткать, тку, ткёшь; -ал, -а́ла, -о** *impf.* (*pf.* **со~**) weave. **тка́цкий** weaver's, weaving; **~ стано́к** loom. **ткач, -а́, ткачи́ха, -и** weaver.

ткну́ть(ся, -у(сь, -ёшь(ся *pf. of* **ты́кать(ся**

тле́ние, -я decay, decomposition, putrefaction; smouldering. **тлеть, -е́ет** *impf.* rot, decay, decompose, putrefy; moulder; smoulder; **~ся** smoulder.

тмин, -a (-у) caraway-seeds.

то *pron.* that; **а не то́** or else, otherwise; **(да) и то́** and even then, and that; **то́ есть** that is (to say); **то и де́ло** every now and then. **то** *conj.* then; **не то..., не то** either ... or; whether ... or; half ..., half; **не то, чтобы...,** **но** it is (was) not that ..., (but); **то..., то** now ..., now; **то ли..., то ли** whether ... or; **то тут, то там** now here, now there.

-то *part.* just, precisely, exactly; **в то́м-то и де́ло** that's just it.

тобо́й *see* **ты**

тов. *abbr.* (*of* **това́рищ**) Comrade.

това́р, -a goods; wares; article; commodity.

това́рищ, -a comrade; friend; companion; colleague; person; assistant, deputy, vice-; **~ по рабо́те** colleague; mate; **~ по шко́ле** schoolfriend; **~ председа́теля** vice-president. **това́рищеск|ий** comradely; friendly; communal; unofficial; **с ~им приве́том** with fraternal greetings.

това́рищество, -a comradeship, fellowship; company; association, society.

това́рность, -и marketability. **това́рный** goods; freight; commodity; marketable; **~ ваго́н** goods truck; **~ склад** warehouse; **~ соста́в** goods train.

това́ро... *in comb.* commodity; goods. **товарообме́н, -a** barter, commodity exchange. **~оборо́т, -a** (sales) turnover; commodity circulation. **~отправи́тель, -я** *m.* consignor, forwarder (*of goods*). **~получа́тель, -я** *m.* consignee.

тогда́ *adv.* then; **~ как** whereas, while. **тогда́шний** of that time, of those days; the then.

того́ *see* **тот**

тожде́ственный identical, one and the same. **то́ждество, -a** identity.

то́же *adv.* also, as well, too.

ток, -a (-у); *pl.* **-и** current.

тока́рный turning; **~ стано́к** lathe. **то́карь, -я;** *pl.* **-я, -ей** *or* **-и, -ей** *m.* turner, lathe operator.

То́кио *m.indecl.* Tokyo.

толк, -a (-у) sense; understanding; use, profit; **бе́з ~у** senselessly, wildly; to no purpose;

знать ~ в+*p.* know what's what in; be a good judge of; **сбить с ~у** confuse, muddle; **с ~ом** sensibly, intelligently.

толка́ть, -а́ю *impf.* (*pf.* **толкну́ть**) push, shove; jog; **~ ло́ктем** nudge; **~ ядро́** put the shot; **~ся** jostle.

то́лки, -ов *pl.* talk; rumours, gossip.

толкну́ть(ся, -ну́(сь, -нёшь(ся *pf. of* **толка́ть(ся**

толкова́ние, -я interpretation; *pl.* commentary. **толкова́ть, -ку́ю** *impf.* interpret; explain; talk; say; **ло́жно ~** misinterpret, misconstrue. **толко́вый** intelligent, sensible; intelligible, clear; **~ слова́рь** defining dictionary. **то́лком** *adv.* plainly, clearly.

толкотня́, -и́ crush, scrum, squash; crowding.

толку́ *etc.: see* **толо́чь**

толку́чий ры́нок flea market. **толку́чка, -и** crush, scrum, squash; crowded place; flea market.

толокно́, -а́ oatmeal.

толо́чь, -лку́, -лчёшь; -ло́к, -лкла́ *impf.* (*pf.* **ис~, рас~**) pound, crush.

толпа́, -ы́; *pl.* **-ы** crowd; throng; multitude. **толпи́ться, -и́тся** *impf.* crowd; throng; cluster.

толсте́ть, -е́ю *impf.* (*pf.* **по~**) grow fat, get stout; put on weight. **толсти́ть, -и́т** *impf.* fatten; make look fat. **толстоко́жий** thick-skinned; pachydermatous. **толстомо́рдый** fat-faced. **то́лстый; -á, -о** fat; stout; thick; heavy. **толстя́к, -á** fat man; fat boy.

толчёный pounded, crushed; ground. **толчёт** *etc.: see* **толо́чь**

толчея́, -и́ crush, scrum, squash.

толчо́к, -чка́ push, shove; put; jolt, bump; shock, tremor; incitement, stimulus.

то́лща, -и thickness; thick. **то́лще** *comp. of* **то́лстый. толщина́, -ы́** thickness; fatness; stoutness.

то́лько *adv.* only, merely; solely; just; **~ что** just, only just; **~~** barely; *conj.* only, but; **(как) ~, (лишь) ~** as soon as; **~ бы** if only.

том, -а; *pl.* **~á** volume. **то́мик, -а** small volume, slim volume.

томи́тельный wearisome, tedious, wearing; tiresome, trying; agonizing. **томи́ть, -млю** *impf.* (*pf.* **ис~**) tire, wear, weary; torment; wear down; stew, steam, braise; **~ся** pine; languish; be tormented. **томле́ние, -я** languor. **томлёный** stewed, steamed, braised. **то́мность, -и** languor. **то́мный; -мен, -мна́, -о** languid, languorous.

тон, -а; *pl.* **-á** *or* **-ы, -о́в** tone; note; shade; tint; **дурно́й ~** bad form; **хоро́ший ~** good form. **тона́льность, -и** key; tonality.

то́ненький thin; slender, slim. **то́нкий; -нок, -нка́, -о** thin; slender, slim; fine; delicate; refined; dainty; subtle; nice; keen; crafty, sly; **~ вкус** refined taste; **~за́пах** delicate perfume; **~ знато́к** connoisseur; **~ слух** good ear; **~ сон** light sleep. **то́нкость, -и** thin-

ness; slenderness, slimness; fineness; subtlety; nice point; nicety.

то́нна, -ы (*metric*) ton, tonne. **тонна́ж, -а** tonnage.

тонне́ль *see* **тунне́ль**

тону́ть, -ну́, -нешь *impf.* (*pf.* **по~, у~**) sink; drown; go down; be lost, be hidden, be covered.

тонфи́льм, -а sound film; (sound) recording.

то́ньше *comp. of* **то́нкий**

то́пать, -аю *impf.* (*pf.* **то́пнуть**) stamp; **~ ного́й** stamp one's foot.

топи́ть¹, -плю́, -пишь *impf.* (*pf.* **по~, у~**) sink; drown; wreck, ruin; **~ся** drown o.s.

топи́ть², -плю́, -пишь *impf.* stoke; heat; melt (down); render; **~ся** burn, be alight; melt. **то́пка, -и** stoking; heating; melting (down); furnace, fire-box.

то́пкий boggy, marshy, swampy.

то́пливн|ый fuel; **~ая нефть** fuel oil. **то́пливо, -а** fuel.

то́пнуть, -ну *pf. of* **то́пать**

топо́граф, -а topographer. **топографи́ческий** topographical. **топогра́фия, -и** topography.

то́полевый poplar. **то́поль, -я;** *pl.* **-я** *or* **-и** *m.* poplar.

топо́р, -á axe. **топо́рик, -а** hatchet. **топори́ще, -а** axe-handle. **топо́рный** axe; clumsy, crude; uncouth.

то́пот, -а tread; tramp; **ко́нский ~** clatter of hooves. **топта́ть, -пчу́, -пчешь** *impf.* (*pf.* **по~**) trample (down); **~ся** stamp; **~ся на ме́сте** mark time.

торг, -а, *loc.* **-у́;** *pl.* **-и́** trading; bargaining, haggling; market; *pl.* auction. **торгова́ть, -гу́ю** *impf.* (*pf.* **с~**) trade, deal; bargain for; be open; +*i.* sell; **~ся** bargain, haggle. **торго́вец, -вца** merchant; trader, dealer; tradesman. **торго́вка, -и** market-woman; stall-holder; street-trader. **торго́вля, -и** trade, commerce. **торго́в|ый** trade, commercial; mercantile; **~ое су́дно** merchant ship; **~ый флот** merchant navy. **торгпре́д, -а** *abbr.* trade representative. **торгпре́дство, -а** *abbr.* trade delegation. **торгфло́т, -а** merchant navy.

торже́ственный solemn; ceremonial; festive; gala. **торжество́, -á** celebration; triumph; exultation; *pl.* festivities, rejoicings. **торжествова́ть, -тву́ю** *impf.* celebrate; triumph, exult. **торжеству́ющий** triumphant, exultant.

торможе́ние, -я braking; deceleration; inhibition. **то́рмоз, -а;** *pl.* **-á** *or* **-ы** brake; drag, hindrance, obstacle. **тормози́ть, -ожу́** *impf.* (*pf.* **за~**) brake, apply the brake(s); hamper, impede, be a drag on; retard, damp; inhibit. **тормозно́й** brake, braking.

тормоши́ть, -шу́ *impf.* pester, plague, worry; torment; bother.

торопи́ть, -плю́, -пишь *impf.* (*pf.* **по~**) hurry; hasten; press; **~ся** hurry, be in a hurry; make haste. **торопли́вый** hurried, hasty.

торпе́да, -ы torpedo. **торпеди́ровать, -рую** *impf. & pf.* torpedo.

торт, -a cake.

торф, -a peat. **торфоболо́тный** peat-moss. **торфяни́стый** peaty. **торфян|о́й** peat; ~о́е боло́то peat-moss, peat-bog.

торча́ть, -чу́ *impf.* stick up, stick out; protrude, jut out; hang about. **торчко́м** *adv.* on end, sticking up.

торше́р, -a standard lamp.

тоска́, -и́ melancholy; anguish; pangs; depression; boredom; nostalgia; ~ по longing for, yearning for; ~ по ро́дине homesickness. **тоскли́вый** melancholy; depressed, miserable; dull, dreary, depressing. **тоскова́ть, -ку́ю** *impf.* be melancholy, depressed, miserable; long, yearn, pine; ~ по miss.

тост, -a toast; toasted sandwich; ~ с сы́ром Welsh rarebit. **то́стер, -a** toaster.

тот *m.*, **та** *f.*, **то** *nt.*, **те** *pl. pron.* that; the former; he, she, it; the other; the opposite; the one; the same; the right; *pl.* those; в том слу́чае in that case; и тому́ подо́бное and so on, and so forth; и ~ и друго́й both; к тому́ же moreover; на той стороне́ on the other side; не ~ the wrong; не ~, так друго́й if not one, then the other; ни с того́ ни с сего́ for no reason at all; without rhyme or reason; ни ~ ни друго́й neither; одно́ и то же one and the same thing, the same thing over again; по ту сто́рону+g. beyond, on the other side of; с тем, что́бы in order to, with a view to; on condition that, provided that; с того́ бе́рега from the other shore; тем вре́менем in the meantime; того́ и гляди́ any minute now; before you know where you are; тот, кто the one who, the person who; э́то не та дверь that's the wrong door. **то́тчас** *adv.* at once; immediately.

точи́лка, -и steel, knife-sharpener; pencil-sharpener. **точи́ло, -a** whetstone, grindstone. **точи́льный** grinding, sharpening; ~ ка́мень whetstone, grindstone. **точи́льщик, -a** (knife-)grinder. **точи́ть, -чу́, -чишь** *impf.* (*pf.* вы́~, на~) sharpen; grind; whet, hone; turn; eat away, gnaw away; corrode; gnaw at, prey upon.

то́чка, -и spot; dot; full stop; point; попа́сть в то́чку hit the nail on the head; ~ в то́чку exactly; to the letter, word for word; ~ зре́ния point of view; ~ с запято́й semi-colon. **то́чно**[1] *adv.* exactly, precisely; punctually; ~ в час at one o'clock sharp. **то́чно**[2] *conj.* as though, as if; like. **то́чность, -и** punctuality; exactness; precision; accuracy; в то́чности exactly, precisely; accurately; to the letter. **то́чн|ый, -чен, -чна́, -о** exact, precise; accurate; punctual; ~ые нау́ки exact sciences; ~ый прибо́р precision instrument. **то́чь-в-то́чь** *adv.* exactly; to the letter; word for word.

тошни́ть, -и́т *impf.*, *impers.+a.*; меня́ тошни́т

I feel sick; меня́ от э́того тошни́т it makes me sick, it sickens me. **тошнота́, -ы́** sickness, nausea. **тошнотво́рный** sickening, nauseating.

тоща́ть, -а́ю *impf.* (*pf.* о~) become thin, get thin. **то́щ|ий; тощ, -а́, -е** gaunt, emaciated; scraggy, skinny, scrawny; lean; empty; poor; ~ая по́чва poor soil.

т.п.: и ~ *abbr.*: (*of* тому́ подо́бное) etc., and so on.

тпру *int.* whoa!

трава́, -ы́; *pl.* **-ы** grass; herb. **трави́нка, -и** blade of grass.

трави́ть, -влю́, -вишь *impf.* (*pf.* вы́~, за~) poison; exterminate, destroy; etch; hunt; persecute, torment; badger; bait; worry the life out of. **травле́ние, -я** extermination, destruction; etching. **тра́вленый** etched. **тра́вля, -и** hunting; persecution, tormenting; badgering.

тра́вма, -ы trauma, injury; shock. **травмати́зм, -а** traumatism; injuries. **травматологи́ческий;** ~ пункт casualty (department).

травокоси́лка, -и lawn mower. **траволече́ние, -я** herbal medicine. **травоя́дный** herbivorous. **травяни́стый** grass; herbaceous; grassy; tasteless, insipid. **травяно́й** grass; herbaceous; herb; grassy.

траге́дия, -и tragedy. **тра́гик, -а** tragic actor; tragedian. **траги́ческий, траги́чный** tragic.

традицио́нный traditional. **тради́ция, -и** tradition.

тракт, -а high road, highway; route; channel. **тракта́т, -а** treatise; treaty.

тракти́р, -а inn, tavern. **тракти́рный** inn. **тракти́рщик, -а, тракти́рщица, -ы** inn-keeper.

трактова́ть, -ту́ю *impf.* interpret; treat, discuss. **тракто́вка, -и** treatment; interpretation.

тра́ктор, -а tractor; гу́сеничный ~ caterpillar tractor. **тракторист, -а, ~ка, -ки** tractor driver.

трал, -а trawl. **тра́лить, -лю** *impf.* (*pf.* про~) trawl; sweep. **тра́льщик, -а** trawler; mine-sweeper.

трамбова́ть, -бу́ю *impf.* (*pf.* у~) ram, tamp. **трамбо́вка, -и** ramming; rammer; beetle.

трамва́й, -я tram-line; tram. **трамва́йный** tram.

трамплин, -а spring-board; ski-jump; trampoline; jumping-off place.

транзи́стор, -а transistor; transistor radio, transistor set. **транзи́сторный** transistor; transistorized.

транзи́т, -а transit.

транквилиза́тор, -а tranquillizer.

транс, -а trance.

трансаге́нтство, -а removal company.

транскриби́ровать, -рую *impf. & pf.* transcribe. **транскри́пция, -и** transcription.

транслировать, -рую *impf. & pf.* broadcast, transmit; relay. **транслятор, -а** repeater. **трансляционный** transmission; broadcasting; relaying. **трансляция, -и** broadcast, transmission; relay.

транспорт, -а transport; transportation, conveyance, consignment; train; supply ship; troopship. **транспортабельный** transportable, mobile. **транспортёр, -а** conveyor; carrier. **транспортир, -а** protractor. **транспортировать, -рую** *impf. & pf.* transport. **транспортник, -а** transport worker; transport plane.

трансформатор, -а transformer; quick-change artist; conjurer, illusionist.

траншейный trench. **траншея, -и** trench.

трап, -а ladder; steps.

трапеза, -ы (*monastery*) dining-table; meal; refectory. **трапезная** *sb.* refectory.

трапеция, -и trapezium; trapeze.

трасса, -ы line, course, direction; route, road. **трассировать, -рую** *impf. & pf.* mark out, trace. **трассирующий** tracer.

трата, -ы expenditure; expense; waste. **тратить, -ачу** *impf.* (*pf.* **ис~, по~**) spend, expend; waste.

траулер, -а trawler.

траур, -а mourning. **траурный** mourning; funeral; mournful, sorrowful.

трафарет, -а stencil; conventional pattern; cliché. **трафаретный** stencilled; conventional, stereotyped; trite, hackneyed.

трачу *etc.*: see **тратить**

требование, -я demand; request; claim; requirement, condition; requisition, order; *pl.* aspirations; needs. **требовательный** demanding, exacting; particular; requisition, order. **требовать, -бую** *impf.* (*pf.* **по~**) send for, call, summon; +*g.* demand, request, require; expect, ask; need, call for; **~ся** be needed, be required; **на это требуется много времени** it takes a lot of time; **что и требовалось доказать** (*math.*) Q.E.D.

тревога, -и alarm; anxiety; uneasiness, disquiet; alert. **тревожить, -жу** *impf.* (*pf.* **вс~, по~**) alarm; disturb; worry, trouble; interrupt; **~ся** worry, be anxious, be alarmed, be uneasy; worry o.s., trouble o.s., put o.s. out. **тревожный** worried, anxious, uneasy, troubled; alarming, disturbing, disquieting; alarm.

трезвенник, -а teetotaller, abstainer. **трезвеннический** temperance. **трезветь, -ею** *impf.* (*pf.* **о~**) sober up, become sober.

трезвон, -а peal (*of bells*); rumours, gossip; row, shindy.

трезвый; -зв, -а, -о sober; teetotal, abstinent.

трейлер, -а trailer.

трель, -и trill, shake; warble.

тренажёр, -а training apparatus; **гребной ~** rowing machine; **лётный ~** flight simulator.

тренер, -а trainer, coach. **тренерский** trainer's, training.

трение, -я friction, rubbing; *pl.* friction.

тренировать, -рую *impf.* (*pf.* **на~**) train, coach; **~ся** train o.s.; be in training. **тренировка, -и** training, coaching. **тренировочный** training; practice.

трепать, -плю, -плешь *impf.* (*pf.* **ис~, по~, рас~**) scutch, swingle; pull about; blow about; dishevel, tousle; tear; wear out; pat; **его треплет лихорадка** he is feverish; **~ся** tear, fray; wear out; flutter, blow about; go round; hang out; blather, talk rubbish; play the fool. **трепет, -а** trembling, quivering; trepidation. **трепетать, -ещу, -ещешь** *impf.* tremble; quiver; flicker; palpitate. **трепетный** trembling; flickering; anxious; timid.

треск, -а crack, crash; crackle, crackling; noise, fuss.

треска, -й cod.

трескаться[1], -ается *impf.* (*pf.* **по~**) crack; chap.

трескаться[2], -аюсь *impf. of* **треснуться**

тресковый cod.

трескотня, -й crackle, crackling; chirring; chatter, blather. **трескучий** crackling; high-falutin(g), high-flown; **~ мороз** hard frost.

треснуть, -нет *pf.* snap, crackle; crack; chap; **~ся** (*impf.* **трескаться**) +*i.* bang.

трест, -а trust.

третейский arbitration; **~ суд** arbitration tribunal.

трет|ий, -ья, -ье third; **в ~ьем часу** between two and three; **половина ~ьего** half past two; **~ьего дня** the day before yesterday; **~ье** *sb.* sweet (course).

третировать, -рую *impf.* slight.

третичный tertiary, ternary. **треть, -и**; *g.pl.* **-ей** third. **третье** *etc.*: see **третий**. **треугольник, -а** triangle. **треугольный** three-cornered, triangular.

трефовый of clubs. **трефы, треф** *pl.* clubs.

трёх... *in comb.* three-, tri-. **трёхгодичный** three-year. **~годовалый** three-year-old. **~голосый** three-part. **~гранный** three-edged; trihedral. **~дневный** three-day; tertian. **~значный** three-digit, three-figure. **~колёсный** three-wheeled. **~летний** three-year; three-year old. **~мерный** three-dimensional. **~местный** three-seater. **~месячный** three-month; quarterly; three-month-old. **~сложный** trisyllabic. **~слойный** three-layered; three-ply. **~сотый** three-hundredth. **~сторонний** three-sided; trilateral; tripartite. **~тонка, -и** three-ton lorry. **~ходовой** three-way, three-pass; three-move. **~цветный** three-coloured; tricolour; trichromatic. **~этажный** three-storey(ed).

трещать, -щу *impf.* crack; crackle; creak; chirr; crack up; jabber, chatter. **трещина, -ы** crack, split; cleft, fissure; chap.

три, трёх, -ём, -емя, -ёх three.

трибуна, -ы platform, rostrum; tribune; stand.

тригонометрия, -и trigonometry.

тридцатилетний thirty-year; thirty-year old.

тридца́тый thirtieth. **три́дцать, -й,** *i.* **-ью** thirty. **три́дцатью** *adv.* thirty times. **три́жды** *adv.* three times; thrice.

трико́ *nt.indecl.* jersey, tricot, stockinet; knitted fabric; tights; pants, knickers. **трико́вый** jersey, tricot. **трикота́ж, -а** jersey, tricot, stockinet; knitted fabric; knitted wear, knitted garments. **трикота́жный** jersey, tricot; knitted.

трило́гия, -и trilogy. **тримара́н, -а** trimaran. **триме́стр, -а** term (*at educational establishment*).

трина́дцатый thirteenth. **трина́дцать, -и** thirteen. **трино́м, -а** trinomial.

трио́ль, -и triplet.

три́ста, трёхсо́т, -ёмста́м, -емяста́ми, -ёхста́х three hundred.

триу́мф, -а triumph; **с ~ом** triumphantly, in triumph. **триумфа́льный** triumphal.

тро́гательный touching, moving, affecting. **тро́гать(ся, -аю(сь** *impf. of* **тро́нуть(ся**

тро́е, -йх *pl.* three. **троебо́рье, -я** triathlon. **троекра́тный** thrice-repeated. **тро́ить, -ою** *impf.* treble; divide into three; **~ся** be trebled; appear treble. **Тро́ица, -ы** Trinity; Whit Sunday. **Тро́ицын день** Whit Sunday. **тро́йка, -и** (*figure*) three; troika; No. 3; three-piece suite; three-man commission. **тройно́й** triple, threefold, treble; three-ply. **тро́йственный** triple; tripartite.

тролле́й, -я trolley. **тролле́йбус, -а** trolley-bus. **тролле́йбусный** trolley-bus.

трон, -а throne. **тро́нный** throne.

тро́нуть, -ну *pf.* (*impf.* **тро́гать**) touch; disturb, trouble; move, affect; start; **~ся** start, set out; go bad; be touched; be moved, be affected; be cracked.

тропа́, -ы́ path.

тро́пик, -а tropic.

тропи́нка, -и path.

тропи́ческий tropical; **~ по́яс** torrid zone.

трос, -а rope, cable, hawser.

тростни́к, -а́ reed, rush. **тростнико́вый** reed.

тро́сточка, -и, трость, -и; *g.pl.* **~е́й** cane, walking-stick.

тротуа́р, -а pavement.

трофе́й, -я trophy; spoils (*of war*), booty; captured material. **трофе́йный** captured.

трою́родн|ый; **~ый брат, ~ая сестра́** second cousin.

тру *etc.: see* **тере́ть**

труба́, -ы́; *pl.* **-ы** pipe; conduit; chimney, flue; funnel, smoke-stack; trumpet; tube; duct. **труба́ч, -а́** trumpeter; trumpet-player. **труби́ть, -блю́** *impf.* (*pf.* **про~**) blow, sound; blare; **~ в+а.** blow. **тру́бка, -и** tube; pipe; fuse; (*telephone*) receiver, handset. **трубны́й** trumpet. **трубопрово́д, -а** pipe-line; piping, tubing; manifold. **трубочи́ст, -а** chimney-sweep. **тру́бочный** pipe; **~ таба́к** pipe tobacco. **тру́бчатый** tubular.

труд, -а́ labour; work; effort; *pl.* works; trans-

actions; **не сто́ит ~а́** it is not worth the trouble; **с ~о́м** with difficulty, hardly. **труди́ться, -ужу́сь, -у́дишься** *impf.* toil, labour, work; trouble. **тру́дно** *pred.* it is hard, it is difficult. **тру́дность, -и** difficulty; obstacle. **тру́дный; -ден, -дна́, -о** difficult; hard; arduous; awkward; serious, grave.

трудо... *in comb.* labour, work. **трудодень, -дня́** *m.* work-day (*unit of payment*). **~лю-би́вый** hard-working, industrious. **~любие, -я** industry, diligence. **~сберега́ющий** labour-saving. **~спосо́бность, -и** ability to work, capacity for work. **~спосо́бный** able-bodied; capable of working.

трудово́й labour, of work; working; earned; hard-earned; **~ стаж** working life. **трудя́щийся** working; **~иеся** *sb.*, *pl.* the workers. **тру́женик, -а, тру́женица, -ы** toiler. **тру́женический** toiling; of toil.

труп, -а dead body, corpse; carcass. **тру́пный** corpse; post-mortem; ptomaine.

тру́ппа, -ы troupe, company.

трус, -а coward.

тру́сики, -ов *pl.* shorts; (*swimming*) trunks.

труси́ть[1], -ушу́ *impf.* trot along, jog along.

труси́ть[2], -у́шу *impf.* (*pf.* **с~**) be a coward; lose one's nerve; quail; be afraid, be frightened. **трусйха, -и** coward. **трусли́вый** cowardly; faint-hearted, timorous; apprehensive. **тру́сость, -и** cowardice.

трусы́, -о́в *pl.* shorts; trunks; pants.

тру́шу́ *etc.: see* **труси́ть, тру́сить**

трущо́ба, -ы slum; godforsaken hole.

трюк, -а feat, stunt; trick. **трю́ковый** trick.

трюм, -а hold.

трюмо́ *nt.indecl.* pier-glass.

тряпи́чный rag; soft, spineless. **тря́пка, -и** rag; duster; spineless creature; *pl.* finery, clothes. **тряпьё, -я́** rags; clothes, things.

тряси́на, -ы bog, swampy ground; quagmire. **тря́ска, -и** shaking, jolting. **тря́ский** shaky, jolty; bumpy. **трясти́, -су́, -сёшь; -яс, -ла́** *impf.*, **тряхну́ть, -ну́, -нёшь** *pf.* (*pf. also* **вы~**) shake; shake out; jolt; +*i.* shake, swing, toss; **~сь** shake; tremble, shiver; quake; bump along, jolt.

тсс *int.* sh! hush!

тт. *abbr.* (*of* **това́рищи**) Comrades; (*of* **тома́**) vols, volumes.

туале́т, -а dress; toilet; dressing; dressing-table; lavatory, cloak-room; **обще́ственный ~** public convenience. **туале́тный** toilet; **~ сто́лик** dressing-table. **туале́тчик, -а, туале́тчица, -ы** lavatory attendant, cloak-room attendant.

туберкулёз, -а tuberculosis, consumption. **туберкулёзник, -а, -ница, -ы** consumptive. **туберкулёзный** tubercular, consumptive; tuberculosis.

ту́го *adv.* tight(ly), taut; with difficulty; **~ наби́ть** pack tight, cram; *pred.*, *impers.* **с деньга́ми у нас ~** money is tight with us, we're strapped for cash; **ему́ ~ прихо́дится**

he is in a (tight) spot. **тугóй; туг, -á, -о** tight; taut; tightly filled, tightly stuffed; blown up hard; close-fisted; difficult; ~ **нá ухо** hard of hearing, **тугоплáвкий** refractory.

тудá *adv.* there, thither; that way; to the right place; **не ~!** not that way!; **ни ~ ни сюдá** neither one way nor the other; ~ **и обрáтно** there and back.

тýже *comp. of* **тýго, тугóй**

тужýрка, -и (*man's*) double-breasted jacket.

туз, -á, *a*. -á ace; dignitary; big name.

тузéмец, -мца, тузéмка, -и native. **тузéмный** native, indigenous.

тýловище, -а trunk; torso.

тулýп, -а sheepskin coat.

тумáн, -а (-у) fog; mist; haze. **тумáнить, -ит** *impf.* (*pf.* **за~**) dim, cloud, obscure; ~**ся** grow misty, grow hazy; be enveloped in mist; be befogged; grow gloomy, be depressed. **тумáнность, -и** fog, mist; nebula; haziness; obscurity. **тумáнный** foggy; misty; hazy; dull, lacklustre; obscure, vague.

тýмба, -ы post; bollard; pedestal. **тýмбочка, -и** bedside table.

тунеядец, -дца parasite, sponger. **тунеядствовать, -твую** *impf.* be a parasite, sponge.

тунúка, -и tunic.

туннéль, -я *m.*, **тоннéль, -я** *m.* tunnel; subway. **туннéльный, тоннéльный** tunnel; subway.

тупéть, -éю *impf.* (*pf.* **о~**) become blunt; grow dull. **тупúк, -á** blind alley, cul-de-sac, dead end; siding; impasse, deadlock; **зайтú в ~** reach a deadlock; **постáвить в ~** stump, nonplus. **тупúть, -плю, -пишь** *impf.* (*pf.* **за~, ис~**) blunt; ~**ся** become blunt. **тупúца, -ы** *c.g.* dimwit, blockhead, dolt. **тупóй; туп, -á, -о** blunt; obtuse; dull; vacant, stupid, meaningless; slow; dim; blind, unquestioning. **тýпость, -и** bluntness; vacancy; dullness; slowness. **тупоýмный** dull, obtuse.

тур, -а turn; round.

турбáза, -ы tourist centre.

турбúна, -ы turbine.

турéцкий Turkish; ~ **барабáн** big drum, bass drum.

турúзм, -а tourism; outdoor pursuits; **вóдный ~** boating; **гóрный ~** mountaineering.

турúст, -а, -úстка, -и tourist; hiker. **турúстский** tourist; ~ **похóд** *see* **турпохóд**

Туркменистáн, -а Turkmenistan.

турнé *nt.indecl.* tour.

турнúк, -á horizontal bar.

турникéт, -а turnstile; tourniquet.

турнúр, -а tournament.

тýрок, -рка Turk. **турчáнка, -и** Turkish woman.

турпохóд, -а *abbr.* (*of* **турúстский похóд**) walking-tour; tourist excursion; outing.

Тýрция, -и Turkey.

тýсклый dim, dull; matt; tarnished; wan; lacklustre; colourless, tame. **тускнéть, -éет** *impf.* (*pf.* **по~**) dim; grow dim, grow dull;

tarnish; pale.

тут *adv.* here; now; ~ **же** there and then. **тýтто** *adv.* just here; there and then.

тýфля, -и *m* shoe; slipper.

тýхлый; -хл, -á, -о rotten, bad. **тýхнуть**[1], **-нет; тух** go bad.

тýхнуть[2], **-нет; тух** *impf.* (*pf.* **по~**) go out.

тýча, -и cloud; storm-cloud; swarm, host. **тучевóй** cloud.

тýчный; -чен, -чнá, -чно fat, obese; rich, fertile; succulent.

туш, -а flourish.

тýша, -и carcass.

тушевáть, -шýю *impf.* (*pf.* **за~**) shade. **тушёвка, -и** shading.

тушёный braised, stewed. **тушúть**[1], **-шý, -шишь** *impf.* (*pf.* **с~**) braise, stew.

тушúть[2], **-шý, -шишь** *impf.* (*pf.* **за~, по~**) extinguish, put out; suppress, stifle, quell.

тушýю *etc.: see* **тушевáть. тушь, -и** Indian ink; ~ **(для реснúц)** mascara.

тчк *abbr.* (*of* **тóчка**) stop (*in telegram*).

тщáтельность, -и thoroughness, carefulness; care. **тщáтельный** thorough, careful; painstaking.

тщедýшный feeble, frail, weak; puny.

тщеслáвие, -я vanity, vainglory. **тщеслáвный** vain, vainglorious. **тщетá, -ы** vanity. **тщéтно** *adv.* vainly, in vain. **тщéтный** vain, futile; unavailing.

ты, тебя, -бé, тобóй, тебé you; thou; **быть на ты с+***i.* be on familiar terms with.

тýкать, тычу *impf.* (*pf.* **ткнуть**) poke; prod; jab; stick; ~ **пáльцем** point; ~**ся** knock (**в+***a.* against, into); rush about, fuss about.

тыква, -ы pumpkin; gourd.

тыл, -а (-у), *loc.* **-ý;** *pl.* **-ы** back; rear; the interior. **тыловóй** rear; ~ **гóспиталь** base hospital. **тыльный** back; rear.

тын, -а paling; palisade, stockade.

тысяча, -и, *i.* **-ей** *or* **-ью** thousand. **тысячелéтие, -я** a thousand years; millennium; thousandth anniversary. **тысячелéтний** thousand-year; millennial. **тысячный** thousandth; of (many) thousands.

тычúнка, -и stamen.

тьма[1], **-ы** dark, darkness.

тьма[2], **-ы;** *g.pl.* **тем** ten thousand; host, swarm, multitude.

тэ *nt.indecl.* the letter **т**.

тюбик, -а tube.

тюк, -á bale, package.

тюлéневый sealskin. **тюлéний** seal. **тюлéнь, -я** *m.* seal.

тюль, -я *m.* tulle.

тюльпáн, -а tulip.

тюрéмн|ый prison; ~**ое заключéние** imprisonment. **тюрéмщик, -а** gaoler, warder; enslaver. **тюрéмщица, -ы** wardress. **тюрьмá, -ы;** *pl.* **-ы, -рем** prison; jail; gaol; imprisonment.

тюфяк, -á mattress. **тюфячный** mattress.

тяга, -и traction; locomotion; locomotives;

thrust; draught; pull, attraction; thirst, craving; taste; **дать тягу** take to one's heels. **тягáться, -áюсь** *impf.* (*pf.* **по~**) measure one's strength (against); vie, contend; have a tug-of-war. **тягáч, -á** tractor.

тя́гостный burdensome, onerous; painful, distressing. **тя́гость, -и** weight, burden; fatigue. **тяготéние, -я** gravity, gravitation; attraction, taste; bent, inclination. **тяготéть, -éю** *impf.* gravitate; be drawn, be attracted; ~ **над** hang over, threaten. **тяготи́ть, -ощу́** *impf.* burden, be a burden on; lie heavy on, oppress.

тягу́чий malleable, ductile; viscous; slow, leisurely, unhurried.

тя́жба, -ы lawsuit; litigation; competition, rivalry.

тяжелó *adv.* heavily; seriously, gravely; with difficulty. **тяжелó** *pred.* it is hard; it is painful; it is distressing; **емý** ~ he feels miserable, he feels wretched. **тяжелоатлéт, -а** weight-lifter. **тяжеловéс, -а** heavy-weight. **тяжеловéсный** heavy; ponderous, clumsy. **тяжеловóз, -а** heavy (draught-)horse; heavy lorry. **тяжёлый; -ёл, -á** heavy; difficult; slow; severe; serious, grave, bad; seriously ill; painful; ponderous, unwieldy. **тя́жесть, -и** gravity; weight; heavy object; heaviness; difficulty; severity. **тя́жкий** heavy, hard; severe; serious, grave.

тяну́ть, -ну́, -нешь *impf.* (*pf.* **по~**) pull; draw; haul; drag; tug; drawl; drag out, protract, delay; weigh, weigh down; draw up; take in; extract; extort; *impers.* (+a.) draw, attract; be tight; **егó тя́нет домóй** he wants to go home; **тя́нет в плечáх** it feels tight across the shoulders; ~ **жрéбий** draw lots; ~ **на буксúре** tow; ~**ся** stretch; extend; stretch out; stretch o.s.; drag on; crawl; drift; move along one after another; last out, hold out; reach (out), strive (**к**+*d.* after); +**за**+*i.* try to keep up with, try to equal.

тяну́чка, -и toffee, caramel.

у *nt.indecl.* the letter **у**.

у *int.* oh.

у *prep.*+*g.* by; at; from, of; belonging to; **спросúте у негó óттиск** ask him to let you have an offprint; **у влáсти** in power; **у ворóт** at the gate; **у меня́**

(есть) I have; **у меня́ к вам мáленькая прóсьба** I have a small favour to ask of you;

у нас at our place, with us; here, in our country; **у неё нет врéмени** she has no time; **у окнá** by the window; **я зáнял дéсять рублéй у сосéда** I borrowed ten roubles from a neighbour.

у... *vbl. pref.* indicating movement away from a place, insertion in something, covering all over, reduction or curtailment, achievement of aim; and, with adjectival roots, forming vv. expressing comp. degree.

убáвить, -влю *pf.*, **убавля́ть, -я́ю** *impf.* reduce, lessen, diminish; ~ **в вéсе** lose weight.

у|баю́кать, -аю *pf.*, **убаю́кивать, -аю** *impf.* lull (to sleep); rock to sleep, sing to sleep.

убегáть, -áю *impf. of* **убежáть**

убеди́тельн|ый convincing, persuasive, cogent; pressing; earnest; **быть ~ым** carry conviction. **убеди́ть, -и́шь** *pf.* (*impf.* **убеждáть**) convince; persuade; prevail on; ~**ся** be convinced; make certain, satisfy o.s.

убежáть, -егу́ *pf.* (*impf.* **убегáть**) run away, run off, make off; escape; boil over.

убеждáть(ся, -áю(сь *impf. of* **убеди́ть(ся.** **убеждéние, -я** persuasion; conviction, belief. **убеждённость, -и** conviction. **убеждённый; -ён, -á** convinced; persuaded; confirmed; staunch, stalwart.

убéжище, -а refuge, asylum; sanctuary; shelter; dug-out; **искáть убéжища** seek refuge; seek sanctuary; **прáво убéжища** right of asylum.

убелённый; -ён, -á whitened, white; ~ **седи́нами** white-haired; ~ **сединóй** white. **убели́ть, -и́т** *pf.* whiten.

уберегáть, -áю *impf.*, **уберéчь, -регу́, -режёшь; -рёг, -глá** *pf.* protect, guard, keep safe, preserve; ~**ся от**+*g.* protect o.s. against, guard against.

уберу́ *etc.*: *see* **убрáть**

убивáть(ся, -áю(сь *impf. of* **убúть(ся.** **убúйственный** deadly; murderous; killing. **убúйство, -а** murder, assassination. **убúйца, -ы** *c.g.* murderer; killer; assassin.

убирáть(ся, -áю(сь *impf. of* **убрáть(ся; убирáйся!** clear off! hop it! **убирáющийся** retractable.

убúтый killed; crushed, broken; *sb.* dead man. **убúть, убью́, -ёшь** *pf.* (*impf.* **убивáть**) kill; murder; assassinate; finish; break, smash; expend; waste; ~**ся** hurt o.s., bruise o.s.; grieve.

убóгий wretched; poverty-stricken, beggarly; squalid; *sb.* pauper, beggar. **убóжество, -а** poverty; squalor; mediocrity; physical disability; infirmity.

убóй, -я slaughter; **корми́ть на ~** fatten; feed up, stuff. **убóйность, -и** effectiveness, destructive power. **убóйный** killing, destructive, lethal; for slaughter.

убóр, -а dress, attire; **головнóй ~** headgear, head-dress.

убóристый close, small.

убóрка, -и harvesting, reaping, gathering in; picking; collection, removal; clearing up, tidying up. **убо́рная** *sb.* lavatory; public convenience; dressing-room. **убо́рочн|ый** harvest, harvesting; ~**ая маши́на** harvester. **убо́рщик**, -а, **убо́рщица**, -ы cleaner. **убра́нство**, -а furniture; appointments; decoration; attire. **убра́ть**, уберу́, -рёшь; -а́л, -а́, -о *pf.* (*impf.* **убира́ть**) remove; take away; kick out; sack; put away, store; harvest, reap, gather in; clear up, tidy up; decorate, adorn; ~ **ко́мнату** do a room; ~ **посте́ль** make a bed; ~ **с доро́ги** put out of the way; ~ **со стола́** clear the table; ~**ся** clear up, tidy up, clean up; clear off, clear out; attire o.s.

убыва́ть, -а́ю *impf.*, **убы́ть**, убу́ду; у́был, -а́, -о *pf.* decrease, diminish; subside, fall, go down; wane; go away, leave. **у́быль**, -и diminution, decrease; subsidence; losses, casualties. **убы́ток**, -тка (-тку) loss; *pl.* damages. **убы́точно** *adv.* at a loss. **убы́точн|ый** unprofitable; ~**ая прода́жа** sale at a loss.

убью́ *etc.*: *see* **убить**

уважа́емый respected, esteemed, honoured; dear. **уважа́ть**, -а́ю *impf.* respect, esteem. **уваже́ние**, -я respect, esteem; **с** ~**м** yours sincerely. **уважи́тельный** valid, good; respectful, deferential.

ува́риваться, -ается *impf.*, **увари́ться**, -а́рится *pf.* be thoroughly cooked; boil down, boil away.

уведоми́тельн|ый notifying, informing; ~**ое письмо́** letter of advice; notice. **уве́домить**, -млю *pf.*, **уведомля́ть**, -я́ю *impf.* inform, notify. **уведомле́ние**, -я information, notification.

уведу́ *etc.*: *see* **увести́**

увезти́, -зу́, -зёшь; увёз, -ла́ *pf.* (*impf.* **увози́ть**) take (away); take with one; steal; abduct, kidnap.

увекове́чивать, -аю *impf.*, **увекове́чить**, -чу *pf.* immortalize; perpetuate.

увёл *etc.*: *see* **увести́**

увеличе́ние, -я increase; augmentation; extension; magnification; enlargement. **увели́чивать**, -аю *impf.*, **увели́чить**, -чу *pf.* increase; augment; extend; enhance; magnify; enlarge; ~**ся** increase, grow, rise. **увели́читель**, -я *m.* enlarger. **увеличи́тельн|ый** magnifying; enlarging; augmentative; ~**ое стекло́** magnifying glass.

у|венча́ть, -а́ю *pf.*, **уве́нчивать**, -аю *impf.* crown; ~**ся** be crowned.

увере́ние, -я assurance; protestation. **уве́ренность**, -и confidence; certitude, certainty; **в по́лной уве́ренности** in the firm belief, quite certain. **уве́ренный** confident; sure; certain; **бу́дь(те) уве́рен(ы)!** you may be sure, you may rely on it. **уве́рить**, -рю *pf.* (*impf.* **уверя́ть**) assure; convince, persuade; ~**ся** assure o.s., satisfy o.s.; be convinced.

уверну́ться, -ну́сь, -нёшься *pf.*, **уве́ртываться**, -аюсь *impf.* от+*g.* dodge; evade. **уве́ртка**, -и dodge, evasion; subterfuge; *pl.*

wiles. **уве́ртливый** evasive, shifty.

увертю́ра, -ы overture.

уверя́ть(ся, -я́ю(сь *impf. of* **уве́рить(ся**

увеселе́ние, -я amusement, entertainment. **увесели́тельн|ый** amusement, entertainment; pleasure; ~**ая пое́здка** pleasure trip. **увеселя́ть**, -я́ю *impf.* amuse, entertain.

уве́систый weighty; heavy.

увести́, -еду́, -едёшь; -ёл, -а́ *pf.* (*impf.* **уводи́ть**) take (away); take with one; carry off, walk off with.

увечить, -чу *impf.* maim, mutilate, cripple. **увечный** maimed, mutilated, crippled; *sb.* cripple. **уве́чье**, -я maiming, mutilation; injury.

уве́шать, -аю *pf.*, **уве́шивать**, -аю *impf.* hang, cover (+*i.* with).

увеща́ние, -я exhortation, admonition. **увеща́ть**, -а́ю *impf.*, **увещева́ть**, -а́ю *impf.* exhort, admonish.

у|ви́дать(ся, -а́ю(сь *pf.* **у|ви́деть(ся**, -и́жу(сь *pf.*

уви́ливать, -аю *impf.*, **увильну́ть**, -ну́, -нёшь *pf.* от+*g.* dodge; evade, shirk; (try to) wriggle out of.

увлажни́ть, -ню́ *pf.*, **увлажня́ть**, -я́ю *impf.* moisten, damp, wet.

увлека́тельный fascinating; absorbing. **увлека́ть**, -а́ю *impf.*, **увле́чь**, -еку́, -ечёшь; -ёк, -ла́ *pf.* carry along; carry away, distract; captivate, fascinate; entice, allure; ~**ся** be carried away; become keen; become mad (+*i.* about); become enamoured, fall (+*i.* for).

уво́д, -а taking away, withdrawal; carrying off; stealing. **уводи́ть**, -ожу́, -о́дишь *impf. of* **увести́**

увожу́ *etc.*: *see* **уводи́ть, увози́ть**

уво́з, -а abduction; carrying off; **сва́дьба** ~**ом** elopement. **увози́ть**, -ожу́, -о́дишь *impf. of* **увезти́**

уво́лить, -лю *pf.*, **увольня́ть**, -я́ю *impf.* discharge, dismiss; retire; sack, fire; ~**ся** retire; resign, leave the service. **увольне́ние**, -я discharge, dismissal; retiring, pensioning off. **увольни́тельный** discharge, dismissal; leave.

увы́ *int.* alas!

увяда́ние, -я fading, withering. **увяда́ть**, -а́ю *impf. of* **увя́нуть. увя́дший** withered.

увяза́ть[1], -а́ю *impf. of* **увя́знуть**

увяза́ть[2], -яжу́, -я́жешь *pf.* (*impf.* **увя́зывать**) tie up; pack up; co-ordinate; ~**ся** pack; tag along. **увя́зка**, -и tying up, roping, strapping; co-ordination.

у|вя́знуть, -ну; -я́з *pf.* (*impf. also* **увяза́ть**) get bogged down, get stuck.

увя́зывать(ся, -аю(сь *impf. of* **увяза́ть(ся**

у|вя́нуть, -ну *pf.* (*impf. also* **увяда́ть**) fade, wither, wilt, droop.

угада́ть, -а́ю *pf.*, **уга́дывать**, -аю *impf.* guess (right).

уга́р, -а charcoal fumes; carbon monoxide (poisoning); ecstasy, intoxication.

уга́рный full of (monoxide) fumes; ~ газ carbon monoxide.

угаса́ть, -а́ет *impf.*, у|га́снуть, -нет; -а́с *pf.* go out; die down.

угле... *in comb.* coal; charcoal; carbon. угле-во́д, -а carbohydrate. ~водоро́д, -а hydrocarbon. ~добы́ча, -и coal extraction. ~жже́ние, -я charcoal burning. ~жёг, -а charcoal-burner. ~кислота́, -ы́ carbonic acid; carbon dioxide. ~ки́слый carbonate (of); ~ки́слый аммо́ний ammonium carbonate. ~ро́д, -а carbon.

углова́тый angular; awkward. угловой corner; angle; angular.

углуби́ть, -блю́ *pf.*, углубля́ть, -я́ю *impf.* deepen; make deeper; sink deeper; extend; ~ся deepen; become deeper; become intensified; go deep; delve deeply; become absorbed. углубле́ние, -я hollow, depression, dip; draught; deepening; extending; intensification. углублённый deepened; deep; profound; absorbed.

угна́ть, угоню́, -о́нишь; -а́л, -а́, -о *pf.* (*impf.* угоня́ть) drive away; send off, despatch; steal; ~ся за+*i.* keep pace with, keep up with.

угнета́тель, -я *m.* oppressor. угнета́тельский oppressive. угнета́ть, -а́ю *impf.* oppress; depress, dispirit. угнете́ние, -я oppression; depression. угнетённый oppressed; depressed; ~ое состоя́ние low spirits, depression.

угова́ривать, -аю *impf.*, уговори́ть, -рю́ *pf.* persuade, induce; urge; talk into; ~ся arrange, agree. угово́р, -а (-у) persuasion; agreement; compact.

уго́да, -ы; в уго́ду+*d.* to please. угоди́ть, -ожу́ *pf.*, угожда́ть, -а́ю *impf.* fall, get; bang; (+*d.*) hit; +*d.* or на+*a.* please, oblige. уго́дливый obsequious. уго́дно *pred.*+*d.*: как вам ~ as you wish, as you please; please yourself; что вам ~? what would you like? what can I do for you?; *part.* кто ~ anyone (you like), whoever you like; что ~ anything (you like), whatever you like. уго́дный pleasing, welcome.

у́гол, угла́, *loc.* -у́ corner; angle; part of a room; place; из-за угла́ (from) round the corner; on the sly; име́ть свой у́гол have a place of one's own; ~ зре́ния visual angle; point of view.

уголо́вник, -а, -ница, -ы criminal. уголо́вный criminal.

уголо́к, -лка́, *loc.* -у́ corner.

у́голь, угля́; *pl.* у́гли, -ей *or* -éй *m.* coal; charcoal.

уго́льник, -а set square; angle iron, angle bracket. уго́льный[1] corner.

у́гольный[2] coal; carbon; carbonic. у́гольщик, -а collier; coal-miner; coal-man; charcoal-burner.

угомони́ть, -ню́ *pf.* calm down, pacify; ~ся calm down.

уго́н, -а driving away; stealing. уго́нщик, -а thief; hijacker; ~ маши́ны car thief.

угоня́ть, -я́ю *impf. of* угна́ть

угора́ть, -а́ю *impf.*, угоре́ть, -рю́ *pf.* get carbon monoxide poisoning; be mad, be crazy. угоре́лый; как ~ like a madman, like one possessed.

у́горь[1], угря́ *m.* eel.

у́горь[2], угря́ *m.* blackhead.

угости́ть, -ощу́ *pf.*, угоща́ть, -а́ю *impf.* entertain; treat. угоще́ние, -я entertaining, treating; refreshments; fare.

угро́бить, -блю *pf.* (*sl.*) do in; ruin, wreck.

угрожа́ть, -а́ю *impf.* threaten. угрожа́ющий threatening, menacing. угро́за, -ы threat, menace.

угрызе́ние, -я pangs; угрызе́ния со́вести remorse.

угрю́мый sullen, morose, gloomy.

уда́в, -а boa, boa-constrictor.

удава́ться, удаётся *impf. of* уда́ться

у|дави́ть(ся, -влю́(сь, -вишь(ся *pf.* уда́вка, -и running-knot, half hitch. удавле́ние, -я strangling, strangulation.

удале́ние, -я removal; extraction; sending away, sending off; moving off. удали́ть, -лю́ *pf.* (*impf.* удаля́ть) remove; extract; send away; move away; ~ся move off, move away; leave, withdraw, retire.

удало́й, уда́лый; -а́л, -а́, -о daring, bold. у́даль, -и, удальство́, -а́ daring, boldness.

удаля́ть(ся, -я́ю(сь *impf. of* удали́ть(ся

уда́р, -а blow; stroke; shock; attack; thrust; seizure; быть в ~е be in good form; нанести́ ~ strike a blow; ~ гро́ма thunder-clap. ударе́ние, -я accent; stress; stress-mark; emphasis. уда́ренный stressed, accented.

уда́рить, -рю *pf.*, ударя́ть, -я́ю *impf.* (*impf. also* бить) strike; hit; sound; beat; attack; set in; ~ся strike, hit; ~ся в бе́гство break into a run; ~ся в слёзы burst into tears.

уда́рник, -а, -ница, -ы shock-worker. уда́рный percussive; percussion; shock; of shock-workers; urgent, rush. ударопро́чный, ударосто́йкий shockproof, shock-resistant.

уда́ться, -а́стся; -адутся; -а́лся, -ла́сь *pf.* (*impf.* удава́ться) succeed, be a success, turn out well, work. уда́ча, -и good luck, good fortune; success. уда́чный successful; felicitous, apt, good.

удва́ивать, -аю *impf.*, удво́ить, -о́ю *pf.* double, redouble; reduplicate. удвое́ние, -я doubling; reduplication. удво́енный doubled, redoubled; reduplicated.

уде́л, -а lot, destiny; apanage; crown lands.

удели́ть, -лю́ *pf.* (*impf.* уделя́ть) spare, devote, give.

уде́льный[1] specific; ~ вес specific gravity.

уде́льный[2] apanage, crown.

уделя́ть, -я́ю *impf. of* удели́ть

у́держ, -у; без ~у unrestrainedly, without restraint, uncontrollably. удержа́ние, -я deduction; retention, keeping, holding. удержа́ть, -жу́, -жишь *pf.*, уде́рживать, -аю *impf.* hold, hold on to, not let go; keep, retain; hold back, keep back; restrain; keep down, suppress; deduct; ~ в па́мяти bear in mind, retain in one's memory; ~ся hold one's ground, hold on, hold out; stand firm; keep one's feet; keep (from), refrain (from); мы не могли́ ~ся от сме́ха we couldn't help laughing; ~ся от собла́зна resist a temptation.

удеру́ *etc.: see* удра́ть

удешеви́ть, -влю́ *pf.*, удешевля́ть, -я́ю *impf.* reduce the price of; ~ся become cheaper. удешевле́ние, -я price-reduction.

удиви́тельный astonishing, surprising, amazing; wonderful, marvellous; не удиви́тельно, что no wonder (that). удиви́ть, -влю́ *pf.*, удивля́ть, -я́ю *impf.* astonish, surprise, amaze; ~ся be astonished, be surprised, be amazed; marvel. удивле́ние, -я astonishment, surprise, amazement; к моему́ удивле́нию to my surprise; на ~ excellently, splendidly, marvellously.

удила́, -и́л *pl.* bit.

уди́лище, -a fishing-rod. уди́льщик, -a, -щица, -ы angler.

удира́ть, -а́ю *impf. of* удра́ть

уди́ть, ужу́, у́дишь *impf.* fish for; ~ ры́бу fish; ~ся bite.

удлине́ние, -я lengthening; extension. удлини́ть, -ню́ *pf.*, удлиня́ть, -я́ю *impf.* lengthen; extend, prolong; ~ся become longer, lengthen; be extended, be prolonged.

удо́бно *adv.* comfortably; conveniently. удо́бн|ый comfortable; cosy; convenient, suitable, opportune; proper, in order; ~ый слу́чай opportunity; ~o+*d.* it is convenient for, it suits.

удобо... *in comb.* conveniently, easily, well. удобовари́мый digestible. ~исполни́мый easy to carry out. ~обтека́емый streamlined. ~перено́симый portable, easily carried. ~поня́тный comprehensible, intelligible. ~произноси́мый easy to pronounce. ~управля́емый easily controlled. ~усво́яемый easily assimilated. ~чита́емый legible, easy to read.

удобре́ние, -я fertilization, manuring; fertilizer. удо́брить, -рю *pf.*, удобря́ть, -я́ю *impf.* fertilize.

удо́бство, -a comfort; convenience; amenity; кварти́ра со все́ми удо́бствами flat with all conveniences.

удовлетворе́ние, -я satisfaction; gratification. удовлетворённый; -рён, -á satisfied, contented. удовлетвори́тельно *adv.* satisfactorily; fair, satisfactory. удовлетвори́тельный satisfactory. удовлетвори́ть, -рю́ *pf.*, удовлетворя́ть, -я́ю *impf.* satisfy; gratify; give satisfaction to; comply with; +*d.* answer, meet; +*i.* supply with, furnish with; ~ жела́ние gratify a wish; ~ потре́бности satisfy the requirements; ~

про́сьбу comply with a request; ~ся content o.s.; be satisfied.

удово́льствие, -я pleasure; amusement. у|дово́льствоваться, -твуюсь *pf.*

удо́й, -я milk-yield; milking. удо́йлив|ый yielding much milk; ~ая коро́ва good milker.

удоста́ивать(ся, -аю(сь *impf. of* удосто́ить(ся

удостовере́ние, -я certification, attestation; certificate; ~ ли́чности identity card. удостове́рить, -рю *pf.*, удостоверя́ть, -я́ю *impf.* certify, attest, witness; ~ ли́чность+*g.* prove the identity of, identify; ~ся make sure (в+*p.* of), assure o.s.

удосто́ить, -о́ю *pf.* (*impf.* удоста́ивать) make an award to; +*g.* award to, confer on; +*i.* favour with, vouchsafe to; ~ся+*g.* receive, be awarded; be favoured with, be vouchsafed; be found worthy.

удосу́живаться, -аюсь *impf.*, удосу́житься, -жусь *pf.* find time.

у́дочка, -и (fishing-)rod.

удра́ть, удеру́, -ёшь; удра́л, -á, -o *pf.* (*impf.* удира́ть) make off, clear out, run away.

удружи́ть, -жу́ *pf.*+*d.* do a good turn.

удруча́ть, -а́ю *impf.*, удручи́ть, -чу́ *pf.* depress, dispirit. удручённый; -чён, -á depressed, despondent.

удуша́ть, -а́ю *impf.*, удуши́ть, -шу́, -шишь *pf.* smother, stifle, suffocate; asphyxiate. удуше́ние, -я suffocation; asphyxiation. уду́шливый stifling, suffocating; asphyxiating. уду́шье, -я asthma; suffocation, asphyxia.

единéние, -я solitude; seclusion. уединённый solitary, secluded; lonely. уедини́ться, -ню́сь *pf.*, уединя́ться, -я́юсь *impf.* retire, withdraw; seclude o.s.

уе́зд, -a uyezd (*administrative unit*).

уезжа́ть, -а́ю *impf.*, уе́хать, уе́ду *pf.* go away, leave, depart.

уж, -á grass-snake.

уж *adv. see* уже́. уж, уже́ *part.* to be sure, indeed, certainly; really.

у|жа́лить, -лю *pf.*

у́жас, -a horror, terror; *pred.* it is awful, it is terrible; ~ (как) awfully, terribly; ~ ско́лько an awful lot of. ужаса́ть, -а́ю *imp.*, ужасну́ть, -ну́, -нёшь *pf.* horrify, terrify; ~ся be horrified, be terrified. ужа́сно *adv.* horribly, terribly; awfully; frightfully. ужа́сный awful, terrible, ghastly, frightful.

у́же *comp. of* у́зкий

уже́, уж *adv.* already; now; by now; ~ давно́ it's a long time ago; ~ не no longer. уже́ *part.: see* уж *part.*

уже́ние, -я fishing, angling.

ужесточа́ться, -а́ется *impf.* become, be made, stricter, tighter, more rigorous. ужесточе́ние, -я tightening up, intensification; making stricter, more rigorous. ужесточи́ть, -чу́ *pf.* make stricter, make more rigorous;

intensify, tighten (up).

уживáться, -áюсь *impf. of* **ужи́ться. ужи́в-чивый** easy to get on with.

ужи́мка, -и grimace.

у́жин, -а supper. **у́жинать, -аю** *impf. (pf.* **по~**) have supper.

ужи́ться, -иву́сь, -ивёшься; -и́лся, -лáсь *pf. (impf.* **уживáться**) get on.

ужу́ *see* **уди́ть**

узаконéние, -я legalization; legitimization; statute. **узакóнивать, -аю** *impf.,* **узакóнить, -ню** *pf.,* **узаконя́ть, -я́ю** *impf.* legalize, legitimize.

Узбекистáн, -а Uzbekistan.

уздá, -ы́; *pl.* **-ы** bridle.

у́зел, узлá knot; bend, hitch; junction; centre; node; bundle, pack; **нéрвный ~** nerve-centre, ganglion.

у́зк|ий; у́зок, узкá, -о narrow; tight; limited; narrow-minded; **~ое мéсто** bottleneck.

узкоколéйка, -и narrow-gauge railway. **узкоколéйный** narrow-gauge.

узловáтый knotty; nodose; gnarled. **узло-в|óй** junction; main, principal, central, key; **~áя стáнция** junction.

узнавáть, -наю́, -наёшь *impf.,* **узнáть, -áю** *pf.* recognize; get to know, become familiar with; learn, find out.

у́зник, -а, у́зница, -ы prisoner.

узóр, -а pattern, design. **узóрный** pattern; patterned. **узóрчатый** patterned.

у́зость, -и narrowness; tightness.

у́зы *pl.* bonds, ties.

уйду́ *etc.: see* **уйти́. уйму́** *etc.: see* **уня́ть**

уйти́, уйду́, -дёшь; ушёл, ушлá *pf. (impf.* **уходи́ть**) go away, leave, depart; escape; get away; evade; retire; sink; bury o.s.; be used up, be spent; pass away, slip away; boil over; spill; **~ (вперёд)** gain, be fast; **на э́то уйдёт мнóго врéмени** it will take a lot of time; **так вы далекó не уйдёте** you won't get very far like that; **~ на пéнсию** retire on a pension; **~ со сцéны** quit the stage; **~ с рабóты** leave work, give up work.

укáз, -а decree; edict, ukase. **указáние, -я** indication, pointing out; instruction, direction. **укáзанный** fixed, appointed, stated. **указáтель, -я** *m.* indicator; marker; gauge; index; guide, directory; **~ направлéния** road-sign. **указáтельн|ый** indicating; demonstrative; **~ый пáлец** index finger, forefinger; **~ая стрéлка** pointer. **указáть, -ажу́, -áжешь** *pf.,* **укáзывать, -аю** *impf.* show; indicate; point; point out; explain; give directions; give orders. **укáзка, -и** pointer; orders; **по чужóй укáзке** at s.o. else's bidding.

укáлывать, -аю *impf. of* **уколóть**

укатáть, -áю *pf.,* **укáтывать[1], -аю** *impf.* roll, roll out; flatten; wear out, tire out; **~ся** become smooth. **укати́ть, -ачу́, -áтишь** *pf.,* **укáтывать[2], -аю** *impf.* roll away; drive off; **~ся** roll away.

укачáть, -áю *pf.,* **укáчивать, -аю** *impf.* rock

to sleep; make sick.

уклáд, -а structure; form; organization, set-up; **~ жи́зни** style of life, mode of life; **общéственно-экономи́ческий ~** social and economic structure. **уклáдка, -и** packing; stacking, piling; stowing; laying; setting, set. **уклáдчик, -а** packer; layer. **уклáды-вать(ся[1], -аю(сь** *impf. of* **уложи́ть(ся**

уклáдываться[2], -аюсь *impf. of* **улéчься**

уклóн, -а slope, declivity; inclination; incline; gradient; bias, tendency; deviation. **уклонéние, -я** deviation; evasion; digression. **уклони́ст, -а** deviationist. **уклони́ться, -ню́сь, -ни́шься** *pf.,* **уклоня́ться, -я́юсь** *impf.* deviate; **+от+g.** turn, turn off, turn aside; avoid; evade. **уклóнчивый** evasive.

уклю́чина, -ы rowlock.

укóл, -а prick; jab; injection; thrust. **уколóть, -лю́, -лешь** *pf. (impf.* **укáлывать**) prick; sting, wound.

укомплектовáние, -я bringing up to strength. **укомплектóванный** complete, at full strength. **укомплектовáть, -тýю** *pf.,* **укомплектóвывать, -аю** *impf.* complete; bring up to (full) strength; man; **+i.** equip with, furnish with.

укóр, -а a reproach.

укорáчивать, -аю *impf. of* **укороти́ть**

укорени́ть, -ню́ *pf.,* **укореня́ть, -я́ю** *impf.* implant, inculcate; **~ся** take root, strike root.

укори́зна, -ы reproach. **укори́зненный** reproachful. **укори́ть, -рю́** *pf. (impf.* **укоря́ть**) reproach (**в+p.** with).

укороти́ть, -очу́ *pf. (impf.* **укорáчивать**) shorten.

укоря́ть, -я́ю *impf. of* **укори́ть**

укóс, -а (hay-)crop.

украдкой *adv.* stealthily, by stealth, furtively. **украду́** *etc.: see* **укрáсть**

Украи́на, -ы (the) Ukraine. **украи́нец, -нца, украи́нка, -и** Ukrainian. **украи́нский** Ukrainian.

украси́ть, -áшу *pf. (impf.* **украшáть**) adorn, decorate, ornament; **~ся** be decorated; adorn o.s.

у|крáсть, -адý, -дёшь *pf.*

украшáть(ся, -áю(сь *impf. of* **украси́ть(ся. украшéние, -я** adorning; decoration; adornment; ornament.

укрепи́ть, -плю́ *pf.,* **укрепля́ть, -я́ю** *impf.* strengthen; reinforce; fix, make fast; fortify; consolidate; brace; enhance; **~ся** become stronger; fortify one's position. **укреплéние, -я** strengthening; reinforcement; consolidation; fortification; work. **укрепля́ющее** *sb.* tonic, restorative.

укрóмный secluded, sheltered, cosy.

укрóп, -а (-у) dill.

укроти́тель, -я *m.* (animal-)tamer. **укроти́ть, -ощу́** *pf.,* **укрощáть, -áю** *impf.* tame; curb, subdue, check; **~ся** become tame, be tamed; calm down, die down. **укрощéние, -я** taming.

укрою etc.: see **укрыть**

укрупнение, -я enlargement, extension; amalgamation. **укрупнить**, -ню pf., **укрупнять**, -яю impf. enlarge, extend; amalgamate.

укрыватель, -я m. concealer, harbourer; ~ краденого receiver (of stolen goods). **укрывательство**, -а concealment, harbouring; receiving. **укрывать**, -аю impf., **укрыть**, -рою pf. cover, cover up; conceal, harbour; give shelter (to); receive, act as receiver of; ~ся cover o.s.; take cover; find shelter; escape notice. **укрытие**, -я cover; concealment; shelter.

уксус, -а (-у) vinegar.

укус, -а bite; sting. **укусить**, -ушу, -усишь pf. bite; sting.

укутать, -аю pf., **укутывать**, -аю impf. wrap up; ~ся wrap o.s. up.

укушу etc.: see **укусить**

ул. abbr. (of **улица**) St., Street; Rd., Road.

улавливать, -аю impf. of **уловить**

уладить, -ажу pf., **улаживать**, -аю impf. settle, arrange; reconcile.

уламывать, -аю impf. of **уломать**

улей, **улья** (bee)hive.

улетать, -аю impf., **улететь**, улечу pf. fly, fly away; vanish. **улетучиваться**, -аюсь impf., **улетучиться**, -чусь pf. evaporate, volatilize; vanish, disappear.

улечься, улягусь; -яжешься; улёгся, -глась pf. (impf. **укладываться**) lie down; find room; settle; subside; calm down.

улизнуть, -ну, -нёшь pf. slip away, steal away.

улика, -и clue; evidence.

улитка, -и snail.

улица, -ы street; **на улице** in the street; out of doors, outside.

уличать, -аю impf., **уличить**, -чу pf. establish the guilt of; ~ в+p. catch out in.

уличный street.

улов, -а catch, take, haul. **уловимый** perceptible; audible. **уловить**, -влю, -вишь pf. (impf. **улавливать**) catch, pick up, locate; detect, perceive; seize. **уловка**, -и trick, ruse, subterfuge.

уложение, -я code. **уложить**, -жу, -жишь pf. (impf. **укладывать**) lay; pack; stow; pile, stack; cover; set; ~ спать put to bed; ~ся pack, pack up; go in; fit in; sink in; +в+a. keep within, confine o.s. to.

уломать, -аю (impf. **уламывать**) talk round, prevail on.

улучать, -аю impf., **улучить**, -чу pf. find, seize, catch.

улучшать, -аю impf., **улучшить**, -шу pf. improve; ameliorate; better; ~ся improve; get better. **улучшение**, -я improvement; amelioration.

улыбаться, -аюсь impf., **улыбнуться**, -нусь, -нёшься pf. smile; +d. appeal to. **улыбка**, -и smile.

ультра... in comb. ultra-. **ультравысокий** ultra-high. ~**звуковой** supersonic, ultra-

sonic. ~**короткий** ultra-short. ~**фиолетовый** ultra-violet.

улягусь etc.: see **улечься**

ум, -á mind, intellect; wits; head; **свести с** ~á drive mad; **склад** ~á mentality; turn of mind; **сойти с** ~á go mad; go crazy.

умаление, -я belittling, disparagement. **умалить**, -лю pf. (impf. **умалять**) belittle, disparage; decrease, lessen.

умалишённый mad, lunatic; sb. lunatic, madman, madwoman.

умалчивать, -аю impf. of **умолчать**

умалять, -яю impf. of **умалить**

умелец, -льца skilled workman, craftsman. **умелый** able, skilful; capable; skilled. **умение**, -я ability, skill; know-how.

уменьшать, -аю impf., **уменьшить**, -шу or -шý pf. reduce, diminish, decrease, lessen; ~ расходы cut down expenditure; ~ скорость slow down; ~ся diminish, decrease, drop, dwindle; abate. **уменьшение**, -я decrease, reduction, diminution, lessening, abatement. **уменьшительный** diminutive.

умеренность, -и moderation. **умеренный** moderate; temperate.

умереть, умру, -рёшь; умер, -лá, -о pf. (impf. **умирать**) die.

умерить, -рю pf. (impf. **умерять**) moderate; restrain.

умертвить, -рщвлю pf., **умерщвлять**, -яю impf. kill, destroy; mortify. **умерший** dead; sb. the deceased. **умерщвление**, -я killing, destruction; mortification.

умерять, -яю impf. of **умерить**

уместить, -ещу pf. (impf. **умещать**) get in, fit in, find room for; ~ся go in, fit in, find room. **уместно** adv. appropriately; opportunely; to the point. **уместный** appropriate; pertinent, to the point; opportune, timely.

уметь, -ею impf. be able, know how.

умещать(ся, -аю(сь impf. of **уместить(ся**

умиление, -я tenderness; emotion. **умилительный** moving, touching, affecting. **умилить**, -лю pf., **умилять**, -яю impf. move, touch; ~ся be moved, be touched.

умирание, -я dying. **умирать**, -аю impf. of **умереть**. **умирающий** dying; sb. dying person.

умнеть, -ею impf. (pf. **по**~) grow wiser. **умник**, -а good boy; clever person. **умница**, -ы good girl; c.g. clever person. **умно** adv. cleverly, wisely; sensibly.

умножать, -аю impf., **у|множить**, -жу pf. multiply; increase; augment; ~ся increase, multiply. **умножение**, -я multiplication; increase, rise. **умножитель**, -я m. multiplier.

умный; умён, умна, умно clever, wise, intelligent; sensible. **умозаключать**, -аю impf., **умозаключить**, -чу pf. deduce; infer, conclude. **умозаключение**, -я deduction; conclusion, inference.

умолить, -лю pf. (impf. **умолять**) move by entreaties.

у́молк, -у; без ~у without stopping, incessantly. **умолка́ть, -а́ю** *impf.*, **умо́лкнуть, -ну; -о́лк** *pf.* fall silent; stop; cease. **умолча́ть, -чу́** *pf.* (*impf.* **ума́лчивать**) pass over in silence, fail to mention, suppress.

умоля́ть, -я́ю *impf. of* **умоли́ть**; beg, entreat, implore, beseech. **умоля́ющий** imploring, pleading.

умопомеша́тельство, -a derangement, madness, insanity.

умори́тельный incredibly funny, killing. **у|мори́ть, -рю́** *pf.* kill; tire out, exhaust.

умо́ю *etc.: see* **умы́ть. умру́** *etc.: see* **умере́ть**

у́мственный mental, intellectual; **~ труд** brainwork.

умудри́ть, -рю́ *pf.*, **умудря́ть, -я́ю** *impf.* make wise, make wiser; **~ся** contrive, manage.

умча́ть, -чу́ *pf.* whirl away, dash away; **~ся** whirl away, dash away.

умыва́льная *sb.* lavatory, cloak-room. **умыва́льник, -a** wash-stand, wash-basin. **умыва́льный** wash, washing. **умыва́ть(ся, -а́ю(сь** *impf. of* **умы́ть(ся**

у́мысел, -сла design, intention; **злой ~** evil intent; **с у́мыслом** of set purpose.

умы́ть, умо́ю *pf.* (*impf.* **умыва́ть**) wash; **~ся** wash (o.s.).

умы́шленный intentional, deliberate.

унаво́живать, -аю *impf.*, **у|наво́зить, -о́жу** *pf.* manure.

у|насле́довать, -дую *pf.*

унести́, -су́, -сёшь; -ёс, -ла́ *pf.* (*impf.* **уноси́ть**) take away; carry off, make off with; carry away, remove; **~сь** whirl away; fly away, fly by; be carried (away).

универма́г, -a *abbr.* department store. **универса́льн|ый** universal; all-round; many-sided; versatile; multi-purpose, all-purpose; **~ магази́н** department store; **~ое сре́дство** panacea. **универса́м, -a** *abbr.* supermarket. **университе́т, -a** university. **университе́тский** university.

унижа́ть, -а́ю *impf.*, **уни́зить, -и́жу** *pf.* humble; humiliate; lower, degrade; **~ся** debase o.s., lower o.s., stoop. **униже́ние, -я** humiliation, degradation, abasement. **уни́женный** humble. **унижённый** oppressed, degraded. **унизи́тельный** humiliating, degrading.

унима́ть(ся, -а́ю(сь *impf. of* **уня́ть(ся**

унита́з, -a lavatory pan.

уничтожа́ть, -а́ю *impf.*, **уничто́жить, -жу** *pf.* destroy, annihilate; wipe out; exterminate; obliterate; abolish; do away with, eliminate; put an end to; crush. **уничтожа́ющий** destructive, annihilating. **уничтоже́ние, -я** destruction, annihilation; extermination, obliteration; abolition, elimination.

уноси́ть(ся, -ошу́(сь, -о́сишь(ся *impf. of* **унести́(сь**

у́нтер, -a, у́нтер-офице́р, -a non-commissioned officer, NCO.

уныва́ть, -а́ю *impf.* be depressed, be dejected. **уны́лый** depressed, dejected, despondent, downcast; melancholy, doleful, cheerless. **уны́ние, -я** depression, dejection, despondency.

уня́ть, уйму́, -мёшь; -я́л, -á, -o *pf.* (*impf.* **унима́ть**) calm, soothe, pacify; stop, check; suppress; **~ся** calm down; stop, abate, die down.

упа́док, -дка decline; decay, collapse; decadence; depression; **~ ду́ха** depression. **упа́дочнический** decadent. **упа́дочный** depressive; decadent. **упаду́** *etc.: see* **упа́сть**

у|пакова́ть, -ку́ю *pf.*, **упако́вывать, -аю** *impf.* pack (up); wrap (up), bale. **упако́вка, -и** packing; wrapping, baling; package. **упако́вочный** packing. **упако́вщик, -a** packer.

упа́сть, -аду́, -адёшь *pf. of* **па́дать**

упере́ть, упру́, -рёшь; -ёр *pf.*, **упира́ть, -а́ю** *impf.* rest, prop, lean (heavily); (*sl.*) pinch, steal; **~ глаза́ в**+a. fix one's eyes on; **~ на**+a. stress, insist on; **~ся** rest, lean, prop o.s.; resist; jib; dig one's heels in; **+в**+a. come up against; run into

упи́танный well-fed; fattened; plump.

упла́та, -ы payment, paying. **у|плати́ть, -ачу́, -а́тишь** *pf.*, **упла́чивать, -аю** *impf.* pay.

уплотне́ние, -я compression; condensation; consolidation; sealing. **уплотни́ть, -ню́** *pf.*, **уплотня́ть, -я́ю** *impf.* condense; consolidate, concentrate, compress; pack (in).

уплыва́ть, -а́ю *impf.*, **уплы́ть, -ыву́, -ывёшь; -ы́л, -á, -o** *pf.* swim away; sail away, steam away; pass, elapse; be lost to sight; vanish, ebb.

уподо́биться, -блюсь *pf.*, **уподобля́ться, -я́юсь** *impf.+d.* become like; be assimilated to. **уподобле́ние, -я** likening, comparison; assimilation.

упое́ние, -я ecstasy, rapture, thrill. **упоённый** intoxicated, thrilled, in raptures. **упои́тельный** intoxicating, ravishing.

уполза́ть, -а́ю *impf.*, **уползти́, -зу́, -зёшь; -о́лз, -зла́** *pf.* creep away, crawl away.

уполномо́ченный *sb.* (authorized) agent, delegate, representative; proxy; commissioner. **уполнома́чивать, уполномо́чивать, -аю** *impf.*, **уполномо́чить, -чу** *pf.* authorize, empower. **уполномо́чие, -я** authorization; authority; credentials.

упомина́ние, -я mention; reference; reminder. **упомина́ть, -а́ю** *impf.*, **упомяну́ть, -ну́, -нешь** *pf.* mention, refer to.

упо́р, -a rest, prop, support; stay, brace; **в ~** point-blank; **сде́лать ~ на**+a. or p. lay stress on; **смотре́ть в ~ на**+a. stare straight at. **упо́рный** stubborn, unyielding, obstinate; dogged, persistent; sustained. **...упо́рный** *in comb.* -resistant. **упо́рство, -a** stubbornness, obstinacy; doggedness, persistence. **упо́рствовать, -твую** *impf.* be stubborn; persist (в+p. in).

упоря́дочивать, -аю *impf.*, **упоря́дочить, -чу** *pf.* regulate, put in (good) order, set to rights.

употреби́тельный (widely-)used; common, generally accepted, usual. **употреби́ть, -блю́** *pf.*, **употребля́ть, -я́ю** *impf.* use; make use of; take. **употребле́ние, -я** use; usage; application; **вы́йти из употребле́ния** go out of use, fall into disuse; **спо́соб употребле́ния** directions for use.

управде́л, -а *abbr.* office manager, business manager. **управдо́м, -а** *abbr.* manager (*of block of flats*), house manager. **управи́тель, -я** *m.* manager; bailiff, steward. **упра́виться, -влюсь** *pf.*, **управля́ться, -я́юсь** *impf.* cope, manage; +c+*i.* deal with. **управле́ние, -я** management; administration; direction; control; driving, piloting, steering; government; authority, directorate, board; controls; **под управле́нием**+*g.* conducted by; ~ **автомоби́лем** driving; ~ **на расстоя́нии** remote control; ~ **по ра́дио** radio control. **управля́емый снаря́д** guided missile. **управля́ть, -я́ю** *impf.*+*i.* manage, administer, direct, run; govern; be in charge of; control, operate; drive, pilot, steer, navigate; ~ **весло́м** paddle. **управля́ющий** control, controlling; *sb.* manager; bailiff, steward; ~ **по́ртом** harbour-master.

упражне́ние, -я exercise. **упражня́ть, -я́ю** *impf.* exercise, train; ~**ся** practise, train.

упраздне́ние, -я abolition; cancellation, annulment. **упраздни́ть, -ню́** *pf.*, **упраздня́ть, -я́ю** *impf.* abolish; cancel, annul.

упра́шивать, -аю *impf. of* **упроси́ть**

упрева́ть, -а́ет *impf. of* **упре́ть**

упрёк, -а reproach, reproof. **упрека́ть, -а́ю** *impf.*, **упрекну́ть, -ну́, -нёшь** *pf.* reproach, reprove; accuse, charge.

у|пре́ть, -е́ет *pf.* (*impf. also* **упрева́ть**) stew.

упроси́ть, -ошу́, -о́сишь *pf.* (*impf.* **упра́шивать**) beg, entreat; prevail upon.

упрости́ть, -ощу́ *pf.* (*impf.* **упроща́ть**) simplify; over-simplify; ~**ся** be simplified, get simpler.

упро́чивать, -аю *impf.*, **упро́чить, -чу** *pf.* strengthen, consolidate; fix; secure; establish firmly; +за+*i.* leave to; establish for, ensure for; ~**ся** be strengthened, be consolidated; become firmer; be firmly established; establish o.s.; settle o.s.; +за+*i.* become attached to, stick to.

упрошу́ *etc.*: *see* **упроси́ть**

упроща́ть(ся, -а́ю(сь *impf. of* **упрости́ть(ся. упроще́ние, -я** simplification. **упрощённый; -щён, -а́** simplified; over-simplified.

упру́ *etc.*: *see* **упере́ть**

упру́гий elastic; resilient, flexible; springy. **упру́гость, -и** elasticity; pressure, tension; spring, bound. **упру́же** *comp. of* **упру́гий**

упря́жка, -и harness, gear; team, relay. **упря́жн|ой** draught; ~**ая ло́шадь** draught-horse, carriage-horse. **у́пряжь, -и** harness, gear.

упря́миться, -млюсь *impf.* be obstinate; persist. **упря́мство, -а** obstinacy, stubbornness.

упря́мый obstinate, stubborn; persistent.

упря́тать, -я́чу *pf.*, **упря́тывать, -аю** *impf.* hide, conceal; put away, banish ~**ся** hide.

упуска́ть, -а́ю *impf.*, **упусти́ть, -ущу́, -у́стишь** *pf.* let go, let slip, let fall; miss; lose; neglect; ~ **из ви́ду** lose sight of, overlook, fail to take account of. **упуще́ние, -я** omission; slip; negligence.

ура́ *int.* hurray!, hurrah!

уравне́ние, -я equalization; equation. **ура́внивать, -аю** *impf.*, **уравня́ть, -я́ю** *pf.* equalize, make equal, make level; equate. **уравни́тельный** equalizing, levelling. **уравнове́сить, -е́шу** *pf.*, **уравнове́шивать, -аю** *impf.* balance; equilibrate; counterbalance; neutralize. **уравнове́шенность, -и** balance, steadiness, composure. **уравнове́шенный** balanced, steady, composed.

урага́н, -а a hurricane; storm.

Ура́л, -а the Urals.

ура́н, -а uranium; Uranus. **ура́новый** uranium; uranic.

урва́ть, -ву́, -вёшь; -а́л, -а́, -о *pf.* (*impf.* **урыва́ть**) snatch, grab.

урегули́рование, -я regulation; settlement, adjustment. **у|регули́ровать, -рую** *pf.*

уре́з, -а a reduction, cut. **уре́зать, -е́жу** *pf.*, **уреза́ть, -а́ю, уре́зывать, -аю** *impf.* cut off; shorten; cut down, reduce; axe.

у́рна, -ы urn; ballot-box; refuse-bin, litter-bin.

у́ровень, -вня *m.* level; plane; standard; grade; gauge.

уро́д, -а freak, monster; deformed person; ugly person; depraved person.

уроди́ться, -ожу́сь *pf.* ripen; grow; be born; +в+*a.* take after.

уро́дливость, -и deformity; ugliness. **уро́дливый** deformed, misshapen; ugly; bad; abnormal; faulty; distorting, distorted. **уро́довать, -дую** *impf.* (*pf.* **из~**) deform, disfigure, mutilate; make ugly; distort. **уро́дство, -а** deformity; disfigurement; ugliness; abnormality.

урожа́й, -я harvest; crop, yield; abundance. **урожа́йность, -и** yield; productivity. **урожа́йный** harvest; productive, high-yield; ~ **год** good year.

урождённый née; inborn, born. **уроже́нец, -нца, уроже́нка, -и** native. **урожу́сь** *see* **уроди́ться**

уро́к, -а a lesson; homework; task.

уро́н, -а losses, casualties; damage. **урони́ть, -ню́, -нишь** *pf. of* **роня́ть**

уро́чный fixed, agreed; usual, established.

урыва́ть, -а́ю *impf. of* **урва́ть. уры́вками** *adv.* in snatches, by fits and starts; at odd moments. **уры́вочный** fitful; occasional.

ус, -а; *pl.* **-ы́** whisker; antenna; tendril; awn; *pl.* moustache.

усади́ть, -ажу́, -а́дишь *pf.*, **уса́живать, -аю** *impf.* seat, offer a seat; make sit down; set; plant; cover; ~ **в тюрьму́** clap in prison. **уса́дьба, -ы;** *g.pl.* **-деб** *or* **-дьб** country es-

tate, country seat; farmstead; farm centre.
усаживаться, -аюсь *impf. of* **усесться**
усатый moustached; whiskery; whiskered.
усваивать, -аю *impf.*, **усвоить, -ою** *pf.* master; assimilate; adopt, acquire; imitate; pick up. **усвоение, -я** mastering; assimilation; adoption.
усеивать, -аю *impf. of* **усеять**
усердие, -я zeal; diligence. **усердный** zealous; diligent, painstaking.
усесться, усядусь; -елся *pf.* (*impf.* **усаживаться**) take a seat; settle; set (to), settle down (to).
усеять, -ею *pf.* (*impf.* **усеивать**) sow; cover, dot, stud; litter, strew.
усидеть, -ижу *pf.* keep one's place, remain seated, sit still; hold down a job. **усидчивость, -и** assiduity. **усидчивый** assiduous; painstaking.
усик, -а tendril; awn; runner; antenna; *pl.* small moustache.
усиление, -я strengthening; reinforcement; intensification; aggravation; amplification. **усиленный** reinforced; intensified, increased; earnest, urgent, importunate; copious. **усиливать, -аю** *impf.*, **усилить, -лю** *pf.* intensify, increase, heighten; aggravate; amplify; strengthen, reinforce; **~ся** increase, intensify; become stronger; become aggravated; swell, grow louder; make efforts, try. **усилие, -я** effort; exertion. **усилитель, -я** *m.* amplifier; booster. **усилительный** amplifying; booster.
ускакать, -ачу, -ачешь *pf.* bound away; skip off; gallop off.
ускользать, -аю *impf.*, **ускользнуть, -ну, -нёшь** *pf.* slip off; steal away; get away; disappear; escape; +**от**+*g.* evade, avoid.
ускорение, -я acceleration; speeding-up. **ускоритель, -я** *m.* accelerator. **ускорить, -рю** *pf.*, **ускорять, -яю** *impf.* quicken; speed up, accelerate; hasten; precipitate; **~ся** accelerate, be accelerated; quicken.
уславливаться *see* **условиться**
усладить, -ажу *pf.*, **услаждать, -аю** *impf.* delight, charm; soften, mitigate.
уследить, -ежу *pf.* +**за**+*i.* keep an eye on; mind; follow.
условие, -я condition; clause, term; stipulation, proviso; agreement; *pl.* conditions; **условия приёма** reception. **условиться, -влюсь** *pf.*, **условливаться, уславливаться, -аюсь** *impf.* agree, settle; arrange, make arrangements. **условленный** agreed, fixed, stipulated. **условность, -и** convention, conventionality; conditional character. **условный** conditional; conditioned; conventional; agreed, prearranged; relative; theoretical; **~ знак** conventional sign.
усложнение, -я complication. **усложнить, -ню** *pf.*, **усложнять, -яю** *impf.* complicate; **~ся** become complicated.
услуга, -и service; good turn; *pl.* service(s),

public utilities; **оказать услугу** do a service.
услуживать, -аю *impf.* **услужить, -жу, -жишь** *pf.* serve, act as a servant; +*d.* do a service, do a good turn. **услужливый** obliging.
услыхать, -ышу *pf.*, **у|слышать, -ышу** *pf.* hear; sense; scent.
усматривать, -аю *impf. of* **усмотреть**
усмехаться, -аюсь *impf.*, **усмехнуться, -нусь, -нёшься** *pf.* smile; grin; sneer; smirk.
усмешка, -и smile; grin; sneer.
усмирение, -я pacification; suppression, putting down. **усмирить, -рю** *pf.*, **усмирять, -яю** *impf.* pacify; calm, quieten; tame; suppress, put down.
усмотрение, -я discretion, judgement; **по усмотрению** at one's discretion, as one thinks best. **усмотреть, -рю, -ришь** *pf.* (*impf.* **усматривать**) perceive, observe; see; regard, interpret.
уснуть, -ну, -нёшь *pf.* go to sleep, fall asleep.
усовершенствование, -я perfecting; finishing, qualifying; advanced studies; improvement, refinement. **усовершенствованный** improved; finished, complete. **у|совершенствовать(ся, -твую(сь** *pf.*
усомниться, -нюсь *pf.* doubt.
усопший *sb.* (the) deceased.
успеваемость, -и progress. **успевать, -аю** *impf.*, **успеть, -ею** *pf.* have time; manage; succeed, be successful. **успеется** *impers.* there is still time, there is no hurry. **успех, -а** success; progress. **успешный** successful.
успокаивать, -аю *impf.*, **успокоить, -ою** *pf.* calm, quiet, soothe; tranquillize; reassure, set one's mind at rest; assuage, deaden; reduce to order, control; **~ся** calm down; compose o.s.; rest content; abate; become still; drop. **успокаивающ|ий** calming, soothing, sedative; **~ее средство** sedative, tranquillizer. **успокоение, -я** calming, quieting, soothing; calm; peace, tranquillity. **успокойтельн|ый** calming, soothing; reassuring; **~ое** *sb.* sedative, tranquillizer.
устав, -а regulations, rules, statutes; service regulations; rule; charter.
уставать, -таю, -ёшь *impf. of* **устать; не уставая** incessantly, uninterruptedly.
уставить, -влю *pf.*, **уставлять, -яю** *impf.* set, arrange, dispose; cover, fill, pile; direct, fix; **~ся** find room, go in; fix one's gaze, stare; become fixed, become steady. **уставный** regulation, statutory, prescribed.
усталость, -и fatigue, tiredness, weariness. **усталый** tired, weary, fatigued.
устанавливать, -аю *impf.*, **установить, -влю, -вишь** *pf.* place, put, set up; install, mount, rig up; adjust, regulate, set; establish; institute; fix, prescribe; secure; obtain; determine; ascertain; **~ся** take position, dispose o.s.; be settled, be established; set in; be formed; be fixed. **установка, -и** placing, putting, setting up, arrangement; installation;

mounting, rigging; adjustment, regulation, setting; plant, unit; directions, directive. **установле́ние, -я** establishment; statute; institution. **устано́вленный** established, fixed, prescribed, regulation.

уста́ну *etc.*: *see* **уста́ть**

устарева́ть, -а́ю *impf.*, **у|старе́ть, -е́ю** *pf.* grow old; become obsolete; become antiquated, go out of date. **устаре́лый** obsolete; antiquated, out-of-date.

уста́ть, -а́ну *pf.* (*impf.* **устава́ть**) become tired, tire; **я уста́ла** I am tired.

у́стно *adv.* orally, by word of mouth. **у́стн|ый** oral, verbal; **~ая речь** spoken language.

усто́й, -я abutment, buttress, pier; foundation, support; *pl.* foundations, bases. **усто́йчивость, -и** stability, steadiness, firmness; resistance. **усто́йчивый** stable, steady, firm; settled; resistant (**к**+*d.* to). **устоя́ть, -ою́** *pf.* keep one's balance, keep one's feet; stand firm, stand one's ground; resist, hold out.

устра́ивать(ся, -аю(сь *impf. of* **устро́ить(ся устране́ние, -я** removal, elimination, clearing. **устрани́ть, -ню́** *pf.*, **устраня́ть, -я́ю** *impf.* remove; eliminate, clear; dismiss; **~ся** resign, retire, withdraw.

устраша́ть, -а́ю *impf.*, **устраши́ть, -шу́** *pf.* frighten; scare; **~ся** be afraid; be frightened, be terrified. **устраша́ющий** frightening; deterrent. **устраше́ние, -я** frightening; fright, fear; **сре́дство устраше́ния** deterrent.

устреми́ть, -млю́ *pf.*, **устремля́ть, -я́ю** *impf.* direct, fix; **~ся** rush; head; be directed, be fixed, be concentrated; concentrate. **устремле́ние, -я** rush; striving, aspiration. **устремлённость, -и** tendency.

у́стрица, -ы oyster. **у́стричный** oyster.

устрое́ние, -я arranging, organization. **устрои́тель, -я** *m.*, **~ница, -ы** organizer. **устро́ить, -о́ю** *pf.* (*impf.* **устра́ивать**) arrange, organize; establish; make; construct; cause, create; settle, order, put in order; place, fix up; get, secure; suit, be convenient; **~ на рабо́ту** find, fix up with, a job; **~ сканда́л** make a scene; **~ся** work out; come right; manage, make arrangements; settle down, get settled; be found, get fixed up. **устро́йство, -а** arrangement, organization; (mode of) construction; layout; apparatus, mechanism, device; structure, system; **запомина́ющее ~** (*comput.*) storage (device), memory; **постоя́нное запомина́ющее ~** (*comput.*) ROM (*read-only memory*).

усту́п, -а shelf, ledge; terrace; bench. **уступа́ть, -а́ю** *impf.*, **уступи́ть, -плю́, -пишь** *pf.* yield; give in; cede; concede; let have, give up; be inferior; take off, knock off; **~ доро́гу** make way; **~ ме́сто** give up one's place, seat. **усту́пка, -и** concession, compromise; reduction. **усту́пчатый** ledged, stepped, terraced. **усту́пчивый** pliant, pliable; compliant, tractable.

устыди́ться, -ыжу́сь *pf.* (+*g.*) be ashamed (of).

у́стье, -я; *g.pl.* **-ьев** mouth; estuary.

усугу́бить, -у́блю *pf.*, **усугубля́ть, -я́ю** *impf.* increase; intensify; aggravate, make worse.

усы́ *see* **ус**

усынови́ть, -влю́ *pf.*, **усыновля́ть, -я́ю** *impf.* adopt. **усыновле́ние, -я** adoption.

усы́пать, -плю *pf.*, **усыпа́ть, -а́ю** *impf.* strew, scatter; cover.

усыпи́тельный soporific. **усыпи́ть, -плю́** *pf.*, **усыпля́ть, -я́ю** *impf.* put to sleep; lull; weaken, undermine, neutralize; **~ боль** deaden pain.

уся́дусь *etc.*: *see* **усе́сться**

ута́ивать, -аю *impf.*, **утаи́ть, -аю́** *pf.* conceal; keep to o.s., keep secret; appropriate.

ута́птывать, -аю *impf. of* **утопта́ть**

ута́скивать, -аю *impf.*, **утащи́ть, -щу́, -щишь** *pf.* drag away, drag off; make off with.

у́тварь, -и utensils, equipment.

утверди́тельный affirmative. **утверди́ть, -ржу́** *pf.*, **утвержда́ть, -а́ю** *impf.* confirm; approve; sanction, ratify; establish; assert, maintain, hold, claim, allege. **утвержде́ние, -я** approval; confirmation; ratification; assertion, affirmation, claim, allegation; establishment.

утека́ть, -а́ю *impf. of* **уте́чь**

утёнок, -нка; *pl.* **утя́та, -я́т** duckling.

утере́ть, утру́, -рёшь; утёр *pf.* (*impf.* **утира́ть**) wipe; wipe off; wipe dry; **~ нос**+*d.* score off.

утерпе́ть, -плю́, -пишь *pf.* restrain o.s.

уте́ря, -и loss. **у|теря́ть, -я́ю** *pf.*

утёс, -а cliff, crag. **утёсистый** steep, precipitous.

уте́чка, -и leak, leakage; escape; loss, wastage, dissipation; **~ га́за** escape of gas. **уте́чь, -еку́, -ечёшь; утёк, -ла́** *pf.* (*impf.* **утека́ть**) flow away; leak, escape; run away; pass, elapse, go by.

утеша́ть, -а́ю *impf.*, **уте́шить, -шу** *pf.* comfort, console; **~ся** console o.s. **утеше́ние, -я** comfort, consolation. **утеши́тельный** comforting, consoling.

утиль, -я *m.*, **утильсырьё, -я́** salvage; scrap; rubbish, refuse. **ути́льный** scrap.

ути́ный duck, duck's.

утира́ть(ся, -а́ю(сь *impf. of* **утере́ть(ся**

утиха́ть, -а́ю *impf.*, **ути́хнуть, -ну; -и́х** *pf.* abate, subside; cease, die away; slacken; drop; become calm, calm down.

у́тка, -и duck; canard.

уткну́ть, -ну́, -нёшь *pf.* bury; fix; **~ся** bury o.s.; **~ся голово́й в поду́шку** bury one's head in the pillow.

утоли́ть, -лю́ *pf.* (*impf.* **утоля́ть**) quench, slake; satisfy; relieve, alleviate, soothe.

утолсти́ть, -лщу́ *pf.*, **утолща́ть, -а́ю** *impf.* thicken, make thicker; **~ся** thicken, become thicker. **утолще́ние, -я** thickening; thickened part, bulge; reinforcement, rib, boss.

утоля́ть, -я́ю *impf. of* **утоли́ть**

утоми́тельный tiresome; tedious; wearisome,

tiring, fatiguing. **утомить, -млю** *pf.*, **утомлять, -яю** *impf.* tire, weary, fatigue; **~ся** get tired. **утомление, -я** tiredness, weariness, fatigue. **утомлённый** tired, weary, fatigued.

у|тонуть, -ну, -нешь *pf.* (*impf. also* **утопать**) drown, be drowned; sink, go down.

утончённость, -и refinement. **утончённый** refined; exquisite, subtle.

утопать, -аю *impf. of* **утонуть** roll, wallow. **у|топить(ся, -плю(сь, -пишь(ся** *pf.* **утопленник, -а** drowned man.

утоптать, -пчу, -пчешь *pf.* (*impf.* **утаптывать**) trample down, pound.

уточнение, -я more precise definition; amplification, elaboration. **уточнить, -ню** *pf.*, **уточнять, -яю** *impf.* define more precisely; amplify, elaborate.

утраивать, -аю *impf. of* **утроить**

у|трамбовать, -бую *pf.*, **утрамбовывать, -аю** *impf.* ram, tamp; **~ся** become flat, become level.

утрата, -ы loss. **утратить, -ачу** *pf.*, **утрачивать, -аю** *impf.* lose.

утренний morning, early. **утренник, -а** morning performance, matinée; early-morning frost.

утрировать, -рую *impf. & pf.* exaggerate; overplay. **утрировка, -и** exaggeration.

утро, -а *or* **-á, -у** *or* **-ý; pl. -а, -ам** *or* **-ám** morning.

утроба, -ы womb; belly.

утроить, -ою *pf.* (*impf.* **утраивать**) triple, treble.

утром *adv.* in the morning; **сегодня ~** this morning.

утру *etc.*: *see* **утереть, утро**

утрудить, -ужу *pf.*, **утруждать, -аю** *impf.* trouble, tire.

утюг, -á iron. **утюжить, -жу** *impf.* (*pf.* **вы~, от~**) iron, press; smooth. **утюжка, -и** ironing, pressing.

ух *int.* oh, ooh, ah.

уха, -и fish soup.

ухаб, -а pot-hole. **ухабистый** full of pot-holes; bumpy.

ухаживать, -аю *impf.* **за**+*i.* nurse, tend; look after; court; pay court to, make advances to.

ухать, -аю *impf. of* **ухнуть**

ухватить, -ачу, -атишь *pf.*, **ухватывать, -аю** *impf.* catch, lay hold of; seize; grasp; **~ся за**+*a.* grasp, lay hold of; set to, set about; seize; jump at; take up. **ухватка, -и** grip; grasp; skill; trick; manner.

ухитриться, -рюсь *pf.*, **ухитряться, -яюсь** *impf.* manage, contrive.

ухлопать, -аю *pf.*, **ухлопывать, -аю** *impf.* squander, waste; (*sl.*) kill.

ухмылка, -и smirk, grin. **ухмыльнуться, -нусь, -нёшься** *pf.*, **ухмыляться, -яюсь** *impf.* smirk, grin.

ухнуть, -ну *pf.* (*impf.* **ухать**) cry out; hoot; crash; bang; rumble; slip, fall; come a crop-

per; come to grief; drop; lose, squander, spend up.

ухо, -а; pl. уши, ушей ear; ear-flap, ear-piece; lug, hanger; **заткнуть уши** stop one's ears; **краем ~а** with half an ear; **по уши** up to one's eyes; **слушать во все уши** be all ears; **тугой на ~** hard of hearing.

уход[1], -а +**за**+*i.* care of; maintenance of; nursing, tending, looking after.

уход[2], -а going away, leaving, departure; withdrawal. **уходить, -ожу, -одишь** *impf. of* **уйти**; stretch, extend.

ухудшать, -аю *impf.*, **ухудшить, -шу** *pf.* make worse, aggravate; **~ся** get worse.

уцелеть, -ею *pf.* remain intact, escape destruction; survive; escape.

уцепить, -плю, -пишь *pf.*, **уцеплять, -яю** *impf.* catch hold of, grasp, seize; **~ся за**+*a.* catch hold of, grasp, seize; jump at.

участвовать, -твую *impf.* take part, participate; have a share, hold shares. **участвующий** *sb.* participant. **участие, -я** participation, taking part; share, sharing; sympathy, concern.

участить, -ащу *pf.* (*impf.* **учащать**) make more frequent, quicken; **~ся** become more frequent, become more rapid.

участливый sympathetic. **участник, -а** participant, member; **~ состязания** competitor. **участок, -тка** plot, strip; allotment; lot, parcel; part, section, portion; length; division; sector, area, zone, district; police district, police-station; field, sphere. **участь, -и** lot, fate, portion.

учащать(ся, -аю(сь *impf. of* **участить(ся. учащённый; -ён, -ена** quickened; faster.

учащийся *sb.* student; pupil. **учёба, -ы** studies; course; studying, learning, drill, training. **учебник, -а** text-book; manual, primer. **учебн|ый** educational; school; training, practice; **~ый год** academic year, school year; **~ые пособия** teaching aids; **~ое судно** training-ship. **учение, -я** learning; studies; apprenticeship; teaching, instruction; doctrine; exercise; *pl.* training. **ученик, -á**, **ученица, -ы** pupil; student; learner; apprentice; disciple, follower. **ученический** pupil's(s); apprentice('s); unskilled; raw, crude, immature. **ученичество, -а** time spent as pupil or student; apprenticeship; rawness, immaturity. **учёность, -и** learning, erudition. **учён|ый** learned, erudite; educated; scholarly; academic; scientific; trained, performing; **~ая степень** (*university*) degree; **~ый** *sb.* scholar; scientist.

учесть, учту, -тёшь; учёл, учла *pf.* (*impf.* **учитывать**) take stock of, make an inventory of; take into account, take into consideration; allow for; bear in mind; discount. **учёт, -а** stock-taking; reckoning, calculation; taking into account; registration; discount, discounting; **без ~а**+*g.* disregarding; **взять на ~** register. **учётн|ый** registration; discount; ~ое отделе́ние records section.

учи́лище, -а school; (training) college.

у|чини́ть, -ню́ *pf.*, **учиня́ть**, -я́ю *impf.* make; carry out, execute; commit.

учи́тель, -я; *pl.* -я́ *m.*, **учи́тельница**, -ы teacher. **учи́тельск|ий** teacher's, teachers'; ~ая *sb.* staff-room.

учи́тывать, -аю *impf. of* **уче́сть**

учи́ть, учу́, у́чишь *impf.* (*pf.* вы́~, на~, об~) teach; be a teacher; learn, memorize; ~ся be a student; +*d. or inf.* learn, study.

учреди́тель, -я *m.* founder. **учреди́тельница**, -ы foundress. **учреди́тельн|ый** constituent; ~ый акт constituent act; ~ое собра́ние constituent assembly. **учреди́ть**, -ежу́ *pf.*, **учрежда́ть**, -а́ю *impf.* found, establish, set up; introduce, institute. **учрежде́ние**, -я founding, setting up; establishment; institution.

учти́вый civil, courteous, polite.

учту́ *etc.*: *see* **уче́сть**

ушёл *etc.*: *see* **уйти́**. **у́ши** *etc.*: *see* **у́хо**

уши́б, -а injury; knock; bruise, contusion. **ушиба́ть**, -а́ю *impf.*, **ушиби́ть**, -бу́, -бёшь; уши́б *pf.* injure; bruise; hurt, shock; ~ся hurt o.s., give o.s. a knock; bruise o.s.

ушко́, -а́; *pl.* -и, -о́в eye; lug; tab, tag.

ушно́й ear, aural.

уще́лье, -я ravine, gorge, canyon.

ущеми́ть, -млю́ *pf.*, **ущемля́ть**, -я́ю *impf.* pinch, jam, nip; limit; encroach on; wound, hurt. **ущемле́ние**, -я pinching, jamming, nipping; limitation; wounding, hurting. **уще́рб**, -а detriment; loss; damage, injury; prejudice; на ~е waning. **уще́рбный** waning.

ущипну́ть, -ну́, -нёшь *pf. of* **щипа́ть**

Уэ́льс, -а Wales.

ую́т, -а cosiness, comfort. **ую́тный** cosy, comfortable.

уязви́мый vulnerable. **уязви́ть**, -влю́ *pf.*, **уязвля́ть**, -я́ю *impf.* wound, hurt.

уясне́ние, -я explanation, elucidation. **уясни́ть**, -ню́ *pf.* **уясня́ть**, -я́ю *impf.* understand, make out; explain.

Ф

ф *letter: see* эф

фа *nt.indecl.* F; fah.

фаб... *abbr.* (*of* **фабри́чный**) *in comb.* factory, works. **фабко́м**, -а works committee.

фа́брика, -и factory, mill, works. **фабрика́нт**, -а manufacturer. **фабрика́т**, -а finished product, manufactured product. **фабрикова́ть**, -ку́ю *impf.* (*pf.* с~) manufacture,

make, fabricate, forge. **фабри́чн|ый** factory; industrial, manufacturing; factory-made; ~ая ма́рка, ~ое клеймо́ trade-mark.

фа́була, -ы plot, story.

фаго́т, -а bassoon. **фаготи́ст**, -а bassoon-player.

фа́за, -ы phase; stage.

фаза́н, -а, **фазани́ха**, -и pheasant. **фаза́ний** pheasant, pheasants'.

фа́зис, -а phase. **фа́зный**, **фа́зовый** phase.

фа́кел, -а torch, flare, flame. **факе́льный** torch(-light). **фа́кельщик**, -а torch-bearer; incendiary.

фа́кс, -а fax; **посла́ть по ~у** to fax. **факси́ми́льный; ~ аппара́т** fax (machine).

факт, -а fact; **соверши́вшийся ~** fait accompli. **факти́чески** *adv.* in fact, actually; practically, virtually, to all intents and purposes. **факти́ческий** actual; real; virtual.

факту́ра, -ы invoice; bill; style, execution, texture; structure.

факультати́вный optional. **факульте́т**, -а faculty, department. **факульте́тский** faculty.

фа́лда, -ы tail, skirt.

фальсифика́тор, -а falsifier, forger. **фальсифика́ция**, -и falsification; forging; adulteration; forgery, fake, counterfeit. **фальсифици́ровать**, -рую *impf. & pf.* falsify; forge; adulterate. **фальши́вить**, -влю *impf.* (*pf.* с~) be a hypocrite, act insincerely; sing or play out of tune. **фальши́вка**, -и forged document. **фальши́вый** false; spurious; forged, fake; artificial, imitation; off-key, out-of-tune; hypocritical, insincere. **фальшь**, -и deception, trickery; falsity; falseness; hypocrisy, insincerity.

фами́лия, -и surname; family, kin. **фами́льный** family. **фамилья́рничать**, -аю be over familiar, take liberties. **фамилья́рность**, -и familiarity; liberty, liberties. **фамилья́рный** (over-)familiar; unceremonious; offhand, casual.

фанати́зм, -а fanaticism. **фана́тик**, -а fanatic. **фанати́ческий** fanatical.

фане́ра, -ы veneer; plywood. **фане́рный** veneer, of veneer; plywood.

фантазёр, -а dreamer, visionary. **фантази́ровать**, -рую *impf.* (*pf.* с~) dream, indulge in fantasies; make up, dream up; improvise. **фанта́зия**, -и fantasy; fancy; imagination; whim; fabrication. **фанта́стика**, -и fiction, fantasy; the fantastic; works of fantasy; **нау́чная ~** science fiction. **фантасти́ческий**, **фантасти́чный** fantastic; fabulous; imaginary.

фа́ра, -ы headlight; **поса́дочные фа́ры** landing-lights.

фарао́н, -а pharaoh; faro. **фарао́нов** pharaoh's.

фарва́тер, -а fairway, channel.

фармазо́н, -а freemason.

фармаце́вт, -а pharmaceutical chemist. **фармацевти́ческий** pharmaceutical.

фарт, -а (*sl.*) luck, success.

фáртук, -а apron; carriage-rug.

фарфóр, -а china; porcelain. **фарфóров|ый** china; ~**ая посýда** china.

фарцóвщик, -а spiv, black marketeer.

фарш, -а stuffing, force-meat; minced meat, sausage-meat. **фарширов́анный** stuffed. **фаршировáть**, -рýю *impf.* (*pf.* **за~**) stuff.

фасовáть, -сýю *impf.* (*pf.* **рас~**) package, pre-pack. **фасóвка**, -и packaging, pre-packing.

фасóль, -и kidney bean(s), French bean(s); haricot beans.

фасóн, -а cut; fashion; style; manner, way; **держáть ~** show off, put on airs. **фасóнистый** fashionable, stylish. **фасóнный** fashioned, shaped; form, forming, shape, shaping.

фаталúст, -а fatalist. **фаталистúческий** fatalistic. **фатáльность**, -и fatality, fate. **фатáльный** fatal, fated; ~ **вид** resigned appearance.

фашúзм, -а Fascism. **фашúст**, -а Fascist. **фашúстский** Fascist.

фаянс, -а faience, pottery. **фаянсовый** pottery.

ФБР *abbr.* (*of* **Федерáльное бюрó расслéдования**) FBI, Federal Bureau of Investigation.

феврáль, -я́ *m.* February. **феврáльский** February.

федератúвный federative, federal. **федерáция**, -и federation.

феерúческий fairy-tale, magical.

фейервéрк, -а firework, fireworks.

фельдмáршал, -а Field Marshal. **фéльдшер**, -а; *pl.* -á, -шерúца, -ы doctor's assistant; (*partly-qualified*) medical attendant; hospital attendant; trained nurse.

фельетóн, -а feuilleton, feature.

фен, -а (hair-)dryer.

фенóмен, -а phenomenon; phenomenal occurrence, person. **феноменáльный** phenomenal.

феодалúзм, -а feudalism. **феодáльный** feudal.

фéрзевый queen's. **ферзь**, -я́ *m.* (*chess*) queen.

фéрма¹, -ы farm.

фéрма², -ы girder, truss. **фéрменный** lattice.

фéрмер, -а farmer.

фестивáль, -я *m.* festival.

фетр, -а felt. **фéтровый** felt.

фехтовáльный fencing, of fencing. **фехтовáльщик**, -а, -щица, -ы fencer. **фехтовáние**, -я fencing. **фехтовáть**, -тýю *impf.* fence.

фéя, -и fairy.

фиáлка, -и violet.

фиберглáс, -а fibreglass. **фиберглáсовый** fibreglass.

фúбра, -ы fibre. **фиброзный** fibrous.

фибролúт, -а chipboard.

фúга, -и fig(-tree).

фигарó *nt.indecl.* bolero.

фигля́р, -а (*circus*) acrobat; clown; mountebank; buffoon. **фигля́рить**, -рю, **фигля́рничать**, -аю, **фигля́рствовать**, -твую *impf.* put on an act.

фигýра, -ы figure; court-card; (chess-)piece. **фигурáльный** figurative, metaphorical; ornate, involved. **фигурáнт**, -а figurant; super, extra. **фигурúровать**, -úрую *impf.* figure, appear. **фигурúст**, -а, -úстка, -и figure-skater. **фигýрка**, -и figurine, statuette; figure. **фигýрн|ый** figured; ornamented, patterned; figure; ~**ое катáние** figure-skating.

фúзик, -а physicist. **фúзика**, -и physics. **физиóлог**, -а physiologist. **физиологúческий** physiological. **физиолóгия**, -и physiology. **физиономúя**, -и physiognomy. **физиотерапéвт**, -а physiotherapist. **физиотерапúя**, -и physiotherapy. **физúческ|ий** physical; physics; ~**ая культýра** physical culture; gymnastics. **физкультýра**, -ы *abbr.* P.E., gymnastics. **физкультýрник**, -а, -ýрница, -ы *abbr.* gymnast, athlete. **физкультýрный** *abbr.* gymnastics; athletic; sports; ~ **зал** gymnasium.

фиксáж, -а fixing; fixer, fixing, solution. **фиксúровать**, -рую *impf. & pf.* (*pf. also* **за~**) fix; record, register.

фиктúвный fictitious. **фúкция**, -и fiction.

филантрóп, -а philanthropist. **филантропúческий** philanthropic. **филантрóпия**, -и philanthropy.

филателúст, -а philatelist, stamp collector. **филателúя**, -и philately.

филé *nt.indecl.* sirloin; fillet; drawn-thread work, filet (lace). **филéй**, -я sirloin. **филéйн|ый** sirloin; filet-lace, drawn-thread; ~**ая рабóта** drawn-thread work, filet.

филиáл, -а branch. **филиáльный** branch.

фúлин, -а eagle-owl.

филúстер, -а philistine. **филúстерский** philistine. **филúстерство**, -а philistinism.

филóлог, -а philologist; student of language and literature. **филологúческий** philological. **филолóгия**, -и philology, study of language and literature.

филóн, -а (*sl.*) skiver, slacker. **филóнить**, -ню *impf.* (*sl.*) slack, skive (off).

филóсоф, -а philosopher. **филосóфия**, -и philosophy. **филосóфский** philosophic(al). **филосóфствовать**, -вую *impf.* philosophize.

фильм, -а film.

фильтр, -а filter. **фильтровáть**, -рую *impf.* (*pf.* **про~**) filter; screen, check.

фин... *abbr.* of **финáнсовый** financial, finance. **фининспéктор**, -а financial officer. ~**отдéл**, -а finance department.

финáл, -а finale; final. **финáльный** final.

финансúровать, -рую *impf. & pf.* finance. **финансúст**, -а financier; financial expert. **финáнсовый** financial. **финáнсы**, -ов *pl.*

finance, fianances; money.
фи́ник, -а date. **фи́никовый** date.
фи́ниш, -а finish; finishing post. **фи́нишный** finishing.
фи́нка, -и Finn; Finnish knife; Finnish cap; Finnish pony. **Финля́ндия, -и** Finland. **финля́ндский** Finnish. **финн, -а** Finn. **фи́нно-уго́рский** Finno-Ugrian. **фи́нский** Finnish.
финт, -а feint.
фиоле́товый violet.
фи́рма, -ы firm; company; combine; large enterprise; trade name; appearance, guise.
фисгармо́ния, -и harmonium.
фити́ль, -я́ *m.* wick; fuse.
флаг, -а flag; **под ~ом** +*g.* flying under the flag of; under the guise of; **приспу́щенные ~и** flags at half-mast; **спусти́ть ~** lower a flag.
флако́н, -а (scent-)bottle, flask.
флама́ндец, -дца, флама́ндка, -и Fleming. **флама́ндский** Flemish.
флане́левый flannel. **флане́ль, -и** flannel.
флегмати́ческий phlegmatic.
фле́йта, -ы flute. **флейти́ст, -а, -и́стка, -и** flautist. **фле́йтовый** flute.
фле́ксия, -и inflexion. **флекти́вный** inflexional; inflected.
фли́гель, -я; *pl.* -я́ *m.* wing; pavilion, extension, annexe.
флирт, -а flirtation. **флиртова́ть, -ту́ю** *impf.* (c+*i.*) flirt (with).
флома́стер, -а felt-tip (pen); marker (pen).
Флоре́нция, -и Florence.
Флори́да, -ы Florida.
флот, -а fleet; **возду́шный ~** air force; aviation. **фло́тский** naval; *sb.* sailor.
флю́гер, -а; *pl.* -а́ weather-vane, weathercock; pennant.
флюс¹, -а gumboil, abscess.
флюс², -а; *pl.* -ы́ flux.
фля́га, -и flask; water-bottle; (milk-)churn, milk-can. **фля́жка, -и** flask.
фойе́ *nt.indecl.* foyer.
фо́кус¹, -а trick; conjuring trick.
фо́кус², -а focus. **фокуси́ровать, -рую** *impf.* focus. **фокуси́ровка, -и** focusing.
фо́кусник, -а conjurer, juggler.
фо́кусный focal.
фольга́, -и́ foil.
фолькло́р, -а folklore.
фо́мка, -и (*sl.*) jemmy.
фон, -а background.
фона́рик, -а small lamp; torch, flashlight. **фона́рный** lamp; **~ столб** lamp-post. **фона́рщик, -а** lamplighter. **фона́рь, -я́** *m.* lantern; lamp; light; skylight; black-eye, shiner.
фонд, -а fund; stock; reserves, resources; stocks; foundation.
фоне́тика, -и phonetics. **фонети́ческий** phonetic.
фонта́н, -а fountain; stream; gusher.
форе́ль, -и trout.
фо́рзац, -а fly-leaf.
фо́рма, -ы form; shape; mould, cast; uniform;

pl. contours; **в пи́сьменной фо́рме** in writing; **в фо́рме** in form; **отли́ть в фо́рму** mould, cast. **форма́льный** formal. **форма́ция, -и** structure; stage; formation; stamp, mentality. **фо́рменный** uniform; regulation; formal; proper, regular, positive. **формирова́ние, -я** forming; organization; unit, formation. **формирова́ть, -рую** *impf.* (*pf.* c~) form; organize; shape; **~ся** form, shape, develop. **формова́ть, -му́ю** *impf.* (*pf.* c~) form, shape; model; mould, cast. **формо́вщик, -а** moulder.
фо́рмула, -ы formula; formulation. **формули́ровать, -рую** *impf.* & *pf.* (*pf. also* c~) formulate. **формулиро́вка, -и** formulation; wording; formula. **формуля́р, -а** record of service; log-book; library card; (*sl.*) dossier.
форпо́ст, -а (*mil.*) advanced post; outpost.
форси́рованный forced; accelerated. **форси́ровать, -рую** *impf.* & *pf.* force; speed up.
фо́рточка, -и fortochka; small hinged window-pane; air vent.
фосфа́т, -а phosphate.
фо́сфор, -а phosphorus. **фо́сфористый** phosphorous.
фо́то *nt.indecl.* photo(graph).
фото... *in comb.* photo-, photo-electric. **фотоаппара́т, -а** camera. **~бума́га, -и** photographic paper. **~гени́чный** photogenic. **фото́граф, -а** photographer. **~графи́ровать, -рую** *impf.* (*pf.* c~) photograph; **~графи́роваться** be photographed, have one's photograph taken. **~графи́ческий** photographic. **~гра́фия, -и** photography; photograph; photographer's studio. **~копи́ровальный; ~ аппара́т** photocopier. **~ко́пия** photocopy. **~ла́мпа, -ы** dark-room lamp; photoelectric cell. **~люби́тель, -я** *m.* amateur photographer. **~набо́р, -а** film-setting; photo typesetting. **~объекти́в, -а** (camera) lens. **~панно́** *nt.indecl.* photo-mural; blow-up. **~репортёр, -а** press photographer. **~хро́ника, -и** news in pictures. **~элеме́нт, -а** a photoelectric cell.
фрагме́нт, -а fragment, detail; **~ фи́льма** film clip.
фра́за, -ы sentence; phrase. **фразёр, -а** phrase-monger.
фрак, -а tail-coat, dress coat, tails; evening dress.
фракцио́нный fractional; factional. **фра́кция, -и** fraction; faction.
франки́ровать, -рую *impf.* & *pf.* prepay, pay the postage (of). **франкиро́вка, -и** prepayment.
франкоязы́чный Francophone.
франкомасо́н, -а Freemason.
франт, -а dandy. **франтовско́й** dandyish, dandified. **франтовство́, -а́** dandyism.
Фра́нция, -и France. **францу́женка, -и** Frenchwoman. **францу́з, -а** Frenchman. **францу́зский** French; **~ ключ** monkey-wrench.

фрахт, -а freight. **фрахтовáть**, -тýю *impf.* (*pf.* за∼) charter.

фрейлúна, -ы maid of honour.

френч, -а service jacket.

фрéска, -и fresco.

фронт, -а; *pl.* -ы, -óв front; **стать во** ∼ stand to attention. **фронтовúк**, -á front-line soldier. **фронтовóй** front(-line).

фронтóн, -а pediment.

фрукт, -а fruit. **фруктóвый** fruit; ∼ **сад** orchard.

фтор, -а fluorine. **фтóристый** fluorine; fluoride. ∼ **кáльций** calcium fluoride.

фу *int.* ugh! oh!

фугáс, -а landmine. **фугáсный** high-explosive.

фундáмент, -а foundation, base; substructure; seating. **фундаментáльный** fundamental; solid, sound; thorough(-going); main; basic.

фундúрованный funded, consolidated.

функционúровать, -рую *impf.* function. **фýнкция**, -и function.

фунт, -а pound. **фýнтик**, -а paper bag, paper cone, screw of paper.

фурáж, -á forage, fodder. **фурáжка**, -и peaked cap, service cap, forage-cap.

фургóн, -а van; estate car, station wagon; caravan; pantechnicon.

фýрия, -и termagant, virago.

фурнитýра, -ы accessories; parts, components; fittings.

фурýнкул, -а furuncle.

фут, -а foot; foot-rule. **футбóл**, -а football, soccer. **футболúст**, -а footballer. **футбóлить**, -лю *impf. & pf.* (*pf. also* от∼) give, be given, the run-around. **футбóлка**, -и football jersey, sports shirt. **футбóльный** football; ∼ **мяч** football.

футля́р, -а case, container; sheath; cabinet; casing, housing.

фýтовый one-foot.

футуролóгия, -и futurology.

фуфáйка, -и jersey; sweater.

фы́ркать, -аю *impf.*, **фы́ркнуть**, -ну *pf.* snort; chuckle; grouse, grumble.

ха *nt.indecl.* the letter **х**.

хаврóнья, -и sow.

хáки *nt.indecl. & adj.* khaki.

халáт, -а robe; dressing-gown; overall. **халáтность**, -и carelessness, negligence. **халáтный** careless, negligent.

халтýра, -ы pot-boiler; hackwork; money made on the side, extra earnings. **халтýрить**, -рю *impf.* do hackwork; earn a little extra. **халтýрщик**, -а hack.

хам, -а boor, lout. **хáмский** boorish, loutish. **хáмство**, -а boorishness, loutishness.

хан, -а khan.

хандрá, -ы́ depression, dejection. **хандрúть**, -рю́ *impf.* suffer from melancholy; be dejected, be depressed.

ханжá, -и́ canting hypocrite, sanctimonious person. **хáнжеский**, **ханжескóй** sanctimonious, hypocritical.

хáнство, -а khanate.

хаóс, -а chaos.

харáктер, -а character; personality; nature; disposition; type. **характеризовáть**, -зýю *impf. & pf.* (*pf. also* о∼) describe; characterize, be characteristic of; ∼**ся** be characterized. **характерúстика**, -и reference; description. **характéрный**[1] characteristic; typical; distinctive; character. **характéрный**[2] of strong character, strong-willed; temperamental; quick-tempered.

хáркать, -аю *impf.*, **хáркнуть**, -ну *pf.* spit, hawk; ∼ **крóвью** spit blood.

хáртия, -и charter.

хáря, -и mug, face.

хáта, -ы peasant hut.

хáять, хáю *impf.* run down; abuse; slate, slang, swear at, curse.

хвалá, -ы́ praise. **хвалéбный** laudatory, eulogistic, complimentary. **хвалёный** highly-praised, much-vaunted. **хвалúть**, -лю́, -лишь *impf.* (*pf.* по∼) praise, compliment; ∼**ся** boast.

хвáстать(ся, -аю(сь *impf.* (*pf.* по∼) boast, brag. **хвастлúвый** boastful. **хвастовствó**, -á boasting, bragging. **хвастýн**, -á boaster, braggart.

хватáть[1], -áю *impf.*, **хватúть**, -ачý, -áтишь *pf.* (*pf. also* схватúть) snatch, seize, catch hold of; grab, grasp; bite; hit, strike, knock; ∼**ся** wake up (to), remember; +*g.* realize the absence of; +за+*a.* snatch at, clutch at; catch at; take up, try out; **пóздно хватúлись** you thought of it too late; ∼**ся за ум** come to one's senses.

хватáть[2], -áет *impf.*, **хватúть**, -áтит *pf.*, *impers.* (+*g.*) suffice, be sufficient, be enough; last out; **врéмени не хватáло** there was not enough time; **мне егó не хватáет** I miss him; **на сегóдня хвáтит** that will do for today, let's call it a day; **у нас не хватáет дéнег** we haven't enough money; **хвáтит!** that will do!; that's enough!; **э́того ещё не хватáло!** that's all we needed!; that's the last straw!; **э́того мне хвáтит на мéсяц** this will last me a month. **хвáтка**, -и grasp, grip; clutch; method, technique; skill. **хвáткий** strong; tenacious; skilful, crafty.

хвóйн|ый coniferous; ∼**ые** *sb.*, *pl.* conifers.

хворáть, -áю *impf.* be ill.

хворост, -а (-у) brushwood; straws. **хворостина**, -ы stick, switch. **хворостяной** brushwood.

хвост, -а *tail*; end, tail-end; train; queue. **хвостик**, -а tail; с ~ом and a bit; сто с ~ом a hundred odd. **хвостовой** tail.

хвоя, -и needle, needles; (*coniferous*) branch(es).

Хельсинки *m.indecl.* Helsinki.

хижина, -ы shack, hut, cabin.

хим... *abbr.* (*of* **химический**) *in comb.* chemical. **химкомбинат**, -а chemical plant. ~**продукты**, -ов chemical products. ~**чистка**, -и dry-cleaning; dry-cleaner's.

химера, -ы chimera. **химерический** chimerical.

химик, -а chemist. **химическ|ий** chemical; ~**ая война** chemical warfare. **химия**, -и chemistry.

химотерапия, -и chemotherapy.

хина, -ы, **хинин**, -а quinine.

хиреть, -ею *impf.* (*pf.* **за~**) grow sickly; wither; decay.

хиропрактик, -а chiropractor.

хирург, -а surgeon. **хирургическ|ий** surgical; ~**ая сестра** theatre nurse, theatre sister. **хирургия**, -и surgery.

хитрец, -а sly, cunning person. **хитрить**, -рю *impf.* (*pf.* **с~**) use cunning, be cunning, be crafty; dissemble. **хитрость**, -и cunning, craftiness; ruse, stratagem; skill, resource; intricacy, subtlety. **хитрый** cunning, sly, crafty, wily; skilful, resourceful; intricate, subtle; complicated.

хихикать, -аю *impf.*, **хихикнуть**, -ну *pf.* giggle, titter, snigger.

хищение, -я theft; embezzlement, misappropriation. **хищник**, -а predator, bird of prey, beast of prey; plunderer, despoiler. **хищнический** predatory, rapacious; destructive; injurious. **хищн|ый** predatory; rapacious, grasping, greedy; ~**ые птицы** birds of prey.

хладнокровие, -я coolness, composure, presence of mind, sang-froid; **сохранять** ~ keep one's head. **хладнокровный** cool, composed, self-possessed. **хладостойкий** cold-resistant; anti-freeze.

хлам, -а rubbish, trash, lumber.

хлеб, -а; *pl.* -ы, -ов *or* -а, -ов bread; loaf; grain, corn, cereal; ~**соль** bread and salt, hospitality. **хлебать**, -аю *impf.*, **хлебнуть**, -ну, -нёшь *pf.* gulp down, drink down; eat; go through, experience. **хлебный** bread; baker's; grain, corn, cereal; rich, abundant; grain-producing.

хлебо... *in comb.* bread; baking; grain. **хлебобулочный** bread. ~**заготовка**, -и grain-procurement. ~**завод**, -а (*mechanized*) bakery. ~**пекарня**, -и; *g.pl.* -рен bakery; bakehouse. ~**поставка**, -и grain delivery. ~**рез**, -а, ~**резка**, -и bread-cutter. ~**родный** grain-growing; rich; ~**родный год** good year (for cereals).

хлев, -а, *loc.* -у; *pl.* -а cow-house, cattle-shed, byre.

хлестать, -ещу, -ещешь *impf.*, **хлестнуть**, -ну, -нёшь *pf.* lash; whip; beat (down), teem, pour; gush, spout.

хлоп *int.* bang! **хлоп**, -а bang, clatter. **хлопать**, -аю *impf.* (*pf.* **хлопнуть**) bang; slap; ~ (**в ладоши**) clap, applaud.

хлопководство, -а cotton-growing. **хлопковый** cotton.

хлопнуть, -ну *pf. of* **хлопать**

хлопок[1], -пка clap.

хлопок[2], -пка cotton.

хлопотать, -очу, -очешь *impf.* (*pf.* **по~**) busy o.s.; bustle about; take trouble, make efforts; +**о**+*p. or* **за**+*a.* petition for, plead for, solicit for. **хлопотливый** troublesome; bothersome; exacting; busy, bustling, restless. **хлопоты**, -от *pl.* trouble; efforts; pains.

хлопчатка, -и cotton. **хлопчатобумажный** cotton.

хлопья, -ьев *pl.* flakes.

хлор, -а chlorine. **хлорвиниловый** vinyl chloride. **хлористый**, **хлорный** chlorine; chloride; **хлорная известь** chloride of lime. **хлорка**, -и bleaching powder, bleach liquor.

хлорофилл, -а chlorophyll.

хлороформ, -а chloroform. **хлороформировать**, -рую *impf. & pf.* (*pf. also* **за~**) chloroform.

хлынуть, -нет *pf.* gush, pour; rush, surge.

хлыст, -а whip, switch.

хмелевод, -а hop-grower. **хмелевой** hop. **хмелеть**, -ею *impf.* (*pf.* **за~, о~**) get tipsy, get tight. **хмель**, -я *loc.* -ю *m.* hop, hops; drunkenness, tipsiness; **во хмелю** tipsy, tight. **хмельн|ой**; -лён, -льна drunken, drunk; tipsy; intoxicating.

хмурить, -рю *impf.* (*pf.* **на~**); ~ **брови** knit one's brows; ~**ся** frown; become gloomy; be overcast, be cloudy. **хмурый** gloomy, sullen; overcast, dull, cloudy; lowering.

хныкать, -ычу *or* -аю *impf.* whimper, snivel; whine.

хобот, -а trunk, proboscis. **хоботок**, -тка proboscis.

ход, -а (-у), *loc.* -у; *pl.* -ы, -ов *or* -ы *or* -а, -ов motion, movement; travel, going; speed, pace; procession; course, progress; work, operation, running; stroke; move; lead; gambit, manoeuvre; entrance; passage, thoroughfare, covered way; wheel-base; runners; **быть в** ~**у** be in demand, be in vogue; **дать задний** ~ back, reverse; **дать** ~ set in motion, set going; **знать все** ~**ы и выходы** know all the ins and outs; **на** ~**у** in transit, on the move, without halting; in motion; in operation; **полным** ~**ом** at full speed, in full swing; **пустить в** ~ start, set in motion, set going; put into operation, put into service; **три часа** ~**у** three hours' journey.

ходатай, -я intercessor, mediator. **ходатайство**, -а petitioning; entreaty, pleading; pe-

tition, application. **ходáтайствовать, -твую**
impf. (*pf.* **по~**) petition, apply.

хóдики, -ов *pl.* wall-clock.

ходи́ть, хожý, хóдишь *impf.* (*pf.* **с~**) walk;
go; run; pass, go round; lead, play; move;
sway, shake; +**в**+*p.* be; wear; +**за**+*i.* look after, take care of, tend; ~ **с пик** lead a spade;
~ **ферзём** move one's queen. **хóдкий; -док,
-дкá, -о** fast; saleable, marketable; popular,
in demand, sought after; current. **ходýли, -
ей** *pl.* stilts. **ходýльный** stilted. **ходьбá, -
ы́** walking; walk; **полчасá ходьбы́** half an
hour's walk. **ходя́чий** walking; able to walk;
popular; current; ~**ая доброде́тель** virtue
personified; ~**ая моне́та** currency.

хозрасчёт, -а *abbr.* (*of* **хозя́йственный расчёт**) self-financing system.

хозя́ин, -а; *pl.* **-я́ева, -я́ев** owner, proprietor;
master; boss; landlord; host; **хозя́ева пóля**
home team. **хозя́йка, -и** owner; mistress;
hostess; landlady; wife, missus. **хозя́йни-
чать, -аю** *impf.* keep house; be in charge;
play the master, take charge. **хозя́йст-
венник, -а** financial manager, economic
manager. **хозя́йственный** economic, of the
economy; management; household; economical, thrifty. **хозя́йство, -а** economy; management; housekeeping; equipment; farm,
holding; **домáшнее** ~ housekeeping; **сéль-
ское** ~ agriculture.

хоккéист, -а (ice-)hockey-player. **хоккéй,
-я** hockey, ice-hockey; **кóнный** ~ polo. **хок-
кéйный** (ice-)hockey.

холéра, -ы cholera.

холестери́н, -а cholesterol. **холестери́но-
вый** cholesteric.

холм, -á hill. **холми́стый** hilly.

хóлод, -а (-у); *pl.* **-á, -óв** cold; coldness; cold
spell, cold weather. **холоди́льник, -а** refrigerator; cooler, condenser; **двухсекцио́н-
ный** ~ fridge-freezer. **холоди́льный** cooling; refrigerating, freezing, freezing. **холо-
ди́ть, -ожý** *impf.* (*pf.* **на~**) cool; chill; produce feeling of cold. **хóлодно** *adv.* coldly.
хóлодность, -и coldness. **холóдн|ый** хó-
лоден, -днá, -о cold; inadequate, thin; ~**ое
ору́жие** side-arms, cold steel; ~**ая** *sb.* cooler,
lock-up.

холóп, -а serf. **холóпий** serf's, of serfdom,
servile.

холостóй; хóлост, -á unmarried, single; bachelor; idle, free; blank, dummy. **холостя́к, -á**
bachelor. **холостя́цкий** bachelor.

холст, -á canvas; sackcloth. **холщóвый** canvas; sackcloth.

хомýт, -á (horse-)collar; burden; clamp, clip.

хор, -а; *pl.* **хóры** choir; chorus.

хорвáт, -а, хорвáтка, -и Croat. **хорвáтский**
Croatian.

хорёк, -рькá polecat.

хори́ст, -а member of choir or chorus. **хорово́д, -а** round dance.

хорони́ть, -ню, -нишь *impf.* (*pf.* **за~, по~,**

с~) bury; hide conceal; ~**ся** hide, conceal o.s.

хорóшенький pretty; nice. **хорóшенько**
adv. properly, thoroughly, well and truly.

хороше́ть, -éю *impf.* (*pf.* **по~**) grow pret-
tier. **хорóший; -óш, -á, -ó** good; nice; pretty,
nice-looking; **хорошó** *pred.* it is good; it is
nice, it is pleasant. **хорошó** *adv.* well; nicely;
all right! very well!; good.

хóры, хор *or* **-ов** *pl.* gallery.

хоте́ние, -я desire, wish. **хоте́ть, хочý, хóчешь, хоти́м** *impf.* (*pf.* **за~**) wish; +*g.* want;
éсли хоти́те perhaps; ~ **пить** be thirsty; ~
сказáть mean; ~**ся** *impers.* +*d.* want; **мне
хоте́лось бы** I should like; **ей хóчется** she
wants; **емý хóчется спать** he is sleepy.

хоть *conj.* although; even if; *part.* at least, if
only; for example, even; ~ **бы** if only. **хотя́**
conj. although, though; ~ **бы** even if; if only.

хохлáтый crested, tufted.

хóхот, -а guffaw, loud laugh. **хохотáть, -очý,
-óчешь** *impf.* guffaw, laugh loudly.

хочý *etc.*: *see* **хоте́ть**

храбрéц, -á brave man. **храбри́ться, -рю́сь**
make a show of bravery; pluck up one's courage. **хрáбрость, -и** bravery, courage. **хрáбрый** brave, courageous, valiant.

храм, -а a temple, church.

хране́ние, -я keeping, custody; storage; conservation; **кáмера хране́ния** cloakroom, left-
luggage office; **сдать на** ~ store, deposit,
leave in a cloakroom. **храни́лище, -а** a storehouse, depository. **храни́тель, -я** *m.* keeper,
custodian; repository; curator. **храни́ть, -ню́**
impf. keep; preserve, maintain; store; ~**ся**
be, be kept; be preserved.

храпе́ть, -плю́ *impf.* snore; snort.

хребéт, -бтá spine; back; (mountain) range;
ridge; crest, peak. **хребто́вый** spinal; range,
ridge, crest.

хрен, -а (-у) horseradish. **хрено́вый** horse-
radish.

хрестомáтия, -и reader.

хрип, -а a wheeze; hoarse sound. **хрипе́ть,
-плю́** *impf.* wheeze. **хри́плый; -пл, -á , -о**
hoarse,wheezing. **хри́пнуть, -ну; хрип** *impf.*
(*pf.* **о~**) become hoarse, lose one's voice.
хрипотá, -ы́ hoarseness.

христиани́н, -а; *pl.* **-áне, -áн, христиáнка, -и**
Christian. **христиáнский** Christian. **христи-
áнство, -а** Christianity; Christendom.
Христóс, -истá Christ.

хром, -а box-calf.

хромáть, -áю *impf.* limp, be lame; be poor,
be shaky. **хроме́ть, -éю** *impf.* (*pf.* **о~**) go
lame. **хромо́й; хром, -á, -о** lame, limping;
game, gammy; shaky, rickety; *sb.* lame man,
woman. **хромотá, -ы́** lameness.

хрóник, -а chronic invalid.

хрóника, -и chronicle; news items; newsreel;
historical film. **хроникáльный** news; documentary.

хрони́ческий chronic.

хронологи́ческий chronological. **хроно-**

ло́гия, -и chronology. **хроно́метр, -а** chronometer. **хронометра́ж, -а** time-study.

хру́пкий; -пок, -пка́, -о fragile; brittle; frail; delicate. **хру́пкость, -и** fragility; brittleness; frailness.

хруст, -а crunch; crackle.

хруста́лик, -а crystalline lens. **хруста́ль, -я́** *m.* cut glass; crystal. **хруста́льный** cut-glass; crystal; crystal-clear.

хрусте́ть, -ущу́ *impf.,* **хру́стнуть, -ну** *pf.* crunch; crackle. **хрустя́щий** crackling; crisp, crunchy; **~ карто́фель** potato crisps.

хрю́кать, -аю *impf.,* **хрю́кнуть, -ну** *pf.* grunt.

хрящ[1], -а́ cartilage, gristle.

хрящ[2], -а́ gravel, shingle. **хрящева́тый[2], хрящево́й[2]** gravelly, shingly.

хрящева́тый[1], хрящево́й[1] cartilaginous, gristly.

худе́ть, -ею *impf. (pf.* **по~)** grow thin.

ху́до, -а harm, ill; evil. **ху́до** *adv.* ill, badly.

худо́жественный art, arts; artistic; aesthetic; **~ фильм** feature film. **худо́жество, -а** art; artistry; *pl.* the arts. **худо́жник, -а** artist.

худо́й[1]; худ, -а́, -о thin, lean.

худо́й[2]; худ, -а́, -о bad; full of holes; worn; tumbledown; **ему́ ху́до** he feels bad; **на ~ коне́ц** if the worst comes to the worst, at (the) worst.

худоща́вый thin, lean.

ху́дший *superl. of* **худо́й, плохо́й** (the) worst. **ху́же** *comp. of* **худо́й, ху́до, плохо́й, пло́хо** worse.

хула́, -ы́ abuse, criticism.

хулига́н, -а hooligan. **хулига́нить, -ню** *impf.* behave like a hooligan. **хулига́нство, -а** hooliganism.

ху́нта, -а junta. **хунти́ст, -а** member of a junta.

ху́тор, -а; *pl.* **-а́** farm; farmstead; small village.

ц *letter: see* **цэ**

ца́пля, -и; *g.pl.* **-пель** heron.

цара́пать, -аю *impf.,* **цара́пнуть, -ну** *pf. (pf. also* **на~, о~)** scratch; scribble; **~ся** scratch; scratch one another; scramble, scrabble. **цара́пина, -ы** scratch; abrasion.

царе́вич, -а tsarevich *(son of a tsar)*. **царе́вна, -ы;** *g.pl.* **-вен** tsarevna *(daughter of a tsar)*. **цари́зм, -а** tsarism. **цари́стский** tsarist. **цари́ть, -рю́** *impf.* be tsar; hold sway; reign, prevail. **цари́ца, -ы** tsarina; queen. **ца́рский** of the tsar, tsar's; royal; tsarist; re-

gal, kingly. **ца́рство, -а** kingdom, realm; reign; domain. **ца́рствование, -я** reign. **ца́рствовать, -твую** *impf.* reign. **царь, -я́** *m.* tsar; king, ruler.

цвести́, -ету́, -ете́шь; -ёл, -а́ *impf.* flower, bloom, blossom; prosper, flourish; grow mouldy.

цвет[1], -а; *pl.* **-а́** colour; **~ лица́** complexion.

цвет[2], -а (-у), *loc.* **-у́;** *pl.* **-ы́** flower; cream, pick; blossom-time; prime; blossom; **во ~е лет** in the prime of life; **во ~е сил** at the height of one's powers; **в цвету́** in blossom.

цветни́к, -а́ flower-bed, flower-garden.

цветно́й coloured; colour; non-ferrous; **~а́я капу́ста** cauliflower; **~ые мета́ллы** non-ferrous metals; **~ое стекло́** stained glass; **~о́й фильм** colour-film.

цветово́дство, -а flower-growing, floriculture.

цветово́й colour; **~а́я слепота́** colour-blindness.

цвето́к, -тка́; *pl.* **цветы́** *or* **цветки́, -о́в** flower. **цвето́чный** flower; **~ магази́н** flower-shop. **цвету́щий** flowering, blossoming, blooming; prosperous, flourishing.

цеди́лка, -и strainer, filter. **цеди́ть, цежу́, це́дишь** *impf.* strain, filter; percolate; say (through clenched teeth).

целе́бный curative, healing.

целево́й special; targeted, earmarked for a specific purpose. **целенапра́вленный** purposeful. **целесообра́зный** expedient. **целеустремлённый; -ён, -ённа** *or* **-ена́** purposeful.

целико́м *adv.* whole; wholly, entirely.

целина́, -ы́ virgin lands, virgin soil. **цели́нн|ый** virgin; **~ые зе́мли** virgin lands.

цели́тельный curative, healing, medicinal.

це́лить(ся, -люсь) *impf. (pf.* **на~)** aim, take aim.

целко́вый *sb.* one rouble.

целлофа́н, -а cellophane. **целлуло́ид, -а** celluloid. **целлюло́за, -ы** cellulose.

целова́ть, -лу́ю *impf. (pf.* **по~)** kiss; **~ся** kiss.

це́лое *sb.* whole; integer. **целому́дренный** chaste. **целому́дрие, -я** chastity. **це́лостность, -и** integrity. **це́лостный** integral; entire, complete. **це́лый; цел, -а́, -о** whole, entire; safe, intact.

цель, -и target; aim, object, goal, end, purpose; **с це́лью** with the object (of), in order to.

цельнометалли́ческий all-metal. **це́льный; -лен, -льна́, -о** one-piece, solid; entire; whole; integral; single; undiluted. **це́льность, -и** wholeness, entirety, integrity.

цеме́нт, -а cement. **цементи́ровать, -рую** *impf. & pf.* cement; case-harden.

цена́, -ы́, *a.* **-у;** *pl.* **-ы** price, cost; worth, value; **цено́й+g.** at the price of, at the cost of; **любо́й цено́й** at any price.

ценз, -а qualification. **це́нзовый** qualifying.

це́нзор, -а censor. цензу́ра, -ы censorship.
цени́тель, -я *m.* judge, connoisseur, expert.
цени́ть, -ню́, -нишь *impf.* value; assess; estimate; appreciate. це́нник, -а price-list.
це́нность, -и value; price; importance; *pl.* valuables; values. це́нный valuable; costly; precious; important.
центр, -а centre. централиза́ция, -и centralization. централизова́ть, -зу́ю *impf. & pf.* centralize. центра́ль, -и main. центра́льный central. центробе́жный centrifugal.
цеп, -á flail.
цепене́ть, -е́ю *impf.* (*pf.* о~) freeze; be numbed; be rooted to the spot. це́пкий tenacious, strong; prehensile; sticky, tacky, loamy; obstinate, persistent, strong-willed. це́пкость, -и tenacity, strength; obstinacy, persistence. цепля́ться, -я́юсь *impf.* за+*a.* clutch at, try to grasp; cling to; stick to.
цепн|о́й chain; ~а́я реа́кция chain reaction. цепо́чка, -и chain; file, series. цепь, -и, *loc.* -й; *g.pl.* -е́й chain; row; series; range; line, file; succession; circuit; *pl.* chains, bonds.
церемо́ниться, -нюсь *impf.* (*pf.* по~) stand on ceremony; be (over-)considerate. церемо́ния, -и ceremony; без церемо́ний informally. церемо́нный ceremonious.
церковнославя́нский Church Slavonic. церко́вный church; ecclesiastical. це́рковь, -кви; *g.pl.* -е́й church.
цех, -а, *loc.* -ý; *pl.* -и *or* -á shop; section; guild, corporation.
цивилиза́ция, -и civilization. цивилизо́ванный civilized. цивилизова́ть, -зу́ю *impf. & pf.*
циге́йка, -и beaver lamb. циге́йковый beaver-lamb.
цика́да, -ы cicada.
цикл, -а cycle. цикли́ческий cyclic(al).
цикло́н, -а cyclone.
циклотро́н, -а cyclotron.
цико́рий, -я chicory. цико́рный chicory.
цили́ндр, -а cylinder; drum; top hat. цилиндри́ческий cylindrical.
цимба́лы, -а́л *pl.* cymbals.
цинга́, -й scurvy. цинго́тный scurvy; scorbutic.
цини́зм, -а cynicism. ци́ник, -а cynic. цини́ческий cynical.
цинк, -а zinc. ци́нковый zinc.
цино́вка, -и mat. цино́вочный mat, of mats.
цирк, -а circus. цирково́й circus.
циркули́ровать, -рует *impf.* circulate. ци́ркуль, -я *m.* (pair of) compasses; dividers. циркуля́р, -а circular.
цирю́льник, -а barber.
цисте́рна, -ы cistern, tank.
цитаде́ль, -и citadel; bulwark, stronghold.
цита́та, -ы quotation. цити́ровать, -рую *impf.* (*pf.* про~) quote.
ци́тра, -ы zither.
ци́трус, -а citrus. ци́трусов|ый citrous; ~ые

sb., pl. citrus plants.
цифербла́т, -а dial, face.
ци́фра, -ы figure; number, numeral. цифров|о́й numerical, in figures; ~а́я за́пись digital recording; ~ы́е да́нные figures.
ЦК *abbr.* (*of* Центра́льный Комите́т) Central Committee.
цо́кать, -аю *impf.*, цо́кнуть, -ну *pf.* clatter, clang; click.
цо́коль, -я *m.* socle, plinth, pedestal. цо́кольный plinth; ~ эта́ж ground floor.
ЦРУ *abbr.* (*of* Центра́льное разве́дывательное управле́ние) CIA, Central Intelligence Agency.
цука́т, -а candied fruit, candied peel.
цыга́н, -а; *pl.* -е, -áн *or* -ы, -ов, цыга́нка, -и gipsy. цыга́нский gipsy.
цыплёнок, -нка *pl.* -ля́та, -ля́т chicken; chick.
цы́почки; на ~, на цы́почках on tip-toe.
цэ *nt.indecl.* the letter ц.
Цю́рих, -а Zurich.

Ч

ч *letter: see* чэ
ч. *abbr.* (*of* час) hour, (*after numerals*) o'clock; (*of* часть) part.
чад, -а (-у) *loc.* -ý fumes, smoke. чади́ть, чажу́ *impf.* (*pf.* на~) smoke. ча́дный smoky, smoke-laden; stupefied, stupefying.
чай, -я (-ю); *pl.* -и́, -ёв tea.
чай *part.* probably, perhaps; no doubt; I suppose; after all.
ча́йка, -и; *g.pl.* ча́ек gull, sea-gull.
ча́йник, -а teapot; kettle. ча́йн|ый tea; ~ая посу́да tea-service; ~ая ро́за tea-rose. чайхана́, -ы́ tea-house.
чалма́, -ы́ turban.
ча́лый roan.
чан, -а, *loc.* -ý; *pl.* -ы́ vat, tub, tank.
ча́рка, -и cup, goblet, small glass.
чарова́ть, -ру́ю *impf.* bewitch; charm, captivate, enchant.
ча́ртерный chartered.
час, -а (-у), with numerals -á, *loc.* -ý; *pl.* -ы́ hours, time, period; *pl.* guard-duty; ~ one o'clock; в два ~á at two o'clock; стоя́ть на ~áх stand guard; ~ы́ пик rush-hour. часо́вня, -и; *g.pl.* -вен chapel. часово́й *sb.* sentry, sentinel, guard. часов|о́й clock, watch; of one hour, an hour's; by the hour; one o'clock; ~о́й переры́в an hour's interval; ~а́я пла́та payment by the hour; ~о́й по́яс time zone; ~а́я стре́лка (hour-)hand.

часовщ**i**к, -**á** watchmaker. ча́сом *adv.* sometimes, at times; by the way.

части́ца, -ы small part, element; particle. части́чно *adv.* partly, partially. части́чный partial.

ча́стность, -и detail; в ча́стности in particular. ча́стн|ый private; personal; particular, individual; local; district; ~ая со́бственность private property.

ча́сто *adv.* often, frequently; close, thickly. частоко́л, -а paling, palisade. частота́, -ы́; *pl.* -ы frequency. часто́тный frequency. часту́шка, -и ditty, folk-song. ча́стый; част, -á, -о frequent; close, close together; dense, thick; close-woven; quick, rapid; ~ гре́бень fine-tooth comb.

часть, -и; *g.pl.* -е́й part; portion; section, department, side; sphere, field; share; unit; ча́сти ре́чи parts of speech.

часы́, -о́в *pl.* clock, watch; нару́чные ~, ручны́е ~ wrist-watch.

ча́хлый stunted; poor, sorry; weakly, sickly, puny. ча́хнуть, -ну; чах *impf.* (*pf.* за~) wither away; become weak, go into a decline. чахо́тка, -и consumption. чахо́точный consumptive; poor, sorry, feeble.

ча́ша, -и cup, bowl; chalice; ~ весо́в scale, pan. ча́шка, -и cup; bowl; scale, pan.

ча́ща, -и thicket.

ча́ще *comp. of* ча́сто, ча́стый; ~ всего́ most often, mostly.

ча́яние, -я expectation; hope. ча́ять, ча́ю *impf.* hope, expect; think, suppose.

чва́ниться, -нюсь *impf.* (+*i.*) boast (of). чва́нство, -а conceit, arrogance, pride.

чего́ *see* что

чей *m.*, чья *f.*, чьё *nt.*, чьи *pl.*, *pron.* whose. чей-либо, чей-нибудь anyone's. чей-то someone's.

чек, -а cheque; check, bill; receipt.

чека́н, -а stamp, die. чека́нить, -ню *impf.* (*pf.* вы́~, от~) mint, coin; stamp, engrave, emboss, chase; ~ слова́ enunciate words clearly; rap out; ~ шаг step out. чека́нный stamping, engraving, embossing; stamped, engraved, embossed, chased; precise, expressive, chiselled; ~ шаг measured tread.

чёлка, -и fringe; forelock.

чёлн, -á; *pl.* чёлны dug-out canoe; boat. челно́к, -á dug-out canoe; shuttle.

челове́к, -а; *pl.* лю́ди; with numerals, *g.* -ве́к, -ам man, person, human being; (man-)servant, waiter.

человеко... *in comb.* man-, anthropo-. челове́ко-де́нь, -дня *m.* man-day. ~люби́вый philanthropic. ~лю́бие, -я philanthropy; humanity; humaneness. ~ненави́стнический misanthropic. ~обра́зный anthropomorphous; anthropoid. челове́ко-ча́с, -а; *pl.* -ы́ man-hour.

челове́чек, -чка little man. челове́ческий human; humane. челове́чество, -а humanity, mankind. челове́чий human.

челове́чный humane.

че́люсть, -и jaw, jaw-bone; denture, dental plate, false teeth.

чем, чём *see* что. чем *conj.* than; +*inf.* rather than, instead of; ~..., тем...+*comp.* the more ..., the more.

чемода́н, -а suitcase.

чемпио́н, -а, чемпио́нка, -и champion(s), title-holder(s). чемпиона́т, -а championship.

чему́ *see* что

чепе́ *nt. indecl.* incident, emergency.

чепуха́, -и́ nonsense, rubbish; trifle, triviality.

че́пчик, -а cap; bonnet.

че́рви, -е́й, че́рвы, черв *pl.* hearts. черво́нн|ый of hearts; red; ~ое зо́лото pure gold; ~ый туз ace of hearts.

червь, -я́; *pl.* -и, -е́й *m.* worm; maggot; bug, virus, germ. червя́к, -á worm; screw.

черда́к, -á attic, loft.

чёред, -á *loc.* -у́ turn; queue; идти́ свои́м ~о́м take its course. чередова́ние, -я alternation, interchange, rotation; (vowel) gradation, ablaut. чередова́ть, -ду́ю *impf.* alternate; ~ся alternate, take turns.

че́рез, чрез *prep.*+*a.* across; over; through; via; in; after; (further) on; every (other); ~ день every other day, on alternate days; ~ полчаса́ in half an hour; ~ три киломе́тра three kilometres further on; ~ ка́ждые три страни́цы every three pages.

чере́муха, -и bird cherry.

че́реп, -а; *pl.* -á skull, cranium.

черепа́ха, -и tortoise; turtle; tortoiseshell. черепа́ховый tortoise; turtle; tortoiseshell. черепа́ший tortoise, turtle; very slow.

черепи́ца, -ы tile. черепи́чный tile; tiled.

черепо́к, -пка́ crock, potsherd, broken piece of pottery.

чересчу́р *adv.* too; too much.

чере́шневый cherry; cherry-wood. чере́шня, -и; *g.pl.* -шен cherry; cherry-tree.

черке́с, -а, черке́шенка, -и Circassian. черке́сский Circassian.

черкну́ть, -ну́, -нёшь *pf.* scrape; leave a mark on; scribble, dash off.

чернеть, -ею *impf.* (*pf.* по~) turn black, go black; show black. черни́ка, -и bilberry, whortleberry. черни́ла, -и́л *pl.* ink. черни́льница, -ы ink-pot, ink-well. черни́льный ink; ~ каранда́ш indelible pencil. черни́ть, -ню́ *impf.* (*pf.* за~, на~, о~) blacken; paint black; slander. черни́чный bilberry.

черно... *in comb.* black; unskilled; rough. чёрно-бе́лый black-and-white. чернобу́рка, -и silver fox (fur). ~бу́рый dark-brown; ~бу́рая лиса́ silver fox; ~волосый black-haired. ~гла́зый black-eyed. ~зём, -а chernozem, black earth. ~зёмный black-earth. ~ко́жий black, coloured; *sb.* Negro; black. ~мо́рский Black-Sea. ~рабо́чий *sb.* unskilled worker, labourer. ~сли́в, -а (-у) prunes. ~сморо́динный blackcurrant.

черновик, -а rough copy, draft. **черновой** rough; draft, preparatory; heavy, dirty; crude. **чернота, -ы** blackness; darkness. **чёрн|ый; -рен, -рна** black; back; heavy, unskilled; ferrous; gloomy, melancholy; **на ~ый день** for a rainy day; **~ые металлы** ferrous metals; **~ый хлеб** black bread, rye-bread; **~ый ход** back way, back door; **~ый** *sb.* Negro, black.

черпак, -а scoop; bucket; grab. **черпалка, -и** scoop; ladle. **черпать, -аю** *impf.*, **черпнуть, -ну, -нёшь** *pf.* draw; scoop; ladle; extract, derive.

черстветь, -ею *impf.* (*pf.* **за~, о~, по~**) grow stale, get stale; become hardened, grow callous. **чёрствый; чёрств, -а, -о** stale; hard, callous.

чёрт, -а; *pl.* **черти, -ей** devil; the devil.

черта, -ы line; boundary; trait, characteristic; **в общих ~х** in general outline; **в черте города** within the town boundary. **чертёж, -а** drawing; blueprint, plan, scheme. **чертёжная** *sb.* drawing-office. **чертёжник, -а** draughtsman. **чертёжный** drawing. **чертить, -рчу, -ртишь** *impf.* (*pf.* **на~**) draw; draw up.

чёртов *adj.* devil's; devilish, hellish. **чертовский** devilish, damnable.

чёрточка, -и line; hyphen. **черчение, -я** drawing. **черчу** *etc.: see* **чертить**

чесать, чешу, -шешь *impf.* (*pf.* **по~**) scratch; comb; card; **~ся** scratch o.s.; comb one's hair; **у него руки чешутся+**inf. he is itching to.

чеснок, -а (-у) garlic. **чесночный** garlic.

чесотка, -и scab; rash; mange; itch.

чествование, -я celebration. **чествовать, -твую** *impf.* celebrate; honour. **честность, -и** honesty, integrity. **честный; -тен, -тна, -о** honest, upright. **честолюбивый** ambitious. **честолюбие, -я** ambition. **честь, -и** *and loc.* **-и** honour; regard, respect; **отдать ~+**d. salute.

четверг, -а Thursday. **четвереньки; на ~, на четвереньках** on all fours, on hands and knees. **четвёрка, -и** figure 4; No. 4; four; (*mark*) good. **четверо, -ых** four. **четвероног|ий** four-legged; **~ое** *sb.* quadruped. **четверостишие, -я** quatrain. **четвёртый** fourth. **четверть, -и;** *g.pl.* **-ей** quarter; quarter of an hour; term; **без четверти час** a quarter to one. **четверть-финал, -а** quarter-final.

чёткий; -ток, -тка, -о precise; clear-cut; clear, well-defined; legible; plain, distinct; articulate. **чёткость, -и** precision; clarity, clearness, definition; legibility; distinctness.

чётный even.

четыре, -рёх, -рьмя, -рёх four. **четыреста, -рёхсот, -ьмястами, -ёхстах** four hundred.

четырёх... *in comb.* four-, tetra-. **четырёхголосный** four-part. **~гранник, -а** tetrahedron. **~кратный** fourfold. **~летие, -я** four-year period; fourth anniversary. **~местный** four-seater. **~моторный** four-engined.

~сотый four-hundredth. **~стопный** tetrameter. **~тактный** four-stroke. **~угольник, -а** square, quadrangle. **~угольный** square, quadrangular. **~часовой** four hours', four-hour; four-o'clock.

четырнадцатый fourteenth. **четырнадцать, -и** fourteen.

чех, -а Czech.

чехарда, -ы leap-frog.

чехлить, -лю *impf.* (*pf.* **за~**) cover. **чехол, -хла** cover, case; loose cover.

Чехословакия, -и Czechoslovakia.

чечевица, -ы lentil; lens. **чечевичн|ый** lentil; **~ая похлёбка** mess of pottage.

чешка, -и Czech. **чешский** Czech.

чешу *etc.: see* **чесать**

чешуйка, -и scale. **чешуя, -й** scales.

чиж, -а, чижик, -а siskin.

чин, -а; *pl.* **-ы** rank; *any of fourteen grades (numbered from the top) of tsarist Civil Service*; official; rite, ceremony, order; **быть в ~ах** hold high rank, be of high rank.

чинить[1], -ню, -нишь *impf.* (*pf.* **по~**) repair, mend.

чинить[2], -ню, -нишь *impf.* (*pf.* **о~**) sharpen.

чинить[3], -ню *impf.* (*pf.* **у~**) carry out, execute; cause; **~ препятствия+**d. put obstacles in the way of.

чиновник, -а civil servant; official, functionary; bureaucrat. **чиновнический, чиновничий** civil-service; bureaucratic.

чипсы, -ов *pl.* (potato) crisps.

чирикать, -аю *impf.*, **чирикнуть, -ну** *pf.* chirp.

чиркать, -аю *impf.*, **чиркнуть, -ну** *pf.*+i. strike; **~ спичкой** strike a match.

численность, -и numbers; strength. **численный** numerical. **числитель, -я** *m.* numerator. **числительное** *sb.* numeral. **числить, -лю** *impf.* count, reckon; **~ся** be; +i. be reckoned, be on paper; be attributed; **за ним числится много недостатков** he has many failings; **~ся больным** be on the sick-list; **~ся в списке** be on the list. **число, -а;** *pl.* **-а, -сел** number; date, day; **в числе+**g. among; **в том числе** including; **единственное ~** singular; **множественное ~** plural; **сегодня восемнадцатое** ~ today is the eighteenth. **числовой** numerical.

чистильщик, -а cleaner; **~ сапог** bootblack, shoeblack. **чистить, чищу** *impf.* (*pf.* **вы~, о~, по~**) clean; brush, scour, sweep; peel, shell; purge; clear; dredge. **чистка, -и** cleaning; purge; **этническая ~** ethnic cleansing; **отдать в чистку** have cleaned, send to the cleaner's. **чисто** *adv.* cleanly, clean; purely, merely; completely. **чистов|ой** fair, clean; **~ая копия, ~ой экземпляр** fair copy, clean copy. **чистокровный** thoroughbred, pure-blooded. **чистописание, -я** calligraphy, (hand)writing. **чистоплотный** clean; neat, tidy; decent. **чистосердечный** frank, sincere, candid. **чистота, -ы** cleanness, cleanliness; neatness, tidiness; purity, innocence. **чи́ст|ый** clean; neat; tidy; pure; unsullied; undiluted; clear; net; utter; mere, sheer; complete, absolute; **на ~ом во́здухе** in the open air; **~ый вес** net weight; **~ые де́ньги** cash; **~ый лист** blank sheet; **~ая при́быль** clear profit; **~ая случа́йность** pure chance.

чита́емый widely-read, popular. **чита́льный** reading. **чита́льня, -и;** g.pl. -лен reading-room. **чита́тель, -я** m. reader. **чита́ть, -а́ю** impf. (pf. **про~, проче́сть**) read; recite, say; **~ ле́кции** lecture, give lectures; **~ с губ** lip-read; **~ся** be legible; be visible, be discernible. **чи́тка, -и** reading; reading through.

чих, -а sneeze. **чиха́ть, -а́ю** impf., **чихну́ть, -ну́, -нёшь** pf. sneeze, cough, splutter.

чи́ще comp. of **чи́сто, чи́стый**

чи́щу etc.: see **чи́стить**

член, -а member; limb; term; part; article. **члене́ние, -я** articulation. **члени́ть, -ню́** impf. (pf. **рас~**) divide; articulate. **членко́р, -а** abbr., (of **член-корреспонде́нт**) abbr. corresponding member, associate. **члено-разде́льный** articulate. **чле́нск|ий** membership; **~ие взно́сы** membership fee, dues. **чле́нство, -а** membership.

чмо́кать, -аю impf., **чмо́кнуть, -ну** pf. make smacking or sucking sound; kiss noisily; **~ губа́ми** smack one's lips.

чо́канье, -я clinking of glasses. **чо́каться, -аюсь** impf., **чо́кнуться, -нусь** pf. clink glasses.

чо́порный prim, stiff; stuck-up, stand-offish.

чрева́тый+i. fraught with, pregnant with. **чре́во, -а** belly, womb. **чревовеща́ние, -я** ventriloquism. **чревовеща́тель, -я** m. ventriloquist.

чрез see **че́рез. чрезвыча́йн|ый** extraordinary; special, extreme; **~ое положе́ние** state of emergency. **чрезме́рный** excessive, inordinate, extreme.

чте́ние, -я reading; reading-matter; **~ с губ** lip-reading. **чтец, -а́, чти́ца, -ы** reader; reciter. **чти́во, -а** (trashy) reading-matter.

чтить, чту impf. honour.

чти́ца see **чтец**

что, чего́, чему́, чем, о чём pron. what?; how?; why?; how much?; which, what, who; anything; **в чём де́ло?** what is the matter? **для чего́?** what ... for? why?; **е́сли ~ случи́тся** if anything happens; **к чему́?** why?; **~ ему́ до э́того?** what does it matter to him?; **~ каса́ется меня́** as for me, as far as I am concerned; **~ с тобо́й?** what's the matter (with you)?; **я зна́ю, ~ вы име́ете в виду́** I know what you mean; **~ ж** yes; all right, right you are; **~ за** what? what sort of?; what (a) ..!; (a) ...!; **~ за ерунда́!** what (utter) nonsense! **что** conj. that. **что (бы) ни** pron. whatever, no matter what; **во что бы то ни ста́ло** at whatever cost.

чтоб, что́бы conj. in order (to), so as; that; to; **он сказа́л, что́бы вы к нему́ зашли́** he

said you were to go and see him; **он хо́чет, что́бы я сде́лал э́то сейча́с же** he wants me to do it at once. **что-ли́бо, что-нибу́дь** prons. anything. **что-то** pron. something. **что-то** adv. somewhat, slightly; somehow, for some reason.

чу́вственность, -и sensuality. **чу́вственный** sensual; perceptible, sensible. **чувстви́тельность, -и** sensitivity, sensitiveness, sensibility; perceptibility; sentimentality; tenderness; feeling; (film) speed. **чувстви́тельный** sensitive, susceptible; sensible, perceptible; sentimental; tender. **чу́вство, -а** feeling; sense; senses; **прийти́ в ~** come round, regain consciousness. **чу́вствовать, -твую** impf. feel; realize; appreciate, have a feeling for; **~ся** be perceptible; make itself felt.

чугу́н, -а́ cast iron. **чугу́нка, -и** (cast-iron) pot; (cast-iron) stove; railway. **чугу́нный** cast-iron.

чуда́к, -а́, чуда́чка, -и eccentric, crank. **чуда́ческий** eccentric, extravagant. **чуда́чество, -а** eccentricity, extravagance.

чудеса́ etc.: see **чу́до. чуде́сный** miraculous; marvellous, wonderful.

чу́диться, -ишься impf. (pf. **по~, при~**) seem.

чу́дно adv. wonderfully, beautifully. **чудно́й; -дён, -дна́** odd, strange. **чу́дный** wonderful, marvellous; beautiful, lovely; magical. **чу́до, -а;** pl. -деса́ miracle; wonder, marvel. **чудо́вище, -а** monster. **чудо́вищный** monstrous; enormous. **чудоде́й, -я, -де́йка, -и** miracle-worker. **чудоде́йственный** miracle-working; miraculous. **чу́дом** adv. miraculously. **чудотво́рный** miraculous, miracle-working.

чужби́на, -ы foreign land, foreign country. **чужда́ться, -а́юсь** impf.+g. shun, avoid; stand aloof from, be untouched by. **чу́жд|ый; -жд, -а́, -о** alien (to); +g. free from, devoid of, a stranger to. **чужезе́мец, -мца, -зе́мка, -и** foreigner, stranger. **чужезе́мный** foreign. **чуж|о́й** someone else's, another's, others'; strange, alien; foreign; **на ~о́й счёт** at s.o. else's expense; **~и́е края́** foreign lands; sb. stranger.

чула́н, -а store-room, lumber-room; larder; built-in-cupboard.

чуло́к, -лка́; g.pl. -ло́к stocking. **чуло́чн|ый** stocking; **~ая вя́зка** stocking-stitch.

чум, -а tent.

чума́, -ы́ plague.

чурба́н, -а block, chock; blockhead. **чу́рка, -и** block, lump.

чу́ткий; -ток, -тка́, -о keen, sharp, quick; sensitive; sympathetic; tactful, delicate, considerate; **~ сон** light sleep. **чу́ткость, -и** keenness, sharpness, quickness; delicacy, tact, consideration.

чу́точка, -и; ни чу́точки not in the least; **чу́точку** a little (bit), a wee bit.

чу́тче comp. of **чу́ткий**

чуть *adv.* hardly, scarcely; just; a little, very slightly; ~ не almost, nearly, all but; ~ свет at daybreak, at first light; ~чуть a tiny bit.

чухо́нец, -нца, чухо́нка, -и Finn. **чухо́н-ск\|ий** Finnish; ~ое ма́сло butter.

чу́чело, -а stuffed animal, stuffed bird; scarecrow.

чушь, -и nonsense, rubbish.

чу́ять, чу́ю *impf.* scent, smell; sense, feel.

чьё *etc.: see* **чей**

чэ *nt.indecl.* the letter ч.

ша *nt.indecl.* the letter ш.

шаба́ш¹, -а a sabbath. **шаба́ш², -а́** end of work, break; finish; ~! that's all! that's enough! that'll do! **шаба́шить, -шу** *impf.* (*pf.* по~) (*sl.*) knock off, stop work; take a break.

шаба́шник, -а moonlighter. **шаба́шничать, -аю** *impf.* moonlight.

шабло́н, -а template, pattern; mould, form; stencil; cliché; routine. **шабло́нный** stencil, pattern; trite, banal; stereotyped; routine.

шаг, -а (-у), with numerals **-а́,** *loc.* **-у́;** *pl.* **-и́** step; footstep; pace; stride.

шага́ть, -а́ю *impf.,* **шагну́ть, -ну́, -нёшь** *pf.* step; walk, stride; pace; go, come; make progress. **ша́гом** *adv.* at walking pace, at a walk; slowly.

ша́йба, -ы washer; puck.

ша́йка¹, -и tub.

ша́йка², -и gang, band.

шака́л, -а jackal.

шала́нда, -ы barge, lighter.

шала́ш, -а cabin, hut.

шали́ть, -лю́ *impf.* be naughty; play up, play tricks. **шаловли́вый** naughty, mischievous, playful. **ша́лость, -и** prank, game; *pl.* mischief, naughtiness. **шалу́н, -а́, шалу́нья, -и;** *g.pl.* **-ний** naughty child.

шаль, -и shawl.

шальн\|о́й mad, crazy; wild; ~ая пу́ля stray bullet.

ша́мкать, -аю *impf.* mumble, lisp.

шампа́нское *sb.* champagne.

шампиньо́н, -а (*cultivated*) mushroom.

шампу́нь, -я *m.* shampoo.

шанс, -а chance.

шансо́н, -а ballad. **шансонье́** *m. indecl.* balladeer; singer-songwriter.

шанта́ж, -а́ blackmail. **шантажи́ровать, -рую** *impf.* blackmail.

ша́пка, -и cap; banner, headline. **ша́почка, -и** cap.

шар, -а, with numerals **-а́;** *pl.* **-ы́** sphere; ball; balloon; ballot; *pl.* (*sl.*) peepers, eyes.

шара́хать, -аю *impf.,* **шара́хнуть, -ну** hit; ~ся rush, dash; shy.

шарж, -а caricature, cartoon. **шаржи́ровать, -рую** *impf.* caricature.

ша́рик, -а ball; corpuscle. **ша́риков\|ый;** ~ая (авто)ру́чка ball-point pen; ~ый подши́пник ball-bearing. **шарикоподши́пник, -а** ball-bearing.

ша́рить, -рю *impf.* grope, feel, fumble; sweep.

ша́ркать, -аю *impf.,* **ша́ркнуть, -ну** *pf.* shuffle; scrape; ~ ного́й click one's heels.

шарма́нка, -и barrel-organ, street organ. **шарма́нщик, -а** organ-grinder.

шарни́р, -а hinge, joint.

шарова́ры, -а́р *pl.* (*wide*) trousers; bloomers.

шарови́дный spherical, globular. **шарово́й** ball; globular. **шарообра́зный** spherical, globular.

шарф, -а scarf.

шассú *nt.indecl.* chassis; undercarriage.

шата́ть, -а́ю *impf.* rock, shake; *impers.+a.* его́ шата́ет he is reeling, staggering; ~ся rock, sway; reel, stagger, totter; come loose, be loose; be unsteady; wander; loaf, lounge about. **шата́ющийся** loose.

шатёр, -тра́ tent; marquee; tent-shaped roof or steeple.

ша́ткий unsteady; shaky; loose; unstable, insecure; unreliable; vacillating.

шатро́вый tent-shaped.

шату́н, -а́ connecting-rod.

ша́фер, -а; *pl.* **-а́** best man.

шафра́н, -а saffron. **шафра́нный, шафра́новый** saffron.

шах¹, -а Shah.

шах², -а check; ~ и мат checkmate. **шахмати́ст, -а** chess-player. **ша́хматн\|ый** chess; chess-board, chequered, check; ~ая па́ртия game of chess. **ша́хматы, -ат** *pl.* chess; chessmen.

ша́хта, -ы mine, pit; shaft. **шахтёр, -а** miner. **шахтёрский** miner's, miners'; mining. **ша́хтный** pit, mine.

ша́шечница, -ы draught-board, chess-board. **ша́шка¹, -и** draught; *pl.* draughts.

ша́шка², -и sabre, cavalry sword.

шашлы́к, -а́ shashlik, kebab.

шва *etc.: see* **шов**

шва́бра, -ы mop, swab.

шваль, -и rubbish; trash; riff-raff.

шварто́в, -а hawser; mooring-line; *pl.* moorings. **швартова́ть, -ту́ю** *impf.* (*pf.* о~, при~) moor; ~ся moor, make fast.

швах *indecl.* weak, poor; bad; in a bad way.

швед, -а, шве́дка, -и Swede. **шве́дский** Swedish.

швейн\|ый sewing; ~ая маши́на sewing-machine. ~ая мастерска́я dress-maker's.

швейца́р, -а (hall-)porter, door-keeper, commissionaire.

швейца́рец, -рца, -ца́рка, -и Swiss. **Швейца́рия**, -и Switzerland. **швейца́рский** Swiss. **Шве́ция**, -и Sweden.

швея́, -и seamstress, machinist.

швырну́ть, -ну́, -нёшь *pf.* **швыря́ть**, -я́ю *impf.* throw, fling, chuck, hurl; ~ся+*i.* throw; throw about, treat carelessly, muck about.

шевели́ть, -елю́, -е́ли́шь *impf.*, **шевельну́ть**, -ну́, -нёшь *pf.* (*pf. also* по~) turn (over); (+*i.*) move, stir, budge; ~ся move, stir, budge.

шевро́ *nt.indecl.* kid.

шеде́вр, -а masterpiece, chef d'oeuvre.

шезло́нг, -а deck-chair; lounger.

шёл *see* идти́

ше́лест, -а rustle, rustling. **шелесте́ть**, -сти́шь *impf.* rustle.

шёлк, -а (-у), *loc.* -ý; *pl.* -á silk. **шелкови́стый** silk, silky. **шелко́вица**, -ы mulberry(-tree). **шелкови́чный** mulberry; ~ червь silkworm. **шёлковый** silk. **шёлкогра́фия**, -и silk-screen printing.

шелохну́ть, -ну́, -нёшь *pf.* stir, agitate; ~ся stir, move.

шелуха́, -и́ skin; peel, peelings; pod; scale. **шелуши́ть**, -шу́ peel; shell; ~ся peel; peel off, flake off.

шепеля́вить, -влю *impf.* lisp. **шепеля́вый** lisping; hissing.

шепну́ть, -ну́, -нёшь *pf.*, **шепта́ть**, -пчу́, -пчешь *impf.* whisper; ~ся whisper (together); **шёпот**, -а whisper. **шёпотом** *adv.* in a whisper.

шере́нга, -и rank; file; column.

шерохова́тый rough; uneven; rugged.

шерсть, -и wool, woollen; fleece; hair, coat. **шерстяно́й** wool, woollen.

шерша́веть, -еет *impf.* become rough, get rough. **шерша́вый** rough.

шест, -á pole; staff.

ше́ствие, -я procession. **ше́ствовать**, -твую walk in procession, process; march, pace, proceed.

шестёрка, -и six; figure 6; No. 6; group of six.

шестерня́, -й; *g.pl.* -рён gear-wheel, cogwheel, pinion.

ше́стеро, -ы́х six.

шести... *in comb.* six-, hexa-, sex(i)-. **шестигра́нник**, -а hexahedron. ~**дне́вка**, -и six-day (*working*) week. ~**деся́тый** sixtieth. ~**кла́ссник**, -а ~**кла́ссница**, -ы sixth-year pupil. ~**ле́тний** six-year; six-year-old. ~**ме́сячный** six-month; six-month-old. ~**сотле́тие**, -я six hundred years; sexcentenary, six-hundredth anniversary. ~**со́тый** six-hundredth. ~**уго́льник**, -а hexagon. ~**уго́льный** hexagonal. ~**часово́й** six-hour; six-o'clock.

шестнадцатиле́тний sixteen-year; sixteen-year old. **шестна́дцатый** sixteenth. **шестна́дцать**, -и sixteen. **шесто́вик**, -á pole-vaulter.

шест|**о́й** sixth; одна́ ~а́я one-sixth. **шесть**, -и́, *i.* -ью́ six. **шестьдеся́т**, -и́десяти, *i.* -ью́десятью sixty. **шестьсо́т**, -исо́т, -иста́м, -ью́ста́ми, -иста́х six hundred. **ше́стью** *adv.* six times.

шеф, -а boss, chief; patron, sponsor, **ше́фский** patronage, sponsorship, adoption; sponsored. **ше́фство**, -а patronage, adoption. **ше́фствовать**, -твую *impf.* +над+*i.* adopt; sponsor.

ше́я, -и neck; **сиде́ть на ше́е у** be a burden to.

шиво́рот, -а collar.

шизофрени́я, -и schizophrenia.

шика́рный chic, smart, stylish; splendid, magnificent; done for effect.

шика́ть, -аю *impf.*, **ши́кнуть**, -ну *pf.*+*d.* hiss, boo; +на+*a.* hush, call 'sh' to.

ши́ло, -а; *pl.* -ья, -ьев awl.

ши́на, -ы tyre; splint.

шине́ль, -и greatcoat, overcoat.

шинко́ванный shredded, chopped. **шинкова́ть**, -ку́ю *impf.* shred, chop.

ши́нный tyre. **шиноремо́нтный** tyre-repairing, tyre-maintenance.

шип, -á thorn, spike, crampon, nail; pin; tenon.

шипе́ние, -я hissing; sizzling; sputtering. **шипе́ть**, -плю́ *impf.* hiss; sizzle; fizz; sputter.

шипо́вник, -а a wild rose, dog-rose.

шипу́чий sparkling; fizzy. **шипу́чка**, -и fizzy drink. **шипя́щий** sibilant.

ши́ре *comp. of* **широ́кий**, **широко́**. **ширина́**, -ы́ width, breadth; gauge. **ши́рить**, -рю *impf.* extend, expand; ~ся spread, extend.

ши́рма, -ы screen.

широ́к|**ий**, -о́к, -á, -око́ wide, broad; **това́ры** ~**ого потребле́ния** consumer goods; ~**ие ма́ссы** the broad masses; ~**ое пла́тье** loose dress; ~**ая пу́блика** the general public; ~**ий экра́н** wide screen. **широко́** *adv.* wide, widely, broadly; extensively, on a large scale; ~ **смотре́ть на ве́щи** be broad-minded.

широко... *in comb.* wide-, broad-. **широковеща́ние**, -я broadcasting. ~**веща́тельный** broadcasting. ~**коле́йный** broad-gauge. ~**ко́стный** big-boned. ~**пле́чий** broad-shouldered. ~**по́лый** wide-brimmed; full-skirted. ~**форма́тный**, ~**экра́нный** wide-screen.

широта́, -ы́; *pl.* -ы width, breadth; latitude. **широ́тный** of latitude; latitudinal. **широча́йший** *superl. of* **широ́кий**. **ширпотре́б**, -а *abbr.* consumption; consumer goods.

ширь, -и (wide) expanse; **во всю** ~ to full width; to the full extent.

ши́тый embroidered. **шить**, шью, шьёшь *impf.* (*pf.* с~) sew; make; embroider. **шитьё**, -я́ sewing, needlework; embroidery.

шифр, -а cipher, code; press-mark; monogram. **шифро́ванный** in cipher, coded. **шифрова́ть**, -ру́ю *impf.* (*pf.* за~) encipher, code. **шифро́вка**, -и enciphering, coding; coded communication, communication in cipher.

шиш, -á fico, fig; nothing; ruffian, brigand; **ни ~á** damn all. **шишка, -и** cone; bump; lump, knob; core; (*sl.*) big shot, big noise. **шишковáтый** knobby, knobbly; bumpy. **шишковúдный** cone-shaped. **шишконóсый** coniferous.

шкалá, -ы́; *pl.* **-ы** scale; dial.

шкатýлка, -и box, casket, case.

шкаф, -а, *loc.* **-ý**; *pl.* **-ы́** cupboard; wardrobe; dresser; **кни́жный ~** bookcase; **несгорáемый ~** safe. **шкáфчик, -а** cupboard, locker.

шквал, -а squall. **шквáлистый** squally.

шкет, -а (*sl.*) boy, lad.

шкив, -а; *pl.* **-ы́** pulley; sheave.

шкóла, -ы school; **~-интернáт** boarding-school. **шкóлить, -лю** *impf.* (*pf.* **вы́~**) train, discipline. **шкóльник, -а** schoolboy. **шкóльница, -ы** schoolgirl. **шкóльный** school; **~ учи́тель** school-teacher, school-master.

шкýра, -ы skin, hide, pelt. **шкýрка, -и** skin; rind; emery paper, sandpaper. **шкýрник, -а, -ница, -ы** self-seeker. **шкýрный** self-centred, selfish.

шла *see* **идти́**

шлагбáум, -а barrier; arm.

шлак, -а slag; dross; cinder; clinker. **шлако-блóк, -а** breeze-block. **шлáковый** slag.

шланг, -а hose.

шлейф, -а train.

шлем, -а helmet; **вя́заный ~** balaclava.

шлёпать, -аю *impf.*, **шлёпнуть, -ну** *pf.* smack, spank; shuffle; tramp; (*sl.*) shoot, execute by shooting; **~ся** fall flat, plop down, plump down.

шли *see* **идти́**

шлифовáльный polishing; grinding; abrasive. **шлифовáть, -фýю** *impf.* (*pf.* **от~**) polish; grind; abrade. **шлифóвка, -и** polishing; grinding; polish.

шло *see* **идти́. шлю** *etc.*: *see* **слать**

шлюз, -а a lock, sluice, floodgate. **шлю́зный, шлюзовóй** lock, sluice.

шлю́пка, -и launch, boat.

шля́па, -ы hat; helpless, feeble creature; **дéло в шля́пе** it's in the bag. **шля́пка, -и** hat; bonnet; head; cap. **шля́пник, -а, шля́пница, -ы** milliner, hatter. **шля́пный** hat.

шмель, -я́ bumble-bee.

шмы́гать, -аю *impf.*, **шмы́гнуть, -ы́гнý, -ы́гнёшь** *pf.* dart, rush, slip, sneak; +*i.* rub, brush; **~ нóсом** sniff.

шнур, -á cord; lace; flex, cable. **шнуровáть, -рýю** *impf.* (*pf.* **за~, про~**) lace up; tie. **шнурóк, -рка́** lace.

шныря́ть, -я́ю *impf.* dart about, run in and out.

шов, шва seam; stitch; suture; joint; weld.

шок, -а shock. **шоки́ровать, -рую** *impf.* shock. **шóков|ый; ~ая терáпия** shock therapy.

шоколáд, -а chocolate. **шоколáдка, -и** chocolate, bar of chocolate. **шоколáдный** chocolate; chocolate-coloured.

шóрох, -а rustle.

шóрты, шорт *pl.* shorts.

шóры, шор *pl.* blinkers.

шоссé *nt.indecl.* highway, main road; (*surfaced*) road.

шотлáндец, -дца Scotsman, Scot. **Шотлáндия, -и** Scotland. **шотлáндка[1], -и** Scot-(swoman). **шотлáндка[2], -и** tartan, plaid. **шотлáндский** Scottish, Scots.

шофёр, -а, driver; chauffeur. **шофёрский** driver's; driving.

шпáга, -и sword.

шпагáт, -а cord; twine; string; splits.

шпаклевáть, -лю́ю *impf.* (*pf.* **за~**) caulk; fill, stop, putty. **шпаклёвка, -и** filling, puttying, stopping; putty.

шпáла, -ы sleeper.

шпанá, -ы́ (*sl.*) hooligan(s), rowdy, rowdies; riff-raff, rabble; petty criminals.

шпаргáлка, -и crib.

шпáрить, -рю *impf.* (*pf.* **о~**) scald.

шпат, -а spar.

шпиль, -я *m.* spire, steeple; capstan, windlass. **шпи́лька, -и** hairpin; hat-pin; tack, brad; stiletto heel.

шпинáт, -а spinach.

шпингалéт, -а bolt; catch, latch.

шпиóн, -а spy. **шпионáж, -а** espionage. **шпиóнить, -ню** *impf.* be a spy; spy (**за**+*i.* on). **шпиóнский** spy's; espionage.

шпóра, -ы spur.

шприц, -а syringe.

шпрóта, -ы sprat; *pl.* smoked sprats in oil.

шпýлька, -и spool, bobbin.

шрам, -а scar.

шрифт, -а; *pl.* **-ы́** type, print; script; **курси́вный ~** italic(s). **шрифтовóй** type.

шт. *abbr.* (*of* **штýка**) item, piece.

штаб, -а; *pl.* **-ы́** staff; headquarters.

штáбель, -я; *pl.* **-я́** *m.* stack, pile.

штаби́ст, -а, штаби́ник, -á staff-officer. **штабнóй** staff headquarters.

штамп, -а die, punch; stamp; impress; letter-head; cliché, stock phrase. **штампóванный** punched, stamped, pressed; trite, hackneyed; stock, standard.

штáнга, -и bar, rod, beam; weight; crossbar. **штангúст, -а** weight-lifter.

штани́шки, -шек *pl.* (*child's*) shorts. **штаны́, -óв** trousers.

штат[1], -а State.

штат[2], -а, штáты, -ов *pl.* staff, establishment. **штати́в, -а** tripod, base, support, stand. **штáтный** staff; established, permanent.

штáтск|ий civilian; **~ое (плáтье)** civilian clothes, mufti, civvies; **~ий** *sb.* civilian.

штемпелевáть, -лю́ю *impf.* (*pf.* **за~**) stamp; frank, postmark. **штéмпель, -я**; *pl.* **-я́** *m.* stamp; **почтóвый ~** postmark.

штéпсель, -я; *pl.* **-я́** *m.* plug, socket. **штéпсельный** plug, socket.

штиль, -я *m.* calm.

штóльня, -и; *g.pl.* **-лен** gallery.

штопáльный darning. **штопаный** darned.

што́пать, -аю *impf.* (*pf.* **за~**) darn. **што́пка,** -и darning; darn; darning wool, darning thread.

што́пор, -а corkscrew; spin.

што́ра, -ы blind.

шторм, -а gale, storm.

штормо́вка, -и anorak; parka.

штраф, -а fine. **штрафно́й** penal; penalty; ~ **батальо́н** penal battalion; ~ **уда́р** penalty kick. **штрафова́ть,** -фу́ю *impf.* (*pf.* **о~**) fine.

штрих, -а́ stroke; hatching; feature, trait. **штрихова́ть,** -ху́ю *impf.* (*pf.* **за~**) shade, hatch.

штуди́ровать, -рую *impf.* (*pf.* **про~**) study.

шту́ка, -и item, one; piece; trick; thing; **вот так ~!** well, I'll be damned! **в том-то и ~!** that's just the point; **пять штук яи́ц** five eggs.

штукату́р, -а plasterer. **штукату́рить,** -рю *impf.* (*pf.* **от~**, **о~**) plaster, parget. **штукату́рка,** -и plastering; plaster; facing, rendering; stucco. **штукату́рный** plaster, stucco.

штурва́л, -а (steering-)wheel, helm; controls. **штурва́льный** steering, control; *sb.* helmsman, pilot.

штурм, -а storm, assault.

штурман, -а; *pl.* -ы *or* -а́ navigator.

штурмова́ть, -му́ю *impf.* storm, assault. **штурмов|о́й** assault; storming; **~а́я авиа́ция** ground-attack aircraft; **~а́я ле́стница** scaling-ladder; **~а́я полоса́** assault course. **штурмовщи́на,** -ы rushed work, production spurt, sporadic effort.

шту́чн|ый piece, by the piece; **~ый пол** parquet floor; **~ая рабо́та** piece-work; **~ый това́р** piece-goods.

штык, -а́ bayonet. **штыково́й** bayonet.

штырь, -я́ *m.* pintle, pin.

шу́ба, -ы winter coat, fur coat.

шу́лер, -а; *pl.* -а́ card-sharper, cheat. **шу́лерство,** -а card-sharping, sharp practice.

шум, -а (-у) noise; din, uproar, racket; sensation, stir; **мно́го ~у из-за ничего́** much ado about nothing; **наде́лать ~у** cause a sensation. **шуме́ть,** -млю́ *impf.* make a noise; row, wrangle; make a stir; make a fuss; cause a sensation. **шу́мный;** -мен, -мна́, -о noisy; loud; sensational. **шумови́к,** -а́ sound effects man.

шумо́вка, -и perforated spoon; skimmer.

шумов|о́й sound, noise; **~ы́е эффе́кты** sound effects. **шумо́к,** -мка́ noise; **под ~** under cover, on the quiet.

шу́рин, -а brother-in-law.

шурша́ть, -шу́ *impf.* rustle, crackle.

шу́стрый; -тёр, -тра́, -о smart, bright, sharp.

шут, -а́ fool; jester; buffoon, clown. **шути́ть,** -чу́, -тишь *impf.* (*pf.* **по~**) joke, jest; play, trifle; **+над**+*i.* laugh at, make fun of. **шу́тка,** -и joke, jest; trick; farce; **без шу́ток, кро́ме шу́ток** joking apart; **в шу́тку** as a joke, in jest; **не на шу́тку** in earnest; **сыгра́ть шу́тку**

с+*i.* play a trick on. **шутли́вый** humorous; joking, light-hearted. **шу́точн|ый** comic; joking; **де́ло не ~ое** it's no joke, no laughing matter. **шутя́** *adv.* for fun, in jest; easily, lightly.

шушу́каться, -аюсь *impf.* whisper together.

шху́на, -ы schooner.

шью *etc.*: *see* **шить**

Щ

ща *nt.indecl.* the letter щ.

щаве́ль, -я́ *m.* sorrel.

щади́ть, щажу́ *impf.* (*pf.* **по~**) spare; have mercy on.

щебёнка, -и, **ще́бень,** -бня *m.* gravel, crushed stone, ballast; road-metal.

ще́бет, -а twitter, chirp. **щебета́ть,** -ечу́, -е́чешь *impf.* twitter, chirp.

щего́л, -гла́ goldfinch.

щёголь, -я *m.* dandy, fop. **щегольну́ть,** -ну́, -нёшь *pf.*, **щеголя́ть,** -я́ю *impf.* dress fashionably; strut about; +*i.* show off, parade, flaunt. **щегольско́й** foppish, dandified.

ще́дрость, -и generosity. **ще́дрый;** -др, -а́, -о generous; lavish, liberal.

щека́, -и́, *a.* щёку; *pl.* щёки, -а́м cheek.

щеко́лда, -ы latch, catch.

щекота́ть, -очу́, -о́чешь *impf.* (*pf.* **по~**) tickle. **щеко́тка,** -и tickling, tickle. **щекотли́вый** ticklish, delicate.

щёлкать, -аю *impf.*, **щёлкнуть,** -ну *pf.* crack; flick, fillip, flip; trill; +*i.* click, snap, pop; **он щёлкает зуба́ми** his teeth are chattering; **~ па́льцами** snap one's fingers.

щёлок, -а lye, liquor. **щелочно́й** alkaline. **щёлочь,** -и; *g.pl.* -е́й alkali.

щелчо́к, -чка́ flick, fillip; slight; blow.

щель, -и; *g.pl.* -е́й crack; chink; slit; fissure, crevice; slit trench; **голосова́я ~** glottis.

щени́ться, -и́тся *impf.* (*pf.* **о~**) pup, whelp, cub. **щено́к,** -нка́; *pl.* -нки́, -о́в *or* -ня́та, -я́т puppy, pup; whelp, cub.

щепа́, -ы́; *pl.* -ы, -а́м, **ще́пка,** -и splinter, chip; kindling; **худо́й как ще́пка** as thin as a rake. **щепа́ть,** -плю́, -плешь *impf.* chip, chop.

щепети́льный punctilious, correct; pernickety, fussy, finicky.

ще́пка *see* **щепа́**

щепо́тка, -и, **щепо́ть,** -и pinch.

щети́на, -ы bristle; stubble. **щети́нистый** bristly, bristling. **щети́ниться,** -ится *impf.* (*pf.* **о~**) bristle. **щётка,** -и brush; fetlock. **щёточный** brush.

щёчный cheek.

щи, щей *or* **щец, щам, ща́ми** *pl.* shchi, cabbage soup.

щи́колотка, -и ankle.

щипа́ть, -плю, -плешь *impf.*, **щипну́ть, -ну́, -нёшь** *pf.* (*pf. also* **об~, о~,** **ущипну́ть**) pinch, nip, tweak; sting, bite; burn; pluck; nibble; **~ся** pinch. **щипко́м** *adv.* pizzicato.

щипо́к, -пка́ pinch, nip, tweak. **щипцы́, -о́в** *pl.* tongs, pincers, pliers; forceps. **щи́пчики, -ов** *pl.* tweezers.

щит, -а́ shield; screen; sluice-gate; (*tortoise*) shell; hoarding; board; panel; **распредели́тельный ~** switchboard; **~ управле́ния** control panel. **щитови́дный** thyroid. **щито́к, -тка́** dashboard.

щу́ка, -и pike.

щуп, -а probe. **щу́пальце, -а;** *g.pl.* **-лец** tentacle; antenna. **щу́пать, -аю** (*pf.* **по~**) feel, touch; feel for; probe.

щу́плый; -пл, -а́, -о weak, puny, frail.

щу́рить, -рю *impf.* (*pf.* **со~**) screw up, narrow; **~ся** screw up one's eyes; narrow.

щу́чий pike's; **(как) по ~ему веле́нью** of its own accord, as if by magic.

Э

э *nt.indecl.*, **э оборо́тное** the letter э.

эвакуацио́нный evacuation. **эвакуа́ция, -и** evacuation. **эвакуи́рованный** *sb.* evacuee. **эвакуи́ровать, -рую** *impf. & pf.* evacuate.

Эвере́ст, -а (Mt.) Everest.

ЭВМ *abbr.* (*of* **электро́нная вычисли́тельная маши́на**) (electronic) computer.

эволюциони́ровать, -рую *impf. & pf.* evolve. **эволюцио́нный** evolutionary. **эволю́ция, -и** evolution; manoeuvre.

эгои́зм, -а egoism, selfishness. **эгои́ст, -а** egoist. **эгоисти́ческий** egoistic, selfish. **эготи́зм, -а** egotism.

Э́динбург, -а Edinburgh.

эй *int.* hi! hey!

Э́йре *nt.indecl.* Eire.

эйтана́зия, -и euthanasia.

Э́йфелева ба́шня, -ой -и the Eiffel Tower.

эква́тор, -а equator. **экваториа́льный** equatorial.

эквивале́нт, -а equivalent. **эквивале́нтный** equivalent.

экз. *abbr.* (*of* **экземпля́р**) copy, specimen.

экза́мен, -а examination, exam; **~ на вожде́ние** driving test; **вы́держать, сдать ~** pass an examination. **экзамена́тор, -а** examiner. **экзаменова́ть, -ну́ю** *impf.* (*pf.*

про~) examine; **~ся** take an examination.

экзе́ма, -ы eczema.

экземпля́р, -а specimen, example; copy.

экипа́ж[1], -а carriage.

экипа́ж[2], -а crew; ship's company. **экипирова́ть, -ру́ю** *impf. & pf.* equip. **экипиро́вка, -и** equipping; equipment.

экологи́ческий ecological. **эколо́гия, -и** ecology.

эконо́м, -а steward, housekeeper; economist. **эконо́мика, -и** economics; economy. **эконо́мить, -млю** *impf.* (*pf.* **с~**) use sparingly, husband; save; economize. **экономи́ческий** economic; economical. **экономи́чный** economical. **эконо́мия, -и** economy; saving. **эконо́мка, -и** housekeeper. **эконо́мный** economical; careful, thrifty.

экосисте́ма, -ы ecosystem.

экра́н, -а screen; **голубо́й ~** television (screen). **экраниза́ция, -и** filming, screening; film version. **экра́нный** on-screen.

экскава́тор, -а excavator, earth-moving machine.

экскурса́нт, -а tourist. **экскурсио́нный** excursion. **экску́рсия, -и** (conducted) tour; excursion, trip; outing; group, party (*of tourists*). **экскурсово́д, -а** guide.

экспанси́вный effusive, expansive, talkative.

экспеди́ровать, -рую *impf. & pf.* dispatch. **экспеди́ция, -и** expedition; dispatch, forwarding; forwarding office.

экспе́рт, -а expert. **эксперти́за, -ы** (expert) examination, expert opinion; commission of experts.

эксплуата́тор, -а exploiter. **эксплуатацио́нн|ый** exploitational, operating; **~ые расхо́ды** running costs; **~ые усло́вия** working conditions. **эксплуата́ция, -и** exploitation; utilization; operation, running. **эксплуати́ровать, -рую** *impf.* exploit; operate, run, work.

экспо́ *f.indecl.* Expo. **экспози́ция, -и** layout; exposition; exposure. **экспона́т, -а** exhibit. **экспоне́нт, -а** exhibitor. **экспони́ровать, -рую** *impf. & pf.* exhibit; expose. **экспоно́метр, -а** exposure meter.

э́кспорт, -а export. **экспортёр, -а** exporter. **экспорти́ровать, -рую** *impf. & pf.* export.

экспре́сс, -а express (*train, coach, etc.*).

экспро́мт, -а impromptu. **экспро́мтом** *adv.* impromptu; suddenly, without warning; **игра́ть ~** improvise.

экстерн, -а external student. **экстерна́т, -а** extramural course(s).

экстравага́нтный extravagant, eccentric, bizarre, preposterous.

экстра́кт, -а (*cul.*) extract; résumé, précis.

экстрасе́нс, -а psychic.

э́кстренн|ый urgent; emergency; extra, special; **~ое заседа́ние** extraordinary session; **~ое изда́ние, ~ый вы́пуск** special edition; **~ые расхо́ды** unforeseen expenses.

эксцентри́чный eccentric.

экю *m. & nt. indecl.* écu.

эласти́чн|ый elastic; springy, resilient; **~ые брю́ки** stretch pants.

элега́нтность, -и elegance. **элега́нтный** elegant, smart.

электризова́ть, -зу́ю *impf. (pf.* **на~)** electrify. **эле́ктрик, -а** electrician. **электрифици́ровать, -рую** *impf. & pf.* electrify. **электри́ческий** electric; **~ фона́рик** torch, flashlight. **электри́чество, -а** electricity; electric light. **электри́чка, -и** electric train. **электро...** *in comb.* electro-, electric, electrical. **электробытово́й** electrical. **~во́з, -а** electric locomotive. **~дви́гатель, -я** *m.* electric motor. **~дина́мика, -и** electrodynamics. **~дугово́й** electric-arc. **~и́згородь, -и** electric fence. **электро́лиз, -а** electrolysis. **~маши́нка, -и** electric typewriter. **~монтёр, -а** electrician. **~одея́ло, -а** electric blanket. **~подогрева́тель, -я** *m.* electric heater. **~по́езд, -а** electric train. **~полоте́нце, -а** hand-drier. **~полотёр, -а** electric floor-polisher. **~прибо́р, -а** electrical appliance. **~про́вод, -а;** *pl.* **-а́** electric cable. **~прово́дка, -и** electric wiring. **~про́игрыватель, -я** *m.* record-player. **~сва́рка, -и** electric welding. **~ста́нция, -и** power-station. **~те́хник, -а** electrical engineer. **~те́хника, -и** electrical engineering. **~тя́га, -и** electric traction. **~шо́к, -а** electric-shock treatment. **~энцефалогра́мма, -ы** (electro-)encephalogram. **~энцефало́граф, -а** (electro-)encephalograph.

электро́н, -а electron. **электро́ника, -и** electronics.

электро́нно- *in comb.* electron, electronic. **электро́нно-лучево́й** electron-beam, cathode-ray. **~микроскопи́ческий** electron-microscope.

электро́нный electron; electronic.

элеме́нт, -а element; cell; type, character. **элемента́рный** elementary; simple.

эль *nt. indecl.* the letter л.

эм *nt. indecl.* the letter м.

эма́левый enamel. **эмали́рованный** enamelled. **эмалирова́ть, -ру́ю** *impf.* enamel. **эма́ль, -и** enamel.

эмансипа́ци|я, -и emancipation; **боре́ц за ~ю же́нщин** women's liberationist. **эмансипи́ровать, -рую** *impf. & pf.* emancipate.

эмба́рго *nt. indecl.* embargo.

эмбле́ма, -ы emblem; insignia.

эмбрио́н, -а embryo.

эмигра́нт, -а emigrant, émigré. **эмигра́ция, -и** emigration. **эмигри́ровать, -рую** *impf. & pf.* emigrate.

эмоциона́льный emotional. **эмо́ция, -и** emotion.

эмпири́зм, -а empiricism. **эмпи́рик, -а** empiricist. **эмпири́ческий** empiricist; empirical.

эму *indecl.* emu.

эму́льсия, -и emulsion.

эн *nt. indecl.* the letter н.

э́ндшпиль, -я *m.* end-game.

энерге́тика, -и power engineering. **энерги́чный** energetic, vigorous, forceful. **эне́ргия, -и** energy; vigour, effort.

энерго... *in comb.* power, energy. **энерговооружённость, -и** power capacity, power supply. **~ёмкий** power-consuming. **~затра́та, -ы** energy expenditure. **~систе́ма, -ы** electric power system.

энтомо́лог, -а entomologist. **энтомологи́ческий** entomological. **энтомоло́гия, -и** entomology.

энтузиа́зм, -а enthusiasm. **энтузиа́ст, -а** (+*g.*) enthusiast (about, for), devotee (of).

энциклопеди́ческий encyclopaedic; **~ слова́рь** encyclopaedia. **энциклопе́дия, -и** encyclopaedia.

эпигра́мма, -ы epigram. **эпи́граф, -а** epigraph.

эпиде́мия, -и epidemic.

эпизо́д, -а episode. **эпизоди́ческий** episodic; occasional, sporadic.

эпикуре́ец, -йца epicurean. **эпикуре́йский** epicurean.

эпиле́псия, -и epilepsy. **эпиле́птик, -а** epileptic. **эпилепти́ческий** epileptic.

эпило́г, -а epilogue. **эпита́фия, -и** epitaph. **эпи́тет, -а** epithet. **эпице́нтр, -а** epicentre.

эпи́ческий epic. **эпопе́я, -и** epic.

эполе́ты, эполе́т *pl.* epaulettes.

эпо́ха, -и epoch, age, era. **эпоха́льный** epoch-making.

эр *nt. indecl.* the letter р.

э́ра, -ы era; **до на́шей э́ры** B.C.; **на́шей э́ры** A.D.

эроге́нн|ый erogenous; **~ые зо́ны** erogenous zones.

эро́тика, -и sensuality. **эроти́ческий, эроти́чный** erotic, sensual.

эруди́ция, -и erudition.

эрцге́рцог, -а archduke. **эрцгерцоги́ня, -и** archduchess. **эрцге́рцогство, -а** archduchy.

эс *nt. indecl.* the letter с.

эска́дра, -ы squadron. **эска́дренный** squadron; **~ миноно́сец** destroyer. **эскадри́льный** squadron. **эскадри́лья, -и;** *g.pl.* **-лий** squadron. **эскадро́н, -а** squadron, troop. **эскадро́нный** squadron, troop.

эскала́тор, -а escalator.

эскало́п, -а cutlet(s).

эски́з, -а a sketch, study; draft, outline. **эски́зный** sketch; sketchy; draft.

эскимо́ *nt. indecl.* choc-ice.

эскимо́с, -а, эскимо́ска, -и Eskimo. **эскимо́сский** Eskimo.

эско́рт, -а (*mil.*) escort. **эскорти́ровать, -рую** *impf. & pf.* (*mil.*) escort.

эсми́нец, -нца *abbr.* (*of* **эска́дренный миноно́сец**) destroyer.

эссе́нция, -и essence.

эстака́да, -ы trestle, platform; trestle bridge; gantry; overpass; pier, boom.

эста́мп, -а print, engraving, plate.

эстафёта, -ы relay race; baton.

эстётика, -и aesthetics; design. **эстети́ческий** aesthetic.

Эсто́ния, -и Estonia.

эстра́да, -ы stage, platform; variety, music hall; **арти́ст эстра́ды** variety performer, artiste; entertainer. **эстра́дный** stage; variety; **~ конце́рт** variety show; entertainment.

эта́ж, -á storey, floor. **этажёрка, -и** shelves; whatnot; stand. **эта́жность, -и** number of storeys.

э́так *adv.* so, thus; about, approximately. **э́такий** such (a), what (a).

этало́н, -a standard.

эта́п, -a stage, phase; lap; halting-place; transport, shipment, of prisoners. **этапи́ровать, -рую** *impf.* ship, transport.

э́тика, -и ethics.

этикёт, -a etiquette.

этикётка, -и label.

этимо́лог, -a etymologist. **этимологи́ческий** etymological. **этимоло́гия, -и** etymology.

эти́ческий, эти́чный ethical.

этни́ческий ethnic.

этногра́фия, -и ethnography.

э́то *part.* this (is), that (is), it (is). **э́тот** *m.*, **э́та** *f.*, **э́то** *nt.*, **э́ти** *pl.* *pron.* this, these.

этю́д, -a study, sketch; étude; exercise; problem.

эф *nt.indecl.* the letter **ф**.

эфёс, -a hilt, handle.

эфио́п, -a, эфио́пка, -и Ethiopian. **эфио́пский** Ethiopian.

эфи́р, -a ether; air. **эфи́рн|ый** ethereal; ether, ester; **~ое ма́сло** essential oil; volatile oil.

эффёкт, -a effect, impact; result, consequences; *pl.* effects; **тепли́чный ~** greenhouse effect. **эффекти́вный** effective; efficient. **эффёктный** effective; striking; done for effect.

эх *int.* eh! oh!

э́хо, -a echo. **эхоло́т, -a** echo-sounder. **эхолока́ция, -и** echo location.

эшафо́т, -a scaffold.

эшело́н, -a echelon; special train, troop-train.

Ю

ю *nt.indecl.* the letter **ю**.

ю. *abbr.* (*of* **юг**) S., south.

ЮАР *abbr.* (*of* **Ю́жно-Африка́нская Респу́блика**) Republic of South Africa.

юбиле́й, -я anniversary; jubilee. **юбиле́йный** jubilee.

ю́бка, -и skirt; **~-брю́ки** split skirt, culottes.

ю́бочка, -и short skirt.

ювели́р, -a jeweller. **ювели́рный** jeweller's, jewellery; fine, intricate; **~ магази́н** jeweller's.

юг, -a south; **на ~е** in the south. **ю́го-восто́к, -a** south-east. **ю́го-за́пад, -a** south-west. **югосла́в, -a, югосла́вка, -и** Yugoslav. **Югосла́вия, -и** Yugoslavia. **югосла́вский** Yugoslav. **южа́нин, -a;** *pl.* **-áне, -áн, южа́нка, -и** southerner. **ю́жный** southern; **Ю~ океа́н** the Antarctic Ocean.

ю́мор, -a humour. **юмори́ска, -и** humoresque. **юмори́ст, -a** humourist. **юмори́стика, -и** humour. **юмористи́ческий** humorous, comic, funny.

юнио́р, -a, юнио́рка, -и junior; junior competitor, player, etc. **юнко́р, -a** *abbr.* youth correspondent.

ю́ность, -и youth. **ю́ноша, -и** *m.* youth. **ю́ношеский** youthful. **ю́ношество, -a** youth; young people. **ю́ный; юн, -á, -o** young; youthful.

юпи́тер, -a floodlight.

юриди́ческ|ий legal, juridical; **~ие нау́ки** jurisprudence, law; **~ий факульте́т** faculty of law. **юрисконсу́льт, -a** legal adviser. **юри́ст, -a** legal expert, lawyer.

ю́ркий; -рок, -рка́, -рко quick-moving, brisk; sharp, smart.

ю́рта, -ы yurt (*nomad's tent in Central Asia*).

юсти́ция, -и justice.

юти́ться, ючу́сь *impf.* huddle (together); take shelter.

Я

я *nt.indecl.* the letter **я**.

я, меня́, мне, мной (-о́ю), (обо) мне *pron.* I.

я́беда, -ы *c.g.*, **я́бедник, -a** sneak, tell-tale; informer. **я́бедничать, -аю** *impf.* (*pf.* **на~**) inform, tell tales, sneak.

я́блоко, -a; *pl.* **-и, -ок** apple; **в я́блоках** dappled, dapple; **глазно́е ~** eyeball. **я́блоневый, я́блонный, я́блочный** apple. **я́блоня, -и** apple-tree.

яви́ться, явлю́сь, я́вишься *pf.*, **явля́ться, -я́юсь** *impf.* appear; present o.s., report; turn up, arrive, show up; arise, occur; +*i.* be, serve as. **я́вка, -и** appearance, attendance, presence; secret rendez-vous; **~ обяза́тельна** attendance obligatory. **явле́ние, -я** phenomenon; appearance; occurrence, happening; scene. **я́вный** obvious, manifest, patent; overt, explicit. **я́вственный** clear, distinct. **я́вствовать, -твует** appear; be clear, be obvious; follow.

ягнёнок, -нка; *pl.* -ня́та, -я́т lamb.

я́года, -ы berry; berries.

я́годица, -ы buttock, buttocks.

яд, -а (-у) poison; venom.

я́дерщик, -а nuclear physicist. **я́дерный** nuclear.

ядови́тый poisonous; venomous; toxic.

ядрёный vigorous, healthy; bracing; sound, crisp, juicy. **ядро́**, -а́; *pl.* -а, я́дер kernel, core; nucleus; main body; (cannon-)ball; shot.

ядротолка́тель, -я *m.* shot-putter.

я́зва, -ы ulcer, sore. **я́звенн|ый** ulcerous; ~ая боле́знь ulcers. **я́звина**, -ы large ulcer; indentation, pit. **язви́тельный** caustic, biting, sarcastic. **язви́ть**, -влю́ *impf.* (*pf.* съ~) wound, sting; be sarcastic.

язы́к, -а́ tongue; clapper; language; **англи́йский** ~ English. **языка́стый** sharp-tongued. **языкове́д**, -а linguist(ician). **языкове́дение**, -я, **языкозна́ние**, -я linguistics. **языково́й** linguistic. **язы́ко́вый** tongue; lingual. **язычко́вый** uvular; reed. **язы́чник**, -а heathen, pagan. **язы́чный** lingual. **язычо́к**, -чка́ tongue; uvula; reed; catch.

яичко, -а; *pl.* -и, -чек egg; testicle. **яи́чник**, -а ovary. **яи́чница**, -ы fried eggs. **яйцеви́дный** oval; oviform, ovoid, egg-shaped. **яйцо́**, -а́; *pl.* я́йца, яи́ц egg; ovum.

як, -а yak.

я́кобы *conj.* as if, as though; *part.* supposedly, ostensibly, allegedly.

я́корн|ый anchor; mooring; ~ая стоя́нка anchorage. **я́корь**, -я; *pl.* -я́ *m.* anchor; armature.

ял, -а whaleboat, whaler; yawl. **я́лик**, -а skiff, dinghy; yawl. **я́личник**, -а ferryman.

Я́лта, -ы Yalta.

я́ма, -ы pit, hole; depression, hollow.

ямщи́к, -а́ coachman.

янва́рский January. **янва́рь**, -я́ *m.* January.

янта́рный amber. **янта́рь**, -я́ *m.* amber.

япо́нец, -нца, **япо́нка**, -и Japanese. **Япо́ния**, -и Japan. **япо́нский** Japanese; ~ лак Japan.

ярд, -а yard (*measure*).

я́ркий; **я́рок**, ярка́, -о bright; colourful, striking; vivid, graphic; ~ приме́р striking example, glaring example.

ярлы́к, -а́ label; tag.

я́рмарка, -и fair. **я́рмарочный** fair, market.

ярмо́, -а́; *pl.* -а yoke.

яровой spring, spring-sown.

я́ростный furious, fierce, savage, frenzied. **я́рость**, -и fury, rage, frenzy.

я́рус, -а circle; tier; layer.

я́рче *comp. of* я́ркий

я́рый vehement, fervent; furious, raging; violent.

я́сельный crèche, day-nursery.

я́сеневый ash. **я́сень**, -я *m.* ash(-tree).

я́сли, -ей *pl.* manger, crib; crèche, day nursery. **ясне́ть**, -е́ет *impf.* become clear, clear. **я́сно** *adv.* clearly. **яснови́дение**, -я clairvoyance. **яснови́дец**, -дца, **яснови́дица**, -ы clairvoyant. **я́сный**; я́сен, ясна́, -о clear; bright; fine; distinct; serene; plain; lucid; precise, logical.

я́ства, яств *pl.* viands, victuals.

я́стреб, -а; *pl.* -а́ hawk. **ястреби́н|ый** hawk; с ~ым взгля́дом hawk-eyed. **ястребо́к**, -бка́ hawk; fighter (*plane*).

я́хта, -ы yacht.

яче́истый cellular, porous. **яче́йка**, -и, **ячея́**, -и́ cell.

ячме́нный barley. **ячме́нь**[1], -я́ *m.* barley. **ячме́нь**[2], -я́ *m.* stye.

я́щерица, -ы lizard.

я́щик, -а box, chest, case; cabinet; drawer; **му́сорный** ~ dustbin; **откла́дывать в до́лгий** ~ shelve, put off.

я́щур, -а foot-and-mouth disease.

A [eɪ] *n.* (*mus.*) ля *nt.indecl.*; **from A to Z** с нача́ла до конца́.

a [ə, eɪ], **an** [æn, ən] *indef. article, not usu. translated*; *adj.* оди́н, не́кий, како́й-то; **fifty miles an hour** пятьдеся́т миль в час; **twice a week** два ра́за в неде́лю.

AA *abbr.* (*of* **Automobile Association**) Ассоциа́ция автомобили́стов.

aback [ə'bæk] *adv.*: **take ~** поража́ть *impf.*, порази́ть *pf.*; засти́гнуть *pf.* враспло́х.

abacus ['æbəkəs] *n.* счёты *m.pl.*

abandon [ə'bænd(ə)n] *v.t.* (*leave*) оставля́ть *impf.*, оста́вить *pf.*; (*desert*) покида́ть *impf.*, поки́нуть *pf.*; (*give up*) броса́ть *impf.*, бро́сить *pf.*; **~ o.s. to** предава́ться (-даю́сь, -даёшься) *impf.*, преда́ться (-а́мся, -а́шься, -а́стся, -ади́мся; -а́лся, -ала́сь) *pf.+d.* **abandoned** *adj.* забро́шенный, поки́нутый; (*profligate*) распу́тный. **abandonment** *n.* (*action*) оставле́ние; (*state*) забро́шенность.

abase [ə'beɪs] *v.t.* унижа́ть *impf.*, уни́зить *pf.* **abasement** *n.* униже́ние.

abate [ə'beɪt] *v.i.* (*lessen*) уменьша́ться *impf.*, уме́ньшиться *pf.*; (*weaken*) слабе́ть *impf.*, о~ *pf.*; (*calm*) успока́иваться *impf.*, успоко́иться *pf.*; (*die down*) затиха́ть *impf.*, зати́хнуть (-х) *pf.* **abatement** *n.* уменьше́ние.

abattoir ['æbə,twɑː(r)] *n.* скотобо́йня (*g.pl.* -бен).

abbess ['æbɪs] *n.* аббати́са. **abbey** ['æbɪ] *n.* абба́тство. **abbot** ['æbət] *n.* абба́т.

abbreviate [ə'briːvɪ,eɪt] *v.t.* сокраща́ть *impf.*, сократи́ть (-ащу́, -ати́шь) *pf.* **abbrevi'ation** *n.* сокраще́ние.

ABC [,eɪbiː'siː] *n.* а́збука, алфави́т.

abdicate ['æbdɪ,keɪt] *v.i.* отрека́ться *impf.*, отре́чься (-еку́сь, -ечёшься; -ёкся, -екла́сь) *pf.* от престо́ла. **abdi'cation** *n.* отрече́ние (от престо́ла).

abdomen ['æbdəmən] *n.* брюшна́я по́лость (*pl.* -ти, -те́й); (*entom.*) брюшко́ (*pl.* -ки́, -ко́в). **abdominal** [æb'dɒmɪn(ə)l] *adj.* брюшно́й.

abduct [əb'dʌkt] *v.t.* наси́льно увози́ть (-ожу́, -о́зишь) *impf.*, увезти́ (увезу́, -зёшь; увёз, -ла́) *pf.* **abduction** *n.* наси́льственный уво́з.

aberration [,æbə'reɪʃ(ə)n] *n.* аберра́ция; (*mental*) помраче́ние ума́.

abet [ə'bet] *v.t.* подстрека́ть *impf.*, подстрекну́ть *pf.* (к соверше́нию преступле́ния *etc.*); соде́йствовать *impf. & pf.* соверше́нию (преступле́ния *etc.*).

abhor [əb'hɔː(r)] *v.t.* пита́ть *impf.* отвраще́ние к+*d.*; (*hate*) ненави́деть (-и́жу, -и́дишь) *impf.* **abhorrence** [əb'hɒrəns] *n.* отвраще́ние. **abhorrent** *adj.* отврати́тельный.

abide [ə'baɪd] *v.t.* (*tolerate*) выноси́ть (-ошу́, -о́сишь) *impf.*, вы́нести (-су́, -сешь; -с) *pf.*; *v.i.* (*remain*) остава́ться (-таю́сь, -таёшься) *impf.*, оста́ться (-а́нусь, -а́нешься) *pf.*; **~ by** (*promise etc.*) выполня́ть *impf.*, вы́полнить *pf.*

ability [ə'bɪlɪtɪ] *n.* спосо́бность; уме́ние.

abject ['æbdʒekt] *adj.* (*miserable*) жа́лкий (-лок, -лка́, -лко); (*low*) ни́зкий (-зок, -зка́, -зко); (*craven*) малоду́шный.

abjure [əb'dʒʊə(r)] *v.t.* отрека́ться *impf.*, отре́чься (-еку́сь, -ечёшься; -ёкся, -екла́сь) *pf.* от+*g.*

ablative ['æblətɪv] *n.* абляти́в.

ablaze [ə'bleɪz] *pred.*: **be ~** горе́ть (-ри́т) *impf.*; сверка́ть *impf.*

able ['eɪb(ə)l] *adj.* спосо́бный, уме́лый; (*talented*) тала́нтливый; **be ~ to** мочь (могу́, мо́жешь; мог, -ла́) *impf.*, с~ *pf.*; быть в состоя́нии; (*know how to*) уме́ть *impf.*, с~ *pf.*

abnormal [æb'nɔːm(ə)l] *adj.* ненорма́льный. **abnormality** [,æbnɔː'mælɪtɪ] *n.* ненорма́льность.

aboard [ə'bɔːd] *adv.* на борт(у́); (*train*) на по́езд(е).

abolish [ə'bɒlɪʃ] *v.t.* отменя́ть *impf.*, отмени́ть (-ню́, -нишь) *pf.*; уничтожа́ть *impf.*, уничто́жить *pf.* **abolition** [,æbə'lɪʃ(ə)n] *n.* отме́на; уничтоже́ние.

abominable [ə'bɒmɪnəb(ə)l] *adj.* отврати́тельный; (*bad*) ужа́сный; **the A~ Snowman** «сне́жный челове́к», йе́ти *m.indecl.* **abomi'nation** *n.* отвраще́ние; (*also object of ~*) ме́рзость.

aboriginal [,æbə'rɪdʒɪn(ə)l] *adj.* исконный, коренно́й; *n.* абориге́н, коренно́й жи́тель *m.* **aborigines** *n.* абориге́ны *m.pl.*, коренны́е жи́тели *m.pl.*

abort [ə'bɔːt] *v.i.* (*med.*) выки́дывать *impf.*, вы́кинуть *pf.*; *v.t.* (*terminate*) прекраща́ть *impf.*, прекрати́ть (-ащу́, -ати́шь) *pf.*; обрыва́ть *impf.*, оборва́ть (-ву́, -вёшь; оборва́л, -а́, -о) *pf.* **abortion** *n.* або́рт, вы́кидыш; **backstreet ~** подпо́льный або́рт. **abortive** *adj.* неуда́вшийся, безуспе́шный.

abound [ə'baʊnd] *v.i.* быть в большо́м коли́честве; **~ in** изоби́ловать *impf.+i.*; **~ with**

кишеть (-шит) *impf.+i.*

about [ə'baut] *adv. & prep.* óколо+*g.*; (*concerning*) о+*p.*, насчёт+*g.*; (*up and down*) по+*d.*; **be ~ to** собираться *impf.*, собраться (соберусь, -рёшся; собрался, -алась, -алóсь) *pf.+inf.*

above [ə'bʌv] *adv.* наверху́; (*higher up*) выше; **from ~** све́рху; свыше; *prep.* над+*i.*; (*more than*) свыше+*g.* **above-board** *adj.* чéстный (-ен, -тна́, -тно), прямóй (прям, -á, -о). **above-mentioned** *adj.* вышеупомя́нутый.

abrasion [ə'breɪʒ(ə)n] *n.* стирáние, истирáние; (*wound*) ссáдина. **abrasive** [ə'breɪsɪv] *adj.* абразивный; *n.* абразив, шлифовáльный материáл.

abreast [ə'brest] *adv.* (*in line*) в ряд, ря́дом; (*on a level*) в уровень.

abridge [ə'brɪdʒ] *v.t.* сокращáть *impf.*, сократить (-ащу́, -атишь) *pf.* **abridgement** *n.* сокраще́ние.

abroad [ə'brɔːd] *adv.* за границей, за границу; **from ~** из-за границы.

abrupt [ə'brʌpt] *adj.* (*steep*) обры́вистый, крутóй (крут, -á, -о, кру́ты); (*sudden*) внезáпный; (*manner*) ре́зкий (-зок, -зкá, -зко).

abscess ['æbsɪs] *n.* абсце́сс, нары́в, гнойни́к (-á).

abscond [əb'skɒnd] *v.i.* скрывáться *impf.*, скры́ться (-рóюсь, -рóешься) *pf.*; бежáть (бегу́, бежи́шь) *impf. & pf.*

absence ['æbs(ə)ns] *n.* отсу́тствие; (*temporary*) отлу́чка; (*from work*) неявка, невы́ход, на рабóту; **~ of mind** рассе́янность.

absent ['æbs(ə)nt; əb'sent] *adj.* отсу́тствующий; в отлу́чке; **be ~** отсу́тствовать *impf.*; *v.t.*: **~ o.s.** отлучáться *impf.*, отлучи́ться *pf.* **absentee** [ˌæbsən'tiː] *n.* отсу́тствующий *sb.*; (*habitual*) прогу́льщик, -ица. **absenteeism** *n.* прогу́л, абсентеи́зм. **absent-minded** *adj.* рассе́янный (-ян, -янна).

absolute ['æbsəˌluːt, -ˌljuːt] *adj.* абсолю́тный; (*complete*) пóлный (-лон, -лнá, пóлнó), соверше́нный (-нен, -нна); (*unrestricted*) безуслóвный, неограни́ченный (-ен, -енна); (*pure*) чи́стый (чист, -á, -о, чи́сты); **~ alcohol** чи́стый спирт (-а(у), *loc.* -е & -ý); **~ pitch** (*of sound*) абсолю́тная высотá; (*in person*) абсолю́тный слух; **~ proof** несомнéнное доказáтельство; **~ zero** абсолю́тный нуль (-ля́) *m.*

absolution [ˌæbsə'luːʃ(ə)n, -'ljuːʃ(ə)n] *n.* отпуще́ние грехóв. **absolve** [əb'zɒlv] *v.t.* прощáть *impf.*, прости́ть *pf.*

absorb [əb'sɔːb, -'zɔːb] *v.t.* (*take in*) впи́тывать *impf.*, впитáть *pf.*; (*swallow, also fig.*) поглощáть *impf.*, поглоти́ть (-ощу́, -óтишь) *pf.*; (*suck in*) всáсывать *impf.*, всосáть (-су́, -сёшь) *pf.*; (*tech.*) абсорби́ровать *impf. & pf.*; (*engross*) захвáтывать *impf.*, захвати́ть (-ачу́, -áтишь) *pf.* **absorbed** *adj.* поглощённый (-ён, -енá), захвáченный (-ен). **absorbent** *adj.* всáсывающий; поглощá-

ющий. **absorption** *n.* впи́тывание; всáсывание; поглоще́ние; абсóрбция; (*mental*) погружённость.

abstain [əb'steɪn] *v.i.* воздéрживаться *impf.*, воздержáться (-жу́сь, -жишься) *pf.* (**from** от+*g.*). **abstemious** [æb'stiːmɪəs] *adj.* воздéржанный (-ан, -анна). **abstention** [əb-'stenʃ(ə)n] *n.* воздержáние; (*from vote*) уклоне́ние, откáз, от голосовáния; (*person*) воздержáвшийся *sb.* **abstinence** ['æbstɪnəns] *n.* воздержáние; (*total ~*) трéзвость. **abstinent** *adj.* воздéржанный (-ан, -анна).

abstract ['æbstrækt; əb'strækt] *adj.* абстрáктный, отвлечённый (-ён, -ённа); *n.* конспéкт, реферáт; **in the ~** абстрáктно, отвлечённо; (*journal of*) **~(s)** реферати́вный журнáл; *v.t.* (*steal*) похищáть *impf.*, похи́тить (-и́щу, -и́тишь) *pf.*; крастъ (-аду́, -адёшь; -ал) *impf.*, у- *pf.*; (*make ~ of*) рефери́ровать *impf. & pf.*, конспекти́ровать *impf.*, за~, про~ *pf.* **ab'stracted** *adj.* погружённый (-ён, -енá) в мы́сли, рассе́янный (-ян, -янна). **ab'straction** *n.* абстрáкция, отвлечённость; (*abstractedness*) погружённость в мы́сли, рассе́янность; (*theft*) похище́ние, крáжа.

absurd [əb'sɜːd] *adj.* нелéпый, абсу́рдный. **absurdity** *n.* нелéпость, абсу́рд(ность).

abundance [ə'bʌnd(ə)ns] *n.* (из)оби́лие. **abundant** *adj.* (из)оби́льный.

abuse [ə'bjuːz; ə'bjuːs] *v.t.* (*revile*) ругáть *impf.*, вы́~, об~, от~ *pf.*; брани́ть *impf.*, вы́~ *pf.*; (*misuse*) злоупотребля́ть *impf.*, злоупотреби́ть *pf.*; *n.* (*curses*) брань, ру́гань, ругáтельства *nt.pl.*; (*misuse*) злоупотребле́ние. **abusive** [ə'bjuːsɪv] *adj.* оскорби́тельный, брáнный.

abut [ə'bʌt] *v.i.* примыкáть *impf.* (**on** к+*d.*). **abutment** *n.* (береговóй) устóй.

abysmal [ə'bɪzm(ə)l] *adj.* бездóнный (-нен, -нна); (*bad*) ужáсный. **abyss** [ə'bɪs] *n.* бéздна, прóпасть. **abyssal** *adj.* абиссáльный.

AC *abbr.* (*of alternating current*) перемéнный ток.

a/c [ə'kaunt] *n. abbr.* (*of account*) теку́щий счёт.

acacia [ə'keɪʃə] *n.* акáция.

academia [ˌækə'diːmɪə] *n.* академи́ческий мир; учёные круги́. **academic** [ˌækə'demɪk] *adj.* академи́ческий, университéтский; (*abstract*) академи́чный. **aca'demician** *n.* акадéмик. **academy** [ə'kædəmɪ] *n.* акадéмия; учéбное заведéние.

accede [æk'siːd] *v.i.* вступáть *impf.*, вступи́ть (-плю́, -пишь) *pf.* (**to** в, на+*a.*); (*assent*) соглашáться *impf.*, согласи́ться *pf.*

accelerate [ək'seləˌreɪt] *v.t. & i.* ускоря́ть(ся) *impf.*, ускóрить(ся) *pf.*; *v.i.* ускоря́ть *impf.*, ускóрить *pf.* ход. **accele'ration** *n.* ускорéние. **accelerator** *n.* ускори́тель *m.*; (*pedal*) акселерáтор.

accent ['æks(ə)nt, -sent; æk'sent] *n.* акце́нт; (*stress*) ударе́ние, знак ударе́ния; *v.t.* де́лать *impf.*, с~ *pf.* ударе́ние на+*a.*; ста́вить *impf.*, по~ *pf.* зна́ки ударе́ния над+*i.* **accentuate** [æk'sentjʊ,eɪt] *v.t.* подчёркивать *impf.*, подчеркну́ть *pf.* **accentu'ation** *n.* подчёркивание.

accept [ək'sept] *v.t.* принима́ть *impf.*, приня́ть (приму́, -мешь; при́нял, -á, -о) *pf.*; (*agree*) соглаша́ться *impf.*, согласи́ться *pf.* **acceptable** *adj.* прие́млемый; (*pleasing*) уго́дный. **acceptance** *n.* приня́тие. **accept'ation** *n.* при́нятое значе́ние. **accepted** *adj.* (обще)при́нятый.

access ['ækses] *n.* до́ступ; (*attack*) при́ступ. **ac'cessary** *n.* (*after the fact*) соуча́стник, -ица (преступле́ния по́сле собы́тия). **ac'cessible** *adj.* досту́пный. **ac'cession** *n.* вступле́ние, восше́ствие (на престо́л); (*acquisition*) приобрете́ние. **ac'cessories** *n.* принадле́жности *f.pl.* **ac'cessory** *adj.* доба́вочный, вспомога́тельный.

accidence ['æksɪd(ə)ns] *n.* морфоло́гия.

accident ['æksɪd(ə)nt] *n.* (*chance*) слу́чай, случа́йность; (*mishap*) несча́стный слу́чай; (*crash*) ава́рия, катастро́фа; **by** ~ случа́йно. **acci'dental** *adj.* случа́йный; *n.* (*mus.*) знак альтера́ции.

acclaim [ə'kleɪm] *v.t.* приве́тствовать *impf.* (*in past also pf.*); *n.* приве́тствие.

acclimatization [ə,klaɪmətaɪ'zeɪʃ(ə)n] *n.* акклиматиза́ция. **a'cclimatize** *v.t.* акклиматизи́ровать *impf.* & *pf.*

accommodate [ə'kɒmə,deɪt] *v.t.* помеща́ть *impf.*, помести́ть *pf.*; размеща́ть *impf.*, размести́ть *pf.* **accommodating** *adj.* услу́жливый. **accommo'dation** *n.* помеще́ние; (*lodging*) жильё; ~ **ladder** нару́жный трап.

accompaniment [ə'kʌmpənɪmənt] *n.* сопровожде́ние; (*mus.*) аккомпанеме́нт. **accompanist** *n.* аккомпаниа́тор. **accompany** *v.t.* сопровожда́ть *impf.*, сопроводи́ть *pf.*; (*mus.*) аккомпани́ровать *impf.*+*d.*

accomplice [ə'kʌmplɪs, -'kɒm-] *n.* соо́бщник, -ица, соуча́стник, -ица.

accomplish [ə'kʌmplɪʃ, ə'kɒm-] *v.t.* соверша́ть *impf.*, соверши́ть *pf.* **accomplished** *adj.* заверше́нный (-ён, -ена́); (*skilled*) превосхо́дный. **accomplishment** *n.* выполне́ние, заверше́ние; *pl.* досто́инства *nt.pl.*, соверше́нства *nt.pl.*

accord [ə'kɔːd] *n.* согла́сие; **of one's own** ~ доброво́льно; **of its own** ~ сам собо́й, сам по себе́; **with one** ~ единогла́сно, единоду́шно. **accordance** *n.*: **in** ~ **with** в соотве́тствии с+*i.*, согла́сно+*d.*, с+*i.* **according** *adv.*: ~ **to** по+*d.*, соотве́тственно+*d.*, с+*i.*; ~ **to him** по его́ слова́м. **accordingly** *adv.* соотве́тственно.

accordion [ə'kɔːdɪən] *n.* гармо́ника, аккордео́н.

account [ə'kaʊnt] *n.* счёт (-a(y); *pl.* -á); расчёт; отчёт; (*description, narrative*) опи-

са́ние, расска́з; **call to** ~ призыва́ть *impf.*, призва́ть (-зову́, -зовёшь; призва́л, -á, -о) *pf.* к отве́ту; **keep** ~ **of** вести́ (веду́, -дёшь; вёл, -á) *impf.* счёт+*d.*; **not on any** ~, **on no** ~ ни в ко́ем слу́чае; **on** ~ в счёт причита́ющейся су́ммы; **on** ~ **of** из-за+*g.*, по причи́не+*g.*; **settle** ~**s with** своди́ть (-ожу́, -о́дишь) *impf.*, свести́ (сведу́, -дёшь; свёл, -á) *pf.* счёты с+*i.*; **take into** ~ принима́ть *impf.*, приня́ть (приму́, -мешь; при́нял, -á) *pf.* во внима́ние, в расчёт; **turn to (good)** ~ обраща́ть *impf.*, обрати́ть (-ащу́, -ати́шь) *pf.* в свою́ по́льзу; *v.i.*: ~ **for** объясня́ть *impf.*, объясни́ть *pf.* **accountable** *adj.* отве́тственный (-ен, -енна), подотчётный. **accountancy** *n.* бухгалте́рия. **accountant** *n.* бухга́лтер.

accredited [ə'kredɪtɪd] *adj.* аккредито́ванный (-ан).

accretion [ə'kriːʃ(ə)n] *n.* прираще́ние, приро́ст.

accrue [ə'kruː] *v.i.* нараста́ть *impf.*, нарасти́ (-тёт; наро́с, -лá) *pf.*; ~**d interest** наро́сшие проце́нты *m.pl.*

accumulate [ə'kjuːmjʊ,leɪt] *v.t.* & *i.* нака́пливать(ся) *impf.*, копи́ть(ся) (-плю, -пит(ся)) *impf.*, на~ *pf.*; *v.i.* ска́пливаться *impf.*, скопи́ться (-ится) *pf.* **accumu'lation** *n.* накопле́ние, скопле́ние. **accumulator** *n.* аккумуля́тор.

accuracy ['ækjʊrəsɪ] *n.* то́чность, ме́ткость. **accurate** *adj.* то́чный (-чен, -чнá, -чно), ме́ткий (-ток, -ткá, -тко).

accursed [ə'kɜːsɪd, ə'kɜːst] *adj.* прокля́тый.

accusation [,ækjuː'zeɪʃ(ə)n] *n.* обвине́ние. **accusative** [ə'kjuːzətɪv] *adj.* (*n.*) вини́тельный (паде́ж (-á)). **accuse** [ə'kjuːz] *v.t.* обвиня́ть *impf.*, обвини́ть *pf.* (**of** в+*p.*); **the** ~**d** обвиня́емый *sb.*, подсуди́мый *sb.*

accustom [ə'kʌstəm] *v.t.* приуча́ть *impf.*, приучи́ть (-учу́, -чишь) *pf.* (**to** к+*d.*). **accustomed** *adj.* привы́чный, обы́чный; **be, get** ~ привыка́ть *impf.*, привы́кнуть (-к) *pf.* (**to** к+*d.*).

ace [eɪs] *n.* (*cards*) туз (-á); (*expert*) ас.

acetic [ə'siːtɪk] *adj.* у́ксусный. **acetylene** [ə'setɪ,liːn] *n.* ацетиле́н; *adj.* ацетиле́новый.

ache [eɪk] *n.* боль; *v.i.* боле́ть (-ли́т) *impf.*

achieve [ə'tʃiːv] *v.t.* достига́ть *impf.*, дости́чь & дости́гнуть (-и́гну, -и́гнешь; -и́г) *pf.*+*g.*; добива́ться *impf.*, доби́ться (-бью́сь, -бьёшься) *pf.*+*g.* **achievement** *n.* достиже́ние.

acid ['æsɪd] *n.* кислота́; *adj.* ки́слый (-сел, -слá, -сло); ~ **rain** кисло́тные дожди́ (*m.pl.*). **a'cidity** *n.* кислота́, кисло́тность.

acknowledge [ək'nɒlɪdʒ] *v.t.* (*admit*) признава́ть (-наю́, -наёшь) *impf.*, призна́ть *pf.*; сознава́ть (-наю́, -наёшь) *impf.*, созна́ть *pf.*; (*express gratitude*) благодари́ть *impf.*, по~ *pf.* за+*a.*; (~ *receipt of*) подтвержда́ть *impf.*, подтверди́ть *pf.* получе́ние+*g.* **acknowledgement** *n.* призна́ние; благода́рность;

подтвержде́ние; **in ~ of** в знак благода́рности за+a.
acme ['ækmɪ] n. верши́на, верх (pl. -и́), вы́сшая то́чка.
acne ['ækni] n. прыщи́ m.pl.
acorn ['eɪkɔːn] n. жёлудь (pl. -ди, -де́й) m.
acoustic [ə'kuːstɪk] adj. (of sound) акусти́ческий, звуково́й; (of hearing) слухово́й; (sound-absorbing) звукопоглоща́ющий. **acoustics** n. аку́стика.
acquaint [ə'kweɪnt] v.t. знако́мить impf., по~ pf.; ознакомля́ть impf., ознако́мить pf. **acquaintance** n. знако́мство; (person) знако́мый sb. **acquainted** adj. знако́мый.
acquiesce [ˌækwɪ'es] v.i. соглаша́ться impf., согласи́ться pf. **acquiescence** n. (молчали́вое, неохо́тное) согла́сие. **acquiescent** adj. (молчали́во) согласа́ющийся.
acquire [ə'kwaɪə(r)] v.t. приобрета́ть impf., приобрести́ (-ету́, -ете́шь; -ёл, -ела́) pf.; (habit etc.) усва́ивать impf., усво́ить pf. **acquired** adj. приобретённый (-ён, -ена́); ~ **taste** благоприобретённый вкус. **acquisition** [ˌækwɪ'zɪʃ(ə)n] n. приобрете́ние. **acquisitive** [ə'kwɪzɪtɪv] adj. жа́дный (-ден, -дна́, -дно).
acquit [ə'kwɪt] v.t. опра́вдывать impf., оправда́ть pf.; ~ **o.s.** вести́ (веду́, -дёшь; вёл, -а́) impf. себя́. **acquittal** n. оправда́ние.
acre ['eɪkə(r)] n. акр; pl. зе́мли (-ме́ль, -мля́м) f.pl., поме́стье. **acreage** ['eɪkərɪdʒ] n. пло́щадь в а́крах.
acrid ['ækrɪd] adj. о́стрый (остр & остёр, остра́, о́стро); е́дкий (е́док, едка́, е́дко).
acrimonious [ˌækrɪ'məʊnɪəs] adj. язви́тельный, жёлчный.
acrobat ['ækrəˌbæt] n. акроба́т. **acro'batic** adj. акробати́ческий. **acro'batics** n. акроба́тика.
acronym ['ækrənɪm] n. акро́ним, аббревиату́ра.
across [ə'krɒs] adv. & prep. че́рез+a.; попере́к (+g.); (to, on, other side) на, по, ту сто́рону (+g.), на той стороне́ (+g.); (crosswise) крест-на́крест. **across-the-board** adj. всео́бщий, всеобъе́млющий, поголо́вный.
acrylic [ə'krɪlɪk] n. акри́л; adj. акри́ловый.
act [ækt] n. (deed) акт, посту́пок (-пка); (law) зако́н; (of play) де́йствие; **A~s (of the Apostles)** Дея́ния nt.pl. апо́столов; v.i. поступа́ть impf., поступи́ть (-плю́, -пишь) pf.; де́йствовать impf., по~ pf.; v.t. игра́ть impf., сыгра́ть pf. **acting** n. игра́ на сце́не; adj. исполня́ющий обя́занности+g. **action** ['ækʃ(ə)n] n. де́йствие, посту́пок (-пка); (leg.) иск, (суде́бный) проце́сс; (battle) бой (loc. бою́). **active** adj. акти́вный, де́ятельный, энерги́чный; ~ **service** действи́тельная слу́жба; ~ **voice** действи́тельный зало́г. **ac'tivity** n. де́ятельность; акти́вность; pl. де́ятельность. **actor** ['æktə(r)] n. актёр. **actress** n. актри́са.
actual ['æktʃʊəl, 'æktjʊəl] adj. действи́тель-

ный, факти́ческий. **actuality** [ˌæktʃʊ'ælɪtɪ, ˌæktjʊ-] n. действи́тельность. **actually** adv. на са́мом де́ле, факти́чески.
actuate ['æktʃʊˌeɪt] v.t. приводи́ть (-ожу́, -о́дишь) impf., привести́ (приведу́, -дёшь; привёл, -а́) pf. в движе́ние.
acuity [ə'kjuːɪtɪ] n. острота́.
acupuncture ['ækjuːˌpʌŋktʃə(r)] n. акупункту́ра, иглоука́лывание.
acute [ə'kjuːt] adj. о́стрый (остр & остёр, остра́, о́стро); (penetrating) проница́тельный; ~ **accent** аку́т.
AD abbr. (of **Anno Domini**) н.э., (на́шей э́ры).
adamant ['ædəmənt] adj. непрекло́нный (-нен, -нна).
adapt [ə'dæpt] v.t. приспособля́ть impf., приспосо́бить pf.; (for stage etc.) инсцени́ровать impf. & pf.; ~ **o.s.** приспособля́ться impf., приспосо́биться pf.; применя́ться impf., примени́ться (-ню́сь, -нишься) pf. **adaptable** adj. приспособля́ющийся. **adap'tation** n. приспособле́ние, адапта́ция, переде́лка; инсцениро́вка.
add [æd] v.t. прибавля́ть impf., приба́вить pf.; добавля́ть impf., доба́вить pf.; ~ **together** скла́дывать impf., сложи́ть (-жу́, -жишь) pf.; ~ **up to** своди́ться (-ится) impf., свести́сь (сведётся; свёлся, -лась) pf. к+d. **addenda** [ə'dendə] n. дополне́ния nt.pl., приложе́ния nt.pl.
adder ['ædə(r)] n. гадю́ка.
addict ['ædɪkt] n. (drug ~) наркома́н, ~ка. **a'ddicted** adj.: **be ~ to** быть рабо́м+g.; ~ **to drink** предаю́щийся пья́нству. **a'ddiction** n. па́губная привы́чка; (to drugs) наркома́ния.
addition [ə'dɪʃ(ə)n] n. прибавле́ние, добавле́ние; дополне́ние; (math.) сложе́ние; **in ~** вдоба́вок, кро́ме того́, к тому́ же. **additional** adj. доба́вочный, дополни́тельный. **'additive** n. доба́вка.
address [ə'dres] n. а́дрес (pl. -а́); (speech) обраще́ние, речь; v.t. адресова́ть impf. & pf.; (apply) обраща́ться impf., обрати́ться (-ащу́сь, -ати́шься) pf. к+d.; ~ **a meeting** выступа́ть impf., вы́ступить pf. с ре́чью на собра́нии. **addre'ssee** n. адреса́т.
adept ['ædept; ə'dept] n. знато́к (-а́), экспе́рт; adj. све́дущий.
adequacy ['ædɪkwəsɪ] n. адеква́тность, доста́точность. **adequate** adj. адеква́тный, доста́точный.
adhere [əd'hɪə(r)] v.i. прилипа́ть impf., прили́пнуть (-нет; прили́п) pf. (to к+d.); (fig.) приде́рживаться impf.+g. **adherence** n. приве́рженность, ве́рность. **adherent** n. приве́рженец (-нца); после́дователь m., ~ница. **adhesion** [əd'hiːʒ(ə)n] n. прилипа́ние, скле́ивание. **adhesive** [əd'hiːsɪv] adj. ли́пкий (-пок, -пка́, -пко), кле́йкий; ~ **tape** скотч; n. клей (-е́я(ю), loc. -ею́; pl. -еи́).
adjacent [ə'dʒeɪs(ə)nt] adj. сме́жный, сосе́дний.

adjectival [ˌædʒɪk'taɪv(ə)l] *adj.* адъекти́вный. **'adjective** *n.* (и́мя *nt.*) прилага́тельное *sb.*

adjoin [ə'dʒɔɪn] *v.t.* прилега́ть *impf.* к+*d.*

adjourn [ə'dʒɜːn] *v.t.* откла́дывать *impf.*, отложи́ть (-жу́, -жишь) *pf.*; *v.i.* объявля́ть *impf.*, объяви́ть (-влю́, -вишь) *pf.* переры́в; (*to another place*) переходи́ть (-ожу́, -о́дишь) *impf.*, перейти́ (перейду́, -дёшь; перешёл, -шла́) *pf.*

adjudicate [ə'dʒuːdɪˌkeɪt] *v.i.* выноси́ть (-ошу́, -о́сишь) *impf.*, вы́нести (-су, -сешь; -с) *pf.* (суде́бное, арбитра́жное) реше́ние; разреша́ть *impf.*, разреши́ть *pf.* спор; рассма́тривать *impf.*, рассмотре́ть (-рю́, -ришь) *pf.* де́ло.

adjust [ə'dʒʌst] *v.t. & i.* приспособля́ть(ся) *impf.*, приспосо́бить(ся) *pf.*; *v.t.* пригоня́ть *impf.*, пригна́ть (-гоню́, -го́нишь; пригна́л, -á, -о) *pf.*; (*regulate*) регули́ровать *impf.*, от~ *pf.* **adjustable** *adj.* регули́руемый; ~ **spanner** разводно́й ключ (-á). **adjustment** *n.* регули́рование, регулиро́вка, подго́нка.

adjutant [ˈædʒʊt(ə)nt] *n.* адъюта́нт.

administer [əd'mɪnɪstə(r)] *v.t.* (*manage*) управля́ть *impf.*+*i.*; (*dispense*) отправля́ть *impf.*; (*give*) дава́ть (даю́, даёшь) *impf.*, дать (дам, дашь, даст, дади́м; дал, -á, да́ло́, -и) *pf.* **admini'stration** *n.* администра́ция, управле́ние; (*government*) прави́тельство. **ad'ministrative** *adj.* администрати́вный, управле́нческий. **ad'ministrator** *n.* администра́тор.

admirable [ˈædmərəb(ə)l] *adj.* похва́льный; (*excellent*) замеча́тельный.

admiral [ˈædmər(ə)l] *n.* адмира́л. **Admiralty** *n.* адмиралте́йство.

admiration [ˌædmɪ'reɪʃ(ə)n] *n.* любова́ние, восхище́ние. **admire** [əd'maɪə(r)] *v.t.* любова́ться *impf.*, по~ *pf.*+*i.*, на+*a.*; восхища́ться *impf.*, восхити́ться (-ищу́сь, -и́тишься) *pf.*+*i.* **admirer** *n.* покло́нник.

admissible [əd'mɪsɪb(ə)l] *adj.* допусти́мый, прие́млемый. **admission** *n.* до́ступ, впуск, вход; (*confession*) призна́ние. **admit** *v.t.* впуска́ть *impf.*, впусти́ть (-ущу́, -у́стишь) *pf.*; (*allow*) допуска́ть *impf.*, допусти́ть (-ущу́, -у́стишь) *pf.*; (*accept*) принима́ть *impf.*, приня́ть (приму́, -мешь; при́нял, -á, -о) *pf.*; (*confess*) признава́ть (-наю́, -наёшь) *impf.*, призна́ть *pf.* **admittance** *n.* до́ступ. **admittedly** *adv.* призна́ться.

admixture [æd'mɪkstʃə(r)] *n.* при́месь.

adolescence [ˌædə'les(ə)ns] *n.* ю́ность. **adolescent** *adj.* подро́стковый; *n.* подро́сток (-тка).

adopt [ə'dɒpt] *v.t.* (*child*) усыновля́ть *impf.*, усынови́ть *pf.*; (*thing*) усва́ивать *impf.*, усво́ить *pf.*; (*approve*) принима́ть *impf.*, приня́ть (приму́, -мешь; при́нял, -á, -о) *pf.* **adopted, adoptive** *adj.* приёмный. **adoption** *n.* усыновле́ние; приня́тие.

adorable [ə'dɔːrəb(ə)l] *adj.* восхити́тельный, преле́стный. **ado'ration** *n.* обожа́ние. **adore** *v.t.* обожа́ть *impf.* **adorer** *n.* обожа́тель *m.*

adorn [ə'dɔːn] *v.t.* украша́ть *impf.*, укра́сить *pf.* **adornment** *n.* украше́ние.

adroit [ə'drɔɪt] *adj.* ло́вкий (-вок, -вка́, -вко, ло́вки́).

adult [ə'dʌlt, ˈædʌlt] *adj. & n.* взро́слый (*sb.*).

adulterate [ə'dʌltəˌreɪt] *v.t.* фальсифици́ровать *impf. & pf.* **adulte'ration** *n.* фальсифика́ция.

adultery [ə'dʌltərɪ] *n.* адюльте́р, внебра́чная связь.

advance [əd'vɑːns] *n.* (*going forward*) продвиже́ние (вперёд); (*progress*) прогре́сс; (*mil.*) наступле́ние; (*rise*) повыше́ние; (*of pay etc.*) ава́нс; (*loan*) ссу́да; **in** ~ зара́нее, вперёд; ава́нсом; **make** ~**s to** уха́живать *impf.* за+*i.*; ~ **information** предвари́тельные све́дения *nt.pl.*; ~ **copy** сигна́льный экземпля́р; *v.i.* (*go forward*) продвига́ться *impf.*, продви́нуться *pf.* вперёд; идти́ (иду́, идёшь; шёл, шла) *impf.* вперёд; (*mil.*) наступа́ть *impf.*, *v.t.* продвига́ть *impf.*, продви́нуть *pf.*; (*put forward*) выдвига́ть *impf.*, вы́двинуть *pf.*; (*promote*) повыша́ть *impf.*, повы́сить *pf.* (*pay in* ~) выпла́чивать *impf.*, вы́платить *pf.* ава́нсом. **advanced** *adj.* передово́й, продви́нутый; ~ **in years** престаре́лый; ~ **studies** вы́сший курс. **advancement** *n.* продвиже́ние, повыше́ние.

advantage [əd'vɑːntɪdʒ] *n.* преиму́щество; (*profit*) вы́года, по́льза; **take** ~ **of** по́льзоваться *impf.*, вос~ *pf.*+*i.*; **to** ~ вы́годно, хорошо́; в вы́годном све́те; **to the best** ~ в са́мом вы́годном све́те. **advan'tageous** *adj.* вы́годный.

adventure [əd'ventʃə(r)] *n.* приключе́ние; ~ **story** приключе́нческий рома́н. **adventurer** *n.* авантюри́ст. **adventuress** *n.* авантюри́стка. **adventurism**. *n.* авантюри́зм. **ad'venturist** *n.* авантюри́ст. **adventurous** *adj.* (*rash*) риско́ванный (-ан, -анна); (*enterprising*) предприи́мчивый.

adverb [ˈædvɜːb] *n.* наре́чие. **adverbial** *adj.* наре́чный, обстоя́тельственный.

adversary [ˈædvəsərɪ] *n.* проти́вник. **adverse** *adj.* неблагоприя́тный; ~ **winds** проти́вные ве́тры *m.pl.* **ad'versity** *n.* несча́стье.

advert [ˈædvɜːt] *abbr.* объявле́ние, рекла́ма. **advertise** *v.t.* реклами́ровать *impf. & pf.*; афиши́ровать *impf. & pf.*; *v.i.* помеща́ть *impf.*, помести́ть *pf.*, дава́ть (даю́, даёшь) *impf.*, дать (дам, дашь, даст, дади́м; дал, -á, да́ло́, -и) *pf.* объявле́ние (**for** о+*p.*). **ad'vertisement** *n.* объявле́ние, рекла́ма.

advice [əd'vaɪs] *n.* сове́т; (*specialist*) консульта́ция; (*notice*) ави́зо *nt.indecl.*; **a piece, word of** ~ сове́т. **advisability** [əd,vaɪzə'bɪlɪtɪ] *n.* жела́тельность. **advisable** *adj.* рекоменду́емый, жела́тельный. **advise** [əd'vaɪz] *v.t.* сове́товать *impf.*, по~ *pf.*+*d. & inf.*; реко мендова́ть *impf. & pf.*, по~ *pf.*+*a. & inf.*; (*notify*) уведомля́ть *impf.*, уве́домить *pf.* ~**dly** *adv.* обду́манно, наме́ренно. **adviser** *n.* сове́тник, -ица; консульта́нт; **legal** ~

юрисконсульт; **medical** ~ врач (-á). **advisory** *adj.* совещáтельный; консультатúвный.

advocacy ['ædvəkəsɪ] *n.* (*profession*) адвокатýра; (*support*) пропагáнда. **advocate** *n.* адвокáт; сторóнник; *v.t.* пропагандúровать *impf.*; выступáть *impf.*, выступить *pf.* в защúту+g.

aerial ['eərɪəl] *n.* антéнна; *adj.* воздýшный.

aero- ['eərəʊ] *in comb.* авиа…, аэро… . **aerobicist** [eə'rəʊbɪsɪst] *n.* аэробúст, ~ка. **ae'robics** *n.* аэрóбика, аэрóбная гимнáстика. **aerodrome** ['eərə,drəʊm] *n.* аэродрóм. **aerody'namics** *n.* аэродинáмика. **aero-engine** *n.* авиациóнный двúгатель *m.* **aero'nautical** *adj.* авиациóнный. **aeroplane** *n.* самолёт. **aerosol** ['eərə,sɒl] *n.* аэрозóль *m.* **aerospace** *adj.* авиациóнно-космúческий.

aesthetic [iːs'θetɪk] *adj.* эстетúческий.

affable ['æfəb(ə)l] *adj.* привéтливый. **affa'bility** *n.* привéтливость.

affair [ə'feə(r)] *n.* (*business*) дéло (*pl.* -лá); (*love*) ромáн.

affect [ə'fekt] *v.t.* дéйствовать *impf.*, по~ *pf.* на+a.; влиять *impf.*, по~ *pf.* на+a.; (*touch*) трóгать *impf.*, трóнуть *pf.*; затрáгивать *impf.*, затрóнуть *pf.*; (*concern*) касáться *impf.*+g.; **it doesn't ~ me** это меня не касáется. **affec'tation** *n.* притвóрство, жемáнство. **affected** *adj.* притвóрный, жемáнный (-нен, -нна). **affecting** *adj.* трóгательный. **affection** *n.* привязанность, любóвь (-бвú, *i.* -бóвью); (*malady*) болéзнь. **affectionate** *adj.* любящий, нéжный (-жен, -жнá, -жно, нéжны), лáсковый.

affiliate [ə'fɪlɪ,eɪt] *v.t.* &*i.* присоединять(ся) *impf.*, присоединúть(ся) *pf.* как филиáл, отделéние. **affiliated** *adj.* филиáльный. **affili'ation** *n.* присоединéние как филиáл; (*of child*) установлéние отцóвства+g.

affinity [ə'fɪnɪtɪ] *n.* (*relationship*) родствó; (*resemblance*) схóдство, блúзость; (*attraction*) увлечéние.

affirm [ə'fɜːm] *v.t.* утверждáть *impf.*; *v.i.* торжéственно заявлять *impf.*, заявúть (-влю, -вишь) *pf.* **affir'mation** *n.* заявлéние. **affirmative** *adj.* утвердúтельный.

affix [ə'fɪks; 'æfɪks] *v.t.* прикреплять *impf.*, прикрепúть *pf.*; *n.* áффикс.

afflict [ə'flɪkt] *v.t.* огорчáть *impf.*, огорчúть *pf.*; причинять *impf.*, причинúть *pf.* страдáния+d. **affliction** *n.* огорчéние.

affluence ['æfluəns] *n.* богáтство. **affluent** *adj.* богáтый; ~ **society** богатéющее óбщество.

afford [ə'fɔːd] *v.t.* позволять *impf.*, позвóлить *pf.* себé; быть в состоянии+*inf.*; (*supply*) предоставлять *impf.*, предостáвить *pf.*; доставлять *impf.*, достáвить *pf.*; **I can't ~ it** мне это не по срéдствам, не по кармáну.

afforest [ə'fɒrɪst, æ-] *v.t.* засáживать *impf.*, засадúть (-ажý, -áдишь) *pf.* лéсом; обле-

сúть *pf.* **affore'station** *n.* лесонасаждéние, облесéние.

affront [ə'frʌnt] *n.* (публúчное) оскорблéние, обúда; *v.t.* оскорблять *impf.*, оскорбúть *pf.*

Afghan (hound) ['æfgæn] *n.* афгáнская борзáя.

afoot [ə'fʊt] *adv.*: **set ~** пускáть *impf.*, пустúть (пущý, пýстишь) *pf.* в ход.

aforesaid [ə'fɔːsed] *adj.* вышеупомянутый.

aforethought [ə'fɔːθɔːt] *adj.* преднамéренный (-ен, -енна).

afraid [ə'freɪd] *pred.*: **be ~** боáться (боюсь, боúшься) *impf.*

afresh [ə'freʃ] *adv.* снóва.

Africa ['æfrɪkə] *n.* Áфрика. **African** *adj.* африкáнский; *n.* африкáнец (-нца), -нка.

Afro-American [,æfrəʊ-] *adj.* афроамерикáнский.

after ['ɑːftə(r)] *adv.* впослéдствии; пóсле, потóм; *prep.* пóсле+g., спустя+a., i.; ~ **all** в концé концóв; **day ~ day** день за днём; **long ~ midnight** далекó за пóлночь.

after- ['ɑːftə(r)] *in comb.* пóсле… . **afterbirth** *n.* послéд. **after-dinner** *adj.* послеобéденный. **afterlife** *n.* загрóбная жизнь. **aftermath** ['ɑːftə,mæθ, -,mɑːθ] *n.* послéдствия *nt.pl.* **afternoon** *n.* вторáя половúна дня; **in the ~** днём, пополýдни. **aftershock** *n.* повтóрные толчкú *m.pl.* **afterthought** *n.* запоздáлая мысль.

afterwards ['ɑːftəwədz] *adv.* впослéдствии; потóм, пóзже.

again [ə'geɪn, ə'gen] *adv.* опять; (*once more*) ещё раз; (*anew*) снóва.

against [ə'geɪnst, ə'genst] *prep.* (*opposed to*) прóтив+g.; (~ *background of*) на фóне+g.

agate ['ægət] *n.* агáт.

age [eɪdʒ] *n.* вóзраст; (*period*) век (на векý; *pl.* -á), эпóха; *v.t.* стáрить *impf.*, со~ *pf.*; *v.i.* старéть *impf.*, по~ *pf.*; стáриться *impf.*, со~ *pf.* **aged** ['eɪdʒɪd] *adj.* стáрый (стар, -á, стáро), престарéлый; **the ~** пожилые люди *m.pl.*, престарéлые *m.pl.* **ageism** *n.* дискриминáция по вóзрасту. **ageist** *n.* сторóнник дискриминáции по вóзрасту.

agency ['eɪdʒənsɪ] *n.* агéнтство; (*mediation*) посрéдничество; **by, through the ~ of** посрéдством, при пóмощи, при содéйствии, +g. **agenda** [ə'dʒendə] *n.* повéстка дня. **agent** *n.* агéнт.

agglomerate [ə'glɒmərət] *n.* агломерáт. **agglome'ration** *n.* скоплéние, агломерáция.

agglutination [ə,gluːtɪ'neɪʃ(ə)n] *n.* агглютинáция. **a'gglutinative** *adj.* агглютинатúвный.

aggravate ['ægrə,veɪt] *v.t.* ухудшáть *impf.*, ухýдшить *pf.*; (*annoy*) раздражáть *impf.*, раздражúть *pf.* **aggra'vation** *n.* ухудшéние; раздражéние.

aggregate ['ægrɪgət] *adj.* совокýпный; *n.* совокýпность, агрегáт; **in the ~** в совокýпности, в цéлом.

aggression [ə'greʃ(ə)n] *n.* агрéссия; агрессúвность. **aggressive** *adj.* агрессúвный.

aggressor *n.* агре́ссор.

aggrieved [ə'gri:vd] *adj.* оби́женный (-ен).

aghast [ə'ga:st] *pred.* поражён (-á) у́жасом; в у́жасе (**at** от+g.).

agile ['ædʒaɪl] *adj.* прово́рный. **agility** [ə'dʒɪlɪtɪ] *n.* прово́рство.

agitate ['ædʒɪteɪt] *v.t.* волнова́ть *impf.*, вз~ *pf.*; *v.i.* агити́ровать *impf.* **agi'tation** *n.* волне́ние; агита́ция.

agnostic [æg'nɒstɪk] *n.* агно́стик; *adj.* агности́ческий. **agnosticism** *n.* агностици́зм.

ago [ə'gəʊ] *adv.* (тому́) наза́д; **long** ~ давно́.

agonizing ['æɡə,naɪzɪŋ] *adj.* мучи́тельный.

agony *n.* мучи́тельная боль; (*of death*) аго́ния.

agrarian [ə'greərɪən] *adj.* агра́рный, земе́льный.

agree [ə'gri:] *v.i.* соглаша́ться *impf.*, согласи́ться *pf.*; усла́вливаться *impf.*, усло́виться *pf.* (**on** o+*p.*); (*reach agreement*) догова́риваться *impf.*, договори́ться *pf.*; (*gram.*) согласова́ться *impf.* & *pf.* **agreeable** *adj.* согла́сный; (*pleasing*) прия́тный. **agreed** *adj.* согласо́ванный (-ан), усло́вленный (-ен). **agreement** *n.* согла́сие, соглаше́ние, догово́р; (*gram.*) согласова́ние; **in** ~ согла́сен (-сна).

agricultural [,ægrɪ'kʌltʃər(ə)l] *adj.* сельскохозя́йственный, земледе́льческий. **'agriculture** *n.* се́льское хозя́йство, земледе́лие; (*science*) агроно́мия.

aground [ə'graʊnd] *pred.* на мели́; *adv.*: **run** ~ сади́ться *impf.*, сесть (ся́ду, -дешь; сел) *pf.* на мель.

ahead [ə'hed] *adv.* (*forward*) вперёд; (*in front*) впереди́; ~ **of time** досро́чно.

aid [eɪd] *v.t.* помога́ть *impf.*, помо́чь (-огу́, -о́жешь; -о́г, -огла́) *pf.*+*d.*; *n.* по́мощь; (*teaching*) посо́бие; ~ **agency** организа́ция по оказа́нию по́мощи; **in** ~ **of** в по́льзу+*g.*; **come to the** ~ **of** прийти́ (приду́, -дёшь; пришёл, -шла́) *pf.* на по́мощь+*d.*

aide-de-camp [,eɪd də 'kã] *n.* адъюта́нт (генера́ла).

AIDS [eɪdz] *n. abbr.* (*of acquired immune deficiency syndrome*) СПИД, (синдро́м приобретённого имму́нного дефици́та).

aileron ['eɪlə,rɒn] *n.* элеро́н.

ailing ['eɪlɪŋ] *adj.* (*ill*) больно́й (-лен, -льна́); (*sickly*) хи́лый (хил, -а́, -о).

ailment ['eɪlmənt] *n.* неду́г.

aim [eɪm] *n.* (*aiming*) прице́л; (*purpose*) цель; наме́рение; *v.i.* це́литься *impf.*, на~ *pf.* (**at** в+*a.*); прице́ливаться *impf.*, прице́литься *pf.* (**at** в+*a.*); (*also fig.*) ме́тить *impf.*, на~ *pf.* (**at** в+*a.*); *v.t.* наце́ливать *impf.*, наце́лить *pf.*; (*also fig.*) наводи́ть (-ожу́, -о́дишь) *impf.*, навести́ (наведу́, наведёшь; навёл, -á) *pf.* **aimless** *adj.* бесце́льный.

air [eə(r)] *n.* во́здух; (*look*) вид; (*mus.*) пе́сня (*g.pl.* -сен), мело́дия; by ~ **crash** авиаката́строфа; ~ **force** ВВС (вое́нно-возду́шные си́лы) *f.pl.*; ~ **hostess** стюарде́сса; ~ **piracy** возду́шный бандити́зм; **by** ~ самолётом; **change of** ~ переме́на обстано́вки; **on the** ~ по ра́дио; *attr.* возду́шный; *v.t.* (*ventilate*) прове́тривать *impf.*, прове́трить *pf.*; (*make known*) выставля́ть *impf.*, вы́ставить *pf.* напока́з; заявля́ть *impf.*, заяви́ть (-влю́, -вишь) *pf.* во всеуслы́шание.

air- [eə(r)] *in comb.* **airborne** ['eəbɔ:n] *adj.* (*mil.*) возду́шно-деса́нтный; *pred.* в во́здухе. **air-conditioner** *n.* кондиционе́р (во́здуха). **air-conditioning** *n.* кондициони́рование во́здуха. **air-cooled** *adj.* с возду́шным охлажде́нием. **aircraft** *n.* самолёт; (*collect.*) самолёты *m.pl.*, авиа́ция. **aircraft-carrier** *n.* авиано́сец (-сца).

airer ['eərə(r)] *n.* (напо́льная) суши́лка.

airless ['eəlɪs] *adj.* (*stuffy*) ду́шный (-шен, -шна́, -шно); безвозду́шный. **airlift** *n.* возду́шные перево́зки *f.pl.*; *v.t.* перевози́ть (-ожу́, -о́зишь) *impf.*, перевезти́ (перевезу́, -зёшь; перевёз, -ла́) *pf.* по во́здуху. **airline** *n.* авиали́ния. **airlock** *n.* возду́шная про́бка. **airmail** *n.* а́виа(по́чта). **airman** *n.* лётчик. **airport** *n.* аэропо́рт (*loc.* -ý). **airship** *n.* дирижа́бль *m.* **airspeed** *n.* возду́шная ско́рость. **airstrip** *n.* лётная полоса́ (*a.* полосу́; *pl.* -осы, -óс, -осáм). **airtight** *adj.* непроница́емый для во́здуха. **airworthy** *adj.* приго́дный к полёту.

aisle [aɪl] *n.* боково́й неф; (*passage*) прохо́д.

alabaster ['ælə,ba:stə(r), -,bæstə(r), ,ælə'b-] *n.* алеба́стр.

alacrity [ə'lækrɪtɪ] *n.* жи́вость; (*readiness*) гото́вность.

alarm [ə'la:m] *n.* трево́га; *v.t.* трево́жить *impf.*, вс~ *pf.*; ~ **clock** буди́льник. **alarming** *adj.* трево́жный. **alarmist** *n.* панике́р; *adj.* панике́рский.

alas [ə'læs, ə'la:s] *int.* увы́!

Alaska [ə'læskə] *n.* Аля́ска.

albatross ['ælbə,trɒs] *n.* альбатро́с.

albino [æl'bi:nəʊ] *n.* альбино́с.

album ['ælbəm] *n.* альбо́м.

alchemist ['ælkəmɪst] *n.* алхи́мик. **alchemy** *n.* алхи́мия.

alcohol ['ælkə,hɒl] *n.* алкого́ль *m.*, спирт (-а(у), *loc.* -е & -ý); спиртны́е напи́тки *m.pl.* **alco'holic** *adj.* алкаго́льский, спиртно́й; *n.* алкаго́лик, -и́чка.

alcove ['ælkəʊv] *n.* алько́в, ни́ша.

alder ['ɔːldə(r)] *n.* ольха́.

alderman ['ɔːldəmən] *n.* о́лдермен.

ale [eɪl] *n.* пи́во, эль *m.*

alert [ə'lɜːt] *adj.* бди́тельный, живо́й (жив, -á, -о); *pred.* на стороже́; *n.* трево́га; *v.t.* предупрежда́ть *impf.*, предупреди́ть *pf.*

algebra ['ældʒɪbrə] *n.* а́лгебра. **algebraic** [,ældʒɪ'breɪɪk] *adj.* алгебраи́ческий. **algorithm** ['ælɡə,rɪð(ə)m] *n.* алгори́тм.

alias ['eɪlɪəs] *adv.* ина́че (называ́емый); *n.* кли́чка, вы́мышленное и́мя *nt.*

alibi ['ælɪ,baɪ] *n.* а́либи *nt.indecl.*

alien ['eɪlɪən] *n.* иностра́нец (-нца), -нка;

(*extraterrestrial*) инопланетя́нин (*pl.* -я́не, -я́н); *adj.* иностра́нный, чужо́й, чу́ждый (чужд, -а́, -о); (*extraterrestrial*) внеземно́й.

alienate *v.t.* отчужда́ть *impf.*; отдаля́ть *impf.*, отдали́ть *pf.* **alie'nation** *n.* отчужде́ние, охлажде́ние; (*insanity*) умопомеша́тельство.

alight¹ [ə'laɪt] *v.i.* сходи́ть (-ожу́, -о́дишь) *impf.*, сойти́ (сойду́, -дёшь; сошёл, -шла́) *pf.*; (*come down*) сади́ться *impf.*, сесть (ся́ду, -дешь; сел) *pf.*; (*dismount*) спе́шиваться *impf.*, спе́шиться *pf.*

alight² [ə'laɪt] *pred.* зажжён (-á); be ~ горе́ть (-ри́т) *impf.*; (*shine*) сия́ть *impf.*

align [ə'laɪn] *v.t.* располага́ть *impf.*, расположи́ть (-жу́, -жишь) *pf.* по одно́й ли́нии; ста́вить *impf.*, по~ *pf.* в ряд. **alignment** *n.* выра́внивание, равне́ние.

alike [ə'laɪk] *pred.* похо́ж, одина́ков; *adv.* одина́ково, то́чно так же.

alimentary [ˌælɪ'mentərɪ] *adj.* пищево́й; ~ **canal** пищевари́тельный кана́л.

alimony ['ælɪmənɪ] *n.* алиме́нты *m.pl.*

alive [ə'laɪv] *pred.* жив (-á, -о), в живы́х; (*brisk*) бодр (-á, -о); ~ **with** кише́ащий+*i.*

alkali ['ælkəˌlaɪ] *n.* щёлочь (*pl.* -чи, -чей). **alkaline** *adj.* щелочно́й.

all [ɔːl] *adj.* весь (вся, всё; все); вся́кий; *n.* всё, все *pl.*; *adv.* всеце́ло, целико́м, по́лностью; совсе́м, соверше́нно; ~ **along** всё вре́мя; ~ **but** почти́, едва́ не; ~ **in** кра́йне утомлён (-á); ~ **over** повсю́ду; ~ **right** хорошо́, ла́дно; (*satisfactory*) так себе́; непло́х (-á, -о); ~ **the same** всё равно́; **in** ~ всего́; **love** ~ по нулю́; **two, etc.,** ~ по́ два и т.д.; **not at** ~ ниско́лько; **on** ~ **fours** на четвере́ньках. **all-in** *adj.*: ~ **wrestling** кетч. **all-round** *adj.* разносторо́нний (-нен, -ння).

allay [ə'leɪ] *v.t.* облегча́ть *impf.*, облегчи́ть *pf.*; успока́ивать *impf.*, успоко́ить *pf.*; утоля́ть *impf.*, утоли́ть *pf.*

allegation [ˌælɪ'geɪʃ(ə)n] *n.* заявле́ние, утвержде́ние. **allege** [ə'ledʒ] *v.t.* заявля́ть *impf.*, заяви́ть (-влю́, -вишь) *pf.*; утвержда́ть *impf.* **allegedly** *adv.* я́кобы.

allegiance [ə'liːdʒ(ə)ns] *adv.* ве́рность.

allegorical [ˌælɪ'gɒrɪk(ə)l] *adj.* аллегори́ческий, иносказа́тельный. **allegory** ['ælɪgərɪ] *n.* аллего́рия, иносказа́ние.

allegretto [ˌælɪ'gretəʊ] *adv.* (*n.*) аллегре́тто (*nt.indecl.*). **allegro** [ə'leɪgrəʊ, ə'leg-] *adv.* (*n.*) алле́гро (*nt.indecl.*).

allergen ['ælədʒ(ə)n] *n.* аллерге́н. **allergic** [ə'lɜːdʒɪk] *adj.* аллерги́ческий. **allergy** *n.* аллерги́я.

alleviate [ə'liːvɪˌeɪt] *v.t.* облегча́ть *impf.*, облегчи́ть *pf.*; смягча́ть *impf.*, смягчи́ть *pf.* **allevi'ation** *n.* облегче́ние, смягче́ние.

alley ['ælɪ] *n.* переу́лок (-лка), прохо́д.

alliance [ə'laɪəns] *n.* сою́з. **allied** ['ælaɪd] *adj.* сою́зный.

alligator ['ælɪˌgeɪtə(r)] *n.* аллига́тор.

alliterate [ə'lɪtəˌreɪt] *v.i.* аллитери́ровать *impf.* **allite'ration** *n.* аллитера́ция.

allocate ['æləˌkeɪt] *v.t.* распределя́ть *impf.*, распредели́ть *pf.*; ассигнова́ть *impf.* & *pf.* **allo'cation** *n.* распределе́ние; ассигнова́ние.

allot [ə'lɒt] *v.t.* предназнача́ть *impf.*, предназна́чить *pf.*; распределя́ть *impf.*, распредели́ть *pf.*; отводи́ть (-ожу́, -о́дишь) *impf.*, отвести́ (отведу́, -дёшь; отвёл, -ла́) *pf.*; выделя́ть *impf.*, вы́делить *pf.* **allotment** *n.* выделе́ние; (*plot of land*) уча́сток (-тка).

allow [ə'laʊ] *v.t.* позволя́ть *impf.*, позво́лить *pf.*; разреша́ть *impf.*, разреши́ть *pf.*; допуска́ть *impf.*, допусти́ть (-ущу́, -у́стишь) *pf.*; ~ **for** принима́ть *impf.*, приня́ть (приму́, -мешь; при́нял, -ла́, -о) *pf.* во внима́ние, в расчёт; учи́тывать *impf.*, уче́сть (учту́, -тёшь; учёл, учла́) *pf.* **allowance** *n.* (*financial*) содержа́ние, посо́бие; (*expenses*) де́ньги (-нег, -ньга́м) *pl.* на расхо́ды; (*deduction, also fig.*) ски́дка; **make** ~(s) **for** принима́ть *impf.*, приня́ть (приму́, -мешь; при́нял, -ла́, -о) *pf.* во внима́ние, в расчёт; де́лать *impf.*, с~ *pf.* ски́дку на+*a.*

alloy ['ælɔɪ; ə'lɔɪ] *n.* сплав; *v.t.* сплавля́ть *impf.*, спла́вить *pf.*

allude [ə'luːd, ə'ljuːd] *v.i.* ссыла́ться *impf.*, сосла́ться (сошлю́сь, -лёшься) *pf.* (**to** на+*a.*); намека́ть *impf.*, намекну́ть *pf.* (**to** на+*a.*).

allure [ə'ljʊə(r)] *v.t.* зама́нивать *impf.*, замани́ть (-ню́, -нишь) *pf.*; завлека́ть *impf.*, завле́чь (-еку́, -ечёшь; -ёк, -екла́) *pf.* **allurement** *n.* прима́нка. **alluring** *adj.* зама́нчивый, завлека́тельный, соблазни́тельный.

allusion [ə'luːʒ(ə)n, ə'ljuː-] *n.* ссы́лка, намёк.

alluvial [ə'luːvɪəl] *adj.* аллювиа́льный, нано́сный.

all-weather *adj.* всепого́дный.

ally ['ælaɪ] *n.* сою́зник; *v.t.* соединя́ть *impf.*, соедини́ть *pf.*

almanac ['ɔːlmənæk, 'ɒl-] *n.* календа́рь (-ря́) *m.*

almighty [ɔːl'maɪtɪ] *adj.* всемогу́щий.

almond ['ɑːmənd] *n.* (*tree; pl. collect.*) минда́ль (-ля́) *m.*; (*nut*) минда́льный оре́х; *attr.* минда́льный.

almost ['ɔːlməʊst] *adv.* почти́, едва́ (ли) не, чуть (бы́ло) не.

alms [ɑːmz] *n.* ми́лостыня. **almshouse** *n.* богоде́льня (*g.pl.* -лен).

aloe(s) ['æləʊ] *n.* ало́э *nt.indecl.*

aloft [ə'lɒft] *adv.* наве́рх (-ý).

alone [ə'ləʊn] *pred.* оди́н (одна́, одно́; одни́); одино́к; *adv.* то́лько; сам по себе́; ~ **with** наедине́ с+*i.*; **leave** ~ оставля́ть *impf.*, оста́вить *pf.* в поко́е; **let** ~ не говоря́ уже́ о+*p.*

along [ə'lɒŋ] *prep.* по+*d.*, вдоль+*g.*, вдоль по+*d.*; *adv.* (*onward*) да́льше, вперёд; (*with o.s.*) с собо́й; **all** ~ всё вре́мя; ~ **with** вме́сте

c+*i*. **along'side** *adv.*, *prep.* ря́дом (с+*i*.), бок
о́ бок (с+*i*.).

aloof [ə'lu:f] *pred.*, *adv.* (*apart*) в стороне́,
вдали́; (*distant*) хо́лоден (-дна́, -дно, хо́лод-
ны́), равноду́шен (-шна).

aloud [ə'laʊd] *adv.* вслух, гро́мко.

alphabet ['ælfəbet] *n.* алфави́т, а́збука.
alpha'betical *adj.* алфави́тный. **alphanumeric** [,ælfənju:'merɪk] *adj.* алфави́тно-
цифрово́й.

alpine ['ælpaɪn] *adj.* альпи́йский.

Alps [ælpz] *n.*: **the ~** А́льпы (-п) *pl.*

already [ɔ:l'redɪ] *adv.* уже́.

also ['ɔ:lsəʊ] *adv.* та́кже, то́же.

altar ['ɔ:ltə(r), 'ɒl-] *n.* алта́рь (-ря́) *m.* **altar-
piece** *n.* запресто́льный о́браз (*pl.* -а́).

alter ['ɔ:ltə(r), 'ɒl-] *v.t.* переде́лывать *impf.*,
переде́лать *pf.*; *v.t.* & *i.* изменя́ть(ся) *impf.*,
измени́ть(ся) (-ню́(сь), -нишь(ся)) *pf.* **alte-
'ration** *n.* переде́лка; переме́на; измене́ние.

altercation [,ɔ:ltə'keɪʃ(ə)n, ,ɒl-] *n.* препира́-
тельство.

alternate [ɔ:l'tɜ:nət, ɒl-; 'ɔ:ltəneɪt, 'ɒl-] *adj.*
череду́ющийся, перемежа́ющийся; *v.t.* & *i.*
чередова́ть(ся) *impf.*; **alternating current**
переме́нный ток; **on ~ days** че́рез день.
alternation [ɔ:ltə'neɪʃ(ə)n, ,ɒl-] *n.* чередо-
ва́ние. **al'ternative** *n.* альтернати́ва; *adj.*
альтернати́вный; **~ medicine** паралле́льная
медици́на; **~ technology** алтернати́вная
техноло́гия.

although [ɔ:l'ðəʊ] *conj.* хотя́.

altimeter ['æltɪ,mi:tə(r)] *n.* альтиме́тр, высо-
томе́р. **altitude** ['æltɪtju:d] *n.* высота́ (*pl.*
-о́ты). **alto** *n.* альт (-а́); контра́льто *f.* &
nt.indecl.; *attr.* альто́вый; контра́льтовый.

altogether [,ɔ:ltə'geðə(r)] *adv.* (*fully*) совсе́м;
(*in total*) всего́; (*wholly*) всеце́ло.

alum ['æləm] *n.* квасцы́ *m.pl.* **aluminium**
[,ælju'mɪnɪəm] *n.* алюми́ний; *attr.* алюми́-
ниевый.

always ['ɔ:lweɪz] *adv.* всегда́; (*constantly*)
постоя́нно.

Alzheimer's disease ['ælts,haɪməz] *n.* боле́знь
Альцге́ймера.

a.m. *abbr.* (*of ante meridiem*) утра́; **6 ~** шесть
часо́в утра́.

amalgamate [ə'mælgəmeɪt] *v.t.* & *i.* амальга-
ми́ровать(ся) *impf.* & *pf.*; объединя́ть(ся)
impf., объедини́ть(ся) *pf.* **amalga'mation** *n.*
амальгами́рование; объедине́ние.

amanuensis [ə,mænju'ensɪs] *n.* перепи́счик,
-ица.

amass [ə'mæs] *v.t.* копи́ть (-плю́, -пишь)
impf., на~ *pf.*

amateur ['æmətə(r)] *n.* люби́тель *m.*, ~ница;
adj. самодея́тельный, люби́тельский. **amateurish** *adj.* люби́тельский.

amatory ['æmətərɪ] *adj.* любо́вный.

amaze [ə'meɪz] *v.t.* удивля́ть *impf.*, удиви́ть
pf.; изумля́ть *impf.*, изуми́ть *pf.* **amazement**
n. удивле́ние, изумле́ние. **amazing** *adj.*
удиви́тельный, изуми́тельный.

Amazon ['æməz(ə)n] *n.* Амазо́нка.

ambassador [æm'bæsədə(r)] *n.* посо́л (-сла́).
ambassadorial [,æmbæsə'dɔ:rɪəl] *adj.* посо́-
льский.

amber ['æmbə(r)] *n.* янта́рь (-ря́) *m.*; *adj.*
янта́рный; (*coloured*) жёлтый (жёлт, -а́,
жёлто́). **ambergris** ['æmbəgrɪs, -,gri:s] *n.*
а́мбра.

ambidextrous [,æmbɪ'dekstrəs] *adj.* одина́-
ково свобо́дно владе́ющий обе́ими рука́ми.

ambiguity [æmbɪ'gju:ɪtɪ] *n.* двусмы́сленность.
am'biguous *adj.* двусмы́сленный (-ен, -енна).

ambition [æm'bɪʃ(ə)n] *n.* честолю́бие. **ambitious** *adj.* честолюби́вый.

amble ['æmb(ə)l] *v.i.* (*horse*) бе́гать *indet.*,
бежа́ть (-жи́т) *det.* и́ноходью; (*ride*) е́здить
indet., е́хать (е́ду, е́дешь) *det.* верхо́м на
иноходце; (*on foot*) ходи́ть (хожу́, хо́дишь)
indet., идти́ (иду́, идёшь; шел, шла) *det.*
неторопли́вым ша́гом; *n.* и́ноходь.

ambrosia [æm'brəʊzɪə, -ʒə] *n.* амбро́зия.

ambulance ['æmbjʊləns] *n.* маши́на ско́рой
по́мощи; ско́рая по́мощь; **air ~** санита́рный
самолёт.

ambush ['æmbʊʃ] *n.* заса́да; *v.t.* напада́ть
impf., напа́сть (-аду́, -адёшь; -а́л) *pf.* из
заса́ды на+*a.*; устра́ивать *impf.*, устро́ить
pf. заса́ду на+*a.*

ameliorate [ə'mi:lɪəreɪt] *v.t.* & *i.* улучша́ть(ся)
impf., улу́чшить(ся) *pf.* **amelio'ration** *n.*
улучше́ние.

amen [ɑː'men, eɪ-] *int.* ами́нь!

amenable [ə'mi:nəb(ə)l] *adj.* усту́пчивый,
сгово́рчивый (**to** +*d.*).

amend [ə'mend] *v.t.* исправля́ть *impf.*, ис-
пра́вить *pf.*; вноси́ть (-ошу́, -о́сишь) *impf.*,
внести́ (внесу́, -сёшь; внёс, -ла́) *pf.* изме-
не́ния, попра́вки, в+*a.* **amendment** *n.*
попра́вка, исправле́ние, поправле́ние.
amends [ə'mendz] *n.*: **make ~ for** загла́-
живать *impf.*, загла́дить *pf.*

amenities [ə'mi:nɪtɪz, ə'menɪtɪz] *n.* пре́лести
f.pl., удо́бства *nt.pl.*

America [ə'merɪkə] *n.* Аме́рика. **American**
adj. америка́нский; *n.* америка́нец (-нца),
-нка. **Americanism** *n.* американи́зм. **Ameri-
canization** [ə,merɪkənaɪ'zeɪʃ(ə)n] *n.* америка-
низа́ция. **A'mericanize** *v.t.* американизи́-
ровать *impf.* & *pf.*

amethyst ['æmɪθɪst] *n.* амети́ст.

amiability [,eɪmɪə'bɪlɪtɪ] *n.* любе́зность. **'amiable**
adj. любе́зный. **amicability** [,æmɪkə'bɪlɪtɪ] *n.*
дружелю́бие. **'amicable** *adj.* дружелю́бный.

amid(st) [ə'mɪdst] *prep.* среди́+*g.*

amiss [ə'mɪs] *adv.* ду́рно, пло́хо; **take it ~** оби-
жа́ться *impf.*, оби́деться (-и́жусь, -и́дишься)
pf.

amity ['æmɪtɪ] *n.* дру́жественные отноше́ния
nt.pl.

ammonia [ə'məʊnɪə] *n.* аммиа́к; (*liquid* ~)
нашаты́рный спирт (-а(у), *loc.* -е & -у́).
ammoniac(al) *adj.* аммиа́чный.

ammunition [,æmjʊ'nɪʃ(ə)n] *n.* боеприпа́сы

m.pl., снаря́ды *m.pl.*, патро́ны *m.pl.*, дробь.
amnesty ['æmnɪstɪ] *n.* амни́стия; **'A~ International'** «Междунаро́дная амни́стия»; *v.t.* амнисти́ровать *impf. & pf.*
among(st) [ə'mʌŋst] *prep.* среди́+*g.*, ме́жду+*i.*
amoral [eɪ'mɒr(ə)l] *adj.* амора́льный.
amorous ['æmərəs] *adj.* влю́бчивый; (*in love*) влюблённый (-ён, -ена́).
amorphous [ə'mɔːfəs] *adj.* амо́рфный, безфо́рменный (-ен, -енна).
amortization [ə,mɔːtaɪ'zeɪʃ(ə)n] *n.* амортиза́ция. **amortize** [ə'mɔːtaɪz] *v.t.* амортизи́ровать *impf. & pf.*
amount [ə'maʊnt] *n.* коли́чество; *v.i.*: ~ **to** составля́ть *impf.*, соста́вить *pf.*; равня́ться *impf.*+*d.*; быть равноси́льным+*d.*
amp [æmp] *n. abbr.* (*of* **ampere**) А, (ампе́р).
ampere ['æmpeə(r)] *n.* ампе́р (*g.pl.* -р).
amphibian [æm'fɪbɪən] *n.* амфи́бия. **amphibious** *adj.* земново́дный.
amphitheatre ['æmfɪ,θɪətə(r)] *n.* амфитеа́тр.
ample ['æmp(ə)l] *adj.* (*enough*) (вполне́) доста́точно; (*abundant*) оби́льный; (*spacious*) обши́рный. **amplification** [,æmplɪfɪ'keɪʃ(ə)n] *n.* усиле́ние. **amplifier** ['æmplɪ,faɪə(r)] *n.* усили́тель *m.* **amplify** *v.t.* (*strengthen*) уси́ливать *impf.*, уси́лить *pf.*; (*enlarge*) расширя́ть *impf.*, расши́рить *pf.* **amplitude** ['æmplɪ,tjuːd] *n.* обши́рность, просто́р. **amply** *adv.* доста́точно.
ampoule ['æmpuːl] *n.* а́мпула.
amputate ['æmpjʊ,teɪt] *v.t.* ампути́ровать *impf. & pf.* **ampu'tation** *n.* ампута́ция.
amuse [ə'mjuːz] *v.t.* забавля́ть *impf.*; развлека́ть *impf.*, развле́чь (-еку́, -ечёшь; -ёк, -екла́) *pf.*; увеселя́ть *impf.* **amusement** *n.* заба́ва, развлече́ние, увеселе́ние; *pl.* аттракцио́ны *m.pl.* **amusing** *adj.* заба́вный; (*funny*) смешно́й (-шо́н, -шна́).
anachronism [ə'nækrə,nɪz(ə)m] *n.* анахрони́зм. **anachro'nistic** *adj.* анахрони́чный, -ческий.
anaemia [ə'niːmɪə] *n.* малокро́вие, анеми́я. **anaemic** *adj.* малокро́вный, анеми́чный, -ческий.
anaesthesia [,ænɪs'θiːzɪə] *n.* анестези́я, обезбо́ливание. **anaesthetic** [,ænɪs'θetɪk] *n.* анестези́рующее, обезбо́ливающее, сре́дство; *adj.* анестези́рующий, обезбо́ливающий. **anaesthetist** [ə'niːsθətɪst] *n.* наркотиза́тор. **anaesthetize** [ə'niːsθə,taɪz] *v.t.* анестези́ровать *impf. & pf.*; обезбо́ливать *impf.*, обезбо́лить *pf.*
anagram ['ænə,græm] *n.* анагра́мма.
anal ['eɪn(ə)l] *adj.* ана́льный.
analogical [,ænə'lɒdʒɪk(ə)l] *adj.* аналоги́ческий. **analogous** [ə'næləgəs] *adj.* аналоги́чный. **analogue** ['ænə,lɒg] *n.* анало́г; ~ **computer** анало́говая вычисли́тельная маши́на, АВМ. **a'nalogy** *n.* анало́гия.
analyse ['ænə,laɪz] *v.t.* анализи́ровать *impf. & pf.*; (*gram.*) разбира́ть *impf.*, разобра́ть (разберу́, -рёшь; разобра́л, -а́, -о) *pf.* **analysis** [ə'næləsɪs] *n.* ана́лиз. **analyst** ['ænəlɪst]

n. анали́тик; психоанали́тик. **analytical** [,ænə'lɪtɪk(ə)l] *adj.* аналити́ческий.
anarchic [æ'nɑːkɪk] *adj.* анархи́чный. **'anarchism** *n.* анархи́зм. **'anarchist** *n.* анархи́ст, ~ка; *adj.* анархи́стский. **'anarchy** *n.* ана́рхия.
anatomical [,ænə'tɒmɪk(ə)l] *adj.* анатоми́ческий. **a'natomist** *n.* ана́том. **a'natomy** *n.* анато́мия.
ancestor ['ænsestə(r)] *n.* пре́док (-дка), пра-роди́тель *m.* **an'cestral** *adj.* родово́й, насле́дственный. **ancestress** *n.* прароди́тельница. **ancestry** *n.* происхожде́ние; пре́дки *m.pl.*, прароди́тели *m.pl.*
anchor ['æŋkə(r)] *n.* я́корь (*pl.* -ря́) *m.*; *v.t.* ста́вить *impf.*, по~ *pf.* на я́корь; *v.i.* станови́ться (-влю́сь, -вишься) *impf.*, стать (ста́ну, -нешь) *pf.* на я́корь. **anchorage** *n.* я́корная стоя́нка. **anchorman** *n.* (*TV, radio*) веду́щий.
anchovy ['æntʃəvɪ, æn'tʃəʊvɪ] *n.* анчо́ус.
ancient ['eɪnʃ(ə)nt] *adj.* анти́чный, дре́вний (-вен, -вня), стари́нный.
and [ænd, ənd] *conj.* и, а; с+*i.*; **you** ~ **I** мы с ва́ми; **my wife** ~ **I** мы с жено́й.
andante [æn'dæntɪ] *adv.* (*n.*) анда́нте (*nt.indecl.*).
Andes ['ændiːz] *n.*: **the** ~ А́нды (-д) *pl.*
anecdotal [,ænɪk'dəʊt(ə)l] *adj.* анекдоти́ческий. **'anecdote** *n.* анекдо́т.
anemometer [,ænɪ'mɒmɪtə(r)] *n.* анемо́метр, ветроме́р.
anemone [ə'nemənɪ] *n.* анемо́н, ве́треница.
aneroid (barometer) ['ænə,rɔɪd] *n.* анеро́ид, баро́метр-анеро́ид.
anew [ə'njuː] *adv.* сно́ва.
angel ['eɪndʒ(ə)l] *n.* а́нгел. **angelic** [æn'dʒelɪk] *adj.* а́нгельский.
anger ['æŋgə(r)] *n.* гнев; *v.t.* серди́ть (-ржу́, -рдишь) *impf.*, рас~ *pf.*
angle[1] ['æŋg(ə)l] *n.* у́гол (угла́); (*fig.*) то́чка зре́ния.
angle[2] ['æŋg(ə)l] *v.i.* уди́ть (ужу́, у́дишь) *impf.* ры́бу. **angler** ['æŋglə(r)] *n.* рыболо́в. **angling** *n.* уже́ние.
Anglican ['æŋglɪkən] *n.* англика́нец (-нца), -нка; *adj.* англика́нский.
anglophile ['æŋgləʊ,faɪl] *n.* англофи́л; *adj.* англофи́льский.
angrily ['æŋgrɪlɪ] *adv.* серди́то, гне́вно. **angry** *adj.* серди́тый, гне́вный (-вен, -вна́, -вно); (*inflamed*) воспалённый (-ён, -ена́).
anguish ['æŋgwɪʃ] *n.* страда́ние, боль. **anguished** *adj.* страда́ющий.
angular ['æŋgjʊlə(r)] *adj.* углово́й; (*sharp*) углова́тый.
aniline ['ænɪ,liːn, -lɪn, -,laɪn] *adj.* анили́новый.
animal ['ænɪm(ə)l] *n.* живо́тное *sb.*; зверь (*pl.* -ри, -ре́й) *m.*; *adj.* живо́тный. **animate** *adj.* живо́й (жив, -á, -о). **animated** ['ænɪ,meɪtɪd] *adj.* оживлённый (-ён, -ена́), живо́й (жив, -á, -о); воодушевлённый (-ён, -ена́); (*film*) мультипликацио́нный; ~ **cartoon** мульт-

фи́льм. **ani'mation** *n.* оживле́ние, жи́вость, воодушевле́ние.

animosity [,ænɪ'mɒsɪtɪ], **animus** ['ænɪməs] *n.* вражде́бность, неприя́знь.

aniseed ['ænɪ,siːd] *n.* ани́совое се́мя *nt.*

ankle ['æŋk(ə)l] *n.* лоды́жка, щи́колотка; ~ **socks** коро́ткие носки́ *m.pl.* **anklet** *n.* ножно́й брасле́т.

annals ['æn(ə)lz] *n.* ле́топись, анна́лы *m.pl.* **'annalist** *n.* летопи́сец (-сца).

annex [æ'neks, ə'n-] *v.t.* аннекси́ровать *impf.* & *pf.*; присоединя́ть *impf.*, присоедини́ть *pf.*; прилага́ть *impf.*, приложи́ть (-жу́, -жишь) *pf.* **anne'xation** *n.* анне́ксия; присоедине́ние. **'annexe** *n.* (*building*) пристро́йка; дополне́ние.

annihilate [ə'naɪə,leɪt, ə'naɪl-] *v.t.* уничтожа́ть *impf.*, уничто́жить *pf.* **annihi'lation** *n.* уничтоже́ние.

anniversary [,ænɪ'vɜːsərɪ] *n.* годовщи́на.

annotate ['ænəʊ,teɪt, 'ænə,teɪt] *v.t.* анноти́ровать *impf.* & *pf.* **annotated** *adj.* снабжённый (-ён, -ена́) примеча́ниями, комментариями. **anno'tation** *n.* примеча́ние, коммента́рий, аннота́ция.

announce [ə'naʊns] *v.t.* объявля́ть *impf.*, объяви́ть (-влю́, -вишь) *pf.*; (*declare*) заявля́ть *impf.*, заяви́ть (-влю́, -вишь) *pf.*; (*radio*) сообща́ть *impf.*, сообщи́ть *pf.*; (*guest*) докла́дывать *impf.*, доложи́ть (-жу́, -жишь) *pf.* о+*p.* **announcement** *n.* объявле́ние; сообще́ние. **announcer** *n.* ди́ктор.

annoy [ə'nɔɪ] *v.t.* досажда́ть *impf.*, досади́ть *pf.*; раздража́ть *impf.*, раздражи́ть *pf.*; **I was ~ed** мне бы́ло доса́дно; **annoyance** *n.* доса́да, раздраже́ние; (*nuisance*) неприя́тность. **annoying** *adj.* доса́дный.

annual ['ænjʊəl] *adj.* ежего́дный, годово́й, годи́чный; (*bot.*) одноле́тний; *n.* ежего́дник; одноле́тник. **annually** *adv.* ежего́дно.

annuity [ə'njuːɪtɪ] *n.* (ежего́дная) ре́нта.

annul [ə'nʌl] *v.t.* аннули́ровать *impf.* & *pf.* **annulment** *n.* аннули́рование.

annunciation [ə,nʌnsɪ'eɪʃ(ə)n] *n.* Благове́щение.

anode ['ænəʊd] *n.* ано́д.

anodyne ['ænə,daɪn] *n.* болеутоля́ющее сре́дство.

anoint [ə'nɔɪnt] *v.t.* пома́зывать *impf.*, пома́зать (-а́жу, -а́жешь) *pf.*

anomalous [ə'nɒmələs] *adj.* анома́льный. **anomaly** *n.* анома́лия.

anon [ə'nɒn] *abbr.*, **anonymous** [ə'nɒnɪməs] *adj.* анони́мный. **anonymity** [,ænə'nɪmɪtɪ] *n.* анони́мность.

anorak ['ænə,ræk] *n.* ку́ртка с капюшо́ном; штормо́вка.

anorexia [,ænə'reksɪə] *n.* анорекси́я. **anorexic** *n.* больно́й анорекси́ей; *adj.* страда́ющий анорекси́ей.

another [ə'nʌðə(r)] *adj.*, *pron.* друго́й; ~ **one** ещё (оди́н); **ask me** ~ почём я зна́ю?; **in ~ ten years** ещё че́рез де́сять лет; **many ~**

мно́гие други́е.

answer ['ɑːnsə(r)] *n.* отве́т; *v.t.* отвеча́ть *impf.*, отве́тить *pf.*+*d.*, на+*a.*; ~ **back** держи́ть *impf.*, на~ *pf.*+*d.*; ~ **for** руча́ться *impf.*, поручи́ться (-чу́сь, -чишься) *pf.* за+*a.*; ~ **the door** отворя́ть *impf.*, отвори́ть (-рю́, -ришь) *pf.* дверь на звоно́к, на стук. **answerable** *adj.* отве́тственный (-ен, -енна). **answerphone** *n.* автоотве́тчик, телефо́н-отве́тчик.

ant [ænt] *n.* мураве́й (-вья́).

antagonism [æn'tægə,nɪz(ə)m] *n.* антагони́зм, вражда́. **antagonist** *n.* антагони́ст, проти́вник. **antago'nistic** *adj.* антагонисти́ческий, вражде́бный. **antagonize** *v.t.* порожда́ть *impf.*, породи́ть *pf.* антагони́зм, вражду́, у+*g.*

Antarctic [ænt'ɑːktɪk] *n.*: **the ~** Анта́рктика; *adj.* антаркти́ческий; ~ **Ocean** Ю́жный океа́н. **Antarctica** *n.* Антаркти́да.

anteater ['ænt,iːtə(r)] *n.* муравье́д.

antecedent [,æntɪ'siːd(ə)nt] *n.* антецеде́нт; *pl.* про́шлое *sb.*; *adj.* антецеде́нтный; предше́ствующий, предыду́щий.

antechamber ['æntɪ,tʃeɪmbə(r)] *n.* пере́дняя *sb.*, прихо́жая *sb.*

antedate [,æntɪ'deɪt] *v.t.* дати́ровать *impf.* & *pf.* за́дним число́м; (*precede*) предше́ствовать *impf.*+*d.*

antediluvian [,æntɪdɪ'luːvɪən, -'ljuːvɪən] *adj.* допото́пный.

antelope ['æntɪ,ləʊp] *n.* антило́па.

antenatal [,æntɪ'neɪt(ə)l] *adj.* дородово́й.

antenna [æn'tenə] *n.* (*zool.*) у́сик, щу́пальце (*g.pl.* -лец & -льцев); (*also radio*) анте́нна.

anterior [æn'tɪərɪə(r)] *adj.* пере́дний; ~ **to** предше́ствующий+*a.*

anteroom ['æntɪ,ruːm, -,rʊm] *n.* пере́дняя.

anthem ['ænθəm] *n.* гимн.

anthill ['ænthɪl] *n.* мураве́йник.

anthology [æn'θɒlədʒɪ] *n.* антоло́гия.

anthracite ['ænθrə,saɪt] *n.* антраци́т; *adj.* антраци́товый.

anthropoid ['ænθrə,pɔɪd] *adj.* человекообра́зный; *n.* антрапо́ид. **anthropological** [,ænθrəpə'lɒdʒɪk(ə)l] *adj.* антропологи́ческий. **anthro'pologist** *n.* антропо́лог. **anthro'pology** антрополо́гия.

anti- ['æntɪ] *in comb.* анти-..., противо-.... ~ **aircraft** *adj.* противовозду́шный, зени́тный. **antibiotic** [,æntɪbaɪ'ɒtɪk] *n.* антибио́тик. **antibody** *n.* антите́ло (*pl.* -ла́). **Antichrist** *n.* анти́христ.

anticipate [æn'tɪsɪ,peɪt] *v.t.* ожида́ть *impf.*+*g.*; (*with pleasure*) предвкуша́ть *impf.*, предвкуси́ть (-ушу́, -уси́шь) *pf.*; (*forestall*) предупрежда́ть *impf.*, предупреди́ть *pf.* **antici'pation** *n.* ожида́ние; предвкуше́ние; предупрежде́ние.

anticlimax [,æntɪ'klaɪmæks] *n.* неосуществлённые ожида́ния *nt.pl.*, антикли́макс.

antics ['æntɪks] *n.* вы́ходки *f.pl.*, ша́лости *f.pl.*

anticyclone [,æntɪ'saɪkləʊn] *n.* антицикло́н.

antide'pressant *n.* антидепресса́нт. **anti-dote** ['æntɪˌdəʊt] *n.* противоя́дие. **anti-fascist** *n.* антифаши́ст. ~ка; *adj.* анти-фаши́стский. **'antifreeze** *n.* антифри́з, хладносто́йкий соста́в. **'antihero** *n.* анти-геро́й. **'antimatter** *n.* антивещество́. **anti-missile missile** *n.* антираке́та.
antimony ['æntɪmənɪ] *n.* сурьма́.
antipathetic [ˌæntɪpə'θetɪk] *adj.* антипати́чный. **antipathy** [æn'tɪpəθɪ] *n.* антипа́тия. **anti'perspirant** *n.* антиперспира́нт, сре́дство от поте́ния. **antipodes** [æn'tɪpəˌdiːz] *n.* антипо́д.
antiquarian [ˌæntɪ'kweərɪən] *adj.* антиква́р-ный; *n.*, **'antiquary** *n.* антиква́р. **antiquated** ['æntɪˌkweɪtɪd] *adj.* устаре́лый. **antique** [æn'tiːk] *adj.* стари́нный; *n.* анти́к; *pl.* старина́. **an'tiquity** *n.* дре́вность, старина́; *pl.* дре́вности *f.pl.*
anti-Semite [ˌæntɪ'siːmaɪt, -semaɪt] *n.* анти-семи́т. **anti-Se'mitic** *adj.* антисеми́тский. **anti-Semitism** [-'semɪtɪz(ə)m] *n.* антисеми-ти́зм. **antiseptic** *adj.* антисепти́ческий; *n.* антисе́птик. **anti-Soviet** *adj.* антисове́т-ский; ~ **propaganda** антисове́тчина; ~ **propagandist** антисове́тчик. **anti-subma-rine** *adj.* противоло́дочный. **anti-tank** *adj.* противота́нковый. **antithesis** [æn'tɪθɪsɪs] *n.* антите́за; (*opposition*) противополо́жность. **antithetical** [ˌæntɪ'θetɪk(ə)l] *adj.* антитети́-ческий; противополо́жный.
antler ['æntlə(r)] *n.* оле́ний рог (*pl.* -á).
anus ['eɪnəs] *n.* за́дний прохо́д.
anvil ['ænvɪl] *n.* накова́льня (*g.pl.* -лен).
anxiety [æŋ'zaɪətɪ] *n.* беспоко́йство, трево́га, озабо́ченность. **anxious** ['æŋkʃəs] *adj.* беспоко́йный, трево́жный, озабо́ченный (-ен, -енна); **be** ~ беспоко́иться *impf.*; трево́житься *impf.*
any ['enɪ] *adj.*, *pron.* како́й-нибудь; ско́лько-нибудь; вся́кий, любо́й; кто́-нибудь, что́-нибудь; (*with neg.*) никако́й, ни оди́н; ни-ско́лько; никто́, ничто́; *adv.* ско́лько-нибудь; (*with neg.*) ниско́лько, ничу́ть. **any-body, anyone** *pron.* кто́-нибудь; вся́кий, любо́й; (*with neg.*) никто́. **anyhow** *adv.* ка́к-нибудь; ко́е-как; (*with neg.*) ника́к; *conj.* во вся́ком слу́чае; всё же, всё равно́. **anyone** *see* **anybody. anything** *pron.* что́-нибудь; всё (*что уго́дно*); (*with neg.*) ничего́. **any-way** *adv.* во вся́ком слу́чае; как бы то ни́ было. **anywhere** *adv.* где, куда́, отку́да, уго́дно; (*with neg., interrog.*) где-, куда́-, отку́да-нибудь.
a.o.b. *abbr.* (*of any other business*) ра́зное.
aorta [eɪ'ɔːtə] *n.* ао́рта.
apart [ə'pɑːt] *adv.* (*aside*) в стороне́, в сто́-рону; (*separately*) разде́льно, врозь; (*into pieces*) на ча́сти; ~ **from** кро́ме+g., не счи-та́я+g.; **take** ~ разбира́ть *impf.*, разо-бра́ть (разберу́, -рёшь; разобра́л, -ла́, -о) *pf.* (на ча́сти); **tell** ~ различа́ть *impf.*, различи́ть *pf.*; отлича́ть *impf.*, отличи́ть

pf. друг от дру́га.
apartheid [ə'pɑːteɪt] *n.* апартеи́д.
apartment [ə'pɑːtmənt] *n.* кварти́ра; *pl.* меблиро́ванные ко́мнаты *f.pl.*
apathetic [ˌæpə'θetɪk] *adj.* апати́чный. **apa-thy** *n.* апа́тия, безразли́чие.
ape [eɪp] *n.* обезья́на; *v.t.* обезья́нничать *impf.*, с~ *pf.* с+g.
aperient [ə'pɪərɪənt] *adj.* слаби́тельный; *n.* слаби́тельное *sb.*
aperture ['æpəˌtjʊə(r)] *n.* отве́рстие.
apex ['eɪpeks] *n.* верши́на.
aphorism ['æfəˌrɪz(ə)m] *n.* афори́зм. **apho-'ristic** *adj.* афористи́чный, -ческий.
apiarist ['eɪpɪərɪst] *n.* пчелово́д. **apiary** ['eɪpɪərɪ] *n.* па́сека, пче́льник.
apiece [ə'piːs] *adv.* (*persons*) на ка́ждого; (*things*) за шту́ку; (*amount*) по+d. *or a.* with 2, 3, 4, 90, 100, *etc.*
Apocalypse [ə'pɒkəlɪps] *n.* Апока́липсис. **apoca'lyptic** *adj.* апокалипти́ческий.
Apocrypha [ə'pɒkrɪfə] *n.* апо́крифы *m.pl.* **apocryphal** *adj.* апокрифи́чный, -ческий.
apogee ['æpəˌdʒiː] *n.* апоге́й.
apolitical [ˌeɪpə'lɪtɪk(ə)l] *adj.* аполити́чный.
apologetic [əˌpɒlə'dʒetɪk] *adj.* извиня́ю-щийся; **be** ~ извиня́ться *impf.*; **feel** ~ чу́вствовать *impf.* свою́ вину́. **apologetics** *n.* апологе́тика. **apologia** [ˌæpə'ləʊdʒɪə] *n.* аполо́гия. **a'pologize** *v.i.* извиня́ться *impf.*, извини́ться *pf.* (**to** пе́ред+i.; **for** за+a.). **a'pology** *n.* извине́ние; ~ **for** жа́лкое подо́-бие+g.
apoplectic [ˌæpə'plektɪk] *adj.* апоплекси́-ческий. **'apoplexy** *n.* апоплекси́я.
apostasy [ə'pɒstəsɪ] *n.* (веро)отсту́пни-чество. **apostate** *n.* (веро)отсту́пник, -ица; *adj.* (веро)отсту́пнический.
apostle [ə'pɒs(ə)l] *n.* апо́стол. **apo'stolic** *adj.* апо́стольский.
apostrophe [ə'pɒstrəfɪ] *n.* апостро́ф.
apotheosis [əˌpɒθɪ'əʊsɪs] *n.* апофео́з, про-славле́ние.
appal [ə'pɔːl] *v.i.* ужаса́ть *impf.*, ужасну́ть *pf.* **appalling** *adj.* ужаса́ющий, ужа́сный.
apparatus [ˌæpə'reɪtəs, 'æp-] аппара́т; прибо́р; (*gymnastic*) гимнасти́ческие снаря́ды *m.pl.*
apparel [ə'pær(ə)l] *n.* одея́ние.
apparent [ə'pærənt] *adj.* (*seeming*) ви́димый; (*manifest*) очеви́дный, я́вный; **heir** ~ пря-мо́й насле́дник. **apparently** *adv.* ка́жется, по-ви́димому; очеви́дно.
apparition [ˌæpə'rɪʃ(ə)n] *n.* виде́ние, при́зрак.
appeal [ə'piːl] *n.* (*request*) призы́в, воззва́-ние, обраще́ние; (*leg.*) апелля́ция, обжа́-лование; (*attraction*) привлека́тельность; ~ **court** апелляцио́нный суд (-á); *v.i.* (*request*) взыва́ть *impf.*, воззва́ть (-зову́, -зовёшь) *pf.* (**to** к+d.; **for** о+p.); обраща́ться *impf.*, обрати́ться (-ащу́сь, -ати́шься) *pf.* (с призы́вом); (*leg.*) апелли́ровать *impf.* & *pf.*; ~ **against** обжа́ловать *pf.*; ~ **to** (*at-tract*) привлека́ть *impf.*, привле́чь (-еку́,

-ечёшь; -ёк, -екла́) *pf.*

appear [ə'pɪə(r)] *v.i.* появля́ться *impf.*, появи́ться (-влю́сь, -ви́шься) *pf.*; выступа́ть *impf.*, вы́ступить *pf.*; (*seem*) каза́ться (ка́жусь, -жешься) *impf.*, по~ *pf.* **appearance** *n.* появле́ние; выступле́ние; (*aspect*) вид, нару́жность; (*pl.*) ви́димость.

appease [ə'piːz] *v.t.* умиротворя́ть *impf.*, умиротвори́ть *pf.* **appeasement** *n.* умиротворе́ние.

appellant [ə'pelənt] *n.* апелля́нт. **appellate** *adj.* апелляцио́нный.

append [ə'pend] *v.t.* прилага́ть *impf.*, приложи́ть (-жу́, -жишь) *pf.*; прибавля́ть *impf.*, приба́вить *pf.* **appendicitis** [ə,pendɪ'saɪtɪs] *n.* аппендици́т. **appendix** *n.* приложе́ние, прибавле́ние; (*anat.*) аппе́ндикс.

appertain [,æpə'teɪn] *v.i.*: ~ **to** принадлежа́ть (-жи́т) *impf.+d.*; относи́ться (-ится) *impf.+d.*

appetite ['æpɪ,taɪt] *n.* аппети́т. **'appetizing** *adj.* аппети́тный.

applaud [ə'plɔːd] *v.t.* аплоди́ровать *impf.+d.*; рукоплеска́ть (-ещу́, -е́щешь) *impf.+d.* **applause** *n.* аплодисме́нты *m.pl.*, рукоплеска́ние.

apple ['æp(ə)l] *n.* я́блоко (*pl.* -ки); *adj.* я́блочный; ~ **charlotte** шарло́тка; ~**-tree** я́блоня.

appliance [ə'plaɪəns] *n.* приспособле́ние, прибо́р. **applicable** ['æplɪkəb(ə)l, ə'plɪkəb(ə)l] *adj.* примени́мый. **'applicant** *n.* пода́тель *m.*, ~ница, заявле́ния; проси́тель *m.*, ~ница; кандида́т. **appli'cation** *n.* (*use*) примене́ние, приложе́ние; (*putting on*) накла́дывание; (*request*) заявле́ние. **applied** *adj.* прикладно́й. **appliqué** [æ'pliːkeɪ] *n.* апплика́ция. **apply** *v.t.* (*use*) применя́ть *impf.*, примени́ть (-ню, -нишь) *pf.*; прилага́ть *impf.*, приложи́ть (-жу́, -жишь) *pf.*; (*put on*) накла́дывать *impf.*, наложи́ть (-жу́, -жишь) *pf.*; *v.i.* (*request*) обраща́ться *impf.*, обрати́ться (-ащу́сь, -ати́шься) *pf.* с про́сьбой (**for** о+*p.*); подава́ть (-даю́, -даёшь) *impf.*, пода́ть (-а́м, -а́шь, -а́ст, -ади́м; по́дал, -ла́, -о) *pf.* заявле́ние.

appoint [ə'pɔɪnt] *v.t.* назнача́ть *impf.*, назна́чить *pf.* **appointment** *n.* назначе́ние; (*office*) до́лжность, пост (-á, *loc.* -ý); (*meeting*) свида́ние.

apposite ['æpəzɪt] *adj.* уме́стный. **appo'sition** *n.* приложе́ние; **in** ~ приложенный (-ен).

appraisal [ə'preɪz(ə)l] *n.* оце́нка. **appraise** *v.t.* оце́нивать *impf.*, оцени́ть (-ню, -нишь) *pf.*

appreciable [ə'priːʃəb(ə)l] *adj.* ощути́мый, ощути́тельный. **appreciate** *v.t.* цени́ть (-ню, -нишь) *impf.*; (*правильно*) оце́нивать *impf.*, оцени́ть (-ню, -нишь) *pf.*; *v.i.* повыша́ться *impf.*, повы́ситься *pf.* **appreciation** [ə,priːʃɪ'eɪʃ(ə)n, ə,priːs-] *n.* (*estimation*) оце́нка; (*recognition*) призна́тельность; (*rise in value*) повыше́ние це́нности, цены́. **appre-**

ciative *adj.* призна́тельный (**of** за+*a.*).

apprehend [,æprɪ'hend] *v.t.* (*arrest*) аресто́вывать *impf.*, арестова́ть *pf.*; (*understand*) понима́ть *impf.*, поня́ть (пойму́, -мёшь; по́нял, -ла́, -о) *pf.*; (*anticipate*) опаса́ться *impf.+g.*, *inf.* **apprehension** *n.* аре́ст; опасе́ние. **apprehensive** *adj.* опаса́ющийся.

apprentice [ə'prentɪs] *n.* учени́к (-á), подмасте́рье (*g.pl.* -в) *m.*; *v.t.* отдава́ть (-даю́, -даёшь) *impf.*, отда́ть (-а́м, -а́шь, -а́ст, -ади́м; о́тдал, -á, -о) *pf.* в уче́ние. **apprenticeship** *n.* учени́чество; обуче́ние.

appro *abbr.* (*of* **approval**): **on** ~ на про́бу.

approach [ə'prəʊtʃ] *v.t.* подходи́ть (-ожу́, -о́дишь) *impf.*, подойти́ (подойду́, -дёшь; подошёл, -шла́) *pf.* к+*d.*; приближа́ться *impf.*, прибли́зиться *pf.* к+*d.*; (*apply to*) обраща́ться *impf.*, обрати́ться (-ащу́сь, -ати́шься) *pf.* к+*d.*; *n.* приближе́ние; подхо́д; подъе́зд, по́дступ.

approbation [,æprə'beɪʃ(ə)n] *n.* одобре́ние.

appropriate [ə'prəʊprɪət; ə'prəʊprɪ,eɪt] *adj.* подходя́щий, соотве́тствующий; *v.t.* присва́ивать *impf.*, присво́ить *pf.*; (*assign money*) ассигнова́ть *impf. & pf.* **appropri-'ation** *n.* присвое́ние, присво́енное *sb.*; ассигнова́ние.

approval [ə'pruːv(ə)l] *n.* одобре́ние; утвержде́ние. **approve** *v.t.* утвержда́ть *impf.*, утверди́ть *pf.*; *v.t. & i.* ~ **of** одобря́ть *impf.*, одо́брить *pf.*

approximate [ə'prɒksɪmət] *adj.* приблизи́тельный; *v.i.* приближа́ться *impf.* (**to** к+*d.*). **approxi'mation** *n.* приближе́ние.

apricot ['eɪprɪ,kɒt] *n.* абрико́с.

April ['eɪprɪl, 'eɪpr(ə)l] *n.* апре́ль *m.*; ~ **Fool!** с пе́рвым апре́ля!; *attr.* апре́льский.

apron ['eɪprən] *n.* пере́дник; (*theatre*) авансце́на; (*airfield*) площа́дка.

apropos ['æprə,pəʊ, -'pəʊ] *adv.* кста́ти; ~ **of** по по́воду+*g.*; относи́тельно+*g.*; что каса́ется+*g.*

apse [æps] *n.* апси́да.

apt [æpt] *adj.* (*suitable*) уда́чный; (*quick*) спосо́бный; (*inclined*) скло́нный (-о́нен, -о́нна, -о́нно). **aptitude** ['æptɪ,tjuːd] *n.* спосо́бность.

aqualung ['ækwə,lʌŋ] *n.* аквала́нг. **aquamarine** [,ækwəmə'riːn] *n.* аквамари́н. **aquarist** ['ækwərɪst] *n.* аквариуми́ст. **aquarium** [ə'kweərɪəm] *n.* аква́риум. **Aquarius** [ə'kweərɪəs] *n.* Водоле́й. **aquatic** [ə'kwætɪk] *adj.* водяно́й, во́дный. **aqueduct** ['ækwɪ,dʌkt] *n.* акведу́к. **aqueous** ['eɪkwɪəs] *adj.* во́дный; (*watery*) водяни́стый.

aquiline ['ækwɪ,laɪn] *adj.* орли́ный.

Arab ['ærəb] *n.* (*person*) ара́б, ~ка; (*horse*) ара́бская ло́шадь (*pl.* -ди, -де́й, -дьми́); *adj.* ара́бский. **arabesque** [,ærə'besk] *n.* арабе́ска. **Arabia** [ə'reɪbɪə] *n.* Ара́вия. **Arabic** *adj.* ара́бский.

arable ['ærəb(ə)l] *adj.* па́хотный.

arbitrary ['ɑːbɪtrərɪ] *adj.* произво́льный.

arbitrate *v.i.* действовать *impf.* в ка́честве тре́тейского судьи́. **arbi'tration** *n.* арбитра́ж, тре́тейское реше́ние. **arbitrator** *n.* арби́тр, тре́тейский судья́ (*pl.* -дьи, -дей, -дьям) *m.*

arboreal [ɑ:'bɔːrɪəl] *adj.* древе́сный; (*living in trees*) обита́ющий на дере́вьях. **arbour** ['ɑːbə(r)] *n.* бесе́дка.

arc [ɑːk] *n.* дуга́ (*pl.* -ги); ~ **lamp** дугова́я ла́мпа. **ar'cade** *n.* арка́да, пасса́ж.

arch[1] [ɑːtʃ] *n.* а́рка, свод, дуга́ (*pl.* -ги); *v.t.* & *i.* выгиба́ть(ся) *impf.*, вы́гнуть(ся) *pf.*; изгиба́ть(ся) *impf.*, изогну́ть(ся) *pf.*

arch[2] [ɑːtʃ] *adj.* игри́вый.

arch- [ɑːtʃ] *in comb.* архи...; эрц... . **archangel** ['ɑːk-] *n.* арха́нгел. **archbishop** *n.* архиепи́скоп. **archdeacon** *n.* архидиа́кон. **archduchess** *n.* эрцгерцоги́ня. **archduchy** *n.* эрцге́рцогство. **archduke** *n.* эрцге́рцог.

archaeological [ˌɑːkɪəˈlɒdʒɪk(ə)l] *adj.* археологи́ческий. **archae'ologist** *n.* архео́лог. **archae'ology** *n.* археоло́гия.

archaic [ɑːˈkeɪɪk] *adj.* архаи́чный. **archaism** *n.* архаи́зм.

archer ['ɑːtʃə(r)] *n.* стрело́к (-лка́) из лу́ка. **archery** *n.* стрельба́ из лу́ка.

archipelago [ˌɑːkɪˈpeləˌgəʊ] *n.* архипела́г.

architect ['ɑːkɪˌtekt] *n.* архите́ктор, зо́дчий *sb.* **archi'tectural** *adj.* архитекту́рный. **architecture** *n.* архитекту́ра.

archives ['ɑːkaɪvz] *n.* архи́в. **archivist** ['ɑːkɪvɪst] *n.* архива́риус, архиви́ст.

archway ['ɑːtʃweɪ] *n.* прохо́д под а́ркой, сво́дчатый прохо́д.

arctic ['ɑːktɪk] *n.*: **the A~** А́рктика; *adj.* аркти́ческий; **A~ Ocean** Се́верный Ледови́тый океа́н.

ardent ['ɑːd(ə)nt] *adj.* горя́чий (-ч, -ча́), пы́лкий (-лок, -лка́, -лко) **ardour** *n.* пыл (-а(у), *loc.* -у́), пы́лкость, рве́ние.

arduous ['ɑːdjʊəs] *adj.* тру́дный (-ден, -дна́, -дно).

area ['eərɪə] *n.* (*extent*) пло́щадь (*pl.* -ди, -дей); (*region*) райо́н, зо́на.

arena [əˈriːnə] *n.* аре́на.

argon ['ɑːgɒn] *n.* арго́н.

arguable ['ɑːgjʊəb(ə)l] *adj.* утвержда́емый, дока́зуемый; (*disputed*) спо́рный. **argue** *v.t.* (*try to prove*) аргументи́ровать *impf.* & *pf.*; (*maintain*) утвержда́ть *impf.*; (*prove*) дока́зывать *impf.*; *v.i.* (*dispute*) спо́рить *impf.*, по~ *pf.* **argument** *n.* аргуме́нт, до́вод; (*dispute*) спор. **argu'mentative** *adj.* лю́бящий спо́рить.

argy-bargy [ˌɑːdʒɪˈbɑːdʒɪ] *n.* (*coll.*) перебра́нка, перепа́лка.

arid ['ærɪd] *adj.* сухо́й (сух, -а́, -о), безво́дный. **a'ridity** *n.* су́хость.

Aries ['eəriːz] *n.* Ове́н (Овна́).

arise [əˈraɪz] *v.i.* возника́ть *impf.*, возни́кнуть (-к) *pf.*; происходи́ть (-ит) *impf.*, произойти́ (-ойдёт; -оше́л, -ошла́) *pf.*

aristocracy [ˌærɪˈstɒkrəsɪ] *n.* аристокра́тия.

'aristocrat *n.* аристокра́т, ~ка. **aristo'cratic** *adj.* аристократи́ческий, -и́чный.

arithmetic [əˈrɪθmətɪk] *n.* арифме́тика. **arith'metical** *adj.* арифмети́ческий. **arithme'tician** *n.* арифме́тик.

ark [ɑːk] *n.* (Но́ев) ковче́г.

arm[1] [ɑːm] *n.* (*of body*) рука́ (*a.* -ку; *pl.* -ки, -к, -ка́м); (*of sea*) морско́й зали́в; (*of chair*) ру́чка; (*of river*) рука́в (-á; *pl.* -á); (*of tree*) больша́я ветвь (*pl.* -ви); ~ **in** ~ под ру́ку; **at** ~'s **length** (*fig.*) на почти́тельном расстоя́нии; **with open** ~s с распростёртыми объя́тиями.

arm[2] [ɑːm] *n.* (*mil.*) род войск; *pl.* (*weapons*) ору́жие; *pl.* (*coat of* ~s) герб (-á); *v.t.* вооружа́ть *impf.*, вооружи́ть *pf.* **armaments** ['ɑːməməntz] *n.* вооруже́ния *nt.pl.*

armature ['ɑːməˌtjʊə(r)] *n.* армату́ра.

armchair *n.* кре́сло (*g.pl.* -сел).

Armenia [ɑːˈmiːnɪə] *n.* Арме́ния.

armful *n.* оха́пка. **armhole** *n.* про́йма.

armistice ['ɑːmɪstɪs] *n.* переми́рие.

armorial [ɑːˈmɔːrɪəl] *adj.* ге́рбовый, геральди́ческий. **armour** ['ɑːmə(r)] *n.* (*hist.*) доспе́хи *m.pl.*; броня́; (*vehicles, collect.*) бронеси́лы *f.pl.* **armoured** *adj.* брониро́ванный (-ан), бронево́й; (*vehicles etc.*) бронета́нковый, броне...; ~ **car** броневи́к (-á), бронеавтомоби́ль *m.*; ~ **forces** бронета́нковые войска́ *nt.pl.*, бронеси́лы *f.pl.* **armourer** *n.* оруже́йник. **armoury** *n.* арсена́л, склад ору́жия.

armpit *n.* подмы́шка.

army ['ɑːmɪ] *n.* а́рмия; *adj.* арме́йский.

aroma [əˈrəʊmə] *n.* арома́т. **aro'matic** *adj.* аромати́чный.

around [əˈraʊnd] *adv.* круго́м, вокру́г; *prep.* вокру́г+*g.*; **all** ~ повсю́ду.

arouse [əˈraʊz] *v.t.* пробужда́ть, буди́ть (бужу́, бу́дишь) *impf.*, про~ *pf.*; возбужда́ть *impf.*, возбуди́ть *pf.*

arraign [əˈreɪn] *v.t.* привлека́ть *impf.*, привле́чь (-еку́, -ече́шь; -ёк, -екла́) *pf.* к суду́. **arraignment** *n.* привлече́ние к суду́.

arrange [əˈreɪndʒ] *v.t.* (*put in order*) приводи́ть (-ожу́, -о́дишь) *impf.*, привести́ (приведу́, -дёшь; привёл, -á) *pf.* в поря́док; расставля́ть *impf.*, расста́вить *pf.*; (*plan*) устра́ивать *impf.*, устро́ить *pf.*; (*mus.*) аранжи́ровать *impf.* & *pf.*; *v.i.*: ~ **for** усла́вливаться *impf.*, усло́виться *pf.* о+*p.*; ~ **to** угова́риваться *impf.*, уговори́ться *pf.*+*inf.* **arrangement** *n.* расположе́ние; устро́йство; (*agreement*) соглаше́ние; (*mus.*) аранжиро́вка; *pl.* приготовле́ния *nt.pl.*

array [əˈreɪ] *v.t.* наряжа́ть *impf.*, наряди́ть (-яжу́, -я́дишь) *pf.*; (*marshal*) стро́ить *impf.*, вы́~ *pf.*; *n.* наря́д; (*series*) совоку́пность.

arrears [əˈrɪəz] *n.* задо́лженность, недои́мка.

arrest [əˈrest] *v.t.* аресто́вывать *impf.*, аресто́вать *pf.*; заде́рживать *impf.*, задержа́ть (-жу́, -жишь) *pf.*; (*attention*) прико́вывать *impf.*, прикова́ть (-кую́, -куёшь) *pf.*;

n. аре́ст, задержа́ние.

arrival [ə'raɪv(ə)l] *n.* прибы́тие, прие́зд; (*new* ~) вновь прибы́вший *sb.*; (*child*) новорождённый *sb.* **arrive** *v.i.* прибыва́ть *impf.*, прибы́ть (прибу́ду, -дешь; при́был, -á, -o) *pf.*; приезжа́ть *impf.*, прие́хать (-е́ду, -е́дешь) *pf.*; (*succeed*) доби́ться (-бью́сь, -бьёшься) *pf.* успе́ха.

arrogance ['ærəgəns] *n.* высокоме́рие, кичли́вость. **arrogant** *adj.* высокоме́рный, кичли́вый.

arrow ['ærəʊ] *n.* стрела́ (*pl.* -лы); (*pointer etc.*) стре́лка. **arrowhead** *n.* наконе́чник стрелы́.

arsenal ['ɑːsən(ə)l] *n.* арсена́л.

arsenic ['ɑːsənɪk] *n.* мышья́к (-á); *adj.* мышья́ковый.

arson ['ɑːs(ə)n] *n.* поджо́г.

art [ɑːt] *n.* иску́сство; ~ **nouveau** стиль *m.* «ар нуво́»; *pl.* гуманита́рные нау́ки *f.pl.*; *adj.* худо́жественный.

arterial [ɑː'tɪərɪəl] *adj.* (*anat.*) артериа́льный; магистра́льный; ~ **road** магистра́ль. **'artery** *n.* (*anat.*) арте́рия; магистра́ль.

artesian [ɑː'tiːzɪən, -ʒ(ə)n] *adj.* артезиа́нский.

artful ['ɑːtfʊl] *adj.* хи́трый (-тёр, -трá, хи́тро́), ло́вкий (-вок, -вка́, -вко, ло́вки́).

arthritic [ɑː'θrɪtɪk] *adj.* артрити́ческий. **arthritis** [ɑː'θraɪtɪs] *n.* артри́т.

artichoke ['ɑːtɪtʃəʊk] *n.* артишо́к; (*Jerusalem* ~) земляна́я гру́ша.

article ['ɑːtɪk(ə)l] *n.* (*literary*) статья́ (*g.pl.* -éй); (*clause*) пункт; (*thing*) предме́т; (*gram.*) арти́кль *m.*, член; *v.t.* отдава́ть (-даю́, -даёшь) *impf.*, отда́ть (-áм, -áшь, -áст, -ади́м; о́тдал, -á, -o) *pf.* в уче́ние.

articulate [ɑː'tɪkjʊlət] *adj.* членоразде́льный, я́сный (я́сен, ясна́, я́сно, я́сны́); *v.t.* произноси́ть (-ошу́, -о́сишь) *impf.*, произнести́ (-есу́, -есёшь; -ёс, -есла́) *pf.*; артикули́ровать *impf.* **articulated** *adj.* сочленённый (-ён, -ена́). **articu'lation** *n.* артикуля́ция; сочлене́ние.

artifice ['ɑːtɪfɪs] *n.* хи́трость, (иску́сная) вы́думка. **artificer** [ɑː'tɪfɪsə(r)] *n.* (вое́нный) те́хник. **artificial** [ˌɑːtɪ'fɪʃ(ə)l] *adj.* иску́сственный (-ен(ен), -енна).

artillery [ɑː'tɪlərɪ] *n.* артилле́рия; *adj.* артиллери́йский. **artilleryman** *n.* артиллери́ст.

artisan [ˌɑːtɪ'zæn, 'ɑː-] *n.* реме́сленник.

artist ['ɑːtɪst] *n.* худо́жник; арти́ст. **artiste** [ɑː'tiːst] *n.* арти́ст, ~ка. **ar'tistic** *adj.* худо́жественный (-ен, -енна); артисти́ческий.

artless ['ɑːtlɪs] *adj.* бесхи́тростный, простоду́шный.

Aryan ['еərɪən] *n.* арие́ц (-и́йца), ари́йка; *adj.* ари́йский.

as [æz, əz] *adv.* как; *conj.* (*time*) когда́; в то вре́мя как; (*cause*) так как; (*manner*) как; (*concession*) как ни; *rel. pron.* како́й; кото́рый; что; **as … as** так (же)… как; **as for, to** относи́тельно+*g.*; что каса́ется+*g.*; **as if** как бу́дто; **as it were** ка́к бы; так сказа́ть; **as soon as** как то́лько; **as well**

та́кже; то́же.

a.s.a.p. *abbr.* (*of as soon as possible*) как мо́жно скоре́е.

asbestos [æz'bestɒs, æs-] *n.* асбе́ст; *adj.* асбе́стовый.

ascend [ə'send] *v.t.* поднима́ться *impf.*, подня́ться (-ниму́сь, -ни́мешься; -я́лся́, -яла́сь) *pf.* на+*a.*; всходи́ть (-ожу́, -о́дишь) *impf.*, взойти́ (взойду́, -дёшь; взошёл, -шла́) *pf.* на+*a.*; *v.i.* возноси́ться (-ошу́сь, -о́сишься) *impf.*, вознести́сь (-есу́сь, -есёшься; -ёсся, -есла́сь) *pf.* **ascendancy** *n.* домини́рующее влия́ние (**over** на+*a.*). **ascendant** *adj.* восходя́щий. **Ascension** *n.* (*eccl.*) Вознесе́ние.

ascent *n.* восхожде́ние (**of** на+*a.*).

ascertain [ˌæsə'teɪn] *v.t.* устана́вливать *impf.*, установи́ть (-влю́, -вишь) *pf.*

ascetic [ə'setɪk] *adj.* аскети́ческий; *n.* аске́т. **asceticism** *n.* аскети́зм.

ascribe [ə'skraɪb] *v.t.* припи́сывать *impf.*, приписа́ть (-ишу́, -и́шешь) *pf.* (**to** +*d.*). **ascription** [ə'skrɪpʃ(ə)n] *n.* припи́сывание.

asepsis [eɪ'sepsɪs, ə-] *n.* асе́птика. **aseptic** *adj.* асепти́ческий.

asexual [eɪ'seksjʊəl, æ-] *adj.* беспо́лый.

ash[1] [æʃ] *n.* (*tree*) я́сень *m.*

ash[2] [æʃ], **ashes** [æʃɪz] *n.* зола́, пе́пел (-пла); (*human remains*) прах.

ashamed [ə'ʃeɪmd] *pred.*: **he is** ~ ему́ сты́дно; **be, feel,** ~ **of** стыди́ться *impf.*, по~ *pf.*+*g.*

ashen ['æʃ(ə)n] *adj.* (*of* **ash**[2]) пе́пельный; (*pale*) мёртвенно-бле́дный.

ashore [ə'ʃɔː(r)] *adv.* на бе́рег(у́).

ashtray ['æʃtreɪ] *n.* пе́пельница.

Asia ['eɪʃə, -ʒə] *n.* А́зия. **Asian, Asiatic** [ˌeɪʃɪ'ætɪk, ˌeɪz-] *adj.* азиа́тский; *n.* азиа́т, ~ка.

aside [ə'saɪd] *adv.* в сто́рону, в стороне́; *n.* слова́ *nt.pl.*, произноси́мые в сто́рону.

asinine ['æsɪnaɪn] *adj.* осли́ный; (*stupid*) глу́пый (глуп, -á, -o).

ask [ɑːsk] *v.t.* (*inquire of*) спра́шивать *impf.*, спроси́ть (-ошу́, -о́сишь) *pf.*; (*request*) проси́ть (-ошу́, -о́сишь) *impf.*, по~ *pf.* (**for** *a.*, *g.*, o+*p.*); (*invite*) приглаша́ть *impf.*, пригласи́ть (-ашу́, -аси́шь) *pf.*; (*demand*) тре́бовать *impf.*+*g.* (**of** от+*g.*); ~ **after** осведомля́ться *impf.*, осве́домиться *pf.* o+*p.*; ~ **a question** задава́ть (-даю́, -даёшь) *impf.*, зада́ть (-áм, -áшь, -áст, -ади́м; за́дал, -á, -o) *pf.* вопро́с; **it's yours for the** ~**ing** сто́ит то́лько попроси́ть.

askance [ə'skæns, -'skɑːns] *adv.* ко́со, с подозре́нием.

askew [ə'skjuː] *adv.* кри́во.

asleep [ə'sliːp] *pred., adv.*: **be** ~ спать (сплю, спишь; спал, -á, -o) *impf.*; **fall** ~ засыпа́ть *impf.*, засну́ть *pf.*; **my foot's** ~ нога́ затекла́.

asp [æsp] *n.* а́спид.

asparagus [ə'spærəgəs] *n.* спа́ржа.

aspect ['æspekt] *n.* аспе́кт, вид (-a(у), на виду́), сторона́ (*a.* -ону; *pl.* -оны, -о́н, -она́м).

aspen ['æspən] *n.* оси́на.

asperity [ə'sperɪtɪ] *n.* рéзкость.

aspersion [ə'spɜ:ʃ(ə)n] *n.* клеветá.

asphalt ['æsfælt] *n.* асфáльт; *adj.* асфáльтовый; *v.t.* асфальтировать *impf. & pf.*

asphyxia [æs'fɪksɪə] *n.* асфиксия, удýшье. asphyxiate *v.t.* удушáть *impf.*, удушить (-шý, -шишь) *pf.*

aspic ['æspɪk] *n.* заливнóе *sb.*; in ~ заливнóй.

aspirant ['æspɪrənt] *n.* претендéнт. aspirate *n.* придыхáтельный *sb.* aspi'ration *n.* (*ling.*) придыхáние; (*desire*) стремлéние. aspire [ə'spaɪə(r)] *v.i.* стремиться *impf.* (to к+*d.*).

aspirin ['æsprɪn] *n.* аспирин; (*tablet*) таблéтка аспирина.

ass [æs] *n.* осёл (ослá).

assail [ə'seɪl] *v.t.* нападáть *impf.*, напáсть (-адý, -адёшь; -áл) *pf.* на+*a.*; (*with questions*) забрáсывать *impf.*, забросáть *pf.* вопрóсами. assailant *n.* нападáющий *sb.*

assassin [ə'sæsɪn] *n.* (наёмный, -ная) убийца *c.g.* assassinate *v.t.* (веролóмно) убивáть *impf.*, убить (убью, убьёшь) *pf.* assassi'nation *n.* (предáтельское) убийство.

assault [ə'sɔ:lt, ə'sɒlt] *n.* нападéние; (*mil.*) штурм; (*rape*) изнасилование; ~ and battery оскорблéние дéйствием; *v.t.* нападáть *impf.*, напáсть (-адý, -адёшь; -áл) *pf.* на+*a.*; штурмовáть *impf.*; насиловать *impf.*, из~ *pf.*

assay [ə'seɪ, 'æseɪ] *n.* прóба; *v.t.* производить (-ожý, -óдишь) *impf.*, произвести (-едý, -едёшь; -ёл, -елá) *pf.* анáлиз+*g.*; прóбовать *impf.*, по~ *pf.*

assemblage [ə'semblɪdʒ] *n.* сбор, собирáние. assemble *v.t.* собирáть *impf.*, собрáть (соберý, -рёшь; собрáл, -á, -о) *pf.*; (*machine*) монтировать *impf.*, с~ *pf.*; *v.i.* собирáться *impf.*, собрáться (-берётся; собрáлся, -алáсь, -алóсь) *pf.* assembly *n.* собрáние, ассамблéя; (*of machine*) сбóрка.

assent [ə'sent] *v.i.* соглашáться *impf.*, согласиться *pf.* (to на+*a.*, *inf.*); *n.* соглáсие; (*royal*) сáнкция.

assert [ə'sɜ:t] *v.t.* утверждáть *impf.*; ~ o.s. отстáивать *impf.*, отстоять (-ою, -оишь) *pf.* свои правá. assertion *n.* утверждéние. assertive *adj.* настóйчивый, самонадéянный (-ян, -янна).

assess [ə'ses] *v.t.* (*amount*) определять *impf.*, определить *pf.*; (*tax*) облагáть *impf.*, обложить (-жý, -жишь) *pf.* налóгом; (*value*) оцéнивать *impf.*, оценить (-ню, -нишь) *pf.* assessment *n.* определéние; обложéние; оцéнка.

asset ['æset] *n.* цéнное кáчество; блáго; *pl.* имýщество; ~s and liabilities актив и пассив.

assiduity [ˌæsɪ'djuːɪtɪ] *n.* прилежáние, усéрдие. assiduous [ə'sɪdjʊəs] *adj.* прилéжный, усéрдный.

assign [ə'saɪn] *v.t.* назначáть *impf.*, назнáчить *pf.*; ассигновáть *impf. & pf.* assignation [ˌæsɪg'neɪʃ(ə)n] *n.* (*meeting*) услóвленная встрéча, свидáние. assignment *n.* (*task*)

assimilate [ə'sɪmɪˌleɪt] *v.t.* ассимилировать *impf. & pf.*; усвáивать *impf.*, усвóить *pf.* assimi'lation *n.* ассимиляция; усвоéние.

assist [ə'sɪst] *v.t.* помогáть *impf.*, помóчь (-огý, -óжешь; -óг, -оглá) *pf.*+*d.*; содéйствовать *impf. & pf.*+*d.* assistance *n.* пóмощь, содéйствие. assistant *n.* помóщник, ассистéнт.

assizes [ə'saɪzɪz] *n.* выезднáя сéссия судá.

associate [ə'səʊʃɪˌeɪt, -sɪˌeɪt; ə'səʊʃɪət, -sɪət] *v.t.* ассоциировать *impf. & pf.*; *v.i.* присоединяться *impf.*, присоединиться *pf.* (with к+*d.*); общáться *impf.* (with с+*i.*); *n.* (*colleague*) коллéга *c.g.*; (*subordinate member*) млáдший член, член-корреспондéнт. associ'ation *n.* óбщество, ассоциáция; присоединéние; A~ football футбóл.

assonance ['æsənəns] *n.* ассонáнс.

assorted [ə'sɔ:tɪd] *adj.* подóбранный (-ан). assortment *n.* ассортимéнт.

assuage [ə'sweɪdʒ] *v.t.* успокáивать *impf.*, успокóить *pf.*; смягчáть *impf.*, смягчить *pf.*

assume [ə'sju:m] *v.t.* (*accept*) принимáть *impf.*, принять (приму, -мешь; принял, -á, -о) *pf.*; (*pretend*) напускáть *impf.*, напустить (-ущý, -ýстишь) *pf.* на себя; (*suppose*) предполагáть *impf.*, предположить (-ожý, -óжишь) *pf.*; ~d name вымышленное имя *nt.* assumption [ə'sʌmpʃ(ə)n] *n.* принятие на себé; (*pretence*) притвóрство; (*supposition*) предположéние, допущéние; (*eccl.*, the A~) Успéние.

assurance [ə'ʃʊərəns] *n.* увéрение; (*self* ~) самоувéренность; (*insurance*) страховáние. assure *v.t.* уверять *impf.*, увéрить *pf.*; гарантировать *impf. & pf.*; (*insure*) страховáть *impf.*, за~ *pf.* (against от+*g.*). assuredly *adv.* несомнéнно.

aster ['æstə(r)] *n.* áстра.

asterisk ['æstərɪsk] *n.* звёздочка.

astern [ə'stɜ:n] *adv.* позади, назáд.

asteroid ['æstəˌrɔɪd] *n.* астерóид.

asthma ['æsmə] *n.* áстма. asth'matic *adj.* астматический.

astigmatic [ˌæstɪg'mætɪk] *adj.* астигматический. a'stigmatism *n.* астигматизм.

astir [ə'stɜ:(r)] *pred.*, *adv.* (*in motion*) в движéнии; (*out of bed*) на ногáх; (*excited*) в возбуждéнии.

astonish [ə'stɒnɪʃ] *v.t.* удивлять *impf.*, удивить *pf.* astonishing *adj.* удивительный. astonishment *n.* удивлéние.

astound [ə'staʊnd] *v.t.* изумлять *impf.*, изумить *pf.* astounding *adj.* изумительный.

astrakhan [ˌæstrə'kæn] *n.* карáкуль *m.*

astral ['æstr(ə)l] *adj.* астрáльный, звёздный.

astray [ə'streɪ] *adv.*: go ~ сбивáться *impf.*, сбиться (собьюсь, собьёшься) *pf.* с пути; lead ~ сбивáть *impf.*, сбить (собью, собьёшь) *pf.* с пути.

astride [ə'straɪd] *adv.* расстáвив нóги; верхóм (of на+*p.*); *prep.* верхóм на+*p.*

astringent [ə'strɪndʒ(ə)nt] *adj.* вя́жущий; *n.* вя́жущее сре́дство.

astro- [æstrəʊ] *in comb.* астро..., звездо... .

astrologer [ə'strɒlədʒə(r)] *n.* астро́лог. **astrological** [ˌæstrə'lɒdʒɪk(ə)l] *adj.* астрологи́ческий. **astrology** [ə'strɒlədʒɪ] *n.* астроло́гия. **astronaut** ['æstrəˌnɔːt] *n.* астрона́вт. **astronomer** [ə'strɒnəmə(r)] *n.* астроно́м. **astronomical** [ˌæstrə'nɒmɪk(ə)l] *adj.* астрономи́ческий. **a'stronomy** *n.* астроно́мия. **astrophysical** *adj.* астрофизи́ческий. **astrophysics** *n.* астрофи́зика.

astute [ə'stjuːt] *adj.* проница́тельный; (*crafty*) хи́трый (хитр, -á, хи́тро).

asunder [ə'sʌndə(r)] *adv.* (*apart*) врозь; (*in pieces*) на ча́сти.

asylum [ə'saɪləm] *n.* психиатри́ческая больни́ца; (*refuge*) убе́жище.

asymmetrical [ˌeɪsɪ'metrɪk(ə)l, ˌæsɪ'metrɪk(ə)l] *adj.* асимметри́ческий. **a'symmetry** *n.* асимметри́я.

at [æt, *unstressed* ət] *prep.* (*position, condition*) на+*p.*, в+*p.*, у+*g.*; (*time, direction*) на+*a.*, в+*a.*; *with vv. etc.*: *see vv. etc.*, *e.g.* **look** смотре́ть (**at** на+*a.*); ~ **all** вообще́; **not** ~ **all** совсе́м не; ~ **first** снача́ла, сперва́; ~ **home** до́ма; ~ **last** наконе́ц; ~ **least** по кра́йней ме́ре; ~ **most** са́мое бо́льшее; ~ **night** но́чью; ~ **once** (*immediately*) сра́зу; (*simultaneously*) одновреме́нно; ~ **present** в настоя́щее вре́мя; ~ **that** на том; (*moreover*) к тому́ же; ~ **work** (*working*) за рабо́той; (~ *place of work*) на рабо́те.

atheism ['eɪθɪˌɪz(ə)m] *n.* атеи́зм. **atheist** *n.* атеи́ст. **athe'istic** *adj.* атеисти́ческий.

Athens ['æθɪnz] *n.* Афи́ны (-н) *pl.*

athlete ['æθliːt] *n.* атле́т; легкоатле́т, ~ка; спортсме́н, ~ка. **athletic** [æθ'letɪk] *adj.* атлети́ческий. **athletics** *n.* (лёгкая) атле́тика.

Atlantic [ət'læntɪk]: ~ **Ocean** Атланти́ческий океа́н.

atlas ['ætləs] *n.* а́тлас.

atmosphere ['ætməsˌfɪə(r)] *n.* атмосфе́ра. **atmospheric** [ˌætməs'ferɪk] *adj.* атмосфе́рный. **atmospherics** *n.* атмосфе́рные поме́хи *f.pl.*

atom ['ætəm] *n.* а́том; ~ **bomb** а́томная бо́мба. **a'tomic** *adj.* а́томный.

atone [ə'təʊn] *v.i.* искупа́ть *impf.*, искупи́ть (-плю́, -пишь) *pf.* (**for** +*a.*). **atonement** *n.* искупле́ние.

atrocious [ə'trəʊʃəs] *adj.* отврати́тельный, ужа́сный. **atrocity** [ə'trɒsɪtɪ] *n.* зве́рство, у́жас.

atrophy ['ætrəfɪ] *n.* атрофи́я, притупле́ние; *v.i.* атрофи́роваться *impf.* & *pf.*

attach [ə'tætʃ] *v.t.* (*fasten*) прикрепля́ть *impf.*, прикрепи́ть *pf.*; (*fig.*) привя́зывать *impf.*, привяза́ть (-яжу́, -я́жешь) *pf.*; (*second*) прикомандиро́вывать *impf.*, прикомандирова́ть *pf.*; (*attribute*) придава́ть (придаю́, -даёшь) *impf.*, прида́ть (-а́м, -а́шь, -а́ст, -ади́м; при́дал, -а́, -о) *pf.* **attaché** [ə'tæʃeɪ] *n.* атташе́ *m.indecl.* **attachment** *n.* прикре-

пле́ние; привя́занность; *pl.* принадле́жности *f.pl.*

attack [ə'tæk] *v.t.* напада́ть *impf.*, напа́сть (-аду́, -адёшь; -а́л) *pf.* на+*a.*; *n.* нападе́ние; (*mil. also*) ата́ка; (*of illness*) припа́док (-дка).

attain [ə'teɪn] *v.t.* достига́ть *impf.*, дости́чь & дости́гнуть (-и́гну, -и́гнешь; -и́г) *pf.*+*g.*, до+*g.*; ~ **the age of** дожива́ть *impf.*, дожи́ть (-иву́, -ивёшь; до́жил, -á, -о) *pf.* до+*g.* **attainment** *n.* достиже́ние.

attempt [ə'tempt] *v.t.* пыта́ться *impf.*, по~ *pf.*+*inf.*; про́бовать *impf.*, по~ *pf.*+*inf.*; *n.* попы́тка; (*on the life of*) покуше́ние (на жизнь+*g.*); **make an** ~ **on the life of** покуша́ться *impf.*, покуси́ться *pf.* на жизнь+*g.*

attend [ə'tend] *v.i.* занима́ться *impf.*, заня́ться (займу́сь, -мёшься; -я́лся, -яла́сь) *pf.* (**to** +*i.*); (*be present*) прису́тствовать *impf.* (**at** на+*p.*); *v.t.* (*accompany*) сопровожда́ть *impf.*, сопроводи́ть *pf.*; (*serve*) обслу́живать *impf.*, обслужи́ть (-жу́, -жишь) *pf.*; (*visit*) посеща́ть *impf.*, посети́ть (-ещу́, -ети́шь) *pf.* **attendance** *n.* (*presence*) прису́тствие; посеща́емость; обслу́живание. **attendant** *adj.* сопровожда́ющий; *n.* (*escort*) провожа́тый *sb.*

attention [ə'tenʃ(ə)n] *n.* внима́ние; **pay** ~ **to** обраща́ть *impf.*, обрати́ть (-ащу́, -ати́шь) *pf.* внима́ние на+*a.*; *int.* (*mil.*) сми́рно! **attentive** *adj.* внима́тельный; (*polite*) ве́жливый.

attenuated [ə'tenjʊˌeɪtɪd] *adj.* утончённый (-ён, -ена́). **attenu'ation** *n.* утонче́ние.

attest [ə'test] *v.t.* заверя́ть *impf.*, заве́рить *pf.*; свиде́тельствовать *impf.*, за~ *pf.*

attic ['ætɪk] *n.* манса́рда, черда́к (-á); (*storey*) мезони́н.

attire [ə'taɪə(r)] *v.t.* наряжа́ть *impf.*, наряди́ть (-яжу́, -я́дишь) *pf.*; *n.* наря́д.

attitude ['ætɪˌtjuːd] *n.* (*posture*) по́за; (*opinion*) отноше́ние (**towards** к+*d.*); (~ *of mind*) склад ума́.

attn. [ə'tenʃ(ə)n] *n. abbr.* (*of for the attention of*) вним., (внима́нию)+*g.*

attorney [ə'tɜːnɪ] *n.* пове́ренный *sb.*; **by** ~ че́рез пове́ренного; **power of** ~ дове́ренность; **A~ General** генера́льный атто́рней.

attract [ə'trækt] *v.t.* притя́гивать *impf.*, притяну́ть (-ну́, -нешь) *pf.*; прельща́ть *impf.*, прельсти́ть *pf.*; привлека́ть *impf.*, привле́чь (-еку́, -ечёшь; -ёк, -екла́) *pf.* **attraction** [ə'trækʃ(ə)n] *n.* притяже́ние; привлека́тельность; (*entertainment*) аттракцио́н. **attractive** *adj.* привлека́тельный, притяга́тельный.

attribute [ə'trɪbjuːt; 'ætrɪˌbjuːt] *v.t.* припи́сывать *impf.*, приписа́ть (-ишу́, -и́шешь) *pf.*; *n.* (*object*) атрибу́т; (*quality*) сво́йство; (*gram.*) определе́ние. **attri'bution** [ˌætrɪ'bjuːʃ(ə)n] *n.* припи́сывание. **a'ttributive** *adj.* атрибути́вный, определи́тельный.

attrition [ə'trɪʃ(ə)n] *n.* истира́ние; **war of** ~

война́ на истоще́ние.
aubergine [ˈəʊbəˌʒiːn] *n.* баклажа́н.
auburn [ˈɔːbən] *adj.* кашта́нового цве́та, рыжева́тый.
auction [ˈɔːkʃ(ə)n] *n.* аукцио́н; *v.t.* продава́ть (-даю́, -даёшь) *impf.*, прода́ть (-а́м, -а́шь, -а́ст, -ади́м; про́дал, -а́, -о) *pf.* с аукцио́на. **auctio'neer** *n.* аукциони́ст.
audacious [ɔːˈdeɪʃəs] *adj.* (*bold*) сме́лый (смел, -а́, -о); (*imprudent*) де́рзкий (-зок, -зка́, -зко) **audacity** [ɔːˈdæsɪtɪ] *n.* сме́лость; де́рзость.
audibility [ˌɔːdɪˈbɪlɪtɪ] *n.* слы́шимость. **'audible** *adj.* слы́шный (-шен, -шна́, -шно). **'audience** *n.* пу́блика, аудито́рия; (радио)слу́шатели *m.pl.*, (теле)зри́тели *m.pl.*; (*interview*) аудие́нция.
audio-lingual [ˌɔːdɪəʊ ˈlɪŋgw(ə)l] *adj.* аудио-речево́й. **audiotape** *n.* плёнка звукоза́писи. **audiotypist** *n.* фономаши́ни́стка. **audiovisual** *adj.* а́удио-визуа́льный.
audit [ˈɔːdɪt] *n.* прове́рка счето́в, реви́зия; *v.t.* проверя́ть *impf.*, прове́рить *pf.* (счета́+g.). **au'dition** *n.* про́ба; *v.t. & i.* устра́ивать *impf.*, устро́ить *pf.* про́бу+g. **'auditor** *n.* ревизо́р. **auditorium** [ˌɔːdɪˈtɔːrɪəm] *n.* зри́тельный зал, аудито́рия. **'auditory** *adj.* слухово́й.
auger [ˈɔːgə(r)] *n.* бура́в (-а́), сверло́ (*pl.* свёрла).
augment [ɔːgˈment] *n.* увели́чивать *impf.*, увели́чить *pf.*; прибавля́ть *impf.*, приба́вить *pf.*+g. **augmen'tation** *n.* увеличе́ние, приба́вка. **augmentative** *adj.* увеличи́тельный.
augur [ˈɔːgə(r)] *v.t. & i.* предвеща́ть *impf.*
August [ˈɔːgəst] *n.* а́вгуст; *attr.* а́вгустовский. **august** [ɔːˈgʌst] *adj.* вели́чественный (-ен, -енна).
aunt [ɑːnt] *n.* тётя (*g.pl.* -тей), тётка. **auntie** *n.* тётушка.
aureole [ˈɔːrɪˌəʊl] *n.* орео́л.
auriferous [ɔːˈrɪfərəs] *adj.* золотоно́сный.
aurochs [ˈɔːrɒks, ˈaʊrɒks] *n.* тур.
aurora [ɔːˈrɔːrə] *n.* авро́ра; ~ **borealis** се́верное сея́ние.
auspices [ˈɔːspɪsɪz] *n.* покрови́тельство. **auspicious** [ɔːˈspɪʃəs] *adj.* благоприя́тный.
austere [ɒˈstɪə(r), ɔːˈstɪə(r)] *adj.* стро́гий (строг, -а́, -о), суро́вый. **austerity** [ɒˈsterɪtɪ, ɔːˈsterɪtɪ] *n.* стро́гость, суро́вость.
austral [ˈɔːstr(ə)l, ˈɒstr(ə)l] *adj.* ю́жный.
Australia [ɒˈstreɪlɪə] *n.* Австра́лия. **Australian** *n.* австрали́ец (-и́йца), -и́йка; *adj.* австрали́йский.
Austria [ˈɒstrɪə] *n.* А́встрия. **Austrian** *n.* австри́ец (-и́йца), -и́йка; *adj.* австри́йский.
authentic [ɔːˈθentɪk] *adj.* (*genuine*) по́длинный (-нен, -нна), аутенти́чный; (*reliable*) достове́рный. **authenticate** *v.t.* удостоверя́ть *impf.*, удостове́рить *pf.*; устана́вливать *impf.*, установи́ть (-влю́, -вишь) *pf.* по́длинность+g. **authen'ticity** *n.* по́длин-

ность, аутенти́чность; достове́рность.
author [ˈɔːθə(r)] *n.* а́втор, писа́тель *m.*, ~ница; *v.t.* писа́ть (пишу́, -шешь) *impf.*, на~ *pf.* **authoress** [ˈɔːθrɪs, ˌɔːθəˈres] *n.* писа́тельница.
authoritarian [ɔːˌθɒrɪˈteərɪən] *adj.* авторита́рный; *n.* сторо́нник авторита́рной вла́сти. **au'thoritative** *adj.* авторите́тный. **au'thority** *n.* (*power*) власть (*pl.* -ти, -те́й), полномо́чие; (*evidence*) авторите́т; (*source*) авторите́тный исто́чник. **'authorize** *v.t.* (*action*) разреша́ть *impf.*, разреши́ть *pf.*; (*person*) уполномо́чивать *impf.*, уполномо́чить *pf.*
authorship [ˈɔːθəʃɪp] *n.* а́вторство.
auto- [ɔːtəʊ] *in comb.* авто... . **autobio'grapher** *n.* автобио́граф. **autobio'graphical** автобиографи́ческий. **autobi'ography** *n.* автобиогра́фия. **autoclave** [ˈɔːtəˌkleɪv] *n.* автокла́в. **autocracy** [ɔːˈtɒkrəsɪ] *n.* автокра́тия. **autocrat** [ˈɔːtəˌkræt] *n.* автокра́т. **auto'cratic** *adj.* автократи́ческий. **autocross** *n.* автокро́сс. **Autocue** *n.* (*propr.*) автосуфлёр. **autograph** *n.* авто́граф; *adj.* напи́санный руко́й а́втора; *v.t.* писа́ть (пишу́, -шешь) *impf.*, на~ *pf.* авто́граф в+p., на+p. **automatic** [ˌɔːtəˈmætɪk] *adj.* автомати́ческий; *n.* автомати́ческий пистоле́т. **auto'mation** *n.* автоматиза́ция. **automaton** [ɔːˈtɒmət(ə)n] *n.* автома́т. **autonomous** [ɔːˈtɒnəməs] *adj.* автоно́мный. **au'tonomy** *n.* автоно́мия. **autopilot** *n.* автопило́т. **autopsy** [ˈɔːtɒpsɪ, ɔːˈtɒpsɪ] *n.* вскры́тие тру́па; аутопсия. **autosuggestion** *n.* самовнуше́ние.
autumn [ˈɔːtəm] *n.* о́сень. **autumn(al)** [ɔːˈtʌmn(ə)l] *adj.* осе́нний.
auxiliary [ɔːgˈzɪljərɪ] *adj.* вспомога́тельный; *n.* помо́щник, -ица; (*gram.*) вспомога́тельный глаго́л; *pl.* вспомога́тельные войска́ *nt.pl.*
avail [əˈveɪl] *n.*: **of no** ~ бесполе́зен (-зна); **to no** ~ напра́сно; *v.t.*: ~ **o.s. of** по́льзоваться *impf.*, вос~ *pf.*+i. **available** [əˈveɪləb(ə)l] *adj.* досту́пный, нали́чный; *pred.* налицо́, в нали́чии.
avalanche [ˈævəˌlɑːnʃ] *n.* лави́на.
avarice [ˈævərɪs] *n.* жа́дность. **avaricious** [ˌævəˈrɪʃəs] *adj.* жа́дный (-ден, -дна́, -дно).
Av(e). [ˈævəˌnjuː] *n. abbr.* (*of* **avenue**) пр., (проспе́кт); авеню́.
avenge [əˈvendʒ] *v.t.* мстить *impf.*, ото~ *pf.* за+a. **avenger** *n.* мсти́тель *m.*
avenue [ˈævəˌnjuː] *n.* (*of trees*) алле́я; (*wide street*) проспе́кт; (*approach*) путь (-ти, -тём) *m.*
aver [əˈvɜː(r)] *v.t.* утвержда́ть *impf.*; заявля́ть *impf.*, заяви́ть (-влю́, -вишь) *pf.*
average [ˈævərɪdʒ] *n.* сре́днее число́ (*pl.* -ла, -сел, -слам), сре́днее *sb.*; **on** ~ в сре́днем; *adj.* сре́дний; *v.t.* составля́ть *impf.* в сре́днем; де́лать *impf.* в сре́днем.
averse [əˈvɜːs] *adj.* нерасположе́нный (-ен,

несклóнный (-нен, -ннá, -нно); **not ~ to** не
прочь+*inf.*, не прóтив+*g.* **aversion** *n.* отвращéние. **avert** *v.t.* (*ward off*) предотвращáть
impf., предотвратить (-ащý, -атишь) *pf.*;
(*turn away*) отводить (-ожý, -óдишь) *impf.*,
отвести (отведý, -дёшь; отвёл, -á) *pf.*
aviary ['eiviəri] *n.* птичник.
aviation [ˌeivi'eiʃ(ə)n] *n.* авиáция. 'a**viator** *n.*
лётчик.
avid ['ævid] *adj.* áлчный, жáдный (-ден, -днá,
-дно). a'**vidity** *n.* áлчность, жáдность.
avionics [ˌeivi'ɒniks] *n.* авиациóнная элект-
рóника.
avoid [ə'vɔid] *v.t.* избегáть *impf.*, избежáть
(-егý, -жишь) *pf.*+*g.*; уклоняться *impf.*,
уклониться (-нюсь, -нишься) *pf.* от+*g.*
avoidance *n.* избежáние, уклонéние.
avoirdupois [ˌævədə'pɔiz; ˌævwɑːdjuː'pwaː] *n.*
эвердьюпóйс.
avowal [ə'vaʊ(ə)l] *n.* признáние.
await [ə'weit] *v.t.* ждать (жду, ждёшь; ждал,
-á, -о) *impf.*+*g.*; '**to ~ arrival**' «до востре-
бования».
awake [ə'weik] *pred.*: **be ~** не спать (сплю,
спишь) *impf.*; **be ~ to** понимáть *impf.*; **stay
~** бóдрствовать *impf.* **awake(n)** *v.t.* про-
буждáть *impf.*, пробудить (-ужý, -удишь)
pf.; *v.i.* просыпáться *impf.*, проснýться *pf.*
award [ə'wɔːd] *v.t.* присуждáть *impf.*, присудить (-ужý, -ýдишь) *pf.*); награждáть
impf., наградить *pf.*; *n.* (*prize*) нагрáда,
прéмия; (*decision*) присуждéние.
aware [ə'weə(r)] *pred.*: **be ~ of** сознавáть
(-аю, -аёшь) *impf.*+*a.*; знать *impf.*+*a.*
away [ə'wei] *adv.* прочь; **far ~** (*from*) далекó
(от+*g.*); **~ game** игрá (*pl.* -ры) на чужóм
пóле; **~ team** комáнда гостéй.
awe [ɔː] *n.* благоговéйный страх; **stand in ~
of** испытывать *impf.* благоговéйный трé-
пет пéред+*i.*; *v.t.* внушáть *impf.*, внушить
pf. (благоговéйный) страх+*d.* **awe-struck**
adj. преисполненный (-ен) благоговéйного
стрáха, благоговéния. **awful** *adj.* ужáсный,
стрáшный (-áшен, -нá, -но, стрáшны́) **awfully** *adv.* ужáсно, óчень, стрáшно.
awkward ['ɔːkwəd] *adj.* нелóвкий (-вок, -вкá,
-вко). **awkwardness** *n.* нелóвкость.
awl [ɔːl] *n.* шило (*pl.* -лья, -льев)
awning ['ɔːniŋ] *n.* навéс, тент.
AWOL ['eiwɒl] *pred. adj. abbr.* (*of absent
without leave*) в самовóльной отлýчке.
awry [ə'rai] *adv.* криво, нáбок; **go ~** прова-
литься (-ится) *pf.*
axe [æks] *n.* топóр (-á); *v.t.* урéзывать, уре-
зáть *impf.*, урéзать (-éжу, -éжешь) *pf.*
axial ['æksiəl] *adj.* осевóй.
axiom ['æksiəm] *n.* аксиóма. **axio'matic** *adj.*
аксиоматический.
axis ['æksis], **axle** *n.* ось (*pl.* óси, осéй)
ay [ai] *int.* да!; *n.* положительный отвéт; (*in
vote*) гóлос (*pl.* -á) „за“; **the ~es have it**
большинствó „за“.
ayatollah [ˌaiə'tɒlə] *n.* аятоллá *m.*

Azerbaijan [ˌæzəbai'dʒɑːn] *n.* Азербайджáн.
azure ['æʒə(r), -zjə(r)] *n.* лазýрь; *adj.* лазýрный.

B [biː] *n.* (*mus.*) си *nt.indecl.* **BA** *abbr.* (*of
Bachelor of Arts*) бакалáвр гуманитáрных
наýк.
babble ['bæb(ə)l] *n.* (*voices*) болтовня; (*water*)
журчáние; *v.i.* болтáть *impf.*; журчáть
(-чит) *impf.*
babel ['beib(ə)l] *n.* галдёж (-á); **tower of B~**
столпотворéние вавилóнское.
baboon [bə'buːn] *n.* павиáн.
baby ['beibi] *n.* младéнец (-нца); *adj.* мáлый
(мал, -á, мáлó, -ы́), дéтский. **babyish** *adj.*
ребяческий. **babysitter** *n.* приходящая няня.
Bacchanalia [ˌbækə'neiliə] *n.* вакханáлия.
Bacchanalian *adj.* вакхический.
bachelor ['bætʃələ(r)] *n.* холостяк (-á); (*degree-
holder*) бакалáвр; *adj.* холостóй (-ост).
bacillus [bə'siləs] *n.* бацилла.
back [bæk] *n.* (*of body*) спинá (*a.* -ну; *pl.*
-ны); (*rear*) зáдняя часть (*pl.* -ти, -тéй);
(*reverse*) оборóт; (*of book*) корешóк (-шкá);
(*of seat*) спинка; (*sport*) защитник; *adj.*
зáдний; (*overdue*) просрóченный (-ен); *v.t.*
поддéрживать *impf.*, поддержáть (-жý,
-жишь) *pf.*; *v.i.* пятиться *impf.*, по~ *pf.*;
отступáть *impf.*, отступить (-плю, -пишь)
pf.; **~ down** уступáть *impf.*, уступить (-плю,
-пишь) *pf.*; **~ out** уклоняться *impf.*, уклониться (-нюсь, -нишься) *pf.* (**of** от+*g.*).
backbiter *n.* клеветник (-á). **backbiting** *n.*
клеветá. **backbone** *n.* позвонóчник; (*support*) глáвная опóра; (*firmness*) твёрдость
харáктера. **backer** *n.* лицó (*pl.* -ца), субси-
дирующее или поддéрживающее пред-
приятие; стóронник. **background** *n.* фон,
зáдний план; (*person's*) воспитáние, происхождéние, окружéние. **backpack** *n.* рюкзáк. **backpacker** *n.* рюкзáчник. **backside**
n. зад (*loc.* -ý; *pl.* -ы́). **backslider** *n.* ренегáт,
рецидивист. **back-up** *adj.* запаснóй; (*comput.*) резéрвный. **backward** *adj.* отстáлый;
adv. назáд. **backwash** *n.* откáт (воды́).
backwater *n.* зáводь, затóн.
bacon ['beikən] *n.* бекóн, грудинка.
bacterium [bæk'tiəriəm] *n.* бактéрия.
bad [bæd] *adj.* плохóй (плох, -á, -о, плóхи);
(*food etc.*) испóрченный (-ен); (*language*)
грýбый (груб, -á, -о); **~ taste** безвкýсица.

badge [bædʒ] *n.* значóк (-чкá), эмблéма.

badger ['bædʒə(r)] *n.* барсýк (-á); *v.t.* пристá вáть (-таю, -таёшь) *impf.*, пристáть (-áну, -áнешь) *pf.* к+*d.*; травúть (-влю, -вишь) *impf.*, за~ *pf.*

badly ['bædlɪ] *adv.* плóхо; (*very much*) óчень, сúльно.

baffle ['bæf(ə)l] *v.t.* стáвить *impf.*, по~ *pf.* в тупúк; приводúть (-ожý, -óдишь) *impf.*, привестú (-едý, -едёшь; привёл, -á) *pf.* в недоумéние; *n.* экрáн.

bag [bæg] *n.* мешóк (-шкá), сýмка; *v.t.* (*game*) убивáть *impf.*, убúть (убью, убь ёшь) *pf.*; *v.i.* (*clothes*) сидéть (сидúт) *impf.*, сесть (сядет; сел) *pf.* мешкóм.

baggage ['bægɪdʒ] *n.* багáж (-á(ý)); *adj.* багá жный.

baggy ['bægɪ] *adj.* мешковáтый.

bagpipe ['bægpaɪp] *n.* волы́нка. **bagpiper** *n.* волы́нщик.

bail[1] [beɪl] *n.* (*security*) поручúтельство, залóг; (*surety*) поручúтель *m.*, -ница; *v.t.* (~ *out*) брать (берý, -рёшь; брал, -á, -о) *impf.*, взять (возьмý, -мёшь; взял, -á, -о) *pf.* на порýки.

bail[2] [beɪl] *n.* (*cricket*) переклáдина ворóт.

bail[3], **bale**[2] [beɪl] *v.t.* вычéрпывать *impf.*, вы́черпнуть *pf.* (вóду из+*g.*); ~ **out** *v.i.* выбрáсываться *impf.*, вы́броситься *pf.* с парашютом. **bailer** *n.* черпáк (-á).

bait [beɪt] *n.* нажúвка; примáнка (*also fig.*); (*fig.*) соблáзн; *v.t.* (*torment*) травúть (-влю, -вишь) *impf.*, за~ *pf.*

baize [beɪz] *n.* бáйка.

bake [beɪk] *v.t.* печь (пекý, печёшь; пёк, -лá) *impf.*, ис~ *pf.*; (*bricks*) обжигáть *impf.*, обжéчь (обожгý, -жжёшь; обжёг, обож глá) *pf.* **baker** *n.* пéкарь *m.*, бýлочник. **bakery** *n.* пекáрня (*g.pl.* -рен), бýлочная *sb.* **baking** *n.* печéние, вы́печка.

Balaclava [,bælə'klɑːvə] *n.*: ~ (**helmet**) вя́за ный шлем.

balance ['bæləns] *n.* (*scales*) весы́ *m.pl.*; (*equilibrium*) равновéсие; (*econ.*) балáнс; (*remainder*) остáток (-тка); ~ **sheet** балáнс; *v.t.* уравновéшивать *impf.*, уравновéсить *pf.*; (*econ.*) балансúровать *impf.*, с~ *pf.*

balcony ['bælkənɪ] *n.* балкóн.

bald [bɔːld] *adj.* лы́сый (лыс, -á, -о), плеши́ вый; ~ **patch** лы́сина.

baldness *n.* плеши́вость.

bale[1] [beɪl] *n.* (*bundle*) тюк (-á), ки́па; *v.t.* уклáдывать *impf.*, уложи́ть (-жý, -жишь) *pf.* в тюки́, ки́пы.

bale[2] [beɪl] *see* **bail**[3]

baleful ['beɪlfʊl] *adj.* пáгубный, мрáчный (-чен, -чнá, -чно).

balk [bɔːk] *n.* бáлка; (*hindrance*) препя́тст вие; *v.t.* препя́тствовать *impf.*, вос~ *pf.*+*d.*

ball[1] [bɔːl] *n.* (*sphere*) мяч (-á), шар (-á *with* 2, 3, 4; *pl.* -ы́); клубóк (-бкá); ~ **and socket** шаровóй шарни́р.

ball[2] [bɔːl] *n.* (*dancing*) бал (*loc.* -ý; *pl.* -ы́)

ballad ['bæləd] *n.* баллáда; шансóн.

ballast ['bæləst] *n.* баллáст; *v.t.* грузи́ть (-ужý, -ýзишь) *impf.*, за~, на~ *pf.* баллáстом.

ball-bearing [,bɔːl'beərɪŋ] *n.* шарикоподши́п ник.

ballerina [,bælə'riːnə] *n.* балери́на.

ballet ['bæleɪ] *n.* балéт. **ballet-dancer** *n.* ар ти́ст, ~ка, балéта, танцóвщик, -ица.

balloon [bə'luːn] *n.* воздýшный шар (-á *with* 2, 3, 4; *pl.* -ы́); *v.t.* раздувáться *impf.*, раз дýться (-ýется) *pf.*

ballot ['bælət] *n.* голосовáние, баллотирóвка. **ballot-paper** *n.* избирáтельный бюллетéнь *m.*; *v.i.* голосовáть *impf.*, про~ *pf.*

ball-point ['bɔːlpɔɪnt] *n.* (*pen*) шáриковая рýчка, шáрик.

ballyhoo [,bælɪ'huː] *n.* шуми́ха.

balm [bɑːm] *n.* бальзáм. **balmy** *adj.* души́ стый.

Baltic ['bɔːltɪk, 'bɒl-] *n.*: the ~ (**Sea**) Балти́й ское мóре; ~ **States** прибалти́йские госу дáрства, Приба́лтика.

baluster ['bæləstə(r)] *n.* баля́сина. **balu'strade** *n.* балюстрáда.

bamboo [bæm'buː] *n.* бамбýк.

bamboozle [bæm'buːz(ə)l] *v.t.* одурáчивать *impf.*, одурáчить *pf.*

ban [bæn] *n.* запрéт, запрещéние; *v.t.* запре щáть *impf.*, запрети́ть (-ещý, -ети́шь) *pf.*

banal [bə'nɑːl] *adj.* банáльный.

banana [bə'nɑːnə] *n.* банáн.

band [bænd] *n.* (*strip*) óбод (*pl.* обóдья, -ьев)), тесьмá, полóска, каймá (*g.pl.* каём); (*of people*) грýппа; (*mus.*) оркéстр; (*radio*) полосá *a.* пóлосу; *pl.* -осы, -óс, -осáм) частóт; *v.i.*: ~ **together** объединя́ться *impf.*, объедини́ться *pf.*

bandage ['bændɪdʒ] *n.* бинт (-á), повя́зка; *v.t.* бинтовáть *impf.*, за~ *pf.*

bandit ['bændɪt] *n.* банди́т.

bandoleer [,bændə'lɪə(r)] *n.* патронтáш.

bandy ['bændɪ] *v.t.* (*throw about*) перебрá сываться *impf.*, переброси́ться *pf.*+*i.*

bandy-legged ['bændɪ,legɪd] *adj.* кривонóгий.

bane [beɪn] *n.* (*ruin*) ги́бель; (*poison*; *fig.*) отрáва. **baneful** *adj.* ги́бельный, ядови́тый.

bang [bæŋ] *n.* (*blow*) (си́льный) удáр; (*noise*) (грóмкий) слух; (*of gun*) вы́стрел; *v.t.* ударя́ть *impf.*, удáрить *pf.*; хлóпать *impf.*, хлóпнуть *pf.*; стучáть (-чý, -чи́шь) *impf.*, стýкнуть *pf.*

bangle ['bæŋg(ə)l] *n.* браслéт.

banish ['bænɪʃ] *v.t.* изгоня́ть *impf.*, изгнáть (-гоню́, -гóнишь; изгнáл, -á, -о) *pf.*; высы лáть *impf.*, вы́слать (вы́шлю, -шлешь) *pf.* **banishment** *n.* изгнáние, вы́сылка, ссы́лка.

banisters ['bænɪstəz] *n.* пери́ла *nt.pl.*

banjo ['bændʒəʊ] *n.* бáнджо *nt.indecl.*

bank[1] [bæŋk] *n.* (*of river*) бéрег (*loc.* -ý; *pl.* -á); (*in sea*) óтмель; (*of earth*) вал (*loc.* -ý; *pl.* -ы́); (*aeron.*) крен; *v.t.* сгребáть *impf.*, сгрести́ (-ебý, -ебёшь; сгрёб, -лá) *pf.* в кýчу.

bank² [bæŋk] *n.* (*econ.*) банк, фонд; ~ **holiday** устано́вленный пра́здник; *v.i.* (*keep money*) держа́ть (-жу́, -жишь) *impf.* де́ньги (в ба́нке); *v.t.* (*put in* ~) класть (кладу́, -дёшь; клал) *impf.*, положи́ть (-жу́, -жишь) *pf.* в банк; ~ **on** полага́ться *impf.*, положи́ться (-жу́сь, -жишься) *pf.* на+*a.*

bankrupt ['bæŋkrʌpt] *n.* банкро́т; *adj.* обанкро́тившийся; *v.t.* доводи́ть (-ожу́, -о́дишь) *impf.*, довести́ (-еду́, -едёшь; -ёл, -ела́) *pf.* до банкро́тства. **bankruptcy** *n.* банкро́тство.

banner ['bænə(r)] *n.* зна́мя (*pl.* -ёна) *nt.*, флаг; ~ **headline** ша́пка.

banquet ['bæŋkwɪt] *n.* банке́т, пир (*loc.* -у́; *pl.* -ы́).

bantam ['bæntəm] *n.* бента́мка. **bantamweight** *n.* легча́йший вес.

banter ['bæntə(r)] *n.* подшу́чивание; *v.i.* шути́ть (шучу́, шу́тишь) *impf.*

baptism ['bæptɪz(ə)m] *n.* креще́ние. **baptize** [bæp'taɪz] *v.t.* крести́ть (-ещу́, -е́стишь) *impf.*, о~ *pf.*

bar [bɑː(r)] *n.* (*beam*) брус (*pl.* -ья, -ьев), полоса́ (*a.* по́лосу́; *pl.* -осы, -о́с, -оса́м); (*of chocolate*) пли́тка; (*of soap*) кусо́к (-ска́); (*barrier*) прегра́да, барье́р; (*leg.*) колле́гия юри́стов; (*counter*) сто́йка; (*room*) бар; (*mus.*) такт; *v.t.* (*obstruct*) прегражда́ть *impf.*, прегради́ть *pf.*; (*prohibit*) запреща́ть *impf.*, запрети́ть (-ещу́, -ети́шь) *pf.*

barb [bɑːb] *n.* зубе́ц (-бца́); ~**ed wire** колю́чая про́волока.

barbarian [bɑː'beərɪən] *n.* ва́рвар; *adj.* ва́рварский. **barbaric** [bɑː'bærɪk], **barbarous** ['bɑːbərəs] *adj.* ва́рварский, гру́бый (груб, -а́, -о).

barber ['bɑːbə(r)] *n.* парикма́хер; ~**'s shop** парикма́херская *sb.*

bar-code ['bɑːkəʊd] *n.* бар-ко́д.

bard [bɑːd] *n.* бард, певе́ц (-вца́).

bare [beə(r)] *adj.* (*naked*) го́лый (гол, -а́, -о); (*barefoot*) босо́й (бос, -а́, -о); (*exposed*) обнажённый (-ён, -ена́); (*unadorned*) неприкра́шенный (-ен); (*scanty*) минима́льный; *v.t.* обнажа́ть *impf.*, обнажи́ть *pf.*; ~ **one's head** снима́ть *impf.*, снять (сниму́, -мешь; снял, -а́, -о) *pf.* шля́пу, ша́пку. **barefaced** *adj.* на́глый (нагл, -а́, -о). **barely** *adv.* едва́, чуть не, е́ле-е́ле, лишь (с трудо́м).

bargain ['bɑːgɪn] *n.* вы́годная сде́лка, дешёвая поку́пка; *v.i.* торгова́ться *impf.*, с~ *pf.*

barge [bɑːdʒ] *n.* ба́ржа, ба́ржа; *v.i.*: ~ **into** ната́лкиваться *impf.*, натолкну́ться *pf.* на+*a.* **bar'gee** *n.* ло́дочник.

baritone ['bærɪ,təʊn] *n.* барито́н.

barium ['beərɪəm] *n.* ба́рий.

bark¹ [bɑːk] *n.* (*sound*) лай; *v.i.* ла́ять (ла́ю, ла́ешь) *impf.*

bark² [bɑːk] *n.* (*of tree*) кора́.

barley ['bɑːlɪ] *n.* ячме́нь (-ня́) *m.*

barm [bɑːm] *n.* заква́ска.

barmaid *n.* буфе́тчица. **barman** *n.* ба́рмен, буфе́тчик.

barn [bɑːn] *n.* амба́р.

barometer [bə'rɒmɪtə(r)] *n.* баро́метр. **barometric(al)** [,bærəʊ'metrɪk] *adj.* барометри́ческий.

baron ['bærən] *n.* баро́н. **baroness** *n.* бароне́сса. **baronet** *n.* бароне́т. **baronial** [bə'rəʊnɪəl] *adj.* баро́нский.

baroque [bə'rɒk] *n.* баро́кко *nt.indecl.*

barrack ['bærək] *n.* каза́рма.

barrack² ['bærək] *v.t.* осви́стывать *impf.*, освиста́ть (-ищу́, -и́щешь) *pf.*

barrage ['bærɑːʒ] *n.* загражде́ние, барра́ж.

barrel ['bær(ə)l] *n.* (*vessel*) бо́чка; (*of gun*) ду́ло; ~ **organ** шарма́нка.

barren ['bærən] *adj.* беспло́дный.

barricade [,bærɪ'keɪd] *n.* баррика́да, прегра́да; *v.t.* баррикади́ровать *impf.*, за~ *pf.*

barrier ['bærɪə(r)] *n.* барье́р, прегра́да, шлагба́ум.

barring ['bɑːrɪŋ] *prep.* за исключе́нием+*g.*

barrister ['bærɪstə(r)] *n.* адвока́т.

barrow¹ ['bærəʊ] *n.* (*tumulus*) курга́н.

barrow² ['bærəʊ] *n.* (*cart*) та́чка.

barter ['bɑːtə(r)] *n.* менова́я торго́вля; *v.i.* обме́ниваться *impf.*, обменя́ться *pf.* това́рами.

base¹ [beɪs] *n.* осно́ва, основа́ние; (*also mil.*) ба́за; *v.t.* осно́вывать *impf.*, основа́ть (-ную́, -нуёшь) *pf.* **baseless** *adj.* необосно́ванный. **baseline** *n.* (*sport*) за́дняя ли́ния площа́дки. **basement** *n.* цо́кольный эта́ж (-а́), подва́л.

base² [beɪs] *adj.* (*low*) ни́зкий (-зок, -зка́, -зко), по́длый (подл, -а́, -о); (*metal, also fig.*) низкопро́бный.

bash [bæʃ] *v.t.* колоти́ть (-очу́, -о́тишь) *impf.*, по~ *pf.*

bashful ['bæʃfʊl] *adj.* засте́нчивый. **bashfulness** *n.* засте́нчивость.

basic ['beɪsɪk] *adj.* основно́й.

basil ['bæz(ə)l] *n.* бази́ли́к.

basin ['beɪs(ə)n] *n.* (*vessel*) ми́ска, таз (*loc.* -у́; *pl.* -ы́); (*geog., geol.*) бассе́йн; (*pool*) водоём.

basis ['beɪsɪs] *n.* ба́зис, осно́ва.

bask [bɑːsk] *v.i.* гре́ться *impf.*; (*fig*) наслажда́ться *impf.*, наслади́ться *pf.* (**in** +*i.*).

basket ['bɑːskɪt] *n.* корзи́на, корзи́нка. **basketball** *n.* баскетбо́л; *adj.* баскетбо́льный.

bas-relief [,bɑː rɪ'liːf] *n.* барелье́ф.

bass¹ [beɪs] *n.* (*mus.*) бас (*pl.* -ы́); *adj.* басо́вый; ~ **drum** большо́й бараба́н.

bass² [bæs] *n.* (*fish*) о́кунь (*pl.* -ни, -не́й) *m.*

bassoon [bə'suːn] *n.* фаго́т.

bastard ['bɑːstəd, 'bæ-] *n.* внебра́чный, побо́чный, ребёнок (-нка; *pl.* де́ти, дете́й); *adj.* незаконорождённый.

baste¹ [beɪst] *v.t.* (*tack*) мета́ть *impf.*, на~, с~ *pf.*

baste² [beɪst] *v.t.* (*cul.*) полива́ть *impf.*, поли́ть (-лью́, -льёшь) *pf.* жи́ром.

bastion ['bæstɪən] *n.* бастио́н.

bat¹ [bæt] *n.* (*zool.*) летучая мышь (*pl.* -ши, -шей).

bat² [bæt] *n.* (*sport*) бита; *v.i.* бить (бью, бьёшь) *impf.*, по~ *pf.* по мячу.

bat³ [bæt] *v.t.* (*wink*) моргать *impf.*, моргнуть *pf.*+*i.*, *abs.*

batch [bætʃ] *n.* пачка; (*of loaves*) выпечка.

bated ['beitid] *adj.* умеренный (-ен); **with ~ breath** затаив дыхание.

bath [bɑːθ] *n.* (*vessel*) ванна; *pl.* плавательный бассейн; **~ robe** купальный халат; *v.t.* купать *impf.*, вы~, ис~ *pf.* **bathe** [beið] *v.i.* купаться *impf.*, вы~, ис~ *pf.*; *v.t.* омывать *impf.*, омыть (омою, омоешь) *pf.* **bather** *n.* купальщик, -ица. **bathhouse** *n.* баня. **bathing** *n.* купание; **~ costume** купальный костюм. **bathroom** *n.* ванная *sb.*

batiste [bə'tiːst] *n.* батист.

batman ['bætmən] *n.* (*mil.*) денщик (-á).

baton ['bæt(ə)n] *n.* (*mil.*) жезл (-á); (*police*) дубинка; (*sport*) эстафета; (*mus.*) дирижёрская палочка.

battalion [bə'tæliən] *n.* батальон.

batten ['bæt(ə)n] *n.* рейка; *v.t.* заколачивать *impf.*, заколотить (-очу, -отишь) *pf.* досками.

batter ['bætə(r)] *n.* жидкое тесто; *v.t.* разбивать *impf.*, разбить (разобью, -ьёшь) *pf.*; размозжить *pf.*; **~ing ram** таран.

battery ['bætəri] *n.* (*mil.*, *tech.*) батарея; (*leg.*) оскорбление действием.

battle ['bæt(ə)l] *n.* битва, сражение, бой (*loc.* бою; *pl.* бои); *adj.* боевой. **battlefield** *n.* поле (*pl.* -ля) боя. **battlement** *n.* зубчатая стена (*a.* -ну; *pl.* -ны, -нам). **battleship** *n.* линейный корабль (-ля) *m.*, линкор.

bauble ['bɔːb(ə)l] *n.* безделушка.

bawdy ['bɔːdɪ] *adj.* непристойный.

bawl [bɔːl] *v.i.* орать (ору, орёшь) *impf.*

bay¹ [bei] *n.* (*bot.*) лавр(овое дерево); *pl.* лавровый венок (-нка), лавры *m.pl.*; *adj.* лавровый.

bay² [bei] *n.* (*geog.*) залив, бухта.

bay³ [bei] *n.* (*recess*) пролёт; **~ window** фонарь (-ря) *m.*; **sick ~** лазарет.

bay⁴ [bei] *v.i.* (*bark*) лаять (лаю, лаешь) *impf.*; (*howl*) выть (вою, воешь) *impf.*; *n.* лай; вой.

bay⁵ [bei] *adj.* (*colour*) гнедой.

bayonet ['beiə,net] *n.* штык (-á); *v.t.* колоть (-лю, -лешь) *impf.*, за~ *pf.* штыком.

bazaar [bə'zɑː(r)] *n.* базар.

BBC *abbr.* (*of British Broadcasting Corporation*) Би-Би-Си *nt. indecl.*.

BC *abbr.* (*of before Christ*) до н.э., до нашей эры.

be¹ [biː, bɪ] *v.* **1.** быть (*fut.* буду, -дешь; был, -á, -о; не был, -á, -о): *usually omitted in pres.*: **he is a teacher** он учитель; +*i. or nom. in past and fut.*: **he was, will ~, a teacher** он был, будет учителем. **2.** (*exist*) существовать *impf.* **3.** (*frequentative*) бывать *impf.* **4.** (**~ situated**) находиться (-ожусь, -одишься)

impf.: **where is the information office?** где находится справочное бюро?; (*upright*) стоять (стою, -оишь) *impf.*: **the piano is against the wall** рояль стоит у стены; (*laid flat*) лежать (-жу, -жишь) *impf.*: **the letter is on the table** письмо лежит на столе. **5.** (*in general definitions*) являться *impf.*+*i.*: **Moscow is the capital of Russia** столицей России является город Москва. **6.**: **there is, are** имеется, имеются; (*emph.*) есть.

be² [biː, bɪ] *v.aux.* **1.** *be*+*inf.*, *expressing duty, plan*: должен (-жна)+*inf.*: **he is to leave on Monday** он должен отправиться в понедельник. **2.** *be*+*past part. pass., expressing passive*: быть+*past part.pass. in short form*: **this was made by my son** это было сделано моим сыном; *impers. construction of 3 pl.*+*a.*: **I was beaten** меня били; *reflexive construction*: **music was heard** слышалась музыка. **3.** *be*+*pres.part. act., expressing continuous tenses*: *imperfect aspect*: **I am reading** я читаю.

beach [biːtʃ] *n.* пляж, берег (*loc.* -ý; *pl.* -á). **beachhead** *n.* плацдарм; *v.t.* вытаскивать *impf.*, вытащить *pf.* на берег.

beacon ['biːkən] *n.* маяк (-á), сигнальный огонь (огня) *m.*

bead [biːd] *n.* бусина; (*of liquid*) капля (*g.pl.* -пель); *pl.* бусы *f.pl.*

beadle ['biːd(ə)l] *n.* церковный сторож (*pl.* -á).

beagle ['biːg(ə)l] *n.* бигль*m.*, английская гончая *sb.*

beak [biːk] *n.* клюв.

beaker ['biːkə(r)] *n.* стакан.

beam [biːm] *n.* (*timber etc.*) балка; (*ray*) луч (-á); (*naut.*) бимс; (*breadth*) ширина; *v.t.* испускать *impf.*, испустить (-ущу, -устишь) *pf.*; *v.i.* (*shine*) сиять *impf.*

bean [biːn] *n.* фасоль, боб (-á).

bear¹ [beə(r)] *n.* медведь *m.*, -дица; **Great, Little, B~** Большая, Малая, Медведица; **~ cub** медвежонок (-жонка; *pl.* -жата, -жат).

bear² [beə(r)] *v.t.* (*carry*) носить (ношу, носишь) *indet.*, нести (несу, -сёшь; нёс, -лá) *det.*, по~ *pf.*; (*support*) поддерживать *impf.*, поддержать (-жу, -жишь) *pf.*; (*endure*) терпеть (-плю, -пишь) *impf.*, выносить (-ошу, -осишь) *impf.*, вынести (-су, -сешь; -с) *pf.*; (*give birth to*) рождать *impf.*, родить *impf. & pf.* (*pf.* родил, -á, -о) *pf.* **bearable** *adj.* сносный, терпимый.

beard ['bɪəd] *n.* борода (*a.* -оду; *pl.* -оды, -бд, -одам). **bearded** *adj.* бородатый.

bearer ['beərə(r)] *n.* носитель *m.*; (*of cheque*) предъявитель *m.*; (*of letter*) податель *m.*

bearing ['beərɪŋ] *n.* ношение; (*behaviour*) поведение; (*relation*) отношение; (*position*) пеленг; (*tech.*) подшипник, опора.

beast [biːst] *n.* животное *sb.*, зверь (*pl.* -ри, -рей) *m.*; (*fig.*) скотина *c.g.* **beastly** *adj.* (*coll.*) противный, отвратительный.

beat [biːt] *n.* бой; (*round*) обход; (*mus.*) такт; *v.t.* бить (бью, бьёшь) *impf.*, по~ *pf.*; (*cul.*)

взбива́ть *impf.*, взбить (взобью́, -ьёшь) *pf.*; ~ **a carpet** выбива́ть *impf.*, вы́бить (-бью, -бьешь) *pf.* ковёр; ~ **off** отбива́ть *impf.*, отби́ть (отобью́, -ьёшь) *pf.*; ~ **time** отбива́ть *impf.*, отбить (отобью́, -ьёшь) *pf.* такт; ~ **up** избива́ть *impf.*, изби́ть (изобью́, -ьёшь) *pf.* **beating** *n.* битьё; (*defeat*) пораже́ние; бие́ние.

beatific [ˌbiːəˈtɪfɪk] *adj.* блаже́нный (-ён, -е́нна). **beatify** [biːˈætɪˌfaɪ] *v.t.* канонизи́ровать *impf.* & *pf.* **be'atitude** *n.* блаже́нство.

beau [bəʊ] *n.* (*fop*) франт; (*ladies' man*) ухажёр.

beautiful [ˈbjuːtɪˌfʊl] *adj.* краси́вый, прекра́сный. **beautify** *v.t.* украша́ть *impf.* укра́сить *pf.* **beauty** *n.* (*quality*) красота́; (*person*) краса́вица.

beaver [ˈbiːvə(r)] *n.* (*animal*) бобр (-а́); (*fur*) бобёр (-бра́), бобро́вый мех (-a(y), *loc.* -е & ý; *pl.* -á).

becalmed [bɪˈkɑːmd] *adj.*: **be** ~ штилева́ть (-лю́ю, -лю́ешь) *impf.*

because [bɪˈkɒz] *conj.* потому́, что; так как; *adv.*: ~ **of** из-за́+g.

beckon [ˈbekən] *v.t.* мани́ть (-ню́, -нишь) *impf.*, по~ *pf.* к себе́.

become [bɪˈkʌm] *v.i.* станови́ться (-влю́сь, -вишься) *impf.*, стать (-а́ну, -а́нешь) *pf.*+i.; ~ **of** ста́ться (-а́нется) *pf.* c+i. **becoming** *adj.* подоба́ющий, иду́щий к лицу́+d.

bed [bed] *n.* крова́ть, посте́ль; (*garden*) гря́дка; (*sea*) дно, *pl.* до́нья, -ьев; (*river*) ру́сло; (*geol.*) пласт (-á, *loc.* -ý). **bedclothes, bedding** *n.* посте́льное бельё. **bedridden** *adj.* прико́ванный (-на) к посте́ли боле́знью. **bedrock** *n.* материко́вая поро́да. **bedroom** *n.* спа́льня (*g.pl.* -лен). **bedtime** *nt.* вре́мя *nt.* ложи́ться спать.

bedeck [bɪˈdek] *v.t.* украша́ть *impf.*, укра́сить *pf.*

bedevil [bɪˈdev(ə)l] *v.t.* терза́ть *impf.*; му́чить *impf.*, за~ *pf.*

bedlam [ˈbedləm] *n.* бедла́м, сумасше́дший дом.

bedraggled [bɪˈdræg(ə)ld] *adj.* заво́женный (-ен).

bee [biː] *n.* пчела́ (*pl.* -ёлы). **beehive** *n.* у́лей (у́лья).

beech [biːtʃ] *n.* бук.

beef [biːf] *n.* говя́дина. **beefburger** *n.* ру́бленый бифште́кс.

beer [bɪə(r)] *n.* пи́во. **beer(y)** *adj.* пивно́й.

beep [biːp] *n.* гудо́к; *v.i.* гуде́ть (-ди́т) *impf.*

beet [biːt] *n.* свёкла.

beetle [ˈbiːt(ə)l] *n.* жук (-á).

beetroot [ˈbiːtruːt] *n.* свёкла.

befall [bɪˈfɔːl] *v.t.* & *i.* случа́ться *impf.*, случи́ться *pf.* (+d.).

befit [bɪˈfɪt] *v.t.* подходи́ть (-ит) *impf.*, подойти́ (-ойдёт; -ошёл, -ошла́) *pf.*+d.

before [bɪˈfɔː(r)] *adv.* пре́жде, ра́ньше; *prep.* пе́ред+i., до+g.; *conj.* до того́ как; пре́жде чем; (*rather than*) скоре́е чем; **the day** ~

yesterday позавчера́. **beforehand** *adv.* зара́нее, вперёд.

befriend [bɪˈfrend] *v.t.* ока́зывать *impf.*, оказа́ть (-ажу́, -а́жешь) *pf.* дру́жескую по́мощь+d.

beg [beg] *v.i.* ни́щенствовать *impf.*; *v.t.* (*ask*) проси́ть (-ошу́, -о́сишь) *impf.*, по~ *pf.*; (*of dog*) служи́ть (-ит) *impf.*; ~ **pardon** проси́ть (-ошу́, -о́сишь) *impf.* проще́ние.

beget [bɪˈget] *v.t.* порожда́ть *impf.*, породи́ть *pf.*

beggar [ˈbegə(r)] *n.* ни́щий *sb.*; *v.t.* разоря́ть *impf.*, разори́ть *pf.* **beggarliness** *n.* нищета́. **beggarly** *adj.* (*poor*) бе́дный (-ден, -дна́, -дно); (*mean*) жа́лкий (-лок, -лка́, -лко).

begin [bɪˈgɪn] *v.t.* начина́ть *impf.*, нача́ть (-чну́, -чнёшь; на́чал, -á, -o) *pf.*; *v.i.* начина́ться *impf.*, нача́ться (-чну́сь, -чнёшься; -ался́, -алáсь) *pf.* **beginner** *n.* начина́ющий *sb.*, новичо́к (-чка́). **beginning** *n.* нача́ло.

begonia [bɪˈgəʊnjə] *n.* бего́ния.

begrudge [bɪˈgrʌdʒ] *v.t.* (*spare*) скупи́ться *impf.*, по~ *pf.* на+a., +inf.

beguile [bɪˈgaɪl] *v.t.* (*amuse*) развлека́ть *impf.*, развле́чь (-еку́ -ечёшь; -ёк, -екла́) *pf.*

behalf [bɪˈhɑːf] *n.*: **on** ~ **of** от и́мени+g.; (*in interest of*) в по́льзу+g.

behave [bɪˈheɪv] *v.i.* вести́ (веду́, -дёшь; вёл, -á) *impf.* себя́. **behaviour** *n.* поведе́ние.

behead [bɪˈhed] *v.t.* обезгла́вливать *impf.*, обезгла́вить *pf.*

behest [bɪˈhest] *n.* заве́т.

behind [bɪˈhaɪnd] *adv.*, *prep.* сза́ди (+g.), позади́ (+g.), за (+a., i.); *n.* зад (*loc.* -ý; *pl.* -ы́). **behold** [bɪˈhəʊld] *int.* ce! **beholden** *pred.*: ~ **to** обя́зан+d.

beige [beɪʒ] *adj.* беж *indecl.*, бе́жевый.

Beijing [beiˈdʒɪŋ] *n.* Пеки́н.

being [ˈbiːɪŋ] *n.* (*existence*) бытие́ (*i.* -ие́м, *p.* -ии́); (*creature*) существо́; **for the time** ~ на не́которое вре́мя; вре́менно.

belabour [bɪˈleɪbə(r)] *v.t.* бить (бью, бьёшь) *impf.*, по~ *pf.*

Belarus [beləˈrʌs] *n.* Белару́сь.

belated [bɪˈleɪtɪd] *adj.* запозда́лый.

belch [beltʃ] *n.* отры́жка; *v.i.* рыга́ть *impf.*, рыгну́ть *pf.*; *v.t.* изверга́ть *impf.*, изве́ргнуть (-г(нул), -гла) *pf.*

beleaguer [bɪˈliːgə(r)] *v.t.* осажда́ть *impf.*, осади́ть *pf.*

belfry [ˈbelfrɪ] *n.* колоко́льня (*g.pl.* -лен).

Belgium [ˈbeldʒəm] *n.* Бе́льгия.

belie [bɪˈlaɪ] *v.t.* противоре́чить *impf.*+d.

belief [bɪˈliːf] *n.* (*faith*) ве́ра; (*confidence*) убежде́ние. **believable** *adj.* вероя́тный, правдоподо́бный. **believe** *v.t.* ве́рить *impf.*, по~ *pf.*+d.; **l** ~ **so** ка́жется так; **l** ~ **not** ду́маю, что нет; едва́ ли.

belittle [bɪˈlɪt(ə)l] *v.t.* умаля́ть *impf.*, умали́ть *pf.*

bell [bel] *n.* ко́локол (*pl.* -á); (*small*) колоко́льчик, бубе́нчик; ~ **tower** колоко́льня (*g.pl.* -лен). **bell-bottomed** *adj.*: ∼ trousers брюки (-к) *pl.* с раструбами.

belle [bel] *n.* красавица.

belles-lettres [bel 'letr] *n.* художественная литература.

bellicose ['belɪˌkəʊz] *adj.* воинственный (-ен, -енна), агрессивный. **belligerency** [bɪ'lɪdʒərənsɪ] *n.* воинственность. **belligerent** *n.* воюющая сторона (*a.* -ону; *pl.* -оны, -он, -онам); *adj.* воюющий.

bellow ['beləʊ] *n.* мычание, рев; *v.t. & i.* мычать (-чу, -чишь *impf.*; реветь (-ву, -вёшь) *impf.*

bellows ['beləʊz] *n.* мехи *m.pl.*

bell-ringer ['belrɪŋə(r)] *n.* звонарь (-ря) *m.*

belly ['belɪ] *n.* живот (-а), брюхо (*pl.* -хи).

belong [bɪ'lɒŋ] *v.i.* принадлежать (-жу, -жишь) *impf.* (**to** (к)+*d.*). **belongings** [bɪ'lɒŋɪŋz] *n.* пожитки (-ков) *pl.*, вещи (-щей) *f.pl.*

beloved [bɪ'lʌvɪd, *pred. also* -lʌvd] *adj.* любимый, возлюбленный (-ен, -енна).

below [bɪ'ləʊ] *adv.* вниз, внизу, ниже; *prep.* ниже+*g.*

belt [belt] *n.* (*strap*) пояс (*pl.* -а), ремень (-мня); (*zone*) зона, полоса (*a.* -осу; *pl.* -осы, -ос, -осам); *v.t.* подпоясывать *impf.*, подпоясать (-яшу, -яшешь) *pf.*

bench [bentʃ] *n.* (*seat*) скамья (*pl.* скамей, -мей), скамейка; (*for work*) станок (-нка); (*court*) полицейские судьи (*g.* -дей) *pl.*; (*parl.*) место (*pl.* -та); **back** ∼**es** скамьи рядовых членов парламента.

bend [bend] *n.* сгиб, изгиб, наклон; *v.t.* сгибать *impf.*, согнуть *pf.*

beneath [bɪ'niːθ] *prep.* под+*i.*

benediction [ˌbenɪ'dɪkʃ(ə)n] *n.* благословение.

benefaction [ˌbenɪ'fækʃ(ə)n] *n.* милость, дар (*pl.* -ы). **benefactor** *n.* благодетель *m.*

benefice ['benɪfɪs] *n.* бенефиция. **be'neficence** *n.* благодеяние, милосердие. **be'neficent** *adj.* благотворный, полезный.

bene'ficial *adj.* полезный, выгодный. **bene'ficiary** *n.* лицо (*pl.* -ца), получающее доходы; (*in will*) наследник. **benefit** *n.* польза, выгода; (*allowance*) пособие; (*theatr.*) бенефис; *v.t.* приносить (-ошу, -осишь) *impf.*, принести (-есу, -есёшь; -ёс, -есла) *pf.* пользу+*d.*; *v.i.* извлекать *impf.*, извлечь (-еку, -ечёшь; -ёк, -екла) *pf.* выгоду.

be'nevolence *n.* благожелательность, благодеяние. **be'nevolent** *adj.* благосклонный (-нен, -нна), благотворительный.

benign [bɪ'naɪn] *adj.* добрый (добр, -а, -о, -ы), мягкий (мягок, мягка, мягко, мягки); (*of tumour*) доброкачественный (-нен, -нна).

bent [bent] *n.* склонность, наклонность.

benumbed [bɪ'nʌmd] *adj.* окоченевший, оцепенелый.

benzene ['benziːn] *n.* бензол.

bequeath [bɪ'kwiːð] *v.t.* завещать *impf. & pf.*

(+*a. & d.*). **bequest** *n.* наследство, посмертный дар (*pl.* -ы).

berate [bɪ'reɪt] *v.t.* ругать *impf.*, вы∼ *pf.*

bereave [bɪ'riːv] *v.t.* лишать *impf.*, лишить *pf.* (**of** +*g.*). **bereavement** *n.* потеря (близкого).

Berlin [bɜː'lɪn] *n.* Берлин.

berry ['berɪ] *n.* ягода.

berserk [bə'sɜːk, -'zɜːk] *adj.* неистовый; **go** ∼ неистовствовать *impf.*

berth [bɜːθ] *n.* (*bunk*) койка; (*naut.*) стоянка; **give a wide** ∼ **to** обходить (-ожу, -одишь) *impf.*; избегать *impf.*, избегнуть (избег(нул), -гла) *pf.*+*g.*; *v.t.* ставить *impf.*, по∼ *pf.* на якорь, на причал.

beryl ['berɪl] *n.* берилл.

beseech [bɪ'siːtʃ] *v.t.* умолять *impf.*, умолить *pf.* **beseeching** *adj.* умоляющий.

beset [bɪ'set] *v.t.* осаждать *impf.*, осадить *pf.*

beside [bɪ'saɪd] *prep.* около+*g.*, возле+*g.*, рядом с+*i.*; ∼ **the point** некстати; ∼ **o.s.** вне себя. **besides** *adv.* кроме того, помимо; *prep.* кроме+*g.*

besiege [bɪ'siːdʒ] *v.t.* осаждать *impf.*, осадить *pf.*

besom ['biːz(ə)m] *n.* садовая метла (*pl.* мётлы, -тел, -тлам), веник.

besotted [bɪ'sɒtɪd] *adj.* одурелый.

bespoke [bɪ'spəʊk] *adj.* заказанный (-ан); ∼ **tailor** портной *sb.*, работающий на заказ.

best [best] *adj.* лучший, самый лучший; *adv.* лучше всего, больше всего; **do one's** ∼ делать *impf.*, с∼ *pf.* всё возможное; ∼ **man** шафер (*pl.* -а). **bestseller** *n.* бестселлер, ходкая книга.

bestial ['bestɪəl] *adj.* скотский, зверский. **bestiality** [ˌbestɪ'ælɪtɪ] *n.* скотство, зверство.

bestow [bɪ'stəʊ] *v.t.* даровать *impf. & pf.*

bestride [bɪ'straɪd] *v.t.* (*sit*) сидеть (сижу, сидишь) *impf.* верхом на+*p.*; (*stand*) стоять (-ою, -оишь) *impf.*, расставив ноги над+*i.*

bet [bet] *n.* пари *nt.indecl.*; (*stake*) ставка; *v.t.* держать (-жу, -жишь) *impf.* пари (на+*a.*). **betting** *n.* заключение пари.

betide [bɪ'taɪd] *v.t. & i.* случаться *impf.*, случиться *pf.* (+*d.*); **whate'er** ∼ что бы ни случилось; **woe** ∼ **you** горе тебе.

betray [bɪ'treɪ] *v.t.* изменять *impf.*, изменить (-ню, -нишь) *pf.*+*d.*; предавать (-даю, -даёшь) *impf.*, предать (-ам, -ашь, -аст, -адим; предал, -а, -о) *pf.* **betrayal** *n.* измена, предательство.

betroth [bɪ'trəʊð] *v.t.* обручать *impf.*, обручить *pf.* **betrothal** *n.* обручение.

better ['betə(r)] *adj.* лучший; *adv.* лучше; (*more*) больше; *v.t.* улучшать *impf.*, улучшить *pf.*; **get the** ∼ **of** брать (беру, -рёшь; брал, -а, -о)) *impf.*, взять (возьму, -мёшь; взял, -а, -о) *pf.* верх над+*i.*; **had** ∼: **you had** ∼ **go** вам (*d.*) лучше бы пойти; **think** ∼ **of** передумывать *impf.*, передумать *pf.* **betterment** *n.* улучшение.

between [bɪ'twiːn] *prep.* между+*i.*

bevel ['bev(ə)l] *n.* (*tool*) маска.

beverage ['bevərɪdʒ] *n.* напиток (-тка).

bevy ['bevɪ] *n.* собрание, компания.

bewail [bɪ'weɪl] *v.t.* сокрушаться *impf.*, сокрушиться *pf.* о+*p.*

beware [bɪ'weə(r)] *v.i.* остерегаться *impf.*, остеречься (-егусь, -ежёшься; -ёгся, -еглась) *pf.* (**of** +*g.*).

bewilder [bɪ'wɪldə(r)] *v.t.* сбивать *impf.*, сбить (собью, -ьёшь) *pf.* с толку. **bewildered** *adj.* смущённый (-ён, -ена), озадаченный (-ен). **bewilderment** *n.* смущение, замешательство.

bewitch [bɪ'wɪtʃ] *v.t.* заколдовывать *impf.*, заколдовать *pf.*; очаровывать *impf.*, очаровать *pf.* **bewitching** *adj.* очаровательный.

beyond [bɪ'jɒnd] *prep.* за+*a.* & *i.*; по ту сторону+*g.*; (*above*) сверх+*g.*; (*outside*) вне+*g.*; **the back of ~** глушь (-ши), край (*loc.* -аю) света.

bias ['baɪəs] *n.* (*inclination*) уклон; (*prejudice*) предупреждение; **to cut on the ~** кроить *impf.*, с~ *pf.* по косой. **biased** *adj.* предупреждённый (-ён, -ена).

bib [bɪb] *n.* нагрудник.

Bible ['baɪb(ə)l] *n.* Библия. **biblical** ['bɪblɪk(ə)l] *adj.* библейский.

bibliography [ˌbɪblɪ'ɒɡrəfɪ] *n.* библиография. **bibliophile** ['bɪblɪəʊˌfaɪl] *n.* библиофил.

bibulous ['bɪbjʊləs] *adj.* пьянствующий.

bicarbonate (of soda) [baɪ'kɑːbənɪt] *n.* сода.

bicentenary [ˌbaɪsen'tiːnərɪ] *n.* двухсотлетие; *adj.* двухсотлетний.

biceps ['baɪseps] *n.* бицепс, двуглавая мышца.

bicker ['bɪkə(r)] *v.i.* пререкаться *impf.*; препираться *impf.* **bickering** *n.* пререкания *nt.pl.*, ссоры *f.pl.* из-за мелочей.

bicycle ['baɪsɪk(ə)l] *n.* велосипед.

bid [bɪd] *n.* предложение цены, заявка; *v.t.* & *i.* предлагать *impf.*, предложить (-жу, -жишь) *pf.* (цену) (**for** за+*a.*); *v.t.* (*command*) приказывать *impf.*, приказать (-ажу, -ажешь) *pf.*+*d.* **bidding** *n.* предложение цены, торги *m.pl.*; (*command*) приказание.

bide [baɪd] *v.t.*: **~ one's time** ожидать *impf.* подходящего момента.

biennial [baɪ'enɪəl] *adj.* двухлетний; *n.* двухлетник.

bier [bɪə(r)] *n.* (*похоронные*) дроги (-г) *pl.*

bifocal [baɪ'fəʊk(ə)l] *adj.* двухфокусный.

big [bɪɡ] *adj.* большой, крупный (-пен, -пна, -пно, крупны); (*important*) важный (-жен, -жна, -жно, важны); ~ **business** дело большого масштаба; ~ **end** большая, нижняя, кривошипная головка; ~ **name** знаменитость; ~ **noise** шишка; ~ **top** цирк; **talk** ~ хвастаться *impf.*

bigamist ['bɪɡəmɪst] *n.* (*man*) двоеженец (-нца); (*woman*) двумужница. **bigamous** *adj.* двубрачный. **bigamy** *n.* двубрачие.

bike [baɪk] *n.* велосипед; (*motorcycle*) мото-

цикл; *v.i.* ездить *indet.*, ехать (еду, едешь) *det.*, по~ на мотоцикле. **biker** *n.* мотоциклист, ~ка. **bikeway** *n.* велосипедная дорожка.

bikini [bɪ'kiːnɪ] *n.* бикини *nt.indecl.*

bilateral [baɪ'lætər(ə)l] *adj.* двусторонний.

bilberry ['bɪlbərɪ] *n.* черника.

bile [baɪl] *n.* желчь. **bilious** ['bɪljəs] *adj.* желчный.

bilge [bɪldʒ] *n.* (*sl.*) ерунда.

bilingual [baɪ'lɪŋɡw(ə)l] *adj.* двуязычный. **bilingualism** *n.* двуязычие.

bill [bɪl] *n.* (*account*) счёт (*pl.* -а); (*draft of law*) законопроект; (~ **of exchange**) весель (*pl.* -ля); (*theatr.*) программа; (*poster*) афиша; *v.t.* (*announce*) объявлять *impf.*, объявить (-влю, -вишь) *pf.* в афишах; расклеивать *impf.*, расклеить *pf.* афиши+*g.*; ~ **of fare** меню *nt.indecl.*; ~ **of health** санитарное удостоверение; ~ **of lading** накладная *sb.*; **B~ of Rights** билль *m.* о правах.

billet ['bɪlɪt] *n.* помещение для постоя, квартиры *f.pl.*; *v.t.* расквартировывать *impf.*, расквартировать *pf.*; ~**ing officer** квартирьер.

billhead ['bɪlhed] *n.* бланк.

billiard-ball ['bɪljəd] *n.* бильярдный шар (-á with 2,3,4; *pl.* -ы). **billiard-cue** *n.* кий (кия; *pl.* кии). **billiard-room** *n.* бильярдная *sb.* **billiard-table, billiards** *n.* бильярд.

billion ['bɪljən] *n.* биллион.

billow ['bɪləʊ] *n.* большая волна (*pl.* -ны, -н, -нам), вал (*loc.* -ý; *pl.* -ы); *v.i.* вздыматься *impf.* **billowy** *adj.* вздымающийся, волнистый.

billposter ['bɪlˌpəʊstə(r)] *n.* расклейщик афиш.

bimonthly [baɪ'mʌnθlɪ] *adj.* (*twice a month*) выходящий два раза в месяц; (*every two months*) выходящий раз в два месяца.

bin [bɪn] *n.* (*refuse*) мусорное ведро (*pl.* вёдра, -дер, -драм); (*corn*) закром (*pl.* -á), ларь (-ря) *m.*

bind [baɪnd] *v.t.* (*tie*) связывать *impf.*, связать (-яжу, -яжешь) *pf.*; (*oblige*) обязывать *impf.*, обязать (-яжу, -яжешь) *pf.*; (*book*) переплетать *impf.*, переплести (-етý, -етёшь; -ёл, -ела) *pf.* **binder** *n.* (*person*) переплётчик, -ица; (*agric.*) вязальщик; (*for papers*) папка. **binding** *n.* (*book*) переплёт; (*braid*) оторочка. **bindweed** *n.* вьюнок (-нка).

binge [bɪndʒ] *n.* кутёж (-á).

bingo ['bɪŋɡəʊ] *n.* бинго *nt.indecl.*

binoculars [bɪ'nɒkjʊləz] *n.* бинокль *m.*

binomial [baɪ'nəʊmɪəl] *adj.* двучленный.

biochemical [ˌbaɪəʊ'kemɪk(ə)l] *adj.* биохимический. **biochemist** *n.* биохимик. **biochemistry** *n.* биохимия. **biographer** [baɪ'ɒɡrəfə(r)] *n.* биограф. **bio'graphical** *adj.* биографический. **biography** *n.* биография, жизнеописание. **biological** [ˌbaɪə'lɒdʒɪk(ə)l] *adj.* биологический. **bi'ologist** *n.* биолог.

bi'ology *n.* биоло́гия.

bipartisan [baɪˈpɑːtɪz(ə)n] *adj.* двухпарти́йный. **bipartite** [baɪˈpɑːtaɪt] *adj.* двусторо́нний. **biped** [ˈbaɪped] *n.* двуно́гое живо́тное *sb.* **biplane** *n.* бипла́н.

birch [bɜːtʃ] *n.* (*tree*) берёза; (*rod*) ро́зга (*g.pl.* -зог); *v.t.* сечь (секу́, сечёшь; сек, -ла́) *impf.*, вы́~ *pf.* ро́згой.

bird [bɜːd] *n.* пти́ца; ~ **of passage** перелётная пти́ца; ~ **of prey** хи́щная пти́ца; ~'**s**-**eye view** вид с пти́чьего полёта.

Biro [ˈbaɪərəʊ] *n.* (*propr.*) ша́риковая ру́чка, ша́рик.

birth [bɜːθ] *n.* рожде́ние; (*origin*) происхожде́ние; ~ **certificate** ме́трика; ~ **control** противозача́точные ме́ры *f.pl.* **birthday** *n.* день (дня) *m.* рожде́ния. **birthplace** *n.* ме́сто (*pl.* -а́) рожде́ния. **birthright** *n.* пра́во по рожде́нию.

biscuit [ˈbɪskɪt] *n.* сухо́е пече́нье.

bisect [baɪˈsekt] *v.t.* разреза́ть *impf.*, разре́зать (-е́жу, -е́жешь) *pf.* попола́м.

bishop [ˈbɪʃəp] *n.* епи́скоп; (*chess*) слон (-а́). **bishopric** *n.* епа́рхия.

bismuth [ˈbɪzməθ] *n.* ви́смут.

bison [ˈbaɪs(ə)n] *n.* бизо́н.

bit[1] [bɪt] *n.* (*piece*) кусо́чек (-чка), до́ля (*pl.* -ли, -ле́й); **a** ~ немно́го; **not a** ~ ничу́ть.

bit[2] [bɪt] *n.* (*tech.*) сверло́ (*pl.* -ёрла), бура́в (-а́); (*bridle*) удила́ (-л) *pl.*

bitch [bɪtʃ] *n.* су́ка.

bite [baɪt] *n.* уку́с; (*fishing*) клёв; *v.t.* куса́ть *impf.*, укуси́ть (-ушу́, -у́сишь) *pf.*; (*fish*) клева́ть (клюёт) *impf.*, клю́нуть *pf.* **biting** *adj.* е́дкий (е́док, -едка́, е́дко), ре́зкий (-зок, -зка́, -зко).

bitter [ˈbɪtə(r)] *adj.* го́рький (-рек, -рька́, -рько). **bitterness** *n.* го́речь.

bittern [ˈbɪt(ə)n] *n.* выпь.

bitumen [ˈbɪtjʊmɪn] *n.* биту́м. **bituminous** [bɪˈtjuːmɪnəs] *adj.* биту́м(инозо)ный.

bivouac [ˈbɪvʊæk] *n.* бива́к.

bi-weekly [baɪˈwiːklɪ] *adj.* (*twice a week*) выходя́щий два ра́за в неде́лю; (*fortnightly*) выходя́щий раз в две неде́ли, двухнеде́льный.

bizarre [bɪˈzɑː(r)] *adj.* стра́нный (-нен, -нна́, -нно), причу́дливый.

blab [blæb] *v.t.* выба́лтывать *impf.*, вы́болтать *pf.*

black [blæk] *adj.* чёрный (-рен, -рна́); (*dark-skinned*) черноко́жий; ~ **eye** подби́тый глаз (*pl.* -а́, глаз, -а́м), фона́рь (-ря́) *m.*; *n.* (*negro*) чёрный *sb.*; (*mourning*) тра́ур. **blackberry** *n.* ежеви́ка (*collect.*). **blackbird** *n.* чёрный дрозд (-а́). **blackboard** *n.* кла́ссная доска́ (*a.* -ску́; *pl.* -ски, -со́к, -ска́м). **black'currant** *n.* чёрная сморо́дина. **blacken** *v.t.* черни́ть *impf.*, за~, на~, (*fig.*) о~ *pf.* **blackguard** [ˈblæɡɑːd, -ɡəd] *n.* подле́ц (-ца́), мерза́вец (-вца). **blackleg** *n.* штрейкбре́хер. **blackmail** *n.* шанта́ж (-а́); *v.t.* шантажи́ровать *impf.*

bladder [ˈblædə(r)] *n.* пузы́рь (-ря́) *m.*

blade [bleɪd] *n.* (*knife etc.*) ле́звие, клино́к (-нка́); (*oar etc.*) ло́пасть (*pl.* -ти, -те́й); (*grass*) были́нка.

blame [bleɪm] *n.* вина́, порица́ние; *v.t.* вини́ть *impf.* (**for** в+*p.*); **be to** ~ быть винова́тым. **blameless** *adj.* безупре́чный, неви́нный (-нен, -нна).

blanch [blɑːntʃ] *v.t.* бели́ть *impf.*, вы́~ *pf.*; (*food*) обва́ривать *impf.*, обвари́ть (-рю́, -ришь) *pf.*; *v.i.* бледне́ть *impf.*, по~ *pf.*

bland [blænd] *adj.* мя́гкий (-гок, -гка́, -гко, мя́гки); (*in manner*) ве́жливый.

blandishment [ˈblændɪʃmənt] *n.*: *pl.* льсти́вые ре́чи (-че́й) *pl.*

blank [blæŋk] *n.* (*space*) пробе́л; (*form*) бланк; (*ticket*) пусто́й биле́т; *adj.* пусто́й (пуст, -а́, -о, -ы́), незапо́лненный (-ен); чи́стый (чист, -а́, -о, чи́сты); ~ **cartridge** холосто́й патро́н; ~ **wall** глуха́я стена́ (*a.* -ну; *pl.* -ны, -н, -на́м); ~ **verse** бе́лый стих (-а́).

blanket [ˈblæŋkɪt] *n.* одея́ло.

blare [bleə(r)] *n.* звук трубы́; *v.i.* труби́ть *impf.*, про~ *pf.*; (*shout*) ора́ть (ору́, орёшь) *impf.*

blasphemous [ˈblæsfɪməs] *adj.* богоху́льный. **blasphemy** *n.* богоху́льство.

blast [blɑːst] *n.* (*wind*) поры́в ве́тра; (*air*) струя́ (*pl.* -у́и); (*sound*) гудо́к (-дка́); (*of explosion*) взрывна́я волна́ (*pl.* -ны, -н, -на́м); *v.t.* взрыва́ть *impf.*, взорва́ть (-ву́, -вёшь; взорва́л, -а́, -о) *pf.*; ~ **off** стартова́ть *impf.* & *pf.*; взлета́ть *impf.*, взлете́ть (-ечу́, -ети́шь) *pf.* **blast-furnace** *n.* до́менная печь (*pl.* -чи, -че́й).

blatant [ˈbleɪt(ə)nt] *adj.* (*clear*) я́вный; (*flagrant*) вопию́щий.

blaze[1] [bleɪz] *n.* (*flame*) я́ркое пла́мя *nt.*; (*light*) я́ркий цвет; *v.i.* (*flame*) пыла́ть *impf.*; (*with light*) сверка́ть *impf.*

blaze[2] [bleɪz] *v.t.* (*mark*) ме́тить *impf.*, на~ *pf.*; ~ **the trail** прокла́дывать *impf.* путь.

blazer [ˈbleɪzə(r)] *n.* спорти́вная ку́ртка.

bleach [bliːtʃ] *n.* хло́рная и́звесть; *v.t.* бели́ть *impf.*, вы́~ *pf.* **bleaching** *n.* отбе́ливание, беле́ние.

bleak [bliːk] *adj.* (*bare*) оголённый (-ён, -ена́); (*dreary*) уны́лый.

bleary [ˈblɪərɪ] *adj.* му́тный (-тен, -тна́, -тно, му́тны́), затума́ненный (-ен). **bleary-eyed** *adj.* с затума́ненными глаза́ми.

bleat [bliːt] *v.i.* бле́ять (-е́ю, -е́ешь) *impf.*; *n.* бле́яние.

bleed [bliːd] *v.i.* кровоточи́ть *impf.*; *v.t.* пуска́ть *impf.*, пусти́ть (пущу́, пу́стишь) *pf.* кровь+*d.*; *n.* кровотече́ние; кровопуска́ние; **my heart** ~**s** се́рдце облива́ется кро́вью.

bleep [bliːp] *n.* бип.

blemish [ˈblemɪʃ] *n.* недоста́ток (-тка), пятно́ (*pl.* -тна, -тен, -тнам), поро́к; **without** ~ непоро́чный, незапя́танный (-ан).

blench [blentʃ] *v.i.* вздро́гнуть *pf.*

blend [blend] *n.* смесь; *v.t.* смéшивать *impf.*, смешáть *pf.*; *v.i.* гармонироáвать *impf.* **blender** *n.* смеситель *m.* (*cul.*) миксер.

bless [bles] *v.t.* благословлять *impf.*, благословить *pf.* **blessed** *adj.* благословéнный (-éн, -éнна), счастливый (счáстлив). **blessing** *n.* (*action*) благословéние; (*object*) блáго.

blind [blaɪnd] *adj.* слепóй (слеп, -á, -о); ~ **alley** тупик (-á); ~ **flying** слепóй полёт; *n.* штóра; *v.t.* ослеплять *impf.*, ослепить *pf.*

blink [blɪŋk] *v.i.* мигáть *impf.*, мигнýть *pf.*; моргáть *impf.*, моргнýть *pf.*; *n.* мигáние. **blinkers** *n.* шóры (-р) *pl.*

blip [blɪp] *n.* сигнáл на экрáне.

bliss [blɪs] *n.* блажéнство. **blissful** *adj.* блажéнный (-éн, -éнна).

blister ['blɪstə(r)] *n.* пузырь (-ря) *m.*, волдырь (-ря) *m.*; *v.i.* покрывáться *impf.*, покрыться (-рóюсь, -рóешься) *pf.* пузырями, волдырями; *v.t.* вызывáть *impf.*, вызвать (-зовет) *pf.* пузырь, волдырь на+*p.*, на кóже+*g.*

blithe [blaɪð] *adj.* весёлый (вéсел, -á, -о, вéселы); (*carefree*) беспéчный.

blitz [blɪts] *n.* стремительное нападéние; (*aerial*) стремительный налёт. **blitzkrieg** ['blɪtskriːg] *n.* молниенóсная войнá.

blizzard ['blɪzəd] *n.* метéль, вьюга.

bloated ['bləʊtɪd] *adj.* надýтый, раздýтый.

bloater ['bləʊtə(r)] *n.* копчёная селёдка.

blob [blɒb] *n.* (*liquid*) кáпля (*g.pl.* -пель); (*spot*) пятнышко (*pl.* -шки, -шек, -шкам).

bloc [blɒk] *n.* блок.

block [blɒk] *n.* (*of wood*) чурбáн, колóда; (*of stone*) глыба; (*obstruction*) затóр; (*traffic*) прóбка; (*tech.*) блок; (~ *of flats*) жилóй дом (*pl.* -á); ~ **and tackle** тáли (-лей) *pl.*; ~ **letters** печáтные бýквы *f.pl.*; *v.t.* преграждáть *impf.*, прегради́ть *pf.*; ~ **out** набрáсывать *impf.*, набросáть *pf.* вчернé.

blockade [blɒˈkeɪd] *n.* блокáда; *v.t.* блокировать *impf.* & *pf.*

blockage ['blɒkɪdʒ] *n.* затóр.

blond [blɒnd] *n.* блондин, ~ка; *adj.* белокýрый.

blood [blʌd] *n.* кровь (*loc.* -ви́; *pl.* -ви, -вéй); (*descent*) происхождéние; ~ **bank** хранилище крóви и плáзмы; ~ **donor** дóнор; ~ **orange** королёк (-лькá); ~ **pressure** кровянóе давлéние; ~ **relation** ближий рóдственник, -ая рóдственница; ~ **transfusion** переливáние крóви. **bloodhound** *n.* ищéйка. **bloodless** *adj.* бескрóвный. **blood-poisoning** *n.* заражéние крóви. **blood-vessel** *n.* кровенóсный сосýд. **bloody** *adj.* кровáвый, окровáвленный (-ен, -енна).

bloom [bluːm] *n.* расцвéт; *v.i.* расцветáть *impf.*, расцвести (-етý, -етёшь; -ёл, -елá) *pf.*

blossom ['blɒsəm] *n.* цветóк (-ткá; *pl.* цветы); *collect.* цвет; **in** ~ в цветý.

blot [blɒt] *n.* клякса; пятнó (*pl.* -тна, -тен, -тнам); *v.t.* промокáть *impf.*, промокнýть *pf.*; пáчкать *impf.*, за~ *pf.*

blotch [blɒtʃ] *n.* пятнó (*pl.* -тна, -тен, -тнам). **blotchy** *adj.* запятнанный (-ан).

blotter ['blɒtə(r)], **blotting-paper** *n.* промокáтельная бумáга.

blouse [blaʊz] *n.* кóфточка, блýзка.

blow¹ [bləʊ] *n.* удáр.

blow² [bləʊ] *v.t.* & *i.* дуть (дýю, дýешь) *impf.*; вéять (вéет) *impf.*; выдувáть *impf.*, выдуть (-ую, -уешь) *pf.*; ~ **away** сносить (-ошý, -óсишь) *impf.*, снести (-есý, -есёшь; снёс, -лá) *pf.*; ~ **down** свáливать *impf.*, свали́ть (-лю, -лишь) *pf.*; ~ **up** взрывáть *impf.*, взорвáть (-вý, -вёшь; взорвáл, -á, -о) *pf.* **blow-lamp** *n.* паяльная лáмпа. **blow-up** *n.* фотопаннó *nt.indecl.*

blubber¹ ['blʌbə(r)] *n.* вóрвань.

blubber² ['blʌbə(r)] *v.i.* ревéть (-вý, -вёшь) *impf.*

bludgeon ['blʌdʒ(ə)n] *n.* дубинка.

blue [bluː] *adj.* (*dark*) синий (-нь, -ня, -не); (*light*) голубóй; *n.* синий, голубóй цвет; (*sky*) нéбо. **bluebell** *n.* колокóльчик. **bluebottle** *n.* синяя мýха. **blueprint** *n.* синька, светокóпия; (*fig.*) проéкт.

bluff¹ [blʌf] *n.* (*deceit*) обмáн, блеф; *v.i.* притворяться *impf.*, притвориться *pf.*

bluff² [blʌf] *n.* (*cliff*) отвéсный бéрег (*loc.* -ý; *pl.* -á); *adj.* (*person*) грубовáто-добродýшный.

blunder ['blʌndə(r)] *n.* грýбая ошибка, оплóшность; *v.i.* ошибáться *impf.*, ошибиться (-бýсь, -бёшься; -бся) *pf.*; (*stumble*) спотыкáться *impf.*, споткнýться *pf.*

blunt [blʌnt] *adj.* (*knife*) тупóй (туп, -á, -о, тýпы); (*person*) прямóй (прям, -á, -о, прямы); (*words*) рéзкий (-зок, -зкá, -зко) *v.t.* тупить (-плю, -пишь) *impf.*, за~, с~ *pf.*; притуплять *impf.*, притупить (-плю, -пишь) *pf.*

blur [blɜː(r)] *n.* расплывчатая фóрма; *v.t.* тумáнить *impf.*, за~ *pf.*; изглáживать *impf.*, изглáдить *pf.*

blurb [blɜːb] *n.* (издáтельская) аннотáция.

blurred ['blɜːd] *adj.* расплывчатый, неясный (-сен, -снá, -сно, неясны).

blurt [blɜːt] *v.t.*: ~ **out** выбáлтывать *impf.*, выболтать *pf.*

blush [blʌʃ] *v.i.* краснéть *impf.*, по~ *pf.*; зардéться *pf.*; *n.* румянец (-нца).

bluster ['blʌstə(r)] *v.i.* бушевáть (-шýю, -шýешь) *impf.*; *n.* пустые угрóзы *f.pl.*

boa ['bəʊə] *n.* боá *m.indecl.* (*snake*), *nt.indecl.* (*wrap*); ~ **constrictor** удáв.

boar [bɔː(r)] *n.* бóров (*pl.* -ы, -óв); (*wild*) вепрь *m.*

board [bɔːd] *n.* доскá (*a.* -ску; *pl.* -ски, -сóк, -скáм); (*table*) стол (-á); (*food*) питáние; (*committee*) правлéние, совéт; *pl.* сцéна, подмóстки (-ков) *pl.*; (*naut.*) борт (*loc.* -ý; *pl.* -á); **on** ~ на борт(ý); *v.i.* столовáться *impf.*; *v.t.* садиться *impf.*, сесть (сяду, -дешь; сел) *pf.* (на корáбль, в пóезд и т.д.); ~**ing**

pass поса́дочный тало́н; (*naut.*) брать (беру́, -рёшь; брал, -á, -о) *impf.*, взять (возьму́, -мёшь; взял, -á, -о) *pf.* на аборда́ж.
boarder *n.* пансионе́р. **boarding-house** *n.* пансио́н. **boarding-school** *n.* интерна́т.
boast [bəʊst] *v.i.* хва́статься *impf.*, по~ *pf.*; *v.t.* горди́ться *impf.*+*i.*; *n.* хвастовство́. **boaster** *n.* хвасту́н (-á). **boastful** *adj.* хвастли́вый.
boat [bəʊt] *n.* ло́дка, су́дно (*pl.* -дá, -до́в), кора́бль (-ля́) *m.*; ~ **building** судострое́ние. **boat-hook** *n.* баго́р (-грá). **boatswain** ['bəʊs(ə)n] *n.* бо́цман.
bob¹ [bɒb] *n.* (*weight*) баланси́р; (*hair*) коро́ткая стри́жка.
bob² [bɒb] *v.i.* подпры́гивать *impf.*, подпры́гнуть *pf.*
bobbin ['bɒbɪn] *n.* кату́шка, шпу́лька.
bobby ['bɒbɪ] *n.* полисме́н, бо́бби *m.indecl.*
bobsleigh ['bɒbsleɪ] *n.* бо́бслей.
bobtail ['bɒbteɪl] *n.* обре́занный хвост (-á).
bode [bəʊd] *v.t.* предвеща́ть *impf.*
bodice ['bɒdɪs] *n.* лиф, корса́ж.
bodily ['bɒdɪlɪ] *adv.* целико́м; *adj.* теле́сный, физи́ческий.
bodkin ['bɒdkɪn] *n.* тупа́я игла́ (*pl.* -лы).
body ['bɒdɪ] *n.* те́ло (*pl.* -лá), ту́ловище; (*corpse*) труп; (*frame*) о́стов; (*troops etc.*) ко́рпус (*pl.* -á); (*carriage*) ку́зов (*pl.* -á); (*main part*) основна́я часть. **body-builder** *n.* культури́ст. **body-building** *n.* культури́зм. **bodyguard** *n.* телохрани́тель *m.*; *collect.* ко́рпус телохрани́телей.
bog [bɒg] *n.* боло́та, тряси́на; **get ~ged down** увяза́ть *impf.*, увя́знуть (-з) *pf.* **boggy** *adj.* боло́тистый.
bogus ['bəʊgəs] *adj.* подде́льный, фальши́вый.
bogy ['bəʊgɪ] *n.* бу́ка, пу́гало.
boil¹ [bɔɪl] *n.* (*med.*) furу́нкул, нары́в.
boil² [bɔɪl] *v.i.* кипе́ть (-пи́т) *impf.*, вс~ *pf.*; *v.t.* кипяти́ть (-пит) *impf.*, с~ *pf.*; (*cook*) вари́ть (-рю́, -ришь) *impf.*, с~ *pf.*; *n.* кипе́ние; **bring to the ~** доводи́ть (-ожу́, -о́дишь) *impf.*, довести́ (-еду́, -дёшь; -ёл, -елá) *pf.* до кипе́ния. **boiled** *adj.* варёный, кипячёный. **boiler** *n.* (*vessel*) котёл (-тлá); (*fowl*) ку́рица го́дная для ва́рки; ~ **suit** комбинезо́н. **boilerhouse** *n.* коте́льная *sb.* **boiling** *n.* кипе́ние; *adj.* кипя́щий; ~ **water** кипято́к (-ткá).
boisterous ['bɔɪstərəs] *adj.* бу́рный (-рен, бу́рнá, -рно), шумли́вый.
bold [bəʊld] *adj.* сме́лый (смел, -á, -о), хра́брый (храбр, -á, -о, хра́бры́), де́рзкий (-зок, -зкá, -зко); (*clear*) чёткий (-ток, -ткá, -тко); (*type*) жи́рный.
bole [bəʊl] *n.* ствол (-á).
bolster ['bəʊlstə(r)] *n.* ва́лик; *v.t.*: ~ **up** подпира́ть *impf.*, подпере́ть (подопру́, -рёшь) подпёр) *pf.*
bolt [bəʊlt] *n.* засо́в, задви́жка; (*tech.*) болт (-á); (*flight*) бе́гство; *v.t.* запира́ть *impf.*,

запере́ть (-пру́, -прёшь; за́пер, -лá, -ло) *pf.* на засо́в; скрепля́ть *impf.*, скрепи́ть *pf.* болта́ми; *v.i.* (*flee*) удира́ть *impf.*, удра́ть (удеру́, -рёшь; удра́л, -лá, -ло) *pf.*; (*horse*) понести́ (-есёт; -ёс, -еслá) *pf.*
bomb [bɒm] *n.* бо́мба; *v.t.* бомби́ть *impf.*; бомбарди́ровать *impf.* **bombard** [bɒm'bɑːd] *v.t.* бомбарди́ровать *impf.* **bombardment** *n.* бомбардиро́вка. **bomber** *n.* бомбардиро́вщик.
bombastic [bɒm'bæstɪk] *adj.* напы́щенный (-ен, -енна).
bonanza [bə'nænzə] *n.* золото́е дно.
bond [bɒnd] *n.* (*econ.*) облига́ция; связь; *pl.* око́вы (-в) *pl.*, (*fig.*) у́зы (уз) *pl.*
bone [bəʊn] *n.* кость (*pl.* -ти, -те́й); *pl.* прах; ~ **of contention** я́блоко раздо́ра.
bonfire ['bɒn,faɪə(r)] *n.* костёр (-трá).
bonnet ['bɒnɪt] *n.* ка́пор, че́пчик; (*car*) капо́т.
bonny ['bɒnɪ] *adj.* здоро́вый, хоро́шенький.
bony ['bəʊnɪ] *adj.* кости́стый.
booby ['buːbɪ] *n.* болва́н, о́лух; ~ **trap** лову́шка.
book [bʊk] *n.* кни́га; *v.t.* (*order*) зака́зывать *impf.*, заказа́ть (-ажу́, -а́жешь) *pf.*; (*reserve*) брони́ровать *impf.*, за~ *pf.* **bookbinder** *n.* переплётчик, -ица. **bookkeeper** *n.* бухга́лтер. **bookmaker**, **bookie** *n.* букме́кер. **booking** *n.* (*order*) зака́з; (*sale*) прода́жа биле́тов; ~ **clerk** касси́р; ~ **office** ка́сса.
boom¹ [buːm] *n.* (*barrier*) бон.
boom² [buːm] *n.* (*sound*) гул; (*econ.*) бум, экономи́ческий подъём; *v.i.* гуде́ть (гужу́, гуди́шь) *impf.*; (*flourish*) процвета́ть *impf.*
boon¹ [buːn] *n.* бла́го.
boon² [buːn] *adj.*: ~ **companion** весёлый друг (*pl.* друзья́, -зе́й).
boor [bʊə(r)] *n.* гру́бый, мужикова́тый челове́к. **boorish** *adj.* мужикова́тый.
boost [buːst] *v.t.* (*raise*) поднима́ть *impf.*, подня́ть (-ниму́, -ни́мешь; по́днял, -á, -о) *pf.*; (*increase*) увели́чивать *impf.*, увели́чить *pf.*
boot [buːt] *n.* боти́нок (-нка; *g.pl.* -нок), сапо́г (-á; *g.pl.* -г); (*football*) бу́тса; *v.t.*: ~ **out** выгоня́ть *impf.*, вы́гнать (вы́гоню, вы́гнишь) *pf.* **boo'tee** *n.* де́тский вя́заный башмачо́к (-чкá). **boots** *n.* коридо́рный *sb.*
booth [buːð, buːθ] *n.* кио́ск, бу́дка; (*polling*) каби́на (для голосова́ния).
bootlegger ['buːtlegə(r)] *n.* торго́вец (-вца) контраба́ндными спиртны́ми напи́тками.
booty ['buːtɪ] *n.* добы́ча; (*mil.*) трофе́и *m.pl.*
booze [buːz] *n.* вы́пивка; *v.i.* выпива́ть *impf.*
boracic [bə'ræsɪk] *adj.* бо́рный. **borax** ['bɔː,ræks] *n.* бура́.
border ['bɔːdə(r)] *n.* (*boundary*) грани́ца; (*edge*) край (*loc.* -аю́; *pl.* -ая́); (*edging*) кайма́, бордю́р; *v.i.* грани́чить *impf.* (**on** с+*i.*); *v.t.* окаймля́ть *impf.*, окайми́ть *pf.* **borderline** *n.* грани́ца.
bore¹ [bɔː(r)] *n.* (*tedium*) ску́ка; (*person*) ну́дный челове́к; *v.t.* надоеда́ть *impf.*,

надое́сть (-е́м, -е́шь, -е́ст, -еди́м; -е́л) *pf.*
boredom *n.* ску́ка. **boring**[1] *adj.* ску́чный (-чен, -чна́, -чно).

bore[2] [bɔː(r)] *n.* (*calibre*) кана́л (ствола́), кали́бр (ору́жия); (*borehole*) бурова́я сква́жина; *v.t.* сверли́ть *impf.*, про~ *pf.* **boring**[2] *adj.* сверля́щий, бурово́й.

born [bɔːn] *adj.* прирождённый; **be ~** роди́ться *impf.*, (-и́лся, -и́ла́сь) *pf.*

borough ['bʌrə] *n.* го́род (*pl.* -а́).

borrow ['bɒrəu] *v.t.* занима́ть *impf.*, заня́ть (займу́, -мёшь; за́нял, -а́, -о) *pf.* (**from** y+g.); заи́мствовать *impf. & pf.*

bosh [bɒʃ] *n.* чепуха́.

bosom ['buz(ə)m] *n.* (*breast*) грудь (-ди́, *i.* -дью; *pl.* -ди, -де́й); (*heart*) се́рдце; (*depths*) не́дра (-р) *pl.*; **~ friend** закады́чный друг (*pl.* друзья́, -зе́й).

boss [bɒs] *n.* хозя́ин (*pl.* -я́ева, -я́ев), шеф; *v.t.* кома́ндовать *impf.*, с~ *pf.*+i. **bossy** *adj.* вла́стный.

botanical [bə'tænɪk(ə)l] *adj.* ботани́ческий. **botanist** ['bɒtənɪst] *n.* бота́ник. **botany** ['bɒtənɪ] *n.* бота́ника.

botch [bɒtʃ] *v.t.* по́ртить *impf.*, ис~ *pf.*

both [bəuθ] *adj., pron.* о́ба (обо́их, -им, -ими *m. & nt.*), о́бе (обе́их, -им, -ими) *f.*; *adv.* то́же; **~ ... and** и... и; не то́лько... но и; как... так и.

bother ['bɒðə(r)] *n.* беспоко́йство, хло́поты (*g.* -о́т) *pl.*; *v.t.* беспоко́ить *impf.*; надоеда́ть *impf.*, надое́сть (-е́м, -е́шь, -е́ст, -еди́м; -е́л) *pf.*

bottle ['bɒt(ə)l] *n.* буты́лка; *v.t.* разлива́ть *impf.*, разли́ть (разолью́, -ьёшь; разли́л, -а́, -о) *pf.* по буты́лкам; **~ up** (*conceal*) зата́ивать *impf.*, затаи́ть *pf.*; (*restrain*) подавля́ть *impf.*, подави́ть (-влю́, -вишь) *pf.* **bottleneck** *n.* у́зкое ме́сто (*pl.* -та́), затор.

bottom ['bɒtəm] *n.* ни́жняя часть (*pl.* -ти, -те́й); (*of river etc.*) дно (*pl.* до́нья, -ьев); (*buttocks*) зад (*loc.* -у́; *pl.* -ы́); *adj.* са́мый ни́жний. **bottomless** *adj.* бездо́нный (-нен, -нна); **~ pit** ад (*loc.* -у́).

bough [bau] *n.* сук (-á, *loc.* -у́; *pl.* -и, -о́в & су́чья, -ьев), ветвь (*pl.* -ви, -ве́й).

boulder ['bəuldə(r)] *n.* валу́н (-á), глы́ба.

bounce [bauns] *n.* прыжо́к (-жка́), скачо́к (-чка́); *v.i.* подпры́гивать *impf.*, подпры́гнуть *pf.* **bouncing** *adj.* ро́слый, здоро́вый.

bound[1] [baund] *n.* (*limit*) преде́л; *v.t.* ограни́чивать *impf.*, ограни́чить *pf.*

bound[2] [baund] *n.* (*spring*) прыжо́к (-жка́), скачо́к (-чка́); *v.i.* пры́гать *impf.*, пры́гнуть *pf.*; скака́ть (-ачу́, -а́чешь) *impf.*

bound[3] [baund] *adj.* (*tied*) свя́занный (-ан); **he is ~ to be there** он объяза́тельно там бу́дет.

bound[4] [baund] *adj.*: **to be ~ for** направля́ться *impf.*, напра́виться *pf.* на+a.

boundary ['baundərɪ, -drɪ] *n.* грани́ца, межа́ (*pl.* -жи, -ж, -жа́м).

bounder ['baundə(r)] *n.* хам.

boundless ['baundlɪs] *adj.* беспреде́льный, безграни́чный.

bounteous ['bauntɪəs], **bountiful** *adj.* (*generous*) ще́дрый (щедр, -а́, -о); (*ample*) оби́льный. **bounty** *n.* ще́дрость; (*gratuity*) пре́мия.

bouquet [buː'keɪ, bəu-] *n.* буке́т.

bourgeois ['buəʒwaː] *n.* буржуа́ *m.indecl.*; *adj.* буржуа́зный. **bourgeoisie** [,buəʒwaː'ziː] *n.* буржуази́я.

bout [baut] *n.* (*of illness*) при́ступ; (*sport*) схва́тка, встре́ча.

boutique [buː'tiːk] *n.* (небольшо́й) мо́дный магази́н.

bovine ['bəuvaɪn] *adj.* быча́чий (-чья, -чье; (*fig.*) тупо́й (туп, -а́, -о, ту́пы).

bow[1] [bəu] *n.* (*weapon*) лук; (*knot*) бант; (*mus.*) смычо́к (-чка́).

bow[2] [bau] *n.* (*obeisance*) покло́н; *v.i.* кла́няться *impf.*, поклани́ться (-ню́сь, -нишься) *pf.*

bow[3] [bau] *n.* (*naut.*) нос (*loc.* -у́; *pl.* -ы́); (*rowing*) пе́рвый но́мер (*pl.* -á).

bowdlerize ['baudlə,raɪz] *v.t.* очища́ть *impf.*, очи́стить *pf.*

bowels ['bauəlz] *n.* кише́чник; (*depths*) не́дра (-р) *pl.*

bower ['bauə(r)] *n.* бесе́дка.

bowl[1] [bəul] *n.* (*vessel*) ми́ска, таз (*loc.* -у́; *pl.* -ы́), ча́ша.

bowl[2] [bəul] *n.* (*ball*) шар (-á with 2,3,4; *pl.* -ы́); *v.i.* мета́ть (мечу́, -чешь) *impf.*, метну́ть *pf.* мяч; подава́ть (-даю́, -даёшь) *impf.*, пода́ть (-а́м, -а́шь, -а́ст, -ади́м; по́дал, -а́, -о) *pf.* мяч. **bowler (hat)** *n.* котело́к (-лка́). **bowling-alley** *n.* кегельба́н. **bowls** *n.* игра́ в шары́; **play ~** игра́ть *impf.*, сыгра́ть *pf.* в шары́.

box[1] [bɒks] *n.* (*container*) коро́бка, я́щик, сунду́к (-á); (*theatr.*) ло́жа; (*coach*) ко́злы (-зел) *pl.*; (*horse*) сто́йло; **~ office** ка́сса; **~ pleat** бантова́я скла́дка.

box[2] [bɒks], **boxwood** *n.* (*bot.*) самши́т.

box[3] [bɒks] *v.i.* бокси́ровать *impf.* **boxer** *n.* боксёр. **boxing** *n.* бокс.

boy [bɔɪ] *n.* ма́льчик, ю́ноша *m.*; **~ scout** бойска́ут. **boyfriend** *n.* друг (*pl.* друзья́, -зе́й). **boyhood** *n.* о́трочество. **boyish** *adj.* мальчи́шеский.

boycott ['bɔɪkɒt] *n.* бойко́т; *v.t.* бойкоти́ровать *impf. & pf.*

bra [braː] *n.* бюстга́лтер.

brace [breɪs] *n.* (*clamp*) скре́па; *pl.* подтя́жки *f.pl.*; (*pair*) па́ра; *v.t.* скрепля́ть *impf.*, скрепи́ть *pf.*; **~ o.s.** напряга́ть *impf.*, напря́чь (-ягу́, -яжешь; -я́г, -ягла́) *pf.* си́лы.

bracelet ['breɪslɪt] *n.* брасле́т.

bracing ['breɪsɪŋ] *adj.* бодря́щий.

bracket ['brækɪt] *n.* (*support*) кронште́йн; *pl.* ско́бки *f.pl.*; (*category*) катего́рия, ру́брика.

brad [bræd] *n.* штифчик. **bradawl** ['brædɔːl] *n.* ши́ло (*pl.* ши́лья, -ьев).

brag [bræg] *v.i.* хва́статься *impf.*, по~ *pf.*

braggart ['brægət] *n.* хвастун (-á).

braid [breɪd] *n.* тесьмá.

Braille [breɪl] *n.* шрифт Брáйля.

brain [breɪn] *n.* мозг (-a(y), *loc.* -e & -ý; *pl.* -й); (*intellect*) ум (-á); ~ **drain** утéчка умóв; *v.t.* размозжи́ть *pf.* гóлову+d. **brainstorm** *n.* припáдок (-дка) безýмия. **brainwashing** *n.* идеологи́ческая обрабóтка. **brainwave** *n.* блестя́щая идéя.

braise [breɪz] *v.t.* туши́ть (-шý, -шишь) *impf.*, с~ *pf.*

brake [breɪk] *n.* тóрмоз (*pl.* -á, *fig.* -ы); *v.t.* тормози́ть *impf.*, за~ *pf.*

bramble ['bræmb(ə)l] *n.* ежеви́ка.

brambling ['bræmblɪŋ] *n.* вьюрóк (-ркá).

bran [bræn] *n.* óтруби (-бéй) *pl.*

branch [brɑːntʃ] *n.* вéтка; (*subject*) óтрасль; (*department*) отделéние, филиáл; *v.i.* разветвля́ться *impf.*, разветви́ться *pf.*

brand [brænd] *n.* (*mark*) клеймó (*pl.* -ма); (*make*) мáрка; (*sort*) сорт (*pl.* -á); *v.t.* клейми́ть *impf.*, за~ *pf.*

brandish ['brændɪʃ] *v.t.* размáхивать *impf.*+i.

brandy ['brændɪ] *n.* коньяк (-á(ý)).

brass [brɑːs] *n.* латýнь, жёлтая медь; (*mus.*) мéдные инструмéнты *m.pl.*; *adj.* латýнный, мéдный; ~ **band** мéдный духовóй оркéстр; **bold as** ~ нáглый (нагл, -á, -о); ~ **hats** начáльство, стáршие офицéры *m.pl.*; **top** ~ вы́сшее начáльство.

brassière ['bræzɪə(r), -sɪˌeə(r)] *n.* бюстгáлтер.

brat [bræt] *n.* ребёнок (-нка; *pl.* дéти, -тéй); (*pej.*) пострéл.

bravado [brə'vɑːdəʊ] *n.* бравáда.

brave [breɪv] *adj.* хрáбрый (храбр, -á, -о, хрáбры), смéлый (смел, -á, -о); *v.t.* хрáбро встречáть *impf.*, встрéтить *pf.* **bravery** *n.* хрáбрость, смéлость.

brawl [brɔːl] *n.* ýличная дрáка, скандáл; *v.i.* дрáться (дерýсь, -рёшься; дрáлся, -алáсь, -áлось) *impf.*, по~ *pf.*; скандáлить *impf.*, на~ *pf.*

brawn [brɔːn] *n.* мýскульная си́ла; (*cul.*) свинóй стýдень (-дня) *m.* **brawny** дюжий (дюж, -á, -е), си́льный (си́лён, -льнá, -льно, си́льны).

bray [breɪ] *n.* крик ослá; *v.i.* кричáть (-чи́т) *impf.*; издавáть (-даю́, -даёшь) *impf.*, издáть (-áм, -áшь, -áст, -ади́м; издáл, -á, -о) *pf.* рéзкий звук.

brazen ['breɪz(ə)n] *adj.* мéдный, брóнзовый; (~-*faced*) бессты́дный.

brazier ['breɪzɪə(r), -ʒə(r)] *n.* жарóвня (*g.pl.* -вен).

breach [briːtʃ] *n.* нарушéние; (*break*) пролóм; (*mil.*) брешь; *v.t.* пролáмывать *impf.*, проломáть, проломи́ть (-млю́, -мишь) *pf.*

bread [bred] *n.* хлеб, (*white*) бýлка. **breadwinner** *n.* корми́лец (-льца).

breadth [bredθ] *n.* ширинá, широтá.

break [breɪk] *n.* пролóм, разры́в; (*pause*) переры́в, пáуза; ~ **of day** рассвéт; *v.t.* ломáть *impf.*, с~ *pf.*; разбивáть *impf.*,

разби́ть (разобью́, -ьёшь) *pf.*; (*violate*) нарушáть *impf.*, нарýшить *pf.*; ~ **in(to)** вламывáться *impf.*, вломи́ться (-млю́сь, -мишься) *pf.* в+a.; ~ **off** отлáмывать *impf.*, отломи́ть (-млю́, -мишь) *pf.*; (*interrupt*) прерывáть *impf.*, прервáть (-вý, -вёшь; -вáл, -валá, -вáло) *pf.*; ~ **out** вырывáться *impf.*, вы́рваться (-вусь, -вешься) *pf.*; ~ **through** пробивáться *impf.*, проби́ться (-бью́сь, -бьёшься) *pf.*; ~ **up** разбивáть(ся) *impf.*, разби́ть(ся) (разобью́, -бьёт(ся) *pf.*; ~ **with** порывáть *impf.*, порвáть (-вý, -вёшь; порвáл, -á, -о) *pf.* с+i. **breakage** *n.* полóмка.

breakdown *n.* авáрия; **nervous** ~ нéрвное расстрóйство. **breaker** *n.* бурýн (-á). **breakfast** ['brekfəst] *n.* ýтренний зáвтрак; *v.i.* зáвтракать *impf.*, по~ *pf.* **breakneck** *adj.*: **at** ~ **speed** сломя́ гóлову. **breakwater** *n.* мол (*loc.* -ý).

breast [brest] *n.* грудь (-ди́, *i.* -дью; *pl.* -ди, -дéй). **breast-feeding** *n.* кормлéние грýдью. **breaststroke** *n.* брасс.

breath [breθ] *n.* дыхáние, дуновéние. **breathalyse** ['breθəlaɪz] *v.t.* проверя́ть *impf.*, провéрить *pf.* на алкогóль *m.* **Breathalyser** *n.* (*propr.*) алкомéтр. **breathe** [briːð] *v.i.* дышáть (-шý, -шишь) *impf.*; ~ **in** вдыхáть *impf.*, вдохнýть *pf.*; ~ **out** выдыхáть *impf.*, вы́дохнуть *pf.* **breather, breathing-space** *n.* передышка. **breathless** *adj.* запыхáвшийся.

breeches [brɪtʃɪz] *n.* бри́джи (-жéй) *pl.*, брю́ки (-к) *pl.*

breed [briːd] *n.* порóда; *v.i.* размножáться *impf.*, размнóжиться *pf.*; *v.t.* разводи́ть (-ожý, -óдишь) *impf.*, развести́ (-едý, -едёшь; -ёл, -елá) *pf.* **breeder** *n.* ...вóд: **cattle** ~ скотовóд; **poultry** ~ птицевóд. **breeding** *n.* разведéние, ...вóдство; (*upbringing*) воспи́танность.

breeze [briːz] *n.* ветерóк (-ркá); (*naut.*) бриз. **breezy** *adj.* свéжий (свеж, -á, -ó, свéжи); (*lively*) живóй (жив, -á, -о).

breviary ['briːvɪərɪ] *n.* трéбник.

brevity ['brevɪtɪ] *n.* крáткость.

brew [bruː] *v.t.* (*beer*) вари́ть (-рю́, -ришь) *impf.*, с~ *pf.*; (*tea*) завáривать *impf.*, завари́ть (-рю́, -ришь) *pf.* **brewer** *n.* пивовáр. **brewery** *n.* пивовáренный завóд.

bribe [braɪb] *n.* взя́тка; *v.t.* давáть (даю́, даёшь) *impf.*, дать (дам, дашь, даст, дади́м; дал, -á, дáлó, -и) *pf.* взя́тку+d.; подкупáть *impf.*, подкупи́ть (-плю́, -пишь) *pf.* **bribery** *n.* пóдкуп.

brick [brɪk] *n.* кирпи́ч (-á) (*also collect.*); (*toy*) (дéтский) кýбик; *adj.* кирпи́чный. **brickbat** *n.* облóмок (-мка) кирпичá. **bricklayer** *n.* кáменщик.

bridal ['braɪd(ə)l] *adj.* свáдебный. **bride** *n.* невéста; (*after wedding*) новобрáчная *sb.* **bridegroom** *n.* жени́х (-á); новобрáчный *sb.* **bridesmaid** *n.* подрýжка невéсты.

bridge[1] [brɪdʒ] *n.* мост (мóстá, *loc.* -ý; *pl.* -ы), мо́стик; (*of nose*) перено́сица; *v.t.* наводи́ть (-жу́, -дишь) *impf.*, навести́ (-еду́, -едёшь; -ёл, -ела́) *pf.* мост че́рез+*a.*; стро́ить *impf.*, по~ *pf.* мост че́рез+*a.* **bridgehead** *n.* плацда́рм.

bridge² [brɪdʒ] *n.* (*cards*) бридж.

bridle ['braɪd(ə)l] *n.* узда́ (*pl.* -ды), узде́чка; *v.t.* обу́здывать *impf.*, обузда́ть *pf.*; *v.i.* возмуща́ться *impf.*, возмути́ться (-ущу́сь, -ути́шься) *pf.*

brief [briːf] *adj.* недо́лгий (-лог, -лга́, -лго), кра́ткий (-ток, -тка́, -тко); *n.* инструкта́ж; *v.t.* инструкти́ровать *impf.* & *pf.* **brief-case** *n.* портфе́ль *m.* **briefing** *n.* инструкти́рование. **briefly** *adv.* кра́тко, сжа́то. **briefs** *n.* трусы́ (-о́в), тру́сики (-ов) *pl.*

brier ['braɪə(r)] *n.* шипо́вник.

brig [brɪg] *n.* бриг.

brigade [brɪ'geɪd] *n.* брига́да. **brigadier** [ˌbrɪgə'dɪə(r)] *n.* бригади́р.

bright [braɪt] *adj.* я́ркий (я́рок, ярка́, я́рко), блестя́щий; (*clever*) смышлёный (-ён). **brighten** *v.i.* проясня́ться *impf.*, проясни́ться *pf.*; *v.t.* придава́ть (-даю́, -даёшь) *impf.*, прида́ть (-а́м, -а́шь, -а́ст, -ади́м; при́дал, -а́, -о) *pf.* блеск, красоту́. **brightness** *n.* я́ркость.

brilliant ['brɪlɪənt] *adj.* блестя́щий.

brim [brɪm] *n.* край (*pl.* -ая́); (*hat*) поля́ (-ле́й) *pl.* **brimful** *adj.* по́лный (-лон, -лна́, полно́) до краёв.

brimstone ['brɪmstəʊn] *n.* саморо́дная се́ра.

brine [braɪn] *n.* рассо́л.

bring [brɪŋ] *v.t.* (*carry*) приноси́ть (-ошу́, -о́сишь) *impf.*, принести́ (-есу́, -есёшь; -ёс, -есла́) *pf.*; (*lead*) приводи́ть (-ожу́, -о́дишь) *impf.*, привести́ (-еду́, -едёшь; -ёл, -ела́) *pf.*; (*transport*) привози́ть (-ожу́, -о́зишь) *impf.*, привезти́ (-езу́, -езёшь; -ёз, -езла́) *pf.*; ~ **about** быть причи́ной+*g.*; ~ **back** возвраща́ть *impf.*, возврати́ть (-ащу́, -ати́шь) *pf.*; ~ **down** сва́ливать *impf.*, свали́ть (-лю́, -лишь) *pf.*; ~ **forward** переноси́ть (-ошу́, -о́сишь) *impf.*, перенести́ (-есу́, -есёшь; -ёс, -есла́) *pf.* на сле́дующую страни́цу; ~ **up** (*educate*) воспи́тывать *impf.*, воспита́ть *pf.*; (*question*) поднима́ть *impf.*, подня́ть (-ниму́, -ни́мешь; по́днял, -а́, -о) *pf.*

brink [brɪŋk] *n.* край (*pl.* -ая́), грань.

brisk [brɪsk] *adj.* (*lively*) живо́й (жив, -а́, -о), оживлённый (-ён, -ённа); (*air etc.*) све́жий (свеж, -а́, -о́, све́жи́), бодря́щий.

brisket ['brɪskɪt] *n.* груди́нка.

brisling ['brɪzlɪŋ, 'brɪs-] *n.* бри́слинг, шпро́та.

bristle ['brɪs(ə)l] *n.* щети́на; *v.i.* ощети́ниваться *impf.*, ощети́ниться *pf.*; ~ **with** изоби́ловать *impf.*+*i.*

Britain ['brɪt(ə)n] *n.* Великобрита́ния, А́нглия. **British** *adj.* брита́нский, англи́йский; ~ **Isles** Брита́нские острова́. **Britisher, Briton** *n.* брита́нец (-нца), -нка; англича́нин (*pl.* -а́не), -а́нка.

brittle ['brɪt(ə)l] *adj.* хру́пкий (-пок, -пка́, -пко).

brittleness *n.* хру́пкость.

broach [brəʊtʃ] *v.t.* начина́ть *impf.*, нача́ть (-чну́, -чнёшь; на́чал, -а́, -о) *pf.* обсужда́ть; затра́гивать *impf.*, затро́нуть *pf.*

broad [brɔːd] *adj.* (*wide*) широ́кий (-о́к, -ока́, -о́ко́); (*general*) о́бщий (общ, -а́); (*clear*) я́сный (я́сен, ясна́, я́сно, я́сны́); **in ~ daylight** средь бе́ла дня; **in ~ outline** в о́бщих черта́х. **broad-minded** *adj.* с широ́кими взгля́дами. **broadly** *adv.*: ~ **speaking** вообще́ говоря́.

broadcast ['brɔːdkɑːst] *n.* ра́дио-, теле-, переда́ча; ра́дио-, теле-, програ́мма; *adj.* ра́дио..., теле...; *v.t.* передава́ть (-даю́, -даёшь) *impf.*, переда́ть (-а́м, -а́шь, -а́ст, -ади́м; пе́редал, -а́, -о) *pf.* по ра́дио, по телеви́дению; (*seed*) се́ять (се́ю, се́ешь) *impf.*, по~ *pf.* вразбро́с. **broadcaster** *n.* ди́ктор. **broadcasting** *n.* ра́дио-, теле-, веща́ние.

brocade [brə'keɪd, brəʊ-] *n.* парча́; *adj.* парчо́вый.

broccoli ['brɒkəlɪ] *n.* спа́ржевая капу́ста.

brochure ['brəʊʃə(r), brəʊ'ʃjʊə(r)] *n.* брошю́ра.

brogue [brəʊg] *n.* (*shoe*) спорти́вный боти́нок (-нка; *g.pl.* -нок); (*accent*) ирла́ндский акце́нт.

broiler ['brɔɪlə(r)] *n.* бро́йлер.

broke [brəʊk] *pred.* разорён (-á); **be ~ to the world** не име́ть *impf.* ни гроша́. **broken** *adj.* сло́манный (-ан), разби́тый, нару́шенный (-ен). **broken-hearted** *adj.* уби́тый го́рем.

broker ['brəʊkə(r)] *n.* бро́кер, ма́клер. **brokerage** *n.* комиссио́нное вознагражде́ние.

bromide ['brəʊmaɪd] *n.* броми́д. **bromine** ['brəʊmiːn] *n.* бром (-a(y)).

bronchitis [brɒŋ'kaɪtɪs] *n.* бронхи́т.

bronze [brɒnz] *n.* бро́нза; *adj.* бро́нзовый; *v.t.* бронзирова́ть *impf.* & *pf.*

brooch [brəʊtʃ] *n.* брошь, бро́шка.

brood [bruːd] *n.* вы́водок (-дка); *v.i.* мра́чно размышля́ть *impf.* **broody** *adj.* сидя́щий на я́йцах; ~ **hen** насе́дка.

brook¹ [brʊk] *n.* руче́й (-чья́).

brook² [brʊk] *v.t.* терпе́ть (-плю́, -пишь) *impf.*

broom [bruːm] *n.* метла́ (*pl.* мётлы, -тел, -тлам); (*plant*) раки́тник, дрок. **broomstick** *n.* (*witches'*) помело́ (*pl.* -лья, -льев).

Bros. *abbr.* (*of* **Brother(s)**) Бра́тья (в назва́нии фи́рмы).

broth [brɒθ] *n.* бульо́н.

brothel ['brɒθ(ə)l] *n.* публи́чный дом (*pl.* -а́).

brother ['brʌðə(r)] *n.* брат (*pl.* -ья, -ьев); ~ **in arms** собра́т (*pl.* -ья, -ьев) по ору́жию. **brother-in-law** *n.* (*sister's husband*) зять (*pl.* -я́, -ёв); (*husband's brother*) де́верь (*pl.* -рья́, -рёй); (*wife's brother*) шу́рин *pl.* (шурья́, -ьёв); (*wife's sister's husband*) своя́к (-á). **brotherhood** *n.* бра́тство. **brotherly** *adj.* бра́тский.

brow [braʊ] *n.* (*eyebrow*) бровь (*pl.* -ви, -вéй); (*forehead*) лоб (лба, *loc.* лбу); (*of cliff*) вы́ступ. **browbeaten** *adj.* запу́ганный (-ан).

brown [braʊn] *adj.* кори́чневый; (*eyes*) ка́рий; ~ **paper** обёрточная бума́га; *v.t.* (*cul.*) подрумя́нивать *impf.*, подрумя́нить *pf.*

browse [braʊz] *v.i.* (*feed*) пасти́сь (пасётся; па́сся, пасла́сь) *impf.*; (*read*) чита́ть *impf.* бессисте́мно.

bruise [bruːz] *n.* синя́к (-á), уши́б; *v.t.* ушиба́ть *impf.*, ушиби́ть (-бу́, -бёшь, -б) *pf.* **bruised** *adj.* (*fruit*) повреждённый (-ён, -ена́).

brunette [bruːˈnet] *n.* брюне́тка.

brush [brʌʃ] *n.* щётка; (*paint*) кисть (*pl.* -ти, -те́й); *v.t.* (*clean*) чи́стить *impf.*, вы́~ *pf.* щёткой; (*touch*) легко́ каса́ться *impf.*, косну́ться *pf.*+*g.*; ~ **one's hair** причёсываться *impf.*, причеса́ться (-ешу́сь, -е́шешься) *pf.* щёткой; ~ **aside** отстраня́ть *impf.*, отстрани́ть *pf.*; ~ **up** собира́ть *impf.*, собра́ть (соберу́, -рёшь; собра́л, -á, -o) *pf.* щёткой; (*renew*) возобновля́ть *impf.*, возобнови́ть *pf.* знако́мство с+*i.* **brush-off** *n.*: **give the** ~ отма́хиваться *impf.*, отмахну́ться *pf.*+*g.*

brushwood [ˈbrʌʃwʊd] *n.* хво́рост (-a(y)).

Brussels [ˈbrʌs(ə)lz] *n.* Брюссе́ль *m.* **Brussels sprouts** *n.* брюссе́льская капу́ста.

brutal [ˈbruːt(ə)l] *adj.* жесто́кий (-о́к, -о́ка́, -о́ко), зве́рский, гру́бый (груб, -á, -o). **bru'tality** *n.* жесто́кость, зве́рство. **brutalize** *v.t.* (*treat brutally*) гру́бо обраща́ться *impf.*, c+*i.*; (*make brutal*) доводи́ть (-ожу́, -о́дишь) *impf.*, довести́ (-еду́, -едёшь; -ёл, -ела́) *pf.* до озвере́ния. **brute** *n.* живо́тное *sb.*; (*person*) скоти́на. **brutish** *adj.* гру́бый (груб, -á, -o), жесто́кий (-о́к, -о́ка́, -о́ко).

B.Sc. *abbr.* (*of Bachelor of Science*) бакала́вр (есте́ственных).

BST *abbr.* (*of British Summer Time*) Брита́нское ле́тнее вре́мя.

bubble [ˈbʌb(ə)l] *n.* пузы́рь (-ря́) *m.*, пузырёк (-рька́); *v.i.* пузы́риться *impf.*; кипе́ть (-пи́т) *impf.*, вс~ *pf.* **bubbly** *n.* шампа́нское *sb.*

buccaneer [ˌbʌkəˈnɪə(r)] *n.* пира́т.

buck [bʌk] *n.* (*male animal*) саме́ц (-мца́); *v.i.* брыка́ться *impf.*

bucket [ˈbʌkɪt] *n.* ведро́ (*pl.* вёдра, -дер, -драм), ведёрко (*pl.* -рки, -рок, -ркам).

buckle [ˈbʌk(ə)l] *n.* пря́жка; *v.t.* застёгивать *impf.*, застегну́ть *pf.* пря́жкой; *v.i.* (*crumple*) коро́биться *impf.*, по~, c~ *pf.*

buckshot [ˈbʌkʃɒt] *n.* карте́чь.

buckskins [ˈbʌkskɪnz] *n.* лоси́ны (-н) *pl.*

buckthorn [ˈbʌkθɔːn] *n.* круши́на.

buckwheat [ˈbʌkwiːt] *n.* гречи́ха.

bucolic [bjuːˈkɒlɪk] *adj.* буколи́ческий, дереве́нский.

bud [bʌd] *n.* по́чка, буто́н; *v.i.* развива́ться *impf.* **budding** *n.* окулиро́вка, почкова́ние.

Buddha [ˈbʊdə] *n.* Бу́дда. **Buddhism** *n.*

будди́зм. **Buddhist** *n.* будди́ст; *adj.* будди́йский.

budge [bʌdʒ] *v.t.* & *i.* шевели́ть(ся) (-елю́(сь), -е́лишь(ся)) *impf.*, по~ *pf.*

budgerigar [ˈbʌdʒərɪˌgɑː(r)] *n.* попуга́йчик.

budget [ˈbʌdʒɪt] *n.* бюдже́т; *v.i.*: ~ **for** предусма́тривать *impf.*, предусмотре́ть (-рю́, -ришь) *pf.* в бюдже́те.

buff [bʌf] *n.* (*leather*) ко́жа; **in, to, the** ~ нагишо́м; *adj.* желтова́то-бе́жевый.

buffalo [ˈbʌfələʊ] *n.* бу́йвол.

buffoon [bəˈfuːn] *n.* шут (-á); **act the** ~ пая́сничать *impf.*

bug [bʌg] *n.* (*bedbug*) клоп (-á); (*virus*) ви́рус; (*microphone*) потайно́й микрофо́н; *v.t.* (*install* ~) устана́вливать *impf.*, установи́ть (-влю́, -вишь) *pf.* аппарату́ру для подслу́шивания в+*p.*; (*listen*) подслу́шивать *impf.*

bugle [ˈbjuːg(ə)l] *n.* рог (*pl.* -á), горн. **bugler** *n.* горни́ст.

build [bɪld] *n.* (*person*) телосложе́ние; *v.t.* стро́ить *impf.*, вы́~, по~ *pf.* **builder** *n.* строи́тель *m.* **building** *n.* (*edifice*) зда́ние; (*action*) строи́тельство; ~ **society** о́бщество, предоставля́ющее сре́дства для поку́пки жилы́х помеще́ний.

bulb [bʌlb] *n.* лу́ковица; (*electric*) ла́мпочка. **bulbous** *adj.* лу́ковичный.

Bulgaria [bʌlˈɡeərɪə] *n.* Болга́рия.

bulge [bʌldʒ] *n.* вы́пуклость, вы́ступ; *v.i.* выпя́чиваться *impf.*; выпира́ть *impf.* **bulging** *adj.* разбу́хший, оттопы́ривающийся; ~ **eyes** глаза́ (-з) *pl.* на вы́кате.

bulk [bʌlk] *n.* (*size*) объём; (*greater part*) бо́льшая часть; (*mass*) основна́я ма́сса; (*large object*) грома́да; ~ **buying** заку́пки *f.pl.* гурто́м; ~ **cargo** груз нава́лом.

bull [bʊl] *n.* (*ox*) бык (-á); (*male animal*) саме́ц (-мца́); *adj.* быча́чий (-чья, -чье). **bulldog** *n.* бульдо́г. **bulldoze** *v.t.* расчища́ть *impf.*, расчи́стить *pf.* бульдо́зером. **bulldozer** *n.* бульдо́зер. **bullfinch** *n.* снеги́рь (-ря́) *m.* **bullock** [ˈbʊlək] *n.* вол (-á). **bull's-eye** *n.* (*target*) я́блоко.

bullet [ˈbʊlɪt] *n.* пу́ля. **bullet-proof** *adj.* пуле-сто́йкий.

bulletin [ˈbʊlɪtɪn] *n.* бюллете́нь *m.*

bullion [ˈbʊlɪən] *n.* сли́ток (-тка).

bully [ˈbʊlɪ] *n.* зади́ра *c.g.*, забия́ка *c.g.*; *v.t.* запу́гивать *impf.*, запуга́ть *pf.*; задира́ть *impf.*

bulrush [ˈbʊlrʌʃ] *n.* камы́ш (-á)

bulwark [ˈbʊlwək] *n.* бастио́н, опло́т.

bum [bʌm] *n.* зад (*loc.* -ý; *pl.* -ы́).

bumble-bee [ˈbʌmb(ə)l,biː] *n.* шмель (-ля́) *m.*

bump [bʌmp] *n.* (*blow*) уда́р, толчо́к (-чка́); (*swelling*) ши́шка; *v.i.* уда́ряться *impf.*, уда́риться *pf.*; ~ **into, against** налета́ть *impf.*, налете́ть (-ечу́, -ети́шь) *pf.* на+*a.*; ната́лкиваться *impf.*, натолкну́ться *pf.* на+*a.* **bumper** *n.* ба́мпер; *adj.* о́чень кру́пный, оби́льный.

bumpkin ['bʌmpkɪn] *n.* неотёсанный па́рень (-рня; *pl.* -рни, -рне́й) *m.*; **country** ~ дереве́нщина *c.g.*

bumptious ['bʌmpʃəs] *adj.* наха́льный, самоуве́ренный (-ен, -енна).

bun [bʌn] *n.* сдо́бная бу́лка.

bunch [bʌntʃ] *n.* пучо́к (-чка́), свя́зка, гроздь (*pl.* -ди, -де́й & -дья, -дьев); *v.t.* собира́ть *impf.*, собра́ть (соберу́, -рёшь; собра́л, -а́, -о) *pf.* в пучки́.

bundle ['bʌnd(ə)l] *n.* у́зел (узла́), узело́к (-лка́); *v.t.* свя́зывать *impf.*, связа́ть (-яжу́, -я́жешь) *pf.* в у́зел; ~ **away, off** спрова́живать *impf.*, спрова́дить *pf.*

bung [bʌŋ] *n.* вту́лка.

bungalow ['bʌŋɡələʊ] *n.* бу́нгало *nt.indecl.*

bungle ['bʌŋɡ(ə)l] *v.t.* по́ртить *impf.*, ис~ *pf.*; *n.* пу́таница. **bungler** *n.* пу́таник.

bunk [bʌŋk] *n.* (*berth*) ко́йка.

bunker ['bʌŋkə(r)] *n.* бу́нкер (*pl.* -á & -ы).

bunkum ['bʌŋkəm] *n.* чепуха́.

buoy [bɔɪ] *n.* буй (*pl.* буй), ба́кен. **buoyancy** *n.* плаву́честь; (*fig.*) бо́дрость, оживле́ние.
buoyant *adj.* плаву́чий; бо́дрый (бодр, -á, -о), жизнера́достный.

bur, burr [bɜ:(r)] *n.* колю́чка.

burden ['bɜːd(ə)n] *n.* бре́мя *nt.*; *v.t.* обременя́ть *impf.*, обремени́ть *pf.*

bureau ['bjʊərəʊ, -'rəʊ] *n.* бюро́ *nt.indecl.* **bureaucracy** [bjʊə'rɒkrəsɪ] *n.* бюрокра́тия (*also collect.*), бюрократи́зм. 'bureaucrat *n.* бюрокра́т. **bureau'cratic** *adj.* бюрократи́ческий.

burger ['bɜːɡə(r)] *n.* га́мбургер, котле́та; ~ **bar** га́мбургерная *sb.*

burglar ['bɜːɡlə(r)] *n.* взло́мщик. **burglary** *n.* кра́жа со взло́мом. **burgle** *v.i.* соверша́ть *impf.*, соверши́ть *pf.* кра́жу со взло́мом; *v.t.* гра́бить *impf.*, о~ *pf.*

burial ['berɪəl] *n.* погребе́ние; ~ **service** заупоко́йная слу́жба.

burlesque [bɜː'lesk] *n.* паро́дия; *v.t.* пароди́ровать *impf.* & *pf.*; *adj.* пароди́ческий, пароди́йный.

burly ['bɜːlɪ] *adj.* здорове́нный.

burn [bɜːn] *v.t.* жечь (жгу, жжёшь, жгут; жёг, жгла) *impf.*, с~ (сожгу́, сожжёшь, сожгу́т; сжёг, сожгла́) *pf.*; *v.t.* & *i.* (*injure*) обжига́ть(ся) *impf.*, обже́чь(ся) (обожгу́(сь), обожжёшь(ся), обожгу́т(ся); обжёг(ся), обожгла́(сь)) *pf.*; *v.i.* горе́ть (-рю́, -ришь) *impf.*, с~ *pf.*; (*by sun*) загора́ть *impf.*, загоре́ть (-рю́, -ри́шь) *pf.*; *n.* ожо́г. **burner** *n.* горе́лка. **burning** *adj.* горя́чий (-ч, -чá).

burnish ['bɜːnɪʃ] *v.t.* полирова́ть *impf.*, на~, от~ *pf.* **burnishing** *n.* полиро́вка; *adj.* полирова́льный.

burr *see* **bur**

burrow ['bʌrəʊ] *n.* норá (*pl.* -ры), но́рка; *v.i.* рыть (ро́ю, ро́ешь) *impf.*, вы~ *pf.* нору́; (*fig.*) ры́ться (ро́юсь, ро́ешься) *impf.*

bursar ['bɜːsə] *n.* казначе́й. **bursary** *n.* стипе́ндия.

burst [bɜːst] *n.* разры́в, вспы́шка; *v.i.* разрыва́ться *impf.*, разорва́ться (-вётся) *impf.*, -валáсь, -валóсь) *pf.*; ло́паться *impf.*, ло́пнуть *pf.*; *v.t.* разрыва́ть *impf.*, разорва́ть (-ву́, -вёшь; разорва́л, -á, -о) *pf.*

bury ['berɪ] *v.t.* (*dead*) хорони́ть (-ню́, -нишь) *impf.*, по~ *pf.*; (*hide*) зарыва́ть *impf.*, зары́ть (-ро́ю, -ро́ешь) *pf.*

bus [bʌs] *n.* авто́бус; ~ **conductor** конду́ктор (*pl.* -á).

bush [bʊʃ] *n.* куст (-á); (*collect.*) куста́рник. **bushy** *adj.* густо́й (густ, -á, -о, гу́сты́).

business ['bɪznɪs] *n.* (*matter*) де́ло; (*occupation*) заня́тие; (*firm*) комме́рческое предприя́тие; (*buying and selling*) би́знес; **big** ~ кру́пный капита́л; **mind your own** ~ не ва́ше де́ло; **no monkey** ~ без фо́кусов; **on** ~ по де́лу. **businessman** *n.* бизнесме́н.

busker [bʌskə(r)] *n.* у́личный музыка́нт.

bust [bʌst] *n.* (*sculpture*) бюст; (*bosom*) грудь (-ди, *i.* -дью; *pl.* -ди, -де́й).

bustle[1] ['bʌs(ə)l] *n.* (*fuss*) сумато́ха, суета́; *v.i.* суети́ться *impf.*

bustle[2] ['bʌs(ə)l] *n.* (*garment*) турню́р.

busy ['bɪzɪ] *adj.* заня́то́й (за́нят, -á, -о); *v.t.*: ~ **o.s.** занима́ться *impf.*, заня́ться (займу́сь, -мёшься; заня́лся́, -ла́сь) *pf.* (**with** +*i.*). **busybody** ['bɪzɪˌbɒdɪ] *n.* челове́к, сую́щий нос в чужи́е дела́.

but [bʌt] *conj.* но, а, кро́ме; ~ **then** но зато́; *prep.* кро́ме+*g.*

butcher ['bʊtʃə(r)] *n.* мясни́к (-á); *v.t.* ре́зать (ре́жу, -жешь) *impf.*, за~ *pf.*; ~'s **shop** мясна́я *sb.* **butchery** *n.* резня́.

butler ['bʌtlə(r)] *n.* дворе́цкий *sb.*

butt[1] [bʌt] *n.* (*cask*) бо́чка.

butt[2] [bʌt] *n.* (*of gun*) прикла́д; (*end*) то́лстый коне́ц (-нцá).

butt[3] [bʌt] *n.* (*target*) мише́нь.

butt[4] [bʌt] *v.t.* бода́ть *impf.*, за~ *pf.*; *v.i.* бода́ться *impf.*

butter ['bʌtə(r)] *n.* (сли́вочное) ма́сло; *v.t.* нама́зывать *impf.*, нама́зать (-ажу́, -а́жешь) *pf.* ма́слом. **buttercup** *n.* лю́тик. **butterfly** *n.* ба́бочка.

buttock ['bʌtək] *n.* я́годица.

button ['bʌt(ə)n] *n.* пу́говица; (*knob*) кно́пка; *v.t.* застёгивать *impf.*, застегну́ть *pf.*

buttress ['bʌtrɪs] *n.* контрфо́рс; *v.t.* подпира́ть *impf.*, подпере́ть (подопру́, -рёшь; подпёр) *pf.*

buy [baɪ] *n.* поку́пка; *v.t.* покупа́ть *impf.*, купи́ть (-плю́, -пишь) *pf.* **buyer** *n.* покупа́тель *m.*

buzz [bʌz] *n.* жужжа́ние; *v.i.* жужжа́ть (-жи́т) *impf.*; гуде́ть (гужу́, гуди́шь) *impf.*

buzzard ['bʌzəd] *n.* каню́к (-á)

buzzer ['bʌzə(r)] *n.* зу́ммер.

by [baɪ] *adv.* ми́мо; ~ **and** ~ вско́ре; *prep.* (*near*) о́коло+*g.* y+*g.*; (*beside*) ря́дом с+*i.*; (*via*) че́рез+*a.*; (*past*) ми́мо+*g.* (*time*) к+*d.*; (*means*) *i. without prep.*; ~ **means of** посре́дством+*g.*

bye-bye ['baɪbaɪ, bə'baɪ] *int.* пока́!; всего́!
by-election ['baɪ,lek(ʃ)(ə)n] *n.* дополни́тельные вы́боры *m.pl.* **bygone** *adj.* пережи́тый, про́шлый; *n.*: *pl.* про́шлое *sb.*; (*objects*) предме́ты *m.pl.*, вы́шедшие из употребле́ния; **let ~s be ~s** что пропа́ло, то быльём поросло́. **by-law** *n.* пастановле́ние ме́стной вла́сти. **bypass** *n.* (*road*) обхо́д, обхо́дный путь (-ти́, -тём) *m.*; (*pipe*) обво́дный кана́л; *v.t.* обходи́ть (-ожу́, -о́дишь) *impf.*, обойти́ (обойду́, -дёшь; обошёл, -шла́) *pf.*; объезжа́ть *impf.*, объе́хать (-е́ду, -е́дешь) *pf.* **by-product** *n.* побо́чный проду́кт. **bystander** *n.* наблюда́тель *m.*
byte [baɪt] *n.* (*comput.*) байт.
byway *n.* просёлочная доро́га. **byword** *n.* (*proverb*) погово́рка; (*example*) приме́р.

C

C¹ [siː] *n.* (*mus.*) до *nt.indecl.*
C² *abbr.* (*of* **Celsius** *or* **centigrade**) (шкала́) Це́льсия; **20°C** 20°Ц (гра́дусов Це́льсия (*or* по Це́льсию)).
c. *abbr.* (*of* **century**) в., век; ст., столе́тие; (*of* **circa**) ок., о́коло; (*of* **cent(s)**) цент.
cab [kæb] *n.* (*taxi*) такси́ *nt.indecl.*; (*of lorry*) каби́на.
cabaret ['kæbə,reɪ] *n.* кабаре́, эстра́дное представле́ние.
cabbage ['kæbɪdʒ] *n.* капу́ста; **~ white** капу́стница.
cabin ['kæbɪn] *n.* (*hut*) хи́жина; (*bathing etc.*) каби́на; (*ship's*) каю́та. **cabin-boy** *n.* ю́нга *m.*
cabinet ['kæbɪnɪt](*pol.*) кабине́т; (*cupboard*) (застеклённый) шкаф (*loc.* -у́; *pl.* -ы́); **C~ Minister** мини́стр-член кабине́та. **cabinet-maker** *n.* краснодере́вец (-вца).
cable ['keɪb(ə)l] *n.* (*rope*) кана́т, трос; (*electric*) ка́бель *m.*; (*cablegram*) каблогра́мма; **~ stitch** жгут (-а́); *v.t. & i.* телеграфи́ровать *impf. & pf.* (по подво́дному ка́белю).
cabotage ['kæbə,tɑːʒ, -tɪdʒ] *n.* каботаж.
cacao [kə'kɑːəʊ, -'keɪəʊ] *n.* кака́о *nt.indecl.*
cache [kæʃ] *n.* укры́тый, та́йный, запа́с.
cackle ['kæk(ə)l] *n.* (*geese*) го́гот, гого́танье; (*hens*) куда́хтанье; *v.i.* гогота́ть (-очу́, -о́чешь) *impf.*; куда́хтать (-хчу, -хчешь) *impf.*
cactus ['kæktəs] *n.* ка́ктус; *adj.* ка́ктусовый.
cad [kæd] *n.* хам.
cadaverous [kə'dævərəs] *adj.* мёртвенно-бле́дный (-ден, -дна́, -дно, -бле́дны́).
caddie ['kædɪ] *n.* челове́к, прислу́живающий при игре́ в гольф.
caddish ['kædɪʃ] *adj.* ха́мский.
caddy ['kædɪ] *n.* (*box*) ча́йница.
cadence ['keɪd(ə)ns] *n.* (*rhythm*) ритм, такт; (*mus.*) каде́нция. **cadenced** *adj.* ме́рный, ритми́чный. **cadenza** [kə'denzə] *n.* каде́нция.
cadet [kə'det] *n.* каде́т (*g.pl.* -т & -тов); *adj.* каде́тский.
cadge [kædʒ] *v.t.* выпра́шивать *impf.*, вы́просить *pf.*
cadre ['kɑːdə(r), 'kɑːdrə] *n.* ка́дры *m.pl.*
Caesarean (section) [sɪ'zeərɪən] *n.* ке́сарево сече́ние.
caesura [sɪ'zjʊərə] *n.* цезу́ра.
cafe ['kæfeɪ, 'kæfɪ] *n.* кафе́ *nt.indecl.* **cafeteria** [,kæfɪ'tɪərɪə] *n.* кафете́рий.
caffeine ['kæfiːn] *n.* кофеи́н.
cage [keɪdʒ] *n.* кле́тка; (*in mine*) клеть (*loc.* -е́ти́; *pl.* -ти, -те́й); *v.t.* сажа́ть *impf.*, посади́ть (-ажу́, -а́дишь) *pf.* в кле́тку; **a ~d lion** лев в кле́тке.
cairn [keən] *n.* гру́да камне́й.
caisson ['keɪs(ə)n, kə'suːn] *n.* кессо́н.
cajole [kə'dʒəʊl] *v.t.* ума́сливать *impf.*, ума́слить *pf.* **cajolery** *n.* лесть, ума́сливание.
cake [keɪk] *n.* торт, пиро́жное *sb.*; (*fruit-~*) кекс; (*soap*) кусо́к (-ска́); *v.i.* твердѣ́ть *impf.*, за~ *pf.*; отвердева́ть *impf.*, отвердѣ́ть *pf.*
calabrese [,kælə'briːz] *n.* спа́ржевая капу́ста.
calamitous [kə'læmɪtəs] *adj.* па́губный, бе́дственный (-ен, -енна). **calamity** *n.* бе́дствие.
calcareous [kæl'keərɪəs] *adj.* известко́вый.
calcium ['kælsɪəm] *n.* ка́льций; *adj.* ка́льциевый.
calculate ['kælkjʊ,leɪt] *v.t.* вычисля́ть *impf.*, вы́числить *pf.*; *v.i.* рассчи́тывать *impf.*, рассчита́ть *pf.* (**on** на+*a.*); **~ing-machine** вычисли́тельная маши́на. **calculated** *adj.* преднаме́ренный (-ен, -енна). **calcu'lation** *n.* вычисле́ние, расчёт. **calculator** *n.* калькуля́тор. **calculus** *n.* (*math.*) исчисле́ние; (*stone*) ка́мень (-мня; *pl.* -мни, -мне́й) *m.*
calendar ['kælɪndə(r)] *n.* календа́рь (-ря́) *m.*; (*register*) спи́сок (-ска).
calf¹ [kɑːf] *n.* (*cow*) телёнок (-нка; *pl.* теля́та, -т); (*other animal*) детёныш; (*leather*) телья́чья ко́жа; **~ love** ребя́ческая любо́вь (-бви, -бо́вью).
calf² [kɑːf] *n.* (*leg*) икра́ (*pl.* -ры).
calibrate ['kælɪ,breɪt] *v.t.* калибри́ровать *impf. & pf.*; калиброва́ть *impf.* **cali'bration** *n.* калибро́вка. **calibre** *n.* кали́бр.
calico ['kælɪ,kəʊ] *n.* коленко́р (-а(у)), митка́ль (-ля́) *m.*
call [kɔːl] *v.* звать (зову́, -вёшь; звал, -а́, -о) *impf.*, по~ *pf.*; (*name*) называ́ть *impf.*, назва́ть (назову́, -вёшь; назва́л, -а́, -о) *pf.*;

(*cry*) крича́ть (-чу́, -чи́шь) *impf.*, кри́кнуть *pf.*; (*wake*) буди́ть (бужу́, бу́дишь) *impf.*, раз~ *pf.*; (*visit*) заходи́ть (-ожу́, -о́дишь) *impf.*, зайти́ (зайду́, -дёшь) зашёл, -шла́) *pf.* (**on** к+*d.*; **at** в+*a.*); (*stop at*) остана́вливаться *impf.*, останови́ться (-вится) *pf.* (**at** в, на, +*p.*); (*summon*) вызыва́ть *impf.*, вы́звать (вы́зову, -вешь; *pf.*; (*ring up*) звони́ть *impf.*, по~ *pf.*+*d.*; ~ **for** (*require*) тре́бовать *impf.*, по~ *pf.*+*g.*; (*fetch*) заходи́ть (-ожу́, -о́дишь) *impf.*, зайти́ (зайду́, -дёшь; зашёл, -шла́) *pf.* за+*i.*; ~ **off** отменя́ть *impf.*, отмени́ть (-ню́, -нишь) *pf.*; ~ **out** вскри́кивать *impf.*, вскри́кнуть *pf.*; ~ **up** призыва́ть *impf.*, призва́ть (призову́, -вёшь; призва́л, -á, -о) *pf.*; *n.* (*cry*) крик; (*summons*) зов, призы́в; (*telephone*) (телефо́нный) вы́зов, разгово́р; (*visit*) визи́т; (*signal*) сигна́л. **call-box** *n.* телефо́н-автома́т. **call-boy** *n.* ма́льчик, вызыва́ющий актёров на сце́ну.

caller *n.* посети́тель *m.*, ~ница; гость (*pl.* -ти, -те́й) *m.*, го́стья (*g.pl.* -тий). **calling** *n.* (*summons*) призва́ние; (*profession*) профе́ссия; (*occupation*) заня́тие; (*trade*) ремесло́. **call-over** *n.* перекли́чка. **call-sign** *n.* позывно́й сигна́л, позывны́е *sb.* **call-up** *n.* призы́в.

callous ['kæləs] *adj.* (*person*) бессерде́чный, бесчу́вственный (-ен(ен), -енна).

callow ['kæləʊ] *adj.* (*unfledged*) неопери́вшийся; (*raw*) нео́пытный.

callus ['kæləs] *n.* мозо́ль.

calm [kɑːm] *adj.* (*tranquil*) споко́йный, хладнокро́вный; (*quiet*) ти́хий (тих, -á, -о); (*windless*) безве́тренный (-ен, -енна); *n.* споко́йствие; безве́трие; *v.t. & i.* (~ *down*) успока́ивать(ся) *impf.*, успоко́ить(ся) *pf.*

calorie ['kælərɪ] *n.* кало́рия.

calumniate [kə'lʌmnɪeɪt] *v.t.* клевета́ть (-ещу́, -е́щешь) *impf.*, на~ *pf.* на+*a.* **calumniation**, **'calumny** *n.* клевета́.

calve [kɑːv] *v.i.* тели́ться (-ится) *impf.*, о~ *pf.*

calypso [kə'lɪpsəʊ] *n.* кали́псо *nt.indecl.*

calyx ['keɪlɪks, 'kæl-] *n.* ча́шечка.

cam [kæm] *n.* кулачо́к (-чка́), кула́к (-á).

camber ['kæmbə(r)] *n.* вы́пуклость. **cambered** *adj.* вы́пуклый.

camcorder ['kæm,kɔːdə(r)] *n.* камко́рдер.

camel ['kæm(ə)l] *n.* верблю́д.

cameo ['kæmɪ,əʊ] *n.* каме́я.

camera ['kæmrə, -ərə] *n.* фотоаппара́т; кино-, теле-, ка́мера. **cameraman** *n.* кинооператор.

camomile ['kæmə,maɪl] *n.* рома́шка.

camouflage ['kæmə,flɑːʒ] *n.* маскиро́вка; камуфля́ж; *adj.* маскиро́вочный; *v.t.* маскирова́ть *impf.*, за~ *pf.*

camp [kæmp] *n.* ла́герь (*pl.* -я, -ей) *m.*; *v.i.* располага́ться *impf.*, расположи́ться (-жу́сь, -жи́шься) *pf.* ла́герем. **camp-bed** *n.* раскладна́я крова́ть, раскладу́шка. **camp-**

chair *n.* складно́й стул (*pl.* -ья, -ьев). **campfire** *n.* бива́чный костёр (-тра́).

campaign [kæm'peɪn] *n.* кампа́ния; похо́д; *v.i.* (*conduct* ~) проводи́ть (-ожу́, -о́дишь) *impf.*, провести́ (-еду́, -едёшь; -ёл, -ела́) *pf.* кампа́нию; (*serve in* ~) уча́ствовать *impf.* в похо́де, в кампа́нии.

campanula [kæm'pænjʊlə] *n.* колоко́льчик.

camphor ['kæmfə(r)] *n.* камфара́. **camphorated oil** *n.* камфо́рное ма́сло.

campus ['kæmpəs] *n.* акеми́ческий городо́к (-дка́), академгородо́к (-дка́).

camshaft ['kæmʃɑːft] *n.* распредели́тельный, кулачко́вый, вал (*loc.* -ý; *pl.* -ы́).

can[1] [kæn] *n.* жестя́нка, (консе́рвная) коро́бка, ба́нка; *v.t.* консерви́ровать *impf.*, за~ *pf.*

can[2] [kæn] *v.aux.* (*be able*) мочь (могу́, мо́жешь; мог, -ла́) *impf.*; с~ *pf.*+*inf.*; (*know how*) уме́ть *impf.*, с~ *pf.*+*inf.*

Canada ['kænədə] *n.* Кана́да. **Canadian** [kə'neɪdɪən] *n.* кана́дец (-дца), -дка; *adj.* кана́дский.

canal [kə'næl] *n.* кана́л.

canary [kə'neərɪ] *n.* канаре́йка.

cancel ['kæns(ə)l] *v.t.* аннули́ровать *impf.* & *pf.*; отменя́ть *impf.*, отмени́ть (-ню́, -нишь) *pf.*; (*math.*) сокраща́ть *impf.*, сократи́ть (-ащу́, -ати́шь) *pf.*; (*print.*) вычёркивать *impf.*, вы́черкнуть *pf.*; (*stamp*) гаси́ть (гашу́, га́сишь) *impf.*, по~ *pf.*; (*print.*) перепеча́танный лист (-á). **cance'llation** *n.* аннули́рование, отме́на; (*math.*) сокраще́ние; (*print.*) перепеча́тка.

cancer ['kænsə(r)] *n.* рак; (**C**~) Рак; *adj.* ра́ковый; ~ **patient** больно́й ра́ком. **cancerous** *adj.* ра́ковый.

candelabrum [,kændɪ'lɑːbrəm] *n.* канделя́бр.

candid ['kændɪd] *adj.* открове́нный (-нен, -нна), и́скренний (-нен, -нна, -нне & -нно); ~ **camera** скры́тый фотоаппара́т.

candidacy ['kændɪdəsɪ] *n.* кандидату́ра. **candidate** *n.* кандида́т. **candidature** *n.* кандидату́ра.

candied ['kændɪd] *adj.* заса́харенный; ~ **peel** цука́т(ы).

candle ['kænd(ə)l] *n.* свеча́ (*pl.* -чи, -че́й); ~ **end** ога́рок (-рка). **candlestick** *n.* подсве́чник. **candlewick** *n.* фити́ль (-ля́) *m.*, вы́шивка фитилька́ми.

candour ['kændə(r)] *n.* открове́нность, и́скренность.

candy ['kændɪ] *n.* сла́дости *f.pl.*; *v.t.* заса́харивать *impf.*, заса́харить *pf.* **candyfloss** *n.* са́харная ва́та.

cane [keɪn] *n.* (*plant*) тростни́к (-á); (*stick*) трость (*pl.* -ти, -те́й), па́лка; ~ **sugar** тростнико́вый са́хар (-a(y)); *v.t.* бить (бью, бьёшь) *impf.*, по~ *pf.* тро́стью, па́лкой.

canine ['keɪnaɪn, 'kæn-] *adj.* соба́чий (-чья, -чье); *n.* (*tooth*) клык (-á).

canister ['kænɪstə(r)] *n.* жестяна́я коро́бка.

canker ['kæŋkə(r)] *n.* рак.

cannibal ['kænɪb(ə)l] *n.* каннибáл, людоéд; *adj.* каннибáльский, людоéдский. **cannibalism** *n.* каннибалúзм, людоéдство. **canniba'listic** *adj.* каннибáльский, людоéдский. **cannibalize** *v.t.* снимáть *impf.*, снять (сниму́, -мешь; снял, -á, -о) *pf.* части с+*g*.

cannon ['kænən] *n.* (*gun*) пу́шка; (*billiards*) карамбóль *m.*; *adj.* пу́шечный; *v.i.*: ~ **into** налетáть *impf.*, налетéть (-лечу́, -летúшь) *pf.* на+*a.*; ~ **off** отскáкивать *impf.*, отскочúть (-очу́, -óчишь) *pf.* от+*g.* **cannon-ball** *n.* пу́шечное ядрó (*pl.* я́дра, я́дер, я́драм); ~ **service** пу́шечная подáча. **cannon-fodder** *n.* пу́шечное мя́со. **canno'nade** *n.* канонáда.

canoe [kə'nu:] *n.* канóэ *nt.indecl.*; челнóк (-á); *v.i.* плáвать *indet.*, плыть (плыву́, -вёшь; плыл, -á, -о) *det.* в челнокé, на канóэ.

canon ['kænən] *n.* канóн; (*person*) канóник; ~ **law** канонúческое прáво. **ca'nonical** *adj.* канонúческий; ~ **hours** устáвные часы́ *m.pl.* молúтв. **ca'nonicals** *n.* церкóвное облачéние. **canoni'zation** *n.* канонизáция. **canonize** *v.t.* канонизовáть *impf. & pf.*

canopy ['kænəpɪ] *n.* балдахúн.

cant¹ [kænt] *n.* (*slant*) наклóн, наклóнное положéние; *v.t.* наклоня́ть *impf.*, наклонúть (-ню́, -ишь) *pf.*; придавáть (-даю́, -даёшь) *impf.*, придáть (-áм, -áшь, -áст, -адúм; прúдал, -á, -о) *pf.*+*d.* наклóнное положéние.

cant² [kænt] *n.* (*hypocrisy*) хáнжество; (*jargon*) жаргóн, аргó *nt.indecl.*

cantaloup ['kæntəˌlu:p] *n.* канталу́па.

cantankerous [kæn'tæŋkərəs] *adj.* ворчлúвый.

cantata [kæn'tɑ:tə] *n.* кантáта.

canteen [kæn'ti:n] *n.* столóвая *sb.*, буфéт; (*case*) я́щик; (*flask*) фля́га.

canter *n.* кéнтер, лёгкий галóп; *v.i.* (*rider*) éздить *indet.*, éхать (éду, éдешь) *det.* лёгким галóпом; (*horse*) ходúть (-дит) *indet.*, идтú (идёт; шёл, шла) *det.* лёгким галóпом; *v.t.* пускáть *impf.*, пустúть (пущу́, пу́стишь) *pf.* лёгким галóпом.

cantilever ['kæntɪˌli:və(r)] *n.* консóль, укóсина; ~ **bridge** консóльный мост (мóстá, *loc.* -ý; *pl.* -ы́).

canto ['kæntəʊ] *n.* песнь.

canton ['kæntɒn] *n.* кантóн.

canvas ['kænvəs] *n.* холст (-á), канвá, паруcúна; (*painting*) картúна; (*sails*) паруcá *m.pl.*; **under** ~ (*on ship*) под парусáми; (*in tent*) в палáтках.

canvass ['kænvəs] *v.i.* собирáть *impf.*, собрáть (соберу́, -рёшь; собрáл, -á, -о) *pf.* голосá; ~ **for** агитúровать *impf.*, c~ *pf.* за+*a.*; *n.* собирáние голосóв; агитáция. **canvasser** *n.* собирáтель *m.* голосóв.

canyon ['kænjən] *n.* каньóн.

cap [kæp] *n.* шáпка, фурáжка; (*cloth*) кéпка; (*woman's*) чепéц (-пцá); (*percussion*) кáпсюль *m.*, пистóн; (*lid*) кры́шка; *v.t.* (*surpass*) перещеголя́ть *pf.*; превосходúть

(-ожу́, -óдишь) *impf.*, превзойтú (-ойду́, -ойдёшь; -ошёл, -ошлá) *pf.*

capability [ˌkeɪpə'bɪlɪtɪ] *n.* спосóбность. **'capable** *adj.* спосóбный; (*skilful*) умéлый; ~ **of** (*admitting*) поддаю́щийся+*d.*; (*able*) спосóбный на+*a.*

capacious [kə'peɪʃəs] *adj.* простóрный, вместúтельный, ёмкий (ёмок, ёмка). **capacitance** [kə'pæsɪt(ə)ns] *n.* ёмкость. **capacity** [kə'pæsɪtɪ] *n.* ёмкость, вместúмость; (*ability*) спосóбность; (*power*) мóщность; **in the** ~ **of** в кáчестве+*g.*

cape¹ [keɪp] *n.* (*geog.*) мыс (*loc.* -е & -ý; *pl.* мы́сы).

cape² [keɪp] *n.* (*cloak*) пелерúна, плащ (-á). **caped** *adj.* с пелерúной.

caper¹ ['keɪpə(r)] *n.* (*plant*) кáперс; *pl.* кáперсы *m.pl.*

caper² ['keɪpə(r)] *n.* (*leap*) прыжóк (-жкá); **cut** ~**s** выдéлывать *impf.* антрашá; *v.i.* дéлать *impf.* прыжкú.

capillary [kə'pɪlərɪ] *n.* капилля́р; *adj.* капилля́рный.

capital ['kæpɪt(ə)l] *adj.* (*city*) столúчный; (*letter*) прописнóй; (*main*) капитáльный; (*excellent*) отлúчный; ~ **goods** срéдства *nt.pl.* произвóдства; ~ **punishment** смéртная казнь; ~ **ship** кру́пный боевóй корáбль (-ля́) *m.*; *n.* (*town*) столúца; (*letter*) прописнáя бу́ква; (*econ.*) капитáл; (*arch.*) капитéль. **capitalism** *n.* капиталúзм. **capitalist** *n.* капиталúст; *adj.* капиталистúческий. **capita'listic** *adj.* капиталистúческий. **capitali'zation** *n.* капитализáция. **capitalize** *v.t.* капитализúровать *impf. & pf.*

capitation [ˌkæpɪ'teɪʃ(ə)n] *attr.* поголóвный.

capitulate [kə'pɪtjʊˌleɪt] *v.i.* капитулúровать *impf. & pf.* **capitu'lation** *n.* капитуля́ция.

capon ['keɪpən] *n.* каплу́н (-á).

caprice [kə'pri:s] *n.* капрúз. **capricious** *adj.* капрúзный.

Capricorn ['kæprɪˌkɔ:n] *n.* Козерóг.

capsize [kæp'saɪz] *v.t. & i.* опрокúдывать(ся) *impf.*, опрокúнуть(ся) *pf.*

capstan ['kæpst(ə)n] *n.* кабестáн.

capsule ['kæpsjuːl] *n.* кáпсула, облáтка.

captain ['kæptɪn] *n.* капитáн; *v.t.* быть капитáном+*g.* **captaincy** *n.* звáние, чин, дóлжность, капитáна.

caption ['kæpʃ(ə)n] *n.* нáдпись, пóдпись; (*cin.*) тúтр.

captious ['kæpʃəs] *adj.* придúрчивый.

captivate ['kæptɪˌveɪt] *v.t.* пленя́ть *impf.*, пленúть *pf.* **captivating** *adj.* пленúтельный. **captive** *adj. n.* плéнный. **cap'tivity** *n.* невóля; (*esp. mil.*) плен (*loc.* -ý). **capture** *n.* взя́тие, захвáт, пой́мка; *v.t.* брать (беру́, -рёшь; брал, -á, -о) *impf.*, взять (возьму́, -мёшь; взял, -á, -о) *pf.* в плен; захвáтывать *impf.*, захватúть (-ачу́, -áтишь) *pf.*

car [kɑ:(r)] *n.* машúна, автомобúль *m.*; ~ **park** пáркинг; *attr.* автомобúльный.

carafe [kə'ræf, -rɑ:f] *n.* графúн.

caramel(s) ['kærə‚mel] *n.* караме́ль.
carat ['kærət] *n.* кара́т (*g.pl.* -т &-тов).
caravan ['kærə‚væn] *n.* (*convoy*) карава́н; (*cart*) фурго́н; (*house*) дом-автоприце́п.
caraway (seeds) ['kærə‚weɪ] *n.* тмин (-а(у)).
carbide ['kɑːbaɪd] *n.* карби́д.
carbine ['kɑːbaɪn] *n.* карби́на.
carbohydrate [‚kɑːbə'haɪdreɪt] *n.* углево́д.
carbolic (acid) [kɑː'bɒlɪk] *n.* карбо́ловая кислота́. **carbon** *n.* углеро́д; ко́пия; ~ **copy** ко́пия (че́рез копи́рку); ~ **dioxide** углеки́слота; ~ **paper** копирова́льная бума́га.
carbonaceous *adj.* (*carbon*) углеро́дистый; (*coal*) у́глистый. '**carbonate** *n.* углеки́слая соль. **carboniferous** [‚kɑːbə'nɪfərəs] *adj.* углено́сный. **carborundum** [‚kɑːbə'rʌndəm] *n.* карбору́нд.
carboy ['kɑːbɔɪ] *n.* буты́ль.
carbuncle ['kɑːbʌŋk(ə)l] *n.* карбу́нкул.
carburettor [‚kɑːbju'retə(r), ‚kɑːbə-] *n.* карбюра́тор.
carcase, carcass ['kɑːkəs] *n.* ту́ша, труп.
carcinogen ['kɑːsɪnədʒ(ə)n] *n.* канцероге́н. **carcino'genic** *n.* канцероге́нный.
card [kɑːd] *n.* ка́рта, ка́рточка; (*ticket*) биле́т; **a house of ~s** ка́рточный до́мик; ~ **index** картоте́ка. **cardboard** *n.* карто́н; *adj.* карто́нный. **card-sharp(er)** *n.* шу́лер (*pl.* -а́). **card-table** *n.* ло́мберный, ка́рточный, стол (-а́).
cardiac ['kɑːdɪ‚æk] *adj.* серде́чный.
cardigan ['kɑːdɪgən] *n.* вя́заная ко́фта, кардига́н.
cardinal ['kɑːdɪn(ə)l] *adj.* (*important*) кардина́льный; ~ **number** коли́чественное числи́тельное *sb.*; *n.* кардина́л.
care [keə(r)] *n.* (*trouble*) забо́та, попече́ние; (*attention*) внима́тельность; (*tending*) ухо́д; **take** ~ осторо́жно!; береги́(те)сь!; смотри́(те)!; **take** ~ **of** забо́титься *impf.*, по~ *pf.* о+*p.*; **I don't** ~ мне всё равно́; **what do I** ~?; **who** ~**s?** а мне всё равно́!; а мне-то что?
career [kə'rɪə(r)] *n.* (*movement*) карье́р; (*profession*) карье́ра; ~ **guidance** профессиона́льная ориента́ция.
carefree ['keəfriː] *adj.* беззабо́тный. **careful** *adj.* (*cautious*) осторо́жный; (*thorough*) тща́тельный. **careless** *adj.* (*negligent*) небре́жный; (*incautious*) неосторо́жный; (*carefree*) беззабо́тный.
caress [kə'res] *n.* ла́ска (*g.pl.* -ск); *v.t.* ласка́ть *impf.*
caretaker ['keə‚teɪkə(r)] *n.* смотри́тель *m.*, ~ница; сто́рож (*pl.* -а́); *attr.* вре́менный.
careworn ['keəwɔːn] *adj.* изму́ченный (-ен) забо́тами.
cargo ['kɑːgəʊ] *n.* груз.
caricature ['kærɪkətjʊə(r)] *n.* карикату́ра; *v.t.* изобража́ть *impf.*, изобрази́ть *pf.* в карикату́рном ви́де.
caries ['keərɪːz, -rɪ‚iːz] *n.* карио́з.
carmine ['kɑːmaɪn] *n.* карми́н, карми́нный цвет; *adj.* карми́нный.
carnage ['kɑːnɪdʒ] *n.* резня́.
carnal ['kɑːn(ə)l] *adj.* пло́тский.
carnation [kɑː'neɪʃ(ə)n] *n.* (садо́вая) гвозди́ка.
carnival ['kɑːnɪv(ə)l] *n.* карнава́л; (*Shrovetide*) ма́сленица.
carnivore ['kɑːnɪ‚vɔː(r)] *n.* плотоя́дное живо́тное *sb.* **car'nivorous** *adj.* плотоя́дный.
carol ['kær(ə)l] *n.* (рожде́ственский) гимн.
carotid artery [kə'rɒtɪd] *n.* со́нная арте́рия.
carousal [kə'raʊzəl] *n.* попо́йка.
carp[1] [kɑːp] *n.* (*wild*) саза́н; (*domesticated*) карп.
carp[2] [kɑːp] *v.i.* придира́ться *impf.*, придра́ться (-деру́сь, -дрёшься; -дра́лся, -драла́сь, -дра́лось) *pf.* (**at** к+*d.*)
carpenter ['kɑːpɪntə(r)] *n.* пло́тник. **carpentry** *n.* пло́тничество.
carpet ['kɑːpɪt] *n.* ковёр (-вра́); *v.t.* устила́ть *impf.*, устла́ть (-телю́, -те́лешь) *pf.* ковра́ми.
carping ['kɑːpɪŋ] *adj.* приди́рчивый; *n.* приди́рки (-рок) *pl.*
carriage ['kærɪdʒ] *n.* (*vehicle*) каре́та, экипа́ж; (*rail.*) ваго́н; (*of machine*) каре́тка; (*conveyance*) прово́з, перево́зка; (*bearing*) оса́нка; ~ **forward** с опла́той доста́вки получа́телем; ~ **free** беспла́тная пересы́лка; ~ **paid** за пересы́лку упла́чено. **carriageway** *n.* проезжа́я часть доро́ги, у́лицы. **carrier** *n.* (*person*) во́зчик; (*object*) бага́жник; ~ **pigeon** почто́вый го́лубь (*pl.* -би, -бе́й) *m.*; ~ **wave** несу́щая волна́ (*pl.* -ны, -н, -на́м).
carrion ['kærɪən] *n.* па́даль; *pl.* чёрная воро́на.
carrot ['kærət] *n.* морко́вка; *pl.* морко́вь (*collect.*).
carry ['kærɪ] *v.t.* (*by hand*) носи́ть (ношу́, но́сишь) *indet.*, нести́ (несу́, -сёшь; нёс, -ла́) *det.*; переноси́ть (-ошу́, -о́сишь) *impf.*, перенести́ (-есу́, -есёшь; -ёс, -есла́) *pf.*; (*in vehicle*) вози́ть (вожу́, во́зишь) *indet.*, везти́ (везу́, -зёшь; вёз, -ла́) *det.*; *v.i.* нести́сь (несётся; нёсся, несла́сь); (*sound*) быть слы́шен (-шна́, -шно); ~ **forward** переноси́ть (-ошу́, -о́сишь) *impf.*, перенести́ (-есу́, -есёшь; -ёс, -есла́) *pf.*; ~ **on** (*continue*) продолжа́ть *impf.*; (*behaviour*) вести́ (веду́, ведёшь; вёл, -а́) *impf.* себя́ несде́ржанно; ~ **out** выполня́ть *impf.*, вы́полнить *pf.*; доводи́ть (-ожу́, -о́дишь) *impf.*, довести́ (-еду́, -едёшь; -ёл, -ела́) *pf.* до конца́; ~ **over** переноси́ть (-ошу́, -о́сишь) *impf.*, перенести́ (-есу́, -есёшь; -ёс, -есла́) *pf.*
cart [kɑːt] *n.* теле́га, пово́зка; *v.t.* вози́ть (вожу́, во́зишь) *indet.*, везти́ (везу́, -зёшь; вёз, -ла́) *det.* в теле́ге. **cartage** *n.* сто́имость перево́зки. **cart-horse** *n.* ломова́я ло́шадь (*pl.* -ди, -де́й, *i.* -дьми́). **cart-load** *n.* воз. **cart-track** *n.* гужева́я доро́га, просёлок (-лка). **cartwheel** колесо́ (*pl.* -ёса) теле́ги;

(*somersault*) переворо́т бо́ком в сто́рону.
cartel [kɑːˈtel] *n.* карте́ль *m.*
cartilage [ˈkɑːtɪlɪdʒ] *n.* хрящ (-á). **cartilaginous** [ˌkɑːtɪˈlædʒɪnəs] *adj.* хрящево́й.
cartographer [kɑːˈtɒɡrəfə(r)] *n.* карто́граф. **carto'graphic** *adj.* картографи́ческий. **cartography** *n.* картогра́фия.
carton [ˈkɑːt(ə)n] *n.* (карто́нная) коро́бка; блок.
cartoon [kɑːˈtuːn] *n.* карикату́ра; (*design*) карто́н; (*cin.*) мультфи́льм. **cartoonist** *n.* карикатури́ст, ~ка.
cartridge [ˈkɑːtrɪdʒ] *n.* патро́н. **cartridge-belt** *n.* патронта́ш.
carve [kɑːv] *v.t.* ре́зать (ре́жу, -жешь) *impf.* по+*d.*; (*wood*) выреза́ть *impf.*, вы́резать (-ежу, -ежешь) *pf.*; (*stone*) высека́ть *impf.*, вы́сечь (-еку, -ечешь; -ек) (*meat etc.*) нареза́ть *impf.*, наре́зать (-éжу, -éжешь) *pf.* **carver** *n.* (*person*) ре́зчик; *pl.* (*cutlery*) большо́й нож (-á) и ви́лка. **carving** *n.* резьба́; резно́й орна́мент; ~ **knife** нож (-á) для наре́зания мя́са.
cascade [kæsˈkeɪd] *n.* каска́д.
case¹ [keɪs] *n.* (*instance*) слу́чай; (*leg.*) де́ло (*pl.* -лá); (*med.*) больно́й *sb.*; (*gram.*) паде́ж (-á); **as the ~ may be** в зави́симости от обстоя́тельств; **in ~** (в слу́чае) е́сли; **in any ~** во вся́ком слу́чае; **in no ~** не в ко́ем слу́чае; **just in ~** на вся́кий слу́чай, на аво́сь.
case² [keɪs] *n.* (*box*) я́щик, коро́бка; (*suitcase*) чемода́н; (*casing*) футля́р, чехо́л; (*print.*) ка́сса; *v.t.* покрыва́ть *impf.*, покры́ть (-ро́ю, -ро́ешь) *pf.* **case-harden** *v.t.* цементи́ровать *impf.* & *pf.*
casement window [ˈkeɪsmənt] *n.* ство́рное окно́ (*pl.* о́кна, о́кон, о́кнам).
cash [kæʃ] *n.* нали́чные *sb.*; де́ньги (-нег, -ньга́м) *pl.*; ка́сса; ~ **and carry** прода́жа за нали́чный расчёт без доста́вки на́ дом; ~ **down** де́ньги на бо́чку; ~ **on delivery** нало́женным платежо́м; ~ **register** ка́сса; *v.t.* превраща́ть *impf.*, преврати́ть (-щу́, -ти́шь) *pf.* в нали́чные *sb.*; ~ **a cheque** получа́ть *impf.*, получи́ть (-чу́, -чишь) *pf.* де́ньги по че́ку. **cashcard** *n.* ка́рточка для де́нежного автома́та. **cashier¹** [kæˈʃɪə(r)] *n.* касси́р. **cashier²** *v.t.* увольня́ть *impf.*, уво́лить *pf.* со слу́жбы.
cashmere [ˈkæʃmɪə(r)] *n.* кашеми́р.
casing [ˈkeɪsɪŋ] *n.* (*tech.*) кожу́х (-á).
casino [kəˈsiːnəʊ] *n.* казино́ *nt.indecl.*
cask [kɑːsk] *n.* бо́чка.
casket [ˈkɑːskɪt] *n.* шкату́лка, ларе́ц (-рцá).
Caspian [ˈkæspɪən] *adj.*: ~ **Sea** Каспи́йское мо́ре.
casserole [ˈkæsərəʊl] *n.* тяжёлая кастрю́ля; блю́до, пригото́вляемое в ней.
cassette [kæˈset, kə-] *n.* кассе́та.
cassock [ˈkæsək] *n.* ря́са.
cast [kɑːst] *v.t.* (*throw*) броса́ть *impf.*, бро́сить *pf.*; (*shed*) сбра́сывать *impf.*, сбро́сить *pf.*; (*theatr.*) распределя́ть *impf.*, распре-

дели́ть *pf.* ро́ли+*d.*; (*found*) лить (лью, льёшь; лил, -á, -о) *impf.*, с~ (со́лью, -льёшь; слил, -á, -о) *pf.*; (*horoscope*) составля́ть *impf.*, соста́вить *pf.*; ~ **ashore** выбра́сывать *impf.*, вы́бросить *pf.* на бе́рег; ~ **off** (*knitting*) спуска́ть *impf.*, спусти́ть (-ущу́, -у́стишь) *pf.* пе́тли; (*naut.*) отплыва́ть *impf.*, отплы́ть (-ыву́, -ывёшь; отплы́л, -á, -о) *pf.*; ~ **on** (*knitting*) набира́ть *impf.*, набра́ть (наберу́, -рёшь; набра́л, -á, -о) *pf.* пе́тли; *n.* (*throw*) бросо́к (-скá), броса́ние; (*of mind etc.*) склад; (*mould*) фо́рма; (*med.*) ги́псовая повя́зка; (*theatr.*) де́йствующие ли́ца (-ц) *pl.*; (*in eye*) лёгкое косогла́зие.
castaway *n.* потерпе́вший *sb.* кораблекруше́ние. **cast iron** *n.* чугу́н (-á). **cast-iron** *adj.* чугу́нный. **cast-offs** *n.* (*clothes*) но́шеное пла́тье.
castanet [ˌkæstəˈnet] *n.* кастанье́та.
caste [kɑːst] *n.* ка́ста; ка́стовая систе́ма.
castigate [ˈkæstɪɡeɪt] *v.t.* бичева́ть *impf.*
castle [ˈkɑːs(ə)l] *n.* за́мок (-мка); (*chess*) ладья́.
castor [ˈkɑːstə(r)] *n.* (*wheel*) ро́лик, колёсико (*pl.* -ки, -ков); ~ **sugar** са́харная пу́дра.
castor oil [ˈkɑːstə(r)] *n.* касто́ровое ма́сло.
castrate [kæˈstreɪt] *v.t.* кастри́ровать *impf.* & *pf.* **castration** *n.* кастра́ция.
casual [ˈkæʒʊəl, -zjʊəl] *adj.* случа́йный; (*careless*) несерьёзный. **casualty** *n.* (*wounded*) ра́неный *sb.*; (*killed*) уби́тый *sb.*; *pl.* поте́ри (-рь) *pl.*; ~ **ward** пала́та ско́рой по́мощи.
casuist [ˈkæzjuːɪst, ˈkæʒʊɪst] *n.* казуи́ст. **casu'istic(al)** *adj.* казуисти́ческий. **casuistry** *n.* казуи́стика.
cat [kæt] *n.* ко́шка; (*tom*) кот (-á). **catcall** *n.* свист, осви́стывание; *v.t.* & *i.* осви́стывать *impf.*, освиста́ть (-ищу́, -и́щешь) *pf.* **cat-o'-nine-tails** *n.* ко́шки *f.pl.* **cat's-eye** *n.* (*min.*) коша́чий глаз (*loc.* -ý; *pl.* -зá, -з); (C~, *propr.*) (*on road*) (доро́жный) рефле́ктор. **catwalk** *n.* у́зкий мо́стик; рабо́чий помо́ст.
cataclysm [ˈkætəˌklɪz(ə)m] *n.* катакли́зм.
catalogue [ˈkætəˌlɒɡ] *n.* катало́г; (*price list*) прейскура́нт; *v.t.* каталогизи́ровать *impf.* & *pf.*
catalysis [kəˈtælɪsɪs] *n.* ката́лиз. **catalyst** [ˈkætəlɪst] *n.* катализа́тор. **cata'lytic** *adj.* катали́тический.
catamaran [ˌkætəməˈræn] *n.* катамара́н.
catapult [ˈkætəˌpʌlt] *n.* (*child's*) рога́тка; (*hist.*, *aeron.*) катапу́льта; *v.t.* катапульти́ровать *impf.* & *pf.*
cataract [ˈkætəˌrækt] *n.* (*waterfall*) водопа́д; (*med.*) катара́кта.
catarrh [kəˈtɑː(r)] *n.* ката́р.
catastrophe [kəˈtæstrəfɪ] *n.* катастро́фа. **catastrophic** [ˌkætəˈstrɒfɪk] *adj.* катастрофи́ческий.
catch [kætʃ] *v.t.* (*captive*) лови́ть (-влю́, -вишь) *impf.*, пойма́ть *pf.*; (*seize*) захва́тывать *impf.*, захвати́ть (-ачу́, -áтишь) *pf.*; (*surprise*)

заставать (-таю, -таёшь) *impf.*, застать (-áну, -áнешь) *pf.*; (*disease*) заражáться *impf.*, заразиться *pf.*+*i.*; (*be in time for*) успевáть *impf.*, успéть *pf.* на+*a.*; ~ **on** зацеплять(ся) *impf.*, зацепить(ся) (-плю(сь), -пишь(ся)) *pf.* за+*a.*; (*v.i.*) (*become popular*) прививáться *impf.*, привиться (-вьётся; -вился, -вилáсь) *pf.*; ~ **up with** догонять *impf.*, догнáть (догоню, -нишь; догнáл, -á, -о) *pf.*; *n.* (*action*) поймка; (*of fish*) улóв; (*trick*) улóвка; (*on door etc.*) защёлка, задвижка; ~ **crops** междупосевные культуры *f.pl.*
catching *adj.* зарáзный; заразительный.
catchment area *n.* водосбóрная плóщадь (*pl.* -ди, -дéй). **catchword** *n.* (*slogan*) лóзунг; (*running title*) колонтитул; (*headword*) заглáвное слóво (*pl.* -вá). **catchy** *adj.* привлекáтельный, легкó запоминáющийся.
catechism ['kætɪ,kɪz(ə)m] *n.* (*eccl.*) катехизис; допрóс. **catechize** ['kætɪ,kaɪz] *v.t.* допрáшивать *impf.*, допросить (-ошу, -óсишь) *pf.*
categorical [,kætɪ'gɒrɪk(ə)l] *adj.* категорический. **'category** *n.* категóрия.
cater ['keɪtə(r)] *v.i.* поставлять *impf.* провизию; ~ **for** снабжáть *impf.*, снабдить *pf.*; обслуживать *impf.*, обслужить (-жу, -жишь) *pf.* **caterer** *n.* поставщик (-á) (провизии).
caterpillar ['kætə,pɪlə(r)] *n.* гусеница; *adj.* гусеничный; **C~ track** (*propr.*) гусеничная лéнта.
caterwaul ['kætə,wɔːl] *v.i.* кричáть (-чý, -чишь) котóм; задавáть (-даёт) *impf.*, задáть (-áст; зáдал, -á, -о) *pf.* кошáчий концéрт. **caterwauling** *n.* кошáчий концéрт.
catgut ['kætgʌt] *n.* кетгýт.
catharsis [kə'θɑːsɪs] *n.* кáтарсис.
cathedral [kə'θiːdr(ə)l] *n.* (кафедрáльный) собóр.
catheter ['kæθɪtə(r)] *n.* катéтер.
cathode ['kæθəʊd] *n.* катóд; ~ **rays** катóдные лучи *m.pl.*
Catholic ['kæθəlɪk, 'kæθlɪk] *adj.* католический; *n.* католик, -ичка. **Ca'tholicism** *n.* католичество, католицизм.
catkin ['kætkɪn] *n.* серёжка.
cattle ['kæt(ə)l] *n.* скот (-á).
Caucasus ['kɔːkəsəs] *n.* Кавкáз.
cauldron ['kɔːldrən] *n.* котёл (-тлá).
cauliflower ['kɒlɪ,flaʊə(r)] *n.* цветнáя капýста.
caulk [kɔːk] *v.t.* конопáтить *impf.*, за~ *pf.*
causal ['kɔːz(ə)l] *adj.* причинный (-нен, -нна). **cau'sality** *n.* причинность. **cau'sation** *n.* причинéние; причинность. **cause** *n.* причина, пóвод; (*leg. etc.*) дéло (*pl.* -лá); *v.t.* причинять *impf.*, причинить *pf.*; вызывáть *impf.*, вызвать (-зову, -зовешь) *pf.*; (*induce*) заставлять *impf.*, застáвить *pf.* **causeless** *adj.* беспричинный (-нен, -нна).
caustic ['kɔːstɪk] *adj.* каустический, éдкий (éдок, едкá, éдко) ~ **soda** éдкий натр; *n.* éдкое существó.
cauterization [,kɔːtəraɪ'zeɪʃ(ə)n] *n.* прижи-

гáние. **'cauterize** *v.t.* прижигáть *impf.*, прижéчь (-жгý, -жжёшь; -жёг, -жглá) *pf.* **'cautery** *n.* термокáутер.
caution ['kɔːʃ(ə)n] *n.* осторóжность; (*warning*) предупреждéние; *v.t.* предостерегáть *impf.*, предостерéчь (-егý, -ежёшь; -ёг, -еглá) *pf.* **cautious** *adj.* осторóжный. **cautionary** *adj.* предостерегáющий.
cavalcade [,kævəl'keɪd] *n.* кавалькáда. **cavalier** [,kævə'lɪə(r)] *adj.* бесцеремóнный (-нен, -нна); (*C~, hist.*) роялистский; роялист.
cavalry ['kævəlrɪ] *n.* кавалéрия. **cavalryman** *n.* кавалерист.
cave [keɪv] *n.* пещéра; *v.i.*: ~ **in** обвáливаться *impf.*, обвалиться (-ится) *pf.*; (*yield*) уступáть *impf.*, уступить (-плю, -пишь) *pf.* **caveman** *n.* пещéрный человéк. **cavern** ['kæv(ə)n] *n.* пещéра. **cavernous** *adj.* пещéристый.
caviare ['kævɪ,ɑː(r)] *n.* икрá.
cavil ['kævɪl] *v.i.* придирáться *impf.*, придрáться (-дерýсь, -дерёшься; -áлся, -алáсь, -áлось) *pf.* (**at** k+*d.*).
cavity ['kævɪtɪ] *n.* впáдина, пóлость (*pl.* -ти, -тéй).
caw ['kɔː] *v.i.* кáркать *impf.*, кáркнуть *pf.*; *n.* кáрканье.
cayman ['keɪmən] *n.* каймáн.
CD *abbr.* (*of compact disk*) компáкт-диск; **CD player** проигрыватель (*m.*) компáкт-дисков.
CD-ROM *abbr.* (*of compact disk — read-only memory*) компáкт-диск ПЗУ; ~ **player** проигрыватель *m.* компáкт-дисков ПЗУ.
cease [siːs] *v.t.* & *i.* прекращáть(ся) *impf.*, прекратить(ся) (-ащý, -атит(ся)) *pf.*; *v.i.* переставáть (-таю, -таёшь) *impf.*, перестáть (-áну, -áнешь) *pf.* (+*inf.*). **cease-fire** *n.* прекращéние огня. **ceaseless** *adj.* непрестáнный (-áнен, -áнна).
cedar ['siːdə(r)] *n.* кедр.
ceiling ['siːlɪŋ] *n.* потолóк (-лкá); (*prices etc.*) максимáльная ценá (*a.* -ну), максимáльный úровень (-вня) *m.*
celandine ['selən,daɪn] *n.* чистотéл.
celebrate ['selɪ,breɪt] *v.t.* прáздновать *impf.*, от~ *pf.*; **be** ~**d** слáвиться *impf.* (**for** +*i.*). **celebrated** *adj.* знаменитый. **cele'bration** *n.* прáзднование. **ce'lebrity** *n.* знаменитость.
celery ['selərɪ] *n.* сельдерéй.
celestial [sɪ'lestɪəl] *adj.* небéсный.
celibacy ['selɪbəsɪ] *n.* безбрáчие. **celibate** *adj.* безбрáчный; (*person*) холостóй (-óст), незамýжняя.
cell [sel] *n.* (*room*) кéлья; (*prison*) тюрéмная кáмера; (*biol.*) клéтка, клéточка; (*pol.*) ячéйка.
cellar ['selə(r)] *n.* подвáл, пóгреб (*pl.* -á); *adj.* подвáльный.
cellist ['tʃelɪst] *n.* виолончелист. **cello** ['tʃeləʊ] *n.* виолончéль.
cellophane ['selə,feɪn] *n.* целлофáн; *adj.*

целлофа́новый. **cellular** ['seljʊlə(r)] *adj.*
кле́точный. **cellule** *n.* кле́точка. **celluloid**
n. целлуло́ид; (кино)фи́льм. **cellulose** *n.*
целлюло́за; клетча́тка.

Celsius ['selsɪəs]: ~ **scale** шкала́ термоме́тра
Це́льсия; ~ **thermometer** термо́метр Це́ль-
сия; **10°** ~ 10° по Це́льсию.

Celt [kelt, selt] *n.* кельт. **Celtic** *adj.* ке́льт-
ский.

cement [sɪ'ment] *n.* цеме́нт; *v.t.* цементи́-
ровать *impf.*, за~ *pf.*

cemetery ['semɪtərɪ] *n.* кла́дбище.

cenotaph ['senə,tɑːf] *n.* кенота́ф.

censer ['sensə(r)] *n.* кади́ло.

censor ['sensə(r)] *n.* це́нзор; *v.t.* подверга́ть
impf., подве́ргнуть (-г) *pf.* цензу́ре. **cen-
sorious** [sen'sɔːrɪəs] *adj.* стро́гий (строг,
-а́, -о); скло́нный (-о́нен, -о́нна́, -о́нно)
осужда́ть. **censorship** *n.* цензу́ра. **censure**
n. осужде́ние; порица́ние; *v.t.* осужда́ть
impf., осуди́ть (-ужу́, -у́дишь) *pf.*; порица́ть
impf.

census *n.* пе́репись (населе́ния).

cent [sent] *n.* цент; **per** ~ проце́нт.

centaur ['sentɔː(r)] *n.* кента́вр.

centenarian [ˌsentɪ'neərɪən] *adj.* столе́тний;
n. столе́тний челове́к, челове́к в во́зрасте
ста лет. **centenary** [sen'tiːnərɪ] *n.* столе́тие.
cen'tennial *adj.* столе́тний; *n.* столе́тняя
годовщи́на; **10°** ~ 10° по Це́льсию. **centigrade** *adj.* стогра́дусный;
10° ~ 10° по Це́льсию. **'centigram** *n.* санти-
гра́мм. **'centilitre** *n.* сантили́тр. **'centimetre**
n. сантиме́тр. **'centipede** *n.* сороконо́жка.

central ['sentr(ə)l] *adj.* центра́льный; ~ **heating** центра́льное отопле́ние. **centralism** *n.*
централи́зм. **centrali'zation** *n.* централи-
за́ция. **centralize** *v.t.* централизова́ть *impf.*
& *pf.* **centre** *n.* центр; середи́на; ~ **back**
центр защи́ты; ~ **forward** центр нападе́ния;
~ **half** центр полузащи́ты; *v.i.* сосредо-
то́чиваться *impf.*, сосредото́читься *pf.*
centri'fugal *adj.* центробе́жный. **centrifuge**
['sentrɪ,fjuːdʒ] *n.* центрифу́га. **cen'tripetal**
adj. центростреми́тельный.

centurion [sen'tjʊərɪən] *n.* центурио́н. **'century** *n.* столе́тие, век (*loc.* в -е, на -ý; *pl.*
-á) (*sport*) сто очко́в.

ceramic [sɪ'ræmɪk, kɪ-] *adj.* керами́ческий.
ceramics *n.* кера́мика.

cereal ['sɪərɪəl] *adj.* хле́бный; *n.:* *pl.* хлеба́
m.pl., хле́бные, зерновы́е, зла́ки *m.pl.*;
breakfast ~**s** зерновы́е хло́пья (-ьев) *pl.*

cerebral ['serɪbr(ə)l] *adj.* мозгово́й.

ceremonial [ˌserɪ'məʊnɪəl] *adj.* форма́льный;
торже́ственный (-ен, -нна), пара́дный; *n.*
церемониа́л. **ceremonious** *adj.* церемо́н-
ный (-нен, -нна). **'ceremony** *n.* церемо́ния.

cerise [sə'riːz, -'riːs] *adj.* (*n.*) све́тло-виш-
нёвый (цвет).

cert [sɜːt] *n.* (*sl.*) ве́рное де́ло. **certain**
['sɜːt(ə)n, -tɪn] *adj.* (*definite*) определённый
(-ёнен, -ённа); (*reliable*) ве́рный (-рен, -рна́,
-рно, ве́рны́); (*doubtless*) несомне́нный

(-нен, -нна); *pred.* уве́рен (-нна); **for** ~
наверняка́. **certainly** *adv.* (*of course*)
коне́чно, безусло́вно; (*without fail*) непре-
ме́нно; (*beyond question*) несомне́нно.
certainty *n.* (*conviction*) уве́ренность; (*undoubted fact*) несомне́нный факт; безус-
ло́вность; **bet on a** ~ держа́ть (-жу́, -жишь)
impf. пари́ наверняка́.

cer'tificate *n.* удостовере́ние, свиде́тельство;
сертифика́т; аттеста́т; **birth** ~ ме́трика.
certify *v.t.* удостоверя́ть *impf.*, удостове́-
рить *pf.*; свиде́тельствовать *impf.*, за~ *pf.*;
(*as insane*) признава́ть (-наю́, -наёшь)
impf., призна́ть *pf.* сумасше́дшим.

certitude *n.* уве́ренность.

cessation [se'seɪʃ(ə)n] *n.* прекраще́ние.

cesspit ['sespɪt] *n.* помо́йная я́ма. **cesspool**
n. выгребна́я я́ма; (*fig.*) клоа́ка.

cf. *abbr.* ср., сравни́.

CFCs *abbr.* (*of chloro-fluorocarbons*) хлори́-
рованные фторуглеро́ды.

chafe [tʃeɪf] *v.t.* (*rub*) тере́ть (тру, трёшь;
тёр) *impf.*; (*rub sore*) натира́ть *impf.*,
натере́ть (-тру́, -трёшь; -тёр) *pf.*; *v.i.* (*fret*)
раздража́ться *impf.*, раздражи́ться *pf.*

chaff [tʃɑːf] *n.* (*husks*) мяки́на; (*chopped
straw*) се́чка; (*banter*) подшу́чивание; *v.t.*
поддра́знивать *impf.*, поддразни́ть (-ню́,
-нишь) *pf.*; подшу́чивать *impf.*, подшути́ть
(-учу́, -у́тишь) *pf.* над+*i.*

chaffinch ['tʃæfɪntʃ] *n.* зя́блик.

chagrin ['ʃægrɪn, ʃə'griːn] *n.* огорче́ние.

chain [tʃeɪn] *n.* цепь (*loc.* -пи́; *pl.* -пи, -пе́й);
(*crochet*) коси́чка; ~ **reaction** цепна́я реа́к-
ция. **chain-stitch** *n.* тамбу́рный шов (шва),
тамбу́рная стро́чка.

chair [tʃeə(r)] *n.* стул (*pl.* -ья, -ьев), кре́сло
(*g.pl.* -сел); (*chairmanship*) председа́тель-
ство; (*chairman*) председа́тель *m.*, ~ница;
(*univ.*) ка́федра; *v.t.* (*preside*) председа́тель-
ствовать *impf.* на+*p.*; (*carry aloft*) под-
нима́ть *impf.*, подня́ть (-ниму́, -ни́мешь;
по́днял, -á, -о) *pf.* и нести́ (несу́, -сёшь; нёс,
-ла́) *impf.* **chairman, -woman** *n.* председа́-
тель *m.*, ~ница.

chalice ['tʃælɪs] *n.* ча́ша.

chalk [tʃɔːk] *n.* мел (-а(у), *loc.* -ý & -е); (*piece
of* ~) мело́к (-лка́); **not by a long** ~ отню́дь
нет, далеко́ не; *v.t.* писа́ть (пишу́, пи́-
шешь) *impf.*, на~ *pf.* ме́лом; черти́ть (-рчу́,
-ртишь) *impf.*, на~ *pf.* ме́лом. **chalky** *adj.*
мелово́й, известко́вый.

challenge ['tʃælɪndʒ] *n.* (*summons*) вы́зов;
(*sentry's call*) о́клик (часово́го); (*leg.*)
отво́д; *v.t.* вызыва́ть *impf.*, вы́звать (-зову,
-вешь) *pf.*; оклика́ть *impf.*, окли́кнуть
pf.; отводи́ть (-ожу́, -о́дишь) *impf.*, отвести́
-еду́, -еде́шь; -ёл, -ела́) *pf.*

chamber ['tʃeɪmbə(r)] *n.* ко́мната; (*pol.*)
пала́та; *pl.* меблиро́ванные ко́мнаты *f.pl.*;
pl. (*judge's*) кабине́т (судьи́); ~ **music**
ка́мерная му́зыка. **chamberlain** ['tʃeɪm-
bəlɪn] *n.* камерге́р; (**C**~) гофме́йстер.

chambermaid *n.* го́рничная *sb.* **chamber-pot** *n.* ночно́й горшо́к (-шка́).

chameleon [kə'mi:liən] *n.* хамелео́н.

chamois ['ʃæmwɑ:; 'ʃæmi] *n.* (*animal*) се́рна; (~-*leather*) за́мша; *adj.* за́мшевый.

champ [tʃæmp] *v.i.* ча́вкать *impf.*, ча́вкнуть *pf.*; ~ **the bit** грызть (-зёт, -з) *impf.* удила́ (*pl.*).

champagne [ʃæm'peɪn] *n.* шампа́нское *sb.*

champion ['tʃæmpɪən] *n.* (*athletic etc.*) чемпио́н, -ка; (*animal, plant etc*) пе́рвый призёр; (*upholder*) побо́рник, -ица; *adj.* получи́вший пе́рвый приз; *v.t.* защища́ть *impf.*, защити́ть (-ищу́, -ити́шь) *pf.* **championship** *n.* пе́рвенство, чемпиона́т; побо́рничество.

chance [tʃɑːns] *n.* случа́йность; (*opportunity*) слу́чай; (*possibility*) шанс; *adj.* случа́йный; *v.i.* (*happen*) случа́ться *impf.*, случи́ться *pf.*; ~ **it** рискну́ть *pf.*

chancel ['tʃɑːns(ə)l] *n.* алта́рь (-ря́) *m.*

chancellery ['tʃɑːnsələrɪ] *n.* канцеля́рия.

chancellor *n.* ка́нцлер; (*univ.*) ре́ктор университе́та; **Lord C~** лорд-ка́нцлер; **C~ of the Exchequer** ка́нцлер казначе́йства. **Chancery** *n.* суд (-а́) ло́рда-ка́нцлера; **c~** канцеля́рия.

chancy ['tʃɑːnsɪ] *adj.* риско́ванный (-ан, -анна).

chandelier [ʃændɪ'lɪə(r)] *n.* лю́стра.

change [tʃeɪndʒ] *n.* переме́на; измене́ние; (*of clothes etc.*) сме́на; (*money*) сда́ча; (*of trains etc.*) переса́дка; ~ **for the better** переме́на к лу́чшему; ~ **of air** переме́на обстано́вки; ~ **of life** климакте́рий; ~ **of scene** переме́на обстано́вки; **for a** ~ для разнообра́зия; *v.t. & i.* меня́ть(ся) *impf.*; изменя́ть(ся) *impf.*, измени́ть(ся) (-ню́(сь), -ни́шь(ся)) *pf.*; *v.i.* (*one's clothes*) переодева́ться *impf.*, переоде́ться (-е́нусь, -е́нешься) *pf.*; (*trains etc.*) переса́живаться *impf.*, пересе́сть (-ся́ду, -ся́дешь; -се́л) *pf.*; *v.t.* (*a baby*) перепелё-нывать *impf.*, перепелена́ть *pf.*; (*give* ~ *for*) разме́нивать *impf.*, разменя́ть *pf.*; ~ **into** превраща́ться *impf.*, преврати́ться (-ащу́сь, -ати́шься) *pf.* в+*a.* **changeable** *adj.* непостоя́нный (-нен, -нна), неусто́йчивый, изме́нчивый. **changeless** *adj.* неизме́нный (-нен, -нна), постоя́нный (-нен, -нна). **changing-room** *n.* раздева́лка; приме́рочная *sb.*

channel ['tʃæn(ə)l] *n.* кана́л, проли́в, прото́к; (*fig.*) ру́сло (*g.pl.* -сл & -сел), путь (-ти́, -тём) *m.*; **the (English) C~** Ла-Ма́нш; **the C~ Islands** Норма́ндские острова́; **C~ tunnel** тонне́ль под Ла-Ма́ншем; *v.t.* пуска́ть *impf.*, пусти́ть (пущу́, пу́стишь) *pf.* по кана́лу; (*fig., direct*) направля́ть *impf.*

chaos ['keɪɒs] *n.* ха́ос. **cha'otic** *adj.* хаоти́чный.

chap¹ [tʃæp] *n.* (*person*) ма́лый *sb.*, па́рень (-рня; *pl.* -рни, -рне́й) *m.*

chap² [tʃæp] *n.* (*crack*) тре́щина; *v.i.* тре́скаться *impf.*, по~ *pf.*

chapel ['tʃæp(ə)l] *n.* часо́вня (*g.pl.* -вен), ка-

пе́лла; моле́льня (*g.pl.* -лен).

chaplain ['tʃæplɪn] *n.* капелла́н.

chapter ['tʃæptə(r)] *n.* глава́ (*pl.* -вы); (*eccl.*) капи́тул; ~ **house** зда́ние капи́тула.

char¹ [tʃɑː(r)] *n.* приходя́щая домрабо́тница.

char² [tʃɑː(r)] *v.t. & i.* обу́гливать(ся) *impf.*, обу́глить(ся) *pf.*

character ['kærɪktə(r)] *n.* хара́ктер; (*testimonial*) рекоменда́ция; (*personage*) персона́ж; (*theatr.*) де́йствующее лицо́ (*pl.* -ца); (*letter*) бу́ква; (*numeral*) ци́фра; (*mark*) знак. **characte'ristic** *adj.* характе́рный; *n.* характе́рная черта́. **characterize** *v.t.* характеризова́ть *impf. & pf.*

charade [ʃə'rɑːd] *n.* шара́да.

charcoal ['tʃɑːkəʊl] *n.* древе́сный у́голь (у́гля) *m.*

charge [tʃɑːdʒ] *n.* (*load*) нагру́зка; (*for gun; elec.*) заря́д; (*fee*) пла́та; (*care*) попече́ние; (*person*) пито́мец (-мца), -мица; (*accusation*) обвине́ние; (*mil.*) ата́ка; **be in** ~ **of** заве́довать *impf.*+*i.*; име́ть *impf.* на попече́нии; in the ~ of на попече́нии+*g.*; *v.t.* (*gun; elec.*) заряжа́ть *impf.*, заряди́ть (-яжу́, -я́ди́шь) *pf.*; (*accuse*) обвиня́ть *impf.*, обвини́ть *pf.* (**with** в+*p.*); (*mil.*) атакова́ть *impf. & pf.*; *v.i.* броса́ться *impf.*, бро́ситься *pf.* в ата́ку; ~ (**for**) брать (беру́, -ерёшь; брал, -а́, -о) *impf.*, взять (возьму́, -мёшь; взял, -а́, -о) *pf.* (за+*a.*); назнача́ть *impf.*, назна́чить *pf.* пла́ту (за+*a.*); ~ **to** (**the account of**) запи́сывать *impf.*, записа́ть (-ишу́, -и́шешь) *pf.* на счёт+*g.*

chargé d'affaires [ˌʃɑːʒeɪ dæ'feə(r)] *n.* пове́ренный *sb.* в дела́х.

chariot ['tʃærɪət] *n.* колесни́ца.

charisma [kə'rɪzmə] *n.* (*divine gift*) бо́жий дар; (*charm*) обая́ние. **charis'matic** *adj.* боговдохнове́нный, вдохнове́нный; с бо́жьей и́скрой; обая́тельный.

charitable ['tʃærɪtəb(ə)l] *adj.* благотвори́тельный; (*merciful*) милосе́рдный; (*lenient*) снисходи́тельный. **charity** *n.* (*kindness*) милосе́рдие; (*leniency*) снисходи́тельность, благотвори́тельность; (*organization*) благотвори́тельное о́бщество; *pl.* благотвори́тельная де́ятельность.

charlatan ['ʃɑːlət(ə)n] *n.* шарлата́н.

charlotte ['ʃɑːlət] *n.*: **apple** ~ шарло́тка.

charm [tʃɑːm] *n.* очарова́ние; пре́лесть; (*spell*) за́говор; *pl.* ча́ры (чар) *pl.*; (*amulet*) талисма́н; (*trinket*) брело́к; **act, work, like a** ~ твори́ть *impf.*, со~ *pf.* чудеса́; *v.t.* очаро́вывать *impf.*, очарова́ть *pf.*; ~ **away** отгоня́ть *impf.*, отогна́ть (отгоню́, -нишь; отогна́л, -а́, -о) *pf.* (как бы) колдовство́м; **bear a** ~**ed life** быть неуязви́мым. **charming** *adj.* очарова́тельный, преле́стный.

charring ['tʃɑːrɪŋ] *n.* рабо́та по до́му; **do, go out,** ~ служи́ть (-жу́, -жишь) *impf.* приходя́щей домрабо́тницей.

chart [tʃɑːt] *n.* (*naut.*) морска́я ка́рта; (*table*) гра́фик; *v.t.* наноси́ть (-ошу́, -о́сишь) *impf.*,

нанести́ (-су́, -сёшь; нанёс, -ла́) *pf.* на
ка́рту; составля́ть *impf.*, соста́вить *pf.*
гра́фик+*g.* **charter** *n.* (*document*) ха́ртия;
(*statutes*) уста́в; (*~-party*) ча́ртер; *v.t.* (*ship*)
фрахтова́ть *impf.*, за~ *pf.*; (*vehicle etc.*)
нанима́ть *impf.*, наня́ть (найму́, -мёшь;
наня́л, -а́, -о) *pf.*
charwoman ['tʃɑːˌwʊmən] *n.* приходя́щая
домрабо́тница.
chase [tʃeɪs] *v.t.* гоня́ться *indet.*, гна́ться
(гоню́сь, го́нишься; гна́лся, -ла́сь, гна́ло́сь)
det. за+*i.*; *n.* (*pursuit*) пого́ня, пресле́до-
вание; (*hunting*) охо́та.
chased [tʃeɪsd] *adj.* укра́шенный (-н) грави-
рова́нием, рельефом.
chasm ['kæz(ə)m] *n.* (*abyss*) бе́здна; (*fissure*)
глубо́кая рассе́лина.
chassis ['ʃæsɪ] *n.* шасси́ *nt.indecl.*
chaste [tʃeɪst] *adj.* целому́дренный (-ен,
-енна).
chastise [tʃæsˈtaɪz] *v.t.* подверга́ть *impf.*,
подве́ргнуть (-г) *pf.* наказа́нию.
chastity ['tʃæstɪtɪ] *n.* целому́дрие.
chat [tʃæt] *n.* бесе́да, разгово́р; *v.i.* бесе́до-
вать *impf.*; разгова́ривать *impf.*
chattels ['tʃæt(ə)lz] *n. pl.* дви́жимость.
chatter ['tʃætə(r)] *n.* болтовня́; трескотня́; *v.i.*
болта́ть *impf.*; треща́ть (-щу́, -щи́шь) *impf.*;
(*of teeth*) стуча́ть (-ча́т) *impf.* **chatterbox**
n. болту́н (-а́). **chatty** *adj.* разгово́рчивый.
chauffeur ['ʃəʊfə(r), -ˈfɜː(r)] *n.* шофёр.
chauvinism ['ʃəʊvɪˌnɪz(ə)m] *n.* шовини́зм.
chauvinist *n.* шовини́ст, ~ка; *adj.* шови-
ни́стский.
cheap [tʃiːp] *adj.* дешёвый (дёшев, -а́, -о).
cheapen *v.t. & i.* обесце́нивать(ся) *impf.*,
обесце́нить(ся) *pf.*; удешевля́ть(ся) *impf.*,
удешеви́ть(ся) *pf.* **cheaply** *adv.* дёшево.
cheapness *n.* дешеви́зна.
cheat [tʃiːt] *v.t.* обма́нывать *impf.*, обману́ть
(-ну́, -нешь) *pf.*; *v.i.* плутова́ть *impf.*, на~,
с~ *pf.*; моше́нничать *impf.*, с~ *pf.*; *n.*
(*person*) обма́нщик, -ица; (*act*) обма́н.
cheating *n.* моше́нничество, плутовство́.
check[1] [tʃek] *n.* контро́ль *m.*, прове́рка;
(*stoppage*) заде́ржка; (*chess*) шах; *adj.*
контро́льный; *v.t.* (*examine*) проверя́ть
impf., прове́рить *pf.*; контроли́ровать *impf.*,
про~ *pf.*; (*restrain*) сде́рживать *impf.*,
сдержа́ть (-жу́, -жишь) *pf.*
check[2] [tʃek] *n.* (*pattern*) кле́тка. **check(ed)**
adj. кле́тчатый.
check-list ['tʃeklɪst] *n.* контро́льный спи́сок
(-ска́). **checkmate** *n.* шах и мат; *v.t.*
наноси́ть (-ошу́, -о́сишь) *impf.*, нанести́
(-су́, -сёшь; нанёс, -ла́) *pf.*+*d.* пораже́-
ние. **checkout** *n.* ка́сса. **checkpoint** *n.* кон-
тро́льно-пропускно́й пункт. **check-up** *n.*
(*med.*) медосмо́тр; (*tech.*) техосмо́тр.
cheek [tʃiːk] *n.* щека́ (*a.* щёку; *pl.* щёки, щёк,
-а́м); (*impertinence*) наха́льство, де́рзость;
v.t. дерзи́ть (-и́шь) *impf.*, на~ *pf.*+*d.* **cheek-
bone** *n.* скула́ (*pl.* -лы). **cheeky** *adj.* дёрз-

кий (-зок, -зка́, -зко), наха́льный.
cheep [tʃiːp] *n.* писк; *v.i.* пища́ть (-щу́, -щи́шь)
impf., пи́скнуть *pf.*
cheer ['tʃɪə(r)] *n.* одобри́тельное воскли-
ца́ние; *pl.* (*applause*) аплодисме́нты (-тов);
pl.; **~s**! за (ва́ше) здоро́вье!; **three ~s
for** ... да здра́вствует (-уют)+*nom.*; *v.t.*
(*applaud*) аплоди́ровать *impf.*+*d.*; **~ up**
ободря́ть(ся) *impf.*, ободри́ть(ся) *pf.* **cheerful** *adj.* весёлый (ве́сел, -а́, -о, ве́селы́),
бо́дрый (бодр, -а́, -о). **cheerless** *adj.* уны́-
лый. **cheery** *adj.* бо́дрый (бодр, -а́, -о).
cheese [tʃiːz] *n.* сыр (-а(у); *pl.* -ы́); **~ straw**
сы́рная па́лочка. **cheesecake** *n.* ватру́шка.
cheesecloth *n.* ма́рля. **cheese-paring** *n.*
ску́пость, грошо́вая эконо́мия; *adj.* скупо́й
(скуп, -а́, -о).
cheetah ['tʃiːtə] *n.* гепа́рд.
chef [ʃef] *n.* (шеф-)по́вар (*pl.* -а́)
chef-d'oeuvre [ʃeɪˈdɜːvr] *n.* шеде́вр.
chemical ['kemɪk(ə)l] *adj.* хими́ческий; **~
warfare** хими́ческая война́; *n.* химика́т; *pl.*
химика́лии (-ий) *pl.* **chemically** *adv.* хими́-
чески. **chemist** *n.* хи́мик; (*druggist*) апте́-
карь *m.*; **~'s (shop)** апте́ка. **chemistry** *n.*
хи́мия. **chemotherapy** [ˌkiːməˈθerəpɪ] *n.* химо-
терапи́я.
chenille [ʃəˈniːl] *n.* сине́ль; *adj.* сине́льный.
cheque [tʃek] *n.* чек. **cheque-book** *n.* че́ко-
вая кни́жка.
chequered ['tʃekə(r)d] *adj.* (*varied*) разно-
обра́зный; (*changing*) изме́нчивый.
cherish ['tʃerɪʃ] *v.t.* (*foster*) леле́ять (-е́ю,
-е́ешь) *impf.*; (*hold dear*) дорожи́ть *impf.*+*i.*;
(*preserve in memory*) храни́ть *impf.* (в па́-
мяти); (*love*) не́жно люби́ть (-блю́, -бишь)
impf. **cherished** *adj.* заве́тный.
cheroot [ʃəˈruːt] *n.* мани́льская сига́ра.
cherry ['tʃerɪ] *n.* ви́шня (*g.pl.* -шен); чере́шня
(*g.pl.* -шен); (*tree*) вишнёвое де́рево (*pl.*
-е́вья, -е́вьев); (*colour*) вишнёвый цвет; *adj.*
вишнёвый, вишнёвого цве́та; (*cherry-
wood*) древеси́на вишнёвого де́рева.
cherub ['tʃerəb] *n.* херуви́м, херуви́мчик.
cherubic *adj.* пу́хлый и розовощёкий.
chervil ['tʃɜːvɪl] *n.* ке́рвель *m.*
chess [tʃes] *n.* ша́хматы (-т) *pl.*; *adj.* ша́х-
матный; **~ champion** чемпио́н по ша́х-
матам; **~ player** шахмати́ст, ~ка. **chess-
board** *n.* ша́хматная доска́ (*a.* -ску; *pl.* -ски,
-со́к, -ска́м). **chessman** *n.* ша́хматная
фигу́ра.
chest [tʃest] *n.* я́щик, сунду́к (-а́); (*anat.*)
грудь (-ди́, *i.* -дью; *pl.* -ди, -де́й); **~ of drawers**
комо́д.
chestnut ['tʃesnʌt] *n.* (*tree, fruit*) кашта́н;
(*colour*) кашта́новый цвет; (*horse*) гнеда́я
sb.; *adj.* кашта́новый; (*horse*) гнедо́й.
chevron ['ʃevrən] *n.* наши́вка.
chew [tʃuː] *v.t.* жева́ть (жую́, жуёшь) *impf.*;
~ over пережёвывать *impf.*, пережева́ть
(-жую́, -жуёшь) *pf.*; **~ the cud** жева́ть
(жую́, жуёшь) *impf.* жва́чку. **chewing** *n.*

жева́ние. **chewing-gum** *n.* жева́тельная
рези́нка, жва́чка.

chicane [ʃɪ'keɪn] *n.* вре́менное и́ли пере-
движно́е препя́тствие на доро́ге, го́ночном
тре́ке. **chicanery** *n.* крючкотво́рство; ма-
хина́ция.

chick [tʃɪk] *n.* цыплёнок (-нка; *pl.* цепля́та,
-т). **chicken** ['tʃɪkɪn] *n.* ку́рица (*pl.* ку́ры,
кур); цыплёнок (-нка; *pl.* цепля́та, -т);
(*meat*) куря́тина; *adj.* трусли́вый. **chicken-
hearted, -livered** *adj.* трусли́вый. **chicken-
pox** *n.* ве́тряная о́спа, ветря́нка.

chicory ['tʃɪkərɪ] *n.* цико́рий.

chief [tʃiːf] *n.* глава́ (*pl.* -вы) *c.g.*; (*mil. etc.*)
нача́льник; (*of tribe*) вождь (-дя́) *m.*; (*robber*) атама́н; *adj.* гла́вный; ста́рший. **chiefly**
adv. гла́вным о́бразом. **chieftain** *n.* вождь
(-дя́) *m.*; (*robber*) атама́н.

chiffon ['ʃɪfɒn] *n.* шифо́н; *adj.* шифо́новый.

child [tʃaɪld] *n.* ребёнок (-нка; *pl.* де́ти, -те́й);
~ **prodigy** вундерки́нд; ~'s **play** де́тские
игру́шки *f.pl.* **childbirth** *n.* ро́ды (-дов) *pl.*
childhood *n.* де́тство. **childish** *adj.* де́тский;
ребя́ческий. **childless** *adj.* безде́тный.
childlike *adj.* де́тский. **child-minder** *n.*
приходя́щая ня́ня. **childrens'** ['tʃɪldrənz] *adj.*
де́тский.

chili ['tʃɪlɪ] *n.* стручко́вый пе́рец (-рца(у)).

chill [tʃɪl] *n.* хо́лод (-а(у); *pl.* -á), охлаж-
де́ние; (*ailment*) просту́да, озно́б; (*fig.*)
холодо́к (-дка́); *v.t.* охлажда́ть *impf.*,
охлади́ть *pf.*; студи́ть (-ужу́, -у́дишь) *impf.*,
о~ *pf.* **chilled** *adj.* охлаждённый (-ён, -ена́),
моро́женый. **chilly** *adj.* холо́дный (хо́ло-
ден, -дна́, -дно, холодны́), прохла́дный.

chime [tʃaɪm] *n.* (*set of bells*) набо́р коло-
коло́в; *pl.* (*sound*) колоко́льный перезво́н;
(*of clock*) бой; *v.t.* звони́ть *impf.*, по~ *pf.*
в+а.; *v.i.* звене́ть (-ни́т) *impf.*, про~ *pf.*;
(*correspond*) соотве́тствовать *impf.* (**to**
+*d.*); ~ **in** вме́шиваться *impf.*, вмеша́ться
pf.

chimera [kaɪ'mɪərə, kɪ-] *n.* химе́ра. **chimerical**
[tʃɪ'merɪk(ə)l] *adj.* химери́ческий.

chimney ['tʃɪmnɪ] *n.* (дымова́я) труба́ (*pl.*
-бы). **chimney-pot** *n.* дефле́ктор. **chimney-
sweep** *n.* трубочи́ст.

chimpanzee [ˌtʃɪmpən'ziː] *n.* шимпанзе́
m.indecl.

chin [tʃɪn] *n.* подборо́док (-дка); *v.t.:* ~ **the
bar, o.s.** подтя́гиваться *impf.*, подтяну́ться
(-ну́сь, -не́шься) *pf.* до у́ровня подборо́дка.

China ['tʃaɪnə] *n.* Кита́й; *adj.* кита́йский.

china ['tʃaɪnə] *n.* (*material*) фарфо́р; (*objects*)
посу́да; *adj.* фарфо́ровый.

chinchilla [tʃɪn'tʃɪlə] *n.* (*animal, fur*) шин-
ши́лла.

Chinese [tʃaɪ'niːz] *n.* (*person*) кита́ец (-а́йца,
-а́йнка; *adj.* кита́йский; ~ **lantern** кита́йский
фона́рик; ~ **white** кита́йские бели́ла (-л)
pl.

chink¹ [tʃɪŋk] *n.* (*sound*) звон; *v.i.* звене́ть
(-и́т) *impf.*, про~ *pf.*

chink² [tʃɪŋk] *n.* (*opening, crack*) щель (*pl.*
-ли, -ле́й), сква́жина.

chintz [tʃɪnts] *n.* глазиро́ванный, ме́бельный
си́тец (-тца(у)).

chip [tʃɪp] *v.t.* отбива́ть *impf.*, отби́ть (ото-
бью́, -ьёшь) края+*g.*; *n.* (*of wood*) щепа́ (*pl.*
-пы, -п, -па́м), ще́пка, лучи́на; щерби́на,
щерби́нка; (*in games*) фи́шка; (*microelectronics*) криста́лл; *pl.* жа́реная карто́-
шка (*collect.*).

chiropody [kɪ'rɒpədɪ] *n.* педикю́р.

chiropractor ['kaɪərəʊˌpræktə(r)] *n.* хиропра́к-
тик.

chirp [tʃɜːp] *v.i.* чири́кать *impf.*

chisel ['tʃɪz(ə)l] *n.* долото́ (*pl.* -та́); стаме́ска;
дуби́ло; резе́ц (-зца́); *v.t.* высека́ть *impf.*,
вы́сечь (-еку, -ечешь; -ек) *pf.*; выреза́ть
impf., вы́резать (-ежу, -ежешь) *pf.* **chiseller**
n. моше́нник.

chit [tʃɪt] *n.* (*note*) запи́ска.

chit-chat ['tʃɪttʃæt] *n.* болтовня́.

chivalrous ['ʃɪvəlrəs] *adj.* ры́царский. **chiv-
alry** *n.* ры́царство.

chive [tʃaɪv] *n.* лук(-а)-ре́занец (-нца).

chloral ['klɔːr(ə)l] *n.* хлоралгидра́т. **chloride**
n. хлори́д. **chlorinate** *v.t.* хлори́ровать *impf.*
& *pf.* **chlorine** *n.* хлор. **chloroform** *n.*
хлорофо́рм; *v.t.* хлороформи́ровать *impf.*
& *pf.* **chlorophyll** *n.* хлорофи́лл.

chock [tʃɒk] *n.* клин (*pl.* -нья, -ьев); (*тормоз-
ная*) коло́дка. **chock-a-block, chock-full**
adj. битко́м наби́тый, перепо́лненный (-ен,
-енна) (**of** +*i.*).

chocolate ['tʃɒkələt, 'tʃɒklət] *n.* шокола́д (-а(у));
(*sweet*) шокола́дка; (*colour*) шокола́дный
цвет; *adj.* шокола́дный; шокола́дного
цве́та.

choice [tʃɔɪs] *n.* вы́бор; *adj.* отбо́рный.

choir ['kwaɪə(r)] *n.* хор (*pl.* хо́ры); хорово́й
ансамбль *m.* **choirboy** *n.* пе́вчий *sb.*, ма́ль-
чик-хори́ст.

choke [tʃəʊk] *n.* (*valve*) дро́ссель *m.*; (*artichoke*) сердцеви́на артишо́ка; *v.i.* дави́ться
(-влю́сь, -вишься) *impf.*, по~ *pf.*; за-
дыха́ться *impf.*, задохну́ться (-о́х(нул)ся,
-о́х(ну́)лась) *pf.*; *v.t.* (*suffocate*) души́ть
(-шу́, -шишь) *impf.*, за~ *pf.*; (*of plants*)
заглуша́ть, глуши́ть *impf.*, за~ *pf.* **choker**
n. (*collar*) высо́кий крахма́льный ворот-
ничо́к (-чка́); (*necklace*) коро́ткое оже-
ре́лье.

cholera ['kɒlərə] *n.* холе́ра.

choleric ['kɒlərɪk] *adj.* вспы́льчивый.

cholesterol [kə'lestərɒl] *n.* холестери́н.

choose [tʃuːz] *v.t.* (*select*) выбира́ть *impf.*,
вы́брать (-беру, -берешь) *pf.*; (*decide*) ре-
ша́ть *impf.*, реши́ть *pf.* **choosy** *adj.* раз-
бо́рчивый.

chop¹ [tʃɒp] *v.t.* руби́ть (-блю́, -бишь) *impf.*,
рубну́ть, рубану́ть *pf.*; (*chop up*) кроши́ть
(-шу́, -шишь) *impf.*, ис~, на~, рас~ *pf.*;
коло́ть (-лю́, -лешь) *impf.*, рас~ *pf.*; ~ **off**
отруба́ть *impf.*, отруби́ть (-блю́, -бишь) *pf.*;

n. (*blow*) рýбящий удáр; (*cul.*) отбивнáя котлéта.

chop² [tʃɒp] *v.i.*: ~ **and change** постоя́нно меня́ться *impf.*; колебáться (-блю́сь, -блешься) *impf.*

chopper ['tʃɒpə(r)] *n.* (*knife*) сéчка, косáрь (-ря́) *m.*; (*axe*) колýн (-á). **choppy** *adj.* неспокóйный; ~ **sea** зыбь нá море.

chops [tʃɒpz] *n.* (*jaws*) чéлюсти (-тей) *pl.*; **lick one's** ~ облизываться *impf.*, облизáться (-жу́сь, -жешься) *pf.*

chop-sticks ['tʃɒpstıkz] *n.* пáлочки *f.pl.* для еды́. **chop-suey** [tʃɒp'suːı] *n.* китáйское parý *nt.indecl.*

choral ['kɔːr(ə)l] *adj.* хоровóй. **chorale** [kɔː'rɑːl] *n.* хорáл.

chord¹ [kɔːd] *n.* (*math.*) хóрда; (*anat.*) свя́зка.

chord² [kɔːd] *n.* (*mus.*) аккóрд.

choreographer [ˌkɒrɪ'ɒɡrəfə(r)] *n.* хореóграф. **choreo'graphic** *adj.* хореографи́ческий. **choreography** *n.* хореогрáфия.

chorister ['kɒrıstə(r)] *n.* пéвчий *sb.*, хори́ст, ~ка.

chortle ['tʃɔːt(ə)l] *v.i.* фы́ркать *impf.*, фы́ркнуть *pf.* от смéха.

chorus ['kɔːrəs] *n.* хор (*pl.* хóры); (*refrain*) припéв; ~ **girl** хори́стка; *v.i.* (*sing*) петь (поёт) *impf.*, про~ *pf.* хóром; (*speak*) говори́ть *impf.*, сказáть (-áжет) *pf.* хóром.

christen ['krıs(ə)n] *v.t.* (*baptise*) крести́ть (-ещу́, -éстишь) *impf.* & *pf.*; (*give name*) давáть (даю́, даёшь) *impf.*, дать (дам, дашь, даст, дади́м; дал, -á, дáло, -и) *pf.*+*d.* и́мя при крещéнии. **Christian** ['krıstıən, 'krıstʃ(ə)n] *n.* христиани́н (*pl.* -áне, -áн), -áнка; *adj.* христиáнский; ~ **name** и́мя *nt.* **Christi'anity** *n.* христиáнство. **Christmas** *n.* Рождествó; ~ **Eve** сочéльник; ~ **tree** ёлка. **Christmastide** *n.* свя́тки (-ток) *pl.*

chromatic [krə'mætık] *adj.* хромати́ческий. **chrome** [krəum] *n.* крон; ~ **leather** хроми́рованная кóжа; ~ **steel** хрóмистая сталь; ~ **yellow** (жёлтый) крон. **chromium** *n.* хром. **chromium-plated** *adj.* хроми́рованный. **chromoli'thograph(y)** *n.* хромолитогрáфия. **chromosome** ['krəuməˌsəum] *n.* хромосóма.

chronic ['krɒnık] *adj.* хрони́ческий.

chronicle ['krɒnık(ə)l] *n.* хрóника, лéтопись; (**Book of) C~s** Паралипоменóн; *v.t.* заноси́ть (-ошý, -óсишь) *impf.*, занести́ (-есý, -есёшь; -ёс, -еслá) *pf.* (в дневни́к, в лéтопись); отмечáть *impf.*, отмéтить *pf.* **chronicler** *n.* летопи́сец (-сца).

chronological [ˌkrɒnə'lɒdʒık(ə)l] *adj.* хронологи́ческий. **chronology** [krə'nɒlədʒı] *n.* хронолóгия. **chronometer** *n.* хрономéтр.

chrysalis ['krısəlıs] *n.* кýколка.

chrysanthemum [krı'sænθəməm] *n.* хризантéма.

chub [tʃʌb] *n.* голáвль (-ля́) *m.*

chubby ['tʃʌbı] *adj.* пýхлый (пухл, -á, -о).

chuck [tʃʌk] *v.t.* бросáть *impf.*, брóсить *pf.*;

~ **it!** брось!; ~ **out** вышибáть *impf.*, вы́шибить (-бу, -бешь; -б) *pf.*; ~ **under the chin** трепáть (-плю, -плешь) *impf.*, по~ *pf.* по подборóдку; ~ **up** бросáть *impf.*, брóсить *pf.* **chucker-out** *n.* вышибáла *m.*

chuckle ['tʃʌk(ə)l] *v.i.* посмéиваться *impf.*

chug [tʃʌɡ] *v.i.* идти́ (идёт) *impf.* с пыхтéнием; ~ **along** пропыхтéть (-ти́т) *pf.*

chum [tʃʌm] *n.* товáрищ.

chump [tʃʌmp] *n.* чурбáн; тóлстый конéц (-нцá); **off one's** ~ спя́тивший с умá.

chunk [tʃʌŋk] *n.* ломóть (-мтя́) *m.*, кусóк (-скá). **chunky** *adj.* корóткий (кóроток, -ткá, -тко, корóтки) и тóлстый (толст, -á, -о, тóлсты); коренáстый.

church [tʃɜːtʃ] *n.* цéрковь (-кви, -ковью; *pl.* -кви, -квéй, -квáм); **C~ of England** англикáнская цéрковь. **churchyard** *n.* (церкóвное) клáдбище.

churlish ['tʃɜːlıʃ] *adj.* грýбый (груб, -á, -о), нелюбéзный.

churn [tʃɜːn] *n.* маслобóйка; *v.t.* сбивáть *impf.*, сбить (собью́, -ьёшь) *pf.*; *v.i.* (*foam*) пéниться *impf.*, вс~ *pf.*; (*seethe*) кипéть (-пи́т) *impf.*, вс~ *pf.*

chute [ʃuːt] *n.* скат, жёлоб (*pl.* -á); (*parachute*) парашю́т.

CIA *abbr.* (*of* **Central Intelligence Agency**) ЦРУ, Центрáльное развéдывательное управлéние.

cicada [sı'kɑːdə, -'keıdə] *n.* цикáда.

CID *abbr.* (*of* **Criminal Investigation Department**) отдéл/департáмент уголóвного рóзыска.

cider ['saıdə(r)] *n.* сидр.

cigar [sı'ɡɑː(r)] *n.* сигáра. **ciga'rette** *n.* сигарéта; папирóса; ~ **lighter** зажигáлка.

cinder ['sındə(r)] *n.* шлак; *pl.* золá; ~ **track** гаревáя дорóжка.

cine-camera ['sını-] *n.* киноаппарáт. **cinema** ['sınıˌmɑː, -mə] *n.* кинó *nt.indecl.*, кинематогрáфия. **cine'matic** *adj.* кинематографи́ческий.

cinnamon ['sınəmən] *n.* кори́ца; (*colour*) свéтло-кори́чневый цвет.

cipher ['saıfə(r)] *n.* (*math.*) ноль (-ля́) *m.*, нуль (-ля́) *m.*; шифр.

circle ['sɜːk(ə)l] *n.* круг (*loc.* -е & -ý; *pl.* -и́); (*theatre*) я́рус; *v.t.* & *i.* кружи́ть(ся) (-ужý(сь), -ýжи́шь(ся)) *impf.*; *v.i.* дви́гаться (-аюсь, -аешься & дви́жусь, -жешься) *impf.*, дви́нуться *pf.* по кругу́. **circlet** *n.* кружóк (-жкá); венóк (-нкá). **circuit** ['sɜːkıt] *n.* кругооборóт; объéзд, обхóд; (*tour*) турнé *nt.indecl.*; (*leg.*) выезднáя сéссия судá; (*elec.*) цепь, кóнтур; **short** ~ корóткое замыкáние. **circuitous** [sɜː'kjuːıtəs] *adj.* крýжный, окóльный. **circular** *adj.* крýглый (кругл, -á, -о, крýглы́), кругово́й; (*circulating*) циркуля́рный; *n.* циркуля́р. **circularize** *v.t.* рассылáть *impf.*, разослáть (-ошлю́, -ошлёшь) *pf.*+*d.* циркуля́ры. **circulate** *v.i.* циркули́ровать *impf.*; *v.t.* рассылáть *impf.*,

разосла́ть (-ошлю́, -ошлёшь) *pf.*; (*spread*) распространя́ть *impf.*, распространи́ть *pf.*
circu'lation *n.* (*movement*) циркуля́ция; (*distribution*) распростране́ние; (*of newspaper*) тира́ж (-а́); (*econ.*) обраще́ние; (*med.*) кровообраще́ние.
circumcise ['sɜ:kəm,saɪz] *v.t.* обреза́ть *impf.*, обре́зать (-е́жу, -е́жешь) *pf.* **circum'cision** *n.* обреза́ние.
circumference [sɜ:'kʌmfərəns] *n.* окру́жность.
circumscribe ['sɜ:kəm,skraɪb] *v.t.* оче́рчивать *impf.*, очерти́ть (-рчу́, -ртишь) *pf.*; (*restrict*) ограни́чивать *impf.*, ограни́чить *pf.*
circumspect ['sɜ:kəm,spekt] *adj.* осмотри́тельный. **circum'spection** *n.* осмотри́тельность.
circumstance ['sɜ:kəmst(ə)ns] *n.* обстоя́тельство; *pl.* (*material situation*) материа́льное положе́ние; **in, under the** ~**s** при да́нных обстоя́тельствах, в тако́м слу́чае; **in, under, no** ~**s** ни при каки́х обстоя́тельствах, ни в ко́ем слу́чае. **circumstantial** [,sɜ:kəm'stænʃ(ə)l] *adj.* (*detailed*) подро́бный; ~ **evidence** ко́свенные доказа́тельства *nt.pl.*
circumvent [,sɜ:kəm'vent] *v.t.* (*outwit*) перехитри́ть *pf.*; (*evade*) обходи́ть (-ожу́, -о́дишь) *impf.*, обойти́ (обойду́, -дёшь; обошёл, -шла́) *pf.*
circus ['sɜ:kəs] *n.* (*show*) цирк; (*arena*) кру́глая пло́щадь (*pl.* -ди, -де́й).
cirrhosis [sɪ'rəʊsɪs] *n.* цирро́з.
CIS *abbr.* (*of Commonwealth of Independent States*) СНГ, Содру́жество незави́симых госуда́рств.
cistern ['sɪst(ə)n] *n.* бак; резервуа́р.
citadel ['sɪtəd(ə)l, -,del] *n.* цитаде́ль.
citation [saɪ'teɪʃ(ə)n] *n.* (*quotation*) ссы́лка, цита́та. **cite** *v.t.* цити́ровать *impf.*, про~ *pf.*; ссыла́ться *impf.*, сосла́ться (сошлю́сь, -лёшься) *pf.* на+*a.*
citizen ['sɪtɪz(ə)n] *n.* граждани́н (*pl.* -а́не, -а́н), -а́нка. **citizenship** *n.* гражда́нство.
citric ['sɪtrɪk] *adj.* лимо́нный. **citron** *n.* цитро́н. **citro'nella** *n.* цитроне́лла. **citrous** *adj.* ци́трусовый. **citrus** *n.* ци́трус; *adj.* ци́трусовый.
city ['sɪtɪ] *n.* го́род (*pl.* -а́).
civet ['sɪvɪt] *n.* (*perfume*) цибети́н; (~ *cat*) виве́рра.
civic ['sɪvɪk] *adj.* гражда́нский. **civil** *adj.* гражда́нский; (*polite*) ве́жливый; ~ **engineer** гражда́нский инжене́р; ~ **engineering** гражда́нское строи́тельство; ~ **servant** госуда́рственный гражда́нский слу́жащий *sb.*; чино́вник; ~ **service** госуда́рственная слу́жба; ~ **war** гражда́нская война́. **ci'vilian** *n.* штатски́й *sb.*; *adj.* штатски́й; гражда́нский. **ci'vility** *n.* ве́жливость. **civili'zation** *n.* цивилиза́ция, культу́ра. **civilize** *v.t.* цивилизова́ть *impf. & pf.*; де́лать *impf.*, с~ *pf.* культу́рным. **civilized** *adj.* цивилизо́ванный; культу́рный.

claim [kleɪm] *n.* (*demand*) тре́бование, притяза́ние, прете́нзия; (*piece of land*) отведённый уча́сток (-тка) *v.t.* заявля́ть *impf.*, заяви́ть (-влю́, -вишь) *pf.* права́ *pl.* на+*a.*; претендова́ть *impf.* на+*a.*
clairvoyance [kleə'vɔɪəns] *n.* ясновиде́ние. **clairvoyant** *n.* ясновиде́ц (-дца), -дица; *adj.* ясновидя́щий.
clam [klæm] *n.* вене́рка, рази́нька.
clamber ['klæmbə(r)] *v.i.* кара́бкаться *impf.*, вс~ *pf.*
clammy ['klæmɪ] *adj.* холо́дный и вла́жный на о́щупь.
clamorous ['klæmərəs] *adj.* крикли́вый. **clamour** *n.* кри́ки *m.pl.*, шум (-а(у)); *v.i.* крича́ть (-чу́, -чи́шь) *impf.*; ~ **for** шу́мно тре́бовать *impf.*, по~ *pf.*+*g.*
clamp[1] [klæmp] *n.* (*clasp*) зажи́м, скоба́ (*pl.* -бы, -б, -ба́м), ско́бка; *v.t.* скрепля́ть *impf.*, скрепи́ть *pf.*
clamp[2] [klæmp] *n.* (*of potatoes*) бурт (бурта́; *pl.* -ы́).
clan [klæn] *n.* клан.
clandestine [klæn'destɪn] *adj.* та́йный.
clang [klæŋ], **clank** [klæŋk] *n.* лязг, бряца́ние; *v.t. & i.* ля́згать *impf.*, ля́згнуть *pf.* (+*i.*); бряца́ть *impf.*, про~ *pf.* (+*i.*, на+*p.*).
clap [klæp] *v.t.* хло́пать *impf.*, хло́пнуть *pf.*+*d.*; аплоди́ровать *impf.*+*d.*; *n.* хлопо́к (-пка́); рукоплеска́ния *nt. pl.*; (*thunder*) уда́р. **clapper** *n.* язы́к (-а́). **claptrap** ['klæptræp] *n.* треску́чая фра́за; (*nonsense*) вздор.
claret ['klærət] *n.* бордо́ *nt.indecl.*
clarification [,klærɪfɪ'keɪʃ(ə)n] *n.* (*explanation*) разъясне́ние; (*of liquid, chem.*) осветле́ние; (*purification*) очище́ние. **'clarify** *v.t.* разъясня́ть *impf.*, разъясни́ть *pf.*; осветля́ть *impf.*, осветли́ть *pf.*; очища́ть *impf.*, очи́стить *pf.*
clarinet [,klærɪ'net] *n.* кларне́т.
clarity ['klærɪtɪ] *n.* я́сность.
clash [klæʃ] *n.* (*conflict*) столкнове́ние; (*disharmony*) дисгармо́ния; (*sound*) гро́хот, лязг; *v.i.* ста́лкиваться *impf.*, столкну́ться *pf.*; (*coincide*) совпада́ть *impf.*, совпа́сть (-адёт; -а́л) *pf.*; не гармони́ровать *impf.*; (*sound*) ля́згать *impf.*, ля́згнуть *pf.*
clasp [klɑːsp] *n.* (*buckle etc.*) пря́жка, застёжка; (*handshake*) пожа́тие руки́; (*embrace*) объя́тие; *v.t.* обнима́ть *impf.*, обня́ть (обниму́, -мешь; обня́л, -а́, -о) *pf.*; сжима́ть *impf.*, сжать (сожму́, -мёшь) *pf.* в объя́тиях. **clasp-knife** *n.* складно́й нож (-а́).
class [klɑːs] *n.* класс; (*category*) разря́д; ~ **war** кла́ссовая борьба́; *v.t.* причисля́ть *impf.*, причи́слить *pf.* (**as** к+*d.*); классифици́ровать *impf. & pf.* **class-conscious** *adj.* (кла́ссово) созна́тельный. **class-consciousness** *n.* кла́ссовое созна́ние.
classic ['klæsɪk] *adj.* класси́ческий; (*renowned*) знамени́тый; *n.* кла́ссик; класси́ческое произведе́ние; *pl.* кла́ссика; класси́-

ческие языки́ *m.pl.* **classical** *adj.* класси́ческий.

classification [ˌklæsɪfɪ'keɪʃ(ə)n] *n.* классифика́ция. **'classify** *v.t.* классифици́ровать *impf. & pf.*; (~ *as secret*) засекре́чивать *impf.*, засекре́тить *pf.*

classroom ['klɑːsruːm, -rʊm] *n.* класс.

classy ['klɑːsɪ] *adj.* кла́ссный, первокла́ссный.

clatter ['klætə(r)] *n.* стук, лязг; *v.i.* стуча́ть (-чу́, -чи́шь) *impf.*, по~ *pf.*; ля́згать *impf.*, ля́згнуть *pf.*

clause [klɔːz] *n.* статья́; (*leg.*) кла́узула; (*gram.*) предложе́ние.

claw [klɔː] *n.* ко́готь (-гтя; *pl.* -гти, -гте́й); (*of crustacean*) клещня́; *v.t.* скрести́ (-ебу́, -ебёшь; ёб, -ебла́) *impf.*

clay [kleɪ] *n.* гли́на; (*pipe*) гли́няная тру́бка; *adj.* гли́няный. **clayey** *adj.* гли́нистый.

clean [kliːn] *adj.* чи́стый (чист, -а́, -о, чи́сты); *adv.* (*fully*) соверше́нно, по́лностью; *v.t.* чи́стить *impf.*, вы́~, по~ *pf.*; очища́ть *impf.*, очи́стить *pf.* **cleaner** *n.* чи́стильщик, -ица; убо́рщик, -ица. **cleaner's** *n.* хими́чистка. **cleaning** *n.* чи́стка, убо́рка; очи́стка. **clean(li)ness** ['klenlɪnɪs] *n.* чистота́. **cleanse** [klenz] *v.t.* очища́ть *impf.*, очи́стить *pf.*

clear [klɪə(r)] *adj.* я́сный (я́сен, ясна́, я́сно, я́сны); (*transparent*) прозра́чный; (*distinct*) отчётливый; (*free*) свобо́дный (of от+g.); *v.t. & i.* очища́ть(ся) *impf.*, очи́стить(ся) *pf.*; *v.t.* (*jump over*) перепры́гивать *impf.*, перепры́гнуть *pf.*; (*acquit*) опра́вдывать *impf.*, оправда́ть *pf.*; ~ **away** убира́ть *impf.*, убра́ть (уберу́, -рёшь; убра́л, -а́, -о) *pf.* со стола́; ~ **off** (*go away*) убира́ться *impf.*, убра́ться (уберу́сь, -рёшься; убра́лся, -ала́сь, -ало́сь) *pf.*; ~ **out** (*v.t.*) вычища́ть *impf.*, вы́чистить *pf.*; (*v.i.*) (*make off*) удира́ть *impf.*, удра́ть (удеру́, -рёшь; удра́л, -а́, -о) *pf.*; ~ **up** (*make tidy*) приводи́ть (-ожу́, -о́дишь) *impf.*, привести́ (-еду́, -едёшь; -ёл, -ела́) *pf.* в поря́док; (*explain*) выясня́ть *impf.*, вы́яснить *pf.* **clearance** *n.* расчи́стка; (*permission*) разреше́ние. **clearing** *n.* расчи́стка; (*in forest*) поля́на. **clearly** *adv.* я́сно; отчётливо.

cleavage ['kliːvɪdʒ] *n.* разделе́ние. **cleaver** ['kliːvə(r)] *n.* нож (-á) мясника́.

clef [klef] *n.* (*mus.*) ключ (-á).

cleft [kleft] *n.* тре́щина, расще́лина; *adj.*: in a ~ **stick** в тупике́.

clematis ['klemətɪs, klə'meɪtɪs] *n.* ломоно́с.

clemency ['klemənsɪ] *n.* милосе́рдие.

clench [klentʃ] *v.t.* (*fist*) сжима́ть *impf.*, сжать (сожму́, -мёшь) *pf.*; (*teeth*) сти́скивать *impf.*, сти́снуть *pf.*

clergy ['klɜːdʒɪ] *n.* духове́нство. **clergyman** *n.* свяще́нник. **clerical** ['klerɪk(ə)l] *adj.* (*of clergy*) духо́вный; (*of clerk*) канцеля́рский.

clerk [klɑːk] *n.* конто́рский служащий *sb.*

clever ['klevə(r)] *adj.* у́мный (умён, -умна́, умно́), спосо́бный. **cleverness** *n.* уме́ние.

cliche ['kliːʃeɪ] *n.* клише́ *nt.indecl.*, изби́тая фра́за.

click [klɪk] *v.t.* щёлкать *impf.*, щёлкнуть *pf.*+*i.*; *n.* щёлк.

client ['klaɪənt] *n.* клие́нт. **clientele** [ˌkliːɒn-'tel] *n.* клиенту́ра.

cliff [klɪf] *n.* утёс, отве́сная скала́ (*pl.* -лы)

climacteric [klaɪ'mæktərɪk, ˌklaɪmæk'terɪk] *n.* климакте́рий; *adj.* климактери́ческий.

climate ['klaɪmɪt] *n.* кли́мат. **climatic** [ˌklaɪ-'mætɪk] *adj.* климати́ческий.

climax ['klaɪmæks] *n.* кульминацио́нный пункт.

climb [klaɪm] *v.t. & i.* ла́зить *indet.*, лезть (ле́зу, -зешь; лез) *det.* на+*a.*; влеза́ть *impf.*, влезть (вле́зу, -зешь, влез) *pf.* на+*a.*; поднима́ться *impf.*, подня́ться (-ниму́сь, -ни́мешься; -ня́лся, -няла́сь) *pf.* на+*a.*; (*aeron.*) набира́ть *impf.*, набра́ть (наберу́, -рёшь; набра́л, -а́, -о) *pf.* высоту́; ~ **down** спуска́ться *impf.*, спусти́ться (-ущу́сь, -у́стишься) *pf.* c+*g.*; (*give in*) уступа́ть *impf.*, уступи́ть (-плю́, -пишь) *pf.* **climber** *n.* (*mountain-~*) альпини́ст, ~ка; (*social ~*) карьери́ст, ~ка; (*plant*) вью́щееся расте́ние. **climbing** *n.* (*sport*) альпини́зм; (*ascent*) восхожде́ние; *adj.* (*plant*) вью́щийся.

clinch [klɪntʃ] *n.* (*boxing*) клинч, захва́т.

cling [klɪŋ] *v.i.* прилипа́ть *impf.*, прили́пнуть (-п) *pf.* (**to** к+*d.*); ~ **to** (*clothes*) облега́ть (-áет) *impf.*

clinic ['klɪnɪk] *n.* (*consultation*) консульта́ция; (*place*) кли́ника. **clinical** *adj.* клини́ческий.

clink [klɪŋk] *v.t. & i.* звене́ть (-ню́, -ни́шь) *impf.*, про~ *pf.* (+*i.*); ~ **glasses** чо́каться *impf.*, чо́кнуться *pf.*; *n.* звон.

clinker ['klɪŋkə(r)] *n.* (*brick*) кли́нкер; (*slag*) шлак.

clip¹ [klɪp] *n.* зажи́м; (*mil.*) обо́йма; *v.t.* скрепля́ть *impf.*, скрепи́ть *pf.*

clip² [klɪp] *v.t.* стричь (стригу́, -ижёшь, -иг) *impf.*, об~, о~ *pf.*; подреза́ть *impf.*, подре́зать (-е́жу, -е́жешь) *pf.* **clipped** *adj.* подре́занный, подстри́женный; ~ **tones** отры́вочная речь. **clipper** *n.* (*naut.*) кли́пер; *pl.* но́жницы *f.pl.* **clipping** *n.* стри́жка; (*newspaper ~*) газе́тная вы́резка; *pl.* настри́г, обре́зки *f.pl.*

clique [kliːk] *n.* кли́ка. **cliquish** *adj.* за́мкнутый.

cloak [kləʊk] *n.* плащ (-á); *v.t.* покрыва́ть *impf.*, покры́ть (-ро́ю, -ро́ешь) *pf.* **cloak-room** *n.* (*for clothing*) гардеро́б; (*for luggage*) ка́мера хране́ния; (*lavatory*) убо́рная *sb.*, туале́т.

clock [klɒk] *n.* часы́ *m.pl.*; ~ **face** цифербла́т; *v.i.*: ~ **in** регистри́ровать *impf.*, за~ *pf.* прихо́д на рабо́ту. **clockmaker** *n.* часовщи́к (-á). **clockwise** *adv.* по часово́й стре́лке. **clockwork** *n.* часово́й механи́зм.

clod [klɒd] *n.* ком (*pl.* -ья, -ьев), глы́ба. **clodhopper** *n.* у́валень (-льня) *m.*, дереве́нщина *c.g.*

clog [klɒg] *n.* башма́к (-á) на деревя́нной подо́шве; *v.t.*: ~ **up** засоря́ть *impf.*, засори́ть *pf.*

cloister ['klɔɪstə(r)] *n. (monastery)* монасты́рь (-ря́) *m.*; *(arcade)* кры́тая арка́да.

clone [kləʊn] *n.* клон; *v.t.* клони́ровать *impf.* & *pf.*

close [kləʊs; kləʊz] *adj. (near)* бли́зкий (-зок, -зка́, -зко, бли́зки́); *(stuffy)* ду́шный (-шен, -шна́, -шно); *(secret)* скры́тый; *v.t. (shut)* закрыва́ть *impf.*, закры́ть *pf.*; *(conclude)* зака́нчивать *impf.*, зако́нчить *pf.*; *adv.* бли́зко (**to** от+*g.*). **closed** *adj.* закры́тый. **closeted** ['klɒzɪtɪd] *adj.*: be ~ **together** совеща́ться *impf.* наедине́. **close-up** *n.* съёмка, сня́тая на кру́пном пла́не; **in** ~ кру́пным пла́ном. **closing** *n.* закры́тие; *adj.* заключи́тельный. **closure** *n.* закры́тие.

clot [klɒt] *n.* сгу́сток (-тка́); *v.i.* сгуща́ться *impf.*, сгусти́ться *pf.* **clotted** *adj.* сгущён- ный; ~ **cream** густы́е топлёные сли́вки (-вок) *pl.*

cloth [klɒθ] *n.* ткань, сукно́ (*pl.* -кна, -кон, -кнам); *(duster)* тря́пка; *(table-~)* ска́терть (*pl.* -ти, -те́й)

clothe [kləʊð] *v.t.* одева́ть *impf.*, оде́ть (-е́ну, -е́нешь) (**in** +*i.*, в+*a.*) *pf.* **clothes** *n.* оде́жда, пла́тье.

cloud [klaʊd] *n.* о́блако (*pl.* -ка́, -ко́в); *(rain, storm* ~) ту́ча; *v.t.* затемня́ть *impf.*, затем- ни́ть *pf.*; омрача́ть *impf.*, омрачи́ть *pf.*; ~ **over** покрыва́ться *impf.*, покры́ться (-ро́ется) *pf.* облака́ми, ту́чами.

clout [klaʊt] *v.t.* ударя́ть *impf.*, уда́рить *pf.*; *n.* затре́щина.

clove [kləʊv] *n.* гвозди́ка; *(garlic)* зубо́к (-бка́). **cloven** ['kləʊv(ə)n] *adj.* раздво́енный (-ен, -енна)

clover ['kləʊvə(r)] *n.* кле́вер (*pl.* -á)

clown [klaʊn] *n.* кло́ун.

club [klʌb] *n. (stick)* дуби́нка; *pl. (cards)* тре́фы *f.pl.*; *(association)* клуб; *v.t. (beat)* бить (бью, бьёшь) *impf.*, по~ *pf.* дуби́нкой; *v.i.*: ~ **together** устра́ивать *impf.*, устро́ить *pf.* скла́дчину.

cluck [klʌk] *v.i.* куда́хтать (-áхчет) *impf.*

clue [klu:] *n. (evidence)* ули́ка; *(to puzzle)* ключ (-á) (**к** разга́дке).

clump [klʌmp] *n.* гру́ппа дере́вьев; *v.i.* тяже- ло́ ступа́ть *impf.*, ступи́ть (-плю́, -пишь) *pf.*

clumsiness ['klʌmzɪnɪs] *n.* неуклю́жесть; беста́ктность. **clumsy** *adj.* неуклю́жий.

cluster ['klʌstə(r)] *n. (bunch)* пучо́к (-чка́); *(group)* гру́ппа; *v.i.* собира́ться *impf.*, со- бра́ться (-берётся; собра́лся, -ала́сь, -áло́сь) *pf.* гру́ппами.

clutch[1] [klʌtʃ] *n. (grasp)* хва́тка; ко́гти (-те́й) *m.pl.*; *(tech.)* сцепле́ние, му́фта; *v.t.* за- жима́ть *impf.*, зажа́ть (зажму́, -мёшь) *pf.*; *v.i.*: ~ **at** хвата́ться *impf.*, хвати́ться (-ачу́сь, -а́тишься) *pf.* за+*a.*

clutch[2] [klʌtʃ] *n. (of eggs)* я́йца *pl.* (я́иц, я́йцам).

clutter ['klʌtə(r)] *n.* беспоря́док (-дка); *v.t.* приводи́ть (-ожу́, -о́дишь) *impf.*, привести́ (-еду́, -еде́шь; ёл, -ела́) *pf.* в беспоря́док.

cm *abbr.* (*of* **centimetre(s)**) см, сантиме́тр.

Co. [kəʊ] *abbr.* (*of* **company**) К°, компа́ния.

c/o *abbr.* (*of* **care of**) по а́дресу+*g.*; че́рез+*a.*

coach [kəʊtʃ] *n. (carriage)* каре́та; *(rail.)* ваго́н; *(bus)* авто́бус; *(tutor)* репети́тор; *(sport)* тре́нер; *v.t.* репети́ровать *impf.*; тре- нирова́ть *impf.*, на~ *pf.*

coagulate [kəʊˈægjʊˌleɪt] *v.i.* сгуща́ться *impf.*, сгусти́ться *pf.*

coal [kəʊl] *n.* у́голь (у́гля́; *pl.* у́гли, угле́й) *m.* **coal-bearing** *adj.* угле́но́сный.

coalesce [ˌkəʊəˈles] *v.i.* соединя́ться *impf.*, соедини́ться *pf.*

coalface *n.* у́гольный забо́й. **coalfield** *n.* каменноу́гольный бассе́йн.

coalition [ˌkəʊəˈlɪʃ(ə)n] *n.* коали́ция.

coalmine *n.* у́гольная ша́хта. **coalminer** *n.* шахтёр. **coal-scuttle** *n.* ведёрко (*pl.* -рки, -рок, -ркам) для у́гля́. **coal-seam** *n.* у́голь- ный пласт (-á).

coarse [kɔ:s] *adj.* гру́бый (груб, -á, -о); *(vulgar)* вульга́рный.

coast [kəʊst] *n.* побере́жье, бе́рег (*loc.* -ý; *pl.* -á); *v.i. (trade)* кабота́жничать *impf.*; *(move without power)* дви́гаться (-и́гается & -и́жется) *impf.*, дви́нуться *pf.* по ине́рции. **coastal** *adj.* береговой, прибре́жный. **coaster** *n.* кабота́жное су́дно (*pl.* -дá, -до́в). **coastguard** *n.* берегова́я охра́на.

coat [kəʊt] *n. (overcoat)* пальто́ *nt.indecl.*; *(jacket)* пиджа́к (-á), ку́ртка; *(layer)* слой (*pl.* слой); *(animal's)* шерсть (*pl.* -ти, -те́й), мех (*loc.* -ý; *pl.* -á); ~ **of arms** герб (-á); *v.t.* покрыва́ть *impf.*, покры́ть (-ро́ю, -ро́ешь) *pf.* (**with** сло́ем+*g.*).

coax [kəʊks] *v.t.* зада́бривать *impf.*, задо́б- рить *pf.*

cob [kɒb] *n. (corn-~)* поча́ток (-тка) куку- ру́зы; *(swan)* ле́бедь(*pl.* -ди, -де́й)-саме́ц (-мца́); *(horse)* ни́зкая верхова́я ло́шадь (*pl.* -ди, -де́й, *i.* -дьми́).

cobalt ['kəʊbɔ:lt, -bɒlt] *n.* ко́бальт.

cobble ['kɒb(ə)l] *n.* булы́жник (*also collect.*); *v.t.* мости́ть *impf.*, вы́, за~ *pf.* булы́жни- ком.

cobbler ['kɒblə(r)] *n.* сапо́жник.

cobra ['kəʊbrə, 'kɒbrə] *n.* очко́вая змея́ (*pl.* зме́и).

cobweb ['kɒbweb] *n.* паути́на.

cocaine [kəˈkeɪn, kəʊ-] *n.* кокаи́н.

cochineal ['kɒtʃɪˌni:l, -'ni:l] *n.* кошени́ль.

cock [kɒk] *n. (bird)* пету́х (-á); *(tap)* кран; *(of gun)* куро́к (-рка́); *v.t. (gun)* взводи́ть (-ожу́, -о́дишь) *impf.*, взвести́ (-еду́, -еде́шь; ёл, -ела́) *pf.* куро́к+*g.*; ~ **a snook** пока́- зывать *impf.*, показа́ть (-ажу́, -а́жешь) *pf.* дли́нный нос. **cocked hat** *n.* треуго́лка.

cockade [kɒˈkeɪd] *n.* кока́рда.

cockatoo [ˌkɒkəˈtu:] *n.* какаду́ *m.indecl.*

cockchafer ['kɒkˌtʃeɪfə(r)] *n.* ма́йский жук (-á).

cockerel ['kɒkər(ə)l] *n.* петушо́к (-шка́).

cockle ['kɒk(ə)l] *n.* съедо́бная сердцеви́дка.

cockney ['kɒknɪ] *n.* уроже́нец (-нца), -нка, Ло́ндона.

cockpit ['kɒkpɪt] *n.* (*arena*) аре́на; (*aeron.*) каби́на.

cockroach ['kɒkrəʊʃ] *n.* тарака́н.

cocktail ['kɒkteɪl] *n.* кокте́йль *m.*

cocky ['kɒkɪ] *adj.* (*cheeky*) де́рзкий (-зок, -зка́, -зко); (*conceited*) чва́нный.

cocoa ['kəʊkəʊ] *n.* кака́о *nt.indecl.*

coco(nut) ['kəʊkəʊ] *n.* коко́с; *adj.* коко́совый.

cocoon [kə'ku:n] *n.* ко́кон.

cod [kɒd] *n.* треска́.

coda ['kəʊdə] *n.* (*mus.*) ко́да.

coddle ['kɒd(ə)l] *v.t.* изне́живать *impf.*, изне́жить *pf.*

code [kəʊd] *n.* (*collection of laws*) ко́декс, зако́ны *m.pl.*; (*cipher*) код, шифр; **civil ~** гражда́нский ко́декс; **~ of honour** зако́ны *m.pl.* че́сти; **penal ~** уголо́вный ко́декс; **Morse ~** а́збука Мо́рзе; *v.t.* шифрова́ть *impf.*, за~ *pf.* **codicil** *n.* припи́ска. **codify** *v.t.* кодифици́ровать *impf. & pf.*

cod-liver ['kɒdlɪvə(r)] *adj.*: **~ oil** ры́бий жир (-a(y)).

co-education [,kəʊedju:'keɪʃ(ə)n] *n.* совме́стное обуче́ние.

coefficient [,kəʊɪ'fɪʃ(ə)nt] *n.* коэффицие́нт.

coerce [kəʊ'ɜ:s] *v.t.* принужда́ть *impf.*, прину́дить *pf.* **coercion** *n.* принужде́ние; **under ~** по принужде́нию.

coexist [,kəʊɪg'zɪst] *v.i.* сосуществова́ть *impf.* **coexistence** *n.* сосуществова́ние.

C. of E. *abbr.* (*of Church of England*) Англика́нская це́рковь.

coffee ['kɒfɪ] *n.* ко́фе *m.* (*nt.* (*coll.*)) *indecl.* **coffee-maker** *n.* кофева́рка. **coffee-mill** *n.* кофе́йница. **coffee-pot** *n.* кофе́йник.

coffer ['kɒfə(r)] *n.* сунду́к(-á); *pl.* казна́.

coffin ['kɒfɪn] *n.* гроб (*loc.* -бу́); *pl.* -ы́).

cog [kɒg] *n.* зубе́ц (-бца́); **~ in the machine** ви́нтик маши́ны. **cogwheel** *n.* зубча́тое колесо́ (*pl.* -ёса), шестерня́ (*g.pl.* -рён).

cogent ['kəʊdʒ(ə)nt] *adj.* убеди́тельный.

cogitate ['kɒdʒ1,teɪt] *v.i.* размышля́ть *impf.*, размы́слить *pf.* **cogi'tation** *n.*: *pl.* мы́сли (-лей) *f.pl.*, размышле́ния *nt.pl.*

cognate ['kɒgneɪt] *n. adj.* ро́дственный (-ен, -енна); *n.* ро́дственное сло́во.

cohabit [kəʊ'hæbɪt] *v.i.* сожи́тельствовать *impf.* **cohabi'tation** *n.* сожи́тельство.

coherence [kəʊ'hɪərəns] *n.* свя́зность. **coherent** *adj.* свя́зный. **cohesion** [kəʊ'hi:ʒ(ə)n] *n.* спло́чённость; сцепле́ние. **cohesive** *adj.* спосо́бный к сцепле́нию.

cohort ['kəʊhɔ:t] *n.* кого́рта.

coil [kɔɪl] *v.t.* свёртывать *impf.*, сверну́ть *pf.* кольцо́м, спира́лью; укла́дывать *impf.*, уложи́ть (-жу́, -ожишь) *pf.* в бу́хту; *n.* кольцо́ (*pl.* -льца, -лец, -льцам), бу́хта; (*elec.*) кату́шка.

coin [kɔɪn] *n.* моне́та; *v.t.* чека́нить *impf.*, от~ *pf.* **coinage** *n.* (*coining*) чека́нка; (*system*) моне́та; моне́тная систе́ма.

coincide [,kəʊɪn'saɪd] *v.i.* совпада́ть *impf.*, совпа́сть (-аду́, -ёшь; -а́л) *pf.* **coincidence** [kəʊ'ɪnsɪd(ə)ns] *n.* совпаде́ние. **coinci'dental** *adj.* случа́йный.

Coke[1] [kəʊk] *n.* (*propr.*) «Ко́ка-ко́ла».

coke[2] [kəʊk] *n.* кокс; *adj.* ко́ксовый; *v.t.* коксова́ть *impf.*; **~ oven** коксова́льная печь (*pl.* -чи, -че́й).

colander ['kʌləndə(r)] *n.* дуршла́г.

cold [kəʊld] *n.* хо́лод (-a(y); *pl.* -á); (*illness*) просту́да, на́сморк; *adj.* холо́дный (хо́лоден, -дна́, -дно, хо́лодны); **~ steel** холо́дное ору́жие; **~ war** холо́дная война́. **cold-blooded** *adj.* жесто́кий (-о́к, -о́ка́, -о́ко); (*zool.*) холоднокро́вный.

colic ['kɒlɪk] *n.* ко́лики *f.pl.*

collaborate [kə'læbə,reɪt] *v.i.* сотру́дничать *impf.* **collabo'ration** *n.* сотру́дничество. **collaborator** *n.* сотру́дник, -ица.

collapse [kə'læps] *v.i.* ру́шиться *impf.*, об~ *pf.*; вали́ться (-лю́сь, -лишься) *impf.*, по~, с~ *pf.*; *n.* паде́ние; крах; прова́л. **collapsible** *adj.* разбо́рный, складно́й, откидно́й.

collar ['kɒlə(r)] *n.* воротни́к (-á), воротничо́к (-чка́); (*dog-~*) оше́йник; (*horse-~*) хому́т (-á); *v.t.* (*seize*) хвата́ть *impf.*, схвати́ть (-ачу́, -а́тишь) *pf.* **collar-bone** *n.* ключи́ца.

collate [kə'leɪt] *v.t.* слича́ть *impf.*, сличи́ть *pf.*

collateral [kə'lætər(ə)l] *adj.* побо́чный, дополни́тельный; *n.* (**~ security**) дополни́тельное обеспе́чение.

collation [kə'leɪʃ(ə)n] *n.* лёгкая заку́ска.

colleague ['kɒli:g] *n.* колле́га *c.g.*

collect [kə'lekt] *v.t.* собира́ть *impf.*, собра́ть (соберу́, -рёшь; собра́л, -á, -о) *pf.*; (*as hobby*) коллекциони́ровать *impf.* **collected** *adj.* со́бранный; **~ works** собра́ние сочине́ний. **collection** *n.* сбор, собира́ние; колле́кция. **collective** *n.* коллекти́в; *adj.* коллекти́вный; **~ farm** колхо́з; **~ farmer** колхо́зник, -ица; **~ noun** собира́тельное существи́тельное *sb.* **collectivization** [kə,lektɪvaɪ'zeɪʃ(ə)n] *n.* коллективиза́ция. **collector** *n.* сбо́рщик; коллекционе́р.

college ['kɒlɪdʒ] *n.* колле́дж. **collegiate** [kə'li:dʒət] *adj.* университе́тский.

collide [kə'laɪd] *v.i.* ста́лкиваться *impf.*, столкну́ться *pf.* **collision** [kə'lɪʒ(ə)n] *n.* столкнове́ние.

collie ['kɒlɪ] *n.* шотла́ндская овча́рка.

collier ['kɒlɪə(r)] *n.* (*miner*) шахтёр; (*ship*) у́гольщик. **colliery** *n.* каменноуго́льная ша́хта.

colloquial [kə'ləʊkwɪəl] *adj.* разгово́рный. **colloquialism** *n.* разгово́рное выраже́ние.

collusion [kə'lu:ʒ(ə)n, -'lju:ʒ(ə)n] *n.* та́йный сго́вор.

Cologne [kə'ləʊn] *n.* Кёльн.

colon¹ ['kəʊlən, -lɒn] *n.* (*anat.*) то́лстая кишка́ (*g.pl.* -шо́к).

colon² ['kəʊlən, -lɒn] *n.* (*punctuation mark*) двоето́чие.

colonel ['kɜːn(ə)l] *n.* полко́вник.

colonial [kə'ləʊnɪəl] *adj.* колониа́льный. **colonialism** *n.* колониали́зм. **colonist** ['kɒlənɪst] *n.* колони́ст, ~ка. **coloni'zation** *n.* колониза́ция. **colonize** *v.t.* колонизова́ть *impf. & pf.* **colony** *n.* коло́ния.

colonnade [,kɒlə'neɪd] *n.* колонна́да.

coloration [,kʌlə'reɪʃ(ə)n] *n.* окра́ска, расцве́тка.

coloratura [,kɒlərə'tʊərə] *n.* (*mus.*) колорату́ра.

colossal [kə'lɒs(ə)l] *adj.* колосса́льный, грома́дный.

colour ['kʌlə(r)] *n.* цвет (*pl.* -а́), кра́ска; (*pl.*) (*flag*) знамя (*pl.* -мена́) *nt.*; ~ **film** цветна́я плёнка; ~ **prejudice** ра́совая дискримина́ция; *v.t.* кра́сить *impf.*, вы́~, о~, по~ *pf.*; раскра́шивать *impf.*, раскра́сить *pf.*; *v.i.* красне́ть *impf.*, по~ *pf.* **colou'ration** *see* **coloration**. **colour-blind** *adj.* страда́ющий дальтони́змом. **coloured** *adj.* цветно́й, раскра́шенный, окра́шенный. **colouring** *n.* кра́сящее вещество́; окра́ска.

colt [kəʊlt] *n.* жеребёнок (-бёнка; *pl.* -бя́та, -бя́т).

column ['kɒləm] *n.* (*archit., mil.*) коло́нна; столб (-а́); (*of print*) столбе́ц (-бца́). **columnist** *n.* обозрева́тель *m.*

coma ['kəʊmə] *n.* ко́ма. **comatose** *adj.* комато́зный.

comb [kəʊm] *n.* гребёнка; гре́бень (-бня *m.*; *v.t.* чеса́ть (чешу́, -шешь) *impf.*; причёсывать *impf.*, причеса́ть (-ешу́, -е́шешь) *pf.*

combat ['kɒmbæt, 'kʌm-] *n.* бой (*loc.* бою́); сраже́ние; *v.t.* боро́ться (-рю́сь, -решься) *impf.* с+*i.*, про́тив+*g.* **'combatant** *n.* комбата́нт; *adj.* строево́й.

combination [,kɒmbɪ'neɪʃ(ə)n] *n.* сочета́ние; соедине́ние; комбина́ция. **combine** ['kɒmbaɪn; kəm'baɪn] *n.* комбина́т; (~*-harvester*) комба́йн; *v.t. & i.* совмеща́ть(ся) *impf.*, совмести́ть(ся) *pf.* **combined** *adj.* совме́стный.

combustible [kəm'bʌstɪb(ə)l] *adj.* горю́чий. **combustion** *n.* горе́ние; internal ~ **engine** дви́гатель *m.* вну́треннего сгора́ния.

come [kʌm] *v.i.* (*on foot*) приходи́ть (-ожу́, -о́дишь) *impf.*, прийти́ (приду́, -дёшь; пришёл, -шла́) *pf.*; (*by transport*) приезжа́ть *impf.*, прие́хать (-е́ду, -е́дешь) *pf.*; ~ **about** случа́ться *impf.*, случи́ться *pf.*; ~ **across** случа́йно ната́лкиваться *impf.*, натолкну́ться *pf.* на+*a.*; ~ **back** возвраща́ться *impf.*, возврати́ться (-ащу́сь, -ати́шься) *pf.*; ~ **from** происходи́ть (-ожу́, -о́дишь) *impf.*, произойти́ (-ойду́, -ойдёшь; -ошёл, -ошла́) *pf.* из, от+*g.*; ~ **in** входи́ть (-ожу́, -о́дишь) *impf.*, войти́ (войду́, -дёшь; вошёл, -шла́)

pf.; ~ **in handy** пригоди́ться *pf.*; ~ **through** проника́ть *impf.*, прони́кнуть (-к) *pf.*; ~ **up to** доходи́ть (-ожу́, -о́дишь) *impf.*, дойти́ (дойду́, -дёшь; дошёл, -шла́) *pf.* до+*g.* **come-back** *n.* возвра́т. **come-down** *n.* паде́ние, ухудше́ние.

comedian [kə'miːdɪən] *n.* комеди́йный актёр, ко́мик. **comedi'enne** *n.* комеди́йная актри́са. **comedy** ['kɒmɪdɪ] *n.* коме́дия.

comet ['kɒmɪt] *n.* коме́та.

comfort ['kʌmfət] *n.* комфо́рт, удо́бство; (*consolation*) утеше́ние; *v.t.* утеша́ть *impf.*, уте́шить *pf.* **comfortable** *adj.* удо́бный. **comforter** *n.* (*person*) утеши́тель *m.*; (*dummy*) со́ска.

comic ['kɒmɪk] *adj.* коми́ческий, юмористи́ческий; ~ **opera** опере́тта; *n.* ко́мик; (*magazine*) ко́микс. **comical** *adj.* смешно́й, коми́чный.

coming ['kʌmɪŋ] *adj.* наступа́ющий.

comma ['kɒmə] *n.* запята́я *sb.*; **inverted** ~ кавы́чка.

command [kə'mɑːnd] *n.* (*order*) прика́з; (*order, authority*) кома́нда; *v.t.* прика́зывать *impf.*, приказа́ть (-ажу́, -а́жешь) *pf.*+*d.*; кома́ндовать *impf.*, с~ *pf.*+*i.*, над (*terrain*) +*i.*; (*have* ~ *of, master*) владе́ть *impf.*+*i.* **'commandant** *n.* комендант. **comman'deer** *v.t.* (*men*) набира́ть *impf.*, набра́ть (наберу́, -рёшь; набра́л, -а́, -о) *pf.* в а́рмию; (*goods*) реквизи́ровать *impf. & pf.* **commander** *n.* команди́р; кома́ндующий *sb.* (**of** +*i.*). **commander-in-chief** *n.* главнокома́ндующий *sb.* **commanding** *adj.* кома́ндующий. **commandment** *n.* за́поведь. **commando** *n.* солда́т деса́нтно-диверсио́нного отря́да.

commemorate [kə'meməˌreɪt] *v.t.* ознаме́новывать *impf.*, ознаменова́ть *pf.* **commemo'ration** *n.* ознаменова́ние. **commemorative** *adj.* па́мятный, мемориа́льный.

commence [kə'mens] *v.t.* начина́ть *impf.*, нача́ть (-чну́, -чнёшь; на́чал, -а́, -о) *pf.* **commencement** *n.* нача́ло.

commend [kə'mend] *v.t.* (*praise*) хвали́ть (-лю́, -лишь) *impf.*, по~ *pf.* **commendable** *adj.* похва́льный. **commen'dation** *n.* похвала́.

commensurable [kə'menʃərəb(ə)l, -sjərəb(ə)l] *adj.* соизмери́мый. **commensurate** *adj.* соразме́рный.

comment ['kɒment] *n.* замеча́ние; *v.i.* де́лать *impf.*, с~ *pf.* замеча́ния; ~ **on** комменти́ровать *impf. & pf.*, про~ *pf.* **commentary** *n.* коммента́рий. **commentator** *n.* коммента́тор.

commerce ['kɒmɜːs] *n.* торго́вля, комме́рция. **co'mmercial** *adj.* торго́вый, комме́рческий; *n.* рекла́мная переда́ча. **commercialize** *v.t.* превраща́ть *impf.*, преврати́ть (-ащу́, -ати́шь) *pf.* в исто́чник дохо́дов.

commiserate [kə'mɪzəˌreɪt] *v.i.*: ~ **with** соболе́зновать *impf.*+*d.* **commise'ration** *n.* соболе́знование.

commissar ['kɒmɪˌsɑː(r)] *n.* комисса́р.

commi'ssariat *n.* (*pol.*) комиссариа́т; (*mil. etc.*) интенда́нтство.

commission [kə'mɪʃ(ə)n] *n.* (*command*) поруче́ние; (*agent's fee*) комиссио́нные *sb.*; (~ *of inquiry etc.*) коми́ссия; (*mil.*) офице́рское зва́ние; **put into ~** вводи́ть (-ожу́, -о́дишь) *impf.*, ввести́ (введу́, -дёшь; ввёл, -а́) *pf.* в строй; *v.t.* поруча́ть *impf.*, поручи́ть (-чу́, -чишь) *pf.*+*d.* **commissio'naire** *n.* швейца́р. **commissioner** *n.* уполномо́ченный представи́тель *m.*; комисса́р.

commit [kə'mɪt] *v.t.* соверша́ть *impf.*, соверши́ть *pf.*; ~ **o.s.** обя́зываться *impf.*, обяза́ться (-яжу́сь, -я́жешься) *pf.*; ~ **to** предава́ть (-даю́, -даёшь) *impf.*, преда́ть (-да́м, -да́шь, -а́ст, -ади́м; пре́дал, -а́, -о) *pf.*+*d.*; ~ **to prison** помеща́ть *impf.*, помести́ть *pf.* в тюрьму́. **commitment** *n.* обяза́тельство.

committee [,kɒmɪ'tiː] *n.* комите́т, коми́ссия.

commodity [kə'mɒdɪtɪ] *n.* това́р; **scarce ~** дефици́тный това́р.

commodore ['kɒmə,dɔː(r)] *n.* (*officer*) коммодо́р.

common ['kɒmən] *adj.* о́бщий, просто́й; обыкнове́нный; *n.* общи́нная земля́ (*a.* -млю; *pl.* -мли, -ме́ль, -млям); ~ **sense** здра́вый смысл. **commonly** *adv.* обы́чно, обыкнове́нно. **commonplace** *n.* изби́тый, бана́льный. **common-room** *n.* о́бщая ко́мната, учи́тельская *sb.* **commonwealth** *n.* содру́жество.

commotion [kə'məʊʃ(ə)n] *n.* сумато́ха, волне́ние.

communal ['kɒmjʊn(ə)l] *adj.* общи́нный, коммуна́льный. **commune** *n.* комму́на; *v.i.* обща́ться *impf.*

communicate [kə'mjuːnɪ,keɪt] *v.t.* передава́ть (-даю́, -даёшь) *impf.*, переда́ть (-да́м, -а́шь, -а́ст, -ади́м; пе́редал, -а́, -о) *pf.*; сообщи́ть *pf.* **communi'cation** *n.* сообще́ние; связь; коммуника́ция. **communicative** *adj.* разгово́рчивый.

communion [kə'mjuːnɪən] *n.* (*eccl.*) прича́стие.

communiqué [kə'mjuːnɪ,keɪ] *n.* коммюнике́ *nt.indecl.*

Communism ['kɒmjʊ,nɪz(ə)m] *n.* коммуни́зм. **Communist** *n.* коммуни́ст, ~ка; *adj.* коммунисти́ческий.

community [kə'mjuːnɪtɪ] *n.* общи́на; содру́жество; о́бщность.

commute [kə'mjuːt] *v.t.* заменя́ть *impf.*, замени́ть (-ню́, -нишь) *pf.* **commuter** *n.* пассажи́р, име́ющий сезо́нный биле́т.

compact¹ ['kɒmpækt] *n.* (*agreement*) соглаше́ние.

compact² [kə'mpækt] *adj.* компа́ктный; пло́тный (-тен, -на́, -тно, пло́тны́); ~ **disk** компа́кт-ди́ск; ~ **disk player** прои́грыватель *m.* компа́кт-ди́сков; *n.* пу́дреница.

companion [kəm'pænjən] *n.* това́рищ; компаньо́н, ~ка; (*fellow traveller*) спу́тник; (*lady's ~*) компаньо́нка; (*handbook*) спра́во-

чник. **companionable** *adj.* общи́тельный, компане́йский. **companionship** *n.* дру́жеское обще́ние. **company** ['kʌmpənɪ] *n.* о́бщество, компа́ния; (*theatr.*) тру́ппа; (*mil.*) ро́та; **ship's ~** экипа́ж.

comparable ['kɒmpərəb(ə)l] *adj.* сравни́мый. **comparative** [kəm'pærətɪv] *adj.* сравни́тельный; *n.* сравни́тельная сте́пень (*pl.* -ни, -не́й). **compare** [kəm'peə(r)] *v.t.* & *i.* сра́внивать(ся) *impf.*, сравни́ть(ся) *pf.* (**to, with** *c+i.*). **comparison** [kəm'pærɪs(ə)n] *n.* сравне́ние.

compartment [kəm'pɑːtmənt] *n.* отделе́ние; (*rail.*) купе́ *nt.indecl.*

compass ['kʌmpəs] *n.* ко́мпас; *pl.* ци́ркуль *m.*; (*extent*) преде́лы *m.pl.*

compassion [kəm'pæʃ(ə)n] *n.* сострада́ние, жа́лость. **compassionate** *adj.* сострада́тельный.

compatibility [kəm,pætə'bɪlɪtɪ] *n.* совмести́мость. **com'patible** *adj.* совмести́мый.

compatriot [kəm'pætrɪət] *n.* соотéчественник, -ица.

compel [kəm'pel] *v.t.* заставля́ть *impf.*, заста́вить *pf.*; принужда́ть *impf.*, прину́дить *pf.* **compelling** *adj.* неотрази́мый.

compendium [kəm'pendɪəm] *n.* кра́ткое руково́дство; конспе́кт.

compensate ['kɒmpen,seɪt] *v.t.*: ~ **for** вознагражда́ть *impf.*, вознагради́ть *pf.* за+*a.*; возмеща́ть *impf.*, возмести́ть *pf.*+*d.*; компенси́ровать *impf.* & *pf.* **compen'sation** *n.* возмеще́ние, вознагражде́ние, компенса́ция.

compère ['kɒmpeə(r)] *n.* конферансье́ *m.indecl.*

compete [kəm'piːt] *v.i.* конкури́ровать *impf.*; соревнова́ться *impf.*; состяза́ться *impf.*

competence ['kɒmpɪt(ə)ns] *n.* компете́нция; компете́нтность; правомо́чие. **competent** *adj.* компете́нтный; правомо́чный.

competition [,kɒmpə'tɪʃ(ə)n] *n.* соревнова́ние, состяза́ние; конкуре́нция; ко́нкурс. **competitive** [kəm'petɪtɪv] *adj.* соревну́ющийся, конкури́рующий; ~ **examination** ко́нкурсный экза́мен. **competitor** *n.* соревну́ющийся *sb.*; конкуре́нт, ~ка.

compilation [,kɒmpɪ'leɪʃ(ə)n] *n.* компиля́ция; составле́ние. **compile** [kəm'paɪl] *v.t.* составля́ть *impf.*, соста́вить *pf.*; компили́ровать *impf.*, *c*~ *pf.* **compiler** *n.* состави́тель *m.*, ~ница; компиля́тор.

complacency [kəm'pleɪsənsɪ] *n.* самодово́льство. **complacent** *adj.* самодово́льный.

complain [kəm'pleɪn] *v.i.* жа́ловаться *impf.*, по~ *pf.* **complaint** *n.* жа́лоба; (*ailment*) боле́знь, неду́г.

complement ['kɒmplɪmənt] *n.* дополне́ние; (*full number*) (ли́чный) соста́в. **comple'mentary** *adj.* дополни́тельный; ~ **medicine** паралле́льная медици́на.

complete [kəm'pliːt] *v.t.* заверша́ть *impf.*, заверши́ть *pf.*; *adj.* по́лный (-лон, -лна́, по́лно); зако́нченный (-ен). **completion** *n.* заверше́ние, оконча́ние.

complex ['kɒmpleks] *adj.* сло́жный (-жен, -жна́, -жно); *n.* ко́мплекс. **com'plexity** *n.* сло́жность.

complexion [kəm'plekʃ(ə)n] *n.* цвет лица́.

compliance [kəm'plaɪəns] *n.* усту́пчивость. **compliant** *adj.* усту́пчивый.

complicate ['kɒmplɪˌkeɪt] *v.t.* осложня́ть *impf.*, осложни́ть *pf.* **complicated** *adj.* сло́жный (-жен, -жна́, -жно). **compli'cation** *n.* осложне́ние.

complicity [kəm'plɪsɪtɪ] *n.* соуча́стие.

compliment ['kɒmplɪmənt] *n.* комплиме́нт; *pl.* приве́т; *v.t.* говори́ть *impf.* комплиме́нт(ы)+*d.*; хвали́ть (-лю́, -лишь) *impf.*, по~ *pf.* **complimentary** [ˌkɒmplɪ'mentərɪ] *adj.* ле́стный, хвале́бный; (*ticket*) беспла́тный.

comply [kəm'plaɪ] *v.i.*: ~ **with** (*fulfil*) исполня́ть *impf.*, испо́лнить *pf.*; (*submit to*) подчиня́ться *impf.*, подчини́ться *pf.*+*d.*

component [kəm'pəʊnənt] *n.* компоне́нт, составна́я часть (*pl.* -ти, -те́й); *adj.* составно́й.

comport [kəm'pɔːt] *v.t.*: ~ **o.s.** вести́ (веду́, -дёшь; вёл, -а́) *impf.* себя́. **comportment** *n.* поведе́ние.

compose [kəm'pəʊz] *v.t.* (*liter., mus.*) сочиня́ть *impf.*, сочини́ть *pf.*; (*institute*) составля́ть *impf.*, соста́вить *pf.*; (*print.*) набира́ть *impf.*, набра́ть (наберу́, -рёшь; набра́л, -а́, -о) *pf.* **composed** *adj.* споко́йный; **be ~ of** состоя́ть (-ои́т) *impf.* из+*g.* **composer** *n.* компози́тор. **composite** ['kɒmpəzɪt, -ˌzaɪt] *adj.* составно́й. **composition** [ˌkɒmpə'zɪʃ(ə)n] *n.* построе́ние; сочине́ние; соста́в. **compositor** [kəm'pɒzɪtə(r)] *n.* набо́рщик.

compost ['kɒmpɒst] *n.* компо́ст.

composure [kəm'pəʊʒə(r)] *n.* самооблада́ние.

compound[1] ['kɒmpaʊnd] *n.* (*mixture*) соедине́ние, соста́в; *adj.* составно́й; сло́жный.

compound[2] ['kɒmpaʊnd] *n.* (*enclosure*) огоро́женное ме́сто (*pl.* -та́).

comprehend [ˌkɒmprɪ'hend] *v.t.* понима́ть *impf.*, поня́ть (пойму́, -мёшь; по́нял, -а́, -о) *pf.* **comprehensible** *adj.* поня́тный. **comprehensive** *adj.* всесторо́нний (-нен, -ння); всеобъе́млющий; ~ **school** общеобразова́тельная шко́ла.

compress [kəm'pres] *v.t.* сжима́ть *impf.*, сжать (сожму́, -мёшь) *pf.*; сда́вливать *impf.*, сдави́ть (-влю́, -вишь) *pf.*; *n.* компре́сс. **compressed** *adj.* сжа́тый. **compression** *n.* сжа́тие. **compressor** *n.* компре́ссор.

comprise [kəm'praɪz] *v.t.* заключа́ть *impf.* в себе́; состоя́ть (-ои́т) *impf.* из+*g.*

compromise ['kɒmprəˌmaɪz] *n.* компроми́сс; *v.t.* компромети́ровать *impf.*, с~ *pf.*; *v.i.* идти́ (иду́, идёшь; шёл, шла) *impf.*, пойти́ (пойду́, -дёшь; пошёл, -шла́) *pf.* на компроми́сс.

compulsion [kəm'pʌlʃ(ə)n] *n.* принужде́ние.

compulsory *adj.* обяза́тельный.

compunction [kəm'pʌŋkʃ(ə)n] *n.* угрызе́ние со́вести.

computation [ˌkɒmpjuː'teɪʃ(ə)n] *n.* вычисле́ние. **compute** [kəm'pjuːt] *v.t.* вычисля́ть *impf.*, вы́числить *pf.* **computer** *n.* вычисли́тельная маши́на; (*electronic*) ЭВМ; компью́тер. **computer-assisted** *adj.* автоматизи́рованный.

comrade ['kɒmreɪd, -rɪd] *n.* това́рищ. **comrade-in-arms** *n.* сора́тник. **comradeship** *n.* това́рищество.

concave ['kɒnkeɪv] *adj.* во́гнутый. **concavity** [kɒn'kævɪtɪ] *n.* во́гнутая пове́рхность.

conceal [kən'siːl] *v.t.* скрыва́ть *impf.*, скрыть (-ро́ю, -ро́ешь) *pf.* **concealment** [kən'siːlmənt] *n.* сокры́тие, ута́ивание.

concede [kən'siːd] *v.t.* уступа́ть *impf.*, уступи́ть (-плю́, -пишь) *pf.*

conceit [kən'siːt] *n.* самомне́ние; чва́нство. **conceited** *adj.* чва́нный (-нен, -нна).

conceivable [kən'siːvəb(ə)l] *adj.* постижи́мый; мы́слимый. **conceive** *v.t.* (*plan, contemplate*) замышля́ть *impf.*, замы́слить *pf.*; (*become pregnant*) зачина́ть *impf.* зача́ть (зачну́, -чнёшь; зача́л, -а́, -о) *pf.*

concentrate ['kɒnsənˌtreɪt] *n.* концентра́т; *v.t.* & *i.* сосредото́чивать(ся) *impf.*, сосредото́чить(ся) *pf.* (**on** на+*p.*); *v.t.* концентри́ровать *impf.*, с~ *pf.* **concentrated** *adj.* концентри́рованный, сосредото́ченный (-ен, -енна) **concen'tration** *n.* сосредото́ченность, концентра́ция.

concentric [kən'sentrɪk] *adj.* концентри́ческий.

concept ['kɒnsept] *n.* поня́тие; конце́пция. **con'ception** *n.* понима́ние; представле́ние; (*physiol.*) зача́тие.

concern [kən'sɜːn] *n.* (*worry*) забо́та; (*business*) предприя́тие; *v.t.* каса́ться *impf.*+*g.*; ~ **s. with** занима́ться *impf.*, заня́ться (займу́сь, -мёшься; заня́лся, -яла́сь) *pf.*+*i.* **concerned** *adj.* озабо́ченный (-ен, -енна) ~ **with** свя́занный (-ан) с+*i.*; за́нятый (-т, -та́, -то)+*i.* **concerning** *prep.* относи́тельно+*g.*

concert ['kɒnsət] *n.* конце́рт; *v.t.* согласо́вывать *impf.*, согласова́ть *pf.* **con'certed** *adj.* согласо́ванный.

concertina [ˌkɒnsə'tiːnə] *n.* гармо́ника.

concession [kən'seʃ(ə)n] *n.* усту́пка; (*econ.*) конце́ссия. **concessio'naire** *n.* концессионе́р.

conch [kɒŋk, kɒntʃ] *n.* ра́ковина.

conciliate [kən'sɪlɪˌeɪt] *v.t.* умиротворя́ть *impf.*, умиротвори́ть *pf.* **concili'ation** *n.* умиротворе́ние. **conciliatory** *adj.* примири́тельный.

concise [kən'saɪs] *adj.* сжа́тый, кра́ткий (-ток, -тка́, -тко). **conciseness** *n.* сжа́тость, кра́ткость.

conclave ['kɒnkleɪv] *n.* конкла́в.

conclude [kən'kluːd] *v.t.* (*complete*) зака́нчивать *impf.*, закончить *pf.*; (*infer, arrange, complete*) заключать *impf.*, заключить *pf.* **concluding** *adj.* заключительный; завершающий. **conclusion** *n.* заключение; окончание; (*deduction*) вывод. **conclusive** *adj.* заключительный; (*decisive*) решающий.

concoct [kən'kɒkt] *v.t.* стряпать *impf.*, со~ *pf.* **concoction** *n.* стряпня.

concomitant [kən'kɒmɪt(ə)nt] *adj.* сопутствующий.

concord ['kɒnkɔːd, 'kɒŋ-] *n.* согласие; согласование. **con'cordance** *n.* согласие; соответствие; (*to Bible etc.*) словарь (-ря) *m.* **con'cordat** *n.* конкордат.

concourse ['kɒnkɔːs, 'kɒŋ-] *n.* скопление; (*area*) открытое место.

concrete ['kɒnkriːt, 'kɒŋ-] *n.* бетон; *adj.* (*made of* ~) бетонный; (*not abstract*) конкретный. **concrete-mixer** *n.* бетономешалка.

concubine ['kɒŋkjʊˌbaɪn] *n.* наложница; младшая жена.

concur [kən'kɜː(r)] *v.i.* соглашаться *impf.*, согласиться *pf.*

concussion [kən'kʌʃ(ə)n] *n.* сотрясение.

condemn [kən'dem] *v.t.* осуждать *impf.*, осудить (-ужу, -удишь) *pf.*; (*as unfit for use*) браковать *impf.*, за~ *pf.* **condem'nation** *n.* осуждение.

condensation [ˌkɒndenˈseɪʃ(ə)n] *n.* конденсация. **con'dense** *v.t.* (*liquid etc.*) конденсировать *impf.* & *pf.*; (*text etc.*) сжато излагать *impf.*, изложить (-жу, -жишь) *pf.* **con'densed** *adj.* сжатый, краткий (-ток, -тка, -тко); сгущённый (-ён, -ена); конденсированный. **con'denser** *n.* конденсатор.

condescend [ˌkɒndɪ'send] *v.i.* снисходить (-ожу, -одишь) *impf.*, снизойти (-ойду, -ойдёшь; -ошёл, -ошла) *pf.* **condescending** *adj.* снисходительный. **condescension** *n.* снисхождение.

condiment ['kɒndɪmənt] *n.* приправа.

condition [kən'dɪʃ(ə)n] *n.* условие; (*state of being*) состояние; положение; *v.t.* обусловливать *impf.*, обусловить *pf.* **conditional** *adj.* условный. **conditioned** *adj.* обусловленный (-ен); ~ **reflex** условный рефлекс.

condole [kən'dəʊl] *v.i.*: ~ **with** соболезновать *impf.*+*d.* **condolence** *n.*: *pl.* соболезнование.

condom ['kɒndɒm] *n.* презерватив.

condone [kən'dəʊn] *v.t.* закрывать *impf.*, закрыть (-рою, -роешь) *pf.* глаза на+*a.*

conduce [kən'djuːs] *v.i.*: ~ **to** способствовать *impf.*+*d.* **conducive** *adj.* способствующий (**to** +*d.*).

conduct ['kɒndʌkt; kən'dʌkt] *n.* ведение; (*behaviour*) поведение; *v.t.* вести (веду, -дёшь; вёл, -а) *impf.*, по~, про~ *pf.*; (*mus.*) дирижировать *impf.*+*i.*; (*phys.*) проводить (-ит) *impf.* **con'duction** *n.* проводимость. **con'ductor** *n.* (*bus, tram*) кондуктор (*pl.* -а); (*phys.*) проводник (-а); (*mus.*) дирижёр.

conduit ['kɒndɪt, -djʊɪt] *n.* трубопровод; (*for wires*) кабелепровод.

cone [kəʊn] *n.* конус; (*of pine, fir*) шишка.

confection [kən'fekʃ(ə)n] *n.* изготовление; кондитерское изделие. **confectioner** *n.* кондитер; ~'**s** (*shop*) кондитерская *sb.* **confectionery** *n.* кондитерские изделия *nt.pl.*

confederacy [kən'fedərəsɪ] *n.* конфедерация. **confederate** *adj.* конфедеративный; *n.* сообщник. **confede'ration** *n.* конфедерация.

confer [kən'fɜː(r)] *v.t.* жаловать *impf.*, по~ *pf.* (+*a.* & *i.*, +*d.* & *a.*); присуждать *impf.*, присудить (-ужу, -удишь) (**on** +*d.*) *pf.*; *v.i.* совещаться *impf.* **conference** ['kɒnfərəns] *n.* совещание; конференция; ~ **hall** конференц-зал. **conferment** [kən'fɜːmənt] *n.* присвоение; присуждение.

confess [kən'fes] *v.t.* (*acknowledge*) признавать (-наю, -наёшь) *impf.*, признать *pf.*; (*eccl., of sinner & priest*) исповедовать *impf.* & *pf.* **confession** *n.* признание; исповедь. **confessor** *n.* духовник (-а).

confidant(e) [ˌkɒnfɪ'dænt, 'kɒn-] *n.* доверенное лицо (*pl.* -ца). **confide** [kən'faɪd] *v.t.* поверять *impf.*, поверить *pf.* **confidence** ['kɒnfɪd(ə)ns] *n.* (*trust*) доверие; (*certainty*) уверенность; ~ **trick** мошенничество; '**confident** *adj.* уверенный (-ен, -енна). **confi'dential** *adj.* секретный; конфиденциальный.

configuration [kənˌfɪgjʊ'reɪʃ(ə)n, -gə'reɪʃ(ə)n] *n.* конфигурация.

confine [kən'faɪn] *v.t.* ограничивать *impf.*, ограничить *pf.*; (*in prison*) заключать *impf.*, заключить *pf.* **confinement** *n.* (*for birth*) роды (-дов) *pl.*; заключение. **confines** ['kɒnfaɪnz] *n.* пределы *m.pl.*

confirm [kən'fɜːm] *v.t.* подтверждать *impf.*, подтвердить *pf.* **confir'mation** *n.* подтверждение; (*eccl.*) конфирмация. **confirmed** *adj.* закоренелый.

confiscate ['kɒnfɪˌskeɪt] *v.t.* конфисковать *impf.* & *pf.* **confis'cation** *n.* конфискация.

conflagration [ˌkɒnflə'greɪʃ(ə)n] *n.* пожарище.

conflict ['kɒnflɪkt; kən'flɪkt] *n.* конфликт; противоречие; *v.i.*: ~ **with** (*contradict*) противоречить *impf.*+*d.* **conflicting** *adj.* противоречивый.

confluence ['kɒnfluəns] *n.* слияние.

conform [kən'fɔːm] *v.i.*: ~ **to** подчиняться *impf.*, подчиниться *pf.*+*d.* **conformity** *n.* соответствие; (*compliance*) подчинение.

confound [kən'faʊnd] *v.t.* сбивать *impf.*, сбить (собью, -ьёшь) *pf.* с толку; ~ **it!** к чёрту! **confounded** *adj.* проклятый.

confront [kən'frʌnt] *v.t.* стоять (-ою, -оишь) *impf.* лицом к лицу с+*i.*; **be confronted with** быть поставленным перед+*i.*

confuse [kən'fjuːz] *v.t.* приводить (-ожу, -одишь) *impf.*, привести (-еду, -едёшь; -ёл,

-ела́) *pf.* в замеша́тельство; пу́тать *impf.*, за~, с~ *pf.* **confusion** *n.* замеша́тельство, пу́таница.

congeal [kən'dʒiːl] *v.t.* застыва́ть *impf.*, засты́(ну)ть (-и́ну, -и́нешь; -ы́(ну)л, -ы́ла) *pf.*

congenial [kən'dʒiːnɪəl] *adj.* бли́зкий (-зок, -зка́, -зко, близки́) по ду́ху.

congenital [kən'dʒenɪt(ə)l] *adj.* врождённый (-ён, -ена́).

conger (eel) ['kɒŋgə(r)] *n.* морско́й у́горь (угря́) *m.*

congested [kən'dʒestɪd] *adj.* перепо́лненный (-ен); (*med.*) засто́йный. **congestion** [kən'dʒestʃ(ə)n] *n.* (*population*) перенаселённость; (*traffic*) зато́р; (*med.*) засто́й кро́ви.

congratulate [kən'grætjʊˌleɪt] *v.t.* поздравля́ть *impf.*, поздра́вить *pf.* (**on** с+*i.*). **congratu-'lation** *n.* поздравле́ние. **congratu'latory** *adj.* поздрави́тельный.

congregate ['kɒŋgrɪˌgeɪt] *v.i.* собира́ться *impf.*, собра́ться (-берётся; -бра́лся, -брала́сь, -бра́ло́сь) *pf.* **congre'gation** *n.* собра́ние; (*eccl.*) прихожа́не (-н) *pl.*

congress ['kɒŋgres] *n.* конгре́сс, съезд. **con'gressional** *adj.* относя́щийся к конгре́ссу. **Congressman** *n.* конгрессме́н.

congruent ['kɒŋgrʊənt] *adj.* конгруэ́нтный. **conic(al)** ['kɒnɪk(ə)l] *adj.* кони́ческий.

conifer ['kɒnɪfə(r), 'kəʊn-] *n.* хво́йное *sb.* **co'niferous** *adj.* хво́йный, шишконо́сный.

conjectural [kən'dʒektʃər(ə)l] *adj.* предположи́тельный. **conjecture** *n.* предположе́ние; *v.t.* предполага́ть *impf.*, предположи́ть (-жу́, -жишь) *pf.*

conjugal ['kɒndʒʊg(ə)l] *adj.* супру́жеский.

conjugate ['kɒndʒʊˌgeɪt] *v.t.* (*gram.*) спряга́ть *impf.*, про~ *pf.* **conju'gation** *n.* (*gram.*) спряже́ние.

conjunction [kən'dʒʌŋkʃ(ə)n] *n.* (*gram.*) сою́з.

conjure ['kʌndʒə(r)] *v.i.*: ~ **up** (*in mind*) вызыва́ть *impf.*, вы́звать (-зову, -зовешь) *pf.* в воображе́нии. **conjurer** *n.* фо́кусник. **conjuring** *n.* пока́зывание фо́кусов; ~ **trick** фо́кус.

conker ['kɒŋkə(r)] *n.* ко́нский кашта́н; *pl.* де́тская игра́ в кашта́ны.

connect [kə'nekt] *v.t.* свя́зывать *impf.*, связа́ть (-яжу́, -я́жешь) *pf.*; соединя́ть *impf.*, соедини́ть *pf.* **connected** *adj.* свя́занный (-ан). **connecting** *adj.* соедини́тельный, свя́зующий. **connecting-rod** *n.* шату́н (-а́). **connection, -exion** *n.* связь (*loc.* связи́).

conning-tower ['kɒnɪŋ] *n.* боева́я ру́бка.

connivance [kə'naɪv(ə)ns] *n.* попусти́тельство. **connive** *v.i.*: ~ **at** попусти́тельствовать *impf.*+*d.*

connoisseur [ˌkɒnə'sɜː(r)] *n.* знато́к (-а́).

conquer ['kɒŋkə(r)] *v.t.* (*country*) завоёвывать *impf.*, завоева́ть (-оюю, -оюешь) *pf.*; (*enemy*) побежда́ть *impf.*, победи́ть (-еди́шь, -еди́т) *pf.*; (*habit*) преодолева́ть

impf., преодоле́ть *pf.* **conqueror** *n.* завоева́тель *m.*; победи́тель *m.* **conquest** ['kɒŋkwest] *n.* завоева́ние; покоре́ние.

consanguinity [ˌkɒnsæŋ'gwɪnɪtɪ] *n.* кро́вное родство́.

conscience ['kɒnʃ(ə)ns] *n.* со́весть; **pangs of** ~ угрызе́ние со́вести. **consci'entious** *adj.* добросо́вестный. **conscious** *adj.* созна́тельный; *pred.* в созна́нии; **be** ~ **of** сознава́ть (-аю, -аёшь) *impf.*+*a.* **consciousness** *n.* созна́ние.

conscript [kən'skrɪpt; 'kɒnskrɪpt] *v.t.* призыва́ть *impf.*, призва́ть (призову́, -вёшь; призва́л, -а́, -о) *pf.* на вое́нную слу́жбу; *n.* новобра́нец (-нца), призывни́к (-а́). **conscription** *n.* во́инская пови́нность.

consecrate ['kɒnsɪˌkreɪt] *v.t.* (*church etc.*) освяща́ть *impf.*, освяти́ть (-ящу́, -яти́шь) *pf.*; (*bishop etc.*) посвяща́ть *impf.*, посвяти́ть (-ящу́, -яти́шь) *pf.* (в епи́скопы и т.д.) **conse'cration** *n.* освяще́ние; посвяще́ние.

consecutive [kən'sekjʊtɪv] *adj.* после́довательный.

consensus [kən'sensəs] *n.* согла́сие.

consent [kən'sent] *v.i.* дава́ть (даю́, даёшь) *impf.*, дать (дам, дашь, даст, дади́м; дал, -а́, да́ло́, -и) *pf.* согла́сие; соглаша́ться *impf.*, согласи́ться *pf.* (**to** +*inf.*, на+*a.*); *n.* согла́сие.

consequence ['kɒnsɪkwəns] *n.* после́дствие; **of great** ~ большо́го значе́ния; **of some** ~ дово́льно ва́жный. **consequent** *adj.* после́довательный; ~ **on** вытека́ющий из+*g.* **consequently** *adv.* сле́довательно. **conse-'quential** *adj.* ва́жный (-жен, -жна́, -жно, -жны́).

conservancy [kən'sɜːvənsɪ] *n.* охра́на (рек и лесов). **conser'vation** *n.* сохране́ние; охра́на приро́ды. **conservative** *adj.* консервати́вный; *n.* консерва́тор. **conservatory** *n.* оранжере́я. **conserve** *v.t.* сохраня́ть *impf.*, сохрани́ть *pf.*

consider [kən'sɪdə(r)] *v.t.* обду́мывать *impf.*, обду́мать *pf.*; рассма́тривать *impf.*, рассмотре́ть (-рю́, -ришь) *pf.*; (*regard as, be of opinion that*) счита́ть *impf.*, счесть (сочту́, -тёшь; счёл, сочла́) *pf.*+*i.*, за+*a.*, что. **considerable** *adj.* значи́тельный. **considerate** *adj.* внима́тельный. **conside'ration** *n.* рассмотре́ние; внима́ние; **take into** ~ принима́ть *impf.*, приня́ть (приму́, -мешь; при́нял, -а́, -о) *pf.* во внима́ние. **considered** *adj.* проду́манный (-ан). **considering** *prep.* принима́я+*a.* во внима́ние.

consign [kən'saɪn] *v.t.* отправля́ть *impf.*, отпра́вить *pf.* **consi'gnee** *n.* грузополуча́тель *m.* **consignment** *n.* (*goods consigned*) па́ртия; (*consigning*) отпра́вка това́ров; ~ **note** накладна́я *sb.* **consignor** *n.* грузоотправи́тель *m.*

consist [kən'sɪst] *v.i.*: ~ **of** состоя́ть *impf.* из+*g.* **consistency, -ce** *n.* после́довательность; консисте́нция. **consistent** *adj.*

после́довательный; ~ **with** совмести́мый c+i. **consistently** adv. после́довательно; согла́сно с+i.

consolation [ˌkɒnsəˈleɪʃ(ə)n] n. утеше́ние. **consolatory** [kənˈsɒlətərɪ] adj. утеши́тельный. **console**[1] [kənˈsəʊl] v.t. утеша́ть impf., уте́шить pf. **consoling** adj. утеши́тельный.

console[2] [ˈkɒnsəʊl] n. пульт управле́ния.

consolidate [kənˈsɒlɪˌdeɪt] v.t. укрепля́ть impf., укрепи́ть pf. **consolidated** adj. (econ.) консолиди́рованный (-ан, -анна). **consoli'dation** n. укрепле́ние; (econ.) консолида́ция.

consonance [ˈkɒnsənəns] n. созву́чие. **consonant** n. согла́сный sb.; adj. созву́чный; согла́сный; совмести́мый.

consort [kənˈsɔːt; ˈkɒnsɔːt] v.i. обща́ться impf.; n. супру́г, ~а; **Prince C~** супру́г ца́рствующей короле́вы.

consortium [kənˈsɔːtɪəm] n. консо́рциум.

conspicuous [kənˈspɪkjʊəs] adj. заме́тный; ви́дный (-ден, -на́, -дно, ви́дны́). **conspicuously** adv. я́сно, заме́тно.

conspiracy [kənˈspɪrəsɪ] n. за́говор. **conspirator** n. загово́рщик, -ица. **conspira'torial** adj. загово́рщицкий. **conspire** [kənˈspaɪə(r)] v.i. устра́ивать impf., устро́ить pf. за́говор.

constable [ˈkʌnstəb(ə)l] n. полице́йский sb. **constabulary** [kənˈstæbjʊlərɪ] n. поли́ция.

constancy [ˈkɒnstənsɪ] n. постоя́нство. **constant** adj. постоя́нный (-нен, -нна); (faithful) ве́рный (-рен, -рна́, -рно, ве́рны́). **constantly** adv. постоя́нно.

constellation [ˌkɒnstəˈleɪʃ(ə)n] n. созве́здие.

consternation [ˌkɒnstəˈneɪʃ(ə)n] n. трево́га.

constipation [ˌkɒnstɪˈpeɪʃ(ə)n] n. запо́р.

constituency [kənˈstɪtjʊənsɪ] n. (area) избира́тельный о́круг (pl. -а́); (voters) избира́тели m.pl. **constituent** n. (component) составна́я часть (pl. -ти, -те́й); (voter) избира́тель m.; adj. составно́й; ~ **assembly** учреди́тельное собра́ние. 'constitute v.t. составля́ть impf., соста́вить pf. **consti'tution** n. (pol., med.) конститу́ция; (composition) составле́ние. **consti'tutional** adj. (med.) конституцио́нный; (pol.) конституциона́льный (-нен, -нна). **consti'tutionally** adv. зако́нно; в соотве́тствии с конститу́цией.

constrain [kənˈstreɪn] v.t. принужда́ть impf., прину́дить pf. **constrained** adj. принужде́нный (-ён, -ена́). **constraint** n. принужде́ние; **without** ~ свобо́дно, непринужде́нно.

constrict [kənˈstrɪkt] v.t. (compress) сжима́ть impf., сжать (сожму́, -мёшь) pf.; (narrow) су́живать impf., су́зить pf. **constriction** n. сжа́тие, суже́ние.

construct [kənˈstrʌkt] v.t. стро́ить impf., по~ pf. **construction** n. стро́ительство; (also gram.) констру́кция; (interpretation) истолкова́ние; ~ **site** стро́йка. **constructional** adj. стро́ительный; (structural) структу́рный. **constructive** adj. конструкти́вный.

constructor n. стро́итель m., констру́ктор.

construe [kənˈstruː] v.t. истолко́вывать impf., истолкова́ть pf.

consul [ˈkɒns(ə)l] n. ко́нсул; **honorary** ~ почётный ко́нсул; ~ **general** генера́льный ко́нсул. **consular** adj. ко́нсульский. **consulate** n. ко́нсульство.

consult [kənˈsʌlt] v.t. консульти́ровать impf., про~ pf. с+i.; сове́товаться impf., по~ pf. с+i. **consul'tation** n. консульта́ция, совеща́ние. **consultative** adj. консультати́вный, совеща́тельный. **consulting** adj. консульти́рующий; ~ **room** враче́бный кабине́т.

consume [kənˈsjuːm] v.t. потребля́ть impf., потреби́ть pf.; расхо́довать impf., из~ pf. **consumer** n. потреби́тель m.; ~ **goods** това́ры m.pl. широ́кого потребле́ния, широ-потре́б; ~ **society** о́бщество потребле́ния.

consummate [kənˈsʌmɪt, ˈkɒnsəmɪt; ˈkɒnsəˌmeɪt] adj. зако́нченный (-ен, -енна); соверше́нный (-нен, -нна); v.t. заверша́ть impf., заверши́ть pf.; доводи́ть (-ожу́, -о́дишь) impf., довести́ (-еду́, -едёшь; довёл, -а́) pf. до конца́. **consu'mmation** n. заверше́ние.

consumption [kənˈsʌmpʃ(ə)n] n. потребле́ние, расхо́д; (disease) чахо́тка. **consumptive** [kənˈsʌmptɪv] adj. чахо́точный, туберкулёзный; n. больно́й sb. чахо́ткой, туберкулёзом.

contact [ˈkɒntækt] n. конта́кт, соприкоснове́ние; v.t. соприкаса́ться impf., соприкосну́ться pf. с+i.; входи́ть (-ожу́, -о́дишь) impf., войти́ (войду́, -дёшь; вошёл, -шла́) pf. в конта́кт с+i.

contagion [kənˈteɪdʒ(ə)n] n. зара́за, инфе́кция. **contagious** adj. зара́зный, инфекцио́нный; ~ **laughter** заразительный смех.

contain [kənˈteɪn] v.t. содержа́ть (-жу́, -жишь) impf.; вмеща́ть impf., вмести́ть pf.; (restrain) сде́рживать impf., сдержа́ть (-жу́, -жишь) pf. **container** n. (vessel) сосу́д; (transport) конте́йнер. **containment** n. сде́рживание.

contaminate [kənˈtæmɪˌneɪt] v.t. заража́ть impf., зарази́ть pf.; загрязня́ть impf., загрязни́ть pf. **contami'nation** n. зараже́ние, загрязне́ние.

contemplate [ˈkɒntəmˌpleɪt] v.t. созерца́ть impf.; размышля́ть impf.; (intend) предполага́ть impf., предположи́ть (-жу́, -жишь) pf. **contem'plation** n. созерца́ние; размышле́ние. **con'templative** adj. созерца́тельный.

contemporary [kənˈtempərərɪ] n. совреме́нник; adj. совреме́нный.

contempt [kənˈtempt] n. презре́ние; ~ **of court** неуваже́ние к суду́; **hold in** ~ презира́ть impf. **contemptible** adj. презре́нный (-ен, -енна). **contemptuous** adj. презри́тельный.

contend [kənˈtend] v.i. (compete) состяза́ться impf.; ~ **for** оспа́ривать impf.; v.t. утвержда́ть impf. **contender** n. соревну́ющийся sb.

content¹ ['kɒntent] *n.* содержа́ние; *pl.* содержи́мое *sb.*; **(table of) contents** содержа́ние.

content² [kən'tent] *n.* дово́льство; *pred.* дово́лен (-льна); *v.t.*: ~ **o.s. with** дово́льствоваться *impf.*, у~ *pf.*+*i.* **contented** *adj.* дово́льный; удовлетворённый (-ён, -ена́).

contention [kən'tenʃ(ə)n] *n.* (*dispute*) спор, разногла́сие; (*claim*) утвержде́ние. **contentious** *adj.* (*disputed*) спо́рный; (*quarrelsome*) вздо́рный.

contest ['kɒntest; kən'test] *n.* соревнова́ние, состяза́ние; *v.t.* оспа́ривать *impf.*, оспо́рить *pf.* **con'testant** *n.* уча́стник, -ица, соревнова́ния; конкуре́нт, ~ка.

context ['kɒntekst] *n.* конте́кст.

contiguity [ˌkɒntɪ'gjuːɪtɪ] *n.* соприкоснове́ние; бли́зость. **con'tiguous** *adj.* (*adjoining*) прилега́ющий (**to** к+*d.*); (*touching*) соприкаса́ющийся (**to** с+*i.*); (*near*) бли́зкий (-зок, -зка́, -зко, бли́зки́) (**to** от+*g.*).

continence ['kɒntɪnəns] *n.* воздержа́ние. **continent¹** *adj.* возде́ржанный (-ан, -анна).

continent² ['kɒntɪnənt] *n.* матери́к (-а́), контине́нт. **conti'nental** *adj.* материко́вый, континента́льный.

contingency [kən'tɪndʒənsɪ] *n.* случа́йность. **contingent** *adj.* случа́йный, непредви́денный (-ен, -енна); ~ **on** в зави́симости от+*g.*; *n.* континге́нт.

continual [kən'tɪnjʊəl] *adj.* непреста́нный (-нен, -нна). **continuance, continu'ation** *n.* продолже́ние. **continue** *v.t.* & *i.* продолжа́ть(ся) *impf.*, продо́лжить(ся) *pf.* **continuous** *adj.* непреры́вный.

contort [kən'tɔːt] *v.t.* искажа́ть *impf.*, искази́ть *pf.* **contortion** *n.* искаже́ние; искривле́ние. **contortionist** *n.* «челове́к-змея́».

contour ['kɒntʊə(r)] *n.* ко́нтур, очерта́ние; ~ **line** горизонта́ль.

contraband ['kɒntrəˌbænd] *n.* контраба́нда; *adj.* контраба́ндный.

contraception [ˌkɒntrə'sepʃ(ə)n] *n.* предупрежде́ние бере́менности. **contraceptive** *n.* противозача́точное сре́дство; *adj.* противозача́точный.

contract ['kɒntrækt; kən'trækt] *n.* контра́кт, догово́р; *v.i.* (*make a* ~) заключа́ть *impf.*, заключи́ть *pf.* контра́кт, догово́р; *v.t.* & *i.* сокраща́ть(ся) *impf.*, сократи́ть(ся) (-ащу́(сь), -ати́шь(ся)) *pf.* **contracting** *adj.* догова́ривающийся; ~ **parties** догова́ривающиеся сто́роны (-о́н, -она́м) *f.pl.* **contraction** *n.* сокраще́ние, сжа́тие. **contractor** *n.* подря́дчик.

contradict [ˌkɒntrə'dɪkt] *v.t.* противоре́чить *impf.*+*d.* **contradiction** *n.* противоре́чие. **contradictory** *adj.* противоречи́вый.

contralto [kən'træltəʊ] *n.* контра́льто (*voice*) *nt.* & (*person*) *f.indecl.*

contraption [kən'træpʃ(ə)n] *n.* штуко́вина; устро́йство.

contrariness ['kɒntrərɪnɪs] *n.* своенра́вие, упря́мство. **contrary** *adj.* (*opposite*) противо-

поло́жный; (*perverse*) упря́мый; ~ **to** вопреки́+*d.*; **on the** ~ наоборо́т.

contrast ['kɒntrɑːst] *n.* контра́ст, противополо́жность; *v.t.* противопоставля́ть *impf.*, противопоста́вить *pf.* (**with** +*d.*).

contravene [ˌkɒntrə'viːn] *v.t.* наруша́ть *impf.*, нару́шить *pf.* **contravention** *n.* наруше́ние.

contribute [kən'trɪbjuːt] *v.t.* (*to fund etc.*) же́ртвовать *impf.*, по~ *pf.* (**to** в+*a.*); ~ **to** (*further*) соде́йствовать *impf.* & *pf.* по~ *pf.*+*d.*; (*to publication etc.*) сотру́дничать *impf.* в+*p.* **contri'bution** *n.* поже́ртвование; вклад. **contributor** *n.* же́ртвователь *m.*; сотру́дник; соуча́стник.

contrite ['kɒntraɪt, kən'traɪt] *adj.* сокруша́ющийся, ка́ющийся. **con'trition** *n.* раска́яние.

contrivance [kən'traɪv(ə)ns] *n.* приспособле́ние; вы́думка. **contrive** *v.t.* умудря́ться *impf.*, умудри́ться *pf.*+*inf.*

control [kən'trəʊl] *n.* (*check*) контро́ль *m.*, прове́рка; (*direction*) управле́ние; (*restraint*) сде́ржанность; (*remote* ~) телеуправле́ние; ~ **point** контро́льный пункт; ~ **tower** диспе́тчерская вы́шка; *v.t.* (*check*) контроли́ровать *impf.*, про~ *pf.*; управля́ть *impf.*+*i.*; ~ **o.s.** сде́рживаться *impf.*, сдержа́ться (-жу́сь, -жишься) *pf.* **control-gear** *n.* механи́зм управле́ния. **controllable, controlled** *adj.* управля́емый, регули́руемый. **controller** *n.* контролёр; (*elec.*) контро́ллер.

controversial [ˌkɒntrə'vɜːʃ(ə)l] *adj.* спо́рный. **controversy** ['kɒntrəˌvɜːsɪ] *n.* спор, диску́ссия.

contuse [kən'tjuːz] *v.t.* конту́зить *pf.* **contusion** *n.* конту́зия.

conundrum [kə'nʌndrəm] *n.* головоло́мка.

convalesce [ˌkɒnvə'les] *v.i.* поправля́ться *impf.* **convalescence** *n.* попра́вка, выздора́вливание. **convalescent** *n.* & *adj.* выздора́вливающий.

convection [kən'vekʃ(ə)n] *n.* конве́кция.

convene [kən'viːn] *v.t.* созыва́ть *impf.*, созва́ть (созову́, -вёшь; созва́л, -а́, -о) *pf.*

convenience [kən'viːnɪəns] *n.* удо́бство; (*public* ~) убо́рная *sb.*; ~ **foods** полуфабрика́ты *m.pl.* **convenient** *adj.* удо́бный.

convent ['kɒnv(ə)nt, -vent] *n.* же́нский монасты́рь (-ря́) *m.*

convention [kən'venʃ(ə)n] *n.* (*assembly*) съезд, собра́ние; (*agreement*) конве́нция; (*practice, use, custom*) обы́чай; (*conventionality*) усло́вность. **conventional** *adj.* общепри́нятый, обы́чный; усло́вный; ~ **weapons** обы́чные ви́ды *m.pl.* ору́жия.

converge [kən'vɜːdʒ] *v.i.* сходи́ться (-дятся) *impf.*, сойти́сь (-йду́тся; сошли́сь) *pf.* в одну́ то́чку. **convergence** *n.* сходи́мость, конверге́нция. **converging** *adj.* сходя́щийся в одно́й то́чке.

conversant [kən'vɜːs(ə)nt] *pred.*: ~ **with** осведемлён (-á) в+*p.*; знако́м с+*i.*

conversation [ˌkɒnvə'seɪʃ(ə)n] *n.* разгово́р,

беседа. **conversational** *adj.* разгово́рный.
con'verse[1] *v.i.* разгова́ривать *impf.*; бесе́довать *impf.*
converse[2] ['kɒnvɜːs] *adj.* обра́тный, противополо́жный. **conversely** *adv.* наоборо́т. **conversion** [kən'vɜːʃ(ə)n] *n.* (*change*) превраще́ние; (*of faith*) обраще́ние; (*of building*) перестро́йка. **con'vert** *v.t.* (*change*) превраща́ть *impf.*, преврати́ть (-ащу́, -ати́шь) *pf.* (**into** в+*a.*); (*to faith*) обраща́ть *impf.*, обрати́ть (-ащу́, -ати́шь) *pf.* (**to** в+*a.*); (*a building*) перестра́ивать *impf.*, перестро́ить *pf.* **con'vertible** *adj.* обрати́мый; *n.* кабриоле́т, фаэто́н.
convex ['kɒnveks] *adj.* вы́пуклый.
convey [kən'veɪ] *v.t.* (*transport*) перевози́ть (-ожу́, -о́зишь) *impf.*, перевезти́ (-езу́, -езёшь; -ёз, -езла́) *pf.*; (*communicate*) сообща́ть *impf.*, сообщи́ть *pf.*; (*transmit*) передава́ть (-даю́, -даёшь) *impf.*, переда́ть (-а́м, -а́шь, -а́ст, -ади́м; пе́редал, -а́, -о) *pf.* **conveyance** *n.* перево́зка, переда́ча. **conveyancing** *n.* оформле́ние перехо́да пра́ва на недви́жимость. **conveyer** *n.* конве́йер, транспортёр.
convict ['kɒnvɪkt; kən'vɪkt] *n.* осуждённый *sb.*, ка́торжник; *v.t.* осужда́ть *impf.*, осуди́ть (-ужу́, -у́дишь) *pf.* **con'viction** *n.* (*leg.*) осужде́ние; (*belief*) убежде́ние. **con'vince** *v.t.* убежда́ть *impf.*, убеди́ть (-и́шь, -и́т) *pf.* **con'vincing** *adj.* убеди́тельный.
convivial [kən'vɪvɪəl] *adj.* компане́йский; весёлый.
convocation [ˌkɒnvə'keɪʃ(ə)n] *n.* созы́в; собра́ние; (*eccl.*) собо́р, сино́д. **convoke** [kən'vəʊk] *v.t.* созыва́ть *impf.*, созва́ть (созову́, -вёшь; созва́л, -а́, -о) *pf.*
convoluted ['kɒnvəˌluːtɪd] *adj.* свёрнутый спира́лью, изви́листый.
convolvulus [kən'vɒlvjʊləs] *n.* вьюно́к (-нка́).
convoy ['kɒnvɔɪ] *n.* конво́й; коло́нна под конво́ем; *v.t.* конвои́ровать *impf.*
convulse [kən'vʌls] *v.t.*: **be convulsed with** содрога́ться *impf.*, содрогну́ться *pf.* от+*g.* **convulsion** *n.* (*med.*) конву́льсия; су́дороги *f.pl.*
coo [kuː] *n.* воркова́ние; *v.i.* воркова́ть *impf.*
cooee ['kuːiː] *int.* ау́!
cook [kʊk] *n.* куха́рка, по́вар (*pl.* -а́), ~иха; *v.t.* стря́пать *impf.*, со~ *pf.*; (*roast*) жа́рить *impf.*, за~, из~ *pf.*; (*boil*) вари́ть (-рю́, -ришь) *impf.*, с~ *pf.* **cooker** *n.* плита́ (*pl.* -ы), печь (*loc.* -чи́; *pl.* -чи, -че́й). **cookery** *n.* кулина́рия, стряпня́. **cooking** *adj.* ку́хонный; ~ **salt** пова́ренная соль.
cool [kuːl] *adj.* прохла́дный; (*of persons*) хладнокро́вный; *v.t.* студи́ть (-ужу́, -у́дишь) *impf.*, о~ *pf.*; охлажда́ть *impf.*, охлади́ть *pf.*; ~ **down, off** остыва́ть *impf.*, осты́(ну)ть (-ы́ну, -ы́нешь; -ы́(ну)л, -ы́ла) *pf.* **coolant** *n.* сма́зочно-охлажда́ющая жи́дкость. **cooler** *n.* охлади́тель *m.* **cooling** *adj.* охлажда́ющий.
coop [kuːp] *n.* куря́тник; *v.t.*: ~ **up** держа́ть

(-жу́, -жишь) *impf.* взаперти́.
cooper ['kuːpə(r)] *n.* бо́ндарь (бо́ндаря́) *m.*, бочар (-а́).
cooperate [kəʊ'ɒpəˌreɪt] *v.i.* сотру́дничать *impf.*; коопери́роваться *impf.* & *pf.* **co-ope'ration** *n.* сотру́дничество; коопера́ция. **cooperative, co-op** *n.* кооперати́в; *adj.* совме́стный, коопери́вный. **co-operator** *n.* коопера́тор.
co-opt [kəʊ'ɒpt] *v.t.* коопти́ровать *impf.* & *pf.*
coordinate [kəʊ'ɔːdɪnət] *v.t.* координи́ровать *impf.* & *pf.*; согласо́вывать *impf.*, согласова́ть *pf.*; *n.* координа́та; *adj.* согласо́ванный (-ан), координи́рованный (-ан, -анна). **coordi'nation** *n.* координа́ция.
coot [kuːt] *n.* лысу́ха.
co-owner [kəʊ'əʊnə(r)] *n.* совладе́лец (-льца).
cop [kɒp] *n.* полице́йский *sb.*; *v.t.* пойма́ть *pf.*
cope[1] [kəʊp] *n.* ри́за.
cope[2] [kəʊp] *v.i.*: ~ **with** справля́ться *impf.*, спра́виться *pf.* с+*i.*
Copenhagen [ˌkəʊpən'heɪgən] *n.* Копенга́ген.
copious ['kəʊpɪəs] *adj.* оби́льный. **copiousness** *n.* изоби́лие.
copper ['kɒpə(r)] *n.* (*metal*) медь; (*vessel*) ме́дный котёл (-тла́); (*coin*) медя́к (-а́); (*policeman*) полице́йский *sb.* **copperplate** *n.* (*handwriting*) каллиграфи́ческий по́черк.
coppice ['kɒpɪs], **copse** [kɒps] *n.* ро́щица.
Copt [kɒpt] *n.* копт. **Coptic** ['kɒptɪk] *adj.* ко́птский.
copulate ['kɒpjʊˌleɪt] *v.i.* спа́риваться *impf.*, спа́риться *pf.* **copu'lation** *n.* копуля́ция.
copy ['kɒpɪ] *n.* ко́пия; (*specimen of book etc.*) экземпля́р; **fair** ~ чистови́к (-а́); **rough** ~ чернови́к (-а́); *v.t.* копи́ровать *impf.*, с~ *pf.*; (*transcribe*) перепи́сывать *impf.*, переписа́ть (-ишу́, -и́шешь) *pf.*. **copybook** *n.* тетра́дь. **copyright** *n.* а́вторское пра́во.
coquetry ['kɒkɪtrɪ, 'kəʊk-] *n.* коке́тство. **coquette** [kɒ'ket, kə'ket] *n.* коке́тка. **coquettish** *adj.* коке́тливый.
coracle ['kɒrək(ə)l] *n.* ло́дка из ивняка́, обтя́нутая ко́жей или паруси́ной.
coral ['kɒr(ə)l] *n.* кора́лл; *adj.* кора́лловый.
corbel ['kɔːb(ə)l] *n.* вы́ступ; консо́ль; кронште́йн.
cord [kɔːd] *n.* шнур (-а́), верёвка; **umbilical** ~ пупови́на; **vocal cords** голосовы́е свя́зки *f.pl.*; *v.t.* свя́зывать *impf.*, связа́ть (-яжу́, -я́жешь) *pf.* верёвкой. **cordage** *n.* сна́сти (-те́й) *pl.*, такела́ж.
cordial ['kɔːdɪəl] *adj.* серде́чный, раду́шный; *n.* (*drink*) фрукто́вый напи́ток (-тка). **cordiality** *n.* серде́чность, раду́шие.
cordless ['kɔːdlɪs] *adj.* беспроводно́й, бесшнурово́й.
corduroy ['kɔːdəˌrɔɪ] *n.* вельве́т (-а(у)) в ру́бчик; плис; *pl.* вельве́товые штаны́ (-но́в) *pl.*
core [kɔː(r)] *n.* сердцеви́на; (*fig.*) суть; *v.t.* удаля́ть *impf.*, удали́ть *pf.* сердцеви́ну из+*g.*

cork [kɔːk] *n.* (*stopper*) пробка; (*float*) поплавок (-вка́); *attr.* пробко́вый; *v.t.* заку́поривать *impf.*, заку́порить *pf.* **corkscrew** *n.* што́пор; *v.i.* дви́гаться (-йгается & -йжется) *impf.*, дви́нуться *pf.* по спира́ли.

corm [kɔːm] *n.* клубнелу́ковица.

cormorant ['kɔːmərənt] *n.* бакла́н.

corn¹ [kɔːn] *n.* зерно́, зерновы́е хлеба́ *m.pl.*; (*wheat*) пшени́ца; (*oats*) овёс (овса́); (*maize*) кукуру́за. **corn-cob** *n.* поча́ток (-тка). **cornflakes** *n.* кукуру́зные хло́пья (-ьев) *pl.* **cornflour** *n.* кукуру́зная мука́. **cornflower** *n.* василёк (-лька́). **corny** *adj.* зерново́й; (*coll.*) бана́льный.

corn² [kɔːn] *n.* (*on foot*) мозо́ль.

corn³ [kɔːn] *v.t.* заса́ливать *impf.*, засоли́ть (-олю́, -о́ли́шь) *pf.*; ~**ed beef** солони́на.

cornea ['kɔːnɪə] *n.* рогова́я оболо́чка.

cornelian [kɔːˈniːliən] *n.* сердоли́к.

corner ['kɔːnə(r)] *n.* у́гол (угла́, *loc.* углу́); *v.t.* загоня́ть *impf.*, загна́ть (-гоню́, -го́нишь; загна́л, -а́, -о) *pf.* в у́гол. **cornerstone** *n.* краеуго́льный ка́мень (-мня; *pl.* -мни, -мней) *m.*

cornet ['kɔːnɪt] *n.* (*mus.*, *mil.*) корне́т; (*paper*) фу́нтик; (*ice-cream*) рожо́к (-жка́).

cornice ['kɔːnɪs] *n.* карни́з.

cornucopia [ˌkɔːnjʊˈkəʊpɪə] *n.* рог изоби́лия.

corolla [kəˈrɒlə] *n.* ве́нчик.

corollary [kəˈrɒlərɪ] *n.* сле́дствие; вы́вод.

corona [kəˈrəʊnə] *n.* коро́на, венёц (-нца́). **coronary (thrombosis)** ['kɒrənərɪ] *n.* венечный тромбо́з. **coro'nation** *n.* корона́ция. **coroner** ['kɒrənə(r)] *n.* сле́дователь *m.* **coronet** ['kɒrənɪt, -ˌnet] *n.* небольша́я коро́на; (*garland*) вено́к (-нка́).

Corp. *abbr.* (*of* **Corporation**) корпора́ция.

corporal¹ ['kɔːpr(ə)l] *n.* капра́л.

corporal² ['kɔːpr(ə)l] *adj.* теле́сный; ~ **punishment** теле́сное наказа́ние.

corporate ['kɔːpərət] *adj.* корпорати́вный. **corpo'ration** *n.* корпора́ция.

corps [kɔː(r)] *n.* ко́рпус (*pl.* -а́).

corpse [kɔːps] *n.* труп.

corpulence ['kɔːpjʊləns] *n.* ту́чность. **corpulent** *adj.* ту́чный (-чен, -чна́, -чно).

corpuscle ['kɔːpʌs(ə)l] *n.* части́ца, те́льце (*pl.* -льца́, -ле́ц, -льца́м); **red, white, ~** кра́сные, бе́лые, ша́рики *m.pl.* **corpuscular** [kɔːˈpʌskjʊlə(r)] *adj.* корпускуля́рный.

corral [kɒˈrɑːl] *n.* заго́н; *v.t.* загоня́ть *impf.*, загна́ть (-гоню́, -го́нишь; загна́л, -а́, -о) *pf.* в заго́н.

correct [kəˈrekt] *adj.* пра́вильный, ве́рный (-рен, -рна́, -рно, ве́рны́); (*conduct*) корре́ктный; *v.t.* исправля́ть *impf.*, испра́вить *pf.* **correction** *n.* исправле́ние; попра́вка. **corrective** *adj.* исправи́тельный. **corrector** *n.* корре́ктор (*pl.* -а́ & -ы́).

correlate ['kɒrəleɪt, 'kɒrɪ-] *v.t.* соотноси́ть (-ошу́, -о́сишь) *impf.*, соотнести́ (-есу́, -есёшь; -ёс, -есла́) *pf.* **corre'lation** *n.* соотноше́ние; корреля́ция.

correspond [ˌkɒrɪˈspɒnd] *v.i.* соотве́тствовать *impf.* (**to, with** +*d.*); (*by letter*) перепи́сываться *impf.* **correspondence** *n.* соотве́тствие; корреспонде́нция. **correspondent** *n.* корреспонде́нт. **corresponding** *adj.* соотве́тствующий (**to** +*d.*).

corridor ['kɒrɪˌdɔː(r)] *n.* коридо́р.

corroborate [kəˈrɒbəˌreɪt] *v.t.* подтвержда́ть *impf.*, подтверди́ть *pf.* **corrobo'ration** *n.* подтвержде́ние.

corrode [kəˈrəʊd] *v.t.* разъеда́ть *impf.*, разъе́сть (-е́ст, -едя́т; -е́л) *pf.* **corrosion** *n.* разъеда́ние, корро́зия. **corrosive** *adj.* е́дкий (е́док, едка́, е́дко); *n.* е́дкое, разъеда́ющее, вещество́.

corrugate ['kɒrʊˌgeɪt] *v.t.* гофрирова́ть *impf.* & *pf.*; ~**d iron** рифлёное желе́зо.

corrupt [kəˈrʌpt] *adj.* испо́рченный (-ен, -енна); развра́тный; *v.t.* развраща́ть *impf.*, разврати́ть (-ащу́, -ати́шь) *pf.*; по́ртить *impf.*, ис~ *pf.* **corruption** *n.* по́рча; развращённость; корру́пция.

corsage [kɔːˈsɑːʒ] *n.* корса́ж.

corsair ['kɔːseə(r)] *n.* корса́р; пира́т.

corset ['kɔːsɪt] *n.* корсе́т.

cortège [kɔːˈteɪʒ] *n.* торже́ственное ше́ствие, корте́ж.

cortex ['kɔːteks] *n.* кора́.

corundum [kəˈrʌndəm] *n.* кору́нд.

corvette [kɔːˈvet] *n.* корве́т.

cos [kɒs] *n.* сала́т ромэ́н.

cosh [kɒʃ] *n.* дуби́нка; *v.t.* ударя́ть *impf.*, уда́рить *pf.* дуби́нкой.

cosine ['kəʊsaɪn] *n.* ко́синус.

cosmetic [kɒzˈmetɪk] *adj.* космети́ческий; *n.* косметическое сре́дство; *pl.* косме́тика.

cosmic ['kɒzmɪk] *adj.* косми́ческий. **cosmonaut** ['kɒzməˌnɔːt] *n.* космона́вт.

cosmopolitan [ˌkɒzməˈpɒlɪt(ə)n] *adj.* космополити́ческий; *n.* космополи́т.

Cossack ['kɒsæk] *n.* каза́к (-а́; *pl.* -а́ки́) -а́чка; *adj.* каза́чий (-чья, -чье), каза́цкий.

cosset ['kɒsɪt] *v.t.* не́жить *impf.*

cost [kɒst] *n.* сто́имость, цена́ (*a.* -ну; *pl.* -ы); *pl.* (*leg.*) суде́бные изде́ржки *f.pl.*; ~ **price** себесто́имость; *v.t.* сто́ить *impf.*

costermonger ['kɒstəˌmʌŋgə(r)] *n.* у́личный торго́вец.

costly ['kɒstlɪ] *adj.* дорого́й (до́рог, -а́, -о), це́нный (-нен, -нна).

costume ['kɒstjuːm] *n.* костю́м, оде́жда; ~ **jewellery** ювели́рное украше́ние без драгоце́нных камне́й; ~ **play** истори́ческая пье́са.

cosy ['kəʊzɪ] *adj.* ую́тный; *n.* тёплая покры́шка.

cot [kɒt] *n.* (*child's*) де́тская крова́тка; (*hospital bed*) ко́йка.

cottage ['kɒtɪdʒ] *n.* котте́дж.

cotton ['kɒt(ə)n] *n.* хло́пок (-пка); (*cloth*) хлопчатобума́жная ткань; (*thread*) (бума́жная) ни́тка; ~ **plant** хлопча́тник; ~ **wool** ва́та; *adj.* хло́пковый, хлопчатобума́жный.

couch [kaʊtʃ] *n.* кушётка, лóже.
couch-grass [kuːtʃ] *n.* пырéй.
cough [kɒf] *n.* кáшель (-шля) *m.*; *v.i.* кáшлять *impf.*
council ['kaʊns(ə)l] *n.* совéт; (*eccl.*) собóр. **councillor** *n.* совéтник; член совéта.
counsel ['kaʊns(ə)l] *n.* (*consultation*) обсуждéние; (*advice*) совéт; (*lawyer*) адвокáт; ~ **for the defence** защи́тник; ~ **for the prosecution** обвини́тель *m.*; *v.t.* совéтовать *impf.*, по~ *pf.*+*d.*
count[1] [kaʊnt] *n.* (*title*) граф.
count[2] [kaʊnt] *v.t.* считáть *impf.*, со~, счесть (сочту́, -тёшь; счёл, сочлá) *pf.*; *n.* счёт (-а(у)), подсчёт. **countdown** *n.* отсчёт врéмени.
countenance ['kaʊntɪnəns] *n.* лицó (*pl.* -ца); *v.t.* одобря́ть *impf.*, одóбрить *pf.*
counter ['kaʊntə(r)] *n.* прилáвок (-вка), стóйка; (*token*) фи́шка, жетóн; *adj.* обрáтный; *adv.*: **run ~ to** дéйствовать *impf.* прóтив+*g.*; *v.t.* пари́ровать *impf.*, от~ *pf.* **counte'ract** *v.t.* противодéйствовать *impf.* **counte'raction** *n.* противодéйствие. **counterbalance** *n.* противовéс; *v.t.* уравновéшивать *impf.*, уравновéсить *pf.* **counterfeit** *adj.* подлóжный, фальши́вый. **counterin'telligence** *n.* контрразвéдка. **counter'mand** *v.t.* отменя́ть *impf.*, отмени́ть (-ню́, -нишь) *pf.* **counterpane** *n.* покрывáло. **counterpart** *n.* соотвéтственная часть (*pl.* -ти, -тéй). **counterpoint** *n.* контрапу́нкт. **counterrevo'lutionary** *n.* контрреволюционéр; *adj.* контрреволюциóнный. **countersign** *n.* парóль *m.*
countess ['kaʊntɪs] *n.* графи́ня.
counting-house ['kaʊntɪŋ] *n.* бухгалтéрия.
countless ['kaʊntlɪs] *adj.* несчётный, бесчи́сленный (-ен, -енна).
countrified ['kʌntrɪˌfaɪd] *adj.* деревéнский.
country *n.* (*nation*) странá; (*land of birth*) рóдина; (*rural areas*) дерéвня; *adj.* деревéнский, сéльский. **countryman, -woman** *n.* земля́к, -я́чка; сéльский жи́тель *m.*, -ая жи́тельница.
county ['kaʊntɪ] *n.* грáфство.
coup (d'état) [ˌkuː deɪ'tɑː] *n.* госудáрственный переворóт; путч.
couple ['kʌp(ə)l] *n.* пáра; два *m.* & *nt.*, две *f.* (двух, двум, двумя́); **married** ~ супру́ги *m.pl.*; *v.t.* сцепля́ть *impf.*, сцепи́ть (-плю́, -пишь) *pf.* **couplet** *n.* двусти́шье. **coupling** *n.* соединéние, сцеплéние.
coupon ['kuːpɒn] *n.* купóн; талóн.
courage ['kʌrɪdʒ] *n.* му́жество, хрáбрость. **courageous** [kə'reɪdʒəs] *adj.* хрáбрый (храбр, -á, -о, хрáбры́).
courier ['kʊrɪə(r)] *n.* (*messenger*) курьéр; (*guide*) гид.
course [kɔːs] *n.* курс, ход, путь (-ти́, -тём) *m.*; (*of meal*) блю́до; **of ~** конéчно; *v.i.* гнáться (гоню́сь, гóнишься; гнáлся, гналáсь, гнáлóсь) *impf.* за+*i.* **coursing** *n.*

охóта с гóнчими.
court [kɔːt] *n.* двор (-á); (*sport*) корт, площáдка; (*law*) суд (-á); ~ **martial** воéнный трибунáл; *v.t.* ухáживать *impf.* за+*i.* **courteous** ['kɜːtɪəs] *adj.* вéжливый, любéзный. **courtesy** ['kɜːtɪsɪ] *n.* вéжливость. **courtier** *n.* придвóрный *sb.*
cousin ['kʌz(ə)n] *n.* двою́родный брат (*pl.* -ья, -ьев)), -ная сестрá (*pl.* сёстры, -тёр, -трам); **second** ~ трою́родный брат (*pl.* -ья, -ьев), -ая сестрá (*pl.* сёстры, -тёр, -трам).
cove [kəʊv] *n.* небольшáя бу́хта.
covenant ['kʌvənənt] *n.* договóр; *v.i.* заключáть *impf.*, заключи́ть *pf.* договóр.
cover ['kʌvə(r)] *n.* покры́шка; покрóв; укры́тие; чехóл (-хлá); (*bed*) покрывáло; (*book*) переплёт, облóжка; **under separate** ~ в отдéльном конвéрте; *v.t.* покрывáть *impf.*, покры́ть (-рóю, -рóешь) *pf.*; скрывáть *impf.*, скрыть (-рóю, -рóешь) *pf.* **coverage** *n.* репортáж, информáция. **covering** *n.* покры́шка, оболóчка; *adj.* покрывáющий; ~ **letter** сопроводи́тельное письмó (*pl.* -сьма, -сем, -сьмам). **covert** *adj.* скры́тый, тáйный.
covet ['kʌvɪt] *v.t.* домогáться *imp.*+*g.*; пожелáть *pf.*+*g.* **covetous** *adj.* зави́стливый, áлчный.
covey ['kʌvɪ] *n.* вы́водок (-дка).
cow[1] [kaʊ] *n.* корóва. **cowboy** *n.* ковбóй. **cowshed** *n.* хлев (*loc.* -е & -ý; *pl.* -á).
cow[2] [kaʊ] *v.t.* запу́гивать *impf.*, запугáть *pf.*
coward ['kaʊəd] *n.* трус. **cowardice** *n.* трусли́вость. **cowardly** *adj.* трусли́вый.
cower ['kaʊə(r)] *v.i.* съёживаться *impf.*, съёжиться *pf.*
cowl [kaʊl] *n.* (*hood*) капюшóн; (*of chimney*) колпáк (-á) дымовóй трубы́.
cowslip ['kaʊslɪp] *n.* первоцвéт.
cox(swain) ['kɒksweɪn, -s(ə)n] *n.* рулевóй *m.*
coxcomb ['kɒkskəʊm] *n.* фат.
coy [kɔɪ] *adj.* скрóмный (-мен, -мнá, -мно).
CPSU *abbr.* (*of* **Communist Party of the Soviet Union**) КПСС, Коммунисти́ческая пáртия Совéтского Сою́за.
crab [kræb] *n.* краб; **catch a** ~ поймáть *pf.* лещá.
crab-apple [kræb] *n.* (*fruit*) ди́кое я́блоко (*pl.* -ки, -к); (*tree*) ди́кая я́блоня.
crack [kræk] *n.* трéщина; треск; удáр; *adj.* первоклáссный, великолéпный; *v.t.* (*break*) колóть (-лю́, -лешь) *impf.*, рас~ *pf.*; *v.i.* (*sound*) трéснуть *pf.*
cracker ['krækə(r)] *n.* (*Christmas* ~) хлопу́шка; (*firework*) фéйерверк. **crackle** *v.i.* потрéскивать *impf.*; хрустéть (-щу́, -сти́шь) *impf.*; *n.* потрéскивание, хруст (-а(у)). **crackpot** *n.* помéшанный *sb.*
cradle ['kreɪd(ə)l] *n.* колыбéль, лю́лька; *v.t.* убаю́кивать *impf.*
craft [krɑːft] *n.* (*trade*) ремеслó (*pl.* -ёсла, -ёсел, -ёслам); (*boat*) су́дно (*pl.* судá, -дóв).

craftiness *n.* хи́трость, лука́вство. **crafts-man** *n.* реме́сленник.

crafty *adj.* хи́трый (-тёр, -тра́, хитро́), кова́рный.

crag [kræg] *n.* утёс. **craggy** *adj.* скали́стый.

cram [kræm] *v.t.* набива́ть *impf.*, наби́ть (набью́, -ьёшь) *pf.*; впи́хивать *impf.*, впихну́ть *pf.*; пи́чкать *impf.*, на~ *pf.*; (*coach*) ната́скивать *impf.*, натаска́ть *pf.* **crammed** *adj.* битко́м наби́тый.

cramp[1] [kræmp] *n.* (*med.*) су́дорога.

cramp[2] [kræmp] *n.* зажи́м, скоба́ (*pl.* -бы, -б, -ба́м); *v.t.* стесня́ть *impf.*, стесни́ть *pf.*; ограни́чивать *impf.*, ограни́чить *pf.* **cramped** *adj.* сти́снутый; ограни́ченный (-ен, -енна).

cranberry ['krænbərɪ] *n.* клю́ква.

crane [kreɪn] *n.* (*bird*) жура́вль (-ля́) *m.*; (*machine*) кран; *v.t.* (& *i.*) вытя́гивать *impf.*, вы́тянуть *pf.* (ше́ю).

cranium ['kreɪnɪəm] *n.* че́реп (*pl.* -а́).

crank[1] [kræŋk] *n.* кривоши́п, заводна́я ру́чка; *v.t.* заводи́ть (-ожу́, -о́дишь) *impf.*, завести́ (-еду́, -еде́шь; -ёл, -ела́) *pf.*

crank[2] [kræŋk] *n.* (*eccentric*) чуда́к (-а́).

crankshaft ['kræŋkʃɑ:ft] *n.* коле́нчатый вал (*loc.* -ý; *pl.* -ы́).

cranky *adj.* чуда́ческий; эксцентри́чный.

cranny ['krænɪ] *n.* щель (*loc.* щели́; *pl.* ще́ли, щеле́й).

crape [kreɪp] *n.* креп; (*mourning*) тра́ур.

crash [kræʃ] *n.* (*noise*) гро́хот, треск; (*accident*) круше́ние, ава́рия; (*financial*) крах, банкро́тство; ~ **helmet** защи́тный шлем; ~ **landing** вы́нужденная поса́дка; *v.i.* ру́шиться *impf.* с тре́ском; разбива́ться *impf.*, разби́ться (разобью́сь, -ьёшься) *pf.*

crass [kræs] *adj.* по́лный (-лон, -лна́, по́лно́), соверше́нный (-нен, -нна).

crate [kreɪt] *n.* упако́вочный я́щик.

crater ['kreɪtə(r)] *n.* кра́тер, жерло́ (*pl.* -ла).

crave [kreɪv] *v.t.* стра́стно жела́ть *impf.*+g.; ~ **for** жа́ждать (-ду, -дешь) *impf.*+g. **craving** *n.* стра́стное жела́ние.

craven ['kreɪv(ə)n] *adj.* трусли́вый, малоду́шный.

crawl [krɔ:l] *v.i.* по́лзать *indet.*, ползти́ (-зу́, -зёшь; -з, -зла́) *det.*; тащи́ться (-щу́сь, -щишься) *impf.*; *n.* полза́ние; ме́дленный ход (-а(у)); (*sport*) кроль *m.*

crayfish ['kreɪfɪʃ] *n.* речно́й рак.

crayon ['kreɪən, -ɒn] *n.* цветно́й мело́к (-лка́), цветно́й каранда́ш (-á); (*drawing*) пасте́ль; *v.t.* рисова́ть *impf.*, на~ *pf.* цветны́м мелко́м, карандашо́м.

craze [kreɪz] *n.* ма́ния. **crazy** *adj.* поме́шанный (-ан).

creak [kri:k] *n.* скрип; *v.i.* скрипе́ть (-плю́, -пи́шь) *impf.* **creaking, creaky** *adj.* скрипу́чий.

cream [kri:m] *n.* сли́вки (-вок) *pl.*, крем; ~ **cheese** сли́вочный сыр (-а(у)); **sour** ~ смета́на; *v.t.* сбива́ть *impf.*, сбить (собью́, -ьёшь) *pf.* **creamed** *adj.* взби́тый, стёртый.

creamy *adj.* сли́вочный, кре́мовый, густо́й.

crease [kri:s] *n.* мя́тая скла́дка; *v.t.* мять (мну, мнёшь) *impf.*, из~ (изомну́, -нёшь), с~ (сомну́, -нёшь) *pf.* **creased** *adj.* мя́тый.

create [kri:'eɪt] *v.t.* создава́ть (-даю́, -даёшь) *impf.*, созда́ть (-а́м, -а́шь, -а́ст, -ади́м; со́здал, -а́, -о) *pf.*; твори́ть *impf.*, со~ *pf.* **creation** *n.* творе́ние; созда́ние. **creative** *adj.* тво́рческий, созда́тельный; *n.* творе́ц (-рца́), созда́тель *m.* **creature** ['kri:tʃə(r)] *n.* существо́; созда́ние; тварь.

crèche [kreʃ, kreɪʃ] *n.* (де́тские) я́сли (-лей) *pl.*

credence ['kri:d(ə)ns] *n.* дове́рие; **letter of** ~ рекоменда́тельное письмо́ (*pl.* -сьма, -сем, -сьмам); **give** ~ ве́рить *impf.* (**to** +*d.*).

credentials [krɪ'denʃ(ə)lz] *n.* манда́т; удостовере́ние ли́чности; вери́тельные гра́моты *f.pl.* **credibility** [ˌkredr'bɪlɪtɪ] *n.* правдоподо́бие. **'credible** *adj.* заслу́живающий дове́рия. **'credibly** *adv.* достове́рно.

credit ['kredɪt] *n.* дове́рие; креди́т; прихо́д; ~ **card** креди́тная ка́рточка, креди́тка; *v.t.*: ~ **with** припи́сывать *impf.*, приписа́ть (-ишу́, -и́шешь) *pf.*+*d.*; **give** ~ кредитова́ть *impf.* & *pf.*+*a.*; отдава́ть (-даю́, -даёшь) *impf.*, отда́ть (-а́м, -а́шь, -а́ст, -ади́м; о́тдал, -а́, -о) *pf.* до́лжное+*d.*; **it is to your** ~ э́то вам де́лает честь. **creditable** *adj.* де́лающий честь. **creditor** *n.* кредито́р. **creditworthy** *adj.* кредитоспосо́бный.

credulity [krɪ'dju:lɪtɪ] *n.* легкове́рие. **'credulous** *adj.* легкове́рный.

creed [kri:d] *n.* убежде́ние; (*eccl.*) вероиспове́дание.

creep [kri:p] *v.i.* по́лзать *indet.*, ползти́ (-зу́, -зёшь; -з, -зла́) *det.*; кра́сться (-аду́сь, -адёшься; -а́лся) *impf.* **creeper** *n.* (*plant*) ползу́чее расте́ние. **creeping** *adj.* ползу́чий; ~ **paralysis** прогресси́вный парали́ч (-á).

cremate [krɪ'meɪt] *v.t.* кремирова́ть *impf.* & *pf.* **cremation** *n.* крема́ция. **crematorium** [ˌkremə'tɔ:rɪəm] *n.* кремато́рий.

Creole ['kri:əʊl] *n.* крео́л, ~ка.

crêpe [kreɪp] *n.* креп; ~ **de Chine** крепдеши́н.

crescendo [krɪ'ʃendəʊ] *adv.*, *adj.* & *n.* креще́ндо *indecl.*

crescent ['krez(ə)nt, 'kres-] *n.* полуме́сяц; *adj.* серпови́дный.

cress [kres] *n.* кресс-(сала́т).

crest [krest] *n.* гре́бень (-бня) *m.*; верши́на. **crestfallen** *adj.* удручённый (-ён, -ённа).

cretin ['kretɪn] *n.* крети́н.

cretonne [kre'tɒn, 'kre-] *n.* крето́н.

crevasse [krə'væs], **crevice** ['krevɪs] *n.* расще́лина, рассе́лина.

crew [kru:] *n.* брига́да; (*of ship*) экипа́ж, кома́нда.

crib [krɪb] *n.* (*bed*) де́тская крова́тка; (*in school*) шпарга́лка; *v.i.* спи́сывать *impf.*, списа́ть (-ишу́, -и́шешь) *pf.* (**from** с+*g.*).

crick [krɪk] *n.* растяже́ние мышц.

cricket[1] ['krɪkɪt] *n.* (*sport*) кри́кет; ~ **bat** бита́.

cricket² ['krɪkɪt] *n.* (*insect*) сверчо́к (-чка́).

crier ['kraɪə(r)] *n.* глаша́тай.

crime [kraɪm] *n.* преступле́ние.

Crimea [kraɪ'mɪə] *n.* Крым.

criminal ['krɪmɪn(ə)l] *n.* престу́пник; *adj.* престу́пный, уголо́вный.

crimp [krɪmp] *v.t.* ме́лко завива́ть *impf.*, зави́ть (-вью́, -вьёшь; зави́л, -а́, -о) *pf.*

crimson ['krɪmz(ə)n] *adj.* мали́новый, карма́зи́нный.

cringe [krɪndʒ] *v.i.* (*cower*) съёживаться *impf.*, съёжиться *pf.*; (*of behaviour*) раболе́пствовать *impf.* **cringing** *adj.* подобостра́стный.

crinkle ['krɪŋk(ə)l] *n.* морщи́на.

crinoline ['krɪnəlɪn] *n.* криноли́н.

cripple ['krɪp(ə)l] *n.* кале́ка *c.g.*; *v.t.* кале́чить *impf.*, ис~ *pf.*; (*fig.*) наноси́ть (-ошу́, -о́сишь) *impf.*, нанести́ (нанесу́, -сёшь; нанёс, -ла́) вред, повреждéние, +*d.*

crisis ['kraɪsɪs] *n.* кри́зис.

crisp [krɪsp] *adj.* (*brittle*) хрустя́щий; (*fresh*) све́жий (свеж, -а́, -о́, свежи́); (*abrupt*) ре́зкий (-зок, -зка́, -зко); *n.*: *pl.* чи́псы (-сов) *pl.*

criss-cross ['krɪskrɒs] *adv.* крест-на́крест.

criterion [kraɪ'tɪərɪən] *n.* крите́рий.

critic ['krɪtɪk] *n.* кри́тик. **critical** *adj.* крити́ческий; (*dangerous*) опа́сный. **criticism** *n.* кри́тика. **criticize** *v.t.* критикова́ть *impf.* **critique** [krɪ'tiːk] *n.* кри́тика.

croak [krəʊk] *n.* ква́канье; *v.i.* ква́кать *impf.*, ква́кнуть *pf.*; хрипе́ть (-плю́, -пи́шь) *impf.*

Croat ['krəʊæt], **Croatian** [krəʊ'eɪʃ(ə)n] *n.* хорва́т, ~ка; *adj.* хорва́тский.

crochet ['krəʊʃeɪ, -ʃɪ] *n.* вяза́ние крючко́м; *v.t.* вяза́ть (вяжу́, вя́жешь) *impf.*, с~ *pf.* (крючко́м).

crock [krɒk] *n.* (*broken pottery*) гли́няный черепо́к (-пка́). **crockery** *n.* гли́няная, фая́нсовая, посу́да.

crocodile ['krɒkədaɪl] *n.* крокоди́л.

crocus ['krəʊkəs] *n.* кро́кус.

croft [krɒft] *n.* ме́лкое хозя́йство. **crofter** *n.* ме́лкий аренда́тор.

croissant ['krwʌsɑ̃] *n.* круасса́н.

crone [krəʊn] *n.* сго́рбленная стару́ха.

crony ['krəʊnɪ] *n.* закады́чный друг (*pl.* друзья́, -зéй, -зья́м).

crook [krʊk] *n.* (*staff*) по́сох; (*bend*) изги́б; (*swindler*) жу́лик, моше́нник; *v.t.* сгиба́ть *impf.*, согну́ть *pf.* **crooked** *adj.* криво́й (крив, -а́, -о); (*dishonest*) нече́стный. **crookedness** *n.* кривизна́; (*dishonesty*) жу́льничество.

croon [kruːn] *v.t.* & *i.* напева́ть *impf.*; мурлы́кать (-ы́чу, -ы́чешь) *impf.* **crooner** *n.* эстра́дный певе́ц (-вца́).

crop [krɒp] *n.* (*yield*) урожа́й; *pl.* культу́ры *f.pl.*; (*bird's*) зоб (*pl.* -ы́); (*haircut*) коро́ткая стри́жка; *v.t.* (*cut*) подстрига́ть *impf.*, подстри́чь (-игу́, -ижёшь; -иг) *pf.*; ~ **up** неожи́данно возника́ть *impf.*, возни́кнуть (-к) *pf.*

croquet ['krəʊkeɪ, -kɪ] *n.* кроке́т.

cross [krɒs] *n.* крест (-á); (*biol.*) (*action*) скре́щивание, (*result*) по́месь; *adj.* (*transverse*) попере́чный; (*angry*) серди́тый; *v.t.* пересека́ть *impf.*, пересе́чь (-еку́ -ечёшь; -éк, -екла́) *pf.*; (*biol.*) скре́щивать *impf.*, скрести́ть *pf.*; ~ **off, out** вычёркивать *impf.*, вы́черкнуть *pf.*; ~ **o.s.** крести́ться (-ещу́сь, -éстишься) *impf.*, пере~ *pf.*; ~ **over** переходи́ть (-ожу́, -о́дишь) *impf.*, перейти́ (-ейду́, -ейдёшь; -ешёл, -ешла́) *pf.* (че́рез)+*a.* **crossbar** *n.* попере́чина. **crossbow** *n.* самостре́л. **cross-breed** *n.* по́месь; *v.t.* скре́щивать *impf.*, скрести́ть *pf.* **cross-country** *adj.*: ~ **race** кросс. **cross-examination** *n.* перекрёстный допро́с. **cross-examine, cross-question** *v.t.* подверга́ть *impf.*, подве́ргнуть (-г) *pf.* перекрёстному допро́су. **cross-eyed** *adj.* косогла́зый. **cross-legged** *adj.*: **sit** ~ сиде́ть (сижу́, сиди́шь) *impf.* по-туре́цки. **cross-reference** *n.* перекрёстная ссы́лка. **crossroad(s)** *n.* перекрёсток (-тка) (*fig.*) распу́тье. **cross-section** *n.* перекрёстное сече́ние. **crossways, crosswise** *adv.* крест-на́крест. **crossword (puzzle)** *n.* кроссво́рд. **crossing** *n.* (*intersection*) перекрёсток (-тка); (*foot*) перехо́д; (*transport; rail.*) перее́зд.

crotch [krɒtʃ] *n.* (*anat.*) проме́жность.

crotchet ['krɒtʃɪt] *n.* (*mus.*) четвертна́я но́та. **crotchety** ['krɒtʃɪtɪ] *adj.* сварли́вый, приди́рчивый.

crouch [kraʊtʃ] *v.i.* пригиба́ться *impf.*, пригну́ться *pf.*

croup [kruːp] *n.* круп.

crow [krəʊ] *n.* воро́на; **as the** ~ **flies** по прямо́й ли́нии; *v.i.* кукаре́кать *impf.*; (*exult*) ликова́ть *impf.* **crowbar** *n.* лом (*pl.* ло́мы, ломо́в).

crowd [kraʊd] *n.* толпа́ (*pl.* -пы); *v.i.* тесни́ться *impf.*, с~ *pf.*; ~ **into** втиски́ваться *impf.*, вти́снуться *pf.*; ~ **out** вытесня́ть *impf.*, вы́теснить *pf.* **crowded** *adj.* перепо́лненный (-ен).

crown [kraʊn] *n.* коро́на, вене́ц (-нца́); (*tooth*) коро́нка; (*head*) маку́шка; (*hat*) тулья́; (*coin*) кро́на; *v.t.* коронова́ть *impf.* & *pf.*; (*fig.*) венча́ть *impf.*, у~ *pf.*; **C~ prince** кронпри́нц.

crucial ['kruːʃ(ə)l] *adj.* (*decisive*) реша́ющий; (*critical*) крити́ческий.

crucible ['kruːsɪb(ə)l] *n.* пла́вильный ти́гель (-гля) *m.*

crucifix ['kruːsɪfɪks], **crucifixion** *n.* распя́тие. **crucify** *v.t.* распина́ть *impf.*, распя́ть (-пну́, -пнёшь) *pf.*

crude [kruːd] *adj.* (*rude*) гру́бый (груб, -а́, -о); (*raw*) сыро́й (сыр, -а́, -о). **crudeness** *n.* гру́бость. **crudity** *n.* гру́бость.

cruel ['kruːəl] *adj.* жесто́кий (-о́к, -о́ка́, -о́ко). **cruelty** *n.* жесто́кость.

cruet ['kruːɪt] *n.* судо́к (-дка́).

cruise [kruːz] *n.* круи́з; морско́е путеше́ствие; *v.i.* крейси́ровать *impf.*; **cruising speed** сре́дняя, экономи́ческая, ско́рость; **cruising taxi** свобо́дное такси́ *nt.indecl.* **cruiser** *n.* крейсер (*pl.* -á & -ы).

crumb [krʌm] *n.* кро́шка; *v.t.* обсыпа́ть *impf.*, обсы́пать (-плю, -плешь) *pf.* кро́шками.

crumble ['krʌmb(ə)l] *v.t.* кроши́ть (-ошу́, -о́шишь) *impf.*, ис~, на~, рас~ *pf.*; *v.i.* обва́ливаться *impf.*, обвали́ться (-ится) *pf.* **crumbling** *adj.* осыпа́ющийся, обва́ливающийся. **crumbly** *adj.* рассы́пчатый, кроша́щийся.

crumpet ['krʌmpɪt] *n.* сдо́бная лепёшка.

crumple ['krʌmp(ə)l] *v.t.* мять (мну, мнёшь) *impf.*, с~ (сомну́, -нёшь) *pf.*; ко́мкать *impf.*, с~ *pf.*

crunch [krʌntʃ] *n.* хруст; треск; *v.t.* грызть (-зу́, -зёшь; -з) *impf.*, раз~ *pf.*; *v.i.* хрустеть (-ущу́, -усти́шь) *impf.*, хру́стнуть *pf.*

crusade [kru:'seɪd] *n.* кресто́вый похо́д; (*fig.*) кампа́ния (в защи́ту+*g.*); *v.i.* боро́ться (-рю́сь, -решься) *impf.* (**for** за+*a.*). **crusader** *n.* крестоно́сец (-сца); (*fig.*) боре́ц (-рца́) (за+*a.*).

crush [krʌʃ] *n.* да́вка, толкотня́; (*infatuation*) си́льное увлече́ние; *v.t.* дави́ть (-влю́, -вишь) *impf.*, раз~, раз~ *pf.*; мять (мну, мнёшь) *impf.*, с~ *pf.*; (*fig.*) подавля́ть *impf.*, подави́ть (-влю́, -вишь) *pf.* **crusher** *n.* дроби́лка. **crushing** *adj.* сокруши́тельный, уничтожа́ющий.

crust [krʌst] *n.* (*of earth*) кора́; (*bread etc.*) ко́рка.

crustacean [krʌ'steɪʃ(ə)n] *n.* ракообра́зное *sb.*

crusty ['krʌstɪ] *adj.* с твёрдой ко́ркой; (*irritable*) сварли́вый, раздражи́тельный.

crutch [krʌtʃ] *n.* косты́ль *m.*

crux [krʌks] *n.* затрудни́тельный вопро́с; ~ **of the matter** суть де́ла.

cry [kraɪ] *n.* плач; крик; **a far ~ to** далеко́ от+*g.*; *v.i.* (*weep*) пла́кать (-а́чу, -а́чешь) *impf.*; (*shout*) крича́ть (-чу́, -чи́шь) *impf.*; ~ **off** отка́зываться *impf.*, отказа́ться (-ажу́сь, -а́жешься) *pf.* (от+*g.*). **crying** *adj.* пла́чущий; вопию́щий; **it's a ~ shame** позо́рно!; жа́лко!

crypt [krɪpt] *n.* склеп. **cryptic** *adj.* зага́дочный. **cryptogram** *n.* та́йнопись.

crystal ['krɪst(ə)l] *n.* криста́лл; (*mineral*) хруста́ль (-ля́) *m.* **crystallize** *v.t.* & *i.* кристаллизова́ть(ся) *impf.* & *pf.*; *v.t.* (*fruit*) заса́харивать *impf.*, заса́харить *pf.*

cub [kʌb] *n.* детёныш (ди́кого зве́ря); **bear ~** медвежо́нок (-жо́нка; *pl.* -жа́та, -жа́т); **fox ~** лисёнок (-нка; *pl.* лися́та, -т); **lion ~** львёнок (-нка; *pl.* льви́та, -т); **wolf ~** волчёнок (-нка; *pl.* волча́та, -т).

cubby-hole ['kʌbɪ] *n.* чула́н.

cube [kju:b] *n.* куб. **cubic** *adj.* куби́ческий.

cubicle ['kju:bɪk(ə)l] *n.* каби́на; бокс.

cuckoo ['kuku:] *n.* (*bird*) куку́шка; (*fool*) глупе́ц (-пца́); *v.i.* кукова́ть *impf.*, про~ *pf.*

cucumber ['kju:kʌmbə(r)] *n.* огуре́ц (-рца́).

cud [kʌd] *n.* жва́чка.

cuddle ['kʌd(ə)l] *v.t.* обнима́ть *impf.*, обня́ть (обниму́, -мешь; о́бнял, -á, -о) *pf.*; *v.i.* обнима́ться *impf.*, обня́ться (обниму́сь, -мешься; обня́лся, -ла́сь) *pf.*

cudgel ['kʌdʒ(ə)l] *n.* дуби́на, дуби́нка.

cue[1] [kju:] *n.* (*theatr.*) ре́плика.

cue[2] [kju:] *n.* (*billiards*) кий (кия́; *pl.* кий).

cuff[1] [kʌf] *n.* манже́та, обшла́г (-á; *pl.* -á); **off the ~** экспро́мтом.

cuff[2] [kʌf] *v.t.* (*hit*) дава́ть (даю́, даёшь) *impf.*, дать (дам, дашь, даст, дади́м; дал, -á, да́ло, -и) *pf.* пощёчину+*d.*

cuff-link ['kʌflɪŋk] *n.* за́понка.

cul-de-sac ['kʌldə.sæk, 'kʊl-] *n.* тупи́к (-á).

culinary ['kʌlɪnərɪ] *adj.* кулина́рный.

cull [kʌl] *v.t.* отбира́ть *impf.*, отобра́ть (отберу́, -рёшь; отобра́л, -á, -о) *pf.*

culminate ['kʌlmɪ.neɪt] *v.i.* достига́ть *impf.*, дости́чь & дости́гнуть (-и́гну, -и́гнешь; -и́г) *pf.* вы́сшей то́чки. **culmi'nation** *n.* кульминацио́нный пункт.

culottes [kju:'lɒts] *n.* ю́бка-брю́ки.

culpability [,kʌlpə'bɪlɪtɪ] *n.* вино́вность. '**culpable** *adj.* вино́вный. '**culprit** *n.* вино́вный *sb.*

cult [kʌlt] *n.* культ; ~ **of personality** культ ли́чности.

cultivate ['kʌltɪ.veɪt] *v.t.* (*land*) обраба́тывать *impf.*, обрабо́тать *pf.*; (*crops*; *fig.*) культиви́ровать *impf.*; (*develop*) развива́ть *impf.*, разви́ть (разовью́, -ьёшь; разви́л, -á, -о) *pf.* **cultivated** *adj.* (*land*) обрабо́танный (-ан); (*plants*) выра́щенный (-ен); (*person*) культу́рный; ~ **crop** пропашна́я культу́ра. **culti'vation** *n.* обрабо́тка, возде́лывание; культива́ция; выра́щивание; **area under ~** посевна́я пло́щадь. **cultivator** *n.* культива́тор.

cultural ['kʌltʃ(ə)r(ə)l] *adj.* культу́рный. **culture** *n.* культу́ра; (*of land*) возде́лывание; (*of animals*) разведе́ние; (*of bacteria*) выра́щивание. **cultured** *adj.* культу́рный; разви́той (ра́звит, -á, -о); ~ **pearls** культиви́рованный же́мчуг (-а(у); *pl.* -á).

culvert ['kʌlvət] *n.* водопропускна́я труба́ (*pl.* -бы).

cumbersome ['kʌmbəsəm] *adj.* обремени́тельный; громо́здкий.

cumulative ['kju:mjʊlətɪv] *adj.* постепе́нно увели́чивающийся. **cumulus** ['kju:mjʊləs] *n.* кучевы́е облака́ (-ко́в) *pl.*

cuneiform ['kju:nɪ.fɔ:m] *adj.* клинообра́зный; *n.* кли́нопись.

cunning ['kʌnɪŋ] *n.* хи́трость, лука́вство; *adj.* хи́трый (-тёр, -тра́, хи́тро́), лука́вый.

cup [kʌp] *n.* ча́шка, ча́ша; (*prize*) ку́бок (-бка).

cupboard ['kʌbəd] *n.* шкаф (*loc.* -у́; *pl.* -ы́).

Cupid ['kju:pɪd] *n.* Купидо́н.

cupidity [kju:'pɪdɪtɪ] *n.* а́лчность.

cupola ['kju:pələ] *n.* ку́пол (*pl.* -á).

cur [kɜː(r)] *n.* (*dog*) дворня́жка; (*person*) гру́бый, ни́зкий, челове́к.

curable ['kjʊərəb(ə)l] *adj.* излечи́мый.

curate ['kjʊərət] *n.* свяще́нник (мла́дшего са́на).

curative ['kjʊərətɪv] *adj.* целе́бный.

curator [kjʊə'reɪtə(r)] *n.* храни́тель *m.* музе́я.

curb [kɜːb] *v.t.* обу́здывать *impf.*, обузда́ть *pf.*; *n.* (*check*) обузда́ние, узда́ (*pl.* -ды); (*kerb*) край (*loc.* кра́ю; *pl.* края́) тротуа́ра.

curd [kɜːd] (*cheese*) *n.* творо́г (творога́(у)) **curdle** *v.t. & i.* свёртывать(ся) *impf.*, сверну́ть(ся) *pf.*; *v.t.* (*blood*) ледени́ть *impf.*, о~ *pf.*

cure ['kjʊə(r)] *n.* (*treatment*) лече́ние; (*means*) сре́дство (**for** про́тив+g.); *v.t.* (*person*) вылё́чивать *impf.*, вы́лечить *pf.*; (*smoke*) копти́ть *impf.*, за~ *pf.*; (*salt*) соли́ть (солю́, со́ли́шь) *impf.*, по~ *pf.*

curfew ['kɜːfjuː] *n.* комендантский час.

curing ['kjʊərɪŋ] *n.* лече́ние; (*cul.*) копче́ние, соле́ние.

curio ['kjʊərɪəʊ] *n.* ре́дкая антиква́рная вещь (*pl.* -щи, -ще́й).

curiosity [ˌkjʊərɪ'ɒsɪtɪ] *n.* любопы́тство. 'curious *adj.* любопы́тный.

curl [kɜːl] *n.* (*hair*) ло́кон; (*spiral; hair*) завито́к (-тка́); *v.t.* завива́ть *impf.*, зави́ть (-вью́, -вьёшь; зави́л, -а́, -о) *pf.*; крути́ть (-учу́, -у́тишь) *impf.*, за~ *pf.*

curlew ['kɜːljuː] *n.* кро́ншнеп.

curling ['kɜːlɪŋ] *n.* кэ́рлинг.

curly ['kɜːlɪ] *adj.* вью́щийся; кудря́вый. **curly-haired, curly-headed** *adj.* курча́вый.

curmudgeon [kə'mʌdʒ(ə)n] *n.* скря́га *c.g.*

currants ['kʌrəntz] *n.* (*collect.*) кори́нка.

currency ['kʌrənsɪ] *n.* валю́та; (*prevalence*) распространённость. **current** *adj.* теку́щий; *n.* тече́ние; (*air*) струя́ (*pl.* -у́и); (*water; elec.*) ток (-а(у)).

curriculum [kə'rɪkjʊləm] *n.* курс обуче́ния. **curriculum vitae** *n.* кра́ткое жизнеописа́ние, биогра́фия.

curry¹ ['kʌrɪ] *n.* кэ́рри *nt.indecl.*

curry² ['kʌrɪ] *v.t.*: ~ **favour with** заи́скивать *impf.* пе́ред+*i.*, у+g.

curse [kɜːs] *n.* прокля́тие, руга́тельство; *v.t.* проклина́ть *impf.*, прокля́сть (-яну́, -янёшь; про́клял, -а́, -о) *pf.*; *v.i.* руга́ться *impf.*, по~ *pf.* **cursed** *adj.* прокля́тый, окая́нный.

cursive ['kɜːsɪv] *n.* ско́ропись; *adj.* скоропи́сный.

cursory ['kɜːsərɪ] *adj.* бе́глый; пове́рхностный.

curt [kɜːt] *adj.* кра́ткий (-ток, -тка́, -тко); ре́зкий (-зок, -зка́, -зко).

curtail [kɜː'teɪl] *v.t.* сокраща́ть *impf.*, сократи́ть (-ащу́, -ати́шь) *pf.* **curtailment** *n.* сокраще́ние.

curtain ['kɜːt(ə)n] *n.* за́навес; занаве́ска. **curtain-call** *n.* вы́зов актёра; *v.t.* занаве́шивать *impf.*, занаве́сить *pf.*

curts(e)y ['kɜːtsɪ] *n.* револя́нс.

curvature ['kɜːvətʃə(r)] *n.* кривизна́; искривле́ние. **curve** [kɜːv] *n.* изги́б; (*math. etc.*) крива́я *sb.*; *v.t.* гну́ть *impf.*, со~ *pf.*; *v.i.* изгиба́ться *impf.*, изогну́ться *pf.* **curvilinear** [ˌkɜːvɪ'lɪnɪə(r)] *adj.* криволине́йный.

cushion ['kʊʃ(ə)n] *n.* поду́шка; *v.t.* смягча́ть *impf.*, смягчи́ть *pf.*

cusp [kʌsp] *n.* о́стрый вы́ступ; (*geom.*) то́чка пересе́чения двух кривы́х.

custard ['kʌstəd] *n.* сла́дкий заварно́й крем, со́ус.

custodian [kʌ'stəʊdɪən] *n.* храни́тель *m.*; сто́рож (*pl.* -á). **custody** ['kʌstədɪ] *n.* опе́ка; хране́ние; (*of police*) аре́ст; **to be in** ~ находи́ться (нахожу́сь, -о́дишься) *impf.* под стра́жей, аре́стом; **to take into** ~ арестова́ть *pf.*

custom ['kʌstəm] *n.* обы́чай; привы́чка; (*customers*) клиенту́ра; *pl.* (*duty*) тамо́женные по́шлины *f.pl.*; **to go through the** ~ проходи́ть (-ожу́, -о́дишь) *impf.*, пройти́ (пройду́, пройдёшь; прошёл, -шла́) *pf.* тамо́женный осмо́тр. **customary** *adj.* обы́чный, привы́чный. **customer** *n.* клие́нт; покупа́тель *m.*; зака́зчик. **custom-house** *n.* тамо́жня.

cut [kʌt] *v.t.* ре́зать (ре́жу, -жешь) *impf.*, по~ *pf.*; (*hair*) стричь (-игу́, -ижёшь; -йг) *impf.*, о~ *pf.*; (*hay*) коси́ть (кошу́, ко́сишь) *impf.*, с~ *pf.*; (*price*) снижа́ть *impf.*, сни́зить *pf.*; (*cards*) снима́ть *impf.*, снять (сниму́, -мешь; снял, -á, -о) *pf.* колоду; ~ **down** сруба́ть *impf.*, сруби́ть (-блю́, -бишь) *pf.* ~ **off** отреза́ть *impf.*, отре́зать (-éжу, -éжешь) *pf.*; (*interrupt*) прерыва́ть *impf.*, прерва́ть (-ву́, -вёшь; -ва́л, -вала́, -ва́ло) *pf.*; ~ **out** выре́зывать *impf.*, вы́резать (-ежу, -ежешь) *pf.*; кро́ить *impf.*, вы́~, с~ *pf.*; ~ **up** разреза́ть *impf.*, разре́зать (-éжу, -éжешь) *pf.*; *n.* поре́з, разре́з; покро́й; сниже́ние; *adj.* разре́занный (-ан); (*glass etc.*) гранёный; ~ **out** скро́енный (-ен); ~ **rate** сни́женная цена́ (a -ну); ~ **up** огорчённый (-ён, -ена́)

cute [kjuːt] *adj.* симпати́чный.

cuticle ['kjuːtɪk(ə)l] *n.* ко́жица.

cutlass ['kʌtləs] *n.* аборда́жная са́бля (*g.pl.* -бель).

cutler ['kʌtlə(r)] *n.* ножо́вщик. **cutlery** *n.* ножевы́е изде́лия *nt.pl.*; ножи́, ви́лки и ло́жки *pl.*

cutlet ['kʌtlɪt] *n.* отбивна́я котле́та.

cut-out ['kʌtaʊt] *n.* (*switch*) предохрани́тель *m.*, выключа́тель *m.*; (*figure*) вы́резанная фигу́ра.

cutter ['kʌtə(r)] *n.* (*tailor*) закро́йщик, -ица; (*naut.*) ка́тер (*pl.* -á).

cutthroat ['kʌtθrəʊt] *n.* головоре́з; *adj.* ожесточённый (-ён, -ённа).

cutting ['kʌtɪŋ] *n.* ре́зание; разреза́ние; (*press*) вы́резка; (*from plant*) черено́к (-нка́); (*rail.*) вы́емка; *adj.* ре́жущий; прони́зывающий; ре́зкий (-зок, -зка́, -зко).

cuttlefish ['kʌt(ə)lfɪʃ] *n.* карака́тица.

c.v. *abbr.* (*of* **curriculum vitae**) кра́ткое жизнеописа́ние, биогра́фия.

cwt ['hʌndrəd,weɪt] *abbr.* (*of* **hundredweight**) (*Imperial* — *approx. 50.8 kg*) англи́йский це́нтнер; (*US* — *approx. 45.4 kg*) америка́нский це́нтнер.

cyanide ['saɪə,naɪd] *n.* циани́д.

cybernetics [,saɪbə'netɪks] *n.* киберне́тика.

cyclamen ['sɪkləmən] *n.* цикламе́н.

cycle ['saɪk(ə)l] *n.* цикл; (*elec.*) герц (*g.pl.* -ц); (*bicycle*) велосипе́д; *v.i.* е́здить *impf.* на велосипе́де. **cyclic(al)** ['saɪklɪk(ə)l, 'sɪk-] *adj.* цикли́ческий. **cycling** *n.* езда́ на велосипе́де; велоспо́рт. **cyclist** *n.* велосипеди́ст.

cyclone ['saɪkləʊn] *n.* цикло́н.

cyclotron ['saɪklə,trɒn] *n.* циклотро́н.

cygnet ['sɪgnɪt] *n.* лебедёнок (-нка; *pl.* лебедя́та, -т).

cylinder ['sɪlɪndə(r)] *n.* цили́ндр. **cy'lindrical** *adj.* цилиндри́ческий.

cymbals ['sɪmb(ə)lz] *n.* таре́лки *f.pl.*

cynic ['sɪnɪk] *n.* ци́ник. **cynical** *adj.* цини́чный. **cynicism** *n.* цини́зм.

cynosure ['saɪnə,zjʊə(r), 'sɪn-] *n.* центр внима́ния.

cypress ['saɪprəs] *n.* кипари́с.

Cypriot ['sɪprɪət] *n.* киприо́т, ~ка; **Greek** (**Turkish**) ~ киприо́т, ~ка, гре́ческого (туре́цкого) происхожде́ния.

Cyprus ['saɪprəs] *n.* Кипр.

Cyrillic [sɪ'rɪlɪk] *n.* кири́ллица.

cyst [sɪst] *n.* киста́.

czar, czarina *see* **tsar, tsarina**

Czech [tʃek] *n.* чех, че́шка; *adj.* че́шский; ~ **Republic** Че́шская Респу́блика.

D

D [diː] *n.* (*mus.*) ре *nt.indecl.*

dab[1] [dæb] *n.* лёгкое каса́ние; мазо́к (-зка́); *v.t.* легко́ прикаса́ться *impf.*, прикосну́ться *pf.* к+*d.*; ~ **on** накла́дывать *impf.*, наложи́ть (-жу́, -жишь) *pf.* мазка́ми.

dab[2] [dæb] *adj.*: **be a** ~ **hand at** соба́ку съесть (-е́м, -е́шь, -е́ст, -еди́м; -ел) *pf.* на+*p.*

dabble ['dæb(ə)l] *v.i.* плеска́ться (-ещу́сь, -е́щешься) *impf.*; ~ **in** пове́рхностно, полюби́тельски, занима́ться *impf.*, заня́ться (займу́сь, -мёшься; -я́лся, -яла́сь) *pf.*+*i.* **dabbler** *n.* дилета́нт.

dachshund ['dækshʊnd] *n.* та́кса.

dad [dæd], **daddy** *n.* па́па. **daddy-long-legs** *n.* долгоно́жка.

dado ['deɪdəʊ] *n.* вну́тренняя пане́ль.

daffodil ['dæfədɪl] *n.* жёлтый нарци́сс.

daft [dɑːft] *adj.* глу́пый (глуп, -а́, -о); бессмы́сленный (-ен, -енна).

dagger ['dægə(r)] *n.* кинжа́л.

dahlia ['deɪlɪə] *n.* георги́н.

daily ['deɪlɪ] *adv.* ежедне́вно; *adj.* ежедне́вный, повседне́вный; ~ **bread** хлеб насу́щный; ~ **dozen** заря́дка; *n.* (*charwoman*) приходя́щая домрабо́тница; (*newspaper*) ежедне́вная газе́та.

daintiness ['deɪntɪnɪs] *n.* изя́щество. **dainty** *adj.* изя́щный; изы́сканный (-ан, -анна).

dairy ['deərɪ] *n.* маслобо́йня; (*shop*) моло́чная *sb.*; ~ **farm** моло́чное хозя́йство. **dairymaid** *n.* доя́рка.

dais ['deɪs] *n.* помо́ст.

daisy ['deɪzɪ] *n.* маргари́тка.

dale [deɪl] *n.* доли́на.

dalliance ['dælɪəns] *n.* пра́здное времяпрепровожде́ние. **dally** *v.i.* развлека́ться *impf.*, развле́чься (-еку́сь, -ечёшься; -ёкся, -екла́сь) *pf.*

Dalmation [dæl'meɪʃ(ə)n] *n.* далма́тский дог.

dam[1] [dæm] *n.* (*barrier*) плоти́на; перемы́чка; *v.t.* прегражда́ть *impf.*, прегради́ть *pf.* плоти́ной; пруди́ть (-ужу́, -у́ди́шь) *impf.*, за~ *pf.*

dam[2] [dæm] *n.* (*animal*) ма́тка.

damage ['dæmɪdʒ] *n.* повреждéние; уще́рб; *pl.* убы́тки *m.pl.*; *v.t.* поврежда́ть *impf.*, повреди́ть *pf.*; по́ртить *impf.*, ис~ *pf.*

damascene ['dæmə,siːn, ,dæmə'siːn] *v.t.* насека́ть *impf.*, насе́чь (-еку́ -ечёшь; -ёк, -екла́) *pf.* зо́лотом, серебро́м.

damask ['dæməsk] *n.* камча́тная ткань; *adj.* дама́сский; камча́тный.

damn [dæm] *v.t.* проклина́ть *impf.*, прокля́сть (-яну́, -янёшь; про́клял, -а́, -о) *pf.*; (*censure*) осужда́ть *impf.*, осуди́ть (-ужу́, -у́дишь) *pf.* **damnable** *adj.* отврати́тельный, прокля́тый. **dam'nation** *n.* прокля́тие. **damned** *adj.* прокля́тый.

damp [dæmp] *n.* сы́рость, вла́жность; *adj.* сыро́й (сыр, -а́, -о); вла́жный (-жен, -жна́, -жно, -жны́); *v.t.* сма́чивать *impf.*, смочи́ть (-чу́, -чишь) *pf.*; увлажня́ть *impf.*, увлажни́ть *pf.* **dampcourse** *n.* гидроизоля́ция. **damp-proof** *adj.* влагонепроница́емый.

damson ['dæmz(ə)n] *n.* терносли́ва.

dance [dɑːns] *v.i.* танцева́ть *impf.*; пляса́ть (-яшу́, -я́шешь) *impf.*, с~ *pf.*; *n.* та́нец (-нца), пля́ска; (*party*) танцева́льный ве́чер (*pl.* -а́). **dancer** *n.* танцо́р, ~ка; (*ballet*) танцо́вщик, -ица; балери́на.

dandelion ['dændɪ,laɪən] *n.* одува́нчик.

dandruff ['dændrʌf] *n.* пе́рхоть.

dandy ['dændɪ] *n.* дэ́нди *m.indecl.*, франт.

Dane [deɪn] *n.* датча́нин (*pl.* -а́не, -а́н), -а́нка; **Great** ~ дог. **Danish** *adj.* да́тский.

danger ['deɪndʒə(r)] *n.* опа́сность. **dangerous** *adj.* опа́сный.

dangle ['dæŋg(ə)l] *v.t.* болта́ть *impf.*+*i.*; *v.i.* болта́ться *impf.*; свиса́ть *impf.*

Danish ['deɪnɪʃ] *adj.* да́тский.

dank [dæŋk] *adj.* вла́жный, сыро́й.

Danube ['dænjuːb] *n.* Дуна́й.

dapper ['dæpə(r)] *adj.* аккура́тный; франтова́тый.

dappled ['dæp(ə)ld] *adj.* пятни́стый. **dapple-grey** *adj.* се́рый (сер, -á, -о) в я́блоках.

dare [deə(r)] *v.i.* сметь *impf.*, по *pf.*; отва́живаться *impf.*, отва́житься *pf.*; **I ~ say** полага́ю; *n.* вы́зов. **daredevil** *n.* сорвиголова́ *c.g.* (*pl.* -овы, -о́в, -ова́м). **daring** *n.* сме́лость; *adj.* сме́лый (смел, -á, -о); де́рзкий (-зок, -зка́, -зко).

dark [dɑːk] *adj.* тёмный (-мен, -мна́); **D~ Ages** ра́ннее средневеко́вье; **~ secret** вели́кая та́йна; *n.* темнота́, тьма, мрак. **darken** *v.t.* затемня́ть *impf.*, затемни́ть *pf.* **darkly** *adv.* мра́чно. **darkness** *n.* темнота́, тьма, мрак. **dark-room** *n.* тёмная ко́мната.

darling ['dɑːklɪŋ] *n.* дорого́й *sb.*, ми́лый *sb.*; люби́мец (-мца); *adj.* дорого́й (до́рог, -á, -о), люби́мый.

darn [dɑːn] *v.t.* што́пать *impf.*, за~ *pf.*; *n.* заштопанное ме́сто (*pl.* -тá). **darning** *n.* што́пка; *adj.* што́пальный; **~ thread, wool** што́пка.

dart [dɑːt] *n.* стрела́ (*pl.* -лы); стре́лка; (*tuck*) вы́тачка; *v.t.* мета́ть (мечу́, ме́чешь) *impf.*; броса́ть *impf.*, бро́сить *pf.*; *v.i.* носи́ться (ношу́сь, но́сишься) *indet.*, нести́сь (несу́сь, -сёшься, несла́сь) *det.*, по~ *pf.*

dash [dæʃ] *n.* (*hyphen*) тире́ *nt.indecl.*; (*admixture*) при́месь; (*rush*) рыво́к (-вка́); *v.t.* швыря́ть *impf.*, швырну́ть *pf.*; *v.i.* броса́ться *impf.*, бро́ситься *pf.*; носи́ться (но́шусь, но́сишься) *indet.*, нести́сь (несу́сь, -сёшься, нёсся, несла́сь) *det.*, по~ *pf.*; мча́ться (мчусь, мчи́шься) *impf.* **dashboard** *n.* прибо́рная доска́ (*a.* -ску; *pl.* -ски, -со́к, -ска́м). **dashing** *adj.* лихо́й (лих, -á, -о, ли́хи́), удало́й (уда́л, -á, -о).

data *n.* да́нные *sb.*; фа́кты *m.pl.* **database** *n.* ба́за да́нных.

date¹ [deɪt] *n.* число́ (*pl.* -сла, -сел, -слам), да́та; (*engagement*) свида́ние; **out of ~** устаре́лый; (*overdue*) просро́ченный (-ен); **up to ~** совреме́нный (-нен, -нна); в ку́рсе де́ла; *v.t. & i.* дати́ровать(ся) *impf. & pf.*; (*make engagement*) назнача́ть *impf.*, назна́чить *pf.* свида́ние с+i.

date² [deɪt] *n.* (*fruit*) фи́ник(овая па́льма).

dative ['deɪtɪv] *adj.* (*n.*) да́тельный (паде́ж (-á)).

daub [dɔːb] *v.t.* ма́зать (ма́жу, -жешь) *impf.*, на~ *pf.*; малева́ть (-лю́ю, -лю́ешь) *impf.*, на~ *pf.*; *n.* плоха́я карти́на.

daughter ['dɔːtə(r)] *n.* дочь (до́чери, *i.* -рью; *pl.* -ри, -ре́й, *i.* -рьми́). **daughter-in-law** *n.* неве́стка (*in relation to mother*), сноха́ (*pl.* -хи) (*in relation to father*).

dauntless ['dɔːntlɪs] *adj.* неустраши́мый.

davit ['dævɪt, 'deɪvɪt] *n.* шлюпба́лка.

dawdle ['dɔːd(ə)l] *v.i.* безде́льничать *impf.*

dawn [dɔːn] *n.* рассве́т; заря́ (*pl.* зо́ри, зорь, зо́рям); *v.i.* (*day*) рассвета́ть *impf.*, рассвести́ (-етёт, -ело́) *pf. impers.*; **~ (up)on** осени́ть *impf.*, осени́ть *pf.*; **it ~ed on me** меня́ осени́ло.

day [deɪ] *n.* день (дня) *m.*; (*working ~*) рабо́чий день (дня) *m.*; (*24 hours*) су́тки (-ток) *pl.*; *pl.* (*period*) пери́од, вре́мя *nt.*; **~ after ~** изо дня́ в де́нь; **the ~ after tomorrow** послеза́втра; **all ~ long** день-денско́й; **the ~ before yesterday** позавчера́; **by ~** днём; **every other ~** че́рез день; **~ off** выходно́й день (дня) *m.*; **one ~** одна́жды; **this ~ week** че́рез неде́лю; **carry, win, the ~** оде́рживать *impf.*, одержа́ть (-жу́, -жишь) *pf.* побе́ду; **lose the ~** потерпе́ть (-плю́, -пишь) *pf.* пораже́ние. **daybreak** *n.* рассве́т. **day-dreams** *n.* мечты́ (*g.* мечта́ний) *f.pl.*, грёзы *f.pl.* **day-labourer** *n.* подёнщик, -ица. **daylight** *n.* дневно́й свет; **in broad ~** средь бе́ла дня́.

daze [deɪz] *v.t.* ошеломля́ть *impf.*, ошеломи́ть *pf.*; *n.* изумле́ние. **dazed** *adj.* изумлённый (-ён. -ена́), потрясённый (-ён, -ена́).

dazzle ['dæz(ə)l] *v.t.* ослепля́ть *impf.*, ослепи́ть *pf.* **dazzling** *adj.* блестя́щий, ослепи́тельный.

DC *abbr.* (*of direct current*) постоя́нный ток.

deacon ['diːkən] *n.* дья́кон (*pl.* -á).

dead [ded] *adj.* мёртвый (мёртв, -а, -о & (*fig.*) -ó), уме́рший; (*animals*) до́хлый; (*plants*) увя́дший; (*numb*) онеме́вший; (*lifeless*) безжи́зненный (-ен, -енна); (*sound*) глухо́й (глух, -á, -о); (*complete*) соверше́нный (-нен, -нна); **~ to** глухо́й (глух, -á, -о) к+d.; *n.*: **the ~** мёртвые *sb.*, уме́ршие *sb.*; **~ of night** глубо́кая ночь (*loc.* -чи́); *adv.* соверше́нно; **~ beat** смерте́льно уста́лый; **~ calm** (*naut.*) мёртвый штиль *m.*; **~ drunk** мертве́цки пья́ный (пьян, -á, -о); **~ end** тупи́к (-á); **~ heat** одновре́менный фи́ниш; **~ march** похоро́нный марш; **~ reckoning** счисле́ние пути́; **~ set** мёртвая сто́йка; **~ weight** мёртвый груз.

deaden ['ded(ə)n] *v.t. & i.* притупля́ть(ся) *impf.*, притупи́ть(ся) (-плю́(сь), -пишь(ся)) *pf.*

dead-end [dedend] *adj.* безвы́ходный. **deadline** (*time*) преде́льный срок (-a(у)). **deadlock** ['dedlɒk] *n.* тупи́к (-á); **reach ~** зайти́ (зайду́, -дёшь; зашёл, -шла́) *pf.* в тупи́к. **deadly** ['dedlɪ] *adj.* смерте́льный, смертоно́сный; **~ nightshade** беллодо́нна; **~ sin** сме́ртный грех (-á). **dead-nettle** ['dednet(ə)l] *n.* глуха́я крапи́ва.

deaf [def] *adj.* глухо́й (глух, -á, -о); **~ and dumb, ~ mute** глухонемо́й (*sb.*). **deafen** *v.t.* оглуша́ть *impf.*, оглуши́ть *pf.* **deafness** *n.* глухота́.

deal¹ [diːl] *n.*: **a great, good, ~** мно́го (+*g.*); (*with comp.*) гора́здо.

deal² [diːl] *n.* (*bargain*) сде́лка; (*cards*) сда́ча; *v.t.* (*cards*) сдава́ть (сдаю́, -аёшь) *impf.*, сдать (-ам, -ашь, -аст, -ади́м; сдал, -á, -о) *pf.*; (*blow*) наноси́ть (-ошу́, -óсишь) *impf.*, нанести́ (-есу́, -есёшь, -ёс, -есла́) *pf.*; ~ **in** торгова́ть *impf.*+*i.*; ~ **out** распределя́ть *impf.*, распредели́ть *pf.*; ~ **with** (*engage in*) занима́ться *impf.*, заня́ться (займу́сь, -мёшься; заня́лся, -ла́сь) *pf.*+*i.*; (*behave towards*) обходи́ться (-ожу́сь, -óдишься) *impf.*, обойти́сь (обойду́сь, -дёшься; обошёлся, -шла́сь) *pf.* с+*i.* **dealer** *n.* (*trader*) торго́вец (-вца) (**in** +*i.*).

deal³ [di:l] *n.* (*wood*) ело́вая, сосно́вая, древеси́на; *adj.* ело́вый, (*pine*) сосно́вый.

dean [di:n] *n.* (*univ.*) дека́н; (*church*) настоя́тель *m.* собо́ра. **deanery** *n.* декана́т.

dear [dɪə(r)] *adj.* дорого́й (до́рог, -á, -о); (*also n.*) ми́лый (мил, -á, -о, ми́лы) (*sb.*).

dearth [dɜ:θ] *n.* недоста́ток (-тка); нехва́тка.

death [deθ] *n.* смерть (*pl.* -ти, -тéй); *adj.* сме́ртный, смерте́льный; **at** ~'s **door** при сме́рти; **put to** ~ казни́ть *impf.* & *pf.*; ~ **certificate** свиде́тельство о сме́рти; ~ **duty** нало́г на насле́дство; ~ **penalty** сме́ртная казнь; ~ **rate** сме́ртность. **deathbed** *n.* сме́ртное ло́же. **deathblow** *n.* смерте́льный уда́р. **deathless** *adj.* бессме́ртный. **deathly** *adj.* сме́ртельный. **death-roll** *n.* спи́сок (-ска) уби́тых. **death-warrant** *n.* сме́ртный пригово́р (*also fig.*).

debar [dɪ'bɑ:(r)] *v.t.* ~ **from** не допуска́ть *impf.* до+*g.*

debase [dɪ'beɪs] *v.t.* понижа́ть *impf.*, пони́зить *pf.* ка́чество+*g.*

debatable [dɪ'beɪtəb(ə)l] *adj.* спо́рный. **debate** *n.* пре́ния (-ий) *pl.*, деба́ты (-тов) *pl.*; *v.t.* обсужда́ть *impf.*, обсуди́ть (-ужу́, -у́дишь) *pf.*; дебати́ровать *impf.*

debauch [dɪ'bɔ:tʃ] *v.t.* развраща́ть *impf.*, разврати́ть (-ащу́, -ати́шь) *pf.*; *n.* о́ргия. **debauched** *adj.* развращённый (-ён, -ённа), развра́тный. **debauchery** *n.* разврат.

debenture [dɪ'bentʃə(r)] *n.* долгово́е обяза́тельство.

debilitate [dɪ'bɪlɪteɪt] *v.t.* рас-, о-, слабля́ть; *impf.*, рас-, о-, слабить *pf.* **debility** *n.* бесси́лие, тщеду́шие.

debit ['debɪt] *n.* дéбет; ~**s and credits** прихо́д и расхо́д; *v.t.* дебетова́ть *impf.* & *pf.*; запи́сывать *impf.*, записа́ть (-ишу́, -и́шешь) *pf.* в дéбет+*d.*

debouch [dɪ'baʊtʃ, -'bu:ʃ] *v.i.* (*mil.*) дебуши́ровать *impf.* & *pf.*; (*river*) впада́ть *impf.*, впасть (впадёт; впал) *pf.*

debris ['debri:, 'deɪ-] *n.* оско́лки *m.pl.*, обло́мки *m.pl.*

debt [det] *n.* долг (-а(у), *loc.* -ý; *pl.* -и́). **debtor** *n.* должни́к (-á)

debunk [di:'bʌŋk] *v.t.* развéнчивать *impf.*, развенча́ть *pf.*

début ['deɪbju:, -bu:] *n.* дебю́т; **make one's** ~ дебюти́ровать *impf.* & *pf.* **debutante** *n.* дебюта́нтка.

deca- *in comb.* дека..., десяти... .

decade ['dekeɪd] *n.* десятилéтие.

decadence ['dekəd(ə)ns] *n.* декадéнтство; упа́дочничество. **decadent** *adj.* декадéнтский; упа́дочный.

decaffeinated [di:'kæfɪˌneɪtɪd] *adj.*: ~ **coffee** бескофеи́новый ко́фе.

decamp [dɪ'kæmp] *v.i.* удира́ть *impf.*, удра́ть (удеру́, -рёшь; удра́л, -á, -о) *pf.*

decant [dɪ'kænt] *v.t.* сцéживать *impf.*, сцеди́ть (-ежу́, -éдишь) *pf.*; (*wine*) перелива́ть *impf.*, перели́ть (-лью́, -льёшь; перели́л, -á, -о) *pf.* (в графи́н). **decanter** *n.* графи́н.

decapitate [dɪ'kæpɪteɪt] *v.t.* обезгла́вливать *impf.*, обезгла́вить *pf.*

decarbonize [di:'kɑ:bənaɪz] *v.t.* очища́ть *impf.*, очи́стить *pf.* от нага́ра.

decathlon [dɪ'kæθlən] *n.* десятибо́рье.

decay [dɪ'keɪ] *v.i.* гнить (-ию́, -иёшь; гнил, -á, -о) *impf.*, с~ *pf.*; *n.* гниéние; распа́д (*also physical*). **decayed** *adj.* прогни́вший, гнило́й (гнил, -á, -о). **decaying** *adj.* гнию́щий.

decease [dɪ'si:s] *n.* кончи́на. **deceased** *adj.* поко́йный; *n.* поко́йник (sb.), поко́йник, -ица.

deceit [dɪ'si:t] *n.* обма́н. **deceitful** *adj.* лжи́вый. **deceive** *v.t.* обма́нывать *impf.*, обману́ть (-ну́, -нешь) *pf.*

deceleration [di:ˌseləˈreɪʃ(ə)n] *n.* замедлéние.

December [dɪ'sembə(r)] *n.* декáбрь (-ря́) *m.*; *attr.* декáбрьский.

decency ['di:sənsɪ] *n.* прили́чие, поря́дочность. **decent** *adj.* прили́чный, поря́дочный.

decentralization [di:ˌsentrəlaɪˈzeɪʃ(ə)n] *n.* децентрализáция. **de'centralize** *v.t.* децентрализовáть *impf.* & *pf.*

deception [dɪ'sepʃ(ə)n] *n.* обмáн. **deceptive** *adj.* обмáнчивый.

deci- [desɪ-] *in comb.* деци... .

decibel ['desɪbel] *n.* децибéл.

decide [dɪ'saɪd] *v.t.* решáть *impf.*, реши́ть *pf.* **decided** *adj.* (*resolute*) реши́тельный; (*definite*) несомнéнный (-нен, -нна). **decidedly** *adv.* реши́тельно, бесспо́рно, я́вно.

deciduous [dɪ'sɪdjʊəs] *adj.* листопáдный.

decimal ['desɪm(ə)l] *n.* десяти́чная дробь (*pl.* -би, -бéй); *adj.* десяти́чный; ~ **point** запятáя sb.

decimate ['desɪˌmeɪt] *v.t.* (*fig.*) коси́ть (-ит) *impf.*, с~ *pf.*

decipher [dɪ'saɪfə(r)] *v.t.* расшифро́вывать *impf.*, расшифровáть *pf.*

decision [dɪ'sɪʒ(ə)n] *n.* решéние. **decisive** [dɪ'saɪsɪv] *adj.* решáющий, реши́тельный.

deck [dek] *n.* пáлуба; (*bus etc.*) этáж (-á); *v.t.*: ~ **out** украшáть *impf.*, укрáсить *pf.* **deck-chair** *n.* шезло́нг. **deck-hand** *n.* пáлубный матро́с. **deckhouse** *n.* рýбка.

declaim [dɪ'kleɪm] *v.t.* декламúровать *impf.*, про~ *pf.*

declaration [ˌdeklə'reɪʃ(ə)n] *n.* объявлéние; (*document*) деклара́ция. **de'clare** *v.t.* за~, объ-, явля́ть *impf.*, за~, объ-, яви́ть (-влю́, -вишь) *pf.*

declassify [di:'klæsɪfaɪ] *v.t.* рассекре́чивать *impf.*, рассекре́чить *pf.*

declension [dɪ'klenʃ(ə)n] *n.* склоне́ние. **decline** [dɪ'klaɪn] *n.* упа́док (-дка); (*price*) пониже́ние; *v.i.* приходи́ть (-ит) *impf.*, прийти́ (придёт; пришёл, -шла́) *pf.* в упа́док; *v.t.* (*refuse*) отклоня́ть *impf.*, отклони́ть (-ню́, -нишь) *pf.*; (*gram.*) склоня́ть *impf.*, про~ *pf.* **declining** *adj.*: ~ **years** прекло́нный во́зраст.

declivity [dɪ'klɪvɪtɪ] *n.* укло́н.

decoction [dɪ'kɒkʃ(ə)n] *n.* отва́р (-a(y)).

decode [di:'kəʊd] *v.t.* расшифро́вывать *impf.*, расшифрова́ть *pf.*

decompose [,di:kəm'pəʊz] *v.t.* разлага́ть *impf.*, разложи́ть (-жу́, -жишь) *pf.*; *v.i.* распада́ться *impf.*, распа́сться (-адётся; -а́лся) *pf.*; (*rot*) гнить (гнию, -иёшь; гнил, -а́, -о) *impf.*, c~ *pf.*

decompress [,di:kəm'pres] *v.t.* снижа́ть *impf.*, сни́зить *pf.* давле́ние на+*a.* **decompression** [,di:kəm'preʃ(ə)n] *n.* декомпре́ссия.

decontaminate [,di:kən'tæmɪ,neɪt] *v.t.* (*gas*) дегази́ровать *impf.* & *pf.*; (*radioactivity*) дезактиви́ровать *impf.* & *pf.*

decontrol [,di:kən'trəʊl] *v.t.* снима́ть *impf.*, снять (сниму́, -мешь; снял, -а́, -о) *pf.* контро́ль *m.* c+*g.*

decorate ['dekə,reɪt] *v.t.* украша́ть *impf.*, укра́сить *pf.*; (*with medal etc.*) награжда́ть *impf.*, награди́ть *pf.* о́рденом (-на́ми). **deco'ration** *n.* украше́ние, отде́лка; о́рден (*pl.* -á). **decorative** *adj.* декорати́вный. **decorator** *n.* маля́р (-á).

decorous ['dekərəs] *adj.* прили́чный; чи́нный (-нен, -нна́, -нно). **decorum** [dɪ'kɔ:rəm] *n.* прили́чие, деко́рум; (*etiquette*) этике́т.

decoy ['di:kɔɪ, dɪ'kɔɪ] *n.* (*trap*) западня́; (*bait*) прима́нка; *v.t.* за~, при~, прима́нивать *impf.*, за~, при~, мани́ть (-ню́, -нишь) *pf.*

decrease ['di:kri:s] *v.t.* & *i.* уменьша́ть(ся) *impf.*, уме́ньшить(ся) *pf.*; *n.* уменьше́ние, пониже́ние.

decree [dɪ'kri:] *n.* ука́з, декре́т, постановле́ние; *v.t.* постановля́ть *impf.*, постанови́ть (-влю́, -вишь) *pf.*

decrepit [dɪ'krepɪt] *adj.* дря́хлый (дряхл, -á, -о); (*dilapidated*) ве́тхий (ветх, -á, -о). **decrepitude** *n.* дря́хлость; ве́тхость.

dedicate ['dedɪ,keɪt] *v.t.* посвяща́ть *impf.*, посвяти́ть (-ящу́, -яти́шь) *pf.* **dedi'cation** *n.* посвяще́ние.

deduce [dɪ'dju:s] *v.t.* заключа́ть *impf.*, заключи́ть *pf.*; де́лать *impf.*, c~ *pf.* вы́вод.

deduct [dɪ'dʌkt] *v.t.* вычита́ть *impf.*, вы́честь (-чту, -чтешь; -чел, -чла) *pf.* **deduction** *n.* (*amount*) вы́чет; (*deducting*) вычита́ние; (*inference*) вы́вод.

deed [di:d] *n.* посту́пок (-пка); (*heroic*) по́двиг; (*leg.*) акт.

deem [di:m] *v.t.* счита́ть *impf.*, счесть (сочту́, -тёшь; счёл, сочла́) *pf.*+*a.* & *i.*

deep [di:p] *adj.* глубо́кий (-о́к, -ока́, -о́ко́);

(*colour*) тёмный (-мен, -мна́); (*sound*) ни́зкий (-зок, -зка́, -зко, ни́зки́); *n.* мо́ре. **deepen** *v.t.* углубля́ть *impf.*, углуби́ть *pf.*; сгуща́ть *impf.*, сгусти́ть *pf.* **deep-rooted** *adj.* закоренѐлый. **deep-seated** *adj.* укорени́вшийся.

deer [dɪə(r)] *n.* оле́нь *m.* **deerskin** *n.* лоси́на. **deer-stalker** *n.* охо́тничья ша́пка.

deface [dɪ'feɪs] *v.t.* по́ртить *impf.*, ис~ *pf.*; (*erase*) стира́ть *impf.*, стере́ть (сотру́, -рёшь; стёр) *pf.* **defacement** *n.* по́рча; стира́ние.

defamation [,defə'meɪʃ(ə)n, ,di:f-] *n.* диффама́ция, клевета́. **de'famatory** *adj.* дискредити́рующий, позо́рящий. **defame** [dɪ'feɪm] *v.t.* поро́чить *impf.*, o~ *pf.*; позо́рить *impf.*, o~ *pf.*

default [dɪ'fɔ:lt, -'fɒlt] *n.* невыполне́ние обяза́тельств; (*leg.*) нея́вка в суд; *v.i.* не выполня́ть *impf.* обяза́тельств.

defeat [dɪ'fi:t] *n.* пораже́ние; *v.t.* побежда́ть *impf.*, победи́ть (-и́шь) *pf.* **defeatism** *n.* пораже́нчество. **defeatist** *n.* пораже́нец (-нца).

defecate ['defɪ,keɪt] *v.i.* испражня́ться *impf.*, испражни́ться *pf.* **defe'cation** *n.* испражне́ние.

defect ['di:fekt; dɪ'fekt] *n.* дефе́кт, недоста́ток (-тка), изъя́н; *v.i.* дезерти́ровать *impf.* & *pf.* **defection** *n.* дезерти́рство. **defective** *adj.* неиспра́вный, повреждённый (-ён, -ена́); дефе́ктный, с изъя́ном. **defector** *n.* дезерти́р, невозвраще́нец (-нца).

defence [dɪ'fens] *n.* защи́та (*also leg.*, *sport*), оборо́на (*also mil.*); *pl.* (*mil.*) закрепле́ния *nt.pl.* **defenceless** *adj.* беззащи́тный. **defend** *v.t.* защища́ть *impf.*, защити́ть (-ищу́, -ити́шь) *pf.*; обороня́ть *impf.*, оборони́ть *pf.*; (*uphold*) подде́рживать *impf.*, поддержа́ть (-жу́, -жишь) *pf.* **defendant** *n.* подсуди́мый *sb.* **defender** *n.* защи́тник. **defensive** *adj.* оборони́тельный.

defer[1] [dɪ'fɜ:(r)] *v.t.* (*postpone*) отсро́чивать *impf.*, отсро́чить *pf.*

defer[2] [dɪ'fɜ:(r)] *v.i.*: ~ **to** подчиня́ться *impf.*+*d.* **deference** ['defərəns] *n.* уваже́ние, почте́ние. **defe'rential** *adj.* почти́тельный.

defiance [dɪ'faɪəns] *n.* откры́тое неповинове́ние; in ~ of вопреки́+*d.*, напепеко́р+*d.* **defiant** *adj.* вызыва́ющий, непоко́рный.

deficiency [dɪ'fɪʃənsɪ] *n.* нехва́тка, дефици́т. **deficient** *adj.* недоста́точный; (*mentally* ~) слабоу́мный. **deficit** ['defɪsɪt] *n.* дефици́т, недочёт.

defile [dɪ'faɪl] *v.t.* оскверня́ть *impf.*, оскверни́ть *pf.* **defilement** *n.* оскверне́ние, профана́ция.

define [dɪ'faɪn] *v.t.* определя́ть *impf.*, определи́ть *pf.* **definite** ['defɪnɪt] *adj.* определённый (-нен, -нна) **definitely** *adv.* несомне́нно. **defi'nition** *n.* определе́ние. **de'finitive** *adj.* оконча́тельный.

deflate [dɪ'fleɪt] *v.t.* & *i.* спуска́ть *impf.*, спусти́ть (-ущу́, -у́стишь) *pf.*; *v.t.* (*person*) сбива́ть *impf.*, сбить (собью́, -ьёшь) *pf.* спесь c+g.; *v.i.* (*econ.*) проводить (-ожу, -одишь) *impf.*, провести (-еду, -едёшь; -ёл, -ела) *pf.* политику дефляции. **deflation** *n.* дефляция.

deflect [dɪ'flekt] *v.t.* отклонять *impf.*, отклонить (-ню, -нишь) *pf.* **deflection** *n.* отклонение.

defoliate [di:'fəʊlɪ,eɪt] *v.t.* уничтожать *impf.*, уничтожить *pf.* растительность+g. **defoli'ation** *n.* дефолиация.

deforest [di:'fɒrɪst] *v.t.* обезлесивать *impf.*, обезлесить *pf.* **deforest'ation** *n.* обезлесение.

deform [dɪ'fɔ:m] *v.t.* уродовать *impf.*, из~ *pf.*; деформировать *impf.* & *pf.* **deformity** *n.* уродство.

defraud [dɪ'frɔ:d] *v.t.* обманывать *impf.*, обмануть (-ну́, -нешь) *pf.*; ~ of выманивать *impf.*, выманить *pf.*+a. & y+g. (*of person*).

defray [dɪ'freɪ] *v.t.* оплачивать *impf.*, оплатить (-ачу, -атишь) *pf.*

defrost [di:'frɒst] *v.t.* размораживать *impf.*, разморозить *pf.*

deft [deft] *adj.* ловкий (-вок, -вка, -вко, ловки).

defunct [dɪ'fʌŋkt] *adj.* усопший.

defy [dɪ'faɪ] *v.t.* (*challenge*) вызывать *impf.*, вызвать (вызову, -вешь) *pf.*; (*resist*) открыто не повиноваться *impf.*+d.

degeneracy [dɪ'dʒenərəsɪ] *n.* вырождение. **degenerate** *n.* дегенерат, выродок (-дка); *adj.* дегенеративный; *v.i.* вырождаться *impf.*, выродиться *pf.* **degenerative** *adj.* дегенеративный.

degradation [ˌdegrə'deɪʃ(ə)n] *n.* деградация; унижение. **degrade** [dɪ'greɪd] *v.t.* унижать *impf.*, унизить *pf.* **degrading** *adj.* унизительный.

degree [dɪ'gri:] *n.* степень (*pl.* -ни, -ней); (*math.etc.*) градус; (*univ.*) учёная степень (*pl.* -ни, -ней).

dehydrate [di:'haɪdreɪt, ˌdi:haɪ'dreɪt] *v.t.* обезвоживать *impf.*, обезводить *pf.* **dehy'dration** *n.* дегидратация.

deify ['di:ɪˌfaɪ, 'deɪɪ-] *v.t.* обожествлять *impf.*, обожествить *pf.*

deign [deɪn] *v.i.* соизволять *impf.*, соизволить *pf.*

deity ['di:ɪtɪ, 'deɪɪ-] *n.* божество.

dejected [dɪ'dʒektɪd] *adj.* удручённый (-ён, -ённа & -ена), унылый. **dejection** *n.* уныние.

delay [dɪ'leɪ] *n.* задержка; замедление; without ~ немедленно; *v.t.* задерживать *impf.*, задержать (-жу, -жишь) *pf.*; замедлять *impf.*, замедлить *pf.*

delegate ['delɪgət] *n.* делегат; *v.t.* делегировать *impf.* & *pf.* **dele'gation** *n.* делегация.

delete [dɪ'li:t] *v.t.* вычёркивать *impf.*, вычеркнуть *pf.*

deliberate [dɪ'lɪbərət; dɪ'lɪbə,reɪt] *adj.* (*intentional*) преднамеренный (-ен, -енна); (*unhurried*) неторопливый; *v.t.* & *i.* размыш-

лять *impf.*, размыслить *pf.* (o+p.). **delibe'ration** *n.* размышление; (*discussion*) обсуждение, совещание.

delicacy ['delɪkəsɪ] *n.* (*tact*) деликатность; (*dainty*) лакомство. **delicate** *adj.* тонкий (-нок, -нка, -нко, тонки); лёгкий (лёгок, -гка, -гко, лёгки); (*health*) болезненный (-ен, -енна).

delicious [dɪ'lɪʃəs] *adj.* восхитительный; (*tasty*) очень вкусный (-сен, -сна, -сно).

delight [dɪ'laɪt] *n.* наслаждение, прелесть. **delightful** *adj.* прелестный.

delimit [dɪ'lɪmɪt] *v.t.* размежёвывать *impf.*, размежевать (-жую, -жуешь) *pf.* **delimi'tation** *n.* размежевание.

delinquency [dɪ'lɪŋkwənsɪ] *n.* правонарушение, преступность. **delinquent** *n.* правонарушитель *m.*, -ница.

delirious [dɪ'lɪrɪəs] *adj.* бредовой; be ~ бредить *impf.* **delirium** *n.* бред (-а(у), *loc.* -ý); ~ tremens белая горячка.

deliver [dɪ'lɪvə(r)] *v.t.* доставлять *impf.*, доставить *pf.*; (*rescue*) избавлять *impf.*, избавить *pf.* (from от+g.); (*lecture*) прочитать *impf.*, прочесть (-чту, -чтёшь; -чёл, -чла) *pf.*; (*letters*) разносить (-ошу, -осишь) *impf.*, разнести (-есу, -есёшь; -ёс, -есла) *pf.*; (*speech*) произносить (-ошу, -осишь) *impf.*, произнести (-есу, -есёшь; -ёс, -есла) *pf.* **deliverance** *n.* избавление, освобождение. **delivery** *n.* доставка.

dell [del] *n.* лощина.

delphinium [del'fɪnɪəm] *n.* дельфиниум.

delta ['deltə] *n.* дельта.

delude [dɪ'lu:d, -'lju:d] *v.t.* вводить (-ожу, -одишь) *impf.*, ввести (-еду, -едёшь; ввёл, -á) *pf.* в заблуждение.

deluge ['delju:dʒ] *n.* (*flood*) потоп; (*rain*) ливень (-вня) *m.*

delusion [dɪ'lu:ʒ(ə)n, -'lju:ʒ(ə)n] *n.* заблуждение; ~s of grandeur мания величия.

demagogue ['demə,gɒg] *n.* демагог. **dema'gogic** *adj.* демагогический. **demagogy** *n.* демагогия.

demand [dɪ'mɑ:nd] *n.* требование; (*econ.*) спрос (for на+a.); *v.t.* требовать *impf.*, по~ *pf.*+g.

demarcate ['di:mɑ:ˌkeɪt] *v.t.* разграничивать *impf.*, разграничить *pf.* **demar'cation** *n.* демаркация; line of ~ демаркационная линия.

demented [dɪ'mentɪd] *adj.* умалишённый (-ён, -ённа). **dementia** *n.* слабоумие.

demi- [demɪ-] *in comb.* полу... .

demigod ['demɪˌgɒd] *n.* полубог (*pl.* -и, -ов).

demilitarization [di:ˌmɪlɪtərər'zeɪʃ(ə)n] *n.* демилитаризация. **de'militarize** *v.t.* демилитаризовать *impf.* & *pf.*

demise [dɪ'maɪz] *n.* кончина.

demobbed [di:'mɒbd] *adj.* демобилизованный (-ан). **demobilization** [di:ˌməʊbɪlaɪ'zeɪʃ(ə)n] *n.* демобилизация. **de'mobilize** *v.t.* демобилизовать *impf.* & *pf.*

democracy [dɪ'mɒkrəsɪ] *n.* демокра́тия. **demo-crat** ['deməˌkræt] *n.* демокра́т. **democratic** *adj.* демократи́ческий, демократи́чный.

demolish [dɪ'mɒlɪʃ] *v.t.* разруша́ть *impf.*, разру́шить *pf.*; (*building*) сноси́ть (-ошу́, -о́сишь) *impf.*, снести́ (-су́, -сёшь; снёс, -ла́) *pf.*; (*refute*) опроверга́ть *impf.*, опрове́ргнуть (-ве́рг(нул), -ве́ргла) *pf.* **demo'lition** *n.* разруше́ние, снос.

demon ['di:mən] *n.* де́мон. **de'monic** *adj.* дья́вольский, демони́ческий.

demonstrable ['demɒnstrəb(ə)l, dɪ'mɒnstrəb(ə)l] *adj.* дока́зуемый. **demonstrably** *adv.* очеви́дно, нагля́дно. **demonstrate** *v.t.* демонстри́ровать *impf.* & *pf.*; *v.i.* уча́ствовать *impf.* в демонстра́ции. **demon'stration** *n.* демонстра́ция, пока́з. **de'monstrative** *adj.* (*behaviour etc.*) экспанси́вный, несде́ржанный (-ан, -анна); (*gram.*) указа́тельный. **demonstrator** *n.* (*laboratory*) демонстра́тор; (*pol.*) демонстра́нт.

demoralization [dɪˌmɒrəlaɪ'zeɪʃ(ə)n] *n.* демо-рализа́ция. **de'moralize** *v.t.* деморализова́ть *impf.* & *pf.*

demote [dɪ'məʊt, di:-] *v.t.* понижа́ть *impf.*, пони́зить *pf.* в до́лжности; (*mil.*) разжа́ловать *pf.* **demotion** *n.* пониже́ние.

demur [dɪ'mɜː(r)] *v.i.* возража́ть *impf.*, возрази́ть *pf.* (**at, to** про́тив+*g.*); *n.*: **without ~** без возраже́ний.

demure [dɪ'mjʊə(r)] *adj.* (притво́рно) скро́мный (-мен, -мна́, -мно).

den [den] *n.* (*animal's*) ло́гово, берло́га; (*thieves' etc.*) прито́н.

denial [dɪ'naɪəl] *n.* отрица́ние, опроверже́ние; (*refusal*) отка́з.

denigrate ['denɪˌgreɪt] *v.t.* черни́ть *impf.*, о~ *pf.*

denim ['denɪm] *adj.* джи́нсовый.

Denmark ['denmaːk] *n.* Да́ния.

denomination [dɪˌnɒmɪ'neɪʃ(ə)n] *n.* (*name*) назва́ние; (*category*) катего́рия; (*relig.*) вероиспове́дание. **de'nominator** *n.* знаме-на́тель *m.*

denote [dɪ'nəʊt] *v.t.* означа́ть *impf.*, озна́чить *pf.*

dénouement [deɪ'nuːmã] *n.* развя́зка.

denounce [dɪ'naʊns] *v.t.* (*accuse*) облича́ть *impf.*, обличи́ть *pf.*; (*inform on*) доноси́ть (-ошу́, -о́сишь) *impf.*, донести́ (-есу́, -есёшь; -ёс, -если́) *pf.* на+*a.*; (*treaty*) денонси́ровать *impf.* & *pf.*

dense [dens] *adj.* (*thick*) густо́й (густ, -а́, -о, гу́сты́); (*stupid*) тупо́й (туп, -а́, -о, ту́пы́). **density** *n.* (*phys. etc.*) пло́тность.

dent [dent] *n.* вы́боина, вмя́тина; *v.t.* вмина́ть *impf.*, вмять (вомну́, -нёшь) *pf.*

dental ['dent(ə)l] *adj.* зубно́й. **dentifrice** ['dentɪfrɪs] *n.* (*paste*) зубна́я па́ста; (*powder*) зубно́й порошо́к (-шка́). **dentist** *n.* зубно́й врач (-а́). **dentistry** *n.* зубоврачева́ние. **denture** *n.* зубно́й проте́з.

denunciation [dɪˌnʌnsɪ'eɪʃ(ə)n *n.* (*accusation*)

обличе́ние; (*informing*) доно́с; (*treaty*) денонса́ция.

deny [dɪ'naɪ] *v.t.* отрица́ть *impf.*; **~ o.s.** отка́зывать *impf.*, отказа́ть (-ажу́, -а́жешь) *pf.* себе́ в+*p.*

deodorant [di:'əʊdərənt] *n.* дезодора́нт.

depart [dɪ'paːt] *v.i.* отбыва́ть *impf.*, отбы́ть (отбу́ду, -дешь; о́тбы́л, -а́, -о) *pf.*; **~ from** отклоня́ться *impf.*, отклони́ться (-ню́сь, -нишься) *pf.* от+*g.*

department [dɪ'paːtmənt] *n.* отде́л; (*government*) департа́мент, ве́домство; (*univ.*) факульте́т, ка́федра; **~ store** универма́г. **depart'mental** *adj.* ве́домственный.

departure [dɪ'paːtʃə(r)] *n.* отбы́тие; отклоне́ние.

depend [dɪ'pend] *v.i.* зави́сеть (-и́шу, -и́сишь) *impf.* (**on** от+*g.*); (*rely*) полага́ться *impf.*, положи́ться (-жу́сь, -жишься) *pf.* (**on** на+*a.*). **dependable** *adj.* надёжный. **dependant** *n.* иждиве́нец (-нца); *pl.* семья́ и дома́шние *sb.* **dependence** *n.* зави́симость. **dependent** *adj.* зави́симый, зави́сящий.

depict [dɪ'pɪkt] *v.t.* изобража́ть *impf.*, изобрази́ть *pf.*; (*in words*) опи́сывать *impf.*, описа́ть (-ишу́, -и́шешь) *pf.*

deplete [dɪ'pliːt] *v.t.* истоща́ть *impf.*, истощи́ть *pf.* **depleted** *adj.* истощённый (-ён, -ённа). **depletion** *n.* истоще́ние.

deplorable [dɪ'plɔːrəb(ə)l] *adj.* приско́рбный, плаче́вный. **deplore** *v.t.* сожале́ть *impf.* о+*p.*

deploy [dɪ'plɔɪ] *v.t.* & *i.* развёртывать(ся) *impf.*, разверну́ть(ся) *pf.* **deployment** *n.* развёртывание.

depopulate [di:'pɒpjʊˌleɪt] *v.t.* истребля́ть *impf.*, истреби́ть *pf.* населе́ние+*g.*

deport [dɪ'pɔːt] *v.t.* высыла́ть *impf.*, вы́слать (вы́шлю, вы́шлешь) *pf.*; (*internal exile*) ссыла́ть *impf.*, сосла́ть (сошлю́, -лёшь) *pf.* **depor'tation** *n.* вы́сылка; ссы́лка. **depor'tee** *n.* высыла́емый *sb.*; ссы́льный *sb.*

deportment [dɪ'pɔːtmənt] *n.* поведе́ние, оса́нка.

depose [dɪ'pəʊz] *v.t.* сверга́ть *impf.*, све́ргнуть (-г(нул), -гла) *pf.* (с престо́ла); *v.i.* (*leg.*) пока́зывать *impf.*, показа́ть (-ажу́, -а́жешь) *pf.* **deposit** [dɪ'pɒzɪt] *n.* (*econ.*) вклад; (*pledge*) взнос; (*sediment*) оса́док (-дка) (*coal etc.*) месторожде́ние; *v.t.* (*econ.*) вноси́ть (-ошу́, -о́сишь) *impf.*, внести́ (-есу́, -есёшь; -ёс, -если́) *pf.*; (*geol.*) отлага́ть *impf.*, отложи́ть (-жу́, -жишь) *pf.* **deposition** [ˌdiːpə'zɪʃ(ə)n, ˌdep-] *n.* сверже́ние (с престо́ла); (*leg.*) показа́ние; (*geol.*) отложе́ние. **depositor** *n.* вкла́дчик. **depository** *n.* храни́лище.

depot ['depəʊ] *n.* склад; депо́ *nt.indecl.*; **~ ship** су́дно-ба́за (*pl.* суда́-ба́зы, судо́в-баз).

deprave [dɪ'preɪv] *v.t.* развраща́ть *impf.*, разврати́ть (-ащу́, -ати́шь) *pf.* **depraved** *adj.* развращённый (-ён, -ённа). **depravity** [dɪ'prævɪtɪ] *n.* развра́т.

deprecate ['deprɪ,keɪt] *v.t.* возража́ть *impf.*, возрази́ть *pf.* про́тив+*g.* **depre'cation** *n.* неодобре́ние.

depreciate [dɪ'priːʃɪ,eɪt, -sɪ,eɪt] *v.t. & i.* обесце́нивать(ся) *impf.*, обесце́нить(ся) *pf.* **depreci'ation** *n.* обесце́нение. **de'preciatory** *adj.* обесце́нивающий.

depress [dɪ'pres] *v.t.* (*lower*) понижа́ть *impf.*, пони́зить *pf.*; (*dispirit*) удруча́ть *impf.*, удручи́ть *pf.* **depressed** *adj.* удручённый (-ён, -ённа & -ена́) **depressing** *adj.* нагоня́ющий тоску́. **depression** *n.* (*hollow*) впа́дина; (*econ., med., meteor., etc.*) депре́ссия.

deprivation [,deprɪ'veɪʃ(ə)n, ,diːpraɪ-] *n.* лише́ние. **deprive** [dɪ'praɪv] *v.t.* лиша́ть *impf.*, лиши́ть *pf.* (**of** +*g.*)

depth [depθ] *n.* глубина́ (*pl.* -ны); ~ **of feeling** си́ла пережива́ния; ~**s of the country** глушь (-ши́); **in the ~ of winter** в разга́ре зимы́. **depth-bomb, depth-charge** *n.* глуби́нная бо́мба.

deputation [,depjʊ'teɪʃ(ə)n] *n.* делега́ция, депута́ция. **depute** [dɪ'pjuːt] *v.t.* делеги́ровать *impf. & pf.* **'deputize** *v.i.* замеща́ть *impf.*, замести́ть *pf.* (**for** +*a.*). **'deputy** *n.* замести́тель *m.*; помо́щник, -ица; (*parl.*) депута́т.

derail [dɪ'reɪl, diː-] *v.t.* спуска́ть *impf.*, спусти́ть (-ущу́, -у́стишь) *pf.* под отко́с; **be derailed** сходи́ть (-ожу́, -о́дишь) *impf.*, сойти́ (сойду́, -дёшь; сошёл, -шла́) *pf.* с ре́льсов. **derailment** *n.* круше́ние, сход с ре́льсов.

derange [dɪ'reɪndʒ] *v.t.* расстра́ивать *impf.*, расстро́ить *pf.* **deranged** *adj.* (*mentally*) душевнобольно́й, ненорма́льный. **derangement** *n.* (психи́ческое) расстро́йство.

derelict ['derəlɪkt, 'derɪ-] *adj.* бро́шенный (-шен). **dere'liction** *n.* упуще́ние; (*of duty*) наруше́ние до́лга.

deride [dɪ'raɪd] *v.t.* высме́ивать *impf.*, вы́смеять (-ею, -еешь) *pf.* **derision** [dɪ'rɪʒ(ə)n] *n.* высме́ивание; **object of** ~ посме́шище. **derisive** *adj.* (*mocking*) насме́шливый. **derisory** *adj.* (*ridiculous*) смехотво́рный.

derivation [,derɪ'veɪʃ(ə)n] *n.* происхожде́ние. **de'rivative** *n.* произво́дное *sb.*; *adj.* произво́дный. **derive** [dɪ'raɪv] *v.t.* извлека́ть *impf.*, извле́чь (-еку́, -ечёшь; -ёк, -екла́) *pf.*; *v.i.*: ~ **from** происходи́ть (-ожу́, -о́дишь) *impf.*, произойти́ (-ойду́, -ойдёшь; -ошёл, -ошла́) *pf.* от+*g.*

dermatitis [,dɜːmə'taɪtɪs] *n.* дермати́т.

derogatory [dɪ'rɒgətərɪ] *adj.* умаля́ющий, унижа́ющий.

derrick ['derɪk] *n.* де́ррик; (*oil-well etc.*) бурова́я вы́шка.

dervish ['dɜːvɪʃ] *n.* де́рви́ш.

descend [dɪ'send] *v.t.* спуска́ться *impf.*, спусти́ться (-ущу́сь, -у́стишься) *pf.* c+*g.*; сходи́ть (-ожу́, -о́дишь) *impf.*, сойти́ (сойду́, -дёшь; сошёл, -шла́) *pf.* c+*g.*; *v.i.* (*go down*) спуска́ться *impf.*, спусти́ться (-ущу́сь, -у́стишься) *pf.*; (*sink*) понижа́ться *impf.*, по-

ни́зиться *pf.*; ~ **on** (*attack*) обру́шиваться *impf.*, обру́шиться *pf.* на+*a.*; ~ **to** (*property; to details etc.*) переходи́ть (-ожу́, -о́дишь) *impf.*, перейти́ (-йду́, -йдёшь; перешёл, -шла́) *pf.* к+*d.*; **be descended from** происходи́ть (-ожу́, -о́дишь) *impf.*, произойти́ (-ойду́, -ойдёшь; -ошёл, -ошла́) *pf.* из, от, +*g.* **descendant** *n.* пото́мок (-мка). **descent** *n.* спуск; (*sinking*) пониже́ние; (*lineage*) происхожде́ние; (*property*) насле́дование.

describe [dɪ'skraɪb] *v.t.* опи́сывать *impf.*, описа́ть (-ишу́, -и́шешь) *pf.* **description** [dɪ'skrɪpʃ(ə)n] *n.* описа́ние. **descriptive** *adj.* описа́тельный.

descry [dɪ'skraɪ] *v.t.* различа́ть *impf.*, различи́ть *pf.*

desecrate ['desɪ,kreɪt] *v.t.* оскверня́ть *impf.*, оскверни́ть *pf.* **dese'cration** *n.* оскверне́ние, профана́ция.

desert[1] ['dezet] *n.* (*wilderness*) пусты́ня; *adj.* пусты́нный (-нен, -нна).

desert[2] [dɪ'zɜːt] *v.t.* покида́ть *impf.*, поки́нуть *pf.*; (*mil.*) дезерти́ровать *impf. & pf.* **deserter** *n.* дезерти́р. **desertion** *n.* дезерти́рство.

desert[3] [dɪ'zɜːt] *n.*: *pl.* заслу́ги *f.pl.* **deserve** *v.t.* заслу́живать *impf.*, заслужи́ть (-жу́, -жишь) *pf.* **deserving** *adj.* заслу́живающий (**of** +*g.*). досто́йный (-о́ин, -о́йна) (**of** +*g.*).

desiccated ['desɪ,keɪtɪd] *adj.* сушёный.

design [dɪ'zaɪn] *n.* (*scheme*) за́мысел (-сла); (*sketch*) рису́нок (-нка); (*model*) констру́кция, прое́кт; **school of** ~ шко́ла изобрази́тельных иску́сств; *v.t.* конструи́ровать *impf.*, c~ *pf.*; создава́ть (-даю́, -даёшь) *impf.*, созда́ть (-а́м, -а́шь, -а́ст, -ади́м; со́зда́л, -а́, -о) *pf.*

designate ['dezɪgnət; 'dezɪg,neɪt] *adj.* назна́ченный (-чен); *v.t.* обознача́ть *impf.*, обозна́чить *pf.*; (*appoint*) назнача́ть *impf.*, назна́чить *pf.* **desig'nation** *n.* обозначе́ние, назва́ние.

designer [dɪ'zaɪnə(r)] *n.* констру́ктор, проекти́ровщик, диза́йнер; (*of clothes*) моделье́р.

desirable [dɪ'zaɪərəb(ə)l] *adj.* жела́тельный. **desire** *n.* жела́ние; *v.t.* жела́ть *impf.*, по~ *pf.*+*g.* **desirous** *adj.* жела́ющий.

desist [dɪ'zɪst] *v.i.* перестава́ть (-таю́, -таёшь) *impf.*, переста́ть (-а́ну, -а́нешь) *pf.*

desk [desk] *n.* пи́сьменный стол (-а́); конто́рка; (*school*) па́рта.

desolate ['desələt] *adj.* (*deserted*) поки́нутый; (*dreary*) уны́лый. **desolation** [,desə'leɪʃ(ə)n] *n.* запусте́ние.

despair [dɪ'speə(r)] *n.* отча́яние; *v.i.* отча́иваться *impf.*, отча́яться (-а́юсь, -а́ешься) *pf.* **despairing** *adj.* отча́янный (-ян, -янна). **desperado** [,despə'rɑːdəʊ] *n.* сорвиголова́ (*pl.* -овы, -о́в, -ова́м). **desperate** ['despərət] *adj.* отча́янный (-ян, -янна). **despe'ration** *n.* отча́яние.

despatch *see* **dispatch**

despicable ['despɪkəb(ə)l, dɪ'spɪk-] *adj.* презре́нный (-ён, -е́нна), жа́лкий (-лок, -лка́, -лко). **despise** [dɪ'spaɪz] *v.t.* презира́ть *impf.*, презре́ть (-рю́, -ри́шь) *pf.*

despite [dɪ'spaɪt] *prep.* вопреки́+d., несмотря́ на+a.

despondency [dɪ'spɒndənsɪ] *n.* уны́ние, пода́вленность. **despondent** *adj.* уны́лый.

despot ['despɒt] *n.* де́спот. **de'spotic** *adj.* деспоти́ческий, деспоти́чный. **despotism** *n.* деспоти́зм, деспоти́чность.

dessert [dɪ'zɜːt] *n.* десе́рт; сла́дкое *sb.*

destination [ˌdestɪ'neɪʃ(ə)n] *n.* ме́сто (*pl.* -та́) назначе́ния, цель. **'destiny** *n.* судьба́, у́часть.

destitute ['destɪˌtjuːt] *adj.* си́льно нужда́ющийся; без вся́ких средств. **desti'tution** *n.* нищета́, нужда́.

destroy [dɪ'strɔɪ] *v.t.* уничтожа́ть *impf.*, уничто́жить *pf.*; губи́ть (-блю́, -бишь) *impf.*, по~ *pf.* **destroyer** *n.* (*naut.*) эсми́нец (-нца). **destruction** [dɪ'strʌkʃ(ə)n] *n.* разруше́ние, уничтоже́ние. **destructive** *adj.* разруши́тельный, уничтожа́ющий.

desultory ['dezəltərɪ] *adj.* беспоря́дочный.

detach [dɪ'tætʃ] *v.t.* отделя́ть *impf.*, отдели́ть *pf.* **detachable** *adj.* съёмный, отделя́емый. **detached** *adj.* отде́льный; ~ **house** особня́к (-а́). **detachment** *n.* отделе́ние, разъедине́ние; (*mil.*) отря́д.

detail ['diːteɪl] *n.* дета́ль, подро́бность; (*mil.*) наря́д; **in detail** подро́бно; *v.t.* подро́бно расска́зывать *impf.*, рассказа́ть (-ажу́, -а́жешь) *pf.*; выделя́ть *impf.*, вы́делить *pf.*; назнача́ть *impf.*, назна́чить *pf.* в наря́д; ~ **for guard duty** назна́чить *pf.* в карау́л. **detailed** *adj.* дета́льный, подро́бный.

detain [dɪ'teɪn] *v.t.* заде́рживать *impf.*, задержа́ть (-жу́, -жишь) *pf.*; аресто́вывать *impf.*, арестова́ть *pf.* **detai'nee** *n.* аресто́ванный *sb.*, (челове́к) под стра́жей.

detect [dɪ'tekt] *v.t.* обнару́живать *impf.*, обнару́жить *pf.* **detection** *n.* обнаруже́ние, рассле́дование. **detective** *n.* сы́щик, детекти́в; *adj.* сыскно́й, детекти́вный; ~ **film, story,** *etc.* детекти́в. **detector** *n.* дете́ктор, обнаружи́тель *m.*

détente [deɪ'tɑːt] *n.* разря́дка.

detention [dɪ'tenʃ(ə)n] *n.* задержа́ние, аре́ст.

deter [dɪ'tɜː(r)] *v.t.* уде́рживать *impf.*, удержа́ть (-жу́, -жишь) *pf.* (**from** от+g.).

detergent [dɪ'tɜːdʒ(ə)nt] *n.* мо́ющее сре́дство; *adj.* мо́ющий, очища́ющий.

deteriorate [dɪ'tɪərɪəˌreɪt] *v.i.* ухудша́ться *impf.*, уху́дшиться *pf.* **deterio'ration** *n.* ухудше́ние.

determination [dɪˌtɜːmɪ'neɪʃ(ə)n] *n.* (*resoluteness*) реши́тельность, реши́мость. **de'termine** *v.t.* устана́вливать *impf.*, установи́ть (-влю́, -вишь) *pf.*; определя́ть *impf.*, определи́ть *pf.* **de'termined** *adj.* (*resolute*) реши́тельный.

deterrent [dɪ'terənt] *n.* уде́рживающее сре́д-

ство, сре́дство устраше́ния; *adj.* сде́рживающий, уде́рживающий.

detest [dɪ'test] *v.t.* ненави́деть (-и́жу, -и́дишь) *impf.* **detestable** *adj.* отврати́тельный. **dete'station** *n.* отвраще́ние, не́нависть.

dethrone [diː'θrəʊn] *v.t.* сверга́ть *impf.*, све́ргнуть (-г(нул), -гла) *pf.* с престо́ла; разве́нчивать *impf.*, развенча́ть *pf.* **dethronement** *n.* сверже́ние с престо́ла; развенча́ние.

detonate ['detəˌneɪt] *v.t. & i.* взрыва́ть(ся) *impf.*, взорва́ть(ся) (-ву́, -вёт(ся); взорва́л(ся), -а́(сь), -о/-а́лось) *pf.* **deto'nation** *n.* детона́ция, взрыв. **detonator** *n.* детона́тор.

detour ['diːtʊə(r)] *n.* обхо́д, объе́зд.

detract [dɪ'trækt] *v.i.*: ~ **from** умаля́ть *impf.*, умали́ть *pf.*+a.

detriment ['detrɪmənt] *n.* уще́рб, вред (-а́). **detri'mental** *adj.* вре́дный (-ден, -дна́, -дно), па́губный.

detritus [dɪ'traɪtəs] *n.* детри́т.

deuce [djuːs] *n.* (*tennis*) ра́вный счёт.

devaluation [diːˌvæljuː'eɪʃ(ə)n] *n.* девальва́ция. **de'value** *v.t.* проводи́ть (-ожу́, -о́дишь) *impf.*, провести́ (-еду́, -едёшь; -ёл, -ела́) *pf.* девальва́цию+g.

devastate ['devəˌsteɪt] *v.t.* опустоша́ть *impf.*, опустоши́ть *pf.* **deva'station** *n.* опустоше́ние.

develop [dɪ'veləp] *v.t. & i.* развива́ть(ся) *impf.*, разви́ть(ся) (разовью́(сь), -вьёшь(ся); разви́л(ся), -а́(сь), -о/-и́лось) *pf.*; *v.t.* (*phot.*) проявля́ть *impf.*, прояви́ть (-влю́, -вишь) *pf.*; (*natural resources*) разраба́тывать *impf.*, разрабо́тать *pf.* **developer** *n.* (*of land etc.*) застро́йщик но́вого райо́на; (*phot.*) прояви́тель *m.* **development** *n.* разви́тие; (*phot.*) проявле́ние.

deviate ['diːvɪˌeɪt] *v.i.* отклоня́ться *impf.*, отклони́ться (-ню́сь, -нишься) *pf.* (**from** от+g.). **devi'ation** *n.* отклоне́ние; (*pol.*) укло́н.

device [dɪ'vaɪs] *n.* устро́йство, прибо́р.

devil ['dev(ə)l] *n.* дья́вол, чёрт (*pl.* че́рти, -те́й), бес. **devilish** *adj.* дья́вольский, чёртовский. **devil-may-care** *adj.* бесшаба́шный.

devious ['diːvɪəs] *adj.* (*indirect*) непрямо́й (-м, -ма́, -мо); (*person*) хи́трый (-тёр, -тра́, хитро́).

devise [dɪ'vaɪz] *v.t.* приду́мывать *impf.*, приду́мать *pf.*

devoid [dɪ'vɔɪd] *adj.* лишённый (-ён, -ена́) (**of**+g.).

devolution [ˌdiːvə'luːʃ(ə)n, -'ljuːʃ(ə)n] *n.* переда́ча; перехо́д. **devolve** [dɪ'vɒlv] *v.t.* передава́ть (-даю́, -даёшь) *impf.*, переда́ть (-а́м, -а́шь, -а́ст, -ади́м; пе́редал, -а́, -о) *pf.*; *v.i.* переходи́ть (-ожу́, -о́дишь) *impf.*, перейти́ (-йду́, -йдёшь; перешёл, -шла́) *pf.*

devote [dɪ'vəʊt] *v.t.* посвяща́ть *impf.*, посвяти́ть (-ящу́, -яти́шь) *pf.* **devoted** *adj.* пре́данный (-ан). **devotion** *n.* пре́данность, приве́рженность; *pl.* религио́зные обя́занности *f.pl.* **devotional** *adj.* религиóзный.

devour [dɪ'vaʊə(r)] *v.t.* пожирáть *impf.*, пожрáть (-рý, -рёшь; пожрáл, -á, -о) *pf.*

devout [dɪ'vaʊt] *adj.* нáбожный, благочестúвый. **devoutness** *n.* нáбожность, благочéстие.

dew [djuː] *n.* росá. **dewdrop** *n.* росúнка. **dewy** *adj.* влáжный (-жен, -жнá, -жно), росúстый.

dexterity [dek'sterɪtɪ] *n.* провóрство, лóвкость; сноровка. **'dext(e)rous** *adj.* провóрный; лóвкий (-вок, -вкá, -вко, лóвкú).

diabetes [ˌdaɪə'biːtiːz] *n.* сáхарная болéзнь, диабéт. **diabetic** [ˌdaɪə'betɪk] *n.* диабéтик; *adj.* диабетúческий.

diabolic(al) [ˌdaɪə'bɒlɪk(l)] *adj.* дья́вольский, звéрский.

diagnose ['daɪəgnəʊz] *v.t.* стáвить *impf.*, по~ *pf.* диáгноз+g. **diag'nosis** *n.* диáгноз.

diagonal [daɪ'ægən(ə)l] *n.* диагонáль; *adj.* диагонáльный. **diagonally** *adv.* по диагонáли.

diagram ['daɪəˌgræm] *n.* диаграмма; чертёж (-á); схéма.

dial ['daɪ(ə)l] *n.* циферблáт; шкалá (*pl.* -лы); (*telephone*) диск нáбора; *v.t.* набирáть *impf.*, набрáть (наберý, -рёшь; набрáл, -á, -о) *pf.*

dialect ['daɪəˌlekt] *n.* диалéкт, нарéчие; *adj.* диалéктный. **dia'lectical** *adj.* диалектúческий.

dialogue ['daɪəˌlɒg] *n.* диалóг.

diameter [daɪ'æmɪtə(r)] *n.* диáметр. **dia'metrical** *adj.* диаметрáльный; ~ly opposed диаметрáльно противополóжный.

diamond ['daɪəmənd] *n.* алмáз, бриллиáнт; (*rhomb*) ромб; (*cards*) бýбна (*pl.* бýбны, бубён, бубнáм); **play a ~** ходúть (хожý, хóдишь) *impf.*, пойтú (пойдý, -дёшь; пошёл, -шлá) *pf.* с бубён; *adj.* алмáзный, бриллиáнтовый; бубнóвый.

diaper ['daɪəpə(r)] *n.* пелёнка.

diaphanous [daɪ'æfənəs] *adj.* прозрáчный.

diaphragm ['daɪəˌfræm] *n.* диафрáгма; мембрáна.

diarrhoea [ˌdaɪə'rɪə] *n.* понóс.

diary ['daɪərɪ] *n.* дневнúк (-á).

diatribe ['daɪəˌtraɪb] *n.* обличúтельная речь (*pl.* -чи, -чéй).

dice *see* **die¹**

dicey ['daɪsɪ] *adj.* рискóванный (-ан, -анна).

dictaphone ['dɪktəˌfəʊn] *n.* диктафóн. **dictate** ['dɪkteɪt; dɪk'teɪt] *n.* велéние; *v.t.* диктовáть *impf.*, про~ *pf.* **dictation** *n.* диктóвка, диктáнт. **dictator** *n.* диктáтор. **dicta'torial** *adj.* диктáторский, повелúтельный. **dictatorship** *n.* диктатýра.

diction ['dɪkʃ(ə)n] *n.* дúкция.

dictionary ['dɪkʃənrɪ, -nərɪ] *n.* словáрь (-ря́) *m.*

dictum ['dɪktəm] *n.* авторитéтное заявлéние; (*maxim*) изречéние.

didactic [daɪ'dæktɪk, dɪ-] *adj.* дидактúческий.

diddle ['dɪd(ə)l] *v.t.* надувáть *impf.*, надýть

(-ýю, -ýешь) *pf.*

die¹ [daɪ] *n.* (*pl.* **dice**) игрáльная кость (*pl.* -ти, -тéй); (*pl.* **dies**) (*stamp*) штамп, штéмпель (*pl.* -ля) *m.*; (*mould*) мáтрица.

die² [daɪ] *v.i.* (*person*) умирáть *impf.*, умерéть (умрý, умрёшь; ýмер, -лá, -ло) *pf.*; (*animal*) дóхнуть (дóх(нул), дóхла) *impf.*, из~, по~ *pf.*; (*plant*) вя́нуть (вя́(ну)л, вя́ла) *impf.*, за~ *pf.*; скончáться *pf.* **die-hard** *adj.* твердолóбый *sb.*

diesel ['diːz(ə)l] *n.* (*engine*) дúзель *m.*; *attr.* дúзельный.

diet ['daɪət] *n.* диéта; (*habitual food*) питáние, стол (-á); *v.i.* соблюдáть *impf.*, соблюстú (-юдý, -юдёшь; -юл, -юлá) *pf.* диéту. **dietary** *adj.* диетúческий. **diet'etics** *n.* диетéтика.

differ ['dɪfə(r)] *v.i.* отличáться *impf.*; различáться *impf.*; (*disagree*) не соглашáться *impf.* **difference** *n.* рáзница; (*disagreement*) разноглáсие. **different** *adj.* разлúчный, рáзный. **diffe'rential** *n.* (*math.*) дифференциáл; рáзница; *adj.* дифференциáльный. **diffe'rentiate** *v.t.* различáть *impf.*, различúть *pf.* **differenti'ation** *n.* различéние; дифференциáция.

difficult ['dɪfɪkəlt] *adj.* трýдный (-ден, -днá, -дно, трýдны), затруднúтельный. **difficulty** *n.* трýдность; затруднéние; **without ~** без трудá.

diffidence ['dɪfɪdəns] *n.* неувéренность в себé. **diffident** *adj.* рóбкий (-бок, -бкá, -бко), неувéренный (-ен) в себé.

diffused [dɪ'fjuːzd] *adj.* рассéянный (-ян, -янна).

dig [dɪg] *n.* (*archaeol.*) раскóпки *f.pl.*; (*poke*) тычóк (-чкá); *pl.* (*lodgings*) квартúра; **give a ~ in the ribs** ткнуть *pf.* лóктем под ребрó; *v.i.* копáть *impf.*, вы́~ *pf.*; рыть (рóю, рóешь) *impf.*, вы́~ *pf.*; (*prod*) ты́кать (ты́чу, -чешь) *impf.*, ткнуть *pf.*

digest ['daɪdʒest; daɪ'dʒest, dɪ-] *n.* (*synopsis*) крáткое изложéние, резюмé *nt.indecl.*; (*collection*) сбóрник резюмé; *v.t.* перевáривать *impf.*, переварúть (-рю́, -ришь) *pf.* **digestible** *adj.* удобоварúмый. **digestion** *n.* пищеварéние. **digestive** *adj.* пищеварúтельный.

digger ['dɪgə(r)] *n.* копáтель *m.*, землекóп. **digging** *n.* копáнье, рытьё; *pl.* земляны́е рабóты *f.pl.*

digit ['dɪdʒɪt] *n.* (*math.*) цúфра, однознáчное числó (*pl.* -сла, -сел, -слам); (*anat.*) пáлец (-льца). **digital** ['dɪdʒɪt(ə)l] *adj.* цифровóй; **~ recording** цифровáя зáпись.

dignified ['dɪgnɪˌfaɪd] *adj.* с чýвством сóбственного достóинства. **dignify** *v.t.* облагорáживать *impf.*, облагорóдить *pf.* **dignitary** *n.* санóвник. **dignity** *n.* достóинство.

digress [daɪ'gres] *v.i.* отклоня́ться *impf.*, отклонúться (-ню́сь, -нúшься) *pf.* (**from** от+g.). **digression** *n.* отступлéние, отклонéние.

dike [daɪk] *n.* насыпь; (*ditch*) ров (рва, *loc.* во рву́).

dilapidated [dɪˈlæpɪˌdeɪtɪd] *adj.* обветша́лый. **dilapi'dation** *n.* (*eccl.*) поврежде́ние.

dilate [daɪˈleɪt] *v.t. & i.* расширя́ть(ся) *impf.*, расши́рить(ся) *pf.*

dilatory ['dɪlətərɪ] *adj.* оття́гивающий.

dilemma [daɪˈlemə, dɪ-] *n.* диле́мма.

dilettante [ˌdɪlɪˈtæntɪ] *n.* дилета́нт; *adj.* дилета́нтский, люби́тельский.

diligence ['dɪlɪdʒ(ə)ns] *n.* прилежа́ние, усе́рдие. **diligent** *adj.* приле́жный, усе́рдный.

dill [dɪl] *n.* укро́п (-a(y)).

dilly-dally [ˌdɪlɪˈdælɪ] *v.i.* ме́шкать *impf.*

dilute [daɪˈljuːt] *v.t.* разбавля́ть *impf.*, разба́вить *pf.*; *adj.* разба́вленный (-ен). **dilution** *n.* разбавле́ние.

dim [dɪm] *adj.* ту́склый (тускл, -á, -о), сму́тный (-тен, -тнá, -тно).

dimension [daɪˈmenʃ(ə)n, dɪ-] *n.* величинá; *pl.* разме́ры *m.pl.*; (*math.*) измере́ние.

diminish [dɪˈmɪnɪʃ] *v.t. & i.* уменьша́ть(ся) *impf.*, уме́ньшить(ся) *pf.* **diminished** *adj.* уме́ньшенный (-ен). **dimi'nution** *n.* уменьше́ние. **diminutive** *adj.* ма́ленький; (*gram.*) уменьши́тельный; *n.* уменьши́тельное *sb.*

dimity ['dɪmɪtɪ] *n.* канифа́с.

dimness ['dɪmnɪs] *n.* ту́склость, полусве́т.

dimple ['dɪmp(ə)l] *n.* я́мочка.

dim-sighted *adj.* недальнови́дный. **dim-witted** *adj.* тупо́й (туп, -á, -о, ту́пы).

din [dɪn] *n.* шум и гам; *v.t.*: ~ **into one's ears** прожужжа́ть (-жу́, -жи́шь) у́ши+*d.*

dine [daɪn] *v.i.* обе́дать *impf.*, по~ *pf.*; *v.t.* угоща́ть *impf.*, угости́ть *pf.* обе́дом. **diner** *n.* обе́дающий *sb.*; (*rail.*) ваго́н(-а)-рестора́н(-а).

ding-dong ['dɪŋdɒŋ] *adj.* череду́ющийся.

dinghy ['dɪŋɪ, 'dɪŋgɪ] *n.* шлю́пка, я́лик.

dingy ['dɪndʒɪ] *adj.* (*drab*) ту́склый (тускл, -á, -о); (*dirty*) гря́зный (-зен, -знá, -зно).

dining-car ['daɪnɪŋ] *n.* ваго́н(-а)-рестора́н(-а). **dining-room** *n.* столо́вая *sb.* **dinner** ['dɪnə(r)] *n.* обе́д. **dinner-hour** *n.* обе́денный переры́в. **dinner-jacket** *n.* смо́кинг. **dinnertime** *n.* обе́денное вре́мя *nt.*

dinosaur ['daɪnəˌsɔː(r)] *n.* диноза́вр.

dint [dɪnt] *n.*: **by** ~ **of** посре́дством+*g.*; с по́мощью+*g.*

diocesan [daɪˈɒsɪs(ə)n] *adj.* епархиа́льный. **diocese** ['daɪəsɪs] *n.* епа́рхия.

diode ['daɪəʊd] *n.* дио́д.

dioxide [daɪˈɒksaɪd] *n.* двуо́кись.

dip [dɪp] *v.t. & i.* окуна́ть(ся) *impf.*, окуну́ть(ся) *pf.*; *v.t.* (*flag*) припуска́ть *impf.*, припусти́ть (-ущу́, -у́стишь) *pf.*; ~ **into** (*book*) перели́стывать *impf.*, перелиста́ть *pf.*; *n.* окуна́ние; (*depression*) впа́дина; (*slope*) укло́н; (*phys., astr.*) наклоне́ние; **have a** ~ (*bathe*) купа́ться *impf.*, вы́~ *pf.*

diphtheria [dɪfˈθɪərɪə] *n.* дифтери́я.

diphthong ['dɪfθɒŋ] *n.* дифто́нг.

diploma [dɪˈpləʊmə] *n.* дипло́м. **diplomacy** *n.* диплома́тия. **'diplomat** *n.* диплома́т. **diplo'matic** *adj.* дипломати́ческий, дипломати́чный; ~ **bag** дипломати́ческая по́чта.

dipper ['dɪpə(r)] *n.* (*ladle*) ковш (-á); (*bird*) оля́пка.

dipsomania [ˌdɪpsəˈmeɪnɪə] *n.* алкоголи́зм.

dire ['daɪə(r)] *adj.* стра́шный (-шен, -шнá, -шно, стра́шны); (*ominous*) злове́щий.

direct [daɪˈrekt, dɪ-] *adj.* прямо́й (прям, -á, -о, пря́мы); непосре́дственный (-ен, -енна); ~ **current** постоя́нный ток (-a(y)); *v.t.* направля́ть *impf.*, напра́вить *pf.*; (*guide, manage*) руководи́ть *impf.*+*i.*; (*film*) режисси́ровать *impf.* **direction** *n.* направле́ние; (*guidance*) руково́дство; (*instruction*) указа́ние; (*film*) режиссу́ра; **stage** ~ рема́рка. **directive** *n.* директи́ва, указа́ние. **directly** *adv.* пря́мо; (*at once*) сра́зу. **director** *n.* дире́ктор (*pl.* -á), член правле́ния; (*film*) режиссёр; **board of directors** правле́ние. **directory** *n.* спра́вочник, указа́тель *m.*; **telephone** ~ телефо́нная кни́га.

dirge [dɜːdʒ] *n.* погреба́льная песнь.

dirt [dɜːt] *n.* грязь (*loc.* -зи́); ~ **cheap** деше́вле па́реной ре́пы; ~ **floor** земляно́й пол (*loc.* -ý; *pl.* -ы́). **dirty** *adj.* гря́зный (-зен, -знá, -зно); (*mean*) по́длый (подл, -á, -о); (*obscene*) непристо́йный; *v.t. & i.* па́чкать(ся) *impf.*, за~ *pf.*

disability [ˌdɪsəˈbɪlɪtɪ] *n.* (*physical*) нетрудоспосо́бность. **disable** [dɪsˈeɪb(ə)l] *v.t.* де́лать *impf.*, с~ *pf.* неспосо́бным; (*cripple*) кале́чить *impf.*, ис~ *pf.* **disabled** *adj.* искале́ченный (-ен); ~ **serviceman** инвали́д войны́. **disablement** *n.* инвали́дность.

disabuse [ˌdɪsəˈbjuːz] *v.t.* выводи́ть (-ожу́, -о́дишь) *impf.*, вы́вести (-еду, -едешь; -ел) *pf.* из заблужде́ния; ~ **of** освобожда́ть *impf.*, освободи́ть *pf.* от+*g.*

disadvantage [ˌdɪsədˈvɑːntɪdʒ] *n.* невы́годное положе́ние; (*defect*) недоста́ток (-тка). **disadvan'tageous** *adj.* невы́годный.

disaffected [ˌdɪsəˈfektɪd] *adj.* недово́льный, нелоя́льный. **disaffection** *n.* недово́льство, нелоя́льность.

disagree [ˌdɪsəˈgriː] *v.i.* не соглаша́ться *impf.*, согласи́ться *pf.*; расходи́ться (-ожу́сь, -о́дишься) *impf.*, разойти́сь (-ойду́сь, -ойдёшься; -ошёлся, -ошла́сь) *pf.* **disagreeable** *adj.* неприя́тный. **disagreement** *n.* расхожде́ние, несогла́сие; (*quarrel*) ссо́ра.

disallow [ˌdɪsəˈlaʊ] *v.t.* отка́зывать *impf.*, отказа́ть (-ажу́, -а́жешь) *pf.* в+*p.*

disappear [ˌdɪsəˈpɪə(r)] *v.i.* исчеза́ть *impf.*, исче́знуть (-ез) *pf.*; пропада́ть *impf.*, пропа́сть (-адý, -адёшь; -áл) *pf.*; скрыва́ться *impf.*, скры́ться (-ро́юсь, -ро́ешься) *pf.* **disappearance** *n.* исчезнове́ние, пропа́жа.

disappoint [ˌdɪsəˈpɔɪnt] *v.t.* разочаро́вывать *impf.*, разочарова́ть *pf.* **disappointed** *adj.* разочаро́ванный (-ан, -ан(н)а). **disappointing** *adj.* вызыва́ющий разочарова́ние. **disappointment** *n.* разочарова́ние; доса́да.

disapproval [ˌdɪsə'pruːvəl] *n.* неодобрение. **disapprove** *v.t.* не одобрять *impf.*

disarm [dɪs'ɑːm] *v.t.* разоружать *impf.*, разоружить *pf.*; обезоруживать *impf.*, обезоружить *pf.* **disarmament** *n.* разоружение.

disarray [ˌdɪsə'reɪ] *n.* беспорядок (-дка), смятение.

disaster [dɪ'zɑːstə(r)] *n.* бедствие, несчастье. **disastrous** *adj.* бедственный (-ен, -енна); гибельный, губительный.

disavow [ˌdɪsə'vaʊ] *v.t.* отрекаться *impf.*, отречься (-екусь, -ечёшься; -ёкся, -еклась) *pf.* от+g.; отрицать *impf.*

disband [dɪs'bænd] *v.t.* распускать *impf.*, распустить (-ущу, -устишь) *pf.*; (*mil.*) расформировывать *impf.*, расформировать *pf.*; *v.i.* расходиться (-ожусь, -одишься) *impf.*, разойтись (-ойдусь, -ойдёшься; -ошёлся, -ошлась) *pf.*

disbelief [ˌdɪsbɪ'liːf] *n.* неверие. **disbelieve** *v.t.* не верить *impf.*+d.

disburse [dɪs'bɜːs] *v.t.* выплачивать *impf.*, выплатить *pf.* **disbursement** *n.* выплата.

disc, disk [dɪsk] *n.* диск, круг (*pl.* -и́); (*gramophone record*) грампластинка; (*comput.*) диск, дискет; ~ **brake** дисковый тормоз (*pl.* -á); ~ **drive** дисковод, накопитель *m.* на дисках; ~ **jockey** диск-жокей.

discard ['dɪskɑːd] *v.t.* отбрасывать *impf.*, отбросить *pf.*; (*cards*) сбрасывать *impf.*, сбросить *pf.*; *n.* (*card*) сброшенная карта.

discern [dɪ'sɜːn] *v.t.* различать *impf.*, различить *pf.*; разглядеть (-яжу, -ядишь) *pf.* **discernible** *adj.* различимый. **discerning** *adj.* проницательный. **discernment** *n.* распознание; умение различать.

discharge [dɪs'tʃɑːdʒ; 'dɪstʃɑːdʒ] *v.t.* (*ship etc.*) разгружать *impf.*, разгрузить (-ужу, -узишь) *pf.* (*gun; elec.*) разряжать *impf.*, разрядить *pf.*; (*dismiss*) увольнять *impf.*, уволить *pf.*; (*prisoner*) освобождать *impf.*, освободить *pf.*; (*debt; duty*) выполнять *impf.*, выполнить *pf.*; (*med.*) выделять *impf.*, выделить *pf.*; *n.* разгрузка; (*gun*) выстрел; (*elec.*) разряд; увольнение; освобождение; выполнение; (*med.*) (*action*) выделение; (*matter*) выделения *nt.pl.*

disciple [dɪ'saɪp(ə)l] *n.* ученик (-á).

disciplinarian [ˌdɪsɪplɪ'neərɪən] *n.* сторонник строгой дисциплины. **disci'plinary** *adj.* дисциплинарный. **'discipline** *n.* дисциплина; *v.t.* дисциплинировать *impf. & pf.*

disclaim [dɪs'kleɪm] *v.t.* отрекаться *impf.*, отречься (-екусь, -ечёшься; -ёкся, -еклась) *pf.* от+g. **disclaimer** *n.* отречение.

disclose [dɪs'kləʊz] *v.t.* обнаруживать *impf.*, обнаружить *pf.* **disclosure** *n.* обнаружение.

discoloured [dɪs'kʌlə(r)d] *adj.* изменивший цвет, обесцвеченный (-ен, -енна), выцветший.

discomfit [dɪs'kʌmfɪt] *v.t.* приводить (-ожу, -одишь) *impf.*, привести (-еду, -едёшь; -ёл, -ела) *pf.* в замешательство. **discomfiture** *n.* замешательство.

discomfort [dɪs'kʌmfət] *n.* неудобство, неловкость.

disconcert [ˌdɪskən'sɜːt] *v.t.* (*plans*) расстраивать *impf.*, расстроить *pf.*; (*person*) смущать *impf.*, смутить (-ущу, -утишь) *pf.*

disconnect [ˌdɪskə'nekt] *v.t.* разъединять *impf.*, разъединить *pf.*; (*elec.*) выключать *impf.*, выключить *pf.* **disconnected** *adj.* (*incoherent*) бессвязный.

disconsolate [dɪs'kɒnsələt] *adj.* неутешный.

discontent [ˌdɪskən'tent] *n.* недовольство. **discontented** *adj.* недовольный.

discontinue [ˌdɪskən'tɪnjuː] *v.t. & i.* прекращать(ся) *impf.*, прекратить(ся) (-ащу, -атит(ся)) *pf.*

discord ['dɪskɔːd] *n.* (*disagreement*) разногласие, разлад; (*mus.*) диссонанс. **dis'cordant** *adj.* несогласующийся, диссонирующий.

discount ['dɪskaʊnt] *n.* скидка; *v.t.* (*econ.*) учитывать *impf.*, учесть (учту, -ёшь; учёл, -чла) *pf.*; (*disregard*) не принимать *impf.*, принять (-иму, -имешь; принял, -á, -o) *pf.* в расчёт, во внимание.

discourage [dɪs'kʌrɪdʒ] *v.t.* обескураживать *impf.*, обескуражить *pf.* **discouragement** *n.* обескураживание.

discourteous [dɪs'kɜːtɪəs] *adj.* нелюбезный, невоспитанный (-ан, -анна). **discourtesy** *n.* нелюбезность, невоспитанность.

discover [dɪ'skʌvə(r)] *v.t.* открывать *impf.*, открыть (-рою, -роешь) *pf.*; обнаруживать *impf.*, обнаружить *pf.* **discoverer** *n.* исследователь *m.* **discovery** *n.* открытие.

discredit [dɪs'kredɪt] *n.* позор; *v.t.* дискредитировать *impf. & pf.*

discreet [dɪs'kriːt] *adj.* осмотрительный, благоразумный. **discretion** [dɪs'kreʃ(ə)n] *n.* усмотрение; (*prudence*) благоразумие; at one's ~ по своему усмотрению.

discrepancy [dɪs'krepənsɪ] *n.* разница, несоответствие.

discriminate [dɪs'krɪmɪˌneɪt] *v.t.* различать *impf.*, различить *pf.*; ~ **against** дискриминировать *impf. & pf.* **discrimi'nation** *n.* дискриминация.

discus ['dɪskəs] *n.* диск; ~ **throwing** метание диска.

discuss [dɪ'skʌs] *v.t.* обсуждать *impf.*, обсудить (-ужу, -удишь) *pf.* **discussion** *n.* обсуждение, дискуссия.

disdain [dɪs'deɪn] *n.* презрение. **disdainful** *adj.* презрительный, надменный (-енен, -енна).

disease [dɪ'ziːz] *n.* болезнь. **diseased** *adj.* больной (-лен, -льна).

disembark [ˌdɪsɪm'bɑːk] *v.t. & i.* высаживать(ся) *impf.*, высадить(ся) *pf.* **disembar'kation** *n.* высадка.

disembodied [ˌdɪsɪm'bɒdɪd] *adj.* бесплотный.

disembowel [ˌdɪsɪm'baʊəl] *v.t.* потрошить *impf.*, вы~ *pf.*

disenchantment [ˌdɪsɪn'tʃɑːntmənt] *n.* разоча-
рова́ние.

disenfranchise [ˌdɪsɪn'fræntʃaɪz] *v.t.* лиша́ть
impf., лиши́ть *pf.* (гражда́нских, избира́-
тельных) прав, привиле́гий. **disenfran-
chisement** *n.* лише́ние гражда́нских, из-
бира́тельных, прав.

disengage [ˌdɪsɪn'geɪdʒ] *v.t.* высвобожда́ть
impf., вы́свободить *pf.*; (*tech.*) разобща́ть
impf., разобщи́ть *pf.*; выключа́ть *impf.*,
вы́ключить *pf.* **disengaged** *adj.* свобо́д-
ный. **disengagement** *n.* освобожде́ние;
разобще́ние, выключе́ние.

disentangle [ˌdɪsɪn'tæŋg(ə)l] *v.t.* распу́тывать
impf., распу́тать *pf.*

disestablishment [ˌdɪsɪ'stæblɪʃmənt] *n.* отде-
ле́ние це́ркви от госуда́рства.

disfavour [dɪs'feɪvə(r)] *n.* неми́лость, не-
прия́знь.

disfigure [dɪs'fɪgə(r)] *v.t.* уро́довать *impf.*,
из~ *pf.*

disgorge [dɪs'gɔːdʒ] *v.t.* изверга́ть *impf.*, из-
ве́ргнуть (-г(нул), -гла) *pf.*

disgrace [dɪs'greɪs] *n.* позо́р; (*disfavour*) не-
ми́лость, опа́ла; *v.t.* позо́рить *impf.*, о~ *pf.*
disgraceful *adj.* позо́рный.

disgruntled [dɪs'grʌnt(ə)ld] *adj.* недово́ль-
ный.

disguise [dɪs'gaɪz] *n.* маскиро́вка; измене́ние
вне́шности; *v.t.* маскирова́ть *impf.*, за~ *pf.*;
изменя́ть *impf.*, измени́ть (-ню́, -нишь) *pf.*
вне́шность+*g.*; (*conceal*) скрыва́ть *impf.*,
скрыть (-ро́ю, -ро́ешь) *pf.* **disguised** *adj.*
замаскиро́ванный (-ан, -анна); ~ **as** пере-
оде́тый в+*a.*

disgust [dɪs'gʌst] *n.* отвраще́ние; *v.t.* внуша́ть
impf., внуши́ть *pf.* отвраще́ние+*d.* **disgusting** *adj.* отврати́тельный, проти́вный.

dish [dɪʃ] *n.* блю́до; *pl.* посу́да *collect.*; *v.t.*:
~ **up** класть (-аду́, -аде́шь; -ал) *impf.*, поло-
жи́ть (-ожу́, -о́жишь) *pf.* на блю́до.

disharmony [dɪs'hɑːmənɪ] *n.* дисгармо́ния;
(*disagreement*) разногла́сие.

dishearten [dɪs'hɑːt(ə)n] *v.t.* обескура́живать
impf., обескура́жить *pf.*

dishevelled [dɪ'ʃev(ə)ld] *adj.* растрёпанный
(-ан, -анна).

dishonest [dɪs'ɒnɪst] *adj.* нече́стный, недо-
бросо́вестный. **dishonesty** *n.* нече́стность.
dishonour *n.* бесче́стье; *v.t.* бесче́стить
impf., о~ *pf.* **dishonourable** *adj.* бесче́ст-
ный, по́длый (подл, -á, -о).

dish-towel ['dɪʃtaʊəl] *n.* ку́хонное полоте́нце
(*g.pl.* -нец). **dish-washer** *n.* (посу́до)мо́ечная
маши́на. **dish-water** *n.* помо́и (-о́ев) *pl.*

disillusion [ˌdɪsɪ'luːʒ(ə)n, -'ljuːʒ(ə)n] *v.t.* разо-
чаро́вывать *impf.*, разочарова́ть *pf.* **dis-
illusionment** *n.* разочаро́ванность.

disinclination [dɪsɪnklɪ'neɪʃ(ə)n] *n.* несклон́-
ность, неохо́та. **disinclined** [ˌdɪsɪn'klaɪnd]
adj. **be** ~ не хоте́ться (хо́чется) *impers.*+*d.*

disinfect [ˌdɪsɪn'fekt] *v.t.* дезинфици́ровать
impf. & *pf.* **disinfectant** *n.* дезинфици́-

ру́ющее сре́дство; *adj.* дезинфици́рующий.
disinfection *n.* дезинфе́кция, обеззара́-
живание.

disingenuous [ˌdɪsɪn'dʒenjʊəs] *adj.* нейскренний (-нен, -нна, -нне & -нно).

disinherit [ˌdɪsɪn'herɪt] *v.t.* лиша́ть *impf.*,
лиши́ть *pf.* насле́дства.

disintegrate [dɪs'ɪntɪˌgreɪt] *v.t.* дезинтегри́-
ровать *impf.* & *pf.*; *v.i.* разлага́ться *impf.*,
разложи́ться (-жу́сь, -жишься); *pf.* **disinte-
'gration** *n.* разложе́ние, дезинтегра́ция,
распа́д.

disinterested [dɪs'ɪntrɪstɪd] *adj.* бескоры́ст-
ный.

disjointed [dɪs'dʒɔɪntɪd] *adj.* бессвя́зный.

disk *see* **disc**

diskette *n.* диске́т.

dislike [dɪs'laɪk] *n.* нелюбо́вь (-бви́, *i.* -бо́вью)
(**for** к+*d.*); нераcположе́ние (**for** к+*d.*); *v.t.*
не люби́ть (-блю́, -бишь) *impf.*

dislocate ['dɪsləˌkeɪt] *v.t.* (*med.*) вывих́ивать
impf., вы́вихнуть *pf.*; расстра́ивать *impf.*,
расстро́ить *pf.* **dislo'cation** *n.* вы́вих; бес-
поря́док (-дка).

dislodge [dɪs'lɒdʒ] *v.t.* смеща́ть *impf.*, смес-
ти́ть *pf.*

disloyal [dɪs'lɔɪəl] *adj.* нелоя́льный, неве́р-
ный (-рен, -рна́, -рно, неве́рны́). **disloyalty**
n. нелоя́льность, неве́рность.

dismal ['dɪzm(ə)l] *adj.* мра́чный (-чен, -чна́,
-чно); уны́лый.

dismantle [dɪs'mænt(ə)l] *v.t.* разбира́ть *impf.*,
разобра́ть (разберу́, -рёшь; разобра́л, -á,
-о) *pf.*; демонти́ровать *impf.* & *pf.*

dismay [dɪs'meɪ] *v.t.* приводи́ть (-ожу́, -о́дишь)
impf., привести́ (-еду́, -едёшь; -ёл, -елá) *pf.*
в у́жас, уны́ние; *n.* (*alarm*) испу́г (-а(у));
(*despair*) уны́ние.

dismember [dɪs'membə(r)] *v.t.* расчленя́ть
impf., расчлени́ть *pf.* **dismemberment** *n.*
расчлене́ние.

dismiss [dɪs'mɪs] *v.t.* (*discharge*) увольня́ть
impf., уво́лить *pf.*; (*disband*) распуска́ть
impf., распусти́ть (-ущу́, -у́стишь) *pf.*; ~!
int. (*mil.*) разойди́сь! **dismissal** *n.* увольне́-
ние; ро́спуск.

dismount [dɪs'maʊnt] *v.i.* (*from horse*) спе́-
шиваться *impf.*, спе́шиться *pf.*

disobedience [ˌdɪsə'biːdɪəns] *n.* непослуша́-
ние. **disobedient** *adj.* непослу́шный. **disobey** [ˌdɪsə'beɪ] *v.t.* не слу́шаться *impf.*+*g.*

disorder [dɪs'ɔːdə(r)] *n.* беспоря́док (-дка).
disordered *adj.* расстро́енный (-ен).
disorderly *adj.* (*untidy*) беспоря́дочный;
(*unruly*) бу́йный (бу́ен, буйна́, -но).

disorganization [dɪsˌɔːgənaɪ'zeɪʃ(ə)n] *n.* де-
зорганиза́ция. **dis'organize** *v.t.* дезоргани-
зова́ть *impf.* & *pf.*

disorientation [dɪsˌɔːrɪən'teɪʃ(ə)n] *n.* дезо-
риента́ция.

disown [dɪs'əʊn] *v.t.* не признава́ть (-наю́,
-наёшь) *impf.*, призна́ть *pf.*; отрица́ть *impf.*

disparage [dɪ'spærɪdʒ] *v.t.* умаля́ть *impf.*,

умали́ть *pf.* **disparagement** *n.* умале́ние.

disparity [dɪ'spærɪtɪ] *n.* нера́венство.

dispassionate [dɪ'spæʃənət] *adj.* беспристра́стный.

dispatch, des- [dɪ'spætʃ] *v.t.* (*send*) отправля́ть *impf.*, отпра́вить *pf.*; (*deal with*) расправля́ться *impf.*, distribute расправиться *pf.* с+*i.*; *n.* отпра́вка; (*message*) донесе́ние; (*rapidity*) быстрота́. **dispatch-box** *n.* вали́за. **dispatch-rider** *n.* мотоцикли́ст свя́зи.

dispel [dɪ'spel] *v.t.* рассе́ивать *impf.*, рассе́ять (-е́ю, -е́ешь) *pf.*

dispensary [dɪ'spensərɪ] *n.* апте́ка.

dispensation [ˌdɪspen'seɪʃ(ə)n] *n.* (*exemption*) освобожде́ние (от обяза́тельства, обе́та). **di'spense** *v.t.* (*distribute*) раздава́ть (-даю́, -даёшь) *impf.*, разда́ть (-а́м, -а́шь, -а́ст, -ади́м; ро́здал & разда́л, раздала́, ро́здало & разда́ло) *pf.*; (*justice, medicine*) отпуска́ть *impf.*, отпусти́ть (-ущу́, -у́стишь) *pf.*; ~ **with** (*do without*) обходи́ться (-ожу́сь, -о́дишься) *impf.*, обойти́сь (-ойду́сь, -дёшься; обошёлся, -шла́сь) *pf.* без+*g.* **di'spenser** *n.* (*person*) фармаце́вт; (*device*) торго́вый автома́т.

dispersal [dɪ'spɜːsəl] *n.* распростране́ние. **disperse** *v.t.* разгоня́ть *impf.*, разогна́ть (разгоню́, -нишь; разогна́л, -а́, -о) *pf.*; рассе́ивать *impf.*, рассе́ять (-е́ю, -е́ешь) *pf.*; *v.i.* расходи́ться (-дится) *impf.*, разойти́сь (-ойдётся; -оше́лся, -ошла́сь) *pf.*

dispirited [dɪ'spɪrɪtɪd] *adj.* удручённый (-ён, -ена́).

displaced [dɪs'pleɪsd] *adj.*: ~ **persons** переме-щённые ли́ца *nt.pl.* **displacement** [dɪs'pleɪs-mənt] *n.* (*of fluid*) водоизмеще́ние.

display [dɪ'spleɪ] *n.* пока́з; проявле́ние; демонстра́ция; *v.t.* пока́зывать *impf.*, показа́ть (-ажу́, -а́жешь) *pf.*; проявля́ть *impf.*, прояви́ть (-влю́, -вишь) *pf.*; демонстри́ровать *impf. &pf.*

displease [dɪs'pliːz] *v.t.* раздража́ть *impf.*, раздражи́ть *pf.* **displeased** *pred.* недово́лен (-льна).

disposable [dɪ'spəʊzəb(ə)l] *adj.* име́ющийся в распоряже́нии; однора́зового по́льзования. **disposal** *n.* удале́ние, избавле́ние (**of** от+*g.*); **at your** ~ (*service*) к ва́шим услу́гам; (*use*) в ва́шем распоряже́нии. **dispose** *v.i.*: ~ **of** избавля́ться *impf.*, изба́виться *pf.* от+*g.* **disposed** *pred.*: ~ **to** скло́нен (-о́нна́, -о́нно) к+*d.*, располо́жен+*inf. or* к+*d.* **dispo'sition** *n.* расположе́ние, скло́нность; (*temperament*) нрав.

disproof [dɪs'pruːf] *n.* опроверже́ние.

disproportionate [ˌdɪsprə'pɔːʃənət] *adj.* непропорциона́льный.

disprove [dɪs'pruːv] *v.t.* опроверга́ть *impf.*, опрове́ргнуть (-г(нул), -гла) *pf.*

dispute [dɪ'spjuːt, 'dɪspjuːt; dɪ'spjuːt] *n.* (*debate*) спор; (*quarrel*) ссо́ра; *v.t.* оспа́ривать *impf.*, оспо́рить *pf.*

disqualification [dɪsˌkwɒlɪfɪ'keɪʃ(ə)n] *n.* дисквалифика́ция. **dis'qualify** *v.t.* лиша́ть *impf.*, лиши́ть *pf.* права́+*inf.*; дисквалифици́ровать *impf. & pf.*

disquiet [dɪs'kwaɪət] *n.* беспоко́йство, трево́га. **disquieting** *adj.* трево́жный.

disregard [ˌdɪsrɪ'gɑːd] *n.* невнима́ние к+*d.*; пренебреже́ние+*i.*; *v.t.* игнори́ровать *impf. & pf.*; пренебрега́ть *impf.*, пренебре́чь (-егу́, -ежёшь; -ёг, -егла́) *pf.*+*i.*

disrepair [ˌdɪsrɪ'peə(r)] *n.* неиспра́вность.

disreputable [dɪs'repjʊtəb(ə)l] *adj.* по́льзующийся дурно́й сла́вой, дурно́й репута́цией. **disre'pute** *n.* дурна́я сла́ва.

disrespect [ˌdɪsrɪ'spekt] *n.* неуваже́ние, непочте́ние. **disrespectful** *adj.* непочти́тельный.

disrupt [dɪs'rʌpt] *v.t.* срыва́ть *impf.*, сорва́ть (-ву́, -вёшь; сорва́л, -á, -о) *pf.* **disruptive** *adj.* подрывно́й, разруши́тельный.

dissatisfaction [ˌdɪsætɪs'fækʃ(ə)n] *n.* неудовлетворённость; недово́льство. **di'ssatisfied** *adj.* неудовлетворённый (-ён, -ена́ & -ённа), недово́льный.

dissect [dɪ'sekt] *v.t.* разреза́ть *impf.*, разре́зать (-е́жу, -е́жешь) *pf.*; (*med. etc.*) вскрыва́ть *impf.*, вскрыть (-ро́ю, -ро́ешь) *pf.*

dissemble [dɪ'semb(ə)l] *v.t.* скрыва́ть *impf.*, скрыть (-ро́ю, -ро́ешь) *pf.*; *v.i.* притворя́ться *impf.*, притвори́ться *pf.*

dissemination [dɪˌsemɪ'neɪʃ(ə)n] *n.* рассе́ивание; распростране́ние.

dissension [dɪ'senʃ(ə)n] *n.* разногла́сие, раздо́р. **dissent** *n.* расхожде́ние, несогла́сие; (*eccl.*) раско́л. **dissenter** *n.* (*eccl.*) раско́льник, секта́нт.

dissertation [ˌdɪsə'teɪʃ(ə)n] *n.* диссерта́ция.

disservice [dɪs'sɜːvɪs] *n.* плоха́я услу́га.

dissident ['dɪsɪd(ə)nt] *n.* диссиде́нт, инакомы́слящий *sb.*

dissimilar [dɪ'sɪmɪlə(r)] *adj.* несхо́дный, непохо́жий, разли́чный. **dissimilation** ['dɪsɪmɪ-'leɪʃ(ə)n] *n.* диссимиля́ция.

dissipate ['dɪsɪpeɪt] *v.t.* (*dispel*) рассе́ивать *impf.*, рассе́ять (-е́ю, -е́ешь) *pf.*; (*squander*) прома́тывать *impf.*, промота́ть *pf.* **dissipated** *adj.* распу́тный, беспу́тный.

dissociate [dɪ'səʊʃɪ,eɪt, -sɪ,eɪt] *v.t.*: ~ **o.s.** отмежёвываться *impf.*, отмежева́ться (-жу́юсь, -жу́ешься) *pf.* (**from** от+*g.*). **dissoci'ation** *n.* разобще́ние, отмежева́ние.

dissolute ['dɪsə,luːt, -,ljuːt] *adj.* распу́щенный (-ен, -енна), развра́тный. **dissolution** *n.* (*treaty etc.*) расторже́ние; (*parl.*) ро́спуск; (*solution*) растворе́ние. **dissolve** [dɪ'zɒlv] *v.t. & i.* (*in liquid*) растворя́ть(ся) *impf.*, раствори́ть(ся) *pf.*; *v.t.* (*annul*) расторга́ть *impf.*, расто́ргнуть (-г(нул), -гла) *pf.*; (*parl.*) распуска́ть *impf.*, распусти́ть (-ущу́, -у́стишь) *pf.*

dissonance ['dɪsənəns] *n.* диссона́нс. **dissonant** *adj.* диссони́рующий.

dissuade [dɪ'sweɪd] *v.t.* отгова́ривать *impf.*, отговори́ть *pf.* **dissuasion** *n.* отгова́ривание.

distaff ['dɪstɑːf] *n.* пря́лка; **on the ~ side** по же́нской ли́нии.

distance ['dɪst(ə)ns] *n.* расстоя́ние; (*distant point*) даль (*loc.* -ли́); (*sport*) диста́нция; **at a great ~** вдали́. **distant** *adj.* да́льний, далёкий (-ёк, -ека́, -ёко́); (*reserved*) сде́ржанный (-ан, -анна).

distaste [dɪs'teɪst] *n.* неприя́знь. **distasteful** *adj.* проти́вный, неприя́тный.

distemper[1] [dɪ'stempə(r)] *n.* (*vet.*) чума́.

distemper[2] [dɪ'stempə(r)] *n.* (*paint*) те́мпера; *v.t.* кра́сить *impf.*, по~ *pf.* те́мперой.

distend [dɪ'stend] *v.t.* расширя́ть *impf.*, расши́рить *pf.*; надува́ть *impf.*, наду́ть (-у́ю, -у́ешь) *pf.* **distension** *n.* расшире́ние, надува́ние.

distil [dɪ'stɪl] *v.t.* перегоня́ть *impf.*, перегна́ть (-гоню́, -го́нишь; перегна́л, -á, -о) *pf.*; дистилли́ровать *impf.* & *pf.* **disti'llation** *n.* перего́нка, дистилля́ция. **distillery** *n.* винокуренный, перего́нный, заво́д.

distinct [dɪ'stɪŋkt] *adj.* (*separate*) отде́льный; (*clear*) отчётливый; (*definite*) определённый (-ёнен, -ённа); **~ from** отлича́ющийся от+*g.* **distinction** *n.* отли́чие, разли́чие. **distinctive** *adj.* осо́бенный, отличи́тельный. **distinctly** *adv.* я́сно, определённо.

distinguish [dɪ'stɪŋgwɪʃ] *v.t.* различа́ть *impf.*, различи́ть *pf.*; **~ o.s.** отлича́ться *impf.*, отличи́ться *pf.* **distinguished** *adj.* выдаю́щийся.

distort [dɪ'stɔːt] *v.t.* искажа́ть *impf.*, искази́ть *pf.*; (*misrepresent*) извраща́ть *impf.*, преврати́ть (-ащу́, -ати́шь) *pf.* **distortion** *n.* искаже́ние, искривле́ние.

distract [dɪ'strækt] *v.t.* отвлека́ть *impf.*, отвле́чь (-еку́, -ечёшь; -ёк, -екла́) *pf.* **distracted** *adj.* (*maddened*) обезуме́вший. **distraction** *n.* (*amusement*) развлече́ние; (*madness*) безу́мие.

distrain [dɪ'streɪn] *v.i.*: **~ upon** накла́дывать *impf.*, наложи́ть (-жу́, -жишь) *pf.* аре́ст на+*a.* **distraint** *n.* наложе́ние аре́ста.

distraught [dɪ'strɔːt] *adj.* обезу́мевший.

distress [dɪ'stres] *n.* (*calamity*) беда́; (*ship etc.*) бе́дствие; (*poverty*) нужда́; (*physical*) недомога́ние; *v.t.* огорча́ть *impf.*, огорчи́ть *pf.*; му́чить *impf.*, из~ *pf.*

distribute [dɪ'strɪbjuːt, 'dɪ-] *v.t.* распределя́ть *impf.*, распредели́ть *pf.* **distri'bution** *n.* распределе́ние, разда́ча. **distributive** *adj.* распредели́тельный. **distributor** *n.* распредели́тель *m.*; (*cin.*) кинопрока́тчик.

district ['dɪstrɪkt] *n.* о́круг (*pl.* -á), райо́н.

distrust [dɪs'trʌst] *n.* недове́рие; *v.t.* не доверя́ть *impf.* **distrustful** *adj.* недове́рчивый.

disturb [dɪ'stɜːb] *v.t.* беспоко́ить *impf.*, о~ *pf.* **disturbance** *n.* наруше́ние поко́я; *pl.* (*pol. etc.*) беспоря́дки *m.pl.*

disuse [dɪs'juːs] *n.* неупотребле́ние; **fall into ~** выходи́ть (-ит) *impf.*, вы́йти (-йдет; вы́шел, -шла) *pf.* из употребле́ния. **disused** *adj.* вы́шедший из употребле́ния.

ditch [dɪtʃ] *n.* кана́ва, ров (рва, *loc.* во рву́).

dither ['dɪðə(r)] *v.i.* колеба́ться (-блю́сь, -блешься) *impf.*; *n.*: **all of a ~** в си́льном возбужде́нии.

ditto ['dɪtəʊ] *n.* то же са́мое; *adv.* так же.

ditty ['dɪtɪ] *n.* пе́сенка.

diuretic [ˌdaɪjʊ'retɪk] *n.* мочего́нное сре́дство; *adj.* мочего́нный.

diurnal [daɪ'ɜːn(ə)l] *adj.* дневно́й.

divan [dɪ'væn, daɪ-, 'daɪ-] *n.* тахта́, дива́н.

dive [daɪv] *v.i.* ныря́ть *impf.*, нырну́ть *pf.*; пры́гать *impf.*, пры́гнуть *pf.* в во́ду; (*aeron.*) пики́ровать *impf.* & *pf.*; (*submarine*) погружа́ться *impf.*, погрузи́ться *pf.*; *n.* ныро́к (-рка́), прыжо́к (-жка́) в во́ду. **dive-bomber** *n.* пики́рующий бомбардиро́вщик. **diver** *n.* водола́з; (*bird*) гага́ра.

diverge [daɪ'vɜːdʒ] *v.i.* расходи́ться (-ится) *impf.*, разойти́сь (-ойдётся -ошёлся, -ошла́сь) *pf.*; (*deviate*) отклоня́ться *impf.*, отклони́ться (-ню́сь, -нишься) *pf.* (**from** от+*g.*). **divergence** *n.* расхожде́ние; отклоне́ние. **divergent** *adj.* расходя́щийся.

diverse [daɪ'vɜːs, 'daɪ-, dɪ-] *adj.* разли́чный, разнообра́зный. **diversifi'cation** *n.* расшире́ние ассортиме́нта. **diversified** *adj.* многообра́зный. **diversify** *v.t.* разнообра́зить *impf.* **diversion** *n.* (*deviation*) отклоне́ние; (*detour*) объе́зд; (*amusement*) развлече́ние; (*mil.*) диве́рсия. **diversionist** *n.* диверса́нт. **diversity** *n.* разнообра́зие, разли́чие. **divert** *v.t.* отклоня́ть *impf.*, отклони́ть (-ню́, -нишь) *pf.*; отводи́ть (-ожу́, -о́дишь) *impf.*, отвести́ (-еду́, -едёшь; -ёл, -ела́) *pf.*; (*amuse*) развлека́ть *impf.*, развле́чь (-еку́, -ечёшь; -ёк, -екла́) *pf.* **diverting** *adj.* заба́вный.

divest [daɪ'vest] *v.t.* (*unclothe*) разоблача́ть *impf.*, разоблачи́ть *pf.*; (*deprive*) лиша́ть *impf.*, лиши́ть *pf.* (**of** +*g.*).

divide [dɪ'vaɪd] *v.t.* дели́ть (-лю́, -лишь) *impf.*, по~ *pf.*; разделя́ть *impf.*, раздели́ть (-лю́, -лишь) *pf.* **dividend** ['dɪvɪˌdend] *n.* дивиде́нд. **dividers** *n.* ци́ркуль *m.*

divination [ˌdɪvɪ'neɪʃ(ə)n] *n.* гада́ние; предсказа́ние. **divine** [dɪ'vaɪn] *adj.* боже́ственный (-ен, -енна); *n.* богосло́в; *v.t.* предска́зывать *impf.*, предсказа́ть (-ажу́, -а́жешь) *pf.* **diviner** [dɪ'vaɪnə(r)] *n.* предсказа́тель *m.*

diving ['daɪvɪŋ] *n.* ныря́ние; (*profession*) водола́зное де́ло; (*aeron.*) пики́рование; (*naut.*) погруже́ние. **diving-board** *n.* трампли́н.

divining-rod [dɪ'vaɪnɪŋ] *n.* волше́бная лоза́ (*pl.* -зы).

divinity [dɪ'vɪnɪtɪ] *n.* божество́; (*theology*) богосло́вие; теоло́гия.

divisible [dɪ'vɪzɪb(ə)l] *adj.* дели́мый. **division** *n.* (*dividing*) деле́ние, разделе́ние; (*section*) отде́л, подразделе́ние; (*mil.*) диви́зия. **divisional** *adj.* дивизио́нный. **divisive** [dɪ'vaɪsɪv] *adj.* разделя́ющий, вызыва́ющий разногла́сия. **divisor** [dɪ'vaɪzə(r)] *n.* дели́тель *m.*

divorce [dɪ'vɔːs] *n.* разво́д; *v.i.* разводи́ться (-ожу́сь, -о́дишься) *impf.*, развести́сь (-еду́сь, -еде́шься; -ёлся, -ела́сь) *pf.* **divorced** *adj.* разведённый (-ён, -ена́).

divor'cee *n.* разведённая жена́ (*pl.* жёны).

divulge [daɪ'vʌldʒ, dɪ-] *v.t.* разглаша́ть *impf.*, разгласи́ть *pf.*

DIY *abbr.* (*of do it yourself*): ~ **store** магази́н «уме́лые ру́ки».

dizziness ['dɪzɪnɪs] *n.* головокруже́ние. **dizzy** *adj.* головокружи́тельный; **I am** ~ у меня́ кру́жится голова́.

DJ *abbr.* (*of disc jockey*) диск-жоке́й.

DNA *abbr.* (*of deoxyribonucleic acid*) ДНК, (*дезоксирибонуклеи́новая кислота́*)

do [du:, də] *v.t.* де́лать *impf.*, c~ *pf.*; вы-полня́ть *impf.*, вы́полнить *pf.*; (*coll.*) (*cheat*) надува́ть *impf.*, наду́ть (-у́ю, -у́ешь) *pf.*; *v.i.* (*be suitable*) годи́ться *impf.*; (*suffice*) быть доста́точным; **that will** ~ хва́тит!; **how** ~ **you** ~**?** здра́вствуйте!; как вы пожива́ете?; ~ **away with** (*abolish*) уничтожа́ть *impf.*, уничто́жить *pf.*; ~ **in** (*kill*) убива́ть *impf.*, уби́ть (убью́, -ьёшь) *pf.*; ~ **up** (*restore*) ремонти́ровать *impf.*, от~ *pf.*; (*wrap up*) завёртывать *impf.*, заверну́ть *pf.*; (*fasten*) застёгивать *impf.*, застегну́ть *pf.*; ~ **without** обходи́ться (-ожу́сь, -о́дишься) *impf.*, обойти́сь (обойду́сь, -дёшься; обошёлся, -шла́сь) *pf.* без+*g.*

docile ['dəʊsaɪl] *adj.* поко́рный. **docility** [də'sɪlɪtɪ] *n.* поко́рность.

dock[1] [dɒk] *n.* (*bot.*) щаве́ль (-ля́) *m.*

dock[2] [dɒk] *v.t.* (*tail*) отруба́ть *impf.*, отру-би́ть (-блю́, -бишь) *pf.*; (*money*) уре́зывать, уреза́ть *impf.*, уре́зать (-е́жу, -е́жешь) *pf.*

dock[3] [dɒk] *n.* (*naut.*) док; *v.t.* ста́вить *impf.*, по~ *pf.* в док; *v.i.* входи́ть (-ожу́, -о́дишь) *impf.*, войти́ (войду́, -дёшь; вошёл, -шла́) *pf.* в док; *v.t. & i.* (*spacecraft*) стыкова́ть(ся) *impf.*, co~ *pf.* **docker** *n.* до́кер, порто́вый рабо́чий *sb.* **docking** *n.* (*ship*) постано́вка в док; (*spacecraft*) стыко́вка. **dockyard** *n.* верфь.

dock[4] [dɒk] *n.* (*leg.*) скамья́ (*pl.* ска́мьи, -ме́й) подсуди́мых.

docket ['dɒkɪt] *n.* квита́нция; (*label*) ярлы́к (-а́), этике́тка.

doctor ['dɒktə(r)] *n.* врач (-а́); (*also univ. etc.*) до́ктор (*pl.* -а́); *v.t.* (*med.*) лечи́ть (-чу́, -чишь) *impf.*; (*falsify*) фальсифици́ровать *impf. & pf.* **doctor(i)al** ['dɒktər(ə)l, ˌdɒk'tɔː-rɪəl] *adj.* до́кторский. **doctorate** *n.* сте́пень (*pl.* -ни, -не́й) до́ктора.

doctrinaire [ˌdɒktrɪ'neə(r)] *n.* доктринёр; *adj.* доктринёрский. **'doctrine** *n.* доктри́на.

document ['dɒkjumənt] *n.* докуме́нт; *v.t.* документи́ровать *impf. & pf.* **docu'mentary** *adj.* документа́льный; *n.* документа́льный фильм. **documen'tation** *n.* документа́ция.

dodder ['dɒdə(r)] *v.i.* дрожа́ть (-жу́, -жи́шь) *impf.* **dodderer** *n.* дря́хлый стари́к.

dodge [dɒdʒ] *n.* (*trick*) ло́вкий приём, уве́ртка; *v.t.* уклоня́ться *impf.*, уклони́ться

(-ню́сь, -ни́шься) *pf.* от+*g.*; уви́ливать *impf.*, увильну́ть *pf.* от+*g.*

doe [dəʊ] *n.* са́мка. **doeskin** *n.* за́мша.

dog [dɒg] *n.* соба́ка, пёс (пса); (*male dog*) кобе́ль (-ля́) *m.*; (*male animal*) саме́ц (-мца́); *v.t.* сле́довать *impf.*, по~ *pf.* по пята́м за+*i.*; (*fig.*) пресле́довать *impf.* **dog-collar** *n.* оше́йник. **dog-fight** *n.* возду́шный бой (*loc.* бою́; *pl.* бои́).

doggerel ['dɒgər(ə)l] *n.* ви́рши (-шей) *pl.*

dogma ['dɒgmə] *n.* до́гма. **dog'matic** *adj.* догмати́ческий.

doing ['duːɪŋ] *n.*: *pl.* дела́ *nt.pl.*; (*events*) собы́тия *nt.pl.*

doldrums ['dɒldrəmz] *n.*: **be in the** ~ хан-дри́ть *impf.*

dole [dəʊl] *n.* посо́бие по безрабо́тице.

doleful ['dəʊlful] *adj.* ско́рбный.

doll [dɒl] *n.* ку́кла (*g.pl.* -кол).

dollar ['dɒlə(r)] *n.* до́ллар.

dollop ['dɒləp] *n.* здоро́вый кусо́к (-ска́).

dolly ['dɒlɪ] *n.* ку́колка; (*stick*) валёк (-лька́); (*cin.*) опера́торская теле́жка.

dolphin ['dɒlfɪn] *n.* дельфи́н, белобо́чка.

dolt [dəʊlt] *n.* болва́н. **doltish** *adj.* тупо́й (туп, -а́, -о, ту́пы).

domain [də'meɪn] *n.* (*estate*) владе́ние; (*field*) о́бласть, сфе́ра.

dome [dəʊm] *n.* ку́пол (*pl.* -а́). **domed** *adj.* с ку́полом.

domestic [də'mestɪk] *adj.* (*of household*; *animals*) дома́шний; (*of family*) семе́йный; (*pol.*) вну́тренний; *n.* прислу́га. **domesticate** *v.t.* прируча́ть *impf.*, приручи́ть *pf.* **domesticity** [ˌdɒmə'stɪsɪtɪ, ˌdəʊ-] *n.* дома́шняя, семе́йная, жизнь.

domicile ['dɒmɪsaɪl, -sɪl] *n.* постоя́нное местожи́тельство; *v.t.* сели́ть *impf.*, по~ *pf.* на постоя́нное жи́тельство. **domiciliary** [ˌdɒmɪ'sɪlɪərɪ] *adj.* дома́шний.

dominance ['dɒmɪnəns] *n.* госпо́дство. **dominant** *adj.* преоблада́ющий; госпо́дствующий; *n.* домина́нта. **dominate** *v.t.* госпо́дствовать *impf.* над+*i.* **domi'neering** *adj.* вла́стный, деспоти́ческий.

dominion [də'mɪnɪən] *n.* доминио́н; влады́-чество.

domino ['dɒmɪnəʊ] *n.* кость (*pl.* -ти, -те́й) домино́; *pl.* (*game*) домино́ *nt.indecl.*

don[1] [dɒn] *n.* (**D**~, *title*) дон; (*univ.*) преподава́тель *m.*

don[2] [dɒn] *v.t.* надева́ть *impf.*, наде́ть (-е́ну, -е́нешь) *pf.*

donate [dəʊ'neɪt] *v.t.* же́ртвовать *impf.*, по~ *pf.* **donation** *n.* дар (*pl.* -ы́), поже́ртвова-ние.

donkey ['dɒŋkɪ] *n.* осёл (-сла́); ~ **engine** вспомога́тельный дви́гатель *m.*

donnish ['dɒnɪʃ] *adj.* педанти́чный.

donor ['dəʊnə(r)] *n.* же́ртвователь *m.*; (*med.*) до́нор.

doom [du:m] *n.* рок, судьба́; (*ruin*) ги́бель; *v.t.* обрека́ть *impf.*, обре́чь (-еку́, -ечёшь;

-ёк, -еклá) *pf.* **doomsday** *n.* стрáшный суд
(-á); конéц (-нцá) свéта.

door [dɔː(r)] *n.* (*house*) дверь (*loc.* -рú; *pl.*
-ри, -рéй, *i.* -рьмú & -рáми); (*smaller*)
двéрца (*g.pl.* -рец). **doorbell** *n.* (двернóй)
звонóк (-нкá). **doorknob** *n.* (двернáя)
рýчка. **doorman** *n.* швейцáр. **doormat** *n.*
половúк (-á). **doorpost** *n.* (двернóй) косáк
(-á). **doorstep** *n.* порóг. **doorway** *n.*
двернóй проём.

dope [dəʊp] *n.* (*drug*) наркóтик; информáция; ~ **fiend** наркомáн, ~ка; *v.t.* давáть
(даю́, даёшь) *impf.*, дать (дам, дашь, даст,
дадúм; дал, -á, дáлó, -и) *pf.* наркóтик+d.

dormant ['dɔːmənt] *adj.* (*sleeping*) спя́щий;
(*inactive*) бездéйствующий.

dormer window ['dɔːmə(r)] *n.* мансáрдное
окнó (*pl.* óкна, óкон, óкнам).

dormitory ['dɔːmɪtərɪ] *n.* дортуáр.

dormouse ['dɔːmaʊs] *n.* сóня.

dorsal ['dɔːs(ə)l] *adj.* спиннóй.

dose [dəʊs] *n.* дóза; *v.t.* давáть (даю́, даёшь)
impf., дать (дам, дашь, даст, дадúм; дал,
-á, дáлó, -и) *pf.* лекáрство+d.

dosh [dɒʃ] *n.* (*sl.*) бáшли (-ей) *pl.*

doss-house [dɒs] *n.* ночлéжный дом (*pl.* -á).

dossier ['dɒsɪə(r), -ɪˌeɪ] *n.* досьé *nt.indecl.*

dot [dɒt] *n.* тóчка; *v.t.* стáвить *impf.*, по~
pf. тóчки на+a.; (*scatter*) усéивать *impf.*,
усéять (-éю, -éешь) *pf.* (**with** +*i.*); **~ted line**
пунктúр.

dotage ['dəʊtɪdʒ] *n.* (стáрческое) слабоýмие.
dotard ['dəʊtəd] *n.* вы́живший из умá
старúк (-á). **dote** *v.i.*: ~ **on** обожáть *impf.*

dotty ['dɒtɪ] *adj.* рехнýвшийся.

double ['dʌb(ə)l] *adj.* двойнóй, пáрный; ~
bed двуспáльная кровáть; (*doubled*)
удвóенный (-ен); *adv.* вдвóе; (*two together*)
вдвоём; *n.* двойнóе колúчество; (*person's*)
двойнúк (-á); (*understudy*) дублёр; *pl.*
(*sport*) пáрная игрá; **at the** ~ бéглым
шáгом; *v.t.* удвáивать *impf.*, удвóить *pf.*;
(*fold*) склáдывать *impf.*, сложúть (-жý,
-жишь) *pf.* вдвóе; ~ **the parts of** (*theatr.*)
игрáть *impf.*, сыгрáть *pf.* рóли+g. **double-
barrelled** *adj.* двуствóльная. **double-bass**
n. контрабáс. **double-breasted** *adj.* дву-
бóртный. **double-cross** *v.t.* обмáнывать
impf., обманýть (-нý, -нешь) *pf.* **double-
dealer** *n.* двурýшник. **double-dealing** *n.*
двурýшничество; *adj.* двурýшнический.
double-decker *n.* двухэтáжный автóбус.
double-edged *adj.* обоюдоóстрый. **double-
faced** *adj.* двулúчный.

doubt [daʊt] *n.* сомнéние; *v.t.* сомневáться
impf. в+*p.* **doubtful** *adj.* сомнúтельный.
doubting *adj.* сомневáющийся. **doubtless**
adv. несомнéнно.

douche [duːʃ] *n.* душ; *v.t.* обливáть *impf.*,
облúть (обольюý, -ьёшь; óблúл, -á, -о) *pf.*
водóй.

dough [dəʊ] *n.* тéсто. **doughnut** *n.* пóнчик,
пы́шка.

dour [dʊə(r)] *adj.* угрю́мый, мрáчный (-чен,
-чнá, -чно).

douse [daʊs] *v.t.* (*light*) тушúть (-шý, -шишь)
impf., за~, по~ *pf.*

dove [dʌv] *n.* гóлубь (*pl.* -би, -бéй) *m.*,
гóрлица. **dove-coloured** *adj.* сúзый (сиз,
-á, -о). **dovecot(e)** *n.* голубя́тня (*g.pl.* -тен).
dovetail *n.* лáсточкин хвост (-á); *v.i.*: ~
(**into one another**) соотвéтствовать *impf.*
друг дрýгу.

Dover ['dəʊvə(r)] *n.* Дувр.

dowager ['daʊədʒə(r)] *n.* вдовá (*pl.* -вы); ~
empress вдóвствующая императрúца.

dowdy ['daʊdɪ] *adj.* безвкýсный, неэлегáнт-
ный.

down[1] [daʊn] *n.* (*geog.*) безлéсная возвы́-
шенность; *pl.* Дáунс.

down[2] [daʊn] *n.* (*fluff*) пух (-a(у), *loc.* -ý),
пушóк (-шкá).

down[3] [daʊn] *adv.* (*motion*) вниз; (*position*)
внизý; **be** ~ **with** (*ill*) болéть *impf.*+*i.*; ~
with (*int.*) долóй+a.; *prep.* вниз с+g., по+d.;
(*along*) (вдоль) по+d.; *v.t.*: ~ **tools** (*strike*)
бастовáть *impf.*, за~ *pf.* **down-and-out** *n.*
бедня́к (-á), оборвáнец (-нца). **downcast,
down-hearted** *adj.* уны́лый. **downfall** *n.*
(*ruin*) гúбель. **downpour** *n.* лúвень (-вня)
m. **downright** *adj.* прямóй (прям, -á, -о,
прáмы́); (*out-and-out*) я́вный; *adv.* совершéнно. **downstream** *adv.* вниз по течéнию.

dowry ['daʊərɪ] *n.* придáное *sb.*

doyen ['dɔɪən, 'dwaːjæ] *n.* старшинá (*pl.* -ны)
m.

doze [dəʊz] *v.i.* дремáть (-млю́, -млешь)
impf.

dozen ['dʌz(ə)n] *n.* дю́жина; **baker's** ~ чёр-
това дю́жина.

Dr. *abbr.* (*of* **Doctor**) д-р, дóктор.

drab [dræb] *adj.* бесцвéтный; (*boring*) скýчный (-чен, -чнá, -чно).

draft [drɑːft] *n.* (*sketch*) черновúк (-á); (*of
document*) проéкт; (*econ.*) трáтта; *see also*
draught; *v.t.* составля́ть *impf.*, состáвить *pf.*
план, проéкт, +g.

drag [dræg] *v.t.* & *i.* тащúть(ся) (-щý(сь),
-щишь(ся)) *impf.*; волочúться (-чý(сь),
-чишь(ся)) *impf.*; *v.t.* (*river etc.*) драгúро-
вать *impf.* & *pf.*; *n.* (*grapnel*) кóшка; (*lure*)
примáнка; (*burden*) обýза; (*brake*) тормоз-
нóй башмáк (-á); (*aeron.*) лобовóе сопротивлéние. **dragnet** *n.* брéдень (-дня) *m.*

dragon ['drægən] *n.* дракóн. **dragonfly** *n.*
стрекозá (*pl.* -зы).

dragoon [drə'guːn] *n.* драгýн (*g.pl.* -н (*collect.*)
& -нов).

drain [dreɪn] *n.* водостóк; (*leakage, also fig.*)
утéчка; *v.t.* осушáть *impf.*, осушúть (-шý,
-шишь) *pf.* **drainage** *n.* сток; канализáция;
дренáж. **drain-pipe** *n.* водостóчная трубá
(*pl.* -бы).

drake [dreɪk] *n.* сéлезень (-зня) *m.*

dram [dræm] *n.* глотóк (-ткá).

drama ['drɑːmə] *n.* дрáма. **dramatic** [drə'mætık] *adj.* драмати́ческий. **dramatis personae** [ˌdræmətıs pɜːˈsəʊnaɪ, -niː] *n.* де́йствующие ли́ца *nt.pl.* **dramatist** ['dræmətıst] *n.* драмату́рг. **dramatize** *v.t.* инсцени́ровать *impf.* & *pf.*; (*fig.*) преувели́чивать *impf.*, преувели́чить *pf.*

drape [dreıp] *v.t.* драпирова́ть *impf.*, за~ *pf.*; *n.* драпиро́вка. **draper** *n.* торго́вец (-вца) тка́нями. **drapery** *n.* драпиро́вка; (*cloth*; *collect.*) тка́ни *f.pl.*

drastic ['dræstık, 'drɑː-] *adj.* круто́й (крут, -á, -о), радика́льный.

drat [dræt] *int.* чёрт возьми́! **dratted** *adj.* прокля́тый.

draught [drɑːft] *n.* (*drink*) глото́к (-ткá); (*air*) тя́га, сквозня́к (-á); (*naut.*) оса́дка; *pl.* (*game*) ша́шки *f.pl.*; *see* **draft**; **be in a ~** быть на сквозняке́; **~ animals** тя́гло *collect.*; **~ beer** пи́во из бо́чки; **~ horse** ломова́я ло́шадь (*pl.* -ди, -де́й, *i.* -дьми́) **draughtsman** *n.* (*person*) чертёжник; (*counter*) ша́шка. **draughty** *adj.*: **it is ~ here** здесь дуёт.

draw [drɔː] *n.* (*action*) вытя́гивание; (*lottery*) лотере́я; (*attraction*) прима́нка; (*drawn game*) ничья́; *v.t.* (*pull*) тяну́ть (тя́ну, -нешь) *impf.*, по~ *pf.*; таска́ть *indet.*, тащи́ть (-щу́, -щишь) *det.*; (*curtains*) заде́ргивать *impf.*, задёрнуть *pf.* (занаве́ски); (*attract*) привлека́ть *impf.*, привле́чь (-еку́, -ече́шь; -ёк, -еклá) *pf.*; (*pull out*) выта́скивать *impf.*, вы́тащить *pf.*; (*sword*) обнажа́ть *impf.*, обнажи́ть *pf.*; (*lots*) броса́ть *impf.*, бро́сить *pf.* (жре́бий); (*water*; *inspiration*) че́рпать *impf.*, черпну́ть *pf.*; (*game*) конча́ть *impf.*, ко́нчить *pf.* (игру́) вничью́; (*evoke*) вызыва́ть *impf.*, вы́звать (вы́зову, -вешь) *pf.*; (*conclusion*) выводи́ть (-ожу́, -о́дишь) *impf.*, вы́вести (-еду, -едешь; -ел) *pf.* (заключе́ние); (*fowl*) потроши́ть *impf.*, вы́~ *pf.*; (*diagram*) черти́ть (-рчу́, -ртишь) *impf.*, на~ *pf.*; (*picture*) рисова́ть *impf.*, на~ *pf.*; **~ aside** отводи́ть (-ожу́, -о́дишь) *impf.*, отвести́ (-еду́, -едёшь; -ёл, -елá) *pf.* в сто́рону; **~ back** (*withdraw*) отступа́ть *impf.*, отступи́ть (-плю́, -пишь) *pf.*; **~ in** (*involve*) вовлека́ть *impf.*, вовле́чь (-еку́, -ече́шь; -ёк, -еклá) *pf.*; **~ up** (*document*) составля́ть *impf.*, соста́вить *pf.* **drawback** *n.* недоста́ток (-тка), поме́ха. **drawbridge** *n.* подъёмный мост (мо́стá, *loc.* -ý; *pl.* -ы́).

drawer *n.* (*person*) чертёжник, рисова́льщик; (*of table etc.*) выдвижно́й я́щик; *pl.* кальсо́ны (-н) *pl.* **drawing** *n.* (*action*) рисова́ние, черче́ние; (*object*) рису́нок (-нка), чертёж(-á). **drawing-board** *n.* чертёжная доска́ (*a.* -ску; *pl.* -ски, -со́к, -скáм). **drawing-pen** *n.* рейсфе́дер. **drawing-pin** *n.* кно́пка. **drawing-room** *n.* гости́ная *sb.*

drawl [drɔːl] *n.* протя́жное, медли́тельное, произноше́ние; *v.i.* растя́гивать *impf.*, растяну́ть (-ну́, -нешь) *pf.* словá.

dray [dreı] *n.* подво́да. **dray-horse** *n.* ломова́я ло́шадь (*pl.* -ди, -де́й, *i.* -дьми́). **drayman** *n.* ломово́й изво́зчик.

dread [dred] *n.* страх; *v.t.* боя́ться (бою́сь, бои́шься) *impf.*+*g.* **dreadful** *adj.* стра́шный (-шен, -шнá, -шно, стра́шны́). **dreadnought** *n.* дредно́ут.

dream [driːm] *n.* сон (сна); мечтá (*g.pl.* -áний); *v.i.* ви́деть (ви́жу, -дишь) *impf.*, у~ *pf.* сон; **~ of** ви́деть (ви́жу, -дишь) *impf.*, у~ *pf.* во сне́; (*fig.*) мечта́ть *impf.* о+*p.* **dreamer** *n.* мечта́тель *m.*, фантазёр.

dreariness ['drıərınıs] *n.* тоскли́вость. **dreary** *adj.* тоскли́вый; ску́чный (-чен, -чнá, -чно).

dredge[1] [dredʒ] *v.t.* (*river etc.*) драги́ровать *impf.* & *pf.* **dredger**[1] *n.* землечерпа́лка; дра́га.

dredge[2] [dredʒ] *v.t.* (*sprinkle*) посыпа́ть *impf.*, посы́пать (-плю, -плешь) *pf.* **dredger**[2] *n.* си́течко (*pl.* -чки, -чек, -чкáм).

dreg [dreg] *n.*:*pl.* оса́дки (-ков) *pl.*, отбро́сы (-сов) *pl.*; **~ of society** подо́нки (-ков) *pl.* о́бщества.

drench [drentʃ] *v.t.* (*wet*) прома́чивать *impf.*, промочи́ть (-чу́, -чишь) *pf.*; **get ~ed** промока́ть *impf.*, промо́кнуть (-к) *pf.*

dress [dres] *n.* пла́тье (*g.pl.* -в), оде́жда; **~ circle** бельэта́ж; **~ coat** фрак; **~ rehearsal** генера́льная репети́ция; *v.t.* & *i.* одева́ть(ся) *impf.*, оде́ть(ся) (-éну(сь), -éнешь(ся)) *pf.*; *v.t.* (*cul.*) приправля́ть *impf.*, припра́вить *pf.*; (*med.*) перевя́зывать *impf.*, перевяза́ть (-яжу́, -я́жешь) *pf.*; *v.i.* (*mil.*) равня́ться *impf.* **dresser**[1] *n.* (*theatr.*) костюме́р; ~шá.

dresser[2] ['dresə(r)] *n.* ку́хонный шкаф (*loc.* -ý; *pl.* -ы́).

dressing ['dresıŋ] *n.* (*cul.*) припра́ва; (*med.*) перевя́зка. **dressing-case** *n.* несессе́р. **dressing-down** *n.* вы́говор. **dressing-gown** *n.* хала́т. **dressing-room** *n.* убо́рная *sb.* **dressing-station** *n.* перевя́зочный пункт. **dressing-table** *n.* туале́тный стол (-á).

dressmaker ['dresˌmeıkə(r)] *n.* портни́ха.

dribble ['drıb(ə)l] *v.i.* (*water*) ка́пать *impf.*; (*child*) пуска́ть *impf.*, пусти́ть (пущу́, пу́стишь) *pf.* слю́ни; (*sport*) вести́ (веду́, -дёшь; вёл, -á) *impf.* мяч. **driblet** ['drıblıt] *n.* ка́пелька.

dried [draıd] *adj.* сушёный. **drier** ['draıə(r)] *n.* суши́лка.

drift [drıft] *n.* тече́ние; (*naut.*) дрейф; (*aeron.*) снос; (*inaction*) безде́йствие; (*purpose*) тенде́нция; (*meaning*) смысл; (*snow*) сугро́б; (*sand*) нано́с; *v.i.* плыть (плыву́, -вёшь; плыл, -á, -о) *impf.* по тече́нию; (*naut.*) дрейфова́ть *impf.*; (*snow etc.*) скопля́ться *impf.*, скопи́ться (-ится) *pf.*; *v.t.* (*snow*) наноси́ть (-ит) *impf.*, нанести́ (-есёт; -ёс, -еслá) *pf.*; заноси́ть (-ит) *impf.*, занести́ (-сёт; -слó) *pf.* (сне́гом, песко́м) *impers.*+*a.*

drill[1] [drıl] *n.* сверло́ (*pl.* ёрла), дрель, бур; *v.t.* сверли́ть *impf.*, про~ *pf.*

drill[2] [drıl] *n.* (*agric. machine*) се́ялка.

drill³ [drɪl] *v.t.* (*mil.*) обучáть *impf.*, обучи́ть (-чý, -чишь) *pf.* стрóю; муштровáть *impf.*, вы́~ *pf.*; *v.i.* проходи́ть (-ожý, -óдишь) *impf.*, пройти́ (-ойдý, -ойдёшь; -ошёл, -ошлá) *pf.* строевýю подготóвку; *n.* строевáя подготóвка.

drink [drɪŋk] *n.* питьё, напи́ток (-тка); (*mouthful*) глотóк (-ткá); (*alcoholic*) спиртнóй напи́ток (-тка); **soft ~** безалкогóльный напи́ток (-тка); *v.t.* пить (пью, пьёшь; пил, -á, -о) *impf.*, вы́~ *pf.* (**to excess** си́льно); (*plants*; *fig.*) впи́тывать *impf.*, впитáть *pf.* **drinking-bout** *n.* запóй. **drinking-song** *n.* застóльная пéсня (*g.pl.* -сен). **drinking-water** *n.* питьевáя водá (*a.* -ду).

drip [drɪp] *n.* (*action*) кáпанье; (*object*) кáпля (*g.pl.* -пель); *v.i.* кáпать *impf.*, кáпнуть *pf.* **drip-dry** *adj.* быстросóхнущий. **dripping** *n.* (*fat*) жир (-а(у), *loc.* -е & -ý); ~ **wet** промóкший насквóзь.

drive [draɪv] *n.* (*journey*) еэдá; (*excursion*) катáнье, прогýлка; (*campaign*) похóд, кампáния; (*energy*) энéргия; (*tech.*) привóд; (*driveway*) подъезднáя дорóга; *v.t.* (*urge*, *chase*) гонять *indet.*, гнать (гоню, -нишь; гнал, -á, -о) *det.*; (*vehicle*) води́ть (вожý, вóдишь) *indet.*, вести́ (ведý, -дёшь; вёл, -á) *det.*; управлять *impf.*+*i.*; (*convey*) вози́ть (вожý, вóзишь) *indet.*, везти́ (везý, -зёшь; вёз, -лá) *det.*, по~ *pf.*; *v.i.* (*travel*) éздить *indet.*, éхать (éду, -éдешь) *det.*, по~ *pf.*; (*compel*) заставлять *impf.*, застáвить *pf.*; (*nail etc.*) вбивáть *impf.*, вбить (вобью, -ьёшь) *pf.* (**into** в+*a.*); (*machine*) приводи́ть (-ожý, -óдишь) *impf.*, привести́ (-едý, -едёшь; -ёл, -елá) *pf.* в движéние (*by steam etc.*, +*i.*); ~ **away** *v.t.* прогонять *impf.*, прогнáть (прогоню, -нишь; прогнáл, -á, -о) *pf.*; *v.i.* уезжáть *impf.*, уéхать (-éду, -éдешь) *pf.*; ~ **out** *v.t.* (*knock out*) выбивáть *impf.*, вы́бить (вы́бью, -ьешь) *pf.*; (*expel*) выгонять *impf.*, вы́гнать (вы́гоню, -нишь) *pf.*; ~ **up** подъезжáть *impf.*, подъéхать (-éду, -éдешь) *pf.* (**to** к+*d.*).

drivel ['drɪv(ə)l] *n.* чепухá; *v.i.* порóть (-рю, -решь) *impf.* чепухý.

driver ['draɪvə(r)] *n.* (*of vehicle*) води́тель *m.*, шофёр. **driving** *n.* вождéние; катáние; *adj.* дви́жущий; ~ **force** дви́жущая си́ла; ~ **school** автошкóла; ~ **test** экзáмен на вождéние. **driving-belt** *n.* приводнóй ремéнь (-мня́) *m.* **driving-licence** *n.* води́тельские правá *nt.pl.* **driving-wheel** *n.* ведýщее колесó (*pl.* -ёса).

drizzle ['drɪz(ə)l] *n.* мéлкий дождь (-дя́) *m.*; *v.i.* мороси́ть *impf.*

droll [drəʊl] *adj.* смешнóй (-шóн, -шнá), забáвный. **drollery** *n.* шýтка.

dromedary ['drɒmɪdərɪ, 'drʌm-] *n.* дромадéр.

drone [drəʊn] *n.* (*bee*; *idler*) трýтень (-тня *m.*; (*buzz*) жужжáние; *v.i.* (*buzz*) жужжáть (-жжý, -жжи́шь) *impf.*; (*mutter*) бубни́ть *impf.*

drool [druːl] *v.i.* пускáть *impf.*, пусти́ть (пущý, пýстишь) *pf.* слюни.

droop [druːp] *v.i.* ни́кнуть (ник) *impf.*, по~, с~ *pf.*

drop [drɒp] *n.* (*of liquid*) кáпля (*g.pl.* -пель); (*pendant*) висю́лька; (*sweet*) леденéц (-нцá); (*fall*) падéние, пониже́ние; *v.t.* & *i.* кáпать *impf.*, кáпнуть *pf.*; (*price*) снижáть(ся) *impf.*, сни́зить(ся) *pf.*; *v.i.* (*fall*) пáдать *impf.*, упáсть (-адý, -адёшь; -áл) *pf.*; *v.t.* роня́ть *impf.*, урони́ть (-ню́, -нишь) *pf.*; (*abandon*) бросáть *impf.*, брóсить *pf.*; (*eyes*) опускáть *impf.*, опусти́ть (-ущý, -ýстишь) *pf.*; ~ **behind** отставáть (-таю́, -таёшь) *impf.*, отстáть (-áну, -áнешь) *pf.*; ~ **in** заходи́ть (-ожý, -óдишь) *impf.*, зайти́ (зайдý, -дёшь; зашёл, -шлá) *pf.* (**on** к+*d.*); ~ **off** (*fall asleep*) засыпáть *impf.*, заснýть *pf.*; ~ **out** выбывáть *impf.*, вы́быть (-буду, -будешь) *pf.* (**of** из+*g.*). **droplet** *n.* кáпелька. **drop-out** *n.* вы́бывший *sb.* **dropper** *n.* пипéтка. **droppings** *n.* помёт, навóз (-а(у)).

dropsy ['drɒpsɪ] *n.* водя́нка.

dross [drɒs] *n.* шлак; (*refuse*) отбрóсы (-сов) *pl.*

drought [draʊt] *n.* зáсуха. **drought-resistant** *adj.* засухоустóйчивый.

drove [drəʊv] *n.* стáдо (*pl.* -дá), гурт (-á). **drover** *n.* гуртовщи́к (-á).

drown [draʊn] *v.t.* топи́ть (-плю́, -пишь) *impf.*, у~ *pf.*; (*sound*) заглушáть *impf.*, заглуши́ть *pf.*; *v.i.* тонýть (-нý, -нешь) *impf.*, у~ *pf.*

drowse [draʊz] *v.i.* дремáть (-млю́, -млешь) *impf.* **drowsiness** *n.* сонли́вость, дремóта. **drowsy** *adj.* сонли́вый, дрéмлющий.

drub [drʌb] *v.t.* порóть (-рю́, -решь) *impf.*, вы́~ *pf.*

drudge [drʌdʒ] *n.* работя́га. **drudgery** *n.* тяжёлая, нýдная, рабóта.

drug [drʌg] *n.* медикамéнт; наркóтик; ~ **addict** наркомáн, ~ка; ~ **trafficker** наркоделéц (-льцá); *v.t.* давáть (даю́, даёшь) *impf.*, дать (дам, дашь, даст, дади́м; дал, -á, дáлó, -и) *pf.* наркóтик+*d.*

druid ['druːɪd] *n.* друи́д.

drum [drʌm] *n.* барабáн; *v.i.* бить (бью, бьёшь) *impf.* в барабáн; барабáнить *impf.* **drummer** *n.* барабáнщик.

drunk [drʌŋk] *adj.* пья́ный (пьян, -á, -о). **drunkard** *n.* пья́ница *c.g.* **drunken** *adj.* пья́ный. **drunkenness** *n.* пья́нство.

dry [draɪ] *adj.* сухóй (сух, -á, -о); ~ **land** сýша; *v.t.* суши́ть (-шý, -шишь) *impf.*, вы́~ *pf.*; (*wipe dry*) вытирáть *impf.*, вы́тереть (-тру, -трешь; -тер) *pf.*; *v.i.* сóхнуть (сох) *impf.*, вы́~, про~ *pf.* **dry-cleaning** *n.* химчи́стка. **drying** *n.* сýшка; *adj.* суши́льный. **dryness** *n.* сýхость.

DSS *abbr.* (*of Department of Social Security*) Министéрство социáльного обеспéчения.

dual ['djuːəl] *adj.* двойнóй, двóйственный (-ен, -енна). **duality** [ˌdjuːˈælɪtɪ] *n.* двóй-

ственность, раздвоенность. **dual-purpose**
adj. двойного назначения.

dub[1] [dʌb] *v.t.* (*nickname*) давать (даю,
даёшь) *impf.*, дать (дам, дашь, даст, дадим;
дал, -а, дало, -и) *pf.* прозвище+*d.*

dub[2] [dʌb] *v.t.* (*cin.*) дублировать *impf.* &
pf. **dubbing** *n.* дубляж.

dubious ['djuːbɪəs] *adj.* сомнительный.

ducal ['djuːk(ə)l] *adj.* герцогский. **duchess**
['dʌtʃɪs] *n.* герцогиня. **duchy** ['dʌtʃɪ] *n.* герцогство.

duck[1] [dʌk] *n.* (*bird*) утка.

duck[2] [dʌk] *v.t.* окунать *impf.*, окунуть *pf.*;
v.i. увёртываться *impf.*, увернуться *pf.* от
удара.

duck[3] [dʌk] *n.* (*cloth*) парусина.

duckling ['dʌklɪŋ] *n.* утёнок (-нка; *pl.* утята,
-т).

duct [dʌkt] *n.* проход, трубопровод; (*anat.*)
проток.

ductile ['dʌktaɪl] *adj.* (*metal*) ковкий (-вок,
-вка, -вко); (*clay*) пластичный. **ductility**
[dʌk'tɪlɪtɪ] *n.* ковкость; пластичность.

dud [dʌd] *n.* (*forgery*) подделка; (*shell*) неразорвавшийся заряд; *adj.* поддельный;
(*worthless*) негодный (-ден, -дна, -дно).

dudgeon ['dʌdʒ(ə)n] *n.* обида, возмущение;
in high ~ в глубоком возмущении.

due [djuː] *n.* должное *sb.*; *pl.* сборы *m.pl.*,
взносы *m.pl.*; *adj.* должный, надлежащий;
pred. должен (-жна); **in** ~ **course** со временем; *adv.* точно, прямо; ~ **to** благодаря+*d.*, вследствие+*g.*

duel ['djuːəl] *n.* дуэль, поединок (-нка).

duet [djuː'et] *n.* дуэт.

duffer ['dʌfə(r)] *n.* дурак (-а), недотёпа *c.g.*

dug-out ['dʌɡaʊt] *n.* (*boat*) челнок (-а); (*mil.*)
блиндаж (-а).

duke [djuːk] *n.* герцог; **Grand D**~ великий
князь (*pl.* -зья, -зей) *m.*

dulcet ['dʌlsɪt] *adj.* сладкий (-док, -дка, -дко),
нежный (-жен, -жна, -жно, нежны).

dulcimer ['dʌlsɪmə(r)] *n.* цимбалы (-л) *pl.*

dull [dʌl] *adj.* тупой (туп, -а, -о, тупы);
(*tedious*) скучный (-чен, -чна, -чно);
(*colour*) тусклый (-л, -ла, -ло), матовый;
(*weather*) пасмурный; *v.t.* притуплять *impf.*,
притупить (-плю, -пишь) *pf.* **dullard** ['dʌləd]
n. тупица *c.g.* **dullness** *n.* тупость; скучность.

duly ['djuːlɪ] *adv.* надлежащим образом;
(*punctually*) в должное время, своевременно.

dumb [dʌm] *adj.* немой (нем, -а, -о); (*taciturn*) молчаливый; **deaf and** ~ глухонемой.
dumb-bell *n.* гантель. **dumb'found** *v.t.*
ошеломлять *impf.*, ошеломить *pf.*

dummy ['dʌmɪ] *n.* макет; (*tailor's*) манекен;
(*cards*) болван; (*baby's*) соска(-пустышка);
adj. ненастоящий, фальшивый.

dump [dʌmp] *n.* свалка; *v.t.* сваливать *impf.*,
свалить (-лю, -лишь) *pf.* **dumping** *n.* (*econ.*)
демпинг, бросовый экспорт.

dumpling ['dʌmplɪŋ] *n.* клёцка.

dumpy ['dʌmpɪ] *adj.* приземистый, коренастый.

dun [dʌn] *adj.* серовато-коричневый.

dunce [dʌns] *n.* болван, тупица *c.g.*

dune [djuːn] *n.* дюна.

dung [dʌŋ] *n.* помёт, навоз (-а(у)).

dungarees [ˌdʌŋɡəˈriːz] *n.* (*рабочий*) комбинезон.

dungeon ['dʌndʒ(ə)n] *n.* темница.

dunk [dʌŋk] *v.t.* макать *impf.*, макнуть *pf.*

dupe [djuːp] *v.t.* обманывать *impf.*, обмануть
(-ну, -нешь) *pf.*; *n.* жертва обмана; простофиля *c.g.*

duplicate ['djuːplɪkət] *n.* дубликат, копия; **in**
~ в двух экземплярах; *adj.* (*double*) двойной; (*identical*) идентичный; *v.t.* дублировать *impf.*; снимать *impf.*, снять (сниму,
-мешь; снял, -а, -о) *pf.* копию с+*g.* **dupli-
cator** *n.* копировальный аппарат.

duplicity [djuːˈplɪsɪtɪ] *n.* двуличность.

durability [ˌdjʊərəˈbɪlɪtɪ] *n.* прочность. **'dura-
ble** *adj.* прочный (-чен, -чна, -чно, прочны). **du'ration** *n.* продолжительность; срок
(-а(у)).

duress [djʊəˈres, ˈdjʊə-] *n.* принуждение; **under**
~ под давлением.

during ['djʊərɪŋ] *prep.* в течение+*g.*, во
время+*g.*

dusk [dʌsk] *n.* сумерки (-рек) *pl.*, сумрак.
dusky *adj.* сумеречный; тёмный (-мен,
-мна); (*complexion*) смуглый (смугл, -а, -о).

dust [dʌst] *n.* пыль (*loc.* -ли); *v.t.* (*clean*)
стирать *impf.*, стереть (сотру, -рёшь; стёр)
pf. пыль с+*g.*; (*sprinkle*) посыпать *impf.*,
посыпать (-плю, -плешь) *pf.*+*i.* **dustbin** *n.*
мусорный ящик. **duster** *n.* пыльная тряпка.
dusting *n.* вытирание, смахивание, пыли.
dust-jacket *n.* суперобложка. **dustman** *n.*
мусорщик. **dustpan** *n.* совок (-вка). **dusty**
adj. пыльный (-лен, -льна, -льно), запылённый (-ён, -ена).

Dutch [dʌtʃ] *adj.* голландский; ~ **courage**
храбрость во хмелью; ~ **treat** складчина;
n.: **the** ~ голландцы *m.pl.* **Dutchman** *n.*
голландец (-дца).

dutiable ['djuːtɪəb(ə)l] *adj.* подлежащий обложению пошлиной. **dutiful** *adj.* послушный.
duty *n.* (*obligation*) долг (-а(у), *loc.* -ý; *pl.* -
и), обязанность; (*office*) дежурство; (*tax*)
пошлина; **on** ~ дежурный; **be on** ~ дежурить *impf.*; **do one's** ~ исполнять *impf.*,
исполнить *pf.* свой долг. **duty-free** *adj.*
беспошлинный. **duty-paid** *adj.* оплаченный
пошлиной.

dwarf [dwɔːf] *n.* карлик, -ица; *adj.* карликовый; *v.t.* (*stunt*) останавливать *impf.*,
остановить (-влю, -вишь) *pf.* рост, развитие+*g.*; (*tower above*) возвышаться *impf.*,
возвыситься *pf.* над+*i.*

dwell [dwel] *v.i.* обитать *impf.*; ~ **upon**
останавливаться *impf.* на+*p.* **dweller** *n.*
житель *m.*, ~ница. **dwelling** *n.* (~-*place*)

местожи́тельство. **dwelling-house** *n*. жило́й дом (-a(y); *pl*. -á).

dwindle ['dwɪnd(ə)l] *v.i.* убыва́ть *impf.*, убы́ть (убу́ду, -дешь; у́был, -á, -о) *pf.*

dye [daɪ] *n.* краси́тель *m.*, кра́ска; *v.t.* окра́шивать *impf.*, окра́сить *pf.* **dyed-in-the-wool** *adj.* (*fig.*) закоренéлый. **dyeing** *n.* кра́шение. **dyer** *n.* краси́льщик. **dye-works** *n.* краси́льня (*g.pl.* -лен).

dying ['daɪɪŋ] *adj.* умира́ющий; (*at time of death*) предсме́ртный; *n.* умира́ние, угаса́ние.

dynamic [daɪ'næmɪk] *adj.* динами́ческий. **dynamics** *n.* дина́мика.

dynamite ['daɪnəmaɪt] *n.* динами́т; *v.t.* взрыва́ть *impf.*, взорва́ть (-ву́, -вёшь; взорва́л, -á, -о) *pf.* динами́том.

dynamo ['daɪnəməʊ] *n.* дина́мо-маши́на.

dynastic [dɪ'næstɪk] *adj.* династи́ческий. **dynasty** *n.* дина́стия.

dysentery ['dɪsəntərɪ, -trɪ] *n.* дизентери́я.

dyspepsia [dɪs'pepsɪə] диспепси́я. **dyspeptic** *n. & adj.* страда́ющий (*sb.*) диспепси́ей.

E

E [iː] *n.* (*mus.*) ми *nt.indecl.*

each [iːtʃ] *adj. & pron.* ка́ждый; ~ **other** друг дру́га (*d.* -гу, *etc.*).

eager ['iːgə(r)] *adj.* стремя́щийся (**for** к+*d.*); (*impatient*) нетерпели́вый. **eagerness** *n.* пыл (-a(y), *loc.* -ý), рве́ние.

eagle ['iːg(ə)l] *n.* орёл (орла́), орли́ца; ~ **owl** фи́лин. **eagle-eyed** *adj.* зо́ркий (-рок, -рка́, -рко). **eaglet** *n.* орлёнок (-нка; *pl.* орля́та, -т).

ear[1] [ɪə(r)] *n.* (*corn*) ко́лос (*pl.* -о́сья, -о́сьев); *v.i.* колоси́ться *impf.*, вы́~ *pf.*

ear[2] [ɪə(r)] *n.* (*organ*) у́хо (*pl.* у́ши, уше́й); (*sense*) слух; ~ **lobe** мо́чка; **by** ~ по слу́ху; **to be all** ~s слу́шать *impf.* во все у́ши. **earache** *n.* боль в у́хе. **eardrum** *n.* бараба́нная перепо́нка.

earl [ɜːl] *n.* граф. **earldom** *n.* гра́фство, ти́тул гра́фа.

earless ['ɪələs] *adj.* безу́хий.

early ['ɜːlɪ] *adj.* ра́нний; (*initial*) нача́льный; *adv.* ра́но.

earmark ['ɪəmɑːk] *n.* клеймо́ (*pl.* -ма); *v.t.* клейми́ть *impf.*, за~ *pf.*; (*assign*) предназнача́ть *impf.*, предназна́чить *pf.*

earn [ɜːn] *v.t.* зараба́тывать *impf.*, зарабо́тать *pf.*; (*deserve*) заслу́живать *impf.*, заслужи́ть (-жу́, -жишь) *pf.* **earnings** *n.* за́работок (-тка).

earnest ['ɜːnɪst] *adj.* серьёзный; *n.*: **in** ~ всерьёз.

earphone ['ɪəfəʊn] *n.* нау́шник. **earplugs** *n.* противошу́мы (-ов) *pl.* **earring** *n.* серьга́ (*pl.* -рьги, -рёг, -рьга́м). **earshot** *n.*: **within** ~ в преде́лах слы́шимости; **out of** ~ вне преде́лов слы́шимости. **ear-splitting** *adj.* оглуши́тельный.

earth [ɜːθ] *n.* земля́ (*a.* -лю); (*soil*) по́чва; (*fox's*) нора́ (*pl.* -ры); (*elec.*) заземле́ние; *v.i.* заземля́ть *impf.*, заземли́ть *pf.*; ~ **up** оку́чивать *impf.*, оку́чить *pf.* **earthen** *adj.* земляно́й. **earthenware** *n.* гли́няная посу́да (*collect.*); *adj.* гли́няный. **earthly** *adj.* земно́й, жите́йский. **earth-moving** *adj.* землеро́йный. **earthquake** *n.* землетрясе́ние. **earthwork** *n.* земляно́е укрепле́ние. **earthworm** *n.* земляно́й червь (-вя́; *pl.* -ви, -ве́й) *m.* **earthy** *adj.* земляно́й, земли́стый; (*coarse*) грубый (груб, -á, -о).

earwig ['ɪəwɪg] *n.* уховёртка.

ease [iːz] *n.* (*facility*) лёгкость; (*unconstraint*) непринуждённость; **at** ~ *int.* во́льно!; **with** ~ легко́, без труда́; *v.t.* облегча́ть *impf.*, облегчи́ть *pf.*

easel ['iːz(ə)l] *n.* мольбе́рт.

east [iːst] *n.* восто́к; (*naut.*) ост; *adj.* восто́чный; о́стовый. **eastern** *adj.* восто́чный. **eastwards** *adv.* на восто́к, к восто́ку.

Easter ['iːstə(r)] *n.* Па́сха.

easy ['iːzɪ] *adj.* лёгкий (-гок, -гка́, -гко, лёгки́); (*unconstrained*) непринуждённый (-ён, -ённа). **easy-going** *adj.* доброду́шный.

eat [iːt] *v.t.* есть (ем, ешь, ест, еди́м; ел) *impf.*, с~ *pf.*; ку́шать *impf.*, по~, с~ *pf.*; ~ **away** разъеда́ть *impf.*, разъе́сть (-е́ст; -е́л) *pf.*; ~ **into** въеда́ться *impf.*, въе́сться (-е́стся; -е́лся) *pf.* в+*a.*; ~ **up** доеда́ть *impf.*, дое́сть (-е́м, -е́шь, -е́ст, -еди́м; -е́л) *pf.* **eatable** *adj.* съедо́бный.

eau-de-Cologne [,əʊdəkə'ləʊn] *n.* одеколо́н.

eaves [iːvz] *n.* стреха́ (*pl.* -и) **eavesdrop** *v.t.* подслу́шивать *impf.*, подслу́шать *pf.*

ebb [eb] *n.* (*tide*) отли́в; (*fig.*) упа́док (-дка).

ebony ['ebənɪ] *n.* чёрное де́рево.

ebullience [ɪ'bʌlɪəns] *n.* кипу́честь. **ebullient** *adj.* кипу́чий.

eccentric [ɪk'sentrɪk, ek-] *n.* чуда́к (-á), -á́чка; (*tech.*) эксце́нтрик; *adj.* эксцентри́чный. **eccen'tricity** *n.* эксцентри́чность, чуда́чество.

ecclesiastic [ɪ,kliːzɪ'æstɪk] *n.* духо́вное лицо́ (*pl.* -ца) **ecclesiastical** *adj.* духо́вный, церко́вный.

echelon ['eʃəlɒn, 'eɪʃə,lɔ̃] *n.* эшело́н; *v.t.* эшелони́ровать *impf. & pf.*

echo ['ekəʊ] *n.* э́хо; (*imitation*) о́тклик;*v.i.* (*resound*) оглаша́ться *impf.*, огласи́ться *pf.* э́хом; *v.t. & i.* (*repeat*) повторя́ть(ся) *impf.*, повтори́ть(ся) *pf.* **echo-sounder** *n.* эхоло́т.

eclipse [ɪ'klɪps] *n.* затме́ние; (*fig.*) упа́док (-дка) *v.t.* затмева́ть *impf.*, затми́ть *pf.*

economic [,iːkə'nɒmɪk, ,ek-] *adj.* экономи́ческий, хозя́йственный; (*profitable*) рента́-

бельный. **economical** *adj.* эконо́мный, бережли́вый. **e'conomist** *n.* экономи́ст. **e'conomize** *v.t.* & *i.* эконо́мить *impf.*, с~ *pf.* **e'conomy** *n.* хозя́йство, эконо́мика; (*saving*) эконо́мия, сбереже́ние.

ecosystem ['i:kəʊ,sɪstəm] *n.* экосисте́ма.

ecstasy ['ekstəsɪ] *n.* экста́з, восхище́ние. **ecstatic** [ɪk'stætɪk] *adj.* исступлённый (-ён, -ённа).

écu ['ekju:] *n.* экю *m.* & *nt.indecl.*

eddy ['edɪ] *n.* (*water*) водоворо́т; (*wind*) вихрь *m.*; *v.i.* (*water*) крути́ться (-ится) *impf.*; (*wind*) клуби́ться *impf.*

edelweiss ['eɪd(ə)l,vaɪs] *n.* эдельве́йс.

edge [edʒ] *n.* край (*loc.* -а́е & аю́; *pl.* -ая́), кро́мка; (*blade*) ле́звие; **on** ~ (*excited*) взволно́ванный (-ан); (*irritable*) раздражён-ный (-ён, -ена́); *v.t.* (*sharpen*) точи́ть (-чу́, -чишь) *impf.*, на~ *pf.*; (*border*) окаймля́ть *impf.*, окайми́ть *pf.*; *v.i.* пробира́ться *impf.*, пробра́ться (-беру́сь, -берёшься; -а́лся, -ала́сь, -ало́сь) *pf.* **edging** *n.* кайма́. **edgy** *adj.* раздражи́тельный.

edible ['edɪb(ə)l] *adj.* съедо́бный.

edict ['i:dɪkt] *n.* ука́з.

edification [,edɪfɪ'keɪʃ(ə)n] *n.* назида́ние. **edi-fice** ['edɪfɪs] *n.* зда́ние, сооруже́ние. **'edify** *v.t.* наставля́ть *impf.*, наста́вить *pf.* **'edify-ing** *adj.* назида́тельный.

Edinburgh ['edɪnbərə, -brə] *n.* Э́динбург.

edit ['edɪt] *v.t.* редакти́ровать *impf.*, от~ *pf.*; (*cin.*) монти́ровать *impf.*, с~ *pf.* **edition** [ɪ'dɪʃ(ə)n] *n.* изда́ние; (*number of copies*) тира́ж (-а́). **editor** *n.* реда́ктор. **edi'torial** *n.* передова́я статья́; *adj.* реда́кторский, редакцио́нный.

educate ['edjʊ,keɪt] *v.t.* воспи́тывать *impf.*, воспита́ть *pf.* **educated** *adj.* образо́ванный (-ан, -анна). **edu'cation** *n.* образова́ние, воспита́ние; (*instruction*) обуче́ние. **edu-'cational** *adj.* образова́тельный, воспита́-тельный; уче́бный.

EEC *abbr.* (*of European Economic Community*) ЕЭС, Европе́йское экономи́ческое соо́б-щество.

eel [i:l] *n.* у́горь (угря́) *m.*

eerie ['ɪərɪ] *adj.* (*gloomy*) мра́чный (-чен, -чна́, -чно); (*strange*) стра́нный (-нен, -нна́, -нно).

efface [ɪ'feɪs] *v.t.* изгла́живать *impf.*, изгла́-дить *pf.*; ~ **o.s.** стушёвываться *impf.*, стушева́ться (-шу́юсь, -шу́ешься) *pf.*

effect [ɪ'fekt] *n.* (*result*) сле́дствие; (*efficacy*) де́йствие; (*impression; theatr., cin.*) эффе́кт; *pl.* иму́щество; (*personal*) ли́чные ве́щи (-ще́й) *f.pl.*; **in** ~ факти́чески; **bring into** ~ осуществля́ть *impf.*, осуществи́ть *pf.*; **take** ~ вступа́ть *impf.*, вступи́ть (-ит) *pf.* в си́лу; *v.t.* производи́ть (-ожу́, -о́дишь) *impf.*, произвести́ (-еду́, -еде́шь; -ёл, -ела́) *pf.* **effective** *adj.* де́йственный (-ен, -енна), эффекти́вный; (*striking*) эффе́ктный; (*actual*) факти́ческий. **effectiveness** *n.* де́йственность, эффекти́вность. **effectual**

adj. де́йственный (-ен, -енна).

effeminate [ɪ'femɪnət] *adj.* изне́женный (-ен, -енна).

effervesce [,efə'ves] *v.i.* пе́ниться *impf.* **effervescent** *adj.* шипу́чий.

efficacious [,efɪ'keɪʃəs] *adj.* де́йственный (-ен, -енна), эффекти́вный. **efficacy** ['efɪkəsɪ] *n.* де́йственность, эффекти́вность. **efficiency** [ɪ'fɪʃənsɪ] *n.* де́йственность, эффекти́вность; (*of person*) уме́ние; (*mech.*) коэффицие́нт поле́зного де́йствия. **efficient** *adj.* де́йст-венный (-ен, -ена), эффекти́вный; (*person*) уме́лый.

effigy ['efɪdʒɪ] *n.* изображе́ние.

effort ['efət] *n.* (*exertion*) уси́лие; (*attempt*) попы́тка.

effrontery [ɪ'frʌntərɪ] *n.* на́глость.

e.g. *abbr.* (*of exempli gratia*) напр., наприме́р.

egg[1] [eg] *n.* яйцо́ (*pl.* я́йца, яи́ц, я́йцам); *attr.* яи́чный.

egg[2] [eg] *v.t.*: ~ **on** подстрека́ть *impf.*, под-стрекну́ть *pf.*

egg-beater ['egbi:tə(r)] *n.* взбива́лка. **eggcup** *n.* рю́мка для яйца́. **eggplant** *n.* баклажа́н. **eggshell** *n.* яи́чная скорлупа́ (*pl.* -пы).

ego ['i:gəʊ] *n.* э́го *indecl.*; я *nt.indecl.* **egoism** *n.* эгои́зм. **egoist** *n.* эгои́ст. **ego'istic** *adj.* эгоисти́ческий. **egotism** *n.* эготи́зм.

egret ['i:grɪt] *n.* бе́лая ца́пля (*g.pl.* -пель).

Egypt ['i:dʒɪpt] *n.* Еги́пет. **Egyptian** [ɪ'dʒɪp-ʃ(ə)n] *n.* египтя́нин (*pl.* -я́не, -я́н), -я́нка; *adj.* еги́петский.

eider ['aɪdə(r)] *n.* (*duck*) га́га; (~-*down*) гага́чий пух (*loc.* -у́). **eiderdown** *n.* (*quilt*) пухо́вое одея́ло.

Eiffel Tower ['aɪf(ə)l] *n.* Э́йфелева ба́шня.

eight [eɪt] *adj.* & *n.* во́семь (-сьми́, -семью́ & -сьмью́); (*collect.*; *8 pairs*) во́сьмеро (-ры́х); (*cards*; *boat*; *number 8*) восьмёрка; (*time*) во́семь (часо́в); (*age*) во́семь лет. **eigh'teen** *adj.* & *n.* восемна́дцать (-ти, -тью); (*age*) восемна́дцать лет. **eigh'teenth** *adj.* & *n.* восемна́дцатый; (*fraction*) восемна́дцатая (часть (*pl.* -ти, -те́й)); (*date*) восемна́дцатое (число́). **eighth** *adj.* & *n.* восьмо́й; (*fraction*) восьма́я (часть (*pl.* -ти, -те́й)); (*date*) восьмо́е (число́). **eightieth** *adj.* & *n.* восьми-деся́тый; (*fraction*) восьмидеся́тая (часть (*pl.* -ти, -те́й)). **eighty** *adj.* & *n.* во́семьдесят (-сьми́десяти, -сьмью́десятью); (*age*) во́семь-десят лет; *pl.* (*decade*) восьмидеся́тые го́ды (-до́в) *m.pl.*

Eire ['eərə] *n.* Э́йре *nt.indecl.*

either ['aɪðə(r), 'i:ðə(r)] *adj.* & *pron.* (*one of two*) оди́н из двух, тот и́ли друго́й; (*each of two*) и тот, и друго́й; о́ба; любо́й; *adv.* & *conj.*: ~ ... **or** и́ли ... и́ли, либо... ли́бо.

eject [ɪ'dʒekt] *v.t.* изверга́ть *impf.*, изве́рг-нуть (-г(ну)л, -гла) *pf.* **ejection** *n.* изве́р-же́ние; ~ **seat** катапульти́руемое кре́сло (*g.pl.* -сел).

eke [i:k] *v.t.*: ~ **out a living** перебива́ться

impf., переби́ться (-бью́сь, -бьёшься) *pf.* кое-как.

elaborate [ɪˈlæbərət; ɪˈlæbəˌreɪt] *adj.* (*complicated*) сло́жный (-жен, -жна́, -жно); (*detailed*) подро́бный; *v.t.* разраба́тывать *impf.*, разрабо́тать *pf.*; уточня́ть *impf.*, уточни́ть *pf.* **elabo'ration** *n.* разрабо́тка; уточне́ние.

elapse [ɪˈlæps] *v.i.* проходи́ть (-о́дит) *impf.*, пройти́ (пройдёт; прошёл, -шла́) *pf.*; истека́ть *impf.*, исте́чь (-ечёт; -ёк, -екла́) *pf.*

elastic [ɪˈlæstɪk, ɪˈlɑːstɪk] *n.* рези́нка; *adj.* эласти́чный, упру́гий. **elas'ticity** *n.* эласти́чность, упру́гость.

elate [ɪˈleɪt] *v.t.* возбужда́ть *impf.*, возбуди́ть *pf.* **elation** *n.* восто́рг.

elbow [ˈelbəʊ] *n.* ло́коть (-ктя; *pl.* -кти, -кте́й) *m.*; *v.t.* толка́ть *impf.*, толкну́ть *pf.* ло́ктем, -тя́ми; ~ **(one's way) through** прота́лкиваться *impf.*, протолкну́ться *pf.* че́рез+*a.*

elder[1] [ˈeldə(r)] *n.* (*tree*) бузина́.

elder[2] [ˈeldə(r)] *n.* (*person*) ста́рец (-рца); *pl.* ста́ршие *sb.*; *adj.* ста́рший. **elderberry** [ˈeldəbərɪ] *n.* я́года бузины́.

elderly *adj.* пожило́й. **eldest** *adj.* ста́рший.

elect [ɪˈlekt] *adj.* и́збранный; *v.t.* выбира́ть *impf.*, вы́брать (вы́беру, -решь) *pf.*; избира́ть *impf.*, избра́ть (изберу́, -рёшь; избра́л, -á, -о) *pf.* **election** *n.* вы́боры *m.pl.*, избра́ние; *adj.* избира́тельный. **elective** *adj.* вы́борный. **elector** *n.* избира́тель *m.* **electoral** *adj.* избира́тельный, вы́борный. **electorate** *n.* избира́тели *m.pl.*

electric(al) [ɪˈlektrɪk(ə)l] *adj.* электри́ческий; ~ **blanket** одея́ло-гре́лка; ~ **shock** уда́р электри́ческим то́ком. **elec'trician** *n.* эле́ктрик, электромонтёр. **elec'tricity** *n.* электри́чество. **electrify** *v.t.* (*convert to electricity*) электрифици́ровать *impf.* & *pf.*; (*charge with electricity; fig.*) электризова́ть *impf.*, на~ *pf.* **electrode** *n.* электро́д. **electron** *n.* электро́н. **elec'tronic** *adj.* электро́нный. **elec'tronics** *n.* электро́ника.

electro- [ɪˈlektrəʊ] *in comb.* электро... . **electrocute** [ɪˈlektrəˌkjuːt] *v.t.* убива́ть *impf.*, уби́ть (убью́, -ьёшь) *pf.* электри́ческим то́ком; (*execute*) казни́ть *impf.* & *pf.* на электри́ческом сту́ле. **electrolysis** [ˌɪlekˈtrɒlɪsɪs, ˌel-] *n.* электро́лиз. **electrolyte** [ɪˈlektrəˌlaɪt] *n.* электроли́т. **electromagnetic** *adj.* электромагни́тный. **electrotype** *n.* (*print.*) гальва́но *nt.indecl.*

elegance [ˈelɪɡəns] *n.* элега́нтность, изя́щество. **elegant** *adj.* элега́нтный, изя́щный.

elegiac [ˌelɪˈdʒaɪək] *adj.* элеги́ческий. **'elegy** *n.* эле́гия.

element [ˈelɪmənt] *n.* элеме́нт; (*4* ~*s*) стихи́я; *pl.* (*rudiments*) нача́тки (-ков) *pl.*; **be in one's** ~ быть в свое́й стихи́и. **ele'mental** *adj.* стихи́йный. **ele'mentary** *adj.* (*rudimentary*) элемента́рный; (*school etc.*) нача́льный.

elephant [ˈelɪfənt] *n.* слон (-á), ~и́ха. **ele'phantine** *adj.* слоно́вый; (*clumsy*) тяжело-ве́сный, неуклю́жий.

elevate [ˈelɪˌveɪt] *v.t.* поднима́ть *impf.*, подня́ть (подниму́, -мешь; по́дня́л, -á, -о) *pf.*; (*in rank*) возводи́ть (-ожу́, -о́дишь) *impf.*, возвести́ (-еду́, -едёшь; -ёл, -ела́) *pf.* **ele'vation** *n.* подня́тие; возведе́ние; (*height*) высота́; (*angle*) у́гол (угла́) возвыше́ния; (*drawing*) вертика́льная прое́кция. **elevator** *n.* подъёмник; (*for grain*) элева́тор.

eleven [ɪˈlev(ə)n] *adj.* & *n.* оди́ннадцать (-ти, -тью); (*time*) оди́ннадцать (часо́в); (*age*) оди́ннадцать лет; (*team*) кома́нда (из оди́ннадцати челове́к). **elevenses** [ɪˈlevənzɪz] *n.* второ́й за́втрак. **eleventh** *adj.* & *n.* оди́ннадцатый; (*fraction*) оди́ннадцатая (часть (*pl.* -ти, -те́й)); (*date*) оди́ннадцатое (числ-о́); **at the** ~ **hour** в после́днюю мину́ту.

elf [elf] *n.* эльф.

elicit [ɪˈlɪsɪt, eˈlɪsɪt] *v.t.* извлека́ть *impf.*, извле́чь (-еку́, -ечёшь; -ёк, -екла́) *pf.* (**from** из+*g.*); (*evoke*) вызыва́ть *impf.*, вы́звать (вы́зову, -вешь) *pf.*

eligibility [ˌelɪdʒɪˈbɪlɪtɪ] *n.* пра́во на избра́ние. **'eligible** *adj.* могу́щий, име́ющий пра́во, быть и́збранным.

eliminate [ɪˈlɪmɪˌneɪt] *v.t.* (*exclude*) устраня́ть *impf.*, устрани́ть *pf.*; (*remove*) уничтожа́ть *impf.*, уничто́жить *pf.* **elimi'nation** *n.* устране́ние; уничтоже́ние.

élite [eɪˈliːt, ɪ-] *n.* эли́та; *adj.* эли́тный.

elk [elk] *n.* лось (*pl.* -си, -се́й) *m.*

ellipse [ɪˈlɪps] *n.* э́ллипс. **ellipsis** *n.* э́ллипсис. **elliptic(al)** *adj.* эллипти́ческий.

elm [elm] *n.* вяз.

elocution [ˌeləˈkjuːʃ(ə)n] *n.* ора́торское иску́сство.

elongate [ˈiːlɒŋˌɡeɪt] *v.t.* удлиня́ть *impf.*, удлини́ть *pf.*

elope [ɪˈləʊp] *v.i.* сбега́ть *impf.*, сбежа́ть (-егу́, -ежи́шь) *pf.* **elopement** *n.* (та́йный) побе́г.

eloquence [ˈeləkwəns] *n.* красноре́чие. **eloquent** *adj.* красноречи́вый, вырази́тельный.

else [els] *adv.* (*besides*) ещё; (*instead*) друго́й; (*with neg.*) бо́льше; **nobody** ~ никто́ бо́льше; **or** ~ ина́че; а (не) то; и́ли же; **s.o.** ~ кто-нибудь друго́й; **something** ~? ещё что-нибудь? **elsewhere** *adv.* (*place*) в друго́м ме́сте; (*direction*) в друго́е ме́сто.

elucidate [ɪˈluːsɪˌdeɪt, ɪˈljuːs-] *v.t.* по-, разъ-ясня́ть *impf.*, по-, разъ-, ясни́ть *pf.* **eluci'dation** *n.* по-, разъ-, ясне́ние.

elude [ɪˈluːd, ɪˈljuːd] *v.t.* избега́ть *impf.*+*g.*; уклоня́ться *impf.*, уклони́ться (-ню́сь, -нишь-ся) *pf.* от+*g.* **elusive** [ɪˈluːsɪv, ɪˈljuːsɪv] *adj.* неулови́мый.

emaciate [ɪˈmeɪsɪˌeɪt, ɪˈmeɪʃɪˌeɪt] *v.t.* истоща́ть *impf.*, истощи́ть *pf.* **emaci'ation** *n.* истоще́ние.

e-mail [ˈiːmeɪl] *n.* электро́нная по́чта.

emanate [ˈeməˌneɪt] *v.i.* исходи́ть (-ит) *impf.*

(from из, от, +g.); (*light*) излуча́ться *impf.*, излучи́ться *pf.* **ema'nation** *n.* излуче́ние, эмана́ция.

emancipate [ɪ'mænsɪ,peɪt] *v.t.* освобожда́ть *impf.*, освободи́ть *pf.*; эмансипи́ровать *impf. & pf.* **emanci'pation** *n.* освобожде́ние, эмансипа́ция.

emasculate [ɪ'mæskjʊ,leɪt] *v.t.* кастри́ровать *impf. & pf.*; (*fig.*) выхола́щивать *impf.*, вы́холостить *pf.* **emascu'lation** *n.* выхола́щивание.

embalm [ɪm'bɑːm] *v.t.* бальзами́ровать *impf.*, на~ *pf.* **embalmer** *n.* бальзамиро́вщик. **embalmment** *n.* бальзамиро́вка.

embankment [ɪm'bæŋkmənt] *n.* (*river*) да́мба, на́бережная *sb.*; (*rail.*) на́сыпь.

embargo [em'bɑːgəʊ, ɪm-] *n.* эмба́рго *nt.indecl.*; *v.t.* накла́дывать *impf.*, наложи́ть (-жу́, -жишь) *pf.* эмба́рго на+a.

embark [ɪm'bɑːk] *v.t.* грузи́ть (-ужу́, -у́зишь) *impf.*, по~ *pf.* на кора́бль; *v.i.* сади́ться *impf.*, сесть (ся́ду, -дешь; сел) *pf.* на кора́бль; ~ **upon** предпринима́ть *impf.*, предприня́ть (-иму́, -и́мешь; предпри́нял, -а́, -о) *pf.* **embar'kation** *n.* поса́дка (на кора́бль).

embarrass [ɪm'bærəs] *v.t.* смуща́ть *impf.*, смути́ть (-ущу́, -ути́шь) *pf.*; (*impede*) затрудня́ть *impf.*, затрудни́ть *pf.*; стесня́ть *impf.*, стесни́ть *pf.* **embarrassing** *adj.* неудо́бный. **embarrassment** *n.* смуще́ние, замеша́тельство.

embassy ['embəsɪ] *n.* посо́льство.

embed [ɪm'bed] *v.t.* вставля́ть *impf.*, вста́вить *pf.*; вдёлывать *impf.*, вде́лать *pf.*

embellish [ɪm'belɪʃ] *v.t.* (*adorn*) украша́ть *impf.*, укра́сить *pf.*; (*story*) прикра́шивать *impf.*, прикра́сить *pf.* **embellishment** *n.* украше́ние; преувеличе́ние.

embers ['embəz] *n.* горя́чая зола́, тле́ющие угольки́ *m.pl.*

embezzle [ɪm'bez(ə)l] *v.t.* растра́чивать *impf.*, растра́тить *pf.* **embezzlement** *n.* растра́та. **embezzler** *n.* растра́тчик.

embitter [ɪm'bɪtə(r)] *v.t.* ожесточа́ть *impf.*, ожесточи́ть *pf.*

emblem ['embləm] *n.* эмбле́ма, си́мвол.

embodiment [ɪm'bɒdɪmənt] *n.* воплоще́ние, олицетворе́ние. **embody** *v.t.* воплоща́ть *impf.*, воплоти́ть (-ощу́, -оти́шь) *pf.*; олицетворя́ть *impf.*, олицетвори́ть *pf.*

emboss [ɪm'bɒs] *v.t.* чека́нить *impf.*, вы́-, от~ *pf.* **embossed** *adj.* чека́ный (-нен, -нна).

embrace [ɪm'breɪs] *n.* объя́тие; *v.i.* обнима́ться *impf.*, обня́ться (обни́мемся, -етесь; -ня́лся, -няла́сь) *pf.*; *v.t.* обнима́ть *impf.*, обня́ть (обниму́, -мешь; о́бнял, -а́, -о) *pf.*; (*accept*) принима́ть *impf.*, приня́ть (приму́, -мешь; при́нял, -а́, -о) *pf.*; (*comprise*) охва́тывать *impf.*, охвати́ть (-ачу́, -а́тишь) *pf.*

embrasure [ɪm'breɪʒə(r)] *n.* амбразу́ра.

embrocation [,embrəʊ'keɪʃ(ə)n] *n.* жи́дкая мазь.

embroider [ɪm'brɔɪdə(r)] *v.t.* (*cloth*) вышива́ть *impf.*, вы́шить (вы́шью, -ьешь) *pf.*; (*story*) прикра́шивать *impf.*, прикра́сить *pf.* **embroidery** *n.* вышива́ние, вы́шивка; преувеличе́ние; ~ **frame** пя́льцы (-лец) *pl.*

embryo ['embrɪəʊ] *n.* заро́дыш, эмбрио́н. **embryonic** *adj.* заро́дышевый, эмбриона́льный; (*fig.*) элемента́рный.

emend [ɪ'mend] *v.t.* исправля́ть *impf.*, испра́вить *pf.* **emen'dation** *n.* исправле́ние.

emerald ['emər(ə)ld] *n.* изумру́д; *adj.* изумру́дный.

emerge [ɪ'mɜːdʒ] *v.i.* появля́ться *impf.*, появи́ться (-влю́сь, -вишься) *pf.* **emergence** *n.* появле́ние. **emergency** *n.* непредви́денный слу́чай; **in case of** ~ в слу́чае кра́йней необходи́мости; **state of** ~ чрезвыча́йное положе́ние; ~ **brake** э́кстренный то́рмоз (*pl.* -а́); ~ **exit** запа́сный вы́ход; ~ **landing** вы́нужденная поса́дка; ~ **powers** чрезвыча́йные полномо́чия *nt.pl.* **emergent** *adj.* появля́ющийся; (*nation*) неда́вно получи́вший незави́симость.

emeritus [ɪ'merɪtəs] *adj.*: ~ **professor** заслу́женный профе́ссор (*pl.* -а́) в отста́вке.

emery ['emərɪ] *n.* нажда́к (-а́); ~ **paper** нажда́чная бума́га.

emetic [ɪ'metɪk] *adj.* рво́тный; *n.* рво́тное *sb.*

emigrant ['emɪgrənt] *n.* эмигра́нт, ~ка. **emigrate** *v.i.* эмигри́ровать *impf. & pf.* **emi'gration** *n.* эмигра́ция. **émigré** ['emɪ,greɪ] *n.* эмигра́нт; *adj.* эмигра́нтский.

eminence ['emɪnəns] *n.* высота́, возвы́шенность; (*title*) высокопреосвяще́нство. **eminent** *adj.* выдаю́щийся. **eminently** *adv.* чрезвыча́йно.

emission [ɪ'mɪʃ(ə)n] *n.* испуска́ние, излуче́ние. **emit** *v.t.* испуска́ть *impf.*, испусти́ть (-ущу́, -у́стишь) *pf.*; (*light*) излуча́ть *impf.*, излучи́ть *pf.*; (*sound*) издава́ть (-даю́, -даёшь) *impf.*, изда́ть (-а́м, -а́шь, -а́ст, -ади́м; изда́л, -а́, -о) *pf.*

emotion [ɪ'məʊʃ(ə)n] *n.* (*state*) волне́ние; (*feeling*) эмо́ция, чу́вство. **emotional** *adj.* эмоциона́льный, волну́ющий.

emperor ['empərə(r)] *n.* импера́тор.

emphasis ['emfəsɪs] *n.* ударе́ние; (*expressiveness*) вырази́тельность. **emphasize** *v.t.* подчёркивать *impf.*, подчеркну́ть *pf.*; выделя́ть *impf.*, вы́делить *pf.* **em'phatic** *adj.* вырази́тельный, подчёркнутый; (*person*) насто́йчивый.

empire ['empaɪə(r)] *n.* импе́рия.

empirical [ɪm'pɪrɪk(ə)l] *adj.* эмпири́ческий, -чный. **empiricism** *n.* эмпири́зм. **empiricist** *n.* эмпи́рик.

employ [ɪm'plɔɪ] *v.t.* (*thing*) по́льзоваться *impf.*+i.; (*person*) нанима́ть *impf.*, наня́ть (найму́, -мёшь; на́нял, -а́, -о) *pf.*; (*busy*) занима́ть *impf.*, заня́ть (займу́, -мёшь; за́нял, -ла́, -о) *pf.*; ~ **o.s.** занима́ться *impf.*, заня́ться (займу́сь, -мёшься; заня́лся, -ла́сь) *pf.* **em'ploy'ee** *n.* сотру́дник, слу́жащий *sb.*

employer *n.* работода́тель *m.* **employment** *n.* рабо́та, слу́жба; испо́льзование; ~ **exchange** би́ржа труда́; **full** ~ по́лная за́нятость.

empower [ɪm'paʊə(r)] *v.t.* уполномо́чивать *impf.*, уполномо́чить *pf.* (**to** на+*a.*).

empress ['emprɪs] *n.* императри́ца.

emptiness ['emptɪnɪs] *n.* пустота́. **empty** *adj.* пусто́й (пуст, -á, -о, пусты́); *v.t.* опорожня́ть *impf.*, опорожни́ть *pf.*; (*solid*) высыпа́ть *impf.*, вы́сыпать (-плю, -плешь) *pf.*; (*liquid*) вылива́ть *impf.*, вы́лить (-лью, -льешь) *pf.*; *v.i.* пусте́ть *impf.*, о~ *pf.*; (*river*) впада́ть *impf.*, впасть (-аде́т, -ал) *pf.* **empty-headed** *adj.* пустоголо́вый.

EMS *abbr.* (*of* **European Monetary System**) ЕВС, Европе́йская валю́тная систе́ма.

emu ['i:mju:] *n.* э́му *m.indecl.*

emulate ['emjʊˌleɪt] *v.t.* соревнова́ться *impf.* с+*i.*; подража́ть *impf.*+*d.* **emu'lation** *n.* соревнова́ние; подража́ние.

emulsion [ɪ'mʌlʃ(ə)n] *n.* эму́льсия.

enable [ɪ'neɪb(ə)l] *v.t.* дава́ть (даю́, даёшь) *impf.*, дать (дам, дашь, даст, дади́м; дал, -á, да́ло, -и) *pf.* возмо́жность+*d. & inf.*

enact [ɪ'nækt] *v.t.* (*ordain*) постановля́ть *impf.*, постанови́ть (-влю, -вишь) *pf.*; (*law etc.*) вводи́ть (-ожу́, -о́дишь) *impf.*, ввести́ (введу́, -дёшь; ввёл, -á) *pf.* в де́йствие; (*part, scene*) игра́ть *impf.*, сыгра́ть *pf.*

enamel [ɪ'næm(ə)l] *n.* эма́ль; *adj.* эма́левый; *v.t.* эмалирова́ть *impf. & pf.*

enamoured [ɪ'næmə(r)d] *pred.*: **be** ~ **of** быть влюблённым (-ён, -ена́) в+*a.*; увлека́ться *impf.*, увле́чься (-еку́сь, -ечёшься; -ёкся, -екла́сь) *pf.*+*i.*

encamp [ɪn'kæmp] *v.i.* располага́ться *impf.*, расположи́ться (-жу́сь, -жишься) *pf.* ла́герем. **encampment** *n.* ла́герь (*pl.* -ря́) *m.*

enchant [ɪn'tʃɑ:nt] *v.t.* (*bewitch*) заколдо́вывать *impf.*, заколдова́ть *pf.*; (*charm*) очаро́вывать *impf.*, очарова́ть *pf.* **enchanting** *adj.* очарова́тельный, волше́бный. **enchantment** *n.* очарова́ние, волшебство́. **enchantress** *n.* волше́бница.

encircle [ɪn'sɜ:k(ə)l] *v.t.* окружа́ть *impf.*, окружи́ть *pf.* **encirclement** *n.* окруже́ние.

enclave ['enkleɪv] *n.* анкла́в.

enclose [ɪn'kləʊz] *v.t.* огора́живать *impf.*, огороди́ть (-ожу́, -о́ди́шь) *pf.*; обноси́ть (-ошу́, -о́сишь) *impf.*, обнести́ (-есу́, -есёшь; -ёс, -есла́) *pf.*; (*in letter*) вкла́дывать *impf.*, вложи́ть (-жу́, -жишь) *pf.*; **please find** ~**d** прилага́ется (-а́ются)+*nom.* **enclosure** *n.* огоро́женное ме́сто (*pl.* -тá); в-, при-, ложе́ние.

encode [ɪn'kəʊd] *v.t.* шифрова́ть *impf.*, за~ *pf.*

encompass [ɪn'kʌmpəs] *v.t.* (*encircle*) окружа́ть *impf.*, окружи́ть *pf.*; (*contain*) заключа́ть *impf.*, заключи́ть *pf.*

encore ['ɒŋkɔ:(r)] *int.* бис!; *n.* вы́зов на бис; **give an** ~ бисирова́ть *impf. & pf.*; *v.t.* вызыва́ть *impf.*, вы́звать (вы́зову, -вешь)

pf. на бис.

encounter [ɪn'kaʊntə(r)] *n.* встре́ча; (*in combat*) столкнове́ние; *v.t.* встреча́ть *impf.*, встре́тить *pf.*; ста́лкиваться *impf.*, столкну́ться *pf.* с+*i.*

encourage [ɪn'kʌrɪdʒ] *v.t.* ободря́ть *impf.*, ободри́ть *pf.*; поощря́ть *impf.*, поощри́ть *pf.* **encouragement** *n.* ободре́ние, поощре́ние, подде́ржка. **encouraging** *adj.* ободри́тельный.

encroach [ɪn'krəʊtʃ] *v.t.* вторга́ться *impf.*, вто́ргнуться (-г(нул)ся, -глась) *pf.* (**on** в+*a.*); (*fig.*) посяга́ть *impf.*, посягну́ть *pf.* (**on** на+*a.*). **encroachment** *n.* вторже́ние; посяга́тельство.

encumber [ɪn'kʌmbə(r)] *v.t.* загромозжда́ть *impf.*, загромозди́ть *pf.*; обременя́ть *impf.*, обремени́ть *pf.* **encumbrance** *n.* обу́за; препя́тствие.

encyclopaedia [enˌsaɪklə'pi:dɪə, ɪn-] *n.* энциклопе́дия. **encyclopaedic** *adj.* энциклопеди́ческий.

end [end] *n* коне́ц (-нца́), край (*loc.* -аю́; *pl.* -ая́); (*conclusion*) оконча́ние; (*death*) смерть; (*purpose*) цель; **an** ~ **in itself** самоце́ль; **in the** ~ в конце́ концо́в; **no** ~ без конца́; **no** ~ **of** ма́сса+*g.*; **on** ~ (*upright*) стоймя́, ды́бом; (*continuously*) подря́д; **at a loose** ~ не у дел; **to the bitter** ~ до после́дней ка́пли кро́ви; **come to the** ~ **of one's tether** дойти́ (дойду́, -дёшь; дошёл, -шла́) *pf.* до то́чки; **make** ~**s meet** своди́ть (-ожу́, -о́дишь) *impf.*, свести́ (сведу́, -дёшь; свёл, -á) *pf.* концы́ с конца́ми; *v.t.* конча́ть *impf.*, ко́нчить *pf.*; зака́нчивать *impf.*, зако́нчить *pf.*; прекраща́ть *impf.*, прекрати́ть (-ащу́, -ати́шь) *pf.*; *v.i.* конча́ться *impf.*, ко́нчиться *pf.*

endanger [ɪn'deɪndʒə(r)] *v.t.* подверга́ть *impf.*, подве́ргнуть (-г) *pf.* опа́сности.

endear [ɪn'dɪə(r)] *v.t.* внуша́ть *impf.*, внуши́ть *pf.* любо́вь к+*d.* (**to** +*d.*). **endearing** *adj.* привлека́тельный. **endearment** *n.* ла́ска (*g.pl.* -ск).

endeavour [ɪn'devə(r)] *n.* попы́тка, стара́ние; *v.i.* стара́ться *impf.*, по~ *pf.*

endemic [en'demɪk] *adj.* эндеми́ческий.

end-game ['endgeɪm] *n.* (*chess*) э́ндшпиль *m.*

ending ['endɪŋ] *n.* оконча́ние (*also gram.*), заключе́ние. **endless** *adj.* бесконе́чный, бесприде́льный.

endorse [ɪn'dɔ:s] *v.t.* (*document*) подпи́сывать *impf.*, подписа́ть (-ишу́, -и́шешь) *pf.*; (*bill*) индосси́ровать *impf. & pf.* (**to** в по́льзу+*g.*); (*approve*) одобря́ть *impf.*, одо́брить *pf.* **endorsement** *n.* по́дпись (на оборо́те+*g.*); индоссаме́нт; одобре́ние.

endow [ɪn'daʊ] *v.t.* обеспе́чивать *impf.*, обеспе́чить *pf.* постоя́нным дохо́дом; (*fig.*) одаря́ть *impf.*, одари́ть *pf.* **endowment** *n.* вклад, поже́ртвование; (*talent*) дарова́ние.

end-product ['endˌprɒdʌkt] *n.* гото́вое изде́лие.

endurance [ɪn'djʊərəns] *n.* (*of person*) вынос-
ливость, терпе́ние; (*of object*) про́чность.
endure *v.t.* выноси́ть (-ошу́, -о́сишь) *impf.*,
вы́нести (-есу, -есешь; -ес) *pf.*; терпе́ть
(-плю́, -пишь) *impf.*, по~ *pf.*; *v.i.* продол-
жа́ться *impf.*, продо́лжиться *pf.*
enema ['enɪmə] *n.* кли́зма.
enemy ['enəmɪ] *n.* враг (-á), проти́вник, не-
прия́тель *m.*; *adj.* вра́жеский.
energetic [,enə'dʒetɪk] *adj.* энерги́чный,
си́льный (си́лён, -льна́, -льно, си́льны).
'**energy** *n.* эне́ргия, си́ла; *pl.* уси́лия *nt.pl.*
enervate ['enə,veɪt] *v.t.* расслабля́ть *impf.*,
рассла́бить *pf.*
enfeeble [ɪn'fiːb(ə)l] *v.t.* ослабля́ть *impf.*,
осла́бить *pf.*
enfilade [,enfɪ'leɪd] *n.* продо́льный ого́нь
(огня́) *m.*; *v.t.* обстре́ливать *impf.*, обстре-
ля́ть *pf.* продо́льным огнём.
enforce [ɪn'fɔːs] *v.t.* принужда́ть *impf.*,
прину́дить *pf.* к+*d.* (**upon** +*a.*); (*law*)
проводи́ть (-ожу́, -о́дишь) *impf.*, провести́
(-еду́, -еде́шь; -ёл, -ела́) *pf.* в жизнь.
enforcement *n.* принужде́ние; (*law etc.*)
осуществле́ние, наблюде́ние за+*i.*, за
соблюде́нием+*g.*
enfranchise [ɪn'fræntʃaɪz] *v.t.* предоставля́ть
impf., предоста́вить *pf.* избира́тельные
права́ (*nt.pl.*)+*d.*; (*set free*) освобожда́ть
impf., освободи́ть *pf.*
engage [ɪn'geɪdʒ] *v.t.* (*hire*) нанима́ть *impf.*,
наня́ть (найму́, -мёшь; на́нял, -á, -о) *pf.*;
(*tech.*) зацепля́ть *impf.*, зацепи́ть (-ит) *pf.*;
~ **the enemy in battle** завя́зывать *impf.*,
завяза́ть (-яжу́, -я́жешь) *pf.* бой с против-
ником. **engaged** *adj.* (*occupied*) за́нятый
(-т, -тá, -то); **be** ~ **in** занима́ться *impf.*,
заня́ться (займу́сь, -мёшься; заня́лся, -ла́сь)
pf.+*i.*; **become** ~ обруча́ться *impf.*, обру-
чи́ться *pf.* (**to** с+*i.*). **engagement** *n.*
(*appointment*) свида́ние; (*obligation*) обязá-
тельство; (*betrothal*) обруче́ние; (*battle*)
бой (*loc.* бою́; *pl.* бои́); ~ **ring** обруча́льное
кольцо́ (*pl.* -льца, -ле́ц, -льцам). **engaging**
adj. привлека́тельный.
engender [ɪn'dʒendə(r)] *v.t.* порожда́ть *impf.*,
породи́ть *pf.*
engine ['endʒɪn] *n.* мото́р, маши́на, дви́-
гатель *m.*; (*rail.*) парово́з. **engine-driver** *n.*
(*rail.*) машини́ст. **engi'neer** *n.* инжене́р; *pl.*
(*mil.*) инжене́рные войска́ (-к) *pl.*; *v.t.*
(*construct*) сооружа́ть *impf.*, сооруди́ть *pf.*;
(*arrange*) устра́ивать *impf.*, устро́ить *pf.*
engi'neering *n.* инжене́рное де́ло, те́хника,
машинострое́ние; *adj.* инжене́рный, тех-
ни́ческий. **engine-room** *n.* маши́нное
отделе́ние.
England ['ɪŋglənd] *n.* А́нглия. **English** *adj.*
англи́йский; *n.*: **the** ~ *pl.* англича́не (-н)
pl.; ~ **Channel** Ла-Ма́нш. **Englishman**,
woman *n.* англича́нин (*pl.* -áне, -áн), -áнка.
engrave [ɪn'greɪv] *v.t.* гравирова́ть *impf.*,
вы́~ *pf.*; (*fig.*) запечатлева́ть *impf.*, запе-

чатле́ть *pf.* **engraver** *n.* гравёр. **engraving**
n. (*picture*) гравю́ра; (*action*) гравиро́вка;
adj. гравирова́льный, гравёрный.
engross [ɪn'grəʊs] *v.t.* завладева́ть *impf.*,
завладе́ть *pf.*+*i.*; поглоща́ть *impf.*, погло-
ти́ть (-ощу́, -о́тишь) *pf.*; **be** ~**ed in** быть
поглощённым+*i.* **engrossing** *adj.* увлека́-
тельный.
engulf [ɪn'gʌlf] *v.t.* заса́сывать *impf.*, засоса́ть
(-су́, -сёшь) *pf.*
enhance [ɪn'hɑːns] *v.t.* увели́чивать *impf.*,
увели́чить *pf.*
enigma [ɪ'nɪgmə] *n.* зага́дка. **enigmatic**
[,enɪg'mætɪk] *adj.* зага́дочный.
enjoin [ɪn'dʒɔɪn] *v.t.* предпи́сывать *impf.*,
предписа́ть (-ишу́, -и́шешь) *pf.*+*d.*; прикáзывать *impf.*, приказа́ть (-ажу́, -а́жешь)
pf.+*d.*; (*leg.*) запреща́ть *impf.*, запрети́ть
(-ещу́, -ети́шь) *pf.*+*d.* (**from** +*inf.*).
enjoy [ɪn'dʒɔɪ] *v.t.* получа́ть *impf.*, получи́ть
(-чу́, -чишь) *pf.* удово́льствие от+*g.*;
наслажда́ться *impf.*, наслади́ться *pf.*+*i.*;
(*have use of*) по́льзоваться *impf.*+*i.*; облá-
да́ть *impf.*+*i.* **enjoyable** *adj.* прия́тный.
enjoyment *n.* удово́льствие, наслажде́ние;
облада́ние (**of** +*i.*).
enlarge [ɪn'lɑːdʒ] *v.t.* & *i.* увели́чивать(ся)
impf., увели́чить(ся) *pf.*; (*widen*) расши-
ря́ть(ся) *impf.*, расши́рить(ся) *pf.*; ~ **upon**
распространя́ться *impf.*, распространи́ться
pf. о+*p.* **enlargement** *n.* увеличе́ние; рас-
шире́ние. **enlarger** *n.* (*phot.*) увеличи́тель *m.*
enlighten [ɪn'laɪt(ə)n] *v.t.* просвеща́ть *impf.*,
просвети́ть (-ещу́, -ети́шь) *pf.*; (*inform*)
осведомля́ть *impf.*, осве́домить *pf.* **enlightenment** *n.* просвеще́ние.
enlist [ɪn'lɪst] *v.i.* поступа́ть *impf.*, поступи́ть
(-плю́, -пишь) *pf.* на вое́нную слу́жбу; *v.t.*
(*mil.*) вербова́ть *impf.*, за~ *pf.*; (*support
etc.*) заруча́ться *impf.*, заручи́ться *pf.*+*i.*
enliven [ɪn'laɪv(ə)n] *v.t.* оживля́ть *impf.*, ожи-
ви́ть *pf.*
enmesh [ɪn'meʃ] *v.t.* опу́тывать *impf.*, опу́-
тать *pf.*
enmity ['enmɪtɪ] *n.* вражда́, неприя́знь.
ennoble [ɪ'nəʊb(ə)l] *v.t.* облагора́живать
impf., облагоро́дить *pf.*
ennui [ɒ'nwiː] *n.* тоска́.
enormity [ɪ'nɔːmɪtɪ] *n.* чудо́вищность. **enormous** *adj.* грома́дный, огро́мный. **enor-
mously** *adv.* кра́йне, чрезвыча́йно.
enough [ɪ'nʌf] *adj.* доста́точный; *adv.* достá-
точно, дово́льно; ~ **money** доста́точно
де́нег (*g.*); **be** ~ хвата́ть *impf.*, хвати́ть
(-ит) *pf.* impers.+*g.*; **I've had** ~ **of him** он
мне надое́л.
enquire, enquiry *see* **inquire, inquiry**
enrage [ɪn'reɪdʒ] *v.t.* беси́ть (бешу́, бе́сишь)
impf., вз~ *pf.*
enrapture [ɪn'ræptʃə(r)] *v.t.* восхища́ть *impf.*,
восхити́ть (-ищу́, -ити́шь) *pf.*
enrich [ɪn'rɪtʃ] *v.t.* обогаща́ть *impf.*, обогa-
ти́ть (-ащу́, -ати́шь) *pf.*

enrol [ɪn'rəʊl] *v.t. & i.* запи́сывать(ся) *impf.*, записа́ть(ся) (-ишу́(сь), -и́шешь(ся)) *pf.*; *v.t.* (*mil.*) вербова́ть *impf.*, за~ *pf.*; *v.i.* (*mil.*) поступа́ть *impf.*, поступи́ть (-плю́, -пишь) *pf.* на вое́нную слу́жбу. **enrolment** *n.* регистра́ция, за́пись.

en route [ɑ̃ 'ruːt] *adv.* по пути́ (**to, for** в+*a.*).

ensconce [ɪn'skɒns] *v.t.:* ~ **o.s.** заса́живаться *impf.*, засе́сть (зася́ду, -дешь; засе́л) *pf.* (**with** за+*a.*).

ensemble [ɒn'sɒmb(ə)l] *n.* (*mus.*) анса́мбль *m.*

enshrine [ɪn'ʃraɪn] *v.t.* (*relic*) класть (кладу́, -дёшь; клал) *impf.*, положи́ть (-жу́, -жишь) *pf.* в ра́ку; (*fig.*) храни́ть *impf.*

ensign ['ensaɪn, -s(ə)n] *n.* (*flag*) флаг; (*rank*) пра́порщик.

enslave [ɪn'sleɪv] *v.t.* порабоща́ть *impf.*, поработи́ть (-ощу́, -оти́шь) *pf.* **enslavement** *n.* порабоще́ние.

ensnare [ɪn'sneə(r)] *v.t.* опу́тывать *impf.*, опу́тать *pf.*

ensue [ɪn'sjuː] *v.i.* сле́довать *impf.*; вытека́ть *impf.* **ensuing** *adj.* после́дующий.

ensure [ɪn'ʃʊə(r)] *v.t.* обеспе́чивать *impf.*, обеспе́чить *pf.*

entail [ɪn'teɪl, en-] *n.* майора́т(ное насле́дование); *v.t.* (*leg.*) определя́ть *impf.*, определи́ть *pf.* насле́дование+*g.*; (*necessitate*) влечь (влечёт; влёк, -ла́) *impf.* за собо́й.

entangle [ɪn'tæŋg(ə)l] *v.t.* запу́тывать *impf.*, запу́тать *pf.*

enter ['entə(r)] *v.t. & i.* входи́ть (-ожу́, -о́дишь) *impf.*, войти́ (войду́, -дёшь; вошёл, -шла́) *pf.* в+*a.*; (*by transport*) въезжа́ть *impf.*, въе́хать (въе́ду, -дешь) *pf.* в+*a.*; *v.i.* (*join*) поступа́ть *impf.*, поступи́ть (-плю́, -пишь) *pf.* в, на, +*a.*; (*competition*) вступа́ть *impf.*, вступи́ть (-плю́, -пишь) *pf.* в+*a.*; (*in list*) вноси́ть (-ошу́, -о́сишь) *impf.*, внести́ (внесу́, -сёшь; внёс, -ла́) *pf.* в+*a.*

enteric [en'terɪk] *adj.* кише́чный. **enteritis** [,entə'raɪtɪs] *n.* энтери́т.

enterprise ['entəpraɪz] *n.* (*undertaking*) предприя́тие; (*initiative*) предприи́мчивость; **free, private,** ~ ча́стное предпринима́тельство. **enterprising** *adj.* предприи́мчивый.

entertain [,entə'teɪn] *v.t.* (*amuse*) развлека́ть *impf.*, развле́чь (-еку́, -ечёшь; -ёк, -екла́) *pf.*; (*guests*) принима́ть *impf.*, приня́ть (приму́, -мешь; при́нял, -á, -o) *pf.*; угоща́ть *impf.*, угости́ть *pf.* (**to** +*i.*); (*hopes*) пита́ть *impf.* **entertaining** *adj.* занима́тельный, развлека́тельный. **entertainment** *n.* развлече́ние; приём; угоще́ние; (*show*) дивертисме́нт.

enthral [ɪn'θrɔːl] *v.t.* порабоща́ть *impf.*, поработи́ть (-ощу́, -оти́шь) *pf.*

enthrone [ɪn'θrəʊn] *v.t.* возводи́ть (-ожу́, -о́дишь) *impf.*, возвести́ (-еду́, -едёшь; -ёл, -ела́) *pf.* на престо́л. **enthronement** *n.* возведе́ние на престо́л. **enthusiasm** [ɪn'θjuːzɪ-,æz(ə)m, -'θuːzɪ,æz(ə)m] *n.* энтузиа́зм, воoду-

шевле́ние. **enthusiast** *n.* энтузиа́ст, ~ка. **enthusi'astic** *adj.* восто́рженный (-ен, -енна), воoдушевлённый (-ён, -ённа).

entice [ɪn'taɪs] *v.t.* зама́нивать *impf.*, замани́ть (-ню́, -нишь) *pf.*; соблазня́ть *impf.*, соблазни́ть *pf.* **enticement** *n.* собла́зн, прима́нка, зама́нивание. **enticing** *adj.* соблазни́тельный, зама́нчивый.

entire [ɪn'taɪə(r)] *adj.* по́лный, це́лый, весь (вся, всё; все). **entirely** *adv.* вполне́, соверше́нно; (*solely*) исключи́тельно. **entirety** *n.* це́льность, полнота́; **in its** ~ по́лностью, в це́лом.

entitle [ɪn'taɪt(ə)l] *v.t.* (*book*) озагла́вливать *impf.*, озагла́вить *pf.*; (*give right to*) дава́ть (даю́, даёшь) *impf.*, дать (дам, дашь, даст, дади́м; дал, -á, да́ло́, -и) *pf.* пра́во+*d.* (**to** на+*a.*); **be** ~**d to** име́ть пра́во на+*a.*

entity ['entɪtɪ] *n.* существо́; (*existence*) бытие́ (*i.* -ие́м, *p.* -ии́).

entomb [ɪn'tuːm] *v.t.* погреба́ть *impf.*, погрести́ (-ебу́, -ебёшь; -ёб, -ебла́) *pf.* **entombment** *n.* погребе́ние.

entomological [,entəmə'lɒdʒɪk(ə)l] *adj.* энтомологи́ческий. **ento'mologist** *n.* энтомо́лог. **ento'mology** *n.* энтомоло́гия.

entrails ['entreɪlz] *n.* вну́тренности (-тей) *pl.*, кишки́ (-шо́к) *pl.*; (*fig.*) не́дра (-р) *pl.*

entrance¹ ['entrəns] *n.* вход, въезд; (*theatr.*) вы́ход; (*into office etc.*) вступле́ние, поступле́ние; ~ **examinations** вступи́тельные экза́мены *m.pl.*; ~ **hall** вестибю́ль *m.*; **back** ~ чёрный вход; **front** ~ пара́дный вход. **entrant** *n.* (*sport*) уча́стник (**for** +*g.*).

entrance² [ɪn'trɑːns] *v.t.* приводи́ть (-ожу́, -о́дишь) *impf.*, привести́ (-еду́, -дёшь; -ёл, -ела́) *pf.* в состоя́ние тра́нса; (*charm*) очаро́вывать *impf.*, очарова́ть *pf.* **entrancing** *adj.* очарова́тельный.

entrap [ɪn'træp] *v.t.* пойма́ть *pf.* в лову́шку; (*fig.*) запу́тывать *impf.*, запу́тать *pf.*

entreat [ɪn'triːt] *v.t.* умоля́ть *impf.*, умоли́ть *pf.* **entreaty** *n.* мольба́, про́сьба.

entrench [ɪn'trentʃ] *v.t.* ока́пывать *impf.*, окопа́ть *pf.*; **be, become** ~**ed** (*fig.*) укореня́ться *impf.*, укорени́ться *pf.*

entropy ['entrəpɪ] *n.* энтропи́я.

entrust [ɪn'trʌst] *v.t.* (*secret*) вверя́ть *impf.*, вве́рить *pf.* (**to** +*d.*); (*object*; *person*) поруча́ть *impf.*, поручи́ть (-чу́, -чишь) *pf.* (**to** +*d.*).

entry ['entrɪ] *n.* вход, въезд; вступле́ние; (*theatr.*) вы́ход; (*in book etc.*) за́пись, статья́; (*sport*) записа́вшийся.

entwine [ɪn'twaɪn] *v.t.* (*interweave*) сплета́ть *impf.*, сплести́ (-ету́, -етёшь; -ёл, -ела́) *pf.*; (*wreathe*) обвива́ть *impf.*, обви́ть (обовью́, -ьёшь; обви́л, -á, -o) *pf.*

enumerate [ɪ'njuːmə,reɪt] *v.t.* перечисля́ть *impf.*, перечи́слить *pf.* **enume'ration** *n.* перечисле́ние, пе́речень (-чня) *m.*

enunciate [ɪ'nʌnsɪ,eɪt] *v.t.* (*proclaim*) объявля́ть *impf.*, объяви́ть (-влю́, -вишь) *pf.*; (*express*) излага́ть *impf.*, изложи́ть (-жу́,

-жи́шь) *pf.*; (*pronounce*) произноси́ть (-ошу́, -о́сишь) *impf.*, произнести́ (-есу́, -есёшь; -ёс, -есла́) *pf.* **enunci'ation** *n.* объявле́ние; изложе́ние; произноше́ние.

envelop [ɪn'veləp] *v.t.* оку́тывать *impf.*, оку́тать *pf.*; завёртывать *impf.*, заверну́ть *pf.*

envelope ['envəˌləʊp, 'ɒn-] *n.* (*letter*) конве́рт; (*other senses*) обёртка, оболо́чка.

enviable ['envɪəb(ə)l] *adj.* зави́дный. **envious** *adj.* зави́стливый.

environment [ɪn'vaɪərənmənt] *n.* окружа́ющая среда́ (*pl.* -ды). **environs** [ɪn'vaɪərənz, 'envɪrənz] *n.* окре́стности *f.pl.*

envisage [ɪn'vɪzɪdʒ] *v.t.* предусма́тривать *impf.*, предусмотре́ть (-рю́, -ришь) *pf.*

envoy ['envɔɪ] *n.* посла́нник, аге́нт.

envy ['envɪ] *n.* за́висть; *v.t.* зави́довать *impf.*, по~ *pf.*+*d.*

enzyme ['enzaɪm] *n.* энзи́м.

epaulette [ˌepə'let] *n.* эполе́т(а).

ephemeral [ɪ'femər(ə)l, ɪ'fiːm-] *adj.* эфеме́рный, недолгове́чный.

epic ['epɪk] *n.* эпи́ческая поэ́ма, эпопе́я; *adj.* эпи́ческий.

epicentre ['epɪˌsentə(r)] *n.* эпице́нтр.

epicure ['epɪˌkjʊə(r)] *n.* эпикуре́ец (-е́йца). **epicu'rean** *adj.* эпикуре́йский.

epidemic [ˌepɪ'demɪk] *n.* эпиде́мия; *adj.* эпидеми́ческий.

epigram ['epɪˌgræm] *n.* эпигра́мма. **epigra'mmatic(al)** *adj.* эпиграммати́ческий.

epigraph ['epɪˌgrɑːf] *n.* эпигра́ф.

epilepsy ['epɪˌlepsɪ] *n.* эпиле́псия. **epi'leptic** *n.* эпиле́птик; *adj.* эпилепти́ческий.

epilogue ['epɪˌlɒg] *n.* эпило́г.

Epiphany [e'pɪfənɪ, ɪ'pɪf-] *n.* (*eccl.*) Богоявле́ние.

episcopal [ɪ'pɪskəp(ə)l] *adj.* епи́скопский. **episcopate** *n.* епи́скопство.

episode ['epɪˌsəʊd] *n.* эпизо́д. **epi'sodic** *adj.* эпизоди́ческий.

epistle [ɪ'pɪs(ə)l] *n.* посла́ние. **epistolary** *adj.* эпистоля́рный.

epitaph ['epɪˌtɑːf] *n.* эпита́фия, надгро́бная на́дпись.

epithet ['epɪˌθet] *n.* эпи́тет.

epitome [ɪ'pɪtəmɪ] *n.* (*summary*) конспе́кт; (*embodiment*) воплоще́ние. **epitomize** *v.t.* конспекти́ровать *impf.*, за~, про~ *pf.*; воплоща́ть *impf.*, воплоти́ть (-ощу́, -оти́шь) *pf.*

epoch ['iːpɒk] *n.* эпо́ха, вех (*pl.* -á), пери́од. ·

equable ['ekwəb(ə)l] *adj.* равноме́рный, ро́вный (-вен, -вна́, -вно).

equal ['iːkw(ə)l] *adj.* ра́вный (-вен, -вна́), одина́ковый; (*capable of*) спосо́бный (**to** на+*a.*, +*inf.*); *n.* ра́вный *sb.*, ро́вня *c.g.*; *v.t.* равня́ться *impf.*+*d.* **equality** [ɪ'kwɒlɪtɪ] *n.* ра́венство, равнопра́вие. **equali'zation** *n.* уравне́ние. **equalize** *v.t.* ура́внивать *impf.*, уравня́ть *pf.*; *v.i.* (*sport*) равня́ть *impf.*, с~ *pf.* счёт. **equally** *adv.* равно́, ра́вным о́бразом.

equanimity [ˌekwə'nɪmɪtɪ, ˌiːk-] *n.* хладно-кро́вие, невозмути́мость.

equate [ɪ'kweɪt] *v.t.* прира́внивать *impf.*, приравня́ть *pf.* (**with** к+*d.*).

equation [ɪ'kweɪʒ(ə)n] *n.* (*math.*) уравне́ние.

equator [ɪ'kweɪtə(r)] *n.* эква́тор. **equatorial** [ˌekwə'tɔːrɪəl, ˌiːk-] *adj.* экваториа́льный.

equestrian [ɪ'kwestrɪən] *n.* вса́дник; *adj.* ко́нный. **equestrianism** *n.* ко́нный спорт. **equestri'enne** *n.* вса́дница.

equidistant [ˌiːkwɪ'dɪst(ə)nt] *adj.* равностоя́щий. **equilateral** [ˌiːkwɪ'lætər(ə)l] *adj.* равносторо́нний (-нен, -ння). **equilibrium** [ˌiːkwɪ'lɪbrɪəm] *n.* равнове́сие.

equine ['iːkwaɪn, 'ek-] *adj.* лошади́ный.

equinox ['iːkwɪˌnɒks, 'ek-] *n.* равноде́нствие.

equip [ɪ'kwɪp] *v.t.* обору́довать *impf.* & *pf.*; снаряжа́ть *impf.*, снаряди́ть *pf.* **equipment** *n.* обору́дование, снаряже́ние.

equitable ['ekwɪtəb(ə)l] *adj.* справедли́вый, беспристра́стный. **equity** *n.* справедли́вость, беспристра́стность; (*econ.*) ма́ржа; *pl.* (*econ.*) обыкнове́нные а́кции *f.pl.*

equivalence [ɪ'kwɪvələns] *n.* эквивале́нтность, равноце́нность. **equivalent** *adj.* эквивале́нтный, равноце́нный (-нен, -нна), равноси́льный; *n.* эквивале́нт.

equivocal [ɪ'kwɪvək(ə)l] *adj.* (*ambiguous*) двусмы́сленный (-ен, -енна); (*suspicious*) сомни́тельный. **equivocate** *v.i.* говори́ть *impf.* двусмы́сленно.

era ['ɪərə] *n.* э́ра, эпо́ха.

eradicate [ɪ'rædɪˌkeɪt] *v.t.* искореня́ть *impf.*, искорени́ть *pf.* **eradi'cation** *n.* искорене́ние.

erase [ɪ'reɪz] *v.t.* стира́ть *impf.*, стере́ть (сотру́, -рёшь; стёр) *pf.*; подчища́ть *impf.*, подчи́стить *pf.* **eraser** *n.* ла́стик. **erasure** *n.* стира́ние, подчи́стка.

erect [ɪ'rekt] *adj.* прямо́й (прям, -á, -о, пря́мы); *v.t.* (*building*) сооружа́ть *impf.*, сооруди́ть *pf.*; воздвига́ть *impf.*, воздви́гнуть (-г) *pf.*; (*straighten*) выпрямля́ть *impf.*, вы́прямить *pf.* **erection** *n.* постро́йка, сооруже́ние; выпрямле́ние.

ermine ['ɜːmɪn] *n.* горноста́й.

erode [ɪ'rəʊd] *v.t.* разъеда́ть *impf.*, разъе́сть (-е́ст, -едя́т; -е́л) *pf.*; (*geol.*) эроди́ровать *impf.* & *pf.*

erogenous [ɪ'rɒdʒɪnəs] *adj.* эроге́нный; ~ **zones** эроге́нные зо́ны.

erosion *n.* разъеда́ние; эро́зия.

erotic [ɪ'rɒtɪk] *adj.* эроти́ческий, любо́вный.

err [ɜː(r)] *v.i.* ошиба́ться *impf.*, ошиби́ться (-бу́сь, -бёшься; -бся) *pf.*; заблужда́ться *impf.*; (*sin*) греши́ть *impf.*, со~ *pf.*

errand ['erənd] *n.* поруче́ние; **run** ~s быть на посы́лках (**for** у+*g.*).

errant ['erənt] *adj.* (*knight*) стра́нствующий; (*thoughts*) блужда́ющий.

erratic [ɪ'rætɪk] *adj.* непостоя́нный (-нен, -нна), изме́нчивый.

erratum [ɪ'rɑːtəm] *n.* (*print*) опеча́тка; (*in writing*) опи́ска. **erroneous** [ɪ'rəʊnɪəs] *adj.* оши́бочный, ло́жный. **error** ['erə(r)] *n.* оши́бка, заблужде́ние.

erudite ['eru:,daɪt] *adj.* учёный. **erudition** [,eru:'dɪʃ(ə)n] *n.* эруди́ция, учёность.

erupt [ɪ'rʌpt] *v.i.* прорыва́ться *impf.*, прорва́ться (-ву́сь, -вёшься; -ва́лся, -вала́сь, -вало́сь) *pf.*; (*volcano*) изверга́ться *impf.*, изве́ргнуться (-гся) *pf.* **eruption** *n.* (*volcano*) изверже́ние; (*mirth*) взрыв; (*med.*) сыпь.

escalator ['eskə,leɪtə(r)] *n.* эскала́тор.

escapade ['eskə,peɪd, ,eskə'peɪd] *n.* вы́ходка, проде́лка. **escape** [ɪ'skeɪp] *n.* (*from prison*) бе́гство, побе́г; (*from danger*) спасе́ние; (*from reality*) ухо́д; (*of gas*) уте́чка; **have a narrow ~** быть на волосо́к (**from** от+g.); *v.i.* (*flee*) бежа́ть (бегу́, бежи́шь) *impf.* & *pf.*; убега́ть *impf.*, убежа́ть (-егу́, -ежи́шь) *pf.*; (*save o.s.*) спаса́ться *impf.*, спасти́сь (-су́сь, -сёшься; -сся, -сла́сь) *pf.*; (*leak*) утека́ть *impf.*, уте́чь (-ечёт; -ёк, -екла́) *pf.*; *v.t.* избега́ть *impf.*, избежа́ть (-егу́, -ежи́шь) *pf.*+g.; (*groan*) вырыва́ться *impf.*, вы́рваться (-вется) *pf.* из, у, +g. **esca'pee** *n.* бегле́ц (-а́).

escort ['eskɔ:t; ɪ'skɔ:t] *n.* конво́й, эско́рт; *v.t.* сопровожда́ть *impf.*, сопроводи́ть *pf.*; (*mil.*) конвои́ровать *impf.*, от~ *pf.*; эскорти́ровать *impf.* & *pf.*

escutcheon [ɪ'skʌtʃ(ə)n] *n.* щит (-а́) герба́.

Eskimo ['eskɪ,məʊ] *n.* эскимо́с, ~ка; *adj.* эскимо́сский.

especial [ɪ'speʃ(ə)l] *adj.* осо́бенный, осо́бый; (*particular*) ча́стный. **especially** *adv.* осо́бенно; в ча́стности.

espionage ['espɪə,nɑːʒ] *n.* шпиона́ж.

espousal [ɪ'spaʊz(ə)l] *n.* (*fig.*) подде́ржка. **espouse** *v.t.* (*fig.*) подде́рживать *impf.*, поддержа́ть (-жу́, -жишь) *pf.*

espy [ɪ'spaɪ] *v.t.* уви́деть (-йжу, -йдишь) *pf.*; (*detect*) замеча́ть *impf.*, заме́тить *pf.*

essay ['eseɪ] *n.* о́черк, эссе́ *nt.indecl.*; (*attempt*) попы́тка, про́ба; *v.t.* пыта́ться *impf.*, по~ *pf.*+*inf.* **essayist** *n.* очерки́ст, ~ка; эссеи́ст.

essence ['es(ə)ns] *n.* су́щность, существо́; (*extract*) эссе́нция. **essential** [ɪ'senʃ(ə)l] *adj.* суще́ственный, необходи́мый, неотъ́ёмлемый; *n.* основно́е *sb.*; *pl.* предме́ты *m.pl.* пе́рвой необходи́мости. **essentially** *adv.* по существу́, в основно́м.

establish [ɪ'stæblɪʃ] *v.t.* (*set up*) учрежда́ть *impf.*, учреди́ть *pf.*; (*fact etc.*) устана́вливать *impf.*, установи́ть (-влю́, -вишь) *pf.*; (*appoint*) устра́ивать *impf.*, устро́ить *pf.*; (*secure*) упро́чивать *impf.*, упро́чить *pf.* **establishment** *n.* (*action*) учрежде́ние, установле́ние; (*institution*) учрежде́ние, заведе́ние; (*staff*) штат.

estate [ɪ'steɪt] *n.* (*property*) поме́стье (*g.pl.* -тий), име́ние; (*class*) сосло́вие; *pl.* недви́жимость; **~ agent** аге́нт по прода́же недви́жимости; **~ duty** нало́г на насле́дство.

esteem [ɪ'sti:m] *n.* уваже́ние, почте́ние; *v.t.* уважа́ть *impf.*; почита́ть *impf.* **estimable**

['estɪməb(ə)l] *adj.* досто́йный (-о́ин, -о́йна) уваже́ния. **estimate** *n.* (*of quality*) оце́нка; (*of cost*) сме́та; *v.t.* оце́нивать *impf.*, оцени́ть (-ню́, -нишь) *pf.* **estimated** *adj.* предполага́емый, приме́рный. **esti'mation** *n.* оце́нка, мне́ние.

Estonia [ɪ'stəʊnɪə] *n.* Эсто́ния.

estrange [ɪ'streɪndʒ] *v.t.* отдаля́ть *impf.*, отдали́ть *pf.* **estrangement** *n.* отчужде́ние, отчуждённость.

estuary ['estjʊərɪ] *n.* у́стье (*g.pl.* -в).

et al [et'æl] *abbr.* (*of et alii*) и др., и други́е.

etc. [et'setərə, 'setrə] *adv. abbr.* (*of et cetera*) и т.д., и так да́лее; и т.п., и тому́ подо́бное. **et cetera** и так да́лее, и тому́ подо́бие.

etch [etʃ] *v.t.* трави́ть (-влю́, -вишь) *impf.*, вы́~ *pf.* **etching** *n.* (*action*) травле́ние; (*object*) офо́рт.

eternal [ɪ'tɜːn(ə)l] *adj.* ве́чный. **eternity** *n.* ве́чность.

ether ['i:θə(r)] *n.* эфи́р. **ethereal** [ɪ'θɪərɪəl] *adj.* эфи́рный.

ethical ['eθɪk(ə)l] *adj.* эти́ческий, эти́чный. **ethics** *n.* э́тика.

ethnic ['eθnɪk] *adj.* этни́ческий; **~ cleansing** этни́ческая чи́стка. **eth'nography** *n.* этногра́фия.

etiquette ['etɪ,ket, -'ket] *n.* этике́т.

étude ['eɪtjuːd, -'tjuːd] *n.* этю́д.

etymological [,etɪmə'lɒdʒɪk(ə)l] *adj.* этимологи́ческий. **etymologist** [,etɪ'mɒlədʒɪst] *n.* этимо́лог. **ety'mology** *n.* этимоло́гия.

eucalyptus [,ju:kə'lɪptəs] *n.* эвкали́пт.

Eucharist ['ju:kərɪst] *n.* евхари́стия, прича́стие.

eulogize ['ju:lə,dʒaɪz] *v.t.* превозноси́ть (-ошу́, -о́сишь) *impf.*, превознести́ (-есу́, -есёшь; -ёс, -есла́) *pf.* **eulogy** *n.* похвала́.

eunuch ['ju:nək] *n.* е́внух.

euphemism ['ju:fɪ,mɪz(ə)m] *n.* эвфеми́зм. **euphe'mistic** *adj.* эвфемисти́ческий.

euphonious [ju:'fəʊnɪəs] *adj.* благозву́чный. **euphony** ['ju:fənɪ] *n.* благозву́чие.

Eurasian [jʊə'reɪʒ(ə)n] *adj.* евразийский.

Europe ['jʊərəp] *n.* Евро́па.

European [,jʊərə'pɪən] *n.* европе́ец (-е́йца), -е́йка; *adj.* европе́йский.

euthanasia [,ju:θə'neɪzɪə] *n.* эйтана́зия.

evacuate [ɪ'vækjʊ,eɪt] *v.t.* (*person*) эвакуи́ровать *impf.* & *pf.*; (*med.*) опорожня́ть *impf.*, опорожни́ть *pf.* **evacu'ation** *n.* эвакуа́ция; опорожне́ние. **evacu'ee** *n.* эвакуи́рованный *sb.*

evade [ɪ'veɪd] *v.t.* уклоня́ться *impf.*, уклони́ться (-ню́сь, -ни́шься) *pf.* от+g.; (*law*) обходи́ть (-ожу́, -о́дишь) *impf.*, обойти́ (обойду́, -дёшь; обошёл, -шла́) *pf.*

evaluate [ɪ'væljʊ,eɪt] *v.t.* оце́нивать *impf.*, оцени́ть (-ню́, -нишь) *pf.* **evalu'ation** *n.* оце́нка.

evangelical [,i:væn'dʒelɪk(ə)l] *adj.* ева́нгельский. **e'vangelist** *n.* евангели́ст.

evaporate [ɪ'væpə,reɪt] *v.t.* & *i.* испаря́ть(ся)

impf., испари́ть(ся) *pf.*; *v.i.* (*lose moisture*) улету́чиваться *impf.*, улету́читься *pf.* **evapo'ration** *n.* испаре́ние.

evasion [ɪ'veɪʒ(ə)n] *n.* уклоне́ние (**of** от+*g.*); (*of law*) обхо́д; (*subterfuge*) увёртка. **evasive** *adj.* укло́нчивый.

eve [iːv] *n.* кану́н; **on the ~** накану́не.

even ['iːv(ə)n] *adj.* ро́вный (-вен, -вна́, -вно) (*uniform*) равноме́рный; (*balanced*) уравнове́шенный; (*number*) чётный; **get ~** расквита́ться *pf.* (**with** c+*i.*); *adv.* да́же; (*just*) как раз; (*with comp.*) ещё; **~ if** да́же е́сли, хотя́ бы и; **~ though** хотя́ бы; **~ so** всё-таки; **not ~** да́же не; *v.t.* выра́внивать *impf.*, вы́ровнять *pf.*

evening ['iːvnɪŋ] *n.* ве́чер (*pl.* -а́); *adj.* вече́рний.

evenly ['iːvənlɪ] *adv.* по́ровну, ро́вно, одина́ково. **evenness** *n.* ро́вность; равноме́рность.

evensong ['iːvən͵sɒŋ] *n.* вече́рня.

event [ɪ'vent] *n.* собы́тие, происше́ствие; **in the ~ of** в слу́чае+*g.*; **at all ~s** во вся́ком слу́чае. **eventual** [ɪ'ventjʊəl] *adj.* (*possible*) возмо́жный; (*final*) коне́чный. **eventu'ality** *n.* возмо́жность. **eventually** *adv.* в конце́ концо́в.

ever ['evə(r)] *adv.* (*at any time*) когда́-либо, когда́-нибудь; (*always*) всегда́; (*emph.*) же; **~ since** с тех пор (как); **~ so** о́чень; **for ~** навсегда́; **hardly ~** почти́ никогда́.

Everest ['evərɪst]: **Mt ~** гора́ Эвере́ст.

evergreen ['evə͵griːn] *adj.* вечнозелёный; *n.* вечнозелёное расте́ние. **ever'lasting** *adj.* ве́чный, постоя́нный. **ever'more** *adv.*: **for ~** навсегда́, наве́ки.

every ['evrɪ] *adj.* ка́ждый, вся́кий, все (*pl.*); **~ now and then** вре́мя от вре́мени; **~ other** ка́ждый второ́й; **~ other day** че́рез день. **everybody, everyone** *pron.* ка́ждый, все (*pl.*). **everyday** *adj.* (*daily*) ежедне́вный; (*commonplace*) повседне́вный. **everything** *pron.* всё. **everywhere** *adv.* всю́ду, везде́.

evict [ɪ'vɪkt] *v.t.* выселя́ть *impf.*, вы́селить *pf.* **eviction** *n.* выселе́ние.

evidence ['evɪd(ə)ns] *n.* свиде́тельство, доказа́тельство, улика; **in ~** (*pred.*) заме́тен (-тна, -тно); **give ~** свиде́тельствовать *impf.* (o+*p.*; +*a.*; +что). **evident** *adj.* очеви́дный, я́сный (я́сен, ясна́, я́сно, я́сны́).

evil ['iːv(ə)l, -ɪl] *n.* зло (*g.pl.* зол), поро́к; *adj.* злой (зол, зла), дурно́й (ду́рён, -рна́, -рно, ду́рны́). **evil-doer** *n.* злоде́й.

evince [ɪ'vɪns] *v.t.* проявля́ть *impf.*, прояви́ть (-влю́, -вишь) *pf.*

evoke [ɪ'vəʊk] *v.t.* вызыва́ть *impf.*, вы́звать (вы́зову, -вешь) *pf.*

evolution [͵iːvə'luːʃ(ə)n, -'ljuːʃ(ə)n] *n.* разви́тие, эволю́ция. **evolutionary** *adj.* эволюцио́нный. **evolve** [ɪ'vɒlv] *v.t. & i.* развива́ть(ся) *impf.*, разви́ть(ся) (разовью́(сь), -ьёшь(ся); разви́л(ся), -ила́(сь), -и́ло́-и́ло́(сь) *pf.*; *v.i.* эволюциони́ровать *impf. &pf.*

ewe [juː] *n.* овца́ (*pl.* о́вцы, ове́ц, о́вцам).

ex- [eks] *in comb.* бы́вший.

exacerbate [ek'sæsə͵beɪt, ɪg-] *v.t.* обостря́ть *impf.*, обостри́ть *pf.* **exacer'bation** *n.* обостре́ние.

exact [ɪg'zækt] *adj.* то́чный (-чен, -чна́, -чно), аккура́тный; *v.t.* взы́скивать *impf.*, взыска́ть (взыщу́, -щешь) *pf.* (**from, of** c+*g.*). **exacting** *adj.* (*person*) взыска́тельный, тре́бовательный; (*circumstance*) суро́вый. **exactitude, exactness** *n.* то́чность. **exactly** *adv.* то́чно, как раз, и́менно.

exaggerate [ɪg'zædʒə͵reɪt] *v.t.* преувели́чивать *impf.*, преувели́чить *pf.* **exagge'ration** *n.* преувеличе́ние.

exalt [ɪg'zɔːlt] *v.t.* возвыша́ть *impf.*, возвы́сить *pf.*; (*extol*) превозноси́ть (-ошу́, -о́сишь) *impf.*, превознести́ (-есу́, -есёшь; -ёс, -есла́) *pf.* **exaltation** [͵egzɔːl'teɪʃ(ə)n] *n.* возвыше́ние; (*elation*) восто́рг.

examination [ɪg͵zæmɪ'neɪʃ(ə)n] *n.* осмо́тр, иссле́дование; (*of knowledge*) экза́мен; (*leg.*) допро́с. **ex'amine** *v.t.* осма́тривать *impf.*, осмотре́ть (-рю́. -ришь) *pf.*; иссле́довать *impf. & pf.*; экзаменова́ть *impf.*, про~ *pf.*; допра́шивать *impf.*, допроси́ть (-ошу́, -о́сишь) *pf.* **examiner** *n.* экзамена́тор.

example [ɪg'zɑːmp(ə)l] *n.* приме́р, образе́ц (-зца́); **for ~** наприме́р.

exasperate [ɪg'zɑːspə͵reɪt] *v.t.* раздража́ть *impf.*, раздражи́ть *pf.* **exasperation** *n.* раздраже́ние.

excavate ['ekskə͵veɪt] *v.t.* выка́пывать *impf.*, вы́копать *pf.*; (*archaeol.*) раска́пывать *impf.*, раскопа́ть *pf.* **exca'vation** *n.* выка́пывание; раско́пки *f.pl.* **excavator** *n.* экскава́тор.

exceed [ɪk'siːd] *v.t.* превыша́ть *impf.*, превы́сить *pf.* **exceedingly** *adv.* чрезвыча́йно.

excel [ɪk'sel] *v.t.* превосходи́ть (-ожу́, -о́дишь) *impf.*, превзойти́ (-ойду́, -ойдёшь; -ошёл, -ошла́) *pf.* (**in** в+*p.*, +*i.*); *v.i.* отлича́ться *impf.*, отличи́ться *pf.* (**at**, **in** в+*p.*). **excellence** ['eksələns] *n.* превосхо́дство. **excellency** *n.* превосходи́тельство. **'excellent** *adj.* превосхо́дный, отли́чный.

except [ɪk'sept] *v.t.* исключа́ть *impf.*, исключи́ть *pf.*; *prep.* исключа́я+*a.*, за исключе́нием+*g.*, кро́ме+*g.* **exception** *n.* исключе́ние; **take ~ to** возража́ть *impf.*, возрази́ть *pf.* про́тив+*g.* **exceptional** *adj.* исключи́тельный.

excerpt ['eksɜːpt] *n.* отры́вок (-вка), вы́держка.

excess [ɪk'ses, 'ekses] *n.* избы́ток (-тка), изли́шек (-шка), изли́шество; **~ fare** допла́та. **excessive** *adj.* чрезме́рный, изли́шний (-шен, -шня).

exchange [ɪks'tʃeɪndʒ] *n.* обме́н (**of** +*i.*); (*of currency*) разме́н; (*rate of* **~**) курс; (*building*) би́ржа; (*telephone*) центра́льная телефо́нная ста́нция; *v.t.* обме́нивать *impf.*, обменя́ть *pf.* (**for** на+*a.*); обме́ниваться *impf.*, обменя́ться *pf.*+*i.*

Exchequer [ɪks'tʃekə(r)] *n.* казначе́йство, казна́.

excise[1] ['eksaɪz] *n.* (*duty*) акци́з(ный сбор); *v.t.* облага́ть *impf.*, обложи́ть (-жу́, -жишь) *pf.* акци́зным сбором.

excise[2] ['eksaɪz] *v.t.* (*cut out*) выреза́ть *impf.*, вы́резать (-ежу, -ежешь) *pf.* **excision** [ɪk'sɪʒ(ə)n] *n.* вы́резка.

excitable [ɪk'saɪtəb(ə)l] *adj.* возбуди́мый. **excite** *v.t.* возбужда́ть *impf.*, возбуди́ть *pf.*; волнова́ть *impf.*, вз~ *pf.* **excitement** *n.* возбужде́ние, волне́ние.

exclaim [ɪk'skleɪm] *v.i.* восклица́ть *impf.*, воскли́кнуть *pf.* **exclamation** [,eksklə'meɪʃ(ə)n] *n.* восклица́ние; ~ **mark** восклица́тельный знак.

exclude [ɪk'sklu:d] *v.t.* исключа́ть *impf.*, исключи́ть *pf.* **exclusion** *n.* исключе́ние. **exclusive** *adj.* исключи́тельный; ~ **of** за исключе́нием+*g.*, не счита́я+*g.*

excommunicate [,ekskə'mju:nɪ,keɪt] *v.t.* отлуча́ть *impf.*, отлучи́ть *pf.* (от це́ркви). **excommuni'cation** *n.* отлуче́ние.

excrement ['ekskrɪmənt] *n.* экскреме́нты (-тов) *pl.*

excrescence [ɪk'skres(ə)ns] *n.* наро́ст.

excrete [ɪk'skri:t] *v.t.* выделя́ть *impf.*, вы́делить *pf.* **excretion** *n.* выделе́ние.

excruciating [ɪk'skru:ʃɪ,eɪtɪŋ] *adj.* мучи́тельный.

exculpate ['ekskʌl,peɪt] *v.t.* опра́вдывать *impf.*, оправда́ть *pf.* **excul'pation** *n.* оправда́ние.

excursion [ɪk'skɜ:ʃ(ə)n] *n.* экску́рсия.

excusable [ɪk'skju:zəb(ə)l] *adj.* извини́тельный, прости́тельный. **excuse** [ɪk'skju:s, ek-] *n.* извине́ние, оправда́ние, отгово́рка; *v.t.* извиня́ть *impf.*, извини́ть *pf.*; проща́ть *impf.*, прости́ть *pf.*; (*release*) освобожда́ть *impf.*, освободи́ть *pf.* (**from** от+*g.*); ~ **me!** извини́те (меня́)!; прости́те (меня́)!; прошу́ проще́ния.

execrable ['eksɪkrəb(ə)l] *adj.* отврати́тельный, ме́рзкий (-ок, -зка́, -зко).

execute ['eksɪ,kju:t] *v.t.* исполня́ть *impf.*, испо́лнить *pf.*; выполня́ть *impf.*, вы́полнить *pf.*; (*criminal*) казни́ть *impf. & pf.* **exe'cution** *n.* выполне́ние, исполне́ние; казнь. **exe'cutioner** *n.* пала́ч (-а́). **e'xecutive** *n.* исполни́тельный о́рган; (*person*) руководи́тель *m.*; *adj.* исполни́тельный; ~ **committee** исполни́тельный комите́т, исполко́м.

exegesis [,eksɪ'dʒi:sɪs] *n.* толкова́ние.

exemplary [ɪg'zemplərɪ] *adj.* приме́рный, образцо́вый. **exemplify** *v.t.* (*illustrate by example*) поясня́ть *impf.*, поясни́ть *pf.* приме́ром, на приме́ре; (*serve as example*) служи́ть (-жу́, -жишь) *impf.*, по~ *pf.* приме́ром+*g.*

exempt [ɪg'zempt] *adj.* освобождённый (-ён, -ена́) (**from** от+*g.*), свобо́дный (**from** от+*g.*);

v.t. освобожда́ть *impf.*, освободи́ть *pf.* (**from** от+*g.*).

exemption *n.* освобожде́ние (**from** от+*g.*).

exercise ['eksə,saɪz] *n.* (*application*) примене́ние, осуществле́ние; (*physical* ~; *task*) упражне́ние; **take** ~ упражня́ться *impf.*; ~ **bicycle** *n.* велотренажёр; ~ **book** тетра́дь; *v.t.* (*apply*) применя́ть *impf.*, примени́ть (-ню́, -нишь) *pf.*; (*employ*) испо́льзовать *impf. & pf.*; (*train*) упражня́ть *impf.*

exert [ɪg'zɜ:t] *v.t.* ока́зывать *impf.*, оказа́ть (-ажу́, -а́жешь) *pf.*; ~ **o.s.** стара́ться *impf.*, по~ *pf.* **exertion** *n.* напряже́ние, уси́лие.

exhalation [,ekshə'leɪʃ(ə)n] *n.* выдыха́ние, вы́дох; (*vapour*) испаре́ние. **exhale** [eks'heɪl, ɪgz-] *v.t.* (*breathe out*) выдыха́ть *impf.*, вы́дохнуть *pf.*; (*as vapour*) испаря́ть *impf.*, испари́ть *pf.*

exhaust [ɪg'zɔ:st] *n.* вы́хлоп; ~ **pipe** вы́хлопна́я труба́ (*pl.* -бы); *v.t.* (*use up*) истоща́ть *impf.*, истощи́ть *pf.*; (*person*) изнуря́ть *impf.*, изнури́ть *pf.*; (*subject*) исче́рпывать *impf.*, исче́рпать *pf.* **exhausted** *adj.*: **be** ~ (*person*) изнемога́ть *impf.*, изнемо́чь (-огу́, -о́жешь; -о́г, -огла́) *pf.* **exhausting** *adj.* изнури́тельный. **exhaustion** *n.* изнуре́ние, истоще́ние, изнеможе́ние. **exhaustive** *adj.* исче́рпывающий.

exhibit [ɪg'zɪbɪt] *n.* экспона́т; (*leg.*) веще́ственное доказа́тельство; *v.t.* (*show*) пока́зывать *impf.*, показа́ть (-ажу́, -а́жешь) *pf.*; (*manifest quality*) проявля́ть *impf.*, прояви́ть (-влю́, -вишь) *pf.*; (*publicly*) выставля́ть *impf.*, вы́ставить *pf.* **exhi'bition** *n.* пока́з, проявле́ние; (*public* ~) вы́ставка. **exhibitor** *n.* экспоне́нт.

exhilarate [ɪg'zɪlə,reɪt] *v.t.* (*gladden*) весели́ть *impf.*, раз~ *pf.*; (*enliven*) оживля́ть *impf.*, оживи́ть *pf.* **exhila'ration** *n.* весе́лье, оживле́ние.

exhort [,egzɔ:t, ,eks-] *v.t.* увещева́ть *impf.* **exhor'tation** *n.* увещева́ние.

exhume [eks'hju:m, ɪg'zju:m] *v.t.* выка́пывать *impf.*, вы́копать *pf.*

exile ['eksaɪl, 'egz-] *n.* изгна́ние, ссы́лка; (*person*) изгна́нник, ссы́льный *sb.*; *v.t.* изгоня́ть *impf.*, изгна́ть (изгоню́, -нишь; изгна́л, -а́, -о) *pf.*; ссыла́ть *impf.*, сосла́ть (сошлю́, -лёшь) *pf.*

exist [ɪg'zɪst] *v.i.* существова́ть *impf.*; (*live*) жить (живу́, -вёшь; жил, -а́, -о) *impf.* **existence** *n.* существова́ние, нали́чие. **existent, existing** *adj.* существу́ющий, нали́чный.

exit ['eksɪt, 'egz-] *n.* вы́ход; (*theatr.*) ухо́д (со сце́ны); (*death*) смерть; ~ **visa** выездна́я ви́за; *v.i.* уходи́ть (-ожу́, -о́дишь) *impf.*, уйти́ (уйду́, -дёшь; ушёл, ушла́) *pf.*

exonerate [ɪg'zɒnə,reɪt] *v.t.* освобожда́ть *impf.*, освободи́ть *pf.* (**from** от+*g.*); (*from blame*) снима́ть *impf.*, снять (сниму́, -мешь; снял, -а́, -о) *pf.* обвине́ние с+*g.*

exorbitant [ɪg'zɔ:bɪt(ə)nt] *adj.* непоме́рный, чрезме́рный.

exorcism ['eksɔːˌsɪz(ə)m] *n.* изгна́ние ду́хов. **exorcize** *v.t.* (*spirits*) изгоня́ть *impf.*, изгна́ть (изгоню́, -нишь; изгна́л, -á, -о) *pf.*

exotic [ɪgˈzɒtɪk] *adj.* экзоти́ческий.

expand [ɪkˈspænd] *v.t. & i.* (*broaden*) расширя́ть(ся) *impf.*, расши́рить(ся) *pf.*; (*develop*) развива́ть(ся) *impf.*, разви́ть(ся) (разовью́(сь), -вьёшь(ся); разви́л(ся), -ила́(сь), -и́ло-и́ло́(сь) *pf.*; (*increase*) увели́чивать(ся) *impf.*, увели́чить(ся) *pf.* **expanse** *n.* простра́нство. **expansion** *n.* расшире́ние; разви́тие; увеличе́ние; (*of territory*) экспа́нсия. **expansive** *adj.* (*extensive*) обши́рный; (*effusive*) экспанси́вный.

expatiate [ɪkˈspeɪʃɪˌeɪt] *v.i.* распространя́ться *impf.*, распространи́ться *pf.* (**on** o+p.).

expatriate [eksˈpætrɪət, -ˈpeɪtrɪət] *n.* экспатриа́нт.

expect [ɪkˈspekt] *v.t.* (*await*) ожида́ть *impf.*+g.; ждать (жду, ждёшь; ждал, -á, -о) *impf.*+g., что; (*anticipate*) наде́яться (-éюсь, -éешься) *impf.*, по~ *pf.*; (*require*) тре́бовать *impf.*+g., что́бы. **expectant** *adj* ожида́ющий (**of** +g.); ~ **mother** бере́менная же́нщина, бу́дущая мать. **expec'tation** *n.* ожида́ние, наде́жда.

expectorant [ekˈspektərənt] *n.* отха́ркивающее (сре́дство) *sb.* **expectorate** *v.t.* отха́ркивать *impf.*, отха́ркать *pf.*

expediency [ɪkˈspiːdɪənsɪ] *n.* целесообра́зность. **expedient** *n.* сре́дство, приём; *adj.* целесообра́зный. **expedite** ['ekspɪˌdaɪt] *v.t.* ускоря́ть *impf.*, уско́рить *pf.*; бы́стро выполня́ть *impf.*, вы́полнить *pf.* **expedition** [ˌekspɪˈdɪʃ(ə)n] *n.* экспеди́ция. **expeditionary** *adj.* экспедицио́нный. **expeditious** *adj.* бы́стрый (быстр, -á, -о, бы́стры).

expel [ɪkˈspel] *v.t.* выгоня́ть *impf.*, вы́гнать (вы́гоню, -нишь) *pf.*; (*from school etc.*) исключа́ть *impf.*, исключи́ть *pf.*

expend [ɪkˈspend] *v.t.* тра́тить *impf.*, ис~, по~ *pf.*; расхо́довать *impf.*, из~ *pf.* **expenditure** *n.* расхо́дование, расхо́д, тра́та. **expense** *n.* расхо́д; *pl.* расхо́ды *m.pl.*, изде́ржки *f.pl.*; **at the** ~ **of** ценою+g., за счёт+g. **expensive** *adj.* дорого́й (до́рог, -á, -о).

experience [ɪkˈspɪərɪəns] *n.* о́пыт, о́пытность; (*incident*) пережива́ние; *v.t.* испы́тывать *impf.*, испыта́ть *pf.*; (*undergo*) пережива́ть *impf.*, пережи́ть (-иву́, -ивёшь; пе́режи́л, -á, -о) *pf.* **experienced** *adj.* о́пытный.

experiment [ɪkˈsperɪmənt, -ˌment] *n.* о́пыт, экспериме́нт; *v.i.* производи́ть (-ожу́, -о́дишь) *impf.*, произвести́ (-еду́, -едёшь; -ёл, -ела́) *pf.* о́пыты (**on** на+a.); эксперименти́ровать *impf.* (**on, with** над, с+i.). **experi'mental** *adj.* эксперимента́льный, о́пытный. **experi- men'tation** *n.* эксперименти́рование.

expert [ˈekspɜːt] *n.* специали́ст (**at, in** в+p., по+d.), знато́к (-á) (+g.); *adj.* о́пытный. **expertise** [ˌekspɜːˈtiːz] *n.* (*opinion*) экспер- ти́за; (*knowledge*) специа́льные зна́ния *nt.pl.*

expiate ['ekspɪˌeɪt] *v.t.* искупа́ть *impf.*, искупи́ть (-плю́, -пишь) *pf.* **expi'ation** *n.* искупле́ние.

expiration [ˌekspɪˈreɪʃ(ə)n] *n.* (*breathing out*) выдыха́ние; (*termination*) истече́ние. **expire** [ɪkˈspaɪə(r)] *v.t.* (*exhale*) выдыха́ть *impf.*, вы́дохнуть *pf.*; *v.i.* (*period*) истека́ть *impf.*, исте́чь (-чёт; -ёк, -екла́) *pf.*; (*die*) умира́ть *impf.*, умере́ть (умру́, -рёшь; у́мер, -ла́, -ло) *pf.* **ex'piry** *n.* истече́ние.

explain [ɪkˈspleɪn] *v.t.* объясня́ть *impf.*, объясни́ть *pf.*; (*justify*) опра́вдывать *impf.*, оправда́ть *pf.* **expla'nation** *n.* объясне́ние. **ex'planatory** *adj.* объясни́тельный.

expletive [ɪkˈspliːtɪv] *adj.* вставно́й; *n.* вставно́е сло́во (*pl.* -вá); (*oath*) бра́нное сло́во (*pl.* -вá).

explicit [ɪkˈsplɪsɪt] *adj.* я́вный, определённый (-ёнен, -ённа).

explode [ɪkˈspləʊd] *v.t. & i.* взрыва́ть(ся) *impf.*, взорва́ть(ся) (-ву́, -вётся; взорва́л(ся), -ала́(сь), -а́ло/-а́ло́(сь) *pf.*; *v.t.* (*discredit*) разоблача́ть *impf.*, разоблачи́ть *pf.*; *v.i.* (*with anger etc.*) разража́ться *impf.*, разрази́ться *pf.*

exploit ['eksplɔɪt; ɪkˈsplɔɪt] *n.* по́двиг; *v.t.* эксплуати́ровать *impf.*; (*mine etc.*) разраба́тывать *impf.*, разрабо́тать *pf.* **exploi'tation** *n.* эксплуата́ция; разрабо́тка. **ex'ploiter** *n.* эксплуата́тор.

exploration [ˌeksplɔˈreɪʃ(ə)n] *n.* иссле́дование. **exploratory** [ɪkˈsplɒrətərɪ] *adj.* иссле́дова- тельский. **explore** [ɪkˈsplɔː(r)] *v.t.* иссле́до- вать *impf. & pf.* **ex'plorer** *n.* иссле́дователь *m.*

explosion [ɪkˈspləʊʒ(ə)n] *n.* взрыв; (*anger etc.*) вспы́шка. **explosive** *n.* взры́вчатое вещество́; *adj.* взры́вчатый, взрывно́й.

exponent [ɪkˈspəʊnənt] *n.* (*interpreter*) истол- кова́тель *m.*; (*representative*) представи́тель *m.*; (*math.*) показа́тель *m.* сте́пени. **exponen- tial** [ˌekspəˈnenʃ(ə)l] *adj.* (*math.*) показа́- тельный.

export ['ekspɔːt; ekˈspɔːt] *n.* вы́воз, э́кспорт; *v.t.* вывози́ть (-ожу́, -о́зишь) *impf.*, вы́везти (-езу, -езешь; -ез) *pf.*; экспорти́ровать *impf. & pf.* **ex'porter** *n.* экспортёр.

expose [ɪkˈspəʊz] *v.t.* (*to risk etc.*) подверга́ть *impf.*, подве́ргнуть (-г) *pf.* (**to** +d.); (*phot.*) экспони́ровать *impf. & pf.*; (*display*) вы- ставля́ть *impf.*, вы́ставить *pf.*; (*discredit*) разоблача́ть *impf.*, разоблачи́ть *pf.*

exposition [ˌekspəˈzɪʃ(ə)n] *n.* изложе́ние, толкова́ние.

exposure [ɪkˈspəʊʒə(r)] *n.* подверга́ние (**to** +d.); (*phot.*) вы́держка; выставле́ние; разо- блаче́ние.

expound [ɪkˈspaʊnd] *v.t.* толкова́ть *impf.*; излага́ть *impf.*, изложи́ть (-жу́, -жишь) *pf.*

express [ɪkˈspres] *n.* (*train*) экспре́сс; (*mes- senger*) на́рочный *sb.*, курье́р; *adj.* (*definite*) определённый (-ёнен, -ённа), то́чный (-чен, -чна́, -чно); *v.t.* выража́ть *impf.*, вы́разить *pf.* **expression** *n.* выраже́ние; (*expressiveness*) вырази́тельность. **expressive** *adj.* вырази́тельный. **expressly** *adv.* наро́чно, наме́ренно.

expropriate [eks'prəυprɪ,eɪt] *v.t.* экспроприи́ровать *impf. & pf.* **expropri'ation** *n.* экспроприа́ция.

expulsion [ɪk'spʌlʃ(ə)n] *n.* изгна́ние; (*from school etc.*) исключе́ние.

expunge [ɪk'spʌndʒ] *v.t.* вычёркивать *impf.*, вы́черкнуть *pf.*

exquisite [ek'skwɪzɪt] *adj.* утончённый (-ён, -ённа).

extant [ek'stænt] *adj.* сохрани́вшийся, существу́ющий.

extemporaneous [ɪk,stempə'reɪnɪəs] *adj.* неподгото́вленный (-ен), импровизи́рованный (-ан). **ex'tempore** *adv.* без подгото́вки, экспро́мптом. **ex'temporize** *v.t. & i.* импровизи́ровать *impf.*, сымпровизи́ровать *pf.*

extend [ɪk'stend] *v.t.* простира́ть *impf.*, простере́ть (-тру́, -трёшь; -тёр) *pf.*; протя́гивать *impf.*, протяну́ть (-ну́, -нешь) *pf.*; (*enlarge*) расширя́ть *impf.*, расши́рить *pf.*; (*prolong*) продлева́ть *impf.*, продли́ть *pf.*; *v.i.* простира́ться *impf.*, простере́ться (-трётся; -тёрся) *pf.*; тяну́ться (-нется) *impf.*, по~ *pf.* **extension** *n.* расшире́ние; продле́ние. **extensive** *adj.* обши́рный, простра́нный (-нен, -нна), протяжённый (-ён, -ённа). **extent** *n.* протяже́ние; (*degree*) сте́пень (*pl.* -ни, -не́й); (*large space*) простра́нство.

extenuate [ɪk'stenjυ,eɪt] *v.t.* уменьша́ть *impf.*, уме́ньшить *pf.*; **extenuating circumstances** смягча́ющие вину́ обстоя́тельства *nt.pl.*

exterior [ɪk'stɪərɪə(r)] *n.* вне́шность, нару́жность; *adj.* вне́шний, нару́жный.

exterminate [ɪk'stɜːmɪ,neɪt] *v.t.* уничтожа́ть *impf.*, уничто́жить *pf.*; истребля́ть *impf.*, истреби́ть *pf.* **extermi'nation** *n.* уничтоже́ние, истребле́ние.

external [ɪk'stɜːn(ə)l] *adj.* вне́шний, нару́жный.

extinct [ɪk'stɪŋkt] *adj.* (*volcano*) поту́хший; (*species*) вы́мерший; **become** ~ ту́хнуть (-x) *impf.*, по~ *pf.*; вымира́ть *impf.*, вы́мереть (-мрет; -мер) *pf.* **extinction** *n.* потуха́ние, вымира́ние.

extinguish [ɪk'stɪŋgwɪʃ] *v.t.* гаси́ть (гашу́, га́сишь) *impf.*, по~ *pf.*; туши́ть (-шу́, -шишь) *impf.*, по~ *pf.*; (*debt.*) погаша́ть *impf.*, погаси́ть (-ашу́, -а́сишь) *pf.* **extinguisher** *n.* гаси́тель *m.*; (*fire* ~) огнетуши́тель *m.*

extirpate ['ekstə,peɪt] *v.t.* истребля́ть *impf.*, истреби́ть *pf.*; искореня́ть *impf.*, искорени́ть *pf.* **extir'pation** *n.* истребле́ние, искорене́ние.

extol [ɪk'stəυl, ɪk'stɒl] *v.t.* превозноси́ть *impf.*, превознести́ (-есу́, -есёшь; -ёс, -есла́) *pf.*

extort [ɪk'stɔːt] *v.t.* вымога́ть *impf.* (**from** y+g.); (*information etc.*) выпы́тывать *impf.*, вы́пытать *pf.* (**from** y+g.). **extortion** *n.* вымога́тельство. **extortionate** *adj.* вымога́-

тельский, граби́тельский.

extra ['ekstrə] *n.* (*theatr.*) стати́ст, ~ка; (*payment*) припла́та, добавле́ние; *adj.* доба́вочный, дополни́тельный, э́кстренный; особый; *adv.* особо, особенно, дополни́тельно.

extra- ['ekstrə] *in comb.* вне… .

extract ['ekstrækt; ɪk'strækt] *n.* экстра́кт; (*from book etc.*) вы́держка; *v.t.* извлека́ть *impf.*, извле́чь (-еку́ -ечёшь; -ёк, -екла́) *pf.*; (*pull out*) выта́скивать *impf.*, вы́тащить *pf.*; (*tooth*) удаля́ть *impf.*, удали́ть *pf.* **ex'traction** *n.* извлече́ние; выта́скивание; удале́ние; (*descent*) происхожде́ние. **extractor (fan)** *n.* вентиля́тор.

extradite ['ekstrə,daɪt] *v.t.* выдава́ть (-даю́, -даёшь) *impf.*, вы́дать (-ам, -ашь, -аст, -адим) *pf.* **extradition** [,ekstrə'dɪʃ(ə)n] *n.* вы́дача.

extraneous [ɪk'streɪnɪəs] *adj.* чу́ждый (чужд, -á, -о) (**to** +*d.*), посторо́нний.

extraordinary [ɪk'strɔːdɪnərɪ, ,ekstrə'ɔːdɪnərɪ] *adj.* необыча́йный, чрезвыча́йный; (*surprising*) удиви́тельный.

extraterrestrial [,ekstrətɪ'restrɪəl] *n.* инопланетя́нин (*pl.* -я́не, -я́н); *adj.* инопланета́рный.

extravagance [ɪk'strævəgəns] *adj.* (*wild spending*) расточи́тельность; (*wildness*) сумасбро́дство. **extravagant** *adj.* расточи́тельный; сумасбро́дный.

extreme [ɪk'striːm] *n.* кра́йность; *adj.* кра́йний, чрезвыча́йный. **extremity** [ɪk'stremɪtɪ] *n.* (*end*) край (*loc.* -áе & -аю́; *pl.* -а́я), коне́ц (-нца́); (*adversity*) кра́йность; *pl.* (*hands & feet*) коне́чности *f.pl.*

extricate ['ekstrɪ,keɪt] *v.t.* (*disentangle*) распу́тывать *impf.*, распу́тать *pf.*; ~ **o.s.** выпу́тываться *impf.*, вы́путаться *pf.*

exuberance [ɪg'zjuːbərəns] *n.* изоби́лие, ро́скошь; (*of person*) жизнера́достность. **exuberant** *adj.* оби́льный, роско́шный; жизнера́достный.

exude [ɪg'zjuːd] *v.t. & i.* выделя́ть(ся) *impf.*, вы́делить(ся) *pf.*

exult [ɪg'zʌlt] *v.i.* ликова́ть *impf.* **exultant** *adj.* лику́ющий. **exul'tation** *n.* ликова́ние.

eye [aɪ] *n.* глаз (*loc.* -зу́; *pl.* -за́, -з, -за́м); (*poet.*) о́ко (*pl.* о́чи, оче́й); (*needle etc.*) ушко́ (*pl.* -ки́, -ко́в); **an eye for an eye** о́ко за о́ко; **up to the eyes in** по́ уши, по го́рло, в+*p.*; *v.t.* всма́триваться *impf.*, всмотре́ться (-рю́сь, -ришься) *pf.* в+*a.* **eyeball** *n.* глазно́е я́блоко (*pl.* -ки, -к). **eyebrow** *n.* бровь (*pl.* -ви, -ве́й). **eye-catching** *adj.* эффе́ктный. **eyelash** *n.* ресни́ца. **eyelid** *n.* ве́ко (*pl.* -ки, -к). **eyepiece** *n.* окуля́р. **eyesight** *n.* зре́ние. **eyewitness** *n.* очеви́дец (-дца).

eyrie ['ɪərɪ] *n.* (орли́ное) гнездо́ (*pl.* -ёзда).

F

F¹ [ef] *n.* (*mus.*) фа *nt.indecl.*

F² ['færən,haɪt] *abbr.* (*of* **Fahrenheit**) °Ф, (шкала́ термо́метра Фаренге́йта); **30°F** 30°Ф (гра́дусов по Фаренге́йту).

fable ['feɪb(ə)l] *n.* ба́сня (*g.pl.* -сен), небыли́ца.

fabric ['fæbrɪk] *n.* (*structure*) структу́ра, устро́йство; (*cloth*) ткань. **fabricate** *v.t.* (*invent*) выду́мывать *impf.*, вы́думать *pf.*; (*forge*) подде́лывать *impf.*, подде́лать *pf.* **fabri'cation** *n.* вы́думка; подде́лка.

fabulous ['fæbjʊləs] *adj.* ска́зочный.

facade [fə'sɑːd] *n.* фаса́д.

face [feɪs] *n.* лицо́ (*pl.* -ца); (*expression*) выраже́ние; (*grimace*) грима́са; (*outward aspect*) вне́шний вид; (*surface*) пове́рхность; (*clock etc.*) цифербла́т; **have the ~** име́ть *impf.* наха́льство; **make faces** ко́рчить *impf.* ро́жи; **~ down** (*cards*) руба́шкой вверх; **~ to ~** лицо́м к лицу́; **in the ~ of** пе́ред лицо́м+*g.*, вопреки́+*d.*; **on the ~ of it** на пе́рвый взгляд; **~ value** номина́льная сто́имость; **take at ~ value** принима́ть *impf.*, приня́ть (приму́, -мешь; при́нял, -а́, -о) *pf.* за чи́стую моне́ту; *v.t.* (*be turned towards*) быть обращённым к+*d.*; (*meet firmly*) смотре́ть (-рю́, -ришь) *impf.* в лицо́+*d.*; (*cover*) облицо́вывать *impf.*, облицева́ть (-цу́ю, -цу́ешь) *pf.*; **~ the music** расхлё́бывать *impf.*, расхлеба́ть *pf.* ка́шу. **faceless** *adj.* безли́чный. **face-lift** *n.* космети́ческий ремо́нт; (*fig.*) вне́шнее обновле́ние.

facet ['fæsɪt] *n.* грань; (*aspect*) аспе́кт.

facetious [fə'siːʃəs] *adj.* шутли́вый.

facial ['feɪʃ(ə)l] *adj.* лицево́й.

facile ['fæsaɪl] *adj.* лёгкий (-гок, -гка́, -гко́, лёгки) свобо́дный; (*pej.*) пове́рхностный. **facilitate** [fə'sɪlɪteɪt] *v.t.* облегча́ть *impf.*, облегчи́ть *pf.* **fa'cility** *n.* (*ease*) лёгкость; (*ability*) спосо́бность; (*opportunity*) возмо́жность.

facing ['feɪsɪŋ] *n.* облицо́вка; (*of garment*) отде́лка, обши́вка.

facsimile [fæk'sɪmɪlɪ] *n.* факси́миле *nt.indecl.*

fact [fækt] *n.* факт; (*reality*) действи́тельность; *pl.* (*information*) да́нные *sb.*; **the ~ is that** ... де́ло в том, что...; **as a matter of ~** со́бственно говоря́; **in ~** действи́тельно, на са́мом де́ле.

faction ['fækʃ(ə)n] *n.* фра́кция. **factional** *adj.* фракцио́нный.

factor ['fæktə(r)] *n.* (*circumstance*) фа́ктор; (*merchant*) комиссионе́р; (*math.*) мно́житель *m.*; (*of safety etc.*) коэффицие́нт.

factory ['fæktərɪ] *n.* фа́брика, заво́д. **factory-ship** *n.* плаву́чий рыбозаво́д.

factual ['fæktjʊəl] *adj.* факти́ческий, действи́тельный.

faculty ['fæk(ə)ltɪ] *n.* спосо́бность, дар (*pl.* -ы́); (*univ.*) факульте́т.

fade [feɪd] *v.i.* вя́нуть (вял) *impf.*, за~ *pf.*; увяда́ть *impf.*, увя́нуть (-я́л) *pf.*; (*colour*) выцвета́ть *impf.*, вы́цвести (-етет, -ел) *pf.*; (*sound*) замира́ть *impf.*, замере́ть (-мрёт; за́мер, -ла́, -ло) *pf.*

faeces ['fiːsiːz] *n.* кал.

fag [fæg] *v.i.* корпе́ть (-плю, -пишь) (**over** над+*i.*); *v.t.* утомля́ть *impf.*, утоми́ть *pf.*; *n.* (*drudgery*) тяжёлая рабо́та; (*cigarette*) сигаре́тка. **fag-end** *n.* оку́рок (-рка).

faggot ['fægət] *n.* (*wood*) вяза́нка хво́роста, -ту.

faience ['faɪɑ̃s] *n.* фая́нс.

fail [feɪl] *n.*: **without ~** обяза́тельно, непреме́нно; *v.t.* & *i.* (*be insufficient*) не хвата́ть *impf.*, не хвати́ть (-ит) *pf. impers.*+*g.* (*subject*) & *y*+*g.* (*object*); *v.i.* (*weaken*) ослабева́ть *impf.*, ослабе́ть *pf.*; *v.i.* (*not succeed*) терпе́ть (-плю́, -пишь) *impf.*, по~ *pf.* неуда́чу; не удава́ться (удаётся) *impf.*, уда́ться (-а́стся; -ало́сь) *pf. impers.*+*d.* (**in** +*inf.*); *v.t.* & *i.* (*examination*) прова́ливать(ся) *impf.*, провали́ть(ся) (-лю́(сь), -лишь(ся)) *pf.* **failing** *n.* недоста́ток (-тка), сла́бость; *prep.* за неиме́нием+*g.*, в слу́чае отсу́тствия+*g.* **failure** *n.* неуда́ча, прова́л; (*person*) неуда́чник, -ица.

faint [feɪnt] *n.* о́бморок; *adj.* (*weak*) сла́бый (слаб, -а́, -о); (*pale*) бле́дный (-ден, -дна́, -дно, бле́дны́); *v.i.* па́дать *impf.*, упа́сть (упаду́, -дёшь; упа́л) *pf.* в о́бморок. **faint-hearted** *adj.* малоду́шный.

fair¹ [feə(r)] *n.* я́рмарка.

fair² [feə(r)] *adj.* (*beautiful*) краси́вый; (*just*) че́стный (-тен, -тна́, -тно), справедли́вый; (*considerable*) поря́дочный; (*blond*) белоку́рый; **~ copy** чистови́к (-а́). **fairly** *adv.* (*tolerably*) дово́льно; (*completely*) соверше́нно. **fairway** *n.* фарва́тер.

fairy ['feərɪ] *n.* фе́я; **~ tale** ска́зка.

faith [feɪθ] *n.* (*belief*) ве́ра; (*trust*) дове́рие; (*loyalty*) ве́рность. **faithful** *adj.* ве́рный (-рен, -рна́, -рно, ве́рны́). **faithless** *adj.* вероло́мный, неве́рный (-рен, -рна́, -рно, -рны́).

fake [feɪk] *n.* подде́лка; *v.t.* подде́лывать *impf.*, подде́лать *pf.*

falcon ['fɔːlkən, 'fɒlkən] *n.* со́кол. **falconry** *n.* соколи́ная охо́та.

fall [fɔːl] *n.* паде́ние; *pl.* водопа́д; *v.i.* па́дать *impf.*, (у)па́сть ((у)паду́, -дёшь; (у)па́л) *pf.*; понижа́ться *impf.*, пони́зиться *pf.*; **~ apart** распада́ться *impf.*, распа́сться (-адётся; -а́лся) *pf.*; **~ asleep** засыпа́ть *impf.*, засну́ть *pf.*; ~ **back on** прибега́ть *impf.*, прибе́гнуть (-г(нул), -гла) *pf.* к+*d.*; ~ **off** отпада́ть *impf.*, отпа́сть (-аду́, -адёшь; -а́л) *pf.*; ~ **over** опроки́дываться *impf.*, опроки́нуться *pf.*; ~ **through** прова́ливаться *impf.*, провали́ться (-ится) *pf.*

fallacious [fə'leɪʃəs] *adj.* оши́бочный, ло́жный. **fallacy** ['fæləsɪ] *n.* оши́бка, заблужде́ние.

fallibility [,fælɪ'bɪlɪtɪ] *n.* оши́бочность. **fallible** *adj.* подве́рженный (-ен) оши́бкам.

fall-out ['fɔːlaʊt] *n.* радиоакти́вные оса́дки (-ков) *pl.*

fallow ['fæləʊ] *n.* пар (*pl.* -ы́), земля́ (*a.* -лю) под па́ром; *adj.* под па́ром; **lie** ~ лежа́ть (-жи́т) *impf.* под па́ром.

fallow deer ['fæləʊ] *n.* лань.

false [fɒls, fɔːls] *adj.* ло́жный, фальши́вый. **falsehood** *n.* ложь (лжи, *i.* ло́жью). **falsetto** [fɒl'setəʊ, fɔːl-] *n.* фальце́т. **falsifi'cation** *n.* фальсифика́ция, подде́лка. **falsify** *v.t.* фальцифици́ровать *impf.* & *pf.*; подде́лывать *impf.*, подде́лать *pf.* **falsity** *n.* ло́жность.

falter ['fɒltə(r), 'fɔːl-] *v.i.* (*stumble*) спотыка́ться *impf.*, споткну́ться *pf.*; (*stammer*) запина́ться *impf.*, запну́ться *pf.*; (*waver*) колеба́ться (-блюсь, -блешься) *impf.*

fame [feɪm] *n.* сла́ва, репута́ция. **famed** *adj.* изве́стный.

familiar [fə'mɪlɪə(r)] *adj.* (*close*) бли́зкий (-зок, -зка́, -зко, бли́зки́); (*well known*) знако́мый; (*usual*) обы́чный; (*informal*) фамилья́рный. **famili'arity** *n.* бли́зость; знако́мство; фамилья́рность. **fa'miliarize** *v.t.* ознакомля́ть *impf.*, ознако́мить *pf.* (**with** c+*i.*).

family ['fæmɪlɪ, 'fæmlɪ] *n.* семья́ (*pl.* -мьи, -ме́й, -мьям); (*lineage etc.*) род (-а(у), *loc.* -у́; *pl.* -ы́); (*generic group*) семе́йство; *attr.* семе́йный, фами́льный; ~ **tree** родосло́вная *sb.*

famine ['fæmɪn] *n.* (*scarcity of food*) го́лод (-а(у)); (*dearth*) недоста́ток (-тка). **famish** ['fæmɪʃ] *v.t.* мори́ть *impf.*, у~ *pf.* го́лодом; *v.i.* **be** ~**ed** голода́ть *impf.*

famous ['feɪməs] *adj.* знамени́тый, изве́стный, просла́вленный.

fan¹ [fæn] *n.* (*device etc.*) ве́ер (*pl.* -á); (*ventilator*) вентиля́тор; *v.t.* обма́хивать *impf.*, обмахну́ть *pf.*; (*flame*) раздува́ть *impf.*, разду́ть (-у́ю, -у́ешь) *pf.*

fan² [fæn] *n.* (*devotee*) боле́льщик, -ица. **fanatic** *n.* фана́тик, -и́чка. **fanatical** [fə'nætɪk(ə)l] *adj.* фанати́ческий.

fanciful ['fænsɪfʊl] *adj.* (*capricious*) прихотли́вый; (*imaginary*) вообража́емый. **fancy** ['fænsɪ] *n.* фанта́зия, воображе́ние; (*whim*) причу́да; *adj.* орнамента́льный; *v.t.* (*imagine*) представля́ть *impf.*, предста́вить *pf.* себе́; (*suppose*) каза́ться (ка́жется; каза́лось) *impf.*, по~ *pf. impers.*+*d.*; (*like*) нра́виться *impf.*, по~ *pf. impers.*+*d.*; ~ **dress** маскара́дный костю́м. **fancy-dress** *adj.* костюми́рованный; ~ **ball** (бал-)маскара́д.

fanfare ['fænfeə(r)] *n.* фанфа́ра.

fang [fæŋ] *n.* клык (-á); (*serpent's*) ядови́тый зуб (*pl.* -ы, -óв).

fantastic [fæn'tæstɪk] *adj.* фантасти́ческий, причу́дливый. '**fantasy** *n.* фанта́зия, воображе́ние.

f.a.o. *abbr.* (*of for the attention of*) вним.+*g.*, внима́нию+*g.*

far [fɑː(r)] *adj.* да́льний, далёкий (-ёк, -ека́, -ёкó); (*remote*) отдалённый; *adv.* далёкó; (*fig.*) намно́го; **as** ~ **as** (*prep.*) до+*g.*; (*conj.*) поско́льку; **by** ~ намно́го; (**in**) **so** ~ **as** поско́льку; **so** ~ до сих пор.

farce [fɑːs] *n.* фарс. **farcical** *adj.* фа́рсовый, смехотво́рный.

fare [feə(r)] *n.* (*price*) проездна́я пла́та; (*passenger*) пассажи́р; (*food*) пи́ща; *v.i.* пожива́ть *impf.* **farewell** *int.* проща́й(те)!; *n.* проща́ние; *attr.* проща́льный; **bid** ~ проща́ться *impf.*, прости́ться *pf.* (**to** c+*i.*).

far-fetched [fɑː'fetʃd] *adj.* натя́нутый; притя́нутый за́ волосы, за́ уши.

farinaceous [,færɪ'neɪʃəs] *adj.* мучни́стый, мучно́й.

farm [fɑːm] *n.* фе́рма, хозя́йство. **farmer** *n.* фе́рмер. **farming** *n.* се́льское хозя́йство.

far-reaching [fɑː'riːtʃɪŋ] *adj.* далеко́ иду́щий.

farrier ['færɪə(r)] *n.* (*smith*) кузне́ц (-á); (*horse-doctor*) конова́л.

far-seeing [fɑː'siːɪŋ] *adj.* дальнови́дный. **far-sighted** *adj.* дальнови́дный; (*physically*) дальнозо́ркий.

farther ['fɑːðə(r)] *comp. adj.* бо́лее отдалённый (-ён, -ённа); дальне́йший; (*additional*) дополни́тельный; *adv.* да́льше. **farthermost** *adj.* са́мый да́льний. **farthest** *superl. adj.* са́мый да́льний, са́мый отдалённый; *adv.* да́льше всего́.

fascicle ['fæsɪk(ə)l] *n.* (*bot.*) пучо́к (-чка́); (*book*) вы́пуск.

fascinate ['fæsɪneɪt] *v.t.* очаро́вывать *impf.*, очарова́ть *pf.* **fascinating** *adj.* очарова́тельный. **fasci'nation** *n.* очарова́ние.

Fascism ['fæʃɪz(ə)m] *n.* фаши́зм. **Fascist** *n.* фаши́ст, ~ка; *adj.* фаши́стский.

fashion ['fæʃ(ə)n] *n.* (*manner*) мане́ра; (*pattern*) фасо́н; (*style*) стиль *m.*; (*style of dress etc.*) мо́да; **after a** ~ не́которым о́бразом; **after the** ~ **of** по образцу́+*g.*; *v.t.* придава́ть (-даю́, -даёшь) *impf.*, прида́ть (-áм, -а́шь, -а́ст, -ади́м; прида́л, -á, -о) *pf.* фо́рму+*d.*; формирова́ть *impf.*, с~ *pf.* **fashionable** *adj.* мо́дный (-ден, -дна, -дно), фешене́бельный.

fast¹ [fɑːst] *n.* пост (-á, *loc.* -у́); *v.i.* пости́ться *impf.*; **break** (**one's**) ~ разговля́ться *impf.*, разгове́ться *pf.*

fast² [fɑːst] *adj.* (*firm*) про́чный (-чен, -чна́, -чно, про́чны́), кре́пкий (-пок, -пка́, -пко), твёрдый (-д, -да́, -до), сто́йкий (-о́ек, -ойка́, -о́йко); (*rapid*) ско́рый (скор, -á, -о), бы́стрый (быстр, -á, -о, бы́стры́); (*immoral*) беспу́тный; **be** ~ (*timepiece*) спеши́ть *impf.*

fasten v.t. (attach) прикрепля́ть impf., прикрепи́ть pf. (**to** к+d.); (tie) привя́зывать impf., привяза́ть (-яжу́, -я́жешь) pf. (**to** к+d.); (garment) застёгивать impf., застегну́ть pf. **fastener, fastening** n. запо́р, задви́жка; (on garment) застёжка.

fastidious [fæ'stɪdɪəs] adj. брезгли́вый.

fat [fæt] n. жир (-a(y), loc. -ý; pl. -ы́), са́ло; adj. (greasy) жи́рный (-рен, -рна́, -рно); (plump) то́лстый (-т, -та́, -то, то́лсты́), ту́чный (-чен, -чна́, -чно); **get, grow ~** толсте́ть impf., по~ pf.

fatal ['feɪt(ə)l] adj. фата́льный, роково́й; (deadly) па́губный, смерте́льный. **fatality** [fə'tælətɪ] n. па́губность, фата́льность; (calamity) несча́стье; (death) смерть. **fate** n. судьба́ (pl. -дьбы, -деб, -дьбам), рок, жре́бий. **fated** pred. обречён (-á). **fateful** adj. роково́й.

father ['fɑ:ðə(r)] n. оте́ц (-тца́). **father-in-law** n. (husband's ~) свёкор (-кра); (wife's ~) тесть m. **fatherland** n. оте́чество. **fatherly** adj. оте́ческий.

fathom ['fæð(ə)m] n. шесть (-ти, -тью) фу́тов (глубины́ воды́); v.t. измеря́ть impf., изме́рить pf. глубину́ (воды́); (understand) понима́ть impf., поня́ть (пойму́, -мёшь; по́нял, -á, -o) pf.

fatigue [fə'ti:g] n. уста́лость, утомле́ние; v.t. утомля́ть impf., утоми́ть pf.

fatness ['fætnɪs] n. ту́чность. **fatten** v.t. отка́рмливать impf., откорми́ть (-млю́, -мишь) pf.; v.i. толсте́ть impf., по~ pf. **fattening** adj. калори́йный. **fatty** adj. жи́рный (-рен, -рна́, -рно), жирово́й.

fatuous ['fætjʊəs] adj. тупо́й (туп, -á, -o, ту́пы́).

fault [fɒlt, fɔ:lt] n. недоста́ток (-тка), дефе́кт; (blame) вина́; (geol.) сброс. **faultless** adj. безупре́чный, безоши́бочный. **faulty** adj. дефе́ктный.

fauna ['fɔ:nə] n. фа́уна.

favour ['feɪvə(r)] n. (goodwill) благоскло́нность; (aid) одолже́ние; **in (s.o.'s) ~ в** по́льзу+g.; **be in ~ of** стоя́ть (-ою́, -ои́шь) impf. за+a.; v.t. благоволи́ть impf. к+d.; благоприя́тствовать impf.+d. **favourable** adj. (propitious) благоприя́тный; (approving) благоскло́нный (-нен, -нна). **favourite** n. люби́мец (-мца), -мица; фавори́т, ~ка; adj. люби́мый.

fawn[1] [fɔ:n] n. оленёнок (-нка; pl. оленя́та, -т); adj. (~-coloured) желтова́то-кори́чневый.

fawn[2] [fɔ:n] v.i. (animal) ласка́ться impf. (**upon** к+d.); (person) подли́зываться impf., подлиза́ться (-ижу́сь, -и́жешься) pf. (**upon** к+d.).

fax [fæks] n. факс; ~ **machine** факси́мильный аппара́т; v.t. передава́ть (-даю́, -даёшь) impf., переда́ть (-а́м, -а́шь, -а́ст, -ади́м; пе́редал, -á, -o) pf. по фа́ксу.

FBI abbr. (of Federal Bureau of Investigation) ФБР, Федера́льное бюро́ рассле́дований.

fealty ['fi:əltɪ] n. (прися́га на) ве́рность.

fear [fɪə(r)] n. страх, боя́знь, опасе́ние; v.t. & i. боя́ться (бою́сь, бои́шься) impf.+g.; опаса́ться impf.+g. **fearful** adj. (terrible) стра́шный (-шен, -шна́, -шно, стра́шны́); (timid) пугли́вый. **fearless** adj. бесстра́шный. **fearsome** adj. гро́зный (-зен, -зна́, -зно).

feasibility [ˌfi:zɪ'bɪlɪtɪ] n. осуществи́мость. **feasible** adj. осуществи́мый, возмо́жный.

feast [fi:st] n. (meal) пир (loc. -e & -ý; pl. -ы́); (festival) пра́здник; v.i. пирова́ть impf.; v.t. угоща́ть impf., угости́ть pf.; **~ one's eyes on** любова́ться impf., по~ pf.+i., на+a.

feat [fi:t] n. по́двиг.

feather ['feðə(r)] n. перо́ (pl. пе́рья, -ьев); pl. (plumage) опере́ние; v.t. оперя́ть impf., опери́ть pf.; **~ bed** перина. **feather-brained** adj. ве́треный. **feathery** adj. перна́тый.

feature ['fi:tʃə(r)] n. осо́бенность, черта́; (newspaper) (темати́ческая) статья́; pl. (of face) черты́ f.pl. лица́; **~ film** худо́жественный фильм; v.t. (in film) пока́зывать impf., показа́ть (-ажу́, -а́жешь) pf. (на экра́не); v.i. (take part) уча́ствовать impf. (**in** в+p.).

febrile ['fi:braɪl] adj. лихора́дочный.

February ['februərɪ] n. февра́ль (-ля́) m.; attr. февра́льский.

fecund ['fi:kənd, 'fek-] adj. плодоро́дный. **fecundity** n. плодоро́дие.

federal ['fedər(ə)l] adj. федера́льный. **federation** n. федера́ция.

fee [fi:] n. гонора́р; (entrance ~ etc.) взнос; pl. (regular payment, school, etc.) пла́та.

feeble ['fi:b(ə)l] adj. сла́бый (слаб, -á, -o), нем́ощный. **feeble-minded** adj. слабоу́мный. **feebleness** n. сла́бость.

feed [fi:d] n. корм (-a(y), loc. -e & -ý; pl. -á); v.t. корми́ть (-млю́, -мишь) impf., на~, по~ pf.; пита́ть impf., на~ pf.; v.i. корми́ться (-млю́сь, -мишься) impf., по~ pf.; пита́ться impf. (**on** +i.); **~ up** (fatten) отка́рмливать impf., откорми́ть (-млю́, -мишь) pf.; **I am fed up with** мне надое́л (-a, -o, -и)+nom. **feedback** n. обра́тная связь; (fig.) о́тклик, реа́кция.

feel [fi:l] v.t. осяза́ть impf.; ощуща́ть impf., ощути́ть (-ущу́, -ути́шь) pf.; чу́вствовать impf., по~ pf.; (undergo) испы́тывать impf., испыта́ть pf.; v.i. (on +i.); **~ bad etc.**) чу́вствовать impf., по~ pf. себя́+adv., +i.; **~ like** хоте́ться (хо́чется) impf. impers.+d. **feeling** n. (sense) ощуще́ние; (emotion) чу́вство; (impression) впечатле́ние; (mood) настрое́ние.

feign [feɪn] v.t. притворя́ться impf., притвори́ться pf.+i. **feigned** adj. притво́рный.

feint [feɪnt] n. ло́жный уда́р; (pretence) притво́рство.

felicitate [fə'lɪsɪˌteɪt] v.t. поздравля́ть impf., поздра́вить pf. (**on** с+i.). **felicitation** n.

поздравле́ние.

felicitous [fə'lɪsɪtəs] *adj.* уда́чный, счастли́вый (сча́стлив). **felicity** *n.* сча́стье, блаже́нство.

feline ['fiːlaɪn] *adj.* коша́чий (-чья, -чье).

fell [fel] *v.t.* (*tree*) сруба́ть *impf.*, сруби́ть (-блю́, -бишь) *pf.*; (*person*) сбива́ть *impf.*, сбить (собью́, -ьёшь) *pf.* с ног.

fellow ['feləʊ] *n.* челове́к, па́рень (-рня; *pl.* -рни, -рне́й) *m.*, това́рищ; член (колле́джа, нау́чного о́бщества и т.п.). **fellowship** *n.* това́рищество, соо́бщество, содру́жество.

felon ['felən] *n.* уголо́вный престу́пник, -ая престу́пница. **felonious** [fɪ'ləʊnɪəs] *adj.* престу́пный. **felony** *n.* углоло́вное преступле́ние.

fel(d)spar ['felspɑː(r)] *n.* полево́й шпат.

felt [felt] *n.* фетр, во́йлок; *adj.* фе́тровый, во́йлочный; ~ **boots** ва́ленки (-нок) *pl.* **felt-tip (pen)** *n.* флома́стер.

female ['fiːmeɪl] *n.* (*animal*) са́мка; (*person*) же́нщина; *adj.* же́нский. **feminine** ['femɪnɪn] *adj.* же́нский, же́нственный (-ен, -енна); (*gram.*) же́нского ро́да.

femoral ['femər(ə)l] *adj.* бе́дренный. **femur** ['fiːmə(r)] *n.* бедро́ (*pl.* бёдра, -дер, -драм).

fen [fen] *n.* боло́то, боло́тистая ме́стность.

fence [fens] *n.* огра́да, забо́р, и́згородь; *v.t.*: ~ **in** огора́живать *impf.*, огороди́ть (-ожу́, -о́ди́шь) *pf.*; ~ **off** отгора́живать *impf.*, отгороди́ть (-ожу́, -о́ди́шь) *pf.*; *v.i.* (*sport*) фехтова́ть *impf.* **fencer** *n.* фехтова́льщик, -ица. **fencing** *n.* огора́живание; (*enclosure*) забо́р, и́згородь; (*sport*) фехтова́ние; *adj.* фехтова́льный.

fend [fend] *v.t.*: ~ **off** отража́ть *impf.*, отрази́ть *pf.*; (*blow*) пари́ровать *impf.*, от~ *pf.*; ~ **for o.s.** забо́титься *impf.*, по~ *pf.* о себе́. **fender** *n.* (*guard*) решётка; (*naut.*) кра́нец (-нца).

fennel ['fen(ə)l] *n.* фе́нхель *m.*

ferment ['fɜːment; fə'ment] *n.* (*substance*) заква́ска; (*action, also fig.*) броже́ние; *v.i.* броди́ть (-дит) *impf.*; *v.t.* ква́сить (-а́шу, -а́сишь) *impf.*, за~ *pf.*; (*excite*) возбужда́ть *impf.*, возбуди́ть *pf.* **fermen'tation** *n.* броже́ние; (*excitement*) возбужде́ние.

fern [fɜːn] *n.* па́поротник.

ferocious [fə'rəʊʃəs] *adj.* свире́пый, лю́тый (лют, -а́, -о). **ferocity** [fə'rɒsɪtɪ] *n.* свире́пость, лю́тость.

ferret ['ferɪt] *n.* хорёк (-рька́); *v.t.*: ~ **out** выгоня́ть *impf.*, вы́гнать (вы́гоню, -нишь) *pf.*; (*search out*) разню́хивать *impf.*, разню́хать *pf.*; *v.i.*: ~ **about** (*rummage*) ры́ться (ро́юсь, ро́ешься) *impf.*

ferro- ['ferəʊ] *in comb.* ферро..., железо... . **ferroconcrete** *n.* железобето́н. **ferrous** ['ferəs] *adj.* желе́зный; ~ **metals** чёрные мета́ллы *m.pl.*

ferry ['ferɪ] *n.* паро́м, перево́з; *v.t.* перево́зи́ть (-ожу́, -о́зишь) *impf.*, перевезти́ (-зу́, -зёшь; -ёз, -езла́) *pf.* **ferryman** *n.* паро́м-

щик, перево́зчик.

fertile ['fɜːtaɪl] *adj.* плодоро́дный, плодови́тый. **fertility** [ˌfɜː'tɪlɪtɪ] *n.* плодоро́дие, плодови́тость. **fertilize** *v.t.* (*soil*) удобря́ть *impf.*, удобри́ть *pf.*; (*egg*) оплодотворя́ть *impf.*, оплодотвори́ть *pf.* **fertilizer** *n.* удобре́ние.

fervent ['fɜːv(ə)nt], **fervid** ['fɜːvɪd] *adj.* горя́чий, пы́лкий (-лок, -лка́, -лко). **fervour** ['fɜːvə(r)] *n.* пыл (-а(у), *loc.* -ý), горя́чность, рве́ние.

festal ['fest(ə)l] *adj.* (*of feast*) пра́здничный; (*gay*) весёлый (ве́сел, -á, -о, весе́лы́).

fester ['festə(r)] *v.i.* гнои́ться *impf.*

festival ['festɪv(ə)l] *n.* пра́здник, фестива́ль *m.* **festive** *adj.* пра́здничный; (*jovial*) весёлый (ве́сел, -á, -о, весе́лы́). **fe'stivity** *n.* весе́лье; *pl.* торжества́ *nt.pl.*

festoon [fe'stuːn] *n.* гирля́нда; (*archit.*) фесто́н; *v.t.* украша́ть *impf.*, укра́сить *pf.* гирля́ндами, фесто́нами.

fetch [fetʃ] *v.t.* (*carrying*) приноси́ть (-ошу́, -о́сишь) *impf.*, принести́ (-есу́, -есёшь; -ёс, -есла́) *pf.*; (*leading*) приводи́ть (-ожу́, -о́дишь) *impf.*, привести́ (-еду́, -едёшь; -ёл, -ела́) *pf.*; (*go and come back with*) (*on foot*) сходи́ть (-ожу́, -о́дишь) *pf.* за+*i.*; заходи́ть (-ожу́, -о́дишь) *impf.*, зайти́ (зайду́, -дёшь; зашёл, -шла́) *pf.* за+*i.*; (*by vehicle*) заезжа́ть *impf.*, зае́хать (-е́ду, -е́дешь) *pf.* за+*i.*; (*cause*) вызыва́ть *impf.*, вы́звать (вы́зову, -вешь) *pf.*; (*price*) выруча́ть *impf.*, вы́ручить *pf.* **fetching** *adj.* привлека́тельный.

fetid ['fetɪd, 'fiːtɪd] *adj.* злово́нный (-нен, -нна).

fetish ['fetɪʃ] *n.* фети́ш.

fetlock ['fetlɒk] *n.* щётка.

fetter ['fetə(r)] *v.t.* ско́вывать *impf.*, скова́ть (скую́, скуёшь) *pf.*; *n.*: *pl.* кандалы́ (-ло́в) *pl.*, око́вы (-в) *pl.*

fettle ['fet(ə)l] *n.* состоя́ние.

feud [fjuːd] *n.* кро́вная месть.

feudal ['fjuːd(ə)l] *adj.* феода́льный. **feudalism** *n.* феодали́зм.

fever ['fiːvə(r)] *n.* (*med.*) жар (-а(у), *loc.* -ý), лихора́дка; (*agitation*) возбужде́ние. **feverish** *adj.* лихора́дочный; возбуждённый (-ён, -ена́).

few, a ~ [fjuː] *adj. & pron.* немно́гие (-их) *pl.*; немно́го+*g.*, ма́ло+*g.*, не́сколько+*g.*; **quite a** ~ нема́ло+*g.*

fez [fez] *n.* фе́ска.

fiancé [fɪ'ɒnseɪ, fɪ'ɑːseɪ] *n.* жени́х (-á). **fiancée** *n.* неве́ста.

fiasco [fɪ'æskəʊ] *n.* прова́л.

fiat ['faɪæt, 'faɪət] *n.* (*sanction*) са́нкция; (*decree*) декре́т.

fib [fɪb] *n.* враньё; *v.i.* привира́ть *impf.*, привра́ть (-ру́, -рёшь; привра́л, -á, -о) *pf.* **fibber** *n.* враль (-ля́) *m.*

fibre ['faɪbə(r)] *n.* фи́бра, волокно́ (*pl.* -о́кна, -о́кон, -о́кнам); (*character*) хара́ктер. **fibreglass** *n.* стекловолокно́. **fibrous** *adj.* фибро́зный, волокни́стый.

fickle ['fɪk(ə)l] *adj.* непостоя́нный (-нен, -нна), изме́нчивый. **fickleness** *n.* непостоя́нство, изме́нчивость.

fiction ['fɪkʃ(ə)n] *n.* (*literature*) беллетри́стика, худо́жественная литерату́ра; (*invention*) вы́думка. **fictional** *adj.* беллетристи́ческий; вы́мышленный. **fic'titious** *adj.* вы́мышленный, фикти́вный.

fiddle ['fɪd(ə)l] *n.* (*violin*) скри́пка; (*swindle*) обма́н; *v.i.* игра́ть *impf.* (with c+*i.*); ~ **about** безде́льничать *impf.*; *v.t.* (*cheat*) надува́ть *impf.*, наду́ть (-у́ю, -у́ешь) *pf.*

fidelity [fɪ'delɪtɪ] *n.* ве́рность.

fidget ['fɪdʒɪt] *n.* непосе́да *c.g.*; *v.i.* ёрзать *impf.*; не́рвничать *impf.* **fidgety** *adj.* непосе́дливый.

field [fiːld] *n.* по́ле (*pl.* -ля́, -ле́й); (*sport*) площа́дка; (*sphere*) о́бласть, сфе́ра; *attr.* полево́й; F~ **Marshal** фельдма́ршал. **field-glasses** *n.* полево́й бино́кль *m.* **field-mouse** *n.* полева́я мышь (*pl.* -ши, -ше́й).

fiend [fiːnd] *n.* (*demon*) дья́вол, де́мон; (*cruel person*) и́зверг. **fiendish** *adj.* дья́вольский.

fierce ['fɪəs] *adj.* свире́пый, лю́тый (лют, -á, -о); (*strong*) си́льный (силён, -льна́, -льно, си́льны).

fiery ['faɪərɪ] *adj.* о́гненный.

fife [faɪf] *n.* ду́дка.

fifteen [fɪf'tiːn, 'fɪf-] *adj. & n.* пятна́дцать (-ти, -тью); (*age*) пятна́дцать лет. **fifteenth** *adj. & n.* пятна́дцатый; (*fraction*) пятна́дцатая (часть (*pl.* -ти, -те́й)); (*date*) пятна́дцатое (число́); **fifth** *adj. & n.* пя́тый; (*fraction*) пя́тая (часть (*pl.* -ти, -те́й)); (*date*) пя́тое (число́); (*mus.*) кви́нта. **fiftieth** *adj. & n.* пятидеся́тый; (*fraction*) пятидеся́тая (часть (*pl.* -ти, -те́й)). **fifty** *adj. & n.* пятьдеся́т (-тидесяти́, -тью́десятью); (*age*) пятьдеся́т лет; *pl.* (*decade*) пятидеся́тые го́ды (-до́в) *m.pl.* **fifty-fifty** *adj.* ра́вный (-вен, -вна́); *adv.* по́ровну.

fig [fɪg] *n.* фи́га, ви́нная я́года, инжи́р.

fig. *abbr.* (*of* **figure**) рис., рису́нок.

fight [faɪt] *n.* дра́ка; (*battle*) бой (*loc.* бою́; *pl.* бои́); (*fig.*) борьба́; *v.t.* боро́ться (-рю́сь, -решься) *impf.* c+*i.*; сража́ться *impf.*, срази́ться *pf.* c+*i.*; *v.i.* дра́ться (деру́сь, -рёшься; дра́лся, -ла́сь, дра́ло́сь) *impf.* **fighter** *n.* бое́ц (бойца́); (*aeron.*) истреби́тель *m.* **fighting** *n.* бой *m.pl.*, сраже́ние, дра́ка; *adj.* боево́й.

figment ['fɪgmənt] *n.* вы́мысел (-сла), плод (-á) воображе́ния.

figuration [fɪgjʊ'reɪʃ(ə)n] *n.* оформле́ние; (*ornamentation*) орнамента́ция. **'figurative** *adj.* о́бразный, перено́сный. **'figure** *n.* (*form, body, person*) фигу́ра; (*number*) ци́фра; (*diagram*) рису́нок (-нка); (*image*) изображе́ние; (*person*) ли́чность; (*of speech*) оборо́т ре́чи; *v.t.* (*represent*) изобража́ть *impf.*, изобрази́ть *pf.*; (*imagine*) представля́ть *impf.*, предста́вить *pf.* себе́; ~ **out** вычисля́ть *impf.*, вы́числить *pf.*

figure-head *n.* (*naut.*) носово́е украше́ние; (*person*) подставно́е лицо́ (*pl.* -ца). **figurine** [ˌfɪgjʊ'riːn] *n.* статуэ́тка.

filament ['fɪləmənt] *n.* волокно́ (*pl.* -о́кна, -о́кон, -о́кнам), нить.

filch [fɪltʃ] *v.t.* стяну́ть (-ну́, -нешь) *pf.*

file¹ [faɪl] *n.* (*tool*) напи́льник; *v.t.* подпи́ливать *impf.*, подпили́ть (-лю́, -лишь) *pf.*

file² [faɪl] *n.* (*folder*) подши́вка, па́пка; (*set of papers*) де́ло (*pl.* -ла́); *v.t.* подшива́ть *impf.*, подши́ть (подошью́, -ьёшь) *pf.*; влага́ть *impf.*, вложи́ть (-жу́, -жишь) *pf.* в па́пки.

file³ [faɪl] *n.* (*row*) ряд (-á with 2,3,4, *loc.* -ý; *pl.* -ы́), шере́нга; **in** (**single**) ~ гусько́м.

filial ['fɪlɪəl] *adj.* (*of son*) сыно́вний; (*of daughter*) дочерний.

filigree ['fɪlɪgriː] *n.* филигра́нь; *adj.* филигра́нный.

fill [fɪl] *v.t. & i.* наполня́ть(ся) *impf.*, напо́лнить(ся) *pf.*; *v.t.* заполня́ть *impf.*, запо́лнить *pf.*; (*tooth*) пломбирова́ть *impf.*, за~ *pf.*; (*occupy*) занима́ть *impf.*, заня́ть (займу́, -мёшь; за́нял, -á, -о) *pf.*; (*satiate*) насыща́ть *impf.*, насы́тить (-ы́щу, -ы́тишь) *pf.*; ~ **in** (*v.t.*) заполня́ть *impf.*, запо́лнить *pf.*; (*words*) впи́сывать *impf.*, вписа́ть (-ишу́, -и́шешь) *pf.*; (*v.i.*) замеща́ть *impf.*, замести́ть *pf.*

fillet ['fɪlɪt] *n.* (*ribbon*) повя́зка; (*cul.*) филе́ *nt.indecl.*

filling ['fɪlɪŋ] *n.* наполне́ние; (*tooth*) пло́мба; (*cul.*) начи́нка.

fillip ['fɪlɪp] *n.* щелчо́к (-чка́); толчо́к (-чка́).

filly ['fɪlɪ] *n.* кобы́лка.

film [fɪlm] *n.* (*haze*) ды́мка; (*layer; phot.*) плёнка; (*cin.*) фильм; ~ **star** кинозвезда́ (*pl.* -ёзды); ~ **studies** *n.* киноведе́ние; *v.t.* экранизи́ровать *impf. & pf.*; *v.i.* производи́ть (-ожу́, -о́дишь) *impf.*, произвести́ (-еду́, -едёшь, -ёл, -ела́) *pf.* киносъёмку; снима́ть *impf.*, снять (сниму́, -мешь; снял, -á, -о) *pf.* фильм. **filmy** *adj.* тума́нный (-нен, -нна).

filter ['fɪltə(r)] *n.* фильтр; *v.t.* фильтрова́ть *impf.*, про~ *pf.*; проце́живать *impf.*, процеди́ть *pf.*; ~ **through, out** проса́чиваться *impf.*, просочи́ться *pf.*

filth [fɪlθ] *n.* грязь (*loc.* -зи́); (*obscenity*) непристо́йность. **filthy** *adj.* гря́зный (-зен, -зна́, -зно); непристо́йный.

fin [fɪn] *n.* плавни́к (-á); (*aeron.*) киль *m.*

final ['faɪn(ə)l] *n.* фина́л; *pl.* выпускны́е экза́мены *m.pl.*; *adj.* после́дний, оконча́тельный. **finale** [fɪ'nɑːlɪ, -leɪ] *n.* фина́л, развя́зка. **fi'nality** *n.* зако́нченность. **finally** *adv.* в конце́ концо́в, оконча́тельно.

finance ['faɪnæns, faɪ'næns] *n.* фина́нсы (-сов) *pl.*; *pl.* дохо́ды *m.pl.*; *v.t.* финанси́ровать *impf. & pf.* **fi'nancial** *adj.* фина́нсовый. **fi'nancier** *n.* финанси́ст.

finch *n. see comb.*, *e.g.* **bullfinch**

find [faɪnd] *n.* нахо́дка; *v.t.* находи́ть (-ожу́, -о́дишь) *impf.*, найти́ (найду́, -дёшь; нашёл,

-шла́) *pf.*; (*person*) заставля́ть (-таю, -таёшь) *impf.*, заста́ть (-а́ну, -а́нешь) *pf.*; ~ **out** узнава́ть (-наю, -наёшь) *impf.*, узна́ть *pf.*; ~ **fault with** придира́ться *impf.*, придра́ться (придеру́сь, -рёшься; придра́лся, -ала́сь, -а́лось) *pf.* к+*d.* **finding** *n.* (*leg.*) пригово́р; *pl.* (*of inquiry*) вы́воды *m.pl.*

fine¹ [faɪn] *n.* (*penalty*) штраф; *v.t.* штрафова́ть *impf.*, о~ *pf.*

fine² [faɪn] *adj.* (*excellent*) прекра́сный, превосхо́дный; (*delicate*) то́нкий (-нок, -нка́, -нко, то́нки́); (*of sand etc.*) ме́лкий (-лок, -лка́, -лко); ~ **arts** изобрази́тельные иску́сства *nt.pl.* **fineness** *n.* то́нкость, изя́щество, острота́. **finery** ['faɪnərɪ] *n.* наря́д, украше́ние. **finesse** [fɪ'nes] *n.* хи́трость.

finger ['fɪŋgə(r)] *n.* па́лец (-льца) (**index** указа́тельный; **middle** сре́дний; **ring** безымя́нный; **little** мизи́нец (-нца)); *v.t.* тро́гать *impf.*, тро́нуть *pf.* **fingerprint** *n.* отпеча́ток (-тка) па́льца. **fingertip** *n.*: have at (one's) ~s знать *impf.* как свои́ пять па́льцев.

finish ['fɪnɪʃ] *n.* коне́ц (-нца́), оконча́ние; (*of furniture etc.*) отде́лка; (*sport*) фи́ниш; *v.t. & i.* конча́ть(ся) *impf.*, ко́нчить(ся) *pf.*; *v.t.* ока́нчивать *impf.*, око́нчить *pf.*; ~**ing** touches после́дние штрихи́ *m.pl.*

finite ['faɪnaɪt] *adj.* определённый (-нен, -нна); (*gram.*) ли́чный.

Finland ['fɪnlənd] *n.* Финля́ндия.

Finn [fɪn] *n.* финн, фи́нка. **Finnish** *adj.* фи́нский.

fir [fɜ:(r)] *n.* ель, пи́хта. **fir-cone** *n.*ело́вая ши́шка.

fire ['faɪə(r)] *n.* ого́нь (огня́) *m.*; (*grate*) ками́н; (*conflagration*) пожа́р; (*bonfire*) костёр (-тра́); (*fervour*) пыл (-а(у), *loc.* -ý); be on ~ горе́ть (-рю́, -ри́шь) *impf.*; catch ~ загора́ться *impf.*, загоре́ться (-рю́сь, -ри́шься) *pf.*; set ~ to, set on ~ поджига́ть *impf.*, подже́чь (подожгу́, -жжёшь; поджёг, подожгла́) *pf.*; *v.t.* зажига́ть *impf.*, заже́чь (-жгу́, -жжёшь; -жёг, -жгла́) *pf.*; воспламеня́ть *impf.*, воспламени́ть *pf.*; (*gun*) стреля́ть *impf.* из+*g.* (at в+*a.*, по+*d.*); (*dismiss*) увольня́ть *impf.*, уво́лить *pf.*; ~ brigade пожа́рная кома́нда; ~ extinguisher огнетуши́тель *m.*; ~ station пожа́рное депо́ *nt.indecl.* **fire-alarm** *n.* пожа́рная трево́га. **firearm(s)** *n.* огнестре́льное ору́жие. **fire-engine** *n.* пожа́рная маши́на. **fire-escape** *n.* пожа́рная ле́стница. **firefly** *n.* светля́к (-а́). **fire-guard** *n.* ками́нная решётка. **fireman** *n.* пожа́рный *sb.*; (*tending furnace*) кочега́р. **fireplace** *n.* ками́н. **fireproof, fire-resistant** *adj.* огнеупо́рный. **fireside** *n.* ме́сто у ками́на. **firewood** *n.* дрова́ (-в) *pl.* **firework** *n.* фейерве́рк. **firing** *n.* (*of gun*) стрельба́.

firm¹ [fɜ:m] *n.* (*business*) фи́рма.

firm² [fɜ:m] *adj.* твёрдый (твёрд, -а́, -о), кре́пкий (-пок, -пка́, -пко), сто́йкий (-о́ек,

-ойка́, -о́йко). **firmament** *n.* небе́сный свод. **firmness** *n.* твёрдость.

first [fɜ:st] *adj.* пе́рвый; (*foremost*) выдаю́щийся; *n.* (*date*) пе́рвое (число́); пе́рвый *sb.*; *adv.* сперва́, снача́ла, в пе́рвый раз; in the ~ place во-пе́рвых; ~ of all пре́жде всего́; at ~ sight на пе́рвый взгляд, с пе́рвого взгля́да; ~ aid пе́рвая по́мощь; give ~ aid ока́зывать *impf.*, оказа́ть (-ажу́, -а́жешь) *pf.* пе́рвую по́мощь (to +*d.*); ~ cousin двою́родный брат (*pl.* -ья, -ьев), двою́родная сестра́ (*pl.* сёстры, сестёр, сёстрам). **first-born** *n.* пе́рвенец (-нца). **first-class** *adj.* первокла́ссный, превосхо́дный. **firsthand** *adv.* из пе́рвых рук. **first-rate** *adj.* первокла́ссный, превосхо́дный.

fiscal ['fɪsk(ə)l] *adj.* фина́нсовый, фиска́льный.

fish [fɪʃ] *n.* ры́ба; *adj.* ры́бный, ры́бий (-бья, -бье); *v.i.* лови́ть (-влю́, -вишь) *impf.* ры́бу; уди́ть (ужу́, у́дишь) *impf.* ры́бу; ~ for (*compliments etc.*) напра́шиваться *impf.*, напроси́ться (-ошу́сь, -о́сишься) *pf.* на+*a.*; ~ out выта́скивать *impf.*, вы́таскать *pf.* **fisherman** *n.* рыба́к (-а́), рыболо́в. **fishery** *n.* ры́бный про́мысел (-сла). **fishing** *n.* ры́бная ло́вля; ~ boat рыболо́вное су́дно (*pl.* суда́, -до́в); ~ line леса́ (*pl.* лёсы); ~ rod уди́лище, у́дочка. **fishmonger** *n.* торго́вец (-вца) ры́бой. **fishy** *adj.* ры́бный, ры́бий (-бья, -бье); (*dubious*) подозри́тельный.

fission ['fɪʃ(ə)n] *n.* расщепле́ние; nuclear ~ деле́ние ядра́; cell ~ деле́ние кле́ток. **fissure** *n.* тре́щина.

fist [fɪst] *n.* кула́к (-а́). **fisticuffs** ['fɪstɪ,kʌfs] *n.* кула́чный бой (*loc.* бою́; *pl.* бои́).

fit¹ [fɪt] *n.*: be a good ~ (*clothes*) хорошо́ сиде́ть (-ди́т, -дя́т) *impf.*; *adj.* подходя́щий, го́дный (-ден, -дна́, -дно); (*healthy*) здоро́вый; *v.t.* (*be suitable*) годи́ться *impf.*+*d.*, на+*a.*, для+*g.*; подходи́ть (-ожу́, -о́дишь) *impf.*, подойти́ (подойду́, -дёшь; подошёл, -шла́) *pf.*+*d.*; (*adjust*) прила́живать *impf.*, прила́дить *pf.* (to к+*d.*); *v.t. & i.* приспоса́бливать(ся) *impf.*, приспосо́бить(ся) *pf.*; ~ out снабжа́ть *impf.*, снабди́ть *pf.*

fit² [fɪt] *n.* (*attack*) припа́док (-дка), при́ступ; (*fig.*) поры́в. **fitful** *adj.* поры́вистый.

fitter ['fɪtə(r)] *n.* монтёр, устано́вщик. **fitting** *n.* (*of clothes*) приме́рка; прила́живание; монта́ж; *pl.* армату́ра; *adj.* подходя́щий, го́дный (-ден, -дна́, -дно). **fitting-room** *n.* приме́рочная *sb.*

five [faɪv] *adj. & n.* пять (-ти́, -тью); (*collect.; 5 pairs*) пя́теро (-ры́х); (*cards; number 5*) пятёрка; (*time*) пять (часо́в); (*age*) пять лет. **five-year** *adj.*: ~ plan пятиле́тка.

fix [fɪks] *n.* (*dilemma*) диле́мма; (*radio etc.*) засе́чка; *v.t.* устана́вливать *impf.*, установи́ть (-влю́, -вишь) *pf.*; (*arrange*) устра́ивать *impf.*, устро́ить *pf.*; (*repair*) поправля́ть *impf.*, попра́вить *pf.*; *v.t. & i.* останавливать(ся) *impf.*, остановить(ся) (-влю(сь), -вишь(ся)) *pf.* (on на+*a.*). **fi'xation** *n.* фиксация. **fixed** *adj.* неподвижный, постоянный (-нен, -нна).

fizz [fɪz] *v.i.* шипеть (-плю, -пишь) *impf.*, зн. (*coll.*) шипучка. **fizzy** *adj.* шипучий.

flabbergast ['flæbə,gɑːst] *v.t.* ошеломлять *impf.*, ошеломить *pf.*

flabby ['flæbɪ], **flaccid** ['flæksɪd, 'flæsɪd] *adj.* дряблый (-л, -ла, -ло), вялый.

flag¹ [flæg] *n.* (*standard*) флаг, знамя (*pl.* -мёна) *nt.*; *v.t.* (*signal*) сигнализировать *impf.* & *pf.*, про~ *pf.* флагами.

flag² [flæg] *n.* (*stone*) плита (*pl.* -ты); *v.t.* мостить *impf.*, вы~, за~ *pf.* плитами.

flag³ [flæg] *v.i.* (*droop*) поникать *impf.*, поникнуть (-к) *pf.*

flagellate ['flædʒɪlɪt] *v.t.* бичевать (-чую, -чуешь) *impf.*

flagon ['flægən] *n.* кувшин.

flagrant ['fleɪgrənt] *adj.* вопиющий, очевидный, скандальный.

flagship ['flægʃɪp] *n.* флагман. **flagstaff** *n.* флагшток.

flail [fleɪl] *n.* цеп (-á).

flair ['fleə(r)] *n.* чутьё.

flake [fleɪk] *n.* слой (*pl.* -ой); *pl.* хлопья (-ьев) *pl.*; *v.i.* слоиться *impf.*, лупиться (-пится) *impf.*, об~ *pf.* **flaky** *adj.* слоистый.

flamboyant [flæm'bɔɪənt] *adj.* цветистый.

flame [fleɪm] *n.* пламя *nt.*, огонь (огня) *m.*; (*passion*) пыл (-a(y), *loc.* -ý); *v.i.* пылать *impf.*; ~ up разгораться *impf.*, разгореться (-рится) *pf.* **flame-thrower** *n.* огнемёт.

flamingo [flə'mɪŋgəʊ] *n.* фламинго *m.indecl.*

flange [flændʒ] *n.* фланец (-нца).

flank [flæŋk] *n.* бок (*loc.* -ý; *pl.* -á), фланг; *v.t.* быть расположенным сбоку, на фланге, +*g.*; (*mil.*) фланкировать *impf.* & *pf.*

flannel ['flæn(ə)l] *n.* фланель; *attr.* фланелевый.

flap [flæp] *n.* мах; (*wings*) взмах; (*board*) откидная доска (*a.* -ску; *pl.* -ски, -сок, -скам); *v.t.* махать (машу, -шешь) *impf.*, махнуть *pf.*+*i.*; взмахивать *impf.*, взмахнуть *pf.*+*i.*; *v.i.* развеваться *impf.*

flare [fleə(r)] *n.* вспышка; (*signal*) световой сигнал; *v.i.* вспыхивать *impf.*, вспыхнуть *pf.*; ~ up вспылить *pf.*

flash [flæʃ] *n.* вспышка, проблеск; in a ~ мигом; *v.i.* сверкать *impf.*, сверкнуть *pf.* · **flashy** *adj.* показной.

flask [flɑːsk] *n.* фляжка.

flat¹ [flæt] *n.* (*dwelling*) квартира.

flat² [flæt] *n.* (~ *region*) равнина; (*mus.*) бемоль *m.*; (*tyre*) спущенная шина; *adj.* плоский (-сок, -ска, -ско), ровный (-вен, -вна, -вно); (*dull*) скучный (-чен, -чна, -чно); ~ foot плоскостопие. **flat-fish** *n.* камбала. **flat-iron** *n.* утюг (-á).

flatmate ['flætmeɪt] *n.* сосед по квартире.

flatten *v.t.* делать *impf.*, с~ *pf.* плоским; *v.i.* становиться (-ится) *impf.*, стать (станет)

pf. плоским; *v.t.* & *i.* выравнивать(ся) *impf.*, выровнять(ся) *pf.*

flatter *v.t.* льстить *impf.*, по~ *pf.*+*d.* **flatterer** *n.* льстец (-á). **flattering** *adj.* льстивый, лестный. **flattery** *n.* лесть.

flaunt [flɔːnt] *v.t.* щеголять *impf.*, щегольнуть *pf.*+*i.*; ~ o.s. выставляться *impf.*, выставиться *pf.*

flautist ['flɔːtɪst] *n.* флейтист.

flavour ['fleɪvə(r)] *n.* аромат, вкус; (*fig.*) привкус, оттенок (-нка); *v.t.* приправлять *impf.*, приправить *pf.* **flavourless** *adj.* безвкусный.

flaw [flɔː] *n.* (*crack*) трещина; (*defect*) изъян.

flax [flæks] *n.* лён (льна). **flaxen** *adj.* льняной; (*colour*) соломенный.

flay [fleɪ] *v.t.* сдирать *impf.*, содрать (сдеру, -рёшь; содрал, -á, -о) *pf.* кожу с+*g.*

flea [fliː] *n.* блоха (*pl.* -хи, -х, -хам). **flea-bite** *n.* блошиный укус.

fleck [flek] *n.* пятно (*pl.* -тна, -тен, -тнам), крапина.

fledge [fledʒ] *v.t.* оперять *impf.*, оперить *pf.*; **be(come) fledged** оперяться *impf.*, оперить-ся *pf.* **fledg(e)ling** *n.* птенец (-нца).

flee [fliː] *v.i.* бежать (бегу, бежишь) *impf.* & *pf.* (**from** от+*g.*); (*vanish*) исчезать *impf.*, исчезнуть (-з) *pf.*

fleece [fliːs] *n.* овечья шерсть, руно (*pl.* -на); *v.t.* обдирать *impf.*, ободрать (обдеру, -рёшь; ободрал, -á, -о) *pf.* **fleecy** *adj.* шерстистый.

fleet [fliːt] *n.* флот (*pl.* -óты, -óтóв); (*vehicles*) парк.

fleeting *adj.* мимолётный.

flesh [fleʃ] *n.* (*as opposed to mind*) плоть; (*meat*) мясо; (*of fruit*) мякоть; in the ~ во плоти. **fleshly** *adj.* плотский. **fleshy** *adj.* мясистый.

flex [fleks] *n.* электрошнур (-á); *v.t.* сгибать *impf.*, согнуть *pf.* **flexibility** *adj.* гибкость, податливость. **flexible** *adj.* гибкий (-бок, -бка, -бко), податливый. **flexion** *n.* сгиб-(áние); (*gram.*) флексия.

flick [flɪk] *n.* щелчок (-чка); *v.t.* & *i.* щёлкать *impf.*, щёлкнуть *pf.* (+*i.*); ~ off смахивать *impf.*, смахнуть *pf.*

flicker ['flɪkə(r)] *n.* мерцание; *v.i.* мерцать *impf.*

flick-knife ['flɪknaɪf] *n.* пружинный нож (-á).

flier *see* **flyer**

flight¹ [flaɪt] *n.* (*fleeing*) бегство; **put to ~** обращать *impf.*, обратить (-ащу, -атишь) *pf.* в бегство.

flight² [flaɪt] *n.* (*flying*) полёт, перелёт; (*trip*) рейс; (*flock*) стая; (*aeron. unit*) звено (*pl.* -нья, -ньев); ~ of stairs лестничный марш. **flighty** *adj.* ветреный.

flimsy ['flɪmzɪ] *adj.* непрочный (-чен, -чна, -чно).

flinch [flɪntʃ] *v.i.* уклоняться *impf.*, уклониться (-нюсь, -нишься) *pf.* (**from** от+*g.*); (*wince*) вздрагивать *impf.*, вздрогнуть *pf.*

fling [flɪŋ] *v.t.* швырять *impf.*, швырнуть *pf.*;

v.i. (*also* ~ *o.s.*) броса́ться *impf.*, бро́ситься *pf.*

flint [flɪnt] *n.* креме́нь (-мня́) *m.*; *attr.* кремнё-вый.

flip [flɪp] *n.* щелчо́к (-чка́); *v.t.* щёлкать *impf.*, щёлкнуть *pf.*+*i.*

flippancy ['flɪpənsɪ] *n.* легкомы́слие. **flippant** *adj.* легкомы́сленный (-ен, -енна).

flipper ['flɪpə(r)] *n.* плавни́к (-а́), ласт.

flirt [flɜːt] *n.* коке́тка; *v.i.* флиртова́ть *impf.* (**with** c+*i.*); (*fig.*) заи́грывать *impf.* (**with** c+*i.*). **flir'tation** *n.* флирт.

flit [flɪt] *v.i.* (*migrate*) переезжа́ть *impf.*, пере-е́хать (-е́ду, -е́дешь) *pf.*; (*fly*) порха́ть *impf.*, порхну́ть *pf.*

float [fləʊt] *n.* поплаво́к (-вка́), плот (-а́); *v.i.* пла́вать *indet.*, плыть (плыву́, -вёшь; плыл, -а́, -о) *det.*; *v.t.* (*loan*) выпуска́ть *impf.*, вы́пустить *pf.*; (*company*) пуска́ть *impf.*, пусти́ть (пущу́, пу́стишь) *pf.* в ход.

flock [flɒk] *n.* (*animals*) ста́до (*pl.* -да́); (*birds*) ста́я; (*people*) толпа́ (*pl.* -пы) *v.i.* стека́ться *impf.*, стечься (стечётся; стёкся, -кла́сь) *pf.*; толпи́ться *impf.*

floe [fləʊ] *n.* плаву́чая льди́на.

flog [flɒg] *v.t.* сечь (секу́, сечёшь; сек, -ла́) *impf.*, вы́~ *pf.*

flood [flʌd] *n.* наводне́ние, разли́в, пото́п; *v.i.* (*river etc.*) выступа́ть *impf.*, вы́ступить *pf.* из берего́в; *v.t.* наводня́ть *impf.*, наводни́ть *pf.*; затопля́ть *impf.*, затопи́ть (-плю́, -пишь) *pf.* **floodgate** *n.* шлюз. **flood-light** *n.* прожёктор (*pl.* -ы & -а́). **flood-tide** *n.* прили́в;

floor [flɔː(r)] *n.* пол (*loc.* -у́; *pl.* -ы́); (*of sea*) дно (*no pl.*); (*storey*) эта́ж (-а́); **ground, first** (*etc.*) ~ пе́рвый, второ́й, (и т.д.) эта́ж (-а́); **take the** ~ брать (беру́, -рёшь; брал, -а́, -о) *impf.*, взять (возьму́, -мёшь; взял, -а́, -о) *pf.* сло́во; *v.t.* настила́ть *impf.*, настла́ть (-телю́, -те́лешь) *pf.* пол+*g.*; (*knock down*) вали́ть (-лю́, -лишь) *impf.*, по~ *pf.* на́ пол; (*confound*) ста́вить *impf.*, по~ *pf.* в тупи́к. **floorboard** *n.* полови́ца. **floorcloth** *n.* поло-ва́я тря́пка. **flooring** *n.* насти́л(ка).

flop [flɒp] *v.i.* шлёпаться *impf.*, шлёпнуться *pf.*; (*fail*) прова́ливаться *impf.*, провали́ть-ся (-ится) *pf.* **floppy** *adj.* вися́щий, болта́ю-щийся; *n.* (*comput.*) ~ (**disk**) ги́бкий диск.

flora ['flɔːrə] *n.* фло́ра. **floral** *adj.* цвето́чный.

Florence ['flɒrəns] *n.* Флоре́нция.

florescence [flɔːˈres(ə)ns, flɒ-] *n.* цвете́ние. **florid** ['flɒrɪd] *adj.* цвети́стый; (*ruddy*) румя́-ный. **'florist** *n.* торго́вец (-вца) цвета́ми.

flotilla [fləˈtɪlə] *n.* флоти́лия.

flotsam ['flɒtsəm] *n.* пла́вающие обло́мки *m.pl.*

flounce[1] [flaʊns] *n.* (*of skirt*) обо́рка.

flounce[2] [flaʊns] *v.i.* броса́ться *impf.*, бро́-ситься *pf.*

flounder[1] ['flaʊndə(r)] *n.* (*fish*) ка́мбала.

flounder[2] ['flaʊndə(r)] *v.i.* бара́хтаться *impf.*; пу́таться *impf.*, с~ *pf.*

flour ['flaʊə(r)] *n.* мука́. **flour-mill** *n.* ме́ль-ница.

flourish ['flʌrɪʃ] *n.* (*movement*) разма́хивание (+*i.*); (*of pen*) ро́счерк; (*mus.*) туш; *v.i.* (*thrive*) процвета́ть *impf.*; *v.t.* (*wave*) разма́-хивать *impf.*, размахну́ть *pf.*+*i.*

floury ['flaʊərɪ] *adj.* мучни́стый.

flout [flaʊt] *v.t.* пренебрега́ть *impf.*, пре-небре́чь (-егу́, -ежёшь; -ёг, -егла́) *pf.*+*i.*

flow [fləʊ] *v.i.* течь (течёт; тёк, -ла́) *impf.*; ли́ться (льётся; ли́лся, лила́сь, лило́сь) *impf.*; *n.* тече́ние, пото́к; (*tide*) прили́в.

flower ['flaʊə(r)] *n.* цвето́к (-тка́; *pl.* -ты́); (*pick*; *prime*) цвет; *v.i.* цвести́ (цветёт; цвёл, -á) *impf.* **flower-bed** *n.* клу́мба. **flowerpot** *n.* цвето́чный горшо́к (-шка́). **flowery** *adj.* покры́тый цвета́ми; (*florid*) цвети́стый.

flu [fluː] *n.* грипп.

fluctuate ['flʌktjʊˌeɪt] *v.i.* колеба́ться (-блюсь, -блешься) *impf.*, по~ *pf.* **fluctu'ation** *n.* колеба́ние.

flue [fluː] *n.* дымохо́д.

fluency ['fluːənsɪ] *n.* пла́вность, бе́глость. **fluent** *adj.* пла́вный, бе́глый. **fluently** *adv.* бе́гло, свобо́дно.

fluff [flʌf] *n.* пух (-а(у), *loc.* -ý), пушо́к (-шка́). **fluffy** *adj.* пуши́стый.

fluid ['fluːɪd] *n.* жи́дкость; *adj.* жи́дкий (-док, -дка́, -дко), теку́чий.

flunkey ['flʌŋkɪ] *n.* лаке́й.

fluorescence [flʊəˈres(ə)ns] *n.* флюоресце́нция. **fluorescent** *adj.* флюоресци́рую-щий.

fluoride ['flʊəraɪd] *n.* фтори́д. **fluorine** ['flʊəriːn] *n.* фтор.

flurry ['flʌrɪ] *n.* (*squall*) поры́в ве́тра; (*commotion*) сумато́ха; *v.t.* (*agitate*) волнова́ть *impf.*, вз~ *pf.*

flush [flʌʃ] *n.* прили́в; (*redness*) румя́нец (-нца); *v.i.* (*redden*) красне́ть *impf.*, по~ *pf.*; *v.t.* спуска́ть *impf.*, спусти́ть (-ущу́, -у́стишь) *pf.* во́ду в+*a.*

fluster ['flʌstə(r)] *n.* волне́ние; *v.t.* волнова́ть *impf.*, вз~ *pf.*

flute [fluːt] *n.* (*mus.*) фле́йта; (*groove*) жело-бо́к (-бка́).

flutter ['flʌtə(r)] *v.i.* порха́ть *impf.*, порхну́ть *pf.*; развева́ться *impf.*; (*with excitement*) тре-пета́ть (-ещу́, -е́щешь) *impf.*; *n.* порха́ние; тре́пет.

fluvial ['fluːvɪəl] *adj.* речно́й.

flux [flʌks] *n.* тече́ние; **in a state of** ~ в со-стоя́нии измене́ния.

fly[1] [flaɪ] *n.* (*insect*) му́ха.

fly[2] [flaɪ] *v.i.* лета́ть *indet.*, лете́ть (лечу́, лети́шь), *det.*, по~ *pf.*; (*flag*) развева́ться *impf.*; (*hasten*) нести́сь (несу́сь, -сёшься; нёсся, несла́сь) *impf.*, по~ *pf.*; (*flee*) бежа́ть (бегу́, бежи́шь) *impf.* & *pf.*; *v.t.* (*aircraft*) управля́ть *impf.*+*i.*; (*transport*) перевози́ть (-ожу́, -о́зишь) *impf.*, перевезти́ (-езу́, -езёшь; -ёз, -езла́) *pf.* (самолётом); (*flag*) поднима́ть *impf.*, подня́ть (-ниму́, -ни́мешь; под-

ня́л, -á, -о) *pf.* **flyer, flier** *n.* лётчик. **flying** *n.* полёт(ы).

flywheel *n.* махови́к (-á).

foal [fəʊl] *n.* (*horse*) жеребёнок (-нка; *pl.* жеребя́та, -т); (*ass*) ослёнок (-нка; *pl.* осля́та, -т); **in ~** жеребая; *v.i.* жереби́ться *impf.*, о~ *pf.*

foam [fəʊm] *n.* пе́на; **~ plastic** пенопла́ст; **~ rubber** пенорези́на; *v.i.* пе́ниться *impf.*, вс~ *pf.* **foamy** *adj.* пени́стый.

focal ['fəʊk(ə)l] *adj.* фо́кусный.

fo'c's'le *see* **forecastle**

focus ['fəʊkəs] *n.* фо́кус, центр; *v.t.* фокуси́ровать *impf.*, с~ *pf.*; (*concentrate*) сосредото́чивать *impf.*, сосредото́чить *pf.*

fodder ['fɒdə(r)] *n.* корм (*loc.* -е & -ý; *pl.* -á), фура́ж (-á).

foe [fəʊ] *n.* враг (-á).

fog [fɒg] *n.* тума́н, мгла. **foggy** *adj.* тума́нный (-нен, -нна), нея́сный (-сен, -сна́, -сно).

foible ['fɔɪb(ə)l] *n.* сла́бость.

foil¹ [fɔɪl] *n.* (*metal*) фо́льга.

foil² [fɔɪl] *v.t.* (*frustrate*) расстра́ивать *impf.*, расстро́ить *pf.* (пла́ны+*g.*).

foil³ [fɔɪl] *n.* (*sword*) рапи́ра.

foist [fɔɪst] *v.t.* навя́зывать *impf.*, навяза́ть (-яжу́, -я́жешь) *pf.* (**on** +*d.*)

fold¹ [fəʊld] *n.* скла́дка, сгиб; *v.t.* скла́дывать *impf.*, сложи́ть (-жу́, -жишь) *pf.*; сгиба́ть *impf.*, согну́ть *pf.* **folder** *n.* па́пка. **folding** *adj.* складно́й, откидно́й, створ́чатый.

fold² [fəʊld] *n.* (*sheep-~*) овча́рня (*g.pl.* -рен).

foliage ['fəʊlɪɪdʒ] *n.* листва́.

folk [fəʊk] *n.* наро́д (-a(y)), лю́ди (-де́й, -дям, -дьми́) *pl.*; *pl.* (*relatives*) родня́; *collect.*; *attr.* наро́дный. **folklore** *n.* фолькло́р.

follow ['fɒləʊ] *v.t.* сле́довать *impf.*, по~ *pf.*+*d.*, за+*i.*; идти́ (иду́, идёшь; шёл, шла) *det.* за+*i.*; следи́ть *impf.* за+*i.* **follower** *n.* после́дователь *m.*, ~ница. **following** *adj.* сле́дующий.

folly ['fɒlɪ] *n.* глу́пость, безу́мие.

fond [fɒnd] *adj.* люби́щий, не́жный; **be ~ of** люби́ть (-блю́, -бишь) *impf.*+*a.*

fondle ['fɒnd(ə)l] *v.t.* ласка́ть *impf.*

fondness ['fɒndnɪs] *n.* не́жность, любо́вь (-бви́, *i.* -бо́вью).

font [fɒnt] *n.* (*eccl.*) купе́ль.

food [fuːd] *n.* пи́ща, еда́; **~ processor** *n.* ку́хонный комба́йн; **~ value** пита́тельность. **foodstuff** *n.* пищево́й проду́кт.

fool [fuːl] *n.* дура́к (-á), глупе́ц (-пца́); *v.t.* дура́чить *impf.*, о~ *pf.*; *v.i.:* **~ about, play the ~** дура́читься *impf.* **foolery** *n.* дура́чество. **foolhardy** *adj.* безрассу́дно хра́брый (храбр, -á, -о). **foolish** *adj.* глу́пый (глуп, -á, -о). **foolishness** *n.* глу́пость.

foot [fʊt] *n.* нога́ (*a.* -гу; *pl.* -ги, -г, -га́м), ступня́; (*measure*) фут; (*of hill etc.*) подно́жие; (*mil.*) пехо́та; **on ~** пешко́м; **put one's ~ in it** сесть (ся́ду, -дешь; сел) *pf.* в лу́жу. **football** *n.* футбо́л; *attr.* футбо́льный. **footballer** *n.* футболи́ст. **footfall** *n.*

по́ступь. footlights *n.* ра́мпа. **footman** *n.* лаке́й. **footnote** *n.* сно́ска, примеча́ние.

footpath *n.* тропи́нка; (*pavement*) тротуа́р.

footprint *n.* след (*pl.* -ы́) (ноги́). **footstep** *n.* (*tread*) шаг (-a(y) & (*with 2,3,4*) -á, *loc.* -ý; *pl.* -и́); (*footprint*) след (*pl.* -ы́) (ноги́).

footwear *n.* о́бувь.

fop [fɒp] *n.* щёголь *m.*, фат. **foppish** *adj.* щегольско́й, фатова́тый.

for [fə(r), fɔː(r)] *prep.* (*of time*) в тече́ние+*g.*, на+*a.*; (*of purpose*) для+*g.*, за+*a.*, +*i.*; (*of destination*) в+*a.*; (*on account of*) из-за+*g.*; (*in place of*) вме́сто+*g.*; **~ the sake of** ра́ди+*g.*; **as ~** что каса́ется+*g.*; *conj.* так как, и́бо.

forage ['fɒrɪdʒ] *n.* фура́ж (-á), корм (*loc.* -е & -ý; *pl.* -á); *v.i.* фуражи́ровать *impf.*

foray ['fɒreɪ] *n.* набе́г.

forbear [fɔː'beə(r)] *v.i.* (*refrain*) возде́рживаться *impf.*, возде́ржа́ться (-жу́сь, -жишься) *pf.* (**from** от+*g.*) **forbearance** *n.* возде́ржанность.

forbid [fə'bɪd] *v.t.* запреща́ть *impf.*, запрети́ть (-ещу́, -ети́шь) *pf.* (+*d.* (*person*) & *a.* (*thing*)); воспреща́ть *impf.*, воспрети́ть (-ещу́, -ети́шь) *pf.*+*a.*, +*inf.*

force [fɔːs] *n.* (*strength*) си́ла; (*violence*) наси́лие; (*meaning*) смысл; *pl.* (*armed* **~**) вооружённые си́лы *f.pl.*; **by ~** си́лой; **by ~ of** в си́лу+*g.*; **in ~** в си́ле; (*in large numbers*) толпа́ми; *v.t.* (*compel*) заставля́ть *impf.*, заста́вить *pf.*; принужда́ть *impf.*, прину́дить *pf.*; (*lock etc.*) взла́мывать *impf.*, взлома́ть *pf.*; (*hasten*) форси́ровать *impf.* & *pf.* **forceful** *adj.* си́льный (силён, -льна́, -льно, си́льны́); (*speech*) убеди́тельный. **forcible** *adj.* наси́льственный.

forceps ['fɔːseps] *n.* щипцы́ (-цо́в) *pl.*

ford [fɔːd] *n.* брод; *v.t.* переходи́ть (-ожу́, -о́дишь) *impf.*, перейти́ (-ейду́, -ейдёшь; -ешёл, -ешла́) *pf.* вброд+*a.*, че́рез+*a.*

fore [fɔː(r)] *n.:* **to the ~** на пере́днем пла́не.

forearm ['fɔːrɑːm] *n.* предплечье (*g.pl.* -чий).

forebear ['fɔːbeə(r)] *n.* (*ancestor*) пре́док (-дка). **forebode** [fɔː'bəʊd] *v.t.* (*betoken*) предвеща́ть *impf.*; (*have presentiment*) предчу́вствовать *impf.* **foreboding** *n.* предчу́вствие. **forecast** *n.* предсказа́ние; (*of weather*) прогно́з; *v.t.* предска́зывать *impf.*, предсказа́ть (-ажу́, -а́жешь) *pf.* **forecastle, fo'c's'le** ['fəʊks(ə)l] *n.* (*naut.*) бак. **forefather** *n.* пре́док (-дка). **forefinger** *n.* указа́тельный па́лец (-льца). **foreground** *n.* пере́дний план. **forehead** ['fɒrɪd, 'fɔːhed] *n.* лоб (лба, *loc.* лбу).

foreign ['fɒrɪn, 'fɒrən] *adj.* (*from abroad*) иностра́нный (-нен, -нна); (*alien*) чужо́й; (*external*) вне́шний; **~ body** иноро́дное те́ло (*pl.* -á). **foreigner** *n.* иностра́нец (-нца).

forelock ['fɔːlɒk] *n.* чёлка. **foreman** *n.* (*jury*) старшина́ (*pl.* -ны) *m.* прися́жных; (*factory*) ма́стер (*pl.* -á).

foremost ['fɔːməʊst] *adj.* передово́й, перед-

ний; (*notable*) выдаю́щийся.
forensic [fə'rensɪk] *adj.* суде́бный.
forerunner ['fɔːrʌnə(r)] *n.* предве́стник. **fore-'see** *v.t.* предви́деть (-йжу, -йдишь) *impf.* **fore'shadow** *v.t.* предвеща́ть *impf.* **foresight** *n.* предви́дение; (*caution*) предусмотри́тельность.
forest ['fɒrɪst] *n.* лес (-а(у), *loc.* -ý; *pl.* -á).
forestall [fɔː'stɔːl] *v.t.* предупрежда́ть *impf.*, предупреди́ть *pf.*
forester ['fɒrɪstə(r)] *n.* лесни́к (-á), лесни́чий *sb.* **forestry** *n.* лесово́дство.
foretaste ['fɔːteɪst] *n.* предвкуше́ние; *v.t.* предвкуша́ть *impf.*, предвкуси́ть (-ушý, -ýсишь) *pf.* **fore'tell** *v.t.* предска́зывать *impf.*, предсказа́ть (-ажý, -а́жешь) *pf.* **forethought** *n.* (*intention*) преднаме́ренность; (*caution*) предусмотри́тельность. **fore'warn** *v.t.* предостерега́ть *impf.*, предостере́чь (-егý, -ежёшь; -ёг, -егла́) *pf.* **foreword** *n.* предисло́вие.
forfeit ['fɔːfɪt] *n.* (*fine*) штраф; (*deprivation*) лише́ние, конфиска́ция; (*in game*) фант; *pl.* (*game*) игра́ в фа́нты; *v.t.* лиша́ться *impf.*, лиши́ться *pf.*+g.; (*pay with*) плати́ться (-ачýсь, -а́тишься) *impf.*, по~ *pf.*+i. **forfeiture** *n.* лише́ние, конфиска́ция, поте́ря.
forge[1] [fɔːdʒ] *n.* (*smithy*) кузни́ца; (*furnace*) горн; *v.t.* кова́ть (кую́, куёшь) *impf.*, вы́~ *pf.*; (*fabricate*) подде́лывать *impf.*, подде́лать *pf.*
forge[2] [fɔːdʒ] *v.i.*: ~ **ahead** продвига́ться *impf.*, продви́нуться *pf.* вперёд.
forger ['fɔːdʒə(r)] *n.* подде́лыватель *m.*; (*of money*) фальшивомоне́тчик. **forgery** *n.* подде́лка, подло́г.
forget [fə'get] *v.t.* забыва́ть *impf.*, забы́ть (забýду, -дешь) *pf.* **forgetful** *adj.* забы́вчивый. **forget-me-not** *n.* незабýдка.
forgive [fə'gɪv] *v.t.* проща́ть *impf.*, прости́ть *pf.* **forgiveness** *n.* проще́ние.
forgo [fɔː'gəʊ] *v.t.* возде́рживаться *impf.*, воздержа́ться (-жýсь, -жишься) *pf.* от+g.
fork [fɔːk] *n.* (*eating*) ви́лка; (*digging*) ви́лы (-л) *pl.*; разветвле́ние; *v.i.* рабо́тать *impf.* ви́лами; (*form* ~) разветвля́ться *impf.*, разветви́ться *pf.*
forlorn [fɔː'lɔːn] *adj.* уны́лый.
form [fɔːm] *n.* фо́рма, вид, фигýра; (*formality*) форма́льность; (*class*) класс; (*document*) бланк, анке́та; (*bench*) скаме́йка; *v.t.* (*shape*) придава́ть (-даю́, -даёшь) *impf.*, прида́ть (-да́м, -да́шь, -да́ст, -дади́м; при́дал, -á, -о) *pf.* фо́рму+d.; (*make up*) составля́ть *impf.*, соста́вить *pf.*; образо́вывать *impf.*, образова́ть *pf.*; формирова́ть *impf.*, с~ *pf.*; *v.i.* принима́ть *impf.*, приня́ть (-и́мет; при́нял, -á, -о) *pf.* фо́рму; образо́вываться *impf.*, образова́ться *pf.* **formal** *adj.* официа́льный, форма́льный. **for'mality** *n.* форма́льность. **for'mation** *n.* образова́ние, формирова́ние, форма́ция.

former ['fɔːmə(r)] *adj.* бы́вший, пре́жний; **the** ~ (*of two*) пе́рвый. **formerly** *adv.* пре́жде.
formidable ['fɔːmɪdəb(ə)l] *adj.* (*dread*) гро́зный (-зен, -зна́, -зно); (*arduous*) трýдный (-ден, -дна́, -дно, трýдны́).
formless ['fɔːmlɪs] *adj.* бесфо́рменный (-ен, -енна).
formula ['fɔːmjʊlə] *n.* фо́рмула. **formulate** *v.t.* формули́ровать *impf.*, с~ *pf.* **formu'lation** *n.* формулиро́вка.
forsake [fə'seɪk, fɔː-] *v.t.* (*desert*) покида́ть *impf.*; (*renounce*) отка́зываться *impf.*, отказа́ться (-ажýсь, -а́жешься) *pf.* от+g.
forswear [fɔː'sweə(r)] *v.t.* отрека́ться *impf.*, отре́чься (-екýсь, -ечёшься; -ёкся, -екла́сь) от+g.
fort [fɔːt] *n.* форт (*loc.* -ý; *pl.* -ы́).
forth [fɔːθ] *adv.* вперёд, да́льше; **back and** ~ взад и вперёд; **and so** ~ и так да́лее. **forthcoming** *adj.* предстоя́щий. **forth'with** *adv.* неме́дленно.
fortieth ['fɔːtɪɪθ] *adj.* & *n.* сороково́й; (*fraction*) сорокова́я (часть (*pl.* -ти, -те́й)).
fortification [ˌfɔːtɪfɪ'keɪʃ(ə)n] *n.* фортифика́ция, укрепле́ние. **fortify** ['fɔːtɪˌfaɪ] *v.t.* укрепля́ть *impf.*, укрепи́ть *pf.*; подкрепля́ть *impf.*, подкрепи́ть *pf.*; (*food*) витамини́зировать *impf.* & *pf.* **'fortitude** *n.* мýжество.
fortnight ['fɔːtnaɪt] *n.* две неде́ли. **fortnightly** *adj.* двухнеде́льный; *adv.* раз в две неде́ли.
fortress ['fɔːtrɪs] *n.* кре́пость.
fortuitous [fɔː'tjuːɪtəs] *adj.* случа́йный.
fortunate ['fɔːtjʊnət, -tʃənət] *adj.* счастли́вый (сча́стлив). **fortunately** *adv.* к сча́стью.
fortune *n.* (*destiny*) судьба́ (*pl.* -дьбы, -деб, -дьбам); (*good* ~) сча́стье; (*wealth*) состоя́ние. **fortune-teller** *n.* гада́льщик, -ица; гада́лка. **fortune-telling** *n.* гада́ние.
forty ['fɔːtɪ] *adj.* & *n.* со́рок (*oblique cases* -á); (*age*) со́рок лет; *pl.* (*decade*) сороковы́е го́ды (-до́в) *m.pl.*
forward ['fɔːwəd] *adj.* пере́дний, передово́й; (*early*) ра́нний; *n.* (*sport*) напада́ющий *sb.*; *adv.* вперёд, да́льше; *v.t.* (*promote*) спосо́бствовать *impf.*, по~ *pf.*+d.; (*letter etc.*) пересыла́ть *impf.*, пересла́ть (перешлю́, -лёшь) *pf.*
fossil ['fɒs(ə)l] *n.* окамене́лость, ископа́емое *sb.*; *adj.* окамене́лый, ископа́емый. **fossilize** *v.t.* & *i.* превраща́ть(ся) *impf.*, преврати́ть(ся) *pf.* (-ащý(сь), -ати́шь(ся)) в окамене́лость.
foster ['fɒstə(r)] *v.t.* воспи́тывать *impf.*, воспита́ть *pf.*; (*feeling*) леле́ять (-е́ю, -е́ешь) *impf.*; *adj.* приёмный. **foster-child** *n.* приёмыш.
foul [faʊl] *adj.* (*dirty*) гря́зный (-зен, -зна́, -зно); (*repulsive*) отврати́тельный; (*obscene*) непристо́йный; (*collision*) столкнове́ние; (*sport*) наруше́ние пра́вил; *v.t.* & *i.* (*dirty*) па́чкать(ся) *impf.*, за~, ис~ *pf.*; (*entangle*) запýтывать(ся) *impf.*, запýтать(ся) *pf.*

found¹ [faʊnd] *v.t.* (*establish*) осно́вывать *impf.*, основа́ть (-ну́ю, -ну́ешь) *pf.*; (*building*) закла́дывать *impf.*, заложи́ть (-жу́, -жишь) *pf.*

found² [faʊnd] *v.t.* (*metal*) отлива́ть *impf.*, отли́ть (отолью́, -ьёшь; о́тлил, -а́, -о) *pf.*

foundation [faʊnˈdeɪʃ(ə)n] *n.* (*of building*) фунда́мент; (*basis*) осно́ва, основа́ние; (*institution*) учрежде́ние; (*funds*) фонд. **'founder¹** *n.* основа́тель *m.*, -ница.

founder² [ˈfaʊndə(r)] *n.* (*of metal*) лите́йщик, плави́льщик.

founder³ [ˈfaʊndə(r)] *v.i.* (*naut.*) идти́ (идёт; шёл, шла) *impf.*, пойти́ (пойдёт; пошёл, -шла́) *pf.* ко дну́.

foundling [ˈfaʊndlɪŋ] *n.* подки́дыш.

foundry [ˈfaʊndrɪ] *n.* лите́йная *sb.*

fount¹ [faʊnt] *n.* (*print.*) компле́кт шрифта́.

fount² [faʊnt] *n.* исто́чник. **fountain** *n.* фонта́н, исто́чник. **fountain-pen** *n.* авторучка.

four [fɔː(r)] *adj. & n.* четы́ре (-рёх, -рём, -рьмя́); (*collect.*; *4 pairs*) че́тверо (-ры́х); (*cards*; *boat*; *number 4*) четвёрка; (*time*) четы́ре (часа́); (*age*) четы́ре го́да; **on all ~s** на четвере́ньках. **four'teen** *adj. & n.* четы́рнадцать (-ти, -тью); (*age*) четы́рнадцать лет. **four'teenth** *adj. & n.* четы́рнадцатый; (*fraction*) четы́рнадцатая (часть (*pl.* -ти, -те́й)); (*date*) четы́рнадцатое (число́). **fourth** *adj. & n.* четвёртый; (*quarter*) че́тверть (*pl.* -ти, -те́й); (*date*) четвёртое (число́); (*mus.*) ква́рта.

fowl [faʊl] *n.* (*bird*) пти́ца; (*domestic*) дома́шняя пти́ца; (*wild*) дичь *collect.*

fox [fɒks] *n.* лиса́ (*pl.* -сы), лиси́ца; *attr.* ли́сий (-сья, -сье); *v.t.* обма́нывать *impf.*, обману́ть (-ну́, -нешь) *pf.* **foxglove** *n.* наперстя́нка. **foxhole** *n.* (*mil.*) яче́йка. **foxy** *adj.* ли́сий (-сья, -сье); (*crafty*) хи́трый (-тёр, -тра́, хи́тро́).

foyer [ˈfɔɪeɪ] *n.* фойе́ *nt.indecl.*

fraction [ˈfrækʃ(ə)n] *n.* (*math.*) дробь (*pl.* -би, -бе́й); (*portion*) части́ца. **fractional** *adj.* дро́бный.

fractious [ˈfrækʃəs] *adj.* раздражи́тельный.

fracture [ˈfræktʃə(r)] *n.* перело́м; *v.t. & i.* лома́ть(ся) *impf.*, с~ *pf.*

fragile [ˈfrædʒaɪl] *adj.* ло́мкий (-мок, -мка́, -мко), хру́пкий (-пок, -пка́, -пко). **fragility** [frəˈdʒɪlɪtɪ] *n.* ло́мкость, хру́пкость.

fragment [ˈfrægmənt] *n.* обло́мок (-мка), оско́лок (-лка; (*of writing etc.*) отры́вок (-вка), фрагме́нт. **fragmentary** *adj.* отры́вочный.

fragrance [ˈfreɪɡrəns] *n.* арома́т. **fragrant** *adj.* арома́тный, души́стый.

frail [freɪl] *adj.* хру́пкий (-пок, -пка́, -пко).

frame [freɪm] *n.* о́стов; (*body*) те́ло (*pl.* -ла́); (*build*) телосложе́ние; (*picture*) ра́ма, ра́мка; (*cin.*) кадр; **~ of mind** настрое́ние; *v.t.* (*devise*) создава́ть (-даю́, -даёшь) *impf.*, созда́ть (-а́м, -а́шь, -а́ст, -ади́м; со́здал, -а́, -о) *pf.*; (*adapt*) приспоса́бливать *impf.*, приспособля́ть *pf.*; (*picture*) вставля́ть

impf., вста́вить *pf.* в ра́му; (*surround*) обрамля́ть *impf.*, обрами́ть *pf.* **framework** *n.* о́стов, структу́ра; (*fig.*) ра́мки *f.pl.*

franc [fræŋk] *n.* франк.

France [frɑːns] *n.* Фра́нция.

franchise [ˈfræntʃaɪz] *n.* (*privilege*) привиле́гия; (*right to vote*) пра́во го́лоса.

frank¹ [fræŋk] *adj.* (*open*) открове́нный (-нен, -нна).

frank² [fræŋk] *v.t.* (*letter*) франки́ровать *impf. & pf.*

frantic [ˈfræntɪk] *adj.* нейстовый, бе́шеный.

fraternal [frəˈtɜːn(ə)l] *adj.* бра́тский. **fraternity** *n.* бра́тство, общи́на. **fraternize** [ˈfrætəˌnaɪz] *v.t.* брата́ться *impf.*, по~ *pf.* (**with** с+i.).

fraud [frɔːd] *n.* (*deception*) обма́н; (*person*) обма́нщик. **fraudulent** *adj.* обма́нный (-нен, -нна).

fraught [frɔːt] *adj.*: **~ with** чрева́тый+i., по́лный (-лон, -лна́, по́лно́)+g. & i.

fray¹ [freɪ] *n.* (*brawl*) дра́ка.

fray² [freɪ] *v.t. & i.* обтрёпывать(ся) *impf.*, обтрепа́ть(ся) (-плю́(сь), -плешь(ся)) *pf.*

freak [friːk] *n.* (*caprice*) причу́да; (*monstrosity*) уро́д.

freckle [ˈfrek(ə)l] *n.* весну́шка. **freckled** *adj.* весну́шчатый.

free [friː] *adj.* свобо́дный, во́льный; (*gratis*) беспла́тный; **of one's own ~ will** по до́брой во́ле; **~ speech** свобо́да сло́ва; **~ thinker** вольноду́мец (-мца); *v.t.* освобожда́ть *impf.*, освободи́ть *pf.* **freedom** *n.* свобо́да. **freelance** *attr.* внешта́тный. **freelancer** *n.* внешта́тник (*coll.*). **Freemason** *n.* франк-масо́н.

freeze [friːz] *v.i.* замерза́ть *impf.*, мёрзнуть (-з) *impf.*, за~ *pf.*; *v.t.* замора́живать *impf.*, заморо́зить *pf.* **freezer** *n.* морози́лка.

freight [freɪt] *n.* фрахт, груз. **freighter** *n.* (*ship*) грузово́е су́дно (*pl.* -да́, -до́в).

French [frentʃ] *adj.* францу́зский; **~ bean** фасо́ль; **~ leave** ухо́д без проща́ния, без разреше́ния. **Frenchman** *n.* францу́з. **Frenchwoman** *n.* францу́женка.

frenetic [frəˈnetɪk] *adj.* нейстовый.

frenzied [ˈfrenzɪd] *adj.* нейстовый. **frenzy** *n.* нейстовство.

frequency [ˈfriːkwənsɪ] *n.* частота́ (*pl.* -ты). **frequent** *adj.* ча́стый (част, -а́, -о); *v.t.* ча́сто посеща́ть *impf.*

fresco [ˈfreskəʊ] *n.* фре́ска.

fresh [freʃ] *adj.* све́жий (свеж, -а́, -о́, све́жи); (*new*) но́вый (нов, -а́, -о); (*vigorous*) бо́дрый (бодр, -а́, -о, бо́дры́); **~ water** пре́сная вода́ (*a.* -ду). **freshen** *v.t.* освежа́ть *impf.*, освежи́ть *pf.*; *v.i.* свеже́ть *impf.*, по~ *pf.* **freshly** *adv.* свежо́; (*recently*) неда́вно. **freshness** *n.* све́жесть; бо́дрость. **freshwater** *adj.* пресново́дный.

fret¹ [fret] *n.* (*irritation*) раздраже́ние; *v.t.* (*eat away*) разъеда́ть *impf.*, разъе́сть (-е́м, -е́шь, -е́ст, -еди́м; -е́л) *pf.*; *v.t. & i.* (*distress*) беспоко́ить(ся) *impf.*, о~ *pf.* **fretful** *adj.*

беспокойный.

fret² [fret] *n.* (*mus.*) лад (*loc.* -ý; *pl.* -ы́).

fretsaw ['fretsɔ:] *n.* лобзик.

friar ['fraɪə(r)] *n.* мона́х. **friary** *n.* мужско́й монасты́рь (-ря́) *m.*

friction ['frɪkʃ(ə)n] *n.* тре́ние; (*fig.*) тре́ния *nt.pl.*

Friday ['fraɪdeɪ, -dɪ] *n.* пя́тница; **Good ~** Вели́кая пя́тница.

fridge [frɪdʒ] *n.* холоди́льник. **fridge-freezer** *n.* двухсекцио́нный холоди́льник.

friend [frend] *n.* друг (*pl.* друзья́, -зе́й), подру́га; прия́тель *m.*, ~ница; (*acquaintance*) знако́мый *sb.* **friendly** *adj.* дру́жеский, дру́жественный. **friendship** *n.* дру́жба.

frigate ['frɪgɪt] *n.* фрега́т.

fright [fraɪt] *n.* испу́г (-a(y)). **frighten** *v.t.* пуга́ть *impf.*, ис~, на~ *pf.* **frightful** *adj.* стра́шный (-шен, -шна́, -шно, стра́шны́), ужа́сный.

frigid ['frɪdʒɪd] *adj.* холо́дный (хо́лоден, -дна́, -дно, хо́лодны́). **fri'gidity** *n.* хо́лодность.

frill [frɪl] *n.* обо́рка.

fringe [frɪndʒ] *n.* бахрома́.

frisk [frɪsk] *n.* (*leap*) прыжо́к (-жка́); *v.i.* (*frolic*) резви́ться *impf.* **frisky** *adj.* игри́вый, ре́звый (резв, -á, -o).

fritter¹ ['frɪtə(r)] *n.* ола́дья (*g.pl.* -дий).

fritter² ['frɪtə(r)] *v.t.*: **~ away** растра́чивать *impf.*, растра́тить *pf.* (по мелоча́м и т.п.).

frivolity [frɪ'vɒlɪtɪ] *n.* легкомы́сленность. **'frivolous** *adj.* легкомы́сленный (-ен, -енна).

fro [frəʊ] *adv.*: **to and ~** взад и вперёд.

frock [frɒk] *n.* пла́тье (*g.pl.* -в). **frock-coat** *n.* сюрту́к (-á).

frog [frɒg] *n.* лягу́шка.

frolic ['frɒlɪk] *v.i.* резви́ться *impf.*; (*play pranks*) прока́зничать *impf.*, на~ *pf.*; *n.* весе́лье; (*prank*) прока́за.

from [frəm, frɒm] *prep. expressing:* **1.** *starting-point:* (*away ~,* ~ *person*) от+g.; (~ *off, down ~; in time*) c+g.; (*out of*) из+g.; **2.** *change of state; distinction:* от+g., из+g.; **3.** *escape, avoidance:* от+g.; **4.** *source:* из+g.; **5.** *giving, sending:* от+g.; (*stressing sense of possession*) y+g.; **6.** *model:* по+d.; **7.** *reason, cause:* от+g.; **8.** *motive:* из-за+g.; **9.:** *in phrasal vv. see vv.*; **10.** ~ ... **to** (*time*) c+g.... до+g.; (*with strictly defined starting point*) от+g.... по+g.; (*up to and including*) c+g.... по+a.; (*space*) (*emphasizing distance*) от+g.... до+g.; (*emphasizing journey*) из+g.... в+a.; **11.** ~ **above** све́рху; ~ **abroad** из-за грани́цы; ~ **afar** и́здали; ~ **among** из числа́+g.; ~ **behind** из-за+g.; ~ **day to day** изо дня в день; ~ **everywhere** отовсю́ду; ~ **here** отсю́да; ~ **long ago** и́здавна; ~ **memory** по па́мяти; ~ **nature** с нату́ры; ~ **now on** отны́не; ~ **off** c+g.; ~ **there** отту́да; ~ **time to time** вре́мя от вре́мени; ~ **under** из-под+g.

front [frʌnt] *n.* фаса́д; пере́дняя сторона́ (a -ону; *pl.* -оны, -он, -она́м); (*mil.*) фронт (*pl.* -ы, -óв); **in ~ of** впереди́+g., пе́ред+i.; *adj.* пере́дний, пара́дный. **frontal** *adj.* (*anat.*)

ло́бный; (*mil.*) лобово́й, фронта́льный.

frontier ['frʌntɪə(r), -'tɪə(r)] *n.* грани́ца; *adj.* пограни́чный.

frost [frɒst] *n.* моро́з. **frost-bite** *n.* отмороже́ние. **frost-bitten** *adj.* отморо́женный (-ен). **frosted** *adj.*: ~ **glass** ма́товое стекло́. **frosty** *adj.* моро́зный; (*fig.*) ледяно́й.

froth [frɒθ] *n.* пе́на; *v.t.* & *i.* пе́нить(ся) *impf.*, вс~ *pf.* **frothy** *adj.* пе́нистый.

frown [fraʊn] *n.* хму́рый взгляд; *v.i.* хму́риться *impf.*, на~ *pf.*

frugal ['fru:g(ə)l] *adj.* (*careful*) бережли́вый; (*scanty*) ску́дный (-ден, -дна́, -дно).

fruit [fru:t] *n.* плод (-á); *collect.* фру́кты *m.pl.* **fruitful** *adj.* плодови́тый, плодотво́рный. **fruition** [fru:'ɪʃ(ə)n] *n.* осуществле́ние; **come to ~** осуществи́ться *pf.* **fruitless** *adj.* беспло́дный, бесполе́зный.

frustrate [frʌ'streɪt, 'frʌs-] *v.t.* расстра́ивать *impf.*, расстро́ить *pf.* **fru'stration** *n.* расстро́йство.

fry¹ [fraɪ] *n.* (*collect., fishes*) малька́ *m.pl.*

fry² [fraɪ] *v.t.* & *i.* жа́рить(ся) *impf.*, за~, из~ *pf.* **frying-pan** *n.* сковорода́ (*pl.* ско́вороды, -óд, -ода́м).

fuel ['fju:əl] *n.* то́пливо, горю́чее *sb.*

fugitive ['fju:dʒɪtɪv] *n.* бегле́ц (-á); *adj.* (*transient*) мимолётный.

fugue [fju:g] *n.* фу́га.

fulcrum ['fʊlkrəm, 'fʌl-] *n.* то́чка опо́ры, враще́ния.

fulfil [fʊl'fɪl] *v.t.* (*perform*) вы́-, ис-, полня́ть *impf.*, вы́-, ис-, по́лнить *pf.*; (*bring about*) осуществля́ть *impf.*, осуществи́ть *pf.* **fulfilment** *n.* вы́-, ис-, полне́ние; осуществле́ние.

full [fʊl] *adj.* по́лный (-лон, -лна́, по́лно́) (*of* +g., *i.*); (*complete*) це́лый; (*abundant*) изоби́лующий, бога́тый; (*replete*) сы́тый (сыт, -á, -o); ~ **back** защи́тник; ~ **stop** то́чка; *n.*: **in ~** по́лностью; **to the ~** в по́лной ме́ре; *adv.* (*very*) о́чень; (*exactly*) пря́мо, как раз. **full-blooded** *adj.* полнокро́вный. **fullness** *n.* полнота́. **fully** *adv.* по́лностью.

fulsome ['fʊlsəm] *adj.* чрезме́рный.

fumble ['fʌmb(ə)l] *v.i.*: ~ **for** нащу́пывать *impf.*+a.; ~ **with** нело́вко обраща́ться *impf.* c+i.

fume [fju:m] *n.* испаре́ние; *v.i.* испаря́ться *impf.*, испари́ться *pf.*; (*with anger*) кипе́ть (-плю́, -пи́шь) *impf.*, вс~ *pf.* от зло́сти.

fumigate ['fju:mɪgeɪt] *v.t.* оку́ривать *impf.*, оку́ри́ть (-рю́, -ришь) *pf.* **fumi'gation** *n.* оку́ривание.

fun [fʌn] *n.* заба́ва, весе́лье; **make ~ of** смея́ться (-ею́сь, -еёшься) *impf.*, по~ *pf.* над+i.

function ['fʌŋkʃ(ə)n] *n.* фу́нкция, назначе́ние; *pl.* (*duties*) обя́занности *f.pl.*; *v.i.* функциони́ровать *impf.*; де́йствовать *impf.* **functional** *adj.* функциона́льный. **functionary** *n.* должностно́е лицо́ (*pl.* -ца).

fund [fʌnd] *n.* запа́с; (*of money*) фонд, капита́л.

fundamental [ˌfʌndəˈment(ə)l] *n.* осно́ва; *adj.* основно́й.

funeral [ˈfjuːnər(ə)l] *n.* по́хороны (-о́н, -она́м) *pl.*; *adj.* похоро́нный, тра́урный. **funereal** [fjuːˈnɪərɪəl] *adj.* (*gloomy*) мра́чный (-чен, -чна́, -чно).

fungoid [ˈfʌŋɡɔɪd] *adj.* грибно́й. **fungus** *n.* гриб (-а́).

funnel [ˈfʌn(ə)l] *n.* воро́нка; (*chimney*) дымова́я труба́ (*pl.* -бы).

funny [ˈfʌnɪ] *adj.* смешно́й (-шо́н, -шна́), заба́вный; (*odd*) стра́нный (-нен, -нна́, -нно).

fur [fɜː(r)] *n.* мех (*loc.* -у́; *pl.* -а́); *pl.* (*collect.*) пушни́на, меха́ *m.pl.*; *attr.* мехово́й; ~ **coat** шу́ба; ~ **farm** зверофе́рма; ~ **farming** зверово́дство.

furious [ˈfjʊərɪəs] *adj.* бе́шеный, я́ростный.

furl [fɜːl] *v.t.* свёртывать *impf.*, сверну́ть *pf.*

furnace [ˈfɜːnɪs] *n.* то́пка, горн.

furnish [ˈfɜːnɪʃ] *v.t.* (*provide*) снабжа́ть *impf.*, снабди́ть *pf.* (**with** c+*i.*); доставля́ть *impf.*, доста́вить *pf.*; (*house*) меблирова́ть *impf.* & *pf.*; обставля́ть *impf.*, обста́вить *pf.* **furniture** *n.* ме́бель, обстано́вка.

furrier [ˈfʌrɪə(r)] *n.* меховщи́к (-а́), скорня́к (-а́).

furrow [ˈfʌrəʊ] *n.* борозда́ (*a.* бо́розду; *pl.* бо́розды, -о́зд, -озда́м); (*wrinkle*) морщи́на; *v.t.* борозди́ть *impf.*, вз~, из~ *pf.*

furry [ˈfɜːrɪ] *adj.* мехово́й, пуши́стый.

further [ˈfɜːðə(r)] *comp. adj.* дальне́йший; (*additional*) доба́вочный; *adv.* да́льше, да́лее; *v.t.* продвига́ть *impf.*, продви́нуть *pf.*; соде́йствовать *impf.* & *pf.*+*d.*; спосо́бствовать *impf.*, по~ *pf.*+*d.* **further'more** *adv.* к тому́ же. **furthest** *superl. adj.* са́мый да́льний.

furtive [ˈfɜːtɪv] *adj.* скры́тый, та́йный. **furtively** *adv.* укра́дкой, кра́дучись.

fury [ˈfjʊərɪ] *n.* я́рость, неи́стовство, бе́шенство.

fuse[1] [fjuːz] *v.t.* & *i.* (*of metal*) сплавля́ть(ся) *impf.*, спла́вить(ся) *pf.*

fuse[2] [fjuːz] *n.* (*in bomb*) запа́л, фити́ль (-ля́) *m.*, взрыва́тель *m.*

fuse[3] [fjuːz] *n.* (*elec.*) пла́вкая про́бка, пла́вкий предохрани́тель *m.*; ~ **wire** пла́вкая про́волока.

fuselage [ˈfjuːzəˌlɑːʒ, -ˌlɪdʒ] *n.* фюзеля́ж.

fusillade [ˌfjuːzɪˈleɪd] *n.* расстре́л.

fusion [ˈfjuːʒ(ə)n] *n.* пла́вка, слия́ние; (*nuclear* ~) си́нтез (я́дер).

fuss [fʌs] *n.* суета́; *v.i.* суети́ться *impf.* **fussy** *adj.* суетли́вый.

fusty [ˈfʌstɪ] *adj.* за́тхлый.

futile [ˈfjuːtaɪl] *adj.* бесполе́зный, тще́тный. **futility** [ˌfjuːˈtɪlɪtɪ] *n.* бесполе́зность, тще́тность.

future [ˈfjuːtʃə(r)] *n.* бу́дущее *sb.*, бу́дущность; (*gram.*) бу́дущее вре́мя *nt.*; *adj.* бу́дущий.

G

G [dʒiː] *n.* (*mus.*) соль *nt.indecl.*

g. *abbr.* (*of* **gram(me)(s)**) гм, (грамм).

gab [ɡæb] *n.* болтовня́.

gabble [ˈɡæb(ə)l] *v.i.* тарато́рить *impf.*

gable [ˈɡeɪb(ə)l] *n.* щипе́ц (-пца́).

gad [ɡæd] *v.i.*: ~ **about** шата́ться *impf.*

gadfly [ˈɡædflaɪ] *n.* о́вод (*pl.* -ы & -а́), слепе́нь (-пня́) *m.*

gadget [ˈɡædʒɪt] *n.* приспособле́ние.

gag [ɡæɡ] *n.* кляп; *v.t.* засо́вывать *impf.*, засу́нуть *pf.* кляп в рот+*d.*

gaggle [ˈɡæɡ(ə)l] *n.* (*flock*) ста́я.

gaiety [ˈɡeɪətɪ] *n.* весе́лье, весёлость. **gaily** *adv.* ве́село.

gain [ɡeɪn] *n.* при́быль; *pl.* дохо́ды *m.pl.*; (*increase*) приро́ст; *v.t.* получа́ть *impf.*, получи́ть (-чу́, -чишь) *pf.*; приобрета́ть *impf.*, приобрести́ (-ету́, -етёшь; -ёл, -ела́) *pf.*; ~ **on** нагоня́ть *impf.*, нагна́ть (нагоню́, -нишь; нагна́л, -а́, -о) *pf.*

gainsay [ɡeɪnˈseɪ] *v.t.* (*deny*) отрица́ть *impf.*; (*contradict*) противоре́чить *impf.*+*d.*

gait [ɡeɪt] *n.* похо́дка.

gala [ˈɡɑːlə] *n.* пра́зднество.

galaxy [ˈɡæləksɪ] *n.* гала́ктика; (**G**~) (*Milky Way*) Мле́чный путь (-ти́, -тём) *m.*; (*fig.*) плея́да.

gale [ɡeɪl] *n.* си́льный ве́тер (-тра; *loc.* на -тру́); (*naut.*) шторм.

gall[1] [ɡɔːl] *n.* (*bile*) жёлчь; (*bitterness*) жёлчность.

gall[2] [ɡɔːl] *n.* (*sore*) сса́дина; (*irritation*) раздраже́ние; *v.t.* (*vex*) раздража́ть *impf.*, раздражи́ть *pf.*

gallant [ˈɡælənt; ɡəˈlænt] *adj.* (*brave*) хра́брый (храбр, -а́, -о); (*courtly*) гала́нтный. **'gallantry** *n.* хра́брость; гала́нтность.

gall-bladder [ˈɡɔːlblædə(r)] *n.* жёлчный пузы́рь (-ря́) *m.*

gallery [ˈɡælərɪ] *n.* галере́я; (*theatr.*) галёрка.

galley [ˈɡælɪ] *n.* (*ship*) гале́ра; (*kitchen*) ка́мбуз.

gallon [ˈɡælən] *n.* галло́н.

gallop [ˈɡæləp] *n.* гало́п; *v.i.* скака́ть (-ачу́, -а́чешь) *impf.* (гало́пом).

gallows [ˈɡæləʊz] *n.* ви́селица.

gallstone [ˈɡɔːlstəʊn] *n.* жёлчный ка́мень (-мня; *pl.* -мни, -мне́й) *m.*

galore [ɡəˈlɔː(r)] *adv.* в изоби́лии.

galosh [ɡəˈlɒʃ] *n.* гало́ша.

galvanic [ɡælˈvænɪk] *adv.* гальвани́ческий.

galvanize ['gælvə‚naɪz] *v.t.* гальванизи́ровать *impf. & pf.*; (*coat with zinc*) оцинко́вывать *impf.*, оцинкова́ть *pf.*

gambit ['gæmbɪt] *n.* гамби́т.

gamble ['gæmb(ə)l] *n.* аза́ртная игра́ (*pl.* -ры); (*undertaking*) риско́ванное предприя́тие; *v.i.* игра́ть *impf.* в аза́ртные и́гры; рискова́ть *impf.* (**with** +*i.*); ~ **away** прои́грывать *impf.*, проигра́ть *pf.* **gambler** *n.* игро́к (-á). **gambling** *n.* аза́ртные и́гры *f.pl.*

gambol ['gæmb(ə)l] *v.i.* резви́ться *impf.*

game [geɪm] *n.* игра́ (*pl.* -ры); (*single* ~) па́ртия; (*collect., animals*) дичь; *adj.* (*ready*) гото́вый. **gamekeeper** *n.* лесни́к (-á). **gaming-house** *n.* иго́рный дом (*pl.* -á). **gaming-table** *n.* иго́рный стол (-á).

gammon ['gæmən] *n.* о́корок.

gamut ['gæmət] *n.* га́мма, диапазо́н.

gander ['gændə(r)] *n.* гуса́к (-á).

gang [gæŋ] *n.* брига́да, ба́нда, ша́йка.

gangrene ['gæŋgriːn] *n.* гангре́на.

gangster ['gæŋstə(r)] *n.* га́нгстер, банди́т.

gangway ['gæŋweɪ] *n.* (*passage*) прохо́д; (*naut.*) схо́дни (-ней) *pl.*

gaol *see* **jail. gaoler** *see* **jailer**

gap [gæp] *n.* (*breach*) брешь, проло́м; (*crack*) щель (*pl.* -ли, -ле́й); (*blank space*) пробе́л.

gape [geɪp] *v.i.* (*person*) разева́ть *impf.*, рази́нуть *pf.* рот; (*chasm*) зия́ть; *impf.*; ~ **at** глазе́ть *impf.*, по~ *pf.* на+*a.*

garage ['gærɑːdʒ, -rɪdʒ] *n.* гара́ж (-á).

garb [gɑːb] *n.* одея́ние.

garbage ['gɑːbɪdʒ] *n.* му́сор; (*fig.*) вздор.

garble ['gɑːb(ə)l] *v.t.* подтасо́вывать *impf.*, подтасова́ть *pf.*

garden ['gɑːd(ə)n] *n.* сад (*loc.* -ý; *pl.* -ы́); (*kitchen* ~) огоро́д; *pl.* парк; *attr.* садо́вый. **gardener** *n.* садо́вник, садово́д. **gardening** *n.* садово́дство.

gargle ['gɑːg(ə)l] *n.* полоска́ние; *v.i.* полоска́ть (-ощу́, -о́щешь) *impf.*, про~ *pf.* го́рло.

gargoyle ['gɑːgɔɪl] *n.* горгу́лья.

garish ['geərɪʃ] *adj.* я́ркий (я́рок, ярка́, я́рко), крича́щий.

garland ['gɑːlənd] *n.* гирля́нда, вено́к (-нка́); *v.t.* украша́ть *impf.*, укра́сить *pf.* гирля́ндами.

garlic ['gɑːlɪk] *n.* чесно́к (-á).

garment ['gɑːmənt] *n.* предме́т оде́жды; *pl.* оде́жда *collect.*

garnish ['gɑːnɪʃ] *n.* (*dish*) гарни́р; (*embellishment*) украше́ние; *v.t.* гарни́ровать *impf. & pf.*; украша́ть *impf.*, укра́сить *pf.*

garret ['gærɪt] *n.* манса́рда.

garrison ['gærɪs(ə)n] *n.* гарнизо́н.

garrulous ['gærʊləs] *adj.* болтли́вый.

garter ['gɑːtə(r)] *n.* подвя́зка.

gas [gæs] *n.* газ (-а(у)); *attr.* га́зовый; ~ **cooker** га́зовая плита́ (*pl.* -ты); ~ **main** газопрово́д; ~ **mask** противога́з; *v.i.* отравля́ть *impf.*, отрави́ть (-влю́, -вишь) *pf.* га́зом. **gaseous** ['gæsɪəs] *adj.* газообра́зный.

gash [gæʃ] *n.* глубо́кая ра́на, разре́з.

gasket ['gæskɪt] *n.* прокла́дка.

gasp [gɑːsp] *v.i.* задыха́ться *impf.*, задохну́ться (-х(ну́)ся, -х(ну́)лась) *pf.*; (*exclaim*) а́хнуть *pf.*

gastric ['gæstrɪk] *adj.* желу́дочный.

gasworks ['gæswɜːks] *n.* га́зовый заво́д.

gate [geɪt] *n.* (*large*) воро́та (-т) *pl.*; (*small*) кали́тка. **gatekeeper** *n.* привра́тник. **gateway** *n.* (*gate*) воро́та (-т) *pl.*; (*entrance*) вход.

gather ['gæðə(r)] *v.t.* на-, со-, бира́ть *impf.*, на-, со-, бра́ть (-беру́, -берёшь; -бра́л, -брала́, -бра́ло) *pf.*; (*infer*) заключа́ть *impf.*, заключи́ть *pf.*; *v.i.* собира́ться *impf.*, собра́ться (-берётся; -бра́лся, -брала́сь, -бра́ло́сь) *pf.* **gathering** *n.* (*action*) собира́ние; (*assembly*) собра́ние.

gaudy ['gɔːdɪ] *adj.* я́ркий (я́рок, ярка́, -я́рко), крича́щий.

gauge [geɪdʒ] *n.* (*measure*) ме́ра; (*instrument*) кали́бр, измери́тельный прибо́р; (*rail.*) коле́я; (*criterion*) крите́рий; *v.t.* измеря́ть *impf.*, изме́рить *pf.*; (*estimate*) оце́нивать *impf.*, оцени́ть (-ню́, -нишь) *pf.*

gaunt [gɔːnt] *adj.* то́щий (тощ, -á, -е).

gauntlet ['gɔːntlɪt] *n.* рукави́ца.

gauze [gɔːz] *n.* ма́рля, газ.

gay [geɪ] *adj.* весёлый (ве́сел, -á, -о, ве́селы́); (*bright*) пёстрый (пёстр, -á, пёстро́); (*homosexual*) гомосексуа́льный; *n.* гомосексуали́ст.

gaze [geɪz] *n.* при́стальный взгляд; *v.t.* при́стально гляде́ть (-яжу́, -яди́шь) *impf.* (**at** на+*a.*).

gazelle [gə'zel] *n.* газе́ль.

gazetteer [‚gæzɪ'tɪə(r)] *n.* географи́ческий спра́вочник.

GB *abbr.* (*of* **Great Britain**) Великобрита́ния.

GCSE *abbr.* (*of* **General Certificate of Secondary Education**) аттеста́т о сре́днем образова́нии.

gear [gɪə(r)] *n.* (*appliance*) приспособле́ние, механи́зм, устро́йство; (*in motor*) переда́ча; (*high, low,* ~ *etc.*) ско́рость (*pl.* -ти, -те́й); **in** ~ включённый (-ён, -ена́) **gearbox** *n.* коро́бка скоросте́й. **gearwheel** *n.* зубча́тое колесо́ (*pl.* -ёса), шестерня́ (*g.pl.* -рён).

geld [geld] *v.t.* кастри́ровать *impf. & pf.* **gelding** *n.* ме́рин.

gelignite ['dʒelɪg‚naɪt] *n.* гелигни́т.

gem [dʒem] *n.* драгоце́нный ка́мень (-мня; *pl.* -мни, -мне́й) *m.*; (*fig.*) драгоце́нность.

Gemini ['dʒemɪ‚naɪ, -‚niː] *n.* Близнецы́ *m.pl.*

gender ['dʒendə(r)] *n.* род (*pl.* -ы́).

gene [dʒiːn] *n.* ген.

genealogical [‚dʒiː‚nɪə'lɒdʒɪk(ə)l] *adj.* генеалоги́ческий. **gene'alogy** *n.* генеало́гия, родосло́вная *sb.*

general ['dʒenər(ə)l] *n.* генера́л; *adj.* о́бщий (общ, -á, -о), всео́бщий; (*chief*) генера́льный, гла́вный; **in** ~ вообще́. **gene'rality** *n.* всео́бщность; (*majority*) большинство́. **generali'zation** *n.* обобще́ние. **generalize** *v.t.* обобща́ть *impf.*, обобщи́ть *pf.*; *v.i.*

говори́ть *impf.* неопределённо. **generally**
adv. обы́чно, вообще́.

generate ['dʒenəˌreɪt] *v.t.* порожда́ть *impf.*,
породи́ть *pf.*; производи́ть (-ожу́, -о́дишь)
impf., произвести́ (-еду́, -еде́шь; -ёл, -ела́)
pf. **gene'ration** *n.* порожде́ние, произво́д-
ство; (*in descent*) поколе́ние. **generator** *n.*
генера́тор.

generic [dʒɪ'nerɪk] *adj.* родово́й; (*general*)
о́бщий (общ, -а́, -о).

generosity [ˌdʒenə'rɒsɪtɪ] *n.* (*magnanimity*)
великоду́шие; (*munificence*) ще́дрость.
'generous *adj.* великоду́шный; ще́дрый
(щедр, -а́, -о); (*abundant*) оби́льный.

genesis ['dʒenɪsɪs] *n.* происхожде́ние; (**G~**)
Кни́га Бытия́.

genetic [dʒɪ'netɪk] *adj.* генети́ческий. **genet-**
ics *n.* гене́тика.

Geneva [dʒɪ'niːvə] *n.* Жене́ва.

genial ['dʒiːnɪəl] *adj.* (*of person*) доброду́-
шный. **geni'ality** *n.* доброду́шие.

genital ['dʒenɪt(ə)l] *adj.* полово́й. **genitals** *n.*
половы́е о́рганы *m.pl.*

genitive ['dʒenɪtɪv] *adj.* (*n.*) роди́тельный
(паде́ж (-а́)).

genius ['dʒiːnɪəs] *n.* (*person*) ге́ний; (*ability*)
гениа́льность; (*spirit*) дух.

genocide ['dʒenəˌsaɪd] *n.* геноци́д.

genre ['ʒɑ̃rə] *n.* жанр.

genteel [dʒen'tiːl] *adj.* благовоспи́танный
(-ан, -анна).

gentian ['dʒenʃ(ə)n, -ʃɪən] *n.* горечавка.

gentile ['dʒentaɪl] *adj.* неевре́йский; *n.*
неевре́й.

gentility [dʒen'tɪlɪtɪ] *n.* благовоспи́танность.

gentle ['dʒent(ə)l] *adj.* (*mild*) мя́гкий (-гок,
-гка́, -гко); (*meek*) кро́ткий (-ток, -тка́,
-тко); (*quiet*) ти́хий (тих, -а́, -о); (*light*)
лёгкий (-гок, -гка́, -гко, лёгки). **gentleman**
n. джентльме́н; господи́н (*pl.* -ода́, -о́д,
-ода́м). **gentleness** *n.* мя́гкость.

genuine ['dʒenjʊɪn] *adj.* (*authentic*) по́длин-
ный (-нен, -нна), настоя́щий; (*sincere*) и́ск-
ренний (-нен, -нна, -нно & -нне). **genuine-**
ness *n.* по́длинность; и́скренность.

genus ['dʒiːnəs, 'dʒenəs] *n.* род (*pl.* -ы́).

geo- ['dʒiːəʊ] *in comb.* гео... . **geographer**
[dʒɪ'ɒɡrəfə(r)] *n.* гео́граф. **geo'graphical** *adj.*
географи́ческий. **ge'ography** *n.* геогра́фия.
geo'logical *adj.* геологи́ческий. **ge'ologist**
n. гео́лог. **ge'ology** *n.* геоло́гия. **geo'me-**
tric(al) *adj.* геометри́ческий. **geome'trician**
n. гео́метр. **ge'ometry** *n.* геоме́трия.

Georgia ['dʒɔːdʒɪə] *n.* Гру́зия. **Georgian** *n.*
(*Caucasian*) грузи́н (*g.pl.* -н), ~ка; *adj.* гру-
зи́нский.

geranium [dʒə'reɪnɪəm] *n.* гера́нь.

germ [dʒɜːm] *n.* микро́б; (*fig.*) заро́дыш.

German ['dʒɜːmən] *n.* не́мец (-мца), не́мка;
adj. неме́цкий; ~ **measles** красну́ха.

germane [dʒɜː'meɪn] *adj.* уме́стный.

Germanic [dʒɜː'mænɪk] *adj.* герма́нский.
Germany ['dʒɜːmənɪ] *n.* Герма́ния.

germinate ['dʒɜːmɪˌneɪt] *v.i.* прораста́ть *impf.*,
прорасти́ (-тёт; проро́с, -ла́) *pf.*

gesticulate [dʒe'stɪkjʊˌleɪt] *v.i.* жестикули́-
ровать *impf.* **gesticu'lation** *n.* жестику-
ля́ция. **'gesture** *n.* жест.

get [ɡet] *v.t.* (*obtain*) достава́ть (-таю́, -таёшь)
impf., доста́ть (-а́ну, -а́нешь) *pf.*; доби-
ва́ться *impf.*, доби́ться (добью́сь, -бёшься)
pf.+g.; (*receive*) получа́ть *impf.*, получи́ть
(-чу́, -чишь) *pf.*; (*understand*) понима́ть
impf., поня́ть (пойму́, -мёшь; по́нял, -а́, -о)
pf.; (*disease*) схва́тывать *impf.*, схвати́ть
(-ачу́, -а́тишь) *pf.*; (*induce*) угова́ривать
impf., уговори́ть *pf.* (**to do** *+inf.*); *v.i.*
(*become*) станови́ться (-влю́сь, -вишься)
impf., стать (ста́ну, -нешь) *pf.+i.*; **have got**
(*have*) име́ть *impf.*; **have got to** быть
до́лжен (-жна́)*+inf.*; ~ **about** (*spread*)
распространя́ться *impf.*, распространи́ться
pf.; ~ **away** ускольза́ть *impf.*, ускользну́ть
pf.; ~ **back** (*recover*) получа́ть *impf.*,
получи́ть (-чу́, -чишь) *pf.* обра́тно; (*return*)
возвраща́ться *impf.*, верну́ться *pf.*; ~ **down**
to принима́ться *impf.*, приня́ться (приму́сь,
-мешься; приня́лся, -ла́сь) *pf.* за+*a.*; ~ **off**
слеза́ть *impf.*, слезть (-зу, -зешь) *pf.* с+*g.*;
~ **on** сади́ться *impf.*, сесть (ся́ду, -дешь; сел)
pf. в, на, +*a.*; (*prosper*) преуспева́ть *impf.*,
преуспе́ть *pf.*; ~ **on with** (*person*) ужи-
ва́ться *impf.*, ужи́ться (уживу́сь, -вёшься;
ужи́лся, -ла́сь) *pf.* с+*i.*; ~ **out of** (*avoid*)
избавля́ться *impf.*, изба́виться *pf.* от+*g.*; ~
to (*reach*) достига́ть *impf.*, дости́гнуть &
дости́чь (-и́гну, -и́гнешь; -и́г) *pf.+g.*; ~ **up**
(*from bed*) встава́ть (-таю́, -таёшь) *impf.*,
встать (-а́ну, -а́нешь) *pf.*

geyser ['ɡaɪzə(r), 'ɡiː-] *n.* (*spring*) ге́йзер;
(*water-heater*) (га́зовая) коло́нка.

ghastly ['ɡɑːstlɪ] *adj.* стра́шный (-шен, -шна́,
-шно, стра́шны), ужа́сный.

gherkin ['ɡɜːkɪn] *n.* огуре́ц (-рца́).

ghetto ['ɡetəʊ] *n.* ге́тто *nt.indecl.*

ghost [ɡəʊst] *n.* привиде́ние, при́зрак, дух,
тень (*pl.* -ни, -не́й). **ghostly** *adj.* при́зрачный.

giant ['dʒaɪənt] *n.* велика́н, гига́нт; *adj.*
грома́дный.

gibberish ['dʒɪbərɪʃ] *n.* тараба́рщина.

gibbet ['dʒɪbɪt] *n.* ви́селица.

gibe [dʒaɪb] *n.* насме́шка; *v.i.* насмеха́ться
impf. (**at** над+*i.*).

giblets ['dʒɪblɪts] *n.* потроха́ (-хо́в) *pl.*

Gibraltar [dʒɪ'brɔːltə] *n.* Гибралта́р; **Strait of**
~ Гибралта́рский проли́в.

giddiness ['ɡɪdɪnɪs] *n.* головокруже́ние; (*fri-*
volity) легкомы́слие. **giddy** *adj.* (*frivolous*)
легкомы́сленный (-ен, -енна); *pred.*: **I am,**
feel, ~ у меня́ кру́жится голова́.

gift [ɡɪft] *n.* (*present*) пода́рок (-рка); (*dona-*
tion; ability) дар (*pl.* -ы́); (*talent*) тала́нт
(к+*d.*); (*ability*) спосо́бность (к+*d.*). **gifted**
adj. одарённый (-ён, -ённа), тала́нтливый.

gig [ɡɪɡ] *n.* (*carriage*) кабриоле́т; (*boat*)
ги́чка.

gigantic [dʒaɪˈgæntɪk] *adj.* гига́нтский, грома́дный.

giggle [ˈgɪg(ə)l] *n.* хихи́канье; *v.i.* хихи́кать *impf.*, хихи́кнуть *pf.*

gild [gɪld] *v.t.* золоти́ть *impf.*, вы́~, по~ *pf.*

gill [gɪl] *n.* (*of fish*) жа́бра.

gilt [gɪlt] *n.* позоло́та; *adj.* золочённый, позоло́ченный.

gimlet [ˈgɪmlɪt] *n.* бура́вчик.

gin[1] [dʒɪn] *n.* (*snare*) западня́; (*winch*) лебёдка; (*cotton-*~) джин.

gin[2] [dʒɪn] *n.* (*spirit*) джин.

ginger [ˈdʒɪndʒə(r)] *n.* имби́рь (-ря) *m.*; *attr.* имби́рный; (*in colour*) ры́жий (рыж, -а́, -е). **gingerbread** *n.* имби́рный пря́ник.

gingerly [ˈdʒɪndʒəlɪ] *adv.* осторо́жно.

gipsy [ˈdʒɪpsɪ] *n.* цыга́н (*pl.* -не, -н), ~ка; *attr.* цыга́нский.

giraffe [dʒɪˈrɑːf, -ˈræf] *n.* жира́ф.

gird [gɜːd] *v.t.* опоя́сывать *impf.*, опоя́сать (-я́шу, -я́шешь) *pf.*; (*encircle*) окружа́ть *impf.*, окружи́ть *pf.* **girder** *n.* ба́лка, фе́рма.

girdle *n.* по́яс (*pl.* -á); *v.t.* подпоя́сывать *impf.*, подпоя́сать (-я́шу, -я́шешь) *pf.*

girl [gɜːl] *n.* де́вочка, де́вушка. **girlfriend** *n.* подру́га. **girlish** *adj.* де́вичий (-чья, -чье).

girth [gɜːθ] *n.* (*band*) подпру́га; (*measurement*) обхва́т.

gist [dʒɪst] *n.* суть, су́щность.

give [gɪv] *v.t.* дава́ть (даю́, даёшь) *impf.*, дать (дам, дашь, даст, дади́м; дал, -á, -да́ло́, -и) *pf.*; дари́ть (-рю́, -ришь) *impf.*, по~ *pf.*; ~ **away** выдава́ть (-даю́, -даёшь) *impf.*, вы́дать (-ам, -ашь, -аст, -адим) *pf.*; ~ **back** возвраща́ть *impf.*, возврати́ть (-ащу́, -ати́шь) *pf.*; ~ **in** (*yield*, *v.i.*) уступа́ть *impf.*, уступи́ть (-плю́, -пишь) *pf.* (**to** +*d.*); (*hand in*, *v.t.*) вруча́ть *impf.*, вручи́ть *pf.*; ~ **out** (*emit*) издава́ть (-даю́, -даёшь) *impf.*, изда́ть (-а́м, -а́шь, -а́ст, -ади́м; изда́л, -á, -о) *pf.*; (*distribute*) раздава́ть (-даю́, -даёшь) *impf.*, разда́ть (-а́м, -а́шь, -а́ст, -ади́м; ро́здал & разда́л, -á, ро́здало & разда́ло) *pf.*; (*cease*) конча́ться *impf.*, ко́нчиться *pf.*; ~ **up** отка́зываться *impf.*, отказа́ться (-ажу́сь, -а́жешься) *pf.* от+*g.*; (*habit etc.*) броса́ть *impf.*, бро́сить *pf.*; ~ **o.s. up** сдава́ться (сдаю́сь, сдаёшься) *impf.*, сда́ться (-а́мся, -а́шься, -а́стся, -ади́мся; сда́лся, -ла́сь, сда́ло́сь) *pf.* **given** *pred.* (*inclined*) скло́нен (-о́нна, -о́нно) (**to** к+*d.*); (*devoted*) пре́дан (-а) (**to** +*d.*).

gizzard [ˈgɪzəd] *n.* (*of bird*) му́скульный желу́док (-дка).

glacial [ˈgleɪʃ(ə)l, -sɪəl] *adj.* леднико́вый; (*fig.*) ледяно́й. **glacier** [ˈglæsɪə(r)] *n.* ледни́к (-á), гле́тчер.

glad [glæd] *adj.* ра́достный, весёлый; *pred.* рад. **gladden** *v.t.* ра́довать *impf.*, об~ *pf.* **gladness** *n.* ра́дость.

glade [gleɪd] *n.* прога́лина, поля́на.

gladiolus [ˌglædɪˈəʊləs] *n.* шпа́жник.

glamorous [ˈglæmərəs] *adj.* (*charming*) обая-

тельный; (*attractive*) привлека́тельный.

glamour [ˈglæmə(r)] *n.* обая́ние; привлека́тельность.

glance [glɑːns] *n.* (*look*) бе́глый взгляд; *v.i.*: ~ **at** взгля́дывать *impf.*, взгляну́ть (-ну́, -нешь) *pf.* на+*a.*; ~ **off** скользи́ть *impf.*, скользну́ть *pf.* по пове́рхности+*g.*

gland [glænd] *n.* железа́ (*pl.* же́лезы, -ёз, -еза́м). **glandular** *adj.* желе́зистый.

glare [gleə(r)] *n.* (*light*) ослепи́тельный блеск; (*look*) при́стальный, свире́пый, взгляд; *v.i.* ослепи́тельно сверка́ть *impf.*; при́стально, свире́по, смотре́ть (-рю́, -ришь) *impf.* (**at** на+*a.*). **glaring** *adj.* (*bright*) я́ркий; (*dazzling*) ослепи́тельный; (*mistake*) гру́бый.

glasnost [ˈglæznɒst, ˈglɑːs-] *n.* гла́сность.

glass [glɑːs] *n.* (*substance*) стекло́; (*drinking vessel*) стака́н, рю́мка; (*glassware*) стекля́нная посу́да; (*mirror*) зе́ркало (*pl.* -лá); *pl.* (*spectacles*) очки́ (-ко́в) *pl.*; *attr.* стекля́нный; ~ **fibre** стекловолокно́. **glass-blower** *n.* стеклоду́в. **glasshouse** *n.* тепли́ца. **glassy** *adj.* (*of glass*) стекля́нный; (*water*) зерка́льный, гла́дкий (-док, -дка́, -дко); (*look*) ту́склый (тускл, -á, -о).

glaze [gleɪz] *n.* глазу́рь; *v.t.* (*picture*) застекля́ть *impf.*, застекли́ть *pf.*; (*cover with* ~) покрыва́ть *impf.*, покры́ть (-ро́ю, -ро́ешь) *pf.* глазу́рью. **glazier** *n.* стеко́льщик.

gleam [gliːm] *n.* сла́бый свет; (*also of hope etc.*) про́блеск; *v.i.* свети́ться (-ится) *impf.*

glean [gliːn] *v.t.* тща́тельно собира́ть *impf.*, собра́ть (соберу́, -рёшь; собра́л, -á, -о) *pf.*; *v.i.* подбира́ть *impf.*, подобра́ть (подберу́, -рёшь; подобра́л, -á, -о) *pf.* коло́сья.

glee [gliː] *n.* весе́лье. **gleeful** *adj.* весёлый (ве́сел, -á, -о, ве́селы́).

glib [glɪb] *adj.* бо́йкий (бо́ек, бойка́, бо́йко).

glide [glaɪd] *v.i.* скользи́ть *impf.*; (*aeron.*) плани́ровать *impf.*, с~ *pf.* **glider** *n.* (*aircraft*) планёр; (*person*) планери́ст.

glimmer [ˈglɪmə(r)] *n.* мерца́ние; *v.i.* мерца́ть *impf.*

glimpse [glɪmps] *n.* (*appearance*) про́блеск; (*view*) мимолётный взгляд; *v.t.* мелько́м ви́деть (ви́жу, ви́дишь) *impf.*, у~ *pf.*

glint [glɪnt] *n.* блеск; *v.i.* блесте́ть (-ещу́, -ести́шь & -е́щешь) *impf.*; сверка́ть *impf.*

glitter [ˈglɪtə(r)] *n.* блеск; *v.i.* блесте́ть (-ещу́, -ести́шь & -е́щешь) *impf.*; сверка́ть *impf.*

gloat [gləʊt] *v.i.* пожира́ть *impf.*, пожра́ть (-ру́, -рёшь; пожра́л, -á, -о) *pf.* глаза́ми (**over** +*a.*); (*maliciously*) злора́дствовать *impf.*

global [ˈgləʊb(ə)l] *adj.* (*world-wide*) мирово́й; (*total*) всео́бщий. **globe** *n.* (*sphere*) шар (-á with 2,3,4; *pl.* -ы́); (*the earth*) земно́й шар; (*chart*) гло́бус.

globular [ˈglɒbjʊlə(r)] *adj.* шарови́дный, сфери́ческий. **globule** *n.* ша́рик.

gloom [gluːm] *n.* мрак. **gloomy** *adj.* мра́чный (-чен, -чна́, -чно).

glorification [ˌglɔːrɪfɪˈkeɪʃ(ə)n] *n.* прославле́ние. **'glorify** *v.t.* прославля́ть *impf.*, прославить *pf.* '**glorious** *adj.* сла́вный (-вен, -вна́, -вно); (*splendid*) великоле́пный. '**glory** *n.* сла́ва; *v.i.* торжествова́ть *impf.*

gloss [glɒs] *n.* (*lustre*) лоск, гля́нец (-нца); (*appearance*) ви́димость; *v.t.* наводи́ть (-ожу́, -о́дишь) *impf.*, навести́ (-еду́, -еде́шь; наве́л, -а́) *pf.* лоск, гля́нец, на+*a.*; ~ **over** зама́зывать *impf.*, зама́зать (-а́жу, -а́жешь) *pf.*

glossary ['glɒsərɪ] *n.* глосса́рий, слова́рь (-ря́) *m.*

glove [glʌv] *n.* перча́тка. **glover** *n.* перча́точник, -ица.

glow [gləʊ] *n.* нака́л, за́рево; (*of cheeks*) румя́нец (-нца); (*ardour*) пыл (-a(y), *loc.* -у́); *v.i.* (*incandescence*) накаля́ться *impf.*, накали́ться *pf.*; (*shine*) сия́ть *impf.* **glow-worm** *n.* светля́к (-а́).

glucose ['glu:kəʊs, -kəʊz] *n.* глюко́за.

glue [glu:] *n.* клей (-е́я (-е́ю), *loc.* -е́е & -ею́; *pl.* -еи́); *v.t.* кле́ить *impf.*, с~ *pf.*; (*attach*) прикле́ивать *impf.*, прикле́ить *pf.* (**to** к+*d.*).

glum [glʌm] *adj.* угрю́мый.

glut [glʌt] *n.* (*surfeit*) пресыще́ние; (*excess*) избы́ток (-тка); (*in market*) затова́ривание (ры́нка); *v.t.* пресыща́ть *impf.*, пресы́тить (-ы́щу, -ы́тишь) *pf.*; (*overstock*) затова́ривать *impf.*, затова́рить *pf.*

glutton ['glʌt(ə)n] *n.* обжо́ра *c.g.* **gluttonous** *adj.* обжо́рливый. **gluttony** *n.* обжо́рство.

GMT *abbr.* (*of Greenwich Mean Time*) вре́мя по Гри́нвичу.

gnarled [nɑ:ld] *adj.* (*hands*) шишкова́тый; (*tree*) сучкова́тый.

gnash [næʃ] *v.t.* скрежета́ть (-ещу́, -е́щешь) *impf.*+*i.* **gnashing** *n.* скре́жет.

gnat [næt] *n.* комар (-а́).

gnaw [nɔ:] *v.t.* глода́ть (-ожу́, -о́жешь) *impf.*, грызть (-зу́, -зёшь; -з) *impf.*

gnome [nəʊm] *n.* гном.

go [gəʊ] *n.* (*movement*) движе́ние; (*energy*) эне́ргия; (*attempt*) попы́тка; **be on the ~** быть в движе́нии; **have a ~** пыта́ться *impf.*, по~ *pf.*; *v.i.* (*on foot*) ходи́ть (хожу́, хо́дишь) *indet.*, идти́ (иду́, идёшь; шёл, шла) *det.*, пойти́ (пойду́, -дёшь; пошёл, -шла́ *pf.*; (*by transport*) е́здить *indet.*, е́хать (е́ду, е́дешь) *det.*, по~ *pf.*; (*work*) рабо́тать *impf.*; (*become*) станови́ться (-влю́сь, -вишься) *impf.*, стать (ста́ну, -нешь) *pf.*+*i.*; **be ~ing** (*to do*) собира́ться *impf.*, собра́ться (собе-ру́сь, -рёшься; собра́лся, -ала́сь, -ало́сь) *pf.* (+*inf.*); ~ **about** (*set to work at*) бра́ться (беру́сь, -рёшься; бра́лся, -ла́сь) *impf.*, взя́ться (возьму́сь, -мёшься; взя́лся, -ла́сь) *pf.* за+*a.*; (*wander*) броди́ть (-ожу́, -о́дишь) *indet.*; ~ **at** (*attack*) набра́сываться *impf.*, набро́ситься *pf.* на+*a.*; ~ **away** (*on foot*) уходи́ть (-ожу́, -о́дишь) *impf.*, уйти́ (уйду́, -дёшь; ушёл, ушла́) *pf.*; (*by transport*) уезжа́ть *impf.*, уе́хать (уе́ду, -дешь) *pf.*; ~ **down** спуска́ться *impf.*, спусти́ться (-ущу́сь, -у́стишься) *pf.*; ~ **into** (*enter*) входи́ть (-ожу́, -о́дишь) *impf.*, войти́ (войду́, -дёшь; вошёл,

-шла́) *pf.* в+*a.*; (*investigate*) рассле́довать *impf.* & *pf.*; ~ **off** (*go away*) уходи́ть (-ожу́, -о́дишь) *impf.*, уйти́ (уйду́, -дёшь; ушёл, ушла́) *pf.*; (*deteriorate*) по́ртиться (-ится) *pf.*; ~ **on** (*continue*) продолжа́ть(ся) *impf.*, продо́лжить(ся) *pf.*; ~ **out** выходи́ть (-ожу́, -о́дишь) *impf.*, вы́йти (вы́йду, -дешь; вы́шел, -шла) *pf.*; (*flame etc.*) га́снуть (-с) *impf.*, по~ *pf.*; ~ **over** (*inspect*) пересма́тривать *impf.*, пересмотре́ть (-рю́, -ришь) *pf.*; (*rehearse*) повторя́ть *impf.*, повтори́ть *pf.*; (*change allegiance etc.*) переходи́ть (-ожу́, -о́дишь) *impf.*, перейти́ (перейду́, -дёшь; перешёл, -шла́) *pf.* (**to** в, на, +*a.*, к+*d.*); ~ **through** (*scrutinize*) разбира́ть *impf.*, разобра́ть (разберу́, -рёшь; разобра́л, -а́, -о) *pf.*; ~ **through with** доводи́ть (-ожу́, -о́дишь) *impf.*, довести́ (-еду́, -едёшь; -ёл, -ела́) *pf.* до конца́; ~ **without** обходи́ться (-ожу́сь, -о́дишься) *impf.*, обойти́сь (обойду́сь, -дёшься; обошёлся, -шла́сь) *pf.* без+*g.*

goad [gəʊd] *v.t.* подгоня́ть *impf.*, подогна́ть (подгоню́, -о́нишь; подогна́л, -а́, -о) *pf.*; ~ **on** (*instigate*) подстрека́ть *impf.*, подстрекну́ть *pf.* (**to** к+*a.*).

go-ahead ['gəʊəhed] *n.* разреше́ние, добро́; *adj.* предприи́мчивый.

goal [gəʊl] *n.* (*aim*) цель; (*sport*) воро́та (-т) *pl.*, (*also point(s) won*) гол (*pl.* -ы́); **score a** ~ забива́ть *impf.*, заби́ть (-бью́, -бьёшь) *pf.* гол. **goalkeeper** *n.* врата́рь (-ря́) *m.*

goat [gəʊt] *n.* коза́ (*pl.* -зы), козёл (-зла́); *attr.* ко́зий (-зья, -зье). **goatherd** *n.* ко́зий пасту́х (-а́).

gobble[1] ['gɒb(ə)l] *v.t.* (*eat*) жрать (жру, жрёшь; жрал, -а́, -о) *impf.*; ~ **up** пожира́ть *impf.*, пожра́ть (-ру́, -рёшь; пожра́л, -а́, -о) *pf.*

gobble[2] ['gɒb(ə)l] *v.i.* (*of turkeys*) кулды́кать *impf.*

go-between ['gəʊbɪˌtwi:n] *n.* посре́дник.

goblet ['gɒblɪt] *n.* бока́л, ку́бок (-бка)

god [gɒd] *n.* бог (*pl.* -и, -о́в); (*idol*) куми́р; (**G**~) Бог (*voc.* Бо́же); *pl.* (*theatr.*) галёрка. **godchild** *n.* кре́стник, -ица. **god-daughter** *n.* кре́стница. **goddess** *n.* боги́ня. **godfather** *n.* кре́стный *sb.* **God-fearing** *adj.* богобоя́зненный (-ен, -енна). **godless** *adj.* безбо́жный. **godlike** *adj.* богоподо́бный. **godly** *adj.* на́божный. **godmother** *n.* кре́стная *sb.* **godparent** *n.* кре́стный *sb.* **godson** *n.* кре́стник.

goggle ['gɒg(ə)l] *v.i.* тара́щить *impf.* глаза́ (**at** на+*a.*). **goggle-eyed** *adj.* пучегла́зый. **goggles** *n.* защи́тные очки́ (-ко́в) *pl.*

going ['gəʊɪŋ] *adj.* де́йствующий. **goings-on** *n.* поведе́ние; дела́ *nt.pl.*

goitre ['gɔɪtə(r)] *n.* зоб (*loc.* -е & -у́; *pl.* -ы́).

gold [gəʊld] *n.* зо́лото; *adj.* золото́й; ~ **leaf** золота́я фо́льга; ~ **plate** золота́я посу́да *collect.* **gold-bearing** *adj.* золотоно́сный. **gold-beater** *n.* золотобо́й. **gold-digger** *n.* золотоиска́тель *m.*; (*sl.*) авантюри́стка.

gold-dust *n.* золотоно́сный песо́к (-ска́ (-ску́)). **golden** *adj.* золото́й, золоти́стый; ~ **eagle** бе́ркут. **gold-field** *n.* золото́й при́иск. **goldfinch** *n.* щего́л (-гла́). **goldfish** *n.* золота́я ры́бка. **gold-mine** *n.* золото́й рудни́к (-а́); (*fig.*) золото́е дно. **gold-plate** *v.t.* золоти́ть *impf.*, по~ *pf.* **goldsmith** *n.* золоты́х дел ма́стер (*pl.* -а́).

golf [gɒlf] *n.* гольф. **golfer** *n.* игро́к (-а́) в гольф.

gondola ['gɒndələ] *n.* гондо́ла. **gondo'lier** *n.* гондолье́р.

gong [gɒŋ] *n.* гонг.

good [gʊd] *n.* добро́, бла́го; *pl.* (*wares*) това́р(ы); **do** ~ (*benefit*) идти́ (идёт; шёл, шла) *impf.*, пойти́ (пойдёт; пошёл, -шла́) *pf.* на по́льзу+*d.*; *adj.* хоро́ший (-ш, -ша́), до́брый (добр, -а́, -о, до́бры́); ~ **morning** до́брое у́тро!; ~ **night** споко́йной но́чи! **good'bye** *int.* проща́й(те)!; до свида́ния! **good-humoured** *adj.* доброду́шный. **good-looking** *adj.* краси́вый. **goodness** *n.* доброта́.

goose [guːs] *n.* гусь (*pl.* -си, -се́й) *m.*, гусы́ня; (*cul.*) гуся́тина. **goose-flesh** *n.* гуси́ная ко́жа.

gooseberry ['gʊzbərɪ] *n.* крыжо́вник (*plant or collect.*) *berries*).

gore[1] [gɔː(r)] *n.* (*blood*) запёкшаяся кровь (*loc.* -ви́).

gore[2] [gɔː(r)] *v.t.* (*pierce*) бода́ть *impf.*, за~ *pf.*

gorge [gɔːdʒ] *n.* гло́тка; (*narrow opening*) уще́лье (*g.pl.* -лий); *v.t.* жрать (жру, жрёшь; жрал, -а́, -о) *impf.*, со~ *pf.*; *v.i.* объеда́ться *impf.*, объе́сться (-е́мся, -е́шься, -е́стся, -еди́мся; -е́лся) *pf.* (**on** +*i.*).

gorgeous ['gɔːdʒəs] *adj.* пы́шный (-шен, -шна́, -шно), великоле́пный.

gorilla [gə'rɪlə] *n.* гори́лла.

gormless ['gɔːmlɪs] *adj.* непоня́тливый, бестолко́вый.

gorse [gɔːs] *n.* утёсник.

gory ['gɔːrɪ] *adj.* окрова́вленный.

gosh [gɒʃ] *int.* бо́же мой!

goshawk ['gɒshɔːk] *n.* большо́й я́стреб (*pl.* -ы & -а́).

gosling ['gɒzlɪŋ] *n.* гусёнок (-нка; *pl.* гуся́та, -т).

Gospel ['gɒsp(ə)l] *n.* Ева́нгелие.

gossamer ['gɒsəmə(r)] *n.* (*web*) паути́на; (*gauze*) то́нкая ткань.

gossip ['gɒsɪp] *n.* (*talk*) болтовня́, спле́тня (*g. pl.* -тен); (*person*) болту́н (-а́), ~ья (*g.pl.* -ний), спле́тник, -ица; *v.i.* болта́ть *impf.*; спле́тничать *impf.*, на~ *pf.*

Goth [gɒθ] *n.* гот. **Gothic** го́тский; (*archit.*; *print.*) готи́ческий.

gouache [gʊ'ɑːʃ, gwɑːʃ] *n.* гуа́шь.

gouge [gaʊdʒ] *v.t.*: ~ **out** выда́лбливать *impf.*, вы́долбить *pf.*; (*eyes*) выка́лывать *impf.*, вы́колоть (-лю, -лешь) *pf.*

goulash ['guːlæʃ] *n.* гуля́ш (-яша́).

gourd [gʊəd] *n.* ты́ква.

gourmand ['gʊəmænd] *n.* лако́мка *c.g.*

gourmet ['gʊəmeɪ] *n.* гурма́н.

gout [gaʊt] *n.* пода́гра. **gouty** *adj.* подагри́ческий.

govern ['gʌv(ə)n] *v.t.* пра́вить *impf.*+*i.*; управля́ть *impf.*+*i.* **governess** *n.* губерна́нтка. **government** *n.* (*of state*) прави́тельство; управле́ние (*of* +*i.*). **govern'mental** *adj.* прави́тельственный. **governor** *n.* прави́тель *m.*, губерна́тор; (*head of institution*) заве́дующий *sb.* (**of** +*i.*).

gown [gaʊn] *n.* (*woman's*) пла́тье (*g.pl.* -в); (*official's*) ма́нтия.

grab [græb] *n.* (*grasp*) захва́т; (*device*) черпа́к (-а́); *v.t.* хвата́ть *impf.*, (с)хвати́ть (-ачу́, -а́тишь) *pf.*; захва́тывать *impf.*, захвати́ть (-ачу́, -а́тишь) *pf.*

grace [greɪs] *n.* (~*fulness*) гра́ция; (*refinement*) изя́щество; (*kindness*) любе́зность; (*favour*) ми́лость; (*theol.*) благода́ть; *v.t.* (*adorn*) украша́ть *impf.*, укра́сить *pf.*; (*confer*) удоста́ивать *impf.*, удосто́ить *pf.* (**with** +*g.*). **graceful** *adj.* грацио́зный, изя́щный.

gracious ['greɪʃəs] *adj.* ми́лостивый, снисходи́тельный.

gradation [grə'deɪʃ(ə)n] *n.* града́ция.

grade [greɪd] *n.* (*level*) сте́пень (*pl.* -ни, -не́й); (*quality*) ка́чество; (*sort*) сорт (*pl.* -а́); (*slope*) укло́н; *v.t.* распределя́ть *impf.*, распредели́ть *pf.* по степеня́м, гру́ппам и т.п.; сортирова́ть *impf.*, рас~ *pf.*; (*road etc.*) нивели́ровать *impf.* & *pf.*

gradient ['greɪdɪənt] *n.* укло́н.

gradual ['grædjʊəl] *adj.* постепе́нный (-нен, -нна).

graduate ['grædjʊət; 'grædjʊˌeɪt] *n.* оконча́вший *sb.* университе́т, вуз; *v.i.* конча́ть *impf.*, око́нчить *pf.* (университе́т, вуз); *v.t.* градуи́ровать *impf.* & *pf.*

graffiti [grə'fiːtiː] *n.* (сте́нные) на́дписи (*f.pl.*).

graft[1] [grɑːft] *n.* (*agric.*) приво́й, приви́вка; (*med.*) переса́дка (живо́й тка́ни); *v.t.* (*agric.*) привива́ть *impf.*, приви́ть (-вью, -вьёшь; приви́л, -а́, -о) *pf.* (**to** +*d.*); (*med.*) переса́живать *impf.*, пересади́ть (-ажу́, -а́дишь) *pf.*

graft[2] [grɑːft] *n.* (*bribe*) взя́тка, по́дкуп; *v.i.* (*give*) дава́ть (даю́, -аёшь) *impf.*, дать (дам, дашь, даст, дади́м; дал, -а́, да́ло́, -и) *pf.* взя́тки; (*take*) брать (беру́, -рёшь; брал, -а́, -о) *impf.*, взять (возьму́, -мёшь; взял, -а́, -о) *pf.* взя́тки.

grain [greɪn] *n.* (*seed*; *collect.*) зерно́ (*pl.* зёрна, -рен, -рнам); (*particle*) крупи́нка; (*of sand*) песчи́нка; (*measure*) гран (*g.pl.* -н); (*smallest amount*) крупи́ца; (*of wood*) (древе́сное) волокно́; **against the** ~ не по нутру́; **not a** ~ **of** ни гра́на+*g.*

gram(me) [græm] *n.* грамм (*g.pl.* -м & -мов).

grammar ['græmə(r)] *n.* грамма́тика; ~ **school** гимна́зия. **grammarian** [grə'meərɪən] *n.* грамма́тик. **gra'mmatical** *adj.* граммати́ческий.

gramophone ['græmə,fəʊn] *n.* граммофо́н, прои́грыватель *m.*; ~ **record** граммпласти́нка.

grampus ['græmpəs] *n.* се́рый дельфи́н.

granary ['grænərɪ] *n.* амба́р.

grand [grænd] *adj.* (*in titles*) вели́кий; (*main*) гла́вный; (*majestic*) вели́чественный (-ен, -енна); (*splendid*) великоле́пный; ~ **duke** вели́кий ге́рцог; (*in Russia*) вели́кий князь (*pl.* -зья́, -зе́й); ~ **master** гроссме́йстер; ~ **piano** роя́ль *m.* **grandchild** *n.* внук, вну́чка; *pl.* внуча́та (-т) *pl.* **granddaughter** *n.* вну́чка. **grandfather** *n.* де́душка *m.* **grandmother** *n.* ба́бушка. **grandparents** *n.* ба́бушка и де́душка. **grandson** *n.* внук. **grandstand** *n.* трибу́на.

grandee [græn'di:] *n.* (*Spanish, Portuguese*) гранд; вельмо́жа *m.*

grandeur ['grændjə(r), -ndʒə(r)] *n.* вели́чие.

grandiloquence [,græn'dɪləkwəns] *n.* напы́щенность. **grandiloquent** *adj.* напы́щенный (-ен, -енна).

grandiose ['grændɪ,əʊs] *adj.* грандио́зный.

grange [greɪndʒ] *n.* фе́рма.

granite ['grænɪt] *n.* грани́т; *attr.* грани́тный.

grannie, granny ['grænɪ] *n.* ба́бушка.

grant [grɑːnt] *n.* дар (*pl.* -ы́); (*financial*) дота́ция, субси́дия; *v.t.* дарова́ть *impf.* & *pf.*; предоставля́ть *impf.*, предоста́вить *pf.*; (*concede*) допуска́ть *impf.*, допусти́ть (-ущу́, -у́стишь) *pf.*; **take for ~ed** счита́ть *impf.*, счесть (сочту́, -тёшь; счёл, сочла́) *pf.* само́ собо́й разуме́ющимся.

granular ['grænjʊlə(r)] *adj.* зерни́стый. **granulate** ['grænjʊ,leɪt] *v.t.* гранули́ровать *impf.* & *pf.*; ~**d sugar** са́харный песо́к (-ска́(у́)). **granule** ['grænju:l] *n.* зёрнышко (*pl.* -шки, -шек, -шкам).

grape [greɪp] *n.* виногра́д (-а(у)) (*collect.*). **grapefruit** *n.* грейпфру́т. **grapeshot** *n.* карте́чь. **grapevine** *n.* виногра́дная лоза́ (*pl.* -зы).

graph [grɑːf, græf] *n.* гра́фик.

graphic ['græfɪk] *adj.* графи́ческий; (*vivid*) я́ркий (я́рок, ярка́, я́рко).

graphite ['græfaɪt] *n.* графи́т.

grapnel ['græpn(ə)l] *n.* дрек, ко́шка.

grapple ['græp(ə)l] *n.* (*grapnel*) дрек, ко́шка; (*grip*) захва́т; *v.i.* сцепля́ться *impf.*, сцепи́ться (-плю́сь, -пишься) *pf.* (**with** с+*i.*); боро́ться (-рю́сь, -решься) *impf.* (**with** с+*i.*); **grappling hook, iron** дрек, ко́шка.

grasp [grɑːsp] *n.* (*grip*) хва́тка; (*control*) власть; (*mental hold*) схва́тывание; *v.t.* (*clutch*) хвата́ть *impf.*, схвати́ть (-ачу́, -а́тишь) *pf.*; (*comprehend*) понима́ть *impf.*, поня́ть (пойму́, -мёшь; по́нял, -а́, -о) *pf.* **grasping** *adj.* жа́дный (-ден, дна́, -дно).

grass [grɑːs] *n.* трава́ (*pl.* -вы), злак; (*pasture*) па́стбище; ~ **snake** уж (-а́); ~ **widow** соло́менная вдова́ (*pl.* -вы). **grasshopper** *n.* кузне́чик. **grassy** *adj.* травяни́стый, травяно́й.

grate[1] [greɪt] *n.* (*in fireplace*) (ками́нная) решётка.

grate[2] [greɪt] *v.t.* (*rub*) тере́ть (тру, трёшь; тёр) *impf.*, на~ *pf.*; *v.i.* (*sound*) скрипе́ть (-плю́) *impf.*; ~ (**up**)**on** (*irritate*) раздража́ть *impf.*, раздражи́ть *pf.*

grateful ['greɪtfʊl] *n.* благода́рный.

grater ['greɪtə(r)] *n.* тёрка.

gratify ['grætɪ,faɪ] *v.t.* удовлетворя́ть *impf.*, удовлетвори́ть *pf.*

grating ['greɪtɪŋ] *n.* решётка.

gratis ['grɑːtɪs] *adv.* беспла́тно, да́ром.

gratitude ['grætɪ,tju:d] *n.* благода́рность.

gratuitous [grə'tju:ɪtəs] *adj.* (*free*) даровой; (*motiveless*) беспричи́нный (-нен, -нна).

gratuity [grə'tju:ɪtɪ] *n.* де́нежный пода́рок (-рка); (*tip*) чаевы́е *sb.*; (*mil.*) наградны́е *sb.*

grave[1] [greɪv] *n.* моги́ла. **gravedigger** *n.* моги́льщик. **gravestone** *n.* надгро́бный ка́мень (-мня; *pl.* -мни, -мне́й) *m.* **graveyard** *n.* кла́дбище.

grave[2] [greɪv] *adj.* (*serious*) серьёзный, ва́жный (-жен, -жна́, -жно, -жны́).

gravel ['græv(ə)l] *n.* гра́вий; ~ **pit** грави́йный карье́р.

gravitate ['grævɪ,teɪt] *v.i.* тяготе́ть *impf.* (**towards** к+*d.*). **gravi'tation** *n.* тяготе́ние.

gravity ['grævɪtɪ] *n.* (*seriousness*) серьёзность; (*force*) тя́жесть; **specific** ~ уде́льный вес.

gravy ['greɪvɪ] *n.* (мясна́я) подли́вка. **gravyboat** *n.* со́усник.

graze[1] [greɪz] *v.t.* & *i.* (*feed*) пасти́ (пасу́(сь), пасёшь(ся); па́с(ся), пасла́(сь)) *impf.*

graze[2] [greɪz] *n.* (*abrasion*) цара́пина; *v.t.* (*touch lightly*) задева́ть *impf.*, заде́ть (-е́ну, -е́нешь) *pf.*; (*abrade*) цара́пать *impf.*, о~ *pf.*

grease [gri:s] *n.* жир (-а(у), *loc.* -е & -ý), то́плёное са́ло; (*lubricant*) сма́зка; *v.t.* сма́зывать *impf.*, сма́зать (-а́жу, -а́жешь) *pf.* **grease-gun** *n.* таво́тный шприц. **greasepaint** *n.* грим. **greasy** *adj.* жи́рный (-рен, -рна́, -рно), са́льный.

great [greɪt] *adj.* (*large*) большо́й; (*eminent*) вели́кий; (*long*) до́лгий (-лог, -лга́, -лго); (*strong*) си́льный (-лён, -льна́, -льно, си́льны́); **G~ Britain** Великобрита́ния; **to a ~ extent** в большо́й сте́пени; **a ~ deal** мно́го (+*g.*); **a ~ many** мно́гие; мно́жество (+*g.*). **great-aunt** *n.* двою́родная ба́бушка. **great-granddaughter** *n.* пра́внучка. **great-grandfather** *n.* пра́дед. **great-grandmother** *n.* праба́бка. **great-grandson** *n.* пра́внук.

greatly ['greɪtlɪ] *adv.* о́чень.

great-uncle [greɪt'ʌŋk(ə)l] *n.* двою́родный де́душка *m.*

Grecian ['gri:ʃ(ə)n] *adj.* гре́ческий. **Greece** *n.* Гре́ция.

greed [gri:d] *n.* жа́дность (**for** к+*d.*), а́лчность. **greedy** *adj.* жа́дный (-ден, -дна́, -дно) (**for** к+*d.*), а́лчный; (*for food*) прожо́рливый.

Greek [gri:k] *n.* грек, греча́нка; *adj.* гре́ческий.

green [gri:n] *n.* (*colour*) зелёный цвет; (*piece of land*) лужо́к (-жка́); *pl.* зе́лень *collect.*; *adj.* зелёный (зе́лен, -а́, -о); (*inexperienced*) нео́пытный. **greenery** *n.* зе́лень. **greenfly** *n.* тля (*g.pl.* тлей). **greengage** *n.* ренкло́д. **greengrocer** *n.* зеленщи́к (-а́). **greenhorn** *n.* новичо́к (-чка́). **greenhouse** *n.* тепли́ца, оранжере́я; ~ **effect** тепли́чный эффе́кт.

greet [gri:t] *v.t.* кла́няться *impf.*, поклони́ться (-ню́сь, -нишься) *pf.*+*d.*; приве́тствовать *impf.* (& *pf. in past tense*). **greeting** *n.* приве́т(ствие).

gregarious [grɪ'geərɪəs] *adj.* ста́дный; (*person*) общи́тельный.

grenade [grɪ'neɪd] *n.* грана́та.

grey [greɪ] *adj.* се́рый (сер, -а́, -о); (*hair*) седо́й (сед, -а́, -о); ~ **hair** седина́ (*pl.* -ы).

greyhound ['greɪhaʊnd] *n.* борза́я *sb.*

grid [grɪd] *n.* (*grating*) решётка; (*network*) сеть (*pl.* -ти, -те́й); (*map*) координа́тная се́тка.

grief [gri:f] *n.* го́ре, печа́ль; **come to** ~ попада́ть *impf.*, попа́сть (попаду́, -дёшь; попа́л) *pf.* в беду́.

grievance ['gri:v(ə)ns] *n.* жа́лоба, оби́да.

grieve [gri:v] *v.t.* огорча́ть *impf.*, огорчи́ть *pf.*; *v.i.* горева́ть (-рю́ю, -рю́ешь) *impf.* (**for** о+*p.*).

grievous ['gri:vəs] *adj.* тя́жкий (-жек, -жка́, -жко); (*flagrant*) вопию́щий.

grill¹ [grɪl] *n.* ра́шпер; *v.t.* (*cook*) жа́рить *impf.*, за~, из~ *pf.* (на ра́шпере); (*question*) допра́шивать *impf.*, допроси́ть (-ошу́, -о́сишь) *pf.*

grille, grill² [grɪl] *n.* (*grating*) решётка.

grim [grɪm] *adj.* (*stern*) суро́вый; (*sinister*) мра́чный (-чен, -чна́, -чно); (*unpleasant*) неприя́тный.

grimace ['grɪməs, grɪ'meɪs] *n.* грима́са; *v.i.* грима́сничать *impf.*

grime [graɪm] *n.* (*soot*) са́жа; (*dirt*) грязь (*loc.* -зи́). **grimy** *adj.* гря́зный (-зен, -зна́, -зно).

grin [grɪn] *n.* усме́шка; *v.i.* усмеха́ться *impf.*, усмехну́ться *pf.*

grind [graɪnd] *v.t.* (*flour etc.*) моло́ть (мелю́, -лешь) *impf.*, с~ *pf.*; (*axe*) точи́ть (-очу́, -чишь) *impf.*, на~ *pf.*; (*oppress*) му́чить *impf.*, за~, из~ *pf.*; ~ **one's teeth** скрежета́ть (-ещу́, -е́щешь) *impf.* зуба́ми.

grip [grɪp] *n.* схва́тывание; (*control*) власть; *v.t.* схва́тывать *impf.*, схвати́ть (-ачу́, -а́тишь) *pf.*

grisly ['grɪzlɪ] *adj.* ужа́сный.

gristle ['grɪs(ə)l] *n.* хрящ (-а́). **gristly** *adj.* хрящева́тый.

grit [grɪt] *n.* кру́пный песо́к (-ска́(у́)); (*firmness*) сто́йкость. **gritty** *adj.* песча́ный.

grizzly ['grɪzlɪ] *adj.* се́рый (сер, -а́, -о); ~ **bear** гри́зли *m.indecl.*

groan [grəʊn] *n.* стон; *v.i.* стона́ть (-ну́, -нешь) *impf.*

grocer ['grəʊsə(r)] *n.* бакале́йщик; ~**'s (shop)** бакале́йная ла́вка, гастроно́м(и́ческий магази́н). **groceries** *n.* бакале́я *collect.*

groin [grɔɪn] *n.* (*anat.*) пах (*loc.* -у́).

groom [gru:m] *n.* грум, ко́нюх; (*bridegroom*) жени́х (-а́); *v.t.* (*horse*) чи́стить *impf.*, вы́~ *pf.*; (*person*) хо́лить *impf.*, вы́~ *pf.*; (*prepare*) гото́вить *impf.*, под~ *pf.* (**for** к+*d.*).

groove [gru:v] *n.* желобо́к (-бка́), паз (*loc.* -у́; *pl.* -ы́); (*routine*) колея́.

grope [grəʊp] *v.i.* нащу́пывать *impf.* (**for, after** +*a.*); ~ **one's way** идти́ (иду́, идёшь; шёл, шла) *impf.*, пойти́ (пойду́, -дёшь; пошёл, -шла́) *pf.* о́щупью.

gross¹ [grəʊs] *n.* (*12 dozen*) гросс; **by the** ~ о́птом.

gross² [grəʊs] *adj.* (*luxuriant*) пы́шный (-шен, -шна́, -шно); (*fat*) ту́чный (-чен, -чна́, -чно); (*coarse*) гру́бый (груб, -а́, -о); (*total*) валово́й; ~ **weight** вес бру́тто.

grotesque [grəʊ'tesk] *adj.* гроте́скный; (*absurd*) неле́пый.

grotto ['grɒtəʊ] *n.* грот, пеще́ра.

ground [graʊnd] *n.* земля́ (*a.* -лю), по́чва, грунт; *pl.* (*dregs*) гу́ща; (*sport*) площа́дка; *pl.* (*of house*) парк; (*background*) фон; (*reason*) основа́ние, причи́на; **break fresh** ~ прокла́дывать *impf.*, проложи́ть (-жу́, -жишь) *pf.* но́вые пути́; **gain** ~ де́лать *impf.*, с~ *pf.* успе́хи; **give, lose,** ~ уступа́ть *impf.*, уступи́ть (-плю́, -пишь) *pf.* (**to** +*d.*); **stand one's** ~ стоя́ть (-ою́, -ои́шь) *impf.* на своём; ~ **floor** цо́кольный, пе́рвый, эта́ж (-а́); *v.t.* (*base*) обосно́вывать *impf.*, обоснова́ть (-ну́ю, -нуёшь) *pf.*; (*instruct*) обуча́ть *impf.*, обучи́ть (-чу́, -чишь) *pf.* осно́вам (**in** +*g.*); *v.i.* (*naut.*) сади́ться *impf.*, сесть (ся́дет; сел) *pf.* на мель. **groundless** *adj.* беспричи́нный (-нен, -нна), необосно́ванный (-ан, -анна). **groundnut** *n.* земляно́й оре́х. **groundsheet** *n.* поло́тнище пала́тки. **groundwork** *n.* фунда́мент, осно́ва, основа́ние.

group [gru:p] *n.* гру́ппа; ~ **captain** полко́вник авиа́ции; *v.t.* & *i.* группирова́ть(ся) *impf.*, с~ *pf.*

grouse¹ [graʊs] *n.* (*bird*) те́терев (*pl.* -а́); (**red**) ~ шотла́ндская куропа́тка.

grouse² [graʊs] *v.i.* (*grumble*) ворча́ть (-чу́, -чи́шь) *impf.*

grove [grəʊv] *n.* ро́ща.

grovel ['grɒv(ə)l] *v.i.* пресмыка́ться *impf.* (**before** пе́ред+*i.*).

grow [grəʊ] *v.i.* расти́ (-ту́, -тёшь; рос, -ла́) *impf.*; (*become*) станови́ться (-влю́сь, -вишься) *impf.*, стать (ста́ну, -нешь) *pf.*+*i.*; *v.t.* (*cultivate*) выра́щивать *impf.*, вы́растить *pf.*; ~ **up** (*person*) выраста́ть *impf.*, вы́расти (-ту, -тешь; вы́рос, -ла) *pf.*; (*custom*) возника́ть *impf.*, возни́кнуть (-к) *pf.*

growl [graʊl] *n.* рыча́ние; *v.i.* ворча́ть (-чу́, -чи́шь) *impf.* (**at** на+*a.*).

grown-up [grəʊn'ʌp] *adj.* взро́слый *sb.*

growth [grəʊθ] *n.* рост (-а(у)); (*tumour*) о́пухоль.

grub [grʌb] *n.* (*larva*) личи́нка; (*sl.*) (*food*) жратва́; *v.i.*: ~ **about** ры́ться (ро́юсь, ро́ешься) *impf.* **grubby** *adj.* гря́зный, чума́зый.

grudge [grʌdʒ] *n.* недово́льство, за́висть; **have a ~ against** име́ть *impf.* зуб про́тив+g.; *v.t.* жале́ть *impf.*, по~ *pf.*+a., +g.; неохо́тно дава́ть (даю́, даёшь) *impf.*, дать (дам, дашь, даст, дади́м; дал, -á, да́ло, -и) *pf.*; неохо́тно де́лать *impf.*, с~ *pf.* **grudgingly** *adv.* неохо́тно.

gruel ['gru:əl] *n.* жи́дкая ка́ша; *v.t.* утомля́ть *impf.*, утоми́ть *pf.* **gruelling** *adj.* изнури́тельный, суро́вый.

gruesome ['gru:səm] *adj.* отврати́тельный.

gruff [grʌf] *adj.* (*surly*) груба́тый; (*voice*) хри́плый (-л, -ла́, -ло).

grumble ['grʌmb(ə)l] *n.* ворча́ние, ро́пот; *v.i.* ворча́ть (-чу́, -чи́шь) *impf.* (**at** на+a.).

grumpy ['grʌmpɪ] *adj.* брюзгли́вый.

grunt [grʌnt] *n.* хрю́канье; *v.i.* хрю́кать *impf.*, хрю́кнуть *pf.*

guarantee [,gærən'ti:] *n.* (*person*) поручи́тель *m.*, ~ница; (*security*) гара́нтия, зало́г; *v.t.* гаранти́ровать *impf.* & *pf.* (**against** от+g.); руча́ться *impf.*, поручи́ться (-чу́сь, -чи́шься) *pf.* за+a. **guarantor** *n.* поручи́тель *m.*, ~ница.

guard [gɑ:d] *n.* (*protection*) охра́на; (*watch*, *body of soldiers*) карау́л; (*sentry*) часово́й *sb.*; (*watchman*) сто́рож (*pl.* -á); (*rail.*) конду́ктор (*pl.* -á); *pl.* (G~) гва́рдия; ~ **of honour** почётный карау́л; *v.t.* охраня́ть *impf.*, охрани́ть *pf.*; *v.i.*: ~ **against** остерега́ться *impf.*, остере́чься (-егу́сь, -ежёшься; -ёгся, -егла́сь) *pf.*+g., *inf.* **guard-house**, **-room** *n.* гауптва́хта. **guardsman** *n.* гварде́ец (-е́йца).

guardian ['gɑ:dɪən] *n.* храни́тель *m.*, ~ница; (*leg.*) опеку́н (-á).

guer(r)illa [gə'rɪlə] *n.* партиза́н; ~ **warfare** партиза́нская война́.

guess [ges] *n.* дога́дка; *v.t.* & *i.* дога́дываться *impf.*, догада́ться *pf.* (о+p.); *v.t.* (~ *correctly*) уга́дывать *impf.*, угада́ть *pf.*

guest [gest] *n.* гость (*pl.* -ти, -те́й) *m.*, ~я (*g.pl.* -ти́й).

guffaw [gʌ'fɔ:] *n.* хо́хот; *v.i.* хохота́ть (-очу́, -о́чешь) *impf.*

guidance ['gaɪd(ə)ns] *n.* руково́дство. **guide** *n.* проводни́к (-á), -и́ца; гид; (*adviser*) сове́тчик; (*manual*) руково́дство; (*guide-book*) путеводи́тель *m.*; *v.t.* води́ть (вожу́, во́дишь) *indet.*, вести́ (веду́, -дёшь; вёл, -á) *det.*; (*direct*) руководи́ть *impf.*+i.; (*control*) управля́ть *impf.*+i.; ~**ed missile** управля́емая раке́та. **guide-dog** *n.* соба́ка-поводы́рь (-ря́). **guide-post** *n.* указа́тельный столб(-á).

guild [gɪld] *n.* ги́льдия, цех.

guile [gaɪl] *n.* кова́рство, хи́трость. **guileful** *adj.* кова́рный. **guileless** *adj.* простоду́шный.

guillotine ['gɪlə,ti:n] *n.* гильоти́на; (*for paper etc.*) бумагоре́зальная маши́на; *v.t.* гильо-

тини́ровать *impf.* & *pf.*

guilt [gɪlt] *n.* вина́, вино́вность. **guiltless** *adj.* неви́нный (-нен, -нна), невино́вный. **guilty** *adj.* вино́вный (**of** в+p.), винова́тый.

guinea ['gɪnɪ] *n.* гине́я. **guinea-fowl** *n.* цеса́рка. **guinea-pig** *n.* морска́я сви́нка; (*fig.*) подо́пытный кро́лик.

guise [gaɪz] *n.* вид, о́блик; **under the ~ of** под ви́дом+g.

guitar [gɪ'tɑ:(r)] *n.* гита́ра.

gulf [gʌlf] *n.* зали́в; (*chasm*) про́пасть; G~ **Stream** гольфстри́м.

gull [gʌl] *n.* ча́йка.

gullet ['gʌlɪt] *n.* пищево́д; (*throat*) го́рло.

gullible ['gʌlɪb(ə)l] *adj.* легкове́рный.

gully ['gʌlɪ] *n.* (*ravine*) овра́г; (*channel*) кана́ва.

gulp [gʌlp] *n.* глото́к (-тка́); *v.t.* жа́дно глота́ть *impf.*

gum[1] [gʌm] *n.* (*anat.*) десна́ (*pl.* дёсны, -сен, -снам).

gum[2] [gʌm] *n.* (*glue*) каме́дь, клей (-е́я(ю), *loc.* -е́е & ею́; *pl.* -еи́); *v.t.* скле́ивать *impf.*, скле́ить *pf.* **gumboot** *n.* рези́новый сапо́г (-á; *g.pl.* -г). **gum-tree** *n.* эвкали́пт.

gumption ['gʌmpʃ(ə)n] *n.* нахо́дчивость.

gun [gʌn] *n.* (*piece of ordnance*) ору́дие, пу́шка; (*rifle etc.*) ружьё (*pl.* -жья, -жей); (*pistol*) пистоле́т; **starting** ~ ста́ртовый пистоле́т; *v.t.*: ~ **down** расстре́ливать *impf.*, расстреля́ть *pf.* **gunboat** *n.* каноне́рская ло́дка. **gun-carriage** *n.* лафе́т. **gunner** *n.* артиллери́ст; (*aeron.*) стрело́к (-лка́). **gunpowder** *n.* по́рох (-а(у)). **gunsmith** *n.* ору́жейный ма́стер (*pl.* -á).

gunwale ['gʌn(ə)l] *n.* планши́рь *m.*

gush [gʌʃ] *n.* си́льный пото́к; излия́ние; *v.i.* хлы́нуть *pf.*; излива́ться *impf.*, изли́ться (изолью́сь, -ьёшься; изли́лся, -ила́сь, -и́ло́сь) *pf.*

gusset ['gʌsɪt] *n.* клин (*pl.* -ья, -ьев), ла́стовица.

gust [gʌst] *n.* поры́в. **gusty** *adj.* поры́вистый.

gusto ['gʌstəʊ] *n.* удово́льствие, смак.

gut [gʌt] *n.* кишка́ (*g.pl.* -шо́к); *pl.* (*entrails*) вну́тренности *f.pl.*; *pl.* (*coll.*, *bravery*) му́жество; *v.t.* потроши́ть *impf.*, вы́~ *pf.*; (*devastate*) опустоша́ть *impf.*, опустоши́ть *pf.*

gutta-percha [,gʌtə'pɜ:tʃə] *n.* гуттапе́рча.

gutter ['gʌtə(r)] *n.* (*водосто́чный*) жёлоб (*pl.* -á), сто́чная кана́ва; ~ **press** бульва́рная пре́сса.

guttural ['gʌtər(ə)l] *adj.* горта́нный, горлово́й.

guy[1] [gaɪ] *n.* (*rope*) оття́жка.

guy[2] [gaɪ] *n.* (*fellow*) па́рень (-рня; *pl.* -рни, -рне́й) *m.*

guzzle ['gʌz(ə)l] *v.t.* (*food*) пожира́ть *impf.*, пожра́ть (-ру́, -рёшь; пожра́л, -á, -о) *pf.*; (*liquid*) хлеба́ть *impf.*, хлебну́ть *pf.*

gym [dʒɪm] *n.* (*gymnasium*) гимнастический зал; (*gymnastics*) гимнастика. **gymnasium** [dʒɪm'neɪzɪəm] *n.* гимнастический зал; (*school*) гимназия. **'gymnast** *n.* гимнаст, ~ка. **gym'nastic** *adj.* гимнастический. **gym'nastics** *n.* гимнастика.

gynaecology [,gaɪnɪ'kɒlədʒɪ] *n.* гинекология.

gypsum ['dʒɪpsəm] *n.* гипс.

gyrate [,dʒaɪə'reɪt] *v.i.* вращаться *impf.* по кругу; двигаться (движется & движется) *impf.* по спирали.

gyro(scope) ['dʒaɪərə,skəʊp] *n.* гироскоп. **gyro-compass** *n.* гирокомпас.

H

ha. *abbr.* (*of* **hectare(s)**) га, гектар.

haberdasher ['hæbə,dæʃə(r)] *n.* торговец (-вца) галантереей. **haberdashery** *n.* (*articles*) галантерея; (*shop*) галантерейный магазин.

habit ['hæbɪt] *n.* привычка; (*dress*) одеяние.

habitable ['hæbɪtəb(ə)l] *adj.* годный (-ден, -дна, -дно) для жилья. **habi'tation** *n.* жилище.

habitual [hə'bɪtjʊəl] *adj.* обычный, привычный. **habitué** *n.* завсегдатай.

hack[1] [hæk] *v.t.* рубить (-блю, -бишь) *impf.*; дробить *impf.*, раз~ *pf.*

hack[2] [hæk] *n.* писака *c.g.* **hackneyed** ['hæknɪd] *adj.* избитый, банальный.

hacksaw ['hæksɔː] *n.* ножовка.

haddock ['hædək] *n.* пикша.

haemophilia [,hiːmə'fɪlɪə] *n.* гемафилия. **haemorrhage** ['hemərɪdʒ] *n.* кровоизлияние, кровотечение. **haemorrhoids** ['hemə,rɔɪdz] *n.* геморрой *collect.*

hag [hæg] *n.* ведьма, карга.

haggard ['hægəd] *adj.* изможденный (-ён, -ена).

haggle ['hæg(ə)l] *v.i.* торговаться *impf.*, с~ *pf.*

hail[1] [heɪl] *n.* град; *v.i.* **it is ~ing** идёт (*past* пошёл) град; *v.t.* осыпать *impf.*, осыпать (-плю, -плешь) *pf.*+*a.* & *i.*; *v.i.* сыпаться (-плется) *impf.* градом. **hailstone** *n.* градина.

hail[2] [heɪl] *v.t.* (*greet*) приветствовать *impf.* (& *pf. in past*); (*call*) окликать *impf.*, окликнуть *pf.*; *v.i.*: **~ from** (*of persons only*) быть родом из+*g.*; происходить (-ожу, -одишь) *impf.*, произойти (произойду, -дёшь; произошёл, -шла) *pf.* из+*g.*

hair [heə(r)] *n.* (*single* ~) волос (*pl.* -осы, -ос, -осам); *collect.* (*human* волосы (-ос,

-осам) *pl.*; (*animal*) шерсть; **do one's ~** причёсываться *impf.*, причесаться (-ешусь, -ешешься) *pf.* **haircut** *n.* стрижка. **hairdo** *n.* причёска. **hairdresser** *n.* парикмахер. **hairspray** *n.* лак для волос. **hairy** *adj.* волосатый.

hake [heɪk] *n.* хек.

halberd ['hælbəd] *n.* алебарда.

hale [heɪl] *adj.* здоровый.

half [hɑːf] *n.* половина; (*sport*) тайм; *in comb.* пол(у)...; *adj.* половинный; **in ~** пополам; **one and a ~** полтора *m.* & *nt.*, -ры́ *f.* +*g.sg.* (*oblique cases:* полу́тора+*pl.*); **~ moon** полумесяц; **~ past** (*one etc.*) половина (второго и т.д.). **half-back** *n.* полузащитник. **half-hearted** *adj.* равнодушный. **half-hour** *n.* полчаса (*oblique cases* получаса). **half-mast** *adv.*: **flag at ~** приспущенный флаг. **half-time** *n.* перерыв между таймами. **halfway** *adv.* на полпути. **halfwitted** *adj.* слабоумный.

halibut ['hælɪbət] *n.* палтус.

hall [hɔːl] *n.* (*large room*) зал; (*entrance* ~) холл, вестибюль *m.*; (*dining* ~) столовая (коллёджа); (~ *of residence*) общежитие.

hallmark *n.* пробирное клеймо (*pl.* -ма); (*fig.*) признак.

hallo *see* **hello**

hallow ['hæləʊ] *v.t.* освящать *impf.*, освятить (-ящу, -ятишь) *pf.*

hallucination [hə,luːsɪ'neɪʃ(ə)n] *n.* галлюцинация.

halo ['heɪləʊ] *n.* гало *nt.indecl.*; (*around Saint*) венчик, нимб; (*fig.*) ореол.

halogen ['hælədʒ(ə)n] *n.* галоген.

⸱¹ [hɒlt, hɔːlt] *n.* (*stoppage*) остановка; (*rail.*) полустанок (-нка) *v.t.* & *i.* останавливать(ся) *impf.*, остановить(ся) (-влю(сь), -вишь(ся)) *pf.*; *int.* (*mil.*) стой(те)!

halt[2] [hɒlt, hɔːlt] *v.i.* (*hesitate*) колебаться (-блюсь, -блешься) *impf.*

halter ['hɒltə(r), 'hɔːl-] *n.* недоуздок (-дка).

halve [hɑːv] *v.t.* делить (-лю, -лишь) *impf.*, раз~ *pf.* пополам.

ham [hæm] *n.* (*cul.*) ветчина, окорок; (*theatr.*) плохой актёр; (*radio* ~) радиолюбитель *m.*; *v.i.* (*theatr.*) переигрывать *impf.*, переиграть *pf.*

hamlet ['hæmlɪt] *n.* деревушка.

hammer ['hæmə(r)] *n.* молот, молоток (-тка); **come under the ~** продаваться (-дается) *impf.*, продаться (-дастся; -дался, -далась) *pf.* с молотка; *v.t.* бить (бью, бьёшь) *impf.* молотом, молотком.

hammock ['hæmək] *n.* гамак (-á); (*naut.*) койка.

hamper[1] ['hæmpə(r)] *n.* (*basket*) корзина с крышкой.

hamper[2] ['hæmpə(r)] *v.t.* (*hinder*) мешать *impf.*, по~ *pf.*+*d.*

hamster ['hæmstə(r)] *n.* хомяк (-á).

hand [hænd] *n.* рука (*a.* -ку; *pl.* -ки, -к, -кам); (*worker*) рабочий *sb.*; (~*writing*) почерк;

(*clock* ~) стрéлка; at ~ под рукóй; on ~s
and knees на четверéньках; *v.t.* передавáть
(-даю́, -даёшь) *impf.*, передáть (-áм, -áшь,
-áст, -адим; -пéредал, -á, -о) *pf.*; вручáть
impf., вручи́ть *pf.* handbag *n.* сýмка,
сýмочка. handball *n.* гандбóл. handbook
n. спрáвочник, руковóдство. handcuffs *n.*
нарýчники *m.pl.* hand-drier, -dryer *n.*
электрополотéнце. handful *n.* горсть (*pl.*
-ти, -тéй).

handicap ['hændɪˌkæp] *n.* (*sport*) гандикáп;
(*hindrance*) помéха. handicapped *adj.*: ~
person инвали́д.

handicraft ['hændɪˌkrɑːft] *n.* ремеслó (*pl.* -ёсла,
-ёсел, -ёслам).

handiwork ['hændɪˌwɜːk] *n.* ручнáя рабóта.

handkerchief ['hæŋkətʃɪf, -ˌtʃiːf] *n.* носовóй
платóк (-ткá).

handle ['hænd(ə)l] *n.* рýчка, рукоя́тка; *v.t.*
(*treat*) обращáться *impf.* c+*i.*; (*manage*)
управля́ть *impf.*+*i.*; (*touch*) трóгать *impf.*,
трóнуть *pf.* рукóй, рукáми. handlebar(s) *n.*
руль (-ля́) *m.*

handsome ['hænsəm] *adj.* краси́вый; (*gener-*
ous) щéдрый (щедр, -á, -о).

handwriting ['hændˌraɪtɪŋ] *n.* пóчерк.

handy ['hændɪ] *adj.* (*convenient*) удóбный;
(*skilful*) лóвкий (-вок, -вкá, -вко, лóвки́);
come in ~ пригоди́ться *pf.*

hang [hæŋ] *v.t.* вéшать *impf.*, повéсить *pf.*;
подвéшивать *impf.*, подвéсить *pf.*; *v.i.* висéть (вишу́, виси́шь) *impf.*; ~ about сло-
ня́ться *impf.*; ~ back колебáться (-блю́сь,
-блешься) *impf.*; ~ on (*remain*) держáться
(-жýсь, -жишься) *impf.* hanger-on *n.*
прижива́льщик. hang-glider *n.* (*craft*)
дельтапла́н; (*operator*) дельтапланери́ст.
hangman *n.* палáч (-á).

hangar ['hæŋə(r)] *n.* ангáр.

hangover ['hæŋˌəʊvə(r)] *n.* похмéлье.

hanker ['hæŋkə(r)] *v.i.*: ~ after стрáстно
желáть *impf.*, по~ *pf.*+*g.*

haphazard [hæp'hæzəd] *adj.* случáйный; *adv.*
случáйно, наудáчу.

hapless ['hæplɪs] *adj.* злополýчный.

happen ['hæpən] *v.i.* (*occur*) случáться *impf.*,
случи́ться *pf.*; происходи́ть (-и́т) *impf.*,
произойти́ (-ойдёт; -ошёл, -шлá) *pf.*; (~ *to*
be somewhere) оказывáться *impf.*, оказáть-
ся (-ажýсь, -áжешься) *pf.*; ~ upon натáлкиваться *impf.*, натолкнýться *pf.* на+*a.*

happiness ['hæpɪnɪs] *n.* счáстье. happy *adj.*
счастли́вый (-сча́стли́в); (*apt*) удáчный; H~
Birthday! (поздравля́ю вас) с днём рож-
дéния!; H~ New Year! с Нóвым гóдом!

harass ['hærəs] *v.t.* беспокóить *impf.*, о~ *pf.*

harbinger ['hɑːbɪndʒə(r)] *n.* предвéстник.

harbour ['hɑːbə(r)] *n.* гáвань, порт (*loc.* -ý;
pl. -ы, -óв); (*shelter*) убéжище; *v.t.* (*person*)
укрывáть *impf.*, укры́ть (-рóю, -рóешь) *pf.*;
(*thoughts*) затаи́вать *impf.*, затаи́ть *pf.*

hard [hɑːd] *adj.* твёрдый (твёрд, -á, -о), жёсткий (-ток, -ткá, -тко); (*difficult*) трýдный

(-ден, -днá, -дно, трýдны́); (*difficult to bear*)
тяжёлый (-л, -лá); (*severe*) сурóвый; ~ copy
(*comput.*) печáтная кóпия; ~ hat защи́тный
шлем. hard-boiled *adj.*: ~ egg яйцó (*pl.*
я́йца, яи́ц, я́йцам) вкрутýю.

harden ['hɑːd(ə)n] *v.t.* дéлать *impf.*, c~ *pf.*
твёрдым, закаля́ть *impf.*, закали́ть *pf.*; *v.i.*
затвердевáть *impf.*, затвердéть *pf.*; (*become*
callous) ожесточáться *impf.*, ожесточи́ться
pf.

hard-headed [hɑːd'hedɪd] *adj.* практи́чный.
hard-hearted *adj.* жестокосéрдный.

hardly ['hɑːdlɪ] *adv.* (*scarcely*) едвá (ли); (*with*
difficulty) с трудóм.

hardship ['hɑːdʃɪp] *n.* (*privation*) нуждá.

hardware ['hɑːdweə(r)] *n.* скобяны́е издéлия
nt.pl.; (*comput.*) аппаратýра, аппарáтное
оборýдование.

hard-working [hɑːd'wɜːkɪŋ] *adj.* прилéжный.

hardy ['hɑːdɪ] *adj.* (*bold*) смéлый (смел, -á,
-о); (*robust*) выносли́вый.

hare [heə(r)] *n.* зáяц (зáйца). hare-brained
adj. опромéтчивый. harelip *n.* зáячья губá.

harem ['hɑːriːm, hɑːˈriːm] *n.* гарéм.

haricot ['hærɪˌkəʊ] *n.* фасóль.

hark [hɑːk] *v.i.*: ~ to, at слýшать *impf.*, по~
pf.+*a.*; ~ back to возвращáться *impf.*, вер-
нýться *pf.* к+*d.*; *int.* чу!

harlot ['hɑːlət] *n.* проститýтка.

harm [hɑːm] *n.* вред (-á), зло; *v.t.* вреди́ть
impf., по~ *pf.*+*d.* harmful *adj.* врéдный
(-ден, -днá, -дно). harmless *adj.* безврéдный.

harmonic [hɑːˈmɒnɪk] *adj.* гармони́ческий.
harmonica *n.* губнáя гармóника. harmonious [hɑːˈməʊnɪəs] *adj.* гармони́чный; (*ami-*
cable) дрýжный (-жен, -жнá, -жно). harmonium *n.* фисгармóния. 'harmonize *v.t.* гар-
монизи́ровать *impf.* & *pf.*; *v.i.* гармони́-
ровать *impf.* (with c+*i.*). 'harmony *n.* гармó-
ния, созвýчие, соглáсие.

harness ['hɑːnɪs] *n.* ýпряжь, сбрýя; *v.t.* за-, в-,
прягáть *impf.*, за-, в-, пря́чь (-ягý, -я́жешь;
-я́г, -яглá) *pf.*; (*fig.*) испóльзовать *impf.* &
pf. как истóчник энéргии.

harp [hɑːp] *n.* áрфа; *v.i.* игрáть *impf.* на
áрфе; ~ on распространя́ться *impf.*, рас-
простраи́ться *pf.* о+*p.* harpist *n.* арфи́ст,
~ка.

harpoon [hɑːˈpuːn] *n.* гарпýн (-á), острогá.

harpsichord ['hɑːpsɪˌkɔːd] *n.* клавеси́н.

harpy ['hɑːpɪ] *n.* гáрпия; (*fig.*) хи́щник.

harridan ['hærɪd(ə)n] *n.* вéдьма, каргá.

harrow ['hærəʊ] *n.* боронá (*a.* -ону; *pl.* -оны,
-óн, -онáм); *v.t.* борони́ть *impf.*, вз~ *pf.*;
(*torment*) терзáть *impf.*

harry ['hærɪ] *v.t.* (*ravage*) опустошáть *impf.*,
опустоши́ть *pf.*; (*worry*) тревóжить *impf.*,
вс~ *pf.*

harsh [hɑːʃ] *adj.* грýбый (груб, -á, -о);
(*sound*) рéзкий (-зок, -зкá, -зко); (*cruel*)
сурóвый.

hart [hɑːt] *n.* олéнь *m.*

harvest ['hɑːvɪst] *n.* жа́тва, сбор (плодо́в); (*yield*) урожа́й; (*fig.*) плоды́ *m.pl.*; *v.t. & abs.* собира́ть *impf.*, собра́ть (соберу́, -рёшь; собра́л, -а́, -о) *pf.* (урожа́й).

hash [hæʃ] *n.* рубле́ное мя́со; (*medley*) мешани́на; **make a ~ of** напу́тать *pf.* +a., в+p.; *v.t.* руби́ть (-блю́, -бишь) *impf.*

hasp [hɑːsp] *n.* застёжка.

hassock ['hæsək] *n.* (*cushion*) поду́шечка; (*tuft of grass*) ко́чка.

haste [heɪst] *n.* поспе́шность, торопли́вость, спе́шка. **hasten** ['heɪs(ə)n] *v.i.* спеши́ть *impf.*, по~ *pf.*; *v.t. & i.* торопи́ть(ся) (-плю́(сь), -пишь(ся)) *impf.*, по~ *pf.*; *v.t.* ускоря́ть *impf.*, уско́рить *pf.* **hasty** *adj.* (*hurried*) поспе́шный; (*rash*) опроме́тчивый; (*quick-tempered*) вспы́льчивый.

hat [hæt] *n.* шля́па; **top** ~ цили́ндр.

hatch¹ [hætʃ] *n.*, **-way** *n.* (*naut.*) люк.

hatch² [hætʃ] *n.* (*brood*) вы́водок (-дка); *v.t.* выси́живать *impf.*, вы́сидеть (-ижу, -идишь) *pf.*; *v.i.* вылу́пливаться, вылупля́ться *impf.*, вы́лупиться *pf.*

hatchback ['hætʃbæk] *n.* пятидве́рная маши́на.

hatchet ['hætʃɪt] *n.* топо́рик.

hate [heɪt] *n.* не́нависть; *v.t.* ненави́деть (-и́жу, -и́дишь) *impf.* **hateful** *adj.* ненави́стный. **hatred** *n.* не́нависть.

haughty ['hɔːtɪ] *adj.* надме́нный (-нен, -нна), высокоме́рный.

haul [hɔːl] *n.* добы́ча; (*distance*) езда́; *v.t.* тяну́ть (-ну́, -нешь) *impf.*; таска́ть *indet.*, тащи́ть (-щу́, -щишь) *det.*; (*transport*) перевози́ть (-ожу́, -о́зишь) *impf.*, перевезти́ (-езу́, -езёшь; -ёз, -езла́) *pf.*

haunch [hɔːntʃ] *n.* бедро́ (*pl.* бёдра, -дер, -драм), ля́жка.

haunt [hɔːnt] *n.* ча́сто посеща́емое ме́сто; (*of criminals*) прито́н; *v.t.* (*frequent*) ча́сто посеща́ть *impf.*

have [hæv, həv] *v.t.* име́ть *impf.*; **I ~** (*possess*) у меня́ (есть; был, -а́, -о)+*nom.*; **I ~ not** у меня́ нет (*past* не́ было)+*g.*; **I ~ (got) to** я до́лжен (-жна́)+*inf.*; **you had better** вам лу́чше бы+*inf.*; **~ on** (*wear*) быть оде́тым в+p.

haven ['heɪv(ə)n] *n.* га́вань; (*refuge*) убе́жище.

haversack ['hævəsæk] *n.* ра́нец (-нца).

havoc ['hævək] *n.* (*devastation*) опустоше́ние; (*disorder*) беспоря́док (-дка).

hawk¹ [hɔːk] *n.* (*bird*) я́стреб (*pl.* -ы & -а́).

hawk² [hɔːk] *v.t.* (*trade*) торгова́ть *impf.* вразно́с+i. **hawker** *n.* разно́счик.

hawser ['hɔːzə(r)] *n.* трос.

hawthorn ['hɔːθɔːn] *n.* боя́рышник.

hay [heɪ] *n.* се́но; **make ~** коси́ть (кошу́, ко́сишь) *impf.*, с~ *pf.* се́но; **~ fever** сенна́я лихора́дка. **haycock** *n.* копна́ (*pl.* -пны, -пён, -пна́м) **hayloft** *n.* сенова́л. **haystack** *n.* стог (*loc.* -е & -у́; *pl.* -а́).

hazard ['hæzəd] *n.* риск; *v.t.* рискова́ть

impf.+i. **hazardous** *adj.* риско́ванный (-ан, -анна).

haze [heɪz] *n.* тума́н, ды́мка.

hazel ['heɪz(ə)l] *n.* лещи́на. **hazelnut** *n.* лесно́й оре́х.

hazy ['heɪzɪ] *adj.* (*misty*) тума́нный (-нен, -нна); (*vague*) сму́тный (-тен, -тна́, -тно).

H-bomb ['eɪtʃbɒm] *n.* водоро́дная бо́мба.

he [hiː, hɪ] *pron.* он (его́, ему́, им, о нём).

head [hed] *n.* голова́ (*a.* -ову; *pl.* -овы, -о́в, -ова́м); (*mind*) ум (-а́); (~ **of cattle**) голова́ скота́; (~ **of coin**) лицева́я сторона́ (*a.* -ону) моне́ты; **~s or tails?** орёл и́ли ре́шка?; (*chief*) глава́ (*pl.* -вы) *m.*, нача́льник; *attr.* гла́вный; *v.t.* (*lead*) возглавля́ть *impf.*, возгла́вить *pf.*; (~ *chapter*) озагла́вливать *impf.*, озагла́вить *pf.*; *v.i.:* ~ **for** направля́ться *impf.*, напра́виться *pf.* в, на, +a., к+d. **headache** *n.* головна́я боль. **head-dress** *n.* головно́й убо́р. **heading** *n.* (*title*) заголо́вок (-вка). **headland** *n.* мыс (*loc.* -е & -у́; *pl.* мы́сы́). **headlight** *n.* фа́ра. **headline** *n.* заголо́вок (-вка). **headlong** *adj.* (*precipitate*) опроме́тчивый; *adv.* стремгла́в. **head'master**, **-'mistress** *n.* дире́ктор (*pl.* -а́) шко́лы. **headphone** *n.* нау́шник. **head'quarters** *n.* штаб-кварти́ра. **head-stone** *n.* надгро́бный ка́мень (-мня, *pl.* -мни, -мне́й) *m.* **headstrong** *adj.* своево́льный. **headway** *n.* движе́ние вперёд. **heady** *adj.* стреми́тельный; (*liquor*) хмельно́й (-лён, -льна́).

heal [hiːl] *v.t.* изле́чивать *impf.*, излечи́ть (-чу́, -чишь) *pf.*; исцеля́ть *impf.*, исцели́ть *pf.*; *v.i.* зажива́ть *impf.*, зажи́ть (-ивёт; зажи́л, -а, -о) *pf.* **healing** *adj.* целе́бный.

health [helθ] *n.* здоро́вье; ~ **foods** натура́льная пи́ща; ~ **food shop** диетети́ческий магази́н. **healthy** *adj.* здоро́вый; (*beneficial*) поле́зный.

heap [hiːp] *n.* ку́ча, гру́да; *v.t.* нагроможда́ть *impf.*, награмозди́ть *pf.*; (*load*) нагружа́ть *impf.*, нагрузи́ть (-ужу́, -у́зи́шь) *pf.* (**with** +i.).

hear [hɪə(r)] *v.t.* слы́шать (-шу, -шишь) *impf.*, у~ *pf.*; (*listen to*) слу́шать *impf.*, по~ *pf.*; (*learn*) узнава́ть (-наю́, -наёшь) *impf.*, узна́ть *pf.*; ~ **out** выслу́шивать *impf.*, вы́слушать *pf.* **hearing** *n.* слух; (*limit*) преде́л слы́шимости; (*leg.*) слу́шание, разбо́р. **hearsay** *n.* слух.

hearken ['hɑːkən] *v.i.* внима́ть *impf.*, внять (*past only:* вня́л, -а́, -о) *pf.* (**to** +d.).

hearse [hɜːs] *n.* катафа́лк.

heart [hɑːt] *n.* (*organ*; *fig.*) се́рдце (*pl.* -дца́, -де́ц, -дца́м); (*fig.*) душа́ (*a.* -шу; *pl.* -ши); (*courage*) му́жество; (*of tree etc.*) сердцеви́на; (*essence*) суть; *pl.* (*cards*) че́рви (-ве́й) *pl.*; **at ~** в глубине́ души́; **by ~** наизу́сть; ~ **attack** серде́чный при́ступ. **heartburn** *n.* изжо́га. **hearten** *v.t.* ободря́ть *impf.*, ободри́ть *pf.* **heartfelt** *adj.* и́скренний (-нен, -нна, -нно & -нне), серде́чный. **heartless**

adj. бессерде́чный. **heart-rending** *adj.* душераздира́ющий. **hearty** *adj.* (*cordial*) серде́чный; (*vigorous*) здоро́вый.

hearth [hɑːθ] *n.* оча́г (-á).

heat [hiːt] *n.* жар (*loc.* -е & -ý), жа́ра; (*phys.*) теплота́; (*of feeling*) пыл (*loc.* -ý); (*sport*) забе́г, зае́зд; *v.t. & i.* нагрева́ть(ся) *impf.*, нагре́ть(ся) *pf.*; *v.t.* топи́ть (-плю́, -пишь) *impf.* **heater** *n.* нагрева́тель *m.* **heating** *n.* отопле́ние.

heath [hiːθ] *n.* пу́стошь.

heathen ['hiːð(ə)n] *n.* язы́чник; *adj.* язы́ческий.

heather ['heðə(r)] *n.* ве́реск.

heave [hiːv] *v.t.* (*lift*) поднима́ть *impf.*, подня́ть (подниму́, -мешь; по́дня́л, -á, -о) *pf.*; (*pull*) тяну́ть (-ну́, -нешь) *impf.*, по~ *pf.*

heaven ['hev(ə)n] *n.* не́бо, рай (*loc.* раю́); *pl.* небеса́ *nt.pl.* **heavenly** *adj.* небе́сный, боже́ственный.

heaviness ['hevɪnɪs] *n.* тя́жесть. **heavy** *adj.* тяжёлый (-л, -ла́); (*strong*) си́льный (си́лён, -льна́, -льно, си́льны́); (*abundant*) оби́льный; (*gloomy*) мра́чный (-чен, -чна́, -чно); (*sea*) бу́рный (-рен, бу́рна́, -рно). **heavyweight** *n.* тяжелове́с.

Hebrew ['hiːbruː] *n.* древнееврейский язык (-á); *adj.* (древне)евре́йский.

heckle ['hek(ə)l] *v.t.* перека́ться *impf.* с+*i.*

hectare ['hekteə(r), -tɑː(r)] *n.* гекта́р.

hectic ['hektɪk] *adj.* лихора́дочный.

hedge [hedʒ] *n.* (*fence*) жива́я и́згородь; (*barrier*) прегра́да; *v.t.* огора́живать *impf.*, огороди́ть (-ожу́, -о́ди́шь) *pf.*; *v.i.* верте́ться (-рчу́сь, -ртишься) *impf.* **hedgerow** *n.* шпале́ра. **hedge-sparrow** *n.* лесна́я завиру́шка.

hedgehog ['hedʒhɒg] *n.* ёж (-á).

heed [hiːd] *n.* внима́ние; *v.t.* обраща́ть *impf.*, обрати́ть (-ащу́, -ати́шь) *pf.* внима́ние на+*a.* **heedful** *adj.* внима́тельный. **heedless** *adj.* небре́жный.

heel [hiːl] *n.* (*of foot*) пята́ (*pl.* -ты, -т, -та́м); (*of foot, sock*) пя́тка; (*of shoe*) каблу́к (-á).

hefty ['heftɪ] *adj.* дю́жий (дюж, -á, -о).

hegemony [hɪ'dʒeməpɪ, -'geməpɪ] *n.* гегемо́ния.

heifer ['hefə(r)] *n.* тёлка.

height [haɪt] *n.* высота́ (*pl.* -ты), вышина́ (*no pl.*); (*elevation*) возвы́шенность. **heighten** *v.t.* повыша́ть *impf.*, повы́сить *pf.*; (*strengthen*) уси́ливать *impf.*, уси́лить *pf.*

heinous ['heɪnəs, 'hiːnəs] *adj.* гну́сный (-сен, -сна́, -сно).

heir [eə(r)] *n.* насле́дник. **heiress** *n.* насле́дница. **heirloom** ['eəluːm] *n.* фами́льная вещь (*pl.* -щи, -ще́й).

helicopter ['helɪkɒptə(r)] *n.* вертолёт.

heliograph ['hiːlɪəgrɑːf] *n.* гелио́граф. **heliotrope** ['hiːlɪətrəʊp, 'hel-] *n.* гелиотро́п.

helium ['hiːlɪəm] *n.* ге́лий.

helix ['hiːlɪks] *n.* спира́ль.

hell [hel] *n.* ад (*loc.* -ý). **hellish** *adj.* а́дский.

hello, hallo [hə'ləʊ] *int.* приве́т!; (*telephone*) алло́!

helm [helm] *n.* руль (-ля́) *m.*, корми́ло (правле́ния). **helmsman** *n.* рулево́й *sb.*; (*fig.*) ко́рмчий *sb.*

helmet ['helmɪt] *n.* шлем.

help [help] *n.* по́мощь; (*person*) помо́щник, -ица; *v.t.* помога́ть *impf.*, помо́чь (-огу́, -о́жешь; -о́г, -огла́) *pf.*+*d.*; (*with negative*) не мочь (могу́, мо́жешь; мог, -ла́) *impf.* не+*inf.*; ~ **o.s.** брать (беру́, -рёшь; брал, -á, -о) *impf.*, взять (возьму́, -мёшь; взял, -á, -о) *pf.* себе́. **helpful** *adj.* поле́зный. **helping** *n.* (*of food*) по́рция. **helpless** *adj.* беспо́мощный.

Helsinki ['helsɪŋkɪ, hel'sɪŋkɪ] *n.* Хе́льсинки *m.indecl.*

helter-skelter [‚heltə'skeltə(r)] *adv.* как попа́ло.

hem [hem] *n.* рубе́ц (-бца́), кайма́ (*g.pl.* каём); *v.t.* подруба́ть *impf.*, подруби́ть (-блю́, -бишь) *pf.*; ~ **about, in** окружа́ть *impf.*, окружи́ть *pf.*

hemisphere ['hemɪsfɪə(r)] *n.* полуша́рие.

hemlock ['hemlɒk] *n.* болиголо́в.

hemp [hemp] *n.* (*plant*) конопля́; (*fibre*) пенька́. **hempen** *adj.* конопля́ный; пенько́вый.

hen [hen] *n.* (*female bird*) са́мка; (*domestic fowl*) ку́рица (*pl.* ку́ры, кур). **henbane** *n.* белена́. **hen-coop** *n.* куря́тник. **henpecked** *adj.*: **be** ~ быть у жены́ под башмако́м, под каблуко́м.

hence [hens] *adv.* (*from here*) отсю́да; (*from this time*) с э́тих пор; (*as a result*) сле́довательно. **hence'forth, hence'forward** *adv.* отны́не.

henchman ['hentʃmən] *n.* приве́рженец (-нца).

henna ['henə] *n.* хна.

her [hɜː(r), hə(r)] *poss. pron.* её; свой (-оя́, -оё; -оя́).

herald ['her(ə)ld] *n.* геро́льд, предве́стник; *v.t.* возвеща́ть *impf.*, возвести́ть *pf.*

herb [hɜːb] *n.* трава́ (*pl.* -вы). **herbaceous** [hɜː'beɪʃəs] *adj.* травяни́стый. **herbal** *adj.* травяно́й. **herbivorous** [‚hɜː'bɪvərəs] *adj.* травоя́дный.

herd [hɜːd] *n.* ста́до (*pl.* -да́); (*of people*) толпа́ (*pl.* -пы); *v.i.* ходи́ть (-ит) *impf.* ста́дом; (*people*) толпи́ться, с~ *pf.*; *v.t.* собира́ть *impf.*, собра́ть (соберу́, -рёшь; собра́л, -á, -о) *pf.* в ста́до. **herdsman** *n.* пасту́х (-á).

here [hɪə(r)] *adv.* (*position*) здесь, тут; (*direction*) сюда́; ~ **is** ~ вот (+*nom.*); ~ **and there** там и сям. **herea'bout(s)** *adv.* побли́зости. **here'after** *adv.* в бу́дущем. **here'by** *adv.* э́тим; таки́м о́бразом. **here-u'pon** *adv.* (*in consequence*) вследствие э́того; (*after*) по́сле э́того. **here'with** *adv.* при сём, при э́том, че́рез э́то.

hereditary [hɪ'redɪtərɪ] *adj.* насле́дственный. **heredity** [hɪ'redɪtɪ] *n.* насле́дственность.

heresy ['herəsɪ] *n.* е́ресь. **heretic** *n.* ерети́к (-á). **he'retical** *adj.* ерети́ческий.

heritable ['herɪtəb(ə)l] *adj.* насле́дуемый.

heritage ['herɪtɪdʒ] *n.* насле́дство, насле́дие.

hermaphrodite [hɜːˈmæfrəˌdaɪt] *n.* гермафроди́т.

hermetic [hɜːˈmetɪk] *adj.* гермети́ческий.

hermit ['hɜːmɪt] *n.* отше́льник, пусты́нник. **hermitage** *n.* пу́стынь; прию́т (отше́льника, пусты́нника).

hernia ['hɜːnɪə] *n.* гры́жа.

hero ['hɪərəu] *n.* геро́й. **heroic** [hɪˈrəuɪk] *adj.* геро́йческий. **heroine** ['herəuɪn] *n.* геро́йня. **heroism** ['herəuˌɪz(ə)m] *n.* геро́йзм.

heron ['herən] *n.* ца́пля (*g.pl.* -пель).

herpes ['hɜːpiːz] *n.* лиша́й (-ая́).

herring ['herɪŋ] *n.* сельдь (*pl.* -ди, -де́й), селё́дка. **herring-bone** *n.* ёлочка; (*attr.*) ёлочкой, в ёлочку.

hers [hɜːz] *poss. pron.* её; свой (-оя́, -оё, -ой).

herself [hɜˈself] *pron.* (*emph.*) (она́) сама́ (-мо́й, *a.* -му́); (*refl.*) себя́ (себе́, собо́й); -ся (*suffixed to v.t.*)

hertz [hɜːts] *n.* герц (*g.pl.* -ц).

hesitant ['hezɪt(ə)nt] *adj.* нереши́тельный.

hesitate *v.i.* колеба́ться (-блюсь, -блешься) *impf.,* по~ *pf.;* (*in speech*) запина́ться *impf.,* запну́ться *pf.* **hesi'tation** *n.* колеба́ние, нереши́тельность.

hessian ['hesɪən] *n.* мешкови́на.

heterogeneous [ˌhetərəuˈdʒiːnɪəs] *adj.* разноро́дный. **heterosexual** *n.* гетеросексуали́ст, ~ка; *adj.* гетеросексуа́льный.

hew [hjuː] *v.t.* руби́ть (-блю́, -бишь) *impf*

hexa- [heksə] *in comb.* шести..., ге́кса... . **hexagon** ['heksəgən] *n.* шестиуго́льник. **hexameter** [hekˈsæmɪtə(r)] *n.* гекза́метр.

hey [heɪ] *int.* эй!

heyday ['heɪdeɪ] *n.* расцве́т.

hi [haɪ] *int.* эй!; приве́т!

hiatus [haɪˈeɪtəs] *n.* пробе́л; (*ling.*) зия́ние.

hibernate ['haɪbəˌneɪt] *v.i.* находи́ться (-ожу́сь, -о́дишься) *impf.* в зи́мней спя́чке; зимова́ть *impf.,* пере~, про~ *pf.* **hiber'nation** *n.* зи́мняя спя́чка, зимо́вка.

hiccough, hiccup ['hɪkʌp] *v.i.* ика́ть *impf.,* икну́ть *pf.; n.: pl.* ико́та.

hide[1] [haɪd] *n.* (*animal's skin*) шку́ра, ко́жа.

hide[2] [haɪd] *v.t. & i.* (*conceal*) пря́тать(ся) (-я́чу(сь), -я́чешь(ся)) *impf.,* с~ *pf.;* скрыва́ть(ся) *impf.,* скрыть(ся) (скро́ю(сь), -о́ешь(ся)) *pf.*

hideous ['hɪdɪəs] *adj.* отврати́тельный, безобра́зный.

hiding ['haɪdɪŋ] *n.* (*flogging*) по́рка.

hierarchy ['haɪəˌrɑːkɪ] *n.* иера́рхия.

hieroglyph ['haɪərəɡlɪf] *n.* иеро́глиф. **hiero'glyphic** *adj.* иероглифи́ческий.

higgledy-piggledy [ˌhɪɡəldɪˈpɪɡəldɪ] *adv.* как придётся.

high [haɪ] *adj.* высо́кий (-о́к, -ока́, -о́ко); (*elevated*) возвы́шенный; (*higher*) вы́сший; (*intense*) си́льный (си́лён, -льна́, -льно, си́льны); **~er education** вы́сшее образова́ние; **~ fidelity** высо́кая то́чность воспроизведе́ния; **~ jump** прыжо́к (-жка́) в

высоту́. **high-class** *adj.* высокока́чественный. **high-handed** *adj.* повели́тельный. **highland(s)** *n.* го́рная страна́. **highly** *adv.* в вы́сшей сте́пени. **highly-strung** *adj.* чувстви́тельный, не́рвный (-вен, нервна́, -вно). **high-minded** *adj.* благоро́дный. **highness** *n.* возвы́шенность; (*title*) высо́чество. **high-pitched** *adj.* высо́кий (-о́к, -ока́, -о́ко). **highway** *n.* больша́я доро́га, шоссе́ *nt.indecl.* **highwayman** *n.* разбо́йник (с большо́й доро́ги)

hijack ['haɪdʒæk] *v.t.* похища́ть *impf.,* похи́тить (-и́щу, -и́тишь) *pf.* **hijacker** *n.* похити́тель *m.*

hike [haɪk] *n.* похо́д.

hilarious [hɪˈleərɪəs] *adj.* весёлый (ве́сел, -о, весела́). **hilarity** [hɪˈlærɪtɪ] *n.* весе́лье.

hill [hɪl] *n.* холм (-а́). **hillock** *n.* хо́лмик. **hilly** *adj.* холми́стый.

hilt [hɪlt] *n.* рукоя́тка.

Himalayas [ˌhɪməˈleɪəz] *n.* Гимала́и (-ев) *pl.*

himself [hɪmˈself] *pron.* (*emph.*) (он) сам (-ого́, -ому́, -и́м, -о́м); (*refl.*) себя́ (себе́, собо́й); -ся (*suffixed to v.t.*).

hind[1] [haɪnd] *n.* (*deer*) са́мка (благоро́дного) оле́ня.

hind[2] [haɪnd] *adj.* (*rear*) за́дний. **hindmost** *adj.* са́мый за́дний.

hinder ['hɪndə(r)] *v.t.* меша́ть *impf.,* по~ *pf.+d.* **hindrance** *n.* поме́ха, препя́тствие.

Hindu ['hɪnduː, -'duː] *n.* инду́с; *adj.* инду́сский.

hinge [hɪndʒ] *n.* шарни́р, пе́тля (*g.pl.* -тель); *v.t.* прикрепля́ть *impf.,* прикрепи́ть *pf.* на пе́тлях; *v.i.* враща́ться *impf.* на пе́тлях; **~ on** (*fig.*) зави́сеть (-сит) *impf.* от+*g.*

hint [hɪnt] *n.* намёк; *v.i.* намека́ть *impf.,* намекну́ть *pf.* (**at** на+*a.*)

hinterland ['hɪntəˌlænd] *n.* глубина́ страны́.

hip[1] [hɪp] *n.* (*anat.*) бедро́ (*pl.* бёдра, -дер, -драм).

hip[2] [hɪp] *n.* (*fruit*) я́года шипо́вника.

hippopotamus [ˌhɪpəˈpɒtəməs] *n.* гиппопота́м.

hire ['haɪə(r)] *n.* наём (на́йма), прока́т; *v.t.* нанима́ть *impf.,* наня́ть (найму́, -мёшь; на́нял, -а́, -о) *pf.;* брать (беру́, -рёшь; брал, -а́, -о) *impf.,* взять (возьму́, -мёшь; взял, -а́, -о) *pf.* напрока́т; **~ out** отдава́ть (-даю́, -даёшь) *impf.,* отда́ть (-а́м, -а́шь, -а́ст, -ади́м; о́тдал, -а́, -о) *pf.* внаймы́, напрока́т.

hireling ['haɪəlɪŋ] *n.* наёмник.

hire-purchase [ˌhaɪəˈpɜːtʃɪs] *n.* поку́пка в рассро́чку.

hirsute ['hɜːsjuːt] *adj.* волоса́тый.

his [hɪz] *poss. pron.* его́; свой (-оя́, -оё; -ой).

hiss [hɪs] *n.* шипе́ние, свист; *v.i.* шипе́ть (-плю́, -пи́шь) *impf.;* свисте́ть (-ищу́, -исти́шь) *impf.; v.t.* освисты́вать *impf.,* освиста́ть (-ищу́, -и́щешь) *pf.*

historian [hɪˈstɔːrɪən] *n.* исто́рик. **historic(al)** [hɪˈstɒrɪk(ə)l] *adj.* истори́ческий. **history** ['hɪstərɪ] *n.* исто́рия.

histrionic [ˌhɪstrɪˈɒnɪk] *adj.* театра́льный.

hit [hɪt] *n.* (*blow*) уда́р; (*on target*) попада́ние (в цель); (*success*) успе́х; *v.t.* (*strike*) уда́рять *impf.*, уда́рить *pf.*; (*target*) попада́ть *impf.*, попа́сть (-аду́, -аде́шь; -а́л) *pf.* (в цель); ~ (up)on находи́ть (-ожу́, -о́дишь) *impf.*, найти́ (найду́, -де́шь; нашёл, -шла́) *pf.*

hitch [hɪtʃ] *n.* (*jerk*) толчо́к (-чка́); (*knot*) у́зел (узла́); (*stoppage*) заде́ржка; *v.t.* (*move*) подта́лкивать *impf.*, подтолкну́ть *pf.*; (*fasten*) зацепля́ть *impf.*, зацепи́ть (-плю́, -пишь) *pf.*; привя́зывать *impf.*, привяза́ть (-яжу́, -я́жешь) *pf.*; ~ up подтя́гивать *impf.*, подтяну́ть (-ну́, -нешь) *pf.* **hitch-hike** *v.i.* голосова́ть *impf.* **hitchhiker** *n.* автостопо́вец (-вца).

hither [ˈhɪðə(r)] *adv.* сюда́. **hither'to** *adv.* до сих пор.

HIV *abbr.* (*of human immunodeficiency virus*) ВИЧ, (*ви́рус иммунодефици́та челове́ка*). **HIV-positive** *adj.* инфици́рованный ВИЧ.

hive [haɪv] *n.* у́лей (у́лья).

hoard [hɔːd] *n.* запа́с; *v.t.* накопля́ть *impf.*, накопи́ть (-плю́, -пишь) *pf.*

hoarding [ˈhɔːdɪŋ] *n.* рекла́мный щит (-а́).

hoar-frost [hɔː(r)] *n.* и́ней.

hoarse [hɔːs] *adj.* хри́плый (-л, -ла́, -ло).

hoary [ˈhɔːrɪ] *adj.* седо́й (сед, -а́, -о).

hoax [həʊks] *n.* мистифика́ция; *v.t.* мистифици́ровать *impf.* & *pf.*

hobble [ˈhɒb(ə)l] *n.* (*for horse*) (ко́нские) пу́ты (-т) *pl.*; *v.i.* прихра́мывать *impf.*; *v.t.* (*horse*) трено́жить *impf.*, с~ *pf.*

hobby [ˈhɒbɪ] *n.* конёк (-нька́), хо́бби *nt.indecl.*

hobnail [ˈhɒbneɪl] *n.* сапо́жный гвоздь (-дя́; *pl.* -ди, -де́й) *m.*

hob-nob [ˈhɒbnɒb] *v.i.* пить (пью, пьёшь) *impf.* вме́сте; ~ with якша́ться *impf.* c+i.

hock [hɒk] *n.* (*wine*) рейнве́йн (-a(y)).

hockey [ˈhɒkɪ] *n.* травяно́й хокке́й; **ice** ~ хокке́й (с ша́йбой); ~ **stick** клю́шка.

hod [hɒd] *n.* (*for bricks*) лото́к (-тка́); (*for coal*) ведёрко (*pl.* -рки, -рок, -ркам).

hoe [həʊ] *n.* моты́га; *v.t.* моты́жить *impf.*

hog [hɒg] *n.* бо́ров (*pl.* -ы, -о́в), свинья́ (*pl.* -ньи, -не́й, -ньям).

hoist [hɔɪst] *n.* подъёмник; *v.t.* поднима́ть *impf.*, подня́ть (-ниму́, -ни́мешь; по́днял, -а́, -о) *pf.*

hold¹ [həʊld] *n.* (*naut.*) трюм.

hold² [həʊld] *n.* (*grasp*) хва́тка; (*influence*) влия́ние (**on** на+a.); *v.t.* (*grasp*) держа́ть (-жу́, -жишь) *impf.*; (*contain*) вмеща́ть *impf.*, вмести́ть *pf.*; (*possess*) владе́ть *impf.*+i.; (*conduct*) проводи́ть (-ожу́, -о́дишь) *impf.*, провести́ (-еду́, -еде́шь; -ёл, -ела́) *pf.*; (*consider*) счита́ть *impf.*, счесть (сочту́, -тёшь; счёл, сочла́) *pf.* (+a. & i., за+a.); *v.i.* держа́ться (-жу́сь, -жишься) *impf.*; (*continue*) продолжа́ться *impf.*, продо́лжиться *pf.*; ~ **back** сде́рживать(ся) *impf.*, сдержа́ть(ся) (-жу́(сь), -жишь(ся)) *pf.*; ~ **forth**

разглаго́льствовать *impf.*; ~ **out** (*stretch out*) протя́гивать *impf.*, протяну́ть (-ну́, -нешь) *pf.*; (*resist*) не сдава́ться (сдаю́сь, сдаёшься) *impf.*; ~ **over** (*postpone*) откла́дывать *impf.*, отложи́ть (-жу́, -жишь) *pf.*; ~ **up** (*support*) подде́рживать *impf.*, поддержа́ть (-жу́, -жишь) *pf.*; (*display*) выставля́ть *impf.*, вы́ставить *pf.*; (*impede*) заде́рживать *impf.*, задержа́ть (-жу́, -жишь) *pf.* **holdall** *n.* портпле́д. **hold-up** *n.* (*robbery*) налёт; (*delay*) заде́ржка.

hole [həʊl] *n.* дыра́ (*pl.* -ры), я́ма, отве́рстие; (*animal's*) нора́ (*pl.* -ры); **full of** ~**s** дыря́вый; **pick** ~**s in** придира́ться *impf.*, придра́ться (придеру́сь, -рёшься; придра́лся, -ала́сь, -а́ло́сь) *pf.* к+d.; *v.t.* (*make a* ~ *in*) продыря́вливать *impf.*, продыря́вить *pf.*

holiday [ˈhɒlɪˌdeɪ, -dɪ] *n.* (*festival*) пра́здник; (*from work*) о́тпуск; *pl.* кани́кулы (-л) *pl.*; **on** ~ в о́тпуске, -ку́.

holiness [ˈhəʊlɪnɪs] *n.* свя́тость; (**H**~, *title*) святе́йшество.

Holland [ˈhɒlənd] *n.* Голла́ндия.

hollow [ˈhɒləʊ] *n.* впа́дина; (*valley*) лощи́на; (*in tree*) дупло́ (*pl.* -пла, -пел, -плам); *adj.* пусто́й (пуст, -а́, -о, пу́сты́), по́лый; (*sunken*) впа́лый; (*sound*) глухо́й (глух, -а́, -о); *v.t.* (~ *out*) выда́лбливать *impf.*, вы́долбить *pf.*

holly [ˈhɒlɪ] *n.* остроли́ст.

holm [həʊm], **-oak** *n.* ка́менный дуб (*loc.* -е & -у́; *pl.* -ы́).

holocaust [ˈhɒləˌkɔːst] *n.* (*sacrifice*) всесожже́ние; (*destruction*) уничтоже́ние (в огне́).

holster [ˈhəʊlstə(r)] *n.* кобура́.

holy [ˈhəʊlɪ] *adj.* свято́й (свят, -а́, -о), свяще́нный (-е́н, -е́нна); **H**~ **Week** Страстна́я неде́ля.

homage [ˈhɒmɪdʒ] *n.* почте́ние, уваже́ние; **do, pay,** ~ **to** отдава́ть (-даю́, -даёшь) *impf.*, отда́ть (-а́м, -а́шь, -а́ст, -ади́м; о́тдал, -а́, -о) *pf.* до́лжное+d.

home [həʊm] *n.* дом (-a(y); *pl.* -а́); (*native land*) ро́дина; **at** ~ до́ма; **feel at** ~ чу́вствовать *impf.* себя́ как до́ма; *adj.* дома́шний, родно́й; ~ **economics** домово́дство; **H**~ **Affairs** вну́тренние дела́ *nt.pl.*; *adv.* (*direction*) домо́й; (*position*) до́ма; (*as aimed*) в цель. **homeland** *n.* ро́дина. **homeless** *adj.* бездо́мный. **home-made** *adj.* дома́шний, самоде́льный. **homesick** *adj.*: **to be** ~ тоскова́ть *impf.* по ро́дине. **homewards** *adv.* домо́й, восвоя́си.

homely [ˈhəʊmlɪ] *adj.* просто́й (прост, -а́, -о, про́сты́).

homoeopath [ˈhəʊmɪəʊˌpæθ, ˈhɒmɪ-] *n.* гомеопа́т. **homoeo'pathic** *adj.* гомеопати́ческий. **homoeopathy** [ˌhəʊmɪˈɒpəθɪ, ˌhɒmɪ-] *n.* гомеопа́тия.

homicide [ˈhɒmɪˌsaɪd] *n.* (*person*) уби́йца *c.g.*; (*action*) уби́йство.

homily [ˈhɒmɪlɪ] *n.* про́поведь, поуче́ние.

homogeneous [ˌhəʊməʊ'dʒiːnɪəs, ˌhɒməʊ-] *adj.* однородный.

homonym ['hɒmənɪm] *n.* омоним.

homosexual [ˌhəʊməʊ'seksjuəl, ˌhɒm-] *n.* гомосексуалист; *adj.* гомосексуальный.

hone [həʊn] *n.* точильный камень (-мня; *pl.* -мни, -мней) *m.*; *v.t.* точить (-чу, -чишь) *impf.*, на~ *pf.*

honest ['ɒnɪst] *n.* (*fair*) честный (-тен, -тна, -тно); (*righteous*) правдивый; (*sincere*) искренний (-нен, -нна, -нне & -нно). **honesty** *n.* честность; правдивость; искренность.

honey ['hʌnɪ] *n.* мёд (-а(у), *loc.* -ý & -е; *pl.* -ы́). **honeycomb** *n.* медовые соты (-тов) *pl.*; *attr.* сотовый, сотовидный. **honeymoon** *n.* медовый месяц; *v.i.* проводить (-ожý, -одишь) *impf.*, провести (-едý, -едёшь; -ёл, -ела) *pf.* медовый месяц. **honeysuckle** *n.* жимолость.

honk [hɒŋk] *v.i.* гоготать (-очý, -очешь) *impf.*; (*siren etc.*) гудеть (-дит) *impf.*

honorarium [ˌɒnə'reərɪəm] *n.* гонорар.

honorary ['ɒnərərɪ] *adj.* почётный.

honour ['ɒnə(r)] *n.* честь, почёт; *pl.* почести *f.pl.*; (**up)on** my ~ честное слово; *v.t.* (*respect*) почитать *impf.*; (*confer*) удостаивать *impf.*, удостоить *pf.* (**with** +*g.*). **honourable** *adj.* честный (-тен, -тна, -тно); (*respected*) почтенный (-нен, -нна).

hood [hʊd] *n.* капюшон.

hoodlum ['huːdləm] *n.* громила *m.*

hoodwink ['hʊdwɪŋk] *v.t.* втирать *impf.*, втереть (вотрý, -рёшь; втёр) *pf.* очки+*d.*

hoof [huːf] *n.* копыто.

hook [hʊk] *n.* крюк (-á, *loc.* -é & -ý), крючок (-чка); (*trap*) ловушка; (*cutting instrument*) серп (-á); *v.t.* зацеплять *impf.*, зацепить (-плю, -пишь) *pf.*; (*catch*) ловить (-влю, -вишь), поймать *pf.*

hookah ['hʊkə] *n.* кальян.

hooligan ['huːlɪgən] *n.* хулиган.

hoop [huːp] *n.* обруч (*pl.* -и, -ей).

hoot [huːt] *v.i.* кричать (-чý, -чишь) *impf.*, крикнуть *pf.*; (*owl*) ухать *impf.*, ухнуть *pf.*; (*horn*) гудеть (-дит) *impf.*

hoover ['huːvə(r)] *n.* (*propr.*) пылесос; *v.t.* пылесосить (-сю, -сишь) *impf.*, про~ *pf.*

hop¹ [hɒp] *n.* (*plant; collect. hops*) хмель (-ля(-лю)) *m.*

hop² [hɒp] *n.* (*jump*) прыжок (-жка); *v.i.* прыгать *impf.*, прыгнуть *pf.* (на одной ноге).

hope [həʊp] *n.* надежда; *v.i.* надеяться (-еюсь, -еешься) *impf.*, по~ *pf.* (**for** на+*a.*). **hopeful** *adj.* (*hoping*) надеющийся; (*promising*) многообещающий. **hopeless** *adj.* безнадёжный.

hopper ['hɒpə(r)] *n.* бункер (*pl.* -á & -ы); (*rail.*) хоппер.

horde [hɔːd] *n.* (*hist., fig.*) орда (*pl.* -ды).

horizon [hə'raɪz(ə)n] *n.* горизонт; (*fig.*) кругозор. **horizontal** [ˌhɒrɪ'zɒnt(ə)l] *n.* горизонталь; *adj.* горизонтальный.

hormone ['hɔːməʊn] *n.* гормон.

horn [hɔːn] *n.* рог (*pl.* -á); (*mus.*) рожок (-жка); (*motor* ~) гудок (-дка); *attr.* роговой. **horn-beam** *n.* граб. **horned** *adj.* рогатый.

hornet ['hɔːnɪt] *n.* шершень (-шня) *m.*

horny ['hɔːnɪ] *adj.* роговой; (*calloused*) мозолистый.

horoscope ['hɒrəˌskəʊp] *n.* гороскоп; **cast a** ~ составлять *impf.*, составить *pf.* гороскоп.

horrible ['hɒrɪb(ə)l] *adj.* ужасный, страшный (-шен, -шна, -шно, страшны). **horrid** *adj.* ужасный, противный. **horrify** *v.t.* ужасать *impf.*, ужаснуть *pf.* **horror** *n.* ужас, отвращение.

hors-d'oeuvre [ɔː'dɜːvr, -'dɜːv] *n.* закуска (*usu. in pl.*).

horse [hɔːs] *n.* лошадь (*pl.* -ди, -дей, *i.* -дьми), конь (-ня; *pl.* -ни, -ней) *m.*; (*collect., cavalry*) конница; *attr.* лошадиный, конский. **horse-chestnut** *n.* конский каштан. **horseflesh** *n.* конина. **horse-fly** *n.* слепень (-пня) *m.* **horsehair** *n.* конский волос. **horseman, -woman** *n.* всадник, -ица. **horseplay** *n.* возня. **horsepower** *n.* лошадиная сила. **horse-radish** *n.* хрен (-а(у)). **horseshoe** *n.* подкова. **horsewhip** *n.* хлыст (-á); *v.t.* хлестать (-ещý, -ещешь) *impf.*, хлестнуть *pf.*

horticulture ['hɔːtɪˌkʌltʃə(r)] *n.* садоводство.

hose [həʊz] *n.* (*stockings*) чулки (*g.* -лок) *pl.*; (~*pipe*) шланг, рукав (-á; *pl.* -á).

hosier ['həʊzɪə(r), 'həʊʒə(r)] *n.* торговец (-вца) трикотажными изделиями. **hosiery** *n.* чулочные изделия *nt.pl.*, трикотаж.

hospitable ['hɒspɪtəb(ə)l, hɒ'spɪt-] *adj.* гостеприимный.

hospital ['hɒspɪt(ə)l] *n.* больница; (*military* ~) госпиталь (*pl.* -ли, -лей) *m.*

hospitality [ˌhɒspɪ'tælɪtɪ] *n.* гостеприимство.

host¹ [həʊst] *n.* (*multitude*) множество; (*army*) войско (*pl.* -ка).

host² [həʊst] *n.* (*landlord etc.*) хозяин (*pl.* -яева, -яев).

host³ [həʊst] *n.* (*eccl.*) облатка.

hostage ['hɒstɪdʒ] *n.* заложник, -ица.

hostel ['hɒst(ə)l] *n.* (*students'*) общежитие; (*tourists'*) турбаза.

hostelry ['hɒstəlrɪ] *n.* постоялый двор (-á).

hostess ['həʊstɪs] *n.* хозяйка; (*air* ~) бортпроводница.

hostile ['hɒstaɪl] *adj.* враждебный. **hostility** [hɒ'stɪlɪtɪ] *n.* враждебность; *pl.* военные действия *nt.pl.*

hot [hɒt] *adj.* горячий (-ч, -чá), жаркий (-рок, -ркá, -рко); (*pungent*) острый (остр & остёр, остра, остро); (*fresh*) свежий (свеж, -á, -ó, свежи); ~ **air** бахвальство. **hotbed** *n.* парник (-á); (*fig.*) рассадник. **hot-blooded** *adj.* пылкий (-лок, -лка, -лко). **hotel** [həʊ'tel] *n.* гостиница, отель *m.* **hotfoot** ['hɒtfʊt] *adv.* поспешно. **hotheaded** *adj.* вспыльчивый. **hothouse** *n.* теплица. **hotplate** *n.* плитка. **hot-water:** ~ **bottle** грелка.

hound [haʊnd] *n.* го́нчая *sb.*; *v.t.* трави́ть (-влю́, -вишь) *impf.*, за~ *pf.*; ~ **on** подстрека́ть *impf.*, подстрекну́ть *pf.*

hour [aʊə(r)] *n.* (*period, specific time*) час (-á with 2,3,4, *loc.* -ý; *pl.* -ы́); (*time in general*) вре́мя *nt.* **hourly** *adj.* ежеча́сный.

house [haʊs] *n.* дом (-a(y); *pl.* -á); (*parl.*) пала́та; (*theatre*) теа́тр; (*audience*) пу́блика; (*performance*) сеа́нс; (*dynasty*) дом (-á), дина́стия; *attr.* дома́шний; *v.t.* помеща́ть *impf.*, помести́ть *pf.*; (*provide houses for*) обеспе́чивать *impf.*, обеспе́чить *pf.* жильём. **housebreaker** *n.* взло́мщик. **household** *n.* (*people*) дома́шние *sb.*; (*establishment*) дома́шнее хозя́йство. **house-keeper** *n.* эконо́мка. **housemaid** *n.* го́рничная *sb.* **house-warming** *n.* новосе́лье. **housewife** *n.* хозя́йка. **housework** *n.* дома́шняя рабо́та.

housing *n.* (*accommodation*) жильё; (*provision of ~*) жили́щное строи́тельство; (*casing*) кожу́х (-á); ~ **estate** жило́й масси́в.

hovel ['hɒv(ə)l] *n.* лачу́га.

hover ['hɒvə(r)] *v.i.* (*bird*) пари́ть *impf.*; (*helicopter*) висе́ть (-си́т) *impf.*; (*hesitate*) колеба́ться (-блюсь, -блешься) *impf.* **hovercraft** *n.* су́дно (*pl.* -дá, -до́в) на возду́шной поду́шке, СВП.

how [haʊ] *adv.* как, каки́м о́бразом; ~ **do you do?** здра́вствуйте!; ~ **many,** ~ **much** ско́лько (+*g.*). **how'ever** *adv.* как бы ни (+*past*); *conj.* одна́ко, тем не ме́нее; ~ **much** ско́лько бы ни (+*g. & past*).

howitzer ['haʊitsə(r)] *n.* гау́бица.

howl [haʊl] *n.* вой, рёв; *v.i.* выть (во́ю, во́ешь) *impf.*; реве́ть (-ву́, -вёшь) *impf.* **howler** ['haʊlə(r)] *n.* (*mistake*) грубе́йшая оши́бка.

h.p. *abbr.* (*of* **horsepower**) л.с., лошади́ная си́ла.

HQ *abbr.* (*of* **headquarters**) штаб, ста́вка.

hub [hʌb] *n.* (*of wheel*) ступи́ца; (*fig.*) центр (внима́ния); ~ **of the universe** пуп (-á) земли́.

hubbub ['hʌbʌb] *n.* шум (-a(y)), гам (-a(y)).

huddle ['hʌd(ə)l] *n.* (*heap*) ку́ча; (*confusion*) сумато́ха; *v.t.* (*heap together*) сва́ливать *impf.*, свали́ть (-лю́, -лишь) *pf.* в ку́чу; *v.i.* ~ **together** съёживаться *impf.*, съёжиться *pf.*

hue [hju:] *n.* (*tint*) отте́нок (-нка).

huff [hʌf] *n.* припа́док (-дка) раздраже́ния; *v.t. & i.* обижа́ть(ся) *impf.*, оби́деть(ся)· (-и́жу(сь), -и́дишь(ся)) *pf.*

hug [hʌg] *n.* объя́тие; (*wrestling*) хва́тка; *v.t.* (*embrace*) обнима́ть *impf.*, обня́ть (обниму́, -мешь; о́бнял, -á, -о) *pf.*; (*keep close to*) держа́ться (-жу́сь, -жишься) *impf.*+*g.*

huge [hju:dʒ] *adj.* огро́мный.

hulk [hʌlk] *n.* ко́рпус (*pl.* -á) (корабля́). **hulking** *adj.* (*bulky*) грома́дный; (*clumsy*) неуклю́жий.

hull[1] [hʌl] *n.* (*of pea etc.*) стручо́к (-чка́); (*of grain*) шелуха́; *v.t.* лущи́ть *impf.*, об~ *pf.*

hull[2] [hʌl] *n.* (*of ship*) ко́рпус (*pl.* -á); (*of*

aeroplane) фюзеля́ж.

hum [hʌm] *n.* жужжа́ние, гуде́ние; *v.i.* жужжа́ть (-жу́, -жи́шь) *impf.*; гуде́ть (гужу́, гуди́шь) *impf.*; *v.t.* напева́ть *impf.*; *int.* гм!

human ['hju:mən] *adj.* челове́ческий, людско́й; *n.* челове́к. **humane** [hju:'mein] *adj.* челове́чный, гума́нный (-нен, -нна). **humanism** *n.* гумани́зм. **humanist** *n.* гумани́ст. **humanity** [hju:'mæniti] *n.* (*human race*) челове́чество; (*humaneness*) гума́нность; **the Humanities** гуманита́рные нау́ки *f.pl.*

humble ['hʌmb(ə)l] *adj.* смире́нный (-ён, -е́нна), скро́мный (-мен, -мна́, -мно); *v.t.* унижа́ть *impf.*, уни́зить *pf.*

humdrum ['hʌmdrʌm] *adj.* (*banal*) бана́льный; (*dull*) ску́чный (-чен, -чна́, -чно).

humid ['hju:mid] *adj.* вла́жный (-жен, -жна́, -жно). **hu'midity** *n.* вла́жность.

humiliate [hju:'milieit] *v.t.* унижа́ть *impf.*, уни́зить *pf.* **humili'ation** *n.* униже́ние. **humility** [hju:'militi] *n.* смире́ние.

humming-bird ['hʌmiŋ] *n.* коли́бри *c.g. indecl.*

hummock ['hʌmək] *n.* (*hillock*) буго́р (-грá); (*in ice*) (ледяно́й) то́рос.

humorist ['hju:mərist] *n.* юмори́ст. **humorous** *adj.* юмористи́ческий. **humour** *n.* ю́мор; (*mood*) настрое́ние; **out of** ~ не в ду́хе; *v.t.* потака́ть *impf.*+*d.*

hump [hʌmp] *n.* горб (-á, *loc.* -ý); (*of earth*) буго́р (-грá); *v.t.* го́рбить *impf.*, с~ *pf.* **humpback** *n.* горб (-á, *loc.* -ý); (*person*) горбу́н (-á), ~ья. **humpbacked** *adj.* горба́тый.

humus ['hju:məs] *n.* перегно́й.

hunch [hʌntʃ] *n.* (*hump*) горб (-á), *loc.* -ý); (*thick piece*) ломо́ть (-мтя́) *m.*; (*suspicion*) подозре́ние; *v.t.* го́рбить *impf.*, с~ *pf.* **hunchback** *n.* горб (-á), *loc.* -ý); (*person*) горбу́н (-á), ~ья. **hunchbacked** *adj.* горба́тый.

hundred ['hʌndrəd] *adj. & n.* сто (*in oblique cases* ста); (*collect.*) со́тня (*g.pl.* -тен); (*age*) сто лет; **two** ~ две́сти (двухсо́т, двумста́м, двумяста́ми, двухста́х); **three** ~ три́ста (трёхсо́т, трёмста́м, тремяста́ми, трёхста́х); **four** ~ четы́реста (-рёхсо́т, -рёмста́м, -рьмяста́ми, -рёхста́х); **five** ~ пятьсо́т (пятисо́т, пятиста́м, пятьюста́ми, пятиста́х). **hundredfold** *adj.* стокра́тный; *adv.* в сто раз. **hundredth** *adj. & n.* со́тый; (*fraction*) со́тая (часть (*pl.* -ти, -те́й)).

Hungarian [hʌŋ'geəriən] *n.* венгр, венге́рка; *adj.* венге́рский. **Hungary** ['hʌŋgəri] *n.* Ве́нгрия.

hunger ['hʌŋgə(r)] *n.* го́лод; (*fig.*) жа́жда (**for** +*g.*); ~ **strike** голодо́вка; *v.i.* голода́ть *impf.*; ~ **for** жа́ждать (-ду, -дешь) *impf.*+*g.* **hungry** *adj.* голо́дный (го́лоден, -дна́, -дно, го́лодны́).

hunk [hʌŋk] *n.* ломо́ть (-мтя́) *m.*

hunt [hʌnt] *n.* охо́та; (*fig.*) по́иски *m.pl.* (**for** +*g.*); *v.t.* охо́титься *impf.* на+*a.*, за+*i.*; трави́ть (-влю́, -вишь) *impf.*, за~ *pf.*; ~

down выследить *pf.*; ~ **out** отыскать (-ыщу, -ыщешь) *pf.* **hunter** *n.* охотник. **hunting** *n.* охота; *attr.* охотничий (-чья, -чье). **huntsman** *n.* охотник, егерь (*pl.* -ря) *m.*

hurdle ['hɜ:d(ə)l] *n.* (*fence*) плетень (-тня) *m.*; (*sport*) барьер; (*fig.*) препятствие. **hurdler** *n.* барьерист. **hurdles, hurdling** *n.* (*sport*) барьерный бег.

hurl [hɜ:l] *v.t.* швырять *impf.*, швырнуть *pf.*

hurly-burly ['hɜ:lɪ,bɜ:lɪ] *n.* суматоха.

hurrah [hʊ'rɑ:], **hurray** [hʊ'reɪ] *int.* ура!

hurricane ['hʌrɪkən, -,keɪn] *n.* ураган.

hurried ['hʌrɪd] *adj.* торопливый. **hurry** *n.* спешка, торопливость; **in a** ~ второпях; *v.t. & i.* торопить(ся) (-плю(сь), -пишь(ся)) *impf.*, по~ *pf.*; *v.i.* спешить *impf.*, по~ *pf.*

hurt [hɜ:t] *n.* вред (-á), ущерб, повреждение; *v.i.* болеть (-лит) *impf.*; *v.t.* повреждать *impf.*, повредить *pf.*; ~ **the feelings of** задевать *impf.*, задеть (-ену, -енешь) *pf.*+*a.*

hurtle ['hɜ:t(ə)l] *v.i.* (*move swiftly*) нестись (несусь, -сёшься; нёсся, -слась) *impf.*, по~ *pf.*

husband ['hʌzbənd] *n.* муж (*pl.* -ья, -ей, -ьям); *v.t.* экономить *impf.*, с~ *pf.*

hush [hʌʃ] *n.* тишина, молчание; *v.t.* успокаивать *impf.*, успокоить *pf.*; *int.* тише!; тсс!

husk [hʌsk] *n.* шелуха; *v.t.* шелушить *impf.*

husky[1] ['hʌskɪ] *adj.* (*voice*) хриплый (хрипл, -á, -о).

husky[2] ['hʌskɪ] *n.* (*dog*) эскимосская лайка.

hussar [hʊ'zɑ:(r)] *n.* гусар (*g.pl.* -p *as collect.*) & -ров.

hustle ['hʌs(ə)l] *n.* толкотня; *v.t. & i.* (*push*) толкать(ся) *impf.*, толкнуть(ся) *pf.*; (*hurry*) торопить(ся) (-плю(сь), -пишь(ся)) *impf.*, по~ *pf.*

hut [hʌt] *n.* хижина, барак.

hutch [hʌtʃ] *n.* клетка.

hyacinth ['haɪəsɪnθ] *n.* гиацинт.

hybrid ['haɪbrɪd] *n.* гибрид; *adj.* гибридный.

hydra ['haɪdrə] *n.* гидра.

hydrangea [haɪ'dreɪndʒə] *n.* гортензия.

hydrant ['haɪdrənt] *n.* гидрант.

hydrate ['haɪdreɪt] *n.* гидрат.

hydraulic [haɪ'drɔ:lɪk, -'drɒlɪk] *adj.* гидравлический; ~ **engineering** гидротехника. **hydraulics** *n.* гидравлика.

hydro- ['haɪdrəʊ] *in comb.* гидро... . **hydro'carbon** *n.* углеводород. **hydro'chloric acid** *n.* соляная кислота. **hydrody'namics** *n.* гидродинамика. **hydroe'lectric** *adj.* гидроэлектрический; ~ **plant** гидроэлектростанция, ГЭС *f.indecl.* **hydrofoil** *n.* подводное крыло (*pl.* -лья, -льев); (*vessel*) судно (*pl.* -да, -дов), корабль (-ля) *m.*, на подводных крыльях, СПК, КПК.

hydrogen ['haɪdrədʒ(ə)n] *n.* водород; ~ **bomb** водородная бомба. **hydrolysis** [haɪ'drɒlɪsɪs] *n.* гидролиз. **hydro'phobia** *n.* водобоязнь. **hydroplane** *n.* (*fin*) горизонтальный руль (-ля) *m.*; (*motor boat*) глиссер; (*seaplane*)

гидросамолёт. **hydroxide** [haɪ'drɒksaɪd] *n.* гидроокись.

hyena [haɪ'i:nə] *n.* гиена.

hygiene ['haɪdʒi:n] *n.* гигиена. **hy'gienic** *adj.* гигиенический.

hymn [hɪm] *n.* гимн.

hyperbola [haɪ'pɜ:bələ] *n.* гипербола. **hyperbolic** [,haɪpə'bɒlɪk] *adj.* гиперболический. **hyperbole** [haɪ'pɜ:bəlɪ] *n.* гипербола. **hyperbolical** [,haɪpə'bɒlɪk(ə)l] *adj.* гиперболический.

hypercritical [,haɪpə'krɪtɪk(ə)l] *adj.* придирчивый.

hypersensitive [,haɪpə'sensɪtɪv] *adj.* сверхчувствительный.

hyphen ['haɪf(ə)n] *n.* дефис. **hyphen(ate)** *v.t.* писать (пишу, -шешь) *impf.*, на~ *pf.* через дефис.

hypnosis [hɪp'nəʊsɪs] *n.* гипноз. **hypnotic** [hɪp'nɒtɪk] *adj.* гипнотический; (*soporific*) снотворный. **'hypnotism** *n.* гипнотизм. **'hypnotist** *n.* гипнотизёр. **'hypnotize** *v.t.* гипнотизировать *impf.*, за~ *pf.*

hypocrisy [hɪ'pɒkrɪsɪ] *n.* лицемерие. **hypocrite** ['hɪpəkrɪt] *n.* лицемер. **hypo'critical** *adj.* лицемерный.

hypodermic [,haɪpə'dɜ:mɪk] *adj.* подкожный. **hypotenuse** [haɪ'pɒtə,nju:z] *n.* гипотенуза. **hypothesis** [haɪ'pɒθɪsɪs] *n.* гипотеза, предположение. **hypothesize** *v.i.* строить *impf.*, по~ *pf.* гипотезу; делать *impf.*, с~ *pf.* предположение. **hypo'thetical** *adj.* гипотетический; предположительный.

hysteria [hɪ'stɪərɪə] *n.* истерия. **hysterical** [hɪ'sterɪk(ə)l] *adj.* истеричный, истерический. **hysterics** *n.* истерика, истерический припадок (-дка).

I

I [aɪ] *pron.* я (меня, мне, мной & мною, обо мне).

iambic [aɪ'æmbɪk] *adj.* ямбический. **iambus** *n.* ямб.

ibid. ['ɪbɪ,dem] *abbr.* (*of ibidem*) там же.

ice [aɪs] *n.* лёд (льда(у), *loc.* льду); (~ *cream*) мороженое *sb.*; ~ **age** ледниковый период; ~ **floe** плавучая льдина; ~ **hockey** хоккей (с шайбой); *v.t.* замораживать *impf.*, заморозить *pf.*; (*cul.*) глазировать *impf.* & *pf.*; *v.i.*: ~ **over, up** обледеневать *impf.*, обледенеть *pf.* **ice-axe** *n.* ледоруб. **iceberg** *n.* айсберг. **ice-boat** *n.* буер (*pl.* -á). **ice-breaker** *n.* ледокол. **ice-cream** *n.* мороженое *sb.*; ~ **parlour** кафе-мороженое *nt.indecl.* **icicle** *n.* сосу́лька. **icing** *n.* (*cul.*) глазу́рь.

icon ['aɪkɒn] *n.* ико́на.

icy ['aɪsɪ] *adj.* ледяно́й; (*also fig.*) холо́дный (хо́лоден, -дна́, -дно, хо́лодны).

ID *abbr.* (*of* **identification**) удостове́рение ли́чности.

idea [aɪ'dɪə] *n.* иде́я, мысль; (*conception*) поня́тие; (*intention*) наме́рение.

ideal [aɪ'diːəl] *n.* идеа́л; *adj.* идеа́льный. **idealism** *n.* идеали́зм. **idealist** *n.* идеали́ст. **idealize** *v.t.* идеализи́ровать *impf. & pf.*

identical [aɪ'dentɪk(ə)l] *adj.* (*of one thing*) тот же са́мый; (*of different things*) тожде́ственный (-ен, -енна), одина́ковый. **identifi'cation** *n.* отождествле́ние; (*recognition*) опозна́ние; (*of person*) установле́ние ли́чности. **identify** *v.t.* отождествля́ть *impf.*, отождестви́ть *pf.*; (*recognize*) опознава́ть (-наю́, -наёшь) *impf.*, опозна́ть *pf.* **identity** *n.* (*sameness*) тожде́ственность; (*of person*) ли́чность; (*math.*) то́ждество; ~ **card** удостове́рение ли́чности.

ideogram ['ɪdɪəˌgræm], **ideograph** ['ɪdɪəˌgrɑːf] *n.* идеогра́мма.

ideological [ˌaɪdɪə'lɒdʒɪk(ə)l] *adj.* идеологи́ческий. **ide'ologist**, **'ideologue** *n.* идео́лог. **ide'ology** *n.* идеоло́гия.

idiocy ['ɪdɪəsɪ] *n.* идиоти́зм.

idiom ['ɪdɪəm] *n.* (*expression*) идио́ма; (*language*) язы́к (-а́), го́вор. **idio'matic** *adj.* идиомати́ческий.

idiosyncrasy [ˌɪdɪəʊ'sɪŋkrəsɪ] *n.* склад ума́, идиосинкрази́я.

idiot ['ɪdɪət] *n.* идио́т. **idiotic** [ɪdɪ'ɒtɪk] *adj.* идио́тский.

idle ['aɪd(ə)l] *adj.* (*vain*) тще́тный; (*useless*) бесполе́зный; (*unoccupied*) неза́нятый; (*lazy*) лени́вый; (*machine*) холосто́й (хо́лост, -á, -о); *v.i.* безде́льничать *impf.*; (*engine*) рабо́тать *impf.* вхолосту́ю; *v.t.*: ~ **away** пра́здно проводи́ть (-ожу́, -о́дишь) *impf.*, провести́ (-еду́, -еде́шь; -ёл, -ела́) *pf.* **idleness** *n.* тще́тность; беспо́лезность; пра́здность, безде́лье. **idler** *n.* безде́льник, -ица.

idol ['aɪd(ə)l] *n.* и́дол, куми́р. **idolater** [aɪ'dɒlətə(r)], **-tress** *n.* идолопокло́нник, -ица. **idolatrous** [aɪ'dɒlətrəs] *adj.* идолопокло́ннический. **idolatry** *n.* идолопокло́нство; (*fig.*) обожа́ние. **idolize** *v.t.* боготвори́ть· *impf.*

idyll ['ɪdɪl] *n.* иди́ллия. **i'dyllic** *adj.* идилли́ческий.

i.e. *abbr.* (*of* **id est**) т.е., то есть.

if [ɪf] *conj.* (*conditions*) е́сли, е́сли бы; (*whether*) ли; **as** ~ как бу́дто; **even** ~ да́же е́сли; ~ **only** е́сли бы то́лько.

igloo ['ɪgluː] *n.* и́глу *nt.indecl.*

igneous ['ɪgnɪəs] *adj.* о́гненный, огнево́й; (*rock*) вулкани́ческий. **ignite** [ɪg'naɪt] *v.t.* зажига́ть *impf.*, заже́чь (-жгу́, -жжёшь; -жёг, -жгла́) *pf.*; *v.i.* загора́ться *impf.*, заго-

ре́ться (-рю́сь, -ри́шься) *pf.* **ignition** [ɪg'nɪʃ(ə)n] *n.* зажига́ние.

ignoble [ɪg'nəʊb(ə)l] *adj.* ни́зкий (-зок, -зка́, -зко).

ignominious [ˌɪgnə'mɪnɪəs] *adj.* позо́рный. **'ignominy** *n.* позо́р.

ignoramus [ˌɪgnə'reɪməs] *n.* неве́жда *m.* **ig'norance** ['ɪgnərəns] *n.* неве́жество, неве́дение. **'ignorant** *adj.* неве́жественный (-ен, -енна); (*uninformed*) несве́дущий (**of** в+*p.*).

ignore [ɪg'nɔː(r)] *v.t.* не обраща́ть *impf.* внима́ния на+*a.*; игнори́ровать *impf. & pf.*

ill [ɪl] *n.* (*evil*) зло; (*harm*) вред (-á); *pl.* (*misfortunes*) несча́стья (-тий) *pl.*; *adj.* (*sick*) больно́й (-лен, -льна́); (*evil*) дурно́й (дурён, -рна́, -рно, ду́рны), злой (зол, зла); *adv.* пло́хо, ду́рно; (*scarcely*) едва́ ли; **fall** ~ заболева́ть *impf.*, заболе́ть *pf.* **ill-advised** *adj.* неблагоразу́мный. **ill-bred** *adj.* невоспи́танный (-ан, -анна). **ill-disposed** *adj.* недоброжела́тельный (**towards** к+*d.*).

illegal [ɪ'liːg(ə)l] *adj.* незако́нный (-нен, -нна), нелега́льный. **illegality** [ˌɪliː'gælɪtɪ] *n.* незако́нность, нелега́льность.

illegible [ɪ'ledʒɪb(ə)l] *adj.* неразбо́рчивый.

illegitimacy [ˌɪlɪ'dʒɪtɪməsɪ] *n.* незако́нность; (*of child*) незаконнорождённость. **illegitimate** *adj.* незако́нный (-нен, -нна); незаконнорождённый (-ён, -ённа).

illiberal [ɪ'lɪbər(ə)l] *adj.* непросвещённый; (*bigoted*) нетерпи́мый; (*stingy*) скупо́й (скуп, -á, -о).

illicit [ɪ'lɪsɪt] *adj.* незако́нный (-нен, -нна), недозво́ленный (-ен, -енна).

illiteracy [ɪ'lɪtərəsɪ] *n.* негра́мотность. **illiterate** *adj.* негра́мотный.

ill-mannered [ɪl'mænəd] *adj.* неве́жливый. **ill-natured** *adj.* зло́бный.

illness ['ɪlnɪs] *n.* боле́знь.

illogical [ɪ'lɒdʒɪk(ə)l] *adj.* нелоги́чный.

ill-tempered [ɪl'tempəd] *adj.* раздражи́тельный. **ill-treat** *v.t.* пло́хо обраща́ться *impf.* с+*i.*

illuminate [ɪ'luːmɪˌneɪt, ɪ'ljuː-] *v.t.* освеща́ть *impf.*, освети́ть (-ещу́, -ети́шь) *pf.*; (*building*) иллюмини́ровать *impf. & pf.*; (*manuscript*) украша́ть *impf.*, укра́сить *pf.* **illumi'nation** *n.* освеще́ние; (*also pl.*) иллюмина́ция; украше́ние (ру́кописи).

illusion [ɪ'luːʒ(ə)n, ɪ'ljuː-] *n.* иллю́зия. **illusory** *adj.* обма́нчивый, иллюзо́рный.

illustrate ['ɪləˌstreɪt] *v.t.* иллюстри́ровать *impf. & pf.*, про~ *pf.* **illu'stration** *n.* иллюстра́ция. **illustrative** *adj.* иллюстрати́вный.

illustrious [ɪ'lʌstrɪəs] *adj.* знамени́тый.

image ['ɪmɪdʒ] *n.* (*statue etc.*) изображе́ние; (*optical* ~) отраже́ние; (*semblance*) подо́бие; (*literary* ~ *etc.*) о́браз. **imagery** *n.* о́бразность.

imaginable [ɪ'mædʒɪnəb(ə)l] *adj.* вообрази́мый. **imaginary** *adj.* вообража́емый, мни́мый. **imagi'nation** *n.* воображе́ние, фанта́-

зия. **imagine** *v.t.* воображáть *impf.*, вообразить *pf.*; (*conceive*) представлять *impf.*, представить *pf.* себé.

imbecile ['ɪmbɪˌsiːl] *n.* слабоýмный *sb.*; (*fool*) глупéц (-пцá); *adj.* слабоýмный.

imbibe [ɪm'baɪb] *v.t.* (*absorb*) впитывать *impf.*, впитáть *pf.*

imbroglio [ɪm'brəʊlɪəʊ] *n.* пýтаница.

imbue [ɪm'bjuː] *v.t.* пропитывать *impf.*, пропитáть *pf.* (**with** +*i.*); внушáть *impf.*, внушить *pf.*+*d.* (**with** +*a.*).

imitate ['ɪmɪˌteɪt] *v.t.* подражáть *impf.*+*d.* **imi'tation** *n.* подражáние (**of** +*d.*), имитáция; *attr.* (*counterfeit*) поддéльный; (*artificial*) искýсственный (-ен(ен), -енна). **imitative** *adj.* подражáтельный.

immaculate [ɪ'mækjʊlət] *adj.* незапятнанный (-ан, -анна); (*irreproachable*) безупрéчный.

immanent ['ɪmənənt] *adj.* присýщий (**in** +*d.*), имманéнтный.

immaterial [ˌɪmə'tɪərɪəl] *adj.* невещéственный (-ен(ен), -енна); (*unimportant*) несущéственный (-ен(ен), -енна).

immature [ˌɪmə'tjʊə(r)] *adj.* незрéлый.

immeasurable [ɪ'meʒərəb(ə)l] *adj.* неизмеримый.

immediate [ɪ'miːdɪət] *adj.* (*direct*) непосрéдственный (-ен, -енна); (*swift*) немéдленный (-ен, -ена). **immediately** *adv.* тóтчас, немéдленно; непосрéдственно.

immemorial [ˌɪmɪ'mɔːrɪəl] *adj.* незапáмятный.

immense [ɪ'mens] *adj.* необъятный, огрóмный.

immerse [ɪ'mɜːs] *v.t.* погружáть *impf.*, погрузить *pf.* **immersion** *n.* погружéние.

immigrant ['ɪmɪgrənt] *n.* иммигрáнт, ~ка. **immigrate** *v.i.* иммигрировать *impf.* & *pf.* **immi'gration** *n.* иммигрáция.

imminent ['ɪmɪnənt] *adj.* близкий (-зок, -зкá, -зко, близки); (*danger*) грозящий.

immobile [ɪ'məʊbaɪl] *adj.* неподвижный. **immobility** [ˌɪməʊ'bɪlɪtɪ] *n.* неподвижность.

immoderate [ɪ'mɒdərət] *adj.* неумéренный (-ен, -енна).

immodest [ɪ'mɒdɪst] *adj.* нескрóмный (-мен, -мнá, -мно).

immolate ['ɪməˌleɪt] *v.t.* приносить (-ошý, -óсишь) *impf.*, принести (-есý, -есёшь; -ёс, -еслá) *pf.* в жéртву; жéртвовать *impf.*, по~ *pf.*+*i.*

immoral [ɪ'mɒr(ə)l] *adj.* безнрáвственный (-ен(ен), -енна). **immorality** [ˌɪmə'rælɪtɪ] *n.* безнрáвственность.

immortal [ɪ'mɔːt(ə)l] *adj.* бессмéртный. **immortality** [ˌɪmɔː'tælɪtɪ] *n.* бессмéртие. **immortalize** *v.t.* обессмéртить *pf.*

immovable [ɪ'muːvəb(ə)l] *adj.* неподвижный, недвижимый; (*steadfast*) непоколебимый.

immune [ɪ'mjuːn] *adj.* (*to illness*) невосприимчивый (**to** к+*d.*); (*free from*) свобóдный (**from** от+*g.*). **immunity** *n.* невосприимчивость (**to** к+*d.*), иммунитéт; освобождéние (**from** от+*g.*); (*diplomatic etc.*) неприкосновéнность.

immure [ɪ'mjʊə(r)] *v.t.* заточáть *impf.*, заточить *pf.*

immutable [ɪ'mjuːtəb(ə)l] *adj.* неизмéнный (-нен, -нна).

imp [ɪmp] *n.* бесёнок (-нка; *pl.* -нята, -нят).

impact ['ɪmpækt] *n.* (*striking*) удáр; (*collision*) столкновéние; (*influence*) влияние.

impair [ɪm'peə(r)] *v.t.* (*damage*) повреждáть *impf.*, повредить *pf.*; (*weaken*) ослаблять *impf.*, ослáбить *pf.*

impale [ɪm'peɪl] *v.t.* прокáлывать *impf.*, проколóть (-лю, -лешь) *pf.*; (*as torture etc.*) сажáть *impf.*, посадить (-ажý, -áдишь) *pf.* нá кол.

impalpable [ɪm'pælpəb(ə)l] *adj.* неосязáемый.

impart [ɪm'pɑːt] *v.t.* делиться (-люсь, -лишься) *impf.*, по~ *pf.*+*i.* (**to** с+*i.*).

impartial [ɪm'pɑːʃ(ə)l] *adj.* беспристрáстный.

impassable [ɪm'pɑːsəb(ə)l] *adj.* непроходимый, непроéзжий.

impasse ['æmpɑːs, 'ɪm-] *n.* тупик (-á).

impassioned [ɪm'pæʃ(ə)nd] *adj.* стрáстный (-тен, -тнá, -тно).

impassive [ɪm'pæsɪv] *adj.* бесстрáстный.

impatience [ɪm'peɪʃəns] *n.* нетерпéние. **impatient** *adj.* нетерпеливый.

impeach [ɪm'piːtʃ] *v.t.* обвинять *impf.*, обвинить *pf.* (**of, with** в+*p.*).

impeccable [ɪm'pekəb(ə)l] *adj.* безупрéчный.

impecunious [ˌɪmpɪ'kjuːnɪəs] *adj.* безденéжный.

impedance [ɪm'piːd(ə)ns] *n.* пóлное сопротивлéние. **impede** *v.t.* препятствовать *impf.*, вос~ *pf.*+*d.*; задéрживать *impf.*, задержáть (-жý, -жишь) *pf.* **impediment** [ɪm'pedɪmənt] *n.* препятствие, задéржка; (*in speech*) заикáние.

impel [ɪm'pel] *v.t.* побуждáть *impf.*, побудить *pf.* (**to** +*inf.*, к+*d.*).

impend [ɪm'pend] *v.i.* нависáть *impf.*, нависнуть *pf.*

impenetrable [ɪm'penɪtrəb(ə)l] *adj.* непроницáемый.

imperative [ɪm'perətɪv] *adj.* (*imperious*) повелительный; (*obligatory*) необходимый; *n.* (*gram.*) повелительное наклонéние.

imperceptible [ˌɪmpə'septɪb(ə)l] *adj.* незамéтный.

imperfect [ɪm'pɜːfɪkt] *n.* имперфéкт; *adj.* (*incomplete*) несовершéнный (-нен, -нна), непóлный (-лон, -лнá, -лно); (*faulty*) дефéктный. **imper'fection** *n.* несовершéнство; (*fault*) недостáток (-тка). **imper'fective** *adj.* (*n.*) несовершéнный (вид).

imperial [ɪm'pɪərɪəl] *adj.* (*of empire*) импéрский; (*of emperor*) императорский. **imperialism** *n.* империализм. **imperialist** *n.* империалист; *attr.* империалистический.

imperil [ɪm'perɪl] *v.t.* подвергáть *impf.*, подвéргнуть (-г) *pf.* опáсности.

imperious [ɪm'pɪərɪəs] *adj.* влáстный.

imperishable [ɪm'perɪʃəb(ə)l] *adj.* вéчный; (*food*) непóртящийся.

impersonal [ɪmˈpɜːsən(ə)l] *adj.* безли́чный.

impersonate [ɪmˈpɜːsəˌneɪt] *v.t.* (*personify*) олицетворя́ть *impf.*, олицетвори́ть *pf.*; (*play part*) исполня́ть *impf.*, испо́лнить *pf.* роль+*g.*; (*pretend to be*) выдава́ть (-даю́, -даёшь) *impf.*, вы́дать (-ам, -ашь, -аст, -адим) *pf.* себя́ за+*a.*

impertinence [ɪmˈpɜːtɪnəns] *n.* де́рзость. **impertinent** *adj.* де́рзкий (-зок, -зка́, -зко).

imperturbable [ˌɪmpəˈtɜːbəb(ə)l] *adj.* невозмути́мый.

impervious [ɪmˈpɜːvɪəs] *adj.* непроница́емый (**to** для+*g.*); (*not responsive*) глухо́й (глух, -а́, -о) (**to** к+*d.*).

impetuous [ɪmˈpetjʊəs] *adj.* стреми́тельный.

impetus [ˈɪmpɪtəs] *n.* дви́жущая си́ла; (*fig.*) и́мпульс.

impiety [ɪmˈpaɪətɪ] *n.* нечести́вость.

impinge [ɪmˈpɪndʒ] *v.i.* & *i.* (**up)on** (*strike*) ударя́ться *impf.*, уда́риться *pf.* о+*a.*; (*encroach*) покуша́ться *impf.*, покуси́ться *pf.* на+*a.*

impious [ˈɪmpɪəs] *adj.* нечести́вый.

impish [ˈɪmpɪʃ] *adj.* прока́зливый.

implacable [ɪmˈplækəb(ə)l] *adj.* неумоли́мый.

implant [ɪmˈplɑːnt] *v.t.* насажда́ть *impf.*, насади́ть *pf.*

implement[1] [ˈɪmplɪmənt] *n.* (*tool*) ору́дие, инструме́нт; *pl.* принадле́жности *f.pl.*

implement[2] [ˈɪmplɪˌment] *v.t.* (*fulfil*) выполня́ть *impf.*, вы́полнить *pf.*

implicate [ˈɪmplɪˌkeɪt] *v.t.* впу́тывать *impf.*, впу́тать *pf.* **impli'cation** *n.* вовлече́ние; (*meaning*) смысл.

implicit [ɪmˈplɪsɪt] *adj.* подразумева́емый; (*absolute*) безогово́рочный.

implore [ɪmˈplɔː(r)] *v.t.* умоля́ть *impf.*

imply [ɪmˈplaɪ] *v.t.* подразумева́ть *impf.*

impolite [ˌɪmpəˈlaɪt] *adj.* неве́жливый.

imponderable [ɪmˈpɒndərəb(ə)l] *adj.* невесо́мый.

import [ˈɪmpɔːt; ɪmˈpɔːt, ˈɪm-] *n.* (*meaning*) значе́ние; (*of goods*) и́мпорт, ввоз; *v.t.* импорти́ровать *impf.* & *pf.*; ввози́ть (-ожу́, -о́зишь) *impf.*, ввезти́ (ввезу́, -зёшь; ввёз, -ла́) *pf.*

importance [ɪmˈpɔːt(ə)ns] *n.* ва́жность. **important** *adj.* ва́жный (-жен, -жна́, -жно, -жны́), значи́тельный.

importunate [ɪmˈpɔːtjʊnət] *adj.* назо́йливый.

impose [ɪmˈpəʊz] *v.t.* (*tax*) облага́ть *impf.*, обложи́ть (-жу́, -жишь) *pf.*+*i.* (**on** +*a.*); (*obligation*) налага́ть *impf.*, наложи́ть (-жу́, -жишь) *pf.* (**on** на+*a.*); (*force* (*o.s.*) *on*) навя́зывать(ся) *impf.*, навяза́ть(ся) (-яжу́(сь), -я́жешь(ся)) *pf.* (**on** +*d.*). **imposing** *adj.* внуши́тельный. **impo'sition** *n.* обложе́ние, наложе́ние.

impossibility [ɪmˌpɒsɪˈbɪlɪtɪ] *n.* невозмо́жность. **im'possible** *adj.* невозмо́жный.

impostor [ɪmˈpɒstə(r)] *n.* самозва́нец (-нца). **imposture** *n.* самозва́нство, обма́н.

impotence [ˈɪmpət(ə)ns] *n.* бесси́лие; (*med.*)

импоте́нция. **impotent** *adj.* бесси́льный; (*med.*) импоте́нтный.

impound [ɪmˈpaʊnd] *v.t.* (*cattle*) загоня́ть *impf.*, загна́ть (загоню́, -нишь; загна́л, -а́, -о) *pf.*; (*confiscate*) конфискова́ть *impf.* & *pf.*

impoverish [ɪmˈpɒvərɪʃ] *v.t.* обедня́ть *impf.*, обедни́ть *pf.*

impracticable [ɪmˈpræktɪkəb(ə)l] *adj.* невыполни́мый.

imprecation [ˌɪmprɪˈkeɪʃ(ə)n] *n.* прокля́тие.

impregnable [ɪmˈpregnəb(ə)l] *adj.* непристу́пный.

impregnate [ˈɪmpregˌneɪt] *v.t.* (*fertilize*) оплодотворя́ть *impf.*, оплодотвори́ть *pf.*; (*saturate*) пропи́тывать *impf.*, пропита́ть *pf.*

impresario [ˌɪmprɪˈsɑːrɪəʊ] *n.* импреса́рио *m.indecl.*, антрепренёр.

impress [ˈɪmpres; ɪmˈpres] *n.* отпеча́ток (-тка), печа́ть; *v.t.* (*imprint*) отпеча́тывать *impf.*, отпеча́тать *pf.*; (*affect person*) производи́ть (-ожу́, -о́дишь) *impf.*, произвести́ (-еду́, -едёшь; -ёл, -ела́) *pf.* (како́е-либо) впечатле́ние на+*a.* **im'pression** *n.* (*notion etc.*) впечатле́ние; (*printing*) о́ттиск; (*reprint*) (стереоти́пное) изда́ние; перепеча́тка.

impressionism [ɪmˈpreʃəˌnɪz(ə)m] *n.* импрессиони́зм.

impressive [ɪmˈpresɪv] *adj.* вырази́тельный; (*producing great effect*) порази́тельный.

imprint [ˈɪmprɪnt; ɪmˈprɪnt] *n.* отпеча́ток (-тка); *v.t.* отпеча́тывать *impf.*, отпеча́тать *pf.*; (*on memory etc.*) запечатлева́ть *impf.*, запечатле́ть *pf.*

imprison [ɪmˈprɪz(ə)n] *v.t.* заключа́ть *impf.*, заключи́ть *pf.* (в тюрьму́). **imprisonment** *n.* тюре́мное заключе́ние.

improbable [ɪmˈprɒbəb(ə)l] *adj.* невероя́тный, неправдоподо́бный.

impromptu [ɪmˈprɒmptjuː] *n.* экспро́мт; *adj.* импровизи́рованный (-ан, -ан(н)а); *adv.* без подгото́вки, экспро́мтом.

improper [ɪmˈprɒpə(r)] *adj.* (*inaccurate*) непра́вильный; (*indecent*) неприли́чный.

improve [ɪmˈpruːv] *v.t.* & *i.* улучша́ть(ся) *impf.*, улу́чшить(ся) *pf.* **improvement** *n.* улучше́ние, усовершенствова́ние.

improvidence [ɪmˈprɒvɪd(ə)ns] *n.* непредусмотри́тельность. **improvident** *adj.* непредусмотри́тельный.

improvisation [ˌɪmprəvaɪˈzeɪʃ(ə)n] *n.* импровиза́ция. **'improvise** *v.t.* импровизи́ровать *impf.*, сымпровизи́ровать *pf.*

imprudence [ɪmˈpruːd(ə)ns] *n.* неосторо́жность. **imprudent** *adj.* неосторо́жный.

impudence [ˈɪmpjʊd(ə)nt] *n.* на́глость. **impudent** *adj.* на́глый (нагл, -а́, -о).

impugn [ɪmˈpjuːn] *v.t.* оспа́ривать *impf.*, оспо́рить *pf.*

impulse [ˈɪmpʌls] *n.* (*push*) толчо́к (-чка́); (*impetus*) и́мпульс; (*sudden tendency*) поры́в. **im'pulsive** *adj.* импульси́вный.

impunity [ɪmˈpjuːnɪtɪ] *n.* безнака́занность;

with ~ безнака́занно.

impure [ɪmˈpjʊə(r)] *adj.* нечи́стый (-т, -та́, -то).

impute [ɪmˈpjuːt] *v.t.* припи́сывать *impf.*, приписа́ть (-ишу́, -и́шешь) *pf.* (**to** +*d.*); (*fault*) вменя́ть *impf.*, вмени́ть *pf.* в+*a.* (**to** +*d.*).

in [ɪn] *prep.* (*place*) в+*p.*, на+*p.*; (*into*) в+*a.*, на+*a.*; (*point in time*) в+*p.*, на+*p.*; ~ **the morning** (*etc.*) у́тром (*i.*); ~ **spring** (*etc.*) весно́й (*i.*); (*at some stage* ~; *throughout*) во вре́мя+*g.*; (*duration*) за+*a.*; (*after interval of*) че́рез+*a.*; (*during course of*) в тече́ние+*g.*; (*circumstance*) в+*p.*, при+*p.*; *adv.* (*place*) внутри́; (*motion*) внутрь; (*at home*) у себя́, до́ма; (~ *fashion*) в мо́де; ~ **here, there** (*place*) здесь, там; (*motion*) сюда́, туда́; *adj.* вну́тренний; (*fashionable*) мо́дный (-ден, -дна́, -дно); *n.*: **the** ~**s and outs** все закоу́лки *m.pl.*; дета́ли *f.pl.*

inability [ˌɪnəˈbɪlɪtɪ] *n.* неспосо́бность, невозмо́жность.

inaccessible [ˌɪnækˈsesɪb(ə)l] *adj.* недосту́пный.

inaccurate [ɪnˈækjʊrət] *adj.* нето́чный (-чен, -чна́, -чно).

inaction [ɪnˈækʃ(ə)n] *n.* безде́йствие. **inactive** *adj.* безде́ятельный. **inac'tivity** *n.* безде́ятельность.

inadequate [ɪnˈædɪkwət] *adj.* недоста́точный, неадеква́тный.

inadmissible [ˌɪnədˈmɪsɪb(ə)l] *adj.* недопусти́мый.

inadvertent [ˌɪnədˈvɜːt(ə)nt] *adj.* (*inattentive*) невнима́тельный; (*unintentional*) ненаме́ренный (-ен, -енна).

inalienable [ɪnˈeɪlɪənəb(ə)l] *adj.* неотъе́млемый, неотчужда́емый.

inane [ɪˈneɪn] *adj.* (*empty*) пусто́й (пуст, -а́, -о, пу́сты́); (*silly*) глу́пый (глуп, -а́, -о).

inanimate [ɪnˈænɪmət] *adj.* (*lifeless*) неодушевлённый (-ён, -ённа); (*dull*) безжи́зненный (-ен, -енна).

inapplicable [ɪnˈæplɪkəb(ə)l, ˌɪnəˈplɪk-] *adj.* неприменимый.

inapposite [ɪnˈæpəzɪt] *adj.* неуме́стный.

inappreciable [ˌɪnəˈpriːʃəb(ə)l] *adj.* незаме́тный.

inappropriate [ˌɪnəˈprəʊprɪət] *adj.* неуме́стный.

inapt [ɪnˈæpt] *adj.* (*unsuitable*) неподходя́щий; (*unskilful*) неиску́сный. **inaptitude** [ɪnˈæptɪˌtjuːd] *n.* неуме́стность; неспосо́бность.

inarticulate [ˌɪnɑːˈtɪkjʊlət] *adj.* (*not jointed*) нечленоразде́льный; (*indistinct*) невня́тный.

inasmuch [ˌɪnəzˈmʌtʃ] *adv.*: ~ **as** так как; ввиду́ того́, что.

inattention [ˌɪnəˈtenʃ(ə)n] *n.* невнима́ние. **inattentive** [ˌɪnəˈtentɪv] *adj.* невнима́тельный.

inaudible [ɪnˈɔːdɪb(ə)l] *adj.* несль́шный.

inaugural [ɪˈnɔːgjʊr(ə)l] *adj.* (*lecture etc.*) вступи́тельный. **inaugurate** *v.t.* (*admit*

to office) торже́ственно вводи́ть (-ожу́, -о́дишь) *impf.*, ввести́ (введу́, -дёшь; ввёл, -а́) *pf.* в до́лжность; (*open*) открыва́ть *impf.*, откры́ть (-ро́ю, -ро́ешь) *pf.*; (*begin*) начина́ть *impf.*, нача́ть (начну́, -нёшь; на́чал, -а́, -о) *pf.* **inaugu'ration** *n.* торже́ственное введе́ние, вступле́ние, в до́лжность; откры́тие.

inauspicious [ˌɪnɔːˈspɪʃəs] *adj.* неблагоприя́тный.

inborn [ˈɪnbɔːn], **inbred** [ɪnˈbred, ˈɪn-] *adj.* врождённый (-ён, -ена́), приро́дный.

incalculable [ɪnˈkælkjʊləb(ə)l] *adj.* неисчисли́мый.

incandesce [ˌɪnkænˈdes] *v.t. & i.* накаля́ть(ся) *impf.*, накали́ть(ся) *pf.* добела́. **incandescence** *n.* бе́лое кале́ние. **incandescent** *adj.* накалённый (-ён, -ена́) добела́.

incantation [ˌɪnkænˈteɪʃ(ə)n] *n.* заклина́ние.

incapability [ɪnˌkeɪpəˈbɪlɪtɪ] *n.* неспосо́бность. **in'capable** *adj.* неспосо́бный (**of** к+*d.*, на+*a.*).

incapacitate [ˌɪnkəˈpæsɪˌteɪt] *v.t.* де́лать *impf.*, с~ *pf.* неспосо́бным.

incapacity [ˌɪnkəˈpæsɪtɪ] *n.* неспосо́бность.

incarcerate [ɪnˈkɑːsəˌreɪt] *v.t.* заключа́ть *impf.*, заключи́ть *pf.* (в тюрьму́). **incarce'ration** *n.* заключе́ние (в тюрьму́).

incarnate [ɪnˈkɑːnət; ˈɪnkɑːˌneɪt, -ˈkɑːneɪt] *adj.* воплощённый (-ён, -ена́); *v.t.* воплоща́ть *impf.*, воплоти́ть (-ощу́, -оти́шь) *pf.* **incar'nation** *n.* воплоще́ние.

incautious [ɪnˈkɔːʃəs] *adj.* неосторо́жный.

incendiary [ɪnˈsendɪərɪ] *adj.* зажига́тельный; *n.* поджига́тель *m.*; (*fig.*) подстрека́тель *m.*; (*bomb*) зажига́тельная бо́мба.

incense[1] [ˈɪnsens] *n.* фимиа́м, ла́дан.

incense[2] [ɪnˈsens] *v.t.* (*enrage*) разъяря́ть *impf.*, разъяри́ть *pf.*

incentive [ɪnˈsentɪv] *n.* побужде́ние.

inception [ɪnˈsepʃ(ə)n] *n.* нача́ло.

incessant [ɪnˈses(ə)nt] *adj.* непреста́нный (-нен, -нна).

incest [ˈɪnsest] *n.* кровосмеще́ние.

inch [ɪntʃ] *n.* дюйм; ~ **by** ~ ма́ло-пома́лу.

incident *n.* слу́чай, инциде́нт. **incidental** [ˌɪnsɪˈdent(ə)l] *adj.* (*casual*) случа́йный; ~ **to** прису́щий+*d.* **inci'dentally** *adv.* случа́йно; (*by the way*) ме́жду про́чим.

incinerate [ɪnˈsɪnəˌreɪt] *v.t.* испепеля́ть *impf.*, испепели́ть *pf.* **incine'ration** *n.* испепеле́ние. **incinerator** *n.* мусоросжига́тельная печь (*pl.* -чи, -че́й).

incipient [ɪnˈsɪpɪənt] *adj.* начина́ющийся.

incise [ɪnˈsaɪz] *v.t.* надре́зывать, надреза́ть *impf.*, надре́зать (-е́жу, -е́зешь) *pf.* **incision** [ɪnˈsɪʒ(ə)n] *n.* надре́з (**in** на+*a.*). **incisive** [ɪnˈsaɪsɪv] *adj.* ре́жущий; (*fig.*) о́стрый (остр & остёр, остра́, о́стро́). **incisor** *n.* резе́ц (-зца́).

incite [ɪnˈsaɪt] *v.t.* побужда́ть *impf.*, побуди́ть *pf.* (**to** к+*d.*, +*inf.*); подстрека́ть *impf.*, подстрекну́ть *pf.* (**to** к+*d.*). **incitement** *n.*

подстрека́тельство.

incivility [ˌɪnsɪ'vɪlɪtɪ] n. невѐжливость.

inclement [ɪn'klemənt] adj. суро́вый.

inclination [ˌɪnklɪ'neɪʃ(ə)n] n. (slope) накло́н; (propensity) скло́нность (for, to к+d.).

incline ['ɪnklaɪn; ɪn'klaɪn] n. накло́н; v.t. & i. склоня́ть(ся) impf., склони́ть(ся) (-ню́(сь), -ни́шь(ся)) pf. **in'clined** adj. (disposed) скло́нный (-о́нен, -о́нна́, -о́нно) (to к+d.).

include [ɪn'kluːd] v.t. включа́ть impf., включи́ть pf. (in в+a.); заключа́ть impf., заключи́ть pf. в себе́. **including** prep. включа́я+a. **inclusion** n. включе́ние. **inclusive** adj. включа́ющий (в себе́); adv. включи́тельно.

incognito [ˌɪnkɒg'niːtəʊ] adv., n. инко́гнито adv., m. & nt.indecl.

incoherence [ˌɪnkəʊ'hɪərəns] n. бессвя́зность. **incoherent** adj. бессвя́зный.

incombustible [ˌɪnkəm'bʌstɪb(ə)l] adj. несгора́емый.

income ['ɪnkʌm, 'ɪnkəm] n. дохо́д; ~ tax подохо́дный нало́г.

incommensurable [ˌɪnkə'menʃərəb(ə)l, -sjərəb(ə)l] adj. несоизмери́мый. **incommensurate** adj. несоразме́рный.

incommode [ˌɪnkə'məʊd] v.t. беспоко́ить impf., o~ pf.

incommodious adj. неудо́бный.

incomparable [ɪn'kɒmpərəb(ə)l] adj. несравни́мый (to, with c+i.); (matchless) несравне́нный (-нен, -нна).

incompatible [ˌɪnkəm'pætɪb(ə)l] adj. несовмести́мый.

incompetence [ɪn'kɒmpɪt(ə)ns] n. неспосо́бность; (leg.) неправомо́чность. **incompetent** adj. неспосо́бный; (leg.) неправомо́чный.

incomplete [ˌɪnkəm'pliːt] adj. непо́лный (-лон, -лна́, -лно), незако́нченный (-ен, -енна).

incomprehensible [ɪnˌkɒmprɪ'hensɪb(ə)l] adj. непоня́тный.

inconceivable [ˌɪnkən'siːvəb(ə)l] adj. невообрази́мый.

inconclusive [ˌɪnkən'kluːsɪv] adj. неубеди́тельный.

incongruity ['ɪnkɒŋ'gruːɪtɪ] n. несоотве́тствие. **in'congruous** adj. несоотве́тственный (-ен, -енна) (with +d.); (out of place) неуме́стный.

inconsequent [ɪn'kɒnsɪkwənt] adj. непосле́довательный. **inconsequential** [ɪnˌkɒnsɪ'kwenʃ(ə)l, ɪnkɒn-] adj. незначи́тельный.

inconsiderable [ˌɪnkən'sɪdərəb(ə)l] adj. незначи́тельный.

inconsiderate [ˌɪnkən'sɪdərət] adj. (person) невнима́тельный; (action) необду́манный (-ан, -анна).

inconsistency [ˌɪnkən'sɪst(ə)nsɪ] n. непосле́довательность; (incompatibility) несовмести́мость. **inconsistent** adj. непосле́довательный; (incompatible) несовмести́мый.

inconsolable [ˌɪnkən'səʊləb(ə)l] adj. безуте́шный.

inconsonant [ɪn'kɒnsənənt] adj. несозву́чный

(with +d.).

inconspicuous [ˌɪnkən'spɪkjʊəs] adj. незаме́тный.

inconstant [ɪn'kɒnst(ə)nt] adj. непостоя́нный (-нен, -нна).

incontestable [ˌɪnkən'testəb(ə)l] adj. неоспори́мый.

incontinence [ɪn'kɒntɪnəns] n. невоздѐржанность; (med.) недержа́ние. **incontinent** adj. невоздѐржанный (-ан, -анна).

incontrovertible [ˌɪnkɒntrə'vɜːtɪb(ə)l] adj. неопровержи́мый.

inconvenience [ˌɪnkən'viːnɪəns] n. неудо́бство; v.t. причиня́ть impf., причини́ть pf. неудо́бство+d. **inconvenient** adj. неудо́бный.

incorporate [ɪn'kɔːpəˌreɪt] v.t. (include) включа́ть impf., включи́ть pf.; v.t. & i. (unite) объединя́ть(ся) impf., объедини́ть(ся) pf.; соединя́ть(ся) impf., соедини́ть(ся) pf.

incorporeal [ˌɪnkɔː'pɔːrɪəl] adj. бестеле́сный.

incorrect [ˌɪnkə'rekt] adj. непра́вильный.

incorrigible [ɪn'kɒrɪdʒɪb(ə)l] adj. неисправи́мый.

incorruptible [ˌɪnkə'rʌptɪb(ə)l] adj. неподку́пный; (not decaying) непо́ртящийся.

increase ['ɪnkriːs; ɪn'kriːs] n. рост, увеличе́ние; (in pay etc.) приба́вка; v.t. & i. увели́чивать(ся) impf., увели́чить(ся) pf.; (intensify) уси́ливать(ся) impf., уси́лить(ся) pf.

incredible [ɪn'kredɪb(ə)l] adj. невероя́тный.

incredulous [ɪn'kredjʊləs] adj. недове́рчивый.

increment ['ɪnkrɪmənt] n. приба́вка; (profit) при́быль.

incriminate [ɪn'krɪmɪˌneɪt] v.t. обвиня́ть impf., обвини́ть pf. (в преступле́нии).

incubate ['ɪnkjʊbeɪt] v.t. (eggs) выводи́ть (-ожу́, -о́дишь) impf., вы́вести (-еду, -едешь; -ел) pf. (в инкуба́торе); (bacteria) выра́щивать impf., вы́растить pf. **incubator** n. инкуба́тор.

inculcate ['ɪnkʌlˌkeɪt] v.t. внедря́ть impf., внедри́ть pf.

incumbent [ɪn'kʌmbənt] adj.: it is ~ (up)on you на вас лежи́т обя́занность.

incur [ɪn'kɜː(r)] v.t. навлека́ть impf., навле́чь (-еку́, -ече́шь; -ёк, -екла́) pf. на себя́.

incurable [ɪn'kjʊərəb(ə)l] adj. неизлечи́мый.

incurious [ɪn'kjʊərɪəs] adj. нелюбопы́тный.

incursion [ɪn'kɜːʃ(ə)n] n. (invasion) вторже́ние; (attack, raid) набе́г.

indebted [ɪn'detɪd] pred. (owing money) в долгу́ (to y+g.); (owing gratitude) обя́зан (-а, -о) (to +d.).

indecency [ɪn'diːs(ə)nsɪ] n. неприли́чие, непристо́йность. **indecent** adj. неприли́чный, непристо́йный.

indecision [ˌɪndɪ'sɪʒ(ə)n] n. нереши́тельность. **indecisive** [ˌɪndɪ'saɪsɪv] adj. нереши́тельный.

indeclinable [ˌɪndɪ'klaɪnəb(ə)l] adj. несклоня́емый.

indecorous [ɪn'dekərəs] adj. неприли́чный.

indecorum [ˌɪndɪ'kɔːrəm] *n.* неприли́чие.

indeed [ɪn'diːd] *adv.* в са́мом де́ле, действи́тельно; (*interrog.*) неуже́ли?

indefatigable [ˌɪndɪ'fætɪgəb(ə)l] *adj.* неутоми́мый.

indefeasible [ˌɪndɪ'fiːzɪb(ə)l] *adj.* неотъе́млемый.

indefensible [ˌɪndɪ'fensɪb(ə)l] *adj.* (*by arms*) непригодный для оборо́ны; (*by argument*) не могу́щий быть опра́вданным.

indefinable [ˌɪndɪ'faɪnəb(ə)l] *adj.* неопредели́мый. **indefinite** [ɪn'defɪnɪt] *adj.* неопределённый (-нён, -нна).

indelible [ɪn'delɪb(ə)l] *adj.* неизглади́мый, несмыва́емый; ~ **pencil** хими́ческий каранда́ш (-а́).

indelicacy [ɪn'delɪkəsɪ] *n.* неделика́тность, беста́ктность. **indelicate** *adj.* неделика́тный, беста́ктный.

indemnify [ɪn'demnɪˌfaɪ] *v.t.*: ~ **against** страхова́ть *impf.*, за~ *pf.* от+g.; обезопа́сить *pf.* от+g.; ~ **for** (*compensate*) компенси́ровать *impf. & pf.* **indemnity** *n.* (*against loss*) гара́нтия от убы́тков; (*compensation*) компенса́ция; (*war* ~) контрибу́ция.

indent [ɪn'dent] *v.t.* (*notch*) зазу́бривать *impf.*, зазубри́ть *pf.*; (*print.*) де́лать *impf.*, с~ *pf.* о́тступ; (*order goods*) зака́зывать *impf.*, заказа́ть (-ажу́, -а́жешь) *pf.* (**for** +*a.*) **inden'tation** *n.* (*notch*) зубе́ц (-бца́); (*print*) о́тступ. **indenture** *n.* контра́кт.

independence [ˌɪndɪ'pend(ə)ns] *n.* незави́симость, самостоя́тельность. **independent** *adj.* незави́симый, самостоя́тельный.

indescribable [ˌɪndɪ'skraɪbəb(ə)l] *adj.* неопису́емый.

indestructible [ˌɪndɪ'strʌktɪb(ə)l] *adj.* неразруши́мый.

indeterminate [ˌɪndɪ'tɜːmɪnət] *adj.* неопределённый (-нен, -нна).

index ['ɪndeks] *n.* и́ндекс, указа́тель *m.*, показа́тель *m.*; (*pointer*) стре́лка; (*finger*) указа́тельный па́лец (-льца); *v.t.* (*provide* ~) снабжа́ть *impf.*, снабди́ть *pf.* указа́телем; (*enter in* ~) заноси́ть (-ошу́, -о́сишь) *impf.*, занести́ (-есу́, есёшь; -ёс, -есла́) *pf.* в указа́тель.

India ['ɪndɪə] *n.* И́ндия. **Indian** *n.* (*from India*) инди́ец (-и́йца), индиа́нка; (*from America*) инде́ец (-е́йца), индиа́нка; *adj.* инди́йский; инде́йский; ~ **club** булава́; ~ **corn** кукуру́за; ~ **ink** тушь; ~ **summer** ба́бье ле́то.

indiarubber [ˌɪndɪə'rʌbə(r)] *n.* каучу́к; (*eraser*) рези́нка.

indicate ['ɪndɪˌkeɪt] *v.t.* ука́зывать *impf.*, указа́ть (-ажу́, -а́жешь) *pf.*; пока́зывать *impf.*, показа́ть (-ажу́, -а́жешь) *pf.* **indi'cation** *n.* указа́ние; (*sign*) при́знак. **in'dicative** *adj.* ука́зывающий; (*gram.*) изъяви́тельный; *n.* изъяви́тельное наклоне́ние. **indicator** *n.* указа́тель *m.*

indict [ɪn'daɪt] *v.t.* обвиня́ть *impf.*, обвини́ть *pf.* (**for** в+*p.*).

indifference [ɪn'dɪfrəns] *n.* равноду́шие, безразли́чие; (*unimportance*) незначи́тельность. **indifferent** *adj.* равноду́шный, безразли́чный; (*mediocre*) посре́дственный (-ен, -енна).

indigenous [ɪn'dɪdʒɪnəs] *adj.* тузе́мный, ме́стный.

indigent ['ɪndɪdʒ(ə)nt] *adj.* нужда́ющийся, бе́дный (-ден, -дна́, -дно, бе́дны́).

indigestible [ˌɪndɪ'dʒestɪb(ə)l] *adj.* неудобовари́мый. **indigestion** *n.* несваре́ние желу́дка.

indignant [ɪn'dɪgnənt] *adj.* негоду́ющий; **be** ~ негодова́ть *impf.* (**with** на+*a.*, **про́тив**+g.). **indig'nation** *n.* негодова́ние.

indignity [ɪn'dɪgnɪtɪ] *n.* оскорбле́ние.

indirect [ˌɪndaɪ'rekt] *adj.* непрямо́й (-м, -ма́, -мо); (*lighting*) отражённый; (*econ.*; *gram.*) ко́свенный.

indiscernible [ˌɪndɪ'sɜːnɪb(ə)l] *adj.* неразличи́мый.

indiscreet [ˌɪndɪ'skriːt] *adj.* нескро́мный (-мен, -мна́, -мно), неосторо́жный. **indiscretion** [ˌɪndɪ'skreʃ(ə)n] *n.* нескро́мность, неосторо́жность, неосмотри́тельность.

indiscriminate [ˌɪndɪ'skrɪmɪnət] *adj.* неразбо́рчивый, огу́льный; (*confused*) беспоря́дочный. **indiscriminately** *adv.* беспоря́дочно; без разбо́ру.

indispensible [ˌɪndɪ'spensəb(ə)l] *adj.* необходи́мый, незамени́мый.

indisposed [ˌɪndɪ'spəʊzd] *pred.* (*unwell*) нездоро́в (-а, -о); (*averse*) не скло́нен (скло́нна́, -но). **indispo'sition** *n.* (*ill health*) нездоро́вье; (*ailment*) неду́г; (*disinclination*) нерасположе́ние.

indisputable [ˌɪndɪ'spjuːtəb(ə)l] *adj.* бесспо́рный.

indissoluble [ˌɪndɪ'sɒljʊb(ə)l] *adj.* неразры́вный; (*in liquid*) нераствори́мый.

indistinct [ˌɪndɪ'stɪŋkt] *adj.* нея́сный (-сен, -сна́, -сно); (*sound only*) невня́тный.

indistinguishable [ˌɪndɪ'stɪŋgwɪʃəb(ə)l] *adj.* неразличи́мый.

individual [ˌɪndɪ'vɪdjʊəl] *n.* индиви́дуум, ли́чность; *adj.* индивидуа́льный, ли́чный. **individualism** *n.* индивидуали́зм. **individualist** *n.* индивидуали́ст. **individua'listic** *adj.* индивидуалисти́ческий. **individu'ality** *n.* индивидуа́льность.

indivisible [ˌɪndɪ'vɪzɪb(ə)l] *adj.* недели́мый.

indoctrinate [ɪn'dɒktrɪˌneɪt] *v.t.* внуша́ть *impf.*, внуши́ть *pf.*+*d.* (**with** +*a.*).

indolence ['ɪndələns] *n.* ле́ность. **indolent** *adj.* лени́вый.

indomitable [ɪn'dɒmɪtəb(ə)l] *adj.* неукроти́мый.

Indonesia [ˌɪndəʊ'niːzɪə] *n.* Индоне́зия.

indoor ['ɪndɔː(r)] *adj.* ко́мнатный, (находя́щийся) внутри́ до́ма. **indoors** *adv.* внутри́ до́ма.

indubitable [ɪn'djuːbɪtəb(ə)l] *adj.* несомне́нный (-е́нен, -е́нна).

induce [ɪn'djuːs] *v.t.* (*prevail on*) заставля́ть *impf.*, заста́вить *pf.*; (*bring about*) вызыва́ть *impf.*, вы́звать (вы́зову, -вешь) *pf.* **inducement** *n.* побужде́ние.

induct [ɪn'dʌkt] *v.t.* вводи́ть (-ожу́, -о́дишь) *impf.*, ввести́ (введу́, -дёшь; ввёл, -а́) *pf.* (в до́лжность).

induction [ɪn'dʌkʃ(ə)n] *n.* инду́кция; (*inducting*) введе́ние в до́лжность.

indulge [ɪn'dʌldʒ] *v.t.* потво́рствовать *impf.*+*d.*; *v.i.* предава́ться (-даю́сь, -даёшься) *impf.*, преда́ться (-а́мся, -а́шься, -а́стся, -ади́мся; -а́лся, -ала́сь) *pf.* (in +*d.*). **indulgence** *n.* снисхожде́ние, потво́рство. **indulgent** *adj.* снисходи́тельный.

industrial [ɪn'dʌstrɪəl] *adj.* промы́шленный. **industrialist** *n.* промы́шленник. **industrious** *adj.* трудолюби́вый, приле́жный. **'industry** *n.* промы́шленность, индустри́я; (*diligence*) приле́жание.

inebriate [ɪ'niːbrɪət; ɪ'niːbrɪ‚eɪt] *n.* пья́ница *c.g.*; *adj.* пья́ный (пьян, -а́, -о); *v.t.* опьяня́ть *impf.*, опьяни́ть *pf.*

inedible [ɪn'edɪb(ə)l] *adj.* несъедо́бный.

ineffable [ɪn'efəb(ə)l] *adj.* несказа́нный.

ineffective [‚ɪnɪ'fektɪv] *adj.* безрезульта́тный; (*person*) неспосо́бный.

ineffectual [ɪnɪ'fektjuəl, -ʃuəl] *adj.* безрезульта́тный.

inefficiency [‚ɪnɪ'fɪʃ(ə)nsɪ] *n.* неэффекти́вность; (*of person*) неспосо́бность. **inefficient** *adj.* неэффекти́вный, неспосо́бный.

inelegant [ɪn'elɪgənt] *adj.* неэлега́нтный.

ineligible [ɪn'elɪdʒɪb(ə)l] *adj.* не могу́щий быть и́збранным.

inept [ɪ'nept] *adj.* (*out of place*) неуме́стный; (*silly*) глу́пый (глуп, -а́, -о); (*unskilful*) неуме́лый.

inequality [‚ɪnɪ'kwɒlɪtɪ] *n.* нера́венство, неро́вность.

inequitable [ɪn'ekwɪtəb(ə)l] *adj.* несправедли́вый.

ineradicable [‚ɪnɪ'rædɪkəb(ə)l] *adj.* неискорени́мый.

inert [ɪ'nɜːt] *adj.* ине́ртный; (*sluggish*) ко́сный. **inertia** [ɪ'nɜːʃə, -ʃɪə] *n.* (*phys.*) ине́рция; (*sluggishness*) ине́ртность.

inescapable [‚ɪnɪ'skeɪpəb(ə)l] *adj.* неизбе́жный.

inessential [‚ɪnɪ'senʃ(ə)l] *adj.* несуще́ственный (-ен(ен), -енна).

inestimable [ɪn'estɪməb(ə)l] *adj.* неоцени́мый.

inevitable [ɪn'evɪtəb(ə)l] *adj.* неизбе́жный.

inexact [‚ɪnɪg'zækt] *adj.* нето́чный (-чен, -чна́, -чно).

inexcusable [‚ɪnɪk'skjuːzəb(ə)l] *adj.* непрости́тельный.

inexhaustible [‚ɪnɪg'zɔːstɪb(ə)l] *adj.* неистощи́мый.

inexorable [ɪn'eksərəb(ə)l] *adj.* неумоли́мый.

inexpedient [‚ɪnɪk'spiːdɪənt] *adj.* нецелесообра́зный.

inexpensive [‚ɪnɪk'spensɪv] *adj.* недорого́й (недо́рог, -а́, -о).

inexperience [‚ɪnɪk'spɪərɪəns] *n.* нео́пытность. **inexperienced** *adj.* нео́пытный.

inexpert [ɪn'ekspɜːt] *adj.* неиску́сный.

inexplicable [‚ɪnɪk'splɪkəb(ə)l, ɪn'eks-] *adj.* необъясни́мый.

inexpressible [‚ɪnɪk'spresɪb(ə)l] *adj.* невырази́мый. **inexpressive** *adj.* невырази́тельный.

inextinguishable [‚ɪnɪk'stɪŋgwɪʃəb(ə)l] *adj.* неугаси́мый.

inextricable [ɪn'ekstrɪkəb(ə)l, ‚ɪnɪk'strɪk-] *adj.* (*of state*) безвы́ходный; (*of problem*) запу́танный (-ан, -анна).

infallible [ɪn'fælɪb(ə)l] *adj.* непогреши́мый.

infamous ['ɪnfəməs] *adj.* (*person*) бессла́вный, гну́сный (-сен, -сна́, -сно); (*action*) позо́рный. **infamy** *n.* позо́р, дурна́я сла́ва.

infancy ['ɪnfənsɪ] *n.* младе́нчество. **infant** *n.* младе́нец (-нца). **infanticide** [ɪn'fæntɪ‚saɪd] *n.* (*action*) детоуби́йство; (*person*) детоуби́йца *c.g.* **infantile** *adj.* младе́нческий, инфанти́льный.

infantry ['ɪnfəntrɪ] *n.* пехо́та; *adj.* пехо́тный. **infantryman** *n.* пехоти́нец (-нца).

infatuate [ɪn'fætju‚eɪt] *v.t.* вскружи́ть (-ужу́, -у́жишь) *pf.* го́лову+*d.* **infatu'ation** *n.* си́льное увлече́ние.

infect [ɪn'fekt] *v.t.* заража́ть *impf.*, зарази́ть *pf.* (with +*i.*). **infection** *n.* зара́за, инфе́кция. **infectious** *adj.* зара́зный; (*fig.*) зарази́тельный.

infelicitous [‚ɪnfɪ'lɪsɪtəs] *adj.* несча́стный, неуда́чный. **infelicity** *n.* несча́стье.

infer [ɪn'fɜː(r)] *v.t.* заключа́ть *impf.*, заключи́ть *pf.*; подразумева́ть *impf.* **inference** ['ɪnfərəns] *n.* заключе́ние.

inferior [ɪn'fɪərɪə(r)] *adj.* ни́зший; (*in quality*) ху́дший, плохо́й (плох, -а́, -о, пло́хи́); *n.* подчинённый *sb.* **inferi'ority** *n.* бо́лее ни́зкое положе́ние, бо́лее ни́зкое ка́чество; ~ **complex** ко́мплекс неполноце́нности.

infernal [ɪn'fɜːn(ə)l] *adj.* а́дский. **inferno** *n.* (*hell*) ад (*loc.* -ý); (*conflagration*) пожа́рище.

infertile [ɪn'fɜːtaɪl] *adj.* неплодоро́дный.

infested [ɪn'festɪd] *adj.*: be ~ with кише́ть (-шу́, -ши́шь) *impf.*+*i.*

infidel ['ɪnfɪd(ə)l] *n.* неве́рный *sb.*, неве́рующий *sb.*; *adj.* неве́рующий. **infidelity** [‚ɪnfɪ'delɪtɪ] *n.* (*disloyalty*) неве́рность; (*disbelief*) неве́рие.

infiltrate ['ɪnfɪl‚treɪt] *v.t.* (*fluid*) фильтрова́ть *impf.*, про~ *pf.*; (*of persons*) постепе́нно проника́ть *impf.*, прони́кнуть (-к) *pf.* в+*a.*

infinite ['ɪnfɪnɪt] *adj.* бесконе́чный, безграни́чный. **infini'tesimal** *adj.* бесконе́чно ма́лый. **in'finitive** *n.* инфинити́в *c.g.* **in'finity** *n.* бесконе́чность, безграни́чность.

infirm [ɪn'fɜːm] *adj.* не́мощный, сла́бый (слаб, -а́, -о). **infirmary** *n.* больни́ца. **infirmity** *n.* не́мощь, сла́бость.

inflame [ɪn'fleɪm] *v.t. & i.* воспламеня́ть(ся) *impf.*, воспламени́ть(ся) *pf.*; (*excite*) возбуждáть(ся) *impf.*, возбудúть(ся) *pf.*; (*med.*) воспалять(ся) *impf.*, воспалúть(ся) *pf.* **inflammable** [ɪnˈflæməb(ə)l] *adj.* огнеопáсный. **infla'mmation** *n.* воспламенéние; (*med.*) воспалéние. **in'flammatory** *adj.* подстрекáтельский; (*med.*) воспалúтельный.

inflate [ɪnˈfleɪt] *v.t.* надувáть *impf.*, надýть (-ýю, -ýешь) *pf.*; (*econ.*) проводúть (-ожý, -óдишь) *impf.*, провестú (-едý, -едёшь; -ёл, -елá) *pf.* инфля́цию+g. **inflated** *adj.* (*bombastic*) напы́щенный (-ен, -енна). **inflation** *n.* надувáние; (*econ.*) инфля́ция.

inflect [ɪnˈflekt] *v.t.* вгибáть *impf.*, вогнýть *pf.*; (*gram.*) изменя́ть *impf.*, изменúть (-ню́, -нúшь) *pf.* (окончáние+g.). **inflection, -xion** *n.* вгибáние; (*gram.*) флéксия.

inflexible [ɪnˈfleksɪb(ə)l] *adj.* негúбкий (-бок, -бкá, -бко); (*fig.*) непреклóнный (-нен, -нна).

inflict [ɪnˈflɪkt] *v.t.* (*blow*) наносúть (-ошý, -óсишь) *impf.*, нанестú (-есý, -есёшь; -ёс, -еслá) *pf.* ((up)on +*d.*); (*suffering*) причиня́ть *impf.*, причинúть *pf.* ((up)on +*d.*); (*penalty*) налагáть *impf.*, наложúть (-жý, -жишь) *pf.* ((up)on на+*a.*); ~ **o.s.** (up)on навя́зываться *impf.*, навязáться (-яжýсь, -я́жешься) *pf.*+*d.*

inflow [ˈɪnfləʊ] *n.* втекáние, притóк.

influence [ˈɪnfluəns] *n.* влия́ние; *v.t.* влия́ть *impf.*, по~ *pf.* на+*a.* **influential** [ˌɪnfluˈenʃ(ə)l] *adj.* влия́тельный.

influenza [ˌɪnfluˈenzə] *n.* грипп.

influx [ˈɪnflʌks] *n.* (*of stream*) впадéние; (*of persons*) наплы́в.

inform [ɪnˈfɔːm] *v.t.* сообщáть *impf.*, сообщúть *pf.*+*d.* (**of, about** +*a.*, о+*p.*); *v.i.* доносúть (-ошý, -óсишь) *impf.*, донестú (-есý, -есёшь; -ёс, -еслá) *pf.* (**against** на+*a.*).

informal [ɪnˈfɔːm(ə)l] *adj.* неофициáльный, неформáльный.

informant [ɪnˈfɔːmənt] *n.* осведомúтель *m.* **infor'mation** *n.* информáция, свéдения *nt.pl.*; ~ **science** информáтика. **informer** *n.* доно́счик.

infraction [ɪnˈfrækʃ(ə)n] *n.* нарушéние.

infra-red [ˌɪnfrəˈred] *adj.* инфракрáсный.

infrequent [ɪnˈfriːkwənt] *adj.* рéдкий (-док, -дкá, -дко).

infringe [ɪnˈfrɪndʒ] *v.t.* (*violate*) нарушáть *impf.*, нарýшить *pf.*; *v.i.*: ~ (up)on посягáть *impf.*, посягнýть *pf.* на+*a.* **infringement** *n.* нарушéние; посягáтельство.

infuriate [ɪnˈfjʊərɪˌeɪt] *v.t.* разъяря́ть *impf.*, разъярúть *pf.*

infuse [ɪnˈfjuːz] *v.t.* вливáть *impf.*, влить (волью́, -ьёшь; влил, -á, -о) *pf.*; (*fig.*) внушáть *impf.*, внушúть *pf.* (**into** +*d.*); (*steep*) настáивать *impf.*, настоя́ть (-ою́, -оúшь) *pf.* **infusion** *n.* вливáние; внушéние; настóй.

ingenious [ɪnˈdʒiːnɪəs] *adj.* изобретáтельный. **inge'nuity** *n.* изобретáтельность.

ingenuous [ɪnˈdʒenjʊəs] *adj.* откровéнный (-нен, -нна), бесхúтростный.

inglorious [ɪnˈɡlɔːrɪəs] *adj.* бесслáвный.

ingot [ˈɪŋɡɒt, -ɡət] *n.* слúток (-тка).

ingrained [ɪnˈɡreɪnd] *adj.* закоренéлый.

ingratiate [ɪnˈɡreɪʃɪˌeɪt] *v.t.* ~ **o.s.** вкрáдываться *impf.*, вкрáсться (-адýсь, -адёшься; -áлся) *pf.* в мúлость (**with** +*d.*).

ingratitude [ɪnˈɡrætɪˌtjuːd] *n.* неблагодáрность.

ingredient [ɪnˈɡriːdɪənt] *n.* составнáя часть (*pl.* -ти, -тéй).

inhabit [ɪnˈhæbɪt] *v.t.* жить (живý, -вёшь; жил, -á, -о) *impf.* в, на, +*p.*; обитáть *impf.* в, на, +*p.* **inhabitant** *n.* жúтель *m.*, ~ница; обитáтель *m.*, ~ница.

inhalation [ˌɪnhəˈleɪʃ(ə)n] *n.* вдыхáние. **inhale** [ɪnˈheɪl] *v.t.* вдыхáть *impf.*, вдохнýть *pf.*

inherent [ɪnˈhɪərənt, ɪnˈherənt] *adj.* присýщий (**in** +*d.*).

inherit [ɪnˈherɪt] *v.t.* наслéдовать *impf. & pf.*, у~ *pf.* **inheritance** *n.* наслéдство. **inheritor** *n.* наслéдник. **inheritress, -trix** *n.* наслéдница.

inhibit [ɪnˈhɪbɪt] *v.t.* (*forbid*) запрещáть *impf.*, запретúть (-ещý, -етúшь) *pf.* (+*d. & inf.*); (*hinder*) препя́тствовать *impf.*, вос~ *pf.*+*d.* **inhi'bition** *n.* запрещéние; сдéрживание; (*psych.*) торможéние.

inhospitable [ˌɪnhɒˈspɪtəb(ə)l, ɪnˈhɒsp-] *adj.* негостеприúмный.

inhuman [ɪnˈhjuːmən] *adj.* (*brutal*) бесчеловéчный; (*not human*) нечеловéческий.

inimical [ɪˈnɪmɪk(ə)l] *adj.* враждéбный; (*harmful*) врéдный (-ден, -днá, -дно).

inimitable [ɪˈnɪmɪtəb(ə)l] *adj.* неподражáемый.

iniquitous [ɪˈnɪkwɪtəs] *adj.* несправедлúвый. **iniquity** *n.* несправедлúвость.

initial [ɪˈnɪʃ(ə)l] *adj.* первоначáльный; *n.* начáльная бýква; *pl.* инициáлы *m.pl.*; *v.t.* стáвить *impf.*, по~ *pf.* инициáлы на+*a.* **initially** *adv.* в начáле.

initiate [ɪˈnɪʃɪˌeɪt] *v.t.* (*begin*) начинáть *impf.*, начáть (начнý, -нёшь; нáчал, -á, -о) *pf.*; (*admit*) посвящáть *impf.*, посвятúть (-ящý, -ятúшь) *pf.* (**into** в+*a.*).

initiative [ɪˈnɪʃətɪv, ɪˈnɪʃɪətɪv] *n.* почúн, инициатúва.

inject [ɪnˈdʒekt] *v.t.* впры́скивать *impf.*, впры́снуть *pf.* **injection** *n.* впры́скивание, инъéкция.

injudicious [ˌɪndʒuːˈdɪʃəs] *adj.* неблагоразýмный.

injunction [ɪnˈdʒʌŋkʃ(ə)n] *n.* предписáние; (*leg.*) судéбное постановлéние, судéбный запрéт.

injure [ˈɪndʒə(r)] *v.t.* вредúть *impf.*, по~ *pf.*+*d.*; повреждáть *impf.*, повредúть *pf.*; (*physically*) рáнить *impf. & pf.* **injurious** [ɪnˈdʒʊərɪəs] *adj.* врéдный (-ден, -днá, -дно); (*insulting*) оскорбúтельный. **injury** *n.* вред (-á); (*physical*) рáна.

injustice [ɪnˈdʒʌstɪs] *n.* несправедлúвость.

ink [ɪŋk] *n.* чернúла (-л) *pl.*; (*printer's* ~) типогрáфская крáска.

inkling ['ɪŋklɪŋ] *n.* (*hint*) намёк (**of** на+*a.*); (*suspicion*) подозрéние.

ink-well ['ɪŋkwel] *n.* чернúльница.

inland ['ɪnlənd, 'ɪnlænd] *adj.* внýтренний; *adv.* (*motion*) внутрь странẃ; (*place*) внутрú странẃ.

inlay [ɪn'leɪ] *n.* инкрустáция; *v.t.* инкрустúровать *impf.* & *pf.*

inlet ['ɪnlet, -lɪt] *n.* (*of sea*) ýзкий залúв; впуск.

inmate ['ɪnmeɪt] *n.* жилéц (-льцá), жилúца; (*of prison*) заключённый *sb.*; (*of hospital*) больнóй *sb.*

inmost ['ɪnməʊst, -məst] *adj.* сáмый внýтренний; (*fig.*) глубочáйший, сокровéнный (-éн, -éнна).

inn [ɪn] *n.* гостúница.

innate [ɪ'neɪt, 'ɪ-] *adj.* врождённый (-ён, -енá).

inner ['ɪnə(r)] *adj.* внýтренний.

innkeeper ['ɪn,kiːpə(r)] *n.* хозя́ин (*pl.* -я́ева, -я́ев) гостúницы.

innocence ['ɪnəs(ə)ns] *n.* невúнность, невинóвность. **innocent** *adj.* невúнный (-нен, -нна), невинóвный (**of** в+*p.*).

innocuous [ɪ'nɒkjʊəs] *adj.* безврéдный.

innovate ['ɪnəveɪt] *v.i.* вводúть (-ожý, -óдишь) *impf.*, ввестú (введý, -дёшь; ввёл, -á) *pf.* нóвшества. **inno'vation** *n.* нововведéние, нóвшество. **innovative** *adj.* новáторский. **innovator** *n.* новáтор.

innuendo [,ɪnjʊ'endəʊ] *n.* намёк, инсинуáция.

innumerable [ɪ'njuːmərəb(ə)l] *adj.* бесчúсленный (-ен, -енна).

inoculate [ɪ'nɒkjʊ,leɪt] *v.t.* прививáть *impf.*, привúть (-вью, -вьёшь; привúл, -á, -о) *pf.*+*d.* (**against** +*a.*). **inocu'lation** *n.* привúвка (**against** от, прóтив+*g.*).

inoffensive [,ɪnə'fensɪv] *adj.* безобúдный.

inoperative [ɪn'ɒpərətɪv] *adj.* недéйствующий.

inopportune [ɪn'ɒpə,tjuːn] *adj.* несвоеврéменный (-нен, -нна).

inordinate [ɪn'ɔːdɪnət] *adj.* чрезмéрный.

inorganic [,ɪnɔː'gænɪk] *adj.* неорганúческий.

in-patient ['ɪn,peɪʃ(ə)nt] *n.* стационáрный больнóй *sb.*

input ['ɪnpʊt] *n.* (*action*) ввод, вход; (*power supplied*) вводúмая мóщность; (*elec. signal*) входнóй сигнáл; (*econ.*) затрáты *f.pl.*; (*data*) входнẃе дáнные *sb.*; (*device*) устрóйство ввóда.

inquest ['ɪnkwest, 'ɪŋ-] *n.* судéбное слéдствие, дознáние.

inquire [ɪn'kwaɪə(r), ɪŋ-] *v.t.* спрáшивать *impf.*, спросúть (-ошý, -óсишь) *pf.*; *v.i.* справля́ться *impf.*, спрáвиться *pf.* (**about** о+*p.*); расслéдовать *impf.* & *pf.* (**into** +*a.*) **inquiry** *n.* вопрóс, спрáвка; (*investigation*) расслéдование; ~ **office** спрáвочное бюрó *nt.indecl.*

inquisition [,ɪnkwɪ'zɪʃ(ə)n, ,ɪŋ-] *n.* расслéдование; **the i~** инквизúция. **in'quisitive** *adj.* пытлúвый, любознáтельный. **in'quisitor** *n.* слéдователь *m.*; (*hist.*) инквизúтор.

inroad ['ɪnrəʊd] *n.* набéг; (*fig.*) посягáтельство (**on, into** на+*a.*).

insane [ɪn'seɪn] *adj.* душевнобольнóй, безýмный. **insanity** [ɪn'sænɪtɪ] *n.* безýмие.

insatiable [ɪn'seɪʃəb(ə)l] *adj.* ненасẃтный.

inscribe [ɪn'skraɪb] *v.t.* надпúсывать *impf.*, надписáть (-ишý, -úшешь) *pf.*; впúсывать *impf.*, вписáть (-ишý, -úшешь) *pf.*; (*dedicate*) посвящáть *impf.*, посвятúть (-ящý, -ятúшь) *pf.* **inscription** [ɪn'skrɪpʃ(ə)n] *n.* нáдпись; посвящéние.

inscrutable [ɪn'skruːtəb(ə)l] *adj.* непостижúмый, непроницáемый.

insect ['ɪnsekt] *n.* насекóмое *sb.* **in'secticide** *n.* инсектицúд. **insec'tivorous** *adj.* насекомоя́дный.

insecure [,ɪnsɪ'kjʊə(r)] *adj.* (*unsafe*) небезопáсный; (*not firm*) непрóчный (-чен, -чнá, -чно).

insensate [ɪn'senseɪt] *adj.* бесчýвственный (-ен, -енна); (*stupid*) глýпый (глуп, -á, -о).

insensibility [ɪn,sensɪ'bɪlɪtɪ] *n.* бесчýвствие. **in'sensible** *adj.* (*inappreciable*) незамéтный; (*unconscious*) потеря́вший сознáние; (*insensitive*) нечувствúтельный.

insensitive [ɪn'sensɪtɪv] *adj.* нечувствúтельный.

inseparable [ɪn'sepərəb(ə)l] *adj.* неотделúмый, неразлýчный.

insert [ɪn'sɜːt] *v.t.* вставля́ть *impf.*, встáвить *pf.*; вклáдывать *impf.*, вложúть (-жý, -óжишь) *pf.*; (*into newspaper etc.*) помещáть *impf.*, поместúть *pf.* (**in** в+*p.*). **insertion** *n.* (*inserting*) вставлéние, вклáдывание; (*thing inserted*) встáвка; (*in newspaper*) объявлéние.

inset ['ɪnset] *n.* (*in book*) вклáдка, вклéйка; (*in dress*) встáвка.

inshore [ɪn'ʃɔː(r), 'ɪn-] *adj.* прибрéжный; *adv.* блúзко к бéрегу.

inside [ɪn'saɪd] *n.* внýтренняя сторонá (*a.* -ону; *pl.* -оны, -óн, -онáм), внýтренность; **turn** ~ **out** вывёртывать *impf.*, вы́вернуть *pf.* наизнáнку; *adj.* внýтренний; ~ **left, right** (*sport*) лéвый, прáвый, полусрéдний *sb.*; *adv.* (*place*) внутрú; (*motion*) внутрь; *prep.* (*place*) внутрú+*g.*, в+*p.*; (*motion*) внутрь+*g.*, в+*a.*

insidious [ɪn'sɪdɪəs] *adj.* ковáрный.

insight ['ɪnsaɪt] *n.* проницáтельность.

insignia [ɪn'sɪgnɪə] *n.* знáки *m.pl.* отлúчия, различия.

insignificant [,ɪnsɪg'nɪfɪkənt] *adj.* незначúтельный.

insincere [,ɪnsɪn'sɪə(r)] *adj.* нейскренний (-нен, -нна).

insinuate [ɪn'sɪnjʊ,eɪt] *v.t.* постепéнно вводúть (-ожý, -óдишь) *impf.*, ввестú (введý, -дёшь; ввёл, -á) *pf.* (*hint*) намекáть *impf.*, намекнýть *pf.* на+*a.*; ~ **o.s.** вкрáдываться *impf.*, вкрáсться (-адýсь, -адёшься; -áлся) *pf.* (**into** в+*a.*). **insinu'ation** *n.* инсинуáция.

insipid [ɪnˈsɪpɪd] *adj.* (*tasteless*) безвку́сный; (*dull*) ску́чный (-чен, -чна́, -чно).

insist [ɪnˈsɪst] *v.t. & i.* утвержда́ть *impf.*; наста́ивать *impf.*, настоя́ть (-ою́, -ои́шь) *pf.* (**on** на+*p.*). **insistent** *adj.* насто́йчивый.

insolence [ˈɪnsələns] *n.* на́глость. **insolent** *adj.* на́глый (нагл, -á, -о).

insoluble [ɪnˈsɒljʊb(ə)l] *adj.* (*problem*) неразреши́мый; (*in liquid*) нераствори́мый.

insolvent [ɪnˈsɒlv(ə)nt] *adj.* несостоя́тельный.

insomnia [ɪnˈsɒmnɪə] *n.* бессо́нница.

insomuch [ˌɪnsəʊˈmʌtʃ] *adv.*: ∼ **that** насто́лько..., что; ∼ **as** ввиду́ того́, что; так как.

inspect [ɪnˈspekt] *v.t.* осма́тривать *impf.*, осмотре́ть (-рю́, -ришь) *pf.*; инспекти́ровать *impf.*, про∼ *pf.* **inspection** *n.* осмо́тр, инспе́кция. **inspector** *n.* инспе́ктор (*pl.* -á), контролёр, ревизо́р.

inspiration [ˌɪnspɪˈreɪʃ(ə)n] *n.* вдохнове́ние; (*breathing in*) вдыха́ние. **inspire** [ɪnˈspaɪə(r)] *v.t.* вдохновля́ть *impf.*, вдохнови́ть *pf.*; внуша́ть *impf.*, внуши́ть *pf.*+*d.* (**with** +*a.*); (*breathe in*) вдыха́ть *impf.*, вдохну́ть *pf.*

instability [ˌɪnstəˈbɪlɪtɪ] *n.* неусто́йчивость.

install [ɪnˈstɔːl] *v.t.* (*person in office*) вводи́ть (-ожу́, -óдишь) *impf.*, ввести́ (введу́, -дёшь; ввёл, -á) *pf.* в до́лжность; (*apparatus*) устана́вливать *impf.*, установи́ть (-влю́, -вишь) *pf.* **installation** [ˌɪnstəˈleɪʃ(ə)n] *n.* введе́ние в до́лжность; устано́вка; *pl.* сооруже́ния *nt.pl.*

instalment [ɪnˈstɔːlmənt] *n.* (*payment*) очередно́й взнос; (*serial publication*) отде́льный вы́пуск; часть (*pl.* -ти, -те́й) *by* ∼**s** в рассро́чку, по частя́м.

instance [ˈɪnst(ə)ns] *n.* приме́р, слу́чай; (*leg.*) инста́нция; **at the** ∼ **of** по тре́бованию+*g.*; **for** ∼ наприме́р.

instant [ˈɪnst(ə)nt] *n.* мгнове́ние, моме́нт; *adj.* (*immediate*) неме́дленный (-ен, -енна); (*urgent*) настоя́тельный; (*of current month*) теку́щего ме́сяца; (*of coffee etc.*) раствори́мый. **instan'taneous** *adj.* мгнове́нный (-нен, -нна). **instantly** *adv.* неме́дленно, то́тчас.

instead [ɪnˈsted] *adv.* вме́сто (**of** +*g.*), взаме́н (**of** +*g.*); ∼ **of going** вме́сто того́, чтобы пойти́.

instep [ˈɪnstep] *n.* подъём.

instigate [ˈɪnstɪɡeɪt] *v.t.* подстрека́ть *impf.*, подстрекну́ть *pf.* (**to** к+*d.*) **insti'gation** *n.* подстрека́тельство. **instigator** *n.* подстрека́тель *m.*, ∼ница.

instil [ɪnˈstɪl] *v.t.* (*liquid*) влива́ть *impf.*, влить (волью́, -ьёшь; влил, -á, -о) *pf.* по ка́пле; (*ideas etc.*) внуша́ть *impf.*, внуши́ть *pf.* (**into** +*d.*).

instinct [ˈɪnstɪŋkt] *n.* инсти́нкт. **in'stinctive** *adj.* инстинкти́вный.

institute [ˈɪnstɪˌtjuːt] *n.* институ́т, (*научное*) учрежде́ние; *v.t.* устана́вливать *impf.*, установи́ть (-влю́, -вишь) *pf.*; учрежда́ть *impf.*,

учреди́ть *pf.*; (*initiate*) начина́ть *impf.*, нача́ть (начну́, -нёшь; на́чал, -á, -о) *pf.* **insti'tution** *n.* установле́ние, учрежде́ние.

instruct [ɪnˈstrʌkt] *v.t.* (*teach*) обуча́ть *impf.*, обучи́ть (-чу́, -чишь) *pf.* (**in** +*d.*); (*inform*) сообща́ть *impf.*, сообщи́ть *pf.*+*d.*; (*command*) прика́зывать *impf.*, приказа́ть (-ажу́, -áжешь) *pf.*+*d.* **instruction** *n.* инстру́кция; (*teaching*) обуче́ние. **instructive** *adj.* поучи́тельный. **instructor** *n.* инстру́ктор.

instrument [ˈɪnstrəmənt] *n.* ору́дие, инструме́нт; (*leg.*) докуме́нт, акт. **instru'mental** *adj.* служа́щий ору́дием; (*mus.*) инструмента́льный; (*gram.*) твори́тельный; **be** ∼ **in** спосо́бствовать *impf.*, по∼ *pf.*+*d.*; *n.* (*gram.*) твори́тельный паде́ж (-á). **instrumen'tation** *n.* (*mus.*) инструменто́вка.

insubordinate [ˌɪnsəˈbɔːdɪnət] *adj.* неподчиня́ющийся.

insufferable [ɪnˈsʌfərəb(ə)l] *adj.* невыноси́мый.

insular [ˈɪnsjʊlə(r)] *adj.* (*of island*) островно́й; (*narrow-minded*) ограни́ченный (-ен, -енна).

insulate [ˈɪnsjʊˌleɪt] *v.t.* изоли́ровать *impf. & pf.*; **insulating tape** изоляцио́нная ле́нта. **insu'lation** *n.* изоля́ция. **insulator** *n.* изоля́тор.

insulin [ˈɪnsjʊlɪn] *n.* инсули́н.

insult [ˈɪnsʌlt; ɪnˈsʌlt] *n.* оскорбле́ние; *v.t.* оскорбля́ть *impf.*, оскорби́ть *pf.* **in'sulting** *adj.* оскорби́тельный.

insurance [ɪnˈʃʊərəns] *n.* страхова́ние; *attr.* страхово́й. **insure** *v.t.* страхова́ть *impf.*, за∼ *pf.* (**against** от+*g.*).

insurgent [ɪnˈsɜːdʒ(ə)nt] *n.* повста́нец (-нца); *adj.* восста́вший.

insurmountable [ˌɪnsəˈmaʊntəb(ə)l] *adj.* непреодоли́мый.

insurrection [ˌɪnsəˈrekʃ(ə)n] *n.* восста́ние, мяте́ж (-á).

intact [ɪnˈtækt] *adj.* (*untouched*) нетро́нутый; (*entire*) це́лый (цел, -á, -о).

intake [ˈɪnteɪk] *n.* (*action*) впуск, вход; (*mechanism*) впускно́е, приёмное, устро́йство; (*of water*) водозабо́р; (*airway in mine*) вентиляцио́нная вы́работка; (*of persons*) набо́р, о́бщее число́; (*quantity*) потребле́ние.

intangible [ɪnˈtændʒɪb(ə)l] *adj.* неосяза́емый.

integral [ˈɪntɪɡr(ə)l] *adj.* неотъе́млемый; (*whole*) це́льный (-лен, -льна́, -льно); (*math.*) интегра́льный; *n.* интегра́л. **integrate** *v.t.* (*combine*) объединя́ть *impf.*, объедини́ть *pf.*; (*math.*) интегри́ровать *impf. & pf.* **inte'gration** *n.* объедине́ние, интегра́ция.

integrity [ɪnˈtegrɪtɪ] *n.* (*wholeness*) це́лостность; (*honesty*) че́стность.

intellect [ˈɪntɪˌlekt] *n.* интелле́кт, ум (-á). **inte'llectual** *n.* интеллиге́нт; *adj.* у́мственный; интеллектуа́льный.

intelligence [ɪnˈtelɪdʒ(ə)ns] *n.* (*intellect*) ум (-á); (*cleverness*) смышлёность; (*information*) све́дения *nt.pl.*; (∼ *service*) разве́дка, разве́ дывательная слу́жба. **intelligent** adj. у́мный (умён, умна́, у́мно́).

intelligentsia [ɪnˌtelɪˈdʒentsɪə] n. интеллиге́нция.

intelligible [ɪnˈtelɪdʒɪb(ə)l] adj. поня́тный.

intemperate [ɪnˈtempərət] adj. невозде́ржанный.

intend [ɪnˈtend] v.t. намерева́ться impf.+inf.; быть наме́ренным (-ен)+inf.; собира́ться impf., собра́ться (соберу́сь, -рёшься; собра́лся, -ала́сь, -а́ло́сь) pf.; (design) предназнача́ть impf., предназна́чить pf. (for для+g., на+a.); (mean) име́ть impf. в виду́.

intense [ɪnˈtens] adj. си́льный (си́лён, -льна́, -льно, -си́льны́), напряжённый (-ён, -ённа). **intensify** v.t. & i. уси́ливать(ся) impf., уси́лить(ся) pf. **intensity** n. интенси́вность, напряжённость, си́ла. **intensive** adj. интенси́вный.

intent [ɪnˈtent] n. наме́рение, цель; adj. (resolved) стремя́щийся (on к+d.); (occupied) погружённый (-ён, -ена́) (on в+a.); (earnest) внима́тельный. **intention** n. наме́рение, цель. **intentional** adj. наме́ренный (-ен, -енна), умы́шленный (-ен, -енна).

inter [ɪnˈtɜː(r)] v.t. (bury) хорони́ть impf., по~ pf.

inter- [ˈɪntə(r)] in comb. (mutually) взаимо…; (between) меж…, между…; (in vv.) пере… .

interact [ˌɪntərˈækt] v.i. взаимоде́йствовать impf. **interaction** n. взаимоде́йствие. **interactive** adj. интеракти́вный, диало́говый.

inter alia [ˌɪntər ˈeɪlɪə, ˈælɪə] adv. ме́жду про́чим.

interbreed [ˌɪntəˈbriːd] v.t. & i. скре́щивать(ся) impf., скрести́ть(ся) pf.

intercede [ˌɪntəˈsiːd] v.i. хода́тайствовать impf., по~ pf. (for за+a.; with пе́ред+i.).

intercept [ˌɪntəˈsept] v.t. перехва́тывать impf., перехвати́ть (-ачу́, -а́тишь) pf.; (cut off) прерыва́ть impf., прерва́ть (-ву́, -вёшь; прерва́л, -а́, -о) pf. **interception** n. перехва́т.

intercession [ˌɪntəˈseʃ(ə)n] n. хода́тайство. **intercessor** n. хода́тай.

interchange [ˈɪntəˌtʃeɪndʒ] n. (exchange) обме́н (of +i.); (alternation) чередова́ние; (road junction) тра́нспортная развя́зка; v.t. обме́ниваться impf., обменя́ться pf.+i.; чередова́ть impf. **interchangeable** adj. взаимозаменя́емый.

inter-city [ˌɪntəˈsɪtɪ] adj. междугоро́дный, межгородско́й.

intercom [ˈɪntəˌkɒm] n. вну́тренняя телефо́нная связь; селе́ктор.

interconnection [ˌɪntəkəˈnekʃ(ə)n] n. взаимосвя́зь.

intercontinental [ˌɪntəˌkɒntɪˈnent(ə)l] adj. межконтинента́льный.

intercourse [ˈɪntəˌkɔːs] n. (social) обще́ние; (trade etc.) сноше́ния nt.pl.; (sexual) половы́е сноше́ния nt.pl.

interdepartmental [ˌɪntəˌdiːpɑːtˈment(ə)l] adj. меж(ду)ве́домственный.

interdependent [ˌɪntədɪˈpendənt] adj. взаимозави́симый.

interdict [ˈɪntədɪkt] n. запреще́ние; v.t. запреща́ть impf., запрети́ть (-ещу́, -ети́шь) pf. (person +d.).

interdisciplinary [ˌɪntəˌdɪsɪˈplɪnərɪ] adj. межотраслево́й.

interest [ˈɪntrəst, -trɪst] n. интере́с (in к+d.); (profit) вы́года; (econ.) проце́нты m.pl.; v.t. интересова́ть impf.; (~ person in) заинтересо́вывать impf., заинтересова́ть pf. (in +i.); be ~ed in интересова́ться impf.+i. **interesting** adj. интере́сный.

interethnic [ˌɪntəˈeθnɪk] adj. межнациона́льный.

interface [ˈɪntəˌfeɪs] n. (comput.) интерфе́йс.

interfere [ˌɪntəˈfɪə(r)] v.i. меша́ть impf., по~ pf. (with +d.); вме́шиваться impf., вмеша́ться pf. (in в+a.). **interference** n. вмеша́тельство; (radio) поме́хи f.pl.

intergovernmental [ˌɪntəɡʌvənˈment(ə)l] adj. межправи́тельственный.

interim [ˈɪntərɪm] n. промежу́ток (-тка) (вре́мени); in the ~ тем вре́менем; adj. промежу́точный; (temporary) вре́менный.

interior [ɪnˈtɪərɪə(r)] n. вну́тренность; (pol.) вну́тренние дела́ nt.pl.; adj. вну́тренний.

interjection [ˌɪntəˈdʒekʃ(ə)n] n. восклица́ние; (gram.) междоме́тие.

interlace [ˌɪntəˈleɪs] v.t. & i. переплета́ть(ся) impf., переплести́(сь) (-ету́(сь), -етёшь(ся); -ёл(ся), -ела́(сь)) pf.

interlinear [ˌɪntəˈlɪnɪə(r)] adj. междустро́чный.

interlock [ˌɪntəˈlɒk] v.t. & i. сцепля́ть(ся) impf., сцепи́ть(ся) (-плю́(сь), -пишь(ся)) pf.

interlocutor [ˌɪntəˈlɒkjʊtə(r)] n. собесе́дник, -ица.

interlope [ˌɪntəˈləʊp] v.i. вме́шиваться impf., вмеша́ться pf. в чужи́е дела́.

interlude [ˈɪntəˌluːd, -ˌljuːd] n. промежу́точный эпизо́д; (theatr.) антра́кт.

intermediary [ˌɪntəˈmiːdɪərɪ] n. посре́дник; adj. посре́днический; (intermediate) промежу́точный.

intermediate [ˌɪntəˈmiːdɪət] adj. промежу́точный.

interment [ɪnˈtɜːmənt] n. погребе́ние.

interminable [ɪnˈtɜːmɪnəb(ə)l] adj. бесконе́чный.

intermission [ˌɪntəˈmɪʃ(ə)n] n. переры́в, па́уза.

intermittent [ˌɪntəˈmɪt(ə)nt] adj. преры́вистый.

intermix [ˌɪntəˈmɪks] v.t. & i. переме́шивать(ся) impf., перемеша́ть(ся) pf.

intern [ɪnˈtɜːn] v.t. интерни́ровать impf. & pf.

internal [ɪnˈtɜːn(ə)l] adj. вну́тренний; ~ combustion engine дви́гатель m. вну́треннего сгора́ния.

international [ˌɪntəˈnæʃən(ə)l] n. (contest) междунаро́дное состяза́ние; adj. междунаро́дный, интернациона́льный. **internationalism** n. интернационали́зм.

internecine [ˌɪntə'niːsaɪn] *adj.* междоусо́бный.
internee [ˌɪntɜː'niː] *n.* интерни́рованный *sb.*
in'ternment *n.* интерни́рование.
interplanetary [ˌɪntə'plænɪtərɪ] *adj.* межпланетный.
interplay ['ɪntəˌpleɪ] *n.* взаимоде́йствие.
interpolate [ɪn'tɜːpəˌleɪt] *v.t.* (*insert*) вставля́ть *impf.*, вста́вить *pf.*; (*math.*) интерполи́ровать *impf.* & *pf.* **interpo'lation** *n.* вста́вка; (*math.*) интерполя́ция.
interpose [ˌɪntə'pəʊz] *v.t.* (*insert*) вставля́ть *impf.*, вста́вить *pf.*; *v.i.* (*intervene*) вме́шиваться *impf.*, вмеша́ться *pf.*
interpret [ɪn'tɜːprɪt] *v.t.* толкова́ть *impf.*; (*speech etc.*) у́стно переводи́ть *impf.*, перевести́ (-еду́, -едёшь; -ёл, -ела́) *pf.* **interpre'tation** *n.* толкова́ние. **interpreter** *n.* толкова́тель *m.*; перево́дчик, -ица.
interregnum [ˌɪntə'regnəm] *n.* междуца́рствие; (*interval*) переры́в.
interrogate [ɪn'terəˌgeɪt] *v.t.* допра́шивать *impf.*, допроси́ть (-ошу́, -о́сишь) *pf.* **interro'gation** *n.* допро́с; (*question*) вопро́с. **inte'rrogative** *adj.* вопроси́тельный.
interrupt [ˌɪntə'rʌpt] *v.t.* прерыва́ть *impf.*, прерва́ть (-ву́, -вёшь; -ва́л, -вала́, -ва́ло) *pf.* **interruption** *n.* переры́в.
intersect [ˌɪntə'sekt] *v.t.* & *i.* пересека́ть(ся) *impf.*, пересе́чь(ся) (-еку́(сь), -ечёшь(ся); -е́к(ся), -екла́(сь)) *pf.* **intersection** *n.* пересече́ние.
intersperse [ˌɪntə'spɜːs] *v.t.* (*scatter*) рассыпа́ть *impf.*, рассы́пать (-плю, -плешь) *pf.* (**between**, **among** ме́жду+*i.*, среди́+*g.*); (*diversify*) разнообра́зить *impf.*
intertwine [ˌɪntə'twaɪn] *v.t.* & *i.* переплета́ть(ся) *impf.*, переплести́(сь) (-ету́(сь), -етёшь(ся); -ёл(ся), -ела́(сь)) *pf.*
interval ['ɪntəv(ə)l] *n.* промежу́ток (-тка); (*also mus.*) интерва́л; (*school*) переме́на.
intervene [ˌɪntə'viːn] *v.i.* (*occur*) происходи́ть (-ит) *impf.*, произойти́ (-ойдёт; -ошёл, -ошла́) *pf.*; ~ in вме́шиваться *impf.*, вмеша́ться *pf.* в+*a.* **intervention** [ˌɪntə'venʃ(ə)n] *n.* вмеша́тельство; (*pol.*) интерве́нция.
interview ['ɪntəˌvjuː] *n.* делово́е свида́ние, встре́ча; (*press* ~) интервью́ *nt.indecl.*; *v.t.* интервьюи́ровать *impf.* & *pf.*, про~ *pf.* **interviewer** *n.* интервьюе́р.
interweave [ˌɪntə'wiːv] *v.t.* вотка́ть (-ку́, -кёшь; -ка́л, -кала́, -ка́ло) *pf.*
intestate [ɪn'testət] *adj.* уме́рший без завеща́ния.
intestinal [ˌɪnte'staɪn(ə)l] *adj.* кише́чный. **intestine** [ɪn'testɪn] *n.* кишка́ (*g.pl.* -шо́к); *pl.* кише́чник.
intimacy ['ɪntɪməsɪ] *n.* инти́мность, бли́зость. **intimate**[1] ['ɪntɪmət] *adj.* инти́мный, бли́зкий (-зок, -зка́, -зко, бли́зки́).
intimate[2] ['ɪntɪˌmeɪt] *v.t.* (*state*) сообща́ть *impf.*, сообщи́ть *pf.*; (*hint*) намека́ть *impf.*, намекну́ть *pf.* на+*a.* **inti'mation** *n.* сообщение; намёк.

intimidate [ɪn'tɪmɪˌdeɪt] *v.t.* запу́гивать *impf.*, запуга́ть *pf.*
into ['ɪntʊ, 'ɪntə] *prep.* в, во+*a.*, на+*a.*
intolerable [ɪn'tɒlərəb(ə)l] *adj.* невыноси́мый. **intolerance** *n.* нетерпи́мость. **intolerant** *adj.* нетерпи́мый.
intonation [ˌɪntə'neɪʃ(ə)n] *n.* интона́ция. **intone** [ɪn'təʊn] *v.t.* интони́ровать *impf.*
intoxicant [ɪn'tɒksɪˌkənt] *adj.* (*n.*) опьяня́ющий (напи́ток (-тка)). **intoxicate** *v.t.* опьяня́ть *impf.*, опьяни́ть *pf.* **intoxi'cation** *n.* опьяне́ние; **in a state of** ~ в нетре́звом состоя́нии.
intra- ['ɪntrə] *pref.* внутри... .
intractable [ɪn'træktəb(ə)l] *adj.* неподатливый.
intransigent [ɪn'trænsɪdʒ(ə)nt, -zɪdʒ(ə)nt] *adj.* непримири́мый.
intransitive [ɪn'trænsɪtɪv, ɪn'trɑːn-, -zɪtɪv] *adj.* непереходный.
intrepid [ɪn'trepɪd] *adj.* неустраши́мый.
intricacy ['ɪntrɪkəsɪ] *n.* запу́танность, сло́жность. **intricate** *adj.* запу́танный (-ан, -анна), сло́жный (-жен, -жна́, -жно).
intrigue [ɪn'triːg, 'ɪn-] *n.* интри́га; *v.i.* интригова́ть *impf.*; *v.t.* интригова́ть *impf.*, за~ *pf.* **intriguer** *n.* интрига́н, ~ка.
intrinsic [ɪn'trɪnzɪk] *adj.* прису́щий, существенный (-ен, -енна).
introduce [ˌɪntrə'djuːs] *v.t.* вводи́ть (-ожу́, -о́дишь) *impf.*, ввести́ (введу́, -дёшь; ввёл, -á) *pf.*; вноси́ть (-ошу́, -о́сишь) *impf.*, внести́ (внесу́, -сёшь; внёс, -ла́) *pf.*; (*person*) представля́ть *impf.*, предста́вить *pf.* **introduction** *n.* введе́ние, внесе́ние; представле́ние; (*to book*) предисло́вие. **introductory** *adj.* вво́дный, вступи́тельный.
introspection [ˌɪntrə'spekʃ(ə)n] *n.* самонаблюде́ние.
intrude [ɪn'truːd] *v.i.* вторга́ться *impf.*, вто́ргнуться (-г(нул)ся, -глась) *pf.* (**into** в+*a.*); *v.t.* & *i.* навя́зывать(ся) *impf.*, навяза́ть(ся) (-яжу́(сь), -я́жешь(ся)) *pf.* (**upon** +*d.*). **intrusion** *n.* вторже́ние.
intuition [ˌɪntjuː'ɪʃ(ə)n] *n.* интуи́ция. **in'tuitive** *adj.* интуити́вный.
inundate ['ɪnənˌdeɪt] *v.t.* наводня́ть *impf.*, наводни́ть *pf.* **inun'dation** *n.* наводне́ние.
inure [ɪ'njʊə(r)] *v.t.* приуча́ть *impf.*, приучи́ть (-чу́, -чишь) *pf.* (**to** к+*d.*, +*inf.*).
invade [ɪn'veɪd] *v.t.* вторга́ться *impf.*, вто́ргнуться (-г(нул)ся, -глась) *pf.* в+*a.* **invader** *n.* захва́тчик.
invalid[1] ['ɪnvəˌliːd, -lɪd] *n.* (*disabled person*) инвали́д, больно́й *sb.*; *adj.* (*disabled*) нетрудоспосо́бный.
invalid[2] [ɪn'vælɪd] *adj.* (*not valid*) недействи́тельный. **invalidate** *v.t.* де́лать *impf.*, с~ *pf.* недействи́тельным.
invaluable [ɪn'væljʊəb(ə)l] *adj.* неоцени́мый.
invariable [ɪn'veərɪəb(ə)l] *adj.* неизме́нный (-нен, -нна); (*math.*) постоя́нный (-нен, -нна).

invasion [ɪn'veɪʒ(ə)n] *n.* вторже́ние (в+*a.*); (*encroachment*) посяга́тельство (на+*a.*).

invective [ɪn'vektɪv] *n.* (*verbal attack*) обличи́тельная речь; (*abuse*) руга́тельства *nt.pl.*

inveigh [ɪn'veɪ] *v.i.* поноси́ть (-ошу́, -о́сишь) *impf.* (**against** +*a.*).

inveigle [ɪn'veɪg(ə)l, -'viːg(ə)l] *v.t.* завлека́ть *impf.*, завле́чь (-еку́, -ече́шь; -ёк, -екла́) *pf.*

invent [ɪn'vent] *v.t.* изобрета́ть *impf.*, изобрести́ (-ету́, -ете́шь; -ёл, -ела́) *pf.*; выду́мывать *impf.*, вы́думать *pf.* **invention** *n.* изобрете́ние; вы́думка. **inventive** *adj.* изобрета́тельный. **inventor** *n.* изобрета́тель *m.*

inventory ['ɪnvəntərɪ] *n.* инвента́рь (-ря́) *m.*, о́пись (иму́щества); *v.t.* инвентаризова́ть *impf.* & *pf.*

inverse ['ɪnvɜːs, -'vɜːs] *adj.* обра́тный. **inversion** *n.* перестано́вка.

invertebrate [ɪn'vɜːtɪbrət, -,breɪt] *adj.* беспозвоно́чный; *n.* беспозвоно́чное *sb.*

invest [ɪn'vest] *v.t.* (*clothe*, *endue*) облека́ть *impf.*, обле́чь (-еку́, -ече́шь; -ёк, -екла́) *pf.* (**in** в+*a.*; **with** +*i.*); (*lay siege to*) осажда́ть *impf.*, осади́ть *pf.*; *v.t.* & *i.* (*econ.*) вкла́дывать *impf.*, вложи́ть (-жу́, -о́жишь) *pf.* (де́ньги) (**in** в+*a.*); инвести́ровать *impf.* & *pf.*

investigate [ɪn'vestɪ,geɪt] *v.t.* иссле́довать *impf.* & *pf.*; (*leg.*) рассле́довать *impf.* & *pf.* **investi'gation** *n.* иссле́дование; рассле́дование. **investigator** *n.* иссле́дователь *m.*; (*leg.*) сле́дователь *m.*

investiture [ɪn'vestɪ,tjʊə(r)] *n.* введе́ние в до́лжность.

investment [ɪn'vestmənt] *n.* (*econ.*) вложе́ние, вклад, инвести́ция; (*mil.*) оса́да. **investor** *n.* вкла́дчик.

inveterate [ɪn'vetərət] *adj.* закорене́лый, застаре́лый.

invigorate [ɪn'vɪgə,reɪt] *v.t.* укрепля́ть *impf.*, укрепи́ть *pf.*; (*animate*) оживля́ть *impf.*, оживи́ть *pf.*

invincible [ɪn,vɪnsɪb(ə)l] *adj.* непобеди́мый.

inviolable [ɪn'vaɪələb(ə)l] *adj.* неприкоснове́нный (-нен, -нна), неруши́мый. **inviolate** *adj.* ненару́шенный.

invisible [ɪn'vɪzɪb(ə)l] *adj.* неви́димый; ~ **ink** симпати́ческие черни́ла (-л) *pl.*

invitation [,ɪnvɪ'teɪʃ(ə)n] *n.* приглаше́ние. **invite** [ɪn'vaɪt] *v.t.* приглаша́ть *impf.*, пригласи́ть *pf.*; (*request*) проси́ть (-ошу́, -о́сишь) *impf.*, по~ *pf.*; (*attract*) привлека́ть *impf.*, привле́чь (-еку́, -ече́шь; -ёк, -екла́) *pf.* **in'viting** *adj.* привлека́тельный.

invocation [,ɪnvə'keɪʃ(ə)n] *n.* призы́в.

invoice ['ɪnvɔɪs] *n.* факту́ра, накладна́я *sb.*

invoke [ɪn'vəʊk] *v.t.* призыва́ть *impf.*, призва́ть (-зову́, -зовёшь; призва́л, -á, -о) взыва́ть *impf.*, воззва́ть (-зову́, -зовёшь) *pf.*

involuntary [ɪn'vɒləntərɪ] *adj.* нево́льный; непроизво́льный.

involve [ɪn'vɒlv] *v.t.* (*entail*) вовлека́ть *impf.*, вовле́чь (-еку́, -ече́шь; -ёк, -екла́) *pf.*; (*include*) включа́ть *impf.*, включи́ть *pf.* в себе́. **involved** *adj.* (*complex*) сло́жный (-жен, -жна́, -жно).

invulnerable [ɪn'vʌlnərəb(ə)l] *adj.* неуязви́мый.

inward ['ɪnwəd] *adj.* вну́тренний. **inwardly** *adv.* внутри́, вну́тренне. **inwards** *adv.* внутрь.

iodine ['aɪə,diːn, -ɪn] *n.* йод; *attr.* йо́дный.

ion ['aɪən] *n.* ио́н. **ionic** [aɪ'ɒnɪk] *adj.* ио́нный.

iota [aɪ'əʊtə] *n.* йо́та; **not an** ~ ни на йо́ту.

IOU [,aɪəʊ'juː] *n.* долгова́я распи́ска.

IQ *abbr.* (*of* **intelligence quotient**) коэффицие́нт у́мственного разви́тия.

Iran [ɪ'rɑːn] *n.* Ира́н.

Iraq [ɪ'rɑːk] *n.* Ира́к.

irascible [ɪ'ræsɪb(ə)l] *adj.* раздражи́тельный.

irate [aɪ'reɪt] *adj.* гне́вный (-вен, -вна́, -вно). **ire** *n.* гнев.

Ireland ['aɪələnd] *n.* Ирла́ндия.

iridescent [,ɪrɪ'des(ə)nt] *adj.* ра́дужный.

iris ['aɪərɪs] *n.* (*anat.*) ра́дужная оболо́чка; (*bot.*) каса́тик.

Irish ['aɪərɪʃ] *adj.* ирла́ндский. **Irishman** *n.* ирла́ндец (-дца). **Irishwoman** *n.* ирла́ндка.

irk [ɜːk] *v.t.* надоеда́ть *impf.*, надое́сть (-е́м, -е́шь, -е́ст, -еди́м; -е́л) *pf.*+*d.* **irksome** *adj.* ску́чный (-чен, -чна́, -чно).

iron ['aɪən] *n.* желе́зо; (*for clothes*) утю́г (-á); *pl.* (*fetters*) кандалы́ (-ло́в) *pl.*; *adj.* желе́зный; *v.t.* (*clothes*) утю́жить *impf.*, вы́~, от~ *pf.*; гла́дить *impf.*, вы́~ *pf.*

ironic(al) [aɪ'rɒnɪkəl] *adj.* ирони́ческий. **irony** ['aɪrənɪ] *n.* иро́ния.

irradiate [ɪ'reɪdɪ,eɪt] *v.t.* (*light up*) освеща́ть *impf.*, освети́ть (-ещу́, -ети́шь) *pf.*; (*subject to radiation*) облуча́ть *impf.*, облучи́ть *pf.* **irradi'ation** *n.* освеще́ние; облуче́ние.

irrational [ɪ'ræʃən(ə)l] *adj.* неразу́мный; (*math.*) иррациона́льный.

irreconcilable [ɪ'rekən,saɪləb(ə)l] *adj.* (*persons*) непримири́мый; (*ideas*) несовмести́мый.

irrecoverable [,ɪrɪ'kʌvərəb(ə)l] *adj.* невозвра́тный.

irredeemable [,ɪrɪ'diːməb(ə)l] *adj.* (*econ.*) не подлежа́щий вы́купу; (*hopeless*) безнадёжный.

irrefutable [ɪ'refjʊtəb(ə)l, ,ɪrɪ'fjuː-] *adj.* неопровержи́мый.

irregular [ɪ'regjʊlə(r)] *adj.* нерегуля́рный; (*gram.*) непра́вильный; (*not even*) неро́вный (-вен, -вна́, -вно); (*disorderly*) беспоря́дочный.

irrelevant [ɪ'relɪv(ə)nt] *adj.* неуме́стный.

irreligious [,ɪrɪ'lɪdʒəs] *adj.* неве́рующий.

irremediable [,ɪrɪ'miːdɪəb(ə)l] *adj.* непоправи́мый, неизлечи́мый.

irremovable [,ɪrɪ'muːvəb(ə)l] *adj.* неустрани́мый; (*from office*) несменя́емый.

irreparable [ɪ'repərəb(ə)l] *adj.* непоправи́мый.

irreplaceable [,ɪrɪ'pleɪsəb(ə)l] *adj.* незамени́мый.

irrepressible [ˌɪrɪ'presɪb(ə)l] *adj.* неудержи́мый.

irreproachable [ˌɪrɪ'prəʊtʃəb(ə)l] *adj.* безупре́чный.

irresistible [ˌɪrɪ'zɪstɪb(ə)l] *adj.* неотрази́мый.

irresolute [ɪ'rezəˌluːt, -ˌljuːt] *adj.* нереши́тельный.

irrespective [ˌɪrɪ'spektɪv] *adj.*: ~ **of** безотноси́тельно к+*d.*, незави́симо от+*g.*

irresponsible [ˌɪrɪ'spɒnsɪb(ə)l] *adj.* (*of conduct etc.*) безотве́тственный (-ен, -енна); (*not responsible*) неотве́тственный (-ен, -енна); (*leg.*) невменя́емый.

irretrievable [ˌɪrɪ'triːvəb(ə)l] *adj.* непоправи́мый, невозвра́тный.

irreverent [ɪ'revərənt] *adj.* непочти́тельный.

irreversible [ˌɪrɪ'vɜːsɪb(ə)l] *adj.* необрати́мый.

irrevocable [ɪ'revəkəb(ə)l] *adj.* неотменя́емый.

irrigate ['ɪrɪˌgeɪt] *v.t.* ороша́ть *impf.*, ороси́ть *pf.* **irri'gation** *n.* ороше́ние, иррига́ция.

irritable ['ɪrɪtəb(ə)l] *adj.* раздражи́тельный. **irritate** *v.t.* раздража́ть *impf.*, раздражи́ть *pf.* **irri'tation** *n.* раздраже́ние.

Islam ['ɪzlɑːm, -læm, -'lɑːm] *n.* исла́м. **Islamic** *adj.* мусульма́нский, исла́мистский.

island ['aɪlənd], **isle** [aɪl] *n.* о́стров (*pl.* -а́); *adj.* островно́й. **islander** *n.* островитя́нин (*pl.* -я́не, -я́н), -я́нка. **islet** *n.* острово́к (-вка́).

iso- ['aɪsəʊ] *in comb.* изо..., равно... **isobar** *n.* изоба́ра. **isosceles** [aɪ'sɒsɪˌliːz] *adj.* равнобе́дренный. **isotherm** *n.* изоте́рма. **isotope** ['aɪsəˌtəʊp] *n.* изото́п.

isolate ['aɪsəˌleɪt] *v.t.* изоли́ровать *impf.* & *pf.*; обособля́ть *impf.*, обосо́бить *pf.*; (*chem.*) выделя́ть *impf.*, вы́делить *pf.* **iso'lation** *n.* изоля́ция; ~ **hospital** инфекцио́нная больни́ца; ~ **ward** изоля́тор.

Israel ['ɪzreɪl] *n.* Изра́иль *m.* **Is'raeli** *n.* израильтя́нин (*pl.* -я́не, -я́н), -я́нка; *adj.* изра́ильский.

issue ['ɪʃuː, 'ɪsjuː] *n.* (*outlet*) вы́ход; (*outflow*) вытека́ние; (*progeny*) пото́мство; (*outcome*) исхо́д, результа́т; (*question*) (спо́рный) вопро́с; (*of book etc.*) вы́пуск, изда́ние; *v.i.* выходи́ть (-ожу́, -о́дишь) *impf.*, вы́йти (вы́йду, -дешь; вы́шел, -шла) *pf.*; (*flow*) вытека́ть *impf.*, вы́течь (-еку, -ечешь; -ек) *pf.*; *v.t.* выпуска́ть *impf.*, вы́пустить *pf.*; выдава́ть (-даю́, -даёшь) *impf.*, вы́дать (-ам, -ашь, -аст, -адим) *pf.*

isthmus ['ɪsməs, 'ɪsθ-] *n.* переше́ек (-е́йка).

it [ɪt] *pron.* он, оно́ (его́, ему́, им, о нём), она́ (её, ей, ей & е́ю, о ней); *demonstrative* э́то.

Italian [ɪ'tæljən] *n.* италья́нец (-нца), -нка; *adj.* италья́нский.

italic [ɪ'tælɪk] *adj.* (**I**~) италий́ский; (*print.*) курси́вный; *n.* курси́в. **italicize** [ɪ'tælɪˌsaɪz] *v.t.* выделя́ть *impf.*, вы́делить *pf.* курси́вом.

Italy ['ɪtəlɪ] *n.* Ита́лия.

itch [ɪtʃ] *n.* зуд, чесо́тка; *v.i.* зуде́ть (-ди́т) *impf.*; чеса́ться (че́шется) *impf.*

item ['aɪtəm] *n.* (*on list*) предме́т; (*in account*) пункт; (*on agenda*) вопро́с; (*in programme*) но́мер (*pl.* -а́); *adv.* та́кже, то́же.

iterate ['ɪtəˌreɪt] *v.t.* повторя́ть *impf.*, повтори́ть *pf.*

itinerant [aɪ'tɪnərənt, ɪ-] *adj.* стра́нствующий. **itinerary** *n.* (*route*) маршру́т; (*guidebook*) путеводи́тель *m.*

its [ɪts] *poss. pron.* его́, её; свой (-оя́, -оё, -ои́).

itself [ɪt'self] *pron.* (*emph.*) (он(о́) сам(о́) (-ого́, -ому́, -им, -о́м), (она́) сама́ (-мо́й, -му́); (*refl.*) себя́ (себе́, собо́й); -ся (*suffixed to v.t.*)

ITV (*abbr. of* **Independent Television**) незави́симое (комме́рческое) телеви́дение.

ivory ['aɪvərɪ] *n.* слоно́вая кость.

ivy ['aɪvɪ] *n.* плющ (-а́).

J

jab [dʒæb] *n.* уко́л, толчо́к (-чка́); *v.t.* ты́кать (ты́чу, -чешь) *impf.*, ткнуть *pf.* (+*i.* в+*a.*; +*a.* в+*a.*).

jabber ['dʒæbə(r)] *n.* болтовня́; *v.t.* & *i.* болта́ть *impf.*

jack [dʒæk] *n.* (*cards*) вале́т; (*lifting machine*) домкра́т; *v.t.* (~ *up*) поднима́ть *impf.*, подня́ть (-ниму́, -ни́мешь; по́днял, -á, -о) *pf.* домкра́том.

jackal ['dʒæk(ə)l] *n.* шака́л.

jackass ['dʒækæs] *n.* осёл (осла́).

jackdaw ['dʒækdɔː] *n.* га́лка.

jacket ['dʒækɪt] *n.* ку́ртка; (*woman's*) жаке́тка; (*tech.*) кожу́х (-а́); (*on boiler*) руба́шка; (*on book*) (супер)обло́жка.

jack-knife ['dʒæknaɪf] *n.* большо́й складно́й нож (-а́).

jaded *adj.* изнурённый (-ён, -ённа).

jade [dʒeɪd] *n.* нефри́т.

jagged ['dʒægɪd] *adj.* зубча́тый, зазу́бренный (-ен, -енна).

jaguar ['dʒægjʊə(r)] *n.* ягуа́р.

jail [dʒeɪl] *n.* тюрьма́ (*pl.* -рьмы, -рем, -рьмам); *v.t.* заключа́ть *impf.*, заключи́ть *pf.* в тюрьму́. **jailer** *n.* тюре́мщик.

jam¹ [dʒæm] *n.* (*crush*) да́вка; (*of machine*) зада́ние, перебо́й; (*in traffic*) про́бка; *v.t.* (*squeeze*) сжима́ть *impf.*, сжать (сожму́, -мёшь) *pf.*; (*thrust*) впи́хивать *impf.*, впихну́ть *pf.* (**into** в+*a.*); (*block*) загроможда́ть *impf.*, загромозди́ть *pf.*; (*radio*) заглуша́ть *impf.*, заглуши́ть *pf.*; *v.i.* (*machine*) заеда́ть *impf.*, зае́сть (-е́ст; -е́ло) *pf. impers.*+*a.*

jam² [dʒæm] *n.* (*conserve*) варе́нье, джем.

jamb [dʒæm] *n.* коса́к (-а́).

jangle ['dʒæŋg(ə)l] *n.* ре́зкий звук; *v.i.* издава́ть (-даю́, -даёшь) *impf.*, изда́ть (-а́м, -а́шь, -а́ст, -ади́м; изда́л, -а́, -о) *pf.* ре́зкие зву́ки.

janitor ['dʒænɪtə(r)] *n.* (*door-keeper*) привра́тник, -ица; (*caretaker*) дво́рник.

January ['dʒænjʊərɪ] *n.* янва́рь (-ря́) *m.*; *attr.* янва́рский.

Japan [dʒə'pæn] *n.* Япо́ния. **Japanese** [,dʒæpə'niːz] *n.* япо́нец (-нца), -нка; *adj.* япо́нский.

jar¹ [dʒɑː(r)] *n.* (*container*) ба́нка.

jar² [dʒɑː(r)] *v.i.* (*sound*) скрипе́ть (-пи́т) *impf.*; (*irritate*) раздража́ть *impf.*, раздражи́ть *pf.* (**upon** +*a.*).

jargon ['dʒɑːgən] *n.* жарго́н.

jasmin(e) ['dʒæsmɪn, 'dʒæz-] *n.* жасми́н.

jasper ['dʒæspə(r)] *n.* я́шма; *attr.* я́шмовый.

jaundice ['dʒɔːndɪs] *n.* желту́ха; (*fig.*) за́висть. **jaundiced** *adj.* желту́шный, больно́й (-лен, -льна́) желту́хой; (*fig.*) зави́стливый.

jaunt [dʒɔːnt] *n.* прогу́лка, прое́здка. **jaunty** *adj.* бо́дрый (бодр, -а́, -о, бо́дры).

javelin ['dʒævəlɪn, -vlɪn] *n.* копьё (*pl.* -пья, -пий, -пьям).

jaw [dʒɔː] *n.* че́люсть; *pl.* пасть, рот (рта, *loc.* во рту́); *pl.* (*of valley etc.*) у́зкий вход; *pl.* (*of vice*) гу́бка.

jay [dʒeɪ] *n.* (*bird*) со́йка; (*fig.*) болту́н (-а́), ~ья.

jazz [dʒæz] *n.* джаз; *adj.* джа́зовый.

jealous ['dʒeləs] *adj.* ревни́вый, зави́стливый; **be ~ of** (*person*) ревнова́ть *impf.*; (*thing*) зави́довать *impf.*, по~ *pf.*+*d.*; (*rights*) ревни́во оберега́ть *impf.*, обере́чь (-егу́, -ежёшь; -ёг, -егла́) *pf.* **jealousy** *n.* ре́вность, за́висть.

jeans [dʒiːnz] *n.* джи́нсы *pl.*

jeep [dʒiːp] *n.* джип.

jeer [dʒɪə(r)] *n.* насме́шка; *v.t. & i.* насмеха́ться *impf.* (**at** +*i.*).

jejune [dʒɪ'dʒuːn] *adj.* (*scanty*) ску́дный (-ден, -дна́, -дно); (*to mind*) неинтере́сный.

jelly ['dʒelɪ] *n.* (*sweet*) желе́ *nt.indecl.*; (*meat, fish*) сту́день (-дня) *m.* **jellyfish** *n.* меду́за.

jemmy ['dʒemɪ] *n.* фо́мка, лом (*pl.* -ы, -ов).

jeopardize ['dʒepə,daɪz] *v.t.* подверга́ть *impf.*, подве́ргнуть (-г) *pf.* опа́сности. **jeopardy** *n.* опа́сность.

jerk [dʒɜːk] *n.* толчо́к (-чка́); (*of muscle*) вздра́гивание; *v.t.* дёргать *impf.*+*i.*; *v.i.* (*twitch*) дёргаться *impf.*, дёрнуться *pf.* **jerky** *adj.* тря́ский (-сок, -ска), отры́вистый.

jersey ['dʒɜːzɪ] *n.* (*garment*) фуфа́йка; (*fabric*) джерси́ *nt.indecl.*

jest [dʒest] *n.* шу́тка, насме́шка; *v.i.* шути́ть (шучу́, шу́тишь) *impf.*, по~ *pf.* **jester** *n.* шутни́к (-а́), -и́ца; (*hist.*) шут (-а́).

Jesuit ['dʒezjʊɪt] *n.* иезуи́т. **Jesu'itical** *adj.* иезуи́тский.

jet¹ [dʒet] *n.* (*stream*) струя́ (*pl.* -у́и); (*nozzle*)

форсу́нка, сопло́ (*pl.* со́пла, со́п(е)л); ~ **engine** реакти́вный дви́гатель *m.*; ~ **plane** реакти́вный самолёт.

jet² [dʒet] *n.* (*min.*) гага́т; *adj.* гага́товый. **jet-black** *adj.* чёрный (-рен, -рна́, -рно) как смоль.

jetsam ['dʒetsəm] *n.* това́ры *m.pl.*, сбро́шенные с корабля́.

jettison ['dʒetɪs(ə)n, -z(ə)n] *v.t.* выбра́сывать *impf.*, вы́бросить *pf.* за́ борт.

jetty ['dʒetɪ] *n.* (*mole*) мол (*loc.* -ý); (*landing pier*) при́стань (*pl.* -ни, -не́й).

Jew [dʒuː] *n.* евре́й. **Jewess** *n.* евре́йка. **Jewish** *adj.* евре́йский. **Jewry** *n.* евре́йство.

jewel ['dʒuːəl] *n.* драгоце́нность, драгоце́нный ка́мень (-мня; *pl.* -мни, -мне́й) *m.* **jeweller** *n.* ювели́р. **jewellery, jewelry** *n.* драгоце́нности *f.pl.*, ювели́рные изде́лия *nt.pl.*

jib [dʒɪb] *n.* (*naut.*) кли́вер (*pl.* -а́ & -ы); (*of crane*) стрела́ (*pl.* -лы) (кра́на).

jigsaw ['dʒɪgsɔː] *n.*: ~ **puzzle** карти́нка-зага́дка.

jingle ['dʒɪŋg(ə)l] *n.* звя́канье; *v.t. & i.* звя́кать *impf.*, звя́кнуть *pf.* (+*i.*).

jingo ['dʒɪŋgəʊ] *n.* ура́-патрио́т. **jingoism** *n.* ура́-патриоти́зм. **jingo'istic** *adj.* ура́-патриоти́ческий.

job [dʒɒb] *n.* (*work*) рабо́та; (*task*) зада́ние; (*position*) ме́сто (*pl.* -а́). **jobless** *adj.* безрабо́тный.

jockey ['dʒɒkɪ] *n.* жоке́й.

jocose [dʒə'kəʊs] *adj.* игри́вый.

jocular ['dʒɒkjʊlə(r)] *adj.* шутли́вый.

jocund ['dʒɒkənd] *adj.* весёлый (ве́сел, -а́, -о, ве́селы).

jog [dʒɒg] *n.* (*push*) толчо́к (-чка́); (*movement*) ме́дленная ходьба́, езда́; *v.t.* толка́ть *impf.*, толкну́ть *pf.*; (*nudge*) подта́лкивать *impf.*, подтолкну́ть *pf.* **jogger** *n.* люби́тель *m.*, ~ница оздорови́тельного бе́га, джо́ггер. **jogging** *n.* оздорови́тельный бег. **jogtrot** *n.* рысца́.

join [dʒɔɪn] *v.t. & i.* соединя́ть(ся) *impf.*, соедини́ть(ся) *pf.*; *v.t.* присоединя́ться *impf.*, присоедини́ться *pf.* к+*d.*; (*become member of*) вступа́ть *impf.*, вступи́ть (-плю́, -пишь) *pf.* в+*a.*; *v.i.*: ~ **up** вступа́ть *impf.*, вступи́ть (-плю́, -пишь) *pf.* в а́рмию.

joiner ['dʒɔɪnə(r)] *n.* столя́р (-а́). **joinery** *n.* (*goods*) столя́рные изде́лия *nt.pl.*; (*work*) столя́рная рабо́та.

joint [dʒɔɪnt] *n.* соедине́ние, ме́сто (*pl.* -а́) соедине́ния; (*anat.*) суста́в; (*tech.*) стык, шов (шва), шарни́р; *adj.* соединённый, о́бщий; совме́стный; ~ **venture** совме́стное предприя́тие; ~ **stock** акционе́рный капита́л; (*attr.*) акционе́рный; *v.t.* (*join*) сочленя́ть *impf.*, сочлени́ть *pf.*; (*divide*) расчленя́ть *impf.*, расчлени́ть *pf.*

joist [dʒɔɪst] *n.* переклади́на.

joke [dʒəʊk] *n.* шу́тка, остро́та, анекдо́т; *v.i.* шути́ть (шучу́, шу́тишь) *impf.*, по~ *pf.* **joker** *n.* шутни́к (-а́), -и́ца.

jollity ['dʒɒlɪtɪ] *n.* весéлье. **jolly** *adj.* весёлый (вéсел, -á, -о, вéселы́); *adv.* óчень.

jolt [dʒəʊlt, dʒɒlt] *n.* тряска; *v.t.* трястú (-сý, -сёшь; -с, -слá) *impf.*

jostle ['dʒɒs(ə)l] *n.* толкотня́; *v.t. & i.* толкáть(ся) *impf.*, толкнýть(ся) *pf.*

jot [dʒɒt] *n.* йóта; **not a** ~ ни на йóту; *v.t.* (~ *down*) бы́стро, крáтко, запи́сывать *impf.*, записáть (-ишý, -и́шешь) *pf.*

joule [dʒuːl] *n.* джóуль *m.*

journal ['dʒɜː(ə)l] *n.* журнáл, дневни́к (-á); (*tech.*) цáпфа, шéйка. **journa'lese** *n.* газéтный язы́к (-á). **journalism** *n.* журнали́стика. **journalist** *n.* журнали́ст.

journey ['dʒɜːnɪ] *n.* путешéствие, поéздка; (*specific ~ of vehicle*) рейс; *v.i.* путешéствовать *impf.*

jovial ['dʒəʊvɪəl] *adj.* (*merry*) весёлый (вéсел, -á, -о, вéселы); (*sociable*) общи́тельный.

jowl [dʒaʊl] *n.* (*jaw*) чéлюсть; (*cheek*) щекá (*a.* щёку; *pl.* щёки, щёк, -áм).

joy [dʒɔɪ] *n.* рáдость. **joyful, joyous** *adj.* рáдостный. **joyless** *adj.* безрáдостный. **joyrider** *n.* автобóр-лихáч (-á). **joystick** *n.* джóйстик.

JP *abbr.* (*of Justice of the Peace*) мировóй судья́.

jubilant ['dʒuːbɪlənt] *adj.* лику́ющий. **jubilate** *v.i.* ликовáть *impf.*

jubilee ['dʒuːbɪˌliː] *n.* юбилéй.

Judaic [dʒuːˈdeɪɪk] *adj.* иудéйский.

judge [dʒʌdʒ] *n.* судья́ (*pl.* -дьи, -дéй, -дьям) *m.*; (*connoisseur*) цени́тель *m.*; *v.t. & i.* суди́ть (сужý, сýдишь) *impf.*; *v.t.* (*appraise*) оцéнивать *impf.*, оцени́ть (-ню́, -нишь) *pf.* **judgement** *n.* (*sentence*) пригово́р; (*decision*) решéние; (*opinion*) мнéние; (*estimate*) оцéнка.

judicature ['dʒuːdɪkətʃə(r), -ˈdɪkətʃə(r)] *n.* отправлéние правосу́дия; (*judiciary*) судéйская корпорáция. **judicial** [dʒuːˈdɪʃ(ə)l] *adj.* (*of law*) судéбный; (*of judge*) судéйский; (*impartial*) беспристрáстный. **ju'dicious** *adj.* здравомы́слящий.

judo ['dʒuːdəʊ] *n.* дзюдó *nt.indecl.*

jug [dʒʌg] *n.* кувши́н; *v.t.* туши́ть (-шý, -шишь) *impf.*, c~ *pf.*

juggle ['dʒʌg(ə)l] *v.i.* жонгли́ровать *impf.* **juggler** *n.* жонглёр.

jugular ['dʒʌgjʊlə(r)] *adj.* шéйный; ~ **vein** ярéмная вéна.

juice [dʒuːs] *n.* сок (-a(y), *loc.* -e & -ý); (*fig.*) сýщность. **juicer** *n.* соковыжимáлка. **juicy** *adj.* сóчный (-чен, -чнá, -чно).

July [dʒuːˈlaɪ] *n.* июль *m.*; *attr.* ию́льский.

jumble ['dʒʌmb(ə)l] *n.* (*disorder*) беспоря́док (-дка); (*articles*) барахлó; *v.t.* перепу́тывать *impf.*, перепу́тать *pf.*

jump [dʒʌmp] *n.* прыжóк (-жкá), скачóк (-чкá); (*in price etc.*) рéзкое повышéние; *v.t.* пры́гать *impf.*, пры́гнуть *pf.*; скакáть (-ачý, -áчешь) *impf.*; (*from shock*) вздрáгивать *impf.*, вздрóгнуть *pf.*; (*of price etc.*) под-

скáкивать *impf.*, подскочи́ть (-ит) *pf.*; *v.t.* (~ *over*) перепры́гивать *impf.*, перепры́гнуть *pf.*; ~ **at** (*accept eagerly*) ухвáтываться *impf.*, ухвати́ться (-ачýсь, -áтишься) *pf.* за+*a.*; ~ **the rails** сходи́ть (-ит) *impf.*, сойти́ (сойдёт; сошёл, -шлá) *pf.* с рéльсов.

jumper ['dʒʌmpə(r)] *n.* (*garment*) джéмпер.

jumpy ['dʒʌmpɪ] *adj.* нéрвный (-вен, нервнá, -вно).

junction ['dʒʌŋkʃ(ə)n] *n.* (*joining*) соединéние; (*rail.*) железнодорóжный ýзел (узлá); (*roads*) перекрёсток (-тка).

juncture ['dʒʌŋktʃə(r)] *n.* (*joining*) соединéние; (*state of affairs*) положéние дел; **at this** ~ в э́тот момéнт.

June [dʒuːn] *n.* ию́нь *m.*; *attr.* ию́нский.

jungle ['dʒʌŋg(ə)l] *n.* джýнгли (-лей) *pl.*

junior ['dʒuːnɪə(r)] *adj.* млáдший.

juniper ['dʒuːnɪpə(r)] *n.* можжевéльник.

junk[1] [dʒʌŋk] *n.* (*rubbish*) барахлó.

junk[2] [dʒʌŋk] *n.* (*ship*) джóнка.

junta ['dʒʌntə] *n.* хýнта.

Jupiter ['dʒuːpɪtə(r)] *n.* Юпи́тер.

jurisdiction [ˌdʒʊərɪsˈdɪkʃ(ə)n] *n.* (*administration of law*) отправлéние правосу́дия; (*legal authority*) юрисди́кция.

jurisprudence [ˌdʒʊərɪsˈpruːd(ə)ns] *n.* юриспрудéнция.

jurist ['dʒʊərɪst] *n.* юри́ст.

juror ['dʒʊərə(r)] *n.* прися́жный *sb.*; (*in competition*) член жюри́. **jury** *n.* прися́жные *sb.*; жюри́ *nt.indecl.*

just [dʒʌst] *adj.* (*fair*) справедли́вый; (*deserved*) заслýженный, дóлжный; *adv.* (*exactly*) тóчно, и́менно; (*barely*) едвá; (*at this, that, moment*) тóлько что; ~ **in case** на вся́кий слýчай.

justice ['dʒʌstɪs] *n.* правосу́дие; (*fairness*) справедли́вость; (*judge*) судья́ (*pl.* -дьи, -дéй, -дьям); (*proceedings*) суд (-á); **bring to** ~ отдавáть (-даю́, -даёшь) *impf.*, отдáть (-áм, -áшь, -áст, -ади́м; óтдал, -á, -о) *pf.* под суд; **do** ~ **to** отдавáть (-даю́, -даёшь) *pf.* отдáть (-áм, -áшь, -áст, -ади́м; óтдал, -á, -о) дóлжное+*d.*

justify ['dʒʌstɪˌfaɪ] *v.t.* опрáвдывать *impf.*, оправдáть *pf.* **justifi'cation** *n.* оправдáние.

jut [dʒʌt] *v.i.* (~ *out, forth*) выдавáться (-даётся) *impf.*, вы́даться (-астся -адутся) *pf.*; выступáть *impf.*

jute [dʒuːt] *n.* джут.

juvenile ['dʒuːvəˌnaɪl] *n.* ю́ноша *m.*, подрóсток (-тка); *adj.* ю́ный (юн, -á, -о), ю́ношеский.

juxtapose [ˌdʒʌkstəˈpəʊz] *v.t.* помещáть *impf.*, помести́ть *pf.* ря́дом; сопоставля́ть *impf.*, сопостáвить *pf.* (**with** c+*i.*).

K

K *abbr.* (*of* **kilobyte**) килобáйт.

k *abbr.* (*of* **kilometre(s)**) км, киломéтр.

kale, kail [keɪl] *n.* кормовáя капýста.

kaleidoscope [kə'laɪdə,skəʊp] *n.* калейдо-скóп.

kangaroo [,kæŋgə'ruː] *n.* кенгурý *m.indecl.*

Kazakhstan [,kɑːzɑːk'stæn, -'stɑːn] *n.* Казах-стáн.

kebab [kɪ'bæb] *n.* кебáб, шашлы́к (-á); ~ **house** кебáбная *sb.*

keel [kiːl] *n.* киль *m.*; *v.t. & i.*: ~ **over** опроки́-дывать(ся) *impf.*, опроки́нуть(ся) *pf.*

keen [kiːn] *adj.* (*sharp*) óстрый (остр & остёр, острá, óстро); (*strong*) си́льный (си́лён, -льнá, -льно, си́льны́); (*penetrating*) прони-цáтельный; (*ardent*) стрáстный (-тен, -тнá, -тно).

keep[1] [kiːp] *n.* (*of castle*) глáвная бáшня (*g.pl.* -шен); (*maintenance*) содержáние; (*food*) пи́ща.

keep[2] [kiːp] *v.t.* (*observe*) соблюдáть *impf.*, соблюсти́ (-юдý, -юдёшь; -юл, -юлá) *pf.* (*the law*); сдéрживать *impf.*, сдержáть (-жý, -жишь) *pf.* (*one's word*); (*celebrate*) прáзд-новать *impf.*, от~ *pf.*; (*possess, maintain*) держáть (-жý, -жишь) *impf.*; храни́ть *impf.*; (*family*) содержáть (-жý, -жишь) *impf.*; (*diary*) вести́ (ведý, -дёшь; вёл, -á) *impf.*; (*detain*) задéрживать *impf.*, задержáть (-жý, -жишь) *pf.*; (*retain, reserve*) сохранять *impf.*, сохрани́ть *pf.*; *v.i.* (*remain*) оставáться (-таю́сь, -таёшься) *impf.*, остáться (-áнусь, -áнешься) *pf.*; (*of food*) не пóртиться *impf.*; ~ **away** держáть(ся) (-жý(сь), -жишь(ся)) *impf.* в отдалéнии; ~ **back** (*hold back*) удéрживать *impf.*, удержáть (-жý, -жишь) *pf.*; (*conceal*) скрывáть *impf.*, скрыть (-рóю, -рóешь) *pf.*; ~ **down** подавля́ть *impf.*, подави́ть (-влю́, -вишь) *pf.*; ~ **from** удéржи-ваться *impf.*, удержáться (-жýсь, -жишься) *pf.* от+*g.*; ~ **on** продолжáть *impf.*, продóл-жить *pf.* (+*inf.*).

keepsake ['kiːpseɪk] *n.* подáрок (-рка) на пáмять.

keg [keg] *n.* бочóнок (-нка).

ken [ken] *n.* (*knowledge*) предéл познáний; (*sight*) кругозóр.

kennel ['ken(ə)l] *n.* конурá.

kerb [kɜːb] *n.* край (*loc.* -аю́; *pl.* -ая́, -аёв) тротуáра. **kerbstone** *n.* бордю́рный кáмень (-мня; *pl.* -мни, -мнéй) *m.*

kerchief ['kɜːtʃiːf, -tʃɪf] *n.* (головнóй) платóк (-ткá).

kernel ['kɜːn(ə)l] *n.* (*nut*) ядрó (*pl.* я́дра, я́дер, я́драм); (*grain*) зернó (*pl.* зёрна, -рен, -рнам); (*fig.*) суть.

kerosene ['kerə,siːn] *n.* кероси́н (-а(у)).

kestrel ['kestr(ə)l] *n.* пустельгá.

kettle ['ket(ə)l] *n.* чáйник. **kettledrum** *n.* литáвра.

key [kiː] *n.* ключ (-á); (*piano, typewriter*) клá-виш(а); (*mus.*) тонáльность; *attr.* ведýщий, ключевóй; *v.t.* (*type*) печáтать *impf.*, на~ *pf.* **keyboard** *n.* клавиатýра. **keyhole** *n.* замóчная сквáжина. **keynote** *n.* (*mus.*) тóника; (*fig.*) тон. **keystone** *n.* (*archit.*) замкóвый кáмень (-мня; *pl.* -мни, -мнéй) *m.*; (*fig.*) основнóй при́нцип.

kg. *abbr.* (*of* **kilogram(me)(s)**) кг, (кило-грáмм).

KGB *abbr.* (*of Russ.*) КГБ, (*Комитéт государ-ственной безопáсности*); ~ **agent** кагебéш-ник, геби́ст.

khaki ['kɑːkɪ] *n. & adj.* хáки *nt.indecl.*, *adj.indecl.*

khan [kɑːn, kæn] *n.* хан. **khanate** *n.* хáнство.

kick [kɪk] *n.* удáр ногóй, пинóк (-нкá); (*recoil of gun*) отдáча; *v.t.* ударять *impf.*, удáрить *pf.* ногóй; пинáть *impf.*, пнуть *pf.*; (*score goal*) забивáть *impf.*, заби́ть (-бью́, -бьёшь) *pf.* (гол, мяч); *v.i.* (*of horse etc.*) лягáться *impf.*; ~ **out** вышвы́ривать *impf.*, вы́швыр-нуть *pf.*

kid[1] [kɪd] *n.* (*goat*) козлёнок (-лёнка; *pl.* -ля́та, -ля́т); (*leather*) лáйка; (*child*) малы́ш (-á).

kid[2] [kɪd] *v.t.* (*deceive*) обмáнывать *impf.*, обманýть (-нý, -нешь) *pf.*; (*tease*) поддрáз-нивать *impf.*, поддразни́ть (-ню́, -нишь) *pf.*

kidnap ['kɪdnæp] *v.t.* похищáть *impf.*, похи́-тить (-и́щу, -и́тишь) *pf.*

kidney ['kɪdnɪ] *n.* пóчка; *attr.* пóчечный; ~ **bean** фасóль.

Kiev ['kiːef] *n.* Ки́ев.

kill [kɪl] *v.t.* убивáть *impf.*, уби́ть (убью́, -ьёшь) *pf.*; (*cattle*) рéзать (рéжу, -жешь) *impf.*, за~ *pf.*; ~ **off** ликвиди́ровать *impf. & pf.* **killer** *n.* уби́йца *c.g.* **killing** *n.* уби́йство; *adj.* (*mur-derous, fig.*) уби́йственный (-ен, -енна); (*amusing, coll.*) уморительный.

kiln [kɪln] *n.* óбжиговая печь (*pl.* -чи, -чéй).

kilo- ['kiːləʊ] *in comb.* кило... . **kilobyte** *n.* килобáйт. **kilocycle, kilohertz** *n.* килогéрц (*g.pl.* -ц). **kilogram(me)** *n.* килогрáмм. **kilometre** *n.* киломéтр. **kiloton(ne)** *n.* килотóнна. **kilowatt** *n.* киловáтт (*g.pl.* -т).

kimono [kɪ'məʊnəʊ] *n.* кимонó *nt.indecl.*

kin [kɪn] *n.* (*family*) семья́ (*pl.* -мьи, -мéй, -мьям); (*collect., relatives*) родня́.

kind[1] [kaɪnd] *n.* сорт (*pl.* -á), род (*pl.* -ы́, -óв); **a** ~ **of** чтó-то врóде+*g.*; **this** ~ **of** такóй; **what** ~ **of** чтó (э́то, *etc.*) за+*nom.*; ~ **of** (*adv.*) как бýдто, кáк-то; **pay in** ~ плати́ть (-ачý, -áтишь) *impf.*, за~ *pf.* натýрой; **return in** ~ отплáчивать *impf.*, отплати́ть (-ачý,

-áтишь) *pf.* той же монéтой+*d.*

kind² [kaɪnd] *adj.* дóбрый (добр, -á, -о, дóбры), любéзный.

kindergarten ['kɪndə,gɑːt(ə)n] *n.* дéтский сад (*loc.* -ý; *pl.* -ы́).

kindle ['kɪnd(ə)l] *v.t.* зажигáть *impf.*, зажéчь (-жгý, -жжёшь; -жёг, -жглá) *pf.*; *v.i.* загорáться *impf.*, загорéться (-рюсь, -ри́шься) *pf.* **kindling** *n.* растóпка.

kindly ['kaɪndlɪ] *adj.* дóбрый (добр, -á, -о, дóбры); *adv.* любéзно; (*with imper.*), (*request*) бýдьте добры́, +*imper.* **kindness** *n.* добротá, любéзность.

kindred ['kɪndrɪd] *n.* (*relationship*) крóвное родствó; (*relatives*) рóдственники *m.pl.*; *adj.* рóдственный (-ен, -енна); (*similar*) схóдный (-ден, -днá, -дно).

kinetic [kɪ'netɪk, kaɪ-] *adj.* кинети́ческий.

king [kɪŋ] *n.* корóль (-ля́) *m.* (*also chess, cards, fig.*); (*fig.*) царь (-ря́) *m.*; (*draughts*) дáмка **kingdom** *n.* корóлевство; (*fig.*) цáрство. **kingfisher** *n.* зиморóдок (-дка). **kingpin** *n.* шквóрень (-рня) *m.*

kink [kɪŋk] *n.* пéтля (*g.pl.* -тель), изги́б.

kinsfolk ['kɪnzfəʊk] *n.* крóвные рóдственники *m.pl.* **kinship** *n.* родствó; (*similarity*) схóдство. **kinsman, -woman** *n.* рóдственник, -ица.

kiosk ['kiːɒsk] *n.* киóск; (*telephone*) бýдка.

kip [kɪp] *v.i.* дры́хнуть (дрых(нул), -хла) *impf.*

kipper ['kɪpə(r)] *n.* копчёная селёдка.

Kirghizia [kɜː'gɪːzɪə] *n.* Кирги́зия.

kiss [kɪs] *n.* поцелýй; *v.t.* целовáть(ся) *impf.*, по~ *pf.*

kit [kɪt] *n.* (*soldier's*) ли́чное обмундировáние; (*clothing*) снаряжéние; (*tools*) комплéкт. **kitbag** *n.* вещевóй мешóк (-шкá).

kitchen ['kɪtʃɪn, -tʃ(ə)n] *n.* кýхня (*g.pl.* -хонь); *attr.* кýхонный; ~ **garden** огорóд. **kitchenmaid** *n.* судомóйка.

kite [kaɪt] *n.* (*bird*) кóршун; (*toy*) бумáжный змей.

kith [kɪθ] *n.*: ~ **and kin** знакóмые *sb.* и родня́.

kitten ['kɪt(ə)n] *n.* котёнок (-тёнка; *pl.* -тя́та, -тят); *v.i.* коти́ться *impf.*, о~ *pf.*

kleptomania [,kleptəʊ'meɪnɪə] *n.* клептомáния. **kleptomaniac** *n.* клептомáн.

km. *abbr.* (*of* **kilometre(s)**) км, километр.

knack [næk] *n.* сноровка, трюк.

knacker ['nækə(r)] *n.* живодёр.

knapsack ['næpsæk] *n.* рюкзáк (-á), рáнец (-нца).

knave [neɪv] *n.* (*rogue*) плут (-á); (*cards*) валéт. **knavery** *n.* плутовствó. **knavish** *adj.* плутовскóй.

knead [niːd] *v.t.* меси́ть (мешý, мéсишь) *impf.*, с~ *pf.*

knee [niː] *n.* колéно (*pl.* (*anat.*) -ни, -ней; (*tech.*) -нья, -ньев). **kneecap** *n.* (*bone*) колéнная чáшка; (*protective covering*) наколéнник. **knee-joint** *n.* колéнный сустáв.

kneel [niːl] *v.i.* стоя́ть (-ою́, -ои́шь) *impf.* на

колéнях; (~ *down*) станови́ться (-влюсь, -вишься) *impf.*, стать (-áну, -нешь) *pf.* на колéни.

knell [nel] *n.* похорóнный звон.

knickers ['nɪkəz] *n.* панталóны (-н) *pl.*

knick-knack ['nɪknæk] *n.* безделýшка.

knife [naɪf] *n.* нож (-á); *v.t.* колóть (-лю́, -лешь) *impf.*, за~ *pf.* ножóм.

knight [naɪt] *n.* ры́царь *m.*; (*holder of order*) кавалéр (óрдена); (*chess*) конь (-ня́; *pl.* -ни, -нéй) *m.* **knighthood** *n.* ры́царство. **knightly** *adj.* ры́царский.

knit [nɪt] *v.t.* (*garment*) вязáть (вяжý, -жешь) *impf.*, с~ *pf.*; (*unite*) свя́зывать *impf.*, связáть (-яжý, -жешь) *pf.*; *v.t. & i.* (*unite*) соединя́ть(ся) *impf.*, соедини́ть(ся) *pf.*; *v.i.* (*bones*) срастáться *impf.*, срасти́сь (-тётся) *pf.*; ~ **one's brows** хмýрить *impf.*, на~ *pf.* брóви. **knitting** *n.* (*action*) вязáние; (*object*) вязáнье. **knittingneedle** *n.* спи́ца. **knitwear** *n.* трикотáж.

knob [nɒb] *n.* ши́шка, кнóпка; (*door handle*) (крýглая) рýчка (двéри). **knobb(l)y** *adj.* шишковáтый.

knock [nɒk] *n.* (*noise*) стук; (*blow*) удáр; *v.t. & i.* (*strike*) ударя́ть *impf.*, удáрить *pf.*; (*strike door etc.*) стучáть (-чý, -чи́шь) *impf.*, по~ *pf.* (**at** в+*a.*); ~ **about** (*treat roughly*) колоти́ть (-очý, -óтишь) *impf.*, по~ *pf.*; (*wander*) шатáться *impf.*; ~ **down** (*person*) сбивáть *impf.*, сбить (сóбью, -ьёшь) *pf.* с ног; (*building*) сноси́ть (-ошý, -óсишь) *impf.*, снести́ (снесý, -сёшь; снёс, -лá) *pf.*; (*at auction*) продавáть (-даю́, -даёшь) *impf.*, продáть (-áм, -áшь, -áст, -ади́м; прóдал, -á, -о) *pf.* с молоткá; ~ **in** вбивáть *impf.*, вбить (вобью́, -ьёшь) *pf.* (в+*a.*); ~ **off** сбивáть *impf.*, сбить (сбью, -ьёшь) *pf.*; (*leave work*) прекращáть *impf.*, прекрати́ть (-ащý, -ати́шь) *pf.* (рабóту); ~ **out** выбивáть *impf.*, вы́бить (-бью, -бьешь) *pf.*; (*sport*) нокаути́ровать *impf. & pf.* **knocker** *n.* (*door-*~) дверной молотóк (-ткá). **knock-out** *n.* нокáут.

knoll [nəʊl] *n.* бугóр (-грá).

knot [nɒt] *n.* ýзел (узлá) (*also fig., naut.*); (*hard lump*) нарóст; (*in wood*) сучóк (-чкá); (*group*) кýчка; *v.t.* завя́зывать *impf.*, завязáть (-яжý, -жешь) *pf.* узлóм. **knotty** *adj.* узловáтый; (*fig.*) запýтанный (-ан, -анна).

knout [naʊt, nuːt] *n.* кнут (-á).

know [nəʊ] *v.t.* знать *impf.*; (~ *how to*) умéть *impf.*, с~ *pf.*+*inf.*; (*be acquainted*) быть знакóмым с+*i.*; (*recognize*) узнавáть (-аю́, -аёшь) *impf.*, узнáть *pf.* **know -all** *n.* всезнáйка *c.g.* **know-how** *n.* умéние. **knowing** *adj.* (*cunning*) хи́трый (-тёр, -трá, хи́трó). **knowingly** *adv.* сознáтельно. **knowledge** ['nɒlɪdʒ] *n.* знáние, познáния (-ний) *pl.*; (*familiarity*) знакóмство (**of** с+*i.*); (*sum of what is known*) наýка; **to my** ~ наскóлько мне извéстно.

knuckle ['nʌk(ə)l] *n.* сустáв пáльца; (*cul.*)

нóжка; *v.i.*: ~ **down to** решúтельно брáться (берýсь, -рёшься; брáлся, -лáсь) *impf.*, взя́ться (возьмýсь, -мёшься; взя́лся, -лáсь) *pf.* за+*a.*; ~ **under** подчиня́ться *impf.*, подчинúться *pf.* (**to** +*d.*).

Korea [kəˈriːə] *n.* Корéя.

kosher [ˈkəʊʃə(r), ˈkɒʃ-] *adj.* кошéрный.

ko(w)tow [kaʊˈtaʊ] *n.* нúзкий поклóн; *v.i.* нúзко кла́няться *impf.*, поклонúться (-ню́сь, -нишься) *pf.*; (*fig.*) раболéпствовать *impf.* (**to** пéред+*i.*).

Kremlin [ˈkremlɪn] *n.* Кремль (-ля́) *m.* **Kremlinologist** [ˌkremlɪnˈɒlədʒɪst] *n.* кремлинóлог. **Kremlinology** *n.* кремлинолóгия.

kudos [ˈkjuːdɒs] *n.* слáва.

kung fu [kʊŋ ˈfuː, kʌŋ] *n.* кун-фý *nt. indecl.*

kW *abbr.* (*of* **kilowatt(s)**) кВт, киловáтт.

L

l. *abbr.* (*of* **litre(s)**) л, литр.

label [ˈleɪb(ə)l] *n.* этикéтка; (*also fig.*) ярлы́к (-á); *v.t.* приклéивать *impf.*, приклéить *pf.* ярлы́к к+*d.*

labial [ˈleɪbɪəl] *adj.* (*n.*) губнóй (звук).

laboratory [ləˈbɒrətərɪ] *n.* лаборатóрия; ~ **assistant, technician** лаборáнт, ~ка.

laborious [ləˈbɔːrɪəs] *adj.* (*arduous*) трýдный (-ден, -днá, -дно, трýдны́); (*of style*) вы́мученный (-ен).

labour [ˈleɪbə(r)] *n.* труд (-á), рабóта; (*workers*) рабóчие *sb.*; (*task*) задáча; (*childbirth*) рóды (-дов) *pl.*; *attr.* трудовóй, рабóчий; ~ **exchange** бúржа трудá; ~ **force** рабóчая сúла; ~ **pains** родовы́е схвáтки *f.pl.*; **L~ Party** лейбори́стская пáртия; *v.i.* трудúться *impf.*; рабóтать *impf.*; *v.t.* (*elaborate*) подрóбно разрабáтывать *impf.*, разрабóтать *pf.* **laboured** *adj.* затруднённый (-ён, -ённа); (*style*) вы́мученный (-ен). **labourer** *n.* чернорабóчий *sb.* **labour-intensive** *adj.* трудоёмкий. **labourite** *n.* лейбори́ст. **labour-saving** *adj.* трудосберегáющий.

laburnum [ləˈbɜːnəm] *n.* золотóй дождь (-дя́) *m.*

labyrinth [ˈlæbərɪnθ] *n.* лабири́нт.

lace [leɪs] *n.* (*fabric*) крýжево; (*cord*) шнур (-á), шнурóк (-ркá); *v.t.* (~ *up*) шнуровáть *impf.*, за~ *pf.*

lacerate [ˈlæsəˌreɪt] *v.t.* рвать (рву, рвёшь; рвал, -á, -о) *impf.*; (*fig.*) раздирáть *impf.* **lace'ration** *n.*(*wound*) рвáная рáна.

lachrymose [ˈlækrɪˌməʊs] *adj.* слезли́вый.

lack [læk] *n.* недостáток (-тка) (**of** +*g.*, в+*p.*),

отсýтствие; *v.t.* испы́тывать *impf.*, испытáть *pf.* недостáток в+*p.*; недоставáть (-таёт) *impf.*, недостáть (-áнет) *pf. impers.* +*d.* (*person*), +*g.* (*object*).

lackadaisical [ˌlækəˈdeɪzɪk(ə)l] *adj.* (*languid*) тóмный (-мен, -мнá, -мно); (*affected*) жемáнный (-нен, -нна).

lackey [ˈlækɪ] *n.* лакéй.

lack-lustre [ˈlæk,lʌstə(r)] *adj.* тýсклый (-л, -лá, -ло).

laconic [ləˈkɒnɪk] *adj.* лакони́чный, -ческий.

lacquer [ˈlækə(r)] *n.* лак; *v.t.* лакировáть *impf.*, от~ *pf.*

lactic [ˈlæktɪk] *adj.* молóчный.

lacuna [ləˈkjuːnə] *n.* пробéл.

lad [læd] *n.* пáрень (-рня; *pl.* -рни, -рнéй) *m.*

ladder [ˈlædə(r)] *n.* лéстница; (*naut.*) трап.

laden [ˈleɪd(ə)n] *adj.* нагружённый (-ён, -енá); (*fig.*) обременённый (-ён, -енá).

ladle [ˈleɪd(ə)l] *n.* (*spoon*) половни́к (*for metal*) ковш (-á); *v.t.* чéрпать *impf.*, черпнýть *pf.*

lady [ˈleɪdɪ] *n.* дáма, лéди *f.indecl.* **ladybird** *n.* бóжья корóвка.

lag¹ [læg] *v.i.*: ~ **behind** отставáть (-таю́, -таёшь) *impf.*, отстáть (-áну, -áнешь) *pf.* (от+*g.*).

lag² [læg] *n.* (*convict*) кáторжник.

lag³ [læg] *v.t.* (*insulate*) покрывáть *impf.*, покры́ть (-рóю, -рóешь) *pf.* изоля́цией. **lagging** *n.* тепловáя изоля́ция.

lagoon [ləˈguːn] *n.* лагýна.

lair [leə(r)] *n.* лóговище, берлóга.

laity [ˈleɪɪtɪ] *n.* (*in religion*) миря́не (-н) *pl.*; (*in profession*) профáны (-нов) *pl.*

lake [leɪk] *n.* óзеро (*pl.* озёра); *attr.* озёрный.

lamb [læm] *n.* ягнёнок (-нка; *pl.* ягня́та, -я́т) (*eccl.*) áгнец (-нца); *v.i.* ягни́ться *impf.*, о~ *pf.*

lame [leɪm] *adj.* хромóй (хром, -á, -о); (*fig.*) неубеди́тельный; **be** ~ хромáть *impf.*; **go** ~ хромéть *impf.*, о~ *pf.*; *v.t.* калéчить *impf.*, о~ *pf.* **lameness** *n.* хромотá.

lament [ləˈment] *n.* плач; *v.t.* оплáкивать *impf.*, оплáкать (-áчу, -áчешь) *pf.* **lamentable** [ˈlæməntəb(ə)l] *adj.* прискóрбный.

lamina [ˈlæmɪnə] *n.* тóнкая пласти́нка, тóнкий слой (*pl.* -ои́). **laminated** *adj.* листовóй, пласти́нчатый.

lamp [læmp] *n.* лáмпа, фонáрь (-ря́) *m.* **lamp-post** *n.* фонáрный столб (-á). **lampshade** *n.* абажýр.

lampoon [læmˈpuːn] *n.* пасквúль *m.*

lamprey [ˈlæmprɪ] *n.* минóга.

lance [lɑːns] *n.* пúка, копьё (*pl.* -пья, -пий, -пьям); (*fish-spear*) острогá; *v.t.* пронзáть *impf.*, пронзúть *pf.* пúкой, копьём; (*med.*) вскрывáть *impf.*, вскрыть (-рóю, -рóешь) *pf.* (ланцéтом). **lance-corporal** *n.* ефрéйтор. **lancer** *n.* улáн (*pl.* -нов & -н (*collect.*)). **lancet** *n.* ланцéт.

land [lænd] *n.* земля́ (*a.* -млю; *pl.* -мли, -мéль, -млям); (*dry* ~) сýша; (*country*) странá (*pl.*

-ы); (*soil*) по́чва; *pl.* (*estates*) поме́стья (-тий) *pl.*; *v.t.* (*unload*) выгружа́ть *impf.*, вы́грузить *pf.*; *v.t. & i.* (*persons*) выса́живать(ся) *impf.*, вы́садить(ся) *pf.*; (*aeron.*) приземля́ть(ся) *impf.*, приземли́ть(ся) *pf.* **landfall** *n.* подхо́д к бе́регу. **landing** *n.* вы́садка; (*aeron.*) поса́дка; (*mil.*) деса́нт; (*on stairs*) ле́стничная площа́дка; ~ **card** *n.* поса́дочный тало́н. **landing-stage** *n.* при́стань (*pl.* -ни, -ней). **landlady** *n.* домовладе́лиц, хозя́йка. **landlord** *n.* землевладе́лец (-льца); (*of house*) домовладе́лец (-льца); (*of inn*) хозя́ин (*pl.* -я́ева, -я́ев). **landmark** *n.* (*boundary stone*; *fig.*) ве́ха; (*conspicuous object*) ориенти́р. **landowner** *n.* землевладе́лец (-льца). **landscape** *n.* ландша́фт; (*also picture*) пейза́ж. **landscape-painter** *n.* пейзажи́ст. **landslide, landslip** *n.* о́ползень (-зня) *m.*

landau ['lændɔ:] *n.* ландо́ *nt.indecl.*

lane [leɪn] *n.* у́зкая доро́га; (*street*) переу́лок (-лка); (*passage*) прохо́д; (*on road*) ряд (-а́ with 2, 3, 4, *loc.* -у́; *pl.* -ы́); (*in race*) доро́жка; (*for ships*) морско́й путь (-ти́, -тём) *m.*; (*for aircraft*) тра́сса полёта.

language ['læŋgwɪdʒ] *n.* язы́к (-а́); (*style, form of speech*) речь.

languid ['læŋgwɪd] *adj.* то́мный (-мен, -мна́, -мно).

languish ['læŋgwɪʃ] *v.i.* (*pine*) томи́ться *impf.*

languor ['læŋgə(r)] *n.* томле́ние, то́мность; (*fatigue*) уста́лость. **languorous** *adj.* то́мный (-мен, -мна́, -мно); уста́лый.

lank [læŋk] *adj.* (*person*) худоща́вый; (*hair*) гла́дкий (-док, -дка́, -дко). **lanky** *adj.* долговя́зый.

lantern ['læntən] *n.* фона́рь (-ря́) *m.*

lap¹ [læp] *n.* (*of person*) коле́ни (-ней) *pl.*; (*racing*) круг (*pl.* -и́).

lap² [læp] *v.t.* (*drink*) лака́ть *impf.*, вы́~ *pf.*; *v.i.* (*water*) плеска́ться (-е́щется) *impf.*

lapel [lə'pel] *n.* отворо́т, ла́цкан.

lapidary ['læpɪdərɪ] *n.* грани́льщик; *adj.* гра́ни́льный; (*fig.*) сжа́тый.

lapse [læps] *n.* (*mistake*) оши́бка; (*of pen*) опи́ска; (*of memory*) прова́л па́мяти; (*decline*) паде́ние; (*expiry*) истече́ние; (*of time*) тече́ние, ход вре́мени; *v.i.* впада́ть *impf.*, впасть (-аду́, -адёшь; -ал) *pf.* (*into* в+*a.*); (*expire*) истека́ть *impf.*, исте́чь (-ечёт, -ёк, -екла́) *pf.*

laptop (computer) ['læptɒp] *n.* наколе́нный, портати́вный компью́тер.

lapwing ['læpwɪŋ] *n.* чи́бис.

larceny ['lɑːsənɪ] *n.* воровство́.

larch [lɑːtʃ] *n.* ли́ственница.

lard [lɑːd] *n.* свино́е са́ло; *v.t.* (*cul.*) шпиго́ва́ть *impf.*, на~ *pf.*; (*fig.*) уснаща́ть *impf.*, уснасти́ть *pf.* (**with** +*i.*).

larder ['lɑːdə(r)] *n.* кладова́я *sb.*

large [lɑːdʒ] *adj.* большо́й, кру́пный (-пен, -пна́, -пно, кру́пны́); (*wide, broad*) широ́кий (-о́к, -ока́, -о́ко́); *n.*: **at** ~ (*free*) на свобо́де;

(*in detail*) подро́бно; (*as a whole*) целико́м. **largely** *adv.* (*to a great extent*) в значи́тельной сте́пени.

largess(e) [lɑː'ʒes] *n.* ще́дрость.

lark¹ [lɑːk] *n.* (*bird*) жа́воронок (-нка).

lark² [lɑːk] *n.* шу́тка, прока́за; *v.i.* (~ *about*) резви́ться *impf.*

larva ['lɑːvə] *n.* личи́нка. **larval** *adj.* личи́ночный.

laryngeal [lə'rɪndʒɪəl] *adj.* горта́нный. **laryngitis** [ˌlærɪn'dʒaɪtɪs] *n.* ларинги́т. **larynx** ['lærɪŋks] *n.* горта́нь.

lascivious [lə'sɪvɪəs] *adj.* похотли́вый.

laser ['leɪzə(r)] *n.* ла́зер; *adj.* ла́зерный.

lash [læʃ] *n.* плеть (*pl.* -ти, -те́й), бич (-а́); (*blow*) уда́р пле́тью, бичо́м; (*eyelash*) ресни́ца; *v.t.* (*beat*) хлеста́ть (хлещу́, -щешь) *impf.*, хлестну́ть *pf.*; (*with words*) бичева́ть (-чу́ю, -чу́ешь) *impf.*; (*fasten*) привя́зывать *impf.*, привяза́ть (-яжу́, -я́жешь) *pf.* (**to** к+*d.*); ~ **together** свя́зывать *impf.*, связа́ть (-яжу́, -я́жешь) *pf.*

lass [læs] *n.* де́вушка, де́вочка.

lassitude ['læsɪtjuːd] *n.* уста́лость.

lasso [læ'suː, 'læsəʊ] *n.* лассо́ *nt.indecl.*; *v.t.* лови́ть (-влю́, -вишь) *impf.*, пойма́ть *pf.* лассо́.

last¹ [lɑːst] *n.* (*cobbler's*) коло́дка.

last² [lɑːst] *adj.* (*final*) после́дний; (*most recent*) про́шлый; (*extreme*) кра́йний; **the year before** ~ позапро́шлый год; ~ **but one** препосле́дний; ~ **but two** тре́тий (-тья, -тье) с конца́; ~ **night** вчера́ ве́чером, но́чью; *n.* (~-*mentioned*) после́дний *sb.*; (*end*) коне́ц (-нца́); **at** ~ наконе́ц, в конце́ концо́в; *adv.* (*after all others*) по́сле все́х; (*on last occasion*) в после́дний раз; (*in last place*) в конце́.

last³ [lɑːst] *v.i.* (*go on*) продолжа́ться *impf.*, продо́лжиться *pf.*; дли́ться *impf.*, про~ *pf.*; (*food, health*) сохраня́ться *impf.*, сохрани́ться *pf.*; (*suffice*) хвата́ть *impf.*, хвати́ть (-ит) *pf.* **lasting** *adj.* (*enduring*) дли́тельный; (*permanent*) постоя́нный (-нен, -нна); (*durable*) про́чный (-чен, -чна́, -чно, про́чны́).

lastly ['lɑːstlɪ] *adj.* в конце́, в заключе́ние, наконе́ц.

latch [lætʃ] *n.* щеко́лда.

late [leɪt] *adj.* по́здний; (*recent*) неда́вний; (*dead*) поко́йный; (*former*) бы́вший; **be** ~ **for** опа́здывать *impf.*, опозда́ть *pf.* на+*a.*; *adv.* по́здно; *n.*: **of** ~ неда́вно, за после́днее вре́мя.

latent ['leɪt(ə)nt] *adj.* скры́тый.

lateral ['lætər(ə)l] *adj.* боково́й. **laterally** *adv.* (*from side*) сбо́ку; (*towards side*) вбок.

latex ['leɪteks] *n.* мле́чный сок (-а(у), *loc.* -е & -у́); (*synthetic*) ла́текс.

lath [lɑːθ] *n.* ре́йка, дра́нка (*also collect.*).

lathe [leɪð] *n.* тока́рный стано́к (-нка́).

lather ['lɑːðə(r), 'læðə(r)] *n.* (мы́льная) пе́на; (*of horse*) мы́ло; *v.t. & i.* мы́лить(ся) *impf.*, на~ *pf.*; (*of horse*) взмы́ливаться *impf.*, взмы́литься *pf.*

Latin ['lætɪn] *adj.* лати́нский; (*Romance*) рома́нский; *n.* лати́нский язы́к (-á); (*when qualified*) латы́нь. **Latin-American** *adj.* латиноамерика́нский.

latitude ['lætɪˌtjuːd] *n.* свобо́да; (*geog.*) широта́.

latrine [lə'triːn] *n.* убо́рная *sb.*; (*esp. in camp*) отхо́жее ме́сто (*pl.* -тá).

latter ['lætə(r)] *adj.* после́дний. **latter-day** *adj.* совреме́нный. **latterly** *adv.* (*towards end*) к концу́; (*of late*) неда́вно.

lattice ['lætɪs] *n.* решётка. **latticed** *adj.* решётчатый.

Latvia ['lætvɪə] *n.* Ла́твия.

laud [lɔːd] *n.* хвала́; *v.t.* хвали́ть (-лю́, -лишь) *impf.*, по~ *pf.* **laudable** *adj.* похва́льный. **laudatory** *adj.* хвале́бный.

laugh [lɑːf] *n.* смех (а(у)), хóхот; *v.i.* сме́яться (-ею́сь, -еёшься) *impf.* (**at** *only+i.*); ~ **it off** отшу́чиваться *impf.*, отшути́ться (-учу́сь, -у́тишься) *pf.* **laughable** *adj.* смешно́й (-шóн, -шна́). **laughing-stock** *n.* посме́шище. **laughter** *n.* смех (-а(у)), хóхот.

launch[1] [lɔːntʃ] *v.t.* броса́ть *impf.*, бро́сить *pf.*; (*ship*) спуска́ть *impf.*, спусти́ть (-ущу́, -у́стишь) *pf.* на́ воду; (*rocket*) запуска́ть *impf.*, запусти́ть (-ущу́, -у́стишь) *pf.*; (*undertake*) предпринима́ть *impf.*, предприня́ть (-ниму́, -ни́мешь; предпри́нял, -á, -о) *pf.*; *n.* спуск на́ воду; за́пуск. **launcher** *n.* (*for rocket*) пусково́е устано́вка. **launching pad** *n.* пускова́я площа́дка.

launch[2] [lɔːntʃ] *n.* (*naut.*) барка́с; (*motor-*~) мото́рный ка́тер (*pl.* -á).

launder ['lɔːndə(r)] *v.t.* стира́ть *impf.*, вы́~ *pf.* **laund(e)'rette** *n.* пра́чечная *sb.* самообслу́живания. **laundress** *n.* пра́чка. **laundry** *n.* (*place*) пра́чечная *sb.*; (*articles*) бельё.

laurel ['lɒr(ə)l] *n.* ла́вр(овое де́рево); (*ornamental plant, Japanese* ~) золото́е де́рево (*pl.* -е́вья, -е́вьев); *pl.* ла́вры *m.pl.*, по́чести *f.pl.*

lava ['lɑːvə] *n.* ла́ва.

lavatory ['lævətərɪ] *n.* убо́рная *sb.*

lavender ['lævɪndə(r)] *n.* лава́нда.

lavish ['lævɪʃ] *adj.* ще́дрый (щедр, -á, -о); (*abundant*) оби́льный; *v.t.* расточа́ть *impf.* (**upon** *+d.*).

law [lɔː] *n.* зако́н, пра́во; (*jurisprudence*) юриспруде́нция; (*rule*) пра́вило; ~ **and order** правопоря́док (-дка). **law-court** *n.* суд (-á). **lawful** *adj.* зако́нный (-нен, -нна). **lawgiver** *n.* законода́тель. **lawless** *adj.* беззако́нный (-нен, -нна).

lawn[1] [lɔːn] *n.* (*fabric*) бати́ст.

lawn[2] [lɔːn] *n.* (*grass*) газо́н. **lawn-mower** *n.* газонокоси́лка.

lawsuit ['lɔːsuːt, -sjuːt] *n.* проце́сс.

lawyer ['lɔːɪə(r), 'lɔːjə(r)] *n.* адвока́т, юри́ст.

lax [læks] *adj.* (*loose*) сла́бый (слаб, -á, -о); (*careless*) небре́жный; (*not strict*) нестро́-

гий. **laxity** *n.* сла́бость; небре́жность; (*moral* ~) распу́щенность.

laxative ['læksətɪv] *adj.* слаби́тельный; *n.* слаби́тельный *sb.*

lay[1] [leɪ] *adj.* (*non-clerical*) све́тский; (*non-professional*) непрофессиона́льный.

lay[2] [leɪ] *n.* (*position*) положе́ние; *v.t.* (*place*) класть (кладу́, -дёшь; клал) *impf.*, положи́ть (-жу́, -жишь) *pf.*; (*impose*) налага́ть *impf.*, наложи́ть (-жу́, -жишь) *pf.*; (*present*) излага́ть *impf.*, изложи́ть (-жу́, -жишь) *pf.*; (*trap etc.*) устра́ивать *impf.*, устро́ить *pf.*; (*crops, dust*) прибива́ть *impf.*, приби́ть (-бью́, -бьёшь) *pf.*; (*calm*) успока́ивать *impf.*, успоко́ить *pf.*; (*ghost*) изгоня́ть *impf.*, изгна́ть (изгоню́, -нишь; изгна́л, -á, -о) *pf.*; (*meal*) накрыва́ть *impf.*, накры́ть (-ро́ю, -ро́ешь) *pf.* стол к+*d.*; (*eggs*) класть (-аде́т; -ал) *impf.*, положи́ть (-ит) *pf.*; *v.abs.* (*lay eggs*) нести́сь (несётся; нёсся, несла́сь) *impf.*, с~ *pf.*; ~ **bare, open** раскрыва́ть *impf.*, раскры́ть (-ро́ю, -ро́ешь) *pf.*; ~ **a bet, wager** держа́ть (-жу́, -жишь) *impf.* пари́ (**on** на+*a.*); ~ **claim to** име́ть пре́тензию на+*a.*; ~ **hands on** (*seize*) завладева́ть *impf.*, завладе́ть *pf.*+*i.*; ~ **siege to** осажда́ть *impf.*, осади́ть *pf.*; ~ **table** накрыва́ть *impf.*, накры́ть (-ро́ю, -ро́ешь) *pf.* стол (**for** *meal*) к+*d.*); ~ **waste** опустоша́ть *impf.*, опустоши́ть *pf.*; ~ **aside** (*put aside*) откла́дывать *impf.*, отложи́ть (-жу́, -жишь) *pf.*; (*save*) прибере́гать *impf.*, прибере́чь (-егу́, -ежёшь; -ёг, -егла́) *pf.*; ~ **down** (*relinquish*) отка́зываться *impf.*, отказа́ться (-ажу́сь, -а́жешься) *pf.* от+*g.*; (*formulate*) составля́ть *impf.*, соста́вить *pf.*; (*rule etc.*) устана́вливать *impf.*, установи́ть (-влю, -вишь) *pf.*; (*ship etc.*) закла́дывать *impf.*, заложи́ть (-жу́, -жишь) *pf.*; ~ **down one's arms** скла́дывать *impf.*, сложи́ть (-жу́, -жишь) *pf.* ору́жие; ~ **down one's life** положи́ть (-жу́, -жишь) *pf.* жизнь (**for** за+*a.*); ~ **in** (*stock of*), запаса́ть *impf.*, запасти́ (-су́, -сёшь; -с, -сла́) *pf.*+*a.*, +*g.*; ~ **off** (*workmen*) вре́менно увольня́ть *impf.*, уво́лить *pf.*; ~ **out** (*spread*) выкла́дывать *impf.*, вы́ложить *pf.*; (*arrange*) разбива́ть *impf.*, разби́ть (разобью́, -ьёшь) *pf.*; (*expend*) тра́тить *impf.*, ис~, по~ *pf.*; ~ **up** запаса́ть *impf.*, запасти́ (-су́, -сёшь; -с, -сла́) *pf.*+*a.*, +*g.*; **be laid up** быть прико́ванным к посте́ли, к до́му.

layabout *n.* безде́льник.

layer ['leɪə(r)] *n.* слой (*pl.* -ои́), пласт (-á, *loc.* -ý); (*hort.*) отво́док (-дка); (*hen*) несу́шка.

layman ['leɪmən] *n.* миря́нин (*pl.* -я́не, -я́н); (*non-expert*) неспециали́ст.

laze [leɪz] *v.i.* безде́льничать *impf.* **laziness** *n.* лень. **lazy** *adj.* лени́вый. **lazy-bones** *n.* лентя́й, ~ка.

lb. [paʊnd(z)] *abbr.* (*of libra*) фунт.

lead[1] [liːd] *n.* (*example*) приме́р; (*leadership*) руково́дство; (*position*) пе́рвое ме́сто;

(*theatr.*) гла́вная роль (*pl.* -ли, -ле́й); (*cards*) пе́рвый ход; (*elec.*) про́вод (*pl.* -а́); (*dog's*) поводо́к (-дка́); *v.t.* води́ть (вожу́, во́дишь) *indet.*, вести́ (веду́, -дёшь; вёл, вла́) *det.*; (*guide*) руководи́ть *impf.*+*i.*; (*army*) кома́ндовать *impf.*, c~ *pf.*+*i.*; (*induce*) заставля́ть *impf.*, заста́вить *pf.*; *v.t. & i.* (*cards*) ходи́ть (хожу́, хо́дишь) *impf.* (c+*g.*); *v.i.* (*sport*) занима́ть *impf.*, заня́ть (займу́, -мёшь; за́нял, -а́, -о) *pf.* пе́рвое ме́сто; ~ **astray** сбива́ть *impf.*, сбить (собью́, -ьёшь) *pf.* c пути́; ~ **away** уводи́ть (-ожу́, -о́дишь) *impf.*, увести́ (-еду́, -еде́шь; увёл, -а́) *pf.*; ~ **on** увлека́ть *impf.*, увле́чь (-еку́, -ече́шь; -ёк, -екла́) *pf.*; ~ **to** (*result in*) приводи́ть (-ит) *impf.*, привести́ (-едёт; -ёл, -ела́) *pf.* к+*d.*

lead² [led] *n.* (*metal*) свине́ц (-нца́); (*naut.*) лот; (*print.*) шпон (-а́). **leaden** *adj.* свинцо́вый.

leader ['li:də(r)] *n.* руководи́тель *m.*, ~ница, ли́дер, вождь (-дя́) *m.*; (*mus.*) концертме́йстер; (*editorial*) передова́я статья́. **leadership** *n.* руково́дство; **under the** ~ **of** во главе́ c+*i.*

lead-free ['ledfri:] *adj.* неэтили́рованный.

leading ['li:dɪŋ] *adj.* веду́щий, выдаю́щийся; ~ **article** передова́я статья́.

leaf [li:f] *n.* лист (-а́; *pl.* (*plant*) -ья, -ьев & (*paper*) -ы́, -о́в); (*of door*) ство́рка; (*of table*) опускна́я доска́ (*a.* -ску; *pl.* -ски, -со́к, -ска́м); *v.i.*: ~ **through** перели́стывать *impf.*, перелиста́ть *pf.* **leaflet** *n.* листо́вка. **leaf-mould** *n.* листово́й перегно́й. **leafy** *adj.* покры́тый ли́стьями.

league [li:g] *n.* ли́га, сою́з; (*sport*) класс.

leak [li:k] *n.* течь, уте́чка; **spring a** ~ дава́ть (даёт) *impf.*, дать (даст; дал, -а́, да́ло́, -и) *pf.* течь; *v.i.* (*escape*) течь (-чёт; тёк, -ла́) *impf.*; (*allow water to* ~) пропуска́ть *impf.* во́ду; ~ **out** проса́чиваться *impf.*, просочи́ться *pf.*

lean¹ [li:n] *adj.* (*thin*) худо́й (худ, -а́, -о); (*meat*) по́стный (-тен, -тна́, -тно); (*meagre*) ску́дный (-ден, -дна́, -дно).

lean² [li:n] *v.t. & i.* прислоня́ть(ся) *impf.*, прислони́ть(ся) (-ню́(сь), -о́ни́шь(ся)) *pf.* (**against** к+*d.*); *v.i.* (~ *on, rely on*) опира́ться *impf.*, опере́ться (обопру́сь, -рёшься; опёрся, опёрла́сь) *pf.* (**on** на+*a.*); (*be inclined*) быть скло́нным (-о́нен, -о́нна́, -о́нно) (**to(wards)** к+*d.*); ~ **back** отки́дываться *impf.*, откину́ться *pf.*; ~ **out of** высо́вываться *impf.*, вы́сунуться *pf.* в+*a.* **leaning** *n.* скло́нность.

leap [li:p] *n.* прыжо́к (-жка́), скачо́к (-чка́); *v.i.* пры́гать *impf.*, пры́гнуть *pf.*; скака́ть (-ачу́, -а́чешь) *impf.*; *v.t.* (~ *over*) перепры́гивать *impf.*, перепры́гнуть *pf.*; ~ **year** високо́сный год (*loc.* -у́; *pl.* -ы & -а́, -о́в). **leap-frog** *n.* чехарда́.

learn [lɜ:n] *v.t.* учи́ться (учу́сь, у́чишься) *impf.*, об~ *pf.*+*d.*; (*find out*) узнава́ть (-наю́, -наёшь) *impf.*, узна́ть *pf.* **learned** ['lɜ:nɪd]

adj. учёный. **learner** *n.* уча́щийся *sb.*, учени́к (-а́). **learning** *n.* (*studies*) уче́ние; (*erudition*) учёность.

lease [li:s] *n.* аре́нда; *v.t.* (*of owner*) сдава́ть (сдаю́, сдаёшь) *impf.*, сдать (-ам, -ашь, -аст, -ади́м; сдал, -а́, -о) *pf.* в аре́нду; (*of tenant*) брать (беру́, -рёшь; брал, -а́, -о) *impf.*, взять (возьму́, -мёшь; взял, -а́, -о) *pf.* в аре́нду. **leaseholder** *n.* аренда́тор.

leash [li:ʃ] *n.* сво́ра, при́вязь.

least [li:st] *adj.* наиме́ньший, мале́йший; *adv.* ме́нее всего́; **at** ~ по кра́йней ме́ре; **not in the** ~ ничу́ть.

leather ['leðə(r)] *n.* ко́жа; *attr.* ко́жаный.

leave¹ [li:v] *n.* (*permission*) разреше́ние; (~ *of absence*) о́тпуск (*loc.* -е & -у́); **on** ~ в о́тпуске, -ку́; **take (one's)** ~ проща́ться *impf.*, прости́ться *pf.* (**of** c+*i.*).

leave² [li:v] *v.t. & i.* оставля́ть *impf.*, оста́вить *pf.*; (*abandon*) покида́ть *impf.*, поки́нуть *pf.*; (*go away*) уходи́ть (-ожу́, -о́дишь) *impf.*, уйти́ (уйду́, -дёшь; ушёл, ушла́) *pf.* (**from** от+*g.*); уезжа́ть *impf.*, уе́хать (уе́ду, -дешь) *pf.* (**from** от+*g.*); (*entrust*) предоставля́ть *impf.*, предоста́вить *pf.* (**to** +*d.*); ~ **out** пропуска́ть *impf.*, пропусти́ть (-ущу́, -у́стишь) *pf.*

leaven ['lev(ə)n] *n.* (*yeast*) дро́жжи (-же́й) *pl.*; заква́ска; *v.t.* ста́вить *impf.*, по~ *pf.* на дрожжа́х; заква́шивать *impf.*, заква́сить *pf.*

leavings ['li:vɪŋz] *n.* оста́тки *m.pl.*; (*food*) объе́дки (-ков) *pl.*

lecherous ['letʃərəs] *adj.* распу́тный.

lectern ['lektɜ:n, -t(ə)n] *n.* анало́й.

lecture ['lektʃə(r)] *n.* (*discourse*) ле́кция; (*reproof*) нота́ция; *v.i.* (*deliver* ~(*s*)) чита́ть *impf.*, про~ *pf.* ле́кцию (-ии) (**on** по+*d.*); *v.t.* (*admonish*) чита́ть *impf.*, про~ *pf.* нота́цию+*d.*; ~ **room** аудито́рия. **lecturer** *n.* ле́ктор; (*univ.*) преподава́тель *m.*, ~ница.

ledge [ledʒ] *n.* вы́ступ; (*under water*) риф.

ledger ['ledʒə(r)] *n.* гла́вная кни́га, гроссбу́х.

lee [li:] *n.* защи́та; ~ **side** подве́тренная сторона́ (*a.* -ону); ~ **shore** подве́тренный бе́рег (*loc.* -у́).

leech [li:tʃ] *n.* (*worm*) пия́вка; (*person*) вымога́тель *m.*

leek [li:k] *n.* лук-поре́й.

leer [lɪə(r)] *v.i.* смотре́ть (-рю́, -ришь) *impf.*, по~ *pf.* и́скоса (**at** на+*a.*).

lees [li:z] *n.* оса́док (-дка), подо́нки (-ков) *pl.*

leeward ['li:wəd, *naut.* 'lu:əd] *n.* подве́тренная сторона́ (*a.* -ону); *adj.* подве́тренный.

leeway ['li:weɪ] *n.* (*naut.*) дрейф.

left [left] *n.* ле́вая сторона́ (*a.* -ону); (**L**~, *pol.*) ле́вые *sb.*; *adj.* ле́вый; *adv.* нале́во, сле́ва (**of** от+*g.*). **left-hander** *n.* левша́ *c.g.*

left-luggage office [left] *n.* ка́мера хране́ния.

leftovers ['left,əuvəz] *n.* оста́тки *m.pl.*; (*food*) объе́дки (-ков) *pl.*

leg [leg] *n.* нога́ (*a.* -гу; *pl.* -ги, -г, -га́м);

(furniture etc.) но́жка; *(support)* подста́вка; *(stage of journey etc.)* эта́п; **pull s.o.'s ~** моро́чить *impf.* го́лову+*d.*

legacy ['legəsɪ] *n.* насле́дство.

legal ['liːg(ə)l] *adj.* *(of the law)* правово́й; *(lawful)* зако́нный; **~ adviser** юриско́нсульт. **legality** [lɪ'gælɪtɪ, liːg-] *n.* зако́нность. **legalize** *v.t.* узако́нивать *impf.*, узако́нить *pf.*

legate [lɪ'geɪt] *n.* лега́т.

legatee [,legə'tiː] *n.* насле́дник.

legation [lɪ'geɪʃ(ə)n] *n.* (дипломати́ческая) ми́ссия.

legend ['ledʒ(ə)nd] *n.* леге́нда. **legendary** *adj.* легенда́рный.

leggings ['legɪŋz] *n.* гама́ши *f.pl.*

legible ['ledʒɪb(ə)l] *adj.* разбо́рчивый.

legion ['liːdʒ(ə)n] *n.* легио́н; *(great number)* мно́жество. **legionary** *n.* легионе́р.

legislate ['ledʒɪs,leɪt] *v.i.* издава́ть (-да́ю, -да́ешь) *impf.*, изда́ть (-а́м, -а́шь, -а́ст, -ади́м; изда́л, -а́, -о) *pf.* зако́ны. **legis'lation** *n.* законода́тельство. **legislative** *adj.* законода́тельный. **legislator** *n.* законода́тель *m.*

legitimacy [lɪ'dʒɪtɪməsɪ] *n.* зако́нность; *(of child)* законнорождённость. **legitimate** *adj.* зако́нный; *(child)* законнорождённый. **legitimize** *v.t.* узако́нивать *impf.*, узако́нить *pf.*

leguminous [lɪ'gjuːmɪnəs] *adj.* бобо́вый, стручко́вый.

leisure ['leʒə(r)] *n.* досу́г; **at ~** на досу́ге. **leisurely** *adj.* неторопли́вый; *adv.* не спеша́.

leitmotiv ['laɪtməʊ,tiːf] *n.* лейтмоти́в.

lemon ['lemən] *n.* лимо́н; *attr.* лимо́нный. **lemo'nade** *n.* лимона́д.

lend [lend] *v.t.* дава́ть (даю́, даёшь) *impf.*, дать (дам, дашь, даст, дади́м; дал, -а́, да́ло, -и) *pf.* взаймы́ **(to** +*d.*); ода́лживать *impf.*, одолжи́ть *pf.* **(to** +*d.*).

length [leŋθ, leŋkθ] *n.* длина́, расстоя́ние; *(duration)* продолжи́тельность; *(of cloth)* отре́з; **at ~** *(at last)* наконе́ц; *(in detail)* подро́бно. **lengthen** *v.t. & i.* удлиня́ть(ся) *impf.*, удлини́ть(ся) *pf.* **lengthways, -wise** *adv.* в длину́, вдоль. **lengthy** *adj.* дли́нный (-нен, -нна́, дли́нно́).

lenience ['liːnɪəns], **-cy** *n.* снисходи́тельность. **lenient** *adj.* снисходи́тельный.

Leningrad ['lenɪn,græd] *n.* Ленингра́д.

lens [lenz] *n.* ли́нза; *(anat.)* хруста́лик гла́за.

Lent [lent] *n.* вели́кий пост (-а́, *loc.* -у́). **Lenten** *adj.* великопо́стный; *(food)* по́стный (-тен, -тна́, -тно).

lentil ['lentɪl] *n.* чечеви́ца.

Leo ['liːəʊ] *n.* Лев (Льва).

leonine ['liːə,naɪn] *adj.* льви́ный.

leopard ['lepəd] *n.* леопа́рд.

leotard ['liːə,tɑːd] *n.* трико́ *nt. indecl.*, леота́рд.

leper ['lepə(r)] *n.* прокажённый *sb.* **leprosy** *n.* прока́за.

lesbian ['lezbɪən] *n.* лесбия́нка; *adj.* лесби́йский.

lesion ['liːʒ(ə)n] *n.* поврежде́ние; *(med.)* пораже́ние.

less [les] *adj.* ме́ньший; *adv.* ме́ньше, ме́нее; *prep.* без+*g.*, за вы́четом+*g.*

lessee [le'siː] *n.* аренда́тор.

lessen ['les(ə)n] *v.t. & i.* уменьша́ть(ся) *impf.*, уме́ньши́ть(ся) *pf.*

lesser ['lesə(r)] *adj.* ме́ньший.

lesson ['les(ə)n] *n.* уро́к.

lest [lest] *conj.* *(in order that not)* чтобы не; *(that)* как бы не.

let [let] *n.* *(lease)* сда́ча в наём; *v.t.* *(allow)* позволя́ть *impf.*, позво́лить *pf.*+*d.*; разреша́ть *impf.*, разреши́ть *pf.*+*d.*; *(allow to escape)* пуска́ть *impf.*, пусти́ть (пущу́, пу́стишь) *pf.*; *(rent out)* сдава́ть (сдаю́, -аёшь) *impf.*, сдать (-а́м, -а́шь, -а́ст, -ади́м; сдал, -а́, -о) *pf.* внаём **(to** +*d.*); *v.aux.* *(imperative) (1st person)* дава́й(те); *(3rd person)* пусть; *(assumption)* допу́стим; **~ alone** оставля́ть *impf.*, оста́вить *pf.* в поко́е; *(in imperative)* не говоря́ уже́ о+*p.*; **~ down** *(lower)* опуска́ть *impf.*, опусти́ть (-ущу́, -у́стишь) *pf.*; *(fail)* подводи́ть (-ожу́, -о́дишь) *impf.*, подвести́ (-еду́, -едёшь; -ёл, -ела́) *pf.*; *(disappoint)* разочаро́вывать *impf.*, разочарова́ть *pf.*; **~ go** выпуска́ть *impf.*, вы́пустить *pf.*; **~'s go** пойдёмте!; пошли́!; поéхали!; **~ in(to)** *(admit)* впуска́ть *impf.*, впусти́ть (-ущу́, -у́стишь) *pf.* в+*a.*; *(into secret)* посвяща́ть *impf.*, посвяти́ть (-ящу́, -яти́шь) *pf.* в+*a.*; **~ know** дава́ть (даю́, даёшь) *impf.*, дать (дам, дашь, даст, дади́м; дал, -а́, да́ло, -и) *pf.* знать+*d.*; *(not punish)* отпуска́ть *impf.*, отпусти́ть (-ущу́, -у́стишь) *pf.* без наказа́ния; **~ off** *(gun)* вы́стрелить *pf.* из+*g.*; **~ out** *(release, loosen)* выпуска́ть *impf.*, вы́пустить *pf.*

lethal ['liːθ(ə)l] *adj.* смертоно́сный.

lethargic [lɪ'θɑːdʒɪk] *adj.* летарги́ческий; *(inert)* вя́лый. **lethargy** ['leθədʒɪ] *n.* летарги́я; вя́лость.

letter ['letə(r)] *n.* *(symbol)* бу́ква; *(print)* ли́тера; *(missive)* письмо́ (*pl.* -сьма, -сем, -сьмам); *pl.* *(literature)* литерату́ра; *pl.* *(erudition)* учёность; **to the ~** буква́льно. **letter-box** *n.* почто́вый я́щик.

lettuce ['letɪs] *n.* сала́т.

leukaemia [luː'kiːmɪə] *n.* лейкеми́я.

level ['lev(ə)l] *n.* у́ровень (-вня) *m.*; *(spirit-~)* ватерпа́с; *(surveyor's)* нивели́р; *(flat country)* равни́на; *adj.* горизонта́льный, ро́вный (-вен, -вна́, -вно); **~ crossing** (железнодоро́жный) перее́зд; *v.t.* *(make ~)* выра́внивать *impf.*, вы́ровнять *pf.*; *(make equal)* ура́внивать *impf.*, уравня́ть *pf.*; *(raze)* ровня́ть *impf.*, с~ *pf.* с землёй; *(gun)* наводи́ть (-ожу́, -о́дишь) *impf.*, навести́ (-еду́, -едёшь; -ёл, -ела́) *pf.* **(at** в, на, +*a.*); *(criticism)* направля́ть *impf.*, напра́вить *pf.* **(at** про́тив+*g.*); *(surveying)* нивели́ровать

impf. & pf. **level-headed** *adj.* уравнове́-
шенный (-ен, -ена).

lever ['li:və(r)] *n.* рыча́г (-а́). **leverage** *n.*
де́йствие рычага́; (*influence*) влия́ние.

leveret ['levərɪt] *n.* зайчо́нок (-чо́нка; *pl.* -ча́та,
-ча́т).

levity ['levɪtɪ] *n.* легкомы́слие.

levy ['levɪ] *n.* (*tax*) сбор; (*mil.*) набо́р; *v.t.* (*tax*)
взима́ть *impf.* (**from** c+g.); (*mil.*) набира́ть
impf., набра́ть (наберу́, -рёшь; набра́л, -а́,
-о) *pf.*

lewd [lju:d] *adj.* (*lascivious*) похотли́вый;
(*indecent*) непристо́йный.

lexicographer [,leksɪ'kɒɡrəfə(r)] *n.* лексико́-
граф. **lexicography** *n.* лексикогра́фия.

lexicon [,leksɪkən] *n.* словарь (-ря́) *m.*

liability [,laɪə'bɪlɪtɪ] *n.* (*responsibility*) отве́тст-
венность (**for** за+a.); (*obligation*) обяза́-
тельство; *pl.* (*debts*) долги́ *m.pl.*; (*susceptibility*) подве́рженность (**to** +d.). **'liable** *adj.*
отве́тственный (-ен, -енна) (**for** за+a.);
обя́занный (-ан); подве́рженный (-ен) (**to**
+d.).

liaison [lɪ'eɪzɒn] *n.* любо́вная связь; (*mil.*)
связь (взаимоде́йствия); ~ **officer** офице́р
свя́зи.

liar ['laɪə(r)] *n.* лгун (-á), ~ья.

libel ['laɪb(ə)l] *n.* клевета́; *v.t.* клевета́ть (-ещу́,
-е́щешь) *impf.*, на~ *pf.* на+a. **libellous**
['laɪbələs] *adj.* клеветни́ческий.

liberal ['lɪbər(ə)l] *n.* либера́л; *adj.* либера́ль-
ный; (*generous*) ще́дрый (щедр, -á, -о);
(*abundant*) оби́льный.

liberate ['lɪbə,reɪt] *v.t.* освобожда́ть *impf.*,
освободи́ть *pf.* **libe'ration** *n.* освобожде́ние;
attr. освободи́тельный. **liberator** *n.* освобо-
ди́тель *m.*

libertine ['lɪbə,ti:n, -tɪn, -,taɪn] *n.* (*profligate*)
распу́тник; (*free-thinker*) вольноду́мец (-мца).

liberty ['lɪbətɪ] *n.* свобо́да, во́льность; **at** ~
на свобо́де.

libidinous [lɪ'bɪdɪnəs] *adj.* похотли́вый.

Libra ['li:brə, 'lɪb-, 'laɪb-] *n.* Весы́ (-со́в) *pl.*

librarian [laɪ'breərɪən] *n.* библиоте́карь *m.*
'library *n.* библиоте́ка.

libretto [lɪ'bretəʊ] *n.* либре́тто *nt.indecl.*

licence[1] ['laɪs(ə)ns] *n.* (*permission, permit*)
разреше́ние, пра́во (*pl.* -вá), лице́нзия;
(*liberty*) (изли́шняя) во́льность. **license,** -
ce[2] *v.t.* (*allow*) разреша́ть *impf.*, разреши́ть
pf.+d.; дава́ть (даю́, даёшь) *impf.*, дать
(дам, дашь, даст, дади́м; дал, -á, -о) *pf.*
пра́во+d.

licentious [laɪ'senʃəs] *adj.* похотли́вый, рас-
пу́щенный.

lichen ['laɪkən, 'lɪtʃ(ə)n] *n.* (*bot.*) лиша́йник;
(*med.*) лиша́й (-áя).

lick [lɪk] *n.* лиза́ние; **go at full** ~ нести́сь
(несу́сь, -сёшься; нёсся, несла́сь) *det.*, по~
pf.; *v.t.* лиза́ть (лижу́, -жешь) *impf.*, лизну́ть
pf.; (~ **all over**) обли́зывать *impf.*, облиза́ть
(-ижу́, -и́жешь) *pf.*; (*thrash*) колоти́ть (-очу́,
-о́тишь) *impf.*, по~ *pf.*; (*defeat*) побежда́ть

impf., победи́ть (-и́шь). **lickspittle** *n.* под-
хали́м.

lid [lɪd] *n.* (*cover*) кры́шка; (*eyelid*) ве́ко (*pl.*
-ки, -к).

lie[1] [laɪ] *n.* (*untruth*) ложь (лжи, *i.* ло́жью);
(*deceit*) обма́н; *v.i.* лгать (лгу, лжёшь; лгал,
-á, -о) *impf.*, со~ *pf.*

lie[2] [laɪ] *n.* (*position*) положе́ние; ~ **of the
land** (*fig.*) положе́ние веще́й; *v.i.* лежа́ть
(-жу́, -жи́шь) *impf.*; (*be situated*) находи́ться
(-ожу́сь, -о́дишься) *impf.*; ~ **down** ложи́ться
impf., лечь (ля́гу, ля́жешь; лёг, -ла́) *pf.*; ~
in wait for подстерега́ть *impf.*, подстере́чь
(-егу́, -ежёшь; -ёг, -егла́) *pf.*+a.

lieu [lju:] *n.*: **in** ~ **of** вме́сто+g.

lieutenant [lef'tenənt] *n.* лейтена́нт. **lieutenant-colonel** *n.* подполко́вник. **lieuten-
ant-general** *n.* генера́л-лейтена́нт.

life [laɪf] *n.* жизнь; (*way of* ~) о́браз жи́зни;
(*energy*) жи́вость; (*biography*) жизнеопи-
са́ние; (*of inanimate object*) срок рабо́ты,
слу́жбы; **for** ~ на всю жизнь; **from** ~ с
нату́ры. **lifebelt** *n.* спаса́тельный по́яс (*pl.*
-á). **lifeboat** *n.* спаса́тельная шлю́пка.
lifebuoy *n.* спаса́тельный буй (*pl.* буй). **life-
guard** *n.* (*bodyguard*) ли́чная охра́на. **Life-
Guards** *n.* лейб-гва́рдия. **life-jacket** *n.*
спаса́тельный жиле́т. **lifeless** *adj.* безжи́-
зненный (-ен, -енна). **lifelike** *adj.* сло́вно
живо́й (жив, -á, -о). **lifelong** *adj.* пожи́знен-
ный (-ен, -енна). **life-size(d)** *adj.* в нату-
ра́льную величину́. **lifetime** *n.* продолжи́-
тельность жи́зни.

lift [lɪft] *n.* подня́тие; (*machine*) лифт, подъ-
ёмная маши́на, подъёмник; (*force*) подъ-
ёмная си́ла; **give a** ~ подвози́ть (-ожу́,
-о́зишь) *impf.*, подвезти́ (-езу́, -езёшь; -ёз,
-езла́) *pf.*; *v.t. & i.* поднима́ть(ся) *impf.*,
подня́ть(ся) (-ниму́(сь), -ни́мешь(ся); по́д-
ня́л/подня́лся, -лá(сь), -ло/ло́сь) *pf.*; *v.t.*
(*steal*) красть (краду́, -дёшь; крал) *impf.*,
у~ *pf.*

ligament ['lɪɡəmənt] *n.* свя́зка.

ligature ['lɪɡətʃə(r)] *n.* лигату́ра; (*mus.*) ли́га.

light[1] [laɪt] *n.* свет, освеще́ние; (*source of* ~)
ого́нь (огня́) *m.*, ла́мпа, фона́рь (-ря́) *m.*;
pl. (*traffic* ~) светофо́р; **bring to** ~ выво-
ди́ть (-ожу́, -о́дишь) *impf.*, вы́вести (-еду,
-едешь; -ел) *pf.* на чи́стую во́ду; **come to** ~
обнару́живаться *impf.*, обнару́житься *pf.*;
shed ~ **on** пролива́ть *impf.*, проли́ть (-лью,
-льёшь; про́ли́л, -á, -о) *pf.* свет на+a.; ~
meter (*phot.*) экспоно́метр; *adj.* (*bright*)
све́тлый (-тел, -тлá, -тло); (*pale*) бле́дный
(-ден, -днá, -дно, бле́дны́); **it is** ~ **in the
room** в ко́мнате светло́; *v.t. & i.* (*ignite*)
зажига́ть(ся) *impf.*, заже́чь(ся) (-жгу́(сь),
-жжёшь(ся); -жёг(ся), -жгла́(сь)) *pf.*; *v.t.*
(*give* ~ *to*) освеща́ть *impf.*, освети́ть (-ещу́
-ети́шь) *pf.*; ~ **up** (*begin to smoke*) закури́ть
(-рю́, -ришь) *pf.*

light[2] [laɪt] *adj.* (*not heavy*) лёгкий (-гок, -гкá,
-гко́, лёгки́); (*unimportant*) незначи́тель-

ный; (*nimble*) бы́стрый (быстр, -á, -о, бы́стры); (*cheerful*) весёлый (ве́сел, -á, -о, ве́селы); ~ **industry** лёгкая промы́шленность; ~ **infantry** лёгкая пехо́та.

light³ [laɪt] *v.i.*: ~ **upon** неожи́данно ната́лкиваться *impf.*, натолкну́ться *pf.* на+*a.*

lighten¹ ['laɪt(ə)n] *v.t. & i.* (*make lighter*) облегча́ть(ся) *impf.*, облегчи́ть(ся) *pf.*; *v.t.* (*mitigate*) смягча́ть *impf.*, смягчи́ть *pf.*

lighten² ['laɪt(ə)n] *v.t.* (*illuminate*) освеща́ть *impf.*, освети́ть (-ещу́, -ети́шь) *pf.*; *v.i.* (*grow bright*) светле́ть *impf.*, по~ *pf.*; (*flash*) сверка́ть *impf.*, сверкну́ть *pf.*; **it is ~ing** сверка́ет мо́лния.

lighter¹ ['laɪtə(r)] *n.* (*cigarette* ~ *etc.*) зажига́лка.

lighter² ['laɪtə(r)] *n.* (*boat*) ли́хтер.

light-fingered [laɪt'fɪŋɡəd] *adj.* нá руку нечи́стый (-т, -тá, -то). **light-headed** *adj.* (*frivolous*) легкомы́сленный (-ен, -енна); (*delirious*) *pred.* в бреду́. **light-hearted** *adj.* беззабо́тный.

lighthouse ['laɪthaʊs] *n.* мая́к (-á).

lighting ['laɪtɪŋ] *n.* освеще́ние; (*lights*) освети́тельные устано́вки *f.pl.*

light-minded [laɪt'maɪndɪd] *adj.* легкомы́сленный (-ен, -енна).

lightning ['laɪtnɪŋ] *n.* мо́лния; **ball** ~ шарова́я мо́лния; **summer** ~ зарни́ца. **lightning-conductor** *n.* молниеотво́д.

lights [laɪts] *n.* (*cul.*) лёгкое *sb.*

lightship ['laɪtʃɪp] *n.* плаву́чий мая́к (-á).

lightweight ['laɪtweɪt] *n.* (*sport*) легкове́с; *adj.* легкове́сный.

light-year ['laɪtjɪə(r)] *n.* световой год (*pl.* го́ды, лет, года́м).

like¹ [laɪk] *adj.* (*similar*) похо́жий (на+*a.*), подо́бный; **what is he ~?** что он за челове́к?; *n.*: **and the ~** и тому́ подо́бное, и т.п.

like² [laɪk] *v.t.* нра́виться *impf.*, по~ *pf. impers.*+*d.*; люби́ть (-блю́, -бишь) *impf.*; (*wish for*) хоте́ть (хочу́, -чешь, хоти́м) *impf.*; **I should ~** я хоте́л бы; **I would ~** мне хо́чется; **as you ~** как вам удо́бно. **likeable** *adj.* симпати́чный.

likelihood *n.* вероя́тность. **likely** *adj.* (*probable*) вероя́тный; (*suitable*) подходя́щий.

liken ['laɪkən] *v.t.* уподобля́ть *impf.*, уподо́бить *pf.* (**to** +*d.*).

likeness ['laɪknɪs] *n.* (*resemblance*) схо́дство; (*semblance*) вид; (*portrait*) портре́т.

likewise ['laɪkwaɪz] *adv.* (*similarly*) подо́бно; (*also*) то́же, та́кже.

liking ['laɪkɪŋ] *n.* вкус (**for** к+*d.*).

lilac ['laɪlək] *n.* сире́нь; *adj.* сире́невый.

lily ['lɪlɪ] *n.* ли́лия; ~ **of the valley** ла́ндыш.

limb [lɪm] *n.* член те́ла; (*of tree*) сук (-á, *loc.* -у́; *pl.* -и, -о́в & су́чья, -ьев).

limber ['lɪmbə(r)] *adj.* (*flexible*) ги́бкий (-бок, -бкá, -бко); (*nimble*) прово́рный; *v.i.*: ~ **up** размина́ться *impf.*, размя́ться (разомну́сь, -нёшься) *pf.*

limbo ['lɪmbəʊ] *n.* преддве́рие а́да; (*fig.*)

забро́шенность, забве́ние; состоя́ние неопределённости.

lime¹ [laɪm] *n.* (*min.*) и́звесть. **limekiln** *n.* печь (*loc.* пе́чи́; *pl.* -чи, -че́й) для о́бжига известняка́. **limelight** *n.*: **in the ~** (*fig.*) в це́нтре внима́ния. **limestone** *n.* известня́к (-á).

lime² [laɪm] *n.* (*fruit*) лайм.

lime³ [laɪm] *n.* (~-*tree*) ли́па.

limit ['lɪmɪt] *n.* грани́ца, преде́л; *v.t.* ограни́чивать *impf.*, ограни́чить *pf.* **limi'tation** *n.* ограниче́ние; (*leg.*) исковáя да́вность. **limitless** *adj.* безграни́чный.

limousine ['lɪmʊziːn, ˌlɪmʊ'ziːn, 'lɪməziːn] *n.* лимузи́н.

limp¹ [lɪmp] *n.* (*lameness*) хромотá; *v.i.* хрома́ть *impf.*

limp² [lɪmp] *adj.* (*not stiff*) мя́гкий (-гок, -гкá, -гко); (*fig.*) вя́лый.

limpet ['lɪmpɪt] *n.* морско́е блю́дечко (*pl.* -чки, -чек, -чкам).

limpid ['lɪmpɪd] *adj.* прозра́чный.

linchpin ['lɪntʃpɪn] *n.* чекá.

linden ['lɪnd(ə)n] *n.* ли́па.

line¹ [laɪn] *n.* ли́ния, чертá; (*cord*) верёвка; (*fishing* ~) лéсá (*pl.* лёсы); (*wrinkle*) морщи́на; (*limit*) грани́ца; (*row*) ряд (-á *with* 2, 3, 4, *loc.* -ý; *pl.* -ы́); (*of words*) строкá (*pl.* -ки, -к, -ка́м); (*of verse*) стих (-á); *v.t.* (*paper*) линова́ть *impf.*, раз~ *pf.*; *v.t. & i.* (~ **up**) выстра́ивать(ся) *impf.*, вы́строить(ся) *pf.* в ряд.

line² [laɪn] *v.t.* (*clothes*) класть (кладу́, -дёшь; клал) *impf.*, положи́ть (-жу́, -жишь) *pf.* на подкла́дку.

lineage ['lɪnɪɪdʒ] *n.* происхожде́ние (по прямо́й ли́нии).

linear ['lɪnɪə(r)] *adj.* лине́йный.

lined¹ [laɪnd] *adj.* (*paper*) лино́ванный; (*face*) морщи́нистый.

lined² [laɪnd] *adj.* (*garment*) на подкла́дке, с подкла́дкой.

linen ['lɪnɪn] *n.* полотно́ (*pl.* -тна, -тен, -тнам); *collect.* бельё; *adj.* льяно́й, полотня́ный.

liner ['laɪnə(r)] *n.* ла́йнер.

linesman ['laɪnzmən] *n.* (*sport*) боково́й судья́ (*pl.* -дьи, -де́й, -дьям).

linger ['lɪŋɡə(r)] *v.i.* ме́длить *impf.*; заде́рживаться *impf.*, задержа́ться (-жу́сь, -жишься) *pf.*

lingerie ['læʒərɪ] *n.* да́мское бельё.

lingering ['lɪŋɡərɪŋ] *adj.* (*illness*) затяжно́й.

lingo ['lɪŋɡəʊ] *n.* (*special language*) жарго́н.

linguist ['lɪŋɡwɪst] *n.* лингви́ст, языкове́д. **lingu'istic** *adj.* лингвисти́ческий. **lingu'istics** *n.* лингви́стика, языкозна́ние.

liniment ['lɪnɪmənt] *n.* жи́дкая мазь.

lining ['laɪnɪŋ] *n.* (*clothing etc.*) подкла́дка; (*tech.*) облицо́вка.

link [lɪŋk] *n.* звено́ (*pl.* -нья, -ньев), связь; *v.t.* соединя́ть *impf.*, соедини́ть *pf.*; свя́зывать *impf.*, связа́ть (свяжу́, -жешь) *pf.*

linnet ['lɪnɪt] *n.* конопля́нка.

lino(leum) ['laɪnəʊ; lɪ'nəʊlɪəm] *n.* линóлеум.

linseed ['lɪnsiːd] *n.* льнянóе сéмя (*g.pl.* -мян) *nt.*; ~ **cake** льнянь́е жмыхи (-хóв) *pl.*; ~ **oil** льнянóе мáсло.

lint [lɪnt] *n.* кóрпия.

lintel ['lɪnt(ə)l] *n.* перемь́чка.

lion ['laɪən] *n.* лев (льва); ~ **cub** львёнок (-нка; *pl.* львя́та, -т). **lioness** *n.* льви́ца.

lip [lɪp] *n.* губá (*pl.* -бы, -б, -бáм); (*of vessel*) край (*loc.* краю́; *pl.* -ая́); (*fig.*) дéрзость. **lipstick** *n.* губнáя помáда.

liquefaction [ˌlɪkwɪ'fækʃ(ə)n] *n.* сжижéние.

liquefy ['lɪkwɪˌfaɪ] *v.t.* & *i.* превращáть(ся) *impf.*, преврати́ть(ся) (-ащý, -ати́т(ся)) *pf.* в жи́дкое состоя́ние.

liqueur [lɪ'kjʊə(r)] *n.* ликёр (-a(y)).

liquid ['lɪkwɪd] *n.* жи́дкость; *adj.* жи́дкий (-док, -дкá, -дко); (*transparent*) прозрáчный; (*ling.*) плáвный; (*econ.*) ликви́дный.

liquidate ['lɪkwɪˌdeɪt] *v.t.* ликвиди́ровать *impf.* & *pf.* **liqui'dation** *n.* ликвидáция; **go into** ~ ликвиди́роваться *impf.* & *pf.*

liquidity [lɪ'kwɪdɪtɪ] *n.* жи́дкое состоя́ние.

liquidizer ['lɪkwɪˌdaɪzə(r)] *n.* (*cul.*) ми́ксер.

liquor ['lɪkə(r)] *n.* (спиртнóй) напи́ток (-тка).

liquorice ['lɪkərɪs, -rɪʃ] *n.* (*plant*) лакри́чник, солóдка; (*root*) лакри́ца, солодкóвый кóрень (-рня) *m.*

lissom ['lɪsəm] *adj.* (*lithe*) ги́бкий (-бок, -бкá, -бко); (*agile*) провóрный.

list[1] [lɪst] *n.* (*roll*) спи́сок (-ска), пéречень (-чня) *m.*; *v.t.* составля́ть *impf.*, состáвить *pf.* спи́сок+*g.*; перечисля́ть *impf.*, перечи́слить *pf.*

list[2] [lɪst] *n.* (*naut.*) крен; *v.i.* накреня́ться *impf.*, крени́ться *impf.*, на~ *pf.*

listen ['lɪs(ə)n] *v.i.* слýшать *impf.*, по~ *pf.* (**to** +*a.*); (*heed*) прислýшиваться *impf.*, прислýшаться *pf.* (**to** к+*d.*); ~ **in** (*telephone*) подслýшивать *impf.*, подслýшать *pf.* (**to** +*a.*); (*radio*) слýшать *impf.* рáдио.

listless ['lɪstlɪs] *adj.* (*languid*) тóмный (-мен, -мнá, -мно); (*indifferent*) безразли́чный.

litany ['lɪtənɪ] *n.* лита́ния.

literacy ['lɪtərəsɪ] *n.* грáмотность.

literal ['lɪtər(ə)l] *adj.* (*in letters*) бýквенный; (*sense etc.*) буквáльный.

literary ['lɪtərərɪ] *adj.* литератýрный.

literate ['lɪtərət] *adj.* грáмотный.

literature ['lɪtərətʃə(r), 'lɪtrə-] *n.* литератýра.

lithe [laɪð] *adj.* ги́бкий (-бок, -бкá, -бко).

lithograph ['lɪθəˌgrɑːf, 'laɪθə-] *n.* литогрáфия; *v.t.* литографи́ровать *impf.* & *pf.* **lithographer** [lɪ'θɒɡrəfə(r)] *n.* литóграф. **lithographic** [ˌlɪθə'ɡræfɪk] *adj.* литографи́ческий. **lithography** [lɪ'θɒɡrəfɪ] *n.* литогрáфия.

Lithuania [ˌlɪθjʊ'eɪnɪə, ˌlɪθuː-] *n.* Литвá.

litigant ['lɪtɪɡənt] *n.* сторонá (*a.* -ону; *pl.* -оны, -óн, -онáм); *adj.* тя́жущийся. **litigate** *v.i.* суди́ться (сужý́сь, сýдишься) *impf.* **liti'gation** *n.* тя́жба. **litigious** [lɪ'tɪdʒəs] *adj.* сутя́жнический.

litmus ['lɪtməs] *n.* лáкмус; ~ **paper** лáкму-

совая бумáга.

litre ['liːtə(r)] *n.* литр.

litter ['lɪtə(r)] *n.* (*vehicle*, *stretcher*) носи́лки (-лок) *pl.*; (*bedding*) подсти́лка; (*disorder*) беспоря́док (-дка); (*rubbish*) сор (-a(y)); (*brood*) помёт; *v.t.* (*make untidy*) сори́ть *impf.*, на~ *pf.* (**with** +*i.*); (*scatter*) разбрá-сывать *impf.*, разбросáть *pf.*

little ['lɪt(ə)l] *n.* немнóгое; ~ **by** ~ мáло-помáлу; **a** ~ немнóго+*g.*; **not a** ~ не-мáло+*g.*; *adj.* мáленький, небольшóй; (*in height*) небольшóго рóста; (*in distance, time*) корóткий (кóроток, короткá, кóрот-кó); (*unimportant*) незначи́тельный; *adv.* мáло, немнóго; (*not at all*) совсéм не.

littoral ['lɪtər(ə)l] *n.* побéрежье; *adj.* при-брéжный.

liturgical [lɪ'tɜːdʒɪk(ə)l] *adj.* литурги́ческий. **'liturgy** *n.* литурги́я.

live[1] [laɪv] *adj.* живóй (жив, -á, -o); (*coals*) горя́щий; (*mil.*) боевóй; (*elec.*) под напря-жéнием; (*active*) дéятельный; (*real*) жи́з-ненный (-ен, -енна); ~ **broadcast** прямáя передáча.

live[2] [lɪv] *v.i.* жить (живý, -вёшь; жил, -á, -o) *impf.*; существовáть *impf.*; ~ **down** заглá-живать *impf.*, заглáдить *pf.*; ~ **on** (*feed on*) питáться *impf.*+*i.*; ~ **through** пережи-вáть *impf.*, пережи́ть (-ивý, -ивёшь; пéрежи́л, -á, -o) *pf.*; ~ **until, to see** дожи-вáть *impf.*, дожи́ть (-ивý, -ивёшь; дóжил, -á, -o) *pf.* до+*g.*; ~ **up to** жить (живý, -вёшь; жил, -á, -o) *impf.* соглáсно+*d.*

livelihood ['laɪvlɪˌhʊd] *n.* срéдства *nt.pl.* к существовáнию.

lively ['laɪvlɪ] *adj.* живóй (жив, -á, -o), весё-лый (вéсел, -á, -o, вéселы).

liven (up) ['laɪv(ə)n] *v.t.* & *i.* оживля́ть(ся) *impf.*, оживи́ть(ся) *pf.*

liver ['lɪvə(r)] *n.* пéчень; (*cul.*) печёнка.

livery ['lɪvərɪ] *n.* ливрéя.

livestock ['laɪvstɒk] *n.* скот (-á), живóй ин-вентáрь (-ря́) *m.*

livid ['lɪvɪd] *adj.* (*colour*) синевáто-сéрый; *pred.* (*angry*) зол (зла).

living ['lɪvɪŋ] *n.* срéдства *nt.pl.* к сущест-вовáнию; (*eccl.*) бенефи́ция; **earn a** ~ зарá-бáтывать *impf.*, зарабóтать *pf.* на жизнь; *adj.* живóй (жив, -á, -o), живý́щий; (*of likeness*) тóчный; ~ **image** кóпия. **living-room** *n.* гости́ная *sb.*

lizard ['lɪzəd] *n.* я́щерица.

lo [ləʊ] *int.* вот!; се!

loach [ləʊtʃ] *n.* голéц (-льцá).

load [ləʊd] *n.* груз; (*also fig.*) брéмя *nt.*; (*tech.*) нагрýзка; *pl.* (*lots*) кýча; *v.t.* на-гружáть *impf.*, грузи́ть (-ужý, -ýжи́шь) *impf.*, на~ *pf.*; (*fig.*) обременя́ть *impf.*, обремени́ть *pf.*; (*gun, camera*) заряжáть *impf.*, заряди́ть (-яжý, -я́ди́шь) *pf.*

loadstar *see* **lodestar. loadstone** *see* **lode-stone.**

loaf[1] [ləʊf] *n.* бухáнка; батóн.

loaf² [ləʊf] *v.i.* бездельничать *impf.*; шататься *impf.* **loafer** *n.* бездельник.

loam [ləʊm] *n.* суглинок (-нка).

loan [ləʊn] *n.* заём (займа); *v.t.* давать (даю, даёшь) *impf.*, дать (дам, дашь, даст, дадим; дал, -а, дало, -и) *pf.* взаймы.

loath [ləʊθ] *pred.*: **be ~ to** не хотеть (хочу, -чешь; хотим) *impf.+inf.*

loathe [ləʊð] *v.t.* питать *impf.* отвращение к+*d.* **loathing** *n.* отвращение. **loathsome** *adj.* отвратительный.

lob [lɒb] *n.* (*sport*) свеча (*pl.* -чи, -чей).

lobby [ˈlɒbɪ] *n.* прихожая *sb.*, вестибюль *m.*; (*parl.*) кулуары *pl.*

lobe [ləʊb] *n.* доля (*pl.* -ли, -лей); (*of ear*) мочка.

lobster [ˈlɒbstə(r)] *n.* омар. **lobster-pot** *n.* верша для омаров.

local [ˈləʊk(ə)l] *adj.* местный; (*train*) пригородный.

locality [ləʊˈkælɪtɪ] *n.* (*site*) местоположение; (*district*) местность.

localize [ˈləʊkəˌlaɪz] *v.t.* (*restrict*) локализовать *impf. & pf.*

locate [ləʊˈkeɪt] *v.t.* (*place*) помещать *impf.*, поместить *pf.*; (*discover*) обнаруживать *impf.*, обнаружить *pf.*; **be ~d** находиться (-ится) *impf.*

location [ləʊˈkeɪʃ(ə)n] *n.* (*position*) местонахождение; определение места; **on ~** (*cin.*) на натуре.

locative [ˈlɒkətɪv] *adj.* (*n.*) местный (падеж (-á)).

loch [lɒk, lɒx] *n.* (*lake*) озеро (*pl.* озёра); (*sea ~*) (узкий) залив.

lock¹ [lɒk] *n.* (*of hair*) локон; *pl.* волосы (волос, -ам) *pl.*

lock² [lɒk] *n.* замок (-мка), запор; (*tech.*) стопор; (*canal*) шлюз; *v.t.* запирать *impf.*, запереть (-пру, -прёшь; запер, -ла, -ло) *pf.*; *v.i.* запираться *impf.*, запереться (-прётся; заперся, -рлась, заперлось) *pf.* **locker** [ˈlɒkə(r)] *n.* шкафчик.

locket [ˈlɒkɪt] *n.* медальон.

lockjaw [ˈlɒkdʒɔː] *n.* столбняк (-á).

lock-keeper [ˈlɒkkiːpə(r)] *n.* начальник шлюза.

lockout [ˈlɒkaʊt] *n.* локаут. **locksmith** *n.* слесарь (*pl.* -ри & -ря) *m.* **lock-up** *n.* (*cell*) арестантская *sb.*

locomotion [ˌləʊkəˈməʊʃ(ə)n] *n.* передвижение. **locomotive** *adj.* движущий(ся); *n.* (*rail.*) локомотив.

locust [ˈləʊkəst] *n.* саранча (*also collect.*; *fig.*).

locution [ləˈkjuːʃ(ə)n] *n.* оборот речи.

lode [ləʊd] *n.* рудная жила. **lodestar**, **load-** *n.* Полярная звезда; (*fig.*) путеводная звезда (*pl.* звёзды). **lodestone**, **load-** *n.* магнитный железняк (-á); (*magnet*) магнит.

lodge [lɒdʒ] *n.* (*hunting*) охотничий домик; (*porter's*) швейцарская *sb.*, сторожка; (*Masonic*) ложа; *v.t.* (*accommodate*) помещать *impf.*, поместить *pf.*; (*deposit*) давать

(даю, даёшь) *impf.*, дать (дам, дашь, даст, дадим; дал, -á, дало, -и) *pf.* на хранение (**with** +*d.*); (*complaint*) подавать (-даю, -даёшь) *impf.*, подать (-ám, -áшь, -áст, -адим; подал, -á, -о) *pf.*; *v.i.* (*reside*) жить (живу, -вёшь; жил, -á, -о) *impf.* (**with** y+*g.*); (*stick*) засаживать *impf.*, засесть (-сядет; -сел) *pf.* **lodger** *n.* жилец (-льца), жилица. **lodging** *n.* (*also pl.*) квартира, (снимаемая) комната.

loft [lɒft] *n.* (*attic*) чердак (-á); (*for hay*) сеновал; (*for pigeons*) голубятня (*g.pl.* -тен); (*gallery*) галерея.

lofty [ˈlɒftɪ] *adj.* очень высокий (-ок, -ока, -око); (*elevated*) возвышенный.

log [lɒg] *n.* бревно (*pl.* брёвна, -вен, -внам); (*for fire*) полено (*pl.* -нья, -ньев); (*naut.*) лаг.

logarithm [ˈlɒgəˌrɪð(ə)m] *n.* логарифм. **loga-'rithmic** *adj.* логарифмический.

log-book [ˈlɒgbʊk] *n.* (*naut.*) вахтенный журнал; (*aeron.*) бортовой журнал; (*registration book*) формуляр.

loggerhead [ˈlɒgəˌhed] *n.*: **be at ~s** ссориться *impf.*, по~ *pf.* (**with** c+*i.*).

logic [ˈlɒdʒɪk] *n.* логика. **logical** *adj.* (*of logic*) логический; (*consistent*) логичный. **logician** [ləˈdʒɪʃ(ə)n] *n.* логик.

logistics [ləˈdʒɪstɪks] *n.* материально-техническое обеспечение.

loin [lɔɪn] *n.* (*pl.*) поясница; (*cul.*) филейная часть.

loiter [ˈlɔɪtə(r)] *v.i.* слоняться *impf.*

London [ˈlʌnd(ə)n] *n.* Лондон. **Londoner** *n.* лондонец, -ка.

lone [ləʊn], **lonely** *adj.* одинокий, уединённый (-ён, -ённа). **loneliness** *n.* одиночество, уединённость.

long¹ [lɒŋ] *v.i.* страстно желать *impf.*, по~ *pf.* (**for** +*g.*); тосковать *impf.* (**for** по+*d.*)

long² [lɒŋ] *adj.* (*space*) длинный (-нен, -нна, длинно); (*time*) долгий (-лог, -лга, -лго); (*protracted*) длительный; (*in measurements*) длиной в+*a.*; **in the ~ run** в конечном счёте; *adv.* долго; **~ after** спустя много времени; **~ ago** (уже) давно; **as ~ as** пока; **~ before** задолго до+*g.* **longboat** *n.* баркас. **longevity** [lɒnˈdʒevɪtɪ] *n.* долговечность.

longing [ˈlɒŋɪŋ] *n.* страстное желание (**for** +*g.*); тоска (**for** по+*d.*)

longitude [ˈlɒŋɡɪˌtjuːd, ˈlɒndʒ-] *n.* долгота (*pl.* -ты).

long-lived [lɒŋˈlɪvd] *adj.* долговечный. **long-sighted** *adj.* дальнозоркий (-рок, -рка); (*fig.*) дальновидный. **long-suffering** *adj.* долготерпеливый; многострадальный. **long-term** *adj.* долгосрочный. **longways** *adv.* в длину. **long-winded** *adj.* многоречивый.

look [lʊk] *n.* (*glance*) взгляд; (*appearance*) вид; (*expression*) выражение; *v.i.* смотреть (-рю, -ришь) *impf.*, по~ *pf.* (**at** на, в, +*a.*); глядеть (-яжу, -ядишь) *impf.*, по~ *pf.* (**at** на+*a.*); (*appear*) выглядеть (-яжу, -ядишь *impf.*+*i.*; (*face*) выходи́ть (-ит) *impf.* (*towards, onto* на+*a.*); ~ **about** осма́триваться *impf.*, осмотре́ться (-рюсь, -ришься) *pf.*; ~ **after** (*attend to*) присма́тривать *impf.*, присмотре́ть (-рю, -ришь) *pf.* за+*i.*; ~ **down on** презира́ть *impf.*; ~ **for** иска́ть (ищу́, и́щешь) *impf.*+*a.*, +*g.*; ~ **forward to** предвкуша́ть *impf.*, предвкуси́ть (-ушу́, -у́сишь) *pf.*; ~ **in on** загля́дывать *impf.*, загляну́ть (-ну́, -нешь) *pf.* к+*d.*; ~ **into** (*investigate*) разбира́ться *impf.*, разобра́ться (разберу́сь, -рёшься; -а́лся, -ала́сь, -а́лось) *pf.* в+*p.*; ~ **like** быть похо́жим на+*a.*; **it** ~s **like rain** похо́же на (то, что бу́дет) дождь; ~ **on** (*regard*) счита́ть *impf.*, счесть (сочту́, -тёшь; счёл, сочла́) *pf.* (**as** +*i.*, за+*i.*); ~ **out** выгля́дывать *impf.*, вы́глянуть *pf.* (в окно́); быть насторожé; *imper.* осторо́жно!; береги́(те)сь!; ~ **over, through** просма́тривать *impf.*, просмотре́ть (-рю, -ришь) *pf.* ~ **up** (*raise eyes*) поднима́ть *impf.*, подня́ть (подниму́, -мешь; по́дня́л, -а́, -о) *pf.* глаза́; (*in dictionary etc.*) иска́ть (ищу́, и́щешь) *impf.*; (*improve*) улучша́ться *impf.*, улу́чшиться *pf.*; ~ **up to** уважа́ть *impf.* **looker-on** *n.* зри́тель *m.*, ~ница. **looking-glass** *n.* зе́ркало (*pl.* -ла́).

loom¹ [luːm] *n.* тка́цкий стано́к (-нка́).

loom² [luːm] *v.i.* нея́сно вырисо́вываться *impf.*, вы́рисоваться; (*fig.*) гото́виться *impf.*

loop [luːp] *n.* пе́тля (*g.pl.* -тель); *v.t.* образо́вывать *impf.*, образова́ть *pf.* пе́тлю; ~ **the** ~ (*aeron.*) де́лать *impf.*, с~ *pf.* мёртвую пе́тлю.

loophole ['luːphəʊl] *n.* бойни́ца; (*fig.*) лазе́йка.

loose [luːs] *adj.* (*free*) свобо́дный; (*not fixed*) неприкреплённый; (*inexact*) нето́чный (-чен, -чна́, -чно); (*not compact*) ры́хлый (рыхл, -а́, -о); (*lax*) распу́щенный (-ен, -енна); **be at a** ~ **end** безде́льничать *impf.*; *v.t.* (*free*) освобожда́ть *impf.*, освободи́ть *pf.*; (*untie*) отвя́зывать *impf.*, отвяза́ть (-яжу́, -я́жешь) *pf.* **loosen** *v.t.* & *i.* ослабля́ть(ся) *impf.*, осла́бить(ся) *pf.*

loot [luːt] *n.* добы́ча; *v.t.* гра́бить *impf.*, о~ *pf.*

lop [lɒp] *v.t.* (*tree*) подреза́ть *impf.*, подре́зать (-е́жу, -е́жешь) *pf.*; (~ **off**) отруба́ть *impf.*, отруби́ть (-блю́, -бишь) *pf.*

lope [ləʊp] *v.i.* бе́гать *indet.*, бежа́ть (бегу́, бежи́шь) *det.* вприпры́жку.

lopsided [lɒp'saɪdɪd] *adj.* кривобо́кий.

loquacious [lɒ'kweɪʃəs] *adj.* болтли́вый. **loquacity** [lɒ'kwæsɪtɪ] *n.* болтли́вость.

lord [lɔːd] *n.* (*master*) господи́н (*pl.* -да́, -д, -да́м), влады́ка *m.*; (**the L**~; *eccl.*) Госпо́дь (-ода, *voc.* -оди); (*peer; title*) лорд; *v.t.*: ~ **it over** помыка́ть *impf.*+*i.* **lordly** *adj.* (*haughty*) высокоме́рный. **lordship** *n.* власть (**over** над+*i.*); (*title*) све́тлость.

lore [lɔː(r)] *n.* зна́ния *nt.pl.*

lorgnette [lɔː'njet] *n.* лорне́т.

lorry ['lɒrɪ] *n.* грузови́к (-á).

lose [luːz] *v.t.* теря́ть *impf.*, по~ *pf.*; (*forfeit*) лиша́ться *impf.*, лиши́ться *pf.*+*g.*; (*game etc.*) прои́грывать *impf.*, проигра́ть *pf.*; *v.i.* (*suffer loss*) терпе́ть (-плю́, -пишь) *impf.*, по~ *pf.* уще́рб (**by** от+*g.*); (*clock*) отстава́ть (-таёт) *impf.*, отста́ть (-а́нет) *pf.* **loss** [lɒs] *n.* поте́ря, уще́рб; (*in game*) про́игрыш; **at a** ~ (*puzzled*) в затрудне́нии.

lot [lɒt] *n.* жре́бий; (*destiny*) у́часть; (*of goods*) па́ртия; **a** ~, ~**s** мно́го, ма́сса; **the** ~ всё (всего́), все (всех) *pl.*

lotion ['ləʊʃ(ə)n] *n.* примо́чка.

lottery ['lɒtərɪ] *n.* лотере́я.

lotto ['lɒtəʊ] *n.* лото́ *nt.indecl.*

lotus ['ləʊtəs] *n.* ло́тос.

loud [laʊd] *adj.* (*sound*) гро́мкий (-мок, -мка́, -мко); (*noisy*) шу́мный (-мен, -мна́, -мно); (*colour*) крича́щий; **out** ~ вслух. **loudspeaker** *n.* громкоговори́тель *m.*; дина́мик.

lounge [laʊndʒ] *n.* фойé *nt.indecl.*; (*sitting room*) гости́ная *sb.*; *v.i.* сиде́ть (сижу́, сиди́шь) *impf.* развали́сь; (*idle*) безде́льничать *impf.* **lounger** *n.* шезло́нг.

lour ['laʊə(r)], **lower**² ['laʊə(r)] *v.i.* (*person, sky*) хму́риться *impf.*, на~ *pf.*

louse [laʊs] *n.* вошь (вши, *i.* во́шью). **lousy** ['laʊzɪ] *adj.* вши́вый; (*coll.*) парши́вый.

lout [laʊt] *n.* у́валень (-льня) *m.*, грубия́н. **loutish** *adj.* неотёсанный (-ан, -анна).

lovable ['lʌvəb(ə)l] *adj.* ми́лый (мил, -á, -о, ми́лы). **love** *n.* любо́вь (-бви́, *i.* любо́вью) (**of, for** к+*d.*); (*sweetheart*) возлю́бленный *sb.*; **in** ~ **with** влюблённый (-ён, -ённа) в+*a.*; *v.t.* люби́ть (-блю́, -бишь) *impf.* **lovely** *adj.* краси́вый; (*delightful*) преле́стный. **lover** *n.* любо́вник, -ица.

low¹ [ləʊ] *n.* (*of cow*) мыча́ние; *v.i.* мыча́ть (-чу́, -чи́шь) *impf.*

low² [ləʊ] *adj.* ни́зкий (-зок, -зка́, -зко), невысо́кий (-о́к, -ока́, -о́ко); (*quiet*) ти́хий (тих, -á, -о); (*coarse*) гру́бый (груб, -á, -о); (*weak*) сла́бый (слаб, -á, -о).

low-alcohol [ˌləʊ'ælkəhɒl] *adj.* слабоалкого́льный. **low-calorie** *adj.* малокалори́йный.

lower¹ ['ləʊə(r)] *v.t.* опуска́ть *impf.*, опусти́ть (-ущу́, -у́стишь) *pf.*; снижа́ть *impf.*, сни́зить *pf.*

lower² *see* **lour**

lower³ ['ləʊə(r)] *adj.* ни́зший, ни́жний.

low-fat ['ləʊfæt] *adj.* маложи́рный.

lowland ['ləʊlənd] *n.* ни́зменность.

lowly ['ləʊlɪ] *adj.* скро́мный (-мен, -мна́, -мно).

low-paid ['ləʊpeɪd] *adj.* малоопла́чиваемый.

loyal ['lɔɪəl] *adj.* ве́рный (-рен, -рна́, -рно, ве́рны́), лоя́льный. **loyalty** *n.* ве́рность, лоя́льность.

lozenge ['lɒzɪndʒ] *n.* (*shape*) ромб; (*tablet*) лепёшка.

LP *abbr.* (*of long-playing record*) долгоигра́ющая пласти́нка.

L-plate ['elpleɪt] *n.* щито́к с на́дписью

«уче́бная» (*на маши́не*).

Ltd. *abbr.* (*of limited liability company*) с ограни́ченной отве́тственностью.

lubricant ['lu:brɪkənt] *n.* сма́зка, сма́зочный материа́л. **lubricate** *v.t.* сма́зывать *impf.*, сма́зать (-а́жу, -а́жешь) *pf.* **lubri'cation** *n.* сма́зка.

lucerne [lu:'sɜːn] *n.* люце́рна.

lucid ['lu:sɪd] *adj.* я́сный (я́сен, ясна́, я́сно, я́сны).

luck [lʌk] *n.* (*chance*) слу́чай; (*good ~*) сча́стье, уда́ча; (*bad ~*) неуда́ча. **luckily** *adv.* к сча́стью. **luckless** *adj.* несча́стный. **lucky** *adj.* счастли́вый (сча́стлив); (*successful*) уда́чный.

lucrative ['lu:krətɪv] *adj.* прибыльный.

lucre ['lu:kə(r)] *n.* прибыль.

ludicrous ['lu:dɪkrəs] *adj.* смехотво́рный.

lug [lʌg] *v.t.* (*drag*) таска́ть *indet.*, тащи́ть (-щу́, -щишь) *det.*

luggage ['lʌgɪdʒ] *n.* бага́ж (-а́).

lugubrious [lu:'gu:brɪəs, lʊ-] *adj.* печа́льный.

lukewarm [lu:k'wɔːm, 'lu:k-] *adj.* теплова́тый; (*fig.*) равноду́шный.

lull [lʌl] *n.* (*in storm*) зати́шье; (*interval*) переры́в; *v.t.* (*to sleep*) убаю́кивать *impf.*, убаю́кать *pf.*; (*suspicions*) усыпля́ть *impf.*, усыпи́ть *pf.*; *v.i.* затиха́ть *impf.*, зати́хнуть (-x) *pf.*

lullaby ['lʌləˌbaɪ] *n.* колыбе́льная пе́сня (*g.pl.* -сен).

lumbago [lʌm'beɪgəʊ] *n.* люмба́го *nt.indecl.*

lumbar ['lʌmbə(r)] *adj.* поясни́чный.

lumber¹ ['lʌmbə(r)] *v.i.* (*move*) дви́гаться (-аюсь, -аешься & дви́жусь, -жешься) *impf.*, дви́нуться *pf.* тяжело́, шу́мно, неуклю́же.

lumber² ['lʌmbə(r)] *n.* (*domestic*) ру́хлядь; (*timber*) лесоматериа́лы *m.pl.*; *v.t.* загроможда́ть *impf.*, загромозди́ть *pf.* **lumberjack** *n.* лесору́б. **lumber-room** *n.* чула́н.

luminary ['lu:mɪnərɪ] *n.* свети́ло.

luminous ['lu:mɪnəs, 'lju:-] *adj.* светя́щийся.

lump [lʌmp] *n.* ком (*pl.* -ья, -ьев), кусо́к (-ска́); (*swelling*) о́пухоль; (*lot*) ку́ча; *v.t.*: ~ **together** сме́шивать *impf.*, смеша́ть *pf.* (в ку́чу).

lunacy ['lu:nəsɪ] *n.* безу́мие.

lunar ['lu:nə(r), 'lju:-] *adj.* лу́нный.

lunatic ['lu:nətɪk] *adj.* (*n.*) сумасше́дший (*sb.*); безу́мный (*sb.*).

lunch [lʌntʃ] *n.* обе́д, второ́й за́втрак; *v.i.* обе́дать *impf.*, по~ *pf.* **lunch-hour, lunch-time** *n.* обе́денный переры́в. **luncheon** ['lʌntʃ(ə)n] *n.* официа́льный обе́д, за́втрак; ~ **voucher** тало́н на обе́д.

lung [lʌŋ] *n.* лёгкое *sb.*

lunge [lʌndʒ, lju:-] *n.* (*sport*) вы́пад; толчо́к (-чка́); *v.i.* (*fencing*) де́лать *impf.*, с~ *pf.* вы́пад; наноси́ть (-ошу́, -о́сишь) *impf.*, нанести́ (-есу́, -есёшь; -ёс, -есла́) *pf.* уда́р (с плеча́) (**at** +*d.*).

lupin(e) ['lu:pɪn] *n.* люпи́н.

lupine ['lu:paɪn] *adj.* во́лчий (-чья, -чье).

lupus ['lu:pəs] *n.* волча́нка.

lurch¹ [lɜːtʃ] *n.*: **leave in the ~** покида́ть *impf.*, поки́нуть *pf.* в беде́.

lurch² [lɜːtʃ] *v.i.* (*stagger*) ходи́ть (хожу́, хо́дишь) *indet.*, идти́ (иду́, идёшь; шёл, шла́) *det.* шата́ясь.

lure [ljʊə(r), lʊə(r)] *n.* прима́нка; *v.t.* прима́нивать *impf.*, примани́ть (-ню́, -нишь) *pf.*

lurid ['ljʊərɪd, 'lʊə-] *adj.* мра́чный (-чен, -чна́, -чно); (*sensational*) сенсацио́нный.

lurk [lɜːk] *v.i.* пря́таться (-я́чусь, -я́чешься) *impf.*, с~ *pf.*; (*fig.*) таи́ться *impf.*

luscious ['lʌʃəs] *adj.* прито́рный.

lush [lʌʃ] *adj.* со́чный (-чен, -чна́, -чно).

lust [lʌst] *n.* по́хоть, вожделе́ние (**of, for** к+*d.*); *v.i.* стра́стно жела́ть *impf.*, по~ *pf.* (**for** +*g.*). **lustful** *adj.* похотли́вый.

lustre ['lʌstə(r)] *n.* (*gloss*) гля́нец (-нца); (*splendour*) блеск; (*chandelier*) лю́стра. **lustrous** *adj.* глянцеви́тый, блестя́щий.

lusty ['lʌstɪ] *adj.* (*healthy*) здоро́вый; (*lively*) живо́й (жив, -á, -о).

lute¹ [lu:t, lju:t] *n.* (*mus.*) лю́тня (*g.pl.* -тен).

lute² [lu:t, lju:t] *n.* (*clay etc.*) зама́зка.

Luxemburg ['lʌksəmˌbɜːg] *n.* Люксембу́рг.

luxuriant [lʌg'zjʊərɪənt, lʌk'sj-, lʌg'ʒʊə-] *adj.* пы́шный (-шен, -шна́, -шно).

luxuriate [lʌg'zjʊərɪˌeɪt, lʌk'sj-, lʌg'ʒʊə-] *v.i.* наслажда́ться *impf.*, наслади́ться *pf.* (**in** +*i.*).

luxurious [lʌg'zjʊərɪəs, lʌk'sj-, lʌg'ʒʊə-] *adj.* роско́шный. **luxury** ['lʌkʃərɪ] *n.* ро́скошь.

lye [laɪ] *n.* щёлок (-а(у)).

lymph [lɪmf] *n.* ли́мфа. **lym'phatic** *adj.* лимфати́ческий.

lynch [lɪntʃ] *v.t.* линчева́ть (-чу́ю, -чу́ешь) *impf. & pf.*; ~ **law** суд (-á) Ли́нча.

lynx [lɪŋks] *n.* рысь.

lyre ['laɪə(r)] *n.* ли́ра.

lyric ['lɪrɪk] *n.* ли́рика; *pl.* слова́ *nt.pl.* пе́сни. **lyrical** *adj.* лири́ческий. **lyricism** ['lɪrɪˌsɪz(ə)m] *n.* лири́зм.

M

m. *abbr.* (*of* **metre(s)**) м, метр; (*of* **mile(s)**) ми́ля; (*of* **million(s)**) млн., миллио́н.

MA *abbr.* (*of Master of Arts*) маги́стр гумани-та́рных нау́к.

macabre [mə'kɑːbr] *adj.* жу́ткий (-ток, -тка́, -тко).

macadam [mə'kædəm] *n.* ще́бень (-бня) *m.* **macadamize** *v.t.* мости́ть *impf.*, вы́~, за~ *pf.* ще́бнем.

macaroni [ˌmækə'rəʊnɪ] *n.* макаро́ны (-н) *pl.*

macaroon [ˌmækə'ru:n] *n.* минда́льное пече́нье.

macaw [mə'kɔ:] *n.* макáо *m.indecl.*
mace [meɪs] *n.* (*weapon*) булавá; (*staff of office*) жезл. **mace-bearer** *n.* жезлонóсец (-сца).
machete [mə'tʃetɪ, mə'ʃetɪ] *n.* мачéте *nt.indecl.*
machination [ˌmækɪ'neɪʃ(ə)n, ˌmæʃ-] *n.* махинáция, интрѝга, кóзни (-ней) *pl.*
machine [mə'ʃiːn] *n.* машѝна, станóк (-нкá); (*state* ~) аппарáт; *attr.* машѝнный; ~ **tool** станóк (-нкá); *v.t.* обрабáтывать *impf.*, обрабóтать *pf.* на станкé; (*sew*) шить (шью, шьёшь) *impf.*, с~ *pf.* (на машѝне).
machine-gun *n.* пулемёт. **machinery** *n.* (*machines*) машѝны *f.pl.*; (*mechanism*) механѝзм; (*of state*) аппарáт. **machinist** *n.* машинѝст; (*sewing*) швéйник, -ица, швея́.
mackerel ['mækr(ə)l] *n.* скýмбрия, макрéль; ~ **sky** нéбо барáшками.
mackintosh ['mækɪn,tɒʃ] *n.* (*material*) прорезѝненная матéрия; (*coat*) непромокáемое пальтó *nt.indecl.*
macrocosm ['mækrəu,kɒz(ə)m] *n.* макрокóсм, вселéнная *sb.*
mad [mæd] *adj.* сумасшéдший, помéшанный (-ан, -анна); (*animal*) бéшеный; (*fig.*) безýмный. **madcap** *n.* сорванéц (-нцá). **madden** *v.t.* сводѝть (-ожý, -óдишь) *impf.*, свестѝ (сведý, -дёшь; свёл, -á) *pf.* с умá; (*irritate*) выводѝть (-ожý, -óдишь) *impf.*, вы́вести (-еду, -едешь; -ел) *pf.* из себя́. **made-to-measure** *adj.* сдéланный (как) на закáз. **madhouse** *n.* сумасшéдший дом (-а(у)); *pl.* -á). **madly** *adv.* безýмно. **madman** *n.* сумасшéдший *sb.*, безýмец (-мца). **madness** *n.* сумасшéствие, безýмие. **madwoman** *n.* сумасшéдшая *sb.*, безýмная *sb.*
made *see* **make**
madder ['mædə(r)] *n.* (*plant*) марéна; (*dye*) крапп.
Madrid [mə'drɪd] *n.* Мадрѝд.
madrigal ['mædrɪg(ə)l] *n.* мадригáл.
maestro ['maɪstrəu] *n.* маэ́стро *m.indecl.*
mafia ['mæfɪə, 'mɑ:-] *n.* мáфия.
magazine [ˌmægə'ziːn] *n.* журнáл; (*mil.*) склад боеприпáсов, вещевóй склад; (*of gun*) магазѝн.
maggot ['mægət] *n.* личѝнка. **maggoty** *adj.* червѝвый.
magic ['mædʒɪk] *n.* мáгия, волшебствó, колдовствó; *adj.* волшéбный, магѝческий. **magician** [mə'dʒɪʃ(ə)n] *n.* волшéбник, колдýн (-á); (*conjurer*) фóкусник.
magisterial [ˌmædʒɪ'stɪərɪəl] *adj.* авторитéтный.
magistracy ['mædʒɪstrəsɪ] *n.* магистратýра. **magistrate** ['mædʒɪstrət] *n.* полицéйский судья́ (*pl.* -дьи, -дéй, -дьям) *m.*
magma ['mægmə] *n.* мáгма.
magnanimous [mæg'nænɪməs] *adj.* великодýшный.
magnate ['mægneɪt, -nɪt] *n.* магнáт.
magnesia [mæg'niːʒə, -ʃə, -zjə] *n.* óкись мáгния. **magnesium** *n.* мáгний.

magnet ['mægnɪt] *n.* магнѝт. **mag'netic** *adj.* магнѝтный; (*attractive*) притягáтельный; ~ **tape** магнитолéнта. **magnetism** *n.* магнетѝзм; притягáтельность. **magnetize** *v.t.* намагнѝчивать *impf.*, намагнѝтить *pf.*
magneto [mæg'niːtəu] *n.* магнéто *nt.indecl.*
magnification [ˌmægnɪfɪ'keɪʃ(ə)n] *n.* увеличéние.
magnificence [mæg'nɪfɪs(ə)ns] *n.* великолéпие, пы́шность. **magnificent** *adj.* великолéпный, пы́шный (-шен, -шнá, -шно).
magnify ['mægnɪ,faɪ] *v.t.* увелѝчивать *impf.*, увелѝчить *pf.*; (*exaggerate*) преувелѝчивать *impf.*, преувелѝчить *pf.*
magnitude ['mægnɪ,tjuːd] *n.* величинá.
magnolia [mæg'nəulɪə] *n.* магнóлия.
magpie ['mægpaɪ] *n.* сорóка.
maharajah [ˌmɑːhə'rɑːdʒə] *n.* магарáджа *m.*
maharanee [ˌmɑːhə'rɑːnɪ] *n.* магарáни *f.indecl.*
mahogany [mə'hɒgənɪ] *n.* крáсное дéрево.
maid [meɪd] *n.* служáнка, гóрничная *sb.*; ~ **of honour** фрéйлина. **maiden** *adj.* незамýжняя, дéвичий; (*first*) пéрвый; ~ **name** дéвичья фамѝлия.
mail¹ [meɪl] *n.* (*letters etc.*) пóчта; (*train*) почтóвый пóезд (*pl.* -á); ~ **order** почтóвый закáз, закáз по пóчте; *v.t.* посылáть *impf.*, послáть (пошлю́, -лёшь) *pf.* по пóчте.
mail² [meɪl] *n.* (*armour*) кольчýга; броня́; ~ed **fist** воéнная, физѝческая, сѝла.
mail-order ['meɪl,ɔ:də(r)] *adj.* торгýющий по почтóвым закáзам; ~ **firm** торгóво-посы́лочная фѝрма.
maim [meɪm] *v.t.* калéчить *impf.*, ис~ *pf.*; увéчить *impf.*
main [meɪn] *n.* (*sea*) откры́тое мóре; (*gas* ~; *pl.*) магистрáль; **in the** ~ в основнóм; **with might and** ~ не щадя́ сил; *adj.* основнóй, глáвный; (*road*) магистрáльный; **by** ~ **force** изо всех сил; **the** ~ **chance** путь (-тѝ, -тём) *m.* к нажѝве; ~ **line** (*rail.*) магистрáль. **mainland** *n.* материк (-á); *attr.* материкóвый. **mainly** *adv.* в основнóм; глáвным óбразом; (*for most part*) бóльшей чáстью. **mainmast** *n.* грот-мáчта. **mainsail** *n.* грот. **mainspring** *n.* ходовáя пружѝна. **mainstay** *n.* грóта-штаг; (*fig.*) глáвная опóра.
maintain [meɪn'teɪn] *v.t.* (*continue*) продолжáть *impf.*, продóлжить *pf.*; (*support*) поддéрживать *impf.*, поддержáть (-жý, -жишь) *pf.*; (*family*) содержáть (-жý, -жишь) *impf.*; (*machine*) обслýживать *impf.*, обслужѝть (-жý, -жишь) *pf.*; (*assert*) утверждáть *impf.*
'maintenance *n.* поддéржка; содержáние; обслýживание, ухóд.
maize [meɪz] *n.* кукурýза.
majestic [mə'dʒestɪk] *adj.* велѝчественный (-ен, -енна). **majesty** ['mædʒɪstɪ] *n.* велѝчественность; (*title*) велѝчество.
major¹ ['meɪdʒə(r)] *n.* (*mil.*) майóр.
major² ['meɪdʒə(r)] *adj.* (*greater*) бóльший; (*more important*) бóлее вáжный; (*main*) глáвный; (*mus.*) мажóрный; (*senior*) стáр-

ший; *n.* совершенноле́тний *sb.*; (*mus.*) мажо́р.

major-general ['meɪdʒə(r)-'dʒenər(ə)l] *n.* генера́л-майо́р.

majority [məˈdʒɒrɪtɪ] *n.* (*greater number*) большинство́; (*full age*) совершенноле́тие.

make [meɪk] *n.* ма́рка, тип, сорт (*pl.* -á); *v.t.* де́лать *impf.*, с~ *pf.* (*create*) создава́ть (-даю́, -даёшь) *impf.*, созда́ть (-áм, -áшь, -áст, -ади́м; со́здал, -á, о) *pf.*; (*produce*) производи́ть (-ожу́, -о́дишь) *impf.*, произвести́ (-еду́, -едёшь; -ёл, -елá) *pf.*; (*compose*) составля́ть *impf.*, соста́вить *pf.*; (*prepare*) гото́вить *impf.*, при~ *pf.*; (*amount to*) равня́ться *impf.*+*d.*; (*become*) станови́ться (-влю́сь, -вишься) *impf.*, стать (ста́ну, -нешь) *pf.*+*i.*; (*earn*) зараба́тывать *impf.*, зарабо́тать *pf.*; (*compel*) заставля́ть *impf.*, заста́вить *pf.*; **made in the USA** изгото́влено в США; **be made of** состоя́ть (-ою́, -ои́шь) *impf.* из+*g.*;~ **as if, though** де́лать *impf.*, с~ *pf.* вид, что; ~ **a bed** стели́ть (стелю́, -лешь) *impf.*, по~ *pf.* посте́ль; ~ **believe** притворя́ться *impf.*, притвори́ться *pf.*; ~ **do with** дово́льствоваться *impf.*, у~ *pf.*+*i.*; ~ **fun of** высме́ивать *impf.*, вы́смеять (-ею, -еешь) *pf.*; ~ **o.s. at home** быть как до́ма; ~ **o.s. scarce** исчеза́ть *impf.*, исче́знуть (-з) *pf.*; ~ **sure of** удостоверя́ться *impf.*, удостове́риться *pf.* в+*p.*; ~ **way for** уступа́ть *impf.*, уступи́ть (-плю́ -пишь) *pf.* доро́гу+*d.*; ~ **away with** поко́нчить *pf.* с+*i.*; ~ **off** удира́ть *impf.*, удра́ть (удеру́, -рёшь; удра́л, -á, -о) *pf.*; ~ **out** (*document*) составля́ть *impf.*, соста́вить *pf.*; (*cheque*) выпи́сывать *impf.*, вы́писать (-ишу, -ишешь) *pf.*; (*understand*) разбира́ть *impf.*, разобра́ть (разберу́, -рёшь; разобра́л, -á, -о) *pf.*; ~ **over** передава́ть (-даю́, -даёшь) *impf.*, переда́ть (-áм, -áшь, -áст, -ади́м; пе́редал, -á, о) *pf.*; ~ **up** (*compound*) составля́ть *impf.*, соста́вить *pf.*; (*theatr.*) гримирова́ть(ся) *impf.*, на(за)~ *pf.*; ~ **it up** мири́ться *impf.*, по~ *pf.* (**with** с+*i.*); ~ **up for** возмеща́ть *impf.*, возмести́ть *pf.*; ~ **up one's mind** реша́ться *impf.*, реши́ться *pf.*; ~ **up to** заи́скивать *impf.* пе́ред+*i.* **make-believe** *n.* притво́рство; *adj.* притво́рный. **makeshift** *adj.* вре́менный. **make-up** *n.* (*theatr.*) грим; (*cosmetics*) косме́тика; (*composition*) соста́в. **makeweight** *n.* дове́сок (-ска).

malachite ['mæləkaɪt] *n.* малахи́т.

maladjusted [ˌmælə'dʒʌstɪd] *adj.* пло́хо приспосо́бленный (-ен).

maladministration [ˌmæləd̩mɪnɪ'streɪʃ(ə)n] *n.* плохо́е управле́ние.

maladroit [ˌmælə'drɔɪt, 'mæl-] *adj.* нело́вкий (-о́вок, -о́вка́, -о́вко); (*tactless*) беста́ктный.

malady ['mælədɪ] *n.* боле́знь.

malaria [mə'leərɪə] *n.* маляри́я.

malcontent ['mælkən̩tent] *n.* недово́льный *sb.*

male [meɪl] *n.* (*animal*) саме́ц (-мца́); (*person*) мужчи́на *m.*; *adj.* мужско́й.

malevolence [mə'levələns] *n.* недоброжела́тельность. **malevolent** *adj.* недоброжела́тельный.

malformation [ˌmælfɔː'meɪʃ(ə)n] *n.* непра́вильное образова́ние.

malice ['mælɪs] *n.* зло́ба; (*leg.*) злой у́мысел (-сла); **with ~ aforethought** со злым у́мыслом. **malicious** [mə'lɪʃəs] *adj.* зло́бный.

malign [mə'laɪn] *adj.* па́губный; *v.t.* клевета́ть (-ещу́, -е́щешь) *impf.*, на~ *pf.* на+*a.* **malignant** [mə'lɪgnənt] *adj.* (*harmful*) зловре́дный; (*malicious*) зло́бный; (*med.*) злока́чественный.

malinger [mə'lɪŋgə(r)] *v.i.* притворя́ться *impf.*, притвори́ться *pf.* больны́м. **malingerer** *n.* симуля́нт.

mallard ['mæləːd] *n.* кря́ква.

malleable ['mælɪəb(ə)l] *adj.* ко́вкий (-вок, -вка́, -вко); (*fig.*) пода́тливый.

mallet ['mælɪt] *n.* (деревя́нный) молото́к (-тка́).

malnutrition [ˌmælnjuː'trɪʃ(ə)n] *n.* недоеда́ние.

malpractice [mæl'præktɪs] *n.* (*wrongdoing*) противозако́нное де́йствие; (*negligence*) престу́пная небре́жность.

malt [mɔːlt, mɒlt] *n.* со́лод; *v.t.* солоди́ть *impf.*, на~ *pf.*

maltreat [mæl'triːt] *v.t.* пло́хо обраща́ться *impf.* с+*i.*

mamba *n.* ма́мба.

mambo ['mæmbə] *n.* ма́мбо *nt.indecl.*

mamma [mə'mɑː] *n.* ма́ма.

mammal ['mæm(ə)l] *n.* млекопита́ющее *sb.* **ma'mmalian** *adj.* млекопита́ющий.

mammary ['mæmərɪ] *adj.* грудно́й.

mammon ['mæmən] *n.* мамо́на, бога́тство.

mammoth ['mæməθ] *n.* ма́монт; *adj.* грома́дный.

man [mæn] *n.* (*human, person*) челове́к (*pl.* лю́ди, -де́й, -дьям, -дьми́); (*human race*) челове́чество; (*male*) мужчи́на *m.*; (*husband*) муж (*pl.* -ья́, -е́й, -ья́м); (*servant*) слуга́ *m.*; (*labourer*) рабо́чий *sb.*; *pl.* (*soldiers*) солда́ты *m.pl.*, рядовы́е *sb.*; *pl.* (*sailors*) матро́сы *m.pl.*; (*draughts*) ша́шка; ~ **in the street** заурядный челове́к; *v.t.* (*furnish with men*) укомплекто́вывать *impf.*, укомплектова́ть *pf.* ли́чным соста́вом; ста́вить *impf.*, по~ *pf.* люде́й к+*d.*; (*act thus*) станови́ться (-влю́сь, -вишься) *impf.*, стать (ста́ну, -нешь) *pf.* к+*d.*

manacle ['mænək(ə)l] *n.* нару́чник; *v.t.* надева́ть *impf.*, наде́ть (-е́ну, -е́нешь) *pf.* нару́чники на+*a.*

manage ['mænɪdʒ] *v.t.* (*control*) управля́ть *impf.*+*i.*; заве́довать *impf.*+*i.*; (*cope*) справля́ться *impf.*, спра́виться *pf.* с+*i.* **management** *n.* управле́ние (**of** +*i.*), заве́дование (**of** +*i.*); (*the* ~) администра́ция, дире́кция.

manager *n.* управля́ющий *sb.* (**of** +*i.*), заве́дующий *sb.* (**of** +*i.*), администра́тор, дире́ктор (*pl.* -á); (*good, bad* ~) хозя́ин; (*in* *entertainment*) импресса́рио *m.indecl.*; (*sport*) ме́неджер. **managerial** [͵mænɪ'dʒɪə-rɪəl] *adj.* административный, дире́кторский.

mandarin ['mændərɪn] *n.* мандари́н.

mandate ['mændeɪt] *n.* манда́т. **mandated** *adj.* подманда́тный. **mandatory** *adj.* обяза́тельный.

mandible ['mændɪb(ə)l] *n.* ни́жняя че́люсть; (*of insect*) жва́ло.

mandolin(e) [͵mændə'lɪn] *n.* мандоли́на.

mane [meɪn] *n.* гри́ва.

manful ['mænfʊl] *adj.* му́жественный (-ен, -енна).

manganese ['mæŋgə͵niːz] *n.* ма́рганец (-нца).

manger ['meɪndʒə(r)] *n.* я́сли (-лей) *pl.*; **dog in the** ~ соба́ка на се́не.

mangle[1] ['mæŋg(ə)l] *n.* (*for clothes*) като́к (-тка́); *v.t.* ката́ть *impf.*, вы́~ *pf.*

mangle[2] ['mæŋg(ə)l] *v.t.* (*mutilate*) кале́чить *impf.*, ис~ *pf.*; (*words*) коверка́ть *impf.*, ис~ *pf.*

mango ['mæŋgəʊ] *n.* ма́нго *nt.indecl.*

mangrove ['mæŋgrəʊv] *n.* ма́нгровое де́рево (*pl.* -е́вья, -е́вьев).

manhandle ['mæn͵hænd(ə)l] *v.t.* передвига́ть *impf.*, передви́нуть *pf.* вручну́ю; (*treat roughly*) гру́бо обраща́ться *impf.* c+i. **manhole** *n.* смотрово́й коло́дец (-дца). **manhood** *n.* возмужа́лость; (*courage*) му́жественность. **man-hour** *n.* челове́ко-час (*pl.* -ы́).

mania ['meɪnɪə] *n.* ма́ния. **maniac** ['meɪnɪæk] *n.* манья́к, -я́чка. **maniacal** *adj.* маниака́льный.

manicure ['mænɪ͵kjʊə(r)] *n.* маникю́р; *v.t.* де́лать *impf.*, c~ *pf.* маникю́р+d. **manicurist** *n.* маникю́рша.

manifest ['mænɪ͵fest] *adj.* очеви́дный; *v.t.* де́лать *impf.*, c~ *pf.* очеви́дным; (*display*) проявля́ть *impf.*, прояви́ть (-влю́, -вишь) *pf.*; *n.* манифе́ст. **manife'station** *n.* проявле́ние. **mani'festo** *n.* манифе́ст.

manifold ['mænɪ͵fəʊld] *adj.* разнообра́зный; *n.* (*tech.*) колле́ктор, трубопрово́д.

manikin ['mænɪkɪn] *n.* (*little man*) челове́чек (-чка); (*lay figure*) манеке́н.

Manil(l)a [mə'nɪlə] *n.* (*hemp*) мани́льская пенька́; (*paper*) мани́льская бума́га.

manipulate [mə'nɪpjʊ͵leɪt] *v.t.* манипули́ровать *impf.*+i. **manipu'lation** *n.* манипуля́ция.

manly ['mænlɪ] *adj.* му́жественный (-ен, -енна).

mankind [mæn'kaɪnd] *n.* челове́чество.

manna ['mænə] *n.* ма́нна (небе́сная).

mannequin ['mænɪkɪn] *n.* манеке́нщица.

manner ['mænə(r)] *n.* спо́соб, о́браз, мане́ра; *pl.* нра́вы *m.pl.*; *pl.* (*good* ~) (хоро́шие) мане́ры *f.pl.* **mannered** *adj.* вы́чурный, мане́рный. **mannerism** *n.* мане́ра; мане́рность.

mannish ['mænɪʃ] *adj.* (*masculine*) мужеподо́бный; (*characteristic of man*) сво́йственный (-ен, -енна) мужчи́не.

manoeuvrable [mə'nuːvrəb(ə)l] *adj.* легко́ управля́емый. **manoeuvre** *n.* манёвр; *v.i.* маневри́ровать *impf.*, c~ *pf.*; проводи́ть (-ожу́, -о́дишь) *impf.*, провести́ (-еду́, -едёшь; -ёл, -ела́) *pf.* манёвры.

man-of-war ['mænəf͵wɔː(r)] *n.* вое́нный кора́бль (-ля́) *m.*

manor ['mænə(r)] *n.* (*estate*) поме́стье (*g.pl.* -тий); (*house*) поме́щичий дом (-а(у); *pl.* -а́). **manorial** [mə'nɔːrɪəl] *adj.* манориа́льный.

manpower ['mæn͵paʊə(r)] *n.* людски́е ресу́рсы *m.pl.*

mansard (roof) ['mænsɑːd] *n.* манса́рдная кры́ша.

manservant ['mæn͵sɜːv(ə)nt] *n.* слуга́ *m.*

mansion ['mænʃ(ə)n] *n.* большо́й дом (*pl.* -а́); *pl.* многокварти́рный дом.

manslaughter ['mæn͵slɔːtə(r)] *n.* человекоуби́йство; (*leg.*) непредумы́шленное уби́йство.

mantelpiece ['mænt(ə)l͵piːs] *n.* ками́нная доска́ (*a.* -ску; *pl.* -ски, -со́к, -ска́м). **mantelshelf** *n.* ками́нная по́лка.

mantis ['mæntɪs] *n.* богомо́л.

mantle ['mænt(ə)l] *n.* (*cloak*) наки́дка; (*gas* ~) газокали́льная се́тка; (*earth's*) ма́нтия.

manual ['mænjʊəl] *adj.* ручно́й; ~ **labour** физи́ческий, ручно́й, труд (-а́); *n.* спра́вочник, руково́дство, уче́бник; (*of organ*) мануа́л. **manually** *adv.* вручну́ю.

manufacture [͵mænjʊ'fæktʃə(r)] *n.* произво́дство, изготовле́ние; *v.t.* производи́ть (-ожу́, -о́дишь) *impf.*, произвести́ (-еду́, -едёшь; -ёл, -ела́) *pf.*; изготовля́ть *impf.*, изгото́вить *pf.*; (*fabricate*) фабрикова́ть *impf.*, c~ *pf.* **manufacturer** *n.* фабрика́нт, промы́шленник, производи́тель *m.*

manure [mə'njʊə(r)] *n.* наво́з; *v.t.* унаво́живать *impf.*, унаво́зить *pf.*

manuscript ['mænjʊskrɪpt] *n.* ру́копись; *adj.* рукопи́сный.

many ['menɪ] *adj. & n.* мно́го+g., мно́гие *pl.*; **how** ~ ско́лько+g.

Maoism ['maʊɪz(ə)m] *n.* маои́зм. **Maoist** *n.* маои́ст; *adj.* маои́стский.

map [mæp] *n.* ка́рта; *v.t.* черти́ть (-рчу́, -ртишь) *impf.*, на~ *pf.* план+g.; ~ **out** составля́ть *impf.*, соста́вить *pf.* план+g.

maple ['meɪp(ə)l] *n.* клён; *attr.* клено́вый.

mar [mɑː(r)] *v.t.* по́ртить *impf.*, ис~ *pf.*

marathon ['mærəθ(ə)n] *n.* марафо́н.

marauder [mə'rɔːdə(r)] *n.* мароде́р. **marauding** *adj.* мародёрский.

marble ['mɑːb(ə)l] *n.* мра́мор; (*toy*) ша́рик; *pl.* (*game*) игра́ в ша́рики; *attr.* мра́морный. **marbled** *adj.* мра́морный.

March[1] [mɑːtʃ] *n.* март; *attr.* ма́ртовский.

march[2] [mɑːtʃ] *v.i.* марширова́ть *impf.*, про~ *pf.*; *n.* марш; ход; ~ **past** прохожде́ние торже́ственным ма́ршем.

mare [meə(r)] *n.* кобы́ла.

margarine [͵mɑːdʒə'riːn] *n.* маргари́н (-a(y)).

margin ['mɑːdʒɪn] *n.* край (*loc.* кра́ю; *pl.*

-ая), кайма́ (*g.pl.* каём); (*on page*) по́ле (*pl.* -ля́); ~ **of error** преде́лы *m.pl.* погре́шности; **profit** ~ при́быль; **safety** ~ запа́с про́чности.

marigold ['mærɪˌgəʊld] *n.* (*Tagetes*) ба́рхатцы (-цев); *pl.*; (*Calendula*) ноготки́ (-ко́в) *pl.*

marijuana [ˌmærɪ'hwɑːnə] *n.* марихуа́на.

marinade [ˌmærɪ'neɪd, 'mæ-] *n.* марина́д; *v.t.* маринова́ть *impf.*, за~ *pf.*

marine [mə'riːn] *adj.* (*maritime*) морско́й; (*naval*) вое́нно-морско́й; *n.* (*fleet*) морско́й флот; (*soldier*) солда́т морско́й пехо́ты; *pl.* морска́я пехо́та. **mariner** ['mærɪnə(r)] *n.* моря́к (-а́), матро́с.

marionette [ˌmærɪə'net] *n.* марионе́тка.

marital ['mærɪt(ə)l] *adj.* супру́жеский, бра́чный.

maritime ['mærɪˌtaɪm] *adj.* морско́й; (*near sea*) примо́рский.

marjoram ['mɑːdʒərəm] *n.* (*Majorana*) майора́н; (*Origanum*) души́ца.

mark[1] [mɑːk] *n.* (*coin*) ма́рка.

mark[2] [mɑːk] *n.* (*target*, *aim*) цель; (*sign*) знак; (*school*) отме́тка; (*numerical*) балл; (*trace*) след (*pl.* -ы́); (*level*) у́ровень (-вня) *m.*; **hit the** ~ попада́ть *impf.*, попа́сть (-аду́, -адёшь; -а́л) *pf.* в то́чку; **make one's** ~ отлича́ться *impf.*, отличи́ться *pf.*; **on your** ~**s** на старт!; *v.t.* отмеча́ть *impf.*, отме́тить *pf.*; ста́вить *impf.*, по~ *pf.* знак, (*goods*) расце́нку, на+*a.*, (*school*) отме́тку, балл, за+*a.*; (*leave trace(s)*) оставля́ть *impf.*, оста́вить *pf.* след(ы́) на+*p.*; (*football*) закрыва́ть *impf.*, закры́ть (-ро́ю, -ро́ешь) *pf.*; ~ **my words** попо́мни(те) мои́ слова́!; ~ **time** топта́ться (-пчу́сь, -пчешься) *impf.* на ме́сте; ~ **off** отделя́ть *impf.*, отдели́ть (-лю́, -лишь) *pf.*; ~ **out** размеча́ть *impf.*, разме́тить *pf.* **marker** *n.* знак, указа́тель *m.*; (*in book*) закла́дка; ~ (**pen**) флома́стер.

market ['mɑːkɪt] *n.* ры́нок (-нка), база́р; (*demand*) спрос; (*trade*) торго́вля; (*conditions*) конъюнкту́ра; **black** ~ чёрный ры́нок (-нка); **buyer's**, **seller's**, ~ конъюнкту́ра ры́нка, вы́годная для покупа́теля, для продавца́; **Common M**~ О́бщий ры́нок (-нка); **find a** ~ находи́ть (-ожу́, -о́дишь) *impf.*, найти́ (найду́, -дёшь; нашёл, -шла́) *pf.* сбыт; ~ **garden** огоро́д; ~ **price** ры́ночная цена́ (*a.* -ну; *pl.* -ы); *v.t.* продава́ть (-даю́, -даёшь) *impf.*, прода́ть (-а́м, -а́шь, -а́ст, -ади́м; про́дал, -а́, -о) *pf.* **marketable** *adj.* хо́дкий (-док, -дка́, -дко); (*econ.*) това́рный. **market-day** *n.* база́рный день (дня) *m.* **marketing** *n.* ма́ркетинг. **market-place** *n.* база́рная пло́щадь (*pl.* -ди, -де́й).

marksman ['mɑːksmən] *n.* ме́ткий стрело́к (-лка́). **marksmanship** *n.* ме́ткая стрельба́.

marmalade ['mɑːməˌleɪd] *n.* апельси́новый джем.

marmoset ['mɑːməˌzet] *n.* игру́нка.

marmot ['mɑːmət] *n.* суро́к (-рка́).

maroon[1] [mə'ruːn] *adj.* (*n.*) (*colour*) тёмно-

бордо́вый (цвет).

maroon[2] [mə'ruːn] *v.t.* (*put ashore*) выса́живать *impf.*, вы́садить *pf.* (на необита́емом о́строве); (*cut off*) отреза́ть *impf.*, отре́зать (-е́жет) *pf.*

marquee [mɑː'kiː] *n.* шатёр (-тра́).

marquis ['mɑːkwɪs] *n.* марки́з.

marriage ['mærɪdʒ] *n.* брак; (*wedding*) сва́дьба; *attr.* бра́чный. **marriageable** *adj.* взро́слый; ~ **age** бра́чный во́зраст. **married** *adj.* (*man*) жена́тый; (*woman*) заму́жняя, за́мужем; (*of* ~ *persons*) супру́жеский.

marrow ['mærəʊ] *n.* ко́стный мозг (*loc.* -у́); (*essence*) су́щность; (*vegetable*) кабачо́к (-чка́). **marrowbone** *n.* мозгова́я кость (*pl.* -ти, -те́й).

marry ['mærɪ] *v.t.* (*of man*) жени́ться (-ню́сь, -нишься) *impf.* & *pf.* на+*p.*; (*of woman*) выходи́ть (-ожу́, -о́дишь) *impf.*, вы́йти (вы́йду, -дешь; вы́шла) *pf.* за́муж за+*a.*; (*give in marriage*) (*man*) жени́ть (-ню́, -нишь) *impf.* & *pf.*, по~ *pf.* (**to** на+*p.*); (*woman*) выдава́ть (-даю́, -даёшь) *impf.*, вы́дать (-ам, -ашь, -аст, -адим) *pf.* за́муж (**to** за+*a.*).

Mars [mɑːz] *n.* Марс.

Marseilles [mɑː'seɪ] *n.* Марсе́ль *m.*

marsh [mɑːʃ] *n.* боло́то. **marsh-gas** *n.* боло́тный газ. **marshy** *adj.* боло́тистый.

marshal ['mɑːʃ(ə)l] *n.* ма́ршал; *v.t.* выстра́ивать *impf.*, вы́строить *pf.*; приводи́ть (-ожу́, -о́дишь) *impf.*, привести́ (-еду́, -едёшь; -ёл, -ела́) *pf.* в поря́док; ~**ling yard** сортиро́вочная ста́нция.

marsupial [mɑː'suːpɪəl] *adj.* су́мчатый; *n.* су́мчатое живо́тное *sb.*

marten ['mɑːtɪn] *n.* куни́ца.

martial ['mɑːʃ(ə)l] *adj.* вое́нный; (*warlike*) во́инский; ~ **law** вое́нное положе́ние.

Martian ['mɑːʃ(ə)n] *n.* марсиа́нин (*pl.* -а́не, -а́н); *adj.* марсиа́нский.

martin ['mɑːtɪn] *n.* стриж (-а́); (*house-*~) городска́я ла́сточка.

martinet [ˌmɑːtɪ'net] *n.* сторо́нник стро́гой дисципли́ны.

martyr ['mɑːtə(r)] *n.* му́ченик, -ца; *v.t.* му́чить *impf.*, за~ *pf.* **martyrdom** *n.* му́ченичество.

marvel ['mɑːv(ə)l] *n.* чу́до (*pl.* -деса́), ди́во; *v.i.* изумля́ться *impf.*, изуми́ться *pf.*; удивля́ться *impf.*, удиви́ться *pf.* **marvellous** *adj.* чуде́сный, изуми́тельный, удиви́тельный.

Marxian ['mɑːksɪən], **Marxist** *n.* маркси́ст; *adj.* маркси́стский. **Marxism** *n.* маркси́зм.

marzipan ['mɑːzɪˌpæn, -'pæn] *n.* марципа́н; *adj.* марципа́нный.

mascara [mæ'skɑːrə] *n.* кра́ска для ресни́ц.

mascot ['mæskɒt] *n.* талисма́н.

masculine ['mæskjʊlɪn, 'mɑːs-] *adj.* мужско́й; (*gram.*) мужско́го ро́да; (*of woman*) мужеподо́бный; *n.* (*gram.*) мужско́й род.

mash [mæʃ] *n.* (*of malt*) су́сло; (*of bran*) по́йло; (*mashed potatoes*) карто́фельное пюре́; *nt.indecl.*; *v.t.* размина́ть *impf.*, размя́ть (разомну́, -нёшь) *pf.*

mask [mɑːsk] *n.* ма́ска; (*gas-~*) противога́з; *v.t.* маскирова́ть *impf.*, за~ *pf.*; **~ed ball** бал-маскара́д.

masochism ['mæsəˌkɪz(ə)m] *m.* мазохи́зм. **masochist** *n.* мазохи́ст. **maso'chistic** *adj.* мазохи́стский.

mason ['meɪs(ə)n] *n.* ка́менщик; (**M~**) масо́н. **Masonic** [mə'sɒnɪk] *adj.* масо́нский. **masonry** ['meɪsənrɪ] *n.* ка́менная кла́дка; (**M~**) масо́нство.

masque [mɑːsk] *n.* ма́ска. **masquer** *n.* уча́стник, -ица, ба́ла-маскара́да. **masquerade** [ˌmɑːskə'reɪd, ˌmæs-] *n.* маскара́д; *v.i.*: **~ as** притворя́ться *impf.*, притвори́ться *pf.*+*i.*; выдава́ть (-даю́, -даёшь) *impf.*, вы́дать (-ам, -ашь, -аст, -адим) *pf.* себя́ за+*a.*

mass[1] [mæs] *n.* (*eccl.*) обе́дня (*g.pl.* -ден), ме́сса.

mass[2] [mæs] *n.* ма́сса; (*majority*) большинство́; (*the ~*) наро́дные ма́ссы *f.pl.*; *attr.* ма́ссовый; **~ media** сре́дства *nt.pl.* ма́ссовой информа́ции; **~ meeting** ми́тинг; **~ production** ма́ссовое произво́дство; *v.t.* масси́ровать *impf.* & *pf.*

massacre ['mæsəkə(r)] *n.* резня́; *v.t.* ре́зать (ре́жу, -жешь) *impf.*, за~ *pf.*

massage ['mæsɑːʒ, -sɑːdʒ] *n.* масса́ж; *v.t.* масси́ровать *impf.* & *pf.* **masseur** [mæ-'sɜː(r)], **-euse** [mæ'sɜːz] *n.* массажи́ст, ~ка.

massif ['mæsiːf, mæ'siːf] *n.* го́рный масси́в.

massive ['mæsɪv] *adj.* масси́вный.

mass-produced [ˌmæsprə'djuːs] *adj.* ма́ссового произво́дства.

mast [mɑːst] *n.* ма́чта.

master ['mɑːstə(r)] *n.* (*owner*) хозя́ин (*pl.* -я́ева, -я́ев), владе́лец (-льца); (*of household, college*) глава́ (*pl.* -вы) *m.* (семьи́, колле́джа); (*of ship*) капита́н; (*teacher*) учи́тель (*pl.* -ля́) *m.*; (**M~**, *univ.*) маги́стр; (*workman; artist*) ма́стер (*pl.* -á); (*of film*) контро́льная ко́пия; (*of record*) пе́рвый оригина́л; **be ~ of** владе́ть *impf.*+*i.*; **M~ of Arts** маги́стр гуманита́рных нау́к; *v.t.* (*overcome*) преодолева́ть *impf.*, преодоле́ть *pf.*; справля́ться *impf.*, спра́виться *pf.* с+*i.*; (*subjugate*) подчиня́ть *impf.*, подчини́ть *pf.* себе́; (*acquire knowledge of*) овладева́ть *impf.*, овладе́ть *pf.*+*i.* **masterful** *adj.* вла́стный. **master-key** *n.* отмы́чка. **masterly** *adj.* мастерско́й. **masterpiece** *n.* шеде́вр. **master-switch** *n.* гла́вный выключа́тель *m.* **mastery** *n.* (*dominion*) госпо́дство; (*skill*) мастерство́; (*knowledge*) соверше́нное владе́ние (**of** +*i.*).

mast-head ['mɑːsthed] *n.* топ ма́чты.

masticate ['mæstɪˌkeɪt] *v.t.* жева́ть (жую́, жуёшь) *impf.*

mastif ['mæstɪf, 'mɑːs-] *n.* масти́фф.

mastodon ['mæstəˌdɒn] *n.* мастодо́нт.

mat [mæt] *n.* ко́врик, полови́к (-á); (*of rushes, straw*) цино́вка; (*under dish etc.*) подста́вка.

match[1] [mætʃ] *n.* спи́чка. **matchbox** *n.* спи́чечная коро́бка.

match[2] [mætʃ] *n.* (*equal*) ро́вня *c.g.*; (*contest*) матч, состяза́ние; (*marriage*) брак; **a ~ for** па́ра+*d.*; **meet one's ~** встреча́ть *impf.*, встре́тить *pf.* ра́вного себе́, досто́йного проти́вника; *v.t.* (*correspond*) соотве́тствовать *impf.*+*d.*; (*of colour*) гармони́ровать *impf.* с+*i.*; (*select*) подбира́ть *impf.*, подобра́ть (подберу́, -рёшь; подобра́л, -á, -о) *pf.* **matchboard** *n.* шпунтова́я доска́ (*a.* -ску; *pl.* -ски, -со́к, -ска́м). **matchless** *adj.* несравне́нный (-нен, -нна). **matchmaker** *n.* сват, сва́тья.

mate[1] [meɪt] *n.* (*chess*) мат; *v.t.* объявля́ть *impf.*, объяви́ть (-влю́, -вишь) *pf.* мат+*d.*

mate[2] [meɪt] *n.* (*one of pair*) саме́ц (-мца́), са́мка; (*fellow worker*) напа́рник, това́рищ; (*assistant*) помо́щник; (*naut.*) помо́щник капита́на; *v.i.* (*of animals*) спа́риваться *impf.*, спа́риться *pf.*

material [mə'tɪərɪəl] *adj.* материа́льный; (*essential*) суще́ственный (-ен, -енна); *n.* материа́л; (*cloth*) мате́рия; *pl.* (*necessary articles*) принадле́жности *f.pl.* **materialism** *n.* материали́зм. **materialist** *n.* материали́ст. **materia'listic** *adj.* материалисти́чный, -ческий. **materiali'zation** *n.* материализа́ция. **materialize** *v.t.* & *i.* материализова́ть(ся) *impf.* & *pf.*; осуществля́ть(ся) *impf.*, осуществи́ть(ся) *pf.*

maternal [mə'tɜːn(ə)l] *adj.* матери́нский; (*kinship*) по ма́тери; **~ grandfather** де́душка с матери́нской стороны́. **maternity** *n.* матери́нство; **~ benefit** посо́бие роже́нице; **~ dress** пла́тье (*g.pl.* -в) для бере́менных; **~ home, hospital** роди́льный дом (-а(у); *pl.* -á); **~ leave** декре́тный о́тпуск (*loc.* -е & -у́); **~ ward** роди́льная пала́та.

mathematical [ˌmæθɪ'mætɪk(ə)l] *adj.* математи́ческий. **mathematician** [ˌmæθɪmə'tɪʃ(ə)n] *n.* матема́тик. **mathematics** *n.* матема́тика.

maths *abbr.* = **mathematics**

matinée ['mætɪˌneɪ] *n.* дневно́й спекта́кль *m.*; **~ coat** распашо́нка.

matins ['mætɪnz] *n.* у́треня.

matriarchal [ˌmeɪtrɪ'ɑːk(ə)l] *adj.* матриарха́льный. **'matriarchy** *n.* матриарха́т. **matricidal** ['meɪtrɪˌsaɪd(ə)l] *adj.* матереуби́йственный. **matricide** *n.* (*action*) матереуби́йство; (*person*) матереуби́йца *c.g.*

matriculate [mə'trɪkjʊˌleɪt] *v.t.* принима́ть *impf.*, приня́ть (приму́, -мешь; при́нял, -á, -о) *pf.* в вуз; *v.i.* быть при́нятым в вуз. **matricu'lation** *n.* зачисле́ние в вуз; (*examination*) вступи́тельный экза́мен в вуз.

matrimonial [ˌmætrɪ'məʊnɪəl] *adj.* супру́жеский. **'matrimony** *n.* брак, супру́жество.

matrix ['meɪtrɪks] *n.* (*womb*) ма́тка; (*rock*) ма́точная поро́да; (*mould*) ма́трица.

matron ['meɪtrən] *n.* заму́жняя же́нщина; (*hospital*) сестра́-хозя́йка; (*school*) заве́дующая *sb.* хозя́йством.

matt [mæt] *adj.* ма́товый.

matted ['mætɪd] *adj.* спу́танный (-ан).

matter ['mætə(r)] *n.* (*substance*) вещество; (*philos.*, *med.*) материя; (*content*) содержание; (*affair*) дело (*pl.* -ла́); (*question*) вопрос; **a ~ of form** формальность; **a ~ of life and death** вопрос жизни и смерти; **a ~ of opinion** спорное дело; **a ~ of taste** дело вкуса; **an easy ~** простое дело; **as a ~ of fact** фактически; собственно говоря; **for that ~** что касается этого; в этом отношении; **money ~s** денежные дела *nt.pl.*; **no laughing ~** не шуточное дело; **what's the ~?** в чём дело?; что случилось?; **what's the ~ with him?** что с ним?; *v.i.* иметь *impf.* значение; (*med.*) гноиться *impf.*; **it doesn't ~** это не имеет значения; **it ~s a lot to me** для меня это очень важно; **what does it ~?** какое это имеет значение? **matter-of-fact** *adj.* прозаичный.

matting ['mætɪŋ] *n.* (*rushes*) циновка; (*bast*) рогожа.

mattock ['mætək] *n.* мотыга.

mattress ['mætrɪs] *n.* матрас, тюфяк (-а́).

mature [mə'tjuə(r)] *adj.* зрелый (зрел, -а́, -о); (*well considered*) хорошо обдуманный (-ан, -анна); *v.i.* зреть *impf.*, со~ *pf.*; *v.t.* доводить (-ожу, -одишь) *impf.*, довести (-еду, -едёшь, -ёл, -ела́) *pf.* до зрелости; (*plan*) обдумывать *impf.*, обдумать *pf.* **maturity** *n.* зрелость.

maul [mɔːl] *v.t.* терзать *impf.*; калечить *impf.*, ис~ *pf.*; (*criticize*) раскритиковать *pf.*

mausoleum [ˌmɔːsə'liːəm] *n.* мавзолей.

mauve [məuv] *adj.* (*n.*) розовато-лиловый (цвет).

maxim ['mæksɪm] *n.* сентенция.

maximum ['mæksɪməm] *n.* максимум; *adj.* максимальный.

May[1] [meɪ] *n.* (*month*) май; **~ Day** Первое *sb.* мая; *attr.* майский.

may[2] [meɪ] *v.aux.* (*possibility, permission*) мочь (могу, можешь; мог, -ла́) *impf.*, с~ *pf.*; (*possibility*) возможно, что+*indicative*; (*wish*) пусть+*indicative*.

maybe ['meɪbiː] *adv.* может быть.

May-bug ['meɪbʌg] *n.* майский жук (-а́). **mayfly** *n.* подёнка.

mayonnaise [ˌmeɪə'neɪz] *n.* майонез.

mayor [meə(r)] *n.* мэр. **mayoress** *n.* жена́ (*pl.* жёны) мэра; женщина-мэр.

maze [meɪz] *n.* лабиринт; (*fig.*) путаница.

mazurka [mə'zɜːkə] *n.* мазурка.

MC *abbr.* (*of* **Master of Ceremonies**) конферансье.

MD *abbr.* (*of* **Doctor of Medicine**) доктор медицины; (*of* **Managing Director**) директор-распорядитель.

mead [miːd] *n.* мёд (-а(у), *loc.* -у́; *pl.* -ы́).

meadow ['medəu] *n.* луг (*loc.* -у́; *pl.* -а́).

meagre ['miːgə(r)] *adj.* скудный (-ден, -дна́, -дно).

meal[1] [miːl] *n.* еда́.

meal[2] [miːl] *n.* (*ground grain*) мука́ крупного помола.

mealtime ['miːltaɪm] *n.*: **at ~s** во время еды.

mealy ['miːlɪ] *adj.* рассыпчатый. **mealy-mouthed** *adj.* сладкоречивый.

mean[1] [miːn] *adj.* (*average*) средний; *n.* (*middle point*) середина, среднее *sb.*; *pl.* (*method*) средство, способ; *pl.* (*resources*) средства *nt.pl.*, состояние; **by all ~s** конечно, пожалуйста; **by ~s of** при помощи+*g.*, посредством+*g.*; **by no ~s** совсем не; **~s test** проверка нуждаемости.

mean[2] [miːn] *adj.* (*ignoble*) подлый (подл, -а́, -о), низкий (-зок, -зка́, -зко); (*miserly*) скупой (скуп, -а́, -о); (*poor*) убогий.

mean[3] [miːn] *v.t.* (*have in mind*) иметь *impf.* в виду; (*intend*) намереваться *impf.*+*inf.*; (*signify*) значить *impf.*

meander [mɪ'ændə(r)] *v.i.* (*stream*) извиваться *impf.*; (*person*) бродить (-ожу, -одишь) *impf.* без цели. **meandering** *adj.* извилистый.

meaning ['miːnɪŋ] *n.* значение, смысл; *adj.* значительный. **meaningful** *adj.* (много)значительный. **meaningless** *adj.* бессмысленный (-ен, -енна).

meantime ['miːntaɪm], **meanwhile** *adv.* тем временем, между тем.

measles ['miːz(ə)lz] *n.* корь. **measly** *adj.* ничтожный.

measurable ['meʒərəb(ə)l] *adj.* измеримый. **measure** *n.* мера; (*size*) мерка; (*degree*) степень (*pl.* -ни, -ней); (*limit*) предел; **made to ~** сшитый по мерке; сделанный (-ан) на заказ; *v.t.* измерять *impf.*, измерить *pf.* мерить *impf.*, с~ *pf.*; (*for clothes*) снимать *impf.*, снять (сниму, -мешь; снял, -а́, -о) *pf.* мерку с+*g.*; (*estimate*) оценивать *impf.*, оценить (-ню, -нишь) *pf.*; *v.i.* (*be of specified size*) иметь *impf.*+*a.*; **the room ~s 30 feet in length** комната имеет тридцать футов в длину; **~ off** отмерять *impf.*, отмерить *pf.*; **~ out** (*deal out*) распределять *impf.*, распределить *pf.*; **~ up to** соответствовать *impf.*+*d.* **measured** *adj.* (*rhythmical*) мерный. **measurement** *n.* (*action*) измерение; *pl.* (*dimensions*) размеры *m.pl.*

meat [miːt] *n.* мясо. **meaty** *adj.* мясной, мясистый.

mechanic [mɪ'kænɪk] *n.* механик. **mechanical** *adj.* механический; (*automatic*) машинальный; **~ engineer** инженер-механик; **~ engineering** машиностроение. **mechanics** *n.* механика. **mechanism** ['mekəˌnɪz(ə)m] *n.* механизм. **mecha'nistic** *adj.* механистический. **mechani'zation** *n.* механизация. **'mechanize** *v.t.* механизировать *impf.* & *pf.*

medal ['med(ə)l] *n.* медаль. **medallion** [mɪ'dæljən] *n.* медальон. **medallist** *n.* (*recipient*) медалист.

meddle ['med(ə)l] *v.i.* вмешиваться *impf.*, вмешаться *pf.* (**in, with** +*a.*).

media ['miːdɪə] *pl. of* **medium**

mediaeval [ˌmedɪ'iːv(ə)l] *adj.* средневековый.

mediate ['miːdɪˌeɪt] *v.i.* посредничать *impf.*

medi'ation *n.* посре́дничество. **mediator** *n.* посре́дник.

medical ['medɪk(ə)l] *adj.* медици́нский; ~ **jurisprudence** суде́бная медици́на; ~ **man** врач (-á); ~ **student** ме́дик, -и́чка. **medicated** *adj.* (*impregnated*) пропи́танный (-ан) лека́рством. **medicinal** [mɪ'dɪsɪn(ə)l] *adj.* (*of medicine*) лека́рственный; (*healing*) целе́бный. **medicine** ['medsɪn, -dɪsɪn] *n.* медици́на; (*substance*) лека́рство. **medicine-man** *n.* зна́харь (-ря́) *m.*, шама́н.

mediocre [,mi:dɪ'əʊkə(r)] *adj.* посре́дственный (-ен, -енна), зауря́дный. **mediocrity** [,mi:dɪ'ɒkrɪtɪ] *n.* посре́дственность.

meditate ['medɪteɪt] *v.i.* размышля́ть *impf.* **medi'tation** *n.* размышле́ние. **meditative** *adj.* заду́мчивый.

Mediterranean [,medɪtə'reɪnɪən] *adj.* средиземномо́рский; *n.* Средизе́мное мо́ре.

medium ['mi:dɪəm] *n.* (*middle*) середи́на; (*means*) сре́дство; (*environment; phys.*) среда́ (*pl.* -ды); (*person*) ме́диум; *pl.* (*mass media*) сре́дства *nt.pl.* ма́ссовой информа́ции; *adj.* сре́дний.

medley ['medlɪ] *n.* смесь, вся́кая вся́чина.

meek [mi:k] *adj.* кро́ткий (-ток, -тка́, -тко), смире́нный (-ён, -е́нна). **meekness** *n.* кро́тость, смире́нность.

meet [mi:t] *v.t. & i.* встреча́ть(ся) *impf.*, встре́тить(ся) *pf.*; *v.t.* (*make acquaintance*) знако́миться *impf.*, по~ *pf.* с+*i.*; *v.i.* (*assemble*) собира́ться *impf.*, собра́ться (соберётся); собра́лся, -ала́сь, -ало́сь) *pf.* **meeting** *n.* встре́ча; собра́ние, заседа́ние, ми́тинг.

mega- ['megə] *in comb.* мега... . **megacycle**, **megahertz** *n.* мегаге́рц (*g.pl.* -ц). **megalith** ['megəlɪθ] *n.* мегали́т. **mega'lithic** *adj.* мегалити́ческий. **megaphone** *n.* мегафо́н. **megaton(ne)** *n.* мегато́нна. **megavolt** *n.* мегаво́льт (*g.pl.* -т). **megawatt** *n.* мегава́тт (*g.pl.* -т). **megohm** ['megəʊm] *n.* мего́м (*g.pl.* -м).

megalomania [,megələ'meɪnɪə] *n.* megaлома́ния.

melancholia [,melən'kəʊlɪə] *n.* меланхо́лия. **melancholic** [,melən'kɒlɪk] *adj.* меланхоли́ческий. **melancholy** ['melənkəlɪ] *n.* грусть, тоска́; *adj.* уны́лый, гру́стный (-тен, -тна́, -тно).

melée ['meleɪ] *n.* сва́лка.

mellow ['meləʊ] *adj.* (*ripe*) спе́лый (спел, -á, -о); (*juicy*) со́чный (-чен, -чна́, -чно); (*soft*) мя́гкий (-гок, -гка́, -гко); (*intoxicated*) подвы́пивший; *v.i.* спеть *impf.*; смягча́ться *impf.*, смягчи́ться *pf.*

melodic [mɪ'lɒdɪk] *adj.* мелоди́ческий. **melodious** [mɪ'ləʊdɪəs] *adj.* мелоди́чный. **melody** ['melədɪ] *n.* мело́дия, напе́в.

melodrama ['melə,drɑːmə] *n.* мелодра́ма. **melodramatic** [,melədrə'mætɪk] *adj.* мелодрамати́ческий.

melon ['melən] *n.* ды́ня; (*water-*~) арбу́з.

melt [melt] *v.t. & i.* раста́пливать(ся) *impf.*, растопи́ть(ся) (-плю́, -пит(ся)) *pf.*; (*smelt*) пла́вить(ся) *impf.*, рас~ *pf.*; (*dissolve*) растворя́ть(ся) *impf.*, раствори́ть(ся) *pf.*; *v.i.* (*thaw*) та́ять (та́ет) *impf.*, рас~ *pf.*; ~**ing point** то́чка плавле́ния.

member ['membə(r)] *n.* член. **membership** *n.* чле́нство; (*number of* ~) коли́чество чле́нов; *attr.* чле́нский.

membrane ['membreɪn] *n.* перепо́нка. **membran(e)ous** *adj.* перепо́нчатый.

memento [mɪ'mentəʊ] *n.* сувени́р. **memoir** ['memwɑː(r)] *n.* кра́ткая биогра́фия; *pl.* мемуа́ры (-ров) *pl.*; воспомина́ния *nt.pl.*

memorable ['memərəb(ə)l] *adj.* достопа́мятный. **memorandum** [,memə'rændəm] *n.* па́мятная запи́ска; (*diplomatic* ~) мемора́ндум. **memorial** [mɪ'mɔːrɪəl] *adj.* па́мятный, мемориа́льный; *n.* па́мятник. **memorize** ['meməraɪz] *v.t.* зау́чивать *impf.*, заучи́ть (-чу́, -чишь) *pf.* наизу́сть. **memory** ['memərɪ] *n.* па́мять; (*recollection*) воспомина́ние; (*comput.*) запомина́ющее устро́йство.

menace ['menɪs] *n.* угро́за; *v.t.* угрожа́ть *impf.*+*d.* **menacing** *adj.* угрожа́ющий.

menagerie [mɪ'nædʒərɪ] *n.* звери́нец (-нца)

mend [mend] *v.t.* чини́ть *impf.*, по~ *pf.*; (*clothes*) штопать *impf.*, за~ *pf.*; (*road*) ремонти́ровать *impf.*, от~ *pf.*; ~ **one's ways** исправля́ться *impf.*, испра́виться *pf.*

mendacious [men'deɪʃəs] *adj.* лжи́вый. **mendacity** [men'dæsɪtɪ] *n.* лжи́вость.

mendicancy ['mendɪkənsɪ] *n.* ни́щенство. **mendicant** *adj.* ни́щий, ни́щенствующий; *n.* ни́щий *sb.*

menial ['mi:nɪəl] *adj.* лаке́йский, ни́зкий (-зок, -зка́, -зко).

meningitis [,menɪn'dʒaɪtɪs] *n.* менинги́т.

menopause ['menəpɔːz] *n.* кли́макс.

menstrual ['menstruəl] *adj.* менструа́льный. **menstru'ation** *n.* менструа́ция.

mental ['ment(ə)l] *adj.* у́мственный, психи́ческий; ~ **arithmetic** счёт в уме́; ~ **deficiency** у́мственная отста́лость; ~ **home, hospital, institution** психиатри́ческая больни́ца. **men'tality** *n.* ум (-á); (*character*) склад ума́. **mentally** *adv.* у́мственно, мы́сленно.

menthol ['menθɒl] *n.* менто́л.

mention ['menʃ(ə)n] *v.t.* упомина́ть *impf.*, упомяну́ть (-ну́, -нешь) *pf.*; **not to** ~ не говоря́ уже́ о+*p.*; *n.* упомина́ние.

mentor ['mentɔː(r)] *n.* ме́нтор.

menu ['menjuː] *n.* меню́ *nt.indecl.*

mercantile ['mɜːkəntaɪl] *adj.* торго́вый; ~ **marine** торго́вый флот.

mercenary ['mɜːsɪnərɪ] *adj.* коры́стный; (*hired*) наёмный; *n.* наёмник.

merchandise ['mɜːtʃəndaɪz] *n.* това́ры *m.pl.* **merchant** *n.* купе́ц (-пца́); торго́вец (-вца); *attr.* торго́вый; ~ **navy** торго́вый флот; ~ **ship** торго́вое су́дно (*pl.* -да́, -до́в).

merciful ['mɜːsɪ,fʊl] *adj.* милосе́рдный. **mercifully** *adv.* к сча́стью. **merciless** *adj.* беспоща́дный.

mercurial [mɜːˈkjʊərɪəl] *adj.* (*person*) живо́й (жив, -а́, -о); (*of mercury*) рту́тный. **'mercury** *n.* (*metal*) ртуть; (**M~**, *planet*) Мерку́рий.

mercy ['mɜːsɪ] *n.* милосе́рдие; поща́да; **at the ~ of** во вла́сти+g.

mere [mɪə(r)] *adj.* просто́й, чи́стый, су́щий; **a ~ child** су́щий ребёнок, всего́ лишь ребёнок. **merely** *adv.* то́лько, про́сто.

meretricious [ˌmerɪˈtrɪʃəs] *adj.* показно́й, мишу́рный.

merge [mɜːdʒ] *v.t. & i.* слива́ть(ся) *impf.*, слить(ся) (солью́(сь), -ьёшь(ся); слил(ся), -ила́(сь), -и́ло/-и́ло́сь) *pf.* **merger** *n.* объедине́ние.

meridian [məˈrɪdɪən] *n.* меридиа́н.

meringue [məˈræŋ] *n.* мере́нга.

merit ['merɪt] *n.* заслу́га, досто́инство; *v.t.* заслу́живать *impf.*, заслужи́ть (-жу́, -жишь) *pf.*+g. **meri'torious** *adj.* похва́льный.

mermaid ['mɜːmeɪd] *n.* руса́лка.

merrily ['merɪlɪ] *adv.* ве́село. **merriment** *n.* весе́лье. **merry** *adj.* весёлый (ве́сел, -а́, -о, ве́селы). **merry-go-round** *n.* карусе́ль. **merry-making** *n.* весе́лье.

mesh [meʃ] *n.* пе́тля (*g.pl.* -тель); *pl.* (*network*) се́ти (-те́й) *pl.*; *pl.* (*fig.*) западня́; *v.i.* сцепля́ться *impf.*, сцепи́ться (-ится) *pf.*

mesmeric [mezˈmerɪk] *adj.* гипноти́ческий. **'mesmerize** *v.t.* гипнотизи́ровать *impf.*, за~ *pf.*

mess [mes] *n.* (*disorder*) беспоря́док (-дка); (*trouble*) беда́; (*eating-place*) столо́вая *sb.*; *v.i.* столова́ться *impf.* (**with** вме́сте с+i.); **~ about** ло́дырничать *impf.*; **~ up** по́ртить *impf.*, ис~ *pf.*

message ['mesɪdʒ] *n.* сообще́ние; (*errand*) поруче́ние. **messenger** *n.* посы́льный *sb.*, курье́р.

Messiah [mɪˈsaɪə] *n.* мессия *m.* **Messianic** [ˌmesɪˈænɪk] *adj.* мессиа́нский.

Messrs ['mesəz] *abbr.* (*of Messieurs*) господа́ (*g.* -д) *m.pl.*

messy ['mesɪ] *adj.* (*untidy*) беспоря́дочный; (*dirty*) гря́зный (-зен, -зна́, -зно).

metabolism [mɪˈtæbə,lɪz(ə)m] *n.* метаболи́зм, обме́н веще́ств.

metal ['met(ə)l] *n.* мета́лл; (*road-~*) ще́бень (-бня) *m.*; (*rail.*) балла́ст; *pl.* (*rails*) ре́льсы *m.pl.*; *adj.* металли́ческий; *v.t.* (*road*) шоссе́ровать *impf. & pf.*; **~ detector** металлоиска́тель *m.*; **~led road** шоссе́ *nt.indecl.* **metallic** [mɪˈtælɪk] *adj.* металли́ческий. **metallurgical** [ˌmetəˈlɜːdʒɪk(ə)l] *adj.* металлурги́ческий. **metallurgy** [mɪˈtælədʒɪ, 'metə,lɜːdʒɪ] *n.* металлу́ргия.

metamorphose [ˌmetəˈmɔːfəʊz] *v.t.* подверга́ть *impf.*, подве́ргнуть (-г) *pf.* метаморфо́зе. **meta'mor'phosis** *n.* метаморфо́за; (*biol.*) метаморфо́з.

metaphor ['metə,fɔː(r)] *n.* мета́фора. **meta'phorical** *adj.* метафори́ческий.

metaphysical [ˌmetəˈfɪzɪk(ə)l] *adj.* метафизи́ческий. **metaphy'sician** *n.* метафи́зик. **metaphysics** *n.* метафи́зика.

meteor ['miːtɪə(r)] *n.* метео́р. **meteoric** [ˌmiːtɪˈɒrɪk] *adj.* метеори́ческий, метео́рный. **meteorite** *n.* метеори́т. **meteoro'logical** *adj.* метеорологи́ческий. **meteo'rologist** *n.* метеоро́лог. **meteo'rology** *n.* метеороло́гия.

meter ['miːtə(r)] *n.* счётчик; *v.t.* измеря́ть *impf.*, изме́рить *pf.* при по́мощи счётчика.

methane ['meθeɪn, 'miːθeɪn] *n.* мета́н.

method ['meθəd] *n.* ме́тод, спо́соб; (*system*) систе́ма. **methodical** [mɪˈθɒdɪk(ə)l] *adj.* системати́ческий, методи́чный.

Methodism ['meθəd,ɪz(ə)m] *n.* методи́зм. **Methodist** *n.* методи́ст; *adj.* методи́стский.

methyl ['meθɪl, 'miːθaɪl] *n.* мети́л; **~ alcohol** мети́ловый спирт. **methylated** ['meθɪ,leɪtɪd] *adj.*: **~ spirit(s)** денатура́т.

meticulous [məˈtɪkjʊləs] *adj.* тща́тельный.

metre ['miːtə(r)] *n.* метр. **metric(al)** ['metrɪk(ə)l] *adj.* метри́ческий.

metronome ['metrə,nəʊm] *n.* метроно́м.

metropolis [mɪˈtrɒpəlɪs] *n.* (*capital*) столи́ца. **metropolitan** [ˌmetrəˈpɒlɪt(ə)n] *adj.* столи́чный; *n.* (*eccl.*) митрополи́т.

mettle ['met(ə)l] *n.* темпера́мент; (*ardour*) пыл (-а(у)). **mettlesome** *adj.* горя́чий (-ч, -ча́).

mew *see* **miaow**

Mexico ['meksɪ,kəʊ] *n.* Ме́ксика.

mezzanine ['metsə,niːn, 'mez-] *n.* антресо́ли *f.pl.*

mezzo-soprano ['metsəʊ] *n.* ме́ццо-сопра́но (*voice*) *nt. & (person*) *f.indecl.*

mg. *abbr.* (*of* **milligram(me)(s)**) мг, милли-гра́м.

miaow [mɪˈaʊ] *int.* мя́у; *n.* мяу́канье; *v.i.* мяу́кать *impf.*, мяу́кнуть *pf.*

mica ['maɪkə] *n.* слюда́.

Michaelmas ['mɪkəlməs] *n.* Миха́йлов день (дня) *m.*

micro- ['maɪkrəʊ] *in comb.* микро... . **microbe** *n.* микро́б. **microcircuit** *n.* микросхе́ма. **microcomponent** *n.* микроэлеме́нт. **microcomputer** *n.* микрокомпью́тер. **microcosm** *n.* микроко́см. **microelectronics** *n.* микроэлектро́ника. **microfiche** *n.* микрофи́ша. **microfilm** *n.* микрофи́льм. **micron** ['maɪkrɒn] *n.* микро́н (*g.pl.* -н). **micro-organism** *n.* микроорганизм. **microphone** *n.* микрофо́н. **microscope** *n.* микроско́п. **micro'scopic** *adj.* микроскопи́ческий. **microsecond** *n.* микросеку́нда. **microwave** *adj.* микроволно́вый; *n.* микроволна́ (*pl.* -о́лны, *d.* -о́лна́м); **~ oven** печь сверхвысо́кой частоты́.

mid [mɪd] *adj.* сре́дний, середи́нный. **midday** *n.* по́лдень (полу́дня & по́лдня) *m.*; *attr.* полу́денный. **middle** *n.* середи́на; *adj.*

сре́дний; **M~ Ages** сре́дние века́ *m.pl.*; ~ **man** посре́дник. **middle-aged** *adj.* сре́дних лет. **middle-sized** *adj.* сре́днего разме́ра. **middleweight** *n.* сре́дний вес.

midge [mɪdʒ] *n.* мо́шка.

midget ['mɪdʒɪt] *n.* ка́рлик, -ица; *adj.* миниатю́рный.

Midlands ['mɪdləndz] *n.* центра́льные гра́фства *nt.pl.* А́нглии. **midnight** *n.* по́лночь (полу́ночи & по́лночи); *attr.* полуно́чный. **midriff** *n.* диафра́гма. **midshipman** *n.* кара́бельный гардемари́н. **midst** *n.* середи́на. **mid'summer** *n.* середи́на ле́та. **midway** *adv.* на полпути́, на полдоро́ге. **mid-week** *n.* середи́на неде́ли. **mid'winter** *n.* середи́на зимы́.

midwife ['mɪdwaɪf] *n.* акуше́рка. **midwifery** ['mɪd,wɪfərɪ] *n.* акуше́рство.

might [maɪt] *n.* мощь, могу́щество; си́ла; **with all one's ~, with ~ and main** не щадя́ сил. **mighty** *adj.* могу́щественный (-ен, -енна), мо́щный (-щен, -щна́, -щно).

migraine ['mi:greɪn, 'maɪ-] *n.* мигре́нь.

migrant ['maɪgrənt] *adj.* кочу́ющий; (*bird*) перелётный; *n.* (*person*) пересе́ленец (-нца); (*bird*) перелётная пти́ца. **mi'grate** *v.i.* мигри́ровать *impf.* & *pf.*; переселя́ться *impf.*, пересели́ться *pf.* **mi'gration** *n.* мигра́ция. **mi'gratory** *adj.* кочу́ющий; (*bird*) перелётный.

mike [maɪk] *n.* микрофо́н.

milch [mɪltʃ] *adj.* моло́чный. **milch-cow** *n.* до́йная коро́ва.

mild [maɪld] *adj.* (*soft*) мя́гкий (-гок, -гка́, -гко); (*light*) лёгкий (-гок, -гка́, -гко́, лёгки); (*not sharp*) неостры́й (не остр & -остёр, остра́, о́стро); (*not strong*) некре́пкий (-пок, -пка́, -пко); ~ **steel** мя́гкая сталь.

mildew ['mɪldju:] *n.* (*fungi*) мильдю́ *nt.indecl.*; (*on paper etc.*) пле́сень.

mile [maɪl] *n.* ми́ля. **mileage** *n.* расстоя́ние в ми́лях; (*distance travelled*) коли́чество про́йденных миль; (*expenses*) де́ньги (-нег, -ньга́м) *pl.* на прое́зд. **milestone** *n.* ми́льный ка́мень (-мня; *pl.* -мни, -мне́й) *m.*; (*fig.*) ве́ха.

militancy ['mɪlɪt(ə)nsɪ] *n.* вои́нственность. **militant** *adj.* вои́нствующий; (*combative*) боево́й; *n.* бое́ц (бойца́); активи́ст. **military** *adj.* вое́нный; ~ **band** духово́й орке́стр; *n.* вое́нные *sb.* **militate** *v.i.*: ~ **against** говори́ть *impf.* про́тив+*g.* **militia** [mɪ'lɪʃə] *n.* ополче́ние; (*in Russia*) мили́ция. **militiaman** *n.* ополче́нец (-нца); (*in Russia*) милиционе́р.

milk [mɪlk] *n.* молоко́; (*of plants*) мле́чный сок; *attr.* моло́чный; *v.t.* дои́ть *impf.*, по-*pf.* **milkmaid** *n.* доя́рка. **milkman** *n.* продаве́ц (-вца́) молока́. **milksop** *n.* тря́пка. **milk-tooth** *n.* моло́чный зуб (*pl.* -ы, -о́в). **milky** *adj.* моло́чный; **M~ Way** Мле́чный Путь (-ти́, -тём) *m.*

mill [mɪl] *n.* ме́льница; (*factory*) фа́брика,

заво́д; (*rolling-~*) прока́тный стан; *v.t.* (*grain etc.*) моло́ть (мелю́, -лешь) *impf.*, с~ *pf.*; (*cloth*) валя́ть *impf.*, с~ *pf.*; (*metal*) фрезерова́ть *impf.*, от~ *pf.*; (*coin*) гурти́ть *impf.*; ~**ed edge** (*of coin*) гурт; *v.i.* кружи́ть (-ужу́, -у́жи́шь) *impf.*

millennium [mɪ'lenɪəm] *n.* тысячеле́тие.

millepede *see* **millipede**

miller ['mɪlə(r)] *n.* ме́льник.

millet ['mɪlɪt] *n.* (*plant*) про́со; (*grain*) пшено́.

mill-hand ['mɪlhænd] *n.* фабри́чный рабо́чий *sb.*

milli- ['mɪlɪ] *in comb.* милли... . **millibar** *n.* миллиба́р. **milligram(me)** *n.* миллигра́мм. **millilitre** *n.* миллили́тр. **millimetre** *n.* миллиме́тр.

milliner ['mɪlɪnə(r)] *n.* моди́стка; шля́пница. **millinery** *n.* да́мские шля́пы *f.pl.*

million ['mɪljən] *n.* миллио́н. **millio'naire** *n.* миллионе́р. **millionth** *adj.* миллио́нный.

millipede ['mɪlɪ,pi:d] *n.* многоно́жка.

mill-pond ['mɪlpɒnd] *n.* ме́льничный пруд (-а́, *loc.* -ý). **mill-race** *n.* ме́льничный лото́к (-тка́). **millstone** *n.* жёрнов (*pl.* -а́); (*fig.*) бре́мя *nt.* **mill-wheel** *n.* ме́льничное колесо́ (*pl.* -ёса).

milt [mɪlt] *n.* моло́ки (-к) *pl.*

mime [maɪm] *n.* ми́м; *v.t.* изобража́ть *impf.*, изобрази́ть *pf.* мими́чески; *v.i.* исполня́ть *impf.*, испо́лнить *pf.* роль в пантоми́ме. **mimic** ['mɪmɪk] *adj.* мими́ческий, подража́тельный; *n.* ми́ми́ст; *v.t.* имити́ровать *impf.*, сымити́ровать *pf.*; (*ape*) обезья́нничать *impf.*, с~ *pf.* c+*g.* **mimicry** *n.* имита́ция.

mimosa [mɪ'məuzə] *n.* мимо́за; (*acacia*) ака́ция.

min. *abbr.* (*of* **minute(s)**) мин., мину́та.

minaret [,mɪnə'ret] *n.* минаре́т.

mince [mɪns] *n.* (*meat*) ру́бленое мя́со, фарш; *v.t.* руби́ть (-блю́, -бишь) *impf.*; (*in machine*) пропуска́ть *impf.*, пропусти́ть (-ущу́, -у́стишь) *pf.* че́рез мясору́бку; *v.i.* (*speak*) говори́ть *impf.* жема́нно; (*walk*) семени́ть *impf.*; **not to ~ matters** говори́ть *impf.* пря́мо, без обиняко́в. **mincemeat** *n.* начи́нка из изю́ма, минда́ля и т.п. **mincer** *n.* мясору́бка.

mind [maɪnd] *n.* ум (-а́), ра́зум; (*memory*) па́мять; (*opinion*) мне́ние; **absence of ~** забы́вчивость, рассе́янность; **bear in ~** име́ть *impf.* в виду́; по́мнить *impf.*; **be in one's right ~** быть в здра́вом уме́; **be out of one's ~** быть не в своём уме́; **change one's ~** переду́мывать *impf.*, переду́мать *pf.*; **make up one's ~** реша́ться *impf.*, реши́ться *pf.*; **presence of ~** прису́тствие ду́ха; *v.t.* (*give heed to*) обраща́ть *impf.*, обрати́ть (-ащу́, -ати́шь) *pf.* внима́ние на+*a.*; (*look after*) присма́тривать *impf.*, присмотре́ть (-рю́, -ришь) *pf.* за+*i.*; **I don't ~** я не возража́ю; я ничего́ не име́ю про́тив; **don't ~ me** не обраща́й(те) внима́ния на меня́!; ~ **you don't forget** смотри́ не забу́дь!; ~ **your own**

business не вмешивайтесь в чужие дела!; **never** ~ не беспокойтесь!; ничего! **minded** adj. (disposed) расположенный (-ен). **mindful** adj. помнящий, внимательный (of к+d.).
mine¹ [maɪn] poss.pron. мой (моя, моё; мой); свой (-оя, -оё; -ой).
mine² [maɪn] n. шахта, рудник (-á); (fig.) источник; (mil.) мина; v.t. (obtain from ~) добывать impf., добыть (добуду, -дешь; добыл, -á, -о) pf.; (mil.) минировать impf. & pf. **minefield** n. минное поле (pl. -ля). **minelayer** n. минный заградитель m. **miner** n. шахтёр, горняк (-á). **minesweeper** n. минный тральщик.
mineral ['mɪnər(ə)l] n. минерал; adj. минеральный; ~ **water** минеральная вода (a. -ду). **mine'ralogist** n. минералог. **mine'ralogy** n. минералогия.
mingle ['mɪŋg(ə)l] v.t. & i. смешивать(ся) impf., смешать(ся) pf.
miniature ['mɪnɪtʃə(r)] n. миниатюра; adj. миниатюрный. **miniaturist** n. миниатюрист.
minibus ['mɪnɪ,bʌs] n. микроавтобус.
minim ['mɪnɪm] n. (mus.) половинная нота. **minimal** adj. минимальный. **minimize** ['mɪnɪ,maɪz] v.t. (reduce) доводить (-ожу, -одишь) impf., довести (-еду, -едёшь; -ёл, -елá) pf. до минимума; (underestimate) преуменьшать impf., преуменьшить pf. **minimum** n. минимум; adj. минимальный.
mining ['maɪnɪŋ] n. горное дело.
miniskirt ['mɪnɪ,skɜːt] n. мини-юбка.
minister ['mɪnɪstə(r)] n. (pol.) министр; (diplomat) посланник; (eccl.) священник. **ministerial** [,mɪnɪ'stɪərɪəl] adj. министерский. **mini'stration** n. помощь. **ministry** n. (pol.) министерство; (eccl.) духовенство.
mink [mɪŋk] n. норка; attr. норковый.
minnow ['mɪnəʊ] n. гольян.
minor ['maɪnə(r)] adj. (lesser) меньший; (less important) второстепенный (-нен, -нна); (mus.) минорный; n. (person under age) несовершеннолетний n.; (mus.) минор. **minority** [maɪ'nɒrɪtɪ] n. (small number) меньшинство (pl. -ва); (age) несовершеннолетие; **national** ~ нацменьшинство (pl. -ва).
minstrel ['mɪnstr(ə)l] n. менестрель m.
mint¹ [mɪnt] n. (plant) мята; (peppermint) перечная мята; attr. мятный.
mint² [mɪnt] n. (econ.) монетный двор (-á); **in** ~ **condition** блестящий, новый (нов, -á, -о); (book etc.) непотрёпанный (-ан); v.t. чеканить impf., от~, вы~ pf.
minuet [,mɪnjʊ'et] n. менуэт.
minus ['maɪnəs] prep. минус+a.; без+g.; n. минус; adj. (math., elec.) отрицательный.
minuscule ['mɪnə,skjuːl] adj. минускульный; (очень) маленький; n. минускул.
minute¹ ['mɪnɪt] n. минута; pl. протокол; v.t. заносить (-ошу, -осишь) impf., занести (-есу, -есёшь; -ёс, -еслá) pf. в протокол.

minute² [maɪ'njuːt] adj. мелкий (-лок, -лкá, -лко), мельчайший. **minutiae** [maɪ'njuːʃɪ,iː, mɪ-] n. мелочи (-чей) f.pl.
minx [mɪŋks] n. кокетка.
miracle ['mɪrək(ə)l] n. чудо (pl. -десá). **miraculous** [mɪ'rækjʊləs] adj. чудесный.
mirage ['mɪrɑːʒ] n. мираж.
mire ['maɪə(r)] n. (mud) грязь (loc. -зи); (swamp) болото. **miry** adj. грязный (-зен, -знá, -зно).
mirror ['mɪrə(r)] n. зеркало (pl. -лá); (fig.) отображение; ~ **image** зеркальное изображение; v.t. отражать impf., отразить pf.
mirth [mɜːθ] n. веселье.
misadventure [,mɪsəd'ventʃə(r)] n. несчастный случай.
misanthrope ['mɪzən,θrəʊp, 'mɪs-] n. мизантроп. **misanthropic** [,mɪzən'θrɒpɪk, 'mɪs-] adj. мизантропический. **mi'santhropy** n. мизантропия.
misapplication [mɪs,æplɪ'keɪʃ(ə)n] n. неправильное использование. **misapply** [,mɪsə'plaɪ] v.t. неправильно использовать impf. & pf. **misapprehend** v.t. неправильно понимать impf., понять (пойму, -мёшь; понял, -á, -о) pf. **misapprehension** n. неправильное понимание. **misappropriate** v.t. незаконно присваивать impf., присвоить pf. **misappropri'ation** n. незаконное присвоение. **misbehave** v.i. дурно вести (веду, -дёшь; вёл, -á) impf. себя.
miscalculate [,mɪs'kælkjʊ,leɪt] v.t. неправильно рассчитывать impf., рассчитать pf.; (fig., abs.) просчитываться impf., просчитаться pf. **miscarriage** n. (mistake) ошибка; (med.) выкидыш; ~ **of justice** судебная ошибка. **miscarry** v.i. терпеть (-плю, -пишь) impf., по~ pf. неудачу; (med.) иметь impf. выкидыш. **miscast** v.t. неправильно распределять impf., распределить pf. роль+d.
miscellaneous [,mɪsə'leɪnɪəs] adj. разный, разнообразный. **mi'scellany** n. (mixture) смесь; (book) сборник.
mischance [mɪs'tʃɑːns] n. несчастный случай. **mischief** ['mɪstʃɪf] n. (harm) вред (-á); (naughtiness) озорство; (pranks) проказы f.pl. **mischievous** adj. озорной. **misconception** n. неправильное представление. **misconduct** n. дурное поведение; (adultery) супружеская неверность; v.t.: ~ **o.s.** дурно вести (веду, -дёшь; вёл, -á) impf. себя. **misconstruction** n. неправильное истолкование. **misconstrue** v.t. неправильно истолковывать impf., истолковать pf. **miscount** n. ошибка при подсчёте; неправильный подсчёт; v.t. ошибаться impf., ошибиться (-бусь, -бёшься; -бся) pf. при подсчёте+g.
misdeal v.i. ошибаться impf., ошибиться (-бусь, -бёшься; -бся) pf. при сдаче карт. **misdeed** n. злодеяние. **misdirect** v.t. неправильно направлять impf., направить pf.;

(*letter*) непра́вильно адресова́ть *impf. & pf.*
misdirection *n.* непра́вильное указа́ние, руково́дство.
miser ['maɪzə(r)] *n.* скупе́ц (-пца́), скря́га *c.g.*
miserable ['mɪzərəb(ə)l] *adj.* (*unhappy*) несча́стный; (*wretched*) жа́лкий (-лок, -лка́, -лко), убо́гий. **miserly** ['maɪzəlɪ] *adj.* скупо́й (скуп, -а́, -о). **misery** ['mɪzərɪ] *n.* страда́ние, несча́стье.
misfire [mɪs'faɪə(r)] *v.i.* дава́ть (даёт) *impf.*, дать (даст; дал, -а́, да́ло́, -и) *pf.* осе́чку; *n.* осе́чка. **misfit** *n.* (*garment*) пло́хо сидя́щее пла́тье (*g.pl.* -в); (*person*) неуда́чник. **misfortune** *n.* несча́стье, беда́. **misgiving** *n.* опасе́ние. **misgovern** *v.t.* пло́хо управля́ть *impf.+i.* **misgovernment** *n.* плохо́е управле́ние. **misguided** *adj.* введённый (-ён, -ена́) в заблужде́ние.
mishap ['mɪshæp] *n.* неуда́ча, несча́стье.
misinform *v.t.* дезинформи́ровать *impf. & pf.* **misinformation** *n.* дезинформа́ция.
misinterpret *v.t.* неве́рно понима́ть *impf.*, поня́ть (пойму́, -мёшь; по́нял, -а́, -о) *pf.*
misjudge *v.t.* неве́рно оце́нивать *impf.*, оцени́ть (-ню́, -нишь) *pf.* **misjudgement** *n.* неве́рная оце́нка. **mislay** *v.t.* класть (-аду́, -адёшь; -ал) *impf.*, положи́ть (-жу́, -жишь) *pf.* не на ме́сто; затеря́ть *pf.* **mislead** *v.t.* вводи́ть (-ожу́, -о́дишь) *impf.*, ввести́ (введу́, -дёшь; ввёл, -а́) *pf.* в заблужде́ние. **mismanage** *v.t.* пло́хо управля́ть *impf.+i.* **mismanagement** *n.* плохо́е управле́ние. **misnomer** [mɪs'nəʊmə(r)] *n.* непра́вильное назва́ние.
misogynist [mɪ'sɒdʒɪnɪst] *n.* женоненави́стник. **misogyny** *n.* женоненави́стничество.
misplace [mɪs'pleɪs] *v.t.* класть (-аду́, -дёшь; -ал) *impf.*, положи́ть (-жу́, -жишь) *pf.* не на ме́сто; **~d confidence** незаслу́женное дове́рие. 'misprint *n.* опеча́тка; *v.t.* непра́вильно печа́тать *impf.*, на~ *pf.* **mispronounce** *v.t.* непра́вильно произноси́ть (-ошу́, -о́сишь) *impf.*, произнести́ (-есу́, -есёшь; -ёс, -сла́) *pf.* **mispronunciation** *n.* непра́вильное произноше́ние. **misquotation** *n.* непра́вильная цита́та; непра́вильное цити́рование. **misquote** *v.t.* непра́вильно цити́ровать *impf.*, про~ *pf.* **misread** *v.t.* непра́вильно чита́ть *impf.*, про~ *pf.* **misrepresent** *v.t.* искажа́ть *impf.*, искази́ть *pf.* **misrepresentation** *n.* искаже́ние.
Miss[1] [mɪs] *n.* (*title*) мисс.
miss[2] [mɪs] *n.* про́мах, неуда́ча; *v.i.* прома́хиваться *impf.*, промахну́ться *pf.*; *v.t.* (*let slip*) упуска́ть *impf.*, упусти́ть (-ущу́, -у́стишь) *pf.*; (*train*) опа́здывать *impf.*, опозда́ть *pf.* на+*a.*; **~ out** пропуска́ть *impf.*, пропусти́ть (-ущу́, -у́стишь) *pf.*; **~ the point** не понима́ть *impf.*, поня́ть (пойму́, -мёшь; по́нял, -а́, -о) *pf.* су́ти.
misshapen [mɪs'ʃeɪpən] *adj.* уро́дливый.
missile ['mɪsaɪl] *n.* снаря́д, раке́та.
missing ['mɪsɪŋ] *adj.* отсу́тствующий, недо-

ста́ющий; (*person*) пропа́вший бе́з вести.
mission ['mɪʃ(ə)n] *n.* ми́ссия; командиро́вка.
missionary *n.* миссионе́р; *adj.* миссионе́рский. **missive** ['mɪsɪv] *n.* письмо́ (*pl.* -сьма, -сем, -сьмам); посла́ние.
misspell [mɪs'spel] *v.t.* непра́вильно писа́ть (пишу́, -шешь) *impf.*, на~ *pf.* **misspelling** *n.* непра́вильное написа́ние. **misspent** *adj.* растра́ченный (-ен) (впусту́ю). **misstatement** *n.* непра́вильное заявле́ние.
mist [mɪst] *n.* тума́н, мгла.
mistake [mɪ'steɪk] *v.t.* непра́вильно понима́ть *impf.*, поня́ть (пойму́, -мёшь; по́нял, -а́, -о) *pf.*; **~ for** принима́ть *impf.*, приня́ть (приму́, -мешь; при́нял, -а́, -о) *pf.* за+*a.*; *n.* оши́бка; **make a ~** ошиба́ться *impf.*, ошиби́ться (-бу́сь, -бёшься; -бся) *pf.* **mistaken** *adj.* оши́бочный; **be ~** ошиба́ться *impf.*, ошиби́ться (-бу́сь, -бёшься; -бся) *pf.*
mistletoe ['mɪs(ə)l,təʊ] *n.* оме́ла.
mistranslate [,mɪstrænz'leɪt, ,mɪstrɑ:-, -s'leɪt] *v.t.* непра́вильно переводи́ть (-ожу́, -о́дишь) *impf.*, перевести́ (-еду́, -едёшь; -ёл, -ела́) *pf.* **mistranslation** *n.* непра́вильный перево́д.
mistress ['mɪstrɪs] *n.* хозя́йка; (*teacher*) учи́тельница; (*lover*) любо́вница.
mistrust [mɪs'trʌst] *v.t.* не доверя́ть *impf.+d.*; *n.* недове́рие. **mistrustful** *adj.* недове́рчивый.
misty ['mɪstɪ] *adj.* тума́нный.
misunderstand [,mɪsʌndə'stænd] *v.t.* непра́вильно понима́ть *impf.*, поня́ть (пойму́, -мёшь; по́нял, -а́, -о) *pf.* **misunderstanding** *n.* непра́вильное понима́ние, недоразуме́ние; (*disagreement*) размо́лвка.
misuse [mɪs'ju:z; mɪs'ju:s] *v.t.* непра́вильно употребля́ть *impf.*, употреби́ть *pf.*; (*ill-treat*) ду́рно обраща́ться *impf.* с+*i.*; *n.* непра́вильное употребле́ние.
mite [maɪt] *n.* (*cheese-~*) (сы́рный) клещ (-а́); (*child*) ма́ленький ребёнок (-нка; *pl.* де́ти, -те́й, -тям, -тьми́), кро́шка.
mitigate ['mɪtɪˌgeɪt] *v.t.* смягча́ть *impf.*, смягчи́ть *pf.* **miti'gation** *n.* смягче́ние.
mitre ['maɪtə(r)] *n.* ми́тра.
mitten ['mɪt(ə)n] *n.* рукави́ца, мите́нка; *pl.* (*boxing-gloves*) боксёрские перча́тки *f.pl.*
mix [mɪks] *v.t.* меша́ть *impf.*, с~ *pf.*; *v.i.* сме́шиваться *impf.*, смеша́ться *pf.*; (*person*) обща́ться *impf.*; **~ up** (*confuse*) пу́тать *impf.*, с~ *pf.*; **get ~ed up in** впу́тываться *impf.*, впу́таться *pf.* в+*a.*; *n.* смесь; (*food ~*) (пищево́й) полуфабрика́т. **mixer** *n.* смеси́тель *m.* **mixture** ['mɪkstʃə(r)] *n.* смесь; (*medicine*) миксту́ра.
ml. *abbr.* (*of* **millilitre(s)**) мл, миллили́тр; (*of* **mile(s)**) ми́ля.
mm. *abbr.* (*of* **millimetre(s)**) мм, миллиме́тр.
mnemonic [nɪ'mɒnɪk] *adj.* мнемони́ческий; *n.* мнемони́ческий приём; *pl.* мнемо́ника.
mo [məʊ] *n.* мину́тка; **half a ~** (одну́) мину́тку!

moan [məʊn] *n.* стон; *v.i.* стона́ть (-ну́, -нешь) *impf.*, про~ *pf.*

moat [məʊt] *n.* (крепостно́й) ров (рва, *loc.* во рву́). **moated** *adj.* обнесённый (-ён, -ена́) рвом.

mob [mɒb] *n.* (*populace*) чернь; (*crowd*) толпа́ (*pl.* -пы); (*gang*) ша́йка; *v.t.* (*attack*) напада́ть *impf.*, напа́сть (-аду́т; -а́л) *pf.* толпо́й на+*a.*; (*crowd around*) толпи́ться *impf.* вокру́г+*g.* **mobster** *n.* га́нгстер.

mobile ['məʊbaɪl] *adj.* подвижно́й, передвижно́й. **mobility** [məʊ'bɪlɪtɪ] *n.* подви́жность. **mobilization** [ˌməʊbɪlaɪ'zeɪʃ(ə)n] *n.* мобилиза́ция. '**mobilize** *v.t. & i.* мобилизова́ть(ся) *impf. & pf.*

moccasin ['mɒkəsɪn] *n.* мокаси́н (*g.pl.* -н).

mocha ['mɒkə] *n.* мо́кко *m. & nt.indecl.*

mock [mɒk] *v.t. & i.* издева́ться *impf.* над+*i.*; осме́ивать *impf.*, осмея́ть (-ею, -еёшь) *pf.*; *adj.* (*sham*) подде́льный; (*pretended*) мни́мый; ~ **turtle soup** суп из теля́чьей головы́.

mockery *n.* (*derision*) издева́тельство, насме́шка; (*travesty*) паро́дия (**of** на+*a.*; +*g.*).

mockingbird *n.* пересме́шник. **mock-up** *n.* маке́т, моде́ль.

mode [məʊd] *n.* (*manner*) о́браз; (*method*) спо́соб.

model ['mɒd(ə)l] *n.* (*representation*) моде́ль, маке́т; (*pattern*) образе́ц (-зца́); (*artist's*) нату́рщик, -ица; (*mannequin*) манеке́нщик, -ица; *adj.* образцо́вый, приме́рный; *v.t.* лепи́ть (-плю, -пишь) *impf.*, вы́~, с~ *pf.*; (*document*) оформля́ть *impf.*, офо́рмить *pf.*; *v.i.* (*act as* ~) быть нату́рщиком, -ицей; быть манеке́нщиком, -ицей; ~ **after, on** создава́ть (-даю́, -даёшь) *impf.*, созда́ть (-а́м, -а́шь, -а́ст, -ади́м; со́зда́л, -а́, -о) *pf.* по образцу́+*g.*; ~ **o.s. on** брать (беру́, -рёшь; брал, -а́, -о) *impf.*, взять (возьму́, -мёшь; взял, -а́, -о) *pf.*+*a.* за образе́ц, приме́р.

modem ['məʊdem] *n.* мо́дем.

moderate ['mɒdərət; 'mɒdəˌreɪt] *adj.* (*var. senses*; *pol.*) уме́ренный (-ен, -енна); (*person, conduct*) сде́ржанный (-ан, -анна); (*quantity*) небольшо́й; *v.t.* умеря́ть *impf.*, уме́рить *pf.*; *v.i.* стиха́ть *impf.*, сти́хнуть (-х) *pf.* **mode'ration** *n.* уме́ренность; **in** ~ уме́ренно.

modern ['mɒd(ə)n] *adj.* совреме́нный (-нен, -нна), но́вый (нов, -а́, -о). **modernism** *n.* модерни́зм. **moder'nistic** *adj.* модерни́стский. **modernity** [mɒ'dɜːnɪtɪ] *n.* совреме́нность. **moderni'zation** *n.* модерниза́ция. **modernize** *v.t.* модернизи́ровать *impf. & pf.*

modest ['mɒdɪst] *adj.* скро́мный (-мен, -мна́, -мно). **modesty** *n.* скро́мность.

modification [ˌmɒdɪfɪ'keɪʃ(ə)n] *n.* видоизмене́ние, модифика́ция. **modify** ['mɒdɪˌfaɪ] *v.t.* (*soften*) смягча́ть *impf.*, смягчи́ть *pf.*; (*partially change*) модифици́ровать *impf. & pf.*

modish ['məʊdɪʃ] *adj.* мо́дный (-ден, -дна́, -дно).

modular ['mɒdjʊlə(r)] *adj.* мо́дульный; бло́чный. **modulate** *v.t.* модули́ровать *impf.* **modu'lation** *n.* модуля́ция. **module** *n.* (*measure*) едини́ца измере́ния; (*unit*) мо́дульный, автоно́мный, отсе́к; **lunar** ~ лу́нная ка́псула. **modulus** *n.* мо́дуль *m.*

mohair ['məʊheə(r)] *n.* мохе́р.

Mohammedan [mə'hæməd(ə)n] *adj.* мусульма́нский; *n.* мусульма́нин (*pl.* -а́не, -а́н), -а́нка. **Mohammedanism** *n.* исла́м.

moiré ['mwɑːreɪ] *adj.* муа́ровый.

moist [mɔɪst] *adj.* сыро́й (сыр, -а́, -о), вла́жный (-жен, -жна́, -жно). **moisten** ['mɔɪs(ə)n] *v.t. & i.* увлажня́ть(ся) *impf.*, увлажни́ть(ся) *pf.* **moisture** *n.* вла́га.

molar ['məʊlə(r)] *n.* (*tooth*) коренно́й зуб (*pl.* -ы, -о́в); *adj.* коренно́й.

molasses [mə'læsɪz] *n.* чёрная па́тока.

Moldavia [mɒl'deɪvɪə] *n.* Молда́вия.

mole[1] [məʊl] *n.* (*on skin*) ро́динка.

mole[2] [məʊl] *n.* (*animal*) крот (-а́). **molehill** *n.* кротови́на. **moleskin** *n.* кро́товый мех; (*fabric*) молески́н; *pl.* молески́новые брю́ки (-к) *pl.*

mole[3] [məʊl] *n.* (*pier*) мол (*loc.* -у́).

molecular [mə'lekjʊlə(r)] *adj.* молекуля́рный. **molecule** ['mɒlɪˌkjuːl] *n.* моле́кула.

molest [mə'lest] *v.t.* пристава́ть (-таю́, -таёшь) *impf.*, приста́ть (-а́ну, -а́нешь) *pf.* к+*d.* **molestation** [ˌməʊle'steɪʃ(ə)n, ˌmɒl-] *n.* пристава́ние.

mollify ['mɒlɪˌfaɪ] *v.t.* смягча́ть *impf.*, смягчи́ть *pf.*

mollusc ['mɒləsk] *n.* моллю́ск.

mollycoddle ['mɒlɪˌkɒd(ə)l] *n.* не́женка *c.g.*; *v.t.* не́жить *impf.*

molten ['məʊlt(ə)n] *adj.* распла́вленный (-ен).

moment ['məʊmənt] *n.* моме́нт, миг, мгнове́ние; (*phys.*) моме́нт; (*importance*) значе́ние; **a** ~ **ago** то́лько что; **at a** ~'**s notice** по пе́рвому тре́бованию; **at the last** ~ в после́днюю мину́ту; **just a** ~ сейча́с!; погоди́! **momen'tarily** *adv.* на мгнове́ние. **momentary** *adj.* преходя́щий, кратковре́менный (-нен, -нна). **momentous** [mə'mentəs] *adj.* ва́жный (-жен, -жна́, -жно, ва́жны́). **mo'mentum** *n.* коли́чество движе́ния; (*impetus*) дви́жущая си́ла; **gather** ~ набира́ть *impf.*, набра́ть (наберу́, -рёшь; набра́л, -а́, -о) *pf.* ско́рость.

monarch ['mɒnək] *n.* мона́рх, ~иня. **monarchical** [mə'nɑːkɪk(ə)l] *adj.* монархи́ческий. **monarchism** *n.* монархи́зм. **monarchist** *n.* монархи́ст. **monarchy** *n.* мона́рхия.

monastery ['mɒnəstərɪ, -strɪ] *n.* (*мужско́й*) монасты́рь (-ря́) *m.* **monastic** [mə'næstɪk] *adj.* (*of monastery*) монасты́рский; (*of monks*) мона́шеский. **mo'nasticism** *n.* мона́шество.

Monday ['mʌndeɪ, -dɪ] *n.* понеде́льник.

monetarist ['mʌnɪtəˌrɪst] *n.* монетари́ст; *adj.* монетари́стский. **monetary** *adj.* де́нежный.

money ['mʌnɪ] *n.* де́ньги (-нег, -ньга́м) *pl.*; ~ **box** копи́лка; ~ **market** де́нежный ры́нок

(-нка); ~ **order** (дéнежный) почтóвый перевóд. **money-changer** *n.* менялa *m.* **moneyed** *adj.* богáтый. **money-grubbing** *adj.* стяжáтельский. **moneylender** *n.* ростовщúк (-á), -úца.

Mongol ['mɒŋg(ə)l] *n.* монгóл, ~ка; *adj.* монгóльский. **Mongolia** [mɒŋ'gəʊlɪə] *n.* Монгóлия.

mongoose ['mɒŋguːs] *n.* мангýста.

mongrel ['mʌŋgr(ə)l, 'mɒŋ-] *adj.* нечистокрóвный, смéшанный; *n.* дворняжка; (*also fig.*) ублюдок (-дка).

monitor ['mɒnɪt(ə)r] *n.* (*school*) стáроста *m.* (клáсса); (*lizard*) варáн; (*naut.*; *TV*) монитóр; (*of broadcasts etc.*) слухáч (-á); (*of radioactivity*) дозимéтр; *v.t.* проверять *impf.*, провéрить *pf.*; контролúровать *impf.*, про~ *pf.*; *v.i.* вестú (ведý, -дёшь; вёл, -á) *impf.* радиоперехвáт. **monitoring** *n.* радиоперехвáт; монитóринг; ~ **station** стáнция радиоперехвáта; **environmental** ~ монитóринг за окружáющей средóй.

monk [mʌŋk] *n.* монáх.

monkey ['mʌŋkɪ] *n.* обезьяна; *v.i.:* ~ **(about) with** неумéло обращáться *impf.* c+*i.*; ~ **business** прокáза; ~ **tricks** шáлости *f.pl.*; ~ **wrench** разводнóй гáечный ключ (-á). **monkey-jacket** *n.* корóткая (матрóсская) кýртка. **monkey-nut** *n.* землянóй орéх. **monkey-puzzle** *n.* араукáрия.

mono- ['mɒnəʊ] *in comb.* одно..., моно..., едино... . **monochrome** ['mɒnəkrəʊm] *adj.* одноцвéтный; *n.* однокрáсочное изображéние. **monocle** ['mɒnək(ə)l] *n.* монóкль *m.* **monogamous** [mə'nɒgəməs] *adj.* единобрáчный. **mo'nogamy** *n.* единобрáчие. '**monogram** *n.* моногрáмма. '**monolith** *n.* монолúт. **mono'lithic** *adj.* монолúтный. '**monologue** *n.* монолóг. **mono'mania** *n.* мономáния. **mono'maniac** *n.* мономáн. '**monoplane** *n.* моноплáн. **mo'nopolist** *n.* монополúст. **mo'nopolize** *v.t.* монополизúровать *impf.* & *pf.* **mo'nopoly** *n.* монопóлия. '**monorail** *n.* монорéльсовая дорóга. **monosy'llabic** *adj.* односложный. '**monosyllable** *n.* односложное слóво (*pl.* -вá). '**monotheism** *n.* единобóжие, монотеúзм. **monothe'istic** *adj.* монотеистúческий. '**monotone** *n.* монотóнность; **in a** ~ монотóнно. **mo'notonous** *adj.* монотóнный, однообрáзный. **mo'notony** *n.* монотóнность, однообрáзие. **mo'noxide** *n.* однóокись.

monsoon [mɒn'suːn] *n.* (*wind*) муссóн; (*rainy season*) дождлúвый сезóн.

monster ['mɒnstə(r)] *n.* чудóвище, урóд; *adj.* громáдный. **monstrosity** [mɒn'strɒsɪtɪ] *n.* урóдство, чудóвищность; чудóвище. **monstrous** *adj.* чудóвищный; (*huge*) громáдный; (*atrocious*) безобрáзный.

montage [mɒn'tɑːʒ] *n.* (*cin.*) монтáж; (*of photographs*) фотомонтáж.

Mont Blanc [mɒn'blɒŋk] *n.* Монблáн.

month [mʌnθ] *n.* мéсяц. **monthly** *adj.* ежемéсячный, мéсячный; *n.* ежемéсячник; *adv.* ежемéсячно.

monument ['mɒnjʊmənt] *n.* пáмятник. **monu'mental** *adj.* монументáльный; (*stupendous*) изумúтельный, колоссáльный.

moo [muː] *v.i.* мычáть (-чý, -чúшь); *n.* мычáние.

mood[1] [muːd] *n.* (*gram.*) наклонéние.

mood[2] [muːd] *n.* настроéние. **moody** *adj.* унылый, в дурнóм настроéнии.

moon [muːn] *n.* (*of earth*) лунá; (*of other planets*) спýтник; *v.i.* бесцéльно слоняться *impf.* **moonlight** *n.* лýнный свет; *v.i.* халтýрить *impf.* **moonshine** *n.* фантáзия; (*liquor*) самогóн. **moonstone** *n.* лýнный кáмень (-мня) *m.* **moonstruck** *adj.* помéшанный (-ан).

Moor[1] [mʊə(r), mɔː(r)] *n.* мавр. **Moorish** *adj.* мавритáнский.

moor[2] [mʊə(r), mɔː(r)] *n.* мéстность, порóсшая вéреском. **moorcock** *n.* самéц (-мцá) шотлáндской куропáтки. **moorhen** *n.* (*water-hen*) водянáя кýрочка. **moorland** *n.* вéресковая пýстошь.

moor[3] [mʊə(r), mɔː(r)] *v.t.* & *i.* швартовáть(ся) *impf.*, при~ *pf.* **mooring** *n.:* *pl.* швартóвы *m.pl.*; (*place*) причáл.

moose [muːs] *n.* америкáнский лось (*pl.* -си, -сéй) *m.*

moot [muːt] *adj.* спóрный.

mop [mɒp] *n.* швáбра; (*of hair*) копнá волóс; *v.t.* протирáть *impf.*, протерéть (-трý, -трёшь; -тёр) *pf.* (швáброй); ~ **one's brow** вытирáть *impf.*, вытереть (-тру, -трешь; -тер) *pf.* лоб; ~ **up** вытирáть *impf.*, вытереть (-тру, -трешь; -тер) *pf.*; (*mil.*) очищáть *impf.*, очúстить *pf.* (от протúвника).

mope [məʊp] *v.i.* хандрúть *impf.*

moped ['məʊped] *n.* мопéд.

moraine [mə'reɪn] *n.* морéна.

moral ['mɒr(ə)l] *adj.* морáльный, нрáвственный (-ен, -енна); *n.* морáль; *pl.* нрáвы *m.pl.*, нрáвственность. **morale** [mə'rɑːl] *n.* морáльное состояние; (*of troops*) боевóй дух. **moralist** *n.* моралúст, ~ка. **mora'listic** *adj.* моралистúческий. **morality** [mə'rælɪtɪ] *n.* нрáвственность, морáль. **moralize** *v.i.* морализúровать *impf.*

morass [mə'ræs] *n.* болóто, трясúна.

moratorium [ˌmɒrə'tɔːrɪəm] *n.* моратóрий.

morbid ['mɔːbɪd] *adj.* болéзненный (-ен, -енна), нездорóвый; (*med.*) патологúческий.

mordant ['mɔːd(ə)nt] *adj.* éдкий (éдок, едкá, éдко).

more [mɔː(r)] *adj.* (*larger*) бóльший; (*greater quantity*) бóльше+*g.*; (*additional*) ещё; *adv.* бóльше; (*in addition*) ещё; (*forming comp.*) бóлее; **and what is** ~ и вдобáвок; и бóльше тогó; ~ **fool you** тем хýже для тебя; ~ **or less** бóлее úли мéнее; **once** ~ ещё раз; **what** ~ **do you want?** что ещё ты хóчешь?; **without** ~ **ado** без дальнéйших церемóний.

mo'reover *adv.* сверх того; кроме того.

mores ['mɔːreɪz, -riːz] *n.* нравы *m.pl.*

morganatic [ˌmɔːgə'nætɪk] *adj.* морганатический.

morgue [mɔːg] *n.* морг; (*journ.*) справочный отдел.

moribund ['mɒrɪˌbʌnd] *adj.* умирающий.

morning ['mɔːnɪŋ] *n.* утро; **in the** ~**s** по утрам; **since** ~ с утра; **towards** ~ к утру; **until** ~ до утра; **at seven o'clock in the** ~ в семь часов утра; *attr.* утренний; ~ **coat** визитка.

morocco [mə'rɒkəʊ] *n.* сафьян; *attr.* сафьяновый.

moron ['mɔːrɒn] *n.* умственно отсталый *sb.* **moronic** [mə'rɒnɪk] *adj.* отсталый.

morose [mə'rəʊs] *adj.* угрюмый.

morpheme ['mɔːfiːm] *n.* морфема.

morphine ['mɔːfiːn] *n.* морфий.

morphology [mɔː'fɒlədʒɪ] *n.* морфология.

Morse (code) [mɔːs] *n.* азбука Морзе.

morsel ['mɔːs(ə)l] *n.* кусочек (-чка).

mortal ['mɔːt(ə)l] *adj.* смертный, смертельный; *n.* смертный *sb.* **mortality** [mɔː'tælɪtɪ] *n.* смертельность; (*death-rate*) смертность.

mortar ['mɔːtə(r)] *n.* (*vessel*) ступа, ступка; (*cannon*) миномёт, мортира; (*cement*) известковый раствор. **mortarboard** *n.* академическая шапочка.

mortgage ['mɔːgɪdʒ] *n.* ипотека; (*deed*) закладная *sb.*; *v.t.* закладывать *impf.*, заложить (-жу, -жишь) *pf.*

mortification [ˌmɔːtɪfɪ'keɪʃ(ə)n] *n.* (*humiliation*) унижение; (*of the flesh*) умерщвление. **mortify** ['mɔːtɪˌfaɪ] *v.t.* унижать *impf.*, унизить *pf.*; умерщвлять *impf.*, умертвить (-рщвлю, -ртвишь) *pf.*

mortise ['mɔːtɪs] *n.* гнездо (*pl.* -ёзда), паз (*loc.* -у́; *pl.* -ы́); ~ **lock** врезной замок (-мка).

mortuary ['mɔːtjʊərɪ] *adj.* похоронный; *n.* морг, покойницкая *sb.*

mosaic [məʊ'zeɪɪk] *n.* мозаика; *adj.* мозаичный.

Moscow ['mɒskəʊ] *n.* Москва; *attr.* московский.

Moslem ['mɒzləm] *n.* мусульманин (*pl.* -ане, -ан), -анка; *adj.* мусульманский.

mosque [mɒsk] *n.* мечеть.

mosquito [mɒs'kiːtəʊ] *n.* москит. **mosquito-net** *n.* москитная сетка.

moss [mɒs] *n.* мох (м(о)ха, *loc.* м(о)хе & мху; *pl.* мхи). **moss-grown** *adj.* поросший мхом. **mossy** *adj.* мшистый.

most [məʊst] *adj.* наибольший; *n.* наибольшее количество; *adj.* & *n.* (*majority*) большинство+*g.*; большая часть+*g.*; *adv.* больше всего, наиболее; (*forming superlative*) самый. **mostly** *adv.* главным образом.

MOT *abbr.* (*of Ministry of Transport*) Министерство транспорта; ~ (**test**) листок (-тка) техосмотра.

mote [məʊt] *n.* пылинка.

motel [məʊ'tel] *n.* мотель *m.*

moth [mɒθ] *n.* моль, ночная бабочка. **moth-ball** *n.* нафталиновый шарик. **moth-eaten** *adj.* изъеденный молью.

mother ['mʌðə(r)] *n.* мать (-тери, *i.* -терью; *pl.* -тери, -терей); *v.t.* относиться (-ошусь, -осишься) *impf.* по-матерински к+*d.*; ~ **country** метрополия; ~ **tongue** родной язык (-á). **motherhood** *n.* материнство. **mother-in-law** *n.* (*wife's* ~) тёща; (*husband's* ~) свекровь. **motherland** *n.* родина. **motherless** *adj.* лишённый (-ён, -ена) матери. **motherly** *adj.* материнский. **mother-of-pearl** *n.* перламутр; *adj.* перламутровый.

motif [məʊ'tiːf] *n.* основная тема.

motion ['məʊʃ(ə)n] *n.* движение, ход; (*gesture*) жест; (*proposal*) предложение; (*of bowels*) испражнение; **in** ~ в движении, на ходу; *v.t.* показывать *impf.*, показать (-ажу, -ажешь) *pf.*+*d.* жестом, чтобы… . **motionless** *adj.* неподвижный. **motivate** ['məʊtɪˌveɪt] *v.t.* побуждать *impf.*, побудить *pf.* **moti'vation** *n.* побуждение. **motive** *n.* повод, мотив; *adj.* движущий, двигательный.

motley ['mɒtlɪ] *adj.* (*in colour*) разноцветный; (*varied*) пёстрый (-р, -á, пёстро); *n.* всякая всячина; (*costume*) шутовской костюм.

motor ['məʊtə(r)] *n.* двигатель *m.*, мотор; *adj.* двигательный, моторный; (*of vehicles*) автомобильный; ~ **boat** моторная лодка; ~ **car** (легковой) автомобиль *m.*; ~ **cycle** мотоцикл; ~ **oil** автол; ~ **racing** автомобильные гонки *f.pl.*; ~ **scooter** мотороллер; ~ **show** *n.* автосалон; ~ **vehicle** автомобиль *m.* **motoring** *n.* автомобилизм. **motorist** *n.* автомобилист, ~ка. **motorize** *v.t.* моторизовать *impf.* & *pf.* **motorway** *n.* автострада.

mottled ['mɒtəld] *adj.* испещрённый (-ён, -ена), крапчатый.

motto ['mɒtəʊ] *n.* девиз.

mould¹ [məʊld] *n.* (*earth*) взрыхлённая земля (*a.* -лю).

mould² [məʊld] *n.* (*shape*) форма, формочка; *v.t.* формовать *impf.*, с~ *pf.*; лепить (-плю, -пишь) *impf.*, вы~, с~ *pf.* **moulding** *n.* (*action*) формовка; (*decoration*) лепное украшение; (*in wood*) багет.

mould³ [məʊld] *n.* (*fungi*) плесень. **mouldy** *adj.* заплесневелый.

moulder ['məʊldə(r)] *v.i.* разлагаться *impf.*, разложиться (-ится) *pf.*

moult [məʊlt] *v.i.* линять *impf.*, вы~ *pf.*; *n.* линька.

mound [maʊnd] *n.* холм (-á); (*heap*) насыпь.

Mount¹ [maʊnt] *n.* (*in names*) гора (*a.* -ру).

mount² [maʊnt] *v.t.* (*ascend*) подниматься *impf.*, подняться (-нимусь, -нимешься; -нялся, -нялась) *pf.* на+*a.*; (~ *a horse etc.*) садиться *impf.*, сесть (сяду, -дешь; сел) *pf.* на+*a.*; (*picture*) наклеивать *impf.*, наклеить *pf.* на картон; (*gem*) вставлять *impf.*, вставить *pf.* в оправу; (*gun*) устанавливать

impf., установи́ть (-влю́, -вишь) *pf.* на
лафе́т; ~ **up** (*accumulate*) нака́пливаться
impf., накопи́ться (-ится) *pf.*; ~ **guard**
стоя́ть (-ою́, -ои́шь) *impf.* на часа́х; *n.* (*for
picture*) карто́н, подло́жка; (*for gem*)
опра́ва; (*horse*) верхова́я ло́шадь (*pl.* -ди,
-дей; *i.* -дьми́).

mountain ['maʊntɪn] *n.* гора́ (*a.* -ру; *pl.* -ры,
-р, -ра́м); *attr.* го́рный; ~ **ash** ряби́на.
mountai'neer *n.* альпини́ст. **mountai'n-
eering** *n.* альпини́зм. **mountainous** *adj.*
гори́стый; (*huge*) грома́дный.

mountebank ['maʊntɪˌbæŋk] *n.* (*clown*) шут
(-а́); (*charlatan*) шарлата́н.

mourn [mɔːn] *v.t.* опла́кивать *impf.*, опла́-
кать (-а́чу, -а́чешь) *pf.*; *v.i.* скорбе́ть (-блю́,
-би́шь) *impf.* (**over** о+*p.*). **mournful** *adj.* пе-
ча́льный, ско́рбный. **mourning** *n.* (*sorrow*)
печа́ль; (*dress*) тра́ур.

mouse [maʊs] *n.* мышь (*pl.* -ши, -ше́й); *v.i.*
лови́ть (-влю́, -вишь) *impf.*, пойма́ть (*pf.*
мыше́й. **mouser** *n.* мышело́в. **mousetrap**
n. мышело́вка.

mousse [muːs] *n.* мусс.

moustache [məˈstɑːʃ] *n.* усы́ (усо́в) *pl.*

mousy ['maʊsɪ] *adj.* мыши́ный; (*timid*)
ро́бкий (-бок, -бка́, -бко).

mouth [maʊθ] *n.* рот (рта, *loc.* во рту́); (*poet.*)
уста́ (-т) *pl.*; (*entrance*) вход; (*of river*) у́стье
(*g.pl.* -в); (*of gun, volcano*) жерло́ (*pl.* -ла);
~ **to feed** едо́к (-а́); **by word of** ~ у́стно; *v.t.*
говори́ть *impf.*, сказа́ть (-ажу́, -а́жешь) *pf.*
напы́щенно. **mouthful** *n.* по́лный рот (рта);
(*small amount*) кусо́к (-ска́), глото́к (-тка́).
mouth-organ *n.* губна́я гармо́ника. **mouthpiece** *n.* мундштук (-а́); (*person*) ру́пор.

movable ['muːvəb(ə)l] *adj.* подвижно́й;
(*property*) дви́жимый.

move [muːv] *n.* (*in game*) ход (-а(у); *pl.*
хо́ды); (*change of location*) переме́на ме́ста;
(*step*) шаг (*loc.* -ý; *pl.* -и́); *v.t. & i.* дви́-
гать(ся) (-аю(сь), -аешь(ся) & дви́жу(сь),
-жешь(ся)) *impf.*, дви́нуться *pf.*; *v.t.* (*affect*)
тро́гать *impf.*, тро́нуть *pf.*; (*propose*)
вноси́ть (-ошу́, -о́сишь) *impf.*, внести́
(внесу́, -сёшь; внёс, -ла́) *pf.*; *v.i.* (*events*)
развива́ться *impf.*, разви́ться (разовьётся;
разви́лся, -ила́сь, -ило́сь) *pf.*; (~ *house*)
переезжа́ть *impf.*, перее́хать (-е́ду, -е́дешь)
pf.; ~ **away** (*v.i.*) уезжа́ть *impf.*, уе́хать
(уе́ду, -дешь) *pf.*; ~ **in** въезжа́ть *impf.*,
въе́хать (-е́ду, -е́дешь) *pf.*; ~ **on** идти́ (иду́,
идёшь; шёл, шла) *impf.*, пойти́ (пойду́,
-дёшь; пошёл, -шла́) *pf.* да́льше; ~ **on!**
проходи́те (да́льше)!; ~ **out** съезжа́ть
impf., съе́хать (-е́ду, -е́дешь) *pf.* (**of** с+*g.*).
movement *n.* движе́ние; (*mus.*) часть (*pl.*
-ти, -те́й). **moving** *n.* дви́жущийся; (*touching*) тро́гательный; ~ **staircase** эскала́тор.

mow [məʊ] *v.t.* (*also* ~ *down*) коси́ть (кошу́,
ко́сишь) *impf.*, с~ *pf.* **mower** *n.* (*person*)
косе́ц (-сца́); (*machine*) коси́лка.

MP *abbr.* (*of Member of Parliament*) член

парла́мента.

mpg *abbr.* (*of miles per gallon*) ми́ли на
галло́н бензи́на.

mph *abbr.* (*of miles per hour*) (сто́лько-то)
миль в час.

Mr *abbr.* (*of mister*) г-н, господи́н, *pl.* -á;
ми́стер.

Mrs ['mɪsɪz] *abbr.* (*of mistress*) г-жа,
госпожа́; ми́ссис *f.indecl.*

MS *abbr.* (*of manuscript*) ру́копись; (*of
multiple sclerosis*) рассе́янный *or* мно́жест-
венный склеро́з.

Ms [mɪz, məz] миз, г-жа, госпожа́.

M.Sc. *abbr.* (*of Master of Science*) маги́стр
(есте́ственных) нау́к.

Mt. *abbr.* (*of Mount, mountain*) г, гора́.

much [mʌtʃ] *adj. & n.* мно́го+*g.*; мно́гое *sb.*;
adv. о́чень (*with comp.adj.*) гора́здо.

muck [mʌk] *n.* (*dung*) наво́з; (*dirt*) грязь (*loc.*
-зи́); *v.t.* (*dirty*) па́чкать *impf.*, за~, ис~ *pf.*;
~ **out** чи́стить *impf.*, вы́~ *pf.*; ~ **up**
изга́живать *impf.*, изга́дить *pf.*

mucous ['mjuːkəs] *adj.* сли́зистый. **mucus**
['mjuːkəs] *n.* слизь.

mud [mʌd] *n.* грязь (*loc.* -зи́). **mudguard** *n.*
крыло́ (*pl.* -лья, -льев). **mudslinger** ['mʌd-
slɪŋə(r)] *n.* клеветни́к (-á).

muddle ['mʌd(ə)l] *v.t.* пу́тать *impf.*, с~ *pf.*;
v.i. ~ **along** де́йствовать *impf.* наобу́м; ~
through ко́е-как доводи́ть (-ожу́, -о́дишь)
impf., довести́ (-еду́, -еде́шь; -ёл, -ела́) *pf.*
де́ло до конца́; *n.* неразбери́ха, пу́таница.
muddle -headed *adj.* бестолко́вый.

muddy ['mʌdɪ] *adj.* гря́зный (-зен, -зна́, -зно);
(*of liquid*) му́тный (-тен, -тна́, -тно); (*of
light*) ту́склый (-л, -ла́, -ло); *v.t.* обры́з-
гивать *impf.*, обры́згать *pf.* гря́зью; (*water*)
мути́ть (мучу́, му́тишь) *impf.*, вз~, за~ *pf.*

muezzin [muːˈezɪn] *n.* муэдзи́н.

muff [mʌf] *n.* му́фта.

muffle ['mʌf(ə)l] *v.t.* заку́тывать *impf.*, заку́-
тать *pf.*; (*sound*) глуши́ть *impf.*, за~ *pf.*;
~**d oars** обмо́танные вёсла (*g.* -сел) *nt.pl.*
muffler *n.* кашне́ *nt.indecl.*, шарф.

mufti ['mʌftɪ] *n.*: **in** ~ в штати́ском.

mug [mʌg] *n.* (*vessel*) кру́жка; (*face*) мо́рда;
v.t. напада́ть, напа́сть (-аду́, -аде́шь; -а́л)
на+*a.* **mugger** *n.* у́личный граби́тель *m.*
mugging *n.* у́личное ограбле́ние.

muggy ['mʌgɪ] *adj.* сыро́й (сыр, -á, -о) и
тёплый (-пел, -пла́).

mulatto [mjuːˈlætəʊ] *n.* мула́т, ~ка.

mulberry ['mʌlbərɪ] *n.* (*tree*) шелкови́ца,
ту́товое де́рево (*pl.* -е́вья, -е́вьев); (*fruit*)
ту́товая я́года.

mulch [mʌltʃ, mʌlʃ] *n.* му́льча; *v.t.* мульчи́-
ровать *impf. & pf.* **mulching** *n.* мульчи́-
рование.

mule [mjuːl] *n.* мул. **mule'teer** *n.* пого́нщик
му́лов. **mulish** *adj.* упря́мый как осёл.

mull [mʌl] *v.t.* подогрева́ть *impf.*, подогре́ть
pf. с пря́ностями; ~**ed wine** глинтве́йн.

mullah ['mʌlə] *n.* мулла́ *m.*

mullet ['mʌlɪt] *n.* (*grey* ~) кефа́ль; (*red* ~) барабу́лька.

mullion ['mʌljən] *n.* сре́дник.

multi- ['mʌltɪ] *in comb.* мно́го... . **multicoloured** *adj.* многокра́сочный. **multifarious** [,mʌltɪ'feərɪəs] *adj.* разнообра́зный. **multilateral** *adj.* многосторо́нний. **multimillionaire** *n.* мультимиллионе́р. **multi-purpose** *adj.* универса́льный, многоцелево́й. **multiracial** *adj.* многора́совый. **multistorey** *adj.* многоэта́жный. **multivitamins** *n.* поливитами́ны (-ов) *pl.*

multiple ['mʌltɪp(ə)l] *adj.* составно́й, сло́жный (-жен, -жна́, -жно); (*varied*) разнообра́зный; (*numerous*) многочи́сленный; (*math.*) кра́тный; ~ **sclerosis** рассе́янный склеро́з; ~ **shop** магази́н с филиа́лами; *n.* кра́тное число́ (*pl.* -сла, -сел, -слам); **least common** ~ о́бщее наиме́ньшее кра́тное *sb.* **multiplication** [,mʌltɪplɪ'keɪʃ(ə)n] *n.* размноже́ние; (*math.*) умноже́ние. **multi'plicity** *n.* многочи́сленность, многообра́зие. **multiply** ['mʌltɪ,plaɪ] *v.t. & i.* размножа́ть(ся) *impf.*, размно́жить(ся) *pf.*; *v.t.* (*math.*) умножа́ть *impf.*, умно́жить *pf.*

multitude ['mʌltɪ,tjuːd] *n.* мно́жество; (*crowd*) толпа́ (*pl.* -пы).

mum[1] [mʌm] *adj.*: ~'s **the word!** (об э́том) ни гугу́!; **keep** ~ молча́ть (-чу́, -чи́шь) *impf.*

mum[2] [mʌm] *n.* (*mother*) ма́ма.

mumble ['mʌmb(ə)l] *v.t. & i.* мя́млить *impf.*, про~ *pf.*

mummify ['mʌmɪ,faɪ] *v.t.* мумифици́ровать *impf. & pf.* **mummy**[1] *n.* му́мия.

mummy[2] ['mʌmɪ] *n.* (*mother*) ма́ма, ма́мочка.

mumps [mʌmps] *n.* свинка.

munch [mʌntʃ] *v.t.* жева́ть (жую́, жуёшь) *impf.*

mundane [mʌn'deɪn] *adj.* земно́й.

Munich ['mjuːnɪk] *n.* Мю́нхен.

municipal [mjuː'nɪsɪp(ə)l] *adj.* муниципа́льный, городско́й. **municipality** [mjuː,nɪsɪ'pælɪtɪ] *n.* муниципалите́т.

munificence [mjuː'nɪfɪs(ə)ns] *n.* ще́дрость. **munificent** *adj.* ще́дрый (щедр, -а́, -о).

munitions [mjuː'nɪʃ(ə)ns] *n.* вое́нное иму́щество.

mural ['mjuər(ə)l] *adj.* стенно́й; *n.* стенна́я ро́спись.

murder ['mɜːdə(r)] *n.* уби́йство; *v.t.* убива́ть *impf.*, уби́ть (убью́, -ьёшь) *pf.*; (*language*) кове́ркать *impf.*, ис~ *pf.* **murderer, murderess** *n.* уби́йца *c.g.* **murderous** *adj.* уби́йственный (-ен, -енна), смертоно́сный.

murky ['mɜːkɪ] *adj.* тёмный (-мен, -мна́), мра́чный (-чен, -чна́, -чно).

murmur ['mɜːmə(r)] *n.* (*of water*) журча́ние; (*of voices*) шёпот; (*of discontent*) ро́пот; **without a** ~ безро́потно; *v.i.* журча́ть (-чи́т) *impf.*; ропта́ть (ропщу́, -щешь) *impf.* (**at** на+*a.*); *v.t.* шепта́ть (шепчу́, -чешь) *impf.*, шепну́ть *pf.*

muscle ['mʌs(ə)l] *n.* мы́шца, му́скул. **muscular** *adj.* мы́шечный, му́скульный; (*person*) мускули́стый.

Muscovite ['mʌskə,vaɪt] *n.* москви́ч (-а́), ~ка.

muse[1] [mjuːz] *v.i.* размышля́ть *impf.*

muse[2] [mjuːz] *n.* му́за.

museum [mjuː'zɪəm] *n.* музе́й.

mushroom ['mʌʃrʊm, -ruːm] *n.* гриб (-а́); (*cultivated*) шампиньо́н; ~ **cloud** грибови́дное о́блако (*pl.* -ка́, -ко́в).

music ['mjuːzɪk] *n.* му́зыка; (*sheet* ~) но́ты *f.pl.*; **play without** ~ игра́ть *impf.*, сыгра́ть *pf.* без нот; ~ **stand** пюпи́тр. **musical** *adj.* музыка́льный; ~ **comedy** музыка́льная коме́дия; *n.* музыка́льная (кино)коме́дия. **musician** [mjuː'zɪʃ(ə)n] *n.* музыка́нт; (*composer*) компози́тор. **music-hall** *n.* мю́зикхо́лл. **musi'cologist** *n.* музыкове́д. **musi'cology** *n.* музыкове́дение. **music-paper** *n.* но́тная бума́га.

musk [mʌsk] *n.* му́скус; ~ **deer** кабарга́ (*g.pl.* -ро́г); ~ **melon** ды́ня.

musket ['mʌskɪt] *n.* мушке́т. **muske'teer** *n.* мушкетёр.

muskrat ['mʌskræt] *n.* онда́тра.

musky ['mʌskɪ] *adj.* му́скусный.

muslin ['mʌzlɪn] *n.* мусли́н, кисея́; *adj.* мусли́новый, кисе́йный.

mussel ['mʌs(ə)l] *n.* съедо́бная ми́дия.

must[1] [mʌst] *n.* муст; (*new wine*) молодо́е вино́.

must[2] [mʌst] *v.aux.* (*obligation*) до́лжен (-жна́) *pred.*+*inf.*; на́до *impers.*+*d. & inf.*; (*necessity*) ну́жно *impers.*+*d. & inf.*; ~ **not** (*prohibition*) нельзя́ *impers.*+*d. & inf.*; *n.* необходи́мость.

mustard ['mʌstəd] *n.* горчи́ца; ~ **gas** горчи́чный газ; ~ **plaster** горчи́чник; ~ **pot** горчи́чница.

musty ['mʌstɪ] *adj.* за́тхлый.

mutant ['mjuːt(ə)nt] *adj.* мута́нтный; *n.* мута́нт. **mu'tation** *n.* мута́ция.

mute [mjuːt] *adj.* (*dumb*) немо́й (нем, -а́, -о); (*silent*) безмо́лвный; *n.* немо́й *sb.*; (*mus.*) сурди́нка. **muted** *adj.* приглушённый (-ён, -ена́); **with** ~ **strings** под сурди́нку.

mutilate ['mjuːtɪ,leɪt] *v.t.* уве́чить *impf.*, из~ *pf.*; кале́чить *impf.*, ис~ *pf.* **muti'lation** *n.* уве́чье.

mutineer [,mjuːtɪ'nɪə(r)] *n.* мяте́жник. '**mutinous** *adj.* мяте́жный. '**mutiny** *n.* мяте́ж (-а́); *v.i.* бунтова́ть *impf.*, взбунтова́ться *pf.*

mutism ['mjuːtɪz(ə)m] *n.* немота́.

mutter ['mʌtə(r)] *v.i.* бормота́ть (-очу́, -о́чешь) *impf.*; ворча́ть (-чу́, -чи́шь) *impf.*; *n.* бормота́ние, ворча́ние.

mutton ['mʌt(ə)n] *n.* бара́нина.

mutual ['mjuːtʃʊəl, -tjʊəl] *adj.* взаи́мный, взаимо...; (*common*) о́бщий; ~ **benefit** ка́сса взаимопо́мощи; ~ **friend** о́бщий друг (*pl.* друзья́, -зе́й).

muzzle ['mʌz(ə)l] *n.* (*animal's*) мо́рда; (*on animal*) намо́рдник; (*of gun*) ду́ло; *v.t.* надева́ть *impf.*, наде́ть (-е́ну, -е́нешь) *pf.* намо́рдник на+*a.*; (*impose silence*) заставля́ть

impf., заста́вить *pf.* молча́ть.
muzzy ['mʌzɪ] *adj.* тума́нный (-нен, -нна).
MW *abbr. (of* **megawatt(s))** МВт, мегава́тт.
my [maɪ] *poss.pron.* мой (моя́, моё; мои́);
свой (своя́, своё; свои́).
myopia [maɪ'əʊpɪə] *n.* близору́кость. **myopic**
[maɪ'ɒpɪk] *adj.* близору́кий.
myriad ['mɪrɪəd] *n.* мириа́ды (-д) *pl.; adj.*
бесчи́сленный (-ен, -енна).
myrrh [mɜ:(r)] *n.* ми́рра.
myrtle ['mɜ:t(ə)l] *n.* мирт; *attr.* ми́ртовый.
myself [maɪ'self] *pron. (emph.)* (я) сам (-ого́,
-ому́, -и́м, -о́м), сама́ (-мо́й, *a.* -му́); *(refl.)*
себя́ (себе́, собо́й); -ся *(suffixed to v.t.).*
mysterious [mɪ'stɪərɪəs] *adj.* таи́нственный
(-ен, -енна). **mystery** ['mɪstərɪ] *n.* та́йна;
(relig. rite; play) мисте́рия.
mystic(al) ['mɪstɪk(ə)l] *adj.* мисти́ческий; *n.*
ми́стик. **mysticism** *n.* мистици́зм. **mystifi-
'cation** *n.* мистифика́ция. **mystify** ['mɪstɪfaɪ]
v.t. озада́чивать *impf.*, озада́чить *pf.*
myth [mɪθ] *n.* миф. **mythical** *adj.* мифи́че-
ский. **mytho'logical** *adj.* мифологи́ческий.
my'thologist *n.* мифо́лог. **my'thology** *n.*
мифоло́гия.

N

nacre ['neɪkə(r)] *n.* перламу́тр. **nacr(e)ous**
adj. перламу́тровый.
nadir ['neɪdɪə(r), 'næd-] *n.* нади́р; *(lowest
point)* са́мый ни́зкий у́ровень (-вня) *m.*
nag¹ [næg] *n. (horse)* ло́шадь *(pl.* -ди, -де́й,
i. -дьми́).
nag² [næg] *v.i.:* ~ **at** пили́ть (-лю́, -лишь)
impf.+a.; (of pain) ныть (но́ет) *impf.*
naiad ['naɪæd] *n.* ная́да.
nail [neɪl] *n. (finger-, toe-~)* но́готь (-гтя; *pl.*
-гти, -гте́й) *m.; (claw)* ко́готь (-гтя; *pl.* -гти,
-гте́й) *m.; (metal spike)* гвоздь (-дя́; *pl.* -ди,
-де́й) *m.;* ~ **varnish** лак для ногте́й; *v.t.*
прибива́ть *impf.*, приби́ть (-бью́ -бьёшь)
pf. (гвоздя́ми). **nail-brush** *n.* щёточка для
ногте́й. **nail-file** *n.* пи́лка для ногте́й. **nail-
scissors** *n.* но́жницы (-ц) *pl.* для ногте́й.
naive [nɑː'iːv, naɪ'iːv] *adj.* наи́вный. **naivety**
n. наи́вность.
naked ['neɪkɪd] *adj.* го́лый (гол, -а́, -о), наго́й
(наг, -а́, -о); обнажённый (-ён, -ена́); ~ **eye**
невооружённый глаз; ~ **light** незащищённый свет; ~ **sword** обнажённый меч (-а́);
~ **truth** чи́стая пра́вда. **nakedness** *n.* на-
гота́.
name [neɪm] *n.* назва́ние; *(forename)* и́мя *nt.;*
(surname) фами́лия; *(reputation)* репута́ция;

what is his ~? как его́ зову́т?; **in the** ~ **of** во
и́мя+g.; *v.t.* называ́ть *impf.*, назва́ть (назову́,
-вёшь; назва́л, -а́, -о) *pf.; (appoint)* назна-
ча́ть *impf.*, назна́чить *pf.* **name-day** *n.* име-
ни́ны (-н) *pl.* **nameless** *adj.* безымя́нный.
namely *adv.* (a) и́менно; то есть. **name-part**
n. загла́вная роль. **name-plate** *n.* доще́чка
с фами́лией. **namesake** *n.* тёзка *c.g.*
nanny ['nænɪ] *n.* ня́ня. **nanny-goat** *n.* коза́
(pl. -зы).
nap¹ [næp] *n. (sleep)* коро́ткий сон (сна); *v.i.*
вздремну́ть *pf.*
nap² [næp] *n. (on cloth)* ворс.
napalm ['neɪpɑːm] *n.* напа́лм.
nape [neɪp] *n.* загри́вок (-вка)
napkin ['næpkɪn] *n.* салфе́тка.
Naples ['neɪp(ə)lz] *n.* Неа́поль *(m.).*
narcissus [nɑː'sɪsəs] *n.* нарци́сс.
narcosis [nɑː'kəʊsɪs] *n.* нарко́з. **narcotic**
[nɑː'kɒtɪk] *adj.* наркоти́ческий; *n.* нарко́тик.
nark [nɑːk] *n. (spy)* лега́вый *sb.*, стука́ч (-а́);
v.t. (irritate) раздража́ть *impf.*, раздражи́ть
pf.
narrate [nə'reɪt] *v.t.* расска́зывать *impf.*, рас-
сказа́ть (-ажу́, -а́жешь) *pf.;* повествова́ть
impf. o+*p.* **narration** *n.* повествова́ние.
narrative ['nærətɪv] *n.* расска́з, по́весть *(pl.*
-ти, -те́й); *adj.* повествова́тельный. **narrator** *n.* расска́зчик, повествова́тель *m.*
narrow ['nærəʊ] *adj.* у́зкий (у́зок, узка́, у́зко;
у́зки́), те́сный (-сен, -сна́, -сно); *(restricted)*
ограни́ченный (-ен, -енна); *n.: pl.* у́зкая
часть; *(strait)* у́зкий проли́в; *v.t. & i.* су́жи-
вать(ся) *impf.*, су́зить(ся) *pf.* **narrow-gauge**
adj. узкоколе́йный. **narrowly** *adv. (hardly)*
чуть, е́ле-е́ле; **he** ~ **escaped drowning** он
чуть не утону́л. **narrow-minded** *adj.* ограни́-
ченный (-ен, -енна). **narrowness** *n.* у́зо-
сть, ограни́ченность.
narwhal ['nɑː(w)ə)l] *n.* нарва́л.
NASA ['næsə] *abbr. (of* **National Aeronautics
and Space Administration)** НАСА.
nasal ['neɪz(ə)l] *adj.* носово́й; *(voice)* гнуса́-
вый.
nascent ['næs(ə)nt, 'neɪs-] *adj.* рожда́ющийся.
nasturtium [nə'stɜːʃəm] *n.* настурция.
nasty ['nɑːstɪ] *adj.* га́дкий (-док, -дка́, -дко),
проти́вный; *(dirty)* гря́зный (-зен, -зна́,
-зно); *(person)* зло́бный.
nation ['neɪʃ(ə)n] *n.* на́ция; *(people)* наро́д;
(country) страна́ *(pl.* -ны). **national** ['næʃə-
n(ə)l] *adj.* национа́льный, наро́дный; *(of the
state)* госуда́рственный; *n.* по́дданный *sb.*
nationalism *n.* национали́зм. **nationalist** *n.*
национали́ст, ~ка. **nationa'listic** *adj.* на-
ционалисти́ческий. **natio'nality** *n.* нацио-
на́льность; *(citizenship)* гражда́нство, по́д-
данство. **nationali'zation** *n.* национали-
за́ция. **nationalize** *v.t.* национализи́ровать
impf. & pf.
native ['neɪtɪv] *n. (~ of)* уроже́нец (-нца), -нка
(+*g.*); тузе́мец (-мца), -мка; *adj. (natural)*
приро́дный; *(of one's birth)* родно́й; *(indig-*

enous) туземный; (*local*) местный; ~ **land** родина; ~ **language** родной язык; ~ **speaker** носитель *m.* языка.

nativity [nə'tɪvɪtɪ] *n.* Рождество (Христово).

NATO ['neɪtəʊ] *abbr.* (*of North Atlantic Treaty Organization*) НАТО; ~ **member** натовец; *adj.* натовский.

natter ['nætə(r)] *v.i.* болтать *impf.*; *n.* болтовня.

natural ['nætʃ(ə)l] *adj.* естественный (-ен, -енна), природный; ~ **death** естественная смерть; ~ **resources** природные богатства *nt.pl.*; ~ **selection** естественный отбор; *n.* (*person*) самородок (-дка); (*mus.*) бекар.

naturalism *n.* натурализм. **naturalist** *n.* натуралист. **natura'listic** *adj.* натуралистический. **naturali'zation** *n.* (*of alien*) натурализация; (*of plant, animal*) акклиматизация. **naturalize** *v.t.* натурализировать *impf.* & *pf.*; акклиматизировать *impf.* & *pf.* **naturally** *adv.* естественно, по природе; (*of course*) конечно, как и следовало ожидать.

nature ['neɪtʃə(r)] *n.* природа; (*character*) характер; **by** ~ по природе; **in the** ~ **of** вроде+g.; **second** ~ вторая натура; **state of** ~ первобытное состояние; ~ **reserve** заповедник. **naturopath** [,neɪtʃərə'pæθ] *n.* натуропат. **naturopathy** [,neɪtʃə'rɒpəθɪ] *n.* натуропатия.

naughtiness ['nɔːtɪnɪs] *n.* (*disobedience*) непослушание; (*mischief*) шалости *f.pl.* **naughty** *adj.* непослушный; шаловливый.

nausea ['nɔːzɪə, -sɪə] *n.* тошнота; (*loathing*) отвращение. **nauseate** *v.t.* тошнить *impf. impers.* от+g.; быть противным+d.; **the idea** ~**s me** меня тошнит от этой мысли; эта мысль мне противна. **nauseous** *adj.* тошнотворный; (*loathsome*) отвратительный.

nautical ['nɔːtɪk(ə)l] *n.* морской.

naval ['neɪv(ə)l] *adj.* (военно-)морской, флотский.

nave [neɪv] *n.* неф.

navel ['neɪv(ə)l] *n.* пупок (-пка).

navigable ['nævɪgəb(ə)l] *adj.* судоходный. **navigate** *v.t.* (*ship*) вести (веду, -дёшь; вёл, -а) *impf.*; (*sea*) плавать *impf.* **navi'gation** *n.* навигация. **navigator** *n.* штурман.

navvy ['nævɪ] *n.* землекоп.

navy ['neɪvɪ] *n.* военно-морской флот (*pl.* -оты, -отов); ~ **blue** тёмно-синий.

Nazi ['nɑːtsɪ, 'nɑːzɪ] *n.* нацист, ~ка; *adj.* нацистский. **Nazism** *n.* нацизм.

NB *abbr.* (*of nota bene*) нотабене.

near [nɪə(r)] *adv.* близко, недалеко; **far and** ~ повсюду; ~ **at hand** под рукой; ~ **by** рядом; *prep.* возле+g., около+g., у+g.; *adj.* близкий; ~ **miss** близкий промах; *v.t.* & *i.*, приближаться *impf.*, приблизиться *pf.* к+d.; подходить (-ожу, -одишь) *impf.*, подойти (-ойду, -ойдёшь; -ошёл, -ошла) *pf.* к+d.

nearly ['nɪəlɪ] *adv.* почти, приблизительно.

near-sighted [nɪə'saɪtɪd] *adj.* близорукий.

neat [niːt] *adj.* (*tidy*) опрятный, аккуратный; (*clear*) чёткий (-ток, -тка, -тко); (*undiluted*)

неразбавленный (-ен, -ена).

nebula ['nebjʊlə] *n.* туманность. **nebular** *adj.* небулярный. **nebulous** *adj.* неясный (-сен, -сна, -сно), туманный (-нен, -нна).

necessarily ['nesəsərɪlɪ, -'serɪlɪ] *adv.* неизбежно. **'necessary** *adj.* нужный (-жен, -жна, -жно, -жны), необходимый; (*inevitable*) неизбежный; *n.* необходимое *sb.* **ne'cessitate** *v.t.* делать *impf.*, с~ *pf.* необходимым; (*involve*) влечь (-ечёт, -екут; влёк, -ла) *impf.* за собой. **ne'cessity** *n.* необходимость; неизбежность; (*object*) предмет первой необходимости; (*poverty*) нужда.

neck [nek] *n.* шея; (*of garment*) вырез; (*of bottle*) горлышко (*pl.* -шки, -шек, -шкам); (*isthmus*) перешеек (-ейка); **get it in the** ~ получить *pf.* по шее; **risk one's** ~ рисковать *impf.* головой; **up to one's** ~ по горло, по уши; ~ **and** ~ голова в голову; ~ **or nothing** либо пан, либо пропал. **neckband** *n.* ворот. **neckerchief** *n.* шейный платок (-тка). **necklace** ['nekləs, -lɪs] *n.* ожерелье (*g.pl.* -лий). **necklet** *n.* ожерелье (*g.pl.* -лий); (*fur*) горжётка. **neckline** *n.* вырез. **necktie** *n.* галстук.

necromancer ['nekrəʊ,mænsə(r)] *n.* колдун (-а). **necromancy** *n.* чёрная магия, колдовство.

nectar ['nektə(r)] *n.* нектар.

née [neɪ] *adj.* урождённая.

need [niːd] *n.* нужда, надобность, потребность; *v.t.* нуждаться *impf.* в+p.; **I** (*etc.*) ~ мне (*d.*) нужен+*nom.*; **I** ~ **five roubles** мне нужно пять рублей.

needle ['niːd(ə)l] *n.* игла (*pl.* -лы), иголка; (*knitting*) спица; (*pointer*) стрелка; *pl.* (*pine-*~) хвоя; *v.t.* раздражать *impf.*, раздражить *pf.*

needless ['niːdlɪs] *adj.* ненужный, излишний; ~ **to say** не приходится и говорить. **needy** *adj.* нуждающийся, бедствующий.

negation [nɪ'geɪʃ(ə)n] *n.* отрицание. **negative** ['negətɪv] *adj.* отрицательный, негативный; ~ **quantity** отрицательная величина; ~ **result** негативный результат; *n.* отрицание; (*gram.*) отрицательное слово (*pl.* -ва); (*phot.*) негатив; **in the** ~ отрицательно; отрицательный.

neglect [nɪ'glekt] *v.t.* пренебрегать *impf.*, пренебречь (-егу, -ежёшь; -ёг, -егла) *pf.*+i.; не заботиться *impf.* о+p.; (*abandon*) забрасывать *impf.*, забросить *pf.*; (*not fulfil*) не выполнять *impf.*+g.; *n.* пренебрежение; (*condition*) заброшенность. **neglectful** *adj.* небрежный, невнимательный (**of** к+d.). **negligence** ['neglɪdʒ(ə)ns] *n.* небрежность, нерадивость. **negligent** *adj.* небрежный, нерадивый. **negligible** *adj.* незначительный.

negotiate [nɪ'gəʊʃɪ,eɪt] *v.i.* вести (веду, -дёшь; вёл, -а) *impf.* переговоры; *v.t.* (*arrange*) заключать *impf.*, заключить *pf.*; (*overcome*) преодолевать *impf.*, преодолеть *pf.*

negoti'ation *n.* (*discussion*) перегово́ры *m.pl.*

Negress ['niːgrɪs] *n.* негритя́нка. **Negro** *n.* негр; *adj.* негритя́нский.

neigh [neɪ] *n.* ржа́ние; *v.i.* ржать (ржу, ржёшь) *impf.*

neighbour ['neɪbə(r)] *n.* сосе́д (*pl.* -и, -ей), ~ка. **neighbourhood** *n.* (*vicinity*) сосе́дство; (*area*) ме́стность; **in the** ~ **of** о́коло+g. **neighbouring** *adj.* сосе́дний. **neighbourly** *adj.* доброcосе́дский.

neither ['naɪðə(r), 'niːð-] *adv.* та́кже не, то́же не; *pron.* ни тот, ни друго́й; ~ ... **nor** ни... ни.

nemesis ['nemɪsɪs] *n.* возме́здие.

neocolonialism [ˌniːəʊkə'ləʊnɪəˌlɪz(ə)m] *n.* неоколониали́зм.

neolithic [ˌniːə'lɪθɪk] *adj.* неолити́ческий.

neologism [niː'ɒlədʒɪz(ə)m] *n.* неологи́зм.

neon ['niːɒn] *n.* нео́н; *attr.* нео́новый.

nephew ['nevjuː, 'nef-] *n.* племя́нник.

nepotism ['nepəˌtɪz(ə)m] *n.* кумовство́.

Neptune ['neptjuːn] *n.* Непту́н.

nerve [nɜːv] *n.* нерв; (*assurance*) самооблада́ние; (*impudence*) на́глость; *pl.* (*nervousness*) нерво́зность; **get on the** ~**s of** де́йствовать *impf.*, по~ *pf.*+d. на не́рвы. **nerveless** *adj.* бесси́льный. **nervous** *adj.* не́рвный (-рвен, -рвна́, -рвно); ~ **breakdown** не́рвное расстро́йство. **nervy** *adj.* нерво́зный.

nest [nest] *n.* гнездо́ (*pl.* -ёзда); ~ **egg** сбереже́ния *nt.pl.*; *v.i.* гнезди́ться *impf.*; вить (вью, вьёшь; вил, -á, -о) *impf.*, свить (совью́, -ьёшь; свил, -á, -о) *pf.* (себе́) гнездо́. **nestle** ['nes(ə)l] *v.i.* льнуть *impf.*, при~ *pf.* **nestling** ['neslɪŋ, 'nest-] *n.* птене́ц (-нца́).

net[1] [net] *n.* сеть (*loc.* се́ти; *pl.* -ти, -те́й), се́тка; *v.t.* (*catch*) лови́ть (-влю́, -вишь) *impf.*, пойма́ть *pf.* сетя́ми; (*cover*) закрыва́ть *impf.*, закры́ть (-ро́ю, -ро́ешь) *pf.* се́ткой.

net[2] [net], **nett** *adj.* не́тто; *indecl.* чи́стый (чист, -á, -о, чи́сты); ~ **price** цена́ не́тто; ~ **profit** чи́стая при́быль; ~ **weight** чи́стый вес, вес не́тто; *v.t.* получа́ть *impf.*, получи́ть (-чу́, -чишь) *pf.* ... чи́стого дохо́да.

Netherlands ['neðələndz] *n.* Нидерла́нды (-ов) *pl.*

nettle ['net(ə)l] *n.* крапи́ва; *v.t.* (*fig.*) раздража́ть *impf.*, раздражи́ть *pf.* **nettle-rash** *n.* крапи́вница.

network ['netwɜːk] *n.* сеть (*loc.* се́ти; *pl.* -ти, -те́й).

neuralgia [njʊə'rældʒə] *n.* невралги́я. **neurasthenia** [ˌnjʊərəs'θiːnɪə] *n.* неврастени́я. **neuritis** *n.* неври́т. **neurologist** *n.* невро́лог. **neurology** *n.* невроло́гия. **neurosis** *n.* невро́з. **neurotic** *adj.* невроти́ческий; *n.* невро́тик, нервнобольно́й *sb.*

neuter ['njuːtə(r)] *adj.* сре́дний, сре́днего ро́да; *n.* (*gender*) сре́дний род; (*word*) сло́во (*pl.* -вá) сре́днего ро́да; (*animal*) кастри-

рованное живо́тное *sb.*; *v.t.* кастри́ровать *impf.* & *pf.* **neutral** *adj.* нейтра́льный; (*indifferent*) безуча́стный; *n.* (*state*) нейтра́льное госуда́рство; (*person*) граждани́н (*pl.* -áне, -áн), -áнка, нейтра́льного госуда́рства; (*gear*) нейтра́льное положе́ние рычага́ коро́бки переда́ч; **in** ~ не включённый (-ён, -ена́). **neutrality** [njuː'trælɪtɪ] *n.* нейтралите́т; безуча́стность. **neutrali'zation** *n.* нейтрализа́ция. **neutralize** *v.t.* нейтрализова́ть *impf.* & *pf.* **neutron** *n.* нейтро́н.

Neva ['niːvə] *n.* Нева́.

never ['nevə(r)] *adv.* никогда́; ~! не мо́жет быть!; ~ **again** никогда́ бо́льше, бо́льше не; ~ **fear!** будь(те) увéрен(ы)!; ~ **mind** ничего́!; всё равно́!; ~ **once** ни ра́зу. **never-never** *n.*: **on the** ~ в рассро́чку. **nevertheless** *conj.*, *adv.* тем не ме́нее.

new [njuː] *adj.* но́вый (нов, -á, -о); (*fresh*) све́жий (свеж, -á, -ó, свéжи́); (*young*) молодо́й (мо́лод, -á, -о); **N**~ **Year** Но́вый год; **N**~ **York** Нью-Йо́рк; **N**~ **Zealand** Но́вая Зела́ндия. **new-born** *adj.* новорождённый. **newcomer** *n.* пришéлец (-льца). **newfangled** *adj.* новомо́дный. **newly** *adv.* (*recently*) неда́вно; (*in new manner*) за́ново, вновь.

newel ['njuːəl] *n.* коло́нка винтово́й ле́стницы.

news [njuːz] *n.* но́вость, -ти *pl.*, извéстие, -ия *pl.*; ~ **agency** агéнтство печа́ти. **newsagent** *n.* газе́тчик. **newsflash** [njuːz] *n.* сро́чное сообще́ние. **newsletter** *n.* информацио́нный бюллете́нь *m.* **newspaper** *n.* газе́та. **newsprint** *n.* газе́тная бума́га. **newsreel** *n.* кинохро́ника. **news-vendor** *n.* газе́тчик, продавéц (-вца́) газе́т.

newt [njuːt] *n.* трито́н.

next [nekst] *adj.* сле́дующий, бу́дущий; *adv.* в сле́дующий раз; пото́м, затéм; ~ **door** по сосéдству; (*house*) в сосéднем до́ме; (*flat*) в сосéдней кварти́ре; ~ **door to** (*fig.*) почти́; ~ **of kin** ближа́йший ро́дственник; ~ **to** ря́дом с+*i.*, о́коло+g.; (*fig.*) почти́. **next-door** *adj.* сосéдний.

nexus ['neksəs] *n.* связь.

NHS *abbr.* (*of National Health Service*) Национа́льная слу́жба здравоохранéния.

nib [nɪb] *n.* перо́ (*pl.* пéрья, -ьев).

nibble ['nɪb(ə)l] *v.t.* & *i.* грызть (-зу́, -зёшь; -з) *impf.*; обгрыза́ть *impf.*, обгры́зть (-зу́, -зёшь; -з) *pf.*; (*grass*) щипа́ть (-плет) *impf.*; (*fish*) клева́ть (клюёт) *impf.*

Nice ['niːs] *n.* Ни́цца.

nice [naɪs] *adj.* (*precise*) то́чный (-чен, -чна́, -чно); (*subtle*) то́нкий (-нок, -нка́, -нко, то́нки́); (*pleasant*) прия́тный (*also iron.*); хоро́ший (-ш, -шá); (*person*) ми́лый (мил, -á, -о, ми́лы́), любéзный. **nicety** ['naɪsɪtɪ] *n.* то́чность; то́нкость; **to a** ~ то́чно, вполнé.

niche [nɪtʃ, niːʃ] *n.* ни́ша; (*fig.*) своё, надлежа́щее, мéсто.

nick [nɪk] *n.* зару́бка, засе́чка; **in the ~ of time** в са́мый после́дний моме́нт; как раз во́время; *v.t.* де́лать *impf.*, с~ *pf.* зару́бку, засе́чку, на+*a.*

nickel ['nɪk(ə)l] *n.* ни́кель *m.*; *attr.* ни́келевый. **nickel-plate** *v.t.* никелирова́ть *impf. & pf.*

nickname ['nɪkneɪm] *n.* про́звище, прозва́ние; *v.t.* прозыва́ть *impf.*, прозва́ть (прозову́, -вёшь; прозва́л, -á, -о) *pf.*

nicotine ['nɪkətiːn] *n.* никоти́н.

niece [niːs] *n.* племя́нница.

niggardly ['nɪgədlɪ] *adj.* (*miserly*) скупо́й (скуп, -á, -о); (*scanty*) ску́дный (-ден, -днá, -дно).

niggling ['nɪglɪŋ] *adj.* ме́лочный.

night [naɪt] *n.* ночь (*loc.* -чи́; *pl.* -чи, -че́й); (*evening*) ве́чер (*pl.* -á); **at ~** но́чью; **first ~** премье́ра; **last ~** вчера́ ве́чером; **~ and day** непреста́нно; *attr.* ночно́й. **nightcap** *n.* ночно́й колпа́к (-á); (*drink*) стака́нчик спиртно́го на́ ночь. **nightclub** *n.* ночно́й клуб. **nightdress** *n.* ночна́я руба́шка. **nightfall** *n.* наступле́ние но́чи. **nightgown** *n.* ночна́я руба́шка. **nightingale** *n.* солове́й (-вья́). **nightjar** *n.* козодо́й. **night-light** *n.* ночни́к (-á). **nightly** *adj.* ночно́й; (*every night*) ежено́щный; *adv.* ежено́щно. **nightmare** *n.* кошма́р. **nightmarish** *adj.* кошма́рный.

nihilism ['naɪɪˌlɪz(ə)m, 'naɪhɪˌlɪz(ə)m] *n.* нигили́зм. **nihilist** *n.* нигили́ст. **nihi'listic** *adj.* нигилисти́ческий.

nil [nɪl] *n.* ноль (-ля́) *m.*

nimble ['nɪmb(ə)l] *adj.* прово́рный; (*mind*) ги́бкий (-бок, -бкá, -бко).

nimbus ['nɪmbəs] *n.* нимб; (*cloud*) дождево́е о́блако (*pl.* -ká, -ко́в).

nine [naɪn] *adj. & n.* де́вять (-ти́, -тью́) (*collect.*; *9 pairs*) де́вятеро (-ры́х); (*cards*; *number 9*) девя́тка; (*time*) де́вять (часо́в); (*age*) де́вять лет. **ninepins** *n.* ке́гли (-лей) *pl.* **nine'teen** *adj. & n.* девятна́дцать (-ти, -тью); (*age*) девятна́дцать лет. **nine'teenth** *adj. & n.* девятна́дцатый; (*fraction*) девятна́дцатая (часть (*pl.* -ти, -те́й)); (*date*) девятна́дцатое (число́). **ninetieth** *adj. & n.* девяно́стый; (*fraction*) девяно́стая (часть (*pl.* -ти, -те́й)). **ninety** *adj. & n.* девяно́сто (-та); (*age*) девяно́сто лет; *pl.* (*decade*) девяно́стые го́ды (-до́в) *m.pl.* **ninth** *adj. & n.* девя́тый; (*fraction*) девя́тая (часть (*pl.* -ти, -те́й)); (*date*) девя́тое (число́); (*mus.*) но́на.

nip[1] [nɪp] *v.t.* (*pinch*) щипа́ть (-плю́, -плешь) *impf.*, щипну́ть *pf.*; (*bite*) куса́ть *impf.*, укуси́ть (-ушу́, -у́сишь) *pf.*; **~ along** слета́ть *pf.*; **~ in the bud** пресека́ть *impf.*, пресе́чь (-еку́, -ечёшь; -ёк, -екла́) *pf.* в ко́рне; *n.* щипо́к (-пка́); уку́с; **there's a ~ in the air** во́здух па́хнет моро́зцем. **nipper** *n.* (*boy*) мальчуга́н.

nip[2] [nɪp] *n.* (*drink*) глото́к (-ткá), рю́мочка. **nipple** ['nɪp(ə)l] *n.* сосо́к (-скá); (*tech.*) ни́п-

пель (*pl.* -ли & -ля́) *m.*

nirvana [nɜːˈvɑːnə, nɪə-] *n.* нирва́на.

nit [nɪt] *n.* гни́да.

nitrate ['naɪtreɪt] *n.* нитра́т. **nitre** *n.* сели́тра. **nitric** *adj.* азо́тный. **nitrogen** *n.* азо́т. **nitrogenous** [ˌnaɪˈtrɒdʒɪnəs] *adj.* азо́тный. **nitroglycerine** *n.* нитроглицери́н. **nitrous** *adj.* азо́тистый; **~ oxide** зáкись азо́та.

nitwit ['nɪtwɪt] *n.* простофи́ля *c.g.*

No. *abbr.* (*of* **number**) №.

no [nəʊ] *adj.* (*not any*) никако́й, не оди́н; (*not a*) (совсе́м) не; *adv.* нет; (*нисколько*) не+*compar.*: *n.* отрица́ние, отка́з; (*in vote*) го́лос (*pl.* -á) „про́тив"; **~ doubt** коне́чно, несомне́нно; **~ fear** коне́чно, нет!; **~ longer** уже́ не, бо́льше не; **~ wonder** не удиви́тельно.

no one ['nəʊ wʌn] *pron.* никто́.

Noah's ark ['nəʊə, nɔː] *n.* Но́ев ковче́г.

nobility [nəʊˈbɪlɪtɪ] *n.* (*class*) дворя́нство; (*quality*) благоро́дство. **noble** ['nəʊb(ə)l] *adj.* дворя́нский, зна́тный; благоро́дный. **nobleman** *n.* дворяни́н (*pl.* -я́не, -я́н).

nobody ['nəʊbədɪ] *pron.* никто́; *n.* ничто́жество.

nocturnal [nɒkˈtɜːn(ə)l] *adj.* ночно́й. **'nocturne** *n.* ноктю́рн.

nod [nɒd] *v.i.* кива́ть *impf.*, кивну́ть *pf.* голово́й; (*drowsily*) клева́ть (клюю́, клюёшь) *impf.* но́сом; **~ding acquaintance** пове́рхностное знако́мство; *n.* киво́к (-вкá).

nodule ['nɒdjuːl] *n.* узело́к (-лкá).

noggin ['nɒgɪn] *n.* кру́жечка.

noise [nɔɪz] *n.* шум (-а(у)); (*radio*) поме́хи *f.pl.* **noiseless** *adj.* бесшу́мный. **noisy** *adj.* шу́мный (-мен, -мнá, -мно).

nomad ['nəʊmæd] *n.* коче́вник. **no'madic** *adj.* кочево́й, кочу́ющий.

nomenclature [nəʊˈmenklətʃə(r), 'nəʊmənˌkleɪtʃə(r)] *n.* номенклату́ра. **nominal** ['nɒmɪn(ə)l] *adj.* номина́льный; (*gram.*) именно́й. **nominate** *v.t.* (*propose*) выдвига́ть *impf.*, вы́двинуть *pf.*; (*appoint*) назнача́ть *impf.*, назна́чить *pf.* **nomi'nation** *n.* выдвиже́ние; назначе́ние. **nominative** *adj.* (*n.*) имени́тельный (паде́ж (-á)). **nomi'nee** *n.* кандида́т.

non- [nɒn] *pref.* не..., без... . **non-acceptance** *n.* неприня́тие.

nonage ['nəʊnɪdʒ, 'nɒn-] *n.* несовершенноле́тие.

nonagenarian [ˌnəʊnədʒɪˈneərɪən, ˌnɒn-] *n.* девяностоле́тний стари́к (-á), -няя стару́ха.

non-aggression [ˌnɒnəˈgreʃ(ə)n] *n.* ненападе́ние; **~ pact** пакт о ненападе́нии. **nonalcoholic** *adj.* безалкого́льный. **non-alignment** *n.* неприсоедине́ние. **non-appearance** *n.* (*leg.*) нея́вка (в суд). **non-arrival** *n.* неприбы́тие.

nonchalance ['nɒnʃələns] *n.* (*indifference*) безразли́чие; (*carelessness*) беспе́чность. **nonchalant** *n.* безразли́чный; беспе́чный.

non-combatant [nɒnˈkɒmbət(ə)nt] *adj.* нестроево́й. **non-commissioned** adj.; ~ officer у́нтер-офице́р. **non-committal** adj. укло́нчивый. **non-conductor** n. непроводни́к (-а́).

non-conformist [ˌnɒnkən'fɔːmɪst] n. дисси-де́нт; adj. диссиде́нтский.

nondescript ['nɒndɪskrɪpt] adj. неопределён-ный (-нен, -нна), неопределённого ви́да.

none [nʌn] pron. (no one) никто́; (nothing) ничто́; (not one) не оди́н; adv. совсе́м не; ничу́ть не; ~ **the less** тем не ме́нее.

nonentity [nɒ'nentɪtɪ] n. ничто́жество.

non-essential [ˌnɒnɪ'senʃ(ə)l] adj. несуще́ст-венный (-ен(ен), -енна). **non-existence** n. небытие́ (i. -ие́м, p. -ии́). **non-existent** adj. несуществу́ющий. **non-ferrous** adj. цветно́й. **non-interference**, **-intervention** n. невмеша́тельство. **non-party** adj. беспарти́йный. **non-payment** n. неплатёж (-а́).

nonplus [nɒn'plʌs] v.t. ста́вить impf., по~ pf. в тупи́к.

non-proliferation [ˌnɒnprəˌlɪfə'reɪʃ(ə)n] n. нераспростране́ние (я́дерного ору́жия). **non-productive** adj. непроизводи́тельный. **non-resident** adj. не прожива́ющий по ме́сту слу́жбы. **non-renewable** adj. невозо-бновля́емый. **non-resistance** n. непротивле́ние.

nonsense ['nɒns(ə)ns] n. вздор, ерунда́, чепуха́. **nonsensical** [nɒn'sensɪk(ə)l] adj. бес-смы́сленный (-ен, -енна).

non sequitur [nɒn 'sekwɪtə(r)] n. нелоги́чное заключе́ние.

non-skid [nɒn'skɪd], **-slip** adj. нескользя́щий. **non-smoker** n. (person) некуря́щий sb.; (compartment) ваго́н, купе́ nt.indecl., для некуря́щих. **non-stick** adj. противоприга́р-ный. **non-stop** adj. безостано́вочный; (flight) беспоса́дочный; adv. без остано́вок; без поса́док. **non-violence** n. ненаси́лие. **non-violent** adj. ненаси́льственный.

noodles ['nuːd(ə)lz] n. лапша́.

nook [nʊk] n. укро́мный уголо́к (-лка́); **every** ~ **and cranny** все углы́ и закоу́лки m.pl.

noon [nuːn] n. по́лдень (-лу́дня & -лдня́) m.; attr. полу́денный.

no one see **no**

noose [nuːs] n. пе́тля (g.pl. -тель); v.t. пойма́ть pf. арка́ном.

nor [nɔː(r), nə(r)] conj. и не; та́кже не, то́же не; **neither** ... ~ ни... ни.

norm [nɔːm] n. но́рма. **normal** adj. норма́ль-ный. **normality** [nɔː'mælɪtɪ] n. норма́ль-ность. **normalize** v.t. нормализова́ть impf. & pf.

north [nɔːθ] n. се́вер; (naut.) норд; adj. се́вер-ный; (naut.) но́рдовый; adv. к се́веру, на се́вер; **N~ Star** Поля́рная звезда́; ~ **wind** норд. **north-east** n. се́веро-восто́к; (naut.) норд-о́ст. **northeaster** n. норд-о́ст. **north-easterly**, **-eastern** adj. се́веро-восто́чный; (naut.) норд-о́стовый. **northerly** ['nɔːðəlɪ] adj. се́верный; (naut.) но́рдовый. **northern**

adj. се́верный; ~ **lights** се́верное сия́ние. **northerner** n. северя́нин (pl. -я́не, -я́н); жи́тель m., ~ница, се́вера. **northernmost** adj. са́мый се́верный. **northward(s)** adv. к се́веру, на се́вер. **north-west** n. се́веро-за́пад; (naut.) норд-ве́ст. **northwester** n. норд-ве́ст. **north-westerly, -western** adj. се́веро-за́падный; (naut.) норд-ве́стовый.

Norway ['nɔːweɪ] n. Норве́гия. **Norwegian** [nɔː'wiːdʒ(ə)n] adj. норве́жский; n. норве́-жец (-жца), -жка.

nose [nəʊz] n. нос (loc. -у́; pl. -ы́); (sense) чутьё; (of ship etc.) носова́я часть (pl. -ти, -те́й); (of rocket) голо́вка; v.t. ню́хать impf., по~ pf.; ~ **out** разню́хивать impf., разню́-хать pf.; v.i. (of ship etc.) осторо́жно про-двига́ться impf., продви́нуться pf. вперёд. **nosebag** n. то́рба. **nosebleed** n. кровоте-че́ние и́з носу. **nosedive** n. пике́ nt.indecl.; v.i. пики́ровать impf. & pf.

nostalgia [nɒ'stældʒɪə, -dʒə] n. тоска́ (по ро́дине, по пре́жнему). **nostalgic** adj. вызыва́ющий тоску́.

nostril ['nɒstrɪl] n. ноздря́ (pl. -ри, -рей).

not [nɒt] adv. не; нет; ни; ~ **at all** ниско́лько, ничу́ть; (reply to thanks) не сто́ит (благо-да́рности); ~ **half** (~ **at all**) совсе́м не; (very much) ужа́сно; ~ **once** ни ра́зу; ~ **that** не то, что́бы; ~ **too** дово́льно+neg.; ~ **to say** что́бы не сказа́ть; ~ **to speak of** не говоря́ уже́ о+p.

notable ['nəʊtəb(ə)l] adj. заме́тный, замеча́-тельный. **notably** adv. осо́бенно, заме́тно.

notary (public) ['nəʊtərɪ] n. нота́риус.

notation [nəʊ'teɪʃ(ə)n] n. нота́ция; (mus.) но́тное письмо́.

notch [nɒtʃ] n. зару́бка; v.t. заруба́ть impf., заруби́ть (-блю, -бишь) pf.

note [nəʊt] n. (record) заме́тка, запи́ска; (annotation) примеча́ние; (letter) запи́ска; (banknote) банкно́т; (mus.; dipl.) но́та; (tone) тон; (attention) внима́ние; ~ **of hand** ве́ксель (pl. -ля́) m.; **man of** ~ выдаю́щийся челове́к; **strike the right (a false)** ~ брать (беру́, -рёшь; брал, -а́, -о) impf., взять (возьму́, -мёшь; взял, -а́, -о) pf. (не)ве́рный тон; **take** ~ **of** обраща́ть impf., обрати́ть (-ащу́, -ати́шь) pf. внима́ние на+a.; v.t. отмеча́ть impf., отме́тить pf.; ~ **down** запи́сывать impf., записа́ть (-ишу́, -и́шешь) pf. **notebook** n. записна́я кни́жка, блокно́т. **notecase** n. бума́жник. **noted** adj. знаме-ни́тый, изве́стный (for +i.). **notepaper** n. почто́вая бума́га. **noteworthy** adj. досто́й-ный (-о́ин, -о́йна) внима́ния.

nothing ['nʌθɪŋ] n. ничто́, ничего́; ~ **but** ничего́ кро́ме+g., то́лько; ~ **of the kind** ничего́ подо́бного; **come to** ~ конча́ться impf., ко́нчиться pf. ниче́м; **for** ~ (free) да́ром; (in vain) зря, напра́сно; **have** ~ **to do with** не име́ть impf. никако́го отно-ше́ния к+d.; **there is (was)** ~ **for it (but to)** ничего́ друго́го не остаётся (остава́лось) (как); придётся (пришлóсь) +*inf.*; **to say ~ of** не говоря ужé о+*p.*

notice ['nəʊtɪs] *n.* (*sign*) объявлéние; (*intimation*) извещéние; (*warning*) предупреждéние; (*attention*) внимáние; (*review*) (печáтный) óтзыв; **at a moment's ~** немéдленно; **give (in) one's ~** подавáть (-даю, -даёшь) *impf.*, подáть (-áм, -áшь, -áст, -адим; пóдал, -á, -о) *pf.* заявлéние об ухóде с рабóты; **give s.o. ~** предупреждáть *impf.*, предупредить *pf.* об увольнéнии; **take no ~ of** не обращáть *impf.* внимáния на+*a.*; *v.t.* замечáть *impf.*, замéтить *pf.*; (*take ~ of*) обращáть *impf.*, обратить (-ащу, -атишь) *pf.* внимáние на+*a.* **noticeable** *adj.* замéтный. **notice-board** *n.* доскá (*a.* -ску; *pl.* -ски, -сóк, -скáм) для объявлéний. **notifiable** ['nəʊtɪˌfaɪəb(ə)l] *adj.* подлежáщий регистрáции. **notification** [ˌnəʊtɪfɪ'keɪʃ(ə)n] *n.* извещéние, уведомлéние; (*of death etc.*) регистрáция. **notify** ['nəʊtɪˌfaɪ] *v.t.* извещáть *impf.*, известить *pf.* (**of** о+*p.*); уведомлять *impf.*, уведомить *pf.* (**of** о+*p.*).

notion ['nəʊʃ(ə)n] *n.* понятие, представлéние.

notoriety [ˌnəʊtə'raɪətɪ] *n.* дурнáя слáва. **notorious** [nəʊ'tɔːrɪəs] *adj.* пресловутый.

notwithstanding [ˌnɒtwɪθ'stændɪŋ, -wɪð'stændɪŋ] *prep.* несмотря на+*a.*; *adv.* тéм не мéнее.

nougat ['nuːgɑː] *n.* нугá.

nought [nɔːt] *n.* (*nothing*) ничтó; (*figure 0*) нуль (-ля) *m.*, ноль (-ля) *m.*; **~s and crosses** крéстики и нóлики *m.pl.*

noun [naʊn] *n.* (*имя nt.*) существительное *sb.*

nourish ['nʌrɪʃ] *v.t.* питáть *impf.*, на~ *pf.* **nourishing** *adj.* питáтельный. **nourishment** *n.* питáние.

nova ['nəʊvə] *n.* нóвая звездá (*pl.* -ёзды).

novel ['nɒv(ə)l] *adj.* нóвый (нов, -á, -о); (*unusual*) необыкновéнный (-нен, -нна); *n.* ромáн. **novelist** *n.* романист. **novelty** *n.* (*newness*) новизнá; (*new thing*) новинка.

November [nə'vembə(r)] *n.* ноябрь (-ря) *m.*; *attr.* ноябрьский.

novice ['nɒvɪs] *n.* (*eccl.*) пóслушник, -ица; (*beginner*) новичóк (-чкá).

now [naʊ] *adv.* тепéрь, сейчáс; (*immediately*) тóтчас же; (*next*) тогдá; *conj.*: **~ (that)** раз, когдá; (**every**) **~ and again, then** врéмя от врéмени; **~ ... ~...** то... то...; **by ~** ужé; **from ~ on** в дальнéйшем, впредь. **nowadays** *adv.* в нáше врéмя.

nowhere ['nəʊweə(r)] *adv.* (*place*) нигдé; (*direction*) никудá; *pron.*: **I have ~ to go** мне нéкуда пойти.

noxious ['nɒkʃəs] *adj.* врéдный (-ден, -днá, -дно).

nozzle ['nɒz(ə)l] *n.* соплó (*pl.* -пла, -п(е)л), форсýнка, пáтрубок (-бка).

nuance ['njuːɑ̃s] *n.* нюáнс.

nuclear ['njuːklɪə(r)] *adj.* ядерный. **nucleus** *n.* ядрó (*pl.* ядра, ядер, ядрам).

nude [njuːd] *adj.* обнажённый (-ён, -енá),

нагóй (наг, -á, -о); *n.* обнажённая фигýра.

nudge [nʌdʒ] *v.t.* подтáлкивать *impf.*, подтолкнуть *pf.* лóктем; *n.* лёгкий толчóк (-чкá).

nudity ['njuːdɪtɪ] *n.* наготá.

nugget ['nʌgɪt] *n.* (*gold*) саморóдок (-дка).

nuisance ['njuːs(ə)ns] *n.* досáда, неприятность; (*person*) раздражáющий, надоéдливый, человéк.

null [nʌl] *adj.*: **~ and void** недействительный. **nullify** ['nʌlɪˌfaɪ] *v.t.* аннулировать *impf.* & *pf.* **nullity** *n.* недействительность.

numb [nʌm] *adj.* онемéлый, оцепенéлый; *v.t.* вызывáть *impf.*, вызвать (-зовет) *pf.* онемéние в+*p.*, у+*g.*

number ['nʌmbə(r)] *n.* (*total*) количество; (*total; symbol; math.; gram.*) числó (*pl.* -сла, -сел, -слам); (*item*) нóмер (*pl.* -á); *v.t.* (*count*) считáть *impf.*, со~, счесть (сочтý, -тёшь; счёл, сочлá) *pf.*; (*assign ~ to*) нумеровáть *impf.*, за~, про~ *pf.*; (*contain*) начитывать *impf.*; **~ among** причислять *impf.*, причислить *pf.* к+*d.*; **his days are ~ed** егó дни сочтены. **numberless** *adj.* бесчисленный (-ен, -енна). **number-plate** *n.* номернáя дощéчка.

numeral ['njuːmər(ə)l] *adj.* числовой, цифровóй; *n.* цифра; (*gram.*) (*имя nt.*) числительное *sb.* **numerator** *n.* числитель *m.* **numerical** *adj.* числовой, цифровóй. **numerous** *adj.* многочисленный (-ен, -енна); (*many*) мнóго+*g.pl.*

numismatic [ˌnjuːmɪz'mætɪk] *adj.* нумизматический. **numismatics** *n.* нумизмáтика. **numismatist** [nju:'mɪzmətɪst] *n.* нумизмáт.

numskull ['nʌmskʌl] *n.* тупица *c.g.*, óлух.

nun [nʌn] *n.* монáхиня. **nunnery** ['nʌnərɪ] *n.* (жéнский) монастырь (-ря) *m.*

nuptial ['nʌpʃ(ə)l] *adj.* брáчный, свáдебный; *n.*: *pl.* свáдьба (*g.pl.* -деб).

nurse [nɜːs] *n.* (*child's*) няня; (*medical*) медсестрá (*pl.* -ёстры, -естёр, -ёстрам), сидéлка; *v.t.* (*suckle*) кормить (-млю, -мишь) *impf.*, на~, по~ *pf.*; (*tend sick*) ухáживать *impf.* за+*i.*; (*treat illness*) лечить (-чý, -чишь) *impf.*; **nursing home** чáстная лечéбница, чáстный санатóрий. **nursery** *n.* (*room*) дéтская *sb.*; (*day ~*) ясли (-лей) *pl.*; (*for plants*) питóмник; **~ rhyme** дéтские стишки *m.pl.*; **~ school** дéтский сад (*loc.* -ý; *pl.* -ы). **nurs(e)ling** *n.* питóмец (-мца), -мица.

nut [nʌt] *n.* орéх; (*for bolt etc.*) гáйка; (*sl., head*) башкá; (*sl., person*) псих. **nutcrackers** *n.* щипцы (-цóв) *pl.* для орéхов. **nuthatch** *n.* пóползень (-зня) *m.* **nutshell** *n.* орéховая скорлупá (*pl.* -пы); **in a ~** в двух словáх. **nut-tree** *n.* орéшник.

nutmeg ['nʌtmeg] *n.* мускáтный орéх.

nutria ['njuːtrɪə] *n.* нýтрия.

nutriment ['njuːtrɪmənt] *n.* питáтельная едá. **nutrition** [njuː'trɪʃ(ə)n] *n.* питáние. **nutritionist** *n.* диетóлог. **nu'tritious** *adj.* питáтельный.

nylon ['naɪlɒn] *n.* нейло́н; *pl.* нейло́новые чулки́ (-ло́к) *pl.*; *attr.* нейло́новый.

nymph [nɪmf] *n.* ни́мфа. **nympho'maniac** *n.* нимфома́нка.

O

O [əʊ] *int.* o!; ax!; ox!

oaf [əʊf] *n.* неуклю́жий, неотёсанный, челове́к. **oafish** *adj.* неуклю́жий.

oak [əʊk] *n.* (*tree*) дуб (*loc.* -e & -ý; *pl.* -ы́); (*wood*) древеси́на ду́ба; *attr.* дубо́вый.

OAP *abbr.* (*of old-age pensioner*) пенсионе́р, ~ка (по ста́рости).

oar [ɔ:(r)] *n.* весло́ (*pl.* вёсла, -сел, -слам). **oarsman** *n.* гребе́ц (-бца́).

oasis [əʊ'eɪsɪs] *n.* оа́зис.

oast-house [əʊst] *n.* хмелесуши́лка.

oat [əʊt] *n.*: *pl.* овёс (овса́) *collect.* **oatcake** *n.* овся́ная лепёшка. **oatmeal** *n.* овся́нка.

oath [əʊθ] *n.* кля́тва, прися́га; (*expletive*) руга́тельство; **on, under,** ~ под прися́гой.

obduracy ['ɒbdjʊərəsɪ] *n.* упря́мство. **obdurate** *adj.* упря́мый.

obedience [əʊ'bi:dɪəns] *n.* послуша́ние. **obedient** *adj.* послу́шный.

obelisk ['ɒbəlɪsk] *n.* обели́ск; (*print.*; *obelus*) крести́к.

obese [əʊ'bi:s] *n.* ту́чный (-чен, -чна́, -чно). **obesity** *n.* ту́чность.

obey [əʊ'beɪ] *v.t.* слу́шаться *impf.*, по~ *pf.*+*g.*; повинова́ться *impf.* (*also pf. in past*)+*d.*

obituary [ə'bɪtjʊərɪ] *n.* некроло́г; *adj.* некрологи́ческий.

object ['ɒbdʒɪkt; əb'dʒekt] *n.* (*thing*) предме́т; (*aim*) цель; (*gram.*) дополне́ние; *v.i.* возража́ть *impf.*, возрази́ть *pf.* (**to** про́тив+*g.*); протестова́ть *impf.* (**to** про́тив+*g.*); **I don't** ~ я не про́тив. **objection** [əb'dʒekʃ(ə)n] *n.* возраже́ние; **I have no** ~ я не возража́ю. **ob'jectionable** *adj.* неприя́тный. **ob'jective** *adj.* объекти́вный; (*gram.*) объе́ктный; *n.* (*mil.*) объе́кт; (*aim*) цель; (*lens*) объекти́в; (*gram.*) объе́ктный паде́ж (-á). **objec'tivity** *n.* объекти́вность. **object-lesson** *n.* (*fig.*) нагля́дный приме́р. **ob'jector** *n.* возража́ющий *sb.*

obligation [ˌɒblɪ'geɪʃ(ə)n] *n.* обяза́тельство; **I am under an** ~ я обя́зан(а). **obligatory** [ə'blɪgətərɪ] *adj.* обяза́тельный. **oblige** [ə'blaɪdʒ] *v.t.* обя́зывать *impf.*, обяза́ть (-яжу́, -я́жешь) *pf.*; заставля́ть *impf.*, заста́вить *pf.*; **be** ~**d to** (*grateful*) быть благода́рным+*d.* **obliging** *adj.* услу́жливый, любе́зный.

oblique [ə'bli:k] *adj.* косо́й (кос, -á, -о); (*indirect*) непрямо́й (-м, -má, -мо); (*gram.*) ко́свенный.

obliterate [ə'blɪtəˌreɪt] *v.t.* (*efface*) стира́ть *impf.*, стере́ть (сотру́, -рёшь; стёр) *pf.*; (*destroy*) уничтожа́ть *impf.*, уничто́жить *pf.* **oblite'ration** *n.* стира́ние; уничтоже́ние.

oblivion [ə'blɪvɪən] *n.* забве́ние. **oblivious** *adj.* (*forgetful*) забы́вчивый; **to be** ~ **of** не замеча́ть *impf.*+*g.*

oblong ['ɒblɒŋ] *adj.* продолгова́тый.

obnoxious [əb'nɒkʃəs] *adj.* проти́вный.

oboe ['əʊbəʊ] *n.* гобо́й.

obscene [əb'si:n] *adj.* непристо́йный. **obscenity** [əb'senɪtɪ] *n.* непристо́йность.

obscure [əb'skjʊə(r)] *adj.* (*dark*) тёмный (-мен, -мна́); (*unclear*) нея́сный (-сен, -сна́, -сно); (*little known*) малоизве́стный; *v.t.* затемня́ть *impf.*, затемни́ть *pf.*; де́лать *impf.*, с~ *pf.* нея́сным. **obscurity** *n.* нея́сность, неизве́стность.

obsequious [əb'si:kwɪəs] *adj.* подобостра́стный.

observance [əb'zɜ:v(ə)ns] *n.* соблюде́ние; (*rite*) обря́д. **observant** *adj.* наблюда́тельный. **observation** [ˌɒbzə'veɪʃ(ə)n] *n.* наблюде́ние; (*remark*) замеча́ние. **observatory** *n.* обсервато́рия. **observe** *v.t.* (*law etc.*) соблюда́ть *impf.*, соблюсти́ (-юду́, -юдёшь; -юл, -юла́) *pf.*; (*watch*) наблюда́ть *impf.*; (*remark*) замеча́ть *impf.*, заме́тить *pf.* **observer** *n.* наблюда́тель *m.*

obsess [əb'ses] *v.t.* пресле́довать *impf.*; му́чить *impf.* **obsession** *n.* одержи́мость; (*idea*) навя́зчивая иде́я. **obsessive** *adj.* навя́зчивый.

obsolescence [ˌɒbsə'les(ə)ns] *n.* устарева́ние. **obsolescent** *adj.* устарева́ющий. **obsolete** ['ɒbsəˌli:t] *adj.* устаре́лый, вы́шедший из употребле́ния.

obstacle ['ɒbstək(ə)l] *n.* препя́тствие, поме́ха. **obstacle-race** *n.* бег с препя́тствиями.

obstetric(al) [əb'stetrɪk(əl)] *adj.* акуше́рский. **obstetrician** [ˌɒbstə'trɪʃ(ə)n] *n.* акуше́р. **obstetrics** *n.* акуше́рство.

obstinacy ['ɒbstɪnəsɪ] *n.* упря́мство. **obstinate** *adj.* упря́мый.

obstreperous [əb'strepərəs] *adj.* бу́йный (бу́ен, буйна́, -но).

obstruct [əb'strʌkt] *v.t.* пре-, за-, гражда́ть *impf.*, пре-, за-, гради́ть *pf.*; (*prevent, impede*) препя́тствовать *impf.*, вос~ *pf.*+*d.*; меша́ть *impf.*, по~ *pf.*+*d.* **obstruction** *n.* пре-, за-, гражде́ние; (*obstacle*) препя́тствие. **obstructive** *adj.* пре-, за-, гражда́ющий; препя́тствующий, меша́ющий.

obtain [əb'teɪn] *v.t.* получа́ть *impf.*, получи́ть (-чу́, -чишь) *pf.*; достава́ть (-таю́, -таёшь) *impf.*, доста́ть (-áну, -áнешь) *pf.*

obtrude [əb'tru:d] *v.t.* навя́зывать *impf.*, навяза́ть (-яжу́, -я́жешь) *pf.* ((up)on +*d.*). **obtrusive** *adj.* навя́зчивый.

obtuse [əb'tju:s] *adj.* тупо́й (туп, -á, -о, ту́пы́).

obverse ['ɒbvɜːs] *n.* (*of coin etc.*) лицевая сторона (*a.* -ону; *pl.* -óны, -óн, -онáм).

obviate ['ɒbvɪeɪt] *v.t.* (*remove*) устранять *impf.*, устранить *pf.*; (*get round*) обходить (-ожý, -óдишь) *impf.*, обойти (обойдý, -дёшь; обошёл, -шлá) *pf.*

obvious ['ɒbvɪəs] *adj.* очевидный, явный.

occasion [ə'keɪʒ(ə)n] *n.* (*juncture*) случай; (*cause*) пóвод (*occurrence*) событие; *v.t.* причинять *impf.*, причинить *pf.* **occasional** *adj.* случáйный, рéдкий (-док, -дкá, -дко). **occasionally** *adv.* иногдá, врéмя от врéмени.

Occident ['ɒksɪd(ə)nt] *n.* Зáпад. **Occidental** [ˌɒksɪ'dent(ə)l] *adj.* зáпадный.

occlude [ə'kluːd] *v.t.* преграждáть *impf.*, преградить *pf.* **occlusion** [ə'kluːʒ(ə)n] *n.* преграждéние.

occult [ɒ'kʌlt, 'ɒkʌlt] *adj.* тáйный, оккýльтный.

occupancy ['ɒkjʊpənsɪ] *n.* зáнятие; (*possession*) владéние (**of** +*i.*). **occupant** ['ɒkjʊpənt] *n.* (*of land*) владéлец (-льца), -лица; (*of house etc.*) жи́тель *m.*, ~ница. **occu'pation** *n.* зáнятие; (*military*) оккупáция; (*profession*) профéссия. **occu'pational** *adj.* профессионáльный; ~ **disease** профессионáльное заболевáние; ~ **therapy** трудотерапия. **occupy** ['ɒkjʊˌpaɪ] *v.t.* занимáть *impf.*, занять (займý, -мёшь; зáнял, -á, -о) *pf.*; (*mil.*) оккупи́ровать *impf. & pf.*

occur [ə'kɜː(r)] *v.i.* (*happen*) случáться *impf.*, случиться *pf.*; (*be met with*) встречáться *impf.*; ~ **to** приходи́ть (-ит) *impf.*, прийти (придёт; пришёл, -шлá) *pf.* в гóлову+*d.* **occurrence** [ə'kʌrəns] *n.* слýчай, происшéствие.

ocean ['əʊʃ(ə)n] *n.* океáн; (*fig.*) мáсса, мóре; *attr.* океáнский. **ocean-going** *adj.* океáнский. **oceanic** [ˌəʊʃɪ'ænɪk, ˌəʊsɪ-] *adj.* океáнский, океани́ческий.

ocelot ['ɒsɪˌlɒt] *n.* оцелóт.

ochre ['əʊkə(r)] *n.* óхра.

o'clock [ə'klɒk] *adv.*: **at six** ~ в шесть часóв.

octagon ['ɒktəgən] *n.* восьмиугóльник. **octagonal** [ˌɒk'tægən(ə)l] *adj.* восьмиугóльный.

octane ['ɒkteɪn] *n.* октáн; ~ **number** октáновое числó.

octave ['ɒktɪv] *n.* (*mus.*) октáва.

octet [ɒk'tet] *n.* октéт.

October [ɒk'təʊbə(r)] *n.* октя́брь (-ря́) *m.*; *attr.* октя́брьский.

octogenarian [ˌɒktəʊdʒɪ'neərɪən] *n.* восьмидесятилéтний стари́к (-á), -няя старýха.

octopus ['ɒktəpəs] *n.* осьмино́г, спрут.

ocular ['ɒkjʊlə(r)] *adj.* глазнóй, окуля́рный. **oculist** *n.* окули́ст.

odd [ɒd] *adj.* (*number*) нечётный; (*not paired*) непáрный; (*casual*) случáйный; (*strange*) стрáнный (-нен, -ннá, -нно); **five hundred** ~ пятьсóт с ли́шним; ~ **job** случáйная рабóта; ~ **man out** (трéтий)

ли́шний *sb.* **oddity** *n.* стрáнность; (*person*) чудáк (-á), -áчка. **oddly** *adv.* стрáнно; ~ **enough** как э́то ни стрáнно. **oddment** *n.* остáток (-тка); *pl.* разрóзненные предмéты *m.pl.* **odds** *n.* (*advantage*) перевéс; (*variance*) разноглáсие; (*chance*) шáнсы *m.pl.*; **be at** ~ **with** (*person*) не лáдить с+*i.*; (*things*) не соотвéтствовать *impf.*+*d.*; **long** (**short**) ~ неравные (почти равные) шáнсы *m.pl.*; **the** ~ **are that** вероя́тнее всегó, что; ~ **and ends** обры́вки *m.pl.*

ode [əʊd] *n.* óда.

odious ['əʊdɪəs] *adj.* ненави́стный, отврати́тельный. **odium** *n.* нéнависть, отвращéние.

odour ['əʊdə(r)] *n.* зáпах; **be in good** (**bad**) ~ **with** быть в (не)ми́лости у+*g.* **odourless** *adj.* без зáпаха.

odyssey ['ɒdɪsɪ] *n.* одиссéя.

oedema [ɪ'diːmə] *n.* отёк.

oesophagus [iː'sɒfəgəs] *n.* пищевóд.

of [ɒv, əv] *prep.* *expressing* **1.** *origin*: из+*g.*: **he comes** ~ **a working-class family** он из рабóчей семьи́; **2.** *cause*: от+*g.*: **he died** ~ **hunger** он ýмер от гóлода; **3.** *authorship*: *g.*: **the works** ~ **Pushkin** сочинéния Пýшкина; **4.** *material*: из+*g.*: **made** ~ **wood** сдéланный из дéрева; *adjective*: **a heart** ~ **stone** кáменное сéрдце; **5.** *identity*: *apposition*: **the city** ~ **Moscow** гóрод Москвá; *adjective*: **the University** ~ **Moscow** Москóвский университéт; **6.** *concern*, *reference*: о+*p.*: **he talked** ~ **the past** он говори́л о прóшлом; **7.** *quality*: *g.*: **a man** ~ **strong character** человéк си́льного харáктера; *adjective*: **a man** ~ **importance** вáжный человéк; **8.** *partition*: *g.* (*often in* -ý(-ю)): **a glass** ~ **milk, tea** стакáн молокá, чáю; из+*g.*: **one** ~ **them** оди́н из них; **9.** *belonging*: *g.*: **the capital** ~ **England** столи́ца Áнглии; *poss. adj.*: **the house** ~ **his father** отцóвский дом; **10.** *following other parts of speech: see individual entries, e.g.* **be afraid** боя́ться (**of** +*g.*); **dispose** ~ избавля́ться от+*g.*

off [ɒf] *adv.*: *in phrasal vv.*, *see v.*, *e.g.* **clear** ~ убирáться; *prep.* (*from surface of*) с+*g.*; (*away from*) от+*g.*; *adj.* (*far*) дáльний; (*right hand*) прáвый; (*free*) свобóдный; ~ **and on** врéмя от врéмени; **on the** ~ **chance** на вся́кий слýчай; ~ **colour** нездорóвый; ~ **the cuff** без подготóвки; ~ **the point** не относя́щийся к дéлу.

offal ['ɒf(ə)l] *n.* (*food*) требухá, потрохá (-хóв) *pl.*; (*carrion*) пáдаль.

offence [ə'fens] *n.* (*attack*) нападéние; (*insult*) оби́да; (*against law*) простýпок (-пка), преступлéние; **take** ~ обижáться *impf.*, оби́деться (-и́жусь, -и́дишься) *pf.* (**at** на+*a.*). **offend** *v.t.* оскорбля́ть *impf.*, оскорби́ть *pf.*; обижáть *impf.*, оби́деть (-и́жу, -и́дишь) *pf.*; ~ **against** нарушáть *impf.*, нарýшить *pf.* **offender** *n.* правонаруши́тель *m.*, ~ница, престýпник, -ица. **offensive** *adj.* (*attacking*) наступáтельный; (*insulting*) оскорби́тельный, оби́дный; (*repulsive*) проти́вный; *n.* нападе́ние.

offer ['ɒfə(r)] *v.t.* предлага́ть *impf.*, предложи́ть (-жу́, -жишь) *pf.*; *n.* предложе́ние; **on** ~ в прода́же.

offhand [ɒf'hænd, 'ɒf,hænd] *adj.* бесцеремо́нный (-нен, -нна), небре́жный; *adv.* (*without preparation*) без подгото́вки, экспро́мтом.

office ['ɒfɪs] *n.* (*position*) до́лжность; (*place, room etc.*) бюро́ *nt.indecl.*, конто́ра, канцеля́рия; (*eccl.*) (церко́вная) слу́жба; ~ **equipment** оргтéхника. **officer** *n.* должностно́е лицо́ (*pl.* -ца); (*mil.*) офице́р. **official** [ə'fɪʃ(ə)l] *adj.* служе́бный, должностно́й; (*authorized*) официа́льный; *n.* должностно́е лицо́ (*pl.* -ца). **o'fficiate** *v.i.* (*eccl.*) соверша́ть *impf.*, соверши́ть *pf.* богослуже́ние. **o'fficious** *adj.* (*intrusive*) навя́зчивый.

offing ['ɒfɪŋ] *n.*: **in the** ~ в недалёком бу́дущем.

offprint ['ɒfprɪnt] *n.* отде́льный о́ттиск. **offscourings** *n.* отбро́сы (-сов) *pl.*, подо́нки (-ков) *pl.* **offset** *n.* (*compensation*) возмеще́ние; (*offshoot*) о́тпрыск; (*in pipe*) отво́д; ~ **process** (*print*) офсе́тный спо́соб; *v.t.* возмеща́ть *impf.*, возмести́ть *pf.* **offshoot** *n.* о́тпрыск. **off'side** *adv.* вне игры́. **offspring** *n.* пото́мок (-мка); (*collect.*) пото́мки *m.pl.*

off-white [ɒf'waɪt] *adj.* не совсе́м бе́лый (бел, -á, бело́).

often ['ɒf(ə)n, 'ɒft(ə)n] *adv.* ча́сто.

ogle ['əʊg(ə)l] *v.t. & i.* стро́ить *impf.* гла́зки+*d.*

ogre ['əʊgə(r)] *n.* велика́н-людое́д. **ogress** *n.* велика́нша-людое́дка.

oh [əʊ] *int.* о!; ах!; ох!

ohm [əʊm] *n.* ом (*g.pl.* ом).

oho [əʊ'həʊ] *int.* ого́!

oil [ɔɪl] *n.* ма́сло (*pl.* -сла́, -сел, -сла́м); (*petroleum*) нефть; (*lubricant*) жи́дкая сма́зка; *pl.* (*paint*) ма́сло, ма́сляные кра́ски *f.pl.*; *v.t.* сма́зывать *impf.*, сма́зать (сма́жу, -жешь) *pf.*; ~ **rig** бурова́я устано́вка; ~ **well** нефтяна́я сква́жина. **oilcake** *n.* жмых (-á). **oilcan** *n.* маслёнка. **oilcloth** *n.* клеёнка. **oilfield** *n.* месторожде́ние не́фти. **oil-paint** *n.* ма́сляная кра́ска. **oil-painting** *n.* карти́на, напи́санная ма́сляными кра́сками. **oilskin** *n.* то́нкая клеёнка; *pl.* дождево́е пла́тье. **oil-tanker** *n.* та́нкер. **oily** *adj.* маслян́и́стый; (*unctuous*) еле́йный.

ointment ['ɔɪntmənt] *n.* мазь.

OK [əʊ'keɪ] *adv.* хорошо́; *int.* ла́дно!; *v.t.* одобря́ть *impf.*, одо́брить *pf.*

okapi [əʊ'kɑːpɪ] *n.* ока́пи *c.g.indecl.*

old [əʊld] *adj.* ста́рый (стар, -á, ста́ро́); (*ancient*; *of long standing*) стари́нный; (*former*) бы́вший; **how** ~ **are you?** ско́лько тебе́, вам, (*d.*) лет?; **she is three years** ~ ей (*d.*) три го́да; **the** ~ старики́ *m.pl.*; ~ **age** ста́рость; **O** ~ **Believer** старообря́дец (-дца); ~ **chap, fellow** *etc.* старина́; **the** ~ **country**

ро́дина, оте́чество; ~ **maid** ста́рая де́ва; ~ **man** (*also father, husband*) стари́к (á); ~ **woman** стару́ха; (*coll.*) стару́шка. **old-age** *adj.*: ~ **pension** пе́нсия по ста́рости. **old-fashioned** *adj.* старомо́дный. **old-time** *adj.* стари́нный, пре́жних времён. **old-world** *adj.* стари́нный.

olfactory [ɒl'fæktərɪ] *adj.* обоня́тельный.

oligarch ['ɒlɪgɑːk] *n.* олига́рх. **oli'garchic(al)** *adj.* олигархи́ческий. **oligarchy** *n.* олига́рхия.

olive ['ɒlɪv] *n.* (*fruit*) масли́на, оли́вка; (*colour*) оли́вковый цвет; *adj.* оли́вковый; ~ **branch** оли́вковая ветвь (*pl.* -ви, -ве́й); ~ **oil** оли́вковое ма́сло; ~ **tree** масли́на, оли́вковое де́рево (*pl.* дере́вья, -ьев).

Olympic [ə'lɪmpɪk] *adj.* олимпи́йский; ~ **games** Олимпи́йские и́гры *f.pl.*

omelet(te) ['ɒmlɪt] *n.* омле́т.

omen ['əʊmən, -men] *n.* предзнаменова́ние. **ominous** ['ɒmɪnəs] *adj.* злове́щий.

omission [ə'mɪʃ(ə)n] *n.* про́пуск; (*neglect*) упуще́ние. **omit** [ə'mɪt] *v.t.* (*leave out*) пропуска́ть *impf.*, пропусти́ть (-ущу́, -у́стишь) *pf.*; (*neglect*) упуска́ть *impf.*, упусти́ть (-ущу́, -у́стишь) *pf.*

omnipotence [ɒm'nɪpət(ə)ns] *n.* всемогу́щество. **omnipotent** *adj.* всемогу́щий. **omni'present** *adj.* вездесу́щий. **omniscient** [ɒm'nɪsɪənt, -ʃɪənt] *adj.* всеве́дующий. **omnivorous** [ɒm'nɪvərəs] *adj.* всея́дный; (*fig.*) всепоглоща́ющий.

on [ɒn] *prep.* (*position*) на+*p.*; ~ **the right of** (*relative position*) с пра́вой стороны́ от+*g.*; (*direction*) на+*a.*; (*time*) в+*a.*; ~ **the next day** на сле́дующий день; ~ **Mondays** (*repeated action*) по понеде́льникам (*d.pl.*); ~ (**the morning of**) **the first of June** (у́тром) пе́рвого ию́ня (*g.*); ~ **arrival** по прибы́тии; (*concerning*) по+*p.*, о+*p.*, на+*a.*; *adv.* да́льше, вперёд; *in phrasal vv., see vv., e.g.* **move** ~ идти́ да́льше; **and so** ~ и так да́лее, и т.д.; **further** ~ да́льше; **later** ~ по́зже.

once [wʌns] *adv.* (*один*) раз; (*on past occasion*) одна́жды; **all at** ~ неожи́данно; **at** ~ сра́зу, неме́дленно; (*if, when*) ~ как то́лько; ~ **again, more** ещё раз; ~ **and for all** раз навсегда́; ~ **or twice** не́сколько раз; ~ **upon a time there lived ...** жил-был... .

oncoming ['ɒn,kʌmɪŋ] *adj.* приближа́ющийся; ~ **traffic** встре́чное движе́ние.

one [wʌn] *adj.* оди́н (одна́, -но́); (*only, single*) еди́нственный; (*unified*) еди́ный; *n.* оди́н (*unit*) едини́ца; *pron.*: *not usu. translated; v. translated in 2nd pers. sg. or by impers. construction*: ~ **never knows** никогда́ не зна́ешь; **where can** ~ **buy this book?** где мо́жно купи́ть э́ту кни́гу?; **chapter** ~ пе́рвая глава́; **I for** ~ что каса́ется меня́; я со свое́й стороны́; ~ **after another** оди́н за други́м; ~ **and all** все до одного́; все как оди́н; ~ **and only** еди́нственный; ~ **and the same** оди́н и тот же; ~ **another** друг дру́га

(d. -гу, etc.); ~ **fine day** в оди́н прекра́сный день; ~ **o'clock** час. **one-armed** adj. однору́кий. **one-eyed** adj. одногла́зый. **one-handed** adj. одноруќий. **one-legged** adj. одноно́гий.

onerous ['ɒnərəs, 'əʊn-] adj. тя́гостный.

oneself [wʌn'self] pron. себя́ (себе́, собо́й); -ся (suffixed to v.).

one-sided ['wʌnsaidid] adj. односторо́нний. **one-time** ['wʌntaim] adj. бы́вший. **one-way** ['wʌnwei] adj. односторо́нний; ~ **street** у́лица односторо́ннего движе́ния.

onion ['ʌnjən] n. (plant; pl. collect.) лук; (single ~) лу́ковица.

onlooker ['ɒn,lʊkə(r)] n. наблюда́тель m., ~ница.

only ['əʊnli] adj. еди́нственный; adv. то́лько; **if** ~ е́сли бы то́лько; ~ **just** то́лько что; conj. но.

onomatopoeia [,ɒnə,mætə'pi:ə] n. звукоподража́ние. **onomatopoeic** adj. звукоподража́тельный.

onset ['ɒnset], **onslaught** ['ɒnslɔ:t] n. на́тиск, ата́ка.

onus ['əʊnəs] n. (burden) бре́мя nt.; (responsibility) отве́тственность.

onward ['ɒnwəd] adj. дви́жущийся вперёд. **onwards** adv. вперёд.

onyx ['ɒniks] n. о́никс; attr. о́никсовый.

ooze [u:z] n. ил, ти́на; v.t. & i. сочи́ться impf. **oozy** adj. и́листый, ти́нистый.

opacity [ə'pæsiti] n. непрозра́чность.

opal ['əʊp(ə)l] n. опа́л; ~ **glass** моло́чное стекло́. **opalescence** [,əʊpə'les(ə)ns] n. опалесце́нция. **opa'lescent** adj. опалесци́рующий. **opaline** ['əʊpə,lain] adj. опа́ловый.

opaque [əʊ'peik] adj. непрозра́чный.

open ['əʊpən] adj. откры́тый; (frank) открове́нный (-нен, -нна); (accessible) досту́пный; (boat) беспалу́бный; **in the** ~ **air** на откры́том во́здухе; v.t. & i. открыва́ть(ся) impf., откры́ть(ся) (-ро́ю(сь), -ро́ешь(ся)) pf.; (~ **wide**) раскрыва́ть (ся) impf., раскры́ть(ся) (-ро́ю(сь), -ро́ешь(ся)) pf.; v.i. (begin) начина́ться impf., нача́ться (-чнётся; начался́, -ла́сь) pf. **opencast** adj.: ~ **mining** откры́тые го́рные рабо́ты f.pl. **open-handed** adj. ще́дрый (щедр, -а́, -о). **opening** n. откры́тие; (aperture) отве́рстие; (beginning) нача́ло; adj. вступи́тельный, нача́льный, пе́рвый. **open-minded** adj. непредупреждённый (-ён, -ённа). **open-mouthed** adj. с рази́нутым ртом. **open-work** n. ажу́рный; ажу́рная рабо́та.

opera ['ɒprə] n. о́пера; attr. о́перный. **opera-glasses** n. бино́кль m. **opera-hat** n. складно́й цили́ндр. **opera-house** n. о́пера, о́перный теа́тр.

operate ['ɒpə,reit] v.i. де́йствовать impf. (**upon** на+a.); ~ pf. опера́цию; (med.) опери́ровать impf. & pf. (**on** +a.); v.t. управля́ть impf.+i.

operatic [,ɒpə'rætik] adj. о́перный.

operating-theatre ['ɒpə,reitiŋ] n. операцио́нная sb. **ope'ration** n. де́йствие; (med.; mil.) опера́ция. **ope'rational** adj. операти́вный. **operative** ['ɒpərətiv] adj. де́йствующий, операти́вный; n. рабо́чий sb. **operator** n. опера́тор; (telephone ~) телефони́ст, ~ка.

operetta [,ɒpə'retə] n. опере́тта.

ophthalmia [ɒf'θælmiə] n. офтальми́я. **ophthalmic** adj. глазно́й.

opiate ['əʊpiət] n. опиа́т.

opine [əʊ'pain] v.t. полага́ть impf. **opinion** [ə'pinjən] n. мне́ние; (expert's ~) заключе́ние (специали́ста); ~ **poll** опро́с обще́ственного мне́ния. **opinionated** adj. упо́рствующий в свои́х взгля́дах.

opium ['əʊpiəm] n. о́пий, о́пиум; ~ **poppy** снотво́рный мак.

opponent [ə'pəʊnənt] n. проти́вник.

opportune ['ɒpə,tju:n] adj. своевре́менный (-нен, -нна). **oppor'tunism** n. оппортуни́зм. **oppor'tunist** n. оппортуни́ст. **oppor'tunity** n. слу́чай, возмо́жность.

oppose [ə'pəʊz] v.t. (contrast) противопоставля́ть impf., противопоста́вить pf. (**to** +d.); (resist) проти́виться impf., вос~ pf.+d.; (speak etc. against) выступа́ть impf., вы́ступить pf. про́тив+g. **opposed** adj. (contrasted) противопоста́вленный (-ен); (of person) про́тив (**to** +g.); **as** ~ **to** в противополо́жность+d. **opposite** ['ɒpəzit] adj. противополо́жный, обра́тный; n. противополо́жность; **just the** ~ как раз наоборо́т; adv. напро́тив; prep. (на)про́тив+g. **oppo'sition** n. (contrast) противопоставле́ние; (resistance) сопротивле́ние; (pol.) оппози́ция.

oppress [ə'pres] v.t. притесня́ть impf., притесни́ть pf.; угнета́ть impf. **oppression** n. притесне́ние, угнете́ние. **oppressive** adj. гнету́щий, угнета́тельский; (weather) ду́шный (-шен, -шна́, -шно). **oppressor** n. угнета́тель m., ~ница.

opprobrious [ə'prəʊbriəs] adj. оскорби́тельный. **opprobrium** n. позо́р.

opt [ɒpt] v.i. выбира́ть impf., вы́брать (вы́беру, -решь) pf. (**for** +a.); ~ **out** не принима́ть impf. уча́стия (**of** в+p.). **optative** (**mood**) ['ɒpteitiv, 'ɒptətiv] n. оптати́в.

optic ['ɒptik] adj. глазно́й, зри́тельный. **optical** adj. опти́ческий. **optician** [ɒp'tiʃ(ə)n] n. о́птик. **optics** n. о́птика.

optimism ['ɒpti,miz(ə)m] n. оптими́зм. **optimist** n. оптими́ст. **opti'mistic** adj. оптимисти́чный, -ческий. **optimum** adj. оптима́льный.

option ['ɒpʃ(ə)n] n. вы́бор; **without the** ~ (**of a fine**) без пра́ва заме́ны штра́фом. **optional** adj. необяза́тельный, факультати́вный.

opulence ['ɒpjʊləns] n. бога́тство. **opulent** adj. бога́тый.

opus ['əʊpəs, 'ɒp-] n. о́пус.

or [ɔ:(r), ə(r)] conj. и́ли; ~ **else** ина́че; ~ **so** приблизи́тельно.

oracle ['ɒrək(ə)l] *n.* ора́кул. **oracular** [ə'rækjulə(r)] *adj.* ора́кульский; (*mysterious*) зага́дочный.

oral ['ɔːr(ə)l] *adj.* у́стный; *n.* у́стный экза́мен.

orange ['ɒrɪndʒ] *n.* (*fruit*) апельси́н; (*colour*) ора́нжевый цвет; *attr.* апельси́нный, апельси́новый; *adj.* ора́нжевый; ~ **blossom** помера́нцевый цвет; (*decoration*) флёрдора́нж; ~ **peel** апельси́новая ко́рка.

orang-(o)utan(g) [ɔː,ræŋuː'tæn] *n.* орангута́нг.

oration [ɔː'reɪʃ(ə)n, ə-] *n.* речь. **orator** ['ɒrətə(r)] *n.* ора́тор. **oratorical** [,ɒrə'tɒrɪk(ə)l] *adj.* ора́торский..

oratorio [,ɒrə'tɔːrɪəʊ] *n.* орато́рия.

oratory[1] ['ɒrətərɪ] *n.* (*chapel*) часо́вня (*g.pl.* -вен).

oratory[2] ['ɒrətərɪ] *n.* (*speech*) ора́торское иску́сство, красноре́чие.

orb [ɔːb] *n.* шар (-á with 2,3,4; *pl.* -ы́); (*part of regalia*) держа́ва.

orbit ['ɔːbɪt] *n.* орби́та; (*eye-socket*) глазна́я впа́дина; **in** ~ на орби́те; *v.t.* враща́ться *impf.* по орби́те вокру́г+*g.* **orbital** *adj.* орбита́льный.

orchard ['ɔːtʃəd] *n.* фрукто́вый сад (*loc.* -у́; *pl.* -ы́).

orchestra ['ɔːkɪstrə] *n.* орке́стр. **orchestral** [,ɔː'kestr(ə)l] *adj.* оркестро́вый. **orchestrate** *v.t.* оркестрова́ть *impf.* & *pf.* **orche'stration** *n.* оркестро́вка.

orchid ['ɔːkɪd] *n.* орхиде́я.

ordain [ɔː'deɪn] *v.t.* предпи́сывать *impf.*, предписа́ть (-ишу́, -и́шешь) *pf.*; (*eccl.*) посвяща́ть *impf.*, посвяти́ть (-ящу́, -яти́шь) *pf.* (в духо́вный сан) (*v.abs.*); в+*nom.-a.pl.* (*of rank*).

ordeal [ɔː'diːl] *n.* испыта́ние.

order ['ɔːdə(r)] *n.* поря́док (-дка); (*system*) строй; (*command*) прика́з; (*for goods*) зака́з; (*document*) о́рдер (*pl.* -á); (*archit.*) о́рдер; (*biol.*) отря́д; (*of monks, knights*) о́рден; (*insignia*) о́рден (*pl.* -á); *pl.* (*holy* ~) духо́вные; **by** ~ по прика́зу; **in** ~ **to** для того́ чтобы; **made to** ~ сде́ланный (-ан) на зака́з; *v.t.* (*command*) прика́зывать *impf.*, приказа́ть (-ажу́, -а́жешь) *pf.+d.*; веле́ть (-лю́, -ли́шь) *impf.* & *pf.+d.*; (*goods etc.*) зака́зывать *impf.*, заказа́ть (-ажу́, -а́жешь) *pf.* **orderly** *adj.* аккура́тный, опря́тный; ~ **officer** дежу́рный офице́р; *n.* (*med.*) санита́р; (*mil.*) ордина́рец (-рца).

ordinal ['ɔːdɪn(ə)l] *adj.* поря́дковый; ~ поря́дковое числи́тельное *sb.*

ordinance ['ɔːdɪnəns] *n.* декре́т.

ordinary ['ɔːdɪnərɪ] *adj.* обыкнове́нный (-нен, -нна), обы́чный; (*mediocre*) заура́дный.

ordination [,ɔːdɪ'neɪʃ(ə)n] *n.* посвяще́ние.

ordnance ['ɔːdnəns] *n.* артилле́рия; *attr.* артилле́рийский.

ore [ɔː(r)] *n.* руда́ (*pl.* -ды).

organ ['ɔːgən] *n.* о́рган; (*mus.*) орга́н. **organ-grinder** *n.* шарма́нщик.

organic [ɔː'gænɪk] *adj.* органи́ческий; ~ **whole** еди́ное це́лое *sb.* '**organism** *n.* органи́зм.

organist ['ɔːgənɪst] *n.* органи́ст.

organization [,ɔːgənaɪ'zeɪʃ(ə)n] *n.* организа́ция. '**organize** *v.t.* организо́вывать *impf.* (*pres. not used*), организова́ть *impf.* (*in pres.*) & *pf.*; устра́ивать *impf.*, устро́ить *pf.* '**organizer** *n.* организа́тор.

orgasm ['ɔːgæz(ə)m] *n.* орга́зм.

orgy ['ɔːdʒɪ] *n.* о́ргия.

oriel ['ɔːrɪəl] *n.* э́ркер; (~ **window**) окно́ (*pl.* о́кна, о́кон, о́кнам) э́ркера.

Orient[1] ['ɔːrɪənt] *n.* Восто́к. **oriental** [,ɔːrɪ'ent(ə)l, ,ɒr-] *adj.* восто́чный.

orient[2] ['ɔːrɪənt], **orientate** *v.t.* ориенти́ровать *impf.* & *pf.* (**o.s.** -ся). **orien'tation** *n.* ориента́ция, ориентиро́вка.

orifice ['ɒrɪfɪs] *n.* отве́рстие.

origin ['ɒrɪdʒɪn] *n.* происхожде́ние, нача́ло. **original** [ə'rɪdʒɪn(ə)l] *adj.* оригина́льный; (*initial*) первонача́льный; (*genuine*) по́длинный (-нен, -нна); *n.* оригина́л, по́длинник. **originality** [ə,rɪdʒɪ'nælɪtɪ] *n.* оригина́льность; по́длинность. **o'riginate** *v.t.* порожда́ть *impf.*, породи́ть *pf.*; *v.i.* происходи́ть (-ожу́, -о́дишь) *impf.*, произойти́ (-ойду́, -ойдёшь; -ошёл, -ошла́) *pf.* (**from, in** от+*g.*); брать (беру́, -рёшь; брал, -á, -о) *impf.*, взять (возьму́, -мёшь; взял, -á, -о) *pf.* нача́ло (**from, in** в+*p.*, от+*g.*). **o'riginator** *n.* а́втор, инициа́тор.

oriole ['ɔːrɪəl] *n.* и́волга.

ornament ['ɔːnəmənt; 'ɔːnə,ment] *n.* украше́ние, орна́мент; *v.t.* украша́ть *impf.*, укра́сить *pf.* **orna'mental** *adj.* орнамента́льный, декорати́вный.

ornate [ɔː'neɪt] *adj.* разукра́шенный (-ен); (*liter. style*) витиева́тый.

ornithological [,ɔːnɪθə'lɒdʒɪk(ə)l] *adj.* орнитологи́ческий. **ornithologist** [,ɔːnɪ'θɒlədʒɪst] *n.* орнито́лог. **orni'thology** *n.* орнитоло́гия.

orphan ['ɔːf(ə)n] *n.* сирота́ (*pl.* -ты) *c.g.*; *v.t.* де́лать *impf.*, с~ *pf.* сирото́й; **be** ~**ed** сироте́ть *impf.*, o~ *pf.* **orphanage** *n.* прию́т, сиро́тский дом (*pl.* -á). **orphaned** *adj.* осироте́лый.

orthodox ['ɔːθə,dɒks] *adj.* ортодокса́льный; (*eccl.*, **O**~) правосла́вный. **orthodoxy** *n.* ортодо́ксия; (**O**~) правосла́вие.

orthographic(al) [,ɔːθə'græfɪk((ə)l)] *adj.* орфографи́ческий. **orthography** [ɔː'θɒgrəfɪ] *n.* орфогра́фия, правописа́ние.

orthopaedic [,ɔːθə'piːdɪk] *adj.* ортопеди́ческий. **orthopaedics** *n.* ортопе́дия.

oscillate ['ɒsɪ,leɪt] *v.i.* вибри́ровать *impf.*; (*also of person*) колеба́ться (-блюсь, -блешься) *impf.*, по~ *pf.* **osci'llation** *n.* вибра́ция, осцилля́ция; колеба́ние. **oscilloscope** [ə'sɪlə,skəʊp] *n.* осциллоско́п.

osier ['əʊzɪə(r)] *n.* (*tree*) и́ва; (*shoot*) лоза́ (*pl.* -зы); *pl.* ивня́к (-á) (*collect*).

osmosis [ɒz'məʊsɪs] *n.* о́смос.

osprey ['ɒspreɪ, -prɪ] *n.* (*bird*) скопа́; (*plume*) эгре́т.

osseous ['ɒsɪəs] *adj.* ко́стный; (*bony*) кости́стый. **ossified** *adj.* окостене́лый.

ostensible [ɒ'stensɪb(ə)l] *adj.* мни́мый. **ostensibly** *adv.* я́кобы.

ostentation [ˌɒsten'teɪʃ(ə)n] *n.* показно́е проявле́ние, выставле́ние напока́з. **ostentatious** *adj.* показно́й.

osteopath ['ɒstɪəˌpæθ] *n.* остеопа́т. **osteopathy** [ˌɒstɪ'ɒpəθɪ] *n.* остеопа́тия.

ostler ['ɒslə(r)] *n.* ко́нюх.

ostracism ['ɒstrəˌsɪz(ə)m] *n.* остраки́зм. **ostracize** ['ɒstrəˌsaɪz] *v.t.* подверга́ть *impf.*, подве́ргнуть (-г) *pf.* остраки́зму.

ostrich ['ɒstrɪtʃ] *n.* стра́ус.

other ['ʌðə(r)] *adj.* друго́й, ино́й; тот; *pl.* други́е *sb.*; **any ~ business** теку́щие дела́ *nt.pl.*, ра́зное *sb.*; **every ~ day** ка́ждый второ́й; **every ~ day** че́рез день; **in ~ words** ины́ми слова́ми; **on the ~ hand** с друго́й стороны́; **on the ~ side** на той стороне́, по ту сто́рону; **one after the ~** оди́н за други́м; **one or the ~** тот и́ли ино́й; **the ~ day** на дня́х, неда́вно; **the ~ way round** наоборо́т; **the ~s** остальны́е. **otherwise** *adv. & conj.* ина́че, а то.

otter ['ɒtə(r)] *n.* вы́дра.

ouch [autʃ] *int.* ай!

ought [ɔːt] *v.aux.* до́лжен (-жна́) (бы) +*inf.*; сле́довало (бы) *impers.*+*d. & inf.*; (*probability*) вероя́тно, по всей вероя́тности+*finite v.*; **~ not** не сле́довало (бы) *impers.*+*d. & inf.*; нельзя́+*d. & inf.*

ounce [auns] *n.* у́нция.

our ['auə(r)], **ours** *poss.pron.* наш (-а, -е; -и); свой (-оя́, -оё; -ои́). **our'selves** *pron.* (*emph.*) (мы) са́ми (-и́х, -и́м, -и́ми); (*refl.*) себя́ (себе́, собо́й); -ся (*suffixed to v.t.*).

oust [aust] *v.t.* вытесня́ть *impf.*, вы́теснить *pf.*

out [aut] *adv.* **1.** нару́жу, вон; **~ with you!** вон отсю́да!; (*to the end*) до конца́; *in phrasal vv. often rendered by pref.* вы- (вы́-*in pf.*), *e.g.* **pull ~** выта́скивать *impf.*, вы́тащить *pf.* **2.: to be ~** *in various senses*: **he is ~** (*not at home*) его́ нет до́ма; (*not in office etc.*) он вы́шел; **the workers are ~** (*on strike*) рабо́чие бастую́т; **the secret is ~** та́йна раскры́та; **the truth will ~** пра́вды не скрыть; **to be ~** *rendered by pf. v. in past* (*English pres., past*) *or fut.* (*English fut.*).: (*be at an end*) ко́нчиться *pf.*; (*be ~ of fashion*) вы́йти (вы́йду, -дешь; вы́шел, -шла) *pf.* из мо́ды; (*of book, be published*) вы́йти (вы́йдет; вы́шел, -шла) *pf.* из печа́ти; (*of candle etc.*) поту́хнуть (-х) *pf.*; (*of flower*) распусти́ться (-ится) *pf.*; (*of person, be unconscious*) потеря́ть *pf.* созна́ние; (*of rash*) вы́ступить *pf.*; **3.: ~ of** из+*g.*, вне+*g.*; **~ of doors** на откры́том во́здухе; **~ of gear** вы́ключенный (-ен); **~ of order** неиспра́вный; **~ of work** безрабо́тный.

out-and-out ['autənd'aut] *adj.* отъя́вленный, соверше́нный.

outbalance [aut'bæləns] *v.t.* переве́шивать *impf.*, переве́сить *pf.* **outbid** *v.t.* предлага́ть *impf.*, предложи́ть (-жу́, -жишь) *pf.* бо́лее высо́кую це́ну, чем+*nom.* **outboard** *adj.*: **~ motor** подвесно́й дви́гатель *m.* **outbreak** *n.* (*of anger, disease*) вспы́шка; (*of war*) нача́ло. **outbuilding** *n.* надво́рная постро́йка. **outburst** *n.* взрыв, вспы́шка. **outcast** *n.* отве́рженец (-нца); *adj.* отве́рженный. **outclass** *v.t.* оставля́ть *impf.*, оста́вить *pf.* далеко́ позади́. **outcome** *n.* результа́т, исхо́д. **outcrop** *n.* обнаже́нная поро́да. **outcry** *n.* (шу́мные) проте́сты *m.pl.* **outdistance** *v.t.* обгоня́ть *impf.*, обогна́ть (обгоню́, -нишь; обогна́л, -á, -о) *pf.* **outdo** *v.t.* превосходи́ть (-ожу́, -о́дишь) *impf.*, превзойти́ (-ойду́, -ойдёшь; -ошёл, -ошла́) *pf.*

outdoor ['autdɔː(r)] *adj.*, **out'doors** *adv.* на откры́том во́здухе, на у́лице.

outer ['autə(r)] *adj.* (*external*) вне́шний, нару́жный; (*far from centre*) отдалённый (от це́нтра). **outermost** *adj.* са́мый да́льний, кра́йний.

outfit ['autfɪt] *n.* снаряже́ние; (*set of things*) набо́р; (*clothes*) оде́жда. **outfitter** *n.* торго́вец (-вца) оде́ждой. **outgoings** *n.* изде́ржки *f.pl.* **out'grow** *v.t.* перераста́ть *impf.*, перерасти́ (-расту́, -растёшь; -ро́с, -росла́) *pf.*; (*clothes*) выраста́ть *impf.*, вы́расти (-ту, -тешь; вы́рос) *pf.* из+*g.*; (*habit*) избавля́ться *impf.*, изба́виться *pf.* с во́зрастом от+*g.* **outhouse** *n.* надво́рная постро́йка.

outing ['autɪŋ] *n.* прогу́лка, экску́рсия.

outlandish [aut'lændɪʃ] *adj.* стра́нный (-нен, -нна́, -нно). **outlast** *v.t.* продолжа́ться *impf.*, продолжи́ться *pf.* до́льше, чем+*nom.* **'outlaw** *n.* лицо́ (*pl.* -ца) вне зако́на; банди́т; *v.t.* объявля́ть *impf.*, объяви́ть (-влю́, -вишь) *pf.* вне зако́на. **'outlay** *n.* изде́ржки *f.pl.*, расхо́ды *m.pl.* **'outlet** *n.* вы́пуск; (*fig.*) вы́ход; (*for goods*) торго́вая то́чка. **'outline** *n.* очерта́ние, ко́нтур; (*sketch, draft*) о́черк; *v.t.* оче́рчивать *impf.*, очерти́ть (-рчу́, -ртишь) *pf.* **outlive** *v.t.* пережи́ть (-иву́, -ивёшь; пе́режи́л, -á, -о) *pf.* **'outlook** *n.* вид, перспекти́вы *f.pl.* **'outlying** *adj.* отдалённый (-ён, -ённа). **outmoded** *adj.* старомо́дный. **outnumber** *v.t.* чи́сленно превосходи́ть (-ожу́, -о́дишь) *impf.*, превзойти́ (-ойду́, -дёшь; -ошёл, -ошла́) *pf.* **'out-of-date** *adj.* устаре́лый, старомо́дный. **'out-of-the-way** *adj.* отдалённый (-ён, -ённа), тру́дно находи́мый. **'out-patient** *n.* амбулато́рный больно́й *sb.* **'outpost** *n.* аванпо́ст. **'output** *n.* вы́пуск, проду́кция.

outrage ['autreɪdʒ] *n.* (*violation of rights*) наси́льственное наруше́ние чужи́х прав; (*gross offence*) надруга́тельство (**upon** над+*i.*); *v.t.* оскорбля́ть *impf.*, оскорби́ть *pf.*; над- руга́ться *pf.* над+*i.*; (*infringe*) наруша́ть *impf.*, нару́шить *pf.* **out'rageous** *adj.* (*immoderate*) возмути́тельный; (*offensive*) оскорби́тельный.

outrigger ['aʊt‚rɪgə(r)] *n.* (*boat*) аутри́гер.
outright *adv.* (*entirely*) вполне́; (*once for all*) раз навсегда́; (*openly*) откры́то; *adj.* прямо́й (прям, -á, -о, пря́мы). **outset** *n.* нача́ло; **at the ~** внача́ле; **from the ~** с са́мого нача́ла. **out'shine** *v.t.* затмева́ть *impf.*, затми́ть *pf.*
outside [aʊt'saɪd, 'aʊtsaɪd] *n.* (*external side*) нару́жная сторона́ (*a.* -ону; *pl.* -оны, -о́н, -она́м); (*exterior, appearance*) нару́жность, вне́шность; **at the ~** са́мое бо́льшее, в кра́йнем слу́чае; **from the ~** извне́; **on the ~** снару́жи; *adj.* нару́жный, вне́шний; (*sport*) кра́йний; *adv.* (*on the ~*) снару́жи; (*to the ~*) нару́жу; (*out of doors*) на откры́том во́здухе, на у́лице; *prep.* вне+*g.*; за+*i.*, за преде́лами+*g.*; (*other than*) кро́ме+*g.*
outsider *n.* посторо́нний *sb.*; (*sport*) аутса́йдер.
outsize ['aʊtsaɪz] *adj.* бо́льше станда́ртного разме́ра. **outskirts** *n.* окра́ина. **out'spoken** *adj.* открове́нный (-нен, -нна), прямо́й (прям, -á, -о, пря́мы). **out'spread** *adj.* распростёртый. **out'standing** *adj.* (*person*) выдаю́щийся; (*debt*) неупла́ченный. **out'stay** *v.t.* переси́живать *impf.*, пересиде́ть (-и́жу, -иди́шь) *pf.*; **~ one's welcome** заси́живаться *impf.*, засиде́ться (-ижу́сь, -ди́шься) *pf.* **out'stretched** *adj.*: **with ~ arms** с распростёртыми объя́тиями. **out'strip** *v.t.* обгоня́ть *impf.*, обогна́ть (обгоню́, -ни́шь; обогна́л, -á, -о) *pf.* **out'vote** *v.t.* побежда́ть *impf.*, победи́ть (-ди́шь) *pf.* большинство́м голосо́в.
outward ['aʊtwəd] *adj.* (*external*) вне́шний, нару́жный; **~ bound** уходя́щий в пла́вание. **outwardly** *adv.* вне́шне, на вид. **outwards** *adv.* нару́жу.
outweigh [aʊt'weɪ] *v.t.* переве́шивать *impf.*, переве́сить *pf.* **outwit** [aʊt'wɪt] *v.t.* перехитри́ть *pf.*
oval ['əʊv(ə)l] *adj.* ова́льный; *n.* ова́л.
ovary ['əʊvərɪ] *n.* яи́чник.
ovation [əʊ'veɪʃ(ə)n] *n.* ова́ция.
oven ['ʌv(ə)n] *n.* печь (*loc.* -чи́; *pl.* -чи, -че́й); духо́вка. **ovenproof** *adj.* жаропро́чный.
over ['əʊvə(r)] *adv. & prep. with vv:* see *vv.*, *e.g.* **jump ~** перепры́гивать *impf.*; **think ~** обду́мывать *impf.*; *adv.* (*in excess*) сли́шком; (*in addition*) вдоба́вок; (*again*) сно́ва; *prep.* (*above*) над+*d.*; (*through; covering*) по+*d.*; (*concerning*) о+*p.*; (*across*) че́рез+*a.*; (*on the other side of*) по ту сто́рону+*g.*; (*more than*) свы́ше+*g.*; бо́лее+*g.*; (*with age*) за+*a.*; **all ~** (*finished*) всё ко́нчено; (*everywhere*) повсю́ду; **all ~ the country** по всей стране́; **~ again** ещё раз; **~ against** напро́тив+*g.*; (*in contrast to*) по сравне́нию с+*i.*; **~ and above** сверх+*g.*; не говоря́ уже́ о+*p.*; **~ the radio** по ра́дио; **~ there** вон там; **~ the way** че́рез доро́гу.
overact [‚əʊvər'ækt] *v.t. & i.* переи́грывать *impf.*, переигра́ть *pf.* **overall** *n.* хала́т; *pl.*

комбинезо́н, спецоде́жда; *adj.* о́бщий.
overawe *v.t.* внуша́ть *impf.*, внуши́ть *pf.* благогове́йный страх+*d.* **overbalance** *v.i.* теря́ть *impf.*, по~ *pf.* равнове́сие. **over'bearing** *adj.* вла́стный, повели́тельный. **'overboard** *adv.* (*motion*) за́ борт; (*position*) за бо́ртом. **'overcast** *adj.* (*sky*) покры́тый облака́ми. **'overcoat** *n.* пальто́ *nt.indecl.* **overcome** *v.t.* преодолева́ть *impf.*, преодоле́ть *pf.*; *adj.* охва́ченный (-ен). **over'crowded** *adj.* перепо́лненный (-ен), перенаселённый (-ён, -ена́). **overcrowding** *n.* перенаселённость. **overdo** *v.t.* (*cook*) пережа́ривать *impf.*, пережа́рить *pf.*; **~ it, things** (*work too hard*) переутомля́ться *impf.*, переутоми́ться *pf.*; (*go too far*) переба́рщивать *impf.*, переборщи́ть *pf.*
overdose ['əʊvə‚dəʊs] *n.* чрезме́рная до́за; передозиро́вка. **overdraft** *n.* превыше́ние креди́та; (*amount*) долг ба́нку. **over'draw** *v.i.* превыша́ть *impf.*, превы́сить *pf.* креди́т (в ба́нке). **overdrive** *n.* ускоря́ющая переда́ча. **over'due** *adj.* просро́ченный (-ен); **be ~** (*late*) запа́здывать *impf.*, запозда́ть *pf.* **over'estimate** *v.t.* переоце́нивать *impf.*, переоцени́ть (-ню́, -нишь) *pf.*; *n.* переоце́нка. **over'flow** *v.i.* перелива́ться *impf.*, перели́ться (-льётся; -лился, -лила́сь, -лило́сь) *pf.*; (*river etc.*) разлива́ться *impf.*, разли́ться (разольётся; разли́лся, -ила́сь, -ило́сь) *pf.*; *n.* разли́в; (*outlet*) переливна́я труба́ (*pl.* -бы). **over'grown** *adj.* заро́сший. **overhang** *v.t. & i.* выступа́ть *impf.* над+*i.*; (*also fig.*) нависа́ть *impf.*, нави́снуть (-с) *pf.* над+*i.*; *n.* свес, вы́ступ.
overhaul [‚əʊvə'hɔːl] *v.t.* разбира́ть *impf.*, разобра́ть (разберу́, -рёшь; разобра́л, -á, -о) *pf.*; (*repair*) капита́льно ремонти́ровать *impf. & pf.*; (*overtake*) догоня́ть *impf.*, догна́ть (догоню́, -нишь; догна́л, -á, -о) *pf.* **'overhead** *adv.* наверху́, над голово́й; *adj.* возду́шный, подвесно́й; (*expenses*) накладно́й; *n.*: *pl.* накладны́е расхо́ды *m.pl.*; **~ projector** графопрое́ктор. **overhear** *v.t.* неча́янно слы́шать (-шу, -шишь) *impf.*, у~ *pf.*; (*eavesdrop*) подслу́шивать *impf.*, подслу́шать *pf.* **overjoyed** *adj.* в восто́рге (**at** от+*g.*), о́чень дово́льный (**at** +*i.*). **'overland** *adj.* сухопу́тный; *adv.* по су́ше. **overlap** *v.t. & i.* (*completely*) перекрыва́ть *impf.*, перекры́ть (-ро́ю, -ро́ешь) *pf.* (друг дру́га); *v.t.* (*in part*) части́чно покрыва́ть *impf.*, покры́ть (-ро́ю, -ро́ешь) *pf.*; *v.i.* части́чно совпада́ть *impf.*, совпа́сть (-адёт; -аде́шь; -а́л) *pf.*
overleaf *adv.* на обра́тной стороне́ (листа́, страни́цы). **overlook** *v.t.* (*look down on*) смотре́ть (-рю́, -ришь) *impf.* све́рху на+*a.*; (*of window*) выходи́ть (-ит) *impf.* на, в, +*a.*; (*not notice*) не замеча́ть *impf.*, заме́тить *pf.*+*g.*; (**~ offence etc.**) проща́ть *impf.*, прости́ть *pf.* **'overlord** *n.* сюзере́н, влады́ка *m.* **overmaster** *v.t.* подчиня́ть *impf.*, подчи-

нить *pf.* себе; (*fig.*) всецело овладевать *impf.*, овладеть *pf.*+*i.* **overnight** *adv.* накануне вечером; (*all night*) с вечера, всю ночь; (*suddenly*) неожиданно, скоро; **stay** ~ ночевать (-чую, -чуешь) *impf.*, переночевать *pf.*; *adj.* ночной. **'overpass** *n.* путепровод. **overpay** *v.t.* переплачивать *impf.*, переплатить (-ачу, -атишь) *pf.*

over-populated [,əʊvə'pɒpjʊ,leɪtɪd] *adj.* перенаселённый (-ён, -ена). **over-popu'lation** *n.* перенаселённость. **overpower** *v.t.* пересиливать *impf.*, пересилить *pf.*; (*heat etc.*) одолевать *impf.*, одолеть *pf.* **over-pro-duction** *n.* перепроизводство. **overrate** *v.t.* переоценивать *impf.*, переоценить (-ню, -нишь) *pf.* **overreach** *v.t.* перехитрить *pf.*; ~ **o.s.** зарываться *impf.*, зарваться (-вусь, -вёшься; -вался, -валась, -валось) *pf.*

override *v.t.* (*fig.*) отвергать *impf*, отвергнуть (-г(нул), -гла) *pf.* **overrule** *v.t.* аннулировать *impf.* & *pf.* **overrun** *v.t.* (*flood*) наводнять *impf.*, наводнить *pf.*; (*ravage*) опустошать *impf.*, опустошить *pf.*

oversea(s) [,əʊvə'si:z; 'əʊvə,si:z] *adv.* за морем, через море; *adj.* заморский. **oversee** [,əʊvə'si:] *v.t.* надзирать *impf.* за+*i.* **'overseer** *n.* надзиратель *m.*, ~ница. **overshadow** *v.t.* затмевать *impf.*, затмить *pf.* **'oversight** *n.* (*supervision*) надзор; (*mistake*) недосмотр, оплошность. **oversleep** *v.i.* просыпать *impf.*, проспать (-плю, -пишь; -пал, -пала, -пало) *pf.* **overstate** *v.t.* преувеличивать *impf.*, преувеличить *pf.* **overstatement** *n.* преувеличение. **overstep** *v.t.* переступать *impf.*, переступить (-плю, -пишь) *pf.*+*a.*, через+*a.*

overt [əʊ'vɜ:t, 'əʊvɜ:t] *adj.* явный, открытый. **overtake** [,əʊvə'teɪk] *v.t.* догонять *impf.*, догнать (догоню, -нишь; догнал, -а, -о) *pf.*; (*of misfortune etc.*) постигать *impf.*, постичь & постигнуть (-йгну, -йгнешь; -иг) *pf.* **overthrow** *v.t.* (*upset*) опрокидывать *impf.*, опрокинуть *pf.*; (*from power*) свергать *impf.*, свергнуть (-г(нул), -гла) *pf.*; *n.* свержение. **'overtime** *n.* (*time*) сверхурочные часы *m.pl.*; (*payment*) сверхурочное *sb.*; *adv.* сверхурочно.

overtone ['əʊvə,təʊn] *n.* (*mus.*) обертон; (*fig.*) скрытый намёк. **overture** ['əʊvə,tjʊə(r)] *n.* предложение, инициатива; (*mus.*) увертюра.

overturn [,əʊvə'tɜ:n] *v.t.* & *i.* опрокидываться(ся) *impf.*, опрокинуть(ся) *pf.*; *v.t.* свергать *impf.*, свергнуть (-г) *pf.* **overweening** *adj.* высокомерный, самонадеянный (-ян, -янна). **overwhelm** *v.t.* подавлять *impf.*, подавить (-влю, -вишь) *pf.*; (*of emotions*) овладевать *impf.*, овладеть *pf.*+*i.* **overwhelming** *adj.* подавляющий. **overwork** *v.t.* & *i.* переутомлять(ся) *impf.*, переутомиться(ся) *pf.*

owe [əʊ] *v.t.* (~ *money*) быть должным (-жен, -жна) +*a.* & *d.*; (*be indebted*) быть обязан-

ным (-ан) +*i.* & *d.*; **he, she,** ~**s me three roubles** он должен, она должна, мне три рубля; **she** ~**s him her life** она обязана ему жизнью. **owing** *adj.*: **be** ~ причитаться *impf.* (**to** +*d.*); ~ **to** из-за+*g.*, по причине+*g.*, вследствие+*g.*

owl [aʊl] *n.* сова (*pl.* -вы). **owlet** *n.* совёнок (-нка; *pl.* совята, -т).

own [əʊn] *adj.* свой (-оя, -оё; -ой); свой (собственный); (*relative*) родной; **on one's** ~ самостоятельно; *v.t.* (*possess*) владеть *impf.*+*i.*; (*admit*) признавать (признаю, -наёшь) *impf.*, признать *pf.*; ~ **up** признаваться (-наюсь, -наёшься) *impf.*, признаться *pf.* **owner** *n.* владелец (-льца), собственник. **ownership** *n.* владение (**of** +*i.*), собственность.

ox [ɒks] *n.* вол (-а). **oxidation** [,ɒksɪ'deɪʃ(ə)n] *n.* окисление. **oxide** ['ɒksaɪd] *n.* окись, оксид (-сла). **oxidize** ['ɒksɪ,daɪz] *v.t.* & *i.* окислять(ся) *impf.*, окислить(ся) *pf.* **oxyacetylene** *adj.* кислородно-ацетиленовый. **oxygen** *n.* кислород; *attr.* кислородный.

oyster ['ɔɪstə(r)] *n.* устрица. **oz.** *abbr.* (*of* **ounce(s)**) унция.

ozone ['əʊzəʊn] *n.* озон; ~ **layer** озонный слой. **ozone-friendly** *adj.* озонобезвредный.

p. *abbr.* (*of* **penny**) пенни *nt. indecl.*, пенс; (*of* **page**) стр, страница. **PA** *abbr.* (*of* **personal assistant**) личный секретарь. **p.a.** [ˌpər 'ænəm] *abbr.* (*of* **per annum**) в год. **pace** [peɪs] *n.* шаг (-а *with* 2, 3, 4, *loc.* -у; *pl.* -й); (*fig.*) темп; **keep** ~ **with** идти (иду, идёшь; шёл, шла) *impf.* в ногу с+*i.*; **set the** ~ задавать (-даю, -даёшь) *impf.*, задать (-ам, -ашь, -аст, -адим; задал, -а, -о) *pf.* темп; *v.i.* шагать *impf.*, шагнуть *pf.*; *v.t.* ~ **out** измерять *impf.*, измерить *pf.* шагами. **pacemaker** *n.* (*sport*) лидер, задающий темп; (*med.*) кардиостимулятор. **pachyderm** ['pækɪ,dɜ:m] *n.* толстокожее (животное) *sb.* **pacific** [pə'sɪfɪk] *adj.* мирный; **P~** тихоокеанский; *n.* Тихий океан. **pacification** [,pæsɪfɪ'keɪʃ(ə)n] *n.* усмирение, умиротворение. **'pacifism** *n.* пацифизм. **'pacifist** *n.* пацифист. **'pacify** *v.t.* усмирять *impf.*, усмирить *pf.*; умиротворять *impf.*, умиротворить *pf.*

pack [pæk] *n.* у́зел (узла́); вьюк (*pl.* -ю́ки); (*soldier's*) ра́нец (-нца); (*hounds*) сво́ра; (*wolves*, *birds*) ста́я; (*cards*) коло́да; ~ **ice** пак, па́ковый лёд (льда, *loc.* льду́); ~ **of lies** сплошна́я ложь (лжи, *i.* ло́жью); *v.t.* накова́ть *impf.*, у~ *pf.*; укла́дывать *impf.*, уложи́ть (-жу́, -жишь) *pf.*; (*cram*) набива́ть *impf.*, наби́ть (-бью, -бьёшь) *pf.* **package** *n.* паке́т, свёрток (-тка); (*packaging*) упако́вка. **packaging** *n.* упако́вка. **packet** *n.* паке́т; па́чка; (*money*) куш. **packhorse** *n.* вью́чная ло́шадь (*pl.* -ди, -дей, *i.* -дьми́). **packing-case** *n.* я́щик. **packing-needle** *n.* упако́вочная игла́ (*pl.* -лы).

pact [pækt] *n.* догово́р, пакт.

pad[1] [pæd] *v.i.* (*walk*) идти́ (иду́, идёшь; шёл, шла) *impf.*, пойти́ (пойду́, -дёшь; пошёл, -шла́) *pf.* неслы́шным ша́гом.

pad[2] [pæd] *n.* (*cushion*) поду́шка, поду́шечка; (*guard*) щито́к (-тка́); (*of paper*) блокно́т; (*paw*) ла́па; *v.t.* набива́ть *impf.*, наби́ть (-бью, -бьёшь) *pf.*; подбива́ть *impf.*, подби́ть (подобью, -ьёшь) *pf.* **padding** *n.* наби́вка.

paddle[1] ['pæd(ə)l] *n.* (*oar*) (байда́рочное) весло́ (*pl.* вёсла, -сел, -слам); (*of* ~ *wheel*) ло́пасть (*pl.* -ти, -те́й); *v.i.* (*row*) грести́ (гребу́, -бёшь; грёб, -ла́) *impf.* байда́рочным весло́м.

paddle[2] ['pæd(ə)l] *v.i.* (*wade*) ходи́ть (хожу́, хо́дишь) *indet.*, идти́ (иду́, идёшь; шёл, шла) *det.*, пойти́ (пойду́, -дёшь; пошёл, -шла́) *pf.* босико́м по воде́; **paddling pool** лягуша́тник.

paddle-boat ['pæd(ə)l,bəʊt] *n.* колёсный парохо́д. **paddle-wheel** *n.* гребно́е колесо́ (*pl.* -ёса).

paddock ['pædək] *n.* небольшо́й луг (*loc.* -у́; *pl.* -а́).

padlock ['pædlɒk] *n.* вися́чий замо́к (-мка́); *v.t.* запира́ть *impf.*, запере́ть (запру́, -рёшь; за́пер, -ла́, -ло) *pf.* на вися́чий замо́к.

paediatric [,pi:dɪˈætrɪk] *adj.* педиатри́ческий. **paediatrician** [,pi:dɪəˈtrɪʃ(ə)n] *n.* педиа́тор. **paediatrics** *n.* педиатри́я.

paella [paɪˈelə] *n.* (*cul.*) пазлья.

pagan ['peɪgən] *n.* язы́чник, -ица; *adj.* язы́ческий. **paganism** *n.* язы́чество.

page[1] [peɪdʒ] *n.* (~*boy*) паж (-а́), ма́льчик-слуга́ *m.*; *v.t.* (*summon*) вызыва́ть *impf.*, вы́звать (вы́зову, -зовешь) *pf.*

page[2] [peɪdʒ] *n.* (*of book*) страни́ца.

pageant ['pædʒ(ə)nt] *n.* пы́шная проце́ссия; великоле́пное зре́лище. **pageantry** *n.* великоле́пие.

paginate ['pædʒɪ,neɪt] *v.t.* нумерова́ть *impf.*, про~ *pf.* страни́цы+*g.*

pagoda [pəˈgəʊdə] *n.* па́года.

paid [peɪd], **paid-up** *adj.* опла́ченный (-ен); *see* **pay**

pail [peɪl] *n.* ведро́ (*pl.* вёдра, -дер, -драм).

pain [peɪn] *n.* боль; *pl.* (*efforts*) уси́лия *nt.pl.*; **on** ~ **of death** под стра́хом сме́рти;

take ~ **over** прилага́ть *impf.*, приложи́ть (-жу́, -жишь) *pf.* уси́лия к+*d.*; *v.t.* причиня́ть *impf.*, причини́ть *pf.* боль+*d.*; (*fig.*) огорча́ть *impf.*, огорчи́ть *pf.* **painful** *adj.* боле́зненный (-ен, -енна); **be** ~ (*part of body*) боле́ть (-ли́т) *impf.* **painkiller** *n.* болеутоля́ющее сре́дство. **painless** *adj.* безболе́зненный (-ен, -енна). **painstaking** *adj.* стара́тельный, усе́рдный.

paint [peɪnt] *n.* кра́ска; *v.t.* кра́сить *impf.*, по~ *pf.*; (*portray*) писа́ть (пишу́, -шешь) *impf.*, на~ *pf.* кра́сками. **paintbrush** *n.* кисть (*pl.* -ти, -те́й). **painter**[1] *n.* (*artist*) худо́жник, -ица; (*decorator*) маля́р (-а́).

painter[2] ['peɪntə(r)] *n.* (*rope*) фа́линь *m.*

painting ['peɪntɪŋ] *n.* (*art*) жи́вопись; (*picture*) карти́на.

pair [peə(r)] *n.* па́ра; *not translated with nn. denoting a single object, e.g.* **a** ~ **of scissors** но́жницы (-ц) *pl.*; **one** ~ **of scissors** одни́ но́жницы *v.t.* & *i.* располага́ть(ся) *impf.*, расположи́ть(ся) (-жу́, -жит(ся)) *pf.* па́рами; ~ **off** уходи́ть (-ожу́, -о́дишь) *impf.*, уйти́ (уйду́, -дёшь; ушёл, ушла́) *pf.* па́рами.

Pakistan [,pɑ:kɪˈstɑ:n, ,pækɪ-] *n.* Пакиста́н.

pal [pæl] *n.* това́рищ, прия́тель *m.*; ~ **up with** дружи́ть (-жу́, -у́жи́шь) *impf.*, подружи́ться (-ужу́сь, -у́жи́шься) *pf.* с+*i.*

palace ['pælɪs] *n.* дворе́ц (-рца́); *attr.* дворцо́вый.

palaeographer [,pælɪˈɒgrəfə(r)] *n.* палео́граф. **palaeography** *n.* палеогра́фия. **palaeolithic** [,pælɪəʊˈlɪθɪk] *adj.* палеолити́ческий. **palaeon'tologist** *n.* палеонто́лог. **palaeon'tology** *n.* палеонтоло́гия. **palaeozoic** [,pælɪəʊˈzəʊɪk] *adj.* палеозо́йский.

palatable ['pælətəb(ə)l] *adj.* вку́сный (-сен, -сна́, -сно); (*fig.*) прия́тный. **palatal** *adj.* нёбный; (*ling. also*) палата́льный; *n.* палата́льный (звук) *sb.* **palatalize** *v.t.* палатализова́ть *impf.* & *pf.* **palate** *n.* нёбо; (*taste*) вкус.

palatial [pəˈleɪʃ(ə)l] *adj.* дворцо́вый; (*splendid*) великоле́пный.

pale[1] [peɪl] *n.* (*stake*) кол (-а́, *loc.* -у́; *pl.* -ья); (*boundary*) грани́ца; (*fig.*) преде́лы *m.pl.*

pale[2] [peɪl] *adj.* бле́дный (-ден, -дна́, -дно, бле́дны); *v.i.* бледне́ть *impf.*, по~ *pf.* **paleface** *n.* бледноли́цый *sb.*

palette ['pælɪt] *n.* пали́тра. **palette-knife** *n.* мастихи́н, шта́пель *m.*

paling(s) ['peɪlɪŋ] *n.* частоко́л.

palisade [,pælɪˈseɪd] *n.* частоко́л, палиса́д.

pall[1] [pɔ:l] *n.* покро́в. **pallbearer** *n.* несу́щий *sb.* гроб.

pall[2] [pɔ:l] *v.i.*: ~ **on** надоеда́ть *impf.*, надое́сть (-е́м, -е́шь, -е́ст, -еди́м; -е́л) *pf.*+*d.*

palliasse ['pælɪ,æs] *n.* соло́менный тюфя́к (-а́).

palliative ['pælɪətɪv] *adj.* смягча́ющий, паллиати́вный; *n.* смягча́ющее сре́дство, паллиати́в.

pallid ['pælɪd] *adj.* бле́дный (-ден, -дна́, -дно,

бле́дный). **pallor** *n.* бле́дность.

palm[1] [pɑ:m] *n.* (*tree*) па́льма; (*branch*) па́льмовая ветвь (*pl.* -ви, -ве́й); (*willow-branch as substitute*) ве́точка ве́рбы; ~ **oil** па́льмовое ма́сло; **P~ Sunday** Ве́рбное воскресе́нье.

palm[2] [pɑ:m] *n.* (*of hand*) ладо́нь; *v.t.* (*conceal*) пря́тать (-я́чу, -я́чешь) *impf.*, c~ *pf.* в руке́; ~ **off** всу́чивать *impf.*, всучи́ть (-учу́, -у́чишь) *pf.* (**on** +*d.*). **palmist** *n.* хирома́нт, ~ка. **palmistry** *n.* хирома́нтия.

palmy ['pɑ:mɪ] *adj.* (*flourishing*) цвету́щий.

palpable ['pælpəb(ə)l] *adj.* осяза́емый.

palpitate ['pælpɪˌteɪt] *v.i.* (*throb*) (си́льно) би́ться (бьётся) *impf.*; (*tremble*) трепета́ть (-ещу́, -е́щешь) *impf.* **palpitations** *n.* (си́льное) сердцебие́ние, пульса́ция.

palsy ['pɔ:lzɪ, 'pɒl-] *n.* парали́ч (-а́).

paltry ['pɔ:ltrɪ, 'pɒl-] *adj.* ничто́жный.

pampas ['pæmpəs] *n.* пампа́сы (-сов) *pl.* **pampas-grass** *n.* пампа́сная трава́.

pamper ['pæmpə(r)] *v.t.* балова́ть *impf.*, из~ *pf.*

pamphlet ['pæmflɪt] *n.* брошю́ра.

pan[1] [pæn] *n.* (*saucepan*) кастрю́ля; (*frying-*~) сковорода́ (*pl.* ско́вороды, -о́д, -ода́м); (*bowl: of scales*) ча́шка; *v.t.*: ~ **off, out** промыва́ть *impf.*, промы́ть (-мо́ю, -мо́ешь) *pf.*

pan[2] [pæn] *v.i.* (*cin.*) панорами́ровать *impf.* & *pf.*

panama (hat) ['pænəˌmɑ:] *n.* пана́ма.

panacea [ˌpænə'si:ə] *n.* панаце́я.

pan-American [ˌpænə'merɪkən] *adj.* панамерика́нский.

pancake ['pænkeɪk] *n.* блин (-а́); *v.i.* (*aeron.*) парашюти́ровать *impf.*, c~ *pf.*

panchromatic [ˌpænkrəʊ'mætɪk] *adj.* панхромати́ческий.

pancreas ['pæŋkrɪəs] *n.* поджелу́дочная железа́ (*pl.* -езы, -ёз, -еза́м).

panda ['pændə] *n.* па́нда; **giant** ~ бамбу́ковый медве́дь *m.*

pandemonium [ˌpændɪ'məʊnɪəm] *n.* гвалт.

pander ['pændə(r)] *n.* сво́дник; *v.i.*: ~ **to** потво́рствовать *impf.*+*d.*

pane [peɪn] *n.* око́нное стекло́ (*pl.* стёкла, -кол, -клам).

panel ['pæn(ə)l] *n.* пане́ль, филёнка; (*control-*~) щит (-а́) управле́ния; (*list of jurors*) спи́сок (-ска) прися́жных; (*jury*) прися́жные *sb.*; (*team in discussion, quiz*) уча́стники *m.pl.* (диску́ссии, виктори́ны); (*team of experts*) гру́ппа специали́стов; *v.t.* обшива́ть *impf.*, обши́ть (обошью́, -ьёшь) *pf.* пане́лями. **panelling** *n.* пане́льная обши́вка.

pang [pæŋ] *n.* о́страя боль; *pl.* му́ки (-к) *pl.*

panic ['pænɪk] *n.* па́ника; *v.i.* впада́ть *impf.*, впасть (-аду́, -адёшь; -ал) *pf.* в па́нику. **panicky** *adj.* пани́ческий.

panicle ['pænɪk(ə)l] *n.* метёлка.

panic-monger ['pænɪkˌmʌŋgə] *n.* паникёр. **panic-stricken** *adj.* охва́ченный (-ен) па́ни-

кой; *adj.* пани́ческий.

pannier ['pænɪə(r)] *n.* корзи́нка.

panorama [ˌpænə'rɑ:mə] *n.* панора́ма. **panoramic** [ˌpænə'ræmɪk] *adj.* панора́мный.

pansy ['pænzɪ] *n.* аню́тины гла́зки (-зок) *pl.*

pant [pænt] *v.i.* задыха́ться *impf.*, задохну́ться (-о́х(ну́л)ся, -о́х(ну́)лась) *pf.*; пыхте́ть (-хчу́, -хти́шь) *impf.*

pantheism ['pænθɪˌɪz(ə)m] *n.* пантеи́зм. **pantheist** *n.* пантеи́ст. **panthe'istic** *adj.* пантеисти́ческий.

panther ['pænθə(r)] *n.* панте́ра, барс.

panties ['pæntɪz] *n.* тру́сики (-ков) *pl.*

pantomime ['pæntəˌmaɪm] *n.* рожде́ственское представле́ние для дете́й; (*dumb show*) пантоми́ма.

pantry ['pæntrɪ] *n.* кладова́я *sb.*; (*butler's*) буфе́тная *sb.*

pants [pænts] *n.* (*trousers*) брю́ки (-к) *pl.*; (*underpants*) кальсо́ны (-н) *pl.*, трусы́ (-со́в) *pl.*

papacy ['peɪpəsɪ] *n.* па́пство. **papal** *adj.* па́пский.

paper ['peɪpə(r)] *n.* бума́га; *pl.* докуме́нты *m.pl.*; (*newspaper*) газе́та; (*wallpaper*) обо́и (-о́ев) *pl.*; (*dissertation*) докла́д; *adj.* бума́жный; *v.t.* окле́ивать *impf.*, окле́ить *pf.* обо́ями. **paperback** *n.* кни́га в бума́жной обло́жке. **paperclip** *n.* скре́пка. **paper-hanger** *n.* обо́йщик. **paper-knife** *n.* разрезно́й нож (-а́). **paper-mill** *n.* бума́жная фа́брика. **paperweight** *n.* пресс-папье́ *nt.indecl.* **papery** *adj.* бума́жный.

papier maché [ˌpæpjeɪ 'mæʃeɪ] *n.* папье́-маше́ *nt.indecl.*

paprika ['pæprɪkə, pə'pri:kə] *n.* кра́сный пе́рец (-рца(у)).

papyrus [pə'paɪərəs] *n.* папи́рус.

par [pɑ:(r)] *n.* (*equality*) ра́венство; (*normal condition*) норма́льное состоя́ние; ~ **of exchange** парите́т; **above, below,** ~ вы́ше, ни́же, номина́льной цены́; **on a** ~ **with** наравне́ c+*i.*

parable ['pærəb(ə)l] *n.* при́тча.

parabola [pə'ræbələ] *n.* пара́бола. **parabolic** [ˌpærə'bɒlɪk] *adj.* параболи́ческий.

parachute ['pærəˌʃu:t] *n.* парашю́т; *v.t.* сбра́сывать *impf.*, сбро́сить *pf.* с парашю́том; *v.i.* спуска́ться *impf.*, спусти́ться (-ущу́сь, -у́стишься) *pf.* с парашю́том. **parachutist** *n.* парашюти́ст.

parade [pə'reɪd] *n.* пара́д; (*display*) выставле́ние напока́з; *v.t. & i.* стро́ить(ся) *impf.*, по~ *pf.*; *v.t.* (*show off*) выставля́ть *impf.*, вы́ставить *pf.* напока́з. **parade-ground** *n.* плац.

paradigm ['pærəˌdaɪm] *n.* паради́гма.

paradise ['pærəˌdaɪs] *n.* рай (*loc.* раю́).

paradox ['pærəˌdɒks] *n.* парадо́кс. **para'doxical** *adj.* парадокса́льный.

paraffin ['pærəfɪn] *n.* парафи́н; (~ *oil*) кероси́н; **liquid** ~ парафи́новое ма́сло; *attr.* парафи́новый; ~ **wax** твёрдый парафи́н.

paragon ['pærəgən] *n.* образе́ц (-зца́).

paragraph ['pærə,grɑ:f] *n.* абза́ц; (*news item*) (газе́тная) заме́тка.

parakeet ['pærə,ki:t] *n.* длиннохво́стый попуга́й.

parallax ['pærə,læks] *n.* паралла́кс.

parallel ['pærə,lel] *adj.* паралле́льный; ~ **bars** паралле́льные бру́сья *m.pl.*; *n.* паралле́ль. **para'llelogram** *n.* параллелогра́мм.

paralyse ['pærə,laiz] *v.t.* парализова́ть *impf.* & *pf.* **paralysis** [pə'rælisis] *n.* парали́ч (-а́). **paralytic** [,pærə'litik] *n.* парали́тик; *adj.* парали́чный.

parameter [pə'ræmitə(r)] *n.* пара́метр.

paramilitary [,pærə'militəri] *adj.* полувое́нный.

paramount ['pærə,maunt] *adj.* (*supreme*) верхо́вный; (*pre-eminent*) первостепе́нный (-нен, -нна).

paranoia [,pærə'nɔiə] *n.* парано́йя.

parapet ['pærəpit] *n.* парапе́т; (*mil.*) бру́ствер.

paraphernalia [,pærəfə'neiliə] *n.* (*personal belongings*) ли́чное иму́щество; (*accessories*) принадле́жности *f.pl.*

paraphrase ['pærə,freiz] *n.* переска́з, парафра́за; *v.t.* переска́зывать *impf.*, пересказа́ть (-ажу́, -а́жешь) *pf.*; парафрази́ровать *impf.* & *pf.*

paraplegia [,pærə'pli:dʒə] *n.* параплеги́я.

parapsychology [,pærəsai'kɒlədʒi] *n.* парапсихоло́гия.

parasite ['pærə,sait] *n.* парази́т; (*person*) туне́ядец (-дца). **parasitic(al)** [,pærə'sitik(ə)l] *adj.* паразити́ческий, парази́тный.

parasol ['pærə,sɒl] *n.* зо́нтик.

paratrooper ['pærə,tru:pə(r)] *n.* парашюти́ст-деса́нтник, авиадеса́нтник. **paratroops** *n.* парашютно-деса́нтные войска́ *nt.pl.*

paratyphoid [,pærə'taifɔid] *n.* парати́ф.

parboil ['pɑ:bɔil] *v.t.* слегка́ отва́ривать *impf.*, отвари́ть (-рю́, -ришь) *pf.*

parcel ['pɑ:s(ə)l] *n.* паке́т, посы́лка; (*of land*) уча́сток (-тка); ~ **post** почто́во-посы́лочная слу́жба; *v.t.*: ~ **out** дели́ть (-лю́, -лишь) *impf.*, раз~ *pf.*; ~ **up** завёртывать *impf.*, заверну́ть *pf.* в паке́т.

parch [pɑ:tʃ] *v.t.* иссуша́ть *impf.*, иссуши́ть (-ит) *pf.*; **become ~ed** пересыха́ть *impf.*, пересо́хнуть (-x) *pf.*

parchment ['pɑ:tʃmənt] *n.* перга́мент; *attr.* перга́мен(т)ный.

pardon ['pɑ:d(ə)n] *n.* проще́ние; извине́ние; (*leg.*) поми́лование; *v.t.* проща́ть *impf.*, прости́ть *pf.*; (*leg.*) поми́ловать *pf.* **pardonable** *adj.* прости́тельный.

pare [peə(r)] *v.t.* обреза́ть *impf.*, обре́зать (-е́жу, -е́жешь) *pf.*; (*fruit*) чи́стить *impf.*, o~ *pf.*; ~ **away, down** (*fig.*) сокраща́ть *impf.*, сократи́ть (-ащу́, -ати́шь) *pf.*

parent ['peərənt] *n.* роди́тель *m.*, ~ница; (*forefather*) пре́док (-дка); (*origin*) причи́на. **parentage** *n.* происхожде́ние. **parental**

[pə'rent(ə)l] *adj.* роди́тельский.

parenthesis [pə'renθəsis] *n.* (*word, clause*) вво́дное сло́во (*pl.* -ва́), предложе́ние; *pl.* (*brackets*) ско́бки *f.pl.*; **in ~** в ско́бках.

pariah [pə'raiə, 'pæriə] *n.* па́рия *c.g.*

parings ['peəriŋz] *n.* обре́зки *f.pl.*

Paris ['pæris] *n.* Пари́ж.

parish ['pæriʃ] *n.* (*area*) прихо́д; (*inhabitants*) прихожа́не *pl.*; *attr.* прихо́дский. **parishioner** [pə'riʃənə(r)] *n.* прихожа́нин (*pl.* -а́не, -а́н), -а́нка.

parity ['pæriti] *n.* ра́венство; (*econ.*) парите́т.

park [pɑ:k] *n.* парк; (*national ~*) запове́дник; (*for cars etc.*) стоя́нка; *v.t.* & *abs.* ста́вить *impf.*, по~ *pf.* (маши́ну); паркова́ть *impf.*, за~ *pf.* (маши́ну). **parking** *n.* стоя́нка. **parking-meter** *n.* парко́вочный автома́т.

parley ['pɑ:li] *n.* перегово́ры (-ров) *pl.*; *v.i.* вести́ (веду́, -дёшь; вёл, -а́) *impf.* перегово́ры.

parliament ['pɑ:ləmənt] *n.* парла́мент. **parliamen'tarian** *n.* знато́к (-а́) парла́ментской пра́ктики. **parlia'mentary** *adj.* парла́ментский.

parlour ['pɑ:lə(r)] *n.* гости́ная *sb.*; приёмная *sb.* **parlourmaid** *n.* го́рничная *sb.*

parochial [pə'rəukiəl] *adj.* прихо́дский; (*fig.*) ограни́ченный (-ен, -енна). **parochialism** *n.* ограни́ченность, у́зкость.

parody ['pærədi] *n.* паро́дия; *v.t.* пароди́ровать *impf.* & *pf.*

parole [pə'rəul] *n.* че́стное сло́во; освобожде́ние под че́стное сло́во; (*password*) паро́ль *m.*; **on ~** освобождённый (-ён, -ена́) под че́стное сло́во.

paroxysm ['pærək,siz(ə)m] *n.* пароксизм, припа́док (-дка).

parquet ['pɑ:ki, -kei] *n.* парке́т; *attr.* парке́тный; *v.t.* устила́ть *impf.*, устла́ть (устелю́, -лешь) *pf.* парке́том.

parricidal [,pæri'said(ə)l] *adj.* отцеуби́йственный (-ен, -енна). **'parricide** *n.* (*action*) отцеуби́йство; (*person*) отцеуби́йца *c.g.*

parrot ['pærət] *n.* попуга́й; *v.t.* повторя́ть *impf.*, повтори́ть *pf.* как попуга́й.

parry ['pæri] *v.t.* пари́ровать *impf.* & *pf.*, от~ *pf.*

parse [pɑ:z] *v.t.* де́лать *impf.*, c~ *pf.* разбо́р+*g.*

parsimonious [,pɑ:si'məuniəs] *adj.* бережли́вый; (*mean*) скупо́й (скуп, -а́, -о). **parsimony** ['pɑ:siməni] *n.* бережли́вость; ску́пость.

parsley ['pɑ:sli] *n.* петру́шка.

parsnip ['pɑ:snip] *n.* пастерна́к.

parson ['pɑ:s(ə)n] *n.* прихо́дский свяще́нник. **parsonage** *n.* дом (*pl.* -а́) прихо́дского свяще́нника.

part [pɑ:t] *n.* часть (*pl.* -ти, -те́й), до́ля (*pl.* -ли, -ле́й); (*taking ~*) уча́стие; (*in play*) роль (*pl.* -ли, -ле́й); (*mus.*) па́ртия; (*in dispute*) сторона́ (*a.* -ону; *pl.* -оны, -о́н, -она́м); **for the most ~** бо́льшей ча́стью; **in**

~ ча́стью; **for my** ~ что каса́ется меня́; **take** ~ **in** уча́ствовать *impf.* в+*p.*; ~ **and parcel** неотъе́млемая часть; *v.t.* & *i.* (*divide*) разделя́ть(ся) *impf.*, раздели́ть(ся) (-лю(сь), -лишь(ся)) *pf.*; *v.i.* (*leave*) расстава́ться (-таю́сь, -таёшься) *impf.*, расста́ться (-а́нусь, -а́нешься) *pf.* (**from, with** с+*i.*); ~ **one's hair** де́лать пробо́р, с~ *pf.* себе́ пробо́р.

partake [pɑ:'teɪk] *v.i.* принима́ть *impf.*, приня́ть (приму́, -мешь; при́нял, -а́, -о) *pf.* уча́стие (**in, of** в+*p.*); (*eat*) есть (ем, ешь, ест, еди́м; ел *impf.*, съ~ *pf.* (**of** +*a.*).

partial ['pɑ:ʃ(ə)l] *adj.* (*incomplete*) части́чный, непо́лный (-лон, -лна́, -лно); (*biased*) пристра́стный; ~ **to** неравноду́шный к+*d.* **partiality** [ˌpɑ:ʃɪ'ælɪtɪ] *n.* пристра́стие (**for** к+*d.*). **partially** *adv.* части́чно.

participant [pɑ:'tɪsɪpənt] *n.* уча́стник, -ица (**in** +*g.*). **participate** *v.i.* уча́ствовать *impf.* (**in** в+*p.*). **partici'pation** *n.* уча́стие (**in** в+*p.*).

participial [ˌpɑ:tɪ'sɪpɪ(ə)l] *adj.* прича́стный. '**participle** *n.* прича́стие.

particle ['pɑ:tɪk(ə)l] *n.* части́ца.

particoloured ['pɑ:tɪˌkʌləd] *adj.* разноцве́тный.

particular [pə'tɪkjʊlə(r)] *adj.* осо́бый, осо́бенный; (*careful*) тща́тельный; *n.* подро́бность; *pl.* подро́бный отчёт; **in** ~ в ча́стности.

parting ['pɑ:tɪŋ] *n.* (*leave-taking*) проща́ние; (*of hair*) пробо́р.

partisan ['pɑ:tɪˌzæn] *n.* (*adherent*) сторо́нник; (*mil.*) партиза́н (*g.pl.* -н); *attr.* узкопарти́йный; партиза́нский.

partition [pɑ:'tɪʃ(ə)n] *n.* разделе́ние, расчлене́ние; (*wall*) перегоро́дка, перебо́рка; *v.t.* разделя́ть *impf.*, раздели́ть (-лю, -лишь) *pf.*; ~ **off** отделя́ть *impf.*, отдели́ть (-лю, -лишь) *pf.* перегоро́дкой.

partitive ['pɑ:tɪtɪv] *adj.* раздели́тельный; ~ **genitive** роди́тельный раздели́тельный *sb.*

partly ['pɑ:tlɪ] *adv.* ча́стью, отча́сти.

partner ['pɑ:tnə(r)] *n.* (со)уча́стник; (*in business*) компаньо́н; (*in dance, game*) партнёр, ~ша. **partnership** *n.* (со)уча́стие, сотру́дничество; (*business*) това́рищество.

partridge ['pɑ:trɪdʒ] *n.* куропа́тка.

part-time [pɑ:t'taɪm] *adj.* (за́нятый (-т, -та́, -то)) непо́лный рабо́чий день.

party ['pɑ:tɪ] *n.* (*pol.*) па́ртия; (*group*) гру́ппа; (*social gathering*) вечери́нка; (*leg.*) сторона́ (*a.* -ону; *pl.* -оны, -о́н, -она́м); (*accomplice*) (со)уча́стник; **be a** ~ **to** принима́ть *impf.*, приня́ть (приму́, -мешь; при́нял, -а́. -о) *pf.* уча́стие в+*p.*; *attr.* парти́йный; ~ **line** (*pol.*) ли́ния па́ртии; (*telephone*) о́бщий телефо́нный про́вод (*pl.* -а́). **party-wall** *n.* о́бщая стена́ (*a.* -ну; *pl.* -ны, -н, -на́м).

pasha ['pɑ:ʃə] *n.* паша́ *m.*

pass [pɑ:s] *v.t.* & *i.* (*go past*) проходи́ть (-ожу́, -о́дишь) *impf.*, пройти́ (пройду́, -дёшь; прошёл, -шла́) *pf.* (**by** ми́мо+*g.*); (*travel past*) проезжа́ть *impf.*,

проє́хать (-е́ду, -е́дешь) *pf.* (**by** ми́мо+*g.*); (*go across; change*) переходи́ть (-ожу́, -о́дишь) *impf.*, перейти́ (-ейду́, -ейдёшь; -ешёл, -ешла́) *pf.* (+*a.*, че́рез+*a.*; **to** в+*a.*, к+*d.*); (*examination*) сдава́ть (сдаю́, -аёшь) *impf.*, сдать (-ам, -ашь, -аст, -ади́м; сдал, -а́, -о) *pf.* (экза́мен); *v.i.* (*happen*) происходи́ть (-ит) *impf.*, произойти́ (-ойдёт; -ошёл, -ошла́) *pf.*; (*cards*) пасова́ть *impf.*, с~ *pf.*; *v.t.* (*sport*) пасова́ть *impf.*, пасну́ть *pf.*; (*overtake*) обгоня́ть *impf.*, обогна́ть (обгоню́, -нишь; обогна́л, -а́, -о) *pf.*; (*time*) проводи́ть (-ожу́, -о́дишь) *impf.*, провести́ (-еду́, -едёшь; -ёл, -ела́) *pf.*; (*hand on*) передава́ть (-даю́, -даёшь) *impf.*, переда́ть (-а́м, -а́шь, -а́ст, -ади́м; пе́редал, -а́, -о) *pf.*; (*law, resolution*) принима́ть *impf.*, приня́ть (приму́, -мешь; при́нял, -а́, -о) *pf.*; (*sentence*) выноси́ть (-ошу́, -о́сишь) *impf.*, вы́нести (-су, -сешь; -с) *pf.* (**upon** +*d.*); ~ **as, for** слыть (слыву́, -вёшь; слыл, -а́, -о) *impf.*, про~ *pf.*+*i.*, за+*a.*; ~ **away** (*die*) сконча́ться *pf.*; ~ **by** (*omit*) пропуска́ть *impf.*, пропусти́ть (-ущу́, -у́стишь) *pf.*; ~ **off** (постепе́нно; хорошо́) проходи́ть (-ит) *impf.*, пройти́ (-йдёт; прошёл, -шла́) *pf.*; ~ **out** (*coll.*) отключа́ться *impf.*, отключи́ться *pf.*; ~ **over** (*in silence*) обходи́ть (-ожу́, -о́дишь) *impf.*, обойти́ (обойду́, -дёшь; обошёл, -шла́) *pf.* молча́нием; ~ **through** (*experience*) пережива́ть *impf.*, пережи́ть (-иву́, -ивёшь; пе́режил, -а́, -о) *pf.*; *n.* (*permit*) про́пуск (*pl.* -а́); (*free* ~) беспла́тный биле́т; (*cards; sport*) пас; (*fencing*) вы́пад; (*juggling*) фо́кус; (*hypnotism*) пасс; (*mountain* ~) перева́л; **bring to** ~ соверша́ть *impf.*, соверши́ть *pf.*; **come to** ~ случа́ться *impf.*, случи́ться *pf.*; **make a** ~ **at** пристава́ть (-таю́, -таёшь) *impf.*, приста́ть (-а́ну, -а́нешь) *pf.* к+*d.*; ~ **degree** дипло́м без отли́чия.

passable ['pɑ:səb(ə)l] *adj.* проходи́мый, прое́зжий; (*fairly good*) неплохо́й (-х, -ха́, -хо).

passage ['pæsɪdʒ] *n.* прохо́д, прое́зд; (*of time*) ход; (*sea trip*) рейс; (*in house*) коридо́р; (*in book*) отры́вок (-вка); (*musical*) пасса́ж.

passenger ['pæsɪndʒə(r)] *n.* пассажи́р.

passer-by [ˌpɑ:sə'baɪ] *n.* прохо́жий *sb.*

passing ['pɑ:sɪŋ] *adj.* (*transient*) мимолётный, преходя́щий; (*cursory*) бе́глый; *n.*: **in** ~ мимохо́дом.

passion ['pæʃ(ə)n] *n.* страсть (*pl.* -ти, -те́й) (**for** к+*d.*); (*attraction*) увлече́ние; (*anger*) вспы́шка гне́ва; **P**~ (*of Christ; mus.*) стра́сти (-те́й) *f.pl.* (Христо́вы). **passionate** *adj.* стра́стный (-тен, -тна́, -тно), пы́лкий. **passion-flower** *n.* страстноцве́т.

passive ['pæsɪv] *adj.* пасси́вный; (*gram.*) страда́тельный; *n.* страда́тельный зало́г. **pa'ssivity** *n.* пасси́вность.

passkey ['pɑ:ski:] *n.* отмы́чка.

passmark ['pɑ:smɑ:k] *n.* посре́дственная оце́нка.

Passover ['pɑ:sˌəʊvə(r)] *n.* евре́йская па́сха.

passport ['pɑːspɔːt] *n.* па́спорт (*pl.* -á).

password ['pɑːswɜːd] *n.* паро́ль *m.*

past [pɑːst] *adj.* про́шлый; (*gram.*) проше́дший; *n.* про́шлое *sb.*; (*gram.*) проше́дшее вре́мя *nt.*; *prep.* ми́мо+*g.*; (*beyond*) за+*i.*; *adv.* ми́мо.

paste [peɪst] *n.* (*of flour*) те́сто; (*similar mixture*) па́ста; (*adhesive*) кле́йстер; (*of imitation gem*) страз; *v.t.* накле́ивать *impf.*, накле́ить *pf.*; ~ up раскле́ивать *impf.*, раскле́ить *pf.* **pasteboard** *n.* карто́н.

pastel ['pæst(ə)l] *n.* (*crayon*) пасте́ль; (*drawing*) рису́нок (-нка) пасте́лью; *attr.* пасте́льный.

pastern ['pæst(ə)n] *n.* ба́бка.

pasteurization [ˌpɑːstjəraɪ'zeɪʃ(ə)n, ˌpæst-] *n.* пастериза́ция. **'pasteurize** *v.t.* пастеризова́ть *impf. & pf.*

pastiche [pæ'stiːʃ] *n.* смесь.

pastille ['pæstɪl] *n.* лепёшка.

pastime ['pɑːstaɪm] *n.* развлече́ние; (*game*) игра́ (*pl.* -ры).

pastor ['pɑːstə(r)] *n.* па́стор. **pastoral** *adj.* (*bucolic*) пастора́льный; (*of pastor*) па́сторский; *n.* пастора́ль.

pastry ['peɪstrɪ] *n.* пече́нье, пиро́жное *sb.*

pasturage ['pɑːstʃərɪdʒ] *n.* пастьба́. **pasture** ['pɑːstʃə(r)] *n.* (*land*) па́стбище; (*herbage*) подно́жный корм (*loc.* -е & -ý); *v.t.* пасти́ (-сý, -сёшь; -с, -слá) *impf.*

pasty[1] ['pæstɪ] *n.* пирожо́к (-жка́).

pasty[2] ['pæstɪ] *adj.* тестообра́зный; (~-faced) бле́дный (-ден, -днá, -дно, бле́дны́).

pat [pæt] *n.* шлепо́к (-пка́); (*of butter etc.*) кусо́к (-ска́); *v.t.* хлопа́ть *impf.*, по~ *pf.*; *adj.* уме́стный; *adv.* кста́ти, своевре́менно.

patch [pætʃ] *n.* запла́та; (*over eye*) повя́зка (на глазу́); (*on face*) му́шка; (*spot*) пятно́ (*pl.* -тна, -тен, -тнам); (*piece of land*) уча́сток (-тка) земли́; ~ pocket накладно́й карма́н; *v.t.* ста́вить *impf.*, по~ *pf.* запла́ту, -ы, на+*a.*; ~ up (*fig.*) ула́живать *impf.*, ула́дить *pf.* **patchwork** *n.* лоску́тная рабо́та; *attr.* лоску́тный. **patchy** *adj.* пёстрый (пёстр, -á, пёстро́); (*uneven*) неро́вный (-вен, -внá, -вно).

pâté ['pæteɪ] *n.* паште́т.

patella [pə'telə] *n.* коле́нная ча́шка.

patent ['peɪt(ə)nt, 'pæt-] *adj.* патенто́ванный (-ан); (*obvious*) я́вный; ~ leather лакиро́ванная ко́жа; *n.* пате́нт; *v.t.* патентова́ть *impf.*, за~ *pf.* **paten'tee** *n.* владе́лец (-льца) пате́нта.

paternal [pə'tɜːn(ə)l] *adj.* отцо́вский; (*fatherly*) оте́ческий; ~ uncle дя́дя *m.* со стороны́ отца́. **paternity** *n.* отцо́вство.

path [pɑːθ] *n.* тропи́нка, тропа́ (*pl.* -пы, -п, тро́пáм); (*way*) путь (-ти́, -тём) *m.*

pathetic [pə'θetɪk] *adj.* жа́лостный, тро́гательный.

pathless ['pɑːθlɪs] *adj.* бездоро́жный.

pathological [ˌpæθə'lɒdʒɪk(ə)l] *adj.* патологи́ческий. **pathologist** [pə'θɒlədʒɪst] *n.*

пато́лог. **pa'thology** *n.* патоло́гия.

pathos ['peɪθɒs] *n.* па́фос.

pathway ['pɑːθweɪ] *n.* тропи́нка, тропа́ (*pl.* -пы, -п, тропа́м).

patience ['peɪʃ(ə)ns] *n.* терпе́ние; (*persistence*) упо́рство; (*cards*) пасья́нс. **patient** *adj.* терпели́вый; (*persistent*) упо́рный; *n.* больно́й *sb.*, пацие́нт, ~ка.

patina ['pætɪnə] *n.* пати́на.

patio ['pætɪəʊ] *n.* (*court*) вну́тренний дво́рик; (*terrace*) терра́са.

patriarch ['peɪtrɪɑːk] *n.* патриа́рх. **patri'archal** *adj.* патриарха́льный; (*relig.*) патриа́рший.

patrician [pə'trɪʃ(ə)n] *n.* аристокра́т, ~ка; (*hist.*) патри́ций; *adj.* аристократи́ческий; (*hist.*) патрициа́нский.

patricidal *etc. see* **parricide**

patrimonial [ˌpætrɪ'məʊnɪəl] *adj.* насле́дственный. **patrimony** ['pætrɪmənɪ] *n.* насле́дство.

patriot ['peɪtrɪət, 'pæt-] *n.* патрио́т, ~ка. **pa'triotic** [ˌpeɪtrɪ'ɒtɪk, ˌpæt-] *adj.* патриоти́ческий. **patriotism** *n.* патриоти́зм.

patrol [pə'trəʊl] *n.* патру́ль (-ля́) *m.*; (*action*) патрули́рование; *v.t. & i.* патрули́ровать *impf.*

patron ['peɪtrən] *n.* покрови́тель *m.*; (*of shop*) клие́нт, ~ка; ~ saint засту́пник, -ица. **patronage** *n.* покрови́тельство. **patroness** *n.* покрови́тельница. **patronize** *v.t.* покрови́тельствовать *impf.*+*d.*; (*shop*) быть клие́нтом, клие́нткой, +*g.*; (*treat condescendingly*) снисходи́тельно относи́ться (-ошу́сь, -о́сишься) *impf.*, к+*d.*

patronymic [ˌpætrə'nɪmɪk] *n.* родово́е и́мя *nt.*; (*Russian name*) о́тчество.

patter[1] ['pætə(r)] *v.i.* (*sound*) посту́кивать *impf.*; *n.* посту́кивание, лёгкий то́пот.

patter[2] ['pætə(r)] *n.* (*speech*) скорогово́рка.

pattern ['pæt(ə)n] *n.* (*paragon*) образе́ц (-зца́); (*model*) моде́ль; (*sewing*) вы́кройка; (*design*) узо́р.

patty ['pætɪ] *n.* пирожо́к (-жка́).

paunch [pɔːntʃ] *n.* брюшко́ (*pl.* -ки́, -ко́в), пу́зо.

pauper ['pɔːpə(r)] *n.* бедня́к (-á), ни́щий *sb.*

pause [pɔːz] *n.* па́уза, переры́в; *v.i.* де́лать *impf.*, с~ *pf.* па́узу; остана́вливаться *impf.*, останови́ться (-влю́сь, -вишься) *pf.*

pave [peɪv] *v.t.* мости́ть *impf.*, вы́~, за~ *pf.*; ~ the way подготовля́ть *impf.*, подгото́вить *pf.* по́чву (for для+*g.*). **pavement** *n.* тротуа́р, пане́ль.

pavilion [pə'vɪljən] *n.* (*building*) павильо́н; (*tent*) пала́тка, шатёр (-трá).

paw [pɔː] *n.* ла́па; *v.t.* тро́гать *impf.* ла́пой; (*horse*) бить (бьёт) *impf.* копы́том.

pawl [pɔːl] *n.* защёлка; (*naut.*) пал.

pawn[1] [pɔːn] *n.* (*chess*) пе́шка.

pawn[2] [pɔːn] *n.*: in ~ в закла́де; *v.t.* закла́дывать *impf.*, заложи́ть (-жý, -жишь) *pf.*; отдава́ть (-даю́, -даёшь) *impf.*, отда́ть (-а́м, -а́шь, -а́ст, -ади́м; о́тдал, -á, -о) *pf.* в зало́г.

pawnbroker *n.* ростовщи́к (-á), -и́ца. **pawnshop** *n.* ломба́рд.

pay [peɪ] *v.t.* плати́ть (-ачу́, -а́тишь) *impf.*, за~, у~ *pf.* (**for** за+*a.*); (*bill etc.*) опла́чивать *impf.*, оплати́ть (-ачу́, -а́тишь) *pf.*; *v.i.* (*be profitable*) окупа́ться *impf.*, окупи́ться (-ится) *pf.*; *n.* (*payment*) упла́та; (*wages*) жа́лованье, зарпла́та. **payable** *adj.* подлежа́щий упла́те. **pa'yee** *n.* получа́тель *m.*, ~ница; (*of cheque etc.*) предъяви́тель *m.*, ~ница. **payload** *n.* поле́зная нагру́зка. **payment** *n.* упла́та, платёж (-á); **by instalments** платёж (-á) в рассро́чку; ~ **in kind** пла́та нату́рой. **pay-packet** *n.* полу́чка. **payroll** *n.* платёжная ве́домость.

PC *abbr.* (*of Police Constable*) полице́йский, конста́бль; (*of personal computer*) ПК, персона́льный компью́тер.

PE *abbr.* (*of physical education*) физкульту́ра.

pea [pi:] *n.* (*also pl., collect.*) горо́х (-a(y)).

peace [pi:s] *n.* мир; (*treaty*) ми́рный догово́р; (*public order; tranquillity*) споко́йствие; (*quiet*) поко́й; *attr.* ми́рный; **at** ~ **with** в ми́ре с+*i.*; **in** ~ в поко́е; **make** ~ заключа́ть *impf.*, заключи́ть *pf.* мир; **make one's** ~ мири́ться *impf.*, по~ *pf.* (**with** с+*i.*); ~ **and quiet** мир и тишина́. **peaceable, peaceful** *adj.* ми́рный. **peace-loving** *adj.* миролюби́вый. **peace-offering** *n.* искупи́тельная же́ртва. **peacetime** *n.* ми́рное вре́мя *nt.*

peach [pi:tʃ] *n.* пе́рсик; (~-*tree*) пе́рсиковое де́рево (*pl.* дере́вья, -ьев).

peacock ['pi:kɒk] *n.* павли́н; ~ **butterfly** дневно́й павли́нный глаз. **peafowl** *n.* павли́н. **peahen** *n.* па́ва.

peak [pi:k] *n.* (*of cap*) козырёк (-рька́); (*summit; highest point*) верши́на; ~ **hour** часы́ *m.pl.* пик. **peak-load** *n.* максима́льная, пи́ковая, нагру́зка.

peaky ['pi:kɪ] *adj.* (*worn out*) изможде́нный (-ён, -ена́).

peal [pi:l] *n.* (*sound*) звон колоколо́в, трезво́н; (*set of bells*) набо́р колоколо́в; (*of thunder*) раска́т; (*of laughter*) взрыв; *v.i.* (*bells*) трезво́нить *impf.*; (*thunder*) греме́ть (-ми́т) *impf.*, по~ *pf.*; ~ **the bells** звони́ть *impf.*, по~ *pf.* в колокола́.

peanut ['pi:nʌt] *n.* земляно́й оре́х, ара́хис.

pear [peə(r)] *n.* гру́ша; (~-*tree*) гру́шевое де́рево (*pl.* дере́вья, -ьев). **pear-shaped** *adj.* грушеви́дный.

pearl [pɜ:l] *n.* же́мчуг (-a(y); *pl.* -á); (*single* ~, *also fig.*) жемчу́жина; ~ **barley** перло́вая крупа́; ~ **button** перламу́тровая пу́говица. **pearl-oyster** *n.* жемчу́жница. **pearly** *adj.* жемчу́жный.

peasant ['pez(ə)nt] *n.* крестья́нин (*pl.* -я́не, -я́н), -я́нка; *attr.* крестья́нский; ~ **woman** крестья́нка. **peasantry** *n.* крестья́нство.

peat [pi:t] *n.* торф (-a(y)). **peatbog** *n.* торфяни́к (-á). **peaty** *adj.* торфяно́й.

pebble ['peb(ə)l] *n.* га́лька. **pebbly** *adj.* по-

кры́тый га́лкой.

peccadillo [ˌpekə'dɪləʊ] *n.* грешо́к (-шка́).

peck [pek] *v.t. & i.* клева́ть (клюю́, клюёшь) *impf.*, клю́нуть *pf.*; *n.* клево́к (-вка́).

pectoral ['pektər(ə)l] *adj.* грудно́й; (*worn on chest*) нагру́дный.

peculiar [pɪ'kju:lɪə(r)] *adj.* (*distinctive*) своеобра́зный; (*special*) осо́бенный; (*strange*) стра́нный (-нен, -нна́, -нно); ~ **to** сво́йственный (-ен(ен), -енна) +*d.* **peculiarity** [pɪˌkju:lɪ'ærɪtɪ] *n.* осо́бенность; стра́нность.

pecuniary [pɪ'kju:nɪərɪ] *adj.* де́нежный.

pedagogical [ˌpedə'gɒgɪk((ə)l), -'gɒdʒɪk((ə)l)] *adj.* педагоги́ческий. **pedagogics** *n.* педаго́гика. 'pedagogue *n.* учи́тель (*pl.* -ля́) *m.*, педаго́г.

pedal ['ped(ə)l] *n.* педа́ль; *v.i.* нажима́ть *impf.*, нажа́ть (-жму́, -жмёшь) *pf.* педа́ль; (*ride bicycle*) е́хать (е́ду, е́дешь) *impf.*, по~ *pf.* на велосипе́де.

pedant ['ped(ə)nt] *n.* педа́нт. **pedantic** [pɪ'dæntɪk] *adj.* педанти́чный. **pedantry** *n.* педанти́чность.

peddle ['ped(ə)l] *v.t.* торгова́ть *impf.* вразно́с+*i.*

pedestal ['pedɪst(ə)l] *n.* пьедеста́л, подно́жие; (*of table*) ту́мба.

pedestrian [pɪ'destrɪən] *adj.* пе́ший, пешехо́дный; (*prosaic*) прозаи́ческий; *n.* пешехо́д; ~ **crossing** перехо́д. **pedestrianization** [pɪˌdestrɪəˌnaɪ'zeɪʃ(ə)n] *n.* созда́ние пешехо́дных зон. **pe'destrianize** *v.t.* запреща́ть *impf.*, запрети́ть (-ещу́, -ети́шь) *pf.* автомоби́льное движе́ние.

pedicure ['pedɪˌkjʊə(r)] *n.* педикю́р.

pedigree ['pedɪgri:] *n.* (*genealogy*) родосло́вная *sb.*; (*descent*) происхожде́ние; *adj.* поро́дистый, племенно́й.

pediment ['pedɪmənt] *n.* фронто́н.

pedlar ['pedlə(r)] *n.* разно́счик.

pedometer [pɪ'dɒmɪtə(r)] *n.* шагоме́р.

peek [pi:k] *v.i.* (~ **in**) загля́дывать *impf.*, загляну́ть (-ну́, -нешь) *pf.*; (~ **out**) выгля́дывать *impf.*, вы́глянуть *pf.*

peel [pi:l] *n.* ко́рка, ко́жица; *v.t.* очища́ть *impf.*, очи́стить *pf.*; *v.i.*: ~ **off** (*detach o.s.*) сходи́ть (-ит) *impf.*, сойти́ (сойдёт; сошёл, -шла́) *pf.* **peelings** *n.* очи́стки (-ков) *pl.*, шелуха́.

peep [pi:p] *v.i.* (~ **in**) загля́дывать *impf.*, загляну́ть (-ну́, -нешь) *pf.*; (~ **out**) выгля́дывать *impf.*, вы́глянуть *pf.*; *n.* (*glance*) бы́стрый взгляд; ~ **of day** рассве́т. **peephole** *n.* глазо́к (-зка́).

peer[1] [pɪə(r)] *v.i.* всма́триваться *impf.*, всмотре́ться (-рю́сь, -ришься) *pf.* (**at** в+*a.*).

peer[2] [pɪə(r)] *n.* (*noble*) пэр, лорд; (*equal*) ра́вный *sb.*, ро́вня *c.g.* **peerage** *n.* (*class*) сосло́вие пэ́ров; (*rank*) зва́ние пэ́ра. **peeress** *n.* (*peer's wife*) супру́га пэ́ра; ле́ди *f.indecl.* **peerless** *adj.* несравне́нный (-е́нен, -е́нна), бесподо́бный.

peeved [pi:vd] *adj.* раздражённый (-ён, -ена́).

peevish *adj.* раздражи́тельный, брюзг-
ли́вый.

peewit ['piːwɪt] *n.* чи́бис.

peg [peg] *n.* ко́лышек (-шка), деревя́нный
гвоздь (-дя́; *pl.* -ди, -де́й) *m.*; (*for hat etc.*)
ве́шалка; (*on violin etc.*) коло́к (-лка́); off
the ~ гото́вый; take down a ~ оса́живать
impf., осади́ть (-ажу́, -а́дишь) *pf.*; *v.t.* при-
крепля́ть *impf.*, прикрепи́ть *pf.* ко́лышком,
-ками; (*price etc.*) иску́сственно поддёр-
живать *impf.*, поддержа́ть (-жу́, -жишь) *pf.*;
v.i.: ~ away приле́жно рабо́тать *impf.* (at
над+*i.*); ~ out (*die*) помира́ть *impf.*, поме-
ре́ть (-мру́, -мрёшь; по́мер, -ла́, -ло) *pf.*

pejorative [pɪ'dʒɒrətɪv, 'piːdʒə-] *adj.* уничижи́-
тельный.

peke [piːk], **Pekin(g)ese** [ˌpiːkɪ'niːz] *n.* кита́й-
ский мопс.

pelican ['pelɪkən] *n.* пелика́н.

pellagra [pɪ'lægrə, -'leɪgrə] *n.* пелла́гра.

pellet ['pelɪt] *n.* ка́тышек (-шка); (*shot*)
дроби́на.

pellicle ['pelɪk(ə)l] *n.* ко́жица, плёнка.

pell-mell [pel'mel] *adv.* (*in disorder*) беспоря́-
дочно; (*headlong*) очертя́, сломя́, го́лову.

pellucid [pɪ'luːsɪd, -'ljuːsɪd] *adj.* (*transparent*)
прозра́чный; (*clear*) я́сный (я́сен, ясна́,
я́сно, я́сны́).

pelmet ['pelmɪt] *n.* ламбреке́н.

pelt[1] [pelt] *n.* (*animal skin*) шку́ра, ко́жа.

pelt[2] [pelt] *v.t.* забра́сывать *impf.*, заброса́ть
pf.; *v.i.* (*rain*) бараба́нить (-ит) *impf.*; *n.*:
(at) full ~ со всех ног.

pelvic ['pelvɪk] *adj.* та́зовый. **pelvis** *n.* таз
(*loc.* -е & -у́; *pl.* -ы́).

pen[1] [pen] *n.* (*for writing*) перо́ (*pl.* -рья, -
рьев); ~ and ink пи́сьменные принадлёж-
ности *f.pl.*; slip of the ~ опи́ска.

pen[2] [pen] *n.* (*enclosure*) заго́н; *v.t.* загоня́ть
impf., загна́ть (загоню́, -нишь; загна́л, -а́,
-о) *pf.*

pen[3] [pen] *n.* (*female swan*) са́мка ле́бедя.

penal ['piːn(ə)l] *adj.* уголо́вный; (*punishable*)
наказу́емый; ~ battalion штрафно́й баталь-
о́н; ~ code уголо́вный ко́декс; ~ servitude
ка́торжные рабо́ты *f.pl.* **penalize** *v.t.*
нака́зывать *impf.*, наказа́ть (-ажу́, -а́жешь)
pf.; (*sport*) штрафова́ть *impf.*, о~ *pf.*
penalty ['pen(ə)ltɪ] *n.* наказа́ние, взыска́ние;
(*sport*) штраф; ~ area штрафна́я пло-
ща́дка; ~ kick штрафно́й уда́р. **penance**
['penəns] *n.* епитимья́ (*g.pl.* -ми́й).

penchant ['pãʃã] *n.* скло́нность (for к+*d.*).

pencil ['pensɪl] *n.* каранда́ш (-а́); *v.t.* (*write*)
писа́ть (пишу́, -шешь) *impf.*, на~ *pf.*
карандашо́м; (*draw*) рисова́ть *impf.*, на~
pf. карандашо́м. **pencil-case** *n.* пена́л.
pencil-sharpener *n.* точи́лка.

pendant ['pend(ə)nt] *n.* подве́ска, куло́н; *adj.*
вися́чий.

pending ['pendɪŋ] *adj.* (*awaiting decision*)
ожида́ющий реше́ния; patent ~ пате́нт
зая́влен; *prep.* (*during*) во вре́мя+*g.*; (*until*)

в ожида́нии+*g.*, до+*g.*

pendulous ['pendjʊləs] *adj.* вися́чий, отви́с-
лый.

pendulum ['pendjʊləm] *n.* ма́ятник.

penetrate ['penɪtreɪt] *v.t.* прони́зывать *impf.*,
пронизáть (-ижу́, -и́жешь) *pf.*; *v.i.* проникáть *impf.*, прони́кнуть (-к) *pf.* (into в+*a.*;
through че́рез+*a.*). **penetrating** *adj.* прони-
цáтельный; (*sound*) пронзи́тельный. **pene-
'tration** *n.* проникнове́ние; (*insight*) прони-
ца́тельность.

pen-friend ['penfrend] *n.* знако́мый *sb.* по
письма́м.

penguin ['peŋgwɪn] *n.* пингви́н.

penicillin [ˌpenɪ'sɪlɪn] *n.* пеницилли́н.

peninsula [pɪ'nɪnsjʊlə] *n.* полуо́стров (*pl.* -á).
peninsular *adj.* полуостровно́й.

penis ['piːnɪs] *n.* муско́й полово́й член.

penitence ['penɪt(ə)ns] *n.* раска́яние, покая́-
ние. **penitent** *adj.* раска́ивающийся; *n.* ка́ю-
щийся гре́шник. **peni'tential** *adj.* покая́н-
ный.

penknife ['pennaɪf] *n.* перочи́нный нож (-á).

pen-name ['penneɪm] *n.* псевдони́м.

pennant ['penənt] *n.* вы́мпел.

penniless ['penɪlɪs] *adj.* безде́нежный; *pred.*
без гроша́; (*poor*) бе́дный (-ден, -дна́, -дно,
бе́дны́).

penny ['penɪ] *n.* пе́нни *nt.indecl.*, пенс.

pension ['penʃ(ə)n] *n.* пе́нсия; *v.t.*: ~ off
увольня́ть *impf.*, уво́лить *pf.* на пе́нсию.
pensionable *adj.* даю́щий, име́ющий, пра́во
на пе́нсию; (*age*) пенсио́нный. **pensioner**
n. пенсионе́р, ~ка.

pensive ['pensɪv] *adj.* заду́мчивый.

penta- ['pentə] *in comb.* пяти..., пента... .
pentacle *n.* маги́ческая фигу́ра. **pentagon**
n. пятиуго́льник; the P~ Пентаго́н. **pen-
tagonal** [pen'tægən(ə)l] *adj.* пятиуго́льный.
pentagram *n.* пентагра́мма. **pentahedron**
[ˌpentə'hiːdrən] *n.* пятигра́нник. **pentameter**
[pen'tæmɪtə(r)] *n.* пента́метр. **pentathlon**
[pen'tæθlən] *n.* пятибо́рье. **pentatonic**
[ˌpentə'tɒnɪk] *adj.* пентато́нный.

Pentecost ['pentɪˌkɒst] *n.* Пятидеся́тница.

penthouse ['penthaʊs] *n.* особня́к (-á) на
кры́ше многоэта́жного до́ма.

pent-up [pent'ʌp] *adj.* (*anger etc.*) сде́рживае-
мый.

penultimate [pɪ'nʌltɪmət] *adj.* (*n.*) предпос-
ле́дний (слог).

penumbra [pɪ'nʌmbrə] *n.* полуте́нь (*loc.* -éни;
pl. -е́ни, -еней).

penurious [pɪ'njʊərɪəs] *adj.* бе́дный (-ден,
-дна́, -дно, бе́дны́); (*stingy*) скупо́й (скуп,
-á, -о). **penury** [pɪ'penjʊrɪ] *n.* нужда́.

peony ['piːənɪ] *n.* пио́н.

people ['piːp(ə)l] *n.* наро́д; (*as pl.*, *persons*)
лю́ди (-де́й, -дям, -дьми́) *pl.*; (*relatives*) род-
ны́е *sb.*; (*occupy*) населя́ть *impf.*, насели́ть
pf.; (*populate*) заселя́ть *impf.*, засели́ть *pf.*

pepper ['pepə(r)] *n.* пе́рец (-рца(у)); *v.t.* пе́р-
чить *impf.*, на~, по~ *pf.*; (*pelt*) забра́сывать

impf., забросáть *pf.* **peppercorn** *n.* пер-
чѝнка. **pepper-pot** *n.* пéречница.
peppermint ['pepəmɪnt] *n.* пéречная мя́та;
(*sweet*) мя́тная конфéта.
peppery ['pepərɪ] *adj.* напéрченный; (*fig.*)
вспы́льчивый.
per [pɜ:(r)] *prep.* (*by means of*) *expressed by
instrumental case* по+d.; (*person*) чéрез+a.;
(*for each*) (*person*) нa+a.; (*time*) в+a.;
(*quantity*) зa+a.; **as** ~ соглáсно+d.; ~ **annum**
ежегóдно, в год; ~ **capita,** ~ **head** на чело-
вéка; ~ **diem** в день; ~ **hour** в час; ~ **se**
сам (-á, -ó) по себé, по существу́.
perceive [pə'si:v] *v.t.* воспринимáть *impf.*,
восприня́ть (-иму́, -ѝмешь; воспрѝнял, -á,
-о) *pf.*
per cent [pə 'sent] *adv.* & *n.* процéнт, на сóт-
ню. **percentage** *n.* процéнтное содержáние,
процéнт.
perceptible [pə'septɪb(ə)l] *adj.* восприни-
мáемый, замéтный. **perception** *n.* восприя́-
тие, понимáние. **perceptive** *adj.* восприни-
мáющий, восприѝмчивый.
perch¹ [pɜ:tʃ] *n.* (*fish*) óкунь (*pl.* -ни, -нéй)
m.
perch² [pɜ:tʃ] *n.* (*roost*) насéст, жёрдочка;
(*fig.*) высóкое, прóчное, положéние; *v.i.*
садѝться *impf.*, сесть (ся́ду, -дешь; сел) *pf.*;
v.t. сажáть *impf.*, посадѝть (-ажу́, -áдишь)
pf. (на насéст); высокó помещáть *impf.*,
поместѝть *pf.* **perched** *adj.* высокó сидя́-
щий, располóженный (-ен).
perchance [pə'tʃɑ:ns] *adv.* быть мóжет.
percussion [pə'kʌʃ(ə)n] *n.* удáр, столкновéние; (*mus. instruments*) удáрные инструмéнты *m.pl.*; ~ **cap** удáрный кáпсюль *m.*
percussive [pə'kʌsɪv] *adj.* удáрный.
perdition [pə'dɪʃ(ə)n] *n.* гѝбель.
peregrine (falcon) ['perɪgrɪn] *n.* сóкол, сап-
сáн.
peremptory [pə'remptərɪ, 'perɪm-] *adj.* пове-
лѝтельный.
perennial [pə'renɪəl] *adj.* вéчный; (*plant*)
многолéтний; *n.* многолéтнее растéние.
perestroika [‚pere'strɔɪkə] *n.* перестрóйка.
perfect ['pɜ:fekt] *adj.* совершéнный (-нен,
-нна); (*exact*) тóчный (-чен, -чнá, -чно);
(*gram.*) перфéктный; (*mus.*) чѝстый; *n.*
перфéкт; *v.t.* совершéнствовать *impf.*, у~
pf. **per'fection** *n.* совершéнство. **per'fective**
adj. (*n.*) совершéнный (вид).
perfidious [‚pɜ:'fɪdɪəs] *adj.* веролóмный, пре-
дáтельский. '**perfidy** *n.* веролóмство, пре-
дáтельство.
perforate ['pɜ:fə‚reɪt] *v.t.* перфорѝровать
impf. & *pf.* **perfo'ration** *n.* перфорáция;
(*hole*) отвéрстие.
perforce [pə'fɔ:s] *adv.* по необходѝмости,
вóлей-невóлей.
perform [pə'fɔ:m] *v.t.* (*carry out*) исполня́ть
impf., испóлнить *pf.*; совершáть *impf.*, со-
вершѝть *pf.*; (*play; music*) игрáть *impf.*,
сыгрáть *pf.*; *v.i.* выступáть *impf.*, вы́ступить

pf. **performance** *n.* исполнéние; (*of play
etc.*) представлéние, спектáкль *m.*; (*of
engine etc.*) эксплуатациóнные кáчества
nt.pl. **performer** *n.* исполнѝтель *m.* **performing** *adj.* (*animal*) дрессирóванный.
perfume ['pɜ:fju:m] *n.* (*sweet smell*) аромáт;
(*smell*) зáпах; (*scent*) духѝ (-хóв) *pl.*; *v.t.*
душѝть (-шу́, -шишь) *impf.*, на~ *pf.* **per-
'fumery** *n.* парфюмéрия.
perfunctory [pə'fʌŋktərɪ] *adj.* повéрхност-
ный.
pergola ['pɜ:gələ] *n.* пéргола.
perhaps [pə'hæps] *adv.* мóжет быть.
peril ['perɪl] *n.* опáсность, риск. **perilous** *adj.*
опáсный, рискóванный (-ан, -анна).
perimeter [pə'rɪmɪtə(r)] *n.* (*geom.*) перѝметр;
(*boundary*) внéшняя гранѝца.
period ['pɪərɪəd] *n.* перѝод; (*term*) срок (-a(y));
(*epoch*) эпóха; (*full stop*) тóчка; *adj.* от-
нося́щийся к определённому перѝоду.
periodic [‚pɪərɪ'ɒdɪk] *adj.* периодѝческий; ~
table периодѝческая систéма элемéнтов
Менделéева. **peri'odical** *adj.* периодѝческий; *n.* периодѝческое издáние, журнáл.
perio'dicity *n.* периодѝчность.
peripheral [pə'rɪfər(ə)l] *adj.* периферѝйный;
n. (*comput.*) периферѝйное устрóйство.
periphery *n.* (*outline*) кóнтур; периферѝя.
periscope ['perɪ‚skəʊp] *n.* перискóп.
perish ['perɪʃ] *v.i.* погибáть *impf.*, погѝбнуть
(-б) *pf.*; (*die*) умирáть *impf.*, умерéть (умру́,
-рёшь; у́мер, -лá, -ло) *pf.*; (*spoil*) пóртиться
impf., ис~ *pf.* **perishable** *adj.* скоропóртя-
щийся; *n.*: *pl.* скоропóртящие товáры *m.pl.*
peritoneum [‚perɪtə'ni:əm] *adj.* брюшѝна.
peritonitis *n.* воспалéние брюшѝны.
periwinkle¹ ['perɪ‚wɪŋk(ə)l] *n.* (*plant*) барвѝ-
нок (-нка)
periwinkle² ['perɪ‚wɪŋk(ə)l] *n.* (*winkle*) лито-
рѝна.
perjure ['pɜ:dʒə(r)] *v.*: ~ **o.s.** нарушáть *impf.*,
нарýшить *pf.* кля́тву. **perjurer** *n.* лжесви-
дéтель *m.*, ~ница. **perjury** *n.* лóжное пока-
зáние под прися́гой, лжесвидéтельство.
perk¹ *see* **perquisite**
perk² [pɜ:k] *v.i.*: ~ **up** оживля́ться *impf.*,
оживѝться *pf.*; приободря́ться *impf.*, при-
ободрѝться *pf.* **perky** *adj.* бóйкий (бóек,
бойкá, -ко); (*pert*) дéрзкий (-зок, -зкá, -зко)
permafrost ['pɜ:mə‚frɒst] *n.* вéчная мерзлотá.
permanence ['pɜ:mənəns] *n.* постоя́нство.
permanency *n.* постоя́нство; (*permanent
employment*) постоя́нная рабóта. **permanent** *adj.* постоя́нный; ~ **wave** перманéнт.
permeable ['pɜ:mɪəb(ə)l] *adj.* проницáемый.
permeate *v.t.* (*penetrate*) проникáть *impf.*,
проникнуть (-к) *pf.* в+a.; (*saturate*) пропѝ-
тывать *impf.*, пропитáть *pf.*; *v.i.* распрост-
раня́ться *impf.*, распространѝться *pf.*
perme'ation *n.* проникáние.
permissible [pə'mɪsɪb(ə)l] *adj.* допустѝмый,
позволѝтельный. **permission** [pə'mɪʃ(ə)n]
n. разрешéние, позволéние. **permissive**

adj. разреша́ющий, позволя́ющий; (*liberal*) либера́льный. **permissiveness** *n.* (сексуа́льная) вседозво́ленность. **permit** [pə'mɪt; 'pɜ:mɪt] *v.t.* разреша́ть *impf.*, разреши́ть *pf.*+*d.*; позволя́ть *impf.*, позво́лить *pf.*+*d.*; *v.i.*: ~ **of** допуска́ть *impf.*, допусти́ть (-ущу́, -у́стишь) *pf.*+*a.*; *n.* про́пуск (*pl.* -а́); (*permission*) разреше́ние.

permutation [,pɜ:mju:'teɪʃ(ə)n] *n.* перестано́вка.

pernicious [pə'nɪʃəs] *adj.* па́губный.

peroration [,perə'reɪʃ(ə)n] *n.* заключи́тельная часть (*pl.* -ти, -те́й) (ре́чи).

peroxide [pə'rɒksaɪd] *n.* пе́рекись; (*hydrogen* ~) пе́рекись водоро́да; ~ **blonde** хими́ческая блонди́нка.

perpendicular [,pɜ:pən'dɪkjʊlə(r)] *adj.* перпендикуля́рный; (*cliff etc.*) отве́сный; *n.* перпендикуля́р.

perpetrate ['pɜ:pɪ,treɪt] *v.t.* соверша́ть *impf.*, соверши́ть *pf.* **perpe'tration** *n.* соверше́ние.

perpetual [pə'petjʊəl] *adj.* ве́чный, бесконе́чный; (*for life*) пожи́зненный; (*without limit*) бессро́чный. **perpetuate** *v.t.* увекове́чивать *impf.*, увекове́чить *pf.* **perpetu'ation** *n.* увекове́чение. **perpe'tuity** *n.* ве́чность, бесконе́чность; **in** ~ навсегда́, наве́чно.

perplex [pə'pleks] *v.t.* приводи́ть (-ожу́, -о́дишь) *impf.*, привести́ (-еду́, -едёшь; -ёл, -ела́) в недоуме́ние; озада́чивать *impf.*, озада́чить *pf.* **perplexity** *n.* недоуме́ние, озада́ченность.

perquisite ['pɜ:kwɪzɪt], **perk**[1] *n.* случа́йный, дополни́тельный, дохо́д.

persecute ['pɜ:sɪ,kju:t] *v.t.* пресле́довать *impf.*; (*pester*) надоеда́ть *impf.*, надое́сть (-е́м, -е́шь, -е́ст, -еди́м; -е́л) *pf.*+*d.* (**with** +*i.*). **persecution** *n.* пресле́дование.

perseverance [,pɜ:sɪ'vɪərəns] *n.* насто́йчивость, сто́йкость. **persevere** *v.i.* сто́йко, насто́йчиво, продолжа́ть *impf.* (**in, at** *etc.* +*a.*, *inf.*).

Persian ['pɜ:ʃ(ə)n] *n.* перс, ~ия́нка; (*cat*) перси́дская ко́шка; *adj.* перси́дский; **P~ lamb** кара́куль *m.*

persist [pə'sɪst] *v.i.* упо́рствовать *impf.* (**in** в+*p.*); насто́йчиво продолжа́ть *impf.* (**in** +*a.*, *inf.*); (*continue to exist*) продолжа́ть *impf.* существова́ть. **persistence** *n.* упо́рство, насто́йчивость. **persistent** *adj.* упо́рный, насто́йчивый.

person ['pɜ:s(ə)n] *n.* челове́к (*pl.* лю́ди, -де́й, -дям, -дьми́), осо́ба; (*appearance*) вне́шность; (*in play*; *gram.*) лицо́ (*pl.* -ца); **in** ~ ли́чно. **personable** *adj.* привлека́тельный. **personage** *n.* осо́ба, (ва́жная) персо́на, выдаю́щаяся ли́чность. **personal** *adj.* ли́чный, персона́льный; ~ **property** дви́жимое иму́щество; ~ **remarks** ли́чности *f.pl.*; ~ **stereo** пле́ер. **personality** [,pɜ:sə'nælɪtɪ] *n.* ли́чность. **personally** *adv.* ли́чно; **I** ~ что каса́ется меня́. **personalty** *n.* дви́жимое иму́щество. **personification** [pə,sɒnɪfɪ'keɪ-

ʃ(ə)n] *n.* олицетворе́ние. **personify** [pə'sɒnɪ,faɪ] *v.t.* олицетворя́ть *impf.*, олицетвори́ть *pf.*

personnel [,pɜ:sə'nel] *n.* ка́дры (-ров) *pl.*, персона́л; (*mil.*) ли́чный соста́в; ~ **carrier** транспортёр; ~ **department** отде́л ка́дров; ~ **manager** нача́льник отде́ла ка́дров.

perspective [pə'spektɪv] *n.* перспекти́ва; *adj.* перспекти́вный.

perspicacious [,pɜ:spɪ'keɪʃəs] *adj.* проница́тельный. **perspicacity** [,pɜ:spɪ'kæsɪtɪ] *n.* проница́тельность.

perspiration [,pɜ:spɪ'reɪʃ(ə)n] *n.* пот (*loc.* -у́; *pl.* -ы́), испа́рина; (*action*) поте́ние. **perspire** [pə'spaɪə(r)] *v.i.* поте́ть *impf.*, вс~ *pf.*

persuade [pə'sweɪd] *v.t.* убежда́ть *impf.*, убеди́ть (-и́шь) *pf.* (**of** в+*p.*); угова́ривать *impf.*, уговори́ть *pf.* **persuasion** *n.* убежде́ние; (*religious belief*) религио́зные убежде́ния *nt.pl.*; (*joc.*) род, сорт. **persuasive** *adj.* убеди́тельный.

pert [pɜ:t] *adj.* де́рзкий (-зок, -зка́, -зко).

pertain [pə'teɪn] *v.i.*: ~ **to** (*belong*) принадлежа́ть *impf.*+*d.*; (*relate*) име́ть *impf.* отноше́ние к+*d.*

pertinence ['pɜ:tɪnəns] *n.* уме́стность. **pertinent** *adj.* уме́стный.

perturb [pə'tɜ:b] *v.t.* (*disturb*) трево́жить *impf.*, вс~ *pf.*; (*agitate*) волнова́ть *impf.*, вз~ *pf.* **perturbation** [,pɜ:tə'beɪʃ(ə)n] *n.* трево́га, волне́ние.

perusal [pə'ru:z(ə)l] *n.* внима́тельное чте́ние. **peruse** *v.t.* (*read*) внима́тельно чита́ть *impf.*, про~ *pf.*; (*fig.*) рассма́тривать *impf.*, рассмотре́ть (-рю́, -ришь) *pf.*

pervade [pə'veɪd] *v.t.* (*permeate*) проника́ть *impf.*, прони́кнуть (-к) *pf.* в+*a.*; (*spread*) распространя́ться *impf.*, распространи́ться *pf.* по+*d.*

perverse [pə'vɜ:s] *adj.* (*persistent*) упря́мый; (*wayward*) капри́зный; (*perverted*) извращённый (-ён, -ённа). **perversion** *n.* извраще́ние. **perversity** *n.* упря́мство; извращённость. **pervert** [pə'vɜ:t; 'pɜ:vɜ:t] *v.t.* извраща́ть *impf.*, изврати́ть (-ащу́, -ати́шь) *pf.*; *n.* извращённый челове́к.

pessimism ['pesɪ,mɪz(ə)m] *n.* пессими́зм. **pessimist** *n.* пессими́ст. **pessi'mistic** *adj.* пессимисти́ческий.

pest [pest] *n.* вреди́тель *m.*; (*fig.*) я́зва. **pester** *v.t.* надоеда́ть *impf.*, надое́сть (-е́м, -е́шь, -е́ст, -еди́м; -е́л) *pf.*+*d.*; (*importune*) пристава́ть (-таю́, -таёшь) *impf.*, приста́ть (-а́ну, -а́нешь) *pf.* к+*d.* **pesticide** *n.* пестици́д. **pestilence** *n.* чума́. **pestilent(ial)** ['pestɪlənt, ,pestɪ'lenʃ(ə)l] *adj.* (*deadly*) смерто́носный; (*injurious*) вре́дный (-ден, -дна́, -дно); (*of pestilence*) чумно́й; (*coll.*) несно́сный, надое́дливый.

pestle ['pes(ə)l] *n.* пест (-а́), пе́стик.

pet [pet] *n.* (*animal*) люби́мое, дома́шнее, живо́тное *sb.*; (*favourite*) люби́мец (-мца), -мица; ба́ловень (-вня) *m.*; *adj.* (*animal*) ко́мнатный, дома́шний; (*favourite*) любимый; ~ **name** ласка́тельное и́мя *nt.*; ~ **shop** зоомагази́н; *v.t.* ласка́ть *impf.*; балова́ть *impf.*, из~ *pf.*

petal ['pet(ə)l] *n.* лепесто́к (-тка́).

peter ['pi:tə(r)] *v.i.*: ~ **out** истоща́ться *impf.*, истощи́ться *pf.*; (*stream*) иссяка́ть *impf.*, исся́кнуть (-к) *pf.*

petition [pɪ'tɪʃ(ə)n] *n.* хода́тайство, проше́ние; (*formal written* ~) пети́ция; (*leg.*) заявле́ние; *v.t.* подава́ть (-даю́, -даёшь) *impf.*, пода́ть (-а́м, -а́шь, -а́ст, -ади́м; по́дал, -а́, -о) *pf.* проше́ние, хода́тайство, +*d.*; обраща́ться *impf.*, обрати́ться (-ащу́сь, -ати́шься) *pf.* с пети́цией в+*a.* **petitioner** *n.* проси́тель *m.*

petrel ['petr(ə)l] *n.* буреве́стник, качу́рка.

petrified ['petrɪˌfaɪd] *adj.* окамене́лый; be ~ (*fig.*) оцепене́ть *pf.* (**with** от+*g.*). '**petrify** *v.t.* превраща́ть *impf.*, преврати́ть (-ащу́, -ати́шь) *pf.* в ка́мень; *v.i.* камене́ть *impf.*, о~ *pf.*

petrochemical [ˌpetrəʊ'kemɪk(ə)l] *adj.* нефтехими́ческий. **petrochemistry** [ˌpetrəʊ'kemɪstrɪ] *n.* нефтехи́мия. **petrodollar** *n.* нефтедо́ллар. **petrol** ['petr(ə)l] *n.* бензи́н; *attr.* бензи́новый; ~ **gauge** бензоме́р; ~ **pipe** бензопрово́д; ~ **pump** (*in engine*) бензонасо́с; (*at* ~ *station*) бензоколо́нка; ~ **station** бензозапра́вочная ста́нция; ~ **tank** бензоба́к; ~ **tanker** бензово́з. **pe'troleum** *n.* нефть.

petticoat ['petɪˌkəʊt] *n.* ни́жняя ю́бка.

pettifogger ['petɪˌfɒgə(r)] *n.* крючкотво́р. **pettifoggery** *n.* крючкотво́рство. **pettifogging** *adj.* кля́узный.

petty ['petɪ] *adj.* ме́лкий (-лок, -лка́, -лко); ~ **bourgeois** мелкобуржуа́зный; ~ **cash** ме́лкие су́ммы *m.pl.*; ~ **officer** старшина́ (*pl.* -ны) *m.*

petulance ['petjʊləns] *n.* нетерпели́вость, раздражи́тельность. **petulant** *adj.* нетерпели́вый, приди́рчивый.

pew [pju:] *n.* церко́вная скамья́ (*pl.* ска́мьй, -ме́й).

pewit *see* **peewit**

pewter ['pju:tə(r)] *n.* сплав о́лова со свинцо́м; (*dishes*) оловя́нная посу́да.

phalanx ['fælæŋks] *n.* фала́нга.

phallic ['fælɪk] *adj.* фалли́ческий. **phallus** *n.* фа́ллос.

phantom ['fæntəm] *n.* фанто́м, при́зрак.

Pharaoh ['feərəʊ] *n.* фарао́н.

Pharisaic(al) [ˌfærɪ'seɪɪk(ə)l] *adj.* фарисе́йский. '**Pharisee** *n.* фарисе́й.

pharmaceutical [ˌfɑːmə'sjuːtɪk(ə)l] *adj.* фармацевти́ческий. '**pharmacist** *n.* фармаце́вт. **pharma'cology** *n.* фармаколо́гия. **pharmacopoeia** [ˌfɑːməkə'piːə] *n.* фармакопе́я. '**pharmacy** *n.* фармаци́я; (*dispensary*) апте́ка.

phase [feɪz] *n.* фа́за, ста́дия.

Ph.D. *abbr.* (*of Doctor of Philosophy*) сте́пень кандида́та нау́к.

pheasant ['fez(ə)nt] *n.* фаза́н.

phenomenal [fɪ'nɒmɪn(ə)l] *adj.* феномена́льный. **phenomenon** *n.* явле́ние; (*also person, event*) феноме́н.

phial ['faɪəl] *n.* скля́нка, пузырёк (-рька́).

philander [fɪ'lændə(r)] *v.i.* волочи́ться (-чу́сь, -чишься) *impf.* (**with** за+*i.*). **philanderer** *n.* воло́кита *m.*

philanthrope ['fɪlən,θrəʊp], **-pist** [fɪ'lænθrəpɪst] *n.* филантро́п. **philanthropic** *adj.* филантропи́ческий. **phi'lanthropy** *n.* филантро́пия.

philatelic [ˌfɪlə'telɪk] *adj.* филателисти́ческий. **philatelist** [ˌfɪ'lætəlɪst] *n.* филатели́ст. **phi'lately** *n.* филатели́я.

philharmonic [ˌfɪlhɑː'mɒnɪk] *adj.* (*in titles*) филармони́ческий.

Philistine ['fɪlɪˌstaɪn] *n.* (*fig.*) фили́стер, меща́нин (*pl.* -а́не, -а́н), -а́нка; *adj.* фили́стерский, меща́нский. **philistinism** ['fɪlɪstɪˌnɪz(ə)m] *n.* фили́стерство, меща́нство.

philological [ˌfɪlə'lɒdʒɪk(ə)l] *adj.* филологи́ческий. **philologist** [fɪ'lɒlədʒɪst] *n.* фило́лог. **phi'lology** *n.* филоло́гия.

philosopher [fɪ'lɒsəfə(r)] *n.* фило́соф. **philosophic(al)** [ˌfɪlə'sɒfɪk(ə)l] *adj.* филосо́фский. **philosophize** *v.i.* филосо́фствовать *impf.* **philosophy** *n.* филосо́фия.

philtre ['fɪltə(r)] *n.* приворо́тное зе́лье (*g.pl.* -лий).

phlegm [flem] *n.* мокрота́; (*quality*) флегма. **phlegmatic** [fleg'mætɪk] *adj.* флегмати́ческий.

phobia ['fəʊbɪə] *n.* фоби́я, страх.

phoenix ['fiːnɪks] *n.* фе́никс.

phone [fəʊn] *n.* телефо́н; *v.t. & i.* звони́ть *impf.*, по~ *pf.*+*d.* (по телефо́ну).

phoneme ['fəʊniːm] *n.* фоне́ма. **pho'nemic** *adj.* фонемати́ческий. **phonetic** [fə'netɪk] *adj.* фонети́ческий. **phonetician** [ˌfəʊnɪ'tɪʃ(ə)n] *n.* фонети́ст. **pho'netics** *n.* фоне́тика.

phone-in ['fəʊnɪn] *n.* радиобесе́да.

phonograph ['fəʊnəˌgrɑːf] *n.* фоно́граф. **phono'logical** *adj.* фонологи́ческий. **pho'nology** *n.* фоноло́гия.

phosphate ['fɒsfeɪt] *n.* фосфа́т. **phosphorescence** [ˌfɒsfə'res(ə)ns] *n.* фосфоресце́нция. **phospho'rescent** *adj.* светя́щийся, фосфоресци́рующий. **phosphorous** *adj.* фо́сфористый. **phosphorus** *n.* фо́сфор.

photo ['fəʊtəʊ] *n.* сни́мок (-мка); *v.t.* снима́ть *impf.*, снять (сниму́, -мешь; снял, -а́, -о) *pf.*; ~ **finish** фотофи́ниш. **photocopier** *n.* фотокопирова́льный аппара́т. **photocopy** *n.* фотоко́пия; *v.t.* ксерокопи́ровать *impf. & pf.* **photoelectric** *adj.* фотоэлектри́ческий; ~ **cell** фотоэлеме́нт. **photogenic** [ˌfəʊtəʊ'dʒenɪk, -'dʒiːnɪk] *adj.* фотогени́чный. **photograph** *n.* фотогра́фия, сни́мок (-мка); *v.t.* фотографи́ровать *impf.*, с~ *pf.*; снима́ть *impf.*, снять (сниму́, -мешь; снял, -а́, о) *pf.* **photographer** [fə'tɒgrəfə(r)] *n.* фото́граф. **photographic** *adj.* фотографи́ческий. **pho-**

tography [fə'tɒgrəfɪ] *n.* фотогра́фия. **photogravure** *n.* фотогравю́ра. **photolithography** *n.* фотолитогра́фия. **photometer** [fəʊ'tɒmɪtə(r)] *n.* фото́метр. **photosynthesis** *n.* фотоси́нтез.

phrase [freɪz] *n.* фра́за; (*diction*) стиль *m.*; (*expression*) оборо́т (ре́чи); *v.t.* выража́ть *impf.*, вы́разить *pf.* слова́ми. **phraseo'logical** *adj.* фразеологи́ческий. **phrase'ology** *n.* фразеоло́гия.

phrenology [frɪ'nɒlədʒɪ] *n.* френоло́гия.

physical ['fɪzɪk(ə)l] *adj.* физи́ческий; ~ **culture** физкульту́ра; ~ **examination** медици́нский осмо́тр; ~ **exercises** заря́дка. **physician** [fɪ'zɪʃ(ə)n] *n.* врач (-а́). **physicist** *n.* фи́зик. **physics** *n.* фи́зика.

physiognomy [,fɪzɪ'ɒnəmɪ] *n.* физионо́мия.

physiological [,fɪzɪə'lɒdʒɪk(ə)l] *n.* физиологи́ческий. **physiologist** [,fɪzɪ'ɒlədʒɪst] *n.* физио́лог. **physi'ology** *n.* физиоло́гия. **physiotherapist** [,fɪzɪəʊ'θerəpɪst] *n.* физиотерапе́вт. **physio'therapy** *n.* физиотерапи́я.

physique [fɪ'ziːk] *n.* телосложе́ние.

pianist ['pɪənɪst] *n.* пиани́ст, ~ка. **piano** [pɪ'ænəʊ] *n.* фортепья́но *nt.indecl.*; (*grand*) роя́ль *m.*; (*upright*) пиани́но *nt.indecl.* **pianoforte** *n.* фортепья́но *nt.indecl.*

piccolo ['pɪkələʊ] *n.* пи́кколо *nt.indecl.*

pick¹ [pɪk] *v.t.* (*ground*) разрыхля́ть *impf.*, разрыхли́ть *pf.*; (*bone*) обгла́дывать *impf.*, обглода́ть (-ожу́ -о́жешь) *pf.*; (*flower*) срыва́ть *impf.*, сорва́ть (-ву́, -вёшь; сорва́л, -á, -о) *pf.*; (*gather*) собира́ть *impf.*, собра́ть (соберу́, -рёшь; собра́л, -á, -о) *pf.*; (*select*) выбира́ть *impf.*, вы́брать (вы́беру, -решь) *pf.*; ~ **s.o.'s brains** присва́ивать *impf.*, присво́ить *pf.* (чужи́е) мы́сли; ~ **a lock** открыва́ть *impf.*, откры́ть (-ро́ю, -ро́ешь) *pf.* замо́к отмы́чкой; ~ **one's nose, teeth** ковыря́ть *impf.*, ковырну́ть *pf.* в носу́, в зуба́х; ~ **a quarrel** иска́ть (ищу́, и́щешь) *impf.* ссо́ры (**with** c+*i.*); ~ **to pieces** (*fig.*) раскритико́вывать *pf.*; ~ **s.o.'s pocket** залеза́ть *impf.*, зале́зть (-зу, -зешь; -з) *pf.* в карма́н+*d.*; ~ **one's way** выбира́ть *impf.*, вы́брать (вы́беру, -решь) *pf.* доро́гу; ~ **off** (*pluck off*) обрыва́ть *impf.*, оборва́ть (-ву́, -вёшь; оборва́л, -á, -о) *pf.*; (*shoot*) перестре́ливать *impf.*, перестреля́ть *pf.* (одного́ за други́м); ~ **on** (*nag*) пили́ть (-лю́, -лишь) *impf.*; ~ **out** отбира́ть *impf.*, отобра́ть (отберу́, -рёшь; отобра́л, -á, -о) *pf.*; ~ **up** (*lift*) поднима́ть *impf.*, подня́ть (подниму́, -мешь; по́днял, -á, -о) *pf.*; (*gain*) добыва́ть *impf.*, добы́ть (добу́ду, -дешь; добы́л, -á, -о) *pf.*; (*fetch*) заезжа́ть *impf.*, зае́хать (зае́ду, -дешь) *pf.* за+*i.*; (*recover*) поправля́ться *impf.*, попра́виться *pf.*; ~ **o.s. up** поднима́ться *impf.*, подня́ться (подниму́сь, -мешься; подня́лся, -ла́сь) *pf.*

pick² [pɪk] *n.* вы́бор; (*best part*) лу́чшая часть, са́мое лу́чшее; **take your** ~ выбира́й(те)!

pick³ [pɪk], **pickaxe** *n.* кирка́ (*pl.* ки́рки́, -рок, ки́рка́м).

picket ['pɪkɪt] *n.* (*stake*) кол (-á, *loc.* -ý; *pl.* -ья, -ьев); (*person*) пике́тчик, -ица; (*collect.*) пике́т; *v.t.* пикети́ровать *impf.*

pickle ['pɪk(ə)l] *n.* (*brine*) рассо́л; (*vinegar*) марина́д; *pl.* соле́нье, марина́ды *m.pl.*, пи́кули (-лей) *pl.*; (*plight*) напа́сть; *v.t.* соли́ть (солю́, со́ли́шь) *impf.*, по~ *pf.*; мариновать *impf.*, за~ *pf.* **pickled** *adj.* солёный (со́лон, -á, -о); марино́ванный; (*drunk*) пья́ный (пьян, -á, -о).

pickpocket ['pɪkˌpɒkɪt] *n.* карма́нник.

pick-up ['pɪkʌp] *n.* (*truck*) пика́п; (*tech.*) звукоснима́тель *m.*

picnic ['pɪknɪk] *n.* пикни́к (-á); *v.i.* уча́ствовать *impf.* в пикнике́.

pictorial [pɪk'tɔːrɪəl] *adj.* изобрази́тельный; (*illustrated*) иллюстри́рованный. **picture** ['pɪktʃə(r)] *n.* карти́на; (~ *of health etc.*) воплоще́ние; (*film*) фильм; **the** ~**s** кино́ *nt.indecl.*; ~ **postcard** худо́жественная откры́тка; ~ **window** целосте́нное окно́ (*pl.* о́кна, о́кон, о́кнам); *v.t.* изобража́ть *impf.*, изобрази́ть *pf.*; (*to o.s.*) представля́ть *impf.*, предста́вить *pf.* себе́. **picture-book** *n.* кни́га с карти́нками. **picture-gallery** *n.* карти́нная галере́я. **pictu'resque** *adj.* живопи́сный; (*language etc.*) о́бразный.

pie [paɪ] *n.* пиро́г (-á), пирожо́к (-жка́).

piebald ['paɪbɔːld] *adj.* пе́гий; *n.* (*horse*) пе́гая ло́шадь (*pl.* -ди, -де́й, *i.* -дьми́).

piece [piːs] *n.* кусо́к (-ска́), часть (*pl.* -ти, -те́й); (*one of set*) шту́ка; (*of land*) уча́сток (-тка); (*of paper*) листо́к (-тка́); (*mus.*, *liter.*) произведе́ние; (*picture*) карти́на; (*drama*) пье́са; (*chess*) фигу́ра; (*coin*) моне́та; **take to** ~**s** разбира́ть *impf.*, разобра́ть (разберу́, -рёшь; разобра́л, -á, -о) *pf.* (на ча́сти); ~ **of advice** сове́т; ~ **of information** све́дение; ~ **of news** но́вость; *v.t.*: ~ **together** собира́ть *impf.*, собра́ть (соберу́, -рёшь; собра́л, -á, -о) *pf.* из кусо́чков; своди́ть (-ожу́, -о́дишь) *impf.*, свести́ (сведу́, -дёшь; свёл, -á) *pf.* воедино. **piecemeal** *adv.* по частя́м. **piece-work** *n.* сде́льщина. **pieceworker** *n.* сде́льщик.

pied [paɪd] *adj.* разноцве́тный.

pier [pɪə(r)] *n.* (*mole*) мол (*loc.* -ý); (*in harbour*) пирс; (*of bridge*) бык (-á); (*between windows etc.*) просте́нок (-нка).

pierce [pɪəs] *v.t.* пронза́ть *impf.*, пронзи́ть *pf.*; прока́лывать *impf.*, проколо́ть (-лю́, -лешь) *pf.*; (*of cold look etc.*) прони́зывать *impf.*, пронизáть (-ижý, -и́жешь) *pf.* **piercing** *adj.* о́стрый (остр & остёр, остра́, о́стро́), пронзи́тельный.

pier-glass ['pɪəɡlɑːs] *n.* трюмо́ *nt.indecl.*

piety ['paɪɪtɪ] *n.* набо́жность.

piffle ['pɪf(ə)l] *n.* чепуха́, вздор. **piffling** *adj.* ничто́жный.

pig [pɪg] *n.* свинья́ (*pl.* -ньи, -не́й, -ньям) (*also of person*); (*of metal*) болва́нка, чу́шка; *v.t.*:

~ **it** жить (живу́, -вёшь; жил, -á, -о) *impf.*
по-сви́нски; *v.abs.* пороси́ться *impf.*, o~ *pf.*
pig'headed *adj.* упря́мый. **pig-iron** *n.* чугу́н
(-á) в чу́шках. **piglet** *n.* поросёнок (-сёнка;
pl. -ся́та, -ся́т). **pigskin** *n.* свина́я ко́жа.
pigsty *n.* свина́рник. **pigswill** *n.* помо́и (-óев)
pl. **pigtail** *n.* коси́чка.
pigeon ['pɪdʒɪn, -dʒ(ə)n] *n.* го́лубь (*pl.* -би,
-бе́й) *m.* **pigeon-hole** (*n.*) отделе́ние для
бума́г; (*v.t.*) раскла́дывать *impf.*, разло-
жи́ть (-ожу́, -о́жишь) *pf.* по отделе́ниям,
по я́щикам; (*put aside*) откла́дывать *impf.*,
отложи́ть (-ожу́, -о́жишь) *pf.* в до́лгий
я́щик.
pigment ['pɪgmənt] *n.* пигме́нт. **pigmen'tation**
n. пигмента́ция.
pigmy *see* **pygmy**
pike[1] [paɪk] *n.* (*weapon*) пи́ка.
pike[2] [paɪk] *n.* (*fish*) щу́ка.
pilaster [pɪ'læstə(r)] *n.* пиля́стр.
pilchard ['pɪltʃəd] *n.* сарди́н(к)а.
pile[1] [paɪl] *n.* (*heap*) ку́ча, ки́па; (*funeral* ~)
погреба́льный костёр (-тра́); (*building*)
огро́мное зда́ние; (*elec.*) батаре́я; (*atomic*
~) я́дерный реа́ктор; *v.t.*: ~ **up** скла́дывать
impf., сложи́ть (-жу́, -жишь) *pf.* в ку́чу; сва́-
ливать *impf.*, свали́ть (-лю́, -лишь) *pf.* в
ку́чу; (*load*) нагружа́ть *impf.*, нагрузи́ть
(-ужу́, -у́зишь) *pf.* (**with** +*i.*); *v.i.*: ~ **in(to)**,
on забира́ться *impf.*, забра́ться (заберу́сь,
-рёшься; забра́лся, -ала́сь, -а́ло́сь) *pf.* в+*a.*;
~ **up** накопля́ться, нака́пливаться *impf.*,
накопи́ться (-ится) *pf.*
pile[2] [paɪl] *n.* (*on cloth etc.*) ворс.
pile[3] [paɪl] *n.* (*support*) свая. **pile-driver** *n.*
копёр (-пра́).
piles [paɪlz] *n.* геморро́й.
pilfer ['pɪlfə(r)] *v.t.* ворова́ть *impf.* **pilfering**
n. ме́лкая кра́жа.
pilgrim ['pɪlgrɪm] *n.* пилигри́м; пало́мник,
-ица. **pilgrimage** *n.* пало́мничество.
pill [pɪl] *n.* пилю́ля; **the** ~ противозача́-
точная пилю́ля.
pillage ['pɪlɪdʒ] *n.* мародёрство; *v.t.* гра́бить
impf., o~ *pf.*; *v.abs.* мародёрствовать *impf.*
pillar ['pɪlə(r)] *n.* столб (-á); (*fig.*) столп (-á).
pillar-box *n.* стоя́чий почто́вый я́щик.
pillion ['pɪljən] *n.* за́днее сиде́нье (мото-
ци́кла).
pillory ['pɪlərɪ] *n.* позо́рный столб (-á); *v.t.*
(*fig.*) пригвожда́ть *impf.*, пригвозди́ть *pf.*
к позо́рному столбу́.
pillow ['pɪləʊ] *n.* поду́шка; *v.t.* подпира́ть
impf., подпере́ть (подопру́, -рёшь; подпёр)
pf. **pillowcase** *n.* на́волочка.
pilot ['paɪlət] *n.* (*naut.*) ло́цман; (*aeron.*)
пило́т, лётчик; *adj.* о́пытный, про́бный; *v.t.*
управля́ть *impf.*+*i.*; (*aeron.*) пилоти́ровать
impf.
pimento [,pɪmɪ'entəʊ, pɪm'jentəʊ] *n.* пе́рец
(-рца(у)).
pimp [pɪmp] *n.* сво́дик, -ица; *v.i.* сво́дничать
impf.

pimpernel ['pɪmpənel] *n.* о́чный цвет.
pimple ['pɪmp(ə)l] *n.* прыщ (-á). **pimpled,
pimply** *adj.* прыща́вый, прыщева́тый.
PIN [pɪn] *abbr.* (*of personal identification
number*) персона́льный код.
pin [pɪn] *n.* була́вка; (*peg*) па́лец (-льца); *v.t.*
прика́лывать *impf.*, приколо́ть (-лю́, -лешь)
pf.; (*press*) прижима́ть *impf.*, прижа́ть (-жму́,
-жмёшь) *pf.* **up** (**against** +*d.*).
pinafore ['pɪnəfɔː(r)] *n.* пере́дник.
pince-nez ['pænsneɪ, pæs'neɪ] *n.* пенсне́
nt.indecl.
pincers ['pɪnsəz] *n.* клещи́ (-ще́й) *pl.*; пинце́т;
(*crab's*) клешни́ *f.pl.*; **pincer movement**
захва́т в клещи́.
pinch [pɪntʃ] *v.t.* щипа́ть (-плю́, -плешь)
impf., (у)щипну́ть *pf.*; прищемля́ть *impf.*,
прищеми́ть *pf.*; (*of shoe*) жать (жмёт)
impf.; (*steal*) стяну́ть (-ну́, -нешь) *pf.*;
(*arrest*) сца́пать *pf.*; *v.i.* скупи́ться *impf.*;
where the shoe ~**es** в чём загво́здка; *n.*
щипо́к (-пка́); (*of salt*) щепо́тка; (*of snuff*)
поню́шка (табаку́); **at a** ~ в кра́йнем
слу́чае.
pinchbeck ['pɪntʃbek] *n.* томпа́к (-á); *adj.*
томпа́ковый.
pincushion ['pɪn,kʊʃ(ə)n] *n.* поду́шечка для
була́вок.
pine[1] [paɪn] *v.i.* томи́ться *impf.*; ~ **for** тоско-
ва́ть *impf.* по+*d.* & *p.*
pine[2] [paɪn] *n.* (*tree*) сосна́ (*pl.* -сны, -сен,
-снам); *attr.* сосно́вый; ~ **cone** сосно́вая
ши́шка; ~ **needles** сосно́вая хвоя *collect.*
pineapple ['paɪn,æp(ə)l] *n.* анана́с.
ping-pong ['pɪŋpɒŋ] *n.* насто́льный те́ннис,
пинг-по́нг.
pinion[1] ['pɪnjən] *n.* (*of wing*) оконе́чность
пти́чьего крыла́; (*flight feather*) махово́е
перо́ (*pl.* -рья, -рьев); *v.t.* подреза́ть *impf.*,
подре́зать (-е́жу, -е́жешь) *pf.* кры́лья+*d.*;
(*person*) свя́зывать *impf.*, связа́ть (-яжу́,
-я́жешь) *pf.* ру́ки+*d.*
pinion[2] ['pɪnjən] *n.* (*cog-wheel*) шестерня́
(*g.pl.* -рён).
pink [pɪŋk] *n.* (*flower*) гвозди́ка; (*colour*)
ро́зовый цвет; **in the** ~ в прекра́сном
состоя́нии; *adj.* ро́зовый.
pinnacle ['pɪnək(ə)l] *n.* (*peak; fig.*) верши́на;
(*turret*) остроконе́чная ба́шенка.
pinpoint ['pɪnpɔɪnt] *v.t.* то́чно определя́ть
impf., определи́ть *pf.* **pinprick** *n.* (*fig.*)
ме́лкая неприя́тность. **pinstripe** *n.* то́нкая
поло́ска.
pint [paɪnt] *n.* пи́нта.
pin-up ['pɪnʌp] *n.* карти́нка (краса́тки), при-
креплённая на сте́ну.
pioneer [,paɪə'nɪə(r)] *n.* пионе́р, ~ка; (*mil.*)
сапёр; *adj.* пионе́рский; сапёрный.
pious ['paɪəs] *adj.* на́божный.
pip[1] [pɪp] *n.* (*on dice etc.*) очко́ (*pl.* -ки́, -ко́в);
(*star*) звёздочка.
pip[2] [pɪp] *n.* (*seed*) зёрнышко (*pl.* -шки, -шек,
-шкам).

pip[3] [pɪp] *n.* (*sound*) бип.

pipe [paɪp] *n.* труба́ (*pl.* -бы); (*mus.*) ду́дка, свире́ль; *pl.* волы́нка; (*for smoking*) тру́бка; *v.t.* (*play on ~*) игра́ть *impf.*, сыгра́ть *pf.* на ду́дке, на свире́ли; (*convey by ~*) пуска́ть *impf.*, пусти́ть (пущу́, пу́стишь) *pf.* по труба́м, по трубопрово́ду; *v.i.* **~ down** замолка́ть *impf.*, замо́лкнуть (-к) *pf.* **pipe-clay** *n.* бе́лая тру́бочная гли́на. **pipedream** *n.* пуста́я мечта́ (*g.pl.* -ний). **pipeline** *n.* трубопрово́д; (*oil ~*) нефтепрово́д. **piper** *n.* волы́нщик. **pipette** [pɪˈpet] *n.* пипе́тка. **piping** *n.* (*on dress etc.*) кант; *adj.* (*voice*) пискли́вый; **~ hot** с пы́лу, с жа́ру.

piquancy [ˈpiːkənsɪ, -kɑːnsɪ] *n.* пика́нтность. **piquant** *adj.* пика́нтный.

piqué [ˈpiːkeɪ] *n.* пике́ *nt.indecl.*

piracy [ˈpaɪrəsɪ] *n.* пира́тство. **pirate** *n.* пира́т; *v.t.* (*book*) самово́льно переиздава́ть (-даю́, -даёшь) *impf.*, переизда́ть (-а́м, -а́шь, -а́ст, -ади́м; -а́л, -ала́, -а́ло) *pf.* **piratical** [paɪəˈrætɪk(ə)l] *adj.* пира́тский.

pirouette [ˌpɪruˈet] *n.* пируэ́т; *v.i.* де́лать *impf.*, с~ *pf.* пируэ́т(ы).

piscatorial [ˌpɪskəˈtɔːrɪəl] *adj.* рыболо́вный.

Pisces [ˈpaɪsiːz, ˈpɪskiːz] *n.* Ры́бы *f.pl.*

pistachio [pɪˈstɑːʃɪəʊ] *n.* фиста́шка; *attr.* фиста́шковый.

pistol [ˈpɪst(ə)l] *n.* пистоле́т.

piston [ˈpɪst(ə)n] *n.* по́ршень (-шня) *m.*; (*in cornet etc.*) писто́н; *adj.* поршнево́й. **piston-ring** *n.* поршнево́е кольцо́ (*pl.* -льца, -ле́ц, -льцам). **piston-rod** *n.* шток по́ршня.

pit [pɪt] *n.* я́ма; (*mine*) ша́хта; (*quarry*) карье́р; (*theatr.*) парте́р; (*in workshop*) ремо́нтная я́ма; (*car-racing*) запра́вочно-ремо́нтный пункт; **the bottomless ~** преиспо́дняя *sb.*; **in the ~ of the stomach** под ло́жечкой; *v.t.*: **~ against** выставля́ть *impf.*, вы́ставить *pf.* про́тив+*g.*

pit-a-pat [ˈpɪtəˌpæt] *adv.* с ча́стым бие́нием; **go ~** (*heart*) затрепета́ть (-е́щет) *pf.*

pitch[1] [pɪtʃ] *n.* (*resin*) смола́; *v.t.* смоли́ть *impf.*, вы́~, о~ *pf.* **pitch-black** *adj.* чёрный (-рен, -рна́) как смоль.

pitch[2] [pɪtʃ] *v.t.* (*camp, tent*) разбива́ть *impf.*, разби́ть (разобью́, -ьёшь) *pf.*; (*ball*) подава́ть (-даю́, -даёшь) *impf.*, пода́ть (-а́м, -а́шь, -а́ст, -ади́м; по́дал, -а́, -о) *pf.* (*fling*) кида́ть *impf.*, ки́нуть *pf.*; *v.i.* (*fall*) па́дать *impf.*, (у)па́сть (-аду́, -адёшь; -а́л) *pf.*; (*ship*) испы́тывать *impf.*, испыта́ть *pf.* килеву́ю ка́чку; **~ into** набра́сываться *impf.*, набро́ситься *pf.* на+*a.*; **~ed battle** генера́льное сраже́ние; *n.* (*of ship*) килева́я ка́чка; (*of ball*) пода́ча; (*football ~ etc.*) площа́дка; (*degree*) у́ровень (-вня) *m.*; (*mus.*) высота́ (*pl.* -ты); (*slope*) укло́н.

pitchblende [ˈpɪtʃblend] *n.* уранини́т.

pitcher[1] [ˈpɪtʃə(r)] *n.* (*sport*) подаю́щий *sb.* (мяч).

pitcher[2] [ˈpɪtʃə(r)] *n.* (*vessel*) кувши́н.

pitchfork [ˈpɪtʃfɔːk] *n.* ви́лы (-л) *pl.*

piteous [ˈpɪtɪəs] *adj.* жа́лостный, жа́лкий (-лок, -лка́, -лко).

pitfall [ˈpɪtfɔːl] *n.* западня́.

pith [pɪθ] *n.* серцеви́на; (*essence*) суть; (*vigour*) си́ла, эне́ргия.

pit-head [ˈpɪthed] *n.* надша́хтный копёр;

pithy [ˈpɪθɪ] *adj.* (*fig.*) сжа́тый, содержа́тельный.

pitiable [ˈpɪtɪəb(ə)l] *adj.* жа́лкий (-лок, -лка́, -лко), несча́стный. **pitiful** *adj.* жа́лостный, жа́лкий (-лок, -лка́, -лко). **pitiless** *adj.* безжа́лостный.

pittance [ˈpɪt(ə)ns] *n.* ску́дное жа́лованье, жа́лкие гроши́ (-ше́й) *pl.*

pitted [ˈpɪtɪd] *adj.* (*of face*) изры́тый, рябо́й (ряб, -а́, -о).

pituitary [pɪˈtjuːɪtərɪ] *adj.* сли́зистый; *n.* (*gland*) гипо́физ.

pity [ˈpɪtɪ] *n.* сожале́ние; **it's a ~** жа́лко, жаль; **take ~ on** сжа́литься *pf.* над+*i.*; **what a ~** как жа́лко!; *v.t.* жале́ть *impf.*, по~ *pf.*; **I ~ you** мне жаль тебя́.

pivot [ˈpɪvət] *n.* сте́ржень (-жня) *m.*; (*fig.*) центр; *v.i.* враща́ться *impf.* **pivotal** *adj.* (*fig.*) центра́льный.

pizza [ˈpiːtsə] *n.* пи́цца; **~ parlour** пиццери́я.

placard [ˈplækɑːd] *n.* афи́ша, плака́т; *v.t.* (*wall*) раскле́ивать *impf.*, раскле́ить *pf.* афи́ши, плака́ты, на+*p.*, по+*d.*

placate [pləˈkeɪt, ˈplæ-, ˈpleɪ-] *v.t.* умиротворя́ть *impf.*, умиротвори́ть *pf.*

place [pleɪs] *n.* ме́сто (*pl.* -та́); **change ~s with** обме́ниваться *impf.*, обменя́ться *pf.* места́ми с+*i.*; **give ~ to** уступа́ть *impf.*, уступи́ть (-плю́, -пишь) *pf.* ме́сто+*d.*; **in ~ of** на ме́сте; (*suitable*) уме́стный; **in ~ of** вме́сто+*g.*; **in the first, second, ~** во-пе́рвых, во-вторы́х; **out of ~** не на ме́сте; (*unsuitable*) неуме́стный; **take ~** случа́ться *impf.*, случи́ться *pf.*; (*pre-arranged event*) состоя́ться (-ои́тся) *pf.*; **take the ~ of** заменя́ть *impf.*, замени́ть (-ню́, -нишь) *pf.*; *v.t.* помеща́ть *impf.*, помести́ть *pf.*; (*stand*) ста́вить *impf.*, по~ *pf.*; (*lay*) класть (кладу́, -дёшь; -ал) *impf.*, положи́ть (-жу́, -жишь) *pf.*; (*determine*) определя́ть *impf.*, определи́ть *pf.* **place-name** *n.* географи́ческое назва́ние.

placenta [pləˈsentə] *n.* плаце́нта.

place-setting [ˈpleɪsˌsetɪŋ] *n.* столо́вый прибо́р.

placid [ˈplæsɪd] *adj.* споко́йный. **placidity** [pləˈsɪdɪtɪ] *n.* споко́йствие.

plagiarism [ˈpleɪdʒəˌrɪz(ə)m] *n.* плагиа́т. **plagiarist** *n.* плагиа́тор. **plagiarize** *v.t.* займствовать *impf.* & *pf.*

plague [pleɪg] *n.* чума́, морова́я я́зва; *v.t.* му́чить *impf.*, за~, из~ *pf.*

plaice [pleɪs] *n.* ка́мбала.

plaid [plæd] *n.* плед; (*cloth*) шотла́ндка; *adj.* в шотла́ндскую кле́тку.

plain [pleɪn] *n.* равни́на; *adj.* (*clear*) я́сный

(я́сен, ясна́, я́сно, ясны́); (*simple*) просто́й (прост, -а́, -о, про́сты́); (*direct*) прямо́й (прям, -а́, -о, пря́мы́); (*ugly*) некраси́вый; ~ **stitch** пряма́я пе́тля. **plain-clothes** *adj.*: ~ **policeman** шпик (-а́). **plain-spoken** *adj.* открове́нный (-нен, -нна).

plaintiff ['pleɪntɪf] *n.* исте́ц (-тца́), исти́ца.

plaintive ['pleɪntɪv] *adj.* жа́лобный.

plait [plæt] *n.* коса́ (*a.* ко́су; *pl.* -сы); *v.t.* плести́ (плету́, -тёшь; плёл, -а́) *impf.*, с~ *pf.*

plan [plæn] *n.* план; *v.t.* плани́ровать *impf.*, за~, с~ *pf.*; (*intend*) намерева́ться *impf.*+*inf.*

plane[1] [pleɪn] *n.* (*tree*) плата́н.

plane[2] [pleɪn] *n.* (*tool*) руба́нок (-нка); *v.t.* строга́ть *impf.*, вы́~ *pf.*

plane[3] [pleɪn] *n.* (*surface*) пло́скость; (*level*) у́ровень (-вня) *m.*; (*aeroplane*) самолёт; *v.i.* плани́ровать *impf.*, с~ *pf.*

plane[4] [pleɪn] *adj.* (*level*) пло́ский (-сок, -ска́, -ско), плоскостно́й.

planet ['plænɪt] *n.* плане́та. **plane'tarium** *n.* планета́рий. **planetary** *adj.* плане́тный, планета́рный.

plank [plæŋk] *n.* доска́ (*a.* -ску; *pl.* -ски, -со́к, -ска́м); (*pol.*) пункт парти́йной програ́ммы; ~ **bed** на́ры (-р) *pl.*; *v.t.* выстила́ть *impf.*, вы́стлать (-телю, -телешь) *pf.* доска́ми. **planking** *n.* насти́л; (*collect.*) до́ски (-со́к, -ска́м) *f.pl.*

plankton ['plæŋkt(ə)n] *n.* планкто́н.

plant [plɑːnt] *n.* расте́ние; (*fixtures*) устано́вка; (*factory*) заво́д; *v.t.* сажа́ть *impf.*, посади́ть (-ажу́, -а́дишь) *pf.*; насажда́ть *impf.*, насади́ть (-ажу́, -а́дишь) *pf.*; (*fix firmly*) про́чно ста́вить *impf.*, по~ *pf.*; (*garden etc.*) заса́живать *impf.*, засади́ть (-ажу́, -а́дишь) *pf.* (**with** +*i.*); (*palm off*) всу́чивать *impf.*, всучи́ть (-учу́, -у́чи́шь) *pf.* (**on** +*d.*); ~ **out** выса́живать *impf.*, вы́садить *pf.* в грунт.

plantain ['plæntɪn] *n.* подоро́жник.

plantation [plæn'teɪʃ(ə)n, plɑːn-] *n.* (*of trees*) (лесо)насажде́ние; (*of cotton etc.*) планта́ция. **planter** ['plɑːntə(r)] *n.* планта́тор.

plaque [plæk, plɑːk] *n.* доще́чка, мемориа́льная доска́ (*a.* -ску; *pl.* -ски, -со́к, -ска́м); (*plate*) декорати́вная таре́лка.

plasma ['plæzmə] *n.* пла́зма; протопла́зма.

plaster ['plɑːstə(r)] *n.* пла́стырь *m.*; (*for walls etc.*) штукату́рка; ~ **of Paris** (*n.*) гипс; (*attr.*) ги́псовый; ~ **cast** (*mould*) ги́псовый слепо́к (-пка); (*for leg etc.*) ги́псовая повя́зка; *v.t.* (*wall*) штукату́рить *impf.*, от~, о~ *pf.*; (*daub*) зама́зывать *impf.*, зама́зать (-а́жу, -а́жешь) *pf.* **plasterboard** *n.* суха́я штукату́рка. **plastered** *adj.* (*drunk*) пья́ный (пьян, -а́, -о). **plasterer** *n.* штукату́р.

plastic ['plæstɪk] *n.* пластма́сса; *adj.* пласти́чный, пласти́ческий; (*made of* ~) пластма́ссовый; ~ **arts** пла́стика; ~ **surgery** пласти́ческая хирурги́я.

plate [pleɪt] *n.* пласти́нка; (*for food*) таре́лка, (*collect.*; *silver, gold* ~) столо́вое серебро́, зо́лото; (*metal sheet*) лист (-а́); (*print.*) печа́тная фо́рма; (*illustration*) (вкладна́я) иллюстра́ция; (*name* ~ *etc.*) доще́чка; (*phot.*) фотопласти́нка; ~ **armour** броневы́е пли́ты *f.pl.*; ~ **glass** зерка́льное стекло́; *v.t.* плакирова́ть *impf.* & *pf.*

plateau ['plætəʊ] *n.* плато́ *nt.indecl.*, плоского́рье.

plateful ['pleɪtfʊl] *n.* по́лная таре́лка. **plate-layer** *n.* путево́й рабо́чий *sb.* **plate-rack** *n.* суши́лка для посу́ды.

platform ['plætfɔːm] *n.* платфо́рма; (*rail.*) перро́н; ~ **ticket** перро́нный биле́т.

platinum ['plætɪnəm] *n.* пла́тина; *attr.* пла́тиновый.

platitude ['plætɪ,tjuːd] *n.* бана́льность, пло́скость. **plati'tudinous** *adj.* бана́льный, пло́ский (-сок, -ска́, -ско).

platoon [plə'tuːn] *n.* взвод.

platypus ['plætɪpəs] *n.* утконо́с.

plaudits ['plɔːdɪts] *n.* аплодисме́нты (-тов) *pl.*

plausibility [,plɔːzɪ'bɪlɪtɪ] *n.* (*probability*) правдоподо́бие; (*speciosity*) благови́дность. **'plausible** *adj.* правдоподо́бный; благови́дный.

play [pleɪ] *v.t.* & *i.* игра́ть *impf.*, сыгра́ть *pf.* (*game*) в+*a.*, (*instrument*) на+*p.*, (*in* ~) в+*p.*, (*for prize*) на+*a.*, (*opponent*) с+*i.*; *v.t.* (~ *part of*; *also fig.*) игра́ть *impf.*, сыгра́ть *pf.* роль+*g.*; (*musical composition*) исполня́ть *impf.*, испо́лнить *pf.*; (*chessman, card*) ходи́ть (хожу́, хо́дишь) *impf.*+*i.*; (*record*) ста́вить *impf.*, по~ *pf.*; (*searchlight*) направля́ть *impf.*, напра́вить *pf.* (**on** на+*a.*); *v.i.* (*frolic*) резви́ться *impf.*; (*fountain*) бить (бьёт) *impf.*; (*light*) перелива́ться *impf.*; ~ **down** преуменьша́ть *impf.*, преуме́ньшить *pf.*; ~ **fair** че́стно поступа́ть *impf.*, поступи́ть (-плю́, -пишь) *pf.*; ~ **false** изменя́ть *impf.*, измени́ть (-ню́, -нишь) *pf.* (+*d.*); ~ **the fool** валя́ть *impf.* дурака́; ~ **into the hands of** игра́ть *impf.*, сыгра́ть *pf.* на́ руку+*d.*; ~ **a joke, trick, on** подшу́чивать *impf.*, подшути́ть (-учу́, -у́тишь) *pf.* над+*i.*; ~ **off** игра́ть *impf.*, сыгра́ть *pf.* реша́ющую па́ртию; ~ **off against** стра́вливать *impf.*, страви́ть (-влю́, -вишь) *pf.* с+*i.*; ~ **safe** де́йствовать *impf.* наверняка́; ~**ed out** измо́танный (-ан); *n.* игра́; (*theatr.*) пье́са.

playbill *n.* театра́льная афи́ша. **playboy** *n.* прожига́тель *m.* жи́зни. **player** *n.* игро́к (-а́); (*actor*) актёр, актри́са; (*musician*) музыка́нт. **playful** *adj.* игри́вый. **playgoer** *n.* театра́л. **playground** *n.* площа́дка для игр. **playhouse** *n.* теа́тр. **playing-card** *n.* игра́льная ка́рта. **playing-field** *n.* спортплоща́дка. **playmate** *n.* друг (*pl.* друзья́, -зе́й) де́тства. **play-off** *n.* реша́ющая встре́ча. **plaything** *n.* игру́шка. **playwright** *n.* драмату́рг.

PLC, plc *abbr.* (*of public limited company*)

общественная компания с ограниченной ответственностью.

plea [pli:] *n.* (*appeal*) обращение; (*entreaty*) мольба; (*statement*) заявление; **on a ~ of** под предлогом+*g.* **plead** *v.i.* умолять *impf.* (**with** +*a.*); *v.t.* ссылаться *impf.*, сослаться (сошлюсь, -лёшься) *pf.* на+*a.*; **~ (not) guilty** (не) признавать (-наю, -наёшь) *impf.*, признать *pf.* себя виновным.

pleasant ['plez(ə)nt] *adj.* приятный. **pleasantry** *n.* шутка. **please** [pli:z] *v.t.* нравиться *impf.*, по~ *pf.*+*d.*; угождать *impf.*, угодить *pf.*+*d.*, на+*a.*; *v.i.*: **as you ~** как вам угодно; **if you ~** пожалуйста, будьте добры; (*iron.*) представьте себе; *imper.* пожалуйста; будьте добры. **pleased** *adj.* довольный; *pred.* рад. **pleasing, pleasurable** ['pleʒərəb(ə)l] *adj.* приятный. **pleasure** *n.* (*enjoyment*) удовольствие; (*will, desire*) воля, желание.

pleat [pli:t] *n.* складка; *pl.* плиссе *nt.indecl.*; *v.t.* делать *impf.*, с~ *pf.* складки на+*p.*; плиссировать *impf.* **pleated** *adj.* плиссе *indecl.* (*follows noun*).

plebeian [plɪ'bi:ən] *adj.* плебейский; *n.* плебей.

plebiscite ['plebɪsɪt, -ˌsaɪt] *n.* плебисцит.

plectrum ['plektrəm] *n.* плектр.

pledge [pledʒ] *n.* (*security*) залог; (*promise*) зарок, обещание; **sign, take, the ~** дать (дам, дашь, даст, дадим; дал, -а, дало, -и) *pf.* зарок не пить; *v.t.* отдавать (-даю, -даёшь) *impf.*, отдать (-ам, -ашь, -аст, -адим; отдал, -а, -о) *pf.* в залог; **~ o.s.** брать (беру, -рёшь; брал, -а, -о) *impf.*, взять (возьму, -мёшь; взял, -а, -о) *pf.* на себя обязательство; **~ one's word** давать (даю, даёшь) *impf.*, дать (дам, дашь, даст, дадим; дал, -а, дало, -и) *pf.* слово.

plenary ['pli:nərɪ] *adj.* полный (-лон, -лна, полно); (*assembly*) пленарный. **plenipotentiary** [ˌplenɪpə'tenʃərɪ] *adj.* (*n.*) полномочный (представитель *m.*). **plenteous** ['plentɪəs], **plentiful** *adj.* обильный. **plenty** *n.* изобилие, избыток (-тка).

plethora ['pleθərə] *n.* изобилие.

pleurisy ['pluərɪsɪ] *n.* плеврит.

pliability [ˌplaɪə'bɪlɪtɪ], '**pliancy** *n.* гибкость; (*fig.*) податливость. '**pliable**, '**pliant** *adj.* гибкий (-бок, -бка, -бко); (*fig.*) податливый.

pliers ['plaɪəz] *n.* плоскогубцы (-цев) *pl.*; клещи (-щей) *pl.*

plight [plaɪt] *n.* (бедственное, трудное) положение.

Plimsoll line ['plɪms(ə)l] *n.* грузовая марка. **plimsolls** *n.* спортивные тапочки *f.pl.*, кеды (-д(ов)) *m.pl.*

plinth [plɪnθ] *n.* плинтус; (*of wall*) цоколь *m.*

plod [plɒd] *v.i.* плестись (плетусь, -тёшься; плёлся, -лась) *impf.*; (*work*) упорно работать *impf.* (**at** над+*i.*). **plodder** ['plɒdə(r)] *n.* работяга *c.g.*

plot [plɒt] *n.* (*of land*) участок (-тка) (земли); (*of book etc.*) фабула; (*conspiracy*) заговор; *v.t.* (*on graph, map, etc.*) наносить (-ошу, -осишь) *impf.*, нанести (-су, -сёшь; нанёс, -ла) на график, на карту; (*a course*) прокладывать *impf.*, проложить (-ожу, -ожишь) *pf.*; *v. abs.* (*conspire*) составлять *impf.*, составить *pf.* заговор. **plotter** *n.* заговорщик, -ица.

plough [plaʊ] *n.* плуг (*pl.* -и); **the P~** (*astron.*) Большая Медведица; (*land*) пашня; *v.t.* пахать (пашу, -шешь) *impf.*, вс~ *pf.*; *v.t. & i.* (*fail in examination*) проваливать(ся) *impf.*, провалить(ся) (-лю(сь), -лишь(ся)) *pf.*; *v.i.*: **~ through** пробиваться *impf.*, пробиться (-бьюсь, -бьёшься) *pf.* сквозь+*a.*

plover ['plʌvə(r)] *n.* ржанка.

ploy [plɔɪ] *n.* уловка.

pluck [plʌk] *n.* (*cul.*) потроха (-хов) *pl.*, ливер; (*courage*) мужество; *v.t.* (*chicken*) щипать (-плю, -плешь) *impf.*, об~ *pf.*; **~ up (one's) courage** собираться *impf.*, собраться (соберусь, -рёшься; собрался, -алась, -алось) *pf.* с духом; *v.i.*: **~ at** дёргать *impf.*, дёрнуть *pf.* **plucky** *adj.* смелый (смел, -а, -о).

plug [plʌg] *n.* пробка; (*elec.*) штепсельная вилка; (*elec. socket*) штепсель (*pl.* -ля) *m.*; (*sparking ~*) (запальная) свеча (*pl.* -чи, -чей); (*tobacco*) прессованный табак (-а(у)); (*advertisement*) реклама; *v.t.* (**~ up**) затыкать *impf.*, заткнуть *pf.*; (*advertise*) рекламировать *impf. & pf.*; **~ in** включать *impf.*, включить *pf.*; *v.i.*: **~ away at** корпеть (-плю, -пишь) *impf.* над+*i.*

plum [plʌm] *n.* (*fruit*) слива; (*colour*) тёмно-фиолетовый цвет; **~ cake** кекс.

plumage ['plu:mɪdʒ] *n.* оперение, перья (-ьев) *nt.pl.*

plumb [plʌm] *n.* отвес; (*naut.*) лот; *adj.* вертикальный; (*fig.*) явный; *adv.* вертикально; (*fig.*) точно; *v.t.* измерять *impf.*, измерить *pf.* глубину+*g.*; (*fig.*) проникать *impf.*, проникнуть (-к) *pf.* в+*a.*

plumber ['plʌmə(r)] *n.* водопроводчик. **plumbing** *n.* (*work*) водопроводное дело; (*system of pipes*) водопроводная система.

plume [plu:m] *n.* (*feather*) перо (*pl.* -рья, -рьев); (*on hat etc.*) султан, плюмаж; **~ of smoke** дымок (-мка); *v.t.*: **~ o.s. on** кичиться *impf.*+*i.*

plummet ['plʌmɪt] *n.* (*plumb*) отвес; (*sounding-line*) лот; (*on fishing-line*) грузило; *v.i.* слетать *impf.*, слететь (-ечу, -етишь) *pf.*

plump[1] [plʌmp] *adj.* полный (-лон, -лна, полно), пухлый (пухл, -а, -о).

plump[2] [plʌmp] *v.t. & i.* бухать(ся) *impf.*, бухнуть(ся) *pf.*; *v.i.*: **~ for** (*vote for*) голосовать *impf.*, про~ *pf.* только за+*a.*; (*fig.*) выбирать *impf.*, выбрать (выберу, -решь) *pf.*

plunder ['plʌndə(r)] *v.t.* грабить *impf.*, о~ *pf.*; *n.* добыча.

plunge [plʌndʒ] *v.t.* & *i.* (*immerse*) погружа́ть(ся) *impf.*, погрузи́ть(ся) *pf.* (**into** в+*a.*); *v.i.* (*dive*) ныря́ть *impf.*, нырну́ть *pf.*; (*rush*) броса́ться *impf.*, бро́ситься *pf.* **plunger** *n.* плу́нжер.

pluperfect [plu:ˈpɜːfɪkt] *adj.* предпрошéдший; *n.* предпрошéдшее врéмя *nt.*

plural [ˈpluər(ə)l] *n.* мнóжественное числó; *adj.* мнóжественный. **pluralism** *n.* плюрали́зм. **plura'listic** *adj.* плюралисти́ческий.

plus [plʌs] *prep.* плюс+*a.*; *adj.* (*additional*) добáвочный; (*positive*) положи́тельный; *n.* (знак) плюс.

plush [plʌʃ] *n.* плюш; *adj.* плю́шевый. **plushy** *adj.* шикáрный.

Pluto [ˈpluːtəʊ] *n.* Плутóн.

plutocracy [pluːˈtɒkrəsɪ] *n.* плутокрáтия. **plutocrat** [ˈpluːtəˌkræt] *n.* плутокрáт. **pluto'cratic** *adj.* плутократи́ческий.

plutonium [pluːˈtəʊnɪəm] *n.* плутóний.

ply¹ [plaɪ] *v.i.* курси́ровать *impf.*; *v.t.* (*tool*) рабóтать *impf.*+*i.*; (*task*) занимáться *impf.*+*i.*; ~ **with questions** засыпáть *impf.*, засы́пать (-плю, -плешь) *pf.* вопрóсами.

ply² [plaɪ] *n.* (*layer*) слой (*pl.* слои́); (*strand*) прядь. **plywood** *n.* фанéра.

PM *abbr.* (*of Prime Minister*) премьéр-мини́стр.

p.m. *abbr.* (*of post meridiem*) пополу́дни.

pneumatic [njuːˈmætɪk] *adj.* пневмати́ческий; ~ **drill** отбóйный молотóк.

pneumonia [njuːˈməʊnɪə] *n.* пневмони́я, воспалéние лёгких.

PO *abbr.* (*of Post Office*) пóчта; (*of postal order*) почтóвый перевóд.

poach¹ [pəʊtʃ] *v.t.* (*cook*) вари́ть (-рю́, -ришь) *impf.*, опускáя в кипятóк; кипяти́ть *impf.* на мéдленном огнé; ~**ed egg** яйцó-пашóт.

poach² [pəʊtʃ] *v.i.* (*hunt*) незакóнно охóтиться *impf.*; (*trespass*) вторгáться *impf.*, вторгнуться (-г(нул)ся, -глась) *pf.* в чужи́е владéния; *v.t.* охóтиться *impf.* на+*a.* на чужóй землé. **poacher** *n.* браконьéр.

pochard [ˈpəʊtʃəd] *n.* нырóк (-ркá).

pocket [ˈpɒkɪt] *n.* кармáн; (*billiards*) лýза; (*air-*~) воздýшная я́ма; **in** ~ в вы́игрыше; **in person's** ~ в рукáх у+*g.*; **out of** ~ в убы́тке; *adj.* кармáнный; *v.t.* класть (-адý, -адёшь; -ал) *impf.*, положи́ть (-жу́, -жишь) *pf.* в кармáн; (*appropriate*) прикармáнивать *impf.*, прикармáнить *pf.*; (*billiards*) загоня́ть (прош. загнáть (загоню́, -нишь; загнáл, -á, -о) *pf.* в лýзу. **pocketful** *n.* пóлный кармáн.

pock-marked [ˈpɒkmɑːkt] *adj.* рябóй (ряб, -á, -о).

pod [pɒd] *n.* стручóк (-чкá), шелухá; *v.t.* лущи́ть *impf.*, об~ *pf.*

podgy [ˈpɒdʒɪ] *adj.* тóлстенький; пýхлый (пухл, -á, о).

podium [ˈpəʊdɪəm] *n.* (*conductor's*) пульт.

poem [ˈpəʊɪm] *n.* стихотворéние; (*longer* ~) поэ́ма. **poet** *n.* поэ́т; **P~ Laureate** поэ́тлауреáт. **poetaster** [ˌpəʊɪˈtæstə(r)] *n.* стихоплёт. **poetess** *n.* поэтéсса. **poetic(al)** [pəʊˈetɪk(ə)l] *adj.* поэти́ческий, поэти́чный; (*in verse*) стихотвóрный. **poetry** *n.* поэ́зия, стихи́ *m.pl.*; (*quality*) поэти́чность.

pogrom [ˈpɒɡrəm, -rɒm] *n.* погрóм.

poignancy [ˈpɔɪnjənsɪ] *n.* остротá. **poignant** *adj.* óстрый (остр & остёр, острá, óстро).

point¹ [pɔɪnt] *n.* тóчка; (*place*; in list; print.) пункт; (*in score*) очкó (*pl.* -ки́, -кóв); (*in time*) момéнт; (*in space*) мéсто (*pl.* -тá); (*essence*) суть; (*sense*) смысл; (*sharp* ~) остриё; (*tip*) кóнчик; (*promontory*) мыс (*loc.* -é & -ý; *pl.* мысы́); (*decimal* ~) запятáя *sb.*; (*power* ~) штéпсель (*pl.* -ля́) *m.*; *pl.* (*rail.*) стрéлка; **be on the** ~ **of** (*doing*) собирáться *impf.*, собрáться (соберу́сь, -рёшься; собрáлся, -алáсь, -алóсь) *pf.*+*inf.*; **beside, off, the** ~ некстáти; **in** ~ **of fact** факти́чески; **that is the** ~ в э́том и дéло; **the** ~ **is that** дéло в том, что; **there is no** ~ (*in doing*) не имéет смы́сла (+*inf.*); **to the** ~ кстáти; ~ **of view** тóчка зрéния.

point² [pɔɪnt] *v.t.* (*wall*) расши́вать *impf.*, расши́ть (разошью́, -ьёшь) *pf.* швы+*g.*; (*gun etc.*) наводи́ть (-ожу́, -óдишь) *impf.*, навести́ (-едý, -едёшь; -ёл, -елá) *pf.* (**at** на+*a.*); *v. abs.* (*dog*) дéлать *impf.*, с~ *pf.* стóйку; *v.i.* (*with finger*) по-, у-, кáзывать *impf.*, по-, у-, казáть (-ажý, -áжешь) *pf.* пáльцем (**at, to** на+*a.*); (*draw attention*; ~ *out*) обращáть *impf.*, обрати́ть (-ащý, -ати́шь) *pf.* внимáние (**to** на+*a.*).

point-blank [pɔɪntˈblæŋk] *adj.* прямóй (прям, -á, -о, пря́мы). **point-duty** *n.* регули́рование движéния.

pointed [ˈpɔɪntɪd] *adj.* (*sharp*) óстрый (остр & остёр, острá, óстро); (*of arch etc.*) стрéльчатый; (*of remark*) кóлкий (-лок, -лкá, -лко). **pointer** *n.* указáтель *m.*; (*of clock etc.*) стрéлка; (*dog*) пóйнтер (*pl.* -ы & -á). **pointless** *adj.* бессмы́сленный (-ен, -енна).

poise [pɔɪz] *v.t.* уравновéшивать *impf.*, уравнóвесить *pf.*; **be** ~**d** (*hover*) висéть (-си́т) *impf.* в вóздухе; *n.* уравновéшенность.

poison [ˈpɔɪz(ə)n] *n.* яд (-a(y)), отрáва; ~ **gas** ядови́тый газ; ~ **ivy** ядонóсный сумáх; *v.t.* отравля́ть *impf.*, отрави́ть (-влю́, -вишь) *pf.* **poisoner** *n.* отрави́тель *m.* **poisonous** *adj.* ядови́тый. **poison-pen** *adj.*: ~ **letter** анони́мка.

poke [pəʊk] *v.t.* ты́кать (ты́чу, -чешь) *impf.*, ткнуть *pf.*; ~ **fun at** подшýчивать *impf.*, подшути́ть (-учý, -ýтишь) *pf.* над+*i.*; ~ **one's nose into** совáть (сую́, суёшь) *impf.*, сýнуть *pf.* нос в+*a.*; ~ **the fire** мешáть *impf.*, по~ *pf.* (кочергóй) ýгли в ками́не; *n.* тычóк (-чкá). **poker¹** *n.* (*metal rod*) кочергá (*g.pl.* -рёг).

poker² [ˈpəʊkə(r)] *n.* (*cards*) пóкер. **pokerface** *n.* бесстрáстное лицó.

poky [ˈpəʊkɪ] *adj.* тéсный (-сен, -снá, -сно).

Poland ['pəʊlənd] *n.* Пóльша.

polar ['pəʊlə(r)] *adj.* поля́рный; (*phys.*) пóлюсный; ~ **bear** бéлый медвéдь *m.* **polarity** [pə'lærɪtɪ] *n.* поля́рность. **polarize** *v.t.* поляризова́ть *impf. & pf.*

pole[1] [pəʊl] *n.* (*geog.; phys.*) пóлюс; ~ **star** Поля́рная звезда́.

pole[2] [pəʊl] *n.* (*rod*) столб (-á), шест (-á).

Pole[3] [pəʊl] *n.* поля́к, пóлька.

pole-axe ['pəʊlæks] *n.* секи́ра, берды́ш (-á).

polecat ['pəʊlkæt] *n.* хорёк (-рька́).

polemic [pə'lemɪk] *adj.* полеми́ческий; *n.* полéмика.

pole-vaulter ['pəʊl,vɔːltə(r), -,vɒltə(r)] *n.* шестови́к. **pole-vaulting** *n.* прыжóк (-жка́) с шестóм.

police [pə'liːs] *n.* поли́ция; (*as pl.*) полицéйские *sb.*; ~ **constable** полицéйский *sb.*; ~ **station** полицéйский уча́сток (-тка). **policeman** *n.* полицéйский *sb.*, полисмéн.

policy[1] ['pɒlɪsɪ] *n.* (*course of action*) поли́тика.

policy[2] ['pɒlɪsɪ] *n.* (*document*) пóлис.

polio(myelitis) [,pəʊlɪəʊ,maɪɪ'laɪtɪs] *n.* полиомиели́т.

Polish[1] ['pəʊlɪʃ] *adj.* пóльский.

polish[2] ['pɒlɪʃ] *n.* (*gloss*) гля́нец (-нца); (*process*) полирóвка; (*substance*) политу́ра; (*fig.*) изы́сканность; *v.t.* полирова́ть *impf.*, на~, от~ *pf.*; ~ **off** расправля́ться *impf.*, распра́виться *pf.* c+*i.* **polished** *adj.* (*refined*) изы́сканный (-ан, -анна).

polite [pə'laɪt] *adj.* вéжливый. **politeness** *n.* вéжливость.

politic ['pɒlɪtɪk] *adj.* полити́чный. **political** [pə'lɪtɪk(ə)l] *adj.* полити́ческий; (*of the state*) госуда́рственный; ~ **economy** политэконóмика; ~ **prisoner** политзаключённый *sb.* **poli'tician** *n.* поли́тик. **politics** *n.* поли́тика.

polka ['pɒlkə, 'pəʊlkə] *n.* пóлька.

poll [pəʊl] *n.* (*voting*) голосова́ние; (*number of votes*) числó голосóв; (*opinion* ~) опрóс; *v.t.* (*receive votes*) получа́ть *impf.*, получи́ть (-чу́, -чишь) *pf.*; *v.i.* голосова́ть *impf.*, про~ *pf.*

pollard ['pɒləd] *v.t.* подстрига́ть *impf.*, подстри́чь (-игу́, -ижёшь; -иг) *pf.*

pollen ['pɒlən] *n.* пыльца́. **pollinate** *v.t.* опыля́ть *impf.*, опыли́ть *pf.*

polling-booth ['pəʊlɪŋbuːð, -,buːθ] *n.* каби́на для голосова́ния. **polling-station** *n.* избира́тельный уча́сток (-тка).

pollutant [pə'luːtənt] *n.* загрязни́тель *m.*, поллюта́нт. **pollute** *v.t.* загрязня́ть *impf.*, загрязни́ть *pf.* **pollution** *n.* загрязнéние.

polo ['pəʊləʊ] *n.* пóло *nt.indecl.*

polonaise [,pɒlə'neɪz] *n.* полонéз.

polo-neck ['pəʊləʊ,nek] *n.* (*garment*) водола́зка.

polyandry ['pɒlɪ,ændrɪ] *n.* полиа́ндрия, многому́жие. **polyester** [,pɒlɪ'estə(r)] *n.* полиэфи́р. **polyethylene** [,pɒlɪ'eθɪ,liːn] *n.* полиэтилéн. **polygamous** [pə'lɪgəməs] *adj.* многобра́чный. **po'lygamy** *n.* многобра́чие. **polyglot** *n.* полиглóт; *adj.* многоязы́чный; (*person*) говоря́щий на мнóгих языка́х. **polygon** *n.* многоугóльник. **polymer** *n.* полимéр.

polyp ['pɒlɪp] *n.* поли́п.

polyphonic [,pɒlɪ'fɒnɪk] *adj.* полифони́ческий. **polyphony** [pə'lɪfənɪ] *n.* полифони́я. **polystyrene** [,pɒlɪ'staɪə,riːn] *n.* полистирóл. **polysy'llabic** *adj.* многослóжный. **polysyllable** *n.* многослóжное слóво (*pl.* -ва́). **poly'technic** *n.* политéхникум. **polytheism** *n.* многобóжие. **polythene** ['pɒlɪ,θiːn] *n.* полиэтилéн. **polyunsaturated** [,pɒlɪʌn'sætʃə,reɪtɪd] *adj.*: ~ **fats** полиненасы́щенные жиры́. **polyurethane** [,pɒlɪ'jʊərə,θeɪn] *n.* полиурета́н. **polyvalent** [,pɒlɪ'veɪlənt] *adj.* многовалéнтный.

pomade [pə'maːd] *n.* пома́да; *v.t.* пома́дить *impf.*, на~ *pf.*

pomegranate ['pɒmɪ,grænɪt, 'pɒm,grænɪt] *n.* грана́т.

Pomeranian [,pɒmə'reɪnɪən] *n.* шпиц.

pommel ['pʌm(ə)l] *n.* (*hilt*) голóвка; (*of saddle*) лука́ (*pl.* -ки).

pomp [pɒmp] *n.* пы́шность, великолéпие. **pom'posity** *n.* напы́щенность. **pompous** *adj.* напы́щенный (-ен, -енна).

pom-pom ['pɒmpɒm] *n.* помпóн.

poncho ['pɒntʃəʊ] *n.* пóнчо *nt.indecl.*

pond [pɒnd] *n.* пруд (-á, *loc.* -ý). **pondweed** *n.* рдест.

ponder ['pɒndə(r)] *v.t.* обду́мывать *impf.*, обду́мать *pf.*; *v.i.* размышля́ть *impf.*, размы́слить *pf.* (**over** o+*p.*).

ponderous ['pɒndərəs] *adj.* тяжеловéсный.

poniard ['pɒnjəd] *n.* кинжа́л.

pontiff ['pɒntɪf] *n.* (*pope*) ри́мский Па́па *m.*; (*bishop*) епи́скоп; (*chief priest*) первосвящéнник.

pontoon[1] [pɒn'tuːn] *n.* понтóн; ~ **bridge** понтóнный мост (мóста́, *loc.* -ý; *pl.* -ы́).

pontoon[2] [pɒn'tuːn] *n.* (*cards*) два́дцать однó.

pony ['pəʊnɪ] *n.* пóни *m.indecl.*

poodle ['puːd(ə)l] *n.* пу́дель (*pl.* -ли & -ля́) *m.*

pooh [puː] *int.* фу! **pooh-pooh** *v.t.* пренебрега́ть *impf.*, пренебрéчь (-егу́, -ежёшь; -ёг, -егла́) *pf.*+*i.*

pool[1] [puːl] *n.* (*of water*) прудóк (-дка́), лу́жа; (*swimming* ~) бассéйн.

pool[2] [puːl] *n.* (*collective stakes*) совоку́пность ста́вок; (*common fund*) óбщий фонд; (*common resources*) объединённые запа́сы *m.pl.*; **car** ~ автоба́за; **typing** ~ машинопи́сное бюрó *nt.indecl.*; *v.t.* объединя́ть *impf.*, объедини́ть *pf.*

poop [puːp] *n.* полуют; (*stern*) корма́.

poor [pʊə(r)] *adj.* бéдный (-ден, -дна́, -дно, бéдны́); (*bad*) плохóй (плох, -á, -о, плóхи); (*scanty*) ску́дный (-ден, -дна́, -дно); (*weak*) сла́бый (слаб, -á, -о) *n.*: **the** ~ беднота́, бедня́к *m.pl.* **poorhouse** *n.* рабóтный дом (*pl.* -á). **poorly** *pred.* нездорóв (-а, -о).

pop[1] [pɒp] *v.i.* хлóпать *impf.*, хлóпнуть *pf.*;

щёлкать *impf.*, щёлкнуть *pf.*; *v.t.* бы́стро всу́нуть *pf.* (into в+a.); ~ in on забега́ть *impf.*, забежа́ть (-егу́, -ежи́шь) *pf.* к+d.; *n.* хлопо́к (-пка́), щёлк; (*drink*) щипу́чий напи́ток (-тка). **popgun** *n.* (*toy*) пуга́ч (-а́).

pop² [pɒp] *adj.* популя́рный, поп-; ~ **art** поп-а́рт; ~ **concert** конце́рт поп-му́зыки; ~ **music** поп-му́зыка.

popcorn ['pɒpkɔːn] *n.* возду́шная кукуру́за.

pope [pəʊp] *n.* Па́па ри́мский *m.* **popery** *n.* папи́зм. **popish** *adj.* папи́стский.

poplar ['pɒplə(r)] *n.* то́поль (*pl.* -ля́) *m.*

poppet ['pɒpɪt] *n.* кро́шка.

poppy ['pɒpɪ] *n.* мак; ~ **seed** (*collect.*) мак (-а(у)).

poppycock ['pɒpɪˌkɒk] *n.* чепуха́.

populace ['pɒpjʊləs] *n.* просто́й наро́д. **popular** *adj.* наро́дный; (*liked*) популя́рный. **popu'larity** *n.* популя́рность. **popularize** *v.t.* популяризи́ровать *impf.* & *pf.* **populate** *v.t.* населя́ть *impf.*, насели́ть *pf.* **popu'lation** *n.* населе́ние. **populous** *adj.* (мно́го)лю́дный.

porcelain ['pɔːsəlɪn] *n.* фарфо́р; *attr.* фарфо́ровый.

porch [pɔːtʃ] *n.* подъе́зд, крыльцо́ (*pl.* -льца, -ле́ц, -льца́м).

porcupine ['pɔːkjʊˌpaɪn] *n.* дикобра́з.

pore¹ [pɔː(r)] *n.* по́ра.

pore² [pɔː(r)] *v.i.*: ~ **over** погружа́ться *impf.*, погрузи́ться (-ужу́сь, -узи́шься) *pf.* в+a.

pork [pɔːk] *n.* свини́на; ~ **pie** пиро́г (-а́) со свини́ной. **pork-butcher** *n.* колба́сник.

pornographic [ˌpɔːnəˈgræfɪk] *adj.* порнографи́ческий. **pornography** [pɔːˈnɒgrəfɪ] *n.* порногра́фия.

porous ['pɔːrəs] *adj.* по́ристый.

porphyry ['pɔːfɪrɪ] *n.* порфи́р.

porpoise ['pɔːpəs] *n.* морска́я свинья́ (*pl.* -ньи, -не́й, -ньям).

porridge ['pɒrɪdʒ] *n.* овся́ная ка́ша.

port¹ [pɔːt] *n.* (*harbour*) порт (*loc.* -у́; *pl.* -ы, -óв); (*town*) порто́вый го́род (*pl.* -а́).

port² [pɔːt] *n.* (*naut.*, *aeron.*) ле́вый борт (*loc.* -у́).

port³ [pɔːt] *n.* (*wine*) портве́йн (-а(у)).

portable ['pɔːtəb(ə)l] *adj.* портати́вный.

portal ['pɔːt(ə)l] *n.* порта́л.

portcullis [pɔːtˈkʌlɪs] *n.* опускна́я решётка.

portend [pɔːˈtend] *v.t.* предвеща́ть *impf.* **portent** ['pɔːtent, -t(ə)nt] *n.* предзнаменова́ние. **por'tentous** *adj.* злове́щий.

porter¹ ['pɔːtə(r)] *n.* (*gate-*, *door-*, *keeper*) швейца́р, привра́тник; ~'s **lodge** швейца́рская *sb.*, до́мик привра́тника.

porter² ['pɔːtə(r)] *n.* (*carrier*) носи́льщик.

portfolio [pɔːtˈfəʊlɪəʊ] *n.* портфе́ль *m.*, па́пка.

porthole ['pɔːthəʊl] *n.* иллюмина́тор.

portico ['pɔːtɪˌkəʊ] *n.* по́ртик.

portion ['pɔːʃ(ə)n] *n.* часть (*pl.* -ти, -те́й), до́ля (*pl.* -ли, -ле́й); (*of food*) по́рция; *v.t.*: ~ **out** разделя́ть *impf.*, раздели́ть *pf.*

portly ['pɔːtlɪ] *adj.* доро́дный.

portmanteau [pɔːtˈmæntəʊ] *n.* чемода́н; ~

word сло́во-гибри́д.

portrait ['pɔːtrɪt] *n.* портре́т. **portraiture** *n.* портре́тная жи́вопись. **portray** [pɔːˈtreɪ] *v.t.* рисова́ть *impf.*, на~ *pf.*; изобража́ть *impf.*, изобрази́ть *pf.* **portrayal** *n.* рисова́ние, изображе́ние.

Portugal ['pɔːtjʊg(ə)l] *n.* Португа́лия. **Portuguese** [ˌpɔːtjʊˈgiːz, ˌpɔːtʃ-] *n.* португа́лец (-льца), -лка; *adj.* португа́льский.

pose [pəʊz] *n.* по́за; *v.t.* (*question*) ста́вить *impf.*, по~ *pf.*; *v.i.* пози́ровать *impf.*; ~ **as** принима́ть *impf.*, приня́ть (приму́, -мешь; при́нял, -а́, -о) *pf.* по́зу+g.

poser ['pəʊzə(r)] *n.* тру́дный вопро́с, тру́дная зада́ча.

poseur [pəʊˈzɜː(r)] *n.* позёр.

posh [pɒʃ] *adj.* шика́рный.

posit ['pɒzɪt] *v.t.* (*assume*) постули́ровать *impf.* & *pf.*

position [pəˈzɪʃ(ə)n] *n.* положе́ние, пози́ция; in a ~ to в состоя́нии+inf.; *v.t.* ста́вить *impf.*, по~ *pf.* **positional** *adj.* позицио́нный.

positive ['pɒzɪtɪv] *adj.* положи́тельный; (*person*) уве́ренный (-ен, -енна); (*proof*) несомне́нный (-нен, -нна); (*phot.*) позити́вный; *n.* (*phot.*) позити́в. **positivism** *n.* позитиви́зм.

posse ['pɒsɪ] *n.* отря́д (шери́фа).

possess [pəˈzes] *v.t.* облада́ть *impf.*+i.; владе́ть *impf.*+i.; (*of feeling etc.*) овладева́ть *impf.*, овладе́ть *pf.*+i. **possessed** *adj.* одержи́мый. **possession** *n.* владе́ние (**of** +i.); *pl.* со́бственность. **possessive** *adj.* со́бственнический; (*gram.*) притяжа́тельный. **possessor** *n.* облада́тель *m.*, ~ница.

possibility [ˌpɒsɪˈbɪltɪ] *n.* возмо́жность. **possible** *adj.* возмо́жный; as much as ~ ско́лько возмо́жно; as soon as ~ как мо́жно скоре́е; *n.* возмо́жное *sb.* **possibly** *adv.* возмо́жно, мо́жет (быть).

post¹ [pəʊst] *n.* (*pole*) столб (-а́); *v.t.* (~ up) выве́шивать *impf.*, вы́весить *pf.*

post² [pəʊst] *n.* (*station*) пост (-а́, *loc.* на -у́); (*trading-~*) факто́рия; *v.t.* (*station*) расставля́ть *impf.*, расста́вить *pf.*; (*appoint*) назнача́ть *impf.*, назна́чить *pf.*

post³ [pəʊst] *n.* (*letters*, ~ *office*, *etc.*) по́чта; by return of ~ с обра́тной по́чтой; *attr.* почто́вый; ~ office по́чта, почто́вое отделе́ние; General P~ Office (гла́вный) почта́мт; *v.t.* (*send by* ~) отправля́ть *impf.*, отпра́вить *pf.* по по́чте; (*put in* ~-*box*) опуска́ть *impf.*, опусти́ть (-ущу́, -у́стишь) в почто́вый я́щик. **postage** *n.* почто́вая опла́та, почто́вые расхо́ды *m.pl.*; ~ **stamp** почто́вая ма́рка. **postal** *adj.* почто́вый; ~ **order** почто́вый перево́д. **postbox** *n.* почто́вый я́щик. **postcard** *n.* откры́тка. **postcode** *n.* почто́вый и́ндекс.

post-date [pəʊstˈdeɪt] *v.t.* дати́ровать *impf.* & *pf.* бо́лее по́здним число́м.

poster ['pəʊstə(r)] *n.* афи́ша, плака́т.

poste restante [ˌpəʊst reˈstɑːt] *n.* (*in address*)

до востре́бования.

posterior [pɒ'stɪərɪə(r)] *adj.* (*later*) после́дующий; (*hinder*) за́дний; *n.* зад (*loc.* -у́; *pl.* -ы́).

posterity [pɒ'sterɪtɪ] *n.* (*descendants*) пото́мство; (*later generations*) после́дующие поколе́ния *nt.pl.*

postern ['pɒst(ə)n, 'pəʊ-] *n.* за́дняя дверь (*loc.* -ри́; *pl.* -ри, -ре́й, *i.* -ря́ми & -рьми́).

post-free [pəʊst'friː] *adj.* без почто́вой опла́ты.

post-graduate [pəʊst'grædjʊət] *n.* аспира́нт; *adj.* аспира́нтский; ~ **course** аспиранту́ра.

posthumous ['pɒstjʊməs] *adj.* посме́ртный.

postman ['pəʊstmən] *n.* почтальо́н. **postmark** *n.* почто́вый штéмпель (*pl.* -ля́) *m.*; *v.t.* штемпелева́ть (-лю́ю, -лю́ешь) *impf.*, за~ *pf.* **postmaster, mistress** *n.* нача́льник почто́вого отделе́ния.

post-mortem [pəʊst'mɔːtəm] *n.* вскры́тие тру́па.

post-paid [pəʊst'peɪd] *adj.* с опла́ченными почто́выми расхо́дами.

postpone [pəʊst'pəʊn, pə'spəʊn] *v.t.* отсро́чивать *impf.*, отсро́чить *pf.* **postponement** *n.* отсро́чка.

postprandial [pəʊst'prændɪəl] *adj.* послеобе́денный.

postscript ['pəʊstskrɪpt, 'pəʊskrɪpt] *n.* постскри́птум.

postulate ['pɒstjʊlət; 'pɒstjʊˌleɪt] *n.* постула́т; *v.t.* постули́ровать *impf. & pf.*

posture ['pɒstʃə(r)] *n.* по́за, положе́ние; *v.i.* рисова́ться *impf.*

post-war [pəʊst'wɔː(r), 'pəʊst-] *adj.* послевое́нный.

posy ['pəʊzɪ] *n.* буке́тик.

pot [pɒt] *n.* горшо́к (-шка́), котело́к (-лка́); (*as prize*) ку́бок (-бка); ~s **of money** ку́ча де́нег; ~ **roast** тушёное мя́со; *v.t.* (*plant*) сажа́ть *impf.*, посади́ть (-ажу́, -а́дишь) *pf.* в горшо́к; (*billiards*) загоня́ть *impf.*, загна́ть (загоню́, -нишь; загна́л, -а́, -о) *pf.* в лу́зу.

potash ['pɒtæʃ] *n.* пота́ш (-á). **potassium** [pə'tæsɪəm] *n.* ка́лий.

potato [pə'teɪtəʊ] *n.* (*plant; pl. collect.*) карто́фель *m.* (*no pl.*); (*plant*) карто́фелина (*also collect.; coll.*); **two** ~**es** две карто́фелины, карто́шки; ~ **peeler** картофелечи́стка.

pot-bellied [pɒt'belɪd] *adj.* пуза́тый. **pot-belly** *n.* пу́зо. **pot-boiler** *n.* халту́ра. (*person*) халту́рщик.

potence ['pəʊt(ə)ns], -**cy** *n.* си́ла, могу́щество; (*of drug etc.*) действенность. **potent** *adj.* (*reason etc.*) убеди́тельный; (*drug etc.*) сильноде́йствующий; (*mighty*) могу́щественный (-ен, -енна). **potentate** *n.* властели́н.

potential [pə'tenʃ(ə)l] *adj.* потенциа́льный, возмо́жный; *n.* потенциа́л, возмо́жность. **potenti'ality** *n.* потенциа́льность.

pot-hole ['pɒthəʊl] *n.* пеще́ра; (*in road*) вы́

бо́ина. **pot-holer** *n.* пеще́рник.

potion ['pəʊʃ(ə)n] *n.* до́за лека́рства, зе́лье.

pot-pourri [pəʊ'pʊərɪ, -'riː] *n.* попурри́ *nt.indecl.*

pot-shot ['pɒtʃɒt] *n.* вы́стрел науга́д.

potter[1] ['pɒtə(r)] *v.i.:* ~ **at, in** рабо́тать *impf.* ко́е-как над+*i.*; ~ **about** ло́дырничать *impf.*

potter[2] ['pɒtə(r)] *n.* гонча́р (-á). **pottery** *n.* (*goods*) гонча́рные изде́лия *nt.pl.*; (*place*) гонча́рная *sb.*

potty[1] ['pɒtɪ] *adj.* (*trivial*) пустяко́вый; (*crazy*) поме́шанный (-ан) (**about** на+*p.*).

potty[2] ['pɒtɪ] *n.* ночно́й горшо́к (-шка́).

pouch [paʊtʃ] *n.* су́мка, мешо́к (-шка́).

pouffe [puːf] *n.* пуф.

poulterer ['pəʊltərə(r)] *n.* торго́вец (-вца) дома́шней пти́цей.

poultice ['pəʊltɪs] *n.* припа́рка; *v.t.* ста́вить *impf.*, по~ *pf.* припа́рку+*d.*

poultry ['pəʊltrɪ] *n.* дома́шняя пти́ца; ~ **farm** птицефе́рма.

pounce [paʊns] *v.i.:* ~ (**up**)**on** налета́ть *impf.*, налете́ть (-ечу́, -ети́шь) *pf.* на+*a.*; набра́сываться *impf.*, набро́ситься *pf.* на+*a.*; (*fig.*) ухвати́ться (-ачу́сь, -а́тишься) *pf.* за+*a.*

pound[1] [paʊnd] *n.* (*measure*) фунт; ~ **sterling** фунт сте́рлингов.

pound[2] [paʊnd] *n.* (*enclosure*) заго́н.

pound[3] [paʊnd] *v.t.* (*crush*) толо́чь (-лку́, -лчёшь; -ло́к, -лкла́) *impf.*, ис~, рас~ *pf.*; (*strike*) колоти́ть (-очу́, -о́тишь) *impf.*, по~ *pf.* по+*d.*, в+*a.*; *v.i.* (*heart*) колоти́ться (-ится) *impf.*; ~ **along** тяжело́ ходи́ть (хожу́, хо́дишь) *impf.*; (*run*) тяжело́ бе́гать *impf.*; ~ **away at** (*with guns*) обстре́ливать *impf.*, обстреля́ть *pf.*

pour [pɔː(r)] *v.t.* лить (лью, льёшь; лил, -á, -о) *impf.*; ~ **out** налива́ть *impf.*, нали́ть (налью́, -ьёшь; на́лил, -á, -о) *pf.*; *v.i.* ли́ться (льётся; ли́лся, лила́сь, ли́ло́сь) *impf.*; **it is** ~**ing** (*with rain*) дождь льёт как из ведра́.

pouring *adj.* (*rain*) проливно́й.

pout [paʊt] *v.t. & i.* надува́ть(ся) *impf.*, наду́ть(ся) (-у́ю(сь), -у́ешь(ся)) *pf.*

poverty ['pɒvətɪ] *n.* бе́дность, убо́гость. **poverty-stricken** *adj.* убо́гий.

POW *abbr.* (*of* **prisoner of war**) военнопле́нный *sb.*

powder ['paʊdə(r)] *n.* порошо́к (-шка́); (*cosmetic*) пу́дра; (*gun-*~) по́рох (-a(y)); ~ **blue** се́ро-голубо́й; ~ **compact** пу́дреница; *v.t.* (*sprinkle with* ~) посыпа́ть *impf.*, посы́пать (-плю, -плешь) *pf.* порошко́м; (*nose etc.*) пу́дрить *impf.*, на~ *pf.*; ~**ed milk** моло́чный порошо́к (-шка́). **powder-keg** *n.* порохова́я бо́чка. **powder-puff** *n.* пухо́вка. **powdery** *adj.* порошкообра́зный.

power ['paʊə(r)] *n.* (*vigour*) си́ла; (*might*) могу́щество; (*ability*) спосо́бность; (*control*) власть; (*authorization*) полномо́чие; (*State*) держа́ва; (*math.*) сте́пень (*pl.* -ни, -не́й); *attr.* силово́й, механи́ческий; **party in** ~ па́ртия у вла́сти; ~ **of attorney** дове́ренность; ~ **cut** прекраще́ние пода́чи эне́ргии; ~

point штепсель (*pl.* -ля́) *m.*; ~ **station** электростанция. **powerful** *adj.* си́льный (си́лён, -льна́, -льно, си́льны́); могу́щественный (-ен, -енна). **powerless** *adj.* бесси́льный.

pp. *abbr.* (*of* **page(s)**) стр, страни́цы.

practicable ['præktɪkəb(ə)l] *adj.* осуществи́мый; (*theatr.*) настоя́щий. **practical** *adj.* (*of practice*) практи́ческий; (*useful in practice*; *person*) практи́чный; ~ **joke** гру́бая шу́тка. **practically** *adv.* (*in effect*) факти́чески; (*almost*) почти́. **practice** *n.* пра́ктика; (*custom*) обы́чай; (*exercise*) упражне́ние; **in** ~ на де́ле; **put into** ~ осуществля́ть *impf.*, осуществи́ть *pf.*; *attr.* уче́бный. **practise** *v.t.* (*carry out*) применя́ть *impf.*, примени́ть (-ню́, -нишь) *pf.* на пра́ктике; (*also abs. of doctor etc.*) практикова́ть *impf.*; (*engage in*) занима́ться *impf.*, заня́ться (займу́сь, -мёшься; заня́лся, -ла́сь) *pf.*+*i.*; упражня́ться *impf.* в+*p.*, (*musical instrument in* игре́ на+*p.*). **practised** *adj.* о́пытный. **prac'titioner** *n.* (*doctor*) практику́ющий врач (-а́); (*lawyer*) практику́ющий юри́ст; **general** ~ врач (-а́) о́бщей пра́ктики.

pragmatic [præg'mætɪk] *adj.* прагмати́ческий. **'pragmatism** *n.* прагмати́зм. **'pragmatist** *n.* прагма́тик.

Prague [prɑːg] *n.* Пра́га.

prairie ['preərɪ] *n.* степь (*loc.* -пи́; *pl.* -пи, -пе́й); (*in N.America*) пре́рия.

praise [preɪz] *v.t.* хвали́ть (-лю́, -лишь) *impf.*, по~ *pf.*; *n.* похвала́. **praiseworthy** *adj.* похва́льный.

pram [præm] *n.* де́тская коля́ска.

prance [prɑːns] *v.i.* (*horse*) станови́ться (-ится) *impf.*, стать (ста́нет) на дыбы́; (*fig.*) задава́ться (-даю́сь, -даёшься) *impf.*

prank [præŋk] *n.* вы́ходка, ша́лость.

prate [preɪt] *v.i.* болта́ть *impf.*

prattle ['præt(ə)l] *v.i.* лепета́ть (-ечу́, -е́чешь); *n.* ле́пет.

prawn [prɔːn] *n.* креве́тка.

pray [preɪ] *v.t.* моли́ть (-лю́, -лишь) *impf.* (**for** o+*p.*); моли́ться (-лю́сь, -лишься) *impf.*, по~ *pf.* (**to** +*d.*; **for** o+*p.*). **prayer** ['preə(r)] *n.* моли́тва. **prayer-book** *n.* моли́твенник.

preach [priːtʃ] *v.t.* пропове́довать *impf.*; *v.i.* произноси́ть (-ошу́, -о́сишь) *impf.*, произнести́ (-есу́, -есёшь; -ёс, -есла́) *pf.* про́поведь. **preacher** *n.* пропове́дник.

preamble [priː'æmb(ə)l, 'priː-] *n.* преа́мбула.

pre-arrange [ˌpriːə'reɪndʒ] *v.t.* зара́нее плани́ровать *impf.*, за~ *pf.* **pre-arrangement** *n.* предвари́тельная договорённость.

precarious [prɪ'keərɪəs] *adj.* ненадёжный; (*insecure*) непро́чный (-чен, -чна́, -чно).

pre-cast ['priːkɑːst] *adj.* сбо́рный.

precaution [prɪ'kɔːʃ(ə)n] *n.* предосторо́жность; (*action*) ме́ра предосторо́жности.

precede [prɪ'siːd] *v.t.* предше́ствовать *impf.*+*d.* **precedence** ['presɪd(ə)ns] *n.* предше́ствование; (*seniority*) старшинство́. **prece-**

dent *n.* прецеде́нт.

precept ['priːsept] *n.* наставле́ние.

precinct ['priːsɪŋkt] *n.* огоро́женное ме́сто; *pl.* окре́стности *f.pl.*; (*boundary*) преде́л.

precious ['preʃəs] *adj.* драгоце́нный (-нен, -нна); (*beloved*) дорого́й (до́рог, -а́, -о); (*refined*) изы́сканный (-ан, -анна); *adv.* о́чень, весьма́.

precipice ['presɪpɪs] *n.* обры́в; (*also fig.*) про́пасть. **precipitate** [prɪ'sɪpɪtət; prɪ'sɪpɪˌteɪt] *n.* оса́док (-дка); *adj.* стреми́тельный; (*person*) опроме́тчивый; *v.t.* (*throw down*) низверга́ть *impf.*, низве́ргнуть (-г) *pf.*; (*hurry*) ускоря́ть *impf.*, ускори́ть *pf.*; (*chem.*) осажда́ть *impf.*, осади́ть (-ажу́, -а́дишь) *pf.* **precipi'tation** *n.* низверже́ние; ускоре́ние; осажде́ние; (*hastiness*) стреми́тельность; (*meteor.*) оса́дки *m.pl.* **pre'cipitous** *adj.* обры́вистый.

précis ['preɪsiː] *n.* конспе́кт.

precise [prɪ'saɪs] *adj.* то́чный (-чен, -чна́, -чно). **precisely** *adv.* то́чно; (*in answer*) и́менно, то́чно так. **precision** [prɪ'sɪʒ(ə)n] *n.* то́чность; *adj.* то́чный.

pre-classical [priː'klæsɪk(ə)l] *adj.* докласси́ческий.

preclude [prɪ'kluːd] *v.t.* предотвраща́ть *impf.*, предотврати́ть (-ащу́, -ати́шь) *pf.*

precocious [prɪ'kəʊʃəs] *adj.* не по года́м разви́той (ра́звит, -а́, -о); ра́но разви́вшийся. **precocity** [prɪ'kɒsɪtɪ] *n.* ра́ннее разви́тие.

preconceived [ˌpriːkən'siːvd] *adj.* предвзя́тый. **preconception** *n.* предвзя́тое мне́ние.

pre-condition [ˌpriːkən'dɪʃ(ə)n] *n.* предпосы́лка.

precursor [priː'kɜːsə(r)] *n.* предте́ча *c.g.*; предше́ственник.

predator ['predətə(r)] *n.* хи́щник. **predatory** *adj.* хи́щнический; (*animal*) хи́щный.

predecease [ˌpriːdɪ'siːs] *v.t.* умира́ть *impf.*, умере́ть (умру́, -рёшь; у́мер, -ла́, -ло) *pf.* ра́ньше+*g.*

predecessor ['priːdɪˌsesə(r)] *n.* предше́ственник, -ица.

predestination [priːˌdestɪ'neɪʃ(ə)n] *n.* предопределе́ние. **pre'destine** *v.t.* предопределя́ть *impf.*, предопредели́ть *pf.*

predetermine [ˌpriːdɪ'tɜːmɪn] *v.t.* предреша́ть *impf.*, предреши́ть *pf.*; предопределя́ть *impf.*, предопредели́ть *pf.*

predicament [prɪ'dɪkəmənt] *n.* затрудни́тельное положе́ние.

predicate ['predɪkət; 'predɪˌkeɪt] *n.* (*gram.*) сказу́емое *sb.*, предика́т; *v.t.* утвержда́ть *impf.* **predicative** [prɪ'dɪkətɪv] *adj.* предикати́вный.

predict [prɪ'dɪkt] *v.t.* предска́зывать *impf.*, предсказа́ть (-ажу́, -а́жешь) *pf.* **prediction** *n.* предсказа́ние.

predilection [ˌpriːdɪ'lekʃ(ə)n] *n.* пристра́стие (**for** к+*d.*).

predispose [ˌpriːdɪ'spəʊz] *v.t.* предрасполага́ть *impf.*, предрасположи́ть (-ожу́, -о́жишь) *pf.* (**to** к+*d.*). **predispo'sition** *n.* предраспо-**

ложе́ние (**to** к+d.).

predominance [prɪˈdɒmɪnəns] *n.* преобла-
да́ние. **predominant** *adj.* преоблада́ющий.
predominate *v.i.* преоблада́ть *impf.*

pre-eminence [priːˈemɪnəns] *n.* превосхо́д-
ство. **pre-eminent** *adj.* выдаю́щийся.

pre-empt [priːˈempt] *v.t.* покупа́ть *impf.*,
купи́ть (-плю́, -пишь) *pf.* пре́жде други́х;
(*fig.*) завладева́ть *impf.*, завладе́ть *pf.*+i.
пре́жде други́х. **pre-emption** *n.* поку́пка
пре́жде други́х; (*right*) преиму́щественное
пра́во на поку́пку. **pre-emptive** *adj.* пре-
иму́щественный; (*mil.*) упрежда́ющий.

preen [priːn] *v.t.* (*of bird*) чи́стить *impf.*, по~
pf. клю́вом; ~ **o.s.** (*smarten*) прихора́-
шиваться *impf.*; (*be proud*) горди́ться *impf.*
собо́й.

pre-fab [ˈpriːfæb] *n.* сбо́рный дом (*pl.* -а́). **prefabricated** [priːˈfæbrɪˌkeɪtɪd] *adj.* заводско́го
изготовле́ния; сбо́рный.

preface [ˈprefəs] *n.* предисло́вие; *v.t.* де́лать
impf., с~ *pf.* преждвари́тельные замеча́ния
к+d. **prefatory** *adj.* вступи́тельный.

prefect [ˈpriːfekt] *n.* префе́кт; (*school*) ста́ро-
ста *m.* **prefecture** *n.* префекту́ра.

prefer [prɪˈfɜː(r)] *v.t.* (*promote*) продвига́ть
impf., продви́нуть *pf.* (по слу́жбе); (*like
better*) предпочита́ть *impf.*, предпоче́сть
(-чту́, -чтёшь; -чёл, -чла́) *pf.*; ~ **a charge
against** выдвига́ть *impf.*, вы́двинуть *pf.*
обвине́ние про́тив+g. **preferable** [ˈprefərə-
b(ə)l] *adj.* предпочти́тельный. **'preference**
n. предпочте́ние; ~ **share** привилегиро́-
ванная а́кция. **prefe'rential** *adj.* предпочти-
ти́тельный; (*econ.*) преференциа́льный.
preferment *n.* продвиже́ние по слу́жбе.

prefiguration [priːˌfɪɡəˈreɪʃ(ə)n] *n.* прообраз.
pre'figure *v.t.* служи́ть (-жу́, -жишь) *impf.*
прообразом+g.

prefix [ˈpriːfɪks] *n.* приста́вка, префикс.

pregnancy [ˈpreɡnənsɪ] *n.* бере́менность.
pregnant *adj.* (*woman*) бере́менная; чре-
ва́тый (**with** +i.), по́лный (-лон, -лна́, -полно́)
(**with** +g.).

prehensile [priːˈhensaɪl] *adj.* хвата́тельный.

prehistoric [ˌpriːhɪˈstɒrɪk] *adj.* доистори́-
ческий. **pre'history** *n.* (*of situation etc.*)
предысто́рия.

pre-ignition [ˌpriːɪɡˈnɪʃ(ə)n] *n.* преждевре́-
менное зажига́ние.

prejudge [priːˈdʒʌdʒ] *v.t.* предреша́ть *impf.*,
предреши́ть *pf.*

prejudice [ˈpredʒʊdɪs] *n.* предрассу́док (-дка)
(*bias*) предупрежде́ние; (*injury*) уще́рб;
without ~ **to** без уще́рба для+g.; *v.t.* наноси́ть (-ошу́, -о́сишь) *impf.*, нанести́ (-есу́,
-есёшь; -ёс, -есла́) *pf.* уще́рб+d.; ~ **against**
восстана́вливать *impf.*, восстанови́ть (-влю́,
-вишь) *pf.* про́тив+g.; ~ **in favour of** распо-
лага́ть *impf.*, расположи́ть (-жу́, -жишь) *pf.*
в по́льзу+g.

prelate [ˈprelət] *n.* прела́т.

prelim [ˈpriːlɪm, prɪˈlɪm] *n.*: *pl.* (*print.*) сбор-

ный лист (-а́). **preliminary** [prɪˈlɪmɪnərɪ] *adj.*
предвари́тельный; *n.*: *pl.* (*discussion*) пред-
вари́тельные перегово́ры *m.pl.*

prelude [ˈpreljuːd] *n.* вступле́ние; (*mus.*; *fig.*)
прелю́дия.

premarital [priːˈmærɪt(ə)l] *adj.* добра́чный.

premature [ˈpremətjʊə(r), -ˈtjʊə(r)] *adj.* преж-
девре́менный (-нен, -нна).

premeditated [priːˈmedɪˌteɪtɪd] *adj.* предна-
ме́ренный (-ен, -енна). **premedi'tation** *n.*
преднаме́ренность.

premier [ˈpremɪə(r)] *adj.* пе́рвый; *n.* премье́р-
мини́стр. **première** [ˈpremɪˌeə(r)] *n.* премье́ра.

premise, premiss [ˈpremɪs] *n.* (*logic*) (пред)-
посы́лка. **premises** *n.* помеще́ние.

premium [ˈpriːmɪəm] *n.* пре́мия.

premonition [ˌpreməˈnɪʃ(ə)n, ˌpriː-] *n.* пред-
чу́вствие. **premonitory** [prɪˈmɒnɪtərɪ] *adj.*
предупрежда́ющий.

prenatal [priːˈneɪt(ə)l] *adj.* предродово́й.

preoccupation [priːˌɒkjʊˈpeɪʃ(ə)n] *n.* озабо́-
ченность. **pre'occupied** *adj.* озабо́ченный
(-ен, -ена). **pre'occupy** *v.t.* поглоща́ть
impf., поглоти́ть (-ощу́, -о́тишь) *pf.* вни-
ма́ние+g.

preordain [ˌpriːɔːˈdeɪn] *v.t.* предопределя́ть
impf., предопредели́ть *pf.*

prep [prep] *n.* приготови́тельная шко́ла; *adj.*:
~ **school** приготови́тельная шко́ла.

pre-pack(age) [priːˈpækɪdʒ] *v.t.* расфасо́вы-
вать *impf.*, расфасова́ть *pf.*

prepaid [priːˈpeɪd] *adj.* опла́ченный (-ен)
вперёд.

preparation [ˌprepəˈreɪʃ(ə)n] *n.* приготов-
ле́ние; *pl.* подгото́вка (**for** к+d.); (*medicine
etc.*) препара́т. **preparatory** [prɪˈpærətərɪ]
adj. под-, при-, готови́тельный; ~ **to**
пре́жде чем. **prepare** [prɪˈpeə(r)] *v.t. & i.*
при-, под-, гота́вливать(ся) *impf.*, при-,
под-, гото́вить(ся) *pf.* (**for** к+d.). **prepared**
adj. гото́вый.

preponderance [prɪˈpɒndərəns] *n.* переве́с.
preponderant *adj.* преоблада́ющий. **pre-
ponderate** *v.i.* име́ть *impf.* переве́с.

preposition [ˌprepəˈzɪʃ(ə)n] *n.* предло́г. **prepositional** *adj.* предло́жный.

prepossessing *adj.* привлека́тельный.

preposterous [prɪˈpɒstərəs] *adj.* (*absurd*)
неле́пый, абсу́рдный.

prepuce [ˈpriːpjuːs] *n.* кра́йняя плоть.

pre-record [ˌpriːrɪˈkɔːd] *v.t.* предвари́тельно
запи́сывать *impf.*, записа́ть (-ишу́, -и́шешь)
pf.

prerequisite [priːˈrekwɪzɪt] *n.* предпосы́лка.

prerogative [prɪˈrɒɡətɪv] *n.* прерогати́ва.

presage [ˈpresɪdʒ] *n.* предве́стник, пред-
знаменова́ние; (*foreboding*) предчу́вствие;
v.t. предвеща́ть *impf.*

presbyter [ˈprezbɪtə(r)] *n.* пресви́тер. **Pres-
byterian** [ˌprezbɪˈtɪərɪən] *n.* пресвитериа́нин
(*pl.* -а́не, -а́н), -а́нка; *adj.* пресвитериа́н-
ский. **presbytery** *n.* пресвите́рия.

prescience [ˈpresɪəns] *n.* предви́дение. **pre-**

scient adj. предви́дящий.

prescribe [prɪ'skraɪb] v.t. устана́вливать impf., установи́ть (-влю, -вишь) pf.; (med.) прописывать impf., прописа́ть (-ишу́, -и́шешь) pf. **(to, for** (person) +d.; **for** (complaint) про́тив+g.). **prescription** [prɪ'skrɪpʃ(ə)n] n. устано́вка; (med.) реце́пт.

presence ['prez(ə)ns] n. прису́тствие; (appearance) (вне́шний) вид; ~ **of mind** прису́тствие ду́ха. **present** adj. прису́тствующий; (being dealt with) да́нный; (existing now) ны́нешний; (also gram.) настоя́щий; pred. налицо́; **be** ~ прису́тствовать impf. (**at** на+p.); n.: **the** ~ настоя́щее sb.; (gram.) настоя́щее вре́мя nt.; (gift) пода́рок (-рка); **at** ~ в настоя́щее, да́нное, вре́мя nt.; **for the** ~ пока́; v.t. (introduce) представля́ть impf., предста́вить pf. (**to** +d.); (hand in) подава́ть (-даю́, -даёшь) impf., пода́ть (-а́м, -а́шь, -а́ст, -ади́м) пода́л, -а́, -о) pf.; (a play) ста́вить impf., по~ pf.; (a gift) подноси́ть (-ошу́, -о́сишь) impf., поднести́ (-есу́, -есёшь; -ёс, -есла́) pf.+d. (**with** +d.); ~ **arms** брать (беру́, -рёшь; брал, -а́, -о) impf., взять (возьму́, -мёшь; взял, -а́, -о) pf. ору́жие на карау́л; (command) на карау́л!; ~ **o.s.** явля́ться impf., яви́ться (явлю́сь, я́вишься) pf. **pre'sentable** adj. прили́чный. **presen'tation** n. представле́ние, подноше́ние. **present-day** adj. ны́нешний, совреме́нный (-нен, -нна).

presentiment [prɪ'zentɪmənt, -'sentɪmənt] n. предчу́вствие.

presently ['prezntlɪ] adv. вско́ре, сейча́с.

preservation [ˌprezə'veɪʃ(ə)n] n. сохране́ние, предохране́ние; (state of ~) сохра́нность; (of game etc.) охра́на. **preservative** [prɪ'zɜːvətɪv] adj. предохрани́тельный; n. предохраня́ющее сре́дство. **pre'serve** v.t. (keep safe) сохраня́ть impf., сохрани́ть pf.; (maintain, ~ fruit etc.) храни́ть impf.; (food) консерви́ровать impf., за~ pf.; (game) охраня́ть impf., охрани́ть pf.; n. (for game, fish) охо́тничий, рыболо́вный, запове́дник; pl. консе́рвы (-вов) pl.; (jam) джем, варе́нье.

preside [prɪ'zaɪd] v.i. председа́тельствовать impf. (**at** на+p.). **presidency** ['prezɪdənsɪ] n. председа́тельство, президе́нтство. **'president** n. председа́тель m., президе́нт. **presi'dential** adj. президе́нтский. **presidium** [prɪ'sɪdɪəm, -'zɪdɪəm] n. прези́диум.

press¹ [pres] n. (of people) толпа́; (of affairs) спе́шка; (machine) пресс; (printing~) печа́тный стано́к (-нка́); (printing firm) типогра́фия; (publishing house) изда́тельство; (the ~) пре́сса, печа́ть; (cupboard) шкаф (loc. -у́; pl. -ы́); ~ **attaché** пресс-атташе́ m.indecl.; ~ **conference** пресс-конфере́нция; ~ **photographer** фотокорреспонде́нт; v.t. жать (жму, жмёшь) impf.; (~ down on) нажима́ть impf., нажа́ть (-жму́, -жмёшь) pf.+a., на+a.; (clasp) прижима́ть

impf., прижа́ть (-жму́, -жмёшь) pf. (**to** к+d.); (with iron) гла́дить impf., вы~ pf.; (oppress, ~ on) тяготи́ть (-ощу́, -оти́шь) impf.; (insist on) наста́ивать impf., настоя́ть (-ою́, -ои́шь) pf. на+p.; ~ **forward** продвига́ться impf., продви́нуться pf. вперёд.

press² [pres] v.t. (hist.) наси́льственно вербова́ть impf., за~, на~ pf. во флот; ~ **into service** по́льзоваться impf.+i. **press-gang** n. отря́д вербо́вщиков.

pressing ['presɪŋ] adj. (urgent) неотло́жный; (persistent) настоя́тельный. **press-stud** n. кно́пка. **pressure** ['preʃə(r)] n. давле́ние, нажи́м; ~ **gauge** мано́метр. **pressure-cooker** n. скорова́рка. **pressurized** adj. (aircraft cabin etc.) гермети́ческий.

prestige [pre'stiːʒ] n. прести́ж.

pre-stressed [priː'strest] adj. предвари́тельно напряжённый (-ён, -ённа).

presumably [prɪ'zjuːməblɪ] adv. вероя́тно, предположи́тельно. **presume** v.t. счита́ть impf. дока́занным; полага́ть impf.; (venture) позволя́ть impf. себе́. **presumption** [prɪ'zʌmpʃ(ə)n] n. предположе́ние; (arrogance) самонаде́янность. **presumptive** adj. предполага́емый. **presumptuous** adj. самонаде́янный (-ян, -янна), наха́льный.

presuppose [ˌpriːsə'pəʊz] v.t. предполага́ть impf.

pretence [prɪ'tens] n. притво́рство. **pretend** v.t. притворя́ться impf., притвори́ться pf. (**to be** +i.); де́лать impf., с~ pf. вид (что); v.i.: ~ **to** претендова́ть impf. на+a. **pretender** n. претенде́нт. **pretension** n. прете́нзия. **pretentious** adj. претенцио́зный.

preternatural [ˌpriːtə'nætʃər(ə)l] adj. сверхъесте́ственный (-ен, -енна).

pretext ['priːtekst] n. предло́г.

pretonic [priː'tɒnɪk] adj. предуда́рный.

prettiness ['prɪtɪnɪs] n. милови́дность. **pretty** adj. милови́дный; (also iron.) хоро́шенький; **a** ~ **penny** кру́гленькая су́мма; adv. дово́льно.

prevail [prɪ'veɪl] v.i. (predominate) преоблада́ть impf.; ~ **(up)on** угова́ривать impf., уговори́ть pf. **prevailing** adj. преоблада́ющий. **prevalent** ['prevələnt] adj. распространённый (-ён, -ённа).

prevaricate [prɪ'værɪˌkeɪt] v.i. говори́ть impf. укло́нчиво.

prevent [prɪ'vent] v.t. предупрежда́ть impf., предупреди́ть pf.; меша́ть impf., по~ pf.+d. **prevention** n. предупрежде́ние. **preventive** adj. предупреди́тельный; (med.) профилакти́ческий; ~ **measures** профила́ктика.

preview ['priːvjuː] n. предвари́тельный просмо́тр.

previous ['priːvɪəs] adj. предыду́щий; adv.: ~ **to** пре́жде чем. **previously** adv. зара́нее, пре́жде.

pre-war [priː'wɔː(r), 'priːwɔː(r)] adj. довое́нный.

prey [preɪ] n. (animal) добы́ча; (victim) же́ртва (**to** +g.); **bird of** ~ хи́щная пти́ца;

v.i.: ~ **(up)on** (*emotion etc.*) мучить *impf.*
price [praɪs] *n.* цена (*a.* -ну; *pl.* -ы); **at any** ~ любой ценой, во что бы то ни стало; **at a** ~ по дорогой цене; **not at any** ~ ни за что; **what** ~ ... какие шансы на+*a.*; *v.t.* назначать *impf.*, назначить *pf.* цену+*g.*; (*fig.*) оценивать *impf.*, оценить (-ню, -нишь) *pf.*
priceless *adj.* бесценный. **price-list** *n.* прейскурант.
prick [prɪk] *v.t.* колоть (-лю, -лешь) *impf.*, укалывать *impf.*, уколоть (-лю, -лешь) *pf.*; (*conscience*) мучить *impf.*; ~ **out** (*plants*) пикировать *impf. & pf.*; ~ **up one's ears** навострить *pf.* уши; *n.* укол. **prickle** *n.* (*thorn*) колючка; (*spine*) игла (*pl.* -лы). **prickly** *adj.* колючий; ~ **heat** потница.
pride [praɪd] *n.* гордость; (*of lions*) прайд; **take a** ~ **in**, ~ **o.s. on** гордиться *impf.+i.*
priest [priːst] *n.* священник; (*non-Christian*) жрец (-á). **priestess** *n.* жрица. **priesthood** *n.* священство. **priestly** *adj.* священнический.
prig [prɪg] *n.* самодовольный педант. **priggish** *adj.* педантичный.
prim [prɪm] *adj.* чопорный.
primacy ['praɪməsɪ] *n.* первенство. **primarily** ['praɪmərɪlɪ, -'meərɪlɪ] *adv.* первоначально; (*above all*) прежде всего. **primary** *adj.* первичный; (*chief*) основной; ~ **colour** основной цвет (*pl.* -á); ~ **feather** маховое перо (*pl.* -рья, -рьев); ~ **school** начальная школа. **primate** *n.* примас; (*zool.*) примат.
prime *n.* расцвет; **in one's** ~, **in the** ~ **of life** в расцвете сил; *adj.* (*chief*) главный; (*excellent*) превосходный; (*primary*) первичный; ~ **cost** себестоимость; ~ **minister** премьер-министр; ~ **number** простое число (*pl.* -сла, -сел, -слам); *v.t.* (*engine*) заправлять *impf.*, заправить *pf.*; (*with information etc.*) заранее снабжать *impf.*, снабдить *pf.* (**with** +*i.*); (*with paint etc.*) грунтовать *impf.*, за~ *pf.* **primer** *n.* букварь (-ря) *m.*; (*textbook*) учебник; (*paint etc.*) грунт. **pri'meval** *adj.* первобытный. **priming** *n.* (*with paint etc.*) грунтовка. **primitive** ['prɪmɪtɪv] *adj.* первобытный, примитивный. **primo'geniture** *n.* первородство. **pri'mordial** *adj.* первобытный; (*original*) исконный.
primrose ['prɪmrəʊz] *n.* первоцвет; (*colour*) бледно-жёлтый цвет.
primula ['prɪmjʊlə] *n.* первоцвет.
Primus (stove) ['praɪməs] *n.* (*propr.*) примус (*pl.* -сы & -á).
prince [prɪns] *n.* принц; (*in Russia*) князь (*pl.* -зья, -зей). **princely** *adj.* княжеский; (*splendid*) великолепный. **princess** *n.* принцесса; (*wife*) княгиня; (*daughter*) княжна (*g.pl.* -жон). **princi'pality** *n.* княжество.
principal *n.* главный, основной; *n.* начальник, -ица; (*of school*) директор (*pl.* -á); (*econ.*) капитал. **principally** *adv.* главным образом, преимущественно.
principle *n.* принцип; **in** ~ в принципе; **on** ~

принципиально. **principled** *adj.* принципиальный.
print [prɪnt] *n.* (*mark*) след (*pl.* -ы); (*also phot.*) отпечаток (-тка); (*fabric*) ситец (-тца(у)); (*print.*) печать; (*picture*) гравюра, эстамп; **in** ~ в продаже; **out of** ~ распроданный (-ан); *v.t.* (*impress*) запечатлевать *impf.*, запечатлеть *pf.*; (*book etc.*) печатать *impf.*, на~ *pf.*; (*write*) писать (пишу, -шешь) *impf.*, на~ *pf.* печатными буквами; (*fabric*) набивать *impf.*, набить (-бью, -бьёшь) *pf.*; (*phot.*) ~ **out**, отпечатывать *impf.*, отпечатать *pf.*; ~ **out** (*of computer etc.*) распечатывать *impf.*, распечатать *pf.*; ~ **run** тираж. **printed** *adj.* печатный; (*fabric*) набивной; ~ **circuit** печатная схема; ~ **matter** бандероль. **printer** *n.* (*person*) печатник, типограф; (*of fabric*) набойщик; (*device*) принтер; ~'s **ink** типографская краска. **printing** *n.* печатание, печать. **printing-press** *n.* печатный станок (-нка). **printout** *n.* распечатка, табулограмма.
prior ['praɪə(r)] *n.* настоятель *m.*; *adj.* (*earlier*) прежний, предшествующий; (*more important*) более важный; *adv.*: ~ **to** до+*g.* **prioress** *n.* настоятельница. **priority** [praɪ'ɒrɪtɪ] *n.* приоритет; **in order of** ~ в порядке очерёдности. **priory** *n.* монастырь (-ря) *m.*
prise [praɪz] *v.t.*: ~ **open** взламывать *impf.*, взломать *pf.* с помощью рычага.
prism ['prɪz(ə)m] *n.* призма. **pris'matic** *adj.* призматический.
prison ['prɪz(ə)n] *n.* тюрьма (*pl.* -рьмы, -рем, -рьмам); *attr.* тюремный; ~ **camp** лагерь (*pl.* -ря) *m.* **prison-break** *n.* побег из тюрьмы. **prisoner** *n.* заключённый *sb.*; (~ *of war*) (военно)пленный *sb.*; ~ **of State** политзаключённый *sb.*
pristine ['prɪstiːn, 'prɪstaɪn] *adj.* (*ancient*) первоначальный; (*untouched*) нетронутый.
privacy ['prɪvəsɪ, 'praɪ-] *n.* (*seclusion*) уединение; (*private life*) частная жизнь. **private** ['praɪvət, -vɪt] *adj.* (*personal*) частный, личный; (*unofficial*) неофициальный; (*confidential*) конфиденциальный; **in** ~ наедине; в частной жизни; ~ **view** закрытый просмотр; *n.* рядовой *sb.* **priva'teer** *n.* капер.
privatization [ˌpraɪvətaɪ'zeɪʃ(ə)n] *n.* приватизация. **'privatize** *v.t.* приватизировать *impf. & pf.*
pri'vation [praɪ'veɪʃ(ə)n] *n.* лишение.
privet ['prɪvɪt] *n.* бирючина.
privilege ['prɪvɪlɪdʒ] *n.* привилегия. **privileged** *adj.* привелигированный.
privy ['prɪvɪ] *adj.* тайный; ~ **to** причастный к+*d.*, посвящённый (-ён, -ённа) в+*a.*; **P~ Council** тайный совет.
prize [praɪz] *n.* (*reward*) премия, приз, награда; *adj.* удостоенный премии, награды; *v.t.* высоко ценить (-ню, -нишь) *impf.* **prizefight** *n.* состязание на приз. **prizefighter** *n.* боксёр-профессионал. **prizewinner** *n.* призёр, лауреат

pro¹ [prəʊ] *n.*: **~s and cons** дóводы *m.pl.* за и прóтив.

pro² [prəʊ] *n.* (*professional*) профессионáл; (спортсмéн-)профессионáл.

probability [ˌprɒbə'bɪlɪtɪ] *n.* вероя́тность, правдоподóбие; **in all ~** по всей вероя́тности. **'probable** *adj.* вероя́тный, правдоподóбный. **'probably** *adv.* вероя́тно.

probate ['prəʊbeɪt, -bət] *n.* утверждéние завещáния.

probation [prə'beɪʃ(ə)n] *n.* испытáние, стажирóвка; (*leg.*) услóвный приговóр. **probationary** *adj.* испытáтельный. **probationer** *n.* стажёр.

probe [prəʊb] *n.* (*med.*) зонд; (*spacecraft*) исслéдовательская ракéта; (*fig.*) расслéдование; *v.t.* зонди́ровать *impf.*; (*fig.*) расслéдовать *impf. & pf.*

probity ['prəʊbɪtɪ, 'prɒ-] *n.* чéстность.

problem ['prɒbləm] *n.* проблéма, вопрóс; (*math., chess, etc.*) задáча; **~ child** трýдный ребёнок (-нка; *pl.* дéти, -тéй, -тям, -тьми́). **proble'matic(al)** *adj.* проблемати́чный, проблемати́ческий.

proboscis [prəʊ'bɒsɪs] *n.* хóбот; (*of insects*) хоботóк (-ткá).

procedural [prə'siːdʒərəl, -dʒərəl] *adj.* процедýрный. **procedure** *n.* процедýра. **proceed** [prə'siːd, prəʊ-] *v.i.* (*go further*) идти́ (иду́, идёшь; шёл, шла) *impf.*, пойти́ (пойду́, -дёшь; пошёл, -шлá) *pf.* дáльше; (*act*) поступáть *impf.*, поступи́ть (-плю́, -пишь) *pf.*; (*abs.*, **~ to say**) продолжáть *impf.*, продóлжить *pf.*; (*of action*) продолжáться *impf.*, продóлжиться *pf.*; **~ against** возбуждáть *impf.*, возбуди́ть *pf.* дéло, процéсс, прóтив+g.; **~ from** исходи́ть (-ожý, -óдишь) *impf.* из, от+g.; **~ in, with** возобновля́ть *impf.*, возобнови́ть *pf.*; продолжáть *impf.*, продóлжить *pf.*; **~ to** приступáть *impf.*, приступи́ть (-плю́, -пишь) *pf.* k+d. **proceeding** *n.* (*action*) посту́пок (-пка); *pl.* (*legal ~*) судопроизвóдство; *pl.* (*published report*) трудьí *m.pl.*, запи́ски *f.pl.* **'proceeds** ['prəʊsiːdz] *n.* вы́ручка.

process ['prəʊses] *n.* (*course*) ход; процéсс; *v.t.* обрабáтывать *impf.*, обрабóтать *pf.*; **~ed cheese** плáвленный сыр (-а(у); *pl.* -ы́). **processing** *n.* обрабóтка. **pro'cession** *n.* процéссия, шéствие. **processor** *n.* (*comput.*) процéссор.

proclaim [prə'kleɪm] *v.t.* провозглашáть *impf.*, провозгласи́ть *pf.*; объявля́ть *impf.*, объяви́ть (-влю́, -вишь) *pf.* **proclamation** [ˌprɒklə'meɪʃ(ə)n] *n.* провозглашéние; объявлéние.

proclivity [prə'klɪvɪtɪ] *n.* наклóнность (**towards**) к+d.).

procrastinate [prəʊ'kræstɪneɪt] *v.i.* мéдлить *impf.* **procrasti'nation** *n.* оття́жка.

procreation [ˌprəʊkrɪ'eɪʃ(ə)n] *n.* деторождéние.

proctor ['prɒktə(r)] *n.* прóктор. **proctorial**

[prɒk'tɔːrɪəl] *adj.* прóкторский.

procuration [ˌprɒkjʊ'reɪʃ(ə)n] *n.* (*obtaining*) получéние; (*pimping*) свóдничество. **pro'cure** *v.t.* добывáть *impf.*, добы́ть (добу́ду, -дешь; дóбы́л, -á, дóбы́ло) *pf.*; доставáть (-таю́, -таёшь) *impf.*, достáть (-áну, -áнешь) *pf.*; *v.i.* (*pimp*) свóдничать *impf.* **pro'curer** *n.* свóдник. **procuress** *n.* свóдница.

prod [prɒd] *v.t.* ты́кать (ты́чу, -чешь) *impf.*, ткнуть *pf.*; *n.* тычóк (-чкá).

prodigal ['prɒdɪg(ə)l] *adj.* (*wasteful*) расточи́тельный; (*lavish*) щéдрый (щедр, -á, -о) (of на+a.); **~ son** блу́дный сын; *n.* мот. **prodigality** [ˌprɒdɪ'gælɪtɪ] *n.* мотовствó; изоби́лие.

prodigious [prə'dɪdʒəs] *adj.* (*amazing*) удиви́тельный; (*enormous*) огрóмный. **prodigy** ['prɒdɪdʒɪ] *n.* чýдо (*pl.* -десá); **infant ~** вундеркинд.

produce [prə'djuːs, 'prɒdjuːs] *v.t.* (*evidence etc.*) представля́ть *impf.*, представить *pf.*; (*ticket etc.*) предъявля́ть *impf.*, предъяви́ть (-влю́, -вишь) *pf.*; (*play etc.*) стáвить *impf.*, по~ *pf.*; (*manufacture; cause*) производи́ть (-ожу́, -óдишь) *impf.*, произвести́ (-еду́, -едёшь; -ёл, -елá) *pf.*; *n.* продýкция; (*collect*) продýкты *m.pl.* **pro'ducer** *n.* (*econ.*) производи́тель *m.*; (*of play etc.*) постанóвщик, режиссёр; **~ gas** генерáторный газ. **'product** *n.* продýкт, фабрикáт; (*result*) результáт; (*math.*) произведéние. **pro'duction** *n.* производство; (*yield*) продýкция; (*artistic ~*) произведéние; (*of play etc.*) постанóвка. **pro'ductive** *adj.* производи́тельный, продукти́вный; (*fruitful*) плодорóдный. **productivity** *n.* производи́тельность.

profanation [ˌprɒfə'neɪʃ(ə)n] *n.* профанáция, осквернéние. **profane** [prə'feɪn] *adj.* свéтский; (*blasphemous*) богоху́льный; *v.t.* оскверня́ть *impf.*, оскверни́ть *pf.* **profanity** [prə'fænɪtɪ] *n.* богоху́льство.

profess [prə'fes] *v.t.* (*pretend*) притворя́ться *impf.*, притвори́ться *pf.* (**to be** +*i.*); (*declare*) заявля́ть *impf.*, заяви́ть (-влю́, -вишь) *pf.*; (*affirm faith*) испове́довать *impf.*; (*engage in*) занимáться *impf.*, заня́ться (займу́сь, -мёшься; заня́лся, -лáсь) *pf.*+*i.* **professed** *adj.* откры́тый; (*alleged*) мни́мый. **profession** *n.* (*declaration*) заявлéние; (*of faith*) испове́дование; (*vocation*) профéссия. **professional** *adj.* профессионáльный; *n.* (спортсмéн-)профессионáл. **professor** *n.* профéссор (*pl.* -á). **profe'ssorial** *adj.* профéссорский.

proffer ['prɒfə(r)] *v.t.* предлагáть *impf.*, предложи́ть (-ожу́, -óжишь) *pf.*

proficiency [prə'fɪʃ(ə)nsɪ] *n.* умéние. **proficient** *adj.* умéлый.

profile ['prəʊfaɪl] *n.* прóфиль *m.*; (*biographical sketch*) крáткий биографи́ческий óчерк.

profit ['prɒfɪt] *n.* (*advantage*) пóльза, вы́года; (*gain*) при́быль; **at a ~** с при́былью; *v.t.* приноси́ть (-ит) *impf.*, принести́ (-есёт; -ёс, -еслá) *pf.* пóльзу+d.; *v.i.* получáть

impf., получи́ть (-чу́, -чишь) *pf.* при́быль; ~ **by** по́льзоваться *impf.*, вос~ *pf.*+*i.*
profitable *adj.* вы́годный, при́быльный.
profi'teer *v.i.* спекули́ровать *impf.*; *n.* спекуля́нт, ~ка. **profi'teering** *n.* спекуля́ция.
profitless *adj.* бесполе́зный.
profligacy ['prɒflɪɡəsɪ] *n.* распу́тство. **profligate** *n.* распу́тник; *adj.* распу́тный.
pro forma [prəʊ 'fɔːmə] *adv.* для проформы.
profound [prə'faʊnd] *adj.* глубо́кий (-о́к, -ока́, -о́ко). **profundity** *n.* глубина́.
profuse [prə'fjuːs] *adj.* (*lavish*) ще́дрый (щедр, -á. -о) (**in** на+*a.*); (*abundant*) изоби́льный. **profusion** *n.* изоби́лие.
progenitor [prəʊ'dʒenɪtə(r)] *n.* прароди́тель *m.* **progeny** ['prɒdʒɪnɪ] *n.* пото́мок (-мка) (*collect.*) пото́мство.
prognosis [prɒɡ'nəʊsɪs] *n.* прогно́з. **prognosticate** [prɒɡ'nɒstɪˌkeɪt] *v.t.* предска́зывать *impf.*, предсказа́ть (-ажу́, -а́жешь) *pf.* **prognosti'cation** *n.* предсказа́ние.
programme ['prəʊɡræm] *n.* програ́мма; *adj.* програ́ммный; *v.t.* программи́ровать *impf.*, за~ *pf.* **programmer** *n.* программи́ст.
progress ['prəʊɡres; prə'ɡres] *n.* прогре́сс; (*success*) успе́хи *m.pl.*; **make** ~ де́лать *impf.*, с~ *pf.* успе́хи; *v.i.* продвига́ться *impf.*, продви́нуться *pf.* вперёд. **pro'gression** *n.* продвиже́ние; (*math.*) прогре́ссия. **pro'gressive** *adj.* прогресси́вный.
prohibit [prə'hɪbɪt] *v.t.* запреща́ть *impf.*, запрети́ть (-ещу́, -ети́шь) *pf.* **prohibition** [ˌprəʊhɪ'bɪʃ(ə)n, ˌprəʊɪ'b-] *n.* запреще́ние; (*on alcohol*) сухо́й зако́н. **prohibitive** *adj.* запрети́тельный; (*price*) недосту́пный.
project [prə'dʒekt; 'prɒdʒekt] *v.t.* (*plan*) проекти́ровать *impf.*, с~ *pf.*; (*cast*) броса́ть *impf.*, бро́сить *pf.*; (*a film*) демонстри́ровать *impf.*, про~ *pf.*; *v.i.* (*jut out*) выступа́ть *impf.*, вы́ступить *pf.* n. прое́кт. **pro'jectile** *n.* снаря́д. **pro'jection** *n.* прое́кция; (*protrusion*) вы́ступ. **pro'jectionist** *n.* киномеха́ник. **pro'jector** *n.* (*apparatus*) проекцио́нный аппара́т.
proletarian [ˌprəʊlɪ'teərɪən] *adj.* пролета́рский; *n.* пролета́рий, -рка. **proletariat** *n.* пролетариа́т.
proliferate [prə'lɪfəˌreɪt] *v.i.* размножа́ться *impf.*, размно́житься; (*spread*) распространя́ться *impf.*, распространи́ться *pf.*
prolific [prə'lɪfɪk] *adj.* плодови́тый; (*abounding*) изоби́лующий (**in** +*i.*).
prolix ['prəʊlɪks, prə'lɪks] *adj.* многосло́вный. **prolixity** *n.* многосло́вие.
prologue ['prəʊlɒɡ] *n.* проло́г.
prolong [prə'lɒŋ] *v.t.* продлева́ть *impf.*, продли́ть *pf.* **prolongation** [ˌprəʊlɒŋ'ɡeɪʃ(ə)n] *n.* продле́ние.
promenade [ˌprɒmɪ'nɑːd] *n.* ме́сто (*pl.* -тá) для гуля́нья; (*at seaside*) на́бережная *sb.*; ~ **deck** ве́рхняя па́луба; *v.i.* прогу́ливаться *impf.*, прогуля́ться *pf.*
prominence ['prɒmɪnəns] *n.* возвыше́ние, вы-

пуклость; (*distinction*) изве́стность. **prominent** *adj.* вы́пуклый; (*conspicuous*) ви́дный; (*distinguished*) выдаю́щийся.
promiscuity [ˌprɒmɪ'skjuːɪtɪ] *n.* разноро́дность; (*sexual* ~) промискуите́т. **promiscuous** [prə'mɪskjʊəs] *adj.* (*varied*) разноро́дный; (*indiscriminate*) беспоря́дочный; (*casual*) случа́йный.
promise ['prɒmɪs] *n.* обеща́ние; *v.t.* обеща́ть *impf.* & *pf.*; ~ed **land** земля́ (*a.* -лю) обето́ванная. **promising** *adj.* многообеща́ющий, перспекти́вный. **promissory** *adj.*: ~ **note** долгово́е обяза́тельство.
promontory ['prɒməntərɪ] *n.* мыс (*loc.* -е & -ý; *pl.* мысы́).
promote [prə'məʊt] *v.t.* (*advance*) продвига́ть *impf.*, продви́нуть *pf.*; (*assist*) спосо́бствовать *impf.* & *pf.*+*d.*; (*product*) соде́йствовать *impf.* & *pf.* прода́же+*g.*; ~ **to** (*mil.*) производи́ть (-ожу́, -о́дишь) *impf.*, произвести́ (-еду́, -едёшь; -ёл, -ела́) *pf.* в+*nom.*-*a.pl.* **promoter** *n.* (*company* ~) учреди́тель *m.*; (*of sporting event etc.*) антрепренёр. **promotion** *n.* продвиже́ние, повыше́ние; соде́йствие.
prompt [prɒmpt] *adj.* бы́стрый (быстр, -á, -о, бы́стры), неме́дленный (-ен, -енна); *adv.* ро́вно; *v.t.* (*incite*) побужда́ть *impf.*, побуди́ть *pf.* (**to** к+*d.*; +*inf.*); (*speaker*; *also* *fig.*) подска́зывать *impf.*, подсказа́ть (-ажу́, -а́жешь) *pf.*+*d.*; (*theatr.*) суфли́ровать *impf.*+*d.*; *n.* подска́зка. **prompt-box** *n.* суфлёрская бу́дка. **prompter** *n.* суфлёр.
promulgate ['prɒməlˌɡeɪt] *v.t.* обнаро́довать *pf.*; публикова́ть *impf.*, о~ *pf.*; (*disseminate*) распространя́ть *impf.*, распространи́ть *pf.* **promul'gation** *n.* обнаро́дование, опубликова́ние; распростране́ние.
prone [prəʊn] *adj.* (*lying*) ничко́м; *pred.*: ~ **to** скло́нен (-о́нна́, -о́нно) к+*d.*
prong [prɒŋ] *n.* зубе́ц (-бца́).
pronominal [prəʊ'nɒmɪn(ə)l] *adj.* местоиме́нный. **pronoun** ['prəʊnaʊn] *n.* местоиме́ние.
pronounce [prə'naʊns] *v.t.* (*declare*) объявля́ть *impf.*, объяви́ть (-влю́, -вишь) *pf.*; (*articulate*) произноси́ть (-ошу́, -о́сишь) *impf.*, произнести́ (-есу́, -есёшь; -ёс, -есла́) *pf.*; *v.i.* (*give opinion*) выска́зываться *impf.*, вы́сказаться (-ажусь, -ажешься) *pf.* **pronounced** *adj.* ре́зко вы́раженный (-ен). **pronouncement** *n.* выска́зывание. **pronunciation** [prəˌnʌnsɪ'eɪʃ(ə)n] *n.* произноше́ние.
proof [pruːf] *n.* доказа́тельство; (*test*) испыта́ние; (*strength of alcohol*) устано́вленный гра́дус; (*print.*) корректу́ра; (*phot.*) про́бный отпеча́ток (-тка); (*of engraving*) про́бный о́ттиск; *adj.* (*impenetrable*) непроница́емый (**against** для+*g.*); (*not yielding*) неподдаю́щийся (**against** +*d.*). **proofreader** *n.* корре́ктор (*pl.* -ы & -á).
prop[1] [prɒp] *n.* (*support*) подпо́рка, сто́йка; (*fig.*) опо́ра; *v.t.* (~ **up**) подпира́ть *impf.*, подпере́ть (-допру́, -допрёшь; -дпёр) *pf.*;

(*fig.*) подде́рживать *impf.*, поддержа́ть (-жу́, -жи́шь) *pf.*

prop² [prɒp] *n.* (*theatr.*): *pl.* (*collect.*) реквизи́т, бутафо́рия.

propaganda [ˌprɒpə'gændə] *n.* пропага́нда. **propagandist** *n.* пропаганди́ст.

propagate ['prɒpəgeɪt] *v.t.* & *i.* размножа́ть(ся) *impf.*, размно́жить(ся) *pf.*; (*disseminate*) распространя́ть(ся) *impf.*, распространи́ть(ся) *pf.* **propa'gation** *n.* размноже́ние; распростране́ние.

propane ['prəupeɪn] *n.* пропа́н.

propel [prə'pel] *v.t.* приводи́ть (-ожу́, -о́дишь) *impf.*, привести́ (-еду́, -еде́шь; -ёл, -ела́) *pf.* в движе́ние; (*fig.*) дви́гать (-аю, -аешь & дви́жу, -жешь *impf.*, дви́нуть *pf.*; ~**ling pencil** автокаранда́ш (-а́). **propellant** *n.* (*in firearm*) по́рох; (*in rocket engine*) то́пливо. **propeller** *n.* (*aeron.*) пропе́ллер; (*aeron.*; *naut.*) винт (-а́).

propensity [prə'pensɪtɪ] *n.* накло́нность (**to** к+*d.*; +*inf.*).

proper ['prɒpə(r)] *adj.* (*characteristic*) сво́йственный (-ен(ен), -енна) (**to** +*d.*); (*gram.*) со́бственный; (*correct*) пра́вильный; (*strictly so called*; *after n.*) в у́зком смы́сле сло́ва; (*suitable*) надлежа́щий, до́лжный; (*decent*) присто́йный; ~ **fraction** пра́вильная дробь (*pl.* -би, -бей). **properly** *adv.* (*fittingly*, *duly*) до́лжным о́бразом, как сле́дует; (*correctly*) со́бственно; (*decently*) прили́чно.

property ['prɒpətɪ] *n.* (*possessions*) со́бственность, иму́щество; (*attribute*) сво́йство; *pl.* (*theatr.*) реквизи́т, бутафо́рия; ~ **man** реквизи́тор, бутафо́р.

prophecy ['prɒfɪsɪ] *n.* проро́чество. **prophesy** ['prɒfɪˌsaɪ] *v.t.* проро́чить *impf.*, на~ *pf.* **prophet** *n.* проро́к. **prophetess** *n.* проро́чица. **prophetic** [prə'fetɪk] *adj.* проро́ческий.

prophylactic [ˌprɒfɪ'læktɪk] *adj.* профилакти́ческий; *n.* профилакти́ческое сре́дство. **prophylaxis** *n.* профила́ктика.

propinquity [prə'pɪŋkwɪtɪ] *n.* (*nearness*) бли́зость; (*kinship*) родство́.

propitiate [prə'pɪʃɪˌeɪt] *v.t.* умиротворя́ть *impf.*, умиротвори́ть *pf.* **propiti'ation** *n.* умиротворе́ние.

propitious [prə'pɪʃəs] *adj.* благоприя́тный.

proponent [prə'pəunənt] *n.* сторо́нник, -ица.

proportion [prə'pɔːʃ(ə)n] *n.* пропо́рция; (*correct relation*) пропорциона́льность; *pl.* разме́ры *m.pl.* **proportional** *adj.* пропорциона́льный; ~ **representation** пропорциона́льное представи́тельство. **proportionate** *adj.* сораз́мерный (**to** +*d.*; с+*i.*).

proposal [prə'pəuz(ə)l] *n.* предложе́ние. **propose** *v.t.* предлага́ть *impf.*, предложи́ть (-жу́, -жишь) *pf.*; (*intend*) предполага́ть *impf.*; *v.i.* ~ (*marriage*) де́лать *impf.*, с~ *pf.* предложе́ние (**to** +*d.*). **proposition** [ˌprɒpə'zɪʃ(ə)n] *n.* (*assertion*) утвержде́ние; (*math.*) теоре́ма; (*proposal*) предложе́ние; (*under*-

taking) (*coll.*) де́ло.

propound [prə'paund] *v.t.* предлага́ть *impf.*, предложи́ть (-жу́, -жишь) *pf.* на обсужде́ние.

proprietary [prə'praɪətərɪ] *adj.* (*of owner*) со́бственнический; (*medicine*) патенто́ванный. **proprietor** *n.* со́бственник, хозя́ин (*pl.* -я́ева, -я́ев). **proprietress** *n.* со́бственница, хозя́йка.

propriety [prə'praɪɪtɪ] *n.* присто́йность, прили́чие.

propulsion [prə'pʌlʃ(ə)n] *n.* движе́ние вперёд; (*fig.*) дви́жущая си́ла.

prorogue [prə'rəug] *v.t.* назнача́ть *impf.*, назна́чить *pf.* переры́в в рабо́те+*g.*

prosaic [prə'zeɪɪk, prəu-] *adj.* прозаи́ческий, прозаи́чный.

proscenium [prə'siːnɪəm, prəu-] *n.* авансце́на.

proscribe [prə'skraɪb] *v.t.* (*put outside the law*) объявля́ть *impf.*, объяви́ть (-влю, -вишь) *pf.* вне зако́на; (*banish*) изгоня́ть *impf.*, изгна́ть (изгоню́, -нишь; изгна́л, -а́, -о)) *pf.*; (*forbid*) запреща́ть *impf.*, запрети́ть (-ещу́, -ети́шь) *pf.*

prose [prəuz] *n.* про́за.

prosecute ['prɒsɪˌkjuːt] *v.t.* (*pursue*) вести́ (веду́, -дёшь; вёл, -а́) *impf.*; (*leg.*) пресле́довать *impf.* **prose'cution** *n.* веде́ние; (*leg.*) суде́бное пресле́дование; (*prosecuting party*) обвине́ние. **prosecutor** *n.* обвини́тель *m.*

proselyte ['prɒsɪˌlaɪt] *n.* прозели́т. **proselytize** ['prɒsɪlɪˌtaɪz] *v.t.* обраща́ть *impf.*, обрати́ть (-ащу́, -ати́шь) *pf.* в другу́ю ве́ру.

prosody ['prɒsədɪ] *n.* просо́дия.

prospect ['prɒspekt; prə'spekt] *n.* вид, перспекти́ва (*v.t.* & *i.* разве́дывать *impf.*, разве́дать *pf.* (**for** на+*a.*). **pro'spective** *adj.* бу́дущий, предполага́емый. **pro'spector** *n.* разве́дчик. **pro'spectus** *n.* проспе́кт.

prosper ['prɒspə(r)] *v.i.* процвета́ть *impf.*; преуспева́ть *impf.* **prosperity** [prɒ'sperɪtɪ] *n.* процвета́ние, преуспева́ние. **prosperous** *adj.* процвета́ющий, преуспева́ющий; (*wealthy*) зажи́точный.

prostate (gland) ['prɒsteɪt] *n.* предста́тельная железа́ (*pl.* же́лезы, -лёз, -леза́м).

prostitute ['prɒstɪˌtjuːt] *n.* проститу́тка; *v.t.* проститу́ировать *impf.* & *pf.* **prosti'tution** *n.* проститу́ция.

prostrate ['prɒstreɪt] *adj.* распростёртый, (лежа́щий) ничко́м; (*exhausted*) обесси́ленный (-ен); (*with grief*) уби́тый (**with** +*i.*); *v.t.* (*exhaust*) истоща́ть *impf.*, истощи́ть *pf.*; ~ **o.s.** па́дать *impf.*, пасть (паду́, -дёшь; пал) *pf.* ниц. **prost'ration** *n.* простра́ция.

protagonist [prəu'tægənɪst] *n.* гла́вный геро́й; (*advocate*) сторо́нник.

protean ['prəutɪən, -'tiːən] *adj.* (*having many forms*) многообра́зный; (*versatile*) многосторо́нний (-нен, -ння).

protect [prə'tekt] *v.t.* защища́ть *impf.*, защити́ть (-ищу́, -ити́шь) *pf.* (**from** от+*g.*; **against**

против+g.). **protection** n. защита, охрана; (patronage) покровительство. **protectionism** n. протекционизм. **protective** adj. защитный, покровительственный. **protector** n. защитник, покровитель m.; (regent) протектор. **protectorate** n. протекторат.

protégé(e) ['prɒtɪˌʒeɪ, -teˌʒeɪ, 'prəʊ-] n. протеже c.g.indecl.

protein ['prəʊtiːn] n. протеин, белок (-лка).

protest ['prəʊtest; prə'test] n. протест; v.i. протестовать impf. & pf.; v.t. (affirm) заявлять impf., заявить (-влю, -вишь) pf.+a., о+p., что.

Protestant ['prɒtɪst(ə)nt] n. протестант, ~ка; adj. протестантский. **Protestantism** n. протестанство.

protestation [ˌprɒtɪ'steɪʃ(ə)n] n. (торжественное) заявление (о+p.; что); (protest) протест.

protocol [ˌprəʊtə'kɒl] n. протокол.

proton ['prəʊtɒn] n. протон.

protoplasm ['prəʊtəˌplæz(ə)m] n. протоплазма.

prototype ['prəʊtəˌtaɪp] n. прототип.

protozoan [ˌprəʊtə'zəʊən] n. простейшее (животное) sb.

protract [prə'trækt] v.t. тянуть (-ну, -нешь) impf.; (plan) чертить (-рчу, -ртишь) impf., на~ pf. **protracted** adj. длительный. **protraction** n. промедление; начертание.

protractor n. (instrument) транспортир; (muscle) разгибательная мышца.

protrude [prə'truːd] v.t. высовывать impf., высунуть pf.; v.i. выдаваться (-даёшься) impf., выдаться (-астся) pf. **protrusion** n. выступ.

protuberance [prə'tjuːbərəns] n. выпуклость, выступ, бугорок (-рка). **protuberant** adj. выпуклый; ~ **eyes** глаза (-з, -зам) m.pl. навыкате.

proud [praʊd] adj. гордый (горд, -а, -о, горды); **be** ~ **of** гордиться impf.+i.

provable ['pruːvəb(ə)l] adj. доказуемый. **prove** v.t. доказывать impf., доказать (-ажу, -ажешь) pf.; удостоверять impf., удостоверить pf.; (a will) утверждать impf., утвердить pf.; v.i. оказываться impf., оказаться (-ажусь, -ажешься) pf. (to be +i.). **proven** adj. доказанный (-ан).

provenance ['prɒvɪnəns] n. происхождение.

provender ['prɒvɪndə(r)] n. корм (loc. -é & -ý; pl. -á).

proverb ['prɒvɜːb] n. пословица. **proverbial** [prə'vɜːbɪəl] adj. вошедший в поговорку; (well known) общеизвестный; ~ **saying** поговорка.

provide [prə'vaɪd] v.t. (stipulate) ставить impf., по~ pf. условием (that что); (supply person) снабжать impf., снабдить pf. (with +i.); обеспечивать impf., обеспечить pf. (with +i.); (supply thing) предоставлять impf., предоставить pf. (to, for +d.); давать (даю, даёшь) impf., дать (дам, дашь, даст,

дадим; дал, -á, дáло, -и) pf. (to, for +d.); v.i.: ~ **against** принимать impf., принять (приму, -мешь; принял, -á, -о) pf. меры против+g.; ~ **for** предусматривать impf., предусмотреть (-рю, -ришь) pf.+a.; (~ for family etc.) содержать (-жу,- жишь) impf.+a. **provided (that)** conj. при условии, что; если только. **providence** ['prɒvɪd(ə)ns] n. провидение; (foresight) предусмотрительность. **provident** adj. предусмотрительный; (thrifty) бережливый. **providential** [ˌprɒvɪ'denʃ(ə)l] adj. (lucky) счастливый (-слив). **providing** see **provided (that)**

province ['prɒvɪns] n. область (pl. -ти, -тей) (also fig.); провинция; pl. (the ~) провинция. **provincial** [prə'vɪnʃ(ə)l] adj. провинциальный; n. провинциал, ~ка. **provincialism** n. провинциальность; (expression) областное выражение.

provision [prə'vɪʒ(ə)n] n. снабжение, обеспечение; pl. провизия; (in agreement etc.) положение; **make** ~ **against** принимать impf., принять (приму, -мешь; принял, -á, -о) pf. меры против+g.; **make** ~ **for** предусматривать impf., предусмотреть (-рю, -ришь) pf.+a.; v.t. снабжать impf., снабдить pf. провизией. **provisional** adj. временный.

proviso [prə'vaɪzəʊ] n. условие, оговорка. **provisory** [prə'vaɪzərɪ] adj. условный.

provocation [ˌprɒvə'keɪʃ(ə)n] n. провокация. **provocative** [prə'vɒkətɪv] adj. провокационный; ~ **of** вызывающий+a. **provoke** [prə'vəʊk] v.t. провоцировать impf., с~ pf.; (call forth, cause) вызывать impf., вызвать (вызову, -вешь) pf.; (irritate) раздражать impf., раздражить pf.

provost ['prɒvəst] n. (univ.) ректор; (mayor) мэр; ~ **marshal** начальник военной полиции.

prow [praʊ] n. нос (loc. -ý; pl. -ы).

prowess ['praʊɪs] n. (valour) доблесть; (skill) умение.

prowl [praʊl] v.i. рыскать (рыщу, -щешь) impf.; v.t. бродить (-ожу, -одишь) impf. по+d.

proximity [prɒk'sɪmɪtɪ] n. близость.

proxy ['prɒksɪ] n. полномочие, доверенность; (person) уполномоченный sb., заместитель m.; **by** ~ по доверенности; **stand** ~ **for** быть impf. заместителем+g.

prude [pruːd] n. скромник, -ица.

prudence ['pruːd(ə)ns] n. благоразумие. **prudent** adj. благоразумный.

prudery ['pruːdərɪ] n. притворная стыдливость. **prudish** adj. ни в меру стыдливый.

prune[1] [pruːn] n. (plum) чернослив(ина); pl. чернослив (-a(y)) (collect.).

prune[2] [pruːn] v.t. (trim) об-, под-, резать impf., об-, под-, резать (-ежу, -ежешь) pf.; (fig.) сокращать impf., сократить (-ащу, -атишь) pf. **pruning-hook** n. прививочный нож (-á).

prurience ['prʊərɪəns] n. похотливость.

prurient *adj.* похотли́вый.
Prussian ['prʌʃ(ə)n] *n.* прусса́к (-á), -áчка; *adj.* пру́сский; ~ **blue** берли́нская лазу́рь.
prussic *adj.*: ~ **acid** сини́льная кислота́.
pry [praɪ] *v.i.* сова́ть (сую́, суёшь) *impf.* нос (into в+*a.*). **prying** *adj.* пытли́вый, любопы́тный.
PS (*abbr. of* **postscript**) постскри́птум, припи́ска.
psalm [sɑːm] *n.* псало́м (-лмá). **psalter** ['sɔːltə(r), 'sɒl-] *n.* псалты́рь (-ри & -рй) *f. & m.*
pseudo- ['sjuːdəʊ] *in comb.* псевдо... . **pseudonym** *n.* псевдони́м.
psyche ['saɪkɪ] *n.* пси́хика. **psychi'atric** *adj.* психиатри́ческий. **psychiatrist** [saɪ'kaɪətrɪst] *n.* психиа́тр. **psy'chiatry** *n.* психиатри́я. **psychic(al)** *adj.* психи́ческий, душе́вный; *n.* экстрасе́нс. **psycho** ['saɪkəʊ] *n.* псих. **psycho-** *in comb.* психо... . **psycho-analyse** *v.t.* подверга́ть *impf.*, подве́ргнуть (-г) *pf.* психоана́лизу. **psycho-analysis** *n.* психоана́лиз. **psycho-analyst** *n.* специали́ст по психоана́лизу. **psycho-analytic(al)** *adj.* психоаналити́ческий. **psychological** *adj.* психологи́ческий. **psy'chologist** *n.* психо́лог. **psy'chology** *n.* психоло́гия; (*coll.*) пси́хика. **psychopath** ['saɪkə,pæθ] *n.* психопа́т. **psycho'pathic** *adj.* психопати́ческий. **psychopathology** *n.* психопатоло́гия. **psy'chosis** *n.* психо́з. **psychotherapy** *n.* психотерапи́я.
pt. *n.* (*abbr. of* **pint(s)**) пи́нта.
ptarmigan ['tɑːmɪgən] *n.* тундря́нка.
pterodactyl [,terə'dæktɪl] *n.* птерода́ктиль *m.*
PTO *abbr.* (*of* **please turn over**) см. на об., смотри́ на оборо́те.
pub [pʌb] *n.* пивна́я *sb.*, каба́к (-á).
puberty ['pjuːbətɪ] *n.* полова́я зре́лость.
public ['pʌblɪk] *adj.* обще́ственный; (*open*) публи́чный, откры́тый; ~ **health** здравоохране́ние; ~ **house** пивна́я *sb.*; ~ **relations officer** слу́жащий *sb.* отде́ла информа́ции; ~ **school** ча́стная сре́дняя шко́ла; ~ **servant** госуда́рственный слу́жащий *sb.*; ~ **spirit** обще́ственный дух; ~ **utility** предприя́тие обще́ственного по́льзования; *n.* пу́блика, обще́ственность; **in** ~ откры́то, публи́чно. **publi'cation** *n.* (*action*) опубликова́ние; (*also book etc.*) изда́ние. **publicist** *n.* публици́ст. **pub'licity** *n.* рекла́ма; ~ **agent** аге́нт по рекла́ме. **publicize** *v.t.* реклами́ровать *impf. & pf.* **publicly** *adv.* публи́чно, откры́то. **publish** *v.t.* публикова́ть *impf.*, о~ *pf.*; (*book*) издава́ть (-даю́, -даёшь) *impf.*, изда́ть (-а́м, -а́шь, -а́ст, -ади́м; изда́л, -á, -о) *pf.* **publisher** *n.* изда́тель *m.* **publishing** *n.* (*business*) изда́тельское де́ло; ~ **house** изда́тельство.
puce [pjuːs] *adj.* (*n.*) краснова́то-кори́чневый (цвет).
puck [pʌk] *n.* (*in ice hockey*) ша́йба.
pucker ['pʌkə(r)] *v.t. & i.* мо́рщить(ся) *impf.*,

с~ *pf.*; *n.* морщи́на.
pudding ['pudɪŋ] *n.* пу́динг, запека́нка.
puddle ['pʌd(ə)l] *n.* лу́жа.
pudgy ['pʌdʒɪ] *adj.* пу́хлый (пухл, -á, -о).
puerile ['pjʊəraɪl] *adj.* ребя́ческий. **puerility** [pjʊə'rɪlɪtɪ] *n.* ребя́чество.
puff [pʌf] *n.* (*of wind*) поры́в; (*of smoke*) дымо́к (-мкá); (*on dress*) бу́фы (-ф) *pl. only*; ~ **pastry** слоёное те́сто; ~ **sleeves** рукава́ *m.pl.* с бу́фами; *v.i.* пыхте́ть (-хчу́, -хти́шь) *impf.*; ~ **at** (*pipe etc.*) попы́хивать *impf.*+*i.*; *v.t.*: ~ **up, out** (*inflate*) надува́ть *impf.*, наду́ть (-у́ю, -у́ешь) *pf.*
puffin ['pʌfɪn] *n.* ту́пик.
pug [pʌg] *n.* (*dog*) мопс.
pugilism ['pjuːdʒɪ,lɪz(ə)m] *n.* бокс. **pugilist** *n.* боксёр.
pugnacious [pʌg'neɪʃəs] *adj.* драчли́вый.
pugnacity [pʌg'næsɪtɪ] *n.* драчли́вость.
pug-nosed [pʌg'nəʊzd] *adj.* курно́сый.
puissant ['pjuːɪs(ə)nt, 'pwiːs-, 'pwɪs-] *adj.* могу́щественный (-ен, -енна).
puke [pjuːk] *v.i.* рвать (рвёт; рва́ло) *impf.*, вы́- *pf. impers.*+*a.*; *n.* рво́та.
pull [pul] *n.* тя́га; (*fig.*) зару́чка; *v.t.* тяну́ть (-ну́, -нешь) *impf.*, по~ *pf.*; таска́ть *indet.*, тащи́ть (-щу́, -щишь) *det.*, по~ *pf.*; (*a muscle*) растя́гивать *impf.*, растяну́ть (-ну́, -нешь) *pf.*; (*a cork*) выта́скивать *impf.*, вы́тащить *pf.*; (*a tooth*) удаля́ть *impf.*, удали́ть *pf.*; *v.t. & i.* дёргать *impf.*, дёрнуть *pf.* (**at** (за)+*a.*); ~ **faces** грима́сничать *impf.*; ~ **s.o's leg** моро́чить *impf.* го́лову+*d.*; ~ **(the) strings, wires** нажима́ть *impf.*, нажа́ть (нажму́, -мёшь) *pf.* на та́йные пружи́ны; ~ **the trigger** спуска́ть *impf.*, спусти́ть (-ущу́, -у́стишь) *pf.* куро́к; ~ **apart, to pieces** разрыва́ть *impf.*, разорва́ть (-ву́, -вёшь; -ва́л, -вала́, -ва́ло) *pf.*; (*fig.*) раскритикова́ть *pf.*; ~ **at** (*pipe etc.*) затя́гиваться *impf.*, затяну́ться (-ну́сь, -нешься) *pf.*+*i.*; ~ **down** (*demolish*) сноси́ть (-ошу́, -о́сишь) *impf.*, снести́ (снесу́, -сёшь; снёс, -ла́) *pf.*; ~ **in** (*earn*) зараба́тывать *impf.*, зарабо́тать *pf.*; (*of train*) прибыва́ть *impf.*, прибы́ть (-бу́дет; при́был, -á, -о) *pf.*; (*of vehicle*) подъезжа́ть *impf.*, подъе́хать (-е́дет) *pf.* к обо́чине доро́ги; ~ **off** (*garment*) стя́гивать *impf.*, стяну́ть (-ну́, -нешь) *pf.*; (*achieve*) успе́шно заверша́ть *impf.*, заверши́ть *pf.*; (*win*) выи́грывать *impf.*, вы́играть *pf.*; ~ **on** (*garment*) натя́гивать *impf.*, натяну́ть (-ну́, -нешь) *pf.*; ~ **out** (*v.t.*) (*remove*) выта́скивать *impf.*, вы́тащить *pf.*; (*v.i.*) (*withdraw*) отка́зываться *impf.*, отказа́ться (-ажу́сь, -а́жешься) *pf.* от уча́стия (**of** в+*p.*); (*of vehicle*) отъезжа́ть *impf.*, отъе́хать (-е́дет) *pf.* от обо́чины (доро́ги); (*of train*) отходи́ть (-ит) *impf.*, отойти́ (-йдёт; отошёл, -шла́) *pf.* (**from** от ста́нции); ~ **through** выжива́ть *impf.*, вы́жить (вы́живу, -вешь) *pf.*; ~ **o.s. together** брать (беру́, -рёшь; брал, -á, -о) *impf.*, взять (возьму́, -мёшь; взял, -á, -о)

pf. себя в руки; ~ **up** (*v.t.*) подтягивать *impf.*, подтянуть (-ну, -нешь) *pf.*; (*v.t. & i.*) (*stop*) останавливать(ся) *impf.*, остановить(ся) (-влю(сь), -вишь(ся)) *pf.*

pullet ['pʊlɪt] *n.* молодка.

pulley ['pʊlɪ] *n.* блок, шкив (*pl.* -ы).

Pullman ['pʊlmən] *n.* пульман(овский вагон).

pullover ['pʊl,əʊvə(r)] *n.* пуловер.

pulmonary ['pʌlmənərɪ] *adj.* лёгочный.

pulp [pʌlp] *n.* (*of fruit*) мякоть; (*anat.*) пульпа; (*of paper*) бумажная масса; *v.t.* превращать *impf.*, превратить (-ащу, -атишь) *pf.* в мягкую массу.

pulpit ['pʊlpɪt] *n.* кафедра.

pulsar ['pʌlsɑ:(r)] *n.* пульсар. **pul'sate** *v.i.* пульсировать *impf.* **pul'sation** *n.* пульсация. **pulse**[1] *n.* (*throbbing*) пульс; *v.i.* пульсировать *impf.*

pulse[2] [pʌls] *n.* (*food*) бобовые *sb.*

pulverize ['pʌlvə,raɪz] *v.t.* размельчать *impf.*, размельчить *pf.*; (*fig.*) сокрушать *impf.*, сокрушить *pf.*

puma ['pju:mə] *n.* пума.

pumice(-stone) ['pʌmɪs] *n.* пемза.

pummel ['pʌm(ə)l] *v.t.* колотить (-очу, -отишь) *impf.*, по~ *pf.*; тузить *impf.*, от~ *pf.*

pump[1] [pʌmp] *n.* (*machine*) насос; *v.t.* (*use* ~) качать *impf.*; (*person*) выпрашивать *impf.*, выпросить *pf.* y+g.; ~ **in(to)** вкачивать *impf.*, вкачать *pf.*; ~ **out** выкачивать *impf.*, выкачать *pf.*; ~ **up** накачивать *impf.*, накачать *pf.*

pump[2] [pʌmp] *n.* (*shoe*) туфля (*g.pl.* -фель).

pumpkin ['pʌmpkɪn] *n.* тыква.

pun [pʌn] *n.* каламбур; *v.i.* каламбурить *impf.*, c~ *pf.*

punch[1] [pʌntʃ] *n.* (*drink*) пунш.

punch[2] [pʌntʃ] *v.t.* (*with fist*) ударять *impf.*, ударить *pf.* кулаком; (*pierce*) пробивать *impf.*, пробить (-бью, -бьёшь) *pf.*; (*a ticket*) компостировать *impf.*, про~ *pf.*; *n.* (*blow*) удар кулаком; (*for tickets*) компостер; (*for piercing*) пробойник; (*for stamping*) пуансон. **punch-ball** *n.* пенчингбол, груша. **punch-up** *n.* драка.

punctilious *adj.* соблюдающий формальности, щепетильный.

punctual ['pʌŋktjʊəl] *adj.* пунктуальный. **punctu'ality** *n.* пунктуальность.

punctuate *v.t.* ставить *impf.*, по~ *pf.* знаки препинания в+a.; прерывать *impf.*, прервать (-ву, -вёшь; прервал, -а, -о) *pf.* **punctu'ation** *n.* пунктуация; ~ **marks** знаки *m.pl.* препинания.

puncture ['pʌŋktʃə(r)] *n.* прокол; *v.t.* прокалывать *impf.*, проколоть (-лю, -лешь) *pf.*; *v.i.* получать *impf.*, получить (-чу, -чишь) *pf.* прокол

pundit ['pʌndɪt] *n.* (*fig.*) знаток (-а).

pungency ['pʌndʒ(ə)nsɪ] *n.* едкость. **pungent** *adj.* едкий (едок, едка, едко).

punish ['pʌnɪʃ] *v.t.* наказывать *impf.*, наказать (-ажу, -ажешь) *pf.* ⌐ **unishable** *adj.*

наказуемый. **punishment** *n.* наказание.

punitive ['pju:nɪtɪv] *adj.* карательный.

punk [pʌŋk] *n.* панк; *adj.* панковый.

punnet ['pʌnɪt] *n.* корзинка.

punster ['pʌnstə(r)] *n.* каламбурист.

punt [pʌnt] *n.* (*boat*) плоскодонка.

punter ['pʌntə(r)] *n.* (*gambler*) игрок (-а).

puny ['pju:nɪ] *adj.* хилый (хил, -а, -о), тщедушный.

pup [pʌp] *n.* щенок (-нка; *pl.* щенки, -ков & щенята, -т); *v.i.* щениться *impf.*, о~ *pf.*

pupa ['pju:pə] *n.* куколка.

pupil ['pju:pɪl, -p(ə)l] *n.* ученик (-а), -ица; (*of eye*) зрачок (-чка).

puppet ['pʌpɪt] *n.* марионетка, кукла (*g.pl.* -кол); ~ **regime** марионеточный режим; ~ **theatre** кукольный театр.

puppy ['pʌpɪ] *n.* щенок (-нка; *pl.* щенки, -ков & щенята, -т).

purblind ['pɜ:blaɪnd] *adj.* близорукий.

purchase ['pɜ:tʃɪs, -tʃəs] *n.* покупка; (*leverage*) точка опоры; *v.t.* покупать *impf.*, купить (-плю, -пишь) *pf.* **purchaser** *n.* покупатель *m.*, -ница.

pure [pjʊə(r)] *adj.* чистый (чист, -а, -о, чисты); (*of science*) теоретический. **pureblooded** *adj.* чистокровный. **pure-bred** *adj.* породистый.

purée ['pjʊəreɪ] *n.* пюре *nt.indecl.*

purely ['pjʊəlɪ] *adv.* чисто; (*entirely*) совершенно.

purgative ['pɜ:gətɪv] *adj.* слабительный; (*purifying*) очистительный; *n.* слабительное *sb.* **purgatory** *n.* чистилище. **purge** [pɜ:dʒ] *v.t.* (*cleanse*) очищать *impf.*, очистить *of.*; (*of medicine; abs.*) слабить *impf.*; (*atone for*) искупать *impf.*, искупить (-плю, -пишь) *pf.*; (~ *party, army etc.*) проводить (-ожу, -одишь) *impf.*, провести (-еду, -едёшь; -ёл, -ела) *pf.* чистку в+a.; *n.* очищение; (*of party, army, etc.*) чистка.

purification [,pjʊərɪfɪ'keɪʃ(ə)n] *n.* очищение, очистка. **purify** ['pjʊərɪ,faɪ] *v.t.* очищать *impf.*, очистить *pf.*

purism ['pjʊərɪz(ə)m] *n.* пуризм. **purist** *n.* пурист.

puritan, P., ['pjʊərɪt(ə)n] *n.* пуританин (*pl.* -ане, -ан), -анка. **puritanical** [,pjʊərɪ'tænɪk(ə)l] *adj.* пуританский.

purity ['pjʊərɪtɪ] *n.* чистота.

purlieu ['pɜ:lju:] *n.*: *pl.* окрестности *f.pl.*

purloin [pə'lɔɪn] *v.t.* похищать *impf.*, похитить (-ищу, -итишь) *pf.*

purple ['pɜ:p(ə)l] *adj.* (*n.*) пурпурный, фиолетовый (цвет)

purport ['pɜ:pɔ:t] *n.* смысл.

purpose ['pɜ:pəs] *n.* цель, намерение; **on** ~ нарочно; **to no** ~ напрасно. **purposeful** *adj.* целеустремлённый (-ён, -ённа). **purposeless** *adj.* бесцельный. **purposely** *adv.* нарочно.

purr [pɜ:(r)] *n.* мурлыканье; *v.i.* мурлыкать (-ычу, -ычешь) *impf.*

purse [pɜːs] *n.* кошелёк (-лька́); *v.t.* поджима́ть *impf.*, поджа́ть (подожму́, -мёшь) *pf.* **purser** *n.* казначе́й.

pursuance [pə'sjuːəns] *n.* выполне́ние. **pursuant** *adv.*: ~ **to** в соотве́тствии с+*i.*; согла́сно+*d.* **pursue** *v.t.* пресле́довать *impf.*

pursuit *n.* пресле́дование; (*occupation*) заня́тие.

purulent ['pjuːrʊlənt] *adj.* гно́йный.

purvey [pə'veɪ] *v.t.* поставля́ть *impf.*, поста́вить *pf.* **purveyor** *n.* поставщи́к (-а́).

purview ['pɜːvjuː] *n.* кругозо́р.

pus [pʌs] *n.* гной (-о́я(ю), *loc.* -о́е & -о́ю).

push [pʊʃ] *v.t.* толка́ть *impf.*, толкну́ть *pf.*; (*goods*) реклами́ровать *impf.* & *pf.*; *v.i.* толка́ться *impf.*; **be ~ed for** име́ть *impf.* ма́ло+*g.*; **he is ~ing fifty** ему́ ско́ро сту́кнет пятьдеся́т; ~ **one's way** проти́скиваться *impf.*, проти́снуться *pf.*; ~ **ahead, on** продвига́ться *impf.*, продви́нуться *pf.*; ~ **around** (*person*) помыка́ть *impf.* +*i.*; ~ **aside** (*also fig.*) отстраня́ть *impf.*, отстрани́ть *pf.*; ~ **away** отта́лкивать *impf.*, оттолкну́ть *pf.*; ~ **into** (*v.t.*) вта́лкивать *impf.*, втолкну́ть *pf.* в+*a.*; (*urge*) толка́ть *impf.*, толкну́ть *pf.* на+*a.*; ~ **off** (*v.i.*) (*in boat*) отта́лкиваться *impf.*, оттолкну́ться *pf.* (от бе́рега); (*go away*) убира́ться *impf.*, убра́ться (уберу́сь, -рёшься; убра́лся, -ала́сь, -а́лось) *pf.*; ~ **through** (*v.t.*) прота́лкивать *impf.*, протолкну́ть *pf.*; (*conclude*) доводи́ть (-ожу́, -о́дишь) *impf.*, довести́ (-еду́, -едёшь; -ёл, -ела́) *pf.* до конца́; *n.* толчо́к (-чка́); (*energy*) эне́ргия. **push-bike** *n.* велосипе́д. **pushchair** *n.* прогу́лочная коля́ска. **pushing** *adj.* (*of person*) напо́ристый.

puss [pʊs], **pussy(-cat)** *n.* ко́шечка, ки́ска.

pustular ['pʌstjʊlə(r)] *adj.* пустулёзный, прыща́вый. **pustule** *n.* пу́стула, прыщ (-а́).

put [pʊt] *v.t.* класть (кладу́, -дёшь; клал) *impf.*, положи́ть (-жу́, -жишь) *pf.*; (*upright*) ста́вить *impf.*, по~ *pf.*; помеща́ть *impf.*, помести́ть *pf.*; (*into specified state*) приводи́ть (-ожу́, -о́дишь) *impf.*, привести́ (-еду́, -едёшь; -ёл, -ела́) *pf.*; (*estimate*) определя́ть *impf.*, определи́ть *pf.* (**at** в+*a.*); (*express*) выража́ть *impf.*, вы́разить *pf.*; (*translate*) переводи́ть (-ожу́, -о́дишь) *impf.*, перевести́ (-еду́, -едёшь; -ёл, -ела́) *pf.* (**into** на+*a.*); (*a question*) задава́ть (-даю́, -даёшь) *impf.*, зада́ть (-а́м, -а́шь, -а́ст, -ади́м; за́дал, -а́, -о) *pf.*; ~ **an end, a stop, to** класть (кладу́, -дёшь; клал) *impf.*, положи́ть (-жу́, -жишь) *pf.* коне́ц+*d.*; ~ **o.s. in another's place** ста́вить *impf.*, по~ *pf.* себя́ на ме́сто+*g.*; ~ **the shot** толка́ть *impf.*, толкну́ть *pf.* ядро́; ~ **to death** казни́ть *impf.* & *pf.*; ~ **to flight** обраща́ть *impf.*, обрати́ть (-ащу́, -ати́шь) *pf.* в бе́гство; ~ **to shame** стыди́ть *impf.*, при~ *pf.*; ~ **about** (*of ship*) лечь (ля́жет, ля́гут; лёг, -ла́) *pf.* на друго́й галс; (*rumour etc.*) распространя́ть *impf.*, распространи́ть *pf.*; ~ **away** (*for future*)

откла́дывать *impf.*, отложи́ть (-жу́, -жишь) *pf.*; (*in prison*) сажа́ть *impf.*, посади́ть (-ажу́, -а́дишь) *pf.*; ~ **back** (*in place*) ста́вить *impf.*, по~ *pf.* на ме́сто; ~ **the clock back** передвига́ть *impf.*, передви́нуть *pf.* стре́лки часо́в наза́д; ~ **by**, (*money*) откла́дывать *impf.*, отложи́ть (-жу́, -жишь) *pf.*; ~ **down** (*suppress*) подавля́ть *impf.*, подави́ть (-влю́, -вишь) *pf.*; (*write down*) запи́сывать *impf.*, записа́ть (-ишу́, -и́шешь) *pf.*; (*passengers*) выса́живать *impf.*, вы́садить *pf.*; (*attribute*) припи́сывать *impf.*, приписа́ть (-ишу́, -и́шешь) *pf.* (**to** +*d.*); ~ **forth** (*of plant*) пуска́ть *impf.*, пусти́ть (-ит) *pf.* (побе́ги); ~ **forward** (*proposal*) предлага́ть *impf.*, предложи́ть (-жу́, -жишь) *pf.*; ~ **the clock forward** передвига́ть *impf.*, передви́нуть *pf.* стре́лки часо́в вперёд; ~ **in** (*install*) устана́вливать *impf.*, установи́ть (-влю́, -вишь) *pf.*; (*a claim*) предъявля́ть *impf.*, предъяви́ть (-влю́, -вишь) *pf.*; (*interpose*) вставля́ть *impf.*, вста́вить *pf.*; (*spend time*) проводи́ть (-ожу́, -о́дишь) *impf.*, провести́ (-еду́, -едёшь; -ёл, -ела́) *pf.*; ~ **in an appearance** появля́ться *impf.*, появи́ться (-влю́сь, -вишься) *pf.*; ~ **off** (*postpone*) откла́дывать *impf.*, отложи́ть (-жу́, -жишь) *pf.*; (*evade*) отде́лываться *impf.*, отде́латься *pf.* от+*g.*; (*dissuade*) отгова́ривать *impf.*, отговори́ть *pf.* от+*g.*, +*inf.*; ~ **on** (*clothes*) надева́ть *impf.*, наде́ть (-е́ну, -е́нешь) *pf.*; (*appearance*) принима́ть *impf.*, приня́ть (приму́, -мешь; при́нял, -а́, -о) *pf.*; (*a play*) ста́вить *impf.*, по~ *pf.*; (*turn on*) включа́ть *impf.*, включи́ть *pf.*; (*add to*) прибавля́ть *impf.*, приба́вить *pf.*; ~ **on airs** важнича́ть *impf.*; ~ **on weight** толсте́ть *impf.*, по~ *pf.*; ~ **out** (*dislocate*) вы́вихнуть *pf.*; (*a fire etc.*) туши́ть (-шу́, -шишь) *impf.*, по~ *pf.*; (*annoy*) раздража́ть *impf.*, раздражи́ть *pf.*; ~ **out to sea** (*of ship*) выходи́ть (-ит) *impf.*, вы́йти (вы́йдет; вы́шел, -шла) *pf.* в мо́ре; ~ **through** (*carry out*) выполня́ть *impf.*, вы́полнить *pf.*; (*on telephone*) соединя́ть *impf.*, соедини́ть *pf.* по телефо́ну; ~ **up** (*building*) стро́ить *impf.*, по~ *pf.*; (*price*) повыша́ть *impf.*, повы́сить *pf.*; (*a guest*) дава́ть (даю́, даёшь) *impf.*, дать (дам, дашь, даст, дади́м; дал, -а́, да́ло, -и) *pf.* прию́т+*g.*; (*as guest*) остана́вливаться *impf.*, останови́ться (-влю́сь, -вишься) *pf.*; ~ **up to** (*instigate*) подстрека́ть *impf.*, подстрекну́ть *pf.* к+*d.*; ~ **up with** терпе́ть (-плю́, -пишь) *impf.*

putative ['pjuːtətɪv] *adj.* предполага́емый.

putrefaction [,pjuːtrɪ'fækʃ(ə)n] *n.* гние́ние. **putrefy** ['pjuːtrɪfaɪ] *v.i.* гнить (-ию, -иёшь; гнил, -а́, -о) *impf.*, с~ *pf.* **putrid** *adj.* гнило́й (гнил, -а́, -о), гни́лостный.

putsch [pʊtʃ] *n.* путч.

puttee ['pʌtɪ] *n.* обмо́тка.

putty ['pʌtɪ] *n.* зама́зка, шпаклёвка; *v.t.* шпаклева́ть (-лю́ю, -лю́ешь) *impf.*, за~ *pf.*

puzzle ['pʌz(ə)l] *n.* (*perplexity*) недоуме́ние;

(*enigma*) зага́дка; (*toy etc.*) головоло́мка; *v.t.* озада́чивать *impf.*, озада́чить *pf.*; ~ **out** разгада́ть *pf.*; *v.i.*: ~ **over** лома́ть *impf.* себе́ го́лову над+*i.*

PVC *abbr.* (*of polyvinyl chloride*) ПХВ, поли-хлорвини́л.

pygmy ['pɪgmɪ] *n.* пигме́й; *adj.* ка́рликовый.

pyjamas [pɪ'dʒɑːməz, pə-] *n.* пижа́м.

pylon ['paɪlən, -lɒn] *n.* пило́н, опо́ра.

pyramid ['pɪrəmɪd] *n.* пирами́да. **pyramidal** [pɪ'ræmɪd(ə)l] *adj.* пирамида́льный.

pyre ['paɪə(r)] *n.* погреба́льный костёр (-тра́).

Pyrenees [ˌpɪrə'niːz] *n.* Пирене́и (-ев) *pl.*

pyromania [ˌpaɪərəʊ'meɪnɪə] *n.* пирома́ния.

pyrotechnic(al) [ˌpaɪərəʊ'teknɪk(ə)l] *adj.* пиротехни́ческий. **pyrotechnics** [ˌpaɪərəʊ-'teknɪks] *n.* пироте́хника.

Pyrrhic ['pɪrɪk] *adj.*: ~ **victory** пи́ррова побе́да.

python ['paɪθ(ə)n] *n.* пито́н.

Q

qua [kwɑː] *conj.* в ка́честве+*g.*

quack[1] [kwæk] *n.* (*sound*) кря́канье; *v.i.* кря́кать *impf.*, кря́кнуть *pf.*

quack[2] [kwæk] *n.* зна́харь *m.*, шарлата́н. **quackery** *n.* зна́харство, шарлата́нство.

quad [kwɒd] *n.* (*quadrangle*) четырёхуго́ль-ный двор (-а́); (*quadrat*) шпа́ция; *pl.* (*quad-ruplets*) че́тверо (-рых) близнецо́в. **quad-rangle** *n.* (*figure*) четырёхуго́льник; (*court*) четырёхуго́льный двор (-а́). **quad'rangular** *adj.* четырёхуго́льный. **quadrant** *n.* квад-ра́нт. **quadrat** ['kwɒdrət] *n.* шпа́ция. **quad-'ratic** *adj.* квадра́тный; ~ **equation** квад-ра́тное уравне́ние. **quadri'lateral** *adj.* четы-рёхсторо́нний.

quadrille [kwɒ'drɪl] *n.* кадри́ль.

quadruped ['kwɒdrʊˌped] *n.* четвероно́гое живо́тное *sb.* **quadruple** ['kwɒdrʊp(ə)l] *adj.* четверно́й, учетверённый (-ён, -ена́); *v.t.* & *i.* учетверя́ть(ся) *impf.*, учетвери́ть(ся) *pf.* **quadruplets** *n.* че́тверо (-ры́х) близ-нецо́в.

quaff [kwɒf, kwɑːf] *v.t.* пить (пью, пьёшь; пил, -а́, -о) *impf.*, вы́~ *pf.* больши́ми глот-ка́ми.

quag [kwɒg], **quagmire** *n.* тряси́на; (*also fig.*) боло́то.

quail[1] [kweɪl] *n.* (*bird*) пе́репел (*pl.* -а́), -ёлка.

quail[2] [kweɪl] *v.i.* (*flinch*) дро́гнуть *pf.*; тру́-сить *impf.*, с~ *pf.* (**before** +*a.*, пе́ред+*i.*).

quaint [kweɪnt] *adj.* причу́дливый, ориги-на́льный.

quake [kweɪk] *v.i.* трясти́сь (трясу́сь, -сёшь-ся; тря́сся, -сла́сь) *impf.*; дрожа́ть (-жу́, -жи́шь) *impf.* (**for, with** от+*g.*); *n.* земле-трясе́ние.

Quaker ['kweɪkə(r)] *n.* ква́кер, ~ка.

qualification [ˌkwɒlɪfɪ'keɪʃ(ə)n] *n.* (*restriction*) ограниче́ние, огово́рка; (*for post etc.*) квалифика́ция; (*for citizenship etc.*) ценз; (*description*) характери́стика. **qualify** ['kwɒ-lɪˌfaɪ] *v.t.* (*describe*) квалифици́ровать *impf.* & *pf.*; (*restrict*) ограни́чивать *impf.*, ограни́чить *pf.*; *v.t.* & *i.* (*prepare for*) гото́-вить(ся) *impf.* (**for** &+*d.*; +*inf.*).

qualitative ['kwɒlɪtətɪv, -ˌteɪtɪv] *adj.* ка́чест-венный. **quality** *n.* ка́чество; сорт; (*excel-lence*) высо́кое ка́чество; (*ability*) спосо́б-ность.

qualm [kwɑːm, kwɔːm] *n.* (*queasiness*) при́-ступ тошноты́; (*doubt, scruple*) колеба́ние, угрызе́ние со́вести.

quandary ['kwɒndərɪ] *n.* затрудни́тельное положе́ние, диле́мма.

quantify ['kwɒntɪˌfaɪ] *v.t.* определя́ть *impf.*, определи́ть *pf.* коли́чество+*g.* **quantitative** *adj.* коли́чественный. **quantity** ['kwɒntɪtɪ] *n.* коли́чество; (*math.*) величина́ (*pl.* -ны).

quantum ['kwɒntəm] *n.* (*amount*) коли́-чество; (*share*) до́ля (*pl.* -ли, -ле́й); (*phys.*) квант; *attr.* ква́нтовый.

quarantine ['kwɒrənˌtiːn] *n.* каранти́н; *v.t.* подверга́ть *impf.*, подве́ргнуть (-г) *pf.* каранти́ну.

quark [kwɑːk] *n.* кварк.

quarrel ['kwɒr(ə)l] *n.* ссо́ра; *v.i.* ссо́риться *impf.*, по~ *pf.* (**with** с+*i.*; **about, for** из-за+*g.*). **quarrelsome** *adj.* вздо́рный.

quarry[1] ['kwɒrɪ] *n.* (*for stone etc.*) камено-ло́мня (*g.pl.* -мен), карье́р; *v.t.* добыва́ть *impf.*, добы́ть (добу́ду, -дешь; до́бы́л, -а́, -о) *pf.*

quarry[2] ['kwɒrɪ] *n.* (*object of pursuit*) пре-сле́дуемый зверь (*pl.* -ри, -ре́й) *m.*

quart ['kwɔːt] *n.* ква́рта. **quarter** *n.* че́тверть (*pl.* -ти, -те́й); (*of year; of town*) кварта́л; (*direction*) сторона́ (*a.* -ону; *pl.* -оны, -о́н, -она́м); (*mercy*) поща́да; *pl.* кварти́ры *f.pl.*; **a** ~ **to one** без че́тверти час; *v.t.* (*divide*) дели́ть (-лю́, -лишь) *impf.*, раз~ *pf.* на четы́ре (ра́вные) ча́сти; (*traitor's body*) четвертова́ть *impf.* & *pf.*; (*lodge*) расквар-тиро́вывать *impf.*, расквартирова́ть *pf.* **quarterdeck** *n.* шка́нцы (-цев) *pl.* **quarter-final** *n.* че́тверть-фина́л(ьная игра́). **quar-terly** *adj.* трёхме́сячный, кварта́льный; *adv.* раз в кварта́л, раз в три ме́сяца; *n.* журна́л, выходя́щий раз в три ме́сяца. **quarter-master** *n.* квартирме́йстер. **quar'tet(te)** *n.* кварте́т. **quarto** *n.* (ин-)ква́рто *nt.indecl.*

quartz [kwɔːts] *n.* кварц.

quasar ['kweɪzɑː(r), -sɑː(r)] *n.* кваза́р.

quash [kwɒʃ] *v.t.* (*annul*) аннули́ровать *impf.* & *pf.*; (*crush*) подавля́ть *impf.*, подави́ть (-влю́, -вишь) *pf.*

quasi *adv.* как бу́дто.
quasi- ['kweɪzaɪ, 'kwɑːzɪ] *in comb.* квази... .
quatercentenary [ˌkwætəsen'tiːnərɪ] *n.* четырёхсотле́тие.
quatrain ['kwɒtreɪn] *n.* четверости́шие.
quaver ['kweɪvə(r)] *v.i.* дрожа́ть (-жу́, -жи́шь) *impf.*; *n.* дрожа́ние; (*mus.*) восьма́я *sb.* но́ты.
quay [kiː] *n.* на́бережная *sb.*
queasy ['kwiːzɪ] *adj.* (*stomach*) сла́бый (слаб, -á, -o); (*person*) испы́тывающий тошноту́.
queen [kwiːn] *n.* короле́ва; (*cards*) да́ма; (*chess*) ферзь (-зя́) *m.*; ~ **bee** ма́тка; ~ **mother** вдо́вствующая короле́ва; *v.t.* (*chess*) проводи́ть (-ожу́, -о́дишь) *impf.*, провести́ (-еду́, -едёшь; -ёл, -ела́) *pf.* в ферзи́. **queenly** *adj.* ца́рственный (-ен(ен), -енна).
queer [kwɪə(r)] *adj.* стра́нный (-нен, -нна́, -нно); **feel** ~ чу́вствовать *impf.* недомога́ние.
quell [kwel] *v.t.* подавля́ть *impf.*, подави́ть (-влю́, -вишь) *pf.*
quench [kwentʃ] *v.t.* (*thirst*) утоля́ть *impf.*, утоли́ть *pf.*; (*fire, desire*) туши́ть (-шу́, -шишь) *impf.*, по~ *pf.*
querulous ['kwerʊləs] *adj.* ворчли́вый.
query ['kwɪərɪ] *n.* вопро́с, сомне́ние; *v.t.* (*express doubt*) выража́ть *impf.* вы́разить *pf.* сомне́ние в+*p.*
quest [kwest] *n.* по́иски *m.pl.*; **in** ~ **of** в по́исках+*g.* **question** *n.* вопро́с; (*doubt*) сомне́ние; **beyond all** ~ вне сомне́ния; **it is** (**merely**) **a** ~ **of** э́то вопро́с+*g.*; де́ло то́лько в том, что́бы+*inf.*; **it is out of the** ~ об э́том не мо́жет быть и ре́чи; **the person in** ~ челове́к, о кото́ром идёт речь; **the** ~ **is this** де́ло в э́том; ~ **mark** вопроси́тельный знак; *v.t.* (*ask*) спра́шивать *impf.*, спроси́ть (-ошу́, -о́сишь) *pf.*; (*doubt*) сомнева́ться *impf.* в+*p.* **questionable** *adj.* сомни́тельный. **questio'nnaire** *n.* анке́та, вопро́сник.
queue [kjuː] *n.* о́чередь (*pl.* -ди, -де́й); *v.i.* стоя́ть (-ою́, -ои́шь) *impf.* в о́череди.
quibble ['kwɪb(ə)l] *n.* софи́зм, увёртка; *v.i.* уклоня́ться *impf.*, уклони́ться (-ню́сь, -ни́шься) *pf.* от су́ти вопро́са, от прямо́го отве́та.
quick [kwɪk] *adj.* ско́рый (скор, -á, -o), бы́стрый (быстр, -á, -o, бы́стры); (*nimble*) прово́рный; (*clever*) смышлёный; *n.*: **to the** ~ за живо́е, до мя́са; **the** ~ **and the dead** живы́е и мёртвые *sb.*; *adv.* ско́ро, бы́стро; *as imper.* скоре́е! **quicken** *v.t.* & *i.* (*accelerate*) ускоря́ть(ся) *impf.*, уско́рить(ся) *pf.*; *v.t.* (*animate*) оживля́ть *impf.*, оживи́ть *pf.* **quicklime** *n.* негашёная и́звесть. **quickness** *n.* быстрота́; прово́рство. **quicksand** *n.* плыву́н (-á), зыбу́чий песо́к (-ска́). **quickset** *n.* (*hedge*) жива́я и́згородь. **quicksilver** *n.* ртуть. **quick-tempered** *adj.* вспы́льчивый. **quick-witted** *adj.* остроу́мный.
quid [kwɪd] *n.* фунт.
quiescence [kwɪ'es(ə)ns] *n.* неподви́жность, поко́й. **quiescent** *adj.* неподви́жный, в

состоя́нии поко́я. **quiet** ['kwaɪət] *n.* (*silence*) тишина́; (*calm*) споко́йствие; *adj.* ти́хий (тих, -á, -o); споко́йный; *int.* ти́ше!; *v.t.* & *i.* успока́ивать(ся) *impf.*, успоко́ить(ся) *pf.*
quill [kwɪl] *n.* (*feather*) перо́ (*pl.* -рья, -рьев); (*spine*) игла́ (*pl.* -лы).
quilt [kwɪlt] *n.* (стёганое) одея́ло; *v.t.* стега́ть *impf.*, вы́~ *pf.* **quilting** *n.* стёжка.
quince [kwɪns] *n.* айва́.
quincentenary [ˌkwɪnsen'tiːnərɪ] *n.* пятисотле́тие.
quinine ['kwɪniːn, -'niːn] *n.* хини́н.
quinquennial [kwɪn'kwenɪəl] *adj.* пятиле́тний.
quintessence [kwɪn'tes(ə)ns] *n.* квинтессе́нция.
quintet(te) [kwɪn'tet] *n.* квинте́т. **quintuple** ['kwɪntjʊp(ə)l] *adj.* пятикра́тный. **quins, quin'tuplets** *n.* пять (-ти́, -тью) близнецо́в.
quip [kwɪp] *n.* острота́.
quire ['kwaɪə(r)] *n.* (*in manuscript*) тетра́дь; (*24 sheets*) ру́сская десть (*pl.* -ти, -те́й).
quirk [kwɜːk] *n.* причу́да.
quisling ['kwɪzlɪŋ] *n.* кви́слинг.
quit [kwɪt] *v.t.* покида́ть *impf.*, поки́нуть *pf.*; (*dwelling*) выезжа́ть *impf.*, вы́ехать (-еду, -едешь) *pf.* из+*g.*
quite [kwaɪt] *adv.* (*wholly*) совсе́м, вполне́; (*somewhat*) дово́льно; ~ **a few** дово́льно мно́го.
quits [kwɪts] *pred.*: **we are** ~ мы с тобо́й кви́ты; **I am** ~ **with him** я расквита́лся (*past*) с ним.
quiver[1] ['kwɪvə(r)] *n.* (*for arrows*) колча́н.
quiver[2] ['kwɪvə(r)] *v.i.* (*tremble*) трепета́ть (-ещу́, -е́щешь) *impf.*; дрожа́ть (-жу́, -жи́шь) *impf.* (мéлкой дро́жью); *n.* тре́пет, ме́лкая дрожь.
quixotic [kwɪk'sɒtɪk] *adj.* донкихо́тский.
quiz [kwɪz] *n.* викторина. **quizzical** *adj.* насмешливый.
quoit [kɔɪt] *n.* мета́тельное кольцо́ (*pl.* -льца, -ле́ц, -льцам); *pl.* (*game*) мета́ние коле́ц в цель.
quorum ['kwɔːrəm] *n.* кво́рум.
quota ['kwəʊtə] *n.* кво́та.
quotation [kwəʊ'teɪʃ(ə)n] *n.* (*quoting*) цити́рование; (*passage quoted*) цита́та; (*estimate*) сме́та; (*of stocks etc.*) котиро́вка; ~ **marks** кавы́чки (-чек) *pl.* **quote** *v.t.* цити́ровать *impf.*, про~ *pf.*; ссыла́ться *impf.*, сосла́ться (сошлю́сь, -лёшься) *pf.* на+*a.*; (*price*) назнача́ть цену́, назна́чить *pf.*
quotidian [kwɒ'tɪdɪən] *adj.* (*daily*) ежедне́вный; (*commonplace*) обы́денный.
quotient ['kwəʊʃ(ə)nt] *n.* ча́стное *sb.*

R

rabbet[1] ['ræbɪt] *n.* шпунт (-á).

rabbi ['ræbaɪ] *n.* раввйн. **rabbinical** [rə'bɪnɪk(ə)l] *adj.* раввйнский.

rabbit ['ræbɪt] *n.* крóлик; ~ **punch** удáр в затьíлок.

rabble ['ræb(ə)l] *n.* сброд, чернь.

rabid ['ræbɪd, 'reɪ-] *adj.* бéшеный. **rabies** ['reɪbiːz] *n.* водобоязнь, бéшенство.

RAC *abbr.* (*of Royal Automobile Club*) Королéвский автомобйльный клуб.

raccoon *see* **racoon**

race[1] [reɪs] *n.* (*ethnic* ~) рáса; род.

race[2] [reɪs] *n.* (*contest*) (*on foot*) бег; (*of cars etc.*; *fig.*) гóнка, гóнки *f.pl.*; (*of horses*) скáчки *f.pl.*; ~ **meeting** скáчки *f.pl.*; **racing driver** автогóнщик; *v.i.* (*compete*) состязáться *impf.* в скóрости; (*rush*) мчáться (мчусь, мчйшься) *impf.*; *v.t.* гнать (гоню, -нишь; гнал, -á, -о) *impf.* **racecard** *n.* прогрáмма скáчек. **racecourse** *n.* ипподрóм. **racehorse** *n.* скаковáя лóшадь (*pl.* -ди, -дéй, *i.* -дьмй). **racer** *n.* (*person*) гóнщик; (*car*) гóночный автомобйль *m.* **racetrack** *n.* трек; автомотодрóм; (*for horse* ~) скаковáя дорóжка.

racial ['reɪʃ(ə)l] *adj.* рáсовый. **rac(ial)ism** *n.* расйзм. **rac(ial)ist** *n.* расйст, ~ка; *adj.* расйстский.

rack[1] [ræk] *n.* (*for fodder*) кормýшка; (*for hats etc.*) вéшалка; (*for plates etc.*) стеллáж (-á); (*in train etc.*) сéтка для вещéй; (*for torture*) дьíба; (*cogged bar*) зубчáтая рéйка; *v.t.* мýчить *impf.*; пытáть *impf.*; ~ **one's brains** ломáть *impf.* себé гóлову.

rack[2] [ræk] *n.*: **go to** ~ **and ruin** разорáться *impf.*, разорйться *pf.*

racket[1] ['rækɪt] *n.* (*bat*) ракéтка.

racket[2] ['rækɪt] *n.* (*uproar*) шум (-a(у)); (*illegal activity*) рэкет. **racke'teer** *n.* рэкетйр.

rac(c)oon [rə'kuːn] *n.* енóт.

racy ['reɪsɪ] *adj.* колорйтный.

radar ['reɪdɑː(r)] *n.* (*system*) радиолокáция; (*apparatus*) радиолокáтор, радáр; *attr.* радиолокациóнный, радáрный.

radial ['reɪdɪəl] *adj.* радиáльный, лучевóй.

radiance ['reɪdɪəns] *n.* сияние. **radiant** *adj.* сияющий; лучйстый; *n.* источник (лучйстого) тепла, свéта. **radiate** *v.t.* излучáть *impf.*; лучйться *impf.+i.*; *v.i.* исходйть (-ит) *impf.* из однóй тóчки; (*diverge*) расходйться

(-ятся) *impf.* лучáми. **radi'ation** *n.* излучéние, радиáция; ~ **sickness** лучевáя болéзнь. **radiator** *n.* радиáтор; (*in central heating*) батерéя.

radical ['rædɪk(ə)l] *adj.* кореннóй; (*pol.*) радикáльный; (*ling.*) корневóй; *n.* (*pol., chem.*) радикáл; (*math., ling.*) кóрень (-рня; *pl.* -рни, -рнéй) *m.* **radically** *adv.* коренным óбразом, совершéнно.

radicle ['rædɪk(ə)l] *n.* корешóк (-шкá).

radio ['reɪdɪəʊ] *n.* рáдио *nt.indecl.*; *adj.* рáдио...; *v.t.* радйровать *impf. & pf.*

radio- ['reɪdɪəʊ] *in comb.* рáдио...; ~ **telescope** радиотелескóп; ~ **wave** радиоволнá (*pl.* -óлны, *d.* -óлнáм). **radioactive** *adj.* радиоактйвный. **radioactivity** *n.* радиоактйвность. **radiocarbon** *n.* радиоактйвный изотóп углербда; ~ **dating** датйрование радиоуглерóдным мéтодом. **radiogram** *n.* (*X-ray picture*) рентгеногрáмма; (~*telegram*) радиогрáмма; (*radio and gramophone*) радиóла. **radiographer** [,reɪdɪ'ɒɡrəfə(r)] *n.* рентгенóлог. **radi'ography** *n.* радиогрáфия; (*spec. X-ray*) рентгеногрáфия. **radioisotope** *n.* радиоизотóп. **radiolocation** *n.* радиолокáция. **radiologist** [,reɪdɪ'ɒlədʒɪst] *n.* радиóлог; (*spec. X-ray*) рентгенóлог. **radi'ology** *n.* радиолóгия; рентгенолóгия. **radi'ometer** *n.* радиомéтр. **radi'oscopy** *n.* рентгеноскопйя. **radiosonde** *n.* радиозóнд. **radiotherapy** *n.* радиотерапйя; (*specifically X-ray*) рентгенотерапйя.

radish ['rædɪʃ] *n.* редйска; редйс (*no pl.*: *plant*; *collect.*).

radium ['reɪdɪəm] *n.* рáдий.

radius ['reɪdɪəs] *n.* (*math.*) рáдиус; (*bone*) лучевáя кость.

RAF *abbr.* (*of Royal Air Force*) ВВС (воéнно-воздýшные сйлы) Великобритáнии.

raffia ['ræfɪə] *n.* рáфия.

raffish ['ræfɪʃ] *adj.* беспýтный.

raffle ['ræf(ə)l] *n.* лотерéя; *v.t.* разьíгрывать *impf.*, разыгрáть *pf.* в лотерéе.

raft [rɑːft] *n.* плот (-á, *loc.* -ý).

rafter ['rɑːftə(r)] *n.* (*beam*) стропйло.

raftsman ['rɑːftsmən] *n.* плотовщйк (-á).

rag[1] [ræg] *v.t.* (*tease*) дразнйть (-ню, -нишь) *impf.*

rag[2] [ræg] *n.* трáпка, лоскýт (-á; *pl.* -á, -óв & -ья, -ьев); *pl.* (*clothes*) лохмóтья (-ьев) *pl.*; ~ **doll** тряпйчная кýкла (*g.pl.* -кол). **rag-muffin** *n.* оборвáнец (-нца). **rag-and-bone man** *n.* старьёвщик.

rage [reɪdʒ] *n.* (*anger*) ярость, гнев; (*desire*) страсть (for, к+*d.*); **all the** ~ послéдний крик мóды; *v.i.* бесйться (бешýсь, бéсишься) *impf.*; (*storm etc.*) свирéпствовать *impf.*

ragged ['rægɪd] *adj.* (*jagged*) зазýбренный (-ен); (*of clothes*) изóдранный (-ан, -анна); (*of person*) в лохмóтьях.

raglan ['ræglən] *n.* реглáн; ~ **sleeve** рукáв (-á; *pl.* -á) реглáн (*indecl.*).

ragout [ræ'guː] *n.* рагу́ *nt.indecl.*

ragtime ['ræɡtaɪm] *n.* ре́гтайм.

ragwort ['ræɡwɜːt] *n.* крестóвник.

raid [reɪd] *n.* набе́г, налёт; (*by police*) обла́ва; *v.t.* де́лать *impf.*, c~ *pf.* налёт на+*a.*

rail [reɪl] *n.* пери́ла (-л) *pl.*; (*rail.*) рельс; (*railway*) желе́зная доро́га; **by** ~ по́ездом, по желе́зной доро́ге; *v.t.*: ~ **in, off** обноси́ть (-ошу́, -о́сишь) *impf.*, обнести́ (-есу́, -есёшь; -ёс, -есла́) *pf.* пери́лами. **railhead** *n.* коне́чный пункт (желе́зной доро́ги). **railing** *n.* пери́ла (-л) *pl.*, огра́да.

raillery ['reɪlərɪ] *n.* доброду́шное подшу́чивание.

railway ['reɪlweɪ] *n.* желе́зная доро́га; *attr.* железнодоро́жный. **railwayman** *n.* железнодоро́жник.

raiment ['reɪmənt] *n.* одея́ние.

rain [reɪn] *n.* дождь (-дя́) *m.*; ~ **forest** тропи́ческий лес; *pl.* (*the* ~) пери́од (тропи́ческих) дожде́й; *v. impers.* **it is (was)** ~**ing** идёт (шёл) дождь; *v.t.* осыпа́ть *impf.*, осы́пать (-плю, -плешь) *pf.*+*i.* (**upon** +*a.*); *v.i.* осыпа́ться *impf.*, осы́паться (-плется) *pf.* **rainbow** *n.* ра́дуга; ~ **trout** ра́дужная форе́ль. **raincoat** *n.* непромока́емое пальто́ *nt.indecl.*, плащ (-а́). **raindrop** *n.* дождева́я ка́пля (*g.pl.* -пель). **rainfall** *n.* (*shower*) ли́вень (-вня) *m.*; (*amount of rain*) коли́чество оса́дков. **rainproof** *adj.* непромока́емый. **rainwater** *n.* дождева́я вода́ (*a.* -ду). **rainy** *adj.* дождли́вый; ~ **day** чёрный день (дня) *m.*

raise [reɪz] *v.t.* (*lift*) поднима́ть *impf.*, подня́ть (подниму́, -мешь; по́днял, -а́, -о) *pf.*; (*heighten*) повыша́ть *impf.*, повы́сить *pf.*; (*erect*) воздвига́ть *impf.*, воздви́гнуть (-г) *pf.*; (*provoke*) вызыва́ть *impf.*, вы́звать (вы́зову, -вешь) *pf.*; (*procure*) добыва́ть *impf.*, добы́ть (добу́ду, -дешь; до́бы́л, -а́, -о) *pf.*; (*children*) расти́ть *impf.*

raisin ['reɪz(ə)n] *n.* изю́минка; *pl.* (*collect.*) изю́м (-a(y)).

raja(h) [ˈrɑːdʒə] *n.* ра́джа (*g.pl.* -же́й) *m.*

rake[1] [reɪk] *n.* (*tool*) гра́бли (-блей & -бель) *pl.*; *v.t.* (~ *together, up*) сгреба́ть *impf.*, сгрести́ (сгребу́, -бёшь; сгрёб, -бла́) *pf.*; (*with shot*) обстре́ливать *impf.*, обстреля́ть *pf.* продо́льным огнём.

rake[2] [reɪk] *n.* (*person*) пове́са *m.* **rakish** *adj.* распу́тный.

rally[1] ['rælɪ] *v.t. & i.* спла́чивать(ся) *impf.*, сплоти́ть(ся) *pf.*; *v.i.* (*after illness etc.*) оправля́ться *impf.*, опра́виться *pf.*; *n.* (*meeting*) слёт; ма́ссовый ми́тинг; (*motoring* ~) (авто)ра́лли *nt.indecl.*; (*tennis*) обме́н уда́рами.

rally[2] ['rælɪ] *v.t.* (*ridicule*) подшу́чивать *impf.*, подшути́ть (-учу́, -у́тишь) *pf.* над+*i.*

RAM [ræm] *n.* (*comput.*) (*abbr. of random-access memory*) ЗУПВ, (запомина́ющее устро́йство с произво́льной вы́боркой).

Ramadan ['ræmə‚dæn] *n.* рамаза́н.

ram [ræm] *n.* (*sheep*) бара́н; (*the Ram, Aries*) Ове́н (Овна́); (*machine*) тара́н; *v.t.* (*beat down*) трамбова́ть *impf.*, у~ *pf.*; (*drive in*) вбива́ть *impf.*, вбить (вобью́, -ьёшь) *pf.*; (*strike with* ~) тара́нить *impf.*, про~ *pf.*

ramble ['ræmb(ə)l] *v.i.* (*walk*) броди́ть (-ожу́, -о́дишь) *impf.*; (*speak*) говори́ть *impf.* несвя́зно; *n.* прогу́лка. **rambler** *n.* (*hiker*) люби́тель *m.* пешехо́дного тури́зма; (*plant*) выо́щаяся ро́за. **rambling** *n.* пешехо́дный тури́зм; *adj.* (*scattered*) разбро́санный; (*incoherent*) бессвя́зный.

ramification [‚ræmɪfɪˈkeɪʃ(ə)n] *n.* разветвле́ние. **ramify** ['ræmɪ‚faɪ] *v.i.* разветвля́ться *impf.*, разветви́ться *pf.*

ramp [ræmp] *n.* скат, укло́н.

rampage ['ræmpeɪdʒ] *v.i.* нейстовствовать *impf.*; *n.* нейстовство.

rampant ['ræmpənt] *adj.* (*of lion etc.*) стоя́щий на за́дних ла́пах; (*raging*) свире́пствующий.

rampart ['ræmpaːt] *n.* вал (*loc.* -у́; *pl.* -ы́).

ramrod ['ræmrɒd] *n.* шо́мпол (*pl.* -а́).

ramshackle ['ræm‚ʃæk(ə)l] *adj.* ве́тхий (ветх, -а́, -о).

ranch [rɑːntʃ] *n.* ра́нчо *nt.indecl.*

rancid ['rænsɪd] *adj.* прого́рклый.

rancour ['ræŋkə(r)] *n.* зло́ба. **rancorous** *adj.* зло́бный.

random ['rændəm] *n.*: **at** ~ науда́чу, науга́д, наобу́м; *adj.* сде́ланный (-ан), вы́бранный (-ан), науга́д; случа́йный.

range [reɪndʒ] *n.* (*of mountains*) цепь (*pl.* -пи, -пе́й); (*grazing ground*) неогоро́женное па́стбище; (*artillery* ~) полиго́н; (*of voice*) диапазо́н; (*scope*) круг (*loc.* -у́; *pl.* -и́), преде́лы *m.pl.*; (*distance*) да́льность; *v.t.* (*arrange in row*) выстра́ивать *impf.*, вы́строить *pf.* в ряд; *v.i.* (*extend*) тяну́ться (-нется) *impf.*; (*occur*) встреча́ться *impf.*, встре́титься *pf.*; (*vary*) колеба́ться (-блется) *impf.*, по~ *pf.*; (*wander*) броди́ть (-ожу́, -о́дишь) *impf.* **rangefinder** *n.* дально́мер.

rank[1] [ræŋk] *n.* (*row*) ряд (-á *with* 2,3,4; *loc.* -у́; *pl.* -ы́); (*taxi* ~) стоя́нка такси́; (*grade*) зва́ние, чин, ранг; *v.t.* (*classify*) классифици́ровать *impf. & pf.*; (*consider*) счита́ть *impf.* (**as** +*i.*); *v.i.*: ~ **with** быть (*fut.* бу́ду, -дешь; был, -á, -о; не́ был, -á, -о) в числе́+*g.*, на у́ровне+*g.*

rank[2] [ræŋk] *adj.* (*luxuriant*) бу́йный (бу́ен, буйна́, -но); (*in smell*) злово́нный (-нен, -нна); (*repulsive*) отврати́тельный; (*clear*) я́вный.

rankle ['ræŋk(ə)l] *v.i.* причиня́ть *impf.*, причини́ть *pf.* боль.

ransack ['rænsæk] *v.t.* (*search*) обша́ривать *impf.*, обша́рить *pf.*; (*plunder*) гра́бить *impf.*, o~ *pf.*

ransom ['rænsəm] *n.* вы́куп; *v.t.* выкупа́ть *impf.*, вы́купить *pf.*

rant [rænt] *v.t. & i.* напы́щенно декламировать *impf.*

rap[1] [ræp] *n.* (*blow*) стук, ре́зкий уда́р; *v.t.*

(ре́зко) ударя́ть *impf.*, уда́рить *pf.*; *v.i.* стуча́ть (-чу́, -чи́шь) *impf.*, сту́кнуть *pf.*; ~ out (*words*) отчека́нивать *impf.*, отчека́нить *pf.*

rap² [ræp] *n.*: not a ~ ниско́лько; I don't care a ~ мне наплева́ть.

rapacious [rə'peɪʃəs] *adj.* неуме́ренно жа́дный (-ден, -дна́, -дно), хи́щнический.

rape¹ [reɪp] *v.t.* наси́ловать *impf.*, из~ *pf.*; *n.* изнаси́лование; (*abduction*) похище́ние.

rape² [reɪp] *n.* (*plant*) рапс. rape-oil *n.* ра́псовое ма́сло.

rapid ['ræpɪd] *adj.* бы́стрый (быстр, -á, -о, бы́стры́); *n.*: *pl.* поро́г, быстрина́ (*pl.* -ны). rapidity [rə'pɪdɪtɪ] *n.* быстрота́.

rapier ['reɪpɪə(r)] *n.* рапи́ра.

rapt [ræpt] *adj.* восхищённый (-ён, -ённа); (*absorbed*) поглощённый (-ен, -ена́). rapture *n.* восто́рг. rapturous *adj.* восто́рженный (-ен, -енна).

rare¹ [reə(r)] *adj.* (*of meat*) недожа́ренный (-ен).

rare² [reə(r)] *adj.* ре́дкий (-док, -дка́, -дко), ре́дкостный. rarefy ['reərɪˌfaɪ] *v.t.* разрежа́ть *impf.*, разреди́ть *pf.* rarity *n.* ре́дкость.

rascal ['rɑːsk(ə)l] *n.* плут (-á).

rase *see* raze

rash¹ [ræʃ] *n.* сыпь.

rash² [ræʃ] *adj.* опроме́тчивый.

rasher ['ræʃə(r)] *n.* ло́мтик (беко́на, ветчины́).

rasp [rɑːsp] *n.* (*file*) ра́шпиль *m.*; (*sound*) ре́жущий звук.

raspberry ['rɑːzbərɪ] *n.* (*plant*) мали́на (*also* collect., *fruit*); *attr.* мали́новый.

rasping ['rɑːspɪŋ] *adj.* (*sound*) ре́жущий, скрипу́чий.

Rastafarian [ˌræstə'feərɪən] *n.* растафа́ри; *adj. indecl.* растафа́ри.

rat [ræt] *n.* кры́са; (*turncoat*) перебе́жчик; ~ race бе́шеная пого́ня за успе́хом; *v.i.*: ~ on предава́ть (-даю́, -даёшь) *impf.*, преда́ть (-а́м, -а́шь, -а́ст, -ади́м; пре́дал, -á, -о) *pf.*+a. rat-catcher *n.* крысоло́в.

ratchet ['rætʃɪt] *n.* храпови́к (-á); *attr.* храпово́й.

rate [reɪt] *n.* но́рма, ста́вка; (*speed*) ско́рость; *pl.* ме́стные нало́ги *m.pl.*; at any ~ во вся́ком слу́чае, по ме́ньшей ме́ре; at the ~ of по+d., со ско́ростью+g.; *v.t.* оце́нивать *impf.*, оцени́ть (-ню́, -нишь) *pf.*; (*consider*) счита́ть *impf.* rateable *adj.* подлежа́щий обложе́нию ме́стным нало́гом; ~ value облага́емая сто́имость. ratepayer *n.* налогоплате́льщик, -ица.

rather ['rɑːðə(r)] *adv.* скоре́е, скоре́й; (*somewhat*) не́сколько, дово́льно; (*as answer*) ещё бы!; he (she) had (would) ~ он (она́) предпочёл (-чла́) бы+inf.; or ~ (и́ли) верне́е (сказа́ть), точне́е (сказа́ть); ~ ... than скоре́е... чем.

ratification [ˌrætɪfɪ'keɪʃ(ə)n] *n.* ратифика́ция. ratify ['rætɪˌfaɪ] *v.t.* ратифици́ровать *impf.* & *pf.*

rating ['reɪtɪŋ] *n.* оце́нка; (*naut.*) рядово́й *sb.*

ratio ['reɪʃɪəʊ] *n.* пропо́рция.

ration ['ræʃ(ə)n] *n.* паёк (пайка́), рацио́н; *v.t.* норми́ровать *impf.* & *pf.*; be ~ed выдава́ться (-даётся) *impf.*, вы́даться (-астся, -адутся) *pf.* по ка́рточкам.

rational ['ræʃən(ə)l] *adj.* разу́мный; (*also* math.) рациона́льный. rationalism *n.* рационали́зм. rationalist *n.* рационали́ст. rationalize *v.t.* дава́ть (даю́, даёшь) *impf.*, дать (дам, дашь, даст, дади́м; дал, -á, да́ло́, -и) *pf.* рационалисти́ческое объясне́ние+g.; (*industry etc.*) рационализи́ровать *impf.* & *pf.*

rattan [rə'tæn] *n.* рота́нг.

rattle ['ræt(ə)l] *v.i.* & *t.* (*sound*) греме́ть (-млю́, -ми́шь) *impf.* (+i.); бряца́ть *impf.* (+i.); *v.i.* (*speak*) болта́ть *impf.*; *v.t.* (*fluster*) смуща́ть *impf.*, смути́ть (-ущу́, -ути́шь) *pf.*; ~ along (*move*) мча́ться (мчусь, мчи́шься) *impf.* с гро́хотом; ~ off (*utter*) отбараба́нить *pf.*; *n.* (*sound*) треск, гро́хот; (*instrument*) трещо́тка; (*toy*) погрему́шка. rattlesnake *n.* грему́чая змея́ (*pl.* -еи, -ей). rattling *adj.* (*brisk*) бы́стрый; ~ good великоле́пный.

rat-trap ['rættræp] *n.* крысоло́вка.

raucous ['rɔːkəs] *adj.* ре́зкий (-зок, -зка́, -зко).

ravage ['rævɪdʒ] *v.t.* опустоша́ть *impf.*, опустоши́ть *pf.*; *n.*: *pl.* разруши́тельное де́йствие.

rave [reɪv] *v.i.* бре́дить *impf.*; (*wind, sea*) реве́ть (-вёт) *impf.*; ~ about бре́дить *impf.*+i., восторга́ться *impf.*+i.

raven ['reɪv(ə)n] *n.* во́рон.

ravenous ['rævənəs] *adj.* прожо́рливый; (*famished*) голо́дный (го́лоден, -дна́, -дно, го́лодны́) как волк; ~ appetite во́лчий аппети́т.

ravine [rə'viːn] *n.* уще́лье (*g.pl.* -лий).

ravioli [ˌrævɪ'əʊlɪ] *n.* равио́ли *sg.* & *pl. indecl.*

ravish ['rævɪʃ] *v.t.* (*rape*) наси́ловать *impf.*, из~ *pf.*; (*charm*) восхища́ть *impf.*, восхити́ть (-ищу́, -ити́шь) *pf.* ravishing *adj.* восхити́тельный.

raw [rɔː] *adj.* сыро́й (сыр, -á, -о); (*brick*) необожжённый; (*alcohol*) неразба́вленный; (*style*) неотде́ланный; (*inexperienced*) нео́пытный; (*stripped of skin*) содра́нный; (*sensitive*) чувстви́тельный; (*edge of cloth*) неподру́бленный; ~ material(s) сырьё (*no pl.*); ~ place (*abrasion*) цара́пина; ~ silk шёлк-сыре́ц (-рца́); ~ wound живая ра́на; *n.* больно́е ме́сто; touch on the ~ задева́ть *impf.*, заде́ть (-е́ну, -е́нешь) *pf.* за живо́е.

rawhide *n.* недублёная ко́жа.

ray¹ [reɪ] *n.* (*beam*) луч (-á); (*fig.*) про́блеск.

ray² [reɪ] *n.* (*fish*) скат.

rayon ['reɪɒn] *n.* виско́за.

raze [reɪz] *v.t.*: ~ to the ground ровня́ть *impf.*, с~ *pf.* с землёй.

razor ['reɪzə(r)] *n.* бри́тва. razor-blade *n.* ле́звие бри́твы.

RC *abbr.* (*of Roman Catholic*) като́лик.

Rd. *abbr.* (*of* **road**) ул., у́лица.
RE *abbr.* (*of Religious Education*) религио́зное обуче́ние.

reach [riːtʃ] *v.t.* (*extend*) протя́гивать *impf.*, протяну́ть (-ну́, -нешь) *pf.*; (*attain, arrive at*) достига́ть *impf.*, дости́чь & дости́гнуть (-и́гну, -и́гнешь; -и́г) *pf.*+g., до+g.; доходи́ть (-ожу́, -о́дишь) *impf.*, дойти́ (дойду́, -дёшь; дошёл, -шла́) *pf.* до+g.; *v.i.* (*extend*) простира́ться *impf.*; *n.* досяга́емость; (*of river*) плёс.
react [rɪˈækt] *v.i.* реаги́ровать *impf.*, от~, про~ *pf.* (**to** на+a.). **reaction** *n.* реа́кция. **reactionary** *adj.* реакцио́нный; *n.* реакционе́р, ~ка. **reactive** *adj.* реаги́рующий; (*tech.*) реакти́вный. **reactor** *n.* реа́ктор.
read [riːd] *v.t.* чита́ть *impf.*, про~, проче́сть (-чту́, -чтёшь; -чёл, -чла́) *pf.*; (*piece of music*) разбира́ть *impf.*, разобра́ть (разберу́, -рёшь; разобра́л, -а́, -о) *pf.*; (*of meter etc.*) пока́зывать *impf.*, показа́ть (-а́жет) *pf.*; (~ *a meter etc.*) снима́ть *impf.*, снять (сниму́, -мешь; снял, -а́, -о) *pf.* показа́ния+g.; (*univ.*) изуча́ть *impf.*; (*interpret*) толкова́ть *impf.*; *v.i.* чита́ться *impf.* **readable** *adj.* интере́сный, хорошо́ напи́санный (-ан); (*legible*) разбо́рчивый. **reader** *n.* чита́тель *m.*, ~ница; (*publisher's* ~) реце́нзе́нт; (*printer's* ~) корре́ктор (*pl.* -ы & -а́); (*univ.*) ста́рший преподава́тель *m.*; (*book*) хрестома́тия.
readily [ˈrɛdɪlɪ] *adv.* (*willingly*) охо́тно; (*easily*) легко́. **readiness** *n.* гото́вность.
reading [ˈriːdɪŋ] *n.* чте́ние; (*erudition*) начи́танность; (*variant*) вариа́нт; (*interpretation*) толкова́ние. **reading-lamp** *n.* насто́льная ла́мпа. **reading-matter** *n.* литерату́ра. **reading-room** *n.* чита́льня (*g.pl.* -лен), чита́льный зал.
ready [ˈrɛdɪ] *adj.* гото́вый (**for** к+d., на+a.); ~ **money** нали́чные де́ньги (-нег, -ньга́м) *pl.*; ~ **reckoner** арифмети́ческие табли́цы *f.pl.* **ready-made** *adj.* гото́вый.
reagent [riːˈeɪdʒ(ə)nt] *n.* реакти́в.
real [riːl] *adj.* настоя́щий, действи́тельный, реа́льный; ~ **estate** недви́жимость. **realism** [ˈriːəˌlɪz(ə)m] *n.* реали́зм. **realist** *n.* реали́ст. **rea'listic** *adj.* реалисти́чный, -и́ческий. **reality** *n.* действи́тельность; **in** ~ действи́тельно. **realization** [ˌriːəlaɪˈzeɪʃ(ə)n] *n.* (*of plan etc.*) осуществле́ние; (*of assets*) реализа́ция; (*understanding*) осозна́ние. **'realize** *v.t.* (*plan etc.*) осуществля́ть *impf.*, осуществи́ть *pf.*; (*assets*) реализова́ть *impf.* & *pf.*; (*apprehend*) осознава́ть (-наю́, -наёшь) *impf.*, осозна́ть *pf.* **really** [ˈrɪəlɪ] *adv.* действи́тельно, в са́мом де́ле.
realm [rɛlm] *n.* (*kingdom*) короле́вство; (*sphere*) о́бласть (*pl.* -ти, -те́й).
ream[1] [riːm] *n.* стопа́ (*pl.* -пы).
ream[2] [riːm] *v.t.* развёртывать *impf.*, разверну́ть *pf.*
reap [riːp] *v.t.* жать (жну, жнёшь) *impf.*,

сжать (сожну́, -нёшь) *pf.*; (*fig.*) пожина́ть *impf.*, пожа́ть (-жну́, -жнёшь) *pf.* **reaper** *n.* (*person*) жнец (-а́), жни́ца; (*machine*) жа́тка. **reaping-hook** *n.* серп (-а́).
rear[1] [rɪə(r)] *v.t.* (*lift*) поднима́ть *impf.*, подня́ть (-ниму́, -ни́мешь; по́днял, -а́, -о) *pf.*; (*children*) воспи́тывать *impf.*, воспита́ть *pf.*; *v.i.* (*of horse*) станови́ться (-ится) *impf.*, стать (-а́нет) *pf.* на дыбы́.
rear[2] [rɪə(r)] *n.* тыл (*loc.* -у́; *pl.* -ы́); **bring up the** ~ замыка́ть *impf.*, замкну́ть *pf.* ше́ствие; *adj.* за́дний; (*also mil.*) ты́льный; (*mil.*) тылово́й; ~ **admiral** контр-адмира́л. **rearguard** *n.* арьерга́рд; ~ **action** арьерга́рдный бой (*pl.* бои́). **rear-light** *n.* (*of car*) за́дний фона́рь (-ря́) *m.*
rearm [riːˈɑːm] *v.t.* & *i.* перевооружа́ть(ся) *impf.*, перевооружи́ть(ся) *pf.* **rearmament** *n.* перевооруже́ние.
rear-view [ˈrɪəvjuː] *adj.*: ~ **mirror** зе́ркало (*pl.* -ла́) за́дней обзо́рности. **rearwards** *adv.* наза́д, в тыл.
reason [ˈriːz(ə)n] *n.* (*cause*) причи́на, основа́ние; (*intellect*) ра́зум, рассу́док (-дка); **it stands to** ~ разуме́ется; **not without** ~ не без основа́ния; *v.t.* (*discuss*) обсужда́ть *impf.*, обсуди́ть (-ужу́, -у́дишь) *pf.*; *v.i.* рассужда́ть *impf.*; ~ **with** (*person*) угова́ривать *impf.*+a. **reasonable** *adj.* (*sensible*) разу́мный; (*well-founded*) основа́тельный; (*inexpensive*) недорого́й (недоро́г, -а́, -о).
reassurance [ˌriːəˈʃʊərəns] *n.* успока́ивание. **reassure** *v.t.* успока́ивать *impf.*, успоко́ить *pf.*
rebate [ˈriːbeɪt] *n.* ски́дка.
rebel [ˈreb(ə)l] *n.* повста́нец (-нца), бунтовщи́к (-а́); *adj.* повста́нческий; *v.i.* бунтова́ть *impf.*, взбунтова́ться *pf.* **rebellion** [rɪˈbeljən] *n.* восста́ние, бунт. **re'bellious** *adj.* мяте́жный, повста́нческий.
rebirth [riːˈbɜːθ, ˈriː-] *n.* возрожде́ние.
rebound [rɪˈbaʊnd] *v.i.* отска́кивать *impf.*, отскочи́ть (-чу́, -чишь) *pf.*; *n.* рикоше́т, отско́к.
rebuff [rɪˈbʌf] *n.* отпо́р; *v.t.* дава́ть (даю́, даёшь) *impf.*, дать (дам, дашь, даст, дади́м; дал, -а́, да́ло, -и) *pf.*+d. отпо́р.
rebuke [rɪˈbjuːk] *v.t.* упрека́ть *impf.*, упрекну́ть *pf.*; *n.* упрёк.
rebut [rɪˈbʌt] *v.t.* (*refute*) опроверга́ть *impf.*, опрове́ргнуть (-г(нул), -гла) *pf.* **rebuttal** *n.* опроверже́ние.
recalcitrant [rɪˈkælsɪtrənt] *adj.* непоко́рный.
recall [rɪˈkɔːl, ˈriːkɔl] *v.t.* (*summon*) призыва́ть *impf.*, призва́ть (призову́, -вёшь; призва́л, -а́, -о) *pf.* обра́тно; (*an official*) отзыва́ть *impf.*, отозва́ть (отзову́, -вёшь; отозва́л, -а́, -о) *pf.*; (*remember*) вспомина́ть *impf.*, вспо́мнить *pf.*; (*remind*) напомина́ть *impf.*, напо́мнить *pf.*; (~ *to life*) возвраща́ть *impf.*, верну́ть *pf.* к жи́зни; *n.* призы́в верну́ться; о́тзыв.
recant [rɪˈkænt] *v.t.* & *i.* отрека́ться *impf.*,

отре́чься (-еку́сь, -ечёшься; -ёкся, -екла́сь) *pf.* (от+*g.*). **recan'tation** *n.* отрече́ние

recapitulate [,ri:kə'pɪtjuˌleɪt] *v.t.* резюми́ровать *impf. & pf.* **recapitu'lation** *n.* резюме́ *nt.indecl.*

recast [ri:'kɑːst] *v.t.* перераба́тывать *impf.*, перерабо́тать *pf.*; переде́лывать *impf.*, переде́лать *pf.*

recede [rɪ'siːd] *v.i.* отходи́ть (-ожу́, -о́дишь) *impf.*, отойти́ (отойду́, -дёшь; отошёл, -шла́) *pf.*; отступа́ть *impf.*, отступи́ть (-плю́, -пишь) *pf.*

receipt [rɪ'siːt] *n.* (*receiving*) получе́ние; *pl.* (*amount*) прихо́д; (*written* ~) распи́ска, квита́нция; *v.t.* распи́сываться *impf.*, расписа́ться (-ишу́сь, -и́шешься) *pf.* на+*p.* **receive** *v.t.* (*accept, admit, entertain*) принима́ть *impf.*, приня́ть (приму́, -мешь; при́нял, -а́, -о) *pf.*; (*acquire, be given, be sent*) получа́ть *impf.*, получи́ть (-чу́, -чишь) *pf.*; (*stolen goods*) укрыва́ть *impf.*, укры́ть (-ро́ю, -ро́ешь) *pf.* **receiver** *n.* (*official* ~) управля́ющий *sb.* иму́ществом (банкро́та); (*of stolen goods*) укрыва́тель *m.* кра́деного; (*radio, television*) приёмник; (*telephone*) тру́бка.

recension [rɪ'senʃ(ə)n] *n.* извод.

recent ['riːs(ə)nt] *adj.* неда́вний; (*new*) но́вый (нов, -á, -о). **recently** *adv.* неда́вно.

receptacle [rɪ'septək(ə)l] *n.* вмести́лище. **reception** *n.* приём; ~ **room** приёмная *sb.* **receptionist** *n.* секрета́рь (-ря́) *m.*, -рша, в приёмной. **receptive** *adj.* восприи́мчивый.

recess [rɪ'ses, 'riːses] *n.* переры́в в рабо́те; (*parl.*) кани́кулы (-л) *pl.*; (*niche*) ни́ша; *pl.* (*of the heart*) тайники́ *m.pl.* **re'cession** *n.* спад.

recidivist [rɪ'sɪdɪvɪst] *n.* рецидиви́ст.

recipe ['resɪpɪ] *n.* реце́пт.

recipient [rɪ'sɪpɪənt] *n.* получа́тель *m.*, ~ница.

reciprocal [rɪ'sɪprək(ə)l] *adj.* взаи́мный; (*corresponding*) соотве́тственный; *n.* (*math.*) обра́тная величина́ (*pl.* -ны). **reciprocate** *v.t.* отвеча́ть *impf.* (взаи́мностью) на+*a.* **reciprocating** *adj.* (*motion*) возвра́тнопоступа́тельный; (*engine*) поршнево́й. **reciprocity** [,resɪ'prɒsɪtɪ] *n.* взаи́мность.

recital [rɪ'saɪt(ə)l] *n.* (*account*) изложе́ние, подро́бное перечисле́ние; (*concert*) (со́льный) конце́рт. **recitation** [,resɪ'teɪʃ(ə)n] *n.* публи́чное чте́ние. **recitative** [,resɪtə'tiːv] *n.* речитати́в. **recite** *v.t.* деклами́ровать *impf.*, про~ *pf.*; чита́ть *impf.*, про~ *pf.* вслух; (*enumerate*) перечисля́ть *impf.*, перечи́слить *pf.*

reckless ['reklɪs] *adj.* (*rash*) опроме́тчивый; (*careless*) неосторо́жный.

reckon ['rekən] *v.t.* подсчи́тывать *impf.*, подсчита́ть *pf.*; (*also regard as*) счита́ть *impf.*, счесть (сочту́, -тёшь; счёл, -сочла́) *pf.* (+*i.*, за+*a.*); *v.i.*: ~ **with** счита́ться *impf.* с+*i.* **reckoning** *n.* счёт, расчёт; **day of** ~ час распла́ты.

reclaim [rɪ'kleɪm] *v.t.* (*reform*) исправля́ть

impf., испра́вить *pf.*; (*land*) осва́ивать *impf.*, осво́ить *pf.*

recline [rɪ'klaɪn] *v.i.* отки́дываться *impf.*, отки́нуться *pf.*; полулежа́ть (-жу́, -жи́шь) *impf.*

recluse [rɪ'kluːs] *n.* затво́рник, -ица.

recognition [,rekəg'nɪʃ(ə)n] *n.* узнава́ние; (*acknowledgement*) призна́ние. **recognize** ['rekəgˌnaɪz] *v.t.* (*know again*) узнава́ть (-наю́, -наёшь) *impf.*, узна́ть *pf.*; (*acknowledge*) признава́ть (-наю́, -наёшь) *impf.*, призна́ть *pf.*

recoil ['riːkɔɪl] *v.i.* отпря́дывать *impf.*, отпря́нуть *pf.*; отша́тываться *impf.*, отшатну́ться *pf.* (**from** от+*g.*); (*of gun*) отдава́ть (-даёт) *impf.*, отда́ть (-а́ст, -аду́т; о́тдал, -а́, -о) *pf.*; *n.* отско́к; отда́ча.

recollect [,rekə'lekt] *v.t.* вспомина́ть *impf.*, вспо́мнить *pf.* **recollection** *n.* воспомина́ние.

recommend [,rekə'mend] *v.t.* рекомендова́ть *impf. & pf.*; (*for prize etc.*) представля́ть *impf.*, предста́вить *pf.* (**for** к+*d.*). **recommen'dation** *n.* рекоменда́ция; представле́ние.

recompense ['rekəmˌpens] *n.* вознагражде́ние; *v.t.* вознагражда́ть *impf.*, вознагради́ть *pf.*

reconcile ['rekənˌsaɪl] *v.t.* примиря́ть *impf.*, примири́ть *pf.*; ~ **o.s.** примиря́ться *impf.*, примири́ться *pf.* (**to** c+*i.*). **reconciliation** [,rekənˌsɪlɪ'eɪʃ(ə)n] *n.* примире́ние.

recondition [,riːkən'dɪʃ(ə)n] *v.t.* приводи́ть (-ожу́, -о́дишь) *impf.*, привести́ (-еду́, -едёшь; -ёл, -ела́) *pf.* в испра́вное состоя́ние.

reconnaissance [rɪ'kɒnɪs(ə)ns] *n.* разве́дка. **reconnoitre** [,rekə'nɔɪtə(r)] *v.t.* разве́дывать *impf.*, разве́дать *pf.*

reconstruct [,riːkən'strʌkt] *v.t.* перестра́ивать *impf.*, перестро́ить *pf.*; реконструи́ровать *impf. & pf.*; воссоздава́ть (-даю́, -даёшь) *impf.* воссозда́ть (-а́м, -а́шь, -а́ст, -ади́м; -а́л, -ала́, -о) *pf.* **reconstruction** *n.* перестро́йка; реконстру́кция; воссозда́ние.

record [rɪ'kɔːd; 'rekɔːd] *v.t.* запи́сывать *impf.*, записа́ть (-ишу́, -и́шешь) *pf.*; *n.* за́пись; (*minutes*) протоко́л; (*gramophone* ~) грампласти́нка; (*sport etc.*) реко́рд; *pl.* архи́в; **off the** ~ неофициа́льно; *adj.* реко́рдный. **record-breaker** *n.* рекордсме́н, ~ка. **re'corder** *n.* (*person who records*) регистра́тор; (*judge*) рико́рдер; (*tech.*) регистри́рующий, самопи́шущий, прибо́р; (*flute*) блок-фле́йта. **record-holder** *n.* рекордсме́н, ~ка. **re'cording** *n.* за́пись; (*sound* ~) звукоза́пись. **record-player** *n.* прои́грыватель *m.*

recount[1] [rɪ'kaʊnt] *v.t.* (*narrate*) переска́зывать *impf.*, пересказа́ть (-ажу́, -а́жешь) *pf.*

re-count[2] [riː'kaʊnt] *v.t.* (*count again*) пересчи́тывать *impf.*, пересчита́ть *pf.*; *n.* пересчёт.

recoup [rɪ'kuːp] *v.t.* возмеща́ть *impf.*, возмести́ть *pf.* (*person* +*d.*; *loss etc.* +*a.*). **re-coupment** *n.* возмеще́ние.

recourse [rɪ'kɔːs] *n.*: have ~ to прибега́ть *impf.*, прибе́гнуть (-г(нул), -гла) *pf.* к по́мощи+*g.*

recover [rɪ'kʌvə(r)] *v.t.* (*regain possession*) получа́ть *impf.*, получи́ть (-чу́, -чишь) *pf.* обра́тно; (*debt etc.*) взы́скивать *impf.*, взыска́ть (-ыщу́, -ы́щешь) *pf.* (from с+*g.*); *v.i.* (~ *health*) поправля́ться *impf.*, попра́виться *pf.* (from по́сле+*g.*). **recovery** *n.* получе́ние обра́тно; выздоровле́ние.

recreate [,riːkrɪ'eɪt] *v.t.* вновь создава́ть (-даю́, -даёшь) *impf.*, созда́ть (-а́м, -а́шь, -а́ст, -ади́м; со́здал, -а́, -о) *pf.*

recreation [,rekrɪ'eɪʃ(ə)n] *n.* развлече́ние, о́тдых.

recrimination [rɪ,krɪmɪ'neɪʃ(ə)n] *n.* взаи́мное обвине́ние.

recruit [rɪ'kruːt] *n.* новобра́нец (-нца); *v.t.* вербова́ть *impf.*, за~ *pf.* **recruitment** *n.* вербо́вка.

rectangle ['rek,tæŋg(ə)l] *n.* прямоуго́льник. **rec'tangular** *adj.* прямоуго́льный.

rectification [,rektɪfɪ'keɪʃ(ə)n] *n.* исправле́ние; (*chem.*) ректифика́ция; (*elec.*) выпрямле́ние. **rectify** ['rektɪ,faɪ] *v.t.* исправля́ть *impf.*, испра́вить *pf.*; ректифици́ровать *impf.* & *pf.*; выпрямля́ть *impf.*, вы́прямить *pf.*

rectilinear [,rektɪ'lɪnɪə(r)] *adj.* прямолине́йный.

rectitude ['rektɪ,tjuːd] *n.* че́стность.

recto ['rektəʊ] *n.* нечётная пра́вая страни́ца; (*of folio*) лицева́я сторона́ (*a.* -ону; *pl.* -оны, -о́н, -она́м).

rector ['rektə(r)] *n.* (*priest*) прихо́дский свяще́нник; (*univ. etc.*) ре́ктор. **rectorship** *n.* ре́кторство. **rectory** *n.* дом (*pl.* -а́) прихо́дского свяще́нника.

rectum ['rektəm] *n.* пряма́я кишка́ (*g.pl.* -шо́к).

recumbent [rɪ'kʌmbənt] *adj.* лежа́чий.

recuperate [rɪ'kuːpə,reɪt] *v.i.* восстана́вливать *impf.*, восстанови́ть (-влю́, -вишь) *pf.* своё здоро́вье. **recupe'ration** *n.* восстановле́ние здоро́вья.

recur [rɪ'kɜː(r)] *v.i.* повторя́ться *impf.*, повтори́ться *pf.*; ~ring decimal периоди́ческая дробь (*pl.* -би, -бе́й). **recurrence** [rɪ'kʌrəns] *n.* повторе́ние. **recurrent** *adj.* повторя́ющийся.

recycle [riː'saɪk(ə)l] *v.t.* рециркули́ровать *impf.* & *pf.*; ~d paper бума́га из ути́ля. **recycling** *n.* повто́рное испо́льзование, перерабо́тка.

red [red] *adj.* (*in colour; fig., pol.*) кра́сный (-сен, -сна́, -сно); (*of hair*) ры́жий (рыж, -а́, -е); *n.* (*colour*) кра́сный цвет; (*fig., pol.*) кра́сный *sb.*; in the ~ в долгу́; ~ admiral адмира́л; ~ cabbage краснокоча́нная капу́ста; ~ deer благоро́дный оле́нь *m.*; ~ herring ло́жный след (*pl.* -ы́); draw a ~ herring across the track сбить (собью́, -ьёшь) *pf.* с то́лку; R~ Indian инде́ец (-е́йца), индиа́нка; ~ lead свинцо́вый су́рик; ~ light кра́сный фона́рь (-ря́)

m.; see the ~ light предчу́вствовать *impf.* приближе́ние опа́сности; ~ pepper стручко́вый пе́рец (-рца); ~ tape волоки́та. **red-blooded** *adj.* энерги́чный. **redbreast** *n.* мали́новка. **redcurrant** *n.* кра́сная сморо́дина (*also collect.*). **redden** *v.t.* окра́шивать *impf.*, окра́сить *pf.* в кра́сный цвет; *v.i.* красне́ть *impf.*, по~ *pf.* **reddish** *adj.* краснова́тый; (*hair*) рыжева́тый.

redeem [rɪ'diːm] *v.t.* (*buy back*) выкупа́ть *impf.*, вы́купить *pf.*; (*from sin*) искупа́ть *impf.*, искупи́ть (-плю́, -пишь) *pf.* **redeemer** *n.* искупи́тель *m.* **redemption** [rɪ'dempʃ(ə)n] *n.* вы́куп; искупле́ние.

red-handed [,red'hændɪd] *adj.* с поли́чным. **red-hot** *adj.* раскалённый (-ён, -ена́) докрасна́.

redolent ['redələnt] *adj.*: ~ of па́хнущий+*i.*; be ~ of па́хнуть (-х(нул), -хла) *impf.*+*i.*

redouble [riː'dʌb(ə)l] *v.t.* удва́ивать *impf.*, удво́ить *pf.*

redoubt [rɪ'daʊt] *n.* реду́т.

redoubtable [rɪ'daʊtəb(ə)l] *adj.* гро́зный (-зен, -зна́, -зно).

redound [rɪ'daʊnd] *v.i.* спосо́бствовать *impf.*, по~ *pf.* (to +*d.*); ~ to s.o.'s credit де́лать *impf.*, с~ *pf.* честь+*d.*

redress [rɪ'dres] *v.t.* исправля́ть *impf.*, испра́вить *pf.*; ~ the balance восстана́вливать *impf.*, восстанови́ть (-влю́, -вишь) *pf.* равнове́сие; *n.* возмеще́ние.

redskin *n.* красноко́жий *sb.*

reduce [rɪ'djuːs] *v.t.* (*decrease*) уменьша́ть *impf.*, уме́ньшить *pf.*; (*lower*) снижа́ть *impf.*, сни́зить *pf.*; (*shorten*) сокраща́ть *impf.*, сократи́ть (-ащу́, -ати́шь) *pf.*; (*bring to*) приводи́ть (-ожу́, -о́дишь) *impf.*, привести́ (-еду́, -едёшь; ёл, -ела́) *pf.* (to в+*a.*); *v.i.* худе́ть *impf.*, по~ *pf.* **reduction** [rɪ'dʌkʃ(ə)n] *n.* уменьше́ние, сниже́ние, сокраще́ние; (*amount of* ~) ски́дка.

redundancy [rɪ'dʌnd(ə)nsɪ] *n.* (*excess of workers*) изли́шек (-шка) рабо́чей си́лы; (*dismissal*) увольне́ние (рабо́чих, слу́жащих). **redundant** *adj.* (*excessive*) изли́шний; (*dismissed*) уво́ленный (-ен) (по сокраще́нию шта́тов).

reduplicate [rɪ'djuːplɪ,keɪt] *v.t.* удва́ивать *impf.*, удво́ить *pf.* **redupli'cation** *n.* удвое́ние.

redwing ['redwɪŋ] *n.* белобро́вик. **redwood** *n.* секво́йя.

reed [riːd] *n.* (*plant*) тростни́к (-а́), камы́ш (-а́); (*in musical instrument*) язычо́к (-чка́); (*mus.*) язычко́вый инструме́нт; a broken ~ ненадёжная опо́ра; *attr.* тростнико́вый, камышо́вый; (*mus.*) язычко́вый. **reed-pipe** *n.* свире́ль. **reedy** ['riːdɪ] *adj.* (*slender*) то́нкий (-нок, -нка́, -нко, то́нки́); (*voice*) пронзи́тельный.

reef [riːf] *n.* (*of sail; ridge*) риф; *v.abs.* брать (беру́, -рёшь; брал, -а́, -о) *impf.*, взять (возьму́, -мёшь; взял, -а́, -о) *pf.* ри́фы.

reefer *n.* (*jacket*) бушла́т; (*cigarette*) сигаре́та с марихуа́ной. **reef-knot** *n.* ри́фовый у́зел (узла́).

reek [riːk] *n.* вонь, дурно́й за́пах; *v.i.*: ~ (of) воня́ть *impf.* (+*i.*).

reel[1] [riːl] *n.* кату́шка; (*of film*) руло́н; (*straight*) **off the** ~ (*fig.*) сра́зу, без переры́ва; *v.t.* (*on to* ~) нама́тывать *impf.*, намота́ть *pf.* на кату́шку; ~ **off** разма́тывать *impf.*, размота́ть *pf.*; (*story etc.*) отбараба́нить *pf.*

reel[2] [riːl] *v.i.* (*be dizzy*) кружи́ться (-и́тся) *impf.*, за~ *pf.*; (*stagger*) поша́тываться *impf.*, пошатну́ться *pf.*

reel[3] [riːl] *n.* (*dance*) рил.

refectory [rɪ'fektərɪ, 'refɪktərɪ] *n.* (*in monastery*) трапе́зная *sb.*; (*in college*) столо́вая *sb.*; ~ **table** дли́нный у́зкий обе́денный стол (-а́).

refer [rɪ'fɜː(r)] *v.t.* (*direct*) отсыла́ть *impf.*, отосла́ть (отошлю́, -лёшь) *pf.* (**to** k+*d.*); *v.i.*: ~ **to** (*cite*) ссыла́ться *impf.*, сосла́ться (сошлю́сь, -лёшься) *pf.* на+*a.*; (*mention*) упомина́ть *impf.*, упомяну́ть (-ну́, -нешь) *pf.*+*a.*; ~ **to drawer** обрати́тесь к чекода́телю. **referee** [,refə'riː] *n.* судья́ (*pl.* -дьи, -де́й, -дьям) *m.*; *v.t.* суди́ть (сужу́, су́дишь) *impf.* '**reference** *n.* (*to book etc.*) ссы́лка; (*mention*) упомина́ние; (*testimonial*) рекоменда́ция; ~ **book** спра́вочник; ~ **library** спра́вочная библиоте́ка (без вы́дачи книг на́ дом). **refe'rendum** *n.* рефере́ндум.

refine [rɪ'faɪn] *v.t.* очища́ть *impf.*, очи́стить *pf.*; рафини́ровать *impf.* & *pf.* **refined** *adj.* (*in style etc.*) утончённый (-ён, -ённа); (*in manners*) культу́рный; ~ **sugar** рафина́д. **refinery** *n.* (*oil* ~) нефтеочисти́тельный заво́д; (*sugar-*~) рафина́дный заво́д.

refit ['riːfɪt; riː'fɪt] *n.* переоборудование; *v.t.* переобору́довать *impf.* & *pf.*

reflect [rɪ'flekt] *v.t.* отража́ть *impf.*, отрази́ть *pf.*; *v.i.* (*meditate*) размышля́ть *impf.*, размы́слить *pf.* (**on** o+*p.*). **reflection** *n.* отраже́ние; размышле́ние; **on** ~ поду́мав. **reflector** *n.* рефле́ктор. **reflex** ['riːfleks] *n.* рефле́кс; *adj.* рефле́кторный; ~ **camera** зерка́льный фотоаппара́т. **reflexive** *adj.* (*gram.*) возвра́тный.

reform [rɪ'fɔːm] *v.t.* реформи́ровать *impf.* & *pf.*; *v.t.* & *i.* (*of people*) исправля́ть(ся) *impf.*, испра́вить(ся) *pf.*; *n.* рефо́рма, исправле́ние. **reformation** [,refə'meɪʃ(ə)n] *n.* рефо́рма; **the R~** Реформа́ция. **reformatory** *adj.* исправи́тельный; *n.* исправи́тельное заведе́ние.

refract [rɪ'frækt] *v.t.* преломля́ть *impf.*, преломи́ть (-ит) *pf.* **refraction** *n.* рефра́кция, преломле́ние. **refractive** *adj.* преломля́ющий. **refractory** *adj.* (*person*) упря́мый, непоко́рный; (*substance*) тугопла́вкий.

refrain[1] [rɪ'freɪn] *n.* припе́в.

refrain[2] [rɪ'freɪn] *v.i.* уде́рживаться *impf.*, удержа́ться (-жу́сь, -жишься) *pf.* (**from** от+*g.*).

refresh [rɪ'freʃ] *v.t.* освежа́ть *impf.*, освежи́ть *pf.*; ~ **o.s.** подкрепля́ться *impf.*, подкрепи́ться *pf.* **refreshment** *n.* (*drink*) освежа́ющий напи́ток (-тка); *pl.* заку́ска; ~ **room** буфе́т.

refrigerate [rɪ'frɪdʒəreɪt] *v.t.* охлажда́ть *impf.*, охлади́ть *pf.* **refrige'ration** *n.* охлажде́ние. **refrigerator** *n.* холоди́льник.

refuge ['refjuːdʒ] *n.* убе́жище, прибе́жище; **take** ~ находи́ть (-ожу́, -о́дишь) *impf.*, найти́ (найду́, -дёшь; нашёл, -шла́) *pf.* убе́жище. **refu'gee** *n.* бе́женец (-нца), -нка.

refund [rɪ'fʌnd; 'riːfʌnd] *v.t.* возвраща́ть *impf.*, возврати́ть (-ащу́, -ати́шь) *pf.*; (*expenses*) возмеща́ть *impf.*, возмести́ть *pf.*; *n.* возмеще́ние.

refusal [rɪ'fjuːz(ə)l] *n.* отка́з; **first** ~ пра́во пе́рвого вы́бора. **refuse**[1] *v.t.* отка́зывать *impf.*, отказа́ть (-ажу́, -а́жешь) *pf.*

refuse[2] ['refjuːs] *n.* отбро́сы (-сов) *pl.*, му́сор.

refusenik [rɪ'fjuːznɪk] *n.* отка́зник, -ица.

refutation [,refjuː'teɪʃ(ə)n] *n.* опроверже́ние.

refute [rɪ'fjuːt] *v.t.* опроверга́ть *impf.*, опрове́ргнуть (-г(нул), -гла) *pf.*

regain [rɪ'geɪn] *v.t.* (*recover*) сно́ва приобрета́ть *impf.*, приобрести́ (-ету́, -етёшь; -ёл, -ела́) *pf.*; (*reach*) сно́ва достига́ть *impf.*, дости́гнуть & дости́чь (-и́гну, -и́гнешь; -и́г) *pf.*

regal ['riːg(ə)l] *adj.* короле́вский.

regale [rɪ'geɪl] *v.t.* угоща́ть *impf.*, угости́ть *pf.* (**with** +*i.*).

regalia [rɪ'geɪlɪə] *n.* рега́лии *f.pl.*

regard [rɪ'gɑːd] *v.t.* смотре́ть (-рю, -ришь) *impf.*, по~ *pf.* на+*a.*; (*take into account*) счита́ться *impf.* c+*i.*; ~ **as** счита́ть *impf.*+*i.*, за+*i.*; **as** ~**s** что каса́ется+*g.*; *n.* (*esteem*) уваже́ние; (*attention*) внима́ние; *pl.* покло́н, приве́т; **with** ~ **to** относи́тельно+*g.*; что каса́ется+*g.* **regarding** *prep.* относи́тельно+*g.*; что каса́ется+*g.* **regardless** *adv.* не обраща́я внима́ния; ~ **of** не счита́ясь c+*i.*

regatta [rɪ'gætə] *n.* рега́та.

regency ['riːdʒ(ə)nsɪ] *n.* ре́гентство.

regenerate [rɪ'dʒenəreɪt; rɪ'dʒenərət] *v.t.* перерожда́ть *impf.*, переродить *pf.*; *adj.* перерождённый (-ён, -ена́). **regene'ration** *n.* перерожде́ние.

regent ['riːdʒ(ə)nt] *n.* ре́гент.

reggae ['regeɪ] *n.* (*mus.*) ре́гги *m. indecl.*

regicide ['redʒɪsaɪd] *n.* (*action*) цареуби́йство; (*person*) цареуби́йца *c.g.*

régime [reɪ'ʒiːm] *n.* режи́м. **regimen** ['redʒɪ,men] *n.* (*med.*) режи́м; (*gram.*) управле́ние.

regiment ['redʒɪmənt] *n.* полк (-а́, *loc.* -ý). **regimental** [,redʒɪ'ment(ə)l] *adj.* полково́й. **regimen'tation** *n.* регламента́ция.

region ['riːdʒ(ə)n] *n.* о́бласть (*pl.* -ти, -те́й). **regional** *adj.* областно́й, региона́льный, ме́стный.

register ['redʒɪstə(r)] *n.* рее́стр, кни́га за́писей; (*also mus.*) реги́стр; *v.t.* регистри́ровать *impf.*, за~ *pf.*; (*express*) выража́ть *impf.*, вы́разить *pf.*; (*a letter*) отправля́ть *impf.*, отпра́вить *pf.* заказны́м. **registered** *adj.* (*letter*) заказно́й. **registrar** [ˌredʒɪs-ˈtrɑː(r), ˈredʒ-] *n.* регистра́тор. **regi'stration** *n.* регистра́ция, за́пись; ~ **mark** номерно́й знак. **registry** *n.* регистрату́ра; (~ *office*) отде́л за́писей а́ктов гражда́нского состоя́ния, загс.

regression [rɪˈgreʃ(ə)n] *n.* регре́сс. **regressive** *adj.* регресси́вный.

regret [rɪˈgret] *v.t.* сожале́ть *impf.* о+*p.*; **I** ~ **to say** к сожале́нию, до́лжен сказа́ть; ~ *n.* сожале́ние. **regretful** *adj.* по́лный (-лон, -лна́, -лно́) **regrettable** *adj.* приско́рбный.

regular [ˈregjʊlə(r)] *adj.* регуля́рный; (*also gram.*) пра́вильный; (*recurring*) очередно́й; (*of officer*) ка́дровый; *n.* (*coll.*) завсегда́тай. **regularity** [ˌregjʊˈlærɪtɪ] *n.* регуля́рность. **regularize** *v.t.* упоря́дочивать *impf.*, упоря́дочить *pf.* **regulate** *v.t.* регули́ровать *impf.*, y~ *pf.* **regu'lation** *n.* регули́рование; *pl.* пра́вила *nt.pl.*, уста́в; *adj.* устано́вленный.

rehabilitate [ˌriːhəˈbɪlɪteɪt] *v.t.* реабилити́ровать *impf. & pf.* **rehabili'tation** *n.* реабилита́ция.

rehash [riːˈhæʃ, ˈriːhæʃ] *v.t.* переде́лывать *impf.*, переде́лать *pf.*; *n.* переде́лка.

rehearsal [rɪˈhɜːs(ə)l] *n.* репети́ция. **rehearse** *v.t.* репети́ровать *impf.*, от~ *pf.*

reign [reɪn] *n.* ца́рствование; *v.i.* ца́рствовать *impf.*; (*prevail*) цари́ть *impf.*

reimburse [ˌriːɪmˈbɜːs] *v.t.* возмеща́ть *impf.*, возмести́ть *pf.* (+*d. of person*). **reimbursement** *n.* возмеще́ние.

rein [reɪn] *n.* по́вод (*loc.* -ý; *pl.* поводья, -ьев); *pl.* во́жжи (-же́й) *pf.*

reincarnation [ˌriːɪnkɑːˈneɪʃ(ə)n] *n.* перевоплоще́ние.

reindeer [ˈreɪndɪə(r)] *n.* се́верный оле́нь *m.*; ~ **moss** оле́ний мох (м(о́)ха, *loc.* мху & м(о́)хе).

reinforce [ˌriːɪnˈfɔːs] *v.t.* подкрепля́ть *impf.*, подкрепи́ть (-плю́, -пишь) *pf.*; усили́вать *impf.*, уси́лить *pf.*; ~**d concrete** железобето́н. **reinforcement** *n.* (*also pl.*) подкрепле́ние, усиле́ние.

reinstate [ˌriːɪnˈsteɪt] *v.t.* восстана́вливать *impf.*, восстанови́ть (-влю́, -вишь) *pf.* **reinstatement** *n.* восстановле́ние.

reinsurance [ˌriːɪnˈʃʊərəns] *n.* перестрахо́вка. **reinsure** *v.t.* перестрахо́вывать *impf.*, перестрахова́ть *pf.*

reiterate [riːˈɪtəˌreɪt] *v.t.* повторя́ть *impf.*, повтори́ть *pf.* **reite'ration** *n.* повторе́ние.

reject [rɪˈdʒekt] *v.t.* отверга́ть *impf.*, отве́ргнуть (-г(нул), -гла) *pf.*; (*as defective*) бракова́ть *impf.*, за~ *pf.*; *n.* брако́ванное изде́лие. **re'jection** *n.* отка́з (*of* от+*g.*); брако́вка.

rejoice [rɪˈdʒɔɪs] *v.t.* ра́довать *impf.*, об~ *pf.*; *v.i.* ра́доваться *impf.*, об~ *pf.* (**in**, **at** +*d.*). **rejoicing** *n.* ликова́ние.

rejoin [riːˈdʒɔɪn] *v.t.* (вновь) присоединя́ться

impf., присоедини́ться *pf.* к+*d.*

rejoinder [rɪˈdʒɔɪndə(r)] *n.* отве́т.

rejuvenate [rɪˈdʒuːvɪˌneɪt] *v.t. & i.* омола́живать(ся) *impf.*, омолоди́ть(ся) *pf.* **rejuve'nation** *n.* омоложе́ние.

relapse [rɪˈlæps] *n.* рециди́в; *v.i.* сно́ва впада́ть *impf.*, впасть (-аду́, -адёшь; -ал) *pf.* (**into** в+*a.*); (*into illness*) сно́ва заболева́ть *impf.*, заболе́ть *pf.*

relate [rɪˈleɪt] *v.t.* (*narrate*) расска́зывать *impf.*, рассказа́ть (-ажу́, -а́жешь) *pf.*; (*establish relation*) устана́вливать *impf.*, установи́ть (-влю́, -вишь) *pf.* связь ме́жду+*i.*; *v.i.* относи́ться (-ится) *impf.* (**to** к+*d.*). **related** *adj.* ро́дственный (-ен, -енна). **relation** *n.* (*narration*) повествова́ние; (*connection etc.*) связь, отноше́ние; (*person*) ро́дственник; **in** ~ **to** относи́тельно+*g.* **relationship** *n.* родство́. **relative** [ˈrelətɪv] *adj.* относи́тельный; *n.* ро́дственник, -ица. **rela'tivity** *n.* относи́тельность; (*phys.*) тео́рия относи́тельности.

relax [rɪˈlæks] *v.t. & i.* ослабля́ть(ся) *impf.*, осла́бить(ся) *pf.*; смягча́ть(ся) *impf.*, смягчи́ть(ся) *pf.* **rela'xation** *n.* ослабле́ние, смягче́ние; (*rest*) о́тдых.

relay [ˈriːleɪ] *n.* сме́на; (*sport*) эстафе́та; (*elec.*) реле́ *nt.indecl.*; (*broadcast etc.*) трансля́ция; *v.t.* сменя́ть *impf.*, смени́ть (-ню́, -нишь) *pf.*; (*radio*) трансли́ровать *impf. & pf.*

release [rɪˈliːs] *v.t.* (*set free*) освобожда́ть *impf.*, освободи́ть *pf.*; отпуска́ть *impf.*, отпусти́ть (-ущу́, -у́стишь) *pf.*; (*film etc.*) выпуска́ть *impf.*, вы́пустить *pf.*; *n.* освобожде́ние; вы́пуск.

relegate [ˈrelɪˌgeɪt] *v.t.* переводи́ть (-ожу́, -о́дишь) *impf.*, перевести́ (-еду́, -едёшь; -ёл, -ела́) *pf.* в бо́лее ни́зкий класс, (*sport*) в ни́зшую ли́гу). **rele'gation** *n.* перево́д (в бо́лее ни́зкий класс, в ни́зшую ли́гу).

relent [rɪˈlent] *v.i.* смягча́ться *impf.*, смягчи́ться *pf.* **relentless** *adj.* неумоли́мый, непреклóнный (-нен, -нна).

relevance [ˈrelɪv(ə)ns] *n.* уме́стность. **relevant** *adj.* относя́щийся к де́лу; уме́стный.

reliable [rɪˈlaɪəb(ə)l] *adj.* надёжный. **reliance** *n.* дове́рие. **reliant** *adj.* уве́ренный (-ен, -енна).

relic [ˈrelɪk] *n.* оста́ток (-тка), рели́квия; *pl.* (*of saint*) мо́щи (-ще́й) *pf.*

relief[1] [rɪˈliːf] *n.* (*art, geol.*) релье́ф.

relief[2] [rɪˈliːf] *n.* (*alleviation*) облегче́ние; (*assistance*) по́мощь; (*in duty*) сме́на; (*raising of siege*) сня́тие оса́ды. **relieve** *v.t.* (*alleviate*) облегча́ть *impf.*, облегчи́ть *pf.*; (*help*) ока́зывать *impf.*, оказа́ть (-ажу́, -а́жешь) *pf.* по́мощь+*d.*; (*replace*) сменя́ть *impf.*, смени́ть (-ню́, -нишь) *pf.*; (*raise siege*) снима́ть *impf.*, снять (сниму́, -мешь; снял, -á, -о) *pf.* оса́ду с+*g.*

religion [rɪˈlɪdʒ(ə)n] *n.* рели́гия. **religious** *adj.* религио́зный.

relinquish [rɪ'lɪŋkwɪʃ] *v.t.* оставля́ть *impf.*, оста́вить *pf.*; (*right etc.*) отка́зываться *impf.*, отказа́ться (-ажу́сь, -а́жешься) *pf.* от+*g.*

reliquary ['relɪkwərɪ] *n.* ра́ка.

relish ['relɪʃ] *n.* (*enjoyment*) смак, наслажде́ние; (*condiment*) припра́ва; *v.t.* смакова́ть *impf.*

reluctance [rɪ'lʌkt(ə)ns] *n.* неохо́та. **reluctant** *adj.* неохо́тный; **be ~ to** не жела́ть *impf.*+*inf.*

rely [rɪ'laɪ] *v.i.* полага́ться *impf.*, положи́ться (-жу́сь, -жи́шься) *pf.* (**on** на+*a.*).

remain [rɪ'meɪn] *v.i.* остава́ться (-аю́сь, -аёшься) *impf.*, оста́ться (-а́нусь, -а́нешься) *pf.* **remainder** *n.* оста́ток (-тка); (*books*) кни́жные оста́тки *m.pl.*; *v.t.* распродава́ть (-даю́, -даёшь) *impf.*, распрода́ть (-а́м, -а́шь, -а́ст, -ади́м; распро́дал, -а́, -о) *pf.* по дешёвой цене́. **remains** *n.* оста́тки *m.pl.*; (*human ~*) оста́нки (-ков) *pl.*

remand [rɪ'mɑːnd] *v.t.* отсыла́ть *impf.*, отосла́ть (отошлю́, -лёшь) *pf.* под стра́жу; *n.* отсы́лка под стра́жу; **prisoner on ~** подсле́дственный *sb.*

remark [rɪ'mɑːk] *v.t.* замеча́ть *impf.*, заме́тить *pf.*; *n.* замеча́ние. **remarkable** *adj.* замеча́тельный.

remedial [rɪ'miːdɪəl] *adj.* лече́бный. **remedy** ['remɪdɪ] *n.* сре́дство (**for** от, про́тив+*g.*); *v.t.* исправля́ть *impf.*, испра́вить *pf.*

remember [rɪ'membə(r)] *v.t.* вспомина́ть *impf.*, вспо́мнить *pf.* о+*p.*; по́мнить *pf.* *impers.*+*d.*; (*greet*) передава́ть (-даю́, -даёшь) *impf.*, переда́ть (-а́м, -а́шь, -а́ст, -ади́м; пе́редал, -а́, -о) *pf.* приве́т от+*g.* (**to** +*d.*).

remembrance [rɪ'membrəns] *n.* па́мять; *pl.* приве́т.

remind [rɪ'maɪnd] *v.t.* напомина́ть *impf.*, напо́мнить *pf.*+*d.* (**of** +*a.*, о+*p.*). **reminder** *n.* напомина́ние.

reminiscence [ˌremɪ'nɪs(ə)ns] *n.* воспомина́ние. **reminiscent** *adj.* напомина́ющий.

remiss [rɪ'mɪs] *pred.* небре́жен (-жна). **remission** *n.* отпуще́ние. **remit** [rɪ'mɪt] *v.t.* пересыла́ть *impf.*, пересла́ть (-ешлю́, -ешлёшь) *pf.* **remittance** *n.* пересы́лка; (*money*) де́нежный перево́д.

remnant ['remnənt] *n.* оста́ток (-тка).

remonstrance [rɪ'mɒnstrəns] *n.* проте́ст. **remonstrate** ['remənˌstreɪt] *v.i.*: **~ with** увещева́ть *impf.*+*a.*

remorse [rɪ'mɔːs] *n.* угрызе́ния *nt.pl.* со́вести. **remorseful** *adj.* по́лный (-лон, -лна́, по́лно́) раска́яния. **remorseless** *adj.* беспоща́дный.

remote [rɪ'məʊt] *adj.* да́льний, отдалённый (-ён, -ённа); **~ control** дистанцио́нное управле́ние, телеуправле́ние.

removal [rɪ'muːv(ə)l] *n.* смеще́ние, устране́ние; (*change of house*) перее́зд; **~ firm** трансаге́нтство. **remove** *v.t.* смеща́ть *impf.*, смести́ть *pf.*; устраня́ть *impf.*, устрани́ть *pf.*; *v.i.* переезжа́ть *impf.*, перее́хать (-е́ду, -е́дешь) *pf.*; *n.* шаг, сте́пень (*pl.* -ни, -не́й)

(отдале́ния). **removed** *adj.* далёкий (-ёк, -ека́, -еко́); **once ~** двою́родный; **twice ~** трою́родный.

remuneration [rɪˌmjuːnə'reɪʃ(ə)n] *n.* вознагражде́ние. **re'munerative** *adj.* вы́годный.

renaissance [rɪ'neɪs(ə)ns, rə'n-, -sɑ̃s] *n.* возрожде́ние; **the R~** Ренесса́нс.

renal ['riːn(ə)l] *adj.* по́чечный.

renascence [rɪ'næs(ə)ns] *n.* возрожде́ние.

render ['rendə(r)] *v.t.* воздава́ть (-даю́, -даёшь) *impf.*, возда́ть (-а́м, -а́шь, -а́ст, -ади́м; возда́л, -а́, -о) *pf.*; (*help etc.*) ока́зывать *impf.*, оказа́ть (-ажу́, -а́жешь) *pf.*; (*role etc.*) исполня́ть *impf.*, испо́лнить *pf.*; (*transmit*) передава́ть (-даю́, -даёшь) *impf.*, переда́ть (-а́м, -а́шь, -а́ст, -ади́м; пе́редал, -а́, -о) *pf.*; (*fat*) топи́ть (-плю́, -пишь) *impf.*; (*stone*) штукату́рить *impf.*, о~, от~ *pf.* **rendering** *n.* исполне́ние; переда́ча; выта́пливание.

rendezvous ['rɒndɪˌvuː, -deɪˌvuː] *n.* (*meeting*) свида́ние, встре́ча; (*meeting-place*) ме́сто (*pl.* -та́) свида́ния, встре́чи; *v.i.* встреча́ться *impf.*, встре́титься *pf.*; собира́ться *impf.*, собра́ться (-берётся; собра́лся, -ала́сь, -а́ло́сь) *pf.*

renegade ['renɪˌgeɪd] *n.* ренега́т, ~ка.

renew [rɪ'njuː] *v.t.* (воз)обновля́ть *impf.*, (воз)обнови́ть *pf.*; (*of agreement etc.*) продлева́ть *impf.*, продли́ть *pf.* срок де́йствия+*g.* **renewable** *adj.* возобновля́емый; **~ resources** возобновля́емые ресу́рсы. **renewal** *n.* (воз)обновле́ние; продле́ние (сро́ка де́йствия).

rennet ['renɪt] *n.* сычу́жина.

renounce [rɪ'naʊns] *v.t.* отка́зываться *impf.*, отказа́ться (-ажу́сь, -а́жешься) *pf.* от+*g.*; отрека́ться *impf.*, отре́чься (-еку́сь, -ечёшься, -ёкся, -екла́сь) *pf.* от+*g.*

renovate ['renəˌveɪt] *v.t.* ремонти́ровать *impf.*, от~ *pf.*; реставри́ровать *impf.* & *pf.* **reno'vation** *n.* ремо́нт.

renown [rɪ'naʊn] *n.* изве́стность, сла́ва. **renowned** *adj.* изве́стный; **be ~ for** сла́виться *impf.*+*i.*

rent [rent] *n.* (*for premises*) аре́нда; аре́ндная, кварти́рная, пла́та; (*for land*) ре́нта; *v.t.* (*of tenant*) арендова́ть *impf.* & *pf.*; брать (беру́, -рёшь; брал, -а́, -о) *impf.*, взять (возьму́, -мёшь; взял, -а́, -о) *pf.* в аре́нду; (*of owner*) сдава́ть (сдаю́, сдаёшь) *impf.*, сдать (-ам, -ашь, -аст, -ади́м; сдал, -а́, -о) *pf.* в аре́нду.

renunciation [rɪˌnʌnsɪ'eɪʃ(ə)n] *n.* отка́з, отрече́ние (**of** от+*g.*).

rep¹ [rep], **repp** *n.* (*fabric*) репс.

rep² [rep] *n.* (*commercial traveller*) коммивояжёр.

repair¹ [rɪ'peə(r)] *v.i.* (*resort*) направля́ться *impf.*, напра́виться *pf.*

repair² [rɪ'peə(r)] *v.t.* (*restore*) ремонти́ровать *impf.*, от~ *pf.*; (*clothing etc.*) чини́ть (-ню́, -нишь) *impf.*, по~ *pf.*; (*error etc.*) исправля́ть *impf.*, испра́вить *pf.*; *n.* (*also pl.*) ремо́нт (*only sg.*), почи́нка; (*good condition*)

испра́вность; **out of** ~ в неиспра́вном
состоя́нии; *attr.* ремо́нтный; почи́ночный.
reparation [ˌrepəˈreɪʃ(ə)n] *n.* возмеще́ние; *pl.*
репара́ции *f.pl.*
repartee [ˌrepaːˈtiː] *n.* остроу́мный, нахо́дчи-
вый, отве́т.
repatriate [riːˈpætrɪˌeɪt] *v.t.* репатрии́ровать
impf. & pf. **repatri'ation** *n.* репатриа́ция.
repay [riːˈpeɪ] *v.t.* отпла́чивать *impf.*, отпла-
ти́ть (-ачу́, -а́тишь) *pf.* (*person +d.*); вознаг-
ражда́ть *impf.*, вознаградить *pf.* (*action*
за+*i.*). **repayment** *n.* отпла́та; вознаграж-
де́ние.
repeal [rɪˈpiːl] *v.t.* отменя́ть *impf.*, отмени́ть
(-ню́, -ни́шь) *pf.*; *n.* отме́на.
repeat [rɪˈpiːt] *v.t. & i.* повторя́ть(ся) *impf.*,
повтори́ть(ся) *pf.*; *n.* повторе́ние. **repeatedly** *adv.* неоднокра́тно.
repel [rɪˈpel] *v.t.* отта́лкивать *impf.*, оттолк-
ну́ть *pf.*; отража́ть *impf.*, отрази́ть *pf.*
repent [rɪˈpent] *v.i.* раска́иваться *impf.*, раска-
я́ться (-а́юсь, -а́ешься) *pf.* (**of** в+*p.*).
repentance *n.* раска́яние. **repentant** *adj.*
раска́ивающийся.
repercussion [ˌriːpəˈkʌʃ(ə)n] *n.* (*of event*)
после́дствие.
repertoire [ˈrepəˌtwaː(r)] *n.* репертуа́р. **rep-
ertory** [ˈrepətərɪ] *n.* (*store*) запа́с; (*repertoire*)
репертуа́р; ~ **company** постоя́нная тру́ппа.
repetition [ˌrepɪˈtɪʃ(ə)n] *n.* повторе́ние. **repe-
titious, repetitive** [rɪˈpetɪtɪv] *adj.* (беспре-
ста́нно) повторя́ющийся.
replace [rɪˈpleɪs] *v.t.* (*put back*) класть (-аду́,
-аде́шь; -ал) *impf.*, положи́ть (-жу́, -жишь)
pf. обра́тно (на ме́сто); (*substitute*) заме-
ня́ть *impf.*, замени́ть (-ню́, -нишь) *pf.* (**by**
+*i.*); замеща́ть *impf.*, замести́ть *pf.* **replacement** [rɪˈpleɪsmənt] *n.* заме́на, заме-
ще́ние.
replay [ˈriːpleɪ; riːˈpleɪ] *n.* (*of a game*) пере-
игро́вка; **action** ~ повто́р; *v.t.* переи́гры-
вать *impf.*, переигра́ть *pf.*
replenish [rɪˈplenɪʃ] *v.t.* пополня́ть *impf.*,
попо́лнить *pf.* **replenishment** *n.* пополне́-
ние.
replete [rɪˈpliːt] *adj.* пресы́щенный (-ен);
(*sated*) сы́тый (сыт, -а́, -о).
replica [ˈreplɪkə] *n.* то́чная ко́пия.
reply [rɪˈplaɪ] *v.t. & i.* отвеча́ть *impf.*, отве́-
тить *pf.* (**to** на+*a.*); *n.* отве́т; ~ **paid** с
опла́ченным отве́том.
report [rɪˈpɔːt] *v.t.* (*relate*) сообща́ть *impf.*,
сообщи́ть *pf.*; (*formally*) докла́дывать
impf., доложи́ть (-жу́, -жишь) *pf.*; *v.i.* (*present o.s.*) явля́ться *impf.*, яви́ться (явлю́сь,
я́вишься) *pf.*; *n.* сообще́ние; докла́д;
(*school*) та́бель *m.* успева́емости; (*sound*)
звук взры́ва, вы́стрела. **reporter** *n.* репортёр, корреспонде́нт.
repose [rɪˈpəʊz] *v.i.* (*lie*) лежа́ть (-жу́, -жи́шь)
impf.; (*rest*) отдыха́ть *impf.*, отдохну́ть *pf.*;
n. (*rest*) о́тдых; (*peace*) поко́й.
repository [rɪˈpɒzɪtərɪ] *n.* храни́лище.

repp *see* **rep**[1]
reprehensible [ˌreprɪˈhensɪb(ə)l] *adj.* предосу-
ди́тельный.
represent [ˌreprɪˈzent] *v.t.* представля́ть *impf.*;
(*portray*) изобража́ть *impf.*, изобрази́ть
pf. **represen'tation** *n.* представи́тельство,
представле́ние; изображе́ние. **repre'sent-
ative** *adj.* изобража́ющий (**of** +*a.*); (*typical*)
типи́чный; (*pol.*) представи́тельный; *n.*
представи́тель *m.*
repress [rɪˈpres] *v.t.* подавля́ть *impf.*, пода-
ви́ть (-влю́, -вишь) *pf.*; репресси́ровать
impf. & pf. **repression** *n.* подавле́ние, реп-
ре́ссия. **repressive** *adj.* репресси́вный.
reprieve [rɪˈpriːv] *v.t.* отсро́чивать *impf.*,
отсро́чить *pf.*+*d.* приведе́ние в исполне́ние
(сме́ртного) пригово́ра; *n.* отсро́чка приве-
де́ния в исполне́ние (сме́ртного) при-
гово́ра.
reprimand [ˈreprɪˌmaːnd] *n.* вы́говор; *v.t.* де́-
лать *impf.*, с~ *pf.* вы́говор+*d.*
reprint [riːˈprɪnt; ˈriːprɪnt] *v.t.* переиздава́ть
(-даю́, -даёшь) *impf.*, переизда́ть (-а́м, -а́шь,
-а́ст, -ади́м; -а́л, -ала́, -а́ло) *pf.*; перепе-
ча́тывать *impf.*, перепеча́тать *pf.*; *n.* пере-
изда́ние; перепеча́тка.
reprisal [rɪˈpraɪz(ə)l] *n.* репресса́лия.
reproach [rɪˈprəʊtʃ] *v.t.* упрека́ть *impf.*,
упрекну́ть *pf.* (**with** в+*p.*); укоря́ть *impf.*,
укори́ть *pf.* (**with** в+*p.*); *n.* упрёк, уко́р.
reproachful *adj.* укори́зненный.
reproduce [ˌriːprəˈdjuːs] *v.t.* воспроизводи́ть
(-ожу́, -о́дишь) *impf.*, воспроизвести́ (-еду́,
-еде́шь; -ёл, -ела́) *pf.* **reproduction**
[ˌriːprəˈdʌkʃ(ə)n] *n.* (*action*) воспроизведе́-
ние; (*object*) ко́пия, репроду́кция. **reproductive** *adj.* воспроизводи́тельный.
reproof [rɪˈpruːf] *n.* порица́ние. **reprove**
[rɪˈpruːv] *v.t.* порица́ть *impf.*
reptile [ˈreptaɪl] *n.* пресмыка́ющееся *sb.*
republic [rɪˈpʌblɪk] *n.* респу́блика. **republican**
adj. республика́нский; *n.* республика́нец
(-нца), -нка.
repudiate [rɪˈpjuːdɪˌeɪt] *v.t.* отка́зываться *impf.*,
отказа́ться (-ажу́сь, -а́жешься) *pf.* от+*g.*;
(*reject*) отверга́ть *impf.*, отве́ргнуть (-г(нул),
-гла) *pf.* **repudi'ation** *n.* отка́з (**of** от+*g.*).
repugnance [rɪˈpʌgnəns] *n.* отвраще́ние.
repugnant *adj.* проти́вный.
repulse [rɪˈpʌls] *v.t.* отража́ть *impf.*, отрази́ть
pf. **repulsion** *n.* отвраще́ние. **repulsive** *adj.*
отврати́тельный, проти́вный.
reputable [ˈrepjʊtəb(ə)l] *adj.* по́льзующийся
хоро́шей репута́цией. **repu'tation, repute**
[rɪˈpjuːt] *n.* репута́ция, сла́ва. **re'puted** *adj.*
предполага́емый.
request [rɪˈkwest] *n.* про́сьба; **by, on,** ~ по
про́сьбе; **in (great)** ~ в (большо́м) спро́се;
~ **stop** остано́вка по тре́бованию; *v.t.*
проси́ть (-ошу́, -о́сишь) *impf.*, по~ *pf.*+*a.*,
+*g.*, о+*p.* (*person +a.*).
requiem [ˈrekwɪˌem] *n.* ре́квием.
require [rɪˈkwaɪə(r)] *v.t.* (*demand; need*) тре́-

бовать *impf.*, по~ *pf.*+*g.*; (*need*) нужда́ться *impf.* в+*p.* **requirement** *n.* тре́бование; (*necessity*) потре́бность. **requisite** ['rekwɪzɪt] *adj.* необходи́мый; *n.* необходи́мое *sb.*, необходи́мая вещь (*pl.* -щи, -ще́й). **requi'sition** *n.* реквизи́ция *v.t.* реквизи́ровать *impf.* & *pf.*

requite [rɪ'kwaɪt] *v.t.* отпла́чивать *impf.*, отплати́ть (-ачу́, -а́тишь) *pf.* (**for** за+*a.*; **with** +*i.*).

rescind [rɪ'sɪnd] *v.t.* отменя́ть *impf.*, отмени́ть (-ню́, -нишь) *pf.*

rescue ['reskju:] *v.t.* спаса́ть *impf.*, спасти́ (-су́, -сёшь; -с, -сла́) *pf.*; *n.* спасе́ние; *attr.* спаса́тельный. **rescuer** *n.* спаси́тель *m.*

research [rɪ'sɜ:tʃ] *n.* иссле́дование (+*g.*); (*occupation*) нау́чно-иссле́довательская рабо́та; *v.i.* занима́ться *impf.*, заня́ться (займу́сь, -мёшься; заня́лся́, -ла́сь) *pf.* иссле́дованиями, нау́чно-иссле́довательской рабо́той; ~ **into** иссле́довать *impf.* & *pf.*+*a.* **researcher** *n.* иссле́дователь *m.*

resemblance [rɪ'zembləns] *n.* схо́дство. **resemble** *v.t.* походи́ть (-ожу́, -о́дишь) *impf.* на+*a.*

resent [rɪ'zent] *v.t.* (*be indignant*) негодова́ть *impf.* на+*a.*, про́тив+*g.*; (*take offence*) обижа́ться *impf.*, оби́деться (-и́жусь, -и́дишься) *pf.* на+*a.* **resentful** *adj.* оби́дчивый. **resentment** *n.* негодова́ние; оби́да.

reservation [,rezə'veɪʃ(ə)n] *n.* (*proviso etc.*) огово́рка; (*booking*) предвари́тельный зака́з; (*tract of land*) резерва́ция. **reserve** [rɪ'zɜ:v] *v.t.* (*postpone*) откла́дывать *impf.*, отложи́ть (-жу́, -жишь) *pf.*; (*keep in stock*) резерви́ровать *impf.* & *pf.*; (*book*) зара́нее зака́зывать *impf.*, заказа́ть (-ажу́, -а́жешь) *pf.*; брони́ровать *impf.*, за~ *pf.*; *n.* (*stock*; *mil.*) запа́с; (*sport*) запасно́й игро́к (-а́); (*nature* ~ *etc.*) запове́дник; (*proviso*) огово́рка; (~ *price*) ни́зшая отплатна́я цена́ (*a.* -ну); (*self-restraint*) сде́ржанность; *attr.* запасно́й, запа́сный, резе́рвный. **re'served** *adj.* (*person*) сде́ржанный (-ан, -анна). **re'servist** *n.* резерви́ст. **reservoir** ['rezə,vwɑ:(r)] *n.* резервуа́р, водохрани́лище; (*of knowledge etc.*) запа́с.

reside [rɪ'zaɪd] *v.i.* прожива́ть *impf.*; (*of right etc.*) принадлежа́ть (-жи́т) *impf.* (**in** +*d.*). **residence** ['rezɪd(ə)ns] *n.* (*residing*) прожива́ние; (*abode*) местожи́тельство; (*official* ~ *etc.*) резиде́нция. **'resident** *n.* (постоя́нный) жи́тель *m.*, ~ница; *adj.* прожива́ющий; (*population*) постоя́нный; ~ **physician** врач, живу́щий при больни́це. **resi'dential** *adj.* жило́й; ~ **qualification** ценз осе́длости.

residual [rɪ'zɪdjʊəl] *adj.* оста́точный. **residuary** *adj.* (*of estate*) оста́вшийся. **residue** ['rezɪ,dju:] *n.* оста́ток (-тка); (*of estate*) оста́вшееся насле́дство.

resign [rɪ'zaɪn] *v.t.* отка́зываться *impf.*, отказа́ться (-ажу́сь, -а́жешься) *pf.* от+*g.*; *v.i.* уходи́ть (-ожу́, -о́дишь) *impf.*, уйти́ (уйду́,

-дёшь; ушёл, ушла́) *pf.* в отста́вку; (*chess*) сдава́ть (сдаю́, сдаёшь) *impf.*, сдать (-а́м, -а́шь, -а́ст, -ади́м; сдал, -а́, -о) *pf.* па́ртию; ~ **o.s.** то покоря́ться *impf.*, покори́ться *pf.*+*d.* **resignation** [,rezɪg'neɪʃ(ə)n] *n.* отста́вка, заявле́ние об отста́вке; (*being resigned*) поко́рность; (*chess*) сда́ча. **resigned** *adj.* поко́рный.

resilient [rɪ'zɪliənt] *adj.* упру́гий; (*person*) неуныва́ющий.

resin ['rezɪn] *n.* смола́ (*pl.* -лы). **resinous** *adj.* смоли́стый.

resist [rɪ'zɪst] *v.t.* сопротивля́ться *impf.*+*d.*; поддава́ться (-даю́сь, -даёшься) *impf.*+*d.* **resistance** *n.* сопротивле́ние; (~ *movement*) движе́ние сопротивле́ния. **resistant** *adj.* про́чный (-чен, -чна́, -чно, про́чны). **resistor** *n.* рези́стор.

resolute ['rezə,lu:t, -,lju:t] *adj.* реши́тельный. **reso'lution** *n.* (*character*) реши́тельность, реши́мость; (*at meeting etc.*) резолю́ция; (*of problem*; *mus.*) разреше́ние. **resolve** [rɪ'zɒlv] *v.t.* реша́ть *impf.*, реши́ть *pf.*; разреша́ть *impf.*, разреши́ть *pf.*; *v.i.* & *i.* (*decide*) реша́ться *impf.*, реши́ться *pf.*+*inf.*, на+*a.*; (*of meeting etc.*) выноси́ть (-ит) *impf.*, вы́нести (-сет; -с) *pf.* резолю́цию; *n.* реше́ние.

resonance ['rezənəns] *n.* резона́нс. **resonant** *adj.* раздаю́щийся; зву́чный (-чен, -чна́, -чно). **resonate** *v.i.* резони́ровать *impf.*

resort [rɪ'zɔ:t] *v.i.*: ~ **to** прибега́ть *impf.*, прибе́гнуть (-г(нул), -гла) *pf.* к+*d.*; (*visit*) (ча́сто) посеща́ть *impf.*+*a.*; *n.* (*expedient*) сре́дство; (*health* ~ *etc.*) куро́рт; **in the last** ~ в кра́йнем слу́чае; **without** ~ **to** не прибега́я к+*d.*

resound [rɪ'zaʊnd] *v.i.* (*of sound etc.*) раздава́ться (-даётся) *impf.*, разда́ться (-а́стся, -аду́тся; -а́лся, -ала́сь) *pf.*; (*of place etc.*) оглаша́ться *impf.*, огласи́ться *pf.* (**with** +*i.*).

resource [rɪ'sɔ:s, -'zɔ:s] *n.* (*usu. pl.*) ресу́рс; сре́дство; (*expedient*) сре́дство, возмо́жность; (*ingenuity*) нахо́дчивость. **resourceful** *adj.* нахо́дчивый.

respect [rɪ'spekt] *n.* (*relation*) отноше́ние; (*esteem*) уваже́ние; **in** ~ **of**, **with** ~ **to** что каса́ется+*g.*, в отноше́нии+*g.*; *v.t.* уважа́ть *impf.*; почита́ть *impf.* **respecta'bility** *n.* почте́нность, респекта́бельность. **respectable** *adj.* почте́нный (-нен, -нна), респекта́бельный. **respectful** *adj.* почти́тельный. **respective** *adj.* соотве́тственный (-ен, -енна). **respectively** *adv.* соотве́тственно.

respiration [,respɪ'reɪʃ(ə)n] *n.* дыха́ние; **artificial** ~ иску́сственное дыха́ние. **'respirator** *n.* респира́тор.

respite ['respaɪt, -pɪt] *n.* переды́шка.

resplendent [rɪ'splend(ə)nt] *adj.* блестя́щий; сверка́ющий.

respond [rɪ'spɒnd] *v.i.*: ~ **to** отзыва́ться *impf.*, отозва́ться (отзову́сь, -вёшься; отозва́лся, -ала́сь, -а́лось) *pf.* на+*a.*; реаги́ровать *impf.*, про~, от~ *pf.* на+*a*. **respondent** *n.* отве́тчик, -ица. **response** *n.* отве́т; о́тклик. **responsi'bility** *n.* отве́тственность, обя́занность. **responsible** *adj.* отве́тственный (-ен, -енна) (**to** перед+*i.*; **for** за+*a.*). **responsive** *adj.* отзы́вчивый.

rest[1] [rest] *v.i.* отдыха́ть *impf.*, отдохну́ть *pf.*; поко́иться *impf.* (**upon** на+*p.*); *v.t.* (*place*) класть (-аду́, -аде́шь) *impf.*, положи́ть (-жу́, -жишь) *pf.*; (*allow to* ~) дава́ть (даю́, дае́шь) *impf.*, дать (дам, дашь, даст, дади́м; дал, -а́, да́ло́, -и) *pf.* о́тдых+*d.*; *n.* (*repose*) о́тдых; (*peace*) поко́й; (*mus.*) па́уза; (*support*) опо́ра, подста́вка.

rest[2] [rest] *n.* (*the remainder*) оста́ток (-тка), остально́е *sb.*; (*the others*) остальны́е *sb.*, други́е *sb.*; **for the** ~ что каса́ется остально́го, что до остально́го.

restaurant ['restəront, -,rɔ̃] *n.* рестора́н.

restful ['restful] *adj.* споко́йный, ти́хий (тих, -á, -о); (*soothing*) успока́ивающий.

restitution [,resti'tju:ʃ(ə)n] *n.* (*restoring*) возвраще́ние; (*reparation*) возмеще́ние убы́тков.

restive ['restiv] *adj.* (*horse*) норови́стый; (*person*; *restless*) беспоко́йный; (*wilful*) своенра́вный.

restless ['restlis] *adj.* беспоко́йный; (*uneasy*) неспоко́йный, трево́жный.

restoration [,restə'reiʃ(ə)n] *n.* реставра́ция, восстановле́ние. **restore** [ri'stɔ:(r)] *v.t.* реставри́ровать *impf.* & *pf.*; восстана́вливать *impf.*, восстанови́ть (-влю́, -вишь) *pf.*

restrain [ri'strein] *v.t.* сде́рживать *impf.*, сдержа́ть (-жу́, -жишь) *pf.*; уде́рживать *impf.*, удержа́ть (-жу́, -жишь) *pf.* (**from** от+*g.*). **restraint** *n.* (*reserve*) сде́ржанность; (*restriction*) ограниче́ние; (*confinement*) заключе́ние; **without** ~ свобо́дно, без у́держу.

restrict [ri'strikt] *v.t.* ограни́чивать *impf.*, ограни́чить *pf.* **restriction** *n.* ограниче́ние. **restrictive** *adj.* ограничи́тельный.

result [ri'zʌlt] *v.i.* сле́довать *impf.*; происходи́ть (-ит) *impf.*, произойти́ (-ойде́т; -ошёл, -ошла́) *pf.* в результа́те; ~ **in** конча́ться *impf.*, ко́нчиться *pf.*+*i.*; *n.* результа́т.

resume [ri'zju:m] *v.t.* возобновля́ть *impf.*, возобнови́ть *pf.* **résumé** ['rezju,mei] *n.* резюме́ *nt.indecl.* **resumption** [ri'zʌmpʃ(ə)n] *n.* возобновле́ние.

resurrect [,rezə'rekt] *v.t.* воскреша́ть *impf.*, воскреси́ть *pf.* **resurrection** *n.* (*of the dead*) воскресе́ние; (*to memory etc.*) воскреше́ние.

resuscitate [ri'sʌsi,teit] *v.t.* приводи́ть (-ожу́, -о́дишь) *impf.*, привести́ (-еду́, -еде́шь; -ёл, -ела́) *pf.* в созна́ние.

retail ['ri:teil] *n.* ро́зничная прода́жа; *attr.* ро́зничный; *adv.* в ро́зницу; *v.t.* продава́ть (-даю́, -дае́шь) *impf.*, прода́ть (-а́м, -а́шь, -а́ст, -ади́м; про́дал, -а́, -о) *pf.* в ро́зницу; *v.i.* продава́ться (-дае́тся) *impf.* в ро́зницу.

retailer *n.* ро́зничный торго́вец (-вца).

retain [ri'tein] *v.t.* уде́рживать *impf.*, удержа́ть (-жу́, -жишь) *pf.*; (*preserve*) сохраня́ть *impf.*, сохрани́ть *pf.*

retaliate [ri'tæli,eit] *v.i.* отпла́чивать *impf.*, отплати́ть (-ачу́, -а́тишь) *pf.* тем же (са́мым); (*make reprisals*) применя́ть *impf.*, примени́ть (-ню́, -нишь) *pf.* репресса́лии. **retali'ation** *n.* отпла́та, возме́здие.

retard [ri'ta:d] *v.t.* замедля́ть *impf.*, заме́длить *pf.* **retarded** *adj.* отста́лый.

retch [retʃ, ri:tʃ] *v.i.* рвать (рвёт; рва́ло) *impf. impers.*+*a.*

retention [ri'tenʃ(ə)n] *n.* удержа́ние; (*preservation*) сохране́ние. **retentive** *adj.* уде́рживающий; (*memory*) хоро́ший.

reticence ['retis(ə)ns] *n.* (*restraint*) сде́ржанность; (*secretiveness*) скры́тность. **reticent** *adj.* сде́ржанный (-ан, -анна); скры́тный.

reticulated [ri'tikju,leitid] *adj.* се́тчатый. **reticu'lation** *n.* се́тчатый узо́р, се́тчатое строе́ние.

retina ['retinə] *n.* сетча́тка.

retinue ['reti,nju:] *n.* сви́та.

retire [ri'taiə(r)] *v.i.* (*withdraw*) уединя́ться *impf.*, уедини́ться *pf.*; (*from office etc.*) уходи́ть (-ожу́, -о́дишь) *impf.*, уйти́ (уйду́, -дёшь; ушёл, ушла́) *pf.* в отста́вку. **retired** *adj.* отставно́й, в отста́вке. **retirement** *n.* отста́вка; ~ **age** пенсио́нный во́зраст. **retiring** *adj.* скро́мный (-мен, -мна́, -мно).

retort[1] [ri'tɔ:t] *v.t.* отвеча́ть *impf.*, отве́тить *pf.* тем же (**on** на+*a.*); *v.i.* возража́ть *impf.*, возрази́ть *pf.*; *n.* возраже́ние; (*reply*) нахо́дчивый отве́т, остроу́мная ре́плика.

retort[2] [ri'tɔ:t] *n.* (*vessel*) рето́рта.

retouch [ri:'tʌtʃ] *v.t.* ретуши́ровать *impf.* & *pf.*, от~ *pf.*

retrace [ri'treis] *v.t.*: ~ **one's steps** возвраща́ться *impf.*, возврати́ться (-ащу́сь, -ати́шься) *pf.*

retract [ri'trækt] *v.t.* (*draw in*) втя́гивать *impf.*, втяну́ть (-яну́, -я́нешь) *pf.*; (*take back*) брать (беру́, -рёшь; брал, -á, -о) *impf.*, взять (возьму́, -мёшь; взял, -á, -о) *pf.* наза́д.

retread [ri:'tred; 'ri:tred] *v.t.* (*tyre*) возобновля́ть *impf.*, возобнови́ть *pf.* протéктор+*g.*; *n.* ши́на с возобновлённым протéктором.

retreat [ri'tri:t] *v.i.* отступа́ть *impf.*, отступи́ть (-плю́, -пишь) *pf.*; *n.* отступле́ние; (*signal*) отбо́й; (*withdrawal*) уедине́ние; (*refuge*) убе́жище.

retrench [ri'trentʃ] *v.t.* & *i.* сокраща́ть *impf.*, сократи́ть (-ащу́, -ати́шь) *pf.* (расхо́ды). **retrenchment** *n.* сокраще́ние расхо́дов.

retribution [,retri'bju:ʃ(ə)n] *n.* возме́здие, ка́ра.

retrieval [ri'tri:v(ə)l] *n.* (*recovery*) восстановле́ние; (*comput.*) по́иск (информа́ции); (*repair*) исправле́ние; *v.t.* восстана́вливать *impf.*, восстанови́ть (-влю́, -вишь) *pf.*; (*repair*) исправля́ть *impf.*, испра́вить *pf.*

retroactive [,retrəu'æktiv] *adj.* (*leg.*) име́ющий обра́тную си́лу. **'retrograde** *adj.* ретрогра́дный. **retrogress** *v.i.* дви́гаться (-аюсь, -аешься & дви́жусь, -жешься) *impf.* наза́д; регресси́ровать *impf.* **'retrorocket** *n.* ретрораке́та. **'retrospect** *n.* ретроспекти́вный взгляд; **in** ~ ретроспекти́вно. **retrospective** *adj.* обращённый (-ён, -ена́) в про́шлое, ретроспекти́вный; (*leg.*) име́ющий обра́тную си́лу.

return [rɪ'tɜːn] *v.t.* & *i.* (*give back*; *come back*) возвраща́ть(ся) *impf.*, возврати́ть(ся) (-ащу́(сь), -ати́шь(ся)) *impf.*, верну́ть(ся) *pf.*; *v.t.* (*reply to*) отвеча́ть *impf.*, отве́тить *pf.* на+*a.*; (*elect*) избира́ть *impf.*, избра́ть (изберу́, -рёшь; избра́л, -а́, -о) *pf.*; *n.* возвраще́ние; возвра́т; (*proceeds*) при́быль; **by** ~ обра́тной по́чтой; **in** ~ взаме́н (**for** +*g.*); ~ **match** отве́тный матч; ~ **ticket** обра́тный биле́т.

reunion [riː'juːnjən, -nɪən] *n.* встре́ча (друзе́й и т. п.); **family** ~ сбор всей семьёй. **reunite** [ˌriːjuː'naɪt] *v.t.* воссоединя́ть *impf.*, воссоедини́ть *pf.*

rev [rev] *n.* оборо́т; *v.t.* & *i.*: ~ **up** ускоря́ть *impf.*, уско́рить *pf.* (дви́гатель *m.*).

revanchism [rɪ'væntʃɪs(ə)m] *n.* реванши́зм. **revanchist** *n.* реванши́ст.

reveal [rɪ'viːl] *v.t.* обнару́живать *impf.*, обнару́жить *pf.*; раскрыва́ть *impf.*, раскры́ть (-ро́ю, -ро́ешь) *pf.*

reveille [rɪ'vælɪ, rɪ'velɪ] *n.* подъём.

revel ['rev(ə)l] *v.i.* пирова́ть *impf.*; ~ **in** наслажда́ться *impf.*+*i.*

revelation [ˌrevə'leɪʃ(ə)n] *n.* открове́ние; откры́тие; **R**~ (*eccl.*) апока́липсис.

revenge [rɪ'vendʒ] *v.t.*: ~ **o.s.** мстить *impf.*, ото~ *pf.* (**for** за+*a.*; **on** +*d.*); *n.* месть; мще́ние. **revengeful** *adj.* мсти́тельный.

revenue ['revənjuː] *n.* дохо́д; *adj.* тамо́женный.

reverberate [rɪ'vɜːbəˌreɪt] *v.i.* & *i.* отража́ть(ся) *impf.* **reverbe'ration** *n.* отраже́ние; (*fig.*) о́тзвук.

revere [rɪ'vɪə(r)] *v.t.* почита́ть *impf.*, глубоко́ уважа́ть *impf.* **reverence** ['revərəns] *n.* благогове́ние; почте́ние. **'reverend** *adj.* (*in title*) (его́) преподо́бие. **reve'rential** *adj.* благогове́йный.

reverie ['revərɪ] *n.* мечты́ (*g.* -та́ний) *f.pl.*

reversal [rɪ'vɜːs(ə)l] *n.* по́лное измене́ние; (*of decision*) отме́на. **reverse** *adj.* обра́тный; ~ **gear** за́дний ход; *v.t.* изменя́ть *impf.*, измени́ть (-ню́, -нишь) *pf.* на обра́тный; (*revoke*) отменя́ть *impf.*, отмени́ть (-ню́, -нишь) *pf.*; *v.i.* дава́ть (даю́, даёшь) *impf.*, дать (дам, дашь, даст, дади́м; дал, -а́, да́ло, -и) *pf.* за́дний ход; *n.* (*the* ~) обра́тное *sb.*, противополо́жное *sb.*; (~ *gear*) за́дний ход; (~ *side*) обра́тная сторона́ (*a.* -ону, *pl.* -оны, -о́н, -она́м); (*misfortune*) неуда́ча; (*defeat*) пораже́ние. **reversible** *adj.* обрати́мый; (*cloth*) двусторо́нний. **reversion** *n.* возвраще́ние, реве́рсия. **revert** *v.i.* возвраща́ться (-аю́сь, -ати́шься) *impf.* (**to** в+*a.*, к+*d.*); (*leg.*) переходи́ть (-ит) *impf.*,

перейти́ (-йдёт; -ешёл, -ешла́) *pf.* к пре́жнему владе́льцу.

review [rɪ'vjuː] *n.* (*leg.*) пересмо́тр; (*mil.*) смотр, пара́д; (*survey*) обзо́р, обозре́ние; (*criticism*) реце́нзия; (*periodical*) журна́л; *v.t.* (*leg.*) пересма́тривать *impf.*, пересмотре́ть (-рю́, -ришь) *pf.*; (*survey*) обозрева́ть *impf.*, обозре́ть (-рю́, -ри́шь) *pf.*; (*of troops etc.*) принима́ть *impf.*, приня́ть (приму́, -мешь; при́нял, -а́, -о) *pf.* пара́д+*g.*; (*book etc.*) рецензи́ровать *impf.*, про~ *pf.* **reviewer** *n.* реце́нзент.

revise [rɪ'vaɪz] *v.t.* пересма́тривать *impf.*, пересмотре́ть (-рю́, -ришь) *pf.*; исправля́ть *impf.*, испра́вить *pf.*; *n.* втора́я корректу́ра. **revision** [rɪ'vɪʒ(ə)n] *n.* пересмо́тр, исправле́ние.

revival [rɪ'vaɪv(ə)l] *n.* возрожде́ние; (*to life etc.*) оживле́ние. **revive** *v.t.* возрожда́ть *impf.*, возроди́ть *pf.*; оживля́ть *impf.*, оживи́ть *pf.*; *v.i.* ожива́ть *impf.*, ожи́ть (оживу́, -вёшь; о́жил, -а́, -о) *pf.*

revocation [ˌrevə'keɪʃ(ə)n] *n.* отме́на. **revoke** [rɪ'vəʊk] *v.t.* отменя́ть *impf.*, отмени́ть (-ню́, -нишь) *pf.*; *v.i.* (*cards*) объявля́ть *impf.*, объяви́ть (-влю́, -вишь) *pf.* рено́нс.

revolt [rɪ'vəʊlt] *n.* бунт, мяте́ж (-а́); *v.t.* вызыва́ть *impf.*, вы́звать (вы́зову, -вешь) *pf.* отвраще́ние у+*g.*; *v.i.* бунтова́ть *impf.*, взбунтова́ться *pf.* **revolting** *adj.* отврати́тельный.

revolution [ˌrevə'luːʃ(ə)n] *n.* (*motion*) враще́ние; (*single turn*) оборо́т; (*pol. etc.*) револю́ция. **revolutionary** *adj.* революцио́нный; *n.* революционе́р. **revolutionize** *v.t.* революциони́зировать *impf.* & *pf.* **revolve** [rɪ'vɒlv] *v.t.* & *i.* враща́ть(ся) *impf.* **revolver** *n.* револьве́р.

revue [rɪ'vjuː] *n.* ревю́ *nt.indecl.*

revulsion [rɪ'vʌlʃ(ə)n] *n.* (*change*) внеза́пное ре́зкое измене́ние; (*dislike*) отвраще́ние.

reward [rɪ'wɔːd] *n.* награ́да, вознагражде́ние; *v.t.* (воз)награжда́ть *impf.*, (воз)награди́ть *pf.*

rewrite [riː'raɪt] *v.t.* (*recast*) переде́лывать *impf.*, переде́лать *pf.*

rhapsodize ['ræpsəˌdaɪz] *v.i.*: ~ **over** восторга́ться *impf.*+*i.* **rhapsody** *n.* (*mus.*) рапсо́дия; *pl.* восхище́ния.

rhesus ['riːsəs] *n.* ре́зус; *in comb.* ре́зус-.

rhetoric ['retərɪk] *n.* рито́рика. **rhetorical** [rɪ'tɒrɪk(ə)l] *adj.* ритори́ческий.

rheumatic [ruː'mætɪk] *adj.* ревмати́ческий. **rheumatism** ['ruːməˌtɪz(ə)m] *n.* ревмати́зм. **'rheumatoid** *adj.* ревмато́идный.

Rhine [raɪn] *n.* Рейн.

rhinestone ['raɪnstəʊn] *n.* иску́сственный бриллиа́нт.

rhino ['raɪnəʊ], **rhinoceros** [raɪ'nɒsərəs] *n.* носоро́г.

rhizome ['raɪzəʊm] *n.* ризо́ма, корневи́ще.

rhododendron [ˌrəʊdə'dendrən] *n.* рододе́ндрон.

rhomb [rɒmb] *n.* ромб. **rhombic** *adj.* ромбический. **rhomboid** *n.* ромбоид. **rhombus** *n.* ромб.

Rhone [rəʊn] *n.* Рона.

rhubarb ['ruːbɑːb] *n.* ревень (-ня) *m.*

rhyme [raɪm] *n.* рифма; *pl.* (*verse*) рифмованные стихи *m.pl.; v.t.* рифмовать *impf.,* c~ *pf.; v.i.* рифмоваться *impf.*

rhythm ['rɪð(ə)m] *n.* ритм, ритмичность. **rhythmic(al)** *adj.* ритмический, -чный.

rib [rɪb] *n.* ребро (*pl.* рёбра, -бер, -брам); (*of umbrella*) спица; (*knitting etc.*) рубчик; (*of leaf*) жилка; (*of ship*) шпангоут (*also collect.*).

ribald ['rɪb(ə)ld] *adj.* непристойный.

ribbon ['rɪbən] *n.* лента; *pl.* (*reins*) вожжи (-жей) *pl.; pl.* (*shreds*) клочья (-ьев) *m.pl.; ~* **development** ленточная застройка.

riboflavin [ˌraɪbəʊ'fleɪvɪn] *n.* рибофлавин.

ribonucleic [ˌraɪbənjuː'kliːɪk] *adj.* рибонуклеиновый.

rice [raɪs] *n.* рис; *attr.* рисовый.

rich [rɪtʃ] *adj.* богатый; (*soil*) тучный (-чен, -чна, -чно); (*food*) жирный (-рен, -рна, -рно); (*amusing*) забавный. **riches** *n.* богатство. **richly** *adv.* (*fully*) вполне.

rick[1] [rɪk] *n.* стог (*loc.* -е & -ý; *pl.* -á), скирд(á) (á & -ы; *pl.* скирды, -д(óв), -дáм).

rick[2] [rɪk] *v.t.* растягивать *impf.,* растянуть (-ну, -нешь) *pf.*

rickets ['rɪkɪts] *n.* рахит. **rickety** *adj.* рахитичный; (*shaky*) расшатанный.

rickshaw ['rɪkʃɔː] *n.* рикша.

ricochet ['rɪkəʃeɪ, -ˌʃet] *n.* рикошет; *v.i.* рикошетировать *impf. & pf.*

rid [rɪd] *v.t.* освобождать *impf.,* освободить *pf.* (**of** от+*g.*); **get ~ of** избавляться *impf.,* избавиться *pf.* от+*g.* **riddance** *n.*: **good ~!** скатертью дорога!

riddle[1] ['rɪd(ə)l] *n.* (*enigma*) загадка.

riddle[2] ['rɪd(ə)l] *n.* (*sieve*) грохот; *v.t.* (*sift*) грохотить *impf.,* про~ *pf.;* (*with bullets etc.*) изрешечивать *impf.,* изрешетить *pf.*

ride [raɪd] *v.i.* ездить *indet.,* ехать (éду, éдешь) *det.,* по~ *pf.* (*on horseback,* верхóм); (*lie at anchor*) стоять (-ою́т) *impf.* на якоре; *v.t.* ездить *indet.,* ехать (éду, éдешь) *det.,* по~ *pf.* в, на+*p.;* п. поездка, езда. **rider** *n.* всадник, -ица; (*clause*) дополнение.

ridge [rɪdʒ] *n.* хребет (-бта), гребень (-бня) *m.;* (*of roof*) конёк (-нька). **ridge-pole** *n.* (*of tent*) растяжка. **ridge-tile** *n.* коньковая черепица.

ridicule ['rɪdɪˌkjuːl] *n.* насмешка; *v.t.* осмеивать *impf.,* осмеять (-ею́, -еёшь) *pf.* **ri'diculous** *adj.* нелепый, смешной (-шóн, -шна́).

riding[1] ['raɪdɪŋ] *n.* (*division of county*) райдинг.

riding[2] ['raɪdɪŋ] *n.* (*horse-~*) (верховая) езда; *~* **habit** амазонка. **riding-light** *n.* якорный огонь (огня) *m.*

Riesling ['riːzlɪŋ, -slɪŋ] *n.* рислинг (-а(у)).

rife [raɪf] *pred.* широко распространён (-á), обычен (-чна); **be ~ with** изобиловать *impf.+i.*

riff-raff ['rɪfræf] *n.* подонки (-ков) *pl.*

rifle ['raɪf(ə)l] *v.t.* (*search*) обыскивать *impf.,* обыскать (-ыщу́, -ы́щешь) *pf.;* (*a gun*) нарезать *impf.,* нарезать (-éжу, -éжешь) *pf.; n.* винтовка; *pl.* стрелки *m.pl.* **rifle-range** *n.* стрельбище.

rift [rɪft] *n.* трещина; (*dispute*) разрыв.

rig [rɪg] *v.t.* оснащать *impf.,* оснастить *pf.; ~* **out** наряжать *impf.,* нарядить (-яжу́, -ядишь) *pf.; ~* **up** стройть *impf.,* по~ *pf.* из чего попало; *n.* буровая установка.

Riga ['riːgə] *n.* Рига.

rigging ['rɪgɪŋ] *n.* такелаж.

right [raɪt] *adj.* (*position*; *justified*; *pol.*) правый (прав, -á, -о); (*correct*) правильный; (*appropriate*) нужный (-жен, -жна́, -жно, -жны́); (*suitable*) подходящий; **in one's ~ mind** в здравом умé; *~* **angle** прямой угол (угла); *~* **side** (*of cloth*) лицевая сторона (*a.* -ону); *v.t.* исправлять *impf.,* исправить *pf.; n.* право (*pl.* -вá); (*~ side*) правая сторона (*a.* -ону); (**R~;** *pol.*) правые *sb.;* **be in the ~** быть (*fut.* буду, -дешь; был, -á, -о; не был, -á, -о) правым; **by ~ of** по праву+*g.;* **by ~s** по праву, по справедливости; **reserve the ~** оставлять *impf.,* оставить *pf.* за собой право; **set to ~s** приводить (-ожу́, -одишь) *impf.,* привести (-еду́, -едёшь; -ёл, -елá) *pf.* в порядок; *~* **of way** право прохода, проезда; *adv.* (*straight*) прямо; (*exactly*) точно, как раз; (*to the full*) совершенно; (*correctly*) правильно; как следует; (*on the ~*) справо (**of** от+*g.*); (*to the ~*) направо.

righteous ['raɪtʃəs] *adj.* (*person*) праведный; (*action*) справедливый.

rightful ['raɪtfʊl] *adj.* законный.

rigid ['rɪdʒɪd] *adj.* жёсткий (-ток, -ткá, -тко), негнущийся; (*strict*) строгий (-г, -гá, -го). **ri'gidity** *n.* жёсткость; строгость.

rigmarole ['rɪgməˌrəʊl] *n.* бессмысленная, несвязная болтовня.

rigor mortis [ˌrɪgə 'mɔːtɪs] *n.* трупное окоченéние.

rigorous ['rɪgərəs] *adj.* строгий (-г, -гá, -го), суровый. **rigour** *n.* строгость, суровость.

rill [rɪl] *n.* ручеёк (-ейкá).

rim [rɪm] *n.* (*of wheel*) обод (*pl.* ободья, -ьев); (*spectacles*) оправа. **rimless** *adj.* без оправы.

rind [raɪnd] *n.* кожура, корка.

ring[1] [rɪŋ] *n.* кольцо (*pl.* -льца, -лéц, -льцам); (*circle*) круг (*loc.* -ý; *pl.* -и); (*boxing*) ринг; (*circus*) цирковая арéна; *~* безымянный палец (-льца); *~* **road** кольцевая дорога; *v.t.* (*encircle*) окружать *impf.,* окружить *pf.* (кольцóм).

ring[2] [rɪŋ] *v.i.* (*sound*) звенеть (-нит) *impf.,* про~ *pf.;* звонить *impf.,* по~ *pf.;* (*of shot etc.*) раздаваться (-даётся) *impf.,* раздаться (-астся; -адутся; áлся, -алась) *pf.;* (*of place*) оглаша́ться *impf.*, огласи́ться *pf.* (**with** +*i.*); *v.t.* звони́ть *impf.*, по~ *pf.* в+*a.*; ~ **off** дава́ть (даю́, даёшь) *impf.*, дать (дам, дашь, даст, дади́м; дал, -а́, да́ло́, -и) *pf.* отбо́й; ~ **up** звони́ть *impf.*, по~ *pf.*+*d.*; *n.* звон, звоно́к (-нка́).

ring-dove ['rɪŋdʌv] *n.* вя́хирь *m.*

ringleader ['rɪŋˌliːdə(r)] *n.* глава́рь (-ря́) *m.*, зачи́нщик.

ringlet ['rɪŋlɪt] *n.* (*of hair*) ло́кон.

ringmaster ['rɪŋˌmɑːstə(r)] *n.* инспе́ктор (*pl.* -á & -ы) мане́жа.

ringworm ['rɪŋwɜːm] *n.* стригу́щий лиша́й (-áя).

rink [rɪŋk] *n.* като́к (-тка́).

rinse [rɪns] *v.t.* полоска́ть (-ощу́, -о́щешь) *impf.*, вы́~, про~ *pf.*; *n.* полоска́ние; (*for hair*) кра́ска для воло́с.

riot ['raɪət] *n.* бунт; **run** ~ бу́йствовать *impf.*; переступа́ть *impf.*, переступи́ть (-плю́, -пишь) *pf.* все грани́цы; (*of plants*) бу́йно разраста́ться *impf.*, разрасти́сь (-тётся; разро́сся, -сла́сь) *pf.*; *v.i.* бунтова́ть *impf.*, взбунтова́ться *pf.* **riotous** *adj.* бу́йный (бу́ен, бу́йна́, -но).

RIP *abbr.* (*of rest in peace*) мир пра́ху (*кого*).

rip [rɪp] *v.t. & i.* рва́ть(ся) (рву, рвёт(ся); -а́л(ся), -ала́(сь), -а́ло́/а́ло́сь) *impf.*, поро́ть(ся) (-рю́, -рет(ся)) *impf.*; *v.t.* (*tear up*) разрыва́ть *impf.*, разорва́ть (-ву́, -вёшь; разорва́л, -а́, -о) *pf.*; *v.i.* (*rush*) мча́ться (мчи́тся) *impf.*; *n.* проре́ха, разре́з. **rip-cord** *n.* вытяжно́й трос.

ripe [raɪp] *adj.* зре́лый (зрел, -á, -о), спе́лый (спел, -á, -о). **ripen** *v.t.* де́лать *impf.*, с~ *pf.* зре́лым; *v.i.* созрева́ть *impf.*, созре́ть *pf.* **ripeness** *n.* зре́лость.

ripple ['rɪp(ə)l] *n.* рябь; *v.t. & i.* покрыва́ть(ся) *impf.*, покры́ть(ся) (-ро́ет(ся)) *pf.* ря́бью.

rise [raɪz] *v.i.* поднима́ться *impf.*, подня́ться (-ниму́сь, -ни́мешься; -ня́лся, -няла́сь) *pf.*; повыша́ться *impf.*, повы́ситься *pf.*; (*get up*) встава́ть (-таю́, -таёшь) *impf.*, встать (-а́ну, -а́нешь) *pf.*; (*rebel*) восстава́ть (-таю́, -таёшь) *impf.*, восста́ть (-а́ну, -а́нешь) *pf.*; (*sun etc.*) в(о)сходи́ть (-ит) *impf.*, взойти́ (-йдёт; взошёл, -шла́) (*wind*) усиливаться *impf.*, уси́литься *pf.*; *n.* подъём, возвыше́ние; (*in pay*) приба́вка; (*of sun etc.*) восхо́д. **riser** *n.* (*of stairs*) подступень; **he is an early** ~ он ра́но встаёт. **rising** *n.* (*revolt*) восста́ние.

risk [rɪsk] *n.* риск; *v.t.* рискова́ть *impf.*, рискну́ть *pf.*+*i.* **risky** *adj.* риско́ванный (-ан, -анна).

risqué ['rɪskeɪ, -'keɪ] *adj.* непристо́йный.

rissole ['rɪsəʊl] *n.* котле́та.

rite [raɪt] *n.* обря́д. **ritual** ['rɪtjʊəl] *n.* ритуа́л; *adj.* ритуа́льный, обря́довый.

rival ['raɪv(ə)l] *n.* сопе́рник, -ица; конкуре́нт, ~ка; *adj.* сопе́рничающий; *v.t.* сопе́рничать *impf.* с+*i.*; конкури́ровать *impf.* с+*i.* **rivalry**

---

n. сопе́рничество.

river ['rɪvə(r)] *n.* река́ (*a.* ре́ку́; *pl.* ре́ки, рек, ре́ка́м); *adj.* речно́й. **riverside** *n.* прибре́жная полоса́ (*a.* по́лосу́; *pl.* -осы, -о́с, -оса́м); *attr.* прибре́жный.

rivet ['rɪvɪt] *n.* заклёпка; *v.t.* клепа́ть *impf.*; за~, с~, клёпывать *impf.*, за~, с~, клепа́ть *pf.*; (*attention etc.*) прико́вывать *impf.*, прикова́ть (-кую́, -куёшь) *pf.* (**on** к+*d.*).

rivulet ['rɪvjʊlɪt] *n.* ре́чка, ручеёк (-ейка́).

RN *abbr.* (*of Royal Navy*) английский ВМФ (военно-морской флот).

roach [rəʊtʃ] *n.* (*fish*) плотва́.

road [rəʊd] *n.* доро́га, путь (-ти́, -тём) *m.*; (*highway*) шоссе́ *nt.indecl.*; (*central part, carriageway*) мостова́я *sb.*; (*street*) у́лица; (*naut.; usu.pl.*) рейд; ~ **sense** чу́вство доро́ги; ~ **sign** доро́жный знак. **roadblock** *n.* загражде́ние на доро́ге. **road-hog** *n.* лиха́ч (-á). **road-house** *n.* придоро́жный буфе́т, придоро́жная гости́ница. **road-map** *n.* а́тлас автомоби́льных доро́г. **roadman** *n.* доро́жный рабо́чий *sb.* **roadside** *n.* обо́чина; *attr.* придоро́жный. **roadstead** *n.* рейд. **roadway** *n.* мостова́я *sb.*

roam [rəʊm] *v.t. & i.* броди́ть (-ожу́, -о́дишь) *impf.* (по+*d.*); скита́ться *impf.* (по+*d.*).

roan [rəʊn] *adj.* ча́лый.

roar [rɔː(r)] *n.* (*animal's*) рёв; (*other noise*) гро́хот, шум; *v.i.* реве́ть (-ву́, -вёшь) *impf.*; грохота́ть (-очу́, -о́чешь) *impf.*, про~ *pf.*

roast [rəʊst] *v.t. & i.* жа́рить(ся) *impf.*, за~, из~ *pf.*; *adj.* жа́реный; ~ **beef** ро́стбиф *n.* жарко́е *sb.*, жа́реное *sb.*

rob [rɒb] *v.t.* гра́бить *impf.*, о~ *pf.*; красть (-аду́, -адёшь; -ал) *impf.*, у~ *pf.* у+*g.* (**of** +*a.*); (*deprive*) лиша́ть *impf.*, лиши́ть *pf.* (**of** +*g.*). **robber** *n.* граби́тель *m.* **robbery** *n.* грабёж (-á).

robe [rəʊb] *n.* (*also pl.*) ма́нтия.

robin ['rɒbɪn] *n.* мали́новка.

robot ['rəʊbɒt] *n.* ро́бот. **ro'botics** *n.* робо(то)те́хника.

robust [rəʊ'bʌst] *adj.* здоро́вый (-в, -ва́), кре́пкий (-пок, -пка́, -пко).

rock[1] [rɒk] *n.* (*geol.*) (го́рная) поро́да; (*cliff etc.*) скала́ (*pl.* -лы); (*large stone*) большо́й ка́мень (-мня; -мни, -мне́й) *m.*; **on the** ~**s** на мели́; (*drink*) со льдом.

rock[2] [rɒk] *v.t. & i.* кача́ть(ся) *impf.*, качну́ть(ся) *pf.*; (*sway*) колеба́ть(ся) (-блю(сь), -блешь(ся)) *impf.*, по~ *pf.*; ~ **to sleep** ука́чивать *impf.*, укача́ть *pf.*; ~ **and roll** рок-н-ро́лл.

rock-bottom [ˌrɒk'bɒtəm] *adj.* са́мый ни́зкий. **rock-crystal** *n.* го́рный хруста́ль (-ля́) *m.* **'rockery** *n.* сад (*loc.* -у́; *pl.* -ы́) ка́мней.

rocket ['rɒkɪt] *n.* раке́та. **rocketry** *n.* раке́тная те́хника.

rocking-chair [ˈrɒkɪŋ-ˌtʃeə(r)] *n.* (кре́сло-)кача́лка. **rocking-horse** *n.* конь-кача́лка.

rock-salt ['rɒksɔːlt] *n.* ка́менная соль. **rocky** *adj.* скали́стый; (*unsteady*) неусто́йчивый.

rococo [rə'kəʊkəʊ] *n.* рококо́ *nt.indecl.*; в

стиле рококо.

rod [rɒd] n. прут (-á; pl. -ья, -ьев); (for caning) рóзга; (tech.) стéржень (-жня) m.; (fishing- ~) ýдочка.

rodent ['rəʊd(ə)nt] n. грызýн (-á).

rodeo ['rəʊdɪəʊ, rə'deɪəʊ] n. родéо nt.indecl.

roe¹ [rəʊ] n. (hard) икрá; (soft) молóки (-óк) pl.

roe² (-deer) [rəʊ] n. косýля. **roebuck** n. самéц (-мцá) косýли.

rogue [rəʊg] n. плут (-á). **roguish** adj. плу-товскóй; (mischievous) прокáзливый.

role [rəʊl] n. роль (pl. -ли, -лéй).

roll¹ [rəʊl] n. (cylinder) рулóн; (document) свитóк (-тка); (register) спúсок (-ска), реéстр; (bread ~) бýлочка.

roll² [rəʊl] v.t. & i. катáть(ся) indet., ка-тúть(ся) (качý(сь), кáтишь(ся)) det., по~ pf.; (~ up) свёртывать(ся) impf., свер-нýть(ся) pf.; v.t. (road) укáтывать impf., укатáть pf.; (metal) прокáтывать impf., прокатáть pf.; (dough) раскáтывать impf., раскатáть pf.; v.i. (sound) гремéть (-мит) impf., за~ катáние; (of thunder) раскáт.

roll-call ['rəʊlkɔːl] n. переклúчка.

roller ['rəʊlə(r)] n. вáлик; (wave) вал (loc. -ý; pl. -ы́); pl. (for hair) бигудú nt.indecl.; ~ **bearing** рóликовый подшúпник; ~ **towel** полотéнце на рóлике. **roller-skate** v.i. ка-тáться impf. на рóликах; **roller-skating rink** роликодрóм. **roller-skates** n. рóлики m.pl., конькú m.pl. на рóликах.

rollicking ['rɒlɪkɪŋ] adj. разухáбистый.

rolling ['rəʊlɪŋ] adj. (of land) холмúстый. **rolling-mill** n. прокáтный стан. **rolling-pin** n. скáлка. **rolling-stock** n. подвижнóй со-стáв.

ROM [rɒm] (comput.) abbr. (of **read only memory**) ПЗУ, (постоянное запоминáю-щее устройство).

Roman ['rəʊmən] n. рúмлянин (pl. -яне, -ян), -янка; adj. рúмский; ~ **alphabet** латúнский алфавúт; ~ **Catholic** (n.) катóлик, -úчка; (adj.) рúмско-католúческий; ~ **type** пря-мóй, свéтлый шрифт.

romance [rəʊ'mæns] n. (tale; love affair) ро-мáн; (quality) ромáнтика; (mus.) ромáнс; R~ **languages** ромáнские языкú m.pl.

Romanesque [ˌrəʊmə'nesk] adj. ромáнский.

Romania [rəʊ'meɪnɪə] n. Румы́ния. **Romanian** n. румы́н (g.pl. -н), ~ка; adj. румы́нский.

romantic [rəʊ'mæntɪk] adj. романтúчный, -чес-кий. **romanticism** n. романтúзм.

Rome [rəʊm] n. Рим.

romp [rɒmp] v.i. возúться (вожýсь, вóзишь-ся) impf.; ~ **home** с лёгкостью вы́играть pf.

rondo ['rɒndəʊ] n. (mus.) рóндо nt.indecl.

rood [ruːd] n. распя́тие. **rood-loft** n. хóры (-р & -ров) pl. в цéркви. **rood-screen** n. пере-горóдка в цéркви.

roof [ruːf] n. кры́ша, крóвля (g.pl. -вель); ~ **of the mouth** нёбо; v.t. крыть (крóю, -óешь

impf., покрывáть impf., покры́ть (-рóю, -рóешь) pf.

rook¹ [rʊk] n. (chess) ладья́.

rook² [rʊk] n. (bird) грач (-á). **rookery** n. грачóвник.

room [ruːm, rʊm] n. (in house) кóмната; pl. помещéние; (space) мéсто; (opportunity) возмóжность. **roomy** adj. простóрный.

roost [ruːst] n. насéст.

root¹ [ruːt] n. (var. senses) кóрень (-рня; pl. -рни, -рнéй) m.; (mus.) основнóй тон (аккóрда); (plant) корнеплóд; ~ **and branch** коренны́м óбразом; v.i. пускáть impf., пустúть (-úт) pf. кóрни; ~ **to the spot** при-гвождáть impf., пригвоздúть pf. к мéсту.

root² [ruːt] v.i. (rummage) ры́ться (рóюсь, рóешься) impf.

rootstock ['ruːtstɒk] n. корневúще.

rope [rəʊp] n. верёвка, канáт, трос; v.t. при-вя́зывать impf., привязáть (-яжý, -я́жешь) pf.; ~ **in, off** о(т)горáживать impf., о(т)го-родúть (-ожý, -óдишь) pf. канáтом. **rope-dancer** n. канатохóдец (-дца). **rope-ladder** n. верёвочная лéстница.

rosary ['rəʊzərɪ] n. (eccl.) чётки (-ток) pl.

rose [rəʊz] n. рóза; (nozzle) сéтка; pl. (com-plexion) румя́нец (-нца). **rosebud** n. бутóн рóзы. **rose-coloured** adj. рóзовый.

rosemary ['rəʊzmərɪ] n. розмарúн.

rosette [rəʊ'zet] n. розéтка. **rose-water** n. рóзовая водá (a. -ду). **rose-window** n. розéтка. **rosewood** n. рóзовое дéрево.

rosin ['rɒzɪn] n. канифóль; v.t. натирáть impf., натерéть (-трý, -трёшь; -тёр) pf. канифóлью.

roster ['rɒstə(r), 'rəʊstə(r)] n. расписáние (нарядов, дежýрств).

rostrum ['rɒstrəm] n. трибýна, кáфедра.

rosy ['rəʊzɪ] adj. рóзовый; (complexion) румя́ный.

rot [rɒt] n. гниль; (nonsense) вздор; v.i. гнить (-úю, -úёшь; гнил, -á, -о) impf., с~ pf.; v.t. гноúть impf., с~ pf.

rota ['rəʊtə] n. расписáние дежýрств. **rotary** adj. вращáтельный, ротациóнный. **ro'tate** v.t. & i. вращáть(ся) impf. **ro'tation** n. вращéние; **in** ~ по óчереди.

rote [rəʊt] n.: **by** ~ наизýсть.

rotten ['rɒt(ə)n] adj. гнилóй (гнил, -á, -о). **rotter** n. дрянь.

rotund [rəʊ'tʌnd] adj. (round) крýглый (-л, -лá, -ло, крýглы́); (plump) пóлный (-лон, -лнá, полнó). **rotunda** n. ротóнда. **rotundity** n. округлённость, полнотá.

rouble ['ruːb(ə)l] n. рубль (-ля́) m.

rouge [ruːʒ] n. румя́на (-н) pl.; v.t. & i. румя́нить(ся) impf., на~ pf.

rough [rʌf] adj. (uneven) нерóвный (-вен, -внá, -вно); (coarse) грýбый (груб, -á, -о); (sea) бýрный (-рен, бýрнá, -но); (approximate) приблизúтельный; ~ **copy** черновúк (-á) n. (~ **ground**) нерóвное пóле; (person) хулигáн. **roughage** n. грýбая пúща. **rough-**

and-ready *adj.* гру́бый но эффекти́вный.
roughcast *n.* га́лечная штукату́рка. **roughly** *adv.* гру́бо; ~ **speaking** приме́рно.
roulette [ru:'let] *n.* руле́тка.
round [raund] *adj.* кру́глый (-л, -ла́, -ло,
кру́глы́); (*plump*) по́лный (-лон, -лна́,
по́лно); ~ **dance** кругово́й та́нец; **in** ~
figures приблизи́тельно; *n.* (~ *object*) круг
(*loc.* -у́; *pl.* -и́); (*circuit*; *also pl.*) обхо́д;
(*sport*) тур, ра́унд; (*series*) ряд (*pl.* -ы́);
(*ammunition*) патро́н, снаря́д; (*of applause*)
взрыв; *adv.* вокру́г; (*in a circle*) по кругу́;
all ~ круго́м; **all the year** ~ кру́глый год;
prep. вокру́г+g.; круго́м+g.; по+d.; ~ **the
corner** (*motion*) за́ угол, (*position*) за угло́м;
v.t. & *i.* округля́ть(ся) *impf.*, округли́ть(ся)
pf.; *v.t.* (*pass* ~) огиба́ть *impf.*, обогну́ть
pf.; ~ **off** (*complete*) заверша́ть *impf.*, за-
верши́ть *pf.*; ~ **up** сгоня́ть *impf.*, согна́ть
(сгоню́, -нишь; согна́л, -а́, -о) *pf.* **roundabout** *n.* (*merry-go-round*) карусе́ль; (*road
junction*) кольцева́я тра́нспортная раз-
вя́зка; *adj.* око́льный; **in a** ~ **way** око́льным
путём. **round-shouldered** *adj.* суту́лый.
round-up *n.* заго́н; (*police*) обла́ва.
rouse [rauz] *v.t.* буди́ть (бужу́, бу́дишь)
impf., раз~ *pf.*; (*to action etc.*) побужда́ть
impf., побуди́ть (-ужу́, -уди́шь) *pf.* (**to** к+d.).
rousing *adj.* возбужда́ющий.
rout [raut] *n.* (*defeat*) разгро́м; (*flight*) бес-
поря́дочное бе́гство; *v.t.* обраща́ть *impf.*,
обрати́ть (-ащу́, -ати́шь) *pf.* в бе́гство.
route [ru:t] *n.* маршру́т, путь (-ти́, -тём) *m.*;
~ **march** похо́дное движе́ние; *v.t.* отправ-
ля́ть *impf.*, отпра́вить *pf.* (по определённому маршру́ту).
routine [ru:'ti:n] *n.* заведённый поря́док (-дка),
режи́м; (*pejor.*) рути́на; *adj.* устано́влен-
ный; очередно́й.
rove [rəuv] *v.i.* скита́ться *impf.*; (*of thoughts
etc.*) блужда́ть *impf.* **rover** *n.* скита́лец
(-льца).
row¹ [rəu] *n.* (*line*) ряд (-á with 2,3,4, *loc.* -у́;
pl. -ы́).
row² [rəu] *v.i.* (*in boat*) грести́ (гребу́, -бёшь;
грёб, -ла́) *impf.*; *v.t.* (*convey*) перевози́ть
(-ожу́, -о́зишь) *impf.*, перевезти́ (-езу́, -езёшь;
ёз, -езла́) *pf.* на ло́дке.
row³ [rau] *n.* (*dispute*) ссо́ра; (*brawl*) сканда́л;
v.i. ссо́риться *impf.*, по~ *pf.*; сканда́лить
impf., на~ *pf.*
rowan ['rəuən, 'rau-] *n.* ряби́на.
rowdy ['raudi] *adj.* бу́йный (бу́ен, буйна́, -но);
n. буя́н.
rowlock ['rɒlək, 'rʌlək] *n.* уклю́чина.
royal ['rɔiəl] *adj.* короле́вский, ца́рский;
(*majestic*) великоле́пный. **royalist** ['rɔiəlist]
n. роли́ст; *adj.* роли́стский. **royalty** *n.*
член, чле́ны *pl.*, короле́вской семьи́; (*author's fee*) а́вторский гонора́р; (*patentee's
fee*) отчисле́ние владе́льцу пате́нта.
RSVP *abbr.* (*of répondez, s'il vous plaît*)
бу́дьте любе́зны отве́тить.

rub [rʌb] *v.t.* & *i.* тере́ть(ся) (тру(сь),
трёшь(ся); тёр(ся)) *impf.*; *v.t.* (*polish*; *chafe*)
натира́ть *impf.*, натере́ть (-тру́, -трёшь;
-тёр) *pf.*; (~ *dry*) вытира́ть *impf.*, вы́тереть
(-тру, -трешь; -тер) *pf.*; ~ **in, on** втира́ть
impf., втере́ть (вотру́, -рёшь; втёр) *pf.*; ~
out стира́ть *impf.*, стере́ть (сотру́, -рёшь;
стёр) *pf.*; ~ **it in** растравля́ть *impf.*, раст-
рави́ть (-влю́, -вишь) *pf.* ра́ну; ~ **one's
hands** потира́ть *impf.* ру́ки (**with** (*joy etc.*),
от+g.); ~ **up the wrong way** гла́дить *impf.*
про́тив ше́рсти.
rubber¹ ['rʌbə(r)] *n.* (*cured*) рези́на; (*not cured*)
каучу́к; (*eraser*, *also* ~ *band*) рези́нка, ла́-
стик; *attr.* рези́новый.
rubber² ['rʌbə(r)] *n.* (*cards*) ро́ббер.
rubberize ['rʌbə,raiz] *v.t.* прорези́нивать
impf., прорези́нить *pf.*
rubber-stamp ['rʌbə,stæmp] *v.t.* (*fig.*) штам-
пова́ть *impf.*
rubbish ['rʌbiʃ] *n.* му́сор, хлам; (*nonsense*)
чепуха́, вздор. **rubbishy** *adj.* дрянно́й (-нен,
-нна́, -нно).
rubble ['rʌb(ə)l] *n.* бут.
rubella [ru:'belə] *n.* красну́ха.
rubicund ['ru:bi,kʌnd] *n.* румя́ный.
rubric ['ru:brik] *n.* ру́брика.
ruby ['ru:bi] *n.* руби́н; *adj.* руби́новый.
ruche [ru:ʃ] *n.* рюш.
ruck [rʌk] *v.t.* (~ *up*) мять (мну, мнёшь) *impf.*,
из~ (изомну́, -нёшь), с~ (сомну́, -нёшь) *pf.*
rucksack ['rʌksæk, 'rʊk-] *n.* рюкза́к (-а́).
rudder ['rʌdə(r)] *n.* руль (-ля́) *m.*
ruddy ['rʌdi] *adj.* кра́сный (-сен, -сна́, -сно);
(*face*) невёжливый; (*sl.*, *damnable*) прок-
ля́тый.
rude [ru:d] *adj.* гру́бый (груб, -á, -о); (*impolite also*) невёжливый; ~ **awakening** глу-
бо́кое разочарова́ние; ~ **health** кре́пкое
здоро́вье; ~ **shock** внеза́пный уда́р.
rudimentary [,ru:di'mentəri] *adj.* зача́точный,
рудимента́рный. **'rudiments** *n.* (*elements*)
нача́тки (-ков) *pl.*; (*beginning*) зача́тки
m.pl.
rue¹ [ru:] *n.* (*plant*) ру́та.
rue² [ru:] *v.t.* сожале́ть *impf.* о+p. **rueful** *adj.*
печа́льный, уны́лый.
ruff¹ [rʌf] *n.* (*frill*) бры́жи (-жей) *pl.*; (*of feathers, hair*) кольцо́ (*pl.* -льца, -ле́ц, -льцам)
(пе́рьев, ше́рсти) вокру́г ше́и.
ruff² [rʌf] *v.t.* (*cards*) покрыва́ть *impf.*, по-
кры́ть (-ро́ю, -ро́ешь) *pf.* ко́зырем; *n.* по-
кры́тие ко́зырем; ко́зырь (*pl.* -ри, -рей) *m.*
ruffian ['rʌfiən] *n.* головоре́з, хулига́н. **ruffi-
anly** *adj.* хулига́нский.
ruffle ['rʌf(ə)l] *v.t.* (*hair*) еро́шить *impf.*, взъ~
pf.; (*water*) ряби́ть *impf.*; (*person*) раздра-
жа́ть *impf.*, раздражи́ть *pf.*
rug [rʌg] *n.* (*mat*) ко́врик, ковёр (-вра́);
(*wrap*) плед.
rugby (football) ['rʌgbi] *n.* ре́гби *nt.indecl.*
rugged ['rʌgid] *adj.* (*uneven*) неро́вный (-вен,
-вна́, -вно); (*rocky*) скали́стый; (*rough*)

грýбый (груб, -á, -о).

ruin ['ru:ɪn] *n.* (*downfall*) гúбель; (*destruction*) разорéние; *pl.* развáлины *f.pl.*, руúны *f.pl.*; *v.t.* губúть (-блю́, -бишь) *impf.*, по~ *pf.*; разорáть *impf.*, разорúть *pf.* **ruinous** *adj.* губúтельный, разорúтельный; (*state*) разрýшенный (-ен).

rule [ru:l] *n.* прáвило; (*carpenter's, print*) линéйка; **as a ~** как прáвило, обы́чно; *v.t. & i.* прáвить *impf.* (+i.); (*make lines*) линовáть *impf.*, раз~ *pf.*; (*give decision*) постановля́ть *impf.*, постановúть (-влю́, -вишь) *pf.*; **~ out** исключáть *impf.*, исключúть *pf.* **ruler** *n.* (*person*) правúтель *m.*, ~ница; (*object*) линéйка. **ruling** *n.* (*of court etc.*) постановлéние.

rum[1] [rʌm] *n.* ром.

rum[2] [rʌm] *adj.* стрáнный (-нен, -ннá, -нно), чуднóй (-дён, -днá).

Rumanian *see* **Romanian**

rumba ['rʌmbə] *n.* рýмба.

rumble ['rʌmb(ə)l] *v.i.* громыхáть *impf.*; грохотáть (-óчет) *impf.*; *n.* громыхáние, грóхот.

ruminant ['ru:mɪnənt] *n.* жвáчное (живóтное) *sb.*; *adj.* жвáчный; (*contemplative*) задýмчивый. **ruminate** *v.i.* жевáть (жуёт) *impf.* жвáчку; (*fig.*) размышля́ть *impf.* (**over, on** o+p.). **rumi'nation** *n.* размышлéние.

rummage ['rʌmɪdʒ] *v.i.* ры́ться (рóюсь, рóешься) *impf.*

rumour ['ru:mə(r)] *n.* слух; *v.t.*: **it is ~ed that** хóдят слýхи (*pl.*), что.

rump [rʌmp] *n.* огýзок (-зка); **~ steak** ромштéкс.

rumple ['rʌmp(ə)l] *v.t.* мять (мну, мнёшь) *impf.*, из~ (измнý, -нёшь), с~ (сомнý, -нёшь) *pf.*; (*hair*) ерóшить *impf.*, взъ~ *pf.*

run [rʌn] *v.i.* бéгать *indet.*, бежáть (бегý, бежúшь) *det.*, по~ *pf.*; (*roll along*) катáться *indet.*, катúться (качýсь, кáтишься) *det.*, по~ *pf.*; (*work, of machines*) рабóтать *impf.*; (*ply, of bus etc.*) ходúть (-ит) *indet.*, идтú (идёт; шёл, шла) *det.*; (*compete in race*) учáствовать *impf.* (в бéге); (*seek election*) выставля́ть *impf.*, вы́ставить *pf.* свою́ кандидатýру; (*be valid*) быть действúтельным; (*of play etc.*) идтú (идёт; шёл, шла) *impf.*; (*spread rapidly*) бы́стро распространя́ться *impf.*, распространúться *pf.*; (*of ink, dye*) расплывáться *impf.*, расплы́ться (-ывётся, -ы́лся, -ылáсь) *pf.*; (*flow*) течь (течёт; тёк, -лá) *impf.*; (*of document*) гласúть *impf.*; *v.t.* (*manage; operate a machine*) управля́ть *impf.*+i.; (*a business etc.*) вестú (ведý, -дёшь; вёл, -á) *impf.*; **~ dry, low** иссякáть *impf.*, иссякнуть (-к) *pf.*; **~ errands** быть на посы́лках (**for** y+g.); **~ risks** рисковáть *impf.*; **~ to earth** (*fig.*) отыскáть (отыщý, -щешь) *pf.*; **~ across, into** (*meet*) встречáться *impf.*, встрéтиться *pf.* c+i.; **~ after** (*fig.*) ухáживать *impf.* за+i.; **~ away** (*flee*) убегáть *impf.*, убежáть (-егý, -ежúшь) *pf.*; **~ down** (*knock*

down) задавúть (-влю́, -вишь) *pf.*; (*disparage*) умаля́ть *impf.*, умалúть *pf.*; **be ~ down** (*of person*) переутомúться *pf.* (*in past tense*); **~ in** (*engine*) обкáтывать *impf.*, обкатáть *pf.*; **~ into** *see* **~ across**; **~ out** кончáться *impf.*, кóнчиться *pf.*; **~ out of** истощáть *impf.*, истощúть *pf.* свой запáс+g.; **~ over** (*glance over*) бéгло просмáтривать *impf.*, просмотрéть (-рю́, -ришь) *pf.*; (*injure*) задавúть (-влю́, -вишь) *pf.*; **~ through** (*pierce*) прокáлывать *impf.*, проколóть (-лю́, -лешь) *pf.*; (*money*) промáтывать *impf.*, промотáть *pf.*; **~ over** *see* **~ over**; **~ to** (*reach*) достигáть *impf.*, достúгнуть & достúчь (-úгну, -úгнешь; -úг) *pf.*+g.; (*of money*) хватáть *impf.*, хватúть (-ит) *pf. impers.*+g. на+a.; **the money won't ~ to a car** этих дéнег не хвáтит на машúну; **~ up against** натáлкиваться *impf.*, натолкнýться *pf.* на+a.; (*also distance covered*) пробéг; (*direction*) направлéние; (*course, motion*) ход, течéние; (*regular route*) маршрýт; (*mus.*) рулáда; (*bombing ~*) захóд на цель; **at a ~** бегóм; **on** большóй спрос на+a.; **common ~ of men** обыкновéнные лю́ди (-дéй, -дям, -дьми) *pl.*; **in the long ~** в концé концóв. **run-down** *adj.* (*decayed*) захудáлый.

rung [rʌŋ] *n.* ступéнь, ступéнька.

runner ['rʌnə(r)] *n.* (*also tech.*) бегýн (-á); (*messenger*) посы́льный *sb.*; (*of sledge*) пóлоз (*pl.* полóзья, -ьев); (*cloth*) дорóжка; (*stem*) стéлющийся побéг; **~ bean** фасóль. **runner-up** *n.* учáстник состязáния, заня́вший вторóе мéсто. **running** *n.* бег; (*of machine*) ход, рабóта; **be in the ~** имéть *impf.* шáнсы на вы́игрыш; **make the ~** задавáть (-даю́, -даёшь) *impf.*, задáть (-áм, -áшь, -áсть, -адúм; зáдал, -á, -о) *pf.* темп; *adj.* бегýщий; (*of ~*) беговóй; (*after pl.n., in succession*) подря́д; **~ account** текýщий счёт; **~ commentary** (*радио*)репортáж; **~ title** колонтúтул; **~ water** протóчная водá (a. -ду). **running-board** *n.* поднóжка. **runway** *n.* (*aeron.*) взлётно-посáдочная полосá (a. пóлосу; *pl.* -осы, -óс, -осáм).

rupee [ru:'pi:] *n.* рýпия.

rupture ['rʌptʃə(r)] *n.* разры́в; (*hernia*) гры́жа.

rural ['ruər(ə)l] *adj.* сéльский, деревéнский.

ruse [ru:z] *n.* хúтрость, улóвка.

rush[1] [rʌʃ] *n.* (*plant*) (*also collect.*) камы́ш (-á), трострúк (-á); (*bot.*) сúтник.

rush[2] [rʌʃ] *v.t.* бы́стро проводúть (-ожý, -óдишь) *impf.*, провестú (-едý, -едёшь; -ёл, -елá) *pf.*; торопúть (-плю́, -пишь) *impf.*, по~ *pf.*; *v.i.* бросáться *impf.*, брóситься *pf.*; мчáться (мчусь, мчúшься) *impf.*; *n.* стремúтельное движéние, поры́в; (*influx*) наплы́в; (*of blood etc.*) прилúв; (*hurry*) спéшка; **~ job** аврáл. **rush-hour** *n.* часы́ *m.pl.* пик.

rusk [rʌsk] *n.* сухáрь (-ря́) *m.*

russet ['rʌsɪt] *adj.* красновáто-корúчневый.

Russia ['rʌʃə] *n.* Росси́я; **Holy** ~ Свята́я Русь. **Russian** *n.* ру́сский *sb.*; россия́нин (*pl.* -я́не, -я́н), -я́нка; *adj.* ру́сский; росси́йский; ~ **salad** винегре́т.

rust [rʌst] *n.* ржа́вчина; *v.i.* ржаве́ть *impf.*, за~ *pf.*

rustic ['rʌstɪk] *adj.* дереве́нский; (*unpolished, uncouth*) неотёсанный (-ан, -анна); *n.* дереве́нский, се́льский, жи́тель *m.*, ~ница.

rusticate *v.t.* (*univ.*) вре́менно исключа́ть *impf.*, исключи́ть *pf.* из университе́та; жить (живу́, -вёшь); жил, -á, -о) *impf.* в дере́вне.

rustle ['rʌs(ə)l] *n.* ше́лест, шо́рох, шурша́ние; *v.i.* шелесте́ть (-ти́шь) *impf.*; *v.t. & i.* шурша́ть (-шу́, -ши́шь) *impf.* (+*i.*); *v.t.* (~ *cattle*) красть (-аду́, -адёшь; -áл) *impf.*, у~ *pf.*

rust-proof ['rʌstpruːf] *adj.* нержаве́ющий. **rusty** *adj.* ржа́вый.

rut [rʌt] *n.* (*groove*) колея́.

ruthless ['ruːθlɪs] *adj.* безжа́лостный.

rye [raɪ] *n.* рожь (ржи); *attr.* ржано́й.

S

Sabbath ['sæbəθ] *n.* (*Jewish*) суббо́та; (*Christian*) воскресе́нье; (*witches'*) шаба́ш. **sabbatical** [sə'bætɪk(ə)l] *adj.*: ~ **year** годи́чный о́тпуск.

sable ['seɪb(ə)l] *n.* (*animal; fur*) со́боль (*pl.* (*animal*) -ли, -ле́й & (*fur*) -ля́) *m.*; (*fur*) собо́лий мех (*loc.* -е & -ý; *pl.* -á); *attr.* соболи́ный, собо́лий.

sabotage ['sæbətɑːʒ] *n.* сабота́ж, диве́рсия; *v.t.* саботи́ровать *impf. & pf.* **sabo'teur** *n.* саботажник, диверса́нт.

sabre ['seɪbə(r)] *n.* са́бля (*g.pl.* -бель), ша́шка. **sabre-rattling** *n.* бряца́ние ору́жием.

sac [sæk] *n.* мешо́чек (-чка).

saccharin ['sækərɪn] *n.* сахари́н.

saccharine ['sækə,riːn] *adj.* са́харистый.

sacerdotal [,sækə'dəʊt(ə)l] *adj.* свяще́ннический.

sachet ['sæʃeɪ] *n.* поду́шечка.

sack[1] [sæk] *v.t.* (*plunder*) разгра́бить *pf.*

sack[2] [sæk] *n.* куль (-ля́) *m.*, мешо́к (-шка́); **the** ~ (*dismissal*) увольне́ние; *v.t.* увольня́ть *impf.*, уво́лить *pf.* **sacking** *n.* (*hessian*) мешкови́на.

sacrament ['sækrəmənt] *n.* та́инство; (*Eucharist*) прича́стие. **sacred** ['seɪkrɪd] *adj.* свяще́нный (-éн, -éнна), свято́й (свят, -á, -о). **sacrifice** ['sækrɪ,faɪs] *n.* же́ртва; *v.t.* же́ртвовать *impf.*, по~ *pf.*+*i.* **sacrificial** [,sækrɪ'fɪʃ(ə)l] *adj.* же́ртвенный. **sacrilege** ['sækrɪlɪdʒ] *n.* святота́тство. **sacri'legious**

adj. святота́тственный. **sacristy** *n.* ри́зница. **sacrosanct** *adj.* свяще́нный (-éн, -éнна).

sad [sæd] *adj.* печа́льный, гру́стный (-тен, -тна́, -тно). **sadden** *v.t.* печа́лить *impf.*, о~ *pf.*

saddle ['sæd(ə)l] *n.* седло́ (*pl.* сёдла, -дел, -длам); *v.t.* седла́ть *impf.*, о~ *pf.*; (*burden*) обременя́ть *impf.*, обремени́ть *pf.* (**with** +*i.*). **saddler** *n.* седе́льник, шо́рник.

sadism ['seɪdɪz(ə)m] *n.* сади́зм. **sadist** *n.* сади́ст. **sadistic** [sə'dɪstɪk] *adj.* сади́стский.

sadness ['sædnɪs] *n.* печа́ль, грусть.

s.a.e. *abbr.* (*of* **stamped addressed envelope**) конве́рт с ма́ркой и обра́тным а́дресом.

safari [sə'fɑːrɪ] *n.* сафа́ри *nt. indecl.*; **on** ~ на охо́те; ~ **park** «сафа́ри» зоопа́рк.

safe [seɪf] *n.* сейф, несгора́емый шкаф (*loc.* -ý; *pl.* -ы́); *adj.* (*uninjured*) невреди́мый; (*out of danger*) в безопа́сности; (*secure*) безопа́сный; (*reliable*) надёжный; ~ **and sound** цел (-á, -о) и невреди́м. **safeguard** *n.* предохрани́тельная ме́ра; *v.t.* предохраня́ть *impf.*, предохрани́ть *pf.* **safety** *n.* безопа́сность; ~ **lamp** рудни́чная ла́мпа; ~ **pin** англи́йская була́вка; ~ **razor** безопа́сная бри́тва. **safety-belt** *n.* предохрани́тельный реме́нь (-мня́) *m.* **safety-catch** *n.* предохрани́тель *m.* **safety-valve** *n.* предохрани́тельный кла́пан; (*fig.*) отду́шина.

saffron ['sæfrən] *n.* шафра́н; *adj.* шафра́нный, шафра́новый.

sag [sæg] *v.i.* провиса́ть *impf.*, прови́снуть (-с) *pf.*; прогиба́ться *impf.*, прогну́ться *pf.*; *n.* провес, прогиб.

saga ['sɑːgə] *n.* са́га.

sagacious [sə'geɪʃ(ə)s] *adj.* проница́тельный. **sagacity** [sə'gæsɪtɪ] *n.* проница́тельность.

sage[1] [seɪdʒ] *n.* (*herb*) шалфе́й.

sage[2] [seɪdʒ] *n.* (*person*) мудре́ц (-á); *adj.* му́дрый (мудр, -á, -о).

sage-green [seɪdʒ'griːn] *adj.* серова́то-зелёный.

Sagittarius [,sædʒɪ'teərɪəs] *n.* Стреле́ц (-льца́).

sago ['seɪgəʊ] *n.* са́го *nt.indecl.*; (*palm*) са́говая па́льма.

Sahara [sə'hɑːrə] *n.* Caхápa.

sail [seɪl] *n.* па́рус (*pl.* -á); (*collect.*) паруса́ *m.pl.*; (*of windmill*) крыло́ (*pl.* -лья, -льев); *v.t.* (*a ship*) управля́ть *impf.*+*i.*; *v.i.* пла́вать *indet.*, плыть (плыву́, -вёшь; плыл, -á, -о) *det.*; (*depart*) отплыва́ть *impf.*, отплы́ть (-ыву́, -ывёшь; -ы́л, -ыла́, -ы́ло) *pf.* **sailboard** *n.* доска́ под па́русом. **sailboarder** *n.* виндсёрфинги́ст. **sailboarding** *n.* виндсёрфинг. **sailcloth** *n.* паруси́на. **sailing** *n.* (*sport*) па́русный спорт. **sailing-ship** *n.* па́русное су́дно (*pl.* -дá, -до́в). **sailor** *n.* матро́с, моря́к (-á).

saint [seɪnt, sənt] *n.* свято́й *sb.* **saintly** *adj.* свято́й (свят, -á, -о), безгре́шный.

St Petersburg [sənt' piːtəz,bɜːg] *n.* Санкт-Петербу́рг.

sake [seɪk] *n.*: **for the** ~ **of** ра́ди+*g.*, для+*g.*

salacious [sə'leɪʃəs] *adj.* непристо́йный; (*lustful*) похотли́вый.

salad ['sæləd] *n.* сала́т, винегре́т; ~ **days** зелёная ю́ность; ~ **oil** расти́тельное, оли́вковое, ма́сло. **salad-dressing** *n.* припра́ва к сала́ту.

salamander ['sælə,mændə(r)] *n.* салама́ндра.

salami [sə'lɑːmɪ] *n.* саля́ми *f.indecl*

salaried ['sælərɪd] *adj.* получа́ющий жа́лованье. **salary** *n.* жа́лованье.

sale [seɪl] *n.* прода́жа; (*also amount sold*) сбыт (*no pl.*); (*at reduced price*) распрода́жа по сни́женным це́нам; **be for** ~ продава́ться (-даётся) *impf.* **saleable** *adj.* хо́дкий (-док, -дка́, -дко) **saleroom** *n.* аукцио́нный зал. **salesman** *n.* продаве́ц (-вца́). **saleswoman** *n.* продавщи́ца.

salient ['seɪlɪənt] *adj.* (*projecting*) выдаю́щийся, выступа́ющий; (*conspicuous*) заме́тный, я́ркий; *n.* вы́ступ.

saline ['seɪlaɪn] *adj.* соляно́й.

saliva [sə'laɪvə] *n.* слюна́. **salivary** *adj.* слю́нный. **salivate** ['sælɪ,veɪt] *v.i.* выделя́ть *impf.*, вы́делить *pf.* слюну́. **sali'vation** *n.* слюноотече́ние.

sallow ['sæləʊ] *adj.* желтова́тый.

sally ['sælɪ] *n.* вы́лазка; (*witticism*) острота́; *v.i.*: ~ **forth, out** отправля́ться *impf.*, отпра́виться *pf.*; ~ **out** (*mil.*) де́лать *impf.*, с~ *pf.* вы́лазку.

salmon ['sæmən] *n.* лосо́сь *m.*, сёмга; (*cul.*) лососи́на, сёмга.

salon ['sælɒn, -lɔ̃] *n.* сало́н. **saloon** [sə'luːn] *n.* (*hall*) зал; (*on ship*) сало́н; (*rail.*) сало́н-ваго́н; (*bar*) бар; ~ **deck** па́луба пе́рвого кла́сса.

salt [sɔːlt, sɒlt] *n.* соль; ~ **lake** соляно́е о́зеро (*pl.* -ёра); ~ **mine** соляны́е ко́пи (-пей) *pl.*; ~ **water** морска́я вода́ (*a.* -ду); *adj.* солёный (со́лон, -á, -о); (*preserved in salt also*) засо́ленный (-ен); *v.t.* соли́ть (солю́, со́лишь) *impf.*, по~ *pf.*; заса́ливать *impf.*, засоли́ть (-олю́, -о́лишь) *pf.*; ~ **away** припря́тывать *impf.*, припря́тать (-я́чу, -я́чешь) *pf.* **salt-cellar** *n.* соло́нка. **salt-marsh** *n.* солонча́к (-á). **saltpetre** [,sɒlt'piːtə(r), ,sɔːlt-] *n.* сели́тра. **salt-water** *adj.* морско́й. **salty** *adj.* (*also fig.*) солёный (со́лон, -á, -о).

salubrious [sə'luːbrɪəs, sə'ljuː-] *adj.* здоро́вый.

salutary ['sæljʊtərɪ] *adj.* благотво́рный. **salu'tation** *n.* приве́тствие. **salute** [sə'luːt, -'ljuːt] *n.* приве́тствие; (*mil.*) салю́т; *v.t.* приве́тствовать *impf.* (*in past also pf.*); салютова́ть *impf. & pf.*, от~ *pf.+d.*

salvage ['sælvɪdʒ] *n.* спасе́ние; (*property*) спасённое иму́щество; (*ship*) спасённое су́дно (*pl.* -дá, -до́в); (*cargo*) спасённый груз; (*waste material*) ути́ль; *v.t.* спаса́ть *impf.*, спасти́ (-су́, -сёшь; -с, -слá, -сло) *pf.*

salvation [sæl'veɪʃ(ə)n] *n.* спасе́ние; **S~ Army** А́рмия спасе́ния.

salve [sælv, sɑːv] *n.* мазь, бальза́м; *v.t.*: ~ **one's conscience** успока́ивать *impf.*, успо-

ко́ить *pf.* со́весть.

salver ['sælvə(r)] *n.* подно́с.

salvo ['sælvəʊ] *n.* залп.

sal volatile [,sæl vɒ'lætɪlɪ] *n.* нюха́тельная соль.

same [seɪm] *adj.* (*monotonous*) однообра́зный; **the** ~ тот же са́мый; тако́й же, одина́ковый; **just the** ~ то́чно тако́й же; **much the** ~ почти́ тако́й же; *pron.*: **the** ~ одно́ и то́ же, то же са́мое; *adv.*: **the** ~ таки́м же о́бразом, так же; **all the** ~ всё-таки, тем не ме́нее. **sameness** *n.* однообра́зие.

samovar ['sæmə,vɑː(r)] *n.* самова́р.

sample ['sɑːmp(ə)l] *n.* образе́ц (-зца́), про́ба; *v.t.* про́бовать *impf.*, по~ *pf.* **sampler** *n.* образча́к вы́шивки.

sanatorium [,sænə'tɔːrɪəm] *n.* санато́рий.

sanctify ['sæŋktɪ,faɪ] *v.t.* освяща́ть *impf.*, освяти́ть (-ящу́, -яти́шь) *pf.* **sanctimonious** [,sæŋktɪ'məʊnɪəs] *adj.* ха́нжеский. **sanction** *n.* са́нкция; *v.t.* санкциони́ровать *impf. & pf.* **sanctity** ['sæŋktɪtɪ] *n.* (*holiness*) свя́тость; (*sacredness*) свяще́нность. **sanctuary** ['sæŋktjʊərɪ] *n.* святи́лище, алта́рь (-ря́) *m.*; (*refuge*) убе́жище; (*for animals etc.*) запове́дник. **sanctum** *n.* святая *sb.* святы́х; (*joc.*) рабо́чий кабине́т.

sand [sænd] *n.* песо́к (-скá(ý)); (*grain of* ~, *usu. pl.*) песчи́нка (*shoal, sg. or pl.*) о́тмель; *pl.* (*beach*) пляж; *pl.* (*expanse of* ~) пески́ *m.pl.*; *attr.* песо́чный, песча́ный.

sandal[1] ['sænd(ə)l] *n.* санда́лия.

sandal[2] ['sænd(ə)l], **-wood** *n.* санда́ловое де́рево.

sandbag ['sændbæg] *n.* мешо́к (-шка́) с песко́м; (*as ballast*) балла́стный мешо́к (-шка́); *v.t.* защища́ть *impf.*, защити́ть (-ищу́, -ити́шь) *pf.* мешка́ми с песко́м. **sandbank** *n.* о́тмель. **sand-bar** *n.* песча́ный бар. **sand-blast** *v.t.* обдува́ть *impf.*, обду́ть (-у́ю, -у́ешь) *pf.* песо́чной струёй. **sand-dune** *n.* дю́на. **sand-glass** *n.* песо́чные часы́ (-со́в) *pl.* **sandpaper** *n.* шку́рка; *v.t.* шлифова́ть *impf.*, от~ *pf.* шку́ркой. **sand-piper** *n.* перево́зчик. **sand-pit** *n.* (*children's*) песо́чница. **sandstone** *n.* песча́ник. **sandstorm** *n.* песча́ная бу́ря.

sandwich ['sænwɪdʒ, -wɪtʃ] *n.* са́ндвич, бутербро́д; (*cake*) торт с просло́йкой; ~ **bar** бутербро́дная *sb.*; *v.t.*: ~ **between** вставля́ть *impf.*, вста́вить *pf.* ме́жду+*i.* **sandwich-board** *n.* рекла́мные щиты́ *m.pl.* **sandwich-man** *n.* челове́к-рекла́ма.

sandy ['sændɪ] *adj.* песча́ный, песо́чный; (*hair*) рыжева́тый.

sane [seɪn] *adj.* норма́льный; (*of views*) разу́мный.

sang-froid [sɑ̃'frwɑː] *n.* самооблада́ние.

sanguinary ['sæŋgwɪnərɪ] *adj.* крова́вый. **sanguine** *adj.* сангвини́ческий, оптимисти́ческий.

sanitary ['sænɪtərɪ] *adj.* санита́рный; гигиени́ческий; ~ **towel** гигиени́ческая поду́шка.

sani'tation *n.* санитария; (*disposal of sewage*) водопровод и канализация. **sanity** *n.* нормальная психика; (*good sense*) здравый ум (-á).

Santa Claus ['sæntə ˌklɔːz] *n.* Санта Клаус; (*Russian equivalent*) дед-мороз.

sap¹ [sæp] *n.* (*juice*) сок (*loc.* -e & -ý); *v.t.* (*exhaust*) истощать *impf.*, истощить *pf.* (*cf.* **sap**²).

sap² [sæp] *n.* (*mil.*) сапа; *v.t.* (*undermine*) подрывать *impf.*, подорвать (-ву, -вёшь; -вáл, -валá, -вáло) *pf.* (*cf.* **sap**¹).

sapling ['sæplɪŋ] *n.* молодое деревце (*pl.* -вцá, -вéц, -вцáм).

sapper ['sæpə(r)] *n.* сапёр.

sapphire ['sæfaɪə(r)] *n.* сапфир; *adj.* (*colour*) синий (синь, -ня, -не).

Saracen ['særəs(ə)n] *n.* сарацин (*g.pl.* -н).

sarcasm ['sɑːˌkæz(ə)m] *n.* сарказм. **sar'castic** *adj.* саркастический.

sarcoma [sɑːˈkəʊmə] *n.* саркома.

sarcophagus [sɑːˈkɒfəgəs] *n.* саркофаг.

sardine ['sɑːdaɪn] *n.* сардина.

sardonic [sɑːˈdɒnɪk] *adj.* сардонический.

sari ['sɑːrɪ] *n.* сари *nt.indecl.*

sartorial [sɑːˈtɔːrɪəl] *adj.* портняжный.

SAS *abbr.* (*of* **Special Air Service**) спец-служба ВВС.

sash¹ [sæʃ] *n.* (*scarf*) пояс (*pl.* -á), кушак (-á).

sash² [sæʃ] *n.* (*frame*) скользящая рама. **sash-window** *n.* подъёмное окно (*pl.* окна, окон, окнам).

Satan ['seɪt(ə)n] *n.* сатана *m.* **satanic** [səˈtænɪk] *adj.* сатанинский; (*devilish*) дьявольский.

satchel ['sætʃ(ə)l] *n.* ранец (-нца), сумка.

sate [seɪt] *v.t.* насыщать *impf.*, насытить (-ыщу, -ытишь) *pf.*

sateen [sæˈtiːn] *n.* сатин.

satellite ['sætəlaɪt] *n.* спутник, сателлит (*also fig.*); ~ **television** космическое телевидение.

satiate ['seɪʃɪeɪt] *v.t.* насыщать *impf.*, насытить (-ыщу, -ытишь) *pf.*; **be ~d** пресыщаться *impf.*, пресытиться (-ыщусь, -ытишься) *pf.* **sati'ation** *n.* насыщение. **satiety** [səˈtaɪɪtɪ] *n.* пресыщение, сытость.

satin ['sætɪn] *n.* атлас; *adj.* атласный; ~ **stitch** гладь. **sati'net(te)** *n.* сатинет. **satiny** *adj.* атласный, шелковистый.

satire ['sætaɪə(r)] *n.* сатира. **satirical** [səˈtɪrɪk(ə)l] *adj.* сатирический. **satirist** ['sætərɪst] *n.* сатирик. **satirize** *v.t.* высмеивать *impf.*, высмеять (-ею, -еешь) *pf.*

satisfaction [ˌsætɪsˈfækʃ(ə)n] *n.* удовлетворение. **satisfactory** *adj.* удовлетворительный. **satisfy** ['sætɪsfaɪ] *v.t.* удовлетворять *impf.*, удовлетворить *pf.*; (*hunger, curiosity*) утолять *impf.*, утолить *pf.*

saturate ['sætʃəreɪt, -tjʊreɪt] *v.t.* пропитывать *impf.*, пропитать *pf.*; насыщать *impf.*, насытить (-ыщу, -ытишь) *pf.* **satu'ration** *n.* насыщение, насыщенность.

Saturday ['sætədeɪ, -dɪ] *n.* суббота.

Saturn ['sæt(ə)n] *n.* Сатурн. **saturnine** ['sætəˌnaɪn] *adj.* мрачный (-чен, -чнá, -чно), угрюмый.

satyr ['sætə(r)] *n.* сатир.

sauce [sɔːs] *n.* соус; (*insolence*) наглость; **apple** ~ яблочное пюре *nt.indecl.* **sauce-boat** *n.* соусник. **saucepan** *n.* кастрюля. **saucer** *n.* блюдце (*g.pl.* -дец). **saucy** *adj.* наглый (нагл, -á, -о).

Saudi Arabia ['saʊdɪ] Саудовская Аравия.

sauna ['sɔːnə] *n.* финская баня, сауна.

saunter ['sɔːntə(r)] *v.i.* прогуливаться *impf.*; *n.* прогулка.

sausage ['sɒsɪdʒ] *n.* колбаса (*pl.* -сы), сосиска; ~ **meat** колбасный фарш; ~ **roll** пирожок (-жкá) с колбасным фаршем.

savage ['sævɪdʒ] *adj.* дикий (дик, -á, -о); (*cruel*) жестокий (-ók, -oká, -óко); *n.* дикарь (-ря) *m.*; *v.t.* свирепо нападать *impf.*, напасть (-аду, -адёшь; -áл) *pf.* на+*a.* **sav-agery** *n.* дикость; жестокость.

savanna(h) [səˈvænə] *n.* саванна.

savant ['sæv(ə)nt, sæˈvɑ̃] *n.* учёный *sb.*

save [seɪv] *v.t.* (*rescue*) спасать *impf.*, спасти (-сý, -сёшь; -с, -слá, -сло) *pf.*; (*put aside*) откладывать *impf.*, отложить (-жý, -жишь) *pf.*; (*spare*) беречь (-егý, -ежёшь; -ёг, -еглá) *impf.*; *v.i.*: ~ **up** копить (-плю, -пишь) *impf.*, на~ *pf.* деньги. **savings** *n.* сбережения *nt.pl.*; ~ **bank** сберегательная касса. **saviour** *n.* спаситель *m.*

savour ['seɪvə(r)] *n.* вкус; *v.t.* смаковать *impf.*; наслаждаться *impf.*, насладиться *pf.*+*i.*

savoury ['seɪvərɪ] *adj.* (*sharp*) острый (остр & остёр, острá, óстро); (*salty*) солёный (солон, -á, -о); (*spicy*) пряный.

savoy [səˈvɔɪ] *n.* савойская капуста.

saw [sɔː] *n.* пилá (*pl.* -лы); *v.t.* пилить (-лю, -лишь) *impf.*; ~ **up** распиливать *impf.*, распилить (-лю, -лишь) *pf.* **sawdust** *n.* опилки (-лок) *pl.* **saw-edged** *adj.* пилообразный. **sawfish** *n.* пила-рыба. **sawmill** *n.* лесопильный завод, лесопилка. **sawyer** *n.* пильщик.

saxophone ['sæksəˌfəʊn] *n.* саксофон.

say [seɪ] *v.t.* говорить *impf.*, сказать (-ажý, -áжешь) *pf.*; **to ~ nothing of** не говоря уже о+*p.*; **that is to** ~ то есть; (*let us*) ~ скáжем; **it is said (that)** говорят (что); *n.* слово; (*opinion*) мнение; (*influence*) влияние; **have one's** ~ высказаться (-ажусь, -ажешься) *pf.* **saying** *n.* поговорка.

scab [skæb] *n.* (*on wound*) струп (*pl.* -ья, -ьев), корка; (*mange*) паршá (*strike-breaker*) штрейкбрехер.

scabbard ['skæbəd] *n.* ножны (*g.* -жен) *pl.*

scabies ['skeɪbiːz] *n.* чесотка.

scabious ['skeɪbɪəs] *n.* скабиоза.

scabrous ['skeɪbrəs] *adj.* скабрёзный.

scaffold ['skæfəʊld, -f(ə)ld] *n.* эшафот. **scaffolding** *n.* лесá (-сóв) *pl.*, подмости (-тей) *pl.*

scald [skɔːld] *v.t.* обва́ривать *impf.*, обвари́ть (-рю́, -ришь) *pf.*; *n.* ожо́г.

scale[1] [skeɪl] *n.* (*of fish*) чешу́йка; *pl.* чешуя́ (*collect.*); (*on boiler etc.*) на́кипь; *v.t.* чи́стить *impf.*, о~ *pf.*; соска́бливать *impf.*, соскобли́ть (-облю́, -обли́шь) *pf.* чешую́ с+*g.*; *v.i.* шелуши́ться *impf.*

scale[2] [skeɪl] *n.* (~-*pan*) ча́ша весо́в; *pl.* весы́ (-со́в) *pl.*

scale[3] [skeɪl] *n.* (*relative dimensions*) масшта́б; (*set of marks*) шкала́ (*pl.* -лы); (*mus.*) га́мма; (*math.*; ~ *of notation*) систе́ма счисле́ния; *v.t.* (*climb*) взбира́ться *impf.*, взобра́ться (взберу́сь, -рёшься; взобра́лся, -ала́сь, -а́ло́сь) *pf.* (по ле́стнице) на+*a.*; ~ **down** понижа́ть *impf.*, пони́зить *pf.*; ~ **up** повыша́ть *impf.*, повы́сить *pf.*

scallop ['skæləp, 'skɒl-] *n.* (*mollusc*) гребешо́к (-шка́); *pl.* (*decoration*) фесто́ны *m.pl.*; ~ **shell** ра́ковина гребешка́; *v.t.* (*cook*) запека́ть *impf.*, запе́чь (-еку́, -ечёшь; -ёк, -екла́) *pf.* в ра́ковине; (*decorate*) украша́ть *impf.*, укра́сить *pf.* фесто́нами.

scalp [skælp] *n.* ко́жа че́репа; (*as trophy*) скальп; *v.t.* скальпи́ровать *impf.* & *pf.*

scalpel ['skælp(ə)l] *n.* ска́льпель *m.*

scaly ['skeɪlɪ] *adj.* чешу́йчатый; (*of boiler etc.*) покры́тый на́кипью.

scamp [skæmp] *n.* плути́шка *m.*

scamper ['skæmpə(r)] *v.i.* бы́стро бе́гать *impf.*; (*playfully*) резви́ться *impf.*

scampi ['skæmpɪ] *n.* креве́тки *f.pl.*

scan [skæn] *v.t.* & *i.* (*verse*) сканди́ровать(ся) *impf.*; *v.t.* (*intently*) внима́тельно рассма́тривать *impf.*; (*quickly*) бе́гло просма́тривать *impf.*, просмотре́ть (-рю́, -ришь) *pf.*

scandal ['skænd(ə)l] *n.* сканда́л; (*gossip*) спле́тни (-тен) *pl.* **scandalize** *v.t.* шоки́ровать *impf.* & *pf.* **scandalmonger** *n.* спле́тник, -ица. **scandalous** *adj.* сканда́льный.

Scandinavia [ˌskændɪˈneɪvɪə] *n.* Скандина́вия. **Scandinavian** *adj.* скандина́вский.

scanner *n.* (*comput., med.*) ска́нер.

scansion ['skænʃ(ə)n] *n.* сканди́рование.

scanty ['skæntɪ] *adj.* ску́дный (-ден, -дна, -дно); (*insufficient*) недоста́точный.

scapegoat ['skeɪpɡəʊt] *n.* козёл (-зла́) отпуще́ния.

scapula ['skæpjʊlə] *n.* лопа́тка.

scar [skɑː(r)] *n.* рубе́ц (-бца́), шрам. **scarred** *adj.* обезобра́женный (-ен) рубца́ми, шра́мами.

scarab ['skærəb] *n.* скарабе́й.

scarce [skeəs] *adj.* дефици́тный, недоста́точный; (*rare*) ре́дкий (-док, -дка́, -дко); **make o.s.** ~ улизну́ть *pf.* **scarcely** *adv.* (*only just*) едва́; (*surely not*) едва́ ли. **scarcity** *n.* недоста́ток (-тка), дефици́т.

scare [skeə(r)] *v.t.* пуга́ть *impf.*, ис~, на~ *pf.*; ~ **away, off** отпу́гивать *impf.*, отпугну́ть *pf.*; *n.* па́ника. **scarecrow** *n.* пу́гало, чу́чело. **scaremonger** *n.* паникёр.

scarf [skɑːf] *n.* шарф.

scarlet ['skɑːlɪt] *adj.* (*n.*) а́лый (цвет); ~ **fever** скарлати́на.

scathing ['skeɪðɪŋ] *adj.* е́дкий (е́док, едка́, е́дко), уничтожа́ющий.

scatter ['skætə(r)] *v.t.* & *i.* рассыпа́ть(ся) *impf.*, рассы́пать(ся) (-плю, -плет(ся)) *pf.*; (*disperse*) рассе́ивать(ся) *impf.*, рассе́ять(ся) (-е́ю, -е́ет(ся)) *pf.*; *v.t.* (*disperse, drive away*) разгоня́ть *impf.*, разогна́ть (разгоню́, -нишь; разогна́л, -а́, -о) *pf.*; *v.i.* (*run*) разбега́ться *impf.*, разбежа́ться (-ежи́тся, -егу́тся) *pf.* **scatterbrained** *adj.* легкомы́сленный (-ен, -енна). **scattered** *adj.* разбро́санный (-ан); (*sporadic*) отде́льный.

scavenger ['skævɪndʒə(r)] *n.* (*person*) му́сорщик; (*animal*) живо́тное *sb.*, пита́ющееся па́далью.

scenario [sɪˈnɑːrɪəʊ, -ˈneərɪəʊ] *n.* сцена́рий. **scenarist** *n.* сценари́ст. **scene** [siːn] *n.* сце́на; (*part of play also*) явле́ние; (*place of action*) ме́сто де́йствия; (*scenery*) декора́ция; **behind the** ~**s** за кули́сами; **make a** ~ устра́ивать *impf.*, устро́ить *pf.* сце́ну. **scene-painter** *n.* худо́жник-декора́тор. **scenery** *n.* (*theatr.*) декора́ция; (*landscape*) пейза́ж. **scene-shifter** *n.* рабо́чий *sb.* сце́ны. **scenic** *adj.* сцени́ческий.

scent [sent] *n.* (*smell*) арома́т; (*perfume*) духи́ (-хо́в) *pl.*; (*trail*) след (-а(у); *pl.* -ы́); *v.t.* (*discern*) чу́ять (чу́ю, чу́ешь) *impf.*; (*apply perfume*) души́ть (-шу́, -шишь) *impf.*, на~ *pf.*; (*make fragrant*) наполня́ть *impf.*, напо́лнить *pf.* арома́том.

sceptic ['skeptɪk] *n.* ске́птик. **sceptical** *adj.* скепти́ческий. **scepticism** *n.* скептици́зм.

sceptre ['septə(r)] *n.* ски́петр.

schedule ['ʃedjuːl] *n.* (*timetable*) расписа́ние; (*inventory*) о́пись; *v.t.* составля́ть *impf.*, соста́вить *pf.* расписа́ние, о́пись, +*g.*

schematic [skɪˈmætɪk, skiː-] *adj.* схемати́ческий. **scheme** [skiːm] *n.* (*plan*) прое́кт; (*intention*) за́мысел (-сла); (*intrigue*) махина́ция; *v.i.* стро́ить *impf.*, та́йные пла́ны. **'schemer** *n.* интрига́н. **'scheming** *adj.* интригу́ющий.

scherzo ['skeətsəʊ] *n.* ске́рцо *nt.indecl.*

schism ['sɪz(ə)m, 'skɪ-] *n.* раско́л. **schis'matic** *adj.* раско́льнический; *n.* раско́льник.

schizophrenia [ˌskɪtsəˈfriːnɪə] *n.* шизофрени́я. **schizophrenic** [ˌskɪtsəˈfrenɪk, -ˈfriːnɪk] *adj.* шизофрени́ческий; *n.* шизофре́ник.

scholar ['skɒlə(r)] *n.* учёный *sb.*: (~*ship holder*) стипендиа́т, ~ка. **scholarly** *adj.* учёный, нау́чный. **scholarship** *n.* учёность, нау́ка; (*payment*) стипе́ндия.

school [skuːl] *n.* шко́ла; (*specialist* ~) учи́лище; (*univ.*) факульте́т; *attr.* шко́льный; *v.t.* (*curb*) обу́здывать *impf.*, обузда́ть *pf.*; (*accustom*) приуча́ть *impf.*, приучи́ть (-чу́, -чишь) *pf.* (**to** к+*d.*, +*inf.*). **school-book** *n.* уче́бник. **schoolboy** *n.* шко́льник, учени́к

(-á). **schoolgirl** *n.* шко́льница, учени́ца. **schooling** *n.* обуче́ние. **school-leaver** *n.* выпускни́к (-á), -и́ца. **schoolmaster** *n.* шко́льный учи́тель (*pl.* -ля́) *m.* **schoolmistress** *n.* шко́льная учи́тельница.

schooner ['sku:nə(r)] *n.* шху́на.

sciatic [saɪˈætɪk] *adj.* седа́лищный. **sciatica** *n.* и́шиас.

science ['saɪəns] *n.* нау́ка; (*natural* ~) есте́ственные нау́ки *f.pl.*; ~ **fiction** нау́чная фанта́стика. **scien'tific** *adj.* нау́чный; ~ **calculator** компью́тер-калькуля́тор. **scientist** *n.* учёный *sb.*; (*natural* ~) есте́ственник, -ица.

scintillate ['sɪntɪˌleɪt] *v.i.* и́скри́ться *impf.* **scintillating** *adj.* блиста́тельный.

scion ['saɪən] *n.* о́тпрыск.

scissors ['sɪzəz] *n.* но́жницы (-ц) *pl.*

sclerosis [sklɪəˈrəʊsɪs] *n.* склеро́з.

scoff¹ [skɒf] *v.i.* (*mock*) издева́ться *impf.* (**at** над+*i.*).

scoff² [skɒf] *v.t.* (*eat*) жрать (жру, жрёшь; жрал, -á, -о) *impf.*, со~ *pf.*

scold [skəʊld] *v.t.* брани́ть *impf.*, вы́~ *pf.* **scolding** *n.* нагоня́й.

scollop *see* **scallop**

sconce [skɒns] *n.* (*bracket*) бра *nt.indecl.*; (*candlestick*) подсве́чник.

scone [skɒn, skəʊn] *n.* сдо́бная лепёшка.

scoop [sku:p] *n.* черпа́к (-á), ковш (-á); *v.t.* (~ *out, up*) вычёрпывать *impf.*, вы́черпать *pf.*

scooter ['sku:tə(r)] *n.* (*child's*) самока́т, ро́ллер; (*motor* ~) моторо́ллер.

scope [skəʊp] *n.* преде́лы *m.pl.*, просто́р, разма́х.

scorch [skɔ:tʃ] *v.t.* пали́ть *impf.*, с~ *pf.*; подпа́ливать *impf.*, подпали́ть *pf.*; ~**ed earth policy** та́ктика вы́женной земли́; *n.* **scorching** *adj.* паля́щий, зно́йный.

score [skɔ:(r)] *n.* (*notch*) зару́бка; (*account, number of points etc.*) счёт; (*mus.*) партиту́ра; (*twenty*) два деся́тка; *pl.* (*great numbers*) деся́тки *m.pl.*, мно́жество; *v.t.* (*notch*) де́лать *impf.*, с~ *pf.* зару́бки на+*p.*; (*points etc.*) получа́ть *impf.*, получи́ть (-чу́, -чишь) *pf.*; (*mus.*) оркестрова́ть *impf.* & *pf.*; *v.i.* (*keep* ~) вести́ (веду́, -дёшь; вёл, -á) *impf.*, с~ *pf.* счёт.

scorn [skɔ:n] *n.* презре́ние; *v.t.* презира́ть *impf.* презре́ть (-рю́, -ри́шь) *pf.* **scornful** *adj.* презри́тельный.

Scorpio ['skɔ:pɪəʊ] *n.* Скорпио́н.

scorpion ['skɔ:pɪən] *n.* скорпио́н.

Scot [skɒt] *n.* шотла́ндец (-дца), -дка. **Scotch** *adj.* шотла́ндский; *n.* (*whisky*) шотла́ндское ви́ски; *nt.indecl.*; **the** ~ шотла́ндцы *m.pl.*

scot-free ['skɒtfri:] *adv.* безнака́занно.

Scotland ['skɒtlənd] *n.* Шотла́ндия. **Scots, Scottish** *adj.* шотла́ндский; *see* **Scotch**

scoundrel ['skaʊndr(ə)l] *n.* негодя́й, подле́ц (-á).

scour¹ ['skaʊə(r)] *v.t.* (*cleanse*) отчища́ть *impf.*, отчи́стить *pf.* **scourer** *n.* металли́ческая моча́лка.

scour² ['skaʊə(r)] *v.t.* & *i.* (*rove*) ры́скать (ры́щу, -щешь) *impf.* (по+*d.*).

scourge [skɜ:dʒ] *n.* бич (-á); *v.t.* бичева́ть (-чу́ю, -чу́ешь) *impf.*

scout [skaʊt] *n.* разве́дчик; (**S**~) бойска́ут; *v.i.*: ~ **about** ры́скать (ры́щу, -щешь) *impf.* (**for** в по́исках+*g.*).

scowl [skaʊl] *v.i.* хму́риться *impf.*, на~ *pf.* *n.* хму́рый вид, взгляд.

scrabble ['skræb(ə)l] *v.i.*: ~ **about** ры́ться (ро́юсь, ро́ешься) *impf.*

scramble ['skræmb(ə)l] *v.i.* кара́бкаться *impf.*, вс~ *pf.*; (*struggle*) дра́ться (деру́сь, -рёшься; дра́лся, -ала́сь, -а́лось) *impf.* (**for** за+*a.*); *v.t.* (*mix together*) переме́шивать *impf.*, перемеша́ть *pf.*; ~**d eggs** яи́чница-болту́нья.

scrap¹ [skræp] *n.* (*fragment etc.*) клочо́к (-чка́), обре́зок (-зка), кусо́чек (-чка); *pl.* оста́тки *m.pl.*; *pl.* (*of food*) объе́дки (-ков) *pl.*; ~ **metal** металли́ческий лом, скрап; *v.t.* превраща́ть *impf.*, преврати́ть (-ащу́, -ати́шь) *pf.* в лом; пуска́ть *impf.*, пусти́ть (пущу́, пу́стишь) *pf.* на слом.

scrap² [skræp] *n.* (*fight*) дра́ка; *v.i.* дра́ться (деру́сь, -рёшься; дра́лся, -ала́сь, -а́лось) *impf.*

scrape [skreɪp] *v.t.* скрести́ (скребу́, -бёшь; скрёб, -ла́) *impf.*; скобли́ть (-облю́, -о́бли́шь) *impf.*; ~ **off** отскреба́ть *impf.*, отскрести́ (-ребу́, -ребёшь; -рёб, -ребла́) *pf.*; ~ **through** (*examination*) с трудо́м выде́рживать *impf.*, вы́держать (-жу, -жишь) *pf.*; ~ **together** наскреба́ть *impf.*, наскрести́ (-ребу́, -ребёшь; -рёб, -ребла́) *pf.*

scratch [skrætʃ] *v.t.* цара́пать *impf.*, о~ *pf.*; *v.t.* & *abs.* чеса́ть(ся) (чешу́(сь), -шешь(ся)) *impf.*, по~ *pf.*; *v.abs.* цара́паться *impf.*; *v.t.* (*erase*, ~ **off, through** *etc.*) вычёркивать *impf.*, вы́черкнуть *pf.*; *n.* цара́пина; *adj.* случа́йный.

scrawl [skrɔ:l] *n.* кара́кули *f.pl.*; *v.t.* писа́ть (пишу́, -шешь) *impf.*, на~ *pf.* кара́кулями.

scrawny ['skrɔ:nɪ] *adj.* то́щий (тощ, -á, -е), сухопа́рый.

scream [skri:m] *n.* крик, визг; *v.i.* крича́ть (-чу́, -чи́шь) *impf.*, кри́кнуть *pf.*; *v.t.* выкри́кивать *impf.*, вы́крикнуть *pf.*

screech [skri:tʃ] *n.* визг; *v.i.* визжа́ть (-жу́, -жи́шь) *impf.*

screen [skri:n] *n.* ши́рма; (*cin., television, radio, etc.*) экра́н; (*sieve*) гро́хот; *v.t.* (*shelter*) защища́ть *impf.*, защити́ть (-ищу́, -ити́шь) *pf.*; заслоня́ть *impf.*, заслони́ть *pf.*; (*show film etc.*) демонстри́ровать *impf.* & *pf.*; (*sieve*) просе́ивать *impf.*, просе́ять (-е́ю, -е́ешь) *pf.*; ~ **off** отгора́живать *impf.*, отгороди́ть (-ожу́, -о́ди́шь) *pf.* ши́рмой. **screen-play** *n.* сцена́рий.

screw [skru:] *n.* (*male* ~; *propeller*) винт (-á); (*female* ~) га́йка; (~-*bolt*) болт (-á); *v.t.* (~ *on*) прива́нчивать *impf.*, привинти́ть *pf.*; (~

up) зави́нчивать *impf.*, завинти́ть *pf.*; ~ **up one's eyes** щу́риться *impf.*, со~ *pf.* **screwdriver** *n.* отвёртка.

scribble ['skrɪb(ə)l] *v.t.* небре́жно, бы́стро, писа́ть (пишу́, -шешь) *impf.*, на~ *pf.*; *n.* кара́кули *f.pl.* **scribbler** *n.* писа́ка *c.g.*

scribe [skraɪb] *n.* писе́ц (-сца́); (*bibl.*) кни́жник.

scrimmage ['skrɪmɪdʒ] *n.* сва́лка.

script [skrɪpt] *n.* по́черк, шрифт; (*of film etc.*) сцена́рий.

Scripture ['skrɪptʃə(r)] *n.* свяще́нное писа́ние.

scriptwriter ['skrɪpt,raɪtə(r)] *n.* сценари́ст.

scrofula ['skrɒfjʊlə] *n.* золоту́ха.

scroll [skrəʊl] *n.* сви́ток (-тка); (*design*) завито́к (-тка́). **scrollwork** *n.* орна́мент в ви́де завитко́в.

scrounge [skraʊndʒ] *v.t.* (*steal*) ти́брить *impf.*, с~ *pf.*; (*cadge*) выкля́нчивать *impf.*, вы́клянчить *pf.*; *v.i.* попроша́йничать *impf.*

scrub¹ [skrʌb] *n.* (*brushwood*) куста́рник; (*area*) поро́сшая куста́рником ме́стность.

scrub² [skrʌb] *v.t.* мыть (мо́ю, мо́ешь) *impf.*, вы́~ *pf.* щёткой; *v.i.* чи́стка. **scrubbingbrush** *n.* жёсткая щётка.

scruff [skrʌf] *n.* загри́вок (-вка); **take by the ~ of the neck** брать (беру́, -рёшь; брал, -á, -о) *impf.*, взять (возьму́, -мёшь; взял, -á, -о) *pf.* за ши́ворот.

scruffy ['skrʌfɪ] *adj.* (*of clothes*) потрёпанный (-ан, -анна); (*of person*) неря́шливый.

scrum(mage) ['skrʌmɪdʒ] *n.* схва́тка вокру́г мяча́.

scruple ['skru:p(ə)l] *n.* (*also pl.*) колеба́ние, угрызе́ния *nt.pl.* со́вести; *v.i.* колеба́ться (-блюсь, -блешься) *impf.* **scrupulous** *adj.* скрупулёзный, щепети́вый.

scrutineer [,skru:tɪ'nɪə(r)] *n.* прове́рщик, -ица. **'scrutinize** *v.t.* рассма́тривать *impf.* **'scrutiny** *n.* рассмотре́ние, прове́рка.

scud [skʌd] *v.i.* нести́сь (несётся; нёсся, несла́сь) *impf.*, по~ *pf.*; скользи́ть *impf.*

scuffed [skʌfd] *adj.* потёртый, поцара́панный.

scuffle ['skʌf(ə)l] *n.* сва́лка; *v.i.* дра́ться (деру́сь, -рёшься; дра́лся, -ала́сь, -а́лось) *impf.*

scull [skʌl] *n.* весло́ (*pl.* вёсла, -сел, -слам); (*stern oar*) кормово́е весло́; *v.i.* грести́ (гребу́, -бёшь; грёб, -ла́) *impf.* (па́рными вёслами); гала́нить *impf.*

scullery ['skʌlərɪ] *n.* судомо́йня (*g.pl.* -óен).

sculptor ['skʌlptə(r)] *n.* ску́льптор. **sculptural** ['skʌlptʃərəl] *adj.* скульпту́рный. **sculpture** ['skʌlptʃə(r)] *n.* скульпту́ра.

scum [skʌm] *n.* пе́на, на́кипь; (*fig., people*) подо́нки (-ков) *pl.*

scupper¹ ['skʌpə(r)] *n.* шпига́т.

scupper² ['skʌpə(r)] *v.t.* (*ship*) потопля́ть *impf.*, потопи́ть (-плю́, -пишь) *pf.*

scurf [skɜːf] *n.* пе́рхоть.

scurrility [skʌ'rɪlɪtɪ] *n.* непристо́йность, гру́бость. **'scurrilous** *adj.* непристо́йный, гру́бый (груб, -á, -о).

scurry ['skʌrɪ] *v.i.* поспе́шно, суетли́во, бе́гать *indet.*, бежа́ть (бегу́, -бежи́шь) *det.*

scurvy ['skɜːvɪ] *n.* цинга́; *adj.* по́длый (подл, -á, -о).

scuttle¹ ['skʌt(ə)l] *n.* (*coal-box*) ведёрка (*pl.* -рки, -рок, -ркам) для угля́.

scuttle² ['skʌt(ə)l] *v.t.* (*ship*) затопля́ть *impf.*, затопи́ть (-плю́, -пишь) *pf.*

scuttle³ ['skʌt(ə)l] *v.i.* (*run away*) удира́ть *impf.*, удра́ть (удеру́, -рёшь; удра́л, -á, -о) *pf.*

scythe [saɪð] *n.* коса́ (*a.* ко́су; *pl.* -сы).

sea [si:] *n.* мо́ре (*pl.* -ря́); **at** ~ в (откры́том) мо́ре; **by** ~ мо́рем; *attr.* морско́й; ~ **anchor** плаву́чий я́корь (*pl.* -ря́) *m.*; ~ **anemone** акти́ния; ~ **breeze** ве́тер (-тра) с мо́ря; ~ **dog** (*person*) морско́й волк (*pl.* -и, -óв); ~ **front** на́бережная *sb.*; ~ **horse** морско́й конёк (-нька́); ~ **lane** морско́й путь (-ти́, -тём) *m.*; ~ **level** у́ровень (-вня) *m.* мо́ря; ~ **lion** морско́й лев (льва); ~ **urchin** морско́й ёж (-á); ~ **wall** да́мба. **seaboard** *n.* побере́жье. **seacoast** *n.* побере́жье. **seafaring** *n.* морепла́вание. **seagoing** *adj.* да́льнего пла́вания. **seagull** *n.* ча́йка.

seal¹ [si:l] *n.* (*on document etc.*) печа́ть; *v.t.* скрепля́ть *impf.*, скрепи́ть *pf.* печа́тью; запеча́тывать *impf.*, запеча́тать *pf.*

seal² [si:l] *n.* (*animal*) тюле́нь *m.*; (*fur-*~) ко́тик.

sealing-wax ['si:lɪŋ,wæks] *n.* сургу́ч (-á).

sealskin ['si:lskɪn] *n.* ко́тиковый мех (*loc.* -е & -ý); *attr.* ко́тиковый.

seam [si:m] *n.* шов (шва), рубе́ц (-бца́); (*stratum*) пласт (-á, *loc.* -ý); *v.t.* сшива́ть *impf.*, сшить (сошью́, -ьёшь) *pf.* шва́ми.

seaman ['si:mən] *n.* моря́к (-á); (*also rank*) матро́с.

seamstress ['semstrɪs] *n.* швея́.

seamy ['si:mɪ] *adj.* со шва́ми нару́жу; **the ~ side** (*also fig.*) изна́нка.

seance ['seɪɑ̃s] *n.* спирити́ческий сеа́нс.

seaplane ['si:pleɪn] *n.* гидросамолёт. **seaport** *n.* порто́вый го́род (*pl.* -á).

sear [sɪə(r)] *v.t.* прижига́ть *impf.*, приже́чь (-жгу́, -жжёшь, -жгу́т; -жёг, -жгла́) *pf.*

search [sɜːtʃ] *v.t.* обы́скивать *impf.*, обыска́ть (-ыщу́, -ы́щешь) *pf.*; *v.i.* иска́ть (ищу́, и́щешь) *impf.* (**for** +*a.*); производи́ть (-ожу́, -о́дишь) *impf.*, произвести́ (-еду́, -едёшь; -ёл, -ела́) *pf.* о́быск; *n.* по́иски *m.pl.*; о́быск; ~ **warrant** о́рдер (*pl.* -á) на о́быск. **searching** *adj.* (*thorough*) тща́тельный; (*look*) испыту́ющий. **searchlight** *n.* прожёктор (*pl.* -ы & -á). **search-party** *n.* по́исковая гру́ппа.

seascape ['si:skeɪp] *n.* мари́на. **seashore** *n.* побере́жье. **seasickness** *n.* морска́я боле́знь. **seaside** *n.* бе́рег (*loc.* -ý) мо́ря; (*resort*) морско́й куро́рт.

season ['si:z(ə)n] *n.* сезо́н; (*period in general*) пери́од; (*one of four*) вре́мя *nt.* го́да; **in** ~ по сезо́ну; ~ **ticket** сезо́нный биле́т; *v.t.*

(*mature*) выдéрживать *impf.*, вы́держать (-жу, -жишь) *pf.*; (*flavour*) приправлять *impf.*, приправить *pf.* **seasonable** *adj.* по сезóну; (*timely*) своеврéменный (-нен, -нна). **seasonal** *adj.* сезóнный. **seasoning** *n.* приправа.

seat [si:t] *n.* мéсто (*pl.* -тá), сидéнье; (*chair*) стул (*pl.* -ья, -ьев); (*bench*) скамéйка; (*buttocks*) седáлище; (*of trousers*) зад (*loc.* -ý; *pl.* -ы́); (*country* ~) усáдьба; (*ticket*) билéт; *v.t.* сажáть *impf.*, посадить (-ажý, -áдишь) *pf.*; (*of room etc.*) вмещáть *impf.*, вместить *pf.*; **be** ~**ed** садиться *impf.*, сесть (сяду, -дешь; сел) *pf.* **seat-belt** *n.* привязнóй ремéнь(-мня) *m.*

seaweed ['si:wi:d] *n.* морскáя вóдоросль.

sebaceous [sɪ'beɪʃəs] *adj.* сáльный.

sec [sek] *n.*: **half a** ~! минýтку!; один момéнт.

sec. *abbr.* (*of* second(s)) сек., секýнда.

secateurs [,sekə'tɜ:z] *n.* секáтор.

secede [sɪ'si:d] *v.i.* откáлываться *impf.*, отколóться (-люсь, -лешься) *pf.* **secession** [sɪ'seʃ(ə)n] *n.* откóл.

secluded [sɪ'klu:dɪd] *adj.* укрóмный. **seclusion** *n.* укрóмность; (*place*) укрóмное мéсто.

second[1] ['sekənd] *adj.* вторóй; **be** ~ **to** (*inferior*) уступáть *impf.*, уступить (-плю, -пишь) *pf.*+*d.*; ~ **ballot** перебаллотирóвка; ~ **sight** ясновидение; **on** ~ **thoughts** взвéсив всё ещё раз; **have** ~ **thoughts** передýмывать *impf.*, передýмать *pf.* (**about** +*a.*); ~ **wind** вторóе дыхáние; *n.* вторóй *sb.*; (*date*) вторóе (числó) *sb.*; (*mus.*; *time*; *angle*) секýнда; (*coll.*, *moment*) момéнт; (*in duel*) секундáнт; *pl.* товáр вторóго сóрта; *pl.* (~ *helping*) вторáя пóрция; ~ **in command** заместитель *m.* командира; ~ **hand** (*of clock etc.*) секýндная стрéлка; *v.t.* (*support*) поддéрживать *impf.*, поддержáть (-жý, -жишь) *pf.*

second[2] [sɪ'kɒnd] *v.t.* (*transfer*) откомандирóвывать *impf.* откомандировáть *pf.*

secondary ['sekəndərɪ] *adj.* втори́чный, второстепéнный (-нен, -нна); (*education*) срéдний. **second-best** *adj.* второсóртный. **second-class** *adj.* второклáссный, второсóртный. **second-hand** *adj.* подéржанный (-ан, -анна); (*of information*) из вторы́х рук. **secondly** *adv.* во-вторы́х. **second-rate** *adj.* второразря́дный.

secrecy ['si:krɪsɪ] *n.* секрéтность. **secret** *n.* тáйна, секрéт; *adj.* тáйный, секрéтный; (*hidden*) потайнóй.

secretarial [,sekrɪ'teərɪəl] *adj.* секретáрский. **secretariat** *n.* секретариáт. '**secretary** *n.* секретáрь (-ря́) *m.*, -рша; (*minister*) министр.

secrete [sɪ'kri:t] *v.t.* (*conceal*) прятать (-я́чу, -я́чешь) *impf.*, с~ *pf.*; (*med.*) выделя́ть *impf.*, вы́делить *pf.* **secretion** *n.* укрывáние; (*med.*) секрéция, выделéние.

secretive ['si:krɪtɪv] *adj.* скры́тный.

sect [sekt] *n.* сéкта. **sectarian** [sek'teərɪən] *adj.* сектáнтский; *n.* сектáнт.

section ['sekʃ(ə)n] *n.* сéкция, отрéзок (-зка);

(*of book*) раздéл; (*of solid*) сечéние, прóфиль, разрéз. **sectional** *adj.* секциóнный.

sector *n.* сéктор (*pl.* -ы & -á), учáсток (-тка).

secular ['sekjʊlə(r)] *adj.* свéтский, мирскóй; ~ **clergy** бéлое духовéнство. **seculari'zation** *n.* секуляризáция. **secularize** *v.t.* секуляризовáть *impf.* & *pf.*

secure [sɪ'kjʊə(r)] *adj.* безопáсный, надёжный; *v.t.* (*fasten*) закрепля́ть *impf.*, закрепи́ть *pf.*; (*guarantee*) обеспéчивать *impf.*, обеспéчить *pf.*; (*obtain*) доставáть (-таю, -таёшь) *impf.*, достáть (-áну, -áнешь) *pf.* **security** *n.* безопáсность; (*guarantee*) залóг; *pl.* цéнные бумáги *f.pl.*; **S**~ **Council** Совéт Безопáсности; ~ **guard** охрáнник; ~ **risk** неблагонадёжный человéк (*pl.* лю́ди, -дéй, -дям, -дьми́); **social** ~ социáльное обеспéчение.

sedan(-chair) [sɪ'dæn] *n.* портшéз.

sedate [sɪ'deɪt] *adj.* степéнный (-нен, -нна). **sedation** [sɪ'deɪʃ(ə)n] *n.* успокоéние. **sedative** ['sedətɪv] *adj.* успокáивающий; *n.* успокáивающее срéдство.

sedentary ['sedəntərɪ] *adj.* сидя́чий.

sedge [sedʒ] *n.* осóка.

sediment ['sedɪmənt] *n.* осáдок (-дка), отстóй. **sedi'mentary** *adj.* осáдочный.

sedition [sɪ'dɪʃ(ə)n] *n.* подстрекáтельство к мятежý. **seditious** *adj.* подстрекáтельский, мятéжный.

seduce [sɪ'dju:s] *v.t.* соблазня́ть *impf.*, соблазни́ть *pf.*; совращáть *impf.*, соврати́ть (-ащý, -ати́шь) *pf.* **seducer** *n.* соблазни́тель. **seductive** [sɪ'dʌktɪv] *adj.* соблазни́тельный, обольсти́тельный. **seductress** *n.* соблазни́тельница.

sedulous ['sedjʊləs] *adj.* прилéжный.

see[1] [si:] *n.* епáрхия; **Holy S**~ пáпский престóл.

see[2] [si:] *v.t.* & *i.* ви́деть (ви́жу, ви́дишь) *impf.*, у~ *pf.*; *v.t.* (*watch*, *look*) смотрéть (-рю́, -ришь) *impf.*, по~ *pf.*; (*find out*) узнавáть (-наю́, -наёшь) *impf.*, узнáть *pf.*; (*understand*) понимáть *impf.*, поня́ть (поймý, -мёшь; пóнял, -á, -о) *pf.*; (*meet*) ви́деться (ви́жусь, ви́дишься) *impf.*, у~ *pf.* с+*i.*; (*imagine*) представля́ть *impf.*, представить *pf.* себé; (*escort*) провожáть *impf.*, проводи́ть *pf.*; ~ **about** (*attend to*) забóтиться *impf.*, по~ *pf.* о+*p.*; ~ **over** осмáтривать *impf.*, осмотрéть (-рю́, -ришь) *pf.*; ~ **through** (*fig.*) ви́деть (ви́жу, ви́дишь) *impf.*, насквóзь+*a.*

seed [si:d] *n.* сéмя (*g.pl.* -мя́н) *nt.*; (*grain*) зернó. **seed-bed** *n.* парни́к (-á). **seed-cake** *n.* бýлочка с тми́ном. **seed-corn** *n.* посевнóе зернó. **seedling** *n.* сея́нец (-нца); *pl.* рассáда. **seed-pearl(s)** *n.* мéлкий жéмчуг. **seedy** *adj.* (*shabby*) потрёпанный (-ан, -анна); (*ill*) нездорóвый.

seeing (that) ['si:ɪŋ] *conj.* ввидý тогó, что.

seek [si:k] *v.t.* искáть (ищý, -щешь) *impf.*+*a.* & *g.*

seem [si:m] *v.i.* каза́ться (кажу́сь, -жешься) *impf.*, по~ *pf.* (+*i.*) (*often used parenthetically in impers. forms*). **seeming** *adj.* мни́мый. **seemingly** *adv.* по-ви́димому, на вид.

seemly ['si:mlɪ] *adj.* прили́чный.

seep [si:p] *v.i.* проса́чиваться *impf.*, просочи́ться *pf.* **seepage** *n.* проса́чивание, течь.

seer ['si:ə(r), sɪə(r)] *n.* прови́дец (-дца).

see-saw ['si:sɔ:] *n.* (*game*) кача́ние на доске́; (*board*) де́тские каче́ли (-лей) *pl.*; *v.i.* кача́ться *impf.* (на доске́).

seethe [si:ð] *v.i.* кипе́ть (-плю, -пи́шь) *impf.*, вс~ *pf.*

segment ['segmənt] *n.* отре́зок (-зка); (*of orange etc.*) до́лька; (*geom.*) сегме́нт.

segregate ['segrɪgət] *v.t.* отделя́ть *impf.*, отдели́ть *pf.* **segre'gation** *n.* отделе́ние, сегрега́ция.

Seine [seɪn] *n.* Се́на.

seismic ['saɪzmɪk] *adj.* сейсми́ческий. **seismograph** *n.* сейсмо́граф. **seis'mology** *n.* сейсмоло́гия.

seize [si:z] *v.t.* хвата́ть *impf.*, схвати́ть (-ачу́, -а́тишь) *pf.*; *v.i.*: ~ **up** заеда́ть *impf.*, зае́сть (-е́ст; -е́ло) *pf. impers.*+*a.*; ~ **upon** ухва́тываться *impf.*, ухвати́ться (-ачу́сь, -а́тишься) *pf.* за+*a.* **seizure** *n.* захва́т; заеда́ние; (*stroke*) уда́р.

seldom ['seldəm] *adv.* ре́дко.

select [sɪ'lekt] *adj.* и́збранный; *v.t.* отбира́ть *impf.*, отобра́ть (отберу́, -рёшь; отобра́л, -á, -о) *pf.* выбира́ть *impf.*, вы́брать (вы́беру, -решь) *pf.* **selection** *n.* вы́бор; (*biol.*) отбо́р. **selective** *adj.* селекти́вный.

self [self] *n.* со́бственная ли́чность; (*one's interests*) свои́ ли́чные интере́сы *m.pl.*

self- [self] *in comb.* само... . **self-absorbed** *adj.* эгоцентри́чный. **self-assured** *adj.* самоуве́ренный (-ен, -енна). **self-centred** *adj.* эгоцентри́чный. **self-confidence** *n.* самоуве́ренность. **self-confident** *adj.* самоуве́ренный (-ен, -енна). **self-conscious** *adj.* засте́нчивый. **self-contained** *adj.* отде́льный. **self-control** *n.* самооблада́ние. **self-defence** *n.* самооборо́на, самозащи́та. **self-denial** *n.* самоотрече́ние. **self-determination** *n.* самоопределе́ние. **self-effacing** *adj.* скро́мный (-мен, -мна́, -мно). **self-esteem** *n.* самоуваже́ние. **self-evident** *adj.* очеви́дный. **self-government** *n.* самоуправле́ние. **self-help** *n.* самопо́мощь. **self-importance** *n.* самомне́ние. **self-interest** *n.* своеко́рыстие.

selfish ['selfɪʃ] *adj.* эгоисти́чный, себялюби́вый. **selfless** *adj.* самоотве́рженный (-ен, -енна).

self-made ['selfmeɪd] *adj.* (*man*) вы́бившийся из низо́в. **self-portrait** *n.* автопортре́т. **self-possessed** *adj.* хладнокро́вный. **self-preservation** *n.* самосохране́ние. **self-propelled** *adj.* самохо́дный. **self-reliant** *adj.* наде́ющийся то́лько на себя́. **self-respect** *n.* чу́вство со́бственного досто́инства. **self-**

righteous *adj.* уве́ренный (-ен, -енна) в свое́й правоте́, фарисе́йский. **self-sacrifice** *n.* самопоже́ртвование. **self-satisfied** *adj.* самодово́льный. **self-service** *n.* самообслу́живание (*attr., in g. after n.*). **self-starter** *n.* самопу́ск. **self-styled** *adj.* самозва́нный. **self-sufficient** *adj.* самостоя́тельный. **self-willed** *adj.* самово́льный.

sell [sel] *v.t. & i.* продава́ть(ся) (-даю́, -даёт(ся)) *impf.*, прода́ть(ся) (-а́м, -а́шь, -а́ст(ся), -ади́м; -ал/-а́лся, -ала́(сь), -ало/-ало́сь) *pf.*; *v.t.* (*deal in*) торгова́ть *impf.*+*i.*; ~ **off,** od распродава́ть (-даю́, -даёшь) *impf.*, распрода́ть (-а́м, -а́шь, -а́ст, -ади́м; -ал, -ала́, -ало) *pf.* **seller** *n.* торго́вец (-вца) (**of** +*i.*), продаве́ц (-вца́). **selling** *n.* прода́жа.

Sellotape ['seləˌteɪp] *n.* (*propr.*) скотч.

selvage ['selvɪdʒ] *n.* кро́мка.

semantic [sɪ'mæntɪk] *adj.* семанти́ческий. **semantics** *n.* сема́нтика.

semaphore ['seməˌfɔ:(r)] *n.* семафо́р.

semblance ['sembləns] *n.* вне́шний вид.

semen ['si:mən] *n.* се́мя *nt.*

semi- ['semɪ] *in comb.* полу... . **semibreve** ['semɪˌbri:v] *n.* це́лая но́та. **semicircle** *n.* полукру́г. **semicircular** *adj.* полукру́глый. **semicolon** *n.* то́чка с запято́й. **semiconductor** *n.* полупроводни́к (-á). **semiconscious** *adj.* полубессозна́тельный. **semidetached** *adj.*: ~ **house** дом, разделённый о́бщей стено́й. **semifinal** *n.* полуфина́л. **semifinalist** *n.* полуфинали́ст. **semi-official** *adj.* полуофициа́льный; официо́зный. **semiprecious** *adj.*: ~ **stone** самоцве́т.

seminar ['semɪˌnɑ:(r)] *n.* семина́р. **seminary** ['semɪnərɪ] *n.* (духо́вная) семина́рия.

semiquaver ['semɪˌkweɪvə(r)] *n.* шестна́дцатая но́та.

Semite ['si:maɪt, 'sem-] *n.* семи́т, ~ка. **Semitic** [sɪ'mɪtɪk] *adj.* семити́ческий.

semitone ['semɪˌtəʊn] *n.* полуто́н. **semivowel** ['semɪˌvaʊəl] *n.* полугла́сный *sb.*

semolina [ˌsemə'li:nə] *n.* ма́нная крупа́.

sempstress *see* **seamstress**

senate ['senɪt] *n.* сена́т; (*univ.*) (учёный) сове́т. **senator** ['senətə(r)] *n.* сена́тор. **senatorial** [ˌsenə'tɔ:rɪəl] *adj.* сена́торский.

send [send] *v.t.* посыла́ть *impf.*, посла́ть (пошлю́, -лёшь) *pf.*; ~ **down** (*univ.*) исключа́ть *impf.*, исключи́ть *pf.* из университе́та; ~ **off** отправля́ть *impf.*, отпра́вить *pf.*; ~ **up** (*ridicule*) высме́ивать *impf.*, вы́смеять (-ею, -еешь) *pf.* **sender** *n.* отправи́тель *m.* **send-off** *n.* про́воды (-дов) *pl.*

senile ['si:naɪl] *adj.* ста́рческий, дря́хлый (-л, -ла́, -ло). **senility** [sɪ'nɪlɪtɪ] *n.* ста́рость, дря́хлость.

senior ['si:nɪə(r)] *adj.* (*n.*) ста́рший (*sb.*); ~ **citizen** стари́к (-á), стару́ха; ~ **partner** глава́ (*pl.* -вы) фи́рмы. **seni'ority** *n.* старшинство́.

senna ['senə] *n.* александри́йский лист (-á).

sensation [sen'seɪʃ(ə)n] *n.* сенса́ция; (*feeling*) ощуще́ние, чу́вство. **sensational** *adj.* сенсаци́онный (-нен, -нна).

sense [sens] *n.* чу́вство, ощуще́ние; (*good* ~) здра́вый смысл; (*meaning*) смысл; **in one's** ~s в своём уме́; *v.t.* ощуща́ть *impf.*, ощути́ть (-ущу́, -ути́шь) *pf.*; чу́вствовать *impf.*

senseless *adj.* бессмы́сленный (-ен, -енна).

sensibility [ˌsensɪ'bɪlɪtɪ] *n.* чувстви́тельность.

sensible ['sensɪb(ə)l] *adj.* благоразу́мный.

sensitive ['sensɪtɪv] *adj.* чувстви́тельный; (*touchy*) оби́дчивый. **sensi'tivity** *n.* чувстви́тельность.

sensory ['sensərɪ] *adj.* чувстви́тельный.

sensual ['sensjʊəl, 'senʃʊəl], **sensuous** *adj.* чу́вственный (-ен, -енна).

sentence ['sent(ə)ns] *n.* фра́за; (*gram.*) предложе́ние; (*leg.*) пригово́р; *v.t.* осужда́ть *impf.*, осуди́ть (-ужу́, -у́дишь) *pf.* (**to** к+*d.*); пригова́ривать *impf.*, приговори́ть *pf.* (**to** к+*d.*).

sententious [sen'tenʃəs] *adj.* сентенцио́зный.

sentiment ['sentɪmənt] *n.* (*feeling*) чу́вство; (*opinion*) мне́ние. **sentimental** [ˌsentɪ'ment(ə)l] *adj.* сентимента́льный. **sentimen'tality** *n.* сентимента́льность.

sentinel ['sentɪn(ə)l], **sentry** *n.* часово́й *sb.*

sepal ['sep(ə)l, 'siː-] *n.* чашели́стник.

separable ['sepərəb(ə)l] *adj.* отдели́мый. **separate** ['sepərət; 'sepəˌreɪt] *adj.* отде́льный; (*independent*) самостоя́тельный; *v.t. & i.* отделя́ть(ся) *impf.*, отдели́ть(ся) (-лю́(сь), -лишь(ся)) *pf.* **sepa'ration** *n.* отделе́ние. **separatism** *n.* сепарати́зм. **separatist** *n.* сепарати́ст. **separator** *n.* сепара́тор.

sepia ['siːpɪə] *n.* се́пия.

sepoy ['siːpɔɪ] *n.* сипа́й.

sepsis ['sepsɪs] *n.* се́псис.

September [sep'tembə(r)] *n.* сентя́брь (-ря́) *m.*; *attr.* сентя́брьский.

septet [sep'tet] *n.* септе́т.

septic ['septɪk] *adj.* септи́ческий; ~ **tank** се́птик.

septuple ['septjʊp(ə)l] *adj.* семикра́тный.

sepulchral [sɪ'pʌlkr(ə)l] *adj.* моги́льный, гробово́й. **sepulchre** ['sepəlkə(r)] *n.* моги́ла.

sequel ['siːkw(ə)l] *n.* (*result*) после́дствие; (*continuation*) продолже́ние. **sequence** *n.* после́довательность; (*cin.*) эпизо́д; ~ **of events** ход собы́тий.

sequester [sɪ'kwestə(r)] *v.t.* (*isolate*) уединя́ть *impf.*, уедини́ть *pf.*; (*confiscate*) секвестрова́ть *impf. & pf.* **sequestered** *adj.* уединённый. **sequestration** [ˌsiːkwɪ'streɪʃ(ə)n] *n.* секве́стр.

sequin ['siːkwɪn] *n.* блёстка.

sequoia [sɪ'kwɔɪə] *n.* секво́йя.

seraph ['serəf] *n.* серафи́м.

Serb(ian) ['sɜːbɪən] *adj.* се́рбский; *n.* серб, ~ка. **Serbo-Croat(ian)** [ˌsɜːbəʊkrəʊ'eɪʃ(ə)n] *adj.* сербскохорва́тский.

serenade [ˌserə'neɪd] *n.* серена́да; *v.t.* исполня́ть *impf.*, испо́лнить *pf.* серена́ду+*d.*

serene [sɪ'riːn, sə'riːn] *adj.* (*calm*) споко́йный; (*clear*) я́сный (я́сен, ясна́, я́сно, я́сны). **se-**

renity [sɪ'renɪtɪ, sə'r-] *n.* споко́йствие; я́сность.

serf [sɜːf] *n.* крепостно́й *sb.* **serfdom** *n.* крепостно́е пра́во; крепостни́чество.

serge [sɜːdʒ] *n.* са́ржа.

sergeant ['sɑːdʒ(ə)nt] *n.* сержа́нт. **sergeant-major** *n.* старшина́ (*pl.* -ны) *m.*

serial ['sɪərɪəl] *adj.* сери́йный; (*of story etc.*) выходя́щий отде́льными вы́пусками; *n.* (*story*) рома́н в не́скольких частя́х; (*film*) сери́йный фильм; (*periodical*) периоди́ческое изда́ние. **serialize** *v.t.* издава́ть (-даю́, -даёшь) *impf.*, изда́ть (-а́м, -а́шь, -а́ст, -ади́м; изда́л, -а́, -о) *pf.* вы́пусками, се́риями.

series *n.* ряд (-а́ with 2,3,4, *loc.* -у́; *pl.* -ы́), се́рия.

serious ['sɪərɪəs] *adj.* серьёзный. **seriousness** *n.* серьёзность.

sermon ['sɜːmən] *n.* про́поведь.

serpent ['sɜːpənt] *n.* змея́ (*pl.* -е́и). **serpentine** *adj.* (*coiling*) изви́листый.

serrated [se'reɪtɪd] *adj.* зазу́бренный, зубча́тый.

serried ['serɪd] *adj.* со́мкнутый.

serum ['sɪərəm] *n.* сы́воротка.

servant ['sɜːv(ə)nt] *n.* слуга́ (*pl.* -ги) *m.*, служа́нка. **serve** *v.t.* служи́ть (-жу́, -жишь) *impf.*, по— *pf.*+*d.* (**as, for** +*i.*); (*attend to*) обслу́живать *impf.*, обслужи́ть (-жу́, -жишь) *pf.*; (*food, ball*) подава́ть (-даю́, -даёшь) *impf.*, пода́ть (-а́м, -а́шь, -а́ст, -ади́м; по́дал, -а́, -о) *pf.*; (*period*) отбыва́ть *impf.*, отбы́ть (-бу́ду, -бу́дешь; о́тбыл, -а́, -о) *pf.*; (*writ etc.*) вруча́ть *impf.*, вручи́ть *pf.* (**on** +*d.*); *v.i.* (*be suitable*) годи́ться (for на+*a.*, для+*g.*); (*sport*) подава́ть (-даю́, -даёшь) *impf.*, пода́ть (-а́м, -а́шь, -а́ст, -ади́м; по́дал, -а́, -о) *pf.* мяч; **it** ~**s him right** поде́лом ему́ (*d.*). **service** ['sɜːvɪs] *n.* слу́жба; (*attendance*) обслу́живание; (*set of dishes etc.*) серви́з; (*sport*) пода́ча; (*transport*) сообще́ние; **at your** ~ к ва́шим услу́гам; *v.t.* обслу́живать *impf.*, обслужи́ть (-жу́, -жишь) *pf.* **serviceable** *n.* (*useful*) поле́зный; (*durable*) про́чный (-чен, -чна́, -чно, про́чны). **serviceman** *n.* военнослу́жащий *sb.* **servi'ette** *n.* салфе́тка. **servile** ['sɜːvaɪl] *adj.* ра́бский; (*cringing*) рабо-ле́пный. **servility** [ˌsɜː'vɪlɪtɪ] *n.* раболе́пие. **serving** *n.* по́рция.

sesame ['sesəmɪ] *n.* кунжу́т; **open** ~! сеза́м, откро́йся!

session ['seʃ(ə)n] *n.* заседа́ние, се́ссия.

set[1] [set] *v.t.* (*put*; ~ **trap**) ста́вить *impf.*, по— *pf.*; (*establish*; ~ **clock**) устана́вливать *impf.*, установи́ть (-влю́, -вишь) *pf.*; (*table*) накрыва́ть *impf.*, накры́ть (-ро́ю, -ро́ешь) *pf.*; (*plant*) сажа́ть *impf.*, посади́ть (-ажу́, -а́дишь) *pf.*; (*bone*) вправля́ть *impf.*, впра́вить *pf.*; (*hair*) укла́дывать *impf.*, уложи́ть (-жу́, -жишь) *pf.*; (*jewel*) оправля́ть *impf.*, опра́вить *pf.*; (*print.*, ~ **up**) набира́ть *impf.*, набра́ть (наберу́, -рёшь; набра́л, -а́, -о) *pf.*; (*bring into state*) приводи́ть (-ожу́, -о́дишь) *impf.*, привести́ (-еду́, -едёшь; -ёл, -ела́) *pf.* (**in, to** в+*a.*); (*example*) подава́ть (-даю́, -даёшь) *impf.*, пода́ть (-а́м, -а́шь, -а́ст, -ади́м; по́дал, -а́, -о) *pf.*; (*task*) задава́ть (-аю́, -аёшь) *impf.*, зада́ть (-а́м, -а́шь, -а́ст, -ади́м; за́дал, -а́, -о) *pf.*; *v.i.* (*solidify*) тверде́ть *impf.*, за~ *pf.*; застыва́ть *impf.*, засты́(ну)ть (-ы́нет; -ы́л) *pf.*; (*fruit*) завя́зываться *impf.*, завя́за́ться (-я́жется) *pf.*; (*sun etc.*) заходи́ть (-ит) *impf.*, зайти́ (зайдёт; зашёл, -шла́) *pf.*; сади́ться *impf.*, сесть (ся́дет; сел) *pf.*; ~ **eyes on** уви́деть (-и́жу, -и́дишь) *pf.*; ~ **free** освобожда́ть *impf.*, освободи́ть *pf.*; ~ **one's heart on** стра́стно жела́ть *impf.*+*g.*; ~ **to music** положи́ть (-жу́, -жишь) *pf.* на му́зыку; ~ **sail** пуска́ться *impf.*, пусти́ться (пущу́сь, пу́стишься) *pf.* в пла́вание; ~ **about** (*begin*) начина́ть *impf.*, нача́ть (начну́, -нёшь; на́чал, -а́, -о) *pf.*; (*attack*) напада́ть *impf.*, напа́сть (-аду́, -адёшь; -а́л) *pf.* на+*a.*; ~ **back** (*impede*) препя́тствовать *impf.*, вос~ *pf.*+*d.*; ~ **down** (*passenger*) выса́живать *impf.*, вы́садить *pf.*; (*in writing*) запи́сывать *impf.*, записа́ть (-ишу́, -и́шешь) *pf.*; (*attribute*) припи́сывать *impf.*, приписа́ть (-ишу́, -и́шешь) *pf.* (**to** +*d.*); ~ **forth** (*expound*) излага́ть *impf.*, изложи́ть (-жу́, -жишь) *pf.*; (*on journey*) see ~ **off;** ~ **in** наступа́ть *impf.*, наступи́ть (-ит) *pf.*; ~ **off** (*on journey*) отправля́ться *impf.*, отпра́виться *pf.*; (*enhance*) оттеня́ть *impf.*, оттени́ть *pf.*; ~ **out** (*state*) излага́ть *impf.*, изложи́ть (-жу́, -жишь) *pf.*; (*on journey*) see ~ **off;** ~ **up** (*business*) осно́вывать *impf.*, основа́ть (-ную́, -нуёшь) *pf.*; (*person*) обеспе́чивать *impf.*, обеспе́чить *pf.* (**with** +*i.*).

set² [set] *n.* набо́р, компле́кт, прибо́р; (*of dishes etc.*) серви́з; (*of people*) круг (*loc.* -у́; *pl.* -и́); (*radio*) приёмник; (*television*) телеви́зор; (*tennis*) сет; (*theatr.*) декора́ция; (*cin.*) съёмочная площа́дка.

set³ [set] *adj.* (*established*) устано́вленный (-ен); (*fixed, of smile etc.*) засты́вший; (*of intention*) обду́манный (-ан); ~ **phrase** усто́йчивое словосочета́ние; ~ **square** уго́льник.

set-back ['setbæk] *n.* неуда́ча.

settee [se'ti:] *n.* дива́н.

setter ['setə(r)] *n.* (*dog*) се́ттер; (*person*) устано́вщик.

setting ['setɪŋ] *n.* (*frame*) опра́ва; (*theatr.*) декора́ция, постано́вка; (*mus.*) му́зыка на слова́; (*of sun etc.*) захо́д, зака́т.

settle ['set(ə)l] *v.t.* (*decide*) реша́ть *impf.*, реши́ть *pf.*; (*arrange*) ула́живать *impf.*, ула́дить *pf.*; (*a bill etc.*) опла́чивать *impf.*, оплати́ть (-ачу́, -а́тишь) *pf.*; (*colonize*) заселя́ть *impf.*, засели́ть *pf.*; *v.i.* сели́ться *impf.*, по~ *pf.*; (*subside*) оседа́ть *impf.*, осе́сть (ося́дет; осе́л) *pf.*; ~ **down** уса́живаться *impf.*, усе́сться (уся́дусь, -дешься; усе́лся) *pf.* **settlement** *n.* поселе́ние; (*of dispute*) разреше́ние; (*payment*) упла́та;

(*subsidence*) оса́дка, оседа́ние; **marriage** ~ бра́чный контра́кт. **settler** *n.* поселе́нец (-нца).

seven ['sev(ə)n] *adj. & n.* семь (-ми́, -мью́); (*collect.*; *7 pairs*) се́меро (-ры́х); (*cards*; *number 7*) семёрка; (*time*) семь (часо́в); (*age*) семь лет. **seventeen** *adj. & n.* семна́дцать; (*age*) семна́дцать лет. **seven'teenth** *adj. & n.* семна́дцатый; (*fraction*) семна́дцатая (часть (*pl.* -ти, -те́й)); (*date*) семна́дцатое (число́). **seventh** *adj. & n.* седьмо́й; (*fraction*) седьма́я (часть(*pl.* -ти, -те́й)); (*date*) седьмо́е (число́). **seventieth** *adj. & n.* семидеся́тый; (*fraction*) семидеся́тая (часть (*pl.* -ти, -те́й)). **seventy** *adj. & n.* се́мьдесят (-ми́десяти, -мью́десятью); (*age*) се́мьдесят лет; *pl.* (*decade*) семидеся́тые го́ды *m.pl.*

sever ['sevə(r)] *v.t.* (*cut off*) отреза́ть *impf.*, отре́зать (-е́жу, -е́жешь) *pf.*; (*relations*) разрыва́ть *impf.*, разорва́ть (-ву́, -вёшь; -ва́л, -вала́, -ва́ло) *pf.*; (*friendship*) порыва́ть *impf.*, порва́ть (-ву́, -вёшь; порва́л, -а́, -о) *pf.*

several ['sevr(ə)l] *pron.* (*adj.*) не́сколько (+*g.*).

severance ['sevərəns] *n.* разры́в; ~ **pay** выходно́е посо́бие.

severe [sɪ'vɪə(r)] *adj.* стро́гий (строг, -а́, -о), суро́вый; (*illness etc.*) тяжёлый (-л, -ла́). **severity** [sɪ'verɪtɪ] *n.* стро́гость, суро́вость.

sew [səʊ] *v.t.* шить (шью, шьёшь) *impf.*, с~ (сошью, -ьёшь) *pf.*; ~ **on** пришива́ть *impf.*, приши́ть (-шью, -шьёшь) *pf.*; ~ **up** зашива́ть *impf.*, заши́ть (-шью, -шьёшь) *pf.*

sewage ['su:ɪdʒ, 'sju:-] *n.* сто́чные во́ды *f.pl.*, нечисто́ты (-т) *pl.*; ~ **farm** поля́ *nt.pl.* ороше́ния. **sewer** *n.* сто́чная, канализацио́нная, труба́ (*pl.* -бы). **sewerage** *n.* канализа́ция.

sewing ['səʊɪŋ] *n.* шитьё. **sewing-machine** *n.* швейная маши́на.

sex [seks] *n.* (*gender*) пол; секс; ~ **appeal** сексапи́льность; **extramarital** ~ секс вне бра́ка; *adj.* сексуа́льный.

sexcentenary [ˌseksen'ti:nərɪ] *n.* шестисотле́тие.

se·.ism ['seksɪz(ə)m] *n.* дискримина́ция же́нщин. **sexist** *n.* женофо́б; *adj.* женоненави́стнический.

sextant ['sekst(ə)nt] *n.* секста́нт.

sextet [sek'stet] *n.* сексте́т.

sexton ['sekst(ə)n] *n.* понома́рь (-ря́) *m.*, моги́льщик.

sextuple ['seks,tju:p(ə)l] *adj.* шестикра́тный.

sexual ['seksjʊəl, -ʃʊəl] *adj.* полово́й, сексуа́льный. **sexuality** [ˌseksjʊ'ælɪtɪ, -ʃʊ'ælɪtɪ] *n.* сексуа́льность. **sexy** *adj.* (*alluring*) соблазни́тельный; (*erotic*) эроти́ческий.

sh [ʃ] *int.* ти́ше!; тсс!

shabby ['ʃæbɪ] *adj.* поно́шенный (-ен), потрёпанный (-ан, -анна); (*mean*) по́длый (подл, -а́, -о).

shack [ʃæk] *n.* лачу́га, хи́жина.

shackle ['ʃæk(ə)l] *n.*: *pl.* кандалы́ (-ло́в) *pl.*; (*also fig.*) око́вы (-в) *pl.*; *v.t.* зако́вывать *impf.*, закова́ть (-ку́ю, -ку́ёшь) *pf.*

shade [ʃeɪd] *n.* тень (*loc.* -ни́; *pl.* -ни, -не́й), полумра́к; (*of colour, meaning*) отте́нок (-нка); (*lamp-~*) абажу́р; **a ~** чуть-чу́ть; *v.t.* затеня́ть *impf.*, затени́ть *pf.*; заслоня́ть *impf.* заслони́ть (-оню́, -о́нишь) *pf.*; (*drawing*) тушева́ть (-шу́ю, -шу́ешь) *impf.*, за~ *pf.*; *v.i.* незаме́тно переходи́ть (-ит) *impf.* (**into** в+*a.*). **shadow** ['ʃædəʊ] *n.* тень (*loc.* -ни́; *pl.* -ни, -не́й); *v.t.* (*follow*) та́йно следи́ть *impf.* за+*i.* **shadowy** *adj.* тёмный (-мен, -мна́), нея́сный (-сен, -сна́, -сно). **shady** *adj.* тени́стый; (*suspicious*) подозри́тельный.

shaft [ʃɑːft] *n.* (*of spear*) дре́вко (*pl.* -ки, -ков); (*arrow; fig.*) стрела́ (*pl.* -лы); (*of light*) луч (-а́); (*of cart*) огло́бля (*g.pl.* -бель); (*axle*) вал (*loc.* -у́; *pl.* -ы́); (*mine ~*) ствол (-а́) (ша́хты).

shaggy *adj.* лохма́тый, косма́тый.

shah [ʃɑː] *n.* шах.

shake [ʃeɪk] *v.t. & i.* трясти́(сь) (-су́(сь), -сёшь(ся)) -с(ся), -сла́(сь)) *impf.*; *v.i.* (*tremble*) дрожа́ть (-жу́, -жи́шь) *impf.*; *v.t.* (*impair*) колеба́ть (-блю, -блешь) *impf.*, по~ *pf.*; ~ **hands** пожима́ть *impf.*, пожа́ть (-жму́, -жмёшь) *pf.* ру́ку+*d.*; ~ **one's head** покача́ть *pf.* голово́й; ~ **off** стря́хивать *impf.*, стряхну́ть *pf.*; (*fig.*) избавля́ться *impf.*, изба́виться *pf.* от+*g.*; ~ **up** (*fig.*) встря́хивать *impf.*, встряхну́ть *pf.*

shako ['ʃeɪkəʊ] *n.* ки́вер (*pl.* -а́).

shaky ['ʃeɪkɪ] *adj.* ша́ткий (-ток, -тка), непро́чный (-чен, -чна́, -чно).

shale [ʃeɪl] *n.* сла́нец (-нца).

shallot [ʃə'lɒt] *n.* лук-шало́т.

shallow ['ʃæləʊ] *adj.* ме́лкий (-лок, -лка́, -лко); (*superficial*) пове́рхностный; *n.* мелково́дье, мель (*loc.* -ли́).

sham [ʃæm] *v.t. & i.* притворя́ться *impf.*, притвори́ться *pf.*+*i.*; *n.* притво́рство; (*person*) притво́рщик, -ица; *adj.* притво́рный; (*fake*) подде́льный.

shaman ['ʃæmən] *n.* шама́н.

shamble ['ʃæmb(ə)l] *v.i.* волочи́ть (-чу́, -чишь) *impf.* но́ги.

shambles ['ʃæmb(ə)lz] *n.* бо́йня; (*muddle*) хао́с.

shame [ʃeɪm] *n.* стыд, позо́р; *v.t.* стыди́ть *impf.*, при~ *pf.* **shamefaced** *adj.* стыдли́вый. **shameful** *adj.* позо́рный. **shameless** *adj.* бессты́дный.

shampoo [ʃæm'puː] *v.t.* мыть (мо́ю, мо́ешь) *impf.*, по~ *pf.*; *n.* шампу́нь *m.*

shamrock ['ʃæmrɒk] *n.* трили́стник.

shandy ['ʃændɪ] *n.* смесь (просто́го) пи́ва с лимона́дом, с имби́рным.

shank [ʃæŋk] *n.* (*leg*) нога́ (*a.* -гу; *pl.* -ги, -г, -га́м), го́лень; (*shaft*) сте́ржень (-жня) *m.*

shanty[1] ['ʃæntɪ] *n.* (*hut*) хиба́рка, лачу́га; ~ **town** бидонви́ль, трущо́ба.

shanty[2] ['ʃæntɪ] *n.* (*song*) матро́сская пе́сня (*g.pl.* -сен).

shape [ʃeɪp] *n.* фо́рма, вид, о́браз; *v.t.* придава́ть (-даю́, -даёшь) *impf.*, прида́ть (-а́м, -а́сть, -ади́м; при́дал, -а́, -о) *pf.* фо́рму+*d.*; *v.i.* принима́ть *impf.*, приня́ть (-и́мет; при́нял, -а́, -о) *pf.* фо́рму. **shapeless** *adj.* бесфо́рменный (-ен, -енна). **shapely** *adj.* стро́йный (-о́ен, -о́йна́, -о́йно).

share [ʃeə(r)] *n.* до́ля (*pl.* -ли, -ле́й), часть (*pl.* -ти, -те́й); (*participation*) уча́стие; (*econ.*) а́кция, пай (*pl.* паи́, паёв); *v.t.* дели́ть (-лю́, -лишь) *impf.*, по~ *pf.*; разделя́ть *impf.*, раздели́ть (-лю́, -лишь) *pf.* **shareholder** *n.* акционе́р, ~ка; па́йщик, -ица.

shark [ʃɑːk] *n.* аку́ла.

sharp [ʃɑːp] *adj.* о́стрый (остр & остёр, остра́, о́стро́); (*steep*) круто́й (крут, -а́, -о); (*sudden; harsh*) ре́зкий (-зок, -зка́, -зко); (*fine*) то́нкий (-нок, -нка́, -нко, то́нки́); *n.* (*mus.*) дие́з; *adv.* (*with time*) ро́вно; (*of angle*) кру́то. **sharpen** ['ʃɑːpən] *v.t.* точи́ть (-чу́, -чишь) *impf.*, на~ *pf.*; обостря́ть *impf.*, обостри́ть *pf.*

shatter ['ʃætə(r)] *v.t. & i.* разбива́ть(ся) *impf.*, разби́ть(ся) (разобью́, -ьёт(ся)) *pf.* вдре́безги; *v.t.* (*hopes etc.*) разруша́ть *impf.*, разру́шить *pf.*

shave [ʃeɪv] *v.t. & i.* бри́ть(ся) (бре́ю(сь), -е́ешь(ся)) *impf.*, по~ *pf.*; *v.t.* (*plane*) строга́ть *impf.*, вы́~ *pf.*; *n.* бритьё; **close ~** едва́ избе́гнутая опа́сность. **shaver** *n.* электри́ческая бри́тва.

shawl [ʃɔːl] *n.* шаль.

she [ʃiː] *pron.* она́ (её, ей, ей & е́ю, о ней).

sheaf [ʃiːf] *n.* сноп (-а́); (*of papers etc.*) свя́зка.

shear [ʃɪə(r)] *v.t.* стричь (-игу́, -ижёшь; -иг) *impf.*, о~ *pf.* **shearer** *n.* стрига́льщик. **shears** *n.* но́жницы (-ц) *pl.*

sheath [ʃiːθ] *n.* (*for sword etc.*) но́жны (*g.* -жен) *pl.*; (*anat.*) оболо́чка; (*for cable etc.*) обши́вка. **sheathe** [ʃiːð] *v.t.* вкла́дывать *impf.*, вложи́ть (-жу́, -жишь) *pf.* в но́жны; обшива́ть *impf.*, обши́ть (обошью́, -ьёшь) *pf.* **sheathing** *n.* обши́вка.

sheave [ʃiːv] *n.* шкив (*pl.* -ы́).

shed[1] [ʃed] *n.* сара́й.

shed[2] [ʃed] *v.t.* (*tears, blood, light*) пролива́ть *impf.*, проли́ть (-лью́, -льёшь; про́ли́л, -а́, -о) *pf.*; (*skin, clothes*) сбра́сывать *impf.*, сбро́сить *pf.*

sheen [ʃiːn] *n.* блеск.

sheep [ʃiːp] *n.* овца́ (*pl.* о́вцы, ове́ц, о́вцам). **sheepdog** *n.* овча́рка. **sheepfold** *n.* овча́рня (*g.pl.* -рен). **sheepish** *adj.* (*bashful*) засте́нчивый; (*abashed*) сконфу́женный (-ен). **sheepskin** *n.* овчи́на.

sheer [ʃɪə(r)] *adj.* абсолю́тный, су́щий; (*textile*) прозра́чный; (*rock etc.*) отве́сный.

sheet[1] [ʃiːt] *n.* (*on bed*) простыня́ (*pl.* про́стыни, -ы́нь, -ыня́м); (*of glass, paper, etc.*) лист (-а́); (*wide expanse*) пелена́ (*g.pl.*

-ён); *attr.* (*metal, glass etc.*) листово́й; ~ **lightning** зарни́ца.

sheet[2] [ʃiːt] *n.* (*naut.*) шкот; ~ **anchor** запасно́й станово́й я́корь (*pl.* -ря́) *m.*; (*fig.*) я́корь (*pl.* -ря́) *m.* спасе́ния.

sheikh [ʃeɪk] *n.* шейх.

shelf [ʃelf] *n.* по́лка; (*of cliff etc.*) усту́п. **shelf-life** *n.* срок хране́ния. **shelf-mark** *n.* шифр.

shell [ʃel] *n.* (*of mollusc etc.*) ра́ковина; (*of tortoise*) щит (-á); (*of egg, nut*) скорлупа́ (*pl.* -пы); (*of building etc.*) о́стов; (*explosive* ~) снаря́д; *v.t.* очища́ть *impf.*, очи́стить *pf.*; лущи́ть *impf.*, об~ *pf.*; (*bombard*) обстре́ливать *impf.*, обстреля́ть *pf.*; ~ **out** (*abs.*) раскоше́ливаться *impf.*, раскоше́литься *pf.*

shellac [ʃəˈlæk] *n.* шелла́к.

shellfish [ˈʃelfɪʃ] *n.* (*mollusc*) моллю́ск; (*crustacean*) ракообра́зное *sb.*

shelter [ˈʃeltə(r)] *n.* прию́т, убе́жище, укры́тие; *v.t.* дава́ть (даю́, даёшь) *impf.*, дать (дам, дашь, даст, дади́м; дал, -á, да́ло, -и) *pf.* прию́т+*d.*; служи́ть (-жу́, -жишь) *impf.*, по~ *pf.* убе́жищем, укры́тием+*d.*; *v.t. & i.* укрыва́ть(ся) *impf.*, укры́ть(ся) (-ро́ю(сь), -ро́ешь(ся)) *pf.*

shelve[1] [ʃelv] *v.t.* (*defer*) откла́дывать *impf.*, отложи́ть *pf.* (в до́лгий я́щик).

shelve[2] [ʃelv] *v.i.* (*of land*) отло́го спуска́ться *impf.* **shelving**[1] *adj.* отло́гий.

shelving[2] [ˈʃelvɪŋ] *n.* (*shelves*) стелла́ж (-á).

shepherd [ˈʃepəd] *n.* пасту́х (-á); (*fig.*) па́стырь *m.*; *v.t.* проводи́ть (-ожу́, -о́дишь) *impf.*, провести́ (-еду́, -еде́шь; -ёл, -ела́) *pf.* **shepherdess** *n.* пасту́шка.

sherbet [ˈʃɜːbət] *n.* щербе́т.

sheriff [ˈʃerɪf] *n.* шери́ф.

sherry [ˈʃerɪ] *n.* хе́рес.

shield [ʃiːld] *n.* щит (-á); *v.t.* прикрыва́ть *impf.*, прикры́ть (-ро́ю, -ро́ешь) *pf.*; заслоня́ть *impf.*, заслони́ть *pf.*

shift [ʃɪft] *v.t. & i.* (*change position*) перемеща́ть(ся) *impf.*, перемести́ть(ся) *pf.*; (*change form*) меня́ть(ся) *impf.*; *v.t.* (*move*; ~ *responsibility etc.*) перекла́дывать *impf.*, переложи́ть (-жу́, -жишь) *pf.*; *n.* перемеще́ние; (*of workers*) сме́на. **shiftless** *adj.* неуме́лый. **shifty** *adj.* ненадёжный, нече́стный.

shilly-shally [ˈʃɪlɪˌʃælɪ] *n.* нереши́тельность; *v.i.* колеба́ться (-блюсь, -блешься) *impf.*, по~ *pf.*

shimmer [ˈʃɪmə(r)] *v.i.* мерца́ть *impf.*; *n.* мерца́ние.

shin [ʃɪn] *n.* го́лень; *v.i.*: ~ **up** ла́зить *impf.* по+*d.* **shin-bone** *n.* большеберцо́вая кость (*pl.* -ти, -те́й).

shindy [ˈʃɪndɪ] *n.* шум, сва́лка.

shine [ʃaɪn] *v.i.* свети́ть(ся) (-и́т(ся)) *impf.*; блесте́ть (-ещу́, -е́щешь & -ести́шь) *impf.*; (*of sun etc.*) сия́ть *impf.*; *v.t.* полирова́ть *impf.*, от~ *pf.*; *n.* свет, сия́ние, блеск; (*polish*) гля́нец (-нца).

shingle[1] [ˈʃɪŋg(ə)l] *n.* (*for roof*) (кро́вельная) дра́нка.

shingle[2] [ˈʃɪŋg(ə)l] *n.* (*pebbles*) га́лька.

shingles [ˈʃɪŋg(ə)lz] *n.* опоя́сывающий лиша́й (-ая́).

shin-guard [ˈʃɪngɑːd], **-pad** *n.* щито́к (-тка́).

shining [ˈʃaɪnɪŋ], **shiny** *adj.* блестя́щий.

ship [ʃɪp] *n.* кора́бль (-ля́) *m.*; су́дно (*pl.* -да́, -до́в); *v.t.* (*transport*) перевози́ть (-ожу́, -о́зишь) *impf.*, перевезти́ (-езу́, -езёшь; -ёз, -езла́) *pf.* (по воде́); (*dispatch*) отправля́ть *impf.*, отпра́вить *pf.* (по воде́). **shipbuilding** *n.* судострое́ние. **shipment** *n.* (*loading*) погру́зка; (*consignment*) груз. **shipping** *n.* суда́ (-до́в) *pl.* **shipshape** *adv.* в по́лном поря́дке. **shipwreck** *n.* кораблекруше́ние. **shipwright** *n.* (*shipbuilder*) судострои́тель *m.*; (*carpenter*) корабе́льный пло́тник. **shipyard** *n.* верфь.

shire [ˈʃaɪə(r)] *n.* гра́фство.

shirk [ʃɜːk] *v.t.* уви́ливать *impf.*, увильну́ть *pf.* от+*g.*

shirt [ʃɜːt] *n.* руба́шка. **shirtsleeves** *n.*: in ~ без пиджака́.

shiver [ˈʃɪvə(r)] *v.i.* (*tremble*) дрожа́ть (-жу́, -жишь) *impf.*; *n.* дрожь.

shoal[1] [ʃəʊl] *n.* (*bank*) мель (*loc.* -ли́).

shoal[2] [ʃəʊl] *n.* (*of fish*) ста́я, кося́к (-á).

shock[1] [ʃɒk] *n.* (*impact etc.*) уда́р, толчо́к (-чка́); (*med.*) шок; *attr.* (*troops, brigade, wave*) уда́рный; ~ **absorber** амортиза́тор; ~ **tactics** та́ктика сокруши́тельных уда́ров; ~ **therapy** шокотерапи́я; *v.t.* шоки́ровать *impf.*

shock[2] [ʃɒk] *n.* (*of sheaves*) копна́ (*pl.* -пны, -пён,-пна́м).

shock[3] [ʃɒk] *n.* (*of hair*) копна́ воло́с.

shocking [ˈʃɒkɪŋ] *adj.* возмути́тельный, ужа́сный. **shock-worker** *n.* уда́рник.

shod [ʃɒd] *adj.* обу́тый.

shoddy [ˈʃɒdɪ] *adj.* дрянно́й (-нен, -нна́, -нно).

shoe [ʃuː] *n.* ту́фля (*g.pl.* -фель); (*horse-*~) подко́ва; (*tech.*) башма́к (-á); *v.t.* подко́вывать *impf.*, подкова́ть (-кую́, -куёшь) *pf.* **shoeblack** *n.* чи́стильщик сапо́г. **shoehorn** *n.* рожо́к (-жка́). **shoe-lace** *n.* шнуро́к (-рка́) для боти́нок. **shoemaker** *n.* сапо́жник. **shoe-string** *n.*: on a ~ с небольши́ми сре́дствами.

shoo [ʃuː] *int.* кш!; *v.t.* прогоня́ть *impf.*, прогна́ть (прогоню́, -нишь; прогна́л, -á, -о) *pf.*

shoot [ʃuːt] *v.t. & i.* (*discharge*) стреля́ть *impf.* (*a gun* из+*g.*; **at** в+*a.*, по+*d.*); (*arrow*) пуска́ть *impf.*, пусти́ть (пущу́, пу́стишь) *pf.*; (*kill*) застре́ливать *impf.*, застрели́ть (-лю́, -лишь) *pf.*; (*execute*) расстре́ливать *impf.*, расстреля́ть *pf.*; (*hunt*) охо́титься *impf.* на+*a.*; (*football*) бить (бью, бьёшь) *impf.* (по воро́там); (*cin.*) снима́ть *impf.*, снять (сниму́, -мешь; снял, -á, -о) *pf.* (фильм); *v.i.* (*go swiftly*) проноси́ться (-ошу́сь, -о́сишься) *impf.*, пронести́сь (-есу́сь, -есёшься; -ёсся, -есла́сь) *pf.*; (*of plant*) пуска́ть *impf.*, пустить (-ит) *pf.* ростки; ~ **down** (*aircraft*) сбивать *impf.*, сбить (собью, -бьёшь *pf.*; *n.* (*branch*) росток (-тка), побе́г; (*hunt*) охо́та. **shooting** *n.* стрельба́; (*hunting*) охо́та. **shooting-box** *n.* охо́тничий до́мик. **shooting-gallery** *n.* тир. **shooting-range** *n.* стре́льбище.

shop [ʃɒp] *n.* (*for sales*) магази́н, ла́вка; (*for repairs, manufacture*) мастерска́я *sb.*, цех (*loc.* -е & -у́; *pl.* -и & -а́); **talk** ~ говори́ть *impf.*, на узкопрофессиона́льные те́мы, о дела́х; ~ **assistant** продаве́ц (-вца́) -вщи́ца; ~ **steward** цехово́й ста́роста *m.*; *v.i.* де́лать *impf.*, с~ *pf.* поку́пки (*f.pl.*); *v.t.* (*imprison*) сажа́ть *impf.*, посади́ть (-ажу́, -а́дишь) *pf.* в тюрьму́; (*inform against*) доноси́ть (-ошу́, -о́сишь) *impf.*, донести́ (-су́, -сёшь; донёс, -ла́) *pf.* на+*a.* **shop-floor** *n.* (*fig.*) рабо́чие *sb.pl.* **shopkeeper** *n.* ла́вочник. **shoplifter** *n.* магази́нщик. **shopper** *n.* покупа́тель *m.*, ~ница. **shopping** *n.* поку́пки *f.pl.*; **go, do one's** ~ де́лать *impf.*, с~ *pf.* поку́пки. **shopwalker** *n.* дежу́рный администра́тор магази́на. **shop-window** *n.* витри́на.

shore¹ [ʃɔː(r)] *n.* бе́рег (*loc.* -у́; *pl.* -а́); ~ **leave** о́тпуск на бе́рег.

shore² [ʃɔː(r)] *v.t.*: ~ **up** подпира́ть *impf.*, подпере́ть (подопру́, -рёшь; подпёр) *pf.*

shorn [ʃɔːn] *adj.* остри́женный (-ен).

short [ʃɔːt] *adj.* коро́ткий (ко́роток, -тка́, ко́ро́тко́); (*concise*) кра́ткий (-ток, -тка́, -тко); (*not tall*) ни́зкий (-зок, -зка́, -зко, ни́зки́); (*of person*) ни́зкого ро́ста; (*deficient*) недоста́точный; **be** ~ **of** (*have too little*) испы́тывать *impf.*, испыта́ть *pf.* недоста́ток в+*p.*; (*not amount to*) быть (*fut.* бу́ду, -дешь; был, -á, -о; не́ был, -á, -о) ме́ньше+*g.*; (*uncivil*) гру́бый (груб, -á, -о) (*crumbling*) рассы́пчатый; **in** ~ одни́м сло́вом; ~ (**circuit**) коро́ткое замыка́ние; ~ **cut** коро́ткий путь (-ти́, -тём) *m.*; ~ **list** оконча́тельный спи́сок (-ска); ~ **measure** недоме́р; **at** ~ **notice** неме́дленно; ~ **sight** близору́кость; ~ **story** расска́з, нове́лла; **in** ~ **supply** дефици́тный; ~ **wave** коротково́лновый; ~ **weight** недове́с; *n.* (*film*) короткометра́жный фильм; (*drink*) спиртно́е *sb.*; *pl.* шо́рты (-т) *pl.* **shortage** *n.* недоста́ток (-тка); дефици́т. **shortbread** *n.* песо́чное пече́нье. **short-change** *v.t.* недодава́ть (-даю́, -даёшь) *impf.*, недода́ть (-а́м, -а́шь, -áст, -ади́м; недо́дал, -á, -о) *pf.* сда́чу+*d.* **short(-circuit)** *v.t.* замыка́ть *impf.*, замкну́ть *pf.* на́коротко. **shortcoming** *n.* недоста́ток (-тка). **shorten** *v.t.* & *i.* укора́чивать(ся) *impf.*, укороти́ть(ся) *pf.*; сокраща́ть(ся) *impf.*, сократи́ть(ся) (-ащу́, -ати́т(ся)) *pf.*; ~ **sail** убавля́ть *impf.*, уба́вить *pf.* парусо́в. **shortfall** *n.* дефици́т. **shorthand** *n.* стеногра́фия. **shorthorn** *n.* шортго́рнская поро́да скота́. **short-list** *v.t.* включа́ть *impf.*, включи́ть *pf.* в оконча́тельный спи́сок. **short-lived** *adj.* недол-

гове́чный, мимолётный. **shortly** *adv.*: ~ **after** вско́ре (по́сле+*g.*); ~ **before** незадо́лго (до+*g.*). **short-range** *adj.* краткосро́чный. **short-sighted** *adj.* близору́кий; (*fig.*) недальнови́дный. **short-tempered** *adj.* вспы́льчивый. **short-term** *adj.* краткосро́чный. **short-winded** *adj.* страда́ющий оды́шкой.

shot¹ [ʃɒt] *n.* (*discharge of gun*) вы́стрел; (*for cannon*; *sport*) ядро́ (*pl.* я́дра, я́дер, я́драм) (*pellet*) дроби́нка; (*as pl.*, *collect.*) дробь; (*person*) стрело́к (-лка́); (*attempt*) попы́тка; (*injection*) уко́л; (*phot.*) сни́мок (-мка); (*cin.*) съёмка; **like a** ~ о́чень охо́тно, неме́дленно; **a** ~ **in the arm** (*fig.*) сти́мул.

shot² [ʃɒt] *adj.* (*of material*) перели́вчатый. **shotgun** [ˈʃɒtɡʌn] *n.* дробови́к (-á).

shoulder [ˈʃəʊldə(r)] *n.* плечо́ (*pl.* -чи, -ч, -ча́м); (*cul.*) лопа́тка; (*of road*) обо́чина; **straight from the** ~ спле́ча; ~ **to** ~ плечо́м к плечу́; *v.t.* взва́ливать *impf.*, взвали́ть (-лю́, -лишь) *pf.* на пле́чи. **shoulder-blade** *n.* лопа́тка. **shoulder-strap** *n.* брете́лька; (*on uniform*) пого́н (*g.pl.* -н).

shout [ʃaʊt] *n.* крик; *v.i.* крича́ть (-чу́, -чи́шь) *impf.*, кри́кнуть *pf.*; ~ **down** перекри́кивать *impf.*, перекрича́ть (-чу́, -чи́шь) *pf.*

shove [ʃʌv] *n.* толчо́к (-чка́); *v.t.* & *i.* толка́ть(ся) *impf.*, толкну́ть *pf.*; ~ **off** (*coll.*) убира́ться *impf.*, убра́ться (уберу́сь, -рёшься; убра́лся, -ала́сь, -а́ло́сь) *pf.*

shovel [ˈʃʌv(ə)l] *n.* сово́к (-вка́), лопа́та; *v.t.* копа́ть *impf.*, вы́~ *pf.*; (~ **up**) сгреба́ть *impf.*, сгрести́ (сгребу́, -бёшь; сгрёб, -лá) *pf.*

show [ʃəʊ] *v.t.* пока́зывать *impf.*, показа́ть (-ажу́, -а́жешь) *pf.*; (*exhibit*) выставля́ть *impf.*, вы́ставить *pf.*; (*film etc.*) демонстри́ровать *impf.*, про~ *pf.*; *v.i.* быть ви́дным (-ден, -дна́, -дно, ви́дны́), заме́тным; ~ **off** (*v.i.*) рисова́ться *impf.*; *n.* (*exhibition*) вы́ставка; (*theatr.*) спекта́кль *m.*; (*spectacle*; *pageant*) зре́лище; (*business*) де́ло (*pl.* -лá); (*appearance*) ви́димость; ~ **of hands** голосова́ние подня́тием руки́. **showboat** *n.* плаву́чий теа́тр. **showcase** *n.* витри́на.

shower [ˈʃaʊə(r)] *n.* (*rain*) до́ждик; (*hail*; *fig.*) град; (~-*bath*) душ; *v.t.* осыпа́ть *impf.*, осы́пать (-плю, -плешь) *pf.*+*i.* (**on** +*a.*); *v.i.* принима́ть *impf.*, приня́ть (приму́, -мешь; при́нял, -á, -о) *pf.* душ. **showery** *adj.* дождли́вый.

showgirl [ˈʃəʊɡɜːl] *n.* стати́стка. **showjumping** *n.* соревнова́ние по ска́чкам. **showman** *n.* балага́нщик. **showroom** *n.* сало́н.

showy [ˈʃəʊɪ] *adj.* я́ркий (я́рок, ярка́, я́рко); (*gaudy*) безвку́сный (-сок, -сна́, -сно).

shrapnel [ˈʃræpn(ə)l] *n.* шрапне́ль.

shred [ʃred] *n.* клочо́к (-чка́), лоскуто́к (-тка́); **not a** ~ ни ка́пли; **tear to** ~**s** (*fig.*) по́лностью опроверга́ть *impf.*, опрове́ргнуть (-г(нул), -гла) *pf.*; *v.t.* ре́зать (ре́жу, -жешь) *impf.*, на клочки́; рвать (рву, рвёшь; рвал, -á, -о) *impf.* в клочки́.

shrew [ʃru:] *n.* (*woman*) сварли́вая, стропти́вая, же́нщина; (*animal*) землеро́йка.

shrewd [ʃru:d] *adj.* проница́тельный.

shrewish ['ʃru:ıʃ] *adj.* сварли́вый.

shriek [ʃri:k] *n.* пронзи́тельный крик, визг; *v.i.* визжа́ть (-жу́, -жи́шь) *impf.*; крича́ть (-чу́, -чи́шь) *impf.*, кри́кнуть *pf.*

shrill [ʃrıl] *adj.* пронзи́тельный, ре́зкий (-зок, -зка́, -зко).

shrimp [ʃrımp] *n.* креве́тка.

shrine [ʃraın] *n.* (*casket*) ра́ка; (*tomb*) гробни́ца; (*sacred place*) святы́ня.

shrink [ʃrıŋk] *v.i.* сади́ться *impf.*, сесть (ся́дет; сел) *pf.*; *v.t.* вызыва́ть *impf.*, вы́звать (-зовет) *pf.* уса́дку y+g.; ~ **from** уклоня́ться *impf.* от+g.; избега́ть *impf.*+g. **shrinkage** *n.* уса́дка. **shrink-proof** *adj.* безуса́дочный.

shrivel ['ʃrıv(ə)l] *v.t.* & *i.* съёживать(ся) *impf.*, съёжить(ся) *pf.*

shroud [ʃraud] *n.* са́ван; *pl.* (*naut.*) ва́нты *f.pl.*; *v.t.* (*fig.*) оку́тывать *impf.*, оку́тать *pf.* (in +i.).

Shrovetide ['ʃrəuvtaıd] *n.* Ма́сленица.

shrub [ʃrʌb] *n.* куст (-á), куста́рник. **shrubbery** *n.* куста́рник.

shrug [ʃrʌg] *v.t.* & *i.* пожима́ть *impf.*, пожа́ть (-жму́, -жмёшь) *pf.* (плеча́ми).

shudder ['ʃʌdə(r)] *n.* содрога́ние; *v.i.* содрога́ться *impf.*, содрогну́ться *pf.*

shuffle ['ʃʌf(ə)l] *v.t.* & *i.* (*one's feet*) ша́ркать *impf.* (нога́ми); *v.t.* (*cards*) тасова́ть *impf.*, с~ *pf.*; (*intermingle, confuse*) переме́шивать *impf.*, перемеша́ть *pf.*; ~ **off** (*blame etc.*) сва́ливать *impf.*, свали́ть (-лю́, -лишь) *pf.* (on to на+a.); *n.* ша́рканье; тасо́вка.

shun [ʃʌn] *v.t.* избега́ть *impf.*+g.

shunt [ʃʌnt] *v.i.* (*rail.*) маневри́ровать *impf.*, с~ *pf.*; *v.t.* (*rail.*) переводи́ть (-ожу́, -о́дишь) *impf.*, перевести́ (-еду́, -едёшь; -ёл, -ела́) *pf.* на запа́сный путь.

shut [ʃʌt] *v.t.* & *i.* закрыва́ть(ся) *impf.*, закры́ть(ся) (-ро́ю, -ро́ет(ся)) *pf.*; ~ **in** запира́ть *impf.*, запере́ть (запру́, -рёшь; за́пер, -ла́, -ло) *pf.*; ~ **up** (*v.i.*) замолча́ть (-чу́, -чи́шь) *pf.*; (*imper.*) заткни́сь!

shutter ['ʃʌtə(r)] *n.* ста́вень (-вня) *m.*, ста́вня (*g.pl.* -вен); (*phot.*) затво́р; *v.t.* закрыва́ть *impf.*, закры́ть (-ро́ю, -ро́ешь) *pf.* ста́внями.

shuttle ['ʃʌt(ə)l] *n.* челно́к (-á). **shuttlecock** *n.* вола́н.

shy[1] [ʃaı] *adj.* засте́нчивый, ро́бкий (-бок, -бка́, -бко).

shy[2] [ʃaı] *v.i.* (*in alarm*) пуга́ться *impf.*, ис~ *pf.* (at +g.).

shy[3] [ʃaı] *v.t.* (*throw*) броса́ть *impf.*, бро́сить *pf.*; *n.* бросо́к (-ска́).

Siamese [,saıə'mi:z] *adj.* сиа́мский; ~ **twins** сиа́мские близнецы́ *m.pl.*

Siberia [saı'bıərıə] *n.* Сиби́рь. **Siberian** *adj.* сиби́рский; *n.* сибиря́к (-á), -я́чка.

sibilant ['sıbılənt] *adj.* (*n.*) свистя́щий (звук) (*sb.*).

sic [sık] *adv.* так!

sick [sık] *adj.* больно́й (-лен, -льна́); **be, feel,** ~ тошни́ть *impf. impers.*+a.; то́шно *impers.*+d.; **be** ~ **for** (*pine*) тоскова́ть *impf.* по+d.; **be** ~ **of** надоеда́ть *impf.*, надое́сть (-е́м, -е́шь, -е́ст, -еди́м; -е́л) *pf.*+nom. (*object*) & *d.* (*subject*); **I'm** ~ **of her** она́ мне надое́ла. **sickbed** *n.* посте́ль больно́го. **sick-benefit** *n.* посо́бие по боле́зни. **sicken** *v.t.* вызыва́ть *impf.*, вы́звать (-зовет) *pf.* тошноту́, (*disgust*) отвраще́ние, y+g.; *v.i.* заболева́ть *impf.*, заболе́ть *pf.* **sickening** *adj.* отврати́тельный.

sickle ['sık(ə)l] *n.* серп (-á).

sick-leave ['sıkli:v] *n.* о́тпуск по боле́зни. **sickly** *adj.* (*ailing*) боле́зненный (-ен, -енна), хи́лый (хил, -á, -о); (*nauseating*) тошнотво́рный. **sickness** *n.* боле́знь; (*vomiting*) тошнота́; ~ **benefit** посо́бие по боле́зни.

side [saıd] *n.* сторона́ (*a.* -ону; *pl.* -оны, -о́н, -она́м), бок (*loc.* -ý; *pl.* -á); ~ **by** ~ бок ó бок; ря́дом (with c+i.); **on the** ~ на стороне́, дополни́тельно; *v.i.*: ~ **with** встава́ть (-таю́, -таёшь) *impf.*, встать (-а́ну, -а́нешь) *pf.* на сто́рону+g. **sideboard** *n.* серва́нт, буфе́т; *pl.* ба́ки (-к) *pl.* **side-car** *n.* коля́ска (мотоци́кла). **side-effect** *n.* (*of medicine etc.*) побо́чное де́йствие. **sidelight** *n.* боково́й фона́рь (-ря́) *m.* **sideline** *n.* (*work*) побо́чная рабо́та. **sidelong** *adj.* (*glance*) косо́й.

sidereal [saı'dıərıəl] *adj.* звёздный.

side-saddle ['saıd,sæd(ə)l] *n.* да́мское седло́ (*pl.* сёдла, -дел, -длам) **side-slip** *n.* боково́е скольже́ние; (*aeron.*) скольже́ние на крыло́. **sidestep** *v.t.* (*fig.*) уклоня́ться *impf.*, уклони́ться (-ню́сь, -ни́шься) *pf.* от+g. **side-stroke** *n.* пла́вание на боку́. **sidetrack** *v.t.* (*distract*) отвлека́ть *impf.*, отвле́чь (-еку́, -ечёшь; -ёк, -екла́) *pf.*; (*postpone*) откла́дывать *impf.*, отложи́ть (-жу́, -жишь) *pf.* рассмотре́ние+g. **side-view** *n.* про́филь *m.*, вид сбо́ку.

sideways ['saıdweız] *adv.* бо́ком; (*from side*) сбо́ку.

siding ['saıdıŋ] *n.* запа́сный путь (-ти́, -тём) *m.*

sidle ['saıd(ə)l] *v.i.* ходи́ть (хожу́, хо́дишь) *impf.* бо́ком.

siege [si:dʒ] *n.* оса́да; **lay** ~ **to** осажда́ть *impf.*, осади́ть *pf.*; **raise the** ~ **of** снима́ть *impf.*, снять (сниму́, -мешь; снял, -á, -о) *pf.* оса́ду c+g.

sienna [sı'enə] *n.* сие́на; **burnt** ~ жжёная сие́на.

siesta [sı'estə] *n.* сие́ста.

sieve [sıv] *n.* решето́ (*pl.* -ёта), си́то; *v.t.* просе́ивать *impf.*, просе́ять (-е́ю, -е́ешь) *pf.*

sift [sıft] *v.t.* просе́ивать *impf.*, просе́ять (-е́ю, -е́ешь) *pf.*; (*evidence etc.*) тща́тельно рассма́тривать *impf.*, рассмотре́ть (-рю́, -ришь) *pf.* **sifter** *n.* си́то.

sigh [saı] *v.i.* вздыха́ть *impf.*, вздохну́ть *pf.*; *n.* вздох.

sight [saıt] *n.* (*faculty*) зре́ние; (*view; range*)

вид; (*spectacle*) зрéлище; *pl.* достопримечáтельности *f.pl.*; (*on gun*) прицéл; **at, on** ~ при вйде (*of* +*g.*); **at first** ~ с пéрвого взгля́да; **in** ~ в видý+*g.*; **long** ~ дальнозóркость; **short** ~ близорýкость; **catch** ~ **of** увйдеть (-йжу, -йдишь) *pf.*; **know by** ~ знать *impf.* в лицó; **lose** ~ **of** теря́ть *impf.*, по~ *pf.* йз виду; (*fig.*) упускáть *impf.*, упустйть (-ущý, -ýстишь) *pf.* йз виду. **sightless** *adj.* слепóй (слеп, -á, -о). **sight-reading** *n.* чтéние нот с листá.

sign [saɪn] *n.* знак; (*indication*) прйзнак; (~*board*) вы́веска; *v.t. & abs.* подпйсывать(ся) *impf.*, подписáть(ся) (-ишý(сь), -йшешь(ся)) *pf.*; *v.i.* (*give* ~) подавáть (-даю́, -даёшь) *impf.*, подáть (-áм, -áшь, -áст, -адйм; пóдал, -á, -о) *pf.* знак.

signal[1] ['sɪgn(ə)l] *adj.* выдаю́щийся, замечáтельный.

signal[2] ['sɪgn(ə)l] *n.* сигнáл; *pl.* (*mil.*) связь; *v.t. & i.* сигнализйровать *impf. & pf.*, про~ *pf.* **signal-box** *n.* сигнáльная бýдка. **signalman** *n.* сигнáльщик.

signatory ['sɪgnətərɪ] *n.* подписáвший *sb.*; (*of treaty*) сторонá (*a.* -ону; *pl.* -оны, -óн, -онáм), подписáвшая договóр.

signature ['sɪgnətʃə(r)] *n.* пóдпись; (*print.*) сигнатýра; (*mus.*) ключ (-á); ~ **tune** музыкáльная шáпка.

signboard ['saɪnbɔːd] *n.* вы́веска.

signet ['sɪgnɪt] *n.* печáтка. **signet-ring** *n.* кольцó (*pl.* -льца, -лéц, -льцам) с печáткой.

significance [sɪgˈnɪfɪkəns] *n.* значéние. **significant** *adj.* значйтельный. **signify** ['sɪgnɪˌfaɪ] *v.t* означáть *impf.*; (*express*) выражáть *impf.*, вы́разить *pf.*; *v.i.* быть (*fut.* бýду, -дешь; был, -á, -о; нé был, -á, -о)) *impf.* вáжным.

signpost ['saɪnpəʊst] *n.* указáтельный столб (-á).

Sikh [siːk, sɪk] *n.* сикх; *adj.* сйкхский.

silage ['saɪlɪdʒ] *n.* сйлос.

silence ['saɪləns] *n.* молчáние, тишинá; *v.t.* застáвить *pf.* замолчáть. **silencer** *n.* глушйтель *m.* **silent** *adj.* (*not speaking*) безмóлвный; (*taciturn*) молчалйвый; (*of film*) немóй; (*without noise*) тйхий (тих, -á, -о), бесшýмный; **be** ~ молчáть (-чý, -чйшь) *impf.*

silhouette [ˌsɪluːˈet] *n.* силуэ́т; *v.t.* **be** ~**d** вырисóвываться *impf.*, вы́рисоваться *pf.* (**against** на фóне+*g.*).

silica ['sɪlɪkə] *n.* кремнезём. **silicate** *n.* силикáт. **silicon** *n.* крéмний; *adj.* крéмниевый ~ **chip** крéмниевый кристáлл. **silicone** *n.* силикóн. **sili'cosis** *n.* силикóз.

silk [sɪlk] *n.* шёлк (-а(у), *loc.* -е & -ý; *pl.* -á); **take** ~ станови́ться (-влю́сь, -вишься) *impf.*, стать (-áну, -áнешь) *pf.* королéвским адвокáтом; *attr.* шёлковый; ~ **hat** цилйндр. **silkworm** *n.* шелковйчный червь (-вя́; *pl.* -ви, -вéй) *m.* **silky** *adj.* шелковйстый.

sill [sɪl] *n.* подокóнник.

silly ['sɪlɪ] *adj.* глýпый (глуп, -á, -о).

silo ['saɪləʊ] *n.* сйлос; *v.t.* силосовáть *impf. & pf.*, за~ *pf.*

silt [sɪlt] *n.* ил (-а(у)); *v.i.*: ~ **up** засоря́ться *impf.*, засорйться *pf.* йлом.

silver ['sɪlvə(r)] *n.* серебрó; (*cutlery*) столóвое серебрó; *adj.* (*of* ~) серéбряный; (*silvery*) серебрйстый; (*hair*) седóй (сед, -á, -о); ~ **foil** серéбряная фóльга; ~ **fox** черно-бýрая лисá; ~ **paper** (*tin foil*) станиóль *m.*; ~ **plate** столóвое серебрó; *v.t.* серебрйть *impf.*, вы́~, по~ *pf.*; (*mirror*) покрывáть *impf.*, покры́ть (-рóю, -рóешь) *pf.* амальгáмой ртýти. **silversmith** *n.* серéбряных дел мáстер (*pl.* -á). **silverware** *n.* столóвое серебрó. **silvery** *adj.* серебрйстый; (*hair*) седóй (сед, -á, -о).

silviculture ['sɪlvɪˌkʌltʃə(r)] *n.* лесовóдство.

simian ['sɪmɪən] *adj.* обезья́ний.

similar ['sɪmɪlə(r)] *adj.* подóбный (**to** +*d.*), схóдный (-ден, -днá, -дно) (**to** с+*i.*; **in** по+*d.*). **similarity** [ˌsɪmɪˈlærɪtɪ] *n.* схóдство; (*math.*) подóбие. **similarly** *adv.* подóбным óбразом. **simile** ['sɪmɪlɪ] *n.* сравнéние.

simmer ['sɪmə(r)] *v.t.* кипятйть *impf.* на мéдленном огнé; *v.i.* кипéть (-пйт) *impf.* на мéдленном огнé; ~ **down** успокáиваться *impf.*, успокóиться *pf.*

simper ['sɪmpə(r)] *v.i.* жемáнно улыбáться *impf.*, улыбнýться *pf.*; *n.* жемáнная улы́бка.

simple ['sɪmp(ə)l] *adj.* простóй (прост, -á, -о, прóсты). **simple-hearted** *adj.* простодýшный. **simple-minded** *adj.* туповáтый. **simpleton** *n.* простáк (-á). **sim'plicity** *n.* простотá. **simplify** ['sɪmplɪˌfaɪ] *v.t.* упрощáть *impf.*, упростйть *pf.* **simply** *adv.* прóсто.

simulate ['sɪmjʊˌleɪt] *v.t.* притворя́ться *impf.*, притворйться *pf.*+*i.*; (*conditions etc.*) моделйровать *impf. & pf.* **simulated** *adj.* (*pearls etc.*) искýсственный.

simultaneous [ˌsɪməlˈteɪnɪəs] *adj.* одноврéменный (-нен, -нна).

sin [sɪn] *n.* грех (-á); *v.i.* грешйть *impf.*, со~ *pf.*; ~ **against** нарушáть *impf.*, нарушйть *pf.*

since [sɪns] *adv.* с тех пор; (*ago*) (томý) назáд; *prep.* с+*g.*; *conj.* с тех пор как; (*reason*) так как.

sincere [sɪnˈsɪə(r)] *adj.* йскренний (-нен, -нна, -нно & -нне). **sincerely** *adv.* искренне; **yours** ~ йскренне Ваш. **sincerity** [sɪnˈserɪtɪ] *n.* йскренность.

sine [saɪn] *n.* сйнус.

sinecure ['saɪnɪˌkjʊə(r), 'sɪn-] *n.* синекýра.

sine die [ˌsaɪnɪ ˈdaɪɪ, ˌsɪneɪ ˈdiːeɪ] *adv.* на неопределённый срок.

sine qua non [ˌsɪneɪ kwɑː ˈnəʊn] *n.* обязáтельное услóвие.

sinew ['sɪnjuː] *n.* сухожйлие. **sinewy** *adj.* жйлистый.

sinful ['sɪnfʊl] *adj.* грéшный (-шен, -шнá, -шно, грéшны́). **sinfully** *adv.* грешнó.

sing [sɪŋ] *v.t. & i.* петь (пою́, поёшь) *impf.*, про~, с~ *pf.*

singe [sɪndʒ] *v.t.* пали́ть *impf.*, о~ *pf.*; *n.* ожо́г.

singer ['sɪŋə(r)] *n.* певе́ц (-вца́), -ви́ца.

single ['sɪŋg(ə)l] *adj.* оди́н (одна́); (*unmarried*) холосто́й, незаму́жняя; (*solitary*) одино́кий; (*bed*) односпа́льный; ~ **combat** единобо́рство; ~ **father** оте́ц-одино́чка; ~ **mother** мать-одино́чка; in ~ **file** гусько́м; ~ **room** ко́мната на одного́; *n.* (*ticket*) биле́т в оди́н коне́ц; *pl.* (*tennis etc.*) одино́чная игра́ *v.t.*: ~ **out** выделя́ть *impf.*, вы́делить *pf.* **single-handed** *adj.* без посторо́нней по́мощи. **single-minded** *adj.* целеустремлённый (-ён, -ённа). **single-seater** *n.* одноме́стный автомоби́ль *m.*

singlet ['sɪŋglɪt] *n.* ма́йка.

singsong ['sɪŋsɒŋ] *adj.* моното́нный.

singular ['sɪŋgjʊlə(r)] *n.* еди́нственное число́; *adj.* еди́нственный; (*unusual*) необыча́йный; (*strange*) стра́нный (-нен, -нна́, -нно). **singularity** [ˌsɪŋgjʊˈlærɪtɪ] *n.* (*peculiarity*) своеобра́зие.

sinister ['sɪnɪstə(r)] *adj.* (*ominous*) злове́щий; (*evil*) злой (зол, зла).

sink [sɪŋk] *v.i.* опуска́ться *impf.*, опусти́ться (-ущу́сь, -у́стишься) *pf.*; (*subside*) оседа́ть *impf.*, осе́сть (ося́дет; осе́л) *pf.*; (*of ship*) тону́ть *impf.*, по~ *pf.*; (*of sick person*) умира́ть *impf.*; *v.t.* (*ship*) топи́ть (-плю́, -пишь) *impf.*, по~ *pf.*; (*well*) рыть (ро́ю, ро́ешь) *impf.*, вы́~ *pf.*; (*shaft*) проходи́ть (-ожу́, -о́дишь) *impf.*, пройти́ (пройду́, -дёшь; прошёл, -шла́) *pf.*; *n.* (*also fig.*) клоа́ка; (*basin*) ра́ковина. **sinker** *n.* грузи́ло.

sinner ['sɪnə(r)] *n.* гре́шник, -ица.

Sino- ['saɪnəʊ] *in comb.* кита́йско-. **sinologist** [saɪˈnɒlədʒɪst, sɪ-] *n.* китаеве́д, сино́лог. **si'nology** *n.* китаеве́дение, синоло́гия.

sinuous ['sɪnjʊəs] *adj.* изви́листый.

sinus ['saɪnəs] *n.* (ло́бная) па́зуха. **sinu'sitis** *n.* синуси́т.

sip [sɪp] *v.t.* пить (пью, пьёшь; пил, -а́, -о) *impf.*, ма́ленькими глотка́ми; *n.* ма́ленький глото́к (-тка́).

siphon ['saɪf(ə)n] *n.* сифо́н.

sir [sɜː(r)] *n.* сэр.

sire ['saɪə(r)] *n.* (*as vocative*) сир; (*stallion etc.*) производи́тель *m.*; *v.t.* быть (*fut.* бу́ду, -дешь; был, -а́, -о; не был, -а́, -о) *impf.* производи́телем+*g.*

siren ['saɪərən] *n.* сире́на.

sirloin ['sɜːlɔɪn] *n.* филе́ *nt.indecl.*

sister ['sɪstə(r)] *n.* сестра́ (*pl.* сёстры, -тёр, -трам). **sisterhood** *n.* (*relig.*) сестри́нская общи́на. **sister-in-law** *n.* (*husband's sister*) золо́вка; (*wife's sister*) своя́ченица. (*brother's wife*) неве́стка.

sit [sɪt] *v.i.* (*be sitting*) сиде́ть (сижу́, сиди́шь) *impf.*; (~ *down*) сади́ться *impf.*, сесть (ся́ду, -дешь; сел) *pf.*; (*parl.*, *leg.*) заседа́ть *impf.*; (*pose*) пози́ровать *impf.* (**for** для+*g.*); *v.t.* уса́живать *impf.*, усади́ть (-ажу́, -а́дишь) *pf.*; (*examination*) сдава́ть (сдаю́, -аёшь)

impf.; ~ **back** отки́дываться *impf.*, отки́нуться *pf.*; ~ **down** сади́ться *impf.*, сесть (ся́ду, -дешь; сел) *pf.*; ~ **on** (*committee etc.*) быть (*fut.* бу́ду, -дешь; был, -а́, -о) *impf.* чле́ном+*g.*; ~ **up** приподнима́ться *impf.*, приподня́ться (-ниму́сь, -ни́мешься; -ня́лся, -няла́сь) *pf.*; (*stay out of bed*) не ложи́ться *impf.* спать. **sit-down** *adj.*: ~ **strike** италья́нская забасто́вка.

site [saɪt] *n.* ме́сто (*pl.* -та́), местоположе́ние; **building** ~ строи́тельная площа́дка.

sitter ['sɪtə(r)] *n.* пози́рующий *sb.*; (*model*) нату́рщик, -ица. **sitting** *n.* (*parl. etc.*) заседа́ние; (*for portrait*) сеа́нс; (*for meal*) сме́на; *adj.* сидя́чий, сидя́щий. **sitting-room** *n.* гости́ная *sb.*

situated ['sɪtjʊˌeɪtɪd] *adj.*: be ~ находи́ться (-ожу́сь, -о́дишься) *impf.* **situ'ation** *n.* местоположе́ние; (*circumstances*) положе́ние; (*work etc.*) ме́сто (*pl.* -та́).

six [sɪks] *adj. & n.* шесть (-ти́, -тью́); (*collect.*; *6 pairs*) ше́стеро (-ры́х); (*cards*; *number 6*) шестёрка; (*time*) шесть (часо́в); (*age*) шесть лет. **sixteen** *adj. & n.* шестна́дцать (-ти, -тью); (*age*) шестна́дцать лет. **sixteenth** *adj. & n.* шестна́дцатый; (*fraction*) шестна́дцатая (часть (*pl.* -ти, -те́й)); (*date*) шестна́дцатое (число́). **sixth** *adj. & n.* шесто́й; (*fraction*) шеста́я (часть (*pl.* -ти, -те́й)); (*date*) шесто́е (число́); (*mus.*) се́кста. **sixtieth** *adj. & n.* шестидеся́тый; (*fraction*) шестидеся́тая (часть (*pl.* -ти, -те́й)). **sixty** *adj. & n.* шестьдеся́т (-ти́десяти, -тью́десятью); (*age*) шестьдеся́т лет; *pl.* (*decade*) шестидеся́тые го́ды (-до́в) *m.pl.*

size[1] [saɪz] *n.* (*dimensions*; *of garment etc.*) разме́р; (*magnitude*) величина́; (*capacity*) объём; (*format*) форма́т; *v.t.*: ~ **up** оце́нивать *impf.*, оцени́ть (-ню́, -нишь) *pf.* **sizeable** *adj.* поря́дочных разме́ров.

size[2] [saɪz] *n.* (*solution*) шли́хта; *v.t.* шлихтова́ть *impf.*

sizzle ['sɪz(ə)l] *v.i.* шипе́ть (-пи́т) *impf.*

skate[1] [skeɪt] *n.* (*fish*) скат.

skate[2] [skeɪt] *n.* (*ice-*~) конёк (-нька́); (*roller-*~) конёк (-нька́) на ро́ликах; *v.i.* ката́ться *impf.* на конька́х. **skateboard** *n.* ро́ликовая доска́. **skating-rink** *n.* като́к (-тка́).

skein [skeɪn] *n.* мото́к (-тка́).

skeleton ['skelɪt(ə)n] *n.* скеле́т, о́стов; ~ **key** отмы́чка.

sketch [sketʃ] *n.* набро́сок (-ска), зарисо́вка; (*theatr.*) скетч; *v.t. & i.* де́лать *impf.*, с~ *pf.* набро́сок, -ски (+*g.*). **sketch-book** *n.* альбо́м для зарисо́вок. **sketch-map** *n.* кроки́ *nt.indecl.* **sketchy** *adj.* отры́вочный; (*superficial*) пове́рхностный.

skew [skjuː] *adj.* косо́й; *n.* укло́н; **on the** ~ ко́со; *v.t.* перека́шивать *impf.*, перекоси́ть *pf.*; *v.i.* уклоня́ться *impf.*, уклони́ться (-ню́сь, -нишься) *pf.*

skewbald ['skjuːbɔːld] *adj.* пе́гий.

skewer ['skjuːə(r)] *n.* ве́ртел (*pl.* -а́); *v.t.* наса́живать *impf.*, насади́ть (-ажу́, -а́дишь) *pf.* на ве́ртел.

ski [skiː] *n.* лы́жа; *v.i.* ходи́ть (хожу́, хо́дишь) *impf.* на лы́жах.

skid [skɪd] *n.* зано́с; *v.i.* заноси́ть (-ошу́, -о́сишь) *impf.*, занести́ (-сёт; -сло́) *pf.* *impers.*+*a.*

skier ['skiːə(r)] *n.* лы́жник.

skiff [skɪf] *n.* я́лик, скиф.

skiing ['skiːɪŋ] *n.* лы́жный спорт. **ski-jump** *n.* трамплйн.

skilful ['skɪlfʊl] *adj.* иску́сный, уме́лый. **skill** *n.* мастерство́, иску́сство, уме́ние. **skilled** *adj.* иску́сный; (*worker*) квалифици́рованный.

skim [skɪm] *v.t.* снима́ть *impf.*, снять (сниму́, -мешь; снял, -а́, -о) *pf.* (*cream*) сли́вки *pl.*; (*skin on milk*) пе́нки *pl.*; (*scum*) на́кипь, *c*+*g.*; *v.i.* скользи́ть *impf.* (*over, along* по+*d.*); ~ **through** бе́гло просма́тривать *impf.*, просмотре́ть (-рю́, -ришь) *pf.*; *adj.*: ~(**med**) **milk** снято́е молоко́.

skimp [skɪmp] *v.t.* & *i.* скупи́ться *impf.* (на+*a.*). **skimpy** *adj.* ску́дный (-ден, -дна́, -дно).

skin [skɪn] *n.* ко́жа; (*hide*) шку́ра; (*of fruit etc.*) кожура́; (*on milk*) пе́нка; *v.t.* сдира́ть *impf.*, содра́ть (сдеру́, -рёшь; содра́л, -а́, -о) *pf.* ко́жу, шку́ру, *c*+*g.*; снима́ть *impf.*, снять (сниму́, -мешь; снял, -а́, -о) *pf.* кожуру́ *c*+*g.* **skin-deep** *adj.* пове́рхностный. **skin-diver** *n.* аквалангú́ст. **skinflint** *n.* скря́га *c.g.* **skinny** *adj.* то́щий (тощ, -а́, -е). **skint** [skɪnt] *adj.* без гроша́ в карма́не. **skin-tight** [skɪn'taɪt] *adj.* в обтя́жку.

skip [skɪp] *v.i.* скака́ть (-ачу́, -а́чешь) *impf.*; (*with rope*) пры́гать *impf.* че́рез скака́лку; *v.t.* (*omit*) пропуска́ть *impf.*, пропусти́ть (-ущу́, -у́стишь) *pf.*; ~**ping rope** скака́лка.

skipper ['skɪpə(r)] *n.* (*naut.*) шки́пер (*pl.* -ы & -а́); (*naut.*, *other senses*) капита́н.

skirmish ['skɜːmɪʃ] *n.* схва́тка, сты́чка; *v.i.* сража́ться *impf.*

skirt [skɜːt] *n.* ю́бка; *v.t.* обходи́ть (-ожу́, -о́дишь) *impf.*, обойти́ (обойду́, -дёшь; обошёл, -шла́) *pf.* стороно́й. **skirting-board** *n.* пли́нтус.

ski-run ['skiːrʌn] *n.* лыжня́.

skit [skɪt] *n.* скетч.

skittish ['skɪtɪʃ] *adj.* (*horse*) норови́стый; (*person*) игри́вый.

skittle ['skɪt(ə)l] *n.* ке́гля; *pl.* ке́гли *f.pl.*

skulk [skʌlk] *v.i.* (*hide*) скрыва́ться *impf.*; (*creep*) кра́сться (краду́сь, -дёшься; кра́лся) *impf.*

skull [skʌl] *n.* че́реп (*pl.* -а́). **skullcap** *n.* ермо́лка.

skunk [skʌŋk] *n.* скунс, воню́чка.

sky [skaɪ] *n.* не́бо (*pl.* -беса́). **sky-blue** *adj.* лазу́рный. **skydiving** *n.* парашю́тный спорт. **skyjack** *v.t.* похища́ть *impf.*, похи́тить (-и́щу, -и́тишь) *pf.* **skylark** *n.* жа́воронок (-нка). **skylight** *n.* окно́ (*pl.* о́кна, о́кон, о́кнам) в кры́ше. **skyline** *n.* горизо́нт. **skyscraper** *n.* небоскрёб. **skyway** *n.* авиатра́сса.

slab [slæb] *n.* плита́ (*pl.* -ты); (*of cake etc.*) кусо́к (-ска́).

slack¹ [slæk] *n.* (*coal-dust*) у́гольная пыль.

slack² [slæk] *adj.* (*loose*) сла́бый (слаб, -а́, -о); (*sluggish*) вя́лый; (*inactive*) неакти́вный; (*negligent*) небре́жный; (*of rope*) ненатя́нутый; *n.* (*of rope*) слабина́; *pl.* повседне́вные брю́ки (-к) *pl.* **slacken** *v.t.* ослабля́ть *impf.*, осла́бить *pf.*; *v.t.* & *i.* (*slow down*) замедля́ть(ся) *impf.*, заме́длить(ся) *pf.*; *v.i.* ослабева́ть *impf.*, ослабе́ть *pf.* **slacker** *n.* безде́льник, ло́дырь *m.*

slag [slæg] *n.* шлак.

slake [sleɪk] *v.t.* (*thirst*) утоля́ть *impf.*, утоли́ть *pf.*; (*lime*) гаси́ть (гашу́, га́сишь) *impf.*, по~ *pf.*

slalom ['slɑːləm] *n.* сла́лом.

slam [slæm] *v.t.* & *i.* (*door*) захло́пывать(ся) *impf.*, захло́пнуть(ся) *pf.*; *n.* (*cards*) шлем.

slander ['slɑːndə(r)] *n.* клевета́; *v.t.* клевета́ть (-ещу́, -е́щешь) *impf.*, на~ *pf.* на+*a.* **slanderous** *adj.* клеветни́ческий.

slang [slæŋ] *n.* сленг, жарго́н; *v.t.* брани́ть *impf.*, вы~ *pf.* **slangy** *adj.* жарго́нный, вульга́рный.

slant [slɑːnt] *v.t.* & *i.* наклоня́ть(ся) *impf.*, наклони́ть(ся) (-ню́, -нит(ся)) *pf.*; *n.* укло́н. **slanting** *adj.* пока́тый, косо́й (кос, -а́, -о).

slap [slæp] *v.t.* хло́пать *impf.*, хло́пнуть *pf.*+*a.*, *i.*, по+*d.*; шлёпать *impf.*, шлёпнуть *pf.*; *n.* шлепо́к (-пка́); *adv.* пря́мо. **slapdash** *adj.* поспе́шный, небре́жный. **slapstick** *n.* балага́н.

slash [slæʃ] *v.t.* руби́ть (-блю́, -бишь) *impf.*; (*prices etc.*) ре́зко снижа́ть *impf.*, сни́зить *pf.*; *n.* разре́з, про́рез.

slat [slæt] *n.* пла́нка, филёнка.

slate¹ [sleɪt] *n.* сла́нец (-нца); (*for roofing*) ши́фер (*no pl.*), ши́ферная пли́тка; (*for writing*) гри́фельная доска́ (*a.* -ску; *pl.* -ски, -со́к, -ска́м); *v.t.* (*roof*) крыть (кро́ю, -о́ешь) *impf.*, по~ *pf.* ши́ферными пли́тками.

slate² [sleɪt] *v.t.* (*criticize*) раскритикова́ть *pf.* **slate-pencil** [sleɪt'pensɪl] *n.* гри́фель *m.*

slattern ['slæt(ə)n] *n.* неря́ха. **slatternly** *adj.* неря́шливый.

slaughter ['slɔːtə(r)] *n.* (*of animals*) убо́й; (*massacre*) резня́; *v.t.* ре́зать (ре́жу, -жешь) *impf.*, за~ *pf.*; (*people*) убива́ть *impf.*, уби́ть (убью́, -ьёшь) *pf.* **slaughterhouse** *n.* бо́йня (*g.pl.* бо́ен).

Slav [slɑːv] *n.* славяни́н (*pl.* -я́не, -я́н), -я́нка (*g.pl.* -нок); *adj.* славя́нский.

slave [sleɪv] *n.* раб (-а́), раба́ (*g.pl.* -нь); *v.i.* рабо́тать *impf.* как раб.

slaver ['slævə(r)] *v.i.* пуска́ть *impf.*, пусти́ть (пущу́, пу́стишь) *pf.* слю́ни; *n.* слю́ни (-не́й) *pl.*

slavery ['sleɪvərɪ] *n.* ра́бство. **slave-trade** *n.* работорго́вля.

Slavic ['slɑːvɪk] *adj.* славя́нский.
slavish ['sleɪvɪʃ] *adj.* ра́бский.
Slavonic [sləˈvɒnɪk] *adj.* славя́нский.
slay [sleɪ] *v.t.* убива́ть *impf.*, уби́ть (убью́, -ьёшь) *pf.*
sleazy ['sliːzɪ] *adj.* (*person*) неря́шливый.
sledge [sledʒ] *n.* са́ни (-не́й) *pl.*
sledge-hammer ['sledʒˌhæmə(r)] *n.* кува́лда.
sleek [sliːk] *adj.* гла́дкий (-док, -дка́, -дко).
sleep [sliːp] *n.* сон (сна); **go to** ~ засыпа́ть *impf.*, засну́ть *pf.*; *v.i.* спать (сплю, спишь; спал, -а́, -о) *impf.*; (*spend the night*) ночева́ть (-чу́ю, -чу́ешь) *impf.*, пере~ *pf.* **sleeper** *n.* спя́щий *sb.*; (*rail., beam*) шпа́ла; (*sleeping-car*) спа́льный ваго́н. **sleeping** *adj.* спя́щий, спа́льный; ~ **partner** пасси́вный партнёр; ~ **sickness** со́нная боле́знь. **sleeping-bag** *n.* спа́льный мешо́к (-шка́). **sleeping-car(riage)** *n.* спа́льный ваго́н. **sleeping-pill** *n.* снотво́рная табле́тка. **sleepless** *adj.* бессо́нный (-нен, -нна). **sleepwalker** *n.* луна́тик. **sleepy** *adj.* со́нный (-нен, -нна).
sleet [sliːt] *n.* мо́крый снег (-a(y), *loc.* -ý).
sleeve [sliːv] *n.* рука́в (-á; *pl.* -á); (*tech.*) му́фта; (*of record*) конве́рт.
sleigh [sleɪ] *n.* са́ни (-не́й) *pl.* **sleigh-bell** бубе́нчик.
sleight-of-hand [slaɪt] *n.* ло́вкость рук.
slender ['slendə(r)] *adj.* (*slim*) то́нкий (-нок, -нка́, -нко, то́нки́); (*meagre*) ску́дный (-ден, -дна́, -дно); (*of hope etc.*) сла́бый (слаб, -á, -о).
sleuth [sluːθ] *n.* сы́щик.
slew [sluː] *v.t. & i.* бы́стро повора́чивать(ся) *impf.*, поверну́ть(ся) *pf.*
slice [slaɪs] *n.* ло́мтик, ломо́ть (-мтя́) *m.*; (*share*) часть (*pl.* -ти, -те́й); *v.t.* (~ **up**) наре́зать *impf.*, наре́зать (-е́жу, -е́жешь) *pf.*
slick [slɪk] *adj.* (*dextrous*) ло́вкий (-вок, -вка́, -вко, ло́вки́); (*crafty*) хи́трый (-тёр, -тра́, хитро́); (*sleek*) гла́дкий (-док, -дка́, -дко); *n.* нефтяна́я плёнка.
slide [slaɪd] *v.i.* скользи́ть *impf.*; (*on ice*) кати́ться (качу́сь, ка́тишься) *impf.*, по~ *pf.* по льду; *v.t.* (*drawer etc.*) задвига́ть *impf.*, задви́нуть *pf.* (*into* в+a.); *n.* (*on ice*) ледяна́я гора́ (a. -ру; *pl.* -ры, -ра́м), ледяна́я доро́жка; (*children's* ~) де́тская го́рка; (*chute*) жёлоб (*pl.* -á); (*microscope* ~) предме́тное стекло́ (*pl.* стёкла́, -кол, -клам); (*phot.*) диапозити́в, слайд. **slide-rule** *n.* логарифми́ческая лине́йка. **slide-valve** *n.* золотни́к (á). **sliding** *adj.* скользя́щий; (*door*) задвижно́й; ~ **seat** слайд.
slight[1] [slaɪt] *adj.* (*slender*) то́нкий (-нок, -нка́, -нко, то́нки́); (*inconsiderable*) незначи́тельный; (*light*) лёгкий (-гок, -гка́, -гко, лёгки́); **not the** ~**est** ни мале́йшего, -шей (*g.*); **not in the** ~**est** ничу́ть.
slight[2] [slaɪt] *v.t.* пренебрега́ть *impf.*, пренебре́чь (-егу́, -ежёшь; -ёг, -егла́) *pf.+i.*; *n.* пренебреже́ние, неуваже́ние.

slightly ['slaɪtlɪ] *adv.* слегка́, немно́го.
slim [slɪm] *adj.* то́нкий (-нок, -нка́, -нко, то́нки́); (*chance etc.*) сла́бый (слаб, -á, -о); *v.i.* худе́ть *impf.*, по~ *pf.*
slime [slaɪm] *n.* слизь. **slimy** *adj.* сли́зистый; (*person*) еле́йный.
sling [slɪŋ] *v.t.* (*throw*) броса́ть *impf.*, бро́сить *pf.*; швыря́ть *impf.*, швырну́ть *pf.*; (*suspend*) подве́шивать *impf.*, подве́сить *pf.*; *n.* (*for throwing*) праща́; (*bandage*) пе́ревязь; (*rope*) строп.
slink [slɪŋk] *v.i.* кра́сться (-аду́сь, -адёшься; -а́лся) *impf.* **slinky** *adj.* (*garment*) отлега́ющий.
slip [slɪp] *n.* (*slipping*) скольже́ние; (*mistake*) оши́бка; (*garment*) комбина́ция; (*pillow-case*) на́волочка; (*building* ~) ста́пель (*pl.* -ля́ & -ли); (*landing*) э́ллинг; (*of paper etc.*) поло́ска; (*print.*) гра́нка; (*cutting*) черено́к (-нка́); (*glaze*) полива́я глазу́рь; ~ **of the pen** опи́ска; ~ **of the tongue** обмо́лвка; **give the** ~ ускользну́ть *pf.* от+g.; *v.i.* скользи́ть *impf.*, скользну́ть *pf.*; поскользну́ться *pf.*; (*from hands etc.*) выска́льзывать *impf.*, вы́скользнуть *pf.*; *v.t.* (*let go*) спуска́ть *impf.*, спусти́ть (-ущу́, -у́стишь) *pf.*; (*insert*) сова́ть (сую́, суёшь) *impf.*, су́нуть *pf.*; ~ **off** (*depart, v.i.*) ускольза́ть *impf.*, ускользну́ть *pf.*; (*clothes, v.t.*) сбра́сывать *impf.*, сбро́сить *pf.*; ~ **on** (*clothes*) наки́дывать *impf.*, наки́нуть *pf.*; ~ **up** (*make mistake*) ошиба́ться *impf.*, ошиби́ться (-бу́сь, -бёшься; -бся) *pf.* **slipper** *n.* (дома́шняя) ту́фля (g.pl. -фель) та́почка (*coll.*). **slippery** *adj.* ско́льзкий (-зок, -зка́, -зко); (*fig., shifty*) увёртливый. **slipshod** *adj.* неря́шливый, небре́жный. **slipway** *n.* (*for building*) ста́пель (*pl.* -ля́ & -ли); (*for landing*) э́ллинг.
slit [slɪt] *v.t.* разреза́ть *impf.*, разре́зать (-е́жу, -е́жешь) *pf.*; *n.* щель (*pl.* -ли, -ле́й), разре́з.
slither ['slɪðə(r)] *v.i.* скользи́ть *impf.*
sliver ['slɪvə(r), 'slaɪvə(r)] *n.* ще́пка.
slob [slɒb] *n.* неря́ха *c.g.*
slobber ['slɒbə(r)] *v.i.* пуска́ть *impf.*, пусти́ть (пущу́, пу́стишь) *pf.* слю́ни; *n.* слю́ни (-не́й) *pl.*
sloe [sləʊ] *n.* тёрн.
slog [slɒg] *v.t.* (*hit*) си́льно ударя́ть *impf.*, уда́рить *pf.*; (*work*) упо́рно рабо́тать *impf.*
slogan ['sləʊgən] *n.* ло́зунг.
sloop [sluːp] *n.* шлюп.
slop [slɒp] *n.*: *pl.* (*water*) помо́и (-о́ев) *pl.*; (*food*) жи́дкая пи́ща; *v.t. & i.* выплё́скивать(ся) *impf.*, вы́плескать(ся) (-ещу, -ещет(ся)) *pf.* **slop-basin** *n.* полоска́тельница.
slope [sləʊp] *n.* накло́н, склон; *v.i.* име́ть *impf.* накло́н. **sloping** *adj.* накло́нный (-нен, -нна), пока́тый.
slop-pail ['slɒppeɪl] *n.* помо́йное ведро́ (*pl.* вёдра, -дер, -драм). **sloppy** *adj.* (*ground*) мо́крый (мокр, -á, -о); (*food*) жи́дкий (-док, -дка́, -дко); (*work*) неря́шливый; (*sentimen-*

tal) сентиментáльный.

slot [slɒt] *n.* щель (*pl.* -ли, -лéй), паз (*loc.* -ý; *pl.* -ы́).

sloth [sləʊθ] *n.* лень; (*zool.*) ленивец (-вца). **slothful** *adj.* ленивый.

slot-machine ['slɒtməˌʃiːn] *n.* автомáт.

slouch [slaʊtʃ] *v.i.* (*stoop*) сутýлиться *impf.*

slough [slʌf] *v.t.* сбрáсывать *impf.*, сбрóсить *pf.*

sloven ['slʌv(ə)n] *n.* неряха *c.g.* **slovenly** *adj.* неряшливый.

slow [sləʊ] *adj.* мéдленный (-ен(ен), -енна); (*tardy*) медлительный; (*stupid*) тупóй (туп, -á, -о, тýпы́); (*business*) вялый; **be ~** (*clock*) отставáть (-таёт) *impf.*, отстáть (-áнет) *pf.*; *adv.* мéдленно; *v.t. & i.* (**~ down**, **up**) замедля́ть(ся) *impf.*, замéдлить(ся) *pf.* **slow-coach** *n.* копýн (-á), ~ья.

slow-worm ['sləʊwɜːm] *n.* веретéница, медяни́ца.

sludge [slʌdʒ] *n.* (*mud*) грязь (*loc.* -зи́); (*sediment*) отстóй.

slug [slʌg] *n.* (*zool.*) слизня́к (-á); (*piece of metal*) кусóк (-скá) металла.

sluggard ['slʌgəd] *n.* лентя́й. **sluggish** *adj.* (*inert*) инéртный; (*torpid*) вялый.

sluice [sluːs] *n.* шлюз; *v.t.* заливáть *impf.*, зали́ть (-лью, -льёшь; зáли́л, -á, -о) *pf.*; *v.i.* ли́ться (льётся; ли́лся, лилáсь, ли́лóсь) *impf.*

slum [slʌm] *n.* трущóба.

slumber ['slʌmbə(r)] *n.* сон (сна); *v.i.* спать (сплю, спишь; спал, -á, -о) *impf.*

slump [slʌmp] *n.* рéзкое падéние (цен, спрóса, интерéса); *v.i.* рéзко пáдать *impf.*, (у)пáсть (-адёт; -áл) *pf.*; (*of person*) тяжелó опускáться *impf.*, опусти́ться (-ущýсь, -ýстишься) *pf.*

slur [slɜː(r)] *v.t.* (*speak indistinctly*) невня́тно произноси́ть (-ошý, -óсишь) *impf.*, произнести́ (-есý, -есёшь; -ёс, -еслá) *pf.*; **~ over** обходи́ть (-ожý, -óдишь) *impf.*, обойти́ (обойдý, -дёшь; обошёл, -шлá) *pf.* молчáнием; *n.* (*stigma*) пятнó (*pl.* -тна, -тен, -тнам); (*mus.*) ли́га.

slush [slʌʃ] *n.* сля́коть. **slushy** *adj.* сля́котный; (*fig.*) сентиментáльный.

slut [slʌt] *n.* (*sloven*) неря́ха; (*trollop*) потаскýха. **sluttish** *adj.* неря́шливый; распýщенный.

sly [slaɪ] *adj.* хи́трый (-тёр, -трá, хи́трó); лукáвый; **on the ~** тайкóм.

smack[1] [smæk] *n.* (*flavour*) при́вкус; *v.i.*: **~ of** пáхнуть *impf.*+i.

smack[2] [smæk] *n.* (*slap*) шлепóк (-пкá); *v.t.* шлёпать *impf.*, шлёпнуть *pf.*

smack[3] [smæk] *n.* (*boat*) смэк.

small [smɔːl] *adj.* мáленький, небольшóй, мáлый (мал, -á); (*of agent, particles; petty*) мéлкий (-лок, -лкá, -лко); (*unimportant*) незначи́тельный; **~ capitals** капитéль; **~ change** мéлочь; **~ fry** мéлкая сóшка; **~ talk** свéтская бесéда; *n.*: **~ of the back** поясни́ца;

pl. мéлочь. **small-minded** *adj.* мéлкий (-лок, -лкá, -лко). **small-scale** *adj.* мелкомасштáбный.

smart[1] [smɑːt] *v.i.* сáдни́ть *impf. impers.*

smart[2] [smɑːt] *adj.* (*brisk*) бы́стрый (быстр, -á, -о, бы́стры́); (*cunning*) лóвкий (-вок, -вкá, -вко, лóвки́); (*sharp*) смекáлистый (*coll.*); (*in appearance*) элегáнтный.

smash [smæʃ] *v.t. & i.* разбивáть(ся) *impf.*, разби́ть(ся) (разобью, -ьёт(ся)) *pf.*; *v.i.* (*collide*) стáлкиваться *impf.*, столкнýться *pf.* (**into** c+i.); *n.* (*disaster*) катастрóфа; (*collision*) столкновéние; (*blow*) тяжёлый удáр.

smattering ['smætərɪŋ] *n.* повéрхностное знáние.

smear [smɪə(r)] *v.t.* смáзывать *impf.*, смáзать (-áжу, -áжешь) *pf.*; (*dirty*) пáчкать *impf.*, за~, ис~ *pf.*; (*discredit*) порóчить *impf.*, о~ *pf.*; *n.* (*slander*) клеветá; (*med.*) мазóк (-зкá).

smell [smel] *n.* (*sense*) обоня́ние; (*odour*) зáпах; *v.t.* чýвствовать *impf.* зáпах+g.; нюхать *impf.*, по~ *pf.*; *v.i.*: **~ of** пáхнуть (пáх(нул), пáхла) *impf.*+i.; **~ out** (*also fig.*) разню́хивать *impf.*, разню́хать *pf.*; **~ing salts** нюхательная соль. **smelly** *adj.* воню́чий.

smelt [smelt] *v.t.* (*ore*) плáвить *impf.*; (*metal*) выплавля́ть *impf.*, вы́плавить *pf.*

smile [smaɪl] *v.i.* улыбáться *impf.*, улыбнýться *pf.*; *n.* улы́бка.

smirk [smɜːk] *v.i.* ухмыля́ться *impf.*, ухмыльнýться *pf.*; *n.* ухмы́лка.

smith [smɪθ] *n.* кузнéц (-á).

smithereens [ˌsmɪðə'riːnz] *n.*: **(in)to ~** вдрéбезги.

smithy ['smɪðɪ] *n.* кýзница.

smock [smɒk] *n.* блýза.

smog [smɒg] *n.* тумáн с ды́мом.

smoke [sməʊk] *n.* дым (-a(у), *loc.* -ý); (*cigarette etc.*) кýрево; **~ bomb** дымовáя бóмба; *v.i.* дыми́ть *impf.*, на~ *pf.*; (*of lamp*) копти́ть *impf.*, на~ *pf.*; *v.t. & i.* (*cigarette etc.*) кури́ть (-рю, -ришь) *impf.*, по~ *pf.*; (*cure; colour*) копти́ть *impf.*, за~ *pf.*; **~ out** выкýривать *impf.*, вы́курить *pf.* **smokeless** *adj.* бездымный. **smoker** *n.* кури́льщик, -ица, кýрящий *sb.* **smokescreen** *n.* дымовáя завéса. **smoking** *n.*: **~ compartment** купé *nt.indecl.* для кýрящих. **smoking-room** *n.* кури́тельная *sb.* **smoky** *adj.* дымный; (*room*) прокýренный; (*colour*) дымчатый.

smooth [smuːð] *adj.* (*surface etc.*) глáдкий (-док, -дкá, -дко); (*movement etc.*) плáвный; (*flattering*) льсти́вый; *v.t.* приглáживать *impf.*, приглáдить *pf.*; **~ over** сглáживать *impf.*, сглáдить *pf.*

smother ['smʌðə(r)] *v.t.* (*stifle, also fig.*) души́ть (-шý, -шишь) *impf.*, за~ *pf.*; (*cover*) покрывáть *impf.*, покрыть (-рóю, -рóешь) *pf.*

smoulder ['sməʊldə(r)] *v.i.* тлеть *impf.*

smudge [smʌdʒ] *v.t.* пáчкать *impf.*, за~, ис~ *pf.*

smug [smʌg] *adj.* самодовóльный.

smuggle ['smʌg(ə)l] *v.t.* провозúть (-ожý, -óзишь) *impf.*, провезтú (-езý, -езёшь; -ёз, -езлá) *pf.* контрабáндой; (*convey secretly*) тáйно проносúть (-ошý, -óсишь) *impf.*, пронестú (-есý, -есёшь; -ёс, -еслá) *pf.* **smuggler** *n.* контрабандúст.

smut [smʌt] *n.* частúца сáжи, кóпоти; (*indecency*) непристóйность. **smutty** *adj.* грязный (-зен, -знá, -зно); непристóйный.

snack [snæk] *n.* закýска; ~ **bar** закýсочная *sb.*, буфéт.

snaffle ['snæf(ə)l] *n.* трéнзель (*pl.* -ли & -ля) *m.*; *v.t.* (*steal*) стащúть (-щý, -щишь) *pf.*

snag [snæg] *n.* (*branch*) сучóк (-чкá); (*in river*) корягá; (*fig.*) загвóздка; *v.t.* зацеплять *impf.*, зацепúть (-плю, -пишь) *pf.*

snail [sneɪl] *n.* улúтка; **at a ~'s pace** черепáхой.

snake [sneɪk] *n.* змея (*pl.* -éи). **snake-charmer** *n.* заклинáтель *m.*, ~ница, змей. **snakeskin** *n.* змеúная кóжа. **snaky** *adj.* змеúный; (*winding*) извúлистый.

snap [snæp] *v.i.* (*of dog etc.*) огрызáться *impf.*, огрызнýться *pf.* (**at** на+*a.*); *v.t. & i.* говорúть *impf.* сердúто, раздражённо; (*break*) обрывáть(ся) *impf.*, оборвáть(ся) (-вý, -вёт(ся); -вáл(ся), -валá(сь), -вáло/вáлóсь) *pf.*; *v.t.* (*make sound*) щёлкать *impf.*, щёлкнуть *pf.*+*i.*; ~ **up** (*buy*) расхвáтывать *impf.*, расхватáть *pf.*; *n.* (*sound*) щёлк; **cold** ~ рéзкое внезáпное похолодáние; *adj.* скоропалúтельный; (*parl.*) внеочереднóй. **snapdragon** *n.* львúный зев. **snap-fastener** *n.* кнóпка. **snapshot** *n.* моментáльный снúмок (-мка).

snare [sneə(r)] *n.* ловýшка; *v.t.* ловúть (-влю, -вишь) *impf.*, поймáть *pf.* в ловýшку.

snarl [snɑːl] *v.i.* рычáть (-чý, -чúшь) *impf.*; (*person*) ворчáть (-чý, -чúшь) *impf.*; *n.* рычáние; ворчáние.

snatch [snætʃ] *v.t.* хватáть *impf.*, (с)хватúть (-ачý, -áтишь) *pf.*; (*opportunity etc.*) ухватúться (-ачýсь, -áтишься) *pf.* за+*a.*; *v.i.*: ~ **at** хватáться *impf.*, (с)хватúться (-ачýсь, -áтишься) *pf.* за+*a.*; *n.* попытка схватúть; (*fragment*) обрывок (-вка); **in, by, ~es** урывками.

sneak [sniːk] *v.i.* (*slink*) крáсться (-адýсь, -адёшься; -áлся) *impf.*; (*tell tales*) ябедничать *impf.*, на~ *pf.* (*coll.*); *v.t.* (*steal*) стащúть (-щý, -щишь) *pf.*; *n.* ябедник, -ица (*coll.*). **sneaking** *adj.* (*hidden*) тáйный; (*of feeling etc.*) неосóзнанный. **sneak-thief** *n.* ворúшка *m.*

sneer [snɪə(r)] *v.i.* (*smile*) насмéшливо улыбáться *impf.*; (*speak*) насмéшливо говорúть *impf.*; *n.* насмéшливая улыбка.

sneeze [sniːz] *v.i.* чихáть *impf.*, чихнýть *pf.*; *n.* чихáнье.

snick [snɪk] *n.* зарýбка.

snide [snaɪd] *adj.* (*sneering*) насмéшливый.

sniff [snɪf] *v.i.* шмыгáть *impf.*, шмыгнýть *pf.*

нóсом; *v.t.* нюхать *impf.*, по~ *pf.*

snigger ['snɪgə(r)] *v.i.* хихúкать *impf.*, хихúкнуть *pf.*; *n.* хихúканье.

snip [snɪp] *v.t.* рéзать (рéжу, -жешь) *impf.* (нóжницами); ~ **off** срезáть *impf.*, срéзать (-éжу, -éжешь) *pf.*; *n.* (*purchase*) выгодная покýпка.

snipe [snaɪp] *n.* (*bird*) бекáс; *v.i.* стрелять *impf.* из укрытия (**at** в+*a.*). **sniper** *n.* снáйпер.

snippet ['snɪpɪt] *n.* отрéзок (-зка); *pl.* (*of knowledge etc.*) обрывки *m.pl.*

snivel ['snɪv(ə)l] *v.i.* (*run at nose*) распускáть *impf.*, распустúть (-ущý, -ýстишь) *pf.* сóпли; (*whimper*) хныкать (хнычу, -чешь & хныкаю, -аешь) *impf.*

snob [snɒb] *n.* сноб. **snobbery** *n.* снобúзм. **snobbish** *adj.* снобúстский.

snook [snuːk] *n.*: **cock a ~ at** показáть (-ажý, -áжешь) *pf.* длúнный нос+*d.*

snoop [snuːp] *v.i.* совáть (сую, суёшь) *impf.* нос в чужúе делá; ~ **about** шпиóнить *impf.*

snooty ['snuːtɪ] *adj.* чвáнный (-нен, -нна).

snooze [snuːz] *v.i.* вздремнýть *pf.*; *n.* корóткий сон (сна).

snore [snɔː(r)] *v.i.* храпéть (-плю, -пúшь) *impf.*; *n.* храп.

snorkel ['snɔːk(ə)l] *n.* шнóркель *m.*; (*diver's*) трýбка (акваланга).

snort [snɔːt] *v.i.* фыркать *impf.*, фыркнуть *pf.*; *n.* фырканье.

snot [snɒt] *n.* сóпли (-лéй) *pl.*

snout [snaʊt] *n.* рыло, мóрда.

snow [snəʊ] *n.* снег (-а(у), *loc.* -ý; *pl.* -á); ~ **boot** бот (*g.pl.* -т & -тов); *v.i.*: **it is ~ing** идёт (*past* шёл) снег; ~**ed up, in** занесённый (-ён, -енá) снéгом. **snowball** *n.* снежóк (-жкá). **snow-blindness** *n.* снéжная слепотá. **snowbound** *adj.* заснежённый (-ён, -енá). **snowdrift** *n.* сугрóб. **snowdrop** *n.* подснéжник. **snowflake** *n.* снежúнка. **snowman** *n.* снéжная бáба. **snowplough** *n.* снегоочистúтель *m.* **snowshoes** *n.* снегостýпы (-пов) *pl.* **snowstorm** *n.* метéль, вьюга. **snow-white** *adj.* белоснéжный. **snowy** *adj.* снéжный; (*snow-white*) белоснéжный.

snub[1] [snʌb] *v.t.* относúться (-ошýсь, -óсишься) *impf.*, отнестúсь (-есýсь, -есёшься; -ёсся, -еслáсь) *pf.* пренебрежúтельно к+*d.*; (*humiliate*) унижáть *impf.*, унúзить *pf.*

snub[2] [snʌb] *adj.* вздёрнутый. **snub-nosed** *adj.* курнóсый.

snuff[1] [snʌf] *n.* (*tobacco*) нюхательный табáк (-á(ý)); **take ~** нюхать *impf.*, по~ *pf.* табáк.

snuff[2] [snʌf] *n.* (*on candle*) нагáр на свечé; *v.t.* снимáть *impf.*, снять (сниму, -мешь; снял, -á, -о) *pf.* нагáр с+*g.*; ~ **out** (*candle*) тушúть (-шý, -шишь) *impf.*, по~ *pf.*; (*hopes etc.*) разрушáть *impf.*, разрушить *pf.*

snuffbox ['snʌfbɒks] *n.* табакéрка.

snuffle ['snʌf(ə)l] *v.i.* (*noisily*) сопéть (-плю, -пúшь) *impf.*

snug [snʌg] *adj.* уютный, удóбный.

snuggle ['snʌg(ə)l] *v.i.*: ~ **up to** прижимáться

impf., прижа́ться (-жму́сь, -жмёшься) *pf.*
к+d.

so [səʊ] *adv.* так; (*in this way*) так, таки́м о́бразом; (*thus, at beginning of sentence*) ита́к; (*also*) та́кже, то́же; *conj.* (*therefore*) поэ́тому; **and ~ on** и так да́лее; **if ~** в тако́м слу́чае; **or ~** и́ли о́коло э́того; **~ ... as** так(о́й)... как; **~ as to** с тем что́бы; **~ be it** быть по сему́; **~ far** до сих пор; **(in) ~ far as** насто́лько, поско́льку; **~ long!** пока́!; **~ long as** поско́льку; **~ much** насто́лько; **~ much ~** до тако́й сте́пени; **~ much the better** тем лу́чше; **~ that** что́бы; **~... that** так... что; **~ to say, speak** так сказа́ть; **~ what?** ну и что?

soak [səʊk] *v.t.* & *i.* пропи́тывать(ся) *impf.*, пропита́ть(ся) *pf.* (**in** +*i.*); *v.t.* мочи́ть (-чу́, -чишь) *impf.*, на~ *pf.*; (*drench*) прома́чивать *impf.*, промочи́ть (-чу́, -чишь) *pf.*; **~ up** впи́тывать *impf.*, впита́ть *pf.*; *v.i.*; **~ through** проса́чиваться *impf.*, просочи́ться *pf.*; **get ~ed** промока́ть *impf.*, промо́кнуть (-к) *pf.*; *n.* (*drinker*) пья́ница *c.g.*

so-and-so ['səʊənd,səʊ] *n.* тако́й-то.

soap [səʊp] *n.* мы́ло (*pl.* -ла́); *attr.* мы́льный; *v.t.* мы́лить *impf.*, на~ *pf.*; **~ boiler** мылова́р; **~ bubble** мы́льный пузы́рь (-ря́) *m.*; **~ dish** мы́льница *n.*; **~ flakes** мы́льные хло́пья (-ьев) *pl.*; **~ powder** стира́льный порошо́к (-шка́) *n.*; **~ works** мылова́ренный заво́д. **soapbox** *n.* (*stand*) импровизи́рованная трибу́на. **soapy** *adj.* мы́льный.

soar [sɔː(r)] *v.i.* пари́ть *impf.*; (*aeron.*) плани́ровать *impf.*, с~ *pf.*; (*building etc.*) вы́ситья *impf.*; (*prices*) подска́кивать *impf.*, подскочи́ть *pf.*

sob [sɒb] *v.i.* рыда́ть *impf.*; *n.* рыда́ние.

sober ['səʊbə(r)] *adj.* тре́звый (трезв, -а́, -о); *v.t.* & *i.*: **~ up** (*also fig.*) отрезвля́ться *impf.*, отрезви́ться *pf.*; *v.i.*: **~ up** трезве́ть *impf.*, о~ *pf.* **sobriety** [sə'braɪɪtɪ] *n.* тре́звость.

sobriquet ['səʊbrɪˌkeɪ] *n.* про́звище.

so-called ['sɒkɔːld] *adj.* так называ́емый.

soccer ['sɒkə(r)] *n.* футбо́л.

sociable ['səʊʃəb(ə)l] *adj.* общи́тельный; (*meeting etc.*) дру́жеский. **social** *adj.* обще́ственный, социа́льный; **S~ Democrat** социа́л-демокра́т; **~ sciences** обще́ственные нау́ки *f.pl.*; **~ security** социа́льное обеспе́чение; *n.* вечери́нка. **socialism** *n.* социали́зм. **socialist** *n.* социали́ст; *adj.* социали́сти́ческий. **socialize** *v.t.* социализи́ровать *impf.* & *pf.* **society** [sə'saɪətɪ] *n.* о́бщество; (*beau monde*) свет; *attr.* све́тский. **sociolin'guistics** *n.* социолингви́стика. **socio'logical** *adj.* социологи́ческий. **soci'ologist** *n.* социо́лог. **soci'ology** *n.* социоло́гия.

sock¹ [sɒk] *n.* носо́к (-ска́).

sock² [sɒk] *v.t.* тузи́ть *impf.*, от~ *pf.*

socket ['sɒkɪt] *n.* впа́дина; (*elec.*) штепсель (*pl.* -ля́) *m.*; (*for bulb*) патро́н; (*tech.*) гнездо́ (*pl.* -ёзда), растру́б.

sod [sɒd] *n.* (*turf*) дёрн; (*piece of turf*) дерни́на.

soda ['səʊdə] *n.* со́да; **~ water** со́довая вода́ (*a.* -ду).

sodden ['sɒd(ə)n] *adj.* промо́кший, пропи́танный (-ан) вла́гой.

sodium ['səʊdɪəm] *n.* на́трий.

sodomite ['sɒdəˌmaɪt] *n.* педера́ст. **sodomy** *n.* педера́стия.

sofa ['səʊfə] *n.* дива́н.

soft [sɒft] *adj.* мя́гкий (-гок, -гка́, -гко); (*sound*) ти́хий (тих, -а́, -о); (*colour*) нея́ркий (-рок, -рка́, -рко); (*malleable*) ко́вкий (-вок, -вка́, -вко); (*tender*) не́жный (-жен, -жна́, -жно; не́жны); **~ drink** безалкого́льный напи́ток (-тка); **~ fruit** я́года; **~ goods** тексти́ль *m.*; **~ toy** мягконаби́вна́я игру́шка. **soft-boiled** *adj.*: **~ egg** яйцо́ всмя́тку. **soften** ['sɒf(ə)n] *v.t.* & *i.* смягча́ть(ся) *impf.*, смягчи́ть(ся) *pf.* **soft-headed** *adj.* придурькова́тый. **soft-hearted** *adj.* мягкосерде́чный. **softness** *n.* мя́гкость. **soft-pedal** *v.t.* преуменьша́ть *impf.*, преуме́ньшить *pf.* (значе́ние+g.). **software** *n.* програ́ммное обеспе́чение. **softwood** *n.* хво́йная древеси́на.

soggy ['sɒgɪ] *adj.* пропи́танный (-ан) водо́й; (*ground*) боло́тистый.

soil¹ [sɔɪl] *n.* по́чва; **~ science** почвове́дение.

soil² [sɔɪl] *v.t.* па́чкать *impf.*, за~, ис~ *pf.*

sojourn ['sɒdʒ(ə)n, -dʒɜːn, 'sʌ-] *n.* вре́менное пребыва́ние; *v.i.* вре́менно жить (живу́, -вёшь; жил, -а́, -о) *impf.*

solace ['sɒləs] *n.* утеше́ние; *v.t.* утеша́ть *impf.*, уте́шить *pf.*

solar ['səʊlə(r)] *adj.* со́лнечный.

solarium [sə'leərɪəm] *n.* соля́рий.

solder ['səʊldə(r), 'sɒ-] *n.* припо́й; *v.t.* пая́ть *impf.*; спа́ивать *impf.*, спая́ть *pf.* **soldering-iron** *n.* пая́льник.

soldier ['səʊldʒə(r)] *n.* солда́т (*g.pl.* -т), вое́нный *sb.*; (*toy* **~**) солда́тик; **~ of fortune** кондотье́р. **soldierly** *adj.* во́инский.

sole¹ [səʊl] *n.* (*of foot, shoe*) подо́шва; (*of foot*) ступня́; (*of shoe*) подмётка; *v.t.* ста́вить *impf.*, по~ *pf.* подмётку к+d., на+a.

sole² [səʊl] *n.* (*fish*) морско́й язы́к (-а́).

sole³ [səʊl] *adj.* еди́нственный; (*exclusive*) исключи́тельный.

solecism ['sɒlɪˌsɪz(ə)m] *n.* солеци́зм.

solemn ['sɒləm] *adj.* торже́ственный (-ен, -енна). **solemnity** [sə'lemnɪtɪ] *n.* торже́ственность; (*celebration*) торжество́.

solicit [sə'lɪsɪt] *v.t.* проси́ть (-ошу́, -о́сишь) *impf.*, по~ *pf.*+а.g., о+p.; выпра́шивать *impf.*; (*of prostitute*) пристава́ть (-таю́, -таёшь) *impf.*, приста́ть (-а́ну, -а́нешь) *pf.* к+d. (*v.abs.* к мужчи́нам). **solicitor** *n.* соли́ситор; юрисконсульт. **solicitous** *adj.* забо́тливый. **solicitude** *n.* забо́тливость

solid ['sɒlɪd] *adj.* (*not liquid*) твёрдый (твёрд, -а́, -о); (*not hollow*; *continuous*) сплошно́й; (*of time*) без переры́ва; (*firm*) про́чный

(-чен, -чна́, -чно, про́чны́), пло́тный (-тен, -тна́, -тно, пло́тны́); (*pure*) чи́стый (чист, -а́, -о, чи́сты́); (*of reason etc.*) убеди́тельный; *n.* твёрдое те́ло (*pl.* -ла́); *pl.* твёрдая пи́ща. **solidarity** [ˌsɒlɪˈdærɪtɪ] *n.* солида́рность. **solidify** [səˈlɪdɪˌfaɪ] *v.t. & i.* де́лать(ся) *impf.*, с~ *pf.* твёрдым; *v.i.* затвердева́ть *impf.*, затверде́ть *pf.* **solidity** [səˈlɪdɪtɪ] *n.* твёрдость; про́чность. **solid-state** *adj.*: ~ **physics** фи́зика твёрдого те́ла.

solidus [ˈsɒlɪdəs] *n.* дели́тельная черта́.

soliloquy [səˈlɪləkwɪ] *n.* моноло́г.

solipsism [ˈsɒlɪpˌsɪz(ə)m] *n.* солипси́зм.

solitaire [ˈsɒlɪˌteə(r)] *n.* (*gem*) солите́р.

solitary [ˈsɒlɪtərɪ] *adj.* одино́кий, уединённый (-ён, -ённа); ~ **confinement** одино́чное заключе́ние. **solitude** *n.* одино́чество.

solo [ˈsəʊləʊ] *n.* со́ло *nt.indecl.*; (*aeron.*) самостоя́тельный полёт; *adj.* со́льный; *adv.* со́ло. **soloist** *n.* соли́ст, -ка.

solstice [ˈsɒlstɪs] *n.* солнцестоя́ние.

soluble [ˈsɒljʊb(ə)l] *adj.* раствори́мый. **solution** [səˈluːʃ(ə)n, -ˈljuːʃ(ə)n] *n.* раство́р; (*action*) растворе́ние; (*of puzzle etc.*) реше́ние, разреше́ние. **solve** *v.t.* реша́ть *impf.*, реши́ть *pf.* **solvency** *n.* платёжеспосо́бность. **solvent** *adj.* растворя́ющий; (*financially*) платёжеспосо́бный; *n.* раствори́тель *m.*

sombre [ˈsɒmbə(r)] *adj.* мра́чный (-чен, -чна́, -чно).

sombrero [sɒmˈbreərəʊ] *n.* сомбре́ро *nt.indecl.*

some [sʌm] *adj. & pron.* (*any*) како́й-нибудь; (*a certain*) како́й-то; (*a certain amount or number of*) не́который, *or often expressed by noun in* (*partitive*) *g.*; (*several*) не́сколько+*g.*; (*approximately*) о́коло+*g.*; *often expressed by inversion of noun and numeral*; (~ *people, things*) не́которые *pl.*; ~ **day** когда́-нибудь; ~ **more** ещё; ~ **other day** друго́й раз; ~ **... others** одни́... други́е; **to** ~ **extent** до изве́стной сте́пени. **somebody, someone** *n. & pron.* (*def.*) кто́-то; (*indef.*) кто́-нибудь; (*important pers.*) ва́жная персо́на. **somehow** *adv.* ка́к-то; ка́к-нибудь; (*for some reason*) почему́-то; ~ **or other** так или ина́че.

somersault [ˈsʌməˌsɒlt] *n.* прыжо́к (-жка́) кувырко́м; *v.i.* кувырка́ться *impf.*, кувыр(к)ну́ться *pf.*

something [ˈsʌmθɪŋ] *n. & pron.* (*def.*) что́-то; (*indef.*) что́-нибудь; ~ **like** (*approximately*) приблизи́тельно; (*a thing like*) что́-то вро́де+*g.* **sometime** *adv.* не́когда; *adj.* бы́вший. **sometimes** *adv.* иногда́. **somewhat** *adv.* не́сколько, дово́льно. **somewhere** *adv.* (*position*) (*def.*) где́-то; (*indef.*) где́-нибудь; (*motion*) куда́-то; куда́-нибудь.

somnolent [ˈsɒmnələnt] *adj.* со́нный.

son [sʌn] *n.* сын (*pl.* -овья́, -ове́й).

sonar [ˈsəʊnə(r)] *n.* гидролока́тор.

sonata [səˈnɑːtə] *n.* сона́та.

sonde [sɒnd] *n.* зонд.

song [sɒŋ] *n.* пе́сня (*g.pl.* -сен); (*singing*) пе́ние; ~ **thrush** певчий дрозд (-á). **songbird** *n.* певчая пти́ца.

sonic [ˈsɒnɪk] *adj.* звуково́й, акусти́ческий.

son-in-law [ˈsʌnɪnˌlɔː] *n.* зять (*pl.* -я́, -ёв) *m.*

sonnet [ˈsɒnɪt] *n.* соне́т.

sonny [ˈsʌnɪ] *n.* сыно́к.

sonorous [ˈsɒnərəs, səˈnɔːrəs] *adj.* зву́чный (-чен, -чна́, -чно).

soon [suːn] *adv.* ско́ро, вско́ре; (*early*) ра́но; **as** ~ **as** как то́лько; **as** ~ **as possible** как мо́жно скоре́е; **no** ~**er said than done** ска́зано — сде́лано; ~**er or later** ра́но и́ли по́здно; **the** ~**er the better** чем ра́ньше, тем лу́чше.

soot [sʊt] *n.* са́жа, ко́поть.

soothe [suːð] *v.t.* успока́ивать *impf.*, успоко́ить *pf.*; (*pain*) облегча́ть *impf.*, облегчи́ть *pf.*

soothsayer [ˈsuːθˌseɪə(r)] *n.* предсказа́тель *m.*, ~ница.

sooty [ˈsʊtɪ] *adj.* запа́чканный (-ан) са́жей, закопте́лый.

sophism [ˈsɒfɪz(ə)m] *n.* софи́зм.

sophisticated [səˈfɪstɪˌkeɪtɪd] *adj.* (*person*) искушённый; (*tastes*) изощрённый (-ён, -ённа); (*equipment*) усовершенствованный.

soporific [ˌsɒpəˈrɪfɪk] *adj.* снотво́рный; *n.* снотво́рное *sb.*

soprano [səˈprɑːnəʊ] *n.* сопра́но (*voice*) *nt.* & (*person*) *f.indecl.*, дискант.

sorbet [ˈsɔːbet, -bɪt] *n.* щербе́т.

sorcerer [ˈsɔːsərə(r)] *n.* колду́н (-á). **sorceress** *n.* колду́нья (*g.pl.* -ний). **sorcery** *n.* колдовство́.

sordid [ˈsɔːdɪd] *adj.* (*dirty*) гря́зный (-зен, -зна́, -зно); (*wretched*) убо́гий; (*base*) по́длый (подл, -á, -о).

sore [sɔː(r)] *n.* боля́чка, я́зва; *adj.* больно́й (-лен, -льна́); **my throat is** ~ у меня́ боли́т го́рло.

sorrel[1] [ˈsɒr(ə)l] *n.* (*herb*) щаве́ль (-ля́) *m.*

sorrel[2] [ˈsɒr(ə)l] *adj.* (*of horse*) гнедо́й; *n.* гнеда́я ло́шадь (*pl.* -ди, -де́й, *i.* -дьми́).

sorrow [ˈsɒrəʊ] *n.* печа́ль, го́ре, скорбь. **sorrowful** *adj.* печа́льный, ско́рбный. **sorry** *adj.* жа́лкий (-лок, -лка́, -лко); *pred.*: **be** ~ жале́ть *impf.* (**about** o+*p.*); жаль *impers.*+*d.* (**for** +*g.*); ~! извини́(те)!

sort [sɔːt] *n.* род (*pl.* -ы́), вид, сорт (*pl.* -á); *v.t.* сортирова́ть *impf.*; разбира́ть *impf.*, разобра́ть (разберу́, -рёшь; разобра́л, -á, -о) *pf.* **sorter** *n.* сортиро́вщик, -ица.

sortie [ˈsɔːtɪ] *n.* вы́лазка.

SOS *n.* (ра́дио)сигна́л бе́дствия.

so-so [ˈsəʊsəʊ] *adj.* так себе́.

sot [sɒt] *n.* пья́ница *c.g.*

sotto voce [ˌsɒtəʊ ˈvəʊtʃɪ] *adv.* вполго́лоса.

soubriquet *see* **sobriquet**

soufflé [ˈsuːfleɪ] *n.* суфле́ *nt.indecl.*

soul [səʊl] *n.* душа́ (*a.* -шу; *pl.* -ши); ~ **music** со́ул.

sound[1] [saʊnd] *adj.* (*healthy*) здоро́вый; (*strong; of sleep*) кре́пкий (-пок, -пка́, -пко);

(*firm*) про́чный (-чен, -чна́, -чно, про́чны); *adv.* кре́пко.

sound² [saʊnd] *n.* (*noise*) звук, шум; *attr.* звуково́й; ~ **barrier** звуково́й барье́р; ~ **effects** звуково́е сопровожде́ние; ~ **wave** звукова́я волна́ (*pl.* -ны, -н, волна́м); *v.i.* звуча́ть (-чи́т) *impf.*, про~ *pf.*

sound³ [saʊnd] *v.t.* (*test depth*) измеря́ть *impf.*, изме́рить *pf.* глубину́+*g.*; (*med., fig.*) зонди́ровать *impf.*, по~ *pf.*; *n.* зонд.

sound⁴ [saʊnd] *n.* (*strait*) проли́в.

soundproof ['saʊndpruːf] *adj.* звуконепрони́цаемый. **soundtrack** *n.* звукова́я доро́жка; звуково́е сопровожде́ние.

soup [suːp] *n.* суп (-а(у), *loc.* -е & -ý; *pl.* -ы́); *v.t.*: ~ **up** повыша́ть *impf.*, повы́сить *pf.* мо́щность+*g.* **soup-kitchen** *n.* беспла́тная столо́вая *sb.*

sour ['saʊə(r)] *adj.* ки́слый (-сел, -сла́, -сло); (*of milk etc.*) проки́сший; ~ **cream** смета́на; *v.i.* прокиса́ть *impf.*, проки́снуть (-с) *pf.*; *v.t. & i.* озлобля́ть(ся) *impf.*, озло́бить(ся) *pf.*

source [sɔːs] *n.* исто́чник; (*of river*) исто́ки *m.pl.*

south [saʊθ] *n.* юг; (*naut.*) зюйд; *adj.* ю́жный; (*naut.*) зюйдовый; *adv.* к ю́гу, на юг; ~ **wind** зюйд. **south-east** *n.* ю́го-восто́к; (*naut.*) зюйд-о́ст. **southeaster** *n.* зюйд-о́ст. **south-easterly, -eastern** *adj.* ю́го-восто́чный; (*naut.*) зюйд-о́стовый. **southerly** ['sʌðəlɪ] *adj.* ю́жный; (*naut.*) зюйдо́вый. **southern** ['sʌð(ə)n] *adj.* ю́жный. **southerner** *n.* южа́нин (*pl.* -а́не, -а́н), -а́нка; жи́тель *m.*, ~ница, ю́га. **southernmost** *adj.* са́мый ю́жный. **southpaw** *n.* левша́ *c.g.* **southward(s)** *adv.* к ю́гу, на юг. **south-'west** *n.* ю́го-за́пад; (*naut.*) зюйд-ве́ст. **south'wester** *n.* зюйд-ве́ст. **south-'westerly, -'western** *adj.* ю́го-за́падный; (*naut.*) зюйд-ве́стовый.

souvenir [ˌsuːvə'nɪə(r)] *n.* сувени́р.

sou'wester [saʊ'westə(r)] *n.* (*hat*) зюйдве́стка.

sovereign ['sɒvrɪn] *adj.* сувере́нный; *n.* суваре́н, мона́рх; (*coin*) сове́рен. **sovereignty** *n.* суверените́т.

soviet ['səʊvɪət, 'sɒ-] *n.* сове́т; Supreme S~ Верхо́вный Сове́т; S~ Union Сове́тский Сою́з; *adj.* (S~) сове́тский.

sow¹ [saʊ] *n.* свинья́ (*pl.* -ньи, -не́й, -ньям), свинома́тка.

sow² [səʊ] *v.t.* (*seed*) се́ять (се́ю, се́ешь) *impf.*, по~ *pf.*; (*field*) засе́ивать *impf.*, засе́ять (-е́ю, -е́ешь) *pf.*; ~**ing machine** се́ялка. **sower** *n.* се́ятель *m.*

soy [sɔɪ] *n.* со́евый со́ус, **soya** ['sɔɪə] *n.* со́я; ~ **bean** со́евый боб (-á).

sozzled ['sɒz(ə)ld] *pred.* в до́ску пьян (-á, -о).

spa [spɑː] *n.* во́ды *f.pl.*, куро́рт.

space [speɪs] *n.* простра́нство; (*distance*) протяже́ние; (*interval*) промежу́ток (-тка); (*place*) ме́сто; (*outer* ~) ко́смос; *attr.* косми́ческий; ~ **station** косми́ческая ста́нция;

v.t. расставля́ть *impf.*, расста́вить *pf.* с промежу́тками. **space-bar** *n.* кла́виша для интерва́лов. **spacecraft** *n.* косми́ческий кора́бль (-ля́) *m.* **spaceman** *n.* космона́вт, астрона́вт. **spaceship** *n.* косми́ческий кора́бль (-ля́) *m.* **spacesuit** *n.* скафа́ндр (космона́вта). **spacious** ['speɪʃəs] *adj.* просто́рный, помести́тельный.

spade¹ [speɪd] *n.* (*tool*) лопа́та, за́ступ.

spade² [speɪd] *n.* (*cards*) пи́ка.

spaghetti [spə'getɪ] *n.* спаге́тти *nt.indecl.*

Spain [speɪn] *n.* Испа́ния.

span [spæn] *n.* (*of bridge*) проле́т; (*aeron.*) разма́х; (*as measure*) пядь (*pl.* пя́ди, пя́де́й); *v.t.* (*of bridge*) соединя́ть *impf.*, соедини́ть *pf.* стороны+*g.*, (*river*) берега́+*g.*

spangle ['spæŋg(ə)l] *n.* блёстка.

Spaniard ['spænjəd] *n.* испа́нец (-нца), -нка.

spaniel ['spænj(ə)l] *n.* спание́ль *m.*

Spanish ['spænɪʃ] *adj.* испа́нский.

spank [spæŋk] *v.t.* шлёпать *impf.*, шлёпнуть *pf.*; *n.* шлепо́к (-пка́).

spanner ['spænə(r)] *n.* га́ечный ключ (-á).

spar¹ [spɑː(r)] *n.* (*naut.*) рангоутное де́рево (*pl.* -е́вья, -е́вьев); (*aeron.*) лонжеро́н.

spar² [spɑː(r)] *v.i.* боксировать *impf.*; (*fig.*) препира́ться *impf.*

spare [speə(r)] *adj.* (*in reserve*) запасно́й, запа́сный; (*extra, to* ~) ли́шний; (*of seat, time*) свобо́дный; (*thin*) худоща́вый; ~ **parts** запасны́е ча́сти (-те́й) *f.pl.*; ~ **room** ко́мната для госте́й; *n.*: *pl.* запча́сти (-те́й) *pl.*; *v.t.* (*grudge*) жале́ть *impf.*, по~ *pf.*+*a.*, *g.*; he ~**d no pains** он не жале́л трудо́в; (*do without*) обходи́ться (-ожу́сь, -о́дишься) *impf.*, обойти́сь (обойду́сь, -дёшься) *impf.*; (*time*) уделя́ть *impf.*, удели́ть *pf.*; (*person, feelings, etc.*) щади́ть *impf.*, по~ *pf.*

spare-rib [speə'rɪb] *n.* (*свино́е*) рёбрышко (*pl.* -шки, -шек, -шкам).

spark [spɑːk] *n.* и́скра; *v.i.* искри́ть *impf.*; ~**ing plug** запа́льная свеча́ (*pl.* -чи, -че́й).

sparkle ['spɑːk(ə)l] *v.i.* искри́ться *impf.*; сверка́ть *impf.*

sparrow ['spærəʊ] *n.* воробе́й (-бья́). **sparrowhawk** *n.* перепеля́тник.

sparse [spɑːs] *adj.* ре́дкий (-док, -дка́, -дко); (*population*) разбро́санный (-ан).

spasm ['spæz(ə)m] *n.* спазм, су́дорога. **spasmodic** [spæz'mɒdɪk] *adj.* спазмоди́ческий, су́дорожный.

spastic ['spæstɪk] *adj.* спасти́ческий.

spate [speɪt] *n.* разли́в; (*fig.*) пото́к.

spatial ['speɪʃ(ə)l] *adj.* простра́нственный.

spatter ['spætə(r)] *v.t.* (*liquid*) бры́згать (-зжу, -зжешь) *impf.*+*i.*; (*person etc.*) забры́згивать *impf.*, забры́згать *pf.* (**with** +*i.*); *n.* бры́зги (-г) *pl.*

spatula ['spætjʊlə] *n.* шпа́тель *m.*

spawn [spɔːn] *v.t. & abs.* мета́ть (ме́чет) *impf.* (икру́); *v.t.* (*fig.*) порожда́ть *impf.*, породи́ть *pf.*; *n.* икра́; (*mushroom* ~) грибни́ца; (*offspring*) отро́дье.

speak [spi:k] *v.t. & i.* говори́ть *impf.*, сказа́ть (-ажу́, -а́жешь) *pf.*; *v.i.* (*make speech*) выступа́ть *impf.*, вы́ступить *pf.* (с ре́чью); выска́зываться *impf.*, вы́сказаться (-ажусь, -ажешься) *pf.* (**for** за+*a.*; **against** про́тив+*g.*). **speaker** *n.* ора́тор; (*at conference etc.*) докла́дчик; (**S~**, *parl.*) спи́кер; (*loud-~*) громкоговори́тель *m.* **speaking** *n.*: **not be on ~ terms** не разгова́ривать *impf.* (**with** c+*i.*). **speaking-trumpet** *n.* ру́пор. **speaking-tube** *n.* перегово́рная тру́бка.

spear ['spɪə(r)] *n.* копьё (*pl.* -пья, -пий, -пьям); *v.t.* пронза́ть *impf.*, пронзи́ть *pf.* копьём. **spearhead** *n.* передово́й отря́д.

special ['speʃ(ə)l] *adj.* осо́бый, специа́льный; (*extra*) э́стренный. **specialist** *n.* специали́ст. **speciality** [,speʃɪ'ælɪtɪ] *n.* специа́льность. **speciali'zation** *n.* специализа́ция. **specialize** *v.t. & i.* специализи́ровать(ся) *impf. & pf.* **specially** *adv.* осо́бенно.

species ['spi:ʃɪz, -ʃi:z, 'spi:s-] *n.* вид.

specific [spɪ'sɪfɪk] *adj.* специфи́ческий; (*biol.*) видово́й; (*phys.*) уде́льный. **specification(s)** [,spesɪfɪ'keɪʃ(ə)n] *n.* специфика́ция. '**specify** ['spesɪ,faɪ] *v.t.* (*mention*) специа́льно упомина́ть *impf.*, упомяну́ть (-ну́, -нешь)+*a.*, о+*p.*; (*include in specifications*) специфици́ровать *impf. & pf.*

specimen ['spesɪmən] *n.* образе́ц (-зца́), экземпля́р; **~ page** про́бная страни́ца.

specious ['spi:ʃəs] *adj.* благови́дный, правдоподо́бный.

speck [spek] *n.* кра́пинка, пя́тнышко (*pl.* -шки, -шек, -шкам). **speckled** *adj.* кра́пчатый.

spectacle ['spektək(ə)l] *n.* зре́лище; *pl.* очки́ (-ко́в) *pl.*

spectacular [spek'tækjʊlə(r)] *adj.* эффе́ктный. **spectator** [spek'teɪtə(r)] *n.* зри́тель *m.*, ~ница.

spectral ['spektr(ə)l] *adj.* (*ghostlike*) при́зрачный; (*phys.*) спектра́льный. **spectre** *n.* при́зрак.

spectroscope ['spektrə,skəʊp] *n.* спектроско́п. **spectro'scopic** *adj.* спектроскопи́ческий.

spectrum ['spektrəm] *n.* спектр.

speculate ['spekjʊ,leɪt] *v.i.* (*meditate*) размышля́ть *impf.*, размы́слить *pf.* (**on** о+*p.*); (*in shares etc.*) спекули́ровать *impf.* **specu'lation** *n.* тео́рия, предположе́ние; спекуля́ция. **speculative** *adj.* гипотети́ческий; спекуляти́вный. **speculator** *n.* спекуля́нт, ~ка.

speech [spi:tʃ] *n.* (*faculty*) речь; (*address*) речь (*pl.* -чи, -че́й), выступле́ние (*language*) язы́к (-а́); **~ day** акт; **~ therapy** логопе́дия. **speechify** ['spi:tʃɪ,faɪ] *v.i.* ора́торствовать *impf.* **speechless** *adj.* немо́й (нем, -а́, -о); (*with emotion*) онеме́вший.

speed [spi:d] *n.* ско́рость, быстрота́; (*phot.*) светочувстви́тельность; **at full ~** по́лным хо́дом; **~ limit** дозво́ленная ско́рость; *v.i.* спеши́ть *impf.*, по~ *pf.*; *v.t.*: **~ up** ускоря́ть

impf., уско́рить *pf.* **speedboat** *n.* быстрохо́дный ка́тер (*pl.* -а́). **spee'dometer** *n.* спидо́метр. **speedway** *n.* доро́жка для мотоцикле́тных го́нок. **speedy** *adj.* бы́стрый (быстр, -а́, -о, бы́стры́), ско́рый (скор, -а́, -о).

speleologist [,spi:lɪ'ɒlədʒɪst, ,spe-] *n.* спелео́лог. **speleology** *n.* спелеоло́гия.

spell[1] [spel] *n.* (*incantation*) заклина́ние.

spell[2] [spel] *v.t.* (*write*) писа́ть (пишу́, -шешь) *impf.*, на~ *pf.* по бу́квам; (*say*) произноси́ть (-ошу́, -о́сишь) *impf.*, произнести́ (-есу́, -есёшь; -ёс, -есла́) *pf.* по бу́квам; **how do you ~ that word?** как пи́шется э́то сло́во?

spell[3] [spel] *n.* (*period*) промежу́ток (-тка) вре́мени.

spellbound ['spelbaʊnd] *adj.* зачаро́ванный (-ан, -ан(н)а).

spelling ['spelɪŋ] *n.* правописа́ние.

spend [spend] *v.t.* (*money; effort*) тра́тить *impf.*, ис~, по~ *pf.*; (*time*) проводи́ть (-ожу́, -о́дишь) *impf.*, провести́ (-еду́, -едёшь; -ёл, -ела́) *pf.* **spendthrift** *n.* расточи́тель *m.*, ~ница; мот, ~о́вка.

sperm[1] [spɜ:m] *n.* спе́рма.

sperm[2] **(whale)** [spɜ:m] *n.* кашало́т.

spermaceti [,spɜ:mə'setɪ] *n.* спермаце́т. **spermatic** [spɜ:'mætɪk] *adj.* семенно́й.

spermatozoon [,spɜ:mətəʊ'zəʊən] *n.* спермато́зо́ид.

sphere [sfɪə(r)] *n.* (*var. senses*) сфе́ра; (*ball*) шар (-а́ *with* 2,3,4; *pl.* -ы́). **spherical** ['sferɪk(ə)l] *adj.* сфери́ческий, шарообра́зный. **spheroid** *n.* сферо́ид.

sphincter ['sfɪŋktə(r)] *n.* сфи́нктер.

sphinx [sfɪŋks] *n.* сфинкс.

spice [spaɪs] *n.* спе́ция, пря́ность; *v.t.* приправля́ть *impf.*, припра́вить *pf.* спе́циями.

spick [spɪk] *adj.*: **~ and span** чи́стый (чист, -а́, -о, чи́сты́), опря́тный; (*of person*) оде́тый с иго́лочки.

spicy ['spaɪsɪ] *adj.* пря́ный; (*fig.*) пика́нтный.

spider ['spaɪdə(r)] *n.* пау́к (-а́). **spidery** *adj.* то́нкий (-нок, -нка́, -нко, то́нки́).

spike[1] [spaɪk] *n.* (*bot.*) ко́лос (*pl.* коло́сья, -ьев).

spike[2] [spaɪk] *n.* (*point*) остриё; (*nail*) гвоздь (-дя́ *pl.* -ди, -де́й) *m.*; (*on shoes*) шип (-а́); (*for papers*) на́колка; *v.t.* снабжа́ть *impf.*, снабди́ть *pf.* шипа́ми; (*gun*) заклёпывать *impf.*, заклепа́ть *pf.*; (*drink*) добавля́ть *impf.*, доба́вить *pf.* спиртно́е в+*a.*

spill [spɪl] *v.t. & i.* пролива́ть(ся) *impf.*, проли́ть(ся) (-лью́, -льёт(ся); про́ли́л/проли́лся, -а́(сь), -о/проли́ло́сь) *pf.*; рассыпа́ть(ся) *impf.*, рассы́пать(ся) (-плю, -плет(ся)) *pf.*; *n.* проли́тие, рассы́пка; (*fall*) паде́ние.

spin [spɪn] *v.t.* (*thread etc.*) прясть (пряду́, -дёшь; -ял, -я́ла́, -яло) *impf.*, с~ *pf.*; (*top*) запуска́ть *impf.*, запусти́ть (-ущу́, -у́стишь) *pf.*; (*coin*) подбра́сывать *impf.*, подбро́сить *pf.*; *v.t. & i.* (*turn*) крути́ть(ся) (-учу́(сь), -у́тишь(ся)) *impf.*; кружи́ть(ся) (-ужу́(сь),

-у́жи́шь(ся)) *impf.*; ~ **out** (*prolong*) затя́гивать *impf.*, затяну́ть (-ну́, -нешь) *pf.*; *n.* круже́ние; (*aeron.*) што́пор; (*excursion*) пое́здка; **go for a** ~ прока́тываться *impf.*, прокати́ться (-ачу́сь, -а́тишься) *pf.*

spinach ['spɪnɪdʒ, -ɪtʃ] *n.* шпина́т.

spinal ['spaɪn(ə)l] *adj.* спинно́й; ~ **column** спинно́й хребе́т (-бта́); ~ **cord** спинно́й мозг.

spindle ['spɪnd(ə)l] *n.* веретено́ (*pl.* -ёна); (*axis, pin*) ось (*pl.* о́си, осе́й) *m.*, шпи́ндель *m.* **spindly** *adj.* дли́нный (-нен, -нна́, дли́нно́) и то́нкий (-нок, -нка́, -нко, то́нки́).

spine [spaɪn] *n.* (*backbone*) позвоно́чник, хребе́т (-бта́); (*bot.*) шип (-а́) (*zool.*) игла́ (*pl.* -лы); (*of book*) корешо́к (-шка́). **spineless** *adj.* (*fig.*) мягкоте́лый, бесхара́ктерный.

spinet [spɪ'net, 'spɪnɪt] *n.* спине́т.

spinnaker ['spɪnəkə(r)] *n.* спи́накер.

spinner ['spɪnə(r)] *n.* пряди́льщик, -ица; (*fishing*) блесна́.

spinney ['spɪnɪ] *n.* ро́щица.

spinning ['spɪnɪŋ] *n.* пряде́ние. **spinning-machine** *n.* пряди́льная маши́на. **spinning-top** *n.* волчо́к (-чка́). **spinning-wheel** *n.* пря́лка.

spinster ['spɪnstə(r)] *n.* незаму́жняя же́нщина.

spiny ['spaɪnɪ] *adj.* колю́чий.

spiral ['spaɪər(ə)l] *adj.* спира́льный, винтово́й; *n.* спира́ль.

spire ['spaɪə(r)] *n.* шпиль *m.*

spirit ['spɪrɪt] *n.* дух, душа́; *pl.* (*mood*) настрое́ние; (*liquid*) спирт (*loc.* -е & -у́; *pl.* -ы́); *pl.* (*drinks*) спиртно́е *sb.*; *v.t.*: ~ **away** та́йно уноси́ть (-ошу́, -о́сишь) *impf.*, унести́ (унесу́, -сёшь; унёс, -ла́) *pf.* **spirited** *adj.* энерги́чный, пы́лкий (-лок, -лка́, -лко). **spirit-lamp** *n.* спирто́вка. **spiritless** *adj.* безжи́зненный (-ен, -енна). **spirit-level** *n.* ватерпа́с. **spiritual** *adj.* духо́вный. **spiritualism** *n.* спирити́зм. **spiritualist** *n.* спири́т. **spirituous** *adj.* спиртно́й.

spit[1] [spɪt] *n.* (*skewer*) ве́ртел (*pl.* -а́); (*of land*) стре́лка, коса́ (*a.* ко́су́; *pl.* -сы) *v.t.* наса́живать *impf.*, насади́ть (-ажу́, -а́дишь) *pf.* на ве́ртел; (*fig.*) пронза́ть *impf.*, пронзи́ть *pf.*

spit[2] [spɪt] *v.i.* плева́ть (плюю́, -юёшь) *impf.*, плю́нуть *pf.*; (*of rain*) мороси́ть *impf.*; (*of fire etc.*) шипе́ть (-пи́т) *impf.*; *v.t.*: ~ **out** выплёвывать *impf.*, вы́плюнуть *pf.*; ~**ing image** то́чная ко́пия; *n.* слюна́, плево́к (-вка́).

spite [spaɪt] *n.* зло́ба, злость; **in** ~ **of** несмотря́ на+*a.* **spiteful** *adj.* зло́бный.

spittle ['spɪt(ə)l] *n.* слюна́, плево́к (-вка́).

spittoon [spɪ'tu:n] *n.* плева́тельница.

spitz [spɪts] *n.* шпиц.

splash [splæʃ] *v.t.* (*person*) забры́згивать *impf.*, забры́згать *pf.* (**with** +*i.*); (~ *liquid*) бры́згать (-зжу, -зжешь) *impf.*+*i.*; *v.i.* плеска́ть(ся) (-ещу́(сь), -е́щешь(ся)) *impf.*

-у́жи́шь(ся)) *impf.*; ~ **out** (*prolong*)

плесну́ть *pf.*; (*move*) шлёпать *impf.*, шлёпнуть *pf.* (**through** по+*d.*); ~ **money about** сори́ть *impf.* деньга́ми; *n.* бры́зги (-г) *pl.*, плеск. **splashdown** *n.* приводне́ние.

splatter ['splætə(r)] *v.i.* плеска́ться (-е́щется) *impf.*

spleen [spli:n] *n.* селезёнка; (*spite*) зло́ба.

splendid ['splendɪd] *adj.* великоле́пный. **splendour** ['splendə(r)] *n.* блеск, великоле́пие.

splenetic [splɪ'netɪk] *adj.* жёлчный.

splice [splaɪs] *v.t.* (*ropes*) сра́щивать *impf.*, срасти́ть *pf.* концы́+g.; (*film, tape*) скле́ивать *impf.*, скле́ить *pf.* концы́+g.; *n.* (*naut.*) спле́сень (-сня) *m.*; (*film, tape*) скле́йка, ме́сто скле́йки.

splint [splɪnt] *n.* лубо́к (-бка́), ши́на; *v.t.* накла́дывать *impf.*, наложи́ть (-жу́, -жишь) *pf.* ши́ну на+*a.*; кла́сть (-аду́, -адёшь; -ал) *impf.*, положи́ть (-жу́, -жишь) *pf.* в лубо́к.

splinter ['splɪntə(r)] *n.* оско́лок (-лка), ще́пка; (*in skin*) зано́за; ~ **group** отколо́вшаяся гру́ппа; *v.t.* & *i.* расщепля́ть(ся) *impf.*, расщепи́ть(ся) *pf.*

split [splɪt] *n.* расще́лина, расще́п; (*schism*) раско́л; *pl.* шпага́т; *v.t.* & *i.* расщепля́ть(ся) *impf.*, расщепи́ть(ся) *pf.*; раска́лывать(ся) *impf.*, расколо́ть(ся) (-лю́, -лет(ся)) *pf.*; (*divide*) дели́ть(ся) (-лю́, -лит(ся)) *impf.*, раз- *pf.* (на ча́сти); *v.i.*: ~ **on** доноси́ть (-ошу́, -о́сишь) *impf.*, донести́ (-есу́, -есёшь; -ёс, -есла́) *pf.* на+*a.*; ~ **hairs** спо́рить *impf.* о мелоча́х; ~ **one's sides** надрыва́ться *impf.* от хо́хота; ~ **pea(s)** лущёный горо́х (-а(у)); ~ **personality** раздвое́ние ли́чности; ~ **pin** шплинт (шпли́нта́); ~ **second** мгнове́ние о́ка. **split-level** *adj.* на ра́зных у́ровнях.

splotch [splɒtʃ] *n.* неро́вное пятно́ (*pl.* -тна, -тен, -тнам), мазо́к (-зка́).

splutter ['splʌtə(r)] *v.i.* бры́згать (-зжу, -зжешь) *impf.* слюно́й; *v.t.* (*utter*) говори́ть *impf.* невня́тно.

spoil [spɔɪl] *n.* (*pl. or collect.*) добы́ча; (*of war*) трофе́и *m.pl.*; *v.t.* & *i.* (*damage; decay*) по́ртить(ся) *impf.*, ис- *pf.*; *v.t.* (*indulge*) балова́ть *impf.*, из- *pf.*; **be** ~**ing for a fight** рва́ться (рвусь, рвёшься; рва́лся, -ала́сь, -а́лось) *impf.* в дра́ку.

spoke [spəʊk] *n.* спи́ца.

spoken ['spəʊkən] *adj.* (*language*) у́стный.

spokesman, -woman *n.* представи́тель *m.*, ~ница.

sponge [spʌndʒ] *n.* гу́бка; ~ **cake** бискви́т; ~ **rubber** гу́бчатая рези́на; *v.t.* (*wash*) мыть (мо́ю, мо́ешь) *impf.*, вы́-, по- *pf.* гу́бкой; (*obtain*) выпра́шивать *impf.*, вы́просить *pf.*; *v.i.*: ~ **on** жить (живу́, -вёшь; жил, -а́, -о) *impf.* на счёт+g. **sponger** *n.* прижива́льщик, парази́т. **spongy** *adj.* гу́бчатый.

sponsor ['spɒnsə(r)] *n.* поручи́тель *m.*, ~ница; *v.t.* руча́ться *impf.*, поручи́ться (-чу́сь, -чишься) *pf.* за+*a.*; (*finance*) финансировать *impf.* & *pf.*

spontaneity [͵spɒntə'niːɪtɪ, -'neɪtɪ] *n.* непосредственность, самопроизвольность. **spontaneous** [spɒn'teɪnɪəs] *adj.* непосредственный (-ен, -енна), самопроизвольный.

spoof [spuːf] *n.* (*hoax*) мистификация; (*parody*) пародия.

spook [spuːk] *n.* привидение.

spool [spuːl] *n.* шпулька, катушка.

spoon [spuːn] *n.* ложка; *v.t.* черпать *impf.*, черпнуть *pf.* ложкой. **spoon-bait** *n.* блесна. **spoonbill** *n.* колпица. **spoonful** *n.* полная ложка.

sporadic [spə'rædɪk] *adj.* спорадический.

spore [spɔː(r)] *n.* спора.

sport [spɔːt] *n.* спорт; *pl.* спортивные соревнования *nt.pl.*; (*fun*) забава, потеха; (*person*) славный малый *sb.*; ~s **car** спортивный автомобиль *m.*; ~s **coat** спортивная куртка; *v.t.* щеголять *impf.*, щегольнуть *pf.*+*i.* **sportsman** *n.* спортсмен. **sportsmanlike** *adj.* спортсменский.

spot [spɒt] *n.* (*place*) место (*pl.* -та); (*mark*) пятно (*pl.* -тна, -тен, -тнам) (*also fig.*), крапинка; (*pimple*) прыщик; (*on dice etc.*) очко (*pl.* -ки, -ков); **on the** ~ на месте; (*without delay*) немедленно; ~ **check** выборочная проверка; *v.t.* (*mark*; *fig.*) пятнать *impf.*, за~ *pf.*; (*recognize*) узнавать (-аю, -аёшь) *impf.*, узнать *pf.*; (*notice*) замечать *impf.*, заметить *pf.*; *v.i.*: **it's** ~**ing with rain** накрапывает дождь. **spotless** *adj.* чистый (чист, -а, -о, чисты); (*fig.*) безупречный. **spotlight** *n.* прожектор (*pl.* -ы & -а); *v.t.* освещать *impf.*, осветить (-ещу, -етишь) *pf.* прожектором. **spotty** *adj.* прыщеватый.

spouse [spaʊz, spaʊs] *n.* супруг, -а.

spout [spaʊt] *v.i.* бить (бьёт) *impf.* струёй; хлынуть *pf.*; *v.t.* выпускать *impf.*, выпустить *pf.* струю+*g.*; (*verses etc.*) декламировать *impf.*, про~ *pf.*; *n.* (*tube*) носик; (*jet*) струя (*pl.* -уи).

sprain [spreɪn] *v.t.* растягивать *impf.*, растянуть (-ну, -нешь) *pf.*; *n.* растяжение.

sprat [spræt] *n.* килька, шпрота.

sprawl [sprɔːl] *v.i.* (*of person*) разваливаться *impf.*, развалиться (-люсь, -лишься) *pf.*; (*of town*) раскидываться *impf.*, раскинуться *pf.*

spray[1] [spreɪ] *n.* (*of flowers etc.*) вет(оч)ка.

spray[2] [spreɪ] *n.* (*liquid*) брызги (-г) *pl.*; (*water*) водяная пыль; (*atomizer*) распылитель *m.*; *v.t.* опрыскивать *impf.*, опрыскать *pf.* (**with** +*i.*); (*cause to scatter*) распылять *impf.*, распылить *pf.* **spray-gun** *n.* краскопульт.

spread [spred] *v.t.* & *i.* (~ **out**) расстилать(ся) *impf.*, разостлать(ся) (расстелю, -лет(ся)) *pf.*; (*unfurl*, *unroll*) развёртывать(ся) *impf.*, развернуть(ся) *pf.*; (*rumour*, *disease*, *etc.*) распространять(ся) *impf.*, распространить(ся) *pf.*; *v.i.* (*extend*) простираться *impf.*, простереться (-трётся, -тёрся) *pf.*; *v.t.* (*bread etc.* +*a.*; *butter etc.*

+*i.*) намазывать, мазать (мажу, -жешь) *impf.*, на~ *pf.*; *n.* распространение; (*span*) размах; (*feast*) пир; (*paste*) паста; (*double page*) разворот.

spree [spriː] *n.* (*drinking*) кутёж (-а); **go on the** ~ кутить (кучу, кутишь) *impf.*, кутнуть *pf.*

sprig [sprɪg] *n.* веточка.

sprightly ['spraɪtlɪ] *adj.* бодрый (бодр, -а, -о, бодры).

spring [sprɪŋ] *v.i.* (*jump*) прыгать *impf.*, прыгнуть *pf.*; *v.t.* (*disclose unexpectedly*) неожиданно сообщать *impf.*, сообщить *pf.* (**on** +*d.*); ~ **a leak** давать (даёт) *impf.*, дать (даст, дадут; дал, -а, дало, -и) *pf.* течь; ~ **a surprise on** делать *impf.*, с~ *pf.* сюрприз+*d.*; ~ **from** (*originate*) происходить (-ожу, -одишь) *impf.*, произойти (-ойду, -ойдёшь; -ошёл, -ошла) *pf.* из+*g.*; ~ **up** (*jump up*) вскакивать *impf.*, вскочить (-чу, -чишь) *pf.*; (*arise*) возникать *impf.*, возникнуть (-к) *pf.*; *n.* (*jump*) прыжок (-жка); (*season*) весна (*pl.* вёсны, -сен, -снам); *attr.* весенний; (*source*) источник, ключ (-а), родник (-а); (*elasticity*) упругость; (*coil*) пружина; (*on vehicle*) рессора; (*fig.*, *motive*) мотив; ~ **balance** пружинные весы (-сов) *pl.*; ~ **mattress** пружинный матрас; ~ **tide** сизигийный прилив; ~ **water** ключевая вода (*a.* -ду). **springboard** *n.* трамплин. **springbok** *n.* прыгун (-а). **spring-clean** *n.* генеральная уборка; *v.t.* производить (-ожу, -одишь) *impf.*, произвести (-еду, -едешь; -ёл, -ела) *pf.* генеральную уборку+*g.* **springy** *adj.* упругий.

sprinkle ['sprɪŋk(ə)l] *v.t.* (*with liquid*) опрыскивать *impf.*, опрыскать *pf.* (**with** +*i.*); (*with solid*) посыпать *impf.*, посыпать (-плю, -плешь) *pf.* (**with** +*i.*). **sprinkler** *n.* (*for watering*) опрыскиватель *m.*; (*fire-extinguisher*) спринклер.

sprint [sprɪnt] *v.i.* бежать (бегу, бежишь) *impf.* на короткую дистанцию; *n.* спринт. **sprinter** *n.* спринтер.

sprocket ['sprɒkɪt] *n.* зубец (-бца). **sprocket-wheel** *n.* звёздочка, цепное колесо (*pl.* -ёса).

sprout [spraʊt] *v.i.* пускать *impf.*, пустить (-ит) *pf.* ростки; *n.* росток (-тка), побег; *pl.* брюссельская капуста.

spruce[1] [spruːs] *adj.* нарядный, элегантный; *v.t.*: ~ **o.s. up** принаряжаться *impf.*, принарядиться (-яжусь, -ядишься) *pf.*

spruce[2] [spruːs] *n.* ель.

spry [spraɪ] *adj.* живой (жив, -а, -о), бодрый (бодр, -а, -о, бодры).

spud [spʌd] *n.* (*tool*) мотыга; (*potato*) картошка (*also collect.*).

spume [spjuːm] *n.* пена.

spur [spɜː(r)] *n.* (*rider's*) шпора; (*fig.*) стимул; (*of mountain*) отрог; **on the** ~ **of the moment** экспромтом; *v.t.*: ~ **on** толкать *impf.*, толкнуть *pf.* (**to** на+*a.*).

spurious ['spjʊərɪəs] *adj.* подде́льный, подло́жный.

spurn [spɜːn] *v.t.* отверга́ть *impf.*, отве́ргнуть (-г(нул), -гла) *pf.*

spurt [spɜːt] *n. (jet)* струя́ *(pl. -у́и); (effort)* рыво́к (-вка́); *v.i.* бить (бьёт) *impf.* струёй; де́лать *impf.*, с~ *pf.* рыво́к.

sputter ['spʌtə(r)] *v.i. (utter)* невня́тно говори́ть *impf.*, *v.i.* шипе́ть (-пи́т) *impf.*

sputum ['spjuːtəm] *n.* слюна́.

spy [spaɪ] *n.* шпио́н; *v.i.* шпио́нить *impf.* (**on** за+*i.*). **spyglass** *n.* подзо́рная труба́ *(pl. -бы).* **spyhole** *n.* глазо́к (-зка́).

Sq. *abbr. (of square)* пл., пло́щадь.

squabble ['skwɒb(ə)l] *n.* перебра́нка; *v.i.* вздо́рить *impf.*, по~ *pf.*

squad [skwɒd] *n.* кома́нда, гру́ппа.

squadron ['skwɒdrən] *n. (mil.)* эскадро́н; *(naut.)* эска́дра; *(aeron.)* эскадри́лья; **S~ Leader** майо́р авиа́ции.

squalid ['skwɒlɪd] *adj.* гря́зный (-зен, -зна́, -зно), убо́гий.

squall [skwɔːl] *n.* шквал; *v.i.* визжа́ть (-жу́, -жи́шь) *impf.* **squally** *adj.* шквали́стый.

squalor ['skwɒlə(r)] *n.* грязь *(loc. -зи́),* убо́гость.

squander ['skwɒndə(r)] *v.t.* растра́чивать *impf.*, растра́тить *pf.; (fortune)* прома́тывать *impf.*, промота́ть *pf.*

square [skweə(r)] *n. (math.)* квадра́т; *(in town)* пло́щадь *(pl. -ди, -де́й),* сквер; *(on paper, material)* кле́тка; *(chess)* по́ле; *(mil.)* каре́ *nt.indecl.; (instrument)* науго́льник; **set** ~ угло́льник; *adj.* квадра́тный; *(meal)* пло́тный (-тен, -тна́, -тно, пло́тны); ~ **root** квадра́тный ко́рень (-рня) *m.;* ~ **sail** прямо́й па́рус *(pl. -а́);* *v.t.* де́лать *impf.*, с~ *pf.* квадра́тным; *(math.)* возводи́ть (-ожу́, -о́дишь) *impf.*, возвести́ (-еду́, -едёшь, -ёл, -ела́) *pf.* в квадра́т; *(bribe)* подкупа́ть *impf.*, подкупи́ть (-плю́, -пишь) *pf.;* ~ **accounts with** распла́чиваться *impf.*, расплати́ться (-ачу́сь, -а́тишься) *pf.* с+*i.*

squash [skwɒʃ] *n. (crowd)* толку́чка; *(drink)* (фрукто́вый) сок (-а(у), *loc.* -е & -у́); *v.t.* разда́вливать *impf.*, раздави́ть (-влю́, -вишь) *pf.; (silence)* заставля́ть *impf.*, заста́вить *pf.* замолча́ть; *(suppress)* подавля́ть *impf.*, пода́вить (-влю́, -вишь) *pf.; v.i.* вти́скиваться *impf.*, вти́снуться *pf.*

squat [skwɒt] *adj.* корена́стый, призе́мистый; *v.i.* сиде́ть (сижу́, сиди́шь) *impf.* на ко́рточках; ~ **down** сади́ться *impf.*, сесть (ся́ду, -дешь; сел) *pf.* на ко́рточки.

squatter ['skwɒtə(r)] *n.* лицо́, самово́льно поселя́ющееся в чужо́м до́ме.

squaw [skwɔː] *n.* индиа́нка (в Се́верной Аме́рике).

squawk [skwɔːk] *n.* пронзи́тельный крик; *(of bird)* клёкот; *v.i.* пронзи́тельно крича́ть (-чу́, -чи́шь) *impf.*, кри́кнуть *pf.; (of bird)* клекота́ть (-о́чет) *impf.*

squeak [skwiːk] *n.* писк, скрип; *v.i.* пища́ть

(-щу́, -щи́шь) *impf.*, пи́скнуть *pf.*; скрипе́ть (-плю́, -пи́шь) *impf.*, скри́пнуть *pf.* **squeaky** *adj.* пискли́вый, скрипу́чий.

squeal [skwiːl] *n.* визг; *v.i.* визжа́ть (-жу́, -жи́шь) *impf.*, ви́згнуть *pf.*

squeamish ['skwiːmɪʃ] *adj.* брезгли́вый, привере́дливый.

squeeze [skwiːz] *n. (crush)* да́вка; *(pressure)* сжа́тие; *(hand)* пожа́тие; *v.t.* дави́ть (давлю́, да́вишь) *impf.*; сжима́ть *impf.*, сжать (сожму́, -мёшь) *pf.;* пожима́ть *impf.*, пожа́ть (пожму́, -мёшь) *pf.;* ~ **in** впи́хивать(ся) *impf.*, впихну́ть(ся) *pf.;* вти́скивать(ся) *impf.*, вти́снуть(ся) *pf.;* ~ **out** выжима́ть *impf.*, вы́жать (вы́жму, -мешь) *pf.;* ~ **through** проти́скивать(ся) *impf.*, проти́снуть(ся) *pf.*

squelch [skweltʃ] *n.* хлю́панье; *v.i.* хлю́пать *impf.*, хлю́пнуть *pf.*

squib [skwɪb] *n. (firework)* пета́рда.

squid [skwɪd] *n.* кальма́р.

squiggle ['skwɪg(ə)l] *n. (flourish)* загогу́лина; *(scribble)* кара́кули *f.pl.*

squint [skwɪnt] *n.* косогла́зие; *adj.* косо́й (кос, -а́, -о), косогла́зый; *v.i.* коси́ть *impf.;* смотре́ть (-рю́, -ришь) *impf.*, по- *pf.* и́скоса.

squire ['skwaɪə(r)] *n.* сква́йр, поме́щик.

squirm [skwɜːm] *v.i. (wriggle)* извива́ться *impf.*, изви́ться (изовью́сь, -вьёшься; изви́лся, извила́сь) *pf.; (fidget)* ёрзать *impf.*

squirrel ['skwɪr(ə)l] *n.* бе́лка.

squirt [skwɜːt] *n.* струя́ *(pl. -у́и); v.i.* бить (бьёт) *impf.* струёй; *v.t.* пуска́ть *impf.*, пусти́ть (пущу́, пу́стишь) *pf.* струю́ *(substance* +*g.;* **at** на+*a.*).

St. *abbr. (of street)* ул., у́лица; *(of saint)* св., Свято́й, -а́я.

stab [stæb] *n.* уда́р (ножо́м *etc.*); *(pain)* внеза́пная о́страя боль; *v.i.* носи́ть (-ошу́, -о́сишь) *impf.*, нанести́ (-есу́, -есёшь; -ёс, -есла́) *pf.* уда́р (ножо́м *etc.*) (**at** +*d.*); *v.t.* коло́ть (-лю́, -лешь) *impf.*, кольну́ть *pf.*

stability [stə'bɪlɪtɪ] *n.* усто́йчивость, про́чность, стаби́льность, постоя́нство. **stabilization** [ˌsteɪbɪˌlaɪ'zeɪʃ(ə)n] *n.* стабилиза́ция. **stabilize** ['steɪbɪˌlaɪz] *v.t.* стабилизи́ровать *impf. & pf.* **stabilizer** *n.* стабилиза́тор.

stable ['steɪb(ə)l] *adj. (steady; of prices, family life etc.)* усто́йчивый; *(lasting, durable)* про́чный (-чен, -чна́, -чно, про́чны); *(un-wavering)* стаби́льный; *(psych.)* уравнове́шенный (-ен, -енна); *n.* коню́шня; *v.t.* ста́вить *impf.*, по~ *pf.* в коню́шню.

staccato [stə'kɑːtəʊ] *n. (mus.)* стакка́то *nt.indecl.; adv. (mus.)* стакка́то.

stack [stæk] *n. (hay)* скирд(а́) (-а́ & -ы́; *pl.* скирды́, -д(о́в), -да́м), стог *(loc.* -е & -у́; *pl.* -а́); *(heap)* ку́ча, ки́па; *(building materials etc.)* штабель (*pl.* -ля́) *m.; (chimney)* (дымова́я) труба́ *(pl.* -бы); *(~-room)* (книго)храни́лище; *pl.* ма́сса, мно́жество; *v.t.* скла́дывать *impf.*, сложи́ть (-жу́, -жишь) *pf.* в ку́чу; укла́дывать *impf.*, уложи́ть (-жу́,

-жишь) *pf.* штабеля́ми.

stadium ['steɪdɪəm] *n.* стадио́н.

staff [staːf] *n.* (*personnel*) штат, шта́ты (-тов) *pl.*, персона́л, ка́дры (-ров) *pl.*; (*mil.*) штаб (*pl.* -бы́) (*stick*) посо́х, жезл (-а́); (*mus.*) но́тные лине́йки *f.pl.*; *adj.* шта́тный; (*mil.*) штабно́й.

stag [stæg] *n.* саме́ц-оле́нь (самца́-оле́ня) *m.*; ~ **beetle** рога́ч (-а́).

stage [steɪdʒ] *n.* (*theatr.*) сце́на, подмо́стки (-ков) *pl.*, эстра́да; (*platform*) платфо́рма; (*period*) ста́дия, фа́за, эта́п; *v.t.* (*theatr.*) ста́вить *impf.*, по~ *pf.*; (*dramatize, feign*) инсцени́ровать *impf.* & *pf.*; (*organize*) организова́ть *impf.* & *pf.*; ~ **whisper** театра́льный шёпот. **stage-manager** *n.* режиссёр.

stagger ['stægə(r)] *n.* пош́атывание, шата́ние; *v.i.* шата́ться *impf.*, шатну́ться *pf.*; кача́ться *impf.*, качну́ться *pf.*; *v.t.* (*surprise*) поража́ть *impf.*, порази́ть *pf.*; потряса́ть *impf.*, потрясти́ (-су́, -сёшь; потря́с, -ла́) *pf.*; (*hours of work etc.*) распределя́ть *impf.*, распредели́ть *pf.* **be staggered** *v.i.* поража́ться *impf.*, порази́ться *pf.* **staggering** *adj.* потряса́ющий, порази́тельный.

stagnancy ['stægnənsɪ], **stagnation** [stæg-'neɪʃ(ə)n] *n.* засто́й, ко́сность, ине́ртность. '**stagnant** *adj.* (*water*) стоя́чий; (*fig.*) засто́йный, ко́сный, ине́ртный. **stag'nate** *v.i.* заста́иваться *impf.*, застоя́ться (-ою́сь, -ои́шься) *pf.*; косне́ть *impf.*, за~ *pf.*

stag-party ['stæg,paːtɪ] *n.* вечери́нка без же́нщин.

staid [steɪd] *adj.* степе́нный (-нен, -нна), тре́звый (трезв, -а́, -о), соли́дный.

stain [steɪn] *n.* пятно́ *pl.* (-тна, -тен, -тнам); (*dye*) кра́ска; *v.t.* па́чкать *impf.*, за~, ис~ *pf.*; пятна́ть *impf.*, за~ *pf.*; (*dye*) окра́шивать *impf.*, окра́сить *pf.*; ~**ed glass** цветно́е стекло́. **stainless** *adj.* незапя́тнанный, безупре́чный; ~ **steel** нержаве́ющая сталь.

stair [steə(r)] *n.* ступе́нь, ступе́нька. **staircase, stairs** *n.* ле́стница. **stairwell** *n.* ле́стничная кле́тка. **flight of stairs** *n.* ле́стничный марш.

stake [steɪk] *n.* (*stick*) кол (-а́, *loc.* -у́; *pl.* -ья, -ьев), столб (-а́); (*landmark*) ве́ха; (*bet*) ста́вка, закла́д; **be at** ~ быть поста́вленным на ка́рту; *v.t.* (*mark out*) огора́живать *impf.*, огороди́ть (-ожу́, -о́ди́шь) *pf.* ко́льями; отмеча́ть *impf.*, отме́тить *pf.* ве́хами; (*risk*) ста́вить *impf.*, по~ *pf.* на ка́рту; рискова́ть *impf.*+*i.*

stalactite ['stæləkˌtaɪt, stə'læk-] *n.* сталакти́т.

stalagmite ['stæləgˌmaɪt] *n.* сталагми́т.

stale [steɪl] *adj.* несве́жий (несве́ж, -а́, -е); (*hard, dry*) чёрствый (чёрств, -а́, -о), сухо́й (сух, -а́, -о); (*musty, damp*) за́тхлый; (*hackneyed*) изби́тый; **become, grow** ~ черстве́ть *impf.*, за~, по~ *pf.*

stalemate ['steɪlmeɪt] *n.* пат; (*fig.*) тупи́к (-а́).

stalk [stɔːk] *n.* сте́бель (-ля; *g.pl.* -бле́й) *m.*; *v.t.* высле́живать *impf.*; *v.t* & *i.* (*stride*)

ше́ствовать *impf.* (по+*d.*)

stall [stɔːl] *n.* сто́йло; (*booth*) ларёк (-рька́), кио́ск, пала́тка; (*theatr.*) кре́сло (*g.pl.* -сел) в парте́ре; *pl.* (*theatr.*) парте́р; *v.t* & *i.* остана́вливать(ся) *impf.*, останови́ть(ся) (-влю́(сь), -вишь(ся)) *pf.*; *v.i.* теря́ть *impf.*, по~ *pf.* ско́рость; (*play for time*) оття́гивать *impf.*, оттяну́ть (-ну́, -нешь) *pf.* вре́мя.

stallion ['stæljən] *n.* жеребе́ц (-бца́).

stalwart ['stɔːlwət] *adj.* сто́йкий (-о́ек, -ойка́, -о́йко); *n.* сто́йкий приве́рженец (-нца), -кая приве́рженка.

stamen ['steɪmən] *n.* тычи́нка.

stamina ['stæmɪnə] *n.* выно́сливость.

stammer ['stæmə(r)] *v.i.* заика́ться *impf.*; *n.* заика́ние. **stammerer** *n.* заи́ка *c.g.*

stamp [stæmp] *n.* печа́ть, штамп, ште́мпель (*pl.* -ля́) *m.*; (*hallmark*) клеймо́ (*pl.* -ма); (*postage*) (почто́вая) ма́рка; (*feet*) то́панье; *v.t.* ста́вить *impf.*, по~ *pf.* печа́ть на+*a.*; штампова́ть *impf.*, штемпелева́ть (-лю́ю, -лю́ешь) *impf.*, за~ *pf.*; клейми́ть *impf.*, за~ *pf.*; (*trample*) топта́ть (-пчу́, -пчешь) *impf.*, по~ *pf.*; *v.i.* то́пать *impf.*, то́пнуть *pf.* (нога́ми); ~ **out** подавля́ть *impf.*, подави́ть (-влю́, -вишь) *pf.*; ликвиди́ровать *impf.* & *pf.* **stamp-duty** *n.* ге́рбовый сбор.

stampede [stæm'piːd] *n.* пани́ческое бе́гство; *v.t* & *i.* обраща́ть(ся) *impf.* в пани́ческое бе́гство.

stanch [staːntʃ, stɔːntʃ] *v.t.* остана́вливать *impf.*, останови́ть (-влю́, -вишь) *pf.*

stanchion ['staːnʃ(ə)n] *n.* подпо́рка, сто́йка.

stand [stænd] *n.* (*hat, coat*) ве́шалка; (*music*) пюпи́тр; (*umbrella, support*) подста́вка; (*counter*) сто́йка; (*booth*) ларёк (-рька́), кио́ск; (*taxi, bicycle*) стоя́нка; (*tribune*) ка́федра, трибу́на; (*at stadium*) трибу́на; (*position*) пози́ция, ме́сто (*pl.* -та́), положе́ние; (*resistance*) сопротивле́ние; *v.i.* стоя́ть (-ою́, -ои́шь) *impf.*; (*remain in force*) остава́ться (-аю́сь, -аёшься) *impf.*, оста́ться (-а́нусь, -а́нешься) в си́ле; **the matter ~s thus** де́ло обстои́т так; **it ~s to reason** разуме́ется; *v.t.* (*put*) ста́вить *impf.*, по~ *pf.*; (*endure*) выде́рживать *impf.*, вы́держать (-жу, -жишь) *pf.*; выноси́ть (-ошу́, -о́сишь) *impf.*, вы́нести (-су, -сешь; -с) *pf.*; терпе́ть (-плю́, -пишь) *impf.*, по~ *pf.*; (*treat to*) угоща́ть *impf.*, угости́ть *pf.* (*s.o.* +*a.*; *sth.* +*i.*). ~ **back** отходи́ть (-ожу́, -о́дишь) *impf.*, отойти́ (-йду́, -йдёшь; отошёл, отошла́) *pf.* (**from** от+*g.*); (*not go forward*) держа́ться (-жу́сь, -жишься) *impf.* позади́; ~ **by** (*v.i.*) (*not interfere*) не вме́шиваться *impf.*, вме́шаться *pf.*; (*prepare*) приготовля́ться *impf.*, пригото́виться *pf.*; (*v.t.*) (*support*) подде́рживать *impf.*, поддержа́ть (-жу́, -жишь) *pf.*; (*fulfil*) выполня́ть *impf.*, вы́полнить *pf.*; ~ **for** (*signify*) означа́ть *impf.*; (*tolerate*) **I shall not ~ for it** я не потерплю́; ~ **in** (*for*) замеща́ть *impf.*, замести́ть *pf.*; ~ **out** выдава́ться (выдаётся) *impf.*, выдаться (-астся, -адутся) *pf.*; выделя́ться *impf.*, вы́делиться *pf.*; ~ **up** встава́ть (встаю́, встаёшь) *impf.*, встать (-а́ну, -а́нешь) *pf.*; ~ **up for** (*defend*) отста́ивать *impf.*, отстоя́ть (-ою́, -ои́шь) *pf.*; защища́ть *impf.*, защити́ть (-ищу́, -ити́шь) *pf.*; ~ **up to** (*endure*) выде́рживать *impf.*, вы́держать (-жу, -жишь) *pf.*; (*not give in to*) не пасова́ть *impf.*, с~ *pf.* пе́ред+*i.*

standard ['stændəd] *n.* (*flag*) зна́мя (*pl.* -мёна) *nt.*, штанда́рт; (*norm*) станда́рт, норм; ~ **of living** жи́зненный у́ровень (-вня) *m.*; **of high** ~ высо́кого ка́чества; ~ **lamp** торше́р; *adj.* норма́льный, станда́ртный, нормати́вный; (*generally accepted*) общепри́нятый; (*exemplary*) образцо́вый. **standard-bearer** *n.* знаменосец (-сца). **standardi'zation** *n.* нормализа́ция, стандартиза́ция. **standardize** *v.t.* стандартизи́ровать *impf.* & *pf.*; нормализова́ть *impf.* & *pf.*

stand-by ['stændbaɪ] *n.* (*store*) запа́с; (*reliable person*) надёжный челове́к (*pl.* лю́ди, -де́й, -дям, -дьми́); (*support*) опо́ра. **stand-in** *n.* замести́тель *m.*, ~ница.

standing ['stændɪŋ] *n.* положе́ние, ранг, репута́ция; **to be in good** ~ (**with s.o.**) быть на хоро́шем счету́ (у кого́-л.); *adj.* (*upright*) стоя́чий; (*permanent*) постоя́нный; ~ **army** постоя́нная а́рмия; ~ **committee** постоя́нный комите́т.

standoffish [stænd'ɒfɪʃ] *adj.* высоко́мерный.
stand-pipe ['stændpaɪp] *n.* стоя́к (-á).
standpoint ['stændpɔɪnt] *n.* то́чка зре́ния.

standstill ['stændstɪl] *n.* остано́вка, засто́й, па́уза; **be at a** ~ стоя́ть (-ою́, -ои́шь) *impf.* на мёртвой то́чке; **bring** (**come**) **to a** ~ остана́вливать(ся) *impf.*, останови́ть(ся) (-влю́(сь), -вишь(ся)) *pf.*

stanza ['stænzə] *n.* строфа́ (*pl.* -фы, -ф, -фа́м), станс.

staple[1] ['steɪp(ə)l] *n.* (*fastening*) скоба́ (*pl.* -бы, -б, -ба́м).

staple[2] ['steɪp(ə)l] *n.* (*principal product*) гла́вный проду́кт, основно́й това́р; (*principal element*) гла́вный элеме́нт; *adj.* основно́й, гла́вный.

star [stɑː(r)] *n.* звезда́ (*pl.* звёзды); (*asterisk*) звёздочка; *adj.* звёздный; (*chief*) гла́вный; (*celebrated*) знамени́тый; *v.i.* игра́ть *impf.*, сыгра́ть *pf.* гла́вную роль. **starfish** *n.* морска́я звезда́ (*pl.* звёзды). **star-gazer** *n.* астро́лог, звездочёт.

starboard ['stɑːbəd] *n.* пра́вый борт (*loc.* -ý).

starch [stɑːtʃ] *n.* крахма́л; *v.t.* крахма́лить *impf.*, на~ *pf.* **starched** *adj.* крахма́льный, накрахма́ленный. **starchy** *adj.* крахмали́стый; (*prim*) чо́порный.

stare [steə(r)] *n.* при́стальный взгляд; *v.i.* при́стально смотре́ть (-трю́, -тришь) (**at** на+*a.*); ~ (**one**) **in the face** (*be obvious*) броса́ться *impf.*, бро́ситься *pf.* (+*d.*) в глаза́.

stark [stɑːk] *adj.* (*bare*) го́лый (гол, -á, -о); (*desolate*) пусты́нный (-нен, -нна); (*sharp*)

ре́зкий (-зок, -зка́, -зко); *adv.* соверше́нно.
starling ['stɑːlɪŋ] *n.* скворе́ц (-рца́).
starry ['stɑːrɪ] *adj.* звёздный. **starry-eyed** *adj.* мечта́тельный.

start [stɑːt] *n.* нача́ло; (*setting out*) отправле́ние; (*sport*) старт; (*advantage*) преиму́щество; (*shudder*) рыво́к (-вка́); *v.i.* начина́ться (начнётся; начался́, -ла́сь) *pf.*; (*engine*) заводи́ться (-о́дится) *impf.*, завести́сь (-еде́тся; -ёлся, -ела́сь) *pf.*; (*set out*) отправля́ться *impf.*, отпра́виться *pf.*; (*shudder*) вздра́гивать *impf.*, вздро́гнуть *pf.*; (*sport*) стартова́ть *impf.* & *pf.*; *v.t.* начина́ть *impf.*, нача́ть (-чну́, -чнёшь; на́чал, -á, -о) *pf.* (*gerund, inf.*, +*inf.*; *by*, +*gerund* с того́, что…; **with** +*i.*, с+*g.*; **from the beginning** с нача́ла); (*set in motion*) пуска́ть *impf.*, пусти́ть (пущу́, пу́стишь) *pf.*; запуска́ть *impf.*, запусти́ть (-ущу́, -у́стишь) *pf.* **starter** *n.* (*tech.*) пуска́тель *m.*, ста́ртер; (*sport*) ста́ртер. **starter, starting** *adj.* пусково́й. **starting-point** *n.* отправно́й пункт.

startle ['stɑːt(ə)l] *v.t.* испуга́ть *pf.*; поража́ть *impf.*, порази́ть *pf.* **startled** *adj.* испу́ганный (-ан), потрясённый (-ён, -ена́). **startling** *adj.* порази́тельный, потряса́ющий.

starvation [stɑː'veɪʃ(ə)n] *n.* го́лод, голода́ние. **starve** *v.i.* страда́ть *impf.*, по~ *pf.* от го́лода; (*to death*) умира́ть *impf.*, умере́ть (умру́, -рёшь; у́мер, -лá, -ло) с го́лоду; *v.t.* мори́ть *impf.*, по~, у~ *pf.* го́лодом. '**starving** *adj.* голода́ющий; (*hungry*) голо́дный (го́лоден, -дна́, -дно, го́лодны́).

state [steɪt] *n.* (*condition*) состоя́ние, положе́ние; (*pomp*) великоле́пие, по́мпа; (*nation, government*) госуда́рство, штат; **lie in** ~ поко́иться *impf.* в откры́том гробу́; *adj.* (*ceremonial*) торже́ственный (-ен, -енна); (*apartments*) пара́дный; (*of State*) госуда́рственный; *v.t.* (*announce*) заявля́ть *impf.*, заяви́ть (-влю́, -вишь) *pf.*; (*expound*) излага́ть *impf.*, изложи́ть (-жу́, -жишь) *pf.*; (*maintain*) утвержда́ть *impf.* **stated** *adj.* (*appointed*) назна́ченный. **stateless** *adj.* не име́ющий гражда́нства. **stately** *adj.* вели́чественный (-ен, -енна), велича́вый. **statement** *n.* (*announcement*) заявле́ние; (*exposition*) изложе́ние; (*assertion*) утвержде́ние. **state-of-the-art** *adj.* совреме́нный, нове́йший. **statesman** *n.* госуда́рственный де́ятель *m.*

static ['stætɪk] *adj.* стати́чный, неподви́жный. **statics** *n.* ста́тика.

station ['steɪʃ(ə)n] *n.* (*rail.*) вокза́л, ста́нция; (*position*) ме́сто (*pl.* -тá); (*social*) обще́ственное положе́ние; (*naval etc.*) ба́за; (*meteorological, hydro-electric power, radio etc.*) ста́нция; (*post*) пост (-á, *loc.* -ý); *v.t.* ста́вить *impf.*, по~ *pf.*; помеща́ть *impf.*, помести́ть *pf.*; (*mil.*) размеща́ть *impf.*, размести́ть *pf.* **station-master** *n.* нача́льник вокза́ла, ста́нции.

stationary ['steɪʃənərɪ] *adj.* неподви́жный;

(*tech.*) стациона́рный; (*constant*) постоя́нный (-нен, -нна), усто́йчивый.

stationer ['steɪʃənə(r)] *n.* продаве́ц (-вца́), -вщи́ца канцеля́рского магази́на; ~'s (**shop**) канцеля́рский магази́н. **stationery** *n.* канцеля́рские това́ры *m.pl.*; (*writing-paper*) почто́вая бума́га.

statistic [stə'tɪstɪk] *n.* статисти́ческое да́нное, ци́фра. **statistical** *adj.* статисти́ческий. **statistician** [ˌstætɪ'stɪʃ(ə)n] *n.* стати́стик. **statistics** *n.* стати́стика.

statue ['stætjuː, 'stætʃuː] *n.* ста́туя. **statu'esque** *adj.* велича́вый. **statu'ette** *n.* статуэ́тка.

stature ['stætʃə(r)] *n.* рост, стан; (*merit*) досто́инство, ка́чество.

status ['steɪtəs] *n.* ста́тус; (*social*) обще́ственное положе́ние; (*state*) состоя́ние. **status quo** *n.* ста́тус-кво́ *m.indecl.*

statute ['stætjuːt] *n.* стату́т; законода́тельный акт; *pl.* уста́в. **statute-book** *n.* свод зако́нов.

statutory ['statjʊtərɪ] *adj.* устано́вленный (-ен) зако́ном.

staunch [stɔːntʃ] *v.t. see* **stanch**; *adj.* (*loyal*) ве́рный (-рен, -рна́, -рно); (*steadfast*) сто́йкий (-о́ек, -ойка́, -о́йко), твёрдый (твёрд, -а́, -о); про́чный (-чен, -чна́, -чно, про́чны).

stave [steɪv] *n.* (*of cask*) клёпка; *v.t.* проби́ва́ть *impf.*, проби́ть (-бью, -бьёшь) *pf.*; разбива́ть *impf.*, разби́ть (разобью́, -бьёшь) *pf.*; ~ **off** предотвраща́ть *impf.*, предотврати́ть (-ащу́, -ати́шь) *pf.*

stay[1] [steɪ] *n.* (*time spent*) пребыва́ние; (*suspension*) приостановле́ние; (*postponement*) отсро́чка; *v.i.* (*remain*) остава́ться (-аю́сь, -аёшься) *impf.*, оста́ться (-а́нусь, -а́нешься) *pf.* (**to dinner** обе́дать); (*put up*) остана́вливаться *impf.*, останови́ться (-влю́сь, -вишься) *pf.* (**at** (*place*) в+*p.*; **at** (*friends' etc.*) y+*g.*); гости́ть *impf.* (**with** y+*g.*); (*live*) жить (живу́, живёшь; жил, -а́, -о); ~ **a moment!** подожди́те мину́тку!; ~ **away** отсу́тствовать *impf.*; ~ **behind** остава́ться (-аю́сь, -аёшься) *impf.*, оста́ться (-а́нусь, -а́нешься) *pf.*; *v.t.* (*check*) заде́рживать *impf.*, задержа́ть (-жу́, -жишь) *pf.*; (*hunger, thirst*) утоля́ть *impf.*, утоли́ть *pf.*; (*suspend*) приостана́вливать *impf.*, приостанови́ть (-влю́, -вишь) *pf.*; (*postpone*) отсро́чивать *impf.*, отсро́чить *pf.*; ~ **the course** подде́рживаться *impf.*, (-жу́сь, -жишься) до конца́. **stay-at-home** *n.* домосе́д, ~ка. **staying-power** *n.* выно́сливость.

stay[2] [steɪ] *n.* (*naut.*) штаг; (*support*) подде́ржка; *v.t.* (*support*) подде́рживать *impf.*, подержа́ть (-жу́, -жишь) *pf.* **stays** *n.* корсе́т.

stead [sted] *n.*: **to stand s.o. in good** ~ ока́зываться *impf.*, оказа́ться (-ажу́сь, -а́жешься) *pf.* поле́зным кому́-л.

steadfast ['stedfɑːst, 'stedfəst] *adj.* (*firm, steady*) про́чный (-чен, -чна́, -чно, про́чны); усто́йчивый; (*unshakeable*) сто́йкий (-о́ек, -ойка́, -о́йко), непоколеби́мый.

steady ['stedɪ] *adj.* (*firm*) про́чный (-чен, -чна́, -чно, про́чны), усто́йчивый, твёрдый (твёрд, -а́, -о); (*continuous*) непреры́вный; (*prices*) усто́йчивый; (*wind, temperature*) ро́вный (-вен, -вна́, -вно); (*speed*) постоя́нный (-нен, -нна); (*unshakeable*) непоколеби́мый; (*staid*) степе́нный (-нен, -нна); ~ **hand** твёрдая рука́ (*a.* -ку; *pl.* -ки, -к, -ка́м); *v.t.* (*boat*) приводи́ть (-ожу́, -о́дишь) *impf.*, привести́ (-еду́, -едёшь; -ёл, -ела́) *pf.* в равнове́сие.

steak [steɪk] *n.* (*before cooking*) то́лстый кусо́к (-ска́) мя́са (*meat*), говя́дины (*beef*), ры́бы (*fish*), для жаре́нья; (*dish*) то́лстый кусо́к (-ска́) мя́са (*meat*), жа́реной ры́бы (*fish*); (*beefsteak*) бифште́кс.

steal [stiːl] *v.t.* ворова́ть *impf.*, c~ *pf.*; красть (краду́, -дёшь; крал) *impf.*, y~ *pf.* (*also a kiss*); ~ **a glance** укра́дкой взгля́дывать *impf.*, взгляну́ть (-ну́, -нешь) *pf.* (**at** на+*a.*); *v.i.* кра́сться (краду́сь, -дёшься; -а́лся) *impf.*; подкра́дываться *impf.*, подкра́сться (-аду́сь, -адёшься; -а́лся) *pf.* **stealing** *n.* воровство́. **stealth** [stelθ] *n.* хи́трость, уло́вка; **by** ~ укра́дкой, тайко́м. **stealthy** *adj.* ворова́тый, та́йный, скры́тый.

steam [stiːm] *n.* пар (*loc.* -у́; *pl.* -ы́); **at full** ~ на всех пара́х; **get up** ~ разводи́ть (-ожу́, -о́дишь) *impf.*, развести́ (-еду́, -едёшь; -ёл, -ела́) *pf.* пары́; (*fig.*) собира́ться *impf.*, собра́ться (-берётся; -бра́лся, -брала́сь, -бра́ло́сь) с си́лами; **let off** ~ (*fig.*) дава́ть (даю́, даёшь) *impf.*, дать (дам, дашь, дасть, дади́м; дал, -а́, да́ло́, -и) *pf.* вы́ход свои́м чу́вствам; **under one's own** ~ сам (-а́, -о́, -и); свои́м хо́дом; *adj.* парово́й, паро... *in comb.*; *v.t.* па́рить *impf.*; *v.i.* па́риться *impf.*, по~ *pf.*; (*vessel*) ходи́ть (хо́дит) *indet.*, идти́ (идёт; шёл, шла) *det.* на пара́х; ~ **up** (*mist over*) запотева́ть *impf.*, запоте́ть *pf.*; поте́ть *impf.*, за~, от~ *pf.*; ~ **engine** парова́я маши́на. **steamer** ['stiːmə(r)] *n.* парохо́д. **steaming** *adj.* дымя́щийся. **steam-roller** *n.* парово́й като́к (-тка́). **steamship** *n.* парохо́д.

steed [stiːd] *n.* конь (-ня́, *pl.* -ни, -не́й) *m.*

steel [stiːl] *n.* сталь; *adj.* стально́й; *v.t.* (*make resolute*) ожесточа́ть *impf.*, ожесточи́ть *pf.*; **to** ~ **one's (own) heart** ожесточа́ть *impf.*, ожесточи́ться *pf.*; ~ **foundry** сталелите́йный заво́д. **steel-making** *adj.* сталепла́ви́льный. **steel-rolling** *adj.* сталепрока́тный. **steelworks** *n.* сталеплави́льный заво́д. **steely** *adj.* стально́й; (*cold*) холо́дный (-о́лоден, -дна́, -дно, хо́лодны́); (*stern*) суро́вый. **steelyard** *n.* безме́н.

steep[1] [stiːp] *v.t.* (*immerse*) погружа́ть *impf.*, погрузи́ть *pf.* (**in** в+*a.*); (*saturate*) пропи́тывать *impf.*, пропита́ть *pf.* (**in** +*i.*); **be** ~**ed in** (*also fig.*) погружа́ться *impf.*, погрузи́ться *pf.* (**in** в+*a.*).

steep[2] [stiːp] *adj.* круто́й (крут, -а́, -о); (*excessive*) чрезме́рный; (*improbable*) невероя́тный. **steepness** *n.* крутизна́.

steeple ['sti:p(ə)l] *n.* шпиль *m.* **steeplechase** *n.* скáчки *f.pl.* с препя́тствиями. **steeplejack** *n.* верхолáз.

steer¹ [stɪə(r)] *n.* молодóй вол (-á), бычóк (-чкá).

steer² [stɪə(r)] *v.t.* (*control, navigate*) управля́ть *impf.*, прáвить *impf.*+*i.*; (*guide*) руководи́ть *impf.*+*i.*; прáвить *impf.* рулём; рули́ть *impf.* (*coll.*); ~ **clear of** избегáть *impf.*, избежáть (-егý, -ежи́шь) *pf.*+*g.* **steering-column** *n.* рулевáя колóнка. **steering-wheel** *n.* руль (-ля́) *m.*, барáнка (*coll.*); (*naut.*) штурвáл.

stellar ['stelə(r)] *adj.* звёздный. **stellate** *adj.* звездообрáзный.

stem¹ [stem] *n.* стéбель (-бля; *pl.* -бли, -блéй) *m.*; (*trunk*) ствол (-á); (*wine-glass*) нóжка; (*ling.*) оснóва; (*naut.*) нос (*loc.* -ý; *pl.* -ы́); **from ~ to stern** от нóса до кормы́; *v.i.*: ~ **from** происходи́ть (-ожý, -óдишь) *impf.*, произойти́ (-ойдёт; -ошёл, -ошлá) *pf.* от+*g.*

stem² [stem] *v.t.* (*dam*) запрýживать *impf.*, запруди́ть (-ужý, -ýдишь) *pf.*; (*stop*) останáвливать *impf.*, остановить *pf.*

stench [stentʃ] *n.* зловóние, смрад.

stencil ['stensɪl] *n.* трафарéт; (*tech.*) шаблóн; *v.t.* наноси́ть (-ошý, -óсишь) *impf.*, нанести́ (-есý, -есёшь; -ёс, -еслá) *pf.* узóр по трафарéту. **stencilled** *adj.* трафарéтный.

stentorian [,sten'tɔ:rɪən] *adj.* громоглáсный.

step [step] *n.* (*pace, action*) шаг (-á with 2,3,4, *loc.* -ý; *pl.* -и́); (*gait*) похóдка; (*dance*) *na nt.indecl.*; (*of stairs, ladder*) ступéнь (*g.pl.* -éней); (*measure*) мéра; ~ **by** ~ шаг за шáгом; **in** ~ в нóгу; **out of** ~ не в нóгу; **watch one's** ~ дéйствовать *impf.* осторóжно; **take** ~**s** принимáть *impf.*, приня́ть (приму́, -мешь; при́нял, -á, -о) *pf.* мéры *v.i.* шагáть *impf.*, шагнýть *pf.*; ступáть *impf.*, ступи́ть (-плю́, -пишь) *pf.*; ~ **aside** сторони́ться (-ню́сь, -ни́шься) *impf.*, по~ *pf.*; ~ **back** отступáть *impf.*, отступи́ть (-плю́, -пишь) *pf.*; ~ **down** (*resign*) уходи́ть (-ожý, -óдишь) *impf.*, уйти́ (уйдý, -дёшь; ушёл, ушлá) *pf.* в отстáвку; ~ **forward** выступáть *impf.*, вы́ступить *pf.*; ~ **in** (*intervene*) вмéшиваться *impf.*, вмешáться *pf.*; ~ **on** наступáть *impf.*, наступи́ть (-плю́, -пишь) *pf.* на+*a.* (*s.o.'s foot* кому́-л. нá ногу); ~ **over** перешáгивать *impf.*, перешагну́ть *pf.*+*a.*, чéрез+*a.*; ~ **up** (*increase, promote*) повышáть *impf.*, повы́сить *pf.*; (*strengthen*) уси́ливать *impf.*, уси́лить *pf.* **step-ladder** *n.* стремя́нка. **stepped** *adj.* ступéнчатый. **stepping-stone** *n.* кáмень (-мня; *pl.* -мни, -мнéй) *m.* для перехóда чéрез рéчку *etc.*; (*fig.*) срéдство для достижéнию цéли. **steps** *n.* лéстница.

stepbrother ['step,brʌðə(r)] *n.* свóдный брат (*pl.* -ья, -ьев). **stepdaughter** *n.* пáдчерица. **stepfather** *n.* óтчим. **stepmother** *n.* мáчеха. **stepsister** *n.* свóдная сестрá (*pl.* сёстры, сестёр, сёстрам). **stepson** *n.* пáсынок (-нка).

steppe [step] *n.* степь (*loc.* -пи́; *pl.* -пи, -пéй) *adj.* степнóй.

stereo ['sterɪəʋ, 'stɪə-] *n.* (*record-player*) стереофони́ческий прои́грыватель *n.*; *adj.* (*recorded in* ~) стéрео. **stereophonic** *adj.* стереофони́ческий. **stereoscope** *n.* стереоскóп. **stereoscopic** *adj.* стереоскопи́ческий. **stereotype** *n.* стереоти́п; (*tech.*) шаблóн. **stereotyped** *adj.* (*also banal*) стереоти́пный, шаблóнный.

sterile ['steraɪl] *adj.* (*barren, germ-free*) стери́льный. **sterility** [stə'rɪlɪtɪ] *n.* стери́льность. **sterilization** [,sterɪlaɪ'zeɪʃ(ə)n] *n.* стерилизáция. **sterilize** *v.t.* стерилизовáть *impf.* & *pf.* **sterilizer** *n.* стерилизáтор.

sterling ['stɜ:lɪŋ] *n.* стéрлинг; **pound** ~ фунт стéрлингов; *adj.* стéрлинговый; (*irreproachable*) безупрéчный; (*reliable*) надёжный.

stern¹ [stɜ:n] *n.* кормá.

stern² [stɜ:n] *adj.* сурóвый, стрóгий (-г, -гá, -го).

sternum ['stɜ:nəm] *n.* груди́на.

stethoscope ['steθəskəʊp] *n.* стетоскóп.

stevedore ['sti:vədɔ:(r)] *n.* стивидóр, грýзчик.

stew [stju:] *n.* (*cul.*) мя́со тушёное вмéсте с овощáми; **be in a** ~ (*coll.*) волновáться *impf.*; *v.t.* & *i.* туши́ть(ся) (-шý(сь), -шишь(ся)) *impf.*, с~ *pf.*; томи́ть(ся) *impf.*; **to** ~ **in one's own juice** расхлёбывать *impf.* кáшу, котóрую сам завари́л. **stewed** *adj.* тушёный; ~ **fruit** компóт. **stewpan, stewpot** *n.* кастрю́ля, сотéйник.

steward ['stju:əd] *n.* стю́ард, бортпроводни́к (-á); (*master of ceremonies*) распоряди́тель *m.* **stewardess** *n.* стюардéсса, бортпроводни́ца.

stick¹ [stɪk] *n.* пáлка; (*of chalk etc.*) пáлочка; (*hockey, walking*) клю́шка; ~**s** (*collect.*) хвóрост (-a(y)).

stick² [stɪk] *v.t.* (*spear*) закáлывать *impf.*, заколóть (-лю́, -лешь) *pf.*; (*make adhere*) прикле́ивать *impf.*, прикле́ить *pf.* (**to** к+*d.*); прилепля́ть *impf.*, прилепи́ть (-плю́, -пишь) *pf.* (**to** к+*d.*); (*coll.*) (*put*) стáвить *impf.*, по~ *pf.*; (*lay*) класть (кладý, -дёшь; клал) *impf.*, положи́ть (-жý, -жишь) *pf.*; *v.i.* (*adhere*) ли́пнуть (лип) *impf.*; прилипáть *impf.*, прили́пнуть (-нет; прили́п) *pf.* (**to** к+*d.*); прикле́иваться *impf.*, прикле́иться *pf.* (**to** к+*d.*); ~ **in** (*thrust in*) втыкáть *impf.*, воткнýть *impf.*, вколóть (-лю́, -лешь) *pf.*; **the arrow stuck into the ground** стрелá воткнýлась в зéмлю; (*into opening*) всóвывать *impf.*, всунуть *pf.*; ~ **on** (*glue on*) наклéивать *impf.*, наклéить *pf.*; ~ **out** (*thrust out*) высóвывать *impf.*, высунуть *pf.* (**from** из+*g.*); (*project*) торчáть (-чý, -чи́шь) *impf.*; ~ **to** (*keep to*) приде́рживаться *impf.*, придержáться (-жýсь, -жишься) *pf.*+*g.*; (*remain at*) не отвлекáться *impf.* от+*g.*; ~ **together** держáться (-жимся) *impf.* вмéсте; ~ **up for** защищáть *impf.*, защити́ть (-ищу́, -ити́шь) *pf.*; **be, get, stuck** застрева́ть *impf.*, застря́ть (-я́ну, -я́нешь) *pf.* **sticker** *n.* (*label*) этике́тка, ярлы́к (-а́). **sticking-plaster** *n.* ли́пкий пла́стырь *m.*

stickleback ['stɪk(ə)l‚bæk] *n.* ко́люшка.

stickler ['stɪklə(r)] *n.* (*ярый*) сторо́нник, -ица; приве́рженец (-нца), -нка (**for** +*g.*).

sticky ['stɪkɪ] *adj.* ли́пкий (-пок, -пка́, -пко), кле́йкий; **he will come to a ~ end** он пло́хо ко́нчит.

stiff [stɪf] *adj.* жёсткий (-ток, -тка́, -тко), неги́бкий (-бок, -бка́, -бко); (*with cold*) окочене́лый; (*prim*) чо́порный; (*difficult*) тру́дный (-ден, -дна́, -дно, трудны́); (*breeze*) си́льный (си́лён, -льна́, -льно, си́льны); **be ~** (*ache*) боле́ть (-ли́т) *impf.* **stiffen** *v.t.* де́лать *impf.*, с~ *pf.* жёстким; *v.i.* станови́ться (-влю́сь, -вишься) *impf.*, стать (-а́ну, -а́нешь) *pf.* жёстким. **stiffness** *n.* жёсткость; (*primness*) чо́порность.

stifle ['staɪf(ə)l] *v.t.* души́ть (-шу́, -шишь) *impf.*, за~ *pf.*; (*suppress*) подавля́ть *impf.*, подави́ть (-влю́, -вишь) *pf.*; (*sound*) заглуша́ть *impf.*, заглуши́ть *pf.*; *v.i.* задыха́ться *impf.*, задохну́ться (-о́х(ну́л)ся, -о́х(ну́)лась) *pf.* **stifling** *adj.* уду́шливый, ду́шный (-шен, -шна́, -шно).

stigma ['stɪgmə] *n.* клеймо́ (*pl.* -ма) позо́ра. **stigmatize** *v.t.* клейми́ть *impf.*, за~ *pf.*

stile [staɪl] *n.* ступе́ньки *f.pl.* для перехо́да че́рез забо́р, перела́з (coll.).

stiletto [stɪ'letəʊ] *n.* стиле́т; **~ heels** гво́здики *m.pl.*, шпи́льки *f.pl.*

still¹ [stɪl] *adv.* (всё) ещё, до сих пор, по-пре́жнему; **~ better** ещё лу́чше; (*nevertheless*) всё же, тем не ме́нее, одна́ко; (*motionless*) неподви́жно; (*quietly*) споко́йно; **stand ~** не дви́гаться (-аюсь, -аешься & дви́жусь, -жешься) *impf.*, дви́нуться *pf.*; **time stood ~** вре́мя останови́лось; **sit ~** сиде́ть (сижу́, сиди́шь) *impf.* сми́рно.

still² [stɪl] *n.* (*quiet*) тишина́; (*film*) кадр; *adj.* ти́хий (тих, -а́, -о), споко́йный; (*immobile*) неподви́жный; (*not fizzy*) не шипу́чий; *v.t.* успока́ивать *impf.*, успоко́ить *pf.*

still³ [stɪl] *n.* перего́нный куб (*pl.* -ы́).

still-born ['stɪlbɔːn] *adj.* мертворождённый.

still life ['stɪllaɪf] *n.* натюрмо́рт.

stillness ['stɪlnɪs] *n.* тишина́, споко́йствие; (*immobility*) неподви́жность.

stilt [stɪlt] *n.* ходу́ля; (*tech.*) сто́йка, сва́я. **stilted** *adj.* ходу́льный.

stimulant ['stɪmjʊlənt] *n.* возбужда́ющее сре́дство. **stimulate** *v.t.* возбужда́ть *impf.*, возбуди́ть *pf.*; стимули́ровать *impf.* & *pf.* **stimulating** *adj.* возбуди́тельный. **stimulation** *n.* возбужде́ние. **stimulus** *n.* стиму́л, возбуди́тель *m.*, побуди́тельная причи́на.

sting [stɪŋ] *n.* жа́ло (*also fig.*); уку́с (*also wound*); *v.t.* жа́лить *impf.*, у~ *pf.*; укуси́ть (-ушу́, -у́сишь) *pf.*; *v.i.* (*burn*) жечь (жжёт, жгут; жёг, жгла) *impf.* **stinging** *adj.* (*caustic*) язви́тельный; **~ nettle** жгу́чая

крапи́ва. **sting-ray** *n.* скат дазиа́тис.

stinginess ['stɪndʒɪnɪs] *n.* ску́пость, ска́редность. **stingy** *adj.* скупо́й (скуп, -а́, -о), ска́редный.

stink [stɪŋk] *n.* злово́ние, вонь, смрад; *v.i.* воня́ть *impf.* (**of** +*i.*); смерде́ть (-ржу́, -рди́шь) *impf.* (**of** +*i.*). **stinking** *adj.* воню́чий, злово́нный (-нен, -нна), смра́дный.

stint [stɪnt] *n.* но́рма; *v.t.* скупи́ться *impf.*, по~ *pf.* на+*a.*

stipend ['staɪpend] *n.* (*salary*) жа́лование; (*grant*) стипе́ндия. **stipendiary** [staɪ'pendjərɪ, stɪ-] *adj.* получа́ющий жа́лование.

stipple ['stɪp(ə)l] *n.* рабо́та, гравирова́ние пункти́ром; *v.t.* & *i.* рисова́ть *impf.*, на~ *pf.*, гравирова́ть *impf.*, вы́~ *pf.*, пункти́ром.

stipulate ['stɪpjʊ‚leɪt] *v.i.* ста́вить *impf.*, по~ *pf.* усло́вием (**that** что); *v.t.* обусло́вливать *impf.*, обусло́вить *pf.*+*i.*; (*demand*) тре́бовать *impf.*+*g.* **stipu'lation** *n.* усло́вие.

stir [stɜː(r)] *n.* шевеле́ние, движе́ние; (*uproar*) суматоха; **cause a ~** вызыва́ть *impf.*, вы́звать (вы́зову, -вешь) *pf.* волне́ние; *v.t.* (*move*) шевели́ть (шевелю́, -е́ли́шь) *impf.*, шевельну́ть *pf.*+*i.*; дви́гать *impf.*, дви́нуть *pf.*+*i.*; (*mix*) меша́ть *impf.*, по~ *pf.*; разме́шивать *impf.*, размеша́ть *pf.*; (*excite*) волнова́ть *impf.*, вз~ *pf.*; *v.i.* (*move*) шевели́ться (шевелю́сь, -е́ли́шься) *impf.*, шевельну́ться *pf.*; дви́гаться *impf.*, дви́нуться *pf.*; (*be excited*) волнова́ться; **~ up** возбужда́ть *impf.*, возбуди́ть *pf.* **stirring** *adj.* волну́ющий.

stirrup ['stɪrəp] *n.* стре́мя (-мени; *pl.* -мена́, -мя́н, -мена́м) *nt.*

stitch [stɪtʃ] *n.* стежо́к (-жка́); (*knitting*) пе́тля (*g.pl.* -тель); (*med.*) шов (шва); (*pain*) ко́лотье (coll.); *v.t.* (*embroider, make line of ~es*) строчи́ть (-очу́, -о́чи́шь) *impf.*, про~ *pf.*; (*join by sewing, make, suture*) сшива́ть *impf.*, сшить (сошью́, сошьёшь) *pf.*; (*med.*) накла́дывать *impf.*, наложи́ть (-жу́, -жишь) *pf.* швы на+*a.*; **~ up** заши́ть *impf.*, заши́ть (-шью, -шьёшь) *pf.* **stitching** *n.* (*sewing*) шитьё; (*stitches*) стро́чка.

stoat [stəʊt] *n.* горноста́й.

stock [stɒk] *n.* (*store*) запа́с; (*equipment*) инвента́рь (-ря́) *m.*; (*live~*) скот (-а́); (*cul.*) бульо́н; (*family*) семья́ (*pl.* -мьи, -ме́й, -мьям); (*origin, clan*) род (*loc.* -у́; *pl.* -ы́); (*fin.*) а́кции *f.pl.*; *pl.* (*fin.*) фо́нды *m.pl.*; (*punishment*) коло́дки *f.pl.*; **in ~** в нали́чии; **out of ~** распро́дан; **take ~ of** обду́мывать *impf.*, обду́мать *pf.*; *adj.* станда́ртный; (*banal*) изби́тый; *v.t.* име́ть в нали́чии; **~ up** запаса́ть *impf.*, запасти́ (-су́, -сёшь; запа́с, -сла́) *pf.* **stock-breeder** *n.* скотово́д. **stock-breeding** *n.* скотово́дство. **stockbroker** *n.* биржево́й ма́клер. **stock-exchange** *n.* фондо́вая би́ржа.

Stockholm ['stɒkhəʊm] *n.* Стокго́льм.

stock-in-trade ['stɒkɪn‚treɪd] *n.* (*торго́вый*) инвента́рь (-ря́) *m.* **stockpile** *n.* запа́с; *v.t.*

накáпливать *impf.*, накопи́ть (-плю́, -пишь) *pf.* **stock-still** *adj.* неподви́жный. **stock-taking** *n.* переучёт товáра, провéрка инвентаря́. **stockyard** *n.* скотоприго́нный двор (-á).

stockade [stɒ'keɪd] *n.* частоко́л.

stocking ['stɒkɪŋ] *n.* чуло́к (-лкá; *g.pl.* чуло́к).

stocky ['stɒkɪ] *adj.* приземи́стый, коренáстый.

stodgy ['stɒdʒɪ] *adj.* (*food*) тяжёлый (-л, -лá); (*boring*) скýчный (-чен, -чнá, -чно).

stoic ['stəʊɪk] *n.* сто́ик. **stoic(al)** *adj.* стои́ческий. **stoicism** ['stəʊɪsɪz(ə)m] *n.* стоици́зм.

stoke [stəʊk] *v.t.* топи́ть (-плю́, -пишь) *impf.* **stokehold, stokehole** *n.* кочегáрка.

stoker ['stəʊkə(r)] *n.* кочегáр, истопни́к (-á).

stole [stəʊl] *n.* палантúн.

stolid ['stɒlɪd] *adj.* флегмати́чный.

stomach ['stʌmək] *n.* желýдок (-дка), (*also surface of body*) живóт (-á); *adj.* желýдочный; *v.t.* терпéть (-плю́, -пишь) *impf.*, по~ *pf.* **stomach-ache** *n.* боль в животé.

stone [stəʊn] *n.* (*material, piece of it*) кáмень (-мня; *pl.* -мни, -мнéй) *m.*; (*fruit*) кóсточка; *adj.* кáменный; *v.t.* побивáть *impf.*, поби́ть (-бью́, -бьёшь) *pf.* камня́ми; (*fruit*) вынимáть *impf.*, вы́нуть *pf.* кóсточки из+*g.*; ~ **to death** заби́ть (-бью́, -бьёшь) *pf.* камня́ми нáсмерть. **Stone Age** *n.* кáменный век (*loc.* -ý). **stone-cold** *adj.* совершéнно холóдный (хóлоден, -днá, -дно, холóдны). **stone-deaf** *adj.* совершéнно глухóй (глух, -á, -о). **stone-mason** *n.* кáменщик. **stonewall** *v.i.* устрáивать *impf.*, устрóить *pf.* обстрýкцию; мешáть *impf.*, по~ *pf.* дискýссии. **stonily** *adv.* с кáменным выражéнием, хóлодно. **stony** *adj.* камени́стый; (*fig.*) кáменный, холóдный (хóлоден, -днá, -дно, хóлодны). **stony-broke** *pred.*: **I am** ~ у меня́ нет ни грошá.

stool [stuːl] *n.* табурéт, табурéтка.

stoop [stuːp] *n.* сутýлость; *v.t. & i.* сутýлить(ся) *impf.*, с~ *pf.*; (*bend down*) наклоня́ть(ся) *impf.*, наклони́ть(ся) (-ню́(сь), -нишь(ся)) *pf.*; ~ **to** (*abase o.s.*) унижáться *impf.*, уни́зиться *pf.* до+*g.*; (*condescend*) снисходи́ть (-ожý, -óдишь) *impf.*, снизойти́ (-ойдý, -ойдёшь, -ошёл, -ошлá) *pf.* до+*g.* **stooped, stooping** *adj.* сутýлый.

stop [stɒp] *n.* останóвка; (*discontinuance*) прекращéние; (*organ*) реги́стр; (*full* ~) тóчка; **request** ~ останóвка по трéбованию; *v.t.* останáвливать *impf.*, останови́ть (-влю́, -вишь) *pf.*; (*discontinue*) прекращáть *impf.*, прекрати́ть (-ащý, -ати́шь) *pf.*; (*restrain*) удéрживать *impf.*, удержáть (-жý, -жишь) *pf.* (**from** от+*g.*); *v.i.* останáвливаться *impf.*, останови́ться (-влю́сь, -вишься) *pf.*; (*discontinue*) прекращáться *impf.*, прекрати́ться (-и́тся) *pf.*; (*cease*) перестaвáть (-таю́, -таёшь) *impf.*, перестáть (-áну, -áнешь) *pf.* (+*inf.*); ~ **up** *v.t.* затыкáть *impf.*, заткнýть *pf.*; ~ **at nothing**

ни перед чéм не останáвливаться *impf.*, останови́ться (-влю́сь, -вишься) *pf.* **stopcock** *n.* запóрный кран. **stopgap** *n.* затычка. **stop-light** *n.* стоп-сигнáл. **stoppage** *n.* останóвка; (*strike*) забастóвка. **stopper** *n.* прóбка; (*tech.*) стóпор. **stop-press** *n.* экстренное сообщéние в газéте. **stop-watch** *n.* секундомéр.

storage ['stɔːrɪdʒ] *n.* хранéние. **store** *n.* запáс; (*storehouse*) склад; (*shop*) магази́н; **set** ~ **by** цени́ть (-ню́, -нишь) *impf.*; **what is in** ~ **for me?** что ждёт меня́ впереди́?; *v.t.* запасáть *impf.*, запасти́ (-сý, -сёшь; запáс, -слá) *pf.*; (*put into storage*) сдавáть (сдаю́, сдаёшь) *impf.*, сдать (сдам, сдашь, сдаст, сдади́м; сдал, -á, -о) *pf.* на хранéние. **storehouse** *n.* склад, амбáр, храни́лище. **storeroom** кладовáя. *sb.*

storey ['stɔːrɪ] *n.* этáж (-á).

stork [stɔːk] *n.* áист.

storm [stɔːm] *n.* бýря, грозá (*pl.* -зы); (*naut.*) шторм; (*mil.*) штурм, при́ступ; (*outburst*) взрыв; *v.t.* (*mil.*) штурмовáть *impf.*; брать (берý, берёшь) *impf.*, взять (возьмý, -мёшь; взял, -á, -о) *pf.* при́ступом; *v.i.* бушевáть (-шýю, -шýешь) *impf.* **stormcloud** *n.* тýча. **stormy** *adj.* бýрный (-рен, бýрнá, -рно), бýйный (бýен, бýйнá, -но).

story ['stɔːrɪ] *n.* расскáз, пóвесть; (*anecdote*) анекдóт; (*plot*) фáбула, сюжéт; (*history, event*) истóрия. **story-teller** *n.* расскáзчик.

stout [staʊt] *adj.* (*solid*) плóтный (-тен, -тнá, -тно, плóтны); (*portly*) дородный; *n.* крéпкий пóртер. **stout-hearted** *adj.* отвáжный. **stoutly** *adv.* (*stubbornly*) упóрно; (*energetically*) энерги́чно; (*strongly*) крéпко. **stoutness** *n.* (*strength*) прóчность; (*portliness*) дородство; (*courage*) отвáга; (*firmness*) стóйкость.

stove [stəʊv] *n.* (*with fire inside*) печь (*loc.* -чи́; *pl.* -чи, -чéй); (*cooker*) плитá (*pl.* -ты).

stow [stəʊ] *v.t.* уклáдывать *impf.*, уложи́ть (-жý, -жишь) *pf.*; ~ **away** (*travel free*) éхать (éду, éдешь) *impf.*, по~ *pf.* зáйцем, без билéта. **stowaway** *n.* зáяц (зáйца), безбилéтный пассажи́р.

straddle ['stræd(ə)l] *v.i.* широкó расставля́ть *impf.*, расстáвить *pf.* нóги; *v.t.* (*sit astride*) сидéть (сижý, сиди́шь) *impf.* верхóм на+*p.*; (*stand astride*) стоя́ть (-ою́, -ои́шь) *impf.*, расстáвив нóги над+*i.*

straggle ['stræg(ə)l] *v.i.* (*drop behind*) отставáть (-стаю́, -стаёшь) *impf.*, отстáть (-áну, -áнешь) *pf.* **straggler** *n.* отстáвший *sb.* **straggling** *adj.* (*scattered*) разбрóсанный; (*untidy*) беспоря́дочный.

straight [streɪt] *adj.* (*unbent*) прямóй (-м, -мá, -мо, прямы́); (*honest*) чéстный (-тен, -тнá, -тно); (*undiluted*) неразбáвленный; *pred.* (*properly arranged*) в поря́дке; *adv.* прямо; ~ **away** срáзу. **straighten** *v.t. & i.* выпрямля́ть(ся) *impf.*, вы́прямить(ся) *pf.*; *v.t.* (*smooth out*) расправля́ть *impf.*, распрáвить *pf.* **straightforward** *adj.* прямо́й (-м, -ма́, -мо, пря́мы́); (*simple*) просто́й (-т, -та́, -то); (*honest*) че́стный (-тен, -тна́, -тно). **straightness** *n.* прямизна́.

strain[1] [streɪn] *n.* (*pull, tension*) натяже́ние; (*also sprain*) растяже́ние; (*phys., tech.*) напряже́ние; (*tendency*) скло́нность; (*sound*) напе́в, звук; **in the same** ~ в том же ду́хе; *v.t.* (*stretch*) натя́гивать *impf.*, натяну́ть (-ну́, -нешь) *pf.*; (*also sprain*) растя́гивать *impf.*, растяну́ть (-ну́, -нешь) *pf.*; (*phys., tech.*) напряга́ть *impf.*, напря́чь (-ягу́, -яжёшь; -яг, -ягла́) *pf.*; (*filter*) процежи́вать *impf.*, процеди́ть (-ежу́, -е́дишь) *pf.*; *v.i.* (*also exert o.s.*) напряга́ться *impf.*, напря́чься (-ягу́сь, -яжёшься; -я́гся, -ягла́сь) *pf.* **strained** *adj.* натя́нутый (*also fig.*); растя́нутый (*also sprained*). **strainer** *n.* (*tea* ~) си́течко; (*filter*) фильтр; (*sieve*) си́то.

strain[2] [streɪn] *n.* (*breed*) поро́да; (*hereditary trait*) насле́дственная черта́.

strait(s) [streɪt] *n.* (*geog.*) проли́в. **straiten** *v.t.* ограни́чивать *impf.*, ограни́чить *pf.* **straitened** *adj.*: **in** ~ **circumstances** в стеснённых обстоя́тельствах. **strait-jacket** *n.* смири́тельная руба́шка. **strait-laced** *adj.* пурита́нский. **straits** *n.* (*difficulties*) затрудни́тельное положе́ние.

strand[1] [strænd] *n.* (*hair, rope*) прядь; (*rope, cable*) стре́нга; (*thread, also fig.*) нить.

strand[2] [strænd] *n.* (*of sea etc.*) бе́рег (*loc.* -у́; *pl.* -а́); *v.t.* сажа́ть *impf.*, посади́ть (-ажу́, -а́дишь) *pf.* на мель. **stranded** *adj.* (*fig.*) без средств.

strange [streɪndʒ] *adj.* стра́нный (-нен, -нна́, -нно); (*unfamiliar*) незнако́мый; (*alien*) чужо́й. **strangely** *adv.* стра́нно. **strangeness** *n.* стра́нность. **stranger** *n.* незнако́мец (-мца), -о́мка; неизве́стный *sb.*; чужо́й *sb.*

strangle [ˈstræŋg(ə)l] *v.t.* души́ть (-шу́, -шишь) *impf.*, за- *pf.* **stranglehold** *n.* мёртвая хва́тка. **strangulate** *v.t.* сжима́ть *impf.*, сжать (сожму́, -мёшь) *pf.* **strangu'lation** *n.* (*strangling*) удуше́ние; (*strangulating*) зажима́ние.

strap [stræp] *n.* реме́нь (-мня́) *m.*; *v.t.* (*tie up*) стя́гивать *impf.*, стяну́ть (-ну́, -нешь) *pf.* ремнём. **strapping** *adj.* ро́слый.

stratagem [ˈstrætədʒəm] *n.* стратаге́ма, хи́трость. **strategic** [strəˈtiːdʒɪk] *adj.* стратеги́ческий. **strategist** *n.* страте́г. **strategy** *n.* страте́гия.

stratification [ˌstrætɪfɪˈkeɪʃ(ə)n] *n.* рассло́ение. **stratified** [ˈstrætɪfaɪd] *adj.* сло́истый. '**stratosphere** *n.* стратосфе́ра. **stratum** [ˈstrɑːtəm, ˈstreɪ-] *n.* слой (*pl.* -ои́), пласт (-а́, *loc.* -у́).

straw [strɔː] *n.* соло́ма; (*drinking*) соло́минка; **the last** ~ после́дняя ка́пля; *adj.* соло́менный.

strawberry [ˈstrɔːbərɪ] *n.* клубни́ка; (*wild* ~) земляни́ка *collect.*; *adj.* клубни́чный; земляни́чный.

stray [streɪ] *v.i.* сбива́ться *impf.*, сби́ться (собью́сь, -ьёшься) *pf.*; (*roam*) блужда́ть *impf.*; (*digress*) отклоня́ться *impf.*, отклони́ться (-ню́сь, -ни́шься) *pf.*; *adj.* (*lost*) заблуди́вшийся; (*homeless*) бездо́мный; *n.* (*waif*) беспризо́рный *sb.*; (*from flock*) отби́вшееся от ста́да живо́тное *sb.*; ~ **bullet** шальна́я пу́ля.

streak [striːk] *n.* полоса́ (*a.* по́лосу́; *pl.* -о́сы, -о́с, -оса́м) (**of luck** везе́ния); (*tendency*) жи́лка; (*lightening*) вспы́шка; *v.t.* испещря́ть *impf.*, испещри́ть *pf.*; *v.i.* (*rush*) проноси́ться (-ошу́сь, -о́сишься) *impf.*, пронести́сь (-есу́сь, -есёшься; -ёсся, -есла́сь) *pf.* **streaked** *adj.* с полоса́ми, с прожи́лками (**with** +*g.*). **streaky** *adj.* полоса́тый; (*meat*) с просло́йками жи́ра.

stream [striːm] *n.* (*brook, tears*) руче́й (-чья́); (*brook, flood, tears, people etc.*) пото́к; (*jet*) струя́ (*pl.* -у́и); (*current*) тече́ние; **up/down** ~ вверх/вниз по тече́нию; **with/against the** ~ по тече́нию, про́тив тече́ния; *v.i.* течь (течёт, теку́т; тёк, текла́) *impf.*; стру́иться (-и́тся) *impf.*; (*rush*) проноси́ться (-ошусь, -о́сишься) *impf.*, пронести́сь (-есу́сь, -есёшься; -ёсся, -есла́сь) *pf.*; (*blow*) развева́ться (-а́ется) *impf.* **streamer** *n.* вы́мпел. **stream-lined** *adj.* обтека́емый; (*fig.*) хорошо́ нала́женный.

street [striːt] *n.* у́лица; *adj.* у́личный; ~ **lamp** у́личный фона́рь (-ря́) *m.*

strength [streŋθ, streŋkθ] *n.* си́ла, кре́пость; (*numbers*) чи́сленность; **in full** ~ в по́лном соста́ве; **on the** ~ **of** в си́лу+*g.* **strengthen** *v.t.* уси́ливать *impf.*, уси́лить *pf.*; укрепля́ть *impf.*, укрепи́ть *pf.* **strengthening** *n.* усиле́ние, укрепле́ние.

strenuous [ˈstrenjʊəs] *adj.* тре́бующий уси́лий, энерги́чный.

stress [stres] *n.* (*pressure, fig.*) давле́ние; (*tech.*) напряже́ние; (*emphasis*) ударе́ние; *v.t.* де́лать *impf.*, с~ *pf.* ударе́ние на+*a.*; подчёркивать *impf.* подчеркну́ть *pf.*

stretch [stretʃ] *n.* (*expanse*) протяже́ние, простра́нство; **at a** ~ (*in succession*) подря́д; *v.t. & i.* (*widen, spread out*) растя́гивать(ся) *impf.*, растяну́ть(ся) (-ну́(сь), -нешь(ся)) *pf.*; (*in length,* ~ **out limbs**) вытя́гивать(ся) *impf.*, вы́тянуть(ся) *pf.*; (*tauten, e.g. bow*) натя́гивать(ся) *impf.*, натяну́ть(ся) (-ну́(сь), -нешь(ся)) *pf.*; (*extend, e.g. rope,* ~ **forth limbs**) протя́гивать(ся) *impf.*, протяну́ть(ся) (-ну́(сь), -нешь(ся)) *pf.*; *v.i.* (*material, land*) тяну́ться (-нется) *impf.*; *v.t.* (*exaggerate*) преувели́чивать *impf.*, преувели́чить *pf.*; ~ **a point** допуска́ть *impf.*, допусти́ть (-ущу́, -у́стишь) *pf.* натя́жку; ~ **o.s.** потя́гиваться *impf.*, потяну́ться (-ну́сь, -нешься) *pf.*; ~ **one's legs** (*coll.*) размина́ть *impf.*, размя́ть (разомну́, -нёшь) *pf.* но́ги. **stretcher** *n.* носи́лки (-лок) *pl.*

strew [struː] *v.t.* разбра́сывать *impf.*, разброса́ть *pf.*; ~ **with** посыпа́ть *impf.*, посыпа́ть

(-плю, -плешь) *pf.*+*i.*; усыпа́ть *impf.*, усы́-
пать (-плю, -плешь) *pf.*+*i.*

stricken ['strɪkən] *adj.* поражённый (-ён, -ена́),
охва́ченный (-ен).

strict [strɪkt] *adj.* стро́гий (-г, -га́, -го); (*precise*) то́чный (-чен, -чна́, -чно). **strictly** *adv.*
стро́го, то́чно. **strictness** *n.* стро́гость, то́ч-
ность. **stricture(s)** *n.* (стро́гая) кри́тика,
осужде́ние.

stride [straɪd] *n.* (большо́й) шаг (-а́ with 2,3,4,
loc. -у́; *pl.* -и́); *pl.* (*fig.*) успе́хи *m.pl.*; **to get
into one's ~** принима́ться *impf.*, приня́ться
(приму́сь, -мешься; -ня́лся, -няла́сь) *pf.* за
де́ло; **to take sth. in one's ~** преодолева́ть
impf., преодоле́ть *pf.* что-л. без уси́лий; *v.i.*
шага́ть *impf.* (больши́ми шага́ми).

stridency ['straɪd(ə)nsɪ] *n.* ре́зкость. **strident**
adj. ре́зкий (-зок, -зка́, -зко).

strife [straɪf] *n.* (*conflict*) борьба́; (*discord*)
раздо́р.

strike [straɪk] *n.* (*refusal to work*) забасто́вка,
ста́чка; (*discovery*) откры́тие; (*blow*) уда́р;
adj. забасто́вочный; *v.i.* (be on ~) басто-
ва́ть *impf.*; (go on ~) забастова́ть *pf.*; объя-
вля́ть *impf.*, объяви́ть (-влю́ -вишь) *pf.*
забасто́вку; (*clock*) бить (бьёт) *impf.*, про~
pf.; *v.t.* (*hit*) ударя́ть *impf.*, уда́рить *pf.*;
(*mil., surprise*) поража́ть *impf.*, порази́ть
pf.; (*discover*) открыва́ть *impf.*, откры́ть
(-ро́ю, -ро́ешь) *pf.*; (*match*) зажига́ть *impf.*,
заже́чь (-жгу́, -жжёшь, -жгут; -жёг, -жгла́)
pf.; (*clock*) бить (бьёт) *impf.*, про~ *pf.*; (occur to) приходи́ть (-ит) *impf.*, прийти́ (придёт; пришёл, -шла́) *pf.* в го́лову+*d.*; **~ off**
выче́ркивать *impf.*, вы́черкнуть *pf.*; **~ up**
начина́ть *impf.*, нача́ть (-чну́, -чнёшь; на́-
чал, -а́, -о) *pf.*; **~ upon** напада́ть *impf.*,
напа́сть (-аду́, -адёшь; -а́л) *pf.* на+*a.* **strike-
breaker** *n.* штрейкбре́хер. **striker** *n.* забас-
то́вщик, -ица. **striking** *adj.* порази́тельный;
~ distance досяга́емость.

string [strɪŋ] *n.* бечёвка, верёвка, завя́зка;
(*mus.*) струна́ (*pl.* -ны); (*series*) верени́ца,
ряд (-а́ with 2,3,4, *loc.* -у́; *pl.* -ы́); (*beads*)
ни́тка; *pl.* (*instruments*) стру́нные инстру-
ме́нты *m.pl.*; **second ~** запасно́й ресу́рс;
pull ~s нажима́ть *impf.*, нажа́ть (нажму́,
-мёшь) *pf.* на та́йные пружи́ны; **without ~s
attached** без каки́х-либо усло́вий; *adj.*
стру́нный; *v.t.* (*tie up*) завя́зывать *impf.*,
завяза́ть (-яжу́, -я́жешь) *pf.*; (*thread*) низа́ть
(нижу́, -жешь) *impf.*, на~ *pf.*; (*beans*) чи́с-
тить *impf.*, о~ *pf.*; **~ along** (*coll.*) (*deceive*)
обма́нывать *impf.*, обману́ть (-ну́, -нешь)
pf.; **~ out** (*prolong*) растя́гивать *impf.*,
растяну́ть (-ну́, -нешь) *pf.*; **strung up** (*tense*)
напряжённый; **~ bag** аво́ська; **~ vest**
се́тка. **stringed** *adj.* стру́нный. **stringy** *adj.*
(*fibrous*) волокни́стый; (*meat*) жи́листый.

stringency ['strɪndʒ(ə)nsɪ] *n.* стро́гость. **strin-
gent** *adj.* стро́гий (-г, -га́, -го).

strip¹ [strɪp] *n.* полоса́ (*a.* по́лосу; *pl.* -осы,
-о́с, -оса́м), поло́ска, ле́нта; **~ cartoon** рас-

ска́з в рису́нках; **~ light** ла́мпа дневно́го
све́та.

strip² [strɪp] *v.t.* (*undress*) раздева́ть *impf.*,
разде́ть (-е́ну, -е́нешь) *pf.*; (*deprive*) лиша́ть
impf., лиши́ть *pf.* (**of** +*g.*); (*lay bare*)
обнажа́ть *impf.*, обнажи́ть *pf.*; **~ off** (*tear
off*) сдира́ть *impf.*, содра́ть (сдеру́, -рёшь;
-а́л, -ала́, -а́ло) *pf.*; *v.i.* раздева́ться *impf.*, раз-
де́ться (-е́нусь, -е́нешься) *pf.* **strip-tease** *n.*
стрипти́з.

stripe [straɪp] *n.* полоса́ (*a.* по́лосу; *pl.* -осы,
-о́с, -оса́м). **striped** *adj.* полоса́тый.

stripling ['strɪplɪŋ] *n.* подро́сток (-тка), юно-
ша *m.*

strive [straɪv] *v.i.* (*endeavour*) стара́ться *impf.*,
по~ *pf.*; стреми́ться *impf.* (**for** к+*d.*);
(*struggle*) боро́ться (-рю́сь, -решься) *impf.*
(**for** за+*a.*; **against** про́тив+*g.*).

stroke [strəʊk] *n.* (*blow, med.*) уда́р; (*of oar*)
взмах; (*oarsman*) загребно́й *sb.*; (*drawing*)
штрих (-а́); (*clock*) бой (*pl.* бой); (*piston*)
ход (*pl.* -ы, -о́в); (*swimming*) стиль *m.*; *v.t.*
гла́дить *impf.*, по~ *pf.*

stroll [strəʊl] *n.* прогу́лка; *v.i.* прогу́ливаться
impf., прогуля́ться *pf.*

strong [strɒŋ] *adj.* (*also able; gram.*) си́льный
(си́лён, -льна́, -льно, си́льны́); (*also drinks*)
кре́пкий (-пок, -пка́, -пко); (*healthy*) здоро́-
вый; (*opinion etc.*) твёрдый (-д, -да́, -до).
stronghold *n.* кре́пость; (*fig.*) опло́т. **strong-
minded, strong-willed** *adj.* реши́тельный.
strong-room ко́мната-сейф.

strop [strɒp] *n.* реме́нь (-мня́) *m.* (для пра́вки
бритв); *v.t.* пра́вить *impf.* бри́тву.

structural ['strʌktʃər(ə)l] *adj.* структу́рный;
(*building*) конструкти́вный, строи́тельный.
structure *n.* (*composition, arrangement*)
структу́ра; (*system*) строй, устро́йство;
(*building*) сооруже́ние.

struggle ['strʌg(ə)l] *n.* борьба́; *v.i.* боро́ться
(-рю́сь, -решься) *impf.* (**for** за+*a.*; **against**
про́тив+*g.*); (*writhe*, **~ with** (*fig.*)) би́ться
(бьюсь, бьёшься) (**with** над+*i.*).

strum [strʌm] *v.i.* бренча́ть (-чу́, -чи́шь) *impf.*
(**on** на+*p.*).

strut¹ [strʌt] *n.* (*vertical*) подпо́ра, сто́йка;
(*horizontal*) распо́рка; (*angle brace*) подко́с.

strut² [strʌt] *v.i.* ходи́ть (хожу́, хо́дишь)
indet., идти́ (иду́, идёшь; шёл, шла) *det.*
го́голем.

stub [stʌb] *n.* (*stump*) пень (пня) *m.*; (*pencil*)
огры́зок (-зка); (*cigarette*) окуро́к (-рка);
(*counterfoil*) корешо́к (-шка́); *v.t.*: **~ one's
toe** ударя́ться *impf.*, уда́риться *pf.* ного́й
(**on** на+*a.*); **~ out** (*cigarette*) гаси́ть (гашу́,
га́сишь) *impf.*, по~ *pf.* (сигаре́ту).

stubble ['stʌb(ə)l] *n.* стерня́, жнивьё; (*hair*)
щети́на.

stubborn ['stʌbən] *adj.* упря́мый, упо́рный.
stubbornness *n.* упря́мство, упо́рство.

stucco ['stʌkəʊ] *n.* штукату́рка; *adj.* штука-
ту́рный.

stuck-up [stʌ'kʌp] *adj.* (*coll.*) наду́тый.

stud[1] [stʌd] *n.* (*press-button*) кно́пка; (*collar, cuff*) за́понка; (*large-headed nail*) гвоздь (-дя́; *pl.* -ди, -де́й) *m.* с большо́й шля́пкой; *v.t.* (*set with* ~*s*) обива́ть *impf.*, оби́ть (обью́, -ьёшь) *pf.* гвоздя́ми; (*bestrew*) усе́ивать *impf.*, усе́ять (-е́ю, -е́ешь) *pf.* (with +*i.*).

stud[2] [stʌd] *n.* (*horses*) ко́нный заво́д. **stud-horse** *n.* племенно́й жеребе́ц (-бца́).

student ['stjuːd(ə)nt] *n.* студе́нт, ~ка.

studied ['stʌdɪd] *adj.* обду́манный (-ан, -анна).

studio ['stjuːdɪəʊ] *n.* (*artist's, broadcasting, cinema*) студия; (*artist's*) ателье́ *nt.indecl.*, мастерска́я *sb.*

studious ['stjuːdɪəs] *adj.* (*diligent*) приле́жный; (*liking study*) любя́щий нау́ку.

study ['stʌdɪ] *n.* изуче́ние, иссле́дование; *pl.* заня́тия *nt.pl.*; (*essay*) о́черк; (*art*) эски́з, этю́д; (*mus.*) этю́д; (*room*) кабине́т; *v.t.* изуча́ть *impf.*, изучи́ть (-чу́, -чишь) *pf.*; учи́ться (учу́сь, у́чишься) *impf.*, об~ *pf.+d.*; занима́ться *impf.*, заня́ться (займу́сь, -мёшься; заня́лся, -яла́сь) *pf.+i.*; (*research*) иссле́довать *impf. & pf.*; (*scrutinize*) рассма́тривать *impf.*, рассмотре́ть (-рю́, -ришь) *pf.*; *v.i.* учи́ться (учу́сь, у́чишься) *impf.*, об~ *pf.*

stuff [stʌf] *n.* (*material*) материа́л, (*substance*) вещество́; ((*woollen*) *fabric*) шерстяна́я мате́рия; ~ **and nonsense** вздор; *v.t.* набива́ть *impf.*, наби́ть (набью́, -ьёшь) *pf.*; (*cul.*) начиня́ть *impf.*, начини́ть *pf.*; (*cram into*) запи́хивать *impf.*, запиха́ть *pf.* (into в+*a.*); (*thrust, shove into*) сова́ть (сую́, суёшь) *impf.*, су́нуть *pf.* (into в+*a.*); *v.i.* (*overeat*) объеда́ться *impf.*, объе́сться (-е́мся, -е́шься, -е́стся, -еди́мся, -е́лся) *pf.* **stuffiness** *n.* духота́, спёртость. **stuffing** *n.* наби́вка; (*cul.*) начи́нка. **stuffy** *adj.* спёртый, ду́шный (-шен, -шна́, -шно).

stumble ['stʌmb(ə)l] *v.i.* (*also fig.*) спотыка́ться *impf.*, споткну́ться *pf.* (over о+*a.*); ~ **upon** натыка́ться *impf.*, наткну́ться *pf.* на+*a.* **stumbling-block** *n.* ка́мень (-мня; *pl.* -мни, -мне́й) *m.* преткнове́ния.

stump [stʌmp] *n.* (*tree*) пень (пня) *m.*; (*pencil*) огры́зок (-зка); (*limb*) обру́бок (-бка) культя́; *v.t.* (*perplex*) ста́вить *impf.*, по~ *pf.* в тупи́к; *v.i.* (*coll.*) ковыля́ть *impf.*

stun [stʌn] *v.t.* (*also fig.*) оглуша́ть *impf.*, оглуши́ть *pf.*; (*also fig.*) ошеломля́ть *impf.*, ошеломи́ть *pf.* **stunning** *adj.* (*also fig.*) ошеломи́тельный; (*fig.*) сногсшиба́тельный (*coll.*)

stunt[1] [stʌnt] *n.* трюк; ~ **man** каскадёр, трюка́ч (-а́).

stunt[2] [stʌnt] *v.t.* заде́рживать *impf.*, задержа́ть (-жу́, -жишь) *pf.* рост+*g.* **stunted** *adj.* ча́хлый, низкоро́слый.

stupefaction [ˌstjuːpɪˈfækʃ(ə)n] *n.* ошеломле́ние. **stupefy** ['stjuːpɪˌfaɪ] *v.t.* ошеломля́ть *impf.*, ошеломи́ть *pf.* **stupendous** *adj.* изуми́тельный; (*huge*) грома́дный. 'stupid *adj.* (*foolish*) глу́пый (глуп, -па́, -по), дура́цкий (*coll.*); (*dull-witted*) тупо́й (туп, -а́, -о,

ту́пы). **stu'pidity** *n.* глу́пость, ту́пость. 'stupor *n.* оцепене́ние; (*med.*) сту́пор.

sturdy ['stɜːdɪ] *adj.* (*robust*) кре́пкий (-пок, -пка́, -пко), здоро́вый (-в, -ва́); (*solid, firm*) твёрдый (-д, -да́, -до).

sturgeon ['stɜːdʒ(ə)n] *n.* осётр (-а́); (*dish*) осетри́на.

stutter ['stʌtə(r)] *n.* заика́ние; *v.i.* заика́ться *impf.* **stutterer** *n.* зайка *c.g.*

sty[1] [staɪ] *n.* (*pig*~) свина́рник.

sty[2] [staɪ] *n.* (*on eye*) ячме́нь (-ня́) *m.*

style [staɪl] *n.* стиль *m.*; (*manner*) мане́ра; (*taste*) вкус; (*fashion*) мо́да; (*sort*) род (*pl.* -ы́); **in** (**grand**) ~ с ши́ком; *v.t.* констру́ировать *impf. & pf.* по мо́де. **stylish** *adj.* мо́дный (-ден, -дна́, -дно), шика́рный. **stylist** *n.* стили́ст. **sty'listic** *adj.* стилисти́ческий. **sty'listics** *n.* стили́стика. **stylize** *v.t.* стилизова́ть *impf. & pf.*

stylus ['staɪləs] *n.* (*грамофо́нная*) иго́лка.

suave [swɑːv] *adj.* обходи́тельный. **suavity** *n.* обходи́тельность.

subaltern ['sʌbəlt(ə)n] *n.* (*mil.*) мла́дший офице́р. **subcommittee** *n.* подкоми́ссия, подкомите́т. **subconscious** *adj.* подсозна́тельный; *n.* подсозна́ние. **subcutaneous** [ˌsʌbkjuːˈteɪnɪəs] *adj.* подко́жный. **subdivide** *v.t.* подразделя́ть *impf.*, подраздели́ть *pf.* **subdivision** *n.* подразделе́ние. **subdue** *v.t.* покоря́ть *impf.*, покори́ть *pf.* **subdued** *adj.* (*suppressed, dispirited*) подавленный; (*soft*) мя́гкий (-гок, -гка́, -гко); (*indistinct*) приглушённый. **sub-editor** *n.* помо́щник, -ица реда́ктора. **sub-heading** *n.* подзаголо́вок (-вка). **subhuman** *adj.* не дости́гший челове́ческого у́ровня.

subject ['sʌbdʒɪkt] *n.* (*theme*) те́ма, сюже́т; (*discipline, theme*) предме́т; (*question*) вопро́с; (*logic, philos., bearer of certain characteristic*) субъе́кт; (*thing on to which action is directed*) объе́кт; (*gram.*) подлежа́щее *sb.*; (*national*) по́дданный *sb.*; *adj.* (*subordinate*) подчинённый (-ён, -ена́) (**to** +*d.*); (*dependent*) подвла́стный (**to** +*d.*); ~ **to** (*susceptible to*) подве́рженный+*d.*; (*on condition that*) при усло́вии, что...; е́сли; ~ **to his agreeing** е́сли он согласи́тся, при усло́вии, что он согласи́тся; е́сли он согласи́тся; **be** ~ **to** (*change etc.*) подлежа́ть (-жи́т) *impf.+d.*; *v.t.*: ~ **to** подчиня́ть *impf.*, подчини́ть *pf.+d.*; подверга́ть *impf.*, подве́ргнуть (подве́рг, -ла) *pf.+d.* **subjection** [səbˈdʒekʃ(ə)n] *n.* подчине́ние. **sub'jective** *adj.* субъекти́вный. **subjectivity** [ˌsʌbdʒekˈtɪvɪtɪ] *n.* субъекти́вность. **subject-matter** *n.* (*book, lecture*) содержа́ние, те́ма; (*discussion*) предме́т.

sub judice [sʌb ˈdʒuːdɪsɪ, sʊb ˈjuːdɪkeɪ] *adj.* на рассмотре́нии суда́.

subjugate ['sʌbdʒʊˌɡeɪt] *v.t.* покоря́ть *impf.*, покори́ть *pf.* **subju'gation** *n.* покоре́ние.

subjunctive (**mood**) [səbˈdʒʌŋktɪv] *n.* сослага́тельное наклоне́ние.

sublet ['sʌblet] *v.t.* передава́ть (-даю́, -даёшь)

impf., переда́ть (-а́м, -ашь, -а́ст, -ади́м; пе́редал, -а́, -о) *pf.* в субаре́нду.

sublimate ['sʌblɪˌmeɪt] *v.t. (chem., psych.)* сублими́ровать; *(fig.)* возвыша́ть *impf.*, возвы́сить *pf.* **subli'mation** *n. (chem., psych.)* сублима́ция; *(fig.)* возвыше́ние. **sublime** [sə'blaɪm] *adj.* возвы́шенный.

subliminal [səb'lɪmɪn(ə)l] *adj.* подсозна́тельный. **sub-machine-gun** *n.* пистоле́т-пулеме́т, автома́т. **submarine** *adj.* подво́дный; *n.* подво́дная ло́дка. **submerge** *v.t.* погружа́ть *impf.*, погрузи́ть *pf.*; затопля́ть *impf.*, затопи́ть (-плю́, -пишь) *pf.* **submission** *n.* подчине́ние; *(for inspection)* представле́ние. **submissive** *adj.* поко́рный. **submit** *v.i.* подчиня́ться *impf.*, подчини́ться *pf.* (to +*d.*); покоря́ться *impf.*, покори́ться *pf.* (to +*d.*); *v.t.* представля́ть *impf.*, предста́вить *pf.* (на рассмотре́ние). **subordinate** [sə'bɔːdɪnət; sə'bɔːdɪˌneɪt] *n.* подчинённый *sb.; adj.* подчинённый (-ён, -ена́); *(secondary)* второстепе́нный; *(gram.)* прида́точный; *v.t.* подчиня́ть *impf.*, подчини́ть *pf.* **subordi'nation** *n.* подчине́ние. **suborn** [sə'bɔːn] *v.t.* подкупа́ть *impf.*, подкупи́ть (-плю́, -пишь) *pf.* **subpoena** [səb'piːnə, sə'piːnə] *n.* вы́зов, пове́стка в суд; *v.t.* вызыва́ть *impf.*, вы́звать (-зову, -зовешь) *pf.* в суд. **subscribe** *v.i.* подпи́сываться *impf.*, подписа́ться (-ищу́сь, -и́шешься) *pf.* (to на+*a.*); ~ to *(opinion)* присоединя́ться *impf.*, присоедини́ться *pf.* к+*d.* **subscriber** *n. (to newspaper etc.)* подпи́счик -ица; абоне́нт, ~ка. **subscription** *n. (to newspaper etc.)* подпи́ска, абонеме́нт; *(fee)* взнос. **subsection** *n.* подразде́л. **subsequent** ['sʌbsɪkwənt] *adj.* после́дующий. **subsequently** *adv.* впосле́дствии. **subservience** [səb'sɜːvɪəns] *n.* раболе́пие, раболе́пство. **subservient** *adj.* раболе́пный. **subside** [səb'saɪd] *v.i. (water)* убыва́ть *impf.*, убы́ть (убу́ду, -дешь; у́был, -а́, -о) *pf.*; *(calm down, abate)* укла́дываться *impf.*, уле́чься (уля́жется, уля́гутся; улёгся, улегла́сь) *pf.*; *(soil)* оседа́ть *impf.*, осе́сть (ося́дет; осе́л) *pf.*; *(collapse)* обва́ливаться *impf.*, обвали́ться (-ится) *pf.* **subsidence** [səb'saɪd(ə)ns, 'sʌbsɪd(ə)ns] *n. (abatement)* спад; *(soil)* оседа́ние. **subsidiary** [səb'sɪdɪərɪ] *adj.* вспомога́тельный; *(secondary)* второстепе́нный. **subsidize** ['sʌbsɪˌdaɪz] *v.t.* субсиди́ровать *impf.* & *pf.* **subsidy** *n.* субси́дия, дота́ция. **subsist** [səb'sɪst] *v.i. (exist)* существова́ть *impf.*; *(live)* жить (живу́, -вёшь; жил, -а́, -о) *impf.* (on +*i.*). **subsistence** *n.* существова́ние; *(livelihood)* пропита́ние. **subsoil** *n.* подпо́чва. **subsonic** *adj.* дозвуково́й. **substance** ['sʌbst(ə)ns] *n.* вещество́; *(essence)* су́щность, суть; *(content)* содержа́ние. **substantial** [səb'stænʃ(ə)l] *adj. (durable)* про́чный (-чен, -чна́, -чно, про́чны́); *(considerable)* значи́тельный; *(food)* пло́тный (-тен, -тна́, -тно, плотны́); *(real)* реа́льный; *(material)* веще́ственный. **sub'stan**-

tially *adv. (basically)* в основно́м; *(considerably)* в значи́тельной сте́пени. **sub'stantiate** *v.t.* приводи́ть (-ожу́, -о́дишь) *impf.*, привести́ (-еду́, -едёшь; -ёл, -ела́) *pf.* доста́точные основа́ния+*g.* **sub'stantive** *n. (имя nt.)* существи́тельное. **'substitute** *n. (person)* замести́тель *m.*, ~ница; *(thing)* заме́на; *(tech.)* замени́тель *m.; v.t.* замени́ть *impf.*, замени́ть (-ню, -нишь) *pf.*+*i.* (for +*a.*); I ~ water for milk заменя́ю молоко́ водо́й. **substi'tution** *n.* заме́на, замеще́ние. **substructure** *n.* фунда́мент. **subsume** [səb'sjuːm] *v.t.* относи́ть (-ошу́, -о́сишь) *impf.*, отнести́ (-су́, -сёшь; ёс, -есла́) *pf.* к како́й-л. катего́рии. **subtenant** *n.* субаренда́тор. **subterfuge** ['sʌbtəˌfjuːdʒ] *n.* уве́ртка, отгово́рка, уло́вка. **subterranean** [ˌsʌbtə'reɪnɪən] *adj.* подзе́мный. **subtitle** *n.* подзаголо́вок (-вка); *(cin.)* субти́тр.

subtle ['sʌt(ə)l] *adj. (fine, delicate)* то́нкий (-нок, -нка́, -нко); *(mysterious)* таи́нственный (-ен, -енна); *(ingenious)* иску́сный; *(cunning)* хи́трый (-тёр, -тра́, хи́тро́). **subtlety** *n. (fineness, delicacy)* то́нкость; *(mystery)* таи́нственность; *(ingenuity)* иску́сность; *(cunning)* хи́трость. **subtract** [səb'trækt] *v.t.* вычита́ть *impf.*, вы́честь (-чту, -чтешь; -чел, -чла) *pf.* **subtraction** *n.* вычита́ние. **suburb** ['sʌbɜːb] *n.* при́город. **suburban** [sə'bɜːbən] *adj.* при́городный. **sub'version** *n. (overthrow)* сверже́ние; *(subversive activities)* подрывна́я де́ятельность. **sub'versive** *adj.* подрывно́й. **sub'vert** *v.t.* сверга́ть *impf.*, све́ргнуть (-г(нул), -гла) *pf.* **subway** *n.* тонне́ль *m.*; *(pedestrian ~)* подзе́мный перехо́д.

succeed [sək'siːd] *v.i.* удава́ться (удаётся) *impf.*, уда́ться (уда́стся, удаду́тся; уда́лся, -ла́сь) *pf.*; the plan will ~ план уда́стся; he ~ed in buying the book ему́ удало́сь купи́ть кни́гу; *(be successful)* преуспева́ть *impf.*, преуспе́ть *pf.* (in в+*p.*); *(follow)* сменя́ть *impf.*, смени́ть (-ню, -нишь) *pf.*; *(be heir)* насле́довать *impf.* & *pf.* (to +*d.*). **succeeding** *adj.* после́дующий. **success** [sək'ses] *n.* успе́х, уда́ча. **successful** *adj.* успе́шный, уда́чный. **succession** *n.* прее́мственность; *(sequence)* последова́тельность; *(series)* (непреры́вная) цепь *(loc.* -пи́; *pl.* -пи, -пе́й); *(to throne)* престолонасле́дие; right of ~ пра́во насле́дования; in ~ подря́д, оди́н за други́м. **successive** *adj. (consecutive)* после́довательный. **successor** *n.* насле́дник, -ица; прее́мник, -ица.

succinct [sək'sɪŋkt] *adj.* сжа́тый. **succour** ['sʌkə(r)] *n.* по́мощь; *v.t.* приходи́ть (-ожу́, -о́дишь) *impf.*, прийти́ (приду́, -дёшь; пришёл, -шла́) *pf.* на по́мощь+*g.* **succulent** ['sʌkjʊlənt] *adj.* со́чный (-чен, -чна́, -чно). **succumb** [sə'kʌm] *v.i.* уступа́ть *impf.*, уступи́ть (-плю́, -пишь) *pf.* (to +*d.*); поддава́ться (-даю́сь, -даёшься) *impf.*, подда́ться (-а́мся,

-áшься, -áстся, -адúмся; -áлся, -алáсь) pf. (to +d.).

such [sʌtʃ] adj. такóй, подóбный; ~ **people** такúе лю́ди; **in** ~ **cases** в такúх, в подóбных, слу́чаях; **in** ~ **a way** такúм óбразом, так; ~ **as** (for example) так напримéр; (of ~ a kind as) такóй как; ~ **beauty as yours** такáя красотá как вáша; (that which) тот (та, то, те), котóрый; **I shall read** ~ **books as I like** я бу́ду читáть те кнúги, котóрые мне нрáвятся; ~ **as to such** adj. такóй, чтóбы; **his illness was not** ~ **as to cause anxiety** егó болéзнь былá не такóй (серьёзной), чтóбы вы́звать беспокóйство; pron. такóв (-á, -ó, -ы́); тот (та, то, те), такóй; ~ **was his character** такóв был егó харáктер; ~ **as are of my opinion** те, кто соглáсен со мной; **as** ~ сам по себé, как таковóй, по существу́; ~ **is not the case** э́то не так. **such-and-such** adj. такóй-то. **suchlike** adj. подóбный, такóй; pron. (inanimate) тому́ подóбное; (people) такúе лю́ди (-дéй, -дям, -дьми́) pl.

suck [sʌk] v.t. сосáть (сосу́, сосёшь) impf.; ~ **in** всáсывать impf., всосáть (-су́, -сёшь) pf.; (engulf) засáсывать impf., засосáть (-су́, -сёшь) pf.; ~ **out** высáсывать impf., вы́сосать (-су, -сешь) pf.; ~ **up to** (coll.) подлúзываться impf., подлизáться (-ижу́сь, -úжешься) pf. к+d. **sucker** n. (biol., rubber device) присóска; (bot.) корневóй óтпрыск.

suckle v.t. кормúть (-млю́, -мишь) impf., на~ pf. гру́дью. **suckling** n. груднóй ребёнок (-нка) (pl. дéти, -тéй), сосу́н (-á). **suction** n. сосáние, всáсывание.

sudden ['sʌd(ə)n] adj. внезáпный, неожúданный (-ан, -анна); ~ **death** скоропостúжная смерть. **suddenly** adv. внезáпно, вдруг, неожúданно. **suddenness** n. внезáпность, неожúданность.

suds [sʌdz] n. мы́льная пéна.

sue [suː, sjuː] v.t. преслéдовать impf. судéбным поря́дком; возбуждáть impf., возбудúть pf. дéло прóтив+g. (for o+p.); ~ **s.o. for damages** предъявля́ть impf., предъявúть (-влю́, -вишь) pf. (к) кому́-л. иск о возмещéнии ущéрба.

suede [sweid] n. зáмша; adj. зáмшевый.

suet ['suːit, 'sjuːit] n. пóчечное сáло.

suffer ['sʌfə(r)] v.t. страдáть impf., по~ pf. +i., от+g.; (experience) испы́тывать impf., испытáть pf.; (loss, defeat) терпéть (-плю́, -пишь) impf., по~ pf.; (allow) позволя́ть impf., позвóлить pf. +d.; дозволя́ть impf., дозвóлить pf. +d.; (tolerate) терпéть (-плю́, -пишь) impf.; v.i. страдáть impf., по~ pf. (from +i., от+g.). **sufferance** n. (tacit consent) молчалúвое соглáсие; **he is here on** ~ егó здесь тéрпят. **suffering** n. страдáние.

suffice [sə'fais] v.i. &t. быть достáточным (для+g.); хватáть (-áет) impf., хватúть (-ит) pf. impers. +g. (+d.); **five pounds will** ~ **me** мне хвáтит пятú фу́нтов. **sufficiency** [sə'fi-

ʃənsi] n. (adequacy) достáточность; (prosperity) достáток (-тка). **sufficient** adj. достáточный.

suffix ['sʌfiks] n. су́ффикс.

suffocate ['sʌfəkeit] v.t. удушáть impf., удушúть (-шу́, -шишь) pf.; v.i. задыхáться impf., задохну́ться (-óх(ну́л)ся, -óх(ну́)лась) pf. **suffocating** adj. ду́шный (-шен, -шнá, -шно), уду́шливый. **suffo'cation** n. удушéние; (difficulty in breathing) уду́шье.

suffrage ['sʌfridʒ] n. (right) избирáтельное прáво.

suffuse [sə'fjuːz] v.t. (light, tears) заливáть impf., залúть (-лью́, -льёшь; зáлил, -á, зáлило) pf. (with +i.); (colour) покрывáть impf., покры́ть (-рóю, -рóешь) pf. (with +i.). **suffusion** n. покры́тие; (colour) крáска; (flush) румя́нец (-нца).

sugar ['ʃʊgə(r)] n. сáхар (-a(y)); adj. сáхарный; v.t. подслáщивать impf., подсластúть pf.; ~ **basin** сáхарница; ~ **beet** сáхарная свёкла; ~ **cane** сáхарный трóстник; ~ **refinery** (сáхаро)рафинáдный завóд. **sugary** adj. сáхарный; (sweet) слáдкий (-док, -дкá, -дко); (saccharine) сахарúстый; (sickly sweet) притóрный, слащáвый.

suggest [sə'dʒest] v.t. (propose) предлагáть impf., предложúть (-жу́, -жишь) pf.; (advise) совéтовать impf., по~ pf.; (call up) внушáть impf., внушúть pf.; ~ **itself to** приходúть (-ит) impf., прийтú (придёт; пришёл, -шлá) pf. кому́-л. в гóлову; **a solution** ~ **itself to me** мне пришлó в гóлову решéние. **suggestible** adj. поддаю́щийся внушéнию. **suggesti'bility** n. внушáемость. **suggestion** n. (proposal) предложéние; (psych.) внушéние. **suggestive** adj. вызывáющий мы́сли (of o+p.); (slightly indecent) соблазнúтельный.

suicidal [ˌsuːi'said(ə)l, ˌsjuː-] adj. самоубúйственный; (fig.) губúтельный. **'suicide** n. самоубúйство; (person) самоубúйца c.g.; (fig.) крах по сóбственной винé; **commit** ~ совершáть impf., совершúть pf. самоубúйство; покóнчить pf. с собóй (coll.).

suit [suːt, sjuːt] n. (clothing) костю́м; (request) прóсьба; (cards) масть; **follow** ~ (cards) ходúть (хожу́, хóдишь) impf. в масть; (fig.) слéдовать impf., по~ pf. примéру; **in one's birthday** ~ в чём мать родилá; v.t. (be convenient for) устрáивать impf., устрóить pf.; (accommodate) приспосáбливать impf., приспосóбить pf.; (be ~able for, match) подходúть (-ожу́, -óдишь) impf., подойтú (-йду́, -йдёшь; подошёл, -шлá) pf. (+d.); (look attractive on) идтú (идёт; шёл, шлá) impf.+d.; ~ **o.s.** выбирáть impf., вы́брать (-беру, -берешь) pf. по вку́су. **suita'bility** n. пригóдность. **suitable** adj. (fitting) подходя́щий; (convenient) удóбный. **suitably** adv. соотвéтственно. **suitcase** n. чемодáн.

suite [swiːt] n. (retinue) свúта; (furniture) гарниту́р; (*rooms*) апарта́менты *m.pl.*; (*mus.*) сюи́та.

suitor ['suːtə(r), 'sjuː-] *n.* (*admirer*) покло́нник; (*plaintiff*) исте́ц (истца́); (*petitioner*) проси́тель *m.*, -ница.

sulk [sʌlk] *v.i.* ду́ться *impf.* **sulkiness** *n.* скве́рное настрое́ние. **sulky** *adj.* наду́тый, хму́рый (-р, -ра́, -ро).

sullen ['sʌlən] *adj.* угрю́мый, хму́рый (-р, -ра́, -ро). **sullenness** *n.* угрю́мость.

sully ['sʌlɪ] *v.t.* пятна́ть *impf.*, за~ *pf.*

sulphur *n.* се́ра. **sul'phuric** *adj.* се́рный; ~ **acid** се́рная кислота́.

sultan ['sʌlt(ə)n] *n.* (*sovereign*) султа́н.

sultana [sʌl'tɑːnə] *n.* (*raisin*) изю́мина без семя́н; *pl.* кишми́ш (-йша́) (*collect.*).

sultriness ['sʌltrɪnɪs] *n.* зной, духота́. **sultry** *adj.* зно́йный; ду́шный (-шен, -шна́, -шно); (*passionate*) стра́стный.

sum [sʌm] *n.* су́мма; (*arithmetical problem*) арифмети́ческая зада́ча; *pl.* арифме́тика; *v.t.* (*add up*) скла́дывать *impf.*, сложи́ть (-жу́, -жишь) *pf.*; ~ **up** (*summarize*) сумми́ровать *impf.* & *pf.*; резюми́ровать *impf.* & *pf.*; (*appraise*) оце́нивать *impf.*, оцени́ть (-ню́, -нишь) *pf.* **summing-up** *n.* (*leg.*) заключи́тельная речь (*pl.* -чи, -че́й) судьи́.

summarize ['sʌməraɪz] *v.t.* сумми́ровать *impf.* & *pf.*; резюми́ровать *impf.* & *pf.* **summary** *n.* резюме́ *nt.indecl.*, конспе́кт, сво́дка; *adj.* сумма́рный, ско́рый (-р, -ра́, -ро).

summer ['sʌmə(r)] *n.* ле́то (*pl.* -та́); **Indian** ~ ба́бье ле́то (*pl.* -та́); *attr.* ле́тний; *v.i.* проводи́ть (-ожу́, -о́дишь) *impf.*, провести́ (-еду́, -едёшь; провёл, -а́) *pf.* ле́то (*pl.* -та́). **summer-house** *n.* бесе́дка. **summery** *adj.* ле́тний.

summit ['sʌmɪt] *n.* верши́на, верх (-а(у), *loc.* -у́; *pl.* -и́ & -а́); (*fig.*) зени́т, преде́л; ~ **meeting** совеща́ние на вы́сшем у́ровне.

summon ['sʌmən] *v.t.* вызыва́ть *impf.*, вы́звать (-зову, -зовешь) *pf.*; (*call*) призыва́ть *impf.*, призва́ть (-зову, -зовёшь; призва́л, -а́, -о) *pf.*; ~ **up one's courage** собира́ться *impf.*, собра́ться (-беру́сь, -берёшься; -бра́лся, -брала́сь, -брало́сь) *pf.* с ду́хом. **summons** *n.* вы́зов; (*leg.*) пове́стка в суд; *v.t.* вызыва́ть *impf.*, вы́звать (-зову, -зовешь) *pf.* в суд.

sumptuous ['sʌmptjʊəs] *adj.* роско́шный.

sun [sʌn] *n.* со́лнце; **in the** ~ на со́лнце. **sun-bathe** *v.i.* гре́ться *impf.* на со́лнце, загора́ть *impf.* **sunbeam** *n.* со́лнечный луч (-а́). **sunburn** *n.* зага́р; (*inflammation*) со́лнечный ожо́г. **sunburnt** *adj.* загоре́лый; **become** ~ загора́ть *impf.*, загоре́ть (-рю, -ри́шь) *pf.*

Sunday ['sʌndeɪ, -dɪ] *n.* воскресе́нье; *adj.* воскре́сный.

sundial ['sʌndaɪəl] *n.* со́лнечные часы́ *m.pl.*

sundry ['sʌndrɪ] *adj.* ра́зный; **all and** ~ все вме́сте и ка́ждый в отде́льности.

sunflower ['sʌn,flaʊə(r)] *n.* подсо́лнечник; ~ **seeds** се́мечки *nt.pl.* **sun-glasses** *n.* защи́т-

ные очки́ (-ко́в) *pl.* от со́лнца.

sunken ['sʌŋkən] *adj.* (*hollow*) впа́лый; (*submerged*) погружённый; (*ship*) зато́пленный; (*below certain level*) ни́же (како́го-л. у́ровня).

sunlight ['sʌnlaɪt] *n.* со́лнечный свет. **sunny** *adj.* со́лнечный. **sunrise** *n.* восхо́д со́лнца. **sunset** *n.* захо́д со́лнца, зака́т. **sunshade** *n.* (*parasol*) зо́нтик; (*awning*) наве́с. **sunshine** *n.* со́лнечный свет. **sunstroke** *n.* со́лнечный уда́р. **suntan** *n.* зага́р. **sun-tanned** *adj.* загоре́лый.

superannuated [,suːpər'ænjʊ,eɪtɪd, ,sjuː-] *adj.* (*pensioner*) вы́шедший на пе́нсию; (*obsolete*) устаре́лый. **superb** [suː'pɜːb, sjuː-] *adj.* великоле́пный, превосхо́дный. **supercilious** [,suːpə'sɪlɪəs, ,sjuː-] *adj.* надме́нный (-нен, -нна), презри́тельный. **superficial** [,suːpə'fɪʃ(ə)l, ,sjuː-] *adj.* пове́рхностный; (*outward*) вне́шний. **superfici'ality** *n.* пове́рхностность. **superfluity** [,suːpə'fluːɪtɪ, ,sjuː-] *n.* (*surplus*) изли́шек (-шка); (*abundance*) оби́лие. **superfluous** [suː'pɜːflʊəs, sjuː-] *adj.* ли́шний, нену́жный; (*abundant*) оби́льный. **superhuman** *adj.* сверхчелове́ческий. **superimpose** *v.t.* накла́дывать *impf.*, наложи́ть (-жу́, -жишь) *pf.* **superintend** *v.t.* заве́довать *impf.*+*i.*; (*supervise*) надзира́ть *impf.* за+*i.* **superintendent** *n.* заве́дующий *sb.* (**of** +*i.*), надзира́тель *m.*, ~ница (**of** +*i.*); (*police*) ста́рший полице́йский офице́р. **superior** [suː'pɪərɪə(r), sjuː-, su-] *n.* нача́льник, -ица; ста́рший *sb.*; (*relig.*) настоя́тель *m.*, ~ница; *adj.* (*better*) лу́чший, превосхо́дящий; (*higher*) вы́сший, ста́рший; (*of better quality*) вы́сшего ка́чества; (*haughty*) высокоме́рный. **superi'ority** *n.* превосхо́дство. **superlative** [suː'pɜːlətɪv, sjuː-] *adj.* превосхо́дный; *n.* (*gram.*) превосхо́дная сте́пень. **superman** *n.* сверхчелове́к. **supermarket** *n.* универса́м. **supernatural** *adj.* сверхъесте́ственный (-ен, -енна). **supernumerary** *adj.* сверхшта́тный. **superpower** *n.* одна́ из наибо́лее мо́щных вели́ких держа́в. **supersede** [,suːpə'siːd, ,sjuː-] *v.t.* заменя́ть *impf.*, замени́ть (-ню́, -нишь) *pf.* **supersonic** *adj.* сверхзвуково́й. **superstition** [,suːpə'stɪʃ(ə)n, ,sjuː-] *n.* суеве́рие. **superstitious** *adj.* суеве́рный. **superstructure** *n.* надстро́йка. **supervene** [,suːpə'viːn, ,sjuː-] *v.i.* сле́довать *impf.*, по~ *pf.* **supervise** ['suːpə,vaɪz, 'sjuː-] *v.t.* наблюда́ть *impf.* за+*i.*, надзира́ть *impf.* за+*i.* **super'vision** *n.* надзо́р, наблюде́ние. **supervisor** *n.* надзира́тель *m.*, ~ница; надсмо́трщик, -ица; (*of studies*) нау́чный руководи́тель *m.*

supine ['suːpaɪn, 'sjuː-] *adj.* (*lying on back*) лежа́щий на́взничь; (*indolent*) лени́вый.

supper ['sʌpə(r)] *n.* у́жин; **have** ~ у́жинать *impf.*, по~ *pf.*; **the Last S~** Та́йная ве́черя.

supplant [sə'plɑːnt] *v.t.* вытесня́ть *impf.*, вы́теснить *pf.*

supple ['sʌp(ə)l] *adj.* ги́бкий (-бок, -бка́, -бко).

suppleness *n.* ги́бкость.

supplement ['sʌplɪmənt] *n.* (*to book*) дополне́ние; (*to periodical*) приложе́ние; *v.t.* дополня́ть *impf.*, дополни́ть *pf.* **supplementary** [ˌsʌplɪ'mentərɪ] *adj.* дополни́тельный.

suppliant ['sʌplɪənt] *n.* проси́тель *m.*, ~ница.

supplier [sə'plaɪə(r)] *n.* поставщи́к (-а́) (*animate & inanimate*). **supply** *n.* снабже́ние, поста́вка; (*stock*) запа́с; (*econ.*) предложе́ние; *pl.* припа́сы (-ов) *pl.*, (*provisions*) продово́льствие; ~ **and demand** спрос и предложе́ние; ~ **line** путь (-ти́, -тём) *m.* подво́за; *v.t.* снабжа́ть *impf.*, снабди́ть *pf.* (**with** +*i.*); поставля́ть *impf.*, поста́вить *pf.*

support [sə'pɔ:t] *n.* подде́ржка, опо́ра; *v.t.* подде́рживать *impf.*, поддержа́ть (-жу́, -жишь) *pf.*; (*family*) содержа́ть (-жу́, -жишь) *impf.* **supporter** [sə'pɔ:tə(r)] *n.* сторо́нник, -ица. **supporting** *adj.* (*tech.*) опо́рный; ~ **actor** исполни́тель *m.*, ~ница второстепе́нной ро́ли.

suppose [sə'pəʊz] *v.t.* (*think*) полага́ть *impf.*; (*presuppose*) предполага́ть *impf.*, предположи́ть (-жу́, -жишь) *pf.*; (*assume*) допуска́ть *impf.*, допусти́ть (-ущу́, -у́стишь) *pf.* **supposed** *adj.* (*pretended*) мни́мый. **supposition** [ˌsʌpə'zɪʃ(ə)n] *n.* предположе́ние. **suppo'sitious** *adj.* предположи́тельный.

suppress [sə'pres] *v.t.* (*uprising, feelings*) подавля́ть *impf.*, подави́ть (-влю́, -вишь) *pf.*; (*laughter, tears*) сде́рживать *impf.*, сдержа́ть (-жу́, -жишь) *pf.*; (*forbid*) запреща́ть *impf.*, запрети́ть (-ещу́, -ети́шь) *pf.* **suppression** *n.* (*prohibition*) запреще́ние.

supremacy [suː'preməsɪ, sjuː-] *n.* госпо́дство, главе́нство. **supreme** [suː'priːm, sjuː-] *adj.* верхо́вный, вы́сший; (*greatest*) велича́йший; **S~ Soviet (of the USSR)** Верхо́вный Сове́т (СССР); **S~ Court** Верхо́вный суд (-а́).

surcharge ['sɜːtʃɑːdʒ] *n.* припла́та, допла́та.

sure [ʃʊə(r), ʃɔː(r)] *adj.* (*convinced*) уве́ренный (-ен, -ена) (**of** в+*p.*; **that** что); (*unerring*) уве́ренный (-ен, -енна); (*certain, reliable*) ве́рный (-рен, -рна́, -рно, ве́рны́); (*steady*) твёрдый (твёрд, -а́, -о); ~ **enough** действи́тельно, на са́мом де́ле; **he is** ~ **to come** он обяза́тельно придёт; **make** ~ **of** (*convince o.s.*) убежда́ться *impf.*, убеди́ться (-ди́шься) *pf.* в+*p.*; (*secure*) обеспе́чивать *impf.*, обеспе́чить *pf.*; **make** ~ **that** (*check up*) проверя́ть *impf.*, прове́рить *pf.* что; **for** ~, **surely** *adv.* наверняка́, наве́рное. **surety** *n.* пору́ка; поручи́тель *m.*, ~ница; **stand** ~ **for** руча́ться *impf.*, поручи́ться (-чу́сь, -чишься) *pf.* за+*a.*

surf [sɜːf] *n.* прибо́й; *v.i.* занима́ться *impf.*, заня́ться (займу́сь, -мёшься; заня́лся́, -ла́сь) *pf.* сёрфингом.

surface ['sɜːfɪs] *n.* пове́рхность; (*exterior*) вне́шность; **on the** ~ (*fig.*) вне́шне; **under the** ~ (*fig.*) по существу́; *adj.* пове́рх-

ностный; (*exterior*) вне́шний; (*ground*) назе́мный; *v.i.* всплыва́ть *impf.*, всплыть (-ыву́, -ывёшь; всплыл, -а́, -о) *pf.*

surfeit ['sɜːfɪt] *n.* (*excess*) изли́шество; (*surplus*) изли́шек (-шка); **be** ~**ed** пресыща́ться *impf.*, пресы́титься (-ы́щусь, -ы́тишься) *pf.* (**with** +*i.*).

surge [sɜːdʒ] *n.* прили́в, (*больша́я*) волна́ (*pl.* -ы, волна́м); *v.i.* (*be agitated, choppy*) волнова́ться *impf.*, вз~ *pf.*; (*rise, heave*) вздыма́ться *impf.*; (*rush, gush*) хлы́нуть *pf.*; ~ **forward** ри́нуться *pf.* вперёд.

surgeon ['sɜːdʒ(ə)n] *n.* хиру́рг; (*mil.*) вое́нный врач (-а́). **surgery** *n.* (*treatment*) хирурги́я; (*place*) кабине́т, приёмная *sb.*, (*врача́*); (~ *hours*) приёмные часы́ *m.pl.* (врача́). **surgical** *adj.* хирурги́ческий.

surly ['sɜːlɪ] *adj.* (*morose*) угрю́мый; (*rude*) гру́бый (груб, -а́, -о).

surmise [sə'maɪz] *n.* предположе́ние, дога́дка; *v.t. & i.* предполага́ть *impf.*, предположи́ть (-жу́, -жишь) *pf.*; *v.i.* дога́дываться *impf.*, догада́ться *pf.*

surmount [sə'maʊnt] *v.t.* преодолева́ть *impf.*, преодоле́ть *pf.*

surname ['sɜːneɪm] *n.* фами́лия.

surpass [sə'pɑːs] *v.t.* превосходи́ть (-ожу́, -о́дишь) *impf.*, превзойти́ (-ойду́, -ойдёшь; -ошёл, -ошла́) *pf.*

surplus ['sɜːpləs] *n.* изли́шек (-шка), избы́ток (-тка); *adj.* изли́шний (-шен, -шня), избы́точный.

surprise [sə'praɪz] *n.* удивле́ние, неожи́данность, сюрпри́з; **by** ~ враспло́х; **to my** ~ к моему́ удивле́нию; ~ **attack** внеза́пное нападе́ние; *v.t.* удивля́ть *impf.*, удиви́ть *pf.*; (*come upon suddenly*) застава́ть (-таю́, -таёшь) *impf.*, заста́ть (-а́ну, -а́нешь) *pf.* враспло́х; **be** ~**d** (*at*) удивля́ться *impf.*, удиви́ться *pf.* (+*d.*). **surprising** *adj.* удиви́тельный, неожи́данный (-ан, -анна).

surreal [sə'rɪəl] *adj.* сюрреалисти́ческий. **surrealism** *n.* сюрреали́зм. **surrealist** *n.* сюрреали́ст; *adj.* сюрреалисти́ческий.

surrender [sə'rendə(r)] *n.* сда́ча; (*renunciation*) отка́з; *v.t.* сдава́ть (сдаю́, сдаёшь) *impf.*, сдать (сдам, сдашь, сдаст, сдади́м; сдал, -а́, -о) *pf.* (*renounce*) отка́зываться *impf.*, отказа́ться (-ажу́сь, -а́жешься) *pf.* от+*g.*; *v.i.* сдава́ться (сдаю́сь, сдаёшься) *impf.*, сда́ться (сда́мся, сда́шься, сда́стся, сдади́мся; сда́лся, -ла́сь) *pf.*; ~ **o.s. to** предава́ться (-даю́сь, -даёшься) *impf.*, преда́ться (-да́мся, -да́шься, -да́стся, -дади́мся; -да́лся, -ла́сь) *pf.*+*d.*

surreptitious [ˌsʌrəp'tɪʃəs] *adj.* та́йный, сде́ланный тайко́м. **surreptitiously** *adv.* та́йно, тайко́м, исподти́шка (*coll.*).

surrogate ['sʌrəgət] *n.* (*person*) замести́тель *m.*, ~ница; (*thing*) замени́тель *m.*, суррога́т.

surround [sə'raʊnd] *n.* (*frame*) обрамле́ние; (*edge, selvage*) кро́мка; *v.t.* окружа́ть *impf.*, окружи́ть *pf.* (**with** +*i.*); обступа́ть *impf.*, обступи́ть (-пит) *pf.*; ~ with (*enclose*) обноси́ть (-ошу́, -о́сишь) *impf.*, обнести́ (-есу́, -есёшь; -ёс, -есла́) *pf.+i.* **surrounding** *adj.* окружа́ющий, окре́стный. **surroundings** *n.* (*environs*) окре́стности *f.pl.*; (*milieu*) среда́, окруже́ние; (*locality*) ме́стность.

surveillance [sɜː'veɪləns] *n.* надзо́р, наблюде́ние.

survey ['sɜːveɪ] *n.* обозре́ние, осмо́тр, обзо́р; (*investigation*) обсле́дование; (*geol.*) изыска́ние; (*topog.*) межева́ние; *v.t.* обозрева́ть *impf.*, обозре́ть (-рю́, -ри́шь) *pf.*; осма́тривать *impf.*, осмотре́ть (-рю́, -ришь) *pf.*; (*investigate*) обсле́довать *impf. & pf.*; (*topography*) межева́ть (-жу́ю, -жу́ешь) *impf.* **surveyor** [sə'veɪə(r)] *n.* землеме́р.

survival [sə'vaɪv(ə)l] *n.* (*surviving*) выжива́ние; (*relic*) пережи́ток (-тка). **survive** *v.t.* пережива́ть *impf.*, пережи́ть (-иву́, -ивёшь) *pf.*; *v.i.* выжива́ть *impf.*, вы́жить (-иву, -ивешь) *pf.*; остава́ться (-аю́сь, -аёшься) *impf.*, оста́ться (-а́нусь, -а́нешься) *pf.* в живы́х. **survivor** *n.* оста́вшийся *sb.* в живы́х.

susceptibility [sə‚septɪ'bɪlɪtɪ] *n.* восприи́мчивость; (*sensitivity*) чувстви́тельность. **su'sceptible** *adj.* восприи́мчивый (**to** к+*d.*); (*sensitive*) чувстви́тельный (**to** к+*d.*); (*impressionable*) впечатли́тельный.

suspect ['sʌspekt; sə'spekt] *n.* подозрева́емый *sb.*; *adj.* подозри́тельный; *v.t.* подозрева́ть *impf.* (**of** в+*p.*); (*mistrust*) не доверя́ть *impf.+d.*; (*foresee*) предчу́вствовать *impf.*; (*have reason to believe*) полага́ть *impf.* (**that** что).

suspend [sə'spend] *v.t.* (*hang up*) подве́шивать *impf.*, подве́сить *pf.*; (*call a halt to*) приостана́вливать *impf.*, приостанови́ть (-влю́, -вишь) *pf.*; (*repeal temporarily*) вре́менно отменя́ть *impf.*, отмени́ть (-ню́, -нишь) *pf.*; (*dismiss temporarily*) вре́менно отстраня́ть *impf.*, отстрани́ть *pf.*; ~ed sentence усло́вный пригово́р. **suspender** *n.* (*stocking*) подвя́зка. **suspense** *n.* (*uncertainty*) неизве́стность, неопределённость; (*anxiety*) беспоко́йство; **keep in** ~ держа́ть (-жу́, -жишь) *impf.* в напряжённом ожида́нии. **suspension** *n.* (*halt*) приостано́вка; (*temporary repeal*) вре́менная отме́на; (*temporary dismissal*) вре́менное отстране́ние; (*hanging up*) подве́шивание; (*tech.*) подве́с; ~ **bridge** вися́чий мост (мо́ста́, *loc.* -у́; *pl.* -ы́).

suspicion [sə'spɪʃ(ə)n] *n.* подозре́ние; **on** ~ по подозре́нию (**of** в+*loc.*); (*trace*) отте́нок (-нка). **suspicious** *adj.* подозри́тельный.

sustain [sə'steɪn] *v.t.* (*support*) подде́рживать *impf.*, поддержа́ть (-жу́, -жишь) *pf.*; (*stand up to*) выде́рживать *impf.*, вы́держать (-жу, -жишь) *pf.*; (*suffer*) потерпе́ть (-плю́, -пишь) *pf.* **sustained** *adj.* (*uninterrupted*) непреры́вный. **sustenance** ['sʌstɪnəns] *n.* пи́ща, пита́ние.

swab [swɒb] *n.* шва́бра; (*med.*) тампо́н; (*smear, specimen*) мазо́к (-зка́); *v.t.* мыть (мо́ю, мо́ешь) *impf.*, вы́~, по~ *pf.* шва́брой; ~ **the decks** (*naut.*) дра́ить (-а́ю, -а́ишь) *impf.*, на~ *pf.* па́лубы.

swaddle ['swɒd(ə)l] *v.t.* пелена́ть *impf.*, за~, с~ *pf.* **swaddling-clothes** *n.* пелёнки (*g.* -нок) *pl.*

swagger ['swægə(r)] *v.i.* (*walk with* ~) расха́живать *impf.* с ва́жным ви́дом; (*put on airs*) ва́жничать *impf.*

swallow¹ ['swɒləu] *n.* глото́к (-тка́); *v.t.* глота́ть *impf.*, глотну́ть *pf.*; прогла́тывать *impf.*, проглоти́ть (-очу́, -о́тишь) *pf.*; ~ **up** поглоща́ть *impf.*, поглоти́ть (-ощу́, -о́тишь) *pf.*

swallow² ['swɒləu] *n.* (*bird*) ла́сточка.

swamp [swɒmp] *n.* боло́та, топь *v.t.* залива́ть *impf.*, зали́ть (-лью́, -льёшь; за́ли́л, -á, -о) *pf.*; ~ **with** (*letters etc.*) засыпа́ть *impf.*, засы́пать (-плю, -плешь) *pf.+i.* **swampy** *adj.* боло́тистый, то́пкий (-пок, -пка́, -пко).

swan [swɒn] *n.* ле́бедь (*pl.* -ди, -де́й) *m.*

swank [swæŋk] *v.i.* хва́статься *impf.*, по~ *pf.* (**about** +*i.*); (*coll.*) бахва́литься *impf.* (**about** +*i.*).

swansong ['swɒnsɒŋ] *n.* лебеди́ная песнь.

swap [swɒp] *n.* обме́н; *v.t.* меня́ть *impf.*, об~, по~ *pf.*; обме́нивать *impf.*, обменя́ть *pf.*; обме́ниваться *impf.*, обменя́ться *pf.+i.*

swarm [swɔːm] *n.* рой (ро́я, *loc.* рою́; *pl.* рои́, роёв; (*crowd*) толпа́ (*pl.* -пы); *v.i.* рои́ться (-и́тся) *impf.*; толпи́ться (-и́тся) *impf.*; кише́ть (-ши́т) *impf.* (**with** +*i.*).

swarthy ['swɔːðɪ] *adj.* сму́глый (-л, -ла́, -ло).

swastika ['swɒstɪkə] *n.* сва́стика.

swat [swɒt] *v.t.* прихло́пнуть *pf.*; убива́ть *impf.*, уби́ть (убью́, -ьёшь) *pf.*

swathe [sweɪð] *n.* (*bandage*) бинт (-á); (*puttee*) обмо́тка; *v.t.* (*bandage*) бинтова́ть *impf.*, за~ *pf.*; (*wrap up*) заку́тывать *impf.*, заку́тать *pf.*

sway [sweɪ] *n.* колеба́ние, кача́ние; (*influence*) влия́ние; (*power*) власть *v.t. & i.* колеба́ть(ся) (-блю(сь), -блешь(ся)) *impf.*, по~ *pf.*; кача́ть(ся) *impf.*, качну́ть(ся) *pf.*; *v.t.* (*influence*) име́ть влия́ние на+*a.*

swear [sweə(r)] *v.i.* (*vow*) кля́сться (кляну́сь, -нёшься; кля́лся, -ла́сь) *impf.*, по~ *pf.*; (*curse*) руга́ться *impf.*, ругну́ться *pf.*; *v.t.*: ~ **in** приводи́ть (-ожу́, -о́дишь) *impf.* привести́ (-еду́, -едёшь; -ёл, -ела́) *pf.* к прися́ге. **swear-word** *n.* руга́тельство, бра́нное сло́во (*pl.* -ва́).

sweat [swet] *n.* пот (*loc.* -у́; *pl.* -ы́); (*perspiration*) испа́рина; *v.i.* поте́ть *impf.*, вс~ *pf.* **sweater** *n.* сви́тер. **sweatshirt** *n.* футбо́лка. **sweaty** *adj.* по́тный (-тен, -тна́, -тно).

Swede [swiːd] *n.* швед, ~дка.

swede [swiːd] *n.* брю́ква.

Sweden ['swiːdən] *n.* Шве́ция. **Swedish** *adj.* шве́дский.

sweep [swiːp] *n.* вымета́ние; (*span*) рахма́х;

(*scope*) охва́т; (*chimney-~*) трубочи́ст; *v.t.* мести́ (мету́, -тёшь; мёл, -а́) *impf.*; подмета́ть *impf.*, подмести́ (-ету́, -етёшь; подмёл, -ела́) *pf.*; (*mil.*) обстре́ливать *impf.*, обстреля́ть *pf.*; (*naut.*) (*drag*) тра́лить *impf.*, про~ *pf.*; *v.i.* (*go majestically*) ходи́ть (хожу́, хо́дишь) *indet.*, идти́ (иду́, идёшь; шёл, шла) *det.*, пойти́ (пойду́, -дёшь; пошёл, -шла́) *pf.* велича́во; (*move swiftly*) мча́ться (мчусь, мчи́шься) *impf.*; ~ **away** смета́ть *impf.*, смести́ (смету́, -тёшь; смёл, -а́) *pf.* **sweeping** *n.* подмета́ние; (*naut.*) тра́ление. *adj.* широ́кий (-к, -ка́, -о́ко) (*wholesale*) огу́льный. **sweepstake** *n.* тотализа́тор.

sweet [swiːt] *n.* (*sweetmeat*) конфе́та; (*dessert*) сла́дкое *sb.*; *adj.* сла́дкий (-док, -дка́, -дко) (*fragrant*) души́стый; (*dear*) ми́лый (мил, -а́, -о, ми́лы). **sweetbread** *n.* (*cul.*) сла́дкое мя́со. **sweeten** *v.t.* подсла́щивать *impf.*, подсласти́ть *pf.* **sweetheart** *n.* возлю́бленный, -нная. *sb.* **sweetness** *n.* сла́дость. **sweet'pea** *n.* души́стый горо́шек (-шка(у)) (*collect.*).

swell [swel] *v.i.* (*up*) опуха́ть *impf.*, опу́хнуть (-x) *pf.*; пу́хнуть (-x) *impf.*, вс~, о~ *pf.*; распуха́ть *impf.*, распу́хнуть (-x) *pf.*; (*a sail*) надува́ться *impf.*, наду́ться (-ýется) *pf.*; (*a bud*) набуха́ть *impf.*, набу́хнуть (-нет; -x) *pf.*; (*increase*) увели́чиваться *impf.*, увели́читься *pf.*; (*sound*) нараста́ть *impf.*, нарасти́ (-тёт; наро́с, -ла́) *pf.*; *v.t.* (*a sail*) надува́ть *impf.*, наду́ть (-у́ю, -у́ешь) *pf.*; (*increase*) увели́чивать *impf.*, увели́чить *pf.*; *n.* вы́пуклость; (*naut.*) мёртвая зыбь (*pl.* -би, -бе́й). **swelling** *n.* о́пухоль; (*bud*) набуха́ние; (*increase*) увеличе́ние.

swelter ['sweltə(r)] *v.i.* томи́ться *impf.*, ис~ *pf.* от жары́. **sweltering** *adj.* зно́йный.

swerve [swɜːv] *v.i.* отклоня́ться *impf.*, отклони́ться (-ню́сь, -ни́шься) *pf.*; (*sudden*) ре́зко свора́чивать *impf.*, свороти́ть (-очу́, -о́тишь) *pf.*, сверну́ть *pf.*, в сто́рону.

swift [swift] *n.* стриж (-а́); *adj.* бы́стрый (быстр, -а́, -о, бы́стры). **swiftness** *n.* быстрота́.

swig [swig] *n.* глото́к (-тка́); *v.t.* потя́гивать *impf.* (*coll.*).

swill [swil] *n.* по́йло; *v.t.* (*rinse*) полоска́ть (-ощу́, -о́щешь) *impf.*, вы~ *pf.*; (*sluice*) обли́ва́ть *impf.*, обли́ть (оболью́, -льёшь; о́бли́л, облила́, о́бли́ло) *pf.*

swim [swim] *v.i.* пла́вать *indet.*, плыть (плыву́, -вёшь; плыл, -а́, -о) *det.*; (*head*) кру́жи́ться (кру́жи́тся) *impf.*; *v.t.* (*across*) переплыва́ть *impf.*, переплы́ть (-ыву́, -ыве́шь; переплы́л, -а́, -о) *pf.*+*a.*, че́рез+*a.*; *n.*: **in the ~** в ку́рсе де́ла. **swimmer** *n.* пловец (-вца́), пловчи́ха. **swimming** *n.* пла́вание. **swimming-pool** *n.* бассе́йн для пла́вания.

swindle ['swind(ə)l] *v.t.* обма́нывать *impf.*, обману́ть (-ну́, -нешь) *pf.*; (*coll.*) надува́ть *impf.*, наду́ть (-у́ю, -у́ешь) *pf.*; *n.* обма́н; надува́тельство (*coll.*) **swindler** *n.* плут (-а́)

~о́вка; моше́нник, -ица.

swine [swain] *n.* свинья́ (*pl.* -ньи, -не́й). **swineherd** *n.* свинопа́с.

swing [swiŋ] *v.i.* кача́ться *impf.*, качну́ться *pf.*; колеба́ться (-блюсь, -блешься) *impf.*, по~ *pf.*; раска́чиваться *impf.*, раскача́ться *pf.*; *v.t.* кача́ть *impf.*, качну́ть *pf.*+*a.*, *i.*; (*arms*) разма́хивать *impf.*+*i.*; раска́чивать *impf.*, раскача́ть *pf.*, *n.* кача́ние; (*stroke*) мах (-а(у)); (*seat*) каче́ли (-лей) *pl.*; **in full ~** в по́лном разга́ре. **swing-bridge** *n.* разводно́й мост (моста́, *loc.* -у́; *pl.* -ы́). **swingdoor** *n.* дверь (*loc.* -ри́; *pl.* -ри, -ре́й, *i.* -рьми́ & -ря́ми) открыва́ющаяся в любу́ю сто́рону.

swingeing ['swindʒin] *adj.* (*huge*) грома́дный; (*forcible*) си́льный (силён, -льна́, -льно, си́льны).

swinish ['swainiʃ] *adj.* сви́нский (*coll.*). **swinishness** *n.* сви́нство (*coll.*).

swipe [swaip] *n.* уда́р сплеча́; *v.t.* ударя́ть *impf.*, уда́рить *pf.* сплеча́.

swirl [swɜːl] *v.i.* кружи́ться (-ужу́сь, -у́жи́шься) *impf.*, верте́ться (-рчусь, -ртишься) *impf.*; *v.t.* кружи́ть (-ужу́, -у́жи́шь) *impf.*; *n.* круже́ние; (*whirlpool*) водоворо́т; (*whirlwind*) вихрь *m.*

swish [swiʃ] *v.i.* (*cut the air*) рассека́ть *impf.*, рассе́чь (-секу́, -сечёшь; -сёк, -ла́) *pf.* во́здух со сви́стом; *v.t.* (*brandish*) разма́хивать *impf.*+*i.*; *v.t.* & *i.* (*rustle*) шелесте́ть (-ти́шь) *impf.* (+*i.*); шурша́ть (-шу́, -ши́шь) *impf.* (+*i.*); *n.* (*of whip*) свист; (*of scythe*) взмах со сви́стом; (*rustle*) ше́лест, шурша́ние.

Swiss [swis] *n.* швейца́рец (-рца), -ца́рка; *adj.* швейца́рский; ~ **roll** руле́т (с варе́ньем).

switch [switʃ] *n.* (*elec.*) выключа́тель *m.*, переключа́тель *m.*; (*rail.*) стре́лка; (*change*) измене́ние; (*twig*) прут (пру́та; *pl.* -тья, -тьев); (*whip*) хлыст (-а́); *v.t.* (*whip*) ударя́ть *impf.*, уда́рить *pf.* пруто́м, хлысто́м; (*elec.*; *fig.*; *also ~ over*) переключа́ть *impf.*, переключи́ть *pf.*; (*wave*) маха́ть (машу́, ма́шешь) *impf.*, махну́ть *pf.*+*i.*; (*change direction*) (*of conversation etc.*) направля́ть *impf.*, напра́вить *pf.* (*разгово́р*) в другу́ю сто́рону; (*rail.*) переводи́ть (-ожу́, -о́дишь) *impf.*, перевести́ (-еду́, -еде́шь; перевёл, -а́) *pf.* (**train** по́езд (*pl.* -а́)) на друго́й путь; ~ **off** выключа́ть *impf.*, вы́ключить *pf.*; ~ **on** включа́ть *impf.*, включи́ть *pf.* **switchback** *n.* америка́нские го́ры *f.pl.* **switchboard** *n.* коммута́тор, распредели́тельный щит (-а́).

Switzerland ['switsər.lænd] *n.* Швейца́рия.

swivel ['swiv(ə)l] *v.t.* & *i.* враща́ть(ся) *impf.*; *n.* вертлю́г; ~ **chair** враща́ющийся стул (*pl.* -ья, -ьев).

swollen ['swəʊlən] *adj.* взду́тый. **swollenheaded** *adj.* чванли́вый.

swoon [swuːn] *n.* о́бморок; *v.i.* па́дать *impf.*, упа́сть (упаду́, -дёшь; упа́л) *pf.* в о́бморок.

swoop [swuːp] *v.i.*: ~ **down** налета́ть *impf.*,

налете́ть (-ечу́, -ети́шь) *pf.* (**on** на+*a.*); *n.* налёт; **at one fell ~** одни́м уда́ром, одни́м ма́хом.

sword [sɔːd] *n.* меч (-á), шпа́га. **sword-fish** *n.* меч-ры́ба. **swordsman** *n.* (иску́сно) владе́ющий *sb.* холо́дным ору́жием; (*fencer*) фехтова́льщик.

sworn [swɔːn] *adj.* (*on oath*) под прися́гой; (*enemy*) закля́тый; (*friend*) закады́чный; (*brother*) назва́ный.

sybaritic [ˌsɪbəˈrɪtɪk] *adj.* сибари́тский.

sycamore [ˈsɪkəˌmɔː(r)] *n.* я́вор.

sycophancy [ˈsɪkəˌfænsɪ] *n.* лесть. **sycophant** *n.* льстец (-á). **syco'phantic** *adj.* льсти́вый.

Sydney [ˈsɪdnɪ] *n.* Сидне́й.

syllabic [sɪˈlæbɪk] *adj.* слоговой; (*liter.*) силлаби́ческий. **syllable** [ˈsɪləb(ə)l] *n.* слог (*pl.* -и, -óв).

syllabus [ˈsɪləbəs] *n.* програ́мма.

symbiosis [ˌsɪmbaɪˈəʊsɪs, ˌsɪmbɪ-] *n.* симбио́з.

symbol [ˈsɪmb(ə)l] *n.* си́мвол, знак. **symbolic(al)** [ˌsɪmˈbɒlɪk(ə)l] *adj.* символи́ческий. **symbolism** *n.* символи́зм. **symbolist** *n.* символи́ст. **symbolize** *v.t.* символизи́ровать *impf.*

symmetrical [sɪˈmetrɪk(ə)l] *adj.* симметри́ческий. **symmetry** [ˈsɪmɪtrɪ] *n.* симметри́я.

sympathetic [ˌsɪmpəˈθetɪk] *adj.* сочу́вственный (-ен, -енна); (*well-disposed*) благожела́тельный; (*physiol.*) симпати́ческий; (*likeable*) симпати́чный. **sympathize** [ˈsɪmpəˌθaɪz] *v.i.* сочу́вствовать *impf.* (**with** +*d.*). 'sympathizer *n.* (*supporter*) сторо́нник, -ица. 'sympathy *n.* сочу́вствие; (*condolence*) соболе́знование; (*favour, liking*) симпа́тия.

symphonic [sɪmˈfɒnɪk] *adj.* симфони́ческий. **symphony** [ˈsɪmfənɪ] *n.* симфо́ния.

symposium [sɪmˈpəʊzɪəm] *n.* симпо́зиум, совеща́ние.

symptom [ˈsɪmptəm] *n.* симпто́м, при́знак. **sympto'matic** *adj.* симтомати́ческий.

synagogue [ˈsɪnəˌɡɒɡ] *n.* синаго́га.

synchronism [ˈsɪŋkrəˌnɪz(ə)m] *n.* синхрони́зм. **synchroni'zation** *n.* синхрониза́ция. **synchronize** *v.t.* синхронизи́ровать *impf. & pf.*; (*cin.*) совмеща́ть *impf.*, совмести́ть *pf.* (**with** с+*i.*).

syncopate [ˈsɪŋkəˌpeɪt] *v.t.* (*mus.*) синкопи́ровать *impf. & pf.* **synco'pation** *n.* синко́па.

syndicate [ˈsɪndɪkət, ˈsɪndɪˌkeɪt] *n.* синдика́т; *v.t.* синдици́ровать *impf. & pf.*

syndrome [ˈsɪndrəʊm] *n.* синдро́м.

synod [ˈsɪnəd] *n.* сино́д, собо́р. **synodal** *adj.* синода́льный.

synonym [ˈsɪnənɪm] *n.* сино́ним. **synonymous** [sɪˈnɒnɪməs] *adj.* синоними́ческий.

synopsis [sɪˈnɒpsɪs] *n.* конспе́кт. **synoptic(al)** *adj.* синопти́ческий.

syntactic(al) [sɪnˈtæktɪkəl] *adj.* синтакси́ческий. 'syntax *n.* си́нтаксис.

synthesis [ˈsɪnθɪsɪs] *n.* си́нтез. **synthesize** *v.t.* синтези́ровать *impf. & pf.* **synthesizer** *n.* синтеза́тор. **synthetic(al)** [sɪnˈθetɪk(əl)] *adj.*

синтети́ческий. **synthetics** *n.* синте́тика.

syphilis [ˈsɪfɪlɪs] *n.* си́филис.

Syria [ˈsɪrɪə] *n.* Си́рия. **Syrian** *n.* сири́ец (-и́йца), сири́йка; *adj.* сири́йский.

syringe [sɪˈrɪndʒ, ˈsɪr-] *n.* шприц, спринцо́вка; *v.t.* спринцева́ть *impf.*

syrup [ˈsɪrəp] *n.* сиро́п, па́тока. **syrupy** *adj.* подо́бный сиро́пу.

system [ˈsɪstəm] *n.* систе́ма; (*order*) строй; (*network*) сеть (*loc.* се́ти́; *pl.* -ти, -те́й); (*organism*) органи́зм. **syste'matic** *adj.* системати́ческий. **systematize** *v.t.* систематизи́ровать *impf. & pf.* **sy'stemic** *adj.* относя́щийся к всему́ органи́зму.

T

T [tiː] *n.*: **to a T** точь-в-то́чь (*coll.*), как раз.

tab [tæb] *n.* (*loop*) пе́телька; (*on uniform*) петли́ца; (*of boot*) ушко́ (*pl.* -ки́, -ко́в); **keep ~s on** следи́ть *impf.* за+*i.*

tabby [ˈtæbɪ] *n.* полоса́тая ко́шка.

tabernacle [ˈtæbəˌnæk(ə)l] *n.* (*Jewish hist.*) ски́ния; (*receptacle*) дарохрани́тельница.

table [ˈteɪb(ə)l] *n.* (*furniture, food*) стол (-á); (*company*) о́бщество за столо́м; (*list*) табли́ца; (*slab*) доска́ (*a.* -ску; *pl.* -ски, -со́к, -ска́м), плита́ (*pl.* -ты); **bedside ~** ту́мбочка; **~ of contents** оглавле́ние; **~ tennis** насто́льный те́ннис; *v.t.* (*for discussion*) предлага́ть *impf.*, предложи́ть (-жу́, -жишь) *pf.* на обсужде́ние.

tableau [ˈtæbləʊ] *n.* жива́я карти́на; (*dramatic situation*) драмати́ческая ситуа́ция.

tablecloth [ˈteɪb(ə)lˌklɒθ] *n.* ска́терть. **tableland** *n.* плоского́рье.

tablespoon *n.* столо́вая ло́жка.

tablet [ˈtæblɪt] *n.* (*medicine*) табле́тка; (*memorial ~*) мемориа́льная доска́; (*a.* -ску; *pl.* -ски, -со́к, -ска́м); (*name plate*) доще́чка; (*notebook*) блокно́т; (*of soap*) кусо́к (-ска́).

tabloid [ˈtæblɔɪd] *n.* малоформа́тная газе́та; (*pej.*) бульва́рная газе́та.

taboo [təˈbuː] *n.* табу́ *nt.indecl.*, запреще́ние; *adj.* (*prohibited*) запрещённый (-ён, -ена́); (*consecrated*) свяще́нный (-ён, -е́нна); *v.t.* налага́ть *impf.*, наложи́ть (-жу́, -жишь) *pf.* табу́ на+*a.*

tabular [ˈtæbjʊlə(r)] *adj.* табли́чный; (*flat*) пло́ский (-сок, -ска́, -ско); (*geol.*) сло́истый, пласти́нчатый. **tabulate** *v.t.* располага́ть *impf.*, расположи́ть (-жу́, -жишь) *pf.* в ви́де табли́ц. **tabulator** *n.* (*on typewriter*) табуля́тор; (*person*) состави́тель *m.* табли́ц.

tacit [ˈtæsɪt] *adj.* (*silent; implied*) молчали́вый;

(*implied*) подразумева́емый. **taciturn** ['tæsɪ‚tɜ:n] *adj.* молчали́вый, неразгово́рчивый.

taci'turnity *n.* молчали́вость, неразгово́рчивость.

tack [tæk] *n.* (*nail*) гво́здик; (*stitch*) намётка; (*naut.*) галс; (*fig.*) курс; *v.t.* (*fasten*) прикрепля́ть *impf.*, прикрепи́ть *pf.* гво́здиками; (*stitch*) смётывать *impf.*, сметáть *pf.* на живу́ю ни́тку; (*fig.*) добавля́ть *impf.*, доба́вить *pf.* ((on)to +*d.*); *v.i.* (*naut.; fig.*) лави́ровать *impf.*

tackle ['tæk(ə)l] *n.* (*requisites*) снасть (*collect.*), принадле́жности *f.pl.*; (*equipment*) обору́дование; (*naut.*) такела́ж; (*block and* ~) тáли (-лей) *pl.*; (*tech.*, ~-*block*) полиспáст; (*sport*) блокиро́вка; *v.t.* (*try to overcome*) пытáться *impf.*, по~ *pf.* преодоле́ть; (*get down to*) брáться (беру́сь, -рёшься) *impf.*, взя́ться (возьму́сь, -мёшься; взя́лся, -лáсь) *pf.* за+*a.*; (*work on*) занимáться *impf.*, заня́ться (займу́сь, -мёшься; заня́лся, -лáсь) *pf.*+*i.*; (*sport*) (*intercept*) перехвáтывать *impf.* перехвати́ть (-ачу́, -áтишь) *pf.*; блоки́ровать *impf.* & *pf.*; (*secure ball from*) отнимáть *impf.*, отня́ть (отниму́, -мешь; о́тнял, -á, -о) *pf.* мяч у+*g.*

tacky ['tækɪ] *adj.* ли́пкий (-пок, -пкá, -пко), кле́йкий.

tact [tækt] *n.* такт(и́чность). **tactful** *adj.* такти́чный.

tactical ['tæktɪk(ə)l] *adj.* такти́ческий; (*artful*) ло́вкий (-вок, -вкá, -вко, ло́вки́). **tactician** [tæk'tɪʃ(ə)n] *n.* тáктик. **tactics** *n.* тáктика.

tactile ['tæktaɪl] *adj.* осязáтельный; (*tangible*) осязáемый.

tactless ['tæktlɪs] *adj.* бестáктный.

tadpole ['tædpəʊl] *n.* головáстик.

Tadzhikistan [‚tædʒɪkɪ'stɑːn] *n.* Таджикистáн.

taffeta ['tæfɪtə] *n.* тафтá; *attr.* тафтяно́й.

tag [tæg] *n.* (*label*) ярлы́к (-á), этике́тка, би́рка; (*of lace*) наконе́чник; (*of boot*) ушко́ (*pl.* -ки́, -ко́в); (*quotation*) изби́тая цитáта; *v.t.* (*label*) прикрепля́ть *impf.*, прикрепи́ть *pf.* ярлы́к на+*a.*; *v.i.*: ~ **along** (*follow*) сле́довать *impf.*, по~ *pf.* по пятáм (**after** за+*i.*); **may I** ~ **along?** мо́жно с вáми?

tail [teɪl] *n.* (*of animal, aircraft, kite, procession, etc.*) хвост; (*of shirt*) ни́жний коне́ц (-нцá); (*of hair; of letter*; (*mus.*) *of note*) хво́стик; (*of coat*) фáлда; (*of coin*) обрáтная сторонá (*a.* -ону) моне́ты; **heads or** ~**s?** орёл и́ли ре́шка?; *pl.* (*coat*) фрак; *v.t.* (*shadow*) выслéживать *impf.*; *v.i.*: ~ **away, off** постепе́нно уменьшáться *impf.*; (*disappear*) исчезáть *impf.*; (*grow silent, abate*) затихáть *impf.* **tailboard** *n.* (*of cart*) откиднáя доскá (*a.* -ску; *pl.* -ски, -со́к, -скáм); (*of lorry*) откидно́й борт (*loc.* -ý; *pl.* -á). **tailcoat** *n.* фрак. **tail-lamp, -light** *n.* зáдний фонáрь (-ря́) *m.*

tailor ['teɪlə(r)] *n.* портно́й *sb.*; *v.t.* шить (шью, шьёшь) *impf.*, сшить (сошью́, сошьёшь) *pf.*; *v.i.* портня́жничать *impf.* (*coll.*). **tailor-**ing *n.* портня́жное де́ло. **tailor-made** *adj.* сши́тый, изгото́вленный на закáз; (*fig.*) приспосо́бленный.

tailpiece ['teɪlpiːs] *n.* (*typography*) концо́вка; (*appendage*) зáдний коне́ц (-нцá).

tailspin ['teɪlspɪn] *n.* што́пор. **tailwind** *n.* попу́тный ве́тер (-тра).

taint [teɪnt] *n.* пятно́ (*pl.* -тна, -тен, -тнам), поро́к; (*trace*) налёт; (*infection*) зарáза; *v.t. & i.* (*spoil*) по́ртить(ся) *impf.*, ис~ *pf.*; (*infect*) заражáть(ся) *impf.*, зарази́ть(ся) *pf.* **tainted** *adj.* испо́рченный (-ен).

Taiwan [ˌtaɪ'wɑːn] *n.* Тайвáнь *m.*

take [teɪk] *v.t.* (*var. senses*) брать (беру́, -рёшь; брал, -á, -о) *impf.*, взять (возьму́, -мёшь; взял, -á, -о) *pf.*; (*also seize, capture*) захвáтывать *impf.*, захвати́ть (-ачу́, -áтишь) *pf.*; (*receive, accept*; ~ *breakfast*; ~ *medicine*; ~ *steps*) принимáть *impf.*, приня́ть (приму́, -мешь; при́нял, -á, -о) *pf.*; (*convey, escort*) провожáть *impf.*, проводи́ть (-ожу́, -о́дишь) *pf.*; (*public transport*) éздить *indet.*, éхать (éду, éдешь) *det.*, по~ *pf.*+*i.*, на+*p.*; (*photograph*) снимáть *impf.*, снять (сниму́, -мешь; снял, -á, -о) *pf.*; (*occupy*; ~ *time*) занимáть *impf.*, заня́ть (займу́, -мёшь; зáнял, -á, -о) *pf.*; (*impers.*) **how long does it** ~**?** ско́лько вре́мени ну́жно?; (*size in clothing*) носи́ть (ношу́, но́сишь) *impf.*; (*exam*) сдавáть (сдаю́, сдаёшь) *impf.*; ~ **courage, heart** мужáться *impf.*; ~ **cover** прятáться (-я́чусь, -я́чешься) *impf.*, с~ *pf.*; ~ **to heart** принимáть *impf.*, приня́ть (приму́, -мешь; при́нял, -á, -о) *pf.* бли́зко к се́рдцу; ~ **a liking to** полюби́ться (-блю́сь, -бишься) *pf. impers.*+*d.* (*coll.*); ~ **a turning** свора́чивать *impf.*, сверну́ть *pf.* на у́лицу (*street*), доро́гу (*road*); *v.i.* (*be successful*) имéть *impf.* успéх (*of injection*) прививáться *impf.*, приви́ться (-вьётся; -ви́лся, -вилáсь) *pf.*; ~ **after** походи́ть (-ожу́, -о́дишь) *impf.* на+*a.*; ~ **away** (*remove*) убирáть *impf.*, убрáть (уберу́, -рёшь; убрáл, -á, -о) *pf.*; (*subtract*) вычитáть *impf.*, вы́честь (-чту, -чтешь; -чел, -чла) *pf.*; ~ **back** брать (беру́, берёшь; брал, -á, -о) *impf.*, взять (возьму́, -мёшь; взял, -á -о) *pf.* обрáтно, назáд; ~ **down** (*in writing*) запи́сывать *impf.*, записáть (-ишу́, -и́шешь) *pf.*; ~ **s.o., sth. for, to be** принимáть *impf.*, приня́ть (приму́, -мешь; при́нял, -á, -о) *pf.* за+*a.*; считáть *impf.*, счесть (сочту́, -тёшь; счёл, сочлá) *pf.*+*i.*, за+*i.*; ~ **from** отнимáть *impf.*, отня́ть (отниму́, -мешь; о́тнял, -á, -о) *pf.* у, от+*g.*; ~ **in** (*clothing*) ушивáть *impf.*, уши́ть (ушью́, -ьёшь) *pf.*; (*understand*) понимáть *impf.*, поня́ть (пойму́, -мёшь; по́нял, -á, -о) *pf.*; (*deceive*) обмáнывать *impf.*, обману́ть (-ну́, -нешь) *pf.*; ~ **off** (*clothing*) снимáть *impf.*, снять (сниму́, -мешь; снял, -á,-о) *pf.*; (*mimic*) передрáзнивать *impf.*, передразни́ть (-ню́, -нишь) *pf.*; (*aeroplane*) взлетáть *impf.*, взлетéть (-éчу, -ети́шь) *pf.*; ~ **on** (*undertake*) брать (беру́, -рёшь; брал, -á, -о) *impf.*, взять (возьму́, -мёшь; взял, -á, -о) *pf.* на себя́; (*at game*) сража́ться *impf.*, срази́ться *pf.* c+i. (**at** в+a.); ~ **out** вынима́ть *impf.*, вы́нуть *pf.*; (*dog*) выводи́ть (-ожу́, -о́дишь) *impf.*, вы́вести (-еду, -едешь; -ел) *pf.* (**for a walk** на прогу́лку); (*person*) води́ть (вожу́, во́дишь) *indet.*, вести́ (веду́, -дёшь; вёл, -á) *det.*, по~ *pf.*; (*to theatre, restaurant etc.*) приглаша́ть *impf.*, пригласи́ть *pf.* (**to** в+a.); **we took them out every night** мы приглаша́ли их куда́-нибудь ка́ждый ве́чер; ~ **over** принима́ть *impf.*, приня́ть (приму́, -мешь; при́нял, -á, -о) *pf.*; (*seize*) завладе́вать *impf.*, завладе́ть *pf.*+i.; ~ **to** (*thing*) пристрасти́ться *pf.* к+d.; (*person*) привя́зываться *impf.*, привяза́ться (-яжу́сь, -я́жешься) *pf.* к+d.; ~ **up** (*enter upon*) бра́ться (беру́сь, -рёшься) *impf.*, взя́ться (возьму́сь, -мёшься; взя́лся, -ла́сь) *pf.* за+a.; (*challenge*) принима́ть *impf.*, приня́ть (приму́, -мешь; при́нял, -á, -о) *pf.*; (*time*) занима́ть *impf.*, заня́ть (займу́, -мёшь; за́нял, -á, -о) *pf.*; *n.* (*fishing*) уло́в; (*hunting*) добы́ча; (*cin.*) дубль *m.*, кинока́др. **take-away** *n.* магази́н, где продаю́т на вы́нос. **take-off** *n.* (*imitation*) подража́ние, карикату́ра; (*aeron.*) взлёт.

takings ['teɪkɪŋz] *n.* сбор, бары́ш *m.pl.*

talc(um) ['tælkəm], ~ **powder** *n.* тальк.

tale [teɪl] *n.* расска́з, ска́зка; (*gossip*) спле́тня (*g.pl.* -тен); (*coll.*, *lie*) вы́думка.

talent ['tælənt] *n.* тала́нт. **talented** *adj.* тала́нтливый.

talisman ['tælɪzmən] *n.* талисма́н.

talk [tɔːk] *v.i.* разгова́ривать *impf.* (**to, with** c+i.); (*gossip*) спле́тничать *impf.*, на~ *pf.*; *v.i. & i.* говори́ть *impf.*, по~ *pf.*; ~ **down to** говори́ть *impf.* свысока́ c+i.; ~ **into** угова́ривать *impf.*, уговори́ть *pf.*+inf.; ~ **over** (*discuss*) обсужда́ть *impf.*, обсуди́ть (-ужу́, -у́дишь) *pf.*; ~ **round** (*persuade*) переубежда́ть *impf.*, переубеди́ть *pf.*; (*discuss, reaching no conclusion*) говори́ть *impf.*, по~ *pf.* o+p. простра́нно, не каса́ясь существа́ де́ла; ~ **to** (*reprimand*) выгова́ривать *impf.*+d.; *n.* (*conversation*) разгово́р, бесе́да; (*chatter, gossip*) болтовня́ (*coll.*); (*lecture*) бесе́да; *pl.* перегово́ры (-ров) *pl.* **talkative** *adj.* болтли́вый, разгово́рчивый. **talker** *n.* говоря́щий *sb.*; (*chatterer*) болту́н (-á) (*coll.*); (*orator*) ора́тор. **talking-to** *n.* (*coll.*) вы́говор.

tall [tɔːl] *adj.* высо́кий (-о́к, -ока́, -о́ко) (*in measurements*) высото́й, ро́стом в+a. **tall-boy** *n.* высо́кий комо́д.

Tallin(n) ['tælɪn] *n.* Та́ллин.

tallow ['tæləʊ] *n.* са́ло. **tallowy** *adj.* са́льный.

tally ['tælɪ] *n.* (*score*) счёт (-a(y)); (*label*) би́рка, ярлы́к (-á); (*duplicate*) ко́пия, дуплика́т; *v.i.* соотве́тствовать (**with** +d.); *v.t.* подсчи́тывать *impf.*, подсчита́ть *pf.*

tally-ho [ˌtælɪˈhəʊ] *int.* ату́!

talon ['tælən] *n.* ко́готь (-гтя; *pl.* -гти, -гтей) *m.*

tambourine [ˌtæmbəˈriːn] *n.* бу́бен (-бна), тамбури́н.

tame [teɪm] *adj.* ручно́й, приручённый (-ён, -ена́); (*submissive*) поко́рный; (*insipid*) ску́чный (-чен, -чна́, -чно); *v.t.* прируча́ть *impf.*, приручи́ть *pf.*; (*also curb*) укроща́ть *impf.*, укроти́ть (-ощу́, -оти́шь) *pf.* **tameable** *adj.* укроти́мый. **tamer** *n.* укроти́тель *m.*; (*trainer*) дрессиро́вщик; (*fig.*) усмири́тель *m.*

tamp [tæmp] *v.t.* (*road etc.*) трамбова́ть *impf.*, у~ *pf.*; (*pack full*) набива́ть *impf.*, наби́ть (-бью, -бьёшь) *pf.*

tamper ['tæmpə(r)] *v.i.*: ~ **with** (*meddle*) вме́шиваться *impf.*, вмеша́ться *pf.* в+a.; (*touch*) тро́гать *impf.*, тро́нуть *pf.*; (*forge*) подде́лывать *impf.*, подде́лать *pf.*

tampon ['tæmpɒn] *n.* тампо́н.

tan [tæn] *n.* (*sun~*) зага́р; (*bark*) толчёная дубо́вая кора́; *adj.* желтова́то-кори́чневый; *v.t.* (*of sun*) обжига́ть *impf.*, обже́чь (обожжёт; обжёг, обожгла́) *pf.*; (*hide*) дуби́ть *impf.*, вы́~ *pf.*; (*beat*) (*coll.*) дуба́сить *impf.*, от~ *pf.*; *v.i.* загора́ть *impf.*, загоре́ть (-рю́, -ри́шь) *pf.*

tandem ['tændəm] *n.* (*bicycle*) та́ндем; (*horses*) упря́жка цу́гом; **in** ~ (*horses*) цу́гом; (*single file*) гусько́м.

tang [tæŋ] *n.* (*taste*) ре́зкий при́вкус; (*smell*) о́стрый за́пах.

tangent ['tændʒ(ə)nt] *n.* (*math.*) каса́тельная *sb.*; (*trig.*) та́нгенс; **go off at a** ~ (*in conversation etc.*) отклоня́ться *impf.*, отклони́ться (-ню́сь, -ни́шься) *pf.* от те́мы. **tangential** [tænˈdʒenʃ(ə)l] *adj.* (*diverging*) отклоня́ющийся.

tangerine [ˌtændʒəˈriːn] *n.* мандари́н.

tangible ['tændʒɪb(ə)l] *adj.* осяза́емый.

tangle ['tæŋg(ə)l] *v.t. & i.* запу́тывать(ся) *impf.*, запу́таться *pf.*; *n.* пу́таница.

tango ['tæŋgəʊ] *n.* та́нго *nt.indecl.*

tangy ['tæŋɪ] *adj.* о́стрый (остр & остёр, остра́, о́стро́); ре́зкий (-зок, -зка́, -зко).

tank [tæŋk] *n.* цисте́рна, бак; (*reservoir*) водоём; (*mil.*) танк; *attr.* та́нковый; ~ **engine** танк-парово́з.

tankard ['tæŋkəd] *n.* кру́жка.

tanker ['tæŋkə(r)] *n.* (*sea*) та́нкер; (*road*) автоцисте́рна.

tanner ['tænə(r)] *n.* дуби́льщик. **tannery** *n.* коже́венный заво́д. **tannin** *n.* тани́н. **tanning** *n.* дубле́ние.

tantalize ['tæntəˌlaɪz] *v.t.* дразни́ть (-ню́, -нишь) *impf.* ло́жными наде́ждами; му́чить *impf.*, за~, из~ *pf.*

tantamount ['tæntəˌmaʊnt] *pred.* равноси́лен (-льна, -льно, -льны) (**to** +d.).

tantrum ['tæntrəm] *n.* вспы́шка гне́ва, при́ступ раздраже́ния.

tap[1] [tæp] *n.* (*water etc.*) кран; **on** ~ распи́вочно; *v.t.* (*open*) открыва́ть *impf.*, от-

кры́ть (-ро́ю, -ро́ешь) *pf.*; (*pour out*) на
лива́ть *impf.*, нали́ть (-лью, -льёшь; на́лил,
-а́, -о) *pf.*; (*med.*) выка́чивать *impf.*, вы́
качать *pf.*; (*draw sap from*) подса́чивать
impf., подсочи́ть *pf.*; (*telephone conversation*) подслу́шивать *impf.*; ~ **telegraph
wires** перехва́тывать *impf.*, перехвати́ть
(-ачу́, -а́тишь) *pf.* телегра́фное сообще́ние;
(*make use of*) испо́льзовать *impf.* & *pf.*

tap² [tæp] *n.* (*knock*) лёгкий стук; *v.t.* сту
ча́ть (-чу́, -чи́шь) *impf.*, по~ *pf.* в+*a.*, по+*d.*
tap-dance *v.i.* отбива́ть *impf.*, отби́ть (ото
бью́, -ьёшь) *pf.* чечётку; *n.* чечётка. **tap-
dancer** *n.* чечёточник, -ица.

tape [teɪp] *n.* (*cotton strip*) тесьма́; (*adhesive,
magnetic, measuring, etc.*) ле́нта; (*sport*) лён
точка; ~ **recorder** магнитофо́н; ~ **recording**
за́пись; *v.t.* (*seal*) закле́ивать *impf.*, за
кле́ить *pf.*; (*record*) запи́сывать *impf.*, за
писа́ть (-ишу́, -и́шешь) *pf.* (на магни́тную
ле́нту). **tape-measure** *n.* руле́тка.

taper ['teɪpə(r)] *n.* (*slender candle*) то́нкая
све́чка; (*wick*) вощённый фити́ль (-ля́) *m.*;
v.t. & *i.* су́живать(ся) *impf.*, су́зить(ся) *pf.*
к концу́. **tapering** *adj.* су́живающийся к
одному́ концу́.

tapestry ['tæpɪstrɪ] *n.* гобеле́н.

tapeworm ['teɪpwɜːm] *n.* ле́нточный глист
(-á).

tapioca [ˌtæpɪˈəʊkə] *n.* тапио́ка.

tapir ['teɪpə(r), -pɪə(r)] *n.* тапи́р.

tar [tɑː(r)] *n.* дёготь (-гтя-гтю) *m.*; (*pitch*)
смола́; (*tarmac*) гудро́н; *v.t.* ма́зать (ма́жу,
-жешь) *impf.*, вы́~, на~, по~ *pf.* дёгтем;
смоли́ть *impf.*, вы́~, о~ *pf.*; гудрони́ровать
impf. & *pf.*

tarantula [təˈræntjʊlə] *n.* тара́нтул.

tardiness ['tɑːdɪnɪs] *n.* (*slowness*) медли́тель
ность; (*lateness*) опозда́ние. **tardy** *adj.*
(*slow*) медли́тельный; (*late*) по́здний, за
поздалый.

tare¹ [teə(r)] *n.* (*vetch*) ви́ка; *pl.* (*bibl.*) пле́
велы *m.pl.*

tare² [teə(r)] *n.* (*comm.*) та́ра; (*allowance*)
ски́дка на та́ру.

target ['tɑːgɪt] *n.* мише́нь, цель.

tariff ['tærɪf] *n.* тари́ф; (*price-list*) прейс
кура́нт; *v.t.* тарифици́ровать *impf.* & *pf.*

tarmac ['tɑːmæk] *n.* (*material*) гудро́н; (*road*)
гудрони́рованное шоссе́ *nt.indecl.*; (*runway*)
бетони́рованная площа́дка; *v.t.* гудрони́
ровать *impf.* & *pf.*

tarn [tɑːn] *n.* го́рное озеркó (*pl.* -ки́, -кóв).

tarnish ['tɑːnɪʃ] *v.t.* де́лать *impf.*, с~ *pf.* ту́ск
лым; (*discredit*) поро́чить *impf.*, о~ *pf.*; *v.i.*
тускне́ть *impf.*, по~ *pf.*; *n.* (*dullness*) ту́ск
лость; (*blemish*) пятно́ (*pl.* -тна, -тен, -тнам).
tarnished *adj.* ту́склый (-л, -ла́, -ло).

tarpaulin [tɑːˈpɔːlɪn] *n.* брезе́нт.

tarragon ['tærəgən] *n.* эстраго́н.

tarry ['tærɪ] *v.i.* ме́длить *impf.*

tart¹ [tɑːt] *adj.* (*taste*) ки́слый (-сел, -сла́, -сло),
те́рпкий (-пок, -пка́, -пко); (*biting*) кóлкий

(-лок, -лка́, -лко). **tartness** *n.* кислота́.

tart² [tɑːt] *n.* (*pie*) сла́дкий пиро́г (-á).

tart³ [tɑːt] *n.* (*prostitute*) шлю́ха.

tartan ['tɑːt(ə)n] *n.* шотла́ндка.

tartar ['tɑːtə(r)] *n.* ви́нный ка́мень (-мня) *m.*

Tartar ['tɑːtə(r)] *n.* тата́рин (*pl.* -ры, -р), -рка:
to catch a ~ встреча́ть *impf.*, встре́тить *pf.*
проти́вника не по си́лам.

task [tɑːsk] *n.* зада́ча, зада́ние; **take to** ~ де́
лать *impf.*, с~ *pf.* вы́говор+*d.*; отчи́тывать
impf., отчита́ть *pf.* (*coll.*); ~ **force** опера
ти́вная гру́ппа.

taskmaster ['tɑːskˌmɑːstə(r)] *n.* эксплуата́тор.

TASS [tæs] *abbr.* (*of Telegraph Agency of the
Soviet Union*) ТАСС, (Телегра́фное аге́н
ство Сове́тского Сою́за).

tassel ['tæs(ə)l] *n.* ки́сточка, кисть (*pl.* -ти,
-те́й).

taste [teɪst] *n.* (*also fig.*) вкус; (*liking*) скло́н
ность (**for** к+*d.*); (*sample*) про́ба; (*small
piece*) ма́ленький кусо́к (-ска́); (*sip*)
ма́ленький глото́к (-тка́); ~ **bud** вкусова́я
лу́ковица; *v.t.* чу́вствовать *impf.*, по~ *pf.*
вкус+*g.*; (*sample*) про́бовать *impf.*, по~ *pf.*;
(*fig.*) вкуша́ть *impf.*, вкуси́ть (-ушу́, -у́сишь)
pf.; (*wine etc.*) дегусти́ровать *impf.* & *pf.*;
v.i. име́ть *impf.* вкус, при́вкус (**of** +*g.*).
tasteful *adj.* (*made*) со вку́сом.
tasteless *adj.* безвку́сный. **tasting** *n.*
дегуста́ция. **tasty** *adj.* вку́сный (-сен, -сна́,
-сно).

tatter ['tætə(r)] *n.* (*shred*) лоску́т (-á); *pl.* лох
мо́тья (-ьев) *pl.* **tattered** *adj.* обо́рванный;
в лохмо́тьях.

tattle ['tæt(ə)l] *n.* (*chatter*) болтовня́; (*gossip*)
спле́тни (-тен) *pl.*; *v.i.* (*chatter*) болта́ть
impf.; (*gossip*) спле́тничать *impf.*, на~ *pf.*

tattoo¹ [təˈtuː, tæ-] *n.* (*mil.*) (*in evening*)
сигна́л вече́рней зари́; (*ceremonial*) тор
же́ственная заря́; **to beat the** ~ бить (бью,
бьёшь) *impf.*, по~ *pf.* зóрю; *v.i.* бараба́нить
impf. па́льцами.

tattoo² [təˈtuː, tæ-] *n.* (*design*) татуиро́вка;
v.t. татуи́ровать *impf.* & *pf.*

taunt [tɔːnt] *n.* насме́шка, кóлкость; *v.t.* на
смеха́ться *impf.* над+*i.* **taunting** *adj.* на
сме́шливый.

Taurus ['tɔːrəs] *n.* Теле́ц (-льца́).

taut [tɔːt] *adj.* ту́го натя́нутый; туго́й (туг,
-á, -о); (*nerves*) взви́нченный. **tauten** *v.t.* &
i. ту́го натя́гивать(ся) *impf.*, натяну́ть(ся)
(-ну́(сь), -нешь(ся)) *pf.* **tautness** *n.* натя
же́ние.

tautological [ˌtɔːtəˈlɒdʒɪk(ə)l] *adj.* тавтоло
ги́ческий. **tau'tology** *n.* тавтоло́гия.

tavern ['tæv(ə)n] *n.* таве́рна.

tawdriness ['tɔːdrɪnɪs] *n.* мишура́. **tawdry** *adj.*
мишу́рный; (*showy*) показно́й.

tawny ['tɔːnɪ] *adj.* рыжева́то-кори́чневый; ~
owl нея́сыть.

tax [tæks] *n.* нало́г; (*strain*) напряже́ние;
direct (indirect) ~**es** прямы́е (ко́свенные)
нало́ги; ~ **collector** сбо́рщик нало́гов; ~

dodger неплате́льщик; *v.t.* облага́ть *impf.*, обложи́ть (-жу́, -жишь) *pf.* нало́гом; (*strain*) напряга́ть *impf.*, напря́чь (-ягу́, -яжёшь; напря́г, -ла́) *pf.*; (*tire*) утомля́ть *impf.*, утоми́ть *pf.*; (*patience*) испы́тывать *impf.*, испыта́ть *pf.*; (*charge*) обвиня́ть *impf.*, обвини́ть *pf.* (**with** в+*p.*). **taxable** *adj.* подлежа́щий обложе́нию нало́гом. **ta'xation** *n.* обложе́ние нало́гом. **tax-free** *adj.* освобождённый (-ён, -ена́) от нало́га. **taxpayer** *n.* налогоплате́льщик.

taxi ['tæksɪ] *n.* такси́ *nt.indecl.*; ~ **rank** стоя́нка такси́; *v.i.* (*aeron.*) рули́ть *impf.*

taxidermist ['tæksɪˌdɜːmɪst] *n.* набивщик чу́чел. **taxidermy** *n.* набивка чу́чел.

taxi-driver ['tæksɪˌdraɪvə(r)] *n.* води́тель *m.* такси́. **taximeter** *n.* таксо́метр.

Tbilisi [təbɪˈliːsɪ] *n.* Тбили́си *m.indecl.*

tea [tiː] *n.* чай (ча́я(ю); *pl.* чаи́); *attr.* ча́йный; ~ **bag** мешо́чек с зава́ркой ча́я; ~ **caddy** ча́йница; ~ **cloth**, ~ **towel** полоте́нце для посу́ды; ~ **cosy** стёганый чехо́льщик (для ча́йника); ~ **strainer** ча́йное си́течко.

teach [tiːtʃ] *v.t.* учи́ть (учу́, у́чишь) *impf.*, на~ *pf.* (*person* +*a.*; *subject* +*d.*, *inf.*); обуча́ть *impf.*, обучи́ть (-чу́, -чишь) *pf.* (*person* +*a.*; *subject* +*d.*, *inf.*); преподава́ть (-даю́, -даёшь) *impf.* (*subject* +*a.*); (*coll.*) проу́чивать *impf.*, проучи́ть (-чу́, -чишь) *pf.* **teacher** *n.* учи́тель (*pl.* -ля́ & (*fig.*) -ли) *m.*, -ница; преподава́тель *m.*, -ница. **teacher-training** *adj.*: ~ **college** педагоги́ческий институ́т. **teaching** *n.* (*instruction*) обуче́ние; (*doctrine*) уче́ние.

teacup ['tiːkʌp] *n.* ча́йная ча́шка.

teak [tiːk] *n.* тик; *attr.* ти́ковый.

tea-leaf ['tiːliːf] *n.* ча́йный лист (-á; *pl.* -ья, -ьев).

team [tiːm] *n.* (*sport*) кома́нда; (*of people*) брига́да, гру́ппа; (*of horses etc.*) упря́жка; *v.i.* (~ **up**) объединя́ться *impf.*, объедини́ться *pf.* (в кома́нду *etc.*); *v.t.* запряга́ть *impf.*, запря́чь (-ягу́, -яжешь; -я́г, -ягла́) *pf.* в упря́жку. **team-mate** *n.* (*sport*) игро́к (-á) той же кома́нды; (*at work*) това́рищ по рабо́те, член той же брига́ды. **teamwork** *n.* брига́дная, совме́стная рабо́та; (*co-operation*) взаимоде́йствие, сотрудни́чество.

tea-pot ['tiːpɒt] *n.* ча́йник.

tear¹ [teə(r)] *n.* (*rent*) проре́ха; (*hole*) дыра́ (*pl.* -ры); (*cut*) разре́з; *v.t.* рвать (рву, рвёшь; рвал, -á, -о) *impf.*; (*also* ~ *to pieces*) разрыва́ть *impf.*, разорва́ть (-ву́, -вёшь; -вал, -вала́, -ва́ло) *pf.*; *v.i.* рва́ться (рвётся; рва́лся, -ала́сь, -а́лось) *impf.*; разрыва́ться *impf.*, разорва́ться (-вётся; -вался, -вала́сь, -а́лось) *pf.*; (*rush*) мча́ться (мчусь, мчи́шься) *impf.*; ~ **down**, **off** срыва́ть *impf.*, сорва́ть (-ву́, -вёшь; сорва́л, -á, -о) *pf.*; ~ **away**, **off** отрыва́ть *impf.*, оторва́ть (-ву́, -вёшь; оторва́л, -á, -о) *pf.*; ~ **out** вырыва́ть *impf.*, вы́рвать (-ву, -вешь) *pf.*; ~ **up** изрыва́ть

impf., изорва́ть (-ву́, -вёшь; -ва́л, -вала́, -ва́ло) *pf.*

tear² [tɪə(r)] *n.* (~-*drop*) слеза́ (*pl.* -ёзы, -ёз, -еза́м). **tearful** *adj.* слезли́вый; (*sad*) печа́льный. **tear-gas** *n.* слезоточи́вый газ (-а(у)).

tease [tiːz] *v.t.* дразни́ть (-ню́, -нишь) *impf.*; (*wool*) чеса́ть (чешу́, -шешь) *impf.*; (*cloth*) ворсова́ть *impf.*, на~ *pf.* **teaser** *n.* (*puzzle*) головоло́мка.

teasel ['tiːz(ə)l], **teazle** *n.* (*plant*) ворся́нка; (*device*) ворши́льная ши́шка.

teaspoon ['tiːspuːn] *n.* ча́йная ло́жка.

teat [tiːt] *n.* сосо́к (-ска́).

technical ['teknɪk(ə)l] *adj.* техни́ческий; (*specialist*) специа́льный; (*formal*) форма́льный; ~ **college** техни́ческое учи́лище. **techni'cality** *n.* техни́ческая сторона́ (*a.* -ону; *pl.* -оны, -он, -она́м); форма́льность. **technician** [tek'nɪʃ(ə)n] *n.* те́хник. **tech'nique** *n.* те́хника; (*method*) ме́тод. **tech'nology** *n.* техноло́гия, те́хника. **techno'logical** *adj.* технологи́ческий. **tech'nologist** *n.* техно́лог.

teddy-bear ['tedɪ] *n.* медвежо́нок (-жо́нка; *pl.* -жа́та, -жа́т).

tedious ['tiːdɪəs] *adj.* ску́чный (-чен, -чна́, -чно), утоми́тельный. **tedium** *n.* ску́ка, утоми́тельность.

teem¹ [tiːm] *v.i.* (*abound in*, *be abundant*) кише́ть (-шит) *impf.* (**with** +*i.*); (*abound in*) изоби́ловать *impf.* (**with** +*i.*).

teem² [tiːm] *v.i.*: **it is ~ing (with rain)** дождь льёт как из ведра́.

teenage ['tiːneɪdʒ] *adj.* ю́ношеский. **teenager** *n.* подро́сток (-тка).

teeter ['tiːtə(r)] *v.i.* кача́ться *impf.*, качну́ться *pf.*; пошáтываться *impf.*

teethe [tiːð] *v.i.*: **the child is teething** у ребёнка подре́зываются зу́бы. **teething** *n.* подре́зывание зубо́в; ~ **troubles** (*fig.*) нача́льные пробле́мы. **teething-ring** *n.* де́тское зубно́е кольцо́.

teetotal [tiːˈtəʊt(ə)l] *adj.* тре́звый (-в, -ва́, -во). **teetotalism** *n.* тре́звенность. **teetotaller** *n.* тре́звенник.

tele- ['telɪ] *in comb.* теле... . **telecommunication(s)** *n.* да́льняя связь. **telegram** *n.* телегра́мма. **telegraph** *n.* телегра́ф; *attr.* телегра́фный; *v.t.* телеграфи́ровать *impf.* & *pf.*; ~ **pole** телегра́фный столб (-á). **telepathic** *adj.* телепати́ческий. **telepathy** [tɪˈlepəθɪ] *n.* телепа́тия. **telephone** *n.* телефо́н; *attr.* телефо́нный; *v.t.* (*message*) телефони́ровать *impf.* & *pf.* +*a.*, о+*p.*; (*person*) звони́ть *impf.*, по~ *pf.* (по телефо́ну) +*d.*; ~ **box** телефо́нная бу́дка; ~ **directory** телефо́нная кни́га; ~ **exchange** телефо́нная ста́нция; ~ **number** но́мер (*pl.* -á) телефо́на. **telephonist** [tɪˈlefənɪst] *n.* телефони́ст, ~ка. **telephoto lens** *n.* телеобъекти́в. **teleprinter** *n.* телета́йп. **telescope** *n.* телеско́п; *v.t.* & *i.* телескопи́чески склады-

вать(ся) *impf.*, сложи́ть(ся) (сложу́, сло́-
жишь) *pf.* **telescopic** *adj.* телескопи́ческий.
televise *v.t.* пока́зывать *impf.*, показа́ть
(покажу́, пока́жешь) *pf.* по телеви́дению;
передава́ть (-даю́, -даёшь) *impf.*, переда́ть
(-а́м, -а́шь, -а́ст, -ади́м; пе́редал, -а́, -о) *pf.*
по телеви́дению. **television** *n.* телеви́дение;
(*set*) телеви́зор; *attr.* телевизио́нный. **telex**
n. те́лекс.
tell [tel] *v.t.* (*relate*) расска́зывать *impf.*,
рассказа́ть (-ажу́, -а́жешь) *pf.* (*thing told*
+*a.*; *person told* +*d.*); (*utter, inform*) гово-
ри́ть *impf.*, сказа́ть (скажу́, -жешь) *pf.*
(*thing uttered* +*a.*; *thing informed about* о+*p.*;
person informed +*d.*); (*order*) веле́ть (-лю́,
-ли́шь) *impf.* & *pf.*+*d.*; ~ **one thing from
another** отлича́ть *impf.*, отличи́ть *pf.*+*a.*
от+*g.*; *v.i.* (*have an effect*) ска́зываться
impf., сказа́ться (скажу́сь, -жешься) *pf.* (**on**
на+*p.*); **all told** итого́; ~ **fortunes** гада́ть
impf., по~ *pf.*; ~ **off** (*select*) отбира́ть *impf.*,
отобра́ть (отберу́, -рёшь; отобра́л, -а́, -о)
pf.; (*rebuke*) отде́лывать *impf.*, отде́лать
pf.; ~ **on,** ~ **tales about** ябе́дничать *impf.*,
на~ *pf.* на+*a.* **teller** *n.* (*of story*) расска́зчик,
-ица; (*of votes*) счётчик голосо́в; (*in bank*)
касси́р, ~ша. **telling** *adj.* (*effective*) эффе́кт-
ный; (*significant*) многозначи́тельный.
telling-'off *n.* вы́говор. **telltale** *n.* доно́счик,
спле́тник; *adj.* преда́тельский.
temerity [tı'merıtı] *n.* (*rashness*) безрассу́д-
ство; (*audacity*) дѐрзость.
temper ['tempə(r)] *n.* (*metal*) зака́л; (*character*) нрав, хара́ктер; (*mood*) настрое́ние;
(*anger*) гнев, **lose one's** ~ выходи́ть (-ожу́,
-о́дишь) *impf.*, вы́йти (вы́йду, -дешь; вы́-
шел, -шла) *pf.* из себя́; *v.t.* (*metal*) отпус-
ка́ть *impf.*, отпусти́ть (-ущу́, -у́стишь) *pf.*;
(*moderate*) смягча́ть *impf.*, смягчи́ть *pf.*
temperament ['tempərəmənt] *n.* темпера́мент;
(*mus.*) темпера́ция. **temperamental** [‚tem-
prə'ment(ə)l] *adj.* темпера́ментный.
temperance ['tempərəns] *n.* (*moderation*)
уме́ренность; (*sobriety*) тре́звенность.
temperate ['tempərət] *adj.* уме́ренный (-ен,
-енна).
temperature ['temprıtʃə(r)] *n.* температу́ра;
(*high* ~) повы́шенная температу́ра; **take
s.o.'s** ~ измеря́ть *impf.*, изме́рить *pf.*
температу́ру+*d.*
tempest ['tempıst] *n.* бу́ря. **tempestuous**
[tem'pestjʊəs] *adj.* бу́рный (-рен, бурна́,
-рно), бу́йный (бу́ен, буйна́, -но).
template ['templıt, -pleıt] *n.* шабло́н.
temple¹ ['temp(ə)l] *n.* (*religion*) храм.
temple² ['temp(ə)l] *n.* (*anat.*) висо́к (-ска́).
tempo ['tempəʊ] *n.* темп.
temporal ['tempər(ə)l] *adj.* (*secular*) мирско́й,
све́тский; (*of time*) временно́й.
temporary ['tempərərı] *adj.* вре́менный.
temporize ['tempə‚raız] *v.i.* приспоса́бли-
ваться *impf.*, приспосо́биться *pf.* ко вре́-
мени и обстоя́тельствам; (*hesitate*)

ме́длить *impf.*
tempt [tempt] *v.t.* искуша́ть *impf.*, искуси́ть
pf.; соблазня́ть *impf.*, соблазни́ть *pf.*; ~ **fate**
испы́тывать *impf.*, испыта́ть *pf.* судьбу́.
temp'tation *n.* искуше́ние, собла́зн. **tempter, -tress** *n.* искуси́тель *m.*, ~ница. **tempting** *adj.* зама́нчивый, соблазни́тельный.
ten [ten] *adj.* & *n.* де́сять (-ти́, -тью); (*collect.*;
10 pairs) де́сятеро (-ры́х); (*cards*; *number
10*) деся́тка; (*time*) де́сять часо́в; (*age*)
де́сять лет; (*set of 10*; *10 years, decade*)
деся́ток (-тка); **in** ~**s** деся́тками. **tenth** *adj.*
& *n.* деся́тый; (*fraction*) деся́тая (часть (*pl.*
-ти, -те́й)); (*date*) деся́тое (число́); (*mus.*)
де́цима.
tenable ['tenəb(ə)l] *adj.* (*strong*) про́чный
(-чен, -чна́, -чно, про́чны́); (*logical*) логи́ч-
ный; (*of office*) могу́щий быть за́нятым.
tenacious [tı'neıʃəs] *adj.* це́пкий (-пок, -пка́,
-пко); (*stubborn*) упо́рный. **tenacity** [tı'næ-
sıtı] *n.* це́пкость; упо́рство.
tenancy ['tenənsı] *n.* (*renting of property*)
наём помеще́ния; (*period*) срок (-а(у))
аре́нды. **tenant** *n.* нанима́тель *m.*, ~ница,
аренда́тор.
tend¹ [tend] *v.i.* (*be apt*) име́ть скло́нность
(**to** к+*d.*, +*inf.*); (*move*) направля́ться *impf.*,
напра́виться *pf.*
tend² [tend] *v.t.* (*look after*) (*person*) уха́жи-
вать *impf.* за+*i.*; (*machine*) обслу́живать
impf., обслужи́ть (-жу́, -жишь) *pf.*
tendency ['tendənsı] *n.* тенде́нция, скло́н-
ность. **tendentious** [ten'denʃəs] *adj.* тенден-
цио́зный.
tender¹ ['tendə(r)] *v.t.* (*offer*) предлага́ть
impf., предложи́ть (-жу́, -жишь) *pf.*; (*money*) предоставля́ть *impf.*, предоста́вить *pf.*;
v.i. (*make* ~ *for*) подава́ть (-даю́, -даёшь)
impf., пода́ть (-а́м, -а́шь, -а́ст, -ади́м; по́дал,
-а́, -о) *pf.* зая́вку (на торга́х); *n.* предло-
же́ние; **legal** ~ зако́нное платёжное сре́д-
ство.
tender² ['tendə(r)] *n.* (*rail.*) те́ндер; (*naut.*)
посы́льное су́дно (*pl.* -да́, -до́в).
tender³ ['tendə(r)] *adj.* (*delicate, affectionate*)
не́жный (-жен, -жна́, -жно, не́жны́); (*soft*)
мя́гкий (-гок, -гка́, -гко); (*sensitive*) чувст-
ви́тельный. **tenderness** *n.* не́жность; (*softness*) мя́гкость.
tendon ['tend(ə)n] *n.* сухожи́лие.
tendril ['tendrıl] *n.* у́сик.
tenement ['tenımənt] *n.* (*ubógий*) многоквар-
ти́рный дом (-а(у); *pl.* -á).
tenet ['tenıt, 'ti:net] *n.* до́гмат, при́нцип.
tennis ['tenıs] *n.* те́ннис; *attr.* те́ннисный; ~
player тенниси́ст, ~ка.
tenon ['tenən] *n.* шип (-á).
tenor ['tenə(r)] *n.* (*structure*) укла́д; (*direction*)
направле́ние; (*purport*) о́бщее содержа́ние;
(*mus.*) те́нор.
tense¹ [tens] *n.* вре́мя *nt.*
tense² [tens] *v.t.* напряга́ть *impf.*, напря́чь
(-ягу́, -яжёшь; напря́г, -ла́) *pf.*; *adj.* (*tight*)

натя́нутый; (*strained*) напряжённый (-ён, -ённа); (*excited*) возбуждённый (-ён, -ена́); (*nervous*) не́рвный (не́рвен, нервна́, не́рвно). **tenseness** *n.* натя́нутость, напряжённость. **tensile** *adj.* растяжи́мый. **tension** *n.* напряже́ние (*also fig.; elec.*); натяже́ние.

tent [tent] *n.* пала́тка; ~ **peg** ко́лышек (-шка) для пала́тки; ~ **pole** пала́точная сто́йка.

tentacle ['tentək(ə)l] *n.* щу́пальце (*g.pl.* -лец & -льцев).

tentative ['tentətiv] *adj.* (*experimental*) про́бный; (*preliminary*) предвари́тельный.

tenterhooks ['tentə,hʊks] *n.*: **be on** ~ сиде́ть (сижу́, сиди́шь) *impf.* как на иго́лках.

tenth *see* **ten**

tenuous ['tenjʊəs] *adj.* (*slender, subtle*) то́нкий (-нок, -нка́, -нко, то́нки́); (*flimsy*) непро́чный (-чен, -чна́, -чно); (*insignificant*) незначи́тельный; (*rarefied*) разрежённый.

tenure ['tenjə(r)] *n.* (*possession*) владе́ние; (*office*) пребыва́ние в до́лжности; (*period*) срок (-а(у)) (*of possession*) владе́ния, (*of office*) пребыва́ния в до́лжности.

tepid ['tepɪd] *adj.* теплова́тый.

tercentenary [,tɜːsen'tiːnərɪ, -'tenərɪ, tɜː'sentɪnərɪ], **-ennial** [,tɜːsen'tenɪəl] *n.* трёхсотле́тие; *adj.* трёхсотле́тний.

term [tɜːm] *n.* (*period*) срок (-а(у)); (*univ.*) семе́стр; (*school*) че́тверть (*pl.* -ти, -те́й) (*math.*) член; (*leg.*) се́ссия; (*technical word, expression*) те́рмин; (*expression*) выраже́ние; (*med.*) норма́льный пери́од бере́менности; *pl.* (*conditions*) усло́вия *nt.pl.* (**of payment** опла́ты); (*relations*) отноше́ния *nt.pl.*; **on good** ~**s** в хоро́ших отноше́ниях; (*language*) язы́к (-а́), выраже́ния *nt.pl.*; **come to** ~**s with** (*resign o.s. to*) покоря́ться *impf.*, покори́ться *pf.* к+*d.*; (*come to an agreement with*) приходи́ть (-ожу́, -о́дишь) *impf.*, прийти́ (приду́, -дёшь; пришёл, -шла́) *pf.* к соглаше́нию с+*i.*; *v.t.* называ́ть *impf.*, назва́ть (назову́, -вёшь; назва́л, -а́, -о) *pf.*; **I do not** ~ **impatience a shortcoming** я не называ́ю нетерпе́ние недоста́тком.

termagant ['tɜːməgənt] *n.* сварли́вая же́нщина; меге́ра (*coll.*).

terminable ['tɜːmɪnəb(ə)l] *adj.* ограни́ченный сро́ком, сро́чный (-чен, -чна́, -чно).

terminal ['tɜːmɪn(ə)l] *adj.* коне́чный, заключи́тельный; (*univ.*) семестро́вый; (*school*) четвертно́й; (*leg.*) сессио́нный; *n.* (*elec.*) зажи́м; (*computer*) термина́л; (*terminus*) (*rail.*) коне́чная ста́нция; (*bus etc.*) коне́чная остано́вка; (*aeron.*) (*airport buildings*) зда́ния *nt.pl.*; **air** ~ аэровокза́л.

terminate ['tɜːmɪneɪt] *v.t.* & *i.* конча́ть(ся) *impf.*, ко́нчить(ся) *pf.* (**in** +*i.*). **termi'nation** *n.* коне́ц (-нца́), оконча́ние.

terminology [,tɜːmɪ'nɒlədʒɪ] *n.* терминоло́гия. **termino'logical** *adj.* терминологи́ческий.

terminus ['tɜːmɪnəs] *n.* (*rail.*) коне́чная ста́нция; (*bus etc.*) коне́чная остано́вка.

termite ['tɜːmaɪt] *n.* терми́т.

tern [tɜːn] *n.* кра́чка.

terra [,terə] *n.*: ~ **firma** су́ша; ~ **incognita** неизве́стная страна́.

terrace ['terəs, -rɪs] *n.* терра́са; (*row of houses*) ряд (-а́ *with* 2, 3, 4, *loc.* -у; *pl.* -ы́) домо́в; *v.t.* террасси́ровать *impf.* & *pf.*

terracotta [,terə'kɒtə] *n.* терракота́; *adj.* террако́товый.

terrain [te'reɪn, tə-] *n.* ме́стность.

terrapin ['terəpɪn] *n.* (*turtle*) водяна́я черепа́ха.

terrestrial [tə'restrɪəl, tɪ-] *adj.* земно́й; (*ground*) назе́мный.

terrible ['terɪb(ə)l] *adj.* (*frightening, dreadful, very bad*) ужа́сный; (*excessive*) стра́шный (-шен, -шна́, -шно, стра́шны́) (*coll.*). **terribly** *adv.* ужа́сно, стра́шно.

terrier ['terɪə(r)] *n.* терье́р.

terrific [tə'rɪfɪk] *adj.* (*huge*) огро́мный; (*marvellous*) потряса́ющий. **terrify** ['terɪfaɪ] *v.t.* ужаса́ть *impf.*, ужасну́ть *pf.*

territorial [,terɪ'tɔːrɪəl] *adj.* территориа́льный. **territory** ['terɪtərɪ, -trɪ] *n.* террито́рия, (*fig.*) о́бласть, сфе́ра.

terror ['terə(r)] *n.* у́жас, страх; (*person, thing causing* ~) терро́р. **terrorism** *n.* террори́зм. **terrorist** *n.* террори́ст, ~ка. **terrorize** *v.t.* терроризи́ровать *impf.* & *pf.*

terse [tɜːs] *adj.* сжа́тый, кра́ткий (-ток, -тка́, -тко). **terseness** *n.* сжа́тость, кра́ткость.

tertiary ['tɜːʃərɪ] *adj.* трети́чный; (*education*) вы́сший.

tesselated ['tesə,leɪtɪd] *adj.* мозаи́чный.

test [test] *n.* испыта́ние, про́ба; (*exam*) экза́мен; контро́льная *sb.* (*coll.*); (*standard*) крите́рий; (*analysis*) ана́лиз; (*chem., reagent*) реакти́в; ~ **ban** запреще́ние испыта́ний я́дерного ору́жия; ~ **case** де́ло (*pl.* -ла́) име́ющее принципиа́льное значе́ние для разреше́ния аналоги́чных дел; ~ **flight** испыта́тельный полёт; ~ **paper** (*exam*) экзаменацио́нный биле́т; ~ **pilot** лётчик-испыта́тель *m.*; *v.t.* (*try out*) испы́тывать *impf.*, испыта́ть *pf.*; (*check up on*) проверя́ть *impf.*, прове́рить *pf.*; (*give exam to*) экзаменова́ть *impf.*, про~ *pf.*

testament ['testəmənt] *n.* завеща́ние; **Old, New T**~ Ве́тхий, Но́вый заве́т. **testamentary** [,testə'mentərɪ] *adj.* завеща́тельный. **testator** [te'steɪtə(r)] *n.* завеща́тель *m.*, ~ница.

testicle ['testɪk(ə)l] *n.* яи́чко (*pl.* -чки, -чек).

testify ['testɪfaɪ] *v.i.* свиде́тельствовать *impf.* (**to** в по́льзу+*g.*; **against** про́тив+*g.*); *v.t.* (*declare*) заявля́ть *impf.*, заяви́ть (-влю́, -вишь) *pf.*; (*be evidence of*) свиде́тельствовать о+*p.*

testimonial [,testɪ'məʊnɪəl] *n.* рекоменда́ция, характери́стика. **testimony** ['testɪmənɪ] *n.* показа́ние, -ния *pl.*, свиде́тельство; (*declaration*) заявле́ние.

test-tube ['testtjuːb] *n.* проби́рка.

testy ['testɪ] *adj.* раздражи́тельный.

tetanus ['tetənəs] *n.* столбня́к (-á).

tetchy ['tetʃɪ] *adj.* раздражи́тельный.

tête-à-tête [ˌteɪtɑːˈteɪt] *n. & adv.* тет-а-те́т.

tether ['teðə(r)] *n.* при́вязь; **be at, come to the end of one's ~** дойти́ (дойду́, -дёшь; дошёл, -шла́) *pf.* до то́чки; *v.t.* привя́зывать *impf.*, привяза́ть (-яжу́, -я́жешь) *pf.*

Teutonic [tjuːˈtɒnɪk] *adj.* тевто́нский.

text [tekst] *n.* текст. **textbook** *n.* уче́бник.

textile ['tekstaɪl] *adj.* тексти́льный; *n.* ткань; *pl.* тексти́ль *m.* (*collect*).

textual ['tekstjʊəl] *adj.* тексто́вой.

texture ['tekstʃə(r)] *n.* (*consistency*) консисте́нция; (*structure*) строе́ние.

thalidomide [θəˈlɪdəˌmaɪd] *n.* талидоми́д.

Thames [temz] *n.* Те́мза.

than [ðən, ðæn] *conj.* (*comparison*) чем; **other ~** (*except*) кро́ме+*g.*; **none other ~** не кто ино́й, как; **nothing else ~** не что ино́е, как.

thank [θæŋk] *v.t.* благодари́ть *impf.*, по~ *pf.* (**for** за+*a.*); **~ God** сла́ва Бо́гу; **~ you** спаси́бо; благодарю́ вас; *n.pl.* благода́рность; спаси́бо; **many ~s** большо́е спаси́бо; **~s to** (*good result*) благодаря́+*d.*; (*bad result*) из-за+*g.* **thankful** *adj.* благода́рный. **thankless** *adj.* неблагода́рный. **thank-offering** *n.* благода́рственная же́ртва. **thanksgiving** *n.* (*service of thanks*) благода́рственный моле́бен (-бна); благодаре́ние.

that [ðæt] *demonstrative adj. & pron.* тот (та, то; *pl.* те); э́тот (э́та, э́то; *pl.* э́ти); **~ which** тот (та, то; те) кото́рый; *relative pron.* кото́рый; *conj.* что; (*purpose*) что́бы; *adv.* так, до тако́й сте́пени.

thatch [θætʃ] *n.* (*straw*) соло́менная, (*reed*) тростнико́вая кры́ша; *v.t.* крыть (кро́ю, кро́ешь) *impf.*, по~ *pf.* соло́мой (*straw*), тростнико́м (*reed*).

thaw [θɔː] *v.t.* раста́пливать *impf.*, растопи́ть (-плю, -пишь) *pf.*; *v.i.* та́ять (та́ет) *impf.*, рас~ *pf.*; (*fig.*) смягча́ться *impf.*, смягчи́ться *pf.*; *n.* о́ттепель; (*fig.*) смягче́ние.

the [ðɪ, ðə, ðiː] *def. article, not usu. translated; adv.* тем; **the ... the ...** чем..., тем; **~ more ~ better** чем бо́льше, тем лу́чше.

theatre ['θɪətə(r)] *n.* теа́тр; (*lecture etc.*) аудито́рия; (*operating*) операцио́нная *sb.* **theatre-goer** *n.* театра́л. **theatrical** [θɪˈætrɪk(ə)l] *adj.* театра́льный.

theft [θeft] *n.* воровство́, кра́жа.

their [ðeə(r)], **theirs** *poss. pron.* их; свой (-оя́, -оё; -ои́).

theism ['θiːɪz(ə)m] *n.* тейзм. **theist** *n.* тейст. **the'istic(al)** *adj.* теисти́ческий.

thematic [θɪˈmætɪk] *adj.* темати́ческий. **theme** [θiːm] *n.* те́ма, предме́т.

themselves [ðəmˈselvz] *pron.* (*emph.*) (они́) са́ми (-и́х, -и́м, -и́ми); (*refl.*) себя́ (себе́, собо́й); -ся (*suffixed to v.t.*).

then [ðen] *adv.* (*at that time*) тогда́, в то вре́мя; (*after that*) пото́м, зате́м; **now and ~** вре́мя от вре́мени; *conj.* в тако́м слу́чае, тогда́; *n.* то вре́мя *nt.*; *adj.* тогда́шний.

thence [ðens] *adv.* отту́да; (*from that*) из э́того. **thence'forth, -'forward** *adv.* с того́/э́того вре́мени.

theodolite [θɪˈɒdəˌlaɪt] *n.* теодоли́т.

theologian [θɪəˈləʊdʒɪən, -dʒ(ə)n] *n.* тео́лог. **theo'logical** *adj.* теологи́ческий. **theology** [θɪˈɒlədʒɪ] *n.* теоло́гия.

theorem ['θɪərəm] *n.* теоре́ма. **theo'retical** *adj.* теорети́ческий. **theorist** *n.* теоре́тик. **theorize** *v.i.* теоретизи́ровать *impf.* **theory** *n.* тео́рия.

theosophy [θɪˈɒsəfɪ] *n.* теосо́фия.

therapeutic(al) [ˌθerəˈpjuːtɪk(əl)] *adj.* терапевти́ческий. **therapeutics** *n.* терапе́втика. **'therapist** *n.* терапе́вт. **'therapy** *n.* терапи́я.

there [ðeə(r)] *adv.* (*place*) там; (*direction*) туда́; *int.* вот!; ну!; **~ is, are** есть, име́ется (-е́ются); **~ you are** (*on giving sth.*) пожа́луйста. **thereabouts** *adv.* (*near*) побли́зости; (*approximately*) приблизи́тельно. **there'after** *adv.* по́сле э́того. **thereby** *adv.* таки́м о́бразом. **therefore** *adv.* поэ́тому, сле́довательно. **there'in** *adv.* в э́том; (*in that respect*) в э́том отноше́нии. **thereu'pon** *adv.* зате́м.

thermal ['θɜːm(ə)l] *adj.* теплово́й, терми́ческий; **~ springs** горя́чие исто́чники *m.pl.*; **~ unit** едини́ца теплоты́.

thermo- ['θɜːməʊ] *in comb.* термо..., тепло... . **thermodynamics** *n.* термодина́мика. **thermometer** [θəˈmɒmɪtə(r)] *n.* термо́метр, гра́дусник. **thermonuclear** *adj.* термоя́дерный. **thermos** ['θɜːməs] *n.* термос. **thermostat** *n.* термоста́т.

thesis ['θiːsɪs] *n.* (*proposition*) те́зис; (*dissertation*) диссерта́ция.

they [ðeɪ] *pron.* они́ (их, им, и́ми, о них).

thick [θɪk] *adj.* то́лстый (-т, -та́, -то, то́лсты́); (*in measurements*) толщино́й в+*a.*; (*line*) жи́рный (-рен, -рна́, -рно); (*dense*) пло́тный (-тен, -тна́, -тно, плотны́); густо́й (-т, -та́, -то, густы́); (*turbid*) му́тный (-тен, -тна́, -тно, му́тны́); (*stupid*) тупо́й (туп, -á, -о, ту́пы́); *n.* гу́ща; (*of fight*) разга́р; **through ~ and thin** не коле́блясь; несмотря́ ни на каки́е препя́тствия. **thicken** *v.t. & i.* утолща́ть(ся) *impf.*, утолсти́ть(ся) *pf.*; (*make, become denser*) сгуща́ть(ся) *impf.*, сгусти́ть(ся) *pf.*; *v.i.* (*become more intricate*) усложня́ться *impf.*, усложни́ться *pf.* **thicket** *n.* ча́ща. **thick-headed** *adj.* тупоголо́вый (*coll.*). **thickness** *n.* (*also dimension*) толщина́; (*density*) пло́тность, густота́; (*layer*) слой (*pl.* слои́). **thick'set** *adj.* корена́стый. **thick-skinned** *adj.* толстоко́жий.

thief [θiːf] *n.* вор (*pl.* -ы, -ов), ~о́вка. **thieve** *v.i.* ворова́ть *impf.*; *v.t.* красть (-аду́, -аде́шь; крал) *impf.*, у~ *pf.* **thievery** *n.* воровство́. **thievish** *adj.* ворова́тый.

thigh [θaɪ] *n.* бедро́ (*pl.* бёдра, -дер, -драм). **thigh-bone** *n.* бе́дренная кость (*pl.* -ти, -те́й).

thimble ['θɪmb(ə)l] *n.* напёрсток (-тка).

thin [θɪn] *adj.* (*slender; not thick*) то́нкий

(-нок, -нка́, -нко, то́нки); (*lean*) худо́й (худ, -а́, -о, ху́ды); (*too liquid*) жи́дкий (-док, -дка́, -дко); (*sparse*) ре́дкий (-док, -дка́, -дко); (*weak*) сла́бый (-б, -ба́, -бо); *v.t.* & *i.* де́лать(ся) *impf.*, с~ *pf.* то́нким, жи́дким; *v.i.*: ~ **down** худе́ть *impf.*, по~ *pf.*; ~ **out** реде́ть *impf.*, по~ *pf.*; *v.t.*: ~ **out** проре́живать *impf.*, прореди́ть *pf.*

thing [θɪŋ] *n.* вещь (*pl.* -щи, -ще́й); (*object*) предме́т; (*matter*) де́ло (*pl.* -ла́); **poor** ~ (*person*) бедня́жка *c.g.* (*coll.*); *pl.* (*belongings*) пожи́тки (-ков) *pl.* (*coll.*); (*clothes*) оде́жда; (*implements*) у́тварь (*collect.*); (*affairs*) дела́ *nt.pl.* **thingamy** ['θɪŋəmɪ] *n.* (*person*) как бишь его́?; (*thing*) шту́ка.

think [θɪŋk] *v.t.* & *i.* ду́мать *impf.*, по~ *pf.* (**about, of** o+*p.*, над+*i.*); (*consider*) счита́ть *impf.*, счесть (сочту́, -тёшь; счёл, сочла́) *pf.* (**to be** +*i.*, за+*a.*; **that** что); *v.i.* (*think, reason*) мы́слить *impf.*; (*intend*) намерева́ться *impf.* (*of doing* +*inf.*); ~ **out** проду́мывать *impf.*, проду́мать *pf.*; ~ **over** обду́мывать *impf.*, обду́мать *pf.*; ~ **up, of** приду́мывать *impf.*, приду́мать *pf.* **thinker** *n.* мысли́тель *m.* **thinking** *adj.* мы́слящий; *n.* (*reflection*) размышле́ние; **to my way of** ~ по моему́ мне́нию.

thinly ['θɪnlɪ] *adv.* то́нко. **thinness** *n.* то́нкость; (*leanness*) худоба́. **thin-skinned** *adj.* (*fig.*) оби́дчивый.

third [θɜːd] *adj.* & *n.* тре́тий (-тья, -тье); (*fraction*) треть (*pl.* -ти, -те́й); (*date*) тре́тье (число́); (*mus.*) те́рция; ~ **party** тре́тья сторона́ (*a.* -ону; *pl.* -оны, -он, -она́м); T~ **World** стра́ны *f.pl.* тре́тьего ми́ра. **third-rate** *adj.* третьестепе́нный.

thirst [θɜːst] *n.* жа́жда (**for** +*g.* (*fig.*)); *v.i.* (*fig.*) жа́ждать (-ду, -дешь) *impf.* (**for** +*g.*). **thirsty** *adj.*: be ~ хоте́ть (хочу́, -чешь; хоти́м) *impf.* пить.

thirteen [θɜːˈtiːn, 'θɜː-] *adj.* & *n.* трина́дцать (-ти, -тью); (*age*) трина́дцать лет. **thirteenth** *adj.* & *n.* трина́дцатый; (*fraction*) трина́дцатая (часть (*pl.* -ти, -те́й)); (*date*) трина́дцатое (число́).

thirtieth ['θɜːtɪɪθ] *adj.* & *n.* тридца́тый; (*fraction*) тридца́тая (часть (*pl.* -ти, -те́й)); (*date*) тридца́тое (число́). **thirty** *adj.* & *n.* три́дцать (-ти́, -тью); (*age*) три́дцать лет; *pl.* (*decade*) тридца́тые го́ды (-до́в) *m.pl.*

this [ðɪs] *demonstrative adj.* & *pron.* э́тот (э́та, э́то; *pl.* э́ти); ~ **way** сюда́; **like** ~ вот так.

thistle ['θɪs(ə)l] *n.* чертополо́х.

thither ['ðɪðə(r)] *adv.* туда́.

thong [θɒŋ] *n.* реме́нь (-мня́) *m.*

thorax ['θɔːræks] *n.* грудна́я кле́тка.

thorn [θɔːn] *n.* шип (-а́), колю́чка (*coll.*). **thorny** *adj.* колю́чий; (*fig.*) терни́стый; (*ticklish*) щекотли́вый.

thorough ['θʌrə] *adj.* основа́тельный, тща́тельный; (*complete*) по́лный (-лон, -лна́, полно́), соверше́нный (-нен, -нна). **thor-**

oughbred *adj.* чистокро́вный, поро́дистый.

thoroughfare *n.* прое́зд; (*walking*) прохо́д.

thoroughgoing *adj.* радика́льный. **thoroughly** *adv.* (*completely*) вполне́, соверше́нно. **thoroughness** *n.* основа́тельность, тща́тельность.

though [ðəʊ] *conj.* хотя́; несмотря́ на то, что; **as** ~ как бу́дто; *adv.* одна́ко, всё-таки.

thought [θɔːt] *n.* мысль; (*heed*) внима́ние; (*meditation*) размышле́ние; (*intention*) наме́рение; *pl.* (*opinion*) мне́ние. **thoughtful** *adj.* заду́мчивый; (*considerate*) внима́тельный, забо́тливый. **thoughtless** *adj.* необду́манный (-ан, -анна); (*inconsiderate*) невнима́тельный.

thousand ['θaʊz(ə)nd] *adj.* & *n.* ты́сяча (*i.* -чей & чью). **thousandth** *adj.* & *n.* ты́сячный; (*fraction*) ты́сячная (часть (*pl.* -ти, -те́й).

thraldom ['θrɔːldəm], **thrall** *n.* (*state*) ра́бство; **in** ~ обращённый (-ён, -ена́) в ра́бство.

thrash [θræʃ] *v.t.* бить (бью, бьёшь) *impf.*, по~ *pf.*; ~ **out** (*discuss*) тща́тельно обсужда́ть *impf.*, обсуди́ть (-ужу́, -у́дишь) *pf.*; *v.i.*: ~ **about** мета́ться (мечу́сь, -чешься) *impf.* **thrashing** *n.* (*beating*) взбу́чка (*coll.*).

thread [θred] *n.* ни́тка, нить (*also fig.*); (*of screw etc.*) наре́зка, резьба́; *v.t.* (*needle*) продева́ть *impf.*, проде́ть (-е́ну, -е́нешь) *pf.* ни́тку в+*a.*; (*beads etc.*) нани́зывать *impf.*, наниза́ть (-ижу́, -и́жешь) *pf.*; ~ **one's way** пробира́ться *impf.*, пробра́ться (-беру́сь, -берёшься; -бра́лся, -брала́сь, -бра́ло́сь) *pf.* (**through** че́рез+*a.*). **threadbare** *adj.* (*clothes etc.*) потёртый, изно́шенный; (*hackneyed*) изби́тый.

threat [θret] *n.* угро́за. **threaten** *v.t.* угрожа́ть *impf.*, грози́ть *impf.*, при~ *pf.* (*person* +*d.*; **with** +*i.*; *to do* +*inf.*).

three [θriː] *adj.* & *n.* три (трёх, -ём, -емя́, -ёх); (*collect.*; *3 pairs*) тро́е (-ои́х); (*cards, number 3*) тро́йка; (*time*) три часа́; (*age*) три го́да; ~ **times** три́жды; ~ **times four** три́жды четы́ре. **three-dimensional** *adj.* трёхме́рный. **threefold** *adj.* тройно́й; *adv.* втройне́. **three-ply** *adj.* (*wood*) трёхсло́йный; (*rope*) тройно́й. **three-quarters** *n.* три че́тверти. **threesome** *n.* тро́йка.

thresh [θreʃ] *v.t.* молоти́ть (-очу́, -о́тишь) *impf.* **threshing** *n.* молотьба́. **threshing-floor** *n.* ток (*loc.* -у́; *pl.* -а́). **threshing-machine** *n.* молоти́лка.

threshold ['θreʃəʊld, -həʊld] *n.* поро́г.

thrice [θraɪs] *adv.* три́жды.

thrift [θrɪft] *n.* бережли́вость. **thriftless** *adj.* расточи́тельный. **thrifty** *adj.* бережли́вый.

thrill [θrɪl] *n.* (*trepidation, excitement*) тре́пет, волне́ние; (*sth.* ~*ing*) что-л. захва́тывающее; *v.t.* & *i.* си́льно волнова́ть(ся) *impf.*, вз~ *pf.* **thriller** *n.* приключе́нческий, детекти́вный (*novel*) рома́н, (*film*) фильм. **thrilling** *adj.* волну́ющий, захва́тывающий.

thrive [θraɪv] *v.i.* процвета́ть *impf.*; (*grow*)

разраста́ться *impf.*, разрасти́сь (-тётся; разро́сся, -сла́сь) *pf.*

throat [θrəʊt] *n.* го́рло. **throaty** *adj.* горта́нный; (*hoarse*) хри́плый (-л, -ла́, -ло).

throb [θrɒb] *v.i.* (*heart*) си́льно би́ться (бьётся) *impf.*; пульси́ровать *impf.*; **his head** ~**bed** кровь стуча́ла у него́ в виска́х; *n.* бие́ние; пульса́ция.

throe [θrəʊ] *n.* о́страя боль; *pl.* му́ки *f.pl.*; (*of birth*) родовы́е му́ки *f.pl.*; (*of death*) аго́ния.

thrombosis [θrɒmˈbəʊsɪs] *n.* тромбо́з.

throne [θrəʊn] *n.* трон, престо́л; **come to the** ~ вступа́ть *impf.*, вступи́ть (-плю, -пишь) *pf.* на престо́л.

throng [θrɒŋ] *n.* толпа́ (*pl.* -пы); *v.i.* толпи́ться *impf.*; *v.t.* заполня́ть *impf.*, запо́лнить *pf.* толпо́й.

throttle [ˈθrɒt(ə)l] *n.* (*gullet*) гло́тка; (*tech.*) дро́ссель *m.*; *v.t.* (*strangle*) души́ть (-шу́, -шишь) *impf.*, за~ *pf.*; (*tech.*) дроссели́ровать *impf. & pf.*; ~ **down** сбавля́ть *impf.*, сба́вить *pf.* ско́рость+g.

through [θruː] *prep.* (*across, via,* ~ *opening*) че́рез+a.; (*esp.* ~ *thick of*) сквозь+a.; (*air, streets etc.*) по+d.; (*agency*) посре́дством+g.; (*reason*) из-за+g.; (*from beginning to end*) с нача́ла до конца́; **be** ~ **with** (*sth.*) ока́нчивать *impf.*, око́нчить *pf.*; (*s.o.*) порыва́ть *impf.*, порва́ть (-ву́, -вёшь; порва́л, -а́, -о) *pf.* с+i.; **put** ~ (*on telephone*) соединя́ть *impf.*, соедини́ть *pf.*; ~ **and** ~ до конца́, соверше́нно; *adj.* сквозно́й. **through'out** *adv.* повсю́ду, во всех отноше́ниях; *prep.* по всему́ (всей, всему́); *pl.* всем)+d.; (*from beginning to end*) с нача́ла до конца́+g.

throw [θrəʊ] *n.* бросо́к (-ска́), броса́ние; *v.t.* броса́ть *impf.*, бро́сить *pf.*; кида́ть *impf.*, ки́нуть *pf.*; (*rider*) сбра́сывать *impf.*, сбро́сить *pf.*; (*pottery*) формова́ть *impf.*, с~ *pf.*; (*party*) устра́ивать *impf.*, устро́ить *pf.*; ~ **o.s. at** набра́сываться *impf.*, набро́ситься *pf.* на+a.; ~ **o.s. into** броса́ться *impf.*, бро́ситься *pf.* в+a.; ~ **about** разбра́сывать *impf.*, разброса́ть *pf.*; ~ **money about** сори́ть *impf.* деньга́ми; ~ **aside, away** отбра́сывать *impf.*, отбро́сить *pf.*; ~ **away, out** выбра́сывать *impf.*, вы́бросить *pf.*; ~ **back** отбра́сывать *impf.*, отбро́сить *pf.* наза́д; ~ **down** сбра́сывать *impf.*, сбро́сить *pf.*; ~ **in** (*add*) добавля́ть *impf.*, доба́вить *pf.*; (*sport*) вбра́сывать *impf.*, вбро́сить *pf.*; ~ **off** сбра́сывать *impf.*, сбро́сить *pf.*; ~ **open** распа́хивать *impf.*, распахну́ть *pf.*; ~ **out** (*see also* ~ *away*) (*expel*) выгоня́ть *impf.*, вы́гнать (вы́гоню, -нишь) *pf.*; (*reject*) отверга́ть *impf.*, отве́ргнуть *pf.*; ~ **over, up** (*abandon, renounce*) броса́ть *impf.*, бро́сить *pf.* **throw-back** *n.* регре́сс, возвра́т к про́шлому, атави́зм. **throw-in** *n.* вбра́сывание мяча́.

thrush¹ [θrʌʃ] *n.* (*bird*) дрозд (-а́).

thrush² [θrʌʃ] *n.* (*disease*) моло́чница.

thrust [θrʌst] *n.* (*shove*) толчо́к (-чка́); (*lunge*) вы́пад; (*blow, stroke, mil.*) уда́р; (*tech., of rocket*) тя́га; *v.t.* (*shove*) толка́ть *impf.*, толкну́ть *pf.*; (~ *into, out of; give quickly, carelessly*) сова́ть (сую́, суёшь) *impf.*, су́нуть *pf.*; ~ **one's way** пробива́ть *impf.*, проби́ть (-бью, -бьёшь) *pf.* себе́ доро́гу; ~ **aside** отта́лкивать *impf.*, оттолкну́ть *pf.*; ~ **out** высо́вывать *impf.*, вы́сунуть *pf.*

thud [θʌd] *n.* глухо́й звук, стук; *v.i.* (*fall with* ~) па́дать *impf.*, (у)па́сть ((у)паду́, -дёшь; (у)па́л) *pf.* с глухи́м сту́ком; шлё́паться *impf.*, шлё́пнуться *pf.* (*coll.*).

thug [θʌg] *n.* головоре́з (*coll.*).

thumb [θʌm] *n.* большо́й па́лец (-льца); **under the** ~ **of** под башмако́м у+g.; *v.t.*: ~ **through** перели́стывать *impf.*, перелиста́ть *pf.*; ~ **a lift** голосова́ть *impf.*, про~ *pf.* (*coll.*). **thumbscrew** *n.* тиски́ (-ко́в) *pl.* для больши́х па́льцев.

thump [θʌmp] *n.* (*heavy blow*) тяжёлый уда́р; (*thud*) глухо́й звук, стук; *v.t.* наноси́ть (-ошу́, -о́сишь) *impf.*, нанести́ (-есу́, -есёшь; -ёс, -есла́) *pf.* уда́р+d.; колоти́ть (-очу́, -о́тишь) *impf.*, по~ *pf.* в+a., по+d.; *v.i.* (*strike with* ~) би́ться (бьюсь, бьёшься) *impf.* с глухи́м шу́мом.

thunder [ˈθʌndə(r)] *n.* гром (*pl.* -ы, -о́в); (*fig.*) гро́хот; *v.i.* греме́ть (-млю́, -ми́шь) *impf.*; грохота́ть (-очу́, -о́чешь) *impf.*; (*fulminate* (*fig.*)) мета́ть (мечу́, -чешь) *impf.* гро́мы и мо́лнии; **it is** ~**ing** гром греми́т. **thunderbolt** *n.* уда́р мо́лнии; (*fig.*) гром среди́ я́сного не́ба. **thunderclap** *n.* уда́р гро́ма. **thundercloud** *n.* грозова́я ту́ча. **thunderous** *adj.* громово́й. **thunderstorm** *n.* гроза́ (*pl.* -зы). **thunderstruck** *adj.* (*fig.*) как гро́мом поражённый (-ён, -ена́). **thundery** *adj.* грозово́й.

Thursday [ˈθɜːzdeɪ, -dɪ] *n.* четве́рг (-а́).

thus [ðʌs] *adv.* (*in this way*) так, таки́м о́бразом; (*accordingly*) ита́к; ~ **far** до сих пор.

thwack [θwæk] *n.* си́льный уда́р; *v.t.* бить (бью, бьёшь) *impf.*, по~ *pf.*

thwart [θwɔːt] *v.t.* меша́ть *impf.*, по~ *pf.*+d.; (*plans*) расстра́ивать *impf.*, расстро́ить *pf.*

thyme [taɪm] *n.* тимья́н.

thyroid [ˈθaɪrɔɪd] *n.* (~ *gland*) щитови́дная железа́.

tiara [tɪˈɑːrə] *n.* тиа́ра.

Tibet [tɪˈbet] *n.* Тибе́т.

tibia [ˈtɪbɪə] *n.* больша́я берцо́вая кость (*pl.* -ти, -те́й).

tic [tɪk] *n.* тик.

tick¹ [tɪk] *n.* (*noise*) ти́канье; (*moment*) моме́нт, мину́точка; (*mark*) пти́чка; *v.i.* ти́кать *impf.*, ти́кнуть *pf.*; *v.t.* отмеча́ть *impf.*, отме́тить *pf.* пти́чкой; ~ **off** (*scold*) отде́лывать *impf.*, отде́лать *pf.* (*coll.*).

tick² [tɪk] *n.* (*mite*) клещ (-а́).

tick³ [tɪk] *n.* (*coll.*) креди́т; **on** ~ в креди́т.

ticket ['tɪkɪt] *n.* биле́т; (*label*) ярлы́к (-а́); (*season* ~) ка́рточка; (*cloakroom* ~) номеро́к (-рка́); (*receipt*) квита́нция; ~ **collector** контролёр; ~ **office** (биле́тная) ка́сса; ~ **punch** компо́стер; *v.t.* прикрепля́ть *impf.*, прикрепи́ть *pf.* ярлы́к к+d.

tickle ['tɪk(ə)l] *n.* щеко́тка; *v.t.* щекота́ть (-очу́, -о́чешь) *impf.*, по~ *pf.*; (*amuse*) весели́ть *impf.*, по~, раз~ *pf.*; *v.i.* щекота́ть (-о́чет) *impf.*, по~ *pf. impers.*; **my throat** ~**s** у меня́ щеко́чет в го́рле. **ticklish** *adj.* щекотли́вый (*also fig.*); **to be** ~ боя́ться (бою́сь, бои́шься) *pf.* щеко́тки.

tidal ['taɪd(ə)l] *adj.* прили́во-отли́вный; ~ **wave** прили́вная волна́ (*pl.* -ны, -н, волна́м).

tiddlywinks ['tɪdlɪwɪŋks] *n.* (игра́ в) бло́шки (-шек) *pl.*

tide [taɪd] *n.* прили́в и отли́в; **high** ~ прили́в; **low** ~ отли́в; (*current, tendency*) тече́ние; **the** ~ **turns** (*fig.*) собы́тия принима́ют друго́й оборо́т; *v.t.*: ~ **over** помога́ть *impf.*, помо́чь (-огу́, -о́жешь; -ог, -огла́) *pf.* +d. of *person* спра́виться (*difficulty* с+i.); **will this money** ~ **you over?** вы протя́нете с э́тими деньга́ми? **tidemark** *n.* отме́тка у́ровня по́лной воды́.

tidiness ['taɪdɪnɪs] *n.* опря́тность, аккура́тность. **tidy** *adj.* опря́тный, аккура́тный; (*considerable*) поря́дочный; *v.t.* убира́ть *impf.*, убра́ть (уберу́, -рёшь; убра́л, -а́, -о) *pf.*; приводи́ть (-ожу́, -о́дишь) *impf.*, привести́ (-еду́, -едёшь; -ёл, -ела́) *pf.* в поря́док.

tie [taɪ] *n.* (*garment*) га́лстук; (*string, lace*) завя́зка; (*link, bond, tech.*) связь; (*equal points etc.*) ра́вный счёт; **end in a** ~ зака́нчиваться *impf.*, зако́нчиться *pf.* вничью́; (*match*) матч; (*mus.*) ли́га; (*burden*) обу́за; *pl.* (*bonds*) у́зы (уз) *pl.*; *v.t.* свя́зывать *impf.*, связа́ть (свяжу́, -жешь) *pf.* (*also fig.*); (~ *up*) завя́зывать *impf.*, завяза́ть (-яжу́, -я́жешь) *pf.*; (*restrict*) ограни́чивать *impf.*, ограни́чить *pf.*; ~ **down** (*fasten*) привя́зывать *impf.*, привяза́ть (-яжу́, -я́жешь) *pf.*; ~ **up** (*tether*) привя́зывать *impf.*, привяза́ть (-яжу́, -я́жешь) *pf.*; (*parcel*) перевя́зывать *impf.*, перевяза́ть (-яжу́, -я́жешь) *pf.*; *v.i.* (*be ~d*) завя́зываться *impf.*, завяза́ться (-я́жется) *pf.*; (*sport*) равня́ть *impf.*, с~ *pf.* счёт; сыгра́ть *pf.* вничью́; ~ **in, up, with** совпада́ть *impf.*, совпа́сть *pf.* с+i. **tie-pin** *n.* була́вка для га́лстука.

tier [tɪə(r)] *n.* ряд (-á *with* 2, 3, 4, *loc.* -ý; *pl.* -ы́), я́рус.

tiff [tɪf] *n.* размо́лвка; *v.i.* ссо́риться *impf.*, по~ *pf.* (**with** с+i.).

tiger ['taɪgə(r)] *n.* тигр. **tigress** *n.* тигри́ца.

tight [taɪt] *adj.* (*compact*) пло́тный (-тен, -тна́, -тно, пло́тны́); (*cramped*) те́сный (-сен, -сна́, -сно), у́зкий (-зок, -зка́, -зко); (*impenetrable*) непроница́емый; (*strict*) стро́гий (-г, -а́, -о); (*tense, taut*) туго́й (туг, -а́, -о), натя́нутый; ~ **corner** (*fig.*) тру́дное положе́ние. **tighten** *v.t. & i.* натя́гиваться

impf., натяну́ться *pf.*; (*clench, contract*) сжима́ть(ся) *impf.*, сжа́ться (сожму́(сь), -мёшь(ся)) *pf.*; ~ **one's belt** поту́же затя́гивать *impf.*, затяну́ть *pf.* по́яс (*also fig.*); ~ **up** (*discipline etc.*) подтя́гивать *impf.*, подтяну́ть *pf.* (*coll.*). **tight-fisted** *adj.* скупо́й (-п, -па́, -по). **tightly** *adv.* (*strongly*) про́чно; (*closely, cramped*) те́сно. **tightness** *n.* теснота́; напряжённость. **tightrope** *n.* ту́го натя́нутый кана́т. **tights** *n.* колго́тки (-ток) *pl.*

tilde ['tɪldə] *n.* ти́льда.

tile [taɪl] *n.* (*roof*) черепи́ца (*also collect.*); (*decorative*) ка́фель *m.* (*also collect.*); *v.t.* крыть (кро́ю, кро́ешь) *impf.*, по~ *pf.* черепи́цей, ка́фелем. **tiled** *adj.* (*roof*) черепи́чный; (*floor*) ка́фельный.

till[1] [tɪl] *prep.* до+g.; **not** ~ то́лько (**Friday в** пя́тницу; **the next day** на сле́дующий день); *conj.* пока́ не; **not** ~ то́лько когда́.

till[2] [tɪl] *n.* ка́сса.

till[3] [tɪl] *v.t.* возде́лывать *impf.*, возде́лать *pf.* **tillage** *n.* обрабо́тка земли́.

tiller[1] ['tɪlə(r)] *n.* земледе́лец (-льца).

tiller[2] ['tɪlə(r)] *n.* (*naut.*) ру́мпель *m.*

tilt [tɪlt] *n.* накло́н; (*naut., aeron.*) крен; **on the** ~ в накло́нном положе́нии; **at full** ~ и́зо всех сил; по́лным хо́дом; *v.t. & i.* наклоня́ть(ся) *impf.*, наклони́ть(ся) (-ню́(сь), -нишь(ся)) *pf.*; (*heel (over)*) крени́ть(ся) *impf.*, на~ *pf.*

timber ['tɪmbə(r)] *n.* лесоматериа́л, лес (-а(у)) (*collect.*); (*beam*) ба́лка; (*naut.*) ти́мберс. **timbered** *adj.* общи́тый де́ревом; деревя́нный. **timbering** *n.* (*work*) пло́тничная рабо́та.

timbre ['tæmbə(r), 'tæbrə] *n.* тембр.

time [taɪm] *n.* вре́мя *nt.*; (*occasion*) раз (*pl.* -зы, -з); (*term*) срок (-а(у)); (*period*) пери́од, эпо́ха; (*mus.*) темп, такт; (*sport*) тайм; *pl.* (*period*) времена́ *pl.*; (*in comparison*) раз; **five** ~**s as big** в пять раз бо́льше; (*multiplication*) **four** ~**s four** четы́режды четы́ре; **five** ~**s four** пя́тью четы́ре; ~ **and** ~ **again,** ~ **after** ~ не раз, ты́сячу раз; **at a** ~ ра́зом, одновреме́нно; **at the** ~ в э́то вре́мя; **at** ~**s** по времена́м; **at the same** ~ в то же вре́мя; **before my** ~ до меня́; **for a long** ~ до́лго; (*up to now*) давно́; **for the** ~ **being** пока́; **from** ~ **to** ~ вре́мя от вре́мени; **in** ~ (*early enough*) во́-время; (*with* ~) со вре́менем; **in good** ~ заблаговре́менно; **in** ~ **with** в такт+d.; **in no** ~ момента́льно; **on** ~ во́-время; **one at a** ~ по одному́; **be in** ~ успева́ть *impf.*, успе́ть *pf.* (**for** с+d., на+a.); **I do not have** ~ **for him** (*fig.*) я не хочу́ тра́тить вре́мя на него́; **have** ~ **to** (*manage*) успева́ть *impf.*, успе́ть *pf.* +inf.; **have a good** ~ хорошо́ проводи́ть (-ожу́, -о́дишь) *impf.*, провести́ (-еду́, -едёшь; -ёл, -ела́) *pf.* вре́мя; **it is** ~ пора́ (**to** +inf.); **what is the** ~? кото́рый час?; **kill** ~ убива́ть *impf.*, уби́ть (убью́, -ьёшь) *pf.* вре́мя; **work**

full (part) ~ рабо́тать *impf.* по́лный (непо́л-ный) рабо́чий день; ~ **bomb** бо́мба заме́дленного де́йствия; ~ **off** о́тпуск; ~ **signal** сигна́л вре́мени; ~ **signature** та́ктовый разме́р; *v.t.* (*choose* ~) выбира́ть *impf.*, вы́брать (-беру́, -берешь) *pf.* вре́мя+g.; (*arrange* ~) назнача́ть *impf.*, назна́чить *pf.* вре́мя+g.; (*ascertain* ~) засека́ть *impf.*, засе́чь (-еку́, -ечёшь; засе́к, -ла́, -ло) *pf.* вре́мя; хронометри́ровать *impf. & pf.* **time-consuming** *adj.* отнима́ющий мно́го вре́мени. **time-honoured** *adj.* освящённый века́ми. **timekeeper** *n.* (*person*) та́бельщик; (*sport*) хронометри́ст. **time-lag** отстава́ние во вре́мени; (*tech.*) запа́здывание. **timeless** *adj.* ве́чный. **time-limit** преде́льный срок (-a(y)). **timely** *adj.* своевре́менный. **timepiece** *n.* часы́ (-со́в) *pl.*; хроно́метр. **timetable** *n.* расписа́ние; (*of work*) гра́фик.

timid ['tɪmɪd] *adj.* ро́бкий (-бок, -бка́, -бко), засте́нчивый. **ti'midity** *n.* ро́бкость, засте́нчивость. **timorous** ['tɪmərəs] *adj.* боязли́вый.

tin [tɪn] *n.* (*metal*) о́лово; ~ **plate** бе́лая жесть; *attr.* оловя́нный, жестяно́й; (*container*) (консе́рвная) ба́нка, жестя́нка; (*cake-*~) фо́рма; (*baking* ~) про́тивень (-вня) *m.*; ~ **foil** оловя́нная фо́льга; *v.t.* (*coat with* ~) луди́ть (лужу́, лу́дишь) *impf.*, по~ *pf.*; (*pack in* ~) консерви́ровать *impf. & pf.*; ~**ned food** консе́рвы (-вов) *pl.*

tincture ['tɪŋktʃə(r), -tʃə(r)] *n.* (*colour, fig.*) отте́нок (-нка); (*taste; fig.*) при́вкус; (*fig.*) налёт; *v.t.* (*colour; fig.*) слегка́ окра́шивать *impf.*, окра́сить *pf.*; (*flavour*) придава́ть (-даю́, -даёшь) *impf.*, прида́ть (-а́м, -а́шь, -а́ст, -ади́м; при́дал, -а́, -о) *pf.* вкус+d.

tinder ['tɪndə(r)] *n.* трут. **tinder-box** *n.* тру́тница.

tinge [tɪndʒ] *n.* (*colour; fig.*) отте́нок (-нка); (*taste; fig.*) при́вкус; (*fig.*) налёт; *v.t.* (*also fig.*) слегка́ окра́шивать *impf.*, окра́сить *pf.*

tingle ['tɪŋɡ(ə)l] *n.* пока́лывание; (*from cold*) пощи́пывание; *v.i.* (*sting*) коло́ть (ко́лет) *impf. impers.*; **my fingers** ~ у меня́ ко́лет па́льцы; **his nose** ~**d with the cold** моро́з пощи́пывал ему́ нос; (*burn*) горе́ть (гори́т) *impf.*; (*jingle*) звене́ть (-ни́т) *impf.* в уша́х (*person* y+g.).

tinker ['tɪŋkə(r)] *n.* ме́дник, луди́льщик; *v.i.* (*work as a* ~) рабо́тать *impf.* луди́льщиком; ~ **with** вози́ться (вожу́сь, во́зишься) *impf.* c+i.

tinkle ['tɪŋk(ə)l] *n.* звон, звя́канье; *v.i.*(*t.*) звене́ть (-ню́, -ни́шь) *impf.* (+i.); звя́кать *impf.*, звя́кнуть *pf.* +i.; (*on instrument*) бренча́ть (-чу́, -чи́шь) *impf.* (**on** на+p.).

tinny ['tɪnɪ] *adj.* (*thin*) то́нкий (-нок, -нка́, -нко, то́нки́); (*piano etc.*) издаю́щий металли́ческий звук; (*sound*) металли́ческий. **tin-opener** *n.* консе́рвный нож (-а́).

tinsel ['tɪns(ə)l] *n.* мишура́ (*also fig.*); *attr.* мишу́рный.

tinsmith ['tɪnsmɪθ] *n.* жестя́нщик.

tint [tɪnt] *n.* отте́нок (-нка); (*faint* ~) бле́дный тон (*pl.* -а́); *v.t.* слегка́ окра́шивать *impf.*, окра́сить *pf.* **tinted** *adj.* окра́шенный; ~ **glasses** тёмные очки́ (-ко́в) *pl.*

tiny ['taɪnɪ] *adj.* о́чень ма́ленький; кро́шечный (*coll.*).

tip¹ [tɪp] *n.* (*end*) ко́нчик; (*of stick, spear etc.*) наконе́чник; *v.t.* приставля́ть *impf.*, приста́вить *pf.* наконе́чник к+d.; **be on the ~ of s.o.'s tongue** верте́ться (ве́ртится) *impf.* на языке́ y+g.

tip² [tɪp] *n.* (*money*) чаевы́е (-ы́х) *pl.*; (*advice*) сове́т, намёк; (*private information*) све́дения *nt.pl.*, полу́ченные ча́стным о́бразом; (*dump*) сва́лка; (*slight push*) лёгкий толчо́к (-чка́) *v.t. & i.* наклоня́ть(ся) *impf.*, наклони́ть(ся) (-ню́(сь), -нишь(ся)) *pf.*; *v.t.* (*hit lightly*) слегка́ ударя́ть *impf.*, уда́рить *pf.*; (*give* ~) дава́ть (даю́, даёшь) *impf.*, дать (дам, дашь, даст, дади́м; дал, -ла́, да́ло́, -и) *pf.* (*person* +d.; *money* де́ньги на чай, *information* ча́стную информа́цию); ~ **out** выва́ливать *impf.*, вы́валить *pf.*; ~ **over, up** (*v.t. & i.*) опроки́дывать(ся) *impf.*, опроки́нуть(ся) *pf.*; ~ **up, back** (*seat*) отки́дывать *impf.*, отки́нуть *pf.*; ~ **the scales** (*fig.*) реша́ть *impf.*, реши́ть *pf.* исхо́д де́ла.

tipple ['tɪp(ə)l] *n.* (алкого́льный) напи́ток (-тка); *v.i.* выпива́ть *impf.*; *v.t. & i.* попива́ть *impf.* (*coll.*). **tippler** *n.* пья́ница *c.g.*

tipster ['tɪpstə(r)] *n.* жучо́к (-чка́).

tipsy ['tɪpsɪ] *adj.* подвы́пивший.

tiptoe ['tɪptəʊ] *n.*: **on** ~ на цы́почках.

tip-top ['tɪptɒp] *adj.* первокла́ссный, превосхо́дный.

tip-up ['tɪpʌp] *adj.*: ~ **lorry** самосва́л.

tirade [taɪ'reɪd, tɪ-] *n.* тира́да.

tire¹ ['taɪə(r)] *n.* (*metal*) колёсный банда́ж (-а́).

tire² ['taɪə(r)] *v.t.* (*weary*) утомля́ть *impf.*, утоми́ть *pf.*; (*bore*) надоеда́ть *impf.*, надое́сть (-е́м, -е́шь, -е́ст, -еди́м; -е́л) *pf.* +d.; *v.i.* утомля́ться *impf.*, утоми́ться *pf.*; устава́ть (устаю́, -аёшь) *impf.*, уста́ть (-а́ну, -а́нешь) *pf.* **tired** *adj.* уста́лый, утомлённый; **be** ~ **of, I am** ~ **of him** он мне надое́л; **I am** ~ **of playing** мне надое́ло игра́ть; ~ **out** изму́ченный. **tiredness** *n.* уста́лость. **tireless** *adj.* неутоми́мый. **tiresome** *adj.* утоми́тельный, надое́дливый. **tiring** *adj.* утоми́тельный.

tiro ['taɪə,rəʊ] *n.* новичо́к (-чка́).

tissue ['tɪʃuː, 'tɪsjuː] *n.* ткань; (*handkerchief*) бума́жная салфе́тка. **tissue-paper** *n.* папиро́сная бума́га.

tit¹ [tɪt] *n.* (*bird*) сини́ца.

tit² [tɪt] *n.*: ~ **for tat** зуб за́ зуб.

titanic [taɪ'tænɪk, tɪ-] *adj.* (*huge*) титани́ческий.

titbit ['tɪtbɪt] *n.* ла́комый кусо́к (-ска́); (*news*) пика́нтная но́вость.

tithe [taɪð] *n.* деся́тая часть (*pl.* -ти, -те́й); (*hist.*) десяти́на.

titillate ['tɪtɪ,leɪt] *v.t.* щекота́ть (-очу́, -о́чешь) *impf.*, по~ *pf.*; прия́тно возбужда́ть *impf.*, возбуди́ть *pf.*

titivate ['tɪtɪ,veɪt] *v.t. & i.* (*coll.*) прихора́шивать(ся) *impf.* (*coll.*).

title ['taɪt(ə)l] *n.* (*of book etc.*) назва́ние; (*heading*) загла́вие; (*rank*) ти́тул, зва́ние; (*cin.*) титр; (*sport*) зва́ние чемпио́на; ~ **role** загла́вная роль (*pl.* -ли, -ле́й). **titled** *adj.* титуло́ванный. **title-deed** *n.* докуме́нт, даю́щий пра́во со́бственности. **title-holder** *n.* чемпио́н. **title-page** *n.* ти́тульный лист (*pl.* -ы́).

titter ['tɪtə(r)] *n.* хихи́канье; *v.i.* хихи́кать *impf.*, хихи́кнуть *pf.*

tittle ['tɪt(ə)l] *n.* чу́точка, ка́пелька. **tittle-tattle** *n.* болтовня́ (*coll.*).

titular ['tɪtjʊlə(r)] *adj.* номина́льный; титуло́ванный.

to [tə, *before a vowel* tʊ, *emph.* tuː] *prep.* (*town, a country, theatre, school, etc.*) в+*a.*; (*the sea, the moon, the ground, post-office, meeting, concert, north, etc.*) на+*a.*; (*the doctor, towards, up* ~; ~ *one's surprise etc.*) к+*d.*; (*with accompaniment of*) под+*a.*; (*in toast*) за+*a.*; (*time*): **ten minutes** ~ **three** без десяти́ три; (*compared with*) в сравне́нии с+*i.*; **it is ten** ~ **one that** де́вять из десяти́ за то, что; ~ **the left (right)** нале́во (напра́во); (*in order to*) что́бы+*inf.*; *adv.*: **shut the door** ~ закро́йте дверь; **come** ~ приходи́ть (-ожу́, -о́дишь) *impf.*, прийти́ (-йду́, -йдёшь; пришёл, -шла́) *pf.* в созна́ние; **bring** ~ приводи́ть (-ожу́, -о́дишь) *impf.*, привести́ (-еду́, -едёшь; -ёл, -ела́) *pf.* в созна́ние; ~ **and fro** взад и вперёд.

toad [təʊd] *n.* жа́ба. **toadstool** *n.* пога́нка.

toady ['təʊdɪ] *n.* подхали́м; *v.t.* льсти́ть *impf.*, по~ *pf.* +*d.*; *v.t. & i.* низкопокло́нничать *impf.* (**to** пе́ред+*i.*).

toast [təʊst] *n.* (*bread*) поджа́ренный хлеб; (*drink*) тост; ~ **rack** подста́вка для поджа́ренного хле́ба; *v.t.* (*bread*) поджа́ривать *impf.*, поджа́рить *pf.*; (*drink*) пить (пью, пьёшь; пил, -а́, -о) *impf.*, вы́~ *pf.* за здоро́вье+*g.* **toaster** *n.* то́стер.

toastmaster ['təʊst,mɑːstə(r)] *n.* тамада́ *m.*

tobacco [tə'bækəʊ] *n.* таба́к; *attr.* таба́чный; ~ **pouch** кисе́т. **tobacconist** *n.* торго́вец (-вца) таба́чными изде́лиями; ~'s **(shop)** таба́чный магази́н.

toboggan [tə'bɒgən] *n.* сала́зки (-зок) *pl.*; *v.i.* ката́ться *impf.* на сала́зках.

today [tə'deɪ] *adv.* сего́дня; (*nowadays*) в на́ши дни; *n.* сего́дняшний день (дня) *m.*; ~'s **newspaper** сего́дняшняя газе́та; **the writers of** ~ совреме́нные писа́тели *m.pl.*

toddle ['tɒd(ə)l] *v.i.* ковыля́ть *impf.* (*coll.*); (*learn to walk*) учи́ться (учу́сь, у́чишься) *impf.* ходи́ть; (*stroll*) прогу́ливаться *impf.* **toddler** *n.* ребёнок (-нка; *pl.* де́ти, -те́й), начина́ющий ходи́ть; малы́ш (-а́) (*coll.*).

toddy ['tɒdɪ] *n.* горя́чий пунш.

to-do [tə'duː] *n.* сумато́ха, суета́.

toe [təʊ] *n.* па́лец (-льца) ноги́; (*of sock etc.*) носо́к (-ска́); **from top to** ~ с головы́ до пят; *v.t.* (*touch with* ~) каса́ться *impf.*, косну́ться *pf.* носко́м+*g.*; ~ **the line** (*fig.*) подчиня́ться *impf.*, подчини́ться *pf.* тре́бованиям. **toecap** *n.* носо́к (-ска́).

toffee ['tɒfɪ] *n.* (*substance*) ири́с; (*a* ~) ири́ска (*coll.*).

toga ['təʊgə] *n.* то́га.

together [tə'geðə(r)] *adv.* вме́сте, сообща́; (*simultaneously*) одновреме́нно; ~ **with** вме́сте с+*i.*; **all** ~ все вме́сте; **get** ~ собира́ть(ся) *impf.*, собра́ть(ся) (-беру́, -берёшь; -брал(ся), -брала́(сь), -бра́ло, -бра́ло́сь) *pf.*; **join** ~ объединя́ть(ся) *impf.*, объедини́ть(ся) *pf.* (**with** с+*i.*).

toggle ['tɒg(ə)l] *n.* (*button*) продолгова́тая (деревя́нная) пу́говица.

toil [tɔɪl] *n.* тяжёлый труд; *v.i.* труди́ться (-ужу́сь, -у́дишься) *impf.*; (*drag o.s. along*) тащи́ться (тащу́сь, -щишься) *impf.* **toiler** *n.* тру́женик, -ица.

toilet ['tɔɪlɪt] *n.* туале́т; ~ **paper** туале́тная бума́га; ~ **water** туале́тная вода́ (*a.* во́ду). **toiletries** ['tɔɪlɪtrɪz] *n.pl.* туале́тные принадле́жности *f.pl.*

token ['təʊkən] *n.* (*sign*) знак; (*keepsake*) пода́рок (-рка) на па́мять; (*coupon, counter*) тало́н, жето́н; **as a** ~ **of** в знак+*g.*; *attr.* символи́ческий; ~ **resistance** ви́димость сопротивле́ния; **by the same** ~ (*similarly*) к тому́ же; (*moreover*) кро́ме того́.

Tokyo ['təʊkjəʊ, -kɪ,əʊ] *n.* То́кио *m.indecl.*

tolerable ['tɒlərəb(ə)l] *adj.* (*bearable*) терпи́мый; (*satisfactory*) удовлетвори́тельный, сно́сный (*coll.*). **tolerance** *n.* терпи́мость; (*tech.*) до́пуск; (*med.*) толера́нтность. **tolerant** *adj.* терпи́мый; (*med.*) толера́нтный. **tolerate** *v.t.* терпе́ть (-плю́, -пишь) *impf.*, по~ *pf.*; (*allow*) допуска́ть *impf.*, допусти́ть (-ущу́, -у́стишь) *pf.*; (*med.*) быть толера́нтным. **tole'ration** *n.* терпи́мость.

toll[1] [təʊl] *v.t.* (*медленно и ме́рно*) ударя́ть *impf.*, уда́рить *pf.* в ко́локол; *v.i.* звони́ть *impf.*, по~ *pf.* (ме́дленно и ме́рно).

toll[2] [təʊl] *n.* (*duty*) по́шлина; **take its** ~ наноси́ть (-ошу́, -о́сишь) *impf.*, нанести́ (-сёт; нанёс, -есла́) *pf.* тяжёлый уро́н. **toll-bridge** *n.* пла́тный мост (мо́ста́, *loc.* -у́; *pl.* -ы́). **toll-gate** *n.* заста́ва, где взима́ется сбор.

tom(-cat) [tɒm] *n.* кот (-а́).

tomahawk ['tɒmə,hɔːk] *n.* томага́вк; *v.t.* бить (бью, бьёшь) *impf.*, по~ *pf.* томага́вком.

tomato [tə'mɑːtəʊ] *n.* помидо́р; *attr.* тома́тный.

tomb [tuːm] *n.* моги́ла. **tombstone** *n.* моги́льная плита́ (*pl.* -ты).

tomboy ['tɒmbɔː] *n.* сорване́ц (-нца́).

tome [təʊm] *n.* больша́я (тяжёлая) кни́га.

tomfoolery [tɒm'fuːlərɪ] *n.* дура́чества *nt.pl.*

tommy-gun ['tɒmɪ,gʌn] *n.* автома́т.

tomorrow [tə'mɒrəʊ] *adv.* за́втра; *n.* за́втрашний день (дня) *m.*; ~ **morning** за́втра ýтром; **the day after** ~ послезáвтра; **see you** ~ (*coll.*) до зáвтра.

tom-tit ['tɒmtɪt] *n.* синúца.

tom-tom ['tɒmtɒm] *n.* тамтáм.

ton [tʌn] *n.* тóнна.

tonal ['təʊn(ə)l] *adj.* тонáльный. **tonality** [tə'nælɪtɪ] *n.* тонáльность. **tone** *n.* тон (*pl.* -ы (*mus. & fig.*), -á (*colour*)); (*atmosphere, mood*) атмосфéра, настроéние; (*med.*) тóнус; ~ **control** регуляция тéмбра; *v.t.* придавáть (-даю, -даёшь) *impf.*, придáть (-áм, áшь, -áст, -адúм; прúдал, -á, -о) *pf.* желáтельный тон+*d.*; *v.i.* (*harmonize*) гармонúровать *impf.* (**with** с+*i.*); ~ **down** смягчáть(ся) *impf.*, смягчúть(ся) *pf.*; ~ **up** усúливать *impf.*, усúлить *pf.*; (*med.*) тонизúровать *impf. & pf.* **tone-arm** *n.* звукосъúматель *m.* **tone-deaf** *adj.* с слáбым музыкáльным слýхом.

tongs [tɒŋz] *n.* щипцы (-цóв) *pl.*

tongue [tʌŋ] *n.* (*var. senses*) язы́к (-á); (*of shoe*) язычóк (-чкá); **give** ~ (*of dog*) поддавáть (-даю, -аёшь) *impf.*, поддáть (-áм, -áшь, -áст, -адúм; пóддал, -á, -о) *pf.* гóлос; (*of person*) грóмко говорúть *impf.*; **hold one's** ~ держáть (-жу, -жишь) *impf.* язы́к за зубáми; **lose one's** ~ проглáтывать *impf.*, проглотúть (-очý, -óтишь) *pf.* язы́к; **put out one's** ~ покáзывать *impf.*, показáть (-ажý, -áжешь) *pf.* язы́к. **tongue-in-cheek** *adj.* с насмéшкой, иронúчески. **tongue-tied** *adj.* косноязы́чный. **tongue-twister** *n.* скороговóрка.

tonic ['tɒnɪk] *n.* (*med.*) тонизúрующее срéдство; (*mus.*) тóника; *adj.* (*med.*) тонизúрующий; (*mus.*) тонúческий.

tonight [tə'naɪt] *adv.* сегóдня вéчером; *n.* сегóдняшний вéчер.

tonnage ['tʌnɪdʒ] *n.* тоннáж, грузовместúмость; (*charge*) корáбельный сбор.

tonsil ['tɒns(ə)l, -sɪl] *n.* миндáлина. **tonsi'llitis** *n.* ангúна.

tonsure ['tɒnsjə(r), 'tɒnʃə(r)] *n.* тонзýра; *v.t.* выбривáть *impf.*, вы́брить (-рею, -реешь) *pf.* тонзýру+*d.*

too [tuː] *adv.* слúшком; (*also*) тáкже, тóже; (*very*) óчень; (*indeed*) действúтельно; (*moreover*) к тому же; **none** ~ не слúшком.

tool [tuːl] *n.* инструмéнт; (*machine-*~) станóк (-нкá); (*implement; fig.*) орýдие. **tool-box** *n.* ящик с инструмéнтами.

toot [tuːt] *n.* гудóк (-дкá); *v.i.* гудéть (-дúт) *impf.*; (*give a hoot*) давáть (даю, даёшь) *impf.*, дать (дам, дашь, даст, дадúм; дал, -á, дáло, -и) *pf.* гудóк *v.t.* (*blow*) трубúть *impf.* в+*a.*

tooth [tuːθ] *n.* зуб (*pl.* -ы, -óв); (*tech.*) зубéц (-бцá); *attr.* зубнóй; **false teeth** вставны́е зýбы (-бóв) *pl.*; **first** ~ молóчный зуб (*pl.* -ы, -óв); **loose** ~ шатáющийся зуб (*pl.* -ы, -óв); **second** ~ постоя́нный зуб (*pl.* -ы, -óв); ~ **and nail** (*fiercely*) не на жизнь, а на смерть; (*energetically*) энергúчно; **in the teeth of** (*in*

defiance of) наперекóр+*d.*; (*directly against*) пря́мо прóтив+*g.*; **have one's teeth attended to** лечúть (-чý, -чишь) зýбы (-бóв) *pl.*; **he has cut a** ~ у негó прорéзался зуб. **toothache** *n.* зубнáя боль. **toothbrush** *n.* зубнáя щётка. **tooth-comb** *n.* чáстый гребéнь (-бня) *m.* **toothed** *adj.* зубчáтый. **toothless** *adj.* беззýбый. **toothpaste** *n.* зубнáя пáста. **toothpick** *n.* зубочúстка. **toothy** *adj.* зубáстый (*coll.*).

top¹ [tɒp] *n.* (*toy*) волчóк (-чкá).

top² [tɒp] *n.* (*of object; fig.*) верх (-а(у), *loc.* -ý; *pl.* -ú); (*of hill etc.*) вершúна; (*of tree*) верхýшка; (*of head*) макýшка; (*of milk*) слúвки (-вок) *pl.*; (*lid*) кры́шка; (*upper part*) вéрхняя часть (*pl.* -ти, -тéй); ~ **copy** оригинáл; ~ **drawer** (*fig.*) вы́сшее óбщество; ~ **hat** цилúндр; (**at**) ~ **level** на вы́сшем ýровне; (*of high rank*) высокопостáвленный; **on** ~ **of** (*position*) на+*p.*, сверх+*g.*; (*on to*) на+*a.*; **on** ~ **of everything** сверх всегó; **from** ~ **to bottom** свéрху дóнизу; **at the** ~ **of one's voice** во всё гóрло; **at** ~ **speed** во весь опóр; *adj.* вéрхний, вы́сший, сáмый высóкий; (*foremost*) пéрвый; *v.t.* (*cover*) покрывáть *impf.*, покры́ть (-рóю, -рóешь) *pf.*; (*reach* ~ *of*) поднимáться *impf.*, подня́ться (-нимýсь, -нúмешься; -ня́лся, -ня́лáсь) *pf.* на вершúну+*g.*; (*excel*) превосходúть (-ожý, -óдишь) *impf.*, превзойтú (-ойдý, -ойдёшь; -ошёл, -ошлá) *pf.*; (*cut* ~ *off*) обрезáть *impf.*, обрéзать (-éжу, -éжешь) *pf.* верхýшку+*g.*; ~ **off** завершáть *impf.*, завершúть *pf.*; ~ **up** (*with liquid*) доливáть *impf.*, долúть (-лью, -льёшь; дóлил, -á, -о) *pf.*; (*with grain etc.*) досыпáть *impf.*, досы́пать (-плю, -плешь) *pf.*

topaz ['təʊpæz] *n.* топáз.

topcoat ['tɒpkəʊt] *n.* пальтó *nt.indecl.*

top-heavy [tɒp'hevɪ] *adj.* перевéшивающий в своéй вéрхней чáсти. **top-secret** *adj.* совершéнно секрéтный.

topiary ['təʊpɪərɪ] *n.* искýсство фигýрной стрúжки кустóв.

topic ['tɒpɪk] *n.* тéма, предмéт. **topical** *adj.* актуáльный; ~ **question** злободнéвный вопрóс. **topi'cality** *n.* актуáльность.

topknot ['tɒpnɒt] *n.* (*tuft, crest*) хохóл (-хлá); (*knot*) пучóк (-чкá) лент (*of ribbons*), волóс (*of hair*).

topmost ['tɒpməʊst] *adj.* сáмый вéрхний; сáмый вáжный.

topographer [tə'pɒɡrəfə(r)] *n.* топóграф. **topographic(al)** [ˌtɒpə'ɡræfɪk(ə)l] *adj.* топографúческий. **topography** *n.* топогрáфия.

topology [tə'pɒlədʒɪ] *n.* тополóгия. **toponymy** [tə'pɒnɪmɪ] *n.* топонúмия.

topple ['tɒp(ə)l] *v.t. & i.* опрокúдывать(ся) *impf.*, опрокúнуть(ся) *pf.*; *v.i.* валúться (-люсь, -лишься) *impf.*, по~, с~ *pf.*

topsail ['tɒpseɪl, -s(ə)l] *n.* мáрсель *m.*

topsoil ['tɒpsɔɪl] *n.* вéрхний слой пóчвы.

topsy-turvy [ˌtɒpsɪ'tɜːvɪ] *adj.* повёрнутый

вверх дном; (*disorderly*) беспоря́дочный; *adv.* вверх дном, ши́ворот-навы́ворот.

torch [tɔːʃ] *n.* фа́кел; (*electric* ∼) электри́ческий фона́рик; (*fig.*) све́точ. **torch-bearer** *n.* фа́кельщик, -ица. **torchlight** *n.* свет фа́кела, фона́рика.

toreador ['tɒrɪədɔː(r)] *n.* тореадо́р.

torment ['tɔːment] *n.* муче́ние, му́ка; *v.t.* му́чить *impf.*, за∼, из∼ *pf.* **tor'mentor** *n.* мучи́тель *m.*

tornado [tɔːʹneɪdəʊ] *n.* торна́до; (*fig.*) урага́н.

torpedo [tɔːʹpiːdəʊ] *n.* торпе́да; *v.t.* торпеди́ровать *impf.* & *pf.*; (*fig.*) прова́ливать *impf.*, провали́ть (-лю́, -лишь) *pf.* **torpedo-boat** *n.* торпе́дный ка́тер (*pl.* -а́).

torpid ['tɔːpɪd] *adj.* (*numb*) онеме́лый; (*sluggish*) вя́лый. **torpor** *n.* онеме́лость; апа́тия.

torque [tɔːk] *n.* (*phys., mechanics*) враща́ющий моме́нт.

torrent ['tɒrənt] *n.* стреми́тельный пото́к; (*fig.*) пото́к; *pl.* ли́вень (-вня) *m.* **torrential** [təʹrenʃ(ə)l] *adj.* теку́щий бы́стрым пото́ком; (*of rain*) проливно́й; (*fig.*) оби́льный.

torrid ['tɒrɪd] *adj.* зно́йный.

torsion ['tɔːʃ(ə)n] *n.* скру́ченность; (*tech.*) круче́ние.

torso ['tɔːsəʊ] *n.* ту́ловище; (*of statue*) торс.

tort [tɔːt] *n.* гражда́нское правонаруше́ние.

tortoise ['tɔːtəs] *n.* черепа́ха. **tortoise-shell** *n.* па́нцирь *m.* черепа́хи; (*material*) черепа́ха; *attr.* черепа́ховый; (*cat*) пёстрый.

tortuous ['tɔːtjʊəs] *adj.* изви́листый; (*evasive*) укло́нчивый.

torture ['tɔːtʃə(r)] *n.* пы́тка; *v.t.* пыта́ть *impf.*; (*torment*) му́чить *impf.*, за∼, из∼ *pf.*; (*distort*) искажа́ть *impf.*, искази́ть *pf.* **torturer** *n.* мучи́тель *m.*, пала́ч (-а́).

toss [tɒs] *n.* бросо́к (-ска́), броса́ние; ∼ **of coin** подбра́сывание моне́ты, жеребьёвка (*fig.*); **win (lose) the** ∼ (не) выпада́ть *impf.*, вы́пасть (-адет; -ал) *pf.* жре́бий *impers.* (**I won the** ∼ мне вы́пал жре́бий); *v.t.* броса́ть *impf.*, бро́сить *pf.*; (*coin*) подбра́сывать *impf.*, подбро́сить *pf.*; (*rider*) сбра́сывать *impf.*, сбро́сить *pf.*; (*of bull etc.*) поднима́ть *impf.*, подня́ть (-ниму́, -ни́мешь; по́днял, -а́, -о) *pf.* на рога́; (*head*) вски́дывать *impf.*, вски́нуть *pf.*; (*salad*) переме́шивать *impf.*, перемеша́ть *pf.*; ∼ **a pancake** перевора́чивать *impf.*, переверну́ть *pf.* блин, подбро́сив его́; *v.i.* (*of ship*) кача́ться *impf.*, качну́ться *pf.*; (*in bed*) мета́ться (мечу́сь, -чешься) *impf.*; ∼ **aside, away** отбра́сывать *impf.*, отбро́сить *pf.*; ∼ **off** (*work*) де́лать *impf.*, с∼ *pf.* на́спех; (*drink*) пить (пью, пьёшь) *impf.*, вы́∼ *pf.* за́лпом; ∼ **up** броса́ть *impf.*, бро́сить *pf.* жре́бий. **toss-up** *n.* жеребьёвка; (*doubtful matter*): **it is a** ∼ э́то ещё вопро́с.

tot¹ [tɒt] *n.* (*coll.*) (*child*) малы́ш (-а́) (*coll.*); (*glass*) ма́ленькая рю́мка; (*dram*) ма́ленький глото́к (-тка́).

tot² [tɒt]: ∼ **up** (*coll.*) (*v.t.*) скла́дывать *impf.*,

сложи́ть (-жу́, -жишь) *pf.*; (*v.i.*) равня́ться *impf.* (**to** +*d.*).

total ['təʊt(ə)l] *n.* ито́г, су́мма; *adj.* о́бщий; (*complete*) по́лный (-лон, -лна́, по́лно́); **in** ∼ в це́лом, вме́сте; ∼ **recall** фотографи́ческая па́мять; ∼ **war** тота́льная война́; **sum** ∼ о́бщая су́мма; *v.t.* подсчи́тывать *impf.*, подсчита́ть *pf.*; *v.i.* равня́ться *impf.*+*d.* **totalitarian** [təʊˌtælɪʹteərɪən] *adj.* тоталита́рный. **totality** [təʊʹtælɪtɪ] *n.* вся су́мма целико́м; **the** ∼ **of** весь (вся, всё; все); **in** ∼ в це́лом, вме́сте. **totali'zator** *n.* тотализа́тор. **totalize** *v.t.* соединя́ть *impf.*, соедини́ть *pf.* воеди́но. **totally** *adv.* соверше́нно.

totem ['təʊtəm] *n.* тоте́м. **totem-pole** *n.* тоте́мный столб (-а́).

totter ['tɒtə(r)] *v.i.* (*walk unsteadily*) ходи́ть (хожу́, хо́дишь) *indet.*, идти́ (иду́, идёшь; шёл, шла) *det.*, пойти́ (пойду́, -дёшь; пошёл, -шла́) *pf.* неве́рными шага́ми; (*reel*) шата́ться *impf.*; (*toddle*) ковыля́ть *impf.*; (*perish*) ги́бнуть (-б) *impf.*, по∼ *pf.*

toucan ['tuːkən] *n.* тука́н.

touch [tʌtʃ] *n.* прикоснове́ние; (*sense*) осяза́ние; (*stroke of brush etc.*) штрих (-а́); (*mus. or art style*) туше́; (*of piano etc.*) уда́р; (*shade*) отте́нок (-нка); (*taste*) при́вкус; (*small amount*) чу́точка; (*of illness*) лёгкий при́ступ; (*sport*) пло́щадь (*pl.* -ди, -де́й) за боковы́ми ли́ниями; (*personal*) ли́чный подхо́д; **get in** ∼ **with** свя́зываться *impf.*, связа́ться (-яжу́сь, -я́жешься) *pf.* с+*i.*; **keep in (lose)** ∼ **with** подде́рживать *impf.*, поддержа́ть (-жу́, -жишь) *pf.* (теря́ть *impf.*, по∼ *pf.*) связь, конта́кт с+*i.*; **put the finishing** ∼**es to** отде́лывать *impf.*, отде́лать *pf.*; **common** ∼ чу́вство ло́ктя; **to the** ∼ на о́щупь; *v.t.* (*lightly*) прикаса́ться *impf.*, прикосну́ться *pf.* к+*d.*; каса́ться *impf.*, косну́ться *pf.*+*g.*; (*also disturb; affect*) тро́гать *impf.*, тро́нуть *pf.*; (*momentarily reach*) подска́кивать *impf.*, подскочи́ть (-чит) *pf.* до+*g.* (*coll.*); (*be comparable with*) идти́ (иду́, идёшь; шёл, -шла) *impf.* в сравне́нии с+*i.*; *v.i.* (*be contiguous; come into contact*) соприкаса́ться *impf.*, соприкосну́ться *pf.*; ∼ **down** приземля́ться *impf.*, приземли́ться *pf.*; ∼ **off** (*provoke*) вызыва́ть *impf.*, вы́звать (вы́зову, -вешь) *pf.*; ∼ (**up)on** (*fig.*) каса́ться *impf.*, косну́ться *pf.*+*g.*; ∼ **up** поправля́ть *impf.*, попра́вить *pf.*; ∼ **wood!** не сгла́зить бы! **touchdown** *n.* поса́дка. **touched** *adj.* тро́нутый. **touchiness** *n.* оби́дчивость. **touching** *adj.* тро́гательный. **touch-line** *n.* бокова́я ли́ния. **touchstone** *n.* про́бирный ка́мень (-мня; *pl.* -мни, -мне́й) *m.* **touch-type** *v.i.* печа́тать *impf.*, напеча́тать *pf.* вслепу́ю. **touch-typing** *n.* слепо́й ме́тод машинописи. **touchy** *adj.* оби́дчивый.

tough [tʌf] *adj.* жёсткий (-ток, -тка́, -тко); (*durable*) про́чный (-чен, -чна́, -чно, про́чны́); (*strong*) кре́пкий (-пок, -пка́, -пко);

(*difficult*) трудный (-ден, -дна, -дно, трудны); (*hardy*) выносливый; *n.* хулиган, бандит. **toughen** *v.t.* & *i.* делать(ся) *impf.*, с~ *pf.* жёстким. **toughness** *n.* жёсткость; (*durability*) прочность.

toupee ['tu:peɪ] *n.* небольшой парик (-á).

tour [tʊə(r)] *n.* (*journey*) путешествие, поездка; (*excursion*) экскурсия; (*of artistes*) турне *nt.indecl.*; (*of duty*) объезд; ~ **de force** проявление силы (*strength*), ловкости (*skill*); *v.i.* (*t.*) совершать *impf.*, совершить *pf.* путешествие, турне, объезд (по+*d.*). **tourism** *n.* туризм. **tourist** *n.* турист, -ка; ~ **class** второй класс.

tournament ['tʊənəmənt] *n.* турнир. **tourney** *v.i.* участвовать *impf.* в турнире.

tourniquet ['tʊənɪˌkeɪ] *n.* турникет.

tousle ['taʊz(ə)l] *v.t.* взъерошивать *impf.*, взъерошить *pf.* (*coll.*).

tout [taʊt] *n.* навязчивый торговец (-вца); (*of horses*) человек (*pl.* люди, -дей, -дям, -дьми) добывающий и продающий сведения о лошадях перед скачками; *v.t.* навязывать *impf.*, навязать (-яжу, -яжешь) *pf.* (*thing* +*a.*; *person* +*d.*).

tow[1] [təʊ] *v.t.* буксировать *impf.*; *n.* буксировка; **on** ~ на буксире.

tow[2] [təʊ] *n.* (*textile*) пакля.

towards [tə'wɔ:dz, twəʊdz, tɔ:dz] *prep.* (*in direction of*) (по направлению) к+*d.*; (*fig.*) к+*d.*; (*for*) для+*g.*

towel ['taʊəl] *n.* полотенце. **towelling** *n.* махровая ткань. **towel-rail** *n.* вешалка для полотенец.

tower ['taʊə(r)] *n.* башня; (*tech.*) вышка; (*fig.*): ~ **of strength** надёжная опора; *v.i.* выситься *impf.*, возвышаться *impf.* (**above** над+*i.*). **towering** *adj.* (*high*) высокий (-ок, -ока, -око); (*rising up*) возвышающийся; (*furious*) неистовый.

town [taʊn] *n.* город (*pl.* -á); *attr.* городской; ~ **clerk** секретарь *m.* городской корпорации; ~ **council** городской совет, муниципалитет; ~ **councillor** член городского совета; ~ **crier** глашатай; ~ **hall** ратуша, мэрия; ~ **planning** градостроительство. **townsman, -swoman** *n.* горожанин (*pl.* -áне, -áн), -áнка.

tow-path ['təʊpɑ:θ] *n.* бечевник (-á). **tow-rope** *n.* буксир, бечева *no pl.*

toxic ['tɒksɪk] *adj.* ядовитый, токсический.

toxin ['tɒksɪn] *n.* яд (-a(y)); (*med.*) токсин.

toy [tɔɪ] *n.* игрушка; ~ **dog** маленькая комнатная собачка; ~ **soldier** оловянный солдатик; *v.i.*: ~ **with** (*sth. in hands*) вертеть (верчу, -ртишь) *impf.* в руках; (*trifle with*) играть *impf.* (с)+*i.*

trace[1] [treɪs] *n.* (*track, mark*) след (*pl.* -ы); (*small amount*) небольшое количество; ~ **element** микроэлемент; *v.t.* (*track* (*down*), *trace* (*through*)) прослеживать *impf.*, проследить *pf.*; (*make copy*) калькировать *impf.*, с~ *pf.*; ~ **back** (*v.i.*) восходить (-ожу,

-одишь) *impf.* (**to** к+*d.*); ~ **out** (*plan*) набрасывать *impf.*, набросать *pf.*; (*map, diagram*) чертить (черчу, -ртишь) *impf.*, на~ *pf.*

trace[2] [treɪs] *n.* (*of harness*) постромка.

tracery ['treɪsərɪ] *n.* узор. **tracing** *n.* (*copy*) чертёж (-á) на кальке. **tracing-paper** *n.* калька.

trachea [trə'ki:ə, 'treɪkɪə] *n.* трахея.

track [træk] *n.* (*path*) дорожка, тропинка; (*mark*) след (*pl.* -ы); (*rail.*) путь (-ти, -тём) *m.*, колея; (*sport*) трек, дорожка; (*on tape*) (звуковая) дорожка; (*on record*) запись; ~ **events** соревнования *nt.pl.* по бегу; ~ **suit** тренировочный костюм; **off the** ~ на ложном пути; (*fig.*) отклонившийся от темы; **off the beaten** ~ в глуши; **be on the** ~ **of** преследовать *impf.*; **go off the** ~ (*fig.*) отклоняться *impf.*, отклониться (-нюсь, -нишься) *pf.* от темы; **keep** ~ **of** следить *impf.* за+*i.*; **lose** ~ **of** терять *impf.*, по~ *pf.* след+*g.*; *v.t.* прослеживать *impf.*, проследить *pf.*; ~ **down** выслеживать *impf.*, выследить *pf.*

tract[1] [trækt] *n.* (*expanse*) пространство; (*anat.*) тракт.

tract[2] [trækt] *n.* (*treatise*) трактат; (*pamphlet*) брошюра.

tractability [ˌtræktə'bɪlɪtɪ] *n.* (*of person*) сговорчивость; (*of material*) ковкость. '**tractable** *adj.* (*person*) сговорчивый; (*material*) ковкий (-вок, -вка, -вко). '**traction** *n.* тяга; (*therapy*) тракция. **traction-engine** *n.* трактор-тягач (-á). '**tractor** *n.* трактор; ~ **driver** тракторист.

trade [treɪd] *n.* торговля; (*occupation*) профессия, ремесло (*pl.* -ёсла, -ёсел, -ёслам); (*collect.*) торговцы *m.pl.*; ~ **mark** фабричная марка; (*fig.*) отличительный знак; ~ **name** (*of firm*) название фирмы; ~ **secret** секрет фирмы; ~ **union** профсоюз; ~ **wind** пассат; *v.i.* торговать *impf.* (**in** +*i.*); *v.t.* (*swap like things*) обмениваться *impf.*, меняться *pf.*+*i.*; (~ **for sth. different**) обменивать *impf.*, обменять *pf.* (**for** на+*a.*); ~ **in** сдавать (сдаю, сдаёшь) *impf.*, сдать (сдам, сдашь, сдаст, сдадим; сдал, -á, -o) *pf.* в счёт покупки нового; ~ **on** (*exploit*) использовать *impf.* & *pf.* **trader, tradesman** *n.* торговец (-вца). **trade-unionist** *n.* член профсоюза. **trading** *n.* торговля, коммерция; *attr.* торговый; ~ **station** фактория.

tradition [trə'dɪʃ(ə)n] *n.* традиция; (*legend*) предание. **traditional** *adj.* традиционный (-нен, -нна). **traditionalism** *n.* приверженность к традициям. **traditionally** *adv.* по традиции.

traduce [trə'dju:s] *v.t.* клеветать (-ещу, -ещешь) *impf.*, на~ *pf.* на+*a.* **traducer** *n.* клеветник (-á), -ица.

traffic ['træfɪk] *n.* движение; (*trade*) торговля; (*transportation*) транспорт; ~ **island** островок (-вка) безопасности; ~ **jam** пробка; *v.i.*

торгова́ть *impf.* (in +*i.*). **trafficator** *n.* указа́тель *m.* поворо́та. **trafficker** *n.* торго́вец (-вца) (in +*i.*). **traffic-lights** *n.* светофо́р.

tragedian [trə'dʒi:dɪən] *n.* тра́гик. **tragedy** ['trædʒɪdɪ] *n.* траге́дия. **tragic** ['trædʒɪk] *adj.* траги́ческий. **tragicomedy** [,trædʒɪ'kɒmɪdɪ] *n.* трагикоме́дия.

trail [treɪl] *n.* (*trace, track*) след (*pl.* -ы́); (*path*) тропи́нка; (*course, road*) путь (-ти́, -тём) *m.*; *v.t.* (*track*) высле́живать *impf.*, вы́следить *pf.*; *v.t. & i.* (*drag*) таска́ть(ся) *indet.*, тащи́ть(ся) (-щу́(сь), -щишь(ся)) *det.*; воло-чи́ть(ся) (-чу́(сь), -чишь(ся)) *impf.* **trailer** *n.* (*on vehicle*) прице́п; (*plant*) сте́лющееся расте́ние; (*cin.*) (кино)ро́лик.

train [treɪn] *n.* по́езд (*pl.* -á); (*of dress*) шлейф; (*retinue*) сви́та; (*mil.*) обо́з; (*convoy*) карава́н; (*series*) цепь (*loc.* -пи́; *pl.* -пи, -пе́й); *v.t.* (*instruct*) обуча́ть *impf.*, обучи́ть (-чу́, -чишь) *pf.* (in +*d.*); (*prepare*) гото́вить *impf.* (for к+*d.*); (*sport*) тренирова́ть *impf.*, на~ *pf.*; (*animals*) дрессирова́ть *impf.*, вы́~ *pf.*; (*break in*) объезжа́ть *impf.*, объе́здить *pf.*; (*aim, point*) направля́ть *impf.*, напра́вить *pf.*; (*plant*) направля́ть *impf.*, напра́вить *pf.* рост+*g.*; *v.i.* пригота́вливаться *impf.*, пригото́виться *pf.* (for к+*d.*); (*sport*) тренирова́ться *impf.*, на~ *pf.* **trai'nee** *n.* стажёр, практика́нт. **trainer** *n.* инстру́ктор; (*sport*) тре́нер; (*of animals*) дрессиро́вщик; *pl.* (*shoes*) адида́ски (-сок), кроссо́вки (-вок) *pl.* **training** *n.* обуче́ние; (*sport*) трениро́вка; (*of animals*) дрессиро́вка; ~ **apparatus** тренажёр. **training-college** *n.* (*teachers'*) педагоги́ческий институ́т, пединститу́т. **training-school** *n.* специа́льное учи́лище.

traipse [treɪps] *v.i.* таска́ться *indet.*, тащи́ться (-щу́сь, -щишся) *det.*

trait [treɪ, treɪt] *n.* (характе́рная) черта́; штрих (-á).

traitor ['treɪtə(r)] *n.* преда́тель *m.*, изме́нник. **traitorous** *adj.* преда́тельский. **traitress** *n.* преда́тельница, изме́нница.

trajectory [trə'dʒektərɪ, 'trædʒɪk-] *n.* траекто́рия.

tram [træm] *n.* трамва́й; ~ **driver** вагоновожа́тый *sb.* **tramline** *n.* трамва́йная ли́ния.

trammel ['træm(ə)l] *n.* (*net*) не́вод (*pl.* -á), трал; (*fig.*) поме́ха, препя́тствие; *v.t.* (*fig.*) препя́тствовать *impf.*, вос~ *pf.*+*d.*

tramp [træmp] *n.* (*vagrant*) бродя́га *m.*; (*tread*) то́пот; (*journey on foot*) путеше́ствие пешко́м; *v.i.* (*of vagrant*) бродя́жничать *impf.*; (*go with heavy tread*) то́пать *impf.*; (*go on foot*) ходи́ть (хожу́, хо́дишь) *indet.*, идти́ (иду́, идёшь; шёл, шла) *det.*, пойти́ (пойду́, -дёшь; пошёл, -шла́) *pf.* пешко́м. **trample** *v.t.* топта́ть (топчу́, -чешь) *impf.*, по~, ис~ *pf.*; ~ **down** выта́птывать *impf.*, вы́топтать (-пчу, -пчешь) *pf.*; ~ **on** (*fig.*) попира́ть *impf.*, попра́ть (-ру́, -рёшь) *pf.*

trampoline ['træmpəliːn] *n.* бату́т, бату́д. **trampolining** *n.* бату́тный спорт. **tram-**

polinist *n.* батути́ст, ~ка.

trance [trɑːns] *n.* транс; (*rapture*) состоя́ние экста́за.

tranquil ['træŋkwɪl] *adj.* споко́йный. **tran'quillity** *n.* споко́йствие. **tranquillize** *v.t.* успока́ивать *impf.*, успоко́ить *pf.* **tranquillizer** *n.* транквилиза́тор.

transact [træn'zækt, trɑːn-, -'sækt] *v.t.* (*business*) вести́ (веду́, -дёшь; вёл, -á) *impf.*; (*a deal*) заключа́ть *impf.*, заключи́ть *pf.* **transaction** *n.* де́ло (*pl.* -лá), сде́лка; *pl.* (*publications*) труды́ *m.pl.*; (*minutes*) протоко́лы *m.pl.*

transatlantic [,trænzət'læntɪk, ,trɑːn-, -sət'læntɪk] *adj.* трансатланти́ческий.

Transcaucasia [,trænskɔː'keɪzjə] *n.* Закавка́зье.

transceiver [træn'siːvə(r), trɑːn-] *n.* приёмопереда́тчик.

transcend [træn'send, trɑːn-] *v.t.* преступа́ть *impf.*, преступи́ть (-плю́, -пишь) *pf.* преде́лы+*g.*; (*excel*) превосходи́ть (-ожу́, -о́дишь) *impf.*, превзойти́ (-ойду́, -ойдёшь; -ошёл, -ошла́) *pf.* **transcendency** *n.* превосхо́дство. **transcendent** *adj.* превосхо́дный. **transcen'dental** *adj.* (*philos.*) трансценде́нтальный.

transcontinental [trænz,kɒntɪ'nent(ə)l, trɑːnz, træns-, trɑːns-] *adj.* трансконтинента́льный.

transcribe [træn'skraɪb, trɑːn-] *v.t.* (*copy out*) перепи́сывать *impf.*, переписа́ть (-ишу́, -и́шешь) *pf.*; (*shorthand*) расшифро́вывать *impf.*, расшифрова́ть *pf.*; (*mus.*) аранжи́ровать *impf.*; (*phon.*) транскриби́ровать *impf. & pf.* **transcript** ['trænskrɪpt, 'trɑːn-] *n.* ко́пия; (*shorthand*) расшифро́вка. **tran'scription** *n.* (*copying out*) перепи́сывание; (*copy*) ко́пия; (*mus.*) аранжиро́вка; (*phon.*) транскри́пция.

transducer [trænz'djuːsə(r)] *n.* преобразова́тель *m.*, да́тчик.

transept ['trænsept, 'trɑːn-] *n.* трансе́пт.

transfer ['trænsfɜː(r), 'trɑːns-] *n.* (*of objects*) перено́с, перемеще́ние; (*of money; of people*) перево́д; (*leg.*) переда́ча; (*design*) переводна́я карти́нка; *v.t.* (*objects*) переноси́ть (-ошу́, -о́сишь) *impf.*, перенести́ (-есу́, -есёшь; -ёс, -есла́) *pf.*; перемеща́ть *impf.*, перемести́ть *pf.*; (*money; people; design*) переводи́ть (-ожу́, -о́дишь) *impf.*, перевести́ (-еду́, -едёшь; -ёл, -ела́) *pf.*; (*leg.*) передава́ть (-даю́, -даёшь) *impf.*, переда́ть (-áм, -áшь, -áст, -ади́м; пе́редал, -á, -о) *pf.*; *v.i.* (*to different job*) переходи́ть (-ожу́, -о́дишь) *impf.*, перейти́ (-ейду́, -ейдёшь; -ешёл, -ешла́) *pf.*; (*change trains etc.*) переса́живаться *impf.*, пересе́сть (-ся́ду, -ся́дешь; -се́л) *pf.* **trans'ferable** *adj.* допуска́ющий переда́чу; (*replaceable*) заменя́емый, замени́мый. **transference** *n.* переда́ча.

transfiguration [træns,fɪgjʊ'reɪʃ(ə)n, trɑː-] *n.* преобразова́ние; (*spiritual*) преображе́ние.

trans'figure v.t. преобразо́вывать impf., преобразова́ть pf.; (in spirit) преображать impf., преобрази́ть pf.

transfix [træns'fıks, trɑ:-] v.t. (pierce) пронза́ть impf., пронзи́ть pf.; (fig.) пригвожда́ть impf., пригвозди́ть pf. к ме́сту.

transform [træns'fɔ:m, trɑ:-] v.t. & i. (also elec.) преобразо́вывать(ся) impf., преобразова́ть(ся) pf.; ~ **into** (i.) превраща́ть(ся) impf., преврати́ть(ся) (-ащу́(сь), -ати́шь(ся)) pf. в+a. **transfor'mation** n. преобразова́ние; превраще́ние. **transformer** n. (elec.) трансформа́тор.

transfuse [træns'fju:z, trɑ:-] v.t. (med.) перелива́ть impf., перели́ть (-лью, -льёшь; -ли́л, -лила́) pf.; (steep) пропи́тывать impf., пропита́ть pf. (in +i.); (convey) передава́ть (-даю́, -даёшь) impf., переда́ть (-а́м, -а́шь, -а́ст, -ади́м; пе́редал, -а́, -о) pf. **transfusion** n. перелива́ние (кро́ви).

transgress [trænz'gres, trɑ:-, -s'gres] v.t. переступа́ть impf., переступи́ть (-плю́, -пишь) pf.; наруша́ть impf., нару́шить pf. **transgression** n. просту́пок (-пка), наруше́ние; (sin) грех (-а́). **transgressor** n. правонаруши́тель m.; (sinner) гре́шник, -ица.

transience ['trænzıəns, 'trɑ:-, -sıəns] n. быстроте́чность, мимолётность. **transient** adj. преходя́щий; (fleeting) мимолётный.

transistor [træn'zıstə(r), trɑ:-, -'sıstə(r)] n. транзи́стор; ~ **radio** транзи́сторный приёмник. **transistorized** adj. на транзи́сторах.

transit ['trænzıt, 'trɑ:-, -sıt] n. транзи́т, прохожде́ние; (astron.) прохожде́ние плане́ты; **in** ~ в, по пути́; ~ **camp** ла́герь (pl. -ря́, -рей) m. переме́щенных лиц; ~ **visa** транзи́тная ви́за. **tran'sition** n. перехо́д. **tran'sitional** adj. перехо́дный; (interim) промежу́точный. **transitive** adj. перехо́дный. **transitory** adj. мимолётный; (temporary) вре́менный.

translate [træn'sleıt, trɑ:-, -'zleıt] v.t. переводи́ть (-ожу́, -о́дишь) impf., перевести́ (-еду́, -едёшь; -ёл, -ела́) pf.; (explain) объясня́ть impf., объясни́ть pf. **translation** n. перево́д. **translator** n. перево́дчик, -ица.

transliterate [trænz'lıtəreıt, trɑ:-, -s'lıtəreıt] v.t. транслитери́ровать impf. & pf. **translite'ration** n. транслитера́ция.

translucency [trænz'lu:s(ə)nsı, trɑ:-, -'lju:s(ə)nsı, -s'l-] n. полупрозра́чность. **translucent** adj. просве́чивающий, полупрозра́чный.

transmigration [,trænzmaı'greıʃ(ə)n, ,trɑ:-, -smaı'greıʃ(ə)n] n. переселе́ние.

transmission [trænz'mıʃ(ə)n, trɑ:-, -s'mıʃ(ə)n] n. переда́ча; (tech.) трансми́ссия; attr. переда́точный. **transmit** v.t. передава́ть (-даю́, -даёшь) impf., переда́ть (-а́м, -а́шь, -а́ст, -ади́м; пе́редал, -а́, -о) pf. **transmitter** n. (радио)переда́тчик.

transmutation [,trænz,mju:'teıʃ(ə)n, trɑ:-, -s,mju:-t'eıʃ(ə)n] n. превраще́ние. **trans'mute** v.t. превраща́ть impf., преврати́ть (-ащу́, -ати́шь) pf.

transparency [træns'pærənsı, trɑ:-, -'peərənsı] n. прозра́чность; (picture) транспара́нт; (phot.) диапозити́в. **transparent** adj. прозра́чный; (obvious) очеви́дный; (frank) открове́нный (-нен, -нна).

transpire [træn'spaıə(r), trɑ:-] v.t. & i. испаря́ть(ся) impf., испари́ть(ся) pf.; v.i. (fig.) обнару́живаться impf., обнару́житься pf.; (occur) случа́ться impf., случи́ться pf.

transplant [træns'plɑ:nt, trɑ:-; 'trænsplɑ:nt, 'trɑ:-] v.t. переса́живать impf., пересади́ть (-ажу́, -а́дишь) pf.; (med.) де́лать impf., c~ pf. переса́дку+g.; n. (med.) переса́дка.

transport ['trænspɔ:t, 'trɑ:-; træns'pɔ:t, trɑ:-] n. (var. senses) тра́нспорт; (conveyance) перево́зка; (of rage etc.) поры́в; attr. тра́нспортный; v.t. перевози́ть (-ожу́, -о́зишь) impf., перевезти́ (-езу́, -езёшь; -ёз, -езла́) pf.; (exile) ссыла́ть impf., сосла́ть (сошлю́, -лёшь) pf. **transpor'tation** n. тра́нспорт, перево́зка; (exile) ссы́лка.

transpose [træns'pəuz, trɑ:-, -z'pəuz] v.t. перемеща́ть impf., перемести́ть pf.; (words) переставля́ть impf., переста́вить pf.; (mus.) транспони́ровать impf. & pf. **transpo'sition** n. перемеще́ние, перестано́вка; (mus.) транспониро́вка.

transsexual [trænz'seksjuəl] n. транссексуали́ст; adj. транссексуа́льный.

trans-ship [trænz'ʃıp, trɑ:-, trænz-] v.t. перегружа́ть impf., перегрузи́ть (-ужу́, -у́зи́шь) pf.

transverse ['trænzvɜ:s, 'trɑ:-, -'vɜ:s, -ns-] adj. попере́чный.

transvestism [trænz'vestız(ə)m, trɑ:-, -s'vestız(ə)m] n. трансвести́зм m. **transvestite** n. трансвести́т.

trap [træp] n. лову́шка (also fig.), западня́, капка́н; (tech.) сифо́н; (cart) рессо́рная двуко́лка; v.t. (catch) лови́ть (-влю́, -вишь) impf., пойма́ть pf. (в лову́шку); (fig.) зама́нивать impf., замани́ть (-ню́, -нишь) pf. в лову́шку. **trapdoor** n. люк.

trapeze [trə'pi:z] n. трапе́ция. **trapezium** n. трапе́ция.

trapper ['træpə(r)] n. охо́тник, ста́вящий капка́ны.

trappings ['træpıŋz] n. сбру́я (collect.); (fig.) (exterior attributes) вне́шние атрибу́ты m.pl.; (adornments) украше́ния nt.pl.

trash [træʃ] n. дрянь (coll.) **trashy** adj. adj. дрянно́й (-нен, -нна́, -нно).

trauma ['trɔ:mə, 'trau-] n. тра́вма. **traumatic** [trɔ:'mætık, trau-] adj. травмати́ческий.

travel ['træv(ə)l] n. путеше́ствие; (tech.) передвиже́ние; ~ **bureau** бюро́ nt.indecl. путеше́ствий; ~ **sickness** n. боле́знь движе́ния; v.i. путеше́ствовать impf.; (tech.) передвига́ться impf., передви́нуться pf.; v.t. объезжа́ть impf., объе́хать (-е́ду, -е́дешь) pf. **traveller** n. путеше́ственник, -ица; (salesman) коммивояжёр; ~**'s cheque** доро́жный чек. **travelling** n. путеше́ствие; attr. доро́жный; (itinerant) передвижно́й.

travelogue ['trævə‚lɒg] *n.* (*film*) фильм о путеше́ствиях; (*lecture*) ле́кция о путеше́ствии с диапозити́вами. **travel-sick** *adj.*: **be** ~ ука́чивать *impf.*, укача́ть *pf. impers.+a.*; **I am** ~ **in cars** меня́ в маши́не ука́чивает.

traverse ['trævəs, trə'vɜːs] *v.t.* пересека́ть *impf.*, пересе́чь (-еку́, -ечёшь; -ёк, -екла́) *pf.*

travesty ['trævistɪ] *n.* паро́дия; *v.t.* пароди́ровать *impf. & pf.*

trawl [trɔːl] *n.* трал; *v.t.* тра́лить *impf.*; *v.i.* лови́ть (-влю́, -вишь) *impf.* ры́бу тра́ловой се́тью. **trawler** *n.* тра́улер. **trawling** *n.* трале́ние.

tray [treɪ] *n.* поднос.

treacherous ['tretʃərəs] *adj.* преда́тельский; (*unreliable*) ненадёжный. **treachery** *n.* преда́тельство.

treacle ['triːk(ə)l] *n.* па́тока. **treacly** *adj.* па́точный.

tread [tred] *n.* по́ступь, похо́дка; (*stair*) ступе́нька; (*of tyre*) протёктор; *v.i.* ступа́ть *impf.*, ступи́ть (-плю́, -пишь) *pf.*; шага́ть *impf.*, шагну́ть *pf.*; *v.t.* топта́ть (-пчу́, -пчешь) *impf.*; дави́ть (-влю́, -вишь) *impf.* **treadle** *n.* (*of bicycle*) педа́ль; (*of sewing machine*) подно́жка.

treason ['triːz(ə)n] *n.* изме́на; **high** ~ госуда́рственная изме́на. **treasonable** *adj.* изме́ннический.

treasure ['treʒə(r)] *n.* сокро́вище, клад; ~ **trove** на́йденный клад; *v.t.* (*preserve*) храни́ть *impf.*; (*value*) дорожи́ть *impf.+i.*; высо́ко цени́ть (-ню́, -нишь) *impf.* **treasurer** *n.* казначе́й. **treasury** *n.* (*also fig.*) сокро́вищница; (**T**~) казна́ *no pl.*; **the T**~ госуда́рственное казначе́йство.

treat [triːt] *n.* (*pleasure*) удово́льствие; (*entertainment*) угоще́ние; *v.t.* (*have as guest*) угоща́ть *impf.*, угости́ть *pf.* (**to** +*i.*); (*med.*) лечи́ть (-чу́, -чишь) *impf.* (**for** от+*g.*; **with** +*i.*); (*behave towards*) обраща́ться *impf.* с+*i.*; (*process*) обраба́тывать *impf.*, обрабо́тать *pf.* (**with** +*i.*); (*discuss*) трактова́ть *impf.* о+*p.*; (*regard*) относи́ться (-ошу́сь, -о́сишься) *impf.*, отнести́сь (-есу́сь, -есёшься; -ёсся, -есла́сь) *pf.* к+*d.* (**as** как к+*d.*). **treatise** ['triːtɪs, -ɪz] *n.* тракта́т. **treatment** *n.* (*behaviour*) обраще́ние; (*med.*) лече́ние; (*processing*) обрабо́тка; (*discussion*) тракто́вка. **treaty** *n.* догово́р.

treble ['treb(ə)l] *adj.* тройно́й; (*trebled*) утро́енный (-ен); (*mus.*) дисканто́вый; *adv.* втро́е, втройне́; *n.* тройно́е коли́чество; (*mus.*) дискант; *v.t. & i.* утра́ивать(ся) *impf.*, утро́ить(ся) *pf.*

tree [triː] *n.* де́рево (*pl.* дере́вья, -ьев). **treeless** *adj.* безле́сный.

trefoil ['trefɔɪl, 'triː-] *n.* трили́стник.

trek [trek] *n.* (*migration*) переселе́ние; (*journey*) путеше́ствие; *v.i.* (*migrate*) переселя́ться *impf.*, пересели́ться *pf.*; (*journey*) путеше́ствовать *impf.*

trellis ['trelɪs] *n.* шпале́ра; (*for creepers*) решётка.

tremble ['tremb(ə)l] *v.i.* трепета́ть (-ещу́, -е́щешь) *impf.* (**at** при+*p.*); дрожа́ть (-жу́, -жи́шь) *impf.* (**with** от+*g.*); трясти́сь (-су́сь, -сёшься; -сся, -сла́сь) *impf.* (**with** от+*g.*). **trembling** *n.* тре́пет, дрожь; **in fear and** ~ трепеща́.

tremendous [trɪ'mendəs] *adj.* (*enormous*) огро́мный; (*excellent, remarkable*) потряса́ющий.

tremor ['tremə(r)] *n.* дрожь, тре́пет; (*earthquake*) толчо́к (-чка́). **tremulous** ['tremjʊləs] *adj.* дрожа́щий; (*uneven*) неро́вный (-вен, -вна́, -вно); (*shy*) ро́бкий (-бок, -бка́, -бко).

trench [trentʃ] *n.* кана́ва, ров (рва, *loc.* во рву); (*mil.*) око́п; ~ **coat** тёплая полушине́ль; *v.t.* рыть (ро́ю, ро́ешь) *impf.*, вы~ *pf.* кана́вы, рвы, око́пы в+*p.*; (*dig over*) перека́пывать *impf.*, перекопа́ть *pf.*

trenchant ['trentʃ(ə)nt] *adj.* о́стрый (остр & остёр, остра́, о́стро́); ре́зкий (-зок, -зка́, -зко). **trenchancy** *n.* острота́, ре́зкость.

trend [trend] *n.* направле́ние, тенде́нция. **trendy** *adj.* мо́дный (-ден, -дна́, -дно).

trepidation [‚trepɪ'deɪʃ(ə)n] *n.* (*trembling*) тре́пет; (*alarm*) трево́га.

trespass ['trespəs] *n.* (*on property*) наруше́ние грани́ц; (*misdemeanour*) просту́пок (-пка); *v.i.* наруша́ть *impf.*, нару́шить *pf.* пра́во владе́ния; ~ **on** (*property*) наруша́ть *impf.*, нару́шить *pf.* грани́цу+*g.*; (*selfishly exploit*) злоупотребля́ть *impf.*, злоупотреби́ть *pf.+i.* **trespasser** *n.* наруши́тель *m.*, ~ница грани́ц.

tress [tres] *n.* ло́кон, коса́ (*a.* ко́су́; *pl.* -сы).

trestle ['tres(ə)l] *n.* ко́злы (-зел, -злам) *pl.*

trial ['traɪəl] *n.* (*test*) испыта́ние (*also ordeal*), про́ба; (*leg.*) проце́сс, суд (-а́); (*sport*) попы́тка; **on** ~ (*probation*) на испыта́нии; (*of objects*) взя́тый на про́бу; (*leg.*) под судо́м; ~ **period** испыта́тельный срок (-а(у)); ~ **run** про́бный пробе́г; (*of ship*) про́бное пла́вание; (*of plane*) испыта́тельный полёт; ~ **and error** ме́тод подбо́ра.

triangle ['traɪ‚æŋg(ə)l] *n.* треуго́льник. **triangular** *adj.* треуго́льный; (*three-edged*) трёхгра́нный.

tribal ['traɪb(ə)l] *adj.* племенно́й, родово́й. **tribe** *n.* пле́мя *nt.*, род (-a(y), *loc.* -ý; *pl.* -ы́). **tribesman** *n.* член пле́мени, ро́да.

tribulation [‚trɪbjʊ'leɪʃ(ə)n] *n.* го́ре, несча́стье.

tribunal [traɪ'bjuːn(ə)l, trɪ-] *n.* трибуна́л; (*court*; *fig.*) ка́федра.

tribune[1] ['trɪbjuːn] *n.* (*leader*) трибу́н.

tribune[2] ['trɪbjuːn] *n.* (*platform*) трибу́на; (*throne*) ка́федра.

tributary ['trɪbjʊtərɪ] *n.* (*geog.*) прито́к; (*hist.*) да́нник. **tribute** *n.* дань (*also fig.*); **pay** ~ (*fig.*) отдава́ть (-даю́, -даёшь) *impf.*, отда́ть (-а́м, -а́шь, -а́ст, -ади́м; о́тдал, -а́, -о) *pf.* дань (уваже́ния) (**to** +*d.*).

trice [traɪs] *n.*: **in a ~** мгнове́нно.

trick [trɪk] *n.* (*ruse*) хи́трость; (*deception*) обма́н; (*conjuring ~*) фо́кус; (*feat, stunt*) трюк; (*joke*) шу́тка; (*of trade etc.*) приём; (*habit*) привы́чка; (*cards*) взя́тка; **play a ~ on** игра́ть *impf.*, сыгра́ть *pf.* шу́тку с+*i.*; *v.t.* обма́нывать *impf.*, обману́ть (-ну́, -нешь) *pf.* **trickery** *n.* обма́н, надува́тельство (*coll.*).

trickle ['trɪk(ə)l] *v.i.* ка́пать *impf.*; сочи́ться *impf.*; *n.* стру́йка.

trickster ['trɪkstə(r)] *n.* обма́нщик, -ица.

tricky *adj.* (*complicated*) сло́жный (-жен, -жна́, -жно); (*crafty*) хи́трый (-тёр, -тра́, хитро́).

tricot ['trɪkəʊ, 'triː-] *n.* трико́ *nt.indecl.*

tricycle ['traɪsɪk(ə)l] *n.* трёхколёсный велосипе́д.

trident ['traɪd(ə)nt] *n.* трезу́бец (-бца).

triennial [traɪ'enɪəl] *adj.* трёхле́тний.

trifle ['traɪf(ə)l] *n.* пустя́к (-а́), ме́лочь (*pl.* -чи, -че́й); (*dish*) бискви́т со сби́тыми сли́вками; **a ~** (*adv.*) немно́го+*g.*; *v.i.* шути́ть (шучу́, шу́тишь) *impf.*, по~ *pf.* (**with** с+*i.*); относи́ться (-ошу́сь, -о́сишься) *impf.*, отнести́сь (-есу́сь, -есёшься; -ёсся, -есла́сь) *pf.* несерьёзно (**with** к+*d.*). **trifling** *adj.* пустяко́вый.

trigger ['trɪgə(r)] *n.* (*of gun*) куро́к (-рка́), спусково́й крючо́к (-чка́); (*releasing catch*) защёлка; *v.t.*: **~ off** вызыва́ть *impf.*, вы́звать (вы́зову, -вешь) *pf.*

trigonometry [ˌtrɪgə'nɒmɪtrɪ] *n.* тригономе́трия.

trilby (hat) ['trɪlbɪ] *n.* мя́гкая фе́тровая шля́па.

trilogy ['trɪlədʒɪ] *n.* трило́гия.

trim [trɪm] *n.* поря́док (-дка), гото́вность; **in fighting ~** в боево́й гото́вности; **in good ~** (*sport*) в хоро́шей фо́рме; (*haircut*) подстри́жка; (*clipping, pruning*) подре́зка; *adj.* (*neat*) аккура́тный, опря́тный; (*smart*) наря́дный; *v.t.* (*cut, clip, cut off*) подреза́ть *impf.*, подре́зать (-е́жу, -е́жешь) *pf.*; (*hair*) подстрига́ть *impf.*, подстри́чь (-игу́, -ижёшь; -и́г) *pf.*; (*square*) обтёсывать *impf.*, обтеса́ть (-ешу́, -е́шешь) *pf.*; (*a dress etc.*) отде́лывать *impf.*, отде́лать *pf.*; (*a dish*) украша́ть *impf.*, укра́сить *pf.* **trimming** *n.* (*on dress*) отде́лка; (*to food*) гарни́р, припра́ва.

trimaran ['traɪməræn] *n.* тримара́н.

Trinity ['trɪnɪtɪ] *n.* тро́ица; **~ Sunday** Тро́ицын день (дня) *m.*

trinket ['trɪŋkɪt] *n.* безделу́шка, брело́к.

trio ['triːəʊ] *n.* три́о *nt.indecl.*; (*of people*) тро́йка.

trip [trɪp] *n.* пое́здка, путеше́ствие, экску́рсия; (*business ~*) командиро́вка; (*stumbling*) спотыка́ние; (*sport*) подно́жка; (*light step*) лёгкая похо́дка; (*mistake*) оши́бка; (*tech.*) расцепля́ющее устро́йство; *v.i.* (*run lightly*) бе́гать *indet.*, бежа́ть (бегу́, бежи́шь) *det.*, по~ *pf.* вприпры́жку; (*stumble*) спотыка́ться *impf.*, споткну́ться *pf.* (**over** о+*a.*);

(*make a mistake*) ошиба́ться *impf.*, ошиби́ться (-бу́сь, -бёшься; -бся) *pf.*; *v.t.* подставля́ть *impf.*, подста́вить *pf.* но́жку+*d.* (*also fig.*); (*confuse*) запу́тывать *impf.*, запу́тать *pf.*

tripartite [traɪ'pɑːtaɪt] *adj.* трёхсторо́нний.

tripe [traɪp] *n.* (*dish*) рубе́ц (-бца́).

triple ['trɪp(ə)l] *adj.* тройно́й; (*tripled*) утро́енный (-ен); *v.t. & i.* утра́ивать(ся) *impf.*, утро́ить(ся) *pf.* **triplet** *n.* (*mus.*) трио́ль; (*one of ~s*) близне́ц (-а́) (*из тро́йни*); *pl.* тро́йня. **triplicate** ['trɪplɪkət] *n.*: **in ~** в трёх экземпля́рах.

tripod ['traɪpɒd] *n.* трено́жник.

triptych ['trɪptɪk] *n.* три́птих.

trite [traɪt] *adj.* бана́льный, изби́тый.

triumph ['traɪəmf, -ʌmf] *n.* триу́мф (*also event*), торжество́, побе́да; *v.i.* торжествова́ть *impf.*, вос~ *pf.* (**over** над+*i.*). **triumphal** [traɪ'ʌmf(ə)l] *adj.* триумфа́льный. **tri'umphant** *adj.* (*exultant*) торжеству́ющий, лику́ющий; (*victorious*) победоно́сный.

trivia ['trɪvɪə] *n.* ме́лочи (-че́й) *pl.* **trivial** *adj.* незначи́тельный. **triviality** [ˌtrɪvɪ'ælɪtɪ] *n.* тривиа́льность, бана́льность. **trivialize** *v.t.* упроща́ть *impf.*, упрости́ть *pf.*

troglodyte ['trɒglədaɪt] *n.* троглоди́т.

troika ['trɔɪkə] *n.* тро́йка.

Trojan ['trəʊdʒ(ə)n] *adj.* троя́нский; *n.* **work like a ~** рабо́тать *impf.* как вол.

troll [trəʊl] *n.* (*myth.*) тролль *m.*

trolley ['trɒlɪ] *n.* теле́жка, вагоне́тка; (*table on wheels*) сто́лик на колёсиках. **trolleybus** *n.* тролле́йбус.

trollop ['trɒləp] *n.* (*sloven*) неря́ха; (*prostitute*) потаску́ха.

trombone [trɒm'bəʊn] *n.* тромбо́н.

troop [truːp] *n.* гру́ппа, отря́д; *pl.* (*mil.*) войска́ *nt.pl.*, солда́ты *m.pl.*; *v.i.* (*move in a crowd*) дви́гаться (-ается & дви́жется) *impf.* толпо́й. **trooper** *n.* кавалери́ст. **trooping the colour(s)** *n.* торже́ственный вы́нос зна́мени (знамён). **troop-ship** *n.* войсково́й тра́нспорт.

trophy ['trəʊfɪ] *n.* трофе́й; (*prize*) приз (*pl.* -ы́).

tropic ['trɒpɪk] *n.* тро́пик; **T~ of Cancer** тро́пик Ра́ка; **T~ of Capricorn** тро́пик Козеро́га. **tropical** *adj.* тропи́ческий.

trot [trɒt] *n.* рысь (*loc.* -си́); *v.i.* рыси́ть *impf.*; (*rider*) е́здить *indet.*, е́хать (е́ду, е́дешь) *det.*, по~ *pf.* ры́сью; (*horse*) ходи́ть (-дит) *indet.*, идти́ (идёт; шёл, шла) *det.*, пойти́ (пойду́, -дёшь; пошёл, -шла́) *pf.* ры́сью; **~ out** (*present for inspection*) представля́ть *impf.*, предста́вить *pf.* на рассмотре́ние; (*show off*) щеголя́ть *impf.*, щегольну́ть *pf.*+*i.* **trotter** *n.* (*horse*) рыса́к (-а́); *pl.* (*dish*) но́жки *f.pl.*

troubadour ['truːbədɔː(r)] *n.* трубаду́р.

trouble ['trʌb(ə)l] *n.* (*worry*) беспоко́йство, трево́га; (*misfortune*) беда́ (*pl.* -ды), го́ре; (*unpleasantness*) неприя́тности *f.pl.*; (*effort*, *pains*) хло́поты (-о́т) *pl.*, труд; (*care*) забо́та; (*disrepair*) пробле́ма, неприя́тности *f.pl.* (**with** с+*i.*); неиспра́вность (**with** в+*p.*); (*illness*) боле́знь; **heart** ~ больно́е се́рдце; **ask for** ~ напра́шиваться *impf.*, напроси́ться (-ошу́сь, -о́сишься) *pf.* на неприя́тности; **be in** ~ име́ть *impf.* неприя́тности; **cause** ~ **to** доставля́ть *impf.*, доста́вить *pf.* хло́поты+*d.*; **get into** ~ попа́сть (-аду́, -адёшь; -а́л) *pf.* в беду́; **make** ~ **for** причиня́ть *impf.*, причини́ть *pf.* неприя́тности+*d.*; **take** ~ стара́ться *impf.*, по~ *pf.*; **take the** ~ труди́ться (-ужу́сь, -у́дишься) *impf.*, по~ *pf.* (**to** +*inf.*); **the** ~ **is** (**that**) беда́ в том, что; *v.t.* (*make anxious, disturb, give pain*) беспоко́ить *impf.*; **may I** ~ **you for ...?** мо́жно попроси́ть у вас +*a.*?; **may I** ~ **you to ...?** мо́жно попроси́ть вас+*inf.*?; *v.i.* (*worry*) беспоко́иться *impf.*; (*take the* ~) труди́ться (тружу́сь, тру́дишься) *impf.* **troubled** *adj.* беспоко́йный. **troublemaker** *n.* нару́шитель *m.*, ~ница споко́йствия. **troubleshooter** *n.* авари́йный монтёр. **troublesome** *adj.* (*restless, fidgety*) беспоко́йный; (*capricious*) капри́зный; (*difficult*) тру́дный (-ден, -дна́, -дно, тру́дны).

trough [trɒf] *n.* (*for food*) корму́шка, коры́то; (*gutter*) жёлоб (*pl.* -а́); (*of wave*) подо́шва; (*meteor.*) ложби́на ни́зкого давле́ния.

trounce [traʊns] *v.t.* (*beat*) бить (бью, бьёшь) *impf.*, по~ *pf.*; (*punish*) суро́во нака́зывать *impf.*, наказа́ть (-ажу́, -а́жешь) *pf.*; (*scold*) суро́во брани́ть *impf.*, вы́~ *pf.* (*coll.*).

troupe [truːp] *n.* тру́ппа.

trouser-leg ['traʊzə(r)] *n.* штани́на (*coll.*). **trousers** *n.* брюки (-к) *pl.*, штаны́ (-но́в) *pl.* **trouser-suit** *n.* брю́чный костю́м.

trousseau ['truːsəʊ] *n.* прида́ное *sb.*

trout [traʊt] *n.* форе́ль.

trowel ['traʊəl] *n.* (*for plastering etc.*) лопа́тка; (*garden* ~) садо́вый сово́к (-вка́).

truancy ['truːənsɪ] *n.* прогу́л. **truant** *n.* прогу́льщик, -ица; **play** ~ прогу́ливать *impf.*, прогуля́ть *pf.*; *adj.* пра́здный.

truce [truːs] *n.* переми́рие; (*respite*) переды́шка.

truck[1] [trʌk] *n.*: **have no** ~ **with** избега́ть *impf.*, избежа́ть (-егу́, -ежи́шь) *pf.* +*g.*

truck[2] [trʌk] *n.* (*lorry*) грузови́к (-а́); (*rail.*) ваго́н-платфо́рма.

truckle ['trʌk(ə)l] *v.i.* раболе́пствовать *impf.* (**to** пе́ред+*i.*).

truculence ['trʌkjʊləns] *n.* свире́пость. **truculent** *adj.* свире́пый.

trudge [trʌdʒ] *n.* утоми́тельная прогу́лка; *v.i.* уста́ло тащи́ться (-щу́сь, -щишься) *impf.*

true [truː] *adj.* (*faithful, correct*) ве́рный (-рен, -рна́, -рно, ве́рны́); (*correct*) пра́вильный; (*genuine*) по́длинный (-нен, -нна); (*exact*) то́чный (-чен, -чна́, -чно); **come** ~ сбыва́ться *impf.*, сбы́ться (сбу́дется; сбы́лся, -ла́сь) *pf.* **true-to-life** *adj.* реалисти́ческий.

truffle ['trʌf(ə)l] *n.* трю́фель (*pl.* -ли, -ле́й) *m.*

truism ['truːɪz(ə)m] *n.* трюи́зм. **truly** *adv.* (*sincerely*) и́скренне; (*faithfully*) ве́рно; (*really, indeed*) действи́тельно, пои́стине; (*accurately*) то́чно; **yours** ~ пре́данный Вам.

trump [trʌmp] *n.* ко́зырь (*pl.* -ри, -ре́й) *m.* (*also fig.*); *v.i.* козыря́ть *impf.*, козырну́ть *pf.* (*coll.*); *v.t.* бить (бью, бьёшь) *impf.*, по~ *pf.* ко́зырем; ~ **up** выду́мывать *impf.*, вы́думать *pf.*; фабрикова́ть *impf.*, с~ *pf.*

trumpery *n.* мишура́; (*rubbish*) дрянь (*coll.*).

trumpet ['trʌmpɪt] *n.* труба́ (*pl.* -бы); *v.i.* труби́ть *impf.* (**on** в+*a.*); (*elephant*) реве́ть (-ву́, -вёшь) *impf.*; *v.t.* (*proclaim*) возвеща́ть *impf.*, возвести́ть *pf.* **trumpeter** *n.* труба́ч (-а́).

truncate [trʌŋ'keɪt, 'trʌŋ-] *v.t.* усека́ть *impf.*, усе́чь (-еку́, -ечёшь; усёк, -ла́) *pf.*; (*cut top off*) среза́ть *impf.*, сре́зать (-е́жу, -е́жешь) *pf.* верху́шку+*g.*; (*abbreviate*) сокраща́ть *impf.*, сократи́ть (-ащу́, -ати́шь) *pf.*

truncheon ['trʌntʃ(ə)n] *n.* (*police*) дуби́нка; (*staff, baton*) жезл (-а́).

trundle ['trʌnd(ə)l] *v.t. & i.* ката́ть(ся) *indet.*, кати́ть(ся) (качу́(сь), ка́тишь(ся)) *det.*, по~ *pf.*

trunk [trʌŋk] *n.* (*stem*) ствол (-а́); (*anat.*) ту́ловище; (*elephant's*) хо́бот; (*box*) сунду́к (-а́); *pl.* (*swimming*) пла́вки (-вок) *pl.*; (*boxing etc.*) трусы́ (-со́в) *pl.*; ~ **call** вы́зов по междугоро́дному телефо́ну; ~ **line** маги-стра́льная ли́ния; ~ **road** магистра́льная доро́га.

truss [trʌs] *n.* (*girder*) ба́лка, фе́рма; (*med.*) грыжево́й банда́ж (-а́); (*sheath, bunch*) свя́зка; *v.t.* (*tie up*, *bird*) свя́зывать *impf.*, связа́ть (-яжу́, -я́жешь) *pf.*; (*reinforce*) укрепля́ть *impf.*, укрепи́ть *pf.*

trust [trʌst] *n.* дове́рие, ве́ра; (*body of* ~*ees*) опе́ка; (*property held in* ~) дове́рительная со́бственность; (*econ.*) трест; (*credit*) креди́т; (*responsibility*) отве́тственность; **breach of** ~ злоупотребле́ние дове́рием; **on** ~ (*credit*) в креди́т; **take on** ~ принима́ть *impf.*, приня́ (приму́, -мешь; при́нял, -а́, -о) *pf.* на ве́ру; *v.t.* доверя́ть *impf.*, дове́рить *pf.*+*d.* (**with** +*a.*; **to** +*inf.*); ве́рить *impf.*, по~ *pf.*+*d.*, в+*a.*; (*entrust*) (*object*) поруча́ть *impf.*, поручи́ть (-чу́, -чишь) *pf.* (**to** +*d.*); (*a secret etc.*) вверя́ть *impf.*, вве́рить *pf.* (**to** +*d.*); *v.i.* (*hope*) наде́яться *impf.*, по~ *pf.* **trus'tee** *n.* попечи́тель *m.*, ~ница, опеку́н, ~ша. **trustful, trusting** *adj.* дове́рчивый. **trustiness** *n.* ве́рность; (*reliability*) надёжность. **trustworthy, trusty** *adj.* надёжный, ве́рный (-рен, -рно, ве́рны́).

truth [truːθ] *n.* и́стина, пра́вда; **tell the** ~ говори́ть *impf.*, сказа́ть (скажу́, -жешь) *pf.* пра́вду; **to tell you the** ~ по пра́вде говоря́. **truthful** *adj.* правди́вый.

try [traɪ] *n.* (*attempt*) попы́тка; (*test, trial*) испыта́ние, про́ба; *v.t.* (*taste; examine effectiveness of*) про́бовать *impf.*, по~ *pf.*; (*test*) испы́тывать *impf.*, испыта́ть *pf.*; (*leg.*)

судить (сужу, судишь) *impf.* (**for** за+*a.*); *v.i.* (*endeavour*) стараться *impf.*, по~ *pf.*; (*make an attempt*) пытаться *impf.*, по- *pf.*; ~ **on** (*clothes*) примерять *impf.*, примерить *pf.* **trying** *adj.* тяжёлый (-л, -ла); (*tiresome*) докучливый (*coll.*).

tsar [za:(r)] *n.* царь (-ря) *m.* **tsarina** [za:'ri:nə] *n.* царица.

T-shirt ['ti:ʃз:t] *n.* тенниска (*coll.*). **T-square** *n.* рейсшина.

tub [tʌb] *n.* кадка, лохань.

tuba ['tju:bə] *n.* туба.

tubby ['tʌbɪ] *adj.* толстенький.

tube [tju:b] *n.* трубка, труба (*pl.* -бы); (*toothpaste etc.*) тюбик; (*underground*) метро *nt.indecl.*; **cathode-ray** ~ элероннолучевая трубка; **inner** ~ камера.

tuber ['tju:bə(r)] *n.* клубень (-бня) *m.* **tubercular** [tju'bз:kjʊlə(r)] *adj.* туберкулёзный. **tuberculosis** *n.* туберкулёз.

tubing ['tju:bɪŋ] *n.* трубы *m.pl.* **tubular** *adj.* трубчатый.

tuck [tʌk] *n.* (*in garment*) складка; *v.t.* (*make ~s in*) делать *impf.*, c~ *pf.* складки на+*loc.*; (*thrust into*, ~ *away*) засовывать *impf.*, засунуть *pf.*; (*hide away*) прятать (-ячу, -ячешь) *impf.*, c~ *pf.*; ~ **in** (*shirt etc.*) заправлять *impf.*, заправить *pf.*; ~ **in, up** (*blanket, skirt*) подтыкать *impf.*, подоткнуть *pf.*; ~ **up** (*sleeves*) засучивать *impf.*, засучить (-чу, -чишь) *pf.*; (*in bed*) укрывать *impf.*, укрыть (-рою, -роешь) *pf.*; (*hair etc. out of the way*) подбирать *impf.*, подобрать (подберу, -рёшь; подобрал, á, -о) *pf.*

Tuesday ['tju:zdeɪ, -dɪ] *n.* вторник.

tuft [tʌft] *n.* пучок (-чка). **tufted** *adj.* с хохолком.

tug [tʌg] *v.t.* (*sharply*) дёргать *impf.*, дёрнуть *pf.*; (*pull*) тянуть (-ну, -нешь) *impf.*, по~ *pf.*; (*tow*) буксировать *impf.*; *n.* рывок (-вка); (*tugboat*) буксирное судно (*pl.* -да, -дов); ~ **of war** перетягивание на канате.

tuition [tju:'ɪʃ(ə)n] *n.* обучение (**in** +*d.*).

tulip ['tju:lɪp] *n.* тюльпан.

tulle [tju:l] *n.* тюль *m.*

tumble ['tʌmb(ə)l] *v.i.* (*fall*) падать *impf.*, (у)пасть ((у)паду, -дёшь; (у)пал) *pf.*; (*go head over heels*) кувыркаться *impf.*, кувыркнуться *pf.*; (*rush headlong*) бросаться *impf.*, броситься *pf.*; *v.t.* (*disarrange*) приводить (-ожу, -одишь) *impf.*, привести (-еду, -едёшь; -ёл, -ела) *pf.* в беспорядок; *n.* падение; кувырканье. **tumbledown** *adj.* полуразрушенный (-ен), развалившийся. **tumbler** *n.* (*acrobat*) акробат; (*glass*) стакан.

tumour ['tju:mə(r)] *n.* опухоль.

tumult ['tju:mʌlt] *n.* (*uproar*) суматоха, шум (-a(y)); (*agitation*) волнение. **tumultuous** [tjʊ'mʌltjʊəs] *adj.* шумный (-мен, -мна, -мно).

tumulus ['tju:mjʊləs] *n.* курган, могильный холм (-á).

tuna ['tju:nə] *n.* тунец (-нца).

tundra ['tʌndrə] *n.* тундра.

tune [tju:n] *n.* мелодия, мотив; **in** ~ в тон, (*of instrument*) настроенный (-ен); **out of tune** не в тон, фальшивый, (*of instrument*) расстроенный (-ен); **be in** ~ **with** (*fig.*) гармонировать *impf.* c+*i.*; **be out of** ~ **with** (*fig.*) (*thing*) идти (иду, идёшь; шёл, шла) *impf.* вразрез c+*i.*; (*person*) быть не в ладу c+*i.*; **call the** ~ распоряжаться *impf.*; **change one's** ~ (пере)менять *impf.*, переменить (-ню, -нишь) *pf.* тон; *v.t.* (*instrument; radio*) настраивать *impf.*, настроить *pf.*; (*engine etc.*) регулировать *impf.*, от~ *pf.*; (*fig.*) приспособлять *impf.*, приспособить *pf.*; ~ **in** настраивать *impf.*, настроить (*radio*) радио (**to** на+*a.*); *v.i.*: ~ **up** настраивать *impf.*, настроить *pf.* инструмент(ы). **tuneful** *adj.* мелодичный, гармоничный. **tuneless** *adj.* немелодичный. **tuner** *n.* настройщик.

tungsten ['tʌŋst(ə)n] *n.* вольфрам.

tunic ['tju:nɪk] *n.* туника; (*of uniform*) китель (*pl.* -ля & -ли) *m.*

tuning ['tju:nɪŋ] *n.* настройка; (*of engine*) регулировка. **tuning-fork** *n.* камертон.

tunnel ['tʌn(ə)l] *n.* туннель *m.*; *v.i.* прокладывать *impf.*, проложить (-жу, -жишь) *pf.* туннель *m.*

tunny ['tʌnɪ] *n.* тунец (-нца).

turban ['tз:bən] *n.* тюрбан, чалма.

turbid ['tз:bɪd] *adj.* мутный (-тен, -тна, -тно); (*fig.*) туманный (-нен, -нна).

turbine ['tз:baɪn] *n.* турбина. **turbo-jet** *adj.* (*n.*) турбореактивный (самолёт). **turbo-prop** *adj.* (*n.*) турбовинтовой (самолёт).

turbot ['tз:bət] *n.* тюрбо *nt.indecl.*

turbulence ['tз:bjʊləns] *n.* буйность, бурность; (*tech.*) турбулентность. **turbulent** *adj.* буйный (буен, буйна, -но), бурный (-рен, бурна, -но); (*tech.*) турбулентный.

tureen [tjʊə'ri:n, tə-] *n.* супник, супница.

turf [tз:f] *n.* дёрн; **the** ~ (*track*) беговая дорожка; (*races*) скачки *f.pl.*; *v.t.* дерновать *impf.*

turgid ['tз:dʒɪd] *adj.* (*swollen*) опухший; (*pompous*) напыщенный (-ен, -енна).

Turk [tз:k] *n.* турок (-рка), турчанка. **Turkey** *n.* Турция.

turkey ['tз:kɪ] *n.* индюк (-á), -юшка; (*dish*) индейка.

Turkic ['tз:kɪk] *adj.* тюркский. **Turkish** *adj.* турецкий; ~ **bath** турецкие бани *f.pl.*; ~ **delight** рахат-лукум.

Turkmenistan [tз:kmenɪ'sta:n] *n.* Туркменистан. **Turkoman** *n.* туркмен, ~ка; *adj.* туркменский.

turmoil ['tз:mɔɪl] *n.* (*disorder*) беспорядок (-дка); (*uproar*) суматоха, шум (-a(y)).

turn [tз:n] *n.* (*change of direction*) поворот; (*revolution*) оборот; (*service*) услуга; (*change*) изменение; **one's** ~ **to do sth.**) очередь; (*character*) склад характера; (*circus, variety*) номер (*pl.* -á); ~ **of phrase** оборот речи; **at every** ~ на каждом шагу; **by, in turn(s)** по очереди; **to a** ~ как раз в меру; **take a bad**

~ принима́ть *impf.*, приня́ть (приму́, -мешь; при́нял, -а́, -о) *pf.* дурно́й оборо́т: take a ~ for the worse изменя́ться *impf.*, измени́ться (-ню́сь, -нишься) *pf.* к ху́дшему; *v.t.* (*handle, key, car around etc.*) повора́чивать *impf.*, поверну́ть *pf.*; (*revolve, rotate*) враща́ть *impf.*, (*spin, twirl*) верте́ть (-рчу́, -ртишь) *impf. +a.* & *i.*; (*page on its face*) перевёртывать *impf.*, перевернуть *pf.*; (*direct*) направля́ть *impf.*, напра́вить *pf.*; (*cause to become*) де́лать *impf.*, c~ *pf. +i.*; (*on lathe*) точи́ть (-чу́, -чишь) *impf.*; ~ s.o.'s head кружи́ть (кружу́, кру́жишь) *impf.*, вс~ *pf.* го́лову+*d.*; ~ one's stomach: that ~ my stomach меня́ от э́того тошни́т; *v.i.* (*change direction*) повора́чивать *impf.*, поверну́ть *pf.*; завёртывать *impf.*, заверну́ть *pf.*; (*rotate*) враща́ться *impf.*; (~ round) повора́чиваться *impf.*, поверну́ться *pf.*; (*become*) станови́ться (-влю́сь, -вишься) *impf.*, стать (ста́ну, -нешь) *pf. +i.*; ~ against ополча́ться *impf.*, ополчи́ться *pf.* на+*a.*, про́тив+*g.*; ~ around *see* ~ round; ~ away (*v.i.* & *i.*) отвора́чивать(ся) *impf.*, отверну́ть(ся) *pf.*; ~ back (*v.i.*) повора́чивать *impf.*, поверну́ть *pf.* наза́д; (*v.t.*) (*bend back*) отгиба́ть *impf.*, отогну́ть *pf.*; ~ down (*refuse*) отклоня́ть *impf.*, отклони́ть (-ню́, -нишь) *pf.*; (*collar*) отгиба́ть *impf.*, отогну́ть *pf.*; (*make quieter*) де́лать *impf.*, c~ *pf.* ти́ше; ~ grey (*v.i.*) седе́ть *impf.*, по~ *pf.*; ~ in (*v.t.*) (*hand back*) возвраща́ть *impf.*, верну́ть *pf.*; (*so as to face inwards*) повора́чивать *impf.*, поверну́ть *pf.* вовну́трь; ~ inside out вывора́чивать *impf.*, вы́вернуть *pf.* наизна́нку; ~ into (*change into*) (*v.t.* & *i.*) превраща́ть(ся) *impf.*, преврати́ть(ся) (-ащу́(сь), -ати́шь(ся)) *pf.* в+*a.*; (*street*) свора́чивать *impf.*, сверну́ть *pf.* на+*a.*; ~ off (*light, radio etc.*) выключа́ть *impf.*, вы́ключить *pf.*; (*tap*) закрыва́ть *impf.*, закры́ть (-ро́ю, -ро́ешь) *pf.*; (*branch off*) свора́чивать *impf.*, сверну́ть *pf.*; ~ on (*light, radio etc.*) включа́ть *impf.*, включи́ть *pf.*; (*tap*) открыва́ть *impf.*, откры́ть (-ро́ю, -ро́ешь) *pf.*; (*attack*) напада́ть *impf.*, напа́сть (-аду́, -адёшь; -ал) *pf.*; ~ out (*light etc.*) *see* ~ off; (*prove to be*) ока́зываться *impf.*, оказа́ться (-ажу́сь, -а́жешься) *pf.* (to be +*i.*); (*drive out*) выгоня́ть *impf.*, вы́гнать (вы́гоню, -нишь) *pf.*; (*pockets*) вывёртывать *impf.*, вы́вернуть *pf.*; (*be present*) приходи́ть (-ожу́, -о́дишь) *impf.*, прийти́ (приду́, -дёшь; пришёл, -шла́) *pf.*; (*product*) выпуска́ть *impf.*, вы́пустить *pf.*; ~ over (*egg, page, on its face, roll over*) (*v.t.* & *i.*) перевёртывать(ся) *impf.*, переверну́ть(ся) *pf.*; (*hand over*) передава́ть (-даю́, -даёшь) *impf.*, переда́ть (-а́м, -а́шь, -а́ст, -ади́м; переда́л, -а́, -о) *pf.*; (*think about*) обду́мывать *impf.*, обду́мать *pf.*; (*overturn*) (*v.t.* & *i.*) опроки́дывать(ся) *impf.*, опроки́нуть(ся) *pf.*; (*switch over*) переключа́ть

impf., переключи́ть *pf.* (to на+*a.*); ~ pale бледне́ть *impf.*, по~ *pf.*; ~ red красне́ть *impf.*, по~ *pf.*; ~ round (*v.i.*) (*rotate*; ~ one's back*; ~ to face sth.*) повёртываться *impf.*, поверну́ться *pf.*; (~ to face) обора́чиваться *impf.*, оберну́ться *pf.*; (*v.t.*) повёртывать *impf.*, поверну́ть *pf.*; ~ sour скиса́ть *impf.*, ски́снуть (скис) *pf.*; ~ to обраща́ться *impf.*, обрати́ться (-ащу́сь, -ати́шься) *pf.* к+*d.* (for за+*i.*); ~ up (*appear*) появля́ться *impf.*, появи́ться (-влю́сь, -вишься) *pf.*; (*be found*) находи́ться (-ожу́сь, -о́дишься) *impf.*, найти́сь (-йду́сь, -йдёшься; нашёлся, -шла́сь) *pf.*; (*shorten garment*) подшива́ть *impf.*, подши́ть (-шью́, -шьёшь) *pf.*; (*crop up*) подвёртываться *impf.*, подверну́ться *pf.*; (*bend up; stick up*) (*v.t.* & *i.*) загиба́ть(ся) *impf.*, загну́ть(ся) *pf.*; (*make louder*) де́лать *impf.*, c~ *pf.* гро́мче; ~ up one's nose вороти́ть (-очу́, -о́тишь) *impf.* нос (at от+*g.*) (*coll.*); ~ upside down перевора́чивать *impf.*, переверну́ть *pf.* вверх дном. **turn-out** *n.* коли́чество приходя́щих. **turn-up** *n.* (*on trousers etc.*) отворо́т, обшла́г (-á; *pl.* -á).

turncoat ['tɜːnkəʊt] *n.* ренега́т, перебе́жчик.

turner ['tɜːnə(r)] *n.* то́карь (*pl.* -ри & -ря́) *m.*

turning ['tɜːnɪŋ] *n.* (*road*) поворо́т. **turning-point** *n.* поворо́тный пункт.

turnip ['tɜːnɪp] *n.* ре́па.

turnover ['tɜːnˌəʊvə(r)] *n.* (*turning over*) опроки́дывание; (*econ.*) оборо́т; (*fluctuation of manpower*) теку́честь рабо́чей си́лы; (*pie*) полукру́глый пиро́г (-á) с начи́нкой.

turnpike ['tɜːnpaɪk] *n.* (*toll gate*) заста́ва (где взима́ется подоро́жный сбор).

turnstile ['tɜːnstaɪl] *n.* турнике́т.

turntable ['tɜːnteɪbl] *n.* (*rail.*) поворо́тный круг (*loc.* -е & -у́; *pl.* -и́); (*of record player*) прои́грыватель *m.*, верту́шка.

turpentine ['tɜːpənˌtaɪn] *n.* скипида́р.

turpitude ['tɜːpɪˌtjuːd] *n.* ни́зость, поро́чность.

turquoise ['tɜːkwɔɪz, -kwɑːz] *n.* (*material, stone*) бирюза́; *adj.* бирюзо́вый.

turret ['tʌrɪt] *n.* ба́шенка; (*gun* ~) оруди́йная ба́шня.

turtle ['tɜːtl] *n.* (морска́я) черепа́ха.

turtle-dove ['tɜːt(ə)l] *n.* го́рлица.

tusk [tʌsk] *n.* би́вень (-вня) *m.*, клык (-á).

tussle ['tʌs(ə)l] *n.* дра́ка; *v.i.* дра́ться (деру́сь, -рёшься; дра́лся, -ла́сь, дра́ло́сь) *impf.* (for за+*a.*).

tut [tʌt] *int.* ах ты!

tutelage ['tjuːtɪlɪdʒ] *n.* (*guardianship*) опеку́нство; (*instruction*) обуче́ние. **tutelar(y)** *adj.* опеку́нский. **tutor** *n.* (*private teacher*) ча́стный дома́шний учи́тель (*pl.* -ля́) *m.*, ~ница; (*coach*) репети́тор; (*univ.*) руководи́тель *m.*, ~ница; (*primer*) уче́бник; (*mus. primer*) шко́ла игры́; *v.t.* (*instruct*) обуча́ть *impf.*, обучи́ть (-чу́, -чишь) *pf.* (in +*d.*); (*give lessons to*) дава́ть (даю́, даёшь) *impf.*, дать (дам, дашь, даст, дади́м; дал, -á, да́ло́, -и) *pf.* уро́ки+*d.*; (*guide*) руководи́ть *impf. +i.*

tutorial [tjuːˈtɔːrɪəl] *n.* консультация, встреча с руководителем.

tutu [ˈtuːtuː] *n.* (*ballet*) пачка.

TV *abbr.* (*of* **television**) ТВ, телевидение; (*set*) телевизор; ~ **addict** телеман, ~ка; **closed-circuit** ~ замкнутое телевидение.

twaddle [ˈtwɒd(ə)l] *n.* пустая болтовня, чепуха.

twang [twæŋ] *n.* (*string*) резкий звук (натянутой струны); (*voice*) гнусавость; *v.i.* (*string*) звучать (-чу, -чишь) *impf.*, про~ *pf.*; (*voice*) гнусавить; *v.t.* (*pluck*) перебирать *impf.*

tweak [twiːk] *n.* щипок (-пка); *v.t.* щипать (-плю, -плешь) *impf.*, (у)щипнуть *pf.*

tweed [twiːd] *n.* твид.

tweet [twiːt] *n.* щёбет; *v.i.* щебетать (-ечу, -ечешь) *impf.*

tweezers [ˈtwiːzəz] *n.* пинцет.

twelfth [twelfθ] *adj. & n.* двенадцатый; (*fraction*) двенадцатая (часть (*pl.* -ти, -тей)); (*date*) двенадцатое (число); **T~ Night** канун Крещения. **twelve** *adj. & n.* двенадцать (-ти, -тью); (*time*) двенадцать (часов); (*age*) двенадцать лет.

twentieth [ˈtwentɪɪθ] *adj. & n.* двадцатый; (*fraction*) двадцатая (часть (*pl.* -ти, -тей)); (*date*) двадцатое (число). **twenty** *adj. & n.* двадцать (-ти, -тью); (*age*) двадцать лет; *pl.* (*decade*) двадцатые годы (-дов) *m.pl.*

twice [twaɪs] *adv.* (2 *times, on 2 occasions*) дважды; ~ **as** вдвое, в два раза+*comp.*

twiddle [ˈtwɪd(ə)l] *v.t.* (*turn, twirl*) вертеть (-рчу, -ртишь) *impf.* +*a.*, *i.*; (*toy with*) играть *impf.* +*i.*; ~ **one's thumbs** (*fig.*) бездельничать *impf.*

twig [twɪg] *n.* веточка, прут (прута; *pl.* -тья, -тьев).

twilight [ˈtwaɪlaɪt] *n.* сумерки (-рек) *pl.*; (*decline*) упадок (-дка). **twilit** *adj.* сумеречный.

twill [twɪl] *n.* твил, саржа.

twin [twɪn] *n.* близнец (-а); *pl.* (*Gemini*) Близнецы *m.pl.*; ~ **beds** пара односпальных кроватей; ~ **brother** брат (*pl.* -ья, -ьев)-близнец (-а); ~ **town** город (*pl.* -а)-побратим; *v.t.* (*unite*) соединять *impf.*, соединить *pf.*

twine [twaɪn] *n.* бечёвка, шпагат; *v.t.* (*twist, weave*) вить (вью, вьёшь; вил, -а, -о) *impf.*, с~ *pf.*; *v.t. & i.* (~ *round*) обвивать(ся) *impf.*, обвить(ся) (обовью(сь), -ьёшь(ся)) обвил(ся), -ла(сь), -ло(сь)) *pf.*

twin-engined [ˌtwɪnˈendʒɪnd] *adj.* двухмоторный.

twinge [twɪndʒ] *n.* приступ (боли), острая боль; (*of conscience*) угрызение.

twinkle [ˈtwɪŋk(ə)l] *n.* мерцание; (*of eyes*) огонёк (-нька); *v.i.* мерцать *impf.*, сверкать *impf.* **twinkling** *n.* мерцание; **in the ~ of an eye** в мгновение ока.

twirl [twɜːl] *n.* вращение, кручение; (*flourish*) росчерк; *v.t. & i.* (*twist, turn*) вертеть(ся) (-рчу(сь), -ртишь(ся)) *impf.*; (*whirl, spin*)

кружить(ся) (-жу́(сь), кружишь(ся)) *impf.*

twist [twɪst] *n.* (*bend*) изгиб, поворот; (~*ing*) кручение; (*distortion*) искажение; (*sprain*) вывих; (*dance*) твист; (*characteristic*) характерная особенность; (*in story*) поворот фабулы; *v.t.* скручивать *impf.*, крутить (-учу, -утишь) *impf.*, с~ *pf.*; (*wind together*) вить (вью, вьёшь; вил, -а, -о) *impf.*, с~ *pf.*; (*distort*) искажать *impf.*, исказить *pf.*; (*sprain*) вывихивать *impf.*, вывихнуть *pf.*; *v.i.* (*bend, curve*) изгибаться *impf.*, изогнуться *pf.*; (*climb, meander, twine*) виться (вьётся) *impf.* **twisted** *adj.* (*bent, distorted*) искривлённый (-ён, -ена) (*also fig.*). **twister** *n.* обманщик, -ица.

twit [twɪt] *n.* глупец (-пца).

twitch [twɪtʃ] *n.* (~*ing, jerk*) подёргивание; (*spasm*) судорога; *v.t. & i.* дёргать(ся) *impf.*, дёрнуть(ся) *pf.* (**at** за+*a.*).

twitter [ˈtwɪtə(r)] *n.* щёбет; *v.i.* щебетать (-ечу, -ечешь) *impf.*, чирикать *impf.*

two [tuː] *adj. & n.* два, две (*f.*) (двух, -ум, -умя, -ух); (*collect.*; 2 *pairs*) двое (-ойх); (*cards, number* 2) двойка; (*time*) два (часа); (*age*) два года; ~ **times** дважды; ~ **times four** дважды четыре; **in** ~ (*in half*) надвое, пополам. **two-dimensional** *adj.* двухмерный. **two-edged** *adj.* обоюдоострый (*also fig.*); (*ambiguous*) двусмысленный (-ен, -енна). **twofold** *adj.* двойной; *adv.* вдвойне. **two-ply** *adj.* (*wood*) двухслойный; (*rope*) двойной. **two-seater** *n.* двухместный (автомобиль). **twosome** *n.* пара, двойка. **two-stroke** *adj.* двухтактный. **two-way** *adj.* двусторонний.

tycoon [taɪˈkuːn] *n.* магнат.

tympanum [ˈtɪmpənəm] *n.* (*anat.*) барабанная перепонка.

type [taɪp] *n.* (*var. senses*) тип; (*model*) типичный образец (-зца); (*sort, kind*) род (*pl.* -ды); (*letter*) литера; (*collect.*) шрифт (*pl.* -ы); **true to** ~ типичный; *v.t.* писать (пишу, -шешь) *impf.*, на~ *pf.* на машинке. **typescript** *n.* машинопись. **typewriter** *n.* пишущая машинка. **typewritten** *adj.* машинописный.

typhoid fever [ˈtaɪfɔɪd] *n.* брюшной тиф.

typhoon [taɪˈfuːn] *n.* тайфун.

typhus [ˈtaɪfəs] *n.* сыпной тиф.

typical [ˈtɪpɪk(ə)l] *adj.* типичный. **typify** [ˈtɪpɪˌfaɪ] *v.t.* служить (-жу, -жишь) *impf.*, по~ *pf.* типичным примером+*g.*; (*personify*) олицетворять *impf.*, олицетворить *pf.*

typist [ˈtaɪpɪst] *n.* машинистка.

typographical [ˌtaɪpəˈgræfɪk(ə)l] *adj.* типографский, книгопечатный. **ty'pography** *n.* книгопечатание; (*style*) оформление.

tyrannical [tɪˈrænɪk(ə)l] *adj.* тиранический, деспотичный. **tyrannize** [ˈtɪrəˌnaɪz] *v.i.* (*t.*) тиранствовать *impf.* (над+*i.*). **tyrant** [ˈtaɪərənt] *n.* тиран, деспот.

tyre [ˈtaɪə(r)] *n.* шина. **tyre-gauge** *n.* манометр для шин.

U

U-boat ['juːbəut] *n.* немецкая подводная лодка.
ubiquitous [juːˈbɪkwɪtəs] *adj.* вездесущий.
ubiquity *n.* вездесущность.
udder ['ʌdə(r)] *n.* вымя *nt.*
UFO *abbr.* (*of unidentified flying object*) НЛО, неопознанный летающий объект.
ugh [əх, ʌg, ʌх] *int.* тьфу!
ugliness ['ʌglɪnɪs] *n.* уродство. **ugly** *adj.* некрасивый, уродливый, безобразный; (*unpleasant*) неприятный; (*repulsive*) противный; ~ **duckling** (*fig.*) гадкий утёнок (-нка; *pl.* утята, -т).
неопознанный летающий объект.
UK *abbr.* (*of United Kingdom*) Соединённое Королевство (Великобритании и Северной Ирландии); *adj.* (велико)британский.
Ukraine [juːˈkreɪn] *n.* Украина. **Ukrainian** *n.* украинец (-нца), -нка; *adj.* украинский.
ukulele [juːkəˈleɪlɪ] *n.* гавайская гитара.
ulcer ['ʌlsə(r)] *n.* язва. **ulcerate** *v.t. & i.* изъязвлять(ся) *impf.*, изъязвить(ся) *pf.* **ulcered, ulcerous** *adj.* изъязвлённый.
ulna ['ʌlnə] *n.* локтевая кость (*pl.* -ти, -тей).
ulterior [ʌlˈtɪərɪə(r)] *adj.* скрытый.
ultimate ['ʌltɪmət] *adj.* (*final*) последний, окончательный; (*fundamental*) основной. **ultimately** *adv.* в конечном счёте, в конце концов. **ultimatum** [ˌʌltɪˈmeɪtəm] *n.* ультиматум.
ultra- ['ʌltrə] *in comb.* ультра..., сверх(ъ).... .
ultramarine [ˌʌltrəməˈriːn] *n.* ультрамарин; *adj.* ультрамариновый. **ultra-violet** [ˌʌltrəˈvaɪələt] *adj.* ультрафиолетовый.
umbilical [ʌmˈbɪlɪk(ə)l, ˌʌmbɪˈlaɪk(ə)l] *adj.* пупочный; ~ **cord** пуповина.
umbra ['ʌmbrə] *n.* полная тень (*loc.* -ни; *pl.* -ни, -ней). **umbrage** *n.* обида; **take** ~ обижаться *impf.*, обидеться (обижусь, -йдишься) *pf.* (**at** на+*a.*).
umbrella [ʌmˈbrelə] *n.* зонтик, зонт (-á); ~ **stand** подставка для зонтов!
umpire ['ʌmpaɪə(r)] *n.* судья (*pl.* -дьи, -дей, -дьям) *m.*; *v.t. & i.* судить (сужу, судишь) *impf.*
UN *abbr.* (*of United Nations* (*Organization*)): **the** ~ ООН *f. indecl.*, Организация Объединённых Наций; *adj.* (*coll.*) оонский.
unabashed [ʌnəˈbæʃt] *adj.* нерастерявшийся; без всякого смущения. **unabated** *adj.* неослабленный, неослабный. **unable** *adj.*: **be** ~ **to** не мочь (могу, можешь; мог, -ла)

impf., с~ *pf.*; быть не в состоянии; (*not know how to*) не уметь *impf.*, с~ *pf.* **unabridged** *adj.* несокращённый, без сокращений. **unaccompanied** *adj.* несопровождаемый; (*mus.*) без аккомпанемента. **unaccountable** *adj.* (*inexplicable*) необъяснимый. **unaccustomed** *adj.* (*not accustomed*) непривыкший (**to** к+*d.*); (*unusual*) непривычный. **unadulterated** *adj.* настоящий, нефальсифицированный; чистейший. **unaffected** *adj.* искренний (-нен, -нна, -нне & -нно); (*not affected*) незатронутый. **unaided** *adj.* без помощи, самостоятельный.
unalloyed *adj.* беспримесный, чистый (чист, -á, -о, чисты). **unalterable** *adj.* неизменяемый, неизменный (-нен, -нна). **unambiguous** *adj.* недвусмысленный (-ен, -енна).
unanimity [juːnəˈnɪmɪtɪ] *n.* единодушие. **unanimous** [juːˈnænɪməs] *adj.* единодушный.
unanswerable *adj.* (*irrefutable*) неопровержимый. **unapproachable** *adj.* неприступный; (*unmatched*) несравнимый. **unarmed** *adj.* безоружный, невооружённый. **unashamed** *adj.* бессовестный, наглый (нагл, -á, -о). **unasked** *adj.* добровольный, непрошеный (*coll.*). **unassailable** *adj.* неприступный; (*irrefutable*) неопровержимый. **unassuming** *adj.* скромный (-мен, -мна, -мно), непритязательный. **unattainable** *adj.* недосягаемый. **unattended** *adj.* (*unaccompanied*) несопровождаемый. **unattractive** *adj.* непривлекательный. **unauthorized** *adj.* неразрешённый; (*person*) неправомочный. **unavailable** *adj.* не имеющийся в наличии, недоступный; **be** ~ в наличии нет+*g.* **unavailing** *adj.* бесполезный, тщетный. **unavoidable** *adj.* неизбежный, неминуемый. **unaware** *pred.*: **be** ~ **of** не сознавать (-аю, -аёшь) *impf.*+*a.*; не знать *impf.* о+*p.* **unawares** *adv.* врасплох, неожиданно; (*unintentionally*) нечаянно. **unbalance** *v.t.* (*psych.*) лишать *impf.*, лишить *pf.* душевного равновесия. **unbalanced** *adj.* (*psych.*) неуравновешенный (-ен, -енна). **unbearable** *adj.* невыносимый. **unbeatable** *adj.* (*unsurpassable*) не могущий быть превзойдённым; (*invincible*) непобедимый. **unbeaten** *adj.* (*unsurpassed*) непревзойдённый (-ен, -енна). **unbecoming** *adj.* (*inappropriate*) неподходящий; (*unseemly*) неприличный; **be** ~ быть не к лицу (**to** +*d.*). **unbelief** *n.* неверие. **unbelievable** *adj.* невероятный. **unbeliever** *n.* неверующий *sb.* **unbend** *v.t. & i.* (*straighten*) выпрямлять(ся) *impf.*, выпрямить(ся) *pf.*; разгибать(ся) *impf.*, разогнуть(ся) *pf.*; *v.i.* (*become affable*) становиться (-влюсь, -вишься) *impf.*, стать (-ану, -анешь) *pf.* приветливым. **unbending** *adj.* непреклонный (-нен, -нна). **unbias(s)ed** *adj.* беспристрастный. **unblemished** *adj.* незапятнанный. **unblushing** *adj.* беззастенчивый. **unbolt** *v.t.*

отпира́ть *impf.*, отпере́ть (отопру́, -рёшь; о́тпер, -ла́, -ло) *pf.* **unborn** *adj.* ещё не рождённый (-ён, -ена́). **unbosom** *v.t.*: ~ **o.s.** открыва́ть *impf.*, откры́ть (-ро́ю, -ро́ешь) *pf.* ду́шу. **unbound** *adj.* (*free*) свобо́дный; (*book*) непереплетённый. **unbounded** *adj.* (*not limited*) неограни́ченный (-ен, -енна); (*joy*) безме́рный; (*infinite*) безграни́чный. **unbreakable** *adj.* небью́щийся. **unbridled** *adj.* разну́зданный (-ан, -анна). **unbroken** *adj.* (*intact*) неразби́тый, це́лый; (*continuous*) непреры́вный; (*unsurpassed*) непоби́тый; (*horse*) необъе́женный. **unbuckle** *v.t.* расстёгивать *impf.*, расстегну́ть *pf.* **unburden** *v.t.*: ~ **o.s.** отводи́ть (-ожу́, -о́дишь) *impf.*, отвести́ (-еду́, -едёшь; -ёл, -ела́) *pf.* ду́шу. **unbutton** *v.t.* расстёгивать *impf.*, расстегну́ть *pf.*

uncalled-for [ʌnˈkɔːldfɔː(r)] *adj.* неуме́стный. **uncanny** *adj.* жу́ткий (-ток, -тка́, -тко), сверхъесте́ственный (-ен, -енна). **uncared-for** *adj.* забро́шенный. **unceasing** *adj.* непреры́вный, безостано́вочный. **unceremonious** *adj.* бесцеремо́нный (-нен, -нна). **uncertain** *adj.* (*not certainly known*) то́чно неизве́стный, нея́сный (-сен, -сна́, -сно); (*indecisive, hesitating*) неуве́ренный (-ен, -на); (*lacking belief, confidence*) неуве́ренный (-ен, -на); (*indeterminate*) неопределённый (-нен, -нна); (*changeable*) изме́нчивый; **be** ~ (*not know for certain*) то́чно не знать *impf.*; **in no** ~ **terms** в недвусмы́сленных выраже́ниях. **uncertainty** *n.* неизве́стность; неуве́ренность; неопределённость; изме́нчивость. **unchain** *v.t.* спуска́ть *impf.* спусти́ть (-ущу́, -у́стишь) *pf.* с це́пи. **unchallenged** *adj.* не вызыва́ющий возраже́ний. **unchangeable** *adj.* неизмени́мый, неизменя́емый. **unchanged** *adj.* неизмени́вшийся. **unchanging** *adj.* неизменя́ющийся. **uncharacteristic** *adj.* нетипи́чный, нехаракте́рный. **uncharitable** *adj.* немилосе́рдный, жесто́кий (-о́к, -о́ка́, -о́ко). **uncharted** *adj.* (*fig.*) неиссле́дованный. **unchecked** *adj.* (*unrestrained*) необу́зданный (-ан, -анна). **uncivil** *adj.* неве́жливый. **uncivilized** *adj.* нецивилизо́ванный. **unclaimed** *adj.* невостре́бованный. **unclassified** *adj.* некласси́фицированный; (*not secret*) несекре́тный.

uncle [ˈʌŋk(ə)l] *n.* дя́дя (*pl.* -ди, -дей & -дья, -дьёв) *m.*

unclean [ʌnˈkliːn] *adj.* (*not clean; bibl. of food*) нечи́стый (-т, -та́, -то). **unclear** *adj.* нея́сный (-сен, -сна́, -сно), непоня́тный. **uncoil** *v.t.* & *i.* разма́тывать(ся) *impf.*, размота́ть(ся) *pf.* **uncomfortable** *adj.* неудо́бный; (*awkward*) нело́вкий (-вок, -вка́, -вко). **uncommon** *adj.* (*unusual, remarkable*) необыкнове́нный (-нен, -нна), замеча́тельный; (*rare*) ре́дкий (-док, -дка́, -дко). **uncommunicative** *adj.* необщи́тельный, молчали́вый. **uncomplaining** *adj.* безро́пот-

ный. **uncompleted** *adj.* неоко́нченный, незако́нченный. **uncomplimentary** *adj.* неле́стный. **uncompromising** *adj.* не иду́щий на компроми́ссы; (*inflexible*) непрекло́нный (-нен, -нна). **unconcealed** *adj.* нескрыва́емый. **unconcern** *n.* (*freedom from anxiety*) беззабо́тность; (*indifference*) равноду́шие. **unconcerned** *adj.* беззабо́тный; равноду́шный. **unconditional** *adj.* безогово́рочный, безусло́вный. **unconfirmed** *adj.* неподтверждённый. ~ **with** не свя́занный (-ан) с+*i.* **unconquerable** *adj.* непобеди́мый. **unconscionable** *adj.* бессо́вестный; (*excessive*) неуме́ренный (-ен, -енна). **unconscious** *adj.* (*also unintentional*) бессозна́тельный; *pred.* без созна́ния; (*unintentional*) нево́льный; **be** ~ **of** не сознава́ть (-аю́, -аёшь) *impf.*+*g.*; *n.* подсозна́тельное *sb.* **unconsciousness** *n.* бессозна́тельное состоя́ние; бессозна́тельность. **unconstitutional** *adj.* неконституцио́нный (-нен, -нна). **unconstrained** *adj.* непринуждённый (-ён, -ённа). **uncontrollable** *adj.* неудержи́мый, неукроти́мый. **uncontrolled** *adj.* (*unbridled*) необу́зданный (-ан, -анна). **unconventional** *adj.* чу́ждый (-д, -да́, -до) усло́вности; необы́чный. **unconvincing** *adj.* неубеди́тельный. **uncooked** *adj.* сыро́й (-р, -ра́, -ро). **uncooperative** *adj.* неотзы́вчивый, безуча́стный. **uncork** *v.t.* отку́поривать *impf.*, отку́порить *pf.* **uncouple** *v.t.* расцепля́ть *impf.*, расцепи́ть (-плю́, -пишь) *pf.* **uncouth** [ʌnˈkuːθ] *adj.* гру́бый (-б, -ба́, -бо). **uncover** *v.t.* (*remove cover from*) снима́ть *impf.*, снять (сниму́, -мешь; снял, -а́, -о) *pf.* кры́шку с+*g.*; (*reveal*) открыва́ть *impf.*, откры́ть (-ро́ю, -ро́ешь) *pf.*; (*disclose*) обнару́живать *impf.*, обнару́жить *pf.* **uncovered** *adj.* незакры́тый, откры́тый. **uncritical** *adj.* некрити́чный.

unction [ˈʌŋkʃ(ə)n] *n.* (*ceremony*) пома́зание; (*process*) втира́ние ма́зи; (*ointment*) мазь; (*balm*) еле́й; (*piety*) на́божность; (*affectedness*) еле́йность; **extreme** ~ собо́рование. **unctuous** *adj.* еле́йный.

uncultivated [ʌnˈkʌltɪˌveɪtɪd] *adj.* (*land*) невозде́ланный; (*talent*) неразвито́й (неразвит, -а́, -о); (*uncultured*) некульту́рный. **uncultured** *adj.* некульту́рный. **uncurl** *v.t.* & *i.* развива́ть(ся) *impf.*, разви́ть(ся) (разовью́, -ьёт(ся); разви́л(ся), -ла́(сь), разви́ло́(сь)) *pf.* **uncut** *adj.* (*unabridged*) несокращённый, без сокраще́ний.

undamaged [ʌnˈdæmɪdʒd] *adj.* неповреждённый, неиспо́рченный. **undaunted** *adj.* бесстра́шный. **undeceive** *v.t.* выводи́ть (-ожу́, -о́дишь) *impf.*, вы́вести (-еду, -едешь; -ел) *pf.* из заблужде́ния. **undecided** *adj.* (*not settled*) нереши́мый; (*irresolute*) нереши́тельный. **undemanding** *adj.* нетребова́тельный. **undemocratic** *adj.* недемократи́ческий, антидемократи́ческий. **undemonstrative** *adj.* сде́ржанный (-ан, -анна).

undeniable *adj.* неоспори́мый, несомне́нный (-нен, -нна).

under [ˈʌndə(r)] *prep.* (*position*) под+*i.*; (*direction*) под+*a.*; (*fig.*) под+*i.*; (*less than*) ме́ньше+*g.*, ни́же+*g.*; (*according to*) по+*d.*; (*in view of, in the reign, time of*) при+*p.*; ∼ **repair** в ремо́нте; ∼ **way** на ходу́; **from** ∼ из-под+*g.*; *adv.* (*position*) внизу́, ни́же; (*direction*) вниз; (*less*) ме́ньше; *adj.* ни́жний; (*subordinate*) ни́зший. **under-age** *adj.* несовершенноле́тний.

undercarriage [ˈʌndəˌkærɪdʒ] *n.* шасси́ *nt.indecl.* **underclothes, underclothing** *n.* ни́жнее бельё. **undercoat** *n.* (*of paint*) грунто́вка. **undercover** *adj.* та́йный, секре́тный. **undercurrent** *n.* подво́дное тече́ние; (*fig.*) скры́тая тенде́нция. **undercut** *v.t.* (*cut away*) подреза́ть *impf.*, подре́зать (-е́жу, -е́жешь) *pf.*; (*price*) назнача́ть *impf.*, назна́чить *pf.* бо́лее ни́зкую це́ну чем+*nom.* **underdeveloped** *adj.* недора́звитый, слабора́звитый; (*phot.*) недопроя́вленный. **underdog** *n.* неуда́чник.

underdone [ˈʌndəˈdʌn, -ˈdʌn-] *adj.* недожа́ренный (-ен). **underemployment** *n.* непо́лная за́нятость. **underestimate** *v.t.* недооце́нивать *impf.*, недооцени́ть (-ню́, -нишь) *pf.*; *n.* недооце́нка. **underexpose** *v.t.* недоде́рживать *impf.*, недодержа́ть (-жу́, -жишь) *pf.* **underfed** *adj.* недоко́рмленный. **underfelt** *n.* грунт ковра́. **underfloor** *adj.* находя́щийся под по́лом. **underfoot** *adv.* под нога́ми. **undergarment** *n.* предме́т ни́жнего белья́.

undergo [ˈʌndəˈɡəʊ] *v.t.* подверга́ться *impf.*, подве́ргнуться (-гся) *pf.*+*d.*; (*endure*) переноси́ть (-ошу́, -о́сишь) *impf.*, перенести́ (-есу́, -есёшь; -ёс, -есла́) *pf.* **undergraduate** *n.* студе́нт, ∼ка. **underground** *n.* (*rail.*) метро́ *nt.indecl.*; (*fig.*) подпо́лье; *adj.* подзе́мный; (*fig.*) подпо́льный; *adv.* под землёй; (*fig.*) подпо́льно; **go** ∼ уходи́ть (-ожу́, -о́дишь) *impf.*, уйти́ (уйду́, -дёшь; ушёл, ушла́) *pf.* в подпо́лье. **undergrowth** *n.* подле́сок (-ска). **underhand** *adj.* закули́сный, та́йный. **underlie** *v.t.* (*fig.*) лежа́ть (-жи́т) *impf.* в осно́ве+*g.* **underline** *v.t.* подчёркивать *impf.*, подчеркну́ть *pf.*

underling *n.* подчинённый *sb.*

undermanned [ˈʌndəˈmænd] *adj.* испы́тывающий недоста́ток в рабо́чей си́ле. **undermentioned** *adj.* нижепомя́нутый. **undermine** *v.t.* де́лать *impf.*, c∼ *pf.* подко́п под+*i.*; (*wash away*) подмыва́ть *impf.*, подмы́ть (-мо́ю, -мо́ешь) *pf.*; (*authority*) подрыва́ть *impf.*, подорва́ть (-ву́, -вёшь; подорва́л, -а́, -о) *pf.*; (*health*) разруша́ть *impf.*, разру́шить *pf.*

underneath [ˈʌndəˈniːθ] *adv.* (*position*) внизу́; (*direction*) вниз; *prep.* (*position*) под+*i.*; (*direction*) под+*a.*; *n.* ни́жняя часть (*pl.* -ти, -те́й); *adj.* ни́жний.

undernourished *adj.* недоко́рмленный; **be**

∼ недоеда́ть *impf.* **undernourishment** *n.* недоеда́ние.

underpaid [ˈʌndəˈpeɪd] *adj.* низкоопла́чиваемый. **underpants** *n.* кальсо́ны (-н) *pl.*, трусы́ (-со́в) *pl.* **underpass** *n.* прое́зд под полотно́м доро́ги, тонне́ль *m.* **underpin** *v.t.* подводи́ть (-ожу́, -о́дишь) *impf.*, подвести́ (-еду́, -едёшь; -ёл, -ела́) *pf.* фунда́мент под+*a.* **underpopulated** *adj.* малонаселённый (-ён, -ённа). **underprivileged** *adj.* по́льзующийся ме́ньшими права́ми; (*poor*) бе́дный (-ден, -дна́, -дно, бе́дны). **underrate** *v.t.* недооце́нивать *impf.*, недооцени́ть *pf.* **under-secretary** *n.* замести́тель *m.* мини́стра.

undersell [ˈʌndəˈsel] *v.t.* продава́ть (-даю́, -даёшь) *impf.*, прода́ть (-а́м, -а́шь, -а́ст, -ади́м; про́дал, -а́, -о) *pf.* дешевле+*g.* **underside** *n.* ни́жняя пове́рхность. **undersigned** *adj.* (*n.*) нижеподписа́вшийся (*sb.*). **undersized** *adj.* маломе́рный, нестанда́ртный; (*dwarfish*) ка́рликовый. **underskirt** *n.* ни́жняя ю́бка. **understaffed** *adj.* неукомплекто́ванный.

understand [ˈʌndəˈstænd] *v.t.* понима́ть *impf.*, поня́ть (пойму́, -мёшь; по́нял, -а́, -о) *pf.*; (*have heard say*) слы́шать *impf.* **understandable** *adj.* поня́тный. **understanding** *n.* понима́ние; (*intellect*) ра́зум; (*mutual* ∼) взаимопонима́ние; (*agreement*) соглаше́ние; (*harmony*) согла́сие; *adj.* (*sympathetic*) чу́ткий (-ток, -тка́, -тко), отзы́вчивый.

understate [ˈʌndəˈsteɪt] *v.t.* преуменьша́ть *impf.*, преуме́ньшить *pf.* **understatement** *n.* преуменьше́ние.

understudy [ˈʌndəˌstʌdɪ] *n.* дублёр; *v.t.* дубли́ровать *impf.* роль+*g.*

undertake [ˈʌndəˈteɪk] *v.t.* (*engage in, enter upon*) предпринима́ть *impf.*, предприня́ть (-иму́, -и́мешь; предпри́нял, -а́, -о) *pf.*; (*responsibility*) брать (беру́, берёшь) *impf.*, взять (возьму́, -мёшь; взял, а́, -о) *pf.* на себя́; (+*inf.*) обя́зываться *impf.*, обяза́ться (-жу́сь, -жешься) *pf.*; (*guarantee*) руча́ться *impf.*, поручи́ться (-чу́сь, -чишься) *pf.* (*that* что). 'undertaker *n.* гробовщи́к (-а́). **undertaking** *n.* предприя́тие; (*obligation*) обяза́тельство.

undertone [ˈʌndəˌtəʊn] *n.* (*half-tint*) полуто́н (*pl.* -ы & -а́); (*nuance*) отте́нок (-нка); **speak in** ∼**s** говори́ть *impf.* вполго́лоса. **undertow** *n.* глуби́нное тече́ние, противополо́жное пове́рхностному; подво́дное тече́ние. **underwater** *adj.* подво́дный. **underwear** *n.* ни́жнее бельё. **underworld** *n.* (*myth.*) преиспо́дняя *sb.*; (*criminals*) престу́пный мир (*pl.* -ы́). **underwrite** *v.t.* (*sign*) подпи́сывать *impf.*, подписа́ть (подпишу́, -шешь) *pf.*; (*accept liability for*) принима́ть *impf.*, приня́ть (приму́, -мешь; при́нял, -а́, -о) *pf.* на страх; (*guarantee*) гаранти́ровать *impf.* & *pf.* **underwriter** *n.* подпи́счик; страхо́вщик; (*company*) страхова́я компа́ния.

undeserved [ˌʌndɪˈzɜːvd] adj. незаслуженный (-ен, -енна). undeserving adj. незаслуживающий; ~ of не заслуживающий+g. undesirable adj. нежелательный; n. нежелательное лицо (pl. -ца). undeveloped adj. неразвитый; (land) незастроенный. undignified adj. недостойный (-оин, -ойна). undiluted adj. неразбавленный. undisciplined adj. недисциплинированный (-ан, -анна). undiscovered adj. неоткрытый; (unknown) неизвестный. undiscriminating adj. непроницательный, неразборчивый. undisguised adj. открытый, явный. undismayed adj. необескураженный. undisputed adj. бесспорный. undistinguished adj. невыдающийся. undisturbed adj. (untouched) нетронутый; (peaceful) спокойный; (in order) в порядке. undivided adj. (unanimous) единодушный; give ~ attention посвящать impf., посвятить (-ящу, -ятишь) pf. все силы (to +d.). undo v.t. (open) открывать impf., открыть (-рою, -роешь) pf.; (untie) развязывать impf., развязать (-яжу, -яжешь) pf.; (unbutton, unhook, unbuckle) расстёгивать impf., расстегнуть pf.; (destroy, cancel) уничтожать impf., уничтожить pf.; (be the ~ing of) губить (гублю, -бишь) impf., по~ pf. undoing n. (ruin, downfall) гибель; (destruction) уничтожение. undoubted adj. несомненный (-нен, -нна). undoubtedly adv. несомненно. undress v.t. & i. раздевать(ся) impf., раздеть(ся) (-ену(сь), -енешь(ся)) pf. undrinkable adj. негодный (-ден, -дна, -дно) для питья. undue adj. чрезмерный. unduly adv. чрезмерно.

undulate [ˈʌndjʊˌleɪt] v.i. быть волнистым, холмистым. undulating adj. волнистый. undu'lation n. волнистость; (motion) волнообразное движение; (of surface) неровность поверхности.

undying [ʌnˈdaɪɪŋ] adj. (eternal) вечный.

unearned [ʌnˈɜːnd] adj. незаработанный; (undeserved) незаслуженный (-ен, -енна); ~ income нетрудовой доход. unearth v.t. (dig up) выкапывать impf., выкопать pf. из земли; (fox etc.) выгонять impf., выгнать (выгоню, -нишь) pf. из норы; (fig.) раскапывать impf., раскопать pf. unearthly adj. неземной, сверхъестественный (-ен, -енна); (inconvenient) крайне неудобный. uneasiness n. (anxiety) беспокойство, тревога; (awkwardness) неловкость. uneasy adj. беспокойный, тревожный; неловкий (-вок, -вка, -вко). uneatable adj. несъедобный. uneconomic adj. нерентабельный, неэкономичный. uneconomical adj. (car etc.) неэкономичный; (person) неэкономный. uneducated adj. необразованный (-ан, -анна). unemployed adj. безработный; (unoccupied) незанятый (-т, -та, -то); (unused) -неиспользованный. unemployment n. безработица; ~ benefit пособие по безработице. unending adj. бесконечный,

нескончаемый. unenlightened adj. непросвещённый (-ён, -ённа); (uninformed) неосведомлённый. unenterprising adj. непредприимчивый, безынициативный. unenviable adj. незавидный. unequal adj. неравный; (of ~ value) неравноценный (-нен, -нна); (unjust) несправедливый; (inadequate) неадекватный; ~ to неподходящий для+g. unequalled adj. бесподобный, непревзойдённый (-ён, -ённа). unequivocal adj. недвусмысленный (-ен, -енна). unerring adj. безошибочный.

uneven [ʌnˈiːv(ə)n] adj. неровный (-вен, -вна, -вно). uneventful adj. не богатый событиями, тихий (тих, -а, -о). unexceptionable adj. безукоризненный (-ен, -енна). unexceptional adj. обычный. unexpected adj. неожиданный (-ан, -анна); (sudden) внезапный. unexplainable adj. необъяснимый. unexplored adj. неисследованный. unexpurgated adj. без купюр, неподвергшийся цензуре.

unfailing [ʌnˈfeɪlɪŋ] adj. неизменный (-нен, -нна); (faithful) верный (-рен, -рна, -рно); (reliable) надёжный; (inexhaustible) неисчерпаемый.

unfair adj. несправедливый; (dishonest) нечестный (-тен, -тна, -тно). unfaithful adj. неверный (-рен, -рна, -рно, неверны); (treacherous) вероломный. unfamiliar adj. незнакомый; (unknown) неведомый. unfashionable adj. немодный (-ден, -дна, -дно). unfasten v.t. (detach, untie) открепять impf., открепить pf.; (detach, unbutton) отстёгивать impf., отстегнуть pf.; (undo, unbutton, unhook) расстёгивать impf., расстегнуть pf. unfathomable adj. (immeasurable) неизмеримый, бездонный; (incomprehensible) непостижимый. unfavourable adj. неблагоприятный; (not approving) неблагосклонный (-нен, -нна). unfeeling adj. бесчувственный (-ен, -енна). unfeigned adj. истинный (-нен, -нна), неподдельный. unfinished adj. незаконченный; (crude) необработанный (-ан, -анна). unfit adj. негодный (-ден, -дна, -дно), непригодный, неподходящий; (unhealthy) нездоровый. unfix v.t. открепять impf., открепить pf. unflagging adj. неослабевающий. unfledged adj. неоперившийся (also fig.). unfold v.t. & i. развёртывать(ся) impf., развернуть(ся) pf.; (open up) раскрывать(ся) impf., раскрыть(ся) (-рою(сь), -роешь(ся)) pf. unforeseen adj. непредвиденный. unforgettable adj. незабываемый. unforgivable adj. непростительный. unforgiving adj. непрощающий. unfortunate adj. несчастливый, несчастный; (regrettable) неудачный; n. несчастливец (-вца) неудачник, -ица. unfortunately adv. к несчастью, к сожалению. unfounded adj. необоснованный (-ан, -анна). unfreeze v.t. & i. размораживать(ся) impf., разморозить(ся) pf. un-

friendly *adj.* недружелюбный, неприветливый. **unfrock** *v.t.* лишать *impf.*, лишить *pf.* духовного сана. **unfruitful** *adj.* бесплодный. **unfulfilled** *adj.* (*promise etc.*) невыполненный; (*hopes etc.*) неосуществлённый. **unfurl** *v.t. & i.* развёртывать(ся) *impf.*, развернуть(ся) *pf.* **unfurnished** *adj.* немеблированный.

ungainly [ʌn'geɪnlɪ] *adj.* нескладный, неуклюжий. **ungentlemanly** *adj.* неблагородный, невежливый. **ungodliness** *n.* безбожие. **ungodly** *adj.* (*also outrageous*) безбожный. **ungovernable** *adj.* необузданный (-ан, -анна), неукротимый. **ungracious** *adj.* нелюбезный. **ungrammatical** *adj.* грамматически неправильный. **ungrateful** *adj.* неблагодарный. **unguarded** *adj.* (*incautious*) неосторожный.

unguent ['ʌŋgwənt] *n.* мазь.

unhappiness [ʌn'hæpɪnɪs] *n.* несчастье. **unhappy** *adj.* несчастливый, несчастный. **unharmed** *adj.* невредимый. **unhealthy** *adj.* (*in var. senses*) нездоровый, болезненный (-ен, -енна); (*harmful*) вредный (-ден, -дна, -дно). **unheard-of** *adj.* неслыханный (-ан, -анна). **unheeded** *adj.* незамеченный. **unheeding** *adj.* невнимательный. **unhelpful** *adj.* бесполезный. **unhesitating** *adj.* решительный. **unhesitatingly** *adv.* без колебания. **unhinge** *v.t.* снимать *impf.*, снять (сниму, -мешь; снял, -á, -о) *pf.* с петли; (*fig.*) расстраивать *impf.*, расстроить *pf.* **unholy** *adj.* (*impious*) нечестивый; (*awful*) ужасный. **unhook** *v.t.* снимать *impf.*, снять (сниму, -мешь; снял, -á, -о) *pf.* с крючка; (*undo hooks*) расстёгивать *impf.*, расстегнуть *pf.*; (*uncouple*) расцеплять *impf.*, расцепить (-плю, -пишь) *pf.* **unhoped-for** *adj.* неожиданный (-ан, -анна). **unhorse** *v.t.* сбрасывать *impf.*, сбросить *pf.* с лошади. **unhurt** *adj.* невредимый.

unicorn ['ju:nɪ,kɔːn] *n.* единорог.

unification [ju:nɪfɪ'keɪʃ(ə)n] *n.* объединение, унификация (*also standardization*).

uniform ['ju:nɪ,fɔːm] *n.* форма, форменная одежда; *adj.* единообразный; (*homogeneous*) однородный; (*of ~*) форменный. **uni'formity** *n.* единообразие, однородность.

unify ['ju:nɪ,faɪ] *v.t.* объединять *impf.*, объединить *pf.*; унифицировать *impf. & pf.* (*also standardize*).

unilateral [ju:nɪ'lætər(ə)l] *adj.* односторонний.

unimaginable [ʌnɪ'mædʒɪnəb(ə)l] *adj.* невообразимый. **unimaginative** *adj.* лишённый (-ён, -ена) воображения, прозаичный. **unimpeachable** *adj.* безупречный. **unimportant** *adj.* неважный. **uninformed** *adj.* (*ignorant*) несведущий (**about** в+*p.*); (*ill-informed*) неосведомлённый. **uninhabitable** *adj.* непригодный для жилья. **uninhabited** *adj.* необитаемый. **uninitiated** *adj.* непосвящённый. **uninspired** *adj.* банальный. **unintelligible** *adj.* неразборчивый. **unin-**

tentional *adj.* неумышленный (-ен, -енна). **unintentionally** *adv.* неумышленно. **uninterested** *adj.* незаинтересованный. **uninteresting** *adj.* неинтересный. **uninterrupted** *adj.* непрерывный. **uninviting** *adj.* непривлекательный.

union ['ju:njən, -nɪən] *n.* (*alliance*) союз; (*joining together, alliance*) объединение; (*combination*) соединение; (*marriage*) брачный союз; (*harmony*) согласие; (*trade ~*) профсоюз. **unionist** *n.* член профсоюза; (*pol.*) унионист.

unique [ju'ni:k, ju:'ni:k] *adj.* единственный (в своём роде), уникальный.

unison ['ju:nɪs(ə)n] *n.* (*mus.*) унисон; (*fig.*) согласие; **in ~** (*mus.*) в унисон; (*fig.*) в согласии.

unit ['ju:nɪt] *n.* единица; (*mil.*) часть (*pl.* -ти, -тей).

unite [ju'naɪt, ju:-] *v.t. & i.* соединять(ся) *impf.*, соединить(ся) *pf.*; объединять(ся) *impf.*, объединить(ся) *pf.* **united** *adj.* соединённый, объединённый; **U~ Kingdom** Соединённое Королевство; **U~ Nations** Организация Объединённых Наций; **U~ States** Соединённые Штаты *m.pl.* Америки. **unity** ['ju:nɪtɪ] *n.* единство; (*cohesion*) сплочённость; (*math.*) единица.

universal [ju:nɪ'vɜːs(ə)l] *adj.* (*general*) всеобщий; (*world-wide*) всемирный; (*many-sided*) универсальный. **'universe** *n.* вселенная *sb.*; (*world*) мир (*pl.* -ы); (*cosmos*) космос.

university [ju:nɪ'vɜːsɪtɪ] *n.* университет; *attr.* университетский.

unjust [ʌn'dʒʌst] *adj.* несправедливый. **unjustifiable** *adj.* не имеющий оправдания. **unjustified** *adj.* неоправданный.

unkempt [ʌn'kempt] *adj.* нечёсаный (-ан); (*untidy*) неопрятный. **unkind** *adj.* недобрый, злой (зол, зла, зло). **unknown** *adj.* неизвестный.

unlace [ʌn'leɪs] *v.t.* расшнуровывать *impf.*, расшнуровать *pf.* **unlawful** *adj.* незаконный (-нен, -нна). **unleaded** *adj.* неэтилированный. **unlearn** *v.t.* разучиваться *impf.*, разучиться (-чусь, -чишься) *pf.* (**how to** +*inf.*); *v.t.* забывать *impf.*, забыть (забуду, -дешь) *pf.* **unleash** *v.t.* (*dog*) спускать *impf.*, спустить (-ущу, -устишь) *pf.* с привязи; (*also fig.*) развязывать *impf.*, развязать (-яжу, -яжешь) *pf.* **unleavened** *adj.* бездрожжевой, пресный (-сен, -сна, -сно).

unless [ʌn'les, ən'les] *conj.* если... не.

unlike [ʌn'laɪk] *adj.* непохожий (на+*a.*); (*in contradistinction to*) в отличие от+*g.* **unlikely** *adj.* маловероятный, неправдоподобный; **it is ~ that** вряд ли, едва ли. **unlimited** *adj.* (*unrestricted*) неограниченный (-ен, -енна); (*boundless*) безграничный. **unlined** *adj.* (*clothing*) без подкладки. **unload** *v.t.* (*remove load from*) разгружать *impf.*, разгрузить (-ужу, -узишь) *pf.*; (*remove load from,* *remove from*) выгружа́ть *impf.*, вы́грузить *pf.*; (*gun*) разряжа́ть *impf.*, разряди́ть *pf.* **unlock** *v.t.* отпира́ть *impf.*, отпере́ть (отопру́, -рёшь; о́тпер, -ла́, -ло) *pf.*; открыва́ть *impf.*, откры́ть (-ро́ю, -ро́ешь) *pf.* **unlucky** *adj.* несчастли́вый; (*unsuccessful, unfortunate*) неуда́чный.

unmake [ʌn'meɪk] *v.t.* (*destroy*) уничтожа́ть *impf.*, уничто́жить *pf.*; (*annul*) аннули́ровать *impf. & pf.*; (*depose*) понижа́ть *impf.*, пони́зить *pf.* **unmanageable** *adj.* тру́дно поддаю́щийся контро́лю; (*of child*) тру́дный (-ден, -дна́, -дно, тру́дны́). **unmanly** *adj.* недосто́йный (-о́ин, -о́йна) мужчи́ны. **unmarketable** *adj.* него́дный (-ден, -дна, -дно) для прода́жи. **unmarried** *adj.* холосто́й (хо́лост, -а́, -о); (*of man*) жена́тый; (*of woman*) незаму́жняя. **unmask** *v.t.* (*fig.*) разоблача́ть *impf.*, разоблачи́ть *pf.* **unmentionable** *adj.* незатра́гиваемый, необсужда́емый. **unmerciful** *adj.* безжа́лостный. **unmerited** *adj.* незаслу́женный (-ен, -енна). **unmethodical** *adj.* несистемати́ческий, неметоди́чный. **unmindful** *adj.* невнима́тельный (**of** к+*d.*). **unmistakable** *adj.* несомне́нный (-нен, -нна), я́сный (я́сен, ясна́, я́сно, я́сны́). **unmitigated** *adj.* несмягчённый; (*absolute*) абсолю́тный; (*thorough*) отъя́вленный. **unmoved** *adj.* (*indifferent*) равноду́шный; (*adamant*) непрекло́нный (-нен, -нна).

unnatural [ʌn'nætʃər(ə)l] *adj.* неесте́ственный (-ен, -енна), противоесте́ственный (-ен, -енна). **unnecessary** *adj.* ну́жный, изли́шний (-шен, -шня). **unnerve** *v.t.* лиша́ть *impf.*, лиши́ть *pf.* реши́мости, му́жества. **unnoticed** *adj.* незаме́ченный.

unobjectionable [ˌʌnəb'dʒekʃənəb(ə)l] *adj.* прие́млемый. **unobservant** *adj.* невнима́тельный, ненаблюда́тельный. **unobserved** *adj.* незаме́ченный. **unobtainable** *adj.* тако́й, кото́рого нельзя́ доста́ть; недосту́пный. **unobtrusive** *adj.* ненавя́зчивый. **unoccupied** *adj.* неза́нятый (-т, -та́, -то), свобо́дный; (*uninhabited*) необита́емый. **unofficial** *adj.* неофициа́льный. **unopposed** *adj.* не встре́тивший сопротивле́ния. **unorthodox** *adj.* неортодокса́льный.

unpack [ʌn'pæk] *v.t.* распако́вывать *impf.*, распакова́ть *pf.* **unpaid** *adj.* (*not receiving pay*) не получа́ющий пла́ты; (*work*) беспла́тный. **unpalatable** *adj.* невку́сный; (*unpleasant*) неприя́тный. **unpardonable** *adj.* непрости́тельный. **unpin** *v.t.* отка́лывать *impf.*, отколо́ть (-лю́, -лешь) *pf.* **unpleasant** *adj.* неприя́тный. **unpleasantness** *n.* неприя́тельность; (*also occurrence*) неприя́тность; (*quarrel*) ссо́ра. **unpopular** *adj.* непопуля́рный. **unprecedented** *adj.* беспрецеде́нтный, беспримерный. **unpredictable** *adj.* не могу́щий быть предска́занный. **unprejudiced** *adj.* беспристра́стный. **unpremeditated** *adj.* непреднаме́ренный (-ен, -енна). **unprepared** *adj.* неподгото́влен-

ный, негото́вый. **unprepossessing** *adj.* непривлека́тельный. **unpretentious** *adj.* просто́й (прост, -а́, -о, про́сты́), без прете́нзий. **unprincipled** *adj.* беспринци́пный; (*immoral*) безнра́вственный (-ен(ен), -енна). **unprintable** *adj.* нецензу́рный. **unproductive** *adj.* непродукти́вный. **unprofitable** *adj.* невы́годный. **unpromising** *adj.* не обеща́ющий ничего́ хоро́шего. **unpronounceable** *adj.* непроизноси́мый. **unpropitious** *adj.* неблагоприя́тный. **unprotected** *adj.* (*defenceless*) беззащи́тный; (*area*) откры́тый. **unproven** *adj.* недока́занный. **unprovoked** *adj.* ниче́м не вы́званный, непровоци́рованный. **unpublished** *adj.* неопублико́ванный, неи́зданный. **unpunctual** *adj.* непунктуа́льный. **unpunished** *adj.* безнака́занный (-ан, -анна).

unqualified [ʌn'kwɒlɪˌfaɪd] *adj.* неквалифици́рованный (-ан, -анна); (*unconditional*) безоговорочный. **unquenchable** *adj.* неутоли́мый; (*fig.*) неугаси́мый. **unquestionable** *adj.* несомне́нный (-нен, -нна), неоспори́мый. **unquestionably** *adv.* несомне́нно. **unquestioned** *adj.* не вызыва́ющий сомне́ния.

unravel [ʌn'ræv(ə)l] *v.t. & i.* распу́тывать(ся) *impf.*, распу́тать(ся) *pf.*; *v.t.* (*solve*) разга́дывать *impf.*, разгада́ть *pf.* **unread** [ʌn'red] *adj.* (*book etc.*) непрочи́танный. **unreadable** *adj.* (*illegible*) неразбо́рчивый; (*boring*) ску́чный (-чен, -чна́, -чно). **unready** *adj.* негото́вый; (*slow-witted*) несообрази́тельный. **unreal** *adj.* ненастоя́щий. **unrealistic** *adj.* нереа́льный. **unreasonable** *adj.* (*unwise*) неблагоразу́мный; (*excessive*) непоме́рный; (*expensive*) непоме́рно дорого́й (до́рог, -а́, -о); (*of price*) непоме́рно высо́кий (-о́к, -ока́, -о́ко́); (*unfounded*; *of demand*) необосно́ванный (-ан, -анна). **unreasoned** *adj.* непроду́манный. **unreasoning** *adj.* немы́слящий. **unreceptive** *adj.* невосприи́мчивый. **unrecognizable** *adj.* неузнава́емый. **unrecognized** *adj.* непри́знанный. **unrefined** *adj.* неочи́щенный; (*manners etc.*) гру́бый (груб, -а́, -о). **unrelenting** *adj.* (*ruthless*) безжа́лостный; (*unremitting*) неосла́бный; (*not abating*) неуменьша́ющийся. **unreliable** *adj.* ненадёжный. **unremitting** *adj.* неосла́бный; (*incessant*) беспреста́нный (-нен, -нна). **unremunerative** *adj.* невы́годный. **unrepeatable** *adj.* (*unique*) неповтори́мый; (*indecent*) неприли́чный. **unrepentant** *adj.* нераска́явшийся. **unrepresentative** *adj.* нехаракте́рный. **unrequited** *adj.*: ~ **love** любо́вь без взаи́мности. **unreserved** *adj.* (*full*) по́лный (-лон, -лна́, полно́); (*open*) открове́нный (-нен, -нна); (*unconditional*) безоговоро́чный; ~ **seats** незаброни́рованные места́ *nt.pl.* **unresisting** *adj.* несопротивля́ющийся. **unrest** *n.* беспоко́йство; (*pol.*) беспоря́дки *m.pl.*, волне́ния *nt.pl.* **unrestrained** *adj.* несде́ржанный (-ан, анна). **unrestricted** *adj.* неограни́ченный (-ен, -енна). **unripe** adj. незре́лый, неспе́лый. **unrivalled** adj. беспод́обный. **unroll** v.t. & i. развёртывать(ся) impf., разверну́ть(ся) pf. **unruffled** adj. (smooth) гла́дкий (-док, -дка́, -дко); (calm) споко́йный. **unruly** [ʌn'ruːlɪ] adj. (wild) бу́йный (бу́ен, буйна́, -но), (disobedient) непослу́шный.

unsafe [ʌn'seɪf] adj. опа́сный; (insecure) ненадёжный. **unsaid** [ʌn'sed] adj.: leave ~ молча́ть (-чу́, -чи́шь) impf. o+p. **unsaleable** adj. нехо́дкий. **unsalted** adj. несолёный (несо́лон, -á, -o). **unsatisfactory** adj. неудовлетвори́тельный. **unsatisfied** adj. неудовлетворённый (-ён, -ена́ & -енна). **unsatisfying** adj. неудовлетворя́ющий; (food) сы́тный (-тен, -тна́, -тно). **unsavoury** adj. невку́сный; (distasteful) проти́вный. **unscathed** adj. невреди́мый; (fig.) жив и невреди́м. **unscheduled** adj. внеочередно́й. **unscientific** adj. ненау́чный. **unscrew** v.t. & i. отви́нчивать(ся) impf., отвинти́ть(ся) pf. **unscrupulous** adj. неразбо́рчивый в сре́дствах, беспринци́пный, бессо́вестный. **unseasonable** adj. не по сезо́ну; (inopportune) несвоевре́менный (-нен, -нна). **unseasoned** adj. (food) неприпра́вленный; (wood) невы́держанный; (unaccustomed) непривы́кший. **unseat** v.t. (of horse) сбра́сывать impf., сбро́сить pf. с седла́; (parl.) лиша́ть impf., лиши́ть pf. парла́ментского манда́та. **unseemly** adj. неподоба́ющий, непристо́йный. **unseen** adj. неви́данный; ~ translation перево́д с листа́. **unselfish** adj. бескоры́стный, неэгоисти́чный. **unserviceable** adj. неприго́дный. **unsettle** v.t. наруша́ть impf., наруши́ть pf. распоря́док+g., выбива́ть impf., вы́бить (-бью, -бьешь) pf. из коле́й; (upset) расстра́ивать impf., расстро́ить pf. **unsettled** adj.: the weather is ~ пого́да не установи́лась. **unshakeable** adj. непоколеби́мый. **unshaven** adj. небри́тый. **unsheathe** v.t. вынима́ть impf., вы́нуть pf. из ножен. **unship** v.t. (cargo) выгружа́ть impf., вы́грузить pf.; (passenger) выса́живать impf., вы́садить pf. на бе́рег. **unsightly** adj. непригля́дный, уро́бливый. **unskilful** adj. неуме́лый. **unskilled** adj. неквалифици́рованный (-ан, -анна). **unsociable** adj. необщи́тельный. **unsold** adj. непро́данный. **unsolicited** adj. непро́шеный. **unsolved** adj. нерешённый. **unsophisticated** adj. просто́й (прост, -á, -о, про́сты́), безыску́ственный (-ен, -енна). **unsound** adj. (unhealthy, unwholesome) нездоро́вый; (rotten, also fig.) гнило́й (гнил, -á, -o); (unreliable) ненадёжный; (unfounded) необосно́ванный (-ан, -анна); (faulty) дефе́ктный; of ~ mind душевнобольно́й. **unsparing** adj. (lavish) ще́дрый (щедр, -á, -o); (merciless) беспща́дный. **unspeakable** adj. (inexpressible) невырази́мый; (very bad) отврати́тельный. **unspecified** adj. то́чно не устано́вленный

(-ен), неопределённый (-нен, -нна). **unspoilt** adj. неиспо́рченный. **unspoken** adj. невы́сказанный. **unsporting, unsportsmanlike** adj. неспорти́вный, недосто́йный (-о́ин, -о́йна) спортсме́на. **unstable** adj. неусто́йчивый; (emotionally) неуравнове́шенный (-ен, -енна). **unsteady** adj. неусто́йчивый. **unsuccessful** adj. неуда́чный, безуспе́шный. **unsuitable** adj. неподходя́щий, неподоба́ющий. **unsuited** adj. (incompatible) несовмести́мый. **unsullied** adj. незапя́тнанный. **unsupported** adj. неподдержанный. **unsure** adj. (not convinced) неуве́ренный (-ен, -ена) (of o.s. в себе́); (hesitating) неуве́ренный (-ен, -енна). **unsurpassed** adj. непревзойдённый (-ён, -ённа). **unsuspected** adj. не вызыва́ющий подозре́ний; (unforeseen) непредви́денный. **unsuspecting** adj. неподозрева́ющий. **unsweetened** adj. неподслащённый. **unswerving** adj. непоколеби́мый. **unsymmetrical** adj. несимметри́ческий. **unsympathetic** adj. несочу́вствующий; (unattractive) несимпати́чный. **unsystematic** adj. несистемати́чный.

untainted adj. неиспо́рченный. **untalented** adj. нетала́нтливый. **untameable** adj. не поддаю́щийся прируче́нию; (indomitable) неукроти́мый. **untapped** adj.: ~ resources неиспо́льзованные ресу́рсы m.pl. **untarnished** adj. непотускне́вший; (fig.) незапя́тнанный. **untenable** adj. несостоя́тельный. **unthinkable** adj. (inconceivable) невообрази́мый; (unlikely) невероя́тный; (out of the question) исключённый (-ён, -ена́). **unthinking** adj. легкомы́сленный (-ен, -енна). **unthread** v.t. вынима́ть impf., вы́нуть pf. ни́тку из+g. **untidiness** n. неопря́тность; (disorder) беспоря́док (дка). **untidy** adj. неопря́тный; (in disorder) в беспоря́дке. **untie** v.t. развя́зывать impf., развяза́ть (-яжу́, -я́жешь) pf.; (set free) освобожда́ть impf., освободи́ть pf.

until [ən'tɪl, ʌn-] prep. до+g.; not ~ не ра́ньше+g.; ~ then до тех пор; conj. пока́, пока́… не; not ~ то́лько когда́.

untimely [ʌn'taɪmlɪ] adj. (premature) безвре́менный; (inopportune) несвоевре́менный (-нен, -нна); (inappropriate) неуме́стный. **untiring** adj. неутоми́мый. **untold** adj. (innumerable) бессчётный, несме́тный; (inexpressible) невырази́мый. **untouched** adj. (also pure) нетро́нутый; (indifferent) равноду́шный. **untoward** [ˌʌntə'wɔːd, ʌn'təʊəd] adj. (unfavourable) неблагоприя́тный; (refractory) непоко́рный. **untrained** adj. необу́ченный. **untranslatable** adj. непереводи́мый. **untried** adj. неиспы́танный. **untroubled** adj. споко́йный. **untrue** adj. (incorrect, disloyal) неве́рный (-рен, -рна́, -рно, неве́рны); (incorrect) непра́вильный; (false) ло́жный. **untrustworthy** adj. ненадёжный. **untruth** n. непра́вда, ложь. **untruthful** adj. лжи́вый.

unusable [ʌn'juːzəb(ə)l] *adj.* непригóдный.
unused *adj.* (*not employed*) неиспóльзованный; (*not accustomed*) непривы́кший
(**to** к+*d.*). **unusual** *adj.* необыкновéнный
(-нен, -нна), необы́чный. **unusually** *adv.*
необыкновéнно. **unutterable** *adj.* невырази́мый.

unvarnished [ʌn'vɑːnɪʃt] *adj.* (*fig.*) неприкрáшенный. **unvarying** *adj.* неизменя́ющийся.
unveil *v.t.* снимáть *impf.*, снять (сниму́,
-мешь; снял, -á, -о) *pf.* покрывáло с+*g.*;
(*statue*) торжéственно открывáть *impf.*, откры́ть (-рóю, -рóешь) *pf.*; (*disclose*) открывáть *impf.*, откры́ть (-рóю, -рóешь) *pf.* **unversed** *adj.* несвéдущий (**in** в+*p.*); (*inexperienced*) нео́пытный (**in** в+*p.*).

unwanted [ʌn'wɒntɪd] *adj.* нежелáнный. **unwarranted** *adj.* (*unjustified*) неоправданный. **unwary** *adj.* неосторóжный. **unwavering** *adj.* непоколеби́мый. **unwelcome** *adj.*
нежелáнный, нежелáтельный; (*unpleasant*)
неприя́тный. **unwell** *adj.* нездорóвый. **unwholesome** *adj.* нездорóвый, врéдный (-ден,
-днá, -дно). **unwieldy** *adj.* громóздкий, неуклю́жий. **unwilling** *adj.* нерасполóженный.
unwillingly *adv.* неохóтно, прóтив желáния. **unwillingness** *n.* неохóта. **unwind** *v.t. & i.* размáтывать(ся)
impf., размотáть(ся) *pf.*; (*rest*) отдыхáть
impf., отдохну́ть *pf.* **unwise** *adj.* не(благо)-
разу́мный. **unwitting** *adj.* невóльный, нечáянный. **unwittingly** *adv.* невóльно, нечáянно. **unwonted** [ʌn'wəʊntɪd] *adj.* непривы́чный, необы́чный. **unworkable** *adj.* неприменимый. **unworldly** *adj.* не от ми́ра
сегó; (*spiritual*) духóвный. **unworthy** *adj.*
недостóйный (-óин, -óйна). **unwrap** *v.t.* развёртывать *impf.*, развернуть *pf.* **unwritten**
adj.: ~ **law** непи́саный закóн.

unyielding [ʌn'jiːldɪŋ] *adj.* упóрный, неподáтливый.

unzip [ʌn'zɪp] *v.t.* расстёгивать *impf.*, расстегну́ть *pf.* (мóлнию+*g.*).

up [ʌp] *adv.* (*motion*) навéрх, вверх; (*position*) наверху́, вверху́; ~ **and down** вверх и
вниз (*back and forth*) взад и вперёд; ~ **to**
(*towards*) к+*d.*; (*time*) вплоть до+*g.*; ~ **to**
now до сих пор; **be** ~ **against** имéть *impf.*
дéло с+*i.*; **it is** ~ **to you**+*inf.*, э́то вам+*inf.*,
вы должны́+*inf.*; **not** ~ **to much** невáжный
(-жен, -жнá, -жно); **what's** ~? что случи́-
лось?; в чём дéло?; **your time is** ~ вáше
врéмя истеклó; ~ **and about** на ногáх; **he**
isn't ~ **yet** он ещё не встал; **he isn't** ~ **to**
this job он не годи́тся для э́той рабóты;
prep. вверх по+*d.*; (*along*) (вдоль) по+*d.*;
v.t. & i. поднимáть(ся) *impf.*, подня́ть(ся)
(-ниму́(сь), -ни́мешь(ся); пóднял/подня́лся,
-лá(сь), -ло́/ло́сь) *pf.*; (*leap* ~) вскáкивать
impf., вскочи́ть (-чу́, -чишь) *pf.*; *n.*: ~**s and**
downs (*fig.*) преврáтности *f.pl.* судьбы́. **up-**
and-coming *adj.* напóристый, многообе-
щáющий.

upbraid [ʌp'breɪd] *v.t.* брани́ть *impf.*, вы́~ *pf.*
(**for** за+*a.*).
upbringing ['ʌp,brɪŋɪŋ] *n.* воспитáние.
update [ʌp'deɪt] *v.t.* модернизи́ровать *impf.*
& *pf.*; (*book*) дополня́ть *impf.*, дополнить
pf.
upgrade ['ʌpgreɪd] *v.t.* повышáть *impf.*, повы́сить *pf.* (по слу́жбе).
upheaval [ʌp'hiːv(ə)l] *n.* сдвиг; (*revolution*)
переворóт; (*geol.*) смещéние пластóв.
uphill ['ʌphɪl] *adj.* иду́щий в гóру; (*fig.*) тяжёлый (-л, -лá); *adv.* в гóру.
uphold [ʌp'həʊld] *v.t.* поддéрживать *impf.*,
поддержáть (-жу́, -жишь) *pf.*; ~ **a view** придéрживаться *impf.* взгля́да. **upholder** *n.*
стóронник.
upholster [ʌp'həʊlstə(r)] *v.t.* обивáть *impf.*,
оби́ть (обобью́, -ьёшь) *pf.* (**with, in** +*i.*). **upholsterer** *n.* обóйщик. **upholstery** *n.* оби́вка.
upkeep ['ʌpkiːp] *n.* (*maintenance, support*) содержáние; (*repair(s)*) ремóнт; (*cost of* ~)
стóимость содержáния.
upland ['ʌplənd] *n.* гори́стая часть (*pl.* -ти,
-тéй) страны́, нагóрная странá (*pl.* -ны);
adj. нагóрный; (*inland*) лежáщий внутри́
страны́.
uplift [ʌp'lɪft; 'ʌplɪft] *v.t.* поднимáть *impf.*, подня́ть (-ниму́, -ни́мешь; пóдня́л, -á, -о) *pf.*;
n. подъём.
upon [ə'pɒn] *prep.* (*position*) на+*p.*, (*motion*)
на+*a.*; *see* **on**
upper ['ʌpə(r)] *adj.* вéрхний; (*socially, in*
rank) вы́сший; **gain the** ~ **hand** одéрживать
impf., одержáть (-жу́, -жишь) *pf.* верх (**over**
над+*i.*); ~ **crust** верху́шка óбщества; **the**
U~ **House** вéрхняя палáта; *n.* передóк (-дкá).
uppermost *adj.* сáмый вéрхний, вы́сший;
be ~ **in person's mind** бóльше всегó занимáть *impf.*, заня́ть (займу́, -мёшь; зáнял, -á,
-о) *pf.* мы́сли когó-л.
uppish ['ʌpɪʃ] *adj.* спеси́вый, высокомéрный.
upright ['ʌpraɪt] *n.* подпóрка, стóйка; *adj.*
вертикáльный; (*straight*) прямóй (-м, -мá,
-мо, пря́мы́); (*honest*) чéстный (-тен, -тнá,
-тно); ~ **piano** пиани́но *nt.indecl.*; *adv.*
вертикáльно, прямо, стоймя́.
uprising ['ʌp,raɪzɪŋ] *n.* восстáние, бунт.
uproar ['ʌprɔː(r)] *n.* шум (-а(у)), гам. **up-**
'roarious *adj.* шу́мный (-мен, -мнá, -мно),
бу́йный (бу́ен, буйнá, -но).
uproot [ʌp'ruːt] *v.t.* вырывáть *impf.*, вы́рвать
(-ву, -вешь) *pf.* с кóрнем; (*eradicate*) искореня́ть *impf.*, искорени́ть *pf.*
upset ['ʌpset] *n.* (*disorder, confusion, discomposure*) расстрóйство; *v.t.* (*disorder, discompose, spoil (plans etc.)*) расстрáивать *impf.*,
расстрóить *pf.*; *v.t. & i.* (*overturn*) опрокидывать(ся) *impf.*, опроки́нуть(ся) *pf.*; *adj.*
(*miserable*) расстрóенный (-ен); ~ **stomach**
расстрóйство желу́дка.
upshot ['ʌpʃɒt] *n.* развя́зка, результáт.
upside-down [,ʌpsaɪd 'daʊn] *adj.* перевёр-

нутый вверх дном; *adv.* вверх дном; (*in disorder*) в беспоря́дке.

upstairs [ʌp'steəz] *adv.* (*position*) наверху́; (*motion*) наве́рх; *n.* ве́рхний эта́ж (-а́); *adj.* находя́щийся в ве́рхнем этаже́.

upstart ['ʌpstɑːt] *n.* вы́скочка *c.g.*

upstream ['ʌpstriːm] *adv.* про́тив тече́ния; (*situation*) вверх по тече́нию.

upsurge ['ʌpsɜːdʒ] *n.* подъём, волна́ (*pl.* -ны, -н, волна́м).

uptake ['ʌpteɪk] *n.*: **be quick on the ~** бы́стро соображать *impf.*, сообрази́ть *pf.*

up-to-date [ʌptə'deɪt] *adj.* совреме́нный (-нен, -нна); (*fashionable*) мо́дный (-ден, -дна́, -дно).

upturned ['ʌptɜːnd] *adj.* (*face etc.*) по́днятый (по́днят, -а́, -о) кве́рху; (*inverted*) переверну́тый.

upward ['ʌpwəd] *adj.* напра́вленный (-ен) вверх, дви́жущийся вверх. **upwards** *adv.* вверх; **~ of** свы́ше+*g.* **upwind** *adv.* про́тив ве́тра.

Urals ['jʊər(ə)lz] *n.* Ура́л.

uranium [jʊ'reɪnɪəm] *n.* ура́н; *attr.* ура́новый.

urban ['ɜːbən] *adj.* городско́й.

urbane [ɜː'beɪn] *adj.* ве́жливый, с изы́сканными мане́рами. **urbanity** [ɜː'bænɪtɪ] *n.* ве́жливость.

urchin ['ɜːtʃɪn] *n.* мальчи́шка *m.*

urge [ɜːdʒ] *n.* (*incitement*) побужде́ние, толчо́к (-чка́); (*desire*) жела́ние; *v.t.* (*impel*, **~ on**) подгоня́ть *impf.*, подогна́ть (подгоню́, -нишь; подогна́л, -а́, -о) *pf.*; (*induce, prompt*) побужда́ть *impf.*, побуди́ть *pf.*; (*advocate*) насто́йчиво убежда́ть *impf.*; (*give as reason*) обраща́ть *impf.*, обрати́ть (-ащу́, -ати́шь) *pf.* внима́ние на+*a.* **urgency** *n.* (*also insistence*) настоя́тельность; (*immediate importance*) безотлага́тельность; **a matter of great ~** сро́чное де́ло (*pl.* -ла́). **urgent** *adj.* сро́чный (-чен, -чна́, -чно); (*also insistent*) настоя́тельный; (*absolutely essential*) кра́йне необходи́мый. **urgently** *adv.* сро́чно.

uric ['jʊərɪk] *adj.* мочево́й. **urinal** [jʊə'raɪn(ə)l, 'jʊərɪn(ə)l] *n.* писсуа́р. **urinate** *v.i.* мочи́ться (-чу́сь, -чишься) *impf.*, по~ *pf.* **uri'nation** *n.* мочеиспуска́ние. **urine** ['jʊərɪn] *n.* моча́.

urn [ɜːn] *n.* у́рна.

US(A) *abbr.* (*of* **United States of America**) США *pl.*, *indecl.*, Соединённые Шта́ты Аме́рики; *adj.* америка́нский.

usable ['juːzəb(ə)l] *adj.* го́дный (-ден, -дна́, -дно) к употребле́нию. **usage** ['juːsɪdʒ] *n.* употребле́ние; (*custom*) обы́чай; (*treatment*) обраще́ние. **use** *n.* (*also benefit*) по́льза; (*application*) употребле́ние, примене́ние, испо́льзование; **it is of no ~** бесполе́зно; **make ~ of** испо́льзовать *impf. & pf.*; по́льзоваться *impf.*+*i.*; *v.t.* употребля́ть *impf.*, употреби́ть *pf.*; по́льзоваться *impf.*+*i.*; применя́ть *impf.*, примени́ть (-ню́, -нишь) *pf.*; (*treat*) обраща́ться *impf.* с+*i.*; **I ~d to see him often** я ча́сто его́ встреча́л; **be, get, ~d to** привыка́ть *impf.*, пр ивы́кнуть (-к)

pf. (**to** к+*d.*) **~ up** расхо́довать *impf.*, из~ *pf.* **used** *adj.* (*second-hand*) поде́ржанный, ста́рый (стар, -а́, ста́ро). **useful** *adj.* поле́зный; **come in ~, prove ~** пригоди́ться *pf.* (**to** +*d.*) **useless** *adj.* бесполе́зный, ни куда́ не го́дный (-ден, -дна́, -дно). **user** *n.* потреби́тель *m.* **user-friendly** *adj.* удо́бный в употребле́нии.

usher ['ʌʃə(r)] *n.* (*door-keeper*) швейца́р; (*theatr.*) билетёр; *v.t.* (*lead in*) вводи́ть (ввожу́, -о́дишь) *impf.*, ввести́ (-еду́, -едёшь; -ёл, -ела́) *pf.*; (*proclaim*, **~ in**) возвеща́ть *impf.*, возвести́ть *pf.* **usherette** *n.* билетёрша.

USSR *abbr.* (*of* **Union of Soviet Socialist Republics**) СССР, Сою́з Сове́тских Социалисти́ческих Респу́блик.

usual ['juːʒʊəl] *adj.* обыкнове́нный (-нен, -нна), обы́чный; **as ~** как обы́чно. **usually** *adv.* обыкнове́нно, обы́чно.

usurer ['juːʒərə(r)] *n.* ростовщи́к (-а́). **usurious** [jʊ'ʒʊərɪəs] *adj.* ростовщи́ческий.

usurp [jʊ'zɜːp] *v.t.* узурпи́ровать *impf. & pf.*; незако́нно захва́тывать *impf.*, захвати́ть (-ачу́, -а́тишь) *pf.* **usurper** *n.* узурпа́тор, захва́тчик.

usury ['juːʒərɪ] *n.* ростовщи́чество.

utensil [juː'tens(ə)l] *n.* инструме́нт, ору́дие; *pl.* у́тварь; принадле́жности *f.pl.*; (*kitchen* **~s**) посу́да.

uterine ['juːtəraɪn, -rɪn] *adj.* ма́точный; (*of one mother*) единоутро́бный. **uterus** *n.* ма́тка.

utilitarian [ˌjuːtɪlɪ'teərɪən] *adj.* утилита́рный; *n.* утилитари́ст. **utilitarianism** *n.* утилитари́зм. **utility** [juː'tɪlɪtɪ] *n.* поле́зность; (*profitableness*) вы́годность; *adj.* утилита́рный; (*practical*) практи́чный. **utilize** ['juːtɪˌlaɪz] *v.t.* испо́льзоваться *impf. & pf.*; утилизи́ровать *impf. & pf.*

utmost ['ʌtməʊst] *adj.* (*extreme*) кра́йний, преде́льный; (*furthest*) са́мый отдалённый (-ён, -ённа); **this is of the ~ importance to me** э́то для меня́ кра́йне ва́жно; *n.*: **do one's ~** де́лать *impf.*, с~ *pf.* всё возмо́жное.

Utopia [juː'təʊpɪə] *n.* уто́пия. **utopian** *adj.* утопи́ческий; *n.* утопи́ст.

utter ['ʌtə(r)] *attr.* по́лный, соверше́нный, абсолю́тный; (*out-and-out*) отъя́вленный (*coll.*); *v.t.* произноси́ть (-ошу́, -о́сишь) *impf.*, произнести́ (-есу́, -есёшь; -ёс, -есла́) *pf.*; (*let out*) издава́ть (-даю́, -даёшь) *impf.*, изда́ть (-а́м, -а́шь, -а́ст, -ади́м; изда́л, -а́, -о) *pf.* **utterance** *n.* (*uttering*) произнесе́ние; (*pronouncement*) выска́зывание; (*diction*) ди́кция; (*pronunciation*) произноше́ние; **gift of ~** дар сло́ва; **give ~ to** выража́ть *impf.*, вы́разить *pf.* слова́ми. **utterly** *adv.* кра́йне, соверше́нно.

U-turn ['juːtɜːn] *n.* разворо́т; (*fig.*) поворо́т на 180°.

uvula [ju:'vjʊlə] *n.* язычо́к (-чка́).

Uzbek ['ʌzbek, 'ʊz-] *n.* узбе́к, -е́чка; *adj.* узбе́кский. **Uzbekistan** [ˌʌzbekɪ'stɑːn, ˌʊz-] *n.* Узбекиста́н.

V

про́тив+g.; **England** ~ **France** А́нглия про́тив Фра́нции.

vacancy ['veɪkənsɪ] n. (for job) вака́нсия, свобо́дное ме́сто (pl. -та́); (at hotel) свобо́дный но́мер (pl. -а́); (emptiness) пустота́; (apathy) безуча́стность; (absent-mindedness) рассе́янность. **vacant** adj. (post) вака́нтный; (post; not engaged, free) свобо́дный; (empty) пусто́й (пуст, -а́, -о, пу́сты́); (look) рассе́янный (-ян, -янна); '~ **possession**' «помеще́ние гото́во для въе́зда». **vacantly** adv. рассе́янно. **vacate** [vəˈkeɪt, veɪ-] v.t. освобожда́ть impf., освободи́ть pf.; покида́ть impf., поки́нуть pf. **va'cation** n. (school, univ.) кани́кулы (-л) pl.; (leave) о́тпуск; (vacating) оставле́ние, освобожде́ние.

vaccinate ['væksɪˌneɪt] v.t. привива́ть impf., приви́ть (-вью́, -вьёшь; приви́л, -а́, -о) pf.+d. (against +a.). **vacci'nation** n. приви́вка (against от, про́тив+g.). **vaccine** ['væksiːn] n. вакци́на.

vacillate ['væsɪˌleɪt] v.i. колеба́ться (-блюсь, -блешься) impf. **vaci'llation** n. колеба́ние; (inconstancy) непостоя́нство.

vacuity [vəˈkjuːɪtɪ] n. пустота́. **vacuous** ['vækjʊəs] adj. пусто́й (пуст, -а́, -о, пу́сты́); (foolish) бессмы́сленный (-ен, -енна). **vacuum** n. ва́куум; (fig.) пустота́; ~ **cleaner** пылесо́с; ~ **flask** те́рмос. **vacuum-clean** v.t. чи́стить impf., вы́~, по~ pf. пылесо́сом.

vade-mecum [ˌvɑːdɪˈmeɪkəm, ˌveɪdɪˈmiːkəm] n. путеводи́тель m.

vagabond ['væɡəˌbɒnd] n. бродя́га m.; attr. бродя́чий. **vagabondage** n. бродя́жничество. **vagabondize** v.i. скита́ться impf., бродя́жничать impf.

vagary ['veɪɡərɪ] n. капри́з, причу́да.

vagina [vəˈdʒaɪnə] n. влага́лище. **vaginal** adj. влага́лищный.

vagrancy ['veɪɡrənsɪ] n. бродя́жничество. **vagrant** adj. бродя́чий; n. бродя́га m.

vague [veɪɡ] adj. (indeterminate, uncertain) неопределённый (-нен, -нна); (unclear) нея́сный (-сен, -сна́, -сно); (dim) сму́тный (-тен, -тна́, -тно); (absent-minded) рассе́янный (-ян, -янна). **vagueness** n. неопределённость, нея́сность; (absent-mindedness) рассе́янность.

vain [veɪn] adj. (futile) тще́тный, напра́сный; (empty) пусто́й (пуст, -а́, -о, пу́сты́); (con-

ceited) самовлюблённый, тщесла́вный; **in** ~ напра́сно, тще́тно, зря. **vain'glorious** adj. тщесла́вный, хвастли́вый. **vain'glory** n. тщесла́вие, хвастли́вость.

valance ['væləns] n. подзо́р, обо́рка, за́навеска.

vale [veɪl] n. дол, доли́на.

valediction [ˌvælɪˈdɪkʃ(ə)n] n. проща́ние. **valedictory** adj. проща́льный.

valency ['veɪlənsɪ] n. вале́нтность.

valentine ['vælənˌtaɪn] n. (sweetheart) возлю́бленный, -нная; (card) любо́вное посла́ние.

valerian [vəˈlɪərɪən] n. валериа́на; (med.) валериа́новые ка́пли (-пель) pl.

valet ['vælɪt, -leɪ] n. камерди́нер, слуга́ (pl. -ги) m.

valiant ['væljənt] adj. хра́брый (храбр, -а́, -о), до́блестный.

valid ['vælɪd] adj. действи́тельный, име́ющий си́лу; (weighty) ве́ский. **validate** v.t. (ratify) утвержда́ть impf., утверди́ть pf.; (declare valid) объявля́ть impf., объяви́ть (-влю́, -вишь) pf. действи́тельным. **validity** [vəˈlɪdɪtɪ] n. действи́тельность; (weightiness) ве́скость.

valise [vəˈliːz] n. саквоя́ж, чемода́н.

valley ['vælɪ] n. доли́на.

valorous ['vælərəs] adj. до́блестный. **valour** n. до́блесть.

valuable ['væljʊəb(ə)l] adj. це́нный (-нен, -нна); (costly) дорого́й (до́рог, -а́, -о); pl. це́нные ве́щи (-ще́й) pl., драгоце́нности f.pl. **valu'ation** n. оце́нка. **value** n. це́нность; (cost, worth) цена́ (pl. -ны); (worth, econ.) сто́имость; (significance) значе́ние; (math.) величина́; (mus.) дли́тельность; pl. це́нности f.pl.; ~ **judgement** субъекти́вная оце́нка; v.t. (estimate) оце́нивать impf., оцени́ть (-ню́, -нишь) pf.; (hold dear) цени́ть (-ню́, -нишь) impf., дорожи́ть impf.+i. **value-added:** ~ **tax** нало́г на доба́вленную сто́имость. **valueless** adj. бесполе́зный, ничего́ не сто́ящий. **valuer** n. оце́нщик.

valve [vælv] n. (tech., med., mus.) кла́пан; (tech.) ве́нтиль m.; (bot.) ство́рка; (radio) электро́нная ла́мпа.

vamp[1] [væmp] n. (of shoe) передо́к (-дка́); (patched-up article) что-л. почи́ненное на ско́рую ру́ку; (mus.) импровизи́рованный аккомпанеме́нт; v.t. (repair) чини́ть (-ню́, -нишь) impf., по~ pf.; (mus.) импровизи́ровать impf., сымпровизи́ровать pf. аккомпанеме́нт k+d.

vamp[2] [væmp] n. (flirt) соблазни́тельница.

vampire ['væmpaɪə(r)] n. (also fig.; also ~ **bat**) вампи́р.

van[1] [væn] n. (road vehicle, caravan) фурго́н; (rail.) бага́жный (luggage), това́рный (goods), служе́бный (guard's), ваго́н.

van[2] [væn] n. (vanguard) аванга́рд.

vandal ['vænd(ə)l] n. ванда́л, хулига́н. **vandalism** n. вандали́зм, варва́рство. **vandalize** v.t. разруша́ть impf., разру́шить pf.

vane [veɪn] n. (weathercock) флю́гер (pl. -а́);

(of windmill) крыло́ *(pl.* -лья, -льев); *(of propeller)* ло́пасть *(pl.* -ти, -те́й); *(of turbine)* лопа́тка.

vanguard ['vænɡɑːd] *n.* авангард.

vanilla [və'nɪlə] *n.* вани́ль; *attr.* вани́льный.

vanish ['vænɪʃ] *v.i.* исчеза́ть *impf.*, исче́знуть (-е́з) *pf.*; пропада́ть *impf.*, пропа́сть (-аду́, -аде́шь; -а́л) *pf.*; ~**ing point** то́чка схо́да.

vanity ['vænɪtɪ] *n. (futility)* тщета́, суета́; *(vainglory)* тщесла́вие; ~ **bag** су́мочка, несессе́р.

vanquish ['væŋkwɪʃ] *v.t. (enemy)* побежда́ть *impf.*, победи́ть (-еди́шь, -еди́т) *pf.*; *(fig.)* преодолева́ть *impf.*, преодоле́ть *pf.*

vantage ['vɑːntɪdʒ] *n.* преиму́щество; ~ **point** вы́годная пози́ция; *(for observation)* пункт наблюде́ния.

vapid ['væpɪd] *adj.* безвку́сный; *(also fig.)* пре́сный (-сен, -сна́, -сно); *(fig.)* ску́чный (-чен, -чна́, -чно).

vaporize ['veɪpəraɪz] *v.t. & i.* испаря́ть(ся) *impf.*, испари́ть(ся) *pf.* **vaporizer** *n.* испари́тель *m.* **vaporous** *adj.* парообра́зный; *(vague)* тума́нный (-нен, -нна). **vapour** *n. (steam etc.)* пар *(loc.* -у́; *pl.* -ы́); *(mist, haze)* тума́н.

variable ['veərɪəb(ə)l] *adj.* изме́нчивый, непостоя́нный (-нен, -нна); *(weather)* неусто́йчивый, *(also math.)* переме́нный; *n. (math.)* переме́нная (величина́). **variance** *n. (disagreement)* разногла́сие; *(change)* измене́ние; *(disparity)* несоотве́тствие; **be at ~ with** расходи́ться (-ожу́сь, -о́дишься) *impf.*, разойти́сь (-ойду́сь, -ойде́шься; -оше́лся, -ошла́сь) *pf.* во мне́ниях с+*i.* **variant** *n.* вариа́нт; *adj.* ра́зный. **vari'ation** *n. (varying)* измене́ние, переме́на; *(variant)* вариа́нт; *(variety)* разнови́дность; *(mus., math.)* вариа́ция.

varicose ['værɪkəʊs] *adj.:* ~ **veins** расшире́ние вен.

variegate ['veərɪɡeɪt, -rɪəɡeɪt] *v.t.* де́лать *impf.*, с~ *pf.* пёстрым; *(diversify)* разнообра́зить *impf.* **variegated** *adj.* разноцве́тный, пёстрый (-р, -ра́, пёстро́); *(diverse)* разнообра́зный. **variety** [və'raɪətɪ] *n.* разнообра́зие; *(sort)* разнови́дность; *(multitude)* мно́жество; ~ **show** варьете́ *nt.indecl.*, эстра́дный конце́рт. **various** *adj. (of several kinds)* разли́чный; *(different, several)* ра́зный; *(diverse)* разнообра́зный.

varnish ['vɑːnɪʃ] *n.* лак; *(fig.)* лоск; *v.t.* лакирова́ть *impf.*, от~ *pf. (also fig.).* **varnishing** *n.* лакиро́вка.

vary ['veərɪ] *v.t.* разнообра́зить *impf.*, меня́ть *impf.*; *v.i. (change)* меня́ться *impf.*, измени́ться *impf.*, измени́ться (-ню́сь, -ни́шься) *pf.*; *(differ)* ра́зниться *impf.*; *(disagree)* не соглаша́ться *impf.*

vase [vɑːz] *n.* ва́за.

vaseline ['væsɪˌliːn] *n.* вазели́н.

vassal ['væs(ə)l] *n.* васса́л.

vast [vɑːst] *adj.* грома́дный, обши́рный. **vastly**

adv. значи́тельно. **vastness** *n.* грома́дность, обши́рность.

VAT *abbr. (of value added tax)* нало́г на доба́вленную/прира́щённую сто́имость.

vat [væt] *n.* чан *(pl.* -ы́), бак.

Vatican ['vætɪkən] *n.* Ватика́н.

vaudeville ['vɔːdəvɪl, 'vəʊ-] *n.* водеви́ль *m.*; *(variety)* варьете́ *nt.indecl.*

vault[1] [vɔːlt, vɒlt] *n. (leap)* прыжо́к (-жка́); *v.t.* перепры́гивать *impf.*, перепры́гнуть *pf.*; *v.i.* пры́гать *impf.*, пры́гнуть *pf.* **vaulting-horse** *n.* гимнасти́ческий конь (-ня́; *pl.* -ни, -не́й) *m.*

vault[2] [vɔːlt, vɒlt] *n. (arch, covering)* свод; *(cellar)* по́греб, подва́л; *(burial ~)* склеп; *v.t.* возводи́ть (-ожу́, -о́дишь) *impf.*, возвести́ (-еду́, -еде́шь; -ёл, -ела́) *pf.* свод над+*i.* **vaulted** *adj.* сво́дчатый.

VCR *abbr. (of video cassette recorder)* видеомагнитофо́н.

VD *abbr. (of venereal disease)* венери́ческая боле́знь.

VDU *abbr. (of visual display unit)* дисплей.

veal [viːl] *n.* теля́тина; *attr.* теля́чий.

vector ['vektə(r)] *n. (math.)* ве́ктор; *(carrier of disease)* перено́счик инфе́кции.

veer [vɪə(r)] *v.i. (change direction)* изменя́ть *impf.*, измени́ть (-ню́, -нишь) *pf.* направле́ние; *(turn)* повора́чивать *impf.*, повороти́ть (-очу́, -о́тишь) *pf.*; ~ **away from** отша́тываться *impf.*, отшатну́ться *pf.* от+*g.*

vegetable ['vedʒɪtəb(ə)l, 'vedʒtəb(ə)l] *n.* о́вощ; *adj.* расти́тельный; *(of vegetables)* овощно́й. **vegetarian** [ˌvedʒɪ'teərɪən] *n.* вегетариа́нец, -нка; *attr.* вегетариа́нский. **vege'tarianism** *n.* вегетариа́нство. **vegetate** *v.i.* расти́ (-ту́, -тёшь; рос, -ла́) *impf.*; *(fig.)* прозяба́ть *impf.* **vege'tation** *n.* расти́тельность; *(fig.)* прозяба́ние. **vegetative** *adj.* расти́тельный; *(biol.)* вегетати́вный; *(fig.)* прозяба́ющий.

vehemence ['viːɪməns] *n. (force)* си́ла; *(passion)* стра́стность. **vehement** *adj. (forceful)* си́льный (силён, -льна́, -льно, си́льны́); *(passionate)* стра́стный (-тен, -тна́, -тно).

vehicle ['viːɪk(ə)l, 'vɪək(ə)l] *n.* сре́дство передвиже́ния/перево́зки; *(motor ~)* автомоби́ль *m.*; *(medium)* сре́дство; *(chem.)* носи́тель *m.* **vehicular** [vɪ'hɪkjʊlə(r)] *adj. (conveying)* перево́зочный; *(of motor transport)* автомоби́льный; ~ **transport** автогужево́й тра́нспорт.

veil [veɪl] *n.* вуа́ль, покрыва́ло; *(fig.)* заве́са, покро́в; *(pretext)* предло́г; *v.t.* покрыва́ть *impf.*, покры́ть (-ро́ю, -ро́ешь) *pf.* вуа́лью, покрыва́лом; *(fig.)* скрыва́ть *impf.*, скрыть (-ро́ю, -ро́ешь) *pf.*

vein [veɪn] *n.* ве́на; *(of leaf; streak)* жи́лка; **in the same ~** в том же ду́хе. **veined** *adj.* испещрённый (-ён, -ена́) жи́лками.

veld [velt] *n.* вельд.

vellum ['veləm] *n. (parchment)* то́нкий перга́мент; *(paper)* веле́невая бума́га.

velocity [vɪ'lɒsɪtɪ] *n.* ско́рость.

velour(s) [və'luə(r)] *n.* велю́р; (*attr.*) велю́ровый.

velvet ['velvɪt] *n.* барха́т; *adj.* барха́тный. **velveteen** *n.* вельве́т. **velvety** *adj.* бархати́стый.

venal ['viːn(ə)l] *adj.* прода́жный, подку́пный. **venality** [,viː'nælɪtɪ] *n.* прода́жность.

vend [vend] *v.t.* продава́ть (-даю́, -даёшь) *impf.*, прода́ть (-а́м, -а́шь, а́ст, -ади́м; про́дал, -а́, -о) *pf.* **vending-machine** *n.* торго́вый автома́т. **vendor** ['vendə(r), -dɔ:(r)] *n.* продаве́ц (-вца́), -вщи́ца.

vendetta [ven'detə] *n.* венде́тта, кро́вная месть.

veneer [vɪ'nɪə(r)] *n.* фанеро́вка; (*fig.*) лоск; *v.t.* фанерова́ть *impf.*

venerable ['venərəb(ə)l] *adj.* почте́нный (-нен, -нна); (V∼) преподо́бный. **venerate** *v.t.* благогове́ть *impf.* пе́ред+*i.* **veneˈration** *n.* благогове́ние, почита́ние. **venerator** *n.* почита́тель *m.*

venereal [vɪ'nɪərɪəl] *adj.* венери́ческий.

venetian blind [vɪ'niːʃ(ə)n] *n.* жалюзи́ *nt.indecl.*

vengeance ['vendʒ(ə)ns] *n.* месть, мще́ние; **take** ∼ мстить *impf.*, ото∼ *pf.* (**on** +*d.*; **for** за+*a.*); **with a** ∼ в по́лном смы́сле сло́ва; (*with might and main*) вовсю́. **vengeful** *adj.* мсти́тельный.

venial ['viːnɪəl] *adj.* прости́тельный.

Venice ['venɪs] *n.* Вене́ция.

venison ['venɪs(ə)n, -z(ə)n] *n.* оле́нина.

venom ['venəm] *n.* яд (-а(у)). **venomous** *adj.* ядови́тый.

vent[1] [vent] *n.* (*opening*) вы́ход (*also fig.*), отве́рстие; (*air-hole*) отду́шина; *v.t.* (*feelings*) дава́ть (даю́, даёшь) *impf.*, дать (дам, дашь, даст, дади́м; дал, -а́, да́ло, -и) *pf.* вы́ход+*d.*; излива́ть *impf.*, изли́ть (-лью́, -льёшь; изли́л, -а́, -о) *pf.* (**on** на+*a.*); (*smoke etc.*) выпуска́ть *impf.*, вы́пустить *pf.*; (*opinion*) выска́зывать *impf.*, вы́сказать (-ажу, -ажешь) *pf.*

vent[2] [vent] *n.* (*slit*) разре́з.

ventilate ['ventɪ,leɪt] *v.t.* прове́тривать *impf.*, прове́трить *pf.*; (*fig.*) обсужда́ть *impf.*, обсуди́ть (-ужу́, -у́дишь) *pf.* **ventiˈlation** *n.* вентиля́ция, прове́тривание. **ventilator** *n.* вентиля́тор.

ventral ['ventr(ə)l] *adj.* брюшно́й.

ventricle ['ventrɪk(ə)l] *n.* желу́дочек (-чка).

ventriloquism [ven'trɪlə,kwɪz(ə)m], **ventriloquy** *n.* чревовеща́ние. **ventriloquist** *n.* чревовеща́тель *m.* **ventriloquize** *v.i.* чревовеща́ть *impf.*

venture ['ventʃə(r)] *n.* риско́ванное предприя́тие; (*speculation*) спекуля́ция; **at a** ∼ науда́чу; *v.i.* (*hazard, dare*) отва́живаться *impf.*, отва́житься *pf.*; *v.t.* (*risk*) рискова́ть *impf.*+*i.*; ста́вить *impf.*, по∼ *pf.* на ка́рту; ∼ **an opinion, guess** осме́ливаться *impf.*, осме́литься *pf.* вы́сказать мне́ние, дога́дку. **venturesome** *adj.* (*person*) сме́лый (смел, -а́, -о); (*enterprise*) риско́ванный (-ан, -анна).

venue ['venjuː] *n.* ме́сто (*pl.* -та́) сбо́ра.

veracious [və'reɪʃəs] *adj.* правди́вый. **veracity** [və'ræsɪtɪ] *n.* правди́вость.

veranda(h) [və'rændə] *n.* вера́нда.

verb [vɜːb] *n.* глаго́л. **verbal** *adj.* (*oral*) у́стный; (*relating to words*) слове́сный; (*gram.*) отглаго́льный. **verbalize** *v.t.* выража́ть *impf.*, вы́разить *pf.* слова́ми; *v.i.* быть многосло́вным. **verbatim** [vɜː'beɪtɪm] *adj.* досло́вный; *adv.* досло́вно. **verbiage** *n.* многосло́вие, пустосло́вие. **verbose** [vɜː'bəʊs] *adj.* многосло́вный. **verbosity** [vɜː'bɒsɪtɪ] *n.* многосло́вие.

verdant ['vɜːd(ə)nt] *adj.* зелёный (зе́лен, -á, -о).

verdict ['vɜːdɪkt] *n.* верди́кт, реше́ние; (*opinion*) мне́ние.

verdigris ['vɜːdɪgrɪs, -,griːs] *n.* я́рь-медя́нка.

verdure ['vɜːdjə(r)] *n.* зе́лень.

verge[1] [vɜːdʒ] *n.* (*also fig.*) край (*loc.* -áe & -аю́; *pl.* -ая́); (*of road*) обо́чина; (*fig.*) грань; (*eccl.*) жезл; **on the** ∼ **of** на гра́ни+*g.*; **he was on the** ∼ **of telling all** он чуть не расска́зал всё.

verge[2] [vɜːdʒ] *v.i.* клони́ться (-ню́сь, -нишься) *impf.* (**towards** к+*d.*); ∼ **on** грани́чить *impf.* с+*i.*

verger ['vɜːdʒə(r)] *n.* церко́вный служи́тель *m.*; (*bearer of staff*) жезлоно́сец (-сца).

verification [,verɪfɪ'keɪʃ(ə)n] *n.* прове́рка; (*confirmation*) подтвержде́ние. **verify** ['verɪ,faɪ] *v.t.* проверя́ть *impf.*, прове́рить *pf.*; (*confirm*) подтвержда́ть *impf.*, подтверди́ть *pf.* **verisimilitude** [,verɪsɪ'mɪlɪ,tjuːd] *n.* правдоподо́бие. **ˈveritable** *adj.* настоя́щий. **ˈverity** *n.* и́стина.

vermicelli [,vɜːmɪ'selɪ, -'tʃelɪ] *n.* вермише́ль.

vermilion [və'mɪljən] *adj.* я́рко-кра́сный (-сен, -сна́, -сно); *n.* ки́новарь.

vermin ['vɜːmɪn] *n.* вреди́тели *m.pl.*, парази́ты *m.pl.*; (*fig.*) подо́нки (-ков) *pl.* **verminous** *adj.* киша́щий парази́тами; (*fig.*) отврати́тельный.

vermouth ['vɜːməθ, və'muːθ] *n.* ве́рмут.

vernacular [və'nækjʊlə(r)] *adj.* (*native, of language*) родно́й; (*local, of dialect*) ме́стный; (*national, folk*) наро́дный; (*colloquial*) разгово́рный; *n.* родно́й язы́к (-á); ме́стный диале́кт; (*homely language*) разгово́рный язы́к (-á).

vernal ['vɜːn(ə)l] *adj.* весе́нний.

verruca [və'ruːkə] *n.* борода́вка.

Versailles [veə'saɪ] *n.* Верса́ль.

versatile ['vɜːsə,taɪl] *adj.* многосторо́нний; (*flexible, of mind*) ги́бкий (-бок, -бкá, -бко). **versaˈtility** *n.* многосторо́нность; ги́бкость.

verse [vɜːs] *n.* (*also bibl.*) стих (-á); (*stanza*) строфа́ (*pl.* -фы́); (*poetry*) стихи́ *m.pl.*, поэ́зия. **versed** *adj.* о́пытный, све́дущий (**in** в+*p.*). **versify** ['vɜːsɪ,faɪ] *v.i.* писа́ть (пишу́, -шешь) *impf.*, на∼ *pf.* стихи́; *v.t.* перелага́ть *impf.*, переложи́ть (-жу́, -жишь) *pf.* в стихи́.

version ['vɜːʃ(ə)n] *n.* (*variant*) вариа́нт; (*interpretation*) ве́рсия; (*text*) текст.

versus ['vɜːsəs] *prep.* про́тив+g.

vertebra ['vɜːtɪbrə] *n.* позвоно́к (-нка́); *pl.* позвоно́чник. **vertebral** *adj.* позвоно́чный.

vertebrate *n.* позвоно́чное живо́тное *sb.*

vertex ['vɜːteks] *n.* верши́на; (*anat.*) маку́шка. **vertical** *adj.* вертика́льный; *n.* вертика́ль.

vertiginous [vəˈtɪdʒɪnəs] *adj.* (*dizzy*) головокружи́тельный; (*rotating*) крутя́щийся. **vertigo** ['vɜːtɪgəʊ] *n.* головокруже́ние.

verve [vɜːv] *n.* подъём, энтузиа́зм.

very ['verɪ] *adj.* (*that ~ same*) тот са́мый; (*this ~ same*) э́тот са́мый; **at that ~ moment** в тот са́мый моме́нт; (*precisely*) как раз; **you are the ~ person I was looking for** как раз вас я иска́л; **the ~** (*even the*) да́же, оди́н; **the ~ thought frightens me** одна́, да́же, мысль об э́том меня́ пуга́ет; (*the extreme*) са́мый; **at the ~ end** в са́мом конце́; *adv.* о́чень; **~ much** о́чень; **~ much**+*comp.* гора́здо+*comp.*; **~**+*superl.*, *superl.*; **~ first** са́мый пе́рвый; **~ well** (*agreement*) хорошо́, ла́дно; **not ~** не о́чень, дово́льно+*neg.*

vesicle ['vesɪk(ə)l] *n.* пузырёк (-рька́).

vespers ['vespəz] *n.* вече́рня.

vessel ['ves(ə)l] *n.* сосу́д; (*ship*) кора́бль (-бля́) *m.*, су́дно (*pl.* суда́, -до́в).

vest¹ [vest] *n.* ма́йка; (*waistcoat*) жиле́т.

vest² [vest] *v.t.* (*with power*) облека́ть *impf.*, обле́чь (-еку́, -ечёшь; -ёк, -екла́) *pf.* (**with** +*i.*); (*rights*) наделя́ть *impf.*, надели́ть *pf.*+*i.* (**in** +*a.*). **vested** *adj.*: **~ interest** ли́чная заинтересо́ванность; **~ interests** (*property rights*) иму́щественные права́ *nt.pl.*; (*entrepreneurs*) кру́пные предпринима́тели *m.pl.*; **~ rights** безусло́вные права́ *nt.pl.*

vestal (virgin) ['vest(ə)l] *n.* веста́лка.

vestibule ['vestɪbjuːl] *n.* вестибю́ль *m.*, пере́дняя *sb.*

vestige ['vestɪdʒ] *n.* (*trace*) след (*pl.* -ы́); (*sign*) при́знак.

vestments ['vestmənts] *n.* одея́ние, оде́жда; (*eccl.*) облаче́ние. **vestry** *n.* ри́зница.

Vesuvius [vɪˈsuːvɪəs] *n.*: **Mt ~** Везу́вий.

vet [vet] *n.* ветерина́р; *v.t.* (*fig.*) проверя́ть *impf.*, прове́рить *pf.*

vetch [vetʃ] *n.* ви́ка *collect.*

veteran ['vetərən] *n.* ветера́н; *adj.* ста́рый (стар, -а́, ста́ро́).

veterinary ['vetərɪnərɪ] *adj.* ветерина́рный; *n.* ветерина́р.

veto ['viːtəʊ] *n.* ве́то *nt.indecl.*, запреще́ние; *v.t.* налага́ть *impf.*, наложи́ть (-жу́, -жишь) *pf.* ве́то на+*a.*; запреща́ть *impf.*, запрети́ть (-ещу́, -ети́шь) *pf.*

vex [veks] *v.t.* досажда́ть *impf.*, досади́ть *pf.*+*d.* **ve'xation** *n.* доса́да. **vexed** *adj.* (*annoyed*) раздоса́дованный (-ан); (*question*) спо́рный. **ve'xatious, vexing** *adj.* доса́дный.

via ['vaɪə] *prep.* че́рез+*a.*

viable ['vaɪəb(ə)l] *adj.* жизнеспосо́бный; (*practicable*) осуществи́мый.

viaduct ['vaɪədʌkt] *n.* виаду́к.

vial ['vaɪəl] *n.* пузырёк (-рька́).

vibrant ['vaɪbrənt] *adj.* (*vibrating*) вибри́рующий; (*resonating*) резони́рующий; (*trembling*) дрожа́щий (**with** от+*g.*). **vibraphone** *n.* вибрафо́н. **vi'brate** *v.i.* вибри́ровать *impf.*, дрожа́ть (-жу́, -жи́шь) *impf.*; (*to sound*) звуча́ть (-чу́, -чи́шь) *impf.*, про~ *pf.*; *v.t.* (*make ~*) вызыва́ть *impf.*, вы́звать (вы́зову, -вешь) *pf.* вибра́цию в+*p.* **vi'bration** *n.* вибра́ция, дрожа́ние. **vibrato** [vɪˈbrɑːtəʊ] *n.* вибра́то *nt.indecl.*

vicar ['vɪkə(r)] *n.* прихо́дский свяще́нник. **vicarage** *n.* дом (*pl.* -а́) свяще́нника.

vicarious [vɪˈkeərɪəs] *adj.* (*deputizing for another*) замеща́ющий друго́го; (*indirect*) ко́свенный.

vice¹ [vaɪs] *n.* (*evil*) поро́к, зло; (*shortcoming*) недоста́ток (-тка).

vice² [vaɪs] *n.* (*tech.*) тиски́ (-ко́в) *pl.*

vice- [vaɪs] *in comb.* ви́це-, замести́тель *m.*; **~ admiral** ви́це-адмира́л. **vice-chairman** *n.* замести́тель *m.* председа́теля. **vice-chancellor** *n.* (*univ.*) проре́ктор. **vice-president** *n.* ви́це-президе́нт. **viceroy** *n.* ви́це-коро́ль (-ля́) *m.*

vice versa [ˌvaɪsɪ ˈvɜːsə] *adv.* наоборо́т.

vicinity [vɪˈsɪnɪtɪ] *n.* окре́стности *f.pl.*, сосе́дство, бли́зость; **in the ~** побли́зости (**of** от+*g.*).

vicious ['vɪʃəs] *adj.* поро́чный; (*spiteful*) зло́бный; (*cruel*, *brutal*) жесто́кий (-о́к, -ока́, -о́ко); **~ circle** поро́чный круг (*loc.* -е & -у́; *pl.* -и́). **viciousness** *n.* поро́чность; зло́бность.

vicissitude [vɪˈsɪsɪˌtjuːd, vaɪ-] *n.* превра́тность.

victim ['vɪktɪm] *n.* же́ртва. **victimi'zation** *n.* пресле́дование. **victimize** *v.t.* (*harass*) му́чить *impf.*, за~, из~ *pf.*; (*persecute*) пресле́довать *impf.*

victor ['vɪktə(r)] *n.* победи́тель *m.*

Victorian [vɪkˈtɔːrɪən] *adj.* викториа́нский; (*fig.*) старомо́дный.

victorious [vɪkˈtɔːrɪəs] *adj.* (*army*) победоно́сный; (*procession etc.*) побе́дный. **victory** ['vɪktərɪ] *n.* побе́да.

victual ['vɪt(ə)l] *v.t.* снабжа́ть *impf.*, снабди́ть *pf.* прови́зией. **victualler** ['vɪtlə(r)] *n.* поставщи́к продово́льствия. **victuals** *n.* пи́ща, прови́зия *collect.*

vide ['vɪdeɪ, 'viː-, 'vaɪdɪ] *imper.* смотри́.

video (recorder) *n.* видеомагнитофо́н; **~ cassette** видеокассе́та; **~ recording** видеоза́пись; *v.t.* запи́сывать *impf.*, записа́ть (-ишу́, -и́шешь) *pf.* (на ви́део). **videotape** *n.* видеоле́нта; видеоза́пись.

vie [vaɪ] *v.i.* сопе́рничать *impf.* (**with** с+*i.*; **for** в+*p.*).

Vienna [vɪˈenə] *n.* Ве́на.

Vietnam [ˌvjetˈnæm] *n.* Вьетна́м.

view [vjuː] *n.* (*prospect*, *picture*) вид; (*opinion*) взгляд, мне́ние; (*viewing*) просмо́тр; (*inspection*) осмо́тр; **in ~ of** ввиду́+*g.*; **on ~** вы́ставленный (-ен) для обозре́ния; **with a ~ to** с це́лью+*g.*, +*inf.*; *v.t.* (*pictures etc.*)

рассма́тривать *impf.*; (*inspect*) осма́тривать *impf.*, осмотре́ть (-рю́, -ришь) *pf.*; (*mentally*) смотре́ть (-рю́, -ришь) *impf.* на+*a.*; *v.i.* смотре́ть (-рю́, -ришь) *impf.*, по~ *pf.* телеви́зор. **viewer** *n.* зри́тель *m.*, ~ница; (*for slides*) прое́ктор. **viewfinder** *n.* видоиска́тель *m.* **viewpoint** *n.* то́чка зре́ния.

vigil ['vɪdʒɪl] *n.* бо́дрствование; **keep** ~ бо́дрствовать *impf.*, дежу́рить *impf.* **vigilance** *n.* бди́тельность. **vigilant** *adj.* бди́тельный.

vigilante [ˌvɪdʒɪ'læntɪ] *n.* дружи́нник.

vignette [viː'njet] *n.* винье́тка.

vigorous ['vɪɡərəs] *adj.* си́льный (силён, -льна́, -льно, си́льны), энерги́чный. **vigour** *n.* си́ла, эне́ргия.

vile [vaɪl] *adj.* (*base*) по́длый (подл, -а́, -о), ни́зкий (-зок, -зка́, -зко); (*disgusting*) отврати́тельный. **vileness** *n.* по́длость; отврати́тельность. **vilify** ['vɪlɪˌfaɪ] *v.t.* черни́ть *impf.*, о~ *pf.*

villa ['vɪlə] *n.* ви́лла.

village ['vɪlɪdʒ] *n.* дере́вня, село́; *attr.* дереве́нский, се́льский. **villager** *n.* дереве́нский, се́льский жи́тель *m.*

villain ['vɪlən] *n.* злоде́й. **villainous** *adj.* злоде́йский; (*foul*) ме́рзкий (-зок, -зка́, -зко). **villainy** *n.* злоде́йство.

Vilnius ['vɪlnɪəs] *n.* Ви́льнюс.

vim [vɪm] *n.* эне́ргия.

vinaigrette [ˌvɪnɪ'ɡret] *n.* (*dressing*) припра́ва из у́ксуса и оли́вкового ма́сла.

vindicate ['vɪndɪˌkeɪt] *v.t.* (*justify*) опра́вдывать *impf.*, оправда́ть *pf.*; (*stand up for*) отста́ивать *impf.*, отстоя́ть (-ою́, -ои́шь) *pf.* **vindi'cation** *n.* (*justification*) оправда́ние; (*defence*) защи́та.

vindictive [vɪn'dɪktɪv] *adj.* мсти́тельный.

vine [vaɪn] *n.* виногра́дная лоза́ (*pl.* -зы).

vinegar ['vɪnɪɡə(r)] *n.* у́ксус; *attr.* у́ксусный. **vinegary** *adj.* ки́слый (-сел, -сла́, -сло).

vineyard ['vɪnjɑːd, -jəd] *n.* виногра́дник.

vintage ['vɪntɪdʒ] *n.* сбор, урожа́й, виногра́да; (*wine*) вино́ из сбо́ра определённого го́да; *attr.* (*wine*) ма́рочный; (*car*) ста́рый (стар, -а́, старо́).

viola ['vaɪəʊlə] *n.* (*mus.*) альт.

violate ['vaɪəˌleɪt] *v.t.* (*treaty, privacy*) наруша́ть *impf.*, нару́шить *pf.*; (*grave*) оскверня́ть *impf.*, оскверни́ть *pf.*; (*rape*) наси́ловать *impf.*, из~ *pf.* **vio'lation** *n.* наруше́ние; оскверне́ние; наси́лие. **violator** *n.* наруши́тель *m.*

violence ['vaɪələns] *n.* (*physical coercion, force*) наси́лие; (*strength, force*) си́ла. **violent** *adj.* (*person*) свире́пый, жесто́кий (-о́к, -ока́, -ко); (*storm etc.*) си́льный (си́лён, -льна́, -льно, си́льны); (*quarrel*) бу́рный (бу́рен, бу́рна́, -но), свире́пый; (*pain*) си́льный (си́лён, -льна́, -льно, си́льны); (*epoch*) бу́рный (бу́рен, бу́рна́, -но), жесто́кий (-о́к, -ока́, -ко); (*death*) наси́льственный. **violently** *adv.* си́льно, о́чень.

violet ['vaɪələt] *n.* (*bot.*) фиа́лка; (*colour*) фио-

ле́товый цвет; *adj.* фиоле́товый.

violin [ˌvaɪə'lɪn] *n.* скри́пка. **violinist** *n.* скрипа́ч (-а́), ~ка.

VIP *abbr.* (*of very important person*) высоко-поста́вленное лицо́ (*pl.* -ца), высо́кий гость.

viper ['vaɪpə(r)] *n.* гадю́ка; (*fig.*) змея́ (*pl.* -е́и). **viperous** *adj.* ядови́тый.

virago [vɪ'rɑːɡəʊ, -'reɪɡəʊ] *n.* меге́ра.

viral ['vaɪər(ə)l] *adj.* ви́русный.

virgin ['vɜːdʒɪn] *n.* де́вственник, -ица; **V~ Mary** де́ва Мари́я; *adj.* (*also fig.*) де́вственный (-ен, -енна); ~ **lands, soil** целина́. **virginal** *adj.* де́вственный (-ен, -енна); (*innocent*) неви́нный (-нен, -нна). **vir'ginity** *n.* де́вственность. **Virgo** ['vɜːɡəʊ] *n.* Де́ва.

virile ['vaɪraɪl] *adj.* (*mature*) возмужа́лый; (*manly*) му́жественный (-ен, -енна). **virility** [vɪ'rɪlɪtɪ] *n.* возмужа́лость; му́жество.

virtual ['vɜːtjʊəl] *adj.* факти́ческий. **virtually** *adv.* факти́чески. **virtue** ['vɜːtjuː, -tʃuː] *n.* (*excellence*) доброде́тель; (*merit*) досто́инство; **by ~ of** посре́дством+*g.*, благодаря́+*d.* **virtu'osity** *n.* виртуо́зность. **virtuoso** [ˌvɜːtjʊ'əʊsəʊ, -zəʊ] *n.* виртуо́з. **virtuous** *adj.* доброде́тельный; (*chaste*) целому́дренный (-ен, -енна).

virulence ['vɪrʊləns, 'vɪrjʊ-] *n.* (*toxicity*) ядови́тость; (*power*) си́ла; (*med.*) вируле́нтность; (*fig.*) зло́ба. **virulent** *adj.* (*poisonous*) ядови́тый; (*of disease*) опа́сный; (*fig.*) зло́бный.

virus ['vaɪərəs] *n.* ви́рус.

visa ['viːzə] *n.* ви́за; *v.t.* визи́ровать *impf.* & *pf.*, за~ *pf.*

visage ['vɪzɪdʒ] *n.* лицо́ (*pl.* -ца); (*aspect*) вид.

vis-à-vis [ˌviːzɑː'viː] *adv.* визави́, напро́тив; *n.* визави́ *nt.indecl.*; *prep.* (*with regard to*) в отноше́нии+*g.*; (*opposite*) напро́тив+*g.*

viscera ['vɪsərə] *n.* вну́тренности *f.pl.*

viscose ['vɪskəʊz, -kəʊs] *n.* виско́за.

viscosity [vɪ'skɒsɪtɪ] *n.* вя́зкость.

viscount ['vaɪkaʊnt] *n.* вико́нт. **viscountess** *n.* виконте́сса.

viscous ['vɪskəs] *adj.* вя́зкий (-зок, -зка́, -зко).

visibility [ˌvɪzɪ'bɪlɪtɪ] *n.* ви́димость. **'visible** *adj.* ви́димый. **'visibly** *adv.* я́вно, заме́тно.

vision ['vɪʒ(ə)n] *n.* (*sense*) зре́ние; (*apparition*) виде́ние; (*insight*) проница́тельность; (*foresight*) предви́дение; (*on television screen*) изображе́ние. **visionary** *adj.* (*spectral; illusory*) при́зрачный; (*imaginary, fantastic*) вообража́емый, фантасти́ческий; (*impracticable*) неосуществи́мый; (*given to having visions*) скло́нный (-о́нен, -о́нна́, -о́нно) к галлюцина́циям; *n.* (*dreamer*) мечта́тель *m.*, ~ница, фантазёр; (*one who has visions*) визионе́р.

visit ['vɪzɪt] *n.* посеще́ние, визи́т; (*trip*) пое́здка; *v.t.* навеща́ть *impf.*, навести́ть *pf.*; посеща́ть *impf.*, посети́ть (-ещу́, -ети́шь) *pf.*; (*call on*) заходи́ть (-ожу́, -о́дишь) *impf.*, зайти́ (-йду́, -йдёшь; зашёл, -шла́) *pf.* к+*d.*; ходи́ть (хожу́, хо́дишь) *indet.*, идти́ (иду́, идёшь; шёл, шла) *det.*, пойти́ (пойду́, -дёшь;

пошёл, -шла́) pf. в го́сти k+d.; be ~ing быть в гостя́х y+g. **visi'tation** n. (official visit) официа́льное посеще́ние; (eccl.) бо́жье-наказа́ние. **visiting-card** n. визи́тная ка́рточка. **visitor** n. гость (pl. -ти, -те́й) m., посети́тель m.

visor ['vaizə(r)] n. (of cap) козырёк (-рька́); (in car) солнцезащи́тный щито́к (-тка́); (of helmet) забра́ло.

vista ['vistə] n. перспекти́ва, вид.

visual ['vizjuəl, 'viʒj-] adj. (of vision) зри́тельный; (graphic) нагля́дный; ~ **aids** нагля́дные посо́бия nt.pl. **visualize** v.t. представля́ть impf., предста́вить pf. себе́.

vital ['vait(ə)l] adj. (also fig.) жи́зненный (-ен, -енна); (fig.) суще́ственный (-ен, -енна); (lively) живо́й (жив, -а́, -о); ~ **statistics** стати́стика есте́ственного движе́ния населе́ния. **vitality** [vai'tæliti] n. жизнеспосо́бность; (liveliness) жи́вость. **vitalize** v.t. оживля́ть impf., оживи́ть pf. **vitals** n. жи́зненно ва́жные о́рганы m.pl.

vitamin ['vitəmin, 'vait-] n. витами́н.

vitiate ['viʃɪˌeit] v.t. по́ртить impf., ис~ pf.; (invalidate) де́лать impf., с~ pf. недействи́тельным; лиша́ть impf., лиши́ть pf. си́лы. **viti'ation** n. по́рча; (leg.) лише́ние си́лы; призна́ние недействи́тельным.

viticulture ['viti,kʌltʃə(r)] n. виногра́дарство.

vitreous ['vitriəs] adj. стеклови́дный; (of glass) стекля́нный. **vitrify** ['vitri,fai] v.t. & i. превраща́ть(ся) impf., преврати́ть(ся) (-ащу́(сь), -ати́шь(ся)) pf. в стекло́, в стеклови́дное вещество́.

vitriol ['vitriəl] n. купоро́с; (fig.) язви́тельность. **vitriolic** [,vitri'blik] adj. купоро́сный; (fig.) язви́тельный.

vituperate [vi'tju:pə,reit, vai-] v.t. брани́ть impf., вы́~ pf. **vitupe'ration** n. брань.

vivacious [vi'veiʃəs] adj. живо́й (жив, -а́, -о), оживлённый (-ён, -ена́). **vivacity** [vi'væsiti] n. жи́вость, оживлённость.

viva voce [,vaivə 'vəutʃi, 'vəusi] adj. у́стный; n. у́стный экза́мен.

vivid ['vivid] adj. (bright) я́ркий (я́рок, ярка́, я́рко); (lively) живо́й (жив, -а́, -о); (imagination) пы́лкий (пы́лок, -лка́, -лко). **vividness** n. я́ркость; жи́вость; пы́лкость.

vivify ['vivi,fai] v.t. оживля́ть impf., оживи́ть pf.

vivisection [,vivi'sekʃ(ə)n] n. вивисе́кция.

vixen ['viks(ə)n] n. лиси́ца-са́мка; (fig.) мегера́.

viz. [viz] adv. то есть, а и́менно.

vizier [vi'ziə(r), 'viziə(r)] n. визи́рь m.

V-neck [vi:'nek, 'vi:-] n. вы́рез в ви́де бу́квы V.

vocabulary [və'kæbjuləri] n. слова́рь (-ря́) m.; (range of language) запа́с слов; (of a language) слова́рный соста́в.

vocal ['vəuk(ə)l] adj. голосово́й; (mus.) вока́льный; (noisy) шу́мный (шу́мен, -мна́, -мно); ~ **chord** голосова́я свя́зка. **vocalic** [və'kælik] adj. гла́сный. **vocalist** n. певе́ц (-вца́), -ви́ца.

vocation [və'keiʃ(ə)n] n. призва́ние; (profession) профе́ссия. **vocational** adj. профессиона́льный. **vocative** ['vɒkətiv] adj. (n.) зва́тельный (паде́ж -á).

vociferate [və'sifə,reit] v.t. крича́ть (-чу́, -чи́шь) impf., кри́кнуть pf. **vociferous** adj. (clamorous) крикли́вый; (noisy) шу́мный (шу́мен, -мна́, -мно).

vodka ['vɒdkə] n. во́дка.

vogue [vəug] n. мо́да; (popularity) популя́рность; in ~ в мо́де.

voice [vɔis] n. го́лос; (gram.) зало́г; v.t. (express) выража́ть impf., вы́разить pf. **voiced** adj. (phon.) зво́нкий (-нок, -нка́, -нко).

voiceless adj. (phon.) глухо́й (глух, -á, -о).

void [vɔid] n. пустота́; adj. пусто́й (пуст, -á, -о, пусты́); (invalid) недействи́тельный; ~ **of** лишённый (-ён, -ена́) +g.; v.t. (render invalid) де́лать impf., с~ pf. недействи́тельным; (excrete) опорожня́ть impf., опорожни́ть pf.

volatile ['vɒlə,tail] adj. (chem.) лету́чий; (inconstant) непостоя́нный (-нен, -нна); (elusive) неулови́мый. **vola'tility** n. лету́честь; непостоя́нство.

vol-au-vent ['vɒləu,vɑ̃] n. слоёный пирожо́к (-жка́).

volcanic [vɒl'kænik] adj. вулкани́ческий (also fig.). **volcano** [vɒl'keinəu] n. вулка́н.

vole [vəul] n. (zool.) полёвка.

Volga ['vɒlgə] n. Во́лга.

volition [və'liʃ(ə)n] n. во́ля; of one's own ~ по свое́й во́ле.

volley ['vɒli] n. (missiles) залп; (fig.; of arrows etc.) град; (sport) уда́р с лёта; v.t. (sport) ударя́ть impf., уда́рить pf. с лёта. **volley-ball** n. волейбо́л.

volt [vəult] n. вольт. **voltage** n. вольта́ж, напряже́ние.

volte-face [vɒlt'fɑ:s] n. (fig.) ре́зкая переме́на.

volubility [,vɒlju'biliti] n. говорли́вость. **'voluble** adj. говорли́вый.

volume ['vɒlju:m] n. (book) том (pl. -á); (capacity, bulk; also fig.) объём; (loudness) гро́мкость; (mus., strength) си́ла. **voluminous** [və'lju:minəs, və'lu:-] adj. (bulky) объёмистый, обши́рный; (of writer) плодови́тый; (of many volumes) многото́мный.

voluntary ['vɒləntəri] adj. доброво́льный; (deliberate) умы́шленный (-ен, -енна); n. (mus.) со́ло nt.indecl. на орга́не. **volun'teer** n. доброво́лец (-льца); v.t. предлага́ть impf., предложи́ть (-жу́, -жишь) pf.; v.i. (offer) вызыва́ться impf., вы́зваться (вы́зовусь, -вешься) pf. (inf., +inf.); for в+a.); (mil.) идти́ (иду́, идёшь; шёл, шла) impf., пойти́ (пойду́, -дёшь; пошёл, -шла́) pf. доброво́льцем.

voluptuary [və'lʌptjuəri] n. сластолю́бец (-бца). **voluptuous** adj. сластолюби́вый, чу́вственный (-ен, енна). **voluptuousness** n. сластолю́бие.

vomit ['vɒmit] n. рво́та; v.t. рвать (рвёт)

impf., вы́рвать (-вет) *pf. impers.*+*i.*; **he was ~ing blood** его́ рва́ло кро́вью; (*fig.*) изверга́ть *impf.*, изве́ргнуть *pf.*

voracious [vəˈreɪʃəs] *adj.* прожо́рливый; (*fig.*) ненасы́тный. **voracity** [vəˈræsɪtɪ] *n.* прожо́рливость; ненасы́тность.

vortex [ˈvɔːteks] *n.* (*whirlpool; also fig.*) водоворо́т; (*whirlwind; also fig.*) вихрь *m.*

votary [ˈvəʊtərɪ] *n.* почита́тель *m.*, ~ница; сторо́нник, -ица.

vote [vəʊt] *n.* (*poll*) голосова́ние; (*individual ~*) го́лос (*pl.* -á); **the ~** (*suffrage*) пра́во го́лоса; (*resolution*) во́тум *no pl.*; **~ of no confidence** во́тум недове́рия (**in** +*d.*); **~ of thanks** выраже́ние благода́рности; *v.i.* голосова́ть *impf.*, про~ *pf.* за+*a.*; **against** про́тив+*g.*); *v.t.* (*grant by ~*) ассигнова́ть *impf. & pf.*; (*deem*) признава́ть *impf.*, призна́ть *pf.*; **the film was ~d a failure** фильм был при́знан неуда́чным; **~ in** избира́ть *impf.*, избра́ть (изберу́, -рёшь; избра́л, -á, -о) *pf.* голосова́нием. **voter** *n.* избира́тель *m.* **voting-paper** *n.* избира́тельный бюллете́нь *m.*

votive *adj.* испо́лненный по обе́ту; **~ offering** приноше́ние по обе́ту.

vouch [vaʊtʃ] *v.i.*; **~ for** руча́ться *impf.*, поручи́ться *pf.* за+*a.* **voucher** *n.* (*receipt*) распи́ска; (*coupon*) тало́н. **vouch'safe** *v.t.* удоста́ивать *impf.*, удосто́ить+*i.* (*person to whom granted* +*a.*).

vow [vaʊ] *n.* кля́тва, обе́т; *v.t.* кля́сться (кляну́сь, -нёшься; кля́лся, -ла́сь) *impf.*, по~ *pf.* в+*p.*

vowel [ˈvaʊəl] *n.* гла́сный *sb.*

voyage [ˈvɔɪdʒ] *n.* путеше́ствие; *v.i.* путеше́ствовать *impf.*

V-sign [ˈviːsaɪn] *n.* (*victory*) знак побе́ды

vulgar [ˈvʌlgə(r)] *adj.* вульга́рный, гру́бый (груб, -á, -о), по́шлый (пошл, -á, -о); (*of the common people*) простонаро́дный. **vulgarism** *n.* вульга́рное выраже́ние. **vulgarity** [vʌlˈgærɪtɪ] *n.* вульга́рность, по́шлость. **vulgari'zation** *n.* вульгариза́ция. **vulgarize** *v.t.* вульгаризи́ровать *impf. & pf.*

vulnerable [ˈvʌlnərəb(ə)l] *adj.* уязви́мый.

vulture [ˈvʌltʃə(r)] *n.* гриф; (*fig.*) хи́щник.

vulva [ˈvʌlvə] *n.* ву́льва.

W

wad [wɒd] *n.* кусо́к (-ска́) ва́ты; (*in gun*) пыж (-á); **~ of money** па́чка бума́жных де́нег; *v.t.* (*stuff with wadding*) набива́ть *impf.*, наби́ть (набью́, -ьёшь) *pf.* ва́той. **wadding**

ва́та; (*padding, packing*) наби́вка.

waddle [ˈwɒd(ə)l] *v.i.* ходи́ть (хожу́, хо́дишь) *indet.*, идти́ (иду́, идёшь; шёл, шла) *det.*, пойти́ (пойду́, -дёшь; пошёл, -шла́) *pf.* вперева́лку (*coll.*).

wade [weɪd] *v.t. & i.* (*river*) переходи́ть (-ожу́, -о́дишь) *impf.*, перейти́ (-йду́, -йдёшь; перешёл, -шла́) *pf.* вброд; *v.i.*: **~ through** (*mud etc.*) пробира́ться *impf.*, пробра́ться (проберу́сь, -рёшься; пробра́лся, -ала́сь, -а́лось) *pf.* по+*d.*; (*sth. boring etc.*) одолева́ть *impf.*, одоле́ть *pf.* **wader** *n.* (*bird*) боло́тная пти́ца; (*boot*) боло́тный сапо́г (-á; *g.pl.* -г).

wafer [ˈweɪfə(r)] *n.* ва́фля (*g.pl.* -фель); (*eccl.; paper seal*) обла́тка.

waffle[1] [ˈwɒf(ə)l] *n.* (*dish*) ва́фля (*g.pl.* -фель).

waffle[2] [ˈwɒf(ə)l] *n.* (*blather*) трёп; *v.i.* трепа́ться (-плю́сь, -плешься) *impf.*

waft [wɒft, wɑːft] *v.t. & i.* нести́(сь) (несу́(сь), -сёшь(ся); нёс(ся), несла́(сь)) *impf.*, по~ *pf.*

wag[1] [wæg] *n.* (*wave*) взмах; (*of tail*) виля́ние; *v.t.* (*tail*) виля́ть *impf.*, вильну́ть *pf.*+*i.*; (*finger*) грози́ть *impf.*, по~ *pf.*+*i.*; *v.i.* кача́ться *impf.*, качну́ться *pf.*

wag[2] [wæg] *n.* (*joker*) шутни́к (-á).

wage[1] [weɪdʒ] *v.t.*: **~ war** вести́ (веду́, -дёшь; вёл, -á) *impf.*, про~ *pf.* войну́.

wage[2] [weɪdʒ] *n.* за́работная пла́та; **~ freeze** замора́живание за́работной пла́ты; **living ~** прожи́точный ми́нимум. **wage-earner** *n.* рабо́чий *sb.*; (*bread-winner*) корми́лец (-льца).

wager [ˈweɪdʒə(r)] *n.* пари́ *nt.indecl.*; (*stake*) ста́вка; *v.i.* (*t.*) держа́ть (-жу́, -жишь) *impf.* пари́ (на+*a.*) (**that** что).

wages *n. see* **wage**[2]

waggish [ˈwægɪʃ] *n.* шаловли́вый.

wag(g)on [ˈwægən] *n.* (*carriage*) пово́зка; (*cart*) теле́га; (*rail.*) ваго́н-платфо́рма; (*van*) фурго́н; (*trolley*) вагоне́тка. **wag(g)oner** *n.* во́зчик.

wagtail [ˈwægteɪl] *n.* трясогу́зка.

waif [weɪf] *n.* беспризо́рник.

wail [weɪl] *n.* вопль *m.*; *v.i.* вопи́ть *impf.* (*coll.*), выть (во́ю, во́ешь) *impf.* (*coll.*).

wainscot [ˈweɪnskət] *n.* пане́ль; *v.t.* обшива́ть *impf.*, обши́ть (обошью́, -ьёшь) *pf.* пане́лью.

waist [weɪst] *n.* та́лия; (*level of ~*) по́яс (*pl.* -á). **waistband** *n.* по́яс (*pl.* -á). **waistcoat** *n.* жиле́т. **waist-deep** *n.* (*adv.*) по по́яс. **waistline** *n.* та́лия.

wait [weɪt] *n.* ожида́ние; **lie in ~** быть в заса́де; **lie in ~ (for)** поджида́ть *impf.*; *v.i.*(*t.*) (*also ~ for*) ждать (жду, ждёшь; ждал, -á, -о) *impf.* (+*g.*); *v.i.* (*be a ~er, ~ress*) быть официа́нтом, -ткой; **~ on** обслу́живать *impf.*, обслужи́ть (-жу́, -жишь) *pf.* **waiter** *n.* официа́нт. **waiting** *n.* ожида́ние. **waiting-list** *n.* спи́сок (-ска) кандида́тов. **waiting-room** *n.* прие́мная *sb.*; (*rail.*) зал ожида́ния. **waitress** *n.* официа́нтка.

waive [weɪv] *v.t.* отка́зываться *impf.*, отказа́ться (-ажу́сь, -а́жешься) *pf.* от+*g.*

wake[1] [weɪk] *n.* (*at funeral*) поми́нки (-нок) *pl.*

wake[2] [weɪk] *n.* (*naut.*) кильва́тер; **in the ~ of** в кильва́тере+*d.*, по пята́м за+*i.*

wake[3] [weɪk] *v.i.* (*also ~ up*) буди́ть (бужу́, бу́дишь) *impf.*, раз~ *pf.*; *v.i.* (*also ~ up*) просыпа́ться *impf.*, просну́ться *pf.*; *v.t. & i.* (*also fig.*) пробужда́ть(ся) *impf.*, пробуди́ть(ся) (-ужу́(сь), -у́дишь(ся)) *pf.* **wakeful** *adj.* (*sleepless*) бессо́нный; (*vigilant*) бди́тельный. **wakefulness** *n.* бди́тельность. **waken** *see* **wake**[3]

Wales [weɪlz] *n.* Уэ́льс.

walk [wɔːk] *n.* (*walking*) ходьба́; (*gait*) похо́дка; (*stroll*) прогу́лка пешко́м; (*path, avenue*) тропа́ (*pl.* -пы, -п, тро́па́м), алле́я; **ten minutes' ~ from here** де́сять мину́т ходьбы́ отсю́да; **go for a ~** идти́ (иду́, идёшь; шёл, шла) *impf.*, пойти́ (пойду́, -дёшь; пошёл, -шла́) *pf.* гуля́ть; **from all ~s of life** всех слоёв о́бщества; *v.i.* ходи́ть (хожу́, хо́дишь) *indet.*, идти́ (иду́, идёшь; шёл, шла) *det.*, пойти́ (пойду́, -дёшь; пошёл, -шла́) *pf.*; гуля́ть *impf.*, по~ *pf.*; **~ away, off** уходи́ть (ухожу́, -о́дишь) *impf.*, уйти́ (уйду́, -дёшь; ушёл, ушла́) *pf.*; **~ in** входи́ть (вхожу́, -о́дишь) *impf.*, войти́ (войду́, -дёшь; вошёл, -шла́) *pf.*; **~ out** выходи́ть (-ожу́, -о́дишь) *impf.*, вы́йти (-йду, -йдешь; вы́шел, -шла) *pf.*; *v.t.* (*traverse*) обходи́ть (-ожу́, -о́дишь) *impf.*, обойти́ (-йду́, -йдёшь; обошёл, -шла́) *pf.*; (*take for ~*) выводи́ть (-ожу́, -о́дишь) *impf.*, вы́вести (-еду, -едешь; -ел) *pf.* гуля́ть. **walker** *n.* ходо́к (-а́). **walkie-talkie** [ˌwɔːkɪˈtɔːkɪ] *n.* (перено́сная) ра́ция. **walking** *n.* ходьба́; *adj.* гуля́ющий; (*med.*; *encyclopaedia*) ходя́чий. **walking-stick** *n.* трость (*pl.* -ти, -те́й).

Walkman [ˈwɔːkmən] *n.* (*propr.*) во́кмен, пле́ер.

walk-on: **~ part** роль (*pl.* -ли, -ле́й) без слов. **walk-out** *n.* (*strike*) забасто́вка; (*exit*) демонстрати́вный ухо́д. **walk-over** *n.* лёгкая побе́да.

wall [wɔːl] *n.* стена́ (*a.* -ну; *pl.* -ны, -н, -на́м); (*of object*) сте́нка; *attr.* стенно́й *v.t.* обноси́ть (-ошу́, -о́сишь) *impf.*, обнести́ (-есу́, -есёшь; -ёс, -есла́) *pf.* стено́й; **~ up** (*door, window*) заде́лывать *impf.*, заде́лать *pf.*; (*brick up*) замуро́вывать *impf.*, замурова́ть *pf.*

wallet [ˈwɒlɪt] *n.* бума́жник.

wallflower [ˈwɔːlˌflaʊə(r)] *n.* желтофио́ль.

wallop [ˈwɒləp] *n.* си́льный уда́р; *v.t.* си́льно ударя́ть *impf.*, уда́рить *pf.*; бить (бью, бьёшь) *impf.*, по~ *pf.*

wallow [ˈwɒləʊ] *v.i.* валя́ться *impf.*, бара́хтаться; **~ in** (*give o.s. up to*) предава́ться (-даю́сь, -даёшься) *impf.*, преда́ться (-а́мся, -а́шься, -а́стся, -ади́мся; преда́лся, -ла́сь) *pf.*+*d.*

wallpaper [ˈwɔːlˌpeɪpə(r)] *n.* обо́и (обо́ев) *pl.*

walnut [ˈwɔːlnʌt] *n.* гре́цкий оре́х; (*wood, tree*) оре́ховое де́рево (*pl.* (*tree*) -е́вья, -е́вьев), оре́х.

walrus [ˈwɔːlrəs, ˈwɒl-] *n.* морж (-а́).

waltz [wɔːls, wɔːlts, wɒ-] *n.* вальс; *v.i.* вальси́ровать *impf.*

wan [wɒn] *adj.* (*pale*) бле́дный (-ден, -дна́, -дно, бле́дны́); (*faint*) ту́склый (-л, -ла́, -ло).

wand [wɒnd] *n.* (*of conductor, magician*) па́лочка; (*of official*) жезл (-а́).

wander [ˈwɒndə(r)] *v.i.* броди́ть (брожу́, -о́дишь) *impf.*; (*also of thoughts etc.*) блужда́ть *impf.*; **~ from the point** отклоня́ться *impf.*, отклони́ться (-ню́сь, -ни́шься) *pf.* от те́мы. **wanderer** *n.* стра́нник, скита́лец (-льца). **wandering** *adj.* бродя́чий; блужда́ющий; (*winding*) изви́листый.

wane [weɪn] *n.* убыва́ние; *v.i.* убыва́ть *impf.*, убы́ть (убу́дет; у́был, -а, -о) *pf.*; (*diminish*) уменьша́ться *impf.*, уме́ньши́ться *pf.*; (*weaken*) ослабева́ть *impf.*, ослабе́ть *pf.*

wangle [ˈwæŋg(ə)l] *v.t.* ухитря́ться *impf.*, ухитри́ться *pf.* получи́ть.

want [wɒnt] *n.* (*lack*) недоста́ток (-тка); (*need*) нужда́; (*requirement*) потре́бность; (*desire*) жела́ние; *v.t.* хоте́ть (хочу́, -чешь, хоти́м) *impf.*, за~ *pf.*+*g. & a.*; (*need*) нужда́ться *impf.* в+*p.*; **I ~ you to come at six** я хочу́, что́бы ты пришёл в шесть. **wanting** *adj.* (*absent*) отсу́тствующий; **be ~** недостава́ть (-таёт) *impf.* (*impers.*+*g.*); **experience is ~** недостаёт о́пыта.

wanton [ˈwɒnt(ə)n] *adj.* (*licentious*) распу́тный; (*senseless*) бессмы́сленный (-ен, -енна); (*luxuriant*) бу́йный (бу́ен, буйна́, -но).

war [wɔː(r)] *n.* война́ (*pl.* -ны); (*attr.*) вое́нный (*in ~ crime, ~ correspondent, ~ debts, ~ loan etc.*); **at ~** в состоя́нии войны́; **~ cry** боево́й клич; **~ dance** вои́нственный та́нец (-нца); **~ memorial** па́мятник па́вшим в войне́; *v.i.* воева́ть (вою́ю, -ю́ешь) *impf.*

warble [ˈwɔːb(ə)l] *n.* трель; *v.i.* издава́ть (-даю́, -даёшь) *impf.*, изда́ть (-а́м, -а́шь, -а́ст, -ади́м; и́зда́л, -а́, -о) *pf.* тре́ли.

ward[1] [wɔːd] *n.* (*hospital*) пала́та; (*child etc.*) подопе́чный *sb.*; (*district*) администрати́вный райо́н го́рода; избира́тельный о́круг (*pl.* -а́).

ward[2] [wɔːd] *v.t.*: **~ off** отража́ть *impf.*, отрази́ть *pf.*

warden [ˈwɔːd(ə)n] *n.* (*prison*) нача́льник; (*college*) ре́ктор.

warder [ˈwɔːdə(r)] *n.* тюре́мщик.

wardrobe [ˈwɔːdrəʊb] *n.* гардеро́б.

warehouse [ˈweəhaʊs] *n.* склад, пакга́уз.

wares [weəz] *n.* изде́лия *nt.pl.*, това́ры *m.pl.*

warfare [ˈwɔːfeə(r)] *n.* война́. **war-game** *n.* вое́нная игра́. **warhead** *n.* боева́я голо́вка. **warhorse** *n.* боево́й конь (-ня́; *pl.* -ни, -не́й) *m.*

warily [ˈweərɪlɪ] *adv.* осторо́жно. **wariness** *n.* осторо́жность.

warlike [ˈwɔːlaɪk] *adj.* вои́нственный (-ен, -енна).

warm [wɔːm] *n.* тепло́; *adj.* (*also fig.*) тёплый (тёпел, -пла́, -пло́, -плы́); *v.t. & i.* гре́ть(ся) *impf.*; согрева́ть(ся) *impf.*, согре́ть(ся) *pf.*;

~ **up** (*food etc.*) подогрева́ть(ся) *impf.*, подогре́ть(ся) *pf.*; (*liven up*) оживля́ть(ся) *impf.*, оживи́ть(ся) *pf.*; (*sport*) размина́ться *impf.*, размя́ться (разомну́сь, -нёшься) *pf.*; (*mus.*) разы́грываться *impf.*, разыгра́ться *pf.* **warmth** *n.* тепло́; (*cordiality*) серде́чность.

warmonger [ˈwɔːmʌŋɡə(r)] *n.* поджига́тель *m.* войны́.

warn [wɔːn] *v.t.* предупрежда́ть *impf.*, предупреди́ть *pf.* (**about** о+*p.*). **warning** *n.* предупрежде́ние.

warp [wɔːp] *n.* (*of cloth*) осно́ва; (*of wood*) коробле́ние *v.t. & i.* (*wood*) коро́бить(ся) *impf.*, по~, с~ *pf.*; *v.t.* (*pervert, distort*) извраща́ть *impf.*, изврати́ть (-ащу́, -ати́шь) *pf.*

warpaint [ˈwɔːpeɪnt] *n.* раскра́ска те́ла пе́ред похо́дом. **warpath** *n.* (*fig.*): **be on the** ~ быть в вои́нственном настрое́нии.

warrant [ˈwɒrənt] *n.* (*for arrest etc.*) о́рдер (*pl.* -а́); (*justification*) оправда́ние; (*proof*) доказа́тельство; *v.t.* (*justify*) опра́вдывать *impf.*, оправда́ть *pf.*; (*guarantee*) гаранти́ровать *impf. & pf.*; руча́ться *impf.*, поручи́ться (-чу́сь, -чишься) *pf.* за+*a.* **warranty** *n.* (*basis*) основа́ние; (*guarantee*) гара́нтия.

warren [ˈwɒrən] *n.* кро́личий садо́к (-дка́).

warrior [ˈwɒrɪə(r)] *n.* во́ин, бое́ц (бойца́).

Warsaw [ˈwɔːsɔː] *n.* Варша́ва.

warship [ˈwɔːʃɪp] *n.* вое́нный кора́бль (-ля́) *m.*

wart [wɔːt] *n.* борода́вка. **wart-hog** *n.* борода́вочник.

wartime [ˈwɔːtaɪm] *n.*: **in** ~ во вре́мя войны́.

warty [ˈwɔːtɪ] *adj.* борода́вчатый.

wary [ˈweərɪ] *adj.* осторо́жный.

wash [wɒʃ] *n.* мытьё; (*thin layer*) то́нкий слой (*pl.* -ои́); (*lotion*) примо́чка; (*surf*) прибо́й; (*backwash*) попу́тная струя́ (*pl.* -у́и); **at the** ~ в сти́рке; **have a** ~ мы́ться (мо́юсь, мо́ешься) *impf.*, по~ *pf.*; *v.t. & i.* мыть(ся) (мо́ю(сь), мо́ешь(ся)) *impf.*, вы́~ *pf.*; *v.t.* (*clothes*) стира́ть *impf.*, вы́~ *pf.*; (*of sea*) омыва́ть *impf.*; *v.i.* (*clothes*) стира́ться *impf.*; ~ **ashore: the body was** ~ed **ashore** труп приби́ло к бе́регу (*impers.*); ~ **away, off, out** смыва́ть(ся) *impf.*, смыть(ся) (смо́ю, -бешь -бет(ся)) *pf.*; (*carry away*) сноси́ть (-ошу́, -о́сишь) *impf.*, снести́ (-есу́, -есёшь; -ёс, -есла́) *pf.*; ~ **out** (*rinse*) спола́скивать *impf.*, сполосну́ть *pf.*; ~ **up** (*dishes*) мыть (мо́ю, мо́ешь) *impf.*, вы́~, по~ *pf.* (посу́ду); ~ **one's hands (of it)** умыва́ть *impf.*, умы́ть (умо́ю, -о́ешь) *pf.* ру́ки. **wash-basin** *n.* умыва́льник. **washed-out** *adj.* (*exhausted*) утомлённый. **washer** *n.* (*tech.*) ша́йба. **washerwoman** *n.* пра́чка. **washing** *n.* (*of clothes*) сти́рка; (*clothes*) бельё. **washing-machine** *n.* стира́льная маши́на. **washing-powder** *n.* стира́льный порошо́к (-шка́).

Washington [ˈwɒʃɪŋt(ə)n] *n.* Вашингто́н.

washing-up [ˌwɒʃɪŋˈʌp] *n.* (*action*) мытьё посу́ды; (*dishes*) гря́зная посу́да. **wash-house** *n.* пра́чечная. **wash-out** *n.* (*fiasco*) прова́л. **washroom** *n.* умыва́льная *sb.* **washtub** *n.* лоха́нь для сти́рки.

wasp [wɒsp] *n.* оса́ (*pl.* о́сы); ~'s **nest** оси́ное гнездо́ (*pl.* -ёзда). **waspish** *adj.* (*irritable*) раздражи́тельный; (*caustic*) язви́тельный.

wastage [ˈweɪstɪdʒ] *n.* уте́чка. **waste** *n.* (*desert*) пусты́ня; (*wastage*) уте́чка; (*refuse*) отбро́сы *m.pl.*; (*of time, money etc.*) (бесполе́зная) тра́та; **go to** ~ пропада́ть *impf.*, пропа́сть (-аду́, -адёшь; -а́л) *pf.* да́ром; ~ **pipe** сто́чная труба́ (*pl.* -бы); *adj.* (*desert*) пусты́нный (-нен, -нна); (*superfluous*) нену́жный; (*uncultivated*) невозде́ланный; **lay** ~ опустоша́ть *impf.*, опустоши́ть *pf.*; ~ **paper** нену́жная бума́га *f.pl.*; (*for recycling*) макулату́ра; ~ **products** отхо́ды (-дов) *pl.*; *v.t.* тра́тить *impf.*, по~, ис~ *pf.*; (*time*) теря́ть *impf.*, по~ *pf.*; *v.t. & i.* (*weaken*) истоща́ть(ся) *impf.*, истощи́ть(ся) *pf.*; *v.i.*; ~ **away** ча́хнуть (-х) *impf.*, за~ *pf.* **wasteful** *adj.* расточи́тельный. **wasteland** *n.* пусты́рь (-ря́) *m.* **waste-paper:** ~ **basket** корзи́на для (нену́жных) бума́г. **wastrel** *n.* (*idler*) безде́льник.

watch [wɒtʃ] *n.* (*timepiece*) часы́ (-со́в) *pl.*; (*duty*) дежу́рство; (*naut.*) ва́хта; **keep** ~ **over** наблюда́ть *impf.* за+*i.*; *v.t.* наблюда́ть *impf.*; следи́ть *impf.* за+*i.*; (*guard*, ~ **over**) охраня́ть *impf.*, охрани́ть *pf.*; (*look after*) смотре́ть (-рю́, -ришь) *impf.*, по~ *pf.* за+*i.*; ~ **television, a film** смотре́ть (-рю́, -ришь) *impf.*, по~ *pf.* телеви́зор, фильм; ~ **out!** осторо́жно! **watch-chain** цепо́чка для часо́в. **watchdog** *n.* сторожево́й пёс (пса). **watchful** *adj.* бди́тельный. **watchmaker** *n.* часовщи́к (-а́). **watchman** *n.* (*ночно́й*) сто́рож (*pl.* -а́, -е́й). **watch-spring** *n.* часова́я пружи́на. **watch-tower** *n.* сторожева́я ба́шня (*g.pl.* -шен). **watchword** *n.* ло́зунг.

water [ˈwɔːtə(r)] *n.* вода́ (*a.* -ду; *pl.* -ды, -д, во́да́м); *attr.* водяно́й, во́дный; ~ **bird** водяна́я пти́ца; ~ **bottle** графи́н для воды́; ~ **bus** речно́й трамва́й; ~ **jump** во́дное препя́тствие; ~ **lily** водяна́я ли́лия; ~ **main** водопрово́дная магистра́ль; ~ **melon** арбу́з; ~ **polo** во́дное по́ло *nt.indecl.*; ~ (*flowers etc.*) полива́ть *impf.*, поли́ть (-лью́, -льёшь; по́ли́л, -а́, -о) *pf.*; (*animals*) пои́ть (пою́, по́ишь) *impf.*, на~ *pf.*; (*irrigate*) ороша́ть *impf.*, ороси́ть (-ишу́, -иси́шь) *pf.*; (*eyes*) слези́ться *impf.*; (*mouth*): **my mouth** ~s у меня́ слю́нки теку́т; ~ **down** разбавля́ть *impf.*, разба́вить *pf.* **water-butt** *n.* бо́чка для дождево́й воды́. **water-closet** *n.* убо́рная *sb.* **water-colour** *n.* акваре́ль. **watercourse** *n.* (*brook*) руче́й (-чья́); (*bed*) ру́сло (*g.pl.* -л); (*channel*) кана́л. **watercress** *n.* кресс водяно́й. **waterfall** *n.* водопа́д. **waterfront** *n.* часть (*pl.* -ти, -те́й) го́рода примыка́ющая к бе́регу. **water-heater** *n.* кипяти́льник. **water-hole** *n.* (*in desert*) ключ (-а́). **watering-can** *n.* ле́йка. **water-level** *n.* у́ровень (-ня) *m.* воды́. **water-**

line *n.* ватерли́ния. **waterlogged** *adj.* забо-ло́ченный (-ен); пропи́танный (-ан) водо́й. **watermark** *n.* (*in paper*) водяно́й знак. **water-mill** *n.* водяна́я ме́льница. **water-pipe** *n.* водопрово́дная труба́ (*pl.* -бы). **water-power** *n.* гидроэне́ргия. **waterproof** *adj.* не-промока́емый; *n.* непромока́емый плащ (-а́). **water-rat** *n.* водяна́я кры́са. **watershed** *n.* водоразде́л. **waterside** *n.* бе́рег (*loc.* -у́; *pl.* -а́). **water-ski** (*n.*) во́дная лы́жа. **water-supply** *n.* водоснабже́ние. **watertight** *adj.* водонепроница́емый; (*hermetic*) гермети́ческий. **water-tower** *n.* водонапо́рная ба́шня (*g.pl.* -шен). **waterway** *n.* во́дный путь (-ти́, -тём) *m.* **water-weed** *n.* во́доросль. **water-wheel** *n.* водяно́е колесо́ (-ёса). **waterworks** *n.* водопрово́дные сооруже́ния *nt.pl.* **watery** *adj.* водяни́стый; (*pale*) блё́дный (-ден, -дна́, -дно, бле́дны).

watt [wɒt] *n.* ватт.

wattle ['wɒt(ə)l] *n.* (*fencing*) плете́нь (-тня́) *m.*; *attr.* плетёный.

wave [weɪv] *v.t.* (*hand etc.*) маха́ть (машу́, -шешь) *impf.*, махну́ть *pf.*+*i.*; (*hair*) зави-ва́ть *impf.*, зави́ть (-вью, -вьёшь; зави́л, -а́, -о) *pf.*; *v.i.* (*flutter*) развева́ться *impf.*; (*rock, swing*) кача́ться *impf.*, качну́ться *pf.*; ~ **aside** (*spurn*) отверга́ть *impf.*, отве́ргнуть (-г) *pf.*; ~ **down** дава́ть (даю́, даёшь) *impf.*, дать (дам, дашь, даст, дади́м; дал, -а́, да́ло́, -ли) *pf.* знак останови́ки+*d.*; *n.* (*in var. senses*) волна́ (*pl.* -ны, -н, во́лна́м); (*of hand*) взмах; (*in hair*) зави́вка. **wavelength** *n.* дли-на́ волны́. **waver** *v.i.* (*also fig.*) колеба́ться (-блюсь, -блешься) *impf.*; (*flicker, flutter*) ко-лыха́ться (-ы́шется)*impf.*, колыхну́ться *pf.* **wavy** *adj.* волни́стый.

wax [wæks] *n.* воск; (*in ear*) се́ра; *attr.* воско-во́й; *v.t.* вощи́ть *impf.*, на- *pf.* **waxen, waxy** *adj.* восково́й; (*like wax*) похо́жий на воск. **waxwork** *n.* восково́я фигу́ра; *pl.* галере́я восковы́х фигу́р.

way [weɪ] *n.* (*road, path, route*; *fig.*) доро́га, путь (-ти́, -тём) *m.*; (*manner*) о́браз; (*method*) спо́соб; (*condition*) состоя́ние; (*respect*) отноше́ние; (*habit*) привы́чка; **by the** ~ (*fig.*) кста́ти, ме́жду про́чим; **on the** ~ по доро́ге, по пути́; **this** ~ (*direction*) сюда́; (*in this* ~) таки́м о́бразом; **the other** ~ **round** наоборо́т; **under** ~ на ходу́; **be in the** ~ меша́ть *impf.*; **get out of the** ~ уходи́ть (-ожу́, -о́дишь) *impf.*, уйти́ (уйду́, -дёшь; ушёл, ушла́) *pf.* с доро́ги; **give** ~ (*yield*) поддава́ться (поддаю́сь, -аёшься) *impf.*, подда́ться (-а́мся, -а́шься, -а́стся, -ади́мся; подда́лся, -ла́сь) *pf.* (**to** +*d.*); (*collapse*) обру́шиваться *impf.*, обру́шиться *pf.*; **go out of one's** ~ стара́ться *impf.*, по- *pf.* изо всех сил+*inf.*; **have it one's own** ~ де́йст-вовать *impf.* по-сво́ему; **make** ~ уступа́ть *impf.*, уступи́ть (-плю́, -пишь) *pf.* доро́гу (**for** +*d.*). **wayfarer** *n.* пу́тник. **way'lay** *v.t.* (*lie in wait for*) подстерега́ть *impf.*, под-

стере́чь (-егу́, -ежёшь; подстерёг, -ла́) *pf.*; (*stop*) перехва́тывать *impf.*, перехвати́ть (-ачу́, -а́тишь) *pf.* по пути́. **wayside** *n.* обо́-чина; *adj.* придоро́жный.

wayward ['weɪwəd] *adj.* своенра́вый, капри́з-ный. **waywardness** *n.* своенра́вие, капри́з-ность.

WC *abbr.* (*of water-closet*) убо́рная *sb.*

we [wiː, wɪ] *pron.* мы (нас, нам, на́ми, нас).

weak [wiːk] *adj.* (*in var. senses*) сла́бый (слаб, -а́, -о); (*indecisive*) нереши́тельный; (*uncon-vincing*) неубеди́тельный. **weaken** *v.t.* ослабля́ть *impf.*, осла́бить *pf.*; *v.i.* слабе́ть *impf.*, o~ *pf.* **weakling** *n.* сла́бый челове́к (*pl.* лю́ди, -де́й, -дям, -дьми́). **weakness** *n.* сла́бость; **have a** ~ **for** име́ть *impf.* сла́бость к+*d.*

weal [wiːl] *n.* (*mark*) рубе́ц (-бца́).

wealth [welθ] *n.* бога́тство; (*abundance*) изо-би́лие. **wealthy** *adj.* бога́тый, состоя́тель-ный.

wean [wiːn] *v.t.* отнима́ть *impf.*, отня́ть (от-ниму́, -мешь) *pf.* от груди́; (*fig.*) отуча́ть *impf.*, отучи́ть (-чу́, -чишь) *pf.* (**of, from** от+*g.*).

weapon ['wepən] *n.* ору́жие. **weaponless** *adj.* безору́жный. **weaponry** *n.* вооруже́ние, ору́жие.

wear [weə(r)] *n.* (*wearing*) но́ска; (*clothing*) оде́жда; (~ **and tear**) изна́шивание; *v.t.* носи́ть (ношу́, но́сишь) *impf.*; быть в+*pr.*; *v.i.* носи́ться (но́сится) *impf.*; ~ **off** (*cease to have effect*) перестава́ть (-таю́, -таёшь) *impf.*, переста́ть (-а́ну, -а́нешь) *pf.* де́йст-вовать; ~ **out** (*clothes*) изна́шивать(ся) *impf.*, износи́ть(ся) (-ошу́(сь), -о́сишь(ся)) *pf.*; (*exhaust, become exhausted*) исто-ща́ть(ся) *impf.*, истощи́ть(ся) *pf.*

weariness ['wɪərɪnɪs] *n.* (*tiredness*) уста́лость, утомле́ние; (*tedium*) утоми́тельность. **wearing** ['weərɪŋ], **wearisome** *adj.* утоми́-тельный. **weary** *adj.* уста́лый, утомлённый (-ён, -ена́); *v.t. & i.* утомля́ть(ся) *impf.*, уто-ми́ть(ся) *pf.*

weasel ['wiːz(ə)l] *n.* ла́ска (*g.pl.* -сок).

weather ['weðə(r)] *n.* пого́да; ~ **forecast** про-гно́з пого́ды; ~ **station** метеорологи́ческая ста́нция; *v.t.* (*storm etc.*) выде́рживать *impf.*, вы́держать (-жу, -жишь) *pf.*; (*expose to atmosphere*) подверга́ть *impf.*, под-ве́ргнуть *pf.* атмосфе́рным влия́ниям. **weather-beaten** *adj.* повреждённый (-ён, -ена́) бу́рями; (*of face*) обве́тренный (-ен); (*of person*) закалённый(-ён, -ена́). **weather-chart** *n.* синопти́ческая ка́рта. **weather-cock, weathervane** *n.* флю́гер (*pl.* -а́). **weatherman** *n.* метеоро́лог.

weave[1] [wiːv] *v.t. & i.* (*fabric*) ткать (тку, ткёшь; ткал, -а́, -о) *impf.*, co~ *pf.*; *v.t.* (*fig.*; *also wreath etc.*) плести́ (плету́, -тёшь; плёл, -а́) *impf.*, c~ *pf.*; *n.* узо́р тка́ни. **weaver** *n.* ткач, -и́ха. **weaving** *n.* (*the art of* ~) тка́чество; (*the* ~) тканьё.

weave² [wiːv] *v.i.* (*sway*) покачиваться *impf.*
web [web] *n.* (*cobweb, gossamer; fig.*) паутина; (*membrane*) перепонка; (*tissue*) ткань; (*fig.*) сплетение. **webbed** *adj.* перепончатый. **webbing** *n.* тканая лента, тесьма.
wed [wed] *v.t.* (*of man*) жениться (-нюсь, -нишься) *impf.* & *pf.* на+*p.*; (*of woman*) выходить (-ожу, -одишь) *impf.*, выйти (выйду, -дешь; вышла) *pf.* замуж за+*a.*; (*unite*) сочетать *impf.* & *pf.*; *v.i.* жениться (-нюсь, -нишься) *pf.* (*coll.*); вступать *impf.*, вступить (-плю, -пишь) *pf.* в брак. **wedded** *adj.* супружеский; ~ **to** (*fig.*) преданный (-ан) +*d.* **wedding** *n.* свадьба, бракосочетание; ~ **cake** свадебный торт; ~ **day** день (дня) *m.* свадьбы; ~ **dress** подвенечное платье (*g.pl.* -в); ~ **ring** обручальное кольцо (*pl.* -льца, -лец, -льцам).
wedge [wedʒ] *n.* клин (*pl.* -ья, -ьев); *v.t.* (~ *open*) заклинивать *impf.*, заклинить *pf.*; *v.t.* & *i.*: ~ **in(to)** вклинивать(ся) *impf.*, вклинить(ся) *pf.* (в+*a.*).
wedlock ['wedlɒk] *n.* брак, супружество; **born out of** ~ рождённый (-ён, -ена) вне брака, внебрачный.
Wednesday ['wenzdeɪ, -dɪ] *n.* среда (*a.* -ду; *pl.* -ды, -д, -дам).
weed [wiːd] *n.* сорняк (-а); *v.t.* полоть (полю, -лешь) *impf.*, вы~ *pf.*; ~ **out** удалять *impf.*, удалить *pf.* **weed-killer** *n.* гербицид. **weedy** *adj.* заросший сорняками; (*person*) тощий (тощ, -а, -е).
week [wiːk] *n.* неделя. **weekday** *n.* будний день (дня) *m.* **weekend** *n.* суббота и воскресенье, уикэнд. **weekly** *adj.* еженедельный; (*wage*) недельный; *adv.* раз в неделю; еженедельно; *n.* еженедельник.
weep [wiːp] *v.i.* плакать (плачу, -чешь) *impf.*; ~ **over** оплакивать *impf.*, оплакать *pf.* **weeping** *n.* плач; *adj.*: ~ **willow** плакучая ива. **weepy** *adj.* слезливый.
weevil ['wiːvɪl] *n.* долгоносик.
weft [weft] *n.* уток (утка).
weigh [weɪ] *v.t.* (*also fig.*) взвешивать *impf.*, взвесить *pf.*; (*consider*) обдумывать *impf.*, обдумать *pf.*; *v.t.* & *i.* (*so much*) весить *impf.*; ~ **down** отягощать *impf.*, отяготить (-ощу, -отишь) *pf.*; ~ **on** тяготить (-ощу, -отишь) *impf.*; ~ **out** отвешивать *impf.*, отвесить *pf.*; ~ **up** (*appraise*) оценивать *impf.*, оценить (-ню, -нишь) *pf.* **weight** *n.* (*also authority*) вес (*pl.* -а); (*load, also fig.*) тяжесть; (*sport*) гиря, штанга; (*influence*) влияние; **lose** ~ худеть *impf.*, по~ *pf.*; **put on** ~ толстеть *impf.*, по~ *pf.*; прибавлять *impf.*, прибавить *pf.* в весе; *v.t.* (*make heavier*) утяжелять *impf.*, утяжелить *pf.* **weightless** *adj.* невесомый. **weightlessness** *n.* невесомость. **weightlifter** *n.* гиревик (-а), штангист. **weightlifting** *n.* поднятие тяжестей. **weighty** *adj.* (*also fig.*) веский; (*heavy*) тяжёлый (-л, -ла); (*important*) важный (-жен, -жна, -жно, -жны).

weir [wɪə(r)] *n.* плотина, запруда.
weird [wɪəd] *adj.* (*strange*) странный (-нен, -нна, -нно).
welcome ['welkəm] *n.* (*greeting*) приветствие; (*reception*) приём; *adj.* желанный (-ан); (*pleasant*) приятный; **you are** ~ (*don't mention it*) не стоит благодарности, пожалуйста; **you are** ~ **to use my bicycle** мой велосипед к вашим услугам; **you are** ~ **to stay the night** вы можете переночевать у меня/ нас; *v.t.* приветствовать *impf.* (& *pf.* in past tense); *int.* добро пожаловать!
weld [weld] *n.* сварной шов (шва); *v.t.* & *i.* сваривать(ся) *impf.*, сварить(ся) *pf.*; (*fig.*) сплачивать *impf.*, сплотить *pf.* **welder** *n.* сварщик. **welding** *n.* сварка.
welfare ['welfeə(r)] *n.* благосостояние, благополучие; W~ **State** государство всеобщего благосостояния; ~ **work** работа по социальному обеспечению.
well¹ [wel] *n.* колодец (-дца); (*for stairs*) лестничная клетка.
well² [wel] *v.i.*: ~ **forth, up** бить (бьёт) *impf.* ключом; хлынуть *pf.*
well³ [wel] *adj.* (*healthy*) здоровый; **feel** ~ чувствовать *impf.*, по~ *pf.* себя хорошо, здоровым; **get** ~ поправляться *impf.*, поправиться *pf.*; **look** ~ хорошо выглядеть (-яжу, -ядишь) *impf.*; **all is** ~ всё в порядке; *int.* ну(!); *adv.* хорошо; (*very much*) очень; **as** ~ тоже; **as** ~ **as** (*in addition to*) кроме+*g.*; **it may be true** вполне возможно, что это так; **very** ~! хорошо!; ~ **done!** молодец!; ~ **done** (*cooked*) (хорошо) прожаренный (-ен). **well-advised** *adj.* благоразумный. **well-balanced** *adj.* уравновешенный (-ен, -енна). **well-behaved** *adj.* благонравный. **well-being** *n.* благополучие. **well-bred** *adj.* благовоспитанный (-ан, -анна). **well-built** *adj.* крепкий (-пок, -пка, -пко). **well-defined** *adj.* чёткий (-ток, -тка, -тко). **well-disposed** *adj.* благосклонный (-нен, -нна), благожелательный. **well-fed** *adj.* откормленный (-ен). **well-groomed** *adj.* (*person*) холеный. **well-grounded** *adj.* обоснованный (-ан, -анна); (*versed*) сведущий (**in** в+*p.*). **well-informed** *adj.* (хорошо) осведомлённый (-ён, -ена) (**about** в+*p.*). **well-known** *adj.* известный.
wellington (**boot**) ['welɪŋt(ə)n] *n.* резиновый сапог (-а; *g.pl.* -г).
well-mannered [ˌwel'mænəd] *adj.* воспитанный (-ан). **well-meaning** *adj.* имеющий хорошие намерения. **wellnigh** ['welnaɪ] *adv.* почти. **well-paid** *adj.* хорошо оплачиваемый. **well-preserved** *adj.* хорошо сохранившийся. **well-proportioned** *adj.* пропорциональный. **well-read** *adj.* начитанный (-ан, -анна). **well-spoken** *adj.* умеющий изысканно говорить. **well-timed** *adj.* своевременный (-нен, -нна). **well-wisher** *n.* доброжелатель *m.* **well-worn** *adj.* (*fig.*) избитый.
welsh¹ [welʃ] *v.t.*: ~ **on** (*swindle*) надувать

impf., наду́ть (-у́ю, -у́ешь) *pf.* (*coll.*); (*fail to keep*) не сде́рживать *impf.*, сдержа́ть (-жу́, -жишь) *pf.*+g.

Welsh² [welʃ] *adj.* валли́йский, уэ́льский. **Welshman** *n.* валли́ец. **Welshwoman** *n.* валли́йка.

welt [welt] *n.* (*of shoe*) рант (*loc.* -у́); (*weal*) рубе́ц (-бца́).

welter ['weltə(r)] *n.* (*confusion*) сумбу́р, пу́таница; *v.i.* валя́ться *impf.*

wench [wentʃ] *n.* де́вка.

wend [wend] *v.t.* ∼ one's way держа́ть (-жу́, -жишь) *impf.* путь.

wer(e)wolf ['wɪəwʊlf, 'weə-] *n.* оборотень (-тня) *m.*

west [west] *n.* за́пад; (*naut.*) вест; *adj.* за́падный; *adv.* на за́пад, к за́паду. **westerly** *adj.* за́падный; *n.* за́падный ве́тер (-тра). **western** *adj.* за́падный; *n.* (*film*) ве́стерн. **westernize** *v.t.* европеизи́ровать *impf.* & *pf.* **westward(s)** *adv.* на за́пад, к за́паду.

wet [wet] *adj.* мо́крый (-р, -ра́, -ро); (*paint*) непросо́хший; (*rainy*) дождли́вый; 'W∼ Paint' «осторо́жно, окра́шено»; ∼ through промо́кший до ни́тки; ∼ suit водонепроница́емый костю́м; *n.* (*dampness*) вла́жность; (*rain*) дождь (-дя́) *m.*; *v.t.* мочи́ть (-чу́, -чишь) *impf.*, на∼ *pf.* **wetness** *n.* вла́жность. **wet-nurse** *n.* корми́лица.

whack [wæk] *n.* (*blow*) си́льный уда́р; *v.t.* колоти́ть (-очу́, -о́тишь) *impf.*, по∼ *pf.*

whale [weɪl] *n.* кит (-а́).

wharf [wɔːf] *n.* при́стань (*pl.* -ни, -не́й).

what [wɒt] *pron.* (*interrog., int.*) что (чего́, чему́, чем, чём); (*how much*) ско́лько; (*rel.*) (то,) что (чего́, чему́, чем, чём); ∼ (...) for заче́м; ∼ if а что е́сли; ∼ is your name как вас зову́т?; *adj.* (*interrog., int.*) како́й; ∼ kind of како́й. **whatever** *pron.* что бы ни+*past* (∼ you think что бы вы ни ду́мали); всё, что (take ∼ you want возьми́те всё, что хоти́те); *adj.* како́й бы ни+*past* (∼ books he read(s) каки́е бы ни кни́ги он ни прочита́л); (*at all*): there is no chance ∼ нет никако́й возмо́жности; is there any chance ∼? есть ли хоть кака́я-нибу́дь возмо́жность?

wheat [wiːt] *n.* пшени́ца. **wheaten** *adj.* пшени́чный.

wheedle ['wiːd(ə)l] *v.t.* (*coax into doing*) угова́ривать *impf.*, уговори́ть *pf.* с по́мощью ле́сти; ∼ out of выма́нивать *impf.*, вы́манить *pf.* у+g. **wheedling** *adj.* вкра́дчивый, льсти́вый.

wheel [wiːl] *n.* колесо́ (*pl.* -ёса); (*steering* ∼, *helm*) руль (-ля́) *m.*, штурва́л; (*potter's*) гонча́рный круг; *v.t.* (*push*) ката́ть *indet.*, кати́ть (качу́, ка́тишь) *det.*, по∼ *pf.*; *v.t. & i.* (*turn*) повёртывать(ся) *impf.*, поверну́ть(ся) *pf.*; *v.i.* (*circle*) кружи́ться (-ужу́сь, -у́жишься) *impf.* **wheelbarrow** *n.* та́чка. **wheelchair** *n.* инвали́дное кре́сло (*g.pl.* -сел) (на колёсах). **wheelwright** *n.* коле́сник.

wheeze [wiːz] *n.* сопе́ние, хрип; *v.i.* сопе́ть (-плю́, -пи́шь) *impf.*, хрипе́ть (-плю́, -пи́шь) *impf.* **wheezy** *adj.* хри́плый (-л, -ла́, -ло).

whelk [welk] *n.* (*mollusc*) брюхоно́гий моллю́ск.

when [wen] *adv.* когда́; *conj.* когда́, в то вре́мя как; (*whereas*) тогда́ как; (*although*) хотя́. **whence** *adv.* отку́да. **whenever** *adv.* когда́ же; *conj.* (*every time*) вся́кий раз когда́; (*at any time*) в любо́е вре́мя, когда́; (*no matter when*) когда́ бы ни+*past*; we shall have dinner ∼ you arrive во ско́лько бы вы ни прие́хали, мы пообе́даем.

where [weə(r)] *adv.* & *conj.* (*place*) где; (*whither*) куда́; from ∼ отку́да. **whereabouts** [,weərə'baʊts; 'weərə,baʊts] *adv.* где; *n.* местонахожде́ние. **where'as** *conj.* тогда́ как; хотя́; (*official*) поско́льку. **where'by** *adv.* & *conj.* посре́дством чего́. **wher'ever** *adv.* & *conj.* (*place*) где бы ни+*past*; (*whither*) куда́ бы ни+*past*; ∼ he goes куда́ бы он ни пошёл. **wherewithal** ['weəwɪˌðɔːl] *n.* сре́дства *nt.pl.*

whet [wet] *v.t.* точи́ть (-чу́, -чишь) *impf.*, на∼ *pf.*; (*stimulate*) возбужда́ть *impf.*, возбуди́ть *pf.* **whetstone** *n.* точи́льный ка́мень (-мня; *pl.* -мни, -мне́й) *m.*

whether ['weðə(r)] *conj.* ли; I don't know ∼ he will come я не зна́ю, придёт ли он; ∼ he comes or not придёт (ли) он и́ли нет.

whey [weɪ] *n.* сы́воротка.

which [wɪtʃ] *adj.* (*interrog., rel.*) како́й; *pron.* (*interrog.*) како́й; (*person*) кто; (*rel.*) кото́рый; (*rel. to whole statement*) что; ∼ is ∼? (*persons*) кто из них кто?; (*things*) что-что? **which'ever** *adj.* & *pron.* како́й бы ни+*past* (∼ book you choose каку́ю бы кни́гу ты ни вы́брал); любо́й (take ∼ book you want возьми́те любу́ю кни́гу).

whiff [wɪf] *n.* (*wind*) дунове́ние; (*smoke*) дымо́к (-мка́); (*odour*) за́пах.

while [waɪl] *n.* вре́мя *nt.*; промежу́ток (-тка) вре́мени; a little ∼ недо́лго; a long ∼ до́лго; for a long ∼ (*up to now*) давно́; for a ∼ на вре́мя; in a little ∼ ско́ро; once in a ∼ вре́мя от вре́мени; it is worth ∼ сто́ит э́то сде́лать; *v.t.*: ∼ away проводи́ть (-ожу́, -о́дишь) *impf.*, провести́ (-еду́, -еде́шь; -ёл, -ела́) *pf.*; *conj.* пока́; в то вре́мя как; (*although*) хотя́; несмотря́ на то, что; (*contrast*) а; we went to the cinema ∼ they went to the theatre мы ходи́ли в кино́, а они́ в теа́тр. **whilst** *see* while

whim [wɪm] *n.* при́хоть, причу́да, капри́з.

whimper ['wɪmpə(r)] *n.* хны́канье; *v.i.* хны́кать (хны́чу, -чешь & хны́каю, -аешь) *impf.*

whimsical ['wɪmzɪk(ə)l] *adj.* капри́зный; (*odd*) причу́дливый. **whimsy** *n.* капри́з, при́хоть, причу́да.

whine [waɪn] *n.* (*wail*) вой; (*whimper*) хны́канье; *v.i.* скули́ть *impf.*; (*wail*) выть (во́ю, во́ешь); (*whimper*) хны́кать *impf.*

whinny ['wɪnɪ] *n.* ти́хое ржа́ние; *v.i.* ти́хо

ржать (ржу, ржёшь) *impf.*

whip [wɪp] *n.* кнут (-á), хлыст (-á); ~ **hand** контрóль (-ля) *m.*; *v.t.* (*lash*) хлестáть (-ещý, -éщешь) *impf.*, хлестнýть *pf.*; (*urge on*) подгонять *impf.*, подогнáть (подгоню, -нишь; подогнáл, -á, -ó) *pf.*; (*cream*) сбивáть *impf.*, сбить (собью, -ьёшь) *pf.*; ~ **off** скидывать *impf.*, скинуть *pf.*; ~ **out** выхвáтывать *impf.*, выхватить *pf.*; ~ **round** быстро повёртываться *impf.*, повернýться *pf.*; ~ **up** (*stir up*) разжигáть *impf.*, разжéчь (разожгý, -ожжёшь; разжёг, разожглá) *pf.* **whipper-snapper** *n.* ничтóжество. **whipping** *n.* побóи (-óев) *pl.* **whip-round** *n.* сбор дéнег.

whirl [wɜːl] *n.* кружéние; (*of dust etc.*) вихрь (-ря) *m.*; (*turmoil*) суматóха, смятéние; *v.t. & i.* кружить(ся) (кружý(сь), крýжишь(ся)) *impf.*, за~ *pf.* **whirlpool** *n.* водоворóт. **whirlwind** *n.* вихрь (-ря) *m.*

whirr [wɜː(r)] *n.* жужжáние; *v.i.* жужжáть (жужжý, -жишь) *impf.*

whisk [wɪsk] *n.* (*of twigs etc.*) вéничек (-чка); (*utensil*) мутóвка; (*movement*) помáхивание; *v.t.* (*cream etc.*) сбивáть *impf.*, сбить (собью, -ьёшь) *pf.*; (*wag, wave*) махáть (машý, -шешь) *impf.*, махнýть *pf.*+*i.*; ~ **away, off** (*brush off*) смáхивать *impf.*, смахнýть *pf.*; (*take away*) быстро уносить (-ошý, -óсишь) *impf.*, унести (-есý, -есёшь; -ёс, -еслá) *pf.*; *v.i.* (*scamper away*) юркнýть *pf.*

whisker [ˈwɪskə(r)] *n.* (*human*) вóлос (*pl.* -осы, -óс, -осáм) на лицé; (*animal*) ус (*pl.* -ы); *pl.* (*human*) бакенбáрды *f.pl.*

whisky [ˈwɪskɪ] *n.* виски *nt.indecl.*

whisper [ˈwɪspə(r)] *n.* шёпот; (*rustle*) шéлест; *v.t. & i.* шептáть (шепчý, -чешь) *impf.*, шепнýть *pf.*; (*rustle*) шелестéть (-тишь) *impf.*

whist [wɪst] *n.* вист.

whistle [ˈwɪs(ə)l] *n.* (*sound*) свист; (*instrument*) свистóк (-ткá); *v.i.* свистéть (-ищý, -истишь) *impf.*, свистнуть *pf.* (*also to dog etc.*); *v.t.* насвистывать *impf.* **whistler** *n.* свистýн (-á) (*coll.*).

whit [wɪt] *n.*: **not a** ~ ничýть, нискóлько.

white [waɪt] *adj.* бéлый (бел, -á, бéло); (*hair*) седóй (сед, -á, -о); (*pale*) блéдный (-ден, -днá, -дно, блéдны); (*transparent*) прозрáчный; (*with milk*) с молокóм; **paint** ~ крáсить *impf.*, по~ *pf.* в бéлый свет; **W~ House** Бéлый дом; ~ **lie** невинная ложь (лжи, *i.* лóжью); **W~ Russian** (*n.*) белорýс, ~ка; (*adj.*) белорýсский; *n.* (*colour*) бéлый цвет; (*egg, eye*) белóк (-лкá); (~ **man**) бéлый *sb.* **white-collar** *adj.* контóрский; ~ **worker** слýжащий *sb.* **white-hot** *adj.* раскалённый добелá. **whiten** *v.t.* белить (белю, бéлишь) *impf.*, на~, по~, вы́~ *pf.*; (*blanch, bleach*) отбéливать *impf.*, отбелить *pf.*; *v.i.* белéть *impf.*, по~ *pf.* **whiteness** *n.* белизнá. **whitewash** *n.* раствóр для побéлки; *v.t.* белить (белю, бéлишь) *impf.*, по~ *pf.*; (*fig.*) обелять *impf.*, обелить *pf.*

whither [ˈwɪðə(r)] *adv. & conj.* кудá.

Whitsun [ˈwɪts(ə)n] *n.* недéля пóсле Трóицы.

whittle [ˈwɪt(ə)l] *v.t.* строгáть *impf.*, вы́~ *pf.* ножóм; ~ **down** (*decrease*) уменьшáть *impf.*, умéньшить *pf.*

whiz(z) [wɪz] *n.* свист; *v.i.* свистéть (-ищý, -истишь) *impf.*

who [huː] *pron.* (*interrog.*) кто (когó, комý, кем, ком); (*rel.*) котóрый.

whoa [wəʊ] *int.* тпру!

whoever [huːˈevə(r)] *pron.* кто бы ни+*past*; (*he who*) тот, кто.

whole [həʊl] *adj.* (*entire*) весь (вся, всё, все), цéлый; (*intact, of number*) цéлый; *n.* (*thing complete*) цéлое *sb.*; (*all there is*) весь (вся, всё; все) *sb.*; (*sum*) сýмма; **as a** ~ в цéлом; **on the** ~ в óбщем. **wholefood** *n.* натурáльные продýкты *m.pl.*; *adj.* натурáльный. **whole-hearted** *adj.*: ~ **support** горячая поддéржка. **whole-heartedly** *adv.* от всей душ, от всего сéрдца. **wholemeal** *n.* непросéянная мукá. **wholesale** *adj.* оптóвый; (*fig.*) мáссовый; *n.* оптóвая торгóвля; *adv.* оптом. **wholesaler** *n.* оптóвый торгóвец (-вца). **wholesome** *adj.* здорóвый, благотвóрный. **wholly** *adv.* пóлностью, целикóм.

whom [huːm] *pron.* (*interrog.*) когó *etc.* (*see* **who**); (*rel.*) котóрого *etc.*

whoop [huːp, wuːp] *n.* крик, гиканье (*coll.*); *v.i.* кричáть (-чý, -чишь) *impf.*, крикнуть *pf.*; гикать *impf.*, гикнуть *pf.* (*coll.*); ~**ing cough** коклюш.

whore [hɔː(r)] *n.* проститýтка.

whorl [wɔːl, wɜːl] *n.* (*bot.*) мутóвка; (*on shell*) завитóк (-ткá); (*of spiral*) витóк (-ткá).

whose [huːz] *pron.* (*interrog., rel.*) чей (чья, чьё, чьи); (*rel.*) котóрого.

why [waɪ] *adv.* почемý; *n.* причина; *int.* (*surprise*) да ведь!; (*impatience*) ну!

wick [wɪk] *n.* (*of lamp etc.*) фитиль (-ля) *m.*

wicked [ˈwɪkɪd] *adj.* злой (зол, зла); (*immoral*) безнрáвственный (-нен, -нна). **wickedness** *n.* злóбность.

wicker [ˈwɪkə(r)] *n.* прýтья *m.pl.* для плетéния; *attr.* плетёный.

wicket [ˈwɪkɪt] *n.* калитка; (*cricket*) ворóтца.

wide [waɪd] *adj.* ширóкий (-к, -кá, ширóко); (*extensive*) обширный; (*in measurements*) в+*a.* ширинóй; ~ **awake** бóдрствующий; (*wary*) бдительный; ~ **open** ширóко открытый; (*defenceless*) незащищённый; *adv.* (*off target*) мимо цéли. **widely** *adv.* ширóко. **widen** *v.t. & i.* расширять(ся) *impf.*, расширить(ся) *pf.* **widespread** *adj.* ширóко распространённый (-ён, -ená).

widow [ˈwɪdəʊ] *n.* вдовá (*pl.* -вы). **widowed** *adj.* овдовéвший. **widower** *n.* вдовéц (-вцá). **widowhood** *n.* вдовствó.

width [wɪtθ, wɪdθ] *n.* ширинá; (*fig.*) широтá; (*of cloth*) полóтнище.

wield [wiːld] *v.t.* держáть (-жý, -жишь) *impf.* в рукáх; владéть+*i.*

wife [waɪf] *n.* женá (*pl.* жёны).

wig [wɪg] *n.* парик (-á).

wiggle ['wɪg(ə)l] *v.t. & i.* (*move*) шевели́ть(ся) *impf.*, по~, шевельну́ть(ся) *pf.*

wigwam ['wɪgwæm] *n.* вигва́м.

wild [waɪld] *adj.* ди́кий (дик, -á, -о); (*flower*) полевóй; (*uncultivated*) невозде́ланный; (*tempestuous*) бу́йный (бу́ен, буйнá, -но); (*furious*) нейстовый; (*ill-considered*) необду́манный (-ан, -анна); **be ~ about** быть без ума́ от+g.; *n.*: *pl.* пусты́ня, де́бри (-рей) *pl.* **wildcat** *adj.* (*reckless*) рискóванный; (*unofficial*) неофициáльный. **wilderness** ['wɪldənɪs] *n.* ди́кая ме́стность; (*desert*) пусты́ня. **wildfire** *n.*: **spread like ~** распространя́ться *impf.*, распространи́ться *pf.* со сверхъесте́ственный быстротóй. **wild-goose: ~ chase** сумасбрóдная зате́я. **wildlife** *n.* живáя прирóда. **wildness** *n.* ди́кость.

wile [waɪl] *n.* хи́трость, улóвка.

wilful ['wɪlfʊl] *adj.* (*obstinate*) упря́мый; (*deliberate*) преднаме́ренный (-ен, -енна), умы́шленный (-ен, -енна). **wilfulness** *n.* упря́мство; преднаме́ренность.

will [wɪl] *n.* вóля; (~-*power*) си́ла вóли; (*desire*) вóля, жела́ние; (*at death*) завеща́ние; **against one's ~** прóтив вóли; **at ~** по жела́нию; **of one's own free ~** добровóльно; **with a ~** с энтузиáзмом; **good ~** дóбрая вóля; **make one's ~** писáть (пишу́, -шешь) *impf.*, на~ *pf.* завеща́ние; *v.t.* (*want, desire*) хоте́ть (хочу́, -чешь, хоти́м) *impf.*, за~ *pf.*+g., *a.*; жела́ть *impf.*, по~ *pf.*+g.; (*order*) веле́ть (-лю́, -ли́шь) *impf. & pf.*; (*compel by one's* ~) заставля́ть *impf.*, застáвить *pf.*; (*bequeath*) завеща́ть *impf. & pf.* **willing** *adj.* готóвый, соглáсный; (*assiduous*) старáтельный. **willingly** *adv.* охóтно. **willingness** *n.* готóвность.

will-o'-the-wisp [ˌwɪləðə'wɪsp] *n.* блуждáющий огонёк (-нькá).

willow ['wɪləʊ] *n.* и́ва.

willy-nilly [ˌwɪlɪ'nɪlɪ] *adv.* вóлей-невóлей.

wilt [wɪlt] *v.i.* вя́нуть (вял) *impf.*, за~ *pf.*; поникáть *impf.*, пони́кнуть *pf.*; (*weaken*) слабе́ть *impf.*, о~ *pf.*

wily ['waɪlɪ] *adj.* хи́трый (-тёр, -трá, хи́трó), ковáрный.

wimp [wɪmp] *n.* хлю́пик, сопля́к (-кá). **wimpish** *adj.* бесхарáктерный.

win [wɪn] *n.* вы́игрыш, побéда; *v.t. & i.* вы́игрывать *impf.*, вы́играть *pf.*; *v.t.* (*obtain*) добивáться *impf.*, доби́ться (-бью́сь, -бьёшься) *pf.*+g.; ~ **over** (*convince*) убеждáть *impf.*, убеди́ть (-ди́шь) *pf.*; (*gain favour of*) располагáть *impf.*, расположи́ть (-жу́, -жишь) *pf.* к себе́; ~ **through** (*overcome*) преодолевáть *impf.*, преодоле́ть *pf.*

wince [wɪns] *n.* содрогáние, вздрáгивание; *v.i.* вздрáгивать *impf.*, вздрóгнуть *pf.*

winch [wɪntʃ] *n.* (*windlass*) лебёдка.

wind[1] [wɪnd] *n.* (*air*) ве́тер (-тра) (*breath*) дыхáние; (*flatulence*) ве́тры *m.pl.*; ~ **instrument** духовóй инструме́нт; **get ~ of** проню́хивать *impf.*, проню́хать *pf.*; *v.t.* (*make*

gasp) заставля́ть *impf.*, застáвить *pf.* задохну́ться.

wind[2] [waɪnd] *v.i.* (*meander*) ви́ться (вьюсь, вьёшься; ви́лся, -лáсь) *impf.*; извивáться *impf.*; *v.t. & i.* (*coil*) намáтывать(ся) *impf.*, намотáть(ся) *pf.*; *v.t.* (*watch*) заводи́ть (-ожу́, -óдишь) *impf.*, завести́ (-еду́, -едёшь; -ёл, -елá) *pf.*; (*wrap*) уку́тывать *impf.*, уку́тать *pf.*; ~ **down** (*v.t. & i.*) размáтывать(ся) *impf.*, размотáть(ся) *pf.*; ~ **up** (*v.t.*) (*reel*) смáтывать *impf.*, смотáть *pf.*; (*watch*) *see* **wind**[2]; (*v.t. & i.*) (*end*) кончáть(ся) *impf.*, кóнчить(ся) *pf.* **winding** *adj.* (*twisted*) витóй, спирáльный; (*meandering*) изви́листый.

windfall ['wɪndfɔːl] *n.* плод (-á), сби́тый ве́тром; (*fig.*) неожи́данное счáстье. **windmill** *n.* ветрянáя ме́льница.

window ['wɪndəʊ] *n.* окнó (*pl.* óкна, óкон, óкнам); (*of shop*) витри́на. **window-box** *n.* нару́жный я́щик для растéний. **window-dressing** *n.* украше́ние витри́н. **window-frame** *n.* окóнная рáма. **window-ledge** *n.* подокóнник. **window-pane** *n.* окóнное стеклó (*pl.* стёкла, -кол, -клам). **window-shopping** *n.* рассмáтривание витри́н. **window-sill** *n.* подокóнник.

windpipe ['wɪndpaɪp] *n.* дыхáтельное гóрло, трахе́я. **windscreen** *n.* пере́днее/ветровóе стеклó (*pl.* стёкла, -кол, -клам); ~ **wiper** стеклоочисти́тель *m.*, двóрник (*coll.*). **windsurfer** *n.* виндсёрфинги́ст. **windsurfing** *n.* виндсёрфинг. **wind-swept** *adj.* откры́тый ветрáм. **windward** *n.* наве́тренная сторонá (*a.* -ону); *adj.* наве́тренный. **windy** *adj.* ве́треный; (*verbose*) многословный.

wine [waɪn] *n.* винó (*pl.* -на); ~ **bottle** ви́нная буты́лка; ~ **cellar** ви́нный пóгреб (*pl.* -á); ~ **list** кáрта вин; ~ **merchant** торгóвец (-вца) винóм; *v.i.* пить (пью, пьёшь; пил, -á, -о) *impf.*, вы́~ *pf.* винó; *v.t.* угощáть *impf.*, угости́ть *pf.* винóм. **wineglass** *n.* рю́мка. **wine-grower** *n.* виногрáдарь *m.* **wine-growing** *n.* виногрáдарство. **winery** *n.* ви́нный завóд. **wine-tasting** *n.* дегустáция вин.

wing [wɪŋ] *n.* (*also pol.*) крылó (*pl.* -лья, -льев); (*archit.*) флигель (*pl.* -ля, -лéй) *m.*; (*sport*) фланг; *pl.* (*theatr.*) кули́сы *f.pl.*; *v.i.* летáть *indet.*, лете́ть (лечу́, лети́шь) *det.* по~ *pf.*; *v.t.* (*provide with wings*) снабжáть *impf.*, снабди́ть *pf.* кры́льями; (*quicken*) ускоря́ть *impf.*, ускóрить *pf.*; (*inspire*) окрыля́ть *impf.*, окрыли́ть *pf.* **winged** *adj.* крылáтый. **wing-nut** *n.* крылáтая гáйка. **wing-span** *n.* размáх кры́льев.

wink [wɪŋk] *n.* (*blink*) моргáние; (*as sign*) подми́гивание; **in a ~** моментáльно; *v.i.* моргáть *impf.*, моргну́ть *pf.*; мигáть *impf.*, мигну́ть *pf.* (**at** +d.); подми́гивать *impf.*, подмигну́ть *pf.* (**at** +d.); (*fig.*) смотре́ть (-рю́, -ришь) *impf.*, по~ *pf.* сквозь пáльцы на+a.

winkle ['wɪŋk(ə)l] *n.* береговáя ули́тка; *v.t.*:

~ **out** выко́вывать *impf.*, вы́ковырять *pf.*
winner ['wɪnə(r)] *n.* победи́тель *m.*, ~ница.
winning *adj.* выи́грывающий, побежда́ющий; (*of shot etc.*) реша́ющий; (*charming*) обая́тельный; *n.*: *pl.* вы́игрыш. **winning-post** *n.* фи́нишный столб (-á).
winnow ['wɪnəʊ] *v.t.* (*grain*) ве́ять (ве́ю, ве́ешь) *impf.*; (*sift*) просе́ивать *impf.*, просе́ять (-е́ю, -е́ешь) *pf.*
winsome ['wɪnsəm] *adj.* привлека́тельный, обая́тельный.
winter ['wɪntə(r)] *n.* зима́; *attr.* зи́мний; *v.i.* проводи́ть (-ожу́, -о́дишь) *impf.*, провести́ (-еду́, -еде́шь; -ёл, -елá) *pf.* зи́му; зимова́ть *impf.*, пере~ *pf.* **wintry** *adj.* зи́мний; (*cold*) холо́дный (-ден, -днá, -дно, холо́дны).
wipe [waɪp] *v.t.* (*also* ~ **out inside of**) вытира́ть *impf.*, вы́тереть (вы́тру, -решь; вы́тер, -ла) *pf.*; ~ **away, off** стира́ть *impf.*, стере́ть (сотру́, -ре́шь; стёр, -ла) *pf.*; ~ **out** (*exterminate*) уничтожа́ть *impf.*, уничто́жить *pf.*; (*disgrace etc.*) смыва́ть *impf.*, смыть (смо́ю, -о́ешь) *pf.*
wire ['waɪə(r)] *n.* про́волока; (*carrying current*) про́вод (*pl.* -á); (*telegram*) телегра́мма; *attr.* про́волочный; ~ **netting** про́волочная сеть; *v.t.* (*elec.*) де́лать *impf.*, с~ *pf.* электри́ческую прово́дку в+*a.*; (*telegraph*) телеграфи́ровать *impf.* & *pf.* **wireless** *n.* ра́дио *nt.indecl.*; ~ **set** радиоприёмник. **wiring** *n.* элекропрово́дка. **wiry** *adj.* жи́листый.
wisdom ['wɪzdəm] *n.* му́дрость; ~ **tooth** зуб (*pl.* -ы, -о́в) му́дрости. **wise** [waɪz] *adj.* му́дрый (-р, -рá, -ро); (*prudent*) благоразу́мный.
wish [wɪʃ] *n.* жела́ние; **with best ~es** всего́ хоро́шего, с наилу́чшими пожела́ниями; *v.t.* хоте́ть (хочу́, -чешь, хоти́м) *impf.*, за~ *pf.* (**I ~ I could see him** мне хоте́лось бы его́ ви́деть; **I ~ to go** я хочу́ пойти́; **I ~ you to come early** я хочу́, что́бы вы ра́но пришли́; **I ~ the day were over** хорошо́ бы день уже́ ко́нчился); жела́ть *impf.*+*g.* (**I ~ you luck** жела́ю вам уда́чи; **I ~ to congratulate on**) поздравля́ть *impf.*, поздра́вить *pf.* (**I ~ you a happy birthday** поздравля́ю тебя́ с днём рожде́ния); *v.i.*: ~ **for** жела́ть *impf.*+*g.*; хоте́ть (хочу́, -чешь, хоти́м) *impf.*, за~ *pf.*+*g.* & *a.* **wishbone** *n.* ду́жка. **wishful** *adj.* жела́ющий; ~ **thinking** самообольще́ние; приня́тие жела́емого за действи́тельное.
wishy-washy ['wɪʃɪ,wɒʃɪ] *adj.* (*too liquid*) жи́дкий (-док, -дкá, -лко); (*fig.*) слáбый (слаб, -á, -о), бесцве́тный.
wisp [wɪsp] *n.* (*of straw*) пучо́к (-чкá); (*hair*) клочо́к (-чкá); (*smoke*) стру́йка.
wistful ['wɪstfʊl] *adj.* (*pensive*) заду́мчивый; (*melancholy*) тоскли́вый.
wit[1] [wɪt] *n.* (*mind*) ум (-á); (*wittiness*) остро́умие; (*person*) остря́к (-á); **be at one's ~'s end** не знать *impf.* что де́лать.
wit[2] [wɪt] *v.i.*: **to ~** то́ есть, а и́менно.

witch [wɪtʃ] *n.* ве́дьма, колду́нья (*g.pl.* -ний). **witchcraft** *n.* колдовство́. **witch-doctor** *n.* знáхарь *m.* **witch-hunt** *n.* охо́та за ведьм.
with [wɪð] *prep.* (*in company of, together* ~) (вме́сте) с+*i.*; (*as a result of*) от+*g.*; (*at house of, in keeping of*) у+*g.*; (*by means of*) +*i.*; (*in spite of*) несмотря́ на+*a.*; (*including*) включа́я+*a.*; ~ **each/one another** друг с дру́гом.
withdraw [wɪð'drɔ:] *v.t.* (*retract*) брать (беру́, -рёшь; брал, -á, -о) *impf.*, взять (возьму́, -мёшь; взял, -á, -о) *pf.* назáд; (*curtain, hand*) отдёргивать *impf.*, отдёрнуть *pf.*; (*cancel*) снимáть *impf.*, снять (сниму́, -мешь; снял, -á, -о) *pf.*; (*mil.*) отводи́ть (-ожу́, -о́дишь) *impf.*, отвести́ (-еду́, -едёшь; -ёл, -елá) *pf.*; (*money from circulation*) изымáть *impf.*, изъя́ть (изыму́, -ы́мешь) из обраще́ния; (*diplomatic representative*) отзывáть *impf.*, отозвáть (отзову́, -вёшь; отозвáл, -á, -о) *pf.*; (*from bank*) брать (беру́, -рёшь; брал, -á, -о) *impf.*, взять (возьму́, -мёшь; взял, -á, -о) *pf.*; *v.i.* удаля́ться *impf.*, удали́ться *pf.*; (*mil.*) отходи́ть (-ожу́, -о́дишь) *impf.*, отойти́ (-йду́, -йдёшь; отошёл, -шлá) *pf.* **withdrawal** *n.* (*retraction*) взя́тие назáд; (*cancellation*) сня́тие; (*mil.*) отхо́д; (*money from circulation*) изъя́тие; (*departure*) ухо́д; ~ **symptoms** абстине́нтный синдро́м. **withdrawn** *adj.* зáмкнутый.
wither ['wɪðə(r)] *v.i.* вя́нуть (вял) *impf.*, за~ *pf.*; высыхáть *impf.*, вы́сохнуть (-х) *pf.*; *v.t.* иссушáть *impf.*, иссуши́ть (-шу́, -шишь) *pf.* **withering** *adj.* (*fig.*) испепеля́ющий.
withers ['wɪðəz] *n.* хо́лка.
withhold [wɪð'həʊld] *v.t.* (*refuse to grant*) не давáть (даю́, даёшь) *impf.*, дать (дам, дашь, даст, дади́м; дал, -á, дáло, -и) *pf.*+*g.*; (*hide*) скрывáть *impf.*, скрыть (скро́ю, -о́ешь) *pf.*; (*restrain*) уде́рживать *impf.*, удержáть (-жу́, -жишь) *pf.*
within [wɪ'ðɪn] *prep.* (*inside*) внутри́+*g.*, в+*p.*; (~ *the limits of*) в предéлах+*g.*; (*time*) в тече́ние+*g.*; *adv.* внутри́; (*at home*) до́ма.
without [wɪ'ðaʊt] *prep.* без+*g.*; (*outside*) вне+*g.*, за+*i.*; ~ **saying good-bye** не прощáясь; **do ~** обходи́ться (-ожу́сь, -о́дишься) *impf.*, обойти́сь (-йду́сь, -йдёшься; обошёлся, -ошлáсь) *pf.* без+*g.*
withstand [wɪð'stænd] *v.t.* противостоя́ть (-ою́, -ои́шь) *impf.*+*d.*; выде́рживать *impf.*, вы́держать (-жу, -жишь) *pf.*
witless ['wɪtlɪs] *adj.* глу́пый (-п, -пá, -по).
witness ['wɪtnɪs] *n.* (*person*) свиде́тель *m.*; (*eye-*~) очеви́дец (-дца); (*to signature etc.*) завери́тель *m.*; (*evidence*) свиде́тельство; **bear ~ to** свиде́тельствовать *impf.*, за~ *pf.*; *v.t.* быть свиде́телем+*g.*; (*document etc.*) заверя́ть *impf.*, заве́рить *pf.* **witness-box** *n.* ме́сто (*pl.* -á) для свиде́телей.
witticism ['wɪtɪ,sɪz(ə)m] *n.* острóта. **wittiness** *n.* остроу́мие. **witty** *adj.* остроу́мный.
wizard ['wɪzəd] *n.* волше́бник, колду́н (-á). **wizardry** *n.* колдовство́.

wizened ['wɪz(ə)nd] *adj.* (*wrinkled*) морщи́нистый.

wobble ['wɒb(ə)l] *v.t. & i.* шата́ть(ся) *impf.*, шатну́ть(ся) *pf.*; кача́ть(ся) *impf.*, качну́ть(ся) *pf.*; *v.i.* (*voice*) дрожа́ть (-жу́, -жи́шь) *impf.* **wobbly** *adj.* ша́ткий.

woe [wəʊ] *n.* го́ре; ~ **is me!** го́ре мне! **woebegone** ['wəʊbɪgɒn] *adj.* удручённый, мра́чный (-чен, -чна́, -чно). **woeful** *adj.* скорбный, го́рестный.

wolf [wʊlf] *n.* волк (*pl.* -и, -о́в); ~ **cub** волчо́нок (-нка; *pl.* волча́та, -т) *v.t.* пожира́ть *impf.*, пожра́ть (-ру́, -рёшь; пожра́л, -а́, -о) *pf.* (*coll.*) **wolfhound** *n.* волкода́в.

woman ['wʊmən] *n.* же́нщина. **womanhood** *n.* (*maturity*) же́нская зре́лость. **womanish** *adj.* женоподо́бный. **womanly** *adj.* же́нственный (-ен, -енна).

womb [wuːm] *n.* ма́тка; (*fig.*) чре́во.

womenfolk ['wɪmɪnfəʊk] *n.* же́нщины *f.pl.*; (*of one's family*) же́нская полови́на семьи́. **Women's Liberation** *n.* эмансипа́ция же́нщин; ~ **movement** движе́ние за эмансипа́цию же́нщин.

wonder ['wʌndə(r)] *n.* чу́до (*pl.* -деса́, -де́с); (*amazement*) изумле́ние; (**it's**) **no** ~ неудиви́тельно; *v.t.* интересова́ться *impf.* (**I** ~ **who will come** интере́сно, кто придёт); *v.i.*: **I shouldn't** ~ **if** неудиви́тельно бу́дет, е́сли; **I** ~ **if you could help me** не могли́ бы вы мне помо́чь?; ~ **at** удивля́ться *impf.*, удиви́ться *pf.+d.* **wonderful, wondrous** *adj.* замеча́тельный, удиви́тельный, чуде́сный.

wont [wəʊnt] *n.*: **as is his** ~ по своему́ обыкнове́нию; *pred.*: **be** ~ **to** име́ть привы́чку+*inf.* **wonted** *adj.* привы́чный.

woo [wuː] *v.t.* уха́живать *impf.* за+*i.*; (*fig.*) добива́ться+*g.*

wood [wʊd] *n.* (*forest*) лес (-а(у), *loc.* -ý; *pl.* -á); (*material*) де́рево; (*firewood*) дрова́ (-в, -ва́м) *pl.*; ~ **pulp** древе́сная ма́сса. **woodbine** *n.* жи́молость. **woodcock** *n.* вальдшне́п. **woodcut** *n.* гравю́ра на де́реве. **wooded** *adj.* леси́стый. **wooden** *adj.* (*also fig.*) деревя́нный. **woodland** *n.* леси́стая ме́стность; *attr.* лесно́й. **woodlouse** *n.* мокри́ца. **woodman** *n.* лесни́к (-á). **woodpecker** *n.* дя́тел (-тла). **woodpigeon** *n.* лесно́й го́лубь (*pl.* -би, -бе́й) *m.* **woodshed** *n.* сара́й для дров. **woodwind** *n.* деревя́нные духовы́е инстру́менты *m.pl.* **woodwork** *n.* столя́рная рабо́та; (*wooden articles*) деревя́нные изде́лия *nt.pl.*; (*wooden parts of sth.*) деревя́нные ча́сти (-те́й) *pl.* (строе́ния). **woodworm** *n.* (жук-)древото́чец (-чца). **woody** *adj.* (*plant etc.*) деревяни́стый; (*wooded*) леси́стый.

wool [wʊl] *n.* шерсть (*pl.* -ти, -те́й). **woollen** *adj.* шерстяно́й. **woolly** *adj.* (*covered with* ~) покры́тый ше́рстью; (*fleecy*) шерсти́стый; (*indistinct*) нея́сный (-сен, -сна́, -сно); ~ **mind, thinking** пу́таница в голове́; *n.* (*coll.*) сви́тер.

word [wɜːd] *n.* (*unit of language*; *utterance*; *promise*) сло́во (*pl.* -вá); (*remark*) замеча́ние; (*news*) изве́стие; **have a** ~ **with** поговори́ть *pf.* с+*i.*; **by** ~ **of mouth** на слова́х, у́стно; **in a** ~ одни́м сло́вом; **in other** ~**s** други́ми слова́ми; ~ **for** ~ сло́во в сло́во; *v.t.* выража́ть *impf.*, вы́разить *pf.* слова́ми; формули́ровать *impf.*, с~ *pf.* **wordiness** *n.* многосло́вие. **wording** *n.* формулиро́вка, реда́кция. **wordy** *adj.* многосло́вный.

work [wɜːk] *n.* рабо́та; (*labour*; *toil*; *scholarly* ~) труд (-á); (*occupation*) заня́тие; (*studies*) заня́тия *nt.pl.*; (*of art*) произведе́ние; (*book*) сочине́ние; *pl.* (*factory*) заво́д; (*mechanism*) механи́зм; **at** ~ (*doing*~) за рабо́той; (*at place of* ~) на рабо́те; **out of** ~ безрабо́тный; *v.i.* (*also function*) рабо́тать *impf.* (**at, on** над+*i.*); (*study*) занима́ться *impf.*, заня́ться (займу́сь, -мёшься; за́нялся́, -ла́сь, -лось) *pf.*; (*also toil, labour*) труди́ться (-ужу́сь, -у́дишься) *impf.*; (*function*) де́йствовать *impf.*; ~ **to rule** рабо́тать *impf.*, выполня́я сли́шком пунктуа́льно все пра́вила, с це́лью уме́ньшить производи́тельность; *v.t.* (*operate*) управля́ть *impf.+i.*; обраща́ться *impf.* с+*i.*; (*wonders*) твори́ть *impf.*, со~ *pf.*; (*soil*) обраба́тывать *impf.*, обрабо́тать *pf.*; (*mine*) разраба́тывать *impf.*, разрабо́тать *pf.*; (*compel to* ~) заставля́ть *impf.*, заста́вить *pf.* рабо́тать; ~ **in** вставля́ть *impf.*, вста́вить *pf.*; ~ **out** (*solve*) реша́ть *impf.*, реши́ть *pf.*; (*plans etc.*) разраба́тывать *impf.*, разрабо́тать *pf.*; (*exhaust*) истоща́ть *impf.*, истощи́ть *pf.*; **everything** ~**ed out well** всё ко́нчилось хорошо́; ~ **out at** (*amount to*) составля́ть *impf.*, соста́вить *pf.*; ~ **up** (*perfect*) обраба́тывать *impf.*, обрабо́тать *pf.*; (*excite*) возбужда́ть *impf.*, возбуди́ть *pf.*; (*appetite*) нагу́ливать *impf.*, нагуля́ть *pf.* **workable** *adj.* осуществи́мый, реа́льный. **workaday** *adj.* бу́дничный. **workaholic** [ˌwɜːkəˈhɒlɪk] *n.* работома́н. **workbench** верста́к (-á). **worker** *n.* рабо́чий *sb.*; рабо́тник, -ица. **workforce** рабо́чая си́ла. **working** *adj.*: ~ **class** рабо́чий класс; ~ **conditions** усло́вия *nt.pl.* труда́; ~ **day** рабо́чий день (дня) *m.*; ~ **hours** рабо́чее вре́мя; *nt.*; ~ **party** коми́ссия. **workload** нагру́зка. **workman** *n.* рабо́чий *sb.*, рабо́тник. **workmanlike** *adj.* иску́сный. **workmanship** *n.* иску́сство, мастерство́. **workroom** рабо́чая ко́мната. **workshop** *n.* мастерска́я *sb.* **work-shy** лени́вый.

world [wɜːld] *n.* мир (*pl.* -ы́), свет; *attr.* мирово́й; ~ **war** мирова́я война́ (*pl.* -ны). **world-famous** *adj.* всеми́рно изве́стный. **worldly** *adj.* (*earthly*) земно́й; (*temporal*) мирско́й; (*experienced*) о́пытный. **world-view** *n.* мировоззре́ние. **world-weary** *adj.* уста́вший от жи́зни. **worldwide** *adj.* распространённый (-ён, -ена́) по всему́ ми́ру; всеми́рный.

worm [wɜːm] *n.* червь (-вя́; *pl.* -ви, -ве́й) *m.*; (*also tech.*) червя́к (-á); (*intestinal*) глист

(-á); *v.t.*: ~ **o.s. into** вкра́дываться *impf.*, вкра́сться (-аду́сь, -аде́шься; -а́лся) *pf.* в+*a.*; ~ **out** выве́дывать *impf.*, вы́ведать *pf.* (**of** у+*g.*); ~ **one's way** пробира́ться *impf.*, пробра́ться (-беру́сь, -берёшься; -бра́лся, -брала́сь, -бра́ло́сь) *pf.* **worm-eaten** *adj.* исто́ченный (-ен) червя́ми. **wormwood** *n.* полы́нь.

worry ['wʌrɪ] *n.* (*anxiety*) беспоко́йство, трево́га; (*care*) забо́та; *v.t.* беспоко́ить *impf.*, о~ *pf.*; трево́жить *impf.*, вс~ *pf.*; (*of dog*) терза́ть *impf.*; *v.i.* беспоко́иться *impf.*, о~ *pf.* (**about** о+*p.*); му́читься *impf.*, за~, из~ *pf.* (**about** из-за+*g.*).

worse [wɜːs] *adj.* ху́дший; *adv.* ху́же; *n.*: **from bad to** ~ всё ху́же и ху́же. **worsen** *v.t. & i.* ухудша́ть(ся) *impf.*, уху́дшить(ся) *pf.*

worship ['wɜːʃɪp] *n.* поклоне́ние (**of** +*d.*); (*relig.*) богослуже́ние; *v.t.* поклоня́ться *impf.*+*d.*; (*adore*) обожа́ть *impf.* **worshipper** *n.* покло́нник, -ица.

worst [wɜːst] *adj.* наиху́дший, са́мый плохо́й; *adv.* ху́же всего́; *n.* са́мое плохо́е; *v.t.* побежда́ть *impf.*, победи́ть (-и́шь) *pf.*

worsted ['wʊstɪd] *n.* шерстяна́я/камво́льная пря́жа.

worth [wɜːθ] *n.* (*value*) цена́ (*a.* -ну; *pl.* -ны); (*fig.*) це́нность; (*merit*) досто́инство; **give me a pound's** ~ **of apples** да́йте мне я́блок на фунт; *adj.*: **be** ~ (*of value equivalent to*) сто́ить *impf.* (**what is it** ~? ско́лько э́то сто́ит?); (*deserve*) сто́ить *impf.*+*g.* (**is this film** ~ **seeing?** сто́ит посмотре́ть э́тот фильм?); **for all one is** ~ изо всех сил. **worthless** *adj.* ничего́ не сто́ящий; (*useless*) бесполе́зный. **worthwhile** *adj.* сто́ящий. **worthy** ['wɜːðɪ] *adj.* досто́йный (-о́ин, -о́йна).

would-be ['wʊdbɪ] *adj.*: ~ **actor** челове́к (*pl.* лю́ди, -де́й, -дьям, -дьми́) мечта́ющий стать актёром.

wound [wuːnd] *n.* ра́на, ране́ние; (*fig.*) оби́да; *v.t.* ра́нить *impf. & pf.*; (*fig.*) обижа́ть *impf.*, оби́деть (-и́жу, -и́дишь) *pf.* **wounded** *adj.* ра́неный.

WPC *abbr.* (*of woman police constable*) же́нщина-полице́йский.

wraith [reɪθ] *n.* виде́ние.

wrangle ['ræŋg(ə)l] *n.* пререка́ние, спор; *v.i.* пререка́ться *impf.*; спо́рить *impf.*, по~ *pf.*

wrap [ræp] *n.* (*shawl*) шаль; (*stole*) палантѝн; *v.t.* (*also* ~ *up*) завёртывать *impf.*, заверну́ть *pf.*; ~ **up** (*v.t. & i.*) (*in wraps*) заку́тывать(ся) *impf.*, заку́тать(ся) *pf.*; (*v.t.*) (*conclude*) заверша́ть *impf.*, заверши́ть *pf.*; ~**ped up in** (*fig.*) поглощённый (-ён, -ена́) +*i.* **wrapper** *n.* обёртка. **wrapping** *n.* обёртка; ~ **paper** обёрточная бума́га.

wrath [rɒθ, rɔːθ] *n.* гнев, я́рость. **wrathful** ['rɒθfʊl] *adj.* гне́вный (-вен, -вна́, -вно).

wreak [riːk] *v.t.*: ~ **havoc** производи́ть (-ожу́, -о́дишь) *impf.*, произвести́ (-еду́, -еде́шь; -ёл, -ела́) *pf.* ужа́сные разруше́ния; ~ **vengeance** мстить *impf.*, ото~ *pf.* (**on** +*d.*).

wreath [riːθ] *n.* вено́к (-нка́); (*of smoke*) кольцо́ (*pl.* -льца, -ле́ц, -льцам). **wreathe** [riːð] *v.t.* (*form into wreath*) сплета́ть *impf.*, сплести́ (-ету́, -етёшь; -ёл, -ела́) *pf.*; (*encircle*) обвива́ть *impf.*, обви́ть (обовью́, -ьёшь; обви́л, -ла́, -ло) *pf.* (**with** +*i.*); *v.i.* (*wind round*) обвива́ться *impf.*, обви́ться (обовью́сь, -ьёшься; обви́лся, -ла́сь) *pf.*; (*of smoke*) клуби́ться *impf.*

wreck [rek] *n.* (*destruction*) круше́ние, ава́рия; (*wrecked ship*) о́стов разби́того су́дна; (*vehicle, person, building etc.*) разва́лина; *v.t.* (*cause destruction of*) вызыва́ть *impf.*, вы́звать (вы́зову, -вешь) круше́ние+*g.*; (*ship*) топи́ть (топлю́, -пишь) *impf.*, по~ *pf.*; (*destroy, also hopes etc.*) разруша́ть *impf.*, разру́шить *pf.*; **be** ~**ed** терпе́ть (-плю́ -пишь) *impf.*, по~ *pf.* круше́ние; (*of plans etc.*) ру́хнуть *pf.* **wreckage** *n.* обло́мки *m.pl.* круше́ния.

wren [ren] *n.* крапи́вник.

wrench [rentʃ] *n.* (*jerk*) дёрганье; (*sprain*) растяже́ние; (*tech.*) га́ечный ключ (-á); (*fig.*) боль; *v.t.* (*snatch, pull out*) вырыва́ть *impf.*, вы́рвать (-ву, -вешь) *pf.* (**from** у+*g.*); (*sprain*) растя́гивать *impf.*, растяну́ть (-ну́, -нешь) *pf.*; ~ **open** взла́мывать *impf.*, взлома́ть *pf.*

wrest [rest] *v.t.* (*wrench*) вырыва́ть *impf.*, вы́рвать (-ву, -вешь) *pf.* (**from** у+*g.*); (*agreement etc.*) исторга́ть *impf.*, исто́ргнуть (-г) *pf.* (**from** у+*g.*); (*distort*) искажа́ть *impf.*, искази́ть *pf.*

wrestle ['res(ə)l] *v.i.* боро́ться (-рю́сь, -решься) *impf.* **wrestler** *n.* боре́ц (-рца́). **wrestling** *n.* борьба́.

wretch [retʃ] *n.* несча́стный *sb.*; (*scoundrel*) негодя́й. **wretched** *adj.* жа́лкий (-лок, -лка́, -лко); (*unpleasant*) скве́рный (-рен, -рна́, -рно).

wriggle ['rɪg(ə)l] *v.i.* извива́ться *impf.*, изви́ться (изовью́сь, -ьёшься; изви́лся, -ла́сь) *pf.*; (*fidget*) ёрзать *impf.*; *v.t.* виля́ть *impf.*, вильну́ть *pf.*+*i.*; ~ **out of** уви́ливать *impf.*, увильну́ть от+*g.*

wring [rɪŋ] *v.t.* (*also* ~ *out*) выжима́ть *impf.*, вы́жать (вы́жму, -мешь) *pf.*; (*extort*) исторга́ть *impf.*, исто́ргнуть (-г) *pf.* (**from** у+*g.*); (*hand*) кре́пко пожима́ть *impf.*, пожа́ть (пожму́, -мёшь) *pf.* (**of** +*d.*); (*neck*) свёртывать *impf.*, сверну́ть *pf.* (**of** +*d.*); ~ **one's hands** лома́ть *impf.*, с~ *pf.* ру́ки. **wringer** *n.* маши́на для отжима́ния белья́.

wrinkle ['rɪŋk(ə)l] *n.* морщи́на; *v.t. & i.* мо́рщить(ся) *impf.*, с~ *pf.*

wrist [rɪst] *n.* запя́стье. **wrist-watch** *n.* нару́чные часы́ (-со́в) *pl.*

writ [rɪt] *n.* пове́стка, предписа́ние.

write [raɪt] *v.t. & i.* (*also fig.*) писа́ть (пишу́, -шешь) *impf.*, на~ *pf.*; ~ **down** запи́сывать *impf.*, записа́ть (запишу́, -шешь) *pf.*; ~ **off** (*cancel*) аннули́ровать *impf. & pf.*; (*dispatch letter*) отсыла́ть *impf.*, отосла́ть (отошлю́,

-шлёшь] *pf.*; ~ **out** выпи́сывать *impf.*, вы́-
писать (-ишу, -ишешь) *pf.* (**in full** по́лностью);
~ **up** (*account of*) подро́бно опи́сывать
impf.; опис́ать (-ишу́, -и́шешь) *pf.*; (*notes*)
перепи́сывать *impf.*, переписа́ть (-ишу́,
-и́шешь) *pf.* **write-off** *n.*: **the car was a** ~
маши́на была́ соверше́нно испо́рчена. **writer**
n. писа́тель *m.*, ~ница. **write-up** *n.* (*report*)
отчёт.
writhe [raɪð] *v.i.* (*from pain*) ко́рчиться *impf.*,
с~ *pf.*; (*fig.*) му́читься *impf.*, за~, из~ *pf.*
writing ['raɪtɪŋ] *n.* (*handwriting*) по́черк; (*work*)
произведе́ние; **in** ~ в пи́сьменной фо́рме;
the ~ **on the wall** злове́щее предзнамено-
ва́ние. **writing-case** *n.* несессе́р для пи́сь-
менных принадле́жностей. **writing-desk** *n.*
пи́сьменный стол (-а́). **writing-paper** *n.*
почто́вая бума́га.
wrong [rɒŋ] *adj.* (*incorrect*) непра́вильный,
неве́рный (-рен, -рна́, -рно, неве́рны́), оши́-
бочный; не тот (**I have bought the** ~ **book**
я купи́л не ту кни́гу; **you've got the** ~
number (*telephone*) вы не туда́ попа́ли);
(*mistaken*) непра́вый (-в, -ва́, -во) (**you are**
~ ты непра́в); (*unjust*) несправедли́вый;
(*sinful*) дурно́й (дурён, -рна́, -рно, ду́рны́);
(*defective*) неиспра́вный; (*side of cloth*)
ле́вый; ~ **side out** наизна́нку; ~ **way round**
наоборо́т; *n.* зло; (*injustice*) несправедли́-
вость; **be in the** ~ быть непра́вым; **do** ~
греши́ть *impf.*, со~ *pf.*; *adv.* непра́вильно,
неве́рно; **go** ~ не получа́ться *impf.*,
получи́ться (-ится) *pf.*; *v.t.* (*harm*) вреди́ть
impf., по~ *pf.*+*d.*; обижа́ть *impf.*, оби́деть
pf.; (*be unjust to*) быть несправедли́вым
к+*d.* **wrongdoer** ['rɒŋ,duːə(r)] *n.* престу́пник,
гре́шник, -ица. **wrongful** *adj.* несправед-
ли́вый, непра́вильный. **wrongly** *adv.* непра́-
вильно, неве́рно.
wrought [rɔːt] *adj.*: ~ **iron** сва́рочное желе́зо.
wry [raɪ] *adj.* криво́й (-в, -ва́, -во), переко́-
шенный; ~ **face** грима́са.

xenophobia [ˌzenə'fəʊbɪə] *n.* ксенофо́бия.
Xerox ['zɪərɒks, 'ze-] *v.t.* размножа́ть *impf.*
размно́жить *pf.* на ксе́роксе. **Xerox copy**
n. ксероко́пия.
X-ray ['eksreɪ] *n.* (*picture*) рентге́н(овский
сни́мок (-мка)); *pl.* (*radiation*) рентге́новы
лучи́ *m.pl.*; *v.t.* (*photograph*) де́лать *impf.*,
с~ *pf.* рентге́н+*g.*; (*examine*) иссле́довать
impf. & *pf.* рентге́новыми луча́ми.
xylophone ['zaɪlə,fəʊn] *n.* ксилофо́н.

yacht [jɒt] *n.* я́хта. **yacht-club** *n.* яхт-клу́б.
yachting *n.* па́русный спорт. **yachtsman** *n.*
яхтсме́н.
yak [jæk] *n.* як.
Yale lock [jeɪl] *n.* (*propr.*) америка́нский за-
мо́к (-мка́).
Yalta ['jæltə] *n.* Я́лта.
yam [jæm] *n.* ям.
yank [jæŋk] *n.* рыво́к (-вка́); *v.t.* рвану́ть *pf.*
yap [jæp] *n.* тя́вканье; *v.i.* тя́вкать *impf.*, тя́в-
кнуть *pf.*
yard[1] [jɑːd] *n.* (*piece of ground*) двор (-а́).
yard[2] [jɑːd] *n.* (*measure*) ярд; (*naut.*) рей.
yardstick *n.* (*fig.*) мери́ло.
yarn [jɑːn] *n.* пря́жа; (*story*) расска́з.
yashmak ['jæʃmæk] *n.* чадра́.
yawl [jɔːl] *n.* ял.
yawn [jɔːn] *n.* зево́к (-вка́); *v.i.* (*person*) зева́ть
impf., зевну́ть *pf.*; (*chasm etc.*) зия́ть *impf.*
year [jɪə(r), jɜː(r)] *n.* год (*loc.* -ý; *pl.* -ы & -а́, -о́в
& лет, -а́м); **from** ~ **to** ~ год о́т году; ~ **in**,
~ **out** из го́да в год. **yearbook** *n.* ежего́д-
ник. **yearly** *adj.* ежего́дный, годово́й; *adv.*
ежего́дно, раз в год.
yearn [jɜːn] *v.i.* тоскова́ть *impf.* (**for** по+*d.* &
p.). **yearning** *n.* тоска́ (**for** по+*d.* & *p.*).
yeast [jiːst] *n.* дро́жжи (-жей) *pl.*
yell [jel] *n.* крик; *v.i.* крича́ть (-чý, -чи́шь)
impf., кри́кнуть *pf.*; *v.t.* выкри́кивать *impf.*,
вы́крикнуть *pf.*
yellow ['jeləʊ] *adj.* жёлтый (-т, -та́, жёлто́);
(*cowardly*) трусли́вый; *n.* жёлтый цвет; *v.i.*
желте́ть *impf.*, по~ *pf.* **yellowish** *adj.* жел-
това́тый.
yelp [jelp] *n.* визг; *v.i.* визжа́ть (-жý, -жи́шь)
impf., ви́згнуть *pf.*
yen [jen] *n.* (*currency*) ие́на.
yes [jes] *adv.* да; *n.* утвержде́ние, согла́сие;
(*in vote*) го́лос (*pl.* -а́) «за». **yes-man** *n.*
подпева́ла *c.g.* (*coll.*).
yesterday ['jestə,deɪ] *adv.* вчера́; *n.* вчера́ш-
ний день (дня) *m.*; ~ **morning** вчера́ у́тром;
the day before ~ позавчера́; ~'s **newspaper**
вчера́шняя газе́та.
yet [jet] *adv.* (*still*) ещё; (*so far*) до сих пор;
(*with comp.*) да́же, ещё; (*in questions*) уже́;
(*nevertheless*) тем не ме́нее; **as** ~ пока́, до
сих пор; **not** ~ ещё не; *conj.* одна́ко, но.
yeti ['jetɪ] *n.* йе́ти *m.indecl.*
yew [juː] *n.* тис.
Yiddish ['jɪdɪʃ] *n.* и́диш.

yield [ji:ld] *n.* (*harvest*) урожа́й; (*econ.*) дохо́д; *v.t.* (*fruit, revenue, etc.*) приноси́ть (-ошу́, -о́сишь) *impf.*, принести́ (-есу́, -есёшь; -ёс, -есла́) *pf.*; дава́ть (даю́, даёшь) *impf.*, дать (дам, дашь, даст, дади́м; дал, -а́, да́ло, -и) *pf.*; (*give up*) сдава́ть (сдаю́, сдаёшь) *impf.*, сдать (-ам, -ашь, -асть, -ади́м; сдал, -а́, -о) *pf.*; *v.i.* (*give in*) (*to enemy etc.*) уступа́ть *impf.*, уступи́ть (-плю́, -пишь) *pf.* (**to** +*d.*); (*to temptation etc.*) поддава́ться (-даю́сь, -даёшься) *impf.*, подда́ться (-а́мся, -а́шься, -а́стся, -ади́мся; -а́лся, -ала́сь) *pf.* (**to** +*d.*).

yodel ['jəʊd(ə)l] *n.* йодль *m.*; *v.i.* петь (пою́, поёшь) *impf.*, про~, с~ *pf.* йо́длем.

yoga ['jəʊgə] *n.* йо́га. **yogi** ['jəʊgɪ] *n.* йог.

yog(h)urt ['jɒgət] *n.* йо́гурт.

yoke [jəʊk] *n.* (*also fig.*) ярмо́ (*pl.* -ма); (*fig.*) и́го; (*for buckets.*) коромы́сло (*g.pl.* -сел); (*of dress*) коке́тка; ~ **of oxen** па́ра запря-жённых воло́в; *v.t.* впряга́ть *impf.*, впрячь (-ягу́, -яжёшь; -яг, -ягла́) *pf.* в ярмо́.

yokel ['jəʊk(ə)l] *n.* дереве́нщина *c.g.*

yolk [jəʊk] *n.* желто́к (-тка́).

yonder ['jɒndə(r)] *adv.* вон там; *adj.* вон тот (та, то; *pl.* те).

yore [jɔ:(r)] *n.*: **in days of** ~ во вре́мя о́но.

you [ju:] *pron.* (*familiar sg.*) ты (тебя́, тебе́, тобо́й, тебе́); (*familiar pl., polite sg. & pl.*) вы (вас, вам, ва́ми, вас); (*one*) *not usu. translated*; *v. translated in 2nd pers. sg. or by impers. construction*: ~ **never know** никогда́ не зна́ешь.

young [jʌŋ] *adj.* молодо́й (мо́лод, -а́, -о); ю́ный (юн, -а́, -о); (*new*) но́вый (нов, -а́, -о); (*inexperienced*) нео́пытный; **the** ~ молодёжь; *n.* (*collect.*) молодня́к (-а́), детёныши *m.pl.* **youngish** *adj.* моложа́вый. **youngster** *n.* ма́льчик, ю́ноша *m.*

your(s) [jɔ:(r), jʊə(r)] *poss. pron.* (*familiar sg.*; *also in letter*) твой (-оя́, -оё; -ой); (*familiar pl., polite sg. & pl.*; *also in letter*) ваш; свой (-оя́, -оё; -ой). **yourself** *pron.* (*emph.*) (*familiar sg.*) (ты) сам (-ого́, -ому́, -и́м, -о́м) (*m.*), сама́ (-мо́й, *a.* -му́) (*f.*); (*familiar pl., polite sg. & pl.*) (вы) са́ми (-и́х, -и́м, -и́ми); (*refl.*) себя́ (себе́, собо́й); -ся (*suffixed to v.t.*); **by** ~ (*independently*) самостоя́тельно, сам (-а́; -и); (*alone*) оди́н (одна́; одни́).

youth [ju:θ] *n.* (*age*) мо́лодость, ю́ность; (*young man*) ю́ноша *m.*; (*collect., as pl.*) молодёжь; *attr.* молодёжный; ~ **club** моло-

дёжный клуб; ~ **hostel** молодёжная тур-ба́за. **youthful** *adj.* ю́ношеский.

yo-yo ['jəʊjəʊ] *n.* йо-йо́.

Yugoslavia [ˌjuːgəˈslɑːvɪə] *n.* Югосла́вия. **Yugo-slav(ian)** *adj.* югосла́вский; *n.* югосла́в, ~ка.

Z

zany ['zeɪnɪ] *adj.* смешно́й (-шо́н, -шна́).

zeal [zi:l] *n.* рве́ние, усе́рдие. **zealot** ['zelət] *n.* фана́тик. **zealous** ['zeləs] *adj.* ре́вност-ный, усе́рдный.

zebra ['zebrə, 'zi:-] *n.* зе́бра.

zenith ['zenɪθ, 'zi:-] *n.* зени́т.

zephyr ['zefə(r)] *n.* зефи́р.

zero ['zɪərəʊ] *n.* нуль (-ля́) *m.*, ноль (-ля́) *m.*; ~ **option** (*pol.*) нулево́й вариа́нт.

zest [zest] *n.* (*piquancy*) пика́нтность; (*ardour*) жар, энтузиа́зм; ~ **for life** жизнелю́бие.

zigzag ['zɪgzæg] *n.* зигза́г; *adj.* зигзаго-обра́зный; *v.i.* де́лать *impf.*, с~ *pf.* зигза́ги.

zinc [zɪŋk] *n.* цинк; *attr.* ци́нковый.

Zionism ['zaɪə,nɪz(ə)m] *n.* сиони́зм. **Zionist** *n.* сиони́ст.

zip [zɪp] *n.* (~ *fastener*) (застёжка-)мо́лния; *v.t. & i.*: ~ **up** застёгивать(ся) *impf.*, застег-ну́ть(ся) *pf.* на мо́лнию.

zither ['zɪðə(r)] *n.* ци́тра.

zodiac ['zəʊdɪ,æk] *n.* зодиа́к; **sign of the** ~ знак зодиа́ка. **zodiacal** [zəˈdaɪək(ə)l] *adj.* зодиака́льный.

zonal ['zəʊnəl] *adj.* зона́льный. **zone** *n.* зо́на; (*geog.*) по́яс (*pl.* -а́).

zoo [zu:] *n.* зоопа́рк. **zoological** [ˌzəʊəˈlɒdʒɪk(ə)l] *adj.* зоологи́ческий; ~ **garden(s)** зоопа́рк, зоологи́ческий сад (*loc.* -ý; *pl.* -ы́). **zoʻologist** *n.* зоо́лог. **zoʻology** *n.* зооло́гия.

zoom [zu:m] *v.i.* (*aeron.*) де́лать *impf.*, с~ *pf.* го́рку; *n.* го́рка; ~ **lens** объекти́в с пере-ме́нным фо́кусным расстоя́нием.

Zulu ['zu:lu:] *adj.* зулу́сский; *n.* зулу́с, ~ка.

Zurich ['zjʊərɪk] *n.* Цю́рих.